The Bibliography of Crime Fiction 1749-1975

The Bibliography of Crime Fiction 1749-1975

Listing all mystery, detective, suspense, police, and gothic fiction in book form published in the English language.

ALLEN J. HUBIN

A Publication of
University Extension
University of California,
San Diego

In Cooperation With

Publisher's Inc.
Del Mar, California

Copyright ©1979 by Allen J. Hubin. All rights reserved. No part of this publication may be reproduced or used in any form or by any means—graphic, electronic, or mechanical, including photocopying, recording, taping, or information storage and retrieval systems—without written permission of the publisher, Publisher's Inc., Drawer P, Del Mar, CA 92014.

Library of Congress Cataloging in Publication Data
Hubin, Allen J
   The bibliography of crime fiction, 1749–1975.

   Includes indexes.
   1. English fiction—Bibliography. 2. Detective and mystery stories—Bibliography. 3. American fiction—Bibliography. 4. Crime and criminals—Fiction—Bibliography. I. Title.
Z2014.F4H82 [PR830.D4] 016.832'0872 78-23929
ISBN 0-89163-048-1

79 80 81 82 83 84   10 9 8 7 6 5 4 3 2 1

DEDICATION

To Marilyn, my wife, whose patience
with this criminous project lasted
(just barely!) through its completion.

CONTENTS

Preface ix
Introduction xi
Author Index 1
Title Index 451
Series Index 685

PREFACE

My pleasures in crime fiction began in my youth in the late 1940s with the discovery of Sherlock Holmes and Perry Mason. In succeeding years I continued to cast my net for reading material more and more widely within the field. In 1958 I began to convert a sizeable accumulation of crime fiction books into a collection by adding to my holdings diligently and systematically. Then followed reviewing, editing, and publishing (*The Armchair Detective*, 1967–   ) and the compiling of anthologies.

With this increasingly serious dedication to the genre came a growing awareness of the absence of specialized bibliographies. Ordean A. Hagen, under a similar conviction, took action: his *Who Done It?* (1969) was the first (and only previous) attempt to provide a comprehensive bibliography of the entire wide range of crime fiction. This was a courageous and pioneering effort in a field of such size and complexity as to leave doubt that it could be approached bibliographically.

Hagen resolved that doubt, but the inadequacies of his work quickly became apparent: errors too abundant for the data to be used with confidence, too many omissions, and an organization not—to my mind, at least—user oriented.

Hagen chose to list all works under authors' real names, no matter how obscure those names and no matter what bylines were used on the authors' crime fiction. I felt that listing by actual byline would present the information in a fashion more convenient to use by readers, collectors, librarians, book dealers, publishers, and authors. Moreover, I was certain that additional useful data could be supplied in a compact format.

And so I made a fresh bibliographic start serially in the pages of my quarterly, *The Armchair Detective*, beginning with the January 1971 issue. In spite of the effort involved, this six-year project produced what I still regarded as an intermediate version—one in which to test the different organization of data, to correct previous errors, and to encourage comment and correction by the many knowledgeable people who saw *The Armchair Detective*.

I then spent an additional twenty months in intensive research and data checking. The cumulative result is before you.

INTRODUCTION

INTENT

The intent of this bibliography is to list all adult crime fiction in book form in the English language published anywhere in the world through December 31, 1975. Thus included are:
1) novels, hardcover and paperback originals, both those first appearing in English and those published in English translations;
2) plays; and
3) short story collections (not anthologies), in which at least one story is crime fiction.

Magazine and dime novel crime fiction is not included.

"Crime fiction" is understood to comprise that fiction in which crime or the threat of crime is a principal plot element. Thus included are mystery, detective, police (procedural), suspense, thriller, and gothic (romantic suspense) fiction. (The question of categorization is discussed in more detail later under "Thematic Challenges.")

ORGANIZATION

The principal section of this bibliography is the author index, and the subsequent title and series indexes provide access to that section. The Author Index has these characteristics:

Byline identification. Each title is listed under the byline appearing on the title page of the first book appearance of that work. Each such byline entry is fully cross-referenced to the real name and/or pseudonym(s) under which the author issued book crime fiction. In each place in which the author's name is cited, it is given in full, and any portion of the name not used in book bylines is enclosed in parentheses.

Title identification. All book titles first issued under a given byline are grouped together under that byline. Republications of any of these titles with altered byline or title are identified in the original byline listing; publisher and date information is also provided for such republications. Titles whose thematic qualifications for inclusion are marginal or unconfirmed are each prefaced with a dash.

Titles under a few bylines are given special treatment, consistent with the intended user orientation of this work and with the nature of the data. When this is the case, the byline headnote describes that treatment (for example, the Georges Simenon, James Reach, and Peter Cheyney entries).

Publishers and dates. For each title the first American publisher and year of first American edition are cited, if the work appeared in the U.S. Similar treatment is given to those works appearing in Britain. If the author was writing primarily for American readers (which means, in most cases, that he was an American) and the book appeared in both the U.S. and Britain, the U.S. edition is cited first; the converse is also true.

If an American (British) edition appeared before the end of 1975, any British (American) edition, or reissue under altered byline or title, including any appearing after 1975, is identified.

Series characters. Many authors have unified their works and provided identification for their readers through the use of recurring or series characters. Each major character appearing in more than one book is identified by name at the head of the byline entry under which books about that character were issued. Each book containing the character is identifed with a code (usually the initials of the character).

When it is believed that every book appearance of the character has been identified, the byline headnote conveys that certainty (for example, "Series character: Perry Mason = PM"; or, "Series character: Lt. Kerrigan, in all titles"). When unidentified appearances of the character may exist, the headnote conveys that uncertainty (as in "Series character: Pete Heysen, in at least those marked PH").

Occasionally, books about a given character were issued under more than one byline. In such cases appropriate cross-references are provided, either in the byline headnotes or (in the case of television novelizations) through the series index.

A recurring major character is usually accompanied by a cadre of associates, antagonists, and/or relatives, who also reappear, sometimes irregularly, from book to book. In most cases only the major character is identified in this bibliography.

Birth and death dates. When known, the years of birth and death of an author are cited immediately following the author's real name, wherever it appears.

Translations. When crime fiction has been published in English translation, the work is listed by the translation title under the byline used on the title page of the first translation edition. When known, the original untranslated title is given parenthetically, along with the city (or country) and year of original publication.

Novelizations. In this century a common practice has been to issue novelizations of successful plays, movies, and television series. Such derivations are identified, along with their source works.

Short story collections. Books known to be collections of short stories are identified with the abbreviation "ss." Books comprising collections of several novelets are also identified.

Plays. Plays published in book form are listed and are identified as such, with the number of acts in each play given when known. When such a play is a dramatization of a novel or short story, both this fact and the source work are noted.

Alphabetization. Concern for convenience to the user has produced only one significant departure from common practice: Mac-, Mc-, and M'- words, considered the same, are alphabetized together as a separate letter of the alphabet coming before M. This practice is followed in all three listings (author, title, series).

Abbreviations. Relatively few are used:
    ss = short stories
    PB = Pocket Books (publisher)
    GM = Gold Medal (publisher)
  WDL = World Distributors Ltd. (publisher)
  NAL = New American Library (publisher)

The Title Index is an alphabetical listing of all titles (including reprint retitlings) identified in the Author Index. Each title is followed by the byline under which the book is entered in the Author Listing.

The Series Index is an alphabetical listing of all series and series characters identified in the Author Listing. Each series (character) is followed by the byline under which books about the series appeared, thus providing ready access to the respective entry in the author section.

STRATEGY

The approach taken throughout the development of this bibliography was to seek the greatest convenience and reliability for the user. To what extent this objective has been realized remains now to be seen; comments and suggestions are invited.

A further point of strategy involved the 1975 cut-off date. This was chosen for two reasons: primary references were only available through 1975 when the last stage of research was begun, and such a cut-off permits convenient five-year supplements to this bibliography.

Work goes forward toward the first of these supplements, covering 1976–1980. This supplement should serve two major functions: to list the new crime fiction of the period and to correct errors and omissions in this bibliography.

Despite what sometimes seemed an endless process of checking and rechecking data, errors—with their remarkable persistence and vigor—doubtless remain. All corrections, especially those with supporting information, are welcome. In addition, many of the decisions to include or exclude marginal material unavoidably were highly personal and subjective, and many were based on second-hand information. Here too recommendations for change based on superior knowledge or information will be very welcome.

THEMATIC CHALLENGES

The greatest challenge in compiling a bibliography of this kind lies in making thematic (or taxonomical) distinctions. All of literature can be viewed as a continuum, at least a thematic continuum. If so, then the carving out of a particular portion—as this bibliography seeks to do—is by definition impossible.

To be sure, substantially universal agreement will exist on the inclusion of most of the works cited—the Nero Wolfe stories by Rex Stout, for example.

But what of westerns? Crime fiction, surely. But also generally regarded as a separate genre of popular fiction, and therefore mostly excluded from this work. But what of westerns with a strong detective element? I have followed my own inclinations and moved a sufficient distance into western fiction to include western detective fiction (the Gregory Quist stories of William Colt MacDonald, for instance).

Stories about Mounties—Royal Canadian Mounted Police—seem to fall into a sort of limbo, sometimes appearing to belong with westerns, other times not. Because of this confusion and because such fiction, with its emphasis on crime and its solution by an organized law enforcement body, seems to fit with (contemporary) police fiction, I have included Mountie fiction.

Gothic (romantic suspense) fiction provides a particularly difficult selection challenge. Gothics are included in this bibliography, but their merging into historical, supernatural (occult), and romantic fiction (all excluded) is so gradual that troublesome marginal material abounds.

In a similar fashion, adult crime fiction merges with juvenile literature, science fiction, fantasy, nonfiction, the mainstream novel, pornography, and even poetry. This bibliography contains entries that move what seem appropriate distances into many of these intermediary regions. Hence, books are included in which important crime (detective) fiction elements appear together with the expected elements of these separate types of work.

ACKNOWLEDGEMENTS

My resources in compiling this bibliography were:

1) Reference works. All data from other sources were checked against two or more such works, and when such checking produced conflicts, the crime fiction books themselves were frequently used to resolve them. References consulted include *The National Union Catalog, Cumulative Book Index, Paperback Books in Print, Cumulative Paperback Index, Forthcoming Books, British Museum Catalogue, English Catalogue, British National Bibliography, British Books in Print, Whitaker's Cumulative Book Lists, Contemporary Authors, A Catalogue of Crime* by Barzun and Taylor, *The Encyclopedia of Science Fiction and Fantasy* by Donald H. Tuck, *Encyclopedia of Mystery and Detection* by Penzler and Steinbrunner, *The Men Behind Boys' Fiction* by Lofts and Adley, *The Detective Short Story* by Ellery Queen, *Victorian Detective Fiction* by Eric Osborne, *A Gothic Bibliography* by Montague Summers, and *The*

Detective Short Story: A Bibliography and Index by Mundell and Rausch.

2) Copies of books by listed authors, principally the approximately 25,000 volumes in my own collection.

3) Assistance from individuals in this country and abroad. I will risk overlooking someone and identify those who made important contributions to the completeness and accuracy of this bibliography. First and foremost, my thanks to Francis M. Nevins Jr. for his extensive and meticulously accurate help throughout the development of this work. I am grateful also to R. C. S. Adey, John Ball, R. Jeff Banks, Jacques Barzun, Peter E. Blau, E. F. Bleiler, Jon L. Breen, Robert E. Briney, J. Randolph Cox, Bill Crider, Michael Cropper, Richard Deming, Theodore Dukeshire, Bill Dunn, L. Foulkes, Brian Garfield, Marilyn Granbeck, Douglas Greene, Mary Groff, Iwan Hedman, Edward D. Hoch, Don Ireland, Nancy Kingman, Marvin Lachman, Robert Lauritzen, Vernon Lay, Dennis Lein, Steve Lewis, Ethel Lindsay, George Locke, W.O.G. Lofts, Michael L. Masliah, Stephen Mertz, Nigel Morland, Stanley Pachon, Lauran Paine, Otto Penzler, B. A. Pike, Bill Pronzini, N. C. Ravenscroft, W. E. D. Ross, Tom and Enid Schantz, Stephen Schultheis, Charles Shibuk, Aaron Marc Stein, Steven A. Stilwell, Wendell H. Taylor, Michael J. Tolley, John D. Vining, Howard Waterhouse, Hillary Waugh, J. F. Whitt, Camille Wolff, Neville W. Wood, and George Wuyek.

Finally, with great pleasure I also acknowledge the work of Loren Hubin, my son, whose months of painstaking effort produced the Title Index.

Allen J. Hubin
3656 Midland Ave.
White Bear Lake, Minnesota 55110

November 2, 1978

Author Index

A

AARONS, EDWARD S(IDNEY). 1916-1975.
Pseudonyms: Paul Ayres, Edward Ronns, qq.v. Many titles published originally as by Ronns were later reprinted as by Aarons. Series character: Sam Durell = SD.
Assignment—Amazon Queen. GM, 1974; Coronet, 1975 SD
Assignment—Angelina. GM, 1958; Fawcett (London), 1959 SD
Assignment—Ankara. GM, 1961; Muller pb, 1962 SD
Assignment—Bangkok. GM, 1972; Coronet, 1972 SD
Assignment—Black Gold. GM, 1975; Coronet, 1977 SD
Assignment—Black Viking. GM, 1967; Coronet, 1968 SD
Assignment—Budapest. GM, 1957; Fawcett (London), 1959 SD
Assignment—Burma Girl. GM, 1961; Muller pb, 1962 SD
Assignment—Carlotta Cortez. GM, 1959; Muller pb, 1960 SD
Assignment—Ceylon. GM, 1973; Coronet, 1974 SD
Assignment—Cong Hai Kill. GM, 1966 SD
Assignment—Golden Girl. GM, 1972; Coronet, 1972 SD
Assignment—Helene. GM, 1959; Muller pb, 1960 SD
Assignment—Karachi. GM, 1962; Muller pb, 1963 SD
Assignment—Lili Lamaris. GM, 1959; Muller pb, 1960 SD
Assignment—Lowlands. GM, 1961 SD
Assignment—Madeleine. GM, 1958; Muller pb, 1960 SD
Assignment—Maltese Maiden. GM, 1972; Coronet, 1973 SD
Assignment—Manchurian Doll. GM, 1963; Muller pb, 1964 SD
Assignment—Mara Tirana. GM, 1960; Jenkins, 1966 SD
Assignment—Moon Girl. GM, 1968 SD
Assignment—Nuclear Nude. GM, 1968; Coronet, 1969 SD
Assignment—Palermo. GM, 1966; Coronet, 1967 SD
Assignment—Peking. GM, 1969; Coronet, 1970 SD
Assignment—Quayle Question. GM, 1975; Coronet, 1976 SD
Assignment—School for Spies. GM, 1966; Coronet, 1967 SD
Assignment—Silver Scorpion. GM, 1973; Coronet, 1974 SD
Assignment—Sorrento Siren. GM, 1963; Muller pb, 1963 SD
Assignment—Star Stealers. GM, 1970; Coronet, 1970 SD
Assignment—Stella Marni. GM, 1957; Fawcett (London), 1958 SD
Assignment—Suicide. GM, 1956; Fawcett (London), 1958 SD
Assignment—Sulu Sea. GM, 1964 SD
Assignment—Sumatra. GM, 1974; Coronet, 1975 SD
Assignment—The Cairo Dancers. GM, 1965 SD
Assignment—The Girl in the Gondola. GM, 1964; Coronet, 1969 SD
Assignment to Disaster. GM, 1955; Fawcett (London), 1956 SD
Assignment—Tokyo. GM, 1971; Coronet, 1971 SD
Assignment—Treason. GM, 1956; Fawcett (London), 1957 SD
Assignment—White Rajah. GM, 1970; Coronet, 1970 SD
Assignment—Zoraya. GM, 1960; Muller pb, 1961 SD
Come Back, My Love. GM, 1953; Fawcett (London), 1954
The Defenders. GM, 1961; Jenkins, 1962. (Novelization of the TV series.)
Escape to Love. GM, 1952; Fawcett (London), 1957
Girl on the Run. GM, 1954
Nightmare. McKay, 1948
The Sinners. GM, 1953; Fawcett (London), 1954

ABBEY, EDWARD. 1927-   .
The Monkey Wrench Gang. Lippincott, 1975

ABBEY, KIERAN. Pseudonym of Helen Reilly, 1891-1962, q.v.
And Let the Coffin Pass. Scribner, 1942
Beyond the Dark. Scribner, 1944
Run with the Hare. Scribner, 1941

ABBEY, RUTH. Pseudonym: Ruth Pattison, q.v.
Bridge of Tears. Hale, 1974; Ace, 1975
Evil at Nunnery Manor. Ace, 1973. (British title?)
Girl from the Sea. Hale, 1973
House by the Tarn. Hale, 1975
Portrait of Doubt. Ace, 1973. (British title?)
Prisoner of the Manor. Hale, 1971; Ace, 1973
The Story of Rachel. Hale, 1972

ABBOT, ANTHONY. Pseudonym of (Charles) Fulton Oursler, 1893-1952, q.v. See also: ANONYMOUS (Dark Masquerade). Series character: Thatcher Colt, in all titles.
About the Murder of a Man Afraid of Women. Farrar, 1937. British title: The Murder of a Man Afraid of Women. Collins, 1937
About the Murder of a Startled Lady. Farrar, 1935. British title: The Murder of a Startled Lady. Collins, 1936
About the Murder of Geraldine Foster. Covici, 1930. British title: The Murder of Geraldine Foster. Collins, 1931
About the Murder of the Circus Queen. Covici, 1932. British title: The Murder of the Circus Queen. Collins, 1933
About the Murder of the Clergyman's Mistress. Covici, 1931. British title: The Crime of the Century. Collins, 1931. Also published as: Murder of the Clergyman's Mistress. Popular Library, 1950
About the Murder of the Night Club Lady. Covici, 1931. British title: The Murder of the Night Club Lady. Collins, 1932. Also published as: The Night Club Lady. Grosset, 1932; Collins, 1932
The Creeps. Farrar, 1939. British title: Murder at Buzzards Bay. Collins, 1940
The Crime of the Century; see About the Murder of the Clergyman's Mistress
Deadly Secret; see The Shudders
Murder at Buzzards Bay; see The Creeps
The Murder of a Man Afraid of Women; see About the Murder of a Man Afraid of Women
The Murder of a Startled Lady; see About the Murder of a Startled Lady
The Murder of Geraldine Foster; see About the Murder of Geraldine Foster
Murder of the Clergyman's Mistress; see About the Murder of the Clergyman's Mistress
The Murder of the Circus Queen; see About the Murder of the Circus Queen
The Murder of the Night Club Lady; see About the Murder of the Night Club Lady
The Night Club Lady; see About the Murder of the Night Club Lady
The Shudders. Farrar, 1943. British title: Deadly Secret. Collins, 1943

ABBOT, WILLIS J(OHN). 1863-1934.
Philip Derby, Reporter. Dodd, 1922; Hurst, 1923

ABBOTT, ALICE IRVING
Circumstantial Evidence. Smith, 1882

ABBOTT, ROSA [ROSA ABBOTT PARKER]
The Young Detective; or, Which Won? Lee & Shepard, 1870

ABBOTT, SANDRA
Castle of Evil. Avon, 1973
Castle of Fear. Avon, 1974
The River and the Rose. Signet, 1967
Whispering Gables. Paperback Library, 1970

ABDULLAH, ACHMED. Pseudonym of Alexander Nicholayevitch Romanoff, 1881-1945.
-Alien Souls. McCann, 1922; Hutchinson, 1923 ss
The Benefactors' Club. Lloyd, 1921 (U.S. title?)
The Blue-Eyed Manchu. Shores, 1917; Hutchinson, 1923
-A Buccaneer in Spats. Hutchinson, 1924 (U.S. title?)
The Bungalow on the Roof. Mystery League, 1931
-Fighting Through. Warne, 1933 (U.S. title?)
The Honorable Gentleman and others. Putnam, 1919 ss
The Lady in the Veil; see The Veiled Woman
The Man on Horseback. McCann, 1919
-The Mating of the Blades. McCann, 1920; Hutchinson, 1921
-Night Drums. McCann, 1921; Hutchinson, 1922
The Red Stain. Hearst, 1915; Simpkin Marshall, 1916
The Remittance-Woman. Garden City, 1924
-Steel and Jade. Doran, 1927 ss
The Trail of the Beast. McCann, 1919; Hutchinson, 1921
-The Veiled Woman. Liveright, 1931. British title: The Lady in the Veil. Hurst, 1931
-Wings. McCann, 1920 ss

ABE, KOBO. 1924-   .
The Ruined Map. Knopf, 1969; Cape, 1972

A'BECKETT, ARTHUR W(ILLIAM). 1844-1909.
Fallen Among Thieves. Chapman, 1870
The Ghost of Greystone Grange. Bradbury Agnew, 1878
Hard Luck; or, A Murder at Monte Carlo. Arrowsmith, 1890
The Mystery of Mostyn Manor. Moxon's Christmas Annual, 1878
Tracked Out: A Secret of the Guillotine. Arrowsmith, 1888
The Tunnel Mystery and Its Solution. Routledge, 1905

ABEL, JOEL S.
The Jonah Game. Curtis, 1973

ABRAHAMS, DORIS CAROLINE. 1901-   .
Pseudonym: Caryl Brahms, q.v.

ABRAHAMS, GERALD. 1907-   .
Conscience Makes Heroes. Eyre, 1945

2/ Abrahams, Robert D. — Bibliography of Crime Fiction

ABRAHAMS, ROBERT D(AVID). 1905-   .
  Series character: Pete Taylor, in both titles.
  Death After Lunch. Phoenix, 1941
  Death in 1-2-3. Phoenix, 1942

ABRO, BEN. Pseudonym.
  July 14 Assassination. Cape, 1963. U.S. title: Assassination. Morrow, 1963

ABROJAL, TULIS. Pseudonym.
  An Index Finger. Fenno, 1898

ACHARD, MARCEL. Pseudonym of Marcel Auguste Ferreol, 1899-   . See: Harry Kurnitz, 1907-1968.

ACHESON, EDWARD (CAMPION). 1902-   .
  The Grammarian's Funeral. Macrae, 1935; Hutchinson, 1935
  Murder by Suggestion; see Red Herring
  Murder to Hounds. Harcourt, 1939; Harrap, 1939
  Red Herring. Morrow, 1932. British title: Murder by Suggestion. Hutchinson, 1933

ACKLAND, RODNEY. 1908-   .
  Crime and Punishment. Marston, 1948; Holt, 1948. (A play based on the novel by Fedor Mikhailovich Dostoevskii, 1821-1881, q.v.)
  A Dead Secret. French (London), 1959. (Play.)

ACOTT, J. H.
  The Rawdon Murder Case. Thacker, ca. 1944

ACRE, STEPHEN. Pseudonym of Frank Gruber, 1904-1969, q.v. Other pseudonyms: Charles K. Boston, John K. Vedder, qq.v.
  Fall Guy for a Killer; see The Yellow Overcoat
  The Yellow Overcoat. Dodd, 1942; Boardman, 1945. Also published as: Fall Guy for a Killer, as by Frank Gruber. Jonathan Press, 1955; reprinted under original title as by Frank Gruber: Popular Library, 1949

ACTON, HAROLD (MARIO MITCHELL). 1904-   .
  The Betrayal and other stories. [Author], no date. ss, some criminous

ADAIR, DENNIS. Pseudonym of Bernard (Charles) Cronin, 1884-   . Other pseudonym: Eric North, q.v.
  Death Rides the Desert. Hutchinson, 1940

ADAM, MICHAEL
  The Admiralty Murders. Sentinel, 1947

ADAM, ROBIN
  Stalk to Kill. Hodder, 1970

ADAM, RUTH (AUGUSTA). 1907-   .
  Look Who's Talking. Muller, 1960
  Murder in the Home Guard. Chapman, 1942

ADAMS, CHRISTOPHER. Pseudonym of (Hector) Kenneth Hopkins, 1914-   , q.v.
  Amateur Agent. Boardman, 1964

ADAMS, CLEVE F(RANKLIN). 1895-1949. Pseudonym: John Spain, q.v. Joint pseudonym with Robert Leslie Bellem, q.v.: Franklin Charles, q.v. Series characters: Rex McBride = RM; John J. Shannon = JS.
  And Sudden Death. Dutton, 1940 RM
  The Black Door. Dutton, 1941
  Borderline Cases; see Contraband
  Contraband. Knopf, 1950. British title: Borderline Cases. Cassell, 1952
  The Crooking Finger. Reynal, 1944 RM
  Death at the Dam; see Sabotage
  Death Before Breakfast; see Sabotage
  Decoy. Dutton, 1941 RM
  Murder All Over; see Up Jumped the Devil
  No Wings on a Cop. Handi-Books, 1950. (Expanded by Robert Leslie Bellem, q.v., from a pulp novelet by Adams.) JS
  The Private Eye. Reynal, 1942 JS
  Sabotage. Dutton, 1940. British title: Death at the Dam. Cassell, 1946. Also published as: Death Before Breakfast. Mystery Novel of the Month, 1942 RM
  Shady Lady. Ace, 1955 RM
  Up Jumped the Devil. Reynal, 1943. Also published as: Murder All Over. Signet, 1950 RM
  What Price Murder. Dutton, 1942

ADAMS, CLIFTON. 1919-   . Pseudonym: Jonathan Gant, q.v.
  Death's Sweet Song. GM, 1955
  The Very Wicked. Berkley, 1960
  Whom Gods Destroy. GM, 1953; Red Seal, 1958

ADAMS, ELIHU
  Operation Homicide. Mill, 1947

ADAMS, EUSTACE L(ANE). 1891-   .
  Death Charter. Coward, 1943; Crowther, 1945
  Gambler's Throw. Dial, 1930; Hamilton, 1931
  Murder in the Hurricane. Methuen, 1938

ADAMS, FRANCIS (WILLIAM LAUDERDALE). 1862-1893.
  John Webb's End; see Strong as Death
  Madeline Brown's Murderer. Kemp, 1887
  Strong as Death. Also published as: John Webb's End. Remington, 1891

ADAMS, FRANK R(AMSAY). 1883-1963.
  For Valour. Paul, 1933
  Help Yourself to Happiness. Macaulay, 1929; Newnes, 1929
  King's Crew. Long & Smith, 1932; Constable, 1932
  The Long Night. Paul, 1932
  -Men on Foot. Newnes, 1937
  -Pleasure Island. Paul, 1935
  -The Secret Attic. Paul, 1930

ADAMS, FREDERICK UPHAM. 1859-1921.
  The Bottom of the Well. Dillingham, 1906; Unwin, 1906
  The Kidnapped Millionaires. Lothrop, 1901; Kelly, 1901

ADAMS, GERALD. See: CORTLAND FITZSIMMONS, 1893-1949.

ADAMS, HERBERT. 1874-1958. Pseudonym: Jonathan Gray, q.v. Series characters: Roger Bennion = RB; Jimmie Haswell = JH.
  The Araway Oath. Collins, 1942 RB
  Black Death. Collins, 1939 RB
  The Bluff. Collins, 1938 RB
  The Body in the Bunker. Collins, 1935; Lippincott, 1935
  By Order of the Five. Methuen, 1925
  Caroline Ormesby's Crime. Methuen, 1929; Lippincott, 1929
  The Case of the Stolen Bridegroom. Collins, 1940 RB
  The Chief Witness. Collins, 1940 RB
  Comrade Jill. Methuen, 1926; Lippincott, 1927
  The Crime in the Dutch Garden. Methuen, 1931; Lippincott, 1930 JH
  Crime Wave at Little Cornford. Macdonald, 1948 RB
  The Crooked Lip. Methuen, 1926; Lippincott, 1926 JH
  The Damned Spot. Collins, 1938 RB?
  The Dean's Daughters. Macdonald, 1950 RB
  Death of a Viewer. Macdonald, 1958 RB
  Death Off the Fairway. Collins, 1936 RB
  Death on the First Tee. Macdonald, 1957 RB
  Diamonds are Trumps. Macdonald, 1947 RB
  The Empty Bed. Methuen, 1928; Lippincott, 1928 JH
  Exit the Skeleton. Macdonald, 1952 RB
  Fate Laughs. Collins, 1935; Lippincott, 1935
  Four Winds. Collins, 1944 RB
  The Golden Ape. Methuen, 1930; Lippincott, 1930 JH
  The Golf House Murder; see John Brand's Will
  John Brand's Will. Methuen, 1933. U.S. title: The Golf House Murder. Lippincott, 1933
  The Judas Kiss. Macdonald, 1955 RB
  The Knife. Collins, 1934. U.S. title: The Strange Murder of Hatton, K.C. Lippincott, 1933
  -A Lady So Innocent. Methuen, 1932
  Murder Without Risk; see A Word of Six Letters
  Mystery and Minette. Collins, 1934; Lippincott, 1934
  The Nineteenth Hole Mystery. Collins, 1939 RB
  Oddways. Methuen, 1930; Lippincott, 1929
  The Old Jew Mystery. Collins, 1936 RB
  One to Play. Macdonald, 1949 RB
  The Paulton Plot. Methuen, 1932; Lippincott, 1931 JH
  The Perfect Round. Methuen, 1927 ss, some criminous
  The Queen's Gate Mystery. Methuen, 1927; Lippincott, 1927 JH
  -Queen's Mate. Methuen, 1931; Lippincott, 1931
  Roger Bennion's Double. Collins, 1941 RB
  Rogues Fall Out. Methuen, 1928; Lippincott, 1928 JH
  -The Scarlet Feather. Cherry Tree, 1943
  The Secret of Bogey House. Methuen, 1924; Lippincott, 1925 JH
  Signal for Invasion. Collins, 1942 RB
  A Single Hair. Collins, 1937 RB
  The Sleeping Draught. Macdonald, 1951 RB
  Slippery Dick. Macdonald, 1954 RB
  The Sloan Square Mystery. Methuen, 1925; Dial, 1926
  The Spectre in Brown. Macdonald, 1953 RB
  Stab in the Back. Collins, 1941 RB
  The Strange Murder of Hatton, K.C.; see The Knife
  Victory Song. Collins, 1943 RB
  Welcome Home! Macdonald, 1946 RB
  The Woman in Black. Methuen, 1933; Lippincott, 1932 JH
  A Word of Six Letters. Collins, 1936. U.S. title: Murder Without Risk. Lippincott, 1936
  The Writing on the Wall. Collins, 1945 RB

ADAMS, J. T.
  Mountain Murder. Pan, 1945

ADAMS, JOEY. 1911-   .
  You Could Die Laughing, and The Swingers. Bobbs, 1968

ADAMS, JOHN F(ESTUS). 1930-   .
  Two Plus Two Equals Minus Seven. Macmillan, 1969; Joseph, 1969

ADAMS, LETA ZOE. 1902-   .
  The Mirror Murder. Phoenix, 1937

ADAMS, NATHAN M(ILLER). 1934-   .
  The Fifth Horseman. Random, 1967; Macmillan (London), 1968

ADAMS, O. S. Pseudonym: Old Hutch, q.v.

ADAMS, REX
  The Star of Persia. Harrap, 1942

ADAMS, ROBERT JAMES. Pseudonym: Paul MacTyre, q.v.

ADAMS, SAMUEL HOPKINS. 1871-1958. See also: STEWART EDWARD WHITE, 1873-1946.
  Average Jones. Bobbs, 1911; Palmer, 1913 ss
  The Flying Death. McClure, 1908
  The Secret of Lonesome Cove. Bobbs, 1912; Hodder, 1913

ADAMS, SHIPLEY. Series character: Inspector Harrow, in at least those marked H.
  Money by Menaces. Fiction House, 1948
  Murder in the First Person. Boardman, 1948 H
  Murder Unsolved. Boardman, 1947
  Murder Well Begun. Boardman, 1950 H

ADAMS, WILLIAM T(AYLOR). 1822-1897. Pseudonym: Warren J. Ashton, q.v.
  Living Too Fast; or, The Confessions of a Bank Officer. Lee, 1876
  Three Millions! or, The Way of the World; see The Way of the World
  -The Way of the World. Lee, 1867. Also published as: Three Millions! or, The Way of the World. Lee, 1891

ADDEO, EDMOND G. See: RICHARD M(cCLELLAN) GARVIN, 1934-   .

ADDIS, ERIC ELRINGTON. Pseudonym: Peter Drax, q.v.

ADDIS, HUGH
  Dark Voyage. Dodd, 1944; Jarrolds, 1947
  Night Over the Wood. Dodd, 1943; Jarrolds, 1944

ADDISCOMBE, JOHN. Pseudonym of (Alfred) John Hunter, 1891-1961, q.v. Other pseudonyms: L. H. Brenning, Anthony Dax, Anthony Drummond, Peter Meriton, qq.v.
  Drums of Death. Hurst, 1929
  Fighting Blood. Mowl, 1935
  Marked Cards. Gramol, 1935
  The Secret of the Graveyard. Gramol, 1937
  The Silk Scarf Murders. Gramol, 1937
  The Speed King. Gramol, 1935
  The Triangle of the Grey Wolf. Gramol, 1937

ADDISON, GWEN. Joint pseudonym of Alfred Harris, 1928-   , q.v., and Arthur Moore, q.v. For Arthur Moore, see also: Don Hoyt. Joint pseudonyms of Arthur Moore and Marilyn Granbeck: Adam Hamilton, Van Saxon, qq.v.
  Storm over Fox Hill. PB, 1974

ADDISON, H(ENRY) R(OBERT). 1805?-1876.
  Behind the Curtain. Maxwell, 1865
  Diary of a Judge, Being Trials of Life Compiled from the Note-Book of a Recently Deceased Judge. Ward, 1860 ss
  Recollections of an Irish Police Magistrate and Other Reminiscences of the South of Ireland. Ward, 1862 ss

ADE, GEORGE. 1866-1944.
  Bang! Bang! Sears, 1928 ss

ADEE, DAVID GRAHAM
  The Blue Scarab. Laird, 1892. Also published as: The Lost Diamond. Laird, 1899
  The Lost Diamond; see The Blue Scarab
  No. 19 State Street. Cassell, 1888

ADKINS, CLEO
  The Case of the Ebony Queen. Arcadia, 1955

ADLEMAN, ROBERT H. 1919-   .
  Annie Deane. World, 1971
  The Bloody Benders. Stein, 1970; Joseph, 1971

ADSIT, BYRON D.
  A Mystery of the Fast Mail. Lovell, 1890
  The P.O. Detective; see Uncle Sam's Bad Boys
  Uncle Sam's Bad Boys; or, Leaves from a Diary of a Post-Office Inspector. Eagle, 1888. Also published as: The P.O. Detective. Eagle, 1891

ADYE, MAJOR GENERAL SIR JOHN. 1857-1930. Pseudonym: John Daye, q.v.
  At the House of the Priest. Jenkins, 1925
  A Flash of Lightning. Methuen, 1927
  The Golden Scarab. Jenkins, 1926

AEBY, JACQUELYN
  Linnet's Folly. Dell, 1973

AESCULAPIUS. Pseudonym.
  The Magnetism of Sin. Greening, 1901

AFFORD, MAX. 1906-   . Series character: Jeffery Blackburn, in all novels.
  Blood on His Hands! Long, 1936
  The Dead are Blind. Long, 1937
  Death's Mannikins. Long, 1937; Appleton, 1937
  Fly by Night. Long, 1942. Also published as: The Owl of Darkness. Angus, 1942
  Lady in Danger. Mulga (Sydney), 1944; with Alexander Kirkland and some variations in text: French, 1946. (3-act play.)
  The Owl of Darkness; see Fly by Night

AFGHAN. Pseudonym. Series character: Asaf Khan, in both titles.
  -Exploits of Asaf Khan. Jenkins, 1922 ss
  -The Wanderings of Asaf. Jenkins, 1923

AFTEREM, GEORGE. Pseudonym of Harold Williams, 1853-   .
  Silken Threads. Cupples, 1885

AGNIEL, LUCIEN D. 1919-   .
  Code Name "Icy". Paperback Library, 1970
  Pressure Point. Paperback Library, 1970

AIDE, (CHARLES) HAMILTON. 1826-1906.
  The Cliff Mystery. Arrowsmith, 1888
  Morals and Mysteries. Smith, Elder, 1872 ss

AIKEN, ALBERT W. 1846-1894. Series character: Joe Phoenix = JP.
  Chin Chin, the Chinese Detective; or, The Dark Work of the Black Hands. Westbrook, 1927
  Joe Phoenix, the Police Spy. Westbrook, 1927 JP
  Joe Phoenix, Private Detective; or, The League of the Skeleton Keys. Westbrook, 1927 JP
  The Wolves of New York; or, The King of Detectives. Westbrook, 1927

AIKEN, EDNAH
  -Love and I. Dodd, 1928

AIKEN, GEORGE L. 1830-1876.
  -The Household Skeleton. American News, 1865

AIKEN, JOAN (DELANO). 1924-   .
  Beware of the Bouquet; see The Trouble with Product X
  The Butterfly Picnic. Gollancz, 1972. U.S. title: A Cluster of Separate Sparks. Doubleday, 1972
  A Cluster of Separate Sparks; see The Butterfly Picnic
  The Crystal Crow; see The Ribs of Death
  Dark Interval; see Hate Begins at Home
  Died on a Rainy Sunday. Gollancz, 1972; Holt, 1972
  The Embroidered Sunset. Gollancz, 1970; Doubleday, 1970
  The Fortune Hunters. Cape, 1965; Doubleday, 1965
  The Green Flash and other tales of horror, suspense and fantasy; see The Windscreen Weepers and other stories of horror and suspense
  Hate Begins at Home. Gollancz, 1967. U.S. title: Dark Interval. Doubleday, 1967
  The Ribs of Death. Gollancz, 1967. U.S. title: The Crystal Crow. Doubleday, 1968
  The Silence of Herondale. Gollancz, 1965; Doubleday, 1964
  The Trouble with Product X. Gollancz, 1966. U.S. title: Beware of the Bouquet. Doubleday, 1966
  The Windscreen Weepers and other stories of horror and suspense. Gollancz, 1969. U.S. title: The Green Flash and other tales of horror, suspense and fantasy. Holt, 1971 ss

AIKEN, JOHN. 1913-   .
  The Lid Off. Hale, 1969
  Nightly Deadshade. Macmillan (London), 1971

AIKEN, RALPH
  The Ghost Hunters. McBride, 1934

AINSWORTH, CYRUS
  The Disappearance of Nicholson. Ouseley, 1908

AINSWORTH, ED(WARD MADDIN). 1902-1968.
  Death Cues the Pageant. Arcadia, 1954

AINSWORTH, HARRIET. Pseudonym of (Violet) Elizabeth Cadell, 1903-   , q.v.
  Consider the Lilies. Hodder, 1955
  Death Among Friends. Hodder, 1964
  Shadow on the Water. Hodder, 1958. U.S. title: Shadows on the Water, as by Elizabeth Cadell. Morrow, 1958

AINSWORTH, MILO. Pseudonym of Peter Fison.
  Murder is Catching. Hammond, 1959

AINSWORTH, PATRICIA
  The Devil's Hole. Hale, 1971

AINSWORTH, W(ILLIAM) HARRISON. 1805-1882.
  Jack Sheppard. Bentley, 1839; Colyer, 1839. Also published as: King of Crooks. Collins, 1930

AIRD, CATHERINE. Pseudonym of Kinn Hamilton McIntosh, 1930-   . Series character: Inspector Sloan = S.
  The Complete Steel. Macdonald, 1969. U.S. title: The Stately Home Murder. Doubleday, 1970 S
  Henrietta Who? Macdonald, 1968; Doubleday, 1968 S
  His Burial Too. Collins, 1973; Doubleday, 1973 S
  A Late Phoenix. Collins, 1970; Doubleday, 1971 S
  A Most Contagious Game. Macdonald, 1967; Doubleday, 1967
  The Religious Body. Macdonald, 1966; Doubleday, 1966 S
  Slight Mourning. Collins, 1975; Doubleday, 1976 S

AIRTH, RENNIE. 1935-   .
  Snatch. Simon, 1969; Cape, 1969

AITKEN, ROBERT. 1872-   . Pseudonym: Hudson Douglas, q.v.
  -Beyond the Skyline. Murray, 1909 ss
  The Golden Horseshoe. Greening, 1908; McBride, 1907
  -A Maid of Honour. Greening, 1908
  -The Redding Straik. Morton, 1905

AIX. Pseudonym of Frederick Bausman, 1861-1931.
  Adventures of a Nice Young Man. Duffield, 1908; Richards, 1909
  Thieves. Duffield, 1911; Palmer, 1912

ALAIS, E(RNEST) W. 1864-1922. All titles were published by Amalgamated Press and feature Sexton Blake.
  Camouflage! 1918
  A Case of Blackmail. 1917
  The Doctor's Double. 1921
  In the Shadow of Night. 1922
  The Lease of Convict 308. 1916

ALAN, A. J. Pseudonym of Leslie Harrison Lambert,   -1940.
  A. J. Alan's Second Book. Hutchinson, 1933 ss, some criminous

ALAN, MARJORIE. Pseudonym of Doris Marjorie Bumpus, 1905-   , q.v.
  Dark Legacy. Hale, 1953
  Dark Prophecy; see Masked Murder
  The Ivory Locket. Hale, 1951
  Masked Murder. Hale, 1945. U.S. title: Dark Prophecy. Mill, 1945
  Murder at Puck's Cottage. Hale, 1951
  Murder in a Maze. Hale, 1955
  Murder in November. Hale, 1946. U.S. title: Rue the Day. Mill, 1946
  Murder Looks Back. Hale, 1955
  Murder Next Door. Hale, 1950
  Rue the Day; see Murder in November

ALAN, RAY. Pseudonym of Joseph Lawrence Valls-Russell.
  My Bonny Lies Under the Sea. Joseph, 1963

ALBERT, ANDREW I. Series character: Paul Decker, in both titles.
  The Maori Murder Case. Vulcan, 1944
  Murder for a Hollow Shell. Vulcan, 1945

ALBERT, EDWARD. 1890-   .
  As Good as a Mile. Nicholson, 1934

ALBERT, MARVIN (H.). Pseudonyms: Nick Quarry, Anthony Rome, qq.v.
  The Gargoyle Conspiracy. Doubleday, 1975; Deutsch, 1975
  Party Girl. GM, 1958; Fawcett (London), 1959. (Novelization of the movie.)
  The Pink Panther. Bantam, 1964. (Novelization of the movie.)

ALBRAND, MARTHA. Pseudonym of Heidi Huberta Freybe Loewengard, 1914-   .
  After Midnight. Random, 1949; Chatto, 1949
  A Call from Austria. Random, 1963; Hodder, 1963
  A Day in Monte Carlo. Random, 1959; Hodder, 1959
  Desperate Moment. Random, 1951; Chatto, 1951
  A Door Fell Shut. NAL, 1966; Hodder, 1966
  Endure No Longer. Little, 1944; Chatto, 1945
  The Hunted Woman. Random, 1952; Hodder, 1953
  The Linden Affair. Random, 1956. British title: The Story That Could Not Be Told. Hodder, 1956
  Manhattan North. Coward, 1971; Hodder, 1972
  The Mask of Alexander. Random, 1955; Hodder, 1956
  Meet Me Tonight. Random, 1960; Hodder, 1961. Also published as: Return to Terror. Ace, 1964
  Nightmare in Copenhagen. Random, 1954; Hodder, 1954
  No Surrender. Little, 1942; Chatto, 1943
  None Shall Know. Little, 1945; Chatto, 1946
  Remembered Anger. Little, 1946
  Return to Terror; see Meet Me Tonight
  Rhine Replica. Random, 1969; Hodder, 1970
  The Story That Could Not Be Told; see The Linden Affair
  Wait for the Dawn. Random, 1950; Chatto, 1950
  Whispering Hill. Random, 1947; Chatto, 1948
  Without Orders. Little, 1943; Chatto, 1944
  Zurich/AZ 900. Holt, 1974; Hodder, 1975

ALCANTER DE BRAHM, JEANNE ICHORD. 1890-   . Pseudonym: Jean Rosmer, q.v.

ALCOTT, LOUISA MAY. 1832-1888.
  Behind a Mask: The Unknown Thrillers of Louisa May Alcott. Morrow, 1975; Allen, 1976 (4 novelets.)

ALDANOV, MARK. Pseudonym of Mark Aleksandrovich Landau, 1886-1957.
  -The Escape. Scribner, 1950; Cape, 1952
  The Fifth Seal. Scribner, 1943; Cape, 1945. (Translation of Nachalo Kontsa. Paris, 1939.)
  The Key. Harrap, 1931
  Nightmare and Dawn. Duell, 1957
  -The Scoundrel. Barker, 1960

ALDEN, WINTHROP. Pseudonym.
  The Lost Million. Dodd, 1913

ALDERSON, A. J.
  The Harding Mystery. Falcon, 1949

ALDERSON, ALEXANDER
  The Subtle Minotaur. Gifford, 1954

ALDERSON, ALFRED JAMES
  The Crime of Wilfred Hanson. Stockwell, 1942

ALDHOUSE, ERIC
  The Crime at the Quay Inn. Allan, 1934

ALDING, PETER. Pseudonym of Roderic (Graeme) Jeffries, 1926-   , q.v. Other pseudonyms: Jeffrey Ashford, Roderic Graeme, Graham Hastings, qq.v. Series characters: Constable Kerr and Inspector Fusil, in all titles.
  All Leads Negative; see The C.I.D. Room
  Call Back to Crime. Long, 1972
  The C.I.D. Room. Long, 1967. U.S. title: All Leads Negative. Harper, 1967
  Circle of Danger. Long, 1968
  Despite the Evidence. Long, 1971; Saturday Review Press, 1972
  Field of Fire. Long, 1973
  Guilt Without Proof. Long, 1970; McCall, 1971
  Murder Among Thieves. Long, 1969; McCall, 1970
  The Murder Line. Long, 1974
  Six Days to Death. Long, 1975

ALDIS, DOROTHY (KEELEY). 1896-1966.
  Murder in a Haystack. Farrar, 1931; Cassell, 1931

ALDOUS, ALLAN
  Danger on the Map. Cheshire (Melbourne), 1947
  It's Murder If You Say So! Skeffington, 1952
  The Lady's Eyes were Green. Skeffington, 1951

ALDRICH, EARL AUGUSTUS. 1886-   . Pseudonym: A. B. Leonard, q.v.

ALDRICH, THOMAS BAILEY. 1836-1907.
  Marjorie Daw and Other People. Osgood, 1873; Routledge, 1873. Also published as (with altered contents): Marjorie Daw and other stories. Houghton, 1885; Douglas, 1894. And as (with differently altered contents): Marjorie Daw and other tales. Tauchnitz, 1879 ss
  Marjorie Daw and other stories; see Marjorie Daw and Other People
  Marjorie Daw and other tales; see Marjorie Daw and Other People
  Out of His Head. Carleton, 1862
  The Stillwater Tragedy. Houghton, 1880; Douglas, 1886

ALDRIDGE, (HAROLD EDWARD) JAMES. 1918-   . Series characters: Kit Quayle = KQ; Rupert Royce = RR.
  -A Captive in the Land. H. Hamilton, 1962; Doubleday, 1963 RR
  -The Diplomat. Bodley Head, 1949; Little, 1950
  -Mockery in Arms. Joseph, 1974; Little, 1974
  -A Sporting Proposition. Joseph, 1973; Little, 1973 KQ
  -The Statesman's Game. H. Hamilton, 1966; Doubleday, 1966 RR
  -The Untouchable Juli. Joseph, 1975; Little, 1976 KQ

ALEXANDER, MRS. Pseudonym of Annie French Hector, 1825-1902.
  -At Bay. Warne, 1885; Holt, 1885
  -A Choice of Evils. White, 1894
  The Crumpled Leaf. Drane, 1911
  -A False Scent. White, 1889; Lovell, 1889
  The Yellow Fiend. Unwin, 1901; Dodd, 1901

ALEXANDER, COLIN JAMES. 1920-   . Pseudonym: Simon Jay, q.v.

ALEXANDER, DAIR
Penelope's Daughter. Hale, 1975

ALEXANDER, DAVID. 1907-1973. Series characters: Bart Hardin = BH; Marty Land = ML; Tommy Twotoes = TT.
Bloodstain. Lippincott, 1961; Boardman, 1962 ML
The Corpse in My Bed; see Most Men Don't Kill
Dead, Man, Dead. Lippincott, 1959; Boardman, 1960 BH
The Death of Daddy-O. Lippincott, 1960; Boardman, 1960 ML
The Death of Humpty-Dumpty. Random, 1957; Boardman, 1959 BH
Die, Little Goose. Random, 1956; Boardman, 1957 BH
Hangman's Dozen. Roy, 1961; Boardman, 1961 ss
Hush-a-Bye Murder. Random, 1957; Boardman, 1958 BH
The Madhouse in Washington Square. Lippincott, 1958; Boardman, 1959
Most Men Don't Kill. Random, 1951; Hammond, 1953. Also published as: The Corpse in My Bed. Ace, 1954 TT
Murder in Black and White. Random, 1951; Hammond, 1954 TT
The Murder of Whistler's Brother. Random, 1956; Boardman, 1958 BH
Murder Points a Finger. Random, 1953; Boardman, 1955
Paint the Town Black. Random, 1954; Boardman, 1957 BH
Pennies from Hell. Lippincott, 1960; Boardman, 1961
Shoot a Sitting Duck. Random, 1955; Boardman, 1957 BH
Terror on Broadway. Random, 1954; Boardman, 1956 BH

ALEXANDER, GRACE
Prince Cinderella. Bobbs, 1921

ALEXANDER, HOLMES (ROSS). 1906- .
Shall Do No Murder. Regnery, 1959; Hammond, 1960

ALEXANDER, IAN
The Disappearance of Archibald Forsyth. Hutchinson, 1933

ALEXANDER, IRENE
Crooked Alley. Penn, 1933
Ninth Week. Penn, 1935
Revenge Can Wait. Putnam, 1941
Villa Caprice. Penn, 1932

ALEXANDER, JAN
The Bishop's Palace. Popular Library, 1972
Blood Moon. Lancer, 1970
Blood Ruby. Ballantine, 1975
Darkwater. PB, 1975
The Girl Who Never Was. Lancer, 1972
Glass House. Popular Library, 1971
The Glass Painting. Popular Library, 1972
The Haunting of Helen Wren. PB, 1975
The House at Rose Point. Avon, 1972
House of Fools. Lancer, 1971
The Jade Figurines. Curtis, 1973
Moon Garden. Popular Library, 1972
Second House. Beagle, 1972
Shadows. Lancer, 1970
White Jade. Popular Library, 1971
Wolves of Craywood. Lancer, 1970

ALEXANDER, JOAN
One Sunny Day. Coward, 1974; Heinemann, 1974

ALEXANDER, JOHN. Pseudonym of John Alexander Vlasto, 1877-1958. Other pseudonym: John Remenham, q.v.
The House of Shayle. Low, 1933
Murder at the Eclipse. Low, 1934

ALEXANDER, MARTIN
Death is Too Good for You. Hale, 1969
A Dream Before Dying. Hale, 1970

ALEXANDER, ROBERT WILLIAM. 1905- .
Pseudonym: Joan Butler, q.v.

ALEXANDER, ROSS
The Mask of Fear. Blackfriars, 1948

ALEXANDER, RUTH. Pseudonym of Ruth Rogers, 1890- .
Blackmail. Readers Library, 1929. (Novelization of the play by Charles Bennett.)
The Ghost Train. Arrowsmith, 1927; Small, 1926. (Novelization of the play by Arnold Ridley, 1896- , q.v.)
The Man Who Knew Too Much. Arrowsmith, 1936. (Novelization of the movie.)
Rome Express. Readers Library, 1932. (Novelization of the movie.)
The Wrecker. Selwyn, 1928. (Novelization of the play by Arnold Ridley, 1896- , q.v., and Bernard Merivale, 1882-1939.)

ALGER, HORATIO, JR. 1832-1899.
Dan, the Detective. Carleton, 1884
Dean Dunham; or, The Waterford Mystery. U.S. Book Co., 1891
$500; or, Jacob Marlowe's Secret. U.S. Book Co., 1890

ALGIE, JAMES. Pseudonym: Wallace Lloyd, q.v.

ALINGTON, ADRIAN (RICHARD). 1895- .
The Amazing Test Match Crime. Chatto, 1939
The Vanishing Celebrities. Chatto, 1938

ALINGTON, CYRIL A(RGENTINE). 1872-1955.
Pseudonym: S. C. Westerham, q.v. Series characters: John Craggs and James Castleton, in at least those marked C&C; Mr. Birtley, in at least those marked B.
The Abbot's Cup. Jenkins, 1930
Archdeacons Afloat. Faber, 1946 C&C, B
Archdeacons Ashore. Faber, 1947 C&C
Blackmail in Blankshire. Faber, 1949 C&C
The Count in Kensington. Jenkins, 1926
Crime on the Kennet. Collins, 1939
Gold and Gaiters. Faber, 1950 C&C, B
Midnight Wireless. Macdonald, 1947 B
Mr. Evans: A Cricketo-Detective Story. Macmillan (London), 1922
The Nabob's Jewel. Faber, 1953
Ten Crowded Hours. Macdonald, 1944

ALLAIN, MARCEL. 1885- . Series character: Fantomas, in all titles (a continuation of the series begun by Pierre Souvestre, 1874-1914, q.v., in collaboration with Allain).
Bulldog and Rats. Paul, 1928
Fantomas Captured. Paul, 1926; McKay, 1926
Juve in the Dock. Paul, 1925; McKay, 1926
The Lord of Terror. Paul, 1925; McKay, 1925
The Revenge of Fantomas. Paul, 1927; McKay, 1927
The Yellow Document; or, "Fantomas of Berlin." Paul, 1920; Brentano's, 1919

ALLAN, A. W.
-Devil's Drive: A Tale of Four Bad'uns. Dodd, Eyton, 1910

ALLAN, DENNIS. Pseudonym of Elinore Denniston, 1900- . Other pseudonym: Rae Foley, q.v.
Born to be Murdered. Mill, 1945; Hammond, 1952
Brandon is Missing. Mill, 1940; Hamilton, 1938
The Case of the Headless Corpse. Mill, 1945
Dead to Rights. Mill, 1946; Hammond, 1953
House of Treason. Greystone, 1936

ALLAN, FRANCIS (K.)
First Come, First Kill. Reynal, 1945; Boardman, 1947
The Invisible Bridge. Reynal, 1947

ALLAN, HENRY
The Tragic Case of John Renold. Dorrance, 1935

ALLAN, LUKE. Pseudonym of William Lacey Amy. Series characters: Gordon Muldrew, in at least those marked GM; Blue Pete (who appears in at least 20 volumes, of which most appear to be westerns without sufficient detective content to be included here) = BP.
Behind the Wire Fence. Arrowsmith, 1935 GM
Beyond the Locked Door. Jenkins, 1938
The Black Opal. Arrowsmith, 1935
Blue Pete. Jenkins, 1938 BP
Blue Pete: Detective. Jenkins, 1928 BP
The Blue Wolf. Jenkins, 1921
The Case of the Open Drawer. Arrowsmith, 1936
The Dark Spot. Arrowsmith, 1932
The End of the Trail. Arrowsmith, 1931 GM
Five for One. Arrowsmith, 1934
The Fourth Dagger. Arrowsmith, 1932
The Ghost Murder. Arrowsmith, 1937
The Jungle Crime. Arrowsmith, 1931 GM
The Man on the Twenty-Fourth Floor. Jenkins, 1937
The Many-Coloured Thread. Jenkins, 1932
The Masked Stranger. Arrowsmith, 1930 GM
Murder at Midnight. Arrowsmith, 1930
Murder at the Club. Arrowsmith, 1933 GM
Scotland Yard Takes a Holiday. Arrowsmith, 1934
The Traitor. Arrowsmith, 1933
The Vengeance of Blue Pete. Jenkins, 1939 BP

ALLAN, MABEL ESTHER. 1915- .
Murder at the Flood. Paul, 1957

ALLARDYCE, PAULA. Pseudonym of Ursula Torday. Other pseudonyms: Charity Blackstock, q.v., Lee Blackstock.
-Adam and Evelina. Ward, 1956
-Adam's Rib. Hodder, 1963
-After the Lady. Ward, 1954
-Beloved Enemy. Ward, 1958
-Death, My Lover. Ward, 1959
-The Doctor's Daughter. Ward, 1955
-A Game of Hazard. Ward, 1955
-The Gentle Highwayman. Ward, 1961
The Ghost of Archie Gilroy. Hodder, 1970
-Johnny Danger. Ward, 1960
-The Lady and the Pirate. Ward, 1957
-The Man of Wrath. Ward, 1956
-A Marriage has been Arranged. Ward, 1959
-My Dear Miss Emma. Ward, 1958
-The Respectable Miss Parkington-Smith. Hodder, 1964
-Southarn Folly. Ward, 1957
Witches' Sabbath. Hodder, 1961; Macmillan, 1962

A

ALLBEURY, TED [THEODORE EDWARD LE BOU-
THILLIER ALLBEURY]. 1917-   .
A Choice of Enemies. Davies, 1973; St.
Martin's, 1973
Omega-Minus; see Palomino Blonde
Palomino Blonde. Davies, 1975. U.S.
title: Omega-Minus. Viking, 1975
Snowball. Davies, 1974; Lippincott,
1974
The Special Collection. Davies, 1975

ALLEN, ADDISON J.
New England Gothic. Chilton, 1960. Also
published as: Thunder Over South
Parish. Dell, 1964

ALLEN, AUSTEN. 1887-   . Series charac-
ter: Inspector Ord, in all titles.
The Dead Mouse. Bles, 1930
Live Wire. Bles, 1931
The Loose Rib. Bles, 1932; Kinsey, 1933
Menace to Mrs. Kershaw. Bles, 1929;
Harper, 1930

ALLEN, A. WHATOFF
Exit an Admiral. Low, 1938

ALLEN, ARTHUR BRUCE. 1903-1975. Pseudonym: Borough Trice, q.v.

ALLEN, CLIFFORD (EDWARD). 1902-   .
The Dark Places. Redman, 1958

ALLEN, E. C. Pseudonym of Elizabeth C.
Ward, 1936-   .
The Laguna Contracts. Pyramid, 1973

ALLEN, ELISABETH OFFUTT. 1895-   .
The Hounds of the Moon. Popular Li-
brary, 1974
This Tangled Web. Bouregy, 1966

ALLEN, ERIC. Pseudonym of Eric Allen-
Ballard.
Canaries Also Sing. Hammond, 1960
Death on Delivery. Hammond, 1958
Eric Allen's Broadcast Stories. Cowan,
1947 ss, some criminous
The Man Who Chose Death. Hammond, 1959
Passport to Murder; see Perilous Pass-
port
Perilous Passport. Hammond, 1958. Also
published as: Passport to Murder.
Corgi, 1959

ALLEN, ERIC VAUGHN. Pseudonym: Erika
Vaughan Allen, q.v.

ALLEN, ERIKA VAUGHAN. Pseudonym of Eric
Vaughn Allen.
Voices in the Wind. Signet, 1967

ALLEN, F.
The Whitechapel Murder. Ogilvie

ALLEN, GERTRUDE M.
House of Dark Secrets. Rich, 1934
Nightshade. Rich, 1934; Macaulay, 1935

ALLEN, (CHARLES) GRANT (BLAIRFINDIE).
1848-1899.
An African Millionaire. Richards, 1897;
Arnold, 1897 ss
-An Army Doctor's Romance. Tuck (Lon-
don), 1894; Tuck (New York), 1893
-At Market Value. Chatto, 1894; Neely,
1894
-Babylon. Chatto, 1885; Appleton, 1885
-The Backslider. Lewis Scribner (London
& New York), 1901 ss
The Beckoning Hand and other stories.
Chatto, 1887 ss
-Blood Royal. Chatto, 1893; Cassell (New
York), 1892
A Bride from the Desert. Fenno, 1896
(3 stories, one or two criminous.)
The Cruise of the Albatross; see Wed-
nesday the Tenth
-Desire of the Eyes and other stories.
Digby, 1895; Fenno, 1895 ss
The Devil's Die. Chatto, 1888; Lovell,
1888
-The Duchess of Powysland. Chatto, 1892;
U.S. Book Co., 1891
-Dr. Palliser's Patient. Mullen, 1889
-Dumaresq's Daughter. Chatto, 1891; Har-
per, 1891
-For Maimie's Sake: A Tale of Love and
Dynamite. Chatto, 1886; Appleton,
1886
-The General's Will. Butterworth, 1892
ss
-The Great Taboo. Chatto, 1890; Harper,
1891
Hilda Wade. Richards, 1900; Harper,
1900 ss
-In All Shades. Chatto, 1886; Rand, 18??
-The Incidental Bishop. Pearson, 1898;
Appleton, 1898
The Indian Mystery; or, Kalee's Shrine;
see Kalee's Shrine
Ivan Greet's Masterpiece. Chatto, 1893
ss
The Jaws of Death. Simpkin Marshall,
1889; New Amsterdam, 1896
Kalee's Shrine, with May Cotes. Arrow-
smith, 1886; New Amsterdam, 1897.
Also published as: The Indian Mys-
tery; or, Kalee's Shrine. New Amster-
dam, 1902
-Linnet. Richards, 1898; New Amsterdam,
1900
Michael's Crag. Leadenhall, 1893; Rand,
1893
Miss Cayley's Adventures. Richards,
1899; Putnam, 1899 ss
Recalled to Life. Arrowsmith, 1891;
Holt, 1891
The Reluctant Hangman and other stories
of crime. Aspen Press, 1975 ss
The Scallywag. Chatto, 1893; Cassell
(New York), 1893
Sir Theodore's Guest and other stories.
Arrowsmith, 1902 ss
A Splendid Sin. White, 1896; Buckles,
1899
-Strange Stories. Chatto, 1894 ss
-The Tents of Shem. Chatto, 1889; Rand,
1889
A Terrible Inheritance. SPCK, 1887;
Crowell, 18??
This Mortal Coil. Chatto, 1888; Apple-
ton, 1889
Twelve Tales. Richards, 1899 ss
Under Sealed Orders. Chatto, 1895;
Collier, 1894
-Wednesday the Tenth. Lothrop, 1890.
Also published as: The Cruise of the
Albatross. Lothrop, 1898. (British
title?)
What's Bred in the Bone. Tit-Bits,
1891; Tucker, 1891

ALLEN, LESLIE. Pseudonym of Horace Brown,
1908-   , q.v.
Murder in the Rough. Five Star, 1946;
Boardman, 1948, as by Horace Brown

ALLEN, LUCY DOREEN
Innocent Murder. Stockwell, 1953

ALLEN, MARCUS. See: ANNE FULLER.

ALLEN, ROBERT. Pseudonym of Allen Robert
Dodd, 1887-   .
Captain Gardiner of the International
Police. Dodd, 1916; Hodder, 1917

ALLEN, TREVOR
Jade Elephants. Bles, 1934

ALLEN, (HERBERT) WARNER. 1881-   . See
also: E(DMUND) C(LERIHEW) BENTLEY,
1875-1956.
Death Fungus. Constable, 1937
The Devil That Slumbers. Hamilton, 1925
Mr. Clerihew: Wine Merchant. Methuen,
1933
The Uncounted Hour. Constable, 1936

ALLEN, WILL
Contraband Cruises. Heritage, 1935

ALLEN, WILLIS BOYD. 1855-1938.
The Head of Pasht. Dutton, 1900

ALLEN-BALLARD, ERIC. Pseudonym: Eric
Allen, q.v.

ALLERTON, BERRIDGE
Who Killed Roger Whitely? Georgian
House, 1946

ALLERTON, MARK. Pseudonym of William
Ernest Cameron, 1881-   .
The Case of Richard Eden. Hodder, 1918
-False Witness. Thomson, 1921
-The Girl in the Web. Thomson, 1927
Let Justice Be Done. Hurst, 1912
The Maitland Street Murder. Skeffing-
ton, 1919
The Mill. Skeffington, 1919
The Mystery of Beaton Craig. Skeffing-
ton, 1919
-The Woman in the Case. Thomson, 1924

ALLERTON, MARY. Pseudonym of (Mary)
Christine Noble Govan, 1898-   ,
q.v. Other pseudonym: J. N. Darby,
q.v.
The Shadow and the Web. Bobbs, 1940;
Hale, 1942

ALLINGHAM, MARGERY (LOUISE). 1904-1966.
Series character: Albert Campion =
AC (continued by Youngman Carter,
1904-1970, q.v.).
The Allingham Case-Book. Chatto, 1969;
Morrow, 1969 ss, some about AC
The Allingham Minibus. Chatto, 1973;
Morrow, 1973 ss, some about AC
The Beckoning Lady. Chatto, 1955. U.S.
title: The Estate of the Beckoning
Lady. Doubleday, 1955 AC
The Black Dudley Murder; see The Crime
at Black Dudley
Black Plumes. Heinemann, 1940; Double-
day, 1940
Cargo of Eagles. Chatto, 1968; Morrow,
1968 AC
The Case Book of Mr. Campion. Mercury,
1947. (ss, many of which also appear
in the 1950 edition of Mr. Campion
and Others, q.v.) AC
The Case of the Late Pig. Hodder, 1937.
(A long novelet published in Britain
as a separate volume and in the U.S.
as part of Mr. Campion: Criminolo-
gist, q.v.) AC
The China Governess. Chatto, 1963;
Doubleday, 1962 AC
Coroner's Pidgin. Heinemann, 1945. U.S.
title: Pearls Before Swine. Double-
day, 1945 AC
The Crime at Black Dudley. Jarrolds,
1929. U.S. title: The Black Dudley
Murder. Doubleday, 1930 AC
Dancers in Mourning. Heinemann, 1937;
Doubleday, 1937. Also published as:
Who Killed Chloe? Avon, 1943 AC
Deadly Duo; see Take Two at Bedtime
Death of a Ghost. Heinemann, 1934;
Doubleday, 1934 AC
The Estate of the Beckoning Lady; see
The Beckoning Lady

The Fashion in Shrouds. Heinemann, 1938; Doubleday, 1938. Revised edition: Heinemann, 1965 AC
The Fear Sign; see Sweet Danger
Flowers for the Judge. Heinemann, 1936; Doubleday, 1936. Also published as: Legacy in Blood. Mercury, 1949 AC
The Gyrth Chalice Mystery; see Look to the Lady
Hide My Eyes. Chatto, 1958. U.S. title: Tether's End. Doubleday, 1958. Also published as: Ten Were Missing. Dell, 1959 AC
Kingdom of Death; see Sweet Danger
Legacy in Blood; see Flowers for the Judge
Look to the Lady. Jarrolds, 1931. U.S. title: The Gyrth Chalice Mystery. Doubleday, 1931 AC
The Mind Readers. Chatto, 1965; Morrow, 1965 AC
Mr. Campion and Others. Heinemann, 1939; Penguin, 1950. (The Penguin edition differs in contents from the Heinemann; while the Heinemann overlaps but does not completely correspond to Mr. Campion: Criminologist, below, the Penguin overlaps but does not completely correspond to The Case Book of Mr. Campion, above.) AC
Mr. Campion: Criminologist. Doubleday, 1937. (Includes the novelet The Case of the Late Pig, above, and several short stories.) AC
More Work for the Undertaker. Heinemann, 1948; Doubleday, 1949. Revised edition: Heinemann, 1964 AC
Mystery Mile. Jarrolds, 1930; Doubleday, 1930. Revised edition: Penguin, 1968 AC
No Love Lost. World's Work, 1954; Doubleday, 1954. (Two novelets.)
Pearls Before Swine; see Coroner's Pidgin
Police at the Funeral. Heinemann, 1931; Doubleday, 1932 AC
The Sabotage Murder Mystery; see Traitor's Purse
Sweet Danger. Heinemann, 1933. U.S. title: Kingdom of Death. Doubleday, 1933. Also published as: The Fear Sign. Macfadden, 1961 AC
Take Two at Bedtime. World's Work, 1950. U.S. title: Deadly Duo. Doubleday, 1949. (Two novelets.)
Ten Were Missing; see Hide My Eyes
Tether's End; see Hide My Eyes
The Tiger in the Smoke. Chatto, 1952; Doubleday, 1952 AC
Traitor's Purse. Heinemann, 1941; Doubleday, 1941. Also published as: The Sabotage Murder Mystery. Avon, 1942 AC
Wanted: Someone Innocent. Pony Books, 1946. (A rare paperback, containing the title novelet, also found in Take Two at Bedtime, and three short stories uncollected until the appearance of The Allingham Minibus, q.v.)
The White Cottage Mystery. Jarrolds, 1928. Revised edition: Chatto, 1975
Who Killed Chloe?; see Dancers in Mourning

ALLIS, SARAH
Nightwind. Bobbs, 1975

ALLISON, CLYDE
Have Nude, Will Travel. Berkley, 1962

ALLISON, WILLIAM
Alias Richard Power. Doubleday, 1921
A Secret of the Sea. Doubleday, 1920
The Turnstile of Night. Doubleday, 1920

ALLSOP, KENNETH. 1920-1973.
-The Leopard-Paw Orchid. Quality, 1954

ALLWRIGHT, MICHAEL
The Roundabout. Macmillan (London), 1968. U.S. title: Neighbors. Walker, 1968

ALLYSON, ALAN
Bright as a Diamond. Hale, 1973
Don't Mess With Murder. Hale, 1972
Do You Deal in Murder? Hale, 1972
The Lady Said No. Hale, 1972; Drake, 1972

ALMHAIN. Pseudonym.
The Jewels of Prince de Janville. Swan, 1888

ALNER, JAMES Z.
The Capital Murder. Knopf, 1932; Hurst, 1933

ALONSO, RICARDO
The Candidate. PB, 1972

ALPERT, HOLLIS. 1916-   . Pseudonym: Robert Carroll, q.v.

ALROY, LIONEL
-Shut Out the Sun. Longmans, 1955

ALTER, ROBERT EDMOND. 1925-1965.
Carny Kill. GM, 1966
The Red Fathom. Avon, 1967
Swamp Sister. GM, 1961; Muller, 1963
Thieves Like Us. Avon, 1968

ALVERSON, CHARLES. 1935-   .
Fighting Back. Bobbs, 1973; H. Hamilton, 1978
Goodey's Last Stand. Houghton, 1975; H. Hamilton, 1976

AMBERLEY, RICHARD. Series character: Inspector Martin, in at least those marked M.
Dead on the Stone. Hale, 1969 M
Incitement to Murder. Hale, 1968 M
An Ordinary Accident. Hale, 1971

AMBLER, DAIL. Pseudonym: Danny Spade, q.v. Series character: Danny Spade, in many (all?) titles.
A Curtain of Glass. Milestone, 1954
Danny Spade Sees Red. Milestone, 1954
Danny Spade Spells Danger. Milestone, 1953
Duet for Two Guns. Scion, 1952
Hold That Tiger. Scion, 1952
Johnny Gets His! Scion, 1952
The Lady Says When. Scion, 1952
Not Killed, Just Dead. Scion, 1952
Someone Falling. Milestone, 1954
Three Men for the Job. Hale, 1975
The Virgin Collector. New English Library pb, 1971
What's With You? Scion, 1952
Wildcat. Comyns, 1952

AMBLER, ERIC. 1909-   . Joint pseudonym with (Percival) Charles Rodda, 1891-   , q.v.: Eliot Reed, q.v. Series characters: Arthur Abdel Simpson = AS; Charles Latimer = CL.
Background to Danger; see Uncommon Danger
Cause for Alarm. Hodder, 1938; Knopf, 1939
A Coffin for Dimitrios; see The Mask of Dimitrios
The Dark Frontier. Hodder, 1936
Dirty Story. Bodley Head, 1967; Atheneum, 1967 AS

Doctor Frigo. Weidenfeld, 1974; Atheneum, 1974
Epitaph for a Spy. Hodder, 1938; Knopf, 1952
The Intercom Conspiracy. Weidenfeld, 1970; Atheneum, 1969 CL
Journey into Fear. Hodder, 1940; Knopf, 1940
Judgment on Deltchev. Hodder, 1951; Knopf, 1951
A Kind of Anger. Bodley Head, 1964; Atheneum, 1964
The Levanter. Weidenfeld, 1972; Atheneum, 1972
The Light of Day. Heinemann, 1962; Knopf, 1963. Also published as: Topkapi. Bantam, 1964 AS
The Mask of Dimitrios. Hodder, 1939. U.S. title: A Coffin for Dimitrios. Knopf, 1939 CL
The Night-Comers. Heinemann, 1956. U.S. title: State of Siege. Knopf, 1956
Passage of Arms. Heinemann, 1959; Knopf, 1960
The Schirmer Inheritance. Heinemann, 1953; Knopf, 1953
State of Siege; see The Night-Comers
Topkapi; see The Light of Day
Uncommon Danger. Hodder, 1937. U.S. title: Background to Danger. Knopf, 1937

AMBLER, JOHN
The Hunters. Exposition, 1969

AMES, CLYDE
Gorgonzola, Won't You Please Come Home? Lancer, 1967

AMES, DELANO (L.). 1906-   . Series characters: Jane and Dagobert Brown = B; Juan Llorca = JL.
The Body on Page One. Hodder, 1951; Rinehart, 1951 B
Coffin for Christopher; see Crime, Gentlemen, Please
The Cornish Coast Conspiracy. Amalgamated Press, 1942 (Sexton Blake)
Corpse Diplomatique. Hodder, 1950; Rinehart, 1951 B
Crime, Gentlemen, Please. Hodder, 1954. U.S. title: Coffin for Christopher. Ives Washburn, 1954 B
Crime Out of Mind. Hodder, 1956; Ives Washburn, 1956 B
Death of a Fellow Traveller. Hodder, 1950; Rinehart, 1950. Also published as: Nobody Wore Black. Dell, 1951 B
For Old Crime's Sake; see Lucky Jane
He Found Himself Murdered. Swan, 1947
Landscape with Corpse. Hodder, 1955; Ives Washburn, 1955 B
Lucky Jane. Hodder, 1959. U.S. title: For Old Crime's Sake. Lippincott, 1959 B
The Man in the Tricorn Hat. Methuen, 1960; Regnery, 1966 JL
The Man with Three Chins. Methuen, 1965; Regnery, 1968 JL
The Man with Three Jaguars. Methuen, 1961; Regnery, 1967 JL
The Man with Three Passports. Methuen, 1967 JL
Murder Begins at Home. Hodder, 1949; Rinehart, 1950 B
Murder, Maestro, Please. Hodder, 1952; Rinehart, 1952 B
Nobody Wore Black; see Death of a Fellow Traveller
No Mourning for the Matador. Hodder, 1953; Ives Washburn, 1953 B
No Traveller Returns. Nicholson, 1934
Not in Utter Nakedness; see They Journey by Night
She Shall Have Murder. Hodder, 1948; Rinehart, 1949 B
She Wouldn't Say Who. Hodder, 1957; Ives Washburn, 1958 B

A

They Journey by Night. Hodder, 1932.
U.S. title: Not in Utter Nakedness. Dial, 1932
-Uneasily to Bed. Grayson, 1934

AMES, JENNIFER. Pseudonym of Maysie Greig, 1902- , q.v.
Danger in Eden; see Danger Wakes My Heart
Danger Wakes My Heart. Collins, 1949. U.S. title: Danger in Eden. Bouregy, 1950
Dark Carnival. Collins, 1951; Random, 1950, as by Maysie Greig
Date with Danger; see Frightened Heart
Fear Kissed My Lips. Collins, 1947
The Fearful Paradise. Collins, 1953. U.S. title: This Fearful Paradise. Random, 1953, as by Maysie Greig
Flight into Fear. Collins, 1954; Bouregy, 1954
The Frightened Heart. Collins, 1952. U.S. title: Date with Danger. Random, 1952, as by Maysie Greig
I Married Mr. Richardson. Collins, 1945
Journey in the Dark. Collins, 1945
Lovers in the Dark. Collins, 1946
Rough Seas to Sunrise. Collins, 1955. U.S. title: Winds of Fear. Avalon, 1956, as by Maysie Greig
This Fearful Paradise; see The Fearful Paradise
Winds of Fear; see Rough Seas to Sunrise

AMES, JOSEPH B(USHNELL). 1878-1928.
The Emerald Buddha. Small, 1921

AMES, LESLIE. Pseudonym of Orlando Joseph Rigoni, 1897- .
The Angry Wind. Lenox Hill, 1970
Bride of Donnybrook. Arcadia, 1966
Castle on the Island. Arcadia, 1969; Hale, 1970
The Hidden Chapel. Arcadia, 1967
The Hill of Ashes. Arcadia, 1968
The House of Haddon. Arcadia, 1969
The Hungry Sea. Arcadia, 1967
Journey to Romance. Hale, 1966. (U.S. title?)
King's Castle. Lenox Hill, 1970
The Phantom Bride. Lenox Hill, 1972
Sinister Love. Hale, 1968. (U.S. title?)
To Shadow Our Love. Hale, 1968. (U.S. title?)
Wind Over the Citadel. Lenox Hill, 1971

AMES, NORMA. 1920- .
My Path Belated. Avon, 1970
Whisper in the Forest. Avon, 1971

AMES, ROBERT. Pseudonym of Charles Clifford.
Awake and Die. GM, 1955
The Dangerous One. GM, 1954; Fawcett (London), 1959
The Devil Drives. GM, 1952; Red Seal, 1959

AMHERST, FRANCES. See: HELEN (ROSEN) WOODWARD, 1882- .

AMINO, L.
Death is So Lonely. Scion, 1954
Masks of Malevolence. Scion, 1953

AMIS, KINGSLEY (WILLIAM). 1922- .
Pseudonym: Robert Markham, q.v.
The Anti-Death League. Gollancz, 1966; Harcourt, 1966
The Riverside Villas Murder. Cape, 1973; Harcourt, 1973

AMOS, ALAN. Pseudonym of Kathleen Moore Knight, q.v.
Borderline Murder. Doubleday, 1947

Fatal Harvest. Doubleday, 1957; Hammond, 1958, as by Kathleen Moore Knight
Jungle Murder; see Pray for a Miracle
Panic in Paradise. Doubleday, 1951
Pray for a Miracle. Duell, 1941. Also published as: Jungle Murder. Adventure Novel Classic, 194?

AMOS, RUSSELL BOOTH. 1928- .
Perhaps I Look Simple. Longmans, 1960
Wasp in the Web. Longmans, 1961

AMY, WILLIAM LACEY. Pseudonym: Luke Allan, q.v.

ANDERS, E. J.
-Behind the Door. Philosophical Library, 1966

ANDERSCH, ALFRED. 1914- .
-Flight to Afar. Coward, 1958; Gollancz, 1958. (Translation of Sansibar; oder, Der Letzte Grund. Germany, 1957.)
The Redhead. Pantheon, 1961; Heinemann, 1961. (Translation of Die Rote. Germany, 1960.)

ANDERSEN, U(ELL) S(TANLEY). 1917- .
Hard and Fast. Popular Library, 1956
-The Smoldering Sea. Wyn, 1953

ANDERSON, BETTY. Pseudonym: Claudia Canyon, q.v.

ANDERSON, EDWARD. 1905- .
Thieves Like Us. Stokes, 1937; Heinemann, 1937. Also published as: Your Red Wagon. Bantam, 1948

ANDERSON, FREDERICK IRVING. 1877-1947.
Series character: Deputy Parr = DP.
Adventures of the Infallible Godahl. Crowell, 1914 ss
The Book of Murder. Dutton, 1930 ss DP
The Notorious Sophie Lang. Heinemann, 1925 ss DP

ANDERSON, GEORGE
The Sit-In. Ace, 1970

ANDERSON, IAIN F(LEMING). 1902- .
The Commerce Patrol. Jenkins, 1937 ss
Cypher 8. Heath Cranston, 1939

ANDERSON, J(OHN) R(ICHARD) L(ANE). 1911- . Series character: Major Peter Blair, in at least those marked PB.
Death in the North Sea. Gollancz, 1975; Stein, 1976 PB
Death in the Thames. Gollancz, 1974; Stein, 1975 PB
Death on the Rocks. Gollancz, 1973; Stein, 1975 PB
The Nine-Spoked Wheel. Gollancz, 1975
Reckoning in Ice. Gollancz, 1971

ANDERSON, JAMES. 1936- .
The Abolition of Death. Constable, 1974; Walker, 1975
The Affair of the Blood-Stained Egg-Cosy. Constable, 1975; McKay, 1977
The Alpha List. Constable, 1972; Walker, 1973
Assassin. Constable, 1969; Simon, 1971

ANDERSON, JESSICA (MARGARET QUEALE)
The Last Man's Head. Macmillan (London), 1970
An Ordinary Lunacy. Macmillan (London), 1963; Scribner, 1964

ANDERSON, M(ARY) D(ESIREE). 1902- .
Grey Sisters. Chatto, 1972

ANDERSON, MARY
Tales of the Rock. Downey, 1897 ss

ANDERSON, MAXWELL. 1888-1959.
The Bad Seed. Dodd, 1955. (2-act play based on the novel by William March, q.v.)

ANDERSON, POUL (WILLIAM). 1926- .
Series character: Trygve Yamamura, in all titles.
Murder Bound. Macmillan, 1962
Murder in Black Letter. Macmillan, 1960
Perish by the Sword. Macmillan, 1959

ANDERSON, REX
Cover Her with Roses. Simon, 1969; Hale, 1973

ANDERSON, W(ALTER) W(ADSLEY). 1904- .
Kill 1 Kill 2. Morrow, 1940

ANDERSON, WILLIAM C(HARLES). 1920- .
Penelope, the Damp Detective. Crown, 1974

ANDOM, R. Pseudonym of Alfred Walter Barrett, 1869- .
The Burglings of Tutt. Jarrolds, 1905
-The Enchanted Ship. Cassell, 1908
The Strange Adventure of Roger Wilkins and other stories. Tylston, 1895 ss

ANDOVER, HENRY. Pseudonym of Henry Hope.
Death on the Pack Road. Eyre, 1931
The Dennisdale Tragedy. Eyre, 1936

ANDRE, R(ICHARD) and G. LEITCH WALKER
The Ace of Spades. Ward, 1900

ANDREAE, PERCY. 1858- .
-A Life at Stake. Ward, 1902
-The Mask and the Man. Smith, 1894
-The Signora. Smith, 1895
Stanhope of Chester. Smith, 1894; Rand, 1896
The Vanished Emperor. Ward, 1896; Rand, 1896

ANDREAS, FRED. 1898- .
Alias. Bles, 1933. U.S. title: Death at Heel. Holt, 1933. (Translation of Der Mann der Zweimal Leben Wollte. Germany, 1932.)
Captain Overboard. Bles, 1936. (Translation of Einer Zuviel an Bord. Germany, 1935
Death at Heel; see Alias
In Court. Bles, 1931. U.S. title: The Trial of Gregor Kaska. Holt, 1932. (Translation of Prozess Gregor Kaska. Germany, 1930.)
The Theatre Crime. Bles, 1932. (Translation of Die Flucht ins Dunkle. Germany, 1927.)
The Trial of Gregor Kaska; see In Court

ANDREWS, CHARLTON. 1874-1939. Series character: Drexel Ware = DW.
The Affair of the Malacca Stick. Washburn, 1936 DW
The Affair of the Syrian Dagger. Washburn, 1937 DW
The Butterfly Murder. Sears, 1932; Allan, 1934
Murder at the Class Reunion. Denison, 1938. (1-act play.)
The Resources of Mycroft Holmes. Aspen Press, 1973 ss

ANDREWS, DOROTHY C(RAIGHEAD)
Death at Springtime. Empire, 1935

ANDREWS, HORACE J.
    The Indian Idol Mystery. Modern, 1938
    -The Luck of the Golden Star. Mellifont, 1934. (64 pp.)

ANDREWS, MICHAEL
    Caracol Reef. Hale, 1972

ANDREWS, PETER J.
    Hoods Incorporated. Badger, 1958

ANDREWS, (CHARLES) R(OBERT) D(OUGLAS). 1903- .
    The Stolen Husband. Grosset, 1931

ANDREZEL, PIERRE. Pseudonym of Baroness Karen Christence Blixen-Finecke, 1885-1962. Other pseudonym: Isak Dinesen, q.v.
    The Angelic Avengers. Putnam (London), 1946; Random, 1947

ANDRZEYEVSKI, JERZY (GEORGE)
    -Ashes and Diamonds. Weidenfeld, 1962. (Translation of Popiol i Diament. Warsaw, 1960.)

ANGEL, ROSS
    Bullet Proof. Scion, 1951
    Call Me Sometime. Scion, 1953
    The Dame Came Late. Scion, 1952
    Dame Trouble There. Scion, 1953
    Dames Don't Dictate. Scion, 1953
    Dead Easy. Scion, 1950
    Drop That Gun. Scion, 1951
    Excuse My Gun. Scion, 1951
    Get Out and Stay Out. Scion, 1952
    Give Me a Gun. Scion, 1952
    Hot Ice. Scion, 1951
    I'll Fry Yet. Scion, 1951
    It's All Yours. Scion, 1952
    It's Murder She Says. Scion, 1951
    Jail Bait! Milestone, 1953
    K.O. for Keeps. Scion, 1950
    Let's Shoot This Out. Scion, 1951
    Live Till You Die. Scion, 1952
    Luger Lullaby. Scion, 1951
    Misguided Angel. Scion, 1954
    Mr. Forty-Five. Scion, 1951
    No Percentage in Death. Scion, 1953
    One-Way Trip. Scion, 1953
    Over My Dead Body. Scion, 1950
    Reckless. Scion, 1954
    Tomorrow—the Chair. Scion, 1950
    To Sleep No More. Scion, 1951
    Voice of Vice. Scion, 1953
    You Don't Die Twice. Scion, 1952

ANGELL, BRYAN MARY. 1877- . Pseudonym: H. Ripley Cromarsh, q.v.

ANGELLOTTI, MARION POLK
    Three Black Bags. Century, 1922

ANGELO, TONY
    Honey, Hold That Scream. Harborough, 1952
    Satan's Sister. Archer, 1951
    Sinner's Shroud. Archer, 1950

ANGUS, DOUGLAS (ROSS). 1909- .
    Death on Jerusalem Road. Random, 1963

ANGUS, JOHN and FIELDING HOPE, 1897- , q.v.
    The Scorpion's Nest. Selwyn, 1929

ANGUS, SYLVIA. 1921- .
    Arson and Old Lace. World, 1972
    Death of a Hittite. Macmillan, 1969

ANKER, JENS. Pseudonym of Robert Hansen, 1883-1957.
    Two Dead Men. Knopf, 1922

ANNE-MARIEL. Pseudonym of Anne Goud, 1917- .
    Murder in Venice. Pinnacle, 1974
    One Evening I Shall Return. Pinnacle, 1973. (Translation of Un Soir, Je Reviendrai. Paris, 1963.)
    Rendezvous in Peking. Pinnacle, 1974

ANNESLEY, MICHAEL. Series character: Lawrie Fenton, in at least those marked LF.
    An Agent Intervenes. Paul, 1944 LF
    Fenton of the Foreign Office; see Room 14
    The Lights That Did Not Fail. Paul, 1949
    The Missing Agent. Harrap, 1938 LF
    Room 14. Harrap, 1935. U.S. title: Fenton of the Foreign Office. Speller, 1937 LF
    Spies Abounding. Paul, 1945 LF
    Spies in Action. Harrap, 1937 LF
    Spies in the Web. Harrap, 1936 LF
    Spy Against the Reich. Harrap, 1940 LF
    Spy Corner. Paul, 1948
    Spy-Counter Spy. Paul, 1946 LF
    Spy Island. Paul, 1950
    Suicide Spies. Paul, 1944 LF
    They Won't Lie Down. Paul, 1947 LF
    Unknown Agent. Harrap, 1940 LF
    The Vanished Vice-Counsel. Harrap, 1939 LF

ANONYMOUS. See also: CHARLES BROCKDEN BROWN, 1771-1810; ANTHONY BERKELEY; (FRANK) GELETT BURGESS, 1866-1951.
    The Actress Detective; or, The Invisible Hand. Aldine
    Adventures of an Attorney in Search of Practice. Saunders, 1839; Lea, 1839. ss (Variously ascribed to Sir George Stephen, 1794-1879, Sir James Stephen, 1789-1859, and Samuel Warren, 1807-1877.)
    -All for Him. Carleton, 1877; Low, 1877. Also published as: Sweetheart and Wife. Carleton, 1882; Low, 1882
    The Artist Detective. Aldine
    The Attorney; or, The Correspondence of John Quod. Hueston, 1853
    Autobiography of an Italian Detective. Maxwell, 18?? ss
    The Bat of the Battery; or, Joe Phoenix, King of Detectives. Aldine
    Beautiful Jack, the Double-Edged Detective. Aldine
    Begumbagh; A Tale of the Indian Mutiny and other stories. Chambers, 1888 ss, at least one criminous
    Belle Starr, the Bandit Queen; or, The Female Jesse James. Fox, 1889
    Benjamin Butts Junr. Aldine
    Binnacle Jack; or, The Cavern of Death. DeWitt, 1876
    The Black Band; or, Mysteries of Midnight. Blackett
    The Black Box Murder. Remington, 1889; Lovell, 1890. (By Maarten Maartens, pseudonym of Joost Marius Willem van der Poorten Schwartz, 1858-1915, q.v.) Reprinted as by William Ward, q.v.: Westbrook, 192?
    The Black Monk; or, The Secret of the Grey Turret. Peirce, 1842
    -The Black Troopers and other stories. Religious Tract Society, 1862
    The Blind Beggar of Bethnal Green and Bessy. (London), 1848
    Bob Bridger, Detective. Aldine
    Bob Younger's Fate. Aldine
    Born Bad; or, The Countess and the Convict. DeWitt, 1876
    The Bottle; or, The First Step to Crime. DeWitt, 1876

Brant Adams, the Emperor of Detectives. Aldine
Broadway Bob, the Bounder Detective. Aldine
Bruce Angelo, the Old Time Detective. Aldine
The California Detective. Aldine
Captain Clew, the Flying Detective. Aldine
Caught in Mid-Ocean. Ogilvie, 1903
The Celebrated Detective. Aldine
The Champion Clue-Finder. Aldine
Charley Hunter; or, The Fate of a Forger. Dick, 1876
A Chase Around the World. Aldine
Chillers and Thrillers. Street, 1945. (11 dramatzied puzzle problems.)
The Chosen Man. Aldine
The Circus Detective. Aldine
-The City of Purple Dreams. Browne, 1913
Columbia; or, Among the Corsican Bandits. Donohue, ca.1897
The Combination-Lock Mystery; or, Little Lightning. Aldine
The Convict's Sweetheart. Ogilvie
The Crackshot Detective. Aldine
The Crime Club. Stevens, ca.1907
The Crime of Monte Carlo. Stevens, ca. 1906
A Cruel Secret. Carleton, ca.1883
Dark Masquerade. Green Circle, 1936. (By Fulton Oursler, 1893-1952, q.v.)
The Dastard "Dr." Aldine
Dead or Alive. Stevens, ca.1904
The Death Deal. Aldine
The Death Trust. [Author], 1889. (by Laura Eugenia Newhall.)
The Decoy Detective. Aldine
The Demon Detective; or, The Gypsy Gentleman. Aldine
Detective Burr's Seven Clues. Aldine
Detective Fleet of London. Aldine
The Detective for Vengeance. Aldine
Detective Gordon's Grip. Aldine
Detective Sketches. Tousey, 1881 ss
Detective Stories. Henderson   ss (5 different volumes bear this title.)
The Detective's Notebook. Ward, 1860
The Detective's Victory. Aldine
Diary of a Great French Detective. Tousey, 188? ss
Dixon Hawke's Case Book. Nos. 1-20. Thomson
Doc Grip, the Sporting Detective. Aldine
The Dog Detective. Aldine
A Double Tragedy. Aldine
The Dream of Raven. Theosophical Publishing Co., 1895
The Drop Detective. Aldine
The Dumb Detective. Boys of England, 1887
The East Side Detective. Aldine
Eileen the Spy. Aldine
Eliza Grimwood. (London), 1844
The Emperor of Detectives. Aldine
Eugenia; or, A Friend's Victim. Minerva, 1889
Euthanasia; or, Turf, Text and Tomb. Routledge, 1893
The Experiences of a Lady Detective. Clarke, 1884. (by William Stephens Hayward, q.v.) ss
Experiences of an American Detective. Infield, 1883. (by William Stephens Hayward, q.v.) ss
The Fair Mystery. Brett, 1870
The Famous Burdick Case. Ogilvie, ca. 1895
-Fanny White and her Friend Jack Rawlings. Vickers
The Far West Detective. Aldine
The Fatal Secret; or, Crime and Retribution. Jay, 1852; Barclay, 1852

10/ Anonymous

Female Depravity; or, The House of Death. DeWitt, 1876
The Ferret Detective. Aldine
Fireside Omnibus. Hutchinson, 1937. (Puzzle ss.)
Five Hundred Pounds Reward. Bentley, 1867. (by A Barrister.)
Foiled. Clark, 1885
The Four Pools Mystery. Century, 1908
The Frisco Detective. Aldine
The Gambler's Last Throw. Ward
Gasparoni Detective. Aldine
The Georgia Detective. Aldine
The Giant City Swindle. Amalgamated, 1927
The Giant Detective. Aldine
The Giant Detective in Ireland. Aldine
The Gold Star Detective from Kentucky. Aldine
The Government Special Detective. Aldine
-The Grasp of the Sultan. Houghton, 1916
The Great Buxton Mystery. 1889. (by William Thomas Standen.)
The Great Cronin Mystery; or, The Irish Patriot's Fate. Laird, ca.1888. (by A Chicago Detective.)
-Greyslaer. Harper, 1840; Bentley, 1840. (by Charles Fenno Hoffman, 1806-1884.)
The Gypsy Detective. Aldine
Hidden, Not Lost. Newnes, 1903
A Hidden Terror. Stevens, ca.1904
The Hollywood Mystery. Stevens, ca.1905
The Hypnotist Detective. Aldine
The Idol of Lost Chance. Aldine
The "Impenetrable Mystery" of Zora Burns. (Chicago), 1888. (by Will Bone, Jr.)
In the Force; or, Confessions of a Policeman. Bryce   ss
The Independent Detective. Aldine
The Irish Detective. Aldine
Iron Burgess, the Government Detective. Aldine
Ironsides Abroad. Aldine
Jack o' the Cudgel; or, The Hero of a Hundred Fights. (London), 18??
Jack Shepard, the Bandit King. Ogilvie, 1903
Jack Vinton, the Boy Detective. Aldine
The Jew Detective; or, The Beautiful Convict. Aldine
Joe Phoenix Puzzled; or, The League of the Skeleton Keys. Aldine
Kate Scott, the Decoy Detective; or, Joe Phoenix's Still Hunt. Aldine
The Kentucky Detective. Aldine
The King of Detectives. Aldine
Kinks. Mystery House, 1927
The Lady Detective; see Revelations of a Lady Detective
Lady Kate, the Dashing Female Detective. Aldine
Leaves from the Notebook of a New York Detective. Dick, 1876 ss
The Library of Fiction. Routledge, 1841 ss, some criminous
The Life, Adventure and Opinions of a Liverpool Policeman and his Contemporaries. Matthews, 1841
The Life and Anecdotes of the Black Dwarf. (Edinburgh), 1820
The Life of Anson Bunker, "The Bloody Hand." Barclay, 1886
London by Night. Oliver
A London Detective's Thrilling Adventures. Tousey, 1883 ss
The Long Branch Detective. Aldine
The Loom and the Law. Stevenson, 1923
Love and Death in a Barn. Old Franklin, 1876
-A Love Spell. Carleton, 1883
The Magic Change Detective. Aldine
The Magnate Detective. Aldine
The Man Trap. Riverton, 1910

Manfred the Magic Trick Detective. Aldine
The Mantrapper. Aldine
Marianne the Outcast: The Sorrowful Tale of a Betrayed Woman Taken from the Diary of Detective Thorn. Eichler, ca.1880. (Issued in 100 parts, totalling 3200 pages.)
The Masked Detective; or, The Dead Alive. Aldine
The Masked Motorist. Thomson
The Matchless Detective; or, Thad Burr's Marvellous Case. Aldine
A Maze of Crime. Aldine
A Midnight Mystery; or, The Double Detective. Aldine
The Midnight Queen. Dick, 1876
The Miner Detective. Aldine
The Mountaineer Detective. Aldine
Mrs. Druse's Case, and Maggie Houghtaling. Old Franklin, 1877
The Muddles of Solon Mudhen, the Blacksmith Detective. Tydfil, 1902 ss
Mura, the Western Lady Detective. Aldine
My Fourteen Cases. Tousey, 1887 ss
The Mysteries of Chicago. Rand, 1889 (by A Reporter)
Mysteries of Crime, as Shown in Remarkable Capital Crimes. Walker, 1870
The Mysteries of Nashua; or, Revenge Punished and Constancy Rewarded. Gill, 1844
The Mysteries of New Orleans. Peterson, 1876
The Mysteries of Oakendale Abbey. Perry, 1856
The Mysterious Crime at Burleigh Mansion. Barclay, 1887
The Mysterious Dagger; or, The Avengers. Peirce, 1842
The Mysterious Marksman; or, The Outlaws of New York. James, 1876
The Mysterious Murder of Pearl Bryan; or, The Headless Horror. Barclay
Mystery Crime Cases. Spencer, 1949
The Mystery of a Madstone. Aldine
The Mystery of Black Pit. Stevens, 1907
The Mystery of Lady Chetwynd's Spectre. Henderson
The Mystery of Woodcroft. Stevens, ca. 1906
The Mystery of Woodleigh Grange. Donohue, ca.1906
The Mystery; or, Forty Years Ago. (London), 1820 (by Thomas Gaspey)
The Naval Detective's Chase. Aldine
The Nevada Detective. Aldine
Nicky Nimble; or, The Night Prowlers. DeWitt, 1876
Nighthawk the Mountain Detective. Aldine
Norma Danton; or, The Lighthouse Murder. Hurst, 1876
Not Guilty. Ogilvie, 1888
Obi; or, Three Fingered Jack. Peterson, 1876
The Old Detective's Pupil. Aldine
Old Electricity, the Lightning Detective. Aldine
Old Harry Hawks. Aldine
Old Puritan, the Old Time Detective. Aldine
Old Sleuth, Detective; or, The Bay Ridge Mystery. Aldine
Old Stonewall, the "Shadower". Aldine
Old Terrible, the Iron Arm Detective. Aldine
Old Transform, the Secret Special Detective. Aldine
On Her Majesty's Secret Service. Maxwell, 1878

On the Scent; or, Hawkeye the London Detective. Aldine
On Trial for His Life. Ogilvie, 1903
O'Neil McDarragh. Aldine
Paul Deverell; or, Two Judgments for One Crime. Dick, 1876
Paul Ferroll. Saunders, 1855; Redfield, 1856. (by Mrs. Archer Clive.)
Phantasmagoria; or, The Development of Magical Deception. Tegg, ca.1825
Piping a Detective. Aldine
Pitiless as Death; or, Crowningshield the Detective. Aldine
Plot and Counterplot. Aldine
The Poisoned Letter; or, The Lost and the Redeemed. DeWitt, 1876
The Post Office Detective. Aldine
The Prairie Detective. Aldine
The President Vanishes. Farrar, 1934. (by Rex Stout, 1886-1975, q.v.)
The Princely Detective. Butler
-The Queen of the Outlaw's Camp. Ogilvie, 1903
The Queen of the Secret Seven. Ogilvie, 1903
A Race for Life and other tales. Leisure Hour, ca.1872 ss, at least one criminous
The Railway Detective. Butler
Ralph Wildhawk; or, Alone Among the Brigands. (London), 18??
Reaping the Whirlwind. Aldine
Red-Light Will, the River Detective. Aldine
Reminiscences of a Great French Detective. Tousey, 188? ss
The Return of Dick Barton. Atlas, 1952
Revelations of a Lady Detective. Vickers, 1864. Also published as: The Lady Detective.
The Revenue Detective; or, Old Rattlesnake. Aldine
Richmond; or, Scenes in the Life of a Bow Street Runner. Colburn, 1827; Dover, 1976
Rival Lovers; or, The Midnight Murder. DeWitt, 1876
-Road to Ruin; or, The Dangers of the Tongue. James, 1876
-Robert Macaire. Routledge, 1888
The Rookery Detective. Aldine
Romances of Mayfair. Paul, 1925 ss, some criminous
Round the Block. Appleton, 1864. (by John Bell Bouton, 1830-1902.)
Running Down a Double; or, Lynx-Eye, the Pacific 'Tec. Aldine
Sarah Brown, Detective; or, The Mystery of the Pavilion. Aldine
The Secret of the Black Mere. Aldine
The Secretary; or, Circumstantial Evidence. DeWitt, 1852
Sergeant Von; or, A Long Chase. Cassell, 1889
The Shadow on the Purple. Lynwood, 1911. (by A Peeress = Kate Everest.)
The Sham Detective. Aldine
Silas Sharp, the Silent Detective. Aldine
Silver Tom, the Detective. Aldine
Slick Detective Yarns. Swan, 1951 ss
The Smiling Corpse. Farrar, 1935. (by Philip Wylie, 1902-1971, q.v., and Bernard A. Bergman.)
The Society Detective. Aldine
Some Queer Stories. Tousey, 1888 ss
Something Better. Lee, 1878
The Spies Abroad; or, The Perils of the Gold Coast. (London), 18??
Stories of a World Renown Detective. Tousey, 188? ss
A Strange Case. Tinsley, 1870
Strange Stories of a Detective; or, Curiosities of Crime by a Retired Member of the Detective Force. Dick, 1863 ss
Struck Dead. Boys of England, 1888

Suppressed Sensations; or, Leaves from the Note Book of a Chicago Reporter. Rand, 1879 ss (by James Maitland, q.v.)
The Suspected Governess. Aldine
Sweetheart and Wife; see All for Him
Tales of Heroism, and Records of Strange and Wonderful Adventures. 1847
Tales of the Coastguard and other stories. Chambers ss, at least one criminous
Tales of the R.I.C. Blackwood ss
The Thrilling Adventures of a New York Detective. Lupton, 1893 ss
Thrilling Stories. Tousey, 1886 ss
Through a Glass Darkly. Aldine
-The Toltec Cup. Vanderpoole, 1890. (by Andrew Carpenter Wheeler.)
Tom and Jerry; or, The Double Detective. Aldine
Tom Fox; or, The Revelations of a Detective. Vickers, 1860 ss
The Trail of the Barrow; or, The Brother's Revenge. International
Trench's Wives; or, The Carrington Mystery. Pollard, 1887. (by The Family Lawyer.)
-Trial and Triumph; or, A Fortune at Stake. MacCrellish, 1868
Trials of a City Detective. Munro, 1883 ss
Tried for his Life; or, The Charles River Mystery Solved. Aldine
-The Truly Remarkable Life of the Beautiful Helen Jewett. Barclay, 1878
The Twin Detectives. Aldine
The Unclaimed Daughter. Binns, ca.1852
Under His Thumb. Aldine
The Van Peltz Diamonds; or, 'Tec Against 'Tec. Aldine
A Wall Street Haul. Aldine
Was It a Ghost? The Murders in Bussey's Wood: An Extraordinary Narrative. Loring, 1868
The White Witch's Warning; or, The League of Three. Aldine
Who Did It; or, Austin, the Detective. Aldine
Who Killed Peter Trueman? Brett, 1900
Who Shot the Spy? Boys of England, 1887
The Widow's Walk; or, The Mysteries of Crime. Garrett, 1852
The Wolves of Washington. Aldine, 1895
The Woman with the Yellow Hair and Other Modern Mysteries. Saunders, 1862 ss
XX—A Fatal Clue; or, Detective Burr's Master Case. Aldine

ANSLE, DOROTHY PHOEBE. Pseudonyms: Laura Conway, Hebe Elsna, Lyndon Snow, qq.v.

ANSON, LINDSAY. Series character: Peter Allen = PA.
Even Doctors Die; see Such Natural Deaths
Hung by an Eyelash. Collins, 1939
I Don't Like Cats. Collins, 1940; Doubleday, 1940 PA
Such Natural Deaths. Collins, 1938. U.S. title: Even Doctors Die. Doubleday, 1939 PA

ANSTEY, EDGAR (CARNEGIE). 1882-   .
The Mystery of the Blue Inns. Longmans, 1937
The Vanishing Yacht. Longmans, 1936

ANTHEIL, GEORGE JOHANN CARL. 1900-1959. Pseudonym: Stacey Bishop, q.v.

ANTHONY, DAVID. Pseudonym of William Dale Smith, 1929-   .
Blood on a Harvest Moon. Coward, 1972; Collins, 1972

The Midnight Lady and the Mourning Man. Bobbs, 1969; Collins, 1970
The Organization. Coward, 1970; Collins, 1971

ANTHONY, ELIZABETH
Dramatic Murder. Hodder, 1948
Made for Murder. Hodder, 1950

ANTHONY, EVELYN. Pseudonym of Evelyn Bridget Patricia Stephens Ward-Thomas, 1928-   .
The Assassin. Hutchinson, 1970; Coward, 1970
The Legend. Hutchinson, 1969; Coward, 1969
The Malaspiga Exit. Hutchinson, 1974. U.S. title: Mission to Malaspiga. Coward, 1974
Mission to Malaspiga; see The Malaspiga Exit
The Occupying Power. Hutchinson, 1973. U.S. title: Stranger at the Gates. Coward, 1973
The Persian Price; see The Persian Ransom
The Persian Ransom. Hutchinson, 1975. U.S. title: The Persian Price. Coward, 1975
The Poellenberg Inheritance. Hutchinson, 1972; Coward, 1972
The Rendezvous. Hutchinson, 1967; Coward, 1968
Stranger at the Gates; see The Occupying Power
The Tamarind Seed. Hutchinson, 1971; Coward, 1971

ANTHONY, MICHAEL
-Her Own Affair. Methuen, 1944
Men Need Sympathy. Methuen, 1943

ANTHONY, NORMAN
The Diamond Racket. Low, 1937
Who is the Ace? Low, 1938

ANTHONY, WILDER
Deep Valley. Dorrance, 1940
Hidden Gold. Macaulay, 1922; Collins, 1924
Men of Mystery. Macaulay, 1926; Collins, 1925

ANTILL, ELIZABETH. Pseudonym of Elizabeth Middleton. Series character: Detective Inspector Simon Ashton, in both titles.
Death on the Barrier Reef. Hammond, 1952
Murder in Mid-Atlantic. Hammond, 1950

ANTONIO, SAN. See: SAN ANTONIO.

ANTONY, PETER. Joint pseudonym of Anthony (Joshua) Shaffer, 1926-   , q.v., and Peter (Levin) Shaffer, 1926-   .
How Doth the Little Crocodile? Evans, 1952; Macmillan, 1957, as by Anthony and Peter Shaffer
The Woman in the Wardrobe. Evans, 1951

APPEL, BENJAMIN. 1907-1977.
-Alley Kids. Lion, 1956
-A Big Man, a Fast Man. Morrow, 1961
Brain Guy. Knopf, 1934; Constable, 1937. Also published as: The Enforcer. Belmont, 1972
But Not Yet Slain. Wyn, 1947
The Dark Stain. Dial, 1943
The Death Master. Popular Library, 1974
-Dock Walloper. Lion, 1953

The Enforcer; see Brain Guy
Four Roads to Death. Knopf, 1935. Also published as: Gold and Flesh. Macfadden, 1972
The Funhouse. Ballantine, 1959
Gold and Flesh; see Four Roads to Death
-Hell's Kitchen. Lion, 1952
Life and Death of a Tough Guy. Avon, 1955. Also published as: Teen-Age Mobster. Avon, 1957
Plunder. GM, 1952
The Power-House. Dutton, 1939
-The Raw Edge. Random, 1958
-Sweet Money Girl. GM, 1954
Teen-Age Mobster; see Life and Death of a Tough Guy
-A Time of Fortune. Morrow, 1963

APPLE, A. E. Series character: Mr. Chang, in both titles.
Mr. Chang of Scotland Yard. Chelsea, 1926
Mr. Chang's Crime Ray. Chelsea, 1928

APPLEBY, JOHN
Aphrodite Means Death. Laurie, 1951. U.S. title: The Arms of Venus. Coward, 1951
The Arms of Venus; see Aphrodite Means Death
The Bad Summer. Hodder, 1958; Washburn, 1958
Barbary Hoard; see The Singing Cave
The Captive City. Hodder, 1955; Sloane, 1955
The Dark Corsican. Laurie, 1953
Grounds for Murder; see Stars in the Water
The Secret Mountains. Hodder, 1955; Washburn, 1957
The Singing Cave. Laurie, 1952. U.S. title: Barbary Hoard. Coward, 1952
Stars in the Water. Laurie, 1952; Coward, 1953. Also published as: Grounds for Murder. Dell, 1958
The Stuffed Swan. Hodder, 1956
Tin Trumpets at Dawn. Laurie, 1950
Venice Preserve Me. Hodder, 1954

APPLETON, G(EORGE) W(EBB). 1845-1909.
-Catching a Tartar. Tinsley, 1879
-A Comedy of the Unexpected. Long, 1910
-The Co-Respondent. Downey, 1894
-Doctor Dale's Dilemma. Long, 1909
The Down Express. Long, 1908
The Duchess of Pontifex Square. Long, 1907
Francois the Valet. Pearson, 1899
-Frozen Hearts. Tinsley, 1878; Appleton, 1890
The House on the Thames. Long, 1907
The Ingenious Captain Cobbs. Long, 1906
-Jack Allyn's Friends. Tinsley, 1880
The Lady in Sables. Chatto, 1904
The Luck of Bella Barton. Digby, 1905
-Miss White of Mayfair. Digby, 1906
The Mysterious Miss Cass. Long, 1904
Rash Conclusions. Chatto, 1902
-The Rook's Nest. Long, 1905
The Silent Passenger. Long, 1905
-A Terrible Legacy. Ward, 1887; Appleton, 1887
The Willoughby Affair. Long, 1908

APPLIN, ARTHUR. 1883-1948?
The Actress. Hurst, 1927; Duffield, 1930
-Adventure for Two. Wright, 1930
-Belle of the Ballet. Leng, 1938
The Black Nail. Hurst, 1932
Blackmailed. Everett, 1915
-The Butcher of Bruton Street. Richards, 1908. Rewritten and published as: The Nursing Home. Mills, 1915
-The Children of the Gutter. Richards, 1908
The Chinese Cabinet. Ward, 1921
Cold Cream. Hurst, 1933

A

Applin, Arthur (continued)
Crash! Wright, 1935
The Dangerous Game. Mellifont, 1935
-Dangerous Lovers. Mellifont, 1933
Daring Anna Alcott. Wright, 1935
Death in the Limelight. Mellifont, 1939
The Death Mask. Hurst, 1928; Duffield, 1930
-Diana Defiant. Mellifont, 1934. (64 pp)
-Diana's Luck. Leng, 1939
-The Eternal Instinct. Wright, 1931
Fallen Among Thieves. Ward, 1914
The Fatal Ace. Hale, 1936
-The Fearless Lovers. Ward, 1922
-Fedora of the Halls. White, 1911
-The Final Payment. Hurst, 1927
-Footlights. Mellifont, 1934
-The Gamble of Life. Pearson, 1922
-The Gay Adventure. Wright, 1939
-The Gold Trap. Hurst, 1930
-The Greater Claim. Mills, 1919
-Her Sacrifice. Ward, 1912
-His Final Choice. Wright, 1933
-His Mexican Wife. Ward, 1917
-The Immediate Jewel. Bohemian, 1910
-Into Thy Hands. White, 1912
-The Irresistable Stranger. Leng, 1931
-Ladies Prefer Bruisers. Wright, 1936
-Lady Dorothy's Indiscretion. Ward, 1912
-The Man Pays. Everett, 1912
-The Marriage of Margot. Ward, 1921
-No Limit. White, 1911
The Nursing Home; see The Butcher of Bruton Street
-The Pantomime Girl. Everett, 1911
-The Path of a Star. Long, 1928
-The Pearl Necklace. Ward, 1911
Picked Up. Hurst, 1935
-The Price of Love. Readers Library, 1930
-The Priest of Piccadilly. White, 1910
-Rags. White, 1910
-The Revue Girl. Hurst, 1927
-The Scared Nymph. Wright, 1934
-The Secret Sister. Ward, 1924
-Shadowed Lives. Long, 1928
-She Asked for Adventure. Hurst, 1939
-Sin. Everett, 1912
-The Sins of the Fathers. Long, 1928
-Sister Susie—Spinster. Mills, 1915. Also published as (abridged): Wilful Susie. Mellifont, 1933
-The Stage Door. White, 1909
-Stage-Struck. Leng, 1935
Storm Driven. Mellifont, 1933
Sweeter Than Honey. Hurst, 1936; Green Circle, 1936
-Tempting Anne Brayton. Long, 1929
-Too Married. Wright, 1931
-The Unforgivable Sin. Long, 1930
The Van Dylk Diamonds. Ward, 1909
-Where are You Going? Wright, 1931
Wicked. Mills, 1920
Wilful Susie; see Sister Susie—Spinster
-Winning Through. Wright, 1933
-The Woman Who Was Not. Ward, 1917

ARANA, RIC
Big Dano. Powell, 1969

ARBUTHNOT, K(ATHLEEN) P(HYLLIS)
"...And Hang Him." Skeffington, 1936

ARCH, E. L. Pseudonym of Rachel (Ruth) C(osgrove) Payes, 1922- , q.v.
The Deathstone. Avalon, 1964
The First Immortals. Avalon, 1965

ARCHER, A. A. Pseudonym of Archie (Lynn) Joscelyn, 1899- , q.v.
Three Men Murdered. Phoenix, 1936
The Week-End Murders. Phoenix, 1938

ARCHER, FRANK. Pseudonym of Richard O'Connor, 1915-1975. Other pseudonym: Patrick Wayland, q.v. Series character: Joe Delaney = JD.
The Malabang Pearl. Doubleday, 1964; Hale, 1966 JD
-The Naked Crusader. Brandon, 1972
Out of the Blue. Doubleday, 1964; Hale, 1966
The Turquoise Spike. GM, 1967; Jenkins, 1968 JD
The Widow Watchers. Doubleday, 1965; Hale, 1967

ARCHER, LANE. Pseudonym of Louise Platt Hauck, 1883-1943. Other pseudonym: Louise Landon, q.v.
Mystery Mansion. Penn, 1931

ARCHER, MARGARET
Canter's Chase. Jarrolds, 1945
Flowers for Teacher. Jarrolds, 1948
The Gentle Rain. Jarrolds, 1952
Gull Yard. Jarrolds, 1947
Jonathan Guest. Jarrolds, 1952
The Silent Sisters. Jarrolds, 1950

ARCHER, MARY
The Body on the Line. Blackfriars, 1947
Concerning Miss Duncan. Cosmo, 1945
What—No Body? Blackfriars, 1947
What—No Witnesses? Locker, 1947

ARCHER, ROBERT
The Case of the Vanishing Women. Howell, 1942; Swan, 1950
Death on the Waterfront. Doubleday, 1941; Swan, 1948

ARCHIBALD, WILLIAM. 1924-1970.
The Innocents. Coward, 1950. (Play based on The Turn of the Screw by Henry James, 1843-1916, q.v.)

ARCTANDER, JOHN W(ILLIAM). 1849-1920.
Guilty? Cochrane, 1910

ARD, WILLIAM (THOMAS). 1922-1960. Pseudonyms: Ben Kerr, Mike Moran, Thomas Wills, qq.v. Series characters: Timothy Dane = TD; Danny Fontaine = DF; Lou Largo = LL.
All I Can Get. Monarch, 1959 LL
And So to Bed. Monarch, 1962 LL
As Bad as I Am. Rinehart, 1959; Boardman, 1960. Also published as: Wanted: Danny Fontaine. Dell, 1960 DF
Babe in the Woods. Monarch, 1961 LL
Cry Scandal. Rinehart, 1956; Digit, 1960 TD
Deadly Beloved; see The Root of His Evil
The Diary. Rinehart, 1952; Hammond, 1954 TD
Don't Come Crying to Me. Rinehart, 1954 TD
A Girl for Danny. Popular Library, 1953
Give Me This Woman. Monarch, 1962 LL
Hell is a City. Rinehart, 1955 TD
Like Ice She Was. Monarch, 1960 LL
Make Mine Mavis. Monarch, 1961 LL
Mr. Trouble. Rinehart, 1954 TD
The Naked and the Innocent. Digit, 1960. (U.S. title?)
No Angels for Me. Popular Library, 1954
The Perfect Frame. Mill, 1951; Hammond, 1953 TD
A Private Party. Rinehart, 1953. British title: Rogue's Murder. Hammond, 1955 TD
Rogue's Murder; see A Private Party
The Root of His Evil. Rinehart, 1957; Boardman, 1958. Also published as: Deadly Beloved. Dell, 1958 TD
The Sins of Billy Serene. Monarch, 1960
.38. Rinehart, 1952. British title: This is Murder. Hammond, 1954. Also published as: You Can't Stop Me. Popular Library, 1953 TD
This is Murder; see .38
Wanted: Danny Fontaine; see As Bad as I Am
When She Was Bad. Dell, 1960 DF
You Can't Stop Me; see .38

ARDEN, ANDREW
The Motive Not the Deed. Talmy Franklin, 1975

ARDEN, WILLIAM. Pseudonym of Dennis Lynds, 1924- , q.v. Other pseudonyms: Michael Collins, John Crowe, Carl Dekker, Maxwell Grant, Mark Sadler, qq.v. Series character: Kane Jackson, in all titles.
A Dark Power. Dodd, 1968; Hale, 1970
Deadly Legacy. Dodd, 1973; Hale, 1974
Deal in Violence. Dodd, 1969; Hale, 1971
Die to a Distant Drum. Dodd, 1972. British title: Murder Underground. Hale, 1974
The Goliath Scheme. Dodd, 1970; Hale, 1973
Murder Underground; see Die to a Distant Drum

ARDIES, TOM. 1931- .
Kosygin is Coming. Doubleday, 1974; Angus, 1975
Pandemic. Doubleday, 1973; Angus, 1974
Russian Roulette. Panther, 1975. (U.S. title?)
Their Man in the White House. Doubleday, 1971; Macmillan (London), 1971
This Suitcase is Going to Explode. Doubleday, 1972; Macmillan (London), 1972

ARDMAN, HARVEY
Endgame. Avon, 1975

ARENT, ARTHUR. 1904-1972.
Gravedigger's Funeral. Grossman, 1967; Macdonald, 1968
The Laying On of Hands. Little, 1969; Joseph, 1971

ARESBYS, THE. Pseudonym of Helen R. Bamberger, 1888- , and Raymond S. Bamberger. Series character: Parrish Darby = PD.
The Mark of the Dead. Washburn, 1929; Skeffington, 1929 PD
Murder at Red Pass. Washburn, 1930
Who Killed Coralie? Washburn, 1927; Skeffington, 1929 PD

ARKINS, FRANK J. [FRANCIS JOSEPH ARKINS]. 1866- .
The Mystery of the Bonanza Trail. General Publishing Syndicate, 1910

ARKWRIGHT, RICHARD
The Queen Anne's Gate Mystery. White, 1889; Arno, 1976

ARLEN, MICHAEL. 1895-1956.
The Crooked Coronet. Heinemann, 1937; Doubleday, 1937 ss
The Flying Dutchman. Heinemann, 1939; Book League, 1939
Hell! Said the Duchess. Heinemann, 1934; Doubleday, 1934

ARLEO, JOSEPH. 1933- .
The Grand Street Collector. Walker, 1970; Sphere, 1972

ARLEY, CATHERINE. 1932- .
Dead Man's Bay. Collins, 1959; Award, 1971

A Matter of Opportunity. Putnam, 1968
Ready Revenge. Collins, 1960; Random, 1961. (Translation of Le Talion.)
Woman of Straw. Collins, 1957; Random, 1958. (Translation of La Femme de Paille. Paris, 1956.)

ARMAT, MRS. MARY
River House. Dorrance, 1958

ARMFELT, ROGER
County Affairs. Pilot, 1945
-Village Affairs. Pilot, 1946

ARMISTEAD, LORNA MARGARET
Death of Henrietta. Cape, 1934

ARMITAGE, FLORA
The Five Deceivers. Dodd, 1963

ARMONT, PAUL. See: LOUISE JORDAN MILN, 1864-1933.

ARMOUR, JOHN. Pseudonym of Lauran Bosworth Paine, 1916- . Other pseudonyms: Reg Batchelor, Kenneth Bedford, Frank Bosworth, Mark Carrel, Robert Clarke, Richard Dana, J. F. Drexler, Troy Howard, Jared Ingersol, John Kilgore, Hunter Liggett, J. K. Lucas, John Morgan, qq.v.
Death of a Doctor. Hale, 1969
A Killer's Category. Hale, 1973
Murder in Hawthorn. Hale, 1975
Run with the Killer. Hale, 1969

ARMOUR, R. C(OUTTS). Pseudonym: Coutts Brisbane, q.v. All titles below were published by Amalgamated Press and feature Sexton Blake.
The Adventure of the Egyptian Student. 1925
The Adventure of the Oil Pirates. 1924
The Adventure of the Silk Smugglers. 1926
The Affair of the Atlantic Mail Robbery. 1929
The Affair of the Crook Explorer. 1928
The Affair of the Trade Rivals. 1926
The Baboon's Paw. 1922
The Bootlegger's Victim. 1929
By the Skin of His Teeth. 1922
The Case of the Eccentric Will. 1924
The Case of the Island Princess. 1923
The Case of the Kidnapped Legatee. 1924. Also published as: The Secret of the Gold Locket. 1935, as by Pierre Quiroule.
The Case of the Millionaire Newspaper Owner. 1924
The Case of the Mysterious Germs. 1923
Certified Insane. 1924
The Clue of the Cloakroom Ticket. 1925
Dead Man's Shoes. 1927
The Desert Trail. 1923
The Diamond Flood. 1922
The Episode of the Stolen Voice. 1921
In Savage Hayti. 1923
The Leopard Man. 1921
The Lighthouse Mystery. 1922
The Man Who Forgot. 1921
The Masked Raiders. 1930
The Movie Mystery. 1927
The Mystery of Bullen Point. 1926
The Mystery of the Isle of Fortune. 1928
The Mystery of the Sunken Road. 1922
The Pirates of the Air Way. 1927
The Platinum Smugglers. 1924
The Prisoner of the Buddha. 1927
The Riddle of the Dead Man's Pit. 1929
The Riddle of the Great Art Exhibition. 1929
The Riddle of the Lost Emigrant. 1926
The Secret of the Cask. 1929
The Secret of the Gold Locket; see The Case of the Kidnapped Legatee
The Secret of the Lagoon. 1923

The Secret of Torre Island. 1926
The Studio Mystery. 1922
The Sun God. 1923
Terror Island. 1921
Through Fire and Water. 1921
The Trail of Doom. 1928
The Trail of the Tiger. 1924
The Treasure of the Manchus. 1926
The Werewolf of Elphinstone. 1922
The White Refugees. 1922

ARMOUR, TOBY
Blood Tells. Curtis, 1973

ARMSTRONG, ANNE (WETZELL). See: G(UY) C(AMERON) POLLOCK.

ARMSTRONG, ANTHONY. Pseudonym of George Anthony Armstrong Willis, 1897-1976. Series character: Jimmie Rezaire = JR.
-The Eleventh Hour. London Play Co., 1933. (Play.)
-The End of the Road. Todd, 1943 (16 pp.)
-The Garden. Todd, 1943 (19 pp.)
He was Found in the Road. Methuen, 1952
-In the Dentist's Chair. French, 1933 (Play.)
Jimmie Rezaire. Paul, 1927. U.S. title: The Trail of Fear. Macrae-Smith, 1927 JR
Mile-Away Murder. London Play Co., 1937. (Play.)
No Higher Mountain. Methuen, 1951
One Jump Ahead. Eyre, 1972
The Poison Trail. Benn, 1932 JR
A Room at the Hotel Ambre; see Spies in Amber
The Secret Trail. Methuen, 1928; Macrae-Smith, 1929 JR
Spies in Amber. Methuen, 1956. U.S. title: A Room at the Hotel Ambre. Doubleday, 1956
The Strange Case of Mr. Pelham. Methuen, 1957; Doubleday, 1957
Ten Minute Alibi. Gollancz, 1933. (Play; novelization with Herbert Shaw: Methuen, 1934.)
The Trail of Fear; see Jimmie Rezaire
The Trail of the Black King. Methuen, 1931; Macrae-Smith, 1931 JR
The Trail of the Lotto. Methuen, 1929; Macrae-Smith, 1930 JR
Well Caught. Butler & Tanner, 1932. (Play.)
-When the Bells Rang, with Bruce Graeme. Harrap, 1943
Without Witness, with Harold Simpson. Gollancz, 1934. (Play.)

ARMSTRONG, CHARLOTTE. 1905-1969. Pseudonym: Jo Valentine, q.v. Series character: MacDougal Duff = MD.
The Albatross. Coward, 1957; Davies, 1958 ss (The title novelet in this collection was reprinted separately as: Mask of Evil. Crest, 1958.)
Alibi for Murder; see The Dream Walker
The Balloon Man. Coward, 1968; Collins, 1968
The Better to Eat You. Coward, 1954; Davies, 1954. Also published as: Murder's Nest. PB, 1955
The Black-Eyed Stranger. Coward, 1951; Davies, 1952
The Case of the Weird Sisters. Coward, 1943; Gifford, 1944 MD
Catch-as-Catch-Can. Coward, 1952; Davies, 1953. Also published as: Walk Out on Death. PB, 1954

The Chocolate Cobweb. Coward, 1948; Davies, 1952
Death Filled the Glass; see The Innocent Flower
A Dram of Poison. Coward, 1956; Davies, 1956
Dream of Fair Woman. Coward, 1966; Collins, 1966
The Dream Walker. Coward, 1955; Davies, 1955. Also published as: Alibi for Murder. PB, 1956
Duo. Coward, 1959; Davies, 1960. (Two novelets, each reprinted separately: The Girl with a Secret. Crest, 1960; Incident at a Corner. Ace, 1963.)
The Gift Shop. Coward, 1967; Collins, 1967
The Girl with a Secret; see Duo
I See You. Coward, 1966 ss
Incident at a Corner; see Duo
The Innocent Flower. Coward, 1945. British title: Death Filled the Glass. Cherry Tree, 1945 MD
Lay On, MacDuff! Coward, 1942; Gifford, 1943 MD
Lemon in the Basket. Coward, 1967; Collins, 1968
A Little Less Than Kind. Coward, 1963; Collins, 1964
The Mark of the Hand. Ace, 1963
Mask of Evil; see The Albatross
Mischief. Coward, 1950; Davies, 1951
The One-Faced Girl. Ace, 1963
The Protege. Coward, 1970; Collins, 1970
Seven Seats to the Moon. Coward, 1969; Collins, 1969
The Seventeen Widows of Sans Souci. Coward, 1959; Davies, 1959
Something Blue. Ace, 1962
Then Came Two Women. Ace, 1962
The Turret Room. Coward, 1965; Collins, 1965
The Unsuspected. Coward, 1946; Harrap, 1946
Walk Out on Death; see Catch-as-Catch-Can
Who's Been Sitting in My Chair? Ace, 1962
The Witch's House. Coward, 1963; Collins, 1964

ARMSTRONG, LEROY. 1854- .
-Dan Gunn, the Man from Mauston, A Countryman Who Did Up the Town. Rand, 1898

ARMSTRONG, MARGARET (NEILSON). 1867-1944.
The Blue Santo Murder Mystery. Random, 1941; Hale, 1943
The Man with No Face. Random, 1940; Hale, 1941
Murder in Stained Glass. Random, 1939; Hale, 1939

ARMSTRONG, RAYMOND. Pseudonym of Norman Lee, 1905-1962. Other pseudonyms: Mark Corrigan, Robertson Hobart, qq.v. Series characters: Laura Scudamore = LS; J. Rockingham Stone, in at least those marked JS.
Cavalier of the Night. Long, 1956 JS
Dangerous Limelight. Long, 1947
Midnight Cavalier. Long, 1954 JS
Murder of a Marriage. Long, 1960
Sinister Playhouse. Long, 1949
The Sinister Widow. Long, 1951 LS
The Sinister Widow Again. Long, 1952 LS
The Sinister Widow at Sea. Long, 1959 LS
The Sinister Widow Comes Back. Long, 1957 LS
The Sinister Widow Down Under. Long, 1958 LS

The Sinister Widow Returns. Long, 1953 LS
They Couldn't Go Wrong. Long, 1951
The Widow and the Cavalier. Long, 1956

ARNALDI, JEAN. Pseudonym: Jean Arnold, q.v.

ARNAUD, GEORGES. Pseudonym of Henri Georges Girard, 1917-   .
-Flesh and Fire. Avon, 1958
-Journey Past Repentance. Bodley Head, 1953. (Translation of Le Voyage du Mauvais Larron. Paris, 1951.)
The Wages of Fear. Bodley Head, 1952; Farrar, 1952. (Translation of Le Salaire de la Peur. Paris, 1950.)

ARNOLD, A(DELAIDE) V(ICTORIA). Byline also: Mrs. J. O. Arnold, q.v.
The Clue. Arnold, 1927

ARNOLD, ALEX S.
His Fortunate Foe. Earle, 1915

ARNOLD, SIR EDWIN. 1832-1904.
The Queen's Justice. Burleigh, 1899

ARNOLD, ELLIOTT. 1912-   .
Code of Conduct. Scribner, 1970; Longmans, 1970
Forests of the Night. Scribner, 1971; Longmans, 1972

ARNOLD, JEAN. Pseudonym of Jean Arnaldi.
Prettybelle. Dial, 1970

ARNOLD, MRS. J. O. Byline also: A(delaide) V(ictoria) Arnold, q.v.
The Merlewood Mystery. Nelson, 1928

ARNOLD, JOHN. 1903-   .
The London Bridge Mystery. Jenkins, 1932
Murder! Jenkins, 1926; Small, 1927
The Murders in Surrey Wood; see The Surrey Wood Mystery
The Surrey Wood Mystery. Jenkins, 1928. U.S. title: The Murders in Surrey Wood. Dutton, 1928
Tumult in San Benito. Jenkins, 1934
What Happened at Andals? Jenkins, 1929; Dutton, 1930

ARNOLD, RALPH (CRISPIAN MARSHALL). 1906-   .
Death of a Sinner. Heinemann, 1933
-Despair and Delight. Constable, 1939
-Fire on the Seven Peaks. Blackie, 1938
Fish and Company. Heinemann, 1951; Macmillan, 1951
-Fortune Favors Fools. Heinemann, 1932
-The Hundred of Hoo. Constable, 1947
Jenkin's Green. Heinemann, 1953
The Kidnapped King. Blackie, 1937
On Secret Service. Blackie, 1935
The Pelican Strikes Back. Nicholson, 1936
Skeletons and Cupboards. Heinemann, 1952; Macmillan, 1951

ARNOT, ALLEN
The Dempsey Diamonds. Lane (London & New York), 1912

ARNOTHY, CHRISTINE. 1930-   .
The Black Garden. Holt, 1969; H. Hamilton, 1969. (Translation of Le Jardin Noir. Paris, 1966.)

ARONSON, HARVEY and MIKE McGRADY
Establishment of Innocence. Putnam, 1975

ARPINO, GIOVANNI. 1927-   .
A Crime of Honor. Braziller, 1963; Weidenfeld, 1963. (Translation of Un Delitto d'Onore. Milan, 1961.)

ARRE, HELEN. Pseudonym of Z(ola) H(elen) Girdey) Ross, 1912-   , q.v. Other pseudonym: Bert Iles, q.v.
The Corpse by the River. Arcadia, 1953
The Golden Shroud. Arcadia, 1958
Murder by the Book. Arcadia, 1960
No Tears at the Funeral. Arcadia, 1954
Write It Murder. Arcadia, 1956

ARRIGHI, MEL. 1933-   .
The Death Collection. Curtis, 1973; Hale, 1976
Freak-Out. Putnam, 1968. British title: A Wild Trip. Hale, 1969
The Hatchet Man. Harcourt, 1975; Hale, 1976
An Ordinary Man. Weyden, 1970; Wingate, 1970
A Wild Trip; see Freak-Out

ARRIGIO, FRANK
Mobster. Belmont, 1975

ARTHUR, BUDD
The Big Squeeze. Bouregy, 1956
Swiftly to Evil. World Distributors, 1958

ARTHUR, FRANK. Pseudonym of Arthur Frank Ebert, 1902-   . Series character: Inspector Spearpoint = IS.
Another Mystery in Suva. Heinemann, 1956 IS
Confession to Murder. United Writers, 1974
Murder in the Tropic Night. Jenkins, 1961 IS
The Suva Harbour Mystery; see Who Killed Netta Maul?
The Throbbing Dark. Jenkins, 1963 IS
Who Killed Netta Maul? Gollancz, 1940. Also published as: The Suva Harbour Mystery. Penguin, 1948 IS

ARTHUR, HARRY. Pseudonym of Harry Arthur Bates.
Summer Showers. Pageant, 1952

ARTHUR, ROBERT. 1909-1969.
Somebody's Walking Over My Grave. Ace, 1961

ARTHUR, WILLIAM. Pseudonym of W(illiam Arthur) Howard Baker, 1925-   , q.v. Other pseudonyms: W. A. Ballinger, Peter Saxon, Richard Williams, qq.v.
Murder with Variety. Amalgamated Press, 1957. (Sexton Blake.)

ARVAY, HARRY. 1925-   .
Eleven Bullets for Mohammed. Corgi, 1975; Bantam, 1975
The Meirovitz Plan. Corgi, 1975
The Moscow Intercept. Corgi, 1975; Bantam, 1975
Operation Kuwait. Corgi, 1975; Bantam, 1975
The Piraeus Plot. Corgi, 1975; Bantam, 1975

ARVONEN, HELEN
A Choice of Angels. Ace, 1974
Circle of Death. Ace, 1967
Doorway to Death. Ace, 1973
Garden of Grief. Ace, 1974
Least of All Evils. Ace, 1970
Outpost of Eternity. Tower, 1969
Remember with Tears. Ace, 1968
Rickshaw Bend. Ace, 1973
Shadow of the Truth. Paperback Library, 1973

A Sorrow for Angels. Ace, 1973
Stranger in Her House. Paperback Library, 1970
The Summer of Evil. Ace, 1965
The Two Mrs. Carrolls. Tower, 1967. (Novelization of the movie.)
Whistle at My Window. Ace, 196?
Witches of Brimstone Hill. GM, 1971

ASBURY, HERBERT. 1891-1963.
The Crimson Rope; see The Devil of Pei-Ling
The Devil of Pei-Ling. Macy-Masius, 1927. British title: The Crimson Rope. Jarrolds, 1928
The Tick of the Clock. Macy-Masius, 1928; Brentano's (London), 1928

ASCHER, EUGENE. Series character: Lucian Carolus, in all titles.
The Grim Caretaker. Everybody's, 1944
There were No Asper Ladies. Mitre, 1944. Also published as: To Kill a Corpse. World Distributors, 1959
To Kill a Corpse; see There were No Asper Ladies
Uncanny Adventures. Everybody's, 1944 ss (48 pp.)

ASCOTT, JOHN. Pseudonym of John William Bobin,   -1935, q.v. Other pseudonym: Mark Osborne, q.v.
The Great Shipyard Mystery. Amalgamated Press, 1931. (Sexton Blake.)

ASH, WILLIAM (FRANKLIN). 1917-
Ride a Paper Tiger. Hutchinson, 1968; Walker, 1969
Take-Off. Hutchinson, 1969; Walker, 1970

ASHBAUGH, NANCY
Turn Left or Be Killed. Vanguard, 1973

ASHBROOK, H(ARRIETTE CORA). 1896-1946. Pseudonym: Susannah Shane, q.v. Series character: Philip "Spike" Tracy, in all titles.
A Most Immoral Murder. Coward, 1935; Eyre, 1935
Murder Comes Back. Coward, 1940; Eyre, 1942
Murder Makes Murder. Coward, 1937
The Murder of Cecily Thane. Coward, 1930; Eyre, 1930
The Murder of Sigurd Sharon. Coward, 1933; Eldon, 1934
The Murder of Steven Kester. Coward, 1931; Eyre, 1933
Murder on Friday; see The Purple Onion Mystery
The Purple Onion Mystery. Coward, 1941; Eyre, 1950. Also published as: Murder on Friday. Arrow, 194?

ASHBY, R(UBIE) C(ONSTANCE). 1899-   .
Death on Tiptoe. Hodder, 1930
He Arrived at Dusk. Hodder, 1933; Macmillan, 1933
Out Went the Taper. Hodder, 1934; Macmillan, 1934
Plot Against a Widow. Hodder, 1932

ASHCROFT, GENE
The Black Vulture. Burnett, 1941

ASHDOWN, CLIFFORD. Pseudonym of R(ichard) Austin Freeman, 1862-1943, q.v., and John James Pitcairn, 1860-1936. Series character: Romney Pringle = RP.
The Adventures of Romney Pringle. Ward, 1902; Train, 1968 ss RP
From a Surgeon's Diary. Ferret Fantasy, 1975; Train, 1977 ss

The Further Adventures of Romney
   Pringle. Train, 1970 ss RP
-The Queen's Treasure. Train, 1975

ASHE, B. D.
  Test Case. Dell, 1970. (Novelization of
  The Young Lawyers TV series.)

ASHE, DOUGLAS. Pseudonym of John Franklin
  Bardin, 1916-   , q.v. Other pseudo-
  nym: Gregory Tree, q.v.
  A Shroud for Grandmama. Scribner, 1951;
  Gollancz, 1951, as by Gregory Tree.
  Also published as: The Longstreet
  Legacy. Paperback Library, 1970

ASHE, GORDON. Pseudonym of John Creasey,
  1908-1973, q.v. Other pseudonyms: M.
  E. Cooke, Norman Deane, Robert Caine
  Frazer, Patrick Gill, Michael Halli-
  day, Charles Hogarth, Brian Hope,
  Colin Hughes, Kyle Hunt, Abel Mann,
  Peter Manton, J. J. Marric, Richard
  Martin, Rodney Mattheson, Anthony
  Morton, Jeremy York, qq.v. Series
  characters: Patrick Dawlish = PD;
  Patrick Dawlish and the Crime Haters
  = PD*.
The Big Call. Long, 1964; Holt, 1975
  PD*
A Blast of Trumpets. Long, 1975; Holt,
  1976 PD*
A Clutch of Coppers. Long, 1967; Holt,
  1969 PD*
Come Home to Death. Long, 1958. U.S.
  title: The Pack of Lies. Doubleday,
  1959 PD
The Crime Haters. Long, 1961; Double-
  day, 1960 PD*
The Croaker; see The Speaker
The Dark Circle. Evans, 1950 PD
Dark Mystery. Long, 1948 PD
Day of Fear. Long, 1956; Holt, 1978 PD
Death from Below. Long, 1963; Holt,
  1968 PD*
Death in a Hurry. Evans, 1952 PD
Death in Diamonds. Evans, 1951 PD
Death in Flames. Long, 1943 PD
Death in High Places. Long, 1942 PD
Death in the Trees. Long, 1954 PD
Death on Demand. Long, 1939 PD
Death on the Move. Long, 1945 PD
Don't Let Him Kill. Long, 1960. U.S.
  title: The Man Who Laughed at Murder.
  Doubleday, 1960 PD
Double for Death. Long, 1954; Holt,
  1969 PD
Drop Dead; see The Long Search
Elope to Death. Long, 1959; Holt, 1977
  PD
Engagement with Death. Long, 1948 PD
Give Me Murder. Long, 1947 PD
A Herald of Doom. Long, 1974; Holt,
  1975 PD*
Here is Danger. Long, 1946 PD
Invitation to Adventure. Long, 1945 PD
The Kidnapped Child. Long, 1955; Holt,
  1971. Also published as: The Snatch.
  Corgi, 1965 PD
Kill or Be Killed. Evans, 1949 PD
A Life for a Death. Long, 1973; Holt,
  1973 PD*
The Long Search. Long, 1953. U.S.
  title: Drop Dead. Ace, 1954 PD
The Man Who Laughed at Murder; see
  Don't Let Him Kill
The Man Who Stayed Alive. Long, 1955
The Masked Gunman; see Who Was the
  Jester?
Missing or Dead. Evans, 1952 PD
Murder Most Foul. Long, 1942 PD
Murder Too Late. Long, 1947 PD
Murder with Mushrooms. Evans, 1950;
  Holt, 1974 PD
A Nest of Traitors. Long, 1970; Holt,
  1971 PD*

No Need to Die. Long, 1956. U.S.
  title: You've Bet Your Life. Ace,
  1957
The Pack of Lies; see Come Home to
  Death
A Promise of Diamonds. Long, 1965;
  Dodd, 1964 PD*
A Puzzle in Pearls. Long, 1949 PD
A Rabble of Rebels. Long, 1971; Holt,
  1972 PD*
Rogues Rampant. Long, 1944 PD
Rogue's Ransom. Long, 1962; Doubleday,
  1961 PD*
A Scream of Murder. Long, 1969; Holt,
  1970 PD*
Secret Murder. Long, 1940 PD
A Shadow of Death. Long, 1968; Holt,
  1976 PD*
Sleepy Death. Long, 1953 PD
The Snatch; see The Kidnapped Child
The Speaker. Long, 1939. U.S. title:
  The Croaker. Holt, 1973 PD
A Taste of Treasure. Long, 1966; Holt,
  1966 PD*
Terror by Day. Long, 1940 PD
There Goes Death. Long, 1942 PD
Two Men Missing. Long, 1943 PD
Wait for Death. Long, 1957; Holt, 1972
  PD
'Ware Danger. Long, 1941 PD
Who Was the Jester? Newnes, 1940. Also
  published as: The Masked Gunman
You've Bet Your Life; see No Need to
  Die

ASHE, NICHOLAS
  Danger Aft. Low, 1935
  Preface to a Killing; see Prelude to a
  Killing
  Prelude to a Killing. Low, 1936. U.S.
  title: Preface to a Killing. Macau-
  lay, 1937

ASHE, SAXON. Pseudonym. Series character:
  Saxon Ashe, in both titles.
  I am Saxon Ashe. Hodder, 1940; Alli-
  ance, 1941
  Saxon Ashe...Secret Agent. Hodder,
  1941; Alliance, 1942

ASHENHURST, JOHN
  The World's Fair Murders. Houghton,
  1933

ASHER, MIRIAM
  Nightmare in Eden. PB, 1974

ASHFORD, F(RANCIS) U(RQUHART)
  A Packet of Trouble. Hale, 1971

ASHFORD, JEFFREY. Pseudonym of Roderic
  (Graeme) Jeffries, 1926-   , q.v.
  Other pseudonyms: Peter Alding,
  Roderic Graeme, Graham Hastings,
  qq.v. Series character: Detective
  Inspector Don Kerry = DK.
  Bent Copper. Long, 1971; Walker, 1971
  The Burden of Proof. Long, 1962; Har-
  per, 1963
  The Colour of Violence. Long, 1974;
  Walker, 1974
  Consider the Evidence. Long, 1966;
  Walker, 1966
  Counsel for the Defense. Long, 1960;
  Harper, 1961
  The D.I.; see Investigations are Pro-
  ceeding
  The Double Run. Long, 1973; Walker,
  1973
  Enquiries are Continuing. Long, 1964.
  U.S. title: The Superintendent's
  Room. Harper, 1965 DK

Forget What You Saw. Long, 1967;
  Walker, 1967
The Hands of Innocence. Long, 1965;
  Walker, 1966
Hit and Run; see Will Anyone Who Saw
  the Accident...
Investigations are Proceeding. Long,
  1961. U.S. title: The D.I. Harper,
  1962 DK
A Man Will Be Kidnapped Tomorrow.
  Long, 1972; Walker, 1972
Prisoner at the Bar. Long, 1969;
  Walker, 1969
The Superintendent's Room; see
  Enquiries are Continuing
Three Layers of Guilt. Long, 1975;
  Walker, 1976
To Protect the Guilty. Long, 1970;
  Walker, 1970
Will Anyone Who Saw the Accident...
  Long, 1963; Harper, 1964. Also
  published as: Hit and Run. Arrow,
  1966

ASHLEY, ARTHUR ERNEST. 1906-   . Pseudonym: Francis Vivian, q.v.

ASHLEY, KATE
  The Cinnabar Shroud. Long, 1956

ASHLEY, KENNETH H.
  Death of a Curate. Lane, 1932

ASHLEY, LANE
  Skeleton's Holiday. Long, 1940

ASHLEY, MARTIN
  Checkmate and Deathmate. Vantage, 1973

ASHLEY, STEVEN
  Caleb, Who is Hotter Than a $2 Pistol.
  McKay, 1975

ASHTON, CHARLES. 1884-   .
  Calamity Comes to Flenton. Nicholson,
  1936
  Dance for a Dead Uncle. Museum, 1948
  Death for Two. Hale, 1940
  Death Greets a Guest. Nicholson, 1936
  Fate Strikes Twice. Cherry Tree, 1944
  (96 pp.)
  Here's Murder Done. Hale, 1943
  Murder at Melton Peveril. Hale, 1946
  Murder in Make-Up. Nicholson, 1934
  Stone Dead. Hale, 1939
  Tragedy After Tea. Nicholson, 1935

ASHTON, HELEN (ROSALINE). 1891-   .
  People in Cages. Macmillan, 1937; Collins, 1937

ASHTON, HERBERT, JR.
  The Locked Room. French (New York),
  1934. (3-act play.)

ASHTON, SHARON
  The Santa Ana Wind. Doubleday, 1974;
  New English Library, 1975

ASHTON, WARREN J. Pseudonym of William
  T(aylor) Adams, 1822-1897, q.v.
  -Hatchie, the Guardian Slave; or, The
  Heiress of Bellevue. Mussey, 1852

ASHTON, WINIFRED. Pseudonym: Clemence
  Dane, q.v.

ASIMOV, ISAAC. 1920-   . Series charac-
  ter: Elijah Baley = EB.
  Asimov's Mysteries. Doubleday, 1968;
  Rapp, 1968 ss
  The Caves of Steel. Doubleday, 1954;
  Boardman, 1954 EB
  The Death Dealers. Avon, 1958. Also
  published as: A Whiff of Death.
  Walker, 1968; Gollancz, 1968

The Naked Sun. Doubleday, 1957; Joseph, 1958 EB
Tales of the Black Widowers. Doubleday, 1974; Gollancz, 1975 ss
A Whiff of Death; see The Death Dealers

ASINOF, ELIOT. 1919- .
The Name of the Game is Murder. Simon, 1968

ASKEW, ALICE and ASKEW, CLAUDE, 18 - 1917.
-The Actor Manager. Newnes, 1913
The Adventures of Police Constable Vane, M.A. Hutchinson, 1908
-Anna of the Plains. White, 1906
-The Apache. Everett, 1912
-Araby's Husband. Hurst, 1914
-The Baxter Family. White, 1907
-Behind Shuttered Windows. C. H. White, 1910
-Bess of Bentley's. White, 1912
The Blue Diamond. C. H. White, 1909
-The Bride in Black. Ward, 1918
-By Order of the King. Aldine, 1914
A Deadly Revenge. Mellifont, 1934
-Destiny. Hurst, 1911
-The Devil and the Crusader. White, 1909
-The Dream Daughter. Ward, 1912
-The Englishwoman. Cassell, 1912
-The Etonian. White, 1906; Bell, 1906
-Eve—and the Law. Chapman, 1905
-Evelyn. Long, 1923
-Fate—and Drusilla. Everett, 1910
-Felix Stone. Everett, 1909
-The Footlight Glare. Ward, 1916
-Freedom. Hurst, 1914
-The Garment of Immortality. Long, 1917
-Gilded London. Ward, 1915
-God's Clay. Unwin, 1913
-The Golden Girl. Ward, 1913
-The Golden Quest. Ward, 1915
-The Grip of Sin. Lloyds, 1920
Helen of the Moor. Ward, 1911
-Her Empty Triumph. Leng, 1926
-Her Father's Daughter. Ward, 1916
-Her Mother's Child. Ward, 1915
-The House Next Door. Ward, 1911
-In Lovers' Lane. Ward, 1912
-In Strange Shoes. Ward, 1914
-The Inscrutable Miss Stone. Long, 1917
-Jennifer Pontefracte. Hurst, 1906
-John Heriot's Wife. White, 1909
-The King's Signature. Chapman, 1912
Kitty Shafton—Swindler. Ward, 1911
-Lady Borradale's Ordeal. Ward, 1918
Lavender's Inheritance. United Press, 1922
-The Legacy. Ward, 1914
-The Lily and the Devil. Everett, 1912
The Lost Idol. Ward, 1917
-The Love Stone. Sisley's 1907
-Love the Jester. Ward, 1914
The Lurking Shadow. Ward, 1915
-Master and Man. Aldine, 1915
-Milly the Actress. Aldine, 1913
The Missing Million. Ward, 1915
The Mystery of Helmsley Grange. Pearson, 1913
Not Proven. Ward, 1908
-Nurse. Hodder, 1916
-The Orchard Close. Hurst, 1908
-The Ordeal of Ann Curtis. Jarrolds, 1918
Out of the Running. Everett, 1907
-Outlaw Jess. Ward, 1912
-The Paignton Honour. Ward, 1917
-The Path of Lies. White, 1908
-The Pearl of Great Price. White, 1911
-The Plains of Silence. Cassell, 1907
-Poison. Nash, 1913
-A Preacher of the Lord. Cassell, 1913
-The Premier's Daughter. White, 1905
-The Quest of El Dorado. Cassell, 1910
-The Rod of Justice. Unwin, 1910; Brentano's, 1910
-Salvation. Chapman, 1917
-The Scarlet Sin. Ward, 1913
-Scarlet Town. C. H. White, 1910
-The Secret Pathway. Collins, 1919
-The Shulamite. Chapman, 1904. Revised edition: Unwin, 1907; Brentano's, 1907
-A Society Marriage. Ward, 1911
-Souls Adrift. Ward, 1913
-The Sporting Chance. Ward, 1910
-The Stolen Lady. Ward, 1911
The Sword of Peace: The Story of a Secret Society. Everett, 1907
-The Telephone Girl. Ward, 1918
-The Tempting of Paul Chester. Unwin, 1908; Fenno, 1910
-Through Folly's Mill. Ward, 1914
-The Tocsin. Long, 1915
-Trespass. Chapman, 1915
-Two Apaches of Paris. Rickey, 1911 (British title?)
-The Weavers. Ward, 1915
-Wild Sheba. Ward, 1910
-A Woman's World. Leng, 1926
-The Work of Her Hands. Chapman, 1918
-The Yellow Yoke. Aldine, 1919

ASPINALL, (HONOR) RUTH (ALASTAIR). 1922- .
The Dark Side of Magic. Harrap, 1971

ASPINWALL, MARGUERITE. See: ELSIE JANIS, 1889-1956.

ASQUITH, HERBERT. 1881-1947.
Wind's End. Hutchinson, 1924; Scribner, 1924

ASTERLEY, H(UGH) C(ECIL)
Tale of Two Murders. Jarrolds, 1932. U.S. title: Mortmain. Sears, 1932

ASTLEY, JULIET
The Fall of Midas. Coward, 1975

ASWELL, MARY LOUISE (WHITE). 1902- .
See also: Q. PATRICK.
Far to Go. Farrar, 1957

ATCHESON, GEORGE. 1923- .
The Peking Incident. Prentice-Hall, 1973; Bantam (London), 1974

ATHEN, ASTOR
The Ladies Leave the Castle. Gifford, 1948

ATHERTON, GERTRUDE (FRANKLIN HORN). 1857-1948.
The Avalanche. Stokes, 1919; Murray, 1919
The Foghorn: Stories. Houghton, 1934. British title: The Foghorn and other stories. Jarrolds, 1935 ss
Mrs. Balfame. Stokes, 1916; Murray, 1916
-The Sophisticates. Liveright, 1931; Chapman, 1931

ATHOLL, JUSTIN. All titles are booklets of less than 70 pages.
Death in the Green fields. Mitre, 1944
The Grey Beast. Everybody's, 1944
Land of Hidden Death. Everybody's, 1944
The Man Who Tilted the Earth. Mitre, 1943
The Oasis of Sleep. Mitre, 1944
The Perfect Murder. Everybody's, 1943
There Goes His Ghost. Everybody's, 1944
The Trackless Thing. Everybody's, 1944

ATIYAH, EDWARD (SELIM). 1903-1964.
-Black Vanguard. Davies, 1952
The Crime of Julian Masters. Hale, 1959
The Cruel Fire; see Donkey from the Mountains
Donkey from the Mountains. Hale, 1961. U.S. title: The Cruel Fire. Doubleday, 1962
-The Eagle Flies from England. Hale, 1960
-Lebanon Paradise. Davies, 1953
Murder, My Love; see The Thin Line
The Thin Line. Davies, 1951; Harper, 1951. Also published as: Murder, My Love. Avon, 1957

ATKEY, BERTRAM. 1880-1952. Series characters: Smiler Bunn = SB; Prosper Fair = PF.
The Amazing Mr. Bunn. Newnes, 1912 SB ss
Arsenic and Gold. Jenkins, 1939; Penn, 1939 SB
Crooks' Castle. Newnes, 1935
-The Golden Lady. Ward, 1914
-Harvest of Javelins. Cassell, 1922; Brentano's, 1923
-Hercules—Sportsman. Robinson & Birch, 1922
The House of Clystevill. Jenkins, 1940 SB
The House of Strange Victims. Appleton, 1930. (British title?) PF
The Man with Yellow Eyes. Newnes, 1923; Dial, 1927
The Midnight Mystery. Appleton, 1928. (British title?) PF
Mr. Dass. Hodder, 1929
The Mystery of the Glass Bullet. Appleton, 1931. (British title?) SB
The Pyramid of Lead. Hutchinson, 1924; Appleton, 1925 PF
The Smiler Bunn Brigade. Hodder, 1916 SB ss
Smiler Bunn, Byewayman. Newnes, 1925 SB ss
Smiler Bunn, Gentleman-Adventurer. Dial, 1927. (= Smiler Bunn, Gentleman-Crook?) SB ss
Smiler Bunn, Gentleman-Crook. Newnes, 1923 SB ss
Smiler Bunn, Manhunter. Newnes, 1920 SB ss

ATKEY, PHILIP. 1908- . Pseudonym: Barry Perowne, q.v.
Blue Water Murder. Cassell, 1935
Heirs of Merlin. Cassell, 1945
Juniper Rock. Cassell, 1952

ATKINS, FRANCIS HENRY. 1840-1927. Pseudonym: Frank Aubrey, q.v.

ATKINS, HAROLD
Sinister Smith. Duckworth, 1938

ATKINS, MEG ELIZABETH
By the North Door. Harper, 1975
Secret Loving Shadows; see The Shadows of the House
The Shadows of the House. Viking, 1969; Hodder, 1969. Also published as: Secret Loving Shadows. Ballantine, 1977

ATKINSON, ALEX. 1916-1962.
Exit Charlie. Davies, 1955; Knopf, 1956

ATKINSON, HUGH. 1923- .
Crack-Up. Hart-Davis, 1974
-Low Company. Cheshire, 1961
The Man in the Middle. Hart-Davis, 1973; Putnam, 1973

The Most Savage Animal. Hart-Davis, 1972; Simon, 1973
-The Pink and the Brown. Gollancz, 1957
The Reckoning. Bodley Head, 1965

ATLEE, BENGE. 1890-   .
Black Feather. Scribner, 1939

ATLEE, PHILIP. Pseudonym of James Atlee Phillips, 1915-   , q.v. Series character: Joe Gall = JG.
The Black Venus Contract. GM, 1975 JG
The Canadian Bomber Contract. GM, 1971 JG
The Death Bird Contract. GM, 1966; Coronet, 1968 JG
The Fer-de-Lance Contract. GM, 1970 JG
The Green Wound. GM, 1963; Muller, 1964. Also published as: The Green Wound Contract. GM, 1967 JG
The Green Wound Contract; see The Green Wound
The Ill Wind Contract. GM, 1969 JG
The Irish Beauty Contract. GM, 1966; Coronet, 1968 JG
The Judah Lion Contract. GM, 1972 JG
The Kiwi Contract. GM, 1972 JG
The Kowloon Contract. GM, 1974 JG
-The Naked Year. Lion, 1954
The Paper Pistol Contract. GM, 1966; Coronet, 1968 JG
The Rockabye Contract. GM, 1968 JG
The Shankill Road Contract. GM, 1973 JG
The Silken Baroness. GM, 1964. Also published as: The Silken Baroness Contract. GM, 1966; Coronet, 1967 JG
The Silken Baroness Contract; see The Silken Baroness
The Skeleton Coast Contract. GM, 1968 JG
The Spice Route Contract. GM, 1973 JG
The Star Ruby Contract. GM, 1967; Coronet, 1969 JG
The Trembling Earth Contract. GM, 1969; Coronet, 1970 JG
The Underground Cities Contract. GM, 1974 JG
The White Wolverine Contract. GM, 1971 JG

ATTIWILL, KEN(NETH). See also: EVADNE PRICE.
Sky Steward. Long, 1936

ATWATER, MARY M(EIGS). 1878-1956.
Crime in Corn-Weather. Houghton, 1935. British title: Murder in Midsummer. Gollancz, 1935

AUBREY, FRANK. Pseudonym of Francis Henry Atkins, 1840-1927.
A Studio Mystery. Jarrolds, 1897

AUBREY-FLETCHER, HENRY LANCELOT. 1887-1969. Pseudonym: Henry Wade, q.v.

AUDEMARS, PIERRE. 1909-   . Series characters: Monsieur Pinaud, in at least those marked MP; Hercule Renard, in at least those marked HR.
And One for the Dead. Long, 1975 MP
The Confession of Hercule. Low, 1947 HR
The Crown of Night. Long, 1962; Harper, 1962 MP
Dead with Sorrow. Long, 1965. U.S. title: A Woven Web. Doubleday, 1965 MP
The Delicate Dust of Death. Long, 1973 MP
The Dream and the Dead. Long, 1963 MP
Fair Maids Missing. Long, 1964; Doubleday, 1965 MP
-Fate and Fernand. Polybooks, 1945. (16 pp.)
The Fire and the Clay. Long, 1959 MP
The Flame in the Mist. Long, 1969; Curtis, 1971 MP

Hercule and the Gods. Pilot, 1944; Rinehart, 1946 HR
A Host for Dying. Long, 1970; Curtis, 1972 MP
Nightmare in Rust. Long, 1975 MP
Night Without Darkness. Selwyn, 1936
No Tears for the Dead. Long, 1974 MP
The Obligations of Hercule. Low, 1947 HR
Stolen Like Magic Away. Long, 1971 MP
The Street of Grass; see The Wings of Darkness
The Temptations of Hercule. Pilot, 1945 HR
Thieves of Enchantment. Chambers, 1956
A Thorn in the Dust. Long, 1967 MP
Time of Temptation. Long, 1966; Doubleday, 1966 MP
The Turns of Time. Long, 1961; Harper, 1962 MP
The Two Imposters. Long, 1958 MP
The Veins of Compassion. Long, 1967 MP
-When the Gods Laughed. Foster, 1946
The White Leaves of Death. Long, 1968 MP
The Wings of Darkness. Long, 1963. U.S. title: The Street of Grass. Harper, 1963 MP
A Woven Web; see Dead with Sorrow

AUDOUARD, YVAN
-Little Pig-Alee. Ace, 1961

AUFRICHT-RUDA, HANS. 1899-   .
The Case for the Defendant. Allen, 1929; Little, 1929

AUGUST, JOHN. Pseudonym of Bernard Augustine DeVoto, 1897-1955.
Advance Agent. Little, 1941; Selwyn, 1943
Rain Before Seven. Little, 1940
Troubled Star. Little, 1939
The Woman in the Picture. Little, 1944; Selwyn, 1944

AUGUST, LEO
Superdoll. Award, 1970

AUGUSTA, CLARA. Pseudonym of Clara Augusta Jones. Other pseudonym: Hero Strong, q.v.
-The Adventures of a Bashful Bachelor. Ogilvie, 1890
The Fatal Glove. Lupton, 1892
The Lost Bride; or, The Price of Silence. Street, 1889
Nobody's Daughter; or, The Hidden Crime at Fernwood. Street, 1891
-Patience Pettigrew's Perplexities. Burt, 1887

AUMONIER, STACY. 1887-1928.
The Baby Grand and other stories. Heinemann, 1926; Holt, 1927 ss
Miss Bracegirdle and others. Hutchinson, 1923; Doubleday, 1923 ss

AUSLANDER, JOSEPH. 1897-   .
Hell in Harness. Doubleday, 1929. (Short crime story in verse.)

AUSTEN-LEIGH, LOIS (E.)
The Gobblecock Mystery. Jenkins, 1938
The Haunted Farm. Jenkins, 1932
The Incredible Crime. Jenkins, 1931
Rude Justice. Jenkins, 1936

AUSTIN, ALEX
Salt and Pepper. Popular Library, 1968. (Novelization of the movie.)

AUSTIN, ANNE. 1895-   . Series character: James F. ("Bonnie") Dundee = JD.
The Avenging Parrot. Greenberg, 1930; Skeffington, 1931 JD
The Black Pigeon. Greenberg, 1929; Skeffington, 1932
Murder at Bridge. Macmillan, 1931; Skeffington, 1931 JD
Murder Backstairs. Macmillan, 1930; Skeffington, 1930 JD
Murdered But Not Dead. Macmillan, 1939 JD
One Drop of Blood Macmillan, 1932; Skeffington, 1932 JD
A Wicked Woman. Macmillan, 1933; Hurst, 1934

AUSTIN, BENJAMIN FISH. 1852-1930. Pseudonym: Benjamin Nitsua, q.v.

AUSTIN, F(REDERICK) BRITTEN. 1885-1941.
According to Orders. Melrose, 1918; Doran, 1918 ss
On the Borderland. Hurst, 1922; Doubleday, 1923 ss
Thirteen. Doubleday, 1925. (ss culled from According to Orders, On the Borderland, and Under the Lens, qq.v.)
Told in the Marketplace. Butterworth, 1935 ss
Under the Lens. Hurst, 1924 ss

AUSTIN, HUGH. Pseudonym of Hugh Austin Evans. Series characters: Peter Quint = PQ; Wm. Sultan (Sultan's Harem) = WS.
The Cock's Tail Murder. Doubleday, 1938 PQ
Death has Seven Faces. Scribner, 1949
Drink the Green Water. Scribner, 1948 WS
It Couldn't Be Murder. Doubleday, 1935; Heinemann, 1936 PQ
Lilies for Madame. Doubleday, 1938; Heinemann, 1938
The Milkmaid's Millions. Scribner, 1948 WS
Murder in Triplicate. Doubleday, 1935; Heinemann, 1936 PQ
Murder of a Matriarch. Doubleday, 1936; Heinemann, 1937 PQ
The Upside Down Murders. Doubleday, 1937; Heinemann, 1938 PQ

AUSTIN, LILIAN EDNA
Shudders. Meador, 1931 ss

AUSTIN, PHYLLIS. 1888-   .
Concerto. Nicholson, 1934

AUSTWICK, JOHN. Pseudonym of Austin Lee, 1904-1965, q.v. Other pseudonym: Julian Callender, q.v. Series character: Inspector Parker, in at least those marked P.
The Borough Council Murders. Hale, 1965
The County Library Murders. Hale, 1962
Highland Homicide. Hale, 1957 P
The Hubberthwaite Horror. Hale, 1958
The Mobile Library Murders. Hale, 1964
Murder in the Borough Library. Hale, 1959 P

AUTUMN, AGNESE
The Gold and Copper Delamonds. Methuen, 1930

AVALLONE, MICHAEL (ANGELO, JR.). 1924-   . Pseudonyms: Priscilla Dalton, Mark Dane, Jean-Anne de Pre, Dora Highland, Steve Michaels, Dorothea Nile, Edwina Noone, Sidney Stuart, Max Walker, qq.v. Series characters: Ed Noon = EN; Napoleon Solo (The Man from U.N.C.L.E., novels

A

based on the TV series, with many other authors) = NS; Satan Sleuth = SS; April Dancer (The Girl from U.N.C.L.E., novels based on the TV series) = AD.
The Alarming Clock. Curtis, 1973; Allen, 1961 EN
Assassins Don't Die in Bed. Signet, 1968 EN
The Bedroom Bolero. Belmont, 1963; Digit, 1964. Also published as: The Bolero Murders. Hale, 1972 EN
The Birds of a Feather Affair. Signet, 1966; Four Square, 1967 AD
The Blazing Affair. Signet, 1966 AD
The Bolero Murders; see The Bedroom Bolero
The Brutal Kook; see Lust is No Lady
A Bullet for Pretty Boy. Curtis, 1970. (Novelization of the movie.)
The Case of the Bouncing Betty. Ace, 1957; Allen, 1959 EN
The Case of the Violent Virgin. Ace, 1957; Allen, 1960 EN
The Coffin Things. Lancer, 1968
The Crazy Mixed-Up Corpse. GM, 1957; Fawcett (London), 1959 EN
Dead Game. Holt, 1954; Allen, 1959 EN
Death Dives Deep. Signet, 1971; Hale, 1971 EN
Devil, Devil. Warner, 1975; New English Library pb, 1976 SS
The Doomsday Bag. Signet, 1969. British title: Killer's Highway. Hale, 1970 EN
Ed Noon in London; see London, Bloody London
Fallen Angel. Warner, 1974; New English Library pb, 1976 SS
The Fat Death. Curtis, 1972; Allen, 1966 EN
The February Doll Murders. Signet, 1967; Allen, 1966 EN
The Felony Squad. Popular Library, 1967 (Novelization of the TV series.)
The Flower-Covered Corpse. Curtis, 1972; Hale, 1969 EN
The Girl in the Cockpit. Curtis, 1972; Hale, 1974 EN
Hawaii Five-O. Signet, 1968. (Novelization of the TV series.)
The Horrible Man. Curtis, 1972; Hale, 1968 EN
The Hot Body. Curtis, 1973 EN
The Incident. Popular Library, 1968. (Novelization of the movie.)
Kaleidoscope. Popular Library, 1966. (Novelization of the movie.)
Killer on the Keys. Curtis, 1973 EN
Kill Her—You'll Like It! Curtis, 1973; Hale, 1974 EN
Killer's Highway; see The Doomsday Bag
The Killing Star. Hale, 1969
Little Miss Murder. Signet, 1971. British title: The Ultimate Client. Hale, 1971 EN
The Living Bomb. Curtis, 1972; Allen, 1963 EN
London, Bloody London. Curtis, 1972. British title: Ed Noon in London. Hale, 1974 EN
Lust is No Lady. Belmont, 1964. British title: The Brutal Kook. Allen, 1965 EN
Madame X. Popular Library, 1966. (Novelization of the movie.)
The Man from AVON. Avon, 1967
The Man from U.N.C.L.E.; see The Thousand Coffins Affair
Mannix. Popular Library, 1968. (Novelization of the TV series.)
Meanwhile Back at the Morgue. GM, 1960; Muller, 1961
Missing! Signet, 1969
The Moving Graveyard; see Shoot It Again, Sam
One More Time. Popular Library, 1970. (Novelization of the movie.)
Shock Corridor. Belmont, 1963. (Novelization of the movie.)
Shoot It Again, Sam. Curtis, 1972. British title: The Moving Graveyard. Hale, 1973 EN
The Spitting Image. Holt, 1953; Barker, 1957 EN
The Tall Dolores. Holt, 1953; Barker, 1956 EN
Terror in the Sun. Signet, 1969. (Novelization of the Hawaii Five-O TV series.)
There is Something About a Dame. Belmont, 1963 EN
The Thousand Coffins Affair (The Man from U.N.C.L.E.). Ace, 1965; Four Square, 1965 NS
The Ultimate Client; see Little Miss Murder
Violence in Velvet. Signet, 1956; Allen, 1958 EN
The Voodoo Murders. GM, 1957; Fawcett (London), 1959 EN
The Werewolf Walks Tonight. Warner, 1974 SS
The X-Rated Corpse. Curtis, 1973 EN

AVELINE, CLAUDE. 1901-   . Series character: Inspector Frederic Belot = FB.
Carriage 7 Seat 15. Dobson, 1968; Doubleday, 1969. (Translation of Voiture 7, Place 15. Paris, 1937.)
The Cat's Eye. Dobson, 1972; Doubleday, 1973. (Translation of L'Oeil-de-Chat. Paris, 1970.) FB
The Double Death of Frederic Belot. Dobson, 1949; Holt, 1940. (Translation of La Double Mort de Frederic Belot. Paris, 1932.) FB
The Fountain at Marlieux. Dobson, 1954; Roy, 1954. (Translation of Le Jet d'Eau.) FB
The Passenger on the U. Dobson, 1968; Doubleday, 1969. (Translation of L'Abonne de la Ligne U. Paris, 1963.) FB
Prisoner Born. Hutchinson, 1950; Doubleday, 1971. (Translation of Le Prisonnier. Paris, 1936.)

AVERILL, CHARLES E.
-The Secret Service Ship; or, The Fall of San Juan d'Ulloa. Gleason, 1848

AVERY, A. A. 1895-   .
Anything for a Quiet Life. Farrar, 1942

AVERY, ROBERT. Series character: Joe Kelly, in at least those marked JK.
The Corpse in Company K. Swift, 1942 JK
A Fast Man with a Dollar. Arcadia, 1947
A Murder a Day! Mystery House, 1940 JK
Murder on the Downbeat. Mystery House, 1943

AVRACH, JOSEPH
Murder in Oil. Westhouse, 1948

AXELROD, GEORGE. 1922-   .
Blackmailer. GM, 1952; Fawcett (London), 1959

AYER, FREDERICK, JR. 1916-1974.
The Man in the Mirror. Regnery, 1965; Gollancz, 1965
Where No Flags Fly. Regnery, 1960

AYLING, KAYE
Who was Ellen Smith? Lancer, 1967

AYLING, KEITH (OLIVER). 1898-1976.
The Last Enemy. Pyramid, 1971

AYRES, PAUL. Pseudonym of Edward S(idney) Aarons, 1916-1975, q.v. Other pseudonym: Edward Ronns, q.v.
Dead Heat. Bell, 1950. (Based on the radio series Casey, Crime Photographer and on the character of Flash Casey, created by George Harmon Coxe, 1901-   , q.v.)

AYRTON, ELIZABETH (WALSHE)
The Cretan. Hodder, 1963. U.S. title: Silence in Crete. Morrow, 1964

AYVAZIAN, L. FRED. 1919-   . Pseudonym: Fred Levon, q.v.

B

B. and R.
Helen Elwood, the Female Detective; or, A Celebrated Forger's Fate. Ogilvie, 1885

B., C. R. Pseudonym of Charles Hull.
-Redeemed. Dillingham, 1894

B., M. A. A.
Clouded in Mystery. McKinney, 1874

BABBIN, JOSEPHINE
Prime Time Corpse. Curtis, 1972

BABCOCK, DWIGHT V(INCENT). 1909-   . Series character: Hannah Van Doren, in all titles.
The Gorgeous Ghoul. Knopf, 1941; United Authors, 1947. Also published as: The Gorgeous Ghoul Murder Case. Avon, 1943
The Gorgeous Ghoul Murder Case; see The Gorgeous Ghoul
Hannah Says Foul Play. Avon, 1946
A Homicide for Hannah. Knopf, 1941. British title: Murder for Hannah. Hale, 1941
Murder for Hannah; see A Homicide for Hannah

BABER, DOUGLAS GORDON. 1918-   . Pseudonym: John Ritson, q.v.

BABSON, MARIAN. Series character: Douglas Perkins, in at least those marked DP.
Cover-Up Story. Collins, 1971 DP
Murder on Show. Collins, 1972 DP
Murder Sails at Midnight. Collins, 1975
Pretty Lady. Collins, 1973
The Stalking Lamb. Collins, 1974
There Must Be Some Mistake. Collins, 1975
Unfair Exchange. Collins, 1974

BACHELLER, IRVING A(DDISON). 1859-1950.
The House of the Three Ganders. Bobbs, 1928; Hutchinson, 1929

BACHMANN, LAWRENCE P(AUL). 1912-   . See also: HANNAH LEES.
The Kiss of Death. Knopf, 1946
The Legend of Joseph Nokato. Little, 1971
The Lorelei. Doubleday, 1958; Collins, 1957
The Phoenix. Collins, 1955. Revised edition: Ten Seconds to Hell. GM, 1958
Ten Seconds to Hell; see The Phoenix
The Ultimate Act. Atheneum, 1972; Collins, 1972

BACKHOUSE, (ENID) ELIZABETH
Death Came Uninvited. Hale, 1957
Death Climbs a Hill. Hale, 1963

Death of a Clown. Hale, 1962
The Mists Came Down. Hale, 1959
The Night has Eyes. Hale, 1961
The Web of Shadows. Hale, 1960

BACKUS, JEAN LOUISE. 1914-   . Pseudonym: David Montrose, q.v.

BACON, JOSEPHINE DASKAM. 1876-1961.
Medusa's Head. Appleton, 1926
The Strange Cases of Dr. Stanchon. Appleton, 1913 ss

BACON, PEGGY [MARGARET FRANCES BACON BROOK].
The Inward Eye. Scribner, 1952. Also published as: Lady Marked for Murder. Mercury, 1953

BACON, ADMIRAL SIR REGINALD. 1863-1947.
A Social Sinner. Nash, 1928
The Stolen Submarine. Nash, 1926

BADGER, ALEXANDER
Quickie Mysteries. Citadel, 1960. (50 mini-ss mystery puzzles.)

BAER, HOWARD. 1921-   .
-O Huge Angel. Roy, 1949

BAER, MRS. LUCY A. 1844?-1925. Pseudonym: K(ate) F. Hill, q.v.

BAGBY, GEORGE. Pseudonym of Aaron Marc Stein, 1906-   , q.v. Other pseudonym: Hampton Stone, q.v. Series character: Inspector Schmidt, in all titles.
Another Day—Another Death. Doubleday, 1968; Hale, 1968
Bait for a Killer; see Dirty Pool
A Big Hand for the Corpse; see Give the Little Corpse a Great Big Hand
Bird Walking Weather. Doubleday, 1939; Cassell, 1940
Blood Will Tell. Doubleday, 1950
The Bloody Wig Murders; see The Corpse Wore a Wig
A Body for the Bride; see The Original Carcase
The Body in the Basket. Doubleday, 1954; Macdonald, 1956
Coffin Corner. Doubleday, 1949
Cop Killer. Doubleday, 1956; Boardman, 1957
Corpse Candle. Doubleday, 1967; Hale, 1968
The Corpse with the Sticky Fingers. Doubleday, 1952
The Corpse with the Purple Thighs. Doubleday, 1939
The Corpse Wore a Wig. Doubleday, 1940. Also published as: The Bloody Wig Murders. Best Detective Selection, 1942
Dead Drunk. Doubleday, 1953; Macdonald, 1954
Dead on Arrival. Doubleday, 1946
Dead Storage. Doubleday, 1956; Boardman, 1959
Dead Wrong. Doubleday, 1957; Boardman, 1958
Death Ain't Commercial. Doubleday, 1951
Dirty Pool. Doubleday, 1966. British title: Bait for a Killer. Hammond, 1967
A Dirty Way to Die. Doubleday, 1955; Macdonald, 1956. Also published as: Shadow on the Window. Detective Book Club, 1955
Drop Dead. Doubleday, 1949
Evil Genius. Doubleday, 1961; Hammond, 1964

Give the Little Corpse a Great Big Hand. Doubleday, 1953; Macdonald, 1954. Also published as: A Big Hand for the Corpse. Detective Book Club, 1953
Here Comes the Corpse. Doubleday, 1941; Long, 1943
Honest Reliable Corpse. Doubleday, 1969; Hale, 1969
In Cold Blood. Doubleday, 1948
Killer Boy was Here. Doubleday, 1970; Hale, 1971
Murder at the Piano. Covici, 1935; Low, 1936
Murder Calling "50". Doubleday, 1942
Murder Half Baked. Covici, 1937; Cassell, 1938
Murder in Wonderland; see Mysteriouser and Mysteriouser
Murder on the Nose. Doubleday, 1938; Cassell, 1939
Murder's Little Helper. Doubleday, 1963; Hammond, 1964
Mysteriouser and Mysteriouser. Doubleday, 1965. British title: Murder in Wonderland. Hammond, 1965
The Original Carcase. Doubleday, 1946; Aldor, 1947. Also published as: A Body for the Bride. Jonathan Press, 1954 (abridged)
The Real Gone Goose. Doubleday, 1959. British title: A Real Gone Goose. Boardman, 1960
Red is for Killing. Doubleday, 1941; Long, 1944
Ring Around a Murder. Covici, 1936
Scared to Death. Doubleday, 1952
Shadow on the Window; see A Dirty Way to Die
The Starting Gun. Doubleday, 1948
The Three-Time Losers. Doubleday, 1958; Boardman, 1958
The Twin Killing. Doubleday, 1947

BAGLEY, DESMOND. 1923-   .
The Freedom Trap. Collins, 1971; Doubleday, 1972. Also published as: The Mackintosh Man. Crest, 1973. Revised edition: Fontana, 1973
The Golden Keel. Collins, 1963; Doubleday, 1964
High Citadel. Collins, 1965; Doubleday, 1965
Landslide. Collins, 1967; Doubleday, 1967
The Mackintosh Man; see The Freedom Trap
Running Blind. Collins, 1970; Doubleday, 1971
The Snow Tiger. Collins, 1975; Doubleday, 1975
The Spoilers. Collins, 1969; Doubleday, 1970
The Tightrope Men. Collins, 1973; Doubleday, 1973
The Vivero Letter. Collins, 1968; Doubleday, 1968
Wyatt's Hurricane. Collins, 1966; Doubleday, 1966

BAGNOLD, ENID
The Chalk Garden. Heinemann, 1956; French, 1956. (Play.)

BAGOT, RICHARD. 1860-1921.
The House at Serraville. Methuen, 1910; Lane (New York), 1911
The Passport. Methuen, 1905; Harper, 1905
A Roman Mystery. Digby, 1899

BAHARAV, I. D.
-The Winds of April. Primary Sources, 1965

BAHR, EDITH-JANE. 1926-   .
Help, Please. Doubleday, 1975; Collins, 1975
A Nice Neighborhood. Dell, 1975; Collins, 1973

BAHR, JEROME. 1909-   .
Holes in the Wall. Luce, 1970

BAILEY, ALICE WARD. 1857-   .
-Mark Heffron. Harper, 1896

BAILEY, ANTHONY
Making Progress. Dial, 1959; Joseph, 1959

BAILEY, CHARLES W(ALDO), II. 1929-   .
See: FLETCHER KNEBEL, 1911-   .

BAILEY, ELLIOT. 1887-   . Series character: Detective-Inspector Geoffrey Fraser, in at least those marked GF.
The Campden Hill Mystery. Bles, 1926
The Cheng Ling Mystery. Gramol, 1937
Death in Piccadilly. Gramol, 1936
Death in Quiet Places. Eldon, 1933 GF
The Maplethorpe Tangle. Bles, 1926
The Metcalfe Mystery. Bles, 1928
Mr. Benson's Business. Bles, 1925
No Crime So Great. Eldon, 1936 GF
Revenge at Nightfall. Eldon, 1937 GF
The Secret Valley. Bles, 1927
The Spider. Gramol, 1936

BAILEY, ERIC. 1933-   .
Cradle's Revenge. Long, 1969
Leave of Absence. Long, 1968

BAILEY, H(ENRY) C(HRISTOPHER). 1878-1961. Series characters: Reggie Fortune = RF; Joshua Clunk = JC.
The Apprehensive Dog; see No Murder
The Best of Mr. Fortune. PB, 1943. (A paperback original consisting of 12 ss from earlier hardcover collections.) RF
The Bishop's Crime. Gollancz, 1940; Doubleday, 1941 RF
Black Land, White Land. Gollancz, 1937; Doubleday, 1937 RF
Call Mr. Fortune. Methuen, 1920; Dutton, 1920 RF ss
Case for Mr. Fortune. Ward, 1932; Doubleday, 1932 RF ss
The Cat's Whisker; see Dead Man's Effects
A Clue for Mr. Fortune. Gollancz, 1936; Doubleday, 1936 RF ss
Clunk's Claimant. Gollancz, 1937. U.S. title: The Twittering Bird Mystery. Doubleday, 1937 JC
Dead Man's Effects. Macdonald, 1945. U.S. title: The Cat's Whisker. Doubleday, 1944 RF
Dead Man's Shoes. Gollancz, 1942. U.S. title: Nobody's Vineyard. Doubleday, 1942 JC
The Garston Murder Case; see Garstons
Garstons. Methuen, 1930. U.S. title: The Garston Murder Case. Doubleday, 1930 JC
The Great Game. Gollancz, 1939; Doubleday, 1939 RF (JC in very minor role)
Honour Among Thieves. Macdonald, 1947; Doubleday, 1947 JC
The Life Sentence. Macdonald, 1946; Doubleday, 1946 RF
The Little Captain. Gollancz, 1941. U.S. title: Orphan Ann. Doubleday, 1941 JC

B

BAILEY, H. C.
The Man in the Cape. Benn, 1933
Meet Mr. Fortune. Doubleday, 1942. (An omnibus comprising The Bishop's Crime, q.v., and 12 RF ss from earlier collections.)
Mr. Clunk's Text; see The Veron Mystery
Mr. Fortune Explains. Ward, 1930; Dutton, 1931 RF ss
Mr. Fortune Finds a Pig. Gollancz, 1943; Doubleday, 1943 RF
Mr. Fortune Here. Gollancz, 1940; Doubleday, 1940 RF ss
Mr. Fortune Objects. Gollancz, 1935; Doubleday, 1935 RF ss
Mr. Fortune, Please. Methuen, 1928; Dutton, 1928 RF ss
Mr. Fortune Speaking. Ward, 1930; Dutton, 1931 RF ss
Mr. Fortune Wonders. Ward, 1933; Doubleday, 1933 RF ss
Mr. Fortune's Practice. Methuen, 1923; Dutton, 1924 RF ss
Mr. Fortune's Trials. Methuen, 1925; Dutton, 1926 RF ss
No Murder. Gollancz, 1942. U.S. title: The Apprehensive Dog. Doubleday, 1942 RF
Nobody's Vineyard; see Dead Man's Shoes
Orphan Ann; see The Little Captain
The Queen of Spades; see Slippery Ann
The Red Castle. Ward, 1932. U.S. title: The Red Castle Mystery. Doubleday, 1932 JC
The Red Castle Mystery; see The Red Castle
Save a Rope; see Saving a Rope
Saving a Rope. Macdonald, 1948. U.S. title: Save a Rope. Doubleday, 1948 RF
Shadow on the Wall. Gollancz, 1934; Doubleday, 1934 RF
Shrouded Death. Macdonald, 1950 JC
Slippery Ann. Gollancz, 1944. U.S. title: The Queen of Spades. Doubleday, 1944 JC
The Sullen Sky Mystery. Gollancz, 1935; Doubleday, 1935 JC
This is Mr. Fortune. Gollancz, 1938; Doubleday, 1938 RF ss
The Twittering Bird Mystery; see Clunk's Claimant
The Veron Mystery. Gollancz, 1939. U.S. title: Mr. Clunk's Text. Doubleday, 1939 JC
The Wrong Man. Macdonald, 1946; Doubleday, 1945 JC

BAILEY, HILEA. Pseudonym of Ruth Lenore Marting, 1907-   . Series characters: Hilea Bailey and Hilary Dunsany Bailey III, in all titles.
Breathe No More, My Lady. Doubleday, 1946
Give Thanks to Death. Doubleday, 1940
The Smiling Corpse. Doubleday, 1941
What Night Will Bring. Doubleday, 1939; Davies, 1940

BAILEY, PAUL (DAYTON). 1906-   .
Deliver Me From Eva. Murray, 1946

BAILEY, SETH
The Hand in the Cobbler's Safe. Bart, 1944

BAILIE, ALEXANDER DUKE. Pseudonym: Inspector Murray, q.v.

BAILLIE-SAUNDERS, MARGARET (ELSIE CROWTHER). 1873-1949.
Answer That Bell! Hutchinson, 1935
-The Sign of the Swan. Hutchinson, 1938

BAIN, GRAHAM WARD
Round Robin. Harrap, 1937; Lippincott, 1937

BAINES, CUTHBERT (EDWARD)
-The Black Circle. Hodder, 1921
The Blue Poppy. Arnold, 1926
A Drug in the Market. Arnold, 1928
The Slip Coach. Arnold, 1927

BAIR, PATRICK
Gargantua Falls. Eyre, 1951
The Gypsum Flower. Eyre, 1959
Open Your Hand and Close Your Eyes. Eyre, 1964
The Tribunal. Macdonald, 1970

BAIRD, EDWIN. 1886-   .
The Mystery of the Locked Door. Sales Tales, 1928
Paul Pry's Poison Pen. Grafton, 1945. (with The Castle of Death by J. B. O'Sullivan, 1919-   , q.v.)

BAKER, AGNES MONICA. 1899-   . Pseudonym: Monica Hill, q.v.

BAKER, AMY J(OSEPHINE). 1895-   .
-The Dangerous Age. Long, 1933

BAKER, ASA. Pseudonym of Davis Dresser, 1904-1977. Other pseudonym: Brett Halliday, q.v. Joint pseudonym with Kathleen Rollins: Hal Debrett, q.v. Joint pseudonym with (Walter) Ryerson Johnson, 1901-   , q.v.: Matthew Blood, q.v. Series character: Jerry Burke, in both titles.
The Kissed Corpse. Carlyle, 1939
Mum's the Word for Murder. Stokes, 1938; Gollancz, 1939. (Dell pb reprints as by Brett Halliday.)

BAKER, BETH
Mystery Evans. DeWolfe, 1890

BAKER, CARLOS (HEARD). 1909-   .
The Gay Head Conspiracy. Scribner, 1973

BAKER, ELLIOTT
-Pocock & Pitt. Putnam, 1971; Joseph, 1974

BAKER, HUGH. Pseudonym.
Cartwright is Dead, Sir! Houghton, 1934

BAKER, IVON. 1928-   .
Days Among the Dead. Hale, 1971
Death in Sanctuary. Hale, 1970
Grave Doubt. Hale, 1972; Washburn, 1972
Justice for Judas. Hale, 1974
The Pandora Feature. Hale, 1973

BAKER, LEDRU, JR.
And Be My Love. GM, 1951
The Cheaters. GM, 1952
The Preying Streets. Ace, 1955

BAKER, MARC(EIL GENEE KOLSTAD). 1911-   . Pseudonym: Marc Miller, q.v.
The Hilltop Murders. Avalon, 1965

BAKER, (HOWELL) NORTH, 1912-   , and **WILLIAM BOLTON**
Dead to the World. Doubleday, 1944

BAKER, PETER. 1921-   .
A Killing Affair. Houghton, 1971

BAKER, RICHARD M(ERRIAM). 1896-   . Series character: Franklin Russell, in all titles.
Death Stops the Bells. Scribner, 1938
Death Stops the Manuscript. Scribner, 1936
Death Stops the Rehearsal. Scribner, 1937; Cassell, 1937

BAKER, ROBERT (MELVILLE), 1868-1929, and **JOHN EMERSON,** 1874-   .
The Conspiracy. Rosenfield, 1912; Dramatic Typing, 1912. (Play.) The novel: Duffield, 1913

BAKER, SAMM SINCLAIR. 1909-   . Series character: Clark Clark Clark, in both titles.
Murder, Very Dry! Graphic, 1956
One Touch of Blood. Graphic, 1955

BAKER, SIDNEY J.
Time is an Enemy. Mystery House, 1958

BAKER, W(ILLIAM ARTHUR) HOWARD. 1925-   . Pseudonyms (not necessarily exclusively held): William Arthur, W. A. Ballinger, Peter Saxon, Richard Williams, qq.v. Series characters: Richard Quintain, in at least those marked RQ; Sexton Blake (with many other authors) = SB. Note: Many of the books under this byline were actually written by Wilfred (Glassford) McNeilly, 1921-   , q.v. Other McNeilly pseudonyms: W. A. Ballinger, Errol Lecale, Desmond Reid, qq.v.
The Angry Night. Amalgamated, 1960. Revised edition: Fire Over India. Mayflower, 1966 SB
Appointment with Danger. Amalgamated, 1958 SB
Battle Song. Amalgamated, 1956 SB
The Big Smear. Amalgamated, 1962 SB
The Big Steal. Mayflower, 1964
Blood Trail. Mayflower, 1966
Brussels Dossier. Lancer, 1968. (British title?)
The Cellar Boys. Consul, 1965
The Charge is Treason. Baker, 1973; Lancer, 1971 RQ
Crime is my Business. Amalgamated, 1958 SB
Cry from the Dark. Consul, 1965
Dark Mambo. Amalgamated, 1956 SB
The Dead and the Damned. Mayflower, 1967
Departure Deferred. Consul, 1965; Macfadden, 1965. (Novelization of the Secret Agent TV series.)
Destination Dieppe. Mayflower, 1965 RQ
Devil's Can-Can. Amalgamated, 1956 SB
The Dirty Game; see The Guardians
The Dogs of War. Mayflower, 1966
Every Man an Enemy; see Walk in Fear
Expresso Jungle. Amalgamated, 1959 SB
Fire Over India; see The Angry Night
The Frightened Lady. Amalgamated, 1956. Revised edition: The Fugitive. Mayflower, 1965 SB
The Fugitive; see The Frightened Lady
The Girl, the City, and the Soldier; see The Rape of Berlin
The Girl in Asses' Milk. Mayflower, 1967
The Guardians. Mayflower, 1967. U.S. title: The Dirty Game. Lancer, 1967 RQ
The Hero Game. Lancer, 1965. (U.S. title?)
The Imposter, with Peter Chambers. Amalgamated, 1963 SB
The Inexpendable. Consul, 1965
It Happened in Hamburg. Amalgamated, 1956 SB
The Judas Diary. Baker, 1969; Lancer, 1969 RQ
The Man Who Knew Too Much. Amalgamated, 1955 SB
Murder Most Intimate. Amalgamated, 1958 SB
Night of the Wolf. Baker, 1969; Lancer, 1967 RQ
No Place for Strangers. Consul, 1965 RQ
No Time to Live. Amalgamated, 1958 SB

Passport into Fear. Amalgamated, 1959 SB
The Rape of Berlin. Consul, 1965; Lancer, 1967. Also published as: The Girl, the City, and the Soldier. Baker, 1968
The Reluctant Gunman. Amalgamated, 1962 SB
Requiem for Redheads. Amalgamated, 1956 SB
Scandal Street. Consul, 1963
Shoot When Ready. Amalgamated, 1957 SB
Storm Over Rockall. Consul, 1965; Macfadden, 1966. (Novelization of the Secret Agent TV series.)
Strike North. Mayflower, 1965; Lancer, 1968 RQ
Take Death for a Lover. Consul, 1965
Traitor! Lancer, 1967. (British title?)
Treason by Truth. (London), 1964
Treason Remembered. Mayflower, 1967 SB
The Treasure Hunters. Mayflower, 1970
Walk in Fear. Amalgamated, 1957. Revised edition: Every Man an Enemy. Mayflower, 1966; Macfadden, 1967 SB
Without Warning. Amalgamated, 1955 SB

BALCHIN, NIGEL (MARLIN). 1908-1970.
-The Borgia Testament. Collins, 1948; Houghton, 1949
-Darkness Falls from the Air. Collins, 1942
-The Fall of the Sparrow. Collins, 1955; Rinehart, 1956, as The Fall of a Sparrow
In the Absence of Mrs. Petersen. Collins, 1966; Simon, 1966
-Lightbody on Liberty. Collins, 1936
-Lord, I Was Afraid. Collins, 1947
Mine Own Executioner. Collins, 1945; Houghton, 1946
-No Sky. H. Hamilton, 1934
-Seen Dimly Before Dawn. Collins, 1962; Simon, 1962
-Simple Life. H. Hamilton, 1935
-The Small Back Room. Collins, 1943; Houghton, 1945
A Sort of Traitors. Collins, 1949. U.S. title: Who is My Neighbor? Houghton, 1950
Who is My Neighbor?; see A Sort of Traitors

BALDRY, W(ALTER) B(URTON), 1888- , and H(ERBERT) SLADE
The Brooklands Mystery. Car Publishing, 1911

BALDWIN, AUDREY. See: J(AMES) M(ORGAN) WALSH, 1897- .

BALFOUR, EVA. Joint pseudonym with Beryl Hearnden: Hearnden Balfour, q.v.

BALFOUR, F.
The League of Crime; or, The Twelve Temptations. Brady, 1870

BALFOUR, HEARNDEN. Joint pseudonym of Eva Balfour and Beryl Hearnden. Series character: Detective-Inspector Jack Strickland, in all titles.
Anything Might Happen. Hodder, 1931. U.S. title: Murder and the Red-Haired Girl. Houghton, 1933
The Enterprising Burglar. Hodder, 1928; Houghton, 1928
A Gentleman from Texas; see The Paper Chase
Murder and the Red-Haired Girl; see Anything Might Happen
The Paper Chase. Hodder, 1927. U.S. title: A Gentleman from Texas. Houghton, 1927

BALFOUR, JAMES
Court Short. Hutchinson, 1969 ss

BALL, BRIAN (NEVILLE). 1932- .
Death of a Low-Handicap Man. Barker, 1974
Keegan: The No-Option Contract. Barker, 1975
Montenegrin Gold. Barker, 1974; St. Martin's, 1978

BALL, DORIS BELL COLLIER. 1897- .
Pseudonym: Josephine Bell, q.v.

BALL, EUSTACE HALE. 1881-1931.
The Scarlet Fox. Grosset, 1927
Traffic in Souls. Dillingham, 1914
The Voice on the Wire. Hearst's, 1915

BALL, JOHN (DUDLEY, JR.). 1911- . Series character: Virgil Tibbs = VT.
The Cool Cottontail. Harper, 1966; Joseph, 1967 VT
Death for a Playmate; see Johnny Get Your Gun
The First Team. Little, 1971; Joseph, 1972
Five Pieces of Jade. Little, 1972; Joseph, 1972 VT
In the Heat of the Night. Harper, 1965; Joseph, 1966 VT
Johnny Get Your Gun. Little, 1969; Joseph, 1970. Revised edition: Death for a Playmate. Bantam, 1972 VT
Mark One: The Dummy. Little, 1974

BALLANTYNE, R(OBERT) M(ICHAEL). 1825-1894.
-The Iron Horse; or, Life on the Line. Nisbet, 1871

BALLARD, ERIC ALAN. Pseudonym: Edwin Harrison, q.v.

BALLARD, HELEN MABRY
To the Tune of Murder. Mill, 1952

BALLARD, K. G. Pseudonym of Holly Roth, 1916-1964, q.v. Other pseudonym: P. J. Merrill, q.v.
Bar Sinister. Doubleday, 1960; Boardman, 1961
The Coast of Fear. Doubleday, 1957. British title: Five Roads to S'Agaro. Boardman, 1958
Five Roads to S'Agaro; see The Coast of Fear
Gauge of Deception. Doubleday, 1963; Boardman, 1964
Trial by Desire. Boardman, 1960

BALLARD, P. D. Pseudonym of W(illis) T(odhunter) Ballard, 1903- , q.v. Other pseudonyms: Neil MacNeil, John Shepherd, qq.v. Joint pseudonym with Norbert Davis, q.v.: Harrison Hunt, q.v.
Age of the Junkman. GM, 1963; Muller pb, 1964
Angel of Death. GM, 1973
Brothers in Blood. GM, 1972
The Death Brokers. GM, 1973
End of a Millionaire. GM, 1964

BALLARD, W(ILLIS) T(ODHUNTER). 1903- .
Pseudonyms: P. D. Ballard, Neil MacNeil, John Shepherd, qq.v. Joint pseudonym with Norbert Davis, q.v.: Harrison Hunt, q.v. Series characters: Bill Lennox = BL (see also the John Shepherd byline); Max Hunter = MH.
Chance Elson. Cardinal, 1958
Dealing Out Death. McKay, 1948 BL

The Demise of a Louse; see Say Yes to Murder
Murder Can't Stop. McKay, 1946 BL
Murder Las Vegas Style. Tower, 1967
Pretty Miss Murder. Permabooks, 1961 MH
Say Yes to Murder. Putnam, 1942. Also published as: The Demise of a Louse, as by John Shepherd. Belmont, 1962 BL
The Seven Sisters. Permabooks, 1962 MH
Three for the Money. Permabooks, 1963 MH
Walk in Fear. GM, 1952; Red Seal, 1957

BALLEM, JOHN (BISHOP)
The Devil's Lighter. General (Ontario), 1974
The Dirty Scenario. General (Ontario), 1974

BALLENGER, DEAN. Series character: Mike Gannon, in all titles.
Blood Beast. Manor, 1974
The Blood Fix. Manor, 1974
Blood for Breakfast. Manor, 1973

BALLEW, CHARLES. Pseudonym of Charles H(orace) Snow, 1877- , q.v. The character Rim-Fire appears in at least 23 of Bellew's 55 western novels; the title below appears to have the strongest detective interest.
Rim-Fire, Detective. Wright, 1936

BALLINGER, BILL S(ANBORN). 1912- .
Pseudonyms: Frederic Freyer, B. X. Sanborn, qq.v. Series characters: Barr Breed = BB; Joaquin Hawks = JH.
Beacon in the Night. Harper, 1958; Boardman, 1960
The Beautiful Trap; see Rafferty
The Body Beautiful. Harper, 1949; World Distributors, 1960 BB
The Body in the Bed. Harper, 1948; World Distributors, 1960 BB
The Chinese Mask. Signet, 1965 JH
The Corsican. Dodd, 1974; Hale, 1976
The Darkening Door. Harper, 1952
The Deadlier Sex; see Portrait in Smoke
Formula for Murder. Signet, 1958
The 49 Days of Death. Sherbourne, 1969
The Fourth of Forever. Harper, 1963; Boardman, 1963
The Heir Hunters. Harper, 1966; Boardman, 1967
Heist Me Higher. Signet, 1969; Hale, 1971
The Law. Warner, 1975. (Novelization of the TV movie.)
The Longest Second. Harper, 1957; Reinhardt, 1958
The Lopsided Man. Pyramid, 1969
Not I, Said the Vixen. GM, 1965
Portrait in Smoke. Harper, 1950; Reinhardt, 1951. Also published as: The Deadlier Sex. Corgi, 1958
Rafferty. Harper, 1953; Reinhardt, 1953. Also published as: The Beautiful Trap. Signet, 1955
The Source of Fear. Signet, 1968; Hale, 1971
The Spy at Angkor Wat. Signet, 1966 JH
The Spy in Bangkok. Signet, 1965 JH
The Spy in the Java Sea. Signet, 1966 JH
The Spy in the Jungle. Signet, 1965 JH
The Tooth and the Nail. Harper, 1955; Reinhardt, 1955
The Wife of the Red-Haired Man. Harper, 1957; Reinhardt, 1957

BALLINGER, W. A. Pseudonym, apparently used by W(illiam Arthur) Howard Baker, 1925- , q.v., and Wilfrid (Glassford) McNeilly, 1921- , q.v.

Other Baker pseudonyms: William Arthur, Peter Saxon, Richard Williams, qq.v. Other McNeilly pseudonyms: W. Howard Baker, Errol Lecale, Desmond Reid, qq.v. Series characters: Sexton Blake (with many other authors) = SB; Richard Quintain (also under the Baker byline) = RQ.
-Call It Rhodesia. Mayflower, 1966
-The Carrion Eaters. Joseph, 1971
-Congo. Mayflower, 1970
A Corpse for Christmas. Amalgamated, 1962 SB
Down Among the Ad Men. Mayflower, 1968 SB
Drums of the Dark Gods. Mayflower, 1966 RQ
Epitaph to Treason. Amalgamated, 1960 SB
The Exterminator. Consul, 1966; Macfadden, 1966. (Novelization of the Secret Agent TV series.)
-The Galaxy Lot. Mayflower, 1968
-The Green Grassy Slopes. Corgi, 1969
I, the Hangman. Mayflower, 1965; Macfadden, 1967 SB
The Last Tiger. Amalgamated, 1963 SB
Murder in Camera. Amalgamated, 1962 SB
Murderer at Large. Mayflower, 1965 SB
Murder in Camera. Amalgamated, 1962 SB
-Naked from a Well. Mayflower, 1967
-Rebellion. Mayflower, 1966
Savage Venture. Amalgamated, 1962 SB
-The Shark Hunters. Baker, 1970
-Six-Day Loving. Mayflower, 1970
A Starlet for a Penny. Mayflower, 1966 SB
The Strange Face of Murder. Mayflower, 1965 SB
Studio One Murder. Amalgamated, 1962 SB
The Television Murders. Amalgamated, 1961 SB
This Man Must Die! Amalgamated, 1960 SB
Unfriendly Persuasion. Consul, 1964 RQ
-The Waters of Madness. New English Library, 1974
The Witches of Notting Hill. Mayflower, 1965; Macfadden, 1967 SB
-Women's Battalion. Mayflower, 1967

BALMER, EDWIN. 1883-1959. See also: WILLIAM (BRIGGS) MacHARG, 1872-1951.
The Breath of Scandal. Little, 1922; Arnold, 1923
-The Candle of the Wicked. Longmans, 1956
Dangerous Business. Dodd, 1927; Long, 1928
Dragons Drive You. Dodd, 1934
Five Fatal Words, with Philip (Gordon) Wylie, 1902-1971, q.v. Smith, 1932; Paul, 1933
Flying Death. Dodd, 1927
The Golden Hoard, with Philip (Gordon) Wylie, 1902-1971, q.v. Stokes, 1934
-Her Great Moment. Paul, 1921. (U.S. title?)
Keeban. Little, 1923; Arnold, 1923
-Resurrection Rock. Little, 1920; Hodder, 1920
-Ruth of the U.S.A. McClurg, 1919
The Shield of Silence, with Philip (Gordon) Wylie, 1902-1971, q.v. Stokes, 1936; Collins, 1937
That Royle Girl. Dodd, 1925
The Torn Letter. Dodd, 1941; Nicholson, 1943
Waylaid by Wireless. Small, 1909

BALNEAVES, ELIZABETH
Murder in the Zoo. Chivers, 1975

BALZAC, HONORÉ DE. 1799-1850. Although crime and mystery elements are scattered throughout Balzac's work, it seems appropriate to mention only the following. (Note that since English translations and editions of Balzac's fiction form an impenetrable maze, the list below keys to the original French title and omits U.S. and British first edition data.)
Histoire des Treize. Published in English in various forms, including in total as: The Thirteen; part one as Ferragus, and as The Mystery of the Rue Soly; part two as The Duchesse de Langeais; and part three as The Girl with the Golden Eyes.
Le Père Goriot. Published in English under titles including: Daddy Goriot; Father Goriot; Old Goriot; Old Man Goriot; Pere Goriot; and Unrequited Affection.
Une Ténébreuse Affaire. Published in English as: The (A) Gondreville Mystery.

BAMBERGER, HELEN R. 1888- . Joint pseudonym with Raymond S. Bamberger: The Aresbys, q.v.

BAMBERGER, RAYMOND S. Joint pseudonym with Helen R. Bamberger, 1888- : The Aresbys, q.v.

BAMBURG, LILIAN. Series character: Septimus March = SM.
Beads of Silence. Selwyn, 1926; Dutton, 1927 SM
Rays of Darkness. Selwyn, 1927 SM
The Riddle of the Dead, with Charles Platt. Gardner, 1930

BAMFORD, FRANCIS
A Question of Taste. Longmans, 1949
Return to Cottington. Longmans, 1946
This Chequered Floor. Longmans, 1941
What Stranger Cause? Longmans, 1944

BANBURY, G(EORGE) A(LEXANDER) LETHBRIDGE
The Lumley Wood Mystery. Hutchinson, 1890

BANCAL, J(EAN). See: J. GUIL.

BANCROFT, GEORGE PLEYDELL. 1868- . Pseudonym: George Pleydell, q.v.

BANDOLIER, STEPHEN
Murder Manana. Duell, 1941

BANDY, EUGENE FRANKLIN, JR. 1914- . Pseudonym: Eugene Franklin, q.v.

BANGS, JOHN KENDRICK. 1862-1922.
The Dreamers. Harper, 1899 ss
The Enchanted Type-Writer. Harper, 1899 ss
Ghosts I Have Met and Some Others. Harper, 1898 ss
Mrs. Raffles. Harper, 1905 ss
The Pursuit of the House Boat. Harper, 1897 ss
R. Holmes & Co. Harper, 1906 ss
Shylock Holmes: His Posthumous Memoirs. Dispatch-Box Press, 1973 ss

BANIM, JOHN. Joint pseudonym with Michael Banim: The O'Hara Family, q.v.

BANIM, MICHAEL. Joint pseudonym with John Banim: The O'Hara Family, q.v.

BANKO, DANIEL
Not Dead Yet. GM, 1972
Very Dry with a Twist. Saturday Review, 1975

BANKOFF, GEORGE ALEXIS. 1903- . Pseudonym: George Braddon, q.v.

BANKS, ELIZABETH (L.)
The Mystery of Frances Farrington. Hutchinson, 1909

BANKS, RAYMOND E. 1918?- . Series character: Sam King, in both titles.
The Computer Kill. Popular Library, 1961
Meet Me in Darkness. Popular Library, 1961

BANNER, HUBERT STEWART. 1891-1964.
Hell's Harvest. Hurst, 1934
The Mountain of Terror. Butterworth, 1928
Red Cobra. Butterworth, 1929
Terror Wave. Hurst, 1935

BANNER, MICHAEL
Q37. Knopf, 1937

BANNERMAN, W. B. Series character: Santos = S.
Bad End Valley. Low, 1937 S
Legionnaire Spy. Low, 1939
Santos, Border Detective. Quality, 1940 S
The Whispering Riders. Low, 1937 S

BANNISTER, PAT
Seven Votes for Death. GM, 1964

BANNISTER, WILLIAM
Counterfeit Murder. Lancer, 1967
Portrait of Death. Lancer, 1966

BANNON, DON
Killer at Large. Pinnacle, 1975

BANNON, PETER. Pseudonym of Paul Durst, 1921- , q.v. Other pseudonym: John Chelton, q.v.
If I Should Die. Jenkins, 1958
They Want Me Dead. Jenkins, 1958
Whisper Murder Softly. Jenkins, 1963

BANVILLE, JOHN
Birchwood. Secker, 1973; Norton, 1973
-Long Lankin. Secker, 1970 ss
-Nightspawn. Secker, 1971; Norton, 1971

BAOL, SAM
The Man from the Diner's Club. Lancer, 1963. (Novelization of the movie.)

BARBER, ALEX. 1906- .
Room with No Escape. Hutchinson, 1932

BARBER, D(ONALD) H(ERBERT). 1907- .
Fortune for Four. Barker, 1937 ss, some criminous

BARBER, DULAN F. 1940- . Pseudonym: David Fletcher, q.v.

BARBER, MARCIN
Britz of Headquarters. Moffat, 1910

BARBER, WILLETTA ANN, 1911- , and R(UDOLPH) F(REDERICK) SCHABELITZ, 1884-1959. Series character: Christopher Storm, in all titles.
The Deed is Drawn. Scribner, 1949
Drawback to Murder. Scribner, 1947
Drawn Conclusion. Doubleday, 1942
Murder Draws a Line. Doubleday, 1940
Murder Enters the Picture. Doubleday, 1942
The Noose is Drawn. Scribner, 1945
Pencil Points to Murder. Doubleday, 1941

BARBETTE, JAY. Joint pseudonym of Bart Spicer, 1918-   , q.v., and Betty Coe Spicer.
The Deadly Doll. Dodd, 1958; Long, 1959
Dear, Dead Days. Dodd, 1953; Barker, 1954. Also published as: Death's Long Shadow. Bantam, 1955
Death's Long Shadow; see Dear, Dead Days
Final Copy. Dodd, 1950; Barker, 1952
Look Behind You. Dodd, 1960; Long, 1961

BARBOUR, A(NNA) MAYNARD. Pseudonym of Anna Mary Barbour, 186?-1941.
At the Time Appointed. Lippincott, 1903
The Award of Justice; see Told in the Rockies
Breakers Ahead. Lippincott, 1906
That Mainwaring Affair. American News, 1900; Ward, 1901
Told in the Rockies. Rand, 1897. Also published as: The Award of Justice. Rand, 1901

BARBOUR, ANNA MARY. 186?-1941. Pseudonym: A(nna) Maynard Barbour, q.v.

BARBOUR, MILDRED
Sybil, Trapper of Men. Grosset, 1927

BARBOUR, R(ALPH) H(ENRY). 1870-1944.
Death in the Virgins. Appleton, 1940

BARCLAY, BILL [WILLIAM EWERT BARCLAY]. 1940-   .
Printer's Devil. Compact, 1966
Somewhere in the Night. Compact, 1966

BARCLAY, JOHN (FRANCIS ST. BARBE). 1902-   .
The Gilchrist Case. Methuen, 1930
The Unknown. London Book Co., 1928

BARCLAY, WILFRID
The Club of Skulls. Modern, 1938
The Secret Menace. Modern, 1938
Tracked Across the Seas. Modern, 193?

BARCLAY, WILSON
The Seventh Man. Ward, 1933; Dial, 1935

BARD, DANIEL
The Aquanauts. Popular Library, 1961. (Novelization of the TV series.)

BARDIN, JOHN FRANKLIN. 1916-   . Pseudonyms: Douglas Ashe, Gregory Tree, qq.v.
The Deadly Percheron. Dodd, 1946; Gollancz, 1946
Devil Take the Blue-Tail Fly. Macfadden, 1967; Gollancz, 1948
The Last of Philip Banter. Dodd, 1947; Gollancz, 1947

BARDON, MINNA
Blood Red Death. Phoenix, 1947
The Case of the Advertised Murder. Hillman-Curl, 1939
The Case of the Blood-Stained Dime; see Murder Does Light Housekeeping
The Case of the Dead Grandmother. Phoenix, 1937
Murder Does Light Housekeeping. Phoenix, 1941. Also published as: The Case of the Blood-Stained Dime. Bleak House, 194?
Murder for Real. Black Knight, 194? (Retitled reprint of ?)

BARDOS, MARIE (DUPUIS). 1935-   .
Nightlight. Doubleday, 1964; Gollancz, 1965

BARDSLEY, MICHAEL
Caught in Terror. Hale, 1969
Hit It Rich. Hale, 1972
Murder for Sale. Hale, 1970; Roy, 1971
Murder on Fire. Hale, 1969
Murder on Ice. Hale, 1972

BARGONE, FREDERIC CHARLES EDOUARD. 1876-1957. Pseudonym: Claude Farrere, q.v.

BARK, CONRAD VOSS. Series character: William Holmes, in all titles.
Mr. Holmes and the Fair Armenian. Macdonald, 1964
Mr. Holmes and the Love Bank. Macdonald, 1964
Mr. Holmes at Sea. Macdonald, 1962; Macmillan, 1962
Mr. Holmes Goes to Ground. Macdonald, 1963; Macmillan, 1964
The Second Red Dragon. Gollancz, 1968; Walker, 1968
See the Living Crocodiles. Gollancz, 1967; Walker, 1968
The Shepherd File. Gollancz, 1966; Dutton, 1966

BARKER, ALBERT. Series characters: Reefe King, in at least those marked RF; Hawk Macrae, in at least those marked HM.
The Apollo Legacy. Award, 1970 RK
The Big Fix. Curtis, 1973 HM
The Blood of Angels. Curtis, 1973
The Dragon in Spring. Curtis, 1973
Gift from Berlin. Award, 1969 RK
If Anything Should Happen to Me. Curtis, 1973 HM
The Straw Virgin. Popular Library, 1975

BARKER, C(LARENCE) HEDLEY. Pseudonyms: Seafarer, Frank Hedley, qq.v.
Blue Water. Cassell, 1933
The Case of the Secret Plans. Lloyds, 1921
Dark Road of Danger. Cherry Tree, 1943
Devil's Brood. Cassell, 1941
Eight Went Cruising. Hale, 1946
The Hallam Moor Mystery. Cherry Tree, 1944
Hangman's Honeymoon. Hale, 1943
They Stole a Ship. Hale, 1945
The Wayward Nymph. Cassell, 1933

BARKER, DUDLEY. 1910-   . Pseudonyms: Lionel Black, q.v., Anthony Matthews.

BARKER, ELSA. 1869-1954. Series character: Dexter Drake, in all titles.
The C.I.D. of Dexter Drake. Sears, 1929; Hamilton, 1931 ss
The Cobra Candlestick. Sears, 1928; Hamilton, 1930
The Redman Cave Murder. Sears, 1930

BARKER, LEONARD NOEL. 1882-   . Pseudonym: L. Noel, q.v.

BARKER, PATRICK
Carver. Popular Library, 1973

BARKER, RONALD (ERNEST). 1920-1976. Pseudonym: E. B. Ronald, q.v.
Clue for Murder. Abelard (London & New York), 1962
The Days are Long. Cassell, 1959; British Book Service, 1959
Tendency to Corrupt. Cassell, 1957; British Book Service, 1957

BARLAY, BENNETT. Pseudonym of Kendell Foster Crossen, 1910-   , q.v. Other pseudonyms: M. E. Chaber, Richard Foster, Christopher Monig, Clay Richards, qq.v.
Satan Comes Across. Eerie, 1945

BARLING, CHARLES. Pseudonym of Muriel Vere Mant Barling, 1904-   . Other pseudonym: Pamela Barrington, q.v. Series character: Inspector George Marshall, in at least those marked GM (see also the Barrington byline).
Afternoon of Violence. Hale, 1963
Appointment with Death. Hale, 1964 GM
Confession of Murder. Hale, 1967 GM
The Crime Against Judy Bishop. Hale, 1966
Death of a Shrew. Hale, 1968
A Marked Man. Hale, 1968
Motive for Murder. Hale, 1963
Time to Kill. Hale, 1965 GM

BARLING, MURIEL VERE MANT. 1904-   . Pseudonyms: Charles Barling, Pamela Barrington, qq.v.

BARLING, TOM
Bergman's Blitz. Allen, 1973
The Shooter Man. Allen, 1974

BARLOW, JAMES (HENRY STANLEY). 1921-   .
The Burden of Proof. H. Hamilton, 1968; Simon, 1968
The Hour of Maximum Danger. H. Hamilton, 1962; Simon, 1963
The Man with Good Intentions. Cassell, 1958
One Half of the World. Cassell, 1957; Harper, 1957
-One Man in the World. H. Hamilton, 1966; Simon, 1966
The Patriots. H. Hamilton, 1960; Harper, 1960
The Protagonists. Cassell, 1956; Harper, 1956
Term of Trial. H. Hamilton, 1961; Simon, 1962
-This Side of the Sky. H. Hamilton, 1964; Simon, 1964

BARMBY, CUTHBERT
James Cope; The Confessions of a United States District Attorney. Ward, 1899; New Amsterdam, 1899

BARNARD, MELVILLE CLEMENS
The Mystery of the Sandal-Wood Box. Mayhew, 1907

BARNARD, ROBERT
Death of an Old Goat. Collins, 1974

BARNES, DALLAS. Series character: Det. Sgt. John Stryker, in both titles.
Badge of Honor. Signet, 1974; Hodder, 1976
"See the Woman". Signet, 1973; Hodder, 1974

BARNES, JAMES. 1866-1936.
The Clutch of Circumstance. Appleton, 1908
Outside the Law. Appleton, 1906

BARNES, MARGARET AYER. See: HENRY KITCHELL WEBSTER, 1875-1932.

BARNES, MICHAEL. Pseudonym: Ricky Drayton, q.v.
Landscape with Corpses. Merit, 1954
You Can Run So Far. Scion, 1952

BARNES, RONALD GORELL. 1884-   . See: LORD GORELL.

BARNETT, GLYN. Series character: Inspector Gramport, in at least those marked G.
The Call-Box Murder. Low, 1935 G
Death Calls Three Times. Low, 1936
Find the Lady. Low, 1946 G

I Knew Mrs. Lang. Low, 1937 G
Murder on Monday. Low, 1936 G
The Silent Street. Barker, 1958
There's Money in Murder. Chapman, 1939

BARNETT, REGINALD
The Devil's Whisper. Walter Scott, 1889
Police Sergeant C21. Walter Scott, 1888
Rubbed Out. Everett, 1904

BARNS, GLENN M(ILLER). Series character: Jonathan Marks, in at least those marked JM.
Deadly Summer. Lippincott, 1957; Hale, 1959
Lawyers Don't Hang. Arcadia, 1953
Masquerade in Blue. Ace, 1956
Murder is a Gamble. Phoenix, 1952; Foulsham, 1954 JM
Murder is Insane. Lippincott, 1956; Foulsham, 1958 JM
Murder Walks the Stairs. Arcadia, 1954; Foulsham, 1955
Murderous Suspense. Foulsham, 1960. (U.S. title?)
Only the Losers Win. GM, 1968

BARON. Pseudonym of Benjamin Anthony Ronzone, 1848- .
The Marquis of Murray Hill. Roxburgh, 1909

BARON, PETER. Pseudonym of Leonard Worswick Clyde, 1906- .
Jerry the Lag. Selwyn, 1928. U.S. title: Murder in Wax. Macaulay, 1931
Murder in Wax; see Jerry the Lag
The Opium Murders; see Who?
The Poacher. Selwyn, 1929. U.S. title: The Round Table Murders. Macaulay, 1931
The Round Table Murders; see The Poacher
Who? Selwyn, 1927. U.S. title: The Opium Murders. Macaulay, 1930

BARON, STANLEY (WADE). 1922- .
All My Enemies. Hart-Davis, 1952; Ballantine, 1952
End of the Line. Hart-Davis, 1951; Knopf, 1951

BARONE, MIKE
Crazy Joe. Bantam, 1974. (Novelization of the movie.)

BARONI, M.
Wreath for a Lady. Spencer, 1957

BARR, A. J.
Let Tomorrow Come. Norton, 1929

BARR, DENNIS. Pseudonym of Felix Denny.
The Crimson Quest; see A Dock Brief
A Dock Brief. Cape, 1928. U.S. title: The Crimson Quest. Sears, 1928
A Rope Broke. Jarrolds, 1932

BARR, ROBERT. 1850-1912. Pseudonym: Luke Sharp.
-A Chicago Princess. Stokes, 1904
-The Face and the Mask. Stokes, 1895; Hutchinson, 1894
From Whose Bourne? Stokes, 1896; Chatto, 1893, as by Luke Sharp
The Girl in the Case. Nash, 1910. (U.S. title?)
Jennie Baxter, Journalist. Stokes, 1899; Methuen, 1899
Lady Eleanor, Lawbreaker. Rand, 1911
-The Mutable Many. Stokes, 1896; Methuen, 1897
-Over the Border. Stokes, 1903; Isbister, 1903
-A Prince of Good Fellows. Stokes, 1902; Chatto, 1902
Revenge! Stokes, 1896; Chatto, 1896 ss

-A Rock in the Baltic. Authors & Newspapers, 1906
-The Strong Arm. Stokes, 1899; Methuen, 1900
Tales of Two Continents. Mills, 1920 ss
The Triumphs of Eugene Valmont. Appleton, 1906; Hurst, 1906 ss
The Watermead Affair. Altemus, 1906
A Woman Intervenes. Stokes, 1896; Chatto, 1896
-The Woman Wins. Stokes, 1904 ss

BARR, ROBERT
The Dark Island. Allen, 1972; Bobbs, 1973
The Edge of the Forest. Allen, 1973

BARRATT, ROBERT
The Fatal Entrance. Hale, 1975

BARRETT, ALFRED WALTER. 1869- . Pseudonym: R. Andom, q.v.

BARRETT, ALFRED WILSON. 1871- .
-The Blue Taxi. Ward, 1915
Father Pink. Ward, 1907; Small, 1906
The French Master. Ward, 1903
-The Golden Lotus. Macqueen, 1901
-The House over the Way. Ward, 1906
-The Jew of Prague. White, 1912
Justus Wise. Ward, 1911
The Man with the Opals, with Austin Fryers. Ward, 1906
The Secret Marriage. Ward, 1912
The Shadow on the House. Everett, 1909
The Silver King. Everett, 1914; Dillingham, 1914
The Silver Pin. Ward, 1905; Saalfield, 1905
-A Soldier's Love. Everett, 1912
-The Third Mistake. Aldine, 1917
The Tower Hill Mystery. Ward, 1912

BARRETT, FRANK. 1848-1926.
-The Admirable Lady Biddy Fane. Cassell (London), 1888; Cassell (New York), 1889
Between Life and Death. Chatto, 1890; U.S. Book Co., 1890
Breaking the Shackles. Macqueen, 1900; Page, 1900
By Misadventure. Rand, 1888 (British title?)
-The Error of Her Ways. Chatto, 1905
-Fantoccini. Tinsley, 1874
Fettered for Life. Chatto, 1889; Munro, 1889. Also published as: Kit Wyndham; or, Fettered for Life. Lovell, 1889
-Folly Morrison. Bentley, 1881
For Love and Honour. Chatto, 1892; U.S. Book Co., 1892
Found Guilty. Ward, 1887; Lovell, 1892
The Great Hesper. Ward, 1887; Appleton, 1887
-The Harding Scandal. Chatto, 1896
-Hidden Gold. Digby Long, 1904
-His Helpmate. Ward, 1887; Appleton, 1887
His Own Law. Ward, 1914
-Honest Davie. Bentley, 1883; Harper, 1883
-Jockey Club Stories. Fun, 1888 ss
-John Ford: His Faults and His Follies. Ward, 1885
The Justification of Andrew Lebrun. Heinemann, 1894; Appleton, 1894
Kit Wyndham; or, Fettered for Life; see Fettered for Life
Kitty's Father. Heinemann, 1893; U.S. Book Co., 1892
Lady Judas. Chatto, 1903

-Lieutenant Barnabas. Bentley, 1881; Lovell, 1888
-Little Lady Linton. Bentley, 1884
-Maggie? Tinsley, 1876
A Missing Witness. Chatto, 1897
The Night of Reckoning. Long, 1905
-The Obliging Husband. Chatto, 1907
Olga's Crime; see The Sin of Olga Zassoulich
Out of the Jaws of Death. Cassell (London & New York), 1892
-Perfidious Lydia. Chatto, 1910
-A Prodigal's Progress. Bentley, 1882
A Recoiling Vengeance. Ward, 1888; Appleton, 1888
A Set of Rogues. Innes, 1895; Macmillan, 1895
The Sin of Olga Zassoulich. Chatto, 1891. U.S. title: Olga's Crime. Lovell, 1891
The Smuggler's Secret. Griffith, 1893; Lovell, 1890
Two Knaves and a Queen. Tinsley, 1877
Under a Strange Mask. Cassell, 1889; Lovell, 1889
-Was She Justified? Chatto, 1898
The Woman of the Iron Bracelets. Chatto, 1893; Tait, 1893

BARRETT, G(EOFFREY) J(OHN)
Concerto of Death. Hale, 1969
A Cup That Kills. Hale, 1969
Danger in Diamonds. Hale, 1968
The Evil Ones. Hale, 1968
Guilty Be Damned. Hale, 1969
He Died Twice. Hale, 1968
A Hearse for McNally. Hale, 1969
His Own Funeral. Hale, 1972
Lonely is the Grave. Hale, 1968
Murder Road. Hale, 1968

BARRETT, GRADY
The Barker Case. Vantage, 1966

BARRETT, JOAN
Monte Carlo Stories. Chatto, 1896 ss, some criminous

BARRETT, MARIANNE. See: THE EDINGTONS.

BARRETT, MARY ELLIN. 1927- .
-Castle Ugly. Dutton, 1966

BARRETT, MICHAEL (JOHN). 1924- .
Appointment in Zahrein. Joseph, 1960. U.S. title: Escape from Zahrein. GM, 1960
Escape from Zahrein; see Appointment in Zahrein
-The Gold of Lubra Rock. Hale, 1967
-The Heroes of Yuca. Hale, 1968
-The Hunt at Desolacion. Hale, 1969
-The Last Flowers. Longmans, 1956; Farrar, 1957
The Man in the Spike. Joseph, 1961
The Return of the Cornish Soldier. Joseph, 1962
The Reward. Longmans, 1955; Farrar, 1956
Stranger in Galah. Longmans, 1958; Norton, 1959
Task of Destruction. Joseph, 1963
Ten Against Nura. Hale, 1965
-Tonight in Sacarra. Hale, 1972
-Zakari's Skull. Hale, 1966

BARRETT, MONTE. 1897?-1949. Series character: Peter Cardigan = PC.
Knotted Silk; see Murder Off Stage
Murder at Belle Camille. Bobbs, 1943; Boardman, 1946
Murder Off Stage. Bobbs, 1931. British title: Knotted Silk. Paul, 1932 PC

The Pelham Murder Case. White House, 1930 PC
The Wedding March Murder. Bobbs, 1933; Paul, 1933 PC

BARRETT, SUSAN
Rubbish. Joseph, 1974

BARRETT, WILLIAM E(DMUND). 1900- .
The Shape of Illusion. Heinemann, 1972; Doubleday, 1972

BARRIE, JAMES M(ATTHEW). 1860-1937.
Better Dead. Sonnenschein, 1888; Lovell, 1892

BARRINGTON, CHARLES F.
Emily; or, The Orphan Sisters. French, 1853

BARRINGTON, HOWARD. 1906- . Pseudonym: Simon Stone, q.v.

BARRINGTON, JOHN H. Pseudonym of John Henry Harvey. Other pseudonym: Operator 1384, q.v.
The Moving Finger. Langdon, 1947
Murder in White Pit. Langdon, 1947

BARRINGTON, MAURICE. Pseudonym of Denis William Brogan, 1900-1974.
Stop on the Green Light! H. Hamilton, 1941; Harper, 1942

BARRINGTON, P. V. See: PAMELA BARRINGTON

BARRINGTON, PAMELA. Byline sometimes: P. V. Barrington. Pseudonym of Muriel Vere Mant Barling, 1904- . Other pseudonym: Charles Barling, q.v. Series character (also under the Charles Barling byline): Inspector George Marshall, in at least those marked GM.
Accessory to Murder. Hale, 1968
Account Rendered. Barker, 1953
Among Those Present. Barker, 1953
By Some Person Unknown. Hammond, 1960 GM
Cage Without Bars. Hale, 1966 GM
The Changing Heart. Long, 1948
Final Judgement. Hale, 1964
Forty-Three Candles for Mr. Beamish. Evans, 1950
The Fourth Victim. Barker, 1958
A Game of Murder. Hale, 1967 GM
The Gentle Killer. Hammond, 1961
Mr. Hedley's Private Hell. Long, 1950
The Mortimer Story. Barker, 1952
My Friend Judas. Hale, 1968
Night of Violence (by P. V. Barrington). Hammond, 1959
The Rest is Silence. Evans, 1951
Saga of a Scoundrel. Long, 1947
Slow Poison. Hale, 1967
The Triangle has Four Sides. Evans, 1949
-White Pierrot. Long, 1932

BARRON, ANN (FORMAN)
Bride of Menace. GM, 1973
Dark Vengeance. GM, 1972
Gentle Kiss of Murder; see Murder is a Gentle Kiss
Maybe It's Murder; see Murder is a Gentle Kiss
Murder is a Gentle Kiss. Bouregy, 1960. British title: Maybe It's Murder. Hammond, 1963. Also published as: Gentle Kiss of Murder. Tower, 1966
Serpent in the Shadows. Berkley, 1973
Spin a Dark Web. Bouregy, 1961
Strange Legacy. GM, 1969

BARRON, DONALD G(ABRIEL). 1922- .
The Man Who Was There. Chatto, 1969; Atheneum, 1969
The Zilov Bombs. Deutsch, 1962; Norton, 1963

BARRON, ELWYN (ALFRED). 1855-1929.
Marcel Levignet. Duffield, 1906

BARRON, HUGH
Bonnie. New English Library pb, 1970
The Corrupter. New English Library pb, 1969
Doll Baby. New English Library pb, 1969
Fun City. New English Library pb, 1969
The Goddess Game. New English Library pb, 1971
High Cost of Murder. New English Library pb, 1971
The Love Thing. New English Library pb, 1971
The Mercenary. New English Library, 1970

BARRY, CHARLES. Pseudonym of Charles Bryson, 1877- . Series character: (Supt.) Lawrence Gilmartin, in at least those marked LG.
The Avenging Ikon. Methuen, 1930; Dutton, 1930 LG
The Boat Train Mystery. Hurst, 1938
A Case Dead and Buried. Hurst, 1938 LG
The Case for Tressider. Hodder, 1937
The Clue of the Clot. Hutchinson, 1928; Dutton, 1929 LG
The Corpse on the Bridge. Methuen, 1927; Dutton, 1928 LG
The Dead Have No Mouths. Hurst, 1940
Death in Darkness. Hurst, 1933; Dutton, 1933
Death of a First Mate. Hurst, 1935; Dutton, 1935
Death Overseas. Hurst, 1937
The Detective's Holiday. Methuen, 1926; Dutton, 1926 LG
The Ghost of a Clue. Methuen, 1931 LG
The Mouls House Mystery. Methuen, 1926; Dutton, 1927 LG
Murder on Monday..? Eyre, 1932; Dutton, 1932
Nicholas Lattermole's Case. Hurst, 1939
Poison in Public. Hurst, 1936
The Red Star Mystery. Mellifont, 1933
Secrecy at Sandhurst. Hurst, 1951
The Shot from the Door. Hurst, 1934; Dutton, 1934 LG
The Smaller Penny. Holden, 1925; Dutton, 1928 LG
The Thirteenth House. Mellifont, 1935
The Witness at the Window. Methuen, 1927; Dutton, 1927 LG
The Wrong Murder Mystery. Hurst, 1933; Dutton, 1933 LG

BARRY, IRIS. 1895- .
The Darkness at Mantia. Berkley, 1973
The House of Deadly Night. Belmont, 1970
The Mandura Mystery. Hale, 1966
Seven Guests of Fear. Hale, 1970. (U.S. title?)
The Unprotected. Berkley, 1973; Remploy, 1974

BARRY, JEROME (BENEDICT). 1894-1975. Series character: Chick Varney = CV.
The Cat's Cradle Murder; see Leopard Cat's Cradle
Extreme License. Doubleday, 1958; Boardman, 1959. Also published as: Murder is No Accident. Dell, 1960
Fall Guy. Doubleday, 1960
Lady of Night. Doubleday, 1944; Boardman, 1945 CV
Leopard Cat's Cradle. Doubleday, 1942; Boardman, 1943. Also published as: The Cat's Cradle Murder. Mystery Novel Classic, 1944 CV
Malignant Stars. Doubleday, 1960
Murder is No Accident; see Extreme License
Murder with Your Malted. Doubleday, 1941; Boardman, 1942 CV
Strange Relations. Doubleday, 1962; Boardman, 1963

BARRY, JO HANNOLD
Murder Mansion. Exposition, 1959

BARRY, JOE. Pseudonym of Joe Barry Lake. Series character: Rush Henry, in at least those marked RH.
The Clean Up. Arcadia, 1947
The Fall Guy. Mystery House, 1945 RH
Homicide Hotel. Phantom, 1951
Kiss and Kill. Ace, 1954
The Pay-Off. Mystery House, 1943 RH
The Third Degree. Mystery House, 1943 RH
Three for the Money. Handi-Books, 1950
The Triple Cross. Mystery House, 1946 RH

BARRY, JOHN BROOKS
The Michaelmas Girls. Deutsch, 1975

BARRY, JOHN E(VARTS). 1906- .
Skeleton in Concrete. Gifford, 1952
The Uranium Murders. Long, 1951

BARRY, LORETTA
Sudden Silence. Zebra, 1975

BARRY, MIKE. Pseudonym of Barry N. Malzberg, 1939- . Series character: Burt Wulff (The Lone Wolf), in all titles.
Bay Prowler. Berkley, 1973
Boston Avenger. Berkley, 1973
Chicago Slaughter. Berkley, 1974
Desert Stalker. Berkley, 1974
Detroit Massacre. Berkley, 1975
Harlem Showdown. Berkley, 1975
Havana Hit. Berkley, 1974
The Killing Run. Berkley, 1975
Los Angeles Holocaust. Berkley, 1974
Miami Marauder. Berkley, 1974
Night Raider. Berkley, 1973
Peruvian Nightmare. Berkley, 1974
Philadelphia Blow-Up. Berkley, 1975
Phoenix Inferno. Berkley, 1975

BARRY, WILLIAM EDWIN
The Jade God. French (New York), 1932. (3-act play based on the novel by Alan Sullivan, 1868-1947, q.v.)

BARTH, LOIS. Pseudonym of Lois Diane Freihofer, 1933- .
Dark Labyrinth. Lenox Hill, 1971
Epitaph for a Teddy Bear. Lenox Hill, 1973
Run from the River. Bouregy, 1965

BARTLETT, E(RIC) G(EORGE). 1920- .
The Case of the 13th Coach. Staples, 1958

BARTLETT, E. DE VERE
Why? Stock, 1917

BARTLETT, FREDERICK ORIN. 1876- .
-The Web of the Golden Spider. Small, 1909; Palmer, 1912

BARTLETT, VERNON. 1894- . Joint pseudonym with Per Jacobsson, 1894-1963: Peter Oldfeld, q.v.

BARTON, D.
Black Panther. Paladin, 1953
Jail Break. Paladin, 1953

BARTON, GEORGE. 1866-1940. Series character: Bromley Barnes = BB.
The Ambassador's Trunk. Page, 1919
The Mystery of the Red Flame. Page, 1918 BB
The Pembroke Mason Affair. Page, 1920 BB
The Strange Adventures of Bromley Barnes. Page, 1918 ss BB
The True Stories of Celebrated Crimes. Winston, 1909 ss, of true crime in fictionalized form

BARTON, J. C.
The Corrupt Ones. Badger, 1961
The Pay-Off. Badger, 1960

BARTON, ROBERT EUSTACE. 1868-1943. Pseudonym (?): Robert Eustace, q.v. See also: L. T. Meade, Dorothy L(eigh) Sayers, 1893-1957, and Gertrude Warden.

BARTRAM, A. V.
Purple Shadows. Modern, 1935

BARTRAM, GEORGE. 1931- .
Fair Game. Macmillan, 1973; Millington, 1976
A Job Abroad. Macmillan, 1975

BAR-ZOHAR, MICHAEL. 1938-
The Spy Who Died Twice. Houghton, 1975; Weidenfeld, 1976. (Translation of Ha-Ish She-met Pa'a Mayim. Israel, 1973.)
The Third Truth. Houghton, 1973; Hodder, 1973. (Translation of La Troisieme Verite. Paris, 1972.)

BASHFORD, H(ENRY) H(OWARTH). 1880-1961.
Behind the Fog. Heinemann, 1926; Harper, 1927

BASIL, DON
Cat and Feather. Earle, 1931; Holt, 1931

BASINGER, DONALD
The Devil Within Us. Dobson, 1963; London House, 1964

BASINSKY, EARLE. 1921- .
The Big Steal. Dutton, 1955; Boardman, 1956
Death is a Cold, Keen Edge. Signet, 1956

BASKERVILLE, BEATRICE and MONK, ELLIOT
The Amethyst Button. Hutchinson, 1926
By Whose Hand? Hutchinson, 1922
The St. Cloud Affair. Hutchinson, 1931

BASS, CHARLES BECK
Head Held High. Vantage, 1958

BATCHELOR, DENZIL (STANLEY). 1906- .
Everything Happens to Hector. Heinemann, 1958
The Man Who Loved Chocolates. Heinemann, 1961
On the Brink. Macdonald, 1964
The Sedulous Ape. Macdonald, 1965
The Taste of Blood. Heinemann, 1958
The Test Match Murder. Angus, 1936

BATCHELOR, REG. Pseudonym of Lauran Bosworth Paine, 1916- . Other pseudonyms: John Armour, Kenneth Bedford, Frank Bosworth, Mark Carrel, Robert Clarke, Richard Dana, J. F. Drexler, Troy Howard, Jared Ingersol, John Kilgore, Hunter Liggett, J. K. Lucas, John Morgan, qq.v.
-Achilles' Isle. Hale, 1974
-Blue Sea & Yellow Sun. Hale, 1967
Inspector Cole. Hale, 1970
-A Legacy of Shadows. Hale, 1972
The Murder Game. Hale, 1970
Murderer's Row. Hale, 1970
-The Time of Assassins. Hale, 1969
The Triangle Murder. Hale, 1973
The Twilight People. Hale, 1970

BATES, H(ERBERT) E(RNEST). 1905- .
-Dear Life. Little, 1949; Joseph, 1950

BATES, HARRY ARTHUR. Pseudonym: Harry Arthur, q.v.

BATESON, DAVID. 1921- . Series character: Larry Vernon, in at least those marked LV.
The Big Tomorrow. Hale, 1956
I'll Do Anything. Hale, 1960
I'll Go Anywhere. Hale, 1959
It's Murder, Senorita. Hale, 1954 LV
The Man from the Rock. Hale, 1955
Night is for Violence. Hale, 1958
The Soho Jungle. Hale, 1958 LV
This Side of Terror. Hale, 1959

BATISTA-OLIVIERI, ISRAEL
Hurt Me No More. Vantage, 1970

BATSON, GEORGE. 1916?-1977.
Dangerous Nan McCrew. French (New York & London), 1949. (3-act play.)
Design for Murder. French, 1960. (3-act play.)
Hangman's Noose. French, 1947. (3-act play.)
House on the Cliff. French, 1957. (3-act play.)
Miss Private Eye. French, 1951. (3-act play.)
Murder on Arrival. French (New York), 1960; French (London), 1958. (3-act play.)
Ramshackle Inn. Dramatists Play Service, 1944. (3-act play.)
Rehearsal for Death. French, 1949. (3-act play.)

BATTYE, GLADYS STARKEY. 1915- . Pseudonym: Margaret Lynn, q.v.

BAUBIE, WILLIAM EDW(ARD)
-The Man Condemned. Stratford, 1936

BAULSIR, EDITH
Within Four Walls. Century, 1921

BAUSMAN, FREDERICK. 1861-1931. Pseudonym: Aix, q.v.

BAVIN, BILL
Dead Regimental. Jarrolds, 1968
The Extortionists. Tandem, 1973
One Man's War. Jarrolds, 1968

BAWDEN, NINA. Pseudonym of Nina Mary Mabey Kark, 1925- .
Change Here for Babylon. Collins, 1955
Devil by the Sea. Collins, 1957; Lippincott, 1959
Eyes of Green; see Who Calls the Tune
The Odd Flamingo. Collins, 1954
The Solitary Child. Collins, 1956; Lancer, 1966
Who Calls the Tune. Collins, 1953. U.S. title: Eyes of Green. Morrow, 1953

BAX, ROGER. Pseudonym of Paul Winterton, 1908- . Other pseudonyms: Andrew Garve, Paul Somers, qq.v.
Blueprint for Murder. Hutchinson, 1948. U.S. title: The Trouble with Murder. Harper, 1948
Came the Dawn. Hutchinson, 1949. U.S. title: Two If by Sea. Harper, 1949
Death Beneath Jerusalem. Nelson, 1938
Disposing of Henry. Hutchinson, 1947; Harper, 1947
A Grave Case of Murder. Hutchinson, 1951; Harper, 1951
Red Escapade. Skeffington, 1940
The Trouble with Murder; see Blueprint for Murder
Two If by Sea; see Came the Dawn

BAXT, GEORGE. 1923- . Series characters: Sylvia Plotkin and Max Van Larsen = P&L; Pharoah Love = PL.
The Affair at Royalties. Scribner, 1972; Macmillan (London), 1971
Burning Sappho. Macmillan, 1972; Macmillan (London), 1972
"I!" Said the Demon. Random, 1969; Cape, 1969 P&L
A Parade of Cockeyed Creatures. Random, 1967; Cape, 1968 P&L
A Queer Kind of Death. Simon, 1966; Cape, 1967 PL
Swing Low, Sweet Harriet. Simon, 1967 PL
Topsy and Evil. Simon, 1968 PL

BAXTER, GREGORY. Joint pseudonym of John Sellar Mathison Ressich, 1877- , and Eric de Banzie, 1894- . Series character: Superintendent Daniels, in at least those marked SD.
The Aincesworth Mystery. Benn, 1929; Appleton, 1930 SD
Blue Lightning. Cassell, 1926
Calamity Comes of Age. Hutchinson, 1936; Macaulay, 1935 SD
Climax at the Falls. Benn, 1932
Death Strikes at Six Bells. Benn, 1930; Macaulay, 1934 SD
Murder Could Not Kill. Benn, 1932; Macaulay, 1934
The Narrowing Lust. Selwyn, 1928 SD

BAXTER, J. K.
The Big Frame. Badger, 1960
Gun Fury. Badger, 1962
The Set-Up. Badger, 1962

BAXTER, OLIVE. Pseudonym of Helen Baker Eastwood, 1892- .
The Jewel in the Crypt. Hale, 1969

BAY, ROGER
Deadly Jigsaw. Hale, 1971
Paid in Full. Hale, 1970

BAYARD, FRED. Joint pseudonym of Margaret Elizabeth Baird Campbell and Johanna Frederika Jansen.
Death and Lilacs. Phoenix, 1948; Modern Publishing, 1950

BAYER, ELEANOR ROSENFELD. Joint pseudonym with Leo Grossberg Bayer, 1908- : Oliver Weld Bayer, q.v.

BAYER, LEO GROSSBERG. 1908- . Joint pseudonym with Eleanor Rosenfeld Bayer: Oliver Weld Bayer, q.v.

BAYER, OLIVER WELD. Joint pseudonym of Eleanor Rosenfeld Bayer, and Leo Grossberg Bayer, 1908- .
Brutal Question. Doubleday, 1947
An Eye for an Eye. Doubleday, 1945
No Little Enemy. Doubleday, 1944; Hutchinson, 1945
Paper Chase. Doubleday, 1943; Hutchinson, 1944

BAYFIELD, WILLIAM J(OHN). 1871-1958. Pseudonyms: Allan Blair, Allan Maxwell, qq.v. All titles below were published by Amalgamated Press and feature Sexton Blake (with many other authors).

The Adventure of the Man "On Bail."
  1928
The Adventure of the Red-Headed Man.
  1926
The Affair of the Demobilized Soldier.
  1919
The Affair of the Family Diamonds. 1921
The Affair of the Seven Mummy Cases.
  1923
All Suspected. 1927
The Architect's Secret. 1921
The "Black Maria" Mystery. 1929
The Bungalow Tragedy. 1919
The Case of the Bogus Ingots. 1920
The Case of the Deported Aliens. 1925
The Case of the Deserted Wife. 1921
The Case of the Double Tangle. 1921
The Case of the Income-Tax Frauds. 1924
The Case of the Millionaire's Black-
  mail. 1924
The Case of the Press Photographer.
  1925
The Case of the Vanished Husband. 1922
The City of Horrors. 1927
The Clue of the Charred Diary. 1919
The Council of Crooks. 1926
The Covent Garden Mystery. 1929
The Crook's Double. 1926
The Crumblerock Crime! 1925
The Death Duty Swindle. 1926
The Death of Duboyne. 1929
The Doctor's Secret. 1923
Down and Out. 1929
False Scents. 1921
The Farrowshot Park Affair. 1924
Flat No. 4. 1924
The "Flying Squad" Tragedy. 1928
The Fourth Theory. 1919
The Home of His Children. 1920
The Last Clue. 1923
The Lincoln's Inn Tragedy. 1920
The Marble Arch Mystery. 1920
The Masked Dancer. 1930
The Masked Forgers. 1929
A Matter of Millions. 1918
The Mint Mystery. 1929
The Mystery of Hanging Sword Alley.
  1926
The Mystery of the Missing Journalist.
  1922
The Mystery of the Pot-Bank. 1925
The Mystery of the Seaside Hotel. 1926
The Oath of Fear. 1927
The Old Tollgate Mystery. 1924
The Riddle of the Million Pound Bet.
  1928
The Secret of the Mansions. 1925
The Secret of the Tomb. 1927
The Strange Case of Habberton's Mile.
  1924
The Trail of the Old Lag. 1927
The Twist in the Trail. 1920
When Conscience Sleeps. 1917
Whose was the Hand? 1918

BAYLY, A. ERIC
  The House with Strange Secrets. Sands,
    1899; Dutton, 1899
  The Man with the Parrots. Sands, 1901
  The Secret of Scotland Yard. Sands,
    1900

BAYNE, ISABELLA. Series character: Bene-
    dict Breeze, in both titles.
  Cruel as the Grave. Jarrolds, 1956
  Death and Benedict. Laurie, 1952

BAYNE, SPENCER. Pseudonym. Series char-
    acter: Hendrik Van Kill, in all
    titles.
  Agent Extraordinary. Dutton, 1942;
    Eyre, 1944
  Murder Recalls Van Kill. Harper, 1939
  The Turning Sword. Harper, 1941

BAYNE-POWELL, ISABELLA
  Death Enters the Ward. Francis James,
    1947

BAYNE-POWELL, ROSAMOND. 1879-   .
  Crime at Cloysters. Murray, 1947
  Crime at Porches Hill. Macdonald, 1950

BAYNES, JACK. Series character: Morocco
    Jones, in all titles.
  Hand of the Mafia. Crest, 1958
  Meet Morocco Jones. Crest, 1956
  Meet Morocco Jones in the Case of the
    Syndicate Hoods. Crest, 1957
  Morocco Jones and the Case of the Gol-
    den Angel. Crest, 1959
  The Peeping Tom Murders. Crest, 1958

BAZAN, EMILIA PARDO. 1852-1921.
  -The Mystery of the Lost Dauphin. Funk,
    1906

BEACH, EDGAR R(ICE). 1841-   .
  Hands of Clay; see Stranded: A Story of
    the Garden City
  -Joshua Humble; A Tale of Old St. Louis.
    Eddins, 1889
  -Stranded: A Story of the Garden City.
    Donohue, 1890. Also published as:
    Hands of Clay. Eddins, 1904

BEAM, MAURICE and BRITTON, SUMNER,
    1902-   .
  Murder in a Shell. Messner, 1939

BEARD, MAY
  The Murder at Chartres Towers. Mitre,
    1943

BEARDMORE, GEORGE. 1908-   . Pseudonyms:
    Cedric Stokes, George Wolfenden,
    qq.v.
  -A Tale of Two Thieves. Macdonald, 1947
  -A Thousand Witnesses. Macdonald, 1953

BEARE, GEORGE. Series characters: Vincent
    Stallard and Cynthia Godwin, in at
    least those marked S&G.
  The Bee Sting Deal. Long, 1972; Hough-
    ton, 1972 S&G
  The Bloody Sun at Noon. Long, 1970;
    Houghton, 1971 S&G
  Chain of Infamy. Long, 1972
  The Snake on the Grave. Long, 1973;
    Houghton, 1974
  The Very Breath of Hell. Long, 1971;
    Houghton, 1971 S&G

BEARE, PETER
  Devil or Man? Jenkins, 1932

BEATTY, ELIZABETH. Pseudonym of Teresa
    Bragunier Holloway, 1906-   .
  The Jupiter Missile Mystery. Bouregy,
    1960
  Murder at Auction. Bouregy, 1961

BEATY, BETTY. 1922-   . Pseudonym:
    Karen Campbell, q.v.

BEATY, (ARTHUR) DAVID. 1919-   . Pseudo-
    nym: Paul Stanton, q.v.
  Cone of Silence. Secker, 1959; Morrow,
    1959
  -Electric Train. Secker, 1975
  -The Proving Flight. Secker, 1956; Mor-
    row, 1957
  The Siren Song. Secker, 1964; Morrow,
    1964
  -Sword of Honour. Secker, 1965; Morrow,
    1966
  The Temple Tree. Secker, 1971; Morrow,
    1971
  The Wind Off the Sea. Secker, 1962;
    Morrow, 1962

BEAUCHAMP, HENRY
  The Lost Emeralds of Zarinthia. Sands,
    1899; Knight, 1900

BEAUMONT, CHARLES. 1929-1967. Joint pseu-
    donym with John (E.) Tomerlin,
    1930-   , q.v.: Keith Grantland,
    q.v.
  The Hunger and other stories. Putnam,
    1957 ss, some criminous
  Night Ride and Other Journeys. Bantam,
    1960 ss, some criminous

BEAUMONT, GERMAINE. 1891-   .
  -Within This Circle. Laurie, 1950

BECHDOLT, FREDERICK R(ITCHIE). 1874-   .
  See also: James (Marie) Hopper,
    1876-   .
  -Mutiny. Chelsea, 1927

BECHDOLT, JACK [JOHN ERNEST BECHDOLT].
    1884-1953.
  The Wages of Peril. Altemus, 1927

BECK, HENRY CHARLTON. 1902-   .
  Cakes to Kill. Dutton, 1932
  Death by Clue. Dutton, 1933
  Murder in the News Room. Dutton, 1931
  Murder in the Newspaper Guild. Dutton,
    1937
  Society Editor. Dutton, 1932

BECKE, (GEORGE) LOUIS. 1855-1913.
  Tom Gerrard. Unwin, 1905

BECKER, STEPHEN (DAVID). 1927-   .
  Pseudonym: Steve Dodge, q.v.
  A Covenant with Death. Atheneum, 1964;
    H. Hamilton, 1965
  -Juice. Simon, 1958; Muller, 1959
  Season of the Stranger. Dell, 1966;
    Panther, 1967

BECKETT, CHARLES HENRY. 1859-   .
  Who is John Noman? Cassell, 1887

BECKETT, JENIFER
  The Trap. St. Martin's, 1975

BECKETT, MARK. Pseudonym of Marcus George
    Truman, 1890-   . Series character:
    Major Burton, in at least those
    marked B.
  The Bullet in the Cornice. Eldon, 1937
    B
  The Dower House Mystery. Eldon, 1935 B
  Escape from Dartmoor. Eldon, 1936
  The Murder at the Flower Show. Eldon,
    1933 B
  The Murder of a Magnate. Eldon, 1934 B
  Tea Time Tragedy. Eldon, 1935 B

BEDFORD, KENNETH
  The Mathematics of Murder. Hale, 1969;
    Roy, 1969

BEDFORD, KENNETH. Pseudonym of Lauran
    Bosworth Paine, 1916-   . Other
    pseudonyms: John Armour, Reg Batche-
    lor, Frank Bosworth, Mark Carrel,
    Robert Clarke, Richard Dana, J. F.
    Drexler, Troy Howard, Jared Ingersol,
    John Kilgore, Hunter Liggett, J. K.
    Lucas, John Morgan, qq.v.
  The Merchant of Menace. Hale, 1969

BEDFORD, SIDNEY
  The Man Who Escaped. Paul, 1940

BEDFORD-JONES, H(ENRY JAMES O'BRIEN).
    1887-1949.
  The Mardi-Gras Mystery. Doubleday, 1921
  The Shadow. Fiction League, 1930
  The Trail of the Shadow. Hurst, 1924.
    (U.S. title?)

B

BEDWELL, BETTINA
Yellow Dusk. Hurst, 1937

BEEBY, OTTO
A Blank Cheque for Murder. Long, 1968
The Faceless Men. Long, 1969
-The Lovely and the Damned. Hale, 1961
No Profit in Dying. Long, 1970
Too Many Innocents. Long, 1972

BEECH, WEBB. Pseudonym of W(illiam) E(dmund) Butterworth (III), 1929-   , q.v.
Article 92: Murder-Rape. GM, 1964

BEECHAM, JOHN CHARLES
-The Argus Pheasant. Watt, 1918; Methuen, 1920
The Yellow Spider. Watt, 1920; Methuen, 1921

BEECHING, JACK
The Dakota Project. Delacorte, 1968; Cape, 1968

BEECHWOOD. Pseudonym.
The Burglar's Accomplice. SPCK, 1894

BEECKMAN, ROSS
The Last Woman. Watt, 1909; Greening, 1912
-Princess Zara. Watt, 1909; Greening, 1912

BEEDING, FRANCIS. Joint pseudonym of John (Leslie) Palmer, 1885-1944, q.v., and Hilary (Aiden) St. George Saunders, 1898-1951, q.v. Pseudonym of John (Leslie) Palmer: Christopher Haddon, q.v. Joint pseudonym of Saunders and Geoffrey Dennis: Barum Browne, q.v. Series characters: Colonel Granby = CG; Professor Kreutzemark = PK; Inspector George Martin = GM.
The Big Fish. Hodder, 1938. U.S. title: Heads Off at Midnight. Harper, 1938
The Black Arrows. Hodder, 1938; Harper, 1938 CG
Coffin for One; see The Eight Crooked Trenches
Death in Four Letters. Hodder, 1935; Harper, 1935
Death Walks in Eastrepps. Hodder, 1931; Mystery League, 1931
The Eight Crooked Trenches. Hodder, 1936; Harper, 1936. Also published as: Coffin for One. Avon, 1943 CG
Eleven were Brave. Hodder, 1940; Harper, 1941 CG
The Emerald Clasp. Hodder, 1933; Little, 1933
The Erring Under-Secretary. Hodder pb, 1937. (A separately published pb novelet, in the same series with Allingham's The Case of the Late Pig and Carr's The Third Bullet, qq.vv.)
The Five Flamboys. Hodder, 1929; Little, 1929 CG
The Four Armourers. Hodder, 1930; Little, 1930 CG
He Could Not Have Slipped. Hodder, 1939; Harper, 1939
Heads Off at Midnight; see The Big Fish
Hell Let Loose. Hodder, 1937; Harper, 1937 CG
The Hidden Kingdom. Hodder, 1927; Little, 1927 PK
The House of Dr. Edwardes. Hodder, 1927; Little, 1928. Also published as: Spellbound. World, 1945
The League of Discontent. Hodder, 1930; Little, 1930 CG
The Little White Hag. Hutchinson, 1926; Little, 1926
Mr. Bobadil. Hodder, 1934. U.S. title: The Street of the Serpents. Harper, 1934
Murder Intended. Hodder, 1932; Little, 1932
Murdered: One by One; see No Fury
The Nine Waxed Faces. Hodder, 1936; Harper, 1936 CG
No Fury. Hodder, 1937. U.S. title: Murdered: One by One. Harper, 1937 GM
The Norwich Victims. Hodder, 1935; Harper, 1935 GM
Not a Bad Show. Hodder, 1940. U.S. title: The Secret Weapon. Harper, 1940 CG
The One Sane Man. Hodder, 1934; Little, 1934 CG
Pretty Sinister. Hodder, 1929; Little, 1929 CG
The Secret Weapon; see Not a Bad Show
The Seven Sleepers. Hutchinson, 1925; Little, 1925 PK
The Six Proud Walkers. Hodder, 1928; Little, 1928 CG
Spellbound; see The House of Dr. Edwardes
The Street of the Serpent; see Mr. Bobadil
Take It Crooked. Hodder, 1932; Little, 1932 CG
The Ten Holy Horrors. Hodder, 1939; Harper, 1939 CG
There are Thirteen. Hodder, 1946; Harper, 1946 CG
The Three Fishers. Hodder, 1931; Little, 1931
The Twelve Disguises. Hodder, 1942; Harper, 1942 CG
The Two Undertakers. Hodder, 1933; Little, 1933 CG

BEESTON, L. J.
Every Night About Half Past Eight, and other stories. Hutchinson, 1923 ss

BEEVOR, ANTONY. 1946-   .
The Violent Brink. Murray, 1975

BEGBIE, ERNEST
The Mystery of the Three B Syndicate. Houghton (London), 1933

BEGBIE, GARSTIN. Series character: Supt. Samuel Quan, in at least those marked SQ.
Murder Mask. Jenkins, 1934 SQ
Sudden Death at Scotland Yard. Jenkins, 1933 SQ
Trailing Death. Jenkins, 1932

BEHN, NOEL
The Kremlin Letter. Simon, 1966; Allen, 1966
The Shadowboxer. Simon, 1969; Hart-Davis, 1970

BEHREND, ARTHUR
The House of the Spaniard. Heinemann, 1935; Doubleday, 1936
The Samarai Affair. Eyre, 1973
Unlucky for Some. Eyre, 1955

BEKESSY, JEAN. 1911-1977. Pseudonym: Hans Habe, q.v.

BELASYSE, E.
The Ventriloquist. Davies, 1935

BELGRAVE, DALRYMPLE J.
A Great Turf Fraud. Hogg, 1888
Jack Warleigh: A Tale of the Turf and the Law. Chapman, 1891
Turf and Veldt. Marsden, 1893 ss

BELL, ABBAN
Out of Circulation. Popular Library, 1965

BELL, GERARD
Villains Galore. Cassell, 1972; PB, 1976

BELL, J(OHN) J(OY). 1871-1934.
Till the Clock Stops. Hodder, 1917; Duffield, 1917

BELL, JAY
One More Time. GM, 1969

BELL, JOHN
In the Shadow of the Bush. Sands, 1899

BELL, JOHN KEBLE. 1875-1928. Pseudonym: Keble Howard, q.v.

BELL, JOSEPHINE. Pseudonym of Doris Bell Collier Ball, 1897-   . Series characters: Dr. Henry Frost = HF; Inspector Steven Mitchell = SM; Claude Warrington-Reeve = CW; Dr. David Wintringham = DW.
Adventure with Crime. Hodder, 1962
The Alien. Bles, 1964
All is Vanity. Longmans, 1940 DW
The Backing Winds. Methuen, 1951
Bones in the Barrow. Methuen, 1953; Macmillan, 1955 DW, SM
The Catalyst. Hodder, 1966; Macmillan, 1967
The China Roundabout. Hodder, 1956. U.S. title: Murder on the Merry-Go-Round. Ballantine, 1965 DW, SM
Curtain Call for a Corpse; see Death at Half-Term
Death at Half-Term. Longmans, 1939. U.S. title: Curtain Call for a Corpse. Macmillan, 1965 DW, SM
Death at the Medical Board. Longmans, 1944; Ballantine, 1964 DW
Death in Clairvoyance. Longmans, 1949 DW, SM
Death in Retirement. Methuen, 1956; Macmillan, 1956
Death of a Con Man. Hodder, 1968; Lippincott, 1968
Death of a Poison-Tongue. Hodder, 1972; Stein, 1977
Death on the Borough Council. Longmans, 1937 DW
Death on the Reserve. Hodder, 1966; Macmillan, 1967 HF
Double Doom. Hodder, 1957; Macmillan, 1958
Easy Prey. Hodder, 1959; Macmillan, 1959 CW, SM
Fall Over Cliff. Longmans, 1938; Macmillan, 1956 DW, SM
The Fennister Affair. Hodder, 1969; Stein, 1978
Fiasco in Fulham; see A Flat Tyre in Fulham
Fires at Fairlawn. Methuen, 1954
A Flat Tyre in Fulham. Hodder, 1963. U.S. title: Fiasco in Fulham. Macmillan, 1963. Also published as: Room for a Body. Ballantine, 1964 CW, SM
From Natural Causes. Longmans, 1939 DW
A Hole in the Ground. Hodder, 1971; Ace, 1973
The House Above the River. Hodder, 1959
The Hunter and the Trapped. Hodder, 1963
A Hydra with Six Heads. Hodder, 1970; Stein, 1978
Murder in Hospital. Longmans, 1937 DW, SM
Murder on the Merry-Go-Round; see The China Roundabout
New People at the Hollies. Hodder, 1961; Macmillan, 1961
No Escape. Hodder, 1965; Macmillan, 1966
A Pigeon Among the Cats. Hodder, 1974; Stein, 1978

The Port of London Murders. Longmans, 1938; Macmillan, 1958 SM
Room for a Body; see A Flat Tyre in Fulham
The Seeing Eye. Hodder, 1958 DW,SM
Stranger on the Cliff; see To Let, Furnished
The Summer School Mystery. Methuen, 1950 DW,SM
To Let, Furnished. Methuen, 1952. U.S. title: Stranger on the Cliff. Ace, 1964
Trouble at Wrekin Farm. Longmans, 1942 DW
The Upfold Witch. Hodder, 1964; Macmillan, 1964 HF
Victim. Hodder, 1975; Walker, 1976
A Well-Known Face. Hodder, 1960; Washburn, 1960 CW,SM
The Wilberforce Legacy. Hodder, 1969; Walker, 1969

BELL, LESLIE. 1916- .
The Laughing Fish. Meridian, 1952
Ring the Bell, Sister! Laurie, 1956

BELL, MALCOLM
His Fatal Success; Being the Strange Adventures of John Stuart. Belford, 1889

BELL, MARY HAYLEY
Duet for Two Hands. French (London), 1947. (Play.)

BELL, NEIL. Pseudonym of Stephen Southwold, 1887-1964. Other pseudonym: Paul Martens, q.v.
Corridor of Venus. Redman, 1960 ss, some criminous
-The Dark Page. Eyre, 1951
The Disturbing Affair of Noel Blake. Gollancz, 1932; Putnam, 1932
The Endless Chain. Redman, 1956
The House at the Crossroads. Redman, 1966 ss, some criminous
The Ninth Earl of Whitby. Redman, 1966 ss, some criminous
Precious Porcelain. Gollancz, 1931; Putnam, 1931
-Thy First Begotten. Redman, 1957
-Who Walk in Fear. Redman, 1953 (3 stories.)

BELL, RAMSEY. Joint pseudonym of Agnes Rosemary Cooper and Mary Elizabeth Phyllis Weller.
Dangerous Promise. Hodder, 1939

BELL, VICARS (WALKER). 1904- . Series character: Dr. Baynes, in all titles.
Death and the Night Watches. Faber, 1955; British Book Centre, 1962
Death Darkens Council. Faber, 1952
Death has Two Doors. Faber, 1950
Death Under the Stars. Faber, 1949
Death Walks by the River. Faber, 1959
Two by Day and One by Night. Faber, 1950

BELL, WYATT
The Magnolia Murder. GM, 1961

BELLAH, JAMES. See: ROBERT G. STIMSON.

BELLAH, JAMES WARNER. 1899-1976.
The Bones of Napoleon. Appleton, 1940
The Brass Gong Tree. Appleton, 1936
7 Must Die. Appleton, 1938

BELLAIRS, GEORGE. Pseudonym of Harold Blundell, 1902- . Series character: Superintendent (Chief Inspector, Detective Inspector) Thomas Littlejohn, in all the following except Turmoil in Zion.)
The Body in the Dumb River. Gifford, 1961
Bones in the Wilderness. Gifford, 1959
Calamity at Harwood. Gifford, 1943; Macmillan, 1945
The Case of the Demented Spiv. Gifford, 1949; Macmillan, 1950
The Case of the Famished Parson. Gifford, 1949; Macmillan, 1949
The Case of the Headless Jesuit. Gifford, 1950. U.S. title: Death Brings in the New Year. Macmillan, 1951
The Case of the Scared Rabbits. Gifford, 1947
The Case of the Seven Whistlers. Gifford, 1948; Macmillan, 1948
Corpse at the Carnival. Gifford, 1958
Corpses at Enderby. Gifford, 1954
The Crime at Halfpenny Bridge. Gifford, 1946
Crime in Lepers' Hollow. Gifford, 1952
The Cursing Stones Murder. Gifford, 1954
Dead March for Penelope; see Dead March for Penelope Blow
Dead March for Penelope Blow. Gifford, 1951; Macmillan, 1951. Also published as: Dead March for Penelope. Viking (London), 1956
The Dead Shall be Raised. Gifford, 1942. U.S. title: Murder Will Speak. Macmillan, 1943
Death Before Breakfast. Gifford, 1962; British Book Centre, 1962
Death Brings in the New Year; see The Case of the Headless Jesuit
Death Drops the Pilot. Gifford, 1956
Death in Dark Glasses. Gifford, 1952; Macmillan, 1952
Death in Desolation. Gifford, 1967
Death in Despair. Gifford, 1960
Death in High Provence. Gifford, 1957
Death in Room Five. Gifford, 1955
Death in the Fearful Night. Gifford, 1960
Death in the Night Watches. Gifford, 1945; Macmillan, 1946
Death in the Wasteland. Gifford, 1963; British Book Centre, 1964
Death of a Busybody. Gifford, 1942; Macmillan, 1943
Death of a Shadow. Gifford, 1964
Death of a Tin God. Gifford, 1961
Death on the Last Train. Gifford, 1948; Macmillan, 1949
Death Sends for the Doctor. Gifford, 1957
Death Spins the Wheel. Gifford, 1965
Death Stops the Frolic; see Turmoil in Zion
Death Treads Softly. Gifford, 1956
Devious Murder. Gifford, 1973
Fatal Alibi. Gifford, 1968
Fear Round About. Gifford, 1975
The Four Unfaithful Servants. Gifford, 1942
Half-Mast for the Deemster. Gifford, 1953
He'd Rather be Dead. Gifford, 1945
Intruder in the Dark. Gifford, 1966
A Knife for Harry Dodd. Gifford, 1953
Littlejohn on Leave. Gifford, 1941
Murder Adrift. Gifford, 1972
Murder Gone Mad. Gifford, 1968
Murder Makes Mistakes. Gifford, 1958
Murder of a Quack. Gifford, 1943; Macmillan, 1944
Murder Will Speak; see The Dead Shall be Raised
The Night They Killed Joss Varran. Gifford, 1970
Outrage on Gallows Hill. Gifford, 1949
Pomeroy, Deceased. Gifford, 1971
Single Ticket to Death. Gifford, 1967
Strangers Among the Dead. Gifford, 1966
Surfeit of Suspects. Gifford, 1964
Toll the Bell for Murder. Gifford, 1959
The Tormentors. Gifford, 1962
Turmoil in Zion. Gifford, 1943. U.S. title: Death Stops the Frolic. Macmillan, 1944
Tycoon's Death-Bed. Gifford, 1970

BELLAMANN, HENRY. 1882-1945.
The Gray Man Walks. Doubleday, 1936

BELLAMY, CHARLES JOSEPH. 1852-1910.
-A Moment of Madness. Burt, 1888

BELLAMY, JEAN
Mistress of Ghosthaven. Lancer, 1969
The Prisoner of Ingecliff. Dell, 1971

BELLAMY, R(OBERT) L(OWE). Series character: Scout Grey, in both titles.
The Adventures of Scout Grey. Low, 1924
Scout Grey—Detective. Low, 1927

BELLEM, ROBERT LESLIE. Joint pseudonym with Cleve F(ranklin) Adams, 1895-1949, q.v.: Franklin Charles, q.v.
Blue Murder. Phoenix, 1938
The Window with the Sleeping Nude. Handi-Books, 1950

BELLINGER, MARTHA (IDELL FLETCHER). 1870- .
The Stolen Singer. Bobbs, 1911

BELLOC, (JOSEPH) HILAIRE (PIERRE RENE). 1870-1953.
But Soft—We are Observed. Arrowsmith, 1928. U.S. title: Shadowed! Harper, 1929
The Emerald of Catherine the Great. Arrowsmith, 1926; Harper, 1926
The Green Overcoat. Arrowsmith, 1912; McBride, 1912
The Haunted House. Arrowsmith, 1927; Harper, 1928
The Missing Masterpiece. Arrowsmith, 1929; Harper, 1929
Shadowed!; see But Soft—We are Observed

BELMAR, CHARLES. 1890- .
Finnegan's Dilemma. Vantage, 1950

BELOT, ADOLPHE. 1829-1890.
Alphonsine; or, The Criminal Charm. General Publishing, 1888
The Drama of the Rue de la Paix; see Men are What Women Make Them
Fedora; or, The Tragedy in the Rue de la Paix; see Men are What Women Make Them
Flower of Crime. Newberry, 1892
Men are What Women Make Them; or, The Drama of Rue de la Paix. Peterson, 1872. British title: A Tragedy Indeed. Remington, 1878. Also published as: Fedora; or, The Tragedy in the Rue de la Paix. Rand, 1883. And as: The Drama of the Rue de la Paix. Vizetelly, 1880. And as: The Tragedy in the Rue de la Paix. Street, 1891
The Tragedy in the Rue de la Paix; see Men are What Women Make Them
A Tragedy Indeed; see Men are What Women Make Them

BELVEDERE, LEE. Pseudonym of V(alerie) Merle (Spanner) Grayland, q.v.
Meet a Dark Stranger. Dell, 1973

BENCHLEY, NATHANIEL (GODDARD). 1915-
Catch a Falling Spy. McGraw, 1963
The Hunter's Moon. Little, 1972

-The Off-Islanders. McGraw, 1961; Hutchinson, 1962
Sail a Crooked Ship. McGraw, 1960; Hutchinson, 1961
Sweet Hostage; see Welcome to Xanadu
The Wake of the Icarus. Atheneum, 1969
Welcome to Xanadu. Atheneum, 1968; Hutchinson, 1968. Also published as: Sweet Hostage. PB, 1977

BENDER, WILLIAM
Tokyo Intrigue. Digit, 1958

BENEDICT, GERALD
The Case of the Deadly Drops. Phoenix, 1941

BENEDICT, LYNN
Bloodstone. Beagle, 1973
The Fatal Flower. Avon, 1973
The Lucifer Cult. PB, 1974
Whisper of Heather. PB, 1974

BENET, JAMES (WALKER). 1914- .
The Knife Behind You. Harper, 1950
A Private Killing. Harper, 1949; Corgi, 1951

BENET, WILLIAM ROSE. 1886-1950.
The First Person Singular. Doran, 1922

BENFIELD, ERIC
Poison in the Shade. Heinemann, 1953

BENJAMIN, EDLA
Murder Without Makeup. Random, 1940
A Well-Born Corpse. Random, 1939

BENNET, ROBERT AMES. 1870-1954.
Which One? McClurg, 1912

BENNET-THOMPSON, LILIAN, 1883-1942, and HUBBARD, GEORGE, 1884- .
The Beak of Death. Chelsea, 1929
The Death Fire. Chelsea, 1929
The Golden Ball. Chelsea, 1929

BENNETT, (ENOCH) ARNOLD. 1867-1931.
The Ghost. Chatto, 1907; Turner, 1907
The Grand Babylon Hotel. Chatto, 1902; Doran, 1902. Also published as: T. Racksole and Daughter. New Amsterdam, 1902
-The Grim Smile of the Five Towns. Chapman, 1907 ss
The Loot of Cities. Rivers, 1904; Train, 1972 ss (British reprint editions contain an additional 7 stories.)
The Night Visitor and other stories. Cassell, 1931; Doubleday, 1931 ss
T. Racksole and Daughter; see The Grand Babylon Hotel
-The Woman Who Stole Everything and other stories. Cassell, 1927; Doran, 1927 ss

BENNETT, CHARLES. See: RUTH ALEXANDER.

BENNETT, DOROTHEA [DOROTHEA BENNETT YOUNG]. 1924- .
The Dry Taste of Fear. Barker, 1960
Under the Skin. Barker, 1961; Mill, 1962

BENNETT, DOROTHY. 1906- .
Come and Be Killed. Select, 1942
How Strange a Thing. Caxton, 1935. (A detective novel in verse.)
Murder Unleashed. Doubleday, 1935

BENNETT, DOROTHY
The Carrion Crows. Hutchinson, 1950
The Curious were Killed. Hutchinson, 1947
Game Without Winners. Hale, 1972
State Puppet. Hale, 1971
Stranger in His Grave. Hale, 1966

BENNETT, EDWIN. See: SYLVIA (G. L.) DANNETT.

BENNETT, EMERSON. 1822-1905.
The Female Spy; or, Treason in the Camp. Stratton, 1851
The Forged Will; or, Crime and Retribution; see Oliver Goldfinch; or, The Hypocrite
The Heiress of Bellefront; see Walde-Warren; a Tale of Circumstantial Evidence
Oliver Goldfinch; or, The Hypocrite. Stratton, 1850. Also published as: The Forged Will; or, Crime and Retribution. Peterson, 1853
Rosalie Du Pont. Stratton, 1851. (Sequel to The Female Spy.)
The Unknown Countess; or Crime and Its Results. Peterson, 1852
Walde-Warren; a Tale of Circumstantial Evidence. Peterson, 1852. Also published as: The Heiress of Bellefront. Peterson, 1855

BENNETT, ERIC
Murder at the Admiralty. Hutchinson, 1941

BENNETT, F. E.
Fred Bennett, the Mormon Detective. Laird, 1888

BENNETT, GEOFFREY MARTIN. 1909- .
Pseudonym: Sea-Lion, q.v.

BENNETT, HAL (ZINA). 1930- .
Wait Until the Evening. Doubleday, 1974

BENNETT, JACK. 1934- .
Dragon. Joseph, 1969
Ocean Road. Joseph, 1966; Little, 1966

BENNETT, JAMES (WILLIAM). 1891- .
-Chinese Blake. Skeffington, 1930
Spinach Jade. Skeffington, 1939
The Yellow Corsair. Hamilton, 1928; Duffield, 1927

BENNETT, JANICE
The Haunted. Ace, 1974
House of Athena. Ace, 1970

BENNETT, JAY. 1912- . Pseudonym: Steve Rand, q.v.
Catacombs. Abelard, 1959
Death is a Silent Room. Abelard, 1965
Murder for Money; see Murder Money
Murder Money. Crest, 1962. British title: Murder for Money. Muller pb, 1963

BENNETT, KEM(YS DEVERELL). 1919- .
Dangerous Knowledge. Collins, 1955. U.S. title: Passport for a Renegade. Doubleday, 1955
The Devil's Current. Collins, 1953; Doubleday, 1953
The Fabulous Wink; see The Wink
Passport for a Renegade; see Dangerous Knowledge
-The Wink. Hart-Davis, 1951. U.S. title: The Fabulous Wink. Pellegrini, 1951

BENNETT, MARGOT. 1912- .
Away Went the Little Fish. Nicholson, 1946; Doubleday, 1947
Farewell Crown and Goodbye King. Eyre, 1953; Walker, 1961
The Golden Pebble. Nicholson, 1948

The Man Who Didn't Fly. Eyre, 1955; Harper, 1956
Someone from the Past. Eyre, 1958; Dutton, 1958
That Summer's Earthquake. Eyre, 1964
Time to Change Hats. Nicholson, 1945; Doubleday, 1946
The Widow of Bath. Eyre, 1952; Doubleday, 1952

BENNETT, MARY
The Broken Heart; or, The Village Bridal. Lofts, ca.1880

BENNETT, RICHARD (LAURENCE)
The Whispering Money. Heinemann, 1953

BENNETT, ROLF
The Web. Hodder, 1917

BENNETT, W(ILLIAM) R(OBERT). 1921- .
Dossier on a Mantis. Hale, 1972
The Man from Checkmate. Hale, 1971

BENNEY, MARK. Pseudonym of Henry Ernest Degras, 1910- .
The Scapegoat Dances. Davies, 1938

BENOIT, PIERRE. 1886-1962.
Count Philip. Hutchinson, 1920. U.S. title: The Secret Spring. Dodd, 1920. Also published as: Konigsmark. Hutchinson, 1924
Konigsmark; see Count Philip
The Secret Spring; see Count Philip

BENSON, B(LACKWOOD) K(ETCHUM). 1845- .
Who Goes There? Macmillan, 1900

BENSON, BEN(JAMIN). 1915-1959. Series characters: Captain Wade Paris = WP; Ralph Lindsay = RL.
The Affair of the Exotic Dancer. Mill, 1958 WP
Alibi at Dusk. Mill, 1951; Corgi, 1952 WP
Beware the Pale Horse. Mill, 1951; Muller, 1952 WP
The Black Mirror. Mill, 1957; Collins, 1958
The Blonde in Black. Mill, 1958; Collins, 1959 WP
Broken Shield. Mill, 1955; Collins, 1957 RL
The Burning Fuse. Mill, 1954; Collins, 1956 WP
The End of Violence. Mill, 1959; Collins, 1959 RL
The Frightened Ladies. Mill, 1960. (Two novelets.)
The Girl in the Cage. Mill, 1954; Collins, 1955 RL
The Huntress is Dead. Mill, 1960 WP
Lily in Her Coffin. Mill, 1952; Boardman, 1954 WP
The Ninth Hour. Mill, 1956; Collins, 1957 WP
The Running Man. Mill, 1957; Collins, 1958 RL
Seven Steps East. Mill, 1959 RL
The Silver Cobweb. Mill, 1955; Collins, 1956 RL
Stamped for Murder. Mill, 1952; Gannet, 1955 WP
Target in Taffeta. Mill, 1953; Collins, 1955 WP
The Venus Death. Mill, 1953; Muller, 1954 WP

BENSON, E(DWARD) F(REDERIC). 1867-1940.
The Blotting Book. Heinemann, 1908; Doubleday, 1908
The Countess of Lowndes Square. Cassell, 1920 ss, some criminous

The Room in the Tower and other stories. Mills, 1912; Knopf, 1929 ss, some criminous
Visible and Invisible. Hutchinson, 1923; Doran, 1924 ss, some criminous

BENSON, GODFREY R(ATHBONE) [LORD CHARNWOOD]. 1864-1945.
Tracks in the Snow. Longmans, 1906; Dial, 1928, as by Lord Charnwood

BENSON, JOHN R.
Death Opens the Ball. Cassell, 1935

BENSON, MATTHEW
Crimson Poppies. Detective Tales

BENSON, O. G.
Cain's Woman. Dell, 1960

BENSON, (ELEANOR) THEODORA (ROBY). 1906- .
Rehearsal for Death. Gollancz, 1954

BENSON, THERESE. Pseudonym of Emilie Benson Knipe, 1870-1958.
Death Wears a Mask. Harper, 1935
Gallant Adventuress. Dodd, 1933
Strictly Private. Dodd, 1931

BENSTEAD, C(HARLES) R(ICHARD). 1896- .
The Strange Adventures of Richard Conway Bowen. Hurst, 1927

BENT, SILAS. 1882-1945.
Buchanan of "The Press." Vanguard, 1932

BENTINCK, HENRY
Isoworg. Joseph, 1971

BENTLEY, E(DMUND) C(LERIHEW). 1875-1956. Series character: Philip Trent = PT.
The Chill; see Elephant's Work
Elephant's Work. Hodder, 1950; Knopf, 1950. Also published as: The Chill. Dell, 1953
Trent Intervenes. Nelson, 1938; Knopf, 1938 ss PT
Trent's Last Case. Nelson, 1913. U.S. title: The Woman in Black. Century, 1913. (Later U.S. editions had the British title.) PT
Trent's Own Case, with H(erbert) W(arner) Allen, 1881- , q.v. Constable, 1936; Knopf, 1936 PT
The Woman in Black; see Trent's Last Case

BENTLEY, H. CUMBERLAND
-A Dream's Fulfillment. Macqueen, 1895

BENTLEY, JOHN. Series characters: Glen Gibson = GG; Sir Richard Herrivell = RH; Dick Marlow = DM.
The Berg Case. Eldon, 1934. U.S. title: The Eyes of Death. Doubleday, 1934 RH
Bullets Make Holes. Hutchinson, 1945 GG
Call Off the Corpse. Hutchinson, 1947. U.S. title: Kill Me Again. Dodd, 1947 GG
Dangerous Waters. Hutchinson, 1939 DM
Dark Disguise. Hutchinson, 1946
The Dead Do Talk. Hutchinson, 1944 DM
The Eyes of Death; see The Berg Case
The Fairbairn Case. Chapman, 1936 RH
Front Page Murder. Hutchinson, 1940. U.S. title: Mr. Marlow Stops for Brandy. Houghton, 1940 DM
The Griffith Case. Eldon, 1935 RH
The Hartland Case. Chapman, 1939 RH
The Iron Orchid. Hutchinson, 1950
It was Murder, They Said. Hutchinson, 1948 GG
Kill Me Again; see Call Off the Corpse
The Landor Case. Chapman, 1937 RH
The L'Estrange Case. Eldon, 1935 RH
Macedonian Mixup. Hutchinson, 1943 DM
Mr. Marlow Chooses Wine. Houghton, 1941 DM (British title?)
Mr. Marlow Stops for Brandy; see Front Page Murder
Mr. Marlow Takes to Rye. Houghton, 1942 DM (British title?)
Obsession for Two. Hutchinson, 1949
The Opperman Case. Chapman, 1936 RH
Pattern for Perfidy. Hutchinson, 1946 GG
Prelude to Trouble. Hutchinson, 1939 DM
The Radcliffe Case. Chapman, 1938 RH
Rendezvous with Death. Hutchinson, 1941 DM
The Whitney Case. Chapman, 1937 RH

BENTLEY, NICOLAS (CLERIHEW). 1907- .
The Events of that Week. Collins, 1972; St. Martin's, 1972
The Floating Dutchman. Joseph, 1950; Duell, 1951
Gammon and Espionage. Cresset, 1938
Inside Information. Deutsch, 1974; Penguin (U.S.), 1978
Third Party Risk. Joseph, 1953
The Tongue-Tied Canary. Joseph, 1948; Duell, 1949

BENTLEY, PHYLLIS (ELEANOR). 1894-1977.
The House of Moreys. Gollancz, 1953; Macmillan, 1953

BENTLEY, ROBERT
Here There be Dragons. Ontario, 1972

BENTON, JOHN L. Pseudonym of Thomas Albert Curry, 1900-1976. Other pseudonym: Albert Jeffers, q.v. Series character: Stephen Duane = SD.
The Art Treasure Murders. Gateway, 1940. British title: Duane and the Art Murders. Cassell, 1939 SD
Duane and the Art Murders; see The Art Treasure Murders
Duane of the FBI. Dodge, 1937. British title: Duane of the G-Men. Cassell, 1938 SD
Duane of the G-Men; see Duane of the FBI
Talent for Murder. Gateway, 1942

BENTON, KENNETH (CARTER). 1909- . Series character: Peter Craig, in all titles.
Craig and the Jaguar. Macmillan (London), 1973; Walker, 1974
Craig and the Midas Touch. Macmillan (London), 1975; Walker, 1976
Craig and the Tunisian Tangle. Macmillan (London), 1974; Walker, 1975
Sole Agent. Collins, 1970; Walker, 1974
Spy in Chancery. Collins, 1972; Walker, 1973
24th Level. Collins, 1969; Dodd, 1970

BERARD, L.
A Servant of Satan. Street, 1889

BERCKMAN, EVELYN (DOMENICA). 1900- .
The Beckoning Dream. Dodd, 1955; Eyre, 1956. Also published as: Worse Than Murder. PB, 1957
Blind Girl's Buff. Dodd, 1962; Eyre, 1962
The Blind Villain. Dodd, 1957; Eyre, 1957. Also published as: House of Terror. Dell, 1960
A Case in Nullity. Doubleday, 1968; Eyre, 1967
Do You Know This Voice? Dodd, 1960; Eyre, 1961
The Evil of Time. Dodd, 1954; Eyre, 1955
A Finger to Her Lips. Doubleday, 1971; Hale, 1971
The Fourth Man on the Rope. Doubleday, 1972; H. Hamilton, 1972
The Heir of Starvelings. Doubleday, 1967; Eyre, 1968
House of Terror; see The Blind Villain
The Hovering Darkness. Dodd, 1957; Eyre, 1958
Indecent Exposure; see The Nightmare Chase
Jewel of Death; see The Strange Bedfellow
Keys from a Window; see A Thing That Happens to You
Lament for Four Brides. Dodd, 1959; Eyre, 1960
The Long Arm of the Prince. Hale, 1968
The Nightmare Chase. Doubleday, 1975. British title (?): Indecent Exposure. H. Hamilton, 1975
No Known Grave. Dodd, 1958; Eyre, 1959
She Asked for It. Doubleday, 1969; H. Hamilton, 1970
A Simple Case of Ill-Will. Dodd, 1965; Eyre, 1964
The Stake in the Game. Doubleday, 1973; H. Hamilton, 1971
Stalemate. Doubleday, 1966; Eyre, 1966
The Strange Bedfellow. Dodd, 1956; Eyre, 1957. Also published as: Jewel of Death. Pyramid, 1968
A Thing That Happens to You. Dodd, 1964. British title: Keys from a Window. Eyre, 1965
The Victorian Album. Doubleday, 1973; H. Hamilton, 1973
The Voice of Air. Doubleday, 1970; Hale, 1971
Wait; see Wait, Just You Wait
Wait, Just You Wait. Doubleday, 1974. British title: Wait. H. Hamilton, 1972
Worse Than Murder; see The Beckoning Dream

BERCOVICI, ALFRED
The Falmont Claiments. Curtis, 1973

BERESFORD, J(OHN) D(AVYS). 1873-1947.
The Decoy. Collins, 1927
An Innocent Criminal. Collins, 1931; Dutton, 1931
The Instrument of Destiny. Collins, 1928; Bobbs, 1928
The Meeting Place and other stories. Faber, 1929 ss
Nineteen Impressions. Sidgwick, 1918 ss

BERESFORD, LESLIE (GEORGE). 1899- .
Murder Can Be Such Fun! Long, 1947
The Other Mr. North. Long, 1926
The Way of Deception. Odhams, 1922
The Web of Wan Li. Gramol, 1935
What's at the End? Jenkins, 1937

BERESFORD, MARCUS. 1919- . Pseudonym: Marc Brandel, q.v.

BERGER, THOMAS (LOUIS). 1924- .
Killing Time. Dial, 1967; Eyre, 1968
Sneaky People. Simon, 1975

BERGES, MAX L.
Woman of Shanghai. Digit, 1959

BERGMAN, ANDREW. Series character: Jack LeVine, in both titles.
The Big Kiss-Off of 1944. Holt, 1974; Hutchinson, 1975
Hollywood and LeVine. Holt, 1975; Hutchinson, 1976

BERGMAN, LEE
  Walk Softly, Walk Deadly. Belmont, 1963

BERGNER, JAY
  A Terrible Performance. Tandem, 1967

BERGQUIST, LILLIAN and IRVING MOORE
  Your Shot, Darling! Morrow, 1948; Low, 1949

BERGSON, LEO and ROBERT McMAHON. Leo Bergson is the pseudonym of S(idney) L(eo) Stebel, 1924- , q.v.
  The Widowmaster. GM, 1967

BERGSTROM, LOUISE. 1914- .
  The Pink Camellia. Bouregy, 1968
  Strange Legacy. Bouregy, 1968

BERKELEY, ANTHONY. Pseudonym of A(nthony) B(erkeley) Cox, 1893-1970, q.v. Other pseudonym: Francis Iles, q.v. Series character: Roger Sheringham = RS.
  Dead Mrs. Stratton; see Jumping Jenny
  Death in the House. Hodder, 1939; Doubleday, 1939
  Jumping Jenny. Hodder, 1933. U.S. title: Dead Mrs. Stratton. Doubleday, 1933 RS
  The Layton Court Mystery. Jenkins, 1925, as by "?"; Doubleday, 1929
  Mr. Pidgeon's Island; see Panic Party
  Murder in the Basement. Hodder, 1932; Doubleday, 1932 RS
  The Mystery at Lover's Cave; see Roger Sheringham and the Vane Mystery
  Not To Be Taken. Hodder, 1938. U.S. title: A Puzzle in Poison. Doubleday, 1938
  Panic Party. Hodder, 1934. U.S. title: Mr. Pidgeon's Island. Doubleday, 1934 RS
  The Piccadilly Murder. Collins, 1929; Doubleday, 1930
  The Poisoned Chocolates Case. Collins, 1929; Doubleday, 1929 RS
  A Puzzle in Poison; see Not To Be Taken
  Roger Sheringham and the Vane Mystery. Collins, 1927. U.S. title: The Mystery at Lover's Cave. Simon, 1927 RS
  The Second Shot. Hodder, 1930; Doubleday, 1931 RS
  The Silk Stocking Murders. Collins, 1928; Doubleday, 1928 RS
  Top Storey Murder. Hodder, 1931. U.S. title: Top Story Murder. Doubleday, 1931 RS
  Trial and Error. Hodder, 1937; Doubleday, 1937
  The Wychford Poisoning Case. Collins, 1926; Doubleday, 1930 RS

BERKELEY, AUGUST
  A Modern Quixote. American Publishing, 1884

BERNANOS, GEORGES. 1888-1948.
  A Crime. Dutton, 1936. British title: The Crime. Hale, 1936

BERNARD, JAY. Pseudonym of Raymond H. Sawkins, 1923- , q.v. Other pseudonyms: Colin Forbes, Richard Raine, qq.v.
  The Burning Fuse. Harcourt, 1970

BERNARD, JOEL
  The Thinking Machine Affair. Ace, 1970. (Novelization of Man from U.N.C.L.E. TV series.)

BERNARD, ROBERT. Pseudonym of Robert Bernard Martin, 1918- .
  Deadly Meeting. Norton, 1970
  Death Takes a Sabbatical. Norton, 1967. British title: Death Takes the Last Train. Constable, 1967

Death Takes the Last Train; see Death Takes a Sabbatical
  Illegal Entry. Norton, 1972; Faber, 1973

BERNEDE, A(RTHUR). 1871-1937. Series character: Chantecoq, in both titles.
  The Haunted House. Reader's Library, 1930
  The Mystery of the Louvre. Reader's Library, 1929; World Wide, 1929

BERNERS, LORD
  The Camel. Constable, 1936

BERNHARD, ROBERT
  The Ullman Code. Putnam, 1975

BERNSTEIN, KEN
  Intercept. Coward, 1971
  The Senator's Ransom. Coward, 1971

BERRIDGE, ELIZABETH. 1921- .
  Across the Common. Heinemann, 1964; Coward, 1965

BERROW, NORMAN. Series characters: Detective-Inspector Courtenay, in at least those marked C; Michael Revel, in at least those marked MR; Detective-Inspector Lancelot Carolus Smith, in at least those marked LS.
  The Bishop's Sword. Ward, 1948
  The Claws of the Cougar. Ward, 1957
  Don't Go Out After Dark. Ward, 1950 LS
  Don't Jump, Mr. Boland! Ward, 1954
  The Eleventh Plague. Ward, 1953
  Fingers for Ransom. Ward, 1939 MR
  The Footprints of Satan. Ward, 1950 LS
  Ghost House. Ward, 1940
  It Howls at Night. Ward, 1937
  The Lady's in Danger. Ward, 1955
  Murder in the Melody. Ward, 1940 MR
  Oil Under the Window. Ward, 1936
  One Thrilling Night. Ward, 1937 C
  The Secret Dancer. Ward, 1936 C
  The Singing Room. Ward, 1948 MR
  The Smokers of Hashish. Eldon, 1934
  The Spaniard's Thumb. Ward, 1949
  The Terror in the Fog. Ward, 1938
  The Three Tiers of Fantasy. Ward, 1947 LS
  Words Have Wings. Ward, 1946 MR

BERRY, ARTHUR
  Take Death for a Lover. Five Star, ca. 1946

BERRY, J(OHN) L(OUIS)
  A Close Call. Ogilvie, 1888
  -Linked with Fate. H. J. Smith, 1892

BERRY, JOHN (EDGAR)
  Don't Betray Me. Signet, 1963; Jenkins, 1964

BERTHOLD, MARY PADDOCK. 1909- .
  A Local Call. Vantage, 1969

BERTON, GUY. Pseudonym of Guy Robert La Coste and Eadfrid A. Bingham.
  Art Thou the Man? Dodd, 1905

BESSELL, J. PERCIVAL
  John Rutland's Romance. Low, 1921; Macaulay, 1921
  Paid Out. Low, 1919; Macaulay, 1919
  The Price of an Impulse. Palmer, 1927

BEST, (OSWALD) HERBERT. 1894- .
  The Mystery of the Flaming Hut. Cassell, 1932; Harper, 1932
  The Skull Beneath the Eaves. Grayson, 1933

BESTE, R(AYMOND) VERNON. 1908- .
  Faith Has No Country. Hodder, 1961. U.S. title: The Moonbeams. Harper, 1961
  The Moonbeams; see Faith Has No Country
  Next Time I'll Pay My Own Fare. Allen, 1969; Simon, 1969
  Repeat the Instructions. Allen, 1968; Harper, 1967
  Seeds of Destruction. Hodder, 1964

BESTER, ALFRED. 1913- .
  The Demolished Man. Shasta, 1953; Sidgwick, 1953

BESTOR, CLINTON. See: GEORGE CLINTON BESTOR.

BESTOR, GEORGE CLINTON
  The Corpse Came Calling (by Clinton Bestor). Phoenix, 1941
  Postage Stamp Murder. Dial, 1935; Low, 1936
  Prelude to Murder. Dial, 1936; Low, 1936

BETHUNE, J. G. Pseudonym of Edward S(ylvester) Ellis, 1840-1916, q.v.
  The "F" Cipher. Price McGill, 1892
  The Great Berwyck Bank Burglary; see Hands Up!
  Hands Up!; or, The Great Bank Burglary. U.S. Book Co., 1890. Also published as: The Great Berwyck Bank Burglary. Collier, 1893
  The Third Man. Cassell (New York), 1893

BETTANY, GEORGE (KERNAHAN GWYNNE). 1891- .
  Dangerous Haven. Skeffington, 1949
  Man Hunt. Skeffington, 1951
  Murder at Benfleet. Skeffington, 1946
  Scarbrow. Skeffington, 1934
  The Secret of the Swamp. Skeffington, 1931
  Silent Mountain. Skeffington, 1935
  Valley of Lost Gold. Skeffington, 1934
  Villainy. Skeffington, 1936

BETTERIDGE, ANNE. Pseudonym of Margaret (Edith) Newman, 1926- , q.v.
  Sirocco. Hurst, 1970

BETTERIDGE, DON. Pseudonym of Bernard (Charles) Newman, 1897-1968, q.v.
  Balkan Spy. Jenkins, 1942
  The Case of the Berlin Spy. Hale, 1954
  Cast Iron Alibi. Jenkins, 1939
  Contact Man. Hale, 1960
  Dictator's Destiny. Jenkins, 1945
  The Escape of General Gerard. Jenkins, 1943
  The Gibraltar Conspiracy. Hale, 1955
  Not Single Spies. Hale, 1951
  The Package Holiday Spy Case. Hale, 1962
  The Potsdam Murder Plot. Jenkins, 1947
  Scotland Yard Alibi. Jenkins, 1938
  Spies Left! Hale, 1950
  The Spies of Peenemunde. Hale, 1958
  Spy—Counter Spy. Hale, 1953

BEVERLEY, BARRINGTON
  The Air Devil. Allan, 1934
  The Space Raiders. Allan, 1936

BEVIS, JAMES. See: MARTEN CUMBERLAND, 1892- .

BEYER, WILLIAM GRAY
  Death of a Puppeteer. Mystery House, 1946

Eenie, Meenie, Minie—Murder! Mystery House, 1945. British title: Murder by Arrangement. Partridge, 1948. Also published as: Murder Secretary. Bart, 1946
Murder by Arrangement; see Eenie, Meenie, Minie—Murder!
Murder Secretary; see Eenie, Meenie, Minie—Murder!

BEYMER, WILLIAM GILMORE. 1881- .
The Middle of Midnight. Whittlesey, 1947

BEYNON, JANE. 1915- . Pseudonym: Lange Lewis, q.v.
Cypress Man. Bobbs, 1944

BEYNON, JOHN. Pseudonym of John Wyndham Parkes Lucas Beynon Harris, 1903-1969.
Foul Play Suspected. Newnes, 1935

BEYNON-HARRIS, VIVIAN
Trouble at Hanard. Partridge, 1948

BICKEL, MARY (DUPUY)
Brassbound. Coward, 1934. British title: The Trial of Linda Stuart. H. Hamilton, 1935

BICKERS, RICHARD (LESLIE) TOWNSHEND. 1917- . Pseudonym: David Richards, q.v. Series character: Mark Stratton, in at least those marked MS.
The Hellions. Hale, 1965 MS
Hunt and Kill. Hale, 1969
Maraskar Bound. Hale, 1969
Scent of Mayhem. Hale, 1965 MS

BICKERTON, DEREK. 1926- .
The Gold Run. Eyre, 1960
Payroll. Eyre, 1959

BICKNELL, FRANK MARTIN. 1854-1916.
The Bicycle Highwayman. Estes, 1900

BIDDLE, A(NTHONY) J(OSEPH) DREXEL. 1874-1948.
Word for Word and Letter for Letter. Gay & Bird, 1898

BIDMEAD, CHARLES
The Man in the Shadows. Rich, 1954
The Silent Men. Rich, 1955

BIDSTON, LESTER. 1884- . All titles below feature Sexton Blake and were published by Amalgamated Press.
Crooks Ltd. 1929
The Cup Final Crime. 1932
The Fatal Alibi. 1931
Gang's Prisoners. 1931
The Mill of Fear. 1932
The Motor Coach Murder. 1933
The Mystery of Oldham. 1930
The Phantom of the Mill. 1927
The Silent Syndicate. 1931

BIDWELL, MARGARET. Series character: Mr. Hodson, in both titles.
Death and His Brother. Hurst, 1940
Death on the Agenda. Hurst, 1939

BIDWELL, MARJORY E. S. Pseudonym: Mary Anne Gibbs, q.v.

BIER, JESSE. 1925- .
-Trial at Bannock. Harcourt, 1963

BIERSTADT, EDWARD HALE
Satan was a Man. Doubleday, 1935. British title: Murder by Inspiration. Chapman, 1935

BIGDEN, HENRY
Late into the Night. Cassell, 1962

BIGELOW, JOHN MASON
Death is an Early Riser. Scribner, 1940

BIGGERS, EARL DERR. 1884-1933. See also: GEORGE M(ICHAEL) COHAN, 1879-1942. Series character: Charlie Chan = CC (continued by Dennis Lynds, 1924- , q.v.).
The Agony Column. Bobbs, 1916. Also published as: Second Floor Mystery. Grosset, 1930
Behind That Curtain. Bobbs, 1928; Harrap, 1928 CC
The Black Camel. Bobbs, 1929; Cassell, 1930 CC
Charlie Chan Carries On. Bobbs, 1930; Cassell, 1931 CC
The Chinese Parrot. Bobbs, 1926; Harrap, 1927 CC
Earl Derr Biggers Tells Ten Stories. Bobbs, 1933 ss
Fifty Candles. Bobbs, 1926
The House Without a Key. Bobbs, 1925; Harrap, 1926 CC
Inside the Lines, with Robert Welles Ritchie. Bobbs, 1915
Keeper of the Keys. Bobbs, 1932; Cassell, 1932 CC
Love Insurance. Bobbs, 1914
Second Floor Mystery; see The Agony Column
Seven Keys to Baldpate. Bobbs, 1913; Mills, 1914

BIGGS, JOHN (JR.)
-Seven Days Whipping. Scribner, 1928; Heinemann, 1929

BILLANY, DAN. 1913-1945.
It Takes a Thief; see The Opera House Murders
The Opera House Murders. Faber, 1940. U.S. title: It Takes a Thief. Harper, 1940
-The Trap. Faber, 1950

BILLETT, MABEL (BROUGHTON). 1892- .
Calamity House. Hutchinson, 1927
The Robot Detective. Hutchinson, 1932
The Shadow on the Steppe. Hutchinson, 1930
Smooth Silence. Ryerson, 1936

BILLING, GRAHAM
The Alpha Trip. Allen, 1969

BINDLOSS, HAROLD (EDWARD). 1866-1945.
-The Broken Net. Ward, 1925. U.S. title: Prairie Gold. Stokes, 1925
The Broken Trail; see Sour Grapes
Carmen's Messenger. Ward, 1917; Stokes, 1917
The Coast of Adventure; see A Risky Game
-The Firm Hand. Ward, 1928. U.S. title: The Lone Hand. Stokes, 1928
The Frontiersman; see Frontiersmen
Frontiersmen. Ward, 1929. U.S. title: The Frontiersman. Stokes, 1929
-Halford's Adventure. Ward, 1928. U.S. title: Mystery Reef. Stokes, 1928
Harden's Escape. Ward, 1930. U.S. title: The Man at Willow Ranch. Stokes, 1930
The Lean Years. Ward, 1931. U.S. title: The Prairie Patrol. Stokes, 1931
The Lone Hand; see The Firm Hand
The Long Portage; see The Pioneer
The Man at Willow Ranch; see Harden's Escape

-The Mistress of Bonaventure. Chatto, 1903; Stokes, 1907
-The Mountaineers. Ward, 1922. U.S. title: Northwest! Stokes, 1922
Mystery Reef; see Halford's Adventure
Northwest!; see The Mountaineers
-The Pioneer. Ward, 1912. U.S. title: The Long Portage. Stokes, 1912
Prairie Gold; see The Broken Net
The Prairie Patrol; see The Lean Years
-A Risky Game. Ward, 1915. U.S. title: The Coast of Adventure. Stokes, 1915
Sour Grapes. Ward, 1926. U.S. title: The Broken Trail. Stokes, 1926
The Wilderness Patrol. Ward, 1923; Stokes, 1923
-Winston of the Prairie. Stokes, 1907 (British title?)
Wyndham's Pal; see Wyndham's Partner
-Wyndham's Partner. Ward, 1919. U.S. title: Wyndham's Pal. Stokes, 1919

BINGHAM, CARSON. Pseudonym of Bruce (Bingham) Cassiday, 1920- , q.v. Other pseudonyms: Mary Anne Drew, Annie Laurie McMurdie, Michael Stratford, qq.v.
The Gang Girls. Monarch, 1963
It Happened in Hawaii. Monarch, 1962

BINGHAM, EADFRID A. Joint pseudonym with Guy Robert La Coste: Guy Berton, q.v.

BINGHAM, JOHN (MICHAEL WARD). 1908- .
A Case of Libel. Gollancz, 1963
The Double Agent. Gollancz, 1966; Dutton, 1967
Five Roundabouts to Heaven. Gollancz, 1953. U.S. title: The Tender Poisoner. Dodd, 1953
A Fragment of Fear. Gollancz, 1965; Dutton, 1966
Good Old Charlie; see I Love, I Kill
I Love, I Kill. Gollancz, 1968. U.S. title: Good Old Charlie. Simon, 1969
Inspector Morgan's Dilemma; see The Paton Street Case
Marion. Gollancz, 1958. U.S. title: Murder Off the Record. Dodd, 1957
Murder is a Witch; see The Third Skin
Murder Off the Record; see Marion
Murder Plan Six. Gollancz, 1958; Dodd, 1959
My Name is Michael Sibley. Gollancz, 1952; Dodd, 1952
Night's Black Agent. Gollancz, 1961; Dodd, 1961
The Paton Street Case. Gollancz, 1955. U.S. title: Inspector Morgan's Dilemma. Dodd, 1956
The Tender Poisoner; see Five Roundabouts to Heaven
The Third Skin. Gollancz, 1954; Dodd, 1954. Also published as: Murder is a Witch. Dell, 1957
Vulture in the Sun. Gollancz, 1971

BINGLEY, D(AVID) E(RNEST). 1920- .
Pseudonyms: Henry Chesham, George Fallon, qq.v.
-Caribbean Crisis. Hale, 1966
The Elusive Witness. Hale, 1966

BINKLEY, ANNE
-What Shall I Cry. Harcourt, 1968; Gollancz, 1968

BINNS, OTTWELL. 1872- . Pseudonym: Ben Bolt, q.v.
An Adventurer of the Bay. Ward, 1926
Behind the Ranges. Ward, 1928
The Blue Sash. Ward, 1935
By Papuan Waters. Ward, 1938
Clancy of the Mounted Police. Ward, 1923

B

The Diamond Trail. Ward, 1928
Doc Churston. Ward, 1933
The Drums of Doom. Ward, 1927
The Far Pursuit. Ward, 1936
The Flaming Crescent. Ward, 1931
Flotsam of the Line. Ward, 1926
Forest Exile. Ward, 1933
A Gipsy of the North. Ward, 1924
Gold is King. Ward, 1934
The Grey Rat. Ward, 1931
A Hazard of the Snows. Ward, 1921
In the Flashlight. Ward, 1937
Java Jack. Ward, 1925
Jim Trelawney. Ward, 1930
The Lady of the Miniature. Ward, 1918
The Lady of the North Star. Ward, 1919; Knopf, 1922
The Last Door. Ward, 1935
The Law of the Hills. Ward, 1925
The Lifting of the Shadow. Ward, 1921
The Love That Believeth. Ward, 1920
The Man from Maloba. Ward, 1917
A Man of Dartmoor. Ward, 1939
-A Mating in the Wilds. Ward, 1920; Knopf, 1920
The Mystery of the Heart. Ward, 1919
The Nets of Fate. Mellifont, 1932
The Poisoned Pen. Ward, 1937
The Red Token. Ward, 1934
Ringing Sands. Ward, 1927
The Secret Adventure. Ward, 1933
The Secret Pearls. Ward, 1930
The Shining Trail. Ward, 1935
A Shot in the Woods. Ward, 1938
A Sin of Silence. Ward, 1918
Snowbird. Ward, 1931
A Soldier of the Legion. Ward, 1937
A Tamer of Men. Ward, 1929
The Three Black Dots. Ward, 1929
The Three Blue Anchors. Ward, 1934
Trader Random. Ward, 1932
The Trail of Adventure. Ward, 1923
The Treasure of Christophe. Ward, 1922
The Vanished Guest. Ward, 1930
Weeds of Hate. Ward, 1936
White Gold. Ward, 1932
The White Hands of Justice. Ward, 1922

BIOY-CASARES, ADOLFO. 1914- .
A Plan for Escape. Dutton, 1975

BIRCH, BRUCE
Subway in the Sky. Four Square, 1959. (Novelization of the movie.)

BIRD, BRANDON. Joint pseudonym of George Bird Evans, 1906- , and Kay Harris Evans, 1906- . Other joint pseudonym: Harris Evans, q.v.
Dead and Gone; see Downbeat for a Dirge
Death in Four Colors. Dodd, 1950; Constable, 1951
Downbeat for a Dirge. Dodd, 1952. Also published as: Dead and Gone. Dell, 1955
Hawk Watch. Dodd, 1954; Boardman, 1955
Never Wake a Dead Man. Dodd, 1950; Constable, 1952

BIRD, KENNETH
Bishop Must Move. Cassell, 1967
The Mozart Fiddle. Hale, 1969
Murder in Vision. Hale, 1969
The Rainbow Coloured Hearse. Hale, 1970
Smash a Glass Image. Cassell, 1968

BIRKIN, CHARLES (LLOYD). 1907- .
Dark Menace. Tandem, 1968 ss
-Devil's Spawn. Allan, 1934 ss
The Kiss of Death. Tandem, 1964; Award, 1969 ss
My Name is Death. Panther, 1966; Award, 1970 ss
The Smell of Evil. Tandem, 1965; Award, 1969 ss
So Pale, So Cold, So Fair. Tandem, 1970 ss
Spawn of Satan. Award, 1970 ss
Where Terror Stalked. Tandem, 1966 ss

BIRKLEY, DOLAN. Pseudonym of (Julia Clara Catherine) Dolores (Birk Olsen) Hitchens, 1907-1972, q.v. Other pseudonyms: Noel Burke, D. B. Olsen, qq.v.
The Blue Geranium. Simon, 1941
The Unloved. Doubleday, 1965; Hale, 1967

BIRMINGHAM, GEORGE A. Pseudonym of James Owen Hannay, 1865-1950.
-Adventurers of the Night. Doran, 1921. (British title?)
-Fed Up. Methuen, 1931; Bobbs, 1931
-Fidgets. Hodder, 1927. U.S. title: Gold, Gore and Gehenna. Bobbs, 1927
Gold, Gore and Gehenna; see Fidgets
The Hymn Tune Mystery. Methuen, 1930; Bobbs, 1931
-The Island Mystery. Methuen, 1918; Doran, 1918
-The Lost Lawyer. Methuen, 1921
-The Major's Candlesticks. Methuen, 1929; Bobbs, 1929
-Miss Maitland's Spy. Methuen, 1940
The Search Party. Methuen, 1909; Doran, 1911
Wild Justice. Methuen, 1930; Bobbs, 1930

BIRMINGHAM, MAISIE
You Can Help Me. Collins, 1974

BIRMINGHAM, STEPHEN. 1932- .
-The Towers of Love. Little, 1961; Collins, 1962

BIRNEY, HERMAN HOFFMAN. 1891-1958. Pseudonym: David Kent, q.v.

BISHOP, CECIL
Adventures of Ah Foo, the Chinese Sherlock Holmes. Mitre, 1943
The Blackmail Gang. Mellifont, 1937
Black Terror. Miller, 1945
Chinese Brown of Scotland Yard. Mellifont, 1937
Claws of the Red Dragon. Mellifont, 1937
Crime and the Underworld. Mitre, 1944 ss
Crime in a Big Way. Mitre, 1944 ss
The Kidnapper. Mellifont, 1937
Murder on the Second Floor. Everybody's, 1944
The Prince of Blackmail. Miller, 1945
The Shadow of Li Tong Su. Miller, 1945
Terror Comes to London. Everybody's, 1944

BISHOP, MALDEN GRANGE
Scylla. Ace, 1954

BISHOP, MARY
Killraven. Dell, 1975
Widow's Walk. Dell, 1975

BISHOP, MORRIS GILBERT. 1893-1973. Pseudonym: W. Bolingbroke Johnson, q.v.

BISHOP, R. F.
Camerton Slope; A Story of Mining Life. Cranston, 1893

BISHOP, SHEILA
-Goldsmith's Row. Hurst, 1969
-The House with Two Faces. Hurst, 1960; Ace, 1960

BISHOP, STACEY. Pseudonym of George Johann Carl Antheil, 1900-1959.
Death in the Dark. Faber, 1930

BISS, GERALD
Branded. Greening, 1908
The Door of the Unreal. Nash, 1919; Putnam, 1920
The Dupe. Greening, 1907; Brentano's, 1909
The Fated Five. Greening, 1910
The House of Terror. Greening, 1909
The White Rose Mystery. Greening, 1907

BISSAGAR, FREDERICK GEORGE
Entrapped; or, Charlie's First Crime. Aldine, 1894

BITTLE, CAMILLA R.
The Boy in the Pool. Lippincott, 1962

BJERKE, ANDRE. 1918- . Pseudonym: Bernhard Borge, q.v.

BLACK, CAMPBELL
Assassins and Victims. Macmillan (London), 1969; Harper's Magazine Press, 1970
Death's Head. Collins, 1972; Lippincott, 1972
The Punctual Rape. Macmillan (London), 1970; Lippincott, 1971

BLACK, DAVID
The Strangler. Manor, 1974

BLACK, E(LIZABETH) BEST. 1894- .
Series character: Peter Strangely, in both titles.
The Crime of the Chromium Bowl. Loring, 1934; Newnes, 1937
The Ravenelle Riddle. Loring, 1933

BLACK, GAVIN. Pseudonym of Oswald (Morris) Wynd, 1913- , q.v. Series character: Paul Harris, in at least those marked PH.
A Big Wind for Summer. Collins, 1975; Harper, 1976 PH
The Bitter Tea. Collins, 1973; Harper, 1972 PH
The Cold Jungle. Collins, 1969; Harper, 1969 PH
Dead Man Calling. Collins, 1962; Harper, 1962
A Dragon for Christmas. Collins, 1963; Harper, 1963 PH
The Eyes Around Me. Collins, 1964; Harper, 1964 PH
The Golden Cockatrice. Collins, 1974; Harper, 1975 PH
Suddenly, at Singapore... Collins, 1961 PH
A Time for Pirates. Collins, 1971; Harper, 1971 PH
A Wind of Death. Collins, 1967; Harper, 1967 PH
You Want to Die, Johnny? Collins, 1966; Harper, 1966 PH

BLACK, HAZELTON. Pseudonym: Scott Graham, q.v.

BLACK, HERMINA
Enmeshed. Eldon
-Romance Comes to Scotland Yard. Hodder, 1969

BLACK, IAN STUART. 1915- .
-The High Bright Sun. Hutchinson, 1962
In the Wake of a Stranger. Dakers, 1953
The Man on the Bridge. Constable, 1975; St. Martin's, 1977
-The Passionate City. Heinemann, 1958; Viking, 1958
-The Yellow Flag. Hutchinson, 1959

BLACK, JOHN D.
  Trouble Man. Dell, 1972. (Novelization of the movie.)

BLACK, LADBROKE (LIONEL DAY). 1877-1940. Pseudonym: Paul Urquhart, q.v. See also: T. C. St. C. Morton. Series characters: Sexton Blake (with many other authors) = SB; Mr. Preed, in at least those marked P.
  The Case of the Crook Banker. Amalgamated, 1930 SB
  -The Gorgon's Head. Low, 1932
  -Her Convict Husband. Tinling, 1941
  The Informer. Amalgamated, 1930 SB
  The Killer at Large. Paul, 1937 P
  Mr. Preed Investigates. Nelson, 1939 P
  Mr. Preed's Gangster. Nelson, 1939 P
  The Mystery Militiaman. Amalgamated, 1940 SB
  -The Poison War. Paul, 1933
  The Prince of Poisoners. Nicholson, 1932; Dial, 1932

BLACK, LIONEL. Pseudonym of Dudley Barker, 1910- . Other pseudonym: Anthony Matthews. Series character: Emma Greaves, in at least those marked EG.
  Arafat is Next! Collins, 1975; Stein, 1975
  The Bait. Cassell, 1966 EG
  Breakaway. Collins, 1970. U.S. title: Flood. Stein, 1971
  Chance to Die. Cassell, 1965 EG
  Death by Hoax. Collins, 1974
  Death has Green Fingers. Collins, 1971; Walker, 1971, as by Anthony Matthews
  Flood; see Breakaway
  The Lady is a Spy; see Two Ladies in Verona
  The Life and Death of Peter Wade. Collins, 1973; Stein, 1974
  Outbreak. Cassell, 1968; Stein, 1968
  A Provincial Crime. Cassell, 1960
  Ransom for a Nude. Collins, 1972; Stein, 1972
  Swinging Murder. Cassell, 1969; Walker, 1969, as by Anthony Matthews
  Two Ladies in Verona. Cassell, 1967. U.S. title: The Lady is a Spy. Paperback Library, 1969 EG

BLACK, MANSELL. Pseudonym of Elleston Trevor, 1920- , q.v. Name originally: Trevor Dudley Smith, q.v. Other pseudonyms: Adam Hall, Simon Rattray, Warwick Scott, Caesar Smith, qq.v. Series character: Richard Vaness, in all titles.
  Dead on Course. Hodder, 1951. Reprinted as by Elleston Trevor: White Lion, 1974
  Shadow of Evil. Hodder, 1953
  Sinister Cargo. Hodder, 1951
  Steps in the Dark. Hodder, 1954

BLACK, PETER. Pseudonym.
  Which of Them? Benn, 1932

BLACK, R(OBERT) JERE. 1892- .
  The Killing of the Golden Goose. Loring, 1934

BLACK, THOMAS B. 1910- . Series character: Al Delaney, in all titles.
  Four Dead Mice. Rinehart, 1954. Also published as: Million Dollar Murder. Bantam, 1955
  Million Dollar Murder; see Four Dead Mice
  The Pinball Murders. Reynal, 1947
  The 3-13 Murders. Reynal, 1946
  The Whitebird Murders. Reynal, 1946

BLACK, VERONICA. Pseudonym of Maureen Peters, 1935- .

A Footfall in the Mist. Hale, 1971
Master of Malcarew. Hale, 1971; Lenox Hill, 1972

BLACKBURN, (EVELYN) BARBARA. 1898- .
  City of Forever. Hale, 1963; Ace, 1966

BLACKBURN, JOHN (FENWICK). 1923- .
  Blow the House Down. Cape, 1970
  Blue Octavo. Cape, 1963. U.S. title: Bound to Kill. Mill, 1963
  Bound to Kill; see Blue Octavo
  Broken Boy. Secker, 1959; Mill, 1962
  Bury Him Darkly. Cape, 1969; Putnam, 1970
  Children of the Night. Cape, 1966; Putnam, 1969
  Colonel Bogus. Cape, 1964. U.S. title: Packed for Murder. Mill, 1964
  Dead Man Running. Secker, 1960; Mill, 1961
  Deep Among the Dead Men. Cape, 1973
  Devil Daddy. Cape, 1972
  The Flame and the Wind. Cape, 1967
  For Fear of Little Men. Cape, 1972
  The Gaunt Woman. Cape, 1962; Mill, 1962
  The Household Traitors. Cape, 1971
  Mister Brown's Bodies. Cape, 1975
  Murder at Midnight; see Winds of Midnight
  Nothing But the Night. Cape, 1968
  Our Lady of Pain. Cape, 1974
  Packed for Murder; see Colonel Bogus
  The Reluctant Spy; see A Scent of New-Mown Hay
  A Ring of Roses. Cape, 1965. U.S. title: A Wreath of Roses. Mill, 1965
  A Scent of New-Mown Hay. Secker, 1958; Mill, 1958. Also published as: The Reluctant Spy. Lancer, 1966
  A Sour Apple Tree. Secker, 1958; Mill, 1959
  The Winds of Midnight. Cape, 1964. U.S. title: Murder at Midnight. Mill, 1964
  A Wreath of Roses; see A Ring of Roses
  The Young Man from Lima. Cape, 1968

BLACKBURN, THOMAS
  A Good Day to Die. Popular Library, 1967

BLACKER, IRWIN R(OBERT). 1919- .
  Chain of Command. Cassell, 1965
  The Kilroy Gambit. World, 1960
  Search and Destroy. Random, 1966. British title: The Valley of Hanoi. Cassell, 1966
  To Hell in a Basket. Cassell, 1967
  The Valley of Hanoi; see Search and Destroy

BLACKLEDGE, LEONARD
  Behind the Evidence. Hutchinson, 1935

BLACKLEDGE, W(ILLIAM) J(AMES). 1886- .
  A Girl in the Spy Racket. Laurie, 1939

BLACKMON, ANITA. 1893- . Series character: Adelaide Adams, in both titles.
  The Hotel Richelieu Murders; see Murder a la Richelieu
  Murder a la Richelieu. Doubleday, 1937. British title: The Hotel Richelieu Murders. Heinemann, 1938
  The Riddle of the Dead Cats; see There is No Return
  There is No Return. Doubleday, 1938. British title: The Riddle of the Dead Cats. Butterworth, 1939

BLACKMORE, JANE. The books below, published at least for the most part as romances in England, have at least mostly been identified as gothics in U.S. editions.
  And Then There was Georgia. Collins, 1975; Ace, 1975
  Angel's Tear. Ace, 1974. (British title?)
  Beloved Stranger. Collins, 1953; Dell, 1973
  Beware the Night. Collins, 1958; Ace, 1968
  Bitter Honey. Collins, 1960
  Bitter Love. Collins, 1956
  The Bridge of Strange Music. Collins, 1952
  Broomstick in the Hall. Collins, 1971; Ace, 1970
  The Closing Door. Collins, 1955
  The Cresselly Inheritance. Collins, 1973; Ace, 1974
  Dance on a Hornet's Nest. Collins, 1970
  Dangerous Love. Collins, 1958
  The Dark Between the Stars. Collins, 1961; Ace, 1967
  Deed of Innocence; see Gold for My Girl
  The Deep Pool. Collins, 1972; Ace, 1972
  Flight into Love. Collins, 1964
  Girl Alone. Collins, 1965
  Gold for My Girl. Collins, 1967. U.S. title: Deed of Innocence. Ace, 1969
  Hunter's Mate. Collins, 1971
  It Couldn't Happen to Me. Collins, 1962; Dell, 1972
  It Happened to Susan. Collins, 1944; Dell, 1973
  Joanna. Collins, 1963
  The Lilac is for Sharing. Collins, 1969
  The Lonely House. Collins, 1957
  A Love Forbidden; see The Other Room
  Man of Power. Collins, 1966
  Miranda. Collins, 1966
  The Missing Hour. Collins, 1959; Ace, 1975
  My Sister Erica. Collins, 1973; Ace, 1975
  Night of the Bonfire. Collins, 1974; Ace, 1974
  The Night of the Stranger. Collins, 1961; Ace, 1967
  The Nine Commandments. Collins, 1950
  The Other Room. Collins, 1968; Ace, 1969. Also published as: A Love Forbidden. Coronet, 1974
  Perilous Waters. Collins, 1954; Dell, 1973
  Raw Summer. Collins, 1967; Dell, 1972
  Return to Love. Collins, 1964
  The Room in the Tower. Collins, 1972; Ace, 1973
  Snow in June. Collins, 1947
  So Dark the Mirror. Collins, 1949
  The Square of Many Colours. Collins, 1948; Ace, 1975
  Storm in the Family. Collins, 1956
  Tears in Paradise. Collins, 1959; Dell, 1973
  That Night. Collins, 1963; Lancer, 1969
  They Carry a Torch. Collins, 1943
  Three Letters to Pan. Collins, 1955
  Towards Tomorrow. Collins, 1941
  A Trap for Lovers. Collins, 1960. U.S. title (?): The Velvet Trap. Ace, 1969
  Two in Shadow. Collins, 1962
  The Velvet Trap; see A Trap for Lovers
  A Woman on Her Own. Collins, 1957; Ace, 1971

BLACKSTOCK, CHARITY. Pseudonym of Ursula Torday. Other pseudonyms: Paula Allardyce, q.v., Lee Blackstock.
  All Men are Murderers; see The Shadow of Murder

The Bitter Conquest. Hodder, 1959
The Briar Patch. Hodder, 1960. U.S.
    title: Young Lucifer. Lippincott,
    1960
Dewey Death. Heinemann, 1956; London
    House, 1958
The English Wife; see The Factor's Wife
The Exorcism. Hodder, 1961. U.S.
    title: A House Possessed. Lippincott,
    1962
The Factor's Wife. Hodder, 1964. U.S.
    title: The English Wife. Coward, 1964
The Foggy, Foggy Dew. Hodder, 1958;
    London House, 1959
The Gallant. Hodder, 1962; Ballantine,
    1966
A House Possessed; see The Exorcism
The Knock at Midnight. Hodder, 1966;
    Coward, 1967
The Lemmings; see The Melon in the
    Cornfield
The Melon in the Cornfield. Hodder,
    1969. U.S. title (?): The Lemmings.
    Coward, 1969
Miss Fenny. Hodder, 1957. U.S. title:
    The Woman in the Woods, as by Lee
    Blackstock. Doubleday, 1958
Mr. Christopoulos. Hodder, 1963; London
    House, 1964
Monkey on a Chain; see When the Sun
    Goes Down
Party in Dolly Creek. Hodder, 1967.
    U.S. title: The Widow. Coward, 1967
The Shadow of Murder. Hodder, 1959.
    U.S. title: All Men are Murderers,
    as by Lee Blackstock. Doubleday, 1958
When the Sun Goes Down. Hodder, 1965.
    U.S. title: Monkey on a Chain.
    Coward, 1965
The Widow; see Party in Dolly Creek
The Woman in the Woods; see Miss Fenny
Young Lucifer; see The Briar Patch

BLACKSTOCK, LEE. See: CHARITY BLACKSTOCK.

BLACKWOOD, ALGERNON (HENRY). 1869-1951.
    Series character: John Silence (JS),
    in both titles.
    Day and Night Stories. Cassell, 1917;
        Dutton, 1917 ss, including one about
        JS
    John Silence. Nash, 1908; Luce, 1909 ss

BLACKWOOD, JOY ANN
    The Ghost of Lost Lover's Lake. Popular
        Library, 1973

BLADES, J. K.
    The Norwood Mystery. Stockwell, 1933

BLAIR, ALLAN. Pseudonym of William J(ohn)
    Bayfield, 1871-1958, q.v. Other pseu-
    donym: Allan Maxwell, q.v. All titles
    feature Sexton Blake and were pub-
    lished by Amalgamated Press (one ex-
    ception noted).
    The Arterial Road Murder. 1933
    The Bathing Pool Mystery. 1935
    The Blazing Garage Crime. 1934
    The Case of the Blackmailed Banker.
        1937
    The Case of the Crook Councilor. 1935
    The Case of the Dictator's Double. 1940
    The Case of the Kidnapped Prisoner.
        1939
    The Case of the Murdered Taxi Driver.
        1935
    The Case of the Stolen Police Dossier.
        1939
    The Crime at the Quay. 1936
    The Crime at the Seaside Hotel. 1934
    Crooks Convoy. 1938
    The Death Ship. Red Mask, 194?. (Bri-
        tish title?)
    Exhumed! 1931
    The Fatal Wager. 1931
    The Great Tunnel Mystery. 1931
    The Great Turf Fraud. 1933
    The Kidnapped Witness. 1931
    The Law Courts Mystery. 1930
    The Lincoln's Inn Tragedy. 1932
    The Lombard Street Mystery. 1930
    The Lord Mayor's Show Mystery. 1933
    The Man from Dublin. 1933
    The Man with the Glaring Eyes. 1936
    The Murder of Constable Cartwright.
        1930
    The Mystery of Beckers' Brook. 1935
    The Mystery of the Missing Constable.
        1938
    The Mystery of the Monument. 1930
    The Old Bailey Mystery. 1936
    The Policeboat Mystery. 1932
    The Riddle of Five Needle Creek. 1937
    The Secret Inquest. 1935
    The Town Hall Crime. 1932
    The Waiting Room Mystery. 1932

BLAIR, CHARLES (RAWDON)
    The Malefactors. Everett, 1903

BLAIR, CHARLES F., JR. See: A(RTHUR)
    J(AMES) WALLIS.

BLAIR, DOROTHY. 1903-   . Joint pseudo-
    nym with Evelyn Page, 1902-   :
    Roger Scarlett, q.v.

BLAIR, E. P. See: H. L. BLAIR.

BLAIR, H. L. and E. P. BLAIR
    Three Saw the Murder. Spiller, 1938

BLAIR, JENNIFER
    Assignment in the Islands. Dell, 1970
    Danger at Olduvai. Dell, 1972
    Dangerous Assignment. Dell, 1975
    Evil Island. Dell, 1974
    Kanesbrake. Dell, 1974
    Skye Manor. Dell, 1972

BLAISDELL, ANNE. Pseudonym of (Barbara)
    Elizabeth Linington, 1921-   , q.v.
    Other pseudonyms: Lesley Egan, Dell
    Shannon, qq.v. All U.S. titles pub-
    lished as by Elizabeth Linington are
    issued in England as by Anne Blais-
    dell.
    Nightmare. Harper, 1961; Gollancz, 1962

BLAISDELL, E(LIJAH) W(HITTIER). 1825-
    1900.
    The Hidden Record; or, The Old Sea Mys-
        tery. Peterson, 1882

BLAKE, ELEANOR. Pseudonym of Eleanor
    Blake Atkinson Cox Pratt, 1899-   .
    Death Down East. Putnam, 1940
    The Jade Green Cats. McBride, 1931

BLAKE, KATHERINE
    -My Sister, My Friend. Reynal, 1965
    Night Stands at the Door. Stein, 1974;
        Hutchinson, 1975

BLAKE, LESLIE
    The Wapping Butt. Allen, 1964

BLAKE, LILLIE D(EVEREUX). 1835-1913.
    A Daring Experiment and other stories.
        Lovell, 1892 ss

BLAKE, NICHOLAS. Pseudonym of Cecil Day-
    Lewis, 1904-1972. Series character:
    Nigel Strangeways = NS.
    The Beast Must Die. Collins, 1938; Har-
        per, 1938 NS
    The Case of the Abominable Snowman.
        Collins, 1941. U.S. title: The Corpse
        in the Snowman. Harper, 1941 NS
    Catch and Kill; see The Whisper in the
        Gloom
    The Corpse in the Snowman; see The Case
        of the Abominable Snowman
    The Deadly Joker. Collins, 1963
    Death and Daisy Bland; see A Tangled
        Web
    The Dreadful Hollow. Collins, 1953;
        Harper, 1953 NS
    End of Chapter. Collins, 1957; Harper,
        1957 NS
    Head of a Traveler. Collins, 1949; Har-
        per, 1949 NS
    Malice in Wonderland. Collins, 1940.
        U.S. title: The Summer Camp Mystery.
        Harper, 1940. Also published as:
        Malice with Murder. Pyramid, 1964 NS
    Malice with Murder; see Malice in
        Wonderland
    Minute for Murder. Collins, 1947; Har-
        per, 1948 NS
    The Morning After Death. Collins, 1966;
        Harper, 1966 NS
    A Penknife in My Heart. Collins, 1958;
        Harper, 1959
    The Private Wound. Collins, 1968; Har-
        per, 1968
    A Question of Proof. Collins, 1935;
        Harper, 1935 NS
    The Sad Variety. Collins, 1964; Harper,
        1964 NS
    Shell of Death; see Thou Shell of Death
    The Smiler with the Knife. Collins,
        1939; Harper, 1939 NS
    The Summer Camp Mystery; see Malice in
        Wonderland
    A Tangled Web. Collins, 1956; Harper,
        1956. Also published as: Death and
        Daisy Bland. Dell, 1960
    There's Trouble Brewing. Collins, 1937;
        Harper, 1937 NS
    Thou Shell of Death. Collins, 1936.
        U.S. title: Shell of Death. Harper,
        1936 NS
    The Whisper in the Gloom. Collins,
        1954; Harper, 1954. Also published
        as: Catch and Kill. Bestseller, 1955
        NS
    The Widow's Cruise. Collins, 1959; Har-
        per, 1959 NS
    The Worm of Death. Collins, 1961; Har-
        per, 1961 NS

BLAKE, ROGER
    Stripped for Murder. Comet, 1963?
        (Mark Sade is given as author on the
        cover.)

BLAKE, STACEY. 1878-1964. All titles fea-
    ture Sexton Blake and were published
    by Amalgamated Press.
    The City of Crooks. 1930
    On Ticket of Leave. 1933
    Prisoners of the Desert. 1929

BLAKE, VANESSA
    Blood Emerald. Hale, 1970; PB, 1975
    Bride of Chance. Hale, 1972. U.S.
        title: Bride of Misfortune. PB, 1974
    Bride of Misfortune; see Bride of
        Chance
    The Dark Guardian. Hale, 1973; PB, 1974
    The Gay Gallant. Hale, 1971. U.S.
        title: Master of Evrington. PB, 1974
    The Lady from Lisbon. Hale, 1971. U.S.
        title: Pentallion. PB, 1974
    Master of Evrington; see The Gay
        Gallant
    Pentallion; see The Lady from Lisbon

BLAKEMAN, WILBERT C.
    The Black Hand. Broadway, 1908

BLAKEMORE, TREVOR (RAMSEY VILLIERS)
    -Through a Glass Darkly. Gay, 1913

BLAKER, RICHARD. 1893-1940.
    The Jefferson Secret. Doubleday, 1929
    Night Shift. Appleton, 1934; Heinemann, 1934

BLAKESLEY, STEPHEN. Pseudonym of F. Bond. All titles feature Sexton Blake and were published by Amalgamated Press.
    The Man with a Number. 1952
    The Riddle of the Blazing Bungalow. 1951
    The Trail of Raider No. 1. 1952

BLAKESTON, OSWELL. 1907-   . Joint pseudonym with Roger d'Este Burford, 1904-   : Simon, q.v.
    And Then the Screaming Started. Hutchinson, 1968
    Ever Singing Die Oh! Die. Hutchinson, 1970
    For Crying Out Shroud. Hutchinson, 1969
    Hop Thief. Blond, 1959
    The Night's Moves. Gaberbocchus, 1961
    Pink Ribbon, as Told to the Police. Quality, 1950

BLANC, SUZANNE. Series character: Inspector Menendez = M.
    The Green Stone. Harper, 1961; Cassell, 1962 M
    The Rose Window. Doubleday, 1967; Cassell, 1968 M
    The Sea Troll. Doubleday, 1969
    The Yellow Villa. Doubleday, 1964; Cassell, 1965 M

BLANCO, L. W.
    Spy Kill. Lancer, 1966

BLAND, E. A. Pseudonym: E. A. B. D., q.v.

BLAND, EDITH NESBIT. 1858-1924. Joint pseudonym with Hubert Bland, 1856-1914: Fabian Bland, q.v.

BLAND, FABIAN. Joint pseudonym of Edith Nesbit Bland, 1858-1924, and Hubert Bland, 1856-1914.
    The Prophet's Mantle. Drane, 1889; Belford, 1889

BLAND, HUBERT. 1856-1914. Joint pseudonym with Edith Nesbit Bland, 1858-1924: Fabian Bland, q.v.

BLAND, JENNIFER. Pseudonym of Jean Bowden, 1925-   . Other pseudonym: Avon Curry, q.v.
    Accomplice. Barker, 1974
    Death in Waiting. Barker, 1975; St. Martin's, 1975

BLAND, OLIVER
    Outwitted. Odhams, 1921

BLANE, FERGUS. Pseudonym.
    Money-Lender in Gloves. Newnes, 1939

BLANEY, CHARLES E. 1865(6)-1944. Pseudonym: Harry Clay Blaney, q.v.
    -Across the Pacific. Ogilvie, 1904
    The Boy Behind the Gun. Ogilvie, 1905
    The Boy Detective. Ogilvie, 1907
    -A Child of the Regiment. Ogilvie
    The Child Slaves of New York, with Howard Hall. Ogilvie, 1904
    -The Curse of Drink. Ogilvie, 1904
    -The Dancer and the King, with J. S. Dawley. Ogilvie, 1907
    -Dion O'Dare. Ogilvie, 1907
    -The Factory Girl. Ogilvie, 1904
    For His Brother's Crime. Ogilvie, 1904
    The Girl and the Detective, with J. Searle Dawley. Ogilvie, 1908
    -The Girl from Texas. Ogilvie, 1909
    The Girl Raffles. Ogilvie, 1906
    -The Hired Girl's Millions. Ogilvie, 1907
    His Terrible Secret; or, The Man Monkey. Ogilvie, 1907
    Kidnapped for Revenge, with Will H. Vedder. Ogilvie, 1907
    The King of the Opium Ring. Ogilvie, 1905
    -The Little Terror. Ogilvie, 1909
    -Lottie, the Poor Saleslady. Ogilvie, 1907
    The Millionaire Detective, with Howard Hall. Ogilvie, 1905
    -Mrs. Blarney from Ireland. Ogilvie, 1905
    -More to be Pitied Than Scorned. Ogilvie, 1904
    -My Tom-Boy Girl. Ogilvie, 1906
    -Old Isaacs from the Bowery. Ogilvie, 1905
    -The Sheriff of Angel Gulch. Ogilvie, 1908
    -The Sporting Deacon. Ogilvie, 1909
    -Tennessee Tess. Ogilvie, 1909
    -Young Buffalo. Ogilvie, 1905
    -Young Buffalo in New York. Ogilvie, 1909

BLANEY, HARRY CLAY. Pseudonym of Charles E. Blaney, 1865(6)-1944, q.v.
    From Sing Sing to Liberty. Ogilvie, 1907

BLANKENSHIP, WILLIAM D(OUGLAS). 1934-   .
    The Helix File. Walker, 1972
    The Leavenworth Irregulars. Bobbs, 1974; Barker, 1975
    The Programmed Man. Walker, 1973; Barker, 1975

BLANKFORT, DOROTHY and MICHAEL (SEYMOUR) BLANKFORT, 1907-   , q.v.
    Monique. French (New York and London), 1957. (2-act play based on the novel Celle qui n'Etait Plus by Pierre Boileau, 1906-   , q.v., and Thomas Narcejac.)

BLANKFORT, MICHAEL (SEYMOUR). 1907-   . See also: DOROTHY BLANKFORT.
    -Behold the Fire. NAL, 1965; Heinemann, 1966
    -I Met a Man. Bobbs, 1937; Hale, 1938
    The Widow-Makers. Simon, 1946; Dobson, 1949

BLASSINGAME, WYATT (RAINEY). 1909-   .
    John Smith Hears Death Walking. Bart, 1944 ss

BLATCHFORD, ROBERT. 1851-1943.
    Tales for the Marines. Clarion, 1901 ss, some criminous

BLAU, ERNEST E.
    The Queen's Falcon. McKay, 1947

BLAYN, HUGO. Pseudonym of John Russell Fearn, 1908-1960, q.v. Other pseudonym: John Slate, q.v. Series character: Inspector Garth, in all titles.
    Except for One Thing. Paul, 1947
    The Five Matchboxes. Paul, 1948
    Flashpoint. Paul, 1950
    The Silvered Cage. Dragon, 1955
    What Happened to Hammond? Paul, 1951

BLAYNE, SEBASTIAN
    Gay Ghastly Holiday. GM, 1951
    Terror in the Night. GM, 1953; Muller pb, 1954

BLAZER, J. S. Pseudonym of Justin (Blazer) Scott, q.v. Series characters: Donald Bracken and James Rowland Woodward VII, in both titles.
    Deal Me Out. Bobbs, 1973
    Lend a Hand. Bobbs, 1975

BLEACKLEY, HORACE (WILLIAM). 1868-1931.
    -A Gentleman of the Road. Lane (New York & London), 1911
    -The Lost Diary. Nash, 1919
    Night of Peril. Lane, 1926

BLEECK, OLIVER. Pseudonym of Ross Thomas, 1926-   , q.v. Series character: Philip St. Ives, in all titles.
    The Brass Go-Between. Morrow, 1969; Hodder, 1970
    The Highbinders. Morrow, 1974; H. Hamilton, 1974
    The Procane Chronicle. Morrow, 1972. British title: The Thief Who Painted Sunlight. Hodder, 1972. Also published as: St. Ives. PB, 1976
    Protocol for a Kidnapping. Morrow, 1971; Hodder, 1971
    St. Ives; see The Procane Chronicle
    The Thief Who Painted Sunlight; see The Procane Chronicle

BLIGH, G.
    Death Came by Night. Pemberton, 1951

BLIGH, GORDON
    The Curse of Scotland. French, 1939. (One-act play.)

BLINKHOOLIE. Pseudonym.
    "Blairmount?" International Horse Agency, 1909

BLISS, ADAM. Joint pseudonym of Robert Ferdinand Burkhardt, 1892-1947, and Eve Burkhardt, 1899-   . Other pseudonym: Rex Jardin, q.v. Series character: Mrs. Penny = P.
    The Camden Ruby Murder. Barse, 1931; Rich, 1934
    Four Times a Widower. Macrae, 1936; Hamilton, 1938 P
    Murder Upstairs. Macrae, 1934; Hamilton, 1935 P

BLISS, EDGAR JANES
    The Peril of Oliver Sargent. Webster, 1891

BLISS, TIP
    The Broadway Butterfly Murders. Greenberg, 1930

BLIXEN-FINECKE, BARONESS KAREN CHRISTENCE. 1885-1962. Pseudonyms: Pierre Andrezel, Isak Dinesen, qq.v.

BLIZARD, MARIE. Series character: Eve MacWilliams = EM.
    Conspiracy of Silence. Mill, 1954; Hammond, 1957
    The Dark Corner. Mill, 1950; Hammond, 1956
    The Late, Lamented Lady. Mystery House, 1946 EM
    The Men in Her Death. Mystery House, 1947 EM
    The Watch Sinister. Mill, 1951; Hammond, 1956

BLOCH, BLANCHE. 1890-   .
    The Bach Festival Murders. Harper, 1942

BLOCH, ROBERT. 1917-   . See also: COLLIER YOUNG.
    American Gothic. Simon, 1974; Allen, 1975

Bloch, Robert

Atoms and Evil. GM, 1962; Muller pb, 1963 ss
Blood Runs Cold. Simon, 1961; Hale, 1962 ss
Bogey Men. Pyramid, 1963 ss
Chamber of Horrors. Award, 1966 ss
The Couch. GM, 1962. (Novelization of the movie.)
The Dead Beat. Simon, 1960; Hale, 1961
Even More Nightmares. Belmont, 196?. (Stories from Pleasant Dreams—Nightmares, q.v., and/or The Opener of the Way, q.v.) ss
Fear Today—Gone Tomorrow. Award, 1975
Firebug. Lancer, 1961; Corgi, 1977
Horror-7. Belmont, 1963; Four Square, 1964. (7 ss from Pleasant Dreams—Nightmares, q.v., and The Opener of the Way, q.v.) ss
The House of the Hatchet and other tales of horror; see Yours Truly, Jack the Ripper: Tales of Horror
The Kidnapper. Lion, 1954
The Living Demons. Belmont, 1967; Sphere, 1970 ss
More Nightmares. Belmont, 1962. (10 ss from Pleasant Dreams—Nightmares, q.v., and The Opener of the Way, q.v.) ss
Nightmares. Belmont, 1961. (10 ss from Pleasant Dreams—Nightmares, q.v.) ss
Night-World. Simon, 1972; Hale, 1974
The Opener of the Way. Arkham, 1945 ss
Pleasant Dreams—Nightmares. Arkham, 1959; Whiting, 1967; Hale, 1960
Psycho. Simon, 1959; Hale, 1960
The Scarf. Dial, 1947. Also published as: Scarf of Passion. Avon, 1948; New English Library, 1972
Scarf of Passion; see The Scarf
Shooting Star. Ace, 1958
The Skull of the Marquis de Sade and other stories. Pyramid, 1961 ss
Spiderweb. Ace, 1954
The Star Stalker. Pyramid, 1968
Tales in a Jugular Vein. Pyramid, 1965; Sphere, 1970 ss
Terror. Belmont, 1962; Corgi, 1964
Terror in the Night and other stories. Ace, 1958 ss
This Crowded Earth & Ladies' Day. Belmont, 1968. (Two novelets.)
The Will to Kill. Ace, 1954
Yours Truly, Jack the Ripper: Tales of Horror. Belmont, 1962. British title: The House of the Hatchet and other tales of horror. Tandem, 1965. (9 stories from Pleasant Dreams—Nightmares, q.v., and The Opener of the Way, q.v.) ss

BLOCHMAN, LAWRENCE G(OLDTREE). 1900-1975. Series characters: Inspector Leonidas Prike = LP; Dr. Coffee = C.
Bengal Fire. Dell, 1948; Collins, 1937 LP
Blow-Down. Harcourt, 1939; Collins, 1940
Bombay Mail. Little, 1934; Collins, 1934 LP
Clues for Dr. Coffee. Lippincott, 1964 C ss
Death Walks in Marble Halls. Dell, 1951. (A novelet, published separately in Dell's 10¢ pb series.)
Diagnosis: Homicide. Lippincott, 1950 C ss
Menace; see Pursuit
Midnight Sailing. Harcourt, 1938; Collins, 1939
Pursuit. Handi-Books, 1951. British title: Menace. Comyns, 1951
Rather Cool for Mayhem. Lippincott, 1951; Cassell, 1952
Recipe for Homicide. Lippincott, 1952; Hammond, 1954 C
Red Snow at Darjeeling. Saint Mystery Library, 1960; Collins, 1938 LP
See You at the Morgue. Duell, 1941; Cassell, 1946
Wives to Burn. Harcourt, 1940; Collins, 1940

BLOCK, LAWRENCE. 1938-   . Pseudonyms: Chip Harrison, Paul Kavanagh, qq.v. Series character: Evan Tanner = ET.
After the First Death. Macmillan, 1969
The Canceled Czech. GM, 1966 ET
The Case of the Pornographic Photos. Belmont, 1961; Consul, 1965. (Novelization of the Markham TV series.)
Deadly Honeymoon. Macmillan, 1967
Death Pulls a Doublecross. GM, 1961
The Girl with the Long Green Heart. GM, 1965; Muller, 1967
Here Comes a Hero. GM, 1968 ET
Me Tanner, You Jane. Macmillan, 1970 ET
Mona. GM, 1961; Muller, 1963
-Ronald Rabbit is a Dirty Old Man. Manor, 1974
The Specialists. GM, 1969
Tanner's Tiger. GM, 1968 ET
Tanner's Twelve Swingers. GM, 1967; Coronet, 1968 ET
The Thief Who Couldn't Sleep. GM, 1966 ET
Two for Tanner. GM, 1967 ET

BLOCK, LIBBIE. 1910?-1972.
Bedeviled. Doubleday, 1947

BLOM, ERIC WALTER. 1888-1959. Pseudonym: Sebastian Farr, q.v.

BLOOD, ADELE and TAM MARRIOTT
The Jade Rabbit. Diamond, 1926; Dial, 1927

BLOOD, MATTHEW. Joint pseudonym of Davis Dresser, 1904-1977, and (Walter) Ryerson Johnson, 1901-   , q.v. Pseudonyms of Davis Dresser: Asa Baker, Brett Halliday, qq.v. Joint pseudonym with Kathleen Rollins: Hal Debrett, q.v. Series character: Morgan Wayne, in both titles.
The Avenger. GM, 1952
Death is a Lovely Dame. GM, 1954

BLOODWORTH, DENNIS
Any Number Can Play. Secker, 1972; Farrar, 1973
The Clients of Omega. Secker, 1975

BLOOM, ROLFE. See: ALLAN ULLMAN.

BLOOMFIELD, ANTHONY. 1922-   .
Delinquents. Hogarth, 1958
Life for a Life. Hogarth, 1971; Scribner, 1971
Russian Roulette. Hogarth, 1955; Harcourt, 1956
The Tempter. Hogarth, 1961; Scribner, 1962
Throw. Hogarth, 1965; Scribner, 1965

BLOOMFIELD, ROBERT. Pseudonym of Leslie Edgley, 1912-   , q.v. Joint pseudonym with Mary Edgley: Brook Hastings, q.v.
From This Death Forward. Doubleday, 1952
Kill with Kindness. Doubleday, 1962
Lust for Vengeance; see Vengeance Street
The Shadow of Guilt. Doubleday, 1947
Stranger in Town. Doubleday, 1953; Boardman, 1954
Vengeance Street. Doubleday, 1952. Also published as: Lust for Vengeance. Bestseller, 1953
When Strangers Meet. Doubleday, 1956; Boardman, 1957

BLORE, TREVOR
The House of Living Death. Aldor, 1946

BLOUNDELLE-BURTON, JOHN EDWARD. 1850-1917.
A Dead Reckoning. White, 1904
Mystery of St. James' Park; see The Silent Shore
The Silent Shore. Maxwell, 1886; Munro, 1887. Also published as: Mystery of St. James' Park. Ivers, 1888

BLOUNT, MARGARET. Pseudonym of Mary O'Francis.
A Dangerous Woman. Brady, 1864
Downe Reserve; or, The Mystery of Wishing Well. Brady, 1864
Hollow Ash Hall. Brady, 1864
Kitty Atherton; or, A Broken Life. Brady, 1863

BLOW, LYNTON
The Bournewick Murders. Butterworth, 1935
The "Moth" Murder. Alexander-Ouseley, 1931; Holt, 1932

BLOXHAM, PETER
Death for a Dropout. Hale, 1970
Funeral for a Physicist. Hale, 1966

BLUM, RALPH. 1932-   .
The Simultaneous Man. Little, 1970; Deutsch, 1970

BLUM, RICHARD (HOSMER ADAMS). 1927-   .
Death and Festivals. Hale, 1968

BLUMBERG, GARY. 1938-   . Pseudonym: Michael Bradley, q.v.
Glover Undercover. Dell, 1973
Hit Woman. Dell, 1975
A Killer in My Mind. Warner, 1975
Two in the Bush. Medallion, 1973

BLUMGARTEN, JAMES
The Astronaut. Warner, 1974

BLUNDELL, HAROLD. 1902-   . Pseudonym: George Bellairs, q.v.

BLUNT, DON. Pseudonym of Edwin Booth, 1906-   , q.v.
Dead Giveaway. Avalon, 1963
Short Cut. Avalon, 1962

BLY, NELLIE. Pseudonym of Elizabeth J. Cochrane, 1867-1922.
The Mystery of Central Park. Dillingham, 1889

BLYTH, JAMES. 1864-1915. See also: BARRY (ERIC ODELL) PAIN, 1864-1928.
The Aerial Burglars. Ward, 1906
Brumblingham Hall. White, 1911
The Diamond and the Lady. Digby, 1908
The Expropriators. Digby, 1919
The Fight for the Luck. Ward, 1921
The Golden Hole. White, 1913
The Hidden Fear. White, 1912
Jack Ranworth. Ward, 1919
The Mystery of the Common. Ward, 1920
The Riddle of the Marsh. Ward, 1922
-The Weird Sisters. Ward, 1918
With a View to Matrimony, and other stories. Richards, 1904 ss, at least one criminous

BLYTHE, E. J. See: J(AMES) M(ORGAN) WALSH, 1897- .

BOARDMAN, NEIL S(ERVIS). 1907- .
The Wine of Violence. Simon, 1964; Cape, 1965

BOBIN, JOHN WILLIAM. -1935. Pseudonyms: John Ascott, Mark Osborne, qq. v. All titles below feature Sexton Blake and were published by Amalgamated Press.
The Banker's Trust. 1916
The Boy Without a Memory. 1919
The Case of the Bogus Laird. 1922
The Case of the Bookmaker Baronet. 1926
The Case of the Cultured Pearls. 1922
The Case of the Girl Reporter. 1918
The Case of the Head Dispenser. 1924
The Case of the International Adventurer. 1917
The Case of the Island Trader. 1921
The Case of the Long-Firm Frauds. 1926. Reprinted in 1936 as by Mark Osborne.
The Case of the Trade Secret. 1922
The Case of the Two Bankers. 1918
Daylight Robbery. 1919
The Fatal Pit. 1927. Reprinted in 1938 as by Mark Osborne.
The Great Diamond Bluff. 1920
The Great "Tote" Fraud. 1929
The Grip of the Law. 1916
The Hidden Menace! 1919
His Son's Honour. 1920
The Hooded Riders. 1922
In the Grip of the Tong. 1922
In the Shadow of the Guillotine. 1918
The Island Mystery. 1919
A Legacy of Shame. 1917
A Legacy of Vengeance. 1923
Link by Link. 1920
The Matador's Fortune. 1919
The Merchant's Secret. 1916
The Mystery Mandarin. 1923
The Mystery of the "Agony". 1919
The Mystery of the Grey Car. 1919
The Only Son. 1920
Out of Reach of the Law. 1920
Payment in Full. 1916
Payment Suspended! 1921
The Problem of the Derby Favorite. 1919
The Riddle of Riverdale. 1919
The Secret of the Surgery. 1929
Sexton Blake—Special Constable. 1917. Reprinted in 1940 as by Mark Osborne.
The Shadow of His Crime. 1915
The Stolen Crown. 1918
The Stolen Partnership Papers. 1919
Ten Years After. 1917
The Tour of Terror. 1927. Reprinted in 1939 as by Mark Osborne.
Twice Wronged! 1920

BOCCA, AL. Pseudonym of Bevis Winter, 1918- , q.v. Other pseudonyms: Peter Cagney, Gordon Shayne, qq.v.
All or Nothing. Milestone, 1953
Any Minute Now. Scion, 1952
Black Morning. Scion, 1952
Blonde Dynamite. Scion, 1950
City Limit Blonde. Scion, 1950
The Coffin Fits. Scion, 1950
A Corner in Corpses. Milestone, 1954
Curves for Danger. Scion, 1950
A Dame Ain't Safe. Scion, 1950
Dead on Delivery. Scion, 1950
Dead on Time. Scion, 1950
Deadly Ernest. Scion, 1951
Double Trouble. Milestone, 1953
Dressed to Kill. Milestone, 1952
Easy Come, Easy Go. Scion, 1951
A Gun for Company. Scion, 1952
The Harder They Fall. Scion, 1951
It's Your Funeral. Scion, 1950
Let's Face It. Scion, 1951
Let's Not Get Smart. Scion, 1952
The Long Sleep. Scion, 1950
No Dice! Scion, 1951
No Room at the Morgue. Milestone, 1954
Requiem for a Redhead. Milestone, 1953
She was No Lady. Scion, 1950
Sinner Takes All. Scion, 1950
Slaughter in Satin. Scion, 1950
The Slick and the Dead. Milestone, 1953
Sorry You've Been Shot. Scion, 1952
Sudden Death! Scion, 1951
Ticket to San Diego. Scion, 1953
Trouble Calling. Milestone, 1953
Wait for It, Pal. Scion, 1951

BOCCA, GEOFFREY
Nadine. Putnam, 1974

BODELSEN, ANDERS. 1937- .
Hit and Run, Run, Run; see One Down
One Down. Harper, 1970. British title: Hit and Run, Run, Run. Joseph, 1970. (Translation of Haedeligt Uheld. Copenhagen, 1968.)
Straus. Harper, 1974. (Translation of Straus. Copenhagen, 1971.)
Think of a Number. Harper, 1969; Joseph, 1969. (Translation of Taenk pa et Tal. Copenhagen, 1968.)

BODEN, L.
And the Body Came Too. Hamilton & Co., 1946

BODINGTON, NANCY HERMIONE. 1912- .
Pseudonym: Shelley Smith, q.v.

BODKIN, M(ATTHIAS) McDONNELL. 1850-1933. Series character: Paul Beck = PB.
Behind the Picture. Ward, 1914
The Capture of Paul Beck. Unwin, 1909; Little, 1911 PB
Dora Myrl, the Lady Detective. Chatto, 1900 ss
Guilty or Not Guilty? Talbot, 1929
-His Brother's Keeper. Hurst, 1913
-Kitty the Madcap. Talbot, 1927
A Modern Robyn Hood. Ward, 1903 ss
-Old Rowley. Holden, 1917
Pat o' Nine Tales. Gill, 1894 ss, some criminous
Paul Beck, Detective. Talbot, 1929 PB ss
Paul Beck, the Rule of Thumb Detective. Pearson, 1898 PB ss
Pigeon Blood Rubies. Nash, 1915
The Quests of Paul Beck. Unwin, 1908; Little, 1910 PB ss
A Stolen Life. Ward, 1898
The Test. Everett, 1914
White Magic. Chapman, 1897
Young Beck. Unwin, 1911; Little, 1912 PB

BODWELL, RICHARD. Pseudonym of Gerald Max Spring, 1897- .
The Mystery of Fernridge Manor. Vantage, 1974

BOGAR, JEFF. Pseudonym of Ronald Wills Thomas, 1910- . Other pseudonym: Ronald Wills, q.v.
Concrete Curtain. Hamilton & Co., 1954
Dinah for Danger. Hamilton & Co., 1952. U.S. title: My Gun, Her Body. Lion, 1952
Fire Zone. Hamilton & Co., 1954
Hoodmen's Bait. Hamilton & Co., 1953
The Land Pirate. Hamilton & Co., 1955
My Gun, Her Body; see Dinah for Danger
Painted on a Donkey Cart. Hamilton & Co., 1955
Pink Film. Hamilton & Co., 1954
The Speed Queens. Hamilton & Co., 1955
The Tigress. Lion, 1952. (British title?)
Undercurrent. Hamilton & Co., 1953

BOGARD, D.
Double Kill. World Distributors, 1952
It's Lonely on the Sidewalk. World Distributors, 1952
Lead Her Gently to the Grave. World Distributors, 1951
Make Sure I'm Dead. World Distributors, 1951
Nobody Died for Honnie. World Distributors, 1952
Pardon My Body. Harlequin, 1951
Speak Softly to the Dead. World Distributors, 1951

BOGART, WILLIAM (G.). 1903-1977. Series character: Johnny Saxon, in at least those marked JS.
Hell on Friday. Swift, 1941 JS
Murder is Forgetful. Mystery House, 1944 JS
Murder Man. Swift, 1941 JS
The Queen City Murder Case. Mystery House, 1946 JS
Sands Street. Swift, 1942
Singapore. Century, 1947. (Novelization of the movie.)

BOGGON, MARTYN
-The Inevitable Hour. Tandem, 1968
Undercurrent. Tandem, 1967

BOGGS, WINIFRED
Murder on the Underground. Jenkins, 1929

BOGUE, HOGAN
The Dog and Duck Mystery. Jarrolds, 1931
-The Golden Helmet. Hodder, 1928

BOHLE, EDGAR (HENRY). 1909- .
The Man Who Disappeared. Random, 1958; Boardman, 1960
The Wife Who Died Twice. Random, 1962; Boardman, 1962

BOHNSTEDT, HANS
No Corpus Delecti. Exposition, 1962

BOILEAU, PIERRE (PROSPER), 1906- , and THOMAS NARCEJAC, 1908- . See also: DOROTHY BLANKFORT.
Choice Cuts. Barker, 1966; Dutton, 1966. (Translation of Et Mon Tout est un Homme. Paris, 1965.)
The Evil Eye. Hutchinson, 1959. (Translation of Le Mauvais Oeil. Paris, 1956.)
Faces in the Dark. Hutchinson, 1955. (Translation of Les Visages de L' Ombre. Paris, 1953.)
The Fiends; see The Woman Who Was
Heart to Heart. H. Hamilton, 1959. (Translation of A Coeur Perdu. Paris, 1959.)
The Living and the Dead. Hutchinson, 1956; Washburn, 1957. Also published as: Vertigo. Dell, 1958. (Translation of D'Entre les Morts. Paris, 1954.)
The Prisoner. Hutchinson, 1957. (Translation of Les Louves. Paris, 1955.)
Sleeping Beauty. Hutchinson, 1959. (Translation of Au Bois Dormant. Paris, 1956.)
Spells of Evil. H. Hamilton, 1961. (Translation of Malefices. Paris, 1961.)
The Tube. H. Hamilton, 1960. (Translation of L'Ingenieur Aimait Trop les Chiffres. Paris, 1959.)
Vertigo; see The Living and the Dead
The Victims; see Who Was Claire Jallu?
Who Was Claire Jallu? Barker, 1965. Also published as: The Victims. Panther, 1967. (Translation of Les Victims. Paris, 1964.)

Boileau, Pierre

The Woman Who Was. Hutchinson, 1954. U.S. title: The Woman Who Was No More. Rinehart, 1954. (Translation of Celle Qui N'Etait Plus. Paris, 1952.)
The Woman Who Was No More; see The Woman Who Was

BOISSIERE, ALBERT. 1866- .
The Man Without a Face, with Florence Crew-Jones. Dillingham, 1911; Unwin, 1911. (Translation of L'Homme Sans Figure. Paris, 1909.)
The Missing Finger. Dodd, 1911. (Translation of Un Crime a ete Commis. Paris, 1908.)

BOK. Pseudonym.
Dragons to Slay. Jenkins, 1937
Piracies, Ltd. Jenkins, 1938
Tong. Jenkins, 1933
-Vampires of the China Coast. Jenkins, 1932

BOLAND, (BERTRAM) JOHN. 1913- . Series character: Kim Smith = KS.
The Big Job. Cassell, 1970
Bitter Fortune. Boardman, 1959
Breakdown. Cassell, 1968
The Catch. Harrap, 1964; Holt, 1966
Counterpol. Harrap, 1963; Walker, 1965 KS
Counterpol in Paris. Harrap, 1964; Walker, 1965 KS
The Disposal Unit. Harrap, 1966
Fatal Error. Boardman, 1962
The Fourth Grave. Cassell, 1969
The Gentlemen at Large. Boardman, 1962; Award, 1968
The Gentlemen Reform. Boardman, 1961; Macmillan, 1964
The Golden Fleece. Boardman, 1961
The Good Citizens. Harrap, 1965
The Gusher. Harrap, 1967
Inside Job. Boardman, 1961
Kidnap. Cassell, 1970
The League of Gentlemen. Boardman, 1958; Beacon, 1961
The Midas Touch. Boardman, 1960
The Mysterious Way. Boardman, 1959
Negative Value. Boardman, 1960
No Refuge. Joseph, 1956
Operation Red Carpet. Boardman, 1959
Painted Lady. Cassell, 1967
Queer Fish. Boardman, 1958
The Shakespeare Curse. Cassell, 1969; Walker, 1970
Vendetta. Boardman, 1961
White August. Joseph, 1955; Arcadia, 1955

BOLDREWOOD, ROLF. Pseudonym of Thomas Alexander Browne, 1826-1915.
Robbery Under Arms. Remington, 1888

BOLES, PAUL DARCY. 1919- .
The Limner. Crowell, 1975

BOLT, BEN. Pseudonym of Ottwell Binns, 1872- , q.v.
The Avenham Mystery. Ward, 1933
The Badge. Ward, 1928
The Buccaneer's Pride. Ward, 1929
The Burnt Caravan. Ward, 1934
The Bushmaster. Ward, 1932
By Breathless Ways. Ward, 1937
Captain Lucifer. Ward, 1928
The Coil of Mystery. Ward, 1930
The Crooked Sign. Ward, 1935
A Desperate Remedy. Ward, 1938
The Diamond-Buckled Shoe. Robinson, 1921
Diane of the Islands. Robinson, 1921
The Empty House Mystery. Ward, 1936
The Five Red Stars. Ward, 1936
The Forest Ranger. Ward, 1931
The Gay Pilgrimage. Jenkins, 1924
The Girl in the Train. Ward, 1939
The Green Arrow. Ward, 1933
The Green Lantern. Ward, 1935
The Impossible Lover. Robinson, 1921
The Jewels of Sin. Ward, 1928
The Lavenham Mystery. Ward, 1933
Linked by Peril. Ward, 1939
Masked Danger. Ward, 1937
A Modern Delilah. Mellifont, 1943
The Mystery Hand. Ward, 1932
The Mystery of Airedale Hall. Mellifont, 1944
The Mystery of Belvoir Mansions. Ward, 1927
The Other Three. Ward, 1929
The Pride of the Ring. Robinson, 1921
The Sealed Envelope. Ward, 1931
The Shadow of the Yemen. Robinson, 1921
A Shot in the Night. Ward, 1934
The Snapshot Mystery. Ward, 1933
The Subway Mystery. Ward, 1930
The Sundial Clue. Ward, 1937
The Sword of Fortune. Ward, 1927
The Unseen Witness. Ward, 1935
Wayland of the Guides. Ward, 1934

BOLTON, GEORGE G.
A Specialist in Crime. Richards, 1904

BOLTON, GUY. 1884- . See also: MAX MARCIN, 1879-1948.
The Enchantress. Doubleday, 1964; Hale, 1966

BOLTON, JOHN
The Air Sleuth. Wright, 1936
The Air Smugglers. Wright, 1938
The Desert Flyer. Wright, 1936
The Island Mystery. Wright, 1938
The Mystery Plane. Wright, 1935
Perils in Persia. Wright, 1939
The Spy Hunters. Wright, 1943
The Swimming Pool Murder. Wright, 1940

BOLTON, MAISIE SHARMAN. 1915- . Pseudonyms: Stratford Davis, Miriam Sharman, qq.v.

BOLTON, WILLIAM. See: (HOWELL) NORTH BAKER, 1912- .

BOMBAL, MARIA LUISA. 1910- .
House of Mist. Farrar, 1947
The Shrouded Woman. Farrar, 1948; Cassell, 1950

BOMMART, JEAN (EMILE GEORGES). 1894- .
The Chinese Fish. Longmans, 1935

BOND, A. CURTIS. -1923.
Mrs. Sparks of Paris. Pollard, 1888

BOND, EVELYN. Pseudonym of Morris Hershman, 1920- , q.v. Other pseudonym: Jess Wilcox, q.v.
Beloved Traitor. Lancer, 1967
Bride of Terror. Lancer, 1968
Clouded Mirror. Lancer, 1967
The Crimson Candle. Avon, 1973
Dark Sonata. Beagle, 1972
The Devil's Footprints. Beagle, 1972
Doomway. Beagle, 1971
Evil in the House. Lancer, 1965
The Girl from Nowhere. Beagle, 1972
Heritage of Fear. Belmont, 1966
Hornet's Nest. Avon, 1972
House of Distant Voices. Belmont, 1965
House of Shadows. Lancer, 1965
Imperial Blue. Beagle, 1973
Lady in Darkness. Lancer, 1965
Lady of Storm House. Lancer, 1965
Raven's Eye. Avon, 1972
Thirteen O'Clock. Berkley, 1970
The Venetian Secret. Lancer, 1967
Widow in White. Lancer, 1967

BOND, F. Pseudonym: Stephen Blakesley, q.v.

BOND, FLORENCE DEMAREST FOOS. Pseudonym: Anne Demarest, q.v.

BOND, J. HARVEY. Pseudonym of Russell Robert Winterbotham, 1904-1971. Series character: Mike Lanson, in all titles.
Bye, Bye, Baby! Ace, 1958
If Wishes Were Hearses. Ace, 1961
Kill Me With Kindness. Ace, 1959; Digit, 1960
Murder Isn't Funny. Ace, 1958; Digit, 1958

BOND, NOREEN
Hide Away. Hodder, 1936
Take Care. Hodder, 1938

BOND, RUSKIN. 1934- .
An Axe for the Rani. Hind Pocket Books, 1972

BOND, WALTER
The Kill Squad. Lancer, 1968

BONETT, EMERY. Pseudonym of Felicity Winifred Carter Coulson, 1907- . See also: BONETT, JOHN and EMERY.
High Pavement. Heinemann, 1944. U.S. title: Old Mrs. Camelot. Blakiston, 1944
-Make Do with Spring. Heinemann, 1942
-Never Go Dark. Heinemann, 1940
Old Mrs. Camelot; see High Pavement

BONETT, JOHN and EMERY. Joint pseudonym of John Hubert Arthur Coulson, 1906- , and Felicity Winifred Carter Coulson, 1907- . See also: EMERY BONETT. Series characters: Inspector Borges = B; Professor Mandrake = M.
A Banner for Pegasus. Joseph, 1951. U.S. title: Not in the Script. Doubleday, 1951 M
Better Dead. Joseph, 1964. U.S. title: Better Off Dead. Doubleday, 1964 B
Dead Lion. Joseph, 1949; Doubleday, 1949 M
Murder on the Costa Brava; see This Side Murder
No Grave for a Lady. Joseph, 1960; Doubleday, 1959 M
No Time to Kill. Harrap, 1972; Walker, 1972 B
Not in the Script; see A Banner for Pegasus
The Private Face of Murder. Joseph, 1966; Doubleday, 1966 B
The Sound of Murder. Harrap, 1970; Walker, 1971 B
This Side Murder. Joseph, 1967. U.S. title: Murder on the Costa Brava. Walker, 1968 B

BONFIGLIOLI, KYRIL
Don't Point That Thing at Me. Weidenfeld, 1972. U.S. title: Mortdecai's Endgame. Simon, 1973

BONHAM, FRANK. 1914- .
By Her Own Hand. Monarch, 1963
One for Sleep. GM, 1960; Muller pb, 1961
The Skin Game. GM, 1962; Muller pb, 1963

BONHAM, MARGARET. 1913- .
The House Across the River. Joseph, 1950; Macmillan, 1951

BONIFACE, MARJORIE. Series character: Sheriff Hiram Odom, in all titles.
Murder as an Ornament. Doubleday, 1940
Venom in Eden. Doubleday, 1942
Wings of Death. McBride, 1946

BONNAMY, FRANCIS. Pseudonym of Audrey Walz. Series character: Peter Shane, in all titles.
Blood and Thirsty. Duell, 1949; Murray, 1952
Dead Reckoning. Duell, 1943
Death by Appointment. Doubleday, 1931
Death on a Dude Ranch. Doubleday, 1937
The King is Dead on Queen Street. Duell, 1945
The Man in the Mist. Duell, 1951; Murray, 1952
Murder as a Fine Art; see Portrait of the Artist as a Dead Man
Portrait of the Artist as a Dead Man. Duell, 1947. British title: Self-Portrait of Murder. Murray, 1951. Also published as: Murder as a Fine Art. Signet, 1949
A Rope of Sand. Duell, 1944
Self-Portrait of Murder; see Portrait of the Artist as a Dead Man

BONNECARRERE, PAUL. 1925?-1977. See: JOAN HEMINGWAY, 1951-   .

BONNELL, JAMES FRANCIS
Death Flies West. Scribner, 1941
Death Over Sunday. Scribner, 1940

BONNER, GERALDINE. 1870-1930. Series character: Molly Morganthau, in at least those marked MM.
The Black Eagle Mystery. Appleton, 1916 MM
The Castlecourt Diamond Case. Funk, 1906
The Girl at Central. Appleton, 1915 MM
The Leading Lady. Bobbs, 1926
Miss Maitland, Private Secretary. Appleton, 1919
-Taken at the Flood. Bobbs, 1927; Mathews, 1928

BONNER, MARGERIE [MRS. MALCOLM LOWRY].
The Last Twist of the Knife. Scribner, 1946
The Shapes That Creep. Scribner, 1946

BONNER, PAUL HYDE. 1893-   .
-S.P.Q.R. Scribner, 1952; Verschoyle, 1953

BONNEY, JOSEPH L. Series character: Simon Rolfe = SR.
Death by Dynamite. Carrick, 1940 SR
Look to the Lady! Lippincott, 1947
Murder Without Clues. Carrick, 1940. British title: No Man's Hand. Heinemann, 1940 SR
No Man's Hand; see Murder Without Clues

BOOCOCK, D. E.
Murder for Love. Long, 1939

BOORE, W(ALTER) H(UGH). 1904-   .
Cry on the Wind. Collins, 1967
The Valley and the Shadow. Heinemann, 1963

BOOTH, CHARLES G(ORDON). 1896-1949.
At Ten Paces; see Those Seven Alibis
The Cat and the Clock. Doubleday, 1935; Cassell, 1938
The General Died at Dawn. PB, 1941; Bell, 1937
Gold Bullets. Morrow, 1929; Hodder, 1929
Kings Die Hard. Hammond, 1949 (U.S. title?)
Mr. Angel Comes Aboard. Doubleday, 1944; Hammond, 1946
Murder at High Tide. Morrow, 1930; Hodder, 1930
Murder Strikes Thrice. Bond, 1946
Sinister House. Morrow, 1926; Hodder, 1927
Those Seven Alibis. Morrow, 1932. British title: At Ten Paces. Hodder, 1933

BOOTH, CHRISTOPHER B. See also: ISABEL (EGENTON) OSTRANDER, 1883-1924. Series character: Amos Clackworthy = AC.
The Amateur Detectives. Chelsea, 1926
Deceiver's Door. Chelsea, 1929
The Fatal Record. Hutchinson, 1929. (U.S. title?)
The House of Rogues. Chelsea, 1923; Hutchinson, 1927
The Kidnaping Syndicate. Chelsea, 1925; Skeffington, 1926
Killing Jazz. Chelsea, 1928
Mr. Clackworthy. Chelsea, 1926 AC ss
Mr. Clackworthy, Con Man. Chelsea, 1927 AC ss
A Seaside Mystery. Chelsea, 1925
The Telltale Print. Chelsea, 1927
$10,000 Reward. Chelsea, 1926

BOOTH, CLARE [CLARE BOOTH LUCE]. 1903-   .
Margin for Error. Dramatists Play Service, 1940. (Play.)

BOOTH, EDWIN. 1906-   . Pseudonym: Don Blunt, q.v.
The Broken Window. Arcadia, 1960
Death on a Summer Day. Arcadia, 1960

BOOTH, ERNEST. 1899-   .
With Sirens Screaming. Doubleday, 1945

BOOTH, J. W.
Murder by Stealth. Cole, 1943
Queen of the Underworld. Cole, 1943
Riddle of Crooked Creek. Cole, 1944
Science Traps the Criminal. Cole, 1943

BOOTH, LOUIS F. Series character: Maxwell Fenner, in both titles.
The Bank Vault Mystery. Dodd, 1933; Hutchinson, 1933
Broker's End. Dodd, 1935; Hutchinson, 1935

BOOTH, MAUD BALLINGTON CHARLESWORTH. 1865-   . Pseudonym: M. E. Charlesworth, q.v.

BOOTHBY, BEN
The Centipede. Ward, 1907

BOOTHBY, GUY (NEWELL). 1867-1905. Series characters: Dr. Nikola = N; Jacob Burrell = JB.
-Across the World for a Wife. Ward, 1898
The Beautiful White Devil. Ward, 1896; Appleton, 1897
A Bid for Fortune; or, Dr. Nikola's Vendetta. Ward, 1895; Appleton, 1895. Also published as: Enter Dr. Nikola. Newcastle, 1975 N
A Bid for Freedom. Ward, 1904
-Billy Binks, Hero, and other stories. Chambers, 1898 ss
-A Bride from the Sea. Long, 1904
A Brighton Tragedy. White, 1905
-Bushigrams. Ward, 1897 ss
A Cabinet Secret. White, 1901; Lippincott, 1901
The Childerbridge Mystery. White, 1902
-Connie Burt. Ward, 1903
A Consummate Scoundrel. White, 1904
The Countess Londa. White, 1903 ss
A Crime of the Under-Seas. Ward, 1905
The Curse of the Snake. White, 1902
A Desperate Conspiracy. White, 1904
Doctor Nikola. Ward, 1896; Appleton, 1896. Also published as: Dr. Nikola Returns. Newcastle, 1976 N
Dr. Nikola Returns; see Doctor Nikola
Dr. Nikola's Experiment. Hodder, 1899; Appleton, 1899 N
Enter Dr. Nikola; see A Bid for Fortune
Farewell Nikola. Ward, 1901; Lippincott, 1901 N
For Love of Her. Ward, 1905 ss, some criminous
-In Spite of the Czar. Long, 1905
In Strange Company. Ward, 1894; Neely, 1894
The Kidnapped President. Ward, 1902; Munro, 1902
The Lady of the Island. Long, 1904 ss
The League of Twelve. White, 1903
Long Live the King. Ward, 1900; Stone, 1900
-A Lost Endeavor. Dent, 1895; Macmillan, 1895
-Love Made Manifest. Ward, 1899; Stone, 1899
The Lust of Hate. Ward, 1898; Warwick House, 1898 N
A Maker of Nations. Ward, 1900; Appleton, 1900
-The Man of the Crag. White, 1907
The Marriage of Esther. Ward, 1895; Appleton, 1895
A Millionaire's Love Story. White, 1901; Buckles, 1901 JB
-My Indian Queen. Ward, 1901; Appleton, 1901
My Strangest Case. Ward, 1902; Page, 1901
The Mystery of the Clasped Hands. White, 1901; Appleton, 1901 JB
An Ocean Secret. White, 1904
-The Phantom Stockman. Phono, 1897. (A ss printed in shorthand!)
Pharos, the Egyptian. Ward, 1899; Appleton, 1899
A Prince of Swindlers. Ward, 1900. U.S. title: The Viceroy's Protege. New Amsterdam, 1903 ss
A Queer Affair. White, 1903
The Race of Life. Ward, 1906; Buckles, 1906
The Red Rat's Daughter. Ward, 1899; New Amsterdam, 1900
-A Royal Affair and other stories. White, 1906 ss
-A Sailor's Bride. White, 1899
Sheilah McLeod. Skeffington, 1897; Stokes, 1897
A Stolen Peer. White, 1906
A Two-Fold Inheritance. Ward, 1903
-Uncle Joe's Legacy and other stories. White, 1902 ss
The Viceroy's Protege; see A Prince of Swindlers
The Woman of Death. Pearson, 1900

BOOTON, (CATHERINE) KAGE. 1919-   .
Andrew's Wife. Doubleday, 1964
Lady in Darkness. Berkley, 1974
Place of Shadows. Dodd, 1959; Gollancz, 1960
Quite by Accident. Doubleday, 1972; Davies, 1974
Runaway Home! Doubleday, 1967; Hale, 1968
Time Running Out. Doubleday, 1968; Hale, 1969
The Toy. Doubleday, 1975
The Troubled House. Dodd, 1958; Gollancz, 1959

BORBOLLA, BARBARA MARTYN. Pseudonym: Don Martyn, q.v.

BORDEAUX, DELMAR E(MIL). 1912-   .
So Thin is the Veil. Bellevue, 1948

BORDEAUX, HENRY (CAMILLE). 1870-1963.
The House That Died. Duffield, 1922; Unwin, 1923. (Translation of La Maison Morte. Paris, 1922.)
Murder Party. Dial, 1931; Gollancz, 1931. (Translation of Murder-Party; ou, Celle Qui N'Etait Pas Invitee. Paris, 1931.)

BORDEN, LEE. Pseudonym of Borden Deal, 1922-   , q.v.
The Devil's Whisper. Avon, 1961
The Secret of Sylvia. GM, 1958

BORDEN, LOWELL MASON
The Counterfeit Bridegroom. Vantage, 1956

BORGE, BERNHARD. Pseudonym of Andre Bjerke, 1918-   .
Death in the Blue Lake. Macdonald, 1961. (Translation of De Dødes Tjern. Oslo, 1942.)

BORGEN, JOHAN. 1902-   .
The Red Mist. Calder, 1973. (Translation of Den Rode Taken. Oslo, 1967.)

BORGENICHT, MIRIAM. 1915-   .
A Corpse in Diplomacy. Mill, 1949; Panther, 1956
Don't Look Back. Doubleday, 1956; Hale, 1958
Extreme Remedies. Doubleday, 1967; Hale, 1968
Margin for Doubt. Doubleday, 1968; Hale, 1969
No Bail for Dalton. Bobbs, 1974
Ring and Walk In. Harper, 1952; H. Hamilton, 1952
Roadblock. Bobbs, 1973
To Borrow Trouble. Doubleday, 1965; Hale, 1966
The Tomorrow Trap. Doubleday, 1969; Hale, 1970
A Very Thin Line. Doubleday, 1970; Hale, 1972

BORGES, JORGE LUIS. 1899-   .
Ficciones. Grove, 1962; Weidenfeld, 1962 ss
Labyrinths. New Directions, 1962   ss

BORNEMAN, ERNEST (WILLIAM JULIUS). 1915-   . Pseudonym: Cameron McCabe, q.v.
Tremolo. Jarrolds, 1948; Harper, 1948

BORTH, WILLAN G. Pseudonym of Willan George Bosworth, 1904-   . Joint pseudonym with Maurce H. B. Mash: Maurice Worth, q.v.
The Monk's Bridge Mystery. Selwyn, 1929

BORTNER, NORMAN STANLEY. Series character: Professor Clifford Wells, in both titles.
Bond Grayson Murdered! Macrae, 1936
Death of a Merchant of Death. Macrae, 1937

BOSSE, M(ALCOLM) J(OSEPH). 1926-   .
The Incident at Naha. Simon, 1972; Macmillan (London), 1972
The Man Who Loved Zoos. Putnam, 1974; Gollancz, 1975. Also published as: Stricken. Dell, 1977
Stricken; see The Man Who Loved Zoos

BOSTON, CHARLES K. Pseudonym of Frank Gruber, 1904-1969, q.v. Other pseudonyms: Stephen Acre, John K. Vedder, qq.v. Series character (continued under the Frank Gruber byline): Otis Beagle = OB.
The Silver Jackass. Reynal, 1941; Cherry Tree, 1952, as by Frank Gruber. Reprinted in the U.S. as by Gruber. OB

BOSWELL, JOHN. Series character: Christopher Kent, in both titles.
The Blue Pheasant. Collins, 1958
Lost Girl. Collins, 1959

BOSWORTH, ALLAN R(UCKER). 1901-   .
Full Crash Dive. Duell, 1942. British title: Murder Goes to Sea. Bodley Head, 1948. Also published as: The Submarine Signalled...Murder! Select, 1942 (abridged)
Murder Goes to Sea; see Full Crash Dive
The Submarine Signalled...Murder!; see Full Crash Dive

BOSWORTH, FRANK. Pseudonym of Lauran Bosworth Paine, 1916-   . Other pseudonyms: John Armour, Reg Batchelor, Kenneth Bedford, Mark Carrel, Robert Clarke, Richard Dana, J. F. Drexler, Troy Howard, Jared Ingersol, John Kilgore, Hunter Liggett, J. K. Lucas, John Morgan, qq.v.
Murder Now, Pay Later. Hale, 1969

BOSWORTH, WILLAN GEORGE. 1904-   . Pseudonym: Willan G. Borth, q.v. Joint pseudonym with Maurce H. B. Mash: Maurice Worth, q.v.

BOTEIN, BERNARD. 1900-1974.
The Prosecutor. Simon, 1956

BOTTOME, PHYLLIS. 1884-1963.
Danger Signal; see Murder in the Bud
-The Lifeline. Faber, 1946; Little, 1946
-The Mortal Storm. Faber, 1937; Little, 1938
Murder in the Bud. Faber, 1939. U.S. title: Danger Signal. Little, 1939
The Rat. Allan, 1927; Doran, 1927. (Novelization of the play by Ivor Novello.)

BOUCHER, ANTHONY. Pseudonym of William Anthony Parker White, 1911-1968. Other pseudonym: H. H. Holmes, q.v. See also: THEO DURRANT. Series character: Fergus O'Breen = FO.
Blood on Baker Street; see The Case of the Baker Street Irregulars
The Case of the Baker Street Irregulars. Simon, 1940. Also published as: Blood on Baker Street. Mercury, 1953 FO
The Case of the Crumpled Knave. Simon, 1939; Harrap, 1939 FO
The Case of the Seven of Calvary. Simon, 1937; H. Hamilton, 1937
The Case of the Seven Sneezes. Simon, 1942; United Authors, 1946 FO
The Case of the Solid Key. Simon, 1941 FO
The Complete Werewolf and other tales of fantasy and science fiction. Simon, 1969; Allen, 1970 ss, including two FO tales and two others combining fantasy and murder
Far and Away. Ballantine, 1955 ss, including one FO tale and others combining science fiction and detection

BOUCHIER, WILLIAM
The Exploits of Black Thumb. Bles, 1936
The Little Grey Man. Bles, 1935
The Strange Fellowship of Maxwell Gale. Pawling, 1934

BOUCICAULT, DION(YSIUS LARDNER), 1820-1890. See: CHARLES READE, 1814-1884.

BOULGER, THEODORA HAVERS.   -1887.
Pseudonym: Theo Gift, q.v.

BOULLE, PIERRE. 1912-   .
The Chinese Executioner; see The Executioner
Desperate Games. Vanguard, 1973. (Translation of Les Jeux d'Esprit. Paris, 1973.)
Ears of the Jungle. Vanguard, 1972; Cassell, 1974. (Translation of Les Oreilles de Jungle. Paris, 1972.)
The Executioner. Vanguard, 1961. British title: The Chinese Executioner. Secker, 1962. (Translation of Le Bourreau. Paris, 1954.)
Face of a Hero. Vanguard, 1956. British title: Saving Face. Secker, 1956. (Translation of La Face. Paris, 1953.)
For a Noble Cause; see A Noble Profession
An Impartial Eye; see The Photographer
A Noble Profession. Vanguard, 1960. British title: For a Noble Cause. Secker, 1961. (Translation of Un Metier de Seigneur. Paris, 1960.)
Not the Glory. Vanguard, 1955. British title: William Conrad. Secker, 1955. Also published as: Spy Converted. Fontana, 1960. (Translation of William Conrad. Paris, 1950.)
The Photographer. Vanguard, 1968. British title: An Impartial Eye. Secker, 1968. (Translation of Le Photographe. Paris, 1967.)
Saving Face; see Face of a Hero
Spy Converted; see Not the Glory
The Virtues of Hell. Vanguard, 1974; Cassell, 1975. (Translation of Les Vertus de l'Enfer. Paris, 1974.)
William Conrad; see Not the Glory

BOURGET, PAUL (CHARLES JOSEPH). 1852-1935.
Andre Cornelis. Spencer Blackett, 1889; Brentano's, 1909

BOURNE, HESTER
After the Island. Hurst, 1969. U.S. title: Haunted Island. Pyramid, 1971
Haunted Island; see After the Island
-The House Across the Water. Hurst, 1972
In the Event of My Death. Hurst, 1964; Doubleday, 1964
-The Red Raincoat. Hurst, 1970
-A Scent of Roses. Hurst, 1971; Pyramid, 1976
The Spanish House. Hurst, 1962; Pyramid, 1965
-Where is Evie Alton? Hurst, 1968

BOURNE, LAWRENCE R.
Stark Naked. Muller, 1934

BOUSFIELD, H(ENRY) T(HOMAS) W(ISHART)
The God with Four Arms and other stories. Barker, 1939 ss, some criminous
Vinegar—and Cream. Murray, 1941 ss

BOUTELL, ANITA (DAY KEARNEY). 1895-   .
Cradled in Fear. Putnam, 1942; Joseph, 1943
Death Brings a Storke. Putnam, 1938
Death has a Past. Putnam, 1939; Joseph, 1939
Tell Death to Wait. Putnam, 1939; Joseph, 1938

BOUTELLE, CLARENCE (MILES)
An Artificial Fate. Ivers, 1891
-Beyond the End. Lupton, 1892
The Grave Between Them. Ivers, 1891

BOUTON, JOHN BELL. 1830-1902. See: ANONYMOUS.

BOUVIER, ALEXIS. 1836-1892.
The Convict's Marriage. Vizetelly, 1888
A Wily Widow. Vizetelly, 1888

BOVE, EMMANUEL. 1898-1945.
The Murder of Suzy Pommier. Little, 1934

BOWDEN, JEAN. 1925-   . Pseudonyms: Jennifer Bland, Avon Curry, qq.v.

BOWEN, E. M.
Murder Will Out. Fiction House, 1945
On the Run. Fiction House, 1946
Ticket for Death. Fiction House, 1946

BOWEN, IAN. Joint pseudonym with John Creasey, 1908-1973, q.v.: Charles Hogarth, q.v.

BOWEN, JOSEPH
The Man Without a Head. Covici, 1936; Butterworth, 1937

BOWEN, MARJORIE. Pseudonym of Gabrielle Margaret Vere Campbell Long, 1886-1952. Other pseudonyms: George R. Preedy, Joseph Shearing, qq.v., Margaret Campbell.
The Bishop of Hell. Bodley Head, 1949 ss
-Old Patch's Medley. Selwyn, 1930 ss
The Shadow on Mockways. Collins, 1932
Withering Fires. Collins, 1931

BOWEN, NAN
Hear No Evil. Macmillan, 1968

BOWEN, ROBERT SIDNEY. 1900-1977. Series character: Gerry Barnes, in both titles.
Make Mine Murder. Crown, 1946
Murder Gets Around. Crown, 1947

BOWEN-JUDD, SARA HUTTON. 1922-   .
Pseudonym: Sara Woods, q.v.

BOWEN-ROWLANDS, ERNEST (BROWN). 1866   .
You Can't Kill the Dead. Allan, 1937

BOWER, B. M. Pseudonym of Bertha Muzzy Bowen Sinclair Cowan, 1874-1940.
The Haunted Hills. Little, 1934; Hodder, 1935
The Voice at Johnnywater. Little, 1923; Hodder, 1923

BOWER, MARIAN and LEON M. LION
The Chinese Puzzle. Hutchinson, 1919; Holt, 1919

BOWERS, DOROTHY (VIOLET). 1904-   .
Series character: Chief Inspector Pardoe = P.
The Bells at Old Bailey. Hodder, 1947; Doubleday, 1947, as The Bells of Old Bailey
A Deed Without a Name. Hodder, 1940; Doubleday, 1940 P
Fear and Miss Betony; see Fear for Miss Betony
Fear for Miss Betony. Hodder, 1941. U.S. title: Fear and Miss Betony. Doubleday, 1942 P
Postscript to Poison. Hodder, 1938 P
Shadows Before. Hodder, 1939; Doubleday, 1940 P

BOWICK, DOROTHY MULLER
Tapestry of Death. Hale, 1973; Walker, 1975

BOWMAN, GERALD.   -1967. Series character: Michael Shannon = MS.
The Devil's Own. Amalgamated, 1937. (Sexton Blake.)
The Hunchback of Hatton Garden. Amalgamated, 1934. (Sexton Blake.)
The Iron Apple. Amalgamated, 1935
Pattern in Poison-Ivy. Laurie, 1948 MS
The Quick and the Wed. Laurie, 1950 MS
Sawdust Angel. Laurie, 1949 MS

BOX, EDGAR. Pseudonym of Eugene Gore Vidal, 1925-   . Series character: Peter Sargeant, in all titles.
Death Before Bedtime. Dutton, 1953; Heinemann, 1954
Death in the Fifth Position. Dutton, 1952; Heinemann, 1954
Death Likes It Hot. Dutton, 1954; Heinemann, 1955

BOX, MURIEL. 1905-   . See: SYDNEY BOX, 1907-   .

BOX, SYDNEY, 1907-   , and MURIEL BOX, 1905-   .
Forbidden Cargo. Heinemann, 1957

BOYD, AUBREY
No Man's Woman. Dutton, 1931; Hutchinson, 1934

BOYD, CATHERINE BRADSHAW
Revenge in a Convent. Exposition, 1955

BOYD, DEREK
The Man Who was Bormann. Hale, 1970

BOYD, DON
Fear Stalks the Footlights. Stanley Baker, 1952

BOYD, EDWARD. See also: BILL KNOX, 1928-   .
The Dark Number, with Roger Parkes, 1933-   , q.v. Constable, 1973; Walker, 1974

BOYD, ERIC FORBES
-The House of Whipplestaff. Hodder, 1924
Merlin Hold. Jarrolds, 1927
-A Stranger in These Parts. Skeffington, 1952

BOYD, EUNICE MAYS. Series character: F. Millard Smyth, in all titles.
Doom in the Midnight Sun. Farrar, 1944
Murder Breaks Trail. Farrar, 1943
Murder Wears Mukluks. Farrar, 1945

BOYD, FRANK. Pseudonym of Frank Kane, 1912-1968, q.v.
The Flesh Peddlers. Monarch, 1959
Johnny Staccato. GM, 1960; Consul, 1964. (Novelization of the TV series.)

BOYD, HAMISH
One Night of Murder. Mystery House, 1958; Ward, 1959

BOYD, JANE. Pseudonym.
Murder in the King's Road. Harvill, 1953; British Book Centre, 1954

BOYD, MARION [MARION MARGARET BOYD HAVIGHURST]
Murder in the Stacks. Lothrop, 1934

BOYD, MARY STUART
Backwaters. Chapman, 1906
-The First Stone. Hodder, 1909
-The Man in the Wood. Chapman, 1904
The Mystery of the Castle. Nisbet, 1911
-With Clipped Wings. Hutchinson, 1902

BOYD, OSCAR
The Case of the Poisoned Cocktails. Modern Fiction, 1946

BOYD, PETER
Slips Sees Red. Melrose, 1950

BOYD, R(OBERT) S. 1928-   . See: DAVID KRASLOW, 1926-   .

BOYD, RAYMOND. Series character: Paul Scarf = PS.
Death Joins the Party. Mellifont, 1944
Fetch Me a Rope. Hammond, 1947 PS
Murder is a Furtive Thing. Hammond, 1950 PS

BOYER, BRIAN (D.). 1939-   . See: JOHN WEISMAN, 1942-   .

BOYER, COLUMBIA. Pseudonym of Nell Columbia Boyer Martin, 1890-   .
The Mosaic Earring. Henkle, 1927. Reprinted as by Nell Martin: International Fiction, 1927

BOYERS, AUDREY. See: BETTINA BOYERS.

BOYERS, BETTINA
Murder by Proxy, with Audrey Boyers. Doubleday, 1945
The White Mazurka. Doubleday, 1946

BOYLAN, MALCOLM STUART. 1897-   .
The Passion of Gabrielle. Crown, 1961; Gollancz, 1962

BOYLE, C(ONSTANCE ANTO)NINA. 1865-   .
Anna's. Allen, 1925; Seltzer, 1925
A Desperate Expedient. Paul, 1932
-Good Old Potts! Paul, 1934
How Could They? Paul, 1932
The Late Unlamented. Paul, 1931
-Moteley's Concession. Allen, 1926
-My Lady's Bath. Paul, 1930
Out of the Frying Pan. Allen, 1920; Seltzer, 1923
-The Rights of Mallaroche. Allen, 1927
The Stranger Within the Gates. Allen, 1926; Seltzer, 1926
What Became of Mr. Desmond. Allen, 1922; Seltzer, 1922

BOYLE, DENIS
Death at Devil-Fish Point. Hale, 1961
Strange Corpse on Murder Mile. Hale, 1960

BOYLE, JACK
Boston Blackie. Fly, 1919

BOYLE, KAY. 1903-   .
Avalanche. Simon, 1944; Faber, 1944
A Frenchman Must Die. Simon, 1946; Faber, 1946
Monday Night. Harcourt, 1938; Faber, 1938

BOYLE, ROBERT
The Baby Sitter. Macdonald, 1975; Walker, 1976

BRACE, TIMOTHY. Pseudonym of Theodore Pratt, 1901-1969. Series character: Anthony Adams, in all titles, which were published in Britain as by Theodore Pratt.
Murder Goes Fishing. Dutton, 1936; Selwyn, 1936
Murder Goes in a Trailer. Dutton, 1937; Eldon, 1951
Murder Goes to the Dogs. Dutton, 1938; Readers Library, 1939
Murder Goes to the World's Fair. Dutton, 1939; Eldon, 1951

BRACEY, AXEL
Public Enemies. Rich, 1934
School for Scoundrels. Rich, 1934

BRACKEEN, STEVE
  Baby Moll. Crest, 1958; Fawcett (London), 1959
  The Body on the Beach. Mystery House, 1957
  Danger in My Blood. Crest, 1959
  Delfina. GM, 1962; Muller pb, 1963
  The Guardians. Holt, 1964; Hale, 1966

BRACKEN, C(ATHERINE) P(HILIPPA). 1918-   .
  Roman Ring. Cassell, 1968

BRACKETT, LEIGH (DOUGLAS) [MRS. EDMOND HAMILTON]. 1915-1978. See also: GEORGE SANDERS, 1906-1972.
  An Eye for an Eye. Doubleday, 1957; Boardman, 1958
  Fear No Evil; see The Tiger Among Us
  No Good from a Corpse. Coward, 1944
  Silent Partner. Putnam, 1969
  13 West Street; see The Tiger Among Us
  The Tiger Among Us. Doubleday, 1957; Boardman, 1958. Also published as: 13 West Street. Bantam, 1962. And as: Fear No Evil. Corgi, 1960

BRADBURY, OSGOOD
  -The Banker's Victim; or, The Betrayed Seamstress. DeWitt, 1857
  -The Fair Quakeress; or, The Perjured Lawyer. DeWitt, 1857
  Female Depravity; or, The House of Death. DeWitt, 1857
  -The Flower of the Forest; or, The Discarded Daughter. DeWitt, 1857
  The Haunted Castle; or, The Abducted Niece. DeWitt, 1857
  Julia Bicknell; or, Love and Murder. Williams, 1845
  -Louise Martin, the Village Maiden; or, The Dangers of City Life. Williams, 1853
  The Rival Lovers; or, The Midnight Murder. DeWitt, 1857

BRADBY, G(ODFREY) F(OX). 1863-   .
  The Face in the Mirror. Hodder, 1923

BRADDON, GEORGE. Pseudonym of George Alexis Bankoff, 1903-   . Series character: Michael Gaunt, in at least those marked MG.
  Death Doubles Death. Jenkins, 1952 MG
  Death in the Picture. Jenkins, 1951
  Death Rings No Bell. Jenkins, 1951 MG
  The Dog It Was That Died. Garnett, 1948
  Judgment Deferred. Trelawney, 1948
  Lady Death. Regular Publications, 1955
  Microbe's Kiss. Faber, 1940
  Murdered Sleep. Garnett, 1949
  That He May Die. Cassell, 1945
  They Stand Accused. Cassell, 1945
  Time Off for Death. Jenkins, 1952; Roy, 1958 MG

BRADDON, M(ARY) E(LIZABETH) [MRS. JOHN MAXWELL]. 1837-1915. Here listed is the book fiction attributed to this British author. No attempt has been made to distinguish among her works on the basis of criminous content. Note that a number of U.S. titles remain uncorrelated with their British originals. Series character: Valentine Hawkehurst = VH.
  All Along the River. Simpkin, 1893; Cassell (New York), 1893
  Asphodel. Maxwell, 1881; Harper, 1881
  Aurora Floyd. Tinsley, 1863; Harper, 1863
  Barbara; or, Splendid Misery; see The Story of Barbara
  Beyond These Voices. Hutchinson, 1910
  Birds of Prey. Ward, 1867; Harper, 1867 VH
  The Black Band; or, The Mysteries of Midnight. De Witt, 1869. (British title?)
  The Blue Hand; or, A Story of a Woman's Vengeance. De Witt, 187?. (British title?)
  Bound to John Company; or, The Adventures and Misadventures of Robert Ainsleigh; see Robert Ainsleigh
  The Captain of the Vulture. Ward, 1862. U.S. title: Darrell Markham; or, The Captain of the Vulture. Dick, 1863
  Charlotte's Inheritance. Ward, 1868; Harper, 1868 VH
  The Christmas Hirelings. Simpkin, 1894; Harper, 1894
  The Cloven Foot. Maxwell, 1879; Harper, 1879
  The Conflict. Simpkin, 1903
  Cut by the County; see One Thing Needful
  Darrell Markham; or, The Captain of the Vulture; see The Captain of the Vulture
  The Day Will Come. Simpkin, 1889; Harper, 1889
  Dead Love Has Chains. Hurst, 1907
  Dead Men's Shoes. Maxwell, 1876; Harper, 1876
  Dead Sea Fruit. Ward, 1868; Harper, 1868
  Diavolo; or, Nobody's Daughter. Dick, 1867. (British title?)
  The Doctor's Wife. Maxwell, 1864; Dick, 1864
  Dudley Carleon; see Ralph the Bailiff
  During Her Majesty's Pleasure. Hurst, 1908
  Eleanor's Victory. Tinsley, 1863; Harper, 1863
  The Factory Girl; or, All is Not Gold That Glitters. De Witt, 1869. (British title?)
  The Fatal Marriage; or, The Shadow in the Corner. Munro, 1885. (British title?)
  The Fatal Three. Simpkin, 1888; Harper, 1888
  Fenton's Quest. Ward, 1871; Harper, 1871
  Figure in the Corner and other stories; see Shadow in the Corner
  Flower and Weed. Maxwell, 1884; Harper, 1882
  George Caulfield's Journey. Munro, 1879 (British title?)
  Gerard; or, The World, the Flesh and the Devil. Simpkin, 1891
  The Golden Calf. Maxwell, 1883; Lovell, 1883
  Great Journey and other stories. Ogilvie, 1882 ss (British title?)
  The Green Curtain. Hutchinson, 1911
  Henry Dunbar; the Story of an Outcast. Maxwell, 1864; Dick, 186?
  Her Convict. Hurst, 1907
  His Darling Sin. Simpkin, 1899
  His Secret. Ogilvie, 1881. (British title?)
  Hostages to Fortune. Maxwell, 1875; Harper, 1875
  In High Places. Hutchinson, 1898
  The Infidel. Simpkin, 1900; Harper, 1900
  Ishmael. Maxwell, 1884; Munro, 1884. Also published as: An Ishmaelite. Lovell, 1884
  An Ishmaelite; see Ishmael
  Jasper Dane's Secret. Peterson, 1885. (British title?)
  John Marchmont's Legacy. Tinsley, 1863; Harper, 1863
  Joshua Haggard's Daughter. Maxwell, 1876; Harper, 1877
  Just As I Am. Maxwell, 1880; Harper, 1880
  Lady Audley's Secret. Tinsley, 1862; Dick, 1863
  The Lady Lisle. Ward, 1862; Dick, 1863
  The Lady's Mile. Ward, 1866; Dick, 1878
  The Lawyer's Secret. Peterson, 1864. (British title?)
  Leighton Grange; or, Who Killed Edith Woodville? De Witt, 187?. Also published as: The Mystery of Leighton Grange. Munro, 1878. (British title?)
  Like and Unlike. Blackett, 1887; Munro, 1887
  The Little Woman in Black. Dunn, 1886. (British title?)
  London Pride; or, When the World was Younger. Simpkin, 1896. U.S. title: When the World was Younger. Fenno, 1897. Reprinted under British title: Fenno, 1898
  A Lost Eden. Hutchinson, 1904
  Lost for Love. Chatto, 1874; Harper, 1875
  The Lovels of Arden. Maxwell, 1871; Harper, 1872
  Lucius Davoreen; or, Publicans and Sinners. Maxwell, 1873; U.S. title: Publicans and Sinners; or, Lucius Davoreen. Harper, 1874
  Married in Haste. Munro, 1883. (British title?)
  Mary. Hutchinson, 1916
  Meeting Her Fate; see Milly Darrell and other tales
  Milly Darrell and other tales. Maxwell, 1873; Carleton, 1877. Also published as: Meeting Her Fate. Carleton, 1881 ss
  Miranda. Hutchinson, 1913
  The Missing Witness. Maxwell, 1880. (A play.)
  Mohawks. Maxwell, 1886; Harper, 1886
  Mount Royal. Maxwell, 1882; Harper, 1882
  My Sister's Confession and other stories. Gill, 1876 ss (British title?)
  The Mystery of Leighton Grange; see Leighton Grange; or, Who Killed Edith Woodville?
  The Octoroon; or, The Lily of Louisiana. De Witt, 1869. (British title?)
  One Life, One Love. Simpkin, 1890
  One Thing Needful, and Cut by the County. Maxwell, 1886; Harper, 1885. Also published as: Penalty of Fate; or, The One Thing Needful. Illustrated Publishing, 1886
  Only a Clod. Maxwell, 1865; Dick, 1865
  Only a Woman. Munro, 1885. (British title?)
  An Open Verdict. Maxwell, 1878; Harper, 1878
  Oscar Bertrand. De Witt, 1869. (British title?)
  Our Adversary. Hutchinson, 1909
  The Outcast; or, The Brand of Society. Dick, 1864. (British title?)
  Penalty of Fate; or, The One Thing Needful; see One Thing Needful, and Cut of the County
  Phantom Fortune. Maxwell, 1883; Harper, 1883
  Ralph the Bailiff and other tales. Ward, 1862. U.S. title: Dudley Carleon. Dick, 1864 ss
  Robert Ainsleigh. Maxwell, 1872. U.S. title: Bound to John Company; or, The Adventures and Misadventures of Robert Ainsleigh. Harper, 187?
  The Rose of Life. Hutchinson, 1905; Brentano's, 1905
  Rough Justice. Simpkin, 1898
  Run to Earth. Ward, 1868
  Rupert Godwin. Ward, 1867; Dick, 1867

Shadow in the Corner. Munro, 1879. Also
  published as: Figure in the Corner
  and other stories. Ogilvie, 1881 ss
  (British title?)
Sir Jasper's Tenant. Maxwell, 1865;
  Dick, 1865
Sons of Fire. Simpkin, 1895
The Story of Barbara. Maxwell, 1880.
  U.S. title: Barbara; or, Splendid
  Misery. Harper, 1880
A Strange World. Maxwell, 1875; Harper,
  1875
Strangers and Pilgrims. Maxwell, 1873;
  Harper, 1873
Taken at the Flood. Maxwell, 1874;
  Harper, 1874
Thou Art the Man. Simpkin, 1894
Three Times Dead; or, The Secret of the
  Heath; see The Trail of the Serpent;
  or, The Secret of the Heath
To the Bitter End. Maxwell, 1872; Harper, 1875
The Trail of the Serpent; or, The
  Secret of the Heath. Ward, 1861. U.S.
  title: Three Times Dead; or, The Se-
  cret of the Heath. Dick, 1864. Re-
  printed in Britain under the U.S.
  title: Clark, 1861
Under Love's Rule. Simpkin, 1897
Under the Red Flag. Maxwell, 1883;
  Harper, 1883
The Venetians. Simpkin, 1892; Harper,
  1892
Vixen. Maxwell, 1879; Harper, 1879
Wages of Sin. Ogilvie, 1881. (British
  title?)
Weavers and Weft, and other tales. Max-
  well, 1877; Harper, 1877 ss
What is this Mystery? Hilton, 1866.
  (British title?)
When the World was Younger; see London
  Pride; or, When the World was Younger
The White House. Hurst, 1906
The White Phantom. Williams, 1868.
  (British title?)
Whose Was the Hand? Munro, 1889. (Bri-
  tish title?)
The World, the Flesh, and the Devil.
  Lovell, 1891. (British title?)
Wyllard's Weird. Maxwell, 1885; Harper,
  1885

BRADDON, RUSSELL (READING). 1921- .
Committal Chamber. Hutchinson, 1966;
  Norton, 1967
End Play. Joseph, 1972. U.S. title:
  The Thirteenth Trick. Norton, 1973
-Gabriel Comes to 24. Hutchinson, 1958
-Out of the Storm. Hutchinson, 1956
The Thirteenth Trick; see End Play
-Will You Walk a Little Faster? Joseph,
  1969

BRADFORD, ERNLE (DUSGATE SELBY)
The Touchstone. Cassell, 1962

BRADLEY, CHARLES
The Belgrade Case. Mills (Melbourne),
  1891
The Red Cripple. Robertson (Melbourne),
  1891

BRADLEY, J(OHN JAMES) FOVARGUE
The Black Abolitionist. Greening, 1910
-The Passing of Night. Long, 1907

BRADLEY, JACK
If Hate Could Kill. Ace, 1960

BRADLEY, MARION ZIMMER. 1930- .
Castle Terror. Lancer, 1966
Souvenir of Monique. Ace, 1967

BRADLEY, MARY (WILHELMINA) HASTINGS.
  188?- .
A Hanging Matter. Appleton, 1937
Murder in Room 700. Appleton, 1931
Murder in the Family. Longmans, 1951

Nice People Murder. Longmans, 1952
Nice People Poison. Longmans, 1952
The Road to Desperation. Appleton, 1932
Unconfessed. Appleton, 1934

BRADLEY, MICHAEL. Pseudonym of Gary Blumberg, 1938- , q.v. Series character: Johnny Adrano, in all titles.
The Blood Bargain. Paperback Library,
  1974
The Corsican Cross. Paperback Library,
  1974
Kill the Hack! Paperback Library, 1974
The Swiss Shot. Paperback Library, 1974

BRADLEY, MURIEL (DEMENS)
Affair at Ritos Bay. Doubleday, 1947;
  Harborough, 1953
Death for My Neighbor. Doubleday, 1951;
  Hammond, 1954
Devil in the Sky. Doubleday, 1948; Ham-
  mond, 1955
Murder in Montana. Doubleday, 1950;
  Foulsham, 1951
Murder Twice Removed. Doubleday, 1951;
  Hammond, 1954
Waltz in Scarlet. Hammond, 1958

BRADSHAW, MRS. ALBERT S. Byline also:
  Annie (Cropper) Bradshaw, q.v.
Murder at the Boarding House. Allan,
  1936

BRADSHAW, ANNIE (CROPPER). Byline also:
  Mrs. Albert S. Bradshaw, q.v.
A Crimson Stain. Cassell, 1885; Munro,
  1885

BRADSHAW, GEORGE (FLOING). 1907- .
Practice to Deceive. Harcourt, 1962;
  Hart-Davis, 1962

BRADSHAW, HOWARD
The Pasha's Web. Watt, 1921

BRADSHAW, OLIVE
Dead Man's Booty. Diamond, 1927

BRADSHAW-JONES, MALCOLM HENRY. Pseudonym:
  Bradshaw Jones, q.v.

BRADY, CYRUS TOWNSEND. 1861-1920.
-The Corner in Coffee. Dillingham, 1904;
  Unwin, 1904
Secret Service. Dodd, 1912; Hodder,
  1916. (Novelization of the play by
  William Gillette, 1855-1937, q.v.)

BRADY, LEO. 1917- .
Brother Orchid. French (New York and
  London), 1940. (3-act play based on a
  ss by Richard Connell, 1893-1949,
  q.v.)
The Edge of Doom. Dutton, 1949; Cresset, 1950

BRADY, MATT
Take Your Last Look. GM, 1954; Red
  Seal, 1959

BRADY, NICHOLAS. Pseudonym of J(ohn)
  V(ictor) Turner, 1900-1945, q.v.
  Other pseudonym: David Hume, q.v.
  Series character: Ebenezer Buckle,
  in at least those marked EB.
The Carnival Murder; see Fair Murder
Coupons for Death. Hale, 1944
Ebenezer Investigates. Bles, 1934 EB
Fair Murder. Bles, 1933. U.S. title:
  The Carnival Murder. Holt, 1933 EB
The House of Strange Guests. Bles,
  1932; Holt, 1932 EB
Week-End Murder. Bles, 1933

BRAEME, CHARLOTTE M(ONICA). 1836-1884.
  Pseudonym: Bertha Clay, q.v.
The Mystery of Colde Fell; or, Not
  Proven. Munro, 1887. Also published
  as by Bertha M. Clay: Lovell, 1887

BRAHAM, HAL. Pseudonyms: Mel Colton, Merrill Trask, qq.v.
Call Me Deadly. Graphic, 1957

BRAHMS, CARYL and S. J. SIMON. Caryl
  Brahms is the pseudonym of Doris
  Caroline Abrahams, 1901- ; S. J.
  Simon is the pseudonym of Simon Jasha
  Skidelsky. Series character: Inspec-
  tor Quill, in at least those marked
  Q.
A Bullet in the Ballet. Joseph, 1937;
  Doubleday, 1938 Q
Casino for Sale. Joseph, 1938. U.S.
  title: Murder a la Stroganoff.
  Doubleday, 1938 Q
Envoy on Excursion. Joseph, 1940 Q
Murder a la Stroganoff; see Casino for
  Sale
Six Curtains for Stroganova. Joseph,
  1945

BRAIN, LEONARD. Pseudonym of Leonard
  Peck, 1906- , q.v.
A Case of Identity. Hale, 1971
-It's a Free Country. Longmans, 1965;
  Coward, 1966

BRAINE, JOHN (GERARD). 1922- .
The Pious Agent. Eyre, 1975; Atheneum,
  1976

BRAINERD, MRS. EDITH RATHBONE JACOBS.
  Joint pseudonym with J. Chauncey
  Corey Brainerd: E. J. Rath, q.v.

BRAINERD, J. CHAUNCEY COREY. Joint pseudonym with Edith Rathbone Jacobs
  Brainerd: E. J. Rath, q.v.

BRALY, MALCOLM. 1925- .
Felony Tank. GM, 1961
It's Cold Out There. GM, 1966
The Master. Paperback Library, 1973.
  (Novelization of the movie Lady Ice.)
On the Yard. Little, 1967
Shake Him Till He Rattles. GM, 1963

BRAMAH, ERNEST. Pseudonym of Ernest Bra-
  mah Smith, 1868-1942. Series char-
  acter: Max Carrados = MC.
The Bravo of London. Cassell, 1934 MC
The Eyes of Max Carrados. Richards,
  1923; Doran, 1924 MC ss
Max Carrados. Methuen, 1914 MC ss
Max Carrados Mysteries. Hodder, 1927
  MC ss
The Specimen Case. Hodder, 1924; Doran,
  1925 ss, including some crime and
  out about MC

BRAMBLE, FORBES. 1939- .
The Strange Case of Deacon Brodie.
  H. Hamilton, 1975

BRAMHALL, MARION. Series character: Kit
  (Marsden) Acton, in all titles.
Button, Button. Doubleday, 1944
Murder is an Evil Business. Doubleday,
  1948
Murder is Contagious. Doubleday, 1949
Murder Solves a Problem. Doubleday,
  1944
Tragedy in Blue. Doubleday, 1945

BRAMLETT, JOHN. Pseudonym of John Leonard Pierce, Jr., 1921- .
The Devil in Broad Daylight. GM, 1967

BRAMLETTE, PAULA. 1917- . See:
  MARGARET (POLK) YATES, 1915- .

BRAMLEY, CHARLES
  The Adventures of a Social Detective. Diprose, 18?? ss

BRAMPTON, JOAN
  Dilemma. Dramatists Play Service, 1958. (3-act play.)

BRAMSON, KAREN (ADLER). 1875-1936.
  The Case of Dr. Morel. Philpot, 1926. U.S. title: Dr. Morel. Greenberg, 1927

BRAMWELL, CHARLOTTE. Pseudonym of John M. Kimbro, 1929- . Other pseudonym: Katheryn Kimbrough, q.v.
  Brother Sinister. Beagle, 1973
  Cousin to Terror. Beagle, 1972
  Stepmother's House. Beagle, 1972

BRANCH, PAMELA (JEAN). 1920-1967.
  Lion in the Cellar. Hale, 1951
  Murder Every Monday. Hale, 1954
  Murder's Little Sister. Hale, 1958
  The Wooden Overcoat. Hale, 1951

BRAND, CHRISTIANNA. Pseudonym of Mary Christianna Milne Lewis, 1907- . Other pseudonym: China Thompson, q.v. Series characters: Inspector Cockrill = C; Inspector Charlesworth = Ch.
  Brand X. Joseph, 1974 ss
  Cat and Mouse. Joseph, 1950; Knopf, 1950
  The Crooked Wreath; see Suddenly at His Residence
  Death in High Heels. Lane, 1941; Scribner, 1954 Ch
  Death of Jezebel. Bodley Head, 1949; Dodd, 1948 C, Ch
  Fog of Doubt; see London Particular
  Green for Danger. Lane, 1945; Dodd, 1944 C
  Heads You Lose. Lane, 1942; Dodd, 1942 C
  London Particular. Joseph, 1952. U.S. title: Fog of Doubt. Scribner, 1953 C, Ch
  Suddenly at His Residence. Bodley Head, 1947. U.S. title: The Crooked Wreath. Dodd, 1946 C
  Tour de Force. Joseph, 1955; Scribner, 1955 C
  What Dread Hand. Joseph, 1968 ss C

BRAND, MAX. Pseudonym of Frederick Schiller Faust, 1892-1944. Other pseudonyms: Walter C. Butler, Frederick Frost, qq.v.
  Big Game. Paperback Library, 1973
  Dead Man's Treasure. White Lion, 1975
  The Granduca. Paperback Library, 1973
  The Phantom Spy. Dodd, 1973; White Lion, 1975
  Six Golden Angels. Dodd, 1937; Hodder, 1938

BRAND, (CHARLES) NEVILLE. 1895- .
  Death in the Forest. Lane, 1933; Kendall, 1933
  Death of a Designer. Lane, 1938
  The Winning Trick. Lane, 1931; Putnam, 1932
  Winter Landscape. Hale, 1949

BRANDE, DOROTHEA [DOROTHEA THOMPSON BRANDE COLLINS]. 1893-1948.
  Most Beautiful Lady. Farrar, 1935. British title: Beauty Vanishes. Bell, 1935

BRANDEL, MARC. Pseudonym of Marcus Beresford, 1919- .
  The Choice. Dial, 1950; Eyre, 1952. Also published as: The Moron. Avon, 1951
  Maniac Rendezvous; see Rain Before Seven
  The Moron; see The Choice
  -Rain Before Seven. Harper, 1945. Also published as: Maniac Rendezvous. Avon, 1951
  The Time of the Fire. Random, 1954; Eyre, 1954

BRANDES, RHODA. Pseudonym: Diana Ramsay, q.v.

BRANDNER, GARY. 1933- . Series character: Big Brain, in both titles.
  The Aardvark Affair. Zebra, 1975; New English Library pb, 1976
  The Beelzebub Business. Zebra, 1975; New English Library pb, 1976

BRANDON, BEATRICE
  The Cliffs of Night. Doubleday, 1974; Hodder, 1975

BRANDON, CHARLES. Series character: John Fortescue, in all titles.
  The Missing Banker. Jenkins, 1927
  The Mystery of King's Everard. Jenkins, 1924
  The Phantom Musketeer. Jenkins, 1929

BRANDON, GORDON. Series characters: Arthur Stukeley Pennington and Insp. Patrick Aloysius McCarthy (following John G. Brandon, 1879-1941, q.v.), in at least those titles marked ASP, PAM; Michael and "Terry" Terrence, in at least those marked T.
  Death of a Mermaid. Wright, 1960 ASP, PAM
  Here Comes the Corpse. Wright, 1949
  Homicidal Holiday. Wright, 1954 T
  A Mild Case of Murder. Wright, 1951 T
  Murder and Marigold. Wright, 1956
  Murder Comes Smiling. Wright, 1959 ASP, PAM
  Murder in Maytime. Wright, 1950 T
  A Swell Night for Murder! Wright, 1947

BRANDON, JOHN G. 1879-1941. All titles below without indication of publisher feature Sexton Blake and were published by Amalgamated Press; many were retitled and given a new chief character and reissued by Wright, but correlations are not available. Series characters (see also Gordon Brandon): Arthur Stukeley Pennington, in at least those marked ASP; Sgt./Det. Insp. Patrick Aloysius McCarthy, in at least those marked PAM.
  The Big City. Methuen, 1931; Brentano's, 1930
  The Big Heart. Methuen, 1924; Brentano's, 1923
  The Black Joss. Methuen, 1931 PAM
  The Black Swastika. 1940
  The Blue Print Murders. Wright, 1942 PAM
  The Bond Street Murder. Wright, 1937 ASP, PAM
  The Bond Street Raiders. 1937
  Bonus for Murder. Wright, 1938
  By Order of the Tong. 1935
  The Call Girl Murders. Wright, 1954 ASP, PAM
  Candidate for a Coffin. Wright, 1946 PAM
  The Case of the Gangster's Moll. 1934
  The Case of the Murdered Commissionaire. 1935
  The Case of the Night Club Queen. 1936
  The Case of the Withered Hand. Wright, 1936
  The Case of the Would-Be Widow. Wright, 1950 ASP
  The Championship Crime. 1934
  The Chink's Victim. 1934
  The Clue of the Tattooed Man. 1938
  The Cork Street Crime. Wright, 1938 ASP, PAM
  The Corpse from "The City". Wright, 1958 ASP, PAM
  The Corpse Rode On. Wright, 1951 ASP, PAM
  The Crime in the Kiosk. 1937
  The Crooked Five! Wright, 1939 PAM
  Crook's Cargo. 1940
  Dead Man's Evidence. 1936
  Death Comes Swiftly. Wright, 19?? PAM
  Death in "D" Division. Wright, 1943 ASP, PAM
  Death in Downing Street. Wright, 1937 ASP, PAM
  Death in Duplicate. Wright, 1945
  Death in Jermyn Street. Wright, 1942 ASP, PAM
  Death in the Ditch. Wright, 1940 ASP
  The Death in the Quarry. Wright, 1941 PAM
  Death of a Greek. Wright, 1955 ASP, PAM
  Death of a Socialite. Wright, 1957 ASP, PAM
  Death on Delivery. Wright, 1939 PAM
  Death Stalks in Soho. Wright, 1959 ASP, PAM
  Death Tolls the Gong. Wright, 1936 ASP, PAM
  The Diamond of Ti Lingo. 1937
  The Downing Street Discovery. 1935
  The Dragnet. Wright, 1936 PAM
  The Espionage Killings. Wright, 19?? PAM
  The False Alibi. 1938
  Fatal Forgery. 1939
  The Ł50 Marriage Case. Wright, 1938. Also published as: The Ł250 Marriage Case. Mellifont, 1954
  Finger-Prints Never Lie! Wright, 1938 PAM
  The Frame-Up. Wright, 1938 PAM
  Gang War. Wright, 1940
  The Girl Who Knew Too Much, 1936
  The Glass Dagger. 1934
  The Great Taxi-Cab Ramp. 1939
  The Gunboat Mystery. 1939
  The Hand of Seeta. Wright, 1937 PAM
  In the Hands of Spies. 1939
  The Joy Ride. Methuen, 1927
  McCarthy, C.I.D. Wright, 1936 PAM
  M for Murder. Wright, 1949
  The Mail Van Mystery. Wright, 1937 PAM
  The Man from Italy. 1937
  The Man from Singapore. 1939
  The Man with Jitters. 1939
  The Mark of the Tong. Wright, 1938 PAM
  The Melbourne Mystery. 1937
  Mr. Pennington Barges In. Wright, 1941 ASP, PAM
  Mr. Pennington Comes Through. Wright, 1939 ASP, PAM
  Mr. Pennington Goes Nap. Wright, 1940 ASP, PAM
  Mr. Pennington Sees Red. Wright, 1942 ASP, PAM
  Murder at the Yard! Wright, 1936 PAM
  Murder for a Million. Wright, 1942
  Murder in Mayfair. Methuen, 1934
  Murder in Pimlico. Wright, 1958 ASP, PAM
  Murder in Soho. Wright, 1937
  Murder in Y Division. 1935
  Murder on the Beam. Wright, 1956 ASP, PAM
  Murder on the Fourth Floor. 1936

Murder on the High Seas. 1938
Murder on the Ice Rink. 1939
Murder on the Stage. 1934
Murderer's Stand-In. Wright, 1953 ASP, PAM
The Mystery of the Dead Man's Wallet. 1938
The Mystery of the Green Bottle. 1939
The Mystery of the Murdered Blonde. 1936
The Mystery of the Murdered Ice Cream Man. 1938
The Mystery of the Murdered Sentry. 1937
The Mystery of the Street Musician. 1938
The Mystery of the Three Acrobats. 1936
The Mystery of the Three City's. 1934
The Mystery of X20. 1937
The Night Club Murder. Wright, 1938 PAM
Nighthawks! Methuen, 1929; Brentano's, 1930
On the Midnight Beat. 1934
On Ticket of Leave. 1940
The One-Minute Murder. Methuen, 1934; Dial, 1935 ASP, PAM
The Pawnshop Murder. Methuen, 1936 ASP, PAM
The Pigeon Loft Crime. 1938
Red Altars. Cassell, 1928 PAM
The Red Boomerang. 1935
The Regent Street Raid. Wright, 1938 ASP, PAM
The Riddle of the Dead Man's Bay. 1940
The Riddle of the Greek Financier. 1940
The Riverside Mystery. Methuen, 1935 ASP, PAM
The Roadhouse Mystery. 1938
A Scream in Soho. Wright, 1940
The Secret Brotherhood. Dial, 1928. (British title?)
The Silent House. Cassell, 1928; Dial, 1928. (Novelization of the play by John G. Brandon and George Pickett.)
The Snatch Game. Wright, 1936 ASP, PAM
The Spy from Spain. 1937
The Survivor's Secret. 1933
The Tattooed Triangle. 1937
The Taxi-Cab Murder. 1933
The Terror of the Pacific. 1940
The Tragedy of the West End Actress. 1933
The Transport Murders. Wright, 1942 PAM
The ₤250 Marriage Case; see The ₤50 Marriage Case
Under Police Protection. 1934
Under Secret Orders. 1941
The Victim of the Secret Service. 1937
The Victim of the Thieves' Den. 1936
West End. Methuen, 1933 ASP, PAM
Yellow Gods. Wright, 1940 PAM
The Yellow Mask. 1935
-Young Love. Methuen, 1925

BRANDON, MARGARET
Hypnotized; or, The Doctor's Confession. Hutchinson, 1891

BRANDON, WILLIAM (E.)
The Dangerous Dead. Dodd, 1943

BRANDRETH, CHARLES A.
A Fenland Mystery. Jarrolds, 1925
-The Honourable Roger. Hutchinson, 1926
-The Lady of the Swamp. Hutchinson, 1927
-Under the Goad. Hutchinson, 1926

BRANDT, TOM. Pseudonym of Thomas B(lanchard) Dewey, 1915-   , q.v.
Kiss Me Hard. Popular Library, 1954
Run, Brother, Run! Popular Library, 1954; Consul, 1961

BRANSCOMB, ALEXANDER C.
-Mystic Romances of the Blue and Grey. Mutual Publishing, 1883 ss

BRANSON, H(ENRY) C. Series character: John Bent, in all titles.
Beggar's Choice. Simon, 1953
Case of the Giant Killer. Simon, 1944; Bodley Head, 1949
The Fearful Passage. Simon, 1943; Bodley Head, 1950
I'll Eat You Last. Simon, 1941; Lane, 1953. Also published as: I'll Kill You Last. Mystery Novel of the Month. 1942
I'll Kill You Last; see I'll Eat You Last
Last Year's Blood. Simon, 1947; Bodley Head, 1950
The Leaden Bubble. Simon, 1949; Bodley Head, 1951
The Pricking Thumb. Simon, 1942; Bodley Head, 1949

BRAUN, LILIAN JACKSON. Series character: Jim Qwilleran, in all titles.
The Cat Who Ate Danish Modern. Dutton, 1967; Collins, 1968
The Cat Who Could Read Backwards. Dutton, 1966; Collins, 1967
The Cat Who Turned On and Off. Dutton, 1968; Collins, 1968

BRAUN, M. G. Series character: Al Glenne, in all titles.
Apostles of Violence. Berkley, 1966
Operation Atlantis. Berkley, 1966
Operation Jealousy. Berkley, 1966
That Girl from Istanbul. Berkley, 1966

BRAUN, MATTHEW
Bloody Hand. Popular Library, 1975

BRAUN, R(EINHARD) A.
Murder, Four Miles High. Arcadia, 1954

BRAUTIGAN, RICHARD. 1935-   .
The Hawkline Monster. Simon, 1974; Cape, 1975
Willard and His Bowling Trophies. Simon, 1975; Cape, 1976

BRAY, ARTHUR
The Clue of the Postage Stamp. Thom, 1913

BRAYSHAW, EILEEN RUTH
The Eye of Kali. Waterloo (Calcutta), 1934

BRAZA, DAVID
The Man of Many Colours. Modern Fiction, 1953

BREAN, HERBERT. 1907-1973. Series character: Reynold Frame = RF.
The Clock Strikes Thirteen. Morrow, 1952; Heinemann, 1954 RF
Collar for the Killer; see A Matter of Fact
The Darker the Night. Morrow, 1949; Heinemann, 1950 RF
Dead Sure; see A Matter of Fact
Hardly a Man is Now Alive. Morrow, 1950; Heinemann, 1952. Also published as: Murder Now and Then. Macmillan (London), 1965 RF
A Matter of Fact. Morrow, 1956. British title: Collar for the Killer. Heinemann, 1957. Also published as: Dead Sure. Dell, 1958
Murder Now and Then; see Hardly a Man is Now Alive
The Traces of Brillhart. Harper, 1960; Heinemann, 1961
The Traces of Merrilee. Harper, 1966
Wilders Walk Away. Morrow, 1948; Heinemann, 1949 RF

BREBNER, PERCY (JAMES). 1864-1922. Pseudonym: Christian Leys, q.v. Series character: Christopher Quarles = CQ.
The Black Card. Lawrence, 1899
The Brown Mask. Cassell, 1911
Christopher Quarles, College Professor and Master Detective. Holden, 1921; Dutton, 1914 ss CQ
The Crucible of Circumstance. Warne, 1906
The Fountain of Green Fire. Hutchinson, 1923; Moffat Yard, 1923
-The Gate of Temptation. Long, 1920
-A Gentleman of Virginia. Macmillan (London), 1910
The Ivory Disc. Duffield, 1920. (British title?)
-The Light That Lures. Fly, 1911. (British title?)
The Little Grey Shoe. Hodder, 1913; Little, 1913
A London Cobweb. Trischler, 1892
The Master Detective. Holden, 1922; Dutton, 1916 ss CQ
Mr. Quixley of the Gate House. Warne, 1904
The Mystery of Ladyplace. Warne, 1900
Peril Island. Hutchinson, 1924
Princess Maritza. Cassell, 1907; McBride, 1906
The Silver Medallion. Mills, 1912
Suspicion. Ward, 1889
The Testing of Olive Vaughn. Doscher, 1909. (British title?)
-The Top Landing. Unwin, 1921
-The Turbulent Duchess. Hodder, 1915; Little, 1915
-The White Gauntlet. Cassell, 1912

BRECHIN, DAVID
Nic Barker I.D.B. Nasionale Boekhandel (Cape Town), 1963
Uncut Diamonds. Nasionale Boekhandel (Cape Town), 1969

BREDE, ARNOLD. Series character: Bull Rogers, in at least those marked BR.
The Climbing Corpse. Cooper, 1952 BR
An Outside Job. Cooper, 1952 BR
Vintage Stuff. Cooper, 1952

BREMNER, MARJORIE (K.). 1916-   .
Murder Amid Proofs. Hodder, 1955
Murder Most Familiar. Hodder, 1953; Detective Book Club, 1954

BRENN, GEORGE J.
Disappearing Bullets. Detective Tales, n.d. (A 61 page mini-paperback.)
Voices. Century, 1923; Jenkins, 1925

BRENNAN, ALICE
The Brooding House. Lancer, 1965
Castle Mirage. Belmont, 1971
Devil Take All. Popular Library, 1974
Devil's Dreamer. Lancer, 1971
Fear No Evil. Lancer, 1967
Ghost at Stagmere. Paperback Library, 1973
House of the Fiery Cauldron. Berkley, 1975
Litany of Evil. Lancer, 1970
A Matter of Witchcraft. Berkley, 1975
Never to Die. Lancer, 1971
Sleep Well, Christine. Avon, 1973
Thirty Days Hath July. Avon, 1975
To Kill a Witch. Lancer, 1973

BRENNAN, BILL
The Faster We Live. Monarch, ca.1962

BRENNAN, DAN
The Badge of Honor. Belmont, 1974
The Godfather Killer. Belmont, 1973
Insurrection! Belmont, 1970
Lay-Over Town. Caravelle, 1968
Operation Sky Drop. Tower, 1975

BRENNAN, FREDERICK HAZLITT. 1901-1962.
  Memo to a Firing Squad. Knopf, 1943
  One of Our H-Bombs is Missing. GM, 1955

BRENNAN, JOHN NEEDHAM HUGGARD. Pseudonym:
  John Welcome, q.v.

BRENNAN, JOSEPH PAYNE. 1918-   .
  The Casebook of Lucius Leffing. Macabre House, 1973 ss
  The Dark Returners. Macabre House, 1959
    ss, some criminous
  Nine Horrors and a Dream. Arkham, 1958
    ss, some criminous
  Scream at Midnight. Macabre House, 1963
    ss, some criminous
  Stories of Darkness and Dread. Arkham, 1973 ss, some criminous

BRENNAN, LOUIS A(RTHUR). 1911-   .
  Death at Flood Tide. Dell, 1958
  More Than Flesh. Dell, 1957

BRENNAN, ROBERT. 1881-   .
  The Man Who Walked Like a Dancer. Rich, 1951
  The Toledo Dagger. Hamilton, 1927

BRENNING, L. H. Pseudonym of (Alfred)
  John Hunter, 1891-1961, q.v. Other
  pseudonyms: John Addiscombe, Anthony
  Dax, Anthony Drummond, Peter Meriton, qq.v.
  Boulevard. Cassell, 1931
  The Butterfly of Paris. Cassell, 1925
  Cabaret; see Parisian Adventure
  The Channel Mystery. Gramol, 1935
  The Death Plot. Cassell, 1931
  Devil's Laughter. Cassell, 1929
  Parisian Adventure. Cassell, 1934. U.S. title: Cabaret. Greenberg, 1934
  Parisian Love. Cassell, 1926

BRENT, LORING. Pseudonym of George
  F(rank) Worts, 1892-   , q.v.
  No More a Corpse. King, 1932
  The Return of George Washington. Hodder, 1928. (U.S. title?)

BRENT, LYNTON WRIGHT
  Daughter of Bonnie & Clyde. Producer Books, 1971. (Novelization of the movie.)
  Death of a Detective. Powell, 1969
  One Man's Crime. Powell, 1969

BRENT, MADELEINE
  Moonraker's Bride. Doubleday, 1973; Souvenir, 1973
  Tregaron's Daughter. Doubleday, 1971; Souvenir, 1971

BRENT, NIGEL. Pseudonym of Cecil Gordon
  Eugene Wimhurst. Series character:
  Barney Hyde, in all titles.
  Badger in the Dusk. Muller, 1959
  Blood in the Bank. Muller, 1954
  Dig the Grave Deep. Muller, 1955
  The Golden Angel. Muller, 1958
  The Leopard Died Too. Muller, 1957
  Motive for Murder. Muller, 1954
  Murder Swings High. Muller, 1956
  No Space for Murder. Muller, 1960
  The Scarlet Lily. Muller, 1953
  Spider in the Web. Muller, 1960

BRENT, PETER (LUDWIG). 1931-   . Pseudonym: Ludovic Peters, q.v.
  No Way Back from Prague. Hodder, 1970

BRENT, R. L. Series character: Jake Brand, in all titles
  The Cocaine Connection. Award, 1974; Tandem, 1975
  Contract for a Killing. Award, 1974; Tandem, 1974
  Invitation to a Strangling. Award, 1975
  The Liquidator. Award, 1974; Tandem, 1974

BRENTER, JAY G.
  Blood on the Shrine. Brandon, 1967

BRENTFORD, BURKE. Pseudonym of Nathan
  D(ane) Urner, 1839-1893, q.v.
  Gold Dust Darrell; or, The Wizard of the Mines. Street, 1890

BRESLIN, HOWARD. Pseudonym: Michael Niall, q.v.

BRESLIN, JIMMY
  The Gang That Couldn't Shoot Straight. Viking, 1969; Hutchinson, 1970

BRETON, FREDERIC
  -The Black Mass. Hutchinson, 1897
  The Crime of Maunsell Grange. Osgood, 1893

BRETT, JOHN MICHAEL. Pseudonym of Miles
  (Barton) Tripp, 1923-   , q.v. Other pseudonym: Michael Brett, q.v.
  A Cargo of Spent Evil. Barker, 1966

BRETT, MARTIN. Pseudonym of (Ronald)
  Douglas Sanderson, 1922-   , q.v.
  Other pseudonym: Malcolm Douglas,
  q.v. Series character: Mike Garfin,
  in at least those marked MG.
  Blondes are My Trouble; see The Darker Traffic
  The Darker Traffic. Dodd, 1954; Reinhardt, 1954. Also published as: Blondes are My Trouble. Popular Library, 1955 MG
  A Dum-Dum for the President. Hammond, 1961. (= Flee from Terror?)
  Exit in Green. Dodd, 1953. British title: Murder Came Tumbling. Hammond, 1959
  Flee from Terror. Popular Library, 1957
  Hot Freeze. Dodd, 1954; Reinhardt, 1954 MG
  Murder Came Tumbling; see Exit in Green

BRETT, MICHAEL. Pseudonym of Miles (Barton) Tripp, 1923-   , q.v. Other pseudonym: John Michael Brett, q.v.
  Series characters: Hugo Baron = HB;
  Pete McGrath = PM.
  Another Day, Another Stiff. PB, 1968 PM
  Cry Uncle!; see Lie a Little, Die a Little
  Dead, Upstairs in the Tub. PB, 1967 PM
  Death of a Hippie. PB, 1968 PM
  Diecast. GM, 1963; Barker, 1964 HB
  An Ear for Murder. PB, 1967 PM
  The Flight of the Stiff. PB, 1967 PM
  Kill Him Quickly, It's Raining. PB, 1966 PM
  Lie a Little, Die a Little. PB, 1968. Also published as: Cry Uncle! PB, 1971 PM
  A Plague of Dragons. Barker, 1965 HB
  Slit My Throat, Gently. PB, 1968 PM
  Turn Blue, You Murderers. PB, 1967 PM
  We, the Killers. PB, 1967 PM

BRETT, MIKE. Series character: Sam Dakkers, in both titles.
  The Guilty Bystander. Ace, 1959; Digit, 1960
  Scream Street. Ace, 1959; Digit, 1960

BRETT, SIMON (ANTHONY LEE). 1945-   .
  Cast, in Order of Disappearance. Gollancz, 1975; Scribner, 1976

BREUER, GUSTAV J. Joint pseudonym with
  Gwen Leys Davenport, 1910-   :
  Michael Hardt, q.v.

BREWER, GIL. Series character: Al Mundy
  (in novelizations of It Takes a Thief TV series) = AM.
  —And the Girl Screamed. Crest, 1956; Fawcett (London), 1959
  Angel. Avon, 1960
  The Angry Dream. Bouregy, 1957
  Appointment in Cairo. Ace, 1970 AM
  Appointment in Hell. Monarch, 1961
  Backwoods Teaser. GM, 1960
  The Bitch. Avon, 1958
  The Brat. GM, 1957; Fawcett (London), 1958
  The Devil in Davos. Ace, 1969 AM
  Flight to Darkness. GM, 1952
  The Girl from Hateville. Zenith, 1958
  Hell's Our Destination. GM, 1953; Fawcett (London), 1955
  The Hungry One. GM, 1966
  A Killer is Loose. GM, 1954; Moring, 1956
  Little Tramp. Crest, 1957; Red Seal, 1959
  Mediterranean Caper. Ace, 1969 AM
  Memory of Passion. Lancer, 1963
  Nude on Thin Ice. Avon, 1960
  Play It Hard. Monarch, 1964
  The Red Scarf. Mystery House, 1958; Digit, 1959
  Satan is a Woman. GM, 1951; New Fiction, 1952
  77 Rue Paradis. GM, 1955; Red Seal, 1959
  Sin for Me. Banner, 1967
  So Rich, So Dead. GM, 1951; New Fiction, 1952
  Some Must Die. GM, 1954; Moring, 1956
  The Squeeze. Ace, 1955
  Sugar. Avon, 1959
  A Taste of Sin. Berkley, 1961
  The Tease. Banner, 1967
  13 French Street. GM, 1951; New Fiction, 1952
  The Three-Way Split. GM, 1960
  The Vengeful Virgin. Crest, 1958; Muller pb, 1960
  Wild. Crest, 1958; Fawcett (London), 1959
  Wild to Possess. Monarch, 1959

BREWER, JORDAN
  Get Dumm! Banner, 1967

BREWER, MIKE
  Man Against Fear. Hale, 1966

BRICE, MONICA
  Green Wood Burns Slow. Lothrop, 1938

BRICKHILL, PAUL (CHESTER JEROME). 1916-   .
  The Deadline. Collins, 1962. U.S. title: War of Nerves. Morrow, 1963

BRIDGE, ANN. Pseudonym of Lady Mary Dolling Saunders O'Malley, 1889-1974.
  Series character: Julia Probyn (Jamieson), in all titles.
  The Dangerous Islands. Chatto, 1964; McGraw, 1963
  Emergency in the Pyrenees. Chatto, 1965; McGraw, 1965
  The Episode at Toledo. Chatto, 1967; McGraw, 1966
  The Lighthearted Quest. Chatto, 1956; Macmillan, 1956
  The Malady in Madeira. Chatto, 1970; McGraw, 1969
  The Numbered Account. Chatto, 1960; McGraw, 1960
  The Portuguese Escape. Chatto, 1958; Macmillan, 1958
  The Tightening String. Chatto, 1962; McGraw, 1962

BRIDGES, HILDA
    House of Storms. Wright, 1931
    The House with Black Blinds. Popular
        Publications (Melbourne), 193?

BRIDGES, ROY(AL). 1885-1952.
    The Alden Case. Hutchinson, 1937
    -And All That Beauty—. Hutchinson, 1929
    -The Black House. Hodder, 1920
    -The Bubble Moon. Hodder, 1915
    The Case for Mrs. Heydon. Hutchinson,
        1945
    -Cloud. Hutchinson, 1932
    -Dead Man's Gold. Hodder, 1916
    -The Fires of Hate. Hodder, 1915
    -The Fugitive. Hodder, 1914
    -Gates of Birth. Hutchinson, 1926
    -The House of Fendon. Hutchinson, 1936
    -The Immortal Dawn. Hodder, 1917
    -Legion: For We are Many. Hutchinson,
        1928
    -Merchandise. Hodder, 1918
    -A Mirror of Silver. Hutchinson, 1927
    -Negrohead. Hutchinson, 1930
    Old Admiral Death. Hutchinson, 1940
    The Owl is Abroad. Hutchinson, 1941
    -Rats' Castle. Hutchinson, 1924; Apple-
        ton, 1924
    Rogues' Haven. Hodder, 1922; Appleton,
        1922
    -Soul of the Sword. Hutchinson, 1933
    This House is Haunted. Hutchinson, 1939
    Through Another Gate. Hutchinson, 1927
    -Trinity. Hutchinson, 1931
    -The Vats of Tyre. Hodder, 1921

BRIDGES, T(HOMAS) C(HARLES). 1868-1944.
    The Crime on the Moore. Amalgamated,
        1935. (Sexton Blake.)
    Criminal Yarns. Hutchinson, 1925 ss
    Killer's Contract. Amalgamated, 1934
    -The Mystery Message. Harrap, 1927
    -The Secret of the Baltic. Collins, 1919

BRIDGES, VICTOR (GEORGE DeFREYNE)
    Accidents Will Happen. Macdonald, 1948
    All Very Irregular. Macdonald, 1953
    Another Man's Shoes. Hodder, 1913;
        Doran, 1913
    Blue Silver. Hodder, 1936
    The Creaking Gate. Macdonald, 1958
    Dusky Night. Hodder, 1940
    Exit Mr. Marlowe. Macdonald, 1957
    The Girl from Belfast. Macdonald, 1961
    The Girl in Black. Mills, 1926; Lippin-
        cott, 1927
    Greensea Island. Mills, 1922; Putnam,
        1922
    The Gulls Fly Low. Hodder, 1943
    The Happy Murderers. Hodder, 1933
    The House on the Saltings. Hodder, 1941
    I Did Not Kill Osborne; see Three Blind
        Mice
    It Happened in Essex. Hodder, 1938
    It Never Rains—. Macdonald, 1944
    Jetsam. Mills, 1914 ss
    The King Comes Back. Hodder, 1930
    The Lady from Long Acre. Mills, 1918;
        Putnam, 1919
    The Man from Nowhere. Mills, 1913
    The Man Who Butted In. Hodder, 1942
    The Man Who Limped. Macdonald, 1947
    The Man Who Vanished. Macdonald, 1954
    Mr. Lyndon at Liberty. Mills, 1915
    Peter in Peril. Hodder, 1935; Penn,
        1935
    Quite Like Old Days. Macdonald, 1949
    The Red Lodge. Mills, 1924; Doubleday,
        1924
    A Rogue by Compulsion. Putnam, 1935.
        (British title?)
    Secrecy Essential. Macdonald, 1959
    The Secret of the Creek. Hodder, 1930;
        Houghton, 1930
    The Secret of the Saltings. Macdonald,
        1955
    The Seven Stars. Hodder, 1939
    The Tenth Commandment. Macdonald, 1951
    Three Blind Mice. Hodder, 1933. U.S.
        title: I Did Not Kill Osborne. Penn,
        1934
    Trouble on the Thames. Macdonald, 1945
    We Don't Want to Lose You. Macdonald,
        1952
    What the Doctor Ordered. Macdonald,
        1956

BRIDGMONT, (JAMES) LESLIE. 1901-   .
    Unbriefed Mission. Falcon, 1953

BRIGHT, ALREDE
    The Golden Earnest. Hocage, 1938

BRIGHT, JOHN. See: KUBEC GLASMON.

BRILLANT, J. MAURICE
    Vision of Murder. Comet, 1954

BRINCHMANN, ALEXANDER. 1888-   . Pseudo-
    nym: Roy Roberts, q.v.

BRINGLE, MARY
    The Footpath Murder. Doubleday, 1975

BRINKWORTH, IAN. Pseudonym: Ian Brook,
    q.v.

BRINTON, HENRY. 1901-   . Pseudonym:
    Alex Fraser, q.v. Series characters:
    John and Sally Strang, in at least
    those marked S.
    An Apple a Day. Hutchinson, 1958; Wash-
        burn, 1959
    Apprentice to Fear; see An Ordinary Day
    Can Death Be Sleep? Hutchinson, 1965
    Coppers and Gold. Hutchinson, 1957;
        Macmillan, 1958 S
    Death to Windward. Hutchinson, 1954
    Drug on the Market. Hutchinson, 1956;
        Macmillan, 1957 S
    Ill Wind. Hutchinson, 1957 S
    Now Like to Die. Hutchinson, 1955
    One Down and Two to Slay. Hutchinson,
        1954. Also published as: Two to Slay.
        Arrow, 1959 S
    An Ordinary Day. Hutchinson, 1959. U.S.
        title: Apprentice to Fear. Macmillan,
        1961 S
    Purple-6. Hutchinson, 1962; Walker,
        1962
    Rude Awakening. Hutchinson, 1961
    Two to Slay; see One Down and Two to
        Slay

BRISBANE, COUTTS. Pseudonym of R.
    C(outts) Armour, q.v. All books fea-
    ture Sexton Blake and were published
    by Amalgamated Press.
    Blind Man's Secret. 1936
    The Case of the Three Absconding Swin-
        dlers. 1936
    The Crime of Gunga Dass. 1936
    Dead Man's Peak. 1933
    The Death House. 1931
    Dr. Ferraro's Frame-Up. 1933
    The Fatal Talisman. 1932
    The Gang's Deserter. 1930
    The Masked Man of the Desert. 1937
    The Middle of the Negro's Head. 1939
    Murder in the Air. 1932
    The Mystery of the Missing Doctor. 1938
    The Mystery of the Rajah's Son. 1935
    The Mystery of the Red Tower. 1940
    The Mystery of the Tramp Steamer. 1933
    The Nursing Home Crime. 1935
    The Secret of the Balkan Heiress. 1936
    The Secret of the Glen. 1935
    The Secret of the Loch. 1933
    The Secret of the Sanatorium. 1931
    The Secret Temple. 1934
    The Trafalgar Square Mystery. 1932
    The Trail of the White Turban. 1936
    The Trapper's Victim. 1930

BRISCO, PATTY. Joint pseudonym of Clayton
    (Hartley) Matthews, 1918-   , q.v.,
    and Patricia Matthews, 1927-   .
    The Crystal Window. Avon, 1973
    Horror at Gull House. Belmont, 1972
    House of Candles. Manor, 1973

BRISTOL, PEGGY. See: IRVING SHULMAN,
    1913-   .

BRISTOW, GWEN [MRS. BRUCE MANNING],
    1903-   , and BRUCE MANNING.
    Series character: Captain Murphy = M.
    The Gutenberg Murders. Mystery League,
        1931 M
    The Invisible Host. Mystery League,
        1930. Also published as: The Ninth
        Guest. Popular Library, 1975. Play
        based on this novel: The Ninth
        Guest. French, 1932
    The Mardi Gras Murders. Mystery
        League, 1932 M
    The Ninth Guest; see The Invisible Host
    Two and Two Make Twenty-Two. Mystery
        League, 1932

BRISTOWE, ANTHONY (LYNN). 1921-   .
    The Tunnel. Belmont, 1965

BRITTON, KENNETH PHILLIPS and ROY HAR-
    GRAVE
    Houseparty. French (New York), 1930.
        (3-act play.)

BRITTON, SUMNER. 1902-   . See: MAURICE
    BEAM.

BROAD, PETER
    Death on the Beach. Cassell, 1959

BROADBRIDGE, HUGH
    Moorland Terror. Butterworth, 1930

BROADHURST, GEORGE. See: ARTHUR HORNBLOW,
    1865-   .

BROADLEY, PHILIP
    In the Key of Black. Hodder, 1963

BROCHET, JEAN ALEXANDRE. 1921-1963. Pseu-
    donym: Jean Bruce, q.v.

BROCK, ALAN (ST. HILL). 1886-   . Pseu-
    donym: Peter Dewdney, q.v.
    After the Fact. Nicholson, 1935
    The Browns of the Yard. Harrap, 1952
    By Misadventure. Nicholson, 1934
    A Casebook of Crime. Rockliff, 1948
    Earth to Ashes. Nicholson, 1939
    Further Evidence. Nicholson, 1934
    Inquiries by the Yard. Harrap, 1950
    Miss Hamblett's Ghost. Macdonald, 1946
    Suspicion was Aroused. Nicholson, 1936

BROCK, EDWIN
    -The Little White God. Hutchinson, 1962

BROCK, LYNN. Pseudonym of Alister McAl-
    lister, 1877-1943. Series character:
    Colonel Gore = G.
    The Barrington Mystery; see The Deduc-
        tions of Colonel Gore
    Colonel Gore's Second Case. Collins,
        1925; Harper, 1926 G
    Colonel Gore's Third Case. Collins,
        1927. U.S. title: The Kink. Harper,
        1927 G
    The Dagwort Coombe Murder. Collins,
        1929. U.S. title: The Stoke Silver
        Case. Harper, 1929

The Deductions of Colonel Gore. Collins, 1924; Harper, 1925. Also published as: The Barrington Mystery. Collins, 1932 G
Fourfingers. Collins, 1939
The Kink; see Colonel Gore's Third Case
The Mendip Mystery. Collins, 1929. U.S. title: Murder at the Inn. Harper, 1929 G
Murder at the Inn; see The Mendip Mystery
Murder on the Bridge; see Q.E.D.
Nightmare. Collins, 1932
Q.E.D. Collins, 1930. U.S. title: Murder on the Bridge. Harper, 1930. Reprinted in England under the U.S. title: Collins, 1932 G
The Riddle of the Roost. Collins, 1939
The Silver Sickle Case. Collins, 1938
The Slip-Carriage Mystery. Collins, 1928; Harper, 1928 G
The Stoat. Collins, 1940 G
The Stoke Silver Case; see The Dagwort Coombe Murder
The Two of Diamonds. Collins, 1926

BROCK, ROSE. Pseudonym of Joseph Hansen, 1923- , q.v.
Long Leaf. Harper, 1974
Tarn House. Avon, 1971; Harrap, 1975

BROCK, STUART. Pseudonym of Louis (Preston) Trimble, 1917- , q.v. Other pseudonym: Gerry Travis, q.v.
Bring Back Her Body. Ace, 1953
Death is My Lover. Mill, 1948
Just Around the Coroner. Mill, 1948
Killer's Choice. Graphic, 1956

BRODE, ROBERT
The Clue of the Curious Cat. Empire, 1935

BRODERICK, GERRY P. See: ERWIN N. NISTLER.

BRODEUR, PAUL (ADRIAN, JR.). 1931- .
-The Sick Fox. Little, 1963; Gollancz, 1963
The Stunt Man. Atheneum, 1970; Bodley Head, 1970

BRODIE, GORDON
The Lady Had a Tiger. Hale, 1968
The Poison of Poppies. Hale, 1968
The Will to Kill. Hale, 1969
Who Called Diamonds? Hale, 1970

BRODIE, JULIAN PAUL. 1908- . Joint pseudonym with Alan (Baer) Green, 1906-1975, q.v.: Roger Denbie, q.v.

BRODIE-INNES, JOHN WILLIAM. 1848- .
-The Devil's Mistress. Rider, 1915
The Golden Rope. Lane (London & New York), 1919
The Tragedy of an Indiscretion. Lane (London & New York), 1916

BRODY, MARC. Pseudonym of R(ichard) Wilkes-Hunter, q.v. Other pseudonyms: Tod Conrad, Alex Crane, qq.v. Series character: Marc Brody, in most (all?) titles. These books were first published in Australia, probably all as Horwitz paperbacks, but detailed information is lacking.
Baby, Your Type's Murder.
Blonde at Bay. Horwitz, 1959
Blueprints for a Blonde.
Book Her for Murder.
Dame on a Death Round.
Hers is a Hearse.
High Tide Temptress.
Hot Line for a Honey.
Lady, Don't Shroud Me! Horwitz, 1958
Late Final Blonde.
Move On, Miss Mayhem.
Murder is a Maiden's Handicap.
One Shot for Sadie.
Penthouse Preview.
Red Hot and Morgue Bound.
Second Storey Sinner.
Sinister Sister. Horwitz, 1959
Siren on the Skids.
Stop Press in Scarlet.
Sugar, You're a Scoop!
Teaser Set to Kill.
Undercover Cutie.
Write Off the Redhead.

BROEMEL, ROSE
The Elusive Criminal. Murray, 1930

BROGAN, COLM. Series character: Patrick Heron, in both titles.
The Ghost Walks. Skeffington, 1932
The Plunge. Skeffington, 1933

BROGAN, DENNIS WILLIAM. 1900-1974. Pseudonym: Maurice Barrington, q.v.

BROGAN, JAMES. Pseudonym of (John) Christopher (Glazebrook) Hodder-Williams, 1926- , q.v.
The Cummings Report. Hodder, 1958. (Later reprinted as by Christopher Hodder-Williams.)

BROINOWSKI, ALISON
Take One Ambassador. Macmillan (London), 1973

BROME, VINCENT. 1910- .
The Embassy. Cassell, 1972. U.S. title: The Ambassador and the Spy. Crown, 1973

BROMIGE, IRIS (AMY EDNA). 1910- .
-Rosevean. Hodder, 1962; Chilton-Musson, 1962

BROMLEY, GORDON. Series character: Inspector Severn, in both titles.
The Chance to Poison. Collins, 1973
In the Absence of the Body. Collins, 1972

BRONSON, F(RANCIS) W(OOLSEY). 1901-1966.
The Bulldog has the Key. Farrar, 1949
Nice People Don't Kill. Farrar, 1940
The Uncas Island Murders. Farrar, 1942

BRONSON-HOWARD, GEORGE (FITZALAN). 1883-1922. See also: ETHEL WATTS MUMFORD, 1878-1940. Series character: Yorke Norroy = YN.
-Birds of Prey. Watt, 1918
The Black Book. Watt, 1920 YN
The Devil's Chaplain. Watt, 1922; Paul, 1924
An Enemy to Society. Doubleday, 1911; Laurie, 1911
The Green-Eyed Monster. Detective Tales, 19??. (63 pp. mini-paperback.)
Norroy, Diplomatic Agent. Saalfield, 1907 ss YN
Slaves of the Lamp. Watt, 1917 YN

BRONTE, LOUISA. Pseudonym of Janet Louise Roberts, 1925- , q.v. Other pseudonyms: Rebecca Danton, Janette Radcliffe, qq.v.
Greystone Tavern. Ballantine, 1975
Her Demon Lover. Avon, 1972
Lord Satan. Avon, 1973

BROOCKS, SCHUYLER
Murder Makes a Marriage. Mystery House, 1946

BROOK, IAN. Pseudonym of Ian Brinkworth.
The Golden Bull. Cassell, 1968

BROOKE, HUGH (FELIX CONRAD). 1902- .
-The Mad Shepherdess. Longmans, 1930
Man Made Angry. Longmans, 1932; Long & Smith, 1932
Miss Mitchell. Heinemann, 1934. U.S. title: The Web. Doubleday, 1934
The Web; see Miss Mitchell

BROOKE, JUSTIN
The Clue of the Golden Tooth. Modern, 193?
Death at Dale's End. Modern, 1935
Gangster's Isle. Modern, 1937
The Limping Sailor. Modern, 193?
Murder in the Temple. Modern, 193?
The Mystery at Folly Mill. Modern, 193?
The Secret of the Siding. Modern, 1935
The Sinister Encounter. Modern, 1938
Who Killed Mr. Fisk? Modern, 1935

BROOKER, BERTRAM. 1888-1955. Pseudonym: Huxley Herne, q.v.

BROOKER, CLAIRE
Dark Mosaic. Arcadia, 1957

BROOKS, (WILLIAM) COLLIN. 1893- . Series characters: O. Swete McTavish, in at least those marked OSM; Raeburn Steel, in at least those marked RS.
Account Paid. Hutchinson, 1930
The Body Snatchers. Hutchinson, 1927 RS
The Catspaws. Hutchinson, 1929
Found Dead. Hutchinson, 1930 OSM
Frame-Up. Hutchinson, 1935
The Ghost Hunters. Hutchinson, 1928; Sears, 1928 RS
-Mad-Doctor Merciful. Hutchinson, 1932
Mr. Daddy-Detective. Hutchinson, 1933
Mr. X. Hutchinson, 1927 RS
O Sweet McTavish. Hutchinson, 1930 OSM
Seven Hells. Hutchinson, 1929
The Swimming Frog. Hutchinson, 1951
Three Yards of Cord. Hutchinson, 1931 OSM

BROOKS, EDWY SEARLES. 1889-1965. Pseudonyms: Berkeley Gray, Victor Gunn, Carlton Ross, qq.v. Series characters: Sexton Blake (with many other authors), in those titles listed without publisher (which was Amalgamated Press); Chief Detective-Inspector William Beeke (The Grouser) = WB.
The Black Dagger. 1933
The Boarding-House Mystery. 1924
The Brixham Manor Mystery. 1924
The Case of the Sleeping Partner. 1924
The Case of the Twin Detectives. 1916
The Green Eyes. 1923
The Grouser Investigates. Harrap, 1936 WB
The House with the Double Moat. 1917
The Human Bloodhound. 1924
The Impersonators. 1926
In the Night Watch. 1925
The Midnight Lorry Crime. 1937
Midst Balkan Perils. 1916
The Mystery of Rodney's Cove. 1924
On the Bed of the Ocean. 1922
The Peril of the Prince! 1916
The Red Spider. 1916
The Riddle of the Body on the Road. 1941
The Strange Case of the Antlered Man. Harrap, 1935 WB

BROOKS, HENRY S. -1910.
A Catastrophe in Bohemia and other stories. Webster, 1893 ss, one criminous

BROOKS, HILDEGARD. 1875- .
  Without a Warrant. Scribner, 1901

BROOKS, JAMES J.
  Whiskey Drips: A Series of Interesting Sketches, Illustrating the Operations of the Whiskey Thieves in Their Evasions of the Law and Its Penalties. Evans, 1873. Also published as: The Adventures of a U.S. Detective. Souder, 1876 ss

BROOKS, LEONARD HAROLD. -1950. All titles feature Sexton Blake and were published by Amalgamated Press.
  The Affair of the Blackfriars Financier. 1920
  The Avenging Seven. 1920
  Fingerprints of Fate! 1922
  The Gnat. 1921
  The House of Ghosts. 1922
  The Mystery of Glyn Castle. 1923
  The Riddle of the Lascar's Head. 1926
  The Secret of Thurlston Towers. 1923

BROOKS, VIVIAN COLLIN. 1922- . Pseudonym: Osmington Mills, q.v.

BROOME, ADAM. Pseudonym of Godfrey Warden James, 1888- . Series character: Captain (Commissioner) Denzil Grigson, in at least those marked DG.
  The Black Mamba. Bles, 1936
  The Cambridge Murders. Bles, 1936
  The Crocodile Club. Bles, 1935 DG
  Crowner's Quest. Benn, 1930 DG
  Dream Murder. Macdonald, 1946
  -Flame of the Forest. Bles, 1943
  The Island of Death. Bles, 1932 DG
  The Oxford Murders. Bles, 1929
  The Porro Palaver. Bles, 1928
  The Queen's Hall Murder. Bles, 1933 DG
  The Red Queen Club. Bles, 1939
  Snakes and Ladders. Bles, 1938 DG

BROPHY, JOHN. 1899-1965.
  Behold the Judge. Collins, 1937
  The Day They Robbed the Bank of England. Chatto, 1959
  The Front Door Key. Heinemann, 1960
  I Let Him Go. Cape, 1935
  Solitude Island. Collins, 1941

BROSTER, D(OROTHY) K(ATHLEEN). 1877-1950.
  Crouching at the Door. Heinemann, 1942 ss
  World Under Snow, with G. Forester. Heinemann, 1935

BROTHERS, JAY
  Ox. Bobbs, 1975

BROTHERS, WILLIAM P.
  Morocco Episode. Hillman-Curl pb, 1959

BROUGHTON, F. LUSK
  Harry Williams, the New York Detective. Ogilvie, 1887
  Nemo, the Shadow Detective. Ogilvie, 1885
  A Victim of Villainy. Street (Magnet)

BROUGHTON, MARY
  Prisoners of Fear. Joseph, 1933

BROUN, DANIEL. Series character: Harry Egypt = HE.
  Counterweight. Holt, 1962
  Egypt's Choice. Holt, 1963; Gollancz, 1964 HE
  From 9 O'Clock to Jamaica Bay. Holt, 1964
  The Subject of Harry Egypt. Holt, 1963; Gollancz, 1963 HE

BROWN, ALEC (JOHN CHARLES). 1900-1962.
  Green Lane; or, Murder at Moat Farm. Cape, 1930
  The Hollow Mountain. Macmillan (London), 1939
  A Time to Kill. Cape, 1930. (2 stories.)

BROWN, ALICE. 1857-1948.
  The Mysteries of Ann. Macmillan, 1925

BROWN, ALYS
  The Pearls of Pilolu. Eldon, 1933

BROWN, ANDREW CASSELS. 1875- .
  Birds of Prey. Methuen, 1929
  Dark Dealing. Methuen, 1930
  Dr. Glazebrook's Revenge. Mills, 1928; Dodd, 1928
  Josselin Takes a Hand. Mills, 1927; Dodd, 1927

BROWN, ANTONY
  Slay Me Suddenly. Long, 1968; Walker, 1969

BROWN, CARNABY
  The Man on the Stairs. Boardman, 1957
  The Small Change. Boardman, 1958; Roy, 1958

BROWN, CARTER. Pseudonym of Alan Geoffrey Yates, 1923- , q.v. Other pseudonym: Caroline Farr, q.v. Earliest books published as by Peter Carter-Brown (PC-B), then as by Peter Carter Brown (PCB), then as by Carter Brown. There are probably uncorrelated rewrites and title changes in this list. Series characters: Larry Baker = LB; Danny Boyd, in at least those marked DB; Paul Donavan = PD; Mike Farrell, in at least those marked MF; Rick Holman = RH; Andy Kane, in at least those marked AK; Randy Roberts = RR; Mavis Seidlitz, in at least those marked MS; Al Wheeler, in at least those marked AW.
  And the Undead Sing. Signet, 1974 MS
  Angel! Horwitz, 1962; Signet, 1962 AW
  The Angry Amazons. Horwitz, 1972; Signet, 1972 RR, DB
  The Aseptic Murders. Horwitz, 1972; Signet, 1972 AW
  Baby, You're Guilt-Edged. Horwitz-Transport, 1956, as by PCB
  The Ballad of Loving Jenny. Horwitz, 1963. US & British title: The White Bikini. Signet, 1963; Four Square, 1965 RH
  Bella Donna was Poison. Horwitz-Transport, 1957, as by PCB
  Bid the Babe Bye-Bye. Horwitz-Transport, 1956, as by PCB
  Bird in a Guilt-Edged Cage. Horwitz, 1963. U.S. & British title: The Guilt-Edged Cage. Signet, 1962; Four Square, 1963. (Rewritten reissue of: That's Piracy, My Pet, q.v.) AK
  The Black Lace Hangover. Horwitz, 1966; Signet, 1966; Four Square, 1969 DB
  Black Widow Weeps. Transport, 1953?, as by PC-B?
  The Blonde. Horwitz-Transport?, 1958; Signet, 1958; Four Square, 1964 AW
  Blonde, Bad and Beautiful. Horwitz-Transport, 1957?, as by PCB. (Rewritten and reissued as: The Hong Kong Caper, q.v.)
  Blonde, Beautiful and—BLAM! Horwitz-Transport, 1956, as by PCB
  Blonde on a Broomstick. Horwitz, 1966; Signet, 1966; Four Square, 1966 RH
  Blonde on the Rocks. Horwitz, 1963; Signet, 1963; Four Square, 1964 RH
  Blonde Verdict. Horwitz-Transport, 1956, as by PCB AW
  The Body. Horwitz, 1961; Signet, 1958; Four Square, 1963. (Rewritten reissue of: No Law Against Angels, q.v.) AW
  The Bombshell. Horwitz, 1960; Signet, 1960; Four Square, 1968. (Rewritten reissue of: Doll for the Big House, q.v.) AW
  Booty for a Babe. Horwitz-Transport, 1956, as by PCB
  The Born Loser. Horwitz, 1973; Signet, 1973 AW
  The Brazen. Horwitz, 1960; Signet, 1960; Four Square, 1962 AW
  The Bribe was Beautiful. Horwitz-Transport, 1956, as by PCB
  A Bullet for My Baby. Horwitz-Transport, 1955, as by PCB MS
  The Bump and Grind Murders. Horwitz, 1965; Signet, 1964; Four Square, 1965 MS
  Burden of Guilt. Horwitz, 1971; Signet, 1970 AW
  Caress Before Killing. Horwitz-Transport, 1956, as by PCB
  Catch Me a Phoenix! Horwitz, 1965; Signet, 1965; Four Square, 1966 AW
  Charlie Sent Me! Horwitz, 1963; Signet, 1963; Four Square, 1965. (Rewritten reissue of: Swan Song for a Siren, q.v.) LB
  Charmer Chased. Horwitz-Transport, 1958?, as by PCB
  Chorine Makes a Killing. Horwitz-Transport, 1957, as by PCB AW
  The Clown. Horwitz, 1973; Signet, 1972 AW
  The Coffin Bird. Horwitz, 1971; Signet, 1970 DB
  The Corpse. Horwitz, 1960; Signet, 1958; Four Square, 1963. (Rewritten reissue of: Death on the Downbeat, q.v.) AW
  A Corpse for Christmas. Horwitz, 1965; Signet, 1965; Four Square, 1966 AW
  The Coven. Horwitz, 1971; Signet, 1971 RH
  The Creative Murders. Horwitz, 1971; Signet, 1971 AW
  Curtains for a Chorine. Horwitz-Transport, 1955, as by PCB
  Curves for a Coroner. Horwitz-Transport, 1955, as by PCB
  Cutie Cashed His Chips. Horwitz-Transport, 1955, as by PCB. (Rewritten and reissued as: The Million Dollar Babe, q.v.)
  Cutie Takes the Count. Horwitz-Transport, 1958, as by PCB?
  Cutie Wins a Corpse. Horwitz-Transport, 1957?, as by PCB. (Rewritten and reissued as: Graves, I Dig!, q.v.)
  The Dame. Horwitz, 1959; Signet, 1959; Four Square, 1966 AW
  The Dance of Death. Horwitz, 1964; Signet, 1964; Four Square, 1965 AW
  Darling You're Doomed. Horwitz-Transport, 1956, as by PCB
  The Deadly Kitten. Horwitz, 1968; Signet, 1967 RH
  Deadly Miss. Horwitz-Transport, 1958, as by PCB
  Death of a Doll. Horwitz-Transport, 1956, as by PCB. (Rewritten and reissued under the same title: Horwitz, 1960. U.S. title: The Ever-Loving Blues. Signet, 1961 RH)
  Death on the Downbeat. Horwitz-Transport, 1958, as by PCB. (Rewritten and reissued as: The Corpse, q.v.)
  The Deep Cold Green. Horwitz, 1968; Signet, 1968 AW
  Delilah was Deadly. Horwitz-Transport, 1956, as by PCB

52/ Brown, Carter

The Desired. Horwitz, 1959; Signet, 1960; Four Square, 1966 AW
Die Anytime, After Tuesday! Horwitz, 1969; Signet, 1969 RH
Doll for the Big House. Horwitz-Transport, 1957, as by PCB. (Rewritten and reissued as: The Bombshell, q.v.)
Donavan. Horwitz, 1974; Signet, 1974 PD
Donavan's Day. Horwitz, 1975?; Signet, 1975 PD
Donna Died Laughing. Horwitz-Transport, 1956, as by PCB
The Dream is Deadly. Horwitz, 1960; Signet, 1960; Four Square, 1962 DB
The Dumdum Murder. Horwitz, 1962; Signet, 1962; Four Square, 1963 AW
The Early Boyd. Horwitz, 1975; Signet, 1975 DB
Eve—It's Extortion. Horwitz-Transport, 1957, as by PCB. (Rewritten and reissued in Australia as: Walk Softly Witch!, q.v., and in the U.S. as: The Victim.)
The Eve of His Dying. Horwitz-Transport, 1956, as by PCB
The Ever-Loving Blues; see Death of a Doll
The Exotic. Horwitz, 1961; Signet, 1961; Four Square, 1962 AW
The Fabulous; see None But the Lethal Heart
Felon Angel; see Homicide Harem and Felon Angel
The Flagellator. Horwitz, 1969; Signet, 1969 RH
The Frame is Beautiful. Transport, 1953, as by PC-B
Fraulein is Feline. Transport, 1953, as by PC-B
The Girl from Outer Space. Horwitz, 1966; Signet, 1965; Four Square, 1966 RH
Girl in a Shroud. Horwitz, 1963; Signet, 1963; Four Square, 1964 AW
The Girl Who was Possessed; see The Sinners
Goddess Gone Bad. Horwitz-Transport, 1958, as by PCB?
Good Morning, Mavis. Horwitz-Transport, 1957?, as by PCB MS
A Good Year for Dwarfs? Horwitz, 1971; Signet, 1970 RH
Graves, I Dig! Horwitz, 1960; Signet, 1960. (Rewritten reissue of: Cutie Wins a Corpse, q.v.)
The Guilt-Edged Cage; see Bird in a Guilt-Edged Cage
Had I But Groaned. Horwitz, 1968; Signet, 1968. British title: The Witches. Four Square, 1969 LB
The Hammer of Thor. Horwitz, 1967; Signet, 1965 AW
The Hang-Up Kid. Horwitz, 1970; Signet, 1970 RH
The Hellcat. Horwitz, 1962; Signet, 1962; Four Square, 1962 AW
Hi-Fi Fadeout. Horwitz-Transport, 1958, as by PCB?
Hi-Jack for a Jill. Horwitz-Transport, 1956, as by PCB
High Fashion in Homicide. Horwitz-Transport, 1958, as by PCB
Homicide Harem and Felon Angel. Horwitz, 1965
Homicide Hoyden. Horwitz-Transport?, 1954, as by PCB?
Honey, Here's Your Hearse! Horwitz-Transport, 1955, as by PCB MS
The Hong Kong Caper. Horwitz, 1962; Signet, 1962; Four Square, 1963. (Rewritten reissue of: Blonde, Bad and Beautiful, q.v.) AK
The Hoodlum was a Honey. Horwitz-Transport, 1956, as by PCB
Hot Seat for a Honey; see Penthouse Passout
House of Sorcery. Horwitz, 1968; Signet, 1967; Four Square, 1968 DB

Ice Cold in Ermine. Horwitz-Transport, 1958, as by PCB
The Ice-Cold Nude. Horwitz, 1962; Signet, 1962; Four Square, 1962 DB
The Invisible Flamini. Horwitz, 1972; Signet, 1971 RH
The Iron Maiden. Horwitz, 1975; Signet, 1975 LB
The Jade-Eyed Jinx. Horwitz, 1963. U.S. and British title: The Jade-Eyed Jungle. Signet, 1963; Four Square, 1964 RH
The Jade-Eyed Jungle; see The Jade-Eyed Jinx
The Killer is Kissable. Horwitz-Transport?, 1954, as by PCB?
Kiss and Kill. Horwitz-Transport, 1955, as by PCB
Kiss Me Deadly. Horwitz-Transport, 1955, as by PCB
The Lady Has No Convictions. Horwitz-Transport, 1956, as by PCB
The Lady is Available; see The Lady is Not Available
The Lady is Chased. Transport, 1953, as by PC-B
The Lady is Not Available. Horwitz, 1963. U.S. and British title: The Lady is Available. Signet, 1963; Four Square, 1964 AW
The Lady is Transparent. Horwitz, 1962; Signet, 1962; Four Square, 1963 AW
Lament for a Lousy Lover. Horwitz, 1961; Signet, 1960; Four Square, 1968 MS, AW
Last Note for a Lovely. Horwitz-Transport, 1957, as by PCB
Lead Astray. Horwitz-Transport, 1955, as by PCB
Lethal in Love. Transport, 1953?, as by PC-B? Also published as: The Minx is Murder. Horwitz-Transport, 1957, as by PCB
Lipstick Larceny. Horwitz-Transport, 1955, as by PCB
Long Time No Leola. Horwitz, 1967; Signet, 1967 RH
The Lover. Horwitz-Transport, 1958; Signet, 1959; Four Square, 1963 AW
Lover, Don't Come Back! Horwitz, 1962; Signet, 1962; Four Square, 1963 DB
The Loving and the Dead. Horwitz, 1959; Signet, 1959; Four Square, 1966 MS
Luck was No Lady. Horwitz-Transport, 1958?, as by PCB
Madam You're Mayhem. Horwitz-Transport, 1957, as by PCB
Maid for Murder. Transport, 1954, as by PCB
Manhattan Cowboy. Horwitz, 1973; Signet, 1973 DB
The Master. Horwitz, 1973; Signet 1973 RH
Meet Murder, My Angel. Horwitz-Transport, 1956, as by PCB
The Million Dollar Babe. Horwitz, 1962; Signet, 1961. (Rewritten reissue of: Cutie Cashed His Chips, q.v.)
The Mini-Murders. Horwitz, 1968; Signet, 1968 DB
The Minx is Murder; see Lethal in Love
Miss Called Murder. Horwitz-Transport, 1955, as by PCB
The Mistress. Horwitz-Transport?, 1958; Signet, 1959; Four Square, 1963 AW
Model of No Virtue. Horwitz-Transport, 1956, as by PCB
Moonshine Momma; see A Siren Signs Off
A Morgue Amour. Horwitz-Transport?, 1954, as by PCB?
Murder by Miss-Demeanour. Horwitz-Transport, 1956, as by PCB

Murder in the Family Way. Horwitz, 1972; Signet, 1971 RR
Murder in the Harem Club. Horwitz, 1962. U.S. and British title: Murder in the Key Club. Signet, 1962; Four Square, 1962 RH
Murder in the Key Club; see Murder in the Harem Club
Murder is a Package Deal. Horwitz, 1964; Signet, 1964; Four Square, 1965 RH
Murder is My Mistress. Associated General Publications, 1954, as by PC-B. (Rewritten and reissued as: The Savage Salome, q.v.)
Murder is So Nostalgic! Horwitz, 1973; Signet, 1972 MS
Murder is the Message. Horwitz, 1970; Signet, 1969 DB
Murder on High. Horwitz, 1973; Signet, 1973 RR
Murder—Paris Fashion. Transport, 1954, as by PC-B
Murder Wears a Mantilla. Horwitz-Transport, 1957, as by PCB. (Revised and reissued under the same title: Horwitz, 1963; Signet, 1962; Four Square, 1962 MS
The Murderer Among Us. Horwitz, 1962. U.S. and British title: A Murderer Among Us. Signet, 1962; Four Square, 1964 RH
My Darling is Deadpan. Horwitz-Transport, 1956, as by PCB
My Mermaid Murmurs Murder. Transport, 1953, as by PC-B
The Myopic Mermaid. Horwitz, 1962; Signet, 1961. (Rewritten reissue of: A Siren Signs Off, q.v.)
Negative in Blue. Horwitz, 1975; Signet, 1974 RH
Nemesis Wore Nylons. Transport, 1954, as by PC-B
The Never-Was Girl. Horwitz, 1964; Signet, 1964; Four Square, 1965 RH
Night Wheeler. Signet, 1974 AW
No Blonde is an Island. Horwitz, 1965; Signet, 1965; Four Square, 1965 LB
No Body She Knows. Horwitz-Transport, 1958, as by PCB. (Carter Brown Collectors' Series edition, Horwitz, 1960, also includes: Slaughter in Satin.)
No Future Fair Lady. Horwitz-Transport, 1958, as by PCB
No Halo for Hedy. Horwitz-Transport, 1956, as by PCB
No Harp for My Angel. Horwitz-Transport, 1956, as by PCB
No Law Against Angels. Horwitz-Transport, 1957, as by PCB. (Rewritten and reissued as: The Body, q.v.)
No Tears from the Widow. Horwitz, 1966; Signet, 1966; Four Square, 1968 RH
None But the Lethal Heart. Horwitz, 1959; Signet, 1959; Four Square, 1967. Also published as: The Fabulous. Horwitz, 1961 MS
Nude—with a View. Horwitz, 1965; Signet, 1965; Four Square, 1966 RH
Nymph to the Slaughter. Horwitz, 1963; Signet, 1963; Four Square, 1964 DB
Only the Very Rich? Horwitz, 1969; Signet, 1969 DB
The Passionate. Horwitz, 1959; Signet, 1959; Four Square, 1966 AW
The Passionate Pagan. Horwitz, 1963; Signet, 1963; Four Square, 1964 DB
Penthouse Passout. Transport, 1953?, as by PC-B?. Also published as: Hot Seat for a Honey. Horwitz-Transport, 1956, as by PCB
Phreak-Out! Horwitz, 1975; Signet, 1973 RH
Play Now—Kill Later! Horwitz, 1966; Signet, 1966 RH

The Plush-Lined Coffin. Horwitz, 1967;
  Signet, 1967; Four Square, 1968 AW
Poison Ivy; see Yogi Shrouds Yolanda
  and Poison Ivy
The Pornbroker. Horwitz, 1972; Signet,
  1972 RH
Ride the Roller Coaster. Horwitz,
  1975?; Signet, 1975 RH
The Sad-Eyed Seductress; see The Seductress
The Savage Salome. Horwitz, 1961; Signet, 1961. (Rewritten reissue of:
  Murder is My Mistress, q.v.) DB
The Scarlet Flush. Horwitz, 1963; Signet, 1963; Four Square, 1965 MF
The Seductress. Horwitz, 1961. U.S.
  and British title: The Sad-Eyed
  Seductress. Signet, 1961; Four
  Square, 1962 DB
Seidlitz and the Super-Spy. Horwitz,
  1967; Signet, 1967. British title:
  The Super Spy. Four Square, 1969 MS
The Seven Sirens. Horwitz, 1972; Signet, 1972 RR
The Sex Clinic. Horwitz, 1971; Signet,
  1972 DB
Sex Trap. Horwitz, 1975; Signet, 1975
  RR
Shady Lady. Transport, 1953?, as by
  PC-B?
Shamus, Your Slip is Showing. Horwitz-Transport, 1955, as by PCB
Shroud for My Sugar. Horwitz-Transport,
  1955, as by PCB
The Silken Nightmare. Horwitz, 1963;
  Signet, 1963; Four Square, 1964 DB
Sinfully Yours. Horwitz-Transport,
  1958?, as by PCB?
Sinner, You Slay Me! Horwitz-Transport,
  1957, as by PCB
The Sinners. Horwitz, 1963. U.S. and
  British title: The Girl Who Was Possessed. Signet, 1963; Four Square,
  1963 AW
A Siren Signs Off. Horwitz-Transport,
  1958, as by PCB. [Carter Brown Collectors' Series edition, Horwitz,
  1960, also includes: Moonshine Momma.] (Rewritten and reissued as: The
  Myopic Mermaid, q.v.)
Slaughter in Satin; see No Body She
  Knows
So Deadly, Sinner! Horwitz, 1959. U.S.
  and British title: Walk Softly,
  Witch. Signet, 1959; Four Square,
  1965 DB
So Lovely She Lies. Horwitz-Transport,
  1958, as by PCB?
So Move the Body. Horwitz, 1973; Signet, 1973 DB
So What Killed the Vampire? Horwitz,
  1966; Signet, 1966; Four Square, 1967
  LB
Sob-Sister Cries Murder. Horwitz-Transport, 1955, as by PCB
The Sometime Wife. Horwitz, 1966; Signet, 1965; Four Square, 1966 DB
The Star-Crossed Lover. Signet, 1974 RH
The Streaked-Blond Slave. Horwitz,
  1970; Signet, 1969 RH
Strictly for Felony. Horwitz-Transport,
  1956, as by PCB
Strip Without Tease. Transport, 1953?,
  as by PC-B?
The Stripper. Horwitz, 1961; Signet,
  1961; Four Square, 1962 AW
Stripper, You've Sinned. Horwitz-Transport, 1957?, as by PCB
Suddenly by Violence. Horwitz, 1959;
  Signet, 1959 DB
The Super Spy; see Seidlitz and the
  Super-Spy
Swan Song for a Siren. Horwitz-Transport, 1955, as by PCB. (Rewritten and
  reissued as: Charlie Sent Me!, q.v.)
Sweetheart, This is Homicide. Horwitz-Transport, 1956, as by PCB

Target for Their Dark Desire. Horwitz,
  1967; Signet, 1966; Four Square, 1968
  AW
Tempt a Tigress. Horwitz-Transport,
  1958?, as by PCB
The Temptress. Horwitz, 1960; Signet,
  1960; Four Square, 1964 AW
Ten Grand Tallulah and Temptation. Horwitz-Transport, 1957, as by PCB
Terror Comes Creeping. Horwitz, 1959;
  Signet, 1959; Four Square, 1967 DB
That's Piracy, My Pet. Horwitz-Transport, 1957?, as by PCB. (Rewritten
  and reissued in Australia as: Bird in
  a Guilt-Edged Cage, q.v., and in the
  U.S. and Britain as: The Guilt-Edged
  Cage.)
The Tigress. Horwitz, 1961; Signet,
  1961. British title: Wildcat. Four
  Square, 1962 AW
Tomorrow is Murder. Horwitz, 1960; Signet, 1960 MS
Trouble is a Dame. Transport, 1953?, as
  by PC-B?
True Son of the Beast! Signet, 1970 LB
The Two-Timing Blonde. Horwitz-Transport, 1955, as by PCB
The Unorthodox Corpse. Horwitz-Transport, 1957, as by PCB. (Rewritten and
  reissued under the same title: Horwitz, 1961; Signet, 1961 AW)
Until Temptation Do Us Part. Horwitz,
  1967; Signet, 1967; Four Square, 1968
  AW
The Up-Tight Blonde. Horwitz, 1970;
  Signet, 1969 AW
The Velvet Vixen; see The Vixen
Venus Unarmed. Transport, 1953, as by
  PC-B
The Victim!; see Walk Softly Witch!
The Vixen. Horwitz, 1964. U.S. and
  British title: The Velvet Vixen. Signet, 1964; Four Square, 1965 AW
Walk Softly, Witch; see So Deadly,
  Sinner! (This is a completely different book from the following
  entry.)
Walk Softly Witch! Horwitz, 1959. U.S.
  title: The Victim. Signet, 1959. (Rewritten reissue of: Eve—It's Extortion, q.v.) AW
The Wanton. Horwitz, 1959; Signet,
  1959; Four Square, 1968 AW
The Wayward; see The Wayward Wahine
The Wayward Wahine. Horwitz, 1960; Signet, 1960; Four Square, 1966. Also
  published as: The Wayward. Horwitz,
  1962 DB
The Wench is Wicked. Horwitz-Transport,
  1955, as by PCB
Wheeler, Dealer! Horwitz, 1975; Signet,
  1975 AW
Wheeler Fortune. Signet, 1974 AW
Where Did Charity Go? Horwitz, 1971;
  Signet, 1970 RH
The White Bikini; see The Ballad of
  Loving Jenny
Who Killed Dr. Sex? Horwitz, 1965; Signet, 1964; Four Square, 1965 RH
W.H.O.R.E. Horwitz, 1972; Signet, 1971
  AW
Widow Bewitched. Horwitz-Transport,
  1958?, as by PCB
Wildcat; see The Tigress
The Wind-Up Doll. Horwitz, 1963; Signet, 1964; Four Square, 1965 RH
The Witches; see Had I But Groaned
Wreath for a Redhead. Horwitz-Transport, 1957, as by PCB
Wreath for Rebecca. Transport, 1953?,
  as by PC-B?
Yogi Shrouds Yolanda and Poison Ivy.
  Horwitz, 1965
Zelda. Horwitz, 1961; Signet, 1961;
  Four Square, 1962 RH

BROWN, CHARLES BROCKDEN. 1771-1810. These
  titles originally appeared anonymously.
  Arthur Mervyn; or, Memoirs of the Year
    1793. H. Maxwell, 1799-1800
  Edgar Huntley; or, The Memoirs of a
    Sleepwalker. H. Maxwell, 1799;
    Colburn, 1831
  Ormond; or, The Secret Witness. Caritat, 1799
  Wieland; or, The Transformation. Caritat, 1798; Colburn, 1811

BROWN, DEE A(LEXANDER). 1908-   .
  They Went Thataway. Putnam, 1960

BROWN, DOROTHY FOSTER
  Grimm Death. Smith, 1946

BROWN, EDNA A(DELAIDE). 1875-   .
  That Affair at St. Peter's. Lothrop,
  1920

BROWN, EDWARD. Series character: Major
  Adrian Titterton, in at least those
  marked AT.
  The Big Man. Harrap, 1965
  A Penny to Spend. Harrap, 1966 AT
  Vandersley. Harrap, 1967 AT

BROWN, ELIJAH. 1867-   . Pseudonym:
  Alan Raleigh, q.v.

BROWN, ELIZABETH (LOUISE). 1924-   .
  The Candle of the Wicked. Zondervan,
  1972

BROWN, ELWOOD S.
  The Elephant Murders. Vantage, 1955

BROWN, FREDRIC. 1906-1972. Series characters: Ed and Am Hunter = H.
  The Bloody Moonlight. Dutton, 1949.
    British title: Murder in the Moonlight. Boardman, 1950 H
  The Case of the Dancing Sandwiches.
    Dell, 1951. (A novelet, published
    separately in Dell's short-lived 10¢
    pb series.)
  Compliments of a Fiend. Dutton, 1950;
    Boardman, 1951 H
  The Dead Ringer. Dutton, 1948; Boardman, 1950 H
  Death Has Many Doors. Dutton, 1951;
    Boardman, 1952 H
  The Deep End. Dutton, 1952; Boardman,
    1953
  The Fabulous Clipjoint. Dutton, 1947;
    Boardman, 1949 H
  The Far Cry. Dutton, 1951; Boardman,
    1952
  The Five-Day Nightmare. Dutton, 1963;
    Boardman, 1963
  Here Comes a Candle. Dutton, 1950;
    Boardman, 1951
  His Name was Death. Dutton, 1954;
    Boardman, 1955
  Knock Three-One-Two. Dutton, 1959;
    Boardman, 1959
  The Late Lamented. Dutton, 1959; Boardman, 1959 H
  The Lenient Beast. Dutton, 1956; Boardman, 1957
  Madball. Dell, 1953; Muller, 1962
  Mrs. Murphy's Underpants. Dutton, 1963;
    Boardman, 1965 H
  Mostly Murder. Dutton, 1953; Boardman,
    1954 ss
  Murder Can Be Fun. Dutton, 1948; Boardman, 1951. Also published as: A Plot
    for Murder. Bantam, 1949

Murder in the Moonlight; see The Bloody Moonlight
The Murderers. Dutton, 1961; Boardman, 1962
Night of the Jabberwock. Dutton, 1950; Boardman, 1951
Nightmares and Geezenstacks. Bantam, 1961. (A collection of short-shorts, some fantasy, some sf, some mystery, some all three.)
One for the Road. Dutton, 1958; Boardman, 1959
A Plot for Murder; see Murder Can Be Fun
The Screaming Mimi. Dutton, 1949; Boardman, 1950
The Shaggy Dog and Other Murders. Dutton, 1963. British title: The Shaggy Dog and other stories. Boardman, 1964 ss
We All Killed Grandma. Dutton, 1952; Boardman, 1953
The Wench is Dead. Dutton, 1955

BROWN, GEORGE DOUGLAS. 1869-1902. Pseudonym: George Douglas, q.v.

BROWN, GERALD. Series character: Duke McCale, in both titles.
Murder in Plain Sight. Phoenix, 1945
Murder on Beacon Hill. Phoenix, 1941

BROWN, HARRY JOE, JR.
Duffy. Dell, 1968. (Novelization of the movie.)

BROWN, HORACE. 1908- . Pseudonym: Leslie Allen, q.v.
The Corpse was a Blonde. Boardman, 1960. (= The Penthouse Killings?)
The Penthouse Killings. News Stand, 1950

BROWN, J(OHN) E(DWARD). 1920- .
Incident at 125th Street. Doubleday, 1970

BROWN, JAMES AMBROSE. 1919- .
The Pact. Putnam, 1966. (Original title and publication probably: The Assassins. Johannesburg, 1965.)
The Snare. Macdonald, 1975

BROWN, JOHN
Death Gets a Place. Allen, 1951
Death in the Silver Ring. Background Books, 1948
Murder Each Way. Allen, 1953

BROWN, JOHN. 1924- .
The Chancer. Macmillan (London), 1972

BROWN, JOY
Night of Terror. Harlequin, 1950

BROWN, PETER CARTER. Pseudonym of Alan Geoffrey Yates, 1923- , q.v. See: CARTER BROWN. Other pseudonym: Caroline Farr, q.v.

BROWN, RICHARD (BLAKE). 1902?- .
The Blank Cheque. Fortune, 1934
Rococo Coffin. Fortune, 1936

BROWN, ROBERT CARLTON. 1886-1959.
The Remarkable Adventures of Christopher Poe. Browne, 1913 ss
What Happened to Mary? Clode, 1913

BROWN, ROYAL
Escape. Dutton, 1938

BROWN, VINCENT
The Chief Constable. Chapman, 1912; Brentano's, 1912

BROWN, W(ILLIAM) P(ERRY)
The Great Baruma Mystery. Henderson, 1904

BROWN, WALTER C. Series character: Detective-Sergeant Stephen Harper, in all titles.
Laughing Death. Lippincott, 1932
Murder at Mocking House. Lippincott, 1933
The Second Guess. Lippincott, 1929

BROWN, WENZELL. 1912- .
An Act of Passion. Monarch, 1962
The Big Rumble. Popular Library, 1955
Cry Kill. GM, 1959
Gang Girl. Avon, 1954
Hong Kong Aftermath. Smith, 1943
The Hoods Ride In. Pyramid, 1959
Jailbait Jungle. Belmont, 196?
The Murder Kick. GM, 1960; Muller pb, 1961
Murder Seeks an Agent. Five Star, 1945; Curzon, 1947
The Naked Hours. Popular Library, 1956
Possess and Conquer. Warner, 1975
Prison Girl. Pyramid, 1958
The Rum and Coca-Cola Murders. Saint Mystery Library, 1960. (Also contains a ss, "Calypsonian", by Samuel Selvon.)
Run, Chico, Run. GM, 1953; Fawcett (London), 1959
-Teen-Age Mafia. GM, 1959
Teen-Age Terror. GM, 1958
The Wicked Streets. GM, 1957

BROWN, WHITNEY
And So to Eternity. Merit, 1954

BROWN, WILL(IAM) H(ERBERT). 1864-1929.
The Legacy of the Golden Key. Standard, 1914

BROWN, ZENITH JONES. 1898- . Pseudonyms: Leslie Ford, David Frome, qq.v.

BROWNE, BARUM. Joint pseudonym of Geoffrey Dennis and Hilary (Aiden) St. George Saunders, 1898-1951, q.v. Joint pseudonym of Saunders with John (Leslie) Palmer, 1885-1949, q.v.: Francis Beeding, q.v.
The Devil and X.Y.Z. Gollancz, 1931; Doubleday, 1931

BROWNE, COURTNEY. Pseudonym of Reginald David Stanley Courtney-Browne, 1915- .
-The Ancient Pond. Hale, 1967; Harper, 1967

BROWNE, COWDRAY
Oliver Quendon's First Case. Hutchinson, 1927

BROWNE, DOUGLAS G(ORDON). 1884- .
Series characters: Inspector Thew, in at least those marked T; Harvey Tuke, in at least those marked HT; Major Maurice Hemyock, in at least those marked MH.
The Cotfold Conundrums. Methuen, 1933 T
The Dead Don't Bite. Methuen, 1933 MH
Death in Perpetuity. Macdonald, 1950 HT
Death in Seven Volumes. Macdonald, 1958 HT
Death Wears a Mask. Hutchinson, 1940; Macmillan, 1954 HT
The House of the Sword. Hutchinson, 1939
The Looking-Glass Murders. Methuen, 1935
The May-Week Murders. Longmans, 1937 MH
Plan XVI. Methuen, 1934; Doubleday, 1934 T
Rustling End. Macdonald, 1948 HT
Sergeant Death. Macdonald, 1955 HT
The Stolen Boat-Train. Methuen, 1935
Too Many Cousins. Macdonald, 1946; Macmillan, 1953 HT
Uncle William and other stories. Blackwood, 1930 ss
What Beckoning Ghost. Macdonald, 1947 HT

BROWNE, ELEANORE
Murder by Appointment. Macaulay, 1934

BROWNE, GERALD A.
11 Harrowhouse. Arbor, 1972; Deutsch, 1973
Hazard. Arbor, 1973; Hart-Davis, 1974

BROWNE, HOWARD. 1908- . Pseudonym: John Evans, q.v. Series character: Paul Pine = PP, who appears also in books under the John Evans byline.
The Taste of Ashes. Simon, 1957; Gollancz, 1958 PP
Thin Air. Simon, 1954; Gollancz, 1955

BROWNE, K(ENNETH) R(OBERT) G(ORDON). 1895- .
Following Ann. Cassell, 1925. U.S. title: The Cheerful Fraud. Putnam, 1925

BROWNE, ROBERT GORE. 1893- . See: ROBERT GORE-BROWNE.

BROWNE, THOMAS ALEXANDER. 1826-1915. Pseudonym: Rolf Boldrewood, q.v.

BROWNING, GARETH H. Pseudonym of George Henry Browning, 1887- .
The Black Ink Mystery. Hutchinson, 1927

BROWNING, GEORGE HENRY. 1887- . Pseudonym: Gareth H. Browning, q.v.

BROWNING, JOHN
If Your Cover is Blown. Hale, 1970
A Quiet War. Hale, 1974
The Saffron Robe. Hale, 1970
The Sleeper. Hale, 1974

BROWNING, STERRY. Pseudonym of Leonard (Reginald) Gribble, 1908- , q.v. Other pseudonyms: Leo Grex, Louis Grey, Dexter Muir, qq.v. See also: JANET GREEN.
Crime at Cape Folly. Clerke, 1951
Sex Marks the Spot. Long, 1954

BROXHOLME, JOHN FRANKLIN. 1930- . Pseudonym: Duncan Kyle, q.v.

BRUCE, GEORGE. 1898- .
Claim of the Fleshless Corpse. Dodge, 1937. British title: Corpse Without Flesh. Jenkins, 1938
Corpse Without Flesh; see Claim of the Fleshless Corpse
Too Tough to Die. Caslon, 1936; Long, 1937

BRUCE, JEAN. Pseudonym of Jean Alexandre Brochet, 1921-1963. Series character: Hubert Bonisseur de la Bath, in all titles, except possibly Corpses Galore.
Cold Spell. Corgi, 1967. (Translation of Cinq Gars pour Singapore. Paris, 1957.)

Corpses Galore. Archer, 1951
Dead Silence. Corgi, 1967
Deep Freeze. Cassell, 1963. (Translation of Tactique Artique. Paris, 1960.)
Double Take. Cassell, 1964. (Translation of Rentre dans la Dans. Paris, 1961.)
Flash Point. Cassell, 1965. (Translation of Moche Coup a Moscou. Paris, 1958.)
High Treason. Corgi, 1967. (Translation of Trahison. Paris, 1965.)
Hot Line. Corgi, 1967. U.S. title: Trouble in Tokyo. Crest, 1965. (Translation of A Tout Coeur a Tokie. Paris, 1958.)
The Last Quarter Hour; see Live Wire
Live Wire. Corgi, 1965. U.S. title: The Last Quarter Hour. Crest, 1965. (Translation of De Dernier Quart d'Heure. Paris, 1955.)
Photo Finish. Corgi, 1965. (Translation of O.S.S. 117 a l'Ecole. Paris, 1961.)
Pole Reaction. Cassell, 1965. (Translation of O.S.S. 117 Repond Toujours. Paris, 1953.)
Shock Tactics. Cassell, 1965. (Translation of Ombres sur la Bosphore. Paris, 1954.)
Short Wave. Cassell, 1964. (Translation of Affaire No. 1. Paris, 1954.)
Soft Sell. Corgi, 1965. (Translation of Plan de Bataille pour O.S.S. 117. Paris, 1957.)
Strip Tease. Corgi, 1968. (Translation of Strip Tease pour O.S.S. 117. Paris, 1962.)
Top Secret. Corgi, 1967
Trouble in Tokyo; see Hot Line

BRUCE, KENNEDY
The Fakir's Curse. Jenkins, 1931
The Poisoned Fang. Jenkins, 1930
The Sliding Death. Jenkins, 1933

BRUCE, LEO. Pseudonym of Rupert Croft-Cooke, 1903- , q.v. Series characters: Sergeant Beef = SB; Carolus Deene = CD.
At Death's Door. H. Hamilton, 1955 CD
A Bone and a Hank of Hair. Davies, 1961; British Book Centre, 1961 CD
Case for Sergeant Beef. Nicholson, 1947 SB
Case for Three Detectives. Bles, 1936; Stokes, 1937 SB
Case with Four Clowns. Davies, 1939; Stokes, 1939 SB
Case with No Conclusion. Bles, 1939 SB
Case with Ropes and Rings. Nicholson, 1940 SB
Case without a Corpse. Bles, 1937; Stokes, 1937 SB
Cold Blood. Gollancz, 1952 SB
Crack of Doom. Davies, 1963. U.S. title: Such is Death. London House, 1963 CD
Dead for a Ducat. Davies, 1956 CD
Dead Man's Shoes. Davies, 1958 CD
Death at Hallows End. Allen, 1965; British Book Centre, 1966 CD
Death at St. Asprey's School. Allen, 1967 CD
Death by the Lake. Allen, 1971 CD
Death in Albert Park. Allen, 1964 CD
Death in the Middle Watch. Allen, 1974 CD
Death of a Bovver Boy. Allen, 1974 CD
Death of a Commuter. Allen, 1967 CD
Death of Cold. Davies, 1956 CD
Death on Allhallowe'en. Allen, 1970 CD
Death on Romney Marsh. Allen, 1968 CD
Death on the Black Sands. Allen, 1966 CD
Death with Blue Ribbon. Allen, 1969; London House, 1970 CD
Die All, Die Merrily. Davies, 1961; British Book Centre, 1961 CD
The Furious Old Women. Davies, 1960 CD
Jack on the Gallows Tree. Davies, 1960 CD
A Louse for the Hangman. Davies, 1958 CD
Neck and Neck. Gollancz, 1951 SB
Nothing Like Blood. Davies, 1962 CD
Our Jubilee is Death. Davies, 1959 CD
Such is Death; see Crack of Doom

BRUCKER, MARGARETTA
Death in the Dormitory. Phoenix, 1937
Murder at Lover's Lake. Phoenix, 1943
Poison Party. Phoenix, 1938

BRULLER, JEAN MARCEL. 1902- . Pseudonym: Vercors, q.v.

BRUN, T.
The Haunted Heart. Westhouse, 1946

BRUNNER, BERNARD
The Face of Night. Fell, 1967

BRUNNER, JOHN (KILIAN HOUSTON). 1934- . Series character: Max Curfew, in at least those marked MC.
Blacklash; see A Plague on Both Your Causes
The Gaudy Shadows. Constable, 1970
Good Men Do Nothing. Hodder, 1970; Pyramid, 1971 MC
Honky in the Woodpile. Constable, 1971 MC
A Plague on Both Your Causes. Hodder, 1969. U.S. title: Blacklash. Pyramid, 1969 MC
Wear the Butcher's Medal. PB, 1965

BRUSSEL, JAMES A(RNOLD). 1905- .
Just Murder, Darling. Scribner, 1959

BRUTON, ERIC (MOORE). 1915- . Series character: Inspector George Judd = GJ.
Death in Ten Point Bold. Jenkins, 1957
The Devil's Pawn. Boardman, 1962
Die, Darling, Die. Boardman, 1959
The Finsbury Mob. Boardman, 1964 GJ
The Fire Bug. Boardman, 1967 GJ
The Hold Out. Boardman, 1961
King Diamond. Boardman, 1961
The Laughing Policeman. Boardman, 1963 GJ
The Smithfield Slayer. Boardman, 1965 GJ
Violent Brothers. Boardman, 1960
The Wicked Saint. Boardman, 1965 GJ

BRYAN, FRANK
The Long Shadow. Comet, 1954

BRYAN, JOHN. Pseudonym of Josephine Delves-Broughton, 191(- . Series character: Richard Sarel, in all titles.
The Contessa Came Too. Faber, 1957
The Difference to Me. Faber, 1957; British Book Centre, 1960
The Man Who Came Back. Faber, 1958; London House, 1959

BRYAN, MICHAEL
Intent to Kill. Dell, 1956; Eyre, 1956
Murder in Majorca. Dell, 1957; Eyre, 1958

BRYAN, SOFI O.
The Secret of the Priory. Dell, 1975

BRYANT, M(ARGUERITE) and G(EORGE) H. MacANALLY. See also: MARGUERITE BRYANT.
Breakfast for Three. Methuen, 1930

BRYANT, MARGUERITE. See also: M(ARGUERITE) BRYANT.
The Adventures of Louis Dural. Brown Langham, 1905
Mrs. Fuller. Hurst, 1925; Duffield, 1925
The Redemption of Richard. Hurst, 1922. U.S. title: Richard. Duffield, 1922
Richard; see The Redemption of Richard

BRYANT, MATT
Cue for Murder. Vanguard, 1954; Barker, 1956

BRYANT, PETER. Pseudonym of Peter (Bryan) George, 1924-1966, q.v. Other pseudonym: Bryan Peters, q.v.
Dr. Strangelove; see Two Hours to Doom
Red Alert; see Two Hours to Doom
Two Hours to Doom. Boardman, 1958. (Suppressed by British Intelligence under the Official Secrets Act.) U.S. title: Red Alert. Ace, 1958. Also published as: Dr. Strangelove, as by Peter George. Corgi, 1963; Bantam, 1963.

BRYANT, ROY
Clouds of Fear. Hammond, 1966

BRYCE, MRS. CHARLES
The Ashiel Mystery. Bodley Head, 1915
The Long Spoon. Bodley Head, 1917
Mrs. Vanderstein's Jewels. Bodley Head, 1914

BRYCE, LLOYD (STEPHENS). 1851-1917.
Romance of an Alter Ego. Brentano's, 1889; Routledge, 1891. Also published as: An Extraordinary Experience; or, The Romance of an Alter Ego. Brentano's, 1891

BRYDON, STANLEY
The Death Cap. Wright, 1962
Guns Over the Border. Wright, 1962
Harvest of Violence. Wright, 1960
Manhunt in Sicily. Wright, 1960
Nightmare Incident. Wright, 1963
Penman's Progress. Wright, 1961
Saraband for a Smuggler. Wright, 1961

BRYSON, CHARLES. 1887- . Pseudonym: Charles Barry, q.v.

BRYSON, LEIGH. Pseudonym of Nancy Rutledge, q.v.
The Gloved Hand. Handi-Books, 1947

BUCHAN, JOHN. 1875-1940. Series characters: Richard Hannay = RH; Edward Leithen = EL; Duncan McCunn = DM.
Castle Gay. Hodder, 1930; Houghton, 1930 DM
The Courts of Morning. Hodder, 1929; Houghton, 1929
The Dancing Floor. Hodder, 1926; Houghton, 1926 EL
The Gap in the Curtain. Hodder, 1932; Houghton, 1932 EL
Greenmantle. Hodder, 1916; Doran, 1915 RH
The House of the Four Winds. Hodder, 1935; Houghton, 1935 DM
Huntingtower. Hodder, 1922; Doran, 1922 DM
The Island of Sheep. Hodder, 1936. U.S. title: The Man from the Norlands. Houghton, 1936

Buchan, John

John Macnab. Hodder, 1925; Houghton, 1925 EL
The Man from the Norlands; see The Island of Sheep
Mr. Standfast. Hodder, 1919; Doran, 1919 RH
The Moon Endureth. Blackwood, 1912; Sturgis, 1912 ss, EL in one story
Mountain Meadow; see Sick Heart River
The Power-House. Blackwood, 1916; Doran, 1916 EL
-The Prince of the Captivity. Hodder, 1933; Houghton, 1933
The Runagates Club. Hodder, 1928; Houghton, 1928 ss, EL in one story
Sick Heart River. Hodder, 1941. U.S. title: Mountain Meadow. Houghton, 1941 EL
The Thirty-Nine Steps. Blackwood, 1915; Doran, 1915 RH
The Three Hostages. Hodder, 1924; Houghton, 1924 RH
The Watcher by the Threshold. Blackwood, 1902; Doran, 1918

BUCHAN, SINCLAIR
Singleton's Mill. Hodder, 1975

BUCHAN, STUART. 1942- .
Fleeced. Putnam, 1975; Hale, 1976

BUCHAN, WILLIAM (JAMES DE L'AIGLE). 1916- .
-The Blue Pavilion. Duckworth, 1966; Morrow, 1966
Helen All Alone. Duckworth, 1961; Morrow, 1961

BUCHANAN, B. J. Pseudonym: Joan Shepherd, q.v.

BUCHANAN, CARL
The Black Cloak Murders. Pearson, 1936
Night of Horror. Mellifont, 1939
The Red Scorpion. Mellifont, 1939

BUCHANAN, HUGH
The Masterful Voice. Hutchinson, 1927

BUCHANAN, JAMES DAVID
The Professional. Constable, 1972; Coward, 1972

BUCHANAN, MADELEINE SHARPS. -1940.
The Black Pearl Murders. McClurg, 1930
The Crimson Blade. Chelsea, 1926
Haunted Bells. Chelsea, 1929; Skeffington, 1930
The Poison Eye. Chelsea, 1928; Skeffington, 1930
Powdered Proof. Chelsea, 1927
The Subway Murder. McClurg, 1930

BUCHANAN, PATRICK. Joint pseudonym of Edwin Corley, 1931- , q.v., and Jack Murphy. Corley pseudonyms: David Harper, William Judson, qq.v. Series characters: Ben Shock and Charity Tucker, in all titles.
A Murder of Crows. Stein, 1970; Hale, 1973
A Parliament of Owls. Stein, 1971; Hale, 1973
A Requiem of Sharks. Dodd, 1973; H. Hamilton, 1975
A Sounder of Swine. Dodd, 1974

BUCHANAN, ROBERT (WILLIAM). 1841-1901.
-Foxglove Manor. Chatto, 1884
-The Moment After. Heinemann, 1890; Munro, 1890
The Strange Adventures of Miss Brown, with Charles Marlowe (pseudonym of Harriett Jay, 1857-1932). Buchanan, 1897; French, 1909

BUCHARD, ROBERT. 1931- .
Thirty Seconds Over New York. Morrow, 1970; Collins, 1970. (Translation of Trente Secondes sur New York. Paris, 1969.)

BUCK, CHARLES NEVILLE. 1879- .
Alias Red Ryan. Doubleday, 1923
A Gentleman in Pajamas. Century, 1924
Iron Will. Doubleday, 1927; Heinemann, 1927
Marked Men. Doubleday, 1929
Mountain Justice. Houghton, 1935
Portuguese Silver. Century, 1925
The Rogue's Badge. Doubleday, 1924; Heinemann, 1924

BUCK, PAUL. 1946- .
The Honeymoon Killers. Award, 1970; Sphere, 1970. (Novelization of the movie.)

BUCK, PEARL S(YDENSTRICKER). 1892-1973.
Death in the Castle. Day, 1965; Methuen, 1966

BUCKINGHAM, BRUCE. Joint pseudonym of Peter Lilley and Anthony Stansfeld. Series character: Don Pancho, in both titles.
Boiled Alive. Joseph, 1957
Three Bad Nights. Joseph, 1956

BUCKINGHAM, DAVID. Pseudonym of David Hugh Villiers. Series character: Sam Wharton, in both titles.
The Cliff Face. Macdonald, 1960
The Wind Tunnel. Macdonald, 1959

BUCKINGHAM, NANCY. Joint pseudonym of John and Nancy Sawyer.
Call of Glengarron. Ace, 1969; Hale, 1969
Cloud Over Malverton. Ace, 1967
Dark Summer. Ace, 1968
The Hour Before Moonrise. Ace, 1967
The House Called Edenhythe. Hawthorn, 1972
The Jade Dragon. Hawthorn, 1975; Hale, 1976
The Legend of Baverstock Manor. Ace, 1968
Quest for Alexis. Hawthorn, 1973
Return to Vienna. Dell, 1971
The Secret of the Ghostly Shroud. Lancer, 1969
Shroud of Silence. Hale, 1970. (U.S. title?)
Storm in the Mountains. Ace, 1967
Valley of the Ravens. Hawthorn, 1973; Hale, 1975

BUCKLEY, CHRISTOPHER
Rain Before Seven. Hodder, 1947
-Royal Chase. Hodder, 1949

BUCKLEY, EDITH E.
The Snare of Circumstance. Little, 1910

BUCKLEY, R(OBERT) J(OHN)
The Master Spy. Ward, 1902

BUCKMASTER, HENRIETTA. Pseudonym.
The Walking Trip. Harcourt, 1972; Gollancz, 1972

BUCKROSE, J. E. Pseudonym of Mrs. Annie Edith Foster Jameson, 1868-1931.
The Good-Natured Lady. Hodder, 1927

BUDD, JACKSON. Pseudonym of William John Budd, 1898- . Other pseudonyms: Wallace Jackson, q.v.
A Convict Has Escaped. Joseph, 1941
-The Dark Horseman. Joseph, 1939
Daughter of Illusion. Low, 1934
The Gallows Waits; see I Stood in the Shadow of the Black Cap
The Gold Express. Low, 1947
I Stood in the Shadow of the Black Cap. Low, 1932. U.S. title: The Gallows Waits. Putnam, 1932
John Lisbon, Agent. Joseph, 1942
Precious Company. Joseph, 1938
-The Princely Quartet. Low, 1932
The Story of Professor X. Stonevale, 1951
-The Three Jolly Vagabonds. Low, 1935
Tragedy in a Brick Box. Low, 1933
-A Wife in Toledo. Low, 1938

BUDD, JOHN. Pseudonym: Julian Prescot, q.v.

BUDD, WILLIAM JOHN. 1898- . Pseudonyms: Jackson Budd, Wallace Jackson, qq.v.

BUDE, JOHN. Pseudonym of Ernest Carpenter Elmore, 1901-1957. Series character: Inspector Meredith, in at least those marked M.
Another Man's Shadow. Macdonald, 1957
The Cheltenham Square Murder. Skeffington, 1937 M
The Constable and the Lady. Macdonald, 1951 M
The Cornish Coast Murder. Skeffington, 1935
Dangerous Sunlight. Macdonald, 1948
Death Deals a Double. Cassell, 1943
Death in Ambush. Macdonald, 1945 M
Death in White Pajamas. Cassell, 1944
Death Knows No Calendar. Cassell, 1942
Death Makes a Prophet. Macdonald, 1947 M
Death of a Cad. Hale, 1940
Death on Paper. Hale, 1940
Death on the Riviera. Macdonald, 1952
Death Steals the Show. Macdonald, 1950 M
A Glut of Red Herrings. Macdonald, 1949 M
Hand on the Alibi. Skeffington, 1939
The Lake District Murder. Skeffington, 1935 M
Loss of a Head. Skeffington, 1938
Murder in Montparnasse. Brown, 1949
The Night the Fog Came Down. Macdonald, 1958; Washburn, 1958
A Shift of Guilt. Macdonald, 1956
Slow Vengeance. Hale, 1941
So Much in the Dark. Macdonald, 1954
The Sussex Downs Murder. Skeffington, 1936 M
A Telegram from Le Touquet. Macdonald, 1956
Trouble A-Brewing. Macdonald, 1946 M
Twice Dead. Macdonald, 1953
A Twist of the Rope. Macdonald, 1958
Two Ends to the Town. Macdonald, 1955
When the Case was Opened. Macdonald, 1952

BUDRYS, ALGIS [ALGIRDAS JONAS BUDRYS]. 1931- .
Who? Pyramid, 1958; Badger, 1960

BUELL, JOHN (EDWARD). 1927- .
The Chosen Girl; see The Pyx
Four Days. Farrar, 1962; Macmillan (London), 1962
The Pyx. Farrar, 1959; Secker, 1960. Also published as: The Chosen Girl. Four Square, 1964
The Shrewsdale Exit. Farrar, 1972; Angus, 1973

BUFFER, JOE
Skull. Pinnacle, 1975

BUHET, GIL. 1908- .
-The Grand Catch. Cape, 1957. (Translation of Pierrot a la Belle Croche. Paris, 1956.)
-The Honey Siege. Cape, 1953. (Translation of Le Chevalier Pierrot. Paris, 1951.)
-Mamizelle Bon Voyage. Cape, 1960
-The Story Teller. Cape, 1955. (Translation of La Romanciere. Paris, 1954.)

BULL, LOIS. 1900- . Pseudonym: Melville Burt, q.v.
Broadway Virgin. Macaulay, 1931; Queensway, 1936

BULLETT, GERALD (WILLIAM). 1894-1958. Pseudonym: Sebastian Fox, q.v. See also: J(OHN) B(OYNTON) PRIESTLEY, 1894- .
Judgment in Suspense. Dent, 1946
The Jury. Dent, 1935; Knopf, 1935
A Man of Forty. Dent, 1940; Knopf, 1940
The Trouble at Number Seven. Joseph, 1952
When the Cat's Away. Dent, 1940; Knopf, 1941

BULLEY, H. A.
-The Seal of Confession. Greening, 1906

BULLIET, RICHARD WILLIAMS. 1940- . Pseudonym: Clarence J.-L. Jackson, q.v.

BULLIVANT, CECIL H(ENRY). 1882- . Series character: Garnett Bell, in at least those marked GB.
-Because of the Woman. Pearson, 1922
Blood Money. Long, 1924 GB
-A Broken Honeymoon. Wright, 1931
-The Call of the World. Wright, 1933
-A Daughter of Allah. Jarrolds, 1922
-A Desert Wooing. Aldine, 1923
-Destiny's Daughter. Wright, 1933
-The Devil's Double. Wright, 1932
-The Enchantress. Wright, 1932
-Eyes of Desire. Wright, 1931
-Fatal Power. Wright, 1934
The Fringe of the Law. Wright, 1931
Garnett Bell, Detective. Odhams, 1920 GB ss
-The Great Alternative. Lloyds, 1921
-The Hammer of God. Mellifont, 1935
-Innocence. Jarrolds, 1923
Jim the Penman. Mellifont, 1935
Judge Not. Long, 1926
A King of Crooks. Wright, 1932
-Love's Great Surrender. Wright, 1932
Millie Lynn, Shop Investigator. Odhams, 1920
-Naomi, the Modern. Long, 1925
-Quicksands of London. Aldine, 1917
-The Rose of Algiers. Long, 1924
-A Strong Man's Way. Odhams, 1919
The Ticket-of-Leave Man. Mellifont, 1935
-The Unbarred Door. Long, 1927
-White Raiment. Wright, 1930
Whose Wife? Jenkins, 1918
The Wife Whom God Forgot. Odhams, 1919
The Woman Always Wins; see The Woman Wins
The Woman Wins. Pearson, 1919. Also published as: The Woman Always Wins. Hale, 1937

BULLOCK, LOTTE
Aquarius Angel. Macmillan (London), 1970

BULWER-LYTTON, EDWARD (GEORGE EARLE). 1803-1873.
Alice; or, The Mysteries. Saunders, 1838; Harper, 1838
Ernest Maltravers. Saunders, 1837; Harper, 1837
Eugene Aram. Colburn, 1832; Harper, 1832. Also published as: The Strange Case of Eugene Aram. Collins, 1930
Godolphin. Bentley, 1833; Carey, 1833
Lucretia; or, The Children of the Night. Saunders, 1846; Harper, 1846
Pelham; or, The Adventures of a Gentleman. Colburn, 1828; Collins and Haunay, 1828
The Strange Case of Eugene Aram; see Eugene Aram
A Strange Story. Low, 1862; Lippincott, 1879

BUMPUS, DORIS MARJORIE. 1905- . Pseudonym: Marjorie Alan, q.v.
-Pattern in Beads. Hale, 1944

BUNCE, FRANK (DAVID). 1907- .
Rehearsal for Murder. Abelard (New York and London), 1956
So Young a Body. Simon, 1950; News of the World, 1952

BUNCE, SYDNEY (GEORGE)
No Sainted City. Angus, 1961
Take This Life. Angus, 1960

BUNKER, EDWARD. 1933- .
No Beast So Fierce. Norton, 1973. Also published as: Straight Time. Dell, 1978

BUNKER, JANE
Diamond Cut Diamond. Bobbs, 1912

BUNNELL, RICHARD D(AY)
Terror by Night. Naylor, 1957

BUNTLINE, NED. Pseudonym of Edward Zane Carroll Judson, 1821-1886.
The Battle of Hate; or, Hearts Are Trumps. Brady, 1865
The Convict; or, The Conspirator's Victim. Dick, 1863
The Curse! Roberts, 1847
The Death-Mystery. Brady, 1861
Eldrida, the Red Rover's Daughter. Brady, 1860
The Grossbeak Mansion. Brady, 1862
Hilliare Henderson; or, The Secret Revealed. Brady, 1861
The Mysteries and Miseries of New Orleans. Berford, 1848
The Mysteries and Miseries of New York. Judson, 1848
The Naval Detective's Chase; or, Nick the Steepleclimber. Street, 1889
Rose Seymour; or, The Ballet Girl's Revenge. Hilton, 1865
Three Years After. Burgess, 1849
The White Cruiser; or, The Fate of the Unheard-Of. Garrett, 1853
The White Wizard; or, The Great Prophet of the Seminoles. Brady, 1858

BURANELLI, PROSPER. 1890-1960. Joint pseudonym with John Chipman Farrar, 1896-1974: John Prosper, q.v.
Big Nick. Doubleday, 1931
The Happy Nightmare. Crown, 1953
News Reel Murder. Funk, 1940

BURBRIDGE, EDITH JOAN. 1919- . Pseudonym: Joan Cockin, q.v.

BURCHELL, SIDNEY HERBERT
The Grip of Fear. Hurst, 1906

BURDETT, CHARLES. 1815- .
The Gambler; or, The Policeman's Story. Baker and Scribner, 1848

BURDON, FREDERICK
The Squire of Kilderman; or, The Snake Bracelet. Henderson

BURFORD, ROGER D'ESTE. 1904- . Pseudonym: Roger East, q.v. Joint pseudonym with Oswell Blakeston, 1907- , q.v.: "Simon", q.v.

BURGE, MILWARD RODON KENNEDY. 1894- . Pseudonyms: Evelyn Elder, Milward Kennedy, qq.v. Joint pseudonym with (Archibald) Gordon McDonell, 1905- , q.v.: Robert Milward Kennedy, q.v.

BURGER, ROSAYLMER. Pseudonym: C. H. Wallace, q.v. Joint pseudonym with Julia Perceval: Jessyca Paull, q.v.

BURGESS, ANTHONY. Pseudonym of John Anthony Burgess Wilson, 1917- .
A Clockwork Orange. Heinemann, 1962; Norton, 1962
-The Doctor is Sick. Heinemann, 1960; Norton, 1960
Tremor of Intent. Heinemann, 1966; Norton, 1966

BURGESS, ERIC (ALEXANDER). 1912- . Series character: Harry Tong, in at least those marked HT.
Accident to Adeline. Joseph, 1952
Closely Confined. Hale, 1962 HT
Deadly Deceit. Hale, 1963 HT
Divided We Fall. Collins, 1959
Exit Pretty Poll. Hale, 1968
A Killing Frost. Collins, 1961 HT
A Knife for Celeste. Joseph, 1949
The Malice of Monday. Joseph, 1950

BURGESS, (FRANK) GELETT. 1866-1951.
Find the Woman. Bobbs, 1911
Ladies in Boxes. Alliance, 1942
The Master of Mysteries. Bobbs, 1912 ss (Published anonymously.)
A Murder at the Dome. Book Club of California, 1937. (26 pp.)
The Picaroons, with Will(iam Henry) Irwin, 1873-1948, q.v. McClure, 1904; Chatto, 1904 ss
Two O'Clock Courage. Bobbs, 1934; Nicholson, 1934
The White Cat. Bobbs, 1907; Chapman, 1908

BURGESS, HELEN STEERS. Pseudonym: Helen Steers, q.v.

BURGESS, WILLIAM WATSON. 1855- .
Life Sentence; or, Duty in Dealing with Crime. Badger, 1905

BURKE, CHARLES RUSSELL
-Thistle Sifters. Neely, 1898

BURKE, J(ACKSON) F. 1915- . Series character: Samuel Moses Kelly, in both titles.
Death Trick. Harper, 1975; Constable, 1976
Location Shots. Harper, 1974; Constable, 1974

BURKE, JAMES WAKEFIELD. 1916- .
Three Day Pass—to Kill. World Wide, 1954

BURKE, JOHN (FREDERICK). 1922- . Pseudonyms: Jonathan Burke, Harriet Esmond, Martin Sands, qq.v. Joint pseudonym with George Theiner, 1927- : Jonathan George, q.v.
The Angry Silence. Hodder, 1961. (Novelization of the movie.)

-Another Chorus. Laurie, 1949
-Chastity House. Laurie, 1952
-Expo 80. Cassell, 1972
Guilty Party. Elek, 1962. (Novelization of the play by George Ross and Campbell Singer.)
The Man Who Finally Died. Pan, 1963. (Novelization of the movie.)
-The Outward Walls. Laurie, 1952
The Poison Cupboard. Secker, 1956
Privilege. Pan, 1967; Avon, 1967. (Novelization of the movie.)
Strange Report. Hodder, 1970; Lancer, 1970. (Novelization of the TV series.)
-Swift Summer. Laurie, 1949
-These Haunted Streets. Laurie, 1950
The Trap. Pan, 1966. (Novelization of the movie.)

BURKE, JONATHAN. Pseudonym of John (Frederick) Burke, 1922-   , q.v. Other pseudonyms: Harriet Esmond, Martin Sands, qq.v. Joint pseudonym with George Theiner, 1927-   : Jonathan George, q.v.
Corpse to Copenhagen. Amalgamated, 1957 (Sexton Blake)
Deadly Downbeat. Long, 1962
Echo of Barbara. Long, 1959
Echo of Treason; see The Twisted Tongues
Fear by Instalments. Long, 1960
Four Stars for Danger. Long, 1970
Goodbye, Gillian; see The Weekend Girls
Gossip to the Grave. Long, 1967. U.S. title: The Gossip Truth. Doubleday, 1968
The Gossip Truth; see Gossip to the Grave
Only the Ruthless Can Play. Long, 1965
Rob the Lady. Long, 1969
Someone Lying, Someone Dying. Long, 1968
Teach Yourself Treachery. Long, 1962
The Twisted Tongues. Long, 1964. U.S. title (?): Echo of Treason. Dodd, 1966
The Weekend Girls. Long, 1966; Doubleday, 1967. Also published as: Goodbye, Gillian. Ace, 196?. Reprinted as by John Burke: Pan, 1968

BURKE, LEDA. Pseudonym of David Garnett, 1892-   , q.v.
Dope-Darling. Laurie, 1919

BURKE, MARGARET ISABEL
When Duty Calls. Dorrance, 1966

BURKE, NOEL. Pseudonym of (Julia Clara Catherine) Dolores (Birk Olsen) Hitchens, 1907-1972, q.v. Other pseudonyms: Dolan Birkley, D. B. Olsen, qq.v.
The Shivering Bough. Dutton, 1942

BURKE, RICHARD. 1886-   . Series character: Quinny Hite = QH.
Barbary Freight. Putnam, 1943; Boardman, 1945
Chinese Red. Putnam, 1942 QH
The Dead Take No Bows. Houghton, 1941 QH
The Fourth Star. Mystery House, 1946 QH
The Frightened Pigeon. Putnam, 1944; Jarrolds, 1946
Here Lies the Body. Putnam, 1942 QH
Murder on High Heels. Gateway, 1940
The Red Gate. Ziff-Davis, 1947
Reluctant Hussy. Curl, 1946; Jarrolds, 1947
Sinister Street. Ziff-Davis, 1948 QH

BURKE, SIMON
Death is the Pay-Off. Scion, 1949

BURKE, THOMAS. 1886-1945.
Abduction. Jenkins, 1939
The Bloomsbury Wonder. Mandrake, 1929
Broken Blossoms. Richards, 1920. (A selection of ss from Limehouse Nights, q.v.)
Dark Nights. Jenkins, 1944 (ss, including The Bloomsbury Wonder, q.v.)
East of Mansion House. Cassell, 1928; Doran, 1926 ss
In Chinatown. Richards, 1921. (A selection of ss from Limehouse Nights, q.v.)
Limehouse Nights. Richards, 1916; McBride, 1917 ss
More Limehouse Nights; see Whispering Windows
Murder at Elstree. Longmans, 1936
Night Pieces. Constable, 1935; Appleton, 1936 ss
The Pleasantries of Old Quong. Constable, 1931. U.S. title: A Tea-Shop in Limehouse. Little, 1931 ss
A Tea-Shop in Limehouse; see The Pleasantries of Old Quong
Whispering Windows. Richards, 1921. U.S. title: More Limehouse Nights. Doran, 1921 ss

BURKHARDT, EVE. 1899-   . Joint pseudonyms with Robert Ferdinand Burkhardt, 1892-1947: Adam Bliss, Rex Jardin, qq.v.

BURKHARDT, ROBERT FERDINAND. 1892-1947. Joint pseudonyms with Eve Burkhardt, 1899-   : Adam Bliss, Rex Jardin, qq.v.

BURKHOLZ, HERBERT. 1932-   .
Mulligan's Seed. Harcourt, 1975

BURKS, ALLISON L.
Tight Rope. Duell, 1945; Heinemann, 1947

BURLAND, HARRIS. See: J(OHN) B(URLAND) HARRIS-BURLAND, 1870-   .

BURLEIGH, DONALD Q(UIMBY). 1894-   .
The Kristiana Killers. Dutton, 1937

BURLEIGH, FLORENCE (S. HOWARD)
The Applewood Mystery. Fiction House, 1942

BURLEIGH, HILARY
Murder at Maison Manche. Hurst, 1948

BURLEY, W(ILLIAM) J(OHN). 1914-   . Series characters: Henry Pym = HP; Superintendent Charles Wycliffe = CW.
Death in a Salubrious Place. Gollancz, 1973; Walker, 1973 CW
Death in Stanley Street. Gollancz, 1974; Walker, 1974 CW
Death in Willow Pattern. Gollancz, 1969; Walker, 1970 HP
Guilt Edged. Gollancz, 1971; Walker, 1972 CW
A Taste of Power. Gollancz, 1966 HP
Three-Toed Pussy. Gollancz, 1968 CW
To Kill a Cat. Gollancz, 1970; Walker, 1970 CW
Wycliffe and the Pea-Green Boat. Gollancz, 1975; Walker, 1975 CW

"BURMAR". Pseudonym of Richard Marr.
The Smith Slayer. Gardner, 1939. Reprinted as by Richard Marr: Big Ben, 1940

BURMEISTER, JON. 1933-   .
Running Scared. Joseph, 1972; St. Martin's, 1973
Someone Else's War. Joseph, 1973; St. Martin's, 1974
The Weatherman Guy. Joseph, 1975; St. Martin's, 1975

BURNABY, NIGEL. Pseudonym of Harold Pincton Ellett, 1882-   . Series character: Chief Inspector Drewry = D.
The Clue of the Green-Eyed Girl. Ward, 1935 D
The Forest Mystery. Ward, 1934
The Secret of Matchams. Ward, 1934
Two Deaths for a Penny. Ward, 1935 D

BURNE, GLEN. Joint pseudonym of Alan (Baer) Green, 1906-1975, q.v., and Gladys Elizabeth Blun Green, 1908-   . Joint pseudonym of Alan (Baer) Green and Julian P. Brodie: Roger Denbie, q.v.
Murder to Music. Dodd, 1934

BURNETT, GEORGE (STANLEY)
Dead Account. Hodder, 1966
The Finsbury Lot. Hodder, 1963
The Sheep and the Wolves. Hodder, 1962
Violent Security. Hodder, 1962

BURNETT, HALLIE (SOUTHGATE). 1908-   .
Watch on the Wall. Morrow, 1965

BURNETT, W(ILLIAM) R(ILEY). 1899-   . Pseudonym: John Monahan, q.v.
The Asphalt Jungle. Knopf, 1949; Macdonald, 1950
Conant. Popular Library, 1961
The Cool Man. GM, 1968
Dark Hazard. Harper, 1933; Heinemann, 1934
High Sierra. Knopf, 1940; Heinemann, 1940
King Cole. Harper, 1936. British title: Six Days' Grace. Heinemann, 1937
Little Caesar. Dial, 1929; Cape, 1929
Little Men, Big World. Knopf, 1951; Macdonald, 1952
Nobody Lives Forever. Knopf, 1943; Heinemann, 1944
The Quick Brown Fox. Knopf, 1942; Heinemann, 1943
Romelle. Knopf, 1946; Heinemann, 1947
Round the Clock at Volari's. GM, 1961
The Silver Eagle. Dial, 1931; Heinemann, 1932
Six Days' Grace; see King Cole
Tomorrow's Another Day. Knopf, 1945; Heinemann, 1946
Underdog. Knopf, 1957; Macdonald, 1957
Vanity Row. Knopf, 1952; Macdonald, 1953
The Widow Barony. Macdonald, 1962 (U.S. title?)

BURNHAM, CLARA LOUISE (ROOT). 1854-1927.
Tobey's First Case. Houghton, 1926

BURNHAM, DAVID. 1907-   .
Last Act in Bermuda. Scribner, 1940

BURNHAM, HELEN. Series character: "One Week" Wimble, in both titles.
The Murder of Lalla Lee. McBride, 1931; Arrowsmith, 1931
The Telltale Telegram. McBride, 1932

BURNING, MICHAEL and ALTHEA GREY
Dusty Death. Jenkins, 1949

BURNS, MARY LOVELAND
Murder at Crawford Notch. Humphries, 1944

BURNS, REX
 The Alvarez Journal. Harper, 1975; Hale, 1976

BURNS, WILLIAM J., 1861-1932, and ISABEL (EGENTON) OSTRANDER, 1883-1924, q.v. Pseudonyms of Isobel Ostrander: Robert Orr Chipperfield, David Fox, Douglas Grant, qq.v.
 The Crevice. Watt, 1915. British title: The Lawton Mystery. Nash, 1917

BURR, ANNA (ROBESON BROWN). 1873-1941.
 -Alain of Halfdene. Lippincott, 1895
 The Bottom of the Matter. Appleton, 1935
 The Great House in the Park. Duffield, 1924
 -The House on Charles Street. Duffield, 1921
 The House on Smith Square. Duffield, 1923
 -The Jessop Bequest. Houghton, 1907
 Palludia. Duffield, 1928; Melrose, 1929
 West of the Moon. Duffield, 1926; Melrose, 1927
 Wind in the East. Duffield, 1933
 The Wrong Move. Macmillan, 1923; Brentano's (London), 1924

BURRAGE, A(LFRED) M(cLELLAND). 1889- .
 Courtland's Crime. Long, 1928
 Don't Break the Seal. Swan, 1946
 -The Golden Barrier. Leng, 1925
 -Poor Dear Esme. Newnes, 1925
 Seeker to the Dead. Swan, 1942
 -The Smokes of Spring. Long, 1926

BURRAGE, ALFRED S.
 The Man with the Yellow Eyes; or, The Woman of Mystery. Henderson

BURRAGE, E(DWIN) HARCOURT
 Ching Ching on the Trail. Lucas, 1892
 The Fatal Nugget. Partridge, 1900
 The Missing Million. Partridge, 1897
 The Vanished Yacht. Nelson, 1898

BURREN, MICHAEL. See: GEORGE MARTON, 1900- .

BURROUGHS, EDGAR RICE. 1875-1950.
 The Oakdale Affair. Burroughs, 1937

BURROWS, JULIE
 Like an Evening Gone. Macmillan (London), 1973
 No Need for Violence. Cassell, 1970

BURT, K(ATHERINE) N(EWLIN). 1882-1977.
 Beggars All. Houghton, 1933
 Captain Millett's Island. Macrae-Smith, 1944
 -Rapture Beyond. Scribner, 1935
 The Red Lady. Houghton, 1920; Constable, 1920
 -Safe Road. Macrae-Smith, 1938
 Still Water. Macrae-Smith, 1948; Coker, 1951
 -When Beggars Choose. Macrae-Smith, 1937

BURT, MELVILLE. Pseudonym of Lois Bull, 1900- , q.v.
 The Granville Crypt Murders. Macaulay, 1936
 The Yellow Robe Murders. Macaulay, 1935

BURT, MICHAEL. 1900- . Series character: Roger Poynings = RP.
 The Case of the Angels' Trumpets. Ward, 1947 RP
 The Case of the Fast Young Lady. Ward, 1942 RP
 The Case of the Laughing Jesuit. Ward, 1948 RP
 Catch-'Em-Alive-O! Chambers, 1938
 The House of Sleep. Ward, 1945
 Secret Orchards. Ward, 1938

BURTIS, THOMSON. 1896- .
 Flying Blood. Fiction League, 1932

BURTON, CARL D. 1913- .
 -The Long Goodnight. Morrow, 1961

BURTON, EDMUND
 The Riddle of the Cloisters. Pendulum, 1946
 The Royal Special, and other stories. Century, 1947 ss

BURTON, EDWARD J. 1917- . Pseudonym: Michael Carey, q.v.

BURTON, FREDERICK R(USSELL). 1861-1909.
 A Seven Day's Mystery. Street (Magnet), 1900

BURTON, MAX
 The Mound Hill Mystery. Fortuny's, 1938

BURTON, MILES. Pseudonym of Cecil John Charles Street, 1884-1961. Other pseudonym: John Rhode, q.v. Series characters: Inspector Arnold and Desmond Merrion, almost always together, in all titles except The Hardway Diamonds Mystery and Murder at the Moorings.
 Accidents Do Happen; see Early Morning Murder
 Beware Your Neighbor. Collins, 1951
 Bones in the Brickfield. Collins, 1958
 The Cat Jumps. Collins, 1946
 The Charabanc Mystery. Collins, 1934
 The Chinese Puzzle. Collins, 1957
 The Clue of the Fourteen Keys; see Death at the Club
 The Clue of the Silver Brush; see The Milk Churn Murder
 The Clue of the Silver Cellar; see Where is Barbara Prentice?
 A Crime in Time. Collins, 1955
 Dark is the Tunnel; see Death in the Tunnel
 Dead Stop. Collins, 1943
 Death at Ash House; see This Undesirable Residence
 Death at Low Tide. Collins, 1938
 Death at the Club. Collins, 1937. U.S. title: The Clue of the Fourteen Keys. Doubleday, 1937
 Death at the Crossroads. Collins, 1933
 Death in a Duffle Coat. Collins, 1956
 Death in Shallow Water. Collins, 1948
 Death in the Tunnel. Collins, 1936. U.S. title: Dark is the Tunnel. Doubleday, 1936
 Death Leaves No Card. Collins, 1939
 Death of Mr. Gantley. Collins, 1932
 Death of Two Brothers. Collins, 1941
 Death Paints a Picture. Collins, 1960
 Death Takes a Detour. Collins, 1958
 Death Takes a Flat. Collins, 1940. U.S. title: Vacancy with Corpse. Doubleday, 1941
 Death Takes the Living. Collins, 1949. U.S. title: The Disappearing Parson. Doubleday, 1949
 Death Visits Downspring; see Up the Garden Path
 The Devereux Court Mystery. Collins, 1935
 Devil's Reckoning. Collins, 1948; Doubleday, 1949
 The Disappearing Parson; see Death Takes the Living
 Early Morning Murder. Collins, 1945. U.S. title: Accidents Do Happen. Doubleday, 1946
 Fate at the Fair. Collins, 1933
 Found Drowned. Collins, 1956
 Four-Ply Yarn. Collins, 1944. U.S. title: The Shadow on the Cliff. Doubleday, 1944
 Ground for Suspicion. Collins, 1950
 The Hardway Diamonds Mystery. Collins, 1930; Mystery League, 1930
 Heir to Lucifer. Collins, 1947
 Heir to Murder. Collins, 1953
 Legacy of Death. Collins, 1960
 Look Alive. Collins, 1949; Doubleday, 1950
 The Man with the Tattooed Face; see Murder in Crown Passage
 The Menace on the Downs. Collins, 1931
 The Milk Churn Murder. Collins, 1935. U.S. title: The Clue of the Silver Brush. Doubleday, 1936
 Mr. Babbacombe Dies. Collins, 1939
 Mr. Westerby Missing. Collins, 1940; Doubleday, 1940
 The Moth-Watch Murder. Collins, 1957
 Murder at the Moorings. Collins, 1932; Sears, 1934
 Murder in Absence. Collins, 1954
 Murder in Crown Passage. Collins, 1937. U.S. title: The Man with the Tattooed Face. Doubleday, 1937
 Murder in the Coalhole. Collins, 1940. U.S. title: Written in Dust. Doubleday, 1940
 Murder M.D. Collins, 1943. U.S. title: Who Killed the Doctor? Doubleday, 1943
 Murder of a Chemist. Collins, 1936
 Murder on Duty. Collins, 1952
 Murder Out of School. Collins, 1951
 Murder Unrecognized. Collins, 1955
 The Mystery of High Eldersham; see The Secret of High Eldersham
 Not a Leg to Stand On. Collins, 1945; Doubleday, 1945
 The Platinum Cat. Collins, 1938; Doubleday, 1938
 Return from the Dead. Collins, 1959
 The Secret of High Eldersham. Collins, 1930; Mystery League, 1931. Also published as: The Mystery of High Eldersham. Collins, 1933
 The Shadow on the Cliff; see Four-Ply Yarn
 Situation Vacant. Collins, 1946
 A Smell of Smoke. Collins, 1959
 Something to Hide. Collins, 1953
 This Undesirable Residence. Collins, 1942. U.S. title: Death at Ash House. Doubleday, 1942
 The Three Corpse Trick. Collins, 1944
 The Three Crimes. Collins, 1931
 To Catch a Thief. Collins, 1934
 Tragedy at the Thirteenth Hole. Collins, 1933
 Unwanted Corpse. Collins, 1954
 Up the Garden Path. Collins, 1941. U.S. title: Death Visits Downspring. Doubleday, 1941
 Vacancy with Corpse; see Death Takes a Flat
 A Village Afraid. Collins, 1950
 Where is Barbara Prentice? Collins, 1936. U.S. title: The Clue of the Silver Cellar. Doubleday, 1937
 Who Killed the Doctor?; see Murder M.D.
 A Will in the Way. Collins, 1947; Doubleday, 1947
 Written in Dust; see Murder in the Coalhole

BURTON, MINA E.
 Ruling the Planets. Bentley, 1891; Harper, 1892

BUSBY, ROGER. Series character: Detective-Inspector Leric = L.
 Deadlock. Collins, 1971 L
 The Frighteners. Collins, 1970 L

Main Line Kill, with Gerald Holtham. Cassell, 1968; Walker, 1968
Pattern of Violence. Collins, 1973 L
A Reasonable Man. Collins, 1972 L
Robbery Blue. Collins, 1969 L

BUSCHLEN, JOHN PRESTON. 1888-   . Pseudonym: Jack Preston, q.v.

BUSH, CHRISTOPHER. 1885-1973. Pseudonym: Michael Home, q.v. Series character: Ludovic Travers, in all titles.
The Body in the Bonfire; see The Case of the Bonfire Body
The Case of the Amateur Actor. Macdonald, 1955; Macmillan, 1956
The Case of the April Fools. Cassell, 1933; Morrow, 1933
The Case of the Benevolent Bookie. Macdonald, 1955; Macmillan, 1956
The Case of the Bonfire Body. Cassell, 1936. U.S. title: The Body in the Bonfire. Holt, 1936
The Case of the Burnt Bohemian. Macdonald, 1953; Macmillan, 1954
The Case of the Careless Thief. Macdonald, 1959; Macmillan, 1960
The Case of the Chinese Gong. Cassell, 1935; Holt, 1935
The Case of the Climbing Rat. Cassell, 1940
The Case of the Corner Cottage. Macdonald, 1951; Macmillan, 1952
The Case of the Corporal's Leave. Cassell, 1945
The Case of the Counterfeit Colonel. Macdonald, 1952; Macmillan, 1953
The Case of the Curious Client. Macdonald, 1947; Macmillan, 1948
The Case of the Dead Man Gone. Macdonald, 1961; Macmillan, 1962
The Case of the Dead Shepherd. Cassell, 1934. U.S. title: The Tea Tray Murders. Morrow, 1934
The Case of the Deadly Diamonds. Macdonald, 1967; Macmillan, 1968
The Case of the Extra Grave. Macdonald, 1961; Macmillan, 1962
The Case of the Extra Man. Macdonald, 1956; Macmillan, 1957
The Case of the Fighting Soldier. Cassell, 1942
The Case of the Flowery Corpse. Macdonald, 1956; Macmillan, 1957
The Case of the Flying Ass. Cassell, 1939
The Case of the Fourth Detective. Macdonald, 1951
The Case of the Frightened Mannequin; see The Case of the Happy Warrior
The Case of the Good Employer. Macdonald, 1966; Macmillan, 1966
The Case of the Grand Alliance. Macdonald, 1964; Macmillan, 1965
The Case of the Green Felt Hat. Cassell, 1939; Holt, 1939
The Case of the Hanging Rope. Cassell, 1937. U.S. title: The Wedding Night Murder. Holt, 1937
The Case of the Happy Medium. Macdonald, 1952; Macmillan, 1952
The Case of the Happy Warrior. Macdonald, 1950. U.S. title: The Case of the Frightened Mannequin. Macmillan, 1951
The Case of the Haven Hotel. Macdonald, 1948
The Case of the Heavenly Twin. Macdonald, 1963; Macmillan, 1964
The Case of the Housekeeper's Hair. Macdonald, 1948; Macmillan, 1949
The Case of the Jumbo Sandwich. Macdonald, 1965; Macmillan, 1966
The Case of the Kidnapped Colonel. Cassell, 1942
The Case of the Leaning Man. Cassell, 1938. U.S. title: The Leaning Man. Holt, 1938
The Case of the Magic Mirror. Cassell, 1943
The Case of the Missing Men. Macdonald, 1946; Macmillan, 1947
The Case of the Missing Minutes. Cassell, 1937. U.S. title: Eight O'Clock Alibi. Holt, 1937
The Case of the Monday Murders. Cassell, 1936. U.S. title: Murder on Monday. Holt, 1936
The Case of the Murdered Major. Cassell, 1941
The Case of the 100% Alibis. Cassell, 1934. U.S. title: The Kitchen Cake Murder. Morrow, 1934
The Case of the Platinum Blonde. Cassell, 1944; Macmillan, 1949
The Case of the Prodigal Daughter. Macdonald, 1968; Macmillan, 1969
The Case of the Purloined Picture. Macdonald, 1949; Macmillan, 1951
The Case of the Red Brunette. Macdonald, 1954; Macmillan, 1955
The Case of the Running Man. Macdonald, 1958; Macmillan, 1959
The Case of the Running Mouse. Cassell, 1944
The Case of the Russian Cross. Macdonald, 1957; Macmillan, 1958
The Case of the Sapphire Brooch. Macdonald, 1960; Macmillan, 1961
The Case of the Second Chance. Macdonald, 1946; Macmillan, 1947
The Case of the Seven Bells. Macdonald, 1949; Macmillan, 1950
The Case of the Silken Petticoat. Macdonald, 1953; Macmillan, 1954
The Case of the Three Lost Letters. Macdonald, 1954; Macmillan, 1955
The Case of the Three-Ring Puzzle. Macdonald, 1962; Macmillan, 1963
The Case of the Three Strange Faces. Cassell, 1933. U.S. title: The Crank in the Corner. Morrow, 1933
The Case of the Treble Twist. Macdonald, 1958. U.S. title: The Case of the Triple Twist. Macmillan, 1958
The Case of the Triple Twist; see The Case of the Treble Twist
The Case of the Tudor Queen. Cassell, 1938; Holt, 1938
The Case of the Unfortunate Village. Cassell, 1932
The Crank in the Corner; see The Case of the Three Strange Faces
Cut Throat. Heinemann, 1932; Morrow, 1932
Dancing Death. Heinemann, 1931; Doubleday, 1931
Dead Man Twice. Heinemann, 1930; Doubleday, 1930
Dead Man's Music. Heinemann, 1931; Doubleday, 1932
The Death of Cosmo Revere; see Murder at Fenwold
Eight O'Clock Alibi; see The Case of the Missing Minutes
The Kitchen Cake Murder; see The Case of the 100% Alibis
The Leaning Man; see The Case of the Leaning Man
Murder at Fenwold. Heinemann, 1930. U.S. title: The Death of Cosmo Revere. Doubleday, 1930
Murder on Monday; see The Case of the Monday Murders
The Perfect Murder Case. Heinemann, 1929; Doubleday, 1929
The Plumley Inheritance. Jarrolds, 1926
The Tea Tray Murders; see The Case of the Dead Shepherd
The Wedding Night Murder; see The Case of the Hanging Rope

BUSH-FEKETE, MARY. Pseudonym: M. Fagyas, q.v.

BUSNACH, WILLIAM (BERTRAND), 1832-1907, and CHABRILLAT, HENRI
Lecoq, the Detective's Daughter. Vizetelly, 1888. (Translation of La Fille de M. Lecoq.)

BUSSELL, CHASE
The Mountain Cabin Mystery. Dorrance, 1935

BUTCHER, MARGARET
Comet's Hair. Skeffington, 1939
Destiny on Demand. Skeffington, 1938
Hogdown Farm Mystery. Skeffington, 1950
Vacant Possession. Skeffington, 1940

BUTLER, ELLIS PARKER. 1869-1937.
Philo Gubb, Correspondence School Detective. Houghton, 1919 ss

BUTLER, EWAN
Conspiracy of Silence. Hodder, 1950
Strange Sanctuary. Hodder, 1949

BUTLER, GEORGE (FRANK). 1857-1921.
The Exploits of a Physician Detective. Clinic, 1908 ss

BUTLER, GERALD (ALFRED). 1907-   .
Blow Hot, Blow Cold; see Choice of Two Women
Choice of Two Women. Jarrolds, 1951. U.S. title: Blow Hot, Blow Cold. Rinehart, 1951
Dark Rainbow; see Their Rainbow Had Black Edges
Kiss the Blood Off My Hands. Nicholson, 1940; Rinehart, 1946. Also published as: The Unafraid. Dell, 1948
The Lurking Man; see Mad with Much Heart
Mad with Much Heart. Jarrolds, 1945; Rinehart, 1946. Also published as: The Lurking Man. Lion, 1952
Slippery Hitch. Jarrolds, 1948; Rinehart, 1949
Their Rainbow Had Black Edges. Jarrolds, 1943. U.S. title: Dark Rainbow. Farrar, 1945
There is a Death, Elizabeth. Hale, 1972
They Cracked Her Glass Slipper. Jarrolds, 1941
The Unafraid; see Kiss the Blood Off My Hands

BUTLER, GWENDOLINE (WILLIAMS). 1922-   . Pseudonym: Jennie Melville, q.v. Series character: Inspector John Coffin, in at least those marked JC.
Coffin Following. Bles, 1968 JC
Coffin for Baby. Bles, 1963; Walker, 1963 JC
A Coffin for Pandora. Macmillan (London), 1973 JC
A Coffin for the Canary. Macmillan (London), 1974 JC
A Coffin from the Past. Bles, 1970 JC
Coffin in Malta. Bles, 1964; Walker, 1965 JC
Coffin in Oxford. Bles, 1962 JC
Coffin Waiting. Bles, 1963; Walker, 1963 JC
Coffin's Dark Number. Bles, 1969 JC
Dead in a Row. Bles, 1957 JC
Death Lives Next Door. Bles, 1960. U.S. title: Dine and Be Dead. Macmillan, 1960 JC
Dine and Be Dead; see Death Lives Next Door
The Dull Dead. Bles, 1958; Walker, 1962
The Interloper. Bles, 1959
Make Me a Murderer. Bles, 1961 JC

The Murdering Kind. Bles, 1958; Roy,
   1964
A Nameless Coffin. Bles, 1966; Walker,
   1967 JC
Olivia. Coward, 1974. (British title?)
Receipt for Murder. Bles, 1956
Sarsen Place. Coward, 1974. (British
   title?)
The Vesey Inheritance. Macmillan (London), 1976; Coward, 1975

BUTLER, IVAN. See: A(RTHUR) A(LEXANDER
   MALCOLM) THOMSON, 1884-   .

BUTLER, JOAN. Pseudonym of Robert William
   Alexander, 1905-   .
Rapid Fire. Paul, 1939
Something Rich. Paul, 1937

BUTLER, K(ATHARINE) R(OSEMARY)
A Desert of Salt. Hodder, 1965; Mill,
   1964
The Evil Damp. Bles, 1966
A Fall of Rock. Bles, 1967
Kanaga. Bles, 1971
Quirindi. Bles, 1970

BUTLER, LESLIE
The Man Who Crawled Away. Hale, 1966
Night and the Judgement. Hale, 1964
Recover or Kill. Hale, 1965

BUTLER, RICHARD. 1925-   .
The Buffalo Hook. Long, 1974
Fingernail Beach. Long, 1964
More Dangerous Than the Moon; see South
   of Hell's Gates
Sharkbait. Long, 1970
South of Hell's Gates. Long, 1967. U.S.
   title: More Dangerous Than the Moon.
   Walker, 1968
Where All the Girls are Sweeter.
   Davis, 1975

BUTLER, WALTER C. Pseudonym of Frederick
   Schiller Faust, 1892-1944. Other
   pseudonyms: Max Brand, Frederick
   Frost, qq.v.
Cross Over Nine. Macaulay, 1935
The Night Flower. Macaulay, 1936

BUTLER, WILLIAM. 1929-   .
-The Bone House. Owen, 1972
-The Butterfly Revolution. Owen, 1962;
   Putnam, 1967
-Cire Perdue. Owen, 1965
-A Danish Gambit. Owen, 1966
-The Experiment. Owen, 1961
-Man in a Net. Owen, 1971
-Mr. Three. Owen, 1964; Putnam, 1966
-The Ring in Meiji. Owen, 1965; Putnam,
   1965
-Spying at the Fountain of Youth. Owen,
   1968

BUTTENSHAW, DIANA (MARGUERITE)
-Chain of Command. Hodder, 1950
-Violence in Paradise. Hodder, 1957

BUTTERWORTH, MICHAEL. 1924-   . Pseudonym: Carola Salisbury, q.v.
The Black Look. Collins, 1972; Doubleday, 1972
Flowers for a Dead Witch. Collins,
   1971; Doubleday, 1971
The Man in the Sopwith Camel. Collins,
   1974; Doubleday, 1974
The Soundless Scream. Long, 1967;
   Doubleday, 1967
The Uneasy Sun; see Vanishing Act
Vanishing Act. Collins, 1970. U.S.
   title: The Uneasy Sun. Doubleday,
   1970
Villa on the Shore. Collins, 1973;
   Doubleday, 1974
Walk Softly in Fear. Long, 1968

BUTTERWORTH, W(ILLIAM) E(DMUND III).
   1929-   . Pseudonym: Webb Beech,
   q.v.
Hot Seat. Signet, 1961

BUXTON, ANNE. Pseudonyms: Anne Maybury,
   Katherine Troy, qq.v.

BYERS, BRUCE
Agent of the Id. Hale, 1974
All My Dead Men. Hale, 1973

BYERS, C(HARLES) A(LMA)
The Inverness Murder. Dial, 1935

BYFIELD, BARBARA NINDE and TEDESCHI,
   FRANK L.
Solemn High Murder. Doubleday, 1975;
   Davies, 1976

BYFORD-JONES, W(ILFRED)
Death by Order. Modern, 193?

BYRNE, MARY
Murder at the "Signal". Long, 1936

BYROM, JAMES. Pseudonym of James Guy
   Bramwell, 1911-   .
Or Be He Dead. Chatto, 1958
Take Only as Directed. Chatto, 1959

BYRON, JAMES
TNT for Two. Ace, 1956

C

C. R. B. Pseudonym of Charles Hull.
-Redeemed. Dillingham, 1894

CABALLERO, ANN
Stranger in the House. Coward, 1965

CABLE, BOYD. Pseudonym of Ernest Andrew
   Ewart, 1878-1943.
-A Double Scoop. Hutchinson, 1924
The Flying Courier. Wright, 1936

CABOT, ISABEL
The Missing Witness. Avalon, 1961
Murder is a House Guest. Avalon, 1962

CABOT, JOAN
Vail's Gate. Lenox Hill, 1970

CADE, ALEXANDER. Pseudonym of Kenneth
   (Walter) Methold, 1931-   , q.v.
Turn Up a Stone. Bles, 1969

CADE, COULSON T.
-The Cornish Penny. Richards, 1922;
   Stokes, 1922

CADE, PAUL
Death Slams the Door. Modern Age, 1937

CADE, ROBIN. Pseudonym of Christopher
   Robin Nicole, 1930-   . Other pseudonym: Andrew York, q.v.
The Fear Dealers. Cassell, 1974; Simon,
   1974

CADELL, (VIOLET) ELIZABETH. 1903-   .
   Pseudonym: Harriet Ainsworth, q.v.
Alice, Where Art Thou? Hodder, 1959
Canary Yellow. Hodder, 1965; Morrow,
   1965
Crystal Clear; see Journey's Eve
Deck with Flowers. Hodder, 1973; Morrow, 1974
The Fox from his Lair. Hodder, 1965;
   Morrow, 1966
-Journey's Eve. Hodder, 1953. U.S.
   title: Crystal Clear. Morrow, 1953
The Yellow Brick Road. Hodder, 1960;
   Morrow, 1960

CADETT, HERBERT
The Adventures of a Journalist. Sands,
   1900 ss

CADMAN, JOHN
With Dead Bodies. Stockwell, 1957 ss

CAGNEY, PETER. Pseudonym of Bevis Winter,
   1918-   , q.v. Other pseudonyms: Al
   Bocca, Gordon Shayne, qq.v.
A Grave for Madam. Jenkins, 1961
Hear the Stripper Scream. Jenkins,
   1960; Roy, 1962
No Diamonds for a Doll. Jenkins, 1960;
   Roy, 1961

CAIDIN, MARTIN. 1927-   . Series character: Steve Austin, in at least those
   marked SA.
Almost Midnight. Morrow, 1971; Bantam
   (London), 1974
Anytime, Anywhere. Dutton, 1969; Allen,
   1970
-The Cape. Doubleday, 1971
Cyborg. Arbor, 1972; Allen, 1973 SA
Cyborg IV. Arbor, 1975; Allen, 1977 SA
Devil Take All. Dutton, 1966; Allen,
   1968
-Four Came Back. McKay, 1968
-The God Machine. Dutton, 1968
High Crystal. Arbor, 1974; Allen, 1975
   SA
The Last Fathom. Meredith, 1967;
   Joseph, 1969
-Marooned. Dutton, 1964; Hodder, 1964
Maryjane Tonight at Angels Twelve.
   Doubleday, 1972
The Mendelov Conspiracy. Meredith,
   1969; Allen, 1971
-No Man's World. Dutton, 1967
Operation Nuke. Arbor, 1973; Allen,
   1974 SA
Three Corners to Nowhere. Bantam, 1975;
   Corgi, 1975

CAILLOU, ALAN. Pseudonym of Allan Lyle-Smythe, 1914-   . Series characters:
   Cabot Cain = CC; Mike Benasque = MB.
Alien Virus. Davies, 1957
Assault on Aimata. Avon, 1975 CC
Assault on Agathon. Avon, 1972 CC
Assault on Fellawi. Avon, 1972 CC
Assault on Kolchak. Avon, 1969 CC
Assault on Loveless. Avon, 1969 CC
Assault on Ming. Avon, 1970 CC
A Journey to Orassia. Doubleday, 1965;
   Allen, 1966
Marseilles. PB, 1964 MB
The Mindanao Pearl. Davies, 1959
The Plotters. Harper, 1960; Davies,
   1960
Rogue's Gambit. Davies, 1955
Who'll Buy My Evil? PB, 1966 MB

CAIN, JAMES M(ALLAHAN). 1892-1977.
The Butterfly. Knopf, 1947. British
   publication in: Three of Hearts, q.v.
Career in C Major and other stories.
   Avon, 1943. British publication of
   title story in: Three of Hearts, q.v.
   ss
Double Indemnity. Avon, 1943. British
   publication, and American republication, in: Three of a Kind, q.v.
The Embezzler. Avon, 1944. British publication, and American republication,
   in: Three of a Kind, q.v.
Galatea. Knopf, 1953; Hale, 1954
Jealous Woman. Avon, 1948; Hale, 1955,
   also containing the first British
   publication of Sinful Woman, q.v.
Love's Lovely Counterfeit. Knopf, 1942.
   British publication in: Three of
   Hearts, q.v.
The Magician's Wife. Dial, 1965; Hale,
   1966
Mignon. Dial, 1962; Hale, 1963
Mildred Pierce. Knopf, 1941; Hale, 1943

The Moth. Knopf, 1948; Hale, 1950
Past All Dishonor. Knopf, 1946. British publication in: Three of Hearts, q.v.
The Postman Always Rings Twice. Knopf, 1934; Cape, 1934
Rainbow's End. Mason/Charter, 1975; Allen, 1975
The Root of His Evil. Avon, 1952; Hale, 1954. Also published as: Shameless. Avon, 1958
Serenade. Knopf, 1937; Cape, 1938
Shameless; see The Root of His Evil
Sinful Woman. Avon, 1948; Hale, 1955, in Jealous Woman, q.v.
Three of a Kind. Knopf, 1944; Hale, 1945. (Contents: Career in C Major, The Embezzler, and Double Indemnity, qq.v.)
Three of Hearts. Hale, 1949. (Contents: Love's Lovely Counterfeit, Past All Dishonor, and The Butterfly, qq.v.)

CAIN, PAUL. Pseudonym of George Sims, 1902-1966.
Fast One. Doubleday, 1933; Constable, 1936
Seven Slayers. Saint Enterprises, 1946 ss

CAINE, (THOMAS HENRY) HALL. 1853-1931.
The Shadow of a Crime. Chatto, 1885; Harper, 1885

CAIRD, JANET (HINSHAW). 1913-   .
In a Glass Darkly; see Murder Reflected
The Loch. Bles, 1968; Doubleday, 1969
Murder Reflected. Bles, 1965. U.S. title: In a Glass Darkly. Morrow, 1966
Murder Remote. Doubleday, 1973. Also published as: The Shrouded Way. Signet, 1973
Murder Scholastic. Bles, 1967; Doubleday, 1968
Perturbing Spirit. Bles, 1966; Doubleday, 1967
The Shrouded Way; see Murder Remote

CAIRNS, CICELY
Murder Goes to Press. Constable, 1950; Macmillan, 1951

CAIRNS, COLLEEN
Great Gorme. Weybright, 1975

CAIRO, JACK
Cocksure Dame. Scion, 1952
Dames for Danger. Scion, 1953
You've Had Your Chance. Scion, 1950

CALDWELL, ALFRED BETTS. Series character: Freddy Philpotts = FP.
Coffee for None. Mathews, 1934
Death Rattle. Doubleday, 1940 FP
No Tears Shed. Doubleday, 1937 FP
Turquoise Hazard. Doubleday, 1936 FP

CALDWELL, GEORGE S.
Gristmill. H. Hamilton, 1975

CALDWELL, (JANET MIRIAM) TAYLOR (HOLLAND). 1900-   .
The Late Clara Beame. Doubleday, 1963; Collins, 1964
Wicked Angel. Reback, 1965; Coronet, 1966

CALEF, NOEL. 1907-   .
Frantic. GM, 1961. (Translation of Ascenseur pour l'Echafaud. Paris, 1956.)
The Snare. Souvenir, 1969. (Translation of La Nasse. Paris, 1966.)

CALIN, ANNE
Decision at Dawn. Lancer, 1967
A Multitude of Shadows. Lancer, 1966

CALIN, HAL JASON
Rocks and Ruin. Vanguard, 1954. Also published as: Payoff in Blood. Jonathan, 1955

CALL, WILLIAM TIMOTHY. 1856-1917.
Blackmail. Call, 1915

CALLAGHAN, MORLEY. 1903-   .
-Strange Fugitive. Scribner, 1928

CALLAND, MARY
The Billion-Dollar Hold-Up. Hale, 1969

CALLAS, THEO. Pseudonym of Shaun Lloyd McCarthy, 1928-   . Other pseudonym: Desmond Cory, q.v.
The City of Kites. Muller, 1955; Walker, 1964

CALLAWAY, SLOANE
The Crime at the Conquistador. Phoenix, 1938

CALLENDER, JULIAN. Pseudonym of Austin Lee, 1904-1965, q.v. Other pseudonym: John Austwick, q.v.
Corpse Too Many. Jenkins, 1965

CALLISON, BRIAN. 1934-   .
A Flock of Ships. Collins, 1970; Putnam, 1970
A Plague of Sailors. Collins, 1971; Putnam, 1971
A Web of Salvage. Collins, 1973; Putnam, 1974

CALMER, NED. 1907-   .
The Avima Affair. Doubleday, 1973
Madam Ambassador. Doubleday, 1975

CALNAN, T(HOMAS) D(ANIEL). 1915-   .
The Reluctant Spy. Curtis, 1973

CALTHROP, DION (WILLIAM PALGRAVE) CLAYTON. 1878-1937. See also: (CHAMBERS) HALDANE (COOKE) MacFALL, 1860-1928.
The Lavender Dagger. Hodder, 1931

CALVERT, WALTER
Justine; or, A Woman's Honour. Eden Remington, 1891

CALVIN, HENRY. Pseudonym of Clifford Hanley, 1922-   .
Boka Lives!; see The Chosen Instrument
The Chosen Instrument. Hutchinson, 1969. U.S. title: Boka Lives! Harper, 1969
The D.N.A. Business. Hutchinson, 1967
The Italian Gadget. Hutchinson, 1966
It's Different Abroad. Hutchinson, 1963; Harper, 1963
Miranda Must Die. Hutchinson, 1968
A Nice Friendly Town. Hutchinson, 1967
The Poison Chasers. Hutchinson, 1971
The System. Hutchinson, 1962
Take Two Popes. Hutchinson, 1972

CAMBRIDGE, ADA. [ADA CAMBRIDGE CROSS]. 1844-   .
At Midnight and other stories. Ward, 1897 ss, criminous in part

CAMERON, DONALD CLOUGH. Series character: Abelard Voss = AV.
And So He Had to Die. Holt, 1941 AV
Death at Her Elbow. Holt, 1940
Dig Another Grave. Mystery House, 1946
Grave Without Grass. Holt, 1940 AV
Murder's Coming. Holt, 1939 AV
White for a Shroud. Mystery House, 1947; Boardman, 1949

CAMERON, ELEANOR ELFORD
Box for a Long Journey. Dell, 1973
The Curse of the Casa Del Monte. Dell, 1975
House on the Beach. PB, 1972
The Spider Stone. Dell, 1973
The Young Widow. Dell, 1974

CAMERON, EVELYN. Series character: Sheriff Jake Thompson, in both titles.
Dead Man's Shoes. Doubleday, 1939
Malice Domestic. Doubleday, 1940

CAMERON, JOHN. Pseudonym of Archibald Gordon MacDonell, 1895-1941. Other pseudonym: Neil Gordon, q.v. Series character: Inspector Fleming, in both titles.
Body Found Stabbed. Methuen, 1932
Seven Stabs. Gollancz, 1929; Doubleday, 1930

CAMERON, KATE
The Awakening Dream. Leisure, 1974
Deadly Nightshade. Leisure, 1975
Legacy of Terror. Leisure, 1974
Music from the Past. Leisure, 1975
Portraits of the Past. Leisure, 1975
Voices in the Fog. Leisure, 1975

CAMERON, LOU. 1924-   .
The Amphorae Pirates. Random, 1970; Hodder, 1971
Angel's Flight. GM, 1960
Barca. Berkley, 1974; Ellis, 1974
Before It's Too Late. GM, 1970
Behind the Scarlet Door. GM, 1971
The Closing Circle. Berkley, 1974; Ellis, 1975
Devil in the Pines. Berkley, 1975
The Dragon's Spine. Avon, 1968
The Empty Quarter. GM, 1962
File on a Missing Redhead. GM, 1968; Coronet, 1969
The Girl with the Dynamite Bangs. Lancer, 1973
The Outsider. Popular Library, 1969. (Novelization of the TV series.)
The Sky Divers. GM, 1962
Tancredi. Berkley, 1975; Ellis, 1976

CAMERON, MONTGOMERY
The Ugly Woman. Vantage, 1966

CAMERON, OWEN. 1905-   .
The Antagonists. Doubleday, 1946
The Butcher's Wife. Simon, 1954; Hammond, 1955
Catch a Tiger. Simon, 1952; Hammond, 1954
The Demon Stirs; see The Fire Trap
The Fire Trap. Simon, 1957; Hammond, 1958. Also published as: The Demon Stirs. Dell, 1958
Man Hunt; see The Mountains Have No Shadow
The Mountains Have No Shadow. Harper, 1952. British title: Man Hunt. Hammond, 1958
The Owl and the Pussycat. Harper, 1949
The Silent One. Random, 1958; Hammond, 1960

CAMERON, WILLIAM ERNEST. 1881-   . Pseudonym: Mark Allerton, q.v.

CAMP, (CHARLES) WADSWORTH. 1879-1936.
The Abandoned Room. Doubleday, 1917; Jarrolds, 1919
The Communicating Door. Doubleday, 1923 ss
-The Forbidden Years. Doubleday, 1930
The Gray Mask. Doubleday, 1920
The House of Fear. Doubleday, 1916;

Hodder, 1917. Also published as: The
Last Warning. Readers Library, 1929
The Last Warning; see The House of
Fear
Sinister Island. Dodd, 1915

CAMPBELL, ALICE (ORMOND). 1887- .
Series characters: Inspector Head-
corn = H; Tommy Rostetter = TR.
The Bloodstained Toy. Collins, 1948 TR
The Borrowed Cottage; see No Murder of
Mine
Child's Play. Collins, 1947. U.S.
title: Veiled Murder. Random, 1949
(revised)
The Click of the Gate. Collins, 1932;
Farrar, 1931 TR
The Cockroach Sings. Collins, 1946.
U.S. title: With Bated Breath. Ran-
dom, 1946 H
The Corpse Had Red Hair. Collins, 1950
Death Framed in Silver. Collins, 1937 H
Desire to Kill. Collins, 1934; Farrar,
1934 TR
A Door Closed Softly. Collins, 1939
Flying Blind. Collins, 1938 TR
Juggernaut. Hodder, 1928; Doubleday,
1928
Keep Away from Water! Collins, 1935;
Farrar, 1935
Murder in Paris; see Spiderweb
The Murder of Caroline Bundy. Collins,
1933; Farrar, 1932
No Light Came On. Collins, 1942; Scrib-
ner, 1945
No Murder of Mine. Collins, 1941;
Scribner, 1941. Also published as:
The Borrowed Cottage. H
Ringed with Fire. Collins, 1943; Ran-
dom, 1942
Spiderweb. Hodder, 1930. U.S. title:
Murder in Paris. Farrar, 1930
They Hunted a Fox. Collins, 1940;
Scribner, 1940 H
Traveling Butcher. Collins, 1944
Veiled Murder; see Child's Play
Water Weed. Hodder, 1929; Farrar, 1929
With Bated Breath; see The Cockroach
Sings

CAMPBELL, COLIN. Pseudonym of Douglas
Christie, 1894- , q.v. Other pseu-
donym: Lynn Durie, q.v.
-Caught in the Machine. Rich, 1936
-Fool's Fair. Hurst, 1932
Murder on the Moors. Rich, 1934
Murder Up the Glen. Rich, 1933
Out of Wild Hills. Hurst, 1932
The Red Glen. Rich, 1936

CAMPBELL, D(ONALD) FREDERICK. 1906- .
See: B(URTON) S(EELY) KEIRSTEAD,
1907- .

CAMPBELL, SIR GILBERT (EDWARD). 1838-
1899.
A Fair Freelance. Routledge, 1891
-From Shadow to Light. Ward, 1889
The Mystery of Mandeville Square. Ward,
1888
New Detective Stories. Ward, 1891 ss
-The Romance of the Ruby. Ward, 1891.
U.S. title: A Ruby Beyond Price.
Minerva, 1891
A Ruby Beyond Price; see The Romance of
the Ruby
The Vanishing Diamond. Ward, 1891
Wild and Weird; or, Remarkable Stories
of Russia. Ward, 1889 ss, some
criminous

CAMPBELL, HARRIETTE R(USSELL). 1883- .
Series character: Simon Brade = SB.
Crime in Crystal. Harper, 1946 SB
Magic Makes Murder. Harper, 1943 SB

The Moor Fires Mystery. Harper, 1939;
Heinemann, 1938 SB
Murder Set to Music. Harper, 1941 SB
The Porcelain Fish Mystery. Knopf,
1937. British title: The Porcelain
Fish. Heinemann, 1937 SB
The String Glove Mystery. Knopf, 1936;
Heinemann, 1936 SB
Three Lost Ladies. Heinemann, 1949
(U.S. title?)
Three Names for Murder. Harper, 1940;
Collins, 1940 SB

CAMPBELL, HAZEL
The Burqa. Long, 1930
The Makra Mystery. Long, 1931
Olga Knaresbrook, Detective. Long, 1933
The Secret Brotherhood. Long, 1929
-The Servants of the Goddess. Long, 1928

CAMPBELL, KAREN. Pseudonym of Betty
Beaty, 1922- .
The Brocken Spectre; see Suddenly, in
the Air
Suddenly, in the Air. Collins, 1969;
Stein, 1969. Also published as: The
Brocken Spectre. Fontana, 1972
Thunder on Sunday. Collins, 1972;
Bobbs, 1972
Wheel Fortune. Collins, 1973. U.S.
title: The Wheel of Fortune. Bobbs,
1973
The Wheel of Fortune; see Wheel Fortune

CAMPBELL, KEITH. Pseudonym of Keith Camp-
bell West-Watson. Series character:
Mike Brett, in at least those marked
MB.
Born Beautiful. Macdonald, 1951 MB
The Broken Branch. Rich, 1944
Darling, Don't. Macdonald, 1950 MB
Goodbye Gorgeous. Macdonald, 1947 MB
The Last Journey. Rich, 1941
Listen, Lovely. Macdonald, 1949 MB
Pardon My Gun. Macdonald, 1954
That was No Lady. Macdonald, 1952

CAMPBELL, SIR MALCOLM. 1885-1948.
Salute to the Gods. Cassell, 1934;
Putnam, 1935
-Thunder Ahead. Cassell, 1934

CAMPBELL, MARGARET. Pseudonym of Gabrielle Margaret Vere Campbell Long,
1886-1952. Other pseudonyms: Marjorie Bowen, George Preedy, Joseph
Shearing, qq.v. For titles (re)pub-
lished under the Margaret Campbell
byline, see: JOSEPH SHEARING.

CAMPBELL, MARGARET ELIZABETH BAIRD.
Joint pseudonym with Johanna
Frederika Jansen: Fred Bayard, q.v.

CAMPBELL, MARY E(LIZABETH). 1903- .
Scandal Has Two Faces. Doubleday, 1943
The White Hand Mystery. Renaissance,
1936

CAMPBELL, R. T. Pseudonym of Ruthven
Todd, 1914- . Series character:
Professor John Stubbs = JS.
Adventures with a Goat. Westhouse, 1946
JS
Apollo Wore a Wig. Westhouse, 1946
Bodies in a Bookshop. Westhouse, 1946
JS
The Death Cap. Westhouse, 1946 JS
Death for Madame. Westhouse, 1946 JS
Swing Low, Sweet Death. Westhouse, 1946
JS
Take Thee a Sharp Knife. Westhouse,
1946 JS
Unholy Dying. Westhouse, 1945 JS

CAMPBELL, R. WRIGHT, 1927- .
The Spy Who Sat and Waited. Putnam,
1975; Weidenfeld, 1975

CAMPBELL, REGINALD (WILFRID). 1894-1950.
See also: PETER MOTTE (pseudonym of
Richard Harrison, 1901- , q.v.).
The Abominable Twilight. Cassell, 1948
The Admiralty Regrets—. Cassell, 1937
The Bangkok Murders. Cassell, 1939
Brainstorm. Cassell, 1950
Coffin for a Murderer. Cassell, 1947
Cruiser in Action. Cassell, 1940
Death by Apparition. Cassell, 1949
-Death in Tiger Valley. Hodder, 1931
-Fear in the Forest. Hodder, 1932
The Haunting of Kathleen Saunders. Cas-
sell, 1938
-Jungle Night. Hodder, 1933
-The King's Enemies. Chapman, 1927
Married into Murder. Cassell, 1951
Murder of My Wife. Cassell, 1952
Murder She Says!, with Peter Motte.
Cassell, 1952
-Striped Majesty. Heinemann, 1947
-This Animal is Dangerous. Hodder, 1934
-Uneasy Virtue. Chapman, 1926

CAMPBELL, RONALD
Marked for Murder. Hammond, 1958

CAMPBELL, SCOTT. Pseudonym of Frederick
William Davis, 1858-1933. Series
character: Felix Boyd = FB.
The Adventures of Felix Boyd. Street
(New Magnet #603), 1909 FB ss
A Battle of Wits. Street (Magnet #449),
190?
Below the Dead-Line. Street (Magnet
#428), 1906 ss FB
A Bid for Life. Street (Magnet #373),
190?
The Doctor's Secret; or, The Shadow on
the Wall. Street (Magnet #170), 1901
Driven to the Wall; or, A Forced Con-
fession. Street (Magnet #154), 1897
Exploits of a Private Detective.
Street (New Magnet #591), 1909 ss FB
The Fate of Austin Craige. Street
(Magnet #190), 190?
Felix Boyd's Final Problems. Street
(New Magnet #627), 1909 ss FB
Felix Boyd's Revelations. Street (New
Magnet #615), 1909 ss FB
The Honor of a Black Sheep. Street
(Magnet #173), 190?
The Links in the Chain; or, Who Killed
Judge Noble? Street (Magnet #167),
190?
The Lion of the Law; or, The Helena
Street Puzzle. Street (Magnet #154)
The Man Outside. Street (Magnet #181),
1901
On the Trail of "Big Finger". Street
(Magnet #429), 1906 ss FB
A Plot for Millions; or, A Game of
Cross Purposes. Street (Magnet #161),
1900
The Red Stain. Street (Magnet #404),
190?
The Reporter's Triumph; or, The Mystery
of the Missing Bride. Street (Magnet
#164), 1900
Sealed Lips. Street (Magnet #195), 190?
A Supernatural Clue. Street (Magnet
#185), 190?
The Tragedy of Ascot Mills. Street
(Magnet #176), 190?
An Unexpected Move. Street (Magnet
#355), 190?
Union Down; A Signal of Distress.
Arena, 1893
Woman in Red. Street (Magnet #335),
190?

CAMPBELL, MRS. VERE [JOSEPHINE ELISABETH
CAMPBELL].
The Crime of Keziah Keene. Ward, 1889

-The Master Schemer. Greening, 1909
-Of This Death. Ward, 1891

CAMPBELL, WALTER STANLEY. 1887-   .
    Pseudonym: Stanley Vestal, q.v.

CAMPBELL, WILLIAM EDWARD MARCH. 1894-
    1954. Pseudonym: William March, q.v.

CAMPDEN, JOHN
    The Hundredth Acre. Ward, 1906

CAMPERT, REMCO
    The Gangster Girl. Hart-Davis, 1968.
    (Translation of Het Gangstermeisje.
    Amsterdam, 1968.)

CAMPION, PETER
    Diamonds Worth a Death or Two. Arco,
    1955
    Model for Murder. Arco, 1955

CAMPION, SARAH. Pseudonym of Mary Rose
    Coulton.
    Unhandsome Corpse. Davies, 1938

CANADAY, JOHN EDWIN. 1907-   . Pseudo-
    nym: Matthew Head, q.v.

CANARY, GLEN
    The Perfect Plot. Pinnacle, 1974
    A Walk in the Jungle. Pinnacle, 1975

CANDY, EDWARD. Pseudonym of Barbara
    Alison Boodson Neville, 1925-   .
    Bones of Contention. Gollancz, 1954
    Which Doctor? Gollancz, 1953; Rinehart,
    1954
    Words for Murder Perhaps. Gollancz,
    1971

CANELSTEIN, HARRY
    A Dull Tree. Vantage, 1970

CANFIELD, MIRIAM
    The Tuscany Madonna. Lancer, 1965

CANLER, M. (LOUIS). 1797-1865.
    Autobiography of a French Detective.
    Ward, 1862. U.S. title (?): Memoirs
    of a Veteran Detective. Munro, 1882
    ss (Translation of Memoires de Can-
    ler, Ancien Chef du Service de Sûr-
    eté. Paris, 1862.)

CANNAN, JOANNA. Pseudonym of Joanna Max-
    well Cannan Pullein-Thompson, 1898-
    . Series character: Inspector
    Ronald Price = RP.
    All is Discovered. Gollancz, 1962 RP
    And Be a Villain. Gollancz, 1958 RP
    Body in the Beck. Gollancz, 1952 RP
    Death at the Dog. Gollancz, 1940; Rey-
    nal, 1941
    Long Shadows. Gollancz, 1955 RP
    Murder Included. Gollancz, 1950. U.S.
    title: Poisonous Relations. Morrow,
    1950. Also published as: The Taste of
    Murder. Dell, 1951 RP
    No Walls of Jasper. Benn, 1930; Double-
    day, 1931
    Poisonous Relations; see Murder In-
    cluded
    The Taste of Murder; see Murder In-
    cluded
    They Rang Up the Police. Gollancz, 1939

CANNELL, CHARLES. Pseudonym of E(velyn)
    Charles (H.) Vivian, 1882-1947, q.v.
    Other pseudonym: Jack Mann, q.v.
    -And the Devil. Lane, 1931
    -Ash. Hutchinson, 1925
    -Barker's Drift. Hutchinson, 1924
    The Guarded Woman. Hutchinson, 1923
    -The Guardian of the Cup. Hodder, 1925
    -The Passionless Quest. Hodder, 1926

CANNELL. J(OHN) C(LUCAS)
    100 Mysteries for Arm-Chair Detectives.
    Long, 1932 quiz ss

CANNING, VICTOR. 1911-   . Series char-
    acter: Rex Carver = RC.
    Bird of Prey; see Venetian Bird
    Black Flamingo. Hodder, 1962; Sloane,
    1963
    Burden of Proof; see Hidden Face
    The Burning Eye. Hodder, 1960; Sloane,
    1960
    The Captives of Mora Island; see The
    Dragon Tree
    Castle Minerva. Hodder, 1955. U.S.
    title: A Handful of Silver. Sloane,
    1954
    The Chasm. Hodder, 1947; Mill, 1947
    A Delivery of Furies. Hodder, 1961;
    Sloane, 1961
    Doubled in Diamonds. Heinemann, 1966;
    Morrow, 1967 RC
    The Dragon Tree. Hodder, 1958; Sloane,
    1958. Also published as: The Captives
    of Mora Island. Permabooks, 1959
    Family Plot; see The Rainbird Pattern
    The Finger of Saturn. Heinemann, 1973;
    Morrow, 1974
    Firecrest. Heinemann, 1971; Morrow,
    1972
    The Forbidden Road; see The Manasco
    Road
    A Forest of Eyes. Hodder, 1950; Mill,
    1950
    The Golden Salamander. Hodder, 1949;
    Mill, 1949
    The Great Affair. Heinemann, 1970;
    Morrow, 1971
    A Handful of Silver; see Castle Minerva
    Hidden Face. Hodder, 1956. U.S. title:
    Burden of Proof. Sloane, 1956
    His Bones are Coral. Hodder, 1955. U.S.
    title: Twist of the Knife. Sloane,
    1955
    The House of the Seven Flies. Hodder,
    1952; Mill, 1952
    The Kingsford Mark. Heinemann, 1975;
    Morrow, 1976
    The Limbo Line. Heinemann, 1963;
    Sloane, 1964
    The Man from the Turkish Slave.
    Hodder, 1954; Sloane, 1954
    The Manasco Road. Hodder, 1957; Sloane,
    1957. Also published as: The For-
    bidden Road. Permabooks, 1959
    The Mask of Memory. Heinemann, 1974;
    Morrow, 1975
    The Melting Man. Heinemann, 1968;
    Morrow, 1969 RC
    Oasis Nine; see Young Man on a Bicycle
    Panther's Moon. Hodder, 1948; Mill,
    1948
    The Python Project. Heinemann, 1967;
    Morrow, 1968 RC
    Queen's Pawn. Heinemann, 1969; Morrow,
    1970
    The Rainbird Pattern. Heinemann, 1972;
    Morrow, 1973. Also published as:
    Family Plot. Award, 1976
    The Scorpio Letters. Heinemann, 1964;
    Sloane, 1964
    Twist of the Knife; see His Bones are
    Coral
    Venetian Bird. Hodder, 1951. U.S.
    title: Bird of Prey. Mill, 1951
    The Whip Hand. Heinemann, 1965; Sloane,
    1965 RC
    Young Man on a Bicycle. Hodder, 1958.
    U.S. title: Oasis Nine. Sloane, 1959.
    (4 novelets.)

CANNON, CURT. Pseudonym of Evan Hunter,
    1926-   , q.v. Other pseudonyms:
    Hunt Collins, Ezra Hannon, Ed McBain,
    Richard Marsten, qq.v. Series charac-
    ter: Curt Cannon, in both titles.
    I Like 'Em Tough. GM, 1958 ss

I'm Cannon—for Hire. GM, 1958; Fawcett
    (London), 1959

CANNON, ELLIOTT
    Breakaway. Hale, 1973
    The Dumbo Dossier. Hale, 1975
    Element of Risk. Hale, 1975
    A Kind of Nightmare. Hale, 1975
    A Piece of Action. Hale, 1973
    A Sense of Danger. Hale, 1973
    Stand By to Shoot. Hale, 1973

CANYON, CLAUDIA. Pseudonym of Betty An-
    derson.
    The Junior League Murders. Arcadia,
    1954

CAPEK, KAREL. 1890-1938.
    Tales from Two Pockets. Faber, 1932;
    Macmillan, 1943 ss

CAPELLI, ACE
    Chicago Payoff. Gaywood, 1949
    The Double Cross. Gaywood, 1950
    Frisco Hi-Jack. Gaywood, 1950
    Get Me Headquarters. Kaye, 1949
    Never Turn Your Back. Gaywood, 1950
    This Man is Death. Gaywood, 1949

CAPES, BERNARD (EDWARD JOSEPH).
       -1918.
    Bag and Baggage. Constable, 1913
    ss, some criminous
    The Fabulists. Mills, 1915 ss, some
    criminous
    Gilead Balm, Knight Errant. Unwin,
    1911; Baker, 1911 ss
    The Great Skene Mystery. Methuen, 1907
    -The Green Parrot. Smith Elder, 1918
    The House of Many Voices. Unwin, 1911
    The Lake of Wine. Heinemann, 1898
    Loaves and Fishes. Methuen, 1906 ss
    The Mill of Silence. Long, 1902; Rand,
    1897
    The Mystery of the Skeleton Key; see
    The Skeleton Key
    -Our Lady of Darkness. Blackwood, 1899;
    Dodd, 1899
    A Rogue's Tragedy. Methuen, 1906
    The Secret in the Hill. Elder, 1903
    The Skeleton Key. Collins, 1919. U.S.
    title: The Mystery of the Skeleton
    Key. Doran, 1918. Reprinted in Bri-
    tain under the U.S. title: Collins,
    1929
    The Vanishing Cheques. Daily Mail, 1904
    Why Did He Do It? Methuen, 1910; Bren-
    tano's, 1910
    The Will and the Way. Murray, 1910

CAPETO, ISABEL
    A Few Drops of Murder. Arcadia, 1955

CAPIT, ELINE
    Run from the Sheep. Arcadia, 1955

CAPON, (HARRY) PAUL. 1912-   .
    -Amongst Those Missing. Heinemann, 1959
    Battered Caravanserai. Heinemann, 1942
    -Brother Cain. Heinemann, 1945
    Dead Man's Chest. Nicholson, 1947
    Death at Shinglestrand. Ward, 1951
    Death on a Wet Sunday. Ward, 1952
    Delay of Doom. Ward, 1952
    -Fanfare for Shadows. Boardman, 1947
    The Hosts of Midian. Nicholson, 1946
    Image of a Murder. Boardman, 1949
    -In All Simplicity. Heinemann, 1953
    Malice Domestic. Ward, 1954
    Margin of Terror. Ward, 1955
    The Murder of Jacob Canansey. Heine-
    mann, 1947
    No Time for Death. Ward, 1951
    -O Clouds Unfold. Ward, 1948

The Seventh Passenger. Ward, 1953
Thirty Days Hath September. Ward, 1955
-Threescore Years. Ward, 1950
-Toby Scuffell. Ward, 1949

CAPOTE, TRUMAN. 1924- .
In Cold Blood. Random, 1965; H. Hamilton, 1966

"CAPSTAN". Pseudonym of Rex Hardinge, 1904- , q.v.
Black Magic. Wright, 1941
Broadcast Murder. Mellifont, 1939 (64 pp.)
Cap'n Luke, Filibuster. Wright, 1937
Carver of the Swamp. Wright, 1938
The Chinese Cabinet. Mellifont, 1941 (48 pp.)
The Feud. Wright, 1950
Forbidden Territory. Wright, 1949
The Hole in the Mountain. Wright, 1939
Inkosi-Carver Investigates. Wright, 1943
Murder of a Musician. Brown Watson, 1949
The Night Coach. Mellifont, 1938
Operation Diamond. Wright, 1951
The Polite Pirate. Wright, 1938
The Problem in Ciphers. Wright, 1952

CARANE, MICHAEL
Why Jane Matcham Disappeared. Ward, 1907

CARCO, FRANCIS. Pseudonym of Francis Carcopino-Tusoli, 1886-1958.
The Noose of Sin. Cape, 1923. U.S. title: The Hounded Man. Seltzer, 1924. (Translation of L'Homme Traque. Paris, 1922.)

CARCOPINO-TUSOLI, FRANCIS. 1886-1958.
Pseudonym: Francis Carco, q.v.

CARDEN, PERCY T(HEODORE)
The Murder of Edwin Drood. Palmer, 1920; Putnam, 1920. (Completion of The Mystery of Edwin Drood by Charles Dickens, 1812-1870, q.v.)

CARDIFF, SARA
Fool's Apple. Random, 1971
The Inner Steps. Random, 1973
The Severing Line. Random, 1974

CARDWELL, ANN. Pseudonym of Jean Powley.
Crazy to Kill. Mystery House, 1941
Murder at Calamity House. Arcadia, 1947

CAREW, DUDLEY
The Puppets Part. Home, 1948

CAREW, HENRY
-The Secret of the Sphinx. Hodder, 1923
-The Vampire of the Andes. Hodder, 1925

CAREW, JACK
The Secret of the Stargazer's Club. Aldine, 1926

CAREW, JEAN. Pseudonym of Jane (Irenita) Corby, 1899- , q.v.
-Samantha. Arcadia, 1966

CAREY, ALFRED EDWARD
-Sealed Orders. Greening, 1909
-Time's Hour Glass. Greening, 1914

CAREY, BASIL
-Captain Christine. Jarrolds, 1932
The Dangerous Isles. Constable, 1926; Dial, 1927
Dead Man's Shadow. Constable, 1931

-The Dreaming God. Constable, 1927
Gray Amber. Clode, 1930. (British title?)
-Isle of Desire. Clode, 1931. (British title?)
Left for Dead. Jarrolds, 1934
-Mountain Gold. Constable, 1929; Clode, 1930
The Secret Enterprise. Jarrolds, 1932
-The Secret of Ayanora. Hale, 1937
-Secret Voyage. King, 1933. (British title?)

CAREY, BERNICE
The Beautiful Stranger. Doubleday, 1951
The Body on the Sidewalk. Doubleday, 1950
The Fatal Picnic. Doubleday, 1955
The Frightened Widow; see Their Nearest and Dearest
The Man Who Got Away With It. Doubleday, 1950
The Missing Heiress. Doubleday, 1952
The Reluctant Murderer. Doubleday, 1949
Their Nearest and Dearest. Doubleday, 1953. Also published as: The Frightened Widow. Mercury, 1954
The Three Widows. Doubleday, 1952

CAREY, CHARLES. Pseudonym of C(harles) C(arey) Waddell, 1868-1930, q.v.
The Van Suyden Sapphires. Dodd, 1905. British title (?): The Motor Cracksman. Unwin, 1905

CAREY, CONSTANCE
The Chekhov Proposal. Putnam, 1975

CAREY, DONNELL
Kisses Can Kill. Phantom, 1951

CAREY, DOUGLAS
The Raven's Feathers. Graphic (Ottawa), 1930
The Scorpion. Graphic (Ottawa), 1931

CAREY, ELIZABETH. Joint pseudonym with Marion Austin White Magoon, 1885- : Carey Magoon, q.v.

CAREY, HELEN A. See: DOUGLAS STAPLETON, 1904- .

CAREY, MICHAEL. Pseudonym of Edward J. Burton, 1917- .
Vice Net. Avon, 1958
Vice Squad Cop. Avon, 1957

CAREY, ROSA NOUCHETTE. 1840-1890. Pseudonym: Le Voleur, q.v.
-Barbara Heathcote's Trial. Bentley, 1883; Munro, 1885
-The Search for Basil Lyndhurst. Bentley, 1889; Lovell, 1889

CAREY, WEBSTER
Walking Tall: Part 2. Bantam, 1975. (Novelization of the movie.)

CAREY, WYMOND
"No. 101." Putnam, 1905; Blackwood, 1906

CARFAX, CATHERINE. Pseudonym of Eleanor Fairburn, 1928- .
The Locked Tower; see To Die a Little
The Semper Inheritance. Hale, 1972
A Silence with Voices. Macmillan (London), 1969
The Sleeping Salamander. Macmillan (London), 1973; Stein, 1973
To Die a Little. Hale, 1972. U.S. title: The Locked Tower. GM, 1974

CARGILL, LESLIE. Series characters: Major Mosson, in at least those marked M; Morrison Sharpe, in at least those marked MS.

Beyond the Frontiers. Jenkins, 1940
Cherry's Choice. Pemberton, 1948
Death Goes by Bus. Jenkins, 1936 MS
Death Sets the Pace. Jenkins, 1950
Death Walks in Scarlet. Jenkins, 1941
Fortune's Apprentice. Jenkins, 1946
Gestapo Gauntlet. Jenkins, 1939
Heads You Lose. Jenkins, 1938 MS
It Might Have Meant Murder. Jenkins, 1940 M
The Lady Was Elusive. Jenkins, 1952
The Man from the Rhine. Jenkins, 1943
The Man Who Wasn't Himself. Jenkins, 1947
Matrimony Most Dangerous. Jenkins, 1949; Roy, 1958
The Missing Background. Jenkins, 1942
Motley Menace. Jenkins, 1949
Murder in the Procession. Jenkins, 1937 M
Next Door to Murder. Jenkins, 1948 M
The Surprising Sanctuary. Jenkins, 1945
Was It Montelli? Jenkins, 1947
The Yellow Phantom. Fiction House, 1935

CARGILL, MORRIS. 1914- . Joint pseudonym with John Hearne: John Morris, q.v.

CARHART, ARTHUR HAWTHORNE. 1892- .
Pseudonym: V. A. Van Sickle, q.v.

CARLE, C. E. Joint pseudonym with Dean M. Dorn: Michael Morgan, q.v.

CARLETON, COUSIN MAY. Pseudonym of May Agnes Fleming, 1840-1880, q.v. Other pseudonym: M(ay) A(gnes) Earlie, q.v.
La Masque; or, The Midnight Queen. Brady, 1863

CARLETON, MARJORIE (C.) 1897-1964.
The Bride Regrets. Morrow, 1950; Joseph, 1951. (Novel is based on an earlier play of the same title, published by Baker in 1944.)
Cry Wolf. Morrow, 1945. Also published as: The Demarest Inheritance. Pyramid, 196?
The Demarest Inheritance; see Cry Wolf
Dread the Sunset. Morrow, 1962; Joseph, 1963. Also published as: Shadows on the Hill. Pyramid, 1966
The Night of the Good Children. Morrow, 1957; Joseph, 1958. Also published as: One Night of Terror. Pyramid, 1960
One Night of Terror; see The Night of the Good Children
Shadows on the Hill; see Dread the Sunset
The Swan Sang Once. Morrow, 1947; Joseph, 1948
Vanished. Morrow, 1955

CARLETON, S. Pseudonym of Susan Carleton Jones, 1864- .
The LaChance Mine Mystery. Little, 1920; Duckworth, 1921

CARLING, JOHN R.
-The Shadow of the Czar. Little, 1902; Ward, 1902
The Viking's Skull. Little, 1904; Ward, 1904
The Weird Picture. Little, 1905; Ward, 1905

CARLINO, LEWIS JOHN
The Brotherhood. Signet, 1968. (Novelization of the movie.)
The Mechanic. Signet, 1972. (Novelization of the movie.)

CARLISLE, D. M.
Althea's Falcon. Barker, 1974

CARLISLE, HELEN GRACE. 1898- .
   The Tiger Sniffs the Rose. Doubleday, 1958

CARLISLE, HENRY (COFFIN). 1926- .
   The Contract. Bobbs, 1968

CARLON, PATRICIA (BERNARDETTE)
   Betray Me—If You Dare. Hodder, 1966
   Circle of Fear. Ward, 1961
   Crime of Silence. Hodder, 1965
   Danger in the Dark. Ward, 1962
   Death by Demonstration. Hodder, 1970
   Forty Pieces of Alloy. Hodder, 1968
   Hush, It's a Game. Hodder, 1967
   The Price of an Orphan. Hodder, 1964
   The Running Woman. Hodder, 1966
   See Nothing—Say Nothing. Hodder, 1967; Walker, 1968
   The Souvenir. Hodder, 1970
   The Unquiet Night. Hodder, 1965
   The Whispering Wall. Hodder, 1969
   Who are You, Linda Condrick? Ward, 1962

CARLSON, NATALIE (SAVAGE). 1906- .
   Old Murders Never Die. Arcadia, 1960

CARLTON, LEWIS. ca.1886- . All titles were published by Amalgamated Press and feature Sexton Blake.
   The Case of the Stranded Touring Company. 1933
   The Monomark Mystery. 1928
   The Night Safe Mystery. 1932

CARLTON, LIEUT.
   The Arm of the Law. Street, ca.1900
   After the Bribe Takers. Street, ca.1900
   The Bank Note Plates. Street, ca.1900
   The Corridor of Death. Street, ca.1900
   A Counterfeiter's Wake. Street, ca.1900
   A Government Spy. Street, ca.1900
   The Haunt of the "Queen" Makers. Street, ca.1900
   The Man in Mail. Street, ca.1900
   The Man in Stripes. Street, ca.1900
   The Man with a Gun. Street, ca.1900
   The Moonshiner's Dupe. Street, ca.1900
   The Pirate's Retreat. Street, ca.1900
   The Poisoned Arrow. Street, ca.1900

CARLYLE, ANTHONY. Pseudonym of Gladys Alexandra Milton.
   Children of Chance. Mills, 1923; Houghton, 1923
   The Fugitive Millionaire; see The Tavern and the Arrows
   The Law of Nemesis. Mills, 1924
   The Tavern and the Arrows. Mills, 1922. U.S. title: The Fugitive Millionaire. Houghton, 1922
   A Vow of Vengeance. Mellifont, 1940

CARMACK, JESSE
   The Tell-Tale Clock Mystery. Stokes, 1937

CARMEL, KATHLEEN
   "S-S-S-Sh!" Nicholson, 1948

CARMICHAEL, ARCHIBALD
   Personal Adventures of a Detective. Morison, 1892 ss

CARMICHAEL, HARRY. Pseudonym of Leopold Horace Ognall, 1908- . Other pseudonym: Hartley Howard, q.v. Series characters: John Piper = JP, and/or Quinn = Q, in virtually all titles and certainly in those so marked.
   Alibi. Collins, 1961; Macmillan, 1962 JP, Q
   Candles for the Dead. Collins, 1973; Saturday Review Press, 1976 JP, Q
   The Condemned. Collins, 1967
   Confession. Collins, 1961
   The Dead of the Night. Collins, 1956 JP, Q
   Deadly Night-Cap. Collins, 1953 JP, Q
   Death Counts Three. Collins, 1954. U.S. title: The Screaming Rabbit. Simon, 1955 JP
   Death Leaves a Diary. Collins, 1952 JP, Q
   Death Trap. Collins, 1970; McCall, 1971 JP, Q
   Emergency Exit. Collins, 1957 JP
   Flashback. Collins, 1964
   Into Thin Air; see Put Out That Star
   James Knowland: Deceased. Collins, 1958
   Justice Enough. Collins, 1956 JP
   The Late Unlamented; see Requiem for Charles
   The Link. Collins, 1962
   Marked Man; see Stranglehold
   Money for Murder. Collins, 1955 JP, Q
   Most Deadly Hate. Collins, 1971; Saturday Review Press, 1974 JP, Q
   The Motive. Collins, 1974; Dutton, 1977 JP, Q
   Murder by Proxy. Collins, 1967 JP, Q
   Naked to the Grave. Collins, 1972; Saturday Review Press, 1973 JP, Q
   Noose for a Lady. Collins, 1955 JP, Q
   Of Unsound Mind. Collins, 1962; Doubleday, 1962 JP, Q
   ...Or Be He Dead. Collins, 1959; Doubleday, 1958 JP, Q
   Post Mortem. Collins, 1965; Doubleday, 1966 JP, Q
   Put Out That Star. Collins, 1957. U.S. title: Into Thin Air. Doubleday, 1958 JP, Q
   A Question of Time. Collins, 1958
   The Quiet Woman. Collins, 1971; Saturday Review Press, 1972 JP, Q
   Remote Control. Collins, 1970; McCall, 1971 JP, Q
   Requiem for Charles. Collins, 1960. U.S. title: The Late Unlamented. Doubleday, 1961 Q
   Safe Secret. Collins, 1964; Macmillan, 1965 JP, Q
   School for Murder. Collins, 1953 JP
   The Screaming Rabbit; see Death Counts Three
   The Seeds of Hate. Collins, 1960
   A Slightly Bitter Taste. Collins, 1968 Q
   Stranglehold. Collins, 1959. U.S. title: Marked Man. Doubleday, 1959 JP, Q
   Suicide Clause. Collins, 1966 JP, Q
   Too Late for Tears. Collins, 1973; Saturday Review Press, 1975 JP, Q
   The Vanishing Trick. Collins, 1952 JP
   Vendetta. Collins, 1963; Macmillan, 1963 JP, Q
   Why Kill Johnny? Collins, 1954 JP, Q

CARNAC, CAROL. Pseudonym of Edith Caroline Rivett, 1894-1958. Other pseudonym: E. C. R. Lorac, q.v. Series characters: Chief Inspector Julian Rivers = JR; Inspector Ryvet = R.
   Affair at Helen's Court; see Long Shadows
   The Burning Question. Collins, 1957
   The Case of the First-Class Carriage. Davies, 1939 R
   Clue Sinister. Macdonald, 1947 JR
   Copy for Crime. Macdonald, 1950; Doubleday, 1951 JR
   Crossed Skis. Collins, 1952 JR
   Death in the Diving Pool. Davies, 1940 R
   Death of a Lady Killer. Collins, 1959
   A Double for Detection. Macdonald, 1945 JR
   The Double Turn. Collins, 1956. U.S. title: The Late Miss Trimming. Doubleday, 1957 JR
   Impact of Evidence. Collins, 1954; Doubleday, 1954 JR
   It's Her Own Funeral. Collins, 1951; Doubleday, 1952 JR
   The Late Miss Trimming; see The Double Turn
   Long Shadows. Collins, 1958. U.S. title: Affair at Helen's Court. Doubleday, 1958 JR
   The Missing Rope. Skeffington, 1937 R
   Murder Among Members. Collins, 1955 JR
   Murder as a Fine Art. Collins, 1953 JR
   Murder at Mornington. Skeffington, 1937
   Over the Garden Wall. Macdonald, 1948; Doubleday, 1949 JR
   A Policeman at the Door. Collins, 1953; Doubleday, 1954 JR
   Rigging the Evidence. Collins, 1955 JR
   The Striped Suitcase. Macdonald, 1946; Doubleday, 1947 JR
   Triple Death. Butterworth, 1936
   Upstairs, Downstairs. Macdonald, 1950. U.S. title: Upstairs and Downstairs. Doubleday, 1950 JR
   When the Devil was Sick. Davies, 1939 R

CARNAHAN, WALTER H(ERVEY). 1891- .
   -Hoffman's Row. Bobbs, 1963

CARNAY, DANIEL
   Whispering Death. Pan, 1972

CARNEY, (JOHN) OTIS. 1922- .
   -The Paper Bullet. Morrow, 1966

CARNI, ROSS
   Against the F.B.I. Hamilton Stafford, 1952
   Date for Homicide. Hamilton Stafford, 1952
   Death Called China. Hamilton Stafford, 1951
   No Time for Corpses. Hamilton Stafford, 1952
   The Set-Up. Hamilton Stafford, 1952
   The Showdown. Hamilton Stafford, 1952

CAROL, J.
   Spin Your Crime. Warren, 1952

CAROL, ROBIN
   Ancestor. Paperback Library, 1969
   Gwenyth. Paperback Library, 1969
   The Gypsy's Curse. Award, 1971

CARPENTER, CARLETON. Series character: Chester Long = CL.
   Cat Got Your Tongue? Curtis, 1973
   Deadhead. Curtis, 1974 CL
   Games Murderers Play. Curtis, 1973
   Only Her Hairdresser Knew. Curtis, 1973 CL
   Sleight of Hand. Popular Library, 1975

CARPENTER, DON(ALD RICHARD). 1931- .
   Blade of Light. Barker, 1967; Harcourt, 1968

CARPENTER, EDWARD CHILDS. See: REGINALD WRIGHT KAUFFMAN, 1877- ; also: HELEN (ALDEN) K(NIPE) CARPENTER; also: LAURENCE GROSS.

CARPENTER, GRANT
   The Night Tide. Fly, 1920

CARPENTER, HELEN (ALDEN) K(NIPE)
   Whistling in the Dark. Dodd, 1932. (Novelization of the play by Laurence Gross, q.v., and Edward Childs Carpenter.)

CARPENTER, MARGARET. 1893-   .
  Experiment Perilous. Little, 1943;
    Harrap, 1943

CARPENTIER, CHARLES
  Flight One. Simon, 1972; Eyre, 1973

CARR, A(LBERT) H. Z(OLOTKOFF). 1902-1971.
  Finding Maubee. Putnam, 1970. British
    title: The Calypso Murders. Hale,
    1973

CARR, ANTONY (JOHN EDWIN)
  Candles in the Night. Cassell, 1956
  A Comedy of Terrors. Cassell, 1955
  The Girl in Green. Cassell, 1959
  The Man in Room 3. Cassell, 1958
  Strange Harmony. Earl, 1948

CARR, GLYN. Pseudonym of (Frank) Showell
    Styles, 1908-   , q.v. Series character: Abercrombie Lewker, in all
    titles (and also in titles under the
    Showell Styles byline).
  A Corpse at Camp Two. Bles, 1955
  The Corpse in the Crevasse. Bles, 1952
  Death Finds a Foothold. Bles, 1961
  Death of a Weirdy. Bles, 1965
  Death on Milestone Buttress. Bles, 1951
  Death under Snowdon. Bles, 1954
  Fat Man's Agony. Bles, 1969
  Holiday with Murder. Bles, 1960
  The Ice-Axe Murders. Bles, 1958
  Lewker in Norway. Bles, 1963
  Lewker in Tyrol. Bles, 1967
  Murder of an Owl. Bles, 1956
  Murder on the Matterhorn. Bles, 1951;
    Dutton, 1953
  Swing Away, Climber. Bles, 1956; Washburn, 1959
  The Youth Hostel Murders. Bles, 1952;
    Dutton, 1953

CARR, JOHN DICKSON. 1905-1977. Pseudonyms: Carr Dickson, Carter Dickson,
    Roger Fairbairn, qq.v. See also:
    ADRIAN CONAN DOYLE, 1911-1970; and:
    JOHN RHODE. Series characters: Henri
    Bencolin = HB; Patrick Butler = PB;
    Dr. Gideon Fell = GF; Colonel March
    (also under the Carter Dickson byline) = CM; Sir Henry Merrivale
    (also under the Carter Dickson byline) = HM.
  The Arabian Nights Murder. Harper,
    1936; H. Hamilton, 1936 GF
  Below Suspicion. Harper, 1949; H. Hamilton, 1950 GF, PB
  The Black Spectacles; see The Problem
    of the Green Capsule
  The Blind Barber. Harper, 1934; H. Hamilton, 1934 GF
  The Bride of Newgate. Harper, 1950;
    H. Hamilton, 1950
  The Burning Court. Harper, 1937; H.
    Hamilton, 1937
  Captain Cut-Throat. Harper, 1955; H.
    Hamilton, 1955
  The Case of the Constant Suicides. Harper, 1941; H. Hamilton, 1941 GF
  Castle Skull. Harper, 1931; Severn
    House, 1976 HB
  The Corpse in the Waxworks. Harper,
    1932. British title: The Waxworks
    Murder. H. Hamilton, 1932 HB
  The Crooked Hinge. Harper, 1938; H.
    Hamilton, 1938 GF
  Dark of the Moon. Harper, 1967; H. Hamilton, 1968 GF
  The Dead Man's Knock. Harper, 1958; H.
    Hamilton, 1958 GF
  Deadly Hall. Harper, 1971; H. Hamilton,
    1971
  Death Turns the Tables. Harper, 1941.
    British title: The Seat of the Scornful. H. Hamilton, 1942 GF

  Death-Watch. Harper, 1935; H. Hamilton,
    1935 GF
  The Demoniacs. Harper, 1962; H. Hamilton, 1962
  The Devil in Velvet. Harper, 1951; H.
    Hamilton, 1951
  Dr. Fell, Detective, and other stories. Mercury, 1947. (Mixed ss and
    radio plays, five about GF.)
  The Eight of Swords. Harper, 1934; H.
    Hamilton, 1934 GF
  The Emperor's Snuff-Box. Harper, 1942;
    H. Hamilton, 1943
  Fire, Burn! Harper, 1957; H. Hamilton,
    1957
  The Four False Weapons. Harper, 1937;
    H. Hamilton, 1938 HB
  The Ghosts' High Noon. Harper, 1969; H.
    Hamilton, 1970
  Hag's Nook. Harper, 1933; H. Hamilton,
    1933 GF
  He Who Whispers. Harper, 1946; H. Hamilton, 1946 GF
  The Hollow Man; see The Three Coffins
  The House at Satan's Elbow. Harper,
    1965; H. Hamilton, 1965 GF
  The Hungry Goblin. Harper, 1972; H.
    Hamilton, 1972
  In Spite of Thunder. Harper, 1960;
    H. Hamilton, 1960 GF
  It Walks by Night. Harper (New York &
    London), 1930 HB
  The Lost Gallows. Harper (New York &
    London), 1931 HB
  The Mad Hatter Mystery. Harper, 1933;
    H. Hamilton, 1933 GF
  The Man Who Could Not Shudder. Harper,
    1940; H. Hamilton, 1940 GF
  The Men Who Explained Miracles. Harper,
    1963; H. Hamilton, 1964. (7 ss, 2
    about CM, 2 about GF, and one about
    HM.)
  Most Secret. Harper, 1964; H. Hamilton,
    1964. (Revision of Devil Kinsmere, as
    by Roger Fairbairn, q.v.)
  The Murder of Sir Edmund Godfrey. Harper, 1936; H. Hamilton, 1936
  The Nine Wrong Answers. Harper, 1952;
    H. Hamilton, 1952
  Panic in Box C. Harper, 1966; H. Hamilton, 1966 GF
  Papa La-Bas. Harper, 1968; H. Hamilton,
    1969
  Patrick Butler for the Defense. Harper,
    1956; H. Hamilton, 1956 PB
  Poison in Jest. Harper, 1932; H. Hamilton, 1932
  The Problem of the Green Capsule. Harper, 1939. British title: The Black
    Spectacles. Harper, 1939 GF
  The Problem of the Wire Cage. Harper,
    1939; H. Hamilton, 1940 GF
  Scandal at High Chimneys. Harper, 1959;
    H. Hamilton, 1959
  The Seat of the Scornful; see Death
    Turns the Tables
  The Sleeping Sphinx. Harper, 1947; H.
    Hamilton, 1947 GF
  The Third Bullet and other stories.
    Harper, 1954; H. Hamilton, 1954.
    (Contains the title novelet, published separately in England under
    the Carter Dickson byline, plus 7
    ss, including 3 about GF and one
    about HM.)
  The Three Coffins. Harper, 1935. British title: The Hollow Man. H. Hamilton, 1935 GF
  Till Death Do Us Part. Harper, 1944;
    H. Hamilton, 1944 GF
  To Wake the Dead. Harper, 1938; H. Hamilton, 1938 GF
  The Waxworks Murder; see The Corpse in
    the Waxworks

  The Witch of the Low-Tide. Harper,
    1961; H. Hamilton, 1961

CARR, JOLYON
  Death Comes by Post. Jenkins, 1940
  Freedom for Two. Jenkins, 1939
  Masters of the Parachute Mail. Jenkins,
    1940
  Murders in the Dispensary. Jenkins,
    1938

CARR, JOSEPH BAKER. Series character:
    Oceola Archer, in both titles.
  Death Whispers. Viking, 1933; Cassell,
    1933
  Man with Bated Breath. Viking, 1934;
    Cassell, 1935

CARR, KIRBY. Series character: Mike Ross
    = MR.
  Alice Dies Twice. Major, 1975
  Don't Bet on Living, Alice. Major, 1975
    MR
  The Girls Who Came to Murder. Canyon,
    1974 MR
  Let Me Kill You Sweetheart. Canyon,
    1974 MR
  They're Coming to Kill You, Jane. Canyon, 1975 MR
  Who Killed You, Cindy Castle? Canyon,
    1974 MR
  You Die Next, Jill Baby! Major, 1975 MR
  You're Hired: You're Dead. Major, 1975

CARR, MARGARET. Pseudonym: Martin Carroll, q.v.
  Blood Will Out. Hale, 1975
  Sitting Duck. Hale, 1972
  Too Close for Comfort. Hale, 1975
  Tread Warily at Midnight. Hale, 1971
  Wait for the Wake. Hale, 1974
  Who's the Target? Hale, 1974

CARR, PHILIPPA. Pseudonym of Eleanor
    Burford Hibbert, 1906-   . Other
    pseudonyms: Elbur Ford, Victoria
    Holt, Kathleen Kellow, qq.v.
  The Lion Triumphant. Collins, 1974;
    Putnam, 1974
  The Witch from the Sea. Collins, 1975;
    Putnam, 1975

CARR, RAY. Pseudonym of Emile Charles
    Victor Foucar, 1894-   .
  The Cluster of Gems. Skeffington, 1930
  -Love in Burma. Bles, 1928
  -Moonshine. Howe, 1932
  The Red Tiger. Skeffington, 1929

CARR, WILLIAM H(ENRY) A(LEXANDER).
    1924-   .
  Medical Examiner. Lancer, 1963

CARREL, FREDERIC
  -The Adventures of John Johns. Bliss
    Sands, 1897. U.S. title: John Johns.
    Kennerley, 1908
  John Johns; see The Adventures of John
    Johns
  The Methods of Mr. Ames. Laurie, 1908;
    Kennerley, 1908
  -The Realization of Justus Moran. Long,
    1900

CARREL, MARK. Pseudonym of Lauran Bosworth Paine, 1916-   . Other pseudonyms: John Armour, Reg Batchelor,
    Kenneth Bedford, Frank Bosworth,
    Robert Clarke, Richard Dana, J. F.
    Drexler, Troy Howard, Jared Ingersol,
    John Kilgore, Hunter Liggett, J. K.
    Lucas, John Morgan, qq.v. Series

character: Andrew McCall, in at least those marked AM.
Assignment for Trouble. Hale, 1974
The Blood Pit. Hale, 1967 AM
Case of the Hollow Man. Foulsham, 1958
Case of the Innocent Witness. Foulsham, 1959
The Case of the Perfect Alibi. Foulsham, 1960
Counsel for the Killer. Hale, 1972
The Dark Edge of Violence. Hale, 1967 AM
The Emerald Heart. Hale, 1971
Kill and Be Damned. Hale, 1970
Murder Without Motive. Hale, 1974
The Octopus' Shadow. Hale, 1974
One Last Time. Hale, 1973
Shadow of a Hawk. Hale, 1967
The Steel Mask. Hale, 1968
A Sword of Silk. Hale, 1967
Tears of Blood. Hale, 1967 AM
The Underground Men. Hale, 1975

CARRICK, JOHN. Pseudonym of Hugh Provan Crosbie, 1912- .
Beware the Shadows. Hale, 1967
Bond of Hate. Hale, 1966
Fairways and Foul. Hale, 1964
The Killer Conference. Hale, 1968
Mario. Hale, 1965
The Vulture. Hale, 1964
The Young and Deadly. Hale, 1969

CARRIER, WARREN (PENDLETON). 1918- .
Bay of the Damned. Day, 1957; Cassell, 1958. Also published as: A Hell of a Murder. Avon, 1958
A Hell of a Murder; see Bay of the Damned
The Hunt. New Directions, 1952; Owen, 1952
The Lost and the Damned. Berkley, 1957

CARRINGTON, ELAINE STERNE. 1892-1958.
The Crimson Goddess. Appleton, 1936

CARRINGTON, V. Pseudonym of Valerie Anne Hughes.
One Man's Awe. Barker, 1956

CARROLL, LESLIE
The Blackmailer and the Blonde. Mitre, 1944 (32 pp.)
The Lamp Burns Blood. Mitre, 1944 (34 pp.)
You Can't Hang the Dead. Mitre, 1944 (31 pp.)

CARROLL, LOREN. 1904- .
Wild Onion. Dodd, 1930

CARROLL, MARTIN. Pseudonym of Margaret Carr, q.v.
Bait. Hale, 1970
Begotten Murder. Hale, 1967
Blood Vengeance. Hale, 1968
Dead Trouble. Hale, 1968
Goodbye is Forever. Hale, 1968
Hear No Evil. Hale, 1971
Miranda Said Murder. Hale, 1970
Too Beautiful to Die. Hale, 1969

CARROLL, ROBERT. Pseudonym of Hollis Alpert, 1916- .
A Disappearance. Dial, 1975. British title: The Budapest Tradeoff. Harwood, 1976

CARROLL, THOMAS D. 1926-1975.
Grounds for Murder. Lancer, 1966
A Plastic Kind of Death. Lancer, 1968

CARRUTHERS, ANNIE
A Left-Handed Murder. Gale & Polden, 1892

CARRYL, CHARLES E. 1841-1920.
The River Syndicate. Harper (New York & London), 1899 ss

CARSON, BART
Bread for the Dead. Hamilton Stafford, 1954
Cuban Heel. Hamilton Stafford, 1953
The Lady is a Spitfire. Hamilton Stafford, 1953
The Late Demented. Hamilton Stafford, 1955
Murder Matinee. Hamilton Stafford, 1953
Phone for a Hearse. Hamilton Stafford, 1953
She Died Downtown. Hamilton Stafford, 1953
Ten Grand Story. Hamilton Stafford, 1951
There Could be Trouble. Hamilton Stafford, 1954
Torment was a Woman. Hamilton Stafford, 1953

CARSON, ROBERT. 1909- .
The Golden Years Caper. Little, 1970; Allen, 1972
The Quality of Mercy. Holt, 1954; Hale, 1955

CARSTAIRS, HENRY. Series character: Lydford Long, in at least those marked LL.
Black Burying. Ward, 1945 LL
Blackdrop Hall. Ward, 1950
Blood, M'Lud. Ward, 1948 LL
Cruel Dart. Ward, 1947 LL
Death's Duet. Ward, 1954
Drifting Death. Ward, 1944 LL
Harpinger's Hunch. Ward, 1943
Lying Down Below. Ward, 1951
Oh, No, You Don't. Ward, 1952
Secretary of State for Death. Ward, 1946 LL
When Three Makes Two. Ward, 1953
Who Lies Bleeding? Ward, 1949 LL
The Winton Street Mystery. Ward, 1955

CARSTAIRS, JOHN PADDY. Series character: Garaway Trenton, in all titles.
The Concrete Kimono. Allen, 1965; Walker, 1965
Gardenias Bruise Easily. Allen, 1958; British Book Centre, 1959
No Thanks for the Shroud. Allen, 1967
No Wooden Overcoat. Allen, 1959
Pardon My Gun. Allen, 1962
A Smell of Peardrops. Allen, 1966
Touch a French Pom-Pom. Allen, 1960

CARSTARPHEN, FRANK E. See: FRANCES (NEWBOLD) NOYES HART, 1890-1943.

CARTER, ALBERTA SIMPSON
An Adopted Face. Popular Library, 1975
Fool's Proof. Popular Library, 1975

CARTER, DIANA
The Ghost Writer. Cassell, 1974; Macmillan, 1975

CARTER, HERBERT
Never Look Back. Vantage, 1966

CARTER, JOHN FRANKLIN. 1897-1967. Pseudonym: Diplomat, q.v.

CARTER, MAX
Call Me Killer! Avon, 1953

CARTER, NICHOLAS. House name. The characterization of Nick Carter began well before the turn of the century and he appeared abundantly in dime novels, which are not listed here. Beginning with the Magnet (M) and New Magnet (NM) Libraries of Street and Smith, the Nicholas Carter byline and characterization appeared in book form in tales as before authored by many different writers. Below are listed these book appearances, some of which were reprints of dime novels. Separately listed, at the end of the entry, are several later American volumes and three British collections.
M-NM Libraries. The stories were written by John R. Coryell, Frederick van Rensselaer Dey, W. Bert Foster, George C. Jenks, Thomas C. Harbaugh, Eugene T. Sawyer, William Wallace Cook, and Samuel C. Spaulding.
Accident or Murder? 1906
An Accidental Password. 1898
The Adder's Brood. 1917
The Adventures of Harrison Keith, Detective. 1899 ss
After the Verdict. 1914
Against Desperate Odds. 1904
Ahead of the Game. 1904
An Amazing Scoundrel. 1907
The American Marquis. 1887 in Secret Service Series; 1897 in M
Among the Counterfeiters. 1898
Among the Nihilists. 1898
The Amphitheatre Plot. 1918
The Angel of Death. 1913
An Artful Schemer. 1908
As a Crook Sows. 1915
At Face Falue. 1911
At Mystery's Threshold. 1909
At Odds with Scotland Yard. 1898
At the Knife's Point. 1902
At Thompson's Ranch. 1898
An Australian Klondike. 1897
The Babbington Case. 1913
Baffled, But Not Beaten. 1906
A Baffled Oath. 1905
Bandits of the Air. 1912
The Bank Draft Puzzle. 1907
A Bargain in Crime. 1907
The Barrel Mystery. 1903
A Battle for the Right. 1919
Behind a Mask. 1902
Behind a Throne. 1906
Behind Closed Doors. 1910
Behind the Black Mask. 1910
Beyond Pursuit. 1904
Birds of Prey. 1914
A Bite of an Apple, and other stories. 1899 ss
A Blackmailer's Bluff. 1903
The Blind Man's Daughter. 1914
A Blindfold Mystery. 1909
The Blood-Red Badge. 1903
Blood Will Tell. 1918
The Bloodstone Terror. 1905
A Blow for Vengeance. 1903
The Blow of a Hammer and other stories. 1901 ss
A Bogus Clew. 1901
Bolts from Blue Skies. 1914
A Bonded Villain. 1903
The Bottle with the Black Label. 1901
The Boulevard Mutes. 1905
The Broadway Cross. 1906
Broken Bars. 1917
A Broken Bond. 1919
Broken on Crime's Wheel. 1911
A Broken Trail. 1904
The Brotherhood of Death. 1907
Brought to Bay. 1900
Brought to the Mark. 1913
The Bullion Mystery. 1914
A Bundle of Clews. 1904
The Burden of Proof. 1916
The Buried Secret. 1912
By an Unseen Hand. 1912
The Cab Driver's Secret. 1904

A Call in the Night. 1912
A Call on the Phone. 1911
Called to Account. 1914
Captain Sparkle, Pirate. 1906
A Carnival of Crime. 1910
The Case of Many Clues. 1916
The Case of the Two Doctors. 1912
A Case Without a Clue. 1906
The Cashier's Secret. 1903
Caught in a Whirlpool. 1913
Caught in the Toils. 1897
The Certified Check. 1904
The Chain of Clues. 1907
The Chain of Evidence. 1903
A Chance Discovery. 1898
A Chase for Millions. 1911
A Chase in the Dark. 1907
Check No. 777. 1898
A Checkmated Scoundrel. 1903
A Cigarette Clew. 1905
Circumstantial Evidence. 1903
The Claws of the Tiger. 1902
The Clever Celestial. 1899
Clew Against Clew. 1918
Clew by Clew. 1912
The Cloak of Guilt. 1903
A Clue from the Unknown. 1916
The Clutch of Dread. 1913
Comrades of the Right Hand. 1911
The Confidence King. 1911
The Connecting Link. 1912
A Conspiracy of Rumors. 1916
Cornered at Last. 1913
The Council of Death. 1903
The Crescent Brotherhood. 1899
The Crime and the Motive. 1908
A Crime in Paradise. 1914
The Crime of the Century. 1912
The Crime of a Countess. 1888 in
  Secret Service Series; 1897 in M
The Crime of the Camera. 1905
The Crime of the French Cafe and
  other stories. 1900 ss
The Criminal Link. 1904
The Crimson Flash. 1912
The Crook's Blind. 1914
The Crook's Double. 1918
The Crossed Needles. 1918
Crossed Wires. 1900
The Crown Diamond. 1903
A Cry for Help. 1907
The Crystal Mystery. 1910
The Danger of Folly. 1915
The Day of Reckoning. 1913
The Dead Accomplice. 1912
A Dead Man's Grip. 1899
The Dead Stranger. 1907
The Deadly Scarab. 1912
A Deal in Diamonds. 1902
Death at the Feast. 1909
The Death Circle. 1906
Death in Life. 1918
The Deeper Game. 1914
The Demon's Eye. 1907
The Demons of the Night. 1907
A Deposit Vault Puzzle. 1898
A Desperate Chance. 1901
The Detective's Pretty Neighbor and
  other stories. 1899 ss
A Detective's Theory. 1904
The Devil's Son. 1911
Diamond Cut Diamond. 1913
The Diamond Mine Case. 1899
The Diamond Trail. 1905
The Disappearing Princess. 1910
A Disciple of Satan. 1909
Doctor Quartz, Magician. 1906
Doctor Quartz's Quick Move. 1906
The Doctor's Strategem. 1908
Dodging the Law. 1914
Done in the Dark. 1907
The Doom of the Reds. 1910
Doomed to Failure. 1913
The Door of Doubt. 1914
A Double-Handed Game. 1902
A Double Identity. 1913
A Double Mystery. 1912

A Double Plot. 1909
The Double Shuffle Club. 1898
Down and Out. 1905
Driven from Cover. 1904
Driven to Desperation. 1913
A Duel of Brains. 1913
The Dumb Witness and other stories.
  1901 ss
The Dynamite Trap. 1907
The Elevated Railroad Mystery and other
  stories. 1900 ss
An Elusive Knave. 1911
Evidence by Telephone. 1898
The Evil Formula. 1916
The Face in the Shadow. 1911
A Fair Criminal. 1898
The False Claimant. 1908
A False Combination. 1902
A Fatal Bargain. 1911
A Fatal Falsehood. 1911
The Fatal Hour. 1912
The Fatal Prescription. 1903
A Fight for a Throne. 1907
A Fight for Right. 1914
A Fight with a Fiend. 1908
Fighting Against Millions. 1888 in
  Secret Service Series; 1897 in M
The Finger of Suspicion. 1907
The Finish of a Rascal. 1913
The Fixed Alibi. 1914
Following a Chance Clew. 1904
For a Madman's Millions. 1911
For a Pawned Crown. 1917
For the Sake of Revenge. 1913
Found in the Jungle. 1917
Found on the Beach. 1898
The Four-Fingered Glove. 1905
The Four Hoodoo Charms. 1911
A Framework of Fate. 1900
From a Prison Cell. 1906
From Clue to Clue. 1916
From Peril to Peril. 1908
The Gambler's Syndicate. 1897
A Game of Craft. 1900
A Game of Plots. 1907
A Game Well Played. 1908
The Gargoni Girdle. 1915
Gideon Drexel's Millions and other
  stories. 1899 ss
The Gift of the Gods. 1911
The Girl in the Case. 1908
The Girl Prisoner. 1915
The Gloved Hand. 1914
The Grafters. 1914
A Great Conspiracy. 1903
The Great Diamond Syndicate. 1910
The Great Enigma. 1888 in Secret Ser-
  vice Series; 1897 in M
The Great Money Order Swindle. 1899
The Great Opium Case. 1916
The Guilty Governor. 1903
The Hand That Won. 1908
Hand to Hand. 1908
The Handcuff Wizard. 1911
Harrison Keith and the Phantom Heiress.
  1909
Harrison Keith at Bay. 1909
Harrison Keith, Magician. 1909
Harrison Keith, Sleuth. 1909
Harrison Keith—Star Reporter. 1910
Harrison Keith's Abduction Tangle. 1909
Harrison Keith's Battle of Nerve. 1909
Harrison Keith's Big Stakes. 1907
Harrison Keith's Cameo Case. 1909
Harrison Keith's Chance Clue. 1907
Harrison Keith's Chance Shot. 1908
Harrison Keith's Close Quarters. 1909
Harrison Keith's Crooked Trail. 1908
Harrison Keith's Cyclone Clue. 1910
Harrison Keith's Danger. 1907
Harrison Keith's Death Compact. 1909
Harrison Keith's Death Watch. 1910
Harrison Keith's Diamond Case. 1908
Harrison Keith's Dilemma. 1907
Harrison Keith's Double Cross. 1909

Harrison Keith's Double Mystery. 1908
Harrison Keith's Drag Net. 1908
Harrison Keith's Dual Role. 1909
Harrison Keith's Fight for Life. 1908
Harrison Keith's Greatest Task. 1907
Harrison Keith's Green Diamond. 1909
Harrison Keith's Haunted Client. 1909
Harrison Keith's Labyrinth. 1910
Harrison Keith's Lucky Strike. 1909
Harrison Keith's Mummy Mystery. 1909
Harrison Keith's Mystic Letter. 1908
Harrison Keith's Oath. 1907
Harrison Keith's Padlock Mystery. 1909
Harrison Keith's Perilous Contact. 1910
Harrison Keith's Poison Problem. 1910
Harrison Keith's Queer Clue. 1908
Harrison Keith's River Front Ruse. 1909
Harrison Keith's River Mystery. 1910
Harrison Keith's Sparkling Trail. 1909
Harrison Keith's Strange Summons. 1908
Harrison Keith's Struggle. 1907
Harrison Keith's Studio Crime. 1910
Harrison Keith's Tact. 1908
Harrison Keith's Time Lock Case. 1908
Harrison Keith's Triple Tragedy. 1909
Harrison Keith's Triumph. 1907
Harrison Keith's Wager. 1910
Harrison Keith's Warning. 1907
Harrison Keith's Weird Partner. 1908
Harrison Keith's Wireless Message. 1908
The Hate That Kills. 1917
Heard in the Dark. 1903
The Heart of the Underworld. 1913
Held for Trial. 1900
Held in Suspense. 1915
A Herald Personal and other stories.
  1899 ss
A Heritage of Trouble. 1914
Hidden Foes. 1919
The Hole in the Vault. 1903
The "Hot Air" Clew. 1904
Hounded to Death. 1902
The House Across the Street. 1913
The House of Doom. 1911
The House of the Yellow Door. 1911
The House of Whispers. 1912
The Human Fiend. 1907
A Hunter of Men. 1908
In Death's Grip. 1908
In Letters of Fire. 1901
In Queer Quarters. 1912
In Record Time. 1915
In Search of Himself. 1909
In Suspicion's Shadow. 1913
In the Face of Evidence. 1912
In the Gloom of Night. 1904
In the Grip of Fate. 1916
In the Lap of Danger. 1906
In the Nick of Time. 1912
In the Shadow of Fear. 1913
In the Toils of Fear. 1914
An Ingenious Stratagem. 1904
Instinct at Fault. 1914
The International Crook League. 1913
Into Nick Carter's Web. 1908
The Jeweled Mummy. 1911
The Just and the Unjust. 1914
Just One Slip. 1915
The Keeper of Black Hounds. 1914
The Key Ring Clew. 1905
King of the Underworld. 1911
The King's Prisoner. 1910
A Klondike Claim. 1897
Knaves in High Places. 1914
Knots in the Noose. 1913
The Kregoff Necklace. 1913
The Lady of Shadows. 1911
Lady Velvet. 1900
The Last Call. 1914
The Last Move in the Game. 1910
A Legacy of Hate. 1907
The "Limited" Hold-Up. 1906
A Live Wire Clue. 1911
The Living Mask. 1905
The Lost Chittendens. 1910
The Lure of Gold. 1906

C

Carter, Nicholas (continued)

Madame "Q". 1911
The Magic Necklace. 1916
Man Against Man. 1902
The Man and his Price. 1902
The Man at the Window. 1901
The Man from India. 1898
The Man from London. 1901
The Man in the Auto. 1911
The Man of Iron. 1907
The Man of Many Faces. 1916
The Man of Mystery. 1901
The Man of Riddles. 1914
The Man They Held Back. 1917
A Man to be Feared. 1909
The Man Who Changed Faces. 1914
The Man Who Fainted. 1913
The Man Who Paid. 1914
The Man Who Stole Millions and other stories. 1900 ss
The Man Who Vanished. 1899
The Man Who was Cursed. 1906
The Man with a Crutch. 1912
The Man with a Double. 1912
The Man Without a Conscience. 1907
The Man Without a Will. 1916
Marked for Death. 1906
The Marked Hand. 1905
A Master Criminal. 1912
A Master of Deviltry. 1909
The Master Villain. 1904
A Masterly Trick. 1911
A Masterpiece of Crime. 1903
A Matter of Skill. 1911
A Maze of Motives. 1913
The Microbe of Crime. 1914
The Middle Link. 1915
The Midnight Message. 1913
A Million in Diamonds. 1912
A Millionaire Partner. 1898
A Millionaire's Mania. 1913
Millions at Stake and other stories. 1901 ss
The Mills of the Law. 1913
A Miscarriage of Justice. 1914
The Missing Cotton King. 1901
The Missing Deputy Chief. 1912
A Missing Man. 1904
A Mixed-Up Mess. 1916
A Move in the Dark. 1902
A Moving Picture Mystery. 1913
The Murray Hill Mystery. 1901
The Mysterious Castle. 1911
The Mysterious Cavern. 1912
A Mysterious Foe. 1904
A Mysterious Game. 1903
A Mysterious "Graft". 1905
The Mysterious Mail Robbery. 1897
The Mystic Diagram. 1904
Nabob and Knave. 1908
A Nation's Peril. 1910
The Needy Nine. 1917
A Network of Crime. 1918
A New Serpent in Eden. 1915
Nick Carter and the Green Goods Men. 1899
Nick Carter and the Red Button. 1913
Nick Carter Down East. 1900
Nick Carter's Auto Trail. 1910
Nick Carter's Chance Clue. 1912
Nick Carter's Chinese Puzzle. 1907
Nick Carter's Cipher. 1908
Nick Carter's Clever Protege. 1899
Nick Carter's Clever Ruse. 1900
Nick Carter's Close Call. 1907
Nick Carter's Close Finish. 1912
Nick Carter's Convict Client. 1910
Nick Carter's Counterplot. 1912
Nick Carter's Death Warrant. 1902
Nick Carter's Double Catch. 1905
Nick Carter's Egyptian Clew. 1912
Nick Carter's Fall. 1906
Nick Carter's Girl Detective. 1900
Nick Carter's Intuition. 1911
Nick Carter's Last Card. 1912
Nick Carter's Masterpiece. 1906
Nick Carter's Menace. 1912
Nick Carter's New Assistant. 1913
Nick Carter's Persistence. 1910
Nick Carter's Promise. 1908
Nick Carter's Retainer. 1900
Nick Carter's Roundup. 1911
Nick Carter's Star Pupils. 1900
Nick Carter's Subtle Foe. 1912
Nick Carter's Swim to Victory. 1909
Nick Carter's Treasure Chest Case. 1913
Nick Carter's Wildest Chase. 1910
Not on the Records. 1914
The Old Detective's Pupil. 1887 in Secret Service Series; 1898 in M
On a Crimson Trail. 1912
On a Million-Dollar Trail. 1915
On the Eve of Triumph. 1913
On the Ragged Edge. 1914
The $100,000 Kiss. 1915
One Object in Life. 1914
One Shipwreck Too Many. 1915
One Step Too Far. 1910
Out for Vengeance. 1912
Out of Crime's Depths. 1909
Out of Death's Shadow. 1906
Out with the Tide. 1913
Outlaws of the Blue. 1917
Over the Edge of the World. 1916
Paid with Death. 1903
Partners in Peril. 1919
The Path of the Spendthrift. 1912
Pauline—A Mystery. 1911
Paying the Price. 1917
A Perilous Parole. 1914
The Photographer's Evidence. 1903
The Piano Box Mystery. 1888 in Secret Service Series; 1897 in M
A Play for Millions. 1912
Played to a Finish. 1902
Playing a Bold Game. 1897
Playing a Lone Hand. 1904
Playing for a Fortune. 1905
A Plaything of Fate. 1909
Plea for Justice. 1913
A Plot for a Warship. 1912
A Plot for an Empire. 1911
The Plot That Failed. 1905
A Plot Uncovered. 1909
A Plot Within a Plot. 1906
A Plunge into Crime. 1908
Pointers to Crime. 1913
The Poisons of Exili. 1913
A Pressing Peril. 1917
The Pretty Stenographer Mystery. 1905
The Price of a Secret. 1901
The Price of Treachery. 1905
The Prince of Liars. 1908
A Prince of Rogues. 1901
A Princess of Crime. 1900
The Purple Spot. 1913
The Puzzle of the Five Pistols and other stories. 1899 ss
The Queen of Diamonds. 1904
The Queen of Knaves and other stories. 1901 ss
The Quest of "The Lost Hope". 1911
A Question of Time. 1911
A Race for Ten Thousand. 1902
A Race Track Gamble. 1903
The Rajah's Ruby. 1910
A Rascal of Quality. 1914
Rascals and Co. 1915
Reaping the Whirlwind. 1909
The Red God of Tragedy. 1914
The Red League. 1907
The Red Plague. 1916
The Red Signal. 1902
The Red Triangle. 1912
Repaid in Like Coin. 1913
A Riddle of Identities. 1913
A Ring of Dust. 1903
A Ring of Rascals. 1908
A Rogue of Quality. 1913
A Rogue Worth Trapping. 1914
The Rogue's Reach. 1912
The Room of Mirrors. 1911
A Rope of Slender Threads. 1914
Round the World for a Quarter. 1916
A Royal Thief. 1905
The Ruby Pin. 1904
Run to Earth. 1902
The Sandal Wood Slipper. 1914
Satan's Apt Pupil. 1915
Saved by a Ruse. 1909
A Scientific Forger. 1904
Scoundrels Rampant. 1916
The Scourge of the Wizard. 1910
Scourged by Fear. 1915
A Scrap of Black Lace. 1901
The Sea Fox. 1919
The Seal of Death. 1903
The Seal of Silence. 1901
The Sealed Door. 1916
Sealed Orders. 1899
The Second Mr. Carstairs. 1911
The Secret of the Marble Mantle. 1920
The Secret Panel. 1904
The Senator's Plot. 1911
The Seven Schemers. 1912
A Sharper's Downfall. 1903
Shown on the Screen. 1911
The Sign of the Coin. 1913
The Sign of the Crossed Knives. 1899
The Sign of the Dagger. 1906
The Silent Guardian. 1907
The Silent Partner. 1908
The Silent Passenger. 1900
The Silver Hair Clue. 1912
A Skyline Message. 1914
The Slave of Crime. 1914
The Snare and the Game. 1908
Snarled Identities. 1918
The Soul Destroyers. 1915
The Spider's Parlor. 1913
A Spinner of Death. 1920
Spoilers and the Spoils. 1914
The Spoils of Chance. 1914
The Steel Casket and other stories. 1901 ss
The Sting of the Adder. 1913
The Stolen Brain. 1916
The Stolen Horse Race. 1899 ss
A Stolen Identity. 1888 in Secret Service Series; 1897 in M
A Stolen Name. 1912
The Stolen Pay Train and other stories. 1899 ss
The Streaked Peril. 1911
A Strike for Freedom. 1908
A Stroke of Policy. 1902
A Struggle with Destiny. 1914
A Submarine Trail. 1911
The Sultan's Pearls. 1917
The Sway of Sin. 1913
A Syndicate of Rascals. 1902
Talika, the Geisha Girl. 1910
A Tangled Case. 1905
Tangled in Crime. 1912
A Tangled Skein. 1914
Tangled Threads. 1908
The Taxicab Riddle. 1912
The Tell-Tale Photographs. 1902
The Temple of Vice. 1909
The Terrible Thirteen. 1905
The Terrible Threat. 1904
A Test of Courage. 1915
The Thief in the Night. 1913
The Thief Who was Robbed. 1914
A Threefold Disappearance. 1919
Through the Cellar Wall. 1906
A Titled Counterfeiter. 1888 in Secret Service Series; 1897 in M
To the Ends of the Earth. 1915
Too Late to Talk. 1915
Tooth and Nail. 1912
The Toss of a Coin. 1902
The Toss of a Penny. 1904
A Tower of Strength. 1913
Toying with Fate. 1913
Tracked Across the Atlantic. 1897

The Trail of a Human Tiger. 1910
The Trail of the Catspaw. 1910
The Trail of the Fingerprints. 1914
The Trail of the Yoshiga. 1912
A Trap of Tangled Wire. 1908
Trapped by a Woman. 1906
Trapped in his own Net. 1905
A Triple Crime. 1901
A Triple Identity. 1905
A Triple Knavery. 1912
The Triple Knock. 1911
A Trusted Rogue. 1902
The Turn of a Card. 1913
Twelve in a Grave. 1916
The Twelve Tin Boxes. 1899
The Twelve Wise Men. 1899
The Twin Mystery. 1903
Two Plus Two. 1899
Two Villains in One. 1902
The Unaccountable Crook. 1906
Under a Black Veil. 1905
Under False Colors. 1903
Under the Tiger's Claws. 1906
The Unfinished Letter. 1913
Unseen Foes. 1914
A Vain Sacrifice. 1912
The Vampire's Trail. 1912
The Van Alstine Case. 1899
The Vanishing Emerald. 1911
The Vanishing Heiress. 1912
The Vial of Death. 1902
A Victim of Circumstances. 1900
A Victim of Deceit. 1905
A Villainous Scheme. 1905
A Voice from the Past. 1906
The Wages of Rascality. 1914
A Wall Street Haul. 1887 in Secret Service Series; 1897 in M
Wanted: A Clew. 1914
Wanted by Two Clients. 1899
A War of Brains. 1911
The Way of the Wicked. 1911
A Weak-Kneed Rogue. 1911
Weaving the Web. 1902
Weighed in the Balance. 1913
A Weird Treasure. 1915
When a Man Yields. 1911
When a Rogue's in Power. 1913
When All is Staked. 1913
When Brave Men Tremble. 1915
When Clews are Hidden. 1913
When Destruction Threatens. 1914
When Honors Fall. 1915
When Jealousy Spurs. 1912
When Necessity Drives. 1911
When Rogues Conspire. 1916
When the Trap was Sprung. 1908
When the Wicked Prosper. 1909
Where Peril Beckons. 1915
While the Fetters were Forged. 1913
The Whirling Death. 1911
Whom the Gods Would Destroy. 1913
Wildfire. 1920
With Links of Steel. 1905
With Shackles of Fire. 1914
Without a Clue. 1908
The Wizard of the Cue. 1904
The Wolf Within. 1914
A Woman at Bay. 1909
The Woman in Black. 1912
The Woman of Evil. 1907
A Woman of Mystery. 1912
The Woman of Steel. 1907
A Woman's Hand. 1888 in Secret Service Series as by John R. Coryell; 1897 in M
Won by Magic. 1917
The Worst Case on Record. 1907
Written in Blood. 1912
The Yellow Brand. 1915
The Yellow Label. 1918
Vital Publications issued the following digest-size reprints from Nick Carter Magazine, usually with a change in title. The original titles as well as the authors' real names are given below in parenthesis.
Death has Green Eyes! 1946 (Richard Wormser)
Empire of Crime. 1945 (Crooks' Empire; Richard Wormser)
Murder Unlimited. 1945 (Bid for a Railroad; Richard Wormser)
Park Avenue Murder! 1946 (Death on Park Avenue; Richard Wormser)
Rendezvous with a Dead Man. 1948 (Murder on Skull Island; John Chambliss)
The Yellow Disc Murder. 1948 (Power; T. C. McClary)

The following titles were published by juvenile fiction publisher Whitman; the stories were reprinted from dime novels.
Gideon Drexel's Millions. 1930
The Man Who Stole Millions. 1930
The Secret Agents of Brazil. 1930
The Stolen Pay Train. 1930
The Stolen Race Horse. 1930
A Triple Crime. 1930

These three collections of short stories, presumably taken from American editions, were published by Pearson in England.
Final Exploits of Nick Carter.
Further Exploits of Nick Carter, Detective. 1920
New Exploits of Nick Carter.

And finally, this collection of three novelets.
Nick Carter, Detective. Macmillan, 1963

CARTER, NICK. House name. Although the Nick Carter characterization appearing above purports to continue in the books below, Carter has been transformed from a private detective into an oversexed superspy.
Agent Counter Agent. Award, 1973; Tandem, 1975
The Amazon. Award, 1969; Tandem, 1969
Amsterdam. Award, 1968; Tandem, 1969
The Arab Plague. Award, 1970. British title: The Slavemaster. Tandem, 1970
Assassin—Code Name Vulture. Award, 1974; Tandem, 1977
Assassination Brigade. Award, 1973; Tandem, 1974
Assault on England. Award, 1972; Tandem, 1973
Assignment: Israel. Award, 1967; Tandem, 1968
The Aztec Avenger. Award, 1974; Tandem, 1976
Beirut Incident. Award, 1974
Berlin. Award, 1969; Tandem, 1971
The Black Death. Award, 1970; Tandem, 1972
The Bright Blue Death. Award, 1967; Tandem, 1968
Butcher of Belgrade. Award, 1973; Tandem, 1974
The Cairo Mafia. Award, 1972; Tandem, 1972
Cambodia. Award, 1970; Tandem, 1971
Carnival for Killing. Award, 1969; Tandem, 1969
The Casbah Killers. Award, 1969; Tandem, 1970
Checkmate in Rio. Award, 1964; Digit, 1965
The China Doll. Award, 1964; Digit, 1965
The Chinese Paymaster. Award, 1967; Tandem, 1968
The Cobra Kill. Award, 1969; Tandem, 1970
The Code. Award, 1973; Tandem, 1975
Code Name: Werewolf. Award, 1973; Tandem, 1973
Counterfeit Agent. Award, 1975
Danger Key. Award, 1966; Tandem, 1968
Death of the Falcon. Award, 1974
The Death Strain. Award, 1970; Tandem, 1971
The Death's Head Conspiracy. Award, 1973
The Defector. Award, 1968; Tandem, 1969
The Devil's Cockpit. Award, 1967; Tandem, 1968
The Devil's Dozen. Award, 1973; Tandem, 1974
Doctor Death. Award, 1975
The Doomsday Formula. Award, 1969; Tandem, 1970
Double Identity. Award, 1967; Tandem, 1969
Dragon Flame. Award, 1966; Tandem, 1968
The Executioners. Award, 1970; Tandem, 1971
Eyes of the Tiger. Award, 1965; Mayflower, 1967
The Filthy Five. Award, 1967; Tandem, 1968
14 Seconds to Hell. Award, 1968; Tandem, 1969
Fraulein Spy. Award, 1964; Digit, 1965
The Golden Serpent. Award, 1967; Mayflower, 1968
Hanoi. Award, 1966; Mayflower, 1968
Hood of Death. Award, 1968; Tandem, 1970
Hour of the Wolf. Award, 1973; Tandem, 1975
The Human Time Bomb. Award, 1969; Tandem, 1970
Ice Bomb Zero. Award, 1971; Tandem, 1972
Ice Trap Terror. Award, 1974; Tandem, 1977
The Inca Death Squad. Award, 1972; Tandem, 1973
Istanbul. Award, 1965; Tandem, 1969
The Jerusalem File. Award, 1975
Jewel of Doom. Award, 1970
The Judas Spy. Award, 1968; Tandem, 1970
The Katmandu Contract. Award, 1975; Tandem, 1977
A Korean Tiger. Award, 1967; Tandem, 1968
Kremlin File. Award, 1973; Tandem, 1976
The Liquidator. Award, 1973; Tandem, 1974
The Living Death. Award, 1969; Tandem, 1970
Macao. Award, 1968; Tandem, 1968
The Man Who Sold Death. Award, 1974
The Mark of Cosa Nostra. Award, 1971; Tandem, 1972
Massacre in Milan. Award, 1974; Tandem, 1977
The Mind Killers. Award, 1970; Tandem, 1971
The Mind Poisoners. Award, 1966; Tandem, 1968
Mission to Vengeance. Award, 1967; Tandem, 1970
Moscow. Award, 1970
Night of the Avenger. Award, 1973; Tandem, 1974
The N3 Conspiracy. Award, 1974; Tandem, 1977
The Omega Terror. Award, 1972; Tandem, 1973
Operation Che Guevara. Award, 1969; Tandem, 1970
Operation Moon Rocket. Award, 1968; Tandem, 1968
Operation Snake. Award, 1969; Tandem, 1970
Operation Starvation. Award, 1966; Tandem, 1968

Our Agent in Rome is Missing. Award, 1973; Tandem, 1976
Peking Dossier. Award, 1974
Peking/The Tulip Affair. Award, 1969; Tandem, 1973
The Red Guard. Award, 1967; Tandem, 1968
The Red Rays. Award, 1969; Tandem, 1969
The Red Rebellion. Award, 1970; Tandem, 1970
Rhodesia. Award, 1968; Tandem, 1969
Run, Spy, Run. Award, 1964; Tandem, 1969
Safari for Spies. Award, 1964; Digit, 1965
Saigon. Award, 1964; Digit, 1965
The Sea Trap. Award, 1969; Tandem, 1969
Seven Against Greece. Award, 1967; Tandem, 1968
Sign of the Cobra. Award, 1974; Tandem, 1977
Six Bloody Summer Days. Award, 1975; Tandem, 1978
The Slavemaster; see The Arab Plague
The Spanish Connection. Award, 1973; Tandem, 1976
Spy Castle. Award, 1966; Tandem, 1968
Strike Force Terror. Award, 1973; Tandem, 1973
Target Doomsday Island. Award, 1973; Tandem, 1974
Temple of Fear. Award, 1968; Tandem, 1969
The Terrible Ones. Award, 1966; Mayflower, 1968
The 13th Spy. Award, 1965; Digit, 1965
Time Clock of Death. Award, 1970; Tandem, 1971
The Ultimate Code. Award, 1975
Vatican Vendetta. Award, 1974; Tandem, 1977
The Weapon of Night. Award, 1968; Mayflower, 1968
Web of Spies. Award, 1966; Mayflower, 1967
The Z Document. Award, 1975; Tandem, 1978

CARTER, WINIFRED
The Dead Return. Rivers, 1929
Marriage by Mistake. Modern

CARTER, (P.) YOUNGMAN. 1904-1970. Husband of Margery Allingham, 1904-1966, q.v.; continued her Albert Campion series with the following titles.
Mr. Campion's Falcon. Heinemann, 1970. U.S. title: Mr. Campion's Quarry. Morrow, 1971
Mr. Campion's Farthing. Heinemann, 1969; Morrow, 1969
Mr. Campion's Quarry; see Mr. Campion's Falcon

CARTER-BROWN, PETER. Pseudonym of Alan Geoffrey Yates, 1923- , q.v. See also: CARTER BROWN. Other pseudonym: Caroline Farr, q.v.

CARTLEDGE, H(ORACE) A(VRON)
Peloton, Detective. Arnold, 1937

CARTLIDGE, ALICE
Murder at Moreby. Stockwell, 1935

CARTMILL, CLEVE. 1908-1964. See: GEORGE SANDERS, 1906-1972.

CARVALHO, CLAIRE and BOYDEN SPARKES
Crime in Ink. Scribner, 1929. (Somewhat fictionalized true crime accounts.)

CARVER, STEWART
Died O' Wednesday. Melrose, 1953
Sneeze on Monday. Melrose, 1951
Trouble on Tuesday. Melrose, 1952

CARVIC, HERON. Series character: Miss Seeton, in all titles.
Miss Seeton Bewitched. Bles, 1971. U.S. title: Witch Miss Seeton. Harper, 1971
Miss Seeton Draws the Line. Bles, 1969; Harper, 1970
Miss Seeton Sings. Davies, 1974; Harper, 1973
Odds on Miss Seeton. Davies, 1976; Harper, 1975
Picture Miss Seeton. Bles, 1968; Harper, 1968
Witch Miss Seeton; see Miss Seeton Bewitched

CARY, (THOMAS) FALKLAND L(ITTON). See also: A. A. THOMSON.
The Artist's Murder. Lewis, 1944. (3-act play.)
Burning Gold, with A. A. Thomson. French, 1943. (3-act play.)
Doctor—There's Danger. French, 1938. (3-act play.)
Murder at the Varsity, with A. A. Thomson. French, 1942. (3-act play.)
Murder Out of Tune. Thornley, 1944; revised: French, 1953. (3-act play.)
Murder Party. Garamond, 1935. (3-act play.)
Open Verdict, with Philip Weathers. French, 1952. (3-act play.)

CASE, DAVID. 1937- .
And Now the Screaming Starts; see Fengriffin
The Cell: Three Tales of Horror. Hill, 1969; Macdonald, 1969
Fengriffin. Hill, 1970; Macdonald, 1971. Also published as: And Now the Screaming Starts. Macdonald, 1971

CASE, FRANCES POWELL. Pseudonym: Frances Powell, q.v.

CASELEYR, CAMILLE AUGUST MARIE. 1909- . Pseudonym: Jack Danvers, q.v.

CASEY, BERNARD L. See: SHARON (B.) WAGNER, 1936- .

CASEY, KEVIN. 1940- .
A Sense of Survival. Faber, 1974

CASEY, PATRICK and TERENCE
-The Gay-Cat. Fly, 1921

CASEY, ROBERT J. 1890-1962. Series character: Jim Sands = JS.
Cambodian Quest. Bobbs, 1931; Mathews, 1932
Four Faces of Siva. Bobbs, 1929; Harrap, 1929
Hot Ice. Greenberg, 1933; Mathews, 1933 JS
News Reel. Bobbs, 1932. British title: The Secret of the Dark Room. Mathews, 1932 JS
The Secret of the Bungalow. Bobbs, 1930; Mathews, 1931 JS
The Secret of the Dark Room; see News Reel
The Secret of Thirty-Seven Hardy Street. Bobbs, 1929; Mathews, 1930 JS
The Third Owl. Bobbs, 1934; Nicholson, 1934 JS
The Voice of the Lobster. Bobbs, 1930

CASEY, TERENCE. See: PATRICK CASEY.

CASHMAN, JOHN
The Cook General. Harper, 1974; H. Hamilton, 1975

The Gentleman from Chicago. Harper, 1973; H. Hamilton, 1974

CASPARY, VERA. 1904- . See also: FREDERICK GOLDSMITH; and: (WILLIAM CANTWELL) FRANK (THORPE) VREELAND, 1891- .
Bedelia. Houghton, 1945; Eyre, 1945
A Chosen Sparrow. Putnam, 1964; Allen, 1964
Death Wish; see The Weeping and the Laughter
Evvie. Harper, 1960; Allen, 1960
False Face. Allen, 1954
Final Portrait. Allen, 1971
The Husband. Harper, 1957; Allen, 1957
Lady in Mink; see The Murder in the Stork Club
Laura. Houghton, 1943; Eyre, 1944
The Man Who Loved His Wife. Putnam, 1966; Allen, 1966
The Murder in the Stork Club. Detective Book Club, 1946. British title: Lady in Mink. Gordon Martin, 1946
The Rosecrest Cell. Putnam, 1967; Allen, 1968
Ruth. Pockettes, 1972
Stranger Than Truth. Random, 1946; Eyre, 1947
Thelma. Little, 1952; Allen, 1953
The Weeping and the Laughter. Little, 1950. British title: Death Wish. Eyre, 1951

CASS, ZOE
Island of the Seven Hills. Random, 1974; Cassell, 1975

CASSELLS, JOHN. Pseudonym of W(illiam) Murdoch Duncan, 1909-1975, q.v. Other pseudonyms: John Dallas, Neill Graham, Martin Locke, Peter Malloch, Lovat Marshall, qq.v. Series characters: Inspector Flagg, in at least those marked F; The Picaroon (Ludovic Saxon), in at least those marked P.
Action for the Picaroon. Long, 1975 P
Again Inspector Flagg. Muller, 1956 F
The Audacious Picaroon. Long, 1967 P
The Avenging Picaroon. Muller, 1955 P
The Bastion of the Damned. Melrose, 1946
The Benevolent Picaroon. Long, 1965 P
Beware! the Picaroon. Muller, 1957 P
Blackfingers. Long, 1966 F
Blue Mask. Long, 1964 F
The Brothers of Benevolence. Long, 1962 F
Call for Superintendent Flagg. Long, 1968 F
Case for Inspector Flagg. Muller, 1954 F
Case 29. Long, 1958 F
The Castle of Sin. Melrose, 1949
Challenge for the Picaroon. Long, 1964 P
The Circle of Dust. Melrose, 1950 F
The Clue of the Purple Asters. Melrose, 1949 F
The Council of the Rat. Long, 1963 F
The Double-Crosser. Long, 1969 F
The Elusive Picaroon. Long, 1968 P
The Enforcer. Long, 1973 F
The Engaging Picaroon. Long, 1958 P
Enter Superintendent Flagg. Long, 1959 F
Enter the Picaroon. Muller, 1954 P
The Enterprising Picaroon. Long, 1959 P
Exit Mr. Shane. Melrose, 1951 F
The Grafter. Long, 1970 F
Grey Face. Long, 1965 F
The Grey Ghost. Melrose, 1951 F
The Hatchet Man. Long, 1971 F
Inspector Flagg and the Scarlet Skeleton. Muller, 1955 F
Killer's Rope. Long, 1974 F

The League of Nameless Men. Melrose, 1948
The Mark of the Leech. Melrose, 1947
Master of the Dark. Melrose, 1948
Meet the Picaroon. Long, 1957 P
Murder Comes to Rothesay. Melrose, 1946
Night of the Picaroon. Long, 1969 P
The Picaroon Collects. Long, 1970 P
The Picaroon Goes West. Long, 1962 P
The Picaroon Laughs Last. Long, 1973 P
Plunder for the Picaroon. Long, 1966 P
Presenting Inspector Flagg. Muller, 1957 F
Prey for the Picaroon. Long, 1963 P
Problem for Superintendent Flagg. Long, 1961 F
Profit for the Picaroon. Long, 1972 P
Quest for Superintendent Flagg. Long, 1975 F
Quest for the Picaroon. Long, 1970 P
The Rattler. Melrose, 1952 F
The Room in Quiver Court. Long, 1967 F
Salute Inspector Flagg. Muller, 1953 F
Salute the Picaroon. Long, 1960 P
Score for Superintendent Flagg. Long, 1960 F
The Second Mrs. Locke. Melrose, 1952
The Sons of the Morning. Melrose, 1946
The Waters of Sadness. Melrose, 1950

CASSELS, LOUIS
A Bad Investment. Pyramid, 1974

CASSERA, NORA
The Blue Flower Mystery. Heath, 1930

CASSERLY, GORDON
The Elephant God. Allan, 1920; Putnam, 1921

CASSIDAY, BRUCE (BINGHAM). 1920- .
Pseudonyms: Carson Bingham, Mary Anne Drew, Annie Laurie McMurdie, Michael Stratford, qq.v.
The Brass Shroud. Ace, 1956
The Buried Motive. Ace, 1957
The Corpse in the Picture Window. Ace, 1961
The Floater. Abelard (New York & London), 1960
Operation Goldkill. Award, 1967
While Murder Waits. Graphic, 1957

CASSILIS, INA L(EON)
Between Midnight and Dawn. Vizetelly, 1885
Blind Justice. Aldine, 1926
Martyr or Criminal? Aldine, 1925

CASSILL, R(ONALD) V(ERLIN). 1919- .
-Doctor Cobb's Game. Geis, 1970
Dormitory Women. Lion, 1954
The Hungering Shame. Avon, 1956
-Lustful Summer. Avon, 1958
-Naked Morning. Avon, 1957
-A Taste of Sin. Ace, 1955
-Tempest. GM, 1959
The Wife Next Door. GM, 1959
-The Wound of Love. Avon, 1956

CASSON, STANLEY. 1889-1944.
Murder by Burial. H. Hamilton, 1938; Harper, 1938

CASTANG, VIOLA
The Invisible Cord. Allen, 1958
A Smell of Garbage. Hale, 1972

CASTIER, JULES
Rather Like. Jenkins, 1920; Lippincott, 1920 ss, at least one criminous

CASTILLOU, HENRY. 1921- .
The Night of the Rose. Redman, 1958. (Translation of Le Nuit de la Rose. Paris, 1957.)

CASTLE, AGNES (SWEETMAN), -1922, and EGERTON CASTLE, 1858-1920.
Flower o' the Orange, and other stories. Methuen, 1908; Macmillan, 1908 ss, some criminous

CASTLE, DENNIS
The Fourth Gambler. Muller, 1964

CASTLE, EGERTON. 1858-1920. See: AGNES (SWEETMAN) CASTLE, -1922.

CASTLE, FRANK. Pseudonym: Steve Thurman, q.v.
Dead and Kicking. GM, 1956; Fawcett (London), 1957
Hawaiian Eye. Dell, 1962. (Novelization of the TV series.)
Lovely and Lethal. GM, 1957; Red Seal, 1959
Move Along, Stranger. GM, 1954; Fawcett (London), 1954
Murder in Red. GM, 1957; Fawcett (London), 1959
Vengeance Under Law. GM, 1957
The Violent Hours. GM, 1956; Fawcett (London), 1956

CASTLE, JOHN. Joint pseudonym of John William Garrod and Ronald Charles Payne.
Flight into Danger, with Arthur Hailey, 1920- . Souvenir, 1958. U.S. title: Runway Zero-Eight. Doubleday, 1959
Runway Zero-Eight; see Flight into Danger
The Seventh Fury. Souvenir, 1961; Walker, 1963

CASWELL, HELEN (RAYBURN). 1923- .
Never Wed an Old Man. Doubleday, 1975

CATALAN, HENRI. Pseudonym of Henri Dupuy-Mazuel, 1885- . Series character: Soeur Angele, in all titles.
Soeur Angele and the Bell Ringer's Niece. Sheed, 1957
Soeur Angele and the Embarrassed Ladies. Sheed, 1955. (Translation of Le Cas de Soeur Angele. Paris, 1953.)
Soeur Angele and the Ghosts of Chambord. Sheed, 1956. (Translation of Soeur Angele et les Fantomes de Chambord. Paris, 1953.)

CATHER, GEORGE P.
Dora's Device. Peterson, 1885

CATTO, MAX(WELL JEFFREY). 1909- .
Pseudonym: Simon Kent, q.v.
-All or Nothing. Popular Library, 1956. (British title?)
-The Killing Frost. Heinemann, 1950. Also published as: Trapeze. Four Square, 1959
-A Prize of Gold. Heinemann, 1953
Sam Casanova. Heinemann, 1973; Signet, 1977
The Tiger in the Bed. Heinemann, 1962; Morrow, 1963
Trapeze; see The Killing Frost

CAUNTER, CYRIL F(RANCIS). 1899- .
Death to the Killer. Eldon, 1935
Ex-Gangster. Eldon, 1933
Madness Opens the Door. Butterworth, 1932

CAUSEY, JAMES O.
The Baby Doll Murders. GM, 1957; Fawcett (London), 1959

Frenzy. Crest, 1960
Killer Take All! Graphic, 1957; Hale, 1960

CAVANAGH, ARTHUR. 1926- .
The Children are Gone. Simon, 1966; Heinemann, 1966

CAVE, HUGH B(ARNETT). 1910- .
Run, Shadow, Run. Hale, 1968

CAVENDISH, CHARLES
The Lure. Collins, 1930. (Novelization of the film adapted from the play by Major J. S. Clair.)

CAVERHILL, WILLIAM MELVILLE. 1910- .
Pseudonym: Alan Melville, q.v.

CAYWOOD, MARK. Pseudonym.
Paradise Island. Bles, 1927. U.S. title: Rainbow Island. Viking, 1927
-Virginia's Quest. Gray, 1934

CEARLEY, J. B.
A Touch of Murder. Caravelle, 1968

CEARNACH, CONALL. See; CEARNACH CONALL.

CECIL, ALLAN
Turquoise Clues. Rich, 1949

CECIL, HENRY. Pseudonym of Henry Cecil Leon, 1902-1976. Series character: Roger Thursby = RT.
According to the Evidence. Chapman, 1954; Harper, 1954
Alibi for a Judge. Joseph, 1960
The Asking Price. Joseph, 1966; Harper, 1966
The Blackmailers; see No Fear or Favour
Brief Tales from the Bench. BBC, 1968; Simon, 1972 ss
Brothers in Law. Joseph, 1955; Harper, 1955. Play version, by Ted Willis, 1918- , and Henry Cecil: French (London), 1957 RT
A Child Divided; see Fathers in Law
Daughters in Law. Joseph, 1961; Harper, 1961
Fathers in Law. Joseph, 1965. U.S. title: A Child Divided. Harper, 1965
Friends at Court. Joseph, 1956; Harper, 1956 RT
Full Circle. Chapman, 1948
Independent Witness. Joseph, 1963
Juror in Waiting. Joseph, 1970
The Long Arm; see Much in Evidence
Much in Evidence. Joseph, 1957. U.S. title: The Long Arm. Harper, 1957
Natural Causes. Chapman, 1953
No Bail for the Judge. Chapman, 1952; Harper, 1952
No Fear or Favour. Joseph, 1968. U.S. title: The Blackmailers. Simon, 1969
The Painswick Line. Chapman, 1951
Portrait of a Judge and other stories. Joseph, 1964; Harper, 1965 ss
Settled Out of Court. Joseph, 1959; Harper, 1959. Play version, by William Saroyan, 1908- , and Henry Cecil: French (London), 1962
Sober as a Judge. Joseph, 1958; Harper, 1959 RT
Tell You What I'll Do. Joseph, 1969; Simon, 1970
Truth with her Boots On. Joseph, 1974
Unlawful Occasions. Joseph, 1962
The Wanted Man. Joseph, 1972
Ways and Means. Chapman, 1952; British Book Service, 1952
A Woman Named Anne. Joseph, 1967; Harper, 1967

CECIL, OLIVE
Behold the Body! Long, 1932
Four Women Went. Long, 1931

74/ Cecil, Olive

-Lighter of Candles. Nash, 1930
The Pepper-Pot Problem. Long, 1933

CELLO, J.
Corruption's Tutor. Scion, 1953
Crisis. Scion, 1953
Duet to Corruption. Scion, 1953
A Guy Gets His. Scion, 1950
Jeanie with the Light Brown Corpse. Scion, 1952
Lights Out. Scion, 1953
Sin has no Future. Scion, 1954
Sin is Her Mantle. Scion, 1953
They Don't Live Long. Scion, 1951

CENNI, JOSEPH
Mafia Women. Tandem, 1974

CERF, CHRISTOPHER BENNETT. 1941- .
Joint pseudonym with Michael K. Frith: I*n Fl*m*ng, q.v.

CERRA, GERDA ANN
A Darker Heritage. Lancer, 1972

CERVUS, G. I. Pseudonym of William James Roe, 1843- .
-White Feathers. Lippincott, 1885

CHABER, M. E. Pseudonym of Kendell Foster Crossen, 1910- , q.v. Other pseudonyms: Bennett Barlay, Richard Foster, Christopher Monig, Clay Richards, qq.v. Series character: Milo March, in all titles.
All the Way Down; see No Grave for March
As Old as Cain. Holt, 1954. Also published as: Take One for Murder. Bestseller, 1955
The Bonded Dead. Holt, 1971; Hale, 1973
Born to be Hanged. Holt, 1973
The Day It Rained Diamonds. Holt, 1966; Macdonald, 1968
Don't Get Caught; see Hangman's Harvest
The Flaming Man. Holt, 1969; Hale, 1970
The Gallows Garden. Rinehart, 1958; Boardman, 1958. Also published as: The Lady Came to Kill. PB, 1959
Green Grow the Graves. Holt, 1970; Hale, 1971
Hangman's Harvest. Holt, 1952. Also published as: Don't Get Caught. Popular Library, 1953
A Hearse of Another Color. Rinehart, 1958; Boardman, 1959
Jade for a Lady. Rinehart, 1962; Boardman, 1962
The Lady Came to Kill; see The Gallows Garden
A Lonely Walk. Rinehart, 1956; Boardman, 1957
A Man in the Middle. Holt, 1967
The Man Inside. Holt, 1954; Eyre, 1955. Also published as: Now It's My Turn. Popular Library, 1954
No Grave for March. Holt, 1953; Eyre, 1954. Also published as: All the Way Down. Popular Library, 1953
Now It's My Turn; see The Man Inside
Six Who Ran. Holt, 1964; Boardman, 1965
So Dead the Rose. Rinehart, 1959; Boardman, 1960
Softly in the Night. Holt, 1963; Boardman, 1963
The Splintered Man. Rinehart, 1955; Boardman, 1957
Take One for Murder; see As Old as Cain
Uneasy Lies the Dead. Holt, 1964; Boardman, 1964
Wanted: Dead Men. Holt, 1965; Boardman, 1966
Wild Midnight Falls. Holt, 1968

CHABREY, F.
The Invisible Image. International, 1969

CHABRILLAT, HENRI. See: WILLIAM (BERTRAND) BUSNACH, 1832-1907.

CHACKO, DAVID. 1942- .
Gage. St. Martin's, 1974; Panther, 1976
Price. St. Martin's, 1973; Gollancz, 1974

CHADWICK, CHARLES. 1874-1953.
The Cactus. Crowell, 1925
The Moving House of Foscaldo. Cassell, 1926

CHADWICK, JOSEPH. Pseudonyms: John Conway, John Creighton, qq.v.
The Golden Frame. GM, 1955

CHADWICK, PAUL. Pseudonym: Brant House, q.v.

CHALLIS, SIMON
Death on a Quiet Beach. Hale, 1968

CHALMERS, STEPHEN. 1880-1935.
The Affair of the Gallows Tree. Doubleday, 1930; Selwyn, 1931
Blood on the Heather. Doubleday, 1932; World's Work, 1935
The Crime in Car 13. Doubleday, 1930
The Greater Punishment. Doubleday, 1920; Bale, 1923
House of Two Green Eyes. Doubleday, 1928
The Vanishing Smuggler. Clode, 1909; Mills, 1910
The Whispering Ghost. Doubleday, 1932

CHAMBERLAIN, ANNE
The Tall Dark Man. Bobbs, 1955; Hart-Davis, 1955

CHAMBERLAIN, ELINOR. 1901- .
Appointment in Manila. Dodd, 1945; Eyre, 1949
Manila Hemp. Dodd, 1947
Snare for Witches. Dodd, 1948; Gollancz, 1949

CHAMBERLAIN, ESTHER and LUCIA. See also: LUCIA CHAMBERLAIN.
The Coast of Chance. Bobbs, 1908

CHAMBERLAIN, GEORGE AGNEW. 1879- .
The Great Van Suttart Mystery. Putnam, 1925
In Defense of Mrs. Maxon. Bobbs, 1938
Night at Lost End. Brewer, 1931
The Red House. Bobbs, 1945
The Silver Cord. Putnam, 1927

CHAMBERLAIN, LUCIA. See also: ESTHER CHAMBERLAIN.
The Other Side of the Door. Bobbs, 1909

CHAMBERLAIN, WILLIAM
Red January. Paperback Library, 1964

CHAMBERS, DANA. Pseudonym of Albert Leffingwell, 1895-1946, q.v. Other pseudonym: Giles Jackson, q.v. Series character: Jim Steele = JS.
The Blonde Died First. Dial, 1941; Hale, 1943 JS
The Case of Caroline Animus. Dial, 1946; Hale, 1951. Also published as: Dear, Dead Women. Jonathan, 1948 JS
Darling, This is Death. Dial, 1945; Hale, 1951
Dear, Dead Women; see The Case of Caroline Animus
Death Against Venus. Dial, 1946; Hale, 1953
The Frightened Man. Dial, 1942; Hale, 1945 JS
The Last Secret. Dial, 1943; Hale, 1949 JS
Rope for an Ape. Dial, 1947; Hale, 1952
She'll be Dead by Morning. Dial, 1940; Hale, 1941 JS
Some Day I'll Kill You. Dial, 1939; Hale, 1939 JS
Too Like the Dead; see Too Like the Lightning
Too Like the Lightning. Dial, 1939; Hale, 1940. Also published as: Too Like the Dead. Bestseller, 1951 JS

CHAMBERS, DEREK HYDE. Pseudonym: D. Herbert Hyde, q.v.

CHAMBERS, MARY (STROTHER). 1899- .
See: (ELWYN) WHITMAN CHAMBERS, 1896- .

CHAMBERS, PETER. Pseudonym of Dennis (John Andrew) Phillips, 1924- , q.v. Other pseudonym: Peter Chester, q.v. See also: W(illiam Arthur) Howard Baker, 1925- . Series character: Mark Preston, in all titles.
Always Take the Big Ones. Hale, 1965
The Bad Die Young. Hale, 1967; Roy, 1968
The Big Goodbye. Hale, 1962
The Blonde Wore Black. Hale, 1968; Roy, 1968
Dames can be Deadly. Hale, 1963; Abelard, 1963
Don't Bother to Knock. Hale, 1966
Down-Beat Kill. Hale, 1963; Abelard, 1964
Lady, This is Murder. Hale, 1963
Murder is for Keeps. Hale, 1961; Abelard, 1962
No Gold When You Go. Hale, 1966
No Peace for the Wicked. Hale, 1968; Roy, 1968
Nobody Lives Forever. Hale, 1964
Somebody Has to Lose. Hale, 1975
Speak Ill of the Dead. Hale, 1968; Roy, 1969
They Call It Murder. Hale, 1973
This'll Kill You. Hale, 1964
Wreath for a Redhead. Hale, 1962; Abelard, 1962
You're Better Off Dead. Hale, 1965

CHAMBERS, PHILIP. 1936- . All titles feature Sexton Blake and were published by Amalgamated Press.
Bullets to Baghdad. 1960
Dangerous Playmate. 1962
Keep It a Secret. 1961
Lotus Leaves and Larceny. 1963
Moscow Manhunt. 1962
Shot from the Dark. 1961

CHAMBERS, ROBERT. 1933- .
Divide by Seven. Bobbs, 1969. British title: The Lesser Evil. Hale, 1971
The Lesser Evil; see Divide by Seven
Moth in a Rag Shop. Bobbs, 1968; Hale, 1969. Also published as: Village East. Dell, 1970
Village East; see Moth in a Rag Shop

CHAMBERS, ROBERT W(ILLIAM). 1865-1933.
The Dark Star. Appleton, 1917
The Flaming Jewel. Doran, 1922; Hodder, 1922
In Secret. Doran, 1919; Hodder, 1919
-The Laughing Girl. Appleton, 1918
Marie Halkett. Appleton, 1937; Unwin, 1925
The Moonlit Way. Appleton, 1919
The Mystery Lady. Grosset, 1925

The Mystery of Choice. Appleton (New York and London), 1897
Secret Service Operator 13. Appleton, 1934. British title: Spy No. 13. Allan, 1935
Spy No. 13; see Secret Service Operator 13
The Tracer of Lost Persons. Appleton, 1906; Murray, 1907 ss

CHAMBERS, (ELWYN) WHITMAN. 1896-   .
Action at World's End. Dutton, 1945
Bright Star of Danger. Doubleday, 1940
Bring Me Another Murder. Dutton, 1942
The Campanile Murders. Appleton, 1933
The Coast of Intrigue. Henkle, 1928. British title: Contraband Coast. Nelson, 1928
-The Come-On. Pyramid, 1953
Contraband Coast; see The Coast of Intrigue
Dangerous Water. Doubleday, 1941. Also published as: Deadly Lure. Jonathan, 1955 (abridged)
Deadly Lure; see Dangerous Water
Dead Men Leave No Fingerprints. Doubleday, 1935; Cassell, 1935
Dog Eat Dog. Doubleday, 1938. British title: Murder in the Mist. Cassell, 1938
Dry Tortugas. Doubleday, 1940
-In Savage Surrender. Monarch, 1959
-Manhandled. Monarch, 1960
Murder for a Wanton. Doubleday, 1934; Melrose, 1936
Murder in the Mist; see Dog Eat Dog
Murder Lady; see Once Too Often
The Navy Murders. Dodd, 1932; Hutchinson, 1931, as by Mary (Strother) Chambers (1899-   ) and Whitman Chambers
Once Too Often. Doubleday, 1938. British title: Murder Lady. Cassell, 1938
-Season for Love. Monarch, 1959
Thirteen Steps. Doubleday, 1935
You Can't Get Away by Running. Doubleday, 1939; Cassell, 1939

CHAMIER, JOHN (EDWIN DesCHAMPS)
Cannonball. Cassell, 1966

CHAMPAGNE, PAUL
A Fair Affair. Greywood, 1967

CHAMPION, JOAN
Incidental Murder. Macdonald, 1946

CHAMPION DE CRESPIGNY, ROSE.   -1935.
See: MRS. PHILIP CHAMPION DE CRESPIGNY.

CHAMPLIN, VIRGINIA. Pseudonym of Grace Virginia Lord,   -1885.
Shadowed by a Detective; or, The Woman in Wax. Ogilvie, 1885

CHANCE, JOHN NEWTON. 1911-   . Pseudonyms: J. Drummond, John Lymington, qq.v. Series characters: Supt. Black, in at least those marked B; Jonathan Blake, in at least those marked JB; John Newton Chance, in at least those marked JNC; Mr. DeHavilland, in at least those marked D; Jason, in at least those marked J.
The Abel Coincidence. Hale, 1969 JB
The Affair at Dead End. Hale, 1966 JB
Affair with a Rich Girl. Hale, 1958
Alarm at Black Brake. Hale, 1960
Aunt Miranda's Murder. Macdonald, 1951; Dodd, 1951
A Bad Dream of Death. Hale, 1972
The Black Highway. Macdonald, 1947 D
The Brandy Pole. Macdonald, 1949 D
The Canterbury Kilgrims. Hale, 1974
The Case of the Death Computer. Hale, 1967
The Case of the Fear Makers. Hale, 1967
The Cat Watchers. Hale, 1971
Commission for Disaster. Hale, 1964
Coven Gibbet. Macdonald, 1948
The Crimes at Rillington Place. Hodder, 1961
Dead Man's Knock. Hale, 1957
Dead Man's Shoes. Hale, 1968 JB
The Dead Tale-Tellers. Hale, 1972
Death of an Innocent. Gollancz, 1938 B,D
Death of a Wild Bird. Hale, 1968
Death Stalks the Cobbled Square; see Screaming Fog
Death Under Desolate. Hale, 1964
The Death Woman. Hale, 1967 JB
The Devil Drives. Gollancz, 1936
The Devil in Greenlands. Gollancz, 1939
The Devil's Edge. Hale, 1975
The Double Death. Hale, 1966
The Eye in Attendance. Macdonald, 1946 JNC
The Faces of a Bad Girl. Hale, 1971
The Farm Villains. Hale, 1973
The Fatal Fascination. Hale, 1959
Fate of the Lying Jade. Hale, 1968
The Forest Affair. Hale, 1963
The Ghost of Truth. Gollancz, 1939 B
The Girl in the Crime Belt. Hale. 1974
The Grab Operators. Hale, 1973
The Halloween Murders. Hale, 1968
Hill Fog. Hale, 1975 JB
The Hurricane Drift. Hale, 1967 JB
The Ice Maidens. Hale, 1969 JB
Import of Evil. Hale, 1961
Involvement in Austria. Hale, 1969
The Jason Affair. Macdonald, 1953. U.S. title: Up to Her Neck. Popular Library, 1955 J
Jason and the Sleep Game. Macdonald, 1954 J
Jason Goes West. Macdonald, 1955 J
The Jason Murders. Macdonald, 1954 J
The Killer Reaction. Hale, 1969 JB
The Killing Experiment. Hale, 1969 JB
The Knight and the Castle. Macdonald, 1946 D
Lady in a Frame. Hale, 1960
The Last Seven Hours. Macdonald, 1956
Last Train to Limbo. Hale, 1972
The Little Crime. Hale, 1957
The Love-Hate Relationship. Hale, 1973
Maiden Possessed. Gollancz, 1937
The Man Behind Me. Hale, 1963
The Man in my Shoes. Macdonald, 1952 JNC
The Man with No Face. Hale, 1959
Man with Three Witches. Hale, 1958
The Man with Two Heads. Hale, 1972
Mantrap. Hale, 1968
The Mask of Pursuit. Hale, 1967 JB
The Mirror Train. Hale, 1970
The Mists of Treason. Hale, 1970 JB
The Monstrous Regiment. Hale, 1975
Murder in Oils. Gollancz, 1935
The Night of the Full Moon. Macdonald, 1950 D
The Night of the Settlement. Hale, 1961
The Randy Inheritance. Macdonald, 1953
The Red Knight. Macdonald, 1945; Macmillan, 1945 JNC,B,D
Rhapsody in Fear. Gollancz, 1937
A Ring of Liars. Hale, 1970
The Rogue Aunt. Hale, 1968 JB
The Screaming Fog. Macdonald, 1944. U.S. title: Death Stalks the Cobbled Square. McBride, 1946 JNC
A Shadow Called Janet. Macdonald, 1956
The Shadow of the Killer. Hale, 1974
The Starfish Affair. Hale, 1974
Stormlight. Hale, 1965
The Three Masks of Death. Hale, 1970 JB
The Thug Executive. Hale, 1967
Triangle of Fear. Hale, 1962
The Twopenny Box. Macdonald, 1952
Up to Her Neck; see The Jason Affair
Wheels in the Forest. Gollancz, 1935 D, B
A Wreath of Bones. Hale, 1971

CHANCE, ROGER (JAMES FERGUSON)
Be Absolute for Death. Davies, 1964

CHANCE, SIMON
Death of a Tax Inspector. Staples, 1941

CHANCE, STEPHEN. Pseudonym of Philip Turner. Series character: Rev. Septimus Treloar, in both titles.
Septimus and the Minister Ghost. Bodley Head, 1972
Septimus and the Danedyke Mystery. Bodley Head, 1971

CHANCELLOR, JOHN. Pseudonym of Charles de Balzac Rideaux, 1900-1971. Series character: Frass, in at least those marked F.
-Another Man's Wife. Newnes, 1931
The Dark God. Hutchinson, 1927; Century, 1928
-Desert Desire. Gramol, 1932
-The Farther Off from England. Cassell, 1969
Frass. Hutchinson, 1929 F
-Her Garden of Eden. Newnes, 1926
The Jersey Plunder. Cassell, 1970
-The Knave of Hearts. Gramol, 1937
The Ladder of Cards. Hutchinson, 1926
The Murder Syndicate. Eldon, 1949
Mystery at Angel's End. Long, 1930
The Mystery of Norman's Court. Hutchinson, 1923; Small, 1924
-The Prim Windows. Cape, 1967
The Return of Frass. Hutchinson, 1930 F
Stolen Gold. Hutchinson, 1932

CHANDLER, DAVID (LEON)
The Gangsters. Morrow, 1975; Allen, 1975
The Glass Totem. Appleton, 1962
The Ramsden Case. Simon, 1967

CHANDLER, NOEL
Satan in High Heels. Belmont, 1963. (Novelization of the movie.)

CHANDLER, RAYMOND (THORNTON). 1888-1959. Series character: Philip Marlowe = PM.
The Big Sleep. Knopf, 1939; H. Hamilton, 1939 PM
Farewell, My Lovely. Knopf, 1940; H. Hamilton, 1940 PM
Finger Man and other stories. Avon, 1946. (Three pulp novelets from the 1930's, later included in hardcover in The Simple Art of Murder, q.v.)
Five Murderers. Avon, 1944. (Five pulp stories, all but one included later in hardcover in The Simple Art of Murder, q.v.)
Five Sinister Characters. Avon, 1945. (Five pulp stories, all included later in hardcover in The Simple Art of Murder, q.v.)
The High Window. Knopf, 1942; H. Hamilton, 1943 PM
Killer in the Rain. Houghton, 1964; H. Hamilton, 1964. (Eight pulp stories, six in their first book appearances and all adapted into the first four PM novels.)
The Lady in the Lake. Knopf, 1943; H. Hamilton, 1944 PM
The Little Sister. Houghton, 1949; H. Hamilton, 1949. Also published as: Marlowe. PB, 1969 PM

CHANDLER, RAYMOND

The Long Goodbye. Houghton, 1954; H. Hamilton, 1953 PM
Marlowe; see The Little Sister
Pearls are a Nuisance. H. Hamilton, 1953 (ss, none in first book appearances.)
Pick-Up on Noon Street; see The Simple Art of Murder
Playback. Houghton, 1958; H. Hamilton, 1958 PM
Red Wind. World, 1946. (Five pulp stories, none in first book appearance, and all but one later included in hardcover in The Simple Art of Murder, q.v.)
The Simple Art of Murder. Houghton, 1950; H. Hamilton, 1950. (Twelve pulp stories and an essay. The stories include all but two of the combined contents of Finger Man, Five Murderers, Five Sinister Characters, Red Wind and Spanish Blood, qq.v. However, this large collection was itself broken into three paperbacks, all issued by PB: Pick-Up on Noon Street, 1952, The Simple Art of Murder, 1953, and Trouble is My Business, 1951.)
Smart-Aleck Kill. H. Hamilton, 1953. (ss, none in first book appearances.)
The Smell of Fear. H. Hamilton, 1965. (Another collection of pulp writings, but here including one story in its first book appearance.)
Spanish Blood. World, 1946. (Five pulp stories, none in first book appearance, and all included later in hardcover in The Simple Art of Murder, q.v.)
Trouble is My Business; see The Simple Art of Murder

CHANNING, B.
Dressed to Kill. World Distributors, 1952

CHANNON, E(THEL) M(ARY) [MRS. FRANCIS CHANNON]. 1875- .
The Chimney Murder. Benn, 1929; Little, 1930
The Gilt-Edge Mystery. Benn, 1932
Golden Glory. Benn, 1931
The House with No Address. Benn, 1931
Twice Dead. Benn, 1930

CHANSLOR, ROY. 1899- .
Hazard. Simon, 1947
Lowdown. Farrar, 1931

CHANSLOR, (MARJORIE) TORREY (HOOD). 1899- . Series characters: Lutie and Amanda Beagle, in both titles.
Our First Murder. Stokes, 1940
Our Second Murder. Stokes, 1941

CHAPIN, ANNA ALICE. 1880- . See: GEORGE C(HARLES) JENKINS, 1850-1929. Pseudonym (?): Harry Coverdale, q.v.

CHAPIN, CARL M(ATTISON). 1879- .
Three Died Beside the Marble Pool. Doubleday, 1936; World's Work, 1937

CHAPMAN, GEORGE WARREN VERNON. 1925- .
Pseudonym: Vernon Warren, q.v.

CHAPMAN, H. E.
The Heseltine Mystery. Crowther, 1944

CHAPMAN, HESTER W(OLFERSTAN). 1899-1976.
Limmerston Hall. Coward, 1973

CHAPMAN, RAYMOND. 1924- . Pseudonym: Simon Nash, q.v.

CHAPMAN, ROBERT (ALEC MARK). 1916- . Series character: Rex Banner, in at least those marked RB.
Be My Ghost. Hale, 1963
Behind the Headlines. Laurie, 1955 RB
Crime on My Hands. Laurie, 1952 RB
Deep Secret. Rich, 1939
The Downward Path. Hale, 1959 RB
The Frozen Stiff. Laurie, 1956 RB
The Hot Half-Million. Hale, 1963
Murder for the Million. Laurie, 1953 RB
One Jump Ahead. Laurie, 1951 RB
The Seven Sisters. Crowther, 1945
Winter Wears a Shroud. Laurie, 1952 RB
Wish You were Dead. Hale, 1960

CHAPPELL, MOLLIE
Murder Comes Home. Collins, 1967

CHARBONNEAU, LOUIS (HENRY). 1924- .
And Hope to Die. Ace, 1970
From a Dark Place. Dell, 1974
Night of Violence. Dodd, 1959. British title: The Trapped Ones. Barker, 1960
Nor All Your Tears. Dodd, 1959
The Trapped Ones; see Night of Violence

CHARLES, ERNEST F. Series character: Dick Torreyton, in at least those marked DT.
-Before the Wind. Nelson, 1938
Death Comes Ashore. Nelson, 1938 DT
Death Crosses the Line. Nelson, 1937 DT

CHARLES, FRANKLIN. Joint pseudonym of Cleve F(ranklin) Adams, 1895-1949, q.v., and Robert Leslie Bellem, q.v. Other Adams pseudonym: John Spain, q.v.
The Vice Czar Murders. Funk, 1941

CHARLES, JOHN
The Man Without a Mouth. Stockwell, 1935

CHARLES, MOIE and BARBARA TOY
The Murder at the Vicarage. French (London), 1950. (A play adapted from the novel by Agatha Christie, 1890-1976, q.v.)

CHARLES, ROBERT. Pseudonym of Robert Charles Smith, 1938- . Other pseudonym: Charles Leader, q.v. Series character: Simon Larren, in at least those marked SL.
Arctic Assignment. Hale, 1966 SL
Assassins for Peace. Hale, 1967
The Big Fish. Hale, 1969
A Clash of Hawks. Hale, 1976; Pinnacle, 1975
Dark Vendetta. Hale, 1964 SL
Dead Before Midnight. Hale, 1975
The Faceless Fugitive. Hale, 1963
The Flight of the Raven. Hale, 1975; Pinnacle, 1975
The Fourth Shadow. Hale, 1966
The Hour of the Wolf. Hale, 1974; Pinnacle, 1975
Mission of Murder. Hale, 1965 SL
Nothing to Lose. Hale, 1963
One Must Survive. Hale, 1964
The Scream of the Dove. Hale, 1976; Pinnacle, 1975
Sea Vengeance. Hale, 1974
Stamboul Intrigue. Hale, 1968; Roy, 1968
Strikefast. Hale, 1969
The Sun Virgin. Hale, 1974
This Side of Hell. Hale, 1965
Three Days to Live. Hale, 1968; Roy, 1968

CHARLES, THERESA. Joint pseudonym of Charles Swatridge and Irene Maude Mossop Swatridge. Pseudonym of Irene Swatridge alone: Jan Tempest, q.v. These titles were apparently published in England as romances and in the U.S. as gothics.
The Burning Beacon. Cassell, 1956; Lancer, 1966
Dark Legacy; see Happy Now I Go
Fairer Than She. Cassell, 1953; Dell, 1968
Happy Now I Go. Longmans, 1947. U.S. title: Dark Legacy. Dell, 1968
House on the Rocks. Hale, 1962; Paperback Library, 1966
Lady in the Mist; see Nurse Alice in Love
The Man for Me. Hale, 1965. U.S. title: The Shrouded Tower. Ace, 1966
Nurse Alice in Love. Hale, 1964. U.S. title: Lady in the Mist. Ace, 1966
Proud Citadel. Hale, 1967; Dell, 1967
Return to Terror; see Widower's Wife
The Shrouded Tower; see The Man for Me
Widower's Wife. Hale, 1963. U.S. title: Return to Terror. Paperback Library, 1966

CHARLES, WILL. Pseudonym of Charles Willeford.
The Hombre from Sonora. Lenox Hill, 1971

CHARLESWORTH, M. E. Pseudonym of Maud Ballington Charlesworth Booth, 1865- .
The Relentless Current. Putnam, 1912. Also published as: Was It Murder?; or, The Relentless Current. Putnam, 1912, as by Maud Ballington Booth

CHARLTON, MARJORY
Death of a Fashion Writer. Murray, 1940

CHARNWOOD, LORD. See: GODFREY R(ATHBONE) BENSON, 1864-1945.

CHARTERIS, LESLIE. 1907- . Name originally: Leslie Charles Bowyer Yin. Series character: Simon Templar (The Saint) = ST.
The Ace of Knaves. Hodder, 1937; Doubleday, 1937. Also published as: The Saint in Action. Sun Dial, 1938; and as: The Saint: Ace of Knaves. Avon, 1955. (Three ST novelets.)
Alias the Saint. Hodder, 1931. (Three ST novelets, all included in the U.S. collection Wanted for Murder, q.v. Note that there are two U.S. paperbacks entitled Alias the Saint, one published by Bonded, 1945, the other by Avon, 1957; each contains only two stories from the British edition.)
Angels of Doom; see She was a Lady
Arrest the Saint; see The First Saint Omnibus
The Avenging Saint; see Knight Templar
The Bandit. Ward, 1929; Doubleday, 1930
Boodle. Hodder, 1934. U.S. title: The Saint Intervenes. Doubleday, 1934. (14 ST ss. Note that some Avon paperback reprint editions are incomplete.)
The Brighter Buccaneer. Hodder, 1933; Doubleday, 1933. Also published as: The Saint—The Brighter Buccaneer. Avon, 1957. (ST ss. Note again that the Avon reprint is incomplete.)
Call for the Saint. Hodder, 1948; Doubleday, 1948. (2 ST novelets.)
Catch the Saint. Hodder, 1975; Doubleday, 1975. (2 ST novelets, adapted by Fleming Lee from original stories by Norman Worker.)

Concerning the Saint. Avon, 1958. (One of two reprints comprising tales omitted from Avon editions of ST ss volumes.)
Daredevil. Ward, 1929; Doubleday, 1929
Enter the Saint. Hodder, 1930; Doubleday, 1931. (3 ST novelets.)
Featuring the Saint. Hodder, 1931. (3 ST novelets, all included in the U.S. collection Wanted for Murder, q.v. Note that the Avon reprint entitled Featuring the Saint, 1958, contains only 2 novelets.)
The First Saint Omnibus. Hodder, 1939; Doubleday, 1939. Also published as: Arrest the Saint! Permabooks, 1951. (A large collection taken from the many pre-1939 volumes of ST ss and novelets, each tale prefaced with extensive commentary by Charteris written especially for this omnibus.)
Follow the Saint. Hodder, 1939; Doubleday, 1938. (3 ST novelets.)
Getaway. Hodder, 1932; Doubleday, 1933. Also published as: Saint's Getaway. Sun Dial, 1943
The Happy Highwayman. Hodder, 1939; Doubleday, 1939. Also published as: The Saint—The Happy Highwayman. Avon, 1955. (9 ST ss. Note that the Avon reprint is incomplete.)
The Holy Terror. Hodder, 1932. U.S. title: The Saint vs. Scotland Yard. Doubleday, 1932. (3 ST novelets.)
Knight Templar. Hodder, 1930. U.S. title: The Avenging Saint. Doubleday, 1931 ST
Lady on a Train. Shaw, 1945. (Novelization of the movie.)
The Last Hero. Hodder, 1930; Doubleday, 1930. Also published as: The Saint Closes the Case. Sun Dial, 1941; and as: The Saint and the Last Hero. Avon, 1953 ST
Meet the Tiger. Ward, 1928; Doubleday, 1929. Also published as: The Saint Meets the Tiger. Sun Dial, 1940 ST
The Misfortunes of Mr. Teal. Hodder, 1934; Doubleday, 1934. Also published as: The Saint in England. Sun Dial, 1941. (3 ST novelets.)
Once More the Saint. Hodder, 1933. U.S. title: The Saint and Mr. Teal. Doubleday, 1933. (3 ST novelets)
Prelude for War. Hodder, 1938; Doubleday, 1938. Also published as: The Saint Plays with Fire. Triangle, 1942 ST
The Saint Abroad. Hodder, 1970; Doubleday, 1969. (2 ST short novels adapted by Fleming Lee from ST teleplays by Michael Pertwee, with final manuscript revision by Charteris.)
The Saint: Ace of Knaves; see The Ace of Knaves
The Saint and Mr. Teal; see Once More the Saint
The Saint and the Fiction Makers. Hodder, 1969; Doubleday, 1968. (Adapted by Fleming Lee from a ST teleplay by John Kruse, with final manuscript revision by Charteris.)
The Saint and the Last Hero; see The Last Hero
The Saint and the People Importers. Hodder pb, 1971; Doubleday, 1971. (Adapted by Fleming Lee from his own ST teleplay, with final manuscript revision by Charteris.)
The Saint and the Sizzling Saboteur; see The Saint on Guard
The Saint Around the World. Hodder, 1957; Doubleday, 1956. (6 ST ss.)
The Saint at a Thieves' Picnic; see Thieves' Picnic

The Saint at Large. Sun Dial, 1943. (A collection of ST ss, all from the three prior ss volumes, with some new introductory matter by Charteris.)
The Saint Bids Diamonds; see Thieves' Picnic
The Saint—The Brighter Buccaneer; see The Brighter Buccaneer
The Saint Cleans Up. Avon, 1959 (One of two reprints comprising tales omitted from Avon editions of ST ss volumes. The other is Concerning the Saint, q.v.)
The Saint Closes the Case; see The Last Hero
Saint Errant. Hodder, 1949; Doubleday, 1948. (9 ST ss.)
The Saint Goes On. Hodder, 1934; Doubleday, 1935. (3 ST novelets.)
The Saint Goes West. Hodder, 1942; Doubleday, 1942. (3 ST novelets. Note that most U.S. reprints contain only two of the three, whereas British paperback reprints are generally complete.)
The Saint—The Happy Highwayman; see The Happy Highwayman
The Saint in Action; see The Ace of Knaves
The Saint in England; see The Misfortunes of Mr. Teal
The Saint in Europe. Hodder, 1954; Doubleday, 1953. (7 ST ss.)
The Saint in Miami. Hodder, 1941; Doubleday, 1940 ST
The Saint in New York. Hodder, 1935; Doubleday, 1935 ST
The Saint in Pursuit. Hodder, 1971; Doubleday, 1970. (Based on an ST comic strip from 1959-60.)
The Saint Intervenes; see Boodle
The Saint in the Sun. Hodder, 1964; Doubleday, 1963. (7 ST ss.)
The Saint Meets his Match; see She Was a Lady
The Saint Meets the Tiger; see Meet the Tiger
The Saint on Guard. Hodder, 1945; Doubleday, 1944. (2 ST novelets. Each was published by Avon in a separate reprint volume: The Avon title The Saint on Guard, 1958, contains only "The Black Market", while The Saint and the Sizzling Saboteur, 1956, contains only "The Sizzling Saboteur.")
The Saint on the Spanish Main. Hodder, 1956; Doubleday, 1955. (6 ST ss.)
The Saint on TV. Hodder, 1968; Doubleday, 1968. (2 ST novelets, adapted by Fleming Lee from teleplays, with final manuscript revisions by Charteris.)
Saint Overboard. Hodder, 1936; Doubleday, 1936 ST
The Saint Plays with Fire; see Prelude for War
The Saint Returns. Hodder, 1969; Doubleday, 1968. (2 ST short novels adapted by Fleming Lee from teleplays, with final manuscript revision by Charteris.)
The Saint Sees It Through. Hodder, 1947; Doubleday, 1946 ST
The Saint Steps In. Hodder, 1944; Doubleday, 1943 ST
The Saint to the Rescue. Hodder, 1961; Doubleday, 1959. (6 ST ss.)
The Saint: Two in One. Sun Dial, 1942. (The Ace of Knaves, and The Happy Highwayman, qq.v., bound together in one volume.)
The Saint vs. Scotland Yard; see The Holy Terror
The Saint—Wanted for Murder; see Wanted for Murder.
Saint's Getaway; see Getaway

The Second Saint Omnibus. Hodder, 1952; Doubleday, 1951. (A collection taken from the volumes of ST ss and novelets published between 1939 and 1951, with extensive commentary by Charteris written especially for this volume.)
Senor Saint. Hodder, 1959; Doubleday, 1958. (4 ST ss.)
She was a Lady. Hodder, 1931. U.S. title: Angels of Doom. Doubleday, 1932. Also published as: The Saint Meets His Match. Avon, 1953 ST
Thanks to the Saint. Hodder, 1958; Doubleday, 1957. (6 ST ss.)
Thieves' Picnic. Hodder, 1937; Doubleday, 1937. Also published as: The Saint Bids Diamonds. Triangle, 1942; and as: The Saint at a Thieves' Picnic. Avon, 1951 ST
Trust the Saint. Hodder, 1962; Doubleday, 1962. (6 ST ss.)
Vendetta for the Saint. Hodder, 1965; Doubleday, 1964 ST
Wanted for Murder. Doubleday, 1931. (A volume of 6 ST novelets, including the complete contents of the two British collections entitled Alias the Saint, and Featuring the Saint, qq.v. The entire volume was also published as: The Saint—Wanted for Murder. Sun Dial, 1943. The 6 novelets were reprinted by Avon in three paperbacks of two tales each, these three volumes being confusingly entitled Alias the Saint, 1958, Featuring the Saint, 1958, and The Saint—Wanted for Murder, 1956.)
The White Rider. Ward, 1928; Doubleday, 1930
X Esquire. Ward, 1927

CHARYN, JEROME
Blue Eyes. Simon, 1975

CHASE, ALAN (LOUIS). 1929- .
The Kidneyed Caper. Simon, 1960

CHASE, ALLAN. 1913- .
The Five Arrows. Random, 1944
Shadow of a Hero. Little, 1949

CHASE, ARTHUR M(INTURN). 1875-1947.
Danger in the Dark. Dodd, 1933; Eldon, 1934
Murder of a Missing Man. Dodd, 1934
No Outlet. Dodd, 1940
The Party at the Penthouse. Dodd, 1932
Peril at the Spy Nest. Dodd, 1943
Twenty Minutes to Kill. Dodd, 1936

CHASE, BORDEN
Diamonds of Death. Hart, 1947

CHASE, JAMES HADLEY. Pseudonym of Rene Brabazon Raymond, 1906- . Other pseudonyms: James L. Docherty, Ambrose Grant, Raymond Marshall, qq.v. Series characters: Al Barney = AB; Dave Fenner = DF; Mark Girland = MG; Steve Harmas = SH; Vic Malloy = VM; Herman Radnitz = HR; Helga Rolfe = HR*; Lu Silk = LS; Frank Terrell = FT.
An Ace Up My Sleeve. Hale, 1971 HR*
Believe This...You'll Believe Anything. Hale, 1975
Believed Violent. Hale, 1968 MG, FT, HR, LS
Cade. Hale, 1966; PB, 1973
The Case of the Strangled Starlet; see Not Safe to be Free
A Coffin from Hong Kong. Hale, 1962
Come Easy—Go Easy. Hale, 1960; PB, 1974
Dead Ringer; see Safer Dead
The Dead Stay Dumb. Jarrolds, 1939.

U.S. title: Kiss My Fist! Eton, 1952.
Reprinted in U.S. under British
title: PB, 1973
The Doll's Bad News; see Twelve Chinks
and a Woman
The Double Shuffle. Hale, 1952; Dutton,
1953 SH
An Ear to the Ground. Hale, 1968 AB,
SH, FT
-Eve. Jarrolds, 1945
The Fast Buck. Hale, 1952
Figure It Out for Yourself. Hale, 1950;
Duell, 1951. Also published as: The
Marijuana Mob. Eton, 1952 VM
The Flesh of the Orchid. Jarrolds,
1948; PB, 1972
Goldfish Have No Hiding Place. Hale,
1974
The Guilty are Afraid. Hale, 1957; Signet, 1959
Have a Change of Scene. Hale, 1973
Have This One on Me. Hale, 1967 MG
I Would Rather Stay Poor. Hale, 1962;
PB, 1974
I'll Bury My Dead. Hale, 1953; Dutton,
1954
I'll Get You for This. Jarrolds, 1946;
Avon, 1951
The Joker in the Pack. Hale, 1975 HR*
Just a Matter of Time. Hale, 1972
Just Another Sucker. Hale, 1961; PB,
1974
Kiss My Fist!; see The Dead Stay Dumb
Knock, Knock! Who's There? Hale, 1973
Last Page. French (London), 1947. (3-
act play.)
Lay Her Among the Lilies. Hale, 1950.
U.S. title: Too Dangerous to be Free.
Duell, 1951 VM
Like a Hole in the Head. Hale, 1970
A Lotus for Miss Quon. Hale, 1961
The Marijuana Mob; see Figure It Out
for Yourself
Miss Callaghan Comes to Grief. Jarrolds, 1941
-Miss Shumway Waves a Wand. Jarrolds,
1944
No Orchids for Miss Blandish. Jarrolds,
1939; Howell Soskin, 1942. Also published as: The Villain and the Virgin. Avon, 1948. Revised edition,
under original title: Panther, 1961;
Avon, 1961 DF
Not Safe to be Free. Hale, 1958. U.S.
title: The Case of the Strangled
Starlet. Signet, 1958
One Bright Summer Morning. Hale, 1963;
PB, 1974
Safer Dead. Hale, 1954. U.S. title:
Dead Ringer. Ace, 1955
Shock Treatment. Hale, 1959; Signet,
1959 SH
So What Happens to Me? Hale, 1974
The Soft Centre. Hale, 1964 FT
Strictly for Cash. Hale, 1951; PB,
1973
Tell It to the Birds. Hale, 1963; PB,
1974 SH
There's a Hippie on the Highway. Hale,
1970 FT
There's Always a Price Tag. Hale, 1956;
PB, 1973 SH
This is for Real. Hale, 1965; Walker,
1967 MG, HR
This Way for a Shroud. Hale, 1953
Tiger by the Tail. Hale, 1954
Too Dangerous to be Free; see Lay Her
Among the Lilies
Twelve Chinamen and a Woman; see Twelve
Chinks and a Woman
Twelve Chinks and a Woman. Jarrolds,
1940; Howell Soskin, 1941. Also published, in revised form, as: Twelve
Chinamen and a Woman. Novel Library,
1950; and as: The Doll's Bad News.
Panther, 1970 DF

The Villain and the Virgin; see No Orchids for Miss Blandish
The Vulture is a Patient Bird. Hale,
1969
Want to Stay Alive? Hale, 1971
The Way the Cookie Crumbles. Hale,
1965; PB, 1974 FT
Well Now, My Pretty—. Hale, 1967; PB,
1972 FT
What's Better Than Money? Hale, 1960;
PB, 1972
The Whiff of Money. Hale, 1969; PB,
1972 MG, HR, LS
The World in my Pocket. Hale, 1959;
Popular Library, 1962
You Have Yourself a Deal. Hale, 1966;
Walker, 1968 MG
You Never Know with Women. Jarrolds,
1949; PB, 1972
You're Dead Without Money. Hale, 1972
AB, HR
You're Lonely When You're Dead. Hale,
1949; Duell, 1950 VM
You've Got It Coming. Hale, 1955; PB,
1973

CHASE, JOSEPHINE.   -1931.
Behind the Purple Mask. Penn, 1932
The Blue Shadow Mystery. Penn, 1935
The Golden Imp. Penn, 1933
The Green Jade Necklace. Penn, 1931
The Mark of the Red Diamond. Penn, 1929

CHASE, KIP. Pseudonym of Trevett Coburn
Chase. Series character: Justine Carmichael = JC.
Killer Be Killed. Hammond, 1963
Murder Most Ingenious. Hammond, 1962 JC
Where There's a Will. Hammond, 1961 JC

CHASE, TREVETT COBURN. Pseudonym: Kip
Chase, q.v.

CHASTAIN, THOMAS
Pandora's Box. Mason/Charter, 1974;
Cassell, 1975

CHATTERTON, E(DWARD) KEBLE. 1878-1944.
-Below the Surface. Hurst, 1934
Sea Spy. Hurst, 1937
Secret Ship. Hurst, 1939

CHAVETTE, EUGENE. Pseudonym of Eugene
Vachette, 1827-1902.
Mystery of Hotel Brichet. Bonner, 1894

CHAVIS, ROBERT
The Terror Package. Ace, 1957

CHAYES, SALLY
Jail Bait. Godwin, 1933

CHAYTOR, LEE
A Course in Murder. Transition, 1969

CHAZE, (LEWIS) ELLIOT
Black Wings Has my Angel. GM, 1953;
Red Seal, 1957. Also published as:
One for My Money. Berkley, 1962
One for My Money; see Black Wings Has
my Angel
Wettermark. Scribner, 1969

CHEAME, WILLIS
"When First We Practise." Long, 1936

CHEATHAM, LILLIAN
The Marriage Pact. Doubleday, 1974
Portrait of Emma. Doubleday, 1975

CHELLIS, MARY DWINELL
Mystery of the Lodge. Lothrop, 1873

CHELTON, JOHN. Pseudonym of Paul Durst,
1921-   , q.v. Other pseudonym:
Peter Bannon, q.v.
My Deadly Angel. GM, 1955

CHESHAM, HENRY. Pseudonym of D(avid)
E(rnest) Bingley, 1920-   , q.v.
Other pseudonym: George Fallon, q.v.
Naples, or Die! Hale, 1965
Skyborne Sapper. Hale, 1966

CHESNEY, MICHAEL. Series character:
Colonel "Steel" Callaghan, in all
titles.
Callaghan Meets his Fate. Jenkins, 1939
Callaghan of Intelligence. Jenkins,
1938
"Steel" Callaghan. Jenkins, 1939

CHESNEY, WEATHERBY. Pseudonym of
C(harles) J(ohn) Cutcliffe (Wright)
Hyne, 1865-1944, q.v.
The Adventures of a Solicitor. Bowden,
1898 ss, some criminous
The Adventures of an Engineer. Bowden,
1898 ss, some criminous
The Baptist Ring. Methuen, 1903
The Branded Prince. Methuen, 1902
The Cable-Man. Chatto, 1907
-The Claimant. Chatto, 1908
The Dilemma of Commander Brett. Bowden,
1899
-The Foundered Galleon. Methuen, 1902
-Four Red Nightcaps. Macqueen, 1900
-John Topp, Pirate. Methuen, 1901
The Mystery of a Bungalow. Methuen,
1904
-The Romance of a Queen. Chatto, 1908
The Tragedy of the Great Emerald.
Methuen, 1904

CHESSMAN, CARYL (WHITTIER). 1921-1960.
The Kid was a Killer. GM, 1960;
Muller pb, 1960

CHESTER, ALFRED. 1929?-1971.
The Exquisite Corpse. Deutsch, 1970

CHESTER, ANN
Slightly Imperfect. Arcadia, 1956

CHESTER, GEORGE RANDOLPH. 1869-1924.
Series character: James Rufus Wallingford, in all titles.
Get-Rich-Quick Wallingford. Altemus,
1908; Richards, 1908
The Son of Wallingford, with Lillian
Eleanor Chester (1888-   ). Small,
1921
Wallingford and Blackie Daw. Bobbs,
1913; Hodder, 1918
Wallingford in his Prime. Bobbs, 1913;
Newnes, 1916
Young Wallingford. Bobbs, 1910; Hodder,
1917

CHESTER, GILBERT. Pseudonym of H(arry)
H(ornaby) Clifford Gibbons, 1888-
1958, q.v. With the one exception
noted, all the following were published by Amalgamated Press and feature Sexton Blake.
The Abyssinian Mystery. 1935
The Beauty Parlor Murder. 1935
The Black-Out Crime. 1940
The Caravan Crime. 1934
The Case of the Bogus Prince. 1933
The Case of the Brass-Bound Chest. 1936
The Case of the Deportee. 1934
The Case of the Man on Leave. 1940
The Case of the Repatriated Prisoner.
1943
The Charity Fund Mystery. 1937
The Coronation Mystery. 1937

The Crime of Corporal Sherwood. 1941
The Crime on the Clyde. 1933
A Date with Danger. 1947
Death Walks In. Wright, 1938 (not Sexton Blake)
The Depository Mystery. 1939
Doctor Sinister. 1943
Dr. Duvene's Crime. 1932
The Great Currency Racket. 1947
The Green Room Crime. 1930
The Hire Purchase Crime. 1938
The House in the Wood. 1945
The House on the Cliffs. 1937
The Man from Moscow. 1937
The Man from Norway. 1941
The Man They Couldn't Buy. 1944
The Man Who Bailed Out. 1942
The Man Who Wouldn't Quit. 1944
The Monastery Mystery. 1939
The Murder on the Broads. 1932
Murder on the Marshes. 1931
Murder on the Pier. 1935
Murder to Music. 1933
The Mystery Gangster. 1931
The Mystery of the Condemned Cottage. 1939
The Mystery of the Confiscated Ship. 1945
The Mystery of the Crashed Air Liner. 1947
The Mystery of the Demobilized Soldier. 1944
The Mystery of the Double Burglary. 1946
The Mystery of the Greek Exile. 1936
The Mystery of the Hush-Hush Factory. 1941
The Mystery of the Kidnapped Munition Worker. 1943
The Mystery of the Old Curiosity Shop. 1936
The Mystery of the Underground Factory. 1942
The Palais de Danse Tragedy. 1932
The Paper Salvage Crime. 1942
Previously Reported Missing—Now? 1944
The Red Van Mystery. 1946
The Riddle of the Gas Meter. 1940
The Riddle of the Kidnapped Pensioner. 1944
The Riddle of the Missing Fire Watcher. 1941
The Riddle of the Murdered Fisherman. 1940
The Riddle of the Night Garage. 1949
The Salvage Pirates. 1934
The Secret of the Farm. 1932
The Secret of the Snows. Dean, 1968
The Secret of the Steps. 1936
The Secret of Stillwater Mere. 1943
The Secret of the Sunken Ships. 1938
The Silk Stocking Murders. 1942
The Soldier Who Came Back. 1943
The Stage Door Crime. 1936
The Strange Case of the Footman's Crime. 1944
The Studio Crime. 1932
The Sword of Vengeance. 1945
The Taxi Man's Quest. 1936
The Tithe War Mystery. 1935
Under Police Observation. 1945
The Victim of the Combine. 1942

CHESTER, LILLIAN ELEANOR. 1888- .
See: GEORGE RANDOLPH CHESTER, 1869-1924.

CHESTER, PETER. Pseudonym of Dennis (John Andrew) Phillips, 1924- , q.v. Other pseudonym: Peter Chambers, q.v. See also: W(illiam Arthur) Howard Baker, 1925- . Series character: Johnny Preston, in at least those marked JP.
Blueprint for Larceny. Jenkins, 1964
Killing Comes Easy. Jenkins, 1958; Roy, 1959 JP

Murder Forestalled. Jenkins, 1960; Roy, 1961 JP
The Pay-Grab Murders. Jenkins, 1962
The Traitors. Jenkins, 1964

CHESTERTON, G(ILBERT) K(EITH). 1874-1936. Series character: Father Brown = FB.
The Club of Queer Trades. Harper (London & New York), 1905 ss
The Ecstatic Thief; see Four Faultless Felons
The Father Brown Omnibus. Dodd, 1935. (This volume contains the entire contents of all five books of FB short stories. A new edition, Dodd, 1951, also includes one FB story that is not in any of the earlier 5 volumes.)
Four Faultless Felons. Cassell, 1930; Dodd, 1930. (Four novelets. Note that prior to this collection there were two small Dodd volumes containing three of the quartet in book form: The Moderate Murderer and The Honest Quack, 1929, 68 pp; and The Ecstatic Thief, 1930, 68 pp.)
The Incredulity of Father Brown. Cassell, 1926; Dodd, 1926 ss FB
The Innocence of Father Brown. Cassell, 1911; Lane, 1911 ss FB
The Man Who Knew Too Much and other stories. Cassell, 1922; Harper, 1922 ss
The Man Who was Thursday. Simpkin, 1908; Dodd, 1908
The Moderate Murderer and The Honest Quack; see Four Faultless Felons
The Paradoxes of Mr. Pond. Cassell, 1936; Dodd, 1937 ss
The Poet and the Lunatics. Cassell, 1929; Dodd, 1929 ss
The Scandal of Father Brown. Cassell, 1935; Dodd, 1935 ss FB
The Secret of Father Brown. Cassell, 1927; Harper, 1927 ss FB
The Wisdom of Father Brown. Cassell, 1914; Lane, 1915 ss FB

CHETTUR, S(ANKARA) K(RISHNA)
The Cobras of Dhermashevi. Higginsbotham, 1937 ss
Muffled Drums. Ganeson, 1927 ss

CHETWYND, BRIDGET. Series characters: Petunia Best & Max Frend, in at least those marked B&F.
Death has Ten Thousand Doors. Hutchinson, 1951 B&F
Rubies, Emeralds and Diamonds. Hutchinson, 1952 B&F
-Uneasy Street. Hutchinson, 1952

CHETWYND-HAYES, R(ONALD HENRY GLYNN). 1919- .
Cold Terror. Tandem, 1973; Pyramid, 1975
The Dark Man. Sidgwick, 1964
-The Elemental. Fontana, 1974
-The Man from the Bomb. Spencer, 1959
-The Monster Club. New English Library pb, 1975
-The Night Ghouls. Fontana, 1975
Terror by Night. Tandem, 1974; Pyramid, 1976 ss
-The Unbidden. Tandem, 1971; Pyramid, 1975

CHEVALIER, HAAKON (MAURICE). 1902- .
For Us the Living. Knopf, 1949; Secker, 1949

CHEVIOT, ANDREW
Trick, Trial and Triumph. Morison, 1891

CHEYNEY, PETER [REGINALD SOUTHOUSE CHEYNEY]. 1896-1951. See also: GERALD VERNER. Series characters: Lemmy Caution = LC; Slim Callaghan = SC; Michael Kells = MK; Alonzo MacTavish = AM; Shaun O'Mara = SO; Johnny Vallon = JV. Note: Cheyney appeared in numerous WWII pamphlets; these are grouped together at the end of the listing.
The Adventures of Julia and two other spy stories. Todd, 1954. U.S. title: The Killing Game. Belmont, 1975. (ss, all or most of which apparently appeared first in Britain in pamphlet form.)
Another Little Drink. Collins, 1940. U.S. title: A Trap for Bellamy. Dodd, 1941. Also published as: Premeditated Murder. Avon, 1943
The Best Stories of Peter Cheyney. Collins, 1954 ss
Callaghan; see Dangerous Curves
Calling Mr. Callaghan. Todd, 1953. (12 ss, at least some first published in pamphlet form.)
Can Ladies Kill? Collins, 1938 LC
The Case of the Dark Hero; see Dark Hero
Case of the Dark Wanton; see Dark Wanton
Cocktails and the Killer; see Ladies Won't Wait
The Counterspy Murders; see Dark Duet
The Curiosity of Etienne MacGregor. Locke, 1947. (Note that a later edition, Todd, 1952, is 43 pages longer and may contain new material.) Also published as: The Sweetheart of the Razors. Four Square, 1952
Dames Don't Care. Collins, 1937; Coward, 1938 LC
Dance Without Music. Collins, 1947; Dodd, 1948
Dangerous Curves. Collins, 1939. U.S. title: Callaghan. Belmont, 1973 SC
Dark Bahama. Collins, 1950; Dodd, 1951. Also published as: I'll Bring Her Back. Eton, 1952 JV
Dark Duet. Collins, 1942; Dodd, 1943. Also published as: The Counterspy Murders. Avon, 1944
Dark Hero. Collins, 1946; Dodd, 1946. Also published as: The Case of the Dark Hero. Avon, 1947
Dark Interlude. Collins, 1947; Dodd, 1947. Also published as: The Terrible Night. Avon, 1959 SO
Dark Street. Collins, 1944; Dodd, 1944. Also published as: The Dark Street Murders. Avon, 1946
The Dark Street Murders; see Dark Street
Dark Wanton. Collins, 1948; Dodd, 1949. Also published as: Case of the Dark Wanton. Avon, 1958
Don't Get Me Wrong. Collins, 1939 LC
Dressed to Kill. Todd, 1952. (ss, at least some first published in pamphlet form.)
Farewell to the Admiral; see Sorry You've Been Troubled
Fast Work; see The Mystery Blues and other stories
G Man at the Yard. Poynings, 1946 LC
G Man at the Yard. Todd, 1953. (ss about LC, SC and MA, all or most of the tales having first been published in pamphlet form.)
He Walked in her Sleep. Todd, 1954. U.S. title: MacTavish. Belmont, 1973 AM ss
I'll Bring Her Back; see Dark Bahama
I'll Say She Does! Collins, 1945; Dodd, 1946 LC

It Couldn't Matter Less. Collins, 1941;
  Arcadia, 1943 SC
The Killing Game; see The Adventures of
  Julia and two other spy stories
Knave Takes Queen. Collins, 1939 ss
Ladies Won't Wait. Collins, 1951; Dodd,
  1951. Also published as: Cocktails
  and the Killer. Avon, 1957 MK
Lady, Behave! Collins, 1950. U.S.
  title: Lady Beware. Dodd, 1950 JV
Lady Beware; see Lady, Behave!
The London Spy Murders; see The Stars
  are Dark
MacTavish; see He Walked in her Sleep
Making Crime Pay. Faber, 1944. (ss,
  articles and radio plays.)
The Man Nobody Saw; see You Can Call It
  a Day
Mr. Caution—Mr. Callaghan. Collins,
  1941 ss LC,SC
Mistress Murder; see One of Those
  Things
The Mystery Blues and other stories.
  Todd, 1954. Also published as: Fast
  Work. Four Square, 1964 ss
Never a Dull Moment. Collins, 1942 LC
No Ordinary Cheyney. Faber, 1948
  ss and articles
One of Those Things. Collins, 1949;
  Dodd, 1950. Also published as: Mis-
  tress Murder. Avon, 1951
Poison Ivy. Collins, 1937 LC
Premeditated Murder; see Another Little
  Drink
Set-Up for Murder. Pyramid, 1950. (Ori-
  ginal title?)
Sinister Errand. Collins, 1945; Dodd,
  1945. Also published as: Sinister
  Murders. Avon, 1957 MK
Sinister Murders; see Sinister Errand
Sorry You've been Troubled. Collins,
  1942. U.S. title: Farewell to the
  Admiral. Dodd, 1943 SC
The Stars are Dark. Collins, 1943;
  Dodd, 1943. Also published as: The
  London Spy Murders. Avon, 1944
The Sweetheart of the Razors; see The
  Curiosity of Etienne MacGregor
The Terrible Night; see Dark Interlude
They Never Say When. Collins, 1944;
  Dodd, 1945 SC
This Man is Dangerous. Collins, 1936;
  Coward, 1938 LC
A Trap for Bellamy; see Another Little
  Drink
Try Anything Twice. Collins, 1948;
  Dodd, 1948. Also published as: Un-
  dressed to Kill. Avon, 1959
Undressed to Kill; see Try Anything
  Twice
Uneasy Terms. Collins, 1946; Dodd, 1947
  SC
The Unscrupulous Mr. Callaghan. Handi-
  Books, 1943 SC (British title?)
The Urgent Hangman. Collins, 1938;
  Coward, 1939 SC
Velvet Johnnie and other stories. Col-
  lins, 1952. (ss, at least some of
  which were probably first published
  in pamphlets.)
You Can Always Duck. Collins, 1943 LC
You Can Call It a Day. Collins, 1949.
  U.S. title: The Man Nobody Saw. Dodd,
  1949 JV
You Can't Hit a Woman and other sto-
  ries. Collins, 1937. (ss, at least
  some later reprinted in pamphlets.)
You Can't Keep the Change. Collins,
  1940; Dodd, 1944 SC
You'd Be Surprised. Collins, 1940
Your Deal, My Lovely. Collins, 1941 LC

Account Rendered. Polybooks, 1944
The Adventures of Alonzo MacTavish.
  Polybooks, 1943 AM
The Adventures of Julia. Poynings, 1945
Alonzo MacTavish Again. Polybooks, 1943
  AM
Cocktail for Cupid and other stories.
  Bantam (London), 1948 ss
Cocktail Party and other stories. Ban-
  tam (London), 1948 ss
Dance Without Music. Polybooks, 1945
Date After Dark and other stories.
  Polybooks, 1944 ss
Escape for Sandra. Poynings, 1945
Fast Work and other stories. Bantam
  (London), 1948. (This volume almost
  certainly differs from that with a
  similar title in the first section
  for this has 48 pages and that has
  188 pages.) ss
He Walked in her Sleep and other sto-
  ries. Polybooks, 1946 ss (This
  almost certainly differs from the
  volume with a similar title in the
  first section, since this has 62
  pages and that has 187 pages.)
Information Received and other stories.
  Bantam (London), 1947 ss
Lady in Green and other stories. Ban-
  tam (London), 1947 ss
The Lady in Tears and other stories.
  Bantam (London), 1948 ss
Love with a Gun and other stories.
  Polybooks, 1943 (16 pp.); Polybooks,
  1946 (62 pp.)
The Man with the Red Beard. Todd, 1943.
  (From: You Can't Hit a Woman and
  other stories, q.v.)
The Man with Two Wives and other sto-
  ries. Polybooks, 1946 ss
A Matter of Luck and other stories.
  Bantam (London), 1947
The Murder of Alonzo. Polybooks, 1943
  AM
Night Club. Poynings, 1945
A Spot of Murder and other stories.
  Polybooks, 1946 ss
Time for Caution. Foster, 1946 LC
A Tough Spot for Cupid and other sto-
  ries. Vallancey, 1945 ss
The Unhappy Lady and other stories.
  Bantam (London), 1948 ss
Vengeance with a Twist and other sto-
  ries. Vallancey, 1946 ss
You Can't Trust Duchesses and other
  stories. Vallancey, 1946 ss

CHICHESTER, HUGH
  The Mystery Man in the Tower. Burns,
  1938

CHICHESTER, JOHN JAY. Series characters:
  Maxwell Sanderson = MS; Jimmy "Wig-
  gly" Price = JP.
  The Bigamist. Chelsea, 1925; Hutchin-
  son, 1927 JP
  The House of the Moving Room. Chelsea,
  1926; Hutchinson, 1926 JP
  The King of Diamonds. Chelsea, 1930;
  Hutchinson, 1931 MS
  The Porcelain Mask. Chelsea, 1924;
  Jenkins, 1925
  Rogues of Fortune. Chelsea, 1929;
  Hutchinson, 1930 MS
  Sanderson: Master Rogue. Chelsea, 1929;
  Hutchinson, 1930 MS
  Sanderson's Diamond Loot. Chelsea,
  1935; Hutchinson, 1935 MS
  The Silent Cracksman. Chelsea, 1929;
  Hutchinson, 1929 MS

CHIDSEY, DONALD BARR. 1902-   .
  Nobody Heard the Shot. Bantam (Los
  Angeles), 1941

CHILD, NELLISE. Series character: Jeremiah Irish, in both titles.
The Diamond Ransom Murders. Knopf,
  1935; Collins, 1934
Murder Comes Home. Knopf, 1933; Collins, 1933

CHILD, RICHARD WASHBURN. 1881-1935.
  -The Blue Wall: A Story of Strangeness
  and Struggle. Houghton, 1912;
  Constable, 1912
  Fresh Waters and other stories. Dutton,
  1924; Hodder, 1925 ss
  The Vanishing Men. Dutton, 1920
  The Velvet Black. Dutton, 1921; Hodder,
  1921 ss

CHILD, RODERICK. 1949-   .
  The Carrington Assignment. Hale, 1968
  Claustrophobia. Hale, 1971
  Spy on Approval. Hale, 1969

CHILDERNESS, GEORGE. Series character:
  Chet Phelps, in both titles.
  Murder in False Face. Phoenix, 1943
  Too Many Murderers. Phoenix, 1944; Pem-
  berton, 1946

CHILDERS, (ROBERT) ERSKINE. 1870-1922.
  The Riddle of the Sands. Smith Elder,
  1903; Dodd, 1915

CHILDERS, JAMES SAXON. 1899-   .
  The Bookshop Mystery. Appleton, 1930

CHILDS, MARQUIS (WILLIAM). 1903-   .
  Taint of Innocence. Harper, 1967;
  Cassell, 1968

CHIPPERFIELD, ROBERT ORR. Pseudonym of
  Isabel (Egenton) Ostrander, 1883-
  1924, q.v. Other pseudonyms: David
  Fox, Douglas Grant, qq.v. See also:
  William J. Burns, 1861-1932. Series
  character: Barry O'Dell = BO.
  Above Suspicion. McBride, 1923; Hurst,
  1923
  Bright Lights. McBride, 1924; Hurst,
  1924
  The Man in the Jury Box. McBride, 1921;
  Hurst, 1921 BO
  The Second Bullet. McBride, 1919;
  Skeffington, 1920
  The Trigger of Conscience. McBride,
  1921; Hurst, 1922
  Unseen Hands. McBride, 1920; Hurst,
  1921 BO

CHITTENDEN, F(RANK) A(LBERT). 1910-   .
  Darkness Over Hycroft. Gifford, 1947
  The Four Cornered Story. Boardman, 1951
  Strange Welcome. Boardman, 1949; Cow-
  ard, 1949
  The Uninvited. Boardman, 1954
  The Widow in White. Gifford, 1949

CHITTY, SIR THOMAS WILLES. 1926-   .
  Pseudonym: Thomas Hinde, q.v.

CHODOROV, EDWARD. 1904-   .
  Decision. French (New York), 1946.
  (3-act play.)
  Kind Lady. French (New York), 1936.
  (Play based on the ss "The Silver
  Mask" from All Souls' Night by Hugh
  Walpole, 1884-1941, q.v.)

CHOLMONDELEY, MARY. 1859-1925.
  The Danvers Jewels. Bentley, 1887;
  Harper, 1890 (bound with Sir Charles
  Danvers, as by "The Author of The
  Danvers Jewels")
  -Prisoners. Hutchinson, 1906; Dodd,
  1906

CHRISTIAN, JOHN. Pseudonym of Roger
  Dixon, 1930-   .

Five Gates to Armageddon. Harwood-Smart, 1975; St. Martin's, 1975

CHRISTIAN, KIT. Joint pseudonym of Delos Russell Thorson, 1906-   , and Sara Winfree Thorson, 1906-   .
Death and Bitters. Dutton, 1943

CHRISTIANSEN, SIGURD (WESLEY). 1891-1948.
Two Living and One Dead. Gollancz, 1932; Liveright, 1932. (Translation of To Levende og en Død. Stockholm, 1932.)

CHRISTIANSON, BARBARA
A Triumphant Defeat. Neely, 1901

CHRISTIE, AGATHA. 1890-1976. See also: MOIE CHARLES, G. R(OY) McRAE, MICHAEL MORTON, ARNOLD RIDLEY, GERALD VERNER, FRANK VOSPER. Series characters: Supt. Battle = B; Tuppence & Tommy Beresford = T&T; Jane Marple = JM; Hercule Poirot = HP; Parker Pyne = PP; Harley Quin = HQ. Grouped separately at the end of the listing are some WWII pamphlets.
The ABC Murders. Collins, 1936; Dodd, 1936. Also published as: The Alphabet Murders. PB, 1966 HP
The Adventure of the Christmas Pudding. Collins, 1960. (6 ss, 5 with HP, 1 with JM. 5 of the 6 are spread throughout the U.S. collections entitled The Regatta Mystery, Three Blind Mice, The Under Dog, and Double Sin, qq.v. An earlier and shorter version of the 6th, "The Mystery of the Spanish Chest," appeared in The Regatta Mystery as "The Mystery of the Baghdad Chest.")
After the Funeral. Collins, 1953. U.S. title: Funerals are Fatal. Dodd, 1953. Also published as: Murder at the Gallop. Fontana, 1963 HP
Afternoon at the Seaside. French, 1963. (1-act play.)
The Alphabet Murders; see The ABC Murders
And Then There were None; see Ten Little Niggers
Appointment with Death. Collins, 1938; Dodd, 1938 HP (Also a play by this title, but without HP: French, 1956.)
At Bertram's Hotel. Collins, 1965; Dodd, 1966 JM
The Big Four. Collins, 1927; Dodd, 1927 HP (A "novel" incorporating 10 HP ss.)
Black Coffee. Ashley, 1934; Baker, 1934. (Play.)
Blood will Tell; see Mrs. McGinty's Dead
The Body in the Library. Collins, 1942; Dodd, 1942 JM
The Boomerang Clue; see Why Didn't They Ask Evans?
By the Pricking of my Thumbs. Collins, 1968; Dodd, 1968 T&T
Cards on the Table. Collins, 1936; Dodd, 1937 HP, SB
A Caribbean Mystery. Collins, 1964; Dodd, 1965 JM
The Case of the Moving Finger; see The Moving Finger
Cat Among the Pigeons. Collins, 1959; Dodd, 1960 HP
The Clocks. Collins, 1963; Dodd, 1964 HP
Crooked House. Collins, 1949; Dodd, 1949
Curtain. Collins, 1975; Dodd, 1975 HP
Dead Man's Folly. Collins, 1956; Dodd, 1956 HP
Dead Man's Mirror; see Murder in the Mews

Death Comes as the End. Collins, 1945; Dodd, 1944
Death in the Air; see Death in the Clouds
Death in the Clouds. Collins, 1935. U.S. title: Death in the Air. Dodd, 1935 HP
Death on the Nile. Collins, 1937; Dodd, 1938 HP
Destination Unknown. Collins, 1954. U.S. title: So Many Steps to Death. Dodd, 1955
Double Sin and other stories. Dodd, 1961. (8 ss, 4 with HP, 2 with JM. Two of the 8 appear in the British collection The Adventure of the Christmas Pudding and one in The Hound of Death, qq.v.; 3 appear later in Poirot's Early Cases, q.v.; 2 remain uncollected in Britain.)
Dumb Witness. Collins, 1937. U.S. title: Poirot Loses a Client. Dodd, 1937 HP
Easy to Kill; see Murder is Easy
Elephants can Remember. Collins, 1972; Dodd, 1972 HP
Endless Night. Collins, 1967; Dodd, 1968
Evil Under the Sun. Collins, 1941; Dodd, 1941 HP
Five Little Pigs. Collins, 1943. U.S. title: Murder in Retrospect. Dodd, 1942 HP
4.50 from Paddington. Collins, 1957. U.S. title: What Mrs. McGillicuddy Saw! Dodd, 1957. Also published as: Murder, She Said. Cardinal, 1961 JM
Funerals are Fatal; see After the Funeral
Go Back for Murder. French, 1960. (A play based on the novel Five Little Pigs, q.v., but without HP.)
The Golden Ball and other stories. Dodd, 1971. (15 ss, none with a series character. 8 are from the British collection The Listerdale Mystery, 5 from The Hound of Death, qq.v.; 2 remain uncollected in Britain.)
Hallowe'en Party. Collins, 1969; Dodd, 1969 HP
Hercule Poirot's Christmas. Collins, 1938. U.S. title: Murder for Christmas. Dodd, 1939. Also published as: A Holiday for Murder. Avon, 1947 HP
Hercule Poirot's Early Cases; see Poirot's Early Cases
Hickory Dickory Death; see Hickory Dickory Dock
Hickory Dickory Dock. Collins, 1955. U.S. title: Hickory Dickory Death. Dodd, 1955 HP
A Holiday for Murder; see Hercule Poirot's Christmas
The Hollow. Collins, 1946; Dodd, 1946. Also published as: Murder After Hours. Dell, 1954 HP Also a play, without HP: French, 1952
The Hound of Death and other stories. Odhams, 1933. (12 ss, none with a series character. 6 appear in the U.S. collection The Witness for the Prosecution, 1 in Double Sin, and 5 in The Golden Ball and other stories, qq.v.)
The Incredible Theft; see Murder in the Mews
The Labours of Hercules. Collins, 1947; Dodd, 1947 12 ss with HP
The Listerdale Mystery. Collins, 1934. (12 ss, none with a series character. 2 appear in the U.S. collection The

Witness for the Prosecution and other stories, 8 in The Golden Ball and other stories, 1 in Surprise! Surprise!, qq.v.; the remaining story is uncollected in the U.S.)
Lord Edgware Dies. Collins, 1933. U.S. title: Thirteen at Dinner. Dodd, 1933 HP
The Man in the Brown Suit. Lane, 1924; Dodd, 1924
The Mirror Crack'd; see The Mirror Crack'd from Side to Side
The Mirror Crack'd from Side to Side. Collins, 1962. U.S. title: The Mirror Crack'd. Dodd, 1963 JM
Miss Marple and the Thirteen Problems; see The Thirteen Problems
The Mousetrap; see Three Blind Mice
The Moving Finger. Collins, 1943; Dodd, 1942. Also published as: The Case of the Moving Finger. Avon, 1948 HP
Mr. Parker Pyne, Detective; see Parker Pyne Investigates
Mrs. McGinty's Dead. Collins, 1952; Dodd, 1952. Also published as: Blood will Tell. Detective Book Club, 1952 HP
Murder After Hours; see The Hollow
Murder at Hazelmoor; see The Sittaford Mystery
Murder at the Gallop; see After the Funeral
The Murder at the Vicarage. Collins, 1930; Dodd, 1930
Murder for Christmas; see Hercule Poirot's Christmas
Murder in Mesopotamia. Collins, 1936; Dodd, 1936 HP
Murder in Retrospect; see Five Little Pigs
Murder in the Calais Coach; see Murder on the Orient Express
Murder in the Mews. Collins, 1937. U.S. title: Dead Man's Mirror. Dodd, 1937. (4 HP stories. One of these was later published separately as: The Incredible Theft. Mercury, 194?. Note that most U.S. paperback editions contain only three of the 4 stories, whereas British paperback reprints are generally complete.)
Murder in Three Acts; see Three Act Tragedy
A Murder is Announced. Collins, 1950; Dodd, 1950 JM
Murder is Easy. Collins, 1939. U.S. title: Easy to Kill. Dodd, 1939 SB
The Murder of Roger Ackroyd. Collins, 1926; Dodd, 1926 HP
The Murder on the Links. Lane, 1923; Dodd, 1923 HP
Murder on the Nile. French, 1948. (A play based on the novel Death on the Nile, q.v., but without HP.)
Murder on the Orient Express. Collins, 1934. U.S. title: Murder in the Calais Coach. Dodd, 1934 HP
Murder, She Said; see 4.50 from Paddington
Murder with Mirrors; see They Do It with Mirrors
The Mysterious Affair at Styles. Lane, 1920; Dodd, 1927 HP
The Mysterious Mr. Quin. Collins, 1930; Dodd, 1930. (12 ss with HQ.)
The Mystery of the Blue Geranium, and other Tuesday Club Murders. Bantam (New York), 1940. (Evidently ss taken from The Thirteen Problems, q.v.)
The Mystery of the Blue Train. Collins, 1928; Dodd, 1928 HP
N or M? Collins, 1941; Dodd, 1941 T&T
Nemesis. Collins, 1971; Dodd, 1971 JM
One, Two, Buckle My Shoe. Collins, 1940. U.S. title: The Patriotic Mur-

ders. Dodd, 1941. Also published as: An Overdose of Death. Dell, 1953 HP
Ordeal by Innocence. Collins, 1958; Dodd, 1959
An Overdose of Death; see One, Two, Buckle my Shoe
The Pale Horse. Collins, 1961; Dodd, 1962
Parker Pyne Investigates. Collins, 1934. U.S. title: Mr. Parker Pyne: Detective. Dodd, 1934. (12 ss with PP.)
Partners in Crime. Collins, 1929; Dodd, 1929. (17 ss about T&T, disguised as a novel, the second half of which was reprinted separately as: The Sunningdale Mystery. Collins, 1933.)
Passenger to Frankfurt. Collins, 1970; Dodd, 1970
The Patient. French, 1963. (1-act play.)
The Patriotic Murders; see One, Two, Buckle my Shoe
Peril at End House. Collins, 1932; Dodd, 1932 HP
A Pocket Full of Rye. Collins, 1953; Dodd, 1954 JM
Poirot Investigates. Lane, 1924; Dodd, 1925. (The British edition has 11 HP ss; the American adds 3 more. Note that some U.S. paperback editions are incomplete.)
Poirot Loses a Client; see Dumb Witness
Poirot's Early Cases. Collins, 1974. U.S. title: Hercule Poirot's Early Cases. Dodd, 1974. (18 HP ss reshuffled from earlier collections.)
Postern of Fate. Collins, 1973; Dodd, 1973 T&T
The Rats. French, 1963. (1-act play.)
The Regatta Mystery. Dodd, 1939. (9 ss, 5 with HP, 2 with PP, 1 with JM, 1 supernatural. Several appeared in Britain in "raid library" pamphlets during WWII but three remain uncollected in hardcover British Christie volumes.)
Remembered Death; see Sparkling Cyanide
Sad Cypress. Collins, 1940; Dodd, 1940 HP
The Secret Adversary. Lane, 1922; Dodd, 1922 T&T
The Secret of Chimneys. Lane, 1925; Dodd, 1925 SB
The Seven Dials Mystery. Collins, 1929; Dodd, 1929 SB
The Sittaford Mystery. Collins, 1931. U.S. title: Murder at Hazelmoor. Dodd, 1931
So Many Steps to Death; see Destination Unknown
Sparkling Cyanide. Collins, 1945. U.S. title: Remembered Death. Dodd, 1945
Spider's Web. French, 1957. (A play.)
The Sunningdale Mystery; see Partners in Crime
Surprise! Surprise! Dodd, 1965. (A reshuffling of ss from earlier Christie hardcover collections.)
Taken at the Flood. Collins, 1948. U.S. title: There is a Tide... Dodd, 1948 HP
Ten Little Indians; see Ten Little Niggers
Ten Little Niggers. Collins, 1939. U.S. title: And Then There were None. Dodd, 1940. Also published as: Ten Little Indians. PB, 1965. Also a play under the original British title: French (London), 1944; and as Ten Little Indians. French (New York), 1946.
There is a Tide...; see Taken at the Flood
They Came to Baghdad. Collins, 1951; Dodd, 1951
They Do It with Mirrors. Collins, 1952. U.S. title: Murder with Mirrors. Dodd, 1952 JM
Third Girl. Collins, 1966; Dodd, 1967 HP
Thirteen at Dinner; see Lord Edgware Dies
13 Clues for Miss Marple. Dodd, 1966. (A reshuffling of JM ss from prior hardcover Christie collections.)
13 for Luck! Collins, 1966; Dodd, 1961. (A reshuffling of ss from prior hardcover Christie collections.)
The Thirteen Problems. Collins, 1932. U.S. title: The Tuesday Club Murders. Dodd, 1933. Also published as: Miss Marple and the Thirteen Problems. Penguin, 1953. (13 ss about JM.)
Three Act Tragedy. Collins, 1935. U.S. title: Murder in Three Acts. Dodd, 1934 HP
Three Blind Mice. Dodd, 1950. Also published as: The Mousetrap. Dell, 19??. (A "novelettization" of the famous Christie stage play, plus 8 ss, 3 with HP, 4 with JM, 1 with HQ. 5 of the 9 tales have not been collected in any British Christie volume.) The play was published separately: The Mousetrap. French, 1954
Towards Zero. Collins, 1944; Dodd, 1944. Also as a play (with Gerald Verner): French, 1957; Dramatists Play Service, 1957 SB
The Tuesday Club Murders; see The Thirteen Problems
The Under Dog and other stories. Dodd, 1951. (A novelet and 8 ss, all about HP, all subsequently appearing in Christie collections in Britain. The title novelet appeared in book form in Britain, bound together with Blackman's Wood by E. Phillips Oppenheim. Reader's Library, 1929. This volume was reprinted as: Two Thrillers. London Daily Express Fiction Library, 1936.)
The Unexpected Guest. French, 1958. (A play.)
Verdict. French, 1958. (2-act play.)
What Mrs. McGillicuddy Saw!; see 4.50 from Paddington
Why Didn't They Ask Evans? Collins, 1934. U.S. title: The Boomerang Clue. Dodd, 1935
The Witness for the Prosecution. Dodd, 1948. (9 ss, one with HP. All but the HP story are collected in Britain, 6 in The Hound of Death, 2 in The Listerdale Mystery, qq.v. The title story also as a play: French, 1954.)
The Crime in Cabin 66; see The Mystery of the Crime in Cabin 66
The Mystery of the Baghdad Chest. Bantam (London), 1943. (HP story from The Regatta Mystery, q.v.)
The Mystery of the Crime in Cabin 66. Bantam (London), 1943. Also published as: The Crime in Cabin 66. Vallancey, 1944. (HP story from The Regatta Mystery, q.v., where it is titled "Problem at Sea.")
Poirot and the Regatta Mystery. Bantam (London), 1943. (HP story, modified from the PP tale, "The Regatta Mystery," in the book of that title, q.v.)
Poirot Knows the Murderer. Polybooks, 1946. (3 HP stories reshuffled from earlier pamphlets: The Mystery of the Baghdad Chest; The Crime in Cabin 66; and Christmas Adventure.)
Poirot Lends a Hand. Polybooks, 1946. (3 HP stories, the first two as published in the pamphlets Problem at Pollensa Bay and Christmas Adventure, and Poirot and the Regatta Mystery, qq.v.; the third as published in the U.S. edition of Poirot Investigates, q.v.)
Poirot on Holiday. Polybooks, 1943. (2 HP stories contained in other pamphlets: The Regatta Mystery, and The Crime in Cabin 66.)
Problem at Pollensa Bay and Christmas Adventure. Polybooks, 1943. (HP stories, the first modified from the PP tale of the same title in The Regatta Mystery, q.v., the second not previously published in book form.)
The Veiled Lady and The Mystery of the Baghdad Chest. Polybooks, 1944. (HP stories from the U.S. edition of Poirot Investigates and from The Regatta Mystery, qq.v.)

CHRISTIE, DOUGLAS. 1894-   . Pseudonyms: Colin Campbell, Lynn Durie, qq.v.
-Isle of Confusion. Hurst, 1930
-Isle of Desire. Hurst, 1929
The Rajah's Casket. Hurst, 1933
-The Striking Force. Rich, 1934
-Terry of Tangistan. Hurst, 1932
Trouble on the Frontier. Rich, 1935
-Under Observation. Hurst, 1931
-"Yellow—Like Gold!" Hurst, 1931

CHRISTIE, KATE
Child's Play. Macmillan (London), 1968; Harcourt, 1969

CHRISTIE, LOUIS
Better Than Weapons. Rich, 1935

CHRISTIE, STEPHEN. Series character (with many other authors): Sexton Blake, in both titles.
Crash and Carry. Mayflower, 1967
Slaughter in the Sun. Baker, 1969

CHRISTOPHER, EDGAR EARL
The Invisibles. Saalfield, 1903

CHRISTOPHER, JOHN. Pseudonym of (Christopher) Samuel Youd, 1922-   , q.v.
The Caves of Night. Eyre, 1958; Simon, 1958
-The Little People. Hodder, 1967; Simon, 1967
Pendulum. Hodder, 1968; Simon, 1968
A Scent of White Poppies. Eyre, 1959; Simon, 1959

CHRISTOPHER, MATTHEW F. 1917-   .
Look for the Body. Phoenix, 1952

CHRISTY, HELEN
Mr. Ace. Bart, 1946. (Novelization of the movie.)

CHURCH, GRANVILLE. Pseudonym of Granville Church People.
Bombs Burst Once. Mill, 1941. Also published as: Wings Over Panama. Adventure Novel Classic, 194?
Race with the Sun. Mill, 1944
Wings Over Panama; see Bombs Burst Once

CHURCHER, W. R. M.
Benevolent Blackmail. Mortiboy's, 1930

CHURCHILL, EDWARD
Menace of Death. Dodge, 1937

CHURCHILL, LUANNA. Pseudonym.
Bride of the Unliving. Lenox Hill, 1975; Remploy, 1975

Craven Castle. Lenox Hill, 1972; Remploy, 1973
Death Rides a Black Steed. Lenox Hill, 1975
Glowering Gables. Lenox Hill, 1974; Remploy, 1974
The Grinning Ghoul. Lenox Hill, 1974; Remploy, 1974
Macabre Mansion. Lenox Hill, 1973; Remploy, 1973
Moonlake Manor. Lenox Hill, 1972
Shades and Shadows. Lenox Hill, 1973; Remploy, 1974
Shadow on the Moon. Lenox Hill, 1974; Remploy, 1974
Witch Haven. Lenox Hill, 1973; Remploy, 1974
Wraithwood. Lenox Hill, 1973; Remploy, 1974

CHUTE, M(ARY) G(RACE). 1907-   .
Sheriff Olson. Appleton, 1942 ss

CHUTE, VERNE. 1917-   .
Blackmail; see Wayward Angel
Flight of an Angel. Morrow, 1946; Museum Press, 1950
Sweet and Deadly; see Wayward Angel
Wayward Angel. Knopf, 1948. British title: Blackmail. Museum Press, 1951. Also published as: Sweet and Deadly. Popular Library, 1952

CICELLIS, KAY [CATHERINE-MATHILDA CICELLIS]. 1926-   .
-The Day the Fish Came Out. Bantam, 1967. (Novelization of the movie.)

CLAD, NOEL. 19 -1963.
The Mafia; see The Savage
The Savage. Simon, 1958; Gollancz, 1958. Also published as: The Mafia. Belmont, 1970
A Taste for Brilliants. Random, 1964; Hammond, 1965

CLAIRE, MARVIN
The Drowning Wire. Ace, 1953

CLANCY, EUGENE A.
Fast Money. Chelsea, 1926
-Red Mountain, Limited. Chelsea, 1926; Hutchinson, 1927
Watched Out. Chelsea, 1925

CLANDON, HENRIETTA. Pseudonym of John (George) Hazlette Vahey, 1881-   , q.v. Other pseudonyms: John Haslette, Anthony Lang, Vernon Loder, John Mowbray, Walter Proudfoot, qq.v. Series characters: Penny & Vincent Mercer = M; William Power = WP.
Fog Off Weymouth. Bles, 1938 M
The Ghost Party. Bles, 1934
Good by Stealth. Bles, 1936 WP
Inquest. Bles, 1933
Power on the Scent. Bles, 1937 WP,M
Rope by Arrangement. Bles, 1935 M,WP
This Delicate Murder. Bles, 1936 M,WP

CLAPP, EVA CATHARINE
A Dark Secret. Laird, 1888

CLAPPEN, JOHN
Snow in Essex. Eldon, 1933

CLAPPERTON, RICHARD. 1934-   .
No News on Monday. Constable, 1968. U.S. title: You're a Long Time Dead. Putnam, 1968
Victims Unknown. Constable, 1970
You're a Long Time Dead; see No News on Monday

CLARE, JOHN
The Passionate Invaders. Doubleday, 1965

CLARE, MARGUERITE. Pseudonym of Mary Heppell.
-Barefoot Witch. Wright, 1968
-Blaze at Noon. Hale, 1966
-Candle of the Night. Wright, 1963
-Chariot of the Sun. Hale, 1965
-The Cintra Story. Wright, 1960
-Deadline for Loren. Wright, 1962
-Deep is the Lake. Wright, 1967
Fear Treads Soft Shod. Wright, 1956
-Golden Enchantress. Wright, 1967
-The Lane of Darkness. Wright, 1949
The Mask of Danger. Wright, 1952
-Pierce the Gloom. Wright, 1958
-Pillar of Fire. Hale, 1964
-Smouldering Fire. Wright, 1959
Spin a Dark Web. Wright, 1961
-Star of the Goddess. Wright, 1968
-The Wild Secret. Wright, 1961

CLARE, T.
The Nine Club. Hutchinson, 1929

CLARETIE, JULES [ARSENE ARNAUD CLARETIE]. 1840-1913.
The Crime of the Boulevard. Fenno, 1897
For Jacques' Sake. Vizetelly, 1888

CLARK, AL C. Series character: Kenyatta, in at least those marked K.
Cry Revenge! Holloway, 1974
Death List. Holloway, 1974
Kenyatta's Escape. Holloway, 1974 K
Kenyatta's Last Hit. Holloway, 1975 K

CLARK, ALFRED ALEXANDER GORDON. 1900-1958. Pseudonym: Cyril Hare, q.v.

CLARK, CHRISTOPHER. 1911-   .
-The Unleashed Will. Little, 1947

CLARK, DALE. Pseudonym of Ronal Kayser.
The Blonde, the Gangster and the Private Eye; see The Red Rods
Country Coffins. Boureqy, 1961
Death Wore Fins. Mystery House, 1959
Focus on Murder. Lippincott, 1943
Mambo to Murder. Ace, 1955
The Narrow Cell. Lippincott, 1944
The Red Rods. Messner, 1946. Also published as: The Blonde, the Gangster and the Private Eye. Avon, 1949
A Run for the Money. Ace, 1956

CLARK, DOROTHY PARK. 1899-   .
Just for the Bride. Doubleday, 1950
Poison Speaks Softly. Doubleday, 1947
Roll, Jordan, Roll. Doubleday, 1947

CLARK, DOUGLAS. Series character: Chief Inspector George Masters, in at least those marked GM.
Deadly Pattern. Cassell, 1970; Stein, 1970 GM
Death After Evensong. Cassell, 1969; Stein, 1970 GM
Nobody's Perfect. Cassell, 1969; Stein, 1969 GM
Premeditated Murder. Gollancz, 1975; Scribner, 1976 GM
Sick to Death. Cassell, 1971; Stein, 1971 GM
Sweet Poison. Cassell, 1970
Three Days to Catastrophe. Hammond, 1966

CLARK, EDWARD C.
The Fatal Element. Empire, 1934

CLARK, ELLERY H(ARDING). 1874-   .
The Carleton Case. Bobbs, 1910
Loaded Dice. Bobbs, 1909

CLARK, EVERT and NICHOLAS HORROCK
Corsican Contract. Bantam (London), 1974

CLARK, FRANCES BETTY
Darken the Moon. Blackwood, 1953
Night on Penwith. Hammond, 1961

CLARK, LAURENCE (WALTER). 1914-   .
Murder of the Prime Minister. Veracity, 1965

CLARK, MABEL MARGARET COWIE. Pseudonym: Lesley Storm, q.v.

CLARK, MARIAN B(UXTON)
The Model Corpse. Hale, Cushman & Flint, 1942; Boardman, 1945

CLARK, MARY HIGGINS
Where are the Children? Simon, 1975; Talmy Franklin, 1975

CLARK, PHILIP
The Dark River. Simon, 1949; Wingate, 1950
Flight into Darkness. Simon, 1948

CLARK, ROSY LEE WINIFRED CECILIA. 1909-   . Pseudonym: Scott Finley, q.v.

CLARK, W(ESLEY) C(LARKE). 1907-   .
Murder Goes to Bank Night. Hale, Cushman & Flint, 1940

CLARK, WILLIAM (DONALDSON). 1916-   .
Special Relationship. Heinemann, 1968; Houghton, 1969

CLARKE, ANNA. 1919-   .
The Darkened Room. Long, 1968
The End of a Shadow. Chatto, 1972
A Mind to Murder. Chatto, 1971
My Search for Ruth. Collins, 1975
Plot Counter-Plot. Collins, 1974; Walker, 1975

CLARKE, DONALD HENDERSON. 1887-1958.
Confidential. Vanguard, 1936; Laurie, 1937
Louis Beretti. Vanguard, 1929; Knopf (London), 1930
Murderer's Holiday. Vanguard, 1940; Laurie, 1941

CLARKE, DUDLEY (WRANGEL). 1899-1974.
Golden Arrow. Hodder, 1955

CLARKE, EDWARD
The Best Will Always Do. Standfast, 1973

CLARKE, IDA CLYDE (GALLAGHER). 1878-
-Record No. 33. Appleton, 1915

CLARKE, JOHN BOYD
Findings is Keepings. Clode, 1927

CLARKE, JOSEPH CALVITT. 1888-   . Pseudonym: Richard Grant, q.v.

CLARKE, LAURENCE (AYSCOUGH)
Bernard Treve's Boots. Hodder, 1920
-The Borrowed Liner. Mills, 1916
-The Call of the People. Hodder, 1926
The Lady in the Blue Veil. Hodder, 1923
The Mayfair Mystery. Hutchinson, 1927
-Millions of Money. Hodder, 1925
-Murray of the Scots Greys. Jarrolds, 1906
-A Prince of India. Hodder, 1915
-The Sport of Fate. Hodder, 1925

CLARKE, MARCUS (ANDREW HISLOP). 1846-1881.
 His Natural Life. Robertson (Melbourne), 1874; Bentley, 1875. U.S. title: For the Term of His Natural Life. Weeks, 1893.

CLARKE, PERCY A. Pseudonym: Martin Frazer, q.v.

CLARKE, ROBERT. Pseudonym of Lauran Bosworth Paine, 1916- . Other pseudonyms: John Armour, Reg Batchelor, Kenneth Bedford, Frank Bosworth, Mark Carrel, Richard Dana, J. F. Drexler, Troy Howard, Jared Ingersol, John Kilgore, Hunter Liggett, J. K. Lucas, John Morgan, qq.v.
 The Case of the Gambler's Corpse. Hale, 1969
 Death of a Flower Child. Hale, 1970
 Murderers are Silent. Hale, 1969
 A Synonym for Murder. Hale, 1972
 The Thirteenth Lover. Hale, 1970

CLARKE, T(HOMAS) E(RNEST) B(ENNETT). 1907- .
 -The Trail of the Serpent. Joseph, 1968
 Two and Two Make Five. Long, 1938
 The Wide Open Door. Joseph, 1966
 The Wrong Turning. Hale, 1971

CLARKE, WILLIAM JAMES. 1872- . Pseudonym: G. F. Monkshood, q.v.

CLARKSON, L. Pseudonym of Louise Clarkson Whitelock, 1865- .
 The Shadow of John Wallace. White, Stokes & Allen, 1884

CLASON, CLYDE B. Series character: Theocritus Lucius Westborough, in all titles.
 Blind Drifts. Doubleday, 1937
 Clue to the Labyrinth; see Murder Gone Minoan
 The Death Angel. Doubleday, 1936; Heinemann, 1937
 Dragon's Cave. Doubleday, 1939; Heinemann, 1940
 The Fifth Tumbler. Doubleday, 1936; Heinemann, 1937
 Green Shiver. Doubleday, 1941; Heinemann, 1948
 The Man from Tibet. Doubleday, 1938; Heinemann, 1938
 Murder Gone Minoan. Doubleday, 1939. British title: Clue to the Labyrinth. Heinemann, 1939
 Poison Jasmine. Doubleday, 1940
 The Purple Parrot. Doubleday, 1937; Heinemann, 1937
 The Whispering Ear. Doubleday, 1938; Heinemann, 1939

CLAUDE, M.
 Memoirs of Monsieur Claude. Munro, 1892 ss

CLAUDIA, SUSAN. Pseudonym of William Johnston, 1924- , q.v.
 Clock and Bell. Doubleday, 1974
 Madness at the Castle. Signet, 1966
 The Searching Spectre. Signet, 1967
 The Silent Voice. Signet, 1967

CLAUSON, CARL
 The Gloyne Murder. Dodd, 1930
 Jaws of Circumstance. Dodd, 1931; Lane, 1931

CLAWSON, PETER. See: J(OHN) T(HOMAS) EDSON.

CLAY, BERTHA M. Pseudonym of Charlotte M(onica) Braeme, 1836-1884, q.v., and others.
 -Crime or Folly? Wright, 1939
 A Fair Mystery. Munro, 1885
 Her Hidden Past. Modern, 1935
 The Moat House Mystery. Wright, 1938
 -The Mysterious Mrs. Nutford. Modern, 1935
 -The Shadow of Tarleton Manor. Wright, 1943

CLAY, ROBERT (KEATING)
 By Night. Blackwood, 1927; Lippincott, 1927

CLAY, WILLIAM AUSTIN. Pseudonym: Austin Fryers. See: EDGAR WINCH.

CLAYDON, STELLA
 Lesson in Murder. Long, 1960

CLAYMORE, TOD. Pseudonym of Hugh Clevely, q.v. See also: EDGAR (ALFRED) JEPSON, 1863-1938. Series character: Tod Claymore, in at least those marked TC.
 Appointment in New Orleans. Cassell, 1950 TC
 Dead Men Don't Answer. Cassell, 1954 TC
 Nest of Vipers. Cassell, 1948 TC
 Rendezvous on an Island. Cassell, 1957 TC
 Reunion in Florida. Cassell, 1952 TC
 -Speedwell. Cassell, 1946
 This is What Happened; see You Remember the Case
 You Remember the Case. Nelson, 1939. U.S. title: This is What Happened. Simon, 1939 TC
 -What Else Could I Do? Cassell, 1948

CLAYTON, RICHARD HENRY MICHAEL. 1907-
 Pseudonym: William Haggard, q.v.

CLEARY, C. P.
 Death in the Life Department. Metropolitan, 1947
 Flower-Bed Murder. Morris, 1945
 The Widow Wore White. Mitre, 1946

CLEARY, JON. 1917- . Series character: Scobie Malone = SM.
 The Climate of Courage. Collins, 1954. U.S. title: Naked in the Night. Popular Library, 1955
 Dust in the Sun; see Justin Bayard
 The Fall of an Eagle. Collins, 1965; Morrow, 1964
 A Flight of Chariots. Collins, 1964; Morrow, 1963
 Forests of the Night. Collins, 1963; Morrow, 1963
 Helga's Web. Collins, 1970; Morrow, 1970 SM
 The High Commissioner. Collins, 1966; Morrow, 1966 SM
 Just Let Me Be. Laurie, 1950
 Justin Bayard. Collins, 1955; Morrow, 1956. Also published as: Dust in the Sun. Four Square, 1960; Popular Library, 1957
 The Liberators; see Mask of the Andes
 The Long Pursuit. Collins, 1967; Morrow, 1967
 The Long Shadow. Laurie, 1949
 -Man's Estate. Collins, 1972. U.S. title: The Ninth Marquess. Morrow, 1972
 Mask of the Andes. Collins, 1971. U.S. title: The Liberators. Morrow, 1971
 Naked in the Night; see The Climate of Courage
 The Ninth Marquess; see Man's Estate
 North from Thursday. Collins, 1960; Morrow, 1961
 Peter's Pence. Collins, 1974; Morrow, 1974
 The Pulse of Danger. Collins, 1966; Morrow, 1966
 Ransom. Collins, 1973; Morrow, 1973
 The Safe House. Collins, 1975; Morrow, 1975
 Season of Doubt. Collins, 1968; Morrow, 1968
 These Small Glories. Angus, 1946
 You Can't See Around Corners. Angus, 1948; Scribner, 1947

CLEATON, IRENE
 The Outsider. Little, 1944

CLEAVER, H(YLTON) R(EGINALD)
 Danger at Ringside. Hutchinson, 1952

CLEEVE, BRIAN (TALBOT). 1921- . Series character: Sean Ryan = SR.
 Assignment to Vengeance. Collins, 1961
 Birth of a Dark Soul. Jarrolds, 1953. U.S. title: The Night Winds. Houghton, 1954
 Counterspy; see Vote X for Treason
 Dark Blood, Dark Terror. Hammond, 1966; Random, 1965 SR
 Death of a Painted Lady. Hammond, 1962; Random, 1963
 Death of a Wicked Servant. Hammond, 1963; Random, 1964
 Escape from Prague; see Exit from Prague
 Exit from Prague. Corgi, 1970. U.S. title: Escape from Prague. Pinnacle, 1973
 The Judas Goat. Hammond, 1966. U.S. title: Vice Isn't Private. Random, 1966 SR
 The Night Winds; see Birth of a Dark Soul
 Tread Softly in this Place. Cassell, 1972; Day, 1972
 Vice Isn't Private; see The Judas Goat
 Violent Death of a Bitter Englishman. Corgi, 1969; Random, 1967 SR
 Vote X for Treason. Collins, 1964; Random, 1965. Also published as: Counterspy. Lancer, 1966 SR
 You Must Never Go Back. Random, 1968

CLEEVE, LUCAS. Pseudonym of Adelina Georgina Isabella Kingscote, -1908.
 The World's Blackmail. White, 1900

CLEFT-ADDAMS, J(ULIA)
 The Secret Deed; see A Woman Always Knows
 The Wasp. Wright, 1932
 A Woman Always Knows. Hurst, 1925. U.S. title (?): The Secret Deed. McBride, 1926

CLEGG, THOMAS BAILEY. 1857- .
 The Bishop's Scapegoat. Lane (London & New York), 1908
 -Joan of the Hills. Lane (London & New York), 1909
 -The Love Child. Lane, 1906
 -The Wilderness. Lane, 1907

CLEIFE, (KENNETH) PHILIP (HUBERT). Series character: Martyn Finch, in both titles.
 The Pinchbeck Masterpiece. Macmillan (London), 1970. U.S. title: Tour de Force. Harper, 1971
 The Slick and the Dead. Macmillan (London), 1972
 Tour de Force; see The Pinchbeck Masterpiece

CLEM, EMERSON S.
　Which—Innocent or Guilty? Comet, 1955
　ss

CLEMENS, BRIAN. See: TED HART.

CLEMENS, NANCY. Pseudonym. See: VANCE
　RANDOLPH, 1892- .

CLEMENS, SAMUEL LANGHORNE. 1835-1910.
　Pseudonym: Mark Twain, q.v.

CLEMENS, WILL(IAM) M(ONTGOMERY). 1860-
　1931.
　The Gilded Lady. Dillingham, 1903;
　　Unwin, 1903

CLEMENT, FRANK A. Series character:
　Superintendent Mersey, in all titles.
　No End of a Rogue. Longmans, 1936
　Picture Him Dead. Longmans, 1935
　Scandal at the Home Office, Longmans,
　　1937

CLEMENT, HENRY
　Any Old Port in a Storm. Popular Li-
　　brary, 1975. (Novelization of the
　　Columbo TV series.)
　By Dawn's Early Light. Popular Library,
　　1975. (Novelization of the Columbo
　　TV series.)
　Dillinger. Curtis, 1973. (Novelization
　　of the movie.)
　A Quiet Place in the Country. Signet,
　　1969. (Novelization of the movie.)
　Slaughter. Curtis, 1972. (Novelization
　　of the movie.)

CLEMENTS, ABIGAIL
　Christabel's Room. GM, 1974
　Mistress of the Moor. GM, 1974

CLEMENTS, CALVIN
　-Barge Girl. GM, 1953
　-Dark Night of Love. Popular Library,
　　1956
　Hell Ship to Kuma. GM, 1954
　Satan Takes the Helm. GM, 1952

CLEMENTS, COLIN (CAMPBELL). 1894- .
　See: FLORENCE RYERSON, 1894- .

CLEMENTS, E(ILEEN) H(ELEN). 1905- .
　Series character: Alister Woodhead,
　　in at least those marked AW.
　Back in Daylight. Hodder, 1957 AW
　Berry Green. Hodder, 1945 AW
　Chair-Lift. Hodder, 1955 AW
　Cherry Harvest. Hodder, 1943; Messner,
　　1944 AW
　Discord in the Air. Hodder, 1955 AW
　High Tension. Hodder, 1959 AW
　Honey for the Marshal. Hodder, 1960 AW
　Let Him Die. Hodder, 1939; Dutton, 1940
　　AW
　Let or Hindrance. Hale, 1963 AW
　Make Fame a Monster. Hodder, 1940
　A Note of Enchantment. Hodder, 1961 AW
　The Other Island. Hodder, 1956 AW
　Over and Done With. Hodder, 1952
　Parcel of Fortune. Hodder, 1954
　Perhaps a Little Danger. Hodder, 1942;
　　Dutton, 1942
　Sea Change. Hodder, 1951
　Uncommon Cold. Hodder, 1958 AW
　Weathercock. Hodder, 1949 AW

CLEMOW, VALENTINE
　Chinese Chanty. Hurst, 1938

CLERI, MARIO. Pseudonym of Mario Puzo,
　1920- , q.v.
　Six Graves to Munich. Banner, 1967

CLERK, ERNIE
　Do You Like Tahiti? International, 1969

CLEVELAND, CYNTHIA E(LOISE)
　-His Honor; or, Fate's Mysteries. Amer-
　　ican News, 1889

CLEVELAND, JOHN. Pseudonym of John Deane
　Hilton, 1855- .
　Hustler Paul. Sidgwick, 1914

CLEVELAND, JOHN. Pseudonym of (Elizabeth)
　Adeline McElfresh, 1918- , q.v.
　Minus One Corpse. Arcadia, 1954

CLEVELY, HUGH. Pseudonym of Tod Claymore,
　q.v. See also: EDGAR (ALFRED) JEPSON,
　1863-1938. Series characters: Maxwell
　Archer, in at least those marked MA;
　John Martinson = JM; Chief Inspector
　Williams = W; and Sexton Blake (with
　many other authors) = SB.
　Amateur Crook. Hutchinson, 1936 W
　Archer Plus Twenty. Cassell, 1938 MA
　Blood and Thunder. Cassell, 1951 MA
　Call the Yard!; see Hell to Pay!
　Calling Whitehall 1212. Amalgamated,
　　1952 SB
　The Case of the Criminal's Daughter.
　　Amalgamated, 1954 SB
　The Case of the Legion Deserter. Amal-
　　gamated, 1955 SB
　The Case of the Smuggled Currency.
　　Amalgamated, 1953 SB
　The Case of the Three Survivors. Amal-
　　gamated, 1954 SB
　The Crime at 3 a.m. Amalgamated, 1954
　　SB
　Dark Eyes and Danger. Hutchinson, 1934
　Death's Counterfeit. Hutchinson, 1937 W
　Fraser Butts In. Hutchinson, 1929;
　　Clode, 1931 W
　Further Outlook Unsettled. Hutchinson,
　　1932 W
　Gang Law. Hutchinson, 1931
　The Gang Smasher. Hutchinson, 1928;
　　Clode, 1930 JM
　The Gang Smasher Again. Cassell, 1938
　　JM
　The Girl from Toronto. Amalgamated,
　　1953 SB
　The Heir of Tower House. Amalgamated,
　　1954 SB
　Hell to Pay! Hutchinson, 1930. U.S.
　　title: Call the Yard! Doubleday, 1930
　　W
　The House of Evil. Amalgamated, 1955 SB
　More Trouble for Archer. Cassell, 1949
　　MA
　Mr. Munt Carries On. Hutchinson, 1934
　The Nightclub Mystery. Amalgamated,
　　1953 SB
　No Peace for Archer. Cassell, 1947 MA
　Not Nice People. Cassell, 1950 MA
　Public Enemy. Cassell, 1953
　Somebody Killed Kelvin. Cassell, 1953
　The Strange Affair of the Widow's Dia-
　　monds. Amalgamated, 1955 SB
　Three Wooden Overcoats. Cassell, 1939
　　MA
　Turning Point; see The Wolf That Fol-
　　lows
　-The Wind was Cold. Cassell, 1955; Mor-
　　row, 1956
　The Wolf That Follows. Cassell, 1955.
　　U.S. title: Turning Point. Morrow,
　　1955
　The Wrong Murderer. Hutchinson, 1935
　Zero the 14th. Cassell, 1937 MA

CLEWES, HOWARD (CHARLES VIVIAN).
　1916- .
　An Epitaph for Love. Macmillan (Lon-
　　don), 1952; Doubleday, 1953

The Libertines; see Man on a Horse
The Long Memory. Macmillan (London),
　1951; Doubleday, 1952
-Man on a Horse. Cape, 1964. U.S.
　title: The Libertines. Doubleday,
　1964

CLIFFORD, CHARLES. Pseudonym: Robert
　Ames, q.v.

CLIFFORD, CHARLES L.
-Too Many Boats. Little, 1934; Heine-
　mann, 1935
Sword of Allah; see While the Bells
　Rang
While the Bells Rang. Doubleday, 1941.
　British title: Sword of Allah. Heine-
　mann, 1941

CLIFFORD, FRANCIS. Pseudonym of Arthur
　Leonard Bell Thompson, 1917-1975.
　Act of Mercy. H. Hamilton, 1959;
　　Coward, 1960. Also published as: Guns
　　of Darkness. Dell, 1962
　All Men are Lonely Now. Hodder, 1967;
　　Coward, 1967
　Amigo, Amigo. Hodder, 1973; Coward,
　　1973
　Another Way of Dying. Hodder, 1968;
　　Coward, 1969
　The Blind Side. Hodder, 1971; Coward,
　　1971
　Good-Bye and Amen; see The Grosvenor
　　Square Goodbye
　The Green Fields of Eden. Hodder, 1963;
　　Coward, 1963
　The Grosvenor Square Goodbye. Hodder,
　　1974. U.S. title: Good-Bye and Amen.
　　Harcourt, 1974
　Guns of Darkness; see Act of Mercy
　The Hunting-Ground. Hodder, 1964;
　　Coward, 1964
　The Naked Runner. Hodder, 1966; Coward,
　　1966
　Overdue. H. Hamilton, 1957; Dutton,
　　1958
　Spanish Duet. Coward, 1966. (A 2-in-1
　　containing U.S. editions of Time is
　　an Ambush and The Trembling Earth,
　　qq.v.)
　The Third Side of the Coin. Hodder,
　　1965; Coward, 1965
　Time is an Ambush. Hodder, 1962. U.S.
　　edition in Spanish Duet, q.v.
　-The Trembling Earth. H. Hamilton, 1955.
　　U.S. edition in Spanish Duet, q.v.
　A Wild Justice. Hodder, 1972; Coward,
　　1972

CLIFFORD, GUY. Pseudonym of Arthur Guy
　Roberts, 1903- .
　Michael Intervenes. Methuen, 1927

CLIFFORD, READ
　Guard the Girl. Mills, 1939
　Hunt the Evidence. Mills, 1938

CLIFT, DENNISON (HALLEY). 1885- .
　The Spy in the Room. Mystery House,
　　1944

CLIFTON, BUD. Pseudonym of David Stac-
　ton.
　-The Bad Girls. Pyramid, 1958
　-D for Delinquent. Ace, 1958
　Let Him Go Hang. Ace, 1961
　The Murder Specialist. Ace, 1959
　-Muscle Boy. Ace, 1958
　-The Power Gods. Pyramid, 1959; Eyre,
　　1958

CLINE, LEONARD (LANSON). 1893-1929.
　-The Dark Chamber. Viking, 1927

CLINTEN, MAX
  The Dead were Strangers. Comyns, 1952
  Don't Make Me Kill. Comyns, 1953
  No Dame Wants to Die. Comyns, 1952
  No Place for a Dame. Comyns, 1953
  Red, Hot and Deadly. Comyns, 1953
  So Long, Sucker. Comyns, 1953
  Strictly Illegal. Comyns, 1952

CLINTON, DANIEL JOSEPH. 1900-   . Pseudonym: Thomas Rourke, q.v.

CLINTON, DOROTHY RANDLE
  The Maddening Scar. Christopher, 1962

CLINTON-BADDELEY, V(ICTOR VAUGHAN REYNOLDS GERAINT) C(LINTON). 1900-1970. Series character: Dr. Davie, in all titles.
  Death's Bright Dart. Gollancz, 1967; Morrow, 1970
  My Foe Outstretch'd Beneath the Tree. Gollancz, 1968; Morrow, 1968
  No Case for the Police. Gollancz, 1970; Morrow, 1970
  Only a Matter of Time. Gollancz, 1969; Morrow, 1970
  To Study a Long Silence. Gollancz, 1972

CLIVE, MRS. ARCHER [CAROLINE WIGLEY CLIVE]. 1801-1873. See: ANONYMOUS.

CLOSE, ROBIN
  The Boheme Combination. Joseph, 1973; Walker, 1974

CLOUSTON, J(OSEPH) STORER. 1870-1944. Series characters: Francis Mandell-Essington = FM; F. T. Carrington = FC.
  -The Adventures of M. D'Haricot. Blackwood, 1902; Harper, 1902
  After the Deed. Blackwood, 1929
  Beastmark the Spy. Blackwood, 1941
  The Best Story Ever. Blackwood, 1932
  Carrington's Cases. Blackwood, 1920 ss FC
  Colonel Dam. Blackwood, 1930
  Count Bunker. Blackwood, 1906; Brentano's, 1907 FM
  -A Country Family. Murray, 1908
  -The Duke. Arnold, 1900; Longmans, 1900
  -Garmiscath. Blackwood, 1904
  His First Offense. Mills, 1912. U.S. title: The Mystery of No. 47. Moffat, 1911
  -The Jade's Progress. Lane, 1928
  The Lunatic at Large. Blackwood, 1899; Appleton, 1900 FM
  The Lunatic at Large Again. Nash, 1922; Dutton, 1923 FM
  The Lunatic in Charge. Bodley Head, 1926; Dutton, 1926 FM
  The Lunatic in Love; see Mr. Essington in Love
  The Lunatic Still at Large. Nash, 1923; Dutton, 1924 FM
  The Man from the Clouds. Blackwood, 1918; Doran, 1919
  -The Man in Steel. Jarrolds, 1939
  Mr. Essington in Love. Lane, 1927. U.S. title: The Lunatic in Love. Dutton, 1927 FM
  The Mystery of No. 47; see His First Offense
  Our Lady's Inn. Blackwood, 1903; Harper, 1903
  -Our Member Mr. Muttlebury. Jenkins, 1935
  Scotland Expects. Jenkins, 1936
  -Scots Wha Ha'e. Jenkins, 1936
  Simon. Blackwood, 1919; Doran, 1919 FC
  The Spy in Black. Blackwood, 1917; Doran, 1918
  The Two Strange Men. Nash, 1924
  Two's Two. Blackwood, 1916
  -The Virtuous Vamp. Blackwood, 1931

CLOUTIER, HELEN (H.). 1909-   .
  Murder, Absolutely Murder. Chicago Paperback, 1962

CLUGSTON, KATE [KATHERINE THATCHER CLUGSTON]. 1892-   .
  A Murderer in the House. Wyn, 1947. Also published as: Twist the Knife Slowly. Ace, 1952

CLUNE, FRANCIS PATRICK. 1893-   .
  The Blue Mountains Murderer. Horwitz, 1959

CLUNE, M. A.
  "Call in the Yard." Mitre, 1946
  Masked Alibi. Rolls, 1945
  Strange Heritage. Rolls, 1945

CLUTTON-BROCK, ALAN (FRANCIS)
  Murder at Liberty Hall. Lane, 1941; Macmillan, 1941

CLYDE, LEONARD WORSWICK. 1906-   . Pseudonym: Peter Baron, q.v.

COATES, JOHN. 1912-   .
  Time for Tea. Methuen, 1948; Macmillan, 1950

COATES, ROBERT M(YRON). 1897-1973.
  The Hour After Westerley. Harcourt, 1947 ss, some criminous
  Wisteria Cottage. Harcourt, 1948; Gollancz, 1949

COBB, (GEOFFREY) BELTON. 1892-   . Series characters: Inspector Cheviot Burmann, in at least those marked CB; Superintendent Manning, in at least those marked M; Bryan Armitage, in at least those marked BA.
  Catch Me—If You Can. Allen, 1970
  Corpse at Casablanca. Allen, 1956; Abelard, 1956 CB
  Corpse in the Cargo. Allen, 1961 CB
  Corpse Incognito. Methuen, 1953
  Dead Girl's Shoes. Allen, 1964 CB
  Death Defies the Doctor. Longmans, 1939 CB
  Death in the 13th Dose. Longmans, 1946 CB
  Death of a Peeping Tom. Allen, 1963 CB
  Death with a Difference. Allen, 1960 CB
  Detective in Distress. Methuen, 1953 CB
  Don't Lie to the Police. Allen, 1960 CB
  Double Detection. Longmans, 1945 CB
  Doubly Dead. Allen, 1957 CB
  Drink Alone and Die. Allen, 1956 CB
  Early Morning Poison. Longmans, 1947 M
  Fatal Dose. Longmans, 1937 CB
  The Fatal Holiday. Longmans, 1938 CB
  Food for Felony. Allen, 1969 BA
  The Framing of Carol Woan. Longmans, 1948 M
  Home Guard Mystery. Longmans, 1942
  The Horrible Man in Heron's Wood. Allen, 1970
  I Fell Among Thieves. Allen, 1971
  I Never Miss Twice. Allen, 1965 CB, BA
  Inspector Burmann's Black-Out. Longmans, 1941 CB
  Inspector Burmann's Busiest Day. Longmans, 1939 CB
  Last Drop. Allen, 1965 CB
  Like a Guilty Thing. Longmans, 1938; British Book Centre, 1959 CB
  Lost Without Trace. Allen, 1967 CB
  The Lunatic, the Lover. Methuen, 1950
  The Missing Scapegoat. Allen, 1958 CB
  Murder: Men Only. Allen, 1962 CB
  Need a Body Tell? Allen, 1954 CB
  Next Door to Death. Methuen, 1952 CB
  No Alibi. Longmans, 1936 CB
  No Charge for the Poison. Methuen, 1950 M
  No Last Words. Longmans, 1949 M
  No Mercy for Margaret. Methuen, 1952 CB
  No Shame for the Devil. Allen, 1964 CB
  Poisoner's Base. Allen, 1957; British Book Centre, 1958
  The Poisoner's Mistake. Longmans, 1936 CB
  Quickly Dead. Longmans, 1937 CB
  Scandal at Scotland Yard. Allen, 1969 BA
  Search for Sergeant Baxter. Allen, 1961 CB
  Secret Inquiry. Allen, 1968 BA, CB
  The Secret of Superintendent Manning. Longmans, 1948 M
  Security Secrets Sold Here. Allen, 1967 CB
  Sergeant Ross in Disguise. Longmans, 1940
  Silence Under Threat. Allen, 1968
  Some Must Watch. Allen, 1966 CB
  Stolen Strychnine. Longmans, 1949 M
  A Stone for his Head. Allen, 1966 CB
  Suspicion in Triplicate. Allen, 1971
  The Willing Witness. Allen, 1955 CB
  With Intent to Kill. Allen, 1958; British Book Centre, 1958 CB

COBB, CLAYTON W. Pseudonym of J. A. Patten.
  The Mountaineer Detective. Street, 1889

COBB, ELIZABETH [MRS. ELIZABETH COBB CHAPMAN] and MARGARET CASE MORGAN
  Murder in Your Home. Long & Smith, 1932. (20 short plays with a quiz after each.)

COBB, IRVIN S(HREWSBURY). 1876-1944. Series character: Judge Priest, at least partially included in titles marked JP.
  -Alias Ben Alibi. Doran, 1925
  -Back Home. Doran, 1912 ss JP
  -Down Yonder with Judge Priest. Long & Smith, 1932 ss JP
  The Escape of Mr. Trimm. Doran, 1913; Hodder, 1914 ss JP
  Faith, Hope and Charity. Bobbs, 1934 ss JP
  Judge Priest Turns Detective. Bobbs, 1937 ss JP
  Murder Day by Day. Bobbs, 1933; Cassell, 1934
  -Old Judge Priest. Doran, 1916 ss JP
  -Snake Doctor and other stories. Doran, 1923 ss JP

COBB, IVO GEIKIE. 1887-   . Pseudonym: Anthony Weymouth, q.v.

COBB, MICHAEL. Pseudonym of Alfred Daniel Wintle.
  -Coldharbour. Selwyn, 1939
  -The Emancipation of Ambrose. Hurst, 1928
  Sholto Budd. Hurst, 1932
  -Sir Peter's Arm. Chapman, 1929

COBB, SYLVANUS, JR. 1823-1887.
  -The Armorer of Tyre. Lupton, 1893
  -The Bandit of Syracuse. Bonner, 1891
  -The Conspirator of Cordova. Bonner, 1896
  -The Council of Ten. Street, 1900
  -A Dark Plot. Ogilvie, 1891
  -The Double Duel. Ogilvie, 1892
  -The Earl's Ward. Gleason, 1852
  -The Fortunes of Conrad. Bonner, 1866
  -The Iron Cross; or, The Countess of Errol. Peterson, 1850

-Ivan the Serf. French, 1853
-The Juggler of Nankin; or, The Grandee's Plot. French, 185?
-Karl, the Lion. Street, 1891
-The King's Talisman; or, The Young Lion of Mt. Hor. Gleason, 1851
-The Lost Heir. Gleason, 1853
-Marco; or, The Female Smuggler. Gleason, 1857
-Orion, the Gold Beater. Cassell (New York), 1888
-The Painter of Parma; or, The Magic of a Masterpiece. Cassell (New York), 1889
-The Queen's Revenge. Lupton, 1892
-Red Hand. Laird, 1893
-The Robber Countess. Bonner, 1891
-Roderick of Kildare. Bonner, 1891
-Rollo of Normandy. Bonner, 1891
-The Royal Outlaw. Bonner, 1891
-The Scourge of Damascus. Bonner, 1891
-The Secrets of the Coast. Donohue, ca. 1897
-The Smuggler of King's Cove; or, The Old Chapel Mystery. Cassell (New York), 1889
-The Spectre's Secret. Bonner, 1892

COBB, THOMAS. 1853-1932. Series character: Inspector Bedison, in at least those marked B.
-The Amateur Emigrants. Rivers, 1907
-Andrew and his Wife. Mills, 1914
-The Anger of Olivia. Mills, 1910
-The Bishop's Gambit. Richards, 1901
-Brownie's Plot. Ward, 1889
-The Busy Whisper. Chapman, 1915
-Captain Marraday's Marriage. Lane (New York & London), 1918
-Carpet Courtship. Lane, 1898
-A Change of Pace. Methuen, 1904
The Chichester Intrigue. Lane (New York & London), 1908
-The Choice of Theodora. Mills, 1911
-Collusion. Rivers, 1906
The Composite Lady. Chapman, 1903
Crime at Keeper's. Benn, 1930
The Crime Without a Clue. Benn, 1929 B
Death on the Cliff. Benn, 1932
-The Deception of Ursula. Paul, 1923
The Disappearance of Mr. Derwent. Ward, 1894; Neely, 1896
-The Dissemblers. Lane, 1901
-Enter Bridget. Mills, 1912
-False Pretences. Nash, 1926
-For Value Received. Ward, 1890
-The Friendship of Veronica. Rivers, 1905
-The Future Mrs. Dering. Laurie, 1908
Getting Rid of Anne. Nash, 1921
-A Giver in Secret. Laurie, 1911
-The Head of the Household. Chapman, 1902
-The Hillerway Letters. Chapman, 1917
The House by the Common. Ward, 1891
-The Impossible Apollo. Lane (New York & London), 1920
Inspector Bedison and the Sunderland Case. Benn, 1931 B
Inspector Bedison Risks It. Benn, 1931 B
-The Intriguers. Nash, 1903
-Joanna Sets to Work. Paul, 1925
-The Judgement of Helen. Lane (New York & London), 1899
-Lady Gwendoline. Richards, 1902
-Lady Sylvia's Imposter. Mills, 1914
The Late Mr. Beverly. Paul, 1924
-A Man of Sentiment. Richards, 1902
-Margaret Rutland. Mills, 1910
-A Marriage of Inconvenience. Mills, 1913
-Masterman's Mistake. Wells Gardner, 1913
The Metal Box. Benn, 1933
-Miss Merewether's Money. Ward, 1892
-Mr. Burnside's Responsibility. Mills, 1909
-Mr. Passingham. Lane, 1899
-Mr. Preston's Daughter. Lane (New York & London), 1920
-Mrs. Belfort's Stratagem. Nash, 1904
-Mrs. Erricker's Reputation. Rivers, 1906. Also published as: Mrs. Pomeroy's Reputation. Lane, 1918
-Mrs. Latham's Extravagance. Chapman, 1915
Mrs. Pomeroy's Reputation; see Mrs. Erricker's Reputation
-Mrs. Whiston's Party. Everett, 1909
-On Trust. Hurst, 1891
-One Who Passed By. Paul, 1924
-An Open Secret. Rand, 1898 (British title?)
-Pat. Chapman, 1916
-Peggy's Dilemma. Nash, 1923
-Phillida. Mills, 1911
-Priscilla to the Rescue. Nash, 1922
The Sark Street Chapel Murder. Benn, 1930
-Scruples. Richards, 1900; Lane (New York), 1900
-Second in the Field. Chapman, 1916
-A Sentimental Season. Laurie, 1907
-Severence. Lane (New York & London), 1901
The Silver Bag. Lane (New York & London), 1919
-Sophy Bunce. Nash, 1905
-The Transformation of Timothy. Mills, 1913
-The Voice of Bethia. Mills, 1912
Wedderburn's Will. Ward, 1892
-The Westlakes. Farran, 1892
-While Guy was in France. Paul, 1918
Who Closed the Casement? Benn, 1932 B
Who Opened the Door? Benn, 1928

COBBAN, J(AMES) MacLAREN. 1849-1903. Series character: Mr. Townshend, in at least those marked T.
-The Angel of the Covenant. Methuen, 1898; Fenno, 1899
The Avenger of Blood. Cassell, 1895
-The Burden of Israel. Chatto, 1893; Harper, 1893
-By Telegraph. SPCK, 1888
-The Cure of Souls. Chatto, 1879
The Golden Tooth. Digby, 1901; Buckles, 1901 T
-The Green Turbans. Long, 1902; Burt, 1902
-Her Royal Highness's Love Affair. Pearson, 1897
The Horned Cat; see Sir Ralph's Secret; or, The Horned Cat
-I'd Crowns Resign. Long, 1900
-The Iron Hand. Long, 1904
Julia Courtney; see Master of His Fate
-The Last Alive. Richards, 1902
-Master of His Fate. Blackwood, 1889; Lovell, 1890. Also published as: Julia Courtney; or, Master of His Fate. Appleton, 1890
Missing Partner; or, Tinted Vapours; see Tinted Vapours; or, A Nemesis
A Nemesis; or, Tinted Vapors; see Tinted Vapours; or, A Nemesis
Pursued by the Law. Long, 1899; Appleton, 1899 T
-The Reverend Gentleman. Methuen, 1891; Lovell, 1891
-A Royal Exchange. Appleton, 1901. (British title?)
Sir Ralph's Secret; or, The Horned Cat. Warne, 1891. U.S. title: The Horned Cat. National Book, 1891
-A Soldier and a Gentleman. Long, 1904; Street, 1901

The Terror by Night. Long, 1905
-Tinted Vapours; or, A Nemesis. Warne, 1885. Also published as: Missing Partner; or, Tinted Vapours. Warne, 1889. U.S. title: A Nemesis; or, Tinted Vapors. Lupton, 1892
-Wilt Thou Have This Woman? Methuen, 1897; Lippincott, 1897

COBDEN, GUY. Series character: John Chadwick, in all titles.
I Saw Murder. Hale, 1962
Murder for her Birthday. Hale, 1960
Murder for his Money. Hale, 1959
Murder Inherited. Hale, 1961
Murder was my Neighbor. Rich, 1955
Murder was Their Medicine. Jarrolds, 1957
My Guess was Murder. Rich, 1956

COBNOR, JOHN
The Four Answers. Cape, 1931

COBURN, ANDREW. 1932- .
The Trespassers. Houghton, 1974

COBURN, SAMMY
Brunettes are no Better. Scion, 1952
Don't Tempt Me. Scion, 1951
Hot Cargo. Scion, 1950
The Lady Pays. Scion, 1951
Uneasy Street. Scion, 1950
You Can't Die Here. Scion, 1950

COCHRAN, RUTH GILBERT. 1893- .
Victoria Pruitt Comes to Town. Mystery House, 1941

COCHRANE, ELIZABETH J. 1867-1922. Pseudonym: Nellie Bly, q.v.

COCKAIN, FRANK
The Inside Out Man. Futura, 1975

COCKBURN, FRANCIS CLAUD. 1904- . Pseudonym: James Helvick, q.v.

COCKIN, JOAN. Pseudonym of Edith Joan Burbridge, 1919- . Series character: Inspector Cam, in at least those marked C.
Curiosity Killed the Cat. Hodder, 1947 C
Deadly Ernest. Hodder, 1952
Villainy at Vespers. Hodder, 1949 C

COCKING, RONALD
Die with Me, Lady. Harlequin, 1953
High Tide at Midnight. Hurst, 1950
The House in Brook Street. Hurst, 1949
Weep No More, Lady. Hurst, 1952

COCKRELL, FRANK and MARIAN (BROWN), 1909- , q.v.
Dark Waters. World, 1944

COCKRELL, MARIAN (BROWN). 1909- . See also: FRANK COCKRELL.
Something Between. Harper, 1946

CODY, C(HARLES) S. Pseudonym of Leslie Waller, 1923- , q.v. Other pseudonym: Patrick Mann, q.v.
Lie Like a Lady. Ace, 1955
The Witching Night. World, 1952; Corgi, 1953

CODY, H(IRAM) A(LFRED)
The Long Patrol. Doran, 1912; Hodder, 1912

CODY, JAMES P. Series character: Brian Petersen, in all titles.
A French Killing. Berkley, 1975
Search and Destroy. Berkley, 1974

Top Secret Kill. Berkley, 1974
Your Daughter will Die! Berkley, 1975

COE, CHARLES FRANCIS. 1890-1956.
About Two A.M. Cosmopolitan, 1931
Ashes, Random, 1952
G Man. Lippincott (Philadelphia & London), 1935
Gunman. Gollancz, 1930 (U.S. title?)
Hooch! Doubleday, 1929
Knockout. Lippincott, 1936; Hutchinson, 1938
Me—Gangster. Putnam (New York & London), 1927
The Other Half. Cosmopolitan, 1930
Pressure. Random, 1951; Allen, 1952
Ransom. Lippincott (Philadelphia & London), 1934
The River Pirate. Putnam (New York & London), 1928
Swag. Putnam (New York & London), 1928
Triumph: The Undoing of Rafferty, Ward Heeler. Sears, 1929

COE, TUCKER. Pseudonym of Donald E(dwin) Westlake, 1933-   , q.v. Other pseudonyms: Timothy J. Culver, Richard Stark, qq.v. Series character: Mitchell Tobin, in all titles.
Don't Lie to Me. Random, 1972; Gollancz, 1974
A Jade in Aries. Random, 1971; Gollancz, 1973
Kinds of Love, Kinds of Death. Random, 1966; Souvenir, 1967
Murder Among Children. Random, 1968; Souvenir, 1968
Wax Apple. Random, 1970; Gollancz, 1973

COFFEY, BRIAN. Pseudonym of Dean R(ay) Koontz, 1945-   , q.v. Other pseudonym: K. R. Dwyer, q.v. Series character: Mike Tucker, in all titles.
Blood Risk. Bobbs, 1973; Barker, 1974
Surrounded. Bobbs, 1974; Barker, 1975
The Wall of Masks. Bobbs, 1975

COFFIN, CARLYN
Dogwatch. Farrar, 1944
Mare's Nest. Farrar, 1941

COFFIN, GEOFFREY. Pseudonym of (Francis) Van Wyck Mason, 1897-   , q.v. Series character: Inspector Scott Stuart, in both titles.
The Forgotten Fleet Mystery. Dodge, 1936; Jarrolds, 1943, as by Van Wyck Mason
Murder in the Senate. Dodge, 1935; Hurst, 1936

COFFIN, PETER. Pseudonym of Jonathan (Wyatt) Latimer, 1906-   , q.v.
The Search for my Great-Uncle's Head. Doubleday, 1937

COFFMAN, VIRGINIA (EDITH). 1914-   .
Pseudonym: Victor Cross, q.v.
-The Affair at Alkali. Arcadia, 1960. British title: Nevada Gunslinger. Gresham, 1962
The Beach House. Signet, 1970
The Beckoning. Ace, 1965
Black Heather. Lancer, 1966
Call of the Flesh. Lancer, 1968
The Candidate's Wife. Lancer, 1968
The Castle at Witch's Coven. Lancer, 1966
Castle Barra. Paperback Library, 1966
Chalet Diabolique. Lancer, 1971
The Chinese Door. Lancer, 1967; Hale, 1971
The Cliffs of Dread. Lancer, 1972
The Curse of the Island Pool. Lancer, 1965
The Dark Beyond Moura; see The Dark Gondola

The Dark Gondola. Ace, 1968. Also published as: The Dark Beyond Moura. Ace, 1977
The Dark Palazzo. Arbor, 1973
The Demon Tower. Signet, 1966
The Devil's Mistress. Lancer, 1969
The Devil's Vicar. Ace, 1966. Revised edition: The Vicar of Moura. Ace, 1972
The Devil's Virgin. Lancer, 1970
The Evil at Queen's Priory. Lancer, 1973
A Fear of Heights. Lancer, 1973
A Few Fiends to Tea. Belmont, 1967
From Satan, with Love. Lancer, 1972
Garden of Shadows. Lancer, 1973
A Haunted Place. Lancer, 1966; Milton House, 1975
The High Terrace. Lancer, 1966. British title: To Love a Dark Stranger. Hale, 1969
The Hounds of Hell. Belmont, 1967
The House at Sandalwood. Arbor, 1974; Milton House, 1975
The House on the Moat. Lancer, 1972
Hyde Place. Arbor, 1974
The Ice Forest. Dell, 1975
Isle of the Undead. Lancer, 1969. British title: Voodoo Widow. Hale, 1970
Masque by Gaslight. Ace, 1970
Masque of Satan. Lancer, 1971
The Master of Blue Mire. Dell, 1971; Milton House, 1975
Mist at Darkness. Signet, 1968
Mistress Devon. Arbor, 1972
Moura. Crown, 1959
Nevada Gunslinger; see The Affair at Alkali
Night at Sea Abbey. Lancer, 1972
Of Love and Intrigue. Signet, 1969
One Man Too Many. Lancer, 1967
Priestess of the Damned. Lancer, 1970
The Rest is Silence. Lancer, 1967
The Richest Girl in the World. Lancer, 1967
The Secret of Shower Tree. Lancer, 1966
The Shadow Box. Lancer, 1967
The Small Tawny Cat. Lancer, 1967. Also published as: The Stalking Terror. Signet, 1977
The Stalking Terror; see The Small Tawny Cat
Survivor of Darkness. Lancer, 1973
To Love a Dark Stranger; see The High Terrace
The Vampyre of Moura. Ace, 1970
Veronique. Arbor, 1975
The Vicar of Moura; see The Devil's Vicar
The Villa Fountains. Belmont, 1967

COFYN, CORNELIUS. Pseudonym.
The Death-Riders. Gollancz, 1935; Knopf, 1936

COGGIN, JOAN
Dancing with Death. Hurst, 1949
The Mystery of Orchard House. Hurst, 1947
Who Killed the Curate? Hurst, 1944
Why Did She Die? Hurst, 1947

COGGINS, PASCHAL HESTON. 1852-1917. Pseudonym: Sidney Marlow, q.v.

COHAN, GEORGE M(ICHAEL). 1879-1942.
The Return of the Vagabond. French, 1940. (Play.)
Seven Keys to Baldpate. French, 1914; Rees, 1914. (Play based on the novel by Earl Derr Biggers, 1884-1933, q.v.)
The Tavern. French, 1933. (Play.)

COHANE, M. E.
Murder One! Pinnacle, 1975

COHEN, ALFRED J. 1861-1928. Pseudonym: Alan Dale, q.v.

COHEN, OCTAVUS ROY. 1891-1959. Series characters: David Carroll = DC; Jim Hanvey = JH.
The Backstage Mystery. Appleton, 1930. Also published as: Curtain at Eight. Grosset, 1933 JH
A Bullet for My Love. Macmillan, 1950; Barker, 1951
-Cameos. Appleton, 1931 ss
Child of Evil. Appleton, 1936
The Corpse That Walked. GM, 1951; Red Seal, 1957
The Crimson Alibi. Dodd, 1919; Nash, 1919
Curtain at Eight; see The Backstage Mystery
Danger in Paradise. Macmillan, 1945; Hale, 1949
Dangerous Lady. Macmillan, 1946; Barker, 1948
-Detours. Little, 1927 ss
Don't Ever Love Me. Macmillan, 1947; Barker, 1948
East of Broadway. Appleton, 1938
Gray Dusk. Dodd, 1920; Nash, 1920 DC
I Love You Again. Appleton, 1937. Also published as: There's Always Time to Die. Popular Library, 1949
The Intruder; see Love can be Dangerous
The Iron Chalice. Little, 1925; Cassell, 1926
Jim Hanvey, Detective. Dodd, 1923; Nash, 1924 ss JH
Lady in Armor. Appleton, 1941
Lost Lady. GM, 1951; Fawcett (London), 1953
Love can be Dangerous. Macmillan, 1955; Barker, 1955. Also published as: The Intruder. Graphic, 1956
Love has no Alibi. Macmillan, 1946; Hale, 1952
The May Day Mystery. Appleton, 1929 JH
Midnight. Dodd, 1922; Nash, 1922 DC
More Beautiful than Murder. Macmillan, 1948; Barker, 1950
Murder in Season; see Romance in Crimson
My Love Wears Black. Macmillan, 1948; Barker, 1949
The Other Woman, with J. U. Giesy. Macaulay, 1917; Gardner, 1920
The Outer Gate. Little, 1927; Hodder, 1927
Romance in Crimson. Appleton, 1940. Also published as: Murder in Season. Popular Library, 1946
Romance in the First Degree. Macmillan, 1944; Hale, 1951
Scrambled Yeggs. Appleton, 1934
Six Seconds of Darkness. Dodd, 1921; Nash, 1921 DC
Sound of Revelry. Macmillan, 1943; Hale, 1945
Star of Earth. Appleton, 1932 JH
There's Always Time to Die; see I Love You Again
The Townsend Murder Mystery. Appleton, 1933. (First radio play published in book form.)

COHEN, STANLEY. 1928-   .
The Abduction; see Taking Gary Feldman
The Diane Game. Stein, 1973; Constable, 1974
Taking Gary Feldman. Putnam, 1970. British title: The Abduction. Constable, 1971

COLBRON, GRACE ISABEL. 1869-1948. Series character (see also: Augusta Groner): Joe Muller = JM.
The Club Car Mystery. Macaulay, 1928

Joe Muller, Detective, with Augusta Groner (1850-). Duffield, 1910 ss JM

COLBY, ROBERT
Beautiful But Bad. Monarch, 1962
The Captain Must Die. GM, 1959; Muller pb, 1960
The Deadly Desire. GM, 1959; Muller pb, 1961
Executive Wife. Monarch, 1964
The Faster She Runs. Monarch, 1963
In a Vanishing Room. Ace, 1961
Kill Me a Fortune. Ace, 1961
Kim. Monarch, 1962
Lament for Julie. Monarch, 1961
Make Mine Vengeance. Avon, 1959
Murder Mistress. Ace, 1959
Murder Times Five. GM, 1972
The Quaking Widow. Ace, 1956
Run for the Money. Avon, 1960
Secret of the Second Door. GM, 1959; Muller pb, 1960
The Star Pad. GM, 1960
These Lonely, These Dead. Pyramid, 1959

COLCORD, LINCOLN. 1883-1947.
The Game of Life and Death. Macmillan (New York & London), 1914 ss, some criminous

COLE, BARRY. 1936- .
The Search for Rita. Methuen, 1970

COLE, BURT. 1930- .
Sahara Survival. Harper's Magazine Press, 1973

COLE, DIANE
Murder at the White Tulip. Arcadia, 1960

COLE, G(EORGE) D(OUGLAS) H(OWARD), 1889-1959, and MARGARET (ISABEL POSTGATE) COLE, 1893- . Series characters: Everard Blatchington = EB; Dr. Tancred = T; Mrs. Warrender = W; Superintendent Wilson = SW. A number of pamphlets are grouped together at the end of the entry.
The Affair at Aliquid. Collins, 1933
The Berkshire Mystery; see Burglars in Bucks
Big Business Murder. Collins, 1935; Doubleday, 1935
The Blatchington Tangle. Collins, 1926; Macmillan, 1926 SW,EB
The Brooklyn Murders. Collins, 1923; Seltzer, 1924. (The first SW novel, written by G.D.H. Cole alone.)
The Brothers Sackville. Collins, 1936; Macmillan, 1937 SW
Burglars in Bucks. Collins, 1930. U.S. title: The Berkshire Mystery. Brewer, 1930 SW
Corpse in Canonicals. Collins, 1930. U.S. title: The Corpse in the Constable's Garden. Morrow, 1931 SW
The Corpse in the Constable's Garden; see Corpse in Canonicals
Counterpoint Murder. Collins, 1940; Macmillan, 1941 SW
Dead Man's Watch. Collins, 1931; Doubleday, 1932
Death in the Quarry. Collins, 1934; Doubleday, 1934 SW,EB
Death of a Millionaire. Collins, 1925; Macmillan, 1925 SW
Death of a Star. Collins, 1932; Doubleday, 1933
Disgrace to the College. Hodder pb, 1937. (A novelet.)
Double Blackmail. Collins, 1939; Macmillan, 1939 SW
Dr. Tancred Begins. Collins, 1935; Doubleday, 1935 T
End of an Ancient Mariner. Collins, 1933; Doubleday, 1934 SW
The Great Southern Mystery. Collins, 1931. U.S. title: The Walking Corpse. Morrow, 1931 SW
Greek Tragedy. Collins, 1939; Macmillan, 1940 SW
Knife in the Dark. Collins, 1941; Macmillan, 1942
Last Will and Testament. Collins, 1936; Doubleday, 1936 T
A Lesson in Crime. Collins, 1933 MW ss
The Man from the River. Collins, 1928; Macmillan, 1928 SW
The Missing Aunt. Collins, 1937; Macmillan, 1938
Mrs. Warrender's Profession. Collins, 1938; Macmillan, 1939 ss W
The Murder at Crome House. Collins, 1927; Macmillan, 1927
The Murder at the Munition Works. Collins, 1940; Macmillan, 1940 SW
Murder in Four Parts. Collins, 1934
Off with her Head! Collins, 1938; Macmillan, 1939 SW
Poison in the Garden Suburb. Collins, 1929. U.S. title: Poison in a Garden Suburb. Payson, 1929 SW
Scandal at School. Collins, 1935. U.S. title: The Sleeping Death. Doubleday, 1936 EB
The Sleeping Death; see Scandal at School
Superintendent Wilson's Holiday. Collins, 1928; Payson, 1929 ss SW
Toper's End. Collins, 1942; Macmillan, 1942 SW
The Walking Corpse; see The Great Southern Mystery
Wilson and Some Others. Collins, 1940 ss, some about SW

Birthday Gifts and other stories. Polybooks, 1946 ss
The Bone of the Dinosaur. Bantam (London), 1943
Death in the Sun. Vallancey, 1945. (From Mrs. Warrender's Profession, q.v.)
Death in the Tankard. Polybooks, 1943
Death of a Bride. Vallancey, 1945. (From Mrs. Warrender's Profession, q.v.)
Fatal Beauty. Locke, 1948. (From Mrs. Warrender's Profession, q.v.)
In a Telephone Cabinet. Polybooks, 1944. (From Superintendent Wilson's Holiday, q.v.)
In Peril of his Life. Locke, 1948. (From Mrs. Warrender's Profession, q.v.)
A Lesson in Crime and other stories. Polybooks, 1946. (From A Lesson in Crime, q.v.) ss
A Lesson in Crime, and The Motive. Polybooks, 1943. (From A Lesson in Crime, q.v.) ss
The Missing Baronet. Polybooks, 1943. (From Superintendent Wilson's Holiday, q.v.)
Murder in Broad Daylight, and Crime at Eslington Hall. Polybooks, 1943. (From Wilson and Some Others, q.v.) ss
The Oxford Mystery. Bantam (London), 1943. (From Superintendent Wilson's Holiday, q.v.)
Strychnine Tonic, and A Dose of Cyanide. Polybooks, 1943 ss
Superintendent Wakley's Mistake. Vallancey, 1944. (From A Lesson in Crime, q.v.)
The Toys of Death. Locke, 1948. (From Mrs. Warrender's Profession, q.v.)
Wilson Calling. Vallancey, 1944. (From A Lesson in Crime, q.v.)

COLE, K(ATHARINE) S.
I'm Afraid I'll Live! Houghton, 1936; Heinemann, 1936

COLE, LOIS DWIGHT. 1902- . Pseudonym: Anne Eliot, q.v.

COLE, MARGARET (ISABEL POSTGATE). 1893- . See: G(EORGE) D(OUGLAS) H(OWARD) COLE, 1889-1959.

COLE, R(OBERT) W(ILLIAM)
-The Artificial Girl. Greening, 1908
The Death Trap. Greening, 1907
-His Other Self. Greening, 1906

COLEMAN, CLARA
A Scent of Sandalwood. Lancer, 1966

COLEMAN, F(RANCIS) X(AVIER) J.
Philip, the Draftsman. Lippincott, 1970

COLERIDGE, GILBERT (JAMES DUKE). 1859- .
An Instinctive Criminal. Treherne, 1905

COLERIDGE, M(ARY) E(LIZABETH). 1861-1907.
-The Shadow on the Wall. Arnold, 1904

COLES, CYRIL HENRY. 1898-1965. Joint pseudonyms with Adelaide Frances Oke Manning, 1891-1959: Manning Coles, Francis Gaite, qq.v.

COLES, MANNING. Joint pseudonym of Adelaide Frances Oke Manning, 1891-1959, and Cyril Henry Coles, 1898-1965. Other joint pseudonym: Francis Gaite, q.v. Series character: Tommy Hambledon = TH. Note that several titles published in the U.S. as by Manning Coles appeared in Britain under the Francis Gaite pseudonym, and are there listed herein.
Alias Uncle Hugo. Hodder, 1953; Doubleday, 1952. Also published as: Operation Manhunt. Jonathan, 1954 TH
All That Glitters; see Not for Export
Among Those Absent. Hodder, 1948; Doubleday, 1948 TH
The Basle Express. Hodder, 1956; Doubleday, 1956 TH
Birdwatcher's Quarry; see The Three Beans
A Brother for Hugh. Hodder, 1947. U.S. title: With Intent to Deceive. Doubleday, 1947 TH
Concrete Crime; see Crime in Concrete
Crime in Concrete. Hodder, 1960. U.S. title: Concrete Crime. Doubleday, 1960 TH
Dangerous by Nature. Hodder, 1950; Doubleday, 1950 TH
Death of an Ambassador. Hodder, 1957; Doubleday, 1957 TH
Diamonds to Amsterdam. Hodder, 1950; Doubleday, 1949 TH
Drink to Yesterday. Hodder, 1940; Doubleday, 1941 TH
The Fifth Man. Hodder, 1946; Doubleday, 1946 TH
Green Hazard. Hodder, 1945; Doubleday, 1945 TH
The House at Pluck's Gutter. Hodder, 1963; Pyramid, 1968 TH
A Knife for the Juggler. Hodder, 1953; Doubleday, 1964. Also published as: The Vengeance Man. Pyramid, 1967 TH
Let the Tiger Die. Hodder, 1948; Doubleday, 1947 TH
The Man in the Green Hat. Hodder, 1955; Doubleday, 1955 TH
The Mystery of the Stolen Plans; see Not for Export
Night Train to Paris. Hodder, 1952; Doubleday, 1952 TH
No Entry. Hodder, 1958; Doubleday, 1958 TH

Not for Export. Hodder, 1954. U.S. title: All That Glitters. Doubleday, 1954. Also published as: The Mystery of the Stolen Plans. Berkley, 1960 TH
Not Negotiable. Hodder, 1949; Doubleday, 1949 TH
Nothing to Declare. Doubleday, 1960 ss TH
Now or Never. Hodder, 1951; Doubleday, 1951 TH
Operation Manhunt; see Alias Uncle Hugo
Pray Silence. Hodder, 1940. U.S. title: A Toast to Tomorrow. Doubleday, 1941 TH
Search for a Sultan. Hodder, 1961; Doubleday, 1961 TH
They Tell No Tales. Hodder, 1941; Doubleday, 1942 TH
This Fortress. Doubleday, 1942
The Three Beans. Hodder, 1957. U.S. title: Birdwatcher's Quarry. Doubleday, 1956 TH
A Toast to Tomorrow; see Pray Silence
The Vengeance Man; see A Knife for the Juggler
With Intent to Deceive; see A Brother for Hugh
Without Lawful Authority. Hodder, 1943; Doubleday, 1943 TH

COLIN, AUBREY. Series character: Insp. Bill Murray, in both titles.
Death Comes to Dinner. Hammond, 1965
Hands of Death. Hammond, 1963

COLIZZI, GIUSEPPE. 1925-   .
The Night has Another Voice. Abelard (London & New York), 1963. (Translation of La Notte ha Un'altra Voce. Milan, 1958.)

COLLES, EDMUND
Fair Exchange. Jenkins, 1931
-A Fool and his Money. Jenkins, 1932

COLLEY, I(SOBEL) B.
Death in the Dimness. Hale, 1974

COLLIER, JOHN. 1901-   .
Fancies and Goodnights. Doubleday, 1951 ss

COLLIER, RICHARD (HUGHESON). 1924-   .
-Beautiful Friend. Pilot, 1947
The Lovely and the Damned. Pilot, 1949
Pay-Off in Calcutta. Pilot, 1948. U.S. title: Solitary Witness. Pellegrini, 1948
Solitary Witness; see Pay-Off in Calcutta

COLLIN, RAYMOND
-Locust in the Wind. Long, 1968
Night of the Eagles. Hammond, 1966

COLLINGWOOD, CHARLES (CUMMINGS). 1917-   .
The Defector. Harper, 1970; Hart-Davis, 1970

COLLINS, CHARLES ALLSTON. 1828-1873.
At the Bar. Chapman, 1866
The Bar Sinister. Smith, Elder, 1864
-Strethcairn. Low, 1864

COLLINS, COLIN
The Blinding Light. Greening, 1910
-Four Million a Year. Greening, 1911
The House of Silence. Lloyd, 1921
The Human Mole. Greening, 1909
Step by Step. Lloyd, 1921

COLLINS, CORNELIUS J.
Bitter is the Fruit. Berkley, 1974

COLLINS, DALE. 1897-1956.
The Fifth Victim. Harrap, 1930
-Ordeal. Heinemann, 1924; Knopf, 1924
Stolen or Strayed. Bookstall (Sydney), 1922
-Vulnerable. Benn, 1933; Bobbs, 1933

COLLINS, MRS. E. BURKE. Pseudonym of Mrs. Emma Augusta Brown Sharkey, 1858-   .
A Debt of Vengeance. Street, 1890
Lillian's Vow; or, The Mystery of Raleigh House. Munro, 1889

COLLINS, FRANK
Here's Why. Constable, 1938

COLLINS, FREDERICK LEWIS. 1882-   .
Pseudonym: Frederick Lewis, q.v.

COLLINS, GILBERT. 1900-   . Series character: Hugh Carding = HC.
The Channel Million. Bles, 1932 HC
Chinese Red. Bles, 1932. U.S. title: Red Death. Holt, 1932
The Dead Walk. Bles, 1933 HC
Death Meets the King's Messenger. Bles, 1934; Doubleday, 1934 HC
The Haven of Unrest. Bles, 1936 HC
Horror Comes to Thripplands. Bles, 1930
The Mongolian Mystery. Ward, 1937
Murder at Brambles; see The Phantom Tourer
Mystery in St. James Square. Ward, 1937
The Phantom Tourer. Bles, 1931. U.S. title: Murder at Brambles. Holt, 1932 HC
Poison Pool. Bles, 1935
Post-Mortem. Bles, 1930 HC
Red Death; see Chinese Red

COLLINS, HUNT. Pseudonym of Evan Hunter, 1926-   , q.v. Other pseudonyms: Curt Cannon, Ezra Hannon, Ed McBain, Richard Marsten, qq.v.
Cut Me In. Abelard, 1954; Boardman, 1960. Also published as: The Proposition. Pyramid, 1955

COLLINS, JACKIE
Lovehead. Allen, 1974

COLLINS, JAMES H(IRAM). 1873-   .
The Great Taxi-Cab Mystery. Lane, 1912

COLLINS, JOHN
Sheer Bluff. Jenkins, 1934

COLLINS, MARY (GARDEN). 1908-   .
Dead Center. Scribner, 1942
Death Warmed Over. Scribner, 1947
Dog Eat Dog. Scribner, 1949
The Fog Comes. Scribner, 1941
Only the Good. Scribner, 1942
The Sister of Cain. Scribner, 1943

COLLINS, MAX (ALLAN). Series character: Frank Nolan, in both titles.
Bait Money. Curtis, 1973; New English Library pb, 1976
Blood Money. Curtis, 1973; New English Library pb, 1977

COLLINS, MICHAEL. Pseudonym of Dennis Lynds, 1924-   , q.v. Other pseudonyms: William Arden, John Crowe, Carl Dekker, Maxwell Grant, Mark Sadler, qq.v. Series character: Dan Fortune, in all titles.
Act of Fear. Dodd, 1967; Joseph, 1968
Blue Death. Dodd, 1975; Hale, 1976
The Brass Rainbow. Dodd, 1969; Joseph, 1970
Night of the Toads. Dodd, 1970; Hale, 1972
Shadow of a Tiger. Dodd, 1972
The Silent Scream. Dodd, 1973; Hale, 1975
Walk a Black Wind. Dodd, 1971; Hale, 1973

COLLINS, (EDWARD JAMES) MORTIMER. 1827-1876.
Who is the Heir? Maxwell, 1865

COLLINS, NORMAN (RICHARD). 1907-   .
The Bat That Flits. Gollancz, 1952; Little, 1952

COLLINS, (WILLIAM) WILKIE. 1824-1889. No attempt has been made to distinguish among Collins' fiction on the basis of criminous content.
After Dark. Smith & Elder, 1856; Dick, 1856
Armadale. Smith & Elder, 1966; Harper, 1866
Basil. Bentley, 1852; Appleton, 1853. Also published as: The Crossed Path; or, Basil. Peterson, 1861
The Black Robe. Chatto, 1881; Belford, 1881
Blind Love. Chatto, 1890; Appleton, 1890. (Completed by Sir Walter Besant.)
The Crossed Path; or, Basil; see Basil
The Dead Secret. Bradbury, 1857; Miller, 1857 ss
The Evil Genius. Chatto, 1886; Harper, 1886
The Fallen Leaves. Chatto, 1879; Rose-Belford, 1879
The Frozen Deep. Bentley, 1874; Gill, 1875 ss
The Ghost's Touch and other stories. Harper, 1885. (ss, taken from other collections.)
The Guilty River. Arrowsmith, 1886; Harper, 1886
The Haunted Hotel. Chatto, 1878; Munro, 18??
Heart and Science. Chatto, 1883; Belford Clarke, 1883
Hide and Seek. Bentley, 1854; Dick, 1858
I Say "No". Chatto, 1884; Harper, 1884
Jezebel's Daughter. Chatto, 1880; Munro, 1880
The Law and the Lady. Chatto, 1875; Harper, 1875
The Legacy of Cain. Chatto, 1889; Lovell, 1888
Little Novels. Chatto, 1887
Man and Wife. Ellis, 1870; Harper, 1870
Miss or Mrs? Bentley, 1873; Peterson, 1872 ss
Mr. Wray's Cash Box; or, The Mask and the Mystery. Bentley, 1852. U.S. title: The Stolen Mask; or, The Mysterious Cash Box. Peterson, 1862
The Moonstone. Tinsley, 1868; Harper, 1868
My Lady's Money. Harper, 1878. (British title?)
My Miscellanies. Low, 1863; Harper, 1874
The New Magdalen. Bentley, 1873; Harper, 1873
No Name. Low, 1862; Harper, 1863
A Plot in Private Life, and other tales. Tauschnitz, 1859. (Stories from The Queen of Hearts, q.v.)
Poor Miss Finch. Bentley, 1872; Harper, 1872
The Queen of Hearts. Hurst, 1859; Harper, 1859 ss
A Rogue's Life. Bentley, 1879; Appleton, 1879
The Stolen Mask; or, The Mysterious Cash Box; see Mr. Wray's Cash Box; or, The Mask and the Mystery

Tales of Suspense. Folio Society, 1954.
  (ss taken from other collections.)
Tales of Terror and the Supernatural.
  Dover, 1972. (ss taken from earlier
  collections.)
The Two Destinies. Chatto, 1876; Harper, 1876
The Woman in White. Low, 1860; Harper, 1860
The Yellow Mask. Popular Library, 1967.
  (ss taken from earlier collections.)

COLLIS, E. T.
  Murder by Warrant. Glen, 1898

COLLIS, LAURISTON
  The Mystery of Holly Tavern. Lippincott, 1873

COLLIS, LOUISE. 1925-   .
  The Great Flood. Macmillan (London), 1966

COLLIS, MAURICE (STEWART). 1889-   .
  The Dark Door. Faber, 1940

COLLISON, WILSON. 1893-1941. Pseudonym:
    Willis Kent, q.v.
  Begins with Murder; see Save a Lady
  Dark Dame. Kendall, 1935
  Diary of Death. McBride, 1930
  Glittering Isle. Covici, 1936
  The Last Witness; see The Murder in the
    Brownstone House
  The Murder in the Brownstone House.
    McBride, 1929. British title: The
    Last Witness. Arrowsmith, 1931
  Murder in the Rain. McBride, 1930
  Red-Haired Alibi. McBride, 1932
  The Second Mrs. Lynton. Kendall, 1935
  Save a Lady. Kendall, 1935. British
    title: Begins with Murder. Long, 1936

COLOMBO, PAT
  Throw Back the Little Ones. Avon, 1963

COLSON, PERCY, 1873-   , and DOUGLAS
    HOARE
  Murder to Music. Gifford, 1945

COLTER, ELI. Series character: Pat Campbell = PC.
  Cheer for the Dead. Mill, 1947; Boardman, 1949 PC
  The Gull Cove Murders. Mill, 1944; Pendulum, 1946 PC
  Rehearsal for the Funeral. Arcadia, 1953

COLTMAN-ALLEN, VIVIAN ERNEST. 1908-   .
  Pseudonym: Ernest Dudley, q.v.

COLTON, A. J. Pseudonym of Alfred Samuel
    Hook.
  The Coatine Case. Hale, 1953

COLTON, JOHN, 1889-1946, and CARLTON
    MILES.
  Nine Pine Street. French (New York),
    1934. (3-act play.)

COLTON, MEL. Pseudonym of Hal Braham,
    q.v. Other pseudonym: Merrill Trask,
    q.v.
  The Big Fix. Ace, 1952
  Big Woman. Magazine Productions, 1953
  Double Take. Ace, 1953
  Never Kill a Cop! Ace, 1953
  Point of No Escape. Ace, 1955

COLVER, ANNE. 1908-   . Pseudonym:
    Colver Harris, q.v.

COLWALL, JAMES. Pseudonym of Gilbert
    Sheldon, 1870-   .
  The Coomsberrow Mystery. Cassell, 1890

COMBER, LEON
  The Strange Cases of Magistrate Pao.
    Tuttle, 1964. (ss, "translated and
    retold" by Comber from ancient
    sources.)

COMLEY, GERTRUDE
  -Fate's Pendulum. Eldon, 1934
  The Mansel Disappearance Mystery.
    Rivers, 1929
  Who Murdered Westaway? Rivers, 1932

COMMORDE, R.
  A Dame is Snatched. Gray, 1952

COMO, LYNN
  Man Hunt! Hamilton Stafford, 1952
  Stuttering Death. Hamilton Stafford, 1953

COMPORT, BRIAN
  Mumsy, Nanny, Sonny, and Girly. Sphere,
    1970; Lancer, 1970. (Novelization of
    the play by Maisie Mosco.)

COMPTON, D(AVID) G(UY). 1930-   . Pseudonym: Frances Lynch, q.v. See also:
    (DAVID) GUY COMPTON.
  -The Palace. Hodder, 1969; Norton, 1969

COMPTON, (DAVID) GUY. 1930-   . Pseudonym: Frances Lynch, q.v. See also:
    D(AVID) G(UY) COMPTON. Series character: Ben Anderson, in at least
    those marked BA.
  And Murder Came Too. Long, 1966
  Dead on Cue. Long, 1964
  Disguise for a Dead Gentleman. Long,
    1964 BA
  High Tide for Hanging. Long, 1965
  Medium for Murder. Long, 1963 BA
  Too Many Murderers. Long, 1962

COMPTON, HERBERT (EASTWICK). 1853-1906.
  The Palace of Spies. Treherne, 1903
  To Defeat the Ends of Justice. Chatto, 1906
  The Undertaker's Field; or, Murder Will
    Out. Bachelor, 1906
  The Wilful Way. Chatto, 1903

COMPTON-RICKETT, ARTHUR. 1869-1937. See
    also: PATRICK LEYTON; and: ERNEST
    (HENRY) SHORT, 1875-1959.
  The Railway Hotel Murder, with Ernest
    (Henry) Short. Jenkins, 1931

COMSTOCK, CAROLINE
  The Bandar-Log Murder. Barker, 1956

CONALL, CEARNACH. Pseudonym of Frederick
    William O'Connell, 1876-1929.
  The Fatal Move, and other stories.
    Gill, 1924 ss, some criminous

CONANT, PAUL
  Dr. Gatskill's Blue Shoes. Wyn, 1952

CONAWAY, JAMES
  The Big Easy. Houghton, 1970; Faber, 1971

CONDE, PHILIP. Series characters: Dick
    Pemberty, in at least those marked
    DP; Irving Todd, in at least those
    marked IT.
  The Case of the Crazy Pilot. Wright,
    1938 DP
  The Corpse in the Clouds. Wright, 1937
  Dead Reckoning. Wright, 1938 IT
  Death from the Air. Wright, 1936 DP
  Death Laughs Aloft. Wright, 1940 DP
  Death Loop. Wright, 1938 DP
  Death Takes the Joystick. Wright, 1937
  The Devil has Wings. Wright, 1937 DP
  The Ghost Plane. Wright, 1936
  Murder at 10,000 Feet. Wright, 1938 IT
  Murder in the Cockpit. Wright, 1936 IT
  Mystery of the Vanishing Aerodrome.
    Wright, 1939
  The Phantom Pilot. Wright, 1936
  Pilot's Graveyard. Wright, 1937
  Secret of the Scarlet Bomber. Wright, 1939
  Skyway Vampire. Wright, 1938 IT
  Spawn of the Hawk. Wright, 1938 DP
  Visibility Nil. Wright, 1940
  Vultures of the Sky. Wright, 1935

CONDON, FRANK and CHARLTON L(AWRENCE)
    EDHOLM
  The Dancing Doll. Barse, 1927; Long, 1928

CONDON, RICHARD (THOMAS). 1915-   .
  Arigato. Dial, 1972; Weidenfeld, 1972
  The Happy Thieves; see The Oldest Confession
  An Infinity of Mirrors. Random, 1964;
    Heinemann, 1967
  The Manchurian Candidate. McGraw, 1959;
    Joseph, 1960
  Mile High. Dial, 1969; Heinemann, 1969
  The Oldest Confession. Appleton, 1958;
    Longmans, 1959. Also published as:
    The Happy Thieves. Bantam, 1962
  Winter Kills. Dial, 1974; Weidenfeld, 1974

CONLY, ROBERT L. 1918-1973. Pseudonym:
    Robert C. O'Brien, q.v.

CONNABLE, ALFRED
  Twelve Trains to Babylon. Little, 1971;
    MacGibbon, 1972

CONNELL, CHARLES
  Catt Among the Pigeons. Jenkins, 1950
  Meet Me at Philippi. Jenkins, 1948
  Most Delicious Poison. Jenkins, 1951

CONNELL, EDWIN
  I Had to Kill Her. Ballantine, 1966

CONNELL, RICHARD (EDWARD). 1893-1949.
    See also: LEO BRADY, 1917-   .
  Mr. Braddy's Safe and other humorous
    tales. Chapman, 1922 ss, some criminous
  Murder at Sea. Minton, 1929; Jarrolds, 1929
  Variety. Minton, 1925; Parsons, 1925
    ss, at least one ("The Most Dangerous
    Game") criminous

CONNELL, VIVIAN. 1903-   .
  Monte Carlo Mission. GM, 1954

CONNELLY, J. H.
  Neila Sen and My Casual Death. Lovell,
    1890. (2 stories.)

CONNELLY, MARC(US COOK). 1890-   .
  A Souvenir from Qam. Holt, 1965

CONNER, REARDEN. 1907-   .
  I am Death. Chapman, 1936. U.S. title:
    Time to Kill. Knopf, 1936

CONNERS, BERNARD F. 1926-   .
  Don't Embarrass the Bureau. Bobbs,
    1972; Allen, 1973

CONNINGTON, J. J. Pseudonym of Alfred
    Walter Stewart, 1880-1947. Series
    characters: Sir Clinton Driffield =
    CD; Mark Brand = MB; Superintendent
    Ross = R.
  The Boat-House Riddle. Gollancz, 1931;
    Little, 1931 CD

C

Connington, J. J. (continued)
The Brandon Case; see The Ha-Ha Case
The Case with Nine Solutions. Gollancz, 1928; Little, 1929   CD
The Castleford Conundrum. Hodder, 1932; Little, 1932   CD
Common Sense is All You Need. Hodder, 1947   CD
The Counsellor. Hodder, 1939; Little, 1939   MB
The Dangerfield Talisman. Benn, 1926; Little, 1927
Death at Swaythling Court. Benn, 1926; Little, 1926
The Eye in the Museum. Gollancz, 1929; Little, 1930   R
For Murder will Speak. Hodder, 1938. U.S. title: Murder will Speak. Little, 1938   CD
The Four Defences. Hodder, 1940; Little, 1940   MB
Gold Brick Island; see Tom Tiddler's Island
Grim Vengeance; see Nemesis at Raynham Parva
The Ha-Ha Case. Hodder, 1934. U.S. title: The Brandon Case. Little, 1934   CD
In Whose Dim Shadow. Hodder, 1935. U.S. title: The Tau Cross Mystery. Little, 1935   CD
Jack-in-the-Box. Hodder, 1944; Little, 1944   CD
A Minor Operation. Hodder, 1937; Little, 1937   CD
Murder in the Maze. Benn, 1927; Little, 1927   CD
Murder will Speak; see For Murder will Speak
Mystery at Lynden Sands. Gollancz, 1928; Little, 1928   CD
Nemesis at Raynham Parva. Gollancz, 1929. U.S. title: Grim Vengeance. Little, 1929   CD
No Past is Dead. Hodder, 1942; Little, 1942   CD
The Sweepstake Murders. Hodder, 1931; Little, 1932   CD
The Tau Cross Mystery; see In Whose Dim Shadow
Tom Tiddler's Island. Hodder, 1933. U.S. title: Gold Brick Island. Little, 1933
Tragedy at Ravensthorpe. Benn, 1927; Little, 1928   CD
Truth Comes Limping. Hodder, 1938; Little, 1938   CD
The Twenty-One Clues. Hodder, 1941; Little, 1941   CD
The Two Tickets Puzzle. Gollancz, 1930. U.S. title: The Two Ticket Puzzle. Little, 1930   SR

CONNOLLY, HENRY
The Finger of Death. Hutchinson, 1929

CONNOLLY, PAUL. Pseudonym of Tom Wicker, 1926-   , q.v.
Get Out of Town. GM, 1951; Fawcett (London), 1959
So Fair, So Evil. GM, 1955; Fawcett (London), 1958
Tears are for Angels. GM, 1952

CONNOLLY, R. P.
Dynamite! Scion, 1951
He Died Laughing. Scion, 1952

CONNOLLY, VIVIAN. 1925-   .
The Fires of Ballymorris. Dell, 1975
South Coast of Danger. Macfadden, 1973

CONNOR, KEVIN
New Departure. Jefferson House, 1962

CONNOR, RALPH. Pseudonym of Charles William Gordon, 1860-1937.
Corporal Cameron. Hodder, 1912. U.S. title: Corporal Cameron of the North West Mounted Police. Doran, 1912

CONNOR, SKID
My Grave is for the Living. Grayling, 1950

CONOT, ROBERT E. 1929-   .
Ministers of Vengeance. Lippincott, 1964; Heinemann, 1965

CONRAD, BRENDA
Caribbean Conspiracy. Scribner, 1942
-Girl with a Golden Bar. Scribner, 1944
The Stars Give Warning. Scribner, 1941

CONRAD, CLIVE. Pseudonym of Frank King, 1892-1958, q.v.
The Crime of his Life. Museum, 1951
Money's Worth of Murder. Museum, 1949
There was a Little Man. Museum, 1948

CONRAD, JOSEPH [JOSEPH CONRAD THEODORE KORZENIOWSKI]. 1857-1924.
The Nature of a Crime, with F(ord) M(adox) Hueffer [Joseph Leopold Ford Hermann Madox Hueffer, 1873-1939]. Duckworth, 1924; Doubleday, 1924, with "Ford Madox Ford"
The Secret Agent. Methuen, 1907; Harper, 1907
A Set of Six. Methuen, 1908; Doubleday, 1915   ss, one criminous
Under Western Eyes. Methuen, 1911; Harper, 1911

CONRAD, CAPT. THOMAS N(ELSON)
A Confederate Spy. Ogilvie, 1892

CONRAD, TOD. Pseudonym of R(ichard) Wilkes-Hunter, q.v. Other pseudonyms: Marc Brody, Alex Crane, qq.v.
The Colonel and the Corpse. Webster, 1958
Kane and Miss Able. Webster, 1958
Rawhide Vixen. Webster, 1958

CONROY, A. L.
The Storefront Lawyers. Bantam, 1970. (Novelization of the TV series.)

CONROY, AL. Series character: Johnny Morini, in all titles.
Death Grip. Lancer, 1972
Murder Mission! Lancer, 1973
Soldato! Lancer, 1972
Strangle Hold! Lancer, 1973

CONROY, ALBERT
The Chiselers. GM, 1953
Devil in Dungarees. Crest, 1960
The Mob Says Murder. GM, 1958; Fawcett (London), 1960
Mr. Lucky. Dell, 1960. (Novelization of the TV series.)
Murder in Room 13. GM, 1958; Fawcett (London), 1960
Nice Guys Finish Dead. GM, 1957; Fawcett (London), 1958
The Road's End. GM, 1952; Fawcett (London), 1958

CONSTABLE, LAWRENCE
House Without Windows. Milton House, 1973

CONSTANTINE, K. C. Pseudonym. Series character: Mario Balzic, in all titles.
The Blank Page. Saturday Review Press, 1974
A Fix Like This. Saturday Review Press, 1975
The Man Who Liked to Look at Himself. Saturday Review Press, 1973
The Rocksburg Railroad Murders. Saturday Review Press, 1972

CONSTINER, (FRANCIS) MERLE
Hearse of a Different Color. Phoenix, 1952

CONTE, CHARLES
The Fear of Death. Hale, 1972
The Spanish Crown Affair. Hale, 1971

CONTE, MANFRED
Cassie. Collins, 1955. U.S. title: Jeopardy. Sloane, 1956. (Translation of Cassia und der Abenteurer. Stuttgart, 1951.)

CONTENT, NIKKI
Hideaway. GM, 1953

CONTY, J. P.
A Big Secret Suzuki. International Publishers, 1969

CONVERSE, FLORENCE. 1871-   .
Into the Void. Little, 1926
Sphinx. Dutton, 1931; Dent, 1931

CONWAY, HUGH. Pseudonym of F(rederick) J(ohn) Fargus, 1840-1885, q.v. Some titles published in the U.S. under the pseudonym appeared in England as by F. J. Fargus.
At What Cost, and other stories. Maxwell, 1885   ss
Bound by a Spell. Lovell, 1887. (British title?)
Bound Together. Remington, 1884; Holt, 1884   ss
Called Back. Arrowsmith, 1883; Holt, 1884
A Cardinal Sin. Eden, 1886; Holt, 1886
Daughter of the Stars and other tales. Munro, 1884. (British title?)
A Family Affair. Macmillan (London), 1885; Holt, 1885
Living or Dead. Macmillan (London), 1886; Holt, 1886
Somebody's Story. Field, 1886; Lovell, 1886

CONWAY, JOAN DITZEL
Island of Fear. GM, 1972

CONWAY, JOHN. Pseudonym of Joseph Chadwick, q.v. Other pseudonym: John Creighton, q.v.
Hell is my Destination. Monarch, 1959
Love in Suburbia. Monarch, 1961
Madigan's Women. Monarch, 1959
Requiem for a Chaser. Monarch, 1960
Sin in Time. Monarch, 1961
This Dark Desire. Monarch, 1960

CONWAY, JOHN W(ILLIAM). 1851-   .
Something or Nothing. Christopher, 1928

CONWAY, KEITH
Hammerhead Reef. Hale, 1971
The Naked Nemesis. Hale, 1970

CONWAY, LAURA. Pseudonym of Dorothy Phoebe Ansle. Other pseudonyms: Hebe Elsna, Lyndon Snow, qq.v. Works of this author appear to have been published in England as romances; those also published in the U.S. as gothics are listed below.
The Abbot's House. Collins, 1969; Saturday Review Press, 1974
Dark Symmetry. Saturday Review Press, 1973   (British title, byline?)
Heiress Apparent. Collins, 1966; McCall, 1970

The Night of the Ruby. Collins, 1969; McCall, 1971
The Unforgotten. Collins, 1967; Saturday Review Press, 1972

CONWAY, NORMAN. Series character: Adam Hunter, in both titles.
The Omega Operation. Canyon, 1974
Operation: Alpha Death. Canyon, 1975

CONWAY, PETER. Pseudonym of George Alexis Bankoff, 1903- .
-A Dark Side Also. Faber, 1940
Expert Witness. Macdonald, 1949
-Hands Without Healing. Macdonald, 1950
-His Hand Betrays. Dakers, 1953
-Miss Pegham. Dakers, 1951
-The Palindrome. Dakers, 1951
Revised Proof. Macdonald, 1947
-The Road Winds Back. Faber, 1942
-Still They Smile. Macdonald, 1946
-Tapestry Odyssey. King, 1944
-Those That Have Eyes. Faber, 1943
-The Unwanted Child. Faber, 1941
-The Weather of my Fate. Macdonald, 1947

CONWAY, PETER. 1929- .
Escape to Danger. Hale, 1974
Hostages to Fortune. Hale, 1975
Motive for Revenge. Hale, 1972
Murder in Duplicate. Hale, 1975
The Padded Cell. Hale, 1973

CONYERS, DOROTHEA (SMYTH). 1873- .
Lady Elverton's Emeralds. Hutchinson, 1909

CONYN, CORNELIUS and JON C(HISHOLM) MARTEN
The Bali Ballet Murder. Harrap, 1961

COOK, ELLA BOOKER. 1886- .
The Ghost of Windy Hill. Vantage, 1964

COOK, EUGENIA
The Forbidden Tower. Dell, 1973

COOK, KENNETH. 1929- .
Bloodhouse. Heinemann, 1974; St. Martin's, 1974
Chain of Darkness. Joseph, 1962
Wake in Fright. Joseph, 1961; St. Martin's, 1962

COOK, MERCER B. Pseudonym of Robert (Harry) Turner, 1915- , q.v.
In Hot Blood. Challenge, 1966. (Suppressed; only 6 copies known.)

COOK, THEODORE KENYON. 1897- .
The Catastrophe at Cliff Haven. Dorrance, 1940

COOK, W(ILLIAM) VICTOR. 1875- .
Ben Hassan's Secret. Aldine, 1922
By Order of the Dead. Aldine, 1923
Grey Fish. Chambers, 1919 ss, some criminous
The Search for Miss Sylvester. Aldine, 1922
Treason Under Seal. Harrap, 1934

COOK, WILFRED
-The Amateurs. Cresset, 1951
Man in the Dark. Cresset, 1959

COOK, WILLIAM WALLACE. 1867-1933.
-His Friend the Enemy. Dillingham, 1903
-A Quarter to Four; or, The Secret of Fortune Island. Dillingham, 1909
A Round Trip in the Year 2000. Street, 1925

COOKE, A(RTHUR) O(WENS). 1867-1930.
-Five Hundred Pounds Reward. Nelson, 1927
The Mellbridge Mystery. Arnold, 1926

COOKE, DAVID C(OXE). 1917- .
c/o American Embassy. Dodd, 1967; Hale, 1968
The 14th Agent. Dodd, 1967; Hale, 1968
Night of the Tiger. Hale, 1970
Sleep with Nightmares. Hale, 1969

COOKE, G(EOFFREY) WALTER. 1924- .
Death can Wait. Bles, 1957
Death is the End. Bles, 1965
Death Takes a Dive. Bles, 1962

COOKE, GRACE MacGOWAN. 1863- .
The Man Behind the Mask. Stokes, 1927; Benn, 1928

COOKE, H. O.
The Sign of the Dagger. Street (Magnet #371)

COOKE, JOHN ESTEN. 1830-1886.
Col. Ross of Piedmont; see The Maurice Mystery
Doctor Vandyke. Appleton, 1872
-The Heir of Greymount. Van Evrie, 1870
-Her Majesty the Queen. Lippincott, 1873
The Maurice Mystery. Appleton, 1885. Also published as: Col. Ross of Piedmont, Dillingham, 188?
-Mr. Grantley's Idea. Harper, 1879
Out of the Foam. Carleton, 1871

COOKE, JOSEPH COTTIN
The Vera Gerard Case. Manthorne, 1937

COOKE, L. A. B.
War in the Gates. Bles, 1937

COOKE, M. E. Pseudonym of John Creasey, 1908-1973, q.v. Other pseudonyms: Gordon Ashe, Norman Deane, Robert Caine Frazer, Patrick Gill, Michael Halliday, Charles Hogarth, Brian Hope, Colin Hughes, Kyle Hunt, Abel Mann, Peter Manton, J. J. Marric, Richard Martin, Rodney Mattheson, Anthony Morton, Jeremy York, qq.v. Some of the titles below may be juveniles or not mysteries.
The Big Radium Mystery. Mellifont, 1936
The Black Heart. Gramol, 1935
The Casino Mystery. Mellifont, 1935
The Crime Gang. Mellifont, 1935
The Day of Terror. Mellifont, 1936
The Death Drive. Mellifont, 1935
The Dummy Robberies. Mellifont, 1936
Fire of Death. Fiction House, 1934
For her Sister's Sake. Fiction House, 1938
The Hadfield Mystery. Mellifont, 1937
The Hypnotic Demon. Fiction House, 1936
The Moat Farm Mystery. Fiction House, 1936
The Mountain Terror. Mellifont, 1938
The Moving Eye. Mellifont, 1937
Number One's Last Crime. Fiction House, 1935
The Raven. Fiction House, 1937
The Secret Fortune. Fiction House, 1936
The Stolen Formula Mystery. Mellifont, 1935
The Successful Alibi. Mellifont, 1936
The Verrall Street Affair. Newnes, 1940

COOKE, MARJORIE BENTON. 1876-1920.
The Clutch of Circumstance. Doran, 1918; Skeffington, 1919

COOKE, RUPERT CROFT-. 1903- . See: RUPERT CROFT-COOKE.

COOKE, W. BOURNE. 1869- .
The Horned Owl. Drane, 1905

COOKSON, CATHERINE (ANN McMULLEN). 1906- . Pseudonym: Catherine Marchant, q.v. These titles are generally published in England as romances, but at least some appear in the U.S. as gothics.
The Blind Miller. Macdonald, 1963; Signet, 1974
Colour Blind. Macdonald, 1953; Beagle, 1971, as by Catherine Marchant
The Devil and Mary Ann. Macdonald, 1958; Morrow, 1976
The Dwelling Place. Macdonald, 1971; Bobbs, 1971
Evil at Roger's Cross, as by Catherine Marchant. Lancer, 1965. (British title?)
Fanny McBride. Macdonald, 1959; Bantam, 1976
Feathers in the Fire. Macdonald, 1971; Bantam, 1973
Fenwick Houses. Macdonald, 1960; Bantam, 1973
The Fifteen Streets. Macdonald, 1952; Bantam, 1973
The Gambling Man. Heinemann, 1975; Morrow, 1975
The Garment. Macdonald, 1962
The Glass Virgin. Macdonald, 1970; Bobbs, 1969
A Grand Man. Macdonald, 1954; Macmillan, 1955
Hannah Massey. Macdonald, 1964; Signet, 1973
The Invisible Cord. Heinemann, 1975; Dutton, 1975
The Invitation. Macdonald, 1970; Signet, 1974
Kate Hannigan. Macdonald, 1950; Bantam, 1972
Katie Mulholland. Macdonald, 1967; Bobbs, 1967
Life and Mary Ann. Macdonald, 1962
The Long Corridor. Macdonald, 1965; Beagle, 1971, as by Catherine Marchant
The Lord and Mary Ann. Macdonald, 1956; Morrow, 1975
Love and Mary Ann. Macdonald, 1961; Morrow, 1976
Maggie Rowan. Macdonald, 1954; Beagle, 1971, as by Catherine Marchant
The Mallen Girl. Heinemann, 1974; Dutton, 1973
The Mallen Litter. Heinemann, 1974. U.S. title: The Mallen Lot. Dutton, 1974
The Mallen Lot; see The Mallen Litter
The Mallen Streak. Heinemann, 1973; Dutton, 1973
Marriage and Mary Ann. Macdonald, 1964
Mary Ann and Bill. Macdonald, 1967
Mary Ann's Angels. Macdonald, 1965
Matty Doolin. Macdonald, 1965
The Menagerie. Macdonald, 1958; Bantam, 1975
The Mists of Memory, as by Catherine Marchant. Lancer, 1967. (British title?)
The Nice Bloke. Macdonald, 1969
Pure as the Lily. Macdonald, 1972; Bobbs, 1973
Rooney. Macdonald, 1957; Bantam, 1976
The Round Tower. Macdonald, 1968; Beagle, 1971, as by Catherine Marchant
Slinky Jane. Macdonald, 1959; Signet, 1976
The Unbaited Trap. Macdonald, 1966; Beagle, 1971, as by Catherine Marchant

COOKSON, GATHORNE
Murder Pays No Dividends. Muller, 1938

COOLIDGE, ERWIN L.
  Gilt-Edge Tom, Conductor; or, The Pride of the Valley Route. Ogilvie, 1896
  The Mountain Limited. Ogilvie, 1893
  The Mystery of the Montauk Mills. Ogilvie, 1893

COOLIDGE-RASK, MARIE
  London After Midnight. Grosset, 1928; Readers Library, 1928. (Novelization of the movie.)

COOM, CHARLES S(LEEMAN). 1851- .
  The Baronet Rag-Picker. Clark, 1905

COOMBS, MURDO. Pseudonym of Frederick C(lyde) Davis, 1902-1977, q.v. Other pseudonym: Stephen Ransome, q.v.
  A Moment of Need. Dutton, 1947

COONEY, MICHAEL. 1921- .
  Doomsday England. Cassell, 1967; Walker, 1968
  Ten Days to Oblivion. Cassell, 1968

COONS, MAURICE. Pseudonym: Armitage Trail, q.v.

COOPER, AGNES ROSEMARY. Joint pseudonym with Mary Elizabeth Phyllis Weller: Ramsay Bell, q.v.

COOPER, (EVELYN) BARBARA. 1915-
  Drown Him Deep. Hale, 1966
  House of Masks. Hale, 1968
  Target for Malice. Hale, 1964
  Who is my Enemy? Hale, 1967

COOPER, BRIAN. 1919- .
  Genesis 38. Heinemann, 1965. U.S. title: The Murder of Mary Steers. Vanguard, 1966
  Giselle; see A Path to the Bridge
  Maria; see Where the Fresh Grass Grows
  A Mission for Betty Smith. Heinemann, 1967. U.S. title: Monsoon Murder. Vanguard, 1968
  Monsoon Murder; see A Mission for Betty Smith
  The Murder of Mary Steers; see Genesis 38
  A Path to the Bridge. Heinemann, 1958. U.S. title: Giselle. Vanguard, 1958
  A Time to Retreat. Heinemann, 1963; Vanguard, 1963
  A Touch of Thunder. Heinemann, 1961; Vanguard, 1962
  The Van Langeren Girl. Heinemann, 1960; Vanguard, 1960
  Where the Fresh Grass Grows. Heinemann, 1955. U.S. title: Maria. Vanguard, 1956

COOPER, CHARLES. Pseudonym of Arnold Charles Cooper Lock.
  The Turkish Spy. Stockwell, 1932

COOPER, CLARENCE L.
  -The Dark Messenger. Regency, 1962
  -Weed. Regency, 1961

COOPER, COLIN
  Outcrop. Faber, 1969

COOPER, COURTNEY RYLEY. 1886-1940.
  Action in Diamonds. Penn, 1942
  -Caged. Little, 1930
  -The Challenge of the Bush. Little, 1929; Collins, 1930
  -The Cross Cut. Little, 1921; Collins, 1922
  -End of Steel. Farrar, 1931
  -The Mystery of the Four Abreast. Collins, 1929 (U.S. title?)
  -Trigger Finger. Collins, 1930 (U.S. title?)
  -The White Desert. Little, 1922; Hurst, 1923

COOPER, CRAIG. Series character: Matt Savage, in at least those marked MS.
  Blackmail is Murder. Hale, 1968
  Catch and Squeeze. Hale, 1968; Roy, 1969 MS
  Dame in Distress. Hale, 1968; Roy, 1968 MS
  No Haloes for Hoods. Hale, 1969; Roy, 1969
  Run with the Fox. Hale, 1971
  Running Scared. Hale, 1972
  Snatch the Lady. Hale, 1970
  Value for Murder. Hale, 1972
  What's Funny About Murder. Hale, 1968; Roy, 1968 MS
  Who Killed Honeybee? Hale, 1968; Roy, 1969 MS
  You'll Die Laughing. Hale, 1968

COOPER, EDWARD H(ERBERT). 1867-1910.
  Resolved to be Rich. Duckworth, 1899; Duffield, 1906

COOPER, H(UGH) H(OMFRAY)
  A Cave with Two Exits. Ross, 1969

COOPER, HENRY ST. JOHN
  -Dangerous Paths. Low, 1933
  -The Golconda Necklace. Low, 1926
  -The Splendid Love. Low, 1932

COOPER, JAMES FENIMORE. 1789-1851.
  The Spy. Wiley, 1821; Whitakker, 1822

COOPER, JAMIE LEE
  Grasshopper Summer. Bobbs, 1975
  The Great Dandelion. Bobbs, 1972

COOPER, JOHN
  Canaries Sometimes Croak. World Distributors, 1952
  Extortion Incorporated. World Distributors, 1952

COOPER, JOHN C.
  The Body was of No Account. Boardman, 1957
  Death in Aberration. Boardman, 1958
  The Grip of the Strangler. Digit, 1958. U.S. title: The Haunted Strangler. Ace, 1959. (Novelization of the movie.)
  The Haunted Strangler; see The Grip of the Strangler

COOPER, JOHN MURRAY. 1908- . Pseudonym: William Sutherland, q.v.

COOPER, KENNETH S.
  Cipher Stories Puzzle Book. Copeland, 1928 puzzle ss

COOPER, LEONARD
  The Accomplices. Cresset, 1960
  Wanted at his Office. Barker, 1953

COOPER, LETTICE (ULPHA). 1897- .
  Tea on Sunday. Gollancz, 1973

COOPER, LYNNA
  The Hour of the Harp. Saturday Review Press, 1975

COOPER, MONTE
  Death Near the River. Holt, 1928

COOPER, MORTON. 1925- .
  -Anything for Kicks. Avon, 1959
  -Come Feed on Me. GM, 1953; Muller pb, 1954
  -Delinquent! Avon, 1958
  -The Flesh and Mr. Rawlie. GM, 1956; Fawcett (London), 1959. Also published as: The Flesh Traders. New English Library pb, 1970
  The Flesh Traders; see The Flesh and Mr. Rawlie
  -Ginny. Avon, 1959
  -High School Confidential. Avon, 1958. (Novelization of the movie.)
  The Innocent and Willing. GM, 1956; Fawcett (London), 1958. Also published as: No Angel. Paperback Library, 1963
  No Angel; see The Innocent and Willing
  -The Ungilded Lily. GM, 1958
  -Young and Wild. Avon, 1958

COOPER, PARLEY J(OSEPH). 1937- .
  The Devil Child. PB, 1972
  Marianne's Kingdom. PB, 1972
  Moonblood. PB, 1975
  My Lady Evil. Simon, 1973
  The Shuddering Fair One. PB, 1974

COOPER, RODERICK
  No Place for a Tickle. Hale, 1975

COOPERSMITH, JEROME
  Baker Street. Doubleday, 1966. (A play)

COPE, HARLEY (FRANCIS). 1898- .
  Death Stalks the Fleet. Lymanhouse, 1939

COPELAND, WILLIAM
  Five Hours from Isfahan. Putnam, 1975; Hart-Davis, 1976

COPP, A. E. See: S. J. STUTLEY.

COPP, DeWITT
  The Pursuit of Agent M. Mill, 1961

COPPEE, FRANCOIS (EDOUARD JOACHIM). 1842-1908.
  The Guilty Man. Dillingham, 1911; Greening, 1912. (Translation of Le Coupable. Paris, 1896.)

COPPEL, ALEC. 1909?-1972.
  The Gazebo. Dramatists Play Service, 1959. (Play.)
  I Killed the Count. Heinemann, 1938. (Play.) Novel based on this play: Blackie, 1939
  -The Last Parable. Barker, 1953
  A Man About a Dog. Harrap, 1947. U.S. title: Over the Line. Doubleday, 1947. Also published as: Obsession. Corgi, 1953
  Moment to Moment. GM, 1966. (Novelization of the movie.)
  Mr. Denning Drives North. Harrap, 1950; Dutton, 1951
  Obsession; see A Man About a Dog
  Over the Line; see A Man About a Dog
  -Tweedledum and Tweedledee. Bles, 1967

COPPEL, ALFRED. 1921- . Pseudonym: A. C. Marin, q.v.
  Thirty-Four East. Harcourt, 1974; Macmillan (London), 1974

COPPER, BASIL. 1924- . Series character: Mike Faraday = MF.
  The Big Chill. Hale, 1972 MF
  The Breaking Point. Hale, 1973 MF
  The Dark Mirror. Hale, 1966 MF
  Dead File. Hale, 1970 MF
  Die Now, Live Later. Hale, 1968 MF
  Don't Bleed on Me. Hale, 1968 MF
  Feedback. Hale, 1974 MF
  A Good Place to Die. Hale, 1975 MF
  A Great Year for Dying. Hale, 1973 MF
  The High Wall. Hale, 1975 MF
  Impact. Hale, 1975 MF
  The Marble Orchard. Hale, 1969 MF

Night Frost. Hale, 1966 MF
No Flowers for the General. Hale, 1967 MF
No Letters from the Grave. Hale, 1971 MF
Ricochet. Hale, 1974 MF
Scratch on the Dark. Hale, 1967 MF
Shock-Wave. Hale, 1973 MF
Strong-Arm. Hale, 1972 MF
A Voice from the Dead. Hale, 1974 MF
When Footsteps Echo. Hale, 1975; St. Martin's, 1975 ss

COPPLESTONE, BENNET. Pseudonym of Frederick Harcourt Kitchin, 1867-1932, q.v. Series character: Chief Inspector Dawson = D.
The Diversions of Dawson. Murray, 1923; Dutton, 1924 D ss
The Last of the Grenvilles. Murray, 1919; Dutton, 1920
The Lost Naval Papers. Murray, 1917; Dutton, 1917 D ss

CORA, JOHN LACEY
They Rubbed Him Out. Everybody's, 1944

CORAM, CHRISTOPHER. Pseudonym of Peter N(orman) Walker, 1936- , q.v. Other pseudonym: Tom Ferris, q.v.
A Call to Danger. Hale, 1968
A Call to Die. Hale, 1969
Death in Ptarmigan Forest. Hale, 1970
Death on the Motorway. Hale, 1973
Murder by the Lake. Hale, 1975

CORBETT, MRS. GEORGE [ELIZABETH BURGOYNE CORBETT]. 1846- .
Adventures of a Lady Detective. Tudor, ca.1890. (Cited by Ellery Queen in The Detective Short Story but not listed in either The English Catalogue or British Museum Catalogue.) ss
The Adventures of an Ugly Girl. Collier, 1893. (British title?)
The Missing Note. Chapman, 1891
Mrs. Grundy's Victim. Tower, 1893
Secrets of a Private Enquiry Office. Routledge, 1891 ss
When the Sea Gives Up Its Dead. Tower, 1894

CORBETT, JAMES
Agent No. 5. Jenkins, 1945
The Air Killer. Jenkins, 1941
At Dawn I Die. Jenkins, 1949
The Body in the Bungalow. Jenkins, 1938
The Carteret Hotel Mystery. Jenkins, 1948; Roy, 1957
Dancing with Death. Jenkins, 1950
Death—by Appointment. Jenkins, 1945
Death Comes to Fanshawe. Jenkins, 1933
Death is my Shadow. Jenkins, 1947
Death Makes a Date. Jenkins, 1950
The Death Pool. Jenkins, 1936
Gallows Wait. Jenkins, 1947
The Ghost Plane. Jenkins, 1939
Her Private Murder. Jenkins, 1932
Her Second Murder. Jenkins, 1940
The Hound of Death. Jenkins, 1944
The Lion's Mouth. Jenkins, 1941
The Man They Could Not Kill. Jenkins, 1935
The Man Who Saw the Devil. Jenkins, 1934
The Man with Nine Lives. Jenkins, 1938
The Merrivale Mystery. Jenkins, 1929; Mystery League, 1931
The Monster of Dagenham Hall. Jenkins, 1935
The Moon Killer. Jenkins, 1938
Murder at Night. Jenkins, 1940
Murder at Pringlehurst. Jenkins, 1933
Murder at Red Grange. Jenkins, 1931
Murder at the Palace. Jenkins, 1937
Murder Begets Murder. Jenkins, 1951
Murder Minus Motive. Jenkins, 1943

Murder While You Wait. Jenkins, 1937
No Other Killer. Jenkins, 1936
Red Dagger. Jenkins, 1934
Red Farm Mystery. Jenkins, 1935
Rendezvous with Danger. Jenkins, 1948
Rendezvous with Death. Jenkins, 1937
The Somerville Case. Jenkins, 1949
Vampire of the Skies. Jenkins, 1932
Wednesday at Noon. Jenkins, 1942
When Death Walks. Jenkins, 1941
The White Angel. Jenkins, 1931
Who was the Killer? Jenkins, 1939
The Winterton Hotel Mystery. Jenkins, 1930

CORBIN, GARY
Cosa Nostra Circus. Nite Time pb, 1961

CORBY, JANE (IRENITA). 1899- . Pseudonym: Jean Carew, q.v.
As Deadly Does. Bouregy, 1961
Farewell to the Castle. Arcadia, 1967
Girl in the Tower. Arcadia, 1966
Peril at Stone House. Arcadia, 1969
Riverwood. Arcadia, 1968
The Shadow and the Fear. Arcadia, 1968

CORCORAN, WILLIAM. 1901- .
The Dark Waters. Appleton, 1936; Hodder, 1936

CORDELL, ALEXANDER. Pseudonym of George Alexander Graber, 1914- .
The Bright Cantonese. Gollancz, 1967. U.S. title: The Deadly Eurasian. Weybright, 1968

CORDER, ERIC
The Bite. Dell, 1975. (U.S. title of Hellbottom?)
Hellbottom. Allen, 1974

CORDER, R. E. Pseudonym of James Dunn.
Tales Told to the Magistrate. Melrose, 1925 ss

CORES, LUCY. 1914- . Series character: Captain Andrew Torrent = AT.
Corpse de Ballet. Duell, 1944; Cassell, 1948 AT
Let's Kill George. Duell, 1946; Cassell, 1950
The Misty Curtain. Harper, 1964; Hale, 1965
Painted for the Kill. Duell, 1943; Cassell, 1946 AT

COREY, FRANK
By Blood Alone. Berkley, 1961

COREY, HERBERT. 1872-1954.
Crime at Cobb's House. Appleton, 1934; Methuen, 1935

COREY, JEAN
The Scar of Crime. Munro, 1891

CORKILL, LOUIS
Fish Lane. Bobbs, 1951

CORLEY, EDWIN. 1931- . Pseudonyms: David Harper, William Judson, qq.v. Joint pseudonym with Jack Murphy: Patrick Buchanan, q.v.
The Jesus Factor. Stein, 1970; Joseph, 1971

CORLISS, ALLENE
Error in Judgment. Bouregy, 1964
Unwelcome Visitor. Bouregy, 1962

CORNE, M(OLLY) E. Series character: Mac McIntyre, in all titles.
Death at a Masquerade. Mill, 1938. Also published as: Death is No Lady. Black Knight, 1946

Death at the Manor. Mill, 1938. Also published as: Death Hides a Mask. Arrow, 194?
Death Hides a Mask; see Death at the Manor
Death is No Lady; see Death at a Masquerade
Jealousy Pulls the Trigger; see A Magnet for Murder
A Magnet for Murder. Mill, 1939. Also published as: Jealousy Pulls the Trigger. Double-Action Detective, 1943

CORNELIUS, OLIVIA SMITH. 1882- .
The Eyes at the Window. Broadway, 1911
-The Persian Tassel. Neale, 1914

CORNELL, LOUIS. Series character: Michael Joyce, in both titles.
Murder Case Number 33. Brentano's, 1932
Poison Case Number 10. Brentano's, 1931

CORNISH, CONSTANCE
Dead of Winter. Simon, 1959; Cassell, 1961

CORNWALLIS, KINAHAN. 1839-1917.
-Adrift with a Vengeance. Carleton, 1870
A Marvellous Coincidence; or, A Chain of Misadventures and Mysteries. Dillingham, 1891. Also published as: Two Strange Adventures; or, A Marvellous Coincidence. Neely, 1897
Two Strange Adventures; or, A Marvellous Coincidence; see A Marvellous Coincidence; or, A Chain of Misadventures and Mysteries

CORNWELL, DAVID JOHN MOORE. 1931- .
Pseudonym: John Le Carre, q.v.

CORRELL, A. BOYD. See also: PHILIP MacDONALD, 1899- .
Murder is an Art. Phoenix, 1950

CORREN, GRACE. Pseudonym of Robert Hoskins, 1933- . Other pseudonym: Susan Jennifer, q.v.
The Darkest Room. Lancer, 1969
Evil in the Family. Lancer, 1972
Mansion of Deadly Dreams. Popular Library, 1973
A Place on Dark Island. Lancer, 1971

CORRIGAN, MARK. Pseudonym of Norman Lee, 1905-1962. Other pseudonyms: Raymond Armstrong, Robertson Hobart, qq.v. Series character: Mark Corrigan, in all titles.
All Brides are Beautiful. Laurie, 1953
Baby Face. Laurie, 1952
Big Boys Don't Cry. Angus, 1956
The Big Squeeze. Angus, 1955
Bullets and Brown Eyes. Laurie, 1948
The Cruel Lady. Angus, 1957
Danger's Green Eyes. Angus, 1962
Dumb as They Come. Angus, 1957
The Girl from Moscow. Angus, 1959
The Golden Angel. Laurie, 1950
Honolulu Snatch. Angus, 1958
I Like Danger. Laurie, 1954
Lady from Tokyo. Angus, 1960
Lady of China Street. Laurie, 1952
Love for Sale. Laurie, 1954
Lovely Lady. Laurie, 1950
Madam and Eve. Laurie, 1955
Madame Sly. Laurie, 1951
Menace in Siam. Angus, 1958
The Naked Lady. Laurie, 1954
Riddle of Double Island. Angus, 1962
The Riddle of the Spanish Circus. Angus, 1964

Shanghai Jezebel. Laurie, 1951
Sin of Hong Kong. Angus, 1960
Singapore Downbeat. Angus, 1959
Sinner Takes All. Laurie, 1949
Sweet and Deadly. Laurie, 1953
Sydney for Sin. Angus, 1956
The Wayward Blonde. Laurie, 1950
Who Do Women?... Angus, 1963

CORY, DESMOND. Pseudonym of Shaun Lloyd McCarthy, 1928- . Other pseudonym: Theo Callas, q.v. Series characters: Johnny Fedora, in at least those marked JF; Mr. Pilgrim = P.
Begin, Murderer! Muller, 1951
A Bit of a Shunt Up the River. Doubleday, 1974
The Circe Complex. Macmillan (London), 1975; Doubleday, 1975
Deadfall. Muller, 1965; Walker, 1965
Dead Man Falling. Muller, 1953. U.S. title: The Hitler Diamonds. Award, 1969 JF
Dead Men Alive; see Height of Day
Even If You Run; see Take My Drum to England
Feramontov. Muller, 1966; Walker, 1966 JF
The Gestapo File; see This Traitor, Death
Hammerhead. Muller, 1963. U.S. title: Shockwave. Walker, 1964 JF
The Head. Muller, 1960
Height of Day. Muller, 1955. U.S. title: Dead Men Alive. Award, 1969 JF
High Requiem. Muller, 1956; Award, 1969 JF
The Hitler Diamonds; see Dead Man Falling
Intrigue. Muller, 1954. U.S. title: Trieste. Award, 1968 JF
Johnny Goes East. Muller, 1958. U.S. title: Mountainhead. Award, 1968 JF
Johnny Goes North. Muller, 1956. U.S. title: The Swastika Hunt. Award, 1969 JF
Johnny Goes South. Muller, 1959; Walker, 1964 JF
Johnny Goes West. Muller, 1959; Walker, 1967 JF
Lady Lost. Muller, 1953
Mountainhead; see Johnny Goes East
The Name of the Game. Muller, 1964
The Nazi Assassins; see Secret Ministry
The Night Hawk. Hodder, 1969; Walker, 1969
The Phoenix Sings. Muller, 1955
Pilgrim at the Gate. Muller, 1957; Washburn, 1958 P
Pilgrim on the Island. Muller, 1959; Walker, 1961 P
Secret Ministry. Muller, 1951. U.S. title: The Nazi Assassins. Award, 1970 JF
The Shaken Leaf. Muller, 1955
Shockwave; see Hammerhead
Stranglehold. Muller, 1961
Sunburst. Hodder, 1971; Walker, 1971 JF
The Swastika Hunt; see Johnny Goes North
Take My Drum to England. Hodder, 1971. U.S. title: Even If You Run. Doubleday, 1972
This is Jezebel. Muller, 1952
This Traitor, Death. Muller, 1952. U.S. title: The Gestapo File. Award, 1971 JF
Timelock. Muller, 1967; Walker, 1967 JF
Trieste; see Intrigue
Undertow. Muller, 1962; Walker, 1963 JF

CORYELL, JOHN R(USSELL). 1851-1924. Pseudonym: Geraldine Fleming, q.v.
A Woman's Hand; or, Detective's Wit Against Lawyer's Wiles. Street, 1890

COSSERY, ALBERT. 1913- .
The House of Certain Death. Hutchinson, 1947; New Directions, 1949. (Translation of La Maison de la Mort Certaine. Paris, 1947.)

COSTELLO, PAUL. Series character: Terence O'Hara, in at least those marked TO.
Blue Diamond. Cassell, 1962 TO
The Cat and the Fiddle. Cassell, 1961
The Long Silence. Hale, 1957 TO
Mortgage for Murder. Cassell, 1960 TO
The Red Beard. Hale, 1958 TO

COSTIGAN, LEE
Never Kill a Cop. PB, 1959
The New Breed. GM, 1962; Muller pb, 1963. (Novelization of the TV series.)

COTLER, GORDON. 1923- . Pseudonym: Alex Gordon, q.v.
The Bottletop Affair. Simon, 1959
Mission in Black. Random, 1967; Heinemann, 1968

COTTAR, GUY. Pseudonym of Clive Garsia.
Tenacity. Jarrolds, 1927

COTTE, JEAN LOUIS. 1923- .
The Trap. Abelard, 1961. (Translation of L'Appat. Paris, 1958.)

COTTERELL, BRIAN. Pseudonym of Aylward Edward Dingle, 1874-1947.
Sinister Eden. Harrap, 1934; Lippincott, 1934

COTTON, JERRY
In the Lion's Den. Three Star, 1965

COTTON, WILL
The Night was Made for Murder. Avon, 1959

COUGHLIN, HANORAH
-Strange Fates; or, Detta. Broadway, 1904

COUGHLIN, WILLIAM J(EREMIAH)
The Destruction Committee. Harrap, 1971
The Dividend was Death. Jenkins, 1968
The Widow Wondered Why. Hammond, 1966

COULSON, FELICITY WINIFRED CARTER. 1907- . Pseudonym: Emery Bonett, q.v. Joint pseudonym with John Hubert Arthur Coulson, 1906- : John and Emery Bonett, q.v.

COULSON, JOHN HUBERT ARTHUR. 1906- . Joint pseudonym with Felicity Winifred Carter Coulson, 1907- : John and Emery Bonett, q.v.

COULSON, JUANITA. 1933- .
Door into Terror. Berkley, 1972
The Secret of Seven Oaks. Berkley, 1972
Stone of Blood. Ballantine, 1975

COULSON, ROBERT STRATTON. 1918- . Joint pseudonym with (Thomas Eu)Gene DeWeese, 1934- , q.v.: Thomas Stratton, q.v.

COULSON, THOMAS. 1886- .
The Queen of Spies. Constable, 1935. (Novelized biography of Louise de Bettignies.)

COULTER, H. G.
Death Comes to Casanova. Manthorne, 1945

COULTER, STEPHEN. 1913- . Pseudonym: James Mayo, q.v.
An Account to Render. Heinemann, 1970
Death in the Sun; see A Stranger Called the Blues
Embassy. Heinemann, 1969; Coward, 1969
-The Loved Enemy. Deutsch, 1952
Offshore! Heinemann, 1965; Morrow, 1966
Players in a Dark Game; see A Stranger Called the Blues
A Stranger Called the Blues. Heinemann, 1968. U.S. title: Players in a Dark Game. Morrow, 1968. Also published as: Death in the Sun. Pan, 1970
Threshold. Heinemann, 1964; Morrow, 1964

COULTON, MARY JANE. Pseudonym: Sarah Campion, q.v.

COUNSEL, FIRTH
Juvenile Jungle. Avon, 1958. (Novelization of the movie.)

COURAGE, JOHN. Pseudonym of Richard Goyne, 1902-1957, q.v. Series characters: William Britain, in at least those marked WB; David Cane, in at least those marked DC.
The Affair Ravel. Paul, 1948 WB
The Buccaneer's Parrot. Puzzle Books, 1933
A Corpse for Charlie. Paul, 1957
Death Goes to the Fair. Paul, 1937 DC
Death of a Gentleman. Paul, 1951
Death of a Village. Paul, 1954
Death on Tour. Paul, 1937 DC
The Dread Cave. Paul, 1952
Four Doors to Death. Paul, 1936 DC
The House with a Past. Paul, 1955
International Commando. Paul, 1944
Lakeland Tragedy. Paul, 1947 WB
Made to Murder. Paul, 1957
Murder Run Riot. Paul, 1940
My Wife's Lover. Paul, 1953
Nightingales Never Sing. Paul, 1950
No Moon Tonight. Paul, 1950
The Obliging Corpse. Paul, 1954
The Parker Case. Paul, 1958
Perhaps the Prodigal. Paul, 1953
Spooks Sometimes Sing. Paul, 1946
They All Came Back. Paul, 1945
We the Unworthy. Paul, 1944
Who Screamed? Paul, 1939 DC
Why Murder Mrs. Hope? Paul, 1940 DC

COURNOS, JOHN. 1881-1966. Pseudonyms: John Courtney, Mark Gault, qq.v.

COURT, S.
The Black Mask. Modern, 193?

COURTENEY, CECIL
Link by Link. Bevington, 1886
-Traced Through a Dream. Arrowsmith, 1887

COURTIER, S(IDNEY) H(OBSON). 1904-1974. Series characters: Inspector "Digger" Haig, in at least those marked DH; Inspector (Supt.) Ambrose Mahon, in at least those marked AM.
Come Back to Murder. Hammond, 1957 AM
A Corpse at Least. Hammond, 1966 DH
A Corpse Won't Sing. Hammond, 1964 AM
Dead If I Remember. Hale, 1972
Death in Dream Time. Hammond, 1959 DH
Gently Dust the Corpse. Hammond, 1960. Also published as: Softly Dust the Corpse. Corgi, 1961
The Glass Spear. Dakers, 1952; Wyn, 1950 AM
Let the Man Die. Hammond, 1961 AM
Ligny's Lake. Hale, 1971; Simon, 1971
Listen to the Mocking Bird. Hale, 1974
Mimic a Murderer. Hammond, 1964 AM
Murder's Burning. Hammond, 1967; Random, 1968

No Obelisk for Emily. Jenkins, 1970 DH
Now Seek my Bones. Hammond, 1957 DH
One Cried Murder. Hammond, 1956; Rinehart, 1954 AM
The Ringnecker. Hammond, 1965 DH
See Who's Dying. Hammond, 1967
A Shroud for Unlac. Hammond, 1958 AM
Softly Dust the Corpse; see Gently Dust the Corpse
Some Village Borgia. Hale, 1971
Swing High, Sweet Murder. Hammond, 1962 DH
Who Dies for Me? Hammond, 1962
A Window in Chungking. Hale, 1975

COURTNEY, JOHN. Pseudonym of John Cournos, 1881-1966. Other pseudonym: Mark Gault, q.v.
Grandmother Martin is Murdered. Skeffington, 1930; Farrar, 1930, as by John Cournos

COURTNEY-BROWNE, REGINALD DAVID STANLEY. 1915-   . Pseudonym: Courtney Browne, q.v.

COUSIN, MICHEL
Where Did the Girls Go? Stein, 1969. (Translation of Detournement de Mineurs. Paris, 1967.)

COUSINS, E(DMUND) G(EORGE). 1893-   .
Series character: Colonel Richard Barne, in at least those marked RB.
Any Kind of Danger. Benn, 1951
Body Behind the Curtain. Gifford, 1966 RB
-Come Like a Storm. Benn, 1950
Death by Marriage. Gifford, 1959 RB
Death by Treble Chance. Gifford, 1959 RB
Death in a Quiet Place. Gifford, 1967 RB
Dressed Up to Kill. Panther, 1961
Fear of Mr. Taltry. Gifford, 1960 RB
-Give Me That Man. Collins, 1955
-Great Elk. Jenkins, 1956
Harlot's House. Panther, 1960
-Moab is my Washpot. Benn, 1952. Also published as: Wine of War. Panther, 1959
Murder in the Top Drawer. Gifford, 1964 RB
Sapphire. Panther, 1959. (Novelization of the movie.)
-To Comfort the Signora. Benn, 1951
-Untimely Frost. Benn, 1953
Weekend with Maxwell. Gifford, 1961
Wine of War; see Moab is my Washpot

COUSINS, MARGARET. 1905-   . Pseudonym: Avery Johns, q.v.

COUSSEAU, JACQUES
Death of Miss Cunningham. Faber, 1962. (Translation of Les Singes. Paris, 1960.)

COVERACK, GILBERT. Pseudonym of J(ohn) Russell Warren, 1886-   , q.v.
Series character: Inspector M'Guire = M; also under the J. Russell Warren byline.
ATS Mystery. Hurst, 1943; Macmillan, 1944
The Magpie Murder. Earl, 1947; Sheridan, 1942, as by J. Russell Warren M
Time for a Murder. Hurst, 1941; Sheridan, 1941, as by J. Russell Warren M

COVERDALE, HARRY. Pseudonym (?) of Anna Alice Chapin, 1880-   .
The Seventh Shot. Chelsea, 1924; Skeffington, 1926
The Unknown Seven. Chelsea, 1923; Unwin, 1924

COWAN, BERTHA MUZZY BOWEN SINCLAIR. 1874-1940. Pseudonym: B. M. Bower, q.v.

COWAN, G. K.
The Cry in the Valley. Jenkins, 1934
The Fanshaw Case. Jenkins, 1933

COWAN, SADA
Bitter Justice. Doubleday, 1943; Gifford, 1946

COWDROY, JOAN. Series characters: Li Moh, in at least those marked LM; Chief Inspector Gorham, in at least those marked G.
Death has No Tongue. Hutchinson, 1938 LM
Disappearance. Hutchinson, 1934 LM
The Flying Dagger Murder; see Watch Mr. Moh
Framed Evidence. Hutchinson, 1936 G
-The Mask. Hutchinson, 1928
Merry-Go-Round. Hutchinson, 1940 LM
Murder of Lydia. Hutchinson, 1933 LM
Murder Out of Court. Hutchinson, 1944 G
Murder Unsuspected. Hutchinson, 1936 LM
Mystery of Sett. Hutchinson, 1930
Nine Green Bottles. Hutchinson, 1939
Watch Mr. Moh. Hutchinson, 1931. U.S. title: The Flying Dagger Murder. McBride, 1932 LM

COWEN, FRANCES. 1915-
The Balcony. Gresham, 1962
The Bitter Reason. Gresham, 1966
The Curse of the Clodaghs. Hale, 1973; Ace, 1974
The Dangerous Child. Hale, 1975
The Daylight Fear. Hale, 1969
The Desperate Holiday. Gresham, 1962
The Edge of Terror. Hale, 1970
The Elusive Quest. Gresham, 1965
The Fractured Silence. Hale, 1969
The Gentle Obsession. Hale, 1968
The Hounds of Carvello. Hale, 1970
Lake of Darkness. Hale, 1971; Ace, 1974
The Little Heiress. Gresham, 1961
The Nightmare Ends. Hale, 1970
The One Between. Hale, 1967
Scented Danger. Gresham, 1966
The Secret of Weir House. Hale, 1975
The Shadow of Polperro. Hale, 1969
Shadow of Theale. Hale, 1974; Ace, 1974
A Step in the Dark. Gresham, 1962
The Unforgiving Moment. Hale, 1971
The Village of Fear. Hale, 1975; Ace, 1974

COWLES, JOHN CLIFFORD
The Whispering Buddha. Hollyway, 1932

COX, A(NTHONY) B(ERKELEY). 1893-1970. Pseudonyms: Anthony Berkeley, Francis Iles, qq.vv.
Mr. Priestley's Problem. Collins, 1927. U.S. title: The Amateur Crime. Doubleday, 1928

COX, ANNE. Pseudonym: Annabel Gray, q.v.

COX, SIR EDMUND C(HARLES). 1856-   .
Series character: John Carruthers = JC.
The Achievements of John Carruthers. Constable, 1911 JC ss
The Exploits of Kesho Naik, Dacoit. Constable, 1912 ss
John Carruthers: Indian Policeman. Cassell, 1905 JC ss

COX, H(ARRY) H(UBERT). See: TOM GURR.

COX, IRVING E., JR.
Murder Among Friends. Abelard, 1957; Nelson, 1957

COX, THOMAS R.
Shadows of One Another. Exposition, 1971

COX, WILLIAM R(OBERT). 1901-   .
Death Comes Early. Dell, 1961
Death on Location. Signet, 1962
Hell to Pay. Signet, 1958
-The Lusty Men. Pyramid, 1957
Make My Coffin Strong. GM, 1954; Fawcett (London), 1955
Murder in Vegas. Signet, 1960
The Tycoon and the Tigress. GM, 1958
Way to Go, Doll Baby! Banner, 1967

COXE, GEORGE HARMON. 1901-   . Series characters: Flash Casey = FC (see also Paul Ayres); Sam Crombie = SC; Jack Fenner = JF; Max Hale = MH; Kent Murdock = KM.
Alias the Dead. Knopf, 1943
Assignment in Guiana. Knopf, 1942; Macdonald, 1943
The Barotique Mystery. Knopf, 1936; Heinemann, 1937. Also published as: Murdock's Acid Test. Dell, 1947 KM
The Big Gamble. Knopf, 1958; Hammond, 1960 KM
The Camera Clue. Knopf, 1937; Heinemann, 1938 KM
The Candid Impostor. Knopf, 1967; Hale, 1969
The Charred Witness. Knopf, 1942; Swan, 1949 KM
The Crimson Clue. Knopf, 1953; Hammond, 1955 KM
Dangerous Legacy. Knopf, 1946; Hammond, 1949
Deadly Image. Knopf, 1964; Hammond, 1964 FC
Death at the Isthmus. Knopf, 1954; Hammond, 1956
Double Identity. Knopf, 1970; Hale, 1971
An Easy Way to Go. Knopf, 1969; Hale, 1969 KM
Error of Judgment. Knopf, 1961; Hammond, 1962. Also published as: One Murder Too Many. Pyramid, 1969 FC
Eye Witness. Knopf, 1950; Hammond, 1963 KM
Fashioned for Murder. Knopf, 1947; Hammond, 1950
Fenner. Knopf, 1971; Hale, 1973 JF, KM
The Fifth Key. Knopf, 1947; Hammond, 1950 KM
Flash Casey, Detective. Avon, 1946. (4 1930's pulp novelets with FC.)
Focus on Murder. Knopf, 1954; Hammond, 1956 KM
Four Frightened Women. Knopf, 1939; Heinemann, 1939 KM, JF
The Frightened Fiancee. Knopf, 1950; Hammond, 1953 SC
The Glass Triangle. Knopf, 1940 KM
The Groom Lay Dead. Knopf, 1944; Hammond, 1946
The Hidden Key. Knopf, 1963; Hammond, 1964 KM
The Hollow Needle. Knopf, 1948; Hammond, 1951 KM
The Impetuous Mistress. Knopf, 1958; Hammond, 1959 SC
Inland Passage. Knopf, 1949; Hammond, 1952
The Inside Man. Knopf, 1974; Hale, 1975
The Jade Venus. Knopf, 1945; Hammond, 1947 KM
The Lady is Afraid. Knopf, 1940; Heinemann, 1940 MH
Lady Killer. Knopf, 1949; Hammond, 1952 KM

Coxe, George Harmon

The Last Commandment. Knopf, 1960; Hammond, 1961 KM
Man on a Rope. Knopf, 1956; Hammond, 1958
The Man Who Died Too Soon. Knopf, 1962; Hammond, 1963 FC
The Man Who Died Twice. Knopf, 1951; Hammond, 1954
Mission of Fear. Knopf, 1962; Hammond, 1963
Moment of Violence. Knopf, 1961; Hammond, 1962
Mrs. Murdock Takes a Case. Knopf, 1941; Swan, 1949 KM
Murder for the Asking. Knopf, 1939; Heinemann, 1940 MH
Murder for Two. Knopf, 1943; Hammond, 1944 FC
Murder in Havana. Knopf, 1943; Hammond, 1945
Murder on Their Minds. Knopf, 1957; Hammond, 1958 KM
Murder with Pictures. Knopf, 1935; Heinemann, 1937 KM
Murdock's Acid Test; see The Barotique Mystery
Never Bet Your Life. Knopf, 1952; Hammond, 1955
No Place for Murder. Knopf, 1975; Hale, 1976 JF
No Time to Kill. Knopf, 1941
One Hour to Kill. Knopf, 1963; Hammond, 1964
One Minute Past Eight. Knopf, 1957; Hammond, 1959
One Murder Too Many; see Error of Judgment
One Way Out. Knopf, 1960; Hammond, 1961
The Reluctant Heiress. Knopf, 1965; Hammond, 1966 KM
The Ring of Truth. Knopf, 1966; Hammond, 1967
Silent are the Dead. Knopf, 1942 FC
The Silent Witness. Knopf, 1973; Hale, 1974 JF
Slack Tide. Knopf, 1959; Hammond, 1960
Suddenly a Widow. Knopf, 1956; Hammond, 1957
Top Assignment. Knopf, 1955; Hammond, 1957
Uninvited Guest. Knopf, 1953; Hammond, 1956
Venturous Lady. Knopf, 1948; Hammond, 1951
The Widow had a Gun. Knopf, 1951; Hammond, 1954 KM
With Intent to Kill. Knopf, 1965; Hammond, 1965
Woman at Bay. Knopf, 1945; Hammond, 1948
Woman with a Gun. Knopf, 1972; Hale, 1974

COXE, KATHLEEN BUDDINGTON. Joint pseudonym of Amelia Reynolds Long, 1904-1978, q.v., and Edna McHugh. Other pseudonyms of Amelia Reynolds Long: Patrick Laing, Adrian Reynolds, Peter Reynolds, qq.v.
Murder Most Foul. Phoenix, 1946

COXE, VIRGINIA ROSALIE
The Embassy Ball. Neely, 1897

COXWELL, HENRY (TRACEY). 1819-1900.
A Knight of the Air; or, The Aerial Rivals. Digby, 1895

COZZENS, JAMES GOULD. 1903-1978.
The Just and the Unjust. Harcourt, 1942; Cape, 1943

CRABB, ARTHUR. Pseudonym. Series character: Samuel Lyle, in both titles.
Ghosts. Century, 1921. British title: Mrs. Brown's Pearls. Page (London), 1921
Mrs. Brown's Pearls; see Ghosts
Samuel Lyle, Criminologist. Century, 1920 ss

CRABTREE, SIMON. Series character: Hector Tumbler (HT), in both titles.
Forgotten Memories. Jarrolds, 1941 ss, including one about HT
Hector Tumbler Investigates. Jarrolds, 1943 ss

CRADDOCK, CHARLES EGBERT. Pseudonym of Mary Noailles Murfree, 1850-1922.
The Mystery of Witch-Face Mountain, and other stories. Houghton, 1895 ss

CRADDOCK, IRVING
The Yazoo Mystery. Britton, 1919

CRADOCK, PHYLLIS NAN SORTAIN. Pseudonym: Frances Dale, q.v.

CRAGG, E. H.
Almack, the Detective. London Literary Society, 1886

CRAIG, BILL. 1930- .
Scobie in September. Hutchinson, 1971. U.S. title: September can be Dangerous in Edinburgh. Walker, 1971

CRAIG, DAVID. Pseudonym of Allan James Tucker, 1929- . Series characters: Stephen Bellecroix and Sheila Roath, in at least those marked B&R; Roy Rickman, in at least those marked RR.
The Albion Case. Macmillan (London), 1975
The Alias Man. Cape, 1968; Stein, 1968 RR
Bolthole. Macmillan (London), 1973. U.S. title: Knifeman. Stein, 1973
Contact Lost. Cape, 1970; Stein, 1970 RR
A Dead Liberty. Macmillan (London), 1974
Double Take. Macmillan (London), 1972; Stein, 1972
Knifeman; see Bolthole
Message Ends. Cape, 1969; Stein, 1969 RR
The Squeeze. Stein, 1974. (British title?)
Up from the Grave. Macmillan (London), 1971
A Walk at Night. Macmillan (London), 1971; Stein, 1971 B&R
Whose Little Girl are You? Macmillan (London), 1974
Young Men May Die. Cape, 1970; Stein, 1970 B&R

CRAIG, JOHN. 1921- .
Close Doesn't Count. Macdonald, 1975. (U.S. title?)
If You Want to See Your Wife Again. Putnam, 1971; Cassell, 1973
In Council Rooms Apart. Putnam, 1971
-Power Play. Paperback Library, 1974
Superdude. Paperback Library, 1974

CRAIG, JONATHAN. Pseudonym of Frank E. Smith, 1919- . Series character: Pete Selby = PS.
Alley Girl. Lion, 1954
The Case of the Beautiful Body. GM, 1957; Fawcett (London), 1958 PS
Case of the Brazen Beauty. GM, 1966 PS
Case of the Cold Coquette. GM, 1957; Fawcett (London), 1958 PS
Case of the Laughing Virgin. GM, 1960 PS
Case of the Nervous Nude. GM, 1959; Muller pb, 1960 PS
Case of the Petticoat Murder. GM, 1958; Fawcett (London), 1960 PS
Case of the Silent Stranger. GM, 1964 PS
Case of the Village Tramp. GM, 1959; Muller pb, 1961 PS
Come Night, Come Evil. GM, 1957; Red Seal, 1959
The Dead Darling. GM, 1955; Red Seal, 1958 PS
Morgue for Venus. GM, 1956; Fawcett (London), 1957
Renegade Cop. Berkley, 1959
So Young, So Wicked. GM, 1957; Fawcett (London), 1958

CRAIG, MARY. Pseudonym of Mary Francis Shura.
The Cranes of Ibycus. Hawthorn, 1974. Also published as: Shadows of the Past. Manor, 1976
Shadows of the Past; see The Cranes of Ibycus
Ten Thousand Several Doors. Hawthorn, 1973

CRAIG, PETER. Pseudonym of Victor MacClure, 1887-1963, q.v.
Conspiracy Island. Harrap, 1933

CRAIG, PHILIP. 1933- .
Gate of Ivory, Gate of Horn. Doubleday, 1969; Macmillan (London), 1970

CRAIG, (CHARLES WILLIAM) THURLOW. 1901- . Series character: Lt. Bunjy Hearne, in at least those marked BH.
-Bitter is the Harvest. Hutchinson, 1949
The Changed Face. Hutchinson, 1939 BH
-Ghost Mesa. Hutchinson, 1944
-Love Under Smoke. Hutchinson, 1937
Plague Over London. Hutchinson, 1939 BH
-The River of Diamonds. Hutchinson, 1945
-The Swamp of Cardelli. Hutchinson, 1947
-West of Rio Grande. Hutchinson, 1948
White Girls Eastward. Hutchinson, 1938 BH

CRAIG, WILLIAM. 1929- .
The Strasbourg Legacy. Reader's Digest, 1975; Hodder, 1976
The Tashkent Crisis. Dutton, 1971; Hodder, 1971

CRANBROOK, SHELDON
The King of the Peak. Wright, 1937
The Spider of Soho. Wright, 1937

CRANDALL, EDWARD
White Violets. Little, 1954

CRANE, ALEX. Pseudonym of R(ichard) Wilkes-Hunter, q.v. Other pseudonyms: Marc Brody, Tod Conrad, qq.v.
Bushman. Horwitz, 1959
One Night of Fear. Horwitz, 1959

CRANE, FRANCES. Series characters: Pat and Jean Abbott, in at least those marked A.
The Amber Eyes. Random, 1962; Hammond, 1962 A
The Amethyst Spectacles. Random, 1944; Hammond, 1946 A
The Applegreen Cat. Lippincott, 1943; Hammond, 1945 A
Black Cypress. Random, 1948; Hammond, 1950 A
Body Beneath a Mandarin Tree. Hammond, 1965 A
The Buttercup Case. Random, 1958; Hammond, 1958 A

The Cinnamon Murder. Random, 1946; Hammond, 1948 A
The Coral Princess Murders. Random, 1954; Hammond, 1955 A
The Daffodil Blonde. Random, 1950; Hammond, 1951 A
Death in Lilac Time. Random, 1955; Hammond, 1955 A
Death in the Blue Hour; see Murder in Blue Street
Death-Wish Green. Random, 1960; Hammond, 1960 A
The Flying Red Horse. Random, 1949; Hammond, 1949 A
The Golden Box. Lippincott, 1942; Hammond, 1944 A
The Gray Stranger; see The Man in Gray
Horror on the Ruby X. Random, 1956; Hammond, 1956 A
The Indigo Necklace. Random, 1945; Hammond, 1947. Also published as: The Indigo Necklace Murders. Bantam, 1949 A
The Indigo Necklace Murders; see The Indigo Necklace
The Man in Gray. Random, 1958. British title: The Gray Stranger. Hammond, 1958 A
Murder in Blue Street. Random, 1951. British title: Death in the Blue Hour. Hammond, 1952 A
Murder in Bright Red. Random, 1953; Hammond, 1954 A
Murder on the Purple Water. Random, 1947; Hammond, 1949 A
The Pink Umbrella. Lippincott, 1943; Hammond, 1944. Also published as: The Pink Umbrella Murder. Popular Library, 1950 A
The Pink Umbrella Murder; see The Pink Umbrella
The Polkadot Murder. Random, 1951; Hammond, 1952 A
The Reluctant Sleuth. Hammond, 1961
The Shocking Pink Hat. Random, 1946; Hammond, 1948 A
13 White Tulips. Random, 1953; Hammond, 1953 A
Three Days in Hong Kong. Hammond, 1965
The Turquoise Shop. Lippincott, 1941; Hammond, 1943 A
The Ultraviolet Widow. Random, 1956; Hammond, 1957 A
A Very Quiet Murder. Hammond, 1966
Worse Than a Crime. Hale, 1968
The Yellow Violet. Lippincott, 1942; Hammond, 1944

CRANE, ROBERT. Series character: Ben Corbin, in at least those marked BC.
Operation Vengeance. Pyramid, 1965 BC
The Paradise Trap. Pyramid, 1967 BC
The Sergeant and the Queen. Pyramid, 1964 BC
Sgt. Corbin's War. Pyramid, 1964 BC
Strikeback! Pyramid, 1965
Time Running Out. Papillon, 1974 BC
Tongue of Treason. Pyramid, 1967 BC

CRANSTON, CLAUDIA. 1886-1947. Series character: Clarice Claremont, in both titles.
Murder Maritime. Lippincott, 1935
The Murder on Fifth Avenue. Lippincott, 1934

CRANSTON, MAURICE (WILLIAM). 1920-   .
Series character: Inspector Mortimer Blunt, in both titles.
Philosopher's Hemlock. Westhouse, 1946
Tomorrow We'll Be Sober. Westhouse, 1946

CRAUFORD, W(ILLIAM) H(AROLD) L(ANE). 1886-   .
And Then There were Nine. Ward, 1945
Another Woman's Poison. Ward, 1954
The Bride Wears Black. Ward, 1948
The Cat Dies First. Ward, 1955
The Crimson Mask. Ward, 1932
A Date with Death. Ward, 1947
-The Dearly Beloved Wives. Ward, 1953
Drakmere Must Die. Ward, 1950
Elementary, My Dear Freddie. Ward, 1950
The Final Curtain. Ward, 1933
The Hawkmoor Mystery. Ward, 1932
-The Ivory Goddess. Ward, 1954
Joseph Proctor's Money. Ward, 1948
A Man's Shadow. Ward, 1951
The Missing Ace. Ward, 1931
Murder of a Dead Man. Ward, 1952
Murder to Music. Ward, 1936
One Man's Meat. Ward, 1952
The Ravencroft Mystery. Ward, 1934
Smooth Killing. Ward, 1949
Till Murder Do Us Part. Ward, 1949
Where is Jenny Willet? Ward, 1953

CRAWFORD, E. M.
She Saw the Murderer. Stanley Smith, 1936

CRAWFORD, IAIN (PADRUIG). 1922-   .
Scare the Gentle Citizen. Hammond, 1966

CRAWFORD, JACK R(ANDALL). 1878-   .
The Philosopher's Murder Case. Sears, 1931; Long, 1932

CRAWFORD, MAX. 1938-   .
Waltz Across Texas. Farrar, 1975

CRAWFORD, PETRINA
Seed of Evil. Lancer, 1973

CRAWFORD, ROBERT. Pseudonym of Hugh C(rauford) Rae, 1935-   , q.v.
The Badger's Daughter. Constable, 1971. Reprinted as by Hugh C. Rae: Sphere, 1974
Cockleburr. Constable, 1969; Putnam, 1970. Also published as: Pay as You Die. Berkley, 1971
Kiss the Boss Goodbye. Constable, 1970; Putnam, 1971. Reprinted as by Hugh C. Rae: Sphere, 1974
Pay as You Die; see Cockleburr
The Shroud Society. Constable, 1969; Putnam, 1969
Whip Hand. Constable, 1972. Reprinted as by Hugh C. Rae: Sphere, 1974

CRAWFORD, STANLEY (G.). 1937-   .
Gascoyne. Putnam, 1966; Cape, 1966

CRAWFORD, WALLACE
Nest of Vipers. Hale, 1969

CRAWFORD, WILLIAM. Series character: Colin Stryker = CS.
The Chinese Connection. Pinnacle, 1973
Cop-Kill. Pinnacle, 1974 CS
Deadly Alliance. Pinnacle, 1975 CS
Drug Run. Pinnacle, 1974 CS
Stryker. Pinnacle, 1973 CS

CRAWFURD, OSWALD (JOHN FREDERICK). 1834-1909.
The League of the White Hand. Chapman, 1909
The Mystery of Myrtle Cottage. Chapman, 1908
The Revelations of Inspector Morgan. Chapman, 1906; Dodd, 1907 ss
Sylvia Arden: A Novel. Kegan Paul, 1888; Lovell, 1889
-The Ways of the Millionaire. Chapman, 1908

CRAWLEY, J. COOPER. Pseudonym.
Investment in Crime. Boardman, 1957
My Rubies are Blood Red. Boardman, 1957

CRAWLEY, RAYBURN. Pseudonym. Series character: Ned Shackleton, in both titles.
-The Chattering Gods. Harper, 1931
-The Valley of Creeping Men. Harper, 1930

CREASEY, JOHN. 1908-1973. Pseudonyms: Gordon Ashe, M. E. Cooke, Norman Deane, Robert Caine Frazer, Patrick Gill, Michael Halliday, Charles Hogarth, Brian Hope, Colin Hughes, Kyle Hunt, Abel Mann, Peter Manton, J. J. Marric, Richard Martin, Rodney Matheson, Anthony Morton, Jeremy York, qq.v. Series characters: Roger West = RW; Dr. Palfrey = P; Department Z = Z; Richard Rollison (The Toff) = RR; Sexton Blake (with many other writers) = SB. Note: Some titles originally published under pseudonyms have been reprinted under the John Creasey byline. These reprints are omitted from the following list, and will be found under the original byline. Also note: A number of paperback originals are grouped at the end of the listing. Finally, many early Creasey novels were revised for republication in the 50's-70's; these revisions are not noted in this or other Creasey lists.
Accident for Inspector West. Hodder, 1957. U.S. title: Hit and Run. Scribner, 1959 RW
Accuse the Toff. Long, 1943; Walker, 1975 RR
Alibi. Hodder, 1971; Scribner, 1971 RW
Battle for Inspector West. Paul, 1948 RW
A Beauty for Inspector West. Hodder, 1954. U.S. title: The Beauty Queen Killer. Harper, 1956. Also published as: So Young, So Cold, So Fair. Dell, 1958 RW
The Beauty Queen Killer; see A Beauty for Inspector West
The Black Spiders. Hodder, 1957; Popular Library, 1975 Z
The Blight. Hodder, 1968; Walker, 1968 P
The Blind Spot; see Inspector West at Bay
Break the Toff; see The Toff Down Under
A Bundle for the Toff. Hodder, 1967; Walker, 1968 RR
Call the Toff. Hodder, 1953; Walker, 1969 RR
Carriers of Death. Melrose, 1937; Popular Library, 1972 Z
The Case Against Paul Raeburn; see Triumph for Inspector West
A Case for Inspector West. Evans, 1951. U.S. title: The Figure in the Dusk. Harper, 1952 RW
The Case of the Acid Throwers; see Inspector West at Bay
The Case of the Innocent Victims. Hodder, 1960; Scribner, 1966 RW
The Case of the Mad Inventor. Amalgamated, 1942 SB
The Case of the Murdered Financier. Amalgamated, 1937 SB
The Children of Despair; see The Children of Hate
The Children of Hate. Evans, 1952. U.S. title: The Killers of Innocence. Walker, 1971. Also published as: The Children of Despair. Jay, 1958 P
The Creepers; see Inspector West Cries Wolf
Dangerous Quest. Long, 1944; Walker, 1974 Z
Dark Harvest. Long, 1947; Walker, 1977 P

Dark Peril. Paul, 1944; Popular Library, 1975 Z
The Dawn of Darkness. Long, 1949 P
The Day of Disaster. Long, 1942 Z
Days of Danger. Melrose, 1937; Popular Library, 1972 Z
Dead or Alive. Evans, 1951; Popular Library, 1974 Z
Death by Night. Long, 1940; Popular Library, 1972 Z
Death in Cold Print. Hodder, 1961; Scribner, 1962 RW
Death in the Rising Sun. Long, 1945; Walker, 1976 P
The Death Miser. Melrose, 1932 Z
Death of an Assassin; see A Prince for Inspector West
Death of a Postman; see Parcels for Inspector West
Death of a Racehorse. Hodder, 1959; Scribner, 1962 RW
Death Round the Corner. Melrose, 1935; Popular Library, 1972 Z
Death Stands By. Long, 1938; Popular Library, 1972 Z
The Department of Death. Evans, 1949 Z
The Depths. Hodder, 1963; Walker, 1967 P
The Dissemblers; see Puzzle for Inspector West
A Doll for the Toff. Hodder, 1963; Walker, 1965 RR
Doorway to Death; see Find Inspector West
Double for the Toff. Hodder, 1959; Walker, 1965 RR
The Drought. Hodder, 1959; Walker, 1967. Also published as: Dry Spell. Four Square, 1967 P
Dry Spell; see The Drought
The Enemy Within. Evans, 1950; Popular Library, 1977 Z
The Executioners. Hodder, 1967; Scribner, 1967 RW
The Extortioners. Hodder, 1974; Scribner, 1975 RW
The Famine. Hodder, 1967; Walker, 1968 P
Feathers for the Toff. Long, 1945; Walker, 1970 RR
The Figure in the Dusk; see A Case for Inspector West
Find Inspector West. Hodder, 1957. U.S. title: The Trouble at Saxby's. Harper, 1959. Also published as: Doorway to Death. Berkley, 1961 RW
First Came a Murder. Melrose, 1934; Popular Library, 1972 Z
The Flood. Hodder, 1956; Walker, 1969 P
Follow the Toff. Hodder, 1961; Walker, 1967 RR
Fool the Toff. Evans, 1950; Walker, 1966 RR
The Foothills of Fear. Hodder, 1961
The Gelignite Gang; see Inspector West Makes Haste
Give a Man a Gun; see A Gun for Inspector West
Go Away Death. Long, 1942; Popular Library, 1976 Z
Go Away to Murder; see Inspector West Leaves Town
The Great Air Swindle. Amalgamated, 1939 SB
A Gun for Inspector West. Hodder, 1953. U.S. title: Give a Man a Gun. Harper, 1954 RW
Hammer the Toff. Long, 1947 RR
Hang the Little Man. Hodder, 1963; Scribner, 1963 RW
Here Comes the Toff. Long, 1940; Walker, 1967 RR
Hit and Run; see Accident for Inspector West
Holiday for Inspector West. Paul, 1946 RW

The Hounds of Vengeance. Long, 1945 P
The House of the Bears. Long, 1947; Walker, 1975 P
Hunt the Toff. Evans, 1952; Walker, 1969 RR
The Inferno. Hodder, 1965; Walker, 1966 P
Inspector West Alone. Evans, 1950; Scribner, 1975 RW
Inspector West at Bay. Evans, 1952. U.S. title: The Blind Spot. Harper, 1954. Also published as: The Case of the Acid Throwers. Avon, 1960 RW
Inspector West at Home. Paul, 1944; Scribner, 1973 RW
Inspector West Cries Wolf. Evans, 1950. U.S. title: The Creepers. Harper, 1952 RW
Inspector West Kicks Off. Paul, 1949. U.S. title: Sport for Inspector West. Lancer, 1971
Inspector West Leaves Town. Paul, 1943. U.S. title: Go Away to Murder. Lancer, 1972 RW
Inspector West Makes Haste. Hodder, 1955. U.S. title: The Gelignite Gang. Harper, 1956. Also published as: Night of the Watchman. Berkley, 196?. And as: Murder Makes Haste. Lancer, 197? RW
Inspector West Regrets. Paul, 1945; Lancer, 1971 RW
Inspector West Takes Charge. Paul, 1942; Scribner, 1972 RW
The Insulators. Hodder, 1972; Walker, 1973 P
Introducing the Toff. Long, 1938 RR
The Island of Peril. Long, 1940; Popular Library, 1976 Z
The Kidnapped Child; see The Toff and the Kidnapped Child
Kill the Toff. Evans, 1950; Walker, 1966 RR
The Killers of Innocence; see The Children of Hate
The Killing Strike; see Strike for Death
A Kind of Prisoner. Hodder, 1954; Popular Library, 1975 Z
Kiss the Toff; see Make-Up for the Toff
A Knife for the Toff. Evans, 1951; Pyramid, 1964 RR
The League of Dark Men. Paul, 1947; Popular Library, 1975 Z
The League of Light. Evans, 1949 P
Leave It to the Toff. Hodder, 1963; Pyramid, 1965 RR
The Legion of the Lost. Long, 1943; Daye, 1944 P
Look Three Ways at Murder. Hodder, 1964; Scribner, 1965 RW
Make-Up for the Toff. Hodder, 1956; Walker, 1967. Also published as: Kiss the Toff. Lancer, 1971
The Man from Fleet Street. Amalgamated, 1940 SB
The Man Who Shook the World. Evans, 1950 P
The Mark of the Crescent. Melrose, 1935; Popular Library, 1972 Z
A Mask for the Toff; see The Toff Goes Gay
The Masters of Bow Street. Hodder, 1974; Simon, 1974
Men, Maids and Murder. Melrose, 1933
Menace! Long, 1938; Popular Library, 1972 Z
The Mists of Fear. Hodder, 1955; Walker, 1977 P
Model for the Toff. Hodder, 1957; Pyramid, 1965 RR

The Mountain of the Blind. Hodder, 1960
Murder, London-Australia. Hodder, 1965; Scribner, 1965 RW
Murder, London-Miami. Hodder, 1969; Scribner, 1969 RW
Murder, London-New York. Hodder, 1958; Scribner, 1961 RW
Murder, London-South Africa. Hodder, 1966; Scribner, 1966 RW
Murder Makes Haste; see Inspector West Makes Haste
Murder Must Wait. Long, 1939; Popular Library, 1972 Z
Murder on the Line. Hodder, 1960; Scribner, 1963 RW
Murder: One, Two, Three; see Two for Inspector West
Murder Out of the Past. Barrington Gray, 1953 RR
Murder Tips the Scales; see Two for Inspector West
Night of the Watchman; see Inspector West Makes Haste
No Darker Crime. Paul, 1943; Popular Library, 1976 Z
The Oasis. Hodder, 1969; Walker, 1970 P
Panic! Long, 1939; Popular Library, 1972 Z
Parcels for Inspector West. Hodder, 1956. U.S. title: Death of a Postman. Harper, 1957 RW
A Part for a Policeman. Hodder, 1970; Scribner, 1970 RW
The Peril Ahead. Paul, 1946; Popular Library, 1974 Z
The Perilous Country; see The Valley of Fear
The Plague of Silence. Hodder, 1958; Walker, 1968 P
Poison for the Toff; see The Toff on Ice
Policeman's Dread. Hodder, 1962; Scribner, 1964 RW
Prepare for Action. Paul, 1942; Popular Library, 1975 Z
A Prince for Inspector West. Hodder, 1956. U.S. title: Death of an Assassin. Scribner, 1960 RW
Private Carter's Crime. Amalgamated, 1943 SB
The Prophet of Fire. Evans, 1951 P
Puzzle for Inspector West. Evans, 1951. U.S. title: The Dissemblers. Scribner, 1967 RW
Redhead. Hurst, 1934 Z
A Rocket for the Toff. Hodder, 1960; Pyramid, 1964 RR
Sabotage. Long, 1941; Popular Library, 1976 Z
Salute the Toff. Long, 1941; Walker, 1971 RR
The Scene of the Crime. Hodder, 1961; Scribner, 1963 RW
A Score for the Toff; see A Six for the Toff
Send Inspector West. Hodder, 1953. U.S. title: Send Superintendent West. Scribner, 1976 RW
Send Superintendent West; see Send Inspector West
Seven Times Seven. Melrose, 1932
Shadow of Doom. Long, 1946 P
A Six for the Toff. Hodder, 1955; Walker, 1969. Also published as: A Score for the Toff. Lancer, 1972 RR
The Sleep. Hodder, 1964; Walker, 1968 P
The Smog. Hodder, 1970; Walker, 1971 P
The Sons of Satan. Long, 1948 P
So Young, So Cold, So Fair; see A Beauty for Inspector West
So Young to Burn. Hodder, 1968; Scribner, 1968 RW
A Splinter of Glass. Hodder, 1972; Scribner, 1972 RW
Sport for Inspector West; see Inspector West Kicks Off

Stars for the Toff. Hodder, 1968;
  Walker, 1968 RR
Strike for Death. Hodder, 1958. U.S.
  title: The Killing Strike. Scribner,
  1961 RW
The Terror. Hodder, 1962; Walker, 1966
  P
Terror for the Toff; see The Toff on
  the Farm
The Terror Trap. Melrose, 1936; Popular Library, 1972 Z
The Theft of Magna Carta. Hodder, 1973;
  Scribner, 1973 RW
Thunder in Europe. Melrose, 1936; Popular Library, 1972 Z
The Toff. Evans, 1963. (A play.) RR
The Toff Among the Millions. Long,
  1943; Walker, 1976 RR
The Toff and Old Harry. Long, 1948;
  Walker, 1970 RR
The Toff and the Curate. Long, 1944;
  Walker, 1969. Also published as: The
  Toff and the Deadly Parson. Lancer,
  1970 RW
The Toff and the Deadly Parson; see The
  Toff and the Curate
The Toff and the Deep Blue Sea. Hodder,
  1955; Walker, 1967 RR
The Toff and the Fallen Angels. Hodder,
  1970; Walker, 1970 RR
The Toff and the Golden Boy. Hodder,
  1969; Walker, 1969 RR
The Toff and the Great Illusion. Long,
  1944; Walker, 1967 RR
The Toff and the Kidnapped Child. Hodder, 1960; Walker, 1965. Also published as: The Kidnapped Child. Popular Library, 1972 RR
The Toff and the Lady. Long, 1946;
  Walker, 1975 RR
The Toff and the Runaway Bride. Hodder,
  1959; Walker, 1964 RR
The Toff and the Sleepy Cowboy. Hodder,
  1974; Walker, 1975 RR
The Toff and the Spider. Hodder, 1965;
  Walker, 1966 RR
The Toff and the Stolen Tresses. Hodder, 1958; Walker, 1965 RR
The Toff and the Teds. Hodder, 1961.
  U.S. title: The Toff and the Toughs.
  Walker, 1968 RR
The Toff and the Terrified Tax Man.
  Hodder, 1973; Walker, 1973 RR
The Tough and the Toughs; see The Toff
  and the Teds
The Toff and the Trip-Trip-Triplets.
  Hodder, 1972; Walker, 1972 RR
The Toff at Butlin's. Hodder, 1954;
  Walker, 1976 RR
The Toff at the Fair. Hodder, 1954;
  Walker, 1968 RR
The Toff Breaks In. Long, 1940 RR
The Toff Down Under. Hodder, 1953;
  Walker, 1969. Also published as:
  Break the Toff. Lancer, 1970 RW
The Toff Goes Gay. Evans, 1951. U.S.
  title: A Mask for the Toff. Walker,
  1966 RR
The Toff Goes On. Long, 1939 RR
The Toff Goes to Market. Long, 1942;
  Walker, 1967 RR
The Toff in New York. Hodder, 1956;
  Pyramid, 1964 RR
The Toff in Town. Long, 1948; Walker,
  1977 RR
The Toff in Wax. Hodder, 1966; Walker,
  1966 RR
The Toff is Back. Long, 1942; Walker,
  1974 RR
The Toff on Board. Evans, 1949; Walker,
  1973 RR
The Toff on Fire. Hodder, 1957; Walker,
  1966 RR
The Toff on Ice. Long, 1947. U.S.
  title: Poison for the Toff. Pyramid,
  1965 RR

The Toff on the Farm. Hodder, 1958;
  Walker, 1964. Also published as:
  Terror for the Toff. Pyramid, 1965 RR
The Toff on the Trail. Everybody's pb,
  194? RR
The Toff Proceeds. Long, 1941; Walker,
  1968 RR
The Toff Steps Out. Long, 1939 RR
The Toff Takes Shares. Long, 1948;
  Walker, 1972 RR
The Touch of Death. Hodder, 1954;
  Walker, 1969 P
Traitor's Doom. Long, 1942; Walker,
  1970 P
Triumph for Inspector West. Paul, 1948.
  U.S. title: The Case Against Paul
  Raeburn. Harper, 1958 RW
The Trouble at Saxby's; see Find Inspector West
Two for Inspector West. Hodder, 1955.
  U.S. title: Murder: One, Two, Three.
  Scribner, 1960. Also published as:
  Murder Tips the Scales. Berkley, 1962
  RW
The Unbegotten. Hodder, 1971; Walker,
  1972 P
The Valley of Fear. Long, 1943. U.S.
  title: The Perilous Country. Walker,
  1973. British reprint editions bear
  the same title as the U.S. edition.
  P
The Voiceless Ones. Hodder, 1973;
  Walker, 1974 P
Vote for the Toff. Hodder, 1971;
  Walker, 1971 RR
The Wings of Peace. Long, 1948; Walker,
  1978 P

The Cinema Crimes. Pemberton, 1945
Dixon Hawke, Secret Agent. Thompson,
  1939
Documents of Death. Mellifont, 1939
The Double Motive. Mellifont, 1938
The Doublecross of Death. Mellifont,
  1938
The Fear of Felix Corder. Fleetway,
  19??
The Hidden Hoard. Mellifont, 1939
John Brand, Fugitive. Fleetway, 19??
The Killer Squad. Newnes, 1936
The Men Who Died Laughing. Thompson,
  1935
The Missing Hoard. Mellifont, 1938
Mottled Death. Thompson, 1939
Murder by Magic. Amalgamated, 1937
The Mysterious Mr. Rocco. Mellifont,
  1937
Mystery at Manby House. Northern
  News, 1938
The Mystery of Blackmoor Prison.
  Mellifont, 1939
The Night of Dread. Fleetway, 19??
The Poison Gas Robberies. Mellifont,
  1940
The Sacred Eye. Thompson, 1939
The Ship of Death. Thompson, 1939

CREBBIN, EDWARD HORACE. Pseudonym: Sea-Wrack, q.v.

CRECY, JEANNE. Pseudonym of Jeanne Williams, 1930- . Other pseudonym:
  Deirdre Rowan, q.v.
Curse of the Wolfskin. Signet, 1975
Evil Among Us. Signet, 1975
Hands of Terror. Berkley, 1972
Lady Gift. Hale, 1973. (U.S. title?)
The Lightning Tree. Berkley, 1973
My Face Beneath the Stone. Signet, 1975
The Night Hunters. Signet, 1975
The Winter Keeper. Signet, 1975

CREED, DAVID. Pseudonym of James Shields
  Guthrie, 1931- .

Trial of Lobo Icheka. Macmillan (London), 1971

CREED, SIBYL
The Shot. Chatto, 1924; Doran, 1924

CREED, WILL. Pseudonym of William Long,
  1922- . Other pseudonym: Peter
  Yates, q.v.
Death Comes Grinning. Five-Star, 1946;
  Edwards, 1947
Death Wears a Green Hat. Five-Star,
  1946; Edwards, 1946

CREIGHTON, JO ANNE
House of Fury. Curtis, 1973
Inn of Evil. Popular Library, 1974

CREIGHTON, JOHN. Pseudonym of Joseph
  Chadwick, q.v. Other pseudonym: John
  Conway, q.v.
The Blonde Cried Murder. Ace, 1961
Destroying Angel. Ace, 1956
Evil is the Night. Ace, 1959
A Half Interest in Murder. Ace, 1960
Not So Evil as Eve. Ace, 1957
Stranglehold. Ace, 1959
Trial by Perjury. Ace, 1958
The Wayward Blonde. Ace, 1958

CRESSWELL, HENRY
Without Issue. Hurst, 1897

CRESSWELL, MAURICE
Murder in a Road Gang. Low, 1936

CREW-JONES, FLORENCE. See: ALBERT BOISSIERE, 1866- .

CRICHTON, LOUISE
-China Rose. Columbine, 1939
-Less Than the Dust. Columbine, 1939
Mandarin's Dagger. Columbine, 1939

CRICHTON, MICHAEL. 1942- . Pseudonyms:
  Jeffery Hudson, John Lange, qq.v.
The Great Train Robbery. Knopf, 1975;
  Cape, 1975

CRISP, FRANK (ROBSON). 1915- .
-The Ape of London. Hodder, 1959
-By Whose Hand. Paul, 1951
-The Chandu Men. Paul, 1955
-Fazackerley's Millions. Paul, 1955
-The Manila Stranger. Long, 1957
-The Nail of Suspicion. Low, 1949
-The Night Callers. Long, 1960
The Voice from Yesterday. Paul, 1948
-Within This House. Paul, 1947

CRISPIN, EDMUND. Pseudonym of Robert
  Bruce Montgomery, 1921- . Series
  character: Gervase Fen, in all
  titles.
Beware of the Trains. Gollancz, 1953;
  Walker, 1962 ss
Buried for Pleasure. Gollancz, 1948;
  Lippincott, 1949
The Case of the Gilded Fly. Gollancz,
  1944. U.S. title: Obsequies at Oxford. Lippincott, 1945
Dead and Dumb; see Swan Song
Frequent Hearses. Gollancz, 1950. U.S.
  title: Sudden Vengeance. Dodd, 1950
Holy Disorders. Gollancz, 1945; Lippincott, 1946
The Long Divorce. Gollancz, 1951; Dodd,
  1951. Also published as: A Noose for
  Her. Mercury, 1952
Love Lies Bleeding. Gollancz, 1948;
  Lippincott, 1948
The Moving Toyshop. Gollancz, 1946;
  Lippincott, 1946
A Noose for Her; see The Long Divorce
Obsequies at Oxford; see The Case of
  the Gilded Fly
Sudden Vengeance; see Frequent Hearses

Swan Song. Gollancz, 1947. U.S. title: Dead and Dumb. Lippincott, 1947

CROCKETT, ANTHONY (JOHN SINCLAIR)
The Perimeter Fence. Hale, 1957
Toys of Desperation. Hale, 1960

CROCKETT, JAMES. Joint pseudonym of Cornelia Warriner and James A. MacPhail.
Lullaby with Lugers. Crown, 1946

CROCKETT, S(AMUEL) R(UTHERFORD). 1860-1914.
Deep Moat Grange. Hodder, 1908; Appleton, 1908
-The Firebrand. Macmillan (London), 1901; McClure, 1901
The Lady of the Hundred Dresses. Nash, 1911 ss

CROFT, D(ESMOND) W(ARRICK). 1894- .
-Frederick Lonton. Longmans (New York & London), 1926

CROFT-COOKE, RUPERT. 1903- . Pseudonym: Leo Bruce, q.v.
Clash by Night. Eyre, 1962
Nasty Piece of Work. Eyre, 1973
Paper Albatross. Eyre, 1965; Abelard, 1968
Pharoah with His Waggons and other stories. Jarrolds, 1937 27 ss, 8 criminous
Seven Thunders. Macmillan (London), 1956; St. Martin's, 1955
Thief. Eyre, 1960; Doubleday, 1961
Three in a Cell. Eyre, 1968

CROFTS, FREEMAN WILLS. 1879-1957. Series character: Inspector Joseph French = JF. Two wartime pamphlets are listed at the end of this entry.
The Affair at Little Wokeham. Hodder, 1943. U.S. title: Double Tragedy. Dodd, 1943 JF
Antidote to Venom. Hodder, 1938; Dodd, 1939 JF
Anything to Declare? Hodder, 1957 JF
The Box Office Murders. Collins, 1929. U.S. title: The Purple Sickle Murders. Harper, 1929 JF
The Cask. Collins, 1920; Seltzer, 1924
The Cheyne Mystery; see Inspector French and the Cheyne Mystery
Circumstantial Evidence; see James Tarrant, Adventurer
Cold-Blooded Murder; see Man Overboard
Crime at Guildford. Collins, 1935. U.S. title: The Crime at Nornes. Dodd, 1935 JF
The Crime at Nornes; see Crime at Guildford
Crime on the Solent; see Mystery on Southampton Water
Dark Journey; see French Strikes Oil
Death of a Train. Hodder, 1946; Dodd, 1947 JF
Death on the Way. Collins, 1932. U.S. title: Double Death. Harper, 1932 JF
Double Death; see Death on the Way
Double Tragedy; see The Affair at Little Wokeham
The End of Andrew Harrison. Hodder, 1938. U.S. title: The Futile Alibi. Dodd, 1938 JF
Enemy Unseen. Hodder, 1945; Dodd, 1945 JF
Fatal Venture. Hodder, 1939. U.S. title: Tragedy in the Hollow. Dodd, 1939 JF
Fear Comes to Chalfont. Hodder, 1942; Dodd, 1942 JF
Found Floating. Hodder, 1937; Dodd, 1937 JF
French Strikes Oil. Hodder, 1952. U.S. title: Dark Journey. Dodd, 1951 JF
The Futile Alibi; see The End of Andrew Harrison

Golden Ashes. Hodder, 1940; Dodd, 1940 JF
The Groote Park Murder. Collins, 1923; Seltzer, 1925
The Hog's Back Mystery. Hodder, 1933. U.S. title: The Strange Case of Dr. Earle. Dodd, 1933 JF
Inspector French and the Cheyne Mystery. Collins, 1926. U.S. title: The Cheyne Mystery. Boni, 1926 JF
Inspector French and the Starvel Tragedy. Collins, 1927. U.S. title: The Starvel Hollow Tragedy. Harper, 1927 JF
Inspector French's Greatest Case. Collins, 1924; Seltzer, 1925 JF
James Tarrant, Adventurer. Hodder, 1941. U.S. title: Circumstantial Evidence. Dodd, 1941 JF
The Losing Game. Hodder, 1941. U.S. title: A Losing Game. Dodd, 1941 JF
The Loss of the Jane Vosper. Collins, 1936; Dodd, 1936 JF
Man Overboard! Collins, 1936; Dodd, 1936. Also published as: Cold-Blooded Murder. Avon, 1947 (abridged) JF
Many a Slip. Hodder, 1955 ss JF
Murderers Make Mistakes. Hodder, 1947 ss JF
Mystery in the Channel. Collins, 1931. U.S. title: Mystery in the English Channel. Harper, 1931 JF
Mystery in the English Channel; see Mystery in the Channel
The Mystery of the Sleeping Car Express, and other stories. Hodder, 1956 ss JF
Mystery on Southampton Water. Hodder, 1934. U.S. title: Crime on the Solent. Dodd, 1934 JF
The Pit-Prop Syndicate. Collins, 1922; Seltzer, 1925
The Ponson Case. Collins, 1921; Boni, 1927
The Purple Sickle Murders; see The Box Office Murders
The Sea Mystery. Collins, 1928; Harper, 1928 JF
Silence for the Murderer. Hodder, 1949; Dodd, 1948 JF
Sir John Magill's Last Journey. Collins, 1930; Harper, 1930 JF
The Starvel Hollow Tragedy; see Inspector French and the Starvel Tragedy
The Strange Case of Dr. Earle; see The Hog's Back Mystery
Sudden Death. Collins, 1932; Harper, 1932 JF
Tragedy in the Hollow; see Fatal Venture
The 12:30 from Croydon. Hodder, 1934. U.S. title: Wilful and Premeditated. Dodd, 1934 JF
Wilful and Premeditated; see The 12:30 from Croydon
The Hunt Ball Murder. Todd, 1943
Mr. Sefton, Murderer. Polybooks, 1944

CROMARSH, H. RIPLEY. Pseudonym of Bryan Mary Angell, 1877- .
The Secret of the Moor Cottage. Small, 1906; Ward, 1907

CROMARTY, NOEL
Ashes for the Living. Hodder, 1949
The Blind Side. Hodder, 1951
An Epitaph for Meredith. Hodder, 1953
Neither Had I Rest. Hodder, 1949
Rogue's Harvest. Hodder, 1950

CROMBIE, MICHAEL
The Awakening of Theodore Wrenn, Gray, 1934

The Frightened Girl. Mystery House, 1941. (British title?)
The Gentleman Crook. Gramol, 1935
The House of Horror. Gray, 193?
Life Must Go On. Gray, 1936
Murder!! Gramol, 1935
The Sealed Room Murder. Gray, 1934

CROMIE, ROBERT. 1856-1907.
-The Crack of Doom. Digby, 1895
El Dorado. Ward, 1904. U.S. title: From the Cliffs of Croaghaun. Saalfield, 1904
From the Cliffs of Croaghaun; see El Dorado
The Lost Liner. Newnes, 1899
The Romance of Poisons: Being Weird Episodes from Life. Jarrolds, 1903 ss

CROMWELL, A. G. E. Series chracter: Rodney Wayne, in both titles.
Death in the Copse. Wright, 1940
Murder in Flat 14. Wright, 1939

CRONIN, A(RCHIBALD) J(OSEPH). 1896- .
Beyond This Place. Gollancz, 1953; Little, 1953

CRONIN, BERNARD CHARLES. 1884- . Pseudonyms: Dennis Adair, Eric North, qq.v.

CRONIN, BRENDAN LEO. 1907- . Pseudonyms: Michael Cronin, David Miles, qq.v.

CRONIN, MICHAEL. Pseudonym of Brendan Leo Cronin, 1907- . Other pseudonym: David Miles, q.v. Series character: Richard Maidment, in many titles at least including those marked RM.
Ask for Trouble. Hale, 1963
Begin with a Gun. Hale, 1960; Walker, 1961 RM
The Big C. Hale, 1973
The Big Tickle. Hale, 1974
A Black Leather Case. Hale, 1971
By His Own Hand. Hale, 1969
Caribbean Kidnap. Hale, 1969
Climb the Wall. Museum, 1956; Washburn, 1957 RM
The Con Game. Hale, 1972
Curtain Call. Hale, 1961
The Dangerous Lady. Hale, 1962
Dead, and Done With. Hale, 1959
Dead in Transit. Hale, 1974
Dead Loss. Hale, 1970
Duet for Death. Hale, 1973
The Elusive Lady. Hale, 1957
Emergency Exit. Hale, 1970
Escape at Sunrise. Hale, 1972
The Fast Exit. Hale, 1962
The Girl on the Beach. Hale, 1967
I Can Cope. Museum, 1955
The Intruder. Hale, 1966
Jump the Gun. Hale, 1966
The Killing is Easy. Hale, 1975
The Last Indictment. Hale, 1964
Leave It to Me. Museum, 1953
The Long Memory. Hale, 1971
The Loose End. Hale, 1961
Loser Takes Nothing. Museum, 1955
Man Alive. Hale, 1968
Man at Large. Hale, 1962
Marked to Die. Hale, 1967
The Marksman. Hale, 1974
Murder Incidental. Hale, 1965
Murder Mislaid. Hale, 1963
The Night of the Party. Hale, 1957; Washburn, 1958
No Sale. Ward, 1950
Nobody Needs a Corpse. Hale, 1972
Pacific Pearl. Museum, 1954
Paid in Full. Museum, 1953
A Proper Carve-Up. Hale, 1970
The Second Bounce. Hale, 1959

The Spanish Lady. Hale, 1960
Strictly Legitimate. Ward, 1951
Strictly Private Business. Hale, 1975
Sweet Water. Museum, 1957; Washburn, 1957 RM
The Unquiet Night. Hale, 1958
You Never Learn. Museum, 1952
You Pay Your Money. Museum, 1954

CROOKENDEN, ISAAC
Horrible Revenge; or, The Monster of Italy! Harrild, 1812

CROOKER, HERBERT. Series character: Clay Brooke, in at least those marked CB.
The Crime in Washington Mews. Macaulay, 1931 CB
The Hollywood Murder Mystery. Macaulay, 1930; Long, 1930 CB
-The Sweet Cheat. Macaulay, 1932

CROSBIE, HUGH PROVAN. 1912- . Pseudonym: John Carrick, q.v.

CROSBIE, JOHN
The Gun Runners. Low, 1937
-The Lion Men. Low, 1938

CROSBY, G(EORGE) S.
-The Mystery; or, Platonic Love. Lippincott, 1875

CROSBY, JOHN
Death by Proxy. Langdon, 1948

CROSBY, JOHN (CAMPBELL). 1912- .
An Affair of Strangers. Stein, 1975; Cape, 1975
Contract on the President. Dell, 1973

CROSBY, KINGSLAND
The Strange Case of Eleanor Cuyler. Dodd, 1910

CROSBY, LEE. Pseudonym of Ware Torrey, 1905-1967. Series character: Eric Hazard, in at least those marked EH.
Bridge House. Belmont, 1965
Doors to Death; see Too Many Doors
Midsummer's Night Murder. Dutton, 1942
Night Attack. Dutton, 1943
Terror by Night. Dutton, 1938 EH
Too Many Doors. Dutton, 1941. Also published as: Doors to Death. Thriller Novel Classic, 194? EH

CROSLAND, T(HOMAS) W(ILLIAM) H(ODGSON). 1865-1924.
The Rogue. Paul, 1926

CROSS, AMANDA. Pseudonym of Carolyn Gold Heilbrun, 1926- . Series character: Kate Fansler, in all titles.
In the Last Analysis. Macmillan, 1964; Gollancz, 1964
The James Joyce Murder. Macmillan, 1967; Gollancz, 1967
Poetic Justice. Knopf, 1970; Gollancz, 1970
The Theban Mysteries. Knopf, 1971; Gollancz, 1972

CROSS, (ALAN) BEVERLEY. 1931- .
The Nightwalkers. Hart-Davis, 1956; Little, 1957

CROSS, JAMES. Pseudonym of Hugh Jones Parry, 1916- .
The Dark Road. Messner, 1959; Heinemann, 1960
The Grave of Heroes. GM, 1961; Heinemann, 1961
Root of Evil. Messner, 1957; Heinemann, 1958
To Hell for Half-a-Crown. Random, 1967; Constable, 1968

CROSS, JOHN KEIR. 1914- .
The Other Passenger. Westhouse, 1944; Lippincott, 1946 ss

CROSS, LAURENCE
The Dope Dealers. Jarrolds, 1928
The White Chalet. Jarrolds, 1929

CROSS, MARK. Pseudonym of Archibald Thomas Pechey, 1876-1961. Other pseudonym: Valentine, q.v. Series characters: Daphne Wrayne and the Four Adjusters, in all titles (see also the Valentine entry).
The Best-Laid Schemes. Ward, 1955
The Black Spider. Ward, 1953
Challenge to the Four. Ward, 1939
The Circle of Freedom. Ward, 1953
Desperate Steps. Ward, 1957
Find the Professor. Ward, 1940
Foul Deeds Will Arise. Ward, 1958
The Four at Bay. Ward, 1939
The Four Get Going. Ward, 1938
The Four Make Holiday. Ward, 1938
The Four Strike Home. Ward, 1937
The Green Circle. Ward, 1942
The Grip of the Four. Ward, 1934
The Hand of the Four. Ward, 1935
How Was It Done? Ward, 1941
In the Dead of Night. Ward, 1955
It Couldn't Be Murder. Ward, 1940
The Jaws of Darkness. Ward, 1952
The Mark of the Four. Ward, 1936
Missing from his Home. Ward, 1949
Murder as Arranged. Ward, 1943
Murder in Black. Ward, 1944
Murder in the Air. Ward, 1943
Murder in the Pool. Ward, 1941
Murder will Speak. Ward, 1954
The Mystery of Gruden's Gap. Ward, 1942
The Mystery of Joan Marryat. Ward, 1945
The Mystery of the Corded Box. Ward, 1956
Not Long to Live. Ward, 1959
Once Too Often. Ward, 1960
Once Upon a Crime. Ward, 1961
On the Night of the 14th. Ward, 1950
Other than Natural Causes. Ward, 1949
Over Thin Ice. Ward, 1958
Perilous Hazard. Ward, 1961
The Secret of the Grange. Ward, 1946
The Shadow of the Four. Ward, 1934
The Strange Affair at Greylands. Ward, 1948
The Strange Case of Pamela Wilson. Ward, 1954
Surprise for the Four. Ward, 1937
Third Time Unlucky. Ward, 1959
Wanted for Questioning. Ward, 1960
The Way of the Four. Ward, 1936
When Danger Threatens. Ward, 1959
When Thieves Fall Out. Ward, 1956
Who Killed Henry Wickenstrom. Ward, 1951

CROSS, MARK S.
To the Dark Tower. Kenedy, 1922

CROSS, MARY
-False Witness. Oliphant, 1891
-Under Sentence. Ward, 1890

CROSS, SETON
The Twelfth Crime. Newnes, 1916

CROSS, VICTOR. Pseudonym of Virginia (Edith) Coffman, 1914- , q.v.
Blood Sport. Award, 1967; Tandem, 1967

CROSSEN, KENDELL FOSTER. 1910- . Pseudonyms: Bennett Barlay, M. E. Chaber, Richard Foster, Christopher Monig,
Clay Richards, qq.v. Series character: Kim Locke = KL.
The Big Dive. Dutton, 1959; Eyre, 1959 KL
The Case of the Curious Heel (by Ken Crossen). Vulcan, 1944
The Case of the Phantom Fingerprints (by Ken Crossen). Vulcan, 1945
Murder Out of Mind (by Ken Crossen). Five Star, 1945
The Tortured Path. Dutton, 1957; Eyre, 1958 KL

CROSSLEY, MAUDE. 1879- . Series character: Guy Bannister, in at least those marked GB.
A Box of Secrets. Jenkins, 1933
The Crimson Feather, with Charles (Thomas) King, 1868- . Jenkins, 1926
Crookery Inn. Jenkins, 1931 GB
The Forbidden Hour, with Charles (Thomas) King, 1868- . Jenkins, 1925 GB
The Lilac Bride Mystery. Mellifont, 1933
Murder in the Vestry. Mellifont, 1935
Secrecy Street. Mellifont, 1933
Shackled. Mellifont, 1934

CROUCH, J. M.
Corpse from the Sky. Gulliver, 1950

CROUDACE, GLYNN. 1917- .
-The Black Rose. Hale, 1968
Blackadder. Macmillan (London), 1969
-The Dark Tide. Hale, 1967
Motives for Murder. Central News Agency (South Africa), 1957
The Scarlet Bikini. Macmillan (London), 1970
-The Silver Grass. Hale, 1968

CROWCRAFT, PETER
That Man Bolt. PB, 1974. (Novelization of the movie.)

CROWE, CECILY
Northwater. Holt, 1968
The Tower of Kilraven. Holt, 1965

CROWE, JOHN. Pseudonym of Dennis Lynds, 1924- , q.v. Other pseudonyms: William Arden, Michael Collins, Carl Dekker, Maxwell Grant, Mark Sadler, qq.v. Series character: Lee Beckett, in all titles.
Another Way to Die. Random, 1972
Bloodwater. Dodd, 1974
Crooked Shadows. Dodd, 1975
A Touch of Darkness. Random, 1972

CROWE, PAT(RICK T.). 1869-1938.
Society's Prodigal. Crowe, 1906

CROWELL, WILL
Murder in Mocking Valley. Eerie Series, 194?

CROWTHER, JOHN
Firebase. Constable, 1975

CROYLAND, WILLIAM
Sinister Civility. Nash, 1924

CROZIER, ALFRED O(WEN). 1863-1939.
The Magnet. Funk, 1908

CROZIER, JOHN. Series character: Falcon, in both titles.
Kidnapped Again. Hutchinson, 1935
Murder in Public. Hutchinson, 1934; Houghton, 1935

CRUGER, JULIE GRINNELL. Pseudonym: Julien Gordon, q.v.

CRUMLEY, JAMES. 1939- .
  The Wrong Case. Random, 1975; Hart-Davis, 1976

CRUMP, LOUISE (ESKRIGGE)
  The Face of Fear. Longmans, 1954; Foulsham, 1956

CRUMP, PAUL
  Burn, Killer, Burn. Johnson, 1962

CRUNDEN, ALLEN B., 1878-   , and ROBERT MORSE CRUNDEN
  Chicago Winter's Tale. Vantage, 1960

CRUNDEN, ROBERT MORSE. See: ALLEN B. CRUNDEN, 1878- .

CSIDA, JOE
  Crime is of the Essence. Five Star, 1946

CULLEN, ANTHONY
  Studd. Avon, 1972

CULLEN, CARTER. Joint pseudonym of Mildred and Richard Macaulay.
  The Deadly Chase. GM, 1957; Fawcett (London), 1958
  Don't Get Caught. GM, 1951; Fawcett (London), 1959

CULLEY, CHRISTOPHER
  The Green Mountain Murders. Ward, 1937
  The Texas Bank Murders. Eldon, 1938

CULLINAN, THOMAS
  The Besieged. Horizon, 1970

CULLINGFORD, GUY. Pseudonym of C(onstance) Lindsay Taylor, 1907-   , q.v.
  Brink of Disaster. Bles, 1964; Roy, 1966
  Conjurer's Coffin. Hammond, 1954; Lippincott, 1954
  Framed for Hanging. Hammond, 1956; Lippincott, 1956
  If Wishes were Hearses. Hammond, 1952; Lippincott, 1953
  Post Mortem. Hammond, 1953; Lippincott, 1953
  The Stylist. Bles, 1968
  Third Party Risk. Bles, 1962
  A Touch of Drama. Hammond, 1960
  The Whipping Boys. Hammond, 1958

CULLUM, RIDGWELL. 1867-1943.
  -The Brooding Wild. Chapman, 1905
  -The Bull Moose. Chapman, 1931; Lippincott, 1931
  -The Candy Man. Palmer, 1926. U.S. title: Child of the North. Doran, 1926
  Child of the North; see The Candy Man
  -The Compact. Chapman, 1926
  -The Devil's Keg. Chapman, 1903. U.S. title: The Story of the Foss River Ranch. Page, 1903. Also published as: Foss River Ranch; or, The Devil's Keg. Newnes, 1927
  -The Flaming Wilderness. Chapman, 1934; Lippincott, 1934
  The Forfeit; see The Purchase Price
  Foss River Ranch; or, The Devil's Keg; see The Devil's Keg
  -The Golden Woman. Chapman, 1913; Jacobs, 1913
  -The Heart of Unaga. Chapman, 1920; Putnam, 1920
  -The Hound from the North. Chapman, 1904; Page, 1904
  -In the Brooding Wild. Page, 1905. (British title?)
  -The Law of the Gun. Chapman, 1918; Jacobs, 1918
  -The Law Breakers. Chapman, 1914; Jacobs, 1914
  -The Luck of the Kid. Palmer, 1923; Putnam, 1923
  The Man from the Lias River; see The Saint of the Speedway
  -The Man in the Twilight. Palmer, 1922; Putnam, 1923
  -The Men Who Wrought. Chapman, 1916; Jacobs, 1916
  -The Mystery of the Barren Lands. Cassell, 1928; Lippincott, 1928
  -The Night Riders. Chapman, 1906; Jacobs, 1913
  One Who Kills. Chapman, 1938; Lippincott, 1938
  -The One-Way Trail. Chapman, 1911; Jacobs, 1911
  -The Purchase Price. Chapman, 1917. U.S. title: The Forfeit. Jacobs, 1917
  -The Riddle of Three-Way Creek. Palmer, 1925; Doran, 1925
  -The Saint of the Speedway. Palmer, 1924; Doran, 1924. Also published as: The Man from the Lias River. Brown Watson, 1950
  -Sheets in the Wind. Chapman, 1932; Lippincott, 1932
  -The Sheriff of Dyke Hole. Chapman, 1909; Jacobs, 1909
  -The Son of his Father. Chapman, 1915; Jacobs, 1915
  The Story of the Foss River Ranch; see The Devil's Keg
  -The Tiger of Cloud River. Cassell, 1929; Lippincott, 1929
  -The Trail of the Axe. Chapman, 1910; Jacobs, 1910
  -The Treasure of Big Waters. Cassell, 1930; Lippincott, 1930
  -The Triumph of John Kars. Chapman, 1917; Jacobs, 1917
  -The Twins of Suffering Creek. Chapman, 1912; Jacobs, 1912
  -The Vampire of N'Gobi. Chapman, 1935; Lippincott, 1936
  -The Watchers of the Plains. Chapman, 1908; Jacobs, 1909
  -The Way of the Strong. Chapman, 1914; Jacobs, 1914
  -The Wolf Pack. Palmer, 1927; Lippincott, 1927

CULPAN, MAURICE. 1918-   . Series character: Chief Inspector Bill Houghton, in at least those marked BH.
  Bloody Success. Collins, 1969 BH
  In a Deadly Vein. Collins, 1967
  The Minister of Injustice. Collins, 1966; Walker, 1966 BH
  A Nice Place to Die. Collins, 1965 BH
  The Vasiliko Affair. Collins, 1968 BH

CULVER, TIMOTHY J. Pseudonym of Donald E(dwin) Westlake, 1933-   , q.v. Other pseudonyms: Tucker Coe, Richard Stark, qq.v.
  -Ex Officio. Evans, 1970. Also published as: Power Play. Dell, 1971

CUMBERLAND, GERALD. Pseudonym of Charles Frederick Kenyon, 1879-1926.
  The Cypress Chest. Richards, 1927
  -Tales of a Cruel Country. Richards, 1919; Brentano's, 1919 ss

CUMBERLAND, MARTEN. 1892-   . Pseudonym: Kevin O'Hara, q.v. Series character: Saturnin Dax, in at least those marked SD.
  And Then Came Fear. Hurst, 1949; Doubleday, 1948 SD
  And Worms Have Eaten Them. Hurst, 1948. U.S. title: Hate Will Find a Way. Doubleday, 1947 SD
  Attention! Saturnin Dax. Hutchinson, 1962 SD
  Bird of Prey. Gramol, 1937
  Booked for Death. Hurst, 1952. U.S. title: Grave Consequences. Doubleday, 1952 SD
  The Charge is Murder. Hurst, 1953 SD
  Confetti can be Red. Hurst, 1951. U.S. title: The House in the Forest. Doubleday, 1950 SD
  The Crime School. Eldon, 1949
  The Dark House. Gramol, 1935
  Darkness as a Bride. Hurst, 1947
  Devil's Snare. Gramol, 1935
  The Dice were Loaded. Hutchinson, 1965 SD
  A Dilemma for Dax; see Hearsed in Death
  Etched in Violence. Hurst, 1953 SD
  Everything He Touched. Macdonald, 1945
  Fade Out the Stars. Hurst, 1952; Doubleday, 1952 SD
  Far Better Dead! Hutchinson, 1957 SD
  The Frightened Brides. Hurst, 1954 SD
  Grave Consequences; see Booked for Death
  Hate Finds a Way. Hutchinson, 1964 SD
  Hate for Sale. Hutchinson, 1957; British Book Centre, 1957 SD
  Hate Will Find a Way; see And Worms Have Eaten Them
  Hearsed in Death. Hurst, 1947. U.S. title: A Dilemma for Dax. Doubleday, 1946 SD
  The House in the Forest; see Confetti can be Red
  The Imposter. Gramol, 1935
  The Knife will Fall. Hurst, 1943; Doubleday, 1944 SD
  Loaded Dice, with B. V. Shann. Methuen, 1926. Also published as by James Bevis: Gramol, 1933
  A Lovely Corpse. Hurst, 1946 SD
  Lying at Death's Door. Hurst, 1956 SD
  The Man Who Covered Mirrors. Hurst, 1951; Doubleday, 1949 SD
  Murder at Midnight, with B. V. Shann. Mellifont, 1935
  Murmurs in the Rue Morgue. Hutchinson, 1959; British Book Centre, 1959 SD
  No Sentiment in Murder. Hutchinson, 1966 SD
  Nobody is Safe; see Which of Us is Safe?
  Not Expected to Live. Hurst, 1945 SD
  On the Danger List. Hurst, 1950 SD
  One Foot in the Grave. Hurst, 1952 SD
  Out of This World. Hutchinson, 1958; British Book Centre, 1959 SD
  The Perilous Way. Jarrolds, 1926
  Policeman's Nightmare. Hurst, 1950; Doubleday, 1949 SD
  Postscript to a Death. Hutchinson, 1963 SD
  Questionable Shape. Hurst, 1941 SD
  Quislings over Paris. Hurst, 1942 SD
  Remains to be Seen. Hutchinson, 1960 SD
  Shadowed. Mellifont, 1936
  -The Sin of David. Selwyn, 1932
  Someone Must Die. Hurst, 1940 SD
  Steps in the Dark. Hurst, 1945; Doubleday, 1945 SD
  The Testing of Tony. Macdonald, 1943
  There Must be Victims. Hutchinson, 1961 SD
  Unto Death Utterly. Hurst, 1954 SD
  Which of Us is Safe? Hurst, 1953. U.S. title: Nobody is Safe. Doubleday, 1953 SD

CUMBERLAND, STEWART C. Pseudonym of Charles Garner.

-A Fatal Affinity. Blackett, 1889
-Marked for a Victim: A Tale of Modern Black Magic. Ogilvie, 1889. (British title?)
-The Vasty Deep. Low, 1889

CUMMINGS, SCOTT
The Rexworth Mystery. Philadelphia Suburban, 1911

CUMMINS, R(OBERT) E(MMET). 1849-
A Perfect Score. Stratford, 1925

CUNNINGHAM, A(LBERT) B(ENJAMIN). 1888-1962. Pseudonym: Estil Dale, q.v. Series character: Sheriff Jess Roden, in all titles.
The Affair at the Boat Landing. Dutton, 1943
The Bancock Murder Case. Dutton, 1942
Blood Runs Cold; see The Hunter is the Hunted
The Cane-Patch Mystery. Dutton, 1944; Swan, 1953
Death at "The Bottoms". Dutton, 1942
Death Haunts the Dark Lane. Dutton, 1948
Death of a Bullionaire. Dutton, 1947
The Death of a Worldly Woman. Dutton, 1948
Death Rides a Sorrel Horse. Dutton, 1946
Death Visits the Apple Hole. Dutton, 1945
The Great Yant Mystery. Dutton, 1943; Swan, 1959
The Hunter is the Hunted. Dutton, 1950. Also published as: Blood Runs Cold. Mercury, 1954 (abridged)
The Killer Watches the Manhunt. Dutton, 1950; Boardman, 1951
Murder at Deer Lick. Dutton, 1939
Murder at the Schoolhouse. Dutton, 1940
Murder Before Midnight. Dutton, 1945
Murder Without Weapons. Dutton, 1949; Mellifont, 1955
One Man Must Die. Dutton, 1946
Skeleton in the Closet. Dutton, 1951
The Strange Death of Manny Square. Dutton, 1941
Strange Return. Dutton, 1952
Who Killed Pretty Becky Low? Dutton, 1951

CUNNINGHAM, E. V. Pseudonym of Howard (Melvin) Fast, 1914-   , q.v. Other pseudonym: Walter Ericson, q.v. Series character: Harvey Krim, in at least those marked HK.
Alice. Doubleday, 1963; Deutsch, 1965
The Assassin Who Gave Up His Gun. Morrow, 1969
Cynthia. Morrow, 1968; Deutsch, 1969 HK
Helen. Doubleday, 1966; Deutsch, 1967
Lydia. Doubleday, 1964; Deutsch, 1965 HK
Margie. Morrow, 1966; Deutsch, 1968
Millie. Morrow, 1973; Deutsch, 1974
Penelope. Doubleday, 1965; Deutsch, 1966
Phyllis. Doubleday, 1962; Deutsch, 1963
Sally. Morrow, 1967; Deutsch, 1967
Samantha. Morrow, 1967; Deutsch, 1968
Shirley. Doubleday, 1964; Deutsch, 1964
Sylvia. Doubleday, 1960; Deutsch, 1962

CUNNINGHAM, LOUIS ARTHUR. 1900-1954.
Discords of the Deep. Quality, 1938 ss, some criminous
-Fog Over Fundy. Penn, 1936
-The Sign of the Burning Ship. Penn, 1940

CUNNINGHAM, WILLIAM. 1901-   .
Pretty Boy. Vanguard, 1936. British title: Tough Guy. Long, 1938

CUOMO, GEORGE (MICHAEL). 1929-   .
-Among Thieves. Doubleday, 1968; Hodder, 1969

CURLE, RICHARD (HENRY PARNELL). 1883-   .
Corruption. Bobbs, 1933; Constable, 1933
Who Goes Home? Bobbs, 1935; Constable, 1935

CURLEY, THOMAS
-It's a Wise Child. New Author's Guild, 1960; Barker, 1961. Also published as: The Crooked Road. Avon, 1962

CURRIE, BARTON (WOOD), 1878-   , and AUGUSTIN McHUGH
Officer 666. Fly, 1912; Paul, 1912

CURRIER, JAY L. Pseudonym of James Leal Henderson, 1913-   , q.v.
Cargo of Fear. Messner, 1947

CURRINGTON, O. J. 1924-   .
A Bad Night's Work. Deutsch, 1974

CURRY, AVON. Pseudonym of Jean Bowden, 1925-   . Other pseudonym: Jennifer Bland, q.v. Series character: Jerome Aylwin, in at least those marked JA.
Derry Down Death. Allen, 1960 JA
Dying High. Allen, 1961 JA
The Fetish Murders. Ace, 1973. (British title?)
The Girl in the Killer's Bed; see Shack-Up
Hunt for Danger. Milton House, 1974
A Place of Execution. Long, 1969
Shack-Up. Long, 1971. U.S. title: The Girl in the Killer's Bed. Ace, 1972

CURRY, ELLSWORTH
The Happening. Bantam, 1967. (Novelization of the movie.)

CURRY, G. LEA
A Portrush Mystery. Baird, 1909

CURRY, MARIAN STEARNS
Come Sweet Death. Cherry Tree, 1946

CURRY, THOMAS ALBERT. 1900-1976. Pseudonyms: John L. Benton, Albert Jeffers, qq.v.

CURTIES, CAPTAIN HENRY. 1860-   .
-The Blood Bond. White, 1910
-Idina's Lover. Ouseley, 1912
Love and the Law. Jenkins, 1925
Out of the Shadows. Greening, 1908
-A Queen's Error. White, 1911
The Queen's Gate Mystery. Rivers, 1908; Estes, 1908
The Scales of Chance. Constable, 1911
The Silver Shamrock. Greening, 1911
Tears of Angels. Sisley's, 1907
-When England Slept. Everett, 1909

CURTIS, FREDERICK
Vivian Morgan's First Case. Western Mail, 19??

CURTIS, GEORGE and JOSEPHINE DENVER CURTIS
-Chivalry and the Gibbet. Devin-Adair, 1926

CURTIS, JAMES. Pseudonym.
-The Gilt Kid. Cape, 1936
There Ain't No Justice. Cape, 1937; Knopf, 1937

-They Drive by Night. Cape, 1938
What Immortal Hand. Nicholson, 1939
You're in the Racket, Too. Cape, 1937; Knopf, 1938

CURTIS, JEAN LOUIS. 1917-   .
Lucifer's Dream. Lehmann, 1952; Putnam, 1953. (Translation of Gibier de Potence. Paris, 1949.)

CURTIS, JOSEPHINE DENVER. See: GEORGE CURTIS.

CURTIS, MARJORIE. Pseudonym of Marjorie Mary Curtis Prebble, 1912-   .
Dew in the Morning. Hale, 1975

CURTIS, PETER. Pseudonym of Norah (Robinson) Lofts, 1904-   , q.v.
The Bride of Moat House. Dell, 1969. (British title?)
Dead March in Three Keys. Davies, 1940. Reprinted as by Norah Lofts: Hodder, 1970. U.S. title: No Question of Murder. Doubleday, 1959
The Devil's Own. Macdonald, 1960; Doubleday, 1960. Also published as: The Witches. Pan, 1966; and as: The Little Wax Doll. Hodder, 1971; Doubleday, 1970
Lady Living Alone. Macdonald, 1945
The Little Wax Doll; see The Devil's Own
No Question of Murder; see Dead March in Three Keys
The Witches; see The Devil's Own

CURTIS, RICHARD. Series character: Dave Bolt (The Pro), in all titles.
Death in the Crease. Warner, 1975
Strike Zone. Warner, 1975
The Suicide Squad. Warner, 1975
The $3 Million Turn-Over. Warner, 1974

CURTIS, ROBERT
Curiosities of Detection; or, The Sea-Coast Station and Other Tales. Ward, 1862 ss
The Irish Police Officer. Ward, 1861 ss

CURTIS, ROBERT (G.)
The Children of Light. Hutchinson, 1935
Corpses Can't Walk. Hutchinson, 1936
The Green Pack. Hutchinson, 1933; Doubleday, 1933, as by Edgar Wallace and R. G. Curtis. (Novelization of the play by Edgar Wallace, 1875-1932, q.v.)
Invitation to Murder. Hutchinson, 1936
The Man Who Changed His Name. Hutchinson, 1934; Doubleday, 1934, as by Edgar Wallace and R. G. Curtis. (Novelization of the play by Edgar Wallace, 1875-1932, q.v.)
The Mouthpiece. Hutchinson, 1935; Dodge, 1936, as by Edgar Wallace and Robert Curtis. (Novelization of the play by Edgar Wallace, 1875-1932, q.v.)
Sanctuary Island. Hutchinson, 1936. (Novelization of the play by Edgar Wallace, 1875-1932, q.v.)
Smoky Cell. Hutchinson, 1935. (Novelization of the play by Edgar Wallace, 1875-1932, q.v.
The Table. Hutchinson, 1936. (Novelization of the play by Edgar Wallace, 1875-1932, q.v.

CURTIS, SPENCER
A Picture of Murder. Hale, 1972
Step into Murder. Hale, 1971

CURTIS, SUSANNAH
The Monk's Retreat. Hurst, 1973

CURTIS, WADE. Pseudonym of Jerry E. Pournelle. Series character: Paul Crane, in both titles.
Red Dragon. Berkley, 1971
Red Heroin. Berkley, 1969

CURTIS, WARDON ALLAN. 1867- .
The Strange Adventures of Mr. Middleton. Stone, 1903 ss

CURTISS, E(LIZABETH) M(ANGAM). Series character: Dr. Bunce, in both titles.
Dead Dogs Bite. Simon, 1939
Nine Doctors and a Madman. Simon, 1937; Jenkins, 1938

CURTISS, PHILIP EVERETT. 1855-1964.
Crater's Gold. Harper, 1919; Butterworth, 1920
The Gay Conspirators. Harper, 1924
The Mysterious Mr. Pickering; see Wanted: A Fool
Wanted: A Fool. Harper, 1920. British title: The Mysterious Mr. Pickering. Butterworth, 1921

CURTISS, URSULA (REILLY). 1923- .
Catch a Killer; see The Noonday Devil
Child's Play; see Out of the Dark
Danger: Hospital Zone. Dodd, 1966; Hodder, 1967
The Deadly Climate. Dodd, 1954; Eyre, 1955
Don't Open the Door. Dodd, 1968; Hodder, 1969
The Face of the Tiger. Dodd, 1958; Eyre, 1960
The Forbidden Garden. Dodd, 1962; Eyre, 1963. Also published as: Whatever Happened to Aunt Alice? Ace, 1969
The Hollow House; see The Second Sickle
Hours to Kill. Dodd, 1961; Eyre, 1962
The Iron Cobweb. Dodd, 1953; Eyre, 1953
Letter of Intent. Dodd, 1971; Macmillan (London), 1972
The Noonday Devil. Dodd, 1951; Eyre, 1953. Also published as: Catch a Killer. PB, 1953
Out of the Dark. Dodd, 1964. British title: Child's Play. Eyre, 1965
The Second Sickle. Dodd, 1950. British title: The Hollow House. Evans, 1951
So Dies the Dreamer. Dodd, 1960; Eyre, 1960
The Stairway. Dodd, 1957; Eyre, 1958
Voice Out of Darkness. Dodd, 1948; Evans, 1949
The Wasp. Dodd, 1963; Eyre, 1964
Whatever Happened to Aunt Alice?; see The Forbidden Garden
Widow's Web. Dodd, 1956; Eyre, 1956

CURTOIS, M(ARGARET) A(NNE)
In Minden Town. Faber and Gwyer, 1926

CURWOOD, JAMES OLIVER. 1878-1927.
Philipp Steele of the Royal Northwest Mounted Police. Bobbs, 1911; Everett, 1912

CURZON, COLIN. Series character: Mark Antony, in both titles.
The Body in the Barrage Balloon; or, Who Killed the Corpse? Hurst, 1941; Macmillan, 1942
The Case of the Eighteenth Ostrich. Hurst, 1943; Macmillan, 1944

CUSACK, (ELLEN) DYMPHNA
Say No to Death. Heinemann, 1951

CUSHING, E. LOUISE. Series character: Inspector MacKay, in at least those marked M.
Blood on My Rug. Arcadia, 1956 M
Murder Without Regret. Arcadia, 1954 M
Murder's No Picnic. Arcadia, 1953; Wright, 1956
The Unexpected Corpse. Arcadia, 1957 M

CUSHMAN, CLARISSA FAIRCHILD. 1889-
The Fatal Step. Little, 1953
I Wanted to Murder. Farrar, 1940; Methuen, 1941

CUSHMAN, DAN. 1909- . Series character: Crawford, in at least those marked C.
-The Fabulous Finn. GM, 1954; Fawcett (London), 1955
-The Forbidden Land. GM, 1958; Fawcett (London), 1959
Jewel of the Java Sea. GM, 1951; Red Seal, 1957
-Jungle She. GM, 1953; Fawcett (London), 1954
Naked Ebony. GM, 1951; Fawcett (London), 1953 C
Opium Flower. Bantam, 1963; Hammond, 1964
Port Orient. GM, 1955
Savage Interlude. GM, 1952; Fawcett (London), 1953 C
-Timberjack. GM, 1953; Fawcett (London), 1955
-Tongking! Ace, 1954

CUSSLER, CLIVE (ERIC). 1931- .
Iceberg. Dodd, 1975; Sphere, 1976
The Mediterranean Caper. Pyramid, 1973

D

D., A. E. Pseudonym of Alice Elizabeth Dracott.
A Mystery at King's Grant. SPCK, 1896

D., E. A. B. Pseudonym of E. A. Bland.
Constable 42Z. Religious Tract Society, 1888

DABBS, GEORGE H(ENRY) R(OQUE)
The Manor Inn. Deacon, 1899

DA CRUZ, DANIEL (JR.). 1921- . Series characters: Jock Sargent = JS; Ape Swain = AS.
Deep Kill. GM, 1974 JS
Double Kill. GM, 1973; Coronet, 1973 JS
The Landfall Finesse. Ballantine, 1975 AS
The Pipe Dream Finesse. Ballantine, 1975 AS
Sky Kill. GM, 1974; Coronet, 1976 JS
Vulcan's Hammer. New American Library, 1967

DAEMER, WILL. Joint pseudonym of Robert Wade, 1920- , q.v., and Bill Miller, 1920-1961. Other joint pseudonyms: Whit Masterston, Wade Miller, Dale Wilmer. See also: Bob Wade.
The Case of the Lonely Lovers. Farrell, 1951

DAGLESS, THOMAS
The Light in Dends Wood, and other stories. Greening, 1903 ss, some criminous

DAHL, ROALD. 1916- .
Kiss Kiss. Knopf, 1960; Joseph, 1960 ss
Someone Like You. Knopf, 1953; Secker, 1954. Revised and expanded edition: Joseph, 1961 ss

DAHLGREN, MADELEINE VINTON. 1825-1898.
The Woodley Lane Ghost and other stories. Drexel Biddle, 1899 ss, some criminous

DAIGER, K(ATHERINE) S. Series character: Insp. Everett Anderson, in both titles.
Fourth Degree. Macrae Smith, 1931; Harrap, 1932
Murder on Ghost Tree Island. Macrae Smith, 1934; Harrap, 1934

DAINGERFIELD, FOXHALL (ALEXANDER). 1887-1933.
Ghost House. Appleton, 1926
The House Across the Way. Appleton, 1928
The Linden Walk Tragedy. Appleton, 1929
The Silver Urn. Appleton, 1927
That Gay Nineties Murder. Doubleday, 1928

DAINTON, WILLIE. Pseudonym.
-Blind Quest. Nicholson, 1944
The Matsu Dossier. Nicholson, 1948

DAKERS, ANDREW HERBERT. 1887- . Pseudonym: Andrew Stewart, q.v.

DALE, ALAN. Pseudonym of Alfred J. Cohen, 1861-1928.
Ned Bachman, the New Orleans Detective. Ogilvie, 1887

DALE, CELIA (MARJORIE). 1912- .
A Dark Corner. Macmillan (London), 1971
A Helping Hand. Macmillan (London), 1966; Walker, 1966

DALE, DARLEY. Pseudonym of Francesca Maria Steele.
-The Village Blacksmith. Hutchinson, 1892. U.S. title: Reuben Foreman, the Village Blacksmith. Bonner's, 1892

DALE, ESTIL. Pseudonym of A(lbert) B(enjamin) Cunningham, 1888-1962, q.v.
The Last Survivor. Dutton, 1952

DALE, FRANCES. Pseudonym of Phyllis Nan Sortain Cradock.
-Scorpion's Suicide. Hurst, 1942

DALE, HENRY
Adventurous Exploits of the Younger Brothers. Street, 1890

DALE, OLIVER
A Bit of Red May. Allen, 1896
Strange Stories of Strange People. Henry, 1894 ss, some criminous

DALE, VIRGINIA
They Waited for the Night. Doubleday, 1939

DALE, WILLIAM
John Doe—Murderer. Gateway, 1942; United Authors, 1946
Outside the Law. Dodge, 1938
The Terror of the Handless Corpse. Gateway, 1939

DALEY, JOSEPH A(NDREW). 1927- .
Spicy Lady. St. Martin's, 1973; Macdonald, 1974

DALHEATH, DAVID
The Shadow of the Cobra. Hale, 1975

DALL, JACK
Death of a Revolutionist. Gateway, 1940. Also published as: Murder Moves On. Green Dragon, 194? (abridged)

DALLAS, DUNCAN
  "I.L.F." Ouseley, 1909
  Paul Richards—Detective. Ouseley, 1908 ss

DALLAS, JOHN. Pseudonym of W(illiam) Murdoch Duncan, 1909-1975, q.v. Other pseudonyms: John Cassells, Neill Graham, Martin Locke, Peter Malloch, Lovat Marshall, qq.v.
  The Night of the Storm. Jenkins, 1961
  Red Ice. Hale, 1973

DALLAS, OSWALD (C. C.). See: DRAYCOT (MONTAGU) DELL, 1888- .

DALLAS, RICHARD. Pseudonym of Nathan Winslow Williams, 1860-1924.
  A Master Hand. Putnam, 1903

DALMAINE, JAMES
  The Vengeance of Science. Stockwell, 1927

DALMAN, MAX
  Buried Once. Ward, 1946
  The Burnt Bones Mystery. Ward, 1940
  Death Before Day. Ward, 1942
  Death Disposes. Ward, 1945
  Death on May Morning. Ward, 1938
  Doctor Disappears. Ward, 1941
  The Elusive Nephew. Ward, 1948
  Herald of Death. Ward, 1943
  The Hidden Light. Ward, 1937
  Mask for Murder. Ward, 1940
  The Missing Grave. Ward, 1939
  Poison Unknown. Ward, 1939
  Third Alibi. Ward, 1942
  Three Strangers. Ward, 1937
  Vampire Abroad. Ward, 1938

DALMAS, HERBERT
  Exit Screaming. Walker, 1966
  The Fowler Formula. Doubleday, 1967; Gollancz, 1968

D'ALPINS, MARCHIONESS
  The House of the Lost Court. Hodder, 1908

DALTON, EMMETT. 1871- .
  Beyond the Law. Ogilvie, 1916

DALTON, MORAY. Series character: Inspector Hugh Collier, in at least those marked HC.
  The Art School Murders. Low, 1943
  The Belfry Murder. Low, 1933 HC
  The Belgrave Manor Crime. Low, 1935 HC
  The Black Death. Low, 1934
  The Black Wings. Jarrolds, 1927
  The Body in the Road. Low, 1931; Harper, 1930
  The Case of Alan Copeland. Low, 1937
  The Case of the Dark Stranger. Low, 1948 HC
  The Condamine Case. Low, 1947 HC
  Death at the Villa. Low, 1946
  Death in the Cup. Low, 1932
  Death in the Dark. Low, 1938 HC
  Death in the Forest. Low, 1939 HC
  Death of a Spinster. Low, 1951 HC
  The Edge of Doom. Low, 1934
  The Harvest of Tares. Low, 1933 HC
  The House of Fear. Low, 1951
  Inquest on Miriam. Low, 1949 HC
  The Kingsclere Mystery. Jarrolds, 1924
  The Longbridge Murders. Low, 1945 HC
  The Murder of Eve. Low, 1945
  The Mystery of the Kneeling Woman. Low, 1936 HC
  The Night of Fear. Low, 1931; Harper, 1931 HC
  One by One They Disappeared. Jarrolds, 1929; Harper, 1929 HC
  The Price of Silence. Low, 1939
  The Shadow on the Wall. Jarrolds, 1926
  The Strange Case of Harriet Hall. Low, 1936 HC
  The Stretton Darknesse Mystery. Jarrolds, 1927
  The Wife of Baal. Low, 1932

DALTON, PRISCILLA. Pseudonym of Michael (Angelo) Avallone (Jr.), 1924- , q.v. Other pseudonyms: Mark Dane, Jean-Anne de Pre, Steve Michaels, Dorothea Nile, Dora Highland, Edwina Noone, Sidney Stuart, Max Walker, qq.v.
  The Darkening Willows. Paperback Library, 1965
  90 Gramercy Park. Paperback Library, 1965
  The Silent, Silken Shadows. Paperback Library, 1965

DALY, CARROLL JOHN. 1889-1958. Series characters: Vee Brown, in at least those marked VB; Satan Hall, in at least those marked SH; Race Williams, in at least those marked RW.
  The Amateur Murderer. Washburn, 1933; Hutchinson, 1933 RW
  Better Corpses. Hale, 1940
  Death's Juggler; see The Mystery of the Smoking Gun
  Emperor of Evil. Stokes, 1937; Hutchinson, 1936 VB
  The Hidden Hand. Clode, 1929; Hutchinson, 1930 RW
  The Man in the Shadows. Clode, 1928; Hutchinson, 1929
  Mr. Strang. Stokes, 1936; Hale, 1937
  Murder at Our House. Museum, 1950
  Murder from the East. Stokes, 1935; Hutchinson, 1935 RW
  Murder Won't Wait. Washburn, 1933; Hutchinson, 1934 VB
  The Mystery of the Smoking Gun. Stokes, 1936. British title: Death's Juggler. Hutchinson, 1935 SH
  Ready to Burn. Museum, 1951 SH
  The Snarl of the Beast. Clode, 1927; Hutchinson, 1928
  The Tag Murders. Clode, 1930; Hutchinson, 1931 RW
  Tainted Power. Clode, 1931; Hutchinson, 1931 RW
  The Third Murderer. Farrar, 1931; Hutchinson, 1932 RW
  The White Circle. Clode, 1926; Hutchinson, 1927

DALY, ELIZABETH. 1878-1967. Series character: Henry Gamadge, in all titles.
  And Dangerous to Know. Rinehart, 1949; Hammond, 1952
  Any Shape or Form. Farrar, 1945; Hammond, 1949
  Arrow Pointing Nowhere. Farrar, 1944; Hammond, 1946. Also published as: Murder Listens In. Bantam, 1949
  The Book of the Crime. Rinehart, 1951; Hammond, 1954
  The Book of the Dead. Farrar, 1944; Hammond, 1946
  The Book of the Lion. Rinehart, 1948; Hammond, 1951
  Deadly Nightshade. Farrar, 1940; Hammond, 1948
  Death and Letters. Rinehart, 1950; Hammond, 1953
  Evidence of Things Seen. Farrar, 1943; Hammond, 1946
  The House Without the Door. Farrar, 1942; Hammond, 1945
  Murder Listens In; see Arrow Pointing Nowhere
  Murders in Volume 2. Farrar, 1941; Eyre, 1943
  Night Walk. Rinehart, 1947; Hammond, 1950
  Nothing Can Rescue Me. Farrar, 1943; Hammond, 1945
  Shroud for a Lady; see The Wrong Way Down
  Somewhere in the House. Rinehart, 1946; Hammond, 1949
  Unexpected Night. Farrar, 1940; Gollancz, 1940
  The Wrong Way Down. Rinehart, 1946; Hammond, 1950. Also published as: Shroud for a Lady. Bestseller, 1956

DAMER, ANNE and JACK DENTON SCOTT, 1915- , q.v.
  Too Lively to Live. Doubleday, 1945

DAMIEN, CHRISTINE
  Appleshaw. Ballantine, 1975

DANA, FRANCIS
  The Decoy. Lane, 1902

DANA, FREEMAN
  Murder at the New York World's Fair. Random, 1938

DANA, MARVIN. 1867- .
  The Lake Mystery. McClurg, 1923
  The Master Mind. Fly, 1913. (Novelization of the play by Daniel D. Carter.)
  The Mystery of the Third Parrot. McClurg, 1924; Hodder, 1925
  Paid; see Within the Law
  Within the Law. Fly, 1913; Mills, 1913, as by Marvin Dana and Esme Forest. Also published as: Paid. Grosset, 1930. (Novelization of the play by Bayard Veiller, 1869-1943, q.v.)

DANA, RICHARD. Pseudonym of Lauran Bosworth Paine, 1916- . Other pseudonyms: John Armour, Reg Batchelor, Kenneth Bedford, Frank Bosworth, Mark Carrel, Robert Clarke, J. F. Drexler, Troy Howard, Jared Ingersol, John Kilgore, Hunter Liggett, J. K. Lucas, John Morgan, qq.v.
  Death of a Millionaire. Hale, 1969
  Death was the Echo. Hale, 1975
  Murder in Paradise. Hale, 1969
  Murderer's Moon. Hale, 1969

DANA, ROSE. Pseudonym of W(illiam) E(dward) D(aniel) Ross, 1912- , q.v. Other pseudonyms: Jan Daniels, Ellen Randolph, Clarissa Ross, Dan Ross, Dana Ross, Marilyn Ross, qq.v.
  Brooding Mist. Hale, 1967

DANBY, FRANK. Pseudonym of Julia Davis Frankau, 1864-1916.
  -The Sphinx's Lawyer. Heinemann, 1906; Stokes, 1906
  The Story Behind the Verdict. Cassell, 1915; Dodd, 1915

DANBY, H. C.
  -Clang on the Anvil. Jarrolds, 1946
  -Sleeping Dogs Laugh. Jarrolds, 1948

DANE, CLEMENCE and HELEN (De GUERRY) SIMPSON, 1897-1940, q.v. Clemence Dane is the pseudonym of Winifred Ashton. Series character: Sir John Saumarez = JS.
  Author Unknown; see Printer's Devil
  Enter Sir John. Hodder, 1928; Cosmopolitan, 1928 JS
  Printer's Devil. Hodder, 1930. U.S. title: Author Unknown. Cosmopolitan, 1930

Re-Enter Sir John. Hodder, 1932; Farrar, 1932 JS

DANE, DANIEL. Pseudonym of Ernest S. Hanson.
Vengeance is Mine. Cassell (New York & London), 1890. Also published as: Is She Not a Woman?; or, Vengeance is Mine. Cassell (New York), 1895

DANE, ELLIOTT
Crime Takes the Count. Background, 1948

DANE, EVA
Shadows in the Fire. Macdonald, 1975

DANE, JOEL Y. Pseudonym of Joseph Francis Delany, 1905- . Series character: Sergeant Cass Harty = CH.
The Cabana Murders. Doubleday, 1937 CH
The Christmas Tree Murders. Doubleday, 1938 CH
Grasp at Straws. Doubleday, 1938 CH
Murder Cum Laude. Smith & Haas, 1935. British title: Murder in College. Bell, 1935
Murder in College; see Murder Cum Laude

DANE, JOHN COLIN
The Hidden House. Cassell, 1906

DANE, MARK. Pseudonym of Michael (Angelo) Avallone (Jr.), 1924- , q.v. Other pseudonyms: Priscilla Dalton, Jean-Anne de Pre, Dora Highland, Steve Michaels, Dorothea Nile, Edwina Noone, Sidney Stuart, Max Walker, qq.v.
Felicia. Belmont, 1964. (Novelization of the movie.)

DANE, MARY. Pseudonym of Nigel Morland, 1905- , q.v. Other pseudonyms: John Donavan, Norman Forrest, Roger Garnett, Neal Shepherd, Vincent McCall, qq.v.
Death Traps the Killer. Wright, 1938

DANIEL, F(ERDINAND) E(UGENE). 1839-1914.
-The Strange Case of Dr. Bruno. Guarantee, 1906

DANIEL, GLYN (EDMUND). 1914- . Pseudonym: Dilwyn Rees, q.v. Series character: Sir Richard Cherington, in the title below and that published as by Dilwyn Rees.
Welcome Death. Gollancz, 1954; Dodd, 1955

DANIEL, ROBIN
Death by Drowning. Gollancz, 1960; Walker, 1961

DANIEL, (WILLIAM) ROLAND. 1880-1969.
Series characters: Wu Fang, in at least those marked WF; Michael Grant, in at least those marked MG; John Hopkins, in at least those marked JH; Buddy Mustard, in at least those marked BM; Brian O'Malley, in at least those marked BO; Jack Pearson, in at least those marked JP; The Remover, in at least those marked R; Bill Saville, in at least those marked BS; Michael Wallace, in at least those marked MW.
Again the Remover. Wright, 1939 R, BS
All Thugs are Dangerous. Wright, 1958
Amber Eyes. Wright, 1935
Ann Turns Detective. Wright, 1932
The Arch-Criminal. Wright, 1933
Arrested for Murder. Wright, 1950 BO
The Arrow of Death. Wright, 1951 BM
At the Silver Butterfly. Wright, 1938
The Big Racket. Wright, 1955
The Big Shot. Wright, 1962 BM
The Big Squeal. Wright, 1940
The Black Eagle. Wright, 1950
The Black Market. Wright, 1943
The Black Raven. Wright, 1939
The Blackmailer. Wright, 1934 R, BS
The Blonde Murder Case. Wright, 1939
The Brown Murder Case. Shaylor, 1930
Brunettes are Dangerous. Wright, 1960 MG
The Buddha's Secret. Wright, 1937
A Bunch of Crooks. Wright, 1946
The Case of the Blackmailed King; see The Case of the King of Montavia
The Case of the King of Montavia. Wright, 1953. Also published as: The Case of the Blackmailed King. Mellifont, 1955
The Crackswoman. Wright, 1932 JP
The Crawshay Jewel Mystery. Wright, 1941 BM
The Crimson Shadow. Wright, 1935 JP
Dangerous Mission. Wright, 1959
Dangerous Moment. Wright, 1957
Deadly Mission. Wright, 1961 BO
A Dead Man Sings. Wright, 1949 BM
Dead Man's Corner. Wright, 1932
Dead Man's Vengeance. Shaylor, 1931
Death by the Lake. Wright, 1963 MG
The Death House. Wright, 1941
The Desert Crime. Wright, 1946
The Devil Woman. Wright, 1964 BO
The Doublecrosser. Wright, 1942
A Double-Crossing Traitor. Wright, 1959
The Dragon's Claw. Wright, 1934
Evil Eyes. Wright, 1942
Evil Shadows. Wright, 1944 BM
The Female Spy. Wright, 1964 BO
Frightened Eyes. Wright, 1956 MG
The Gangster. Wright, 1932
The Gangster's Daughter. Wright, 1965 BM
The Gangster's Last Shot. Wright, 1939 JP
The Girl by the Roadside. Wright, 1942
The Girl in the Dark. Wright, 1945
The Great Secret. Wright, 1958
The Green Jade God. Wright, 1932
The Hangman Waits. Wright, 1963 BM
The Haughton Diamond Robbery. Wright, 1947
Human Vultures. Wright, 1939
The Hunchback of Soho. Wright, 1943
Husky Voice. Wright, 1932
It Happened at Night. Wright, 1952
The Jail-Breakers. Wright, 1934
The Kenya Tragedy. Wright, 1948
Kidnapped Wife. Wright, 1965
The Kidnappers. Wright, 1959 MG
The Killer. Wright, 1935
Killers Must Die. Wright, 1955
The Lady in Scarlet. Wright, 1947 BM
The Lady Turned Traitor. Wright, 1961
The Lady was a Spy. Wright, 1962 MW
The Langley Murder Case. Wright, 1938
The Little Old Lady. Wright, 1950
The 'Lo Sweeny Gang. Wright, 1935
Lovely But Dangerous. Wright, 1960 MW
The Man from Paris. Wright, 1958 BM
The Man from Prison. Wright, 1949
The Man Who Sold Secrets. Wright, 1948
The Man Who Sought Trouble. Wright, 1935
The Man with the Magnetic Eyes. Wright, 1938
The Millionaire Crook. Wright, 1944
The Missing Body. Wright, 1961 BM
The Missing Heiress. Wright, 1942
The Missing Lady. Wright, 1937
Mrs. Greystone—Murdered. Wright, 1947
Murder at a Cottage. Wright, 1949 BM
Murder at Little Malling. Wright, 1946 JP
The Murder Gang. Wright, 1954 BM
Murder Goes Free. Wright, 1954
Murder in Dawson City. Wright, 1957
Murder in Ocean Drive. Wright, 1964 MG
Murder in Piccadilly. Wright, 1950
Murder of a Bookmaker. Wright, 1953
Murder of Guy Thorpe. Wright, 1956
The Murphy Gang. Wright, 1934
The Mystery of Mary Hamilton. Wright, 1932
Night Club Murder. Wright, 1963 MW
On the Run. Wright, 1955
The Princess' Own. Wright, 1933
The Prisoner. Wright, 1965 MW
The Professor. Wright, 1944 BM
Quicksilver. Wright, 1953
Red-Headed Dames and Murder. Wright, 1960 MG
Red Murchison. Wright, 1936
The Remover. Wright, 1933 R, BS
The Remover Returns. Wright, 1935 R, BS
The Return of Wu Fang. Wright, 1937 WF
The River Gang. Wright, 1938
The Rosario Murder Case. Brentano's, 1930 JH
Ruby of a Thousand Dreams. Wright, 1933
Sally of the Underworld. Wright, 1934
Scarthroat. Wright, 1934; Godwin, 1935
The Secret Hand. Wright, 1936
The Secret Service Girl. Wright, 1966
Shattered Hopes. Wright, 1941
The Shooting of Sergius Leroy. Wright, 1932 JH
The Signal. Wright, 1932
Singapore Kate. Wright, 1943
Slant Eye. Wright, 1940
The Slayer. Wright, 1936
Slick-Fingered Kate. Wright, 1936
Snake Face. Wright, 1936
The Snide Man. Wright, 1937
The Society of the Spiders. Brentano's, 1928 BS
The Son of Wu Fang. Wright, 1935 WF
Special Agent. Wright, 1957
Spencer Blair, G-Man. Wright, 1949
The Spider's Web. Wright, 1943
The Stedman Gang. Wright, 1936
The Stolen Necklace. Wright, 1954
The Stool Pigeon. Wright, 1936
The Stop-at-Nothing Man. Wright, 1950
Suicide can be Murder. Wright, 1956
This Woman is Wanted. Wright, 1940
Three Sundays to Live. Wright, 1952 BM
"The Tipster." Wright, 1937
Trouble at the Inn. Wright, 1953
The Twenty-Two Windows. Wright, 1942
The Undercover Girl. Wright, 1951
White Eagle. Wright, 1933
Women—Dope—and Murder. Wright, 1962 MG
Wu Fang. Brentano's, 1929 WF, BS
Wu Fang's Revenge. Wright, 1934 WF
The Yellow Devil. Wright, 1932
The "Z" Case. Wright, 1947

DANIELS, CORA LINN. 1852- .
The Bronze Buddha. Little, 1899; Gay & Bird, 1899
-Sardia. Lee, 1891

DANIELS, DOROTHY
Affair in Hong Kong. Pyramid, 1969
Affair in Marakesh. Pyramid, 1968
The Angry Scar; see Journey into Terror
The Apollo Fountain. Paperback Library, 1974
The Attic Rope. Lancer, 1970
The Beaumont Tradition. Paperback Library, 1971
Bed of Ashes; see The Last of the Mansions
The Bell. Paperback Library, 1971
Blackthorn. PB, 1975
Blue Devil Suite. Belmont, 1968
The Caldwell Shadow. Paperback Library, 1973
Candle in the Sun. Lancer, 1968

The Carson Inheritance. Paperback Library, 1969
Castle Morvant. Paperback Library, 1972
Child of Darkness. PB, 1974
Cliffside Castle. Lancer, 1965
Conover's Folly. Paperback Library, 1972
The Curse of Mallory Hall. GM, 1970; Coronet, 1972
Dance in Darkness. Lancer, 1965
Danger Mansion; see Nurse at Danger Mansion
Dark Island. Paperback Library, 1972
The Dark Stage. Paperback Library, 1970
Dark Villa. Lancer, 1966
Darkhaven. Paperback Library, 1965
Diablo Manor. Paperback Library, 1971; Star, 1977
Duet. Lancer, 1968
The Duncan Dynasty. Paperback Library, 1973
The Eagle's Nest. Lancer, 1967
Emerald Hill. Paperback Library, 1970
The Exorcism of Jenny Slade. PB, 1974
Ghost Song. PB, 1974
The Guardian of Willow House. PB, 1975; Magna, 1977
Hills of Fire. Paperback Library, 1973
The House of Broken Dolls. Paperback Library, 1972
House of False Faces. Paperback Library, 19??
The House of Many Doors. Paperback Library, 19??
House of Stolen Memories. Lancer, 1967. Also published as: Mansion of Lost Memories. Lancer, 1969
House of the Seven Courts. Lancer, 1967
The House on Circus Hill. Paperback Library, 1972
Illusion at Haven's Edge. PB, 1975; Magna, 1977
Image of a Ghost. Paperback Library, 1973
Island of Bitter Memories. Paperback Library, 1974
Island of Evil. Paperback Library, 1970. (Novelization of the Strange Paradise TV series.)
Jade Green. Paperback Library, 1973
Journey into Terror. Pyramid, 1970. Orig. title: The Angry Scar.
Key Diablo. Paperback Library, 1971
Knight in Red Armor. Lancer, 1966
Lady of the Shadows. Paperback Library, 1968
The Lanier Riddle. Paperback Library, 1972
The Larrabee Heiress. Paperback Library, 1972
The Last of the Mansions. Lancer, 1966. Also published as: Survivors of Darkness. Lancer, 1969. Orig. title: Bed of Ashes
The Leland Legacy. Pyramid, 1965
The Lily Pond. Paperback Library, 1965
The Man from Yesterday. Paperback Library, 1970
Mansion of Lost Memories; see House of Stolen Memories
The Marble Angel; see The Marble Leaf
The Marble Hills. Warner, 1975
The Marble Leaf. Warner, 1966. Also published as: The Marble Angel. Lancer, 1970
Marriott Hall. Paperback Library, 1965
Maya Temple. Paperback Library, 1972
Midday Moon. Lancer, 1966
The Mistress of Falcon Hill. Pyramid, 1965
Mostly by Moonlight. Lancer, 1968
Mystic Manor. Paperback Library, 1966
Nurse at Danger Mansion. Lancer, 1966. Also published as: Danger Mansion. Lancer, 19??

The Possessed. PB, 1975
Possession of Tracy Corbin. Paperback Library, 1973
The Prisoner of Malville Hall. Paperback Library, 1973
The Raging Waters. Pyramid, 1970
Raxl, Voodoo Princess. Paperback Library, 1970. (Novelization of the Strange Paradise TV series.)
The Sevier Secrets. Lancer, 1967
Shadow Glen. Paperback Library, 1965
Shadow of a Man. Popular Library, 1975
Shadows from the Past. Paperback Library, 1972
Shadows of Tomorrow. Paperback Library, 19??
The Silent Halls of Ashenden. Paperback Library, 1973
The Spanish Chapel. Belmont, 1972
The Stone House. Paperback Library, 1973
Survivor of Darkness; see The Last of the Mansions
The Templeton Memoirs. Lancer, 1966
This Ancient Evil. Lancer, 1966
The Tidemill. Popular Library, 1975
The Tormented. Paperback Library, 1969
The Tower Room. Lancer, 1965
Traitor's Road. Lancer, 1967
The Two Worlds of Peggy Scott. PB, 1974; Magna, 1977
The Unearthly. Lancer, 1970
The Unguarded. Lancer, 1965
The Unlamented. PB, 1975
Voice on the Wind. Paperback Library, 1969
The Watcher in the Dark. Ballantine, 1973
A Web of Peril. Pyramid, 1974
Willow Weep. Pyramid, 1970
Witch's Castle. Paperback Library, 1971
Witch's Island. Paperback Library, 1972

DANIELS, HAROLD R(OBERT). 1919- .
The Accused. Dell, 1958; Deutsch, 1961
For the Asking. GM, 1962; Muller pb, 1963
The Girl in 304. Dell, 1956
House on Greenapple Road. Random, 1966; Deutsch, 1967
In his Blood. Dell, 1955
The Snatch. Dell, 1958; Deutsch, 1960

DANIELS, J(EFFERY) R(OBERT)
Crash Programme. Macmillan (London), 1973. U.S. title: First Flight. Coward, 1973
Firegold. Macmillan (London), 1975
First Flight; see Crash Programme

DANIELS, JAN. Pseudonym of W(illiam) E(dward) D(aniel) Ross, 1912- , q.v. Other pseudonyms: Rose Dana, Ellen Randolph, Clarissa Ross, Dan Ross, Dana Ross, Marilyn Ross, qq.v.
Bride for Arundel. Hale, 1966

DANIELS, MAX
Passport to Terror. Avon, 1960

DANIELS, NORMAN (A.). Series characters: Bruce Baron = BB; Kelly Carvel = KC; John Keith = JK.
Arrest and Trial. Lancer, 1963. (Novelization of the TV series.)
The Baron of Hong Kong. Lancer, 1967 BB
Baron's Mission to Peking. Lancer, 196? BB
The Captive. Avon, 1959
Chase. Berkley, 1974. (Novelization of the TV series.)
The Deadly Game. Avon, 1959
The Detectives. Lancer, 1962. (Novelization of the TV series.)
The Hunt Club. Pyramid, 1964 JK
A Killing in the Market. Lancer, 1967
The Kono Diamond. Berkley, 1969
Lady for Sale. Avon, 1960

License to Kill. Pyramid, 1972 KC
Lover, Let Me Live. Avon, 1960
The Magnetic Man. Berkley, 1968. (Novelization of The Avengers TV series.)
The Mausoleum Key. Gateway, 1942
Meet the Smiths. Berkley, 1971. (Novelization of the Smith Family TV series.)
The Missing Witness. Lancer, 1964. (Novelization of the Arrest and Trial TV series.)
Moon Express. Berkley, 1969. (Novelization of The Avengers TV series.)
One Angry Man. Pyramid, 1971 KC
Operation K. Pyramid, 1965 JK
Operation N. Pyramid, 1966 JK
Operation S-L. Pyramid, 1971 JK
Operation T. Pyramid, 1967 JK
Operation VC. Pyramid, 1967 JK
Overkill. Pyramid, 1964 JK
The Rape of a Town. Pyramid, 1970 KC
The Secret War. Pyramid, 1964
Some Die Running. Avon, 1960
Something Burning. GM, 1963; Muller pb, 1963
Spy Ghost. Pyramid, 1965 JK
Spy Hunt. Pyramid, 1960
Suddenly by Shotgun. GM, 1961

DANNAY, FREDERIC. 1905- . Joint pseudonyms with Manfred Bennington Lee, 1905-1971: Ellery Queen, Barnaby Ross, qq.v.

DANNE, MAX HALLAN
Premature Burial. Lancer, 1962. (Novelization of the movie.)

DANNETT, SYLVIA (G. L.). 1909- .
Defy the Tempest, with Edwin Bennett. Messner, 1944
The Door to the Tower. Lancer, 1966
Nor Iron Bars, with Edwin Bennett. Fortuny, 1940

DANNING, MELROD. Pseudonym of Sinclair Gluck, 1887- , q.v.
The Majesty of the Law. Hodder, 1916

DANTON, REBECCA. Pseudonym of Janet Louise Roberts, 1925- , q.v. Other pseudonyms: Louisa Bronte, Janette Radcliffe, qq.v.
Black Horse Tavern. Popular Library, 1972
Sign of the Golden Goose. Popular Library, 1972

DANVERS, JACK. Pseudonym of Camille Auguste Marie Caseleyr, 1909- .
-The End of It All. Heinemann, 1962
-The Living Come First. Heinemann, 1961

DANVERS, MILTON. Series character: Robert Spicer, in at least those marked RS.
A Desperate Dilemma; or, An Unheard of Crime. Diprose, 1892 RS
The Detective's Honeymoon; or, The Doctor of the "Pinjarrah". Diprose, 1894 RS
The Doctor's Crime; or, Simply Horrible! Diprose, 1891
The Fatal Finger Mark, Rose Courtenay's First Case. Diprose, 1895
The Grantham Mystery; or, Confidence and Crime. Diprose, 1893 RS
The "Lone Cross Manor" Mystery; or, Hugh Darrill's Confession. Diprose, 1896
Mysterious Disappearance of a Bride; or, Who was She? Diprose, 1895 RS
The Squire's Fatal Will; or, Twenty Years of Plot and Crime. Diprose, 1897

D'APERY, HELEN BURRELL GIBSON. 1842-1915.
Pseudonym: Olive Harper, q.v.

DARBY, EMMA
A Conflict of Women. Hale, 1971; St. Martin's, 1972
-Into the Arena. Hale, 1969; St. Martin's, 1972

DARBY, J. N. Pseudonym of (Mary) Christine Noble Govan, 1898- , q.v. Other pseudonym: Mary Allerton, q.v.
Murder in the House with the Blue Eyes. Bobbs, 1939

DARBY, RUTH. Series characters: Peter and Janet Barron, in all titles.
Beauty Sleep. Doubleday, 1942
Death Boards the Lazy Lady. Doubleday, 1939
Death Conducts a Tour. Doubleday, 1940
If This be Murder. Doubleday, 1941
Murder with Orange Blossoms. Doubleday, 1943; Muller, 1947

D'ARCY, EDGAR
The Morton Mystery. Popular, 1880

DARD, F(REDERIC). Pseudonym: San Antonio, q.v.
The Man of the Avenue. International, 1969. (Translation of L'Homme de l'Avenue. Paris, 1962.)

DARE, ALAN. Pseudonym of George Goodchild, 1888- , q.v. Other pseudonym: Jesse Templeton, q.v.
-Body and Soul. Jarrolds, 1929
-The Eye of Abu. Jenkins, 1927. Reprinted as by George Goodchild: Newnes, 1934
-The Guarded Soul. Jenkins, 1928
-The Isle of Hate. Jenkins, 1924. Reprinted as by George Goodchild: Newnes, 1935
-Killigrew. Jenkins, 1922
-Out of the Desert. Jenkins, 1925. Reprinted as by George Goodchild: Newnes, 1934

DARE, MICHAEL
Murder Incognito. Partridge, 1947

DARGON. Pseudonym.
The Nameless Order. Lane, 1924

DARK, JAMES. Most if not all of these titles were originally published by Horwitz in Australia. Series character: Mark Hood = MH.
Assignment Hong Kong. Horwitz, 19??. U.S. title: Hong Kong Incident. Signet, 1966 MH
Assignment Tokyo. Signet, 1966 MH
The Bamboo Bomb. Signet, 1965 MH
Come Die with Me. Signet, 1965 MH
Dame on the Lam. Milestone, 1952
A Guy Must Live. Milestone, 1954
Hong Kong Incident; see Assignment Hong Kong
The Invisibles. Signet, 1969 MH
Operation Ice Cap. Signet, 1969 MH
Operation Octopus. Signet, 1968 MH
Operation Scuba. Signet, 1967 MH
Sea Scrape. Signet, 1971 MH
Spy from the Grave. Horwitz, 1964
Spying Blind. Signet, 1968 MH
The Squealer. Milestone, 1954
The Sword of Genghis Khan. Signet, 1967 MH
The Throne of Satan. Signet, 1967 MH

DARK, JOHNNY. Pseudonym of Victor (George Charles) Norwood, 1920- , q.v. Other pseudonyms: Mark Hampton, Hank Janson, Nat Karta, Mark Shane, qq.v.
Snake Walk. Scion, 1951

DARK, REX. Series character: Bartholomew Dane, in at least those marked BD.
The Channing Affair. Wright, 1937 BD
Dead Men Tell... Wright, 1937 BD
The Invisible Hand. Wright, 1937 BD
The Ming Vase Mystery. Wright, 1936 BD
Murder in Berkeley Square. Wright, 1938
The Prison Murder. Wright, 1939
Spy 222. Wright, 1940 BD
The Tremlow Murder Case. Wright, 1938
The Uranian Jewel Case. Wright, 1939 BD
The Wardour Street Mystery. Wright, 1936 BD

DARK, RICHARD. 1876- .
Dibchick. Moray, 1937

DARLINGTON, W(ILLIAM) A(UBREY CECIL). 1890- .
Mr. Cronk's Cases. Jenkins, 1931 ss

DARRELL, GRATIANA
The Haunted Looking Glass. Digby, 1897

DARRELL, STANLEY
Inquest—Eleven Thirty. Crowther, 1947

DARWENT, GEORGE
Mystery in the Snow. Rich, 1935

DAVENPORT, FRANCINE. Pseudonym of Velma Tate, 1913- .
The Secret of the Bayou. Ace, 1966

DAVENPORT, GWEN LEYS. 1910- . Joint pseudonym with Gustav J. Breuer: Michael Hardt, q.v.

DAVEY, JOCELYN. Pseudonym of Chaim Raphael, 1908- . Series character: Ambrose Usher, in all titles.
A Capitol Offense; see The Undoubted Deed
A Killing in Hats. Chatto, 1965
The Naked Villany. Chatto, 1958; Knopf, 1958
A Touch of Stagefright. Chatto, 1960
The Undoubted Deed. Chatto, 1956. U.S. title: A Capitol Offense. Knopf, 1956

DAVID, D(AVID) L(AWRENCE)
This Man is a Spy. Rich, 1948

DAVID, K.
Born to Die. Warren, 1952
I was Alone. Warren, 1952
It's Easier for Homicide. Warren, 1952
The Man Who Went Away. Warren, 1952
Now We are Free. Warren, 1952

DAVIDSON, ANDREW
The Golden Lode. Hutchinson, 1956; Abelard, 1957
-The Wilderness Road. Jarrolds, 1958; Roy, 1959

DAVIDSON, BASIL. 1914- .
-Golden Horn. Cape, 1952

DAVIDSON, DAVID (ALBERT). 1908- .
The Quest of Juror 19. Doubleday, 1971

DAVIDSON, DIANE. 1924- .
-Feversham. Crown, 1969

DAVIDSON, HUGH COLEMAN. 1852- .
The Gargrave Mystery. Warne, 1889
-The Queen of the Black Hand. Trischler, 1890

DAVIDSON, LIONEL. 1922-
A Long Way from Shiloh. Gollancz, 1966. U.S. title: The Menorah Men. Harper, 1966
Making Good Again. Cape, 1968; Harper, 1968
The Menorah Men; see A Long Way from Shiloh
Night of Wenceslas. Gollancz, 1960; Harper, 1960
The Rose of Tibet. Gollancz, 1962; Harper, 1962

DAVIDSON, T. L. Pseudonym of David Landsborough Thomson, 1901-1964.
The Murder in the Laboratory. Methuen, 1929; Dutton, 1929

DAVIES. House name.
The Warehouse Murder. Amalgamated, 1930

DAVIES, A. A. T.
The Horses of Winter. Weidenfeld, 1967

DAVIES, BETTY EVELYN. Pseudonym: Pauline Warwick, q.v.

DAVIES, ERNEST. 1873- . Pseudonym: Oliver Martin, q.v.
-Dives and Son. Rivers, 1910
-The Moment. Rivers, 1911
The Widow's Necklace. Duckworth, 1913; Devin-Adair, 1913

DAVIES, FREDRIC. Joint pseudonym of Ron Ellik, 1938-1968, and Frederic Langley.
The Cross of Gold Affair. Ace, 1968. (Novelization of The Man from U.N.C.L.E. TV series.)

DAVIES, G(EOFFREY) H(OWARD)
Justice by Proxy. Hale, 1967

DAVIES, HUGH SYKES. 1909- .
Full Fathom Five. Lane, 1956
No Man Pursues. Lane, 1950
The Papers of Andrew Melmoth. Methuen, 1960; Morrow, 1961

DAVIES, JOHN
Mystery Flight. Ward, 1956
Sabotage at Sea. Ward, 1959
See Naples and Die. Ward, 1961

DAVIES, JOHN EVAN WESTON. Pseudonym: Berkley Mather, q.v.

DAVIES, KENDAL
Nine Bells. Hutchinson, 1947

DAVIES, L(ESLIE) P(URNELL). 1914- . Pseudonym: Leslie Vardre, q.v.
The Artificial Man. Jenkins, 1965; Doubleday, 1967
Assignment Abacus. Barrie, 1975; Doubleday, 1975
Give Me Back Myself. Barrie, 1972; Doubleday, 1971
The Lampton Dreamers. Jenkins, 1966; Doubleday, 1967
Man Out of Nowhere. Jenkins, 1965. U.S. title: Who is Lewis Pinder? Doubleday, 1966
The Paper Dolls. Jenkins, 1964; Doubleday, 1966
The Shadow Before. Barrie, 1971; Doubleday, 1970
Stranger to Town. Jenkins, 1969; Doubleday, 1969
What Did I Do Tomorrow? Barrie, 1972; Doubleday, 1973
The White Room. Barrie, 1970; Doubleday, 1969
Who is Lewis Pinder?; see Man Out of Nowhere

DAVIES, N. E.
Doctor Cockaigne. Methuen, 1930

DAVIES, RHYS. 1903- .
Nobody Answered the Bell. Heinemann, 1971; Dodd, 1971

DAVIOT, GORDON. Pseudonym of Elizabeth MacKintosh, 1896-1952. Other pseudonym: Josephine Tey. Series character: Inspector Alan Grant = AG, whose cases are continued under the Josephine Tey byline.
The Man in the Queue. Methuen, 1929; Dutton, 1929. Reprinted as by Josephine Tey: Macmillan, 1953. Also published as: Killer in the Crowd, as by Josephine Tey. Mercury, 1954

DAVIS, ANDREW JACKSON. 1826-1910.
Tale of a Physician; or, The Seeds and Fruits of Crime. White, 1869

DAVIS, BERRIE
The Fourth Day of Fear. Putnam, 1973; Barker, 1974

DAVIS, BURTON. 1893- . Joint pseudonym with Clare Ogden Davis, 1892- : Lawrence Saunders, q.v.

DAVIS, CHARLES. 1923- .
Two Weeks to Find a Killer. Carlton, 1966

DAVIS, CLARE OGDEN. 1892- . Joint pseudonym with Burton Davis, 1893- : Lawrence Saunders, q.v.

DAVIS, DOROTHY SALISBURY. 1916- .
Series characters: Mrs. Norris and Jasper Tully = N&T.
Black Sheep, White Lamb. Scribner, 1963; Boardman, 1964
The Clay Hand. Scribner, 1950
Death of an Old Sinner. Scribner, 1957; Secker, 1958 N&T
Enemy and Brother. Scribner, 1967; Hodder, 1967
A Gentle Murderer. Scribner, 1951
A Gentleman Called. Scribner, 1958; Secker, 1958 N&T
God Speed the Night, with Jerome Ross. Scribner, 1968; Hodder, 1969
The Judas Cat. Scribner, 1949
The Little Brothers. Scribner, 1973; Barker, 1974
Old Sinners Never Die. Scribner, 1959; Secker, 1960
The Pale Betrayer. Scribner, 1965; Hodder, 1967
Shock Wave. Scribner, 1972; Barker, 1974
A Town of Masks. Scribner, 1952
Where the Dark Streets Go. Scribner, 1969; Hodder, 1970

DAVIS, DUANE
Bedroom Bang Bang. Series 70, 1968

DAVIS, ELIZABETH
Along Came a Spider. Signet, 1970
My Soul to Keep. Pyramid, 1970
Suffer a Witch to Die. Signet, 1970
There was an Old Woman. Doubleday, 1971; Hale, 1972

DAVIS, FRANKLIN M(ILTON), JR., 1918- .
Series character: Quinn Leland = QL.
Kiss the Tiger. Pyramid, 1961 QL
The Naked and the Lost. Lion, 1954
Secret: Hong Kong. Pyramid, 1962 QL
-Spearhead. Permabooks, 1958

DAVIS, FREDERICK C(LYDE). 1902-1977.
Pseudonyms: Murdo Coombs, Stephen Ransome, qq.v. Series characters: Cyrus Hatch = CH; Schyler Cole & Luke Speare = C&S.
Another Morgue Heard From. Doubleday, 1954. British title: Deadly Bedfellows, as by Stephen Ransome. Gollancz, 1955 C&S
Coffins for Three. Doubleday, 1938. British title: One Murder Too Many. Heinemann, 1938 CH
Deadly Bedfellows; see Another Morgue Heard From
The Deadly Miss Ashley. Doubleday, 1950; Gollancz, 1950, as by Stephen Ransome C&S
Deep Lay the Dead. Doubleday, 1942
Detour to Oblivion. Doubleday, 1947 CH
Drag the Dark. Doubleday, 1953; Gollancz, 1954, as by Stephen Ransome C&S
Gone Tomorrow. Doubleday, 1948 CH
The Graveyard Never Closes. Doubleday, 1940 CH
He Wouldn't Stay Dead. Doubleday, 1939; Heinemann, 1939 CH
High Heel Homicide. Ace, 1961
Let the Skeletons Rattle. Doubleday, 1944 CH
Lilies in Her Garden Grew. Doubleday, 1951; Gollancz, 1951, as by Stephen Ransome C&S
Murder Doesn't Always Out; see Poor, Poor Yorick
Night Drop. Doubleday, 1955; Gollancz, 1956, as by Stephen Ransome C&S
One Murder Too Many; see Coffins for Three
Poor, Poor Yorick. Doubleday, 1939. British title: Murder Doesn't Always Out. Heinemann, 1939 CH
Thursday's Blade. Doubleday, 1947 CH
Tread Lightly, Angel. Doubleday, 1952; Gollancz, 1952, as by Stephen Ransome C&S

DAVIS, FREDERICK WILLIAM. 1858-1933.
Pseudonym: Scott Campbell, q.v.

DAVIS, GEORGE. Series character: Simon Good, in at least those marked SG.
The Crime in Threadneedle Street. Collins, 1968
Death of a Fire-Raiser. Collins, 1974
Friday Before Bank Holiday. Collins, 1964
The Killer Grew Tired. Collins, 1971
Roag's Syndicate. Chapman, 1960 SG
Toledano. Chapman, 1962 SG

DAVIS, GORDON. Pseudonym of (Everette) Howard Hunt, 1918- , q.v. Other pseudonyms: Robert Dietrich, John Q, David St. John, qq.v.
Counterfeit Kill. GM, 1963; Muller pb, 1964. Reprinted as by E. Howard Hunt: Pinnacle, 1975
House Dick. GM, 1961; Muller pb, 1962. Also published as: Washington Payoff. Pinnacle, 1975, as by E. Howard Hunt
I Came to Kill. GM, 1953; Fawcett (London), 1955
Ring Around Rosy. GM, 1964
Washington Payoff; see House Dick
Where Murder Waits. GM, 1965. Reprinted as by E. Howard Hunt: GM, 1973

DAVIS, HARRY. Pseudonym of Elizabeth Roberta Sebenthal, 1917- . Other pseudonym: Paul Kruger, q.v.
My Brother's Wife. Greenberg, 1956
Portrait of Rene. Greenberg, 1956

DAVIS, HELEN
"For So Little": The Story of a Crime. Swan, 1890

DAVIS, HOWARD CHARLES. 1909- . Series characters: Hugh Rudd, in at least those marked HG; Edward Tope, in at least those marked ET.
And Murder Won. Long, 1969
The Big Heist. Long, 1964
The Child Witness. Jarrolds, 1957
Dangerous Twin. Long, 1967
Dead Man's Cross. Long, 1965
Death in the Scillies. Long, 1968
The Death of Laura. Hale, 1963
Desperate Night. Long, 1965
The Gunmen of Gozo. Long, 1970
The Man Who Wasn't Murdered. Jarrolds, 1955
Murder Out of Class. Ward, 1961
Murder Starts from Fishguard. Long, 1966 HR
The Night of the Funeral. Long, 1958
Perhaps to Kill. Hale, 1963
A Pistol for Miss Preedy. Jarrolds, 1956
Renegade from Russia. Long, 1959
The Third Assassin. Long, 1959
The Tortured Boy. Ward, 1961 ET
Trouble in the Bank. Ward, 1960 ET
The Waxworks Spies. Ward, 1962 HR

DAVIS, J(AMES) FRANK. 1870- .
The Chinese Label. Little, 1920

DAVIS, JOHN GORDON
-Years of the Hungry Tiger. Joseph, 1974; Doubleday, 1975

DAVIS, JULIA. 1904- . Pseudonym: F. Draco, q.v.

DAVIS, LAVINIA R(IKER). 1909-1961.
Barren Heritage. Doubleday, 1946
Evidence Unseen. Doubleday, 1945
Reference to Death. Doubleday, 1950
Taste of Vengeance. Doubleday, 1947
Threat of Dragons. Doubleday, 1948; Cherry Tree, 1950

DAVIS, LEOPOLD
Strange Occurrences. Davis, 1877 ss

DAVIS, MARTHA WIRT. Pseudonym: Wirt Van Arsdale, q.v.

DAVIS, MEANS. Series character: Matthew Higgins = MH.
The Chess Murders. Random, 1937
The Hospital Murders. Smith, 1934; Bell, 1934 MH
Murder Without Weapons. Smith, 1934; Bell, 1935 MH

DAVIS, MILDRED (B.)
The Dark Place. Simon, 1955
The Invisible Border. Random, 1974; Hale, 1975
Nightmare of Murder; see Walk into Yesterday
The Room Upstairs. Simon, 1948
The Sound of Insects. Doubleday, 1966; Hodder, 1967
Strange Corner. Doubleday, 1967; Hodder, 1968
Tell Them What's-Her-Name Called. Random, 1975; Hale, 1976
They Buried a Man. Simon, 1953
The Third Half. Doubleday, 1969; Hale, 1970
Three Minutes to Midnight. Random, 1971; Hale, 1973
The Voice on the Telephone. Random, 1964

Walk into Yesterday. Doubleday, 1967. British title: Nightmare of Murder. Hale, 1969

DAVIS, NORBERT. Joint pseudonym with W(illis) T(odhunter) Ballard, 1903- , q.v.: Harrison Hunt, q.v. Series characters: Doan and Carstairs = D&C.
Dead Little Rich Girl; see The Mouse in the Mountain
The Mouse in the Mountain. Morrow, 1943. Also published as: Dead Little Rich Girl. Handi-Books, 1945 D&C
Oh, Murderer Mine. Handi-Books, 1946 D&C
Rendezvous with Fear. Cherry Tree, 1944. (U.S. title?)
Sally's in the Alley. Morrow, 1943; Boardman, 1944

DAVIS, OLIVE BELL
-Exodus: 20. Pageant, 1959

DAVIS, OWEN
At 9:45. French (New York), 1928. British title: 9:45. French (London), 1927. (Play.)
The Donovan Affair. French (New York & London), 1930. (Play.)
The Haunted House. French (New York), 1926. (Play.)
Mr. & Mrs. North. French, 1941. (A play based on stories by Frances & Richard Lockridge, q.v.)
9:45; see At 9:45
The Ninth Guest. French (New York), 1930. (Play based on the novel by Gwen Bristow and Bruce Manning, q.v.)

DAVIS, REGINALD
The Crowing Hen. Bles, 1936; Doubleday, 1936
Nine Days' Panic. Bles, 1937; Doubleday, 1938
Twelve Midnight Street. Bles, 1938

DAVIS, RICHARD HARDING. 1864-1916.
In the Fog. Russell, 1901; Ward, 1901
-The Scarlet Car. Scribner, 1907
-Vera the Medium. Scribner, 1908
-The White Mice. Scribner, 1909

DAVIS, STRATFORD. Pseudonym of Maisie Sharman Bolton, 1915- . Other pseudonym: Maisie Sharman, q.v.
Death in Seven Hours. Melrose, 1952
His Father's Ghost. Abelard (London & New York), 1963
No Tears are Shed. Melrose, 1952
One Man's Secret. Boardman, 1956
The Troubled Mind. Melrose, 1953

DAVIS, TECH. Series character: Aubrey Nash, in all titles.
Full Fare for a Corpse. Doubleday, 1937
Murder on Alternate Tuesdays. Doubleday, 1938
Terror on Compass Lake. Doubleday, 1935

DAVIS, YORKE. Pseudonym.
The Green Cloak. Sturgis, 1910; Sidgwick, 1910

DAVIS, ZEKE
-Invited. Pageant, 1959

DAVISON, G(ILDEROY). 1892- . Series characters: Twisted Face (Straussman) = TF; Peter Castle, in at least those marked PC.
Death in the A.R.P. Jenkins, 1939
The Devil's Apprentice. Jenkins, 1933 TF
The Devil's Diamonds; or, Beauty and the Beast. Jenkins, 1938
A Dog Fight with Death. Jenkins, 1940 TF, PC

Exit Mr. Brent. Jenkins, 1936 PC
Jewel of Destiny. Jenkins, 1938
A Killer at Scotland Yard. Jenkins, 1933
The Lily-Pond Mystery. Jenkins, 1937
The Man with Half a Face. Jenkins, 1936 PC
The Man with the Twisted Face. Jenkins, 1931 TF, PC
Murder in a Muffler; or, Dead Man's Farm. Jenkins, 1937
The Mysterious Mr. Brent. Jenkins, 1935
Mystery of the Red-Haired Valet. Jenkins, 1934 PC
The Prince of Spies. Jenkins, 1932 TF, PC
Robin Hoodwinker, V.C. Jenkins, 1944
Satan's Satellite. Jenkins, 1945
A Traitor Unmasked. Jenkins, 1932 TF
Twisted Face Defends His Title. Jenkins, 1940 TF
Twisted Face Strikes Again. Jenkins, 1939 TF
Twisted Face, the Avenger. Jenkins, 1935 TF

DAVISON, GEOFFREY
The Berlin Spy Trap. Hale, 1974
The Chessboard Spies. Hale, 1969; Roy, 1969
The Fallen Eagles. Hale, 1970
The Honourable Assassins. Hale, 1971
Nest of Spies. Hale, 1968
Spy Puppets. Hale, 1973
The Spy Who Swopped Shoes. Hale, 1967

DAVISON, NORMA
Reivaulx Abbey. Ace, 1975

DAVY, COLIN (KAYSER). 1896- .
Agents of the League. Harrap, 1936
Brown Paper Twice. Collins, 1939
-A Heritage in Trust. Hale, 1957
Mariella—Spy! Harrap, 1935
The Twister's Double. Hale, 1954

DAWE, (WILLIAM) CARLTON. Series character: Colonel Gantian (Leathermouth), in at least those marked G.
The Admiralty's Secret. Long, 1918
After Many Days. Ward, 1928
The Black Spider. Nash, 1911
-A Brush with Fate. Long, 1920
-Captain Castle. Smith Elder, 1897
-The Chief. Ward, 1933
-Claudia Pole. Hutchinson, 1901
-The Confessions of a Currency Girl. Ward, 1894
-The Confessions of Cleodora. Long, 1908
The Crackswoman. Ward, 1914
Crumpled Lilies. Ward, 1933 G
-The Demagogue. Hodder, 1902
-The Desirable Woman. Ward, 1929
-Desperate Love. Ward, 1924
-The Emu's Head. Ward, 1893
-Euryale in London. Ward, 1922 ss
Fifteen Keys. Ward, 1932 G
Fishers of Men. Ward, 1930
-The Forbidden Shrine. Ward, 1926
The Girl from Nippon. Ward, 1915
-The Glare. Ward, 1926
-The Grand Duke. Hutchinson, 1905
The Green Killer. Ward, 1936 G
-Her Highness's Secretary. Nash, 1907
The Knightsbridge Affair. Ward, 1927
-Lammas Grove. Brown, 1904
The Law of the Knife. Ward, 1934 G
Lawless. Ward, 1932
Leathermouth. Ward, 1931 G
Leathermouth's Luck. Ward, 1934 G
-The Life Perilous. Hutchinson, 1907
Live Cartridge. Ward, 1937

The London Plot. Nash, 1908
-The Mighty Arm. Long, 1919
The Missing Clue. Ward, 1930
The Missing Treaty. Ward, 1934 G
-A Morganatic Marriage. Hutchinson, 1906
-Mount Desolation. Cassell, 1892
-The New Andromeda. Nash, 1909
-One Fair Enemy. Long, 1908
-Pacific Blue. Ward, 1928
-The Prime Minister and Mrs. Grantham. Nash, 1903
-The Redemption of Grace Milroy. Lane, 1916
A Royal Alliance. Ward, 1935 G
-A Saint in Mufti. Nash, 1910
The Shadow of Evil. Laurie, 1913
The Sign of the Glove. Ward, 1932 G
-Slings and Arrows. Ward, 1927
-A Strange Destiny. Ward, 1937
-Stranger Than Fiction. Ward, 1923
-Straws in the Wind. Hurst, 1901
-The Super-Barbarians. Lane, 1915
-A Tangled Marriage. Ward, 1921
-The Temptation of Selma. Ward, 1924
Tough Company. Ward, 1936 G
-Virginia. Ward, 1923
Wanted! Ward, 1931
Waste Lands. Ward, 1935 G
-The Way of a Maid. Ward, 1925
-The Winding Road. Ward, 1929
-The Woman, the Man, and the Monster. Stuyvesant Press, 1909. (British title?)
-The Yellow Man. Hutchinson, 1900

DAWE, JOHN STANLEY
Crime Takes Wings. Eldon, 1939

DAWSON, A(LEC) J(OHN). 1872-1951.
The Case Books of X 37. Richards, 1930 ss

DAWSON, CAROLYN BYRD
The Lady Wept Alone. Doubleday, 1940
Remind Me to Forget. Doubleday, 1942

DAWSON, CONINGSBY (WILLIAM). 1883-1959.
-The House of the Weeping Woman. Hodder, 1908. (U.S. title?)
Murder Point. Doran, 1910
The Vanishing Point. Cosmopolitan, 1922; Hutchinson, 1922

DAWSON, FORBES
A Sensational Trance. Downey, 1895

DAWSON, JAMES
Hell Gate. McKay, 1967

DAWSON, JANIS
Mackenzie's Glen. Hale, 1975

DAWSON, MINNIE TWILIGHT. 1876- .
The Stillwell Murder; or, A Society Crime. [Author], 1908

DAWSON, (FRANCIS) WARRINGTON. 1878-1962.
Adventure in the Night. Doubleday, 1924; Unwin, 1924
-The Crimson Pall. Bernard, 1927

DAWSON, WILLIAM JAMES. 1854-1928.
The Borrowdale Tragedy. Lane (London & New York), 1920

DAX, ANTHONY. Pseudonym of (Alfred) John Hunter, 1891-1961. Other pseudonyms: John Addiscombe, L. H. Brenning, Anthony Drummond, Peter Meriton, qq.v.
The Man Behind. World's Work, 1937; Dutton, 1938, as by John Hunter

DAY, ALBERT A.
The Mysterious Beggar. Ogilvie, 1891; Gay & Bird, 1891

DAY, GINA
Tell No Tales. Hart-Davis, 1967; Stein, 1968

DAY, JULIAN
Design for Death. Hale, 1958

DAY, JULIUS E(DGAR). 1884- .
Crooked Money. Barron, 1937

DAY, LILLIAN, 1893- , and NORBERT (LEWIS) LEDERER, 1888-1955. Series character: Frederick Hunt, in both titles.
Death Comes on Friday. Cassell, 1937; Dutton, 1937
Murder in Time. Cassell, 1935; Furman, 1936

DAY, LULA M.
The Mystery of the Red Suitcase. Hip Books, 1946. (Eleven other titles by this author were announced but it is not known if any were published.)

DAY, VALENTINE
That Fatal Tree. Mayne, 1893

DAY, WILL B.
Bravo 9. Caravelle, 1967
The Man from M.O.D. Caravelle, 1967

DAY-LEWIS, CECIL. 1904-1972. Pseudonym: Nicholas Blake, q.v.

DAYE, JOHN. Pseudonym of Major General Sir John Adye, 1857-1930, q.v.
Who Killed Lord Henry Rollestone? Jenkins, 1924

DAYLE, DEXTER
Claws of Fate. Fiction House, 1939
The Crooked Jacket. Fiction House, 1938
Dangerous Love. Fiction House, 1938
The Day of Vengeance. Fiction House, 1940
Death in the Threatre. Fiction House, 1935
Death to the Spy. Fiction House, 1939
Five were Doomed. Fiction House, 1935
Kidnapped for a Million. Fiction House, 1935
Love's Ordeal. Fiction House, 1937
Murder in Mid-Air. Fiction House, 1935
The Purple Threat. Fiction House, 1935
The Torture Machine. Fiction House, 1935
The Towers of Terror. Fiction House, 1935

DAYMONT, J.
Pelota Murder. Gannet, 1954

DEAKIN, H(ILDA) L. See also: GRACE MILLER WHITE.
The Secret of the Cove. Methuen, 1930
The Shot That Killed Graeme Andrews. Nelson, 1931

DEAL, BABS H(ODGES). 1929- .
The Crystal Mouse. Doubleday, 1973; New English Library, 1973
Fancy's Knell. Doubleday, 1966; Gollancz, 1967
Waiting to Hear from William. Doubleday, 1975; New English Library, 1976
The Walls Came Tumbling Down. Doubleday, 1968; Cassell, 1968

DEAL, BORDEN. 1922- . Pseudonym: Lee Borden, q.v.
Killer in the House. Signet, 1957

DEAL, MASON. Pseudonym of Henry Ware Eliot, 1879-1947.
The Rumble Murders. Houghton, 1932

DEAN, AMBER. 1902- . Series character: Albie Harris = AH.
August Incident. Doubleday, 1951
Be Home by Eleven. Putnam, 1973; Hale, 1974
The Blonde is Dead; see Call Me Pandora
Bullet Proof. Doubleday, 1960
Call Me Pandora. Doubleday, 1946. Also published as: The Blonde is Dead. Mystery Novel Classic, 194? AH
Chanticleer's Muffled Crow. Doubleday, 1945 AH
Collector's Item. Doubleday, 1953
Dead Man's Float. Doubleday, 1944 AH
Deadly Contact. Doubleday, 1963; Hale, 1964
The Devil Threw Dice. Doubleday, 1954
The Dower Chest. Putnam, 1970; Hale, 1972
Encounter with Evil. Doubleday, 1961
Foggy Foggy Dew. Doubleday, 1947
No Traveller Returns. Doubleday, 1948 AH
Snipe Hunt. Doubleday, 1949 AH
Something for the Birds. Doubleday, 1959
Ticket to Buffalo. Doubleday, 1951
Wrap It Up. Doubleday, 1946 AH

DEAN, DENNIS
The Emerald Murder Case. Phoenix, 1939

DEAN, DUDLEY. Pseudonym of Dudley Dean MacGaughy. Other pseudonym: Owen Dudley, q.v.
Lila My Lovely. GM, 1960

DEAN, ELIZABETH. Series characters: Emma Marsh and Hank Fairbanks, in all titles.
Murder a Mile High. Doubleday, 1944; Boardman, 1948
Murder is a Collector's Item. Doubleday, 1939; Cassell, 1939
Murder is a Serious Business. Doubleday, 1940; Swan, 1943

DEAN, GRAHAM M. 1904- .
The Front Page Mystery. Appleton, 1931
Gleaming Rails. Appleton, 1930

DEAN, GREGORY. Pseudonym of Jacob D. Posner, 1883- . Series character: Deputy Commissioner Benjamin Simon, in all titles.
The Case of Marie Corwin. Covici, 1933; Nicholson, 1934
The Case of the Fifth Key. Covici, 1934; Nicholson, 1936
Murder on Stilts. Hillman-Curl, 1939

DEAN, HAYDON. Pseudonym of Harry Harding, 1885- , q.v.
The Caves of Blackscar. Nicholson, 1934

DEAN, HOWARD
-The Iron Hand. Abbey, 1898

DEAN, LYN. Pseudonym of Winifred Selina Garrett, 1909- .
Ask No Questions. Melrose, 1937
The Rope Waits. Melrose, 1937

DEAN, ROBERT GEORGE. Pseudonym: George Griswold, q.v. Series character: Tony Hunter = TH.
Affair at Lover's Leap. Doubleday, 1953. British title: Death at Lover's Leap. Boardman, 1954 TH
The Body was Quite Cold. Dutton, 1951 TH
The Case of Joshua Locke. Dutton, 1951 TH
Death at Lover's Leap; see Affair at Lover's Leap
Layoff. Scribner, 1942 TH
A Murder by Marriage. Scribner, 1940 TH
Murder in Mink. Scribner, 1941 TH
Murder Makes a Merry Widow. Doubleday, 1938 TH
Murder Most Opportune. Doubleday, 1939
A Murder of Convenience. Doubleday, 1938 TH
Murder on Margin. Doubleday, 1937
Murder Through the Looking Glass. Doubleday, 1940 TH
On Ice. Scribner, 1942 TH
The Sutton Place Murders. Doubleday, 1936; Heinemann, 1936
Three Lights Went Out. Doubleday, 1937
What Gentleman Strangles a Lady? Doubleday, 1936

DEAN, SPENCER. Pseudonym of Prentice Winchell, 1895- . Other pseudonyms: Jay de Bekker, Stewart Sterling, Dexter St. Clair, Dexter St. Clare, qq.v. Series character: Don Cadee, in all titles.
Credit for a Murder. Doubleday, 1961; Boardman, 1962
Dishonor Among Thieves. Doubleday, 1958; Boardman, 1959
The Frightened Fingers. Washburn, 1954; Boardman, 1955
Marked Down for Murder. Doubleday, 1956; Boardman, 1957
The Merchant of Murder. Doubleday, 1959; Boardman, 1960
Murder After a Fashion. Doubleday, 1960; Boardman, 1961
Murder on Delivery. Doubleday, 1957; Boardman, 1958
Price Tag for Murder. Doubleday, 1959; Boardman, 1960
The Scent of Fear. Washburn, 1954; Boardman, 1956. Also published as: The Smell of Fear. Jonathan, 1956
The Smell of Fear; see The Scent of Fear

DEANE, DONALD
Hidden Clues. Hamilton, 1932
The Luck of Luce. Hamilton, 1931
The Mystery of the Fifth Tulip. Hamilton, 1930

DEANE, EDWIN S.
Bob Younger's Fate. Street, 1890

DEANE, JIM. Series character: Nick Merlotti, in both titles.
The Great Pretender. Signet, 1974
Moon Over Miami. Signet, 1975

DEANE, NORMAN. Pseudonym of John Creasey, 1908-1973, q.v. Other pseudonyms: Gordon Ashe, M. E. Cooke, Robert Caine Frazer, Patrick Gill, Michael Halliday, Charles Hogarth, Brian Hope, Colin Hughes, Kyle Hunt, Abel Mann, Peter Manton, J. J. Marric, Richard Martin, Rodney Mattheson, Anthony Morton, Jeremy York, qq.v. Series characters: Bruce Murdoch = BM; The Liberator = L. Reprinted in England as by John Creasey = *; reprinted there as by Michael Halliday = #.
Come Home to Crime. Hurst, 1945 L
Dangerous Journey. Hurst, 1939; McKay, 1974, as by John Creasey BM *
Death in the Spanish Sun. Hurst, 1954 #
Double for Death. Hurst, 1951
Gateway to Escape. Hurst, 1944 L
Golden Death. Hurst, 1952
I am the Withered Man. Hurst, 1941; McKay, 1973, as by John Creasey BM
Incense of Death. Hurst, 1954 *
Intent to Murder. Hurst, 1948
Look at Murder. Hurst, 1952

Deane, Norman

The Man I Didn't Kill. Hurst, 1950 #
Murder Ahead. Hurst, 1953
No Hurry to Kill. Hurst, 1950
Play for Murder. Hurst, 1946
Return to Adventure. Hurst, 1943 L
Secret Errand. Hurst, 1939; McKay, 1974, as by John Creasey BM *
The Silent House. Hurst, 1947
Unknown Mission. Hurst, 1940; McKay, 1972, as by John Creasey BM
Where is the Withered Man? Hurst, 1942; McKay, 1974, as by John Creasey BM
Why Murder? Hurst, 1948
The Withered Man. Hurst, 1940; McKay, 1974, as by John Creasey BM

DEANE, PHILIP
A Time for Treason. Longmans (Canada), 1966

DEANE, SHIRLEY (JOAN). 1920- .
No Tears for the Dead. Ward, 1968. U.S. title: Corpses in Corsica. Vanguard, 1969

DEARDEN, HAROLD. See: ROLAND PERTWEE, 1885-1963.

DEARDEN, HILDA DANVERS
The Blonde Madonna. Grayson, 1933
"In the King's Name—!" Hurst, 1932
The Mystery of the Skating Rink. Hurst, 1931
Revolt from Bondage. Grayson, 1935
Strange Rendezvous. Grayson, 1934
"This Road is Dangerous!" Hurst, 1930
-The Trappings are Gorgeous. Hale, 1937

DEARDEN, R(ICHARD) L(IONEL). 1883- .
Care of the Commander. Jenkins, 1939

DEASY, MARY (MARGARET). 1914- .
The Corioli Affair. Little, 1954; Heinemann, 1955
Devil's Bridge. Little, 1952; Heinemann, 1956

DEATH, J.
Death Dates a Dame. Gray, 1952
Deep is my Grave. Gray, 1951

DE BANZIE, ERIC. 1894- . Joint pseudonym with John Sellar Matheson Ressich, 1877- : Gregory Baxter, q.v.

DE BEKKER, JAY. Pseudonym of Prentice Winchell, 1895- . Other pseudonyms: Spencer Dean, Dexter St. Clair, Dexter St. Clare, Stewart Sterling, qq.v.
Gutter Gang. Beacon, 1954
Keyhole Peeper. Beacon, 1955

DE BILIO, BETH
Vendetta Con Brio. Bobbs, 1973

DE BLASIS, CELESTE. 1946- .
The Night Child. Coward, 1975

DE BOSSCHERE, JOHN. 1878-
-Marthe and the Madman. Covici, 1928. (Translation of Marthe et L'Enrage. Paris, 1927.)

DE BRA, LEMUEL
Ways That are Wary. Butterworth, 1924; Clode, 1925 ss, some criminous

DE BRAHM, JEANNE ICHORD ALCANTER. 1890- . Pseudonym: Jean Rosmer, q.v.

DEBRETT, HAL. Joint pseudonym of Davis Dresser, 1904-1977, and Kathleen Rollins. Other pseudonyms of Davis Dresser: Asa Baker, Brett Halliday, qq.v. Joint pseudonym with (Walter) Ryerson Johnson, 1901- , q.v.: Matthew Blood, q.v.
Before I Wake. Dodd, 1949; Jarrolds, 1953. Reprinted as by Brett Halliday: Dell, 1955
A Lonely Way to Die. Dodd, 1950; Jarrolds, 1954

DE BRUNE, (CHARLES FRANCIS) AIDAN. 1879- .
The Carson Loan Mystery. Cornstall (Sydney), 1926
The Dagger and Cord. Cornstall (Sydney), 1927
Shadow Crook. Angus (Sydney), 1930

DE CAIRE, EDWIN. Pseudonym of Edwin Alfred Williams.
Death Among the Writers. Hodder, 1952
The Umgasi Diamonds. Hodder, 1954

DECKER, DUANE. 1910-1964.
The Devil's Punchbowl. Ace, 1960

DECOIN, DIDIER. 1945- .
The Case Against Love. NAL, 1967. (Translation of Le Proces d'Amour. Paris, 1966.)

DE CRESPIGNY, MRS. PHILIP CHAMPION [ROSE CHAMPION DE CRESPIGNY]. -1935.
A Case for the C.I.D. Cassell, 1933
-The Coming of Aurora. Nash, 1909
The Dark Sea. Lane, 1927
The Eye of Nemesis. Cassell, 1931
-The Five of Spades. Mills, 1915
-From Behind the Arras. Unwin, 1902
-The Grey Domino. Nash, 1906
-Hester and I. Mills, 1915
-Malloy's Tryst. Mills, 1914
-The Mark. Mills, 1912
-The Mischief of a Glove. Unwin, 1903
The Missing Piece. Cassell, 1927
-My Cousin Cynthia, and others. Nash, 1908 ss
The Riddle of the Emeralds. Cassell, 1929
-The Rose Brocade. Nash, 1905
-The Spanish Prisoner. Nash, 1907
-Stories of Today and Yesterday. Mills, 1917 ss
Straws in the Wind. Cassell, 1928
Tangled Evidence. Cassell, 1924
-The Valley of Achor. Mills, 1910

DECREST, JACQUES. Pseudonym of Jacques Napoleon Faure-Biguet, 1893- . Series character: M. Gilles, in at least those marked G.
Body on the Beach. Hammond, 1953. (Translation of Le Rendez-Vous du Dimanche Soir. Paris, 1935.) G
Meet a Body. Hammond, 1953. (Translation of Hasard. Paris, 1933.)
The Missing Formula. Hammond, 1956. (Translation of Les Trois Jeunes Filles de Vienne. Paris, 1934.) G

DE CROISSET, FRANCIS. See: EDGAR (ALFRED) JEPSON, 1863-1938.

DEDINA, MICHEL. 1933-
The Harm in Trying. Muller, 1964
The Mink Steel. Muller, 1966

DEEGAN, JON J.
Beyond the Fourth Door. Hamilton Stafford, 1954
Reconnoitre Krellig. Hamilton Stafford, 1951
Underworld of Zello. Hamilton Stafford, 1952

DEEMSTER, NICK
Run, Killer, Run. Mitre, 1946

DE FELITTA, FRANK (PAUL). 1921- .
Audrey Rose. Putnam, 1975; Collins, 1976
Oktoberfest. Doubleday, 1973; Collins, 1974

DE FONTMELL, E. V. Pseudonym.
Honour Lost, All Lost. Scholartis, 1929

DE FORD, MIRIAM ALLEN. 1888-1975.
The Theme is Murder. Abelard, 1967 ss

DE FOREST, J(OHN) W(ILLIAM). 1826-1906.
-The Bloody Chasm. Appleton, 1881. Also published as: The Oddest of Courtships; or, The Bloody Chasm. Appleton, 1882
The Oddest of Courtships; see The Bloody Chasm
-Playing the Mischief. Harper, 1875
Seacliffe; or, The Mystery of the Westervelts. Phillips, 1859
The Weatherel Affair. Sheldon, 1873

DE FRAGA, GEOFF. 1913- .
Murder at the Cookout. Cassell, 1968
Murder by Wash of Light. Rigby (Adelaide), 1970; Hale (London), 1971

DE GRAMONT, SANCHE. 1932- .
Lives to Give. Putnam, 1971; Hodder, 1972

DEGRAS, HENRY ERNEST. 1910- . Pseudonym: Mark Benney, q.v.

DE HALSALLE, HENRY. 1872- . See also: R(ICHARD) D('OYLY) HEMINGWAY, 1878- . Series character: Olga von Kopf = OK.
The Life Story of Madame Zelle, the World's Most Beautiful Spy. Skeffington, 1918
A Secret Service Woman. Laurie, 1917 OK
A Woman Spy. Skeffington, 1918 OK

DE HAMEL, HERBERT
Many Thanks, Ben Hassett. Simpkin, 1915; Congreve, 1948

DE HAVILLAND, R(OBERT J.) L(ANGSTAFF)
The Forked Tongue. Vizetelly, 1885

DEIGHTON, LEN [LEONARD CYRIL DEIGHTON]. 1929- . Series character: nameless British agent known from the films as Harry Palmer = HP.
The Billion Dollar Brain. Cape, 1966; Putnam, 1966 HP
An Expensive Place to Die. Cape, 1967; Putnam, 1967 HP
Funeral in Berlin. Cape, 1964; Putnam, 1965 HP
Horse Under Water. Cape, 1963; Putnam, 1968 HP
The Ipcress File. Hodder, 1962; Simon, 1963 HP
Spy Story. Cape, 1974; Harcourt, 1974 HP
Yesterday's Spy. Cape, 1975; Harcourt, 1975

DE JEAN, GEORGES. 1886- .
Who Killed Lord Brixham? Jenkins, 1937

DE JEAN, LOUIS (LEON)
The Girl in Black Velvet. Macaulay, 1937

DEJEANS, ELIZABETH
The Double House. Doubleday, 1924; Hutchinson, 1924

The Moreton Mystery. Bobbs, 1920; Allen & Unwin, 1922
The Romance of a Million Dollars. Bobbs, 1922; Hutchinson, 1926
The Tiger's Coat. Bobbs, 1917; Butterworth, 1923

DE JONG, DOLA. 1911-   .
The Whirligig of Time. Doubleday, 1964

DEKKER, ANTHONY
Divers Diamonds. Collins, 1970
Temptation in a Private Zoo. Constable, 1969; Morrow, 1970

DEKKER, CARL. Pseudonym of John (Alfred Charles) Laffin, 1922-   , q.v. Other pseudonyms: Mark Napier, Dirk Sabre, qq.v.
Don't Bother to Knock. Calvert, 1954
Silence So Deadly. Calvert, 1953

DEKKER, CARL. Pseudonym of Dennis Lynds, 1924-   , q.v. Other pseudonyms: William Arden, Michael Collins, John Crowe, Maxwell Grant, Michael Sadler, qq.v.
Woman in Marble. Bobbs, 1972

DEKKER, J.
Dolls and Dollars. Martin, 1948
Hex Marks the Spot. Martin, 1949
Manhunt in Manhattan. Martin, 1949
Shoot to Kill. Martin, 1949
The Siamese Cat. Martin, 1948
Singapore Set-Up. Martin, 1948
Streetcar to Hell. Martin, 1949

DEKOBRA, MAURICE. Pseudonym of Ernest Maurice Tessier, 1885-1973. Series character: Bradley Adams, in at least those marked BA.
The Bachelor's Widow; see Hell is Sold Out
Blood and Caviar. Laurie, 1937. (Translation of Le Fou de Bassan. Paris, 1935.)
-The Blue Parrot. Laurie, 1948. (Translation of La Perruche Bleue.)
Chinese Puzzle. Allen, 1956
-The Cloven-Footed Angel. Macaulay, 1932
-Confucius in a Tail-Coat. Laurie, 1935; Greenberg, 1935. (Translation of Confucius en Pullover. Paris, 1934.)
Death Requests the Pleasure. Laurie, 1940. (Translation of Meteore 101.)
-Diamond Queen. Allen, 1965. (Translation of L'Amazone de Pretoria.)
-Double or Quits. Allen, 1962. (Translation of Bouddha le Terrible. Paris, 1961.)
-Emigrants de Luxe. Laurie, 1943. (Translation of Emigres de Luxe.)
-Flames of Velvet. Laurie, 1929
The Golden-Eyed Venus. Allen, 1963. (Translation of La Venus aux Yeux d'Or. Paris, 1962.)
-Hamydal, the Vagabond Philosopher. Laurie, 1937. (Translation of Hamydal le Philosophe. Paris, 1918.)
The Hangman Never Waits. Allen, 1960. (Translation of Le Bourreau n'Attend Jamais. Paris, 1959.)
-Hell is Sold Out. Laurie, 1948. U.S. title: The Bachelor's Widow. Ace, 1954
-His Chinese Concubine. Laurie, 1935. (Translation of Madame Joli-Supplice. Paris, 1934.)
-Honeymoon in Shanghai. Laurie, 1946. U.S. title: Shanghai Honeymoon. Philosophical Library, 1946. (Translation of Lune de Miel a Shanghai.)
The Lady is a Vamp. Allen, 1958. (Translation of Vamp ou Vestale. Paris, 1957.) BA

-Love Calling. Laurie, 1933. (Translation of La Volupte Eclairant le Monde. Paris, 1932.)
-The Love Clinic. Payson, 1929
-The Madonna in Hollywood. Laurie, 1945
The Madonna of the Sleeping Cars. Laurie, 1927; Payson, 1927. (Translation of La Madone des Sleepings. Paris, 1925.)
The Man Who Died Twice. Allen, 1954. (Translation of Les Vestales du Veau d'Or. Paris, 1948.)
-Midnight on the Place Pigalle. Laurie, 1932. (Translation of Minuit—Place Pigalle. Paris, 1923.)
Operation Magali. Allen, 1952. (Translation of Operation Magali. Paris, 1951.)
-Passion Lighting the World. Macaulay, 1933
-The Phantom Gondola. Laurie, 1928. (Translation of La Gondola aux Chimeres. Paris, 1926.)
-Phryne; or, Love is a Fine Art. Laurie, 1931. (Translation of Le Geste de Phryne. Paris, 1930.)
Poison at Plessis. Allen, 1953. (Probably a translation of La Pavane des Poisons. Paris, 1950.)
-Prince or Clown. Readers Library, 1928. (Translation of Prince ou Pitre? Paris, 1920.)
-Princess Brinda. Laurie, 1935. (Translation of La Prison des Reves. Paris, 1933.)
-The Romance of a Coward. Laurie, 1943
Serenade to the Hangman. Laurie, 1929; Payson, 1929. (Translation of Serenade au Bourreau. Paris, 1928.)
The Seventh Wife of Prince Hassan. Allen, 1961. (Translation of Les Sept Femmes du Prince Hassan.)
Shanghai Honeymoon; see Honeymoon in Shanghai
She Wore Pink Gloves. Allen, 1958. (Translation of La Veuve aux Gants Roses. Paris, 1956.) BA
-Some Tommies. Paul, 1919. (Translation of Messieurs les Tommies. Paris, 1917.)
-Stars and Stripes. Laurie, 1938. (Translation of Mimi Broadway. Paris, 1936.)
-The Street of Painted Lips. Laurie, 1934; Macaulay, 1934. (Translation of La Rue des Bouches-Peintes.)
-The 13th Lover. Payson, 1928
-Venus on Wheels. Laurie, 1930; Macaulay, 1930. (Translation of La Venus a Roulettes. Paris, 1925.)
The Widow with the Pink Gloves. Laurie, 1938. (Translation of Fusille a l'Aube. Paris, 1937.)
-The Widow's Might. Allen, 1957. (Translation of Les Lotus Dorment la Nuit. Paris, 1956.)
-Wings of Desire. Laurie, 1927; Macaulay, 1925. (Translation of Mon Coeur au Ralenti. Paris, 1924.)

DE KREMER, JEAN RAYMOND. 1887-1964. Pseudonym: Jean Ray, q.v.

DE LAGUNA, FREDERICA. 1906-   .
The Arrow Points to Murder. Doubleday, 1937
Fog on the Mountain. Doubleday, 1938

DELAMARE, GEORGE. 1886-   .
The Midnight King. Henkle, 1927

DE LA MARE, WALTER (JOHN). 1873-1956.
The Riddle, and other stories. Selwyn, 1923; Knopf, 1923 ss

DELANCEY, ROGER
Murder Below Wall Street. Appleton (New York & London), 1934

DELANE, BRIAN
Her Crooked Lover. Fiction House, 1935
Who Killed the Count? Fiction House, 1938

DELANEY, DENIS. Pseudonym of Peter (Morris) Green, 1924-   , q.v.
Cat in Gloves. Gryphon, 1956

DELANEY, M.
Protection for a Lady. Milestone, 1953
She had my Number. Milestone, 1953

DELANNOY, (H.) BURFORD
Beaten at the Post. Digby, 1907
Between the Lines. Ward, 1901
Dead Man's Rooms. Ward, 1905
Denzil's Device. Everett, 1904
The Flat Beneath. Rivers, 1931
The Garden Court Mystery. Street, 1899 (Magnet #112). (British title?)
In Mid-Atlantic. Ward, 1904
The Margate Murder Mystery. Ward, 1902; Brentano's, 1901
The Midnight Special. Milne, 1902
The Missing Cyclist and other stories. Simpkin, 1898 ss
The Money Lender. Ward, 1907
M.R.C.S. Ward, 1903
Nineteen Thousand Pounds. Ward, 1901; Fenno, 1900
The Pound of Flesh. Digby, 1911
The Scales of Justice. Digby, 1908
A Studio Model. Digby, 1909
A Thespian Detective and other theatrical stories. Ellis, 1899 ss

DELANY, JOSEPH FRANCIS. 1905-   . Pseudonym: Joel Y. Dane, q.v.

DE LA TORRE, LILLIAN [LILLIAN DE LA TORRE BUENO McCUE]. 1902-   . Series character: Dr. Sam: Johnson = SJ.
The Detections of Dr. Sam: Johnson. Doubleday, 1960 DJ ss
Dr. Sam: Johnson, Detector. Knopf, 1946; Joseph, 1948 DJ ss
Elizabeth is Missing. Knopf, 1945; Joseph, 1947
Goodbye, Miss Lizzie Borden. Baker, 1948 (1-act play.)
The Heir of Douglas. Knopf, 1952; Joseph, 1953
The Truth about Belle Gunness. GM, 1955; Muller, 1960

DE LAUER, MARJEL JEAN
The Mystery of the Phantom Billionaire. Ashley, 1972

DE LEON, JACK
The Man at Six. Collins, 1930. (Novelization of the play by Jack Celestin and Jack de Leon.)

DELF, T. W. H.
The Man in the Check Suit. Jarrolds, 1897

DELF, THOMAS. 1810-1865. Pseudonym: Charles Martel, q.v.

DE L'ISLE, F. D. A. C.
The Adventures of a Turf Detective. Everett, 1910 ss

DELL, AMEN
Johnny on the Spot. Mystery House, 1943

DELL, DRAYCOT (MONTAGU), 1888-   , and OSWALD (C. C.) DALLAS
The Death Gang. Columbine, 193?

DELLA, LEW
  Dark Angel. Milestone, 1953
  Fast and Loose. Milestone, 1953
  Ladies Sleep Alone. Archer, 19??; Kaywin, 1951
  Life is Short. Milestone, 1953
  Love Comes Lethal. Milestone, 1953
  Risky! Milestone, 1954
  Shadows Sometimes Scream. Milestone, 1954
  Touch and Go. Milestone, 1954

DELLAR, H. J.
  Incident Closed. Quality, 1947

DELLBRIDGE, JOHN. 1887- . Series character: Rupert Hambledon, in at least those marked RH.
  The Lady in the Wood. Hurst, 1950 RH
  The Moles of Death. Diamond, 1927
  Searchlight on Hambledon. Hurst, 1947 RH
  Unfit to Plead. Hurst, 1949

DELMAN, DAVID. Series characters: Jacob & Helen Horowitz = H.
  He Who Digs a Grave. Doubleday, 1973; Hale, 1975
  One Man's Murder. McKay, 1975; Collins, 1975 H
  Sudden Death. Doubleday, 1972; Collins, 1973 H
  A Week to Kill. Doubleday, 1972 H

DEL MAR, DON
  Blood Pearls of Sulu. Vantage, 1972

DELMAS, LEON RENE. 1830-1904. Pseudonym: Rene De Pont-Jest, q.v.

DELMONICO, ANDREA
  Chateau Chaumond. Ace, 1968
  Eyrie of an Eagle. Ace, 1970

DEL REY, LESTER [RAMON FELIPE SAN JUAN MARIO SILVIO ENRICO ALVAREZ DEL REY]. 1915- . Pseudonym: Erik van Lhin, q.v.

DELVES-BROUGHTON, JOSEPHINE. 1916- Pseudonym: John Bryan, q.v.

DELVING, MICHAEL. Pseudonym of Jay Williams, 1914-1978. Series characters: Dave Cannon = DC; Bob Eddison = BE.
  Bored to Death. Scribner, 1975. British title: A Wave of Fatalities. Collins, 1975 DC
  The Devil Finds Work. Scribner, 1969; Collins, 1970 DC, BE
  Die Like a Man. Scribner, 1970; Collins, 1970 DC
  A Shadow of Himself. Scribner, 1972; Collins, 1972 BE
  Smiling the Boy Fell Dead. Scribner, 1967; Macdonald, 1967 DC
  A Wave of Fatalities; see Bored to Death

DE MAR, PAUL. Pseudonym of Pearl Foley, q.v.
  The Gnome Mine Mystery. Hamilton, 1933

DEMAREST, ANNE. Pseudonym of Florence Demarest Foos Bond.
  Murder on Every Floor. Hillman-Curl, 1939
  -She was his Secretary. Gramercy, 1939

DEMARIS, OVID. Pseudonym of Ovide E. Desmarais, 1919- .
  Candyleg. GM, 1961; Muller pb, 1962. Also published as: Machine Gun McCain. GM, 1970; Coronet, 1970
  The Contract; see The Organization
  The Enforcer. GM, 1960
  The Extortioners. GM, 1960; Muller pb, 1961
  The Gold-Plated Sewer. Avon, 1960
  The Hoods Take Over. GM, 1957
  The Long Night. Avon, 1959
  The Lusting Drive. GM, 1958; Muller pb, 1961
  Machine Gun McCain; see Candyleg
  The Organization. Tower, 1965. Also published as: The Contract. Belmont, 1970; Sphere, 1971
  The Overlord. Signet, 1972
  The Parasite. Berkley, 1963
  Ride the Gold Mare. GM, 1957
  The Slasher. GM, 1959

DE MARQUAND, ALIX
  House on Somber Lake. Lancer, 1968

DEMBO, SAMUEL
  The Amber Eyes of the Lion. Redman, 1963
  Kalahari Kill; see The Sands of Lilliput
  The Sands of Lilliput. Redman, 1963. U.S. title: Kalahari Kill. Mill, 1964

DE MEXICO, N. R.
  Madman on a Drum. Cavalcade, 1944. Also published as: Strange Pursuit. Suspense Novel, 194?
  Marijuana Girl. Universal Publishing, 1951
  Strange Pursuit; see Madman on a Drum

DEMIJOHN, THOM. Joint pseudonym of Thomas M(ichael) Disch, 1940- , q.v., and John Sladek, 1937- , q.v.
  Black Alice. Doubleday, 1968; Allen, 1969

DE MILLE, JAMES. 1837-1880.
  The American Baron. Harper, 1872
  -Among the Brigands. Lee, 1872
  -A Castle in Spain. Harper, 1878
  -A Comedy of Terrors. Osgood, 1872
  -Cord and Cheese. Harper, 1869
  The Cryptogram. Harper, 1871
  The Lady of the Ice. Appleton, 1870
  -The Living Link. Harper, 1874
  -An Open Question. Appleton, 1873
  -A Strange Manuscript Found in a Copper Cylinder. Harper, 1888; Chatto, 1888

DE MILLE, NELSON. 1943- . Series characters: Keller = K; Ryker = R (see also: Edson T. Hamill).
  The Agent of Death. Leisure, 1974 R
  The Cannibal. Manor, 1975 K
  The Hammer of God. Leisure, 1974 R
  Night of the Phoenix. Manor, 1975 K
  The Quest. Manor, 1975
  The Smack Man. Manor, 1975 K
  The Sniper. Leisure, 1974 R
  The Terrorists. Leisure, 1974 R

DEMING, RICHARD. 1915- . Pseudonyms: Max Franklin, Emily Moor, qq.v. See also: Nick Marino. Series character: Manville Moon = MM.
  Anything But Saintly. Permabooks, 1963
  Body for Sale. PB, 1962
  The Careful Man. Allen, 1962
  Death of a Pusher. PB, 1964
  Dragnet: The Case of the Courteous Killer. PB, 1958. (Novelization of the TV series.)
  Dragnet: The Case of the Crime King. PB, 1959. (Novelization of the TV series.)
  Edge of the Law. Berkley, 1960
  Fall Girl. Zenith, 1959. British title: Walk a Crooked Mile. Boardman, 1959
  The Gallows in my Garden. Rinehart, 1952; Boardman, 1953 MM
  Give the Girl a Gun; see Whistle Past the Graveyard
  The Greek God Affair. Pyramid, 1968. (Novelization of the Mod Squad TV series.)
  A Groovy Way to Die. Pyramid, 1968. (Novelization of the Mod Squad TV series.)
  Hand-Picked to Die; see Tweak the Devil's Nose
  The Hit. Pyramid, 1970. (Novelization of the Mod Squad TV series.)
  Hit and Run. PB, 1960
  Juvenile Delinquent. Boardman, 1958
  Kiss and Kill. Zenith, 1960; Digit, 1961
  She'll Hate Me Tomorrow. Monarch, 1963
  The Sock-It-to-Em Murders. Pyramid, 1968. (Novelization of the Mod Squad TV series.)
  Spy-In. Pyramid, 1969. (Novelization of the Mod Squad TV series.)
  This Game of Murder. Monarch, 1964
  This is my Night. Monarch, 1961
  Tweak the Devil's Nose. Rinehart, 1953; Boardman, 1953. Also published as: Hand-Picked to Die. Jonathan, 1956 MM
  Vice Cop. Belmont, 1961
  Walk a Crooked Mile; see Fall Girl
  What's the Matter with Helen? Beagle, 1971. (Novelization of the movie.)
  Whistle Past the Graveyard. Rinehart, 1954; Boardman, 1955. Also published as: Give the Girl a Gun. Jonathan, 1955 MM

DE MIRJIAN, ARTO, JR. 1931- .
  Not a Clue. Popular Library, 1974

DE MORGAN, WILLIAM FREND. 1839-1917.
  The Old Madhouse. Heinemann, 1919; Holt, 1919

DENBIE, ROGER. Joint pseudonym of Alan (Baer) Green, 1906-1975, q.v., and Julian Paul Brodie, 1908- . Joint pseudonym of Alan (Baer) Green and Gladys Elizabeth Green, 1908- : Glen Burne, q.v. Series character: Dr. Quentin Pace, in both titles.
  Death Cruises South. Morrow, 1934; Nicholson, 1934
  Death on the Limited. Morrow, 1933. British title: The Timetable Murder. Nicholson, 1934
  The Timetable Murder; see Death on the Limited

DENBY, EDWIN. 1903- .
  Mrs. W's Last Sandwich. Horizon, 1972

DENEVI, MARCO. 1922- .
  Rosa at Ten O'Clock. Holt, 1964. (Translation of Rosaura a las Diez. Buenos Aires, 1957.)

DENHAM, REGINALD. 1894- . See: EDWARD PERCY.

DENHAM, THOMAS S(IDNEY). 1906- .
  Background to Murder, and other stories. Mitre, 1943 ss
  The Grand National Mystery, and other tales. Mitre, 1944 ss

DENISON, DULCIE WINIFRED CATHERINE. 1920- . Pseudonym: Dulcie Gray, q.v.

DENISON, FRANK
　Tales of the Strong Room. Digby, 1899 ss

DENISON, MRS. MARY A(NDREWS). 1826-1911.
　A Brave Little Woman. Lupton, 1892 ss
　-Led to the Light. Claxton, 1867
　The Man in Blue; or, Which Did He Love? Street, 1889
　-Opposite the Jail. Hoyt, 1859
　-Out of Prison. Sheldon, 1864
　-Sequel to Opposite the Jail; or, On Trial for his Life. Bradley, 1883

DENMAN, PETER
　The Man Who Guided Missiles. Hale, 1973

DENNIS, CHARLES. 1946-   .
　The Next-to-Last Train Ride. Macmillan (London), 1974; St. Martin's, 1974
　Somebody Just Grabbed Annie. Macmillan (London), 1975; St. Martin's, 1975
　Stoned Cold Soldier. Bachman, 1973

DENNIS, EVE
　Death for Safety. Gifford, 1949

DENNIS, GEOFFREY. Joint pseudonym with Hilary (Aiden) St. George Saunders, 1898-1951, q.v.: Barum Browne, q.v.

DENNIS, RALPH. Series character: Jim Hardman, in all titles.
　Atlanta Deathwatch. Popular Library, 1974
　The Charleston Knife's in Town. Popular Library, 1974
　Down Among the Jocks. Popular Library, 1974
　The Golden Girl and All. Popular Library, 1974
　Murder's Not an Odd Job. Popular Library, 1974
　Pimp for the Dead. Popular Library, 1974
　Working for the Man. Popular Library, 1974

DENNIS, ROBERT C. Series character: Paul Reeder, in both titles.
　Conversations with a Corpse. Bobbs, 1974; Gollancz, 1974
　The Sweat of Fear. Bobbs, 1973; Gollancz, 1973

DENNISTON, ELINORE. 1900-   . Pseudonyms: Dennis Allan, Rae Foley, qq.v.

DENNY, FELIX. Pseudonym: Dennis Barr, q.v.

DENT, JOHN CHARLES. 1841-1888.
　The Gerrard Street Mystery and other weird tales. Rose (Toronto), 1888 ss

DENT, LESTER. 1905-1959. Pseudonym: Kenneth Robeson, q.v. Series character: Chance Malloy = CM.
　Cry at Dusk. GM, 1952
　Dead at the Take-Off. Doubleday, 1946; Cassell, 1948. Also published as: High Stakes. Ace, 1953 CM
　High Stakes; see Dead at the Take-Off
　Lady Afraid. Doubleday, 1948; Cassell, 1950
　Lady in Peril. Ace, 1959
　Lady So Silent. Cassell, 1951. (U.S. title?)
　Lady to Kill. Doubleday, 1946; Cassell, 1949 CM

DENTON, RALPH
　Charlie Finds a Corpse. Yates, 1949

DENVER, PAUL
　Cannon, the Falling Blonde. Star, 1975
　The Last Laugh, and No Pictures for Cathy. Consul, 1965
　Striptease for Murder. Consul, 1965

DE POLNAY, PETER. 1906-   .
　Blood and Water. Allen, 1975
　The Crow and the Cat. Allen, 1974; St. Martin's, 1975
　A Life of Ease. Allen, 1971

DE PONT-JEST, RENE. Pseudonym of Leon Rene Delmas, 1830-1904.
　Artist and Model; see The Divorced Princess
　The Case of Doctor Plemen. Spencer Blackett, 1888. U.S. title: Rhea; or, The Case of Dr. Plemen. Rand, 1889. Also published as: The Romance of a Pretty Girl. Brandus, 1891. (Translation of Cas du Docteur Plemen. Paris, 1887.)
　The Divorced Princess. Vickers, 1888. U.S. title: Artist and Model. Rand, 1889. (Translation of Divorcee. Paris, 1885.)
　No. 13 Rue Marlot. Lee, 1880. (Translation of Le No. 13 de la Rue Marlot. Paris, 1877.)
　Rhea; see The Case of Doctor Plemen
　The River of Pearls; or, The Red Spider. Page, 1899
　The Romance of a Pretty Girl; see The Case of Doctor Plemen

DE PRE, JEAN-ANNE. Pseudonym of Michael (Angelo) Avallone (Jr.), 1924-   , q.v. Other pseudonyms: Priscilla Dalton, Mark Dane, Dora Highland, Steve Michaels, Dorothea Nile, Edwina Noone, Sidney Stuart, Max Walker, qq.v.
　Aquarius, My Evil. Popular Library, 1972
　Die, Jessica, Die. Popular Library, 1972
　A Sound of Dying Roses. Popular Library, 1972
　The Third Woman. Popular Library, 1971; Sphere, 1973
　Warlock's Woman. Popular Library, 1973

DEPTULA, WALTER. Series character: Frank Arrow, in both titles.
　Naked Mistress. Curtis, 1974
　Wine, Women, and Death. Curtis, 1974

DE PUY, E(DWARD) SPENCE. 1872-   . Series character: Sam Houston = SH.
　Dr. Nicholas Stone. Dillingham, 1905; Unwin, 1905
　The Hospital Homicides. Phoenix, 1937 SH
　The Long Knife. Doubleday, 1936 SH

DERBY, E. C.
　A Counterfeiter's Roguery. Street, ca.1900
　The Crossing of Clues. Street, ca.1900
　The Empty Mail Bags. Street, ca.1900
　Foiling a Counterfeiter. Street, ca.1900
　The Gold Maker's Secret. Street, ca.1900
　The Government's Man. Street, ca.1900
　In League with Counterfeiters. Street, ca.1900
　The Mail Robbers' Syndicate. Street, ca.1900
　The Man on the Couch. Street, ca.1900
　A Master Stroke. Street, ca.1900
　A Nihilist's Vengeance. Street, ca.1900
　The Outlaw's Oath. Street, ca.1900
　A Smuggler's Fate. Street, ca.1900
　The Test of Anarchy. Street, ca.1900

DERBY, MARK. Pseudonym of Harry Wilcox.
　Afraid in the Dark; see Malayan Rose
　The Bad Step; see Out of Asia Alive
　The Big Water. Collins, 1953; Viking, 1953
　The Dark. Collins, 1962
　Echo of a Bomb. Viking, 1957. (British title?)
　Element of Risk. Collins, 1952; Viking, 1952
　Five Nights in Singapore. Collins, 1961
　Ghost Blonde. Viking, 1960. (British title?)
　Malayan Rose. Collins, 1951. U.S. title: Afraid in the Dark. Viking, 1952
　Out of Asia Alive. Collins, 1954. U.S. title: The Bad Step. Viking, 1954
　Sun in the Hunter's Eyes. Collins, 1958; Viking, 1958
　The Sunlit Ambush. Collins, 1955; Viking, 1955
　The Tigress. Collins, 1959. U.S. title: Womanhunt. Viking, 1959
　Womanhunt; see The Tigress

DE RESZKE, DAVID
　Nine Dragon Man. Pyramid, 1975

D'ERIGNY, SIMONE
　The Mysterious Madame S. Lippincott, 1934. (Translation of L'Estrange Volonte du Professeur Lorrain. Paris, 1933.)

DERING, JOAN (ROSALIND CORDELIA). 1917-   .
　-The Caravanners. Hodder, 1959
　Louise. Hodder, 1956; Washburn, 1957
　Marianne. Hodder, 1960
　-Mrs. Winterton's Rebellion. Hodder, 1958
　Not Proven. Hodder, 1966
　Number Two, North Steps. Hodder, 1965
　The Silent Witness. Hodder, 1962

DERLETH, AUGUST. 1909-1971. Pseudonym: Tally Mason, q.v. Series characters: Judge Peck = P; Solar Pons = SP.
　The Adventure of the Orient Express. Candlelight Press, 1965 SP
　The Adventure of the Unique Dickensians. Mycroft, 1968 SP
　The Adventures of Solar Pons; see In re Sherlock Holmes
　The Casebook of Solar Pons. Mycroft, 1965 SP ss
　The Chronicles of Solar Pons. Mycroft, 1973; Robson, 1975 SP ss
　Death by Design. Arcadia, 1953
　Death Stalks the Wakely Family; see Murder Stalks the Wakely Family
　Fell Purpose. Arcadia, 1953 P
　In re Sherlock Holmes: The Adventures of Solar Pons. Mycroft, 1945. British title: The Adventures of Solar Pons. Robson, 1975. Also published as: Regarding Sherlock Holmes. Pinnacle, 1974 SP ss
　The Man on All Fours. Loring, 1934; Newnes, 1936 P
　The Memoirs of Solar Pons. Mycroft, 1951 SP ss
　Mischief in the Lane. Scribner, 1944; Muller, 1948 P
　Mr. Fairlie's Final Journey. Mycroft, 1968 SP
　Murder Stalks the Wakely Family. Loring, 1934. British title: Death Stalks the Wakely Family. Newnes, 1937 P
　The Narracong Riddle. Scribner, 1940 P
　No Future for Luana. Scribner, 1945; Muller, 1948 P
　A Praed Street Dossier. Mycroft, 1968 SP
　Praed Street Papers. Candlelight Press, 1965 SP
　Regarding Sherlock Holmes; see In re Sherlock Holmes
　The Reminiscences of Solar Pons. Mycroft, 1961 SP ss

The Return of Solar Pons. Mycroft, 1958 SP ss
Sentence Deferred. Scribner, 1939; Heinemann, 1939 P
The Seven Who Waited. Scribner, 1943; Muller, 1945 P
Sign of Fear. Loring, 1935; Newnes, 1936 P
Three Problems for Solar Pons. Mycroft, 1952 SP ss
The Three Straw Men. Candlelight Press, 1970
Three Who Died. Loring, 1935 P

DE ROO, EDWARD
  The Little Caesars. Ace, 1961

DERRICK, HENRY. See: GEORGE DOUGLAS (pseudonym of Mrs. George Ferme).

DERRICK, LIONEL. Series character: The Penetrator (Mark Hardin), in all titles.
  Baja Bandidos. Pinnacle, 1974
  Blood on the Strip. Pinnacle, 1973
  Capitol Hell. Pinnacle, 1974
  Dodge City Bombers. Pinnacle, 1975
  The Hellbound Flight. Pinnacle, 1975
  Hijacking Manhattan. Pinnacle, 1974
  Mardi Gras Massacre. Pinnacle, 1974
  Northwest Contract. Pinnacle, 1975
  The Target is H. Pinnacle, 1973
  Terror in Taos. Pinnacle, 1975
  Tokyo Purple. Pinnacle, 1974

DE ST. JORRE, JOHN, 1936-   , and BRIAN SHAKESPEARE
  The Patriot Game. Hodder, 1973; Houghton, 1973

DE SAIX, TYLER. Pseudonym of H(enry) DeVere Stacpoole, 1863-1951, q.v.
  The Man Without a Head. Moffat, 1908
  The Vulture's Prey. Unwin, 1909. Reprinted as by H. DeVere Stacpoole: Unwin, 1918

DE SAVALLO, DONA TERESA. Pseudonym of A(lice) M(uriel Livingston) Williamson, 1869-   , q.v. See also: C(HARLES) N(ORRIS) WILLIAMSON, 1859-1920.
  The House of the Lost Court. McClure, 1908. (British title?)

DES CARS, GUY
  The Brute. Wingate, 1952; Greenberg, 1952. (Translation of La Brute. Paris, 1951.)
  -Chantal. Houghton, 1954. Also published as: Woman of Paris. Popular Library, 1955. (Translation of L'Impure. Paris, 1946.)
  -The Damned One. Pyramid, 1956
  -A Strange Affection. Sidgwick, 1965. (Translation of Cette Etrange Tendresse. Paris, 1960.)
  -The Unclean. Wingate, 1953. (Translation of La Corruptrice. Paris, 1952.)
  Woman of Paris; see Chantal

DES LIGNERIS, FRANCOISE
  Bijoux. Avon, 1963

DESMARAIS, OVIDE E. 1919-   . Pseudonym: Ovid Demaris, q.v.

DESMOND, CLIVE
  Intrigue. Hodder, 1919

DESMOND, COLIN
  -The Secret of Stark Island. Pilgrim, 1928

DESMOND, HUGH. Series character: Alan Fraser, in at least those marked AF.
  Appointment at Eight. Wright, 1957 AF
  Blood Cries for Vengeance. Wright, 1948
  Bluebeard's Wife. Wright, 1947
  Bodies in a Cupboard. Wright, 1963 AF
  Breath of Suspicion. Wright, 1954
  Calling Alan Fraser. Wright, 1951 AF
  The Case of the Blue Orchid. Wright, 1961 AF
  A Clear Case of Murder. Wright, 1950
  Condemned. Wright, 1964 AF
  Dark Deeds. Wright, 1952
  The Dark Shadow. Wright, 1965 AF
  Death at my Elbow. Wright, 1960
  Death in the Shingle. Wright, 1948
  Death Let Loose. Wright, 1956
  The Death Parade. Wright, 1954 AF
  Death Strikes at Dawn. Wright, 1943
  Death Walks in Scarlet. Wright, 1948
  Deliver Us from Evil. Wright, 1953 AF
  A Desperate Gamble. Wright, 1946
  Destination—Death. Wright, 1955 AF
  Doorway to Death. Wright, 1959 AF
  The Edge of Horror. Wright, 1950
  Escape. Wright, 1968
  Fanfare for Murder. Wright, 1961 AF
  Fear Walks the Island. Wright, 1951
  The Fuehrer Dies. Wright, 1944
  Gallows' Fruit. Wright, 1949
  The Hand of Vengeance. Wright, 1945 AF
  The Hangman Waits. Wright, 1955
  Highways of Death. Wright, 1940
  His Reverence the Rogue. Wright, 1946
  Horror at the Moated Mill. Wright, 1967 AF
  Hostage to Death. Wright, 1964 AF
  In Fear of the Night. Wright, 1960 AF
  Intent to Kill. Hale, 1942
  The Jacaranda Murders. Wright, 1951
  The Lady has Claws. Wright, 1966 AF
  Lady in Peril. Wright, 1946
  Lady, Where are You? Wright, 1957 AF
  Look Upon the Prisoner. Wright, 1958
  Mask of Terror. Wright, 1968 AF
  The Misty Pathway. Wright, 1940
  Murder at Midnight. Wright, 1962
  Murder is Justified. Wright, 1951
  Murder on the Moor. Wright, 1967 AF
  Murder Run Wild. Hale, 1941
  Murder Strikes at Dawn. Wright, 1965 AF
  Murderer's Bride. Wright, 1954
  The Mystery Killer. Wright, 1943
  Night of Terror. Wright, 1953
  The Night of the Crime. Wright, 1953
  No Reprieve. Wright, 1957
  Not Guilty, My Lord. Wright, 1965 AF
  Overture to Death. Wright, 1947
  A Pact with the Devil. Wright, 1952 AF
  Poison Pen. Wright, 1958 AF
  Put Out the Light. Wright, 1962
  Reign of Terror. Wright, 1952
  A Scream in the Night. Wright, 1955
  The Secret of the Moat. Wright, 1940
  The Secret Voice. Wright, 1942
  She Met Murder. Wright, 1956 AF
  The Silent Witness. Wright, 1963 AF
  The Slasher. Wright, 1939
  A Slight Case of Murder. Wright, 1963 AF
  Someday I'll Kill You. Wright, 1964 AF
  Stay of Execution. Wright, 1962 AF
  Stella Shall Die. Wright, 1956
  Stranger Than Fiction. Wright, 1961
  The Strangler. Wright, 1947
  A Strong Dose of Poison. Wright, 1959
  Suicide Fleet. Wright, 1959
  Terror Walks by Night. Wright, 1944
  They Lived with Death. Wright, 1945
  Turn Back from Death. Wright, 1960
  The Viper's Sting. Wright, 1946 AF
  We Walk with Death. Wright, 1968 AF
  The Wicked Shall Flourish. Wright, 1959
  A Wife in the Dark. Wright, 1948

DESPARD, LESLIE. Pseudonym of John Leslie Despard Howitt.

The Amazing Adventures of Mr. Henry Button. Hodder, 1927
The Crime Without a Flaw. Nash, 1931
The Mystery of the Tower Room. Hodder, 1925

DESSART, GINA. 1912-   .
  Cry for the Lost. Harper, 1959
  The Last House. Harper, 1950; Hodder, 1951
  A Man Died Here. Harper, 1947; Hodder, 1948

DE STEFANO, ANTHONY
  Mondo. Manor, 1975

DE STEIGUER, WALTER. 1884-   .
  Jewels for a Shroud. Morrow, 1950; Locke, 1951

DE TERAMOND, GUY. Pseudonym of Edmond Gautier Teramond, 1869-   .
  The Mystery of Lucien Delorme. Appleton, 1915. (Translation of L'Homme Qui Voit a Travers les Murailles. Paris, 1913.)

DETZER, KARL (WILLIAM). 1891-   .
  The Broken Three. Bobbs, 1929
  -Contrabando. Bobbs, 1936
  True Tales of the D.C.I. Bobbs, 1925 ss

DE VILLIERS, GERALD. 1929-   . Series character: Malko Linge, in all titles.
  Angel of Vengeance. Pinnacle, 1974
  Checkpoint Charlie. Pinnacle, 1975
  The Countess and the Spy. Pinnacle, 1974
  Death on the River Kwai. Pinnacle, 1975
  Kill Kissinger. Pinnacle, 1974
  The Man from Kabul. Pinnacle, 1973
  Operation New York. Pinnacle, 1973
  Que Viva Guevara. Pinnacle, 1975
  Versus the C.I.A. Pinnacle, 1974
  West of Jerusalem. Pinnacle, 1973

DEVINE, D(AVID) M(cDONALD). 1920-   . Pseudonym: Dominic Devine, q.v.
  Death is my Bridegroom. Collins, 1969; Walker, 1969
  The Devil at Your Elbow. Collins, 1966; Walker, 1967
  Doctors Also Die. Collins, 1962; Dodd, 1963
  The Fifth Cord. Collins, 1967; Walker, 1967
  His Own Appointed Day. Collins, 1965; Walker, 1967
  Illegal Tender. Collins, 1970; Walker, 1970
  My Brother's Killer. Collins, 1961; Dodd, 1962
  The Royston Affair. Collins, 1964; Dodd, 1965
  The Sleeping Tiger. Collins, 1968; Walker, 1968

DEVINE, DOMINIC. Pseudonym of D(avid) M(cDonald) Devine, 1920-   , q.v.
  Dead Trouble. Collins, 1971; Doubleday, 1971
  Three Green Bottles. Collins, 1972; Doubleday, 1972

DEVINE, (VIRGINIA) STEWART
  Even in Death. Doubleday, 1950
  Listen for a Stranger. Doubleday, 1951

DE VOTO, BERNARD AUGUSTINE. 1897-1955. Pseudonym: John August, q.v.

DE WAAL, PHILIP
  The Mystery of the Green Garnet Murder. (No publisher or date given.)

DEWAR, EVELYN
  A Dying Business. Bles, 1974
  Perfumes of Arabia. Bles, 1973; Walker, 1974

DEWDNEY, PETER. Pseudonym of Alan (St. Hill) Brock, 1886- .
  Arising from an Accident. Wright, 1939
  On Appeal. Wright, 1938

DeWEESE, (THOMAS EU)GENE, 1934- , and ROBERT (STRATTON) COULSON, 1918- . Joint pseudonym: Thomas Stratton, q.v. Pseudonym of DeWeese alone: Jean DeWeese, q.v.
  Now You See It-Him-Them. Doubleday, 1975; Hale, 1976

DeWEESE, JEAN. Pseudonym of (Thomas Eu)-Gene DeWeese, 1934- , q.v. Joint pseudonym with Robert (Stratton) Coulson, 1918- : Thomas Stratton, q.v.
  The Carnelian Cat. Ballantine, 1975
  The Moonstone Spirit. Ballantine, 1975
  The Reimann Curse. Ballantine, 1975

DEWES, SIMON. Pseudonym of John St. Clair Muriel, 1909- .
  Cul-de-Sac. Rich, 1941
  Death Stalks the Waterway. Rich, 1946
  Panic in Pursuit. Rich, 1945

DEWEY, THOMAS B(LANCHARD). 1915- . Pseudonym: Tom Brandt, q.v. Series characters: Singer Batts = SB; Mac = M; Pete Schofield = PS.
  And Where She Stops. Popular Library, 1957. British title: I.O.U. Murder. Boardman, 1958 PS
  As Good as Dead. Jefferson, 1946; Dakers, 1952 SB
  The Brave, Bad Girls. Simon, 1956; Boardman, 1957 M
  Can a Mermaid Kill? Tower, 1965
  The Case of the Chased and the Unchaste. Random, 1959; Boardman, 1960 M
  The Case of the Murdered Model; see Prey for Me
  Dame in Danger; see Draw the Curtain Close
  Deadline. Simon, 1966; Boardman, 1967 M
  Death and Taxes. Putnam, 1967; Hale, 1969 M
  Death Turns Right; see The King Killers
  Don't Cry for Long. Simon, 1964; Boardman, 1965 M
  Draw the Curtain Close. Jefferson, 1947; Dakers, 1951. Also published as: Dame in Danger. Signet, 1958 SB
  Every Bet's a Sure Thing. Simon, 1953; Dakers, 1953
  The Girl in the Punchbowl. Dell, 1964; Boardman, 1965 PS
  The Girl Who Never Was; see The Girl Who Wasn't There
  The Girl Who Wasn't There. Simon, 1960; Boardman, 1960. Also published as: The Girl Who Never Was. Mayflower, 1962 M
  The Girl with the Sweet Plump Knees. Dell, 1963; Boardman, 1963 PS
  Go, Honeylou. Dell, 1962; Boardman, 1962 PS
  Go to Sleep, Jeannie. Popular Library, 1959; Boardman, 1960 PS
  The Golden Hooligan. Dell, 1961. British title: Mexican Slayride. Boardman, 1961 PS
  Handle with Fear. Mill, 1951; Dakers, 1955 SB
  How Hard to Kill. Simon, 1962; Boardman, 1963 M
  Hue and Cry. Jefferson, 1944. British title: The Murder of Marion Mason. Dakers, 1951. Also published as: Room for Murder. Signet, 1950 SB
  Hunter at Large. Simon, 1961; Boardman, 1962
  I.O.U. Murder; see And Where She Stops
  The King Killers. Putnam, 1968. British title: Death Turns Right. Hale, 1969 M
  The Love-Death Thing. Simon, 1969 M
  The Mean Streets. Simon, 1955; Boardman, 1955 M
  Mexican Slayride; see The Golden Hooligan
  Mourning After. Mill, 1950; Dakers, 1953 SB
  The Murder of Marion Mason; see Hue and Cry
  My Love is Violent. Popular Library, 1956; Consul, 1961
  Nude in Nevada. Dell, 1965; Boardman, 1966 PS
  Only on Tuesdays. Dell, 1964; Boardman, 1964 PS
  Portrait of a Dead Heiress. Simon, 1965; Boardman, 1966 M
  Prey for Me. Simon, 1954; Boardman, 1954. Also published as: The Case of the Murdered Model. Avon, 1955 M
  Room for Murder; see Hue and Cry
  A Sad Song Singing. Simon, 1963; Boardman, 1964 M
  A Season for Violence. GM, 1966
  The Taurus Trip. Simon, 1970 M
  Too Hot for Hawaii. Popular Library, 1960; Boardman, 1963 PS
  You've Got Him Cold. Simon, 1958; Boardman, 1959 M

DEWHURST, EILEEN
  Death Came Smiling. Hale, 1975

DE WIL, ERNEST
  The Brookham Mystery. International, 1893

DE WITT, JACK
  Murder on Shark Island. Liveright, 1941

DEXTER, BRUCE
  I'll Sing You the Death of Bill Brown. McGraw, 1963; Allen, 1964

DEXTER, (NORMAN) COLIN. 1930- .
  Last Bus to Woodstock. Macmillan (London), 1975; St. Martin's, 1975

DEXTER, LEE
  The Case of the Brooklyn Mobsters. Warren, 1949
  Detective Crime Stories. Warren, 1949 ss
  Police Detective Stories. Warren, 1949 ss

DEY, FREDERICK MERRILL VAN RENSSELAER. 1861-1922. Pseudonyms: Marmaduke Dey, Frederic Ormond, Varick Vanardy, qq.v.

DEY, MARMADUKE. Pseudonym of Frederick Merrill van Rensselaer Dey, 1861-1922. Other pseudonyms: Frederic Ormond, Varick Vanardy, qq.v.
  Muertalma; or, The Poisoned Pen. Street, 1890

DIAMOND, B.
  Redheads Die Young. Spencer, 1950
  Say It with Homicide. Spencer, 1952
  Sister Sinister. Spencer, 1949
  Such Men are Dangerous. Spencer, 1951

DIAMOND, FRANK. Series characters: Ransome Dragoon & Vicky Gaines = D&G.
  Love Me to Death. Ace, 1955

  Murder in Five Columns. Mystery House, 1944 D&G
  Murder Rides a Rocket. Mystery House, 1946; Equerry, 1947 D&G
  The Widow Maker. Ace, 1961

DIBNER, MARTIN. 1911- .
  -A God for Tomorrow. Doubleday, 1961

DICK, ALEXANDRA. Pseudonym of Sibyl Cicely Alexandra Dick Erikson. Other pseudonym: Frances Hay, q.v.
  -And Only Man. Hurst, 1944
  -Comet's Tail. Hodder, 1938
  Crime in the Close. Hale, 1955
  Cross Purposes. Hurst, 1950
  The Curate's Crime. Hurst, 1945; Bouregy, 1946, as by Sibyl Erikson
  -Dear Angel. Hurst, 1946
  Death at the Golden Crown. Hale, 1956
  -The First Man. Hodder, 1937
  -How Can We Sing? Hodder, 1942
  -Imperial Venus. Hale, 1954
  The Innocence of Rosamond Prior. Hale, 1953
  MacAlastair Looks On. Hurst, 1947
  -Many a Flower. Hurst, 1944
  -Never to Me. Hurst, 1943
  -No Sentiment. Hodder, 1939
  An Old-Fashioned Christmas. Hurst, 1944
  -One is One. Hale, 1958
  -A Pack of Cards. Hodder, 1940
  -The Sleeping Beauty's Daughter. Hurst, 1947
  -The Witch's Doing. Hurst, 1951
  -Yellowing Hay. Hodder, 1939

DICK, GEORGE
  -Fitch and his Fortunes. Stock, 1898

DICK, PHILIP K(ENDRED). 1928- .
  -Flow My Tears, the Policeman Said. Doubleday, 1974; Gollancz, 1974
  -A Maze of Death. Doubleday, 1970; Gollancz, 1972

DICK, T. Pseudonym of Eric Richard Osler, 1900- .
  Dark Before Dawn. Long, 1935

DICKENS, CHARLES (JOHN HUFFHAM). 1812-1870.
  Bleak House. Bradbury, 1853; Harper, 1853
  Hunted Down. Hotten, 1871
  The Mystery of Edwin Drood. Chapman, 1870; Fields, 1870

DICKENS, MARY ANGELA
  A Mist of Error. Collier, 1890

DICKENS, MONICA. 1915- .
  The Room Upstairs. Heinemann, 1966; Doubleday, 1966

DICKENSON, FRED
  Kill 'Em with Kindness. Bell, 1950

DICKINSON, PETER. 1927- . Series character: Supt. James Pibble = JP.
  The Glass-Sided Ants' Nest; see Skin Deep
  -The Green Gene. Hodder, 1973; Pantheon, 1973
  The Lively Dead. Hodder, 1975; Pantheon, 1975
  The Lizard in the Cup. Hodder, 1972; Harper, 1972 JP
  The Old English Peep Show; see A Pride of Heroes
  The Poison Oracle. Hodder, 1974; Pantheon, 1974
  A Pride of Heroes. Hodder, 1969. U.S. title: The Old English Peep Show. Harper, 1969 JP
  The Seals. Hodder, 1970. U.S. title: The Sinful Stones. Harper, 1970 JP

The Sinful Stones; see The Seals
Skin Deep. Hodder, 1968. U.S. title: The Glass-Sided Ants' Nest. Harper, 1968 JP
Sleep and His Brother. Hodder, 1971; Harper, 1971 JP

DICKINSON, WEED
Dead Man Talks Too Much. Lippincott (Philadelphia & London), 1937

DICKSON, ARTHUR (PARKINSON). 1888- .
Death Bids for Corners. Humphries, 1941

DICKSON, CARR. Pseudonym of John Dickson Carr, 1905-1977, q.v. Other pseudonyms: Carter Dickson, Roger Fairbairn, qq.v. See also: JOHN RHODE; and: ADRIAN CONAN DOYLE, 1911-1970.
The Bowstring Murders. Morrow, 1933; Heinemann, 1934, as by Carter Dickson. (All reprints as by Carter Dickson.)

DICKSON, CARTER. Pseudonym of John Dickson Carr, 1905-1977, q.v. Other pseudonyms: Carr Dickson, Roger Fairbairn, qq.v. See also: JOHN RHODE; and: ADRIAN CONAN DOYLE, 1911-1970. Series character: Sir Henry Merrivale = HM (see also John Dickson Carr byline).
And So to Murder. Morrow, 1940; Heinemann, 1941 HM
Behind the Crimson Blind. Morrow, 1952; Heinemann, 1952 HM
The Cavalier's Cup. Morrow, 1953; Heinemann, 1954 HM
Cross of Murder; see Seeing is Believing
The Crossbow Murder; see The Judas Window
The Curse of the Bronze Lamp. Morrow, 1945. British title: Lord of the Sorcerers. Heinemann, 1946 HM
Death and the Gilded Man; see The Gilded Man
Death in Five Boxes. Morrow, 1938; Heinemann, 1938 HM
The Department of Queer Complaints. Morrow, 1940; Heinemann, 1940. (11 ss, 7 about Colonel March, 4 non-series. The 7 March stories were reprinted as: Scotland Yard: Department of Queer Complaints. Dell, 1944.)
Fear is the Same. Morrow, 1956; Heinemann, 1956
The Gilded Man. Morrow, 1942; Heinemann, 1942. Also published as: Death and the Gilded Man. PB, 1947 HM
A Graveyard to Let. Morrow, 1949; Heinemann, 1950 HM
He Wouldn't Kill Patience. Morrow, 1944; Heinemann, 1944 HM
The Judas Window. Morrow, 1938; Heinemann, 1938. Also published as: The Crossbow Murder. Berkley, 196? HM
Lord of the Sorcerers; see The Curse of the Bronze Lamp
The Magic Lantern Murders; see The Punch and Judy Murders
Murder in the Atlantic; see Nine—and Death Makes Ten
Murder in the Submarine Zone; see Nine—and Death Makes Ten
My Late Wives. Morrow, 1946; Heinemann, 1947 HM
Night at the Mocking Widow. Morrow, 1950; Heinemann, 1951 HM
Nine—and Death Makes Ten. Morrow, 1940. British title: Murder in the Submarine Zone. Heinemann, 1940. Also published as: Murder in the Atlantic. World Distributors, 1959 HM
The Peacock Feather Murders. Morrow, 1937. British title: The Ten Teacups. Heinemann, 1937 HM
The Plague Court Murders. Morrow, 1934; Heinemann, 1935 HM
The Punch and Judy Murders. Morrow, 1937. British title: The Magic Lantern Murders. Heinemann, 1936 HM
The Reader is Warned. Morrow, 1939; Heinemann, 1939 HM
The Red Widow Murders. Morrow, 1935; Heinemann, 1935 HM
Scotland Yard: Department of Queer Complaints; see The Department of Queer Complaints
Seeing is Believing. Morrow, 1941; Heinemann, 1942. Also published as: Cross of Murder. World Distributors, 1959 HM
She Died a Lady. Morrow, 1943; Heinemann, 1943 HM
The Skeleton in the Clock. Morrow, 1948; Heinemann, 1949 HM
The Ten Teacups; see The Peacock Feather Murders
The Third Bullet. Hodder pb, 1937. (A paperback novelet about Colonel Marquis, a prototype of Colonel March. This novelet is included in hardcover in the collection of the same name as by John Dickson Carr, q.v.)
The Unicorn Murders. Morrow, 1935; Heinemann, 1936 HM
The White Priory Murders. Morrow, 1934; Heinemann, 1935 HM

DICKSON, GRIERSON. Series character: Supt. "Cissie" Marlow, in at least those marked CM.
Design for Treason. Hutchinson, 1937 CM
The Devil's Torch. Hutchinson, 1936 CM
Gun Business. Hutchinson, 1935
Knight's Gambit. Hutchinson, 1950 CM
The Seven Screens. Hutchinson, 1950
Soho Racket. Hutchinson, 1935
Traitor's Market. Hutchinson, 1936 CM

DICKSON, JAMES GRIERSON. Pseudonym: Hilary King, q.v.

DIDELOT, (ROGER) FRANCIS. 1902- .
Series characters: Commissaire Orestes Bignon = OB; Inspector Lecain = L.
Death of the Deputy. Lippincott (Philadelphia & London), 1935. (Translation of L'Assassin du Depute. Paris, 1934.) L
Death on the Champs-Elysees. Macmillan (London), 1965. (Translation of Bignon et la Verite. Paris, 1963.) OB
The Many Ways of Death. Belmont, 1966. (Translation of 6 Heures d'Anguisse. Paris, 1955.) OB
Murder in the Bath. Lippincott (Philadelphia & London), 1933. (Translation from the French.) L
The Seventh Juror. Macdonald, 1960; Belmont, 1963. (Translation of Le Septieme Jure. Paris, 1958.)
The Tenth Leper. Macdonald, 1962. (Translation of Feu Sur le Mage! Paris, 1956.) OB
Warrant for Arrest. Macdonald, 1963. (Translation of Mandat d'Arret. Paris, 1961.) OB

DIEHL, ALICE M(ANGOLD). 1844-1912.
The Desborough Mystery. Digby, 1903
-Entrapped. Long, 1904
-A Mysterious Bohemian. Digby, 1908
-The Secret of Sir George Hartley. Digby, 1910

DIETRICH, ROBERT. Pseudonym of (Everette) Howard Hunt, 1918- , q.v. Other pseudonyms: Gordon Davis, John Q, David St. John, qq.v. Series character: Steve Bentley = SB.
Angel Eyes. Dell, 1961 SB
Be My Victim. Dell, 1956
The Cheat. Pyramid, 1954
Curtains for a Lover. Lancer, 1961 SB
End of a Stripper. Dell, 1959 SB
The House on Q Street. Dell, 1959 SB
Mistress to Murder. Dell, 1960 SB
Murder on her Mind. Dell, 1960 SB
Murder on the Rocks. Dell, 1957; Ward, 1958 SB
My Body. Lancer, 1962. Reprinted as by E. Howard Hunt: Lancer, 1973 SB
One for the Road. Pyramid, 1954
Steve Bentley's Calypso Caper. Dell, 1961 SB

DIETZ, LEW. 1907- .
The Running Man. Avon, 1969

DIGNAM, C. B.
Black Velvet. Hamilton, 1926
The Sons of Seven. Hamilton, 1928

DIKE, DONALD
The Bishop's Park Mystery. Cassell, 1926

DILKE, CHRISTOPHER
-The Guardian. Hale, 1953

DILLON, EILIS. 1920- . Series character: Inspector Mike Kenny = MK.
Death at Crane's Court. Faber, 1953; Walker, 1963 MK
Death in the Quadrangle. Faber, 1956; British Book Centre, 1962 MK
Sent to His Account. Faber, 1954; British Book Centre, 1961

DILLON, JACK
A Great Day for Dying. GM, 1968; Coronet, 1968

DILNOT, FRANK (BUCKLAND). 1875- .
Scoundrel Mark. Blackwood, 1906

DILNOT, GEORGE. 1883-1951. See also: FRANK FROEST. Series characters: Horace Augustus Elver = HE; Val Emery = VE; Jim Strang = JS; Inspector Strickland = S; Sexton Blake (with many other authors) = SB.
The Black Ace. Bles, 1929; Houghton, 1929 S
The Black Ace. Amalgamated, 1938 SB
The Case of the Missing Bridegroom. Amalgamated, 1938 SB
Counter-Spy. Bles, 1942 JS
The Crime Reporter's Secret. Amalgamated, 1937 SB
Crook's Castle. Bles, 1934; Houghton, 1934 HE
The Crooks' Game. Bles, 1927; Houghton, 1927 S
Fighting Fool. Bles, 1939 VE
The Great Mail Racket. Bles, 1936 HE
The Hat-Pin Murder. Bles, 1927. U.S. title: Suspected. Clode, 1920
The Inside Track. Bles, 1935
The Lazy Detective. Bles, 1926
Murder at Scotland Yard. Bles, 1937 HE
Murder Masquerade. Bles, 1935 HE
The Real Detective. Bles, 1933
Rogues' March. Bles, 1934 ss
The Secret Service Man. Nash, 1916 JS
Sister Satan. Bles, 1933; Houghton, 1933
Suspected; see The Hat-Pin Murder
The Thousandth Case. Bles, 1932; Houghton, 1933
Tiger Lily. Bles, 1939 VE

DIMENT, ADAM. Series character: Philip McAlpine, in all titles.
The Bang Bang Birds. Joseph, 1968; Dutton, 1968
The Dolly Dolly Spy. Joseph, 1967; Dutton, 1967

The Great Spy Race. Joseph, 1968;
  Dutton, 1968
Think Inc. Joseph, 1971

DIMMOCK, F(REDERICK) H(AYDN). 1895-
  The Clue of the Ivory Claw, with
    Michael Poole (q.v.; pseudonym of
    Reginald Heber Poole, 1885-   ,
    q.v.). Pearson, 1919
  The Lost Trooper. Pearson, 1920
  The Secret of Gaunt House, with
    Michael Poole (as above). Pearson,
    1931

DI MONA, JOSEPH
  The Last Man at Arlington. Fields,
    1973; Weidenfeld, 1974
  70 Sutton Place. Dodd, 1972

DINELLI, MEL
  The Man. Dramatists Play Service, 1950;
    English Theatre Guild, 1954. (2-act
    play.)

DINES, MICHAEL. 1916-   .
  Operation—Deadline. Ward, 1967
  Operation—Kill or Be Killed. Hale,
    1969
  Operation—To Kill a Man. Ward, 1968

DINESEN, ISAK. Pseudonym of Baroness
  Karen Christence Blixen Finecke,
  1885-1962. Other pseudonym: Pierre
  Andrezel, q.v.
  Last Tales. Random, 1957; Putnam (London), 1957 ss
  Seven Gothic Tales. Smith & Haas, 1934;
    Putnam (London), 1934 ss
  Winter's Tales. Random, 1942; Putnam
    (London), 1943 ss

DINGLE, AYLWARD EDWARD. 1874-1947. Pseudonym: Brian Cotterell, q.v.

DINGWALL, PETER. Pseudonym of Robin Forsythe, 1879-   , q.v.
  The Poison Duel. Methuen, 1934

DINNEEN, JOSEPH F(RANCIS). 1897-   .
  The Alternate Case. Little, 1959; Cassell, 1960. Also published as: The
    Biggest Holdup. Ace, 1961
  The Anatomy of a Crime. Scribner, 1954;
    Cassell, 1955
  The Biggest Holdup; see The Alternate
    Case
  The Merry-Go-Round of Murder. Mystery
    Novel of the Month, 194?

DINNER, WILLIAM, and WILLIAM MORUM. Pseudonym of William Dinner: Surrey
  Smith, q.v.
  The Bluffing of Gaston Leroux. French
    (London), 1949. (1-act play.)
  Ladies' Bar. Deane, 1954. (1-act play.)
  The Late Edwina Black. French (London),
    1950; French (New York), 1951. (3-act
    play.)
  Too Soon for Daisies. Dean, 1964.
    (Play.)

DIPLOMAT. Pseudonym of John Franklin
  Carter, 1897-1967. Series character:
  Dennis Tyler, in all titles.
  The Brain Trust Murder. Coward, 1935
  The Corpse on the White House Lawn.
    Covici, 1932; Hurst, 1933
  Death in the Senate. Covici, 1933
  Murder in the Embassy. Cape & Smith,
    1930; Harrap, 1931
  Murder in the State Department. Cape &
    Smith, 1930
  Scandal in the Chancery. Cape & Smith,
    1931
  Slow Death at Geneva. Coward, 1934

DIPPER, ALAN. 1922-   .
  The Colour of Darkness. Joseph, 1974

The Golden Virgin. Joseph, 1972; Walker, 1973
The Hard Trip. Joseph, 1970
The Paradise Formula. Morrow, 1970
The Wave Hangs Dark. Morrow, 1969

DIRCKX, JOHN H. 1938-   . Series character (following R. Austin Freeman,
  1862-1943, and Norman Donaldson,
  1922-   , qq.v.): Dr. John Thorndyke.
  Dr. Thorndyke's Dilemma. Aspen, 1974

DISCH, THOMAS M(ICHAEL). 1940-   . Joint
  pseudonym with John Sladek, 1937-   :
  Thom Demijohn, q.v.
  The Prisoner. Ace, 1969. (Novelization
    of the TV series.)

DISNEY, DORIS MILES. 1907-1976. Series
  characters: Jeff DiMarco = JM; David
  Madden = DM; Jim O'Neill = JO.
  Appointment at Nine. Doubleday, 1947 JO
  At Some Forgotten Door. Doubleday,
    1966; Hale, 1967
  Black Mail. Doubleday, 1958; Foulsham,
    1960 DM
  The Case of the Straw Man; see Straw
    Man
  The Chandler Policy. Putnam, 1971;
    Hale, 1973 JD
  A Compound for Death. Doubleday, 1943
    JO
  Count the Ways. Doubleday, 1949
  Cry for Help. Doubleday, 1975; Hale,
    1976
  Dark Lady. Doubleday, 1960. British
    title: Sinister Lady. Hale, 1962
  Dark Road. Doubleday, 1946; Nimmo,
    1947. Also published as: Dead Stop.
    Dell, 1956 JD
  The Day Miss Bessie Lewis Disappeared.
    Doubleday, 1972; Hale, 1973
  Dead Stop; see Dark Road
  Death by Computer; see Do Not Fold,
    Spindle or Mutilate
  Death for my Beloved; see Enduring Old
    Charms
  The Departure of Mr. Gaudette. Doubleday, 1964. British title: Fateful
    Departure. Hale, 1965
  Did She Fall or Was She Pushed? Doubleday, 1959; Hale, 1962 JD
  Do Not Fold, Spindle or Mutilate.
    Doubleday, 1970. British title: Death
    by Computer. Hale, 1971
  Do Unto Others. Doubleday, 1953
  Don't Go into the Woods Today. Doubleday, 1974
  Driven to Kill; see The Last Straw
  Enduring Old Charms. Doubleday, 1947.
    Also published as: Death for my Beloved. Bestseller, 1949
  Family Skeleton. Doubleday, 1949 JD
  Fatal Choice; see Two Little Children
    and How They Grew
  Fateful Departure; see The Departure of
    Mr. Gaudette
  Find the Woman. Doubleday, 1962; Hale,
    1964 JD
  Fire at Will. Doubleday, 1950 JO
  Flame of Evil; see Night of Clear
    Choice
  The Halloween Murder; see Trick or
    Treat
  Heavy, Heavy Hangs. Doubleday, 1952
  Here Lies. Doubleday, 1963; Hale, 1964
  The Hospitality of the House. Doubleday, 1964. British title: Unsuspected
    Evil. Hale, 1965
  The Last Straw. Doubleday, 1954. British title: Driven to Kill. Foulsham,
    1957 JO

Look Back on Murder. Doubleday, 1951
The Magic Grandfather. Doubleday, 1966.
  British title: Mask of Evil. Hale,
  1967
Mask of Evil; see The Magic Grandfather
Method in Madness. Doubleday, 1957.
  British title: Quiet Violence. Foulsham, 1959. Also published as: Too
  Innocent to Kill. Avon, 1959 JD
Money for the Taking. Doubleday, 1968;
  Hale, 1968
Mrs. Meeker's Money. Doubleday, 1961;
  Hale, 1963 DM
Murder on a Tangent. Doubleday, 1945 JO
My Neighbor's Wife. Doubleday, 1957;
  Foulsham, 1958
Night of Clear Choice. Doubleday, 1967.
  British title: Flame of Evil. Hale,
  1968
No Next of Kin. Doubleday, 1959; Foulsham, 1961
Only Couples Need Apply. Doubleday,
  1973; Hale, 1974
The Post Office Case; see Unappointed
  Rounds
Prescription: Murder. Doubleday, 1953
Quiet Violence; see Method in Madness
Room for Murder. Doubleday, 1955; Foulsham, 1959
Shadow of a Man. Doubleday, 1965; Hale,
  1966
Should Auld Acquaintance. Doubleday,
  1962; Hale, 1963
Sinister Lady; see Dark Lady
Sow the Wind; see Who Rides a Tiger
Straw Man. Doubleday, 1951. British
  title: The Case of the Straw Man.
  Foulsham, 1958 JD
Testimony by Silence. Doubleday, 1948
That Which is Crooked. Doubleday, 1948
Three's a Crowd. Doubleday, 1971; Hale,
  1972
Too Innocent to Kill; see Method in
  Madness
Trick or Treat. Doubleday, 1955. British title: The Halloween Murder.
  Foulsham, 1957 JD
Two Little Children and How They Grew.
  Doubleday, 1969. British title: Fatal
  Choice. Hale, 1970
Unappointed Rounds. Doubleday, 1956.
  British title: The Post Office Case.
  Foulsham, 1957 DM
Unsuspected Evil; see The Hospitality
  of the House
Voice from the Grave. Doubleday, 1968;
  Hale, 1969
Who Rides a Tiger. Doubleday, 1946.
  British title: Sow the Wind. Nimmo,
  1948

DISNEY, DOROTHY CAMERON
  The Balcony. Random, 1940; Hale, 1941
  Crimson Friday. Random, 1943; Hale,
    1945
  Death in the Back Seat. Random, 1936;
    Hale, 1937
  Explosion. Random, 1948
  The Golden Swan Murder. Random, 1939;
    Hale, 1940
  The Hangman's Tree. Random, 1949
  The 17th Letter. Random, 1945; Hale,
    1948
  Strawstack. Random, 1939; Hale, 1939.
    Also published as: The Strawstack
    Murders. Dell, 1944
  The Strawstack Murders; see Strawstack
  30 Days Hath September, with George
    Sessions Perry (1910-1956). Random,
    1942; Hale, 1950

DITTON, JAMES
  The Bigger They Are. Hale, 1973
  Escapemanship. Hale, 1975
  You're Fairly Welcome. Hale, 1973

DIVEN, ROBERT JOSEPH. 1869- .
  The Black Wolf Mystery. Century, 1931

DIVINE, A(RTHUR) D(URHAM). 1904- .
  Pseudonyms: David Divine, q.v., David Rame.
  Admiral's Million. Methuen, 1936
  Dark Moon. Methuen, 1933
  Escape from Spain. Methuen, 1936
  Fire in the Ice. Blackwell, 1937
  Graveyard Watch. Methuen, 1931
  Lawless Voyage. Hodder pb, 1937
  Pelican Island. Methuen, 1932
  The Pub on the Pool. Collins, 1938
  Sea Loot. Methuen, 1930; McBride, 1931
  Seventy Fathom Treasure. Newnes, 1936
  Slack Water. Collins, 1939
  Terror in the Thames. Collins, 1938
  They Blocked the Suez Canal. Methuen, 1935; Furman, 1936
  Tunnel from Calais. Collins, 1942; Macmillan, 1943, as by David Rame
  U-Boat in the Hebrides. Collins, 1940
  Wings Over the Atlantic. Lane, 1936

DIVINE, DAVID. Pseudonym of A(rthur) D(urham) Divine, 1904- , q.v.
  Other pseudonym: David Rame.
  Atom at Spithead. Hale, 1953; Macmillan, 1953
  -The Blunted Sword. Hutchinson, 1964
  Boy on a Dolphin. Murray, 1955; Macmillan, 1955
  -The Daughter of the Pangaran. Hutchinson, 1963; Little, 1963
  -The Golden Fool. Murray, 1954; Macmillan, 1954

DIX, BEULAH MARIE. 1876- .
  Wedding Eve Murder. McBride, 1941

DIX, MAURICE B(UXTON). 1889-1956. Series characters: Supt. Simon Bullion, in at least those marked B; Tommy Malins, Anthony Mornington and George Hawkins, in at least those marked M&M&H; Inspector James Miller, in at least those marked JM; Sexton Blake (with many other authors) = SB.
  The Affair of the Smuggled Millions. Amalgamated, 1943 SB
  Beacons of Death. Ward, 1937 M&M&H
  The Dartmoor Mystery. Ward, 1935
  Emily Coulton Dies. Ward, 1936
  The Fixer. Ward, 1936
  The Flame of the Khan. Ward, 1934
  The Fleetwood Mansions Mystery. Ward, 1934 JM
  The Golden Fluid. Ward, 1935 M&M&H
  The Great Hush-Hush Mystery. Amalgamated, 1939 SB
  The Kidnapped Scientist. Ward, 1937 M&M&H
  A Lady Richly Left. Staples, 1951
  The Masinglee Murders. Hale, 1947
  Murder at Grassmere Abbey. Ward, 1933 JM
  Murder Strikes Twice. Ward, 1939 B
  The Night Assassin. Hale, 1941
  Prologue to Murder. Ward, 1938
  The Secret of the Dead Convict. Amalgamated, 1937 SB
  The Secret of the Siegfried Line. Amalgamated, 1940 SB
  The Third Degree. Gramol, 1936
  This is my Murder. Ward, 1938 B
  The Treasure of Scarland. Ward, 1936
  Twisted Evidence. Ward, 1933 M&M&H
  The Victim of the Girl Spy. Amalgamated, 1936 SB

DIXON, CHARLES
  A Fortune for the Taking. Hale, 1963
  A Hand in Murder. Hale, 1962
  Ministry Murder. Hale, 1961
  Red Murder File. Hale, 1964
  So Slender a Thread. Hale, 1962
  A Trail to Treason. Hale, 1964

DIXON, H(ARRY) VERNOR. 1908- .
  Cry Blood. GM, 1956
  Deep is the Pit. GM, 1952
  Get Out of Town. GM, 196?
  The Hunger and the Hate. GM, 1955
  Killer in Silk. GM, 1956; Fawcett (London), 1957
  A Lover for Cindy. GM, 1954; Fawcett (London), 1955
  -The Marriage Bed. Red Seal (U.S.), 1952
  The Pleasure Seekers. Monarch, 1963
  The Rag Pickers. McKay, 1966; Hale, 1967
  Something for Nothing. Harper, 1950; H. Hamilton, 1950
  To Hell Together. GM, 1951
  Too Rich to Die. GM, 1953; Fawcett (London), 1956
  Up a Winding Stair. GM, 1953; Fawcett (London), 1954

DIXON, J. EARLE
  Killers in the Sun. Abelard (London), 1960; Abelard (New York), 1961

DIXON, PETER L(EE), 1932- , and LAIRD P. KOENIG, q.v.
  The Children are Watching. Ballantine, 1970; Longmans, 1971

DIXON, ROGER. 1930- . Pseudonym: John Christian, q.v.

DIXON, W(ILLMOTT) WILLMOTT. 1843- .
  Pseudonym: Thormanby, q.v.
  The Adventures of Captain Mounsell. Everett, 1902
  -The Rogue of Rye. Chatto, 1909

DOBBINS, PAUL H. 1916- .
  Death in the Dunes. Phoenix, 1950
  Death Trap. Phoenix, 1951
  Fatal Finale. Phoenix, 1949
  Murder Moon. Murray & Gee, 1949

DOBNER, MAEVA (PARK). 1918- .
  The Gingerbread House. Dell, 1974
  Heather. Dell, 1971
  The Woman in the Maze. Dell, 1970

DOBSON, KENNETH AUSTIN. 1907- .
  Mail Train. Hodder, 1946

DOBYNS, STEPHEN. 1941- .
  A Man of Little Evils. Atheneum, 1973

DOCHERTY, JAMES L. Pseudonym of Rene Brabazon Raymond, 1906- . Other pseudonyms: James Hadley Chase, Ambrose Grant, Raymond Marshall, qq.v.
  He Won't Need It Now. Rich, 1939

DODD, ALLEN ROBERT. 1887- . Pseudonym: Robert Allen, q.v.

DODGE, ALICE M. and MADELEINE SAFONOV
  The Eye of the Peacock. Bouregy, 1966

DODGE, CONSTANCE W(OODBURY). 1896- .
  The Unrelenting. Doubleday, 1950

DODGE, DAVID (FRANCIS). 1919- . Series characters: Al Colby = AC; John Abraham Lincoln = JL; Whit Whitney = WW.
  Angel's Ransom. Random, 1956. British title: Ransom of the Angel. Joseph, 1957
  Bullets for the Bridegroom. Macmillan, 1944; Joseph, 1948 WW
  Carambola. Little, 1961. British title: High Corniche. Joseph, 1961
  Death and Taxes. Macmillan, 1941; Joseph, 1947 WW
  A Drug on the Market; see It Ain't Hay
  Hatchetman; see Hooligan
  High Corniche; see Carambola
  Hooligan. Macmillan, 1969. British title: Hatchetman. Joseph, 1970 JL
  It Ain't Hay. Simon, 1946. British title: A Drug on the Market. Joseph, 1949 WW
  The Lights of Skaro. Random, 1954; Joseph, 1954
  The Long Escape. Random, 1948; Joseph, 1950 AC
  Loo Loo's Legacy. Little, 1961; Joseph, 1961
  Plunder of the Sun. Random, 1949; Joseph, 1950 AC
  Ransom of the Angel; see Angel's Ransom
  The Red Tassel. Random, 1950; Joseph, 1951 AC
  Shear the Black Sheep. Macmillan, 1942; Joseph, 1949 WW
  To Catch a Thief. Random, 1952; Joseph, 1953
  Troubleshooter. Macmillan, 1971; Joseph, 1972 JL

DODGE, LANGDON. Pseudonym of Victor Wolfson, 1910- , q.v.
  Midsummer Madness. Doubleday, 1950

DODGE, LOUIS. 1870- .
  Whispers. Scribner, 1920

DODGE, STEVE. Pseudonym of Stephen (David) Becker, 1927- , q.v.
  Shanghai Incident. GM, 1955; Fawcett (London), 1956. (Later reprints are as by Stephen Becker.)

DODGE, MARY LOUISE
  Tamara. Paperback Library, 1969

DODS, MARCUS. 1874-1935.
  The Bunker at the 5th. Hodge, 1925

DODSON, DANIEL B(OONE)
  The Dance of Love. Mason, 1974; New English Library, 1975
  The Man Who Ran Away. Dutton, 1961; Barker, 1961

DOE, JOHN. Pseudonym of Tiffany (Ellsworth) Thayer, 1902-1959, q.v.
  Eye-Witness! Day, 1931; Hurst, 1931

DOHERTY, EDWARD J. 1890-1975.
  The Broadway Murders. Doubleday, 1929. Also published as: Murder on the Roof. Grosset, 193?
  The Corpse Who Wouldn't Die (as by Ed Doherty). Mystery House, 1945
  Murder on the Roof; see The Broadway Murders

DOLAN, PATRICK
  Poison in the Blood. Hale, 1970

DOLBEY, ETHEL M. Joint pseudonym with Geoffrey May Dolbey: E. M. D. Hawthorne, q.v.

DOLBEY, GEOFFREY MAY. Joint pseudonym with Ethel M. Dolbey: E. M. D. Hawthorne, q.v.

DOLE, JEREMY (HASKELL). 1932- .
  Venus Disarmed. Crown, 1966

DOLINER, ROY. 1932- .
  Sandra Rifkin's Jewels. NAL, 1966

DOLINSKY, MEYER. 1923- .
  Hot Rod Gang Rumble. Avon, 1957. (Novelization of the movie.)
  There is no Silence. Hale, 1959

DOLLOND, JOHN
  A Gentleman Hangs. Longmans, 1940; Macmillan, 1941

DOLPH, JACK. 1894-1962. Series character: Doc Connor, in all titles.
  Dead Angel. Doubleday, 1953; Boardman, 1954
  Hot Tip. Doubleday, 1951; Boardman, 1952
  Murder is Mutuel. Morrow, 1948; Boardman, 1950
  Murder Makes the Mare Go. Doubleday, 1950
  Odds-On Murder. Morrow, 1948; Boardman, 1949

DOLPHIN, REX [REGINALD CHARLES DOLPHIN].
  Series character (with many other authors): Sexton Blake = SB.
  The Devil to Pay. Amalgamated, 1961 SB
  Driven to Kill. Baker, 1969 SB
  Guilty Party. Amalgamated, 1959 SB
  Murder Goes Nap. Mayflower, 1966 SB
  Ride the Man Down. Mayflower, 1967 SB
  Some Died Laughing! Amalgamated, 1960 SB
  Stop Press—Homicide! Amalgamated, 1959 SB
  The Trial of the Golden Girl. Mayflower, 1967 SB
  Trouble is my Name. Amalgamated, 1961 SB
  Walk in the Shadows. Amalgamated, 1959 SB

DOLSON, HILDEGARDE. 1908-   . Series character: Lucy Ramsdale, in all titles.
  A Dying Fall. Lippincott, 1973
  Please Omit Funeral. Lippincott, 1975
  To Spite her Face. Lippincott, 1971

DOMINIC, R. B. Joint pseudonym of Mary J. Latsis and Martha Hennissart. Other joint pseudonym: Emma Lathen, q.v. Series character: Ben Safford = BS.
  Epitaph for a Lobbyist. Doubleday, 1974; Macmillan (London), 1974 BS
  Murder in High Place. Doubleday, 1970; Macmillan (London), 1969 BS
  Murder Out of Court; see There is no Justice
  Murder, Sunny Side Up. Abelard, 1968
  There is no Justice. Doubleday, 1971. British title: Murder Out of Court. Macmillan (London), 1971 BS

DONAHUE, JACKSON
  The Confessor. Barker, 1963; World, 1964
  Erase my Name. Barker, 1964; World, 1964

DONAHUE, MARILYN (CRAM)
  Sutter's Sands. Belmont, 1971

DONALD, STUART
  The Uncertain Agent. Hale, 1970

DONALDSON, NORMAN. 1922-   . Series character (following R. Austin Freeman, 1862-1943, q.v., and preceding John H. Dirckx, 1938-   , q.v.): Dr. John Thorndyke.
  Goodbye, Dr. Thorndyke. Norris, 1972

DONALDSON, ROBERT and MICHAEL JOSEPH
  Wilderness. H. Hamilton, 1975

DONATI, SERGIO
  The Paper Tomb. Collins, 1958

DONAVAN, JOHN. Pseudonym of Nigel Morland, 1905-   , q.v. Other pseudonyms: Mary Dane, Norman Forrest, Roger Garnett, Vincent McCall, Neal Shepherd, qq.v. Series character: Johnny Lamb, in at least those marked JL.
  The Case of the Beckoning Dead. Hale, 1938; Hillman-Curl, 1938. Apparently reprinted as by Nigel Morland: Mystery Novel of the Month, 194? JL
  The Case of the Coloured Wind. Hodder, 1939. U.S. title: The Case of the Violet Smoke. Mystery House, 1940 JL
  The Case of the Plastic Man. Hodder, 1940. U.S. title: The Case of the Plastic Mask. Mystery House, 1941 JL
  The Case of the Plastic Mask; see The Case of the Plastic Man
  The Case of the Rusted Room. Hale, 1937; Hillman-Curl, 1937 JL
  The Case of the Talking Dust. Hale, 1938; Mystery House, 1941 JL
  The Case of the Violet Smoke; see The Case of the Coloured Wind
  The Dead have no Friends. Home & Van Thal, 1952

DONCASTER, (FREDERICK) PATRICK. 1917-   .
  The Devil Held the Aces. Allen, 1944
  The Long Week. Allen, 1951
  A Sigh for a Drum-Beat. Earl, 1947; Dutton, 1948

DONNE, MAXIM. Pseudonym of Madelaine Duke, 1925-   , q.v.
  Claret, Sandwiches and Sin. Heinemann, 1964; Doubleday, 1964, as by Madelaine Duke
  This Business of Bomfog. Heinemann, 1967; Doubleday, 1969, as by Madelaine Duke

DONNEL, C. P(HILIP), JR.
  Murder-Go-Round. McKay, 1945; Boardman, 1948

DONNELLY, ELEANOR C(ECILIA). 1838-1917.
  The Fatal Diamonds. Benziger, 1897

DONOVAN, DICK. Pseudonym of J(oyce) E(mmerson Preston) Muddock, 1843-1934, q.v. Series character: Dick Donovan, in at least those marked DD.
  The Adventures of Tyler Tatlock, Private Detective. Chatto, 1900 ss
  Caught at Last! Leaves from the Notebook of a Detective. Chatto, 1889 ss DD
  The Chronicles of Michael Danevitch of the Russian Secret Service. Chatto, 1897 ss
  The Crime of the Century: Being the Life Story of Richard Piggott. Long, 1904
  Dark Deeds. Chatto, 1895 ss DD
  Deacon Brodie; or, Behind the Mask. Chatto, 1901
  A Detective's Triumphs. Chatto, 1891 ss DD
  Eugene Vidocq: Soldier, Thief, Spy, Detective. Hutchinson, 1895
  The Fatal Ring. Hurst, 1905
  The Fatal Woman. White, 1911
  For Honour or Death. Ward, 1910
  Found and Fettered: A Series of Thrilling Detective Stories. Hutchinson, 1894 ss DD
  From Clue to Capture: A Series of Thrilling Detective Stories. Hutchinson, 1893 ss DD
  From Information Received: Detective Stories. Chatto, 1892 ss DD
  A Gilded Serpent. Ward, 1908
  The Gold-Spinner. White, 1907
  The Great Turf Fraud, and Other Notorious Crimes. Mellifont, 1936 ss
  In the Face of Night. Long, 1908
  In the Grip of the Law. Chatto, 1892 ss DD
  In the Queen's Service. Long, 1907
  Jim the Penman: The Life Story of One of the Most Astounding Criminals That Have Ever Lived. Newnes, 1901
  A Knight of Evil. White, 1905
  The Knutsford Mystery. White, 1906
  Lil of the Slums. Laurie, 1909
  Link by Link: Detective Stories. Chatto, 1893 ss DD
  The Man from Manchester. Chatto, 1890
  The Man-Hunter. Chatto, 1888 ss DD
  The Mystery of Jamaica Terrace. Chatto, 1896
  The Naughty Maid of Mitcham. White, 1910
  Out There: A Romance of Australia. Everett, 1922
  Preaching Jim; see The Sin of Preaching Jim
  The Records of Vincent Trill of the Detective Service. Chatto, 1899 ss
  The Rich Man's Wife, with E(rnest) W(ay) Elkington, 1872-   , q.v. Ham-Smith, 1912
  Riddles Read. Chatto, 1896 ss DD
  The Scarlet Seal: A Tale of the Borgias. Long, 1902
  Scarlet Sinners: Stories of Notorious Criminals and Crimes. Newnes, 1910 ss
  The Shadow of Evil. Everett, 1907
  The Sin of Preaching Jim. Everett, 1908. Also published as: Preaching Jim. Aldine, 1919
  Startling Crimes and Notorious Criminals. Mellifont, 1936 ss
  Stories from the Note-Book of a Detective; see Tracked and Taken
  Suspicion Aroused. Chatto, 1893 ss DD
  Tales of Terror. Chatto, 1899 ss DD
  Tangled Destinies. Laurie, 1908
  Thurtell's Crime. Laurie, 1906
  Tracked and Taken: Detective Sketches. Chatto, 1890. U.S. title: Stories from the Note-Book of a Detective (2 volumes). Street, 1900 ss DD
  Tracked to Doom. Chatto, 1892 DD
  The Trap. White, 1911
  The Triumphs of Fabian Field: Criminologist. White, 1912 ss
  The Turning Wheel: A Story of the Charn Hall Inheritance. White, 1912
  Wanted! A Detective's Strange Adventures. Chatto, 1892 ss DD
  Who Poisoned Hetty Duncan? and other detective stories. Chatto, 1890 ss DD
  A Wild Beauty. White, 1908

DONOVAN, LAURENCE. See: KENNETH ROBESON.

DOOLEY, ROGER (BURKE). 1920-   .
  Flashback. Doubleday, 1969

DORAN, JAMES
  -In the Depths of the First Degree: A Romance of the Battle of Bull Run. Peter Paul, 1898

DORIAN, RAY
  The House of Dread. Paperback Library, 1968

DORLING, HENRY TAPRELL. 1883-1968. Pseudonym: Taffrail, q.v.

DORN, DEAN M. Joint pseudonym with C. E. Carle: Michael Morgan, q.v.

DORRANCE, ETHEL (ARNOLD SMITH), 1880-   , and JAMES (FRENCH) DORRANCE, 1879-   , q.v.
  Get Your Man. Macaulay, 1921. British title: Rawson of the Mounted. Cassell, 1927

-His Robe of Honor. Macaulay, 1916
-Lonesome Town. Macaulay, 1922
Rawson of the Mounted; see Get Your Man

DORRANCE, JAMES (FRENCH). 1879- . See also: ETHEL (ARNOLD SMITH) DORRANCE, 1880- .
-Fighting Hearts. Macaulay, 1932; Wright, 1933
The Golden Alaskan. Macaulay, 1931; Skeffington, 1935
The Long Arm of the Mounted. Macaulay, 1926; Nelson, 1928
Never Fire First. Macaulay, 1924; Nicholson, 1936
The Rio Rustlers. Macaulay, 1928; Hurst, 1928

DORRINGTON, ALBERT
The Fatal Call. Methuen, 1929
The Radium Terrors. Nash, 1912; Doubleday, 1912
The Velvet Claw. Wright, 1932

DORY, JOHN. Pseudonym.
The Casting of the Shadows. Stockwell, 1922
Grip Finds the Lady. Benn, 1932

DOSTOEVSKI, FEDOR MIKHAILOVICH. 1821-1881. See also: RODNEY ACKLAND, 1908- .
Crime and Punishment. Vizetelly, 1886; Crowell, 1886

DOUBLEDAY, ROMAN. Pseudonym of Lily Augusta Long, -1927.
The Fullerton Case; see The Hemlock Avenue Mystery
The Green Tree Mystery. Appleton, 1917
The Hemlock Avenue Mystery. Little, 1908. British title: The Fullerton Case. Nash, 1920
The Red House on Rowan Street. Little, 1910
The Saintsbury Affair. Little, 1912

DOUBTFIRE, DIANNE (ABRAMS). 1918- .
Behind the Screen. Davies, 1969
Escape on Monday. Macmillan (London), 1970
The Flesh is Strong. Davies, 1966
Kick a Tin Can. Davies, 1964
Lust for Innocence. Davies, 1960; Morrow, 1960
Reason for Violence. Davies, 1961

DOUGALL, BERNARD. Series character: Steve Borden, in both titles.
I Don't Scare Easy. Dodd, 1941
The Singing Corpse. Dodd, 1943; Boardman, 1944

DOUGALL, L(ILY). 1858-1923.
The Earthly Purgatory. Hutchinson, 1904. U.S. title: The Summit House Mystery. Funk, 1905

DOUGHERTY, RICHARD
The Commissioner. Doubleday, 1963; Hart-Davis, 1963. Also published as: Madigan. PB, 1968

DOUGLAS, ALECK
The Murder Hole Road. Stockwell, 1940

DOUGLAS, ARTHUR. 1928- . Series character: Mark Register, in all titles.
The Decoy Murders. Milton House, 1975
The Noah's Ark Murders. Milton House, 1974
The Special Murders. Milton House, 1974

DOUGLAS, BILL
Bloody Precinct. Belmont, 1960

DOUGLAS, DAYLE
Haunted Harbor. Mystery House, 1943

DOUGLAS, ELLEN [ELLEN DOUGLAS WILLIAMSON]
Moon of Violence. Avalon, 1960

DOUGLAS, GAVIN. Series character: Captain Samson, in at least those marked S.
Captain Samson, A.B. Collins, 1937; Putnam, 1937 S
The Obstinate Captain Samson. Collins, 1936; Putnam, 1937 S
Rough Passage. Collins, 1936. U.S. title: The Tall Man. Putnam, 1936 S
The Search for the Blue Sedan. Collins, 1938
The Struggle. Hale, 1951
A Tale of Pimlico. Hale, 1948
The Tall Man; see Rough Passage

DOUGLAS, GEORGE. Pseudonym of Mrs. George Ferme.
The Mystery of North Fortune, with Henry Derrick. Oliphant, 1893; Ogilvie, 1895

DOUGLAS, GEORGE. Pseudonym of George Douglas Brown, 1869-1902.
The House with the Green Shutters. Macqueen, 1901

DOUGLAS, GEORGE
The Case of the Greedy Rainmaker. Bouregy, 1963

DOUGLAS, GEORGE. Pseudonym of Douglas (G.) Fisher, 1902- , q.v. Series characters: Inspector Hallan & Sgt. Spratt, in at least those marked H&S.
Crime Most Foul. Hale, 1971
Crime Without Reason. Hale, 1975
Dead on the Dot. Hale, 1974
Dead Reckoning. Hale, 1969
Death in Darkness. Hale, 1973
Death in Duplicate. Hale, 1968
Death on the Doorstep. Hale, 1973
Death Unheralded. Hale, 1967
Death Went Hunting. Hale, 1967 H&S
The Devil to Pay. Hale, 1969
Final Score. Hale, 1975
Gunman at Large. Hale, 1968
Murder Unmourned. Hale, 1970
Odd Woman Out. Hale, 1966 H&S
One to Jump. Hale, 1972
Time to Die. Hale, 1971
Unwanted Witness. Hale, 1966 H&S

DOUGLAS, HUDSON. Pseudonym of Robert Aitken, 1872- , q.v.
The Lantern of Luck. Watt, 1909; Murray, 1910, as by Robert Aitken
A Million a Minute. Watt, 1908; Newnes, 1912
The Man in the Mirror. Watt, 1910; Robert Aitken, 1910, as by Robert Aitken
The White Blackbird. Little, 1912

DOUGLAS, LAURA W.
The Mystery of Arrowhead Hill. Avalon, 1963
The Mystery of Crooknose. Avalon, 1963

DOUGLAS, MALCOLM. Pseudonym of (Ronald) Douglas Sanderson, 1922- , q.v. Other pseudonym: Martin Brett, q.v.
The Deadly Dames. GM, 1956; Consul, 1961
Murder Comes Calling. GM, 1958
Prey by Night. GM, 1955; Fawcett (London), 1957

Pure Sweet Hell. GM, 1957
Rain of Terror. GM, 1956; Fawcett (London), 1956

DOUGLAS, MARY K.
-Beloved Enemy. Fiction House, 1948
-Dangerous Course. Mellifont, 1941
-Dark House. Mellifont, 1939
-Fool's Bet. Mellifont, 1940
-The Gift Horse. Mellifont, 1937
-The Great Deception. Mellifont, 1935
-Heavy Stakes. Mellifont, 1938
One Thrilling Night. Fiction House, 1940
-The Outsider. Mellifont, 1939
Peril of the Course. Mellifont, 1936
-Rival Stables. Mellifont, 1940

DOUGLAS, ROBERT K(ENNAWAY). See: L(ILLIE) T(HOMAS) MEADE.

DOUGLAS, RONALD MacDONALD
-The Closed Door. Modern Age, 1941

DOUGLAS, ROY
Who is Nemo? Harrap, 1937; Lippincott, 1937
Winner Takes All. Mellifont, 1934

DOUGLAS, THEO. Pseudonym of Mrs. H. D. Everett.
-Behind a Mask. Harper (London), 1898
Carr of Dimscaur. Harper (London), 1899
Iris. Blackwood, 1896; Harper (New York), 1896
-A Legacy of Hate. Pearson, 1899
Three Mysteries. Everett, 1904. (3 stories.)
-A White Witch. Hurst, 1908

DOUGLAS, WILLIAM
Money to Burn. Arrowsmith, 1926

DOUGLAS-IRVINE, HELEN. See: HELEN DOUGLAS IRVINE.

DOUGLASS, DONALD McNUTT. 1899- . Series character: Bolivar Manchenil, in all titles.
Many Brave Hearts. Harper, 1958; Eyre, 1959
Rebecca's Pride. Harper, 1956; Eyre, 1956
Saba's Treasure. Harper, 1961; Eyre, 1963

DOUIE, MARJORIE
The Pointing Man. Hutchinson, 1917; Dutton, 1920

DOUTHWAITE, L(OUIS) C(HARLES). 1878- . Series character (with many other authors): Sexton Blake = SB.
The Army Defaulter's Secret. Amalgamated, 1943 SB
The Clean-Up. Gramol, 1933
Crime Limited. Gramol, 1933
Crook Bait. Gramol, 1933
-Diana of the Woods. Brentano's (London), 1929
-Dimbleby's. Parsons, 1924
The Eyes of Omar. Gramol, 1934
Fear! Gramol, 1933
-Fourflush Island. Brentano's (London), 1929
The Ghost Trail. Amalgamated, 1932. Also published as: The Riddle of the Yukon. Amalgamated, 1940 SB
Horror House. Amalgamated, 1930 SB
House of Torture. Mellifont, 1933
The Killer. Gramol, 1933
-The Luck of St. Boniface. Jarrolds, 1925
The Man from Chicago. Gramol, 1934
Murder Goes West. Nelson, 1946

The Riddle of the Yukon; see The Ghost Trail
The Scarlet Scarab. Gramol, 1933
The Secret of Tso Feng. Gramol, 1933
The Silent Terror. Gramol, 1933
Sinister House. Mellifont, 1941
The Terror of the Moat House. Gramol, 1933
-The Third Robin Featherstone. Chambers, 1929
-Warden of the North. Nelson, 1938
-Waters of the North. Duckworth, 1926
-Yellerlegs. Chambers, 1930
Zero Hour. Gramol, 1933

DOW, JOHN
The Little Boy Laughed. Mystery House, 1945. Also published as: The Blonde is Dead. Handi-Books, 1945

DOWLING, RICHARD. 1846-1898.
A Baffling Quest. Ward, 1891; Lovell, 1891
-Below Bridge. Ward, 1895
Catmur's Caves; or, The Quality of Mercy. Black, 1892; National Book, 1891
-The Crimson Chair, and other stories. Ward, 1891 ss
-A Dark Intruder. Downey, 1895
-Fatal Bonds. Ward, 1886
-The Fate of Luke Ormerod. Hurst, 1905
-The Hidden Flame. Tinsley, 1885
-High-Water Mark. Munro, 1880. (British title?)
-The Husband's Secret. Tinsley, 1881; Munro, 188?
An Isle of Surrey. Ward, 1889
-The Last Call. Tinsley, 1884
-Miracle Gold. Ward, 1888; Lovell, 1888
-My Darling's Ransom. Ogilvie, 1881. (British title?)
The Mystery of Killard. Tinsley, 1879
Old Corcoran's Money. Chatto, 1897
-On the Embankment. Tinsley, 1884 ss
-A Sapphire King, and other stories. Tinsley, 1882 ss
The Skeleton Key. Ward, 1886
-The Sport of Fate. Tinsley, 1880 ss
-Sweet Inisfail. Tinsley, 1882; Munro, 1883
-Tempest Driven. Tinsley, 1886; Appleton, 1887
-Under St. Paul's. Tinsley, 1880; Munro, 1881
The Weird Sisters. Tinsley, 1880
While London Sleeps. Ward, 1895
-With the Unhanged. Swan, 1887

DOWNES, DONALD. 1903- .
The Easter Dinner. Rinehart, 1960
Orders to Kill. Rinehart, 1958; Panther, 1960
A Red Rose for Maria. Rinehart, 1959; Panther, 1961
The Scarlet Thread: Adventures in Wartime Espionage. British Book Centre, 1953; Verschoyle, 1953

DOWNES, QUENTIN. Pseudonym of Michael Harrison, 1907- , q.v. Series character: Det. Insp. Abraham Kozminski, in all titles.
Heads I Win. Wingate, 1953; Roy, 1955
No Smoke No Flame. Wingate, 1952; Roy, 1956
They Hadn't a Clue. Arco, 1954

DOWNEY, EDMUND. 1856-1937.
A House of Tears. Ward, 1886; Lovell, 1888

DOWNING, (GEORGE) TODD. 1902- . Series characters: Peter Bounty = PB; Hugh Rennert = HR.
The Case of the Unconquered Sisters. Doubleday, 1936; Methuen, 1937 HR
The Cat Screams. Doubleday, 1934; Methuen, 1935 HR
Death under the Moonflower. Doubleday, 1938 PB
The Last Trumpet. Doubleday, 1937; Methuen, 1938 HR
The Lazy Lawrence Murders. Doubleday, 1941 PB
Murder on the Tropic. Doubleday, 1935; Methuen, 1936 PB
Murder on Tour. Putnam, 1933 HR
Night over Mexico. Doubleday, 1937; Methuen, 1938 HR
Vultures in the Sky. Doubleday, 1935; Methuen, 1936 HR

DOWNING, WARWICK. 1931- .
The Mountains West of Town. Saturday Review, 1975
The Player. Saturday Review, 1974

DOWNS, SARAH ELIZABETH FORBUSH. 1843- . Pseudonym: Mrs. Georgie Sheldon, q.v.

DOYLE, (SIR) A(RTHUR) CONAN. 1859-1930.
See also: WILL SPENCE; (JOHN) MICHAEL (DRINKROW) HARDWICK, 1924- .
Series character: Sherlock Holmes = SH (see also: next entry).
The Adventures of Sherlock Holmes. Newnes, 1892; Harper, 1892 ss SH
The Black Doctor and other tales of terror and mystery. Doran, 1925. (Contains 8 ss from Round the Fire Stories, q.v., and 5 ss from other collections.)
The Captain of the Polestar, and other stories. Longmans, 1890; Munro, 1894 ss, some criminous
The Case-Book of Sherlock Holmes. Murray, 1927; Doran, 1927 ss SH
Danger!, and other stories. Murray, 1918; Doran, 1919 ss, some criminous
The Doings of Raffles Haw. Cassell, 1892; Lovell, 1892
The Green Flag and other stories of war and sport. Smith, 1900; McClure, 1900 ss, some criminous
His Last Bow. Murray, 1917; Doran, 1917 ss SH
The Hound of the Baskervilles. Newnes, 1902; McClure, 1902 SH
-The Last Galley. Smith, 1911; Doubleday, 1911
The Memoirs of Sherlock Holmes. Newnes, 1894; Harper, 1894 ss SH
My Friend the Murderer and other mysteries and adventures. Lovell, 1893 ss, some criminous
Mysteries and Adventures. Scott, 1889 ss, some criminous
The Mystery of Cloomber. Ward, 1889; Fenno, 1895
The Return of Sherlock Holmes. Newnes, 1905; McClure, 1905 ss SH
Round the Fire Stories. Smith Elder, 1908 ss, some criminous
Round the Red Lamp. Methuen, 1894; Appleton, 1894 ss, some criminous
The Sign of the Four. Blackett, 1890; Lippincott, 1890 SH
A Study in Scarlet. Beeton's Christmas Annual, 1887; Lippincott, 1890 SH
The Surgeon of Gaster Fell. Ivers, 1885; Westbrook, ca.1920
Tales of Terror and Mystery. Murray, 1922 ss
The Valley of Fear. Smith Elder, 1915; Doran, 1915 SH

DOYLE, ADRIAN (MALCOLM) CONAN, 1910-1970, and JOHN DICKSON CARR, 1905-1977, q.v. For Carr, see also pseudonyms: Carr Dickson, Carter Dickson, Roger Fairbairn. Series character (following A. Conan Doyle, 1859-1930, q.v.): Sherlock Holmes.
The Exploits of Sherlock Holmes. Murray, 1954; Random, 1954. Reprinted in two volumes: The Exploits of Sherlock Holmes. Murray, 1963; and: More Exploits of Sherlock Holmes. Murray, 1964

DOYLE, DR. C(HARLES) W(ILLIAM). 1852-1903.
The Shadow of Quong Lung. Lippincott, 1900; Constable, 1900 ss

DOYLE, MONTE
Signpost to Murder. French (London), 1963. (Play.)

DRABBLE, J(OHN) F(REDERICK). 1906- .
Death's Second Self. Sidgwick, 1971

DRACHMAN, THEODORE S.
Addicted to Murder; see Something for the Birds
Cry Plague! Ace, 1953
Reason for Madness. Abelard (New York & London), 1970
Something for the Birds. Crown, 1958; Boardman, 1959. Also published as: Addicted to Murder. Avon, 196?

DRACO, F. Pseudonym of Julia Davis, 1904- . Series characters: Lord and Lady (Ginger) Tintagel, in both titles.
Cruise with Death. Rinehart, 1952
The Devil's Church. Rinehart, 1951

DRACOTT, ALICE ELIZABETH. Pseudonym: A. E. D., q.v.

DRAGO, (HARRY) SINCLAIR. 1888- .
-Women to Love. Amour, 1931; Melrose, 1932

DRAKE, ARNOLD
The Steel Noose. Ace, 1954

DRAKE, BURGESS. See: H(ENRY) B(URGESS) DRAKE.

DRAKE, DREXEL. Pseudonym of Charles H. Huff, 1887?-1959. Series character: The Falcon, in all titles.
The Falcon Cuts In. Lippincott, 1937
The Falcon Meets a Lady. Lippincott, 1938
The Falcon's Prey. Lippincott, 1936; Harrap, 1937

DRAKE, H(ENRY) B(URGESS)
Chinese White. Falcon, 1950, as by Burgess Drake
-Cursed be the Treasure. Lane, 1926; Macy-Masius, 1928
-The Shadowy Thing. Macy-Masius, 1928. (British title?)

DRAKE, MAURICE. 1875-1924.
The Coming Back of Laurence Averil; see The Salving of a Derelict
The Doom Window. Hodder, 1923; Dutton, 1925
Galleon Gold. Hodder, 1924
Lethbridge of the Moor. Laurie, 1908; Kearney, 1908
The Mystery of the Mud Flats; see WO_2
The Ocean Sleuth. Methuen, 1915; Dutton, 1916
The Salving of a Derelict. Laurie, 1906. U.S. title: The Coming Back of Laurence Averil. Clode, 1915
WO_2. Methuen, 1913; Dutton, 1913. Also published as: The Mystery of the Mud Flats. Collins, 1930
Wrack. Duckworth, 1910

DRAMOND, ALONZO E.
A Secret of the Midway Plaza. Byron S. Adams, 1890

DRAPER, ALFRED (ERNEST). 1924- .
The Death Penalty. Macmillan (London), 1972
Swansong for a Rare Bird. Macmillan (London), 1970; Coward, 1970

DRATLER, JAY J. 1911- .
-All for a Woman. Popular Library, 1958
-Doctor Paradise. Popular Library, 1957
-Dream of a Woman. Popular Library, 1958
-Ducks in Thunder. Reynal, 1940
The Judas Kiss. Holt, 1955. British title: Without Mercy. Hale, 1957
The Pitfall. Crown, 1947
Without Mercy; see The Judas Kiss

DRAX, PETER. Pseudonym of Eric Elrington Addis. Series character: Chief Inspector Thompson, in at least those marked T.
Crime to Music; see Tune to a Corpse
Crime Within Crime; see Death by Two Hands
Death by Two Hands. Hutchinson, 1937. U.S. title: Crime Within Crime. Appleton, 1938 T
He Shot to Kill. Hutchinson, 1936
High Seas Murder. Hutchinson, 1939
Murder by Chance. Hutchinson, 1936 T
Murder by Proxy. Hutchinson, 1937
Sing a Song of Murder. Hutchinson, 1944
Tune to a Corpse. Hutchinson, 1938. U.S. title: Crime to Music. Appleton, 1939 T

DRAYTON, RICKY. Pseudonym of Michael Barnes, q.v.
Anyone's Grief. Scion, 1951
Crime on my Hands. Scion, 1952
Death Comes Wholesale. Milestone, 1953
Eve was No Lady. Scion, 1952
Get a Load o' Dis. Scion, 1952
Get that Man. Scion, 1952
Grin and Dare It. Milestone, 1953
The Heat's On. Scion, 1952
Hell and High Water. Scion, 1951
Hell's Belles. Milestone, 1953
The Howling Dog. Gannet, 1954
I Don't Die Easy. Scion, 1952
It Doesn't Add Up. Scion, 1952
It's Murder. Milestone, 1953
Make It Lethal. Milestone, 1954
The Midnight Male. Milestone, 1954
The Nude was Framed. Milestone, 1953
One False Move. Milestone, 1954
Stay Dead, Sweetheart. Scion, 1951
Stick or Bust. Milestone, 1953
Stripped to Kill. Scion, 1952
Take It on the Lam. Scion, 1951
Too Late to Shout. Milestone, 1954
Troubled Night. Milestone, 1953

DREISER, THEODORE. 1871-1945.
An American Tragedy. Boni, 1925; Constable, 1926

DRENNEN, RAYMOND
Murder Beat. Mystery House, 1956

DRESSER, DAVIS. 1904-1977. Pseudonyms: Asa Baker, Brett Halliday, qq.v. Joint pseudonym with Kathleen Rollins: Hal Debrett, q.v. Joint pseudonym with (Walter) Ryerson Johnson, 1901- , q.v.: Matthew Blood, q.v.

DREW, MARY ANNE. Pseudonym of Bruce (Bingham) Cassiday, 1920- , q.v. Other pseudonyms: Carson Bingham, Annie Laurie McMurdie, Michael Stratford, qq.v.
The Diabolist. Avon, 1975

DREW, PATRICIA
Deep in a Dark Country. Lancer, 1968

DREW, SIDNEY. Pseudonym of Edgar Joyce Murray, 1878- , q.v. Series character (with many other authors): Sexton Blake, in all titles.
The Fortnight of Fear. Amalgamated, 1931
The Gangster's Deputy. Amalgamated, 1930
The Mansion House Mystery. Amalgamated, 1931

DREWE, MARCUS
The Barber of Littlewick. Jenkins, 1930

DREWRY, EDITH S(TEWART)
-A Death Ring. Moor, 1881
-On Dangerous Ground. White, 1883

DREXLER, J. F. Pseudonym of Lauran Bosworth Paine, 1916- . Other pseudonyms: John Armour, Reg Batchelor, Kenneth Bedford, Frank Bosworth, Mark Carrel, Robert Clarke, Richard Dana, Troy Howard, Jared Ingersol, John Kilgore, Hunter Liggett, J. K. Lucas, John Morgan, qq.v.
The Anonymous Assassin. Hale, 1968
The Fire Ant. Hale, 1975

DRIN, MICHAEL
Signpost to Fear. Ward, 1964

DRISCOLL, PETER. 1942- .
In Connection with Kilshaw. Macdonald, 1974; Lippincott, 1974
The White Lie Assignment. Macdonald, 1971; Lippincott, 1975
The Wilby Conspiracy. Macdonald, 1973; Lippincott, 1972

DRIVER, C(HARLES) J(ONATHAN). 1939- .
Elegy for a Revolutionary. Faber, 1969; Morrow, 1970

DROGE, EDWARD F., JR.
In the Highest Tradition. Atheneum, 1974; Secker, 1975

DRUCE, HUBERT
Henry Cassland. Melrose, 1911

DRUMMOND, A(NDREW) L(EWIS). 1844- .
True Detective Stories. Dillingham, 1909. (Fictionalized true crime ss.)

DRUMMOND, ANTHONY. Pseudonym of (Alfred) John Hunter, 1891-1961, q.v. Other pseudonyms: John Addiscombe, L. H. Brenning, Anthony Dax, Peter Meriton, qq.v.
Blood Money. Gramol, 1935
The Devil's Signpost. Gramol, 1935
The Island of Dangerous Men. Gramol, 1937
The Scented Death. Unwin, 1924

DRUMMOND, CHARLES. Pseudonym of Kenneth Giles, 1922-1972, q.v. Other pseudonym: Edmund McGirr, q.v. Series character: Sergeant Reed, in all titles.
Death and the Leaping Ladies. Gollancz, 1968; Walker, 1969
A Death at the Bar. Gollancz, 1972; Walker, 1973
Death at the Furlong Post. Gollancz, 1967; Walker, 1968
The Odds on Death. Gollancz, 1969; Walker, 1970
Stab in the Back. Gollancz, 1970; Walker, 1970

DRUMMOND, HAMILTON. 1857-1935.
Room Five. Ward, 1904
-The Three Envelopes. Paul, 1912
-The Tournelles Plot. Paul, 1933

DRUMMOND, IVOR. Pseudonym (?) of Roger (Erskine) Longrigg, 1929- , q.v. Series characters: Jennifer Norrington, Alessandro di Ganzarello, and Coleridge Tucker III, in all titles.
The Frog in the Moonflower. Macmillan (London), 1972; St. Martin's, 1973
The Jaws of the Watchdog. Macmillan (London), 1973; St. Martin's, 1973
The Man with the Tiny Head. Macmillan (London), 1969; Harcourt, 1970
The Power of the Bug. Macmillan (London), 1974; St. Martin's, 1974
The Priests of the Abomination. Macmillan (London), 1970; Harcourt, 1971

DRUMMOND, J. Pseudonym of John Newton Chance, 1911- , q.v. Other pseudonym: John Lymington, q.v. Series character (with many other authors): Sexton Blake, in all titles, which were published by Amalgamated Press.
At Sixty Miles Per Hour. 1945
The Case of the "Dead" Spy. 1949
The Case of L.A.C. Dickson. 1950
The Case of the Man with No Name. 1951
The Case of the Two-Faced Swindler. 1955
The Essex Road Crime. 1944
Hated by All! 1951
The House in the Woods. 1950
The House on the Hill. 1945
The House on the River. 1952
The Manor House Menace. 1944
The Mystery of the Deserted Camp. 1948
The Mystery of the Five Guilty Men. 1954
The Mystery of the Haunted Square. 1950
The Mystery of the Sabotaged Jet. 1951
The Painted Dagger. 1944
The Riddle of the Leather Bottle. 1944
The Riddle of the Mummy Case. 1945
The Riddle of the Receiver's Hoard. 1949
The Secret of the Living Skeleton. 1949
The Secret of the Sixty Steps. 1950
The South Coast Mystery. 1949
The Teddy-Boy Mystery. 1955
The Town of Shadows. 1948
The Tragic Case of the Station Master's Legacy. 1944

DRUMMOND, JOHN
Proof Positive. Duckworth, 1956

DRUMMOND, JUNE. 1923- .
Bang! Bang! You're Dead. Gollancz, 1973
The Black Unicorn. Gollancz, 1959
The Boon Companions. Gollancz, 1974. U.S. title: Drop Dead. Walker, 1976
Cable-Car. Gollancz, 1965; Holt, 1967
Drop Dead; see The Boon Companions
Farewell Party. Gollancz, 1971; Dodd, 1973
The Gantry Episode. Gollancz, 1968. U.S. title: Murder on a Bad Trip. Holt, 1968
Murder on a Bad Trip; see The Gantry Episode
The People in Glass House. Gollancz, 1969; Simon, 1970
The Saboteurs. Gollancz, 1967; Holt, 1967
Slowly the Poison. Gollancz, 1975; Walker, 1976
Welcome, Proud Lady. Gollancz, 1964; Holt, 1968

DRUMMOND, WILLIAM
Gaslight. Arrow, 1967; Paperback Library, 1966. (Novelization of the play by Patrick Hamilton, 1904-1962, q.v.)

Life for Ruth. Corgi, 1962. (Novelization of the movie.)
Midnight Lace. Pan, 1960. (Novelization of the movie.)
Night Must Fall. Fontana, 1964; Signet, 1964. (Novelization of the movie.)
Victim. Corgi, 1961. (Novelization of the movie.)

DRURY, REV. SHELDON
The Startling and Thrilling Narrative of the Dark and Terrible Deeds of Henry Medison, and His Associate and Accomplice, Miss Ella Stevens, Who was Executed by the Vigilance Committee of San Francisco, on the 20th September Last. Barclay, 1857

DRURY, W(ILLIAM) P(RICE). 1861- .
"Fightingcocks". Hutchinson, 1939

DRYER, BERNARD VICTOR
The Image Makers. Harper, 1958; Hutchinson, 1959
Murder in Port Afrique; see Port Afrique
Port Afrique. Harper, 1949; Cassell, 1950. Also published as: Murder in Port Afrique. Avon, 1956
The Torch Bearers. Simon, 1968; Heinemann, 1968

DU BOIS, THEODORA (McCORMICK). 1890- .
Series characters: Anne & Jeffrey McNeill = M.
Armed with a New Terror. Houghton, 1936; Heinemann, 1937 M
The Body Goes Round and Round. Houghton, 1942 M
The Case of the Perfumed Mouse. Doubleday, 1944; Boardman, 1946 M
The Cavalier's Corpse. Doubleday, 1952; Boardman, 1953 M
Death Comes to Tea. Houghton, 1940 M
Death Dines Out. Houghton, 1939; Readers Library, 1942 M
Death is Late to Lunch. Houghton, 1941; Boardman, 1943 M
Death Sails in a High Wind. Doubleday, 1945; Boardman, 1946 M
Death Tears a Comic Strip. Houghton, 1939 M
Death Wears a White Coat. Houghton, 1938 M
The Devil and Destiny. Doubleday, 1948; Boardman, 1949 M
The Face of Hate. Doubleday, 1948 M
The Footsteps. Doubleday, 1947; Boardman, 1949 M
Fowl Play. Doubleday, 1951; Boardman, 1952 M
High Tension. Doubleday, 1950; Boardman, 1951
It's Raining Violence. Doubleday, 1949; Boardman, 1950. Also published as: Money, Murder and the McNeills. Lancer, 1969 M
The Late Bride. Washburn, 1965; Hale, 1966
The Listener. Doubleday, 1953
The McNeills Chase a Ghost. Houghton, 1941 M
Money, Murder and the McNeills; see It's Raining Violence
Murder Strikes an Atomic Unit. Doubleday, 1946; Boardman, 1947 M
Rogue's Coat. Doubleday, 1949
Seeing Red. Doubleday, 1954; Collins, 1955 M
Shannon Terror. Washburn, 1964
The Wild Duck Murders. Doubleday, 1943; Boardman, 1948 M

DU BOIS, W.
Pistols with Coffee. Newcoll, 1945

DU BOIS, WILLIAM. 1903- . Series character: Jack Jordan, in all titles.

The Case of the Deadly Diary. Little, 1940. British title: The Deadly Diary. Macdonald, 1947
The Case of the Frightened Fish. Little, 1940; Swan, 1947
The Case of the Haunted Brides. Little, 1941; Swan, 1947
The Deadly Diary; see The Case of the Deadly Diary

DU BOISGOBEY, FORTUNE (HIPPOLYTE AUGUSTE). 1821-1891. Here listed are known English translations of this French author. No attempt has been made to distinguish among his works on the basis of criminous content.
The Ace of Hearts. Munro, 1883; Vizetelly, 1889
The Angel of the Bells. Munro, 1885; Aldine, 1877. Also published as: The Blue Veil; or, The Angel of the Belfry. Laird, 1889; Maxwell, 1886. And as: The Blue Veil; or, The Crime of the Tower. Lovell, 1889. And as: The Angel of the Chimes. Greening, 1903
The Angel of the Chimes; see The Angel of the Bells
Babiole, the Pretty Milliner. Munro, 1885
Bertha's Secret. Lovell, 1888; Vizetelly, 1885
The Blue Veil; or, The Angel of the Belfry; see The Angel of the Bells
The Blue Veil; or, The Crime of the Tower; see The Angel of the Bells
The Bride of a Day; see The Convict Colonel
Cash on Delivery. Munro, 1887; Routledge, 1887
The Cat's-Eye Ring, A Secret of Paris Life. Routledge (London & New York), 1888
Cecile's Fortune; see Merindol
Chevalier Casse-Cou. DeWitt, 1875
The Closed Door. Munro, 1886. British title: The Condemned Door. Routledge, 1887. Also published as: The Condemned Door; or, The Secret of Trigabon Castle. Lovell, 1884
The Condemned Door; see The Closed Door
The Condemned Door; or, The Secret of Trigabon Castle; see The Closed Door
The Consequences of a Duel. Munro, 1885. Also published as: The Results of a Duel. Lovell, 1888; Vizetelly, 1888
The Convict Colonel. Street, 1891; Vizetelly, 1887. Also published as (?): The Bride of a Day. Routledge, 1887
The Coral Pin. Munro, 1883; Vizetelly, 1886
The Count's Millions. Street (Magnet #216)
The Crime of the Opera House. Munro, 1881
The Cry of Blood. Munro, 1886. British title: The Cry of Blood: A Story of Crime and Its Penalty. Maxwell, 1886
The Day of Reckoning. Vizetelly, 1885
The Detective's Crime. Donohue, ca.1897
The Detective's Dilemma. Street, ca. 1888
The Detective's Eye. Lovell, 1888. Also published as: Piedouche, A French Detective. Munro, 1884. And as: The Parisian Detective. Ivers, 1887
The Detective's Triumph. Street, ca. 1888
Doctor Villagos; or, The Nihilist Chief. Street, 1901; Pollard, 1889

An Exchanged Identity. Street, ca.1897
Fernande's Choice, Vizetelly, 1887
The Ferry Boat. Munro, 1882. Also published as: Love's Triumph: The Tragedy of the Ferry. Tousey, 1882. And as: Was It Murder? or, Who is the Heir? McNally, 1883
Fickle Heart. Maxwell, 1890
A Fight for a Fortune. Donohue, ca. 1897; Vizetelly, 1886
Fontenay, the Swordsman: A Military Novel. McNally, 1891
The Golden Pig. Munro, 1882. British title: The Golden Pig; or, The Idol of Modern Paris. Vizetelly, 1886
The Golden Tress. Claxton, 1896
The Great Jewel Mystery. Donohue, ca. 1897
The Half-Sister's Secret. Routledge, 1889
The High Roller; or, Plunging and Honeyfugling on the Race Track: A Sporting Romance. Pollard, 1891
His Great Revenge. Munro, 1882
In the Serpent's Coils. Vizetelly, 1885
The Iron Mask. Munro, 1884
The Jailer's Pretty Wife; see The Pretty Jailer
The Lost Casket. Putnam, 1881. Also published as: The Severed Hand. Munro, 1888; Vizetelly, 1885. And as: The Severed Hand; or, A Terrible Confession. Ogilvie, ca.1895
The Lottery Ticket. Munro, 1885. Also published as: The Red Lottery Ticket. Lovell, 1888; Vizetelly, 1887
Love's Triumph: The Tragedy of the Terry; see The Ferry Boat
Marie-Rose; or, The Mystery. Munro, 1883
Married for Love. Routledge, 1888
The Matapan Affair. Munro, 1880; Vizetelly, 1885. Also published as: The Matapan Jewels. Lotus Library (London), 1902
The Matapan Jewels; see The Matapan Affair
Merindol. Munro, 1884. British title: Cecile's Fortune. Vizetelly, 1886
The Millionaire's Fate. Donohue
The Missing Rubies. Donohue, ca.1897
The Mysterious Juror. Higgins, 1892
The Mystery of an Omnibus. Munro, 1882. British title: An Omnibus Mystery (with: The Old Age of Lecoq, the Detective, q.v.). Vizetelly, 1885
A Mystery Still. Boulevard Novels, 1888; Vizetelly, 1888
The Nameless Man. Westbrook, ca.1920; Vizetelly, 1887
An Ocean Knight; or, The Corsairs and Their Conquerors. Warne (London & New York), 1891
The Old Age of Lecoq, the Detective; see The Old Age of Monsieur Lecoq
The Old Age of Monsieur Lecoq. Munro, 1888. British title: The Old Age of Lecoq, the Detective. Vizetelly (with An Omnibus Mystery), 1885
An Omnibus Mystery; see The Mystery of an Omnibus
The Parisian Detective; see The Detective's Eye
The Phantom Leg. Vizetelly, 1886
Piedouche, A French Detective; see The Detective's Eye
The Pretty Jailer. Munro, 1886. British title: The Jailer's Pretty Wife. Vizetelly, 1886
The Prima Donna's Husband. Munro, 1885
The Privateersman's Legacy. Munro, 1882
A Railway Tragedy. Vizetelly, 1887
The Red Band, The Adventures of a Young Girl During the Siege of Paris. Munro, 1887. British title: The Red Band; or, The Siege and the Commune. Maxwell, 1887

The Red Camelia. Vizetelly, 1887
The Red Lottery Ticket; see The Lottery Ticket
The Results of a Duel; see The Consequences of a Duel
The Robbery of the Orphans; or, JT's Inheritance. Munro, 1882
Satan's Coach. Munro, 1883
Saved from the Harem. Vizetelly, 1888
The Sculptor's Daughter; see The Vitriol Thrower
Sealed Lips. Munro, 1883
The Severed Hand; see The Lost Casket
The Steel Necklace. Street, 1891; Vizetelly, 1886
The Temple of Death. Westbrook, ca.1920
Thieving Fingers. Vizetelly, 1887
The Thumb Stroke. Vizetelly, 1886
The Vitriol Thrower. Tousey, 1884. Also published as: The Sculptor's Daughter. Munro, 1886
Was It Murder? or, Who is the Heir?; see The Ferry Boat
Where's Zenobia?; see Zenobie Capitaine
The Youngest Soldier of the Grand Armee. Higgins, 1892
Zenobie Capitaine. Munro, 1884. British title: Where's Zenobia? Vizetelly, 1888
Zig-Zag the Clown; or, The Steel Gauntlets. Munro, 1885

DU BREUIL, LINDA
Nightmare Baby. Belmont, 1970
The Secret. Lancer, 1972

DU CAMP, ALWYN
Twana. Mercantile (Clairwood, South Africa), 1969?

DU CANN, C(HARLES) G(ARFIELD) L(OTT). 1889- .
The Secret Hand. Methuen, 1929

DUCHESS, THE. Pseudonym of Mrs. (Margaret Wolfe Hamilton) Hungerford, 1855?-1897, q.v.
-A Passive Crime, and other stories. Lovell, 1885 ss

DUDLEY, (HELEN) DOROTHY, 1895- , and JUANITA SHERIDAN, q.v.
What Dark Secret. Morrow, 1943

DUDLEY, ERNEST. Pseudonym of Vivian Ernest Coltman-Allen, 1908- . Series character: Dr. Morelle, in at least those marked M.
The Adventures of Jimmy Strange. Long, 1945 ss
Alibi and Dr. Morelle. Hale, 1959 M
The Blind Beak. Hale, 1954
Callers for Dr. Morelle. Hale, 1957 M
Confess to Dr. Morelle. Hale, 1959 M
The Crooked Inn. Hodder, 1953
The Crooked Straight. Hodder, 1948
The Dark Bureau. Hodder, 1950
Dr. Morelle, with Arthur Watkyn. Evans, 1954. (Play.) M
Dr. Morelle and Destiny. Hale, 1958 M
Dr. Morelle and the Doll. Hale, 1960 M
Dr. Morelle and the Drummer Girl. Hodder, 1950 M
Dr. Morelle at Midnight. Hale, 1959 M
Dr. Morelle Meets Murder and other new adventures. Findon, 1948 M ss
Dr. Morelle Takes a Bow. Hale, 1957 M
The Harassed Hero. Hodder, 1951
Leatherface. Hale, 1958
Look Out for Lucifer! Long, 1951
Meet Dr. Morelle. Long, 1943 M ss
Meet Dr. Morelle Again. Long, 1944 M
Menace for Dr. Morelle. Long, 1947 M
The Mind of Dr. Morelle. Hale, 1958 M
Mr. Walker Wants to Know. Wright, 1939
Nightmare for Dr. Morelle. Hale, 1960 M
Picaroon. Hale, 1952; Bobbs, 1953
The Private Eye. Long, 1950
To Love and To Perish. Hale, 1962
Two-Face. Long, 1951
The Whistling Sands. Hodder, 1956

DUDLEY, FRANK. Pseudonym of Ward Greene, 1892-1956, q.v.
The Havana Hotel Murders. Houghton, 1936; Bell, 1937
King Cobra. Carrick, 1940
Ride the Nightmare. Cape (New York), 1930

DUDLEY, OWEN. Pseudonym of Dudley Dean McGaughy. Other pseudonym: Dudley Dean, q.v.
The Deep End. Ace, 1956
Murder for Charity. Ace, 1957
Run If You Can. Ace, 1960

DUDLEY, OWEN FRANCIS. 1882-1952.
-The Coming of the Monster. Longmans, 1936

DUERRENMATT, FRIEDRICH. 1921- . See also: JAMES YAFFE, 1927- . Series character: Kommissar Hans Barlach = HB.
A Dangerous Game. Cape, 1960. U.S. title: Traps. Knopf, 1960. (Translation of Die Panne. Zurich, 1956.)
End of the Game; see The Judge and His Hangman
The Judge and His Hangman. Jenkins, 1954; Harper, 1955. Also published as: End of the Game. Warner, 1976. (Translation of Der Richter und Sein Henker. Einsiedeln, 1952.) HB
The Pledge. Cape, 1959; Knopf, 1959. (Translation of Das Versprechen. Zurich, 1958.)
The Quarry. Cape, 1962; New York Graphic Society, 1962. (Translation of Der Verdacht. Einsiedeln, 1959.) HB
Traps; see A Dangerous Game

DUFF, BELDON
Ask No Questions. Doubleday, 1930
The Central Park Murder. Doubleday, 1929

DUFF, DAVID. 1912- .
Castle Fell. Burke, 1950
Loch Spy. Burke, 1948
Traitor's Pass. Staples, 1954; Roy, 1955

DUFF, DOUGLAS V(ALDER). 1901- .
Peter Darington. Thames, 19?? ss

DUFF, JAMES P.
Dangerous to Know. Ace, 1959
Run from Death. Mystery House, 1957
Some Die Young. Graphic, 1956
Who Dies There? Graphic, 1956

DUGDALE, (ARTHUR) GILES
Should a Corpse Tell? Earl, 1948

DUGGAN, FLOYD
Pay-Off for a Dumb Dame. Barrington Gray, 1953

DUHART, WILLIAM H.
The Deadly Pay-Off. GM, 1958; Fawcett (London), 1959

DUKE, FRANCIS
The Gold Cup Murder. New English Library pb, 1973

DUKE, MADELAINE. 1925- . Pseudonym: Maxim Donne, q.v.
Death of a Holy Murderer. Joseph, 1975

DUKE, WILL. Pseudonym of William Campbell Gault, 1910- , q.v.
Fair Prey. Graphic, 1956; Boardman, 1958

DUKE, WINIFRED. -1962.
Bastard Verdict. Jarrolds, 1931; Knopf, 1934
-The Black Mirror. Jarrolds, 1948
-Blind Geese. Jarrolds, 1946
-The Cherry-Fair. Hale, 1954
Crookedshaws. Jarrolds, 1936
-The Dancing of the Fox. Hale, 1956
-Death and his Sweetheart. Jarrolds, 1938
-Dirge for a Dead Witch. Jarrolds, 1949
-The Drove Road. Jarrolds, 1930
Funeral March of a Marionette. Jarrolds, 1945
Heir to Kings; see The Laird
-The Hour-Glass. Jarrolds, 1934
-The House of Ogilvie. Long, 1922
-The Laird. Long, 1925. U.S. title (?): Heir to Kings. Stokes, 1926
-The Lost Cause. Hale, 1953
-Madeleine Smith. Hodge, 1928
Murder of Mr. Mallabee. Jarrolds, 1937
-The Needful Journey. Jarrolds, 1950
Room for a Ghost. Jarrolds, 1937
-The Royal Ishmael. Jarrolds, 1943
-Seven Women. Jarrolds, 1947
-Shadows. Jarrolds, 1951
-The Shears of Destiny. Jarrolds, 1942
Skin for Skin. Gollancz, 1935; Little, 1935
-The Spider's Web. Jarrolds, 1945
-Stubble. Jarrolds, 1935
-The Unjust Jury. Jarrolds, 1941
-A Web in Childhood. Hale, 1952
-The Wild Flame. Long, 1923
-Winter Pride. Hale, 1952

DUMAS, CHARLES ROBERT
Second Bureau. Eldon, 1939
Spies Against Them. Eldon, 1940

DU MAURIER, ANGELA
Treveryan. Joseph, 1942; Doubleday, 1942

DU MAURIER, DAPHNE. 1907- .
The Apple Tree. Gollancz, 1952. U.S. title: Kiss Me Again, Stranger. Doubleday, 1953. Also published as: The Birds and other stories. Penguin, 1963 ss
The Birds and other stories; see The Apple Tree
The Blue Lenses and other stories; see The Breaking Point
The Breaking Point. Gollancz, 1959; Doubleday, 1959. Also published as: The Blue Lenses and other stories. Penguin, 1970 ss
Don't Look Now; see Not After Midnight
The Flight of the Falcon. Gollancz, 1965; Doubleday, 1965
The House on the Strand. Gollancz, 1969; Doubleday, 1969
Jamaica Inn. Gollancz, 1936; Doubleday, 1936
Kiss Me Again, Stranger; see The Apple Tree
My Cousin Rachel. Gollancz, 1951; Doubleday, 1952
Not After Midnight. Gollancz, 1971. U.S. title: Don't Look Now. Doubleday, 1971 ss
Rebecca. Gollancz, 1938; Doubleday, 1938
The Scapegoat. Gollancz, 1957; Doubleday, 1957

DU MAURIER, GERALD. See: H(ERMAN) C(YRIL) McNEILE, 1888-1937.

DUN, (MARIE DE) NERVAUD
 Point of Death. Hammond, 1954

DUNBAR, JOHN G.
 -A Way to Adventure, and two other stories. Stockwell, 1942 ss

DUNCAN, ACTEA CAROLINE. 1913-   . Pseudonym: Carolyn Thomas, q.v.

DUNCAN, ALLAN. Series character: Major Charles Douglas Ker(r)wood, in both titles.
 A Cabinet Minister Resigns. Hutchinson, 1939
 An Official Secret. Hutchinson, 1937; Crowell, 1937

DUNCAN, DAVID. 1913-   .
 The Bramble Bush. Macmillan, 1948; Low, 1949. Also published as: Sweet and Deadly. Mercury, 1949
 The Madrone Tree. Macmillan, 1949; Gollancz, 1950. Also published as: Worse Than Murder. PB, 1954
 -The Serpent's Egg. Macmillan, 1950
 The Shade of Time. Random, 1946; Grey Walls, 1948
 Sweet and Deadly; see The Bramble Bush
 Worse Than Murder; see The Madrone Tree

DUNCAN, FRANCIS. Series character: Peter Justice, in at least those marked PJ.
 Behold a Fair Woman. Long, 1954
 Dangerous Mr. X. Jenkins, 1939
 Fear Holds the Key. Jenkins, 1945
 The Hand of Justice. Jenkins, 1945 PJ
 In at the Death. Long, 1952
 Justice Limited. Jenkins, 1941 PJ
 Justice Returns. Jenkins, 1940 PJ
 The League of Justice. Jenkins, 1937 PJ
 Ministers Too are Mortal. Long, 1951
 Murder But Gently. Long, 1953
 Murder for Christmas. Long, 1949
 Murder has a Motive. Long, 1947
 Murder in Man. Long, 1940
 Murderer's Bluff. Jenkins, 1938
 Night Without End. Jenkins, 1943
 A Question of Time. Hale, 1959
 So Pretty a Problem. Long, 1950
 The Sword of Justice. Jenkins, 1937 PJ
 They'll Never Find Out. Jenkins, 1944
 Tigers Fight Alone. Jenkins, 1938

DUNCAN, LOIS. 1934-   .
 I Know What You Did Last Summer. Little, 1973
 Point of Violence. Doubleday, 1966; Hale, 1968

DUNCAN, PETER
 The Tell-Tale Tart. GM, 1961; Muller pb, 1962

DUNCAN, ROBERT L(IPSCOMB). 1927-   .
 Pseudonym: James Hall Roberts, q.v.
 The Day the Sun Fell. Morrow, 1970
 The Dragons at the Gate. Morrow, 1975; Joseph, 1976

DUNCAN, W(ILLIAM) MURDOCH. 1909-1975.
 Pseudonyms: John Cassells, John Dallas, Neill Graham, Martin Locke, Peter Malloch, Lovat Marshall, qq.v.
 Series characters: The Dreamer (Supt. Donald Reamer) = D; Supt. Gaylord, in at least those marked G; Mr. Gilly, in at least those marked MG; Inspector Laurie Hume, in at least those marked LH; Supt. MacNeill, in at least those marked M.
 Again the Dreamer. Long, 1965 D
 The Big Timer. Long, 1973
 The Black Mitre. Melrose, 1951
 The Blackbird Sings of Murder. Melrose, 1948
 The Blood Red Leaf. Melrose, 1952
 The Breath of Murder. Long, 1972
 The Brothers of Judgement. Melrose, 1950
 Case for the Dreamer. Long, 1966 D
 Challenge for the Dreamer. Long, 1969 D
 The Company of Sinners. Melrose, 1951
 Cord for a Killer. Long, 1969
 The Council of Comforters. Long, 1967
 The Crime Master. Long, 1963 MG
 The Cult of the Queer People. Melrose, 1949
 Death and Mr. Gilly. Long, 1974 MG
 Death Beckons Quietly. Melrose, 1946
 Death Comes to Lady's Steps. Melrose, 1952
 Death Stands Round the Corner. Rich, 1955 M
 Death Wears a Silk Stocking. Melrose, 1945
 The Deathmaster. Hutchinson, 1953
 Detail for the Dreamer. Long, 1971 D
 The Doctor Deals with Murder. Melrose, 1944
 The Dreamer at Large. Long, 1972 D
 The Dreamer Deals with Murder. Long, 1970 D
 The Dreamer Intervenes. Long, 1968 D
 The Green Knight. Long, 1964
 The Green Triangle. Long, 1969
 The Hooded Man. Long, 1960 G
 The Hour of the Bishop. Long, 1964
 The House in Spite Street. Long, 1961
 The House of Wailing Winds. Long, 1965
 The Joker Deals with Death. Long, 1958
 Killer Keep. Melrose, 1946
 A Knife in the Night. Rich, 1955 M
 Laurels for the Dreamer. Long, 1975 D
 Meet the Dreamer. Long, 1963 D
 Murder at Marks Caris. Melrose, 1945
 Murder Calls the Tune. Long, 1957 LH
 The Murder Man. Long, 1959 LH
 Mystery on the Clyde. Melrose, 1945
 The Nighthawk. Long, 1962 G
 Pennies for his Eyes. Rich, 1956
 Presenting the Dreamer. Long, 1966 D
 Prey for the Dreamer. Long, 1974 D
 Problem for the Dreamer. Long, 1967 D
 The Puppets of Father Bouvard. Melrose, 1948
 Redfingers. Long, 1962
 Salute the Dreamer. Long, 1968 D
 Straight Ahead for Danger. Melrose, 1946
 The Tiled House Mystery. Melrose, 1947
 The Whisperer. Long, 1970
 The Whispering Man. Long, 1959 LH

DUNCOMBE, MRS. A.
 The Village Gentleman, and The Attorney at Law. (London), 1808

DUNCOMBE, FRANCES (RIKER). 1900-   .
 Death of a Spinster. Scribner, 1958; Secker, 1958

DUNDAS, LAWRENCE [LAURENCE GEORGE DIONICIO DUNDAS]. Series character: Andrew Salmond, in all titles.
 He Liked Them Murderous. Hammond, 1964
 A Spider at the Elvira. Hammond, 1949
 The Strange Smell of Murder. Hammond, 1965

DUNDEE, ROBERT. Pseudonym of Robert R. Kirsch, 1922-   .
 Inferno. Signet, 1962
 Pandora's Box. Signet, 1962

DUNLOP, AGNES MARY ROBERTSON. Pseudonym: Elizabeth Kyle, q.v.

DUNN, DETECTIVE. Pseudonym of Charles E. Pearce, q.v.
 The Beautiful Devil. Paul, 1923
 A Queen of Crooks. Paul, 1924
 The Red Mill Mystery. Paul, 1925

DUNN, DOROTHY. 1913-   .
 Murder's Web. Harper, 1950; Foulsham, 1951

DUNN, IRMA LARAWAY
 A Slightly Disjointed Affair. Vantage, 1963

DUNN, J(OSEPH) ALLAN (ELPHINSTONE). 1872-   .
 -Dead Man's Gold. Hurst, 1921; Doubleday, 1920
 The Death Gamble. Hamilton, 1932
 The Dragon's Claw. Mellifont, 1940
 The Elimination Syndicate. Pemberton, 1949
 -The Flower of Fate. Pearson, 1928
 -The Girl of Ghost Mountain. Pearson, 1927; Small, 1921
 The House on Doubloon Inlet. Earl, 1947
 -The Isle of the Drums. Hurst, 1923
 -Long-Haired Bill. Hurst, 1927
 -Luck and a Lady. Mellifont, 1942
 The Man Trap. Hurst, 1922; Doubleday, 1921
 The Sign of the Skull. Hurst, 192?

DUNN, JAMES. Pseudonym: R. E. Corder, q.v.

DUNN, N. J.
 The Vultures of Erin: A Tale of the Penal Laws. Kenedy, 1886

DUNNETT, ALASTAIR MacTAVISH. 1908-   .
 Pseudonym: Alec Tavis, q.v.

DUNNETT, DOROTHY. U.S. byline of Dorothy Halliday, q.v.

DUNNING, JOHN. 1942-   .
 The Holland Suggestions. Bobbs, 1975

DUNSANY, LORD [EDWARD JOHN MORETON DRAX PLUNKETT]. 1878-1957.
 The Little Tales of Smethers, and other stories. Jarrolds, 1952 ss, some criminous

DUNTON, JAMES G(ERALD)
 The Murders in Lovers' Lane. Small, 1927

DUPREE, MORRISON. Pseudonym of Sherlock Bronson Gass.
 A Tap on the Shoulder. Doubleday, 1929

DUPUY, ELIZA A(NN). 1814?-1881.
 -The Cancelled Will. Peterson, 1872; Halifax, 1878
 -The Dethroned Heiress. Peterson, 1873
 -Florence; or, The Fatal Vow. Stratton, 1852
 -The Gipsy's Warning. Peterson, 1873
 -The Hidden Sin. Harper, 1866
 -How He Did It. Peterson, 1871. Also published as: Was He Guilty? Peterson, 1873
 Was He Guilty?; see How He Did It
 -Who Shall Be Victor? Peterson, 1872; Halifax, 1878

DUPUY, WILLIAM ATHERTON. 1876-1941.
 Uncle Sam, Detective. Stokes, 1916 ss

DUPUY-MAZUEL, HENRI. 1885-   . Pseudonym: Henri Catalan, q.v.

DURAND, ALICE MARIE CELESTE FLEURY. 1842-1902. Pseudonym: Henry Greville, q.v.

DURAND, ROBERT
  Lady in a Cage. Popular Library, 1964. (Novelization of the movie.)

DURBIN, CHARLES
  The Patriot. Coward, 1971; Joseph, 1972
  Vendetta. Coward, 1970; Joseph, 1971

DURBRIDGE, FRANCIS. 1912-   . Joint pseudonym with James Douglas Rutherford McConnell, 1915-   : Paul Temple, q.v. Other McConnell pseudonym: Douglas Rutherford, q.v. Series characters: Paul Temple (also under the Paul Temple byline) = PT; Tim Frazer = TF.
  Another Woman's Shoes. Hodder, 1965
  Back Room Girl. Long, 1950
  Bat Out of Hell. Hodder, 1972
  Beware of Johnny Washington. Long, 1951
  The Case of the Twisted Scarf; see The Scarf
  The Curzon Case. Coronet, 1972 PT
  Dead to the World. Hodder, 1967
  Design for Murder. Long, 1951
  The Desperate People. Hodder, 1966
  A Game of Murder. Hodder, 1975
  The Geneva Mystery. Hodder pb, 1971 PT
  A Man Called Harry Brent. Hodder, 1970. (Novelization of the TV series.)
  My Friend Charles. Hodder, 1963
  My Wife Melissa. Hodder, 1967
  News of Paul Temple. Long, 1940 PT
  The Other Man. Hodder, 1958
  Paul Temple and the Front Page Men. Long, 1939. (Adapted by Francis Durbridge and Charles Hatton from the play by Durbridge.)
  Paul Temple and the Harkdale Robbery. Hodder pb, 1970 PT
  Paul Temple and the Kelby Affair. Hodder pb, 1970 PT
  Paul Temple Intervenes. Long, 1944 PT
  The Pig-Tail Murder. Hodder, 1969
  Portrait of Alison. Hodder, 1962; Dodd, 1962
  The Scarf. Hodder, 1960. U.S. title: The Case of the Twisted Scarf. Dodd, 1961
  Send for Paul Temple. Long, 1938 PT
  Send for Paul Temple Again! Long, 1948 PT
  Tim Frazer Again. Hodder, 1964 TF
  A Time of Day. Hodder, 1959
  The World of Tim Frazer. Hodder, 1962; Dodd, 1962 TF

DURHAM, DAVID. Pseudonym of Roy Vickers, 1888-1965, q.v. Other pseudonyms: Sefton Kyle, John Spencer, qq.v. Series character (also under Kyle and Vickers bylines): Det. Insp. Rason, in at least those marked R.
  Against the Law. Jenkins, 1939
  The Exploits of Fidelity Dove. Hodder, 1924. (Reprinted as by Roy Vickers: Newnes, 1935.) ss R
  The Forgotten Honeymoon. Jenkins, 1935
  The Girl who Dared. Jenkins, 1938
  Hounded Down. Hodder, 1923. (Reprinted as by Roy Vickers: Newnes, 1935.) R
  The Pearl-Headed Pin. Hodder, 1925. (Reprinted as by Roy Vickers: Newnes, 1935.)
  The Woman Accused. Hodder, 1923. (Reprinted as by Roy Vickers: Newnes, 1936.)

DURHAM, MARY. Series character: Inspector York, in at least those marked Y.
  Castle Mandragora. Gifford, 1950
  Cornish Mystery. Crowther, 1946
  Corpse Errant. Skeffington, 1949
  Crime Insoluble. Crowther, 1947 Y
  The Devil was Sick. Gifford, 1952
  Forked Lightning. Gifford, 1951
  Hate is my Livery. Gifford, 1945
  Keeps Death His Court. Crowther, 1946 Y
  Murder by Multiplication. Skeffington, 1948 Y
  Murder Hath Charms. Skeffington, 1948
  Why Pick on Pickles? Crowther, 1945 Y

DURIE, LYNN. Pseudonym of Douglas Christie, 1894-   , q.v. Other pseudonym: Colin Campbell, q.v.
  Paydirt. Ward, 1931
  This Yellow Slave. Ward, 1933
  The Triall Case. Ward, 1932

DURRANT, DIGBY. 1926-   .
  With my Little Eye. Gollancz, 1975

DURRANT, THEO. Byline on a collaborative novel by California members of the Mystery Writers of America, reportedly under the guidance of Anthony Boucher, q.v.
  The Marble Forest. Knopf, 1951; Wingate, 1951. Also published as: The Big Fear. Popular Library, 1953

DURRENMATT, FRIEDRICH. 1921-   . See: FRIEDRICH DUERRENMATT.

DURST, PAUL. 1921-   . Pseudonyms: Peter Bannon, John Chelton, qq.v.
  Backlash. Cassell, 1967
  Badge of Infamy. Cassell, 1968
  Die, Damn You! Lion, 1952

DURSTON, P. E. H.
  Mortissimo. Random, 1967; Macdonald, 1968

DU SOE, ROBERT C.
  The Devil Thumbs a Ride. McBride, 1938

DUSTON, MERLE
  -The Wind in our Hands. Harlo, 1966

DUTHOIT, EUNICE H.
  Death Takes the Stump. Phoenix (London), 1946

DUTTON, CHARLES J(UDSON). 1888-   .
  Series characters: John Bartley = JB; Harley Manners = HM.
  Black Fog. Dodd, 1934; Hurst, 1934 HM
  The Circle of Death. Dodd, 1933; Hurst, 1933 HM
  The Clutching Hand. Dodd, 1928 JB
  The Crooked Cross. Dodd, 1926 JB
  Flying Clues. Dodd, 1927; Lane, 1927 JB
  The House by the Road. Dodd, 1924; Lane, 1924 JB
  Murder in a Library. Dodd, 1931; Hurst, 1931 HM
  Murder in the Dark. Brentano's (London), 1929. (U.S. title?)
  Out of the Darkness. Dodd, 1922; Lane, 1922 JB
  Poison Unknown. Dodd, 1932. British title: The Vanishing Murderer. Hurst, 1932 HM
  The Second Bullet. Dodd, 1925. British title: The Westwood Mystery. Hurst, 1926 JB
  The Shadow of Evil. Dodd, 1930; Hurst, 1930 HM
  The Shadow on the Glass. Dodd, 1923; Jenkins, 1925 JB
  Streaked with Crimson. Dodd, 1929 HM
  The Underwood Mystery. Dodd, 1921; Robinson & Birch, 1922 JB
  The Vanishing Murderer; see Poison Unknown
  The Westwood Mystery; see The Second Bullet

DUVAL, HENRI
  The Devil in Her. Lewis, 1946
  Mayfair Nights. Hamilton, 1946
  Passion's Victim. Curzon, 1947
  Search the Lady. Murray, 1946
  She Vamped a Strangler. Curzon, 1946
  Tortured Love. Curzon, 1946

DWIGHT, OLIVIA. Pseudonym of Mary Hazzard.
  Close His Eyes. Harper, 1961

DWYER, DEANNA
  Children of the Storm. Lancer, 1972
  Dance with the Devil. Lancer, 1973
  The Dark of Summer. Lancer, 1972
  The Demon Child. Lancer, 1971

DWYER, JAMES FRANCIS. 1874-1952.
  Cold Eyes. Methuen, 1934

DWYER, K. R. Pseudonym of Dean R(ay) Koontz, 1945-   , q.v. Other pseudonym: Brian Coffey, q.v.
  Chase. Random, 1972; Barker, 1974
  Dragonfly. Random, 1975
  Shattered. Random, 1973; Barker, 1974

DWYER-JOYCE, ALICE (LOUISE). 1913-   .
  -Cry the Soft Rain. Hale, 1972; St. Martin's, 1973
  -The Moonlit Way. Hale, 1974; St. Martin's, 1974
  The Rainbow Glass. Hale, 1973; St. Martin's, 1973
  Reach for the Shadows. Hale, 1972; St. Martin's, 1973
  -The Strolling Players. Hale, 1975; St. Martin's, 1975

DYAR, C. W. See: CHARLES HOWARD MONTAGUE, 1858-1889.

DYAR, HARRISON GRAY. 1866-1929.
  -Diamonds Going and Coming. Stratford, 1926

DYE, CHARLES. 1927-1960?
  Prisoner in the Skull. Abelard (London), 1960

DYE, WILLIAM H.
  The Devil's Cameo. Exposition, 1956

DYER, CHARLES (RAYMOND). 1928-   .
  Time, Murderer, Please. English Theatre Guild, 1962. (Play.)
  Wanted—One Body! English Theatre Guild, 1961. (Play.)

DYER, GEORGE (BELL). 1903-   . Series: Catalyst Club = CC.
  Adriana. Scribner, 1939. British title: The Mystery of Martha's Vineyard. Heinemann, 1939
  The Catalyst Club. Scribner, 1936; Heinemann, 1937 CC
  The Five Fragments. Houghton, 1932; Skeffington, 1933
  The Long Death. Scribner, 1937; Heinemann, 1938 CC
  The Mystery of Martha's Vineyard; see Adriana
  The People Ask Death. Scribner, 1940; Heinemann, 1940 CC
  A Storm is Rising. Houghton, 1934; Skeffington, 1934
  The Three-Cornered Wound. Houghton, 1931; Skeffington, 1932

DYSON, JOHN
  The Prime Minister's Boat is Missing. Angus, 1974

E

"E.7". Pseudonym.
Romance of a Spy. Hurst, 1947

EADES, M(AUD) L. Series character: Winston Barrows = WB.
The Crown Swindle. Jenkins, 1925 WB
In Another Man's Shoes. Jenkins, 1936
The Torrington Square Mystery. Jenkins, 1932 WB

EADIE, ARLTON
The Carnival of Death. Fiction House, 1935
The Crimson Query. Jarrolds, 1929
The Death Express. Fiction House, 1935
Her Lover's Peril. Fiction House, 1935
Heroine of the Desert. Fiction House, 1935
The League of the Lotus. Fiction House, 1935
Murder Manor. Fiction House, 1935
Murder on the Wing. Fiction House, 1935
The Murillo Mystery. Fiction House, 1935
The Phantom Lover. Fiction House, 1935
The Phantom of the Films. Fiction House, 1935
The Trail of the Cloven Hoof. Skeffington, 1935
The Veiled Vampire. Fiction House, 1937

EAGLE, JOHN
The Hoodlums. Avon, 1953

EAMES, D.
Say It with Violence. Bear Hudson, 1944

EAMES, ROWLAND A.
The Lady is in Danger. Morris, 1947

EARL, LAWRENCE. 1915- .
Risk. Harrap, 1969

EARLIE, M(AY) A(GNES). Pseudonym of May Agnes (Early) Fleming, 1840-1880, q.v. Other pseudonym: Cousin May Carleton, q.v.
Eulalie; or, The Wife's Tragedy. Brady, 1866

EARLY, CHARLES
The Tigers are Hungry. Morrow, 1967; Rapp & Whiting, 1968

EAST, FRED. 1895- . Pseudonym: Fred Orpet, q.v.

EAST, MICHAEL. Pseudonym of Morris L(anglo) West, 1916- , q.v.
The Concubine; see McCreary Moves In
McCreary Moves In. Heinemann, 1958. Reprinted as by Morris L. West: Heinemann, 1974. Also published as: The Concubine. Four Square, 1967. Reprinted under this title as by Morris L. West: New English Library, 1973
The Naked Country. Heinemann, 1960; Dell, 1961. Reprinted as by Morris L. West: Heinemann, 1974

EAST, ROGER. Pseudonym of Roger d'Este Burford, 1904- . Joint pseudonym with Oswell Blakeston, 1907- : "Simon", q.v. Series character: Colin Knowles, in at least those marked CK.
The Bell is Answered. Collins, 1934
Candidate for Lilies. Collins, 1934; Knopf, 1934
Detectives in Gum Boots. Collins, 1936 CK
Kingston Black. Collins, 1960
Murder Rehearsal. Collins, 1933; Knopf, 1934 CK

The Mystery of the Monkey-Gland Cocktail. Putnam (London & New York), 1932
The Pearl Choker. Collins, 1954
The Pin Men. Hodder, 1963
Twenty-Five Sanitary Inspectors. Collins, 1935

EASTMAN, ELIZABETH. 1905- .
The Mouse with Red Eyes. Farrar, 1948; Heinemann, 1950. Also published as: His Dead Wife. Lion, 1950

EASTMAN, ROY O. 1883- .
The Mysteries of Blair House. Conjure House, 1948

EASTON, JOHN
Dog-Face. Allan, 1927. Revised edition: Eyre, 1937
Ferrol Bond. Putnam (London & New York), 1933
-Matheson Fever. Allan, 1928
-Old Granstock. Grayson, 1934
Red Sap. Putnam (London & New York), 1930. Revised edition: Eyre, 1938

EASTON, LAWRENCE
The Driven Flesh. Ace, 1955

EASTON, M. G.
-The House by the Bridge. Lane, 1906

EASTON, MICHAEL
Solent Intrigue. Stockwell, 1969

EASTON, NAT. Series character: Bill Banning = BB.
Always the Wolf. Boardman, 1957 BB
Bill for Damages. Boardman, 1958; Roy, 1958 BB
A Book for Banning. Boardman, 1959; Roy, 1959 BB
Forgive Me, Lovely Lady. Boardman, 1961 BB
Frangipani. Boardman, 1958
Mistake Me Not. Boardman, 1959; Roy, 1959 BB
Moment on Ice. Boardman, 1960
Nothing for Nothing. Boardman, 1958
One Good Turn. Boardman, 1957 BB
Quick Tempo. Boardman, 1960 BB
Right for Trouble. Boardman, 1960 BB

EASTWICK, MRS. EGERTON
The Rubies of Rajmar; or, Mr. Charlecote's Daughters. Newnes, 1895

EASTWOOD, HELEN BAKER. 1892- . Pseudonym: Olive Baxter, q.v.

EASTWOOD, JAMES. 1918- . Series character: Anna Zordan = AZ.
The Chinese Visitor. Cassell, 1965; Coward, 1965 AZ
Come Die with Me. Macmillan (London), 1970. U.S. title: Diamonds are Deadly. McKay, 1969
-Deadline. Dakers, 1952. (Novelization of the movie.)
Diamonds are Deadly; see Come Die with Me
Henry in a Silver Frame. Macmillan (London), 1972; McKay, 1972
Little Dragon from Peking. Cassell, 1967; Coward, 1967. Also published as: Seduce and Destroy. Pan, 1969; Dell, 1968 AZ
Murder Inc. Dakers, 1952
Seduce and Destroy; see Little Dragon from Peking

EATOCK, MARJORIE
The Ivory Tower. Curtis, 1972

EATON, FRANCES U.
A Fearless Investigator. McClurg, 1896

EATON-BACK, MRS. B. Pseudonym: Derek Vane, q.v.

EBERHARD, FREDERICK G(EORGE). 1889- . Series character: Chief of Police Sutherland = S.
The Microbe Murders. Macaulay, 1935 S
The Secret of the Morgue. Macaulay, 1932
The Skeleton Talks. Macaulay, 1933
Super-Gangster. Macaulay, 1932
The 13th Murder. Macaulay, 1931 S

EBERHARDT, WALTER F. 1891?-1935.
A Dagger in the Dark. Morrow, 1932
The Jig-Saw Puzzle Murder. Grosset, 1933

EBERHART, MIGNON G(OOD). 1899- .
Series characters: Sarah Keate & Lance O'Leary = K&O; Sarah Keate = SK.
Another Man's Murder. Random, 1957; Collins, 1958
Another Woman's House. Random, 1947; Collins, 1948
Brief Return. Collins, 1939
Call After Midnight. Random, 1964; Collins, 1965
The Cases of Susan Dare. Doubleday, 1934; Lane, 1935 ss
The Chiffon Scarf. Doubleday, 1939; Collins, 1940
The Crime at Honotassa; see The Cup, the Blade or the Gun
The Crimson Paw. Hammond, 1959. (Three novelets, two included in the U.S. collection Deadly is the Diamond, q.v., the third uncollected in the U.S.)
The Cup, the Blade or the Gun. Random, 1961. British title: The Crime at Honotassa. Collins, 1962
Danger in the Dark. Doubleday, 1937. British title: Hand in Glove. Collins, 1937
Danger Money. Random, 1975; Collins, 1975
The Dark Garden. Doubleday, 1933. British title: Death in the Fog. Lane, 1934
Dead Men's Plans. Random, 1952; Collins, 1953
Deadly is the Diamond. Random, 1958. (Four novelets, two each collected in the British volumes Five of My Best, and The Crimson Paw, qq.v.)
Death in the Fog; see The Dark Garden
El Rancho Rio. Random, 1970; Collins, 1971
Enemy in the House. Random, 1962; Collins, 1963
Escape the Night. Random, 1944; Collins, 1945
Fair Warning. Doubleday, 1936; Collins, 1936
Five of My Best. Collins, 1949. (Five novelets, two included in the U.S. collection Deadly is the Diamond, q.v., the other three uncollected in the U.S.)
Five Passengers from Lisbon. Random, 1946; Collins, 1946
From this Dark Stairway. Doubleday, 1931; Heinemann, 1932 K&O
The Glass Slipper. Doubleday, 1938; Collins, 1938
Hand in Glove; see Danger in the Dark
The Hangman's Whip. Doubleday, 1940; Collins, 1941
Hasty Wedding. Doubleday, 1938; Collins, 1939

The House by the Sea. Pockettes, 1972
House of Storm. Random, 1949; Collins, 1949
The House on the Roof. Doubleday, 1935; Collins, 1935
Hunt with the Hounds. Random, 1950; Collins, 1951
Jury of One. Random, 1960; Collins, 1961
Man Missing. Random, 1954; Collins, 1954 SK
The Man Next Door. Random, 1943; Collins, 1944
Melora. Random, 1959; Collins, 1960. Also published as: The Promise of Murder. Dell, 1961
Message from Hong Kong. Random, 1969; Collins, 1969
Murder by an Aristocrat. Doubleday, 1932. British title: Murder of my Patient. Lane, 1934 K&O
Murder in Waiting. Random, 1973; Collins, 1974
Murder of my Patient; see Murder by an Aristocrat
The Mystery of Hunting's End. Doubleday, 1930; Heinemann, 1931 K&O
Never Look Back. Random, 1951; Collins, 1951
The Patient in Room 18. Doubleday, 1929; Heinemann, 1929 K&O
The Pattern. Doubleday, 1937; Collins, 1937. Also published as: Pattern of Murder. Popular Library, 1948
Pattern of Murder; see The Pattern
Postmark Murder. Random, 1956; Collins, 1956
The Promise of Murder; see Melora
R.S.V.P. Murder. Random, 1965; Collins, 1966
Run Scared. Random, 1963; Collins, 1964
Speak No Evil. Random, 1941; Collins, 1941
Strangers in Flight. Bantam (Los Angeles), 1941
Two Little Rich Girls. Random, 1972; Collins, 1972
Unidentified Woman. Random, 1943; Collins, 1945
The Unknown Quantity. Random, 1953; Collins, 1953
While the Patient Slept. Doubleday, 1930; Heinemann, 1930 K&O
The White Cockatoo. Doubleday, 1933; Lane, 1933
The White Dress. Random, 1946; Collins, 1947
Wings of Fear. Random, 1945; Collins, 1946
With This Ring. Random, 1941; Collins, 1942
Witness at Large. Random, 1966; Collins, 1967
Wolf in Man's Clothing. Random, 1942; Collins, 1943 SK
Woman on the Roof. Random, 1967; Collins, 1968

EBERT, ARTHUR FRANK. 1902- . Pseudonym: Frank Arthur, q.v.

EBY, LOIS (CHRISTINE), 1908- , and JOHN C(HESTER) FLEMING, 1906- .
Blood Runs Cold. Dutton, 1946
The Case of the Malevolent Twin. Dutton, 1946
Death Begs the Question. Abelard, 1952; Abelard-Schuman (London), 1959
Hell Hath No Fury. Dutton, 1947
The Velvet Fleece. Dutton, 1947

ECCLES, CHARLOTTE O'CONOR. Pseudonym: Hal Godfrey, q.v.

ECHARD, MARGARET
Before I Wake. Doubleday, 1943
The Dark Fantastic. Doubleday, 1947
I Met Murder on the Way. Doubleday, 1965; Hale, 1967
If This be Treason. Doubleday, 1944
A Man Without Friends. Doubleday, 1940
Stand-In for Death. Doubleday, 1940
Who Killed Frankie Leash? Curtis, 1973

EDELMAN, MAURICE. 1911-1975.
A Call on Kuprin. Longmans, 1959; Lippincott, 1959
A Dream of Treason. Wingate, 1954; Lippincott, 1955
The Fratricides. H. Hamilton, 1963; Random, 1963

EDELSTEIN, MORTIMER S. See: MARION K. SANDERS, -1977.

EDEN, DOROTHY. 1912- . Pseudonym: Mary Paradise, q.v.
Afternoon for Lizards. Hodder, 1962. U.S. title: Bridge of Fear. Ace, 1966
An Afternoon Walk. Hodder, 1971; Coward, 1971
Bella. Hodder, 1964. U.S. title: Ravenscroft. Coward, 1965
The Bird in the Chimney. Hodder, 1963. U.S. title: Darkwater. Coward, 1964
Bride by Candlelight. Macdonald, 1954; Ace, 1972
Bridge of Fear; see Afternoon for Lizards
The Brooding Lake; see Lamb to the Slaughter
Cat's Prey. Macdonald, 1952; Ace, 1967
Crow Hollow. Macdonald, 1950; Ace, 1967
Darkwater; see The Bird in the Chimney
Darling Clementine. Macdonald, 1955. U.S. title: Night of the Letter. Ace, 1967
The Daughters of Ardmore Hall; see The Schoolmaster's Daughters
The Deadly Travelers. Macdonald, 1959; Ace, 1966
Death is a Red Rose. Macdonald, 1956; Ace, 1970
Lady of Mallow; see Samantha
Lamb to the Slaughter. Macdonald, 1953. U.S. title: The Brooding Lake. Ace, 1966
The Laughing Ghost. Macdonald, 1943; Ace, 1968
-A Linnet Singing. Pockettes, 1972
Listen to Danger. Macdonald, 1958; Ace, 1967
The Marriage Chest. Hodder, 1965; Coward, 1966, as by Mary Paradise
Night of the Letter; see Darling Clementine
The Pretty Ones. Macdonald, 1957; Ace, 1966
Ravenscroft; see Bella
Samantha. Hodder, 1960. U.S. title: Lady of Mallow. Coward, 1962
The Schoolmaster's Daughters. Macdonald, 1946. U.S. title: The Daughters of Ardmore Hall. Ace, 1968
The Shadow Wife. Hodder, 1968; Coward, 1968
Sleep in the Woods. Hodder, 1960; Coward, 1961
The Sleeping Bride. Macdonald, 1959; Ace, 1969
Summer Sunday. Macdonald, 1946
The Vines of Yarrabee. Hodder, 1969; Coward, 1969
The Voice of the Dolls. Macdonald, 1950; Ace, 1971
Waiting for Willa. Hodder, 1970; Coward, 1970
Walk into my Parlour. Macdonald, 1947
We are for the Dark. Macdonald, 1944
Winterwood. Hodder, 1967; Coward, 1967
Yellow is for Fear and other stories. Severn House, 1977; Ace, 1968 ss

EDEN, FRANCIS I. S.
The Ninth Life. Arcadia, 1969

EDEN, MATTHEW. Series character: Mark Savage, in at least those marked MS.
Conquest Before Autumn. Abelard, 1973 MS
Countdown to Crisis. Hale, 1968
Dangerous Exchange. Hale, 1969
Flight of Hawks. Hale, 1969; Abelard, 1970 MS
The Gilt-Edged Traitor. Abelard (London & New York), 1972 MS
The Man Who Fell. Hale, 1970

EDGAR, ALFRED. 1896- . Series character (with many other authors): Sexton Blake, in all titles, all published by Amalgamated Press.
The Cup Final Mystery. 1927
Lawless Justice. 1922
The Power of the Unknown. 1922
The Secret of the Safe. 1923
The Secret of the Tong; see The Sign in the Sky
The Sign in the Sky. 1922. Also published as: The Secret of the Tong, as by H. Gregory. 1936

EDGAR, GEORGE. 1877- .
The Red Colonel. Mills, 1913; Appleton, 1913

EDGAR, JOSEPHINE. Pseudonym of Mary Mussi, 1907- . At least some of these titles were published in England as romances and in the U.S. as gothics.
The Dancer's Daughter. Collins, 1968; Dell, 1970
The Dark Tower. Collins, 1966
The Devil's Innocents. Collins, 1972; Dell, 1975
The Lady of Wildersley. Macdonald, 1975; PB, 1977
My Sister Sophie. Collins, 1964; PB, 1974
Shadows in the Sun. Collins, 1957
The Stranger at the Gate. Collins, 1973; PB, 1973
Time of Dreaming. Collins, 1968; PB, 1974

EDGAR, KEITH
Honduras Double Cross. Howard, 1944
I Hate You to Death. Howard, 1944
Incendiary Blonde. Howard, 1946 ss

EDGE, SPENCER
A Maker of Ware. Cassell, 1913

EDGINTON, MAY [MRS. HELEN MARION EDGINTON BAILEY]. 1883- .
The Adventures of Napoleon Prince. Cassell (London & New York), 1912 ss

EDGLEY, LESLIE. 1912- . Pseudonym: Robert Bloomfield, q.v. Joint pseudonym with Mary Edgley: Brook Hastings, q.v.
The Angry Heart. Doubleday, 1947; Barker, 1949. Also published as: Tracked Down. Ace, 1954
Diamonds Spell Death; see The Runaway Pigeon
A Dirty Business. Putnam, 1969; Hale, 1970
False Face. Simon, 1947; Barker, 1948
Fear No More. Simon, 1946; Barker, 1948
Final Reckoning. Hale, 1971
The Judas Goat. Doubleday, 1952; Barker, 1953
One Blonde Died; see The Runaway Pigeon
The Runaway Pigeon. Doubleday, 1953. British title: Diamonds Spell Death. Barker, 1954. Also published as: One

Blonde Died. Bestseller, 1954
Tracked Down; see The Angry Heart

EDGLEY, MARY. Joint pseudonym with Leslie
   Edgley, 1912-   , q.v.: Brook Hastings, q.v.

EDHOLM, CHARLTON L(AWRENCE). See: FRANK
   CONDON.

EDINGTONS, THE [ARLO CHANNING EDINGTON,
   1890-1953, and CARMEN BALLEN EDING-
   TON, 1894-   ]. Series character:
   Detective Smith, in at least those
   marked S.
   -Drum Madness, with Marianne Barrett.
      Cassell, 1934
   The House of the Vanishing Goblets; see
      Murder to Music
   The Monk's Hood Murders. Collins, 1931;
      Cosmopolitan, 1931 S
   Murder to Music. Collins, 1930. U.S.
      title: The House of the Vanishing
      Goblets. Century, 1930 S
   The Studio Murder Mystery. Collins,
      1929; Reilly & Lee, 1929 S

EDMISTON, HELEN (JEAN MARY). 1913-   .
   Pseudonym: Helen Robertson, q.v.
   The Shake-Up. Macdonald, 1962

EDMONDS, HARY (MORETON SOUTHEY).
   1891-   .
   Across the Frontiers. Ward, 1936
   The Clockmaker of Heidelberg; or, The
      Strange Affair of Hugh Brodie,
      Englishman. Macdonald, 1949
   The Death Ship; or, The Tragedy of the
      "Valmeira". Lane, 1933
   The East Coast Mystery. Ward, 1934
   The North Sea Mystery: A Story of Naval
      Intelligence Work. Ward, 1930
   The Orphans of Brandenburg. Ward, 1953
   The Professor's Last Experiment. Rich,
      1935
   The Red Desert. Ward, 1931
   Red Invader. Ward, 1933
   The Riddle of the Straits. Ward, 1931
   The Rockets—Operation Manhattan. Mac-
      donald, 1951
   The Secret Voyage. Macdonald, 1946
   The Trail of the Lonely River. Ward,
      1934
   Wind in the East. Ward, 1935

EDMUNDS, BRENT
   Beware the Crimson Cord! Laurie, 1956
   A Gun in my Back. Laurie, 1955
   Ride a Dead Horse. Laurie, 1955
   Spiders in the Night. Laurie, 1956

EDQVIST, DAGMAR. 1903-   .
   Black Sister. Doubleday, 1963; Joseph,
      1963. (Translation of Den Svarta Sys-
      tern. Stockholm, 1961.)

EDSON, J(OHN) T(HOMAS), 1928-   , and
   PETER CLAWSON
   Blonde Genius. Corgi, 1973

EDWARD, MARIE ELAINE
   Amberleigh. Paperback Library, 1967
   Lenore. Paperback Library, 1966
   Terror Manor. Paperback Library, 1967

EDWARDS, ALEXANDER
   The Black Bird. Warner, 1975; Star,
      1976. (Novelization of the movie.)
   The Last of Sheila. Paperback Library,
      1973. (Novelization of the movie.)
   McQ. Paperback Library, 1974. (Noveli-
      zation of the movie.)

EDWARDS, ANNE. 1927-   .
   Alexandrovitch is Missing!; see Miklos
      Alexandrovitch is Missing
   Child of Night. Random, 1975
   Haunted Summer. Coward, 1972; Hodder,
      1973
   Miklos Alexandrovitch is Missing.
      Coward, 1970. British title: Alexan-
      drovitch is Missing! Hodder, 1970
   The Survivors. Holt, 1968; Allen, 1968

EDWARDS, BLAIR
   Murder Blues. Modern Fiction, 1946

EDWARDS, CHARMAN. Pseudonym of Frederick
   Anthony Edwards, 1896-   . Other
   pseudonym: Julius Van Dyke, q.v.
   Series character: Percy Aloysius
   Huff, in at least those marked PH.
   -A Big, Strong Man! Low, 1923
   The Blue Macaw. Ward, 1935 PH
   Confetti for a Killing. Ward, 1937 PH
   -Derision. Ward, 1926
   -Dolly's Walk. Ward, 1950
   -Drama of Mr. Dilly. Hale, 1939
   -Drink No Deeper. Ward, 1933
   Fear Haunts the Roses. Ward, 1936 PH
   -Gabriel Sounds for Africa. Hale, 1938
   -High Street. Ward, 1928
   No Coffins in China. Hale, 1937
   -Rainbrother. Ward, 1927
   -Sir Richard Penniless. Ward, 1928
   -Tall Pines in Paddington. Ward, 1949
   Ten Thirteen. Ward, 1936 PH
   Terror Ship. Ward, 1935 PH
   -Windfellow. Ward, 1925
   -The Yellow Wagon. Ward, 1932

EDWARDS, FREDERICK ANTHONY. 1896-   .
   Pseudonyms: Charman Edwards, Julius
   Van Dyke, qq.v.

EDWARDS, GRANT
   The Mystery of the Lyons Mail. Collins,
      1930
   The Office Scandal. London Book Co.,
      1929

EDWARDS, H(ENRY) SUTHERLAND. 1828-1906.
   The Case of Reuben Malachi. Chapman,
      1886; Rand, 1886
   -The Missing Man. Remington, 1885

EDWARDS, HARRY STILLWELL. 1855-1938.
   -The Marbeau Cousins. Rand, 1896

EDWARDS, HUGH. 1878-1952.
   All Night at Mr. Stanyhurst's. Cape,
      1933

EDWARDS, JAMES G. Pseudonym of James
   William MacQueen, 1900-   . Series
   character: Inspector Victor Bondur-
   ant, in all titles.
   But the Patient Died. Doubleday, 1948;
      Cherry Tree, 1949
   Death Among Doctors. Doubleday, 1942
   Death Elects a Mayor. Doubleday, 1939
   F Corridor. Doubleday, 1936
   Murder at Leisure. Doubleday, 1937
   Murder in the Surgery. Doubleday, 1935
   The Odor of Bitter Almonds. Doubleday,
      1938
   The Private Pavilion. Doubleday, 1935

EDWARDS, JANE (CAMPBELL). 1932-   .
   The Houseboat Mystery. Bouregy, 1965

EDWARDS, NORMAN
   Dilemma. Jenkins, 1936
   The Frightened Village. Jenkins, 1937

EDWARDS, PAUL. Series character: John
   Eagle (The Expediter), in all titles.
   Deadly Cyborgs. Pyramid, 1975
   The Death Devils. Pyramid, 1974
   Devil's Island Death Camp. Pyramid,
      1973
   The Fist of Fatima. Pyramid, 1973; New
      English Library pb, 1976
   Glyphs of Gold. Pyramid, 1973
   The Green Goddess. Pyramid, 1975
   The Holocaust Auction. Pyramid, 1975
   The Ice Goddess. Pyramid, 1974
   The Laughing Death. Pyramid, 1973; New
      English Library pb, 1976
   Needles of Death. Pyramid, 1973; New
      English Library pb, 1976
   Operation Weatherkill. Pyramid, 1975
   Poppies of Death. Pyramid, 1975
   Silverskull. Pyramid, 1975
   Valley of Vultures. Pyramid, 1973; New
      English Library pb, 1976

EDWARDS, RICHARD KEMBLE
   The Mystery of the Miniature. Clark,
      1908

EDWARDS, SAMUEL. Pseudonym of Noel B(ertram) Gerson, 1914-   , q.v. Other
   pseudonym: Leon Phillips, q.v.
   The Caves of Guernica. Praeger, 1975
   The Exploiters. Praeger, 1974; Heine-
      mann, 1975

EDWARDS, STAFFORD
   Money Order Murder. Vantage, 1963

EDWARDS, WALTER. Pseudonym of Walter
   Shute,   -ca.1940, q.v. Series
   character (with many other authors):
   Sexton Blake, in all titles, which
   were published by Amalgamated Press.
   The Ambush. 1931
   The Barber's Shop Crime. 1936
   The Case of the Murdered Pawn Broker.
      1935
   The Fatal Memoirs. 1934
   The Great Stores Crime. 1933
   The Great Stores Mystery. 1940
   The Hiker's Secret. 1933
   The Man in Brown. 1935
   The Murder on the Moor. 1932
   The Mystery of the Marchers. 1937
   The Newspaper Seller's Secret. 1938
   The Secret of the Cellar. 1939
   The Secret of the Identification Par-
      ade. 1936

EDWIN, MARIBEL
   Sound Alibi. Ward, 1935; Hillman, 1938
   The Valiant Jester. Ward, 1930
   Windfall Harvest. Ward, 1931

EGAN, LESLEY. Pseudonym of (Barbara) Eli-
   zabeth Linington, 1921-   , q.v.
   Other pseudonyms: Anne Blaisdell,
   Dell Shannon, qq.v. Series charac-
   ters: Jesse Falkenstein = JF; Vic
   Varallo = VV.
   Against the Evidence. Harper, 1962;
      Gollancz, 1963 JF
   The Borrowed Alibi. Harper, 1962; Gol-
      lancz, 1963 VV
   A Case for Appeal. Harper, 1961; Gol-
      lancz, 1962 JF, VV
   Detective's Due. Harper, 1965; Gol-
      lancz, 1966 VV
   In the Death of a Man. Harper, 1970;
      Gollancz, 1970 JF
   Malicious Mischief. Harper, 1971;
      Gollancz, 1972 VV
   My Name is Death. Harper, 1964; Gol-
      lancz, 1964 JF
   The Nameless Ones. Harper, 1967; Gol-
      lancz, 1968 VV
   Paper Chase. Harper, 1972; Gollancz,
      1973 JF
   Run to Evil. Harper, 1963; Gollancz,
      1964 VV
   A Serious Investigation. Harper, 1968;
      Gollancz, 1969 JF

Some Avenger, Rise! Harper, 1966; Gollancz, 1967 JF
The Wine of Violence. Harper, 1969; Gollancz, 1970 VV

EGERTON, DENISE
Design for an Accident. Hodder, 1957; Washburn, 1958
The Hour of Truth. Hodder, 1959; Washburn, 1960
It Couldn't be Caroline. Hodder, 1961
A Man That I Love. Hodder, 1955
No Thoroughfare. Hodder, 1954; Coward, 1955

EGERTON, FRANCIS CHARLES GRANVILLE. Pseudonym: Charles Granville, q.v.

EGERTON, J. KENILWORTH
A Soul Laid Bare. Street, 1906

EGGLESTON, EDWARD. 1837-1902.
The Mystery of Metropolisville. Judd, 1873; Routledge, 1873

EGLETON, CLIVE. 1927-   . Series character: David Garnett = DG.
The Black Windmill; see Seven Days to a Killing
The Bormann Brief; see The October Plot
The Judas Mandate. Hodder, 1972; Coward, 1972 DG
Last Post for a Partisan. Hodder, 1971; Coward, 1971 DG
The October Plot. Hodder, 1974. U.S. title: The Bormann Brief. Coward, 1974
A Piece of Resistance. Hodder, 1970; Coward, 1970 DG
Seven Days to a Killing. Hodder, 1973; Coward, 1973. Also published as: The Black Windmill. Crest, 1974
Skirmish. Hodder, 1975; Coward, 1975

EHRLICH, J. W. See: BRAD WILLIAMS, 1918-   .

EHRLICH, JACK [JOHN GUNTHER EHRLICH]. 1930-   . Series character: Robert Flick, in at least those marked RF.
Bloody Vengeance. PB, 1973
Court Martial. Pyramid, 1959
Cry, Baby. Dell, 1962 RF
The Drowning. PB, 1970; Hale, 1972
The Girl Cage. Dell, 1967 RF
Parole. Dell, 1960 RF
Revenge. Dell, 1958
Slow Burn. Dell, 1961 RF

EHRLICH, MAX (SIMON). 1909-
Dead Letter; see First Train to Babylon
Deep is the Blue. Doubleday, 1963; Gollancz, 1964
First Train to Babylon. Harper, 1955; Gollancz, 1955. Also published as: Dead Letter. Corgi, 1958. And as: The Naked Edge. Corgi, 1961
The Naked Edge; see First Train to Babylon
The Reincarnation of Peter Proud. Bobbs, 1974; Allen, 1975
Spin the Glass Web. Harper, 1952; Corgi, 1957
The Takers. Harper, 1961; Gollancz, 1961

EHRMANN, MAX. 1872-1945.
-A Fearsome Riddle. Bowen-Merrill, 1901; Stevens, 1901
The Mystery of Madeline Le Blanc. Cooperative, 1900

EICHLER, ALFRED. 1908-   . Series characters: Martin Ames = MA; Inspector Knickman = K.
The Big Bruiser. Phoenix, 1941. British title: The Gentle Giant. Swan, 1943
Bury in Haste. Arcadia, 1957 K
Death at the Mike. Lantern, 1946; Hammond, 1954 K, MA
Death of an Ad Man. Abelard, 1954. British title: A Hearse for the Boss. Hammond, 1956 K, MA
Death of an Artist. Arcadia, 1955; Hammond, 1955 K, MA
Election by Murder. Lantern, 1947 MA
The Gentle Giant; see The Big Bruiser
A Hearse for the Boss; see Death of an Ad Man
Moment for Murder. Arcadia, 1956; Hammond, 1957 K
Murder in the Radio Department. Gold Label, 1943; Hammond, 1953 K, MA
Murder Off Stage. Hammond, 1963. (U.S. title?)
Pipeline to Death. Hammond, 1962. (U.S. title?)

EIKER, MATHILDE. 1893-   . Pseudonym: March Evermay, q.v.

EINSTEIN, CHARLES. 1926-   .
The Bloody Spur. Dell, 1953. Also published as: While the City Sleeps. Dell, 1956
-The Last Laugh. Dell, 1956
The Naked City. Dell, 1959; World Distributors, 1960. (ss versions of TV scripts by Stirling Silliphant, q.v.)
No Time at All. Simon, 1957; Davies, 1958
-The Only Game in Town. Dell, 1955
While the City Sleeps; see The Bloody Spur
Wiretap! Dell, 1955

EISINGER, JO
The Walls Came Tumbling Down. Coward, 1943; Jarrolds, 1945

EISNER, SIMON. Pseudonym of C(yril) M. Kornbluth, 1923-1958, q.v. Other pseudonym: Jordan Park, q.v.
The Naked Storm. Lion, 1952

EKBERGH, IDA DIANA
The Mysterious Chinese Mandrake, and other stories. Pageant, 1954 ss

ELAND, CHARLES. Pseudonym of Charles Adolph von Rimanoczy, 1906-   .
The Desperate Search. Hale, 1971
Dossier Closed. Hale, 1970
The Gold Hijack. Hale, 1973

ELDER, EVELYN. Pseudonym of Milward Rodon Kennedy Burge, 1894-   . Other pseudonym: Milward Kennedy, q.v. Joint pseudonym with (Archibald) Gordon McDonell, 1905-   , q.v.: Robert Milward Kennedy, q.v.
Angel in the Case. Methuen, 1932
Murder in Black and White. Methuen, 1931

ELDER, MARK. 1935-   .
-Jedcrow. GM, 1974

ELDER, MICHAEL (AIKEN). 1931-   .
The Phantom in the Wings. Murray, 1957

ELDREDGE, GILBERT. Series characters: Thibault Parew and Chips Carpenter, in both titles.
Death for the Surgeon. Phoenix, 1939
Murder in the Stratosphere. Phoenix, 1940

ELDRIDGE, GEORGE DYRE. 1848-1928.
In the Potter's House. Doubleday, 1908; Methuen, 1908
The Millbank Case. Holt, 1905; Nash, 1907

ELDRIDGE, JIM
Down Payment on Death. Hale, 1972

ELDRIDGE, RUBY
The Legend of the Grey Castle. Vantage, 1969

ELDRIDGE, WILLIAM TILLINGHAST. 1881-1941.
Hilma. Dodd, 1907; Stevens, 1907
Meryl. Dodd, 1908; Stevens, 1908

ELEGANT, ROBERT S(AMPSON). 1928-   .
A Kind of Treason. Holt, 1966

ELGIN, MARY
Highland Masquerade; see Return to Glenshael
A Man from the Mist; see Visibility Nil
Return to Glenshael. Hodder, 1965. U.S. title: Highland Masquerade. Mill, 1966
Visibility Nil. Hodder, 1964. U.S. title: A Man from the Mist. Mill, 1965
The Wood and the Trees. Hodder, 1967; Mill, 1967

ELIADE, MIRCEA. 1907-   .
-Two Tales of the Occult. Herder, 1970. (2 novelets.)

ELIAS, DAVID. Series character: Nell Bartlett, in at least those marked NB.
The Cause of the Screaming. Hammond, 1953 NB
Dress Up and Die. Hammond, 1955
The Gory Details. Hammond, 1954 NB

ELIOT, ANNE. Pseudonym of Lois Dwight Cole, 1902-   .
The Dark Beneath the Pines. Hawthorn, 1974; Hale, 1976
Incident at Villa Rahmana. Hawthorn, 1972; Hale, 1975
Return to Aylforth. Meredith, 1967
Shadows Waiting. Meredith, 1969
Stranger at Pembroke. Hawthorn, 1971

ELIOT, MAJOR GEORGE F(IELDING). 1894-1971. Series character: Dan Fowler, in all titles.
Federal Bullets. Caslon, 1936; Cassell, 1937
The Navy Spy Murders. Dodge, 1937
The Purple Legion. Caslon, 1936; Cassell, 1937

ELIOT, HENRY WARE. 1879-1947. Pseudonym: Mason Deal, q.v.

ELKINGTON, E(RNEST) WAY. 1872-   . See also: DICK DONOVAN.
-The Lucky Shot. Treherne, 1902
The Rugged Way. Drane, 1903
-The Two Forces. Long, 1907

ELLERBECK, ROSEMARY
Inclination to Murder. Hodder, 1965

ELLERTON, EDWARD
A Fatal Resemblance. Lennon, 1885

ELLETT, HAROLD PINCTON. 1882-   . Pseudonym: Nigel Burnaby, q.v.

ELLIK, RONALD D. 1938-1968. Joint pseudonym with Frederic Langley: Frederic Davies, q.v.

ELLIN, STANLEY (BERNARD). 1916-   .
The Big Night; see Dreadful Summit

The Bind. Random, 1970. British title:
  The Man from Nowhere. Cape, 1970
The Blessington Method, and other
  strange tales. Random, 1964; Macdon-
  ald, 1965 ss
Dreadful Summit. Simon, 1948; Boardman,
  1958. Also published as: The Big
  Night. Lion, 1950
The Eighth Circle. Random, 1958; Board-
  man, 1959
House of Cards. Random, 1967; Macdon-
  ald, 1967
The Key to Nicholas Street. Simon,
  1952; Boardman, 1953
Kindly Dig Your Grave, and other wicked
  stories. Davis, 1975 ss
The Man from Nowhere; see The Bind
Mirror, Mirror on the Wall. Random,
  1972; Cape, 1973
Mystery Stories. Simon, 1956; Boardman,
  1957. Also published as: Quiet Hor-
  ror. Dell, 1959 ss
The Panama Portrait. Random, 1962;
  Macdonald, 1963
Quiet Horror; see Mystery Stories
Stronghold. Random, 1975; Cape, 1975
The Valentine Estate. Random, 1968;
  Macdonald, 1968
The Winter After This Summer. Random,
  1960; Boardman, 1961

ELLINGER, GEOFFREY. Series character:
  Roger Hartley = RH.
  Bars of Gold. Heritage, 1935
  The Blasted Acre. Smith, 1936
  The Lyddon House Mystery. Jenkins, 1928
  The Return of Cardannesley. Heritage,
    1934 RH
  The Ricksha Clue. Jenkins, 1931
  The Trap in the Tunnel. Jenkins, 1931
    RH

ELLINGTON, RICHARD. Series character:
  Steve Drake, in all titles.
  Exit for a Dame. Morrow, 1951; Board-
    man, 1954
  It's a Crime. Morrow, 1948; Cassell,
    1956
  Just Killing Time. Morrow, 1953; Board-
    man, 1954. Also published as: Shake-
    down. Bantam, 1955
  Shakedown; see Just Killing Time
  Shoot the Works. Morrow, 1948; Cassell,
    1950
  Stone Cold Dead. Morrow, 1950; Cassell,
    1952

ELLIOTT, BRUCE (WALTER GARDNER LIVELY
  STACY). 1915?-1973.
  One is a Lonely Number. Lion, 1952
  You'll Die Laughing. Five Star, 1945

ELLIOTT, GEORGE
  The Case of the Missing Airmen. Swan,
    1944
  The Mystery of the Missing Corpses.
    Swan, 1945

ELLIOTT, FRANCIS PERRY. 1861-1924.
  The Haunted Pajamas. Bobbs, 1911

ELLIOTT, JANE
  Darkening Night. Popular Library, 1975

ELLIOTT, PEERS
  The Mystery of the Black Dagger. Hale,
    1952
  The Pay Out. Hale, 1940
  The Silent Bullet. Hale, 1941
  Trust the Police. Hale, 1939

ELLIOTT, R. C.
  The Blackmailer. Hornsey, 1938
  The Phantom Bat. Amalgamated, 1930.
    (Sexton Blake.)
  Sabotage. Gray, 1956

ELLIOTT, ROBIN
  -The House of Dogs. Jenkins, 1948

ELLIOTT, SUMNER LOCKE
  Careful, He Might Hear You. Harper,
    1962; Gollancz, 1963
  The Man Who Got Away. Harper, 1972;
    Joseph, 1973

ELLIOTT, W. GERALD
  Treasure on the Broads. Jenkins, 1933

ELLIOTT, WILLIAM J(AMES). 1886-   .
  Series characters: Royston Frere, in
    at least those marked RF; Ed Gunning,
    in at least those marked EG; Bren
    Hardy, in at least those marked BH.
  "And Worms Have Eaten Them..." Swan,
    1940
  Bren Hardy Again. Swan, 1945 BH
  Bren Hardy, Tough Dame. Swan, 1942 BH
  -The Demon of Desire. Swan, 1940
  Dope Devils. Swan, 1942 RF
  False Pretenses. Mellifont, 1934
  Footprints in the Sand. Eldon, 1937
  Freak Racket. Swan, 1941 EG
  Gunning in England. Swan, 1946 EG
  Kissed Corpse. Swan, 1946
  -Lost Souls in Bohemia. Swan, 1941
  Mystery of Me...? Swan, 1944
  £1,000,000. Swan, 1949
  The Running Killer. Swan, 1946 RF
  Sheer Silk. Swan, 1946
  Shot-Silk. Swan, 1943
  "Silk!" Swan, 1942
  The Silver Panther. Gramol, 1934
  Snatched Dame. Swan, 1942 EG
  Spun Silk. Swan, 1947
  The Suicide Circle. Gramol, 1934
  Tough Ghosts. Swan, 1941
  Triggers are Trumps. Swan, 1942 EG
  The Wolf of Corsica. Mellifont, 1932
  The Yellow Fiend. Mellifont, 1932

ELLIOTT-CANNON, ARTHUR ELLIOTT.
  1919-   . Pseudonym: Nicholas
  Forde, q.v.

ELLIS, EDWARD S(YLVESTER). 1840-1916.
  Pseudonym: J. G. Bethune, q.v.
  The Eye of the Sun. Rand, 1897; Weekly
    Telegraph Novels (abridged)
  The Heart of Oak Detective. Westbrook

ELLIS, J. C.
  Black Fame. Hutchinson, 1926 ss
  Blackmailers & Co. Selwyn, 1929
  The Night of Mystery. Selwyn, 1928

ELLIS, J(OHN) BRECKENRIDGE. 1870-1956.
  The Mysterious Dr. Oliver. Macaulay,
    1929
  The Red Box Clue. Revell, 1902
  The Third Diamond. Badger, 1913

ELLIS, JULIE
  The Jeweled Dagger. Dell, 1973
  Kara. Dell, 1974
  Walk a Tightrope. Dell, 1975

ELLIS, KENNETH M.
  Dolores Divine, Guilty or Innocent?
    Grosset, 1931
  The Trial of Vivienne Ware. Grosset,
    1931

ELLIS, N. A. TEMPLE. See: N. A. TEMPLE-
  ELLIS, pseudonym of Neville Aldridge
  Holdaway, 1894-   .

ELLIS, VIRGINIA
  Death Comes Like a Thief. Arcadia, 1952

ELLIS, WILLIAM. 1918-   .
  The Knife Edge. Macmillan (London),
    1972; Walker, 1973
  No Will to Die. Walker, 1975

ELLIS, WILLIAM SENIOR. Joint pseudonym
  with Emeric Hulme-Beaman, q.v.: Ben
  Strong, q.v.

ELLISON, EARL
  The Big Deal. Spencer, 1952
  Corpses Don't Care. Curzon, 1946
  Corrupt City. Spencer, 1953
  Desert Intrigue. Hamilton Stafford,
    1949
  Design for Danger. Spencer, 1952
  Don't Mourn for Me. Spencer, 1953
  Framed. Spencer, 1953
  Gun Fever. Burrell, 1947
  Guns and Saddles. Hamilton Stafford,
    1948
  A Lady on Loan. Spencer, 1950
  Midnight Alibi. Spencer, 1952
  Miss Gloria Gets Wise. Spencer, 1949
  No Escape. Spencer, 1953
  Paid in Full. Spencer, 1953
  Rita Makes a Killing. Spencer, 1949
  Too Much Ambition. Spencer, 1953
  Too Smart to Live. Spencer, 1953
  Undercover Agent. Spencer, 1953
  Unwilling Guest. Spencer, 1952

ELLISON, HARLAN. 1934-   .
  The Deadly Streets. Ace, 1958; Digit,
    1959
  Gentleman Junkie and Other Stories of
    the Hung-Up Generation. Regency, 1961
    ss
  The Juvies. Ace, 1961
  Memos from Purgatory. Regency, 1961
  No Doors, No Windows. Pyramid, 1975 ss
  Rockabilly. GM, 1961; Muller pb, 1963
  Rumble. Pyramid, 1958

ELLSON, HAL. 1910-   .
  Blood on the Ivy. Pyramid, 1971
  Duke. Scribner, 1949
  Games. Ace, 1967. (Novelization of the
    movie.)
  The Golden Spike. Ballantine, 1952.
    British title: Reefer Boy. Spearman,
    1955
  I'll Fix You. Popular Library, 1956
  Jailbait Street. Monarch, 1959
  A Killer's Kiss. Hillman, 1959
  The Knife. 1961
  A Nest of Fear. Ace, 1961
  Nightmare Street. Belmont, 1965
  Reefer Boy; see The Golden Spike
  Rock. Ballantine, 1955
  Stairway to Nowhere. Ballantine, 1959
  Summer Street. Ballantine, 1953
  Tell Them Nothing. Ballantine, 1956 ss
  That Glover Woman. Award, 1967
  This is It. Popular Library, 1956
  Tomboy. Scribner, 1950

ELMONT, LOUISE
  The Egremont Mystery. Stockwell, 1953
    ss

ELSNA, HEBE. Pseudonym of Dorothy Phoebe
  Ansle. Other pseudonyms: Laura Conway, Lyndon Snow, qq.v. Titles by
  this author were apparently published
  in England as romances; one also published in the U.S. as a gothic is
  listed below.
  Strange Visitor. Hale, 1956; Saturday
    Review Press, 1975, as by Laura Con-
    way

ELSTOW, T. FRANCIS
  A Human Vampire. Modern, 193?

ELSTOW, T. FRANCIS
  The Scarlet Gargoyle. Modern, 193?
  Yellow Fangs. Modern, 1938

ELSWORTHY, A(LEXANDER) L(OCKHART)
  -Burdock. Hutchinson, 1937
  Death Glides In. Hutchinson, 1935

ELTON, EDWARD
  The Murder Chase. Hutchinson, 1929
  -She Drew the Bolt. Hutchinson, 1928

ELTON, JAMES T.
  Assignment in Tokyo. Badger, 1960
  The Quest of the Seeker. Badger, 1958

ELVESTAD, SVEN (CHRISTOPHER SVENDSON). 1894-1934. Series character: Asbjorn Krag = Osborne Crag = AK.
  The Case of Robert Robertson. Lane, 1930; Knopf, 1930
  The Man Who Plundered the City. McBride, 1924 AK
  The Mystery of the Abbe Montrose. Jarrolds, 1924 AK

ELWIN, MALCOLM. 1902-   .
  The Little Hangman. Macdonald, 1953

ELY, DAVID. Pseudonym of David Eli Lilienthal, Jr., 1927-   .
  -Poor Devils. Houghton, 1970
  Seconds. Pantheon, 1963; Deutsch, 1964
  Time Out. Delacorte, 1968; Secker, 1968 ss
  The Tour. Delacorte, 1967; Secker, 1967
  Trot. Pantheon, 1963; Secker, 1963

EMERICK, LUCILLE. See also: FRANCIS SWANN.
  -The City Beyond. Holt, 1952
  The Web of Evil. Doubleday, 1948

EMERSON, DAVID. 1900-   .
  A Murder in the Family. Hutchinson, 1970

EMERSON, JOHN. 1874-   . See: ROBERT (MELVILLE) BAKER, 1868-1929.

EMERSON, P(ETER) H(ENRY). 1856-1936.
  The Blood Eagle, and other mystery tales. Melrose, 1925 ss

EMERY, (RUSSELL) GUY. 1908-   .
  Front for Murder. Macrae Smith, 1947; Boardman, 1948

EMERY, J. INMAN
  The Luck of Udaipur. Jarrolds, 1925
  The Tiger of Baragunga. Jarrolds, 1924; Putnam, 1925

EMERY, SAMUEL
  At Nine Bells. Paul, 1932
  The House That Whispered. Paul, 1929; Dutton, 1929

EMSLEY, LLOYD
  False Freedom. Hale, 1971

ENDFIELD, MERCEDES. Series: Ms. Squad, in both titles.
  Lucky Pierre. Bantam, 1975
  On the Brink. Bantam, 1975

ENDICOTT, J(OHN) S.
  Crime Inc. Fiction League, 1932

ENDICOTT, STEPHEN. Pseudonym of W(alter) Adolphe Roberts, 1886-1962, q.v.
  Mayor Harding of New York. Mohawk, 1931
  -The Strange Career of Bishop Sterling. Meteor, 1932

ENDORE, GUY. 1900-1970.
  Detour at Night. Simon, 1959. British title: Detour Through Devon. Gollancz, 1959
  Detour Through Devon; see Detour at Night
  The Man from Limbo. Farrar, 1930; Gollancz, 1931
  Methinks the Lady——. Duell, 1945; Cresset, 1947
  The Werewolf of Paris. Farrar, 1933; Long, 1934

ENEFER, DOUGLAS. Series characters: Sam Bawtry, in at least those marked SB; Dale Shand, in at least those marked DS.
  The Avengers. Consul, 1963
  The Dark Kiss. World Distributors, 1965; Leisure, 1973 DS
  The Days of Vengeance. World Distributors, 1961
  The Deadline Dolly. Hale, 1970
  The Deadly Quiet. World Distributors, 1961; Leisure, 1973 DS
  The Gilded Kiss. Hale, 1969 DS
  The Girl Chase. Hale, 1968 DS
  Girl in a Million. Hale, 1970
  Girl in Arms. Hale, 1968 DS
  Girl on the M6. Hale, 1973
  The Jade Green Judy. Hale, 1974
  Lakeside Zero. Hale, 1973
  The Last Door. World Distributors, 1959
  The Last Train to Rock Ferry. Hale, 1975
  The Long Chance. World Distributors, 1961; Leisure, 1973 DS
  The Long Hot Night. Hale, 1967 DS
  A Long Way to Pitt Street. Hale, 1972
  Pacific North-West. Hale, 1975
  The Painted Death. Hale, 1966 DS
  Pierhead 627. Hale, 1968 SB
  Riverside 90. Hale, 1970; Roy, 1970 SB
  Sammy. World Distributors, 1963
  The Screaming Orchid. Hale, 1972
  The Shining Trap. World Distributors, 1965
  13 Steps to Lime Street. Hale, 1969 SB

ENGLAND, GEORGE ALLAN. 1877-1936.
  -Adventure Isle. Century, 1926
  The Alibi. Small, 1916
  -The Gift Supreme. Doran, 1916
  The Greater Crime. Cassell, 1917. (U.S. title?)
  Pod, Bender & Co. McBride, 1916; Laurie, 1916

ENGLAND, JANE. Pseudonym of Vera Murdock Stuart Jervis, 1897-   .
  -Flight into Danger. Hurst, 1950
  -House of Fears. Hurst, 1951
  -Safe Conduct. Hurst, 1942
  Trader's Licence. Hurst, 1936

ENGLISH, ERNEST I(VAN)
  Killers Come Cheap. Hale, 1967
  Who Needs Forever? Hale, 1974

ENGLISH, RICHARD. Pseudonym of Richard Murray, 1910-1957.
  The Sugarplum Staircase. Simon, 1947

ENGSTRAND, STUART (DAVID). 1905-1955.
  More Deaths Than One. Messner, 1955
  -The Sling and the Arrow. Creative Age, 1947

ENRIGHT, RICHARD E(DWARD). 1871-1953.
  The Borrowed Shield. Watt, 1925
  Vultures of the Dark. Brentano's, 1924; Brentano's (London), 1926

ENSOR, (ALICK CHARLES) DAVID(SON)
  Verdict Afterwards. Jenkins, 1960

EPHESIAN. Pseudonym of Carl Eric Bechhofer Roberts, 1894-1949. See also: GEORGE GOODCHILD, 1888-   . Series character: A.B.C. Hawkes, in all titles.
  A.B.C. Investigates. Jarrolds, 1937 ss
  A.B.C. Solves Five. Hodder, 1937 ss
  A.B.C.'s Test Case. Jarrolds, 1936

EPPLEY, LOUISE and REBECCA GAYTON
  Murder in the Cellar. Morrow, 1931; Grayson, 1932

ERDMAN, PAUL E(MIL). 1932-   .
  The Billion Dollar Killing; see The Billion Dollar Sure Thing
  The Billion Dollar Sure Thing. Scribner, 1973. British title: The Billion Dollar Killing. Hutchinson, 1973
  The Silver Bears. Scribner, 1974; Hutchinson, 1974

ERICKSON, NANCY WATSON
  Splinters of Fear. Avon, 1960

ERICSON, WALTER. Pseudonym of Howard (Melvin) Fast, 1914-   , q.v. Other pseudonym: E. V. Cunningham, q.v.
  Fallen Angel. Little, 1952. Also published as: The Darkness Within. Ace, 1953; and as: Mirage, as by Howard Fast. Crest, 1965

ERIKSON, SIBYL CICELY ALEXANDRA DICK. Pseudonyms: Alexandra Dick, Frances Hay, qq.v.

ERLANGER, MICHAEL. 1915-   .
  Mindy Lindy May Surprise. Random, 1969

ERNST, PAUL. 1886-   . Pseudonym: Kenneth Robeson (The Avenger series), q.v. Series characters: Shirley Leighton (Harper) and Bill Harper = H; Lt. Jim Ryan = JR.
  The Bronze Mermaid. Mill, 1952; Cassell, 1954 JR
  Hangman's Hat. Mill, 1951; Muller, 1952 JR, H
  Lady, Get Your Gun. Mill, 1955. British title: A Rose from the Dead. Cassell, 1956 H
  A Rose from the Dead; see Lady, Get Your Gun
  Short of Murder. Mystery House, 1959

ERSKINE, FIRTH. Joint pseudonym of Gladys Shaw Erskine, 1895-   , and Ivan Eustace Firth, 1891-   .
  Naked Murder. Macaulay, 1933; Butterworth, 1935

ERSKINE, GLADYS SHAW. 1895-   . Joint pseudonym with Ivan Eustace Firth, 1891-   : Firth Erskine, q.v.

ERSKINE, LAURIE YORK. 1894-1976.
  The Coming of Cosgrove. Appleton, 1926
  The Confidence Man. Appleton, 1925
  The Laughing Rider. Appleton, 1924; Hodder, 1927

ERSKINE, MARGARET. Pseudonym of Margaret Wetherby Williams. Series character: Inspector Septimus Finch, in all titles.
  And Being Dead. Bles, 1938. U.S. title: The Limping Man. Doubleday, 1939
  Besides the Wench is Dead. Hodder, 1973; Doubleday, 1973
  The Brood of Folly. Hodder, 1971; Doubleday, 1971
  Caravan of Night; see I Knew MacBean
  The Case of Mary Fielding. Hodder, 1970; Doubleday, 1970

Case with Three Husbands. Hodder, 1967; Doubleday, 1967
Dead by Now. Hammond, 1953; Doubleday, 1954
The Dead Don't Speak; see Fatal Relations
Death of Our Dear One. Hammond, 1952. U.S. title: Look Behind You, Lady. Doubleday, 1952. Also published as: Don't Look Behind You. Ace, 1972
The Disappearing Bridegroom. Hammond, 1950. U.S. title: The Silver Ladies. Doubleday, 1951
Don't Look Behind You; see Death of Our Dear One
The Ewe Lamb. Hodder, 1968; Doubleday, 1968
The Family at Tammerton; see Take a Dark Journey
Fatal Relations. Hammond, 1955. U.S. title: Old Mrs. Ommanney is Dead. Doubleday, 1955. Also published as: The Dead Don't Speak. Detective Book Club, 1955
Give Up the Ghost. Hammond, 1949; Doubleday, 1949
A Graveyard Plot; see The House of the Enchantress
Harriet Farewell. Hodder, 1975; Doubleday, 1975
The House in Belmont Square. Hodder, 1963. U.S. title: No. 9 Belmont Square. Doubleday, 1963
The House of the Enchantress. Hodder, 1959. U.S. title: A Graveyard Plot. Doubleday, 1959
I Knew MacBean. Hammond, 1948; Doubleday, 1948. Also published as: Caravan of Night. Ace, 1972
The Limping Man; see And Being Dead
Look Behind You, Lady; see Death of Our Dear One
No. 9 Belmont Square; see The House in Belmont Square
Old Mrs. Ommanney is Dead; see Fatal Relations
The Silver Ladies; see The Disappearing Bridegroom
Sleep No More. Hodder, 1958; Ace, 1969
Take a Dark Journey. Hodder, 1965. U.S. title: The Family at Tammerton. Doubleday, 1966
The Voice of Murder. Hodder, 1956; Doubleday, 1956
The Voice of the House; see The Whispering House
The Whispering House. Hammond, 1947. U.S. title: The Voice of the House. Doubleday, 1947
The Woman at Belguardo. Hodder, 1961; Doubleday, 1961

ERVIN, MARI
Death in the Yew Alley. Phoenix, 1937. Also published as: If I Die—It's Murder. Green Dragon, 194?

ESHLEMAN, JOHN M(ORTON). Series character: Lt. Larry Koharik, in both titles.
The Deadly Chase; see The Long Chase
Death of a Cheat; see The Long Window
The Long Chase. Washburn, 1954. Also published as: The Deadly Chase. Mercury, 1955
The Long Window. Washburn, 1953. Also published as: Death of a Cheat. Mercury, 1955

ESLER, ANTHONY (JAMES). 1934-   .
The Blade of Castlemayne. Morrow, 1974

ESMOND, HARRIET. Pseudonym of John (Frederick) Burke, 1922-   , q.v. Other pseudonyms: Jonathan Burke, Martin Sands, qq.v. Joint pseudonym with George Theiner, 1927-   : Jonathan George, q.v.
Darsham's Folly. Collins, 1974. U.S. title: Darsham's Tower. Delacorte, 1973
Darsham's Tower; see Darsham's Folly
The Eye Stones. Delacorte, 1975

ESMOND, SIDNEY
The Dead Look Down. Hutchinson, 1945
The Evil Cross. Hutchinson, 1944
The Peacock's Feather. Hutchinson, 1947
Sacrament of Death. Redman, 1950
The Secret Cargo. Hutchinson, 1945
Verboten. Hutchinson, 1940

ESSER, ROBIN. 1933-   .
The Hot Potato. Joseph, 1969
The Paper Chase. Joseph, 1971

ESSEX, DAVID
Betrayed. Warren, 1948
Retribution. Warren, 1949
-Secret Betrothal. Warren, 1949
Star Detective. Warren, 1948

ESSEX, LOUIS. Pseudonym of Levi Isaacs.
The Crook of Crauford Court. Amalgamated Press, 1930. (Sexton Blake.)

ESSEX, RICHARD. Pseudonym of Richard (Henry) Starr, 1878-   , q.v. Series characters: Lessinger = L; John Slade = JS.
Assisted by Lessinger. Jenkins, 1939 L
The Girl in Black. Tallis, 1966. (Retitled reprint of ?) JS, L
Lessinger Comes Back. Jenkins, 1935 L, JS
Lessinger Laughs Last. Jenkins, 1938 L
Marinova of the Secret Service. Jenkins, 1937 L
Murder in the Bank. Jenkins, 1936 L
Slade of the Yard. Jenkins, 1932; McBride, 1933 L, JS
Slade Scores Again. Jenkins, 1933; McBride, 1933 L, JS

ESTABROOKS, G(EORGE) H. 1896?-1973. See: RICHARD (ORSON) LOCKRIDGE, 1898-   .

ESTES, CARROLL COX
Eavesdropping on Death. Arcadia, 1952
Embrace of Death; see The Moon Gate
The Moon Gate. Doubleday, 1954; Barker, 1958. Also published as: Embrace of Death. Bestseller, 1955
Unhappy New Year. Doubleday, 1953

ESTEVEN, JOHN. Pseudonym of Samuel Shellabarger, 1888-1954. Other pseudonym: Peter Loring, q.v. Series characters: Inspector Rae Norse = RN; Miles Le Breton = ML.
Assurance Double Sure. Hodder, 1939
Blind Man's Night. Hodder, 1938
By Night at Dinsmore. Doubleday, 1935; Harrap, 1935 ML
The Door of Death. Century, 1928; Methuen, 1929 RN
Graveyard Watch. Modern Age, 1938
Voodoo. Doubleday, 1930; Hutchinson, 1930 RN
While Murder Waits. Doubleday, 1937; Harrap, 1936 ML

ESTRIDGE, ROBIN. Pseudonym: Philip Loraine, q.v.

ETHAN, JOHN B. Series character: Victor Grant, in all titles.
The Black Gold Murders. Detective Book Club, 1959
Call Girls for Murder. PB, 1960
Murder on Wall Street. Mill, 1960

ETHERIDGE, A. I.
The Elvin Court Mystery. Stockwell, 1929

EUSTACE, ROBERT. Pseudonym of Eustace Rawlins, 1854-   , or Robert Eustace Barton, 1868-1943. See also: L. T. MEADE; DOROTHY L(EIGH) SAYERS, 1893-1957; GERTRUDE WARDEN, with whom he collaborated.
The Human Bacillus. Long, 1907

EUSTIS, HELEN. 1916-   .
The Fool Killer. Doubleday, 1954; Secker, 1955
The Horizontal Man. Harper, 1946; H. Hamilton, 1947

EVANS, ALAN. Pseudonym of Alan Stoker, 1930-   .
Bannon. Cassell, 1968
The Big Deal. Hale, 1971
The End of the Running. Cassell, 1966
Mantrap. Cassell, 1967
Vicious Circle. Hale, 1970

EVANS, ALFRED JOHN. 1889-   .
All's Fair on Lake Garda. Hodder, 1958
The Escaping Club. Lane, 1921
The House of Anna. Hodder, 1953
The V2 Expert. Hodder, 1956
Who's the Guy? Hodder, 1940

EVANS, CICELY LOUISE
Nemesis Wife. Doubleday, 1970

EVANS, CONSTANCE MAY. Pseudonym: Mairi O'Nair, q.v.

EVANS, DEAN
No Slightest Whisper. Abelard, 1955. Also published as: This Kill is Mine. Graphic, 1956

EVANS, VICE ADMIRAL E(DWARD) R(ATCLIFFE) G(ARTH) R(USSELL). 1880-1957.
Spanish Death. Jarrolds, 1933

EVANS, E. EVERETT
-Alien Minds. Fantasy Press, 1955
-Man of Many Minds. Fantasy Press, 1953

EVANS, ELAINE
Black Autumn. Lancer, 1973
A Dark and Deadly Love. Lancer, 1973
Shadowland. Lancer, 1971
Wintershade. Popular Library, 1974

EVANS, (FRANCIS) FALLON. 1925-   .
Pistols and Pedagogues. Sheed, 1963

EVANS, GENE
Murder on Queer Street. Brandon, 1968

EVANS, GEORGE BIRD. 1906-   . Joint pseudonyms with Kay Harris Evans, 1906-   : Brandon Bird, Harris Evans, qq.v.

EVANS, GWYN (FIL ARTHUR). 1899-1938. Series characters: Sexton Blake (with many other authors) = SB (all such titles published by Amalgamated Press); Chester Brett, in at least those marked CB; Quentin Drex, in at least those marked QD; Bill Kellaway, in at least those marked BK; Double O'Day, in at least those marked DO.
The Abandoned Car Crime. 1931 SB
The Barton Manor Mystery. 1925. Also published as: The Curse of the Santyres. 1937 SB
The Black Cap. 1934 SB
Bluebeard's Keys. Wright, 1937 DO
The Case of the Climbing Corpse. Wright, 1939

The Case of the Crimson Conjuror. 1928 SB
The Case of the Jack of Clubs. 1928 SB
The Case of the Man Who Never Slept; see The Man Who Never Slept!
The Case of the Poisoned Pen. 1927 SB
Castle Sinister. Wright, 1936
The Clue of the Missing Link. Wright, 1938 CB
Coffins for Two. Wright, 1939 DO
The Crook of Fleet Street. 1926 SB
The Crystal Cell. 1931 SB
The Curse of the Santyres; see The Barton Manor Mystery
Death in the Jungle. 1933 SB
The Death Sign. 1931 SB
Death Speaking. Wright, 1934
Dr. Sinister. 1933 SB
The Fatal Friendship. 1933 SB
The Great Waxworks Crime. 1932 SB
The Hanging Judge. Wright, 1936
Hercules, Esq. Shaylor, 1930. U.S. title: Mr. Hercules. Dial, 1931 BK
His Majesty—the Crook. Wright, 1935 QD
The Homicide Club. Shaylor, 1931; Dial, 1932 BK
Iron Mask. Wright, 1938
King of the Underworld. 1928 SB
The Man from Dartmoor. 1932 SB
The Man Who Never Slept! 1925. Also published as: The Case of the Man Who Never Slept. 1936 SB
The Man with the Scarlet Skull, and other tales. Wright, 1935 ss
The Mission of Doom. 1930
Mr. Hercules; see Hercules, Esq.
Murderers Meet. Wright, 1934
The Mysterious Miss Death. Wright, 1937 CB
The Mystery of Mitcham Common. 1928
The Prisoners of Peru. 1927
The Return of Hercules, Esq. Wright, 1937
The Riddle of the Red Dragon. Wright, 1935
The Riddle of the Turkish Baths. 1931
Rogue Royal. Wright, 1936 QD
Satan Ltd. Wright, 1935 BK
The Sign of the Saracen. Wright, 1936
The Silent Jury. 1930
Sinister Castle. 1932
The Sleepless Man. Wright, 1940 DO
Steel Face. 1931
The Triangle of Terror. Wright, 1938 CB

EVANS, HARRIS. Joint pseudonym of George Bird Evans, 1906- , and Kay Harris Evans, 1906- . Other joint pseudonym: Brandon Bird, q.v.
The Pink Carrara. Dodd, 1960; Allen, 1960

EVANS, HOWEL
The Actor's Knife. Jarrolds, 1930
Crabtree House. Richards, 1919
A Girl Alone. Richards, 1917; Putnam, 1918
The Murder Club. Jarrolds, 1924; Putnam, 1925
The Murder Trap. Richards, 1929
The Sixth Commandment. Jarrolds, 1925

EVANS, HUGH AUSTIN. Pseudonym: Hugh Austin, q.v.

EVANS, JACKSON
Death Haunts the Charnel Estate. Bear Hudson, 1946

EVANS, JOHN. Pseudonym of Howard Browne, 1908- , q.v. Series character: Paul Pine = PP (also under the Howard Browne byline).
Halo for Satan. Bobbs, 1948; Boardman, 1949 PP
Halo in Blood. Bobbs, 1946 PP
Halo in Brass. Bobbs, 1949; Foulsham, 1951 PP
If You Have Tears. Mystery House, 1947. Also published as: Lona. Lion, 1952
Lona; see If You Have Tears

EVANS, JULIA RENDEL. 1913- . Pseudonym: Polly Hobson, q.v.

EVANS, KAY HARRIS. 1906- . Joint pseudonyms with George Bird Evans, 1906- : Brandon Bird, Harris Evans, qq.v.

EVANS, (CYRIL) KENNETH. 1917- .
Blueprint to Kill. Hale, 1975
No Cause for Dying. Hale, 1969
Oasis of Fear. Hale, 1968; Roy, 1968
A Rich Way to Die. Hale, 1973
Shadows of Violence. Hale, 1971

EVANS, PETER. 1933- .
Twisted Nerve. Sphere, 1969. (Novelization of the movie.)

EVANS, PHILIP. 1944- .
The Bodyguard Man. Hodder, 1973
Next Time, You'll Wake Up Dead. Hodder, 1972

EVANS, SAM
Love, Lust and Larceny. Leason, 1949

EVARTS, HAL G(EORGE). 1915- .
The Turncoat. GM, 1961

EVELYN, CHARLES
I am a Smuggler. Cassell, 1952
The Return of Van Weik. Cassell, 1952

EVELYN, FRANCES and LANGFORD REED
The Prime Minster's Pyjamas. Archer, 1933

EVELYN, JOHN MICHAEL. 1916- . Pseudonym: Michael Underwood, q.v.

EVERETT, MRS. H. D. Pseudonym: Theo Douglas, q.v.

EVERETT, PETER. 1913- .
A Day of Dwarfs. Spearman, 1962
The Fetch. Cape, 1966; Simon, 1967
The Instrument. Hutchinson, 1962
Negatives. Cape, 1964; Simon, 1965

EVERETT-GREEN, E(VELYN). 1856-1932.
-Adventurous Annie. Paul, 1916
-The Back Number. Paul, 1926
-Barbed Wire. Paul, 1914
-Billy's Bargain. Paul, 1920
-Blackladies. Hutchinson, 1914
-Blue Mist and Mystery. Paul, 1928
-The Boys of Red House. Melrose, 1902
-The Chatterton Mystery. Clarke, 1896
-The City of the Golden Gate. Paul, 1909
-Claud the Charmer. Paul, 1927
-Clive Lorimer's Marriage. Paul, 1911
-Co-Heiresses. Paul, 1909
-The Curse of Carlyon. Wright, 1931
-Dare Lorimer's Heritage. Hutchinson, 1891
-Dashing Dick's Daughter. Paul, 1916
-Duckworth's Diamonds. Paul, 1912
-A Fiery Chariot. Hutchinson, 1900
-The Heronstroke Mystery. Religious Tract Society, 1915
-A Holiday in a Manor House; or, Who Solved the Mystery. Biggs, 1892
-The Mystery of Alton Grange. Nelson, 1899
-The Secret Chamber at Chad. Nelson, 1894
-The Secret of Maxshelling. Shaw, 1902
-The Secret of Wold Hall. Hutchinson, 1905; McClurg, 1905
-The Squire's Heir; or, The Secret of Rochester's Will. Melrose, 1903
-Temple's Trial; or, For Life or Death. Nelson, 1887

EVERITT, BRIDGET (MARY). 1924- .
A Cold Front. Davies, 1972; Walker, 1973

EVERMAY, MARCH. Pseudonym of Mathilde Eiker, 1893- . Series character: Inspector Glover, in both titles.
They Talked of Poison. Macmillan, 1938; Jarrolds, 1939
This Death was Murder. Macmillan, 1940; Jarrolds, 1940

EVERTON, FRANCIS. Pseudonym of Francis William Stokes, 1883- . Series characters: Inspector George Annesley = GA; Detective-Inspector Allport = A.
The Dalehouse Murder. Collins, 1927; Bobbs, 1927 A
The Hammer of Doom. Collins, 1928; Bobbs, 1929 A
Insoluble. Collins, 1934
Murder at Plenders. Collins, 1930. U.S. title: Murder Through the Window. Morrow, 1930 GA
Murder May Pass Unpunished. Collins, 1936 GA, A
Murder Through the Window; see Murder at Plenders
The Young Vanish. Collins, 1932; Morrow, 1932 A

EWART, ERNEST ANDREW. 1878-1943. Pseudonym: Boyd Cable, q.v.

EXBRAYAT, CHARLES
The Ravishing Idiot. Popular Library, 1965. (Translation of Une Ravissante Idiote. Paris, 1962.)

EYLES, ALFRED W. Series character: Paul Chisholm, in at least those marked PC.
Mirrored Murder. Fiction House, 1945
Murder at Out-Patients. World's Work, 1948 PC
Murder Brewing. World's Work, 1947 PC
Murder in Hospital. World's Work, 1944 PC

EYLES, (MARGARET) LEONORA (PITCAIRN). 1890- .
Death of a Dog. Hutchinson, 1936
They Wanted Him Dead! Hutchinson, 1936

EYRE, ARCHIBALD
The Girl in Waiting. Luce, 1906; Ward, 1906

EYRE, JOHN R.
Condemned to Death. Ouseley, 1908

EYRE, KATE
A Step in the Dark. Cassell, 1894

EYRE, KATHERINE WIGMORE. 1901-1970.
Amy. Appleton, 1963; Hodder, 1964
The Chinese Box. Appleton, 1959; Hodder, 1960
The Lute and the Glove. Appleton, 1955; Hodder, 1957
Monk's Court. Appleton, 1966
The Sandalwood Fan. Meredith, 1968

EYRE, MARIE
The Absence. Popular Library, 1973
Blackgable Inn. Popular Library, 1971

Bury Me Not at Sea. Popular Library, 1974
Eyrie of the Fox. Popular Library, 1973
The Girl in the Tiffany Dress. Popular Library, 1972
The Omen. Popular Library, 1973
The Presence. Popular Library, 1972
Return to Gravesend. Popular Library, 1972

F

F, INSPECTOR. Pseudonym of William Russell. Other pseudonym: Waters, q.v.
Experiences of a Real Detective. Ward, 1862 ss
Mrs. Waldegrave's Will and other tales. Ward, 1870 ss

FABER, CHRISTINE. Pseudonym.
-A Fatal Resemblance. Kenedy, 1900
The Guardian's Mystery; or, Rejected for Conscience's Sake. Kenedy, 1887
-A Mother's Sacrifice; or, Who was Guilty? Kenedy, 1891

FACOS, JAMES. 1924-   .
The Silver Lady. Atheneum, 1972

FADIMAN, EDWIN, JR. 1925-   .
An Act of Violence. Signet, 1957
The One-Eyed King. Geis, 1971; Allen, 1972
Who will Watch the Watchers. Little, 1970; Allen, 1971

FAGAN, NORBERT
The Crooked Mile. GM, 1953; Fawcett (London), 1955
One Against the Odds. GM, 1954; Fawcett (London), 1955

FAGYAS, M. Pseudonym of Maria Bush-Fekete.
The Devil's Lieutenant. Putnam, 1970; Blond, 1970
The Fifth Woman. Doubleday, 1963; Hodder, 1965
The Widowmaker. Doubleday, 1966; Cassell, 1967

FAHERTY, ROBERT
Better Than Dying. Doubleday, 1935; Gollancz, 1935

FAHRENKOPF, ANNE. Joint pseudonym with Ruth Fox: Alexander Irving, q.v.

FAIR, A. A. Pseudonym of Erle Stanley Gardner, 1889-1970, q.v. Other pseudonyms: Carleton Kendrake, Charles J. Kenny, qq.v. Series characters: Donald Lam and Bertha Cool, in all titles.
All Grass Isn't Green. Morrow, 1970; Heinemann, 1970
An Axe to Grind; see Give 'em the Ax
Bachelors Get Lonely. Morrow, 1961; Heinemann, 1962
Bats Fly at Dusk. Morrow, 1942; Hale, 1951
Bedrooms Have Windows. Morrow, 1949; Heinemann, 1956
Beware the Curves. Morrow, 1956; Heinemann, 1957
The Bigger They Come. Morrow, 1939. British title: Lam to the Slaughter. H. Hamilton, 1939
Cats Prowl at Night. Morrow, 1943; Hale, 1949
The Count of Nine. Morrow, 1958; Heinemann, 1959
Crows Can't Count. Morrow, 1946; Heinemann, 1953
Cut Thin to Win. Morrow, 1965; Heinemann, 1966
Double or Quits. Morrow, 1941; Hale, 1949
Fish or Cut Bait. Morrow, 1963; Heinemann, 1964
Fools Die on Friday. Morrow, 1947; Heinemann, 1955
Give 'em the Ax. Morrow, 1944. British title: An Axe to Grind. Heinemann, 1951
Gold Comes in Bricks. Morrow, 1940; Hale, 1942
Kept Women Can't Quit. Morrow, 1960; Heinemann, 1961
Lam to the Slaughter; see The Bigger They Come
Owls Don't Blink. Morrow, 1942; Hale, 1951
Pass the Gravy. Morrow, 1959; Heinemann, 1960
Shills Can't Cash Chips. Morrow, 1961. British title: Stop at the Red Light. Heinemann, 1962
Some Slips Don't Show. Morrow, 1957; Heinemann, 1959
Some Women Won't Wait. Morrow, 1953; Heinemann, 1958
Spill the Jackpot! Morrow, 1941; Hale, 1948
Stop at the Red Light; see Shills Can't Cash Chips
Top of the Heap. Morrow, 1952; Heinemann, 1957
Traps Need Fresh Bait. Morrow, 1967; Heinemann, 1968
Try Anything Once. Morrow, 1962; Heinemann, 1963
Turn on the Heat. Morrow, 1940; H. Hamilton, 1940
Up for Grabs. Morrow, 1964; Heinemann, 1965
Widows Wear Weeds. Morrow, 1966; Heinemann, 1966
You Can Die Laughing. Morrow, 1957; Heinemann, 1958

FAIRBAIRN, DOUGLAS. 1926-   .
Shoot. Doubleday, 1973; Heinemann, 1974

FAIRBAIRN, ROGER. Pseudonym of John Dickson Carr, 1905-1977, q.v. Other pseudonyms: Carr Dickson, Carter Dickson, qq.v. See also: JOHN RHODE; ADRIAN CONAN DOYLE, 1911-1970.
Devil Kinsmere. Harper, 1934; H. Hamilton, 1934. Revised edition: Most Secret, as by John Dickson Carr. Harper, 1964; H. Hamilton, 1964

FAIRBANK, JANET AYER. See: HENRY KITCHELL WEBSTER, 1875-1932.

FAIRBURN, ELEANOR. 1928-   . Pseudonym: Catherine Carfax, q.v.

FAIRCHILD, WILLIAM
The Sound of Murder. French (London), 1960. (3-act play.)
The Swiss Arrangement. Macmillan (London), 1973; St. Martin's, 1974

FAIRFAX, DENNIS
The Masked Ball Murder. Jenkins, 1934

FAIRFAX-BLAKEBOROUGH, J(OHN FREEMAN). 1883-   .
Beating the Nobblers. Allan, 1933
The Disappearance of Cropton. Allan, 1933
-Gypsy's Luck, with Christopher Somers. Allan, 1932
-A Last Gamble. Allan, 1936
-Nat Wedgewood, Jockey. Allan, 1933 ss
Queen of the Gangsters. Allan, 1936
-A Rank Outsider. Allan, 1933
A Turf Mystery, with Rupert St. Cloud. Allan, 1934
Warned Off. Allan, 1934
Who Maimed Spurto? Allan, 1933

FAIRLIE, GERARD. 1899-   . Series characters: Victor Caryll = VC; Bulldog Drummond (continuing the series created by H. C. McNeile, 1888-1937, q.v.; see also: Henry Reymond) = BD; Johnny Macall = JM; Mr. Malcolm = M.
Birds of Prey. Hodder, 1932
Bulldog Drummond Attacks. Hodder, 1939; Gateway, 1940 BD
Bulldog Drummond on Dartmoor. Hodder, 1938; Hillman-Curl, 1939 BD
Bulldog Drummond Stands Fast. Hodder, 1947 BD
Calling Bulldog Drummond. Hodder, 1951 BD
Captain Bulldog Drummond. Hodder, 1945 BD
Copper at Sea. Hodder, 1934
Deadline for Macall. Hodder, 1956; Mill, 1956 JM
Double the Bluff. Hodder, 1957 JM
The Exquisite Lady. Hodder, 1929. U.S. title: Yellow Munro. Little, 1929
Hands Off Bulldog Drummond. Hodder, 1949 BD
Macall Gets Curious. Hodder, 1959 JM
The Man Who Laughed. Hodder, 1928; Little, 1928 VC
The Man with Talent. Hodder, 1931
Men for Counters. Hodder, 1933 M
Mr. Malcolm Presents. Hodder, 1932 M
The Muster of the Vultures. Hodder, 1929; Little, 1930
No Sleep for Macall. Hodder, 1955 JM
The Pianist Shoots First. Hodder, 1938
Please Kill My Cousin. Hodder, 1961 JM
The Reaper. Little, 1929 (British title?)
The Return of the Black Gang. Hodder, 1954 BD
The Rope Which Hangs. Hodder, 1932
Scissors Cut Paper. Hodder, 1927; Little, 1928 VC
Shot in the Dark. Hodder, 1932; Doubleday, 1932 M
Stone Blunts Scissors. Hodder, 1928; Little, 1929 VC
Suspect. Hodder, 1930; Doubleday, 1930
That Man Returns. Hodder, 1934 VC
They Found Each Other. Hodder, 1946
The Treasure Nets. Hodder, 1933
Unfair Lady. Hodder, 1931
Winner Take All. Hodder, 1953; Dodd, 1953 JM
Yellow Munro; see The Exquisite Lady

FAIRMAN, PAUL W. 1916-1977.
Coffy. Lancer, 1973. (Novelization of the movie.)
-The Cover Girls. Macfadden, 1970
The Ghost of Graveyard Hill. Curtis, 1972
The Glass Ladder. Handi-Books, 1950
-The Joy Wheel. Lion, 1954
Pattern for Destruction. Macfadden, 1970
-Playboy. Macfadden, 1970
Search for a Dead Nympho. Lancer, 1967
That Girl. Popular Library, 1971. (Novelization of the TV series.)
To Catch a Crooked Girl. Pinnacle, 1971
Terror by Night. Curtis, 1972
-The World Grabbers. Monarch, 1964

FAIRWAY, SIDNEY. Pseudonym of Sidney Herbert Daukes, 1879-   .
-A Cuckoo in Harley Street. Paul, 1932. U.S. title: Dr. Falke of Harley Street. Kinsey, 1933

Dr. Falke of Harley Street; see A Cuckoo in Harley Street
-Doctor Severin's Secret. Paul, 1943
-The Doctor's Defence. Paul, 1931; Kinsey, 1932
-He Loved Freedom. Paul, 1947
-It Came to Pass. Paul, 1944
-A Late Recovery. Paul, 1940
-The Long Tunnel. Paul, 1935; Doubleday, 1936
Thanks to Dr. Molly. Paul, 1937
The Yellow Viper. Paul, 1931

FALCON, MARY LEE
The Dungeon. Belmont, 1969

FALK, DAVID G.
Rick; or, The Recidiviste. Trischler, 1891

FALKIRK, RICHARD. Pseudonym of Derek (William) Lambert, 1929-   , q.v. Series character: Blackstone = B.
Beau Blackstone. Eyre, 1973; Stein, 1974 B
Blackstone. Eyre, 1972; Stein, 1973 B
Blackstone and the Scourge of Europe. Eyre, 1974; Stein, 1974 B
Blackstone's Fancy. Eyre, 1973; Stein, 1973 B
The Chill Factor. Joseph, 1971; Doubleday, 1971
The Twisted Wire. Corgi, 1972; Doubleday, 1971

FALKNER, J(OHN) MEADE. 1858-1932.
The Lost Stradivarius. Blackwood, 1895
The Nebuly Coat. Arnold, 1903

FALKNER, LEONARD. 1901?-1977.
M. Holt, 1931
Murder Off Broadway. Holt, 1930; Hamilton, 1930

FALLON, GEORGE. Pseudonym of D(avid) E(rnest) Bingley, 1920-   , q.v. Other pseudonym: Henry Chesham, q.v.
Rendezvous in Rio. Hale, 1967

FALLON, MARTIN. Pseudonym of Henry Patterson, 1929-   . Other pseudonyms: James Graham, Jack Higgins, Hugh Marlowe, Harry Patterson, qq.v. Series character: Paul Chavasse, in all titles.
Dark Side of the Street. Long, 1967; GM, 1974, as by Jack Higgins. Reprinted in England as by Jack Higgins: Coronet, 1973
A Fine Night for Dying. Long, 1969
The Keys of Hell. Abelard (London & New York), 1965. Reprinted as by Jack Higgins: Coronet, 1972; GM, 1976
Midnight Never Comes. Long, 1966; GM, 1975, as by Jack Higgins. Reprinted in Britain as by Jack Higgins: Coronet, 1973
The Testament of Caspar Schultz. Abelard (London & New York), 1962. Reprinted as by Jack Higgins: GM, 1978
Year of the Tiger. Abelard (London), 1963; Abelard (New York), 1964

FALLON, THOMAS
The Last Warning. French, 1935. (Play based on the novel The House of Fear by Wadsworth Camp, 1879-1936, q.v.)

FALSTEIN, LOUIS
Slaughter Street. Lion, 1953; Panther, 1961
Sole Survivor. Dell, 1954

FANE, ANTHONY
The Wycliffe-Pepin Case. Poe, 1931

FANGER, HORST. 1919-   .
A Life for a Life. Ballantine, 1954; Hale, 1956. (Translation of Wir Selber Sind das Rad. Darmstadt, 1952.)

FARAGO, LUCIEN
An Easy Victim. Cape, 1957. (Translation of Un Homme a Devorer. Paris, 1955.)

FARGUS, F(REDERICK) J(OHN). 1840-1885. Pseudonym: Hugh Conway, q.v.
Carriston's Gift and other stories. Arrowsmith, 1884; Holt, 1885, as by Hugh Conway. Also published as: Dead Man's Face. Munro, 1885, as by Hugh Conway ss
Circumstantial Evidence. Bailey, 1887; Ogilvie, 1885, as by Hugh Conway ss
Dark Days. Arrowsmith, 1884
Dead Man's Face; see Carriston's Gift and other stories
Paul Vargas, a Mystery, and other tales. Lovell, 1885, as by Hugh Conway (ss, taken from Carriston's Gift and other stories, q.v.)
Slings and Arrows and other tales. Arrowsmith, 1885; Holt, 1885, as by Hugh Conway

FARHI, (MUSA) MORIS. 1935-   .
The Pleasure of Your Death. Constable, 1972

FARJEON, B(ENJAMIN) L(EOPOLD). 1838-1903.
-The Amblers. Hutchinson, 1904
-Basil and Annette. White, 1890; U.S. Book Co., 1890
-The Bells of Penraven. Tinsley, 1879; Harper, 1879
The Betrayal of John Fordham. Hutchinson, 1896; Fenno, 1896
-Blade-o'-Grass. Hutchinson, 1899
-The Blood White Rose. Trischler, 1889
The Clairvoyante. Hutchinson, 1905
Devlin the Barber. Ward, 1888; Arno, 1976
-Doctor Glennie's Daughter: A Story of Real Life. Hurst, 1889
For the Defense. Trischler, 1891; Lovell, 1891
Gautran; see The House of the White Shadows
The Golden Land; or, Links from Shore to Shore. Ward, 1886
Great Porter Square. Ward, 1885; Harper, 1885. Also published as: 119 Great Porter Square. Munro, 1881?
-Grif. Tinsley, 1870; DeWitt, 1871?
The House of the White Shadows. Tinsley, 1884. U.S. title: Gautran; or, The House of the White Shadows. Lovell, 1883
-In a Silver Sea. Ward, 1886
-Jessie Trim. Tinsley, 1874; Harper, 1875
The Last Tenant. Hutchinson, 1893; Cassell, 1893
-London's Heart. Tinsley, 1873; Harper, 1873
-Love's Harvest. Lovell, 1885. (British title?)
-Love's Victory. Tinsley, 1875; Harper, 1875
-The March of Fate. White, 1893
The Mesmerists. Hutchinson, 1900
Miriam Rozella. White, 1898
-Miser Farebrother. Ward, 1888; Harper, 1887
-Mrs. Dimmock's Worries. Hutchinson, 1906
Mrs. Isaacs; see Solomon Isaacs
The Mystery of M. Felix. White, 1890; Lovell, 1890
The Mystery of Roaring Meg. Tinsley, 1878. U.S. title: The Widow Cherry; or, The Mystery of Roaring Meg. Carleton, 1878
The Mystery of the Royal Mail. Hutchinson, 1902
The Nine of Hearts. Ward, 1886; Harper, 1886
119 Great Porter Square; see Great Porter Square
The Peril of Richard Pardon. White, 1890; Harper, 1888
The Pride of Race. Hutchinson, 1901; Jacobs, 1901
Samuel Boyd of Catchpole Square: A Mystery. Hutchinson, 1899; New Amsterdam, 1899
A Secret Inheritance. Ward, 1887
-Self-Doomed. Farran, 1885; Harper, 1885
-The Shield of Love. Arrowsmith, 1891; Holt, 1891
-Solomon Isaacs. Carleton, 1877. Also published as: Mrs. Isaacs. Carleton, 1883. (British title?)
Something Occurred. Routledge (London & New York), 1893
-A Strange Enchantment. White, 1889
Toilers of Babylon. Ward, 1888; Harper, 1889
The Tragedy of Featherstone. Ward, 1887
-A Very Young Couple. White, 1890; U.S. Book Co., 1890
The Widow Cherry; see The Mystery of Roaring Meg
-A Young Girl's Life. Ward, 1889

FARJEON, J(OSEPH) JEFFERSON. 1883-1955. Pseudonym: Anthony Swift, q.v. Series character: Ben the Tramp = B.
Adventure at Eighty. Macdonald, 1948
Adventure for Nine. Macdonald, 1951
The Appointed Date. Longmans, 1929; Dial, 1930
At the Green Dragon. Harrap, 1927. U.S. title: The Green Dragon. Dial, 1926
Aunt Sunday Sees It Through. Collins, 1940. U.S. title: Aunt Sunday Takes Command. Bobbs, 1940
Aunt Sunday Takes Command; see Aunt Sunday Sees It Through
Back to Victoria. Macdonald, 1947
Ben on the Job. Collins, 1952 B
Ben Sees It Through. Collins, 1932; Dial, 1933 B
Black Castle. Collins, 1944
Bob Hits the Headlines. Bodley Head, 1954
The Caravan Adventure. Macdonald, 1955
Castle of Fear. Collins, 1954
Cause Unknown. Collins, 1950
The Crook's Shadow. Harrap, 1927; Dial, 1927
Dangerous Beauty. Collins, 1936
Dark Lady. Collins, 1938
Dead Man's Heath. Collins, 1933. U.S. title: The Mystery of Dead Man's Heath. Dodd, 1934
Death in Fancy Dress; see The Fancy Dress Ball
Death in the Inkwell; see End of an Author
Death of a World. Collins, 1948
Detective Ben. Collins, 1936 B
The Disappearance of Uncle David. Collins, 1949
The Double Crime. Collins, 1953
End of an Author. Collins, 1938. U.S. title: Death in the Inkwell. Bobbs, 1942
Exit John Horton. Collins, 1939. U.S. title: Friday the 13th. Bobbs, 1940
-Facing Death. Quality, 1940 ss
The Fancy Dress Ball. Collins, 1934. U.S. title: Death in Fancy Dress. Bobbs, 1939
The 5.18 Mystery. Collins, 1929; Dial, 1929
Following Footsteps. Dial, 1930. (British title?)

Friday the 13th; see Exit John Horton
The Green Dragon; see At the Green Dragon
Greenmask. Collins, 1944; Bobbs, 1944
Holiday at Half-Mast. Collins, 1937
Holiday Express. Collins, 1935
The House of Disappearance. Harrap, 1928; Dial, 1927
The House of Shadows. Collins, 1943
The House on the Marsh; see The Mystery of the Creek
The House Opposite. Collins, 1931; Dial, 1931 B
The House over the Tunnel. Collins, 1951
The Impossible Guest. Macdonald, 1949
The Judge Sums Up. Collins, 1942; Bobbs, 1942
Little God Ben. Collins, 1935 B
The Lone House Mystery. Collins, 1949
The Master Criminal. Brentano's (London), 1924; Dial, 1924
Money Walks. Macdonald, 1953
Mountain Mystery. Collins, 1935
Murderer's Trail. Collins, 1931. U.S. title: Phantom Fingers. Dial, 1931 B
Mystery in White. Collins, 1937; Bobbs, 1938
The Mystery of Dead Man's Heath; see Dead Man's Heath
The Mystery of the Creek. Collins, 1933. U.S. title: The House on the Marsh. Dial, 1933
The Mystery on the Moor. Collins, 1930
Mystery Underground; see Underground
Number Nineteen. Collins, 1952 B
No. 17. Hodder, 1926; Dial, 1926 B
Old Man Mystery. Collins, 1933
The Oval Table. Collins, 1946
Peril in the Pyrenees. Collins, 1946
The Person Called "Z". Collins, 1930; Dial, 1929
Phantom Fingers; see Murderer's Trail
Prelude to Crime. Collins, 1948
Room Number 6. Collins, 1941
Seven Dead. Collins, 1939; Bobbs, 1939
The Shadow of Thirteen. Collins, 1949
Shadows by the Sea. Harrap, 1928; Dial, 1928
Sinister Inn. Collins, 1934; Dodd, 1934
-Sometimes Life's Funny. Methuen, 1933
The Third Victim. Collins, 1941
Thirteen Guests. Collins, 1936; Bobbs, 1938
Trunk Call. Collins, 1932. U.S. title: The Trunk Call Mystery. Dial, 1932
The Trunk Call Mystery; see Trunk Call
Underground. Collins, 1929; Dial, 1928. Also published as: Mystery Underground. Collins, 1932
Uninvited Guests. Brentano's (London), 1925; Dial, 1925
The Windmill Mystery. Collins, 1934
Yellow Devil. Collins, 1937
The "Z" Murders. Collins, 1932; Dial, 1932

The following are WWII pamphlets:
Down the Green Stairs and other stories. Todd, 1943 ss
The Invisible Companion and other stories. Todd, 16 pp.; Polybooks, 62 pp., 1946 ss
Midnight Adventure and other stories. Polybooks, 1946 ss
The Twist and other stories. Vallancey, 1944 ss
Waiting for the Police and other stories. Todd, 1943 ss

FARMER, BERNARD J(AMES). 1902-   .
    Series character: P. C. James Wigan, in all titles.
    Death at the Cascades. Heinemann, 1953
    Death of a Bookseller. Heinemann, 1956
    Murder Next Year. Heinemann, 1959
    Once, and Then the Funeral. Heinemann, 1958

FARMER, GEOFFREY NORTON
    Quella. Rivers, 1914

FARMER, LUCY
    The Chronicles of Cardewe Manor. Hutchinson, 1891

FARMER, PATRICIA
    The Legend of Piper's Hole. Popular Library, 1973

FARMER, PHILIP JOSE. 1918-   .
    The Adventure of the Peerless Peer. Aspen, 1974. (Sherlock Holmes.)

FARNDALE, JOHN. Pseudonym of John Wilfred Harvey, 1889-   .
    The Nine Nicks. Methuen, 1930

FARNOL, (JOHN) JEFFERY. 1878-1952. Series character: Sgt. Jasper Shrig, in at least those marked JS.
-The Amateur Gentleman. Low, 1913; Little, 1913
-Another Day. Low, 1929; Little, 1929
-Beltane the Smith. Low, 1915; Little, 1915
-Black Bartlemy's Treasure. Low, 1920; Little, 1920
-The Broad Highway. Low, 1910; Little, 1911
-Charmian, Lady Vibart. Low, 1932; Little, 1932
-The Chronicles of the Imp. Low, 1915
The Crooked Furrow. Low, 1937; Doubleday, 1937 JS
-The Definite Object. Low, 1917; Little, 1917
-The Fool Beloved. Low, 1949
-The Glad Summer. Low, 1951
-Gyfford of Weare. Low, 1928; Little, 1928
The Happy Harvest. Low, 1939; Doubleday, 1940 JS
Heritage Perilous. Low, 1946; McBride, 1947 JS
The High Adventure. Low, 1926; Little, 1926 JS
-The Honourable Mr. Tawnish. Low, 1913; Little, 1913
-The Jade of Destiny. Low, 1931; Little, 1931, as A Jade of Destiny
-John o' the Green. Low, 1935; Little, 1935
Justice by Midnight. Low, 1956
-The Lonely Road. Low, 1938; Doubleday, 1938
The Loring Mystery. Low, 1925; Little, 1925 JS
A Matter of Business and other stories. Low, 1940; Doubleday, 1940 ss, one about JS
-The Money Moon. Low, 1911; Dodd, 1911
-Most Sacred of All. McBride, 1948. (British title?)
Murder by Nail. Low, 1942. U.S. title: Valley of Night. Doubleday, 1942 JS
-My Lady Caprice. Stevens, 1907; Dodd, 1907
The Ninth Earl. Low, 1950 JS
-Our Admirable Betty. Low, 1918; Little, 1925
-Over the Hills. Low, 1930; Little, 1930
-Peregrine's Progress. Low, 1922; Little, 1922
-The "Piping Times." Low, 1945
-The Quest of Youth. Low, 1927; Little, 1927
The Shadow, and other stories. Low, 1929; Little, 1929
-Sir John Dering. Low, 1923; Little, 1923
Valley of Night; see Murder by Nail
Waif of the River. Low, 1952 JS

-The Way Beyond. Low, 1933; Little, 1933
-Winds of Fortune. Low, 1934; Little, 1934

FARNSWORTH, MONA
    Companion to Evil. Ace, 1972
    A Cross for Tomorrow. Pinnacle, 1972
    The Evil That Waited. Pinnacle, 1973
    The Great Stone Heart. Pinnacle, 1971
    House of Deadly Calm. Apollo, 1970
    The Menace of Marble Hill. Manor, 1974
    Ransome Castle. Apollo, 1970
    Starcrossed Road. Pinnacle, 1973
    The Three Sisters of No End House. Ace, 1972

FARR, CAROLINE. Pseudonym of Alan G(eofrey) Yates, 1923-   , q.v. Other pseudonym: Carter Brown, q.v. Most of these titles were probably published in Australia by Horwitz, but complete information is lacking. In addition, this list probably contains uncorrelated title changes.
    The Castle in Canada. Signet, 1972
    A Castle in Spain; see Web of Horror
    Castle of Terror. Horwitz, 1975; Signet, 1975
    Dark Citadel. Horwitz, 1976; Signet, 1971
    Dark Mansion. Signet, 1974
    Granite Folly. Signet, 1967
    House of Dark Illusions. Signet, 1973
    House of Destiny. Signet, 1970
    House of Secrets. Signet, 1973
    The House of Tombs. Horwitz, 1966; Signet, 1966
    The House on the Cliffs. Signet, 1974
    The Intruder. Horwitz, 1966
    The Mansion of Evil. Signet, 1966
    Mansion of Peril. Horwitz, 1966; Signet, 1975
    The Possessed. Horwitz, 1973
    The Scream in the Storm. Signet, 1975
    The Secret of Castle Ferrara. Signet, 1971
    The Secret of the Chateau. Signet, 1967
    So Near and Yet. Signet, 1967
    Terror on Duncan Island. Signet, 1971
    The Towers of Fear. Signet, 1972
    Villa of Shadows. Horwitz, 1966
    Web of Horror. Signet, 1966. Also published as: A Castle in Spain. Signet, 1967
    Witch's Hammer. Horwitz, 1967; Signet, 1967

FARR, FINIS (KING). 1904-   .
    The Elephant Valley. Arlington, 1967

FARR, JOHN. Pseudonym of Jack Webb, 1920-   , q.v.
    The Deadly Combo. Ace, 1958
    Don't Feed the Animals. Abelard-Schuman, 1955. British title: The Zoo Murders. Foulsham, 1956. Also published as: Naked Fear. Jonathan, 1955
    The Lady and the Snake. Ace, 1957
    Naked Fear; see Don't Feed the Animals
-She Shark. Ace, 1956
    The Zoo Murders; see Don't Feed the Animals

FARR, SEBASTIAN. Pseudonym of Eric Walter Blom, 1888-1959.
    Death on the Down Beat. Dent, 1941

FARRAN, ROY (ALEXANDER). 1921-   .
    Never Had a Chance. Bles, 1967

FARRAR, HELEN
    Murder Goes to School. Ziff-Davis, 1948

FARRAR, JOHN CHIPMAN. 1896-1974. Joint pseudonym with Prosper Buranelli, 1890-1960, q.v.: John Prosper, q.v.

FARRAR, STEWART. Series character: Inspector Elwyn Morgan = EW.
 Death in the Wrong Bed. Collins, 1963; Walker, 1964 EM
 The Snake on 99. Collins, 1958; Washburn, 1959 EM
 -The Twelve Maidens. Joseph, 1974; St. Martin's, 1974
 Zero in the Gate. Collins, 1960; Walker, 1961 EM

FARRELL, DAVID. Pseudonym of Frederick E(screet) Smith, 1922-   , q.v.
 The Other Cousin. Gresham, 1962. U.S. title: Dark Cliffs. Paperback Library, 1966, as by Frederick E. Smith

FARRELL, HENRY. Pseudonym: Charles Henry, q.v.
 Death on the Sixth Day. Holt, 1961; Eyre, 1962
 How Awful About Allan. Holt, 1963; Eyre, 1964
 Such a Gorgeous Kid Like Me. Delacorte, 1967
 What Ever Happened to Baby Jane? Rinehart, 1960; Eyre, 1960

FARRER, KATHERINE. 1911-   . Series character: Inspector Richard Ringwood, in all titles.
 The Cretan Counterfeit. Collins, 1954
 Gownsman's Gallows. Hodder, 1957
 The Missing Link. Collins, 1952

FARRERE, CLAUDE. Pseudonym of Frederic Charles Pierre Edouard Bargone, 1876-1957.
 The House of the Secret. Dutton, 1923; Dent, 1923. (Translation of La Maison des Hommes Vivants. Paris, 1911.)
 The Man Who Killed. Brentano's, 1917. (Translation of L'Homme Qui Assassina. Paris, 1907.)

FARRIMOND, JOHN. 1913-   .
 -Dust in my Throat. Harrap, 1963
 -The Hollow Shell. Harrap, 1964
 Kill Me a Priest. Harrap, 1965
 Pick and Run. Harrap, 1966
 -The Unending Track. Harrap, 1970

FARRINGTON, FIELDEN. 1909-   .
 A Little Game. Walker, 1968; Macdonald, 1968
 The Strangers in 7-A. McKay, 1972

FARRINGTON, JOSEPH
 The Hand. Jenkins, 1961
 Night Train to Mombasa. Jenkins, 1962

FARRINGTON, JOSEPH J.
 The Uncrowned Prince; or, The Mystery of the Yellow Manse. (New York), 1900

FARRIS, JOHN. 1936?-   .
 The Captors. Trident, 1969; New English Library, 1971
 The Corpse Next Door. Graphic, 1956
 Happy Anniversary, Harrison High. PB, 1973
 Sharp Practice. Simon, 1974; Weidenfeld, 1975
 The Trouble at Harrison High. PB, 1970
 When Michael Calls. Trident, 1967; New English Library, 1970

FAST, HOWARD (MELVIN). 1914-   . Pseudonyms: E. V. Cunningham, Walter Ericson, qq.v.
 The Winston Affair. Crown, 1959; Methuen, 1960

FAST, JULIUS. 1919-   .
 And Then Murder; see Street of Fear
 The Bright Face of Danger. Rinehart, 1946
 Down Through the Night; see Walk in Shadow
 A Model for Murder. Rinehart, 1956; Hale, 1957
 Street of Fear. Rinehart, 1958; Hale, 1959. Also published as: And Then Murder. Hillman, 1959
 Walk in Shadow. Rinehart, 1947. Also published as: Down Through the Night. Crest, 1956
 Watchful at Night. Farrar, 1945

FAULEY, WILBUR FINLEY. 1872-1942.
 -After Midnight. Ogilvie, 1904
 Burnt Earth. Carlyle, 1936 (3-act play)
 Fires of Fate. Metropolitan, 1923
 -Jenny Be Good. Britton, 1919
 -Mesalliance. Macaulay, 1934
 Queenie: The Adventures of a Nice Young Lady. Macaulay, 1921
 -The Shuddering Castle. Green Circle, 1936

FAULKNER, WILLIAM. 1897-1962. Series character: Gavin Stevens = GS.
 Intruder in the Dust. Random, 1948; Chatto, 1949 GS
 Knight's Gambit. Random, 1949; Chatto, 1951 GS ss
 Sanctuary. Cape & Smith, 1931; Chatto, 1931

FAUR, MICHAEL P., JR.
 A Friendly Place to Die. Signet, 1966; Tandem, 1967

FAURE-BIGUET, JACQUES NAPOLEON. 1893-   . Pseudonym: Jacques Decrest, q.v.

FAUST, FREDERICK SCHILLER. 1892-1944. Pseudonyms: Max Brand, Walter C. Butler, Frederick Frost, qq.v.

FAUST, RON
 Tombs of Blue Ice. Bobbs, 1975

FAWCETT, EDGAR. 1847-1904.
 -The Evil That Men Do. Belford, 1889
 -A Hopeless Case. Houghton, 1880
 -Loaded Dice. Tait, 1891
 Rutherford. Funk, 1884; Hunt, 1887

FAWCETT, F(RANK) DUBREZ. 1891-1968. Pseudonyms: Griff, Spike Gordon (?), Ben Sarto, Elmer Eliot Saks, qq.v.
 Journey to Genoa. Amalgamated, 1960. (Sexton Blake.)

FAWKES, F(RANK) A(TTFIELD)
 Adventures of a Chemist. Simpkin, 1930 ss

FAY, DOROTHY. Pseudonym of Anna Chandler Lindholm, 1870-   .
 The Black Pearl of Passion. Galleon, 1936

FAY, JUDITH. Pseudonym: Kate Nicholson, q.v.

FEAGLES, ANITA MacRAE. 1926-   . Pseudonym: Travis MacRae, q.v.

FEAKES, G. J.
 Moonrakers and Mischief. Chapman, 1961; Washburn, 1962

FEAR, WILLIAM H(ENRY CHARLES)
 The Killers. Digit, 1964

FEARING, KENNETH (FLEXNER). 1902-1961.
 The Big Clock. Harcourt, 1946; Bodley Head, 1947
 Clark Gifford's Body. Random, 1942; Lane, 1943
 Cry Killer!; see Dagger of the Mind
 Dagger of the Mind. Random, 1941; Lane, 1941. Also published as: Cry Killer! Avon, 1958
 The Generous Heart. Harcourt, 1954; Bodley Head, 1955
 The Loneliest Girl in the World. Harcourt, 1951; Bodley Head, 1952. Also published as: The Sound of Murder. Mercury, 1952
 The Sound of Murder; see The Loneliest Girl in the World

FEARN, JOHN RUSSELL. 1908-1960. Pseudonyms: Hugo Blayn, John Slate, qq.v.

FEARNLEY, JOHN BLAKEWAY
 A Corpse to Bury. Jarrolds, 1956
 Murder by Degrees. Hale, 1940

FEARON, DIANA. Series character: Arabella Frant, in at least those marked AF.
 Death Before Breakfast. Hale, 1959 AF
 Murder-on-Thames. Hale, 1960 AF
 Nairobi Nightcap. Hale, 1958
 A Rhino for Rosamund. Hale, 1959

FECHER, CONSTANCE. 1911-   . Pseudonym: Constance Heaven, q.v.

FEEGEL, JOHN R(ICHARD). 1932-   .
 Autopsy. Avon, 1975

FEENY, ALFRED
 By a Vanished Hand. Ward, 1906 ss, some criminous

FEILDING, DOROTHY. 1884-   . Pseudonym: A. Fielding, q.v.

FEIN, HARRY H.
 -The Flying Chinaman. Knopf, 1938

FEIST, AUBREY (NOEL LYDSTON). 1903-   .
 The Eyes of St. Emlyn. Long, 1938
 Key Men. Melrose, 1937

FELIX, CHARLES. Pseudonym.
 The Notting Hill Mystery. Saunders, 1865; Arno, 1976
 -Ram Dass. Tinsley, 1875
 -Velvet Lawn. Saunders, 1864

FELIX, CHRISTOPHER. See: GEORGE MARTON, 1900-   .

FELTNER, BERT, JR.
 Death Comes Easy. Carlton, 1964

FEMLING, JEAN
 Backyard. Harper, 1975

FENISONG, RUTH. Series character: Gridley Nelson, in at least those marked GN.
 Bite the Hand. Doubleday, 1956. British title: The Blackmailer. Foulsham, 1958 GN
 The Blackmailer; see Bite the Hand
 But Not Forgotten. Doubleday, 1960. British title: Sinister Assignment. Foulsham, 1960 GN
 The Butler Died in Brooklyn. Doubleday, 1943; Aldor, 1946 GN
 The Case of the Gloating Landlord; see The Schemers
 Dead Weight. Doubleday, 1962; Hale, 1964 GN
 Dead Yesterday. Doubleday, 1951 GN
 Deadlock. Doubleday, 1952 GN
 Death is a Gold Coin; see The Lost Caesar
 Death is a Lovely Lady; see Jenny Kissed Me

Death of the Party. Doubleday, 1958 GN
Desperate Cure. Doubleday, 1946
The Drop of a Hat. Doubleday, 1970; Hale, 1971
Grim Rehearsal. Doubleday, 1950; Foulsham, 1951 GN
Ill Wind. Doubleday, 1950; Foulsham, 1952
Jenny Kissed Me. Doubleday, 1944. Also published as: Death is a Lovely Lady. Popular Library, 1949
The Lost Caesar. Doubleday, 1945; Aldor, 1946. Also published as: Death is a Gold Coin. Popular Library, 1950
Miscast for Murder. Doubleday, 1954. Also published as: Too Lively to Live. Bestseller, 1955 GN
Murder Needs a Face. Doubleday, 1942 GN
Murder Needs a Name. Doubleday, 1942; Swan, 1950 GN
Murder Runs a Fever. Doubleday, 1943 GN
The Schemers. Doubleday, 1957. British title: The Case of the Gloating Landlord. Foulsham, 1958
Sinister Assignment; see But Not Forgotten
Snare for Sinners. Doubleday, 1949; Foulsham, 1951
Too Lively to Live; see Miscast for Murder
Villainous Company. Doubleday, 1967; Hale, 1968
The Wench is Dead. Doubleday, 1953 GN
Widows' Blackmail; see Widow's Plight
Widow's Plight. Doubleday, 1955. British title: Widows' Blackmail. Foulsham, 1957

FENN, CAROLINE K. Joint pseudonym with Julia McGrew: Fenn McGrew, q.v.

FENN, G(EORGE) MANVILLE. 1831-1909.
-The Adventures of Doc Lavington. Partridge, 1896
Aynsley's Case. Long, 1906
The Bag of Diamonds. Ward, 1887; Lovell, 1887
-Beneath the Sea. Crowell, 1896. (British title?)
-Bent, Not Broken. Tinsley, 1867
-The Black Bar. Low, 1893
Black Blood: A Peculiar Case. Lovell, 1888. (British title?)
Black Shadows. Chatto, 1902
Blind Policy. Long, 1904
-By Birth a Lady. Tinsley, 1871
-The Cankerworm: Being Episodes in a Woman's Life. Chatto, 1901
The Case of Ailsa Gray. White, 1896
The Chaplain's Craze; Being the Mystery of Findon Friars. Ward, 1886; Harper, 1886
-The Clerk of Portwick. Chapman, 1880
-Coming Home to Roost. White, 1904
-Commodore Junk. Cassell, 1888; Munro, 1889
Cormorant Crag: A Tale of the Smuggling Days. Partridge, 1895; Dodd, 1895
-A Country Squire: Being an Impossible Story. White, 1907
A Crimson Crime. Chatto, 1899
The Dark House: A Knot Unravelled. Ward, 1885; Harper, 1885
Double Cunning: A Tale of a Transparent Mystery. Chapman, 1896
A Double Knot. Methuen, 1890; U.S. Book Co., 1891
-Dutch the Diver; or, A Man's Mistake. Cassell, 1883
-Fire Island: Being the Adventures of Uncertain Naturalists in a Unknown Track. Low, 1894
-A Fluttered Dovecote. Ward, 1890
-In an Alpine Valley. Hurst, 1894
In Jeopardy, and other stories of peril. Ward, 1889 ss
-It Came to Pass. White, 1903
-Jack the Rascal. Everett, 1909
-King of the Castle. Ward, 1892
-Lady Maude's Mania. Warne, 1890; U.S. Book Co., 1890
-The Lass That Loved a Soldier. Ward, 1889
-Mad: A Story of Dust and Ashes. Tinsley, 1868
-Mahme Nousie. Hurst, 1891
-The Man with a Shadow. Ward, 1888
-The Master of the Ceremonies. Ward, 1886
-Midnight Webs. Tinsley, 1872
-Morgan's Horror: A Romance of the "West Countree." Cassell (London), 1885; Cassell (New York), 1888
The Mynns' Mystery. Warne, 1890; Lovell, 1889
-The New Mistress. Chatto, 1891
-Nic Revel. Chambers, 1898
-Nurse Elisia. Hurst, 1893; Cassell, 1892
-Of High Descent. Ward, 1889
-Off to the Wilds: Being the Adventures of Two Brothers. Low, 1881
-One Maid's Mischief. Ward, 1887; Appleton, 1888
-The Parson o' Dumford. Chapman, 1879; Cassell, 1883
-The Queen's Scarlet: Being the Adventures and Misadventures of Sir Richard Frayne. Cassell (London), 1895
-The Rajah of Dah. Chambers, 1891
-The Rosery Folk: A Country Tale. Chapman, 1884; Munro, 1884
-Running Amok: A Story of Adventure. Chatto, 1901
-Sappers and Miners; or, The Flood Beneath the Sea. White, 1896
-The Sapphire Cross. Tinsley, 1871
Sawn Off. Henry, 1891
-A Secret Quest. Taylor, 1893. (British title?)
-The Silver Canyon; A Tale of the Western Plains. Low, 1884
-Sir Hilton's Sin. White, 1908
-So Like a Woman. Chatto, 1905
-The Star-Gazers. Methuen, 1894
-The Story of Antony Grace; or, Some Shared Pages. Ward, 1888; Appleton, 1888
-Sweet Mace: A Sussex Legend of the Iron Times. Chapman, 1884; Cassell (New York), 1885
-Thereby Hangs a Tale. Tinsley, 1876
-This Man's Wife. Ward, 1887; Lovell, 1887
-Three People's Secret: A Tale of the Faculty. Simpkin Marshall, 1889
-The Tiger Lily: A Story of Two Passions. Chatto, 1894; Cassell, 1895
-The Traitor's Gate and other stories. Digby Long, 1906 ss
-The Vibart Affair. Pearson, 1899
-The Vicar's People: A Story of a Stain. Chapman, 1881; Munro, 1881
-Webs in the Way. Tinsley, 1867
-The White Virgin. Chatto, 1894; Rand, 1896
Witness to the Deed. Chatto, 1893; Cassell, 1893
-A Woman Worth Winning. Chatto, 1898; Rand, 1898

FENN, LOUIS ANDERSON
The Killing Bottle Murder. Methuen, 1936

FENN, W(ILLIAM) W(ILTHEW). ca.1827- .
After Sundown; or, The Palette and the Pen. Low, 1880 ss, some criminous
Half Hours of a Blind Man's Holiday; or, Summer and Winter Sketches in Black and White. Low, 1878 ss, some criminous

FENNELLY, PARKER (W.)
Cuckoos on the Hearth. Dramatists Play Service, 1942. (3-act play.)

FENNERTON, WILLIAM
-Christmas Without Roddy. Hutchinson, 1965
The Lucifer Cell. Hodder, 1969; Atheneum, 1968
-Old Fox. Davies, 1972
The Potentate. Gollancz, 1963; Harper, 1961
-A Touch of Red. Hutchinson, 1966

FENTON, EDWARD. 1917- .
The Double Darkness. Doubleday, 1947

FENTY, PHILIP
Super Fly. Ballantine, 1972. (Novelization of the movie.)

FENWICK, E. P. [ELIZABETH FENWICK WAY]. 1920- . Byline also: Elizabeth Fenwick, q.v.
The Inconvenient Corpse. Farrar, 1943
Murder in Haste. Farrar, 1944
Two Names for Death. Farrar, 1945; Wells Gardner, 1949

FENWICK, ELIZABETH [ELIZABETH FENWICK WAY]. 1920- . Byline also: E. P. Fenwick, q.v.
Disturbance on Berry Hill. Atheneum, 1968; Gollancz, 1968
A Friend of Mary Rose. Harper, 1961; Gollancz, 1962
Goodbye, Aunt Elva. Atheneum, 1968; Gollancz, 1969
Impeccable People. Gollancz, 1971
The Last of Lysandra. Gollancz, 1973
A Long Way Down. Harper, 1959; Gollancz, 1959
The Make-Believe Man. Harper, 1963; Gollancz, 1964
A Night Run. Gollancz, 1961
The Passenger. Atheneum, 1967; Gollancz, 1967
Poor Harriet. Harper, 1957; Gollancz, 1958
The Silent Cousin. Atheneum, 1966; Gollancz, 1962

FERGUSON, ANTHONY
The Big Snatch. Hale, 1971
A Game of Chance. Hale, 1970
A Running Man. Hale, 1969

FERGUSON, CHRIS(TOPHER WILSON). 1944- .
-The Molting Season. Harper, 1974

FERGUSON, JOHN (ALEXANDER). 1873- .
Series character: Francis MacNab = FM.
The Dark Geraldine. Lane (London & New York), 1921 FM
Death Comes to Perigord. Collins, 1931; Dodd, 1931 FM
Death of Mr. Dodsley. Collins, 1937 FM
The Grouse Moor Murder; see The Grouse Moor Mystery
The Grouse Moor Mystery. Collins, 1934. U.S. title: The Grouse Moor Murder. Dodd, 1934 FM
The Man in the Dark. Lane, 1928; Dodd, 1928 FM
Murder on the Marsh. Lane, 1930; Dodd, 1930 FM
Night in Glengyle. Collins, 1933; Dodd, 1933
The Secret Road. Bodley Head, 1925; Dodd, 1925
Stealthy Terror. Lane (London & New York), 1918

Ferguson, John

Terror on the Island. Collins, 1942; Vanguard, 1942

FERGUSON, MARGARET
The Sign of the Ram. Hale, 1943; Blakiston, 1945

FERGUSON, PAMELA
The Pipe Dream. Everest, 1974

FERGUSON, RUBY (CONSTANCE ANNIE)
A Woman with a Secret. Hodder, 1965

FERGUSON, W(ILLIAM) B(LAIR) M(ORTON). 1882- . Pseudonym: William Morton, q.v.
The Big Take. Long, 1952
-Black Bread. Long, 1933
The Black Company. Jenkins, 1925; Chelsea, 1924
Boss of the Skeletons. Long, 1945
The Clue in the Glass. Jenkins, 1927. U.S. title: The Clew in the Glass. Chelsea, 1926
Crackerjack. Long, 1936
Dog Fox. Long, 1938
Escape to Eternity. Long, 1944
The Island of Surprises. Long, 1935
London Lamb. Long, 1939
Other Folks' Money. Nelson, 1928
Phonies. Long, 1951
Prelude to Horror. Long, 1943
The Riddle of the Rose. Jenkins, 1929; McBride, 1929
Sally. Long, 1940
The Shayne Case. Long, 1947
Somewhere Off Borneo. Long, 1936
The Vanishing Men. Long, 1932
-Wyoming Tragedy. Long, 1935

FERGUSSON, BERNARD (EDWARD). 1911- .
The Rare Adventure. Collins, 1954; Rinehart, 1955

FERM, BETTY. 1926- .
Edge of Beauty. Dell, 1974
Eventide. Dell, 1974
False Idols. Putnam, 1974
The Vengeance of Valdone. Dell, 1973

FERME, MRS. GEORGE. Pseudonym: George Douglas, q.v.

FERNALD, CHESTER BAILEY. 1869-1938.
-Chinatown Stories. Heinemann, 1900 ss

FERNANDES, J. R.
Yokohama Hood. Vantage, 1967

FERNANDEZ, ALONZO
The Castle of Lugas. Jamaica, 1927

FERNEE, HERBERT
The Narrow House. Christophers, 1948
Now, Gentlemen, Please. Faber, 1940
They Wetted His Head. Faber, 1943

FERRAND, GEORGINA
Dangerous Inheritance. Beagle, 1974
House of Glass. Ballantine, 1975
The Thickening Light. Beagle, 1974

FERRARS, ELIZABETH (XAVIA). U.S. byline: FERRARS, E. X. Pseudonym of Morna Doris MacTaggart Brown, 1907- . Series character: Toby Dyke = TD.
Alibi for a Witch. Collins, 1952; Doubleday, 1952
Alive and Dead. Collins, 1974; Doubleday, 1975
Always Say Die. Collins, 1956. U.S. title: We Haven't Seen Her Lately. Doubleday, 1956
Breath of Suspicion. Collins, 1972
The Busy Body. Collins, 1962. U.S. title: Seeing Double. Doubleday, 1962
Cheat the Hangman; see Murder Among Friends
The Clock That Wouldn't Stop. Collins, 1952; Doubleday, 1952
Count the Cost; see Unreasonable Doubt
The Cup and the Lip. Collins, 1975; Doubleday, 1976
Death in Botanist's Bay. Hodder, 1941. U.S. title: Murder of a Suicide. Doubleday, 1941 TD
The Decayed Gentlewoman; see A Legal Fiction
Depart This Life; see A Tale of Two Murders
Don't Monkey with Murder. Hodder, 1942. U.S. title: The Shape of a Stain. Doubleday, 1942 TD
The Doubly Dead. Collins, 1963; Doubleday, 1963
Drowned Rat. Collins, 1975; Doubleday, 1975
Enough to Kill a Horse. Collins, 1955; Doubleday, 1955
Fear the Light. Collins, 1960; Doubleday, 1960
Foot in the Grave. Collins, 1973; Doubleday, 1972
Furnished for Murder. Collins, 1957
Give a Corpse a Bad Name. Hodder, 1940 TD
Hanged Man's House. Collins, 1974; Doubleday, 1974
Hunt the Tortoise. Collins, 1950; Doubleday, 1950
I, Said the Fly. Hodder, 1945; Doubleday, 1945
Kill or Cure; see Murder Moves In
A Legal Fiction. Collins, 1964. U.S. title: The Decayed Gentlewoman. Doubleday, 1963
The Lying Voices. Collins, 1954
The March Hare Murders. Collins, 1949; Doubleday, 1949
Milk of Human Kindness. Collins, 1950
Murder Among Friends. Collins, 1946. U.S. title: Cheat the Hangman. Doubleday, 1946
Murder in Time. Collins, 1953
Murder Moves In. Collins, 1956. U.S. title: Kill or Cure. Doubleday, 1956
Murder of a Suicide; see Death in Botanist's Bay
Neck in a Noose; see Your Neck in a Noose
Ninth Life. Collins, 1965
No Peace for the Wicked. Collins, 1966; Harper, 1966
Rehearsals for Murder; see Remove the Bodies
Remove the Bodies. Hodder, 1940. U.S. title: Rehearsals for Murder. Doubleday, 1941 TD
Seeing Double; see The Busy Body
The Seven Sleepers. Collins, 1970; Walker, 1970
The Shape of a Stain; see Don't Monkey with Murder
Skeleton Staff. Collins, 1969; Walker, 1969
Sleeping Dogs. Collins, 1960; Doubleday, 1960
The Small World of Murder. Collins, 1973; Doubleday, 1973
A Stranger and Afraid. Collins, 1971; Walker, 1971
The Swaying Pillars. Collins, 1968; Walker, 1969
A Tale of Two Murders. Collins, 1959. U.S. title: Depart This Life. Doubleday, 1958
Unreasonable Doubt. Collins, 1958. U.S. title: Count the Cost. Doubleday, 1957
The Wandering Widows. Collins, 1962; Doubleday, 1962
We Haven't Seen Her Lately; see Always Say Die
With Murder in Mind. Collins, 1948
Your Neck in a Noose. Hodder, 1942. U.S. title: Neck in a Noose. Doubleday, 1943 TD
Zero at the Bone. Collins, 1967; Walker, 1968

FERRARS, FRANCIS
Jim Cummings; or, The Crime of the Frisco Express. RR Publishing, 1887. (Later rewritten and published as by Frank Pinkerton.)

FERREOL, MARCEL AUGUSTE. 1899- . Pseudonym: Marcel Achard. See: HARRY KURNITZ, 1907-1968.

FERRIS, JEAN ERSKINE
House of Hate. Remploy, 1974

FERRIS, TOM. Pseudonym of Peter N(orman) Walker, 1936- , q.v. Other pseudonym: Christopher Coram, q.v.
Espionage for a Lady. Hale, 1969

FERRIS, WALLY
Across 110th. Harper, 1970. British title: The Hunt. MacGibbon, 1971

FESSIER, MICHAEL. 1907- .
Fully Dressed and In His Right Mind. Knopf, 1935; Gollancz, 1935

FETHALAND, JOHN
The Murder at Charters. Gollancz, 1939

FETTA, EMMA LOU. Series characters: Lyle Curtis and Susan Yates, in at least those marked C&Y.
Dressed to Kill. Doubleday, 1941
Murder in Style. Doubleday, 1939 C&Y
Murder on the Face of It. Doubleday, 1940 C&Y

FETTER, ELIZABETH HEAD. 1904-1973. Pseudonym: Hannah Lees, q.v.

FFORDE, (ARTHUR) BROWNLOW. 1871- .
The Subaltern, the Policeman, and the Little Girl. Low, 1890
The Trotter: A Poona Mystery. Low, 1890

FIASCHETTI, MICHAEL
You Gotta Be Rough. Doubleday, 1930. British title: The Man They Couldn't Escape. Selwyn, 1928 ss

FICK, CARL
The Danziger Transcript. Putnam, 1971; Deutsch, 1973

FICKLING, FORREST E. 1925- . Joint pseudonym with Gloria Fickling: G. G. Fickling, q.v.

FICKLING, G. G. Joint pseudonym of Gloria Fickling and Forrest E. Fickling, 1925- . Series characters: Honey West = HW; Erik March = EM.
Blood and Honey. Pyramid, 1961 HW
Bombshell. Pyramid, 1964 HW
The Case of the Radioactive Redhead. Belmont, 1963 EM
The Crazy Mixed-Up Nude. Belmont, 1964 EM
Dig a Dead Doll. Pyramid, 1960 HW
Girl on the Loose. Pyramid, 1958 HW
Girl on the Prowl. Pyramid, 1959 HW
A Gun for Honey. Pyramid, 1958 HW
Honey in the Flesh. Pyramid, 1959 HW
Honey on Her Tail. Pyramid, 1971 HW
Kiss for a Killer. Pyramid, 1960 HW
Naughty But Dead. Belmont, 1962 EM
Stiff as a Broad. Pyramid, 1971 HW
This Girl for Hire. Pyramid, 1957 HW

FICKLING, GLORIA. Joint pseudonym with Forrest E. Fickling, 1925-   : G. G. Fickling, q.v.

FIDLER, HENRY J.
Chronicles of Dennis Chetwynd. Hutchinson, 1927 ss

FIELD, HERBERT N.
The Marsh Gang. Jarrolds, 1929
The Needle. Jarrolds, 1929

FIELD, KATHERINE. Series character: Det. Insp. Ross Paterson, in all titles.
Disappearance of a Niece. Murray, 1941
Murder to Follow. Jenkins, 1944
The Two-Five to Mardon. Murray, 1942

FIELD, MEDORA. 1898-   .
Blood on Her Shoe. Macmillan, 1942; Jarrolds, 1943
Who Killed Aunt Maggie? Macmillan, 1939; Jarrolds, 1940

FIELD, MOIRA. Series character: Det. Insp. Flower, in both titles.
Foreign Body. Bles, 1950; Macmillan, 1951
Gunpowder Treason and Plot. Bles, 1951

FIELD, TEMPLE
Five. Farrar, 1931
Killer's Carnival. Farrar, 1932

FIELDING, A. Pseudonym of Dorothy Feilding, 1884-   . Series character: Inspector Pointer = P. (Note: A few U.S. titles have the byline A. E. Fielding.)
Black Cats are Lucky. Collins, 1937; Kinsey, 1938, as by AEF P
The Case of the Missing Diary. Collins, 1935; Kinsey, 1936 P
The Case of the Two Pearl Necklaces. Collins, 1936; Kinsey, 1936, as by AEF P
The Cautley Conundrum. Collins, 1934. U.S. title: The Cautley Mystery. Kinsey, 1934 P
The Cautley Mystery; see The Cautley Conundrum
The Charteris Mystery. Collins, 1925; Knopf, 1925 P
The Clifford Affair. Collins, 1927; Knopf, 1927. Also published as: The Clifford Mystery. Collins, 1933 P
The Clifford Mystery; see The Clifford Affair
The Cluny Problem. Collins, 1928; Knopf, 1929 P
The Craig Poisoning Mystery. Collins, 1930; Cosmopolitan, 1930 P
Death of John Tait. Collins, 1932; Kinsey, 1932 P
Deep Currents. Collins, 1924
The Eames-Erskine Case. Collins, 1924; Knopf, 1925 P
The Footsteps That Stopped. Collins, 1926; Knopf, 1926 P
Murder at the Nook. Collins, 1929; Knopf, 1930 P
Murder in Suffolk. Collins, 1938; Kinsey, 1938, as by AEF
The Mysterious Partner. Collins, 1929; Knopf, 1929 P
Mystery at the Rectory. Collins, 1936; Kinsey, 1937, as by AEF P
The Net Around Joan Ingilby. Collins, 1928; Knopf, 1928 P
The Paper-Chase. Collins, 1934. U.S. title: The Paper-Chase Mystery. Kinsey, 1935 P
The Paper-Chase Mystery; see The Paper Chase
Pointer to a Crime. Collins, 1944; Mystery House, 1945 P
Scarecrow. Collins, 1937; Kinsey, 1937, as by AEF P
The Tall House Mystery. Collins, 1933; Kinsey, 1933 P
Tragedy at Beechcroft. Collins, 1935; Kinsey, 1935 P
The Upfold Farm Mystery. Collins, 1931; Kinsey, 1932 P
The Wedding-Chest Mystery. Collins, 1930; Kinsey, 1932 P
The Westwood Mystery. Collins, 1932; Kinsey, 1933 P

FIELDING, A. E. See: A. FIELDING.

FIELDING, HOWARD. Pseudonym of Charles Witherle Hooke, 1861-1929.
The Confederate; see Hidden Out
Equal Partners. Dillingham, 1901
Hidden Out. Chelsea, 1927. British title: The Confederate. Nelson, 1929
The Housekeeper's Secret. (New York), 1889
Straight Crooks. Chelsea, 1927
-The Victim of his Clothes. Ogilvie, 1890

FIELDING, PETER
Text for Murder. Evans, 1951

FIELDING, WILLIAM
Take Me as I Am. GM, 1952

FILER, TOM. 1925-   .
-The Man on Watch. Harper, 1961; Hutchinson, 1961

FINCH, MATTHEW. Pseudonym of Merton Fink, 1921-   . Series character: a female private eye, in both titles.
Eye Spy. Dobson, 1975
Eye with Mascara. Dobson, 1968

FINDLEY, FERGUSON. Pseudonym of Charles Weiser Frey, 1910-   .
Counterfeit Corpse. Ace, 1956
Dead Ringer; see The Man in the Middle
A Handful of Murder; see The Man in the Middle
Killer Cop; see My Old Man's Badge
The Man in the Middle. Duell, 1952. British title: A Handful of Murder. Reinhardt, 1955. Also published as: Dead Ringer. Bestseller, 1953
Murder Makes Me Mad. Popular Library, 1956
My Old Man's Badge. Duell, 1950; Reinhardt, 1950. Also published as: Killer Cop. Monarch, 1959
Remember That Face!; see Waterfront
Waterfront. Duell, 1951. British title: Remember That Face! Reinhardt, 1951

FINDLEY, TIMOTHY. 1931?-   .
The Butterfly Plague. Viking, 1969; Deutsch, 1970
The Last of the Crazy People. Meredith, 1967; Macdonald, 1967

FINK, MERTON. 1921-   . Pseudonym: Matthew Finch, q.v.

FINLEY, GLENNA [GLENNA FINLEY WHITE]. 1925-   .
Death Strikes Out. Arcadia, 1957

FINLEY, SCOTT. Pseudonym of Rosy Lee Winifred Cecelia Clark, 1909-   .
The Case of the Black Sheep. Phoenix, 1950

FINN, EDMUND. 1819-1898.
The Hordern Mystery. McKinley (Melbourne), 1889
A Priest's Secret; Under Seal of Confession. McKinley (Melbourne), 1888

FINNEGAN, ROBERT. Pseudonym of Paul William Ryan, 1906-1947. Series character: Dan Banion, in all titles.
The Bandaged Nude. Simon, 1946; Boardman, 1949
The Lying Ladies. Simon, 1946; Bodley Head, 1949
Many a Monster. Simon, 1948; Boardman, 1950

FINNEY, JACK. Pseudonym of Walter Braden Finney, 1911-   .
Assault on a Queen. Simon, 1959; Eyre, 1960
Five Against the House. Doubleday, 1954; Eyre, 1954
The House of Numbers. Dell, 1957; Eyre, 1957

FINNEY, R. C. Series character: Inspector Bourne, in at least some of these titles.
The Coleville Skeleton. Scion, 1950
The Crimson Hand. Scion, 1949
Death in the Mist. Burrell, 1947
Death Takes a Ride. Scion, 1951
Find the Lady. Scion, 1949
The Haunted Rock. Century, 1948
Honeymoon Murder. Burrell, 1947
Lover's Feud. Scion, 1949
Love's Prisoner. Scion, 1952
Meet Inspector Bourne. Newcoll, 1945
The "Scarlet Ship." Partridge, 1928
The Secret Tunnel. Mellifont, 1937
Talking Clues. Scion, 1949
Three Point Murder. Scion, 1949

FINNEY, WALTER BRADEN. 1911-   . Pseudonym: Jack Finney, q.v.

FIRTH, ANTHONY. 1937-   .
Tall, Balding, Thirty-Five. Hutchinson, 1966; Harper, 1967. Also published as: The Limbo Affair. Lancer, 1968

FIRTH, IVAN EUSTACE. 1891-   . Joint pseudonym with Gladys Shaw Erskine, 1895-   : Firth Erskine, q.v.

FIRTH, J. W.
Crime Confessions. Spencer, 1948

FIRTH, N. WESLEY
Concerto for Fear. Bear Hudson, 1945
Dames Play Rough. Murray, 1946
-Guns of Calliope. Fiction House, 1948
Lady in Leicester Square. Brown Watson, 1946
Manhattan Bombshell. Hamilton Stafford, 1946
Murder for Sale. Bear Hudson, 1945
Mystery Crime Cases. Spencer, 1948 ss
-Outlawed Guns. Mitre, 1946
Phantom Detective Cases. Spencer, 1948 ss
Spawn of the Vampire. Bear Hudson, 1946
Terror Stalks by Night. Bear Hudson, 1945
This is Murder, Lady! Mitre, 1945 ss
Trouble Buster. Mitre, 1946
When Shall I Sleep Again? Gifford, 1950
The Woman of Danger. Modern Fiction, 1946

FIRTH, VIOLET MARY. 1890-1946. Pseudonym: Dion Fortune, q.v.

FISCHER, BRUNO. 1908-   . Pseudonym: Russell Gray, q.v. Series characters: Ben Helm = BH; Rick Train = RT.
The Angels Fell. Dodd, 1950; Boardman, 1951. Also published as: The Flesh was Cold. Signet, 1950

The Bleeding Scissors. Ziff-Davis, 1948. British title: The Scarlet Scissors. Foulsham, 1950
Croaked the Raven; see Quoth the Raven
The Dead Men Grin. McKay, 1945; Quality, 1947 BH
The Evil Days. Random, 1974; Hale, 1976
The Fast Buck. GM, 1952; Red Seal, 1959
The Fingered Man; see Quoth the Raven
The Flesh was Cold; see The Angels Fell
Fools Walk In. GM, 1951; Red Seal, 1958
The Girl Between. GM, 1960
The Hornet's Nest. Morrow, 1944; Quality, 1947 RT
House of Flesh. GM, 1950; Red Seal, 1958
Kill to Fit. Five Star, 1946; Instructive Arts, 1951 RT
Knee-Deep in Death. GM, 1956; Fawcett (London), 1957
The Lady Kills. GM, 1951
More Deaths Than One. Ziff-Davis, 1947; Foulsham, 1950 BH
Murder in the Raw. GM, 1957; Fawcett (London), 1959
The Paper Circle. Dodd, 1951; Boardman, 1952. Also published as: Stripped for Murder. Signet, 1953 BH
The Pigskin Bag. Ziff-Davis, 1946; Foulsham, 1951
Quoth the Raven. Doubleday, 1944. British title: Croaked the Raven. Quality, 1947. Also published as: The Fingered Man. Ace, 1953
The Restless Hands. Dodd, 1949; Foulsham, 1950 BH
Run for Your Life. GM, 1953; Fawcett (London), 1954
The Scarlet Scissors; see The Bleeding Scissors
Second-Hand Nude. GM, 1959; Muller pb, 1960
The Silent Dust. Dodd, 1950; Boardman, 1951 BH
So Much Blood. Greystone, 1939. Also published as: Stairway to Death. Pyramid, 1951
So Wicked My Love. GM, 1954; Fawcett (London), 1957
The Spider Lily. McKay, 1946; Quality, 1953
Stairway to Death; see So Much Blood
Stripped for Murder; see The Paper Circle

FISCHER, ERWIN. 1928- .
The Berlin Indictment. World, 1971. (Translation of Kameradenessen. Munich, 1970.)

FISCHER, MARJORIE. 1903?-1961.
Embarrassment of Riches. Random, 1944

FISH, ROBERT L(LOYD). 1912- . Pseudonym: Robert L. Pike, q.v. See also: JACK LONDON, 1876-1916. Series characters: Jose da Silva = JdS; Kek Huuygens = KH; Schlock Homes = SH; Carruthers, Simpson and Briggs = CSB.
Always Kill a Stranger. Putnam, 1967 JdS
Brazilian Sleigh Ride. Simon, 1965; Boardman, 1966 JdS
The Bridge That Went Nowhere. Putnam, 1968; Long, 1970 JdS
Death Cuts the Deck; see Rub-a-Dub-Dub
The Diamond Bubble. Simon, 1965; Boardman, 1965 JdS
The Fugitive. Simon, 1962; Boardman, 1963 JdS
The Green Hell Treasure. Putnam, 1971 JdS
A Handy Death, with Henry Rothblatt. Simon, 1973; Hale, 1975
The Hochmann Miniatures. NAL, 1967 KH
The Incredible Schlock Homes. Simon, 1966 SH ss
Isle of the Snakes. Simon, 1963; Boardman, 1964 JdS
The Memoirs of Schlock Homes. Bobbs, 1974 SH ss
The Murder League. Simon, 1968; New English Library, 1970 CSB
Rub-a-Dub-Dub. Simon, 1971. Also published as: Death Cuts the Deck. Ace, 1972 CSB
The Shrunken Head. Simon, 1963; Boardman, 1965 JdS
Trials of O'Brien. Signet, 1965. (Novelization of the TV series.)
The Tricks of the Trade. Putnam, 1972; Hale, 1974 KH
Trouble in Paradise. Doubleday, 1975 JdS
The Wager. Putnam, 1974; Hale, 1976 KH
Whirligig. World, 1970 KH
The Xavier Affair. Putnam, 1969; Hale, 1974 JdS

FISHER, DAVE. See: JOEY.

FISHER, DAVID E(LIMELECH). 1932- .
Crisis. Doubleday, 1971; Allen, 1971

FISHER, DOUGLAS (G.). 1902- . Pseudonym: George Douglas, q.v.
Corpse in Community. Hodder, 1953
Death at Pyford Hall. Hodder, 1952
Poison-Pen at Pyford. Hodder, 1951
What's Wrong at Pyford? Hodder, 1950

FISHER, GERARD
Hospitality for Murder. Hale, 1959; Washburn, 1959
It's Your Turn to Die. Hale, 1960

FISHER, GRAHAM
End of the Line. Macdonald, 1975
Face of Danger. Macdonald, 1974

FISHER, LAINE. Pseudonym of James A(rch) Howard, 1922- , q.v.
Fare Prey. Ace, 1959

FISHER, LAWRENCE (V.). 1923- .
Death by the Day. Berkley, 1961
Die a Little Every Day. Random, 1963; Boardman, 1963

FISHER, NORMAN. 1910- . Series character: Nigel Morrison, in all titles.
The Last Assignment. Triton, 1973; Walker, 1973
Rise at Dawn. Triton, 1971; Walker, 1971
Walk at a Steady Pace. Triton, 1970; Walker, 1971

FISHER, RICHARD. 1899- .
-Crisis Comes to Mister Smith. Selwyn, 1939
Indian Police. Selwyn, 1939
-Out of Evil. Selwyn, 1928

FISHER, RUDOLPH. 1897- .
The Conjure Man Dies. Covici, 1932

FISHER, STEVE [STEPHEN GOULD FISHER]. 1912- . Pseudonyms: Stephen Gould, Grant Lane, qq.v.
The Big Dream. Doubleday, 1970
-Forever Glory. Macaulay, 1936
The Hell-Black Night. Sherbourne, 1970
I Wake Up Screaming. Dodd, 1941; Hale, 1943. Revised edition: Bantam, 1960
Image of Hell. Dutton, 1961
Murder of the Pigboat Skipper. Hillman-Curl, 1937
The Night Before Murder. Hillman-Curl, 1939
No House Limit. Dutton, 1958

Satan's Angel. Macaulay, 1935
Saxon's Ghost. Sherbourne, 1969
The Sheltering Night. GM, 1952
Take All You Can Get. Random, 1955
Winter Kill. Dodd, 1946

FISHTER, J(ACOB) FRANZ. 1904- .
The Ambassador of Death. Macaulay, 1937

FISON, Peter. Pseudonym: Milo Ainsworth, q.v.

FITT, MARY. Pseudonym of Kathleen Freeman, 1897-1959. Other pseudonym: Stuart Mary Wick, q.v. Series character: Inspector Mallett, in at least those marked M.
Aftermath of Murder; see Death and Mary Dazill
The Banquet Ceases. Macdonald, 1949 M
Bulls Like Death. Nicholson, 1937
Case for the Defence. Macdonald, 1958; British Book Centre, 1958
Clues to Christabel. Joseph, 1944; Doubleday, 1944 M
Death and Mary Dazill. Joseph, 1941. U.S. title: Aftermath of Murder. Doubleday, 1941 M
Death and the Bright Day. Macdonald, 1948 M
Death and the Pleasant Voices. Joseph, 1946; Putnam, 1946 M
Death and the Shortest Day. Macdonald, 1952 M
Death at Dancing Stones. Nicholson, 1939 M
Death Finds a Target; see Death on Herons' Mere
Death on Herons' Mere. Joseph, 1941. U.S. title: Death Finds a Target. Doubleday, 1941 M
Death Starts a Rumour. Nicholson, 1940 M
Expected Death. Nicholson, 1938 M
A Fine and Private Place. Macdonald, 1947; Putnam, 1947 M
An Ill Wind. Macdonald, 1951 M
The Late Uncle Max. Macdonald, 1957
Love from Elizabeth. Macdonald, 1954 M
The Man Who Shot Birds and other tales. Macdonald, 1954 M ss
Mizmaze. Joseph, 1959; British Book Centre, 1959 M
Murder Mars the Tour. Nicholson, 1936
Murder of a Mouse. Nicholson, 1939
The Night-Watchman's Friend. Macdonald, 1953
Pity for Pamela. Macdonald, 1950; Harper, 1951
Requiem for Robert. Joseph, 1942 M
Sky-Rocket. Nicholson, 1938 M
Sweet Poison. Macdonald, 1956 M
There are More Ways of Killing... Joseph, 1960; British Book Centre, 1960
The Three Hunting Horns. Nicholson, 1937
Three Sisters Flew Home. Nicholson, 1936; Doubleday, 1936

FITTS, JAMES FRANKLIN. 1840-1890.
A Sharp Night's Work. Laird, 1888

FITZ, JEAN DeWITT. 1912- .
The Devon Maze. Geron-X, 1969
Graven Image. Pyramid, 1975
The Viper's Bite. Geron-X, 1969

FITZGERALD, ARLENE J. Pseudonym: Monica Heath, q.v.
House of Tragedy. Manor, 1973
-Numbers for Lovers. Manor, 1974

Pamela's Palace. Manor, 1972
-Satanic Sex. Manor, 1973

FITZGERALD, KEVIN. 1902- .
Dangerous to Lean Out. Heinemann, 1960; Macmillan, 1961
It's Different in July. Heinemann, 1955
It's Safe in England. Heinemann, 1949
Kill Him Gently, Nurse. Heinemann, 1966
Not So Quickly. Heinemann, 1948
Quiet Under the Sun. Heinemann, 1953; Little, 1954
A Throne of Bayonets. Heinemann, 1952
Trouble in West Two. Heinemann, 1958

FITZGERALD, NIGEL. 1906- . Series characters: Inspector/Superintendent Duffy, in at least those marked D; Alan Russell, in at least those marked AR.
Affairs of Death. Collins, 1967 D
Black Welcome. Collins, 1961; Macmillan, 1962 D
The Candles are All Out. Collins, 1960; Macmillan, 1961 AR
The Day of the Adder. Collins, 1963. U.S. title: Echo Answers Murder. Macmillan, 1965 D
Echo Answers Murder; see The Day of the Adder
Ghost in the Making. Collins, 1960 AR
The House is Falling. Collins, 1955 D
Imagine a Man. Collins, 1956 D
Midsummer Malice. Collins, 1953; Macmillan, 1959 D
The Rosy Pastor. Collins, 1954 D
The Student Body. Collins, 1958 D
Suffer a Witch. Collins, 1958 D
This Won't Hurt You. Collins, 1959; Macmillan, 1960

FITZGERALD, PERCY (HETHERINGTON). 1834-1925.
Chronicles of the Bow Street Police-Office. Chapman, 1888 ss

FITZGERALD, TOM
-Chocolate Charlie. Paperback Library, 1974
A Matter of Scents. Pyramid, 1974

FITZHAMON, LEWIN
The Rival Millionaires. Ward, 1904
The Vixen. Ward, 1915

FITZPATRICK, JANINE
The Dreamwalker. PB, 1975

FITZSIMMONS, CORTLAND. 1893-1949. Series characters: Arthur Martinson = AM; Ethel Thomas = ET.
The Bainbridge Murder. McBride, 1930; Eyre, 1930 AM
Crimson Ice. Stokes, 1935
Death on the Diamond. Stokes, 1934
Death Rings a Bell. Lippincott, 1942; Boardman, 1943
The Evil Men Do. Stokes, 1941; Boardman, 1942 ET
The Girl in the Cage, with John Mulholland (1898-1970). Stokes, 1939
The Manville Murders. McBride, 1930 AM
The Moving Finger. Stokes, 1937 ET
Murder is Swift; see One Man's Poison
Mystery at Hidden Harbor. Stokes, 1938; Lane, 1939 ET
No Witness! Stokes, 1932; Hutchinson, 1933
One Man's Poison. Stokes, 1940. British title (?): Murder is Swift. Boardman, 1944
Red Rhapsody. Stokes, 1933
70,000 Witnesses. McBride, 1931
Sudden Silence. Stokes, 1938; Lane, 1939
This—is Murder!, with Gerald Adams. Stokes, 1941

Tied for Murder. Lippincott, 1943; Boardman, 1945
The Whispering Window. Stokes, 1936; Boardman, 1943 ET

FLAGG, JOHN. Pseudonym of John Gearon, q.v. Series character: Hart Muldoon, in at least those marked HM.
Dear, Deadly Beloved. GM, 1954
Death and the Naked Lady. GM, 1951; Muller, 1953
Death's Lovely Mask. GM, 1958; Fawcett (London), 1960 HM
The Lady and the Cheetah. GM, 1951; Fawcett (London), 1954
Murder in Monaco. GM, 1957; Red Seal, 1959 HM
The Paradise Gun. GM, 1961; Muller pb, 1962 HM
The Persian Cat. GM, 1950
Woman of Cairo. GM, 1953; Muller, 1954

FLAGG, W(ILLIAM) J(OSEPH). 1818-1898.
Wall Street and the Woods; or, Woman the Stronger. Baker, 1885

FLAHERTY, JOE
Fogarty and Co. Coward, 1973

FLANAGAN, T. J.
Harry Blount, the Detective; or, The Martin Mystery Solved. Ogilvie, 1891

FLATAU, HERMIONE
Drama of Mount Street. Hurst, 1930

FLATTERY, M(AURICE) DOUGLAS. 1870-1925.
A Pair of Knaves and A Few Trumps. Abbey, 1900

FLAVIN, MARTIN. 1883- .
Cameron Hill. Harper, 1957; Muller, 1958

FLEETWOOD, HUGH (NIGEL). 1944- .
A Conditional Sentence. H. Hamilton, 1974
Foreign Affairs. H. Hamilton, 1973; Stein, 1974
The Girl Who Passed for Normal. H. Hamilton, 1973; Stein, 1973
A Painter of Flowers. H. Hamilton, 1972; Viking, 1972
A Picture of Innocence. Harrap, 1975

FLEISCHMAN, A(LBERT) S(IDNEY). 1920- .
Series character: Max Brindle = MB.
Chinese Crimson; see Look Behind You, Lady
Counterspy Express. Ace, 1954
Danger in Paradise. GM, 1953; Jenkins, 1964
Look Behind You, Lady. GM, 1952; Fawcett (London), 1953. Also published as: Chinese Crimson. Jenkins, 1962
Malay Manhunt; see Malay Woman
Malay Woman. GM, 1954; Fawcett (London), 1955. Also published as: Malay Manhunt. Jenkins, 1966
Murder's No Accident. Phoenix, 1949 MB
Shanghai Flame. GM, 1951; Fawcett (London), 1957
The Straw Donkey Case. Phoenix, 1948 MB
The Venetian Blonde. GM, 1963; Muller pb, 1964

FLEMING, BRANDON. 1889- .
The Beauty-Killer. White, 1920. U.S. title: The Crooked House. Clode, 1921
The Crime Maker. White, 1923
The Crooked House; see The Beauty-Killer
Masks. Everett, 1913
Pillory. White, 1921

FLEMING, E(DWARD) L(ASCELLES)
Nazi Shadows. Williams, 1935

FLEMING, ETHYL
Murder Takes a Honeymoon. Gateway, 1940

FLEMING, GERALDINE. Pseudonym of John R(ussell) Coryell, 1851-1924, q.v.
-False. Lovell, 1888
$5000 Reward; or, The Missing Bride. Munro, 1887
-How He Won Her, and, A False Friend. Munro, 1885
-A Sinless Crime. Lovell, 1888
-A Sister's Sacrifice. Munro, 1885
-Sunlight and Gloom. Munro, 1885
-A Terrible Secret. Munro, 1885

FLEMING, H(ORACE) K(INGSTON). 1901- .
The Day They Kidnapped Queen Victoria. Frewin, 1969

FLEMING, IAN (LANCASTER). 1908-1964.
Series character: James Bond, in all titles.
Casino Royale. Cape, 1953; Macmillan, 1953. Also published as: You Asked for It. Popular Library, 1955
Diamonds are Forever. Cape, 1956; Macmillan, 1956
Doctor No. Cape, 1958; Macmillan, 1958
For Your Eyes Only. Cape, 1960; Viking, 1960 ss
From Russia, with Love. Cape, 1957; Macmillan, 1957
Goldfinger. Cape, 1959; Macmillan, 1959
Live and Let Die. Cape, 1954; Macmillan, 1954
The Man with the Golden Gun. Cape, 1965; NAL, 1965
Moonraker. Cape, 1955; Macmillan, 1955. Also published as: Too Hot to Handle. Perma, 1957
Octopussy; see Octopussy and The Living Daylights
Octopussy and The Living Daylights. Cape, 1966. U.S. title: Octopussy. NAL, 1966 ss (Note that the paperback edition, Signet, 1967, contains one additional story.)
On Her Majesty's Secret Service. Cape, 1963; NAL, 1963
The Spy Who Loved Me. Cape, 1962; Viking, 1962
Thunderball. Cape, 1961; Viking, 1961
Too Hot to Handle; see Moonraker
You Asked for It; see Casino Royale
You Only Live Twice. Cape, 1964; NAL, 1964

FL*M*NG, I*N. Joint pseudonym of Christopher Bennett Cerf, 1941- , and Michael K. Frith.
Alligator. Vanitas, 1962. (A parody on the James Bond stories of Ian Fleming, 1908-1964, q.v.)

FLEMING, JANE
Hawthorn Wood. Berkley, 1975

FLEMING, JOAN (MARGARET). 1908- .
Series character: Nuri Iskirlak, in at least those marked NI.
Alas, Poor Father. Collins, 1972; Putnam, 1973
Be a Good Boy; see Grim Death and the Barrow Boys
The Chill and the Kill. Collins, 1964; Washburn, 1964
A Cup of Cold Poison; see The Man Who Looked Back
A Daisy-Chain for Satan. Hutchinson, 1950; Doubleday, 1951

Death of a Sardine. Collins, 1963; Washburn, 1964
The Deeds of Dr. Deadcert. Hutchinson, 1955; Washburn, 1957
Dirty Butter for Servants. H. Hamilton, 1972
The Gallows in My Garden. Hutchinson, 1951
The Good and the Bad. Hutchinson, 1953; Doubleday, 1953
Grim Death and the Barrow Boys. Collins, 1971. U.S. title (?): Be a Good Boy. Putnam, 1971
He Ought to be Shot. Hutchinson, 1955; Doubleday, 1955
Hell's Belle. Collins, 1968; Washburn, 1969
How to Live Dangerously. Collins, 1974; Putnam, 1975
In the Red. Collins, 1961; Washburn, 1961
Kill or Cure. Collins, 1968; Washburn, 1968
Maiden's Prayer. Collins, 1957; Washburn, 1958
Malice Matrimonial. Collins, 1959; Washburn, 1959
The Man from Nowhere. Collins, 1960; Washburn, 1961
The Man Who Looked Back. Hutchinson, 1951; Doubleday, 1952. Also published as: A Cup of Cold Poison. H. Hamilton, 1969
Midnight Hag. Collins, 1966; Washburn, 1966
Miss Bones. Collins, 1959; Washburn, 1960
No Bones About It. Collins, 1967; Washburn, 1967
Nothing is the Number When You Die. Collins, 1965; Washburn, 1965 NI
Polly Put the Kettle On. Hutchinson, 1952
Screams from a Penny Dreadful. H. Hamilton, 1971
Too Late! Too Late! The Maiden Cried. H. Hamilton, 1975; Putnam, 1975
Two Lovers Too Many. Hutchinson, 1949
When I Grow Rich. Collins, 1962; Washburn, 1962 NI
You Can't Believe Your Eyes. Collins, 1957; Washburn, 1957
You Won't Let Me Finish. Collins, 1973. U.S. title: You Won't Let Me Finnish. Putnam, 1974
Young Man, I Think You're Dying. Collins, 1970; Putnam, 1970

FLEMING, JOHN C(HESTER). 1906- . See: LOIS (CHRISTINE) EBY, 1908- .

FLEMING, MAY AGNES (EARLY). 1840-1880. Pseudonyms: Cousin May Carleton, M(ay) A(gnes) Earlie, qq.v.
The Actress's Daughter. Carleton, 1886; Milner, 1903
-The Baronet's Bride; or, A Woman's Vengeance. Brady, 1868
-The Dark Secret. Federal Book, 1875
-Ermine; or, The Gipsy's Vow. Brady, 1862
-A Fateful Abduction; or, The Secret Sorrow. Dillingham, 1907
The Heiress of Glen Gower; or, The Hidden Crime. Munro, 1892
-Norine's Revenge, and Sir Noel's Heir. Carleton, 1875
One Night's Mystery. Carleton, 1876; Low, 1876
Sharing Her Crime. Carleton, 1882
A Terrible Secret. Carleton, 1874; Low, 1874
-Who Wins?, or, The Secret of Monkswood Waste. Donohue, 1870

FLEMING, NICHOL. 1939- .
Counter Paradise. Joseph, 1968; Coward, 1968
Czech Point. Joseph, 1970
Hash. Joseph, 1971

FLEMING, OLIVER. Joint pseudonym of Philip MacDonald, 1899- , q.v., and his father, Ronald MacDonald, 1860-1933. Other Philip MacDonald pseudonym: Martin Porlock, q.v.
Ambrotox and Limping Dick. Ward, 1920
The Spandau Quid. Palmer, 1923

FLEMING, (ROBERT) PETER. 1907- .
The Sixth Column. Hart-Davis, 1951; Scribner, 1951
A Story to Tell. Cape, 1942; Scribner, 1942 ss

FLEMING, ROBERT. 1891- .
And Death Drove On; see Night Freight Murders
A Bullet in his Cap; see Night Freight Murders
Murder Comes to Dinner; see Night Freight Murders
Night Freight Murders. Smith & Durrell, 1942. British title: Murder Comes to Dinner. Long, 1943. Also published as: A Bullet in his Cap. Handi-Books, 1942. And as: And Death Drove On. Green Dragon, 194?

FLEMING, RUDD. 1908- .
Cradled in Murder. Simon, 1938; H. Hamilton, 1938

FLEMING, THOMAS J(AMES). 1927- .
A Cry of Whiteness. Morrow, 1967

FLETCHER, DAVID. Pseudonym of Dulan F. Barber, 1940- .
A Lovable Man. Macmillan (London), 1974; Coward, 1975
A Respectable Woman. Macmillan (London), 1975; Coward, 1975

FLETCHER, DOROTHY
Beyond Recall. Lancer, 1971
The Brand Inheritance. Lancer, 1974
Farewell to Vienna. Lancer, 1970
House of Hate. Lancer, 1967
Meeting in Madrid. Lancer, 1970
Shadows on the Water. Beagle, 1972
Still Waters. Paperback Library, 1970

FLETCHER, H(ARRY) L(UFT) V(ERNE). 1902- . Pseudonym: John Garden, q.v.
-The Devil Has the Best Tunes. Macdonald, 1947
-Forest Inn. Macdonald, 1948
-High Pastures. Macdonald, 1957
-The Lonely Island. Macdonald, 1958
Miss Agatha. Gardner, 1946. U.S. title: Miss Agatha Doubles for Death. Messner, 1947
Miss Agatha Doubles for Death; see Miss Agatha
-The Reluctant Prodigal. Macdonald, 1958
-The Rising Sun. Macdonald, 1951
-The Storm. Macdonald, 1954
The Whip and the Tongue. Macdonald, 1949
-The Woman's House. Macdonald, 1944

FLETCHER, J(OSEPH) S(MITH). 1863-1935. Series character: Ronald Camberwell = RC.
The Adventures of Archer Dawe, Sleuth-Hound. Digby Long, 1909. Also published as: The Contents of the Coffin. Novel Library, 1928 ss
The Air-Ship. Digby Long, 1903 ss
The Amaranth Club. Ward, 1918; Knopf, 1926
The Ambitious Lady. Ward, 1923. U.S. title (?): And Sudden Death. Hillman-Curl, 1938. Also published as: Pedigreed Murder Case. Detective Novel Classics, 194?
And Sudden Death; see The Ambitious Lady
Andrewlina. Kegan Paul, 1889
The Annexation Society. Ward, 1916; Knopf, 1925
The Bartenstein Case. Long, 1913. U.S. title: The Bartenstein Mystery. Dial, 1927
The Bartenstein Mystery; see The Bartenstein Case
The Bedford Row Mystery. Hodder, 1925. U.S. title: The Strange Case of Mr. Henry Marchmont. Knopf, 1927
Behind the Monocle. Jarrolds, 1928; Doubleday, 1930 ss
Behind the Panel; see In the Mayor's Parlour
The Black House in Harley Street; see The Million-Dollar Diamond
The Borgia Cabinet. Jenkins, 1932; Knopf, 1930
The Borough Treasurer. Ward, 1919; Knopf, 1921
The Box Hill Murder. Jenkins, 1931; Knopf, 1929
The Burma Ruby. Benn, 1932; Dial, 1933
The Canterbury Mystery; see The Ravenswood Mystery
The Carrismore Ruby. Jarrolds, 1935 ss
The Cartwright Gardens Murder. Collins, 1924; Knopf, 1926
The Charing Cross Mystery. Jenkins, 1923; Putnam, 1923
The Chestermarke Instinct. Allen & Unwin, 1918; Knopf, 1921
The Clue of the Artificial Eye; see Paul Campenhaye, Specialist in Criminologist
Cobweb Castle. Jenkins, 1928; Knopf, 1928
The Contents of the Coffin; see The Adventures of Archer Dawe, Sleuth-Hound
The Copper Box. Hodder, 1923; Doran, 1923
Dead Men's Money; see Droonin' Watter
The Death That Lurks Unseen. Ward, 1899 ss
The Diamond Murders; see The Diamonds
The Diamonds. Digby Long, 1904. U.S. title: The Diamond Murders. Dodd, 1929
The Double Chance. Nash, 1928; Dodd, 1928
The Dressing-Room Murder. Jenkins, 1930; Knopf, 1931
Droonin' Watter. Allen & Unwin, 1919. U.S. title: Dead Men's Money. Knopf, 1930
The Ebony Box. Butterworth, 1934; Knopf, 1934 RC
The Eleventh Hour. Butterworth, 1935; Knopf, 1935 RC
Exterior to the Evidence. Hodder, 1920; Knopf, 1923
False Scent. Jenkins, 1924; Knopf, 1925
-Families Repaired. Allen & Unwin, 1916
The Fear of the Night. Routledge, 1903 ss
Find the Woman. Collins, 1933 ss
The Flamstock Mystery; see The Malachite Jar
The Golden Spur. Long, 1901; Dial, 1928
The Great Brighton Mystery. Hodder, 1925; Knopf, 1926
Green Ink. Jenkins, 1926; Small Maynard, 1926 ss
The Green Rope. Jenkins, 1927; Knopf, 1927

The Guarded Room. Long, 1931; Clode, 1931
Hardican's Hollow. Everett, 1910; Doran, 1927
The Harvest Moon. Nash, 1908; Doran, 1927
The Heaven-Kissed Hill. Hodder, 1922; Doran, 1924
The Heaven-Sent Witness and other stories. Doubleday, 1930. (Contains 14 of the 27 ss in The Ivory God, q.v., and 7 of the ss in The Man in No. 3, q.v.)
The Herapath Property. Ward, 1920; Knopf, 1921
The House in Tuesday Market. Jenkins, 1930; Knopf, 1929
In the Mayor's Parlour. Bodley Head, 1922. Also published as: Behind the Panel. Collins, 1931
The Investigators. Long, 1902; Clode, 1930
The Ivory God. Murray, 1907. (14 of the 27 ss in this volume were included in The Heaven-Sent Witness, q.v.)
The Kang-He Vase. Collins, 1924; Knopf, 1926
The King Versus Wargrave. Ward, 1915; Knopf, 1924
The Lost Mr. Linthwaite. Hodder, 1920; Knopf, 1923
The Lynne Court Spinney. Ward, 1916. U.S. title: The Mystery of Lynne Court. Remington, 1923
The Malachite Jar. Collins, 1930. Also published as: The Flamstock Mystery. Collins, 1932. The first 11 ss also reprinted separately as: The Manor House Mystery. Collins, 1933 ss
Malvery Hold. Ward, 1917. U.S. title: The Mystery of the Hushing Pool. Hillman-Curl, 1938
The Man in No. 3. Collins, 1931. (7 of the ss were included in The Heaven-Sent Witness, q.v.)
The Man in the Fur Coat. Collins, 1932 ss
The Manor House Mystery; see The Malachite Jar
The Mantle of Ishmael. Nash, 1909
Many Engagements. Long, 1923 ss
Marchester Royal. Everett, 1909; Doran, 1926
The Markenmore Mystery. Jenkins, 1922; Knopf, 1923
The Marrendon Mystery, and other stories of crime and detection. Collins, 1930 ss
-The Marriage Lines. Nash, 1914
The Massingham Butterfly. Jenkins, 1926; Small Maynard, 1926 ss
The Matheson Formula. Jenkins, 1930; Knopf, 1929
The Mazaroff Murder. Jenkins, 1923. U.S. title: The Mazaroff Mystery. Knopf, 1924
The Mazaroff Mystery; see The Mazaroff Murder
The Middle of Things. Ward, 1922; Knopf, 1922
The Middle Temple Murder. Ward, 1919; Knopf, 1919
The Mill House Murder; see Todmanhawe Grange
The Mill of Many Windows. Collins, 1925; Doran, 1925
The Million-Dollar Diamond. Jenkins, 1923. U.S. title: The Black House in Harley Street. Doubleday, 1928
The Missing Chancellor; see The Stolen Budget
The Mortover Grange Affair; see The Mortover Grange Mystery
The Mortover Grange Mystery. Jenkins, 1926. U.S. title: The Mortover Grange Affair. Knopf, 1927
Murder at Wrides Park. Harrap, 1931; Knopf, 1931 RC
Murder in Four Degrees. Harrap, 1931; Knopf, 1931 RC
The Murder in Medora Mansions. Collins, 1933 ss
The Murder in the Pallant. Jenkins, 1927; Knopf, 1928
Murder in the Squire's Pew. Harrap, 1932; Knopf, 1932 RC
Murder of a Banker; see The Mystery of the London Banker
Murder of the Lawyer's Clerk; see Who Killed Alfred Snowe?
Murder of the Ninth Baronet. Harrap, 1932; Knopf, 1932 RC
Murder of the Only Witness. Harrap, 1933; Knopf, 1933 RC
Murder of the Secret Agent. Harrap, 1934; Knopf, 1934 RC
The Mysterious Chinaman. Jenkins, 1924. U.S. title: The Rippling Ruby. Putnam, 1923
The Mystery of Lynne Court; see The Lynne Court Spinney
The Mystery of the Hushing Pool; see Malvery Hold
The Mystery of the London Banker. Harrap, 1933. U.S. title: Murder of a Banker. Knopf, 1933 RC
Old Lattimer's Legacy. Jarrolds, 1892; Clode, 1929
The Orange-Yellow Diamond. Newnes, 1920; Knopf, 1921
Paradise Court. Unwin, 1908; Doubleday, 1929
The Paradise Mystery; see The Wrychester Paradise
Pasquinado. Ward, 1898 ss
The Passenger to Folkestone. Jenkins, 1927; Knopf, 1927
Paul Campenhaye, Specialist in Criminology. Ward, 1918. U.S. title: The Clue of the Artificial Eye. Hillman-Curl, 1939 ss
Pedigreed Murder Case; see The Ambitious Lady
The Perilous Crossways. Ward, 1917; Hillman-Curl, 1938
-Perris of the Cherry Trees. Nash, 1913; Doubleday, 1920
-The Queen of a Day. Unwin, 1907; Doubleday, 1929
The Ransom for London. Long, 1914; Dial, 1929
Ravensdene Court. Ward, 1922; Knopf, 1922
The Ravenswood Mystery. Collins, 1929. Also published as: The Canterbury Mystery. Collins, 1933 ss
The Rayner-Slade Amalgamation. Allen & Unwin, 1917; Knopf, 1922
The Rippling Ruby; see The Mysterious Chinaman
The Root of All Evil. Hodder, 1921; Doran, 192?
Safe Number Sixty-Nine. International Pocket Library, 1931 ss
The Safety Pin. Jenkins, 1924; Putnam, 1924
Scarhaven Keep. Ward, 1920; Knopf, 1922
Sea Fog. Jenkins, 1925; Knopf, 1925
The Secret Cargo. Ward, 1913
The Secret of Secrets. Clode, 1929. (British title?)
The Secret of the Barbican. Hodder, 1924; Doran, 1925 ss
The Secret Way. Digby Long, 1903; Small Maynard, 1925
The Seven Days' Secret. Jarrolds, 1919; Clode, 1930
The Shadow of Ravenscliffe. Digby Long, 1914; Clode, 1928

The Solution of a Mystery. Harrap, 1932; Doubleday, 1932
The South Foreland Murder. Jenkins, 1930; Knopf, 1930
The Stolen Budget. Hodder, 1926. U.S. title: The Missing Chancellor. Knopf, 1927
The Strange Case of Mr. Henry Marchmont; see The Bedford Row Mystery
The Talleyrand Maxim. Ward, 1919; Knopf, 1920
The Three Days' Terror. Long, 1901; Clode, 1927
The Threshing Floor. Unwin, 1905
The Time-Worn Town. Collins, 1929; Knopf, 1924
Todmanhawe Grange. Butterworth, 1937. U.S. title: The Mill House Murder. Knopf, 1937. (Completed after JSF's death by Torquemada, pseudonym of Edward Powys Mathers, 1892-   .)
The Valley of Headstrong Men. Hodder, 1919; Doran, 1924
-The Wheatstack. Nash, 1909 ss
Who Killed Alfred Snowe? Harrap, 1933. U.S. title: Murder of the Lawyer's Clerk. Knopf, 1933 RC
-The Winding Way. Kegan Paul, 1890
The Wolves and the Lamb. Ward, 1914; Knopf, 1925
The Wrist Mark. Jenkins, 1929; Knopf, 1928
The Wrychester Paradise. Ward, 1921. U.S. title: The Paradise Mystery. Knopf, 1920
The Yorkshire Moorland Murder. Jenkins, 1930; Knopf, 1930

FLETCHER, LUCILLE [LUCILLE FLETCHER WALLOP]. 1912-   . See also: ALLAN ULLMAN.
...And Presumed Dead. Random, 1963; Eyre, 1963
Blindfold. Random, 1960; Eyre, 1960
Eighty Dollars to Stamford. Random, 1975; Hale, 1977
The Girl in Cabin B54. Random, 1968; Hodder, 1969
Sorry Wrong Number, and The Hitchhiker. Dramatists Play Service, 1952. (Two plays.)
The Strange Blue Yawl. Random, 1964; Eyre, 1965

FLETCHER, MARY MANN
The Devil's Dress. Lancer, 1973
Devil's Instrument. Lancer, 1969
The House Called Whispering Winds. Beagle, 1974
The Scorpion of Chateau Laverria. Beagle, 1970

FLETCHER, R(OBERT) J(AMES). 1877-   .
Series character: Gilbert Davison, in all titles.
By Misadventure. Murray, 1930
Half Devil, Half Tiger, with Alex(ander) McLachlan. Murray, 1929
The Missing Doctor. Murray, 1930

FLETCHER, ROBERT HOWE. 1850-1936.
The Johnstown Stage, and other stories. Appleton, 1891. British title: The Mystery of a Studio and other stories. Lawrence, 1892 ss

FLETCHER, VERNE
Death and the Durlings. Swan, 1942

FLETT, ALFRED
Never Shake a Skeleton. Joseph, 1973

FLINN, JOHN JOSEPH. 1851-1929.
The Mysterious Disappearance of Helen St. Vincent. Hazlitt, 1895

FLINT, ANNIE AUSTIN. 1866-   .
  The Breaking Point. Broadway, 1915

FLOOD, CHARLES BRACELEN. 1929-   .
  Trouble at the Top. McGraw, 1972

FLOOD, ROBERT J.
  The Hit Man. Manor, 1972; Allen, 1974

FLORA, FLETCHER. 1914-1969. See also:
    (CHARLES) STUART PALMER, 1905-1968.
  -The Brass Bed. Lion, 1956
  -Desperate Asylum. Lion, 1955. Also published as: Whisper of Love. Pyramid, 1959
  -The Hotshot. Avon, 1956
  The Irrepressible Peccadillo. Macmillan, 1962; Boardman, 1963
  Killing Cousins. Macmillan, 1960; Cape, 1961
  Leave Her to Hell! Avon, 1958
  Let Me Kill You, Sweetheart! Avon, 1958
  -Most Likely to Love. Monarch, 1960
  -Park Avenue Tramp. GM, 1958; Fawcett (London), 1959
  -The Seducer. Monarch, 1961
  Skuldoggery. Belmont, 1967
  -Strange Sisters. Lion, 1954
  -Take Me Home. Monarch, 1959
  -Wake Up with a Stranger. Signet, 1959
  Whisper of Love; see Desperate Asylum
  -Whispers of the Flesh. Signet, 1958

FLOWER, ELLIOTT. 1863-1920.
  Policeman Flynn. Century, 1902 ss

FLOWER, PAT.   -1978.
  Cat's Cradle. Collins, 1973; Stein, 1978
  Cobweb. Collins, 1972; Stein, 1978
  Fiends of the Family. Hale, 1966
  Goodbye, Sweet William. Angus, 1959
  Hell for Heather. Hale, 1962
  Hunt the Body. Hale, 1968
  Odd Job. Collins, 1974; Stein, 1978
  One Rose Less. Angus, 1961
  Slyboots. Collins, 1974; Stein, 1978
  Term of Terror. Hale, 1963
  Vanishing Point. Collins, 1975; Stein, 1977
  Wax Flowers for Gloria. Angus, 1958
  A Wreath of Water-Lilies. Angus, 1960

FLOWERDEW, HERBERT
  -A Celibate's Wife. Lane (London & New York), 1898
  -In an Ancient Mirror. Unwin, 1897
  Love and a Title. Greening, 1913
  -Maynard's Wives. Nash, 1907
  -Mrs. Gray's Past. Paul, 1913
  The Realist. Lane (London & New York), 1900. Also published as: The Room of Mirrors. Nash, 1912
  -Retaliation. Constable, 1901
  The Room of Mirrors; see The Realist
  -The Second Elopement. Paul, 1910
  The Seventh Postcard. Greening, 1914
  -The Third Kiss. Nash, 1905
  The Villa Mystery. Paul, 1912; Brentano's, 1912
  -The Ways of Men. Unwin, 1908
  -The Woman's View. Richards, 1903

FLOWERS, CHARLES. 1942-
  It Never Rains in Los Angeles. Coward, 1970

FLOYD, LESLIE
  The Case of the Frantic Ladies. Harrap, 1938

FLOYD, LOUISE McKNIGHT
  The Commencement Day Murders. Vantage, 1954

FLOYD, MORDIE
  The Secret of Saraband. Bouregy, 1961

FLYNN, BRIAN. 1885-   . Series character: Anthony Bathurst, in all titles.
  And Cauldron Bubble. Long, 1951
  The Billiard-Room Mystery. Hamilton, 1927; Macrae-Smith, 1929
  Black Agent. Long, 1950
  Black Edged. Long, 1939; Macrae-Smith, 1939
  The Case of Elymas the Sorcerer. Long, 1945
  The Case of the Black Twenty-Two. Hamilton, 1928; Macrae-Smith, 1929
  The Case of the Faithful Heart. Long, 1939
  The Case of the Painted Ladies. Long, 1940
  The Case of the Purple Calf. Long, 1934. U.S. title: The Ladder of Death. Macrae-Smith, 1935
  Cold Evil. Long, 1938
  Conspiracy at Angel. Long, 1947
  The Creeping Jenny Mystery. Long, 1930. U.S. title: The Crime at the Crossways. Macrae-Smith, 1932
  The Crime at the Crossways; see The Creeping Jenny Mystery
  The Dice are Dark. Long, 1956
  The Doll's Done Dancing. Long, 1954
  The Ebony Stag. Long, 1938
  The Edge of Terror. Long, 1932
  Exit Sir John. Long, 1947
  Fear and Trembling. Long, 1936. U.S. title: The Somerset Murder Case. Mill, 1937
  The Feet of Death. Long, 1954
  The Five Red Fingers. Long, 1929; Mill, 1938
  The Fortescue Candle. Long, 1936
  Glittering Prizes. Long, 1942
  The Grim Maiden. Long, 1944
  The Hands of Justice. Long, 1957
  The Horn. Long, 1934
  Invisible Death. Hamilton, 1929
  The Ladder of Death; see The Case of the Purple Calf
  The League of Matthias. Long, 1934
  Men for Pieces. Long, 1949
  The Mirador Collection. Long, 1955
  Murder En Route. Long, 1930; Macrae-Smith, 1932
  The Murders Near Mapleton. Hamilton, 1929; Macrae-Smith, 1930
  The Mystery of the Peacock's Eye. Hamilton, 1928; Macrae-Smith, 1930
  The Nine Cuts. Long, 1958
  The Orange Axe. Long, 1931
  Out of the Dusk. Long, 1953
  The Padded Door. Long, 1932
  Reverse the Charges. Long, 1943
  The Ring of Innocent. Long, 1952
  The Running Nun. Long, 1952
  The Saints are Sinister. Long, 1958
  The Seventh Sign. Long, 1952
  The Shaking Spear. Long, 1955
  The Sharp Quillet. Long, 1947
  The Somerset Murder Case; see Fear and Trembling
  The Spiked Lion. Long, 1933; Macrae-Smith, 1934
  Such Bright Disguises. Long, 1941
  The Sussex Cuckoo. Long, 1935
  The Swinging Death. Long, 1948
  They Never Came Back. Long, 1940
  The Toy Lamb. Long, 1956
  Tread Softly. Long, 1937; Mill, 1938
  The Triple Bite. Long, 1931
  Where There was Smoke. Long, 1951
  The Wife Who Disappeared. Long, 1957

FLYNN, J. M. Also uses byline: Jay Flynn, q.v.
  The Deadly Boodle. Ace, 1958
  Deep Six. Ace, 1961
  Drink with the Dead. Ace, 1959
  The Girl from Las Vegas. Ace, 1961
  The Hot Chariot. Ace, 1960
  One for the Death House. Ace, 1961
  Ring Around a Rogue. Ace, 1960
  The Screaming Cargo. Ace, 1962
  SurfSide 6. Dell, 1962. (Novelization of the TV series.)
  Terror Tournament. Mystery House, 1959

FLYNN, JAY. Also uses byline: J. M. Flynn, q.v. Series character: McHugh, in at least those marked M.
  The Action Man. Avon, 1961
  A Body for McHugh. Avon, 1960; Consul, 1961 M
  The Five Faces of Murder. Avon, 1962; Consul, 1965 M
  It's Murder, McHugh. Avon, 1960; Consul, 1961 M
  McHugh. Avon, 1959; Consul, 1961 M
  Viva McHugh. Avon, 1960 M

FLYNN, T(HOMAS) T(HEODORE). 1902-   .
  It's Murder! Hector Kelly, 1950
  Murder Caravan. Hector Kelly, 1950

FLYNN, WILLIAM J(AMES). 1867-1952.
  The Barrel Mystery. McCann, 1919
  Eagle's Eye. Prospect, 1919

FLYNT, JOSIAH. Pseudonym of Josiah Flynt Willard, 1869-1907.
  Notes of an Itinerant Policeman. Page, 1900
  The Powers That Prey, with Francis Walton (pseudonym of Alfred Hodder, 1866-1907). McClure, 1900; Ward, 1901 ss
  The Rise of Ruderick Clowd. Dodd, 1903; Richards, 1904

FODEN, FREDERICK
  -Denver Lil. Gray, 1953
  -Hick Town Dame. Gray, 1953
  Syndicate of Death. Warren, 1950

FOGARTY, MICHAEL. 1939-   .
  The Achilles Mandate. Davis-Poynter, 1975

FOLDER, LOUIS
  Rocky Libido in San Francisco. Contact, 1962

FOLDES, YOLANDA. 1903-   .
  Mind Your Own Murder. Hutchinson, 1948

FOLEY, PEARL. Pseudonym: Paul De Mar, q.v.
  The Octagon Crystal. Carrier & Isles, 1929; Brentano's (London), 1929
  The Yellow Circle. Lippincott (Philadelphia & London), 1937

FOLEY, RAE. Pseudonym of Elinore Denniston, 1900-   . Other pseudonym: Dennis Allan, q.v. Series characters: John Harland = JH; Hiram Potter = HP.
  An Ape in Velvet. Dodd, 1951; Boardman, 1952 JH
  Back Door to Death. Dodd, 1963; Boardman, 1964. Also published as: Nightmare Honeymoon. Dell, 1976 HP
  The Barclay Place. Dodd, 1975; Hale, 1976
  Bones of Contention. Dodd, 1950
  The Brownstone House. Dodd, 1974. British title: Murder by Bequest. Hale, 1976
  A Calculated Risk. Dodd, 1970; Hale, 1972
  Call It Accident. Dodd, 1965; Hale, 1966 HP
  Curtain Call; see It's Murder, Mr. Potter

Dangerous to Me. Dodd, 1959; Hammond, 1960 HP
The Dark Hill. Dodd, 1975; Hale, 1976
Dark Intent. Dodd, 1954; Boardman, 1955
The Deadly Noose; see Repent at Leisure
Death and Mr. Potter. Dodd, 1955; Boardman, 1955. Also published as: The Peacock is a Bird of Prey. Dell, 1976 HP
Don't Kill, My Love; see Wake the Sleeping Wolf
Fatal Lady. Dodd, 1964; Boardman, 1964 HP
Fear of a Stranger. Dodd, 1967; Hale, 1968
The First Mrs. Winston. Dodd, 1972; Chivers, 1974
The Girl from Nowhere. Dodd, 1949 JH
Girl on a High Wire. Dodd, 1969; Hale, 1971
The Hundredth Door. Dodd, 1950; Boardman, 1951
It's Murder, Mr. Potter. Dodd, 1961; Hammond, 1961. Also published as: Curtain Call. Dell, 1976 HP
The Last Gamble. Dodd, 1956; Boardman, 1957 HP
Malice Domestic. Dodd, 1968; Hale, 1969
The Man in the Shadow. Dodd, 1953; Boardman, 1954
Murder by Bequest; see The Brownstone House
Nightmare Honeymoon; see Back Door to Death
Nightmare House. Dodd, 1968; Hale, 1969
No Hiding Place. Dodd, 1969; Hale, 1970
No Tears for the Dead. Dodd, 1948; Cherry Tree, 1949
Ominous Star. Dodd, 1971; Hale, 1973
One O'Clock at the Gotham. Dodd, 1974; Hale, 1975
The Peacock is a Bird of Prey; see Death and Mr. Potter
Reckless Lady. Dodd, 1973; Hale, 1975
Repent at Leisure. Dodd, 1962. British title: The Deadly Noose. Hammond, 1963 HP
Run for Your Life. Dodd, 1957; Boardman, 1958 HP
Scared to Death. Dodd, 1966; Hale, 1967
The Shelton Conspiracy. Dodd, 1967; Hale, 1968
Sleep Without Morning. Dodd, 1972; Hale, 1974
Suffer a Witch. Dodd, 1965; Hale, 1966
This Woman Wanted. Dodd, 1971; Hale, 1972
Trust a Woman? Dodd, 1973
Wake the Sleeping Wolf. Dodd, 1952; Boardman, 1953. Also published as: Don't Kill, My Love. Bestseller, 1953
Where is Nancy Bostwick? Dodd, 1958; Boardman, 1958 HP
Wild Night. Dodd, 1966; Hale, 1967

FOLLETT, KEN. 1949-   . Pseudonym: Symon Myles, q.v.

FOLLIOTT, DORIA
Signpost to Murder. Popular Library, 1964. (Novelization of the movie.)

FONBLANQUE, ALBANY (DE GRENIER). 1829-1924.
Tom Rocket. Ward, 1860

FONSECA, ESTHER HAVEN. 1900-   .
The Affair at the Grotto. Doubleday, 1939
Death Below the Dam. Doubleday, 1936
The Thirteenth Bed in the Ballroom. Doubleday, 1937

FONTANA, DOROTHY C.
The Questor Tapes. Ballantine, 1974. (Novelization of the TV movie.)

FOOTE, HORTON
Baby, the Rain Must Fall. Popular Library, 1965. (Novelization of the movie.)
The Chase. Rinehart, 1956. Play version: Dramatists Play Service, 1952

FOOTMAN, DAVID (JOHN). 1895-   .
-The Mine in the Desert. Long, 1929
-A Pretty Pass; or, Just a Little Careless. Morrow, 1933. (British title?)
The Yellow Rock. Jenkins, 1929

FOOTNER, (WILLIAM) HULBERT. 1879-1944.
Series characters: Madame Rosika Storey = RS; Amos Lee Mappin = AM.
The Almost Perfect Murder. Lippincott, 1937; Collins, 1933 RS ss
Anybody's Pearls. Doubleday, 1930; Hodder, 1929
-A Backwoods Princess. Doran, 1926; Hodder, 1926
-Cap'n Sue. Doubleday, 1928; Hodder, 1927
The Casual Murderer. Lippincott, 1937; Collins, 1932 RS ss All but the title story reprinted as: The Kidnapping of Madame Storey. Collins, 1936
-The Chase of the Linda Belle. Hodder, 1925. (U.S. title?)
Dangerous Cargo. Harper, 1934; Collins, 1934 RS
The Dark Ships. Harper, 1937; Collins, 1937
Dead Man's Hat. Harper, 1932; Collins, 1932
The Death of a Celebrity. Harper, 1938; Collins, 1938 AM
Death of a Saboteur. Harper, 1943; Collins, 1944 AM
The Deaves Affair. Doran, 1922; Collins, 1922
The Doctor Who Held Hands. Doubleday, 1929; Collins, 1929. Also published as: The Murderer's Challenge. Collins, 1932
Easy to Kill. Harper, 1931; Collins, 1931 RS
The Folded Paper Mystery; see The Mystery of the Folded Paper
The Fugitive Sleuth. Hodder, 1918. (U.S. title?)
-The Fur-Bringers. McCann, 1920; Hodder, 1916
The House with the Blue Door. Harper, 1942; Collins, 1943 AM
-The Huntress. McCann, 1922; Hodder, 1917
The Island of Fear. Harper, 1936; Cassell, 1936
-Jack Chanty. Doubleday, 1913; Hodder, 1917
The Kidnapping of Madame Storey; see The Casual Murderer
Madame Storey. Doran, 1926; Collins, 1926 ss RS
Murder in the Sun; see The Obeah Murders
Murder of a Bad Man. Harper, 1936; Collins, 1935
Murder Runs in the Family. Harper, 1934; Collins, 1934
The Murder That Had Everything. Harper, 1939; Collins, 1939 AM
The Murderer's Challenge; see The Doctor Who Held Hands
Murderer's Vanity. Harper, 1940; Collins, 1941 AM
Mystery at Ramshackle House; see Ramshackle House
The Mystery of the Folded Paper. Harper, 1930. British title: The Folded Paper Mystery. Collins, 1930 AM
The Nation's Missing Guest. Harper, 1939; Collins, 1939 AM
The New Made Grave; see The Whip-Poor-Will Mystery
The Obeah Murders. Harper, 1937. British title: Murder in the Sun. Collins, 1938
Officer! Doran, 1924; Collins, 1924
On Swan River; see The Woman from Outside
Orchids to Murder. Harper, 1945; Collins, 1945 AM
The Owl Taxi. Doran, 1921; Collins, 1922
The Queen of Clubs. Doran, 1927; Collins, 1928
Ramshackle House. Doran, 1922; Collins, 1923. Also published as: Mystery at Ramshackle House. Collins, 1932
The Ring of Eyes. Harper, 1933; Collins, 1933
Scarred Jungle. Harper, 1935; Cassell, 1935
-The Sealed Valley. Doubleday, 1914; Hodder, 1915
A Self-Made Thief. Doubleday, 1929; Collins, 1929
-The Shanty Sled. Doran, 1926; Hodder, 1925
Sinfully Rich. Harper, 1940; Collins, 1940
The Substitute Millionaire. Doran, 1919; Collins, 1921
Thieves' Wit. Doran, 1918; Hodder, 1919
Tortuous Trails. Collins, 1937 ss
Trial by Water. Farrar, 1931; Hodder, 1930
-Two on the Trail. Doubleday, 1911; Methuen, 1911
The Under Dogs. Doran, 1925; Collins, 1925 RS
Unneutral Murder. Harper, 1944; Collins, 1944 AM
The Velvet Hand. Doubleday, 1928; Collins, 1928 RS ss
The Viper. Collins, 1930. (Three stories, 2 from The Velvet Hand, q.v.)
The Whip-Poor-Will Mystery. Harper, 1935. British title: The New Made Grave. Collins, 1935
-The Wild Bird. Doran, 1923; Hodder, 1923
Who Killed the Husband? Harper, 1941; Collins, 1941 AM
-The Woman from Outside. McCann, 1921. British title: On Swan River. Hodder, 1919

FORAN, PHIL. See: ROBERT McLAUGHLIN, 1925-   .

FORAN, W(ILLIAM) ROBERT. 1882-   .
Drums of Sacrifice. Hutchinson, 1934
-The Land of Fear. Hutchinson, 1937
-The Path of Ivory. Hutchinson, 1934
Watchers in the Hills. Hutchinson, 1935

FORBAT, SANDOR. 1890-   . Pseudonym: A. F. Witley, q.v.

FORBES, LADY ANGELA [SELINA BIANCA ST. CLAIR-ERSKINE]. 1876-   .
Should She Have Spoken? Nash, 1923

FORBES, COLIN. Pseudonym of Raymond H. Sawkins, 1923-   , q.v. Other pseudonyms: Jay Bernard, Richard Raine, qq.v.
The Heights of Zervos. Collins, 1970; Dutton, 1971
The Palermo Affair; see The Palermo Ambush
The Palermo Ambush. Collins, 1972. U.S. title: The Palermo Affair. Dutton, 1972

152/ Forbes, Colin

The Stone Leopard. Collins, 1975; Dutton, 1976
Target Five. Collins, 1973; Dutton, 1973
Year of the Golden Ape. Collins, 1974; Dutton, 1974

FORBES, D. R.
Murder of an Unpopular Man. Bles, 1941

FORBES, DANIEL. Pseudonym of Michael Kenyon, 1931- , q.v.

FORBES, DELORIS FLORINE STANTON. 1923- . Pseudonyms: Stanton Forbes, Tobias Wells, qq.v. Joint pseudonym with Helen B. Rydell: Forbes Rydell, q.v.

FORBES, DIANA (R.)
The Man Behind the Tinted Glasses. Holden, 1924
Whose the Hand? Holden, 1925

FORBES, DONALD
The Eleventh Hour. Hutchinson, 1955; Roy, 1955

FORBES, EDMUND
Red Fate. Greening, 1901

FORBES, HAY
A Detective in Italy; or, The Mystery of Berwyn Kennedy. Ward, 1891

FORBES, J. D.
Murder in Full View. Caravelle, 1968

FORBES, MURRAY
Hollow Triumph. Ziff-Davis, 1946; Martin, 1946

FORBES, ROBERT ERSTONE. Pseudonym of Ralph Straus, 1882- , q.v.
The Transactions of Oliver Prince. Chapman, 1924 ss

FORBES, (JOAN) ROSITA (TORR)
The Cavaliers of Death. Butterworth, 1930; Macaulay, 1930

FORBES, STANTON. Pseudonym of DeLoris Florine Stanton Forbes, 1923- . Other pseudonym: Tobias Wells, q.v. Joint pseudonym with Helen B. Rydell: Forbes Rydell, q.v.
All for One and One for Death. Doubleday, 1971; Hale, 1972
Bury Me in Gold Lame. Doubleday, 1974; Hale, 1975
A Business of Bodies. Doubleday, 1966; Hale, 1967
But I Wouldn't Want to Die There. Doubleday, 1972; Hale, 1973
A Deadly Kind of Lonely. Doubleday, 1971; Hale, 1973
Encounter Darkness. Doubleday, 1967; Hale, 1968
Go to Thy Death Bed. Doubleday, 1968; Hale, 1969
Grieve for the Past. Doubleday, 1963; Gollancz, 1964
If Laurel Shot Hardy the World Would End. Doubleday, 1970. British title: Murder Runs Riot. Hale, 1971
If Two of Them are Dead. Doubleday, 1968; Hale, 1968
The Long Hate; see The Terrors of the Earth
Melody of Terror; see The Terrors of the Earth
Murder Runs Riot; see If Laurel Shot Hardy the World Would End
The Name's Death, Remember Me? Doubleday, 1969; Hale, 1970
Relative to Death. Doubleday, 1965; Hale, 1966
The Sad, Sudden Death of My Fair Lady. Doubleday, 1971; Hale, 1971
She was Only the Sheriff's Daughter. Doubleday, 1970; Hale, 1970
Some Poisoned by Their Wives. Doubleday, 1974; Hale, 1975
Terror Touches Me. Doubleday, 1966; Hale, 1966
The Terrors of the Earth. Doubleday, 1964. British title: The Long Hate. Hale, 1966. Also published as: Melody of Terror. Pyramid, 1967
Welcome, My Dear, to Belfry House. Doubleday, 1973; Hale, 1974

FORBES, WILLIAM G. Series character: Ben Bradley, in at least those marked BB.
Ben Bradley's Puzzle. Street (Magnet), 190? BB
Ben Bradley's Weirdest Case. Street (Magnet), 190? BB
Fighting an Unknown Power. Street (Magnet), 190?
Fight to a Finish. Street (Magnet), 190?
From Despair to Triumph. Street (Magnet), 1906
Into the Jaws of Death. Street (Magnet), 190?

FORD, BRYANT
Show Business. Dodd, 1939

FORD, COREY. 1902-1969. Pseudonym: John Riddell, q.v.

FORD, ELBUR. Pseudonym of Eleanor Burford Hibbert, 1906- . Other pseudonyms: Philippa Carr, Victoria Holt, Kathleen Kellow, qq.v.
The Bed Disturbed. Laurie, 1952
Evil in the House; see Such Bitter Business
Flesh and the Devil. Laurie, 1950
Poison in Pimlico. Laurie, 1950
Such Bitter Business. Heinemann, 1953. U.S. title: Evil in the House. Morrow, 1954

FORD, FLORENCE
Fear is a Weapon. Hale, 1969
Laughter in the Night. Hale, 1964
The Ninth Candle. Collins, 1960
Play with Matches. Hale, 1966
Shadow on the House. Collins, 1958

FORD, HARRIET. See also: ARTHUR HORNBLOW, 1865- .
The Argyle Case, with Harvey J(errold) O'Higgins, 1876-1929, q.v. French, 1927. (Play.)

FORD, HILARY
Bella on the Roof. Longmans, 1965
Castle Malindine. Macmillan (London), 1975; Harper, 1975
-Felix Running. Eyre, 1959
-Felix Walking. Eyre, 1958
Sarnia. H. Hamilton, 1974; Doubleday, 1974

FORD, JEREMY
Murder Laughs Last. Bouregy, 1956; Ward, 1959

FORD, LESLIE. Pseudonym of Zenith Jones Brown, 1898- . Other pseudonym: David Frome, q.v. Series characters: Lt. Joseph Kelly = JK; Grace Latham = GL; Col. John Primrose = JP.
All for the Love of a Lady. Scribner, 1944. British title: Crack of Dawn. Collins, 1945 GL & JP
The Bahamas Murder Case. Scribner, 1952; Collins, 1952
Burn Forever. Farrar, 1935. British title: Mountain Madness. Hutchinson, 1935
By the Watchman's Clock. Farrar, 1932
The Capital Crime; see The Murder of the Fifth Columnist
The Clue of the Judas Tree. Farrar, 1933 JK
Crack of Dawn; see All for the Love of a Lady
Date with Death. Scribner, 1949. British title: Shot in the Dark. Collins, 1949
The Devil's Stronghold. Scribner, 1948; Collins, 1948 GL & JP
False to Any Man. Scribner, 1939. British title: Snow-White Murder. Collins, 1940 GL & JP
Footsteps on the Stairs; see The Sound of Footsteps
The Girl from the Mimosa Club. Scribner, 1957; Collins, 1957
Honolulu Murder Story; see Honolulu Story
Honolulu Murders; see Honolulu Story
Honolulu Story. Scribner, 1946. British title: Honolulu Murder Story. Collins, 1947. Also published as: Honolulu Murders. Popular Library, 1967 GL & JP
Ill Met by Moonlight. Farrar, 1937; Collins, 1937 GL & JP
Invitation to Murder. Scribner, 1954; Collins, 1955
The Lying Jade; see Washington Whispers Murder
Mountain Madness; see Burn Forever
Mr. Cromwell is Dead; see Reno Rendezvous
Murder Comes to Eden. Scribner, 1955; Collins, 1956
Murder Down South; see Murder with Southern Hospitality
Murder in Maryland. Farrar, 1932; Hutchinson, 1933 JK
Murder in the O.P.M. Scribner, 1942. British title: The Priority Murder. Collins, 1943 GL & JP
Murder is the Pay-Off. Scribner, 1951; Collins, 1951
The Murder of the Fifth Columnist. Scribner, 1941. British title: The Capital Crime. Collins, 1941 GL & JP
Murder with Southern Hospitality. Scribner, 1942. British title: Murder Down South. Collins, 1943
Old Lover's Ghost. Scribner, 1940 GL & JP
The Philadelphia Murder Story. Scribner, 1945; Collins, 1945 GL & JP
The Priority Murder; see Murder in the O.P.M.
Reno Rendezvous. Farrar, 1939. British title: Mr. Cromwell is Dead. Collins, 1939 GL & JP
Road to Folly. Scribner, 1940; Collins, 1941
Shot in the Dark; see Date with Death
The Simple Way of Poison. Farrar, 1937; Collins, 1938 GL & JP
Siren in the Night. Scribner, 1943; Collins, 1944 GL & JP
Snow-White Murder; see False to Any Man
The Sound of Footsteps. Doubleday, 1931. British title: Footsteps on the Stairs. Gollancz, 1931
The Strangled Witness. Farrar, 1934 JP
Three Bright Pebbles. Farrar, 1938; Collins, 1938 GL

The Town Cried Murder. Scribner, 1939;
    Collins, 1939
Trial by Ambush. Scribner, 1962. British title: Trial from Ambush. Collins, 1962
Trial from Ambush; see Trial by Ambush
Washington Whispers Murder. Scribner, 1953. British title: The Lying Jade. Collins, 1953   GL & JP
The Woman in Black. Scribner, 1947; Collins, 1948   GL & JP

FORD, MARY FORKER. 1905-   .
    The Dude Ranch Murders. Bouregy, 1965
    Long Journey Home. Bouregy, 1966
    Murder, Country Style. Bouregy, 1966
    The Rosewell Heritage. Bouregy, 1968
    Shadow of Murder. Bouregy, 1965
    The Silent Witness. Bouregy, 1964

FORD, PAUL LEICESTER. 1865-1902.
    The Great K & A Train Robbery. Dodd, 1897; Low, 1897

FORDE, DON
    Cocaine. Scion, 1950
    Death Rides the Speedway. Warren, 1949
    Highway to Hell. Scion, 1950

FORDE, NICHOLAS. Pseudonym of Arthur Elliott Elliott-Cannon, 1919-   .
    Urgent Action. Hale, 1974
    Urgent Delivery. Hale, 1975
    Urgent Enquiry. Hale, 1973

FORES, JOHN. 1914-   .
    The Abandoned Power. Hodder, 1970
    Candidates for Glory. Hodder, 1968
    The Desirable Dictator. Hodder, 1967
    The Forgotten Place. Hodder, 1956; Coward, 1956
    The Human Element; see No Mercy in the Sky
    New Man in Lowuni. Hodder, 1961
    No Mercy in the Sky. Hodder, 1957. U.S. title: The Human Element. Doubleday, 1958
    Overload of Hope. Hodder, 1966
    The Secret Island. Hodder, 1959
    The Springboard. Hodder, 1956
    Water for the Fire. Hodder, 1969

FOREST, ESME. See: MARVIN DANA, 1867-   .

FORESTER, C(ECIL) S(COTT). 1899-1966.
    Payment Deferred. Lane, 1926; Little, 1942
    Plain Murder. Lane, 1930; Dell, 1954

FORFEX ET HESTA. Pseudonym of Bessie C. Morris and Anne B. Spear.
    The Lost Key; or, The Mysterious Box. Grant, 1879

FORGIONE, LOUIS
    The Men of Silence. Dutton, 1928; Dent, 1929

FORMA, WARREN. 1923-   .
    The Falling Man. Crowell, 1973

FORMAN, HENRY JAMES. 1879-   .
    Guilt. Boni & Liveright, 1924
    The Rembrandt Murder. Smith, 1931; Paul, 1931

FORMAN, JUSTUS MILES. 1875-1915.
    The Six Rubies. Ward, 1914

FORREST, A(LFRED) E(DGAR). 1863-   .
    Silent Guests. Covici Friede, 1927

FORREST, DAVID. Pseudonym of Robert Forrest-Webb, 1929-   . Other pseudonym: Forrest Webb, q.v.
    The Great Dinosaur Robbery. Hodder, 1970. U.S. title: One of Our Dinosaurs is Missing. Avon, 1975

FORREST, GEORGE F.
    Misfits. Harvey, 1905   ss, some criminous

FORREST, NORMAN. Pseudonym of Nigel Morland, 1905-   , q.v. Other pseudonyms: Mary Dane, John Donavan, Roger Garnett, Vincent McCall, Neal Shepherd, qq.v. Series character: John Finnegan, in both titles.
    Death Took a Greek God. Harrap, 1937; Hillman-Curl, 1938
    Death Took a Publisher. Harrap, 1936; Hillman-Curl, 1938

FORREST, RICHARD (STOCKTON). 1932-   .
    A Child's Garden of Death. Bobbs, 1975
    Who Killed Mr. Garland's Mistress? Pinnacle, 1974

FORREST, WILLIAMS
    -The Great Debauch. GM, 1958
    The Huntress. GM, 1964
    -Seed of Violence. Crest, 1957
    -Stigma for Valor. Crest, 1958
    -The Woman with Claws. GM, 1956

FORREST, WILMA
    Anne of Destiny House. GM, 1973
    Last Hope House. GM, 1968
    Shadow Mansion. GM, 1969

FORREST-WEBB, ROBERT. 1929-   . Pseudonyms: David Forrest, Forrest Webb, qq.v.

FORRESTER, ANDREW, JR.
    The Female Detective. Ward, 1864   ss
    The Private Detective. Ward, 1868   ss
    Revelations of a Detective; see The Revelations of a Private Detective
    The Revelations of a Private Detective. Ward, 1863. Also published as: Revelations of a Detective. Ward, 1868   ss
    Secret Service; or, Recollections of a City Detective. Ward, 1864   ss
    Tales by a Female Detective. Ward, 1868   ss

FORRESTER, IZOLA L(OUISE). 1878-   .
    The Dangerous Inheritance; or, The Mystery of the Tittani Rubies. Houghton, 1920
    The Secret of the Blue Macaw. Macrae, 1936

FORRESTER, LARRY. 1924-   .
    -Battle of the April Storm. Harrap, 1969; Day, 1970
    Diamond Beach. Harrap, 1973; McKay, 1974
    A Girl Called Fathom. Heinemann, 1967; GM, 1967

FORSTER, JOSEPH
    -Studies in Black and Red. Ward, 1896   ss

FORSYTE, CHARLES. Series character: Detective Inspector Richard Left, in at least those marked RL.
    Diplomatic Death. Cassell, 1961; Morrow, 1961   RL
    Dive into Danger; see Diving Death
    Diving Death. Cassell, 1962. U.S. title: Dive into Danger. Morrow, 1962   RL
    Double Death. Cassell, 1965   RL
    Murder with Minarets. Cassell, 1968

FORSYTH, FREDERICK. 1938-   .
    The Day of the Jackal. Hutchinson, 1971; Viking, 1971
    -The Dogs of War. Hutchinson, 1974; Viking, 1974
    The Odessa File. Hutchinson, 1972; Viking, 1972

FORSYTH, PHIL
    The Man Who Feared. Jarrolds, 1927

FORSYTHE, ROBIN. 1879-   . Pseudonym: Peter Dingwall, q.v. Series character: Anthony Vereker, in at least those marked AV.
    The Ginger Cat Mystery. Lane, 1935. U.S. title: Murder at Marston Manor. Appleton, 1935   AV
    The Hounds of Justice. Lane, 1930
    Missing or Murdered. Lane, 1929   AV
    Murder at Marston Manor; see The Ginger Cat Mystery
    Murder on Paradise Island. World's Work, 1937
    The Pleasure Cruise Mystery. Lane, 1933; Appleton, 1934   AV
    The Polo Ground Mystery. Lane, 1932   AV
    The Spirit Murder Mystery. Lane, 1936   AV

FORTUNE, MRS. Pseudonym: W. W., q.v.

FORTUNE, DION. Pseudonym of Violet Mary Firth, 1890-1946.
    The Secrets of Dr. Taverner. Douglas, 1926; Llewellyn, 1962

FOSBURGH, HUGH. 1916-1976.
    -The Drowning Stone. Morrow, 1958; Cape, 1959

FOSS, JOHN. Pseudonym of James Gordon, 1912-   .
    Flesh and Blood. Dobson, 1951
    Plush and Guilt. Dobson, 1953

FOSTER, CHARLES FREEMAN. 1830-   . Pseudonym: Hatherly Sealis, q.v.

FOSTER, DAVID SKAATS. 1852-1920.
    -The Road to London. Franklin, 1914

FOSTER, DIRK
    Blonde Bombshell. Gaywood, 1952
    Don't Scare Me, Sister. Gaywood, 1952
    Lady, Shed Your Head. Gaywood, 1952
    Some Dames Die Young. Gaywood, 1952
    Tough for You, Hazel. Gaywood, 1952

FOSTER, GEORGE C(ECIL). 1893-   . Pseudonym: Seaforth, q.v.
    Cracksmen All. Jenkins, 1943
    -Crocodile Down the River. Jenkins, 1942
    -Green Lipstick. Jenkins, 1940
    Poindexter Crashes the Fifth Column. Jenkins, 1941
    -Say It with Flowers. Jenkins, 1939

FOSTER, GLADYS S.
    Two Tickets to Destruction. Exposition, 1975

FOSTER, IRIS. Pseudonym of Richard Posner, 1944-   , q.v. Other pseudonyms: Beatrice Murray, Paul Todd, qq.v.
    The Crimson Moon. Lancer, 1973
    Deadly Sea, Deadly Sand. Lancer, 1972
    The Moorwood Legacy. Lancer, 1972
    Nightshade. Lancer, 1973
    The Sabath Quest. Lancer, 1973

FOSTER, JAN
    Echo My Tears. Dial, 1948; Muller, 1952

FOSTER, JOHN. 1867-   .
    The Searchers. Hodder, 1919; Doran, 1920

FOSTER, JOHN
    Dark Heritage. GM, 1955; Red Seal, 1959

FOSTER, MAXIMILIAN. 1872-1956.
 -Bubbles. Lippincott, 1929
 -Corrie Who? Small Maynard, 1908
  Crooked. Lippincott, 1928
  Humdrum House. Appleton, 1924
 -I Want to be a Lady. Lippincott, 1926
 -Rich Man, Poor Man. Appleton, 1916
  The Trap. Appleton, 1920
  The Whistling Man. Appleton, 1913

FOSTER, R(EGINALD) FRANCIS. 1896-   .
  Series character: Anthony Ravenhill, in at least those marked AR.
  Anthony Ravenhill, Crime Merchant. Jarrolds, 1926 AR
  The Body in the Shaft; see The Lift Murder
  The Chillery Court Mystery; see Something Wrong at Chillery
  Confession. Nash, 1927
  The Dark Night. Nash, 1930
  The Lift Murder. Jarrolds, 1924. U.S. title: The Body in the Shaft. Siebel, 1925 AR
  The Missing Gates. Jarrolds, 1924; Siebel, 1926 AR
  The Moat House Mystery. Nash, 1928; Macaulay, 1930 AR
  Murder from Beyond. Nash, 1930; Macaulay, 1931 AR
  The Music Gallery Murder. Unwin, 1927 AR
  The Mystery at Chillery; see Something Wrong at Chillery
  The Secret of the White Thug. Amalgamated Press, 1929. (Sexton Blake)
  Something Wrong at Chillery. Nash, 1931. U.S. title: The Mystery at Chillery. Fiction League, 1931. Also published as: The Chillery Court Mystery. Mellifont, 1936 AR

FOSTER, RICHARD. Pseudonym of Kendell Foster Crossen, 1910-   , q.v. Other pseudonyms: Bennett Barlay, M. E. Chaber, Christopher Monig, Clay Richards, qq.v. Series characters: Chin Kwang Kham = CK; Pete Draco, in at least those marked PD.
  Bier for a Chaser. GM, 1959; Muller pb, 1960 PD
  Blonde and Beautiful. Popular Library, 1955
  The Girl from Easy Street. Popular Library, 1952
  The Invisible Man Murders. Five Star, 1945 CK
  The Laughing Buddha Murders. Vulcan, 1944 CK
  The Rest Must Die. GM, 1959; Muller pb, 1960
  Too Late for Mourning. GM, 1960; Muller pb, 1961 PD

FOSTER, ROBERT FREDERICK. 1853-1948.
  Cab No. 44. Stokes, 1910

FOSTER, W(ALTER) BERT(RAM). 1869-1929.
  From Six to Six. Clode, 1927

FOUCAR, EMILE CHARLES VICTOR. 1894-   .
  Pseudonym: Ray Carr, q.v.

FOURNIER, PIERRE. 1916-   . Pseudonym: Pierre Gascar, q.v.

FOUTS, EDWARD LEE. 1902-   . Pseudonym: Edward Lee, q.v.

FOWLER, KEITH
  All the Skeletons in All the Closets. Macaulay, 1934. British title: Skeletons in the Cupboard. Jarrolds, 1935

FOWLER, MARIE LOUISE
  The Toll. Field, 1938

FOWLER, SYDNEY. Pseudonym of Sydney Fowler Wright, 1874-   . U.S. byline: S. Fowler Wright. Series characters: Prof. Blinkwell, in at least those marked B; Insp. Cauldron, in at least those marked IC; Insp. Cleveland, in at least those marked C; Mr. Jellipot, in at least those marked J.
  The Adventure of the Blue Room. Rich, 1945
  Arresting Delia. Jarrolds, 1933; Macaulay, 1933 C
  The Attic Murder. Butterworth, 1936 J
  The Bell Street Murders. Harrap, 1931; Macaulay, 1931 J & B
  A Bout with the Mildew Gang. Eyre, 1941 IC
  By Saturday. Lane, 1931 C
  The Case of Anne Bickerton; see The King Against Anne Bickerton
  Crime and Co.; see The Handprint Mystery
  Dinner in New York. Eyre, 1943 J
  The End of the Mildew Gang. Eyre, 1944 IC
  Four Callers in Razor Street. Jenkins, 1937 J
  The Hand-Print Mystery. Jarrolds, 1932. U.S. title: Crime and Co. Macaulay, 1931 C
  The Hanging of Constance Hillier. Jarrolds, 1931; Macaulay, 1932 C
  The Jordans Murder. Jenkins, 1938; Hillman-Curl, 1939 J
  The King Against Anne Bickerton. Harrap, 1930. U.S. title: The Case of Anne Bickerton. Boni & Liveright, 1930. Also published as: Rex v. Anne Bickerton. Penguin, 1947
  The Murder in Bethnal Square. Jenkins, 1938 J
  Post-Mortem Evidence. Butterworth, 1936 J
  The Rissole Mystery. Rich, 1941
  Second Bout with the Mildew Gang. Eyre, 1942 IC
  The Secret of the Screen. Jarrolds, 1933 B
  Three Witnesses. Butterworth, 1935
  Too Much for Mr. Jellipot. Eyre, 1945 J
  Was Murder Done? Butterworth, 1936
  Who Else But She? Jarrolds, 1934
  Who Murdered Reynard? Jarrolds, 1947 B
  The Wills of Jane Kanwhistle. Jenkins, 1939
  With Cause Enough? Harvill, 1954 J

FOWLES, ANTHONY
  Double Feature. Allen, 1972; Simon, 1973
  Dupe Negative. Allen, 1970; Simon, 1972
  Pastime. Allen, 1974

FOWLES, JOHN. 1926-   .
  The Collector. Cape, 1963; Little, 1963

FOX, CLAYTON
  End of a Big Wheel. Ace, 1962
  Never Forget, Never Forgive. Ace, 1961

FOX, DAVID. Pseudonym of Isabel (Egenton) Ostrander, 1883-1924, q.v. Other pseudonyms: Robert Orr Chipperfield, Douglas Grant, qq.v. See also: WILLIAM J. BURNS, 1861-1932. Series characters: The Shadowers, Inc., in all titles. Note that in England these titles were published as by Robert Orr Chipperfield.
  The Doom Dealer. McBride, 1923; Hurst, 1925
  Ethel Opens the Door. McBride, 1922; Hurst, 1924
  The Handwriting on the Wall. McBride, 1924; Hurst, 1925
  The Man Who Convicted Himself. McBride, 1920; Hurst, 1923

FOX, GARDNER F(RANCIS). 1911-   .
  One Wife's Ways. GM, 1963; Muller pb, 1963
  Terror Over London. GM, 1957
  Witness this Woman. GM, 1959; Muller pb, 1961

FOX, GEORGE (RICHARD). 1934-   .
  Without Music. Holt, 1971

FOX, GEORGE R.
  The Fangs of the Serpent. Minton Balch, 1924

FOX, JAMES M. Pseudonym of James M. W. Knipscheer. Series characters: John & Suzy Marshall, in at least those marked M.
  The Aleutian Blue Mink. Little, 1951; Home and Van Thal, 1952. Also published as: Fatal in Furs. Dell, 1952 M
  Bright Serpent. Little, 1953; Hammond, 1956. Also published as: Rites for a Killer. Jonathan, 1957 M
  Cell Car 54; see Free Ride
  Cheese from a Mousetrap. Davies, 1944
  Code Three. Little, 1953; Hammond, 1956
  Dark Crusade. Little, 1954; Cassell, 1955, as by Grant Holmes
  Dead Pigeon. Hammond, 1967
  Death Commits Bigamy. Coward, 1948; Home & Van Thal, 1950 M
  Don't Try Anything Funny. Davies, 1943
  The Exiles. Weybright, 1970; Cassell, 1970
  Fatal in Furs; see The Aleutian Blue Mink
  Free Ride. Popular Library, 1957; Cassell, 1957. Also published as: Cell Car 54. Manor, 1977
  The Gentle Hangman. Little, 1950; Home & Van Thal, 1951 M
  Hell on the Way. Davies, 1943
  The Inconvenient Bride. Coward, 1948; Home & Van Thal, 1951 M
  The Iron Virgin. Little, 1951; Hammond, 1954 M
  Journey into Danger. Cherry Tree, 1943
  The Lady Regrets. Coward, 1947; Davies, 1947 M
  Operation Dancing Dog. Walker, 1974
  Rites for a Killer; see Bright Serpent
  Save Them for Violence. Monarch, 1959
  The Scarlet Slippers. Little, 1952; Hammond, 1955 M
  A Shroud for Mr. Bundy. Little, 1952; Hammond, 1955 M
  The Wheel is Fixed. Little, 1951; Home & Van Thal, 1952 M

FOX, LESLIE H.
  Design for Murder, and five other stories. Alliance (London), 1945 ss
 -The Heel of Achilles. Pan, 1961 ss
 -Twisted Tales. Alliance (London), 1946 ss
 -The Vampire, and sixteen other stories. Alliance (London), 1945 ss

FOX, MARION
  The Mystery Keepers. Lane (London & New York), 1919

FOX, RUTH. Joint pseudonym with Anne Fahrenkopf: Alexander Irving, q.v.

FOX, SEBASTIAN. Pseudonym of Gerald (William) Bullett, 1894-1958, q.v. See also: J(OHN) B(OYNTON) PRIESTLEY,

1894-   . Series character: George
  Lydney, in both titles.
Odd Woman Out. Dent, 1958
One Man's Poison. Chatto, 1956

FOX-DAVIES, A(RTHUR) C(HARLES). 1871-
  1928.
The Average Man. Routledge, 1907
The Dangerville Inheritance. Lane
  (London & New York), 1907
The Duplicate Death. Long, 1910;
  Macaulay, 1910
The Finances of Sir John Kynnersley.
  Lane (London & New York), 1908 ss
The Mauleverer Murders. Lane (London
  & New York), 1907
The Testament of John Hastings. Long,
  1911
The Troubles of Colonel Marwood. White,
  1909
The Ultimate Conclusion. Long, 1912

FOXALL, ARTHUR J.
-The Singing Soul. Christopher, 1932

FOXALL, P(ETER) A(UGUSTUS)
The Big-Timer. Hale, 1973
Confessions of a Convict. Hale, 1974
Dynasty of Doom. Hale, 1972; Drake,
  1972
Scamp's Law. Hale, 1975
Vultures in the Smoke. Hale, 1972

FOXALL, RAYMOND (JEHOIADA CAMPBELL).
  1916-   . Series character: Harry
  Adkins, in some of these titles.
Brandy for the Parson. Hale, 1970; St.
  Martin's, 1974
The Dark Forest. Hale, 1972; St. Mar-
  tin's, 1974
-The Devil's Smile. Hale, 1960
-The Devil's Spawn. Hale, 1965
-Here Lies the Shadow. Hale, 1957
The Little Ferret. Hale, 1968; St.
  Martin's, 1974
The Silver Goblet. Hale, 1974; St.
  Martin's, 1974
-Song for a Prince. Hale, 1959
-Squire Errant. Hale, 1968
-The Wicked Lord. Hale, 1962

FOXE, ALISON
Heirs to Kildrennan. Melrose, 1951
Winged Danger. Melrose, 1952

FOXX, JACK. Pseudonym of Bill Pronzini,
  1943-   , q.v. Other pseudonym:
  Alex Saxon, q.v. Series character:
  Jim Connell, in both titles.
Dead Run. Bobbs, 1975
The Jade Figurine. Bobbs, 1972

FOY, KENNETH RUSSELL. 1922-   . Pseudonym: Keith Franklin, q.v.

FRANCES, STEPHEN D(ANIEL). Series char-
  acter: John Gail, in at least those
  marked JG.
The Ambassador's Plot; see The Sad and
  Tender Flesh
Bad Boy. Consul, 1964
The Caress of Conquest. Mayflower,
  1968, Award, 1970 JG
Cry for My Lovely. Mayflower, 1971
A Grave for Coyotes. Consul, 1965
Hate is for the Hunted. Mayflower,
  1968; Award, 1970 JG
The Illusionist. Mayflower, 1970
The Sad and Tender Flesh. Mayflower,
  1966. U.S. title: The Ambassador's
  Plot. Award, 1970 JG
The Sweet Shame of Fury. Mayflower,
  1968
This Woman is Death. Mayflower, 1965;
  Award, 1969 JG
To Love and Yet to Die. Mayflower,
  1966; Award, 1970 JG

FRANCILLON, R(OBERT) E(DWARD). 1841-1919.
  Romances of the Law. Chatto, 1889;
  Gebbie, 1889. (12 ss, including 2
  from Romantic Stories of the Legal
  Profession, q.v.)
Romantic Stories of the Legal Profes-
  sion. Low, 1883 7 ss

FRANCIS, BASIL. 1906-   . Series char-
  acter: Detective Sergeant Paul Dean,
  in at least those marked PD.
Death at the Bank. Constable, 1938 PD
Death for Safe Custody. Quality, 1944
  PD
Death in Act IV. Jenkins, 1954
Death on the Atoll. Quality, 1948
Death on the Roof. Quality, 1946 PD
The Holiday Camp Murder. Constable,
  1939 PD
Slender Margin. Constable, 1938 PD

FRANCIS, C. D. E. Pseudonym of Patrick
  John Fielding Howarth, 1916-   ,
  q.v.
Portrait of a Killer. Hammond, 1956

FRANCIS, CAROLINE
Directors' Corridor. Hutchinson, 1936
It Couldn't be Suicide. Hutchinson,
  1936

FRANCIS, DICK [RICHARD STANLEY FRANCIS].
  1920-
Blood Sport. Joseph, 1967; Harper, 1968
Bonecrack. Joseph, 1971; Harper, 1972
Dead Cert. Joseph, 1962; Holt, 1962
Enquiry. Joseph, 1969; Harper, 1970
Flying Finish. Joseph, 1966; Harper,
  1967
For Kicks. Joseph, 1965; Harper, 1965
Forfeit. Joseph, 1969; Harper, 1969
High Stakes. Joseph, 1975; Harper, 1976
Knock Down. Joseph, 1974; Harper, 1975
Nerve. Joseph, 1964; Harper, 1964
Odds Against. Joseph, 1965; Harper,
  1966
Rat Race. Joseph, 1970; Harper, 1971
Slay-Ride. Joseph, 1973; Harper, 1974
Smokescreen. Joseph, 1972; Harper, 1973

FRANCIS, WILLIAM. Pseudonym of William
  Francis Urell. Series character:
  Anthony Martin, in at least those
  marked AM.
Bury Me Not. Morrow, 1943; Boardman,
  1950 AM
The Corruptors. Lion, 1953
Don't Dig Deeper. Lion, 1953
I.O.U.—Murder. Signet, 1951
Kill or Cure. Morrow, 1942; Boardman,
  1951
Rough on Rats. Morrow, 1942 AM

FRANK, E. Z.
-Counter Plot. Fiction House, 1948
-Dead City Round Up. Fiction House, 1949
-Six-Gun Judgment. Fiction House, 1949

FRANK, LEONHARD. 1882-1961.
The Cause of the Crime. Davies, 1928.
  (Translation of Die Ursache. Leipzig,
  1929.)

FRANK, PAT (HARRY HART). 1907-1964.
An Affair of State. Lippincott, 1948;
  Dymock, 1951
Forbidden Area. Lippincott, 1956. Bri-
  tish title: Seven Days to Never.
  Constable, 1957
Seven Days to Never; see Forbidden Area

FRANK, THEODORE. Pseudonym of D(orothea)
  F(rances) Gardiner, 1879-   , q.v.
The Lifted Latch. Butterworth, 1929

FRANK, WALDO (DAVID). 1889-   .
Chalk Face. Boni, 1924

FRANKAU, GILBERT. 1884-1952.
Air Ministry, Room 28; see Winter of
  Discontent
Concerning Peter Jackson and others.
  Hutchinson, 1931 ss, some criminous
Experiments in Crime. Hutchinson, 1937;
  Dutton, 1937 ss
The Lonely Man. Hutchinson, 1932; Dut-
  ton, 1933
Secret Services. Hutchinson, 1934 ss
Winter of Discontent. Hutchinson, 1941.
  U.S. title: Air Ministry, Room 28.
  Dutton, 1942

FRANKAU, JULIA. 1864-1916. Pseudonym:
  Frank Danby, q.v.

FRANKAU, PAMELA. 1908-1967.
Appointment with Death; see A Democrat
  Dies
Colonel Blessington. Bodley Head, 1968;
  Delacorte, 1969. (Completed by Diana
  Raymond.)
A Democrat Dies. Heinemann, 1939. U.S.
  title: Appointment with Death. Dut-
  ton, 1940

FRANKISH, H.
Dr. Cunliffe—Investigator. Heath, 1913
  ss

FRANKLAND, EDWARD PERCY. 1884-   .
-The Half Brothers. Macdonald, 1947
-The Invaders. Redman, 1958
The Murders at Crossby. Dent, 1955
Mystery at Grimsdale. Low, 1929
-The Nymph at Bay. Low, 1930
The Swarthmoor Tragedy. Stockwell, 1922

FRANKLIN, CHARLES. Pseudonym of Frank
  (Hugh) Usher, 1909-   , q.v. Other
  pseudonym: Frank Lester, q.v. Series
  characters: Inspector Burgess, in at
  least those marked B; Maxine Danger-
  field, in at least those marked MD;
  Grant Garfield, in at least those
  marked GG.
The Bath of Acid. Hale, 1962 B
Breathe No More. Hale, 1959 GG
Cocktails with a Stranger. Collins,
  1947
The Dangerous Ones. Hale, 1964 MD
Darling Murderess. Hale, 1957
Death in the East. Hale, 1967 MD
Death on My Shoulder. Hale, 1958 GG
Died in the Grass. Hale, 1971
The Escape. Hale, 1968
Escape to Death. Collins, 1951 GG
Exit Without Permit. Collins, 1946
Face the Music. Hale, 1957
Fear Runs Softly. Hale, 1961 GG
The Fortieth Victim. Hale, 1963
Gallows for a Fool. Collins, 1952 GG
Girl in Shadow. Collins, 1955
Guilt for Innocence. Hale, 1959 B
Guilty You Must Be. Hale, 1959 GG
A Handful of Sinners. Hale, 1960 GG
The Home Secretary Affair. Hale, 1971
The KGB is Here. Hale, 1972
Kill Me and Live. Hale, 1961 B
Maid for Murder. Collins, 1951
The Mark of Kane. Collins, 1949 GG
Murder Before Dinner. Hale, 1963
The Murder Column. Hale, 1970
Murder on My Hands. Hale, 1973
No Other Victim. Collins, 1952
On the Day of the Shooting. Hale, 1965
  MD
One Night to Kill. Collins, 1950

Out of Time. Collins, 1956
Perchance to Kill. Collins, 1954
Play with Death. Collins, 1953
Rope of Sand. Collins, 1948
She'll Love You Dead. Collins, 1950
Stop That Man. Collins, 1954
Storm in an Inkpot. Collins, 1949 GG
The Stranger Came Back. Collins, 1953
The Third Degree. Hale, 1970
The Trembling Thread. Collins, 1955

FRANKLIN, DONALD
Lethal Playground. New English Library pb, 1975
Stray Bullet. New English Library pb, 1975
Two-Way Witness. New English Library pb, 1974
The Velvet Hammer. New English Library pb, 1974

FRANKLIN, EDGAR. Pseudonym of Edgar Franklin Stearns, 1879- .
In and Out. Watt, 1917

FRANKLIN, EUGENE. Pseudonym of Eugene Franklin Bandy, Jr., 1914- . Series characters: Berkeley Barnes and Larry Howe, in all titles.
The Bold House Murders. Stein, 1973; Hale, 1975
The Money Murders. Stein, 1972
Murder Trapp. Stein, 1971

FRANKLIN, GORDON
Smouldering Fire. Heath, 1923

FRANKLIN, HARRY
Crash. Hale, 1968
Don't Go to Ceuta. Chapman, 1970

FRANKLIN, JUNE. 1924- .
The Sugar Man's Dead. Hale, 1972

FRANKLIN, KEITH. Pseudonym of Kenneth Russell Foy, 1922- .
Murder at Shirttail Flats. GM, 1968

FRANKLIN, MAX. Pseudonym of Richard Deming, 1915- , q.v. Other pseudonym: Emily Moor, q.v. See also: NICK MARINO.
The Destructors. Ballantine, 1974. (Novelization of the movie.)
The 5th of November. Ballantine, 1975. British title: Hennessy. Futura, 1975. (Novelization of the movie.)
Hell Street. Rinehart, 1954
Hennessy; see The 5th of November
Justice Has No Sword. Rinehart, 1953; Boardman, 1954. Also published as: Murder Muscles In. Bestseller, 1956
Murder Muscles In; see Justice Has No Sword
99 44/100 % Dead. Award, 1974; Tandem, 1974. (Novelization of the movie.)

FRANKLIN, STEVE. Pseudonym of Franklin Stevens, 1933- .
The Chickens in the Airshaft. Doubleday, 1972
The Malcontents. Doubleday, 1970

FRASER, ALEX. Pseudonym of Henry Brinton, 1901- , q.v. Series character: Inspector Noel Tracy, in at least those marked NT.
Bury Their Dead. Bles, 1959; Roy, 1960 NT
Constables Don't Count. Bles, 1957; Roy, 1960 NT
The Dark Places. Bles, 1960
Death is so Final. Bles, 1958; Roy, 1962
High Tension. Bles, 1959 NT
The Three Wives. Bles, 1957; Roy, 1958

FRASER, ANTHEA (MARY). 1930- .
Home Through the Dark. Milton House, 1974; Dodd, 1976
Laura Possessed. Milton House, 1974; Dodd, 1974
Whistler's Lane. Milton House, 1975; Dodd, 1975

FRASER, COLIN. See: PHILIP RIDGEWAY.

FRASER, ELISE (PARKER). 1903- .
The Emerald Necklace. Van Kampen, 1950
The Jade Elephant. Van Kampen, 1952

FRASER, FERRIN L.
The Screaming Portrait. Sears, 1928

FRASER, HERMIA
One Touch of Murder. Arcadia, 1953

FRASER, J. MALCOLM. See: B(ERTRAM) FLETCHER ROBINSON.

FRASER, JAMES. Pseudonym of Alan White, 1924- , q.v. Other pseudonym: Alec Whitney, q.v. Series character: Insp. William Aveyard, in all titles.
Blood on a Window's Cross. Barrie, 1972
A Cock-Pit of Roses. Jenkins, 1969; Harcourt, 1970
Deadly Nightshade. Jenkins, 1970; Harcourt, 1970
Death in a Pheasant's Eye. Barrie, 1971; Walker, 1972
The Evergreen Death. Jenkins, 1968; Harcourt, 1969
The Five-Leafed Clover. Barrie, 1973
A Wreath of Lords and Ladies. Barrie, 1974; Doubleday, 1975

FRASER, JEAN
The Deadly Nightshade. Hale, 1973
Death on the Piazza. Hale, 1973
The Lone Vendetta. Hale, 1972

FRASER, JOHN
Death the Showman. Unwin, 1901

FRASER, JOHN. 1931- .
Clap Hands if You Believe in Fairies. Collins, 1969. U.S. title: The Babysitter. Putnam, 1969

FRASER, JOHN ARTHUR. Pseudonym: Hawkshaw, q.v.
The Cronin Mystery. Eagle, 1889

FRASER, ROBERT
The Fire Opal. Clode, 1911
Three Men and a Maid. Clode, 1907

FRASER, RON(ALD LESLIE)
The After-Dark. Ward, 1961

FRASER, STUART
The Night in George Square. Long, 1960

FRASER, T. A.
The Eye of Jinas and other stories. Fraser Asher, 1923 ss

FRASER, W. J.
-A Living Skeleton. Neely, 1899

FRASER-SIMSON, C(ICELY DEVENISH)
Count the Hours. Hutchinson, 1940
Danger Follows. Heinemann, 1929
Footsteps in the Night. Methuen, 1926; Dutton, 1927
The Swinging Shutter. Heinemann, 1927; Dutton, 1928

FRAY, AL. Pseudonym of Ralph Salaway.
And Kill Once More. Graphic, 1955
Built for Trouble. Dell, 1958; Hale, 1960
Come Back for More. Dell, 1958; Hale, 1960

The Dame's the Game. Popular Library, 1960
The Dice Spelled Murder. Dell, 1957

FRAYN, MICHAEL. 1933- .
The Russian Interpreter. Collins, 1966; Viking, 1966

FRAZEE, (CHARLES) STEVE. 1909- .
Flight 409. Avon, 1969
Running Target. GM, 1957; Fawcett (London), 1958
The Sky Block. Rinehart, 1953; Bodley Head, 1955

FRAZER, ANDREW. Pseudonym of Milton Lesser, 1928- . Other pseudonyms: Stephen Marlowe, Jason Ridgway, C. H. Thames, qq.v. See also: RICHARD S(COTT) PRATHER, 1921- . Series character: Duncan Pride, in both titles.
The Fall of Marty Moon. Avon, 1960
Find Eileen Hardin—Alive! Avon, 1959

FRAZER, MARTIN. Pseudonym of Percy A. Clarke. Series character (with many other authors): Sexton Blake, in all Amalgamated Press titles.
Acquitted! Wright, 1937
The Case of the Dope Dealers. Amalgamated, 1952
The Case of the Shot Looter. Amalgamated, 1941
The Crime at Crown Inn. Amalgamated, 1936
The Crook Ship. Wright, 1940
Dangerous Waters. Wright, 1951
The Fainting Lady. Wright, 1938
The Fatal V Sign. Amalgamated, 1942
The Four Jealous Men. Wright, 1938
The Mystery of the German Prisoner. Amalgamated, 1940
The Mystery of the Shadowed Footballer. Amalgamated, 1948
The Riddle of Dead Man's Mine. Amalgamated, 1937
Secret in Seven Fathoms. Wright, 1946
The Star in the Forest. Wright, 1940

FRAZER, ROBERT CAINE. Pseudonym of John Creasey, 1908-1973, q.v. Other pseudonyms: Gordon Ashe, M. E. Cooke, Norman Deane, Patrick Gill, Michael Halliday, Charles Hogarth, Brian Hope, Colin Hughes, Kyle Hunt, Abel Mann, Peter Manton, J. J. Marric, Richard Martin, Rodney Mattheson, Anthony Morton, Jeremy York, qq.v. Series character: Mark Kilby, in all titles.
The Hollywood Hoax. PB, 1961; Collins, 1964
Mark Kilby and the Manhattan Murders; see Mark Kilby Stands Alone
Mark Kilby and the Miami Mob. PB, 1960. British title: The Miami Mob, in the double-volume: The Miami Mob and Mark Kilby Stands Alone. Collins, 1965
Mark Kilby and the Secret Syndicate. PB, 1960. British title: The Secret Syndicate. Collins, 1963
Mark Kilby Solves a Murder. PB, 1959. British title: R.I.S.C. Collins, 1962. Also published as: The Timid Tycoon. Fontana, 1965
Mark Kilby Stands Alone. PB, 1962. British edition included in the double-volume: The Miami Mob and Mark Kilby Stands Alone. Collins, 1965. Also published as: Mark Kilby and the Manhattan Murders. Fontana, 1966
Mark Kilby Takes a Risk. PB, 1962
The Miami Mob and Mark Kilby Stands

Alone; see Mark Kilby and the Miami Mob, and Mark Kilby Stands Alone
R.I.S.C.; see Mark Kilby Solves a Murder
The Secret Syndicate; see Mark Kilby and the Secret Syndicate
The Timid Tycoon; see Mark Kilby Solves a Murder

FREDE, RICHARD. Pseudonym of Macdowell Frederics, 1934-   , q.v.
Coming-Out Party. Random, 1969

FREDERICKS, ARNOLD. Pseudonym of Frederick Arnold Kummer, 1873-1943, q.v. Series character: Richard Duvall = RD.
The Blue Lights. Watt, 1915; Simpkin, 1917   RD
The Film of Fear. Watt, 1917; Hayes, 1921   RD
The Ivory Snuff Box. Watt, 1912; Simpkin, 1916   RD
The Little Fortune. Watt, 1915; Simpkin, 1917   RD
The Mark of the Rat. Sears, 1929; Paul, 1930
One Million Francs. Watt, 1912; Nash, 1920   RD
The Spanish Lady. Sears, 1933

FREDERICKS, ERNEST JASON
Cry Flood! Ace, 1959. British title: Murder Matrix. Ward, 1960
Lost Friday; see Shakedown Hotel
Murder Matrix; see Cry Flood!
Shakedown Hotel. Ace, 1958. British title: Lost Friday. Hale, 1959

FREDERICS, JOCKO
Everybody's Ready to Die. Holt, 1966. British title: Ready to Die. Hale, 1968

FREDERICS, MACDOWELL. 1934-   . Pseudonym: Richard Frede, q.v.
Emergency Procedure. Coward, 1970; Hale, 1971

FREDMAN, (HENRY) JOHN. 1927-   . Series character: Charles Dexter, in all titles.
Epitaph to a Bad Cop. Hale, 1973; McKay, 1973
The False Joanna. Hutchinson, 1970; Bobbs, 1971
The Fourth Agency. Hutchinson, 1969; Bobbs, 1970

FREDRICS, GEORGE
Operation Nightmare. Powell, 1969. (Two novelets.)

FREED, DONALD
The Killing of R.F.K. Dell, 1975

FREEDGOOD, MORTON. Pseudonym: John Godey, q.v.

FREELING, NICOLAS. 1927-   . Pseudonym: F. R. E. Nicolas, q.v. Series characters: Henri Castang = HC; Inspector Van Der Valk = V.
Aupres de ma Blonde; see A Long Silence
Because of the Cats. Gollancz, 1963; Harper, 1964   V
The Bugles Blowing; see What are the Bugles Blowing For?
Criminal Conversation. Gollancz, 1965; Harper, 1966   V
Death in Amsterdam; see Love in Amsterdam
Double Barrel. Gollancz, 1964; Harper, 1965   V
The Dresden Green. Gollancz, 1966; Harper, 1967
A Dressing of Diamond. H. Hamilton, 1974; Harper, 1974   HC
Gun Before Butter. Gollancz, 1963. U.S. title: Question of Loyalty. Harper, 1964   V
The King of the Rainy Country. Gollancz, 1966; Harper, 1966   V
A Long Silence. H. Hamilton, 1972. U.S. title: Aupres de ma Blonde. Harper, 1972   V
Love in Amsterdam. Gollancz, 1962; Harper, 1963. Also published as: Death in Amsterdam. Ballantine, 1964   V
The Lovely Ladies; see Over the High Side
Over the High Side. H. Hamilton, 1971. U.S. title: The Lovely Ladies. Harper, 1971   V
Question of Loyalty; see Gun Before Butter
Strike Out Where Not Applicable. Gollancz, 1967; Harper, 1968   V
This is the Castle. Gollancz, 1968; Harper, 1968
Tsing-Boum. H. Hamilton, 1969; Harper (spelled Tsing-Boom), 1969   V
What are the Bugles Blowing For? Heinemann, 1975. U.S. title: The Bugles Blowing. Harper, 1976   HC

FREEMAN, ELIZABETH WOODS. 1888-   .
Murder Sets the Pace. Pageant, 1952

FREEMAN, KATHLEEN. 1897-1959. Pseudonyms: Mary Fitt, Stuart Mary Wick, qq.v.
The Intruder, and other stories. Cape, 1926   ss, some criminous
Gown and Shroud. Macdonald, 1947

FREEMAN, LUCY (GREENBAUM). 1916-   . Series character: Dr. William Ames, in all titles.
The Case on Cloud Nine. Arbor, 1975
The Dream. Arbor, 1971
The Psychiatrist Says Murder. Arbor, 1973

FREEMAN, MARTIN J(OSEPH). 1899-   . Series character: Jerry Todd = JT.
The Case of the Blind Mouse. Dutton, 1935; Eldon, 1936   JT
Murder by Magic. Dutton, 1932
The Murder of a Midget. Dutton, 1931; Eldon, 1934
The Scarf on the Scarecrow. Dutton, 1938   JT

FREEMAN, R(ICHARD) AUSTIN. 1862-1943. Joint pseudonym with John James Pitcairn, 1860-1936: Clifford Ashdown, q.v. Series character: Dr. John Thorndyke = JT (see also: Norman Donaldson, 1922-   ; and: John H. Dirckx, 1938-   ).
The Adventures of Dr. Thorndyke; see The Singing Bone
As a Thief in the Night. Hodder, 1928; Dodd, 1928   JT
The Blue Scarab; see Dr. Thorndyke's Case-Book
The Cat's Eye. Hodder, 1923; Dodd, 1927   JT
A Certain Dr. Thorndyke. Hodder, 1927; Dodd, 1928   JT
The D'Arblay Mystery. Hodder, 1926; Dodd, 1926   JT
Death at the Inn; see Felo De Se?
Dr. Thorndyke Intervenes. Hodder, 1933; Dodd, 1933   JT
Dr. Thorndyke Investigates. Univ. of London Press, 1930. (5 ss culled from prior collections.)
The Dr. Thorndyke Omnibus; see The Famous Cases of Dr. Thorndyke
Dr. Thorndyke's Case-Book. Hodder, 1923. U.S. title: The Blue Scarab. Dodd, 1924   JT
Dr. Thorndyke's Cases; see John Thorndyke's Cases
Dr. Thorndyke's Discovery; see When Rogues Fall Out
The Exploits of Danby Croker. Duckworth, 1916
The Eye of Osiris. Hodder, 1911. U.S. title: The Vanishing Man. Dodd, 1912   JT
The Famous Cases of Dr. Thorndyke. Hodder, 1929. U.S. title: The Dr. Thorndyke Omnibus. Dodd, 1932. (The British edition contains 37 out of the 40 Thorndyke ss, leaving out 3 from John Thorndyke's Cases, q.v. The U.S. edition has 38 of the 40, omitting the two that were originally included in The Great Portrait Mystery, q.v.)   JT   ss
Felo De Se? Hodder, 1937. U.S. title: Death at the Inn. Dodd, 1937   JT
Flighty Phyllis. Hodder, 1928
For the Defence: Dr. Thorndyke. Hodder, 1934; Dodd, 1934   JT
The Great Portrait Mystery. Hodder, 1918   ss, two with JT
Helen Vardon's Confession. Hodder, 1922   JT
The Jacob Street Mystery. Hodder, 1942. U.S. title: The Unconscious Witness. Dodd, 1942   JT
John Thorndyke's Cases. Chatto, 1909. U.S. title: Dr. Thorndyke's Cases. Dodd, 1931   JT   ss
The Magic Casket. Hodder, 1927; Dodd, 1927   JT
Mr. Polton Explains. Hodder, 1940; Dodd, 1940   JT
Mr. Pottermack's Oversight. Hodder, 1930; Dodd, 1930   JT
The Mystery of Angelina Frood. Hodder, 1924; Dodd, 1925   JT
The Mystery of 31, New Inn. Hodder, 1912; Winston, 1913   JT
The Penrose Mystery. Hodder, 1936; Dodd, 1936   JT
Pontifex, Son & Thorndyke. Hodder, 1931; Dodd, 1931   JT
The Puzzle Lock. Hodder, 1925; Dodd, 1926   JT   ss
The Red Thumb Mark. Collingwood, 1907; Newton, 1911   JT
A Savant's Vendetta. Pearson, 1920. U.S. title: The Uttermost Farthing. Winston, 1914
The Shadow of the Wolf. Hodder, 1925; Dodd, 1925   JT
A Silent Witness. Hodder, 1914; Winston, 1915   JT
The Singing Bone. Hodder, 1912; Dodd, 1923. Also published as: The Adventures of Dr. Thorndyke. Popular Library, 1947   JT   ss
The Stoneware Monkey. Hodder, 1938; Dodd, 1939   JT
The Surprising Experiences of Mr. Shuttlebury Cobb. Hodder, 1927
The Unconscious Witness; see The Jacob Street Mystery
The Uttermost Farthing; see A Savant's Vendetta
The Vanishing Man; see The Eye of Osiris
When Rogues Fall Out. Hodder, 1932. U.S. title: Dr. Thorndyke's Discovery. Dodd, 1932   JT

FREEMAN-HILTON, THOMAS
The Sayle Case. Gifford, 1946

FREEMANTLE, BRIAN (HARRY). 1936- .
  Face Me When You Walk Away. Cape, 1974; Putnam, 1975
  Goodbye to an Old Friend. Cape, 1973; Putnam, 1973
  The Man Who Wanted Tomorrow. Cape, 1975; Stein, 1975

FREESTONE, BASIL
  -Crave Pity from the Wind. Dobson, 1962
  -The Golden Drum. Quality, 1954

FREETHY, VERNON F.
  Dangerous Homecoming. McKay, 1962

FREIHOFER, LOIS DIANE. 1933- . Pseudonym: Lois Barth, q.v.

FREMLIN, CECIA. Pseudonym of Celia Margaret Goller, 1914- .
  Appointment with Yesterday. Gollancz, 1972
  By Horror Haunted. Gollancz, 1974 ss
  Don't Go to Sleep in the Dark. Gollancz, 1970; Lippincott, 1970 ss
  The Hours Before Dawn. Gollancz, 1958; Lippincott, 1959
  The Jealous One. Gollancz, 1965; Lippincott, 1965
  The Long Shadow. Gollancz, 1975; Doubleday, 1976
  Possession. Gollancz, 1969; Lippincott, 1969
  Prisoner's Base. Gollancz, 1967; Lippincott, 1967
  Seven Lean Years. Gollancz, 1961. U.S. title: Wait for the Wedding. Lippincott, 1961
  The Trouble Makers. Gollancz, 1963; Lippincott, 1963
  Uncle Paul. Gollancz, 1959; Lippincott, 1960
  Wait for the Wedding; see Seven Lean Years

FRENCH, ALICE. 1850-1934. Pseudonym: Octave Thanet, q.v.

FRENCH, E. T.
  Never Smile at Children. Pyramid, 1959

FRENCH, FERGUS
  Invitation to Die. Hale, 1970
  Smouldering Fuse. Hale, 1970

FRENCH, H(ENRY) W(ILLARD)
  Castle Foam; or, The Heir of Meerschaum. Lee, 1880

FRENCH, RICHARD P.
  A Spy is Forever. Tuttle, 1970

FRETLAND, D. JOHN
  Morning of the Tiger. Exposition, 1969

FREUND, PHILIP. 1909- .
  The Beholder. Allen, 1961; British Book Centre, 1963 ss
  The Devious Ways. Allen, 1962; London House, 1963
  The Spymaster. Allen, 1965; Washburn, 1966

FREY, CHARLES WEISER. 1910- . Pseudonym: Ferguson Findley, q.v.

FREYER, FREDERIC. Pseudonym of Bill S(anborn) Ballinger, 1912- , q.v. Other pseudonym: B. X. Sanborn, q.v.
  The Black, Black Hearse. St. Martin's, 1955; Hale, 1956. Also published as: Case of the Black, Black Hearse. Avon, 1955

FRIEDMAN, BRUCE JAY. 1930- .
  The Dick. Knopf, 1970; Cape, 1971

FRIEDMAN, KEN. See: JONATHAN KAPLAN.

FRIEDMAN, PHILIP
  Rage. Paperback Library, 1973. (Novelization of the movie.)

FRIEDMAN, ROY. 1934- .
  The Insurrection of Hippolytus Brandenberg. Stein, 1968; Macmillan (London), 1968

FRIEDMAN, STUART. 1913- .
  The Bedside Corpse; see The Gray Eyes
  -Come-On Girl. Belmont, 1960
  -Damned are the Meek. Monarch, 1964
  Ex-Con. Pyramid, 1954
  -Fathers and Daughters. Monarch, 1963
  -The Fly Girls. Monarch, 1961
  Free are the Dead. Abelard, 1954
  The Gray Eyes. Abelard, 1955. Also published as: The Bedside Corpse. Lion, 1957
  -Irina. Monarch, 1963
  -The Luscious Puritan. Monarch, 1964
  Nikki. Monarch, 1959
  -Nikki Revisited. Monarch, 1963
  -Ravaged. Monarch, 1962
  -The Revolt of Jill Braddock. Monarch, 1960
  -The Surgeons. Monarch, 1962
  -The Trouble with Ava. Monarch, 1961
  -The Troubles of Doctor Cortland. Monarch, 1965
  -The Way We Love. Monarch, 1960
  The Woman and the Prowler. Avon, 1957

FRIEDRICH, OTTO (ALVA). 1929- .
  The Loner. Crown, 1964; Allen, 1965

FRIEL, ARTHUR O(LNEY). 1885- .
  -King—of Kearsarge. Penn, 1921; Melrose, 1922
  -The Pathless Trail. Harper, 1922
  -Tiger River. Harper, 1923; Long, 1924

FRIEND, ED. Pseudonym of Richard (Edward) Wormser, 1908-1977, q.v.
  The Infernal Light. Dell, 1966. (Novelization of the Green Hornet TV series.)
  The Most Deadly Game. Lancer, 1970. (Novelization of the TV series.)

FRIEND, OSCAR J(EROME). 1897-1963. Pseudonym: Owen Fox Jerome, q.v.
  Domes of Silence. Paul, 1929

FRIERSON, TOMMY R.
  A Six-Letter Word for Death. Vantage, 1970

FRISBIE, CARL
  At War with the Unknown. Street (New Magnet)
  A Flash of Light. Street (New Magnet)
  The Great Turf Mystery. Street (New Magnet)
  Out of Satan's Grip. Street (New Magnet)
  When Cold Steel Clashed. Street (New Magnet)

FRISCHAUER, PAUL. See: ALLEN HADEN.

FRITCH, CHARLES E.
  Negative of a Nude. Ace, 1959

FRITH, MICHAEL K. Joint pseudonym with Christopher Bennett Cerf, 1941- : I*n Fl*m*ng, q.v.

FRITH, WALTER
  The Sack of Monte Carlo. Arrowsmith, 1897; Harper, 1898

FRIZELL, BERNARD
  Timetable for the General. Collins, 1972. U.S. title: The Grand Defiance. Morrow, 1972

FROEST, FRANK
  The Crime Club, with George Dilnot, 1883-1951, q.v. Nash, 1915 ss
  The Grell Mystery. Nash, 1913; Clode, 1914
  The Maelstrom; see The Rogues' Syndicate
  The Rogues' Syndicate, with George Dilnot, 1883-1951, q.v. Nash, 1916. U.S. title: The Maelstrom. Clode, 1916, as by Frank Froest alone

FROME, DAVID. Pseudonym of Zenith Jones Brown, 1898- . Other pseudonym: Leslie Ford, q.v. Series characters: Evan Pinkerton = EP; Major Gregory Lewis = GL.
  Arsenic in Richmond; see Mr. Pinkerton Goes to Scotland Yard
  The Black Envelope. Farrar, 1937. British title: The Guilt is Plain. Longmans, 1938 EP
  The Body in Bedford Square; see Mr. Pinkerton Grows a Beard
  The Body in the Turl; see Mr. Pinkerton Finds a Body
  The By-Pass Murder; see Two Against Scotland Yard
  The Eel Pie Murders. Farrar, 1933. British title: The Eel Pie Mystery. Longmans, 1933 EP
  The Eel Pie Mystery; see The Eel Pie Murders
  The Guilt is Plain; see The Black Envelope
  The Hammersmith Murders. Doubleday, 1930; Methuen, 1930 EP
  Homicide House. Rinehart, 1950. British title: Murder on the Square. Hale, 1951 EP
  In at the Death. Longmans (New York), 1930; Skeffington, 1929
  The Man from Scotland Yard. Farrar, 1932. British title: Mr. Simpson Finds a Body. Longmans, 1933 EP
  Mr. Pinkerton and the Old Angel; see Mr. Pinkerton at the Old Angel
  Mr. Pinkerton at the Old Angel. Farrar, 1939. British title: Mr. Pinkerton and the Old Angel. Longmans, 1939 EP
  Mr. Pinkerton Finds a Body. Farrar, 1934. British title: The Body in the Turl. Longmans, 1935 EP
  Mr. Pinkerton Goes to Scotland Yard. Farrar, 1934. British title: Arsenic in Richmond. Longmans, 1934 EP
  Mr. Pinkerton Grows a Beard. Farrar, 1935. British title: The Body in Bedford Square. Longmans, 1935 EP
  Mr. Pinkerton has the Clue. Farrar, 1936; Longmans, 1936 EP
  Mr. Pinkerton: Passage for One. Royce, 1945
  Mr. Simpson Finds a Body; see The Man from Scotland Yard
  The Murder of an Old Man. Methuen, 1929 GL
  The Murder on the Sixth Hole; see The Strange Death of Martin Green
  Murder on the Square; see Homicide House
  Scotland Yard can Wait! Farrar, 1933. British title: That's Your Man, Inspector! Longmans, 1934
  The Strange Death of Martin Green. Doubleday, 1931. British title: The Murder on the Sixth Hole. Methuen, 1931 GL
  That's Your Man, Inspector!; see Scotland Yard Can Wait!
  Two Against Scotland Yard. Farrar, 1931. British title: The By-Pass Murder. Longmans, 1932 EP

FROST, BARBARA. Series character: Marka de Lancey = ML.
The Corpse Died Twice. Coward, 1951 ML
The Corpse Said No. Coward, 1949 ML
Innocent Bystander. Coward, 1955 ML
The Unwelcome Corpse. Coward, 1947

FROST, C. VERNON
The Crime on the Heath. Amalgamated, 1937. (Sexton Blake.)

FROST, CONRAD
Evidence Before Gabriel. Aldor, 1947

FROST, FREDERICK. Pseudonym of Frederick Schiller Faust, 1892-1944. Other pseudonyms: Max Brand, Walter C. Butler, qq.v. Series character: Anthony Hamilton, in all titles.
The Bamboo Whistle. Macrae, 1937
Secret Agent Number One. Macrae, 1936; Harrap, 1937
Spy Meets Spy. Macrae, 1937; Harrap, 1937

FROST, KELMAN (DALGETY)
Death Registers at the Eagle Arms. Oberon.

FROST, LESLEY. 1899- .
Murder at Large. Coward, 1932

FROST, WALTER ARCHER. 1876-1964.
The Man Between. Doubleday, 1913
The Marworth Mystery. Long, 1930
No Questions Asked. Long, 1927

FROUD, P.
Used in Evidence. Kangaroo, 1947 ss

FRUCHTER, NORMAN. 1937- .
Single File. Knopf, 1970

FRUTTERO, C(ARLO) and LUCENTINI, FRANCO
The Sunday Woman. Harcourt, 1973; Collins, 1974. (Translation of La Donna della Domenica. Milan, 1972.)

FRY, ALAN. 1931- .
-The Revenge of Annie Charlie. Doubleday, 1973

FRY, PETE. Pseudonym of James Clifford King, 1914- . Series character: Pete Fry, in all titles.
The Black Beret. Boardman, 1959; Roy, 1959
The Black Cotton Gloves. Long, 1970
The Bright Green Waistcoat. Long, 1967; Roy, 1967
The Brown Suede Jacket. Long, 1968; Roy, 1968
The Green Scarf. Boardman, 1961
The Grey Sombrero. Boardman, 1958; Roy, 1958
The Long Overcoat. Boardman, 1957
The Orange Necktie. Boardman, 1968
The Paint-Stained Flannels. Boardman, 1965; Roy, 1966
The Purple Dressing Gown. Boardman, 1960
The Red Stockings. Boardman, 1962; Roy, 1962
The Scarlet Cloak. Boardman, 1958
The Thick Blue Sweater. Boardman, 1964; Roy, 1964
The White Crash Helmet. Long, 1969; Roy, 1969
The Yellow Trousers. Boardman, 1963; Roy, 1963

FRYERS, AUSTIN. Pseudonym of William Austin Clay. See: ALFRED WILSON BARRETT, 1871- .

FULLER, ANNE and MARCUS ALLEN
Blood on the Common. Dutton, 1933
Blood on the Outer Shoal. Dutton, 1934

FULLER, BLAIR. 1927- .
A Far Place. Harper, 1957; Secker, 1957

FULLER, H(AROLD) E(DGAR)
A Sickness of the Soul. Hale, 1971

FULLER, HECTOR. 1865-1934.
-Roach & Co., Pirates, and other stories. Bowen-Merrill, 1898 ss

FULLER, LESTER. 1908- . See: EDWIN ROLFE, 1909-1954.

FULLER, ROGER. Pseudonym of Don(ald Fiske) Tracy, 1905- .
All the Silent Voices. PB, 1964. (Novelization of The Defenders TV series.)
Burke's Law; see Who Killed Beau Sparrow?
Eve of Judgment. PB, 1965. (Novelization of The Defenders TV series.)
Fear in a Desert Town. PB, 1964. (Novelization of The Fugitive TV series.)
The Martini Murders; see Who Killed Madcap Millicent?
On the Double. PB, 1961. (Novelization of the movie.)
Ordeal. PB, 1964. (Novelization of The Defenders TV series.)
-The Timeless Serpent. PB, 196?
Who Killed Beau Sparrow? Perma, 1964. British title: Burke's Law. Fontana, 1965. (Novelization of the Burke's Law TV series.)
Who Killed Madcap Millicent? PB, 1964. British title: The Martini Murders. Fontana, 1964. (Novelization of the Burke's Law TV series.)

FULLER, ROY (BROADBENT). 1912- .
Fantasy and Fugue. Verschoyle, 1954; Macmillan, 1956
The Second Curtain. Verschoyle, 1953; Macmillan, 1956
With My Little Eye. Lehmann, 1948; Macmillan, 1957

FULLER, SAMUEL (MICHAEL). 1911- .
Crown of India. Award, 1966
The Dark Page. Duell, 1944. Also published as: Murder Makes a Deadline. Bestseller, 1952
Dead Pigeon on Beethoven Street. Pyramid, 1974
Murder Makes a Deadline; see The Dark Page
The Naked Kiss. Belmont, 1964. (Novelization of the movie.)
144 Piccadilly. Baron, 1971; New English Library, 1972

FULLER, TIMOTHY. 1914- . Series character: Jupiter Jones, in all titles.
Harvard has a Homicide. Little, 1936. British title: J for Jupiter. Collins, 1937
J for Jupiter; see Harvard has a Homicide
Keep Cool, Mr. Jones. Little, 1950; Heinemann, 1951
Reunion with Murder. Little, 1941; Heinemann, 1947
This is Murder, Mr. Jones. Little, 1943; Heinemann, 1944
Three Thirds of a Ghost. Little, 1941; Heinemann, 1947

FULLER, VINCENT. Pseudonym.
The Long Green Gaze. Huebsch, 1925

FULLER, WILLIAM. Series character: Brad Dolan = BD.
Back Country. Dell, 1954 BD
Brad Dolan's Blonde Cargo. Dell, 1957 BD
Brad Dolan's Miami Manhunt. Dell, 1958; World Distributors, 1959 BD
The Girl in the Frame. Dell, 1957; Four Square, 1967 BD
Goat Island. Dell, 1954. Also published as: Local Talent. Dell, 1959 BD
Local Talent; see Goat Island
The Pace That Kills. Dell, 1956
Tight Squeeze. Dell, 1959; World Distributors, 1960 BD

FULTON, CHANDOS. 1839-1904.
The Vidocq of New York. American News, 1891

FURBER, DOUGLAS. Pseudonym of Michael Lewin, 1885-1961.
Just Another Murder. Dakers, 1950

FUREY, MICHAEL. Pseudonym of Arthur Henry Sarsfield Ward, 1883-1959. Other pseudonym: Sax Rohmer, q.v.
Wulfheim. Jarrolds, 1950; Bookfinger, 1972, as by Sax Rohmer

FURMAN, A(BRAHAM) L(OEW). 1902- .
Chief Counsel. Macaulay, 1934

FURNESS, AUDREY
Clue to Danger. Mills, 1966
Debt to Dishonour. Mills, 1969
A Face in the Mirror. Hurst, 1961
The Forbidden Cave. Macdonald, 1964
House of Menace; see Letter to a Ghost
In Search of Emily Crew. Mills, 1971
Letter to a Ghost. Mills, 1962. U.S. title: House of Menace. Paperback Library, 1966
Lonely Heritage. Mills, 1968
The Long Road. Mills, 1962
A Reason for Loving. Mills, 1964
Return to Ballyrock. Mills, 1970
The River of Marriage. Mills, 1969
To Love Again. Mills, 1965
The Young Accused. Mills, 1967

FURNIVALL, GORDON
The Perfect Criminal. Jenkins, 1932
The Tracker Tracked. Jenkins, 1928

FUTRELLE, JACQUES. 1875-1912. Series character: Prof. Augustus S. F. X. Van Dusen (The Thinking Machine) = AV.
Best Thinking Machine Detective Stories. Dover, 1973. (12 ss, 10 taken from The Thinking Machine and The Thinking Machine on the Case, qq.v., the remaining 2 heretofore uncollected in book form.) AV
Blind Man's Buff. Hodder, 1914 (U.S. title?)
The Chase of the Golden Plate. Dodd, 1906 AV
The Diamond Master. Bobbs, 1909; Holden, 1912. (Contains 88-page novelet about AV.)
Elusive Isabel. Bobbs, 1909. British title: The Lady in the Case. Nelson, 1910
The High Hand. Bobbs, 1911. British title: The Master Hand. Hodder, 1914
The Lady in the Case; see Elusive Isabel
The Master Hand; see The High Hand
My Lady's Garter. Rand, 1912; Hodder, 1913
The Problem of Cell 13; see The Thinking Machine
The Professor on the Case; see The Thinking Machine on the Case
The Simple Case of Susan. Appleton, 1908. (See also: Lieutenant What's-His-Name, by May Futrelle.)

The Thinking Machine. Dodd, 1907; Chapman, 1907. Also published as: The Problem of Cell 13. Dodd, 1918 AV ss
The Thinking Machine on the Case. Appleton, 1908. British title: The Professor on the Case. Nelson, 1909 AV ss

FUTRELLE, MAY (PEEL). 1876-   .
Lieutenant What's-His-Name. Bobbs, 1915; Newnes, 1916. (Elaborated from The Simple Case of Susan, by her husband Jacques Futrelle, q.v.)
Secretary of Frivolous Affairs. Bobbs, 1911; Gay, 1912

G

G., M. E.
-The Manoeuvres of Celeste. Beumar, 1912 ss

GABORIAU, EMILE. 1833-1873. Series character: Monsieur Lecoq, in at least those marked L.
An Adventuress of France; see The Marquise de Brinvilliers
Baron Trigault's Vengeance; see The Count's Secret
A Beautiful Scourge; see The Little Old Man of the Batignolles
The Blackmailers; see File No. 113
The Catastrophe. Vizetelly, 1885
Caught in the Net; see The Slaves of Paris
The Champdoce Mystery; see The Slaves of Paris
A Chance Marriage; see Marriages of Adventure
The Clique of Gold. Osgood, 1874; Street, 1891. Also published as: The Gilded Clique. Lovell, 1884; Ward Lock, 1909. (Translation of La Clique Doree. Paris, 1873.)
The Count's Millions; see The Count's Secret
The Count's Secret. Estes, 1881; Routledge, 1888. (A two-part novel, with Part I, "Pascal et Marguerite," published separately as: The Count's Millions. Scribner, 1913; Part II, "Lia d'Argeles", as: Baron Trigault's Vengeance. Scribner, 1913.) (Translation of La Vie Infernale. Paris, 1870.)
Crime at Orcival; see The Mystery of Orcival
Dossier No. 113; see File No. 113
The Downward Path. Estes, 1883; Routledge, 1887. (Translation of La Degringolade. Paris, 1872.)
File No. 113. Lovell, 1883; Routledge, 1887. Also published as: The Blackmailers. Lotus Library, 1907; Collins, 1929. And as: Dossier No. 113. Vizetelly, 1883. And as: File 113. Harvill, 1953. (A brief summary of the book was published as: Warrant No. 113; or, The Mystery of the Steel Safe. Crown, 1884.) (Translation of Le Dossier No. 113. Paris, 1867.)
The Gilded Clique; see The Clique of Gold
The Honor of the Name; see Monsieur Lecoq
In Deadly Peril; see Within an Inch of his Life
In Peril of his Life; see Within an Inch of his Life
The Intrigues of a Prisoner. Vizetelly, 1885
The Lerouge Case; see The Widow Lerouge
The Little Old Man of the Batignolles. Munro, 1880. (Translation of Le Petit Vieux de Batignolles. Paris, 1876.) (The French book contained the title novelet plus five stories. Various assortments of Gaboriau's short stories were published as: Max's Marriage; or, The Viscount's Choice. Munro, 1880. And as: The Little Old Man of Batignolles and other stories. Vizetelly, 1884; Lovell, 1888. And as: A Thousand Francs Reward. Munro, 1887. And as: A Beautiful Scourge. Tousey, 1883.
Marie de Brinvilliers; see The Marquise de Brinvilliers
The Marquise de Brinvilliers. Aldine, 1886. Also published as: Marie de Brinvilliers. Routledge, 1888. And as: An Adventuress of France. Robinson, 1921; Federation Press, 1926. (Translation of Les Amours d'une Empoisonneuse. Paris, 1881.)
Marriage at a Venture; see Marriage of Adventure
Marriage of Adventure. Robins, 1921; Federation Press, 1925. (A two-part novel, with Part I, "M.J.D. de Saint-Roch, Ambassadeur Matrimoniel", published separately as: A Chance Marriage. Privately Printed, 1878. And as: Marriage at a Venture. Munro, 1879. Part II, "Promesses de Mariage," as: Promise of Marriage. Lovell, 1883. And as: Promises of Marriage. Munro, 1884.) (Translation of Les Mariages d'Aventure. Paris, 1862.)
Max's Marriage; or, The Viscount's Choice; see The Little Old Man of the Batignolles
The Men of the Bureau. Munro, 1880. (Translation of Les Gens de Bureau. 1862.)
Monsieur Lecoq. Estes, 1880; Routledge, 1887. (A two-part novel, with Part I, "L'Enquete," published separately as: Monsieur Lecoq: The Detective's Dilemma. Street, 1891; Ward, 1888. And as: Monsieur Lecoq. Scribner, 1900. Part II, "L'Honneur du Nom," as: Monsieur Lecoq: The Detective's Triumph. Street, 1891; Ward, 1888. And as: The Honor of the Name. Scribner, 1900; Hodder, 1920.) (Translation of Monsieur Lecoq. Paris, 1868.) L
Monsieur Lecoq: The Detective's Dilemma; see Monsieur Lecoq
Monsieur Lecoq: The Detective's Triumph; see Monsieur Lecoq
The Mystery of Orcival. Holt, 1871; Routledge, 1887. Also published as: Crime at Orcival. Harvill, 1952 (abr.). (Translation of Le Crime d'Orcival. Paris, 1867.) L
Other People's Money. Osgood, 1875; Routledge, 1888. (Translation of L'Argent des Autres. Paris, 1873.)
Promise(s) of Marriage; see Marriages of Adventure
The Slaves of Paris. Estes, 1882; Routledge, 1887. (A two-part novel, with Part I, "Le Chantage," published separately as: Caught in the Net. Street, 1891. Part II, "Le Secret de Champdoce," as: The Champdoce Mystery. Street, 1891. (Translation of Les Esclaves de Paris. Paris, 1868.) L
A Thousand Francs Reward; see The Little Old Man of the Batignolles
Warrant No. 113; or, The Mystery of the Steel Safe; see File No. 113
The Widow Lerouge. Osgood, 1873; Routledge, 1887. Also published as: The Lerouge Case. Federation Press, 1925.
(Translation of L'Affaire Lerouge. Paris, 1866.) L
Within an Inch of his Life. Osgood, 1874; Routledge, 1888. Also published as: In Peril of his Life. Lovell, 1883. And as: In Deadly Peril. Ward, 1888. (Translation of La Corde au Cou. Paris, 1873.)

GABRIEL, H. WILHELM
A Corpse for a Client. Arcadia, 1961

GADDA, CARLO EMILIO. 1893-   .
That Awful Mess on Via Merulana. Braziller, 1965; Secker, 1966. (Translation of Quer Pasticciaccio Brutto de via Merulana. Milan, 1957.)

GADHART, RINE
Too Tough to Die. Swan, 1942

GADNEY, REG. 1941-   .
Drawn Blanc. Heinemann, 1970; Coward, 1971
Seduction of a Tall Man. Heinemann, 1972
Something Worth Fighting For. Heinemann, 1974
Somewhere in England. Heinemann, 1971; St. Martin's, 1971

GAGE, NICHOLAS. Pseudonym of Nicholas Ngagoyeanes, 1939-   .
Bones of Contention. Berkley/Putnam, 1974

GAGE, WILLIAM H(ENRY), JR. 1915-1973.
Appointment with Dishonor. Little, 1958; Hale, 1959

GAINES, AUDREY. Series character: Chauncey O'Day = CO.
No Crime Like the Present. Arcadia, 1952
The Old Must Die. Crowell, 1939 CO
Omit Flowers, Please. Messner, 1946
The Voodoo Goat. Crowell, 1942 CO
While the Wind Howled. Crowell, 1940 CO

GAINES, ROBERT. 1912-   .
Against the Public Interest. Macdonald, 1959; Walker, 1964
The Cruel Deadline. Macdonald, 1960
Daybreak at Deest. Heinemann, 1951
Final Night. Heinemann, 1950; Doubleday, 1950
The Invisible Evil. Macdonald, 1963; Walker, 1963
A Kind of Justice. Heinemann, 1955
The Name is Judas. Joseph, 1966
The Vain Ambitions. Heinemann, 1953

GAINHAM, SARAH. 1922-   .
Appointment in Vienna; see The Mythmaker
The Cold Dark Night. Barker, 1957; Walker, 1961
Maculan's Daughter. Macmillan (London), 1973; Putnam, 1974
The Mythmaker. Barker, 1957. U.S. title: Appointment in Vienna. Dutton, 1958
Night Falls on the City. Collins, 1967; Holt, 1967
A Place in the Country. Weidenfeld, 1969; Holt, 1969
Private Worlds. Weidenfeld, 1971; Holt, 1971
The Silent Hostage. Eyre, 1960; Dutton, 1960
The Stone Roses. Eyre, 1959; Dutton, 1959
Takeover Bid. Weidenfeld, 1970; Holt, 1972
Time Right Deadly. Barker, 1956; Walker, 1960

GAIR, MALCOLM. Series character: Mark
    Raeburn, in all titles.
  The Bad Dream. Collins, 1960
  The Burning of Troy. Collins, 1959;
    Doubleday, 1958
  A Long Hard Look. Collins, 1958
  Sapphires on Wednesday. Collins, 1957;
    Doubleday, 1957
  The Schultz Money. Collins, 1960;
    Doubleday, 1960
  Snow Job. Collins, 1962; Doubleday,
    1962

GAITE, FRANCIS. Joint pseudonym of Adel-
    aide Frances Oke Manning, 1891-1959,
    and Cyril Henry Coles, 1898-1965.
    Other pseudonym: Manning Coles, q.v.
    All titles below published in the
    U.S. as by Manning Coles. Series
    characters: Charles and James Latim-
    er = L.
  Brief Candles. Hodder, 1954; Doubleday,
    1954 L
  Come and Go. Hodder, 1958; Doubleday,
    1958 L
  Duty Free. Hodder, 1959; Doubleday,
    1959
  A Family Matter. Hodder, 1956. U.S.
    title: Happy Returns. Doubleday, 1955
    L
  The Far Traveller. Hodder, 1957;
    Doubleday, 1956
  Happy Returns; see A Family Matter

GALCOM, G.
  The Green Mandarin Mystery. Warren,
    1950

GALE, ADELA
  Angel Among Witches. Signet, 1969
  Goddess of Terror. Signet, 1967
  Harvest of Terror. Signet, 1969

GALE, JOHN. Pseudonym of Richard Gaze,
    1917-   .
  Death by Chalk Face. Long, 1962
  Death for Short; see The Short Reaction
  The Short Reaction. Long, 1961. U.S.
    title: Death for Short. Macmillan,
    1962
  Spare Time for Murder. Long, 1960;
    Macmillan, 1961

GALLAGHER, GALE. Joint pseudonym of
    Will(iam Charles) Oursler, 1913-   ,
    q.v., and Margaret Scott. Other
    Oursler pseudonym: Nick Marino, q.v.
    Series character: Gale Gallagher, in
    both titles.
  Chord in Crimson. Coward, 1949; Board-
    man, 1950
  I Found Him Dead. Coward, 1947

GALLAGHER, PATRICIA
  Answer to Heaven. Avon, 1964
  Fires of Brimstone. Avon, 1966
  Shannon. Avon, 1967
  The Sons and the Daughters. Bantam,
    1963
  Summer of Sighs. Avon, 1971
  The Thicket. Avon, 1974

GALLAGHER, RICHARD
  The Doomsday Committee. Award, 1971
  Murder by Gemini. Lancer, 1971. (Novel-
    ization of the Cannon TV series.)
  The One-Armed Murder. Lancer, 1971.
    (Novelization of The Most Deadly
    Game TV series.)
  The Stewardess Strangler. Lancer, 1971.
    (Novelization of the Cannon TV
    series.)

GALLETLEY, LEONARD
  -King's Justice. Williams, 1932
  The Yatton Murders. Williams, 1935

GALLICO, PAUL (WILLIAM). 1897-1976.
    Series character: Hiram Holliday =
    HH.
  The Adventures of Hiram Holliday.
    Knopf, 1939; Joseph, 1939 ss HH
  The Boy Who Invented the Bubble Gum.
    Delacorte, 1974; Heinemann, 1974
  The Hand of Mary Constable. Doubleday,
    1964; Heinemann, 1964
  The Secret Front. Knopf, 1944 HH
  Thief is an Ugly Word. Dell 10¢ pb,
    1951
  Too Many Ghosts. Doubleday, 1959;
    Joseph, 1961
  Trial by Terror. Knopf, 1952; Joseph,
    1952
  The Zoo Gang. Coward, 1971; Heinemann,
    1971 ss

GALLIE, MENNA (PATRICIA HUMPHREYS).
    1920-
  Strike for a Kingdom. Gollancz, 1959;
    Harper, 1959
  -Travels with a Duchess. Gollancz, 1968;
    Harper, 1968
  -You're Welcome to Ulster! Gollancz,
    1970; Harper, 1970

GALLIMORE, F. A.
  The Ebony Mirror. Methuen, 1933

GALLON, TOM. 1866-1914.
  -Aunt Phipps. Hutchinson, 1905
  -Boden's Boy. Hutchinson, 1904
  -Brother Rogue and Brother Saint. Paul,
    1909
  -The Charity Ghost. Hutchinson, 1902
  -Christmas at Poverty Castle. Nash, 1907
  -Comethup. Hutchinson, 1899
  The Dead Ingleby. Hutchinson, 1902
  Dead Man's Love. Ward, 1911; Bren-
    tano's, 1910
  -The Diamond Trail. Mills, 1916
  -The Dream—and the Woman. Paul, 1909
  -Fortune A-Begging. Hurst, 1906
  The Girl Behind the Keys. Hutchinson,
    1903 ss
  -The Golden Thread. Nash, 1904
  -The Great Gay Road. Long, 1910; Bren-
    tano's, 1912
  -The Idol of the Blind. Appleton, 1899.
    (British title?)
  -In a Little House. Hutchinson, 1903
  -"It Will Be All Right!" Hutchinson,
    1914
  Jarwick the Prodigal. Ward, 1904
  -Jimmy Quixote. Hurst, 1906
  -Judy—and the Philosopher. Hutchinson,
    1907
  -Kiddy. Hutchinson, 1900; Valentine,
    1900
  The Kingdom of Hate. Hutchinson, 1899;
    Appleton, 1899
  -The Lackey and the Lady. Hurst, 1908
  -The Lady in the Black Mask. Mills, 1917
  -The Lady of the Cameo. Hutchinson, 1903
  -Lagden's Luck. Arrowsmith, 1905
  Levity Hicks. Long, 1912
  -The Man Hunt. Mills, 1916
  -The Man in Motley. Mills, 1915
  Meg the Lady. Hutchinson, 1905
  The Mystery of John Peppercorn. Hutch-
    inson, 1902
  The Mystery of Roger Bullock. Paul,
    1910
  -Peplow's Paper-Chase. Hutchinson, 1904
  -The Prince of Mischance. Hutchinson,
    1897; Appleton, 1898
  -The Princess of Happy Chance. Hutchin-
    son, 1915
  Rickerby's Folly. Methuen, 1901
  A Rogue in Love. Hutchinson, 1900
  -The Rogue's Heiress. Hutchinson, 1910;
    Dillingham, 1910

  The Second Dandy Chater. Hutchinson,
    1901; Dodd, 1901
  Tatterley. Hutchinson, 1897; Appleton,
    1897
  Tinman. Ward, 1908; Small, 1907
  -The Touch of the Child, and other sto-
    ries. Mills, 1918
  -Young Eve and Old Adam. Long, 1913

GALTON, RAY(MOND PERCY) and ALAN (FRAN-
    CIS) SIMPSON, 1929-   .
  The Spy with a Cold Nose. Dell, 1966;
    Arrow, 1967. (Novelization of the
    movie.)

GALWAY, ROBERT CONINGTON
  Assignment Andalusia. Hale, 1965
  Assignment Argentina. Hale, 1969
  Assignment Death Squad. Hale, 1970
  Assignment Fenland. Hale, 1969
  Assignment Gaolbreak. Hale, 1968
  Assignment London. Hale, 1963
  Assignment Malta. Hale, 1966
  Assignment New York. Hale, 1963
  Assignment Sea Bed. Hale, 1969
  Assignment Sydney. Hale, 1970
  The Negative Man. Hale, 1971
  The Timeless Sleep. Hale, 1963

GALWEY, G(EOFFREY) V(ALENTINE). 1912-   .
    Series character: Inspector "Daddy"
    Bourne, in all titles.
  Full Fathom Five. Hodder, 1951
  The Lift and the Drop. Bodley Head,
    1948
  Murder on Leave. Lane, 1946

GAMBIER, JAMES W(ILLIAM). 1841-   .
  -Swifter Than a Weaver's Shuttle. Son-
    nenschein, 1887

GAMBLE, FREDERICK (JOHN). 1904-   .
  The Frightened One. Barker, 1958
  -A Man and a Half. Barker, 1956
  -My Coat is Travel-Stained. Barker, 1957

GAMMON, DAVID J.
  The Getaway Gang. Archer, 1946
  Meet the Falcon. Archer, 1947

GANACHILLY, ALFRED
  The Whispering Dead. Methuen, 1919;
    Knopf, 1920

GANDOLFI, SIMON
  The 100 Kilo Club. Wildwood, 1975

GANNETT, JAMES
  Murder After Dark. Muller, 1956

GANNOLD, JOHN. Pseudonym of John (Frank-
    lin Coasten) Langdon, 1913-   ,
    q.v.
  The Fix. Hale, 1972
  The Night of the Fox. Hale, 1974

GANPAT. Pseudonym of Martin Louis Alan
    Gompertz, 1886-1951.
  -The Marches of Honour. Hodder, 1931
  The One-Eyed Knave. Hodder, 1936
  Out of Evil. Hodder, 1933
  -The Second Tigress. Hodder, 1933
  -The Snow Falcon. Hodder, 1935
  -Stella Nash. Blackwood, 1924; Houghton,
    1924
  The Three R's. Hodder, 1930; Doubleday,
    1931

GANT, JONATHAN. Pseudonym of Clifton
    Adams, 1919-   , q.v.
  The Long Vendetta. Avalon, 1963
  Never Say No to a Killer. Ace, 1956

GANT, MATTHEW. Pseudonym.
Queen Street. Regency, 1963

GANT, NORMAN
Burn. Lancer, 1970. (Novelization of the movie.)

GAR, ROBIN
The Avenger. Gramol, 1934
The Big Boss. Fiction House, 1946
The Dead Ones Don't Talk. Mellifont, 1933
"Hate!" Mellifont, 1933
Jade of Death. Gramol, 1934
"Moon of Death!" Gramol, 1934
Murder on the River. Mellifont, 1935
The Mystery in Minchin Mews. Mellifont, 1946
The Stolen Plans. Mellifont, 1934
The Valley of Fear. Mellifont, 1935

GARBO, NORMAN, 1919-   , and HOWARD GOODKIND
Confrontation. Harper, 1966

GARD, OLIVER
The Seventh Chasm. Dodd, 1953; Boardman, 1954

GARDEN, JOHN. Pseudonym of H(arry) L(uft) V(erne) Fletcher, 1902-   , q.v.
All on a Summer's Day. Joseph, 1949
Day of Reckoning; see Murder Isn't Private
Death in the Village. Hale, 1967
A Little Time to Stay. Joseph, 1953
Murder Isn't Private. Joseph, 1950. U.S. title: Day of Reckoning. Lippincott, 1951
6 to 10. Joseph, 1947

GARDENER, HELEN H(AMILTON CHENOWETH). 1853-1925.
-A Thoughtless Yes. Belford, 1890 ss

GARDENHIRE, SAMUEL M(AJOR). 1855-   .
The Long Arm. Harper (New York & London), 1906 ss
The Silence of Mrs. Harrold. Harper (New York & London), 1905

GARDINER, D(OROTHEA) F(RANCES). 1879-   .
Pseudonym: Theodore Frank, q.v.
Another Night, Another Day. Constable, 1930
The Beguiling Shore. Constable, 1930
Murder at a Dog Show. Muller, 1935
The Prison House. Constable, 1929

GARDINER, DOROTHY. 1894-   . Series characters: Sheriff Moss Magill = MM; Mr. Watson = W.
Beer for Psyche. Doubleday, 1946; Hurst, 1948
The Case of the Hula Clock; see What Crime Is It?
A Drink for Mr. Cherry. Doubleday, 1934. British title: Mr. Watson Intervenes. Hurst, 1935 W
Lion in Wait. Doubleday, 1963. British title: Lion? or Murder? Hammond, 1964 MM
Lion? or Murder?; see Lion in Wait
Mr. Watson Intervenes; see A Drink for Mr. Cherry
The Seventh Mourner. Doubleday, 1958; Hammond, 1960 MM
The Transatlantic Ghost. Doubleday, 1933; Harrap, 1933 W
What Crime is It? Doubleday, 1956. British title: The Case of the Hula Clock. Hammond, 1957 MM

GARDINER, GORDON. 1874-1937.
At the House of Dree. Low, 1928; Houghton, 1928
The Man with a Weak Heart. Low, 1932; Houghton, 1932
The Pattern of Chance. Low, 1929; Houghton, 1930
The Reconnaissance. Chapman, 1914; Macmillan, 1914

GARDINER, HEATHER
Money on Murder. Hutchinson, 1951
Murder in Haste. Hutchinson, 1954; Roy, 1954

GARDINER, LINDA
-His Heritage. Paul, 1888
Mrs. Wylde. Jarrolds, 1897
-The Rev. Miles Latimer. Remington, 1885
-The Sound of a Voice. Hurst, 1897
-Sylvia in Flowerland. Seeley, 1899; Dutton, 1899

GARDINER, STEPHEN
Death is an Artist. Barker, 1958; Washburn, 1959

GARDNER, ALAN (HAROLD). 1925-   . Series character: David Troy, in at least those marked DT.
Assignment Tahiti. Muller, 1965 DT
The Escalator. Muller, 1963 DT
The Hibernation of Ginger Scrubb. Muller, 1968
The Man Who Was Too Much. Muller, 1967 DT
Six-Day Week. Muller, 1966; Coward, 1966 DT

GARDNER, ARTHUR R(OBERT) L(EE)
Lower Underworld. Quality, 1942
Tinker's Kitchen. Allan, 1932

GARDNER, CHARLES W.
-The Doctor and the Devil; or, Midnight Adventures of Dr. Parkhurst. Gardner, 1894

GARDNER, CURTISS T.
Bones Don't Lie. Mill, 1946. Also published as: The Fatal Cast. Graphic, 1954

GARDNER, ERLE STANLEY. 1889-1970. Pseudonyms: A. A. Fair, Carleton Kendrake, Charles J. Kenny, qq.v. Series characters: Perry Mason = PM; Doug Selby = DS; Terry Clane = TC; Sheriff Bill Eldon = BE; Gramps Wiggins = W.
The Case of the Amorous Aunt. Morrow, 1963; Heinemann, 1969 PM
The Case of the Angry Mourner. Morrow, 1951; Heinemann, 1958 PM
The Case of the Backward Mule. Morrow, 1946; Heinemann, 1955 TC
The Case of the Baited Hook. Morrow, 1940; Cassell, 1940 PM
The Case of the Beautiful Beggar. Morrow, 1965; Heinemann, 1972 PM
The Case of the Bigamous Spouse. Morrow, 1961; Heinemann, 1967 PM
The Case of the Black-Eyed Blonde. Morrow, 1944; Cassell, 1948 PM
The Case of the Blonde Bonanza. Morrow, 1962; Heinemann, 1967 PM
The Case of the Borrowed Brunette. Morrow, 1946; Cassell, 1951 PM
The Case of the Buried Clock. Morrow, 1943; Cassell, 1945 PM
The Case of the Calendar Girl. Morrow, 1958; Heinemann, 1964 PM
The Case of the Careless Cupid. Morrow, 1968; Heinemann, 1973 PM
The Case of the Careless Kitten. Morrow, 1942; Cassell, 1944 PM
The Case of the Caretaker's Cat. Morrow, 1935; Cassell, 1936 PM
The Case of the Cautious Coquette. Morrow, 1949; Heinemann, 1955 PM (Note: The Dollar Mystery Guild edition includes two PM novelets, The Case of the Crimson Kiss, and The Case of the Crying Swallow.)
The Case of the Counterfeit Eye. Morrow, 1935; Cassell, 1935 PM
The Case of the Crimson Kiss. Morrow, 1970; Heinemann, 1975. (A collection containing the title novelet, with PM, and four stories with other characters.)
The Case of the Crooked Candle. Morrow, 1944; Cassell, 1947 PM
The Case of the Crying Swallow. Morrow, 1971; Heinemann, 1974. (A collection containing the title novelet, with PM, and three stories with other characters.)
The Case of the Curious Bride. Morrow, 1935; Cassell, 1935 PM
The Case of the Dangerous Dowager. Morrow, 1937; Cassell, 1937 PM
The Case of the Daring Decoy. Morrow, 1957; Heinemann, 1963 PM
The Case of the Daring Divorcee. Morrow, 1964; Heinemann, 1969 PM
The Case of the Deadly Toy. Morrow, 1959; Heinemann, 1964 PM
The Case of the Demure Defendant. Morrow, 1956; Heinemann, 1962 PM
The Case of the Drowning Duck. Morrow, 1942; Cassell, 1944 PM
The Case of the Drowsy Mosquito. Morrow, 1943; Cassell, 1946 PM
The Case of the Dubious Bridegroom. Morrow, 1949; Heinemann, 1954 PM
The Case of the Duplicate Daughter. Morrow, 1960; Heinemann, 1965 PM
The Case of the Empty Tin. Morrow, 1941; Cassell, 1943 PM
The Case of the Fabulous Fake. Morrow, 1969; Heinemann, 1974 PM
The Case of the Fan-Dancer's Horse. Morrow, 1947; Heinemann, 1952 PM
The Case of the Fenced-In Woman. Morrow, 1972; Heinemann, 1976 PM
The Case of the Fiery Fingers. Morrow, 1951; Heinemann, 1957 PM
The Case of the Foot-Loose Doll. Morrow, 1958; Heinemann, 1964 PM
The Case of the Fugitive Nurse. Morrow, 1954; Heinemann, 1959 PM
The Case of the Gilded Lily. Morrow, 1956; Heinemann, 1962 PM
The Case of the Glamorous Ghost. Morrow, 1955; Heinemann, 1960 PM
The Case of the Gold-Digger's Purse. Morrow, 1945; Cassell, 1948 PM
The Case of the Green-Eyed Sister. Morrow, 1953; Heinemann, 1959 PM
The Case of the Grinning Gorilla. Morrow, 1952; Heinemann, 1958 PM
The Case of the Half-Wakened Wife. Morrow, 1945; Cassell, 1949 PM
The Case of the Haunted Husband. Morrow, 1941; Cassell, 1942 PM
The Case of the Hesitant Hostess. Morrow, 1953; Heinemann, 1959 PM
The Case of the Horrified Heirs. Morrow, 1964; Heinemann, 1971 PM
The Case of the Howling Dog. Morrow, 1934; Cassell, 1935 PM
The Case of the Ice-Cold Hands. Morrow, 1962; Heinemann, 1968 PM
The Case of the Irate Witness. Morrow, 1972; Heinemann, 1975. (A collection containing the title story, with PM, and three stories with other characters.)
The Case of the Lame Canary. Morrow, 1937; Cassell, 1937 PM

The Case of the Lazy Lover. Morrow, 1947; Heinemann, 1954 PM
The Case of the Lonely Heiress. Morrow, 1948; Heinemann, 1952 PM
The Case of the Long-Legged Models. Morrow, 1958; Heinemann, 1963 PM
The Case of the Lucky Legs. Morrow, 1934; Harrap, 1934 PM
The Case of the Lucky Loser. Morrow, 1957; Heinemann, 1962 PM
The Case of the Mischievous Doll. Morrow, 1963; Heinemann, 1968 PM
The Case of the Moth-Eaten Mink. Morrow, 1952; Heinemann, 1958 PM
The Case of the Murderer's Bride. Davis pb, 1969. (A collection of 7 ss and novelets, edited by Ellery Queen.)
The Case of the Musical Cow. Morrow, 1950; Heinemann, 1957. (A non-series police procedural.)
The Case of the Mythical Monkeys. Morrow, 1959; Heinemann, 1965 PM
The Case of the Negligent Nymph. Morrow, 1950; Heinemann, 1956 PM
The Case of the Nervous Accomplice. Morrow, 1955; Heinemann, 1961 PM
The Case of the One-Eyed Witness. Morrow, 1950; Heinemann, 1956 PM
The Case of the Perjured Parrot. Morrow, 1939; Cassell, 1939 PM
The Case of the Phantom Fortune. Morrow, 1964; Heinemann, 1970 PM
The Case of the Postponed Murder. Morrow, 1973; Heinemann, 1977 PM
The Case of the Queenly Contestant. Morrow, 1967; Heinemann, 1973 PM
The Case of the Reluctant Model. Morrow, 1962; Heinemann, 1967 PM
The Case of the Restless Redhead. Morrow, 1954; Heinemann, 1960 PM
The Case of the Rolling Bones. Morrow, 1939; Cassell, 1940 PM
The Case of the Runaway Corpse. Morrow, 1954; Heinemann, 1960 PM
The Case of the Screaming Woman. Morrow, 1957; Heinemann, 1963 PM
The Case of the Shapely Shadow. Morrow, 1960; Heinemann, 1966 PM
The Case of the Shoplifter's Shoe. Morrow, 1938; Cassell, 1939 PM
The Case of the Silent Partner. Morrow, 1940; Cassell, 1941 PM
The Case of the Singing Skirt. Morrow, 1959; Heinemann, 1965 PM
The Case of the Sleepwalker's Niece. Morrow, 1936; Cassell, 1936 PM
The Case of the Smoking Chimney. Morrow, 1943; Cassell, 1945 GW
The Case of the Spurious Spinster. Morrow, 1961; Heinemann, 1966 PM
The Case of the Stepdaughter's Secret. Morrow, 1963; Heinemann, 1968 PM
The Case of the Stuttering Bishop. Morrow, 1936; Cassell, 1937 PM
The Case of the Substitute Face. Morrow, 1938; Cassell, 1938 PM
The Case of the Sulky Girl. Morrow, 1933; Harrap, 1934 PM
The Case of the Sun Bather's Diary. Morrow, 1955; Heinemann, 1961 PM
The Case of the Terrified Typist. Morrow, 1956; Heinemann, 1961 PM
The Case of the Troubled Trustee. Morrow, 1965; Heinemann, 1971 PM
The Case of the Turning Tide. Morrow, 1941; Cassell, 1942 GW
The Case of the Vagabond Virgin. Morrow, 1948; Heinemann, 1952 PM
The Case of the Velvet Claws. Morrow, 1933; Harrap, 1933 PM
The Case of the Waylaid Wolf. Morrow, 1959; Heinemann, 1965 PM
The Case of the Worried Waitress. Morrow, 1966; Heinemann, 1972 PM
The D.A. Breaks a Seal. Morrow, 1946; Cassell, 1950 DS

The D.A. Breaks an Egg. Morrow, 1949; Heinemann, 1957 DS
The D.A. Calls a Turn. Morrow, 1944; Cassell, 1947 DS
The D.A. Calls It Murder. Morrow, 1937; Cassell, 1937 DS
The D.A. Cooks a Goose. Morrow, 1942; Cassell, 1943 DS
The D.A. Draws a Circle. Morrow, 1939; Cassell, 1940 DS
The D.A. Goes to Trial. Morrow, 1940; Cassell, 1941 DS
The D.A. Holds a Candle. Morrow, 1938; Cassell, 1939 DS
The D.A. Takes a Chance. Morrow, 1948; Heinemann, 1956 DS
Murder Up My Sleeve. Morrow, 1937; Cassell, 1938 TC
Over the Hump. Gordon Martin (London), 1945. (A 92-page version of the novelet "Death Rides a Boxcar" included in the collection The Case of the Murderer's Bride, q.v.)
Two Clues. Morrow, 1947; Cassell, 1951. (Two novelets about BE.)

GARDNER, JOHN. 1926-   . Series characters: Prof. Moriarty = M; Boysie Oakes = BO; Derek Torry = DT.
Air Apparent; see The Airline Pirates
The Airline Pirates. Hodder, 1970. U.S. title: Air Apparent. Putnam, 1971 BO
Amber Nine. Muller, 1966; Viking, 1966 BO
The Assassination File. Corgi, 1974 ss
-The Censor. New English Library, 1970
A Complete State of Death. Cape, 1969; Viking, 1969. Also published as: The Stone Killer. Award, 1973 DT
The Corner Men. Joseph, 1974; Doubleday, 1976 DT
Founder Member. Joseph, 1969 BO
Hideaway. Corgi, 1968 ss
A Killer for a Song. Hodder, 1975 BO
The Liquidator. Muller, 1964; Viking, 1964 BO
Madrigal. Muller, 1967; Viking, 1968 BO
Moriarty; see The Return of Moriarty
The Return of Moriarty. Weidenfeld, 1974; Putnam, 1974. Also published as: Moriarty. Pan, 1976
The Revenge of Moriarty. Weidenfeld, 1975; Putnam, 1976 M
The Stone Killer; see A Complete State of Death
Traitor's Exit. Muller, 1970 BO
Understrike. Muller, 1965; Viking, 1965 BO

GARDNER, LEE
Calina. Award, 1967

GARDNER, MAURICE B.
-Horrors of Smiling Manor. Forum, 1962

GARDNER, S. A.
Outwitted at Last. Carleton, 1878

GARDNER, WILLIAM HENRY. 1837-   .
The Curious Case of Gen. Delaney Smythe. Abbey, 1900

GARFIELD, BRIAN (FRANCIS WYNNE). 1939-   . Pseudonyms: Drew Mallory, Frank O'Brian, qq.v. See also: DONALD E(DWIN) WESTLAKE, 1934-   . Series characters: Paul Benjamin = PB; Sam Watchman = SW.
Death Sentence. Evans, 1975; Macmillan (London), 1976 PB
Death Wish. McKay, 1972; Hodder, 1973 PB

Deep Cover. Delacorte, 1971; Hodder, 1972
The Hit. Macmillan, 1970
Hopscotch. Evans, 1975; Macmillan (London), 1975
Kolchak's Gold. McKay, 1973; Macmillan (London), 1974
The Last Bridge. McKay, 1966
Line of Succession. Delacorte, 1972; Hodder, 1974
Relentless. World, 1972; Hodder, 1973 SW
The Romanov Succession. Evans, 1974; Macmillan (London), 1974
The Threepersons Hunt. Evans, 1974; Coronet, 1975 SW
Tripwire. McKay, 1973; Coronet, 1976
-The Villiers Touch. Delacorte, 1970
What of Terry Conniston? World, 1971; Coronet, 1976

GARFORTH, JOHN. Series: Novelizations of The Avengers TV series = A.
The Floating Game. Panther, 1967; Berkley, 1967 A
Heil Harris! Panther, 1967; Berkley, 1967 A
The Laugh was on Lazarus. Panther, 1967; Berkley, 1967 A
The Passing of Gloria Munday. Panther, 1967; Berkley, 1967 A
The Sixth Sense is Death. Hodder pb, 1969. (Novelization of The Champions TV series.)
Sleep, and the City Trembles. Panther, 1969

GARLAND, (MARY) ISABEL. 1903-   . Joint pseudonym with Mindret Lord: Garland Lord, q.v.
Abandon Hope. Mystery House, 1941. Also published as: Death Comes Courting. Mystery Novel of the Month, 1942

GARLAND, JOHN
Crime of the Crossword. Columbine, 1939

GARLAND, RODNEY. Pseudonym of Adam Hegedus, 1910-   .
-The Heart in Exile. Allen, 1953
-Hell and High Water. Allen, 1962
Sorcerer's Broth. Allen, 1966
The Troubled Midnight. Allen, 1954; Coward, 1955
-World Without Dreams. Allen, 1961

GARLAND, RUFUS CUMMINS
Zalea: A Psychological Episode and Tale of Love. Neale, 1900

GARLINGTON, PHILIP
Aces & Eights. Evans, 1975; Ellis, 1976

GARNER, CHARLES. Pseudonym: Stewart C. Cumberland, q.v.

GARNER, DAVID
This Fell Sergeant. New English Library pb, 1974

GARNER, HUGH. 1913-   .
Death in Don Mills. McGraw, 1975

GARNER, WILLIAM. 1920-   . Series character: Mick Jagger = MJ.
The Andra Fiasco. Collins, 1971. U.S. title: Strip Jack Naked. Bobbs, 1971
A Big Enough Wreath. Collins, 1974; Putnam, 1975
The Deep, Deep Freeze. Collins, 1968; Putnam, 1968 MJ
Ditto, Brother Rat! Collins, 1972
The Manipulators; see The Puppet-Masters

G

Overkill. Collins, 1966; NAL, 1966 MJ
The Puppet-Masters. Collins, 1970. U.S. title: The Manipulators. Bobbs, 1970
Strip Jack Naked; see The Andra Fiasco
The Us or Them War. Collins, 1969; Putnam, 1969

GARNETT, DAVID. 1892-   . Pseudonym: Leda Burke, q.v.

GARNETT, ROGER. Pseudonym of Nigel Morland, 1905-   , q.v. Other pseudonyms: Mary Dane, John Donavan, Norman Forrest, Vincent McCall, Neal Shepherd, qq.v. Series characters: R. I. Perkins, in at least those marked RP; Chief Inspector Jonathan Black, in at least those marked JB.
The Croaker. Wright, 1938
Danger—Death at Work. Wright, 1939
Death in Piccadilly. Wright, 1937 JB
Death Spoke Sweetly. Wright, 1946
Dusky Death. Wright, 1948
Eve Finds the Killer. Martin & Reid, 1947. (16 pp.)
The Killing of Paris Norton. Wright, 1938 RP
A Man Died Talking. Wright, 1943 JB
Starr Bedford Dies. Wright, 1937 RP

GARRATT, MARIE
And Then Look Down. Hurst, 1964. U.S. title: Dangerous Enchantment. Ace, 1966
Dangerous Enchantment; see And Then Look Down
Festival of Darkness; see Where No Fire Burns
Where No Fire Burns. Hurst, 1963. U.S. title: Festival of Darkness. Ace, 1966

GARRETT, RANDALL (PHILLIPS). Joint pseudonym with Larry M(ark) Harris, 1933-   , q.v.: Mark Phillips, q.v.
Too Many Magicians. Doubleday, 1967; Macdonald, 1968

GARRETT, ROBERT. Series character: Alan Brett, in both titles.
Run Down: The World of Alan Brett. Joseph, 1970; Atheneum, 1972
Spiral: The World of Alan Brett. Joseph, 1971; Atheneum, 1972

GARRETT, TRUMAN. Pseudonym of Margaret (Haddican) Judd, 1906-   , q.v.
Murder—First Edition. Arcadia, 1956

GARRETT, WILLIAM (A.). 1890-1967.
Dr. Ricardo. Hutchinson, 1925; Appleton, 1925
Friday to Monday. Hutchinson, 1923; Appleton, 1923
From Dusk Till Dawn. Lane, 1929; Appleton, 1929
The Professional Guest. Lane, 1928; Appleton, 1928
The Secret of the Hills. Jarrolds, 1920. U.S. title: Treasure Royal. Appleton, 1926
Treasure Royal; see The Secret of the Hills

GARRETT, WINIFRED SELINA. 1909-   . Pseudonym: Lyn Dean, q.v.

GARRIK, IVAN. Pseudonym.
The Cave and the Beast. Vantage, 1966

GARRISON, CHARLES M. Pseudonym: Charles MacDaniel, q.v.

GARRITY. Pseudonym of David James Gerrity, 1923-   . See also: DAVE GERRITY.
Cry Me a Killer. GM, 1961; Muller pb, 1963
Dragon Hunt. Signet, 1967
The Hot Mods. Signet, 1969
Kiss Off the Dead. GM, 1960; Muller pb, 1961

GARROD, JOHN WILLIAM. Joint pseudonym with Ronald Charles Payne: John Castle, q.v.

GARROD, PAT
-Little Doll. Allen, 1963
Man in a Net. Allen, 1966

GARSIA, CLIVE. Pseudonym: Guy Cottar, q.v.

GARSTON, GUY. Pseudonym of Bernard John Hurren.
The Champagne Mystery. Muller, 1935

GARTH, DAVID. 1908-   .
-Angels are Cowards. Dodd, 1934
Appointment with Danger; see The Road to Glenfairlie
Bermuda Calling. Putnam, 1944
Challenge for Three. Kinsey, 1938; Hale, 1939
Eastward in Eden. Kinsey, 1939; Hale, 1940
Fire on the Wind. Putnam (New York), 1951; Putnam (London), 1952
Four Men and a Prayer. Kinsey, 1937
Gray Canaan. Putnam, 1947
A Love Like That. Kinsey, 1937
Manila Masquerade. Kinsey, 1942 ss
-Never Mind the Lady. Dodd, 1935
The Road to Glenfairlie. Kinsey, 1940; Hale, 1942. Also published as: Appointment with Danger. Popular Library, 1948
Three Roads to a Star. Putnam, 1955; Hale, 1956
Thunderbird. Kinsey, 1942; Paul, 1943
Tiger Milk. Kinsey, 1941; Paul, 1942
The Tortured Angel. Putnam, 1948
The Watch on the Bridge. Putnam, 1959

GARTH, ED. Both titles are novelizations of the Matt Lincoln TV series.
The Hostage. Lancer, 1971
The Revolutionist. Lancer, 1970

GARTLAND, HANNAH
The Globe Hollow Mystery. Dodd, 1923
The House of Cards. Dodd, 1922; Jenkins, 1924

GARVE, ANDREW. Pseudonym of Paul Winterton, 1908-   . Other pseudonyms: Roger Bax, Paul Somers, qq.v.
The Ascent of D-13. Collins, 1969; Harper, 1969
The Ashes of Loda. Collins, 1965; Harper, 1965
Boomerang. Collins, 1970; Harper, 1970
By-Line for Murder; see A Press of Suspects
The Case of Robert Quarry. Collins, 1972; Harper, 1972
The Cuckoo Line Affair. Collins, 1953; Harper, 1953
Death and the Sky Above. Collins, 1953; Harper, 1954
The End of the Track. Collins, 1955; Harper, 1956
The Far Sands. Collins, 1961; Harper, 1960
The File on Lester. Collins, 1974. U.S. title: The Lester Affair. Harper, 1974
Fontego's Folly; see No Mask for Murder
Frame-Up. Collins, 1964; Harper, 1964
The Galloway Case. Collins, 1958; Harper, 1958
The Golden Deed. Collins, 1960; Harper, 1960
A Hero for Leanda. Collins, 1959; Harper, 1959
Hide and Go Seek; see Murderer's Fen
A Hole in the Ground. Collins, 1952; Harper, 1952
The House of Soldiers. Collins, 1962; Harper, 1961
The Late Bill Smith. Collins, 1971; Harper, 1971
The Lester Affair; see The File on Lester
The Long Short Cut. Collins, 1968; Harper, 1968
The Megstone Plot. Collins, 1956; Harper, 1957
Murder in Moscow. Collins, 1951. U.S. title: Murder Through the Looking Glass. Harper, 1952
Murder Through the Looking Glass; see Murder in Moscow
Murderer's Fen. Collins, 1966. U.S. title: Hide and Go Seek. Harper, 1966
The Narrow Search. Collins, 1957; Harper, 1957
No Mask for Murder. Collins, 1950. U.S. title: Fontego's Folly. Harper, 1950
No Tears for Hilda. Collins, 1950; Harper, 1950
A Press of Suspects. Collins, 1951. U.S. title: By-Line for Murder. Harper, 1951
Prisoner's Friend. Collins, 1962; Harper, 1962
The Riddle of Samson. Collins, 1954; Harper, 1955
The Sea Monks. Collins, 1963; Harper, 1963
A Very Quiet Place. Collins, 1967; Harper, 1967

GARVICE, CHARLES. 1833-1920.
The Fatal Ruby. Hodder, 1909; Doran, 1909

GARVIN, RICHARD M(cCLELLAN), 1934-   , and EDMUND G. ADDEO.
The FORTEC Conspiracy. Sherbourne, 1968
The Talbott Agreement. Sherbourne, 1968

GASCAR, PIERRE. Pseudonym of Pierre Fournier, 1916-   .
Lambs of Fire. Braziller, 1965. (Translation of Les Moutons de Feu. Paris, 1963.)

GASCOIGNE, PETER. Pseudonym of Peter Townend, 1935-   , q.v.
Zero Always Wins. Collins, 1961

GASK, ARTHUR (CECIL). 1872-   . Series character: Gilbert Larose = GL.
The Beachy Head Murder. Jenkins, 1941 GL
Cloud the Smiter. Jenkins, 1926 GL
Crime Upon Crime. Jenkins, 1952; Roy, 1957 GL
The Dark Highway. Jenkins, 1928 GL
The Dark Mill Stream. Jenkins, 1947 GL
The Fall of a Dictator. Jenkins, 1939
Gentlemen of Crime. Jenkins, 1932; Macaulay, 1933 GL
The Grave-Digger of Monks Arden. Jenkins, 1938 GL
The Hangman's Knot. Jenkins, 1936 GL
The Hidden Door. Jenkins, 1934; Macaulay, 1935 GL
His Prey was Man. Jenkins, 1942 GL
The House on the Fens. Jenkins, 1940 GL
The House on the Island. Jenkins, 1932 GL

The House with the High Wall. Jenkins, 1948 GL
The Judgment of Larose. Jenkins, 1934; Macaulay, 1935 GL
The Lonely House. Jenkins, 1929; Macaulay, 1931 GL
The Man of Death. Jenkins, 1946 GL
Marauders by Night. Jenkins, 1951 GL
The Master Spy. Jenkins, 1937; Macaulay, 1937 GL
Murder in the Night; see The Red Paste Murders
The Mystery of Fell Castle. Jenkins, 1944 GL
Night and Fog. Jenkins, 1951
The Night of the Storm. Jenkins, 1937 GL
The Poisoned Goblet. Jenkins, 1935 GL
The Red Paste Murders. Jenkins, 1924. U.S. title: Murder in the Night. Macaulay, 1932
The Secret of the Garden. Jenkins, 1924
The Secret of the Sandhills. Jenkins, 1923
The Shadow of Larose. Jenkins, 1930 GL
The Silent Dead. Jenkins, 1950 GL
The Storm Breaks. Jenkins, 1949 GL
The Tragedy of the Silver Moon. Jenkins, 1940 GL
The Unfolding Years. Jenkins, 1947 GL
The Vaults of Blackarden Castle. Jenkins, 1950 GL
The Vengeance of Larose. Jenkins, 1939 GL

GASKILL, JANE. 1941-   .
-A Sweet, Sweet Summer. Hodder, 1969

GASKIN, CATHERINE. 1929-   .
Edge of Glass. Collins, 1967; Doubleday, 1967
The File on Devlin. Collins, 1965; Doubleday, 1965
Fiona. Collins, 1970; Doubleday, 1970
The Lynmara Legacy. Collins, 1975; Doubleday, 1976
The Property of a Gentleman. Collins, 1974; Doubleday, 1974
The Tilsit Inheritance. Collins, 1963; Doubleday, 1963

GASS, SHERLOCK BRONSON. Pseudonym: Morrison Dupree, q.v.

GASTON, BILL. Series character: Roy MacLean, in at least those marked RM.
Dark Roots of Fear. Jenkins, 1969
Death Crag. Hammond, 1965 RM
The Death Dealers. Hammond, 1966
Deep Green Death. Hammond, 1963 RM
Drifting Death. Hammond, 1964 RM
Shabby Eagles. Hale, 1973
Zero 08.00. Hammond, 1966

GATCHELL, CHARLES. 1851-1910. Pseudonym: Thorold King, q.v.

GATENBY, ROSEMARY. 1918-   .
Aim to Kill. Morrow, 1968; Hale, 1969
Deadly Relations. Morrow, 1970; Hale, 1971
Evil is As Evil Does. Mill, 1967; Hale, 1968
Hanged for a Sheep. Dodd, 1973; Hale, 1974
The Season of Danger. Dodd, 1974

GATES, CLIFFORD
The Case of the Murdered Caretaker. Amalgamated Press, 1940. (Sexton Blake.)

GATES, H(ENRY) L(EYFORD). 1880-   .
-Born to Sin. Macaulay, 1934
Death Counts Five. Watt, 1934
-The Devil's Lady. Macaulay, 1933
-Even the Rich Girl. Macaulay, 1934
-High Road to Hell. Godwin, 1938
The House of Murder. Fiction League, 1930
The Laughing Peril. Macaulay, 1933
Murder in the Fog. Macaulay, 1932. British title: Murder in the Mist. Hurst, 1933
Murder in the Mist; see Murder in the Fog
The Mystery of the Hope Diamond. International Copyright Bureau, 1921
The Mystery of the 7 Bad Men. Macaulay, 1933
-The Red Dancer of Moscow. Barse, 1928; Readers Library, 1928
The Scarlet Fan. Macaulay, 1932

GATES, NATALIE
Decoy in Diamonds. Putnam, 1971; Hale, 1973
Hush Hush Johnson. Holt, 1967

GATES, TUDOR. Series character: Danny Scipio = DS (novelizations of the TV series Vendetta).
Ancora Scipio. Muller, 1970 DS
I was Walking Down Below. Corgi, 1967
Mister Scipio. Corgi, 1968 DS
Scipio. Corgi, 1967 DS

GATTZDEN, MATT
Black Vendetta. Belmont, 1970
O.D. at Sweet Claude's. Belmont, 1970

GAULDEN, RAY. 1914-   .
A Good Place to Die. Hale, 1965

GAULT, MARK. Pseudonym of John Cournos, 1881-1966. Other pseudonym: John Courtney, q.v.
The Face of Death. Methuen, 1933

GAULT, WILLIAM CAMPBELL. 1910-   .
Pseudonym: Will Duke, q.v. Series characters: Brock (The Rock) Callahan = BC; Joe Puma = JP.
Blood on the Boards. Dutton, 1953; Boardman, 1954
The Bloodstained Bokhara; see The Bloody Bokhara
The Bloody Bokhara. Dutton, 1952. British title: The Bloodstained Bokhara. Boardman, 1953
The Canvas Coffin. Dutton, 1953; Boardman, 1953
Come Die with Me. Random, 1959; Boardman, 1961 BC
The Convertible Hearse. Random, 1957; Boardman, 1958 BC
County Kill. Simon, 1962; Boardman, 1963 BC
Day of the Ram. Random, 1956; Boardman, 1958 BC
Dead Hero. Dutton, 1963; Boardman, 1964 BC
Death Out of Focus. Random, 1959; Boardman, 1959
Don't Call Tonight; see End of a Call Girl
Don't Cry for Me. Dutton, 1952; Boardman, 1952
End of a Call Girl. Crest, 1958. British title: Don't Call Tonight. Boardman, 1960 JP
The Hundred-Dollar Girl. Dutton, 1961; Boardman, 1963 JP
Million Dollar Tramp. Crest, 1960; Boardman, 1962 JP
Murder in the Raw; see Ring Around Rosa
Night Lady. Crest, 1958; Boardman, 1960 JP
Ring Around Rosa. Dutton, 1955; Boardman, 1955. Also published as: Murder in the Raw. Dell, 1956 BC
Run, Killer, Run. Dutton, 1954; Boardman, 1955
Square in the Middle. Random, 1956; Boardman, 1957
The Sweet Blond Trap. Zenith, 1959
Sweet Wild Wench. Crest, 1959; Boardman, 1961 JP
Vein of Violence. Simon, 1961; Boardman, 1962 BC
The Wayward Widow. Crest, 1959; Boardman, 1960 JP

GAUNT, ARTHUR NETTLETON. Pseudonym: Arthur Nettleton, q.v.

GAUNT, JEFFREY. Pseudonym of Geo(rge) E(rnest) Rochester, q.v.
The Haunted Man. Eldon, 1951

GAUNT, M. B. Pseudonym of Richard Henry Horsfield, 1872-1942.
The Leases of Death. Long, 1937

GAUNT, MARY (ELIZABETH BAKEWELL). 1872-1942.
The Mummy Moves. Laurie, 1910; Clode, 1925

GAUTIER, JEAN-JACQUES
-The Bridge of Asses. Barker, 1953
-Skin Deep. Barker, 1955
Triple Mirror. Barker, 1951; Roy, 1954

GAVIN, CATHERINE (IRVINE)
The Devil in Harbour. Hodder, 1968; Morrow, 1968

GAVIN, MARIAN
-Jailer, My Jailer. Doubleday, 1964; Dent, 1964

GAVINE, WILLIAM
Wings of Mystery. Collins, 1929

GAYE, PHOEBE FENWICK. 1905-   .
Treen and Wild Horses. Cassell, 1958; British Book Service, 1958

GAYLE, NEWTON. Joint pseudonym of Maurice C. Guiness and Muna Lee de Munoz Marin, 1895-   . Series character: James Greer, in all titles.
Death Follows a Formula. Scribner, 1935; Gollancz, 1935
Death in the Glass. Scribner, 1937; Gollancz, 1937
Murder at 28:10. Scribner, 1936; Gollancz, 1936
Murder in the Haunted Sentry-Box; see The Sentry-Box Murder
The Sentry-Box Murder. Scribner, 1935. British title: Murder in the Haunted Sentry-Box. Gollancz, 1935
Sinister Crag. Scribner, 1939; Gollancz, 1938

GAYLORD, OTIS H.
The Rise and Fall of Legs Diamond. Bantam, 1960. (Novelization of the movie.)

GAYTON, REBECCA. See: LOUISE EPPLEY.

GAZE, RICHARD. 1917-   . Pseudonym: John Gale, q.v.

GEACH, CHRISTINE. 1930-   . Pseudonym: Anne Loring, q.v.

GEARON, JOHN. Pseudonym: John Flagg, q.v.
The Velvet Well. Duell, 1946; Pilot, 1947

GEDDES, PAUL
The High Game. Joseph, 1968; Weybright, 1968

G

A November Wind. Joseph, 1970; Coward, 1971
The Ottawa Allegation. Faber, 1973; Coward, 1973

GEE, MAURICE
In my Father's Den. Faber, 1972

GEHMAN, RICHARD (BOYD). 1921-1972.
Driven. McKay, 1954; Davies, 1956
Each Life to Live. Red Seal (Fawcett), 1952
The Had. Simon, 1965
The Slander of Witches. Rinehart, 1955

GEIS, GILBERT L. Pseudonym: Gil Lawrence, q.v.

GELLER, ELI
Window Episode. Mystery House, 1958

GELLER, STEPHEN
She Let Him Continue. Dutton, 1966. Also published as: Pretty Poison. Ballantine, 1967

GELLIBRAND, EDWARD
The End of a Cigarette. Long, 1924
The Windblow Mystery. Hamilton, 1926

GELLIS, ROBERTA (LEAH JACOBS). 1927- .
Sing Witch, Sing Death. Bantam, 1975

GEOGHEGAN, LAURENCE
The Breckenridge Enigma. Methuen, 1929
The Double Death Mystery. Mellifont, 1934
The Subterranean Club. Hodder, 1932
The Vagabond Sonata. Hodder, 1930

GEORGE, ALFRED K.
Snow Among the Stars. Paul, 1938

GEORGE, BRIAN
Atom of Doubt. Methuen, 1959

GEORGE, DAVID ROBINSON
Death Meets the Deadline. Vulcan, 1944

GEORGE, JONATHAN. Joint pseudonym of John (Frederick) Burke, 1922- , q.v., and George Theiner, 1927- . Other Burke pseudonyms: Jonathan Burke, Harriet Esmond, Martin Sands, qq.v.
Dead Letters. Macmillan (London), 1972
The Kill Dog. Macmillan (London), 1970; Doubleday, 1970

GEORGE, PETER (BRYAN). 1924-1966. Pseudonyms: Peter Bryant, Bryan Peters, qq.v.
Come Blond, Came Murder. Boardman, 1952
Commander-1. Heinemann, 1965; Delacorte, 1965
Cool Murder. Boardman, 1958. Reprinted as by Bryan Peters: Mayflower, 1965
The Final Steal. Boardman, 1962; Dell, 1965
Pattern of Death. Boardman, 1954

GEORGE, SARA. 1947- .
Acid Drop. Macmillan (London), 1975; Atheneum, 1975

GEORGE, THEODORE. Series character: Lt. Arnold Zimmerman, in both titles.
The Deadly Homecoming. Dodd, 1972; Hale, 1974
The Murders on the Square. Dodd, 1971

GEORGE, W(ALTER) L(IONEL). 1882-1926.
One of the Guilty. Harper, 1923; Chapman, 1923

GEORGIUS. Pseudonym of Georges Guibourg, 1897- .
My Fair Lady. Staples, 1951; Roy, 1954

GERAHTY, DIGBY GEORGE. Pseudonym: Robert Standish, q.v.

GERARD, FRANCIS. 1905- . Series characters: Commissioner Sanders (continuing the character created by Edgar Wallace, 1875-1932, q.v.) = S; Sir John Meredith, in at least those marked JM.
Bare Bodkin. Macdonald, 1951 JM
The Black Emperor. Rich, 1936 JM
Concrete Castle. Rich, 1936. U.S. title: The Concrete Castle Murders. Holt, 1936 JM
The Concrete Castle Murders; see Concrete Castle
The Dictatorship of the Dove. Rich, 1936 JM
Emerald Embassy. Rich, 1939 JM
The Envoy of the Emperor. Macdonald, 1951
Fatal Friday. Rich, 1937; Holt, 1937 JM
-The Flail and the Fish. Macdonald, 1949
Flight into Fear. Macdonald, 1948 JM
Golden Guilt. Rich, 1938; Dutton, 1940 JM
The Justice of Sanders. Rich, 1951 S
The Law of the River. Rich, 1939; Dutton, 1940 S ss
The Mark of the Moon. Macdonald, 1952
The Mind of John Meredith. Macdonald, 1946 JM
Number 1-2-3. Rich, 1936. U.S. title: The 1-2-3 Murders. Holt, 1937 JM
The 1-2-3 Murders; see Number 1-2-3
The Prince of Paradise. Rich, 1938; Dutton, 1941 JM
The Prisoner of the Pyramid. Macdonald, 1948 JM
The Promise of the Phoenix. Macdonald, 1950 JM
Red Rope. Rich, 1937; Dutton, 1939 JM
The Return of Sanders of the River. Rich, 1938; Dutton, 1939 S ss
Secret Sceptre. Rich, 1937; Dutton, 1939 JM
Sinister Secret. Macdonald, 1952
Sorcerer's Shaft. Macdonald, 1947 JM
Transparent Traitor. Macdonald, 1950 JM
Wotan's Wedge. Rich, 1939

GERARD, LOUISE
The Mystery of "Golden Lotus". Mills, 1919
The Strange Young Man. Mills, 1931; Macaulay, 1931

GERARD, MORICE. Pseudonym of John Jessop Teague, 1856-1929.
The Adventures of an Equerry. Cassell, 1905. Also published as: Under the Red Star; or, The Adventures of an Equerry. Cassell, 1911
The Adventures of Marmaduke Clegg. Hodder, 1917
-Beacon Fires. Hodder, 1915
-Black Gull Rock. Nelson, 1897
A Black Vintage. Digby, 1901
-The Broken Sword. Hodder, 1910
-Cast Out. Hurst, 1890
Check to the King. Hodder, 1906
A Corner in Diamonds. Hodder, 1916
-The Countess of Zelle. Odhams, 1919
-Crenland Castle. Hodder, 1912
-The Crowning of Esther. Odhams, 1919
-Danes Abbey. Hodder, 1918
Dr. Manton. Long, 1907
-A Fair Prisoner. Partridge, 1912
-A Fair Refugee. Hodder, 1909
For England. Ward, 1902
-For France. Odhams, 1922
-Fortune's Wheel. Odhams, 1921
-A Gentleman of London. Nash, 1908
-A Grey Fair. Holden, 1924
-The Grip of the Wolf. Marshall, 1900
-The Haunted Shore. Hodder, 1918
-The Heart of a Hero. Hodder, 1913
-A Heather Mixture. Hodder, 1914
A Heather Mystery. Odhams, 1919
-An Interrupted Wedding. Hodder, 1910
-John Montcalm. Long, 1908
-The King's Signet. Hodder, 1909
-The King Waits. Odhams, 1921
-The Last Link. Hodder, 1911
-The League of Life. Jarrolds, 1909
-A Lieutenant of the King. Cassell, 1904
Love in the Purple; see Purple Love
The Man of the Moment. Ward, 1900
The Man with the White Face. Ward, 1903
The Mystery Car. Hodder, 1913
-The New Order. Hodder, 1917
Night Wings. Hodder, 1915
-One of Marlborough's Captains. Hodder, 1912
-Prince Karl. Nelson, 1900
-Purple Love. Hodder, 1908. Also published as: Love in the Purple. Hodder, 1911
-The Prisoner. Nash, 1908
-Queen's Mate. Hodder, 1901
-The Red Seal. Cassell, 1906
-Rose of Blenheim. Hodder, 1907
The Secret of the Moor. Newnes, 1907
-The Shadow of Gilsland. Marshall, 1901
-The Silent Conquest. Century, 1911
-A Snow Heroine. Hodder, 1912
-The Tenant of the Grange. Cassell, 1903
-The Tide of Fortune. Hodder, 1916
Under the Red Star; or, The Adventures of an Equerry; see The Adventures of an Equerry
-The Unseen Barrier. Hodder, 1911
-The Unspoken Word. Hodder, 1910
-The Ward of Navarre. Odhams, 1921

GERMESHAUSEN, ANNA LOUISE
Cats in Crime...and others. Luther Norris, 1970 ss

GEROULD, GORDON HALL. 1877-1953.
A Midsummer Mystery. Appleton (New York & London), 1925

GERRARD, R. J. See: RANDLE McKAY.

GERRITY, DAVE [DAVID JAMES GERRITY]. 1923- . Pseudonym: Garrity, q.v.
The Never Contract. Signet, 1975

GERRY, MARGARITA SPALDING
The Sound of Water. Harper, 1914

GERSHE, LEONARD
Miss Pill is Missing. French (London), 1963. (3-act play.)

GERSON, JACK
Man on the Crater's Edge. Hale, 1972

GERSON, NOEL B(ERTRAM). 1914- . Pseudonyms: Samuel Edwards, Leon Phillips, qq.v.
All That Glitters. Doubleday, 1975
State Trooper. Doubleday, 1973; Barker, 1974
Temptation to Steal. Doubleday, 1972

GHEORGHIU, C(ONSTANTIN) VIRGIL. 1916- .
-The Death of Kyralessa. Regnery, 1968. (Translation of Le Meurtre de Kyralessa. Paris, 1966.)
The Immortals of the Mountain. Regnery, 1969. (Translation of Les Immortels d'Agapia. Paris, 1964.)
-The Twenty-Fifth Hour. Knopf, 1950; Heinemann, 1950. (Translation of La Vingt-Cinquieme Heure. Paris, 1949.)

GIANETTA, SAL
The Capac Legacy. Simon, 1975; Allen, 1975

GIBBON, CHARLES. 1843-1890.
-Amoret. Maxwell, 1886
-Beyond Compare. Low, 1888
-Blood Money, and other stories. Chatto, 1889 ss
-The Braes of Yarrow. Low, 1881; Harper, 1881
-By Mead and Stream. Chatto, 1884; Harper, 1884
-Clare of Claresmede. Low, 1886; Harper, 1886
-Dangerous Connexions. Maxwell, 1864
-The Dead Heart. Maxwell, 1865
-Fancy Free and other stories. Chatto, 1884 ss
-The Flower of the Forest. Chatto, 1882
-For Lack of Gold. Blackie, 1871; Munro, 1880
-Garvock. Maxwell, 1885
-The Golden Knot. Chatto, 1882; Harper, 1882
A Hard Knot. Chatto, 1885; Harper, 1885. (A plagiarized version of Emile Gaboriau's L'Affaire Lerouge, q.v.)
-Heart's Delight. Chatto, 1885; Harper, 1885
-A Heart's Problem. Chatto, 1881; Harper, 1882
-In Cupid's Wars. White, 1884
-In Honour Bound. Chatto, 1874; Munro, 1880
-In Love and War. Chatto, 1877
-In Pastures Green and other stories. Chatto, 1880; Munro, 1883 ss
Lady Grace's Mistake. Modern, 193? (Original title?)
-Loving a Dream, and One of His Inventions. Chatto, 1884
-A Maiden Fair and other stories. Maxwell, 1885; Munro, 1883 ss
Margaret Carmichael; or, A Princess of Jutedom; see A Princess of Jutedom
-Of High Degree. Chatto, 1883; Harper, 1882
-A Princess of Jutedom. Ward, 1886. U.S. title: Margaret Carmichael; or, A Princess of Jutedom. New Amsterdam, 1896
-Queen of the Meadow. Chatto, 1880; Harper, 1880
-Robin Grey. Blackie, 1869; Munro, 1880
-The Shadow of Wrong. Maxwell, 1886
-A Strange Wooing. Ward, 1890. U.S. title: Was Ever Woman in This Humor Wooed? Lovell, 1890
Was Ever Woman in This Humor Wooed?; see A Strange Wooing
-What will the World Say? Bentley, 1875; Munro, 1883

GIBBON, PERCEVAL. 1879-1926.
The Adventures of Miss Gregory. Dent, 1912; Putnam, 1913 ss
-The Dark Places. Methuen, 1926 ss
-Salvator. Blackwood, 1908; Doubleday, 1909
The Second Class Passenger, and other stories. Methuen, 1913 ss
-Souls in Bondage. Blackwood, 1904
-Those Who Smiled, and other stories. Cassell, 1920
Vrouw Grobelaar and Her Leading Cases; see The Vrouw Grobelaar's Leading Cases
The Vrouw Grobelaar's Leading Cases. Blackwood, 1905. U.S. title: Vrouw Grobelaar and Her Leading Cases. McClure, 1906 ss

GIBBONS, CROMWELL, 1893- .
-The Bat Woman. World, 1938
Murder in Hollywood. Kemp, 1936

GIBBONS, H(ARRY) H(ORNABY) CLIFFORD. 1888-1958. Pseudonym: Gilbert Chester, q.v. All titles below feature Sexton Blake and were published by Amalgamated Press.
The Affair of the Country Club. 1924
The Affair of the Cross-Roads. 1926
The Affair of the Diamond Star. 1925
The Affair of the Kidnapped Crook. 1927
The Ballot Box Mystery. 1929
The Case of the Bogus Bride! 1925
The Case of the Old Oak Chest. 1926
The Case of the Red Crimona's. 1925
The Case of the Silent Safe-Cutters. 1926
The Crook of Mayfair. 1925
The Excavator's Secret. 1926. Reprinted in 1938 as by Gilbert Chester.
The Flaming Belt. 1929
The Fur Raiders. 1928. Reprinted in 1939 as by Gilbert Chester.
The Great Revue Mystery. 1923
The Great Salvage Swindle. 1927
The King's Secret. 1924
Limited Liability. 1925
The Motor Show Mystery. 1929
The Mystery of the Four Rooms. 1927
The Mystery of the Mansion Fire. 1927
On the Night Express! 1925
The Riddle of the Garage. 1928
The Riddle of the Registry Office. 1925
The Riddle of the Runaway Cat. 1928
The Riddle of the West End Hairdresser. 1928. Reprinted in 1939 as by Gilbert Chester.
The Secret Millionaire. 1924
The Secret of the Carpathians. 1924
The Secret of the Snows. 1927. Reprinted in 1938 as by Gilbert Chester.
The Secret People. 1924
Solved in Thirty-Six Hours! 1923
The South Coast Mystery. 1926
The Third Key. 1924
Who Killed Carson? 1927
The Yellow Cat. 1925

GIBBONS, JAMES
The Green Jade Buddha. Swan, 1946

GIBBS, ANGELICA
Murder Between Drinks. Morrow, 1932

GIBBS, GEORGE F(ORT). 1870-1942.
Anything Can Happen. Appleton, 1936
The Black Stone. Appleton, 1919
The Castle Rock Mystery. Appleton, 1927
-The Fire Within. Appleton, 1930
Foul Weather. Appleton, 1933
The Golden Bough. Appleton, 1918. British title: Under the Golden Bough. Mellifont, 1944 (abridged)
Hunted. Appleton, 1937
The Joyous Conspirator. Sears, 1927; Hodder, 1927
The Maker of Opportunities. Appleton, 1912
The Medusa Emerald. Appleton, 1907
Out of the Dark. Appleton, 1934
-Paradise Garden. Appleton, 1916
The Road to Bagdad. Appleton, 1938
The Secret Witness. Appleton, 1917
The Silent Battle. Appleton, 1913
The Silver Death. Appleton, 1939
The Sleeper Wakes. Appleton, 1941
The Splendid Outcast. Appleton, 1920
The Triangle Man. Appleton, 1939
Under the Golden Bough; see The Golden Bough
The Vagrant Duke. Appleton, 1921
The Vanishing Idol. Appleton, 1936
The Yellow Diamond. Appleton, 1935
The Yellow Dove. Appleton, 1915

GIBBS, HENRY (ST. JOHN CLAIR). 1909-1975. Pseudonym: Simon Harvester, q.v.

At a Farthing's Rate. Jarrolds, 1943
The Bamboo Prison. Jarrolds, 1961
Blue Days and Fair. Jarrolds, 1946
Cape of Shadows. Jarrolds, 1954
Children's Overture. Jarrolds, 1947
Cream and Cider. Jarrolds, 1952
Disputed Barricade. Jarrolds, 1952
From All Blindness. Jarrolds, 1944
Know Then Thyself. Jarrolds, 1947
The Mortal Fire. Jarrolds, 1963
Not to the Swift. Jarrolds, 1944
The Six-Mile Face. Jarrolds, 1952
The Splendor and the Dust. Jarrolds, 1955
Taps, Colonel Roberts. Jarrolds, 1951
Ten-Thirty Sharp. Jarrolds, 1949
Thunder at Dawn. Jarrolds, 1957
The Tumult and the Shouting. Jarrolds, 1958
The Winds of Time. Jarrolds, 1956
Withered Garland. Jarrolds, 1950

GIBBS, MARY ANNE. Pseudonym of Marjory E. S. Bidwell.
The Amateur Governess. Hurst, 1964. U.S. title: The House of Ravensbourne. Pyramid, 1965

GIBBS, PHILIP (HAMILTON). 1877-1962.
The Ambassador's Wife. Hutchinson, 1956

GIBBS-SMITH, C(HARLES) H(ARVARD). 1909- .
The Caroline Affair; see Operation Caroline
Escape and Be Secret. Hutchinson, 1957
Operation Caroline. Heinemann, 1953. U.S. title: The Caroline Affair. Viking, 1954
-Yankee Poodle. Heinemann, 1955

GIBERSON, DOROTHY (DODDS)
The Echoing Wave. Coward, 1960; Gresham, 1962

GIBNEY, SOMERVILLE
A Charge from the Grave. Ward, 1889
Sentenced! Chatto, 1890
The Trial of Parson Finch. Ward, 1891

GIBSON, WALTER B(ROWN). 1897- . Pseudonym: Maxwell Grant, q.v. Series character: Lamont Cranston (The Shadow) = LC (see also pseudonymous titles).
A Blonde for Murder. Atlas, 1948
Grove of Doom. Tempo, 1969 LC
Looks That Kill! Atlas, 1948
The Mask of Mephisto; see The Shadow
Murder by Magic; see The Shadow
Murder by Moonlight. Tempo, 1969 LC
Return of the Shadow. Belmont, 1963 LC
The Shadow. Doubleday, 1975. (Contains two pulp novels: The Mask of Mephisto, and Murder by Magic.) LC
Voodoo Death. Tempo, 1969 LC

GIDLEY, WILL(IAM) S(ELDEN). 1852- .
A Dicker in Souls, and other stories. Hazen, 1905 ss, some criminous

GIELGUD, VAL (HENRY). 1900- . Series characters: Antony Havilland, in at least those marked AH; Inspector Gregory Pellew and Viscount Clymping, in at least those marked P&C; Inspector Simon Spears, in at least those marked SS.
And Died So? Collins, 1961 P&C
Beyond Dover. Hutchinson, 1940 ss
The Black Sambo Affair. Macmillan (London), 1972 P&C
The Broken Men. Constable, 1932; Houghton, 1933
The Candle-Holders. Macmillan (London), 1970 P&C

Cat. Collins, 1956; Random, 1957
Conduct of a Member. Collins, 1967 P&C
Confident Morning. Collins, 1943
Death of an Extra, with Holt Marvell (pseudonym of Eric Maschwitz, 1901-   , q.v.) Rich, 1935 SS
Death at Broadcasting House, with Holt Marvell (pseudonym of Eric Maschwitz, 1901-   , q.v.). Rich, 1934. U.S. title: London Calling. Doubleday, 1934 SS
Death in Budapest, with Holt Marvell (pseudonym of Eric Maschwitz, 1901-   , q.v.) Rich, 1937 SS
Fall of a Sparrow. Collins, 1949. U.S. title: Stalking Horse. Morrow, 1950 AH
A Fearful Thing. Macmillan (London), 1975 P&C
The First Television Murder, with Eric Maschwitz (1901-   , q.v.). Hutchinson, 1940
Gallows' Foot. Collins, 1958 P&C
The Goggle-Box Affair. Collins, 1963. U.S. title: Through a Glass Darkly. Scribner, 1963 P&C
Gravelhanger. Cassell, 1934. U.S. title: The Ruse of the Vanished Women. Doubleday, 1934 AH
The High Jump. Collins, 1953. U.S. title: Ride for a Fall. Morrow, 1953
Imperial Treasure. Constable, 1931; Houghton, 1931
In Such a Night... Macmillan (London), 1974 P&C
London Calling; see Death at Broadcasting House
A Necessary End. Collins, 1969 P&C
Outrage in Manchukuo. Cassell, 1937 AH
Prinvest-London. Collins, 1965 P&C
The Red Account. Rich, 1938
Ride for a Fall; see The High Jump
The Ruse of the Vanished Women; see Gravelhanger
Special Delivery. Collins, 1950 AH
Stalking Horse; see Fall of a Sparrow
Through a Glass Darkly; see The Goggle-Box Affair
To Bed at Noon. Collins, 1960 P&C
Under London, with Holt Marvell (pseudonym of Eric Maschwitz, 1901-   , q.v.). Rich, 1933

GIFFORD, A(LICE) S(HERMAN)
A Romance of Hellerism. Neely, 1901. (3 novelets, at least one criminous.)

GIFFORD, LEE
Pieces of the Game. GM, 1960

GIFFORD, NICHOLAS
Long Distance—Wrong Number. Jenkins, 1962

GIFFORD, THOMAS
The Wind Chill Factor. Putnam, 1975; H. Hamilton, 1975

GIFT, THEO. Pseudonym of Theodora Havers Boulger,   -1889.
-Victims. Hurst, 1887; Holt, 1887

GILBART-SMITH, MARCUS MERVYN TOBIAS. 1899-   . Pseudonym: Hibbart Gilson, q.v.

GILBERT, ANNA
Images of Rose. Hodder, 1974; Delacorte, 1974
The Look of Innocence. Hodder, 1975

GILBERT, ANTHONY. Pseudonym of Lucy Beatrice Malleson, 1899-1973. Other pseudonyms: J. Kilmeny Keith, Anne Meredith, qq.v. Series characters: Arthur Crook = AC; Scott Egerton = SE; M. Dupuy = D.

After the Verdict; see She Shall Die
And Death Came Too. Collins, 1956; Random, 1956 AC
The Bell of Death. Collins, 1939 AC
Black Death; see Footsteps Behind Me
The Black Stage. Collins, 1945; Smith & Durrell, 1946. Also published as: Murder Cheats the Bride. Bantam, 1948 AC
The Body on the Beam. Collins, 1932; Dodd, 1932 SE
By Hook or by Crook; see The Spinster's Secret
The Case Against Andrew Fane. Collins, 1931; Dodd, 1931
A Case for Mr. Crook; see Miss Pinnegar Disappears
The Case of the Tea-Cosy's Aunt. Collins, 1942. U.S. title: Death in the Blackout. Smith & Durrell, 1943 AC
The Clock in the Hatbox. Collins, 1939; Arcadia, 1943 AC
Courtier to Death. Collins, 1936. U.S. title: The Dover Train Mystery. Dial, 1936 D
Dark Death; see Footsteps Behind Me
Dear Dead Woman. Collins, 1940; Mystery House, 1942. Also published as: Death Takes a Redhead. Arrow, 1944 AC
Death Against the Clock. Collins, 1958; Random, 1958 AC
Death at Four Corners. Collins, 1929; Dial, 1929 SE
Death at the Door; see He Came by Night
Death Casts a Long Shadow; see Death Takes a Wife
Death in Fancy Dress. Collins, 1933
Death in the Blackout; see The Case of the Tea-Cosy's Aunt
Death in the Wrong Room. Collins, 1947; Barnes, 1947 AC
Death Knocks Three Times. Collins, 1949; Random, 1950 AC
Death Lifts the Latch; see Don't Open the Door!
Death Takes a Redhead; see Dear Dead Woman
Death Takes a Wife. Collins, 1959. U.S. title: Death Casts a Long Shadow. Random, 1959 AC
Death Wears a Mask. Collins, 1970. U.S. title: Mr. Crook Lifts the Mask. Random, 1970 AC
Death Won't Wait; see Snake in the Grass
Die in the Dark. Collins, 1947. U.S. title: The Missing Widow. Barnes, 1948 AC
Don't Open the Door! Collins, 1945. U.S. title: Death Lifts the Latch. Barnes, 1946 AC
The Dover Train Mystery; see Courtier to Death
The Fingerprint. Collins, 1964; Random, 1964 AC
Footsteps Behind Me. Collins, 1953. U.S. title: Black Death. Random, 1953. Also published as: Dark Death. Pyramid, 1963 AC
Give Death a Name. Collins, 1957 AC
He Came by Night. Collins, 1944. U.S. title: Death at the Door. Smith & Durrell, 1945 AC
The Innocent Bottle; see Lift Up the Lid
Is She Dead Too? Collins, 1955. U.S. title: A Question of Murder. Random, 1955 AC
Knock, Knock, Who's There? Collins, 1964. U.S. title: The Voice. Random, 1965 AC
Lady Killer. Collins, 1951 AC

Lift Up the Lid. Collins, 1948. U.S. title: The Innocent Bottle. Barnes, 1949
The Long Shadow. Collins, 1932 SE
The Looking Glass Murder. Collins, 1966; Random, 1967 AC
The Man in the Button Boots. Collins, 1934; Holt, 1935 MD
The Man Who was Too Clever. Collins, 1935 SE
The Man Who Wasn't There. Collins, 1937 AC
Miss Pinnegar Disappears. Collins, 1952. U.S. title: A Case for Mr. Crook. Random, 1952 AC
Missing from her Home. Collins, 1969; Random, 1969 AC
The Missing Widow; see Die in the Dark
Mr. Crook Lifts the Mask; see Death Wears a Mask
The Mouse Who Wouldn't Play Ball. Collins, 1943. U.S. title: 30 Days to Live. Smith & Durrell, 1944 AC
Murderous Anonymous; see Night Encounter
Murder by Experts. Collins, 1936; Dial, 1937 AC
Murder Cheats the Bride; see The Black Stage
Murder Comes Home. Collins, 1950; Random, 1951 AC
Murder has no Tongue. Collins, 1937 AC
Murder is Cheap; see The Scarlet Button
The Murder of Mrs. Davenport. Collins, 1928; Dial, 1928 SE
Murder's a Waiting Game. Collins, 1972; Random, 1972 AC
The Musical Comedy Crime. Collins, 1933 SE
Mystery in the Woodshed; see Something Nasty in the Woodshed
The Mystery of the Open Window. Gollancz, 1929; Dodd, 1930 SE
The Mystery of the Woman in Red; see The Woman in Red
A Nice Cup of Tea. Collins, 1950. U.S. title: The Wrong Body. Random, 1951 AC
A Nice Little Killing. Collins, 1974; Random, 1974 AC
Night Encounter. Collins, 1968. U.S. title: Murder Anonymous. Random, 1968 AC
The Night of the Fog. Gollancz, 1930; Dodd, 1930 SE
No Dust in the Attic. Collins, 1962; Random, 1963 AC
An Old Lady Dies. Collins, 1934 SE
Out for the Kill. Collins, 1960; Random, 1960 AC
Passenger to Nowhere. Collins, 1965; Random, 1966 AC
Prelude to Murder; see Third Crime Lucky
A Question of Murder; see Is She Dead Too?
Riddle of a Lady. Collins, 1956; Random, 1957 AC
Ring for a Noose. Collins, 1963; Random, 1964 AC
The Scarlet Button. Collins, 1944; Smith & Durrell, 1945. Also published as: Murder is Cheap. Bantam, 1949 AC
She Shall Die. Collins, 1961. U.S. title: After the Verdict. Random, 1961 AC
She Vanished in the Dawn; see The Vanishing Corpse
Snake in the Grass. Collins, 1954. U.S. title: Death Won't Wait. Random, 1954 AC
Something Nasty in the Woodshed. Collins, 1942. U.S. title: Mystery in the Woodshed. Smith & Durrell, 1942 AC

The Spinster's Secret. Collins, 1946.
U.S. title: By Hook or by Crook.
Barnes, 1947 AC
A Spy for Mr. Crook. Barnes, 1944.
(British title?) AC
Tenant for the Tomb. Collins, 1971;
Random, 1971 AC
Third Crime Lucky. Collins, 1959. U.S.
title: Prelude to Murder. Random,
1959 AC
Thirty Days to Live; see The Mouse Who
Wouldn't Play Ball
The Tragedy at Freyne. Collins, 1927;
Dial, 1927 SE
Treason in my Breast. Collins, 1938 AC
Uncertain Death. Collins, 1961; Random,
1962 AC
The Vanishing Corpse. Collins, 1941.
U.S. title: She Vanished in the Dawn.
Arcadia, 1941 AC
The Visitor. Collins, 1967; Random,
1967 AC
The Voice; see Knock, Knock, Who's
There?
The Woman in Red. Collins, 1941; Smith
& Durrell, 1943. Also published as:
The Mystery of the Woman in Red.
Handi-Books, 1944 AC
The Wrong Body; see A Nice Cup of Tea

GILBERT, BERNARD. 1882- .
-Tattershall Castle. Horncastle, 1913

GILBERT, ELLIOTT
Don't Push Me Around. Popular Library,
1955
The Vice Trap. Avon, 1958

GILBERT, HARRIETT. 1948- .
Hotels with Empty Rooms. Hodder, 1973;
Harper, 1973
An Offense Against the Persons. Hodder,
1974; Harper, 1975

GILBERT, MICHAEL (FRANCIS). 1912- .
Series characters: Inspector Hazel-
rigg = H; Patrick Petrella = PP.
After the Fine Weather. Hodder, 1963;
Harper, 1963
Amateur in Violence. Davis, 1973 PP in
4 ss, H in 3 ss
The Bargain. Constable, 1961. (Play.)
Be Shot for Sixpence. Hodder, 1956;
Harper, 1956
Blood and Judgment. Hodder, 1959; Har-
per, 1959 PP
The Body of a Girl. Hodder, 1972; Har-
per, 1972
A Clean Kill. Constable, 1960. (Play.)
Close Quarters. Hodder, 1947; Walker,
1963 H
The Country-House Burglar; see Sky High
The Crack in the Teacup. Hodder, 1966;
Harper, 1966
The Danger Within; see Death in Cap-
tivity
Death has Deep Roots. Hodder, 1951;
Harper, 1951 H
Death in Captivity. Hodder, 1952. U.S.
title: The Danger Within. Harper,
1952
The Doors Open. Hodder, 1949; Walker,
1962 H
The Dust and the Heat. Hodder, 1967.
U.S. title: Overdrive. Harper, 1968
The Etruscan Net. Hodder, 1969. U.S.
title: The Family Tomb. Harper, 1970
The Family Tomb; see The Etruscan Net
Fear to Tread. Hodder, 1953; Harper,
1953 H
Flash Point. Hodder, 1974; Harper, 1974
Game Without Rules. Hodder, 1968; Har-
per, 1967 ss
He Didn't Mind Danger; see They Never
Looked Inside
The Ninety-Second Tiger. Hodder, 1973;
Harper, 1973
Overdrive; see The Dust and the Heat

The Shot in Question. Constable, 1963.
(Play.)
Sky High. Hodder, 1955. U.S. title:
The Country-House Burglar. Harper,
1955
Smallbone Deceased. Hodder, 1950; Har-
per, 1950 H
Stay of Execution. Hodder, 1971 ss, 2
with H
They Never Looked Inside. Hodder, 1948.
U.S. title: He Didn't Mind Danger.
Harper, 1949 H

GILBERT, NELSON RUST
The Affair at Pine Court. Lippincott,
1907

GILBERT, STEPHEN. 1912- .
Ratman's Notebooks. Joseph, 1968;
Viking, 1969

GILBERT, W(ILLIAM) S(CHWENCK). 1836-1911.
Foggerty's Fairy and other tales.
Routledge, 1890 ss, some criminous

GILCHRIST, R(OBERT) MURRAY. 1868-1917.
The Abbey Mystery. Ward, 1908
-Beggar's Manor. Heinemann, 1903
-The Chase. White, 1914
-The Courtesy Dame. Heinemann, 1900;
Dodd, 1900
-Damosel Croft. Paul, 1912
-The First Born. Laurie, 1911
-The Gentle Thespians. Milne, 1908
-Good-Bye to Market. Moorlands, 1908 ss
-Hercules and the Marionettes. Bliss,
1894
-Honeysuckle Rogue. Westall, 1917
-The Labyrinth. Richards, 1902
-Lords and Ladies. Hurst, 1903 ss
-Passion the Plaything. Heinemann, 1890;
Lovell, 1890
-Pretty Fanny's Way. Everett, 1909
-Roadknight. Holden, 1913
-The Rue Bargain. Richards, 1898
-The Secret Tontine. Long, 1912
-The Stone Dragon and Other Tragic Ro-
mances. Methuen, 1894 ss
-The Two Goodwins. Milne, 1908
Under Cover of Night. Long, 1914
-Weird Wedlock. Long, 1913
-Willowbrake. Methuen, 1908
-Willowford Woods. Ward, 1911

GILES, ELIZABETH. Pseudonym of John
Robert Holt, 1926- . Other pseudo-
nym: Raymond Giles, q.v.
As Darker Grows the Night. Lancer, 1972
Children of the Griffin. Lancer, 1971

GILES, FREDERICK R.
The Mysterious Mr. Jarvis. Rowland,
1892

GILES, GUY ELWYN. 1904- . Series character: Brice Kent, in both titles.
Target for Murder. Morrow, 1943
3 Died Variously. Reynal, 1941

GILES, HERBERT A(LLEN). 1845-1935.
Strange Stories from a Chinese Studio.
de la Rue, 1880 ss

GILES, KENNETH. 1922-1972. Pseudonyms:
Charles Drummond, Edmund McGirr,
qq.v. Series character: Inspector
Harry James, in at least those
marked HJ.
The Big Greed. Gollancz, 1966
Death Among the Stars. Gollancz, 1968;
Walker, 1968 HJ
Death and Mr. Prettyman. Gollancz,
1967; Walker, 1969 HJ

Death Cracks a Bottle. Gollancz, 1969;
Walker, 1970 HJ
Death in Diamonds. Gollancz, 1967;
Simon, 1968 HJ
A Death in the Church. Gollancz, 1970
A File on Death. Gollancz, 1973;
Walker, 1973 HJ
Murder Pluperfect. Gollancz, 1970;
Walker, 1970 HJ
Picture of Death; see A Provenance of
Death
A Provenance of Death. Gollancz, 1966;
Simon, 1967. Also published as: Pic-
ture of Death. Panther, 1970 HJ
Some Beasts No More. Gollancz, 1965;
Walker, 1968 HJ

GILES, NORMAN. Pseudonym of Norman
Robert McKeown.
-Keersbosskloof. Collins, 1929
-The Whips of Time. Collins, 1931

GILES, RAYMOND. Pseudonym of John Robert
Holt, 1926- . Other pseudonym:
Elizabeth Giles, q.v.
Shamus. Lancer, 1973. (Novelization of
the movie.)

GILFORD, C(HARLES) B(ERNARD). 1920- .
The Crooked Shamrock. Doubleday, 1969;
Arlington, 1970

GILL, ELIZABETH. Series character: Benvenuto Brown, in all titles.
The Crime Coast. Doubleday, 1931. British title: Strange Holiday. Cassell,
1931
Crime de Luxe. Doubleday, 1933; Cassell, 1933
Strange Holiday; see The Crime Coast
What Dread Hand? Doubleday, 1932; Cassell, 1932

GILL, HERBERT J.
The Second Knife. Houghton (London),
1935

GILL, JOHN. Pseudonym of John Russell
Gillies, 1920- .
The Last Heroes. Collins, 1973; Random,
1974
The Listener; see The Tenant
The Tenant. Collins, 1972. U.S. title:
The Listener. Stein, 1972

GILL, JOSEPHINE (ECKERT)
Dead of Summer. Doubleday, 1959; Mac-
donald, 1960
The House That Died. Doubleday, 1955;
Collins, 1956

GILL, PATRICK. Pseudonym of John Creasey,
1908-1973, q.v. Other pseudonyms:
Gordon Ashe, M. E. Cooke, Norman
Deane, Robert Caine Frazer, Michael
Halliday, Charles Hogarth, Brian
Hope, Colin Hughes, Kyle Hunt, Abel
Mann, Peter Manton, J. J. Marric,
Richard Martin, Rodney Mattheson,
Anthony Morton, Jeremy York, qq.v.
The Battle for the Cup. Mellifont, 1939
The Fighting Footballers. Mellifont,
1937
The Fighting Tramp. Mellifont, 1939
The Laughing Lightweight. Mellifont,
1937
The Mystery of the Centre-Forward.
Mellifont, 1939
The Secret Super-Charger. Mellifont,
1940
The ₤10,000 Trophy Race. Mellifont,
1939

GILLA, ESKER N.
Cap and Gown for a Shroud. Vantage,
1960

G

GILLEN, MOLLIE. 1908- .
   A Star of Death. Bles, 1960

GILLES, DANIEL
   -The Anthill. Chapman, 1962; Vanguard, 1963

GILLETTE, PAUL J. 1938- .
   The Cat O' Nine Tails. Award, 1971. (Novelization of the movie.)
   Play Misty for Me. Award, 1971; Tandem, 1972. (Novelization of the movie.)

GILLETTE, WILLIAM (HOOKER). 1855-1937.
   See also: CYRUS TOWNSEND BRADY, 1861-1920.
   The Astounding Crime on Torrington Road. Harper, 1927; Cassell, 1928
   -A Legal Wreck. Rockwood, 1888
   The Painful Predicament of Sherlock Holmes. Abramson, 1955. (Play.)
   The Red Owl. French, 1924. (Play.)
   Secret Service. French, 1898. (Play.)
   Sherlock Holmes. French, 1922. (Play.)

GILLIAM, EDWARD W(INSLOW). 1834-1925.
   -Ravenswood. Neale, 1908

GILLIAN, MICHAEL
   Warrant for a Wanton. Mill, 1952

GILLIES, JOHN RUSSELL. 1920- . Pseudonym: John Gill, q.v.

GILLMORE, RUFUS (HAMILTON). 1879-1935.
   The Alster Case. Appleton, 1914
   The Ebony Bed Murder. Mystery League, 1932
   The Mystery of the Second Shot. Appleton, 1912
   The Opal Pin. Appleton, 1914

GILMAN, DOROTHY [DOROTHY GILMAN BUTTERS]. 1923- . Series character: Mrs. Pollifax = P.
   The Amazing Mrs. Pollifax. Doubleday, 1970; Hale, 1971 P
   The Clairvoyant Countess. Doubleday, 1975; Prior, 1976
   The Elusive Mrs. Pollifax. Doubleday, 1971; Hale, 1973 P
   Mrs. Pollifax, Spy; see The Unexpected Mrs. Pollifax
   A Nun in the Closet. Doubleday, 1975. British title: A Nun in the Cupboard. Hale, 1976
   A Nun in the Cupboard; see A Nun in the Closet
   A Palm for Mrs. Pollifax. Doubleday, 1973; Hale, 1974 P
   Uncertain Voyage. Doubleday, 1967; Hale, 1968
   The Unexpected Mrs. Pollifax. Doubleday, 1966; Hale, 1967. Also published as: Mrs. Pollifax, Spy. Tandem, 1971 P

GILMORE, JOSEPH
   Vendetta. Pinnacle, 1973

GILMOUR, R.
   -Bewitched. Mellifont, 1935
   Death in the Ring. Mellifont, 1940
   Double-Cross Murder. Mellifont, 1943
   The Kukri Killer. Mellifont, 1945
   The Missing Rajah. Mellifont, 1946
   Wanted for Murder. Mellifont, 1939

GILRUTH, SUSAN. 1911- . Series character: Liane Cranfurd, in at least those marked LC.
   A Corpse for Charybdis. Hodder, 1956 LC
   Death in Ambush. Hale, 1952
   Drown Her Remembrance. Hodder, 1961 LC
   Postscript to Penelope. Hale, 1954
   The Snake is Living Yet. Hodder, 1963 LC

   Sweet Revenge. Hale, 1951
   To This Favour. Hodder, 1957 LC

GILSON, HIBBART. Pseudonym of Marcus Mervyn Tobias Gilbart-Smith, 1899- .
   The Unaccepted Death. Gill, 1928

GILZEAN, ELIZABETH (HOUGHTON BLANCHET). 1913- .
   Murder on Sundays. Hale, 1967

GIMPEL, ERICH. 1910- .
   Spy for Germany. Hale, 1957. (Translation of Spion fur Deutschland. Munich, 1956. Fictionalized true account.)

GINN, R. C. K.
   Tyger! Tyger! Macmillan, 1968

GIOVANNI, JOSE
   The Break. Cape, 1960. (Translation of Le Trou. Paris, 1957.)

GIRARD, HENRI GEORGES. 1917- . Pseudonym: Georges Arnaud, q.v.

GIRTIN, TOM [THOMAS GIRTIN]. 1913- .
   Unnatural Break. Hutchinson, 1959

GIVENS, CHARLES G(ARLAND). 1899-1964. Series character: Jimmy Hastings, in at least those marked JH
   All Cats are Grey. Bobbs, 1937; Long, 1938
   Devil Takes a Hill Town. Bobbs, 1939
   The Jig-Time Murders. Bobbs, 1936 JH
   The Rose Petal Murders. Bobbs, 1935 JH

GIVINS, ROBERT C. Pseudonym: Snivig C. Trebor, q.v.

GLAENZER, RICHARD B(UTLER). 1876-1937.
   Spoofs. McBride, 1933 ss, at least one criminous

GLANVILLE, ALEC. Pseudonym of Alexander Haig Glanville Grieve, 1902- . Series characters: Insp. "Dusty" Muller and "Tiny" Meldrum = M&M.
   The Body in the Trawl. Harrap, 1938 M&M
   Death Goes Ashore. Harrap, 1936 M&M
   Death in our Wake. Harrap, 1937
   Gunner's Island. Jenkins, 1949
   Out of the Shadow. Jenkins, 1951; Roy, 1958

GLANVILLE, BRIAN (LESTER). 1931- .
   After Rome, Africa. Secker, 1959

GLASKIN, G(ERALD) M(ARCUS). 1923- .
   The Man Who Didn't Count. Barrie, 1965; Delacorte, 1967

GLASMON, KUBEC and JOHN BRIGHT
   The Public Enemy. Grosset, 1931. (Novelization of the movie.)

GLASPELL, SUSAN. 1882-1948.
   A Jury of her Peers. Benn, 1927

GLEIG, CHARLES. 1862- . See also: EDWIN W(ILLIAM) PUGH, 1874-1930.
   -The Edge of Honesty. Lane, 1898
   The Nancy Manoeuvres. Brown Langham, 1907
   -Reeds in the Wind. Brentano's (London), 1927

GLEMSER, BERNARD. 1908- . Pseudonym: Geoffrey Napier, q.v.

GLEN, ELSA
   The Secret of Villa Vanesta. Collins, 1935

GLENDINNING, RICHARD. 1917- .
   -Carnival Girl. Popular Library, 1956
   Mission to Murder. GM, 1954
   Retreat into Night. GM, 1954
   Terror in the Sun. GM, 1952
   -Too Fast We Live. Popular Library, 1954
   Who Evil Thinks. GM, 1952

GLESS, ELEANOR GREEN
   Aunt Ivy Diddit. Chapman, 1948
   Murder at Tall Tip. Avalon, 1964

GLEW, DORIS MURIEL. 1899- .
   The Fourth Matter. Melrose, 1929

GLICK, CARL (CANNON). 1890- .
   Death Sits In. Washburn, 1954
   The Laughing Buddha. Lothrop, 1937; Bell, 1937

GLIDDEN, FREDERICK DILLEY. 1908-1975. Pseudonym: Luke Short, q.v.

GLIDDEN, M(INNA MAUD) W(ESSELHOFT). Series character: Carey Brent, in both titles.
   Death Strikes Home. Phoenix, 1937
   The Long Island Murders. Phoenix, 1937

GLINTO, DARCY. Pseudonym of Harold Ernest Kelly, 1899- . Other pseudonyms: Gordon Holt, Buck Toler, qq.v.
   Blue Blood Flows East. Robin Hood, 1947
   Curtains for Carrie. Robin Hood, 1947
   Dainty was a Jane. Robin Hood, 1948
   Dame Between Two. Robin Hood, 1948
   "Dames are Out." Robin Hood, 1953
   Lady—Don't Turn Over. Wells Gardner, 1940
   The Mannequin Doll. Robin Hood, 1948
   No Come-Back from Connie. Robin Hood, 1948
   No Mortgage on a Coffin. Robin Hood, 1941
   One More Nice White Body. Robin Hood, 1950
   Road Floozie. Robin Hood, 1950
   She Gave Me Hell and... Robin Hood, 1950
   "Snow" Vogue. Wells Gardner, 1941
   Straight-Up Girl. Robin Hood, 1949
   "You Took Me...Keep Me." Robin Hood, 1941

GLOAG, JOHN (EDWARDS). 1896- . Series character: Lionel Buckby, in at least those marked LB.
   -All England at Home. Cassell, 1949
   Documents Marked "Secret". Cassell, 1938
   -I Want an Audience. Cassell, 1941
   In Camera. Cassell, 1945
   -It Makes a Nice Change. Nicholson, 1938 ss
   Kind Uncle Buckby. Cassell, 1946 LB
   Mr. Buckby is Not at Home. Cassell, 1942 LB
   -Not in the Newspapers. Cassell, 1953
   Ripe for Development. Cassell, 1936 LB
   -Rising Suns. Cassell, 1964
   -Sacred Edifice. Cassell, 1937
   -Slow. Cassell, 1954
   Sweet Racket. Cassell, 1936
   Unlawful Justice. Cassell, 1962
   Unwilling Adventurer. Cassell, 1940 LB

GLOAG, JULIAN. 1930- .
   Maundy. Secker, 1969; Simon, 1969
   Our Mother's House. Secker, 1963; Simon, 1963
   A Sentence of Life. Secker, 1966; Simon, 1966
   A Woman of Character. Weidenfeld, 1973; Random, 1973

GLORE, CHARLES
  Moonshine Mountain. Novel Books, 1964. (Novelization of the movie.)

GLOVER, ROBERT. 1913- .
  Lace in the Mews. Elek, 1956
  Murderer's Maze. Elek, 1951
  Things Happen. Elek, 1941

GLUCK, SINCLAIR. 1887- . Pseudonym: Melrod Danning, q.v. Series characters: Paul Bernard = PB; Clayton = C; Ross McCoy = RM.
  The Blind Fury. Mills, 1930; Dodd, 1930 RM
  Come and Kill Me. Mills, 1941
  Death Comes to Dinner. Mills, 1929. U.S. title: Shadow in the House. Dodd, 1929 PB
  The Deeper Scar. Mills, 1927; Dodd, 1927
  A Delicate Case of Murder. Mills, 1937; Macmillan, 1937
  The Dragon in Harness. Mills, 1927; Dodd, 1932 C
  The Four Winds. Mills, 1926; Dodd, 1926
  The Golden Panther. Mills, 1923. U.S. title: The House of the Missing. Dodd, 1924 C
  The Great London Mystery. Mills, 1936
  The Green Blot. Mills, 1925; Dodd, 1925
  Honourable Mister Death and other stories. World's Work, 1942 ss
  The House of the Missing; see The Golden Panther
  The Last Trap. Mills, 1928; Dodd, 1928 PB
  The Man Who Never Blundered. Mills, 1928; Dodd, 1929 RM
  Minus X. Mills, 1933
  Red Emeralds. Mills, 1932
  Sea Shroud. Mills, 1934
  Shadow in the House; see Death Comes to Dinner
  Thieves' Honour. Mills, 1924; Dodd, 1925
  The White Streak. Mills, 1924; Clode, 1924
  The Wildcat. Mills, 1931; Dodd, 1932

GLUYAS, CONSTANCE
  Vantage Hall. Leisure, 1971

"G-MAN". Pseudonym.
  Call in the Feds. Hamilton Stafford, 1951
  F.B.I. Showdown. Hamilton Stafford, 1952
  F.B.I. Special Agent. Hamilton Stafford, 1952
  Federal Agent. Hamilton Stafford, 1952

GOBLE, (LLOYD) NEIL. 1933- .
  Condition Green: Tokyo. Tuttle, 1966

GODDARD, ANTHEA
  The Vienna Pursuit. Milton House, 1974; Walker, 1976

GODDARD, GLORIA. 1897- . Pseudonym: Paul Palmer, q.v.

GODDARD, HARRY
  The Silent Force. Popular Library, 1971. (Novelization of the TV series.)

GODDARD, HENRY. 1800-1883.
  Memoirs of a Bow Street Runner. Museum, 1956; Morrow, 1957. ("Novelized" episodes of true crime.)

GODDARD, NORMAN. 1881-1917.
  The Man with the Green Eyes. Amalgamated, 1917. (Sexton Blake)

GODDEN, JON. 1906- .
  Kitten with Blue Eyes. Chatto, 1971. U.S. title: Mrs. Starr Lives Alone. Knopf, 1972

GODEY, JOHN. Pseudonym of Morton Freedgood. Series character: Jack Albany = JA.
  The Blonde Betrayer; see The Man in Question
  The Blue Hour. Doubleday, 1948; Boardman, 1949. Also published as: Killer at his Back. Bestseller, 1955. And as: The Next to Die. Tandem, 1975
  The Clay Assassin. Boardman, 1959
  The Fifth House. Berkley, 1973; Boardman, 1960
  The Gun and Mr. Smith. Doubleday, 1974; Coronet, 1976
  Killer at his Back; see The Blue Hour
  The Man in Question. Doubleday, 1951; Boardman, 1953. Also published as: The Blonde Betrayer. Bestseller, 1955
  Never Put Off Till Tomorrow What You Can Kill Today. Random, 1970 JA
  The Next to Die; see The Blue Hour
  The Reluctant Assassin. Hale, 1966
  The Taking of Pelham One Two Three. Putnam, 1973; Hodder, 1973
  This Year's Death. Doubleday, 1953; Boardman, 1953
  A Thrill a Minute with Jack Albany. Simon, 1967 JA
  The Three Worlds of Johnny Handsome. Random, 1972; Hodder, 1973

GODFREY, HAL. Pseudonym of Charlotte O'Conor Eccles.
  -The Rejuvenation of Mrs. Semaphore. Jarrolds, 1897; Page, 1898

GODFREY, LIONEL ROBERT HOLCOMBE. 1932- . Pseudonyms: Elliot Kennedy, Scott Mitchell, qq.v.

GODFREY, PETER. 1917- .
  Death Under the Table. Scientific Pub. Co. (Cape Town), 1954

GODLEY, ROBERT. 1908- . Pseudonym: Franklin James, q.v.

GODWIN, JOHN. 1928- .
  Requiem for a Rat. Jenkins, 1963

GODWIN, WILLIAM. 1756-1836.
  Things As They Are; or, The Adventures of Caleb Williams. Crosby, 1794; Rice, 1795. Variously reprinted as: Caleb Williams; and as: The Adventures of Caleb Williams

GODWYN, MARJORIE
  Let's Ask Aunt. Allan, 1936

GOENEY, WILLIAM M(ORTON). 1914- .
  The Moment of Truth. Holt, 1959

GOFF, IVAN and BEN ROBERTS
  Portrait in Black. French (New York & London), 1948. (Play.)

GOFF, OLIVER
  The Eye of the Peacock. Eyre, 1975

GOINES, DONALD
  Black Gangster. Holloway, 1972
  Black Girl Lost. Holloway, 1973
  Daddy Cool. Holloway, 1974
  Dopefiend. Holloway, 1971
  Eldorado Red. Holloway, 1974
  Inner City Hoodlum. Holloway, 1975
  Never Die Alone. Holloway, 1974
  Street Players. Holloway, 1973
  Swamp Man. Holloway, 1974
  White Man's Justice: Black Man's Grief. Holloway, 1973
  Whoreson. Holloway, 1972

GOLDBERG, EDWARD. Pseudonym: "Goldey", q.v.

GOLDBERG, GERALD J(AY). 1929- .
  -The Lynching of Orin Newfield. Dial, 1970

GOLDBERG, HARRY. Pseudonym: Harry Grey, q.v.

GOLDBERG, MARSHALL
  The Anatomy Lesson. Putnam, 1974
  The Karamanov Equations. World, 1972; MacGibbon, 1972

"GOLDEY". Pseudonym of Edward Goldberg.
  Tracked by a Woman; or, The Female Detective. Eagle, 1889

GOLDHURST, RICHARD. 1927- .
  The Deceivers. Signet, 1965

GOLDIE, BERTHA (BARRE). 1871- .
  -The Cotherstones. Melrose, 1926
  -Dahlia. Ward, 1937
  -The Discipline of Christine. Rivers, 1904
  The Green Tablets; see The Green Tabloids
  The Green Tabloids. Hodder, 1929. Also published as: The Green Tablets. Ward, 1939
  -The Hand of the Waverleys. Melrose, 1928
  -Nightlights. Ward, 1936
  -The Piper of Arristoun. Ward, 1935
  -Raven. Ward, 1936
  -The Signature. Ward, 1937
  -Vellum. Ward, 1935
  -The Village Never Knew. Ward, 1938
  -Whispering Galleries. Ward, 1940

GOLDIE, VALENTINE FRANCIS TAUBMAN. See: VALENTINE FRANCIS TAUBMAN-GOLDIE.

GOLDING, LOUIS. 1895-1958.
  The Frightening Talent. Allen, 1973
  Luigi of Catanzaro. Archer, 1926
  Pale Blue Nightgown. Corvinus, 1936
  Pale Blue Nightgown. Hutchinson, 1944 ss
  The Pursuer. Gollancz, 1936; Farrar, 1936

GOLDING, MORTON JAY. 1925- . Pseudonyms: Stephanie Lloyd, Patricia Morton, qq.v.

GOLDMAN, JAMES (A.). 1927- .
  The Man from Greek and Roman. Random, 1974; Hutchinson, 1975

GOLDMAN, LAWRENCE (LOUIS)
  Black Fire. Ace, 1956
  Dangerous Design. Arcadia, 1952
  Fall Guy for Murder. Dutton, 1943; Gifford, 1945
  -The Heart Merchants. Paperback Library, 196?
  Judd for the Defense. Paperback Library, 1968. (Novelization of the TV series.)
  Judd for the Defense #2: The Secret Listeners. Paperback Library, 1968. (Novelization of the TV series.)
  Tiger by the Tail. McKay, 1946
  Wolf Tone. Mill, 1948

GOLDMAN, RAYMOND LESLIE. 1895- .
Series character: Asaph Clune = AC.
Death Plays Solitaire. Coward, 1939;
   Boardman, 1945 AC
The Hartwell Case. Skeffington, 1929
Judge Robinson Murdered! Coward, 1936;
   Boardman, 1937
Murder Behind the Mike. Coward, 1942;
   Boardman, 1943 AC
The Murder of Harvey Blake. Skeffington, 1931 AC
Murder Without Motive. Coward, 1938 AC
Out on Bail. Coward, 1937; Cassell, 1938
The Purple Shells. Ziff-Davis, 1947;
   Boardman, 1948
The Snatch. Coward, 1940; Boardman, 1945 AC

GOLDMAN, WILLIAM (W.). 1931- . Pseudonym: Harry Longbaugh, q.v.
Marathon Man. Delacorte, 1974; Macmillan (London), 1975

GOLDSMITH, FREDERIC
Murder in Mayfair. Allen, 1954. (Novelization of a ss by Vera Caspary, 1904- , q.v.)
The Smugglers. Allen, 1955

GOLDSMITH, GENE
Layout for a Corpse. Mill, 1949; Boardman, 1950
Murder on his Mind. Mill, 1947; Quality, 1954

GOLDSMITH, LOUIS C.
The Streamlined Dragon. World's Work, 1948

GOLDSMITH, MARTIN M.
Detour. Macaulay, 1939; Hurst, 1939
Double Jeopardy. Macaulay, 1938; Hurst, 1938
Shadows at Noon. Ziff-Davis, 1943

GOLDSMITH, NORMAN
The Atlantic City Murder Mystery. Macaulay, 1936

GOLDSTEIN, ARTHUR D. Pseudonyn: Albert Ross, q.v. Series character: Max Guttman, in both titles.
A Person Shouldn't Die Like That. Random, 1972; Prior, 1977
You're Never Too Old to Die. Random, 1974

GOLDSTEIN, WILLIAM (ISAAC). 1932- .
Series character: Dr. Phibes, in both titles, which are novelizations of movies.
Dr. Phibes. Award, 1971
Dr. Phibes Rises Again. Award, 1972

GOLDSTON, ROBERT CONROY. 1927- . Pseudonym: James Stark, q.v.

GOLDSTONE, LAWRENCE ARTHUR. 1903- .
Original name of: Lawrence Treat, q.v.
-Run Far, Run Fast. Greystone, 1937

GOLDTHWAITE, EATON K(ENNETH). 1907- .
Series character: Lt. Joseph Dickerson = JD.
The Body Next Door; see You Did It
Cat and Mouse. Duell, 1946. British title: Cat and Mouse Murder. Jarrolds, 1950. Also published as: Date with Death. Bantam, 1947; Corgi, 1962 JD
Cat and Mouse Murder; see Cat and Mouse
Cut for Partners. Duell, 1951. Also published as: The Scarlet Spade. Ace, 1952
Date with Death; see Cat and Mouse
Death Springs the Trap; see You Did It

Don't Mention My Name. Duell, 1942
The Marble Forest. Doubleday, 1971; Hale, 1973
Once You Stop, You're Dead. Morrow, 1968
Root of Evil. Duell, 1948
Scarecrow. Duell, 1945; Jarrolds, 1948 JD
The Scarlet Spade; see Cut for Partners
The Sixpenny Dame. Dodd, 1953
You Did It. Duell, 1943; Jarrolds, 1945. Also published as: Death Springs the Trap. Death House, 1944. And as: The Body Next Door. Handi-Books, 1946

GOLLER, CELIA MARGARET. 1914- . Pseudonym: Celia Fremlin, q.v.

GOLLOMB, JOSEPH. 1881-1950. Series character: Galt = G.
The Curtain of Storm. Macmillan, 1933 G
The Girl in the Fog. Boni, 1923; Long, 1924
Master Manhunters. Macaulay, 1926. (Novelized true crime accounts.)
The Portrait Invisible. Macmillan, 1928; Heinemann, 1928 G
The Subtle Trail. Macmillan, 1929; Heinemann, 1930 G

GOLSWORTHY, ARNOLD. 1865- .
A Cry in the Night. Greening, 1899
Death and the Woman. Favourite, 1898
-Hands in the Darkness. Pearson, 1899; Fenno, 1900
-The New Master. Pearson, 1901

GOMPERTZ, MARTIN LOUIS ALAN. 1886-1951. Pseudonym: "Ganpat", q.v.

GONZALES, JOHN. Series character: Harry Horne = HH.
Death for Mr. Big. GM, 1951; Fawcett (London), 1953
End of a JD. GM, 1960 HH
Follow That Hearse! GM, 1963 HH
The Magnificent Moll. Red Seal (U.S.), 1952
Someone's Sleeping in my Bed. GM, 1962; Muller pb, 1963 HH

GOOCH, R(ICHARD) H(EATHCOTE)
Her Ladyship's Jewels and What Became of Them. [Author], 1870's

GOODALL, CEDRIC
The Black Chalice. Melrose, 1935; Macaulay, 1935
Death by Appointment. Pemberton, 1950
The Destroyer; or, Adventures of the Scorpion. Modern, 1935
Hidden Death. Blackie, 1935
The House of Death. Gramol, 1934
The Prisoner of the Priory. Gramol, 1934
-The Unicorn. Modern, 1935
Without Trace. Hamilton, 1938

GOODCHILD, GEORGE. 1888- . Pseudonyms: Alan Dare, Jesse Templeton, qq.v. See also next entry. Series characters: Inspector McLean, in at least those marked M; Nigel Rex, in at least those marked NR; Q33 = Q.
Ace High. Hodder, 1927
Again McLean. Hodder, 1939 M ss
The Alaskan. Lloyds, 1921
The Barton Mystery. Jarrolds, 1916. (Novelization of the play by Walter Hackett.)
Behind That Door. Ward, 1943

The Black Orchid. Hodder, 1926
Brave Interlude. Ward, 1942
Call McLean. Hodder, 1937 M ss
Captain Crash. Hayes, 1924
Captain Sinister. Hodder, 1933
Cauldron Bubble. Macdonald, 1946
Chief Inspector McLean. Hodder, 1932 M ss
The Clock Struck Seven. Hale, 1939
-Colorado Jim; or, The Taming of Angela. Hayes, 1920; Watt, 1922
Companion to Sirius. Rich, 1949 M
The Compassionate Rogue. Jarrolds, 1920
The Crimson Domino. Simpkin, 1919. Also published as by Jesse Templeton: Mellifont, 1933 ss
Danger Below. Hodder pb, 1937
The Danger Line. Jarrolds, 1958
Dear Conspirator. Ward, 1948
Death on the Centre Court. Hodder, 1935; Green Circle, 1936 M
Double Acrostic. Rich, 1954 M
-Down "Plug Street" Way, and other stories. Simpkin, 1918 ss
East of Singapore. Mellifont, 1946
The Efford Tangle. Rich, 1950
-The Elephant; or, The Man from Beyond. Hodder, 1929
-The Emperor of Hallelujah Island. Hodder, 1930; Houghton, 1931
False Intruder. Jarrolds, 1960
Final Score. Ward, 1950
Find the Lady. Rich, 1955 M ss
Follow McLean. Jarrolds, 1961 M
-The Footlight's Call. Mellifont, 1945
For Reasons Unknown. Hodder, 1932
Forced Landing. Hodder, 1940
Forever McLean. Jarrolds, 1957 M ss
-The Girl at Pine Creek. Thomson, 1930
-The Girl Who Failed Him. Thomson, 1930
-The Great Alone. Simpkin, 1919 ss
Hail McLean! Hodder, 1945 M ss
Having No Hearts. Hodder, 1937 M
-The Homeward Trail. Newnes, 1935
How Now, McLean? Hodder, 1931 M ss
-Hurricane Tex. Hodder, 1925
Infamous Gentleman. Hale, 1938
Inspector McLean's Casebook. Rich, 1949 M ss
Inspector McLean's Holiday; see McLean Takes a Holiday
Jack O'Lantern. Hodder, 1929; Mystery League, 1930
-Jim Goes North. Hodder, 1926
-Klondyke Kit's Revenge. Jenkins, 1923
Knight Takes Queen. Newnes, 1935
Knock and Come In. Ward, 1935 NR
Known as Z.1. Ward, 1940
Lady Takes Care. Ward, 1946
-The Land of Eldorado. Jarrolds, 1919
-The Last Cruise of the "Majestic". Simpkin, 1917
The Last Ditch. Mellifont, 1944
The Last Redoubt. Rich, 1952 M
The Last Secret. Rich, 1956
Laurels for McLean. Jarrolds, 1964 M ss
Lead On, McLean! Hodder, 1936 M ss
McLean at the Golden Owl. Hodder, 1930 M ss
McLean Carries On. Rich, 1950 M ss
McLean Deduces. Hodder, 1940 M ss
McLean Disposes. Jarrolds, 1958 M ss
McLean Excels. Hodder, 1939 M ss
McLean Finds a Way. Hodder, 1936 M ss
McLean Incomparable. Hodder, 1938 M ss
McLean Intervenes. Hodder, 1939 M ss
McLean Investigates. Hodder, 1930 M ss
McLean Invincible. Jarrolds, 1963 M ss
McLean Keeps Going. Hodder, 1941 M ss
McLean Knows Best. Hodder, 1935 M ss
McLean Knows the Answers. Long, 1967 M ss
McLean: Non-Stop. Hodder, 1941 M ss
McLean of Scotland Yard. Hodder, 1929 M ss

McLean Plays a Hand. Ward, 1934 M
McLean Predominant. Rich, 1951 M ss
McLean Prevails. Ward, 1935 M ss
McLean Remembers! Hodder, 1936 M
McLean Scores Again. Jarrolds, 1959 M ss
McLean Sees It Through. Hodder, 1939 M
McLean Solves It. Rich, 1956 M ss
McLean Steps In. Rich, 1952 M ss
McLean Takes a Holiday. Hodder, 1942. Revised edition: Inspector McLean's Holiday. Pan, 1951 M
McLean Takes Charge. Hodder, 1937 M ss
McLean Takes Over. Long, 1966 M ss
McLean the Magnificent. Hodder, 1940 M ss
McLean to the Dark Tower Came. Rich, 1951 M
Mad Mike. Chapman, 1934
The Man from the West. Thomson, 1929. Reprinted as by Jesse Templeton: Mellifont, 1933
The Man from the West, and other stories of adventure. Newnes, 1935 ss
-Man Peter. Ward, 1941
-The Man Who Wasn't. Jenkins, 1924
Mister Q33. Newnes, 1935 Q
The Monster of Grammont. Hodder, 1927; Mystery League, 1930
-Mountain Gold. Hodder, 1933
A Murder will be Committed. Hale, 1937
-Mushalong. Hayes, 1927
Next of Kin. Jarrolds, 1957 M ss
No Exit. Newnes, 1936
Operator No. 19. Ward, 1937
-Petticoat Lane. Mellifont, 1932
The Public Defender; see The Splendid Crime
Q33. Odhams, 1933 Q
Q33—Spy Catcher. Newnes, 1937 Q ss
Quest of Nigel Rex. Ward, 1934 NR
The Rain on the Roof. Hodder, 1928
-Rivers to Cross. Ward, 1947
The Road to Marrakesh. Hodder, 1931; Houghton, 1932
-Rough Going. Ward, 1936
Safety Last. Ward, 1944
Savage Encounter. Jarrolds, 1962 M
The Spanish Steps. Ward, 1951
The Splendid Crime. Hodder, 1930; Houghton, 1930. Also published as: The Public Defender. Grosset, 1931
The Square Deal. Modern, 193?
-Steve. Hale, 1936
-Stout Cortez. Ward, 1949
-Summer Moon. Leng, 1936
-Tall Timber. Hodder, 1927; Watt, 1924
-The Taming of Nancy. Thomson, 1925
This Woman is Wanted. Newnes, 1936
Tiger, Tiger. Jarrolds, 1959 M ss
The Triumph of McLean. Hodder, 1933 M
Trooper O'Neill. Hayes, 1921; Watt, 1923 ss
Trust McLean. Rich, 1954 M
Uncle Oscar's Niece. Hodder, 1944 M
Up, McLean! Hodder, 1940 M
-The Valley of Lies. Long, 1923
Watch McLean. Rich, 1955 M
Well Caught, McLean! Rich, 1953 M
-Wise Virgin. Mellifont, 1945
-The Woollen Monkey. Lloyds, 1920
-Yellowstones. Ward, 1938
Yes, Inspector McLean. Hodder, 1934 M

GOODCHILD, GEORGE, 1888-   , and (CARL ERIC) BECHHOFER ROBERTS, 1894-1949. See also: previous entry. Pseudonyms of George Goodchild: Alan Dare, Jesse Templeton, qq.v. Pseudonym of Roberts: Ephesian, q.v.
The Dear Old Gentleman. Jarrolds, 1935; Harper, 1936
The Jury Disagree. Jarrolds, 1934; Macmillan, 1955
The Prisoner's Friend. Jarrolds, 1938
Tidings of Joy. Jarrolds, 1936
We Shot an Arrow. Gollancz, 1939

GOODE, BILL. Pseudonym of William F. Goodykoontz.
The Senator's Nude. Ziff-Davis, 1947

GOODE, GEORGE W.
King Dan, the Factory Detective. Katahdin, 1896
The Post-Office Detective; or, A Mystery of the Mails. Street, 1888

GOODFIELD, (GWYNETH) JUNE. 1927-
Courier to Peking. Hart-Davis, 1973; Dutton, 1973

GOODHART, HONOR (MAHON). See: LIONEL (PEEL) YATES.

GOODIS, DAVID. 1917-1967.
Behold This Woman. Appleton, 1947
Black Friday. Lion, 1954
The Blonde on the Street Corner. Lion, 1954
The Burglar. Lion, 1953
Cassidy's Girl. GM, 1951; Red Seal, 1958
Dark Passage. Messner, 1946; Heinemann, 1947
Down There. GM, 1956; Fawcett (London), 1958. Also published as: Shoot the Piano Player. Black Cat, 1962
Fire in the Flesh. GM, 1957; Fawcett (London), 1958
The Moon in the Gutter. GM, 1953
Night Squad. GM, 1961; Fawcett (London), 1962
Nightfall. Messner, 1947; Heinemann, 1948
Of Missing Persons. Morrow, 1950
-Of Tender Sin. GM, 1952
Retreat from Oblivion. Dutton, 1939
Shoot the Piano Player; see Down There
Somebody's Done For. Banner, 1967
Street of No Return. GM, 1954; Red Seal, 1958
Street of the Lost. GM, 1952; Fawcett (London), 1959
The Wounded and the Slain. GM, 1955; Red Seal, 1959

GOODKIND, HOWARD. See: NORMAN GARBO, 1919-   .

GOODMAN, E(DWARD) J(OHN). 1836-   .
The Fate of Herbert Wayne. Chatto, 1892
-His Other Self. Ward, 1889
The Only Witness: What Did She See? Trischler, 1891
-Paid in His Own Coin. Bentley, 1888
-Too Curious. Bentley, 1887; Lippincott, 1888

GOODMAN, G. S.
The Mysterious Abduction. Greening, 1908

GOODMAN, GEORGE (J. W.), 1930-   , and WINTHROP KNOWLTON.
A Killing in the Market. Doubleday, 1958; Macdonald, 1958, as by Winthrop Goodman

GOODMAN, JONATHAN. 1931-   .
Criminal Tendencies. Long, 1964
Hello Cruel World, Goodbye. Long, 1964
Instead of Murder. Hammond, 1961

GOODMAN, WINTHROP. See: GEORGE (J. W.) GOODMAN, 1930-   .

GOODSPEED, EDGAR J(OHNSON). 1871-1962.
The Curse in the Colophon. Willett Clark, 1935

GOODWIN, INGE (DOROTHEA ROSI). 1923-   .
Bury Me in Lead. Wingate, 1952

GOODWIN, JOHN. Pseudonym of Sidney (Floyd) Gowing, 1878-   , q.v. Series character: Det.-Sgt. (Supt.) Scarfe, in at least those marked S.
Above the Law. Jenkins, 1936
The Avenger. Putnam, 1926. (British title?)
Blackmail. Amalgamated, 1910
Blood Money. Putnam (London), 1931; Sears, 1932
Dead Man's Treasure. Putnam (London), 1929. U.S. title: Let It Lie. Putnam (New York), 1929
-Helen of London. Jenkins, 1924
The House of Marney. Jenkins, 1923. U.S. title: The Sign of the Serpent. Putnam (New York), 1923
In Full Cry. Jenkins, 1941 S
Jennifer. Jenkins, 1924
The King's Elm Mystery. Jenkins, 1934
Let It Lie; see Dead Man's Treasure
Mafalda. Hodder, 1925
The Man with the Brooding Eyes; see Paid in Full
Paid in Full. Jenkins, 1921. U.S. title: The Man with the Brooding Eyes. Putnam (New York), 1921
The Shadow Man. Putnam (London), 1932; Sears, 1932 S
The Sign of the Serpent; see The House of Marney
The Spider Woman. Jenkins, 1920
The Stronger Hand. Hodder, 1926
When Dead Men Tell Tales. Putnam (New York), 1928. (British title?)
Without Mercy. Jenkins, 1920; Putnam (New York), 1920

GOODWIN, JOHN C(UTHBERT). 1891-   .
Diamonds and Hearts. Hutchinson, 1927
-The Zig-Zag Man. Hutchinson, 1925

GOODWIN, RALPH A.
The Stoenberg Affair. Sully, 1913

GOODYKOONTZ, WILLIAM F. Pseudonym: Bill Goode, q.v.

GORDON, ALEX. Pseudonym of Gordon Cotler, 1923-   , q.v.
The Cipher. Simon, 1961; Boardman, 1962

GORDON, ARTHUR. 1912-   .
Reprisal. Simon, 1950; H. Hamilton, 1950

GORDON, CHARLES WILLIAM. 1860-1937. Pseudonym: Ralph Connor, q.v.

GORDON, DIANA
A Few Days in Endel. Corgi, 1968; Ace, 1973

GORDON, DONALD. Pseudonym of Donald Gordon Payne, 1924-   .
The Flight of the Bat. Hodder, 1963; Morrow, 1964
The Golden Oyster. Hodder, 1967; Morrow, 1968
Leap in the Dark. Hodder, 1970; Morrow, 1971

GORDON, ETHEL (EDISON). 1915-   .
The Birdwatcher. McKay, 1974; Barker, 1975
The Chaperone. Coward, 1973; Barker, 1974
The Freebody Heiress. McKay, 1975; Barker, 1974
Freer's Cove. Coward, 1972

GORDON, FRITZ. Joint pseudonym of Frederick Gordon Jarvis, Jr., 1930-   , and Robert F. Van Beever. Series character: Schuyler Townsend, in both titles.

GORDON, FRITZ
Flight of the Bamboo Saucer. Award, 1967
Tonight They Die to Mendelssohn. Award, 1968

GORDON, GILES (ALEXANDER ESME). 1940- .
Girl with Red Hair. Hutchinson, 1974

GORDON, GORDON. 1912- . See: THE GORDONS.

GORDON, HAVA
Dead on Arrival. Modern Fiction, 1953
Devil's Coffin. Modern Fiction, 1953

GORDON, IAN (DOUGLAS FELLOWES). 1921- .
After Innocence. Dell, 1955
The Big Success. Dell, 1956; World Distributors, 1957
The Burden of Guilt. Simon, 1951
-Deep is my Desire. Popular Library, 1955
-Harlem is my Heaven. Berkley, 1957
The Night Thorn. Dial, 1952
The Whip Hand. Crown, 1954

GORDON, JAMES. 1912- . Pseudonym: John Foss, q.v.

GORDON, JAN. 1882-1944. Pseudonym: William Gore, q.v.

GORDEN, JULIEN. Pseudonym of Julie Grinnell Cruger.
-A Diplomat's Diary. Lippincott, 1890; Routledge, 1890

GORDON, LESLIE HOWARD
The Camp of Fear. Hodder, 1920
-The Gates of Tien T'ze. Hodder, 1920
-The House of Night. Hodder, 1921; Small, 1921
-The Land of Big Things. Hodder, 1918
-The Little Brother of God. Hodder, 1919
-The Little Lady of the Shot-Gun. Hodder, 1917

GORDON, MAX
The Dead Say No. Warren, 1952
I Never Killed. Warren, 1952
Look Down for Mercy. Warren, 1952
Why Squeal on Me? Warren, 1952

GORDON, MILDRED. 1912- . See also: GORDONS, THE.
The Little Man Who Wasn't There. Doubleday, 1946

GORDON, NEIL. Pseudonym of Archibald Gordon Macdonell, 1895-1941. Other pseudonym: John Cameron, q.v. Series character: Peter Kerrigan, in at least those marked PK.
The Big Ben Alibi. Lane, 1930
The Factory on the Cliff. Longmans, 1928. U.S. title: The New Gun Runners. Harcourt, 1928
Murder in Earl's Court. Lane, 1931 PK
The New Gun Runners; see The Factory on the Cliff
The Professor's Poison. Longmans, 1928; Harcourt, 1928
The Shakespeare Murders. Barker, 1933; Holt, 1933 PK
The Silent Murders. Longmans, 1929; Doubleday, 1930

GORDON, PETER
The Case of the Missing Bullion. Baker, 1969

GORDON, R(ICHARD) L(AURENCE)
The River Gets Wider. Crowell, 1974; Hart-Davis, 1975

GORDON, RICHARD. Pseudonym of Gordon Ostlere, 1921- .
The Medical Witness. Heinemann, 1971. U.S. title: Witness for the Crown. Simon, 1971

GORDON, RUSSELL
Dead Level. Morrow, 1948. Also published as: She Posed for Death. Avon, 1950

GORDON, SAMUEL. 1871-1927.
The Avenger. Macaulay, 1921

GORDON, SPIKE. Pseudonym, possibly of F(rank) Dubrez Fawcett, 1891-1968, q.v. Other pseudonyms: Griff, Ben Sarto, Elmer Eliot Saks, qq.v.
The Big Fix. Modern Fiction, 1953
Doctor Samovar, Crook. Modern Fiction, 1953
Don't Tempt the Hangman. Modern Fiction, 1953
Don't Touch Me. Modern Fiction, 1953
Gale Gallyon Takes a Hand. Modern Fiction, 1951
I Don't Get It. Modern Fiction, 1953
She Means Trouble. Modern Fiction, 1953
Taken for Dollars. Modern Fiction, 1953
Unhappy Hophead. Modern Fiction, 1953
You Take the Rap. Modern Fiction, 1953
You're No Lady. Modern Fiction, 1953

GORDON, WELCHE
Jesse James, and His Band of Notorious Outlaws. Laird, 1890
Jim the Penman. Laird, 1891

GORDONS, THE. Byline of Gordon Gordon, 1912- , and Mildred Gordon, 1912- , q.v. Series characters: D. C. Randall (a cat) = DC; John Ripley = JR.
The Big Frame. Doubleday, 1957; Macdonald, 1957
Campaign Train. Doubleday, 1952; Wingate, 1952. Also published as: Murder Rides the Campaign Train. Bantam, 1956
Captive. Doubleday, 1957; Macdonald, 1958
Case File: FBI. Doubleday, 1953; Macdonald, 1954 JR
The Case of the Talking Bug. Doubleday, 1955. British title: Playback. Macdonald, 1955
Catnapped: The Further Adventures of Undercover Cat. Doubleday, 1974; Macdonald, 1975 DC
Experiment in Terror; see Operation Terror
FBI Story. Doubleday, 1950; Corgi, 1957 JR
The Informant. Doubleday, 1973; Macdonald, 1973
Journey with a Stranger; see Menace
Make Haste to Live. Doubleday, 1950
Menace. Doubleday, 1962. British title: Journey with a Stranger. Macdonald, 1963
Murder Rides the Campaign Train; see Campaign Train
Night Before the Wedding. Doubleday, 1969; Macdonald, 1969
Operation Terror. Doubleday, 1961; Macdonald, 1961. Also published as: Experiment in Terror. Bantam, 1962 JR
Playback; see The Case of the Talking Bug
Power Play. Doubleday, 1965; Macdonald, 1966
That Darn Cat; see Undercover Cat
Undercover Cat. Doubleday, 1963; Macdonald, 1964. Also published as: That Darn Cat. Bantam, 1966; Corgi, 1966 DC
Undercover Cat Prowls Again. Doubleday, 1966; Macdonald, 1967 DC

GORE, MRS. [CATHERINE GRACE FRANCES MOODY]. 1799-1861.
Craigallen Castle; or, The Stolen Will. Garrett, 1852

GORE, WILLIAM. Pseudonym of Jan Gordon, 1882-1944. Series character: Inspector Penk = P.
Death in the Wheelbarrow. Harrap, 1935; Mystery House, 1940, as by Jan Gordon P
Murder Most Artistic. Harrap, 1937. U.S. title: The Mystery of the Painted Nude. Doubleday, 1938 P
The Mystery of the Painted Nude; see Murder Most Artistic
There's Death in the Churchyard. Harrap, 1934

GORE-BROWNE, ROBERT. 1893- . Series character: Lucien Clay, in at least those marked LC.
By Way of Confession; see Death on Delivery
-The Crater. Collins, 1925; Doran, 1926
Death on Delivery. Collins, 1929. U.S. title: By Way of Confession. Doubleday, 1930 LC
-An Imperfect Lover. Collins, 1928; Doubleday, 1929
In Search of a Villain; see Murder of an M.P.
Murder of an M.P. Collins, 1927. U.S. title: In Search of a Villain. Doubleday, 1928 LC

GORELL, LORD [RONALD GORELL BARNES]. 1884- . Series character: Insp. Maurice Hepburn, in at least those marked MH.
D.E.Q. Murray, 1922 MH
Devil's Drum. Murray, 1929
The Devouring Fire. Murray, 1928
Earl's End. Ward, 1951
"He Who Fights..." Murray, 1928
In the Night. Longmans, 1917
Let Not Thy Left Hand. Ward, 1949
Murder at Manor House. Ward, 1954
Murder at Mavering. Murray, 1943 MH
Red Lilac. Murray, 1935 MH
Venturers All. Murray, 1927
Where There's a Head. Ward, 1952

GORES, JOE [JOSEPH N. GORES]. 1931- . Series characters: Daniel Kearney Associates = DKA.
Dead Skip. Random, 1972; Gollancz, 1973 DKA
Final Notice. Random, 1973; Gollancz, 1974 DKA
Hammett. Putnam, 1975; Macdonald, 1976
Interface. Evans, 1974; Futura, 1977
A Time of Predators. Random, 1969; Allen, 1970

GORON, M(ARIE) F(RANCOIS). 1847-1933.
The Red Nights of Paris. Dillingham, 1912
The Truth About the Case. Lippincott, 1907. British title: The World of Crime: True Detective Stories. Hurst, 1907 ss
The World of Crime; see The Truth About the Case

GOSSELIN, LOUIS LEON THEODORE. 1857-1925. Pseudonym: G. Lenotre, q.v.

GOTTFRIED, THEODORE MARK. 1928- . Pseudonyms: Harry Gregory, Katherine Tobias, qq.v.

GOTTLIEB, ANNIE. See: JACQUES SANDULESCU.

GOTTLIEB, PAUL. 1936-   .
  Agency. Musson (Don Mills, Ontario),
    1974; Hale, 1975

GOUD, ANNE. 1917-   . Pseudonym: Anne-
  Mariel, q.v.

GOUGH, GEORGE W(OOLEY). 1869-   .
  -A Daughter of Kings. Skeffington, 1930
  My Lady Vamp. Methuen, 1926
  The Terror by Night. Blackwood, 1922
    ss

GOULART, RON(ALD JOSEPH). 1933-   . See
  also: KENNETH ROBESON. Series charac-
  ters: John Easy = JE; Cleopatra
  Jones (in novelizations of movies) =
  CJ.
  Cleopatra Jones. Paperback Library,
    1973 CJ
  Cleopatra Jones and the Casino of Gold.
    Paperback Library, 1975 CJ
  Ghost Breaker. Ace, 1971 ss
  If Dying was All. Ace, 1971 JE
  Odd Job No. 101, and other future
    crimes and intrigues. Scribner, 1975;
    Hale, 1976 ss
  One Grave Too Many. Ace, 1974 JE
  The Same Lie Twice. Ace, 1973 JE
  The Sword Swallower. Doubleday, 1968
  Too Sweet to Die. Ace, 1972 JE
  What's Become of Screwloose? and other
    stories. Scribner, 1971; Sidgwick,
    1971 ss, criminous in part

GOULD, ANTHONY
  -The Faithful Achates. Judge, 1889
  A Woman of Sorek. American News, 1889

GOULD, CHESTER. 1900-   . Series charac-
  ter: Dick Tracy, in all titles, which
  are collected newspaper comic strips.
  The Celebrated Cases of Dick Tracy,
    1931-1951. Chelsea, 1970
  Dick Tracy and the Woo Woo Sisters.
    Dell, 1947
  Pruneface. GM, 1975
  Snowflake and Shaky. GM, 1975

GOULD, HEYWOOD
  One Dead Debutante. St. Martin's, 1975

GOULD, NAT(HANIEL). 1857-1919.
  Chased by Fire; or, A Stable Mystery.
    Ogilvie, 1905. (British title?)
  -A Dangerous Stable. Long, 1922
  The Dark Horse. Routledge, 1899
  -A Dead Certainty. Routledge, 1900
  The Doctor's Double. Routledge, 1896
  The Exploits of a Race-Course Detec-
    tive. Long, 1927 ss
  -The Jockey's Revenge. Long, 1909
  A Lad of Mettle. Routledge, 1897
  Landed at Last. Routledge, 1899
  -A Racecourse Tragedy. Everett, 1901
  A Stable Mystery, and other stories.
    Robinson, 1921 ss
  -The Stolen Race, Long, 1909
  -A Turf Conspiracy. Long, 1916
  -Warned Off. Everett, 1901
  Who Did It? Routledge, 1896

GOULD, STEPHEN. Pseudonym of Steve
  Fisher (Stephen Gould Fisher),
  1912-   , q.v. Other pseudonym:
  Grant Lane, q.v.
  Homicide Johnny. Mystery House, 1940;
    Pemberton, 1946. Reprinted as by
    Steve Fisher: Popular Library, 1950
  Murder of the Admiral. Macaulay, 1936

GOULDEN, PIERCE
  The Compassionate Crook. Eldon, 1939
  Death Rope Island. Eldon, 1934
  The Golden Scarab. Eldon, 1939

GOUZE, ROGER
  A Quiet Game of Bambu. Doubleday, 1964.
    (Translation of La Partie de Bambu.
    Paris, 1963.)

GOVAN, (MARY) CHRISTINE NOBLE. 1898-   .
  Pseudonyms: Mary Allerton, J. N. Dar-
  by, qq.v.
  Murder on the Mountain. Houghton, 1937
  Plantation Murder. Houghton, 1938

GOVER, (JOHN) ROBERT. 1929-   .
  The Maniac Responsible. Grove, 1963;
    MacGibbon, 1964

GOWING, SIDNEY (FLOYD). 1878-   . Pseu-
  donym: John Goodwin, q.v.
  -Heather-Bells. Hodder, 1927
  Held to Ransom. Jenkins, 1924
  -Kim Ruff. Jenkins, 1925
  -Sea Lavender. Hodder, 1925; Holt, 1925
  Sealed Orders. Putnam (London), 1929;
    Putnam (New York), 1929, as by John
    Goodwin

GOYDER, MARGOT. 1903-   . Joint pseudonym with Aune Neville Goyder Joske,
  1893-   : Margot Neville, q.v.

GOYNE, RICHARD. 1902-1957. Pseudonym:
  John Courage, q.v. Series characters:
  Supt. "Tubby" Greene, in at least
  those marked TG; The Padre, in at
  least those marked P; Paul Templeton,
  in at least those marked PT.
  The Broken Circle. Federation, 1926
  The Cinema Crime. Amalgamated, 1933.
    (Sexton Blake)
  -The Clock. Paul, 1950
  The Courtway Case. Paul, 1951 P
  The Crime Philosopher. Paul, 1945 P
  Danger in Suburbia. Paul, 1939
  The Dark Mind. Paul, 1948 P
  The Darkened Room. Paul, 1952
  Daughter of Darkness. Paul, 1953
  Death by Desire. Paul, 1936; Macaulay,
    1937 PT
  Death in Harbour. Paul, 1937 PT
  Destination Unknown. Paul, 1945
  Fear Haunts the Fells. Paul, 1944 PT
  The Fentons. Paul, 1956
  Five Roads Inn. Paul, 1944 PT
  Fugitive Men. Long, 1957
  The Gravel Patch. Paul, 1953
  The Great Fear. Aldine, 1927
  Hanged I'll Be! Paul, 1946 PT
  Harvest of Hate. Paul, 1952
  In the Last Act. Aldine, 1927
  Introducing the Super. Paul, 1955 TG
  -The Invisible Verdict. Paul, 1950
  The Last Shot and other stories. Feder-
    ation, 1925 ss
  The Kidnapper's Victim. Amalgamated,
    1934. (Sexton Blake)
  The Lipstick Clue. Paul, 1954
  The Man in the Trilby Hat. Paul, 1946
  The Merrylees Mystery. Paul, 1939 PT
  The Missing Minx. Paul, 1957 TG
  Murder at the Inn. Paul, 1935 PT
  Murder Made Easy. Paul, 1944 PT
  Murderer's Moon. Paul, 1949 PT
  Overnight. Paul, 1953
  Parisian Nights. Federation, 1925
  Produce the Body. Paul, 1935 PT
  Savarin's Shadow. Paul, 1947 P
  Seven were Suspect. Paul, 1938 PT
  Strange Motives. Paul, 1934 PT
  Suicide Squad. Paul, 1942
  Traitor's Tide. Paul, 1948 P
  Who Killed My Wife? Paul, 1940 PT
  You Can't Kill Shadows. Paul, 1954

GRAAF, PETER. Series character: Joe Dust,
  in at least those marked JD.
  Daughter Fair. Joseph, 1958; Washburn,
    1958 JD

Dust and the Curious Boy. Joseph, 1957.
  U.S. title: Give the Devil His Due.
  Mill, 1957 JD
Give the Devil His Due; see Dust and
  the Curious Boy
-The Gull's Kiss. Davies, 1962
The Sapphire Conference. Joseph, 1959;
  Washburn, 1959 JD

GRABER, GEORGE ALEXANDER. 1914-   .
  Pseudonym: Alexander Cordell, q.v.

GRABO, CARL. See: HERBERT O(SBORN) YARD-
  LEY, 1889-   .

GRACE, ALICIA
  The Enchanted Circle. Lancer, 1968
  Hawksboll Manor. Lancer, 1967
  The Head of Medusa. Lancer, 1967. Also
    published as: Hour of Evil. Belmont,
    1973
  Hour of Evil; see The Head of Medusa
  Mass for a Dead Witch. Lancer, 1970
  The Terrified Heart; see The Terrified
    Target
  The Terrified Target. Lancer, 1966.
    Also published as: The Terrified
    Heart. Belmont, 1973
  Wharf Sinister. Lancer, 1971

GRADY, FRANK P.
  Sergeant Death. Mussey, 1936

GRADY, JAMES (THOMAS). 1949-   . Series
  character: Richard Malcolm (The Con-
  dor), in both titles.
  Shadow of the Condor. Putnam, 1975;
    Hodder, 1976
  Six Days of the Condor. Norton, 1974;
    Hodder, 1975. Also published as:
    Three Days of the Condor. Dell, 1975
  Three Days of the Condor; see Six Days
    of the Condor

GRADY, RONAN CALISTUS, JR. 1921-   .
  Pseudonym: John Murphy, q.v.

GRAEME, BRUCE. Pseudonym of Graham Mon-
  tague Jeffries, 1900-   . Other
  pseudonyms: David Graeme, Roderic
  Hastings, qq.v. Series characters:
  Blackshirt = B (see also Roderic
  Graeme); Dgt. Sgt. Robert Mather =
  RM; Insps. Stevens & Allain, in at
  least those marked S&A; Theodore I.
  Terhune, in at least those marked TT;
  Lord Blackshirt = LB.
  The Accidental Clue. Hutchinson, 1957
  Adventures of Blackshirt; see Black-
    shirt Again
  Alias Blackshirt. Harrap, 1932; Dodd,
    1932 B
  Almost Without Murder. Hutchinson, 1963
  Always Expect the Unexpected. Hutchin-
    son, 1965
  And a Bottle of Rum. Hutchinson, 1949
    TT
  Blackshirt. Unwin, 1925; Dodd, 1925 B
    ss
  Blackshirt Again. Hutchinson, 1929.
    U.S. title: Adventures of Blackshirt.
    Dodd, 1929 B
  Blackshirt, Counter-Spy. Hutchinson,
    1938 B
  Blackshirt Interferes. Hutchinson, 1939
    B
  Blackshirt Strikes Back. Hutchinson,
    1940 B
  Blackshirt Takes a Hand. Hutchinson,
    1937 B
  Blackshirt the Adventurer. Hutchinson,
    1936 B
  Blackshirt the Audacious. Hutchinson,
    1935; Lippincott, 1936 B

G

Graeme, Bruce (continued)

Blind Date for a Private Eye. Hutchinson, 1969
Body Unknown. Hutchinson, 1939 S&A
Boomerang. Hutchinson, 1959
A Brief for O'Leary, and two other episodes in his career. Hutchinson, 1947 ss
Calling Lord Blackshirt. Hutchinson, 1943 LB
Cardyce for the Defence. Hutchinson, 1936
A Case for Solomon. Hutchinson, 1943 TT
A Case of Books. Hutchinson, 1946
Cherchez la Femme. Hutchinson, 1951
The Coming of Carew. Hutchinson, 1945
The Corporal Died in Bed. Hutchinson, 1940 S&A
The "D" Notice. Hutchinson, 1974 RM
Dead Pigs at Hungry Farm. Hutchinson, 1951 TT
The Devil was a Woman. Hutchinson, 1966
Disappearance of Roger Tremayne. Hutchinson, 1937
Encore Allain! Hutchinson, 1941 S&A
Epilogue. Hutchinson, 1933; Lippincott, 1934 S&A
Fog for a Killer. Hutchinson, 1960
Gigins Court. Hutchinson, 1932
Hate Ship. Hutchinson, 1928; Dodd, 1928
Holiday for a Spy. Hutchinson, 1963
House with Crooked Walls. Hutchinson, 1942 TT
Impeached! Hutchinson, 1933
The Imperfect Crime. Hutchinson, 1932; Lippincott, 1933 S&A
An International Affair. Hutchinson, 1934 S&A
John Jenkin, Public Enemy; see Public Enemy—No. 1
Just an Ordinary Case. Hutchinson, 1956
La Belle Laurine. Unwin, 1926. Revised edition: Laurine. Allan, 1935
The Lady Doth Protest. Hutchinson, 1971
Lady in Black. Hutchinson, 1952
Laurine; see La Belle Laurine
The Long Night. Hutchinson, 1958
Lord Blackshirt. Hutchinson, 1942 LB
Madame Spy. Allan, 1935
The Man from Michigan. Hutchinson, 1938. U.S. title: The Mystery of the Stolen Hats. Lippincott, 1939 S&A
Mr. Whimset Buys a Gun. Hutchinson, 1953
Much Ado About Something. Hutchinson, 1967
A Murder of Some Importance. Hutchinson, 1931; Lippincott, 1931 S&A
The Mystery of the Stolen Hats; see The Man from Michigan
Mystery on the Queen Mary. Hutchinson, 1937; Lippincott, 1938 S&A
Never Mix Business with Pleasure. Hutchinson, 1968
News Travels by Night. Hutchinson, 1943 S&A
No Clues for Dexter. Hutchinson, 1948
Not Proven. Hutchinson, 1935 S&A
The Penance of Brother Alaric. Hutchinson, 1930
Poisoned Sleep. Hutchinson, 1939 S&A
Public Enemy—No. 1. Hutchinson, 1934. U.S. title: John Jenkin, Public Enemy. Lippincott, 1935
The Quiet Ones. Hutchinson, 1970 RM
Racing Yacht Mystery. Hutchinson, 1938
The Return of Blackshirt. Unwin, 1927; Dodd, 1927 B ss
Satan's Mistress. Hutchinson, 1935 S&A
Seven Clues in Search of a Crime. Hutchinson, 1941 TT
So Sharp the Razor. Hutchinson, 1955
Some Geese Lay Golden Eggs. Hutchinson, 1968
Son of Blackshirt. Hutchinson, 1941 LB
Suspense. Hutchinson, 1953
Ten Trails to Tyburn. Hutchinson, 1944 TT
Thirteen in a Fog. Hutchinson, 1940
Through the Eyes of the Judge. Hutchinson, 1930; Lippincott, 1930
Tigers Have Claws. Hutchinson, 1949
Tomorrow's Yesterday. Hutchinson, 1972
The Trail of the White Knight. Harrap, 1926; Doran, 1927
Trouble! Harrap, 1929; Lippincott, 1929
Two and Two Make Five. Hutchinson, 1973 RM
The Undetective. Hutchinson, 1962; London House, 1963
Unsolved. Hutchinson, 1931; Lippincott, 1932
The Way Out. Hutchinson, 1954
Without Malice. Hutchinson, 1946
Work for the Hangman. Hutchinson, 1944 TT

GRAEME, DAVID. Pseudonym of Graham Montague Jeffries, 1900- . Other pseudonyms: Bruce Graeme, Roderic Hastings, qq.v. Series character: Monsieur Blackshirt (an ancestor of Bruce Graeme's character) = MB.

The Drums Beat Red. Harrap, 1963
The Inn of the Thirteen Swords. Harrap, 1938 MB
Monsieur Blackshirt. Harrap, 1933; Lippincott, 1933 MB
The Sword of Monsieur Blackshirt. Harrap, 1936; Lippincott, 1936 MB
The Vengeance of Monsieur Blackshirt. Harrap, 1934; Lippincott, 1935 MB

GRAEME, RODERIC. Pseudonym of Roderic (Graeme) Jeffries, 1926- , q.v. Other pseudonyms: Peter Alding, Jeffrey Ashford, Graham Hastings, qq.v. Series character: Blackshirt (continuation of the character created by his father, Bruce Graeme, q.v.), in all titles.

The Amazing Mr. Blackshirt. Hutchinson, 1955
Blackshirt at Large. Long, 1966
Blackshirt Finds Trouble. Long, 1961
Blackshirt Helps Himself. Long, 1961
Blackshirt in Peril. Long, 1967
Blackshirt Meets the Lady. Long, 1956
Blackshirt on the Spot. Long, 1963
Blackshirt Passes By. Hutchinson, 1953
Blackshirt Saves the Day. Hutchinson, 1964
Blackshirt Sees It Through. Long, 1960
Blackshirt Sets the Pace. Long, 1959
Blackshirt Stirs Things Up. Long, 1969
Blackshirt Takes the Trail. Long, 1962
Blackshirt Wins the Trick. Hutchinson, 1953
Call for Blackshirt. Long, 1963
Concerning Blackshirt. Hutchinson, 1952
Danger for Blackshirt. Long, 1965
Double for Blackshirt. Long, 1958
Paging Blackshirt. Long, 1957
Salute to Blackshirt. Hutchinson, 1954

GRAEME-HOLDER, W.
The Decker. Lane, 1931

GRAFFY, JOSEPH
The Man Who was Not Himself. Hodder, 1958

GRAFTON, C(ORNELIUS) W(ARREN). 1909- . Series character: Gil Henry = GH.
Beyond a Reasonable Doubt. Rinehart, 1950; Heinemann, 1951
The Rat Began to Gnaw the Rope. Farrar, 1943; Gollancz, 1944 GH
The Rope Began to Hang the Butcher. Farrar, 1944; Gollancz, 1945 GH

GRAFTON, SAMUEL. 1907- .
A Most Contagious Game. Doubleday, 1955; Hart-Davis, 1956

GRAHAM, ALAN
-Araminta and the River. Newnes, 1916
Follow the Little Pictures! Blackwood, 1920
The Golden Torrent. Hodder, 1922
Murder Disqualifies. Blackwood, 1922
-The Treasure on Camise. Paul, 1929
-The Voyage Home. Blackwood, 1921
Who Killed Gerald Cruden? Jenkins, 1925
Witch Temple. Paul, 1929

GRAHAM, ANTHONY. Series characters: Eric Marsden, in some titles including that marked EM; Frank Richmond, in at least those marked FR.
Act of Silence. Boardman, 1963
Behind the Arras. Boardman, 1964
The Deadly Lovers. Boardman, 1966 FR
The Death Business. Boardman, 1967 FR
The Desperate Witch. Boardman, 1962
Minus a Shamus. Boardman, 1955
No Sale for Haloes. Boardman, 1954
The Veetols. Boardman, 1965 EM

GRAHAM, BURTON
Spy or Die. Dent, 1972
The Spy Trap. Dent, 1971; Weybright, 1972

GRAHAM, DAVID
Grave of Sand. Hale, 1963
Operation Cleansweep. Hale, 1965

GRAHAM, JAMES. Pseudonym of Henry Patterson, 1929- . Other pseudonyms: Martin Fallon, Jack Higgins, Hugh Marlowe, Harry Patterson, qq.v.
Bloody Passage. Macmillan (London), 1974. U.S. title: The Run to Morning. Stein, 1974
A Game for Heroes. Macmillan (London), 1970; Doubleday, 1970
The Khufra Run. Macmillan (London), 1972
The Run to Morning; see Bloody Passage
The Wrath of God. Macmillan (London), 1971; Doubleday, 1971

GRAHAM, JOHN ALEXANDER. 1941- .
The Aldeburg Cezanne. Atlantic-Little, 1970
Arthur. Harper, 1969
The Involvement of Arnold Wechsler. Atlantic-Little, 1971
Something in the Air. Atlantic-Little, 1970; H. Hamilton, 1970

GRAHAM, NANCY
-The Black Swan. Cassell, 1958
-The Purple Jacaranda. Cassell, 1958

GRAHAM, NEILL. Pseudonym of W(illiam) Murdoch Duncan, 1909-1975, q.v. Other pseudonyms: John Cassells, John Dallas, Martin Locke, Peter Malloch, Lovat Marshall, qq.v. Series characters: Mr. Sandyman, in at least those marked S; James "Solo" Malcolm, in at least those marked SM.
Again, Mr. Sandyman. Jarrolds, 1952 S
The Amazing Mr. Sandyman. Jarrolds, 1952 S
Assignment, Murder. Long, 1974 SM
Blood on the Pavement. Long, 1970 SM
Candidate for a Coffin. Long, 1968 SM
Cop in a Tight Frame. Long, 1973 SM
Death of a Canary. Long, 1969 SM
Frame-Up. Long, 1972 SM
Graft Town. Long, 1963 SM
Hit Me Hard. Jarrolds, 1958 SM
Killers are on Velvet. Long, 1960 SM
Label It Murder. Long, 1963 SM
Make Mine Murder. Long, 1962 SM
A Matter of Murder. Long, 1971 SM
Money for Murder. Long, 1966 SM
Murder, Double Murder. Long, 1971 SM

Murder has been Done. Long, 1967 SM
Murder in a Dark Room. Long, 1973 SM
Murder is my Weakness. Long, 1961 SM
Murder Lies in Waiting. Long, 1969 SM
Murder Made Easy. Long, 1964 SM
Murder Makes a Date. Jarrolds, 1955;
   Roy, 1955 SM
Murder Makes It Certain. Long, 1963 SM
Murder Makes the News. Long, 1967 SM
Murder of a Black Cat. Long, 1964 SM
Murder on Demand. Long, 1966 SM
Murder on my Hands. Long, 1965 SM
Murder on the 'Duchess'. Long, 1961 SM
Murder on the List. Long, 1975 SM
Murder Rings the Bell. Jarrolds, 1959
   SM
Murder Walks on Tiptoe. Melrose, 1951
Murder's Always Final. Long, 1965 SM
One for the Book. Long, 1970 SM
Passport to Murder. Melrose, 1949 S
Pay Off. Long, 1968 SM
Play It Solo. Jarrolds, 1955 SM
The Quest of Mr. Sandyman. Jarrolds,
   1951 S
Salute Mr. Sandyman. Jarrolds, 1953 S
Salute to Murder. Long, 1958 SM
Say It with Murder. Jarrolds, 1956 SM
The Symbol of the Cat. Melrose, 1948 S
The Temple of Slumber. Melrose, 1950
You Can't Call It Murder. Jarrolds,
   1957 SM

GRAHAM, PETER. Pseudonym of Kenneth (Joseph Robb) Langmaid, q.v.
   Tiger Mark. Hamilton, 1928

GRAHAM, PETER
   -The Atom-Busters. Foster, 1948
   Behind the First Wall. Quality, 1946
   The Doctor Detective. Foster, 1946
   -Life is no Bargain. Quality, 1948

GRAHAM, ROSS
   Death on a Smokeboat. Hurst, 1947

GRAHAM, SCOTT. Pseudonym of Hazelton
   Black.
   -A Bolt from the Blue. Long, 1891
   -By Bitter Experience. Partridge, 1906
   -An Earl Without an Earldom. Partridge,
      1908
   -The Golden Milestone. Wyman, 1885
   -A Lost Inheritance. Partridge, 1912
   The Sandcliff Mystery. Oliphant, 1891
   -The Showman's Daughter. Hurst, 1897

GRAHAM, SEAN. 1920-   .
   Hippo's Coup. Weidenfeld, 1968
   A Surfeit of Sun. Weidenfeld, 1964;
      Doubleday, 1965

GRAHAM, VICTORIA
   The Witchstone. Pyramid, 1973

GRAHAM, WHIDDEN
   Crimson Hairs. Greenleaf, 1968

GRAHAM, (MATILDA) WINIFRED (MURIEL).
   Series character: Miss Woolfe, in at
   least those marked W.
   The Frozen Death. Hutchinson, 1938
   -Ghostly Strength. Hutchinson, 1936
   Glenvirgin's Ghost. Hutchinson, 1938
   -Hallowmass Abbey. Hutchinson, 1935
   -Identity. Hutchinson, 1933
   In Fear of a Woman. Hutchinson, 1925
   The Last Laugh. Hutchinson, 1930 W
   -The Life of a Nobody. Hutchinson, 1932
   The Man Behind the Chair. Hutchinson,
      1935
   -The Pit of Corruption. Paul, 1913
   -Sacrifice & Co. Hutchinson, 1940
   -A Spider Never Falls. Hutchinson, 1944
   Unholy Matrimony. Hutchinson, 1927
   -What Next? Hutchinson, 1945
   -What Thinkest Thou, Simon? Hutchinson,
      1936

Wolf-Net. Hutchinson, 1931 W
A Wolf of the Evenings. Hutchinson,
   1930 W

GRAHAM, WINSTON (MAWDSLEY). 1909-   .
   After the Act. Hodder, 1965; Doubleday,
      1966
   Angell, Pearl and Little God. Collins,
      1970; Doubleday, 1970
   Bridge to Vengeance; see The Little
      Walls
   The Dangerous Pawn. Ward, 1937
   The Forgotten Story. Ward, 1945
   Fortune is a Woman. Hodder, 1952;
      Doubleday, 1953
   The Giant's Chair. Ward, 1938
   Greek Fire. Hodder, 1958; Doubleday,
      1958
   The House with the Stained Glass Windows. Ward, 1934
   Into the Fog. Ward, 1935
   The Japanese Girl. Collins, 1971;
      Doubleday, 1972 ss
   Keys of Chance. Ward, 1939
   The Little Walls. Hodder, 1955; Doubleday, 1955. Also published as: Bridge
      to Vengeance. Bestseller (abridged),
      1957
   Marnie. Hodder, 1961; Doubleday, 1961
   The Merciless Ladies. Ward, 1944
   My Turn Next. Ward, 1942
   Night Journey. Ward, 1941; Doubleday,
      1968
   Night Without Stars. Hodder, 1950;
      Doubleday, 1950
   No Exit. Ward, 1940
   The Riddle of John Rowe. Ward, 1935
   The Sleeping Partner. Hodder, 1956;
      Doubleday, 1956
   Strangers Meeting. Ward, 1939
   Take my Life. Ward, 1947; Doubleday,
      1967
   The Tumbled House. Hodder, 1959;
      Doubleday, 1960
   The Walking Stick. Collins, 1967;
      Doubleday, 1967
   Without Motive. Ward, 1936
   Woman in the Mirror. Bodley Head, 1975;
      Doubleday, 1975. (Based in part on
      The Giant's Chair, q.v.)
   The Wreck of the Grey Cat. Doubleday,
      1958 (British title?)

GRAHAME, ARTHUR W.
   -Rabbitfoot. Dorrance, 1967

GRAIGIE, HAMILTON
   Derring-Do. Detective Tales, 19??
      (62 pp. mini-paperback.)

GRAINGER, FRANCIS EDWARD. 1857-1927.
   Pseudonym: Headon Hill, q.v.

GRANBECK, MARILYN. Pseudonyms: Ben Grant,
   Clayton Moore, qq.v. Joint pseudonyms with Arthur Moore, q.v.: Adam
   Hamilton, Van Saxon, qq.v.

GRANBY, GEORGE
   The Secret of Musterton House. Mills,
      1929; Dutton, 1929

GRANGER, HENRY FRANCIS
   The Gray Gull. Garden City, 1924

GRANT, ALAN. Pseudonym of (Gilbert) Alan
   Kennington, 1906-   , q.v.
   It Walks the Woods. Nicholson, 1936.
      Reprinted as by Alan Kennington:
      Mellifont, 1944

GRANT, AMBROSE. Pseudonym of Rene Raymond, 1906-   . Other pseudonyms:
   James Hadley Chase, James L. Docherty, Raymond Marshall, qq.v.

More Deadly Than the Male. Eyre, 1946.
   Reprinted as by James Hadley Chase:
   Panther, 1960

GRANT, BEN. Pseudonym of Marilyn Granbeck. Other pseudonym: Clayton Moore,
   q.v. Joint pseudonyms with Arthur
   Moore, q.v.: Adam Hamilton, Van
   Saxon, qq.v.
   Alice Dies Twice. Major, 1975
   Hitchhike to Hell. Merit, 1963
   Murder in the Raw. Merit, 1964
   One for the Road. Merit, 1966

GRANT, DOUGLAS. Pseudonym of Isabel
   (Egenton) Ostrander, 1883-1924, q.v.
   Other pseudonyms: Robert Orr Chipperfield, David Fox, qq.v. See also:
   WILLIAM J. BURNS, 1861-1932.
   Anything Once. Watt, 1920
   Booty. Watt, 1919; Hurst, 1921
   The Fifth Ace. Watt, 1918; Hurst, 1921.
      Also published as: The Red Glove.
      Grosset, 19??
   The Red Glove; see The Fifth Ace
   The Single Track. Watt, 1919; Hurst,
      1922
   Two-Gun Sue. McBride, 1922; Hurst, 1922

GRANT, DOUGLAS ALLEN
   Monsieur Brunner. Butterworth, 1933

GRANT, (CHARLES) GRAHAM
   The Diary of a Police Surgeon. Pearson,
      1920. (Fictionalized episodes of true
      crime.)

GRANT, HILDA KAY. 1910-   . Pseudonym:
   Jan Hilliard, q.v.

GRANT, JAMES EDWARD
   The Green Shadow. Hartney, 1935

GRANT, JOAN (MARSHALL). 1907-   .
   The Laird and the Lady. Methuen, 1949;
      Ace, 1966

GRANT, MAXWELL. House name under which
   were published the adventures of The
   Shadow. Most of the original Shadow
   stories in the pulps were by Walter
   B(rown) Gibson, 1897-   , q.v. All
   Belmont titles, except that marked
   *, were written by Dennis Lynds,
   1924-   , q.v. Those from other publishers are reprints from 1930's and
   40's pulps. Series character: Lamont
   Cranston (The Shadow), in all titles
   (see also Walter B. Gibson entry).
   The Black Master. Pyramid, 1974; New
      English Library pb, 1975
   The Crime Cult. Pyramid, 1975
   The Crime Oracle. Dover, 1975; Constable, 1975
   Cry Shadow. Belmont, 1965
   The Death Tower. Bantam, 1969
   Double Z. Pyramid, 1975
   Eyes of the Shadow. Street, 1931
   Gangdom's Doom. Bantam, 1970
   The Ghost Makers. Bantam, 1970
   Hands in the Dark. Pyramid, 1975; New
      English Library pb, 1977
   Hidden Death. Bantam, 1970
   The Living Shadow. Street, 1931; New
      English Library pb, 1976
   Mark of the Shadow. Belmont, 1966
   The Mask of Mephisto. Doubleday, 1975
   The Mobsmen on the Spot. Pyramid, 1974;
      New English Library pb, 1976
   Mox. Pyramid, 1975
   Murder by Magic. Doubleday, 1975
   The Night of the Shadow. Belmont, 1966
   The Red Menace. Pyramid, 1975

Grant, Maxwell (continued)

Return of the Shadow. Belmont, 1963 * (Written by Walter B. Gibson, q.v.)
The Romanoff Jewels. Pyramid, 1975
Shadow Beware. Belmont, 1965
The Shadow and the Voice of Murder. Bantam (Los Angeles), 1945
The Shadow—Destination Moon. Belmont, 1967
Shadow—Go Mad! Belmont, 1966
The Shadow Laughs! Street, 1931
The Shadow Strikes. Belmont, 1964
The Shadow's Revenge. Belmont, 1965
The Silent Seven. Pyramid, 1975
The Teeth of the Dragon. Dover, 1975; Constable, 1975
The Weird Adventures of the Shadow. Grosset, 1966. (Reprinting of the pulp novels <u>The Grove of Doom</u>, <u>Voodoo Death</u>, and <u>Murder by Moonlight</u>.)

GRANT, RICHARD. Pseudonym of Joseph Calvitt Clarke, 1888- .
The Case of the Baronet's Memoirs. Long, 1960
Circle of Death. Paul, 1952
The Death Light. Long, 1959
Doom Candle. Paul, 1943
Five Ways to Die. Paul, 1946
Formula for Crime. Paul, 1956
Legacy of Danger. Paul, 1954
Lives in a Box. Paul, 1951
Men in Knots. Paul, 1945
The Serpent Stirs. Paul, 1942
Shoot Your Enemies. Paul, 1948
The Silky Ones Sting. Paul, 1947
The Slaves of Ishtar. Paul, 1951
The Sniper Murders. Long, 1958
The Storm Gang. Paul, 1952
This is Dynamite. Paul, 1955
The Threat of the Cloven Hand. Paul, 1950
Who Strikes by Night. Paul, 1944

GRANT, ROBERT. 1852-1940.
The Law-Breakers and other stories. Scribner, 1906 ss

GRANT, RODERICK
The Stalking of Adrian Lawford. New English Library pb, 1974

GRANTHAM, GERALD
Dope Runners. Popular Publications (Australia), 193?
Mystery of the S. S. Timor. Popular Publications (Australia), 193?

GRANTLAND, KEITH. Joint pseudonym of Charles Beaumont, 1929-1967, q.v., and John (E.) Tomerlin, 1930- , q.v.
Run from the Hunter. GM, 1957; Boardman, 1959

GRANVILLE, AUSTYN
-The Shadow of Shame. Sergel, 1891

GRANVILLE, CHARLES. Pseudonym of Francis Charles Granville Egerton.
-A Broken Stirrup-Leather. Murray, 1888
-Mrs. John Foster. Heinemann, 1897
A Sapphire Ring. Murray, 1895
-Sir Hector's Watch. Murray, 1887

GRANVILLE, EDGAR
The Domino Plan. Bachman, 1975

GRATUS, JACK and T. PRESTON
What the Peeper Saw. Signet, 1972. (Novelization of the movie.)

GRAVES, CHARLES (PATRICK RANKE). 1899- .
Dusk to Dawn. Hutchinson, 1946
-Five Survive. Hutchinson, 1944

GRAVES, RICHARD L(ATSHAW). 1928- .
Series character: De Prundis = D.
The Black Gold of Malverde. Stein, 1973; Hart-Davis, 1974 D
Cobalt 60. Stein, 1975
The Platinum Bullet. Stein, 1974 D

GRAY, ANGELA
The Ashes of Falconwyck. Lancer, 1973
Blackwell's Ghost. Lancer, 1972
The Ghost Dancers. Lancer, 1971
The Golden Packet. Lancer, 1971
The Lattimore Arch. Lancer, 1971
Nightmare at Riverview. Lancer, 1973
Ravenswood Hall. Lancer, 1971
The Warlock's Daughter. Lancer, 1973

GRAY, ANNABEL. Pseudonym of Anne Cox.
The Mystic Number Seven. Simpkin, 1900

GRAY, BERKELEY. Pseudonym of Edwy Searles Brooks, 1889-1965, q.v. Other pseudonyms: Victor Gunn, Carlton Ross, qq.v. Series characters: Norman Conquest, in all except the one noted exception.
Alias Norman Conquest. Collins, 1945
The Big Brain. Collins, 1959
Blonde for Danger. Collins, 1943
Calamity Conquest. Collins, 1965
Call Conquest for Danger. Collins, 1961
Castle Conquest. Collins, 1964
Cavalier Conquest. Collins, 1944
Conquest After Midnight. Collins, 1957
Conquest Calls the Tune. Hale, 1968
Conquest Goes Home. Collins, 1957
Conquest Goes West. Collins, 1954
Conquest in California. Collins, 1958
Conquest in Command. Collins, 1956
Conquest in Ireland. Hale, 1969
Conquest in Scotland. Collins, 1951
Conquest in the Underworld. Collins, 1962
Conquest Likes It Hot. Collins, 1965
Conquest Marches On. Collins, 1939
Conquest on the Run. Collins, 1960
Conquest Overboard. Collins, 1964
Conquest Takes All. Collins, 1940
The Conquest Touch. Collins, 1948
Convict 1066. Collins, 1940
Count Down for Conquest. Collins, 1963
Curtains for Conquest? Collins, 1966
Dare-Devil Conquest. Collins, 1950
Death on the Hit Parade. Collins, 1958
Duel Murder. Collins, 1949
Follow the Lady. Collins, 1954
The Gay Desperado. Collins, 1944
Get Ready to Die. Collins, 1961
The Half-Open Door. Collins, 1953
The House of the Lost. Collins, 1956
Killer Conquest. Collins, 1947
The Lady is Poison. Collins, 1952
Leave It to Conquest. Collins, 1939
Meet the Don. Collins, 1940
Miss Dynamite. Collins, 1939
Mr. Ball of Fire. Collins, 1946
Mr. Mortimer Gets the Jitters. Collins, 1938
Murder & Co. Collins, 1959
Nightmare House. Collins, 1960
Operation Conquest. Collins, 1951
Seven Dawns to Death. Collins, 1950
Six Feet of Dynamite. Collins, 1941
Six to Kill. Collins, 1940
The Spot Marked X. Collins, 1948
Target for Conquest. Collins, 1953
Thank You, Mr. Conquest. Collins, 1941
Three Frightened Men. Amalgamated, 1938. (Sexton Blake)
Turn Left for Danger. Collins, 1955
Vultures, Ltd. Collins, 1938

GRAY, CHARLES EDWARD
Murder Defies the Roman Emperor. Humphries, 1957

GRAY, CURME
Murder in Millenium VI. Shasta, 1951

GRAY, DULCIE. Pseudonym of Dulcie Winifred Catherine Denison, 1920- .
Series character: Inspector Cardiff, in at least those marked C.
Baby Face. Barker, 1959
Dead Give Away. Macdonald, 1974
Deadly Lampshade. Macdonald, 1971
The Devil Wore Scarlet. Macdonald, 1964
Died in the Red. Macdonald, 1968 C
Epitaph for a Dead Actor. Barker, 1960 C
For Richer for Richer. Macdonald, 1970
Murder in Melbourne. Barker, 1958
Murder in Mind. Macdonald, 1963
The Murder of Love. Macdonald, 1967
Murder on Honeymoon. Macdonald, 1969
Murder on a Saturday. Barker, 1961
Murder on the Stairs. Barker, 1957; British Book Centre, 1958
No Quarter for a Star. Macdonald, 1965
Ride on a Tiger. Macdonald, 1975
Understudy to Murder. Macdonald, 1972

GRAY, HILARY
Frightened to Death. Hurst, 1950
Week-End with Death. Hurst, 1951

GRAY, JONATHAN. Pseudonym of Herbert Adams, 1874-1958, q.v.
The Owl. Harrap, 1937; Lippincott, 1937
Safety Last. Muller, 1934

GRAY, JONATHAN. Pseudonym of Jack Taylor.
Untimely Slain. Hutchinson, 1947

GRAY, MICHAEL (WAUDE)
Minutes to Impact. Cassell, 1967

GRAY, OSCAR
The Bagshot Mystery. Selwyn, 1928; Macaulay, 1929
Three Shots. Selwyn, 1929

GRAY, RUSSELL. Pseudonym of Bruno Fischer, 1908- , q.v.
The Lustful Ape. Lion, 1950. Reprinted as by Bruno Fischer: GM, 1959; Red Seal, 1959

GRAY, SIMON JAMES HALLIDAY. 1936- .
Pseudonym: Hamish Reade, q.v.

GRAYDON, ROBERT MURRAY. -1937. All titles below were published by Amalgamated Press and feature Sexton Blake.
The Masked Marauder. 1930
The Masquerader. 1919
The Mysterious Mr. Reece. 1917
The Mystery of the Mandarin's Idol. 1928

GRAYDON, W(ILLIAM) MURRAY. 1864-1946. All titles without publisher below were published by Amalgamated Press and feature Sexton Blake.
The Adventure of the Annamese Prince. 1925
The Adventure of the Rogue's Apprentice. 1927
The Affair of the Missing Witness. 1926
The Affair of the Three Gunmen. 1924
African Gold. 1920
An Amateur in Crime. 1924
The Arctic Trail. 1923
At the Shrine of the Buddha. 1921
Behind the Walls. 1926
Black Cargo. 1925
The Black Streak. 1920
The Blackshirt Mystery. 1926
The Blockade Runners. 1917
The Bloodhound's Revenge. 1926
The Bogus Tourist-Agency. 1929
A Breach of Trust. 1921
The Brigand's Secret. 1922
The Burglar of White Birches. 1927

By Order of the King! 1925
By the Terms of the Will. 1920
Carfax Baines: His Strange and Remarkable Exploits. Henderson   ss
The Case for the Prosecution. 1921
The Case of the Adopted Daughter. 1923
The Case of the Bogus Treasure Hunt. 1926
The Case of the Cashiered Officer. 1916
The Case of the Fatal Taxi Cab. 1928
The Case of the Five Merchants. 1921
The Case of the Four Barons. 1923
The Case of the Human Ape. 1927
The Case of the Mill Owner's Son. 1921
The Case of the Murdered Mahout. 1929
The Case of the Mysterious Jockey. 1919
The Case of the Nabob's Son. 1925
The Case of the Society Blackmailer. 1925
The Case of the Suppressed Will. 1916
The Case of the Theatrical Profiteer. 1926
The Case of the Two Guardians. 1924
The Case of the Two Scapegraces. 1925
The Clause in the Will. 1926
Craft and Cunning, 1917
Crag Island; or, The Mystery of Val Stanlock. Partridge, 1904
The Crime in the Wood. 1927
The Crime of Convict 13. 1930
The Crook of Chinatown. 1927
The Cryptogram. Street, 1899. (British title?)
The Curious Case of the Crook's Memoirs. 1924
Dark Secrets. 1919
The Derelicts. 1922
The Deserter of the Foreign Legion. 1928
The Desert of Doom. 1930
The Doctor Who Wouldn't Tell. 1928
Down East. 1923
The Earl's Return. 1922
The Embassy Detective. 1917
Exiled to Siberia. Penn, 1900. (British title?)
The Feud of Fear. 1930
The Five Diamonds. 1919
Five Years After. 1919
The Four Trails. 1921
From Lake to Wilderness; or, The Cruise of the Yolande. Street, 1899. (British title?)
The Game Keeper's Secret. 1924
Gipsy or Gentleman? 1921
The Great Abduction Mystery. 1918
The Green Turban. 1921
The Hand That Hid in Darkness. 1920
Held in Trust! 1925
His Father's Crime. 1925
In Barracks and Wigwam. Street, 1900. (British title?)
In Double Disguise. 1924
In Fort and Prison; or, The Mystery of Larry Redmayne. Street, 1903. (British title?)
In Friendship's Guise. Street, 1899. (British title?)
In the Hand of the Riffs. 1924
In Triple Disguise. 1916
The Island Secret. Pilgrim, 1935
Lady Sharlow's Secret. 1922
The Lama's Secret. 1922
Lost in Cambodia. 1922
Lost in the Slave Land; or, The Mystery of the Sacred Lamp Rock. Partridge, 1902
The Man Who Came Back. 1929
The Man Who Drove On. 1927
The Masked Dictator. 1927
The Master of Charteris Towers; or, A Rank Imposter. Henderson
The Mystery of Monte Carlo. 1928
The Mystery of the Abandoned Cottage. 1924
The Mystery of the Docks. 1929
The Mystery of the Dover Road. 1923
The Mystery of the Golden Chalice. 1928

The Mystery of the Swamp. 1922
Next O' Kin. 1924
On Winding Waters. Partridge, 1902
One of the Flying Squad. 1921
The Ordeal of Alick Hillersdon. 1918
The Path of Fear. 1923
The Perils of Pekin. Shaw, 1904
Perils of Petrograd. 1917
The Priest's Secret. 1925
The Princess of the Purple Palace. McClure, 1901. (British title?)
The Prisoner of Ellis Island. 1924
The Prisoner of the Mountains. 1926
The Rajah's Fortress. Street, 1900. (British title?)
The Record of the Case. 1919
The Reformation of Royce Remington. 1918
The Riddle of Crocodile Creek. 1928
The Rogue of Afghanistan. 1928
Rogues of the Desert. 1927
Salvage of the Sea. 1919
The Secret of the Flames. 1929
The Secret of the Past. 1917
The Secret of the Russian Refugees. 1928
The Secret of the Two Blackmailed Men. 1928
The Secret of the Vampire Actress. 1929
Sexton Blake in Silesia. 1922
Shadowed Lives. 1920
A Sheep in Wolf's Clothing. 1919
The Shield of the Law. 1923
The Shipwrecked Detective. 1926
The Sign of the Serpent. 1921
The Sixth Victim. 1929
The Taming of Neville Ibbetson. 1922
Ten Day's Leave. 1918
Their Great Adventure. 1916
Thirty Years After. 1921
The Three Trails. 1917
The Trader's Daughter. 1922
The Trail of Death. 1927
The Traitor Dragoon. Aldine, 1897
The Vanishing Death. 1929
The Vengeance of Three. 1920
Wanted. 1927
Where the Trail Ended. 1917
The White Death. 1926
The White King of Africa; or, The Mystery of the Ancient Fort. Street, 1899. (British title?)
With Cossack and Convict. Jarrolds, 1903
Within Fourteen Days. 1921
The Yacht of Mystery. 1926
The Yellow Face. 1921

GRAYLAND, V(ALERIE) MERLE (SPANNER). Pseudonym: Lee Belvedere, q.v. Series character: Hoani Mata, probably in all titles.
The Dead Men of Eden. Hale, 1962
The Grave-Digger's Apprentice. Hale, 1964
Jest of Darkness. Hale, 1965
Night of the Reaper. Hale, 1963

GRAYSON, ELIZABETH
By Demons Possessed. Manor, 1973
Macabre Manor. Manor, 1974
A Token of Evil. Manor, 1974

GRAYSON, PAULINE
Pyrrha: A Story of Two Crimes. American News, 1889. Also published as: Run to Earth; or, The Story of Two Crimes. Donohue, 189?
Run to Earth; see Pyrrha
-The Social Evil; or, The Woman Lalarge. Ogilvie, 1893

GRAYSON, RICHARD. Pseudonym of Richard Grindal. Series character: John Bryant, in at least those marked JB.

Dead So Soon. Hammond, 1960 JB
Death in Melting. Hammond, 1957 JB
Madman's Whisper. Hammond, 1958 JB
Murder Red-Handed. Long, 1965
Play the Roman Fool and Die. Long, 1970
The Spiral Path. Hammond, 1955 JB
Spy in Camera. Long, 1968
A Taste of Death. Hale, 1973

GRAYSON, RUPERT. Series character: Gunston Cotton = GC. (Note that all U.S. titles give the series character in full, Gunston, whereas British titles shorten it to Gun.)
Death Rides the Forest. Nash, 1921; Dutton, 1938 GC
Escape with Gun Cotton. Grayson, 1934 GC
Gun Cotton: A Romance of Secret Service. Nash, 1929. U.S. title: Gunston Cotton: Secret Service Agent. Dutton, 1936 GC
Gun Cotton—Ace High. Grayson, 1937 GC
Gun Cotton—Adventure Nine. Grayson, 1937 GC
Gun Cotton—Adventurer. Grayson, 1933; Dutton, 1937 GC
Gun Cotton at Blind Man's Hood. Grayson, 1938 GC
Gun Cotton Goes to Russia. Grayson, 1936 GC
Gun Cotton in Hollywood. Grayson, 1936 GC
Gun Cotton in Mexico. Grayson, 1937; Dutton, 1940 GC
Gun Cotton—Murder at the Bank. Grayson, 1939 GC
Gun Cotton—Outside the Law. Grayson, 1936 GC
Gun Cotton, Secret Agent. Grayson, 1934 GC
Gun Cotton—Secret Airman. Grayson, 1939; Dutton, 1939 GC
Gunston Cotton: Secret Service Agent; see Gun Cotton: A Romance of Secret Service
Introducing Mr. Robinson. Eldon, 1940
Scarlet Livery. Nash, 1928
Secret Agent in Africa. Dutton, 1939 GC (British title?)

GRAYSON, RUTH
Thieves' Highway. Hale, 1973
Yesterday's Poison. Hale, 1975

GREATOREX, CLIFFORD W(ILLEY). 1896-   .
The Secret of the Diamonds. Fiction House, 1935

GREAVES, RICHARD. Pseudonym of Peter Simonds, 1906-   .
The Case of Constable Shields. Dorrance, 1940

GRECCO, JOHNNY
Call Her Savage. Kaye, 1953
"Emma Slasky." Kaye, 1953
Mexican Deadline. Gaywood, 1950
Million Dollar Snatch. Gaywood, 1952
Send Another Coffin. Gaywood, 1950
She's No Lady. Kaye, 1953

GREEN, ALAN (BAER). 1906-1975. Joint pseudonym with Gladys Elizabeth Blun Green, 1908-   : Glen Burne, q.v. Joint pseudonym with Julian P. Brodie: Roger Denbie, q.v.
They Died Laughing. Simon, 1952; Panther, 1957

GREEN, ANNA KATHARINE. 1846-1935. Series characters: Ebenezer Gryce = EG; Violet Strange = VS.
Agatha Webb. Putnam, 1899; Ward, 1900
The Amethyst Box. Bobbs, 1905; Chatto, 1905

Green, Anna Katharine

Behind Closed Doors. Putnam, 1888; Routledge, 1888 EG
The Chief Legatee. Authors, 1906. British title: A Woman of Mystery. Collier (London), 1909
The Circular Study. McClure, 1900; Ward, 1902 EG
Cynthia Wakeham's Money. Putnam, 1892; Ward, 1904
Dark Hollow. Dodd, 1914; Nash, 1914
A Difficult Problem and other stories. Lupton, 1900; Ward, 1903 six ss, one with EG
The Doctor, His Wife, and the Clock. Putnam, 1895; Unwin, 1895 EG
Doctor Izard. Putnam, 1895; Cassell, 1895
The Filigree Ball. Bobbs, 1903; Unwin, 1904
The Forsaken Inn. Bonner, 1890; Routledge, 1890
The Golden Slipper and Other Problems for Violet Strange. Putnam, 1915 ss VS
Hand and Ring. Putnam, 1883; Ward, 1884 EG
The House in the Mist. Bobbs, 1905. (Contains the title novel and 2 ss.)
The House of the Whispering Pines. Putnam, 1910; Nash, 1910
Initials Only. Dodd, 1911; Nash, 1912 EG
The Leavenworth Case. Putnam, 1878; Routledge, 1878 EG
Lost Man's Lane. Putnam, 1898 EG
Marked "Personal". Putnam, 1893; Ward, 1904
Masterpieces of Mystery. Dodd, 1913. Also published as: Room Number 3 and other stories. Dodd, 1919 ss
A Matter of Millions. Bonner, 1890; Routledge, 1890 EG
The Mayor's Wife. Bobbs, 1907; London Daily Mail, 1909
The Mill Mystery. Putnam, 1886; Routledge, 1886
The Millionaire Baby. Bobbs, 1905; Chatto, 1905
Miss Hurd: An Enigma. Putnam, 1894
The Mystery of the Hasty Arrow. Dodd, 1917 EG
The Old Stone House and other stories. Putnam, 1891 ss
One of my Sons. Putnam, 1901; Ward, 1904 EG
-Risifi's Daughter. Putnam, 1887
Room Number 3 and other stories; see Masterpieces of Mystery
7 to 12. Putnam, 1887; Routledge, 1887
The Step on the Stair. Dodd, 1923; Lane, 1923
A Strange Disappearance. Putnam, 1880; Routledge, 1884 EG
The Sword of Damocles. Putnam, 1881; Ward, 1884
That Affair Next Door. Putnam, 1897; Nash, 1903 EG
Three Thousand Dollars. Badger, 1910
To the Minute and Scarlet and Black: Two of Life's Perplexities. Putnam, 1916
The Woman in the Alcove. Bobbs, 1906; Chatto, 1906
A Woman of Mystery; see The Chief Legatee
XYZ. Putnam, 1883; Ward, 1883

GREEN, CHALMERS
The Scarlet Venus. GM, 1952; Fawcett (London), 1959

GREEN, DANIEL DAVID
Hangman's Noose. Stockwell, 1954

GREEN, EDITH PINERO
The Death Trap. Dell, 1975

GREEN, F(REDERICK) L(AWRENCE). 1902-1953.
Ambush for the Hunter. Joseph, 1952; Random, 1953
-Clouds in the Wind. Joseph, 1950; Coward, 1951
-A Flask for the Journey. Joseph, 1945; Reynal, 1948
-A Fragment of Glass. Joseph, 1947
-Give Us the World. Joseph, 1941
The Magician. Joseph, 1951; Coward, 1951
Mist on the Waters. Joseph, 1948; Harcourt, 1949
Odd Man Out. Joseph, 1945; Reynal, 1947
-On the Edge of the Sea. Joseph, 1944
On the Night of the Fire. Joseph, 1939; Macmillan, 1939
-A Song for the Angels. Joseph, 1943
-The Sound of Winter. Joseph, 1940

GREEN, GERALD. 1922-   .
Faking It; or, The Wrong Hungarian. Trident, 1971

GREEN, GLADYS ELIZABETH BLUN. 1908-   .
Joint pseudonym with Alan (Baer) Green, 1906-1975, q.v.: Glen Burne, q.v.

GREEN, GLINT. Pseudonym of Margaret (Ann) Peterson, 1883-1933, q.v. Series character: Inspector Wield, in all titles.
Beauty—A Snare. Hutchinson, 1933
Devil Spider. Hutchinson, 1932
Poison Death. Hutchinson, 1933
Strands of Red...Hair! Hutchinson, 1931

GREEN, HELEN
-Mr. Jackson. Dodge, 1909

GREEN, JANET. Pseudonym of Victoria McCormick, 1914-
Murder Mistaken, with Leonard (Reginald) Gribble, 1908-   , q.v. Allen, 1953. (Novelization of Janet Green's play.)
My Turn Now. Triton, 1971

GREEN, JULIEN (HARTRIDGE). 1900-   .
The Dark Journey. Heinemann, 1929; Harper, 1929. (Translation of Leviathan. Paris, 1929.)

GREEN, PETER (MORRIS). 1924-   . Pseudonym: Denis Delaney, q.v.
Habeas Corpus and other stories. H. Hamilton, 1962; World, 1963 ss

GREEN, STAGG
-Commando Escape. Hammond, 1943
Fortress of the Maquis. Hammond, 1944

GREEN, STEPHEN
Missing from Home. Redman, 1962

GREEN, WILLIAM M(ARK). 1936-   .
Avery's Fortune. Bobbs, 1972; Hale, 1973
The Plutonium Heist; see Spencer's Bag
The Salisbury Manuscript. Bobbs, 1973; Hale, 1973
Spencer's Bag. Simon, 1971. British title: The Plutonium Heist. Hale, 1973

GREENAN, RUSSELL H(ENRY)
Heart of Gold. Random, 1975
It Happened in Boston. Random, 1968
Nightmare. Random, 1970. British title: Nightmare in Colour. Joseph, 1971
Nightmare in Colour; see Nightmare
The Queen of America. Random, 1972
The Secret Life of Algernon Pendleton. Random, 1973

GREENAWAY, GLADYS
-The Affair at Little Todsham. Hurst, 1964
-Coffee in the Morning. Hurst, 1967
-Devil in the Wind. Hurst, 1966
-Feather Your Nest. Hurst, 1967
-Follow a Shadow. Hale, 1961
-Follow my Leader. Hurst, 1966
-No Looking Back. Hurst, 1963
-Shadows on the Sand. Hurst, 1958
-Sing Softly, Stranger. Hurst, 1963
-Spring Came Late. Hale, 1961
-View of the Mountain. Hurst, 1959
-Week of Suspense. Hurst, 1962

GREENBAUM, LEONARD. 1930-   .
Out of Shape. Harper, 1969; Gollancz, 1970

GREENBURG, DAN
Philly. Simon, 1969; Secker, 1970

GREENE, A(LVIN) C(ARL). 1923-   .
The Santa Claus Bank Robbery. Knopf, 1972

GREENE, E(LIZABETH RUSSELL) PLUNKET. 1899-   . See: R(USSELL GEORGE HERBERT PLUNKET) GREENE, 1901-   .

GREENE, FRANCES NIMMO. 1850-1921.
The Devil to Pay. Scribner, 1918
Into the Night. Crowell, 1909; Methuen, 1910
-One Clear Call. Scribner, 1915

GREENE, GRAHAM. 1904-   .
The Basement Room and other stories. Cresset, 1935 ss
Brighton Rock. Heinemann, 1938; Viking, 1938
A Burnt-Out Case. Heinemann, 1961; Viking, 1961
The Comedians. Bodley Head, 1966; Viking, 1966
The Confidential Agent. Heinemann, 1939; Viking, 1939
The End of the Affair. Heinemann, 1951; Viking, 1951
England Made Me. Heinemann, 1935; Doubleday, 1935. Also published as: The Shipwrecked. Viking, 1953
A Gun for Sale. Heinemann, 1936. U.S. title: This Gun for Hire. Doubleday, 1936
The Heart of the Matter. Heinemann, 1948; Viking, 1948
The Honorary Consul. Bodley Head, 1973; Simon, 1973
It's a Battlefield. Heinemann, 1934; Doubleday, 1934. Revised edition: Heinemann, 1948; Viking, 1952
The Labyrinthine Ways; see The Power and the Glory
Loser Takes All. Heinemann, 1955; Viking, 1957
The Man Within. Heinemann, 1929; Doubleday, 1929
The Ministry of Fear. Heinemann, 1943; Viking, 1943
The Name of Action. Heinemann, 1930; Doubleday, 1931
Nineteen Stories. Heinemann, 1947; Viking, 1949. (Includes 8 ss from The Basement Room, q.v.)
Orient Express; see Stamboul Train
Our Man in Havana. Heinemann, 1958; Viking, 1958
The Potting Shed. French (London & New York), 1957. (3-act play.)
The Power and the Glory. Heinemann, 1940. U.S. title: The Labyrinthine

Ways. Viking, 1940. Reprinted as: The Power and the Glory. Viking, 1946
The Quiet American. Heinemann, 1955; Viking, 1956
The Return of A. J. Raffles. Bodley Head, 1975; Simon, 1976. (Play.)
Rumour at Nightfall. Heinemann, 1931; Doubleday, 1932
A Sense of Reality. Bodley Head, 1963; Viking, 1963 ss
The Shipwrecked; see England Made Me
Stamboul Train. Heinemann, 1932. U.S. title: Orient Express. Doubleday, 1933
The Third Man and The Fallen Idol. Heinemann, 1950. U.S. title: The Third Man. Viking, 1950. (The Fallen Idol does not appear in the U.S. edition but is included under its original title, The Basement Room, in Nineteen Stories, q.v.)
This Gun for Hire; see A Gun for Sale
Travels with my Aunt. Bodley Head, 1969; Viking, 1970
Twenty-One Stories. Heinemann, 1954; Viking, 1962. (Revision of Nineteen Stories, q.v., with 2 tales removed from the earlier edition and 4 new ones added.)

GREENE, HARRIS. 1921-   .
Cancelled Accounts. Doubleday, 1972; New English Library, 1973
-The "Mozart" Leaves at Nine. Doubleday, 1961; Heinemann, 1961

GREENE, JOSIAH E(NSIGN). 1911-1955.
The Laughing Loon. Morrow, 1939
Madmen Die Alone. Morrow, 1938

GREENE, L. PATRICK. (Name originally: Louis Montague Greene.) Series characters: Dynamite Drury, in at least those marked DD; Sgt. Lancey, in at least those marked L; Aubrey St. John Major, in at least 19 titles, including those marked AM
Black Tide Rising. Harrap, 1936
The Devil's Kloof. Hamilton, 1928
Drums Call the Major. Harrap, 1938 AM
Dynamite Drury. Selwyn, 1929 DD
Dynamite Drury Again. Jarrolds, 1930 DD
Dynamite Drury Patrols. Devonshire, 1946 DD
Escape from Liberty. Hamilton, 1939 AM
Face Falue. Hamilton, 1939 AM
The Flame. Hamilton, 1930
Forbidden Valley. Hamilton, 1932
Just Vengeance. Hamilton, 1934
The Lake of the Dead. Hamilton, 1935
Major Adventures. Heinemann, 1928 AM
Major Developments. Hamilton, 1931 AM
The Major—Diamond Buyer. Hamilton, 1926; Doubleday, 1924 AM
Major Exploits. Selwyn, 1930 AM
Major Hazards. Hamilton, 1932 AM
The Major—Knight Errant. Heinemann, 1929 AM
Major Occasions. Hamilton, 1931 AM
Murder Beacon, with Walter S(idney) Masterman, 1876-   , q.v. Low, 1932
The Point of a Thousand Spears. Hamilton, 1934 L
The Red Idol. Hamilton, 1928
Sergeant Lancey Carries On. Hamilton, 1933 L
Sergeant Lancey Reports. Hamilton, 1931 L
Sergeant Lancey Tells the Tale. Devonshire, 1947 L
Sergeant Whatisname. Low, 1933
The Splendid Exile. Hamilton, 1935 AM
Swordsman of Fortune. Mellifont, 1943
White Man's Stride. Hamilton, 1936

GREENE, R(USSELL GEORGE HUBERT PLUNKET), 1901-   , and E(LIZABETH RUSSELL) PLUNKET GREENE, 1899-   .
Eleven-Thirty Till Twelve. Secker, 1934
-Where Ignorance is Bliss. Murray, 1932

GREENE, WARD. 1892-1956. Pseudonym: Frank Dudley, q.v.
Death in the Deep South. Stackpole, 1936; Cassell, 1937

GREENER, WILLIAM OLIVER. 1862-
The Exploits of Jo Salis, a British Spy. Hurst, 1905
A Secret Agent in Port Arthur. Constable, 1905

GREENFIELD, GEORGE
-At Bay. Cassell, 1955
-Desert Episode. Macmillan (London), 1945
-This World is Wide Enough. Laurie, 1948

GREENFIELD, IRVING A. 1928-   .
Clove Crest. Belmont, 1969

GREENFIELD, JOHN
Death in the Library. Kangaroo, 1944

GREENHAM, G(EORGE) H(EPBURN)
Scotland Yard Experiences. Routledge, 1904 ss

GREENING, ARTHUR
The Curse of Kali. Jarrolds, 1922

GREENLAND, WILLIAM KINGSCOTE. Pseudonym: W. Scott King, q.v.

GREENLEAF, SAUL G.
The Three Knaves. Fenno, 1912

GREENLEAVES, WINIFRED
The Trout Inn Tragedy. Collins, 1929. U.S. title: The Trout Inn Mystery. Dial, 1929

GREENLEE, SAM. 1930-   .
The Spook Who Sat by the Door. Baron, 1969; Allison, 1969

GREENOUGH, MRS. (SARA DANA LORING). 1827-1885.
In Extremis. Roberts, 1972
Treason at Home. Newby, 1865; Peterson, 187?

GREENWOOD, EDWIN
Dark Understudy. Hale, 1940
The Deadly Dowager; see Skin and Bone
The Fair Devil; see Pins and Needles
French Farce. Skeffington, 1936; Doubleday, 1937
-Miracle in the Drawing Room. Skeffington, 1935; Doubleday, 1936
Old Goat. Heinemann, 1937
Pins and Needles. Skeffington, 1935. U.S. title: The Fair Devil. Doubleday, 1935
Skin and Bone. Skeffington, 1935. U.S. title: The Deadly Dowager. Doubleday, 1935

GREENWOOD, WALTER. 1903-   .
Only Mugs Work. Hutchinson, 1938

GREET, MRS. (DORA VICTORIA)
Mrs. Greet's Story of the Golden Owl. Leadenhall, 1892

GREGG, CECIL FREEMAN. 1898-   . Series characters: Inspector Cuthbert Higgins, in at least those marked CH; Henry Prince = HP.
Accidental Murder. Methuen, 1952 CH
Airtight Alibi. Methuen, 1956
The Body Behind the Bar. Methuen, 1932 CH
The Body in the Safe; see The Murdered Manservant
The Brazen Confession. Hutchinson, 1930. U.S. title: I Have Killed a Man! Dial, 1931 CH
The Chief Constable. Methuen, 1955 CH
Danger at Cliff House. Methuen, 1935; Dial, 1936 CH
Danger in the Dark. Methuen, 1939 CH
Dead on Time. Methuen, 1956 CH
The Double Solution. Hutchinson, 1931; Dial, 1932 CH
The Duke's Last Trick. Methuen, 1933 CH
The Execution of Diamond Deutsch. Methuen, 1934. U.S. title: Murder in the Park. Dial, 1935 CH
Exit Harlequin. Methuen, 1946 CH
Expert Evidence: Rex v. Marfelt. Methuen, 1938
The Fatal Error. Methuen, 1940 CH
Finlay of the Sentinel. Methuen, 1957
From Information Received. Methuen, 1950 CH
Henry Prince in Action. Methuen, 1936 HP
I Have Killed a Man!; see The Brazen Confession
Inspector Higgins Goes Fishing. Methuen, 1951 CH
Inspector Higgins Hurries. Hutchinson, 1932; Dial, 1932 CH
Inspector Higgins Sees It Through. Methuen, 1934; Appleton, 1934 CH
Justice! Methuen, 1941
The Man with a Monocle. Methuen, 1948
Melander's Millions. Methuen, 1944 CH
Murder at Midnight. Methuen, 1947 CH
Murder in the Park; see The Execution of Diamond Deutsch
The Murder of Estelle Cantor; see The Ten Black Pearls
The Murder on the Bus. Hutchinson, 1930; Dial, 1930 CH
The Murdered Manservant. Hutchinson, 1928. U.S. title: The Body in the Safe. Dial, 1930 CH
Mystery at Moor Street. Methuen, 1938
Night Flight to Zurich. Methuen, 1954 CH
The Obvious Solution. Methuen, 1958 CH
The Old Manor. Methuen, 1945; McNaughton, 1946 CH
Professional Jealousy. Methuen, 1960 CH
The Return of Henry Prince. Methuen, 1943 HP
The Rutland Mystery. Hutchinson, 1931; Dial, 1931 CH
Sufficient Rope. Methuen, 1953 CH
The Ten Black Pearls. Methuen, 1935. U.S. title: The Murder of Estelle Cantor. Dial, 1936 HP
The Three Daggers. Hutchinson, 1929; Dial, 1929 CH
Tragedy at Wembley. Methuen, 1936; Dial, 1936 CH
Two Died at Three. Methuen, 1943; Mystery House, 1944 CH
The Ugly Customer. Methuen, 1949 CH
The Vandor Mystery. Methuen, 1942 CH
Who Dialled 999? Methuen, 1939 CH
The Wrong House. Methuen, 1937

GREGORY, DAN
Three Must Die! Graphic, 1956

GREGORY, F(RANKLIN) L(ONG). 1905-   .
The Cipher of Death. Harper (London & New York), 1934
Murder at Four Dot Ranch. World's Work, 1936
-The White Wolf. Random, 1941

GREGORY, H. Pseudonym. See: ALFRED EDGAR, 1896-   ; REGINALD H(EBER) POOLE, 1885-   .

GREGORY, HARRY. Pseudonym of Theodore Mark Gottfried, 1928-   . Other pseudonym: Katherine Tobias, q.v.
  The Man from MOTHER. PB, 1967

GREGORY, HYLTON. Pseudonym. See: HARRY EGBERT HILL.

GREGORY, JACKSON. 1882-1943. Series character: Paul Savoy = PS.
  A Case for Mr. Paul Savoy. Scribner, 1933. British title: The Second Case of Mr. Paul Savoy. Hodder, 1933   PS
  The Emerald Murder Trap. Scribner, 1934. British title: The Third Case of Mr. Paul Savoy. Hodder, 1934   PS
  The First Case of Mr. Paul Savoy; see The House of the Opal
  The House of the Opal. Scribner, 1932. British title: The First Case of Mr. Paul Savoy. Hodder, 1933   PS
  -Ladyfingers. Scribner, 1920; Melrose, 1921
  Mystery at Spanish Hacienda. Dodd, 1929. British title: Rapidan. Hodder, 1929
  Rapidan; see Mystery at Spanish Hacienda
  The Second Case of Mr. Paul Savoy; see A Case for Mr. Paul Savoy
  The Third Case for Mr. Paul Savoy; see The Emerald Murder Trap

GREGORY, MASON. Joint pseudonym of Doris Meek and Adrienne Jones. Other joint pseudonym: Gregory Mason, q.v.
  If Two of Them are Dead. Arcadia, 1953

GREGORY, SACHA. Pseudonym.
  Yellowleaf. Heinemann, 1919; Lippincott, 1919

GREIG, IAN (BAXTER). Series character: Inspector Swinton, in all titles.
  Baxter's Second Death. Benn, 1932; Kinsey, 1933
  False Scent. Benn, 1933
  The King's Club Murder. Benn, 1930. U.S. title: The Silver King Mystery. Holt, 1930
  Murder at Lintercombe. Benn, 1931
  The Silver King Mystery; see The King's Club Murder
  The Tragedy of the Chinese Mine. Benn, 1930; Holt, 1931

GREIG, MAYSIE. 1902-   . Pseudonyms: Jennifer Ames, q.v., Mary Douglas Warren.
  Cloak and Dagger Lover. Collins, 1955. U.S. title: Moon Over the Water. Arcadia, 1956, as by Mary Douglas Warren
  Moon Over the Water; see Cloak and Dagger Lover
  Whispers in the Sun. Collins, 1949; Random, 1949

GRESHAM, ELIZABETH (F.). 1904-   . Pseudonym: Robin Grey, q.v. Series characters: Jenny Gilette (Lewis) and Hunter Lewis, in all titles (also in those as by Robin Grey).
  Puzzle in Paisley. Curtis, 1972
  Puzzle in Parchment. Curtis, 1973
  Puzzle in Parquet. Curtis, 1973
  Puzzle in Patchwork. Curtis, 1973

GRESHAM, WILLIAM LINDSAY. 1909-1962.
  Nightmare Alley. Rinehart, 1946; Heinemann, 1947

GREVILLE, HENRY. Pseudonym of Alice Marie Celeste Fleury Durand, 1842-1902.
  Un Mystere (A Mystery). Donohue, 1890. Also published as: The Beaurand Mystery. Mershon, 1900. (Translation of Un Mystere. Paris, 1890.)

GREW, WILLIAM. Pseudonym of William O'Farrell, 1904-1962, q.v.
  Doubles in Death. Doubleday, 1953
  Murder has Many Faces. Graphic, 1955

GREX, LEO. Pseudonym of Leonard (Reginald) Gribble, 1908-   , q.v. Other pseudonyms: Sterry Browning, Louis Grey, Dexter Muir, qq.v. See also: JANET GREEN. Series characters: Paul Irving, in at least those marked PI; Phil Sanderson, in at least those marked PS.
  Ace of Danger. Hutchinson, 1952   PI
  The Black-Out Murders. Harrap, 1940
  The Brass Knuckle. Long, 1964
  The Carlent Manor Crime. Hutchinson, 1939. Reprinted as by Leonard Gribble: Cherry Tree, 1946.
  Crooked Sixpence. Harrap, 1949
  Crooner's Swan Song. Hutchinson, 1935
  Die—As in Murder. Hale, 1974
  The Hard Kill. Long, 1969   PS
  Kill Now—Pay Later. Long, 1971
  King Spiv. Harrap, 1948
  Larceny in her Heart. Long, 1959
  The Lonely Inn Mystery. Hutchinson, 1933   PI
  The Madison Murder. Hutchinson, 1933   PI
  The Man from Manhattan. Hutchinson, 1934; Doubleday, 1935
  Murder in the Sanctuary. Hutchinson, 1934   PI
  The Nightborn. Hutchinson, 1931
  The Stalag Mites. Harrap, 1947
  Stolen Death. Hutchinson, 1936
  Terror Wears a Smile. Long, 1962
  Thanks for the Felony. Long, 1958
  The Tragedy at Draythorpe. Hutchinson, 1931
  Transatlantic Trouble. Hutchinson, 1937. Reprinted as by Leonard Gribble: Cherry Tree, 1946.
  Violent Keepsake. Long, 1967   PS

GREY, A. F. Pseudonym of Adeline Phyllis Neal, 1894-1977.
  Momentary Stoppage. Gollancz, 1942

GREY, ALTHEA. See: MICHAEL BURNING.

GREY, ANTHONY. 1938-   .
  Some Put Their Trust in Chariots. Joseph, 1973

GREY, DOUGLAS
  The Tracking of K.K. Chelsea, 1925; Skeffington, 1926

GREY, HARRY. Pseudonym of Harry Goldberg.
  Call Me Duke. Crown, 1955
  The Hoods. Crown, 1952
  Portrait of a Mobster. Signet, 1958

GREY, LOUIS. Pseudonym of Leonard (Reginald) Gribble, 1908-   , q.v. Other pseudonyms: Sterry Browning, Leo Grex, Dexter Muir, qq.v. See also: JANET GREEN.
  The Signet of Death. Nicholson, 1934. Reprinted as by Dexter Muir: Jenkins, 1946

GREY, MAXWELL. Pseudonym of Mary Gleed Tuttiett,   -1923.
  -An Innocent Imposter and other stories. Appleton, 1893   ss

GREY, NAIDRA
  Dark Sun, Pale Shadows. Putnam, 1973. British title: The Quinta Affair. Macmillan (London), 1974

GREY, ROBIN. Pseudonym of Elizabeth (F.) Gresham, 1904-   , q.v. Series characters: Jenny Gilette (Lewis) and Hunter Lewis, in both titles (also in those as by Elizabeth Gresham).
  Puzzle in Pewter. Duell, 1947. Reprinted as by Elizabeth Gresham: Curtis, 1973
  Puzzle in Porcelain. Duell, 1945. Reprinted as by Elizabeth Gresham: Curtis, 1973

GREY, SCARLET. Pseudonym.
  -Golden Hooves. Columbine, 1939
  Jock MacKay, Crook. Columbine, 1939

GRIBBEN, JAMES. 1915-   . Pseudonym: Vincent James, q.v.

GRIBBLE, LEONARD (REGINALD). 1908-   . Pseudonyms: Sterry Browning, Leo Grex, Louis Grey, Dexter Muir, qq.v. See also: JANET GREEN. Series character: Supt. Anthony Slade, in at least those marked AS.
  Alias the Victim. Hale, 1971
  The Arsenal Stadium Mystery. Harrap, 1939. Revised edition: Jenkins, 1950   AS
  Atomic Murder. Harrap, 1947; Ziff-Davis, 1947   AS
  The Case-Book of Anthony Slade. Quality, 1937   AS   ss
  The Case of the Malverne Diamonds. Harrap, 1936; Greenberg, 1937   AS
  The Case of the Marsden Rubies. Harrap, 1929; Doubleday, 1930   AS
  The Death Chime. Harrap, 1934
  Death Pays the Piper. Jenkins, 1956; Roy, 1958   AS
  A Diplomat Dies. Jenkins, 1969
  Don't Argue with Death. Jenkins, 1959; Roy, 1959   AS
  The Frightened Chameleon. Jenkins, 1951; Roy, 1957   AS
  The Gillespie Suicide Mystery. Harrap, 1929. U.S. title: The Terrace Suicide Mystery. Doubleday, 1929   AS
  The Glass Alibi. Jenkins, 1952; Roy, 1956   AS
  The Grand Modena Murder. Harrap, 1930; Doubleday, 1931   AS
  Hangman's Moon. Allen, 1950   AS
  Heads You Die. Jenkins, 1964   AS
  The Inverted Crime. Jenkins, 1954   AS
  Is This Revenge? Harrap, 1931. U.S. title: The Serpentine Murder. Dodd, 1932   AS
  Murder Out of Season. Jenkins, 1952
  Mystery at Tudor Arches. Harrap, 1935   AS
  Mystery Manor. Goulden, 1951
  Programmed for Death. Hale, 1973
  The Riddle of the Ravens. Harrap, 1934   AS
  Riley of the Special Branch. Harrap, 1936
  Sally of Scotland Yard, with Geraldine Laws. Allen, 1954
  The Secret of Tangles. Harrap, 1933; Lippincott, 1934   AS
  The Serpentine Murder; see Is This Revenge?
  She Died Laughing. Jenkins, 1953   AS
  Stand-In for Murder. Jenkins, 1957; Roy, 1958   AS
  The Stolen Home Secretary. Harrap, 1932. U.S. title: The Stolen Statesman. Dodd, 1932   AS
  The Stolen Statesman; see The Stolen Home Secretary
  Strip-Tease Macabre. Jenkins, 1967   AS
  Superintendent Slade Investigates. Jenkins, 1956; Roy, 1957   AS   ss
  The Terrace Suicide Mystery; see The Gillespie Suicide Mystery

They Kidnapped Stanley Matthews. Jenkins, 1950 AS
Tragedy in E Flat. Harrap, 1938; Hillman-Curl, 1939 AS
The Velvet Mask and other stories. Allen, 1952 ss
The Violent Dark. Jenkins, 1965 AS
Wantons Die Hard. Jenkins, 1961; Roy, 1961 AS
Who Killed Oliver Cromwell? Harrap, 1937; Greenberg, 1938 AS
The Yellow Bungalow Mystery. Harrap, 1933 AS
You Can't Die Tomorrow. Hale, 1975

GRIBBON, WILLIAM LANCASTER. 1879-1940. Pseudonym: Talbot Mundy, q.v.

GRIDLEY, THOMAS. Pseudonym: Louis Southworth, q.v.

GRIEG, MICHAEL. 1922- .
A Fire in his Hand. Doubleday, 1963

GRIERSON, EDWARD. 1914-1975.
A Crime of One's Own. Chatto, 1967; Putnam, 1967
The Massingham Affair. Chatto, 1962; Doubleday, 1963
Reputation for a Song. Chatto, 1952; Knopf, 1953
The Second Man. Chatto, 1956; Knopf, 1956

GRIERSON, FRANCIS (DURHAM). 1888- .
Series characters: Supt. Andrew Ash = AA; Chief Det. Insp. George Muir = GM; Det. Insp. Sims and Professor Wells = RF; Richard Furling = RF; Commissaire Patras = P.
The Acrefield Mystery. Butterworth, 1938
Blackmail in Red. Hale, 1954 AA
The Blind Frog. Hale, 1955 AA
The Blue Bucket Mystery. Bles, 1929; Clode, 1930 S&W
Boomerang Murder. Hutchinson, 1951 GM
The Buddha of Fleet Street. Hutchinson, 1949 AA
The Cabaret Crime. Butterworth, 1938 GM
A Covenant with Death. Butterworth, 1938 GM
The Coward's Club. Butterworth, 1937 P
The Crimson Cat. Eyre, 1944 GM
Death on Deposit. Butterworth, 1935 S&W
The Double Thumb. Hodder, 1925 S&W ss
The Empty House. Butterworth, 1933; Appleton, 1934
Entertaining Murder. Eyre, 1945 GM
The Green Diamond Mystery. Collins, 1929
Green Evil. Hale, 1958 AA
He Had It Coming to Him. Eyre, 1948 AA
The Heart in the Box. Butterworth, 1936 P
The Ink Street Murder. Butterworth, 1940 GM
The Jackdaw Mystery. Collins, 1931
Judas C.I.D. Hale, 1954 AA
The Lady of Despair. Collins, 1930 P
The Limping Man. Hodder, 1924; Clode, 1926 S&W
The Lost Pearl. Hodder, 1925; Clode, 1926 S&W
The Mad Hatter Murder. Eyre, 1941 GM
Madame Shadow. Hutchinson, 1952 AA
The Man from Madagascar. Butterworth, 1937 P
The Monkhurst Murder. Collins, 1933 RF
Murder at Lancaster Gate. Butterworth, 1934 S&W
Murder at the Wedding; see The Yellow Rat
Murder in Black. Butterworth, 1935; Appleton, 1935 S&W
Murder in Mortimer Square. Collins, 1932 RF
The Murder in the Garden; see The Zoo Murder
The Mysterious Mademoiselle. Collins, 1930 S&W
Mystery in Red. Collins, 1931
The Mystery of the Golden Angel. Collins, 1933 RF
The Mystery of the Two-Faced Man. Butterworth, 1939 GM
No Wreaths for the Duchess. Hutchinson, 1948 AA
Out of the Ashes. Eyre, 1946 AA
The Red Cobra. Hale, 1960 AA
Secret Judges. Hodder, 1925 S&W
The Sign of the Nine. Hale, 1956 AA
The Smiling Death. Bles, 1927; Clode, 1927 S&W
The Strange Case of Edgar Heriot. Hutchinson, 1950 AA
Thrice Judas. Eyre, 1942 GM
Traitor's Cross. Hutchinson, 1952 AA
The White Camellia. Bles, 1929; Clode, 1929 S&W
The Yellow Rat. Collins, 1929. Also published as: Murder at the Wedding. Collins, 1932 S&W
The Zoo Murder. Bles, 1926. U.S. title: The Murder in the Garden. Clode, 1927 S&W

GRIEVE, ALEXANDER HAIG GLANVILLE. 1902- . Pseudonym: Alec Glanville, q.v.

GRIFF. House name. Some of these titles were written by F(rank) Dubrez Fawcett, 1891-1968, q.v. Other Fawcett pseudonyms: Spike Gordon (?), Elmer Eliot Saks, Ben Sarto, qq.v. Others written by Ernest L(ionel) McKeag, 1896- , q.v. Other McKeag pseudonyms: Mark Grimshaw, Ramon Lacroix, qq.v.
Back-Alley Blond. Modern Fiction, 1952
Brooklyn Moll Shoots Bedmate. Modern Fiction, 1951
Bullets for Snoopers. Modern Fiction, 1953
Cage of Corruption. Modern Fiction, 1953
Caribbean Cutie. Modern Fiction, 1953
The City of Lost Women. Modern Fiction, 1953
Come and Get Me. Modern Fiction, 1949
Crooked Coffins. Modern Fiction, 1952
Curves can Cast Shadows. Modern Fiction, 1953
Dames Don't Forget. Modern Fiction, 195?
Dared by a Dame. Modern Fiction, 1953
Demon Barber of Broadway. Modern Fiction, 1953
Devil's Daughter. Modern Fiction, 1952
Dope is for Dopes. Modern Fiction, 1949
The Doped and the Damned. Modern Fiction, 1953
Eastern Men—Chicago Women. Modern Fiction, 1951
From Dance Hall to Opium Den. Modern Fiction, 1950
Good-Bye Tomorrow. Modern Fiction, 1951
Hank Tries the Sidewalk. Modern Fiction, 1953
Hell-Bomb Floozies. Modern Fiction, 1951
Hi-Jack That Dame. Modern Fiction, 1950
Hot-Shot Rita. Modern Fiction, 1951
I Don't Get It. Modern Fiction, 1953
I Spit on Your Grave. Modern Fiction, 195?
Kiss Tomorrow Goodbye. Modern Fiction, 1952
Liquid Death. Modern Fiction, 1953
Main Street Morgue. Modern Fiction, 1953
Midnight Hostess. Modern Fiction, 1955
Molls Mean Murder. Modern Fiction, 1949
Murder by Contract. Modern Fiction, 1951
Night Patrol. Modern Fiction, 1953
Only Mugs Die Young. Modern Fiction, 1949
Played the Hard Way. Modern Fiction, 1954
Poisonous Angel. Modern Fiction, 1953
The Quick and the Dead. Modern Fiction, 1953
Rackets Incorporated. Modern Fiction, 1949
Rub-Out Specialty. Modern Fiction, 1949
She Had It Coming—. Modern Fiction, 1951
She Paid 'Em Off. Modern Fiction, 1951
Shoot to Live. Modern Fiction, 1953
The Silver Key. Modern Fiction, 1953
Some Rats have Two Legs. Modern Fiction, 1950
Stiffs Can't Squeal. Modern Fiction, 1950
That Room in Camden Town. Modern Fiction, 1952
Too Tough to Live. Modern Fiction, 1952
Trading with Bodies. Modern Fiction, 1950
Vice Queens on Broadway. Modern Fiction, 1951
You Pay the Price. Modern Fiction, 1952

GRIFFIN, A. M.
The Man Who Called Too Soon. Gifford, 1945
Nurse Lester's First Case. Gifford, 1947

GRIFFIN, (EDITHA) ACEITUNA. 1876- .
-Amber and Jade. Longmans, 1928
Commandments Six and Eight. Low, 1936
-Conscience. Murray, 1931
-Genesta. Murray, 1930
-Lady Sarah's Deed of Gift. Blackwood, 1906
Motive for Murder, with Joy Griffin. Low, 1935
-Mrs. Vannock. Nash, 1907
-Pearl and Plain. Longmans, 1927
The Punt Murder. Low, 1936
-A Servant of the King. Blackwood, 1906
Sweets and Sinners. Low, 1937
-The Tavistocks. Laurie, 1908
"Where There is a Will..." Low, 1939

GRIFFIN, FRANK
Appointment with my Lady. Westhouse, 1946
Danger at Midnight. Mellifont, 1948
Death After Dark. Fiction House, 1947
Death Takes a Hand. Bear Hudson, 1945
Killer's Progress. Pendulum, 1947
October Day. Secker, 1939
A Rope for Christmas. Yates, 1951
She Deserved to Die. Yates, 1951
Strumpet's Fool. Westhouse, 1947

GRIFFIN, JOY. See: (EDITHA) ACEITUNA GRIFFIN.

GRIFFIN, LEROY F. [LAROY FREESE GRIFFIN]. 1844-1916.
The Abduction of Princess Chriemhild. Weed, 1898

GRIFFIN, ROBERT J. Series character: Coppersmith, in all titles.
-Coppersmith. Pyramid, 1968
-Coppersmith's Dolls. Pyramid, 1969
-Genghis Coppersmith. Pyramid, 1972
-King Coppersmith. Pyramid, 1971

GRIFFIN, SAMUEL FRANKLIN
  Betencourt Five. Gold Side, 1971
  Little Squaw Big Hurry. Gold Side, 1971

GRIFFITH, MR. and MRS. E. G. Pseudonym: Jason Griffith, q.v.

GRIFFITH, GEORGE (CHETWYND). 1859-1906.
  Brothers of the Chain. White, 1900
  A Conquest of Fortune. White, 1906
  A Criminal Croesus. Long, 1904
  Denver's Double. White, 1901
  -The Great Pirate Syndicate. White, 1899
  -The Great Syndicate. White, 1908
  -The Great Weather Syndicate. White, 1906
  -His Beautiful Client. White, 1906
  -His Better Half. White, 1905
  The Justice of Revenge. White, 1901
  Knaves of Diamonds. Pearson, 1899 ss
  A Mayfair Magician. White, 1905
  -The Sacred Skull. Everett, 1908
  The White Witch of Mayfair. White, 1902
  -The World Masters. Long, 1903

GRIFFITH, (RICHARD) GLYN. 1892-   .
  Fire over Baghdad. Long, 1939
  -Hangman's Tale. Long, 1933

GRIFFITH, JASON. Pseudonym of Mr. & Mrs. E. G. Griffith.
  The Monkey Wrench. Stratford, 1933

GRIFFITHS, (MAJOR) ARTHUR (GEORGE FREDERICK). 1838-1908.
  Agony Terrace: Some Secrets of the Cynosure Club. White, 1907 ss
  The Bank Robbers; see Fast and Loose
  -Before the British Raj: A Story of Military Adventure in India. Everett, 1903
  -A Bid for Empire: A Story of Love and Adventure in Modern Egypt. Digby Long, 1902
  The Brand of the Broad Arrow. Pearson, 1900
  Criminals I Have Known. Chapman, 1895 ss
  -A Duchess in Difficulties: A Story of Modern Manners. White, 1902
  Fast and Loose. Chapman, 1885; Munro, 1886. Also published as: The Bank Robbers; or, Fast and Loose. Munro, 1894
  Forbidden by Law. Jarrolds, 1897
  Ford's Folly, Ltd. Macqueen, 1900
  A Girl of Grit: A Story of the Intelligence Department. Milne, 1898; Fenno, 1899
  The House in Spring Gardens. Nash, 1906
  In Tight Places: Some Experiences of an Amateur Detective. Jarrolds, 1900 ss
  The Lezaire Mystery. Mellifont, 1937
  Locked Up. Blackwood, 1887
  My Peril in a Pullman Car and other tales. Drane, 1893 ss
  No. 99. Chapman, 1885; Munro, 1885. New edition, with another story, Blue Blood: Macqueen, 1901
  The Passenger from Calais. Nash, 1905; Page, 1906
  The Prison Princess: A Romance of Millbank Penitentiary. Cassell, 1893
  The Rome Express. Milne, 1896; Page, 1907
  A Royal Rascal: Episodes in the Career of Colonel Sir Theophilus St. Clair, K.C.B. Unwin, 1905 ss
  A Set of Flats. Milne, 1901
  -The Silver Spoon: The Adventures of a Young Gentleman in Society. White, 1903
  -A Son of Mars. Remington, 1900
  Tales of a Government Official. White, 1902 ss
  -The Thin Red Line. Chapman, 1886
  Thrice Captive. White, 1908
  -Viscount Lacklands: A Tale of Modern Mammon. Remington, 1881; Munro, 1883
  -A Wayward Woman. Smith Elder, 1879; Harper, 1880
  -Winnifred's Way. White, 1905
  A Woman of Business. Long, 1904
  The Wrong Road by Hook or Crook. Blackwood, 1888. Also published as: The Wrong Road. Milne, 1903

GRIFFITHS, THOMAS H. See: ARMSTRONG LIVINGSTON, 1885-   .

GRIMES, LEE. 1920-   .
  -The Ax of Atlantis. Warner, 1975
  The Eye of Shiva. Warner, 1974

GRIMSHAW, BEATRICE (ETHEL).   -1953.
  The Beach of Terror, and other stories. Cassell, 1931 ss
  The Mystery of Tumbling Reef. Cassell, 1932; Houghton, 1932
  -The Sands of Oro. Hurst, 1924; Doubleday, 1924
  South Sea Sarah, and Murder in Paradise. New Century Press (Sydney), 1940. (2 novels.)
  -The Terrible Island. Hurst, 1920
  -The Wreck of the Redwing. Hurst, 1927; Holt, 1927

GRIMSHAW, MARK. Pseudonym of Ernest L(ionel) McKeag, 1896-   , q.v. Other pseudonyms: Griff, Ramon Lacroix, qq.v.
  Colwyn Dane—the Outlawed Detective. Amalgamated, 1937
  The Sign of the Grinning Dragon. Amalgamated, 1938

GRINDAL, RICHARD. Pseudonym: Richard Grayson, q.v.

GRISEWOOD, HARMON (JOSEPH GERARD). 1906-   .
  -The Last Cab on the Rank. Macdonald, 1964
  -The Recess. Macdonald, 1963

GRISEWOOD, R(OBERT) NORMAN. 1876-   .
  -The Venture. Fenno, 1911

GRISON, GEORGES. 1841-1928.
  Dispatch and Secrecy. Vizetelly, 1888

GRISWOLD, GEORGE. Pseudonym of Robert George Dean, q.v. Series character: Mr. Groode, in all titles.
  A Checkmate by the Colonel. Dutton, 1953; Eyre, 1954
  A Gambit for Mr. Groode. Dutton, 1952; Eyre, 1953
  The Pinned Man. Little, 1955; Eyre, 1956
  Red Pawns. Dutton, 1954; Eyre, 1955

GRISWOLD, LATTA. 1876-1931.
  The Inn at the Red Oak. Shores, 1917

GROC, LEON. 1882-   .
  The Bus That Vanished. Macaulay, 1928. (Translation of L'Autobus Evanoui. Paris, 1914.)
  The House of Death. Readers Library, 1921. (Translation of La Maison des Morts. Paris, 19??)

GRONER, AUGUSTA. 1850-   . See also: GRACE ISABEL COLBRON, 1869-1948, translator of Groner's work and sometimes billed as her collaborator. Series character: Joe Muller (see also the Colbron entry), in all titles.
  The Lady in Blue, with Grace Isabel Colbron. Duffield, 1922
  The Man with the Black Cord. Duffield, 1911; Chatto, 1911
  Mene Tekel: A Tale of Strange Happenings. Duffield, 1912

GROOM, K(ATHLEEN) C(LARICE)
  The Folly of Fear. Hurst, 1947
  Phantom Fortune. Hurst, 1948
  The Recoil. Hutchinson, 1952

GROOM, (ARTHUR JOHN) PELHAM. Series character: Peter Mohune, in at least those marked PM.
  "Defend the Rock." Jarrolds, 1945
  The Devil Fish. Ward, 1955
  The Fourth Seal. Jarrolds, 1948 PM
  High Adventure. Ace (London), 1938
  The Little Hanging Men. Jarrolds, 1946
  Mohune's Nine Lives; see What are Your Angels Now?
  Sabotage Unlimited. Hamilton, 1938 PM
  Temperamental Journey. Jarrolds, 1947
  What are Your Angels Now? Jarrolds, 1943. U.S. title: Mohune's Nine Lives. Books, Inc., 1944 PM
  Whistling Wires. Melrose, 1935

GROOM, MRS. SIDNEY
  Detective Sylvia Shale. Hurst, 1923

GROOME, FRANCIS HINDES. 1851-1902.
  -Kriegspiel: The War Game. Ward (London & New York), 1896

GROPPER, MILTON HERBERT, 1897-1955, and SHERRY, EDNA,   -1967, q.v.
  Grounds for Indecency. Macaulay, 1931
  Is No One Innocent? Cosmopolitan, 1930

GROSS, LAURENCE and EDWARD CHILDS CARPENTER. See also: HELEN (ALDEN) K(NIPE) CARPENTER.
  Whistling in the Dark. French (New York & London), 1933. (Play.)

GROTE, WILLIAM
  Cain's Girl Friend. Ace, 1957

GROVE, WALT
  -Down. Dell, 1953; World Distributors, 1961
  Hell-Bent for Danger. GM, 1950
  -The Joy Boys. Dell, 1959; Panther, 1963
  The Man Who Said No. GM, 1950; Fawcett (London), 1954

GROVES, REGINALD. 1908-   .
  The Mystery of Victor Grayson. Pendulum, 1946

GROVES, W(ILLIAM) E.
  Bride of the Wolf. Pearson, 1939
  The Scarlet Mask. Leng, 1938
  The Schemer. Leng, 1936
  The Secret of the Spectre's Nest. Fiction House, 1945

GRUBB, DAVIS (ALEXANDER). 1919-   .
  Fools' Parade. World, 1969
  The Golden Sickle. World, 1968
  The Night of the Hunter. Harper, 1953; H. Hamilton, 1954
  One Foot in the Grave; see Twelve Tales of Suspense and the Supernatural
  -Shadow of my Brother. Holt, 1966; Hutchinson, 1966
  Twelve Tales of Suspense and the Supernatural. Scribner, 1964. British title: One Foot in the Grave. Arrow, 1966

The Watchman. Scribner, 1961; Joseph, 1962

GRUBER, FRANK. 1904-1969. Pseudonyms: Stephen Acre, Charles K. Boston, John K. Vedder, qq.v. Series characters: Otis Beagle = OB (see also Charles K. Boston entry); Johnny Fletcher & Sam Cragg = F&C; Simon Lash = SL; Oliver Quade = OQ.
Beagle Scented Murder. Rinehart, 1946. Also published as: Market for Murder. Penguin (New American Library), 1947 OB
Brass Knuckles. Sherbourne, 1966 OQ ss
Bridge of Sand. Dutton, 1963; Boardman, 1964
Brothers of Silence. Dutton, 1962; Boardman, 1962
The Buffalo Box. Farrar, 1942; Nicholson, 1944 SL
The Corpse Moved Upstairs; see The Mighty Blockhead
Die Like a Dog; see The Hungry Dog
The Etruscan Bull. Dutton, 1969; Hale, 1970
The Fourth Letter. Rinehart, 1947
The French Key. Farrar, 1940; Hale, 1941. Also published as: The French Key Mystery. Avon, 1946; and as: Once Over Deadly. Jonathan (abridged), 1956 F&C
The Gamecock Murders; see The Scarlet Feather
The Gift Horse. Farrar, 1942; Nicholson, 1943 F&C
The Gold Gap. Dutton, 1968; Hale, 1968
The Greek Affair. Dutton, 1964; Boardman, 1965
The Honest Dealer. Rinehart, 1947 F&C
The Hungry Dog. Farrar, 1941; Nicholson, 1950. Also published as: Die Like a Dog. Jonathan, 1953 F&C
A Job of Murder; see The Leather Duke
The Laughing Fox. Farrar, 1940; Nicholson, 1942 F&C
The Leather Duke. Rinehart, 1949; Pemberton, 1950. Also published as: A Job of Murder. Signet, 1950 F&C
The Limping Goose. Rinehart, 1954; Barker, 1955. Also published as: Murder One. Belmont, 1973 F&C
Little Hercules. Dutton, 1965; Boardman, 1966
The Lock and the Key. Rinehart, 1948; World's Work, 1950. Also published as: Too Tough to Die. Jonathan, 1954; and as: Run, Thief, Run. Crest, 1955
The Lonesome Badger. Rinehart, 1954. Also published as: Mood for Murder. Graphic, 1956 OB
The Long Arm of Murder; see Murder '97
Market for Murder; see Beagle Scented Murder
The Mighty Blockhead. Farrar, 1942; Nicholson, 1948. Also published as: The Corpse Moved Upstairs. Belmont, 1964 F&C
Mood for Murder; see The Lonesome Badger
Murder '97. Rinehart, 1948; Barker, 1956. Also published as: The Long Arm of Murder. Jonathan, 1956 SL
Murder One; see The Limping Goose
The Navy Colt. Farrar, 1941; Nicholson, 1942 F&C
Once Over Deadly; see The French Key
Run, Fool, Run. Dutton, 1966; Hale, 1967
Run, Thief, Run; see The Lock and the Key
The Scarlet Feather. Rinehart, 1948; Cherry Tree, 1951. Also published as: The Gamecock Murders. Signet, 1949 F&C
The Silver Tombstone. Farrar, 1945; Nicholson, 1949. Also published as: The Silver Tombstone Mystery. Signet, 1959 F&C
The Silver Tombstone Mystery; see The Silver Tombstone
Simon Lash, Detective; see Simon Lash, Private Detective
Simon Lash, Private Detective. Farrar, 1941. British title: Simon Lash, Detective. Nicholson, 1943 SL
The Spanish Prisoner. Dutton, 1969; Hale, 1970
Swing Low, Swing Dead. Belmont, 1964 F&C
The Talking Clock. Farrar, 1941; Nicholson, 1942 F&C
Too Tough to Die; see The Lock and the Key
Twenty Plus Two. Dutton, 1961; Boardman, 1961
The Twilight Man. Dutton, 1967; Hale, 1967
The Whispering Master. Rinehart, 1947 F&C

GRUPPE, HENRY
The Truxton Cipher. Simon, 1973; Gollancz, 1974

GUENTER, C. H.
Hunter of Men. Pinnacle, 1975

GUEST, FRANCIS HAROLD. 1901- . Pseudonym: James Spenser, q.v.

GUIBOURG, GEORGES. 1897- . Pseudonym: Georgius, q.v.

GUIGO, ERNEST PHILIP. Pseudonym: E. Carleton Holt, q.v.

GUIL, J. and J(EAN) BANCAL. J. Guil is the pseudonym of Jean Guillemonat.
One Crime Too Many. Staples, 1953

GUILD, NICHOLAS
The Lost and Found Man. Harper's Magazine, 1975

GUILDFORD, JOHN. Pseudonym of Bluebell Matilda Hunter, 1887- .
Big Ben Looks On! Grayson, 1933
Death Dams the Tide. Grayson, 1932

GUILLEMONAT, JEAN. Pseudonym: J. Guil, q.v.

GUINESS, MAURICE C. Joint pseudonym with Muna Lee de Munoz Marin, 1895- : Newton Gayle, q.v.

GUINN, WILLIAM
Death Lies Deep. GM, 1955

GUINNESS, K(ATHERINE) D(ORIS)
Fisherman's End. Macdonald, 1958

GUIRDHAM, ARTHUR
-I-A Stranger. Quality, 1949
-The Lights were Going Out. Quality, 1944

GUISE, STANLEY
The Falcon Mystery. Long, 1930
The Green Cat. Long, 1940

GULL, C(YRIL ARTHUR EDWARD) RANGER. 1876-1923. Pseudonym: Guy Thorne, q.v.
The Adventures of Mr. Topham, Comedian. Greening, 1903
The Air Pirate. Hurst, 1919; Harcourt, 1920
Black Honey. Greening, 1913
-The Bridge Players. White, 1908
-The Chain Invisible. Laurie, 1907
Cinema City. Hurst, 1922; Harcourt, 1923
-The Creggan Peerage. Long, 1916
-The Enemies of England. Laurie, 1914
-A Gentleman from Portland. Laurie, 1909
-The Glad Eye. Greening, 1912. (Novelization of the play by Jose Levy.)
-The Harvest of Love. Long, 1905
-House of Torment: Memoirs of the Life of Mr. John Commendone. Greening, 1911
The Hypocrite. Greening, 1898
The Iron Box. Hurst, 1923
The Lost Judge. White, 1914
-Miss Malevolent. Greening, 1899
-The Monstrous Enemy. Laurie, 1915
Murder Limited. Laurie, 1913
The Parrot Faced Man. White, 1912
-The Path of a Hundred Deaths. Fiction Lover's Library, 1913
-The Patron Saint and other stories. White, 1908 ss
-The Price of Pity. White, 1905
The Ravenscroft Affair; see The Ravenscroft Horror
The Ravenscroft Horror. Laurie, 1917. U.S. title: The Ravenscroft Affair, as by Guy Thorne. Clode, 1924
-The Reins of Chance. White, 1910
Retribution. Laurie, 1909
Rogues Ltd. Goodship, 1922
The Snare of the Fowler. Jarrolds, 1917
-The Soul Stealer. White, 1906
A Story of the Stage. White, 1905
The Terror by Night. White, 1909
-When Satan Ruled. Greening, 1914
-Wings of Love. Greening, 1912
The Woman in the Case. Greening, 1909

GULLIVER, HAL. 1935- .
Kill with Style. Scribner, 1974

GULLIVER, SAM
The Vulcan Bulletins. Simon, 1973; Hodder, 1974

GULYASHKI, ANDREI
The Zakhov Mission. Cassell, 1968; Doubleday, 1969. (Translation of Prikliucheniiata na Avakum Zakhov. Sofia, 1963.)

GUMLEY, F. W.
Crime in the Crypt. Swan, 1943
Death Behind the Door. Mitre, 1944
Death Calls the Tune. Mitre, 1945
Death Goes Touring. Mitre, 1945
Death on Delivery. Mitre, 1944
The Death Seance. Mitre, 1945
Death Stills the Brush. Mitre, 1946
Death Visits the Parish. Mitre, 1945
Diary of Death. Mellifont, 1942
The Football Racketeers. Mellifont, 1944
The Ghoul Goalie. Pan, 1945
The Hoodoo Half-Back. Mellifont, 1942
The House of Fatal Mirrors. Grafton, 1944
The Lurking Death. Mitre, 1944
Murder in the Museum. Mellifont, 1944
Mystery of Horseshoe Island. Gordon, 1947
The Phantom Footballer. Mellifont, 1939
The Phantom Greyhound. Pan, 1946
The Toast is Death! Mitre, 1945

GUNN, JAMES (EDWARD) .
Deadlier Than the Male. Duell, 1942

GUNN, JOHN. 1922- .
The Wild Abyss. Hale, 1972

GUNN, ROBERT A(LEXANDER). 1844- .
Bruce Douglas, A Man of the People. Mayhew, 1909

GUNN, VICTOR. Pseudonym of Edwy Searles Brooks, 1889-1965, q.v. Other pseudonyms: Berkeley Gray, Carlton Ross, qq.v. Series character: Bill "Ironsides" Cromwell of Scotland Yard, in all titles.
- Alias the Hangman. Collins, 1950
- All Change for Murder. Collins, 1962
- The Black Cap Murder. Collins, 1965
- The Body in the Boot. Collins, 1963
- The Body Vanishes. Collins, 1952
- The Borgia Head Mystery. Collins, 1951
- Castle Dangerous. Collins, 1957
- The Crippled Canary. Collins, 1954
- The Crooked Staircase. Collins, 1954
- Dead in a Ditch. Collins, 1959
- The Dead Man Laughs. Collins, 1944
- Dead Man's Warning. Collins, 1949
- Dead Men's Bells. Collins, 1956
- Death at Traitor's Gate. Collins, 1960
- Death Comes Laughing. Collins, 1952
- Death on Bodmin Moor. Collins, 1960
- Death on Shivering Sand. Collins, 1946
- Death's Doorway. Collins, 1941
- Devil in the Maze. Collins, 1961
- Footsteps of Death. Collins, 1939
- The Golden Monkey. Collins, 1957
- Ironsides' Lone Hand. Collins, 1941
- Ironsides of the Yard. Collins, 1940
- Ironsides on the Spot. Collins, 1948
- Ironsides Sees Red. Collins, 1957
- Ironsides Smashes Through. Collins, 1940
- Ironsides Smells Blood. Collins, 1946
- The Laughing Grave. Collins, 1955
- Mad Hatter's Rock. Collins, 1942
- Murder at the Motel. Collins, 1964
- Murder on Ice. Collins, 1951
- Murder on Whispering Sands. Collins, 1965
- Murder with a Kiss. Collins, 1963
- The Next One to Die. Collins, 1959
- Nice Day for a Murder. Collins, 1945
- The Painted Dog. Collins, 1955
- The Petticoat Lane Murders. Collins, 1966
- Road to Murder. Collins, 1949
- The 64 Thousand Murder. Collins, 1958
- Sweet Smelling Death. Collins, 1961
- Three Dates with Death. Collins, 1947
- The Treble Chance Murder. Collins, 1958
- The Whistling Key. Collins, 1953

GUNTER, ARCHIBALD CLAVERING. 1847-1907.
- Adrienne de Portalis. Home, 1900
- The Adventures of Dr. Burton. Home, 1905
- Ballyho Bey; or, The Power of Women. Hurst (New York), 1897; Routledge, 1897
- Baron Montez of Panama and Paris. Home, 1893; Routledge, 1893
- Billy Hamilton. Home, 1898; Routledge, 1898
- Bob Covington. Home, 1897; Routledge, 1897
- The Changing Pulse of Madame Touraine. Home, 1905
- The City of Mystery. Home, 1902; French, 1902
- The Conscience of a King. Home, 1903; French, 1903
- Deacon and Actress. White, 1902. (U.S. title?)
- The Deacon's Second Wind. Home, 1901; Routledge, 1901
- Doctor Burton. Ward, 1907. (U.S. title?)
- Doctor Burton's Success. Ward, 1908. (U.S. title?)
- Don Belasco of Key West. Home, 1896; Routledge, 1897
- The Empty Hotel. Ward, 1902. (U.S. title?)
- The Fighting Troubadour. Home, 1899; Routledge, 1899
- The First of the English. Home, 1894; Routledge, 1895
- Her Senator. Home, 1896; Routledge, 1896
- Jack Curzon. Home, 1898; Routledge, 1899
- The King's Stockbroker. Home, 1894; Routledge, 1906
- The Ladies' Juggernaut. Home, 1895; Routledge, 1895
- A Lost American. Home, 1898; Routledge, 1898
- M. S. Bradford, Special. Home, 1899; Routledge, 1899
- The Man Behind the Door. Home, 1904; French, 1904
- A Manufacturer's Daughter; or, Tangled Flags; see Tangled Flags
- Miss Dividends. Home, 1892; Routledge, 1892
- Miss Nobody of Nowhere. Hurst (New York), 1888; Routledge, 1890
- Mr. Barnes of New York. Welch, 1887; Vizetelly, 1887
- Mr. Barnes, American. Dodd, 1907; Stevens, 1907
- Mr. Potter of Texas. Home, 1888; French, 1888
- My Japanese Prince. Home, 1904; French, 1904
- Phil Conway. Home, 1903; French, 1904
- The Power of Woman. Home, 1897; Routledge, 1897. (Contains both Susan Turnbull, and Ballyho Bey, qq.v.)
- A Prince in the Garret. Home, 1905; French, 1905
- Prince Karl. Dillingham, 1907; Ward, 1907
- The Princess of Copper. Home, 1900
- A Princess of Paris. Home, 1894; Routledge, 1894
- The Shadow of a Vendetta. Ward, 1908. (U.S. title?)
- The Spy Company. Hurst (New York), 1900; French, 1903
- The Surprises of an Empty Hotel. Home, 1902; Routledge, 1902
- Susan Turnbull; or, The Power of Woman. Hurst (New York), 1897; Routledge, 1897
- The Sword in the Air. Ward, 1904. (U.S. title?)
- Tangled Flags. Home, 1900; Routledge, 1900. Also published as: A Manufacturer's Daughter; or, Tangled Flags. White, 1902
- That Frenchman. Home, 1889; Routledge, 1889
- Twixt Sword and Glove. French, 1906. (U.S. title?)

GUNTER, MRS. ARCHIBALD CLAVERING. See: RICHARD HENRY SAVAGE, 1846-1903.

GUNTER, JOHN. 1901-1970.
 The Bright Nemesis. Bobbs, 1932; Secker, 1932

GUNTON, ERIC
 Trouble Ahead. Popular Publications (Australia), 193?

GURDON, J(OHN) E(VERARD)
 Banners Yellow. Newnes, 1938
 Feeding the Wind. Chapman, 1924
 The Monkey Trick. Newnes, 1936 ss
- Over and Above. Collins, 1919

GURNEY, PETER
 Queer Things at Queechy. Crowther, 1946

GURR, TOM and H(ARRY) H(UBERT) COX
 Obsessions. Muller, 1958

GUTHRIE, A(LFRED) B(ERTRAM), JR. 1901-
 Murders at Moon Dance. Dutton, 1943. Also published as: Trouble at Moon Dance. Popular Library, 1951
 Trouble at Moon Dance; see Murders at Moon Dance
 Wild Pitch. Houghton, 1973

GUTHRIE, JAMES SHIELDS. 1931- . Pseudonym: David Creed, q.v.

GUTTERIDGE, (THOMAS GORDON) LINDSEY. 1923-
 Cold War in a Country Garden. Cape, 1971; Putnam, 1971
 Killer Pine. Cape, 1973; Putnam, 1973

GWINN, WILLIAM R. Pseudonym: William Randall, q.v.

GWYNNE, ESTELLE
 The Fulfilling of the Law. Epworth, 1924

H

HAAS, BEN(JAMIN LEOPOLD). 1926- .
 Pseudonym: Richard Meade, q.v.
 Daisy Canfield. Simon, 1973; Davies, 1973

HAAS, JOSEPH L. 1929-1971.
 Vendetta. Regnery, 1975

HAASE, JOHN. 1923- .
- The Noon Balloon to Rangoon. Simon, 1967

HABBERTON, JOHN. 1842-1921.
 The Bowsham Puzzle. Funk, 1884; Ward, 1884

HABE, HANS. Pseudonym of Jean Bekessy, 1911-1977.
 Agent of the Devil. Harrap, 1958. U.S. title: The Devil's Agent. Fell, 1958. (Translation of In Namen des Teufels. Vienna, 1956.)
 The Devil's Agent; see Agent of the Devil
 The Poisoned Stream. Harrap, 1969; McGraw, 1969

HACKETT, WALTER. See: LOUISE JORDAN MILN, 1864-1933; and: GEORGE GOODCHILD, 1888- .

HACKFORTH-JONES, (FRANK) GILBERT. 1900- . Series character: Paul Decker, in those marked PD and two others.
 All Stations to Malta. Hodder, 1971
 Chinese Poison. Hodder, 1969
 Crack of Doom. Hodder, 1961
 Danger Below. Hodder, 1963
 Dangerous Trade. Hodder, 1952
 Death of an Admiral. Hodder, 1956
 An Explosive Situation. Hodder, 1973 PD
 Fight to a Finish. Hodder, 1968
 Fish Out of Water. Hodder, 1954
- The Greatest Fool. Hodder, 1948
- I am the Captain. Hodder, 1963
- Life on the Ocean Wave. Hodder, 1960
- No Less Renowned. Blackwood, 1939 ss
- One Man's Wars. Hodder, 1964
- One-One-One. Hodder, 1942 ss
 The Price was High. Hodder, 1946
 The Questing Hound. Hodder, 1947
 Redoubtable Dexter. Hodder, 1975 PD
 Rough Passage. Hodder, 1946
 Second-in-Command. Hodder, 1974 PD
 Security Risk. Hodder, 1970
 Shadow of the Rock. Hodder, 1973 PD

-Sixteen Bells. Hodder, 1946 ss
The Sole Survivor. Hodder, 1953
The Stern Chase. Hodder, 1966
Storm in Harbour. Hodder, 1965
Submarine Flotilla. Hodder, 1940
-Sweethearts and Wives. Hodder, 1949.
(Novelization of the play by Gilbert Hackforth-Jones and Margaret Hackforth-Jones.)
-Warrior's Playtime. Hodder, 1967
The Worst Enemy. Hodder, 1950
Yellow Peril. Hodder, 1972

HACKFORTH-JONES, MARGARET. See: (FRANK) GILBERT HACKFORTH-JONES, 1900- .

HACKSTAFF, RICHARD
Tracked by a Pin. Street (Magnet)

HADATH, JOHN EDWARD GUNBY. -1954.
Pseudonym: Shepherd Pearson, q.v.

HADDAD, C. A.
The Moroccan. Harper, 1975; Allen, 1977

HADDON, CHRISTOPHER. Pseudonym of John (Leslie) Palmer, 1885-1944, q.v. Joint pseudonym with Hilary (Aiden) St. George Saunders, 1898-1951, q.v.: Francis Beeding, q.v.
Under the Long Barrow. Gollancz, 1939. U.S. title: The Man in the Purple Gown. Dodd, 1939, as by John Palmer

HADDOW, DENIS
Hanged by a Thread. Hutchinson, 1947

HADEN, ALLEN
My Enemy—My Wife. Putnam, 1951. (Novelization of a story by Paul Frischauer.)

HADLEY, HAROLD
Come See Them Die. Messner, 1934

HADLEY, MARTIN
He Died Twice. Columbine, 1940

HAEDRICH, MARCEL. Pseudonym.
Crack in the Mirror. Allen, 1960; Dell, 1961. (Translation of Drame dans un Miroir. Paris, 1958.)

HAGAN, ARTHUR P.
The Day the Bookies Took a Bath. Sherbourne, 1971

HAGEN, MIRIAM-ANN. Series character: Hortense Clinton, in all titles.
Dig Me Later. Doubleday, 1949
Murder—But Natch. Doubleday, 1951
Plant Me Now. Doubleday, 1947

HAGERTY, HARRY J.
The Jasmine Trail. Lothrop, 1936

HAGGARD, (SIR) H(ENRY) RIDER. 1856-1925.
Mr. Meeson's Will. Blackett, 1888; Harper, 1888

HAGGARD, PAUL. Pseudonym of Stephen Longstreet, 1907- , q.v. Other pseudonym: Henri Weiner, q.v. Series character: Mike Warlock, in all titles.
Dead is the Door-Nail. Lippincott, 1937
Death Talks Shop. Hillman-Curl, 1938
Death Walks on Cat Feet. Hillman-Curl, 1938
Poison from a Wealthy Widow. Hillman-Curl, 1938

HAGGARD, RAYMOND
Miss Ivory White. Collins, 1970; Dell, 1972

HAGGARD, WILLIAM. Pseudonym of Richard Henry Michael Clayton, 1907- . Series characters: Col. Charles Russell = CR; Paul Martiny = PM.
The Antagonists. Cassell, 1964; Washburn, 1964 CR
The Arena. Cassell, 1961; Washburn, 1961 CR
The Bitter Harvest. Cassell, 1971. U.S. title: Too Many Enemies. Walker, 1971 CR
Closed Circuit. Cassell, 1960; Washburn, 1960
The Conspirators. Cassell, 1967; Walker, 1968 CR
A Cool Day for Killing. Cassell, 1968; Walker, 1968 CR
The Doubtful Disciple. Cassell, 1969 CR
The Hard Sell. Cassell, 1965; Washburn, 1966 CR
The Hardliners. Cassell, 1970; Walker, 1971 CR
The High Wire. Cassell, 1963; Washburn, 1963 CR
The Kinsman. Cassell, 1974; Walker, 1974 PM
The Notch on the Knife; see The Old Masters
The Old Masters. Cassell, 1973. U.S. title: The Notch on the Knife. Walker, 1973 CR
The Powder Barrel. Cassell, 1965; Washburn, 1965 CR
The Power House. Cassell, 1966; Washburn, 1967 CR
The Protectors. Cassell, 1972; Walker, 1972 PM
The Scorpion's Tale. Cassell, 1975; Walker, 1975 CR
Slow Burner. Cassell, 1958; Little, 1958 CR
The Telemann Touch. Cassell, 1958; Little, 1958
Too Many Enemies; see The Bitter Harvest
The Unquiet Sleep. Cassell, 1962; Washburn, 1962 CR
Venetian Blind. Cassell, 1959; Washburn, 1959 CR

HAGUE, JOHN. Pseudonym.
Fillets on the Menu. Hutchinson, 1933

HAIG, ALEC. Series character: Alec Haig, in all titles.
Flight from Montego Bay. Dodd, 1972; Heinemann, 1972
Peruvian Printout. Dodd, 1970; Heinemann, 1974
Sign On for Tokyo. Dodd, 1968; Heinemann, 1968

HAILEY, ARTHUR. 1920- . See: JOHN CASTLE.

HAINES, WILLIAM WISTER. 1908- .
Target. Little, 1964

HAINING, PETER. 1940- .
The Hero. New English Library, 1973

HAKE, THOMAS ST. EDMUND
Within Sound of the Weir. Cassell, 1891

HALDANE, EMMA
Maluti Murder. Eldon, 1933

HALE, ARLENE. 1924- .
One More Bridge to Cross. Little, 1975
Where the Heart Is. Little, 1974

HALE, CHRISTOPHER. Pseudonym of Frances Moyer Ross Stevens, 1895-1948. Series character: Lt. Bill French = BF.
Dead of Winter. Doubleday, 1941. British title (?): Going, Going, Gone. Boardman, 1950 BF
Deadly Ditto. Doubleday, 1948; Boardman, 1949 BF
Exit Screaming. Doubleday, 1942; Boardman, 1943 BF
Ghost River. Doubleday, 1937; Boardman, 1947
Going, Going, Gone; see Dead of Winter
Hangman's Tie. Doubleday, 1943; Boardman, 1946 BF
He's Late This Morning. Doubleday, 1949; Boardman, 1951 BF
Midsummer Nightmare. Doubleday, 1945; Boardman, 1948 BF
Murder in Tow. Doubleday, 1943; Boardman, 1944 BF
Murder on Display. Doubleday, 1939; Boardman, 1947 BF
Rumor Hath It. Doubleday, 1945; Boardman, 1947 BF
Smoke Screen. Doubleday, 1935; Boardman, 1948 BF
Stormy Night. Doubleday, 1937; Heinemann, 1937 BF
Witch Wood. Doubleday, 1940; Boardman, 1946 BF

HALE, EDGAR. Series character: Michael Regan, in at least those marked MR.
Blue Murder. Ward, 1948
Coffee for One. Ward, 1949
Death Came Back. Ward, 1948
Death Dealt the Cards. Ward, 1947
Devil's Tears. Ward, 1946 MR
Never Shoot a Lady. Ward, 1947 MR
So the Lady Died. Ward, 1949

HALE, JENNIFER
The Secret of Devil's Cave. Lancer, 1973
Stormhaven. Lancer, 1970

HALE, JOHN. 1926- .
The Fort. Quartet, 1973

HALE, MRS. MARICE RUTLEDGE GIBSON. 1884- . Pseudonym: Maryse Rutledge, q.v.

HALE, MARTIN
The Empire on Arumac. Cape, 1966
The Fourth Reich. Cape, 1965

HALEGUA, LILLIAN
The Hanging. Owen, 1970

HALES, A(LFRED) G(REENWOOD). 1870-1936.
-Abner Crane's Vengeance. Long, 1932
Marozia. Unwin, 1908 ss, some criminous
The Mystery of Wo-Sing. Long, 1924

HALIDOM, M. Y. Pseudonym.
-The Poet's Curse. Greening, 1911
The Poison Ring. Greening, 1912
A Son of Desolation. Greening, 1909
-The Woman in Black. Greening, 1906
-Zoe's Revenge. Greening, 1908

HALIFAX, CLIFFORD. See: L(ILLIE) T(HOMAS) MEADE.

HALIFAX, ROBERT
-The House of Horror. Digby, 1911
The Jewels of Death. Newnes, 1911

HALKET, ROBERTSON
Documentary Evidence. Nicholson, 1936
Where Every Prospect Pleases. Benn, 1933

HALL, ADAM. Pseudonym of Elleston Trevor, 1920- , q.v. Name originally: Trevor Dudley Smith, q.v. Other pseudonyms: Mansell Black, Simon Rattray, Warwick Scott, Caesar Smith, qq.v. Series character: Quiller = Q.

HALL, ADAM

The Berlin Memorandum. Collins, 1965. U.S. title: The Quiller Memorandum. Simon, 1965 Q
The Mandarin Cypher. Collins, 1975; Doubleday, 1975 Q
The 9th Directive. Heinemann, 1966; Simon, 1966 Q
The Quiller Memorandum; see The Berlin Memorandum
The Striker Portfolio. Heinemann, 1969; Simon, 1969 Q
The Tango Briefing. Collins, 1973; Doubleday, 1973 Q
The Volcanoes of San Domingo. Collins, 1963; Simon, 1964
The Warsaw Document. Heinemann, 1971; Doubleday, 1970 Q

HALL, ANDREW. 1937-
Frost. Cassell, 1966; Putnam, 1967
Man in Aspic. Cassell, 1965
Safe Behind Bars. Cassell, 1968

HALL, ANGUS. 1932-
-The Come-Uppance of Arthur Hearne. Hammond, 1967
Devilday. Sphere, 1969; Ace, 1971
-The Gentle Sex. Sphere, 1972
-The High-Bouncing Lover. Hammond, 1966
-The Late Boy Wonder. Jenkins, 1969; Ace, 1970
-Live Like a Hero. Hammond, 1967
A Long Way to Fall. Allen, 1971
Madhouse. Award, 1974 (British title?)
On the Run. Harrap, 1974
Qualtrough. Jenkins, 1969
-The Scars of Dracula. Sphere, 1971; Beagle, 1971
-To Play the Devil. Sphere, 1971

HALL, DOUGLAS. 1929-
The Brittle Thread. Zondervan, 1968
The Girl in 906. Zondervan, 1970
The Kirsty Affair. Zondervan, 1972
The Long Way Down. Zondervan, 1971

HALL, F. CAMERON
A Country Tragedy. Neely, 1898

HALL, F. H. 1926-
In the Lamb White Days. Bobbs, 1975

HALL, GEOFFREY HOLIDAY
The End is Known. Simon, 1949; Heinemann, 1950
The Watcher at the Door. Simon, 1954

HALL, GIMONE. 1940-
The Blue Taper. Macfadden, 1970
The Juliet Room. Manor, 1974
Witch's Suckling. Macfadden, 1970

HALL, HOLWORTHY. Pseudonym of Harold Everett Porter, 1887-1936.
What He Least Expected. Bobbs, 1917

HALL, HOWARD. See: CHARLES E. BLANEY, 1865(6)-1944.

HALL, JAY
Evidently Murdered. Dorrance, 1943

HALL, JENNI(FER ANTOINETTE). 1939-
-Ask Agamemnon. Cassell, 1964; Atheneum, 1964. Also published as: Goodbye Gemini. Sphere, 1970
-The Diamond Trip. New English Library, 1971
Goodbye Gemini; see Ask Agamemnon
-Mr. Capon. Cassell, 1965; Harcourt, 1965

HALL, LELAND. 1883-
Sinister House. Houghton, 1919

HALL, MARJORY [MARJORY HALL YEAKLEY]. 1908-
Rosamunda. Dell, 1974

HALL, MICHAEL
Once Upon a Crime. Falcon, 1947

HALL, OAKLEY M(AXWELL). 1920- . Pseudonym: Jason Manor, q.v.
A Game for Eagles. Morrow, 1970
Murder City. Farrar, 1949; Barker, 1950
-So Many Doors. Random, 1950

HALL, PATRICK. 1932-
The Power Sellers. Putnam, 1969

HALL, RICHARD
The Butterscotch Prince. Pyramid, 1975

HALL, RICHARD S. S.
Betrayal into Darkness. Vantage, 1967

HALL, ROGER (WOLCOTT). 1919-
19. Norton, 1970

HALL, WARNER
Even Jericho. Macrae Smith, 1944

HALL, WHYTE. Pseudonym of Augustus Alfred Rayner, 1894- .
Crime and a Clock. Harrap, 1936
Death and the Golden Image. Harrap, 1936
Death of the Doctor's Wife. Quality, 1939

HALLAHAN, WILLIAM H.
The Dead of Winter. Bobbs, 1972
The Ross Forgery. Bobbs, 1973
The Search for Joseph Tully. Bobbs, 1974; Macmillan (London), 1975

HALLAS, RICHARD. Pseudonym of Eric Mowbray Knight, 1897-1943.
You Play the Black and the Red Comes Up. McBride, 1938

HALLATT, WILLIAM
Suppression. Skeffington, 1930

HALLERAN, E(UGENE) E(DWARD). 1905- .
Thirteen Toy Pistols. McKay, 1945

HALLEY, LAURENCE
Simultaneous Equations. Cape, 1975

HALLIDAY, BRETT. Pseudonym of Davis Dresser, 1904-1977. Other pseudonym: Asa Baker, q.v. Joint pseudonym with Kathleen Rollins: Hal Debrett, q.v. Joint pseudonym with (Walter) Ryerson Johnson, 1901- , q.v.: Matthew Blood, q.v. See also: JAMES REACH, 1909?-1970. Series character: Michael Shayne, in all titles.
Armed...Dangerous... Dell, 1966
At the Point of a .38. Dell, 1974
The Blonde Cried Murder. Torquil/Dodd, 1956; Jarrolds, 1957
Blood on Biscayne Bay. Ziff-Davis, 1946; Jarrolds, 1950
Blood on the Black Market. Dodd, 1943. In Britain contained in: Michael Shayne Takes a Hand. Jarrolds, 1944. Also published as: Heads You Lose. Dell, 1958
Blood on the Stars. Dodd, 1948. British title: Murder is a Habit. Jarrolds, 1951
Blue Murder. Dell, 1973
Bodies are Where You Find Them. Holt, 1941. In Britain contained in: Michael Shayne Investigates. Jarrolds, 1943
The Body Came Back. Torquil/Dodd 1963
Call for Michael Shayne. Dodd, 1949; Jarrolds, 1951
The Careless Corpse. Torquil/Dodd, 1961
The Case of the Walking Corpse; see The Corpse Came Calling
Caught Dead. Dell, 1972
The Corpse Came Calling. Dodd, 1942. In Britain contained in: Michael Shayne Investigates. Jarrolds, 1943. Also published as: The Case of the Walking Corpse. Handi-Books, 1943
The Corpse That Never Was. Torquil/Dodd, 1963
Count Backwards to Zero. Dell, 1971
Counterfeit Wife. Ziff-Davis, 1947; Jarrolds, 1950
Date with a Dead Man. Torquil/Dodd, 1959; Long, 1960. (Expansion of the novelet "Dead Man's Diary", included in Michael Shayne's Triple Mystery, q.v.)
Dead Man's Diary; see Michael Shayne's Triple Mystery
Death has Three Lives. Torquil/Dodd, 1955; Jarrolds, 1955
Die Like a Dog. Torquil/Dodd, 1959; Long, 1961
Dinner at Dupre's; see Michael Shayne's Triple Mystery
Dividend on Death. Holt, 1939; Jarrolds, 1941
Dolls are Deadly. Torquil/Dodd, 1960
Fit to Kill. Torquil/Dodd, 1958; Long, 1959
Fourth Down to Death. Dell, 1970
Framed in Blood. Dodd, 1951; Jarrolds, 1953
Guilty as Hell. Dell, 1967
Heads You Lose; see Blood on the Black Market
The Homicidal Virgin. Torquil/Dodd, 1960
I Come to Kill You. Dell, 1971
In a Deadly Vein; see Murder Wears a Mummer's Mask
Kill All the Young Girls. Dell, 1973
Killers from the Keys. Torquil/Dodd, 1961
Lady, Be Bad. Dell, 1969
The Lady Came by Night; see One Night with Nora
Last Seen Hitchhiking. Dell, 1974
Marked for Murder. Dodd, 1945; Jarrolds, 1950
Mermaid on the Rocks. Dell, 1967
Michael Shayne Investigates. Jarrolds, 1943. Contains: Bodies are Where You Find Them, and The Corpse Came Calling, qq.v.
Michael Shayne Takes a Hand. Jarrolds, 1944. Contains: Murder Wears a Mummer's Mask, and Blood on the Black Market, qq.v.
Michael Shayne's 50th Case. Torquil/Dodd, 1964
Michael Shayne's Long Chance. Dodd, 1944; Jarrolds, 1945
Michael Shayne's Triple Mystery. Ziff-Davis, 1948. (Three novelets: Dead Man's Diary, A Taste for Cognac, and Dinner at Dupre's. A Dell reprint combined #1 and #3 in 1950; a later Dell reprint, 1959, combined #1 and #2. #2, A Taste for Cognac, was reprinted separately as a Dell 10¢ paperback in 1951. #1 was later expanded into the novel Date with a Dead Man, q.v.)
Murder and the Married Virgin. Dodd, 1944; Jarrolds, 1946
Murder and the Wanton Bride. Torquil/Dodd, 1958; Long, 1959
Murder by Proxy. Torquil/Dodd, 1962; Mayflower, 1968
Murder in Haste. Torquil/Dodd, 1961; Mayflower, 1963
Murder is a Habit; see Blood on the Stars
Murder is my Business. Dodd, 1945; Jarrolds, 1945

Murder Spins the Wheel. Dell, 1966
Murder Takes No Holiday. Torquil/Dodd, 1960
Murder Wears a Mummer's Mask. Dodd, 1943. In Britain contained in: Michael Shayne Takes a Hand. Jarrolds, 1944. Also published as: In a Deadly Vein. Dodd, 1956
Never Kill a Client. Torquil/Dodd, 1962
Nice Fillies Finish Last. Dell, 1965
One Night with Nora. Torquil/Dodd, 1953. British title: The Lady Came by Night. Jarrolds, 1954
Pay-Off in Blood. Torquil/Dodd, 1962
The Private Practice of Michael Shayne. Holt, 1940; Jarrolds, 1941
A Redhead for Mike Shayne. Torquil/Dodd, 1964
She Woke to Darkness. Torquil/Dodd, 1954; Jarrolds, 1955
Shoot the Works. Torquil/Dodd, 1957; Long, 1958
Shoot to Kill. Torquil/Dodd, 1964
Six Seconds to Kill. Dell, 1970
So Lush, So Deadly. Dell, 1968
Stranger in Town. Torquil/Dodd, 1955; Jarrolds, 1956
Target: Mike Shayne. Torquil/Dodd, 1959; Long, 1960
A Taste for Cognac; see Michael Shayne's Triple Mystery
A Taste for Violence. Dodd, 1949; Jarrolds, 1952
This is It, Michael Shayne. Dodd, 1950; Jarrolds, 1952
Tickets for Death. Holt, 1941; Jarrolds, 1942
Too Friendly, Too Dead. Torquil/Dodd, 1963; Mayflower, 1964
The Uncomplaining Corpses. Holt, 1940; Jarrolds, 1942
Violence is Golden. Dell, 1968
The Violent World of Michael Shayne. Dell, 1965
Weep for a Blonde. Torquil/Dodd, 1957; Long, 1958
What Really Happened. Dodd, 1952; Jarrolds, 1953
When Dorinda Dances. Dodd, 1951; Jarrolds, 1953

HALLIDAY, DOROTHY. U.S. byline: Dorothy Dunnett. Series character: Johnson Johnson, in all titles.
Dolly and the Cookie Bird. Cassell, 1970. U.S. title: Murder in the Round. Houghton, 1970
Dolly and the Doctor Bird. Cassell, 1971. U.S. title: Match for a Murderer. Houghton, 1971
Dolly and the Singing Bird. Cassell, 1968. U.S. title: The Photogenic Soprano. Houghton, 1968
Dolly and the Starry Bird. Cassell, 1973. U.S. title: Murder in Focus. Houghton, 1973
Match for a Murderer; see Dolly and the Doctor Bird
Murder in Focus; see Dolly and the Starry Bird
Murder in the Round; see Dolly and the Cookie Bird
The Photogenic Soprano; see Dolly and the Singing Bird

HALLIDAY, FRED. 1937-   .
The Chocolate Mousse Murders. Pinnacle, 1974

HALLIDAY, LEONARD. 1917-   .
The Devil's Door. Hammond, 1959
The Smiling Spider. Hammond, 1955
Stay of Execution. Hammond, 1964
Top Secret. Hammond, 1957

HALLIDAY, MICHAEL. Pseudonym of John Creasey, 1908-1973, q.v. Other pseudonyms: Gordon Ashe, M. E. Cooke, Norman Deane, Robert Caine Frazer, Patrick Gill, Charles Hogarth, Brian Hope, Colin Hughes, Kyle Hunt, Abel Mann, Peter Manton, J. J. Marric, Richard Martin, Rodney Mattheson, Anthony Morton, Jeremy York, qq.v. Some titles originally published under the Norman Deane byline, where they are listed herein, were reprinted as by Michael Halliday. Series characters: Dr. Emmanuel Cellini = EC; Martin & Richard Fane = F.
As Empty as Hate. Hodder, 1972; World, 1972, as by Kyle Hunt   EC
As Lonely as the Damned. Hodder, 1971; World, 1972, as by Kyle Hunt   EC
As Merry as Hell. Hodder, 1973; Stein, 1974, as by Kyle Hunt   EC
Cat and Mouse. Hodder, 1955. U.S. title: Hilda, Take Heed, as by Jeremy York. Scribner, 1957
Come Here and Die; see Death of a Stranger
Crime with Many Voices. Paul, 1945
Cruel as a Cat. Hodder, 1968; Macmillan, 1969, as by Kyle Hunt   EC
Cunning as a Fox. Hodder, 1965; Macmillan, 1965, as by Kyle Hunt   EC
Death of a Stranger. Hodder, 1957. U.S. title: Come Here and Die, as by Jeremy York. Scribner, 1959
Death Out of Darkness. Hodder, 1954; World, 1971, as by John Creasey
Dine with Murder. Evans, 1950
The Dying Witnesses. Evans, 1949
The Edge of Terror. Hodder, 1961; Macmillan, 1963, as by Jeremy York
First a Murder. Paul, 1948; McKay, 1972, as by Jeremy York
Five to Kill. Paul, 1943
Foul Play Suspected. Paul, 1942
Four Find Danger. Cassell, 1937
The Girl with the Leopard-Skin Bag; see How Many to Kill?
Go Ahead with Murder. Hodder, 1960. U.S. title: Two for the Money, as by Jeremy York. Doubleday, 1962
Guilt of Innocence. Hodder, 1964
Hate to Kill. Hodder, 1962
Heir to Murder. Paul, 1940
Hilda, Take Heed; see Cat and Mouse
How Many to Kill? Hodder, 1960. U.S. title: The Girl with the Leopard-Skin Bag. Scribner, 1961
The Lame Dog Murder. Evans, 1952; World, 1972, as by John Creasey   F
Lend a Hand to Murder. Paul, 1947
The Man I Killed. Hodder, 1961; Macmillan, 1963, as by Jeremy York
Man on the Run. Hodder, 1953; World, 1972, as by John Creasey   F
Missing; see Missing from Home
Missing from Home. Hodder, 1959. U.S. title: Missing, as by Jeremy York. Scribner, 1960
Murder Assured. Hodder, 1958
Murder at End House. Hodder, 1955
Murder at King's Kitchen. Paul, 1943
Murder by the Way. Paul, 1941
Murder Come Home. Paul, 1940
Murder in the Stars. Hodder, 1953   F
Murder Makes Murder. Paul, 1946
Murder Week-End. Evans, 1950
Mystery Motive. Paul, 1947; McKay, 1974, as by Jeremy York
No Crime More Cruel. Paul, 1944
No End to Danger. Paul, 1948
Out of the Shadows. Hodder, 1954; World, 1971, as by John Creasey
A Period of Evil. Hodder, 1970; World, 1971, as by Kyle Hunt   EC
Quarrel with Murder. Evans, 1951
The Quiet Fear. Hodder, 1963; Macmillan, 1968, as by Jeremy York

Runaway. Hodder, 1957; World, 1971, as by John Creasey
Sly as a Serpent. Hodder, 1967; Macmillan, 1967, as by Kyle Hunt   EC
Take a Body. Evans, 1951; World, 1972, as by John Creasey   F
Thicker Than Water. Hodder, 1959; Doubleday, 1962, as by Jeremy York
This Man Did I Kill? Hodder, 1974; Stein, 1974, as by Kyle Hunt   EC
Three for Adventure. Cassell, 1937
Too Good to be True. Hodder, 1969; Macmillan, 1969, as by Kyle Hunt   EC
Two for the Money; see Go Ahead with Murder
Two Meet Trouble. Cassell, 1938
Who Died at the Grange? Paul, 1942
Who Killed Rebecca? Paul, 1949
Who Said Murder? Paul, 1944
Who Saw Him Die? Paul, 1941
Wicked as the Devil. Hodder, 1966; Macmillan, 1966, as by Kyle Hunt   EC

HALLS, GERALDINE. Pseudonym of Geraldine Mary Jay, 1919-   , q.v. Other pseudonym: Charlotte Jay, q.v.
The Voice of the Crab. Constable, 1974; Harper, 1974, as by Charlotte Jay

HALSE, A. W.
-The White Crusaders. Jenkins, 1935

HALSEY, FORREST
-The Bawlerout. FitzGerald, 1912
-The Shadow on the Hearth. American, 1914
The Stain. Browne, 1913
-A Term of Silence. FitzGerald, 1913

HALSEY, HARLAN PAGE. 1839?-1898. Pseudonyms: Old Sleuth, Tony Pastor, Judson R. Taylor, qq.v.
-Annie Wallace; or, The Exile of Penang. Miller, 1857
The Chosen Man; or, The Mystery of the Secret Service. Street, 1888
-Her Great Surprise. Parlor Car, 1893
-A Lady Bachelor. Parlor Car, 1892
The Masked Detective. Street, 1888
Van, the Government Detective; or, The Base Metal Coiners. Street, 1888; Aldine, 18??, as by Judson R. Taylor

HALSEY, HELEN NORWOOD
The Child Witness. Neely, 1898

HALSTEAD, ADA L. Pseudonym of Mrs. Laura Eugenia Newhall.
Adopted; or, The Serpent Bracelet. Golden Era, 1886
-After the Night has Passed. Laird, 1896
The Bride of Infelice. Bancroft, 1892
The Death Trust. [Author], 1889. Also published as: Hazel Verne; or, The Death Trust. [Author], 1889
Hazel Verne; or, The Death Trust; see The Death Trust

HALSTEAD, JOHN. Series character: Inspector Todd, in at least those marked T.
The Black Arab. Paul, 1933
The Black Fear. Paul, 1935   T
The Black Flame. Paul, 1936
The Black Hate. Paul, 1937   T
The Black Nat. Paul, 1932
The Black Templar. Paul, 1934   T

HALSTEAD, THAYER
The Godfather Must Live. Dell, 1974

HAMBLEDON, PHYLLIS. Pseudonym of Phyllis MacVean, 1892-   , q.v. Other pseudonym: Philippa Vane, q.v. Series character: Insp. "Tubby" Hall, in at least those marked TH.
Death of an Uncle. Hale, 1962
I Know a Secret. Laurie, 1951
Invitation to Terror. Laurie, 1950

Keys for the Criminal. Hale, 1958 TH
The Listening Boy. Laurie, 1951
Murder and Miss Ming. Hale, 1959 TH
Murder's No Picnic. Hale, 1961
Passports to Murder. Hale, 1959

HAMBLETT, CHARLES
The Crazy Kill. Sidgwick, 1956

HAMILL, EDSON T. Series character: Ryker, in both titles (see also: NELSON DE MILLE, 1943-   ).
Child Killer. Leisure, 1975
Motive for Murder. Leisure, 1975

HAMILL, STUART
China Kill. Harlo, 1974

HAMILTON, ADAM. Joint pseudonym of Marilyn Granbeck and Arthur Moore, q.v. Other joint pseudonym: Van Saxon, q.v. Other Granbeck pseudonyms: Ben Grant, Clayton Moore, qq.v. For Arthur Moore, see also: DON HOYT. Series character: Barrington Hewes-Bradford (The Peacemaker), in all titles.
The Wyss Pursuit. Berkley, 1975
The Xander Pursuit. Berkley, 1974
The Yashar Pursuit. Berkley, 1974
The Zaharan Pursuit. Berkley, 1974

HAMILTON, ALEX
As If She were Mine. New Authors, 1962
Beam of Malice. Hutchinson, 1966; McKay, 1967 ss
The Dead Needle. Hutchinson, 1969
Flies on the Wall. Hutchinson, 1972
Town Parole. Hutchinson, 1964
Wild Track. Hutchinson, 1963

HAMILTON, (ARTHUR DOUGLAS) BRUCE. 1900-   .
The Brighton Murder Trial: Rex v. Rhodes. Boriswood, 1937
Dead Reckoning; see Middle Class Murder
Hanging Judge; see Let Him Have Judgment
Hue and Cry. Collins, 1931
Let Him Have Judgment. Cresset, 1948. U.S. title: Hanging Judge. Harper, 1948
Middle Class Murder. Methuen, 1936. U.S. title: Dead Reckoning. Simon, 1937
Pro: An English Tragedy. Cresset, 1946
So Sad, So Fresh. Cresset, 1952
The Spring Term. Methuen, 1933
To be Hanged. Faber, 1930; Doubleday, 1930
Too Much of Water. Cresset, 1958
Traitor's Way. Cresset, 1938; Bobbs, 1939

HAMILTON, DONALD (BENGTSSON). 1916-   . Series character: Matt Helm = MH.
The Ambushers. GM, 1963; Coronet, 1967 MH
Assassins have Starry Eyes; see Assignment: Murder
Assignment: Murder. Dell, 1956. Also published as: Assassins have Starry Eyes. GM, 1966
The Betrayers. GM, 1966; Coronet, 1968 MH
Date with Darkness. Rinehart, 1947; Wingate, 1951
Death of a Citizen. GM, 1960; Muller, 1960 MH
The Devastators. GM, 1965; Coronet, 1967 MH
The Interlopers. GM, 1969; Coronet, 1969 MH
The Intimidators. GM, 1974; Coronet, 1974 MH
The Intriguers. GM, 1973; Coronet, 1973 MH

Line of Fire. Dell, 1955; Wingate, 1956
The Menacers. GM, 1968; Hodder, 1968 MH
Murder Twice Told. Rinehart, 1950; Wingate, 1952. (2 novelets.)
Murderer's Row. GM, 1962; Muller, 1963 MH
Night Walker. Dell, 1954. British title: Rough Company. Wingate, 1954
The Poisoners. GM, 1971; Coronet, 1971 MH
The Ravagers. GM, 1964 MH
The Removers. GM, 1961; Muller, 1962 MH
Rough Company; see Night Walker
The Shadowers. GM, 1964; Muller, 1964 MH
The Silencers. GM, 1962; Hodder pb, 1966 MH
The Steel Mirror. Rinehart, 1948; Wingate, 1950
The Terminators. GM, 1975; Coronet, 1976 MH
The Wrecking Crew. GM, 1960; Muller, 1961 MH

HAMILTON, EDMOND. 1904-1977.
Murder in the Clinic. Newcoll, 1946

HAMILTON, ELAINE. Series character: Insp. Reynolds, in at least those marked R.
The Casino Mystery. Ward, 1936 R
The Chelsea Mystery. Paul, 1932 R
The Green Death. Paul, 1932 R
Murder Before Tuesday. Ward, 1937 R
Murder in the Fog. Paul, 1931 R
Peril at Midnight. Ward, 1934 R
The Silent Bell. Paul, 1933
Some Unknown Hand. Paul, 1930. U.S. title: The Westminster Mystery. Century, 1931 R
Tragedy in the Dark. Ward, 1935 R
The Westminster Mystery; see Some Unknown Hand

HAMILTON, (LORD) ERNEST (WILLIAM). 1858-1939.
The Four Tragedies of Memworth. Gollancz, 1928
The Perils of Josephine. Unwin, 1899; Stone, 1899

HAMILTON, (LORD) FREDERIC SPENCER. 1856-1928. Series character: P. J. Davenant, in all titles.
The Beginnings of Mr. P. J. Davenant. Hodder, 1917 ss
The Education of Mr. P. J. Davenant. Nash, 1916 ss
The Holiday Adventures of Mr. P. J. Davenant. Nash, 1915 ss
-More about P. J., the Secret Service Boy. Nelson, 1923 ss
Nine Holiday Adventures of Mr. P. J. Davenant in the Year 1915. Newnes, 1916. (A revised edition of The Holiday Adventures of Mr. P. J. Davenant, q.v.)
-P. J., the Secret Service Boy. Nelson, 1922 ss
Some Further Adventures of Mr. P. J. Davenant. Nash, 1915 ss

HAMILTON, HENRIETTA. 1920-   . Series characters: Sally and Johnny Heldar, in all titles.
Answer in the Negative. Hodder, 1959
At Night to Die. Hodder, 1959
Death at One Below. Hodder, 1957
The Two Hundred Ghost. Hodder, 1956

HAMILTON, HENRY. 1853?-1918. See: CECIL RALEIGH.

HAMILTON, IAN. 1935-   . Series character: Pete Heysen, in at least those marked PH.

The Creeping Vicar; see The Man with the Brown Paper Face
The Man with the Brown Paper Face. Constable, 1967. U.S. title: The Creeping Vicar. Lippincott, 1967 PH
Never Die in Honolulu. Mayflower, 1969; Lippincott, 1969 PH
The Persecutor. Constable, 1965; Lippincott, 1965 PH
The Thrill Machine. Collins, 1972

HAMILTON, J. LINDSAY
The Black Asp. Jenkins, 1931
The Gorgon. Jenkins, 1930

HAMILTON, MARY AGNES. 1883-   .
Life Sentence. H. Hamilton, 1935. U.S. title: Sentenced to Life. Houghton, 1935
Murder in the House of Commons. H. Hamilton, 1931; Houghton, 1931
Sentenced to Life; see Life Sentence
-Special Providence: A Tale of 1917. Allen & Unwin, 1930. U.S. title: Three Against Fate: A Tale of 1917. Houghton, 1930
Three Against Fate; see Special Providence

HAMILTON, MOLLIE. Pseudonym of M(ary) M(argaret) Kaye, 1911-   , q.v.

HAMILTON, (ANTHONY WALTER) PATRICK. 1904-1962. Series character: Mr. Gorse, in at least those marked G.
Angel Street; see Gas Light
Gas Light. Constable, 1939. U.S. title: Angel Street. French, 1942. (3-act play.)
Hangover Square; or, The Man with Two Minds. Constable, 1941; Random, 1942
-The Man Upstairs. Constable, 1954 (Play.)
Mr. Stimpson and Mr. Gorse. Constable, 1953 G
Money with Menaces, and To the Public Danger. Constable, 1939 (2 radio plays.)
Rope. Constable, 1929. U.S. title: Rope's End. Smith, 1930. (Play.)
Rope's End; see Rope
Unknown Assailant. Constable, 1955 G
The West Pier. Constable, 1951; Doubleday, 1952 G

HAMILTON, ROGER
Living's a Dying Game. Hale, 1969
Mosquitoes Don't Kill. Hale, 1971
The Rules Don't Apply. Hale, 1968

HAMLEY, MAJOR GENERAL W(ILLIAM) G(EORGE). 1815-1893.
Guilty, or Not Guilty? Blackwood, 1878

HAMMETT, (SAMUEL) DASHIELL. 1894-1961. Series characters: The Continental Op = CO; Sam Spade = SS.
The Adventures of Sam Spade and other stories. Bestseller, 1944. (7 stories, 3 about SS. The complete collection was reprinted as: They Can Only Hang You Once. Mercury, 1949. The 3 SS stories and 2 of the other 4 reprinted as: A Man Called Spade. Dell, 1945.)
The Big Knockover (novelet about CO); see $106,000 Blood Money
The Big Knockover. Random, 1966. British title: The Dashiell Hammett Story Omnibus. Cassell, 1966. (A collection, with introduction by Lillian Hellman, containing 7 CO stories, a chapter from Hammett's unfinished novel, and the CO novelet The Big Knockover, for further data on which see $106,000 Blood Money. This col-

lection was split for paperback reprint into two separate volues, confusingly titled The Big Knockover, Dell, 1967, and The Continental Op, Dell, 1967.)
The Big Knockover (partial paperback reprint of hardcover collection of the same title); see The Big Knockover
Blood Money; see $106,000 Blood Money
The Continental Op. Bestseller, 1945. (4 ss about CO.)
The Continental Op (partial paperback reprint of hardcover collection The Big Knockover); see The Big Knockover
The Continental Op. Random, 1974; Macmillan (London), 1975. (A collection of 7 CO ss taken from earlier collections, with an introduction by Steven Marcus.)
The Creeping Siamese. Jonathan, 1950. (6 ss, 3 about CO)
The Dain Curse. Knopf, 1929; Cassell, 1929 CO
The Dashiell Hammett Omnibus. Cassell, 1950. (Contains all 5 major novels plus 4 ss about CO.)
The Dashiell Hammett Story Omnibus; see The Big Knockover
Dead Yellow Women. Jonathan, 1947. (6 ss, 4 about CO)
The Glass Key. Knopf, 1931; Cassell, 1931
Hammett Homicides. Bestseller, 1946. (6 ss, 4 about CO)
The Maltese Falcon. Knopf, 1930; Cassell, 1930 SS
A Man Called Spade; see The Adventures of Sam Spade and other stories
A Man Named Thin. Mercury, 1962. (8 ss, 1 about CO)
Nightmare Town. Mercury, 1948. (4 ss, 2 about CO)
$106,000 Blood Money. Bestseller, 1943. Also published as: Blood Money. World, 1943; and as: The Big Knockover. Jonathan, 1948. Also included as the title story in the hardcover collection The Big Knockover, q.v. (Note: This novelet was originally published in two parts in Black Mask, February and May 1927, the first part entitled "The Big Knockover" and the second part $106,000 Blood Money.")
Red Harvest. Knopf, 1929; Cassell, 1929 CO
The Return of the Continental Op. Jonathan, 1945. (5 ss about CO)
They Can Only Hang You Once; see The Adventures of Sam Spade and other stories
The Thin Man. Knopf, 1934; Barker, 1934
Woman in the Dark. Jonathan, 1951. (7 ss, 3 about CO)

HAMMOCK, CLAUDE STUART. 1876- .
Why Murder the Judge? Macmillan, 1930

HAMMOND, CLEMENT MILTON. See: CHARLES HOWARD MONTAGUE, 1858-1889.

HAMMOND, GERALD
Fred in Situ. Hodder, 1965
The Loose Screw. Hodder, 1966
Mud in his Eye. Hodder, 1967

HAMMOND, LAWRENCE
A Life to Lose. Allen, 1966

HAMMOND, (DR.) WILLIAM A(LEXANDER), 1828-1900, and CLARA HAMMOND LANZA, 1859- .
Tales in Eccentric Life. Appleton, 1886 ss

HAMMOND-INNES, RALPH. 1913- . See: (RALPH) HAMMOND INNES.

HAMPTON, MARK. Pseudonym of Victor (George Charles) Norwood, 1920- , q.v. Other pseudonyms: Johnny Dark, Nat Karta, Hank Janson, Mark Shane, qq.v.
Killer Take All. Scion, 1953
Raw Deal for Dames. Scion, 1952
That's Her Problem. Scion, 1952

HANCOCK, FRANCES DEAN. Pseudonym of Jeanne Judson, 1890- , q.v.
Legacy of Fear. Avalon, 1969

HANCOCK, HARRIE I(RVING). 1868-1922.
Blackmail: A Central Office Problem. Street, 1899
Detective Johnson of New Orleans: A Tale of Love and Crime. Ogilvie, 1891
His Evil Eye; or, Sybil's Trials. Ogilvie, 1891
Inspector Henderson, the Central Office Detective. Ogilvie, 1892

HANCOCK, SYBIL. 1940- .
Mosshaven. Beagle, 1973

HANDLEY, ALAN
Kiss Your Elbow. McKay, 1948. Also published as: Terror in Times Square. Pyramid, 1950

HANDLEY, LEONARD (MOURANT H.). 1890- .
-Luxury Tour. Long, 1941
Remote Journey. Long, 1939
-There was no Island. Long, 1942

HANKINS, ARTHUR P(RESTON). 1880-1932. Pseudonym: Emart Kinsburn, q.v.
-Cole of Spyglass Mountain. Dodd, 1923
Judy the Torch. Chelsea, 1928
Tong Men and a Million. Chelsea, 1928

HANKINS, R(OBERT) M(AXWELL). 1905- .
-Ace-in-the-Hole Haggerty. Macrae, 1945; Hodder, 1948

HANKINSON, CHARLES JAMES. 1866-1959. Pseudonym: Clive Holland, q.v.

HANLEY, CLIFFORD. 1922- . Pseudonym: Henry Calvin, q.v.

HANNA, FRANCES NICHOLS. Pseudonym: Fan Nichols, q.v.

HANNAH, BARRY
Nightwatchmen. Viking, 1973

HANNAY, J(AMES) F(REDERICK) W(YNNE). 1906- .
Flight of an Angel. Methuen, 1932
Gin and Ginger. Methuen, 1931
Murder and Me. Hutchinson, 1937
-Rebels' Triumph. Methuen, 1933
The Thirteenth Floor. Methuen, 1931
Three Alibis. Hutchinson, 1938
When the Wicked Man... Methuen, 1934

HANNAY, JAMES OWEN. 1865-1950. Pseudonym: George A. Birmingham, q.v.

HANNON, EZRA. Pseudonym of Evan Hunter, 1926- , q.v. Other pseudonyms: Curt Cannon, Richard Marsten, Ed McBain, qq.v.
Doors. Stein, 1975; Macmillan (London), 1976

HANSARD, RENE
The Silver Fox. Morrow, 1938; Heinemann, 1938

HANSEN, JOSEPH. 1923- . Pseudonym: Rose Brock, q.v. Series character: Dave Brandstetter, in all titles.
Death Claims. Harper, 1973; Harrap, 1973
Fadeout. Harper, 1970; Harrap, 1972
Troublemaker. Harper, 1975; Harrap, 1975

HANSEN, ROBERT. 1883-1957. Pseudonym: Jens Anker, q.v.

HANSEN, ROBERT P(OWELL)
Back to the Wall. Mill, 1957; Boardman, 1958
Dead Pigeon. Mill, 1951; Barker, 1953
Deadly Purpose. Mill, 1958; Boardman, 1959
Mark Three for Murder. Mill, 1957; Boardman, 1957
Murder is Where You Find It. Mill, 1956; Boardman, 1957
There's Always a Payoff. Mill, 1959; Boardman, 1960
Trouble Comes Double. Mill, 1954; Barker, 1955
Walk a Crooked Mile. Mill, 1955; Boardman, 1955

HANSHEW, HAZEL PHILLIPS. See also: THOMAS W. HANSHEW, 1857-1914; and: MARY E. HANSHEW. Series character: Hamilton Cleek, in both titles (and under Thomas W. Hanshew and Mary E. Hanshew bylines.
Murder in the Hotel. Long, 1932
The Riddle of the Winged Death. Long, 1931

HANSHEW, MARY E. and THOMAS W. HANSHEW, 1857-1914. Series character: Hamilton Cleek, in all titles; see also Hazel Phillips Hanshew and Thomas W. Hanshew bylines.
The Amber Junk. Hutchinson, 1924. U.S. title: The Riddle of the Amber Ship. Doubleday, 1924. (Actually written by Hazel Phillips Hanshew.)
The Frozen Flame. Simpkin, 1920. U.S. title: The Riddle of the Frozen Flame. Doubleday, 1920. (Actually written by Hazel Phillips Hanshew.)
The House of Discord. Hutchinson, 1922. U.S. title: The Riddle of the Spinning Wheel. Doubleday, 1922. (Actually written by Hazel Phillips Hanshew.)
The House of the Seven Keys. Hutchinson, 1925. (Actually written by Hazel Phillips Hanshew.)
The Riddle of the Amber Ship; see The Amber Ship
The Riddle of the Frozen Flame; see The Frozen Flame
The Riddle of the Mysterious Light. Doubleday, 1921. (Actually written by Hazel Phillips Hanshew.)
The Riddle of the Spinning Wheel; see The House of Discord

HANSHEW, THOMAS W. 1857-1914. Series character: Hamilton Cleek = HC; see also Hazel Phillips Hanshew and Mary E. Hanshew bylines.
Beautiful but Dangerous; or, The Heir of Shadowdene. Street, 1891
Cleek of Scotland Yard. Cassell, 1914; Doubleday, 1914. (An episodic novel incorporating several HC ss.)
Cleek, the Man of the Forty Faces. Cassell (London & New York), 1913. (An episodic novel constituting a revised edition of The Man of the Forty Faces, q.v.) HC
Cleek, the Master Detective; see The Man of the Forty Faces
Cleek's Government Cases; see Cleek's Greatest Riddles

Hanshew, Thomas W.

Cleek's Greatest Riddles. Simpkin, 1916. U.S. title: Cleek's Government Cases. Doubleday, 1917. (An episodic novel incorporating several HC ss.)
Fate and the Man. Cassell, 1910
The Great Ruby. Ward, 1905
The Hoxton Mystery; see The World's Finger
The Mallison Mystery. Ward, 1903
The Man of the Forty Faces. Cassell, 1910. U.S. title: Cleek, the Master Detective. Doubleday, 1918 HC ss
The Riddle of the Night. Simpkin, 1916; Doubleday, 1915. (Actually written by Mary E. Hanshew and Hazel Phillips Hanshew based on notes by Thomas W. Hanshew.) HC
The Riddle of the Purple Emperor, with Mary E. Hanshew. Simpkin, 1918; Doubleday, 1919. (Actually written by Mary E. Hanshew and Hazel Phillips Hanshew.) HC
The Shadow of a Dead Man. Ward, 1906
The World's Finger. Ward, 1901; Irwin, 1901. Also published as: The Hoxton Mystery. Ogilvie, 1905

HANSOM, MARK
The Beasts of Brahm. Wright, 1937
The Ghost of Gaston Revere. Wright, 1935
The Madman. Wright, 1938
Master of Souls. Wright, 1937
The Shadow on the House. Wright, 1934; Godwin, 193?
Sorcerer's Chessman. Wright, 1939
The Wizard of Berner's Abbey. Wright, 1935

HANSON, ERNEST S. Pseudonym: Daniel Dane, q.v.

HANSON, JAMES W.
Brother Berserk. Vantage, 1969

HANSON, V. J.
Death and Little Girl Blue. Amalgamated, 1962. (Sexton Blake)

HANSON, VIRGINIA (L.). 1905-1968. Series characters: Adam Drew and Katherine (Kay) Cornish, in all titles.
Casual Slaughters. Doubleday, 1939
Death Walks the Post. Doubleday, 1938
Mystery for Mary. Doubleday, 1942

HARBAGE, ALFRED BENNETT. 1901-1976. Pseudonym: Thomas Kyd, q.v.

HARBAUGH, THOMAS CHALMERS. 1849-1924. Pseudonym: Captain Howard Holmes, q.v.

HARBEN, WILL(IAM) N(ATHANIEL). 1858-1919.
The Caruthers Affair. Neely (New York & London), 1898
From Clue to Climax. Street, 1902
The North Walk Mystery. Street, 1899

HARCOURT, F(REDERICK) C. VERNON. 1845- .
Bolts and Bars. Digby, 1905 ss
The Devil's Derelicts. Digby, 1905 ss

HARCOURT, PALMA
Climate for Conspiracy. Collins, 1974
A Fair Exchange. Collins, 1975; McKay, 1976

HARDIE, D(AVID) W(ILLIAM) F(ERGUSON). 1906- . Series character: Detective-Inspector Elwyn Hughes, in all titles.
The Case of the Praying Evangelist. Nicholson, 1950
A Grave for Miss Carling. Nicholson, 1952
The Iron Egg. Nicholson, 1947
THe Riddle of the Cambrian Venus. Nicholson, 1949

HARDIN, PETER. Pseudonym of Louis Charles Vaczek, 1913- .
The Frightened Dove. Scribner, 1951; Heinemann, 1952
The Hidden Grave. Harper, 1955; Muller, 1956

HARDING, ALBERT
Death on Raven's Scar. Staples, 1953

HARDING, ANTHONY
Arms for the Love of Allah. Hutchinson, 1939

HARDING, D. E.
How Briggs Died. Harrap, 1940

HARDING, ERIC
Behold! the Executioner! Hutchinson, 1939
Pray for the Dawn. Low, 1946

HARDING, HARRY. 1885- . Pseudonym: Haydon Dean, q.v.
The Beckoning Finger. Methuen, 1926
-The Hawk of Rede. Hodder, 1922

HARDING, RICHARD
Appointment in Tenerife. Hurst, 1966
-Gay Deception. Hale, 1967

HARDING, RONALD S. L.
The Black Bottle. Fiction House, 1935
Castle of Fear. Fiction House, 1938
The Demon of Hong Kong. Mowl, 1934
The Library of Death. Modern, 1938
The Murder Maniac. Fiction House, 1935
"One Dreadful Night." Modern, 1935
Strange Fate. Fiction House, 1937

HARDINGE, GEORGE. Pseudonym: George Milner, q.v.

HARDINGE, REX. 1904- . Pseudonym: "Capstan", q.v. All titles below listed without publisher were published by Amalgamated Press and feature Sexton Blake.
Beyond the Skyline. Eldon, 1933
The Black-Hill Murder Case. 1933
The Blazing Launch Murder. 1934
The Body on the Beach. 1937
By Whose Hand? 1956
The Case of the African Emigrant. 1948
The Case of the African Hoodoo. 1953
The Case of the African Trader. 1949
The Case of the Black Magician. 1935
The Case of the Chinese Courier. 1947
The Case of the Crime Reporter. 1949
The Case of the Frightened Girl. 1951
The Case of the Green Caravan. 1951
The Case of the Kidnapped Specialist. 1938
The Case of the Missing Musician. 1939
The Case of the Murdered Postman. 1938
The Case of the Secret Agent. 1949
The Case of the Stolen Mine. 1948
Consider Your Verdict; see The Mystery of the Devil Mask
The Crime in Carson's Shack. 1935
The Crooked Gambler.
Dangerous Money. 1938
The Ex-Serviceman's Secret. 1936
The Fatal Car. 1930
Found—Adventure. Jenkins, 1938
The Gargoyle of Polgelly. 1948
The Headmaster's Secret. 1951
The Ivory Tusk. 1933
The Legacy of Hate. 1949
The Lodging-House Mystery. 1954
The Man from Chun King. 1946
The Man from Holland. 1934
The Man from Mongolia. 1947
The Man from Space. 1952
The Man from the Jungle. 1940
The Man They Could Not Convict. 1937
The Man with Five Enemies. 1955
The Masked Slayer. 1932
The Midnight Mystery. 1929
The Mission of Menace. 1930
The Mission of Vengeance. 1931
The Motor Show Mystery. 1936
The Murder at Hermit's Cottage. 1936
Murder on the Boat Express. 1936
Murder on the Veld. Wright, 1954
The Mystery of the African Expedition. 1937
The Mystery of the African Farm. 1939
The Mystery of the African Mine. 1936
The Mystery of the Body on the Cliff. 1953
The Mystery of the Devil Mask. 1949. Reprinted in revised version as: Consider Your Verdict. 1959
The Mystery of the Forbidden Territory. 1950
The Mystery of the Murdered Chef. 1934
The Mystery of the Outlawed Black. 1955
The Mystery of the Reunion Dinner. 1932
The Observer Corps Mystery. 1940
One of Seven. 1941
The Police Station Mystery. 1939
The Prisoner of the Manor. 1952
The Problem in Ciphers. Wright, 1952
The Radio Crook. 1931
The Riddle of the Crooked Gambler. 1952
The Riddle of the Highwayman's Stone. 1948
The Riddle of the Invisible Menace. 1954
The Riddle of the Sealed Room. 1948
Safari with Fear! 1959
The Secret of the African Settler. 1948
The Secret of the African Trader. 1932
The Secret of the Dental Surgeon. 1937
The Secret of the Desert. 1951
The Secret of the Fated Family. 1953
The Secret of the Jungle. 1947
The Secret of the Man Who Died. 1955
The Secret of the Sale Room. 1936
The Secret of the Sheba. Wright, 1954
The Secret of the Smuggler's Cove. 1935
The Secret of the Veld. 1947
"Three Rounds Rapid—". Skeffington, 1936
The Tragedy of the Bromleigh's. 1949
The Tragedy of Windyridge. 1950
The Victim of the Devil's Bowl. 1954
The Voyage of Fear. 1954
With Criminal Instinct. 1950
The Yellow Terror. 1947

HARDT, MICHAEL. Joint pseudonym of Gwen Leys Davenport, 1910- , and Gustav J. Breuer.
A Stranger and Afraid. Bobbs, 1943

HARDWICK, (JOHN) MICHAEL (DRINKROW), 1924- , and MOLLIE HARDWICK
The Game's Afoot. Murray, 1969. (Plays from the Sherlock Holmes stories by A. Conan Doyle, 1859-1930, q.v.)
The Private Life of Sherlock Holmes. Mayflower, 1970; Bantam, 1971. (Novelization of the movie.)

HARDWICK, MOLLIE. See: (JOHN) MICHAEL (DRINKROW) HARDWICK, 1924- .

HARDWICK, RICHARD (HOLMES, JR.). 1923- .

Hawk. Belmont, 1966. (Novelization of the TV series.)
The Plotters. Doubleday, 1965; Hale, 1966
The Season to be Deadly. Doubleday, 1966; Hale, 1967

HARDY, A(RTHUR) S(TEFFENS). All titles were published by Amalgamated Press and feature Sexton Blake.
The Bookmaker's Crime. 1935
The Case of the Mystery Champion. 1928
The Crimson Mask. 1919
The Crook of Newmarket. 1931
The Mystery of the Championship Belt. 1926
The Secret of the Mine. 1919
Sexton Blake's Vow. 1918
The Team of Crooks. 1927
The Touring Company Crime. 1935
The Trainer's Secret. 1925
Traitor and Spy. 1917
Who Killed Trainer Lincoln? 1930

HARDY, ARTHUR SHERBURNE. 1847-1930.
Diane and Her Friends. Houghton, 1914 ss
No. 13, Rue du Bon Diable. Houghton, 1917

HARDY, IZA DUFFUS
-A Broken Faith. Hurst, 1879
-Hearts or Diamonds. White, 1885
-His Silence. Digby, 1907
-The Lesser Evil. Chatto, 1901
MacGilleroy's Millions. Simpkin, 1900
The Mystery of a Moonlight Tryst. Digby, 1908
A New Othello. Jarrold, 1890
The Silent Watchers. Digby, 1910
The Strange Disappearance of John Haversham. Digby, 1909
-A Trap of Fate. Digby, 1906
The Westhorpe Mystery. White, 1886

HARDY, J(OCELYN) L(EE). 1894-   .
Everything is Thunder. Lane, 1935; Doubleday, 1935
I Escape. Allied News, 1938
Never in Vain. Collins, 1936; Doubleday, 1936
Pawn in the Game. Collins, 1939
Recoil. Collins, 1936; Doubleday, 1936
The Stroke of Eight. Collins, 1938

HARDY, LINDSAY. Series character: Gregory Keene, in at least those marked GK.
The Faceless Ones. Hale, 1956. (U.S. title?)
The Nightshade Ring. Appleton, 1954; Hale, 1955 GK
Requiem for a Redhead. Appleton, 1953 GK
Show No Mercy. Popular Library, 1955

HARDY, ROBERT. 1917-   .
A Winter's Tale. Chatto, 1959

HARDY, RONALD
The Face of Jalanath. Putnam, 1973

HARDY, WILLIAM (MARION). 1922-   .
The Case of the Missing Co-Ed; see A Little Sin
Lady Killer. Dodd, 1957; H. Hamilton, 1957
A Little Sin. Dodd, 1958; H. Hamilton, 1959. Also published as: The Case of the Missing Co-Ed. Dell, 1960
A Time of Killing. Dodd, 1962; H. Hamilton, 1963

HARE, ARNOLD. 1921-   .
The Man Who Never Laughed. Allen, 1963; Norton, 1963

HARE, CYRIL. Pseudonym of Alfred Alexander Gordon Clark, 1900-1958. Series characters: Inspector Mallett = M; Francis Pettigrew = FP.
Best Detective Stories of Cyril Hare. Faber, 1959; Walker, 1961 ss
The Christmas Murder; see An English Murder
Death is No Sportsman. Faber, 1938 M
Death Walks the Woods; see That Yew Tree's Shade
An English Murder. Faber, 1951; Little, 1951. Also published as: The Christmas Murder. Mercury, 1953
He Should Have Died Hereafter. Faber, 1958. U.S. title: Untimely Death. Macmillan, 1958 M & FP
Suicide Excepted. Faber, 1939; Macmillan, 1954 M
Tenant for Death. Faber, 1937; Dodd, 1937 M
That Yew Tree's Shade. Faber, 1954. U.S. title: Death Walks the Woods. Little, 1954 FP
Tragedy at Law. Faber, 1942; Harcourt, 1943 M & FP
Untimely Death; see He Should Have Died Hereafter
When the Wind Blows. Faber, 1949. U.S. title: The Wind Blows Death. Little, 1950 FP
The Wind Blows Death; see When the Wind Blows
With a Bare Bodkin. Faber, 1946 M & FP

HARE, ROBERT. Pseudonym of Robert Hare Hutchinson, 1887-   , q.v.
The Crime in the Crystal; see Spectral Evidence
The Doctor's First Murder. Hurst, 1933; Longmans, 1933
The Hand of the Chimpanzee. Hurst, 1934; Longmans, 1934
Spectral Evidence. Hurst, 1932. U.S. title: The Crime in the Crystal. Longmans, 1933

HARE, WALTER BEN. 1880-   .
And Billy Disappeared. Baker, 1919. (4-act play.)
And Home Came Ted. Denison, 1917. (3-act play.)
Assisted by Sadie. Denison, 1919. (4-act play.)
Aunt What's-Her-Name! Baker, 1922. (3-act play.)
The Dutch Detective. Baker, 1914. (3-act play.)
The Gold Bug. Denison, 1920. (A play based in part on Edgar Allan Poe's short story.)
Has Anyone Seen Jean? Baker, 1927. (3-act play.)

HARGRAVE, ROY. See: KENNETH PHILLIPS BRITTON.

HARINGTON, DONALD. 1935-   .
Some Other Place, the Right Place. Little, 1972; Cape, 1973

HARKER, CHARLES R.
A Singular Sinner. Abbey, 1900

HARKINS, STERLING
The Butcherknife Killings. Brandon, 1974

HARKNETT, TERRY. 1936-   . Pseudonyms: Joseph Hedges, William Pine, Thomas H. Stone, William Terry, qq.v. Series characters: Chief Supt. John Crown = JC; Steve Wayne, in at least those marked SW.

The Benevolent Blackmailer. Hale, 1962
Crown: Bamboo Shoot-Out. Futura, 1975 JC
Crown: Macao Mayhem. Futura, 1974 JC
Crown: The Sweet and Sour Kill. Futura, 1974; Pinnacle, 1974 JC
Dead Little Rich Girl. Hale, 1963
Death of an Aunt. Hammond, 1967 SW
The Evil Money. Hale, 1964 SW
Invitation to a Funeral. Hale, 1963 SW
The Man Who Did Not Die. Hale, 1964 SW
-Promotion Tour. New English Library pb, 1972
The Scratch on the Surface. Hale, 1962 SW
The Softcover Kill. Hale, 1971
The Two-Way Frame. Hammond, 1967
The Upmarket Affair. Hale, 1973

HARLAND, HENRY. Pseudonym: Sidney Luska, q.v.

HARLING, ROBERT. 1910-   .
The Dark Saviour. Chatto, 1952; Harper, 1953
The Endless Colonnade. Chatto, 1958; Putnam, 1959
The Enormous Shadow. Chatto, 1955; Harper, 1956
The Hollow Sunday. Chatto, 1967
The Paper Palace. Chatto, 1951; Harper, 1951

HARMAN, NEAL
The Case of the Wounded Mastiff. Barker, 1947
-Crown Colony. Barker, 1939
Death and the Archdeacon. Barker, 1949
Peace and Peter Lamont. Barker, 1950
-Rebellion. Barker, 1937
Yours Truly, Angus MacIvor. Barker, 1952

HARNAN, TERRY. Pseudonym: Eric Traviss Hull, q.v.
Signal for Danger. Doubleday, 1946

HARPER, DAVID. Pseudonym of Edwin Corley, 1931-   , q.v. Other pseudonym: William Judson, q.v. Joint pseudonym with Jack Murphy: Patrick Buchanan, q.v.
Hijacked. Dodd, 1970; Souvenir, 1971. Also published as: Skyjacked. Bantam, 1971; Corgi, 1972
The Patchwork Man. Dodd, 1975; Prior, 1975
Skyjacked; see Hijacked

HARPER, E. M.
The Assassin. Berkley, 1960

HARPER, HARRY
File No. 115; or, A Man of Steel. Ogilvie, 1886

HARPER, HARRY
The Sign of the Knotted String. Mellifont, 1944

HARPER, HENRY G.
The Silent Stranger. Street, ca.1900

HARPER, HENRY HOWARD. 1871-   .
-The Devil's Nest. (Boston), 1923

HARPER, OLIVE. Pseudonym of Helen Burrell Gibson D'Apery, 1842-1915.
The Burglar and the Lady. Ogilvie, 1912
-Caught in Mid-Ocean. Ogilvie, 1911
The Chinatown Trunk Mystery. Ogilvie, 1909
The Convict's Sweetheart. Ogilvie, 1909
The Creole Slave's Revenge. Ogilvie, 1908
A Desperate Chance. Ogilvie, 1903
-The Gambler of the West. Ogilvie, 1906

Jack Sheppard, the Bandit King. Ogilvie, 1908
-King of Bigamists. Ogilvie, 1909
Millionaire and the Policeman's Wife. Ogilvie, 1908
A Millionaire's Revenge. Ogilvie, 1906
On Trial for His Life. Ogilvie, 1908
The Opium Smugglers of Frisco; or, The Crimes of a Beautiful Opium Fiend. Ogilvie, 1908
Queen of the Secret Seven. Ogilvie, 1909
-Shadow Behind the Throne. Ogilvie, 1908
-A Slave of the Mill. Ogilvie, 1905
Wanted by the Police. Ogilvie, 1909

HARPER, RICHARD J.
The Dragonhead Deal. Warner, 1975

HARPER, STEPHEN
A Necessary End. Collins, 1975

HARRADEN, BEATRICE. 1864-1935.
Search will Find It Out. Mills, 1928

HARRELL, J.
Death Comes to the Hermit. Pan, 1946 ss

HARRINGTON, JOSEPH. 1903- . Series character: Lt. Kerrigan, in all titles.
Blind Spot. Lippincott, 1966; Hale, 1967
The Last Doorbell. Lippincott, 1969; Hale, 1970
The Last Known Address. Lippincott, 1965; Hale, 1966

HARRINGTON, WILLIAM
The Gospel of Death; see The Power
The Jupiter Crisis. McKay, 1971
Mister Target. Delacorte, 1973; Joseph, 1974
-The Power. Bobbs, 1964. British title: The Gospel of Death. Joseph, 1966
Scorpio 5. Coward, 1975
The Search for Elizabeth Brandt. McKay, 1969
Trial. McKay, 1970; Barrie, 1970
Which the Justice, Which the Thief. Bobbs, 1963; Joseph, 1965
-Yoshar the Soldier. Bobbs, 1966; Eyre, 1967

HARRIS, A. L.
The Fatal Request. Street (Magnet #253)

HARRIS, ALFRED. 1928- . Joint pseudonym with Arthur Moore, q.v.: Gwen Addison, q.v.
Baroni. Putnam, 1975
The Joseph File. Putnam, 1974

HARRIS, CHARLES. 1913- .
Death of a Barrow Boy. Phoenix (London), 1952
Three Ha-Pence to the Angel. Phoenix (London), 1950

HARRIS, COLVER. Pseudonym of Anne Colver, 1908- . Series character: Timothy Fowler, in all titles.
Going to St. Ives. Macrae Smith, 1936
Hide and Go Seek. Minton Balch, 1933
Murder in Amber. Hillman-Curl, 1938

HARRIS, EDWIN
John Jasper's Gatehouse. Mackays, 1931. (A sequel to Charles Dickens' The Mystery of Edwin Drood, q.v.)

HARRIS, H. B.
The Seven Elms Mystery. Stockwell, 1937

HARRIS, HERBERT
Who Kill to Live. Jenkins, 1962

HARRIS, JOEL CHANDLER. 1848-1908.
On the Wing of Occasions. Doubleday, 1900; Murray, 1900. Also published as: The Kidnapping of Lincoln and Other War Detective Stories. Doubleday, 1909 ss

HARRIS, JOHN. 1916- . Pseudonym: Mark Hebden, q.v.
Adventure's End; see Road to the Coast
The Claws of Mercy. Hurst, 1955
Close to the Wind; see Getaway
The Courtney Entry. Hutchinson, 1971; Doubleday, 1970
Covenant with Death. Hutchinson, 1961; Sloane, 1961
The Cross of Lazzaro. Hutchinson, 1965; Morrow, 1965
Getaway. Hurst, 1956. U.S. title: Close to the Wind. Sloane, 1956
Hallelujah Corner. Hurst, 1952
The Jade Wind; see The Mercenaries
A Kind of Courage. Hutchinson, 1972
Light Cavalry Action. Hutchinson, 1967; Morrow, 1967
The Lonely Voyage. Hurst, 1951
The Mercenaries. Hutchinson, 1969. U.S. title: The Jade Wind. Doubleday, 1969
The Mustering of the Hawks. Hutchinson, 1972
The Old Trade of Killing. Hutchinson, 1966; Morrow, 1966
The Professionals. Hutchinson, 1973
Ride Out the Storm. Hutchinson, 1975
Right of Reply. Hutchinson, 1968; Coward, 1968
Road to the Coast. Hutchinson, 1959. U.S. title: Adventure's End. Sloane, 1959
The Sea Shall Not Have Them. Hurst, 1953. U.S. title: The Undaunted. Sloane, 1953
The Sleeping Mountain. Hutchinson, 1958; Sloane, 1958
Smiling Willie and the Tiger. Hutchinson, 1974
The Spring of Malice. Hutchinson, 1962; Sloane, 1962
Sunset at Sheba. Hutchinson, 1960; Sloane, 1960
The Undaunted; see The Sea Shall Not Have Them
The Unforgiving Wind. Hutchinson, 1963; Sloane, 1964
Vardy. Hutchinson, 1964; Sloane, 1965
The Victors. Hutchinson, 1975

HARRIS, JOHN WYNDHAM PARKES LUCAS BEYNON. 1903-1969. Pseudonym: John Beynon, q.v.

HARRIS, JOHN NORMAN. 1915- .
The Weird World of Wes Beattie. Harper, 1963; Faber, 1964

HARRIS, LARRY M(ARK). 1933- . Pseudonym: Laurence M. Janifer, q.v. Joint pseudonym with Randall (Phillips) Garrett: Mark Phillips, q.v.
The Pickled Poodles. Random, 1960; Boardman, 1961. (Novel based on the series character John J. Malone created by Craig Rice, 1908-1957, q.v.)
The Protector. Random, 1961; Boardman, 1962

HARRIS, MARILYN [MARILYN HARRIS SPRINGER]. 1931- .
The Conjurers. Random, 1974

HARRIS, MURIEL
The Clinic of Dr. Aicadre. Harper, 1932. British title: The Scornful Man. Cape, 1932

HARRIS, DETECTIVE NICK [NICHOLAS BOILVIN HARRIS]
In the Shadows. Times Mirror, 1923 ss

HARRIS, (WILLIAM) PETER. 1923- .
Cry Hold! Long, 1970
The Final Set. Long, 1965
Letters of Discredit. Long, 1964
What Became of Alex Bretherton? Long, 1967

HARRIS, REX [REGINALD DUCKETT HARRIS]
A Hand in Diamonds. Constable, 1961

HARRIS, ROGER
The L.S.D. Dossier. Compact, 1966

HARRIS, ROSEMARY (JEANNE). 1923- .
All My Enemies. Faber, 1967; Simon, 1973
The Double Snare. Faber, 1974; Simon, 1975
The Nice Girl's Story. Faber, 1968. U.S. title: Nor Evil Dreams. Simon, 1974
Nor Evil Dreams; see The Nice Girl's Story
A Wicked Pack of Cards. Faber, 1969; Walker, 1970

HARRIS, THOMAS. 1940- .
Black Sunday. Putnam, 1975; Hodder, 1975

HARRIS, TIMOTHY
Steelyard Blues. Bantam, 1972. (Novelization of the movie.)

HARRIS, VIVIAN BEYNON
-Confusion at Campden Trig. Museum, 1948
-One Thing Constant. Museum, 1949
-Song for a Siren. Museum, 1951

HARRIS-BURLAND, J(OHN) B(URLAND). 1870- .
Baldragon. Chapman, 1914
The Black Motor-Car. Richards, 1906; Dillingham, 1905, as by Harris Burland
The Broken Law. Richards, 1906; Cupples, 1908
The Brown Book. Long, 1923
The Curse of Cloud. Chapman, 1914
-Dacobra; or, The White Priests of Ahriman. Everett, 1903
The Disc. Greening, 1909
-The Financier. Greening, 1906; Dillingham, 1906, as by Harris Burland
-The Gold Worshippers. Greening, 1907; Dillingham, 1906
The Grey Cat. Chapman, 1913
The Hidden Hour. Long, 1925
The House of the Soul. Chapman, 1909
-Life's Golden Web. Newnes, 1912
Lord of Irongray. Greening, 1911
Love the Criminal. Greening, 1907; Cupples, 1908
The Poison League. Bale, 1921
-The Red Moon. Long, 1923
-The Secret of Enoch Seal. Chapman, 1910
The Shadow of Malreward. Chapman, 1911; Knopf, 1919
-Sunk Island. Newnes, 1911
The Torhaven Mystery. Chapman, 1910
The White Rook. Chapman, 1917; Knopf, 1918
Workers in Darkness. Greening, 1908

HARRISON, BARBARA. 1941- .
A Cold Night's Death. Award, 1973. (Novelization of the TV movie.)

HARRISON, BRUCE
A-100. Dutton, 1930

HARRISON, MRS. BURTON [CONSTANCE CARY HARRISON]. 1843-1920.
The Carcellini Emerald, with other tales. Stone, 1899; Richards, 1899 ss, some criminous

HARRISON, CHIP. Pseudonym of Lawrence Block, 1938- , q.v. Other pseudonym: Paul Kavanagh, q.v. Series character: Leo Haig, in both titles.
Make Out with Murder. GM, 1974
The Topless Tulip Caper. GM, 1975

HARRISON, E(RNEST) J(OHN). 1873- .
-Rasprava. Bles, 1924
The Red Camarilla. Allen, 1923

HARRISON, EDWIN. Pseudonym of Eric Alan Ballard. All titles below were published by Amalgamated Press and feature Sexton Blake.
Diamonds can be Trouble. 1958
The Fatal Hour. 1958
Killer's Playground. 1959
Witness to Murder. 1959

HARRISON, F(ANNIE) HEWITT. 1878- .
The White Cowl. Burney, 1937

HARRISON, HARRY (MAX). 1925- . Series characters: Slippery Jim Di Griz = JD; Tony Hawkin = TH.
Montezuma's Revenge. Doubleday, 1972 TH
Queen Victoria's Revenge. Doubleday, 1974; Severn House, 1977 TH
The Stainless Steel Rat. Pyramid, 1961; Sphere, 1973 JD
The Stainless Steel Rat Saves the World. Putnam, 1972; Faber, 1973 JD
The Stainless Steel Rat's Revenge. Walker, 1970; Faber, 1971 JD

HARRISON, J. E.
The Kara Yerta Tragedy. Scott, 1889

HARRISON, JIM [JAMES HARRISON]. 1937- .
A Good Day to Die. Simon, 1973; Allen, 1975

HARRISON, LEWIS. Pseudonym of Lewis H. Watson.
-Not to the Swift. Welch, 1891
-A Strange Infatuation. Rand, 1890

HARRISON, MICHAEL. 1907- . Pseudonym: Quentin Downes, q.v.
The Darkened Room. Home & Van Thal, 1952
The Exploits of the Chevalier Dupin. Mycroft, 1968. British title: Murder in the Rue Royale. Stacey, 1972. (The U.S. edition contains 7, the British edition 12, ss based on the character C. Auguste Dupin, created by Edgar A. Poe, 1809-1849, q.v.
Murder in the Rue Royale; see The Exploits of the Chevalier Dupin

HARRISON, RICHARD (MOTTE). 1901- .
Pseudonym: Peter Motte, q.v. See also: REGINALD (WILFRID) CAMPBELL, 1894-1950. Series character: Chief Inspector William Bastion, in at least those marked WB.
Aftermath of Murder. Jarrolds, 1942
Black Widow. Jarrolds, 1946 WB
Bootlaces for Bastion. Jarrolds, 1947 WB
Brickbats for Bastion. Jarrolds, 1948 WB
The Circle of Von Boden. Jarrolds, 1944
The Dog It Was. Jarrolds, 1940
Foul Deeds will Rise. Long, 1958
Murder-on-Sea. Jarrolds, 1949 WB
Our Doom is Gone. Jarrolds, 1951
Rope over Jezebel. Jarrolds, 1950 WB
The Shuttle of Hate. Jarrolds, 1942
Suburban Saraband. Jarrolds, 1952
The Utmost Ebb. Jarrolds, 1944

HARRISON, W. G. A. Pseudonym: A. G. Wilson, q.v.

HARRISON, WHIT. Pseudonym of Harry Whittington, 1915- , q.v.
Swamp Kill. Phantom, 1952
Violent Night. Phantom, 1952

HART, CAROLYN G.
Flee from the Past. Bantam, 1975

HART, FRANCES (NEWBOLD) NOYES. 1890-1943.
The Bellamy Trial. Doubleday, 1927; Heinemann, 1927. A play, with Frank E. Carstarphen: French (New York & London), 1932
Contact and other stories. Doubleday, 1923 ss, some mildly criminous
The Crooked Lane. Doubleday, 1934; Heinemann, 1934
Hide in the Dark. Doubleday, 1929; Heinemann, 1929

HART, I(NNES) R(UTH) G(RAY). 1889- .
Adjustments. Benn, 1931
Coloured Glass. Rich, 1933
The Dead Hand. Benn, 1929
The Double Image. Benn, 1928
Facets. Benn, 1930
Forests of the Night. Benn, 1930
Frontier of Fear. Benn, 1928. U.S. title (?): Torture Island. Simon, 1928
Like Water. Benn, 1931
Torture Island; see Frontier of Fear

HART, JANET
File for Death. Boardman, 1965
Who's been Sleeping in my Grave? Boardman, 1966

HART, L. H.
The Court of Last Resort. Macdonald, 1943
Murder at Cost Price. Swan, 1947
Venus Died at Dawn. Macdonald, 1947
You'll End Up Dead. Macdonald, 1945

HART, TED. Both volumes below are adapted from Brian Clemens' stories for the TV series.
More Stories from Thriller. Fontana, 1975 ss
Thriller. Fontana, 1974 ss

HART-DAVIS, DUFF. 1936- .
The Gold of St. Matthew. Constable, 1970. U.S. title: The Gold-Trackers. Doubleday, 1970
The Gold-Trackers; see The Gold of St. Matthew
The Megacull. Constable, 1968
Spider in the Morning. Constable, 1972; Doubleday, 1972

HARTENFELS, JEROME. 1934- .
Doctor Death. Hill, 1970; Calder, 1971

HARTER, WALTER L.
The Nice Young Man. Holt, 1962. British title: Deadly Reunion. Boardman, 1965

HARTLEY, OLGA
The Malaret Mystery. Methuen, 1925; Small, 1926
-The Witch of Chelsea. Methuen, 1930

HARTMAN, LEE FOSTER. 1879-1941.
The White Sapphire. Harper, 1914

HARTMANN, HELMUT. Pseudonym: H(enry) Seymour, q.v.

HARVESTER, SIMON. Pseudonym of Henry (St. John Clair) Gibbs, 1909-1975, q.v. Series characters: Heron Murmur, in at least those marked HM; Dorian Silk, in at least those marked DS; Malcolm Kenton, in at least those marked MK.
Arrival in Suspicion. Jarrolds, 1953
Assassins Road. Jarrolds, 1965; Walker, 1965 DS
The Bamboo Screen. Jarrolds, 1955; Walker, 1968 MK
Battle Road. Jarrolds, 1967; Walker, 1967 DS
A Breastplate for Aaron. Rich, 1949
Cat's Cradle. Jarrolds, 1952
The Chinese Hammer. Jarrolds, 1960; Walker, 1961 HM
The Copper Butterfly. Jarrolds, 1957; Walker, 1962 MK
A Corner of the Playground. Jarrolds, 1973
Delay in Danger. Jarrolds, 1954
Dragon Road. Jarrolds, 1956; Walker, 1969 DS
Epitaph for Lemmings. Rich, 1943; Macmillan, 1944
Flight in Darkness. Jarrolds, 1964; Walker, 1965
The Flying Horse; see Troika
Forgotten Road. Hutchinson, 1974; Walker, 1974 DS
The Golden Fear. Jarrolds, 1957 MK
Good Men and True. Rich, 1949
An Hour Before Zero. Jarrolds, 1959
A Lantern for Diogenes. Rich, 1946
Let Them Pray. Rich, 1942
Lucifer at Sunset. Jarrolds, 1953
Maybe a Trumpet. Rich, 1945
Moonstone Jungle. Jarrolds, 1961
Moscow Road. Jarrolds, 1970; Walker, 1971 DS
Nameless Road. Jarrolds, 1969; Walker, 1970 DS
Obols for Charon. Jarrolds, 1951
The Paradise Men. Jarrolds, 1956 MK
Red Road. Jarrolds, 1963; Walker, 1964 DS
Sahara Road. Jarrolds, 1972; Walker, 1972 DS
The Sequins Lost Their Lustre. Rich, 1948
Shadows in a Hidden Land. Jarrolds, 1966; Walker, 1966
Sheep May Safely Graze. Rich, 1950
Silk Road. Jarrolds, 1962; Walker, 1963 DS
Spiders' Web. Jarrolds, 1953
Tiger in the North. Jarrolds, 1955; Walker, 1963
Traitors' Gate. Jarrolds, 1952
Treacherous Road. Jarrolds, 1966; Walker, 1967 DS
Troika. Jarrolds, 1962. U.S. title: The Flying Horse. Walker, 1964 HM
Unsung Road. Jarrolds, 1960; Walker, 1961 DS
The Vessel May Carry Explosives. Jarrolds, 1951
Whatsoever Things are True. Rich, 1947
Witch Hunt. Jarrolds, 1951
The Yesterday Walkers. Jarrolds, 1958
Zion Road. Jarrolds, 1968; Walker, 1968 DS

HARVEY, ANNIE JANE TENNANT. -1898.
Pseudonym: Andree Hope, q.v.

HARVEY, JACK. See: MILTON M(ICHAEL) RAISON, 1903- .

HARVEY, JOHN HENRY. Pseudonyms: John H. Barrington, Operator 1384, qq.v.

HARVEY, JOHN WILFRED. 1889- . Pseudonym: John Farndale, q.v.

HARVEY, MARION. Series character: Graydon McKelvie, in at least those marked GM.
Alias the Eagle; see The Clue of the Clock

The Arden Mystery. Brentano's (London), 1925 (U.S. title?)
The Clue of the Clock. Clode, 1929. British title: Alias the Eagle. Brentano's (London), 1928
The Dragon of Lung Wang. Clode, 1928; Wright, 1934 GM
The House of Seclusion. Small, 1925; Wright, 1935 GM
The Inner Circle. Longmans (New York), 1930 (3-act play.)
The Mystery of the Hidden Room. Clode, 1922; Brentano's (London), 1923 GM
The Vengeance of the Ivory Skull. Clode, 1923; Wright, 1935 GM

HARVEY, WILLIAM C(LUNIE). 1900- .
Death's Treasure Hunt. Eldon, 1933
Murder Abroad. Eldon, 1933

HARVEY, WILLIAM F(RYER). 1885-1937.
The Arm of Mrs. Egan and other strange stories. Dent, 1951; Dutton, 1952 ss
-The Beast with Five Fingers. Dent, 1928; Dutton, 1928 ss
-Caprimulgus. Constable, 1936
-Midnight House and other tales. Dent, 1910 ss
-Midnight Tales. Dent, 1946 ss
The Misadventures of Athelstan Digby. Swarthmore, 1920 ss
-Moods and Tenses. Blackwell, 1933 ss
-Mr. Murray and the Boococks. Nelson, 1938
The Mysterious Mr. Badman. Pawling, 1934

HARVEY, WILLIAM W(IRT). 1866- .
-Lige Golden: The Man Who Twinkled. Brimmer, 1924

HARWOOD, RONALD. 1934- .
The Guilt Merchants. Cape, 1963; Holt, 1969

HASLETTE, JOHN. Pseudonym of John (George) Hazlette Vahey, 1881- , q.v. Other pseudonyms: Henrietta Clandon, Anthony Lang, Vernon Loder, John Mowbray, Walter Proudfoot, qq.v.
-The Carven Ball. Digby, 1910
-Desmond Rourke, Irishman. Low, 1911; Appleton, 1911
-Johnnie Madison. Smith Elder, 1914
The Man Who Pulled the Strings. Nash, 1916
-The Mesh. Low, 1912
-The Passion of the President. Everett, 1909
-The Shadow of Salvador. Heath Cranston, 1913

HASLUCK, ALEXANDRA
Of Ladies Dead. Angus (Sydney), 1970 ss of historical mystery

HASTINGS, BROOK. Joint pseudonym of Leslie Edgley, 1912- , q.v., and Mary Edgley. Other pseudonym of Leslie Edgley: Robert Bloomfield, q.v.
The Demon Within. Doubleday, 1953; Boardman, 1954

HASTINGS, D(OROTHY) G(RACE). 1911- .
Death at the Depot. Harper, 1944

HASTINGS, GEORGE
-His Royal Highness. Brandus, 1891
-Mrs. Jonathan Abroad. Argonaut, 1890
Philip Henson M.D. Brandus, 1891; Ward, 1892. Also published as: A Tale of the Town; or, Philip Henson, M.D. Ivers, 1894
A Tale of the Town; see Philip Henson M.D.

HASTINGS, GRAHAM. Pseudonym of Roderic (Graeme) Jeffries, 1926- , q.v. Other pseudonyms: Peter Alding, Jeffrey Ashford, Roderic Graeme, qq.v.
Deadly Game. Hale, 1961
Twice Checked. Hale, 1959

HASTINGS, HARRINGTON. Joint pseudonym of Florence Shepherd and John Marsh, 1907- , q.v.
Criminal Square. Hutchinson, 1929
-The War Dog Stirs. Hutchinson, 1930

HASTINGS, MACDONALD. 1909- . Series character: Montague Cork, in all titles.
Cork and the Serpent. Joseph, 1955
Cork in Bottle. Joseph, 1953; Knopf, 1954
Cork in the Doghouse. Joseph, 1957; Knopf, 1958
Cork on Location; see Cork on the Telly
Cork on the Telly. Joseph, 1966. U.S. title: Cork on Location. Walker, 1967
Cork on the Water. Joseph, 1951; Random, 1951. Also published as: Fish and Kill. Mercury, 1952 (abridged)
Fish and Kill; see Cork on the Water

HASTINGS, MICHAEL
They Killed a Spy. Harrap, 1940

HASTINGS, MICHAEL. 1937- .
The Castle of Vengeance. Macdonald, 1971
The Citadel of the Bats. Macdonald, 1962
The Coast of No Return. Methuen, 1953
Dangerous Oasis. Macdonald, 1968
Death Across the Tamagash. Macdonald, 1965
Death in Deep Green. Methuen, 1952
Desert Convoy. Macdonald, 1975
The Digger of the Pit. Methuen, 1955
Dragon Island. Macdonald, 1974
Fire Mountain. Macdonald, 1970
The Frauds. Allen, 1960
The Game. Allen, 1957
The Green Silence. Macdonald, 1966
An Hour-Glass to Eternity. Macdonald, 1959
Killer Road. Macdonald, 1972
The Killing in Black and White. Macdonald, 1969
The Man Who Came Back. Macdonald, 1957
The Nightcomers. Pan, 1973; Delacorte, 1972. (Novelization of the movie.)
The Port of Lost Cargoes. Macdonald, 1963
The Rising Sea. Macdonald, 1962
The Sands of Khali. Macdonald, 1964
The Snake and the Arrow. Macdonald, 1967
Tiger Reef. Macdonald, 1973
Twelve on Endurance. Macdonald, 1958
The Voyage of the 'San Marcos'. Macdonald, 1960

HASTINGS, PHYLLIS. 1913- .
An Act of Darkness. Hale, 1969. U.S. title: The House on Malador Street. Putnam, 1970
The Conservatory. Hale, 1973; PB, 1974
The Harlot's Daughter; see Their Flowers were Always Black
House of the Twelve Caesars. Hale, 1975
The House on Malador Street; see An Act of Darkness
-The Swan River Story. Hale, 1968
-Their Flowers were Always Black. Hale, 1967. Also published as: The Harlot's Daughter. New English Library pb, 1967
-When the Gallows is High. Hale, 1971

HASTINGS, RODERIC. Pseudonym of Graham Montague Jeffries, 1900- . Other pseudonyms: Bruce Graeme, David Graeme, qq.v.
Naked Tide. Avon, 1958. (British title?)

HASTINGS, ROSLYN. See: KATE KLEIN.
Dead Wrong. Avalon, 1963
Mind Over Murder. Avalon, 1960
Where There's a Will. Avalon, 1960

HASTINGS, W(ELLS) S(OUTHWORTH). 1879- .
The Man in the Brown Derby. Bobbs, 1911
The Professor's Mystery, with Brian Hooker. Bobbs, 1911

HASTY, JOHN EUGENE
Angel with Dirty Wings. GM, 1961; Muller pb, 1962
Man Without a Face. Dodd, 1958; Long, 1960
Some Mischief Still. GM, 1962; Muller pb, 1963

HATCH, (ALDEN) DENISON. 1935- .
The Fingered City. Eriksson, 1973; New English Library, 1975

HATCH, ERIC (STOWE). 1901-1973.
-Crockett's Woman. GM, 1951; Fawcett (London), 1953
-The Golden Woman. GM, 1952; Fawcett (London), 1959

HATCH, MARY R. P(LATT). 1848- .
The Bank Tragedy. Welch Fracker, 1890
The Berkeley Street Mystery. Page, 1928
The Missing Man. Lee & Shepard, 1893
The Strange Disappearance of Eugene Comstocks. Dillingham, 1895
The Upland Mystery. Laird, 1887

HATCH, RICHARD W(ARREN). 1898- .
Delayed Action. Rich, 1951

HATHAWAY, ALAN. See: KENNETH ROBESON.

HATHAWAY, ANN
The Man in the Monkey Suit. Godwin, 1933

HATTON, CHARLES. See: TED WILLIS, 1918- .

HATTON, JOSEPH. 1841-1907.
The Abbey Murder. Blackett, 1888; Lovell, 1888
-Against the Stream. Skeet, 1866
-The Banishment of Jessop Blythe. Hutchinson, 1895; Lippincott, 1895
-Behind a Mask. Dicks, 1886
-By Order of the Czar. Hutchinson, 1890; Lovell, 1890. A play by this title: Hutchinson, 1904
-Captured by Cannibals. Hodder, 1888; Pott, 1889
-Christopher Henrick. Bradbury, 1869; Putnam, 1869
-Clytie. Chapman, 1874; Lovell, 1876
-Cruel London. Chapman, 1878; Lovell, 1883
-The Dagger and the Cross. Hutchinson, 1897; Fenno, 1897
A Daughter of France; see When Greek Meets Greek
The Gay World. Hurst, 1877
-In Male Attire. Hutchinson, 1900
-In the Lap of Fortune. Chapman, 1873
John Needham's Double. Maxwell, 1885; Harper, 1885
-A Modern Ulysses. Chapman, 1883; U.S. Book Co., 1892
The Old House at Sandwich. Low, 1887; Appleton, 1887
The Park Lane Mystery. Arrowsmith, 1887
-The Princess Mazaroff. Hutchinson, 1891; Lovell, 1891

-Provincial Papers. Kent, 1861 ss
-The Queen of Bohemia. Beccles, 1877; Harper, 1882
The Tallants of Barton. Tinsley, 1867
-Three Recruits, and the Girls They Left Behind Them. Hurst, 1880; Harper, 1880
-Tom Chester's Sweetheart. Hutchinson, 1895
Under the Great Seal. Hutchinson, 1893; Cassell (New York), 1893
-The Valley of Poppies. Chapman, 1871
-The Vicar. Hutchinson, 1898; Lippincott, 1898
A Vision of Beauty. Hutchinson, 1902; Burt, 1902
-When Greek Meets Greek. Hutchinson, 1895; Lippincott, 1896. Also published as: A Daughter of France. Hutchinson, 1896
When Rogues Fall Out. Pearson, 1899; Lippincott, 1899

HAUCK, DARBY
The Death Cry. Shores, 1917

HAUCK, LOUISE PLATT. 1883-1943. Pseudonyms: Lane Archer, Louise Landon, qq.v.
The Mystery of Tumult Rock. Burton, 1920

HAWK, JOHN. 1893- . Series character: Mortimer Sark, in at least those marked MS.
The Family Skeleton. Skeffington, 1933
The House of Sudden Sleep. Skeffington, 1930; Mystery League, 1930
It was Locked; see The Locked Door
The Locked Door. Skeffington, 1929. U.S. title: It was Locked. Farrar, 1930
The Lone Lodge Mystery. Hodder, 1926; Doran, 1926 MS
The Mid-Ocean Tragedy. Hodder, 1927; Doran, 1927 MS
Murder at Arondale Farm. Skeffington, 1931; Farrar, 1932
The Murder of a Mystery Writer. Skeffington, 1929; Doubleday, 1929 MS
The Serpent-Headed Stick. Hodder, 1926; Doran, 1927 MS
The Titanic Hotel Mystery. Skeffington, 1928; Doubleday, 1928 MS

HAWKER, BESSY
Overlooked. Wells Gardner, 1898

HAWKES, F. A.
Adventures of a Chemist. 1930 ss

HAWKES, ROBERT. Series character: John Bolt, in all titles.
The Beauty Kill. Signet, 1975
Corsican Death. Signet, 1975
The Death List. Signet, 1974; Star, 1975
Death of a Courier. Signet, 1974
Death Song. Signet, 1975
The Delgado Killings. Signet, 1974
Kill for It. Signet, 1975
Kill the Dragon. Signet, 1974
NARC. Lancer, 1973

HAWKEY, RAYMOND and ROGER BINGHAM
Wild Card. Stein, 1974; Cape, 1974

HAWKINS, SIR ANTHONY HOPE. 1863-1933. Pseudonym: Anthony Hope, q.v.

HAWKINS, DEAN
Headsman's Holiday. Mystery House, 1946
In Memory of Murder. Doubleday, 1937
Skull Mountain. Doubleday, 1941
Walls of Silence. Doubleday, 1943

HAWKINS, EDWARD H.
Prisoners of Devil's Claw. Apollo, 1971
Wellspring. Echo House, 1969

HAWKINS, JOHN, 1910- , and WARD HAWKINS, 1912- .
Broken River. Dutton, 1944; World's Work, 1948
Death Watch. Dodd, 1958; Eyre, 1959. (2 novelets.)
Devil on his Trail. Dutton, 1944
The Floods of Fear. Dodd, 1956; Eyre, 1957. Also published as: A Girl, a Man, and a River. Popular Library, 1957
A Girl, a Man, and a River; see The Floods of Fear
If I Kill Him; see We Will Meet Again
Pilebuck. Dutton, 1943. Also published as: Secret Command. Adventure Novel Classic, 194?
Secret Command; see Pilebuck
Violent City. Dodd, 1957; Eyre, 1958
We Will Meet Again. Dial, 1940. Also published as: If I Kill Him. Handi-Books, 1945 (abridged)

HAWKINS, WARD. 1912- . See: JOHN HAWKINS, 1910- .

HAWKINS, WILLARD E. 1887- .
The Cowled Menace. Sears, 1930

HAWKSHAW. Pseudonym of John Arthur Fraser, q.v.
The Benwell Mystery. Continental, 1891
Blinkey Morgan, the Detective's Foe. Eagle, 1888
Escaped from Sing Sing. Eagle, 1888
The Fatal Chair; see Kemmler
Kemmler; or, The Fatal Chair. Eagle, 1890. Also published as: The Fatal Chair. Donohue, 189?
Shadowed from Europe. Eagle, 1889. Also published as: The Story of a Dark Crime; or, Shadowed from Europe. Donohue, 189?
The Story of a Dark Crime; see Shadowed from Europe
The Swamps of Death. Donohue, 189?
A Wayward Girl's Fate. Eagle, 1890

HAWKWOOD, ALLAN
-John Solomon, Incognito. Hurst, 1925

HAWTHORN, E. M. D. Joint pseudonym of Ethel M. Dolbey and Geoffrey May Dolbey.
Quietly She Lies. H. Hamilton, 1953; Harper, 1953

HAWTHORNE, JULIAN. 1846-1934. Series character: Inspector Byrnes = B.
An American Monte Cristo. Allen, 1893. (U.S. title?)
An American Penman. Cassell, 1887; Cassell (London), 1888 B
Another's Crime. Cassell, 1888; Cassell (London), 1889 B
-Archibald Malmaison. Funk, 1884; Bentley, 1879
-Beatrix Randolph. Osgood, 1884; Chatto, 1884
-Bressant. Appleton, 1873; King, 1873
The Confessions of a Convict. Hartrauft, 1893
-Constance, and Calbot's Rival. Appleton, 1889 ss
David Poindexter's Disappearance, and other tales. Appleton, 1888; Chatto, 1888 ss (British edition has 2 additional ss.)
-A Dream and a Forgetting. Belford, 1888; Chatto, 1888
-Dust. Houghton, 1882; Chatto, 1883
-Ellice Quentin, and other stories. Chatto, 1880 ss (U.S. title?)
A Fool of Nature. Scribner, 1896; Downey, 1896
-Fortune's Fool. Osgood, 1883; Chatto, 1883
Garth. Appleton, 1877; Bentley, 1877
-The Golden Fleece. Lippincott, 1896
The Great Bank Robbery. Cassell (New York), 1887; Cassell (London), 1888 B
John Parmelee's Curse. Cassell (New York & London), 1886
Kildhurm's Oak. Burt, 1889
-The Laughing Mill and other stories. Macmillan (London), 1879 ss (U.S. title?)
-Love is a Spirit. Harper, 1896
-Love—or a Name. Ticknor, 1885; Chatto, 1885
A Messenger from the Unknown. Collier, 1892
-Miss Cadogna. Chatto, 1885. (U.S. title?)
Mr. Dunton's Invention, and other stories; see Six Cent Sam's
-Mrs. Gainsborough's Diamonds. Appleton, 1878; Chatto, 1879
-Noble Blood. Appleton, 1885
-Pauline. U. S. Book Co., 1890
Prince Saroni's Wife. Funk, 1884; Chatto, 1882 ss
-The Professor's Sister. Belford, 1888. British title: The Spectre of the Camera; or, The Professor's Sister. Chatto, 1888
-Sebastian Strome. Appleton, 1880; Bentley, 1879
Section 558; or, The Fatal Letter. Cassell (New York & London), 1888 B
Six Cent Sam's. Price, 1893. Also published as: Mr. Dunton's Invention, and other stories. Merriam, 1896 ss
The Spectre of the Camera; see The Professor's Sister
-The Subterranean Brotherhood. McBride, 1914
A Tragic Mystery. Cassell, 1887; Cassell (London), 1888 B
The Trial of Gideon, and Countess Almara's Murder. Funk, 1886

HAWTHORNE, NATHANIEL. 1804-1864.
Dr. Grimshawe's Secret. Osgood, 1882; Longmans, 1883
Twice-Told Tales. American Stationers, 1837 ss

HAWTHORNE, VIOLET
Diary of Evil. Lancer, 1973
Identical Strangers. Ballantine, 1975

HAWTON, HECTOR. 1901- . Pseudonym: John Sylvester, q.v.
The Case of the Crazy Atom. Ward, 1948
Deadly Nightcap. Ward, 1949
Death of a Witch. Ward, 1952
Frozen Fire. Amalgamated, 1935
The Green Scorpion. Ward, 1957
Murder at H.Q. Ward, 1945
Murder by Mathematics. Ward, 1948
Murder Cave. Amalgamated, 1934
Murder Most Foul. Ward, 1946
The Nine Singing Apes. Ward, 1949
Operation Superman. Ward, 1951
Rope for the Judge. Ward, 1954
The Skeleton in the Cupboard. Ward, 1955
The Tower of Darkness. Hodder, 1949; Roy, 1951
Unnatural Causes. Ward, 1947

HAY, FRANCES. Pseudonym of Sibyl Cicely Alexandra Dick Erikson. Other pseudonym: Alexandra Dick, q.v.
Barbary Kate. Jenkins, 1964
The Lady with a Rose. Jenkins, 1960
There was no Moon. Jenkins, 1957
Traitor's Island. Jenkins, 1956

HAY, JAMES, JR. 1881-1936. Series character: Jefferson Hastings, in at least those marked JH.
The Bellamy Case. Dodd, 1925 JH
The Hidden Woman. Dodd, 1929
The Man Who Forgot. Doubleday, 1915; Curtis Brown, 1915
The Melwood Mystery. Dodd, 1920 JH
Mrs. Marden's Ordeal. Little, 1918
"No Clue!". Dodd, 1920; Jenkins, 1923 JH
That Washington Affair. Dodd, 1926; Jenkins, 1927
The Unlighted House. Dodd, 1921; Jenkins, 1922
The Winning Clue. Dodd, 1919; Jenkins, 1920

HAY, L(INDSAY) F(ITZGERALD). Series characters: Archibald Beldrum and Nigel Blair, in all titles.
It Wasn't a Nightmare. Hutchinson, 1937; Macmillan, 1937
No Mean Tartar. Hutchinson, 1938
The Terrible Hand. Hutchinson, 1937

HAY, M(AVIS) DORIEL
Death on the Cherwell. Skeffington, 1935
Murder Underground. Skeffington, 1934
The Santa Klaus Murder. Skeffington, 1936

HAY, MARIE. Pseudonym of Agnes Blanche Marie von Hindeburg, 1873-   .
The Evil Vanguard. Putnam (London), 1923

HAY, MARY CECIL. 1840?-1886.
-Among the Ruins and other stories. Harper, 1882; Griffith, 1891 ss
-The Arundel Motto. Harper, 1877; Blackett, 1877
-Back to the Old Home. Harper, 1878
-Bid Me Discourse. Harper, 1883; Hurst, 1883 ss
-Brenda Yorke, and other tales. Munro, 1879; Hurst, 1875
-A Dark Inheritance. Harper, 1878
-Dorothy's Venture. Harper, 1882; Hurst, 1882
-For Her Dear Sake. Harper, 1880; Hurst, 1880
Hidden Perils. Harper, 1876; Hurst, 1874
-Into the Shade, and other stories. Harper, 1881 ss
-Lester's Secret. Harper, 1886; Hurst, 1885
Missing! and other tales. Harper, 1880; Hurst, 1881 ss
-Nora's Love Test. Harper, 1877; Hurst, 1876
Old Myddelton's Money. Harper, 1875; Hurst, 1874
-A Shadow on the Threshold. Harper, 1878
-The Sorrow of a Secret. Harper, 1879
-The Squire's Legacy. Harper, 1876; Hurst, 1875
Under the Will, and other tales. Hurst, 1878. (U.S. title?) ss
-Victor and Vanquished. Harper, 1876; Hurst, 1874
-A Wicked Girl. Harper, 1886; Hurst, 1886 ss

HAY, W(ILLIAM) LAING. 1892-   .
Who Cut the Colonel's Throat? Longmans (London), 1931

HAY, WILLIAM (GOSSE). 1875-1945.
The Escape of the Notorious Sir William Heans, and The Mystery of Mr. Daunt. Allen & Unwin, 1918
The Mystery of Alfred Doubt. Allen & Unwin, 1937

HAYCOX, ERNEST. 1899-1950.
Murder on the Frontier. Little, 1952. (Western murder ss.)

HAYES, JOSEPH (ARNOLD). 1918-   .
Calculated Risk. French (New York), 1963. (Play based on another play, Any Other Business, by George Ross and Campbell Singer.)
The Deep End. Viking, 1967; Allen, 1967
The Desperate Hours. Random, 1954; Deutsch, 1954. A play: Random, 1955; revised edition: French (New York & London), 1956
Don't Go Away Mad. Random, 1962; Allen, 1964
The Hours After Midnight. Random, 1958; Deutsch, 1959
Like Any Other Fugitive. Dial, 1971; Deutsch, 1972
The Long Dark Night. Putnam, 1974; Deutsch, 1974
The Third Day. McGraw, 1964; Allen, 1965

HAYES, LEAL
Dark Legend. Belmont, 1973
Harlequin House. Ace, 1967

HAYES, MILTON
-Bad Men Make Good Wives. Hurst, 1930
Cling of the Clay. Hodder, 1925; Adelphi, 1925

HAYES, RALPH. Series characters: Agent of Cominsec = A; Check Force = CF; John Yard (The Hunter) = JY.
The Bloody Monday Conspiracy. Belmont, 1974 A
Clouds of War. Manor, 1975 CF
The Deadly Prey. Leisure, 1975 JY
The Death Makers. Belmont, 1975 A
The Doomsday Conspiracy. Belmont, 1974 A
The Hellfire Conspiracy. Belmont, 1974 A
Night of the Jackals. Leisure, 1975 JY
The Nightmare Conspiracy. Belmont, 1974 A
Nightmare Island. Manor, 1975 CF
100 Megaton Kill. Manor, 1975 CF
The Peking Plot. Manor, 1975 CF
Scavenger Kill. Leisure, 1975 JY
A Taste of Blood. Leisure, 1975 JY
Track of the Beast. Leisure, 1975 JY
The Turkish Mafia Conspiracy. Belmont, 1974 A

HAYES, ROY
The Hungarian Game. Simon, 1973; Secker, 1973

HAYES, WILLIAM EDWARD. 1897-   . Series character: Arthur Halstead, in all titles.
Before the Cock Crowed. Doubleday, 1937
Black Chronicle. Doubleday, 1938
The Black Doll. Doubleday, 1936

HAYFORD, EUGENE. Pseudonym of Richard Hill Wilkinson, 1904-   , q.v. Other pseudonyms: E. Harrison Ott, Paul Pray, qq.v.
One Horrible Night. Drama Guild, 1939. (3-act play.)

HAYLES, KENNETH
The Death-Masque. Hale, 1962; Roy, 1963
The Long Reach. Hale, 1956
The Purple Sheba. Hale, 1959
Trader Brook. Hale, 1957
Volcano. Hale, 1958

HAYNES, ANNIE.   -1929. Series characters: Inspector Furnival, in at least those marked F; Inspector Stoddart, in at least those marked S.
The Abbey Court Murder. Bodley Head, 1923
The Blue Diamond. Bodley Head, 1925
The Bungalow Mystery. Bodley Head, 1923
The Crime at Tattenham Corner. Bodley Head, 1929 S
The Crow's Inn Tragedy. Bodley Head, 1927; Dodd, 1927 F
The Crystal Beads Murder. Bodley Head, 1930 S
The House in Charlton Crescent. Bodley Head, 1926 F
The Man with the Dark Beard. Bodley Head, 1928
The Master of the Priory. Bodley Head, 1927
The Secret of Greylands. Bodley Head, 1924; Watt, 1925
Who Killed Charmian Karslake? Bodley Head, 1929; Dodd, 1930 S
The Witness on the Roof. Bodley Head, 1925

HAYS, H(OFFMAN) R(EYNOLDS). 1904-   .
Lie Down in Darkness. Reynal, 1944; Hale, 1948
Stranger on the Highway. Little, 1943; Hale, 1947

HAYS, LEE
Harry-O. Popular Library, 1975. (Novelization of the TV series.)
Nakia. Popular Library, 1974. (Novelization of the TV series.)

HAYS, PETER. 1927-   . Pseudonym: Ian Jefferies, q.v.

HAYS, SUE BROWN
Go Down, Death. Scribner, 1946; Hammond, 1948

HAYTHORNE, JOHN
None of Us Cared for Kate. Cassell, 1968; Dutton, 1968

HAYWARD, C. F. R.
The Mentons: Was It a Crime? Donnelley, 1887

HAYWARD, RICHARD
The Soft Arms of Death. GM, 1955; Fawcett (London), 1955
Trapped. GM, 1952

HAYWARD, WILLIAM STEPHENS. See also: ANONYMOUS (The Experiences of a Lady Detective).
Eulalie; or, The Red and White Roses. Clarke, 1874
-Hunted to Death; or, Life in Two Hemispheres. (London), 1862
John Hazel's Vengeance. Maxwell, 1880 ss
Love Against the World. Clarke, 1875
The Stolen Will. Maxwell, 1881 ss

HAZARD, FORRESTER. Pseudonym of Alexander (Hazard) Williams, 1894-1952, q.v.
The Hex Murder. Lippincott, 1936

HAZARD, LAURENCE
The Andean Murders. Barker, 1960

HAZELTINE, HORACE. Pseudonym of Charles Stokes Wayne, 1858-   .
Sable Lorcha. McClurg, 1912

HAZZARD, MARY. Pseudonym: Olivia Dwight, q.v.

HEAD, ANN. Pseudonym of Anne Christensen Morse, 1915- .
Always in August. Doubleday, 1961; Hurst, 1963
Everybody Adored Cara. Doubleday, 1963; Hurst, 1964

HEAD, HELEN SMITH
Death Below Zero. Comet, 1954

HEAD, MATTHEW. Pseudonym of John Edwin Canaday, 1907- . Series character: Dr. Mary Finney = MF.
The Accomplice. Simon, 1947
Another Man's Life. Simon, 1953
The Cabinda Affair. Simon, 1949; Heinemann, 1950 MF
The Congo Venus. Simon, 1950; Garland (London), 1976 MF
The Devil in the Bush. Simon, 1945 MF
Murder at the Flea Club. Simon, 1955; Heinemann, 1957 MF
The Smell of Money. Simon, 1943

HEADLAM, CUTHBERT (MORLEY). 1876- .
Knight Reluctant. Murray, 1934

HEALD, TIM(OTHY VILLIERS). 1944- .
Series character: Simon Bognor, in all titles.
Blue Blood will Out. Hutchinson, 1974; Stein, 1974
Deadline. Hutchinson, 1975; Stein, 1975
Unbecoming Habits. Hutchinson, 1973; Stein, 1973

HEALEY, BEN(JAMIN JAMES). 1908- .
Pseudonyms: Jeremy Sturrock, q.v., J. G. Jeffreys. Series characters: Harcourt d'Espinal, in at least those marked HE; Paul Hedley, in at least those marked PH.
Death in Three Masks. Hale, 1967. U.S. title: The Terrible Pictures. Harper, 1967 PH
The Horstmann Inheritance. Hale, 1975
The Millstone Men. Hale, 1966
Murder Without Crime. Hale, 1968
The Red Head Herring. Hale, 1969
The Stone Baby. Hale, 1974; Lippincott, 1973 HE
The Terrible Pictures; see Death in Three Masks
The Trouble with Penelope. Hale, 1972
The Vespucci Papers. Hale, 1972; Lippincott, 1972 HE
Waiting for a Tiger. Hale, 1965; Harper, 1965 PH

HEALEY, EVELYN. See also: ANNE HOCKING.
The Braydon Mystery. Long, 1963
Death in Cold Storage. Long, 1965
Let X Equal Murder. Long, 1961

HEALY, EUGENE P. Series character: Paul Craine, in both titles.
Craine's First Case. Holt, 1938; Hale, 1939
Mr. Sandeman Loses His Life. Holt, 1940

HEARD, H(ENRY) F(ITZGERALD). 1889-1971.
Series character: Mr. Mycroft = M.
The Great Fog and other weird tales. Vanguard, 1944; Cassell, 1947 ss
Murder by Reflection. Vanguard, 1942; Cassell, 1945
The Notched Hairpin. Vanguard, 1949; Cassell, 1951 M
Reply Paid. Vanguard, 1942 M
A Taste for Honey. Vanguard, 1941; Cassell, 1942. Also published as: A Taste for Murder. Avon, 1955 M
A Taste for Murder; see A Taste for Honey

HEARD, NATHAN C(LIFF). 1936- .
-To Reach a Dream. Dial, 1972

HEARNDEN, BERYL. Joint pseudonym with Eva Balfour: Hearnden Balfour, q.v.

HEARNE, JOHN. Joint pseudonym with Morris Cargill, 1914- : John Morris, q.v.

HEATH, CATHERINE
-Stone Walls. Cape, 1973
The Vulture. Cape, 1974

HEATH, ELIZABETH ALDEN. Pseudonym of Edith Austin Holton, 1881- .
The Affair at Tideways. Crowell, 1932

HEATH, ERIC. Series character: Wade Anthony = WA.
Death Takes a Dive. Hillman-Curl, 1938
Murder in the Museum. Hillman-Curl, 1939
Murder of a Mystery Writer. Arcadia, 1955 WA
The Murder Pool. Arcadia, 1954 WA

HEATH, MONICA. Pseudonym of Arlene J. Fitzgerald.
Calderwood. Signet, 1975
Chateau of Shadows. Signet, 1973
Clerycastle. Signet, 1969
Dunleary. Signet, 1967
Duncraig. Signet, 1974
Falconlough. Signet, 1966
The Legend of Crownpoint. Signet, 1974
Mistress of Ravenstone. Signet, 1973
Return to Clerycastle. Signet, 1970
The Secret Citadel. Signet, 1975
The Secret of the Vineyard. Signet, 1970
Secrets can be Fatal. Signet, 1967
Woman in Black. Signet, 1974

HEATH, THOMAS EDWARD
Tales in Prose and Verse. King, 1906 ss, at least one criminous

HEATH, W(ILLIAM) L(EDBETTER). 1924- .
Blood on the River. Long, 1961
The Good Old Boys. McCall, 1971
Ill Wind. Harper, 1957; H. Hamilton, 1957
Violent Saturday. Harper, 1955; H. Hamilton, 1955

HEATTER, BASIL. 1918- .
Act of Violence. Lion, 1954
Any Man's Girl. GM, 1961; Muller pb, 1962
-The Better Part of Valor. Doubleday, 1964
Harry and the Bikini Bandits. GM, 1970
The Mutilators. GM, 1962; Muller pb, 1962
The Naked Island. Trident, 1968; Hale, 1970
-Sailor's Luck. Lion, 1953
The Scarred Man. GM, 1953
-The Trouble with Love. GM, 196?; Muller pb, 1962
Virgin Cay. GM, 1963; Muller pb, 1964

HEAVEN, CONSTANCE. Pseudonym of Constance Fecher, 1911- .
Castle of Eagles. Heinemann, 1974; Coward, 1974

HEBACH, LOUISE
The Murder of Bishop Conrad. Fortuny's, 1940

HEBDEN, MARK. Pseudonym of John Harris, 1916- , q.v. Series character: Colonel Mostyn, in at least those marked M.
The Dark Side of the Island. Joseph, 1973; Harcourt, 1973
The Errant Knights. Harrap, 1968; Harcourt, 1968
The Eyewitness. Harrap, 1966; Harcourt, 1967
Grave Journey; see Portrait in a Dusty Frame
A Killer for the Chairman. Joseph, 1972; Harcourt, 1972
Mask of Violence. Joseph, 1971; Harcourt, 1970 M
Portrait in a Dusty Frame. Harrap, 1969. U.S. title: Grave Journey. Harcourt, 1970
A Pride of Dolphins. Joseph, 1974; Harcourt, 1974 M
What Changed Charley Farthing. Harrap, 1965

HEBERDEN, M(ARY) V(IOLET). 1906- .
Pseudonym: Charles L. Leonard, q.v. Series characters: Desmond Shannon = DS; Rick Vanner = RV.
Aces, Eights, and Murder. Doubleday, 1941 DS
The Case of the Eight Brothers. Doubleday, 1948; Cherry Tree, 1949 DS
Death on the Door Mat. Doubleday, 1939 DS
Drinks on the Victim. Doubleday, 1947 DS
Engaged to Murder. Doubleday, 1949 RV
Exit This Way. Doubleday, 1950; Hale, 1954. Also published as: You'll Fry Tomorrow. Bestseller, 1955 DS
Fugitive from Murder. Doubleday, 1940 DS
Ghosts Can't Kill; see That's the Spirit
The Lobster Pick Murder. Doubleday, 1941 DS
Murder Cancels All Debts. Doubleday, 1946; Edwards, 1947 RV
Murder Follows Desmond Shannon. Doubleday, 1942; Hale, 1949 DS
Murder Goes Astray. Doubleday, 1943; Hale, 1951 DS
Murder Makes a Racket. Doubleday, 1942 DS
Murder of a Stuffed Shirt. Doubleday, 1944 DS
Murder Unlimited. Doubleday, 1953; Hale, 1954 DS
The Sleeping Witness. Doubleday, 1951; Hale, 1955
Subscription to Murder. Doubleday, 1940 DS
That's the Spirit. Doubleday, 1950. British title: Ghosts Can't Kill. Clerke, 1951 DS
They Can't All Be Guilty. Doubleday, 1947 DS
To What Dread End. Doubleday, 1944; Hale, 1952
Tragic Target. Doubleday, 1952; Hale, 1953 DS
Vicious Pattern. Doubleday, 1945; Hale, 1952 DS
You'll Fry Tomorrow; see Exit This Way

HECHT, BEN. 1893-1964.
Actor's Blood. Covici, 1936 ss
Broken Necks and other stories. Haldeman-Julius, 1924. Expanded edition: Covici, 1926 ss
The Champion from Far Away. Covici, 1931 ss
The Collected Stories of Ben Hecht. Crown, 1945; Hammond, 1950. A selection of 8 largely criminous tales from this collection published as: Concerning a Woman of Sin and other stories. Avon, 1947 ss
Concerning a Woman of Sin and other stories; see The Collected Stories of Ben Hecht

Count Bruga. Boni, 1926
The Florentine Dagger. Boni, 1923; Heinemann, 1924
Hollywood Mystery!; see I Hate Actors!
I Hate Actors! Crown, 1944. Also published as: Hollywood Mystery! Bart, 1946
The Sensualists. Messner, 1959; Blond, 1960
A Thousand and One Afternoons in Chicago. Covici, 1922 ss
1001 Afternoons in New York. Viking, 1941 ss

HECKSTALL-SMITH, ANTHONY. 1904- .
The Man with Yellow Shoes. Wingate, 1957; Roy, 1958
Murder on the Brain. Wingate, 1958; Roy, 1958
Where There are Vultures. Wingate, 1958; Roy, 1959

HECTOR, ANNIE FRENCH. 1825-1902. Pseudonym: Mrs. Alexander, q.v.

HECTOR, BARBARA
-As the Stars Fade. Swan, 1947
-No Through Road. Swan, 1942
The Victim's Niece. Swan, 1946

HEDDLE, ETHEL F(ORSTER)
-A Mystery of St. Rule's. Blackie, 1902

HEDGES, JOSEPH. Pseudonym of Terry Harknett, 1936- , q.v. Other pseudonyms: William Pine, Thomas H. Stone, William Terry, qq.v. Series character: John Stark, in all titles.
Arms for Oblivion. Sphere, 1973; Pyramid, 1975
The Chinese Coffin. Sphere, 1975; Pyramid, 1975
Corpse on Ice. Sphere, 1975; Pyramid, 1975
Funeral Rites. Sphere, 1973; Pyramid, 1974
The Gold Plated Hearse. Sphere, 1974; Pyramid, 1975
Mexican Mourning. Sphere, 1975
The Mile Deep Grave. Sphere, 1975
Rainbow Coloured Shroud. Sphere, 1974; Pyramid, 1975
The Stainless Steel Wreath. Sphere, 1975

HEDGES, SID(NEY) G(EORGE). 1897- .
The Channel Tunnel Mystery. Jenkins, 1931
Diamond Duel. Jenkins, 1935
The Malta Mystery. Jenkins, 1932
Mediterranean Mystery. Mellifont, 1940
Plague Panic. Jenkins, 1934
The Venetian Swimmer Mystery. Jenkins, 1933
The Weir Boyd Mystery. Jenkins, 1930

HEDLEY, FRANK. Pseudonym of C(larence) Hedley Barker, q.v. Other pseudonym: Seafarer, q.v.
Cavalier of Crime. Harrap, 1937; Lippincott, 1937

HEED, RUFUS
Ghosts Never Die. Vantage, 1954

HEFFERNAN, DEAN
Murder at Sunset Gables. Duffield, 1932

HEGEDUS, ADAM. 1910- . Pseudonym: Rodney Garland, q.v.

HEGGY, JOE P.
The Grab. Hamilton Stafford, 1953
Make It Nylons. Hamilton Stafford, 1953
Poison Ivy. Hamilton Stafford, 1953
The Trouble with Women. Hamilton Stafford, 1954

HEGNER, WILLIAM
-The Adopters. PB, 1974

HEILBRUN, CAROLYN GOLD. 1926- . Pseudonym: Amanda Cross, q.v.

HEIMER, MEL(VIN LEIGHTON). 1915-1971.
The Empty Man. McCall, 1971

HEINECKE, HAZEL JOAN
And the Winds Blew. Comet, 1957

HEITNER, IRIS. Pseudonym: Robert James, q.v.

HELD, PETER. Pseudonym of John Holbrook Vance, 1916- , q.v. Byline also: Jack Vance, q.v. Other pseudonym: Alan Wade, q.v.
Take My Face. Mystery House, 1957

HELEY, VERONICA
Scream for Sarah. Hale, 1975
Sue for Mercy. Hale, 1974

HELLER, FRANK. Pseudonym of Martin Gunnar Serner, 1886-1947. Series character: Mr. Collin = C.
The Chinese Coats; see The Emperor's Old Clothes
The Emperor's Old Clothes. Crowell, 1923. British title: The Chinese Coats. Jarrolds, 1924
The Grand Duke's Finances. Crowell, 1924; Jarrolds, 1925
Lead Me into Temptation. Crowell, 1927
The London Adventures of Mr. Collin. Crowell, 1924. British title: The Perilous Transactions of Mr. Collin. Lane, 1924 ss C
The Marriage of Yussuf Khan. Crowell, 1923; Hutchinson, 1924
Mr. Collin is Ruined. Crowell, 1925 C
The Perilous Transactions of Mr. Collin; see The London Adventures of Mr. Collin
The Strange Adventures of Mr. Collin. Crowell, 1926 ss C
The Thousand and Second Night. Crowell, 1925; Williams & Norgate, 1926 ss

HELLER, LARRY. Pseudonym of Lorenz Heller, q.v. Other pseudonyms: Larry Holden, Frederick Lorenz, qq.v.
Body of the Crime. Pyramid, 1962
I Get What I Want. Popular Library, 1956

HELLER, LORENZ. Pseudonyms: Larry Heller, Larry Holden, Frederick Lorenz, qq.v.
Murder in Makeup. Messner, 1937

HELLER, MIKE
So I'm a Heel. GM, 1957; Red Seal, 1958

HELLINGER, MARK. 1903-1947.
The Ten Million. Farrar, 1934; Bodley Head, 1935 ss, some criminous

HELM, JEANETTE
The House of the Purple Stairs. Jenkins, 1925
Without Clues. Brentano's (London), 1924; Boni, 1923

HELM, PETER (JAMES). 1916- . Series character: Martin Ridgway, in all titles.
Dead Men's Fingers. Long, 1960. U.S. title: A Walk into Murder. Scribner, 1960
Death has a Thousand Entrances. Long, 1962
The Man with No Bones. Long, 1966
A Walk into Murder; see Dead Men's Fingers

HELMORE, THOMAS
Affair at Quala. Simon, 1964; Cape, 1965

HELSETH, HENRY EDWARD. 1912- .
The Brothers Brannigan. Signet, 1961. (Novelization of the TV series.)
The Chair for Martin Rome. Dodd, 1947; Laurie, 1952
The Devil's Behind You. Harper, 1942
This Man Dawson. Signet, 1962. (Novelization of the TV series.)
The Yellow Angels. Harper, 1940

HELVICK, JAMES. Pseudonym of Francis Claud Cockburn, 1904- .
Beat the Devil. Boardman, 1953; Lippincott, 1951
The Horses. McGibbon, 1961; Walker, 1963

HELWIG, DAVID. 1938- .
The Day Before Tomorrow. Oberon, 1971. Also published as: Message from a Spy. PaperJacks, 1975

HELY, ELIZABETH. Pseudonym of Elizabeth Hely Younger. Series character: Antoine Cirret, in at least those marked AC.
Dominant Third. Heinemann, 1959. U.S. title: I'll be Judge, I'll be Jury. Scribner, 1959 AC
I'll be Judge, I'll be Jury; see Dominant Third
The Long Shot. Heinemann, 1963
A Mark of Displeasure. Heinemann, 1961; Scribner, 1960 AC
Package Deal. Hale, 1965

HEMING, BRACEBRIDGE
Where Angels Fear... Hamilton, 1938

HEMINGWAY, JOAN, 1951- , and PAUL BONNECARRERE, 1925?-1977.
Rosebud. Ellis, 1974; Morrow, 1974. (Translation of Rosebud. Paris, 1973.)

HEMINGWAY, KENNETH
Murder Flight. Quality, 1954

HEMINGWAY, R(ICHARD) D('OYLY), 1878- , and HENRY DE HALSALLE, 1872- , q.v.
Three Gentlemen from New Caledonia. Paul, 1915; Putnam, 1915

HEMPSTEAD, JUNIUS L(ACKLAND). 1842- .
Thompson the Detective. Abbey, 1902

HEMYNG, (SAMUEL) BRACEBRIDGE. 1841-1901.
-The Bondage of Brandon. Maxwell, 1881
A Brighton Mystery; or, The Disappearance of Captain Jarvice. Diprose, 1894
Called to the Bar. Clarke, 1867
Contesting the County, and other tales. Clarke, 1868
Curious Crimes. Clarke, 1871 ss
The Danger Signal and other tales. Ward, 1868 ss
-Dead Heat; or, Neck in Neck. Clarke, 1887
-The Demon Jockey; or, A Run of Luck. Clarke, 1887
-The Favourite Scratched; or, The Spider and the Fly. Clarke, 1869
-Gaspar Trenchard. Maxwell, 1864
-Held in Thrall. Clarke, 1869
In the Force; or, Revelations of a Private Policeman. Maxwell, 1880 ss

On the Line and Danger Signal. Diprose, 1881 ss, some criminous
-On the Rank; or, The Adventures of a Cabman. Maxwell, 1880 ss
-On the Road: Tales Told by a Commercial Traveler. Routledge, 1868 ss
-The Orange Girl. Maxwell, 1865
-River Secrets. Maxwell, 1880 ss
-Secrets of the Dead-Letter Office. Clarke, 1866 ss
Secrets of the River. Berger, 1870 ss
Secrets of the Turf; or, How I Won the Derby. Clarke, 1868 ss
-The Sharks of Society. Diprose, 1888
-The Stockbroker's Wife, and other sensational tales. Maxwell, 1885 ss
-Strange Journeys. Maxwell, 1880 ss
-Telegraph Secrets. Clarke, 1866 ss
-The Toilers of the Thames. Clarke, 1870
-Too Sharp by Half; or, The Man Who Made Millions. Clarke, 1871
Tried for his Life; or, A Mysterious Case and other stories. Diprose, 1885 ss
The Women of London. Vickers, 1884
The Women of Paris. Vicker, 1884

HENDERSON, CECIL
Too Many Clues. Modern, 193?

HENDERSON, DONALD (LANDELS). 1905- .
Goodbye to Murder. Constable, 1946
Mr. Bowling Buys a Newspaper. Constable, 1943; Random, 1944
Murderer at Large. Paul, 1936
Procession—to Prison. Paul, 1937
The Trial of Lizzie Borden and other radio plays. Hurst, 1946

HENDERSON, JAMES. 1934- .
Copperhead. Knopf, 1971; Collins, 1972

HENDERSON, JAMES LEAL. 1913- . Pseudonym: Jay L. Currier, q.v.
-Whirlpool. Prentice-Hall, 1947

HENDERSON, LAURENCE. 1928- . Series character: Det. Sgt. Arthur Milton, in at least those marked AM.
Cage Until Tame. Harrap, 1972; St. Martin's, 1972 AM
Sitting Target. Harrap, 1970; St. Martin's, 1972 AM
With Intent. Harrap, 1968; St. Martin's, 1971

HENDERSON, WILLIAM
Clues; or, Leaves from a Chief Constable's Note Book. Oliphant, 1889; White and Allen, 1890 ss
Detective Stories. Heywood, 1891 ss

HENDRYX, JAMES B(EARDSLEY). 1880- .
These are largely if not completely Northwest, Northwest Mounted Police, or frontier stories. Series characters: Corporal Downey, in at least those marked D; Connie Morgan, in at least those marked CM.
At the Foot of the Rainbow. Putnam, 1924
Badmen on Halfaday Creek. Doubleday, 1950; Hammond, 1956 ss
Beyond the Outposts. Hutchinson, 1924. (U.S. title?)
Black John of Halfaday Creek. Doubleday, 1939; Jarrolds, 1939 ss
Blood of the North. Doubleday, 1938; Jarrolds, 1938
Blood on the Yukon Trail. Doubleday, 1930 D
Connie Morgan Hits the Trail. Doubleday, 1929 CM
Connie Morgan in Alaska. Putnam, 1916; Jarrolds, 1919 CM
Connie Morgan in Barren Lands. Jarrolds, 1934. (U.S. title?) CM
Connie Morgan in the Arctic. Putnam, 1936; Jarrolds, 1936 CM
Connie Morgan in the Cattle Country. Putnam, 1923; Jarrolds, 1927 CM
Connie Morgan in the Fur Country. Putnam, 1921; Jarrolds, 1928 CM
Connie Morgan in the Lumber Camps. Putnam, 1919; Jarrolds, 1928 CM
Connie Morgan, Prospector. Jarrolds, 1930. (U.S. title?) CM
Connie Morgan with the Forest Rangers. Putnam, 1925; Jarrolds, 1926 CM
Connie Morgan with the Mounted. Putnam, 1918; Jarrolds, 1924 CM
Corporal Downey Takes the Trail. Doubleday, 1931; Jarrolds, 1932 D
Courage of the North. Doubleday, 1946; Hammond, 1954
The Czar of Halfaday Creek. Doubleday, 1940; Hammond, 1955 ss
Death Heads North; see Grubstake Gold
Devil's Gold. Jarrolds, 1940. (U.S. title?) D
Downey of the Mounted. Putnam, 1926; Hutchinson, 1926 D
Edge of Beyond. Doubleday, 1939
Frozen Inlet Post. Doubleday, 1927; Hutchinson, 1927
Gambler's Choice. Carlton, 1941; Museum, 1943
Gold and Guns on Halfaday Creek. Carlton, 1942; Hale, 1953 ss
Gold—and the Mounted. Doubleday, 1928; Hutchinson, 1928
The Gold Girl. Putnam, 1920
Gold is Where You Find It. Doubleday, 1953; Hammond, 1957
Good Men and Bad. Doubleday, 1954; Hammond, 1958
Grubstake Gold. Doubleday, 1936; Jarrolds, 1937. Also published as: Death Heads North. Adventure Novel Classic, 194?
The Gun-Brand. Putnam, 1917; Jarrolds, 1921
Hard Rock Man. Carlton, 1940; Hale, 1941
Intrigue on Halfaday Creek. Doubleday, 1953 ss
It Happened on Halfaday Creek. Doubleday, 1944 ss
Justice on Halfaday Creek. Doubleday, 1949; Museum, 1954 ss
Law and Order on Halfaday Creek. Carlton, 1941; Hale, 1954 ss
Man of the North. Doubleday, 1929; Hutchinson, 1930
Murder in the Outlands. Doubleday, 1949; Museum, 1953
Murder on Halfaday Creek. Doubleday, 1951 ss
New Rivers Calling. Doubleday, 1943; Hale, 1952
North. Putnam, 1923
Oak and Iron. Putnam, 1925; Hutchinson, 1925
On the Rim of the Arctic. Doubleday, 1948; Museum, 1952
Outlaws of Halfaday Creek. Doubleday, 1935; Jarrolds, 1935 ss
Prairie Flowers. Putnam, 1920; Jarrolds, 1923
The Promise. Putnam, 1915
Raw Gold. Doubleday, 1933; Jarrolds, 1933
The Saga of Halfaday Creek. Doubleday, 1947; Hammond, 1955 ss
Skullduggery on Halfaday Creek. Doubleday, 1946; Hammond, 1953 ss
Snowdrift. Putnam, 1922
Sourdough Gold. Doubleday, 1952; Hammond, 1957
The Stampeders. Doubleday, 1951; Hammond, 1956
Strange Doings on Halfaday Creek. Doubleday, 1943; Hale, 1952 ss
Terror on Halfaday Creek. Consul, 1963. (U.S. title?)
The Texan. Putnam, 1918; Jarrolds, 1922
The Way of the North. Doubleday, 1945; Edwards, 1946
Without Gloves. Putnam, 1924; Hutchinson, 1924
The Yukon Kid. Doubleday, 1934; Jarrolds, 1934 D

HENISSART, PAUL (HENRI). 1923- .
Narrow Exit. Simon, 1973; Hutchinson, 1974

HENLE, THEDA O. 1918- .
Death Files for Congress. Vanguard, 1971

HENNEKER, PHILIP
And One Must Die. Hale, 1965
Don't be Afraid of the Dark. Hale, 1965
Too Late for Tears. Hale, 1966

HENNESSEY, (JOHN) DAVID. 1847- .
-An Australian Bush Track. Low, 1896. Also published as: The Bush Track. Hodder, 1913
The Bush Track; see An Australian Bush Track
The Caves of Shend. Hodder, 1915
-Cords of Vanity. Hodder, 1920
-The Dis-Honourable. Low, 1896
-A Lost Identity. Warne, 1899
-The Outlaw. Hodder, 1913
-The Tail of Gold. Hodder, 1914
-Wynnum. Low, 1896

HENNISSART, MARTHA. Joint pseudonyms with Mary J. Latsis: R. B. Dominic, Emma Lathen, qq.v.

HENOT, GEORGES. 1848-1918. Pseudonym: Georges Ohnet, q.v.

HENRIQUEZ, RICHARD A.
Four Way Proof. Phoenix, 1951

HENRY, CHARLES. Pseudonym of Henry Farrell, q.v.
The Hostage. Random, 1959. British title: Moving Day. Secker, 1960. Also published as: Ride with Terror, as by Henry Farrell. New English Library, 1972

HENRY, CLAY. Series character: Matt Archer, in at least those marked MA.
Devils Burn Too. Boardman, 1963
Not Dead Enough. Boardman, 1965
Nude on the Rocks. Boardman, 1965 MA
The Third Twin. Boardman, 1966
Welcome Home, Lily Glow. Boardman, 1960 MA

HENRY, JACK
Flannelfoot, Phantom Crook. Hutchinson, 1949
Lucifer and Partner. Modern, 1950

HENRY, MARGARET
-The Householders. Cassell, 1964
Unlucky Dip. Cassell, 1960

HENRY, MICHAEL
Murder in the Old Jail. Hamilton, 1938

HENRY. O. Pseudonym of William Sydney Porter, 1862-1910. Some criminous tales are scattered through the short story collections listed below.
Cabbages and Kings. McClure, 1904
Cops and Robbers. Bestseller, 1948. (A collection of criminous ss taken from the other collections.)

H

Henry, O.
The Four Million. McClure, 1906; Hodder, 1916
The Gentle Grafter. McClure, 1908
Heart of the West. McClure, 1907; Nash, 1912
Roads of Destiny. Doubleday, 1909
Rolling Stones. Doubleday, 1912; Hodder, 1916
Sixes and Sevens. Doubleday, 1911; Hodder, 1916
Strictly Business. Doubleday, 1910
The Trimmed Lamp. McClure, 1907; Hodder, 1915
The Voice of the City. McClure, 1908; Hodder, 1916
Waifs and Strays. Doubleday, 1917; Hodder, 1920
Whirligigs. Doubleday, 1910; Hodder, 1916

HENRY, VERA
Mystery of Cedar Valley. Bouregy, 1964

HENSHAW, (WILLIAM) KEITH
Kath. Collins, 1964
Sea Vermin. Collins, 1963

HENSHAW, NANCY ELY
Worse and More of It. Vantage, 1959

HENSLEY, JOE L. [JOSEPH L. HENSLEY]. 1926- . Series character: Donald Robak = DR.
The Color of Hate. Ace, 1960
Deliver Us to Evil. Doubleday, 1971 DR
Legislative Body. Doubleday, 1972 DR
The Poison Summer. Doubleday, 1974
Song of Corpus Juris. Doubleday, 1974 DR

HENTY, G(EORGE) A(LFRED). 1832-1902.
-Colonel Thorndyke's Secret. Chatto, 1898; Mershon, 1901
-Condemned as a Nihilist. Blackie, 1893; Scribner, 1892
-The Curse of Carne's Hold. Blackett, 1889; Lovell, 1889
-Dorothy's Double. Chatto, 1894; Rand, 1895
-A Hidden Foe. Low, 1891; U.S. Book Co., 1890
-The Lost Heir. Bowden, 1899; New Amsterdam, 1900
-A Search for a Secret. Tinsley, 1867

HEPPELL, MARY. Pseudonym: Marguerite Clare, q.v.

HEPWORTH, GEORGE H(UGHES). 1833-1902.
The Queerest Man Alive, and other stories. Fenno, 1897 ss, some criminous

HERBER, WILLIAM. Series character: Jimmy Rehm = JR.
The Almost Dead. Lippincott, 1957; Foulsham, 1958
Death Paints a Portrait. Lippincott, 1958; Foulsham, 1959
King-Sized Murder. Lippincott, 1954; Foulsham, 1955. Also published as: Some Die Slow. Bantam, 1956 JR
Live Bait for Murder. Lippincott, 1955; Foulsham, 1956 JR
Some Die Slow; see King-Sized Murder

HERBERT, A(LAN) P(ATRICK). 1890- .
The House by the River. Methuen, 1920; Knopf, 1921

HERBERT, BENSON. 1912- .
Murder by Telephone. Newcoll, 1945
The Parcel Post Murder. Cole, 1943
-Strange Romance. Cole, 1943
They Don't Always Hang Murderers. Cole, 1942

HERBERT, CYRIL
The Clue of the Six Kissing Girls. Mitre, 1946
How Dark are the Dunes? Mitre, 1946
How Slow the Snooth. Mitre, 1946
Justice Peeps over the Handkerchief. Mitre, 1946
The Man Who was Ten Years Late for Breakfast. Mitre, 1946
Midnight Minute. Mitre, 1946

HERBERT, FRANK (PATRICK). 1920- .
The Dragon in the Sea. Doubleday, 1956; Gollancz, 1960

HERBRAND, JAN(ICE M.). 1931- .
The Dangerous House. Warner, 1975

HERD, TRAVIS
Death of a Convict. Hale, 1960
Fast Shuffle. Hale, 1961
Guilty Party. Hale, 1961
Snake's Picnic. Hale, 1960

HERE, R. A.
Case of Doctor Tracey. Cranley, 1934

HERFORD, OLIVER. 1863- . See: CLEVELAND MOFFETT, 1863-1926.

HERING, HENRY A(UGUSTUS). 1864- .
The Burglars' Club. Cassell, 1906; Dodge, 1906. Revised edition, with 6 new stories: Cassell, 1910 ss

HERLIN, HANS. 1925- .
Friends. Heinemann, 1975. U.S. title: Commemorations. St. Martin's, 1975. (Translation of Freunde. Munich, 1974.)

HERMAN, HENRY. 1832-1894. See also: David Christie Murray, 1847-1907.
The Crime of a Christmas Toy. Ward, 1893
A Dead Man's Story, and other tales. Warne, 1894 ss
The Great Becklswaithe Mystery. Simpkin, 1896
Hearts of Gold and Hearts of Steel. Newnes, 1893
A King in Bohemia. Remington, 1894
Lady Turpin. Beeton's, 1895
-A Leading Lady. Chatto, 1891
-The Postman's Daughter, and other tales. Warne, 1894 ss
Scarlet Fortune. Trischler, 1891
The Silver King's Vengeance, and other stories. Digby, 1907 ss
The Sword of Fate. Greening, 1899
Woman, the Mystery. Ward, 1894

HERMAN, LOUIS. 1905- . See: William Targ, 1907- .

HERMANN, WALTER. Pseudonym of Walter (Herman) Wager, 1924- , q.v. Other pseudonym: John Tiger, q.v.
Operation Intrigue. Avon, 1956

HERNE, HUXLEY. Pseudonym of Bertram Brooker, 1888-1955.
The Tangled Miracle. Nelson, 1936

HERON-MAXWELL, BEATRICE
The Adventures of a Lady Pearl Broker. New Century, 1899 ss

HERRIES, NORMAN
Death has Two Faces. Ace, 1955
My Private Hangman. Ace, 1956

HERRING, PAUL
-Dragon's Silk. Cassell, 1908
The Midnight Murder; see The Murder of Margot Midnight
The Murder of Margot Midnight. Low, 1932. U.S. title: The Midnight Murder. Lippincott, 1932
-The Wrong Mr. Chamberlain and other stories. Arrowsmith, 1904 ss

HERRINGTON, LEE
Carry My Coffin Slowly. Simon, 1951

HERRIOT, DENYS G.
The Last of Mrs. Cheyney. Collins, 1930. (Adapted from the play by Frederick Lonsdale.)

HERRON, SHAUN. 1912- . Series character: Miro = M.
-The Bird in Last Year's Nest. Evans, 1974; Cape, 1974
The Hound and the Fox and the Harper. Random, 1970. British title: The Miro Papers. Hale, 1972 M
Miro. Random, 1969; Hale, 1971 M
The Miro Papers; see The Hound and the Fox and the Harper
Through the Dark and Hairy Wood. Random, 1972; Cape, 1973 M
The Whore-Mother. Evans, 1973; Cape, 1973

HERSHATTER, RICHARD L. Series character: Rand Stannard, in all titles.
Fallout for a Spy. Ace, 1969
The Spy Who Hated Licorice. Signet, 1966
The Spy Who Liked Fudge. Ace, 1970

HERSHMAN, MORRIS. 1920- . Pseudonyms: Evelyn Bond, Jess Wilcox, qq.v.
Guilty Witness. Belmont, 1964
Target for Terror. Belmont, 1967

HERTZ, GEORGE
The Foreign Harry Complot. Hale, 1972

HERVEY, HARRY (CLAY). 1900-1951.
The Black Parrot. Century (New York & London), 1923
Caravans by Night. Century, 1922; Butterworth, 1925
Red Ending. Liveright, 1929; Allen, 1952
Red Hotel. Jarrolds, 1932 (U.S. title?)

HERVEY, MAURICE H.
-Amyas Egerton, Cavalier. Arrowsmith, 1896; Harper, 1896
Dartmoor. Arrowsmith, 1896; Stokes, 1895
-David Dimsdale, M.D. Redway, 1897
Dead Man's Court. Arrowsmith, 1895; Stokes, 1895
Dr. Somerville's Crime. Arrowsmith, 1901
-Eric the Archer. Arnold, 1895
-The Reef of Gold. Arnold, 1894

HERVEY, MICHAEL. 1920- .
All in Good Crime. Hampton, 1953
Appointment with Death. Newcoll, 1945
Better Luck Next Crime. Forsyte, 1949
The Body in the Drum Mystery. Modern, 1951
The Book of Master Crimes. Mitre, 1945
Brooklyn Angel. Hamilton Stafford, 1947
The Case of the Missing Hand. Hampton, 1946
Corpse Parade. Hampton, 1946
Creeps Medley. Hampton, 1946 ss
Crime a la Carte. Hampton, 1953
Crime Medley. Hampton, 1945
Cut Price Murder. Everybody's, 1944
Dames Spell Trouble. Bear, 1944 ss
Dark Waterfront. Hamilton Stafford, 1947

Death at my Heels, and other stories. Mitre, 1945 ss
Death Tolls the Bell. Mitre, 1944
The Devil and Miss Thrace, and other stories. Pan, 1945 ss
Dumb Witness. Hampton, 1946 ss
G is for Ghoul. Hampton, 1946 ss
Ghost Voice. Hampton, 1946
Gold Digger, and fourteen other short stories. Alliance, 1945 ss
Horror Medley. Hampton, 1945 ss
Imperfect Alibi. Mitre, 1944 ss
Insufficient Evidence. Century, 1946
Laughter in the Ranks. Alliance, 1945 ss
Make Mine Murder. Hampton, 1948. (1-act play.)
Murder at the Movies. Mitre, 1944 ss
Murder by Installment. Everybody's, 1944
Murder Medley. Hampton, 1945 ss
Murder Thy Neighbor. Mitre, 1944
No Crime Like the Present. Mitre, 1944
No Excuse for Murder. Hampton, 1946
No More Love. Hampton, 1945
No Peace for the Living. Hampton, 1947. (A play.)
The Queer Looking Box, and other stories. Everybody's, 1944 ss
Save Your Pity. Mitre, 1943
The Silver Death. Mitre, 1944
Strange Hunger. Hamilton Stafford, 1946
Suspicion. Hampton, 1946 ss
Toughs Afloat. Alliance, 1946
Toughs Ashore. Alliance, 1947
Travel the Hard Way. Mitre, 1944
The Walking Dead. Hampton, 1949
Wanted: Dead or Alive. Hampton, 1948. (1-act play.)
Wide Boy! Hampton, 1945 ss
Wide Girl. Hampton, 1945

HERZOG, DOROTHY
  Undercover Woman. Macaulay, 1937; Brown Watson, 1950

HESKY, OLGA.   -1974. Series character: Inspector Tami Shimoni = TS.
  The Different Night. Long, 1970; Random, 1971 TS
  Life Sentence. Doubleday, 1972
  The Sequin Syndicate. Long, 1969; Dodd, 1969 TS
  The Serpent's Smile. Long, 1966; Dodd, 1967 TS
  Time for Treason. Long, 1967; Dodd, 1968 TS

HESLOP, HAROLD. 1898-   .
  The Crime of Peter Ropner. Fortune, 1934

HETH, EDWARD HARRIS. 1909-   .
  -Any Number Can Play. Harper, 1945. Also published as: The Big Bet. Bantam, 1948

HEWENS, FRANK E(DGAR). 1912-   .
  The Murder of the Dainty-Footed Model. Macmillan, 1968

HEWITT, E. L.
  Dangerous Edge. Hutchinson, 1939

HEWITT, KATHLEEN (DOUGLAS). 1893-   .
  Pseudonym: Dorothea Martin, q.v.
  -Comedian. Nicholson, 1934
  -Decoration. Nicholson, 1935
  -Fetish. Elkin Mathews, 1933
  -Go Find a Shadow. Jarrolds, 1937
  -The Golden Milestone. Jarrolds, 1939
  -Harmony in Autumn. Jarrolds, 1955
  -The House by the Canal. Jarrolds, 1938
  -Lady Gone Astray. Jarrolds, 1939
  -Mardi. Douglas, 1932
  The Mice are Not Amused. Jarrolds, 1942; Mystery House, 1943
  Murder in the Ballroom. Jarrolds, 1948
  -No Time to Play. Jarrolds, 1939
  -One Man's Woman. Jarrolds, 1954
  -A Pattern in Yellow. Douglas, 1932
  -Plenty Under the Counter. Jarrolds, 1943
  -Return to the River. Jarrolds, 1936
  Stand-In for Danger. Jarrolds, 1940
  -Still the World is Young. Jarrolds, 1951
  -Strange Salvation. Elkin Mathews, 1934
  -Thanks for the Apple. Jarrolds, 1947
  -Three Rainbows. Jarrolds, 1952

HEWLETT, WILLIAM
  The Breaking Point. Skeffington, 1936
  -The Child at the Window. Secker, 1915
  The Crimson Claw. Allan, 1936
  -Introducing William Allison. Secker, 1916
  -Is and Was. Skeffington, 1936
  The Pear-Tree. Skeffington, 1938
  The Plot-Maker. Duckworth, 1917
  -Simpson of Snells. Skeffington, 1918
  -Telling the Truth. Secker, 1913
  -Uncle's Advice. Secker, 1913
  -White Stacks. Hurst, 1923
  -Windswept Farm. Routledge, 1918

HEXT, HARRINGTON. Pseudonym of Eden Phillpotts, 1862-1960, q.v.
  The Monster. Macmillan, 1925
  Number 87. Butterworth, 1922; Macmillan, 1922
  The Thing at Their Heels. Butterworth, 1923; Macmillan, 1923
  Who Killed Cock Robin?; see Who Killed Diana?
  Who Killed Diana? Butterworth, 1924. U.S. title: Who Killed Cock Robin? Macmillan, 1924

HEYER, GEORGETTE. 1902-1974. Series characters: Insp. Hemingway = H; Supt. Hannasyde (with Hemingway, as a sergeant, in a supporting role) = H*.
  Behold, Here's Poison! Hodder, 1936; Doubleday, 1936 H*
  A Blunt Instrument. Hodder, 1938; Doubleday, 1938 H*
  Death in the Stocks. Longmans, 1935. U.S. title: Merely Murder. Doubleday, 1935 H*
  Detection Unlimited. Heinemann, 1953; Dutton, 1969 H
  Duplicate Death. Heinemann, 1951; Dutton, 1969 H
  Envious Casca. Hodder, 1941; Doubleday, 1941 H
  Footsteps in the Dark. Longmans, 1932
  Merely Murder; see Death in the Stocks
  No Wind of Blame. Hodder, 1939; Doubleday, 1939 H
  Penhallow. Heinemann, 1942; Doubleday, 1943
  They Found Him Dead. Hodder, 1937; Doubleday, 1937 H*
  The Unfinished Clue. Longmans, 1934; Doubleday, 1937
  Why Shoot a Butler? Longmans, 1933; Doubleday, 1936

HEYES, DOUGLAS
  Goodbye Stranger; see The Kiss-Off
  The Kiss-Off. Simon, 1951. British title: Goodbye Stranger. Redman, 1952
  The 12th of Never. Random, 1963; Boardman, 1964

HEYGATE, BARBARA
  The Crime of Vera Seymour; see "Unless a Child is Born—"
  The Sabbath Slayer. Pearson, 1939
  -Thou Shalt Not Kill. Pearson, 1937
  -"Unless a Child is Born—". Pearson, 1939. Also published as: The Crime of Vera Seymour. Pearson, 1940

HEYM, STEFAN. 1913-   .
  Hostages. Putnam (New York), 1942; Putnam (London), 1943

HEYMAN, EVAN LEE
  Cain's Hundred. Popular Library, 1961. (Novelization of the TV series.)
  Dead Heat on a Merry-Go-Round. Avon, 1966. (Novelization of the movie.)
  Miami Undercover. Popular Library, 1961. (Novelization of the TV series.)
  The Thomas Crown Affair. Avon, 1968; Hodder pb, 1968. (Novelization of the movie.)

HEYWARD, DOROTHY. 1890-1961.
  The Pulitzer Prize Murders. Farrar, 1932

HIBBERT, ELEANOR BURFORD. 1906-   .
  Pseudonyms: Philippa Carr, Elbur Ford, Victoria Holt, Kathleen Kellow, qq.v.

HICHENS, ROBERT (SMYTHE). 1864-1950.
  After the Verdict. Methuen, 1924; Doran, 1924
  Doctor Artz. Hutchinson, 1929
  The Paradine Case. Benn, 1933; Doubleday, 1933
  The Power to Kill. Benn, 1934; Doubleday, 1934
  Secret Information. Hurst, 1938; Doubleday, 1938
  That Which is Hidden. Cassell, 1939; Doubleday, 1940

HICKEY, T(HEODOSIA) F(RANCES) W(YNNE)
  The Corpse in the Church. Methuen, 1930
  The Hand; or, Mystery at Number Ten. Heinemann, 1937
  -The Unexpected Adventure. Heinemann, 1935

HICKMAN, J. M.
  Death on the Run. Brown Watson, 1954
  Missing Witness. Brown Watson, 1955
  Nine O'Clock Curtains. Brown Watson, 1954
  Tide of Death. Brown Watson, 1954

HICKMAN, W(ILLIAM) T(HEODORE)
  The Nick of Time. Maxwell, 1887

HICKOK, FRANCES
  An Eye for an Eye. Paul, 1930

HIGGIN, L(OUIS)
  Lyona Grimswood, Spinster. Pearson, 1900

HIGGINS, GEORGE V(INCENT). 1939-   .
  Cogan's Trade. Knopf, 1974; Secker, 1974
  The Digger's Game. Knopf, 1973; Secker, 1973
  The Friends of Eddie Coyle. Knopf, 1972; Secker, 1972

HIGGINS, JACK. Pseudonym of Henry Patterson, 1929-   . Other pseudonyms: Martin Fallon, James Graham, Hugh Marlowe, Harry Patterson, qq.v. Note that numerous titles originally published under other bylines have later been reprinted as by Jack Higgins.

The Eagle has Landed. Collins, 1975; Holt, 1975
East of Desolation. Hodder, 1968; Doubleday, 1969
In the Hour Before Midnight. Hodder, 1969; Doubleday, 1969. Also published as: The Sicilian Heritage. Lancer, 1970
The Last Place God Made. Collins, 1971; Holt, 1972
Night Judgment at Sinos. Hodder, 1970; Doubleday, 1971
A Prayer for the Dying. Collins, 1973; Holt, 1974
The Savage Day. Collins, 1972; Holt, 1972
The Sicilian Heritage; see In the Hour Before Midnight

HIGGINS, MARGARET
The Changeling. Ace, 1973; Barker, 1974
A Doctor for the Dead. Ace, 1974
Unholy Sanctuary. Ace, 1971; Barker, 1974
A Witch Alone. Ace, 1972; Barker, 1975

HIGGINSON, HAROLD WYNYARD. 1887- .
The Murder by the Arch. Crowell, 1931

HIGHLAND, DORA. Pseudonym of Michael (Angelo) Avallone (Jr.), 1924- , q.v. Other pseudonyms: Priscilla Dalton, Mark Dane, Jean-Anne de Pre, Steve Michaels, Dorothea Nile, Edwina Noone, Sidney Stuart, Max Walker, qq.v.
Death is a Dark Man. Popular Library, 1974
153 Oakland Street. Popular Library, 1973

HIGHSMITH, (MARY) PATRICIA (PLAUGMAN). 1921- . Series character: Tom Ripley = TR.
The Animal-Lover's Book of Beastly Murder. Heinemann, 1975 ss
The Blunderer. Coward, 1954; Cresset, 1956. Also published as: Lament for a Lover. Popular Library, 1956
The Cry of the Owl. Harper, 1962; Heinemann, 1963
Deep Water. Harper, 1957; Heinemann, 1958
A Dog's Ransom. Knopf, 1972; Heinemann, 1972
Eleven; see The Snail-Watcher and other stories
A Game for the Living. Harper, 1958; Heinemann, 1959
The Glass Cell. Doubleday, 1964; Heinemann, 1965
Lament for a Lover; see The Blunderer
Ripley Under Ground. Doubleday, 1970; Heinemann, 1971 TR
Ripley's Game. Knopf, 1974; Heinemann, 1974 TR
The Snail-Watcher and other stories. Doubleday, 1970. British title: Eleven. Heinemann, 1970 ss
The Story-Teller. Doubleday, 1965. British title: A Suspension of Mercy. Heinemann, 1965
Strangers on a Train. Harper, 1950; Cresset, 1950
A Suspension of Mercy; see The Story-Teller
The Talented Mr. Ripley. Coward, 1955; Cresset, 1957 TR
This Sweet Sickness. Harper, 1960; Heinemann, 1961
Those Who Walk Away. Doubleday, 1967; Heinemann, 1967
The Tremor of Forgery. Doubleday, 1969; Heinemann, 1969
The Two Faces of January. Doubleday, 1964; Heinemann, 1964

HILDICK, (EDMUND) WALLACE. 1925- .
Bracknell's Law. Harper, 1975; H. Hamilton, 1976

HILL, AMY HOSKIN
Murder on the Mountain. Arcadia, 1961

HILL, ARCHIE
Cage of Shadows. Hutchinson, 1973
-A Corridor of Mirrors. Hutchinson, 1975

HILL, BENETT
Diamond Crime Detective. Warren, 1950

HILL, BRIAN MERRIKIN. 1896- . Pseudonym: Marcus Magill, q.v.

HILL, CHRISTOPHER. 1928- .
Jackdaw. Collins, 1975; Holt, 1976
Scorpion. Collins, 1974; St. Martin's, 1974

HILL, FREDERICK TREVOR. 1866-1930.
The Accomplice. Harper, 1905
The Case and Exceptions. Stokes, 1900 ss
The Minority. Stokes, 1902; Richards, 1902
Tales Out of Court. Stokes, 1920 ss
The Thirteenth Juror. Century, 1913
The Web. Doubleday, 1903; Heinemann, 1903

HILL, H. HAVERSTOCK. Pseudonym of J(ames) M(organ) Walsh, 1897-1952, q.v. Other pseudonyms: Stephen Maddock, George M. White, qq.v.
-Anne of the Flying Gap. Hodder, 1926
-Golden Harvest. Hodder, 1929
-The Golden Isle. Hodder, 1928
-The Secret of the Crater. Hurst, 1930
-Spoil of the Desert. Hodder, 1927

HILL, HARRY EGBERT. All titles below published by Amalgamated Press and feature Sexton Blake.
The Actor's Secret. 1923
The Blackmailed Baronet. 1926. Reprinted as: The Mystery of the Blackmailed Baronet, as by Hylton Gregory. 1937
The Case of the Rajah's Son. 1922
The Curse of Kali; see The Shrine of Kali
The Golden Goddess. 1922
The Great Museum Mystery. 1924
The Hunchback of Hatton Garden! 1925
The Idol's Eye. 1921
In Darkest Madras. 1923
The Loot of Nana Sahib. 1924
The Mill Pond Mystery. 1922
The Mystery of the Blackmailed Baronet; see The Blackmailed Baronet
The Rajah of Ghanapore. 1922
The Riddle of the Amber Room. 1927. Reprinted as: The Sign of the Black Feather, as by Hylton Gregory. 1939
The Shrine of Kali. 1924. Reprinted as: The Curse of Kali, as by Hylton Gregory. 1935
The Sign of the Black Feather; see The Riddle of the Amber Room

HILL, HEADON. Pseudonym of Francis Edward Grainger, 1857-1927. Series character: Sebastian Zambra, in at least those marked SZ.
Aboard the American Duchess. Putnam, 1903. (British title?)
The Avengers. Ward, 1906; Dodge, 1907
The Broken Seal. Ward, 1917
By a Hair's Breadth. Cassell, 1897; Dodd, 1897
Caged!: The Romance of a Lunatic Asylum. Ward, 1900
The Cliff-Path Mystery. Ward, 1913
Clues from a Detective's Camera. Arrowsmith, 1893 ss SZ
The Comlyn Alibi. Ward, 1915
Coronation Mysteries and other stories. Digby, 1902 ss
The Cottage in the Chine. Ward, 1913
The Crimson Honeymoon. Ward, 1914
The Divinations of Kala Persad and other stories. Ward, 1895 ss SZ
The Duke Decides. Cassell, 1903; Wessels, 1903
The Duplicate Duke. Ward, 1920
The Embassy Case. Ward, 1915
The Epsom Mystery: A Race with Ruin; see A Race with Ruin
Foes of Justice. Ward, 1910. U.S. title: The Monksglade Mystery. Fenno, 1910
The Golden Temptress. Jenkins, 1924
The Great Bluff. Ward, 1925
The Green Shade. Ward, 1924
Guile. Ward, 1920
Guilty Gold. Pearson, 1896
The Hate of Man. Cassell, 1908
Her Grace at Bay. Cassell, 1906
Her Splendid Sin. Ward, 1908
The Hour-Glass Mystery. Ward, 1913
The Jesmond Mystery. Ward, 1919
The Kiss of the Enemy. Cassell, 1904
Links in the Chain. Long, 1909
The Mammoth Mansions Mystery. Ward, 1926
The Man from Egypt. Ward, 1917
Millions of Mischief: The Story of a Great Secret. Ward, 1905; Transatlantic, 1904
The Monksglade Mystery; see Foes of Justice
My Lord the Felon. Ward, 1912
The Narrowing Circle. Jenkins, 1924 SZ
The One Who Saw. Cassell, 1905; Victoria, 1905
The Peer and His Plunder. Ward, 1922
The Peril of the Prince: A Romance of Modern Anarchism. Pearson, 1907
Perils of the Red Box. Ward, 1904 ss
The Plunder Ship. Pearson, 1900
The Queen of Night. Ward, 1896
A Race with Ruin. Ward, 1904. U.S. title: The Epsom Mystery: A Race with Ruin. Fenno, 1908
Radford Shone. Ward, 1908 ss
-The Rajah's Second Wife. Warwick, 1894
The Red Rain Mystery. Ward, 1925
A Rogue in Ambush. Ward, 1911
Seaward for the Foe. Ward, 1903. (2 novelets.)
The Sentence of the Court. Pearson, 1901
The Shadow of the Bear. Pearson, 1899
Sir Vincent's Patient. Ward, 1914
The Skeleton Finger. Ward, 1924
Spectre Gold: A Romance of the Klondyke. Cassell, 1898
The Spies of the Wight. Pearson, 1899
The Split Peas. Paul, 1914
Spriggs the Cracksman. Ogilvie, 1895. (British title?)
Storm-Wrack. Paul, 1926
The Thread of Proof. Paul, 1912 ss
Tracked Down. Pearson, 1902
A Traitor's Wooing. Ward, 1909; Kearney, 1909
Troubled Waters. Paul, 1909
Unmasked at Last. Ward, 1906; Fenno, 1907
Zambra the Detective: Some Clues from his Notebook. Chatto, 1894 ss SZ
The Zone of Fire. Pearson, 1897

HILL, JOHN
Treason-Felony. Chatto, 1892

HILL, JOHN
The Dope Ring. Methuen, 1931

HILL, JOHN A(LEXANDER). 1858-1916.
Stories of the Railroad. Doubleday, 1899 ss, some criminous

HILL, K(ATE) F. Pseudonym of Mrs. Lucy A. Baer, ca.1844-1925.
The Mysterious Case; or, Tracing a Crime. Street, 1889; Ward, 1890
The Mystery of a Madstone; or, The Commercial Traveller Detective. Street, 1889
Sarah Brown, Detective; or, The Mystery of the Pavilion. Westbrook, 19??
The Twin Detectives; or, The Robbers of the Tomb. Street, 1888

HILL, KATHARINE. Series character: Lorna Donahue, in both titles.
Case for Equity. Dutton, 1945
Dear Dead Mother-in-Law. Dutton, 1944

HILL, LAWRENCE. Series character: Insp. Macsporran, in both titles.
Corpse Without Boots. Collins, 1940
Dagger Drawn. Collins, 1939

HILL, MONICA. Pseudonym of Agnes Monica Baker, 1899- .
Smooth Runs the Water. Hutchinson, 1936

HILL, NEWTON
The Body Drank Coffee. Hale, 1951

HILL, PAMELA. 1920- .
The Devil of Aske. Hodder, 1972; St. Martin's, 1973
The Incumbent. Hodder, 1974
The Malvie Inheritance. Hodder, 1973; St. Martin's, 1974
Whitton's Folly. Hodder, 1975; St. Martin's, 1975

HILL, R. LANCE. 1943- .
King of White Lady. Putnam, 1975; Souvenir, 1976
Nails. Lester & Orpen (Toronto), 1974; Souvenir, 1975

HILL, REGINALD (CHARLES). 1936- .
Pseudonym: Patrick Ruell, q.v. Series character: Supt. Andrew Dalziel, in at least those marked AD.
An Advancement of Learning. Collins, 1971 AD
An April Shroud. Collins, 1975
A Clubbable Woman. Collins, 1970 AD
A Fairly Dangerous Thing. Collins, 1972
Fell of Dark. Collins, 1971 AD
Ruling Passion. Collins, 1973; Harper, 1977 AD
A Very Good Hater. Collins, 1974

HILL, SAM
The Nodding Towers. Vantage, 1966

HILL, SUSAN. 1942- .
I'm King of the Castle. H. Hamilton, 1970; Viking, 1970

HILL, VINCENT
Amber to Red. Hodder, 1952
The Cunning Enemy. Hodder, 1957
Lady from Hamburg. Hodder, 1954
The Soft Guy. Hodder, 1953

HILL, WARREN
The Crystal Skull. Jarrolds, 1930
That Which is Crooked. Jarrolds, 1930
The Thumb-Mark. Jarrolds, 1929
Yellow Will Out! Jarrolds, 1929

HILL, WELDON. Pseudonym of William R. Scott.
A Man Could Get Killed That Way. McKay, 1967

HILLARY, MAX
A Deadly Errand; see Hunted Down
Hunted Down. Ward, 1885; Marquis, 1885. Also published as: A Deadly Errand. Ward, 1886
-Once for All. Low, 1885

HILLCOAT, CHARLES H.
A Mystery of the Suez Canal. Bryce, 1896

HILLER, GUY PEMBER. See: GUY PEMBER-HILLER.

HILLERMAN, TONY. 1925- . Series character: Joe Leaphorn = JL.
The Blessing Way. Harper, 1970; Macmillan (London), 1970 JL
The Fly on the Wall. Harper, 1971
Dance Hall of the Dead. Harper, 1973 JL

HILLGARTH, ALAN. 1898- .
Change for Heaven. Chapman, 1929. U.S. title: What Price Paradise? Houghton, 1929
-Davy Jones. Nicholson, 1936
The Passionate Trail. Hutchinson, 1925
-The Prince and the Perjurer. Chapman, 1924
-The War Maker. Nelson, 1926
What Price Paradise?; see Change for Heaven

HILLIARD, A(LEC) R(OWLEY). 1908- . Series character: Judge Manfred, in both titles.
Justice be Damned. Farrar, 1941; Cassell, 1944
Outlaw Island. Farrar, 1942; Cassell, 1947

HILLIARD, JAN. Pseudonym of Hilda Kay Grant, 1910- .
Morgan's Castle. Abelard, 1964

HILLIARD, MAURICE. 1931- .
The Witchfinder. Coward, 1974; Heinemann, 1974

HILLIERS, ASHTON. Pseudonym of Henry Marriage Wallis.
The Walbury Case. Methuen, 1923

HILLMAN, RALF RIDGWAY. -1940.
The Houseboat Enigma. Dorrance, 1937

HILLYARD, WILLIAM HEARD
Recollections of a Physician; or, Episodes of Life During Thirty Years of Practice. Ward, 1861 ss
Reginald Vernon; or, The Fatal Likeness. Routledge, 1888

HILTON, FRANCIS W.
Blazing Trails. Kinsey, 1936; Rich, 1937
Gray Sage. Kinsey, 1938; Rich, 1939
Hell-Crazy Range. Kinsey, 1934
-The Long Rope. Kinsey, 1935
Mad-Gun Mesa. Kinsey, 1937; Rich, 1937
The Manana Kid. Kinsey, 1939; Ward, 1941
-Phantom Rustlers. Kinsey, 1934; Bles, 1934
The Pioneer Herd. Kinsey, 1937; Rich, 1938
Powder River. Kinsey, 1935
Skyline Riders. Kinsey, 1939; Harrap, 1939

HILTON, JAMES. 1900-1954. Pseudonym: Glen Trevor, q.v.

HILTON, JOHN BUXTON. 1921- . Series character: Supt. Kenworthy, in all titles.
Death in Midwinter. Cassell, 1969; Walker, 1969
Death of an Alderman. Cassell, 1968; Walker, 1969
Hangman's Tide. Macmillan (London), 1975; St. Martin's, 1975
No Birds Sang. Macmillan (London), 1975; St. Martin's, 1976

HILTON, JOHN DEANE. 1855- . Pseudonym: John Cleveland, q.v.

HILTON, JOSEPH
-Angels in the Gutter. GM, 1955
-Beyond Mombasa. Avon, 1957
Cry Baby Killer. Avon, 1958. (Novelization of the movie.)
Ship of the Damned. Lancer, 1972
-That French Girl. GM, 1953

HIMES, CHESTER (BOMAR). 1909- . Series characters: Grave Digger Jones & Coffin Ed Johnson = J&J.
All Shot Up. Avon, 1960; Panther, 1969 J&J
The Big Gold Dream. Avon, 1960; Panther, 1968 J&J
Blind Man with a Pistol. Morrow, 1969; Hodder, 1969. Also published as: Hot Day Hot Night. Dell, 1970 J&J
Come Back, Charleston Blue; see The Heat's On
Cotton Comes to Harlem. Putnam, 1965; Muller, 1965 J&J
The Crazy Kill. Avon, 1959; Panther, 1968 J&J
For Love of Imabelle. GM, 1957. Also published as: A Rage in Harlem. Avon, 1965; Panther, 1969 J&J
The Heat's On. Putnam, 1966; Muller, 1966. Also published as: Come Back, Charleston Blue. Berkley, 1970 J&J
Hot Day Hot Night; see Blind Man with a Pistol
A Rage in Harlem; see For Love of Imabelle
The Real Cool Killers. Avon, 1959; Panther, 1969 J&J
Run Man Run. Putnam, 1966; Muller, 1967

HIMMEL, RICHARD. Series character: Johnny Maguire, in at least those marked JM.
Beyond Desire. GM, 1952
The Chinese Keyhole. GM, 1951; Jenkins, 1968 JM
Cry of the Flesh. GM, 1955
I have Gloria Kirby. GM, 1951; Fawcett (London), 1953 JM
I'll Find You. GM, 1950; Fawcett (London), 1958. Also published as: It's Murder, Maguire. Jenkins, 1962 JM
It's Murder, Maguire; see I'll Find You
The Name's Maguire. Jenkins, 1963 JM (Original title?)
The Rich and the Damned. GM, 1958; Fawcett (London), 1960 JM
The Shame. Avon, 1959
The Sharp Edge. GM, 1952
Two Deaths Must Die. GM, 1954; Red Seal, 1957 JM

HINCKLEY, JULIAN. 1905- .
Murder by Schedule. Golden Willow, 1947

HINCKS, CYRIL MALCOLM. 1881-1954.
The Throne of Peril. Amalgamated Press, 1930. (Sexton Blake.)

HINDE, THOMAS. Pseudonym of Sir Thomas Wiles Chitty, 1926- .
Agent. Hodder, 1974
Bird. Hodder, 1970
The Day the Call Came. Hodder, 1964; Vanguard, 1965

Hinde, Thomas

Games of Chance. Hodder, 1965; Vanguard, 1967

HINDS, ROY W.
The Man Called Eighty-Eighty. McBride, 1930
The Treasure of Caricar. Altemus, 1927; Long, 1930
The Tunnel to Doom. Chelsea, 1927; Long, 1929

HINE, AL. 1915-   .
Juggernaut. Bantam, 1974; Corgi, 1974. (Novelization of the movie.)

HINES, JEANNE
The Slashed Portrait. Dell, 1973
Talons of the Hawk. Dell, 1975

HINKEMEYER, MICHAEL T(HOMAS). 1940-   .
The Dark Below. GM, 1974

HINTZE, NAOMI A. 1909-   .
Aloha Means Goodbye. Random, 1972; British title: Hawaii for Danger. Hale, 1973
Cry Witch. Random, 1975; Collins, 1976
Hawaii for Danger; see Aloha Means Goodbye
The House with the Watching Eyes; see You'll Like My Mother
Listen, Please Listen. Random, 1973; Hale, 1975
The Stone Carnation. Random, 1971; Hale, 1973
You'll Like My Mother. Putnam, 1969. British title: The House with the Watching Eyes. Hale, 1970

HIPKINS, CHARLES HAMMOND. 1893-   .
Pseudonym: Carl Talbot, q.v.

HIRAI, TARO. 1894-   . Pseudonym:
Edogawa Rampo, q.v.

HIRD, FRANK. 1873-   .
The Bannantyne Sapphires. Paul, 1930
-Chained. Chapman, 1927
Clipped Hedges. Paul, 1932
The Deeper Stain. Bell, 1909
-The Fourth Road. Paul, 1934
The Golden Crystal. Paul, 1933
-King Fritz's A.D.C. Bell, 1901
The Lustre Jug. Paul, 1931
The Secret Terror. Nash, 1926

HIRSCH, LEE. Pseudonym of Leon David Hirsch, 1881-   .
Murder Steals the Show. Fell, 1946

HIRSCH, LEON DAVID. 1881-   . Pseudonym:
Lee Hirsch, q.v.

HIRSCHBERG, CORNELIUS. 1901-   .
Florentine Finish. Harper, 1963; Gollancz, 1964

HIRSCHFELD, BURT. 1923-   .
Bonnie and Clyde. Lancer, 1967; Hodder pb, 1967. (Novelization of the movie.)
"Father Pig." Arbor, 1972; Allen, 1977
Gas. Curtis, 1970. (Novelization of the movie.)
The Masters Affair. Arbor, 1971; Allen, 1973
Secrets. Simon, 1975; Allen, 1976

HISCOCK, LESLIE. 1902-   . Pseudonym:
Patrick Marsh, q.v.

HISCOCK, ROBIN. 1929-   .
The Killer Wind. Barker, 1958
The Last Run South. Longmans, 1956; Knopf, 1958
The Send-Off. Heinemann, 1967

HISCOTT, LESLIE
The Bishop's Move. Macdonald, 1961
The Margravine. Macdonald, 1966

HITCHCOCK, ALFRED (JOSEPH). 1899-   .
Rope. Dell, 1948. (Novelization of the play by Patrick Hamilton, 1904-1962, q.v.)

HITCHENS, (HU)BERT (ALLEN) and (JULIA CLARA CATHERINE) DOLORES (BIRK OLSEN) HITCHENS, 1907-1972, q.v. Pseudonyms of Dolores Hitchens: Dolan Birkley, Noel Burke, D. B. Olsen, qq.v. Series characters: John Farrel = JF; Collins & McKechnie = C&M.
End of the Line. Doubleday, 1957; Boardman, 1958 JF
F.O.B. Murder. Doubleday, 1955; Boardman, 1957 C&M
The Grudge. Doubleday, 1963; Boardman, 1964 JF
The Man Who Followed Women. Doubleday, 1959; Boardman, 1960 C&M
One-Way Ticket. Doubleday, 1956; Boardman, 1958

HITCHENS, (JULIA CLARA CATHERINE) DOLORES (BIRK OLSEN). 1907-1972. See also: (HU)BERT (ALLEN) HITCHENS. Pseudonyms: Dolan Birkley, Noel Burke, D. B. Olsen, qq.v. Series character: Jim Sader, in at least those marked JS.
The Abductor. Simon, 1962; Boardman, 1962
The Bank with the Bamboo Door. Simon, 1965; Boardman, 1965
The Baxter Letters. Putnam, 1971; Hale, 1973
Beat Back the Tide. Doubleday, 1954; Macdonald, 1955. Also published as: The Fatal Flirt. Bestseller, 1956 (abridged)
Cabin of Fear; see Postscript to Nightmare
A Collection of Strangers. Putnam, 1969; Macdonald, 1971
The Fatal Flirt; see Beat Back the Tide
Fools' Gold. Doubleday, 1958; Boardman, 1958
Footsteps in the Night. Doubleday, 1961; Boardman, 1961
In a House Unknown. Doubleday, 1973; Hale, 1974
The Man Who Cried All the Way Home. Simon, 1966; Hale, 1967
Nets to Catch the Wind. Doubleday, 1952. Also published as: Widows Won't Wait. Dell, 1954
Postscript to Nightmare. Putnam, 1967. British title: Cabin of Fear. Joseph, 1968
Sleep with Slander. Doubleday, 1960; Boardman, 1961 JS
Sleep with Strangers. Doubleday, 1955; Macdonald, 1956 JS
Stairway to an Empty Room. Doubleday, 1951
Terror Lurks in Darkness. Doubleday, 1953
The Watcher. Doubleday, 1959; Boardman, 1959
Widows Won't Wait; see Nets to Catch the Wind

HITTLEMAN, CARL K.
36 Hours. Popular Library, 1965. (Novelization of the movie.)

HIVELY, MILDRED ENGLISH
The Moday Mystery. Vantage, 1966

HOARE, DOUGLAS. See: PERCY COLSON, 1873-   .

HOARE, HUGH ALAN
Now and For Ever. Hale, 1973

HOBART, DONALD BAYNE
The Adventure Trail. Nelson, 1929. (U.S. title?)
The Cell Murder Mystery. Fiction League, 1931
The Clue of the Leather Noose. Whitman, 1929
Double Shuffle. Clode, 1928
Homicide Honeymoon. Arcadia, 1959
Hunchback House. Whitman, 1929

HOBART, ROBERTSON. Pseudonym of Norman Lee, 1905-1962, q.v. Other pseudonyms: Raymond Armstrong, Mark Corrigan, qq.v. Series character: Grant Vickary, in at least those marked GV.
Blood on the Lake. Hale, 1961
The Case of the Shaven Blonde. Hale, 1959 GV
Dangerous Cargoes. Hale, 1960 GV
Death of a Love. Hale, 1961

HOBBS, MARC J.
The Memoirs of J. (Paddy) MacDowell. Vantage, 1970

HOBBS, ROE R.
-The Gates of Flame. Neale, 1908

HOBDAY, WILLIAM ALFRED
-Accessory After the Fact. Clark, 1911

HOBHOUSE, ADAM
The Hangover Murders. Knopf, 1935

HOBHOUSE, CHRISTINA. 1941-   .
A Well-Told Lie. Macmillan (London), 1972; Knopf, 1973

HOBSON, CORALIE VON WERNER. 1891-   . Pseudonym: Sarah Salt, q.v.

HOBSON, FRANCIS
Death on a Back Bench. Eyre, 1959; Harper, 1959

HOBSON, HANK. Pseudonym of Harry Hobson, 1908-   . Other pseudonym: Hank Janson, q.v. Series character: Brad Ford, in at least those marked BF.
Beyond Tolerance. Cassell, 1960 BF
The Big Twist. Cassell, 1959 BF
Death Makes a Claim. Cassell, 1958 BF
The Gallant Affair. Cassell, 1957
The Mission House Murder. Cassell, 1959 BF

HOBSON, HARRY. 1908-   . Pseudonyms: Hank Hobson, Hank Janson, qq.v.

HOBSON, POLLY. Pseudonym of Julia Rendel Evans, 1913-   . Series character: Inspector Basil, in at least those marked B.
Murder Won't Out. Jenkins, 1964 B
The Mystery House. Benn, 1963
A Terrible Thing has Happened to Miss Dupont; see Titty's Dead
The Three Graces. Constable, 1970; British Book Centre, 1971 B
Titty's Dead. Constable, 1968. U.S. title: A Terrible Thing has Happened to Miss Dupont. McCall, 1970 B

HOCH, EDWARD D(ENTINGER). 1930-   . Series characters: Simon Ark = SA; Carl Crader and Earl Jazine = C&J.
City of Brass, and other Simon Ark stories. Leisure, 1971 SA ss
The Fellowship of the Hand. Walker, 1973; Hale, 1976 C&J
The Frankenstein Factory. Warner, 1975; Hale, 1976 C&J

The Judges of Hades, and other Simon
   Ark stories. Leisure, 1971 ss SA
The Shattered Raven. Lancer, 1969;
   Hale, 1970
The Spy and the Thief. Davis pb, 1971
   ss
The Transvection Machine. Walker, 1971;
   Hale, 1974 C&J

HOCKER, GEORG. 1860-   .
   The Tell-Tale Watch. Bonners, 1895.
   (Translation of Der Lebende hat
   Recht.)

HOCKING, ANNE. Pseudonym of Mona (Naomi
   Anne) Messer, 189?-   , q.v. Series
   character: Inspector William Austen,
   in at least those marked WA.
All My Pretty Chickens. (Publisher and
   date unknown). U.S. title: Death
   Loves a Shining Mark. Doubleday, 1943
   WA
And No One Wept. Allen, 1954 WA
As I was Going to St. Ives. Paul, 1937
At "The Cedars". Bles, 1949 WA
The Best Laid Plans. Bles, 1952;
   Doubleday, 1950 WA
Candidates for Murder. Long, 1961 WA
Cat's Paw. Paul, 1933
Deadly is the Evil Tongue; see Old Mrs.
   Fitzgerald
Death Among the Tulips. Allen, 1953 WA
Death at the Wedding. Bles, 1946 WA
Death Disturbs Mr. Jefferson. Bles,
   1951; Doubleday, 1950 WA
Death Duel. Paul, 1933
Death Loves a Shining Mark; see All My
   Pretty Chickens
Epitaph for a Nurse. Allen, 1958. U.S.
   title: A Victim Must be Found.
   Doubleday, 1959 WA
The Evil That Men Do. Allen, 1953
The Finishing Touch; see Prussian Blue
He had to Die. Long, 1962 WA
The House of En-Dor. Paul, 1936
The Hunt is Up. Paul, 1934
Ill Deeds Done. Bles, 1938
Killing Kin; see Mediterranean Murder
The Little Victims Play. Bles, 1938
Mediterranean Murder. Evans, 1951. U.S.
   title: Killing Kin. Doubleday, 1951
   WA
Miss Milverton. Bles, 1941. U.S.
   title: Poison is a Bitter Brew.
   Doubleday, 1942 WA
Murder at Mid-Day. Allen, 1956 WA
Murder Cries Out. Long, 1968. (Com-
   pleted by Evelyn Healey, q.v.) WA
Night's Candles. Bles, 1941
Nile Green. Bles, 1943 WA
Old Mrs. Fitzgerald. Bles, 1939. U.S.
   title: Deadly is the Evil Tongue.
   Doubleday, 1940 WA
One Shall be Taken. Bles, 1942 WA
Poison in Paradise. Allen, 1955;
   Doubleday, 1955 WA
Poison is a Bitter Brew; see Miss Mil-
   verton
Poisoned Chalice. Long, 1959 WA
Prussian Blue. Bles, 1947. U.S. title:
   The Finishing Touch. Doubleday, 1948
   WA
A Reason for Murder. Allen, 1955 WA
Relative Murder. Allen, 1957 WA
The Simple Way of Poison. Allen, 1957;
   Washburn, 1957 WA
Six Green Bottles. Bles, 1943 WA
So Many Doors. Bles, 1939
Stranglehold. Paul, 1936
There's Death in the Cup. Evans, 1952
The Thin-Spun Thread. Long, 1960 WA
To Cease Upon the Midnight. Long, 1959
   WA

A Victim Must be Found; see Epitaph for
   a Nurse
The Vultures Gather. Bles, 1945 WA
Walk into my Parlour. Paul, 1934
What a Tangled Web. Paul, 1937
The Wicked Flee. Bles, 1940
Without the Option. Paul, 1935

HOCKING, JOSEPH. 1860-1937.
-"And Shall Trelawney Die?" Bowden, 1897
The Case of Miss Dunstable. Hodder,
   1923
The Secret of Trescobell. Ward, 1931
The Sign of the Triangle. Ward, 1929
-The Weapons of Mystery. Routledge, 1890

HOCKING, MARY
Ask No Question. Chatto, 1967; Morrow,
   1967
The Bright Day. Chatto, 1975

HOCKING, SILAS (KITTO). 1850-1935.
Adventures of Latimer Field, Curate.
   Warne, 1903 ss
-The Beautiful Alien. Low, 1916
His Own Accuser. Low, 1917
-The Mystery Man. Low, 1930
The Scarlet Clue. Warne, 1904
-The Sinister Shadow. Low, 1926

HODDER, ALFRED. 1866-1907. Pseudonym:
   Francis Walton. See: JOSIAH FLYNT.

HODDER, (WILLIAM) REGINALD. See also:
   EDGAR TURNER.
-The Doubling of Joseph Brereton. Ward,
   1903
-Ultus, the Man from the Dead. Hodder,
   1916; Doran, 1916
-Vampire. Rider, 1913

HODDER-WILLIAMS, (JOHN) CHRISTOPHER
   (GLAZEBROOK). 1926-   . Pseudonym:
   James Brogan, q.v.
Chain Reaction. Hodder, 1959; Double-
   day, 1959
The Egg-Shaped Thing. Hodder, 1967
Final Approach. Hodder, 1960; Double-
   day, 1960
The Higher They Fly. Hodder, 1963;
   Putnam, 1964
The Main Experiment. Hodder, 1964;
   Putnam, 1965
-98.4. Hodder, 1969
Turbulence. Hodder, 1961

HODGE, CHARLES
-The House of the Winds. Faber, 1948
-The Raven's Causeway. Faber, 1946

HODGE, JANE AIKEN. 1917-   .
The Adventurers. Doubleday, 1965; Hod-
   der, 1966
Greek Wedding. Doubleday, 1970; Hodder,
   1970
Here Comes a Candle. Doubleday, 1967;
   Hodder, 1967. Also published as: The
   Master of Penrose. Dell, 1968
Marry in Haste. Doubleday, 1970; Hod-
   der, 1969
The Master of Penrose; see Here Comes a
   Candle
Maulever Hall. Doubleday, 1964; Hale,
   1964
One Way to Venice. Coward, 1975; Hod-
   der, 1974
Savannah Purchase. Doubleday, 1971;
   Hodder, 1971
Strangers in Company. Coward, 1973;
   Hodder, 1973
Watch the Wall, My Darling. Doubleday,
   1966; Hodder, 1967
The Winding Stair. Doubleday, 1969;
   Hodder, 1968

HODGES, A. NOEL
The Bancaster Mystery. Eyre, 1932

HODGES, ARTHUR. 1864-1949.
-Along the Road. Butterworth, 1936
The Body in the Car. Butterworth, 1932
The Embassy Murder. Butterworth, 1931
-The Glittering Hour. Hurst, 1933
-Madame Lucien. Butterworth, 1930
-The Man of Substance. Hurst, 1931
-The Multi-Millionaire. Butterworth,
   1937

HODGES, CARL G. 1902-1964.
Crime on my Hands. Phantom, 1953
Murder by the Pack. Ace, 1953
Naked Villainy. Farrell, 1951

HODGES, DORIS MARJORIE. 1915-   . Pseudonym: Charlotte Hunt, q.v.

HODGKIN, M(ARION DeKAY) P.(OUS)
Dead Indeed. Gollancz, 1955; Macmillan,
   1956
Student Body. Gollancz, 1950; Scribner,
   1949

HODGKINSON, IVAN TATTERSALL. 1891-   .
   Pseudonym: Ivan Tattersall, q.v.

HODGSON, WILLIAM HOPE. 1877-1918.
Captain Gault. Nash, 1917; McBride,
   1918 ss
Carnacki, the Ghost Finder. Nash, 1913;
   Mycroft, 1947 ss (The U.S. edition
   contains 3 ss not in the British edi-
   tion.)
Carnacki, the Ghost Finder, and a Poem.
   Reynolds, 1910. (14 pp.)

HOFFECKER, DOUGLAS M(EADE)
The Wall Street Murders. Fortuny's,
   1936

HOFFMAN, J. A.
A Good Day to Die. Milestone, 1954

HOFFMAN, LOUISE
Conspiracy of Love. Hale, 1971
Fear Among the Shadows. Hale, 1969;
   Ace, 1974
House of Intrigue. Hale, 1970; Dell,
   1972
The Impossible Dream. Hale, 1973
A Quiet Passion. Hale, 1974; St. Mar-
   tin's, 1975
Passing Stranger. Hale, 1974; St. Mar-
   tin's, 1974
To Dream of Evil. Ace, 1975. (British
   title?)
The Unknown Woman. Hale, 1968
Woman Out of Nowhere. Hale, 1968

HOFFMAN, WILLIAM. 1925-   .
A Walk to the River. Doubleday, 1970;
   Hale, 1972

HOGAN, ROBERT J. 189?-1963. Series char-
   acter: G-8, in all titles.
Aces of the White Death. Berkley, 1970
The Bat Staffel. Berkley, 1969
Bombs from the Murder Wolves. Berkley,
   1971
Fangs of the Sky Leopard. Berkley, 1971
Flight from the Grave. Berkley, 1971
The Mark of the Vulture. Berkley, 1971
Purple Aces. Berkley, 1969
Vultures of the White Death. Berkley,
   1971

HOGARTH, CHARLES. Joint pseudonym of John
   Creasey, 1908-1973, q.v., and Ian
   Bowen. Other pseudonyms of John Crea-
   sey: Gordon Ashe, M. E. Cooke, Norman
   Deane, Robert Caine Frazer, Patrick
   Gill, Michael Halliday, Brian Hope,
   Colin Hughes, Kyle Hunt, Abel Mann,
   Peter Manton, J. J. Marric, Richard
   Martin, Rodney Mattheson, Anthony
   Morton, Jeremy York, qq.v.
Murder on Largo Island. Selwyn, 1944

HOGARTH, EMMETT. Joint pseudonym of Mitchell A. Wilson, 1913-1973, q.v., and Abraham Polonsky.
  The Goose is Cooked. Simon, 1940. Also published as: Death by Remote Control. Detective Novel Classics, 194?

HOGARTH, GRACE ALLEN. 1905- . Joint pseudonym with Alice Mary Norton, 1912?- : Allen Weston, q.v.

HOGG, DANIEL
  Murder at the Microphone. Quality, 1949

HOGSTRAND, OLLE (EDVARD). 1933- . Series character: Chief Inspector Lars Kollin, in all titles.
  The Debt. Pantheon, 1975; Hale, 1976. (Translation of Skulden. Stockholm, 1973.)
  The Gambler. Pantheon, 1974; Hale, 1976. (Translation of Spelarna. Stockholm, 1972.)
  On the Prime Minister's Account. Pantheon, 1972; Gollancz, 1972. (Translation of Maskerat Brott. Stockholm, 1971.)

HOGUE, WILBUR OWINGS. 1910?-1952. Pseudonym: Carl Shannon, q.v.

HOHN, GEORGE K.
  The Bleak Strand. Dorrance, 1972

HOLBROOK, J(AMES). 1812-1864.
  Ten Years Among the Mail Bags; or, Notes from the Diary of a Special Agent of the Post-Office Department. Cowperthwait, 1855 ss

HOLBROOK, MARION
  Crime Wind. Dodd, 1945
  Death Writes an Ad; see Suitable for Framing
  Suitable for Framing. Dodd, 1941; Cassell, 1946. Also published as: Death Writes an Ad. Mystery Novel Classic, 1943 (abridged)
  Wanted: A Murderess. Dodd, 1943; Cassell, 1948

HOLCOMBE, W(ILLIAM) H(ENRY), M.D. 1825-1893.
  A Mystery of New Orleans. Lippincott, 1890

HOLDAWAY, NEVILLE ALDRIDGE. 1894- . Pseudonym: N. A. Temple-Ellis, q.v.

HOLDEN, ANNE
  Death After School. Hale, 1968
  -The Empty Hills. Hale, 1967
  The Girl on the Beach. Macmillan (London), 1973; Delacorte, 1973
  The Witnesses. Macmillan (London), 1971; Harper, 1971

HOLDEN, DENIS
  Menace from the East. Long, 1938

HOLDEN, GENEVIEVE. Pseudonym of Genevieve Long Pou, 1919- . Series character: Lt. Al White = AW.
  Deadlier Than the Male. Doubleday, 1961
  Don't Go in Alone. Doubleday, 1965; Hale, 1966
  Killer Loose! Doubleday, 1953 AW
  Something's Happened to Kate. Doubleday, 1958 AW
  Sound an Alarm. Doubleday, 1954 AW
  The Velvet Target. Doubleday, 1956; Muller, 1957 AW

HOLDEN, J. RAILTON
  Death Flies High. Newnes, 1935
  Desert Squadron. Newnes, 1937
  Doomed Flight. Newnes, 1937
  The Hornet's Nest. Hamilton, 1933
  Night Hawk. Newnes, 1938
  Spider Flies Again. Newnes, 1937
  Suez Patrol. Newnes, 1936
  Suez Side Ace. Newnes, 1938
  The Vanished Squadron. Newnes, 1936
  Winged Death. Newnes, 1935
  Wings of Revolution. Hamilton, 1934

HOLDEN, LARRY. Pseudonym of Lorenz Heller, q.v. Other pseudonyms: Larry Heller, Frederick Lorenz, qq.v.
  Crime Cop. Pyramid, 1959
  Dead Wrong. Pyramid, 1957
  Hide-Out. Eton, 1953

HOLDEN, RAYMOND P(ECKHAM). 1894- . Pseudonym: Richard Peckham, q.v.
  Death on the Border. Holt, 1937
  The Penthouse Murders. Doubleday, 1931

HOLDER, WILLIAM
  The Case of the Dead Divorcee. Signet, 1958

HOLDING, ELISABETH SANXAY. 1889-1955.
  The Blank Wall. Simon, 1947
  Dark Power. Vanguard, 1930
  The Death Wish. Dodd, 1934; Nicholson, 1935
  The Girl Who had to Die. Dodd, 1940
  Hostess to Murder. Mystery Novel Classic, 1943. (Retitled reprint of ?)
  The Innocent Mrs. Duff. Simon, 1946
  Kill Joy. Duell, 1942. Also published as: Murder is a Kill-Joy. Dell, 1946
  Lady Killer. Duell, 1942
  Miasma. Dutton, 1929
  Murder is a Kill-Joy; see Kill Joy
  Net of Cobwebs. Simon, 1945; Corgi, 1952
  No Harm Intended; see The Obstinate Murderer
  The Obstinate Murderer. Dodd, 1938. British title: No Harm Intended. Lane, 1939
  The Old Battle Ax. Simon, 1943
  The Party was the Pay-Off; see Too Many Bottles
  Speak of the Devil. Duell, 1941
  The Strange Crime in Bermuda. Dodd, 1937; Lane, 1938
  Too Many Bottles. Simon, 1951; Muller, 1953. Also published as: The Party was the Pay-Off. Mercury, 1952
  Trial by Murder; see Who's Afraid?
  The Unfinished Crime. Dodd, 1935; Newnes, 1936
  The Virgin Huntress. Simon, 1951
  Who's Afraid? Duell, 1940. Also published as: Trial by Murder. Thriller Novel Classic, 194?
  Widow's Mite. Simon, 1953; Muller, 1954

HOLICKER, CHARLOTTE
  A Name my Own. Dell, 1974

HOLLAND, CLIVE. Pseudonym of Charles James Hankinson, 1866-1959.
  The Hidden Submarine; or, The Plot That Failed. Scott, 1917

HOLLAND, HESTER
  -A Man Must Live. Butterworth, 1938
  Week-Ends for Harry. Hurst, 1947

HOLLAND, ISABELLE. 1920- .
  Kilgaren. Weybright, 1974; Collins, 1975
  Moncrieff. Weybright, 1975. British title: The Standish Place. Collins, 1976
  The Standish Place; see Moncrieff
  Trelawny. Weybright, 1974. British title: Trelawny's Fell. Collins, 1976
  Trelawny's Fell; see Trelawny

HOLLAND, MARTY
  Blonde Baggage; see Fallen Angel
  Fallen Angel. Dutton, 1945; Davies, 1946. Also published as: Blonde Baggage. Novel Library, 1950
  The Glass Heart. Messner, 1946; Davies, 1946. Also published as: Her Private Passions. Avon, 1948
  Her Private Passions; see The Glass Heart

HOLLAND, ROBERT. 1940- .
  The Hunter. Stein, 1971; Hale, 1974

HOLLAND, RUPERT SARGENT. 1878-1952.
  Crooked Lanes. Jacobs, 1923
  The House of Delusion. Jacobs, 1922
  How Murder Speaks. Sears, 1933
  The Man in the Moonlight. Jacobs, 1920; Paul, 1925
  Minot's Folly. Macrae, 1925
  The Mystery of the "Opal". Jacobs, 1924; Paul, 1924
  -Neptune's Son. Jacobs, 1919
  The Panelled Room. Jacobs, 1921
  -Peter Cotterell's Treasure. Lippincott, 1922
  -A Race for a Fortune. Lippincott, 1931

HOLLAND, EDITH. 1898- . Pseudonym: Ruth Holland, q.v.

HOLLAND, RUTH and J(OHN) B(OYNTON) PRIESTLEY, 1894- , q.v. Ruth Holland is the pseudonym of Edith Holland, 1898- .
  Dangerous Corner. H. Hamilton, 1932; Doubleday, 1933. (Novelization of the play by J. B. Priestley, q.v.)

HOLLEY, HELEN. Series character: Tessie Venable, in both titles.
  Blood on the Beach. Mystery House, 1946
  Dead Run. Mystery House, 1947

HOLLINGSWORTH, LEONARD. Series character: Insp. (Supt.) Adams, in all titles.
  The Body on the Bus. Murray, 1930
  Dead Man's Alibi. Murray, 1933
  Death Leaves Us Naked. Murray, 1931

HOLLIS, JIM. Joint pseudonym of Hollis Spurgeon Summers, 1915- , and James F. Rourke, 1922- .
  Teach You a Lesson. Harper, 1955; Foulsham, 1956. Also published as: The Case of the Bludgeoned Teacher. Avon, 1956

HOLLOWAY, ELIZABETH HUGHES
  Cobweb House. Dutton, 1931

HOLLOWAY, M.
  Three Keys to Murder. Fiction House, 1950

HOLLOWAY, TERESA BRAGUNIER. 1906- . Pseudonym: Elizabeth Beatty, q.v.

HOLLY, J. HUNTER. Pseudonym of Joan Carol Holly, 1932- .
  The Assassination Affair. Ace, 1967. (Novelization of The Man from UNCLE TV series.)

HOLLY, JOAN CAROL. 1932- . Pseudonym: J. Hunter Holly, q.v.

HOLMAN, (CLARENCE) HUGH. 1914- . Pseudonym: Clarence Hunt, q.v. Series character: Sheriff Macready = M.

Another Man's Poison. Mill, 1947; Foulsham, 1950 M
Death Like Thunder. Phoenix, 1942
Slay the Murderer. Mill, 1946; Foulsham, 1950 M
Trout in the Milk. Mill, 1945; Boardman, 1951 M
Up This Crooked Way. Mill, 1946; Foulsham, 1951 M

HOLMAN, RUSSELL. See: ARTHUR (JOHN ARBUTHNOTT) STRINGER, 1874-1950.

HOLMES, DARRELL FORSYTHE, JR.
Implied Immunity. Vantage, 1963

HOLMES, DAVID C(HARLES). 1919-   .
The Velvet Ape. Mystery House, 1957

HOLMES, GORDON. Pseudonym of Louis Tracy, 1863-1928, q.v., jointly in part with M(atthew) P(hipps) Shiel, 1865-1947, q.v. Series character: Inspector Furneaux = F (see also Louis Tracy entry.)
The Arncliffe Puzzle. Laurie, 1906; Clode, 1906. Revised edition: Jarrolds, 1932, as by Louis Tracy
By Force of Circumstances. Mills, 1910; Clode, 1909. Reprinted as by Louis Tracy: Jarrolds, 1932 F
The de Bercy Affair; see The Feldisham Mystery
The Feldisham Mystery. Amalgamated, 1911. U.S. title: The de Bercy Affair. Clode, 1910 F
The House 'Round the Corner. Ward, 1914; Clode, 1919
The Late Tenant. Cassell, 1907; Clode, 1906. Also published as by Louis Tracy: Jarrolds, 1932

HOLMES, GRANT. Pseudonym of James M. W. Knipscheer. Other pseudonym: James M. Fox, q.v.

HOLMES, H. H. Pseudonym of William Anthony Parker White, 1911-1968. Other pseudonym: Anthony Boucher, q.v. See also: THEO DURRANT. Series character: Sister Ursula, in both titles.
Nine Times Nine. Duell, 1940. Subsequently reprinted as by Anthony Boucher.
Rocket to the Morgue. Duell, 1942. Subsequently reprinted as by Anthony Boucher.

HOLMES, CAPTAIN HOWARD. Pseudonym of Thomas Chalmers Harbaugh, 1849-1924.
The Never-Fail Detective. Westbrook, 1920's

HOLMES, J. GIBB
-Ghosts' Gloom. Sonnenschein, 1889

HOLMES, MRS. M(ICHAEL) A(NGELO)
Woman Against Woman. Ogilvie, 1885
A Woman's Vengeance. Lovell, 1886

HOLMES, MRS. M. E.
Her Fatal Sin. Laird, 1886
The Tragedy of Redmount. Laird, 1886

HOLMES, MRS. MARY J(ANE). 1825-1907.
Chateau d'Or. Carleton, 1880; Low, 1880

HOLMES, PAUL A(LLEN). 1901-   .
Murder Buttoned Up. Dutton, 1948

HOLMES, ROBERT
Fear Comes to Euston Road. Hale, 1941

HOLMES, SAMUEL
Fade into Murder. Langdon, 1947

HOLMGREN, FLORENCE DEPPE
The Mystery of Bent Cove. Bouregy, 1966

HOLT, ALLISON
Bier for a Hussy. Phoenix, 1943. Also published as: Death for a Hussy. Red Dagger, 1946 (abridged)

HOLT, BARRY
The Mowbray Mystery. Stockwell, 1933

HOLT, DEBEN. Pseudonym.
Circle of Shadows. Gifford, 1947
Sinner Takes All. Gifford, 1948

HOLT, E. CARLETON. Pseudonym of Ernest Philip Guigo.
Mystery at Arden Court. Stockwell, 1954

HOLT, GAVIN. Pseudonym of (Percival) Charles Rodda, 1891-   , q.v. Other pseudonym: Gardner Low, q.v. Joint pseudonym with Eric Ambler, 1909-   , q.v.: Eliot Reed, q.v. Series characters: Professor Bastion, in at least those marked B; Joel Saber, in at least those marked JS; Sherrett York, in at least those marked SY.
Begonia Walk. Hodder, 1946. U.S. title: Send No Flowers. Howell Soskin, 1947 JS
Black Bullets. Hodder, 1935 B
Dark Lady. Hodder, 1933 B
The Dark Street. Hodder, 1942
Death Takes the Stage. Hodder, 1934; Little, 1934 B
Drums Beat at Night. Hodder, 1932 B
Dusk at Penarder. Hodder, 1956
The Emerald Spider. Hodder, 1935 B
Eyes in the Night. Hutchinson, 1927
The Garden of Silent Beasts. Hodder, 1931 B
Garlands for Sylvia. Hodder, 1958
Give a Man Rope. Hodder, 1942
The Golden Witch. Hodder, 1933 B
Green for Danger. Gollancz, 1939
Green Talons. Hodder, 1930; Bobbs, 1931 B
Irina. Hale, 1965
Ivory Ladies. Hodder, 1937 SY
Ladies in Ermine. Hodder, 1947 JS
Mark of the Paw. Hodder, 1933 B
Murder at Marble Arch. Hodder, 1931 B
Murder Train. Hodder, 1936 SY
No Curtains for Cora. Hodder, 1950
Pattern of Guilt. Hodder, 1960; Walker, 1962
The Praying Monkey; see The White-Faced Man
Red Eagle. Hodder, 1932 B
-Redemption Range. Gryphon, 1952
Send No Flowers; see Begonia Walk
Six Minutes Past Twelve. Hodder, 1928 B
Sole Survivor. Hale, 1969
Steel Shutters. Hodder, 1936 B
Storm. Hodder, 1931; Swain, 1933, as by Charles Rodda
Swing It, Death. Gollancz, 1940 JS
Take Away the Lady. Hodder, 1954
The Theme is Murder. Gollancz, 1938; Simon, 1939 JS
Tonight is for Death. Hodder, 1952
Trafalgar Square. Hodder, 1934 B
Trail of the Skull. Hodder, 1931 B
Valse Caprice. Hodder, 1932
The White-Faced Man. Hodder, 1929. U.S. title: The Praying Monkey. Dial, 1930 B

HOLT, GORDON. Pseudonym of Harold Ernest Kelly, 1899-   . Other pseudonyms: Darcy Glinto, Buck Toler, qq.v.
The Stables to ₤1,000,000. Hector Kelly, 1948

HOLT, HARRISON JEWELL
Midnight at Mears House. Dodd, 1912; Simpkin, 1916

HOLT, HENRY. Series characters: Inspector Silver, in at least those marked S; Mike Logan, in at least those marked ML.
The Ace of Spades. Harrap, 1930; Dial, 1930 S
Call Out the Flying Squad!; see Gallows Grange
Calling All Cars. Collins, 1934. U.S. title: The Sinister Shadow. Doubleday, 1934 S
Calling Scotland Yard. Hale, 1944 S
Don't Shoot, Darling. Hale, 1961; Roy, 1963 ML & S
Gallows Grange. Harrap, 1933. U.S. title: Call Out the Flying Squad! Doubleday, 1933 S
The Man Who Forgot. Hale, 1943
The Mayfair Murder; see The Mayfair Mystery
The Mayfair Mystery. Harrap, 1929. U.S. title: The Mayfair Murder. Dial, 1929 S
The Midnight Mail. Harrap, 1931; Doubleday, 1931 S
Mink and Murder. Hale, 1958
Motley and Murder. Hale, 1945 S
Murder at the Bookstall. Collins, 1934 S
Murder, My Sweet. Museum, 1950 S
Murder of a Film Star. Collins, 1940
Murderer's Luck. Harrap, 1932; Doubleday, 1932 S
The Mystery of the Smiling Doll. Collins, 1939
The Necklace of Death. Harrap, 1931; Doubleday, 1931 S
No Lilies. Hale, 1947 ML
No Medals for Murder. Museum, 1954
The Scarlet Messenger. Collins, 1933; Doubleday, 1933 S
The Sinister Shadow; see Calling All Cars
There has been a Murder. Collins, 1936 S
Tiger of Mayfair. Collins, 1935 S
Unknown Terror. Collins, 1935
Wanted for Murder. Collins, 1938
The Whispering Man. Collins, 1938
The Wolf; see The Wolf's Claw
The Wolf's Claw. Harrap, 1932. U.S. title: The Wolf. Doubleday, 1932 S
A Wreath for the Lady. Hale, 1959 ML & S

HOLT, JOHN ROBERT. 1926-   . Pseudonyms: Elizabeth Giles, Raymond Giles, qq.v.

HOLT, RICHARD
Money from Rome. Mayflower, 1965

HOLT, THOMAS LITTLETON
John Horsleydown; or, The Confessions of a Thief. Ward, 1860 ss

HOLT, VICTORIA. Pseudonym of Eleanor Burford Hibbert, 1906-   . Other pseudonyms: Philippa Carr, Elbur Ford, Kathleen Kellow, qq.v.
Bride of Pendorric. Collins, 1963; Doubleday, 1963
The Curse of the Kings. Collins, 1973; Doubleday, 1973
The House of a Thousand Lanterns. Collins, 1974; Doubleday, 1974
The King of the Castle. Collins, 1968; Doubleday, 1968
Kirkland Revels. Collins, 1962; Doubleday, 1962
The Legend of the Seventh Virgin. Collins, 1965; Doubleday, 1965
Lord of the Far Island. Collins, 1975; Doubleday, 1975
Menfreya. Collins, 1966. U.S. title: Menfreya in the Morning. Doubleday, 1966

Menfreya in the Morning; see Menfreya
Mistress of Mellyn. Collins, 1961;
  Doubleday, 1960
On the Night of the Seventh Moon. Collins, 1973; Doubleday, 1973
The Secret Woman. Collins, 1971;
  Doubleday, 1970
The Shadow of the Lynx. Collins, 1972;
  Doubleday, 1971
The Shivering Sands. Collins, 1969;
  Doubleday, 1969

HOLT-WHITE, W(ILLIAM EDWARD BRADDON),
    1878- .
  The Crime Club; see The Prime Minister's Secret
  -The Earthquake. Richards, 1906
  -Helen of All Time. Unwin, 1910
  -The Man Who Dreamed Right. Everett,
    1910
  -The Man Who Stole the Earth. Unwin,
    1909
  The Prime Minister's Secret. Unwin,
    1910. U.S. title: The Crime Club.
    Macaulay, 1910
  The Super Spy. Melrose, 1916
  -The Woman Who Saved the World. Everett,
    1914
  -The World Stood Still. Everett, 1912

HOLTHAM, GERALD. See: ROGER BUSBY.

HOLTON, EDITH AUSTIN. 1881- . Pseudonym: Elizabeth Alden Heath, q.v.

HOLTON, LEONARD. Pseudonym of Leonard
    Patrick O'Connor Wibberley, 1915- .
    Series character: Father Joseph
    Bredder, in all titles.
  Deliver Us from Wolves. Dodd, 1963
  The Devil to Play. Dodd, 1974
  Flowers by Request. Dodd, 1964
  The Mirror of Hell. Dodd, 1972
  Out of the Depths. Dodd, 1966; Hammond,
    1967
  A Pact with Satan. Dodd, 1960; Hale,
    1961
  A Problem in Angels. Dodd, 1970
  The Saint Maker. Dodd, 1959; Hale, 1960
  Secret of the Doubting Saint. Dodd,
    1961
  A Touch of Jonah. Dodd, 1968

HOLZER, HANS W. 1920- .
  The Red Chindvit Conspiracy. Award,
    1970

HOME, BERNARD
  Passport to Death. Hutchinson, 1937
  Rogue Haven. Hutchinson, 1938

HOME, MICHAEL. Pseudonym of Christopher
    Bush, 1885-1973, q.v.
  -The Auber File. Methuen, 1953
  -City of the Soul. Methuen, 1943
  -The Cypress Road. Methuen, 1945
  -The Harvest is Past. Rich, 1937
  -July at Fritham. Rich, 1938
  No Snow at Latching. Methuen, 1949
  -The Questing Man. Rich, 1936
  -The Soundless Years. Methuen, 1951
  The Strange Prisoner. Methuen, 1947
  -That was Yesterday. Methuen, 1955

HOME-GALL, EDWARD R(EGINALD)
  The Haunted Ice Rink. New Arts, 1946

HOME-GALL, WILLIAM BENJAMIN. 1861-1936.
  State Secrets. Amalgamated, 1921.
    (Sexton Blake.)

HOMERSHAM, B(ASIL) H(ENRY). 1902- .
  Pseudonym: Basil Manningham, q.v.
  Arsenic on the Menu. Paul, 1936
  Murder of an M.P. Paul, 1935

HOMES, GEOFFREY. Pseudonym of Daniel
    (Geoffrey Homes) Mainwaring, 1902-
    1977, q.v. Series characters: Robin
    Bishop = RB; Humphrey Campbell = HC.
  Build My Gallows High. Morrow, 1946
  The Case of the Mexican Knife; see The
    Street of the Crying Woman
  The Case of the Unhappy Angels; see The
    Six Silver Handles
  Dead as a Dummy; see The Hill of the
    Terrified Monk
  The Doctor Died at Dusk. Morrow, 1936
    RB
  Finders Keepers. Morrow, 1940 HC
  Forty Whacks. Morrow, 1941. Also published as: Stiffs Don't Vote. Bantam,
    1947 HC
  The Hill of the Terrified Monk. Morrow,
    1943. Also published as: Dead as a
    Dummy. Bantam, 1949
  The Man Who Didn't Exist. Morrow, 1937;
    Eyre, 1939 RB
  The Man Who Murdered Goliath. Morrow,
    1938; Eyre, 1940 RB
  The Man Who Murdered Himself. Morrow,
    1936; Lane, 1936 RB
  No Hands on the Clock. Morrow, 1939 HC
  Seven Died. Cherry Tree, 1943. (U.S.
    title?)
  The Six Silver Handles. Morrow, 1944;
    Cherry Tree, 1946. Also published as:
    The Case of the Unhappy Angels. Bantam, 1950 HC
  Stiffs Don't Vote; see Forty Whacks
  The Street of the Crying Woman. Morrow,
    1942. Also published as: The Case of
    the Mexican Knife. Bantam, 1948
  Then There were Three. Morrow, 1938;
    Cherry Tree, 1945 RB & HC

HONE, JOSEPH. 1937- . Series character: Peter Marlow, in both titles.
  The Private Sector. H. Hamilton, 1971;
    Dutton, 1972
  The Sixth Directorate. Secker, 1975;
    Dutton, 1975

HONEYCOMBE, GORDON. 1936- .
  Adam's Tale. Hutchinson, 1974
  Dragon Under the Hill. Hutchinson,
    1972; Simon, 1972
  Neither the Sea nor the Sand. Hutchinson, 1969; Weybright, 1970

HONEYMAN, WILLIAM C. Pseudonym: James
    M'Govan, q.v.

HONIG, DONALD. 1931- .
  Divide the Night. Regency, 1961
  -Judgment Night. Belmont, 1971
  The Operator; see Sidewalk Caesar
  The Severith Style. Scribner, 1972
  Sidewalk Caesar. Pyramid, 1958. Also
    published as: The Operator. Belmont,
    1971

HOOD, CHRISTOPHER
  The Mullenthorpe Thing. Chatto, 1971

HOOD, MARGARET PAGE. 1892- .
  The Bell on Lonely. Coward, 1959
  Drown the Wind. Coward, 1961
  In the Dark Night. Coward, 1957. Also
    published as: The Murders on Fox Island. Dell, 1960
  The Murders on Fox Island; see In the
    Dark Night
  The Scarlet Thread. Coward, 1956
  The Silent Women. Coward, 1954
  The Sin Mark. Coward, 1963

HOOD, STEPHEN. Pseudonym of Jack Lewis,
    q.v. Other pseudonym: Lewis Jackson,
    q.v.
  The Crook from Chicago. Amalgamated
    Press, 1931. (Sexton Blake.)

HOOK, ALFRED SAMUEL. Pseudonym: A. J.
    Colton, q.v.

HOOKE, CHARLES WITHERLE. 1861-1929. Pseudonym: Howard Fielding, q.v.

HOOKE, NINA WARNER. 1907- .
  Darkness I Leave You. Hale, 1956
  Deadly Record. Hale, 1958. Play version: French, 1965

HOOKER, G(WENDA) DALTON
  Smith's Odyssey. Angus, 1962

HOOPER, C(YRUS) LAURON. 1863- .
  A Cloverdale Skeleton. Alden, 1889

HOPE, ANDREE. Pseudonym of Annie Jane
    Tennant Harvey,   -1898.
  The Secret of Wardale Court and other
    stories. Wilsons, 1894 ss, title ss
    criminous
  The Vyvyans; or, The Murder in the Rue
    Bellechasse. Chapman, 1893; Rand,
    1893

HOPE, ANTHONY. Pseudonym of Sir Anthony
    Hope Hawkins, 1863-1933.
  Beaumaroy Home from the Wars. Methuen,
    1919. U.S. title: The Secret of the
    Tower. Appleton, 1919

HOPE, BRIAN. Pseudonym of John Creasey,
    1908-1973, q.v. Other pseudonyms:
    Gordon Ashe, M. E. Cooke, Norman
    Deane, Robert Caine Frazer, Patrick
    Gill, Michael Halliday, Charles Hogarth, Colin Hughes, Kyle Hunt, Abel
    Mann, Peter Manton, J. J. Marric,
    Richard Martin, Rodney Mattheson,
    Anthony Morton, Jeremy York, qq.v.
  Four Motives for Murder. Newnes, 1938

HOPE, CAMILLA. Pseudonym of Grace E.
    Thompson.
  -Curiously Planned. Long, 1928
  Long Shadows. Long, 1928; Fiction Library, 1929
  -Moon of Joy. Long, 1927

HOPE, CHARLES (EVELYN) GRAHAM
  The Second Plan. Hodder, 1938

HOPE, COLIN
  Air Gold. Hamilton, 1935
  The Air Peril. Hamilton, 1937
  Death in the Fens. Hamilton, 1935
  A Ghost from the Past. Fiction House,
    1936
  The Harne Grange Mystery. Mellifont,
    1935
  The House in the Way. Modern, 1935
  The Mystery at Crowstone. Hamilton,
    1936
  "No Honour—." Hamilton, 1935
  The Phantom Killer. Fiction House, 1935
  The Prince of Trouble. Hamilton, 1936
  Vengeance in the Air. Mellifont, 1940

HOPE, FIELDING. 1897- . See also:
    JOHN ANGUS.
  The Guinea Pig's Tail. Selwyn, 1934.
    U.S. title (?): Marie Arnaud, Spy.
    Macaulay, 1934
  Marie Arnaud, Spy; see The Guinea Pig's
    Tail
  The Mystery of the House of Commons.
    Selwyn, 1929; Dial, 1930

HOPE, FRANCES ESSEX THEODORA. Pseudonym:
    Essex Smith, q.v.

HOPE, HENRY. Pseudonym: Henry Andover,
    q.v.

HOPE, MARK. Pseudonym of Eustace Clare
    Grenville Murray, 1824-1881.

Dark and Light Stories. Chapman, 1879
ss, some criminous

HOPE, (WILLIAM EDWARD) STANTON. 1889-1961. All titles were published by Amalgamated Press and feature Sexton Blake.
The Amazing Affair of the Shipyard Sabotage. 1940
The Case of the Missing Ships. 1935
The Case of the Monta Grandee Diamonds. 1945
The Cruise of Terror. 1932
The Death Ship. 1931
The Dockyard Mystery. 1936
In the Grip of the Gestapo. 1940
The Mystery of the Engraved Skull. 1954
The Secret at Sixty-Six Fathoms. 1938
The Sign of the Blue Triangle. 1942
The Stolen Submarine. 1937
The Terror of Thunder Creek. 1936
The Victim of the Red Mask. 1931; Red Mask, 194?

HOPKINS, A. T. Pseudonym of Annette Turngren, 1902- .
Have a Lovely Funeral. Rinehart, 1954

HOPKINS, (HECTOR) KENNETH. 1914- . Pseudonym: Christopher Adams, q.v. Series characters: Dr. Blow = B; Gerry Lee = GL.
Body Blow. Macdonald, 1962; Holt, 1962 B
Campus Corpse. Macdonald, 1963 GL
Dead Against My Principles. Macdonald, 1960; Holt, 1962 B
The Forty-First Passenger. Macdonald, 1958 GL
The Girl Who Died. Macdonald, 1955 GL
Pierce with a Pin. Macdonald, 1960 GL
She Died Because... Macdonald, 1957; Holt, 1964 B

HOPKINS, LINTON C(OOKE). 1872-1943.
Black Buck. Little, 1931
The Candle. Green Circle, 1937; Joseph, 1936

HOPKINS, NEVIL MONROE. 1873-1945. Series character: Mason Brant, in both titles.
The Investigation at Holman Square; see The Strange Cases of Mason Brant
The Racoon Lake Mystery. Lippincott, 1917
The Strange Cases of Mason Brant. Lippincott, 1916 ss; one of the three stories was published separately as: The Investigation at Holman Square. Modern, 193?

HOPKINS, R. THURSTON. See: CLARICE MAYNE.

HOPKINS, ROBERT (S.). Pseudonym: Robert Rostand, q.v.
The Raid on the Villa Joyosa. Putnam, 1973; Barker, 1975

HOPKINS, SEWARD W.
A Baffled Imposter. Henderson, 189?
-On a False Charge. Bonner's, 1895

HOPKINS, STANLEY, JR. Series character: Peter Marrell, in both titles.
Murder by Inches. Harcourt, 1943
The Parchment Key. Harcourt, 1944

HOPKINSON, HENRY THOMAS. 1905- . Pseudonym: Thomas Pembroke. See: MILESON (DENIS JAMES) HORTON, 1899- .

HOPLEY, GEORGE. Pseudonym of Cornell (George Hopley) Woolrich, 1903-1968, q.v. Other pseudonym: William Irish, q.v.
Fright. Rinehart, 1950; Foulsham, 1950

Night has a Thousand Eyes. Farrar, 1945; Penguin, 1949. Reprinted as by William Irish: Dell, 1953. Reprinted as by Cornell Woolrich: Paperback Library, 1967

HOPPER, JAMES (MARIE), 1876- , and FRED(ERICK) R(ITCHIE) BECHDOLT, 1874- , q.v.
9009. McClure, 1908; Heinemann, 1909

HOPWOOD, AVERY. 1884-1928. See: MARY ROBERTS RINEHART, 1876-1958.

HORAN, JAMES D(AVID). 1914- .
The New Vigilantes. Crown, 1975

HORLER, SYDNEY. 1888-1954. Series characters: The "Ace" = A; Sir Harker Bellamy = HB; "Bunny" Chipstead = BC; H. Emp = HE; Sir Brian Fordinghame = BF; Martin Huish = MH; Sir William Kirby = WK; Gerald Lissendale = GL; Chief Constable Meatyard = M; Nighthawk (Gerald Frost) = N; Sebastian Quin = SQ; Peter Scarlett = PS; Tiger Standish = TS; Baron Veseloffsky = BV; Paul Vivanti = PV; Robert Wynnton = RW.
Adventure Calling! Hodder, 1931
Beauty and the Policeman and other stories. Hutchinson, 1933 ss, one about WK
The Black Heart. Hodder, 1927; Doubleday, 1928
The Blade is Bright. Eyre, 1952
The Blanco Case. Quality, 1950
The Breed of the Beverleys. Odhams, 1921
A Bullet for the Countess. Quality, 1945
The Cage. Hale, 1953
Cavalier of Chance. Hodder, 1931. U.S. title: Peril. Mystery League, 1930
The Charlatan; see The Formula
Checkmate. Hodder, 1930
Chipstead of the Lone Hand. Hodder, 1928; Holt, 1929 BC
The Closed Door. Pilot, 1948 GL
Corridors of Fear. Quality, 1947
The Curse of Doone. Hodder, 1928; Mystery League, 1930
Danger Preferred. Hodder, 1942
Danger's Bright Eyes. Hodder, 1930; Harper, 1932
Dark Danger. Arcadia, 1945. (British title?)
The Dark Hostess. Eyre, 1955
Dark Journey. Hodder, 1938
The Dark Night. Hodder, 1953 A
Death at Court Lady. Collins, 1936
Death of a Spy. Museum, 1953
The Destroyer and The Red-Haired Death. Hodder, 1938. (Two novelets, one about HB.)
The Devil and the Deep; see The House in Greek Street
The Devil Comes to Bolobyn. Percival Marshall, 1951
Dying to Live and other stories. Hutchinson, 1935 ss
The Enemy Within the Gates. Hodder, 1940 BC
Enter the Ace. Hodder, 1941 A
The Evil Chateau. Hodder, 1930; Knopf, 1931
The Evil Messenger. Hodder, 1938 SQ
Exit the Disguiser. Hodder, 1948 TS
The Face of Stone. Barker, 1952
False-Face. Hodder, 1926; Doran, 1926 BV & BF
The False Purple; see Princess After Dark

Fear Walked Behind. Hale, 1942 SQ
The Formula. Long, 1933. U.S. title: The Charlatan. Little, 1934
A Gentleman for the Gallows. Hodder, 1938; Hillman-Curl, 1938
Gentleman-in-Waiting. Benn, 1932
Great Adventure and Out of a Dark Sky. Hale, 1946. (Two novelets.)
The Grim Game. Collins, 1936; Little, 1936 TS
Harlequin of Death. Long, 1933; Little, 1933
Heart Cut Diamond. Hodder, 1929
Hell's Brew. Hodder, 1952 A
Here is an S.O.S. Hodder, 1939 M
Here is an S.O.S. Hodder, 1942 (43 pp)
The Hidden Hand. Collins, 1937
The High Game. Redman, 1950
High Hazard. Hodder, 1943
High Stakes. Collins, 1932; Little, 1935 BF
Horror's Head. Hodder, 1932 HE
The Hostage. Quality, 1943
The House in Greek Street. Hodder, 1935. (Four ss. A later edition, Crowther, 1946, contains the title ss and two others, The Devil and the Deep and Knight at Arms, the latter not appearing in the 1935 edition.) 1 ss about SQ; 3 about HB
The House of Jackals. Hodder, 1951 TS
The House of Secrets. Hodder, 1926; Doran, 1927
The House of the Uneasy Dead. Barker, 1950
The House with the Light. Hodder, 1948
Huntress of Death. Hodder, 1933
In the Dark. Hodder, 1927. U.S. title: A Life for Sale. Doubleday, 1928 BC
Instruments of Darkness. Hodder, 1937
Knaves & Co. Collins, 1938 ss, 2 about SQ
Knight at Arms; see The House in Greek Street
Lady of the Night. Hodder, 1929; Knopf, 1930
The Lady with the Limp. Hodder, 1944 TS
The Lessing Murder Case. Collins, 1935 WK
A Life for Sale; see In the Dark
Lord of Terror. Collins, 1935; Hillman-Curl, 1937 PV
Love, the Sportsman. Hodder, 1923. Also published as: The Man with Two Faces. Collins, 1934
The Man from Scotland Yard. Hutchinson, 1934
The Man in the Cloak. Eyre, 1951 RW
The Man in the Hood. Redman, 1955
The Man in the Shadows. Hale, 1955
The Man in White. Staples, 1942
A Man of Affairs. Pilot, 1949
The Man of Evil. Barker, 1951
The Man Who did not Hang. Quality, 1948
The Man Who Died Twice. Hodder, 1939. Play version: Nelson, 1941
The Man Who Loved Spiders. Barker, 1948 M
-The Man Who Mislaid the War. Muller, 1943. (3-act play.)
The Man Who Preferred Cocktails. Crowther, 1943
The Man Who Shook the Earth. Hutchinson, 1933 ss
The Man Who Used Perfume. Wingate, 1952 RW
The Man Who Walked with Death. Hodder, 1941; Knopf, 1931
The Man with Dry Hands. Eyre, 1944
The Man with Two Faces; see Love, the Sportsman
Master of Venom. Hodder, 1949 HE
The Menace. Collins, 1933; Little, 1933
Miss Mystery. Hodder, 1928; Little, 1935 BV
The Mocking Face of Murder. Hale, 1952

Murder for Sale. Vallancey, 1945 (16 pp.)
Murder is so Simple. Eyre, 1943
The Murder Mask. Readers Library, 1930
Murderer at Large. Hodder, 1952 HE
My Lady Dangerous. Collins, 1932; Harper, 1933 HB
The Mystery Mission. Poynings, 1944 (31 pp.)
The Mystery Mission and other stories. Hodder, 1931 ss
The Mystery of Mr. X. Foulsham, 1951
The Mystery of No. 1. Hodder, 1925. U.S. title: The Order of the Octopus. Doran, 1926 PV
The Mystery of the Seven Cafes. Hodder, 1935 TS
Nap On Nighthawk. Hodder, 1950 N
The Night of Reckoning. Eyre, 1942
Nighthawk Mops Up. Hodder, 1944 N
Nighthawk Strikes to Kill. Hodder, 1941 N
Nighthawk Swears Vengeance. Hodder, 1954 N
The Order of the Octopus; see The Mystery of No. 1
Out of a Dark Sky; see Great Adventure
Peril; see Cavalier of Chance
-The Phantom Forward. Hodder, 1939
The Prince of Plunder. Hodder, 1934; Little, 1934 BF
Princess After Dark. Hodder, 1931. U.S. title: The False Purple. Mystery League, 1932
The Red-Haired Death; see The Destroyer
The Return of Nighthawk. Hodder, 1940 N
Ring Up Nighthawk. Hodder, 1947 N
Scarlett Gets the Kidnapper. Foulsham, 1951 PS
Scarlett—Special Branch. Foulsham, 1950 PS
The Screaming Skull and other stories. Hodder, 1930 ss, 2 about HB; 1 about SQ
The Secret Agent. Collins, 1934; Little, 1934 BC
The Secret Hand. Barker, 1954
The Secret Service Man. Hodder, 1929; Knopf, 1930 MH & GL
Sinister Street. Vallancey, 1944. (Taken from The Mystery Mission and other stories, q.v.)
S.O.S. Hutchinson, 1934
The Spy. Hodder, 1931
The Stroke Sinister and other stories. Hutchinson, 1935 ss, one about MH
-The Temptation of Mary Gordon. Newnes, 1931
Terror Comes to Twelvetrees. Eyre, 1945
Terror on Tip-Toe. Hodder, 1939
These Men and Women. Museum, 1951
They Called Him Nighthawk. Hodder, 1937 N
They Thought He was Dead. Hodder, 1949 TS
The 13th Hour. Readers Library, 1928
Tiger Standish. Long, 1932; Doubleday, 1933 TS
Tiger Standish Comes Back. Hutchinson, 1934 TS
Tiger Standish Does His Stuff. Hodder, 1941 (2 novelets.) TS
Tiger Standish has a Party. Todd, 1943 (16 pp.) TS
Tiger Standish Steps on It. Hodder, 1940 TS
Tiger Standish Takes the Field. Hodder, 1939 TS
The Traitor. Collins, 1936; Little, 1936
The Vampire. Hutchinson, 1935; Bookfinger, 1974
Virus X. Quality, 1945 PV
Vivanti. Hodder, 1927; Doran, 1927 PV
Vivanti Returns. Hodder, 1931 PV
The Web. Redman, 1951
-Whilst the Crowd Roared. Archer, 1949

Wolves of the Night. Readers Library, 1931
The Worst Man in the World. Hodder, 1929 PV

HORN, HOLLOWAY. 1886-   .
The Intruder. Collins, 1929
The Murder at Linpara. Collins, 1931
The Neglected Fire. Collins, 1923
The Purple Claw. Muller, 1935

HORNBLOW, ARTHUR. 1865-   .
The Argyle Case. Harper (New York & London), 1913. (Novelization of the play by Harriet Ford, q.v., and Harvey O'Higgins, 1876-1929, q.v.)
Find the Woman; see The Third Degree
-The Lion and the Mouse. Dillingham, 1906. (Novelization of the play by Charles Klein.)
The Mask. Dillingham, 1913
-The Price. Dillingham, 1914. (Novelization of the play by George Broadhurst.)
The Profligate. Dillingham, 1908; Unwin, 1908
The Third Degree, with Charles Klein. Dillingham, 1909. British title: Find the Woman; or, The Third Degree. Bird, 1912
-The Watch Dog. Dillingham, 1915

HORNBY, JOHN WILKINSON. 1913-   .
Alpine Crack-Up. Hamilton Stafford, 1952
Death Pays Dividends. Hamilton Stafford, 1951
Die Quickly, Brother. Hamilton Stafford, 1951
Here Today—Dead Tomorrow. Hamilton Stafford, 1951

HORNE, GEOFFREY. 1916-   . Pseudonym: Gil North, q.v.
-Land of No Escape. Hutchinson, 1958
-The Man Who was Chief. Chapman, 1960
-The Portuguese Diamonds. Chapman, 1961
-Quest for Gold. Hutchinson, 1959
-Winter. Hutchinson, 1957

HORNIMAN, ROY. 1874-1930.
Israel Rank. Chatto, 1907

HORNUNG, E(RNEST) W(ILLIAM). 1866-1921. Series character: Raffles = R.
The Amateur Cracksman. Methuen, 1899; Scribner, 1899. Also published as: Raffles, the Amateur Cracksman. Nash, 1906 R
At Large. Scribner, 1902 (British title?)
The Belle of Toorak. Richards, 1900. U.S. title: The Shadow of a Man. Scribner, 1901
The Black Mask. Richards, 1901. U.S. title: Raffles: Further Adventures of the Amateur Cracksman. Scribner, 1901 R
-The Boss of Taroomba. Bliss, 1894; Scribner, 1900
-A Bride from the Bush. Smith & Elder, 1890; U.S. Book Co., as by "A New Writer"
The Camera Fiend. Unwin, 1911; Scribner, 1911
The Crime Doctor. Nash, 1914; Bobbs, 1914 ss
Dead Men Tell No Tales. Methuen, 1899; Scribner, 1899
Denis Dent. Isbister, 1903; Stokes, 1904
-Irralie's Bushranger. New Vagabond Library, 1896; Scribner, 1896

Mr. Justice Raffles. Smith & Elder, 1909; Scribner, 1909 R
-My Lord Duke. Cassell, 1897; Scribner, 1897
Old Offenders and a Few Old Scores. Murray, 1923 ss
Peccavi. Richards, 1900; Scribner, 1900
Raffles: Further Adventures of the Amateur Cracksman; see The Black Mask
Raffles, the Amateur Cracksman; see The Amateur Cracksman
The Rogue's March. Cassell, 1896; Scribner, 1896
The Shadow of a Man; see The Belle of Toorak
The Shadow of a Rope. Chatto, 1902; Scribner, 1902
Some Persons Unknown. Cassell, 1898; Scribner, 1898 ss
Stingaree. Chatto, 1905; Scribner, 1905 ss
A Thief in the Night. Chatto, 1905; Scribner, 1905 R ss
The Thousandth Woman. Nash, 1913; Bobbs, 1913
-Tiny Luttrell. Cassell (London & New York), 1893
-Under Two Skies. A. & C. Black, 1892
-Witching Hill. Hodder, 1913; Scribner, 1913 ss
-Young Blood. Cassell, 1898; Scribner, 1898

HORROCK, NICHOLAS. See: EVERT CLARK.

HORSEFIELD, L(ESLIE) G(RAHAM)
Murder at No. 3. Swan, 1950
Mystery at Vellum. Scion, 1949

HORSFIELD, RICHARD HENRY. 1872-1942. Pseudonym: M. B. Gaunt, q.v.

HORTON, GEORGE. 1852-   .
The Edge of Hazard. Bobbs, 1906
-A Fair Brigand. Stone, 1899; Ward, 1900
-A Fair Insurgent. Ward, 1906. (U.S. title?)
-Like Another Helen. Bobbs, 1901; Stevens & Brown, 1901
-The Long Straight Road. Bowen-Merrill, 1902; Stevens & Brown, 1902
-Miss Schuyler's Alias. Badger, 1913
The Monk's Treasure. Bobbs, 1905; Ward, 1907
-The Temptation of Father Anthony. McClure, 1901
-The Unspeakable Turk. McClure, 1900

HORTON, MILESON (DENIS JAMES), 1899-   , and THOMAS PEMBROKE (pseudonym of Henry Thomas Hopkinson, 1905-   .)
Photocrimes. Barker, 1936. (Illustrated puzzle ss.)

HOSEGOOD, LEWIS. 1920-   .
The Minotaur Garden. Heinemann, 1972; Delacorte, 1972

HOSKEN, ALICE CECIL SEYMOUR. Pseudonym: Coralie Stanton, q.v.

HOSKEN, CLIFFORD (JAMES WHEELER). 1882-1950. Pseudonym: Richard Keverne, q.v.
Missing from His Home. Putnam (London), 1932. Reprinted as by Richard Keverne: Penguin, 1939
The Pretender. Harrap, 1930
The Shadow Syndicate. Harrap, 1930; Dial, 1930

HOSKEN, (ERNEST CHARLES) HEATH. See: CORALIE STANTON.

HOSKINS, BERTHA LADD
The Double Fortune. Neale, 1909

HOSKINS, ROBERT. 1933- . Pseudonyms: Grace Corren, Susan Jennifer, qq.v.

HOSSENT, HARRY. 1916- . Pseudonym (?): David Savage, q.v. Series character: Max Heald, in all titles.
The Fear Business. Long, 1967
Memory of Treason. Long, 1961
No End to Fear. Long, 1959
Run for Your Death. Long, 1965
Spies Die at Dawn. Long, 1958
Spies have no Friends. Long, 1963

HOSTER, GRACE (MADELEINE JOHNSON). 1893- .
Goodbye, Dear Elizabeth. Farrar, 1943; Hammond, 1948
Trial by Murder. Farrar, 1944; Hammond, 1952

HOSTOVSKY, EGON. 1908-1973.
The Midnight Patient. Appleton, 1954; Heinemann, 1955
Missing. Viking, 1952; Secker, 1952
-The Plot. Doubleday, 1961; Cassell, 1961
-Three Nights. Cassell, 1964

HOTCHKISS, C(HAUNSEY) C(RAFTS). 1852- .
The Ivory Ball. Watt, 1920
-Mavde Baxter. Watt, 1911
-The Red Paper. Watt, 1912
-The Spur of Danger. Watt, 1915

HOTCHNER, A(ARON) E(DWARD). 1920- .
The Dangerous American. Random, 1958; Weidenfeld, 1959
Treasure. Random, 1970; Hodder, 1971

HOUGH, JOHN (T.), JR. 1946- .
The Guardian. Little, 1975

HOUGH, S(TANLEY) B(ENNETT). 1917- .
Pseudonym: Bennett Stanley, q.v.
The Bronze Perseus. Secker, 1959; Walker, 1962. Also published as: The Tender Killer. Avon, 1963; Ian Henry, 1975
Dear Daughter Dead. Gollancz, 1965; Walker, 1966
Extinction Bomber. Bodley Head, 1956
Fear Fortune, Father. Gollancz, 1974
Frontier Incident. Hodder, 1951; Crowell, 1952
Mission in Guemo. Hodder, 1953; Walker, 1964
Moment of Decision. Hodder, 1952
Sweet Sister Seduced. Gollancz, 1968
The Tender Killer; see The Bronze Perseus

HOUGHTON, CLAUDE. Pseudonym of Claude Houghton Oldfield, 1889- .
-All Change, Humanity! Collins, 1942
-At the End of a Road. Hutchinson, 1953
-The Big Trail. Readers Library, 1931. (Novelization of the movie.)
Birthmark. Chatto, 1950
-Captain of the Guard. Readers Library, 1930. (Novelization of the movie.)
-The Clock Ticks. Hutchinson, 1954
The Enigma of Conrad Stone. Collins, 1952
A Hair Divides. Butterworth, 1930; Doubleday, 1931
I am Jonathan Scrivener. Butterworth, 1930; Simon, 1930
-The Last Command. Readers Library, 1929. (Novelization of the movie.)
-The Man Who Could Still Laugh. Todd, 1943. (16 pp.)
-More Lives Than One. Hutchinson, 1957
The Passing of Third Floor Back. Queensway, 1935
-Passport to Paradise. Collins, 1944
-The Quarrel. Collins, 1948
The Riddle of Helena. Holden, 1927
-The Sins of the Fathers. Readers Library, 1930. (Novelization of the movie.)
-Six Lives and a Book. Collins, 1943
-Some Rise by Sin. Hutchinson, 1956
-This was Ivor Trent. Heinemann, 1935; Doubleday, 1935
-Three Fantastic Tales. Joiner, 1934 (79 pp.)
Transformation Scene. Collins, 1946

HOUGRON, JEAN. 1923- .
A Question of Character. Hutchinson, 1957; Farrar, 1958. Also published as: Trapped. Dell, 1959. (Translation of Je Reviendrai a Kandara. Paris, 1955.)

HOULT, NORAH. 1901- .
A Death Occurred. Hutchinson, 1954
-Frozen Ground. Heinemann, 1952
-The Last Days of Miss Jenkinson. Hutchinson, 1962
Scene for Death. Heinemann, 1943
-There were no Windows. Heinemann, 1944

HOUSE, BRANT. Pseudonym of Paul Chadwick. All titles below are in the Secret Agent X series.
City of the Living Dead. Corinth, 1966
Curse of the Mandarin's Fan. Corinth, 1966
The Death-Torch Terror. Corinth, 1966
Octopus of Crime. Corinth, 1966
Servants of the Skull. Corinth, 1966
The Sinister Scourge. Corinth, 1966
The Torture Trust. Corinth, 1966

HOUSEHOLD, GEOFFREY (EDWARD WEST). 1900- .
Arabesque. Chatto, 1948; Little, 1948
The Brides of Solomon and other stories. Joseph, 1958; Little, 1958 ss
The Courtesy of Death. Joseph, 1967; Little, 1967
Dance of the Dwarfs. Joseph, 1968; Little, 1968
Doom's Caravan. Joseph, 1971; Little, 1971
Fellow Passenger. Joseph, 1955; Little, 1955. Also published as: Hang the Man High. Bestseller, 1957
Hang the Man High; see Fellow Passenger
The High Place. Joseph, 1950; Little, 1950
The Lives and Times of Bernardo Brown. Joseph, 1973; Little, 1974
Man Hunt; see Rogue Male
Olura. Joseph, 1965; Little, 1965
Red Anger. Joseph, 1975; Little, 1975
Rogue Male. Chatto, 1939; Little, 1939. Also published as: Man Hunt. Triangle, 1942
A Rough Shoot. Joseph, 1951; Little, 1951 ss
Sabres on the Sand. Joseph, 1966; Little, 1966 ss
The Salvation of Pisco Gabar and other stories. Chatto, 1938; Little, 1940. (The U.S. edition has two more stories than the British.) ss
Tales of Adventurers. Joseph, 1952; Little, 1952 ss
Thing to Love. Joseph, 1963; Little, 1963
The Third Hour. Chatto, 1937; Little, 1938
The Three Sentinels. Joseph, 1972; Little, 1972
A Time to Kill. Joseph, 1952; Little, 1951

Watcher in the Shadows. Joseph, 1960; Little, 1960

HOUSER, LIONEL
Lake of Fire. Kendall, 1933; Jarrolds, 1934

HOUSMAN, LAURENCE. 1865-1959.
Odd Pairs. Cape, 1925 ss, some criminous

HOUSTON, BILLIE
Twice Round the Clock. Hutchinson, 1935

HOUSTON, MARGARET BELLE
-The Witch Man. Hutchinson, 1922; Small, 1922
Yonder. Allen, 1955; Crown, 1955

HOUSTON, R. B.
Two for the Grave. Hale, 1972

HOVICK, ROSE LOUISE. 1914-1970. Pseudonym: Gypsy Rose Lee, q.v.

HOW, BRIAN
Recoil. Hale, 1962

HOWARD, CLARK
The Doomsday Squad. Weybright, 1970; Allen, 1971
The Killings. Dial, 1973; Souvenir, 1974
Last Contract. Pinnacle, 1973
Mark the Sparrow. Dial, 1975; Souvenir, 1976
-A Movement Toward Eden. Moore, 1969
Summit Kill. Pinnacle, 1975

HOWARD, COLIN. 1934- .
Killing No Murder. Hale, 1972

HOWARD, GEORGE (FITZALAN) BRONSON. 1883-1922. See: GEORGE (FITZALAN) BRONSON-HOWARD.

HOWARD, HARTLEY. Pseudonym of Leopold Horace Ognall, 1908- . Other pseudonym: Harry Carmichael, q.v. Series characters: Glenn Bowman, in at least those marked GB; Philip Scott, in at least those marked PS.
The Armitage Secret. Collins, 1959 GB
Assignment K; see Department K
The Big Snatch. Collins, 1958
Bowman at a Venture. Collins, 1954 GB
Bowman on Broadway. Collins, 1954 GB
Bowman Strikes Again. Collins, 1953 GB
The Bowman Touch. Collins, 1956 GB
Count-Down. Collins, 1962 GB
Counterfeit. Collins, 1966
Cry on my Shoulder. Collins, 1970 GB
Dead Drunk. Collins, 1974 GB
Deadline. Collins, 1959 GB
Death of Cecilia. Collins, 1952 GB
Department K. Collins, 1964. U.S. title: Assignment K. Pyramid, 1968 PS
Double Finesse. Collins, 1962
Epitaph for Joanna. Collins, 1972
Extortion. Collins, 1960 GB
The Eye of the Hurricane. Collins, 1968 PS
Fall Guy. Collins, 1960 GB
A Hearse for Cinderella. Collins, 1956 GB
Highway to Murder. Collins, 1973
I'm No Hero. Collins, 1961 GB
Key to the Morgue. Collins, 1957 GB
The Last Appointment. Collins, 1951 GB
The Last Deception. Collins, 1951 GB
The Last Vanity. Collins, 1952 GB
The Long Night. Collins, 1957 GB
Million Dollar Snapshot. Collins, 1971 GB
Murder One. Collins, 1971
Nice Day for a Funeral. Collins, 1972

No Target for Bowman. Collins, 1955 GB
The Other Side of the Door. Collins, 1953
Out of the Fire. Collins, 1965
Portrait of a Beautiful Harlot. Collins, 1966 GB
Room 37. Collins, 1970 GB
Routine Investigation. Collins, 1967 GB
The Secret of Simon Cornell. Collins, 1969 GB
Sleep for the Wicked. Collins, 1955 GB
Sleep, My Pretty One. Collins, 1958 GB
The Stretton Case. Collins, 1963
Time Bomb. Collins, 1961 GB
Treble Cross. Collins, 1975

HOWARD, HERBERT EDMUND. 1900-   . Pseudonym: R. Philmore, q.v.

HOWARD, JAMES A(RCH). 1922-   . Pseudonym: Laine Fisher, q.v. Series character: Steve Ashe = SA.
Blow Out My Torch. Popular Library, 1956; Digit, 1964 SA
The Bullet-Proof Martyr. Dutton, 1961
Die on Easy Street. Popular Library, 1957; Digit, 1964 SA
I Like It Tough. Popular Library, 1955; Digit, 1964 SA
I'll Get You Yet. Popular Library, 1954; Digit, 1964 SA
Murder in Mind. Dutton, 1960
Murder Takes a Wife. Dutton, 1958

HOWARD, KEBLE. Pseudonym of John Keble Bell, 1875-1928.
The Cheerful Knave. Unwin, 1927

HOWARD, KENT
Go South, Go Crazy. Cooper, 1952
Shooting Made Easy. Cooper, 1952
Kearny Died Twice. Cooper, 1952
Small Time Crooks. Cooper, 1952

HOWARD, LEIGH
Blind Date. Longmans, 1955; Simon, 1958. Also published as: Chance Meeting. Avon, 1960

HOWARD, LESLEY
Invitation to Paradise. Coward, 1974

HOWARD, LOUIS G. REDMOND-. See: L(OUIS) G. REDMOND-HOWARD.

HOWARD, TROY. Pseudonym of Lauran Bosworth Paine, 1916-   . Other pseudonyms: John Armour, Reg Batchelor, Kenneth Bedford, Frank Bosworth, Mark Carrel, Robert Clarke, Richard Dana, J. F. Drexler, Jared Ingersol, John Kilgore, Hunter Liggett, J. K. Lucas, John Morgan, qq.v.
The Black Light. Hale, 1968

HOWARD, VECHEL. Pseudonym of Howard Rigsby, 1909-   , q.v.
Murder on her Mind. GM, 1959; Muller pb, 1960
Murder with Love. GM, 1959; Muller pb, 1960

HOWARD, VINCE
Rendezvous in Rio. Nite Time, 1964

HOWARD, WENDELL
The Last Refuge of a Scoundrel and other stories. Exposition, 1952 ss

HOWARTH, CAROLINE M.
Eyes in the Night. Pageant, 1953

HOWARTH, DAVID (ARMINE). 1912-   .
Group Flashing Two. Hale, 1952
One Night in Styria. Hale, 1953
Thieves' Hole. Rinehart, 1954. (British title?)

HOWARTH, PATRICK (JOHN FIELDING). Pseudonym: C. D. E. Francis, q.v.
The Dying Ukranian. Bodley Head, 1953

HOWATCH, SUSAN. 1940-   .
April's Grave. Ace, 1969; H. Hamilton, 1973
Call in the Night. Ace, 1967; H. Hamilton, 1972
Cashelmara. Simon, 1974; H. Hamilton, 1974
The Dark Shore. Ace, 1965; H. Hamilton, 1972
The Devil on Lammas Night. Ace, 1970; H. Hamilton, 1973
Penmarric. Simon, 1971; H. Hamilton, 1971
The Shrouded Walls. Ace, 1968; H. Hamilton, 1972
The Waiting Sands. Ace, 1966; H. Hamilton, 1972

HOWE, EDGAR WATSON. 1853-1937.
The Mystery of the Locks. Osgood, 1885

HOWE, GEORGE (LOCKE). 1898-1977.
Call It Treason. Viking, 1949; Hart-Davis, 1950. Also published as: Decision before Dawn. Digit, 1958

HOWE, MURIEL. Pseudonym of Muriel Smithies.
The Affair at Falconers. Macdonald, 1957
Pendragon. Macdonald, 1958

HOWE, RUSSELL WARREN. 1925-   .
Behold the City. Secker, 1953
-The Light and the Shadows. Secker, 1952 ss

HOWELL, PATRICIA HOGAN
Winds of Terror. Avon, 1975

HOWES, ROYCE. 1901-1973. Series character: Capt. Ben Lucias = BL.
The Callao Clue. Doubleday, 1936
The Case of the Copy-Hook Killing. Dutton, 1945 BL
Death Dupes a Lady. Doubleday, 1937 BL
Death on the Bridge. Doubleday, 1935
Death Rides a Hobby. Doubleday, 1939 BL
Murder at Maneuvers. Doubleday, 1938 BL
The Nasty Name Murders. Doubleday, 1939 BL
Night of the Garter Murder. Doubleday, 1937 BL

HOWIE, EDITH
The Band Played Murder. Mill, 1946; Boardman, 1948
Cry Murder. Mill, 1944; Boardman, 1950
Murder at Stone House. Farrar, 1942; Boardman, 1945
Murder for Christmas. Farrar, 1941; Boardman, 1942
Murder for Tea. Farrar, 1941, in the threesome Three Prize Murders; Boardman, 1942
Murder's So Permanent. Farrar, 1942; Boardman, 1944
No Face to Murder. Mill, 1946; Boardman, 1946

HOWITT, JOHN LESLIE DESPARD. Pseudonym: Leslie Despard, q.v.

HOWLETT, JOHN (REGINALD). 1940-   .
The Christmas Spy. Hutchinson, 1975; Harcourt, 1975

HOXIE, WALTER PALMER. Pseudonym: Alton Hurlba, q.v.

HOYNE, THOMAS TEMPLE. 1875-   .
Intrigue on the Upper Level. Reilly, 1934

HOYT, DON and ART(HUR) MOORE, q.v. Joint pseudonyms of Arthur Moore and Marilyn Granbeck: Adam Hamilton, Van Saxon, qq.v.
Death is a Drag. Powell, 1970

HOYT, EDWIN PALMER (JR.). 1923-   .
-The Ghost Lane. Luce, 1971
A Matter of Conscience. Duell, 1966

HOYT, PAUL
Murderer's Wench. Hale, 1936

HOYT, VICTOR B.
Spin a Coin for Murder. Milestone, 1954

HRABEL, BAHUMIL. 1924-   .
The Death of Mr. Balishberger. Doubleday, 1974. (Translation of Automat Svet.) ss

HUBBARD, GEORGE. 1884-   . See: LILIAN BENNET-THOMPSON, 1883-1942.

HUBBARD, MARGARET ANN. 1909-   .
Murder at St. Dennis. Bruce, 1952
Murder Takes the Veil. Bruce, 1950
Sister Simon's Murder Case. Bruce, 1959
Step Softly on my Grave. Bruce, 1966

HUBBARD, P(HILIP) M(AITLAND). 1910-   .
Cold Waters. Bles, 1970; Atheneum, 1969
The Country of Again; see The Custom of the Country
The Custom of the Country. Bles, 1969. U.S. title: The Country of Again. Atheneum, 1968
The Dancing Man. Macmillan (London), 1971; Atheneum, 1971
Flush as May. Joseph, 1963; London House, 1963
The Graveyard. Macmillan (London), 1975; Atheneum, 1975
High Tide. Macmillan (London), 1971; Atheneum, 1970
A Hive of Glass. Joseph, 1965; Atheneum, 1965
The Holm Oaks. Joseph, 1965; Atheneum, 1966
Picture of Millie. Joseph, 1964; London House, 1964
A Rooted Sorrow. Macmillan (London), 1973; Atheneum, 1973
A Thirsty Evil. Macmillan (London), 1974; Atheneum, 1974
The Tower. Bles, 1968; Atheneum, 1967
The Whisper in the Glen. Macmillan (London), 1972; Atheneum, 1972

HUBBARD, RICHARD
Retake. Signet, 1969. British title: Close-Up of a Killing. New English Library pb, 1970

HUBBELL, WALTER. 1851-   .
The Great Amherst Mystery. Brentano's, 1888; Routledge, 1888

HUBER, BERTRAND
Death and the Dowager. Appleton, 1934. British title: Murder with Gloves. Hale, 1936

HUBLER, RICHARD G(IBSON). 1912-   .
The Chase. Coward, 1952
The Pass. Coward, 1955

HUCH, RICARDA (OCTAVIA). 1864-1947.
The Deruga Trial. Macaulay, 1929; Gerald Howe, 1930. (Translation of Der Fall Deruga. Berlin, 1917.)

HUDIBURG, EDWARD
Killer's Game. Lion, 1956

HUDSON, JEFFERY. Pseudonym of Michael Crichton, 1942- , q.v. Other pseudonym: John Lange, q.v.
A Case of Need. NAL, 1968; Heinemann, 1968

HUDSON, LAURA HOPE
The Cruel Legacy. Lancer, 1969

HUDSON, W(ILLIAM) C(ADWALADER). 1843-1915. Pseudonym: Barclay North, q.v.
-An American Cavalier. Cassell (New York), 1897
The Dugdale Millions. Cassell (New York), 1891. Reprinted as by Barclay North: Cassell (New York), 1892
J. P. Dunbar: A Story of Wall Street. Dodge, 1906
Jack Gordon, Knight Errant. Gotham 1883. Cassell (New York), 1890; Cassell (London), 1890, as by Barclay North
The Man with a Thumb. Cassell (New York), 1891. Reprinted as by Barclay North: Street, 1899
On the Rack. Cassell (New York), 1892. Reprinted as by Barclay North: Street, 1899
-Should She Have Left Him? Cassell (New York), 1894. Reprinted as by Barclay North: Street, 1900
-Vivier of Vivier, Longman & Company, Bankers. Cassell (New York & London), 1890. Reprinted as by Barclay North: Street, 1899

HUESTON, ETHEL. 1889- .
Idle Island. Bobbs, 1927; Hutchinson, 1927

HUFF, AFTON PATRICIA (WALKER). 1928- .
The Key to Hawthorn Heath. Berkley, 1972

HUFF, CHARLES H. 1887?-1959. Pseudonym: Drexel Drake, q.v.

HUFF, T. E.
Meet a Dark Stranger. Hawthorn, 1974. Also published as: Whisper in the Darkness. Dell, 1977
Midnight at Mallyncourt. Berkley/Putnam, 1975
Nine Buck's Row. Hawthorn, 1973
Whisper in the Darkness; see Meet a Dark Stranger

TUFF, TOM. Pseudonym: Beatrice Parker, q.v.

HUFFMAN, LAURIE (NELL ALFORD). 1916- .
-A House Behind the Mint. Doubleday, 1969

HUFFORD, SUSAN. 1940- .
Midnight Sailing. Popular Library, 1975

HUGGINS, ROY. 1914- . Series character: Stuart Bailey = SB.
The Double Take. Morrow, 1946; Cassell, 1947 SB
Lovely Lady, Pity Me. Duell, 1949
77 Sunset Strip. Dell, 1959. (Novelization of the TV series based on Huggins' character.) SB
Too Late for Tears. Morrow, 1947; Cassell, 1950

HUGHES, ALFRED
Leaves from the Note Book of a Chief of Police. Virtue, 1865? ss

HUGHES, BABETTE (PLECHNER). 1906- .
Series character: Professor Craig, in both titles.
Murder in Church. Appleton, 1934
Murder in the Zoo. Appleton, 1932; Benn, 1932

HUGHES, BEATRIX
The Mystery of St. Martin's Copse. Heath, 1929

HUGGINS, ROY. 1914- . Series character: Stuart Bailey = SB.
The Double Take. Morrow, 1946; Cassell, 1947 SB
Lovely Lady, Pity Me. Duell, 1949
77 Sunset Strip. Dell, 1959. (Novelization of the TV series based on Huggins' character.) SB
Too Late for Tears. Morrow, 1947; Cassell, 1950

HUGHES, BABETTE (PLECHNER). 1906- .
Series character: Professor Craig, in both titles.
Murder in Church. Appleton, 1934
Murder in the Zoo. Appleton, 1932; Benn, 1932

HUGHES, BEATRIX
The Mystery of St. Martin's Copse. Heath, 1929

HUGHES, (JOHN) CLEDWYN. 1920- .
The Inn Closes for Christmas. Pilot, 1947. U.S. title: He Dared Not Look Behind. Wyn, 1947

HUGHES, COLIN. Pseudonym of John Creasey, 1908-1973, q.v. Other pseudonyms: Gordon Ashe, M. E. Cooke, Norman Deane, Robert Caine Frazer, Patrick Gill, Michael Halliday, Charles Hogarth, Brian Hope, Kyle Hunt, Abel Mann, Peter Manton, J. J. Marric, Richard Martin, Rodney Mattheson, Anthony Morton, Jeremy York, qq.v.
Triple Murder. Newnes, 1940

HUGHES, DENIS T.
The Aeroplane Mystery. Warren, 1948
-Beautiful Schemer. Hamilton Stafford, 1949
The Case of the River Smugglers. Warren, 1949
The Hidden Gang. Warren, 1948
-Istanbul Elopement. Hamilton Stafford, 1950
Murder by Telecopter. Warren, 1950

HUGHES, DOROTHY B(ELLE FLANAGAN). 1904- . Series character: Inspector Tobin = T.
The Bamboo Blonde. Duell, 1941
The Blackbirder. Duell, 1943; Nicholson, 1948
The Body on the Bench; see The Davidian Report
The Candy Kid. Duell, 1950
The Cross-Eyed Bear. Duell, 1940; Nicholson, 1943. Also published as: The Cross-Eyed Bear Murders. Dell, 1944 T
The Cross-Eyed Bear Murders; see The Cross-Eyed Bear
The Davidian Report. Duell, 1952. Also published as: The Body on the Bench. Dell, 1955
The Delicate Ape. Duell, 1944
Dread Journey. Duell, 1945; Nicholson, 1948
The Expendable Man. Random, 1963; Deutsch, 1964
The Fallen Sparrow. Duell, 1942; Nicholson, 1943 T
In a Lonely Place. Duell, 1947; Nicholson, 1950
Johnnie. Duell, 1944; Nicholson, 1946
Kiss for a Killer. Jonathan, 1954
Ride the Pink Horse. Duell, 1946
The So Blue Marble. Duell, 1940 T

HUGHES, KEN(NETH GRAHAM). 1922- .
High Wray. Gifford, 1952
-The Long Echo. Constable, 1955

HUGHES, RODNEY
The Dragon Keepers. Popular Library, 1974

HUGHES, RUPERT. 1872-1956.
The Amiable Crimes of Dirk Memling. Appleton (New York & London), 1913
Ladies' Man. Harper, 1930; Hurst, 1930

HUGHES, VALERIE ANNE. Pseudonym: V. Carrington, q.v.

HUGHES, WILLIAM
Blind Terror; see See No Evil
Connecting Rooms. Award, 1969; Tandem, 1970. (Novelization of the movie.)
Inside Out. Award, 1976; Tandem, 1975. (Novelization of the movie.)
Secret Ceremony. Award, 1968; Sphere, 1968. (Novelization of the movie.)
See No Evil. Award, 1971. British title: Blind Terror. Sphere, 1971. (Novelization of the movie.)

HUGHES, WILLIAM THOMAS MAINWARING. 1893- . Pseudonym: Main Waring, q.v.

HUGHESTON, JOSEPHINE. See: (MABEL) DANA LYON, 1897- .

HUGHSTON, DANA. Pseudonym.
You Stand Accused. Hillman-Curl, 1937

HUGI, MAURICE G. 1904-1947. Series character: Martin Speed, in at least those marked MS.
The Convict's Hoard. Swan, 1947 MS
He Died Thrice. Swan, 1947
Martin Speed Versus "The Snatcher". Swan, 1946 MS
Murder Begets Murder. Swan, 1947
The Tin Bath Murder. Swan, 1947 MS

HUGILL, ROBERT
Peril in Provence. Barrington Gray, 1953

HULL, CHARLES. Pseudonym: C. R. B., q.v.

HULL, ERIC TRAVISS. Pseudonym of Terry Harnan, 1920- , q.v.
Murder Lays a Golden Egg. Doubleday, 1944; Westhouse, 1946

HULL, HELEN. 1888?-1971.
Close Her Pale Blue Eyes. Dodd, 1963
A Tapping on the Wall. Dodd, 1960; Collins, 1961

HULL, RICHARD. Pseudonym of Richard Henry Sampson, 1896- .
And Death Came Too. Collins, 1939; Messner, 1942
Beyond Reasonable Doubt; see Excellent Intentions
Excellent Intentions. Faber, 1938. U.S. title: Beyond Reasonable Doubt. Messner, 1941
The Ghost It Was. Faber, 1937; Putnam, 1937
Invitation to an Inquest. Collins, 1950
Keep It Quiet. Faber, 1935; Putnam, 1935
Last First. Collins, 1947
Left-Handed Death. Collins, 1946
The Martineau Murders. Collins, 1953
A Matter of Nerves. Collins, 1950
Murder Isn't Easy. Faber, 1936; Putnam, 1936
The Murder of my Aunt. Faber, 1934; Minton Balch, 1934

The Murderers of Monty. Faber, 1937;
Putnam, 1937
My Own Murderer. Collins, 1940; Messner, 1940
The Unfortunate Murderer. Collins, 1941; Messner, 1942
Until She was Dead. Collins, 1949

HULME-BEAMAN, EMERIC. Joint pseudonym with William Senior Ellis: Ben Strong, q.v. Series character; Ozmar, in at least those marked O.
The Experiment of Doctor Nevill. Long, 1900
The Faith That Kills. Hurst, 1899
Ozmar the Mystic. Sands, 1896 O
The Prince's Diamond. Hutchinson, 1898 O

HULTMAN, HELEN JOAN
Death at Windward Hill. Fiction League, 1931
Find the Woman. Doubleday, 1929
Murder in the French Room. Mystery League, 1931
Murder on Route 40. Phoenix, 1940
Ready for Death. Phoenix, 1939
This Murderous Shaft. Phoenix, 1946

HUME, CYRIL, 1900-   , and RICHARD MAIBAUM
Ransom. French (New York), 1963. (Play.)

HUME, DAVID. Pseudonym of J(ohn) V(ictor) Turner, 1900-1945, q.v. Other pseudonym: Nicholas Brady, q.v. Series characters: Mick Cardby, in at least those marked MC; Tony Carter, in at least those marked TC; Detective-Inspector Sanderson = S.
Below the Belt. Collins, 1934 MC
Bring 'Em Back Dead! Collins, 1936; Appleton, 1936 MC
Bullets Bite Deep. Putnam (London), 1932 MC
Call in the Yard. Collins, 1935 ss S
Cemetery First Stop! Collins, 1937 MC
Come Back for the Body. Collins, 1945 MC
Corpses Never Argue. Collins, 1938 MC
The Crime Combine. Collins, 1936 ss S
Crime Unlimited. Collins, 1933; McBride, 1933 MC
Dangerous Mr. Dell. Collins, 1935; Appleton, 1935 MC
Death Before Honour. Collins, 1939 MC
Destiny is my Name. Collins, 1942 MC
Dishonour Among Thieves. Collins, 1943 MC
Eternity, Here I Come! Collins, 1940 MC
Five Aces. Collins, 1940
The Foursquare Murder; see Murders Form Fours
The Gaol Gates are Open. Collins, 1935. U.S. title: The Jail Gates are Open. Appleton, 1935 MC
Get Out the Cuffs. Collins, 1943 MC
Good-Bye to Life. Collins, 1938 MC
Halfway to Horror. Collins, 1937 MC
Heading for a Wreath. Collins, 1946 MC
Heads You Live. Collins, 1939 MC
Invitation to the Grave. Collins, 1940
The Jail Gates are Open; see The Gaol Gates are Open
Make Way for the Mourners. Collins, 1939 MC
Meet the Dragon. Collins, 1936 MC
Mick Cardby Works Overtime. Collins, 1944 MC
Murders Form Fours. Putnam (London), 1933. U.S. title: The Foursquare Murder. McBride, 1933 MC
Never Say Live! Collins, 1942 TC
Requiem for Rogues. Collins, 1942 MC
The Return of Mick Cardby. Collins, 1941 MC
Stand Up and Fight. Collins, 1941

They Called Him Death. Collins, 1934; Appleton, 1935 MC
They Never Came Back. Collins, 1945 MC
Toast to a Corpse. Collins, 1944 MC
Too Dangerous to Live. Collins, 1934 MC
You'll Catch Your Death. Collins, 1940 TC

HUME, DORIS
Dark Purpose. Popular Library, 1960

HUME, FERGUS(ON WRIGHT). 1859-1932. Series character: Octavius Fanks, in at least those marked OF.
Across the Footlights. White, 1912
-Aladdin in London. Black, 1892; Houghton, 1892
The Amethyst Cross. Cassell, 1908
Answered: A Spy Story. White, 1915
-The Best of her Sex. Allen, 1894
Bishop Pendle; or, The Bishop's Secret; see The Bishop's Secret
The Bishop's Secret. Long, 1900. U.S. title: Bishop Pendle; or, The Bishop's Secret. Rand, 1900
The Black Carnation. Gale & Polden, 1892; U.S. Book Co., 1892
The Black Image. Ward, 1918
The Black Patch. Long, 1906
The Blue Talisman. Laurie, 1912; Clode, 1925
The Caravan Mystery. Hurst, 1926
The Carbuncle Clue. Warne, 1896 OF
The Caretaker. Ward, 1916
The Chinese Jar. Low, 1893 OF
Claude Duval of Ninety-Five: A Romance of the Road. Digby Long, 1897; Dillingham, 1897
The Clock Struck One. Warne, 1898
A Coin of Edward VII. Digby Long, 1903; Dillingham, 1903
Crazy-Quilt. Ward, 1919
A Creature of the Night. Low, 1891; Lovell, 1891
The Crime of the Crystal. Digby Long, 1901
The Crime of the 'Liza Jane. Ward, 1895
The Crimson Cryptogram. Long, 1900; Buckles, 1912
The Crowned Skull. Laurie, 1908. U.S. title (?): The Red Skull. Dodge, 1908
The Curse. Laurie, 1915
The Dancer in Red. Digby, 1906 ss
The Dark Avenue. Ward, 1920
The Devil-Stick. Downey, 1898
The Devil's Ace. Everett, 1909
The Disappearing Eye. Digby Long, 1909; Dillingham, 1909
The Dwarf's Chamber and other stories. Ward, 1896 ss
The Fatal Song. White, 1905
The Fever of Life. Low, 1892; Lovell, 1891
Flies in the Web. White, 1908
For the Defense. Rand, 1898. (British title?)
The 4 P.M. Express. White, 1914
From Thief to Detective. Street (Magnet #241).   (British title?)
The Gates of Dawn. Low, 1894; Neely, 1894
The Gentleman Who Vanished. White, 1890. U.S. title: The Man Who Vanished. Liberty Book Co., 1892
The Girl from Malta. Hansom Cab Co., 1889; Lovell, 1889
The Golden Wang-Ho. Long, 1901. U.S. title: The Secret of the Chinese Jar. Westbrook, 1928
The Green Mummy. Long, 1908; Dillingham, 1908
The Grey Doctor. Ward, 1917
The Guilty House. White, 1903
Hagar of the Pawn-Shop. Skeffington, 1898; Buckles, 1898 ss

-The Harlequin Opal. Allen, 1893; Rand, 1893
Heart of Ice. Hurst, 1918
High Water Mark. White, 1911
The Hurton Treasure Mystery. Mellifont, 1937
The Indian Bangle. Low, 1899
In Queer Street. White, 1913
The Jade Eye. Long, 1903
The Jew's House. Ward, 1911
Jonah's Luck. White, 1906
The Lady from Nowhere. Chatto, 1900
Lady Jezebel. Pearson, 1898
Lady Jim of Curzon Street. Laurie, 1905; Dillingham, 1906
The Last Straw. Hutchinson, 1932
The Lone Inn. Jarrolds, 1894; Cassell (New York), 1895
The Lonely Church. Long, 1904
The Lonely Subaltern. White, 1910
The Lost Parchment. Ward, 1914; Dillingham, 1914
Madame Midas. Hansom Cab Co., 1888; Munro, 1888
The Man Who Vanished; see The Gentleman Who Vanished
The Man with a Secret. White, 1890
The Mandarin's Fan. Digby Long, 1904; Dillingham, 1904
A Marriage Mystery: Told from Three Points of View. Digby Long, 1896
The Masquerade Mystery. Digby Long, 1895
The Master-Mind. Hurst, 1919
A Midnight Mystery. Gale & Polden, 1894
The Mikado Jewel. Everett, 1910
The Millionaire Mystery. Chatto, 1901; Buckles, 1901
The Miser's Will. Treherne, 1903
Miss Mephistopheles. White, 1890; Lovell, 1890. (A sequel to Madame Midas, q.v.)
Monsieur Judas. Blackett, 1891 OF
The Moth-Woman. Hurst, 1923
Mother Mandarin. White, 1912
The Mystery of a Hansom Cab. (Hume), 1886; Munro, 1888
The Mystery of a Motor Cab. Everett, 1908
The Mystery of Landy Court. Jarrolds, 1894
The Mystery of the Shadow. Cassell, 1906; Dodge, 1906
The Mystery Queen. Ward, 1912; Dillingham, 1912
Next Door. Ward, 1918
Not Wanted. White, 1914
The Opal Serpent. Long, 1905; Dillingham, 1905
The Other Person. White, 1920
The Pagan's Cup. Digby Long, 1902; Dillingham, 1902
The Peacock of Jewels. Digby Long, 1910; Dillingham, 1910
The Piccadilly Puzzle. White, 1889; Lovell, with 2 additional stories, 1889
The Pink Shop. White, 1911
The Purple Fern. Everett, 1907
The Rainbow Feather. Digby Long, 1898; Dillingham, 1898
The Rectory Governess. White, 1911
The Red Bicycle. Ward, 1916
The Red-Headed Man. Digby Long, 1899
Red Money. Ward, 1912; Dillingham, 1911
The Red Skull; see The Crowned Skull
The Red Window. Digby Long, 1904; Dillingham, 1904
The Sacred Herb. Long, 1908; Dillingham, 1908
The Scarlet Bat. White, 1905
The Sealed Message. Digby Long, 1908; Dillingham, 1907

The Secret of the Chinese Jar; see The
    Golden Wang-Ho
The Secret Passage. Long, 1905; Dil-
    lingham, 1905
Seen in the Shadow. White, 1913
Shylock of the River. Digby Long, 1900
The Silent House; see The Silent House
    in Pimlico
The Silent House in Pimlico. Long,
    1899. U.S. title: The Silent House.
    Doscher, 1907
The Silent Signal. Ward, 1917
The Silver Bullet. Long, 1903
The Singing Head. Hurst, 1920
The Solitary Farm. Ward, 1909; Dilling-
    ham, 1909
A Speck of the Motley. Innes, 1893
The Spider. Ward, 1910
The Steel Crown. Digby Long, 1911;
    Dillingham, 1911
The Third Volume. Cassell (New York),
    1895. (British title?)
The Thirteenth Guest. Ward, 1913
Three. Ward, 1921
The Tombstone Treasure. Daffodil Li-
    brary, 1897
The Top Dog. White, 1909
Tracked by Fate. Street (Magnet #225).
    (British title?)
Tracked by a Tattoo. Warne, 1896
A Traitor in London. Long, 1900;
    Buckles, 1900
A Trick of Time. Hurst, 1922
The Turnpike House. Long, 1902
The Unexpected. Odhams, 1921
The Unwilling Bride. Ogilvie, 1895.
    (British title?)
The Vanishing of Tera. White, 1900
The Wheeling Light. Chatto, 1904
The Whispering Lane. Hurst, 1924;
    Small, 1925
The White Prior. Warne, 1895
-Whom God Hath Joined: A Question of
    Marriage. White, 1891
Woman: The Sphinx. Long, 1902
A Woman's Burden. Jarrolds, 1901
The Woman Who Held On. Ward, 1920
The Wooden Hand. White, 1905
-The Year of Miracle: A Tale of the Year
    One Thousand Nine Hundred. Routledge,
    1891; Lovell, 1891
The Yellow Holly. Digby Long, 1903;
    Dillingham, 1903
The Yellow Hunchback. White, 1907

HUME, ROBERT W.
    My Lodger's Legacy; or, The History of
    a Recluse. Funk, 1886

HUMMEL, GEORGE F(REDERICK). 1882-   .
    Summer Lightning. Liveright, 1929

HUMPHREYS, ELIZA MARGARET J. GOLLAN.
    1860-1938. Pseudonym: Rita, q.v.

HUMPHREYS, RAY
    Hunch. Loring, 1934. British title:
    Death Hunch. Newnes, 1936

HUNGERFORD, MRS. (MARGARET WOLFE HAMIL-
    TON). 1855?-1897. Pseudonym: The
    Duchess, q.v.
    The Red House Mystery. Chatto, 1893.
    U.S. title: The Red House, by "The
    Duchess". Rand, 1894

HUNT, CHARLOTTE. Pseudonym of Doris Mar-
    jorie Hodges, 1915-   . Series char-
    acter: Dr. Paul Holton, in at least
    those marked PH.
    Chambered Tomb. Ace, 1975
    The Cup of Thanatos. Ace, 1968 PH
    Gemini Revenged. Ace, 1973
    The Gilded Sarcophagus. Ace, 1967 PH
    The Lotus Vellum. Ace, 1970 PH
    The Thirteenth Treasure. Ace, 1972
    A Touch of Myrrh. Ace, 1974 PH

Tremayne's Wife. Ace, 1974
A Wreath for Jenny's Grave. Ace, 1975

HUNT, CLARENCE. Pseudonym of (Clarence)
    Hugh Holman, 1914-   , q.v.
    Small Town Corpse. Phoenix, 1951

HUNT, E(VERETTE) HOWARD. 1918-   . See:
    (EVERETTE) HOWARD HUNT, 1918-   .

HUNT, (MARY) EVE(LYN)
    The Danger Game. Hale, 1967
    Girl on the Run. Hale, 1966

HUNT, HARRISON. Joint pseudonym of
    W(illis) T(odhunter) Ballard,
    1903-   , q.v., and Norbert Davis,
    q.v. Other Ballard pseudonyms: P. D.
    Ballard, Neil MacNeil, John Shepherd,
    qq.v.
    Murder Picks the Jury. Curl, 1947

HUNT, (EVERETTE) HOWARD. 1918-   . Pseu-
    donyms: Gordon Davis, Robert Die-
    trich, John Q, David St. John, qq.v.
    Many books originally published pseu-
    donymously were reprinted as by How-
    ard Hunt.
    The Berlin Ending. Putnam, 1973
    -Bimini Run. Farrar, 1949
    Cruel is the Night; see Maelstrom
    Dark Encounter. GM, 1950
    The Judas Hour. GM, 1951; Fawcett (Lon-
        don), 1953
    Lovers are Losers. GM, 1953
    Maelstrom. Farrar, 1948. Also published
        as: Cruel is the Night. Berkley, 1955
    The Violent Ones. GM, 1950; Fawcett
        (London), 1958
    Whisper Her Name. GM, 1952; Fawcett
        (London), 1958

HUNT, KATHERINE CHANDLER. Pseudonym:
    Chandler Nash, q.v.

HUNT, KYLE. Pseudonym of John Creasey,
    1908-1973, q.v. Other pseudonyms:
    Gordon Ashe, M. E. Cooke, Norman
    Deane, Robert Caine Frazer, Patrick
    Gill, Michael Halliday, Charles Ho-
    garth, Brian Hope, Colin Hughes, Abel
    Mann, Peter Manton, J. J. Marric,
    Richard Martin, Rodney Mattheson,
    Anthony Morton, Jeremy York, qq.v.
    NOTE: The Dr. Cellini series was
    published in England as by Michael
    Halliday and is listed in this bi-
    bliography under that byline.
    Kill a Wicked Man. Barker, 1958; Simon,
        1957
    Kill Once, Kill Twice. Barker, 1957;
        Simon, 1956
    Kill My Love. Boardman, 1959; Simon,
        1958
    To Kill a Killer. Boardman, 1960; Ran-
        dom, 1960

HUNT, MARY VINCENT
    Cast a Green Shadow. Avalon, 1961
    The Mystery of Daria Kane. Avalon, 1960

HUNT, PETER. Joint pseudonym of George
    Worthing Yates, q.v., and Charles
    Hunt Marshall. Series character: Alan
    Miller, in all titles
    Murder Among the Nudists. Vanguard,
        1934
    Murder for Breakfast. Vanguard, 1934
    Murders at Scandal House. Appleton,
        1933

HUNT, (ISOBEL) VIOLET. 1866-1942.
    -The House of Many Mirrors. Paul, 1915

-The Last Ditch. Paul, 1918
-More Tales of the Uneasy. Heinemann,
    1925 ss
-Tales of the Uneasy. Heinemann, 1911 ss

HUNT, (JOSEPH) WRAY (ANGUS). 1899-   .
    The Hayes Hall Affair. Fenland, 1932

HUNTER, ALAN (JAMES HERBERT). 1922-   .
    Series character: Inspector/Superin-
    tendent Gently, in all titles.
    Gently at a Gallop. Cassell, 1971
    Gently by the Shore. Cassell, 1956;
        Rinehart, 1956
    Gently Coloured. Cassell, 1969
    Gently Continental. Cassell, 1967
    Gently Does It. Cassell, 1955; Rine-
        hart, 1955
    Gently Down the Stream. Cassell, 1957;
        Roy, 1960
    Gently Floating. Cassell, 1963; Berk-
        ley, 1964
    Gently French. Cassell, 1973
    Gently Go Man. Cassell, 1961; Berkley,
        1964
    Gently in the Highlands; see Gently
        North-West
    Gently in the Sun. Cassell, 1959; Berk-
        ley, 1964
    Gently in Trees. Cassell, 1974. U.S.
        title: Gently Through the Woods. Mac-
        millan, 1975
    Gently North-West. Cassell, 1967. U.S.
        title: Gently in the Highlands. Mac-
        millan, 1975
    Gently Sahib. Cassell, 1964
    Gently Through the Mill. Cassell, 1958;
        St. Martin's, 1971, in an omnibus,
        Gently in an Omnibus, which also con-
        tains Gently Does It and Gently in
        the Sun, qq.v. (British edition of
        Gently in an Omnibus: Cassell, 1966.)
    Gently Through the Woods; see Gently in
        Trees
    Gently to the Summit. Cassell, 1961;
        Berkley, 1965
    Gently Where the Roads Go. Cassell,
        1962; St. Martin's, 1972, in an omni-
        bus: Gently in Another Omnibus (also:
        Cassell, 1969), in which are also:
        Gently Go Man, and Gently Floating,
        qq.v.)
    Gently with Love. Cassell, 1975
    Gently with the Innocents. Cassell,
        1970; Macmillan, 1974
    Gently with the Ladies. Cassell, 1965;
        Macmillan, 1974
    Gently with the Painters. Cassell,
        1960; Macmillan, 1976
    Landed Gently. Cassell, 1957; British
        Book Service, 1957
    Vivienne—Gently Where She Lay. Cas-
        sell, 1975

HUNTER, BLUEBELL MATILDA. 1887-   .
    Pseudonym: John Guildford, q.v.

HUNTER, CLAUDE
    Murders While You Wait. Alliance (Lon-
        don), 1945 ss

HUNTER, EVAN. 1926-   . Pseudonyms: Curt
    Cannon, Hunt Collins, Ezra Hannon, Ed
    McBain, Richard Marsten, qq.v.
    The Big Fix. Falcon, 1952. Also pub-
        lished as: So Nude, So Dead, as by
        Richard Marsten. Crest, 1956
    The Blackboard Jungle. Simon, 1954;
        Constable, 1955
    Don't Crowd Me. Popular Library, 1953;
        World Distributors, 1960. Also pub-
        lished as: The Paradise Party. Four
        Square, 1968
    Every Little Crook and Nanny. Double-
        day, 1972; Constable, 1972

Hunter, Evan

Happy New Year, Herbie and other stories. Simon, 1963; Constable, 1965 ss
A Horse's Head. Delacorte, 1967; Constable, 1968
The Jungle Kids. PB, 1956. (12 ss, of which 6 were included in The Last Spin, q.v.)
The Last Spin and other stories. Constable, 1960. (15 ss, including 6 from The Jungle Kids, q.v.)
A Matter of Conviction. Simon, 1959; Constable, 1959. Also published as: The Young Savages. PB, 1966
Nobody Knew They were There. Doubleday, 1971; Constable, 1971
The Paradise Party; see Don't Crowd Me
So Nude, So Dead; see The Big Fix
The Young Savages; see A Matter of Conviction

HUNTER, HARRIET
A Case for Punishment. Hale, 1967
Inclination to Murder. Hale, 1966

HUNTER, JACK D(AYTON). 1921- .
The Expendable Spy. Dutton, 1965; Muller, 1966
One of Us Works for Them. Dutton, 1967; Muller, 1968
Spies, Inc. Dutton, 1969; Muller, 1970

HUNTER, JAMES H(OGG). 1890- .
Banners of Blood. Evangelical Pub., 1947
The Mystery of Mar Saba. Evangelical Pub., 1940

HUNTER, (ALFRED) JOHN. 1891-1961. Pseudonyms: John Addiscombe, L. H. Brenning, Anthony Dax, Anthony Drummond, Peter Meriton, qq.v. Series character (with many other authors): Sexton Blake, in all titles listed without publisher (which is Amalgamated Press).
The Affair of the Spiv's Secret. 1948
Barred from the West End. 1944
The Case of the American Tourists. 1948
The Case of the Bronze Statue. 1942
The Case of the Crooked Skipper. 1951
The Case of the Defaulting Sailor. 1946
The Case of the Deserted War Bride. 1945
The Case of the Doped Favourite. 1952
The Case of the Double Event. 1947
The Case of the Fatal Film. 1935
The Case of the French Raiders. 1942
The Case of the Girl on Remand. 1952
The Case of the Stolen Ransom. 1954
The Crime on the French Frontier. 1954
The Crime on the Promenade. 1937
Crook Cargo. 1936
The Curse of the Track. 1948
Dead Man's Gate. Cassell, 1931
Dead Man's Island. Newnes, 1932
-Desperado. Cassell, 1932
Destination Unknown. 1953
The Devil of Danehurst. 1943
Fourteen Years After! 1946
Gangster's Girl. 1956
The Great Airport Racket. 1945
The House of Darkness. 1940
It Happened in Melgrove Square. 1951
The Man Behind. Cherry Tree, 1942
The Man from the Far East. 1944
The Man Who Turned King's Evidence. 1938
The Monopoly Menace. 1943
Murder in the Air. 1955
The Mysterious Mr. Maynard. 1940
The Mystery of Moat Farm. 1946
The Mystery of the American Envoy. 1942
The Mystery of the New Tenant. 1951
The Mystery of the Red Chateau. 1945
The Mystery of the Vanished Trainer. 1955
The Prisoner of Lost Island. 1937
Raiders Passed! 1941
The Riddle of the Black Racketeers. 1942
The Riddle of the Italian Prisoner. 1944
The Riddle of the Lost Ship. 1939
The Riddle of the Smiling Man. 1947
The Riddle of the Uncensored Letter. 1942
The Secret of the Demolition Worker. 1942
The Secret of the Grave. 1941
The Secret of the Hold. 1938
Sergeant Gray's Crime. 1945
Silent Witness. 1957
The Spiv's Mistake. 1952
The Thieves of Alexandria. 1953
The Three Crows. Cassell, 1928
Three Die at Midnight. 1934
Thunder Island. Newnes, 1924
The Trail of the Dope Chief. 1936
The Victim of the Crooked Hypnotist. 1952
Warned Off! 1947
When the Gunmen Came. Cassell, 1930
When the Jury Disagreed! 1950
The White Phantom. Cassell, 1934; Smith & Haas, 1935
The Wimbledon Common Trap. 1946
Witness to the Crime. 1950
The Woman on the Spot. 1953

HUNTER, P(ETER) HAY. 1854-1910.
-John Armiger's Revenge. Oliphant, 1897; Bradley, 1897
The Silver Bullet. Oliphant, 1894

HUNTING, (HENRY) GARDNER. 1872-1958.
A Hand in the Game. Holt, 1911

HUNTINGDON, JOHN. Pseudonym of Gerald William Phillips, 1884- .
The Seven Black Chessmen. Holt, 1928; Gerald Howe, 1928

HUNTSBERRY, WILLIAM E(MERY). 1916- .
Dangerous Harbour; see Harbor of the Little Boats
Harbor of the Little Boats. Rinehart, 1958. British title: Dangerous Harbour. Hammond, 1960
Oscar Mooney's Head. Holt, 1961. British title: Whose Head? Hammond, 1961
Whose Head?; see Oscar Mooney's Head

HUNVALD. HENRY
The Masterpiece of Nice Mr. Breen. World, 1972

HURD, DOUGLAS (RICHARD). 1930- .
-Scotch on the Rocks, with Andrew Osmond, 1938- , q.v. Collins, 1971
Send Him Victorious, with Andrew Osmond, 1938- , q.v. Collins, 1968; Macmillan, 1969
The Smile on the Face of the Tiger, with Andrew Osmond, 1938- , q.v. Collins, 1969; Macmillan, 1970
Truth Game. Collins, 1972; St. Martin's, 1972
Vote to Kill. Collins, 1975

HURD, FLORENCE
Curse of the Moors. Manor, 1975
The Gorgon's Head. Macfadden, 1971
House of Shadows. GM, 1973
The House on Trevor Street. Macfadden, 1973
Moorsend Manor. Manor, 1973
Nightmare at Mountain Aerie. Manor, 1974
Possessed. Belmont, 1970
Seance for the Dead. Macfadden, 1972
The Secret of Awen Castle. Avon, 1974
The Secret of Canfield House. GM, 1966; Coronet, 1972
The Secret of Hayworth Hall. Avon, 1975
Storm House. Manor, 1973
Tamarind. GM, 19??
Voyage of the Secret Duchess. Avon, 1975
Wade House. Signet, 1967
The Witches' Pond. Macfadden, 1972

HURLBA, ALTON. Pseudonym of Walter Palmer Hoxie.
-Eugenia. Welles, 1888. British title: A Friend's Victim. Routledge, 1889

HURLBUT, EDWARD H.
Lanagan, Amateur Detective. Sturgis, 1913 ss

HURLEY, GENE
Have You Seen This Man? Bobbs, 1944

HURLEY, T. P.
The Avenging Eagle. Morris, 1946

HURRELL, F(RANCIS) G(ORDON). 1885- .
John Lillibud. Rich, 1934; Kendall, 1935

HURREN, BERNARD JOHN. Pseudonym: Guy Garston, q.v.

HURST, EDWARD H(ARRY). 1868- .
Mystery Island. Page, 1907; Hurst, 1908

HURST, HEATHER SMITH
Dark is my Destiny. Dell, 1974

HURST, J. H.
Four Plus One. Martin, 1946

HURST, NORMAN
The Ivory Queen. Milne, 1899

HURT, FREDA (MARY ELIZABETH). 1911- . Series character: Inspector Herbert Broom, in at least those marked HB.
Acquainted with Murder. Hale, 1962 HB
The Body at Busman's Hollow. Macdonald, 1959 HB
A Cause for Malice. Hale, 1966 HB
Cold and Unhonoured. Hale, 1964 HB
Dangerous Visit. Hale, 1971
Dark Design. Hale, 1972
Death and the Bridegroom. Hale, 1963 HB
Death and the Dark Daughter. Hale, 1966
Death by Bequest. Macdonald, 1960 HB
Death in the Mist. Hale, 1969
Fatal Fortune. Hale, 1975
Return to Terror. Hale, 1974
Seven Year Secret. Hale, 1968
So Dark a Shadow. Hale, 1967
Sweet Death. Macdonald, 1961 HB
A Witch at the Funeral. Hale, 1970

HURWOOD, BERNHARDT J. 1926- .
Born Innocent. Ace, 1975. (Novelization of the movie.)
Rip-Off! GM, 1972

HUSTON, FRAN. Pseudonym of R. S. Miller, 1936- .
The Rich Get It All. Doubleday, 1973; Macmillan (London), 1974

HUSTON, H(OWARD) C(HAUNCEY). Series character: Detective Chief Charles A. Baker, in both titles.
The Blind Saw Murder. Macmillan, 1954; Hodder, 1955
With Murder for Some. Macmillan, 1953; Hodder, 1954

HUTCH, OLD. See: OLD HUTCH

HUTCHESON, J(OHN) C(ONROY)
-Caught in a Trap. Newby, 1870

HUTCHINSON, HORACE (or HORATIO) G(ORDON). 1859-1932.
The Crime and the Confessor. Murray, 1928
-The Eight of Diamonds. Hutchinson, 1914
-Fairway Island. Cassell, 1892
The Fate of Osmund Brett. Hutchinson, 1924
The Foreign Secretary Who Vanished. Hutchinson, 1927
-The Fortnightly Club. Murray, 1922
-Glencairly Castle. Smith Elder, 1904
The Greenwell's Glory Case. Hutchinson, 1924
The Lost Golfer. Murray, 1930
-Mr. Punt of Chelsea. Murray, 1924
Murder in Monk's Wood. Murray, 1927
The Mystery of the Summer-House. Hutchinson, 1925; Doran, 1919
-A Prideful Woman. Hutchinson, 1926
-That Fiddler Fellow. Arnold, 1891
The Twins Murder Case. Murray, 1930
Two Moods of a Man. Smith Elder, 1905; Putnam, 1905
-What Should a Man Do? Hutchinson, 1926

HUTCHINSON, ROBERT HARE. 1887- . Pseudonym: Robert Hare, q.v.
The Fourth Challenge. Hurst, 1932

HUTCHISON, GRAHAM SETON. 1890-1946. Pseudonym: Graham Seton, q.v.

HUTTEN, BETTINA VON. 1874- . See: VON HUTTEN, BETTINA.

HUTTON, BRETT
The Green Death and other stories. Bantam (Los Angeles), 1940 ss

HUTTON, J(OY) F(ERRIS)
Dead Man Friday; see Too Good to be True
The Dolphin Mystery; see Too Good to be True
Too Good to be True. Simon, 1948. British title: The Dolphin Mystery. Foulsham, 1949. Also published as: Dead Man Friday. Ace, 1953

HUTTON, W. R.
Death at the Drome. Fiction House, 1948
Death at the Golden Cockerel. Fiction House, 1947
Death of a Wide-Boy. Fiction House, 1948
Murder in Transit. Fiction House, 1949
Not a Dog's Chance. Fiction House, 1947
Valley of Death. Hamilton & Co., 1949

HUXLEY, ALDOUS (LEONARD). 1894-1963.
Mortal Coils. Chatto, 1922; Doran, 1922 ss, including Huxley's famous and probably only crime story, "The Gioconda Smile."

HUXLEY, ELSPETH (JOCELYN GRANT). 1907- . Series character: Superintendent Vachell = V.
The African Poison Murders; see Death of an Aryan
Death of an Aryan. Methuen, 1939. U.S. title: The African Poison Murders. Harper, 1940 V
The Incident at the Merry Hippo; see The Merry Hippo
A Man from Nowhere. Chatto, 1964; Morrow, 1965
The Merry Hippo. Chatto, 1963. U.S. title: The Incident at the Merry Hippo. Morrow, 1964

Murder at Government House. Methuen, 1937; Harper, 1937 V
Murder on Safari. Methuen, 1938; Harper, 1938 V

HYAMS, EDWARD (SOLOMON). 1910-1975.
-The Death Lottery. Longmans, 1971
The Final Agenda. Allen Lane, 1973

HYATT, BETTY HALE
Ivy Halls. Arcadia, 1966
The Vesper Bells. Arcadia, 1967

HYATT, STANLEY PORTAL. 1877-1914.
-Black Sheep. Laurie, 1909
Fallen Among Thieves. Laurie, 1913
-The Land of Promises. Laurie, 1911
-The Law of the Bolo. Laurie, 1910; Estes, 1910
-The Maker of Mischief. Laurie, 1911
-The Mammoth. Laurie, 1916
-A Man from the Past. Laurie, 1915
-Marcus Hay. Constable, 1907
The Markham Affair. Clode, 1925. (British title?)
-The Way of the Cardines. Laurie, 1913

HYDE, AUSTIN
Killer on the Line. Paxton, 1945
Murders by Moonlight. Paxton, 1945

HYDE, D. HERBERT. Pseudonym of Derek Hyde Chambers.
Dressed to Kill. Amalgamated, 1959 (Sexton Blake)

HYDE, THEODORE. Pseudonym.
After the Execution. Eyre, 1934
Murder in Whitehall. Murray, 1942

HYDER, ALAN
-Black-Girl, White-Lady. Barker, 1934
Prelude to Blue Mountains. Barker, 1936; Kendall, 1936
Vampires Overhead. Allan, 1935

HYLAND, (HENRY) STANLEY. 1914- .
Green Grow the Tresses-O. Gollancz, 1965; Bobbs, 1967
Top Bloody Secret. Gollancz, 1969; Bobbs, 1969
Who Goes Hang? Gollancz, 1958; Dodd, 1959

HYMAN, ANN. 1936- .
The Lansing Legacy. McKay, 1974; Millington, 1975

HYMERS, JOHN
Utter Death. Gifford, 1952; Detective Book Club, 1953

HYND, ALAN. 1908-1974.
'Til Death Do Us Part. Paperback Library, 1962

HYNE, C(HARLES) J(OHN) CUTCLIFFE (WRIGHT). 1865-1944. Pseudonym: Weatherby Chesney, q.v. Series character: Captain Owen Kettle, in at least those marked OK.
-Absent Friends. Ward, 1933
-Admiral Teach. Methuen, 1920
-Adventures of Captain Kettle. Pearson, 1898; Doubleday, 1898 OK
-Beneath Your Very Boots. Digby, 1889
-Captain Kettle, Ambassador. Ward, 1932 OK
-Captain Kettle, K.C.B. Pearson, 1903 OK
-Captain Kettle on the War-Path. Methuen, 1916 OK
-Captain Kettle's Bit. Hodder, 1918 OK

-The Captured Cruiser; or, Two Years from Land. Blackie, 1893
-Currie, Curtis & Co., Crammers. Remington, 1890
The Derelict. Lewis, 1901. (Contains 13 of the 17 ss appearing in Mr. Horrocks, Purser, q.v., including all but one of the 6 Mr. Horrocks ss—missing is "The Looting of the Specie-Room".)
The Escape Agents. Laurie, 1911 ss, some about OK
-The Filibusters. Hutchinson, 1900; Stokes, 1900
-Firemen Hot. Methuen, 1914
-Further Adventures of Captain Kettle. Pearson, 1899. U.S. title: A Master of Fortune. Dillingham, 1901 ss OK
-The Glass Dagger. New Amsterdam, 1899. (British title?)
Honour of Thieves. Chatto, 1895; Fenno, 1899. Also published as: The Little Red Captain. Pearson, 1902 OK
-Ivory Valley. Ward, 1938 OK
Kate Meredith, Financier. Cassell, 1907; Empire, 1906
The Little Red Captain; see Honour of Thieves
-McTodd. Macmillan (London & New York), 1903
The Marriage of Captain Kettle; see The Marriage of Kettle
The Marriage of Kettle. Heinemann, 1912. U.S. title: The Marriage of Captain Kettle. Bobbs, 1912 OK
A Master of Fortune; see Further Adventures of Captain Kettle
-A Matrimonial Mixture. Ward, 1891
Mr. Horrocks, Purser. Methuen, 1902 ss (See also: The Derelict.)
-Mr. Kettle, Third Mate. Ward, 1931 OK
The "Paradise" Coal-Boat, and other tales. Bowden, 1897 ss, including one about OK
-President Kettle. Nash, 1929 OK
The Recipe for Diamonds. Heinemann, 1893; Appleton, 1893
-Red Herrings. Methuen, 1918
-The Rev. Captain Kettle. Harrap, 1925 OK
-Steamboatmen. Penguin, 1943 ss
-Stinson's Reef. Blackie, 1899
-Thompson's Progress. Richards, 1902; Macmillan, 1903
-The Trials of Commander McTurk. Murray, 1906; Dutton, 1906
-West Highland Spirits. Ward, 1932
-The Wild-Catters. Sunday School Union, 1895
-Wishing Smith. Hale, 1939

HYTHE, GABRIEL. Pseudonym.
Death of a Goblin. Macdonald, 1960
Death of a Puppet. Macdonald, 1959
Death of a Scapegoat. Macdonald, 1961

I

IAMS, JACK [SAMUEL H. IAMS, JR.]. 1910- . Series character: Rocky Rockwell = RR.
The Body Missed the Boat. Morrow, 1947; Rich, 1949
A Corpse of the Old School. Gollancz, 1955
Death Draws the Line. Morrow, 1949; Rich, 1951
Do Not Murder Before Christmas. Morrow, 1949 RR
Girl Meets Body. Morrow, 1947; Rich, 1950
Into Thin Air. Morrow, 1952; Gollancz, 1953

Iams, Jack

A Shot of Murder. Morrow, 1950; Gollancz, 1952 RR
What Rhymes with Murder? Morrow, 1950; Gollancz, 1951 RR

IANNUZZI, JOHN NICHOLAS. 1935- .
  Courthouse. Doubleday, 1975
  Part 35. Baron, 1970
  Sicilian Defense. Baron, 1972; Allen, 1973

ILES, BERT. Pseudonym of Z(ola) H(elen Girdey) Ross, 1912- , q.v. Other pseudonym: Helen Arre, q.v.
  Murder in Mink. Arcadia, 1956

ILES, FRANCIS. Pseudonym of A(nthony) B(erkeley) Cox, 1893-1970, q.v. Other pseudonym: Anthony Berkeley, q.v.
  As for the Woman. Jarrolds, 1939; Doubleday, 1939
  Before the Fact. Gollancz, 1932; Doubleday, 1932. Revised edition: Pan, 1958
  Malice Aforethought. Gollancz, 1931; Harper, 1931

IMBER, HUGH
  The House of the Apricots. Heffer, 1934
  On Helle's Wave. Hodder, 1930
  -The Spine. Hodder, 1929

IMBERT-TERRY, SIR HENRY (MACHU). 1854-1938. Series character: Detective-Inspector Du Cas, in at least those marked D.
  Acid. Skeffington, 1928 D
  Clay. Skeffington, 1931 D
  Doom. Skeffington, 1929
  Nightshade. Skeffington, 1930
  Weeds. Skeffington, 1933 D

INCE, DOROTHEA
  In Those Dark Woods. Bell, 1937

INCHBALD, RALPH (MORDAUNT ELLIOT). 1902- . Series character: Colonel Paternoster, in all titles.
  Colonel Paternoster. Hodder, 1951
  The Five Inns. Hodder, 1952
  September Story. Hodder, 1955

IND, ALLISON. 1903-1974.
  The Sino-Variant. McKay, 1969

INGATE, MARY. 1914- .
  The Sound of the Weir. Macmillan (London), 1974; Dodd, 1974

INGERSOL, JARED. Pseudonym of Lauran Bosworth Paine, 1916- . Other pseudonyms: John Armour, Reg Batchelor, Kenneth Bedford, Frank Bosworth, Mark Carrel, Robert Clarke, Richard Dana, J. F. Drexler, Troy Howard, John Kilgore, Hunter Liggett, J. K. Lucas, John Morgan, qq.v.
  The Beautiful Murder. Hale, 1970
  Diamond Fingers. Hale, 1970
  A Fine Day for Murder. Hale, 1974
  A Game Called Murder. Hale, 1969
  The Golden Gloves. Hale, 1973
  The Jade Eye. Hale, 1970
  The Killer's Conscience. Hale, 1971
  The Man Who Made Roubles. Hale, 1972
  The Man Who Stole Heaven. Hale, 1971
  The Money Murder. Hale, 1971
  The Night of the Crisis. Hale, 1968
  The Non-Murder. Hale, 1972
  A Rose can Kill. Hale, 1969
  The Steel Garrotte. Hale, 1970
  The Witchcraft Murder. Hale, 1975

INGHAM, DANIEL. Pseudonym of Isobel (Mary) Lambot, 1926- , q.v.
  Contract for Death. Hale, 1972

INGHAM, H(ENRY) LLOYD
  Bury Me Deep. Hammond, 1963

INGHAM, RICHARD
  Yoris. Allison, 1974

INGRAHAM, CAPTAIN
  The Dancing Star. Donohue, 189?

INGRAM, ELEANOR M(ARIE). 1886-1921.
  -The Game and the Candle. Bobbs, 1909. British title: John Allard; or, The Game and the Candle. Laurie, 1912
  John Allard; see The Game and the Candle
  -Stanton Wins. Bobbs, 1911
  -The Thing from the Lake. Lippincott, 1921
  -The Twice American. Lippincott, 1917
  -The Unafraid. Lippincott, 1913

INGRAM, GEORGE. Pseudonym.
  -Cockney Cavalcade. Archer, 1935
  The Muffled Man. Archer, 1936
  "Stir". Archer, 1933
  -"Stir" Train. Archer, 1935
  -Welded Lives. Duckworth, 1939

INGRAM, (ARCHIBALD) KENNETH. 1882-1965.
  The Ambart Trial. Quality, 1938
  Death Comes at Night. Allan, 1933; Sears, 1934
  -"It is Expedient..." Bles, 1935
  -Return of Yesterday. Quality, 1942
  The Steep Steps. Allan, 1931
  -Storm in a Sanctuary. Benn, 1954
  -The Window. Ouseley, 1922

INGRAMS, RICHARD. Joint pseudonym with Andrew Osmond, 1938- , q.v.: Philip Reid, q.v.

INMAN, H(ERBERT) ESCOTT
  Nancy Lee, Mill Lass. Amalgamated, 1909
  The Quest of Douglas Holmes. Warne, 1908
  What Shall It Profit? Amalgamated, 1910

INMAN, PHILIP (ALBERT). 1892- .
  -The Silent Loom. Bles, 1930 ss

INMAN, ROBERT. 1931- .
  The Torturer's Horse. Bobbs, 1965

INNES, (RALPH) HAMMOND. 1913- . Some of these titles are probably more nearly adventure than crime fiction.
  Air Bridge. Collins, 1951; Knopf, 1952
  Air Disaster. Jenkins, 1937
  All Roads Lead to Friday. Jenkins, 1939
  The Angry Mountains. Collins, 1950; Harper, 1951
  Atlantic Fury. Collins, 1962; Knopf, 1962
  Attack Alarm. Collins, 1941; Macmillan, 1942
  The Blue Ice. Collins, 1948; Harper, 1949
  Campbell's Kingdom. Collins, 1952; Knopf, 1952
  Dead and Alive. Collins, 1946
  The Doomed Oasis. Collins, 1960; Knopf, 1960
  The Doppelganger. Jenkins, 1936
  Fire in the Snow; see The Lonely Skier
  Gale Warning; seee Maddon's Rock
  The Golden Soak. Collins, 1973; Knopf, 1973
  The Killer Mine. Collins, 1947; Harper, 1948. Also published as: Run by Night. Bantam, 1951
  The Land God Gave to Cain. Collins, 1958; Knopf, 1958
  Levkas Man. Collins, 1971; Knopf, 1971
  The Lonely Skier. Collins, 1947. U.S. title: Fire in the Snow. Harper, 1947
  Maddon's Rock. Collins, 1948. U.S. title: Gale Warning. Harper, 1948
  The Mary Deare. Collins, 1956. U.S. title: The Wreck of the Mary Deare. Knopf, 1956
  The Naked Land; see The Strange Land
  North Star. Collins, 1974; Knopf, 1975
  Run by Night; see The Killer Mine
  Sabotage Broadcast. Jenkins, 1938
  The Strange Land. Collins, 1954. U.S. title: The Naked Land. Knopf, 1954
  The Strode Venturer. Collins, 1965; Knopf, 1965
  The Survivors; see The White South
  Trapped; see Wreckers Must Breathe
  The Trojan Horse. Collins, 1940
  The White South. Collins, 1949. U.S. title: The Survivors. Harper, 1950
  The Wreck of the Mary Deare; see The Mary Deare
  Wreckers Must Breathe. Collins, 1940. U.S. title: Trapped. Putnam, 1940

INNES, MICHAEL. Pseudonym of J(ohn) I(nnes) M(ackintosh) Stewart, 1906- , q.v. Series character: John Appleby = JA.
  Appleby at Allington. Gollancz, 1968. U.S. title: Death by Water. Dodd, 1968 JA
  The Appleby File. Gollancz, 1975; Dodd, 1976 JA ss
  Appleby on Ararat. Gollancz, 1941; Dodd, 1941 JA
  Appleby Plays Chicken. Gollancz, 1957. U.S. title: Death on a Quiet Day. Dodd, 1957 JA
  Appleby Talking. Gollancz, 1954. U.S. title: Dead Man's Shoes. Dodd, 1954 JA ss
  Appleby Talks Again. Gollancz, 1956; Dodd, 1957 JA ss
  Appleby's Answer. Gollancz, 1973; Dodd, 1973 JA
  Appleby's End. Gollancz, 1945; Dodd, 1945 JA
  Appleby's Other Story. Gollancz, 1974; Dodd, 1974 JA
  An Awkward Lie. Gollancz, 1971; Dodd, 1971 JA
  The Bloody Wood. Gollancz, 1966; Dodd, 1966 JA
  Candleshoe; see Christmas at Candleshoe
  The Case of Sonia Wayward; see The New Sonia Wayward
  The Case of the Journeying Boy; see The Journeying Boy
  A Change of Heir. Gollancz, 1966; Dodd, 1966
  Christmas at Candleshoe. Gollancz, 1953; Dodd, 1953. Also published as: Candleshoe. Penguin, 1978
  A Comedy of Terrors; see There Came Both Mist and Snow
  A Connoisseur's Case. Gollancz, 1962. U.S. title: The Crabtree Affair. Dodd, 1962 JA
  The Crabtree Affair; see A Connoisseur's Case
  The Daffodil Affair. Gollancz, 1942; Dodd, 1942 JA
  Dead Man's Shoes; see Appleby Talking
  Death at the Chase. Gollancz, 1970; Dodd, 1970 JA
  Death at the President's Lodging. Gollancz, 1936. U.S. title: Seven Suspects. Dodd, 1937 JA
  Death by Moonlight; see The Man from the Sea
  Death by Water; see Appleby at Allington
  Death on a Quiet Day; see Appleby Plays Chicken

A Family Affair. Gollancz, 1969. U.S. title: Picture of Guilt. Dodd, 1969 JA
From London Far. Gollancz, 1946. U.S. title: The Unsuspected Chasm. Dodd, 1946
Hamlet, Revenge! Gollancz, 1937; Dodd, 1937 JA
Hare Sitting Up. Gollancz, 1959; Dodd, 1959 JA
The Journeying Boy. Gollancz, 1949. U.S. title: The Case of the Journeying Boy. Dodd, 1949
Lament for a Maker. Gollancz, 1938; Dodd, 1938 JA
The Long Farewell. Gollancz, 1958; Dodd, 1958 JA
The Man from the Sea. Gollancz, 1955; Dodd, 1955. Also published as: Death by Moonlight. Avon, 1957
Money from Holme. Gollancz, 1964; Dodd, 1965
Murder is an Art; see A Private View
The Mysterious Commission. Gollancz, 1974; Dodd, 1975
The New Sonia Wayward. Gollancz, 1960. U.S. title: The Case of Sonia Wayward. Dodd, 1960
A Night of Errors. Gollancz, 1948; Dodd, 1947 JA
Old Hall, New Hall. Gollancz, 1956. U.S. title: A Question of Queens. Dodd, 1956
One Man Show; see A Private View
The Open House. Gollancz, 1972; Dodd, 1972 JA
Operation Pax. Gollancz, 1951. U.S. title: The Paper Thunderbolt. Dodd, 1951 JA
The Paper Thunderbolt; see Operation Pax
Picture of Guilt; see A Family Affair
A Private View. Gollancz, 1952. U.S. title: One-Man Show. Dodd, 1952. Also published as: Murder is an Art. Avon, 1959 JA
A Question of Queens; see Old Hall, New Hall
The Secret Vanguard. Gollancz, 1940; Dodd, 1941 JA
Seven Suspects; see Death at the President's Lodging
Silence Observed. Gollancz, 1961; Dodd, 1961 JA
The Spider Strikes; see Stop Press
Stop Press. Gollancz, 1939. U.S. title: The Spider Strikes. Dodd, 1939 JA
There Came Both Mist and Snow. Gollancz, 1940. U.S. title: A Comedy of Terrors. Dodd, 1940 JA
The Unsuspected Chasm; see From London Far
The Weight of the Evidence. Gollancz, 1944; Dodd, 1943 JA
What Happened at Hazelwood. Gollancz, 1946; Dodd, 1946

INNES, MURRAY M.
Cosgrove: Detective. Stockwell, 1938 ss

IRALDI, JAMES C.
The Problem of the Purple Maculas. Norris, 1968. (Sherlock Holmes pastiche)

IRELAND, DAVID. 1927-   .
The Chantic Bird. Heinemann, 1968; Scribner, 1968

IRISH, WILLIAM. Pseudonym of Cornell (George Hopley) Woolrich, 1903-1968, q.v. Other pseudonym: George Hopley, q.v.
After-Dinner Story. Lippincott, 1944; Hutchinson, 1947. Also published as: Six Times Death. Popular Library, 1948 ss
And So to Death; see I Wouldn't be in Your Shoes
The Blue Ribbon. Lippincott, 1949; Hutchinson, 1951. Also published as: Dilemma of the Dead Lady. Graphic, 1950 (which omits 2 ss from the hardcover edition) ss
Bluebeard's Seventh Wife. Popular Library, 1952 ss
Borrowed Crime. Avon, 1946 ss
The Dancing Detective. Lippincott, 1946; Hutchinson, 1948 ss
Dead Man Blues. Lippincott, 1948; Hutchinson, 1950 ss
Deadline at Dawn. Lippincott, 1944; Hutchinson, 1947
Deadly Night Call; see Somebody on the Phone
Dilemma of the Dead Lady; see The Blue Ribbon
Eyes That Watch You. Rinehart, 1952 ss
I Married a Dead Man. Lippincott, 1948; Hutchinson, 1950
I Wouldn't be in Your Shoes. Lippincott, 1943; Hutchinson, 1946. Also published as: And So to Death. Jonathan, 1947. And as: Nightmare. Reader's Choice Library, 1950. (Both of these paperback editions omit two stories from the original hardcover.)
If I Should Die Before I Wake. Avon, 1945 ss
Marihuana. Dell 10¢ pb, 1951. (Separate publication of a story first collected in After-Dinner Story, q.v.)
The Night I Died; see Somebody on the Phone
Nightmare; see I Wouldn't be in Your Shoes
Phantom Lady. Lippincott, 1942; Hale, 1945
Six Nights of Mystery. Popular Library, 1950 ss
Six Times Death; see After-Dinner Story
Somebody on the Phone. Lippincott, 1950. British title: The Night I Died. Hutchinson, 1951. Also published as: Deadly Night Call. Graphic, 1951, with two stories omitted ss
Strangler's Serenade. Rinehart, 1951; Hale, 1952
Waltz into Darkness. Lippincott, 1947; Hutchinson, 1948
You'll Never See Me Again. Dell 10¢ pb, 1951. (Separate publication of a novelet later collected in Nightwebs, as by Cornell Woolrich, q.v.)

IRONSIDE, JOHN. Pseudonym of Euphemia Margaret Tait. Series character: Det. Insp. John Freeman, in at least those marked JF.
Blackmail. Mellifont, 1938
The Call-Box Mystery. Methuen, 1923. U.S. title: The Phone Booth Mystery. Holt, 1924
-Chris: A Love Story. Hodder, 1926
The Crime and the Casket. Mellifont, 1945
-Forged in Strong Fires. Methuen, 1912; Little, 1911
Jack of Clubs. Nelson, 1931
Lady Pamela's Pearls. Hodder, 1927
The Marten Mystery. Arrowsmith, 1933 JF
The Phone Booth Mystery; see The Call-Box Mystery
The Red Symbol. Nash, 1911; Little, 1910 JF

IRVINE, HELEN DOUGLAS
Mirror of a Dead Lady. Longmans, 1940

77 Willow Road; see Sweet is the Rose
Sweet is the Rose. Longmans, 1944. U.S. title: 77 Willow Road. Doubleday, 1945

IRVINE, R(OBERT) R.
Jump Cut. Popular Library, 1974

IRVING, ALEXANDER. Joint pseudonym of Ruth Fox and Anne Fahrenkopf.
Bitter Ending. Dodd, 1946
Deadline. Dodd, 1947
Symphony in Two Time. Dodd, 1948

IRVING, CLIFFORD (MICHAEL). 1930-   .
The Losers. Coward, 1957; Heinemann, 1959
The Thirty-Eighth Floor. McGraw, 1965; Heinemann, 1965
-The Valley. McGraw, 1961; Heinemann, 1962

IRVING, PETER HENRY. 1914-   .
-Fully Ripe. Hurst, 1944
-Green for a Season. Hurst, 1947
The Inner Room. Evans, 1952
An Italian Called Mario. Evans, 1954
-The Lady and the Unicorn. Evans, 1953
-One Way Street. Hurst, 1948
-Roger Quinney. Hurst, 1949
-The Triumphal Chariot. Hurst, 1945

IRVING-JAMES, T(HOMAS)
Deserted by the Devil. Hale, 1971
Dinner After Death. Hale, 1964
A Glimpse of Evil. Hale, 1967

IRWIN, F. WILMOT
Black Terror. Fiction House, 1935
A Continental Conspiracy. Mellifont, 1935
A Cup-Tie Mystery. Mellifont, 1933
Death Makes a Date. Fiction House, 1943
Death Visits the Cinema. Fiction House, 1945
Horror Hall. Fiction House, 1938
Murder Makes Merry. Fiction House, 1944
Murder Mission. Fiction House, 1944
Murder on the Mountain! Fiction House, 1935
The Mystery of Moor Manor. Mellifont, 1934
Terror Tower. Fiction House, 1935
The Third Shot. Fiction House, 1937
The Tragic Quest. Mellifont, 1941

IRWIN, H(ARVEY) S(AMUEL)
Helena. Dillingham, 1899

IRWIN, INEZ HAYNES. 1873-   . Series character: Patrick O'Brien, in all titles.
A Body Rolled Downstairs. Random, 1938; Heinemann, 1938
Many Murders. Random, 1941; Swan, 1950
Murder in Fancy Dress; see Murder Masquerade
Murder Masquerade. Smith & Haas, 1935. British title: Murder in Fancy Dress. Heinemann, 1935
The Poison Cross Mystery. Smith & Haas, 1936; Heinemann, 1936
The Women Swore Revenge. Random, 1946; Boardman, 1948

IRWIN, JUDY
Murderous Welcome. Hale, 1967; Roy, 1967

IRWIN, THEODORE D. 1907-   .
Collusion. Godwin, 1932

IRWIN, WALLACE (ADMAH). 1876-1959.
The Julius Caesar Murder Case. Appleton, 1935

IRWIN, WILL(IAM HENRY). 1873-1948. See also: (Frank) Gelett Burgess, 1866-1951.
The Confessions of a Con Man. Huebsch, 1909
The House of Mystery. Century, 1910
The Red Button. Bobbs, 1912

ISAACS, LEVI. Pseudonym: Louis Essex, q.v.

ISELY, REYMOURE KEITH
A Strange Code of Justice. Bobbs, 1974

ISHAM, FREDERIC S(TEWART). 1866-1922.
-Half a Chance. Bobbs, 1909
-A Man and his Money. Bobbs, 1912
The Social Buccaneer. Bobbs, 1910; Everett, 1911

ISLAY, NICHOLAS
A Brace of Rogues. Murray, 1920
The Selicombe Murder. Murray, 1920

ISRAEL, CHARLES E(DWARD)
The Hostages. Simon, 1966; Macmillan (London), 1966
The Mark. Simon, 1958; Macmillan (London), 1958
Shadows on a Wall. Simon, 1965; Macmillan (London), 1965

ISRAEL, PETER
Hush Money. Crowell, 1974; Hodder, 1975

I-TING, WANG
Thirty Famous Chinese Stories. Commercial, 1934 ss, at least one criminous

J

J., R. C.
The Tragedy of Captain Harrison; or, The Brownlow Street Mystery. Nutt, 1890

JACKMAN, STUART (BROOKE). 1922- .
Guns Covered with Flowers. Faber, 1973
Slingshot. Faber, 1974

JACKS, JEFF. Series character: Shep Stone, in both titles.
Find the Don's Daughter. GM, 1974
Murder on the Wild Side. GM, 1971

JACKS, OLIVER. Pseudonym of Kenneth Royce, 1920- , q.v.
Man on a Short Leash. Hodder, 1974; Stein, 1974

JACKSON, ACE
There's Danger, Miss Minden! Brown Watson, 1949

JACKSON, BASIL. 1920- .
Supersonic. Norton, 1975

JACKSON, BLYDEN. 1910- .
Operation Burning Candle. Third Press, 1973

JACKSON, CHARLES ROSS. 1867-1915.
Quintus Oakes. Dillingham, 1904; Unwin, 1904
-The Sheriff of Wasco. Dillingham, 1907
The Third Degree. Dillingham, 1903; Unwin, 1903

JACKSON, CLARENCE J.-L. Pseudonym of Richard Williams Bulliet, 1940- .

Kicked to Death by a Camel. Harper, 1973

JACKSON, EVERATT
The Road to Hell. Hale, 1975

JACKSON, FELIX
So Help Me God. Viking, 1955; Cassell, 1957

JACKSON, FREDERICK. 1886- .
The Cat will Mew. Jarrolds, 1932
The Diamond Necklace. Whitman, 1929. (British title?)
-Intimate Relations. Jarrolds, 1930
-Into this Universe. Jarrolds, 1929
Pantoufle. Jarrolds, 1934; Knopf, 1935

JACKSON, GILES. Pseudonym of Albert Leffingwell, 1895-1946, q.v. Other pseudonym: Dana Chambers, q.v.
Blood on the Blonde; see Witch's Moon
Court of Shadows. Dial, 1943; Museum, 1945
Witch's Moon. Dial, 1941; Museum, 1943. Also published as: Blood on the Blonde, as by Dana Chambers. Jonathan, 1952 (abridged)

JACKSON, JOAN
Murder Makes Me Laugh. Aldor, 1947

JACKSON, KEN. Series character: Jud Blade, in both titles.
The Cutting Edge. Simon, 1970
The Sticking Point. Simon, 1971

JACKSON, LEWIS. Pseudonym of Jack Lewis, q.v. Other pseudonym: Stephen Hood, q.v. All titles were published by Amalgamated Press and feature Sexton Blake.
According to Plan. 1947
The Case of the Biscay Pirate. 1944
The Case of the Discharged Policeman. 1949
The Case of the Doped Heavyweight. 1948
The Case of the Fatal Souvenir. 1946
The Case of the Fighting Padre. 1947
The Case of the Five Fugitives. 1944
The Case of the Five Red Herrings. 1945
The Case of John Muir of Merchant Navy. 1942
The Case of the Missing Stoker. 1942
The Case of the Night Lorry Driver. 1946
The Case of the "Suspect" Watchmaker. 1943
The Crime on the Cliff. 1947
The Death of Mrs. Preedy. 1949
Down East! 1946
The Man from Arnheim. 1945
The Man from Persia. 1951
The Man Who Left Home. 1949
The Man Who Went Wrong. 1948
The Night of the 23rd. 1947
On Compassionate Leave. 1945
The Riddle of the Film Star's Jewels. 1947
The Riddle of the Ruins. 1944
The Riddle of the Workman Squire. 1945
The Tallyman's Fate. 1945
The Tenant of No. 13. 1946
The Woman with a "Record." 1946

JACKSON, MARR
A Dram of Poison. Bell, 1938
Escape into Murder. Cassell, 1939

JACKSON, MARY E.
The Spy of Osawatomie; or, The Mysterious Companions of Old John Brown. Bryan, 1881

JACKSON, O. T.
Dark Love, Dark Magic. Lancer, 1969

JACKSON, RALPH
Violent Night. Ace, 1955

JACKSON, SHIRLEY. 1920-1965. See also: F. ANDREW LESLIE.
The Bird's Nest. Farrar, 1954; Joseph, 1955. Also published as: Lizzie. Signet, 1957 ss
Come Along with Me. Viking, 1968; Joseph, 1969 ss
Hangsaman. Farrar, 1951; Gollancz, 1951
The Haunting of Hill House. Viking, 1959; Joseph, 1960
Lizzie; see The Bird's Nest
The Lottery. Farrar, 1949; Gollancz, 1950 ss
The Road Through the Wall. Farrar, 1949
The Sundial. Farrar, 1958; Joseph, 1958
We Have Always Lived in the Castle. Viking, 1962; Joseph, 1963

JACKSON, WALLACE. Pseudonym of William John Budd, 1898- . Other pseudonym: Jackson Budd, q.v. Series characters: Clancy Martin = CM; Archibald Penny = AP.
The Diamonds of Death. Low, 1936; Hopkins, 1937 CM
The Extraordinary Case of Mr. Bell. Low, 1935; Hopkins, 1936 AP
The Sinister Madonna. Low, 1937; Hopkins, 1937 CM
Two Knocks for Death. Low, 1934; Hopkins, 1935 CM
The Zadda Street Affair. Low, 1934 AP

JACKSON, WILFRID S(CARBOROUGH). 1871- .
Nine Points of the Law. Lane (London & New York), 1903

JACOBS, T(HOMAS) C(URTIS) H(ICKS). Pseudonym of Jacques Pendower, 1899-1976, q.v. Series characters: Chief Inspector Barnard, in at least those marked B; Detective Superintendent John Bellamy, in at least those marked JB; Temple Fortune, in at least those marked TF; Mike Seton, in at least those marked MS; Jim Malone, in at least those marked JM.
Appointment with the Hangman. Paul, 1936; Macaulay, 1936
Ashes in the Cellar. Hale, 1966 TF
The Black Box. Paul, 1946 B
The Black Devil. Hale, 1969 TF
Black Trinity. Long, 1959 JB
Blood and Sun-Tan. Paul, 1952 TF
Broken Alibi. Paul, 1957; Roy, 1957 JB
The Broken Knife. Paul, 1941 B
The Bronkhurst Case. Paul, 1931. U.S. title: Documents of Murder. Macaulay, 1933
Brother Spy. Paul, 1940 B
Cause for Suspicion. Paul, 1956
The Curse of Khatra. Paul, 1947 JB
Danger Money. Hale, 1963 TF
Dangerous Fortune. Paul, 1949 TF
Deadly Race. Long, 1958 TF
Death in the Mews. Paul, 1955 TF
Death of a Scoundrel. Hale, 1967 TF
Documents of Murder; see The Bronkhurst Case
The Elusive Mr. Drago. Hale, 1964 MS
Final Payment. Hale, 1965 TF
Good Knight, Sailor. Paul, 1954 TF
The Grenson Murder Case. Paul, 1943 JB
House of Horror. Hale, 1969 TF
Identity Unknown. Paul, 1938 B
The Kestrel House Mystery. Paul, 1932; Macaulay, 1933 B
Lady, What's Your Game? Paul, 1952 TF
The Laughing Men. Hodder, 1937 B
Let Him Stay Dead. Hale, 1961 JM
Lock the Door, Mademoiselle. Paul, 1951 TF
Murder Market. Hale, 1962 TF
No Sleep for Elsa. Paul, 1953 TF

The Red Eyes of Kali. Paul, 1950 TF
The Red Net. Hale, 1962 JM
Results of an Accident. Paul, 1955 JB
Reward for Treason. Paul, 1944 B
Scorpion's Trail. Paul, 1932; Macaulay, 1934 B
The Secret Power. Hale, 1963
Security Risk. Hale, 1972
Silent Terror. Paul, 1936; Macaulay, 1937 B
Sinister Quest. Paul, 1934; Macaulay, 1934 B
Sweet Poison. Hale, 1966 TF
Target for Terror. Hale, 1961 MS & TF
The Tattooed Man. Hale, 1961
The Terror of Torlands. Paul, 1930
The 13th Chime. Paul, 1935; Macaulay, 1935 B
Traitor Spy. Paul, 1939 B
Wild Week-End. Hale, 1967
With What Motive? Paul, 1948 JB
The Woman Who Waited. Paul, 1954
Women are Like That. Hale, 1960 TF

JACOBS, W(ILLIAM) W(YMARK). 1863-1943.
The Lady of the Barge. Harper (London), 1902; Dodd, 1902 ss, some criminous
Sea Whispers. Hodder, 1926 ss

JACOBSEN, JULIUS
-The Revelations of a Police Court Interpreter. Whitaker, 1866

JACOBSSON, PER. 1894-1963. Joint pseudonym with Vernon Bartlett, 1894-   : Peter Oldfeld, q.v.

JACOLLIOT, J. L(OUIS). 1837-1890.
The Froler Case. Bonner's, 1893. Also published as: The Sign of the Dagger; or, The Froler Case. Street, 1904

JACQUES, NORBERT. 1880-   .
Dr. Mabuse, Master of Mystery. Allen & Unwin, 1923. (Translation of Doktor Mabuse. Berlin, 1920.)

JAEDIKER, KERMIT
Hero's Lust. Lion, 1953
Tall, Dark and Dead. Mystery House, 1947

JAFFE, MICHAEL
Death Goes to a Party. Phoenix, 1942

JAFFEE, MARY and IRVING
Beyond Baker Street. Pontine, 1973 ss

JAHN, MIKE
The Unfortunate Replacement. Popular Library, 1975. (Novelization of the Rockford Files TV series.)

JAKES, JOHN (WILLIAM). 1932-   . Pseudonyms: Alan Payne, Jay Scotland, qq.v. Series character: Johnny Havoc = JH.
The Devil has Four Faces. Mystery House, 1958
The Imposter. Mystery House, 1959
Johnny Havoc. Belmont, 1960 JH
Johnny Havoc and the Doll Who had "It." Belmont, 1963 JH
Johnny Havoc Meets Zelda. Belmont, 1962 JH
A Night for Treason. Mystery House, 1956

JAMES, POLICE CAPTAIN. Pseudonym.
Little Lightning, the Shadow Detective; or, The Twenty-Third Street Mystery. Street, 1888
The Revenue Detective. Street, 1889

JAMES, BARBARA
Beauty That Must Die. Hodder, 1961; Ace, 1967
Bright Deadly Summer. Hodder, 1962; Ace, 1966

JAMES, BRENI. Series character: Sgt. Gunnar Matson, in both titles.
Night of the Kill. Simon, 1961; Hammond, 1963
The Shake-Up. Simon, 1964

JAMES, DON(ALD H.). 1905-   .
Dark Hunger. Monarch, 1963

JAMES, FLORENCE ALICE PRICE. 1857-1929. Pseudonym: Florence Warden, q.v.

JAMES, FRANKLIN. Pseudonym of Robert Godley, 1908-   .
Killer in the Kitchen. Lantern Press, 1947

JAMES, GODFREY WARDEN. 1888-   . Pseudonym: Adam Broome, q.v.

JAMES. HALLAM
Fair-Isle Jumper Mystery. James, 1944

JAMES, HENRY. 1843-1916. See also: MICHAEL REDGRAVE; and: WILLIAM ARCHIBALD, 1924-1970.
The Other House. Macmillan, 1896; Heinemann, 1896
The Turn of the Screw. Macmillan, 1898, in Two Magics; Heinemann, 1898
Two Magics; see The Turn of the Screw

JAMES, HENRY COLBERT
The Girl from Taiping. Jarrolds, 1954
Gold is Where You Find It. Harrap, 1949
The Green Opal. Jarrolds, 1953
The Madness of Charlie Pierce. Jarrolds, 1952

JAMES, LEIGH. Pseudonym. 1918-   .
The Capitol Hill Affair. Weybright, 1968
The Chameleon File. Weybright, 1967; Jenkins, 1968
The Push-Button Spy. Prentice-Hall, 1970
Triple Mirror. Mason, 1973

JAMES, MARYL
Brandy on the Rocks. Lancer, 1967

JAMES, MAX
Death is Where You Meet It. Hamilton & Co., 1952

JAMES, P(HYLLIS) D(OROTHY). 1920-   . Series character: Adam Dalgliesh, in all titles.
The Black Tower. Faber, 1975; Scribner, 1975
Cover Her Face. Faber, 1962; Scribner, 1966
A Mind to Murder. Faber, 1963; Scribner, 1967
Shroud for a Nightingale. Faber, 1971; Scribner, 1971
Unnatural Causes. Faber, 1967; Scribner, 1967
An Unsuitable Job for a Woman. Faber, 1972; Scribner, 1973

JAMES, PAUL
What Became of Eugene Ridgewood? Carleton, 1883

JAMES, REBECCA (SALSBURY)
Storm's End. Doubleday, 1974; New English Library, 1975

JAMES, ROBERT. Pseudonym of Iris Heitner.
Board Stiff. Doubleday, 1951
Death Wears Pink Shoes. Doubleday, 1952

JAMES, STUART
Jack the Ripper. Monarch, 1960. (Novelization of the movie.)
The Stranglers of Bombay. Monarch, 1960. (Novelization of the movie.)

JAMES, VINCENT. Pseudonym of James Gribben, 1915-   .
Island of the Pit. Benn, 1955; Messner, 1956
The Long Ride Out. Benn, 1957; Putnam, 1958
Morgan's Wife. Quality, 1949
Red Sky. Quality, 1953

JAMESON, MRS. ANNIE EDITH FOSTER. 1868-1931. Pseudonym: J. E. Buckrose, q.v.

JAMESON, (MARGARET) STORM
Before the Crossing. Macmillan (London & New York), 1947

JAMIESON, LELAND (SHATTUCK). 1904-1941.
G-Men on Murder Island. Swan, 1947
Murder Island. Melrose, 1935; Greenberg, 1936

JAMISON, AMELIA
The Lairds of Turriff Hall. Popular Library, 1974

JANE, FRED(ERICK) T(HOMAS). 1865-1916.
Ever Mohun. Macqueen, 1901
-The Incubated Girl. Tower, 1896
The Lordship, the Passen, and We. Innes, 1897
-A Royal Bluejacket. Low, 1908
-To Venus in Five Seconds. Innes, 1897

JANIFER, LAURENCE M. Pseudonym of Larry M(ark) Harris, 1933-   , q.v. Joint pseudonym with Randall (Phillips) Garrett: Mark Phillips, q.v.
The Final Fear. Belmont, 1967
The Woman Without a Name. Signet, 1966
You Can't Escape. Lancer, 1967

JANIS, ELSIE, 1889-1956, and MARGUERITE ASPINWALL
Counter Currents. Putnam (New York & London), 1926

JANSEN, JOHANNA FREDERIKA. Joint pseudonym with Margaret Elizabeth Baird Campbell: Fred Bayard, q.v.

JANSEN, LAURA MAY
Bride of the Shadows. Lancer, 1967

JANSON, HANK. Pseudonym used by Harry Hobson, 1908-   , q.v. Other pseudonym: Hank Hobson, q.v. Also used by Victor (George Charles) Norwood, 1920-   , q.v. Other pseudonyms: Johnny Dark, Mark Hampton, Nat Karta, qq.v. Hank Janson byline probably also used by other writers.
Abomination. Roberts, 1965
The Affairs of Paula. Gold Star, 1965
Amorous Captive. Moring, 1958
Angel Astray. Roberts, 1962
Angel, Shoot to Kill. Frances, 1949
Auctioned. New Fiction Press, 1952
Avenging Nymph. Moring, 1958
Baby, Don't Dare Squeal. Frances, 1951
Backlash of Infamy. Roberts, 1965
Bad Girl. Turton, 1959
Beauty and the Beat. Roberts, 1962
Becky. Gold Star, 1965
Beloved Traitor. Roberts, 1960
Bid for Beauty. Roberts, 1966
The Big H. Roberts, 1966
Blonde on the Spot. Gaywood, 1949
Blood Bath. Roberts, 1962
Brand Image. Roberts, 1963

J

Janson, Hank

Brazen Seductress. Gold Star, 1965
Break for a Lovely. Roberts, 1961
The Bride Wore Weeds. Gaywood, 1950
Broads Don't Scare Easy. New Fiction, 1951
Casinopoly. Roberts, 1968
Catch Me a Renegade. Roberts, 1965
Chicago Chick. Roberts, 1962
Cold Dead Coed. Gold Star, 1965
Come Quickly, Honey. Roberts, 1960
Conflict. New Fiction Press, 1952
Contraband. Moring, 1955
Cool Sugar. Roberts, 1960
Counter-Feat. Roberts, 1962
Crime on My Hands. Roberts, 1962
Crime Beat Crisis. Roberts, 1964
Crowns can Kill. Roberts, 1961
Cutie on Call. Roberts, 1960
Darling Delinquent. Roberts, 1966
Dateline Darlene. Roberts, 1963
Dateline Debbie. Roberts, 1963
Dateline Diane. Roberts, 1963
Daughter of Shame. Roberts, 1963
Dead Certainty. Roberts, 1966
Deadly Mission. Moring, 1955
Death Wore a Petticoat. Francis, 1951
Delicious Danger. Roberts, 1961
Desert Fury. New Fiction, 1953
Design for Dupes. Roberts, 1964
Destination Dames. Roberts, 1961
Devil and the Deep. Roberts, 1965
Devil's Highway. Moring, 1956
Dig Those Heels. Roberts, 1962
Doctor Fix. Roberts, 1964
Don't Dare Me, Sugar. Gaywood, 1950
Don't Mourn Me, Toots. Frances, 1951
Don't Scare Easy. Moring, 1958
Double Take. Roberts, 1964
Downtown Doll. Roberts, 1961
Ecstacy. Roberts, 1960
Escalation. Roberts, 1966
Escape. Moring, 1956
Exclusive. Roberts, 1962
The Exotic Seductress. Gold Star, 1965
Expectant Nymph. Gold Star, 1965
Fan Fare. Roberts, 1964
Fanny. Gold Star, 1965
Fast Buck. Roberts, 1963
F.E.U.D. Roberts, 1966
The Filly Wore Red. New Fiction, 1952
Fireball. Roberts, 1961
Flashpoint. Roberts, 1965
Flight from Fear. Moring, 1958
Flower of Desire. Roberts, 1964
48 Hours. Moring, 1955
Frails can be So Tough. New Fiction, 1951
Framed. Moring, 1955
Furtive Flame. Roberts, 1965
A Girl in Hand. Roberts, 1964
Go with a Jerk. Roberts, 1963
Grape Vine. Roberts, 1962
Gun Moll for Hire. Frances, 1948
Gunsmoke in her Eyes. Frances, 1949
Hate. Moring, 1958
Heartache. Roberts, 1963
Helldorado. Roberts, 1966
Hell's Angel. Moring, 1956; Gold Star, 1965
Hell's Belles. Roberts, 1961
Her Weapon is Passion. Gold Star, 1965
Hilary's Terms. Roberts, 1963
Honey for Me. Roberts, 1962
Honey Take My Gun. Frances, 1949
Hot House. Gold Star, 1965
Hot Line. Roberts, 1963
Hotsy, You'll be Chilled. Frances, 1951
I for Intrigue. Roberts, 1963
Invasion. Moring, 1959
It's Always Eve That Weeps. Frances, 1951
It's Bedtime, Baby! Gold Star, 1965
Jack Spot. Moring, 1959
The Jane with Green Eyes. Gaywood, 1950
Janson, Go Home. Roberts, 1961
Jazz Jungle. Roberts, 1965
Junk Market. Roberts, 1965
Kill Her If You Can. New Fiction, 1952
Kill Her with Passion. Gold Star, 1965
Kill Me for Kicks. Roberts, 1962
Kill This Man. Moring, 1958
Krush. Roberts, 1966
The Lady has a Scar. Gaywood, 1950
Lady, Lie Low. Roberts, 1961
Lady, Mind That Corpse. Frances, 1948
Lady, Toll the Bell. Gaywood, 1950
Ladybirds are In. Roberts, 1967
Lake Loot. Roberts, 1964
The Last Lady. Roberts, 1964
Late Night Revel. Roberts, 1961
Like Crazy. Roberts, 1962
Like Lethal. Roberts, 1962
Like Poison. Roberts, 1962
Lilies for my Lovely. Frances, 1949
Limbo Lover. Roberts, 1964
Liquor is Quicker. Roberts, 1966
Lola Brought her Wreath. Gaywood, 1950
Lose This Gun. Moring, 1958
The Love Makers. Roberts, 1963
The Love Secretaries. Roberts, 1964
Lover. Gold Star, 1963
Lust for Vengeance. Roberts, 1965
Make Mine Mink. Roberts, 1966
Master Mind. Roberts, 1961
Mayfair Slayride. Roberts, 1966
Menace. Moring, 1955
Milady Took the Rap. New Fiction, 1951
Missile Mob. Roberts, 1965
Mistress of Fear. Moring, 1958
Model in Mayhem. Roberts, 1965
Murder. New Fiction, 1952
Nefarious Quest. Roberts, 1966
Nerve Centre. Roberts, 1963
A Nice Way to Die. Gold Star, 1963
No Regrets for Clara. Frances, 1949
Nymph in the Night. Roberts, 1962
A Nympho Named Silvia. Gold Star, 1965
One Against Time. Moring, 1956
One Man in his Time. New Fiction, 1953
Outcast. Roberts, 1961
Passion Pact. Roberts, 1963
Passionate Playmate. Gold Star, 1964
Passionate Waif. Roberts, 1960
Pattern of Rape. Roberts, 1964
Physical Attraction. Roberts, 1967
Play It Casual. Roberts, 1962
Playgirl. Roberts, 1963
Prey for a Newshawk. Roberts, 1961
Quiet Waits the Grave. Roberts, 1960
Rave for a Roughneck. Roberts, 1962
Reluctant Hostess. Roberts, 1961
Ripe for Rapture. Roberts, 1960
Riviera Showdown. Roberts, 1967
Roxy by Proxy. Roberts, 1965
Run for Lover. Roberts, 1962
Sadie, Don't Cry Now. New Fiction, 1952
Same Difference. Roberts, 1968
Savage Sequel. Roberts, 1962
Say It with Candy. Roberts, 1965
Scent from Heaven. Roberts, 1961
Second String. Roberts, 1963
Secret Session. Roberts, 1960
Sentence for Sin. Roberts, 1960
Sex Angle. Roberts, 1964
The Sexy Vixen. Gold Star, 1965
She Sleeps to Conquer. Roberts, 1961
Short-Term Wife. Roberts, 1961
Silken Snare. Moring, 1959
Sister, Don't Hate Me. Frances, 1951
Situation, Grave! Moring, 1958
Skirts Bring Me Sorrow. New Fiction, 1952
Slay-Ride for Cutie. Frances, 1949
Smart Girls Don't Talk. Frances, 1949
Soft Cargo. Roberts, 1964
Some Look Better Dead. Frances, 1950
Square One. Roberts, 1964
Strange Ritual. Roberts, 1963
Suddenly It's Sin. Roberts, 1961
Sugar and Vice. Moring, 1958
Sultry Avenger. Moring, 1959
Sweet Talk. Roberts, 1965
Sweetheart, Here's Your Grave! Frances, 1949
Sweetie, Hold Me Tight. Frances, 1952
Tail Sting. Roberts, 1965
Take This—Sweetie. Roberts, 1962
Tension. Frances, 1952
That Brain Again. Roberts, 1964
This Dame Dies Soon. Frances, 1951. Also published as: Too Soon to Die. Moring, 1962
This Hood for Hire. Roberts, 1960
This Woman is Death. Frances, 1948
Tigress. Roberts, 1964
Tomorrow and a Day. Moring, 1955
Too Soon to Die; see This Dame Dies Soon
Top Ten. Roberts, 1964
Torment for Trixy. Gaywood, 1950
Torrid Temptress. Turton, 1959
Twist for Two. Roberts, 1962
Uncommon Market. Roberts, 1962
Uncover Agent. Roberts, 1962
The Unseen Assassin. Moring, 1956
V for Vitality. Roberts, 1963
Vagabond Vamp. Roberts, 1962
Venus Makes Three. Roberts, 1961
Visit from a Broad. Roberts, 1963
Voodoo Violence. Roberts, 1964
Way Out Wanton. Roberts, 1962
When Dames Get Tough. Ward & Hitchon, 1946
Whiplash. New Fiction, 1952
Why Should Sylvia? Roberts, 1965
Wild Girl. Turton, 1959
Will-Power. Roberts, 1964
Women Hate Till Death. New Fiction, 1951
The Young Wolves. Roberts, 1968
Zero Take All. Roberts, 1967

JANSSON, ROBERT
Meet You in Munich. Barker, 1975

JAPRISOT, SEBASTIEN. Pseudonym of Jean Baptiste Rossi, 1931-   .
Goodbye, Friend. Simon, 1969; Souvenir, 1969. (Translation of Adieu L'Ami. Paris, 1968.)
The Lady in the Car with Glasses and a Gun. Simon, 1967; Souvenir, 1968. (Translation of La Dame dans l'Auto avec les Lunettes et un Fusil. Paris, 1966.)
The Sleeping Car Murders; see The 10:30 from Marseilles
The 10:30 from Marseilles. Doubleday, 1963; Souvenir, 1964. Also published as: The Sleeping Car Murders. PB, 1967. (Translation of Compartiment Tueurs. Paris, 1962.)
Trap for Cinderella. Simon, 1964; Souvenir, 1965. (Translation of Piege pour Cendrillon. Paris, 1962.)

JARDIN, REX. Joint pseudonym of Robert Ferdinand Burkhardt, 1892-1947, and Eve Burkhardt, 1899-   . Other joint pseudonym: Adam Bliss, q.v.
The Devil's Mansion. Fiction League, 1931

JARDINE, JACK OWEN. 1931-   . Pseudonym: Larry Maddock, q.v.

JARDINE, WARWICK. Pseudonym of Francis Alister Warwick. All titles below were published by Amalgamated Press and feature Sexton Blake.
The British Museum Mystery. 1934
A Case for M.I.5. 1950
The Case of the Murdered Wedding Guest. 1936

The Cloakroom Murder. 1934
The Crime in Park Lane. 1933
Crook's Loot. 1932
Death her Destination. 1961
Doomed Men. 1932. Revised version: 1940
The Great Dumping Mystery. 1932
The Hailey Street Murder. 1933
The Lift Shaft Crime. 1938
The Madman of the Marshes. 1949
The Man from Algiers. 1948
The Man from Tokyo. 1933
The Man with a Grievance. 1952
The Mystery of the Arab Agent. 1953
The Mystery of the Unknown Victim. 1933
The Old Man of the Moors. 1950
The Pavement Artist Mystery. 1937
The Pleasure Cruise Murder. 1933
The Riddle of the Green Cylinder. 1955
The Riddle of the Ranch. 1939
The Seaside Cafe Crime. 1936
The Seaside Crime. 1936
The Secret of Capri. 1950
The Secret of the Glacier. 1935
The Secret of the Sudan. 1933
The Secret of the Surgery. 1939
The Stolen Test-Tube. 1935
The 13th Code. 1939
Top Secret No. 1. 1951
The Victim of the Cult. 1937

JARRETT, CORA (HARDY). 1877- . Pseudonym: Faraday Keene, q.v.
The Ginkgo Tree. Farrar, 1935; Barker, 1935
Night Over Fitch's Pond. Houghton, 1933; Barker, 1933
Strange Houses. Farrar, 1936; Heinemann, 1937

JARVIE, CLODAGH GIBSON. 1923- .
He Would Provoke Death. Boardman, 1959; Roy, 1959
Variation on a Theme of Murder. Simpkin, 1948
Vicious Circuit. Boardman, 1957

JARVIS, EDWARD
The Big Fix. Hale, 1969; Roy, 1970

JARVIS, FRED(ERICK) G(ORDON, JR.). 1930- . Joint pseudonym with Robert F. Van Beever: Fritz Gordon, q.v.
Murder at the Met. Coward, 1971

JARVIS, H(ENRY) W(OOD)
The House of Silence. Muller, 1959

JASON, STUART. Series character: The Butcher = B.
African Contract. Pinnacle, 1975 B
-Black Emperor. Lancer, 1971
-Black Hercules. Lancer, 1969
-Black Lord. Lancer, 1970; New English Library pb, 1971
-Black Master. Lancer, 1970; New English Library, 1972
-Black Prince. Lancer, 1970
Blood Debt. Pinnacle, 1972 B
Blood Vengeance. Pinnacle, 1975 B
Come Watch Him Die. Pinnacle, 1971 B
Deadly Deal. Pinnacle, 1973 B
The Deadly Doctor. Pinnacle, 1974 B
Death Race. Pinnacle, 1973 B
Fire Bomb. Pinnacle, 1973 B
Keepers of Death. Pinnacle, 1971 B
Kill Gently, But Sure. Pinnacle, 1975 B
Kill Quick or Die. Pinnacle, 1970 B
Kill Time. Pinnacle, 1973 B
Killer's Cargo. Pinnacle, 1974 B
-Kingblood. Paperback Library, 1969; New English Library, 1974
Sealed with Blood. Pinnacle, 1973 B
Suicide in San Juan. Pinnacle, 1975 B
Valley of Death. Pinnacle, 1974 B

JAVOR, F(RANK) A.
The Rim-World Legacy. Signet, 1967

JAY, CHARLOTTE. Pseudonym of Geraldine Mary Jay, 1919- , q.v. Other pseudonym: Geraldine Halls, q.v.
Arms for Adonis. Collins, 1960; Harper, 1961
Beat Not the Bones. Collins, 1952; Harper, 1953
The Fugitive Eye. Collins, 1953; Harper, 1954
A Hank of Hair. Heinemann, 1964; Harper, 1964
The Knife is Feminine. Collins, 1951
The Man Who Walked Away. Collins, 1958. U.S. title: The Stepfather. Harper, 1958
The Stepfather; see The Man Who Walked Away
The Yellow Turban. Collins, 1955; Harper, 1955

JAY, GERALDINE MARY. 1919- . Pseudonyms: Geraldine Halls, Charlotte Jay, qq.v.
The Feast of the Dead. Hale, 1956. U.S. title: The Brink of Silence. Harper, 1957, as by Charlotte Jay

JAY, HARRIETT. 1857-1932. Pseudonym: Charles Marlowe. See: ROBERT (WILLIAM) BUCHANAN, 1841-1901.

JAY, SIMON. Pseudonym of Colin James Alexander, 1920- .
Death of a Skin-Diver. Collins, 1964; Doubleday, 1964
Sleepers Can Kill. Collins, 1968; Doubleday, 1968

JAY, WILLA
Fear in Borzano. Lancer, 1967

JAYE, PETER
The Body's Name was Jones. Ward, 1961

JEAN, (MARIE JOSEPH) ALBERT. 1892- .
See: MAURICE RENARD, 1875-1939.

JEFFERIES, IAN. Pseudonym of Peter Hays, 1927- .
-Dignity and Purity. Cape, 1960
-House-Surgeon. Cape, 1966
-It Wasn't Me! Cape, 1961
-Thirteen Days. Cape, 1959

JEFFERIS, BARBARA
Beloved Lady. Sloane, 1955; Dent, 1956
Contango Day; see Undercurrent
Half Angel. Sloane, 1959; Dent, 1960
One Black Summer. Morrow, 1967; Hart-Davis, 1968
Solo for Several Players. Sloane, 1961; Dent, 1961
Undercurrent. Sloane, 1953. British title: Contango Day. Dent, 1954
The Wild Grapes. Sloane, 1963; Joseph, 1963

JEFFERS, ALBERT. Pseudonym of Thomas Albert Curry, 1900-1976. Other pseudonym: John L. Benton, q.v.
Screen for Murder. Mystery House, 1941. Also published as: Design for Dying. Bleak House, 194? (abridged)

JEFFERSON, BEATRICE W.
Small Town Murder. Dutton, 1941

JEFFERSON, PAUL
The Cuban Heel. Macmillan, 1969

JEFFERY, C. E.
The Vicar's Secret. Murray, 1912

JEFFERY, RANSOM and JOHN KEEBLE, 1944- .
Mine. Grossman, 1974

JEFFREYS, J. G. Pseudonym of Ben(jamin James) Healey, 1908- , q.v., used for U.S. editions of books published in England as by Jeremy Sturrock, q.v.

JEFFRIES, GRAHAM MONTAGUE. 1900- .
Pseudonyms: Bruce Graeme, David Graeme, Roderic Hastings, qq.v.

JEFFRIES, RODERIC (GRAEME). 1926- .
Pseudonyms: Peter Alding, Jeffrey Ashford, Roderic Graeme, Graham Hastings, qq.v.
The Benefits of Death. Collins, 1963; Dodd, 1964
Dead Against the Lawyers. Collins, 1965; Dodd, 1966
Dead Man's Bluff. Collins, 1970
A Deadly Marriage. Collins, 1967
Death in the Coverts. Collins, 1966
An Embarrassing Death. Collins, 1964; Dodd, 1965
Evidence of the Accused. Collins, 1961; London House, 1963
Exhibit No. Thirteen. Collins, 1962
Mistakenly in Mallorca. Collins, 1974
A Traitor's Crime. Collins, 1968

JELLETT, DR. H(ENRY). 1872-1948. See: NGAIO MARSH, 1899- .

JELLEY, SYMMES M. Pseudonym: Le Jemlys, q.v.

JENKINS, CECIL. 1927- .
Message from Sirius. Collins, 1961; Dodd, 1961

JENKINS, (JOHN) EDWARD. 1838-1910.
A Week of Passion. Remington, 1884; Harper, 1885

JENKINS, ELIZABETH
Harriet. Gollancz, 1934; Doubleday, 1934. Also published as: Murder by Neglect. Four Square, 1960

JENKINS, GEOFFREY. 1920- .
A Bridge of Magpies. Collins, 1974; Putnam, 1975
A Cleft of Stars. Collins, 1973; Putnam, 1973
The Disappearing Island; see A Grue of Ice
A Grue of Ice. Collins, 1962; Viking, 1962. Also published as: The Disappearing Island. Avon, 1964
The Hollow Sea; see Scend of the Sea
Hunter-Killer. Collins, 1966; Putnam, 1967
The River of Diamonds. Collins, 1964; Viking, 1964
Scend of the Sea. Collins, 1971. U.S. title: The Hollow Sea. Putnam, 1972
A Twist of Sand. Collins, 1959; Viking, 1960
The Watering Place of Good Peace. Collins, 1960

JENKINS, GEORGE B.
Ten Dangerous Hours. Detective Tales, 19?? (64 pp. mini-paperback.)

JENKINS, HERBERT (GEORGE). 1876-1923.
Series character: Malcolm Sage, in all titles.
John Dene of Toronto. Jenkins, 1920; Doran, 1919
Malcolm Sage, Detective. Jenkins, 1921; Doran, 1921 ss

Jenkins, Herbert

The Stiffsons, and other stories. Jenkins, 1928 ss, including one about MS

JENKINS, (JOHN) ROBIN. 1912- .
-Some Kind of Grace. Macdonald, 1960

JENKINS, WILL(IAM) F(ITZGERALD). 1896-1975. Pseudonym: Murray Leinster, q.v.
Destroy the U.S.A.; see The Murder of the U.S.A.
The Man Who Feared. Gateway, 1942
The Murder of the U.S.A. Crown, 1946. Also published as: Destroy the U.S.A. Ambassador (Toronto), 1946

JENKINSON, ARTHUR
-God's Winepress. Warne, 1896

JENKS, GEORGE C(HARLES). 1850-1929.
-The Climax. Fly, 1909. (Novelization of the play by Edward Locke.)
The Deserters, with Anna Alice Chapin, 1880- , q.v. Fly, 1911
Stop Thief!, with Carlyle Moore, 1875- . Fly, 1913. (Novelization of the play by Carlyle Moore.)

JENNIFER, SUSAN. Pseudonym of Robert Hoskins, 1933- . Other pseudonym: Grace Corren, q.v.
Country of the Kind. Avon, 1975
The House of Counted Hatreds. Avon, 1973

JENNINGS, G. L.
Murders at the Lakes. Mortiboys, 1936

JENSEN, RUBY JEAN
The Girl Who Didn't Die. Warner, 1975
House at River's Bend. Dell, 1975
The House That Samael Built. Paperback Library, 1974
Seventh All Hallow's Eve. Paperback Library, 1974

JENSON, MARTIN
An Odour of Decay. New English Library pb, 1975
Village of Fear. New English Library pb, 1974

JEPSON, EDGAR (ALFRED). 1863-1938.
An Accidental Don Juan. Jenkins, 1935
Alice Devine; see Garthoyle Gardens
Arsene Lupin, with Maurice Leblanc, 1864-1941, q.v. Mills, 1909; Doubleday, 1909. (Novelization of the play by Maurice Leblanc and Francis de Croisset.)
Barradine Detects. Jenkins, 1937 ss
Buried Rubies. Jenkins, 1925; Siebel, 1926
Captain Sentimental and other stories. Mills, 1911 ss, some criminous
The Cuirass of Diamonds. Jenkins, 1928; Macy-Masius, 1929
The Dangerous Twins. Jenkins, 1935
-The Dictator's Daughter. Cassell, 1902
The Emerald Tiger; see The Splendid Adventures of Hannibal Tod
-Esther Lawes. Hutchinson, 1916
The Four Green Fish. Jenkins, 1939
-The Four Philanthropists. Unwin, 1907; Authors & Newspapers Assn., 1907
The Garden at No. 19; see No. 19
Garthoyle Gardens. Hutchinson, 1913. U.S. title: Alice Devine. Bobbs, 1916
Gentle Binns. Jenkins, 1931
The Gillingham Rubies. Hutchinson, 1915
The Girl's Head. Greening, 1910. Also published as: Tracked by the Ogpu. Eric Grant, 1937
The Grinning Avenger. Jenkins, 1934
The House on the Mall. Hutchinson, 1912; Dillingham, 1911
-A Hundred Thousand Guineas. Jenkins, 1931
-James Whitaker's Dukedom. Hutchinson, 1914. U.S. title: Whitaker's Dukedom. Bobbs, 1914
-The Keepers of the People. Pearson, 1898
Kitty Brown's Princes. Jenkins, 1936
-The Knight Errant. Jenkins, 1936
-L.2002. Hutchinson, 1918
-The Lady Noggs, Peeress. Unwin, 1906
The Loudwater Mystery. Odhams, 1919; Knopf, 1920
Lucy and the Dark Gods. Jenkins, 1936
The Man Who Came Back. Hutchinson, 1915
The Man with the Amber Eyes, with Hugh Clevely, q.v. Jenkins, 1928
-Man, Woman and Sin. Readers Library, 1928
The Murder in Romney Marsh. Jenkins, 1929
The Murder of Augustin Dench. Jenkins, 1938
The Mystery of the Myrtles. Hutchinson, 1909
The Night Hawk. Hutchinson, 1916
No. 19. Mills, 1910. U.S. title: The Garden at No. 19. Wessels, 1910
An Obstinate Girl. Jenkins, 1934
-Peter Intervenes. Jenkins, 1926
The Pocket Hercules. Jenkins, 1938
-A Prince in Petrograd. Odhams, 1921
-A Professional Prince. Hutchinson, 1917; Reynolds, 1917
The Secret Square. Jenkins, 1933
-The Sentimental Warrior. Richards, 1902
The Smuggled Masterpiece. Jenkins, 1923
The Splendid Adventure of Hannibal Tod. Jenkins, 1927. U.S. title: The Emerald Tiger. Macy-Macius, 1928
The Sweepstake Winner. Jenkins, 1933
The Theft of the Crown Jewels. Jenkins, 1937
Tracked by the Ogpu; see The Girl's Head
-The Whiskered Footman. Jenkins, 1922

JEPSON, SELWYN. 1899- . Series characters: Eve Gill = EG; Ian MacArthur = IM.
The Angry Millionaire. Macmillan (London), 1969; Harper, 1968
The Assassin. Collins, 1956; Lippincott, 1956
The Black Italian. Collins, 1954; Doubleday, 1954 EG
The Death Gong. Harrap, 1927; Watt, 1927
Fear in the Wind. Allen, 1964 EG
The Golden Dart. Macdonald, 1949; Doubleday, 1949 EG
Golden-Eyes. Harrap, 1924. U.S. title: The Sutton Papers. Dial, 1924
Heads or Tails, with Michael Joseph. Jarrolds, 1933 ss
The Hungry Spider. Macdonald, 1951; Doubleday, 1950 EG
I Met Murder. Hodder, 1930; Harper, 1930
Keep Murder Quiet. Joseph, 1940; Doubleday, 1941
Killer by Proxy; see Man Running
-The King's Red-Haired Girl. Hutchinson, 1923
The Laughing Fish. Hart-Davis, 1960. U.S. title: Verdict in Question. Doubleday, 1960 EG
Letter to a Dead Girl. Macmillan (London), 1971
-Love—and Helen. Harrap, 1928; Watt, 1928
Love in Peril. Mellifont, 1934
Man Dead. Collins, 1951; Doubleday, 1951
Man Running. Macdonald, 1948. U.S. title: Outrun the Constable. Doubleday, 1948. Also published as: Killer by Proxy. Bantam, 1950 EG
Manchu Jade; see The Qualified Adventurer
The Mystery of the Rabbit's Paw; see Rabbit's Paw
A Noise in the Night. Hart-Davis, 1957; Lippincott, 1957
Outrun the Constable; see Man Running
Puppets of Fate. Hutchinson, 1922
The Qualified Adventurer. Hutchinson, 1922; Harcourt, 1922. Also published as: Manchu Jade. Mellifont, 1935 IM
Rabbit's Paw. Hodder, 1932. U.S. title: The Mystery of the Rabbit's Paw. Harper, 1932
-Riviera Love Story. Mellifont, 1948
Rogues and Diamonds. Harrap, 1925; Dial, 1925
Snaggletooth. Harrap, 1926
The Sutton Papers; see Golden-Eyes
-Tempering Steel. Mellifont, 1949
-That Fellow MacArthur. Hutchinson, 1923 IM
The Third Possibility. Allen, 1965
Tiger Dawn. Hodder, 1929
Verdict in Question; see The Laughing Fish
-The Wise Fool. Mellifont, 1934

JEROME, GILBERT. Pseudonym.
The Filibuster's Warning. Street, ca.1900
The Loaded Orange. Street (Magnet #263)

JEROME, JUDSON (BLAIR). 1927- .
The Fell of Dark. Houghton, 1966

JEROME, OWEN FOX. Pseudonym of Oscar J(erome) Friend, 1897-1963, q.v. Series character: Philip MacCray = PM.
The Corpse Awaits. Mystery House, 1946; Wells Gardner, 1948
Double Life. Harlequin, 1950. (U.S. title?)
The Five Assassins. Mystery House, 1958 PM
The Golf Club Murder. Clode, 1929. British title: The Golf-Course Murder. Hutchinson, 1928
The Golf-Course Murder; see The Golf Club Murder
The Hand of Horror. Clode, 1927; Skeffington, 1929 PM
Murder as Usual. Gateway, 1942
The Murder at Avalon Arms. Clode, 1931; Hutchinson, 1930 PM
The Red Kite Clue. Clode, 1928; Skeffington, 1929 PM

JERROLD, IANTHE (BRIDGMAN). 1897- .
Dead Man's Quarry. Chapman, 1930
-Seaside Comedy. Chapman, 1934
The Studio Crime. Chapman, 1929
-Summer's Day. Chapman, 1933

JERVIS, VERA MURDOCK STUART. 1897- . Pseudonym: Jane England, q.v.

JESMER, ELAINE. 1939- .
-Number One with a Bullet. Farrar, 1974; Weidenfeld, 1974

JESSE, F(RYNIWYD) TENNYSON. 1889?-1958. Pseudonym: Beamish Tinker, q.v.
A Pin to See the Peepshow. Heinemann, 1934; Doubleday, 1934
The Solange Stories. Heinemann, 1931; Macmillan, 1931 ss

JESSOP, GEORGE H. See: (JAMES) BRANDER MATTHEWS, 1852-1929.

JESSUP, HENRY WYNANS. 1864-1934.
-Abimelech Pott, the Don Quixote of the Bar. Neale, 1928
The Van Beck Will. Neale, 1928

JESSUP, RICHARD
Cry Passion. Dell, 1956
The Cunning and the Haunted. GM, 1954
The Deadly Duo. Dell, 1959; Boardman, 1961
Lowdown. Dell, 1958; Secker, 1958
The Man in Charge. Secker, 1957. (U.S. title?)
Night Boat to Paris. Dell, 1956; WDL, 1960
Port Angelique. GM, 1961
A Rage to Die. GM, 1955
Wolf Cop. GM, 1961; Muller pb, 1963
The Young Don't Cry. GM, 1957; Red Seal, 1959

JEWELL, DEREK. 1927- .
Come In Number One, Your Time is Up. Macmillan (London), 1971; Doubleday, 1971
Sellout. Macmillan (London), 1973

JEWELL, ROBERT
The Mystery of Orleton House. Blackwood, 1876

JOBSON, HAMILTON. 1914- . Series character: Inspector Anders, in at least those marked A.
Contract with a Killer. Long, 1974
The Evidence You Will Hear. Collins, 1975; Scribner, 1975 A
The House with Blind Eyes. Long, 1971
Naked to my Enemy. Long, 1970
The Sand Pit. Long, 1972
The Shadow That Caught Fire. Long, 1972; Scribner, 1976
The Silent Cry. Long, 1970
Smile and be a Villain. Long, 1969; Abelard-Schuman, 1971
Therefore I Killed Him. Long, 1968 A

JOCELYN, MRS. ROBERT [ADA MARIA JENYNS JOCELYN RODEN]. 1860- .
-A Big Stake. White, 1892; Lippincott, 1892
The Criton Hunt Mystery. Hurst, 1890
-A Dangerous Brute. Hutchinson, 1895
-A Distracting Guest. White, 1889
-Drawn Blank. White, 1892; Lippincott, 1892
-For One Season Only. White, 1893
-Henry Massinger. White, 1899
-Juanita Carrington. Digby, 1896
Lady Mary's Experiences. White, 1897
-The M.F.H.'s Daughter. White, 1890
-Miss Rayburn's Diamonds. White, 1898
-£100,000 versus Ghosts. White, 1888
One of the Bevans; or, Only a Horse Dealer; see Only a Horse Dealer
-Only a Flirt. White, 1897
-Only a Horse Dealer. White, 1893. U.S. title: One of the Bevans; or, Only a Horse Dealer. Lippincott, 1893
-Only a Love Story. Hutchinson, 1897
-Pamela's Honeymoon. Hutchinson, 1894
-A Regular Fraud. White, 1896
-Run to Ground. Hutchinson, 1894
-The Sea of Fortune. Digby, 1901

JOEY and DAVE FISHER
Hit #29. PB, 1975
Joey Kills. PB, 1975

JOHN, E. H.
-Breach of Reason. Gifford, 1953

JOHN, HENDRIX
The Carnellian Circle. Atheneum, 1975

JOHN, KATHARINE. See: ROMILLY JOHN.

JOHN, OWEN. 1918- . Series character: Haggai Godin, in at least those marked HG.
A Beam of Black Light. Joseph, 1968; Paperback Library, 1969 HG
Dead on Time. Joseph, 1969; Paperback Library, 1969
The Diamond Dress. Cassell, 1970
The Disinformer. Joseph, 1967; Paperback Library, 1968 HG
Sabotage. Cassell, 1973; Dutton, 1973 HG
The Shadow in the Sea. Cassell, 1972; Dutton, 1972 HG
Thirty Days Hath September. Joseph, 1966; Dutton, 1967 HG

JOHN, ROMILLY and KATHARINE
Death by Request. Faber, 1935

JOHNS, AVERY. Pseudonym of Margaret Cousins, 1905- .
Traffic with Evil. Doubleday, 1962

JOHNS, FOSTER. Pseudonym of Gilbert Vivian Seldes, 1893-1970.
The Square Emerald. Day, 1928
The Victory Murders. Day, 1927; Harrap, 1927

JOHNS, GILBERT. Pseudonym of James Stagg, q.v. Both titles below were published by Amalgamated Press and feature Sexton Blake.
Thief of Clubs. 1961
Vote for Violence. 1961

JOHNS, RICHARD. Pseudonym of Montague Slater, 1902- .
Man with a Background of Flames. Dobson, 1954; Roy, 1954

JOHNS, VERONICA PARKER. 1907- . Series characters: Webster Flagg = WF; Agatha Welch (Prentiss) = AW.
Hush, Gabriel! Duell, 1940 AW
Murder by the Day. Doubleday, 1953 WF
Servant's Problem. Doubleday, 1958 WF
Shady Doings. Duell, 1941 AW
The Singing Widow. Duell, 1941

JOHNS, W(ILLIAM) E(ARL). 1893-1968. Series character: Steeley, in at least those marked S.
Blue Blood Runs Red. Newnes, 1936
The Camels are Coming. Hamilton, 1932
Desert Night. Hamilton, 1938
The Man Who Lost his Way. Macdonald, 1959
The Murder at Castle Deeping. Hamilton, 1938. Revised edition: Latimer, 1951
Murder by Air. Newnes, 1937. Revised edition: Latimer, 1951
No Motive for Murder. Hodder, 1958; Washburn, 1959
The Raid. Hamilton, 1935
-Sinister Service. Oxford, 1942
Sky Fever, and other stories. Latimer, 1953
-Sky High. Newnes, 1936. Revised edition: Latimer, 1951
The Spy Flyers. Hamilton, 1933
Steeley Flies Again. Newnes, 1936. Revised edition: Latimer, 1951 S
The Unknown Quantity. Hamilton, 1940
Wings of Romance. Newnes, 1939. Revised edition: Latimer, 1951 S

JOHNSON, ADRIAN. See: ELIZABETH JOHNSON.

JOHNSON, B. B. Series character: Richard Spade, in at least those marked RS.
Bad Day for a Black Brother. Paperback Library, 1970 RS
Black is Beautiful. Paperback Library, 1970 RS
Blues for a Black Sister. Paperback Library, 1971
Death of a Blue-Eyed Soul Brother. Paperback Library, 1970 RS
Mother of the Year. Paperback Library, 1970 RS
That's Where the Cat's At, Baby. Paperback Library, 1970 RS

JOHNSON, DIANE. 1934- .
The Shadow Knows. Knopf, 1974; Bodley Head, 1975

JOHNSON, DOROTHY
The Death of a Spinster. Longmans, 1931
-Doris. Jarrolds, 1925
Private Inquiries. Longmans, 1932
-To Meet Mr. Stanley. Longmans, 1926

JOHNSON, DUFF
The Chiseller. Hamilton Stafford, 1951
The Come Back. Hamilton Stafford, 1952
Come Out Fighting. Hamilton Stafford, 1951
The Dead Don't Rise. Hamilton Stafford, 1951
Dynamite on Wheels. Hamilton Stafford, 1952
One-Time Champ. Hamilton Stafford, 1951
Operator from Chicago. Hamilton Stafford, 1950
Racing Crazy. Hamilton Stafford, 1952
Rocky Mountain. Hamilton Stafford, 1951
Sucker Punch. Hamilton Stafford, 1950

JOHNSON, E(MIL) RICHARD. 1929- .
Cage Five is Going to Break. Harper, 1970; Macmillan (London), 1971
The Cardinalli Contract. Pyramid, 1975
Case Load—Maximum. Harper, 1971
The God Keepers. Harper, 1970; Macmillan (London), 1971
The Inside Man. Harper, 1969; Macmillan (London), 1970
The Judas. Harper, 1971
Mongo's Back in Town. Harper, 1969; Macmillan (London), 1970
Silver Street. Harper, 1968. British title: The Silver Street Killer. Hale, 1969
The Silver Street Killer; see Silver Street

JOHNSON, EDGAR. 1901- .
The Praying Mantis. Stackpole, 1937; Cassell, 1938

JOHNSON, ELIZABETH and ADRIAN
The Game of the Golden Ball. Macaulay, 1910

JOHNSON, EVELYN (DAVIES), 1904- , and GRETTA PALMER
Murder. Covici Friede, 1928. British title: Murder and Mystery. Richards, 1929. (Short crime puzzles.)

JOHNSON, EVELYN KIMBALL
Tangles Unravelled; A Realistic Melodrama Spiced with Comedy. Ogilvie, 1884

JOHNSON, GEORGE CLAYTON and JACK GOLDEN RUSSELL
Ocean's 11. Cardinal, 1960. (Novelization of the movie.)

JOHNSON, GRACE (CECELIA TRACY) and HAROLD (NELS) JOHNSON
The Broken Rosary. Bruce, 1959
Roman Collar Detective. Bruce, 1953

JOHNSON, HAROLD (NELS). See: GRACE (CECELIA TRACY) JOHNSON.

JOHNSON, HENRY. Pseudonym: Muirhead Robertson, q.v.

JOHNSON, HENRY T.
The Ape Man. Modern, 193?
-The Devil's Advocate. Mascot, 1916
-A Fairy of the Film. Mascot, 1919
The Murder Link. Modern, 1938
-A Princess in Mufti. Mascot, 1919
When London Sleeps. Modern, 1938
-The World of Sin. Mascot, 1914

JOHNSON, J.
What Befell a Bristol Trader. Drane, 1903

JOHNSON, JAMES L(EONARD). 1927- .
Series character: Sebastian, in all titles.
Code Name Sebastian. Lippincott, 1967
A Handful of Dominoes. Lippincott, 1970
The Nine Lives of Alphonse. Lippincott, 1968
A Piece of the Moon is Missing. Holman, 1974

JOHNSON, LEE. Pseudonym of Lilian Beatrice Johnson.
Heads for Death. Gifford, 1966
Keep It Simple. Gifford, 1963
The Medallion. Gifford, 1962
Murder Began Yesterday. Gifford, 1966

JOHNSON, LILIAN BEATRICE. Pseudonym: Lee Johnson, q.v.

JOHNSON, MAURICE C.
Damning Trifles. Knopf, 1932

JOHNSON, MENDAL W.
Let's Go Play at the Adams'. Crowell, 1974

JOHNSON, OWEN (McMAHON). 1878-1952.
Max Fargus. Barker & Taylor, 1906
Murder in Any Degree. Century, 1913 ss
The Sixty-First Second. Stokes, 1913; Heinemann, 1913

JOHNSON, PAMELA HANSFORD. 1912- .
Joint pseudonym with Neil Stewart: Nap Lombard, q.v.

JOHNSON, PHILIP (EDWARD). 1911- .
Hung Until Dead. Phoenix, 1940

JOHNSON, (WALTER) RYERSON. 1901- .
Joint pseudonym with Davis Dresser, 1904-1977, q.v.: Matthew Blood, q.v.
Lady in Dread. GM, 1955

JOHNSON, STANLEY (PATRICK). 1940- .
God Bless America. Doubleday, 1974. (British title?)
Gold Drain. Heinemann, 1967
Panther Jones for President. Heinemann, 1968. U.S. title: The Presidential Plot. Simon, 1968
The Presidential Plot; see Panther Jones for President
The Urbane Guerilla. Macmillan (London), 1975

JOHNSON, T(HOMAS) M(ARVIN). 1889- .
See: JUDSON (PENTECOST) PHILIPS, 1903- .

JOHNSON, W. BOLINGBROKE. Pseudonym of Morris Gilbert Bishop, 1893-1973.
The Widening Stain. Knopf, 1942; Lane, 1943

JOHNSON, WILHELMINA
The Ranger of the Tomb; or, Gipsy's Prophecy. Lloyd, 1847

JOHNSON, ZOE
At the Sign of the Clove and Hoof. Bles, 1937
Mourning After. Bles, 1939

JOHNSTON, CHRISTOPHER N(ICHOLSON). Pseudonym of Christopher Nicholson Johnston Sands, 1857-1934.
Major Owen, and other tales. Blackwood, 1909 ss, some criminous

JOHNSTON, CLINT
The Kabaka. Avon, 1970

JOHNSTON, FRANK (NORMAN HOWARD). 1900- .
Disqualified. Wright, 1935
The Dope Specialist. Long, 1943
Easy Money: The Amazing Adventures of Tony Denton, the Raffles of the Turf. Wright, 1935
The Fellowship of Five. Long, 1932
Highway Robber's Derby. Long, 1933
Li Kwang's Dagger. Wright, 1936
Million Dollar Gamble. Long, 1946
The Mystery Tipster. Wright, 1934
Prince of Turf Crooks. Long, 1952
Spider Joe. Wright, 1937
The Strangest Grand National. Long, 1947
The Trodmore Turf Mystery. Long, 1944
The Turf Crook. Long, 1937
Turf Racketeers. Long, 1933
A Weird Legacy. Wright, 1936

JOHNSTON, GEORGE H(ENRY). 1912-1970.
Pseudonym: Shane Martin, q.v.
Death Takes Small Bites. Gollancz, 1948; Dodd, 1951

JOHNSTON, GRACE L. KEITH. Pseudonym: Leslie Keith, q.v.

JOHNSTON, J(AMES) WESLEY. 1850- .
The Mystery of Miriam. Turner, 1904; Richards, 1904

JOHNSTON, MADELEINE. Series character: Noah Bradshaw, in both titles.
Comets have Long Tails. Doubleday, 1938; Eyre, 1939
Death Casts a Lure. Doubleday, 1938

JOHNSTON, MYRTLE. 1909- .
A Robin Redbreast in a Cage. Heinemann, 1950; Houghton, 1951

JOHNSTON, NORMA. Pseudonym: Nicole St. John, q.v.

JOHNSTON, RAY(MOND) R. (CAREW)
Maud Blackstone, the Millionaire's Daughter. Henneberry, 1901

JOHNSTON, RONALD. 1926- .
The Angry Ocean. Collins, 1968; Harcourt, 1969
The Black Camels; see The Black Camels of Qashran
The Black Camels of Qashran. Collins, 1970. U.S. title: The Black Camels. Harcourt, 1969
Collision Ahead; see Disaster at Dungeness
Danger at Bravo Key; see Red Sky in the Morning
Disaster at Dungeness. Collins, 1964. U.S. title: Collision Ahead. Doubleday, 1965
The Eye of the Needle. Collins, 1975
Paradise Smith. Collins, 1972; Harcourt, 1972
Red Sky in the Morning. Collins, 1965. U.S. title: Danger at Bravo Key. Doubleday, 1965
The Stowaway. Collins, 1966; Harcourt, 1966
The Wrecking of Offshore Five. Collins, 1967; Harcourt, 1968

JOHNSTON, VELDA
Along a Dark Path. Dodd, 1967; Milton House, 1974
Castle Perilous; see I Came to a Castle
Circle of Evil; see The People on the Hill
The Face in the Shadows. Dodd, 1971; Hale, 1973
House Above Hollywood. Dodd, 1968; Milton House, 1974
The House on the Left Bank. Dodd, 1975
A Howling in the Woods. Dodd, 1968; Hale, 1969
I Came to a Castle. Dodd, 1969. British title: Castle Perilous. Hale, 1971
I Came to the Highlands. Dodd, 1974; Milton House, 1975
The Late Mrs. Fonsell. Dodd, 1972; Milton House, 1974
The Light in the Swamp. Dodd, 1970; Hale, 1972
Masquerade in Venice. Dodd, 1973; Milton House, 1974
The Mourning Trees. Dodd, 1972; Milton House, 1974
The People on the Hill. Dodd, 1971. British title: Circle of Evil. Hale, 1972
The Phantom Cottage. Dodd, 1970; Hale, 1971
A Room with Dark Mirrors. Dodd, 1975; Prior, 1976
The White Pavilion. Dodd, 1973; Milton House, 1974

JOHNSTON, WILLIAM (ANDREW). 1871-1929.
An Accidental Accomplice. Doubleday, 1928
The Affair in Duplex 9B. Doran, 1927
The Apartment Next Door. Little, 1919; Jarrolds, 1923
The House of Whispers. Little, 1918; Jarrolds, 1922
The Innocent Murderers, with Paul West. Duffield, 1910
The Mystery in the Ritsmore. Little, 1920; Jarrolds, 1924
The Tragedy at the Beach Club. Little, 1922; Jarrolds, 1924
The Waddington Cipher. Doubleday, 1923; Paul, 1925
The Yellow Letter. Bobbs, 1911; Greening, 1912

JOHNSTON, WILLIAM. 1924-   . Pseudonym: Susan Claudia, q.v. Series character: Maxwell Smart = MS (in novelizations of the Get Smart TV series).
And Loving It! Grosset, 1967 MS
Angel, Angel, Down We Go. Lancer, 1969. (Novelization of the movie.)
Asylum. Bantam, 1972. (Novelization of the movie.)
Barney. Random, 1970
Banyon. Paperback Library, 1971. (Novelization of the TV series.)
Captain Nice. Grosset, 1967. (Novelization of the TV series.)
Dick Tracy. Grosset, 1970. (Novelization of the comic strip.)
Get Smart! Grosset, 1965 MS
Get Smart Once Again! Grosset, 1966 MS
Home is Where the Quick Is. Pinnacle, 1971. (Novelization of the Mod Squad TV series.)

Klute. Paperback Library, 1971; Sphere, 1971. (Novelization of the movie.)
The Marriage Cage. Stuart, 1960
Max Smart and the Ghastly Ghost Affair. Grosset, 1969 MS
Max Smart and the Perilous Pellets. Grosset, 1966 MS
Max Smart Loses Control. Grosset, 1968 MS
Max Smart—The Spy Who Went Out to the Cold. Grosset, 1968 MS
Missed It by That Much. Grosset, 1967 MS
My Friend Tony. Lancer, 1968. (Novelization of the movie.)
Sorry, Chief. Grosset, 1966 MS
Then Came Bronson. Pyramid, 1970. (Novelization of the TV series.)

JONES, ADRIENNE. Joint pseudonyms with Doris Meek: Mason Gregory, Gregory Mason, qq.v.

JONES, ALICE. 1853-   .
-Bubbles We Buy. Turner, 1903; Richards, 1903. Also published as: Isabel Broderick—"Bubbles We Buy". Lane, 1904
-Gabriel Praed's Castle. Turner, 1904; Richards, 1904
Isabel Broderick—"Bubbles We Buy"; see Bubbles We Buy
-Marcus Holbeach's Daughter. Appleton, 1912

JONES, ARTHUR E. Series character: Felix Holliday, in all titles.
It Makes You Think. Long, 1958
Too Dead to Talk. Hutchinson, 1957
You Know the Way It Is. Hutchinson, 1956

JONES, (MALCOLM HENRY) BRADSHAW. Series characters: Supt. Arthur Carson, in at least those marked AC; James Keen, in at least those marked JK; Claude Ravel, in at least those marked CR.
But Ill He Lived. Long, 1968
The Crooked Phoenix. Long, 1963 JK & CR
The Deadly Trade. Long, 1967
Death Deals in Diamonds. Long, 1965; Walker, 1966
Death on a Pale Horse. Long, 1964 CR
A Den of Savage Men. Long, 1967
The Embers of Hate. Long, 1966
The Hamlet Problem. Long, 1962 JK
Layers of Deceit. Long, 1969; Bobbs, 1970
Murder has no Friends. Long, 1966; Bobbs, 1968 AC
Private Vendetta. Long, 1964
The Shadowless Men. Long, 1970
Taint of Plague. Long, 1970
Testament of Evil. Long, 1966 CR
Tiger from the Shadows. Long, 1963
To Catch a Shadow. Long, 1969; Bobbs, 1970 AC

JONES, C. DAVENPORT
An Excellent Mystery. Sonnenschein, 1886

JONES, CHARLES REED. Series character: Leighton Swift = LS.
The King Murder. Dutton, 1929 LS
The Rum Row Murders. Macaulay, 1931
The Torch Murder. Dutton, 1930 LS
The Van Norton Murders. Macaulay, 1931 LS

JONES, CLARA AUGUSTA. Pseudonyms: Clara Augusta, Hero Strong, qq.v.

JONES, ELWYN. 1923-   . Series character: Supt. Barlow, in all titles (based on the BBC TV series).
The Barlow Casebook, with John Lloyd. Barker, 1975 ss
Barlow Comes to Judgement. Barker, 1974; St. Martin's, 1976
Barlow in Charge. Barker, 1973
The Ripper File, with John Lloyd. Barker, 1975

JONES, EMMA GARRISON. 1838-1898.
A Terrible Crime. Street, 1903

JONES, EUGENE
Who Killed Gregory? Stokes, 1928. British title: The Last Clue. Selwyn, 1931

JONES, G. WAYMAN. House name.
Alias Mr. Death. Fiction League, 1932

JONES, GEORGE E.
Trap. Graphic, 1955

JONES, GLYN. 1905-   .
-The Blue Bed. Cape, 1937; Dutton, 1938

JONES, GREGORY
Prowl Cop. Ace, 1956

JONES, H(ENRY DAVID) LLEWELLIN. 1890- Series character: Fraser Todd, in both titles.
The Case is Altered. Hamilton, 1929
Under the Shadow. Hamilton, 1928

JONES, HANNAH MARIA [HANNAH MARIA JONES LOWNDES].   -1859?
-A Child of Mystery; or, The Cottager's Daughter. Tallis, 1837
Elinor Clare; or, The Haunted Oak; see The Gipsey Chief
-Emily Moreland; or, The Mail of the Valley. Virtue, 1829
-The Forged Note; or, Julian and Marianne. Jacques, 1824
The Gipsey Chief; or, The Haunted Oak. Virtue, 1840. Also published as: Elinor Clare; or, The Haunted Oak. Milner, 1868
The Gipsey Girl; or, The Heir of Hazel Dell. Tallis, 1836
-The Gipsey Mother; or, The Miseries of Enforced Marriage. Virtue, 1833
-Gretna Green; or, The Elopement of Miss D—— with a Gallant Son of Mars. Tallis, 1821
-Katharine Beresford; or, The Shade and Sunshine of Woman's Life. M'Gowan, 1852
-The Outlaw's Bride. Virtue, 1838
-Rosaline Woodbridge; or, The Midnight Visit. Virtue, 1827
-The Scottish Chieftains; or, The Perils of Love and War. Virtue, 1831
-The Stranger of the Glen; or, The Travellers Benighted. Virtue, 1827
-Trials of Love; or, Woman's Reward. M'Gowan, 1849
-The Victim of Fashion; or, A Treacherous Friend. Virtue, 1836
-Village Scandal; or, The Gossip's Tale. Emans, 1835
-The Wedding Ring; or, Married and Single. Virtue, 1824

JONES, HENRY JAMES O'BRIEN BEDFORD-. 1887-1949. See: H(ENRY JAMES O'BRIEN) BEDFORD-JONES.

JONES, INIGO. Pseudonym.
The Albatross Murders. Mystery House, 1941
The Clue of the Hungry Corpse. Arcadia, 1939

JONES, J. G.
The Secret of the Bucket Shop. Amalgamated, 1924. (Sexton Blake.)

JONES, JACK
Journey into Death. GM, 1955

JONES, JAMES. 1921-1977.
A Touch of Danger. Doubleday, 1973; Collins, 1973

JONES, JENNIFER. Series character: Daisy Jane Mott, in all titles.
Dirge for a Dog. Doubleday, 1939
Murder al Fresco. Doubleday, 1939
Murder-on-Hudson. Crowell, 1937

JONES, KEN
Etched in Murder. Zenith, 1959

JONES, L. Q.
The Brotherhood of Satan. Award, 1971. (Novelization of the movie.)

JONES, M. SHERIDAN
Flames of Vengeance. Wright, 1935
A Million to Burn. Wright, 1934
Pay to Bearer. Wright, 1934
The Shanghai Lily. Wright, 1935
Storm Tossed. Wright, 1934

JONES, MADISON. 1925-   .
A Cry in Absence. Crown, 1971; Deutsch, 1972

JONES, MARY TUPPER
The System's Hand. Mid-West, 1920

JONES, (MAY)NARD (BENEDICT). 1904-   .
The Case of the Hanging Lady. Dodd, 1938
I'll Take What's Mine. GM, 1954
Ride the Dark Storm. GM, 1955

JONES, PHILIP (MITCHELL). 1919-   .
The Fifth Defector. Heinemann, 1967
Johnny Lost. Heinemann, 1965; Holt, 1966
La Bora. Angus, 1961
The Month of the Pearl. Heinemann, 1964; Holt, 1965

JONES, ROBERT PAGE
The Heisters. Monarch, 1963

JONES, SUSAN CARLETON. 1864-   . Pseudonym: S. Carleton, q.v.

JONES, (CHARLES) VICTOR. 1919-   .
Monument of Terror. Stuart, 1969

JONES, W(ILFRED) BYFORD. See: W(ILFRED) BYFORD-JONES.

JONES, WILLIAM J.
Real Estate Skeleton Caper. Vantage, 1975

JOPSON, MARION
A Fist in the Sky. Hale, 1970

JORDAN, DAVID. Series characters: Kane & Condon, in both titles.
Black Account. Joseph, 1975
Nile Green. Joseph, 1973; Day, 1974

JORDAN, ELIZABETH (GARVER). 1867-1947.
After the Verdict. Appleton, 1939
The Blue Circle. Century, 1922; Hodder, 1925
The Devil and the Deep Blue Sea. Century, 1929; Hutchinson, 1929
The Life of the Party. Appleton, 1936; Long, 1936
Miss Blake's Husband. Century, 1926; Hutchinson, 1927
The Night Club Mystery. Century, 1930; Hutchinson, 1930
Page Mr. Pomeroy. Appleton, 1934; Long, 1934

-Red Riding Hood. Century, 1925; Hodder, 1926
The Trap. Appleton, 1937

JORDAN, F. P.
Double Dealing. Beck, 1932

JORDAN, J. A.
Death in the Wind. Mellifont, 1935
The Death Singer. Mellifont, 1939
The Devil's Eye. Mellifont, 1942
The Grey Mask Gang. Mellifont, 1938
-Guilty Hands. Pemberton, 1945
The Gunboat Mystery. Mellifont, 1937
The Haunting Shadow. Mellifont, 1938
-The Love Test. Mellifont, 1935
Matched with Mystery. Fiction House, 1940
The Murder Mask. Mellifont, 1942
The Murder Trap. Mellifont, 1940
Night Club Murder. Mellifont, 1939
-Out to Win. Mellifont, 1940
Sterne of the Secret Service. Aldine, 1931

JORDAN, ROBERT FURNEAUX. 1905- . Pseudonym: Robert Player, q.v.

JORGENSEN, H. R(AYMOND). 1898- .
The Red Lacquer Case. World, 1933

JORGENSON, GEORGE E(LLINGTON). See: NORA JORGENSON.

JORGENSON, IVAR
Rest in Agony. Monarch, 1963

JORGENSON, NORA and GEORGE E(LLINGTON) JORGENSON
The Circle of Vengeance. Appleton, 1930

JOSCELYN, ARCHIE (LYNN). 1899- . Pseudonym: A. A. Archer, q.v.
The Golden Bowl. World, 1931. Also published as: Eric Hearle, Detective. World, 1934

JOSEPH, ALAN. Series character: Logan, in both titles.
Killers at Sea. Belmont, 1970
Logan. Belmont, 1970

JOSEPH, GEORGE (ISRAEL). 1912- .
Before I Die. Boardman, 1959
The Curtain has Lace Fringes. Muller, 1954
The Insider. Boardman, 1963
Leave It to Me. Popular Library, 1955. (British title?)
Lie Fallow my Acre. Jenkins, 1957
Murder in Paradise. Boardman, 1958
Needle in a Haystack. Boardman, 1957
Swan Song for a Thrush. Boardman, 1957
Take any City. Hale, 1970
This is for Keeps. Popular Library, 1958. (British title?)
Three Strangers. Boardman, 1956
Venom in the Cup. Boardman, 1958
When the Rainbow is Pale. Hale, 1962

JOSEPH, MICHAEL. See: SELWYN JEPSON, 1899- .

JOSEPH, MICHAEL. See: ROBERT DONALDSON.

JOSEPH, ROBERT. 1912- .
-Berlin at Midnight. Greenberg, 1948

JOSEPH-RENAUD, J(EAN). 1874- .
Doctor Mephisto. Hutchinson, 1930
The Phantom Violin. Metropolitan, 1948

JOSKE, AUNE NEVILLE GOYDER. 1893- .
Joint pseudonym with Margot Goyder, 1903- : Margot Neville, q.v.

JOST, JOHN
This is Harry Flynn. Angus, 1974

JOURNET, TERENCE
The Deathwishers. Hale, 1967
The Godkillers. Hale, 1968
A Troupe of Star-Crossed Killers. Hale, 1973
Victim. Hale, 1974

JOYCE, CYRIL
A Web to Catch a Spider. Hale, 1975

JOYCE, T. ROBERT
S.P.Y.S. PB, 1974; Sphere, 1974. (Novelization of the movie.)

JUDD, HARRISON
Shadow of a Doubt. GM, 1961; Muller pb, 1962

JUDD, MARGARET (HADDICAN). 1906- .
Pseudonym: Truman Garrett, q.v.
Gospel of Death. Arcadia, 1960
Husband of the Corpse. Arcadia, 1958
Murder is a Best Seller. Arcadia, 1959
Murder Makes Its Mark. Arcadia, 1961

JUDE, CHRISTOPHER
The Case of Dan Morris. Low, 1939
The Moorlands Murder. Low, 1938
The Terror of the Shape. Low, 1937

JUDGE, S(IDNEY) W(ALTER)
The Mystery of the Elms. Stockwell, 1944

JUDSON, EDWARD ZANE CARROLL. 1821-1866.
Pseudonym: Ned Buntline, q.v.

JUDSON, JEANNE. 1890- . Pseudonym: Frances Dean Hancock, q.v.
The Island Heirs. Avalon, 1958
The Legacy of Redfern. Bouregy, 1968
Treasure of Wycliffe House. Bouregy, 1967

JUDSON, WILLIAM. Pseudonym of Edwin Corley, 1931- , q.v. Other pseudonym: David Harper, q.v. Joint pseudonym with Jack Murphy: Patrick Buchanan, q.v.
Alice and Me. Fields, 1973; Talmy Franklin, 1973

JUSTIN, DEREK
Shard's Rock. Elek, 1966

K

KAGEY, RUDOLF HORNADAY. 1904-1946. Pseudonym: Kurt Steel, q.v.

KAHLER, HUGH (TORBERT) McNAIR. 1883- .
Bright Danger. Triangle, 1942
-Daniel P. Wack, "Dumb-Bell". Lloyd's, 1922
-Hills were Higher Then. Farrar, 1931 ss
-Local Talent. Lloyd's, 1921
The White Rook. Chelsea, 1927

KAHN, ALEC
-The Menace of X. Newnes, 1936

KALEDIN, VICTOR K. 1887- .
Flash D 13. Coward, 1930; Cassell, 1931 ss

KAMARCK, LAWRENCE
The Bellringer. Random, 1969
The Dinosaur. Random, 1968; Dent, 1970

KAMM, (JAN) DORINDA. 1952- .
Cliff's Head. Lenox, 1972; Remploy, 1974
The Devil's Doorstep. Lenox, 1972; Remploy, 1974

KAMPF, HAROLD B. 1916- . Pseudonym: H. B. Kaye, q.v.

KANE, ABEL
Slaughter's Big Rip-Off. Curtis, 1973. (Novelization of the movie.)

KANE, BOB
Batman. Signet, 1966 ss

KANE, FRANK. 1912-1968. Pseudonym: Frank Boyd, q.v. Series character: Johnny Liddell = JL.
About Face. Mystery House, 1947. Also published as: Death About Face. Handi-Books, 1948; and as: The Fatal Foursome. Dell, 1958 JL
Bare Trap. Washburn, 1952 JL
Barely Seen. Dell, 1964; Mayflower, 1964 JL
Bullet Proof. Washburn, 1951; Mayflower, 1969 JL
The Conspirators. Dell, 1962
Crime of Their Life. Dell, 1962; Mayflower, 1964 JL
Dead Rite. Dell, 1962; Mayflower, 1968 JL
Dead Weight. Washburn, 1951 JL
Death About Face; see About Face
Due or Die. Dell, 1961; Mayflower, 1963 JL
Esprit de Corpse. Dell, 1965 JL
The Fatal Foursome; see About Face
Fatal Undertaking. Dell, 1964; Mayflower, 1965 JL
Final Curtain. Dell, 1964; Mayflower, 1964 JL
Grave Danger. Washburn, 1954 JL
Green Light for Death. Washburn, 1949; Mayflower, 1966 JL
The Guilt-Edged Frame. Dell, 1964 JL
Hearse Class Male. Dell, 1963; Mayflower, 1969 JL
Johnny Come Lately. Dell, 1963; Mayflower, 1964 JL
Johnny Liddell's Morgue. Dell, 1956; WDL, 1958 ss JL
Juke Box King. Dell, 1959
Key Witness. Dell, 1956
The Line-Up. Dell, 1959; WDL, 1960. (Novelization of the TV series.)
The Living End. Dell, 1957 JL
Liz. Beacon, 1958
Maid in Paris. Dell, 1966 JL
Margin for Terror. Dell, 1967 JL
The Mourning After. Dell, 1961 JL
Poisons Unknown. Washburn, 1953 JL
A Real Gone Guy. Rinehart, 1956; Boardman, 1957 JL
Red Hot Ice. Washburn, 1955; Boardman, 1956 JL
Ring-a-Ding-Ding. Dell, 1963; Mayflower, 1964 JL
A Short Bier. Dell, 1960; Mayflower, 1964 JL
Slay Ride. Washburn, 1950 JL
Stacked Deck. Dell, 1961; Mayflower, 1964 ss JL
Syndicate Girl. Dell, 1958
Time to Prey. Dell, 1960; Mayflower, 1964 JL
Trigger Mortis. Rinehart, 1958 JL
Two to Tangle. Dell, 1965 JL

KANE, HENRY. 1918- . Pseudonym: Anthony McCall, q.v. Series characters: Peter Chambers = PC; McGregory = M; Marla Trent = MT.
Armchair in Hell. Simon, 1948; Boardman, 1949 PC
The Avenger. Atheneum, 1975
Better Wed than Dead; see Unholy Trio

The Bomb Job. Lancer, 1970 PC
The Case of the Murdered Madame. Avon, 1955. (Contains the title novelet, "Candlestick" and "Precise Moment.") British title: Triple Terror. Boardman, 1958. (Contains "Candlestick" and "Precise Moment" but uses "The Little Black Bag" instead of "The Case of the Murdered Madame".) PC
Come Kill with Me. Lancer, 1972 PC
Conceal and Disguise. Macmillan, 1966; Boardman, 1966 M
A Corpse for Christmas. Lippincott, 1951; Boardman, 1952. Also published as: Homicide at Yuletide. Signet, 1966 PC
The Crumpled Cup. Signet, 1963; Boardman, 1961
The Dangling Man; see Fistful of Death
Dead in Bed. Lancer, 1961; Boardman, 1963 PC
The Deadly Doll. Zenith, 1959
The Deadly Finger. Popular Library, 1957. British title: The Finger. Boardman, 1957
Death for Sale. Dell, 1957. Revised edition: Sleep Without Dreams. Lancer, 1970; Boardman, 1958
Death is the Last Lover. Avon, 1959. British title: Nirvana can also Mean Death. Boardman, 1959 PC
Death of a Dastard. Signet, 1963; Boardman, 1962 PC
Death of a Flack. Signet, 1961; Boardman, 1961 PC
Death of a Hooker. Avon, 1963; Boardman, 1961 PC
Death on the Double. Avon, 1957; Boardman, 1958. (Two novelets.) PC
Decision. Dial, 1973
The Devil to Pay; see Unholy Trio
Dirty Gertie. Belmont, 1965; Boardman, 1963. Also published as: To Die or Not to Die. Belmont, 1974
Don't Call Me Madame. Lancer, 1969 PC
Don't Go Away Dead. Lancer, 1970 PC
Edge of Panic. Simon, 1950; Boardman, 1951
The Escort Job. Lancer, 1972 PC
The Finger; see The Deadly Finger
Fistful of Death. Avon, 1958. British title: The Dangling Man. Boardman, 1959 PC
Frenzy of Evil. Dell, 1966; Boardman, 1963
The Glow Job. Lancer, 1971 PC
A Halo for Nobody. Simon, 1947; Boardman, 1950. Also published as: Martinis and Murder. Avon, 1956 PC
Hang by Your Neck. Simon, 1949; Boardman, 1950 PC
Homicide at Yuletide; see A Corpse for Christmas
Kill for the Millions. Lancer, 1972 PC
Killer's Kiss; see Kisses of Death
Kiss! Kiss! Kill! Kill! Lancer, 1970. (Four novelets, two from Report for a Corpse, and one each from The Case of the Murdered Madame and Death on the Double, qq.v.) PC
Kisses of Death. Belmont, 1962. British title: Killer's Kiss. Boardman, 1962 PC & MT
Laughter Came Screaming. Avon, 1954; Boardman, 1953. Also published as: A Mask for Murder. Avon, 1957
Laughter in the Alehouse. Macmillan, 1968 M
Lust of Power. Atheneum, 1975
Martinis and Murder; see A Halo for Nobody
A Mask for Murder; see Laughter Came Screaming
The Midnight Man. Macmillan, 1965. British title: Other Sins Only Speak. Boardman, 1965 M
The Moonlighter. Geis, 1971; Hale, 1972

Murder for the Millions; see Never Give a Millionaire an Even Break
Murder of the Park Avenue Playgirl; see Report for a Corpse
My Business is Murder. Avon, 1954. (Two novelets, both included in the British edition of Trinity in Violence, q.v.) PC
My Darlin' Evangeline. Dell, 1961. British title: The Perfect Crime. Boardman, 1961. Reprinted under the British title: Belmont, 1967
The Name is Chambers. Pyramid, 1957. (Six stories, including two from Trinity in Violence and one each from Report for a Corpse and The Case of the Murdered Madame, qq.v.) PC
The Narrowing Lust; see Too French and Too Deadly
Never Give a Millionaire an Even Break. Lancer, 1963. British title: Murder for the Millions. Boardman, 1964 PC
Nirvana can Also Mean Death; see Death is the Last Lover
Nobody Loves a Loser. Belmont, 1963; Boardman, 1964. Also published as: Who Dies There? Lancer, 1969 PC
Other Sins Only Speak; see The Midnight Man
The Perfect Crime; see My Darlin' Evangeline
Peter Gunn. Dell, 1960. (Novelization of the TV series.)
Prey by Dawn. Boardman, 1965. (U.S. title?)
Private Eyeful. Pyramid, 1959; Boardman, 1960 MT
Report for a Corpse. Simon, 1948; Boardman, 1951. Also published as: Murder of the Park Avenue Playgirl. Avon, 1957. (Six stories and novelets, one later reprinted in The Name is Chambers, q.v.) PC
Run for Doom. Signet, 1962; Boardman, 1960
The Schack Job. Lancer, 1969 PC
Sleep Without Dreams; see Death for Sale
Snatch an Eye. Perma, 1964; Boardman, 1963 PC
Sweet Charlie; see Who Killed Sweet Sue?
The Tail Job. Lancer, 1971 PC
To Die or Not to Die; see Dirty Gertie
Too French and Too Deadly. Avon, 1955. British title: The Narrowing Lust. Boardman, 1956. (Reprinted complete, under the British title, in The Locked Room Reader, ed. Hans Stefan Santesson. Random, 1968.) PC
Trilogy in Jeopardy. Boardman, 1955. (Contains 3 novelets, two of which are in the U.S. title Trinity in Violence, q.v.) PC
Trinity in Violence. Avon, 1955. (Contains: "Far Cry", "Slaughter on Sunday" and "Skip a Beat".) British edition: Boardman, 1954. (Contains: "The Big Touch", "Loose End" and "Far Cry"; the first two of these are collected in the U.S. as My Business is Murder, q.v.) PC
Triple Terror; see The Case of the Murdered Madame
Two Must Die. Tower, 1963
Unholy Trio. PB, 1967. British title: The Devil to Pay. Boardman, 1966. Also published as: Better Wed than Dead. Lancer, 1970 PC
Until You are Dead. Simon, 1951; Boardman, 1952 PC
The Violator. Warner, 1974
-The Virility Factor. McKay, 1972
Who Dies There?; see Nobody Loves a Loser

Who Killed Sweet Sue? Avon, 1956. British title: Sweet Charlie. Boardman, 1957 PG

KANE, MARK
 Fit to Kill. Hale, 1972
 Reluctant Transgressor. Hale, 1967
 Sucker Trap. Hale, 1968; Roy, 1968
 Walk of the Devil. Hale, 1968

KANE, WILLIAM R(ENO). 1885-   . See: MASON WRIGHT.

KANER, HYMAN
 An Alibi Too Much. Kaner, 1946
 -Ape-Man's Offering. Kaner, 1946 ss
 The Cynic's Desperate Mission. Kaner, 1946
 Fire-Watcher's Night. Kaner, 1944 ss
 Hot Swag. Kaner, 1945 ss
 A Lady Screams. Kaner, 1946
 The Naked Foot. Kaner, 1946 ss
 Ordeal by Moonlight. Kaner, 1947 ss
 -People of the Twilight. Kaner, 1946
 -Squaring the Triangle, and other short stories. Kaner, 1944 ss
 -The Sun Queen. Kaner, 1946
 The Terror Catches Up. Kaner, 1946

KANTOR, HAL
 The Vegas Trap. Pinnacle, 1970

KANTOR, MacKINLAY. 1904-1977.
 Author's Choice. Coward, 1944 ss, some criminous
 It's About Crime. Signet, 1960 ss
 Signal Thirty-Two. Random, 1950

KAPLAN, BARRY JAY. Pseudonym: Bettina Kingsley, q.v.

KAPLAN, JONATHAN and KEN FRIEDMAN
 White Line Fever. Signet, 1975. (Novelization of the movie.)

KARIG, WALTER. 1898-1956. Pseudonym: Keats Patrick, q.v.

KARK, NINA MARY MABEY. 1925-   . Pseudonym: Nina Bawden, q.v.

KARLOVA, IRINA
 Broomstick. Hurst, 1946
 Dreadful Hollow. Hurst, 1942; Vanguard, 1942
 The Empty House. Hurst, 1944

KARNEY, JACK. 1911-   . Series character: Jim Breen, in at least those marked JB.
 Cop. Holt, 1951
 Cry, Brother, Cry. Popular Library, 1959
 Cut Me In. Pyramid, 1959
 The Knave of Diamonds. Ace, 1959 JB
 Knock 'em Dead. Ace, 1955
 Layout for Murder. Berkley, 1960 JB
 The Ragged Edge. Morrow, 1946. Revised edition: Tough Town. Pyramid, 1961
 Some Like It Tough. Monarch, 1959
 There Goes Shorty Higgins. Morrow, 1945
 Tough Town; see The Ragged Edge
 Work of Darkness. Putnam, 1956
 Yield to the Night. Monarch, 196?

KARP, DAVID. 1922-   .
 -All Honorable Men. Knopf, 1956; Gollancz, 1956
 The Big Feeling. Banner, 1967
 The Brotherhood of Velvet. Lion, 1952
 Cry Flesh. Lion, 1953. Also published as: The Girl on Crown Street. Lion, 1956
 -The Day of the Monkey. Vanguard, 1955; Gollancz, 1955
 Enter Sleeping. Avon, 1961
 Escape to Nowhere. Lion, 1955
 The Girl on Crown Street; see Cry Flesh

Hardman. Lion, 1953
-The Last Believers. Harcourt, 1964; Cape, 1965
One. Vanguard, 1953; Gollancz, 1954

KARSLAND, COLLIS. See: VEVA CARSLAND.

KARSLAND, VEVA and COLLIS
The Witness Box; or, The Murder of Mr. A.B.C. Trischler, 1890

KARTA, NAT. Pseudonym of Victor (George Charles) Norwood, 1920-   , q.v. Other pseudonyms: Johnny Dark, Mark Hampton, Hank Janson, Mark Shane, qq.v.
Big Top Dame. Scion, 1952
Brother Rat. Scion, 1952
Climax. Scion, 1953
The Concrete Nymph. Scion, 1954
Eat Me If You Must. Muir, Watson, 1949
The Elusive Corpse. Scion, 1954
Foolish Cargo. Scion, 1954
The Foolish Virgin. Thorpe, 1950
The Foolish Virgin Returns. Scion, 1953
The Foolish Virgin Says No! Scion, 1953
Jealousy. Scion, 1953
Love Me, Hurt Me. Scion, 1953
Payoff. Scion, 1953
Sinister Lovely. Scion, 1953
Some Dame. Scion, 1953
The Trap. Scion, 1954
Uneasy Alibi. Scion, 1954
We the Condemned. Scion, 1953

KASPER, ROY CHARLES
Love Spy, Love. Caravelle, 1968

KASTLE, HERBERT D(AVID). 1924-   .
Countdown to Murder. Signet, 1961
Cross-Country. Delacorte, 1975; Allen, 1975
Hot Prowl. GM, 1965
The Millionaires. Delacorte, 1972; Allen, 1973

KASTNER, ERICH. 1899-1942?
The Missing Miniature. Cape, 1936; Knopf, 1937. (Translation of Die Verschwundene Miniatur. Berlin, 1936.)

KATCHA, VAHE. Pseudonym of Vaha Katchadourian, 1928-   .
Don't Look Down. Hart-Davis, 1962. (Translation of Ne te Retourne Pas, Kipian. Paris, 1958.)

KATCHADOURIAN, VAHA. 1928-   . Pseudonym: Vahe Katcha, q.v.

KATCHER, LEO
The Blind Cave. Viking, 1966
Hard Man. Macmillan, 1957
Hot Pursuit. Atheneum, 1971
The Money People. Doubleday, 1961
Now is the Time. Macmillan, 1964

KATHRENS, VAUGHAN
Benny Went First. Melrose, 1950
Hit and Run. Melrose, 1951
The Lady Makes News. Melrose, 1952
Violent End. Melrose, 1953

KATZENBERGER, FRANCES I(SABELLA)
The Three Verdicts. Editor Publishing, 1898

KAUFFMAN, (RAY) FRANKLIN
The Coconut Wireless. Macmillan, 1948

KAUFFMAN, REGINALD WRIGHT. 1877-   .
Series character: Frances Baird, in at least those marked FB.
-The Azure Rose. Macaulay, 1919; Laurie, 1918
Beg Pardon, Sir! Penn, 1929
Blind Man. Duffield, 1927; Hurst, 1926
-The Chasm, with Edward Childs Carpenter. Appleton, 1903
-The Dark House in Florissant. Altemus, 1927
-The Free Lovers. Macaulay, 1925; Laurie, 1925
Jarvis; see Jarvis of Harvard
-Jarvis of Harvard. Page, 1901. Also published as: Jarvis. St. Botolph Society, 1923
-Jim. Moffat, 1915. British title: Jim Trent. Laurie, 1929
Jim Trent; see Jim
-The Mark of the Beast. Macaulay, 1916; Gardner, 1919
Miss Frances Baird, Detective. Page, 1906 FB
Money to Burn. Chelsea, 1924; Hurst, 1927
My Heart and Stephanie. Page, 1910; Pitman, 1910 FB
-The Ranger of the Susquehannock. Penn, 1924
Share and Share Alike. Chelsea, 1925
The Spider's Web. Moffat, 1913
-The Things That are Caesar's. Appleton, 1902

KAUFFMANN, LANE. 1921-   .
The Perfectionist. Lippincott, 1954; Macmillan (London), 1955
Waldo. Lippincott, 1960; Gollancz, 1962

KAUFMAN, LOUIS. 1916-   . Pseudonym: Dan Keller, q.v.

KAUFMAN, MICHAEL T.
The Gun. Award, 1974. (Novelization of the movie.)
The Nickel Ride. Award, 1974; Tandem, 1974. (Novelization of the movie.)

KAUFMAN, WOLFE. 1905-1970.
I Hate Blondes. Simon, 1946

KAVANAGH, PAUL. Pseudonym of Lawrence Block, 1938-   , q.v. Other pseudonym: Chip Harrison, q.v.
Not Comin' Home to You. Putnam, 1974; Hodder, 1976
Such Men are Dangerous. Macmillan, 1969; Hodder, 1971
The Triumph of Evil. World, 1971; Hodder, 1972

KAVANAUGH, CYNTHIA
Bride of Lenore. Pyramid, 1966
The Deception. Pyramid, 1966

KAY, CAMERON
Thieves Fall Out. GM, 1953; Red Seal, 1953

KAY, KENNETH (EDMOND). 1915-   .
Trouble in the Air. Eyre, 1959

KAYE, H. B. Pseudonym of Harold B. Kampf, 1916-   .
Death is a Black Camel. Hammond, 1952
The Grave can Wait. Gifford, 1950
The Hungry Heart. Gifford, 1949
The Man in my Chair. Gifford, 1948
Red Rafferty. Gifford, 1949
This Man is a Stranger. Gifford, 1949
A Touch of the Sun. Quality, 1952
You Only Die Once. Gifford, 1950

KAYE, H. R.
The Dark Mansion. Brandon, 1968
Two Gay Sleuths. Brandon, 1968

KAYE, M(ARY) M(ARGARET). 1911-   .
Death Walked in Berlin. Staples, 1955
Death Walked in Cyprus. Staples, 1956
Death Walked in Kashmir. Staples, 1953
The House of Shade. Longmans, 1959; Coward, 1959
It's Later Than You Think; see Later Than You Think
Later Than You Think. Longmans, 1958; Coward, 1959, as by Mollie Hamilton. Also published as: It's Later Than You Think. WDL, 1960
Night on the Island. Longmans, 1960
Trade Wind. Longmans, 1963; Coward, 1964

KAYE, MARVIN (NATHAN). 1938-   . Series character: Hilary Quayle, in both titles.
The Grand Ole Opry Murders. Saturday Review, 1974
A Lively Game of Death. Saturday Review, 1972; Barker, 1974

KAYE, MOLLIE
Six Bars at Seven. Hutchinson, 1940

KAYSER, RONAL. Pseudonym: Dale Clark, q.v.

KEANE, CHRISTOPHER
The Maximus Zone. Pyramid, 1975

KEAREY, CHARLES. 1916-   .
-Last Plane from Uli. Collins, 1972; Holt, 1972

KEARNEY, SELSKAR
The False Finger Tip. Maunsel, 1921

KEATE, E(DITH) M(URRAY)
Demon Again. Eldon, 1937
Demon of the Air. Eldon, 1936
-A Garden of the Gods. Rivers, 1914
The Jackanapes Jacket. Low, 1931
The Mystery of Nelson's Coat. Eldon, 1936
A Wild-Cat Scheme. Rivers, 1930

KEATING, H(ENRY) R(EYMOND) F(ITZWALTER). 1926-   . Series character: Inspector Ganesh Ghote = GG.
Bats Fly Up for Inspector Ghote. Collins, 1974; Doubleday, 1974
Death and the Visiting Firemen. Gollancz, 1959; Doubleday, 1973
Death of a Fat God. Collins, 1963; Dutton, 1964
The Dog It was That Died. Gollancz, 1962
Inspector Ghote Breaks an Egg. Collins, 1970; Doubleday, 1971 GG
Inspector Ghote Caught in Meshes. Collins, 1967; Dutton, 1968 GG
Inspector Ghote Goes by Train. Collins, 1971; Doubleday, 1972 GG
Inspector Ghote Hunts the Peacock. Collins, 1968; Dutton, 1968 GG
Inspector Ghote Plays a Joker. Collins, 1969; Dutton, 1969 GG
Inspector Ghote Trusts the Heart. Collins, 1972; Doubleday, 1973 GG
Inspector Ghote's Good Crusade. Collins, 1966; Dutton, 1966 GG
Is Skin Deep, is Fatal. Collins, 1965; Dutton, 1965
The Perfect Murder. Collins, 1964; Dutton, 1965 GG
A Remarkable Case of Burglary. Collins, 1975; Doubleday, 1976
A Rush on the Ultimate. Gollancz, 1961
-The Strong Man. Heinemann, 1971
Zen There was Murder. Gollancz, 1960

KEATING, JOSEPH. 1871-1934.
The Fairfax Mystery. Wright, 1935

KEATOR, MAUDE C(OLE)
The Eyes Through the Trees. Appleton, 1930

KECK, MAUD and OLIVE ORBISON. Pseudonym: Keck Orbison, q.v.
Behind the Devil Screen. Ives Washburn, 1928; Long, 1929, as by Keck Orbison
Thursday Island. Ives Washburn, 1932

KEDDIE, HENRIETTA. 1827-1914. Pseudonym: Sarah Tytler, q.v.

KEEBLE, JOHN. 1944-   . See: RANSOM JEFFERY.

KEECH, GERTRUDE C.
The Charter Lane Mystery. Mitre, 1967
-The Record of Jeffrye Cranfield. Mitre, 1963

KEELER, HARRY STEPHEN. 1890-1967. Series characters: Angus MacWhorter = AM; Tuddleton Trotter = TT.
The Ace of Spades Murder; see The Case of the Jeweled Ragpicker
The Amazing Web. Dutton, 1930; Ward, 1929
Behind That Mask. Ward, 1933. (Earliest book edition of a story that Keeler later expanded into a two-volume novel published in the U.S. as Finger! Finger! and Behind That Mask, qq.v.)
Behind That Mask. Dutton, 1938. (Second of the two volumes expanded by Keeler from the original English edition of Behind That Mask. The first book of the two-volume novel is Finger! Finger!, q.v.)
The Barking Clock; see The Case of the Barking Clock
The Black Satchel; see The Matilda Hunter Murder
The Blue Spectacles; see The Spectacles of Mr. Cagliostro
The Book with the Orange Leaves. Dutton, 1942; Ward, 1943
The Bottle with the Green Wax Seal. Dutton, 1942. (Third and final novel in the sequence whose first two volumes were The Portrait of Jirjohn Cobb and Cleopatra's Tears, qq.v.)
The Box from Japan. Dutton, 1932; Ward, 1933
By Third Degree; see The Sharkskin Book
The Case of the Barking Clock. Phoenix, 1947. British title: The Barking Clock. Ward, 1951. (The British edition is 5-8,000 words longer than the American.) TT
The Case of the Canny Killer. Phoenix, 1946. British title: Murder in the Mills. Ward, 1946
The Case of the Ivory Arrow. Phoenix, 1945. British title: The Search for X-Y-Z. Ward, 1943. (The British edition is substantially longer than the American.)
The Case of the Jeweled Ragpicker. Phoenix, 1948. British title: The Ace of Spades Murder. Ward, 1949. (The British edition is longer than the American.) AM
The Case of the Lavender Gripsack. Phoenix, 1944. British title: The Lavender Gripsack. Ward, 1941. (Fourth and final volume in the sequence whose first three volumes were The Man with the Magic Eardrums, The Man with the Crimson Box, and The Man with the Wooden Spectacles, qq.v.)
The Case of the Mysterious Moll. Phoenix, 1945. British title: The Iron Ring. Ward, 1944. (The British edition is probably longer than the American.)
The Case of the 16 Beans. Phoenix, 1944. British title: The 16 Beans. Ward, 1945
The Case of the Transposed Legs. Phoenix, 1948; Ward, 1951
The Case of the Two Strange Ladies. Phoenix, 1943. British title: The Two Strange Ladies. Ward, 1945
The Chameleon. Dutton, 1939. (Second of the two volumes expanded by Keeler from the original British edition of The Mysterious Mr. I, q.v. The first of the two U.S. volumes is also entitled The Mysterious Mr. I.)
Cheung, Detective; see Y. Cheung, Business Detective
Cleopatra's Tears. Dutton, 1940; Ward, 1940. (Volume two of the sequence of novels that began with The Portrait of Jirjohn Cobb, q.v., and concluded with The Bottle with the Green Wax Seal, q.v.)
The Crilly Court Mystery; see The Face of the Man from Saturn
The Crimson Box; see The Man with the Crimson Box
The Defrauded Yeggman. Dutton, 1937. (The first book of the two-volume American edition of Keeler's Vagabond Nights, whose parts are scattered over three U.S. and two British titles. For details, see Vagabond Nights, below.)
The Face of the Man from Saturn. Dutton, 1933. British title: The Crilly Court Mystery. Ward, 1933
The Fiddling Cracksman; see The Mystery of the Fiddling Cracksman
Find Actor Hart; see The Portrait of Jirjohn Cobb
Find the Clock. Dutton, 1927; Hutchinson, 1925
Finger! Finger! Dutton, 1938. (The first of two volumes expanded by Keeler from the original British edition of Behind That Mask, q.v. The second book of the two-volume U.S. edition is also titled Behind That Mask, q.v.)
The Five Silver Buddhas. Dutton, 1935; Ward, 1935
The Fourth King. Dutton, 1930; Ward, 1929
The Green Jade Hand. Dutton, 1930; Ward, 1930. (The British edition is cut down from the American.)
The Iron Ring; see The Case of the Mysterious Moll
The Lavender Gripsack; see The Case of the Lavender Gripsack
The Magic Eardrums; see The Man with the Magic Eardrums
The Man with the Crimson Box. Dutton, 1940. British title: The Crimson Box. Ward, 1940. (Second book in the four-volume sequence that began with The Man with the Magic Eardrums, q.v., and went on to include The Man with the Wooden Spectacles and The Case of the Lavender Gripsack, qq.v.)
The Man with the Magic Eardrums. Dutton, 1939. British title: The Magic Eardrums. Ward, 1939. (First book in the four-volume sequence that went on to include The Man with the Crimson Box, The Man with the Wooden Spectacles and The Case of the Lavender Gripsack, qq.v.)
The Man with the Wooden Spectacles. Dutton, 1941. British title: The Wooden Spectacles. Ward, 1941. (Third book of the four-volume sequence that began with The Man with the Magic Eardrums and The Man with the Crimson Box, qq.v., and concluded with The Case of the Lavender Gripsack, q.v.)
The Marceau Case. Dutton, 1936; Ward, 1936. (First book of the trilogy that went on to include X. Jones of Scotland Yard and The Wonderful Scheme of Mr. Christopher Thorne, qq.v.)
The Matilda Hunter Murder. Dutton, 1931. British title: The Black Satchel. Ward, 1931. (The British edition is heavily cut.) TT
The Monocled Monster. Ward, 1947
Murder in the Mills; see The Case of the Canny Killer
The Murder of London Lew. Ward, 1952
The Murdered Mathematician. Ward, 1949
The Mysterious Mr. I. Ward, 1937. (Earliest book edition of a story that Keeler later expanded into a two-volume novel published in the U.S. as The Mysterious Mr. I and The Chameleon, qq.v.)
The Mysterious Mr. I. Dutton, 1938. (First of the two volumes expanded by Keeler from the original British edition of The Mysterious Mr. I. The second of the two U.S. volumes is The Chameleon, q.v.)
The Mystery of the Fiddling Cracksman. Dutton, 1934. British title: The Fiddling Cracksman. Ward, 1934
The Peacock Fan. Dutton, 1941; Ward, 1942
The Portrait of Jirjohn Cobb. Dutton, 1940. British title: Find Actor Hart. Ward, 1939. (First of the three-volume sequence that continued with Cleopatra's Tears, and concluded with The Bottle with the Green Wax Seal, qq.v.)
The Riddle of the Traveling Skull. Dutton, 1934. British title: The Traveling Skull. Ward, 1934
The Riddle of the Yellow Zuri. Dutton, 1930. British title: The Tiger Snake. Ward, 1934
The Search for X-Y-Z; see The Case of the Ivory Arrow
The Sharkskin Book. Dutton, 1941. British title: By Third Degree. Ward, 1948
Sing Sing Nights. Dutton, 1928; Hutchinson, 1927
The 16 Beans; see The Case of the 16 Beans
The Skull of the Waltzing Clown. Dutton, 1935. (For details of the English equivalent of this title, see Vagabond Nights, below.)
The Spectacles of Mr. Cagliostro. Dutton, 1929; Hutchinson, 1926. Also published as: The Blue Spectacles. Ward, 1931
Stand By—London Calling! Ward, 1953 AM
The Steeltown Strangler. Ward, 1950
The Strange Will. Ward, 1949
Ten Hours. Ward, 1934. (The one-volume British edition of Keeler's Vagabond Nights, whose parts are scattered over three U.S. and two British titles. For details, see Vagabond Nights, below.)
10 Hours. Dutton, 1937. (Volume 2 of the two-volume American edition of Vagabond Nights, whose parts are scattered over three U.S. and two English titles. For details, see Vagabond Nights, below.)
Thieves' Nights. Dutton, 1929; Ward, 1930
The Tiger Snake; see The Riddle of the Yellow Zuri

The Traveling Skull; see The Riddle of the Traveling Skull
The Two Strange Ladies; see The Case of the Two Strange Ladies
Under Twelve Stars; see The Washington Square Enigma
Vagabond Nights. (This was Keeler's overall title for a 180,000 word novel built on the same principle of three prisoners telling their stories as was the earlier Sing Sing Nights. The British version of this book was published first, and in a single volume, under the title Ten Hours, q.v. The American version is a two-volume novel, The Defrauded Yeggman and 10 Hours, qq.v. But between the British and American publications Keeler had expanded the tale of the first prisoner in the British version into a complete novel, The Skull of the Waltzing Clown, q.v., which was published only in the U.S. since a precis of the story had already appeared in England in Ten Hours. Finally, after the U.S. two-volume publication of Vagabond Nights as The Defrauded Yeggman and 10 Hours, Keeler expanded the tale of the first prisoner in the American edition—a tale totally different from the corresponding tale in the British edition—into a novel, When Thief Meets Thief, q.v., that was published only in England since a precis had already appeared in the U.S. as part of The Defrauded Yeggman!)
The Vanishing Gold Truck. Dutton, 1941; Ward, 1942 AM
The Voice of the Seven Sparrows. Dutton, 1928; Hutchinson, 1924
The Washington Square Enigma. Dutton, 1933. British title: Under Twelve Stars. Ward, 1933
When Thief Meets Thief. Ward, 1938. (For details on the American equivalent of this novel, see Vagabond Nights, above.)
The Wonderful Scheme; see The Wonderful Scheme of Mr. Christopher Thorne
The Wonderful Scheme of Mr. Christopher Thorne. Dutton, 1937. British title: The Wonderful Scheme. Ward, 1937. (Third book of the trilogy whose first two volumes were The Marceau Case and X. Jones of Scotland Yard, qq.v.
The Wooden Spectacles; see The Man with the Wooden Spectacles
X. Jones; see X. Jones of Scotland Yard
X. Jones of Scotland Yard. Dutton, 1936. British title: X. Jones. Ward, 1936. (Second volume of the trilogy that began with The Marceau Case and ended with The Wonderful Scheme of Mr. Christopher Thorne, qq.v.)
Y. Cheung, Business Detective. Dutton, 1939. British title: Cheung, Detective. Ward, 1938

KEELEY, EDMUND (LEROY). 1928- .
The Imposter. Doubleday, 1970

KEENAN, JAMES
Run, Mann, Run! Major, 1975

KEENAN, WILLIAM. Series character: John Marne, in at least those marked JM.
Lonely Mosaic. Hale, 1967 JM
Mosaic of Death. Hale, 1969 JM
Murder in Melancholy. Hale, 1971

KEENE, DAY
About Doctor Ferrel. GM, 1952; Fawcett (London), 1958
The Big Kiss-Off. Graphic, 1954
The Brimstone Bed. Avon, 1960
Bring Him Back Dead. GM, 1956. Revised edition: Lancer, 1963
Bye, Baby Bunting. Holt, 1963; Allen, 1963
Carnival of Death. Macfadden, 1965
Chautauqua, with Dwight Vincent. Putnam, 1960; Allen, 1961
Chicago 11. Dell, 1966
The Dangling Carrot. Ace, 1955
Dead Dolls Don't Talk. Crest, 1959; Muller, 1963
Dead in Bed. Pyramid, 1959
Death House Doll. Ace, 1954
Evidence Most Blind; see Framed in Guilt
Farewell to Passion. Hanro, 1951. Also published as: The Passion Murders. Avon, 1955
Flight by Night. Ace, 1956; Red Seal, 1960
Framed in Guilt. Mill, 1949. British title: Evidence Most Blind. Hennel Locke, 1949
-His Father's Wife. Pyramid, 1954
Home is the Sailor. GM, 1952
Homicidal Lady. Graphic, 1954
Hunt the Killer. Phantom, 1952
If the Coffin Fits. Graphic, 1952
It's a Sin to Kill. Avon, 1958
Joy House. Lion, 1954; Consul, 1964
-Live Again, Love Again. Signet. 1970
Love Me—and Die! Phantom, 1951
Miami 59. Dell, 1960; Mayflower, 1966
Moran's Woman. Zenith, 1959
Mrs. Homicide. Ace, 1953
Murder on the Side. GM, 1956; Fawcett (London), 1956
My Flesh is Sweet. Lion, 1951
Naked Fury. Phantom, 1952
Notorious. GM, 1954; Fawcett (London), 1955
Passage to Samoa. GM, 1958; Fawcett (London), 1960
The Passion Murders; see Farewell to Passion
Payola. Pyramid, 1960
Seed of Doubt. Simon, 1961; Allen, 1962
Sleep with the Devil. Lion, 1954
So Dead My Lovely. Pyramid, 1959
-Southern Daughter. Macfadden, 1967
Strange Witness. Graphic, 1953
Take a Step to Murder. GM, 1959; Muller pb, 1960
There was a Crooked Man. GM, 1954; Fawcett (London), 1955. Revised edition: Lancer, 1963
This is Murder, Mr. Herbert and other stories. Avon, 1948 ss
To Kiss, or Kill. GM, 1952; Fawcett (London), 1953
-Too Black for Heaven. Croydon, 1959
Too Hot to Hold. GM, 1959; Muller pb, 1960
Wake Up to Murder. Phantom, 1952
Who has Wilma Lathrop? GM, 1955; Jenkins, 1966
-Wild Girl. Macfadden, 1970

KEENE, FARADAY. Pseudonym of Cora (Hardy) Jarrett, 1877- , q.v.
Pattern in Black and Red. Houghton, 1934; Barker, 1934, as by Cora Jarrett
Peccadilloes. Day, 1929; Noel Douglas, 1930 ss

KEENE, ROSWELL W.
The Blue Diamond. Abbey, 1902

KEEPING, TEMPEST
-Diamond Mountain. Eldon, 1935

KEINZLEY, FRANCES
The Cottage at Chapelyard. Bobbs, 1975

Illusion. Allen, 1970; Stein, 1970
A Time to Prey. Allen, 1969; Stein, 1970

KEIRSTEAD, B(URTON) S(EELY), 1907- , and D(ONALD) FREDERICK CAMPBELL, 1906- .
The Brownsville Murders. Macmillan, 1933

KEITH, CARLTON. Pseudonym of Keith Carlton Robertson, 1914- . Series character: Jeff Green = JG.
The Crayfish Dinner. Doubleday, 1966. British title: The Elusive Epicure. Hale, 1968 JG
The Diamond-Studded Typewriter. Macmillan, 1958; Heinemann, 1960. Also published as: A Gem of a Murder. Dell, 1959 JG
The Elusive Epicure; see The Crayfish Dinner
A Gem of a Murder; see The Diamond-Studded Typewriter
The Hiding Place. Doubleday, 1965; Hale, 1966
The Missing Book-Keeper; see A Taste of Sangria
Missing, Presumed Dead. Doubleday, 1961 JG
Rich Uncle. Doubleday, 1963; Hale, 1965 JG
A Taste of Sangria. Doubleday, 1968. British title: The Missing Book-Keeper. Hale, 1969 JG

KEITH, DAVID. Pseudonym of Francis Steegmuller, 1906- . Series character: T. S. Weaver = TW.
Blue Harpsichord. Dodd, 1949; Collins, 1950. Reprinted as by Francis Steegmuller: Dolphin, 1961
A Matter of Accent. Dodd, 1943 TW
A Matter of Iodine. Dodd, 1940; Cassell, 1940 TW

KEITH, J. KILMENY. Pseudonym of Lucy Beatrice Malleson, 1899-1973. Other pseudonyms: Anthony Gilbert, Anne Meredith, qq.v.
The Man Who Saved London. Collins, 1925
-The Sword of Harlequin. Collins, 1927

KEITH, LESLIE. Pseudonym of Grace L. Keith Johnston.
-A Pleasant Rogue. Hurst, 1902

KELLAND, CLARENCE BUDINGTON. 1881-1964. Series character: Scattergood Baines = SB.
The Artless Heiress. Dodd, 1962
The Case of the Nameless Corpse. Harper, 1956; Hale, 1958
The Cat's Paw. Harper, 1934
Conflict. Harper, 1922; Hodder, 1928
Contraband. Harper, 1923; Hodder, 1928
Counterfeit Gentleman. Dodd, 1960; Hale, 1961
Dangerous Angel. Harper, 1953; Hale, 1955
Death Keeps a Secret. Harper, 1956; Hale, 1957
Double Treasure. Harper, 1946; Macdonald, 1949
The Great Mail Robbery. Harper, 1951; Museum, 1954
The Key Man. Harper, 1952; Hale, 1954
-Knuckles. Harper, 1928; Hodder, 1928
The Lady and the Giant. Dodd, 1959; Hale, 1960
Mark of Treachery. Dodd, 1961
The Monitor Affair. Dodd, 1960; Hale, 1961
Murder for a Million. World's Work, 1947. (U.S. title?)

Murder Makes an Entrance. Harper, 1955; Hale, 1956
No Escape. Museum, 1951. (U.S. title?)
Party Man. Dodd, 1962
-Scattergood Baines. Harper, 1921; Hodder, 1942 SB
-Scattergood Baines Pulls the Strings. Harper, 1941 SB ss
-Scattergood Returns. Harper, 1940 SB ss
The Sinister Strangers. Dodd, 1961
Stolen Goods. Harper, 1950; Museum, 1951
Where There's Smoke. Harper, 1959; Hale, 1960

KELLER, BEVERLY (LOU)
The Baghdad Defections. Bobbs, 1973

KELLER, DAN. Pseudonym of Louis Kaufman, 1916- .
Flee the Night in Anger. Popular Library, 1954
One Way Street. Hale, 1960

KELLER, DAVID H(ENRY). 1880-1966.
Wolf Hollow Bubbles. ARRA Printers, 1933

KELLER, H(ARRY) A. 1894- .
Death Sits In. Brentano's, 1932

KELLEY, J(AMES) D(OUGLAS) JERROLD. 1847-1922.
A Desperate Chance. Scribner, 1886

KELLEY, LAMAR
That's No Way to Die. Pyramid, 1970

KELLEY, LEO P.
Deadlocked! GM, 1973

KELLEY, MARTHA MOTT. See: Q. PATRICK.

KELLIHER, DAN T. Joint pseudonym with W. G. Secrist: Kelliher Secrist, q.v.

KELLOW, KATHLEEN. Pseudonym of Eleanor Burford Hibbert, 1906- . Other pseudonyms: Philippa Carr, Elbur Ford, Victoria Holt, qq.v.
-Call of the Blood. Hale, 1956
-Danse Macabre. Hale, 1952
-It Began in Vauxhall Gardens. Hale, 1955
-Lilith. Hale, 1954
-Milady Charlotte. Hale, 1959
-Rooms at Mrs. Oliver's. Hale, 1952
-The World's a Stage. Hale, 1960

KELLY, BILL. Series character: Pepperoni Hero, in all titles.
Peanut Butter & Jelly is Not for Kids. Zebra, 1975
Sandwiches are Not My Business. Zebra, 1975
Tuna is Not for Eating. Zebra, 1975

KELLY, F. J.
The Gates of Brass. Monarch, 1963

KELLY, FLORENCE FINCH. 1858-1939.
The Delafield Affair. McClurg, 1908
The Fate of Felix Brand. Winston, 1913
-Frances. Sanfred, 1899
-On the Inside. Sanford, 1890
-With Hoops of Steel. Bowen-Merrill, 1900; Stevens, 1900

KELLY, HAROLD ERNEST. 1899- . Pseudonyms: Darcy Glinto, Gordon Holt, Buck Toler, qq.v.

KELLY, JUDITH (SAGE). 1908-1957.
A Diplomatic Incident. Houghton, 1949; Gollancz, 1950

KELLY, MARY. 1927- . Series characters: Inspector Nightingale = IN; Nicholson = N.
The Christmas Egg. Secker, 1958; Holt, 1966 IN
A Cold Coming. Secker, 1956; Walker, 1968 IN
Dead Corse. Joseph, 1966; Holt, 1967
Dead Man's Riddle. Secker, 1957; Walker, 1967 IN
The Dead of Summer; see Due to a Death
Due to a Death. Joseph, 1962. U.S. title: The Dead of Summer. Mill, 1963 N
March to the Gallows. Joseph, 1964; Holt, 1965
The Spoilt Kill. Joseph, 1961; British Book Centre, 1961 N
That Girl in the Alley. Macmillan (London), 1974; Walker, 1974
The Twenty-Fifth Hour. Macmillan (London), 1971; Walker, 1972
Write on Both Sides of the Paper. Joseph, 1969; London House, 1970

KELLY, TIM J.
The Burning Man. French (New York), 1962. (2-act play.)

KELLY, VINCE
The Greedy Ones. Angus, 1958
The Shadow: Frank Fahy. Mayflower, 1967

KELLY, W(ILLIAM) P(ATRICK). 1848- .
-The Cuban Treasure Island. Routledge, 1903
-Doctor Baxter's Invention. Greening, 1912
-The Dolomite Cavern; or, Light in the Darkness. Greening, 1899
The Harrington Street Mystery. Simpkin, 1915
-The House at Norwood. Arrowsmith, 1914
-Schoolboys Three. Downey, 1895

KELSEY, VERA
The Bride Dined Alone. Doubleday, 1943
Fear Came First. Doubleday, 1945
The Owl Sang Three Times. Doubleday, 1941
Satan has Six Fingers. Doubleday, 1943
Whisper Murder! Doubleday, 1946

KELSTON, ROBERT
Kill One, Kill Two. Ace, 1958
Murder's End. Graphic, 1956

KELTON, GERALD
-Dolores. Eldon, 1934
Wheels Beneath. Rich, 1935

KEMELMAN, HARRY. 1908- . Series character: Rabbi David Small = DS.
Friday the Rabbi Slept Late. Crown, 1964; Hutchinson, 1965 DS
Monday the Rabbi Took Off. Putnam, 1972; Hutchinson, 1972 DS
The Nine Mile Walk. Putnam, 1967; Hutchinson, 1968 ss
Saturday the Rabbi Went Hungry. Crown, 1966; Hutchinson, 1967 DS
Sunday the Rabbi Stayed Home. Putnam, 1969; Hutchinson, 1969 DS
Tuesday the Rabbi Saw Red. Fields, 1974; Hutchinson, 1974 DS

KEMP, HAROLD (CURRY). 1896- . Series character: Inspector Jimmy Brent, in at least those marked JB.
As the Devil Burned. Hammond, 1949
Dead Snakes' Venom. Hammond, 1948
Death of a Dwarf. Bles, 1955

Heat Not a Furnace. Hammond, 1952 JB
Mark of a Witch. Bles, 1959 JB
Murder Humane. Hammond, 1947 JB
Red for Murder. Bles, 1957 JB

KEMPLEY, WALTER
The Probability Factor. Saturday Review Press, 1972

KENDALL, CAROL (SEEGER). 1917- .
The Baby-Snatcher. Lane, 1952
The Black Seven. Lane, 1950; Harper, 1946
The Other Side of the Tunnel. Lane, 1956; Abelard, 1957

KENDALL, KATHRYA
Black Terrace. Arcadia, 1955
Death Rides the Storm. Arcadia, 1958

KENDALL, RALPH S(ELWOOD). 1878- .
Benton of the Royal Mounted. Lane (New York), 1918; Lane (London), 1919
The Luck of the Mounted. Lane (New York & London), 1920

KENDRAKE, CARLETON. Pseudonym of Erle Stanley Gardner, 1889-1970, q.v. Other pseudonyms: A. A. Fair, Charles J. Kenny, qq.v.
The Clew of the Forgotten Murder. Morrow, 1935; Cassell, 1935. (Reprinted extensively as by Erle Stanley Gardner.)

KENDRICK, BAYNARD (HARDWICK). 1894-1977. Series characters: Capt. Duncan Maclain = DM; Stan Rice = SR.
The Aluminum Turtle. Dodd, 1960. British title: The Spear Gun Murders. Hale, 1961 DM
Blind Allies. Morrow, 1954 DM
Blind Man's Bluff. Little, 1943; Methuen, 1944 DM
Blood on Lake Louisa. Greenberg, 1934; Methuen, 1937
Clear and Present Danger. Doubleday, 1958; Hale, 1959 DM
Death Beyond the Go-Thru. Doubleday, 1938 SR
Death Knell. Morrow, 1945; Methuen, 1946 DM
The Eleven of Diamonds. Greenberg, 1936; Methuen, 1937 SR
Eyes in the Night; see The Odor of Violets
Flight from a Firing Wall. Simon, 1966; Hale, 1968
Frankincense and Murder. Dodd, 1961; Hale, 1962
Hot Red Money. Dodd, 1959; Hale, 1962
The Iron Spiders. Greenberg, 1936; Methuen, 1938. Also published as: The Iron Spiders Murder. Dell, 1944 SR
The Iron Spiders Murder; see The Iron Spiders
The Last Express. Doubleday, 1937; Methuen, 1938 DM
Make Mine Maclain. Morrow, 1947. (Three novelets.) DM
The Murderer Who Wanted More. Dell 10¢ pb, 1951. (Separate publication of one of the three novelets from Make Mine Maclain, q.v.) DM
The Odor of Violets. Little, 1941; Methuen, 1941. Also published as: Eyes in the Night. Grosset, 1942 DM
Out of Control. Morrow, 1945; Methuen, 1947 DM
Reservations for Death. Morrow, 1957; Hale, 1958 DM
The Spear Gun Murders; see The Aluminum Turtle

The Tunnel. Scribner, 1949
The Whistling Hangman. Doubleday, 1937; Hale, 1959 DM
You Die Today. Morrow, 1952; Hale, 1958 DM

KENEALLY, THOMAS. 1935- .
The Chant of Jimmie Blacksmith. Angus, 1972; Viking, 1972
The Fear. Cassell, 1965
The Place at Whitten. Cassell, 1964; Walker, 1965
The Survivor. Angus, 1969; Viking, 1970

KENEALY, ARABELLA
-King Edward Intervenes. Long, 1910

KENLEY, PETER
-Surregar's Raft. Earl, 1948

KENNEDY, ADAM. Pseudonym: John Redgate, q.v.
The Domino Principle. Viking, 1975; New English Library, 1976

KENNEDY, BART. 1861-1930.
The Wandering Romanoff. Burleigh, 1898

KENNEDY, ELLIOT. Pseudonym of Lionel Robert Holcombe Godfrey, 1932- .
Other pseudonym: Scott Mitchell, q.v.
The Big Loser. Hale, 1972; Drake, 1972
Bullets are Final. Hale, 1973
The Dead Sleep Late. Hale, 1975
Never Say Dead. Hale, 1974
That Fatal Feeling. Hale, 1974

KENNEDY, HARVEY J.
Murder and the Shocking Miss Williams. Vantage, 1957

KENNEDY, HOWARD ANGUS. 1861-1938.
Unsought Adventure. Carrier, 1929

KENNEDY, JOHN (BOYD). 1921- .
Paper Chase. Abelard-Schuman, 1956

KENNEDY, JOHN DE N(AVARRE). 1888- .
Crime in Reverse. Nelson, 1939
In the Shadow of the Cheka. Nelson, 1935; Macaulay, 1935
The Rain of Death. Nelson, 1945

KENNEDY, MILWARD. Pseudonym of Milward Rodon Kennedy Burge, 1894- . Other pseudonym: Evelyn Elder, q.v. Joint pseudonym with (Archibald) Gordon McDonell, 1905- , q.v.: Robert Milward Kennedy, q.v. Series characters: Sir George Bull = GB; Inspector Cornford = C.
Bull's Eye. Gollancz, 1933; Kinsey, 1933 GB
Corpse Guards Parade. Gollancz, 1929; Doubleday, 1930 C
Corpse in Cold Storage. Gollancz, 1934; Kinsey, 1934 GB
The Corpse on the Mat. Gollancz, 1929. U.S. title: The Man Who Rang the Bell, as by Robert Milward Kennedy. Doubleday, 1929 C
Death in a Deck-Chair. Gollancz, 1930; Doubleday, 1931
Death to the Rescue. Gollancz, 1931
Escape to Quebec. Gollancz, 1946
Half-Mast Murder. Gollancz, 1930; Doubleday, 1930
I'll be Judge, I'll be Jury. Gollancz, 1937
It Began in New York. Gollancz, 1943
The Man Who Rang the Bell; see The Corpse on the Mat
The Murderer of Sleep. Gollancz, 1932; Kinsey, 1933
Poison in the Parish. Gollancz, 1935
The Scornful Corpse; see Sic Transit Gloria
Sic Transit Gloria. Gollancz, 1936. U.S. title: The Scornful Corpse. Dodd, 1936
The Top Boot. Hale, 1950
Two's Company. Hale, 1952

KENNEDY, ROBERT MILWARD. Joint pseudonym of Milward Rodon Kennedy Burge, 1894- , and (Archibald) Gordon McDonell, 1905- , q.v. Other Burge pseudonyms: Evelyn Elder, Milward Kennedy, qq.v.
The Bleston Mystery. Gollancz, 1928; Doubleday, 1929

KENNEDY, STETSON. 1916- .
Passage to Violence. Lion, 1954

KENNEDY, VAN G.
The Penalty is Death! Fiction House, 1946

KENNEDY, WILLIAM. 1928- .
Legs. Coward, 1975; Cape, 1976

KENNINGTON, (GILBERT) ALAN. 1906- .
Pseudonym: Alan Grant, q.v.
All Fall Down. Jarrolds, 1950. U.S. title: Young Man with a Scythe. Macmillan, 1951
A Bagful of Bones. Jarrolds, 1942
Blood Velvet. Jarrolds, 1954
Death of a Shrew. Jarrolds, 1937
-Desirable Alien. Locker, 1947
Flying Visitor. Jarrolds, 1946
-Fritzi. Dickson, 1932
The Golden Horse. Hale, 1958
Hemlock Galore. Hale, 1974
The Lost One. Jarrolds, 1955
-Love on the Set. Mellifont, 1938
Murder, M.A. Jarrolds, 1941
The Night has Eyes. Jarrolds, 1939
See How They Run. Dickson, 1934
She Died Young. Jarrolds, 1938
Since There's No Help. Jarrolds, 1948
Young Man with a Scythe; see All Fall Down

KENNY, CHARLES J. Pseudonym of Erle Stanley Gardner, 1889-1970, q.v. Other pseudonyms: A. A. Fair, Carleton Kendrake, qq.v.
This is Murder. Morrow, 1935; Methuen, 1936. (Extensively reprinted as by Erle Stanley Gardner.)

KENNY, PAUL
Tanagra Affair. International, 1969

KENRICK, TONY. 1935- .
The Kidnap Kid. Joseph, 1975. U.S. title: Stealing Lillian. McKay, 1975
The Only Good Body's a Dead One. Cape, 1970; Simon, 1971
Stealing Lillian; see The Kidnap Kid
A Tough One to Lose. Joseph, 1972; Bobbs, 1972
Two for the Price of One. Joseph, 1974; Bobbs, 1974

KENT, ARTHUR. Series character: Sexton Blake (with many other authors) = SB.
Action of the Tiger. Consul, 1961
Black Sunday. Hale, 1965
Broken Doll. Digit, 1961
Corpse to Cuba. Mayflower, 1966; Macfadden, 1967 SB
Inclining to Crime. Amalgamated, 1956 SB
Plant Poppies on my Grave. Digit, 1966; Avon, 1967
Red—Red—Red. Compact, 1966
Special Edition—Murder. Amalgamated, 1957 SB
Stairway to Murder. Amalgamated, 1958 SB
Wake Up Screaming! Amalgamated, 1958 SB
The Weak and the Strong. Amalgamated, 1962 SB

KENT, DAVID. Pseudonym of Herman Hoffman Birney, 1891-1958. Series character: Jason Burr, in both titles.
Jason Burr's First Case. Random, 1941
A Knife is Silent. Random, 1947

KENT, EDWARD
A Lawful Crime. Leadenhall, 1899

KENT, ELIZABETH. Pseudonym.
The House Opposite. Putnam (New York & London), 1902
Who? Putnam (New York & London), 1912

KENT, FORTUNE
The House at Canterbury. PB, 1975
House of Masques. Ballantine, 1975
The Isle of the Seventh Sentry. PB, 1974
The Opal Legacy. Ballantine, 1975

KENT, GRAEME
Deadly Company. Hale, 1966
The Foreign Squad. Hale, 1967
Gypsy's Warning. Hale, 1968
The Lurking Policeman. Hale, 1969
-The Monkey Game. Muller, 1964
Nelson's Blood. Hale, 1966
Who Needs Enemies? Hale, 1970

KENT, MARTIN
-The Flying Hooligans. Low, 1936
The Flying Kidnappers. Low, 1937
The Hanging Rope. Eldon, 1944
A Spy for England. Eldon, 1940

KENT, MARY. See: MICHAEL KENT.

KENT, MICHAEL
The Armitage Case, with Mary Kent. Crowther, 1943
Hail, Victor, Hail! Staples, 1946

KENT, NORA. 1899- .
A Hint of Murder. Macdonald, 1967

KENT, OLIVER
-Her Heart's Gift. Dillingham, 1913
-Her Right Divine. Dillingham, 1913

KENT, SIMON. Pseudonym of Max(well Jeffrey) Catto, 1909- , q.v.
The Lions at the Kill. Hutchinson, 1959

KENT, WILLIS. Pseudonym of Wilson Collison, 1893-1941, q.v.
A Woman in Purple Pajamas. McBride, 1931

KENWOOD, CLIVE
The Film Studio Murder. World's Work, 1937

KENYON, CAMILLA. 1876- .
Dark Harvest. Grayson, 1933

KENYON, CHARLES FREDERICK. 1879-1926.
Pseudonym: Gerald Cumberland, q.v.

KENYON, LARRY. House name. Series character: Don Miles, in all titles.
Challenge at Le Mans. Avon, 1967
Countdown at Monaco. Avon, 1967
The Devil's Ring. Avon, 1967
Revenge at Indy. Avon, 1967

KENYON, MICHAEL. 1931- . Series character: Supt. O'Malley, in at least those marked O.
Green Grass. Macmillan (London), 1969
May You Die in Ireland. Collins, 1965; Morrow, 1965
Mr. Big. Collins, 1975; Coward, 1975, as by Daniel Forbes
The 100,000 Welcomes. Collins, 1970; Coward, 1970
Out of Season. Collins, 1968
The Shooting of Dan McGrew. Collins, 1972; McKay, 1975 O
A Sorry State. Collins, 1974; McKay, 1974 O
The Trouble with Series Three; see The Whole Hog
The Whole Hog. Collins, 1967. U.S. title: The Trouble with Series Three. Morrow, 1967

KERKOW, HERBERT
The Fateful Star Murder. Mohawk, 1931

KERNAHAN, (JOHN) COULSON. 1858-1943.
The Apples of Sin. Ward, 1898; Page, 1901. (Taken from A Book of Strange Sins, q.v.)
A Book of Strange Sins. Ward, 1893; Altemus, 1895 ss
Captain Shannon. Ward, 1897; Dodd, 1896
-A Dead Man's Diary. Ward, 1890; Ogilvie, 1905
The Dumpling: A Detective Love Story of a Great Labour Rising. Cassell, 1906; Dodge, 1907
The Jackals. Ward, 1905
-The Lonely God. Ward, 1897; Page, 1901 ss
-The Man of No Sorrows. Cassell (London), 1911; Cassell (New York), 1912
-The Red Peril. Hurst, 1908
Scoundrels & Co. Ward, 1901; Stone, 1899
A Strange Sin. Ward, 1898; Page, 1901. (Taken from A Book of Strange Sins, q.v.)

KERNAHAN, MRS. COULSON [MARY JANE HICKLING GWYNNE KERNAHAN]. 1857- .
The Affair of Maltravers. Mellifont, 1949
-An Artist's Model. White, 1906
The Avenging of Ruthanna. Long, 1900
-A Beautiful Savage. White, 1904
-The Blue Diamond. Everett, 1914
A Case for the Courts. White, 1907
-The Chance Child. Everett, 1914
-Devastation. Long, 1904
The Disappearance of the Duke. White, 1907
-A Fair Sinner. Everett, 1913
The Fate of Felix. Long, 1905
-Frank Redland, Recruit. Long, 1899
The Fraud. Hodder, 1907
-The Gate of Sinners. Everett, 1908
The Go-Between. Everett, 1912
The Graven Image. Milne, 1909
-The Hired Girl. Everett, 1912
-The House of Blight. Everett, 1911
The Mummy's Hand. Mellifont, 1937
The Mystery of Magdalen. Long, 1906
The Mystery of Mere Hall. Everett, 1912
-No Vindication. Long, 1901
-Quixote of Magdalen. Everett, 1909
-The Sinnings of Seraphine. Long, 1906
-The Soul of Phyllis Fabian. Mellifont, 1935
The Stolen Man. Everett, 1915
The Temptation of Gideon Holt. Epworth, 1923
-The Thirteenth Man. Everett, 1910; Dillingham, 1910
The Trap. Everett, 1917
-Trewinnot of Guy's. Long, 1898
-Two Legacies. Ward, 1886
-Under Seal of the Confessional. Everett, 1910

-An Unwise Virgin. Long, 1903
-The Vagrant Bride. Everett, 1911
A Village Mystery. White, 1905
-The Whip of the Will. Epworth, 1927
-The Whisperer. White, 1905
-The Wireless Call. Epworth, 1930
-The Woman Who Understood. Everett, 1916

KERNER, BEN. See: TOM VAN DYCKE.

KERR, BEN. Pseudonym of William (Thomas) Ard, 1922-1960, q.v. Other pseudonyms: Mike Moran, Thomas Wills, qq.v.
The Blonde and Johnny Malloy. Popular Library, 1958
Club 17. Popular Library, 1957
Damned If He Does. Popular Library, 1956
Down I Go. Popular Library, 1955
I Fear You Not. Popular Library, 1956; Digit, 1960
Shakedown. Holt, 1952

KERR, CAROLE
Shadow of the Hunter. Hale, 1975

KERR, GEOFFREY. 1895- .
Under the Influence. Joseph, 1953; Lippincott, 1954

KERR, JAMES. 1923- .
Emergency Room. Delacorte, 1975

KERR, MICHAEL
Benjamin Seven. Secker, 1975

KERR, ORPHEUS C. Pseudonym of Robert Henry Newell, 1836-1901.
The Cloven Foot: Being an Adaptation of the English Novel, "The Mystery of Edwin Drood". Carleton, 1870. British title: The Mystery of Mr. E. Drood. Hotten, 1871

KERR, ROBERT. Pseudonym. 1899- .
The Stuart Legacy. Stein, 1973

KERR, SOPHIE. 1880- .
-The Blue Envelope. Doubleday, 1917; Wayfarer's Library, 1919
-The Man Who Knew the Date. Rinehart, 1951; Allen, 1952

KERRIGAN, M.
Once Upon a Crime. Milestone, 1953
Suddenly a Shroud. Milestone, 1954

KERSEY, JOHN
Night of the Wolf. Cassell, 1968

KERSH, GERALD. 1909-1968.
-The Angel and the Cuckoo. Heinemann, 1967; NAL, 1966
-An Ape, a Dog, and a Serpent. Heinemann, 1945
-Battle of the Singing Men. Everybody's, 1944 ss
-Brain and Ten Fingers. Heinemann, 1943
-The Brazen Bull. Heinemann, 1952
-The Brighton Monster and others. Heinemann, 1946 ss
-Brock. Heinemann, 1969
-Clean, Bright, and Slightly Oiled. Heinemann, 1946 ss
-Clock Without Hands. Heinemann, 1949
The Great Wash. Heinemann, 1953. U.S. title: The Secret Masters. Ballantine, 1953
-Guttersnipe. Heinemann, 1954 ss
-The Horrible Dummy and other stories. Heinemann, 1944 ss

-The Hospitality of Miss Tolliver and other stories. Heinemann, 1965 ss
-The Implacable Hunter. Heinemann, 1961
-Jews Without Jehovah. Wishart, 1934
-A Long Cool Day in Hell. Heinemann, 1965
-Men Without Bones and other stories. Heinemann, 1955; Paperback Library, 1962. (British edition has 22 ss; U.S. edition has 13.)
-More Than Once Upon a Time. Heinemann, 1964 ss
-Neither Man Nor Dog. Heinemann, 1946 ss
Night and the City. Joseph, 1938; Simon, 1946
-Nightshade & Damnations. Coronet, 1969 ss
Prelude to a Certain Midnight. Heinemann, 1947; Doubleday, 1947
-Sad Road to the Sea. Heinemann, 1947
The Secret Masters; see The Great Wash
-The Song of the Flea. Heinemann, 1948; Doubleday, 1948
-The Terribly Wild Flowers. Heinemann, 1962
-The Ugly Face of Love and other stories. Heinemann, 1960 ss

KERSHAW, JOHN
A Meeting in Casa. Hale, 1973

KESSEL, JOSEPH. 1898- .
The Bernan Affair. St. Martin's, 1965. (Translation of L'Affaire Bernan. Paris, 1950.)

KESSELRING, JOSEPH (OTTO). 1902- .
Arsenic and Old Lace. Random, 1941; English Theatre Guild, 1948. (Play.)

KETCHUM, PHILIP. 1902- .
Death at Dusk. Phoenix, 1938. Also published as: Kill at Dusk. Red Dagger, 1946
Death in the Library. Crowell, 1937
Death in the Night. Phoenix, 1939
Kill at Dusk; see Death at Dusk
-The Stalkers. Berkley, 1961

KETTERER, BERNADINE
The Manderley Mystery. Eldon, 1937

KETTERING, RALPH
The Clutching Claw. Dramatists Play Service, 1938. (3-act play.)

KEVERNE, BARBARA. Pseudonym of Donald Lee Shepherd, 1932- .
Dark Eden. PB, 1973
Darkness Falling. Pinnacle, 1974
The Devil's Vineyard. Pinnacle, 1975
The Key. Beagle, 1974

KEVERNE, RICHARD. Pseudonym of Clifford (James Wheeler) Hosken, 1882-1950, q.v. Series characters: Simon Artifex = SA; Inspector Mace = M.
Artifex Intervenes. Constable, 1934 (3 novelets.) SA
At the Blue Gates. Constable, 1932; Doubleday, 1932
The Black Cripple. Collins, 1941
Carteret's Cure. Constable, 1926; Houghton, 1926
Coroner's Verdict: Accident; see The Lady in No. 4
Crook Stuff. Constable, 1935 ss, 3 with SA
Crooks and Vagabonds. Collins, 1941 ss
The Fleet Hall Inheritance. Constable, 1931; Harper, 1931
The Havering Plot. Constable, 1928; Harper, 1929
He Laughed at Murder. Constable, 1934; Holt, 1935

K

The Lady in No. 4. Collins, 1944. U.S. title: Coroner's Verdict: Accident. McKay, 1945
The Man in the Red Hat. Constable, 1930; Harper, 1930
Menace. Constable, 1933
More Crook Stuff. Constable, 1938 ss, one with SA
Open Verdict. Constable, 1940 M
The Sanfield Scandal. Constable, 1929; Harper, 1929
The Strange Case of William Cook; see William Cook—Antique Dealer
White Gas. Constable, 1937 M
William Cook—Antique Dealer. Constable, 1928. U.S. title: The Strange Case of William Cook. Harper, 1928

KEY, (SAM)UEL (WHITTELL). Series character: Professor Arnold Rhymer, in both titles.
The Broken Fang. Hodder, 1920 ss
Yellow Death. Books Limited, 1921

KEYES, FRANCES PARKINSON. 1885-1970.
Dinner at Antoine's. Messner, 1948; Eyre, 1949
The Gold Slippers; see Victorine
The Letter from Spain; see Station Wagon in Spain
The Royal Box. Messner, 1954; Eyre, 1954
Station Wagon in Spain. Farrar, 1959. British title: The Letter from Spain. Eyre, 1959
Victorine. Messner, 1958. British title: The Gold Slippers. Eyre, 1958

KEYES, MICHAEL
The Dead Parrot. Doubleday, 1933. British title: The Murder Cruise. Harrap, 1934

KEYNES, HELEN M(ARY). 1892- .
Murder in Rosemary Lane. Melrose, 1936
Who Killed Jefferson Broome? Melrose, 1937

KEYSTONE, OLIVER. Pseudonym of James M. Mantinband. Series character: Paul Plush, in at least those marked PP.
Arsenic for the Teacher. Phoenix, 1950 PP
Deep as the Grave. Phoenix, 1950 PP
Major Crime. Phoenix, 1948

KEYWORTH, HENRY
The Black Market Murders. Kangaroo, 1944
Death in Gelly Wood. Kangaroo, 1944
Death in the Signal Box. Kangaroo, 1946
Killer by Night. Kangaroo, 1944

KIDDY, MAURICE G(EORGE). 1894- . Series character: Stonewall Steevens, in at least those marked SS.
The Devil's Dagger. Hutchinson, 1928
The House of Faith. Hutchinson, 1928
The Jade Hatpin. Hutchinson, 1933 SS
Killing No Murder. Hutchinson, 1931 SS
The Orange Ray. Hutchinson, 1934
Stonewall Steevens Investigates. Hutchinson, 1933 SS
-The Watcher in the Wood. Hutchinson, 1929

KIEFER, WARREN. 1929- .
The Lingala Code. Random, 1972

KIELLAND, AXEL (ZETLITZ). 1907- .
Dangerous Honeymoon. Collins, 1946; Little, 1946
Live Dangerously. Collins, 1944. U.S. title: Shape of Danger. Little, 1945
Shape of Danger; see Live Dangerously

KIELY, BENEDICT. 1919- .
-The Cards of the Gambler. Methuen, 1953

KIERAN, JAMES
Come Murder Me. GM, 1951

KILGORE, JOHN. Pseudonym of Lauran Bosworth Paine, 1916- . Other pseudonyms: John Armour, Reg Batchelor, Kenneth Bedford, Frank Bosworth, Mark Carrel, Robert Clarke, Richard Dana, J. F. Drexler, Troy Howard, Jared Ingersol, Hunter Liggett, J. K. Lucas, John Morgan, qq.v.
Murder to Music. Hale, 1972
Some Die Young. Hale, 1970

KILPATRICK, SARAH
Wake All the Dead. Doubleday, 1970

KILVINGTON, EDWIN. Series character: Crispin Quane, in both titles.
Mystery in Glass. Houghton (London), 1931
Window in the Dark. Houghton (London), 1932

KIM, DON 'O
Password. Angus, 1975

KIMBERLEY, HUGH
Wreath for a Dead Angel. Clerke, 1951

KIMBRO, JOHN M. 1929- . Pseudonyms: Charlotte Bramwell, Katheryn Kimbrough, qq.v.

KIMBROUGH, KATHERYN. Pseudonym of John M. Kimbro, 1929- . Other pseudonym: Charlotte Bramwell, q.v.
The Broken Sphinx. Popular Library, 1972
The Children of Houndstooth. Popular Library, 1972
The Heiress to Wolfskill. Popular Library, 1973
The House on Windswept Ridge. Popular Library, 1971
The Phantom Flame of Wind House. Popular Library, 1973
The Shadow over Pleasant Heath. Popular Library, 1974
A Shriek in the Midnight Tower. Popular Library, 1975
The Spectre of Dolphin Cove. Popular Library, 1973
Thanesworth House. Popular Library, 1972
The Three Sisters of Briarwick. Popular Library, 1973
The Twisted Cameo. Pouplar Library, 1971
Unseen Torment. Popular Library, 1974

KIMMINS, ANTHONY (MARTIN)
Lugs O'Leary. Heinemann, 1960

KINDON, THOMAS
Murder in the Moor. Methuen, 1929; Dutton, 1929

KING, ALICE
A Strange Tangle. Maxwell, 1888

KING, (WILLIAM BENJAMIN) BASIL. 1859-1928.
The Break of Day. Harper, 1930

KING, BRADLEY. See: TALBOT MUNDY.

KING, C(HARLES) DALY. 1895-1963. Series character: Michael Lord = ML.
Arrogant Alibi. Appleton, 1939; Collins, 1938 ML
Bermuda Burial. Funk, 1941; Collins, 1940 ML
Careless Corpse. Collins, 1937 ML
The Curious Mr. Tarrant. Dover, 1977; Collins, 1935 ss
Obelists at Sea. Knopf, 1933; Heritage, 1932
Obelists en Route. Collins, 1934 ML
Obelists Fly High. H. Smith, 1935; Collins, 1935 ML

KING, CHRISTOPHER
-Operation Mora. Hale, 1974

KING, (JAMES) CLIFFORD. 1914- . Pseudonym: Pete Fry, q.v.
Bitter Springs. Convoy, 1950. (Novelization of the movie.)
End in Sight. Hutchinson, 1956
A Place to Hide. Hart-Davis, 1951
Two Shadows Pass. Hart-Davis, 1952

KING, FRANCIS (HENRY). 1923- .
-An Air That Kills. Home, 1948
-The Brighton Belle and other stories. Longmans, 1968 ss
-The Custom House. Longmans, 1961; Doubleday, 1962
-A Domestic Animal. Longmans, 1969
-The Japanese Umbrella and other stories. Longmans, 1964 ss
-The Last of the Pleasure Gardens. Longmans, 1965
The Needle. Hutchinson, 1975; Mason/Charter, 1976
-Never Again. Home, 1947
-So Hurt and Humiliated and other stories. Longmans, 1959 ss
-To the Dark Tower. Home, 1946
-The Waves Behind the Boat. Longmans, 1967
-The Widow. Longmans, 1957

KING, FRANK. 1892-1958. Pseudonym: Clive Conrad, q.v. Series characters: The Dormouse, in at least those marked D; Dr. Frank King, in at least those marked FK; Inspector/Superintendent Gloom, in at least those marked G; Clarence Knight, in at least those marked CK.
The Big Blackmail. Hale, 1954 D
Candidates for Murder. Hale, 1945
The Case of the Frightened Brother. Hale, 1959 D
The Case of the Painted Girl. Jarrolds, 1931 G
The Case of the Strange Beauties. Hale, 1952 D
The Case of the Vanishing Artist. Hale, 1956 G
The Catastrophe Club. Hale, 1947 D
Crooks' Caravan. Hale, 1955 D
Crooks' Cross. Hale, 1943 D
Death Changes his Mind. Hale, 1953 FK
Death has a Double. Hale, 1955 FK
Death of a Cloven Hoof. Hale, 1951 FK
Death of a Halo. Hale, 1950 FK
Dictator of Death. Jarrolds, 1935
The Dormouse has Nine Lives. Hale, 1938 D
The Dormouse—Peacemaker. Hale, 1938 D
The Dormouse—Undertaker. Hale, 1937 D
Dough for the Dormouse. Hale, 1939 D
The Empty Flat. Hale, 1957 D
Enter the Dormouse. Hale, 1936 D
Gestapo Dormouse. Hale, 1944 D
The Ghoul. Bles, 1928; Watt, 1929 CK
Green Gold. Jarrolds, 1933 G
Greenface. Jarrolds, 1929 CK
The House of Sleep. Jarrolds, 1934
The Midnight Sleep. Hale, 1941
Molly on the Spot. Hale, 1940 ss
Mr. Balkram's Band. Jarrolds, 1934
Night at Krumlin Castle. Jarrolds, 1932
Only Half the Doctor Died. Hale, 1954

Operation Halter. Hale, 1948 D
Operation Honeymoon. Hale, 1950 D
The Owl. Jarrolds, 1930; Watt, 1930 CK
Sinister Light. Hale, 1946 D
The Smiling Mask. Jarrolds, 1935
Terror at Staups House. Bles, 1927; Watt, 1929
That Charming Crook. Hale, 1958 D
They Vanish at Night. Hale, 1941 D
This Doll is Dangerous. Hale, 1940 D
The Two Who Talked. Hale, 1958 D
What Price Doubloons? Hale, 1942 D

KING, HAROLD. 1945- .
Paradigm Red. Bobbs, 1975

KING, HILARY. Pseudonym of James Grierson Dickson. All titles below feature Sexton Blake and were published by Amalgamated Press.
The Big Circus Mystery. 1953
The Crime at the Fair. 1953
The Man from Dieppe. 1952
The Mystery of the Lost Loot. 1951
On the 11:40 Down. 1951
Partners in Crime. 1951

KING, IRENE, 1943- , and CARYL THURMAN, 1938- .
She's a Cop, Ain't She?, with W. Ware Lynch. Dial, 1975

KING, LOUIS
Cornered. Ace, 1958

KING, LOUISE W(OOSTER)
The Rochemer Hag. Doubleday, 1967

KING, O. B.
Five Million in Cash. Doubleday, 1932; Jarrolds, 1933

KING, PHILIP. See: A(RTHUR) A(LEXANDER MALCOLM) THOMSON, 1894- .

KING, R(ICHARD) ASHE. 1839-1932.
-Love's Legacy. Ward, 1890

KING, RUFUS (FREDERICK). 1893-1966.
Series character: Lt. Valcour = V.
The Case of the Constant God. Doubleday, 1936; Methuen, 1938 V
The Case of the Dowager's Etchings. Doubleday, 1944; Methuen, 1946. Also published as: Never Walk Alone. Popular Library, 1951
The Case of the Redoubled Cross. Doubleday, 1949
Crime of Violence. Doubleday, 1937; Methuen, 1938 V
The Deadly Dove. Doubleday, 1945
Design in Evil. Doubleday, 1942
Diagnosis: Murder. Doubleday, 1941; Methuen, 1942 ss
Duenna to a Murder. Doubleday, 1951; Methuen, 1951
The Faces of Danger. Doubleday, 1964 ss
The Fatal Kiss Mystery. Doubleday, 1928
Holiday Homicide. Doubleday, 1940; Methuen, 1941
I Want a Policeman!, with Milton Lazarus. Dramatists' Play Service, 1937. (A play.)
Invitation to a Murder. French, 1934. (3-act play.)
The Lesser Antilles Case. Doubleday, 1934. Also published as: Murder Challenges Valcour. Dell, 1944
Lethal Lady. Doubleday, 1947
Malice in Wonderland. Doubleday, 1958 ss
Murder by Latitude. Doubleday, 1930; Heinemann, 1931 V
Murder by the Clock. Doubleday, 1929; Chapman, 1929 V
Murder Challenges Valcour; see The Lesser Antilles Case

Murder DeLuxe; see Mystery DeLuxe
Murder Masks Miami. Doubleday, 1939; Methuen, 1939 V
Murder in the Willett Family. Doubleday, 1931 V
Murder on the Yacht. Doubleday, 1932; H. Hamilton, 1932 V
A Murderer in This House; see Somewhere in This House
Museum Piece No. 13. Doubleday, 1946. Also published as: Secret Beyond the Door. Triangle, 1947
Mystery DeLuxe. Doran, 1927. British title: Murder DeLuxe. Parsons, 1927
Never Walk Alone; see The Case of the Dowager's Etchings
Profile of a Murder. Harcourt, 1935 V
Secret Beyond the Door; see Museum Piece No. 13
Somewhere in This House. Doubleday, 1930. British title: A Woman is Dead. Chapman, 1929. Also published as: A Murderer in This House. Detective Novel Classic, 1945 (abridged) V
The Steps to Murder. Doubleday, 1960 ss
Valcour Meets Murder. Doubleday, 1932 V
A Variety of Weapons. Doubleday, 1943
A Woman is Dead; see Somewhere in This House

KING, (RAYMOND) SHERWOOD. 1904- .
Between Murders. Appleton, 1935, as by Sherry King. British title: Death Carries a Cane. Cherry Tree, 1941
Death Carries a Cane; see Between Murders
If I Die Before I Wake. Simon, 1938; World's Work, 1938. Also published as: The Lady from Shanghai. World's Work, 1947
The Lady from Shanghai; see If I Die Before I Wake

KING, T. STANLEYAN. Series characters: Dixon Brett, in at least those marked DB; Scarsdale Waring, in at least those marked SW.
Black Magic. Mellifont, 1934 SW
The Call of Death. Mellifont, 1934 SW
The Fatal Image. Mellifont, 1940
The Headless Ghost. Mellifont, 1932
The Kidnapped Prince. Mellifont, 1932
The Missing Mayor. Aldine, 1926 DB
The Monk's Croft Mystery. Mellifont, 1933
The Motor Horn Mystery. Mellifont, 1932
The Mummy's Curse. Mellifont, 1933
Slayer of Souls. Mellifont, 1932
Vampire City. Mellifont, 1935 SW
Viola's Dilemma. Mellifont, 1932
Who Killed Stephen Tennant? Aldine, 1926
The Yellow Wolf. Aldine, 1926 DB

KING, TERRY JOHNSON. 1929-1978.
The Neutron Beam Murder. Abelard (New York & London), 1965
The Noose of Red Beads. Abelard (New York), 1968; Abelard (London), 1969

KING, THOROLD. Pseudonym of Charles Gatchell, 1851-1910.
Hashish. McClurg, 1886

KING, W. SCOTT. Pseudonym of William Kingscote Greenland.
Behind the Granite Gateway. Hodder, 1902
-Hidden Paths. Epworth, 1920

KINGERY, DON
Death Must Wait. GM, 1956
-Paula. Dell, 1959
-Swamp Fire. Popular Library, 1957

KINGSBURY, MYRA
Beware the Bog. Ballantine, 1975
Island of Fog. Ballantine, 1974

KINGSCOTE, ADELINE GEORGINA ISABELLA. -1908. Pseudonym: Lucas Cleeve, q.v.

KINGSLEY, BETTINA. Pseudonym of Barry Jay Kaplan.
The Black Angel. PB, 1974
Blind Chance. Dell, 1974
The Captive. Dell, 1974
Darwich Castle. Dell, 1974
The House on the Drive. Dell, 1975; New English Library pb, 1977
Stages of Terror. Popular Library, 1972
The Stand In. Dell, 1973

KINGSLEY, MICHAEL J. 1917?-1972.
Black Man, White Man, Dead Man. Random, 1970
Branches of Evil; see Shadow over Elveron
Shadow over Elveron. Random, 1963. Also published as: Branches of Evil. Macfadden, 1964

KINGSLEY, SIDNEY. 1906- .
Darkness at Noon. Random, 1951. (Play based on the novel by Arthur Koestler, 1905- , q.v.)
Detective Story. Random, 1949. (Play.)

KINGSLEY-SMITH, TERENCE. 1940- .
The Forsaken. PB, 1975

KINGSTON, CHARLES. Pseudonym of Charles Kingston O'Mahoney. Series character: Inspector Wake, in at least those marked W.
The Brighton Beach Mystery. Ward, 1936 M
Burning Conscience. Ward, 1938
The Circle of Guilt. Ward, 1937 W
Death Came Back. Paul, 1944 W
The Delacott Mystery. Ward, 1941
Fear Followed On. Paul, 1945 W
The Great London Mystery. Lane, 1931
The Guilty House. Lane, 1928; Dutton, 1929
The Highgate Mystery. Lane, 1928
I Accuse. Mellifont, 1939
The Infallible System. Lane, 1929
A Miscarriage of Justice. Paul, 1925
Murder in Disguise. Ward, 1938 W
Murder in Piccadilly. Ward, 1936 W
Murder Tunes In. Ward, 1942
Mystery in the Mist. Ward, 1942
Poison in Kensington. Ward, 1934
The Portland Place Mystery. Paul, 1925
The Rigdale Puzzle. Ward, 1937 W
The Secret Barrier. Ward, 1939
The Shadow of Monte Carlo and other stories. Richards, 1931 ss
Six Under Suspicion. Ward, 1940
Slander Villa. Ward, 1939
-Stolen Virtue. Paul, 1921
-Vain Pride. Ward, 1941

KINGSTON, KEEDY
The Great Pimlico Mystery. Diprose, 1896

KINLAY, ALVIN
Killers Cannot Live. Micron, 1961

KINNELL, GALWAY. 1927- .
Black Light. Houghton, 1966; Hart-Davis, 1967

KINNEY, THOMAS. Pseudonym of Curtis Thomas.
Devil Take the Foremost. Doubleday, 1947

KINSBURN, EMART. Pseudonym of Arthur P(reston) Hankins, 1880-1932, q.v.
  The Wizard's Spyglass. Chelsea, 1926

KINSLEY, PETER
  Pimpernel 60. Joseph, 1968; Dutton, 1968

KIPLEY, JOSEPH
  The Ice Pond Mystery. Laird, 1889

KIPPAX, PETER
  Goring's First Case. Joseph, 1936

KIRBY, ARTHUR. Pseudonym of Arthur (George) MacLean, q.v. Both titles below feature Sexton Blake and were published by Amalgamated Press.
  High Summer Homicide. 1962
  Man on the Run! 1960

KIRBY, DALLAS. Series character: Victor Garrison, in at least those marked VG.
  Carnival of Death. Swan, 1942
  Death at my Heels. Swan, 1942
  Death Man. Swan, 1943
  Victor. Swan, 1942 VG
  Victor Versus Verhasst. Swan, 1943 VG

KIRBY, R.
  East Side Assignment. Hamilton Stafford, 1950
  Newshound's Nemesis. Hamilton Stafford, 1949
  Why Call It Homicide? Hamilton Stafford, 1950

KIRK, LAURENCE. Pseudonym of Eric Andrew Simson, 1895-
  -Dangerous Cross-Roads. Hutchinson, 1928
  The Farm at Paranao; see The Farm at Sante Fe
  The Farm at Sante Fe. Heinemann, 1935. U.S. title: The Farm at Paranao. Doubleday, 1935
  -Flight Errant. Hutchinson, 1929
  -The Gale of the World. Cassell, 1948
  -Halfway to Paradise. Blackwood, 1951
  -Matrimonial Causes. Cassell, 1949 ss
  -Mushrooms on Toast. Heinemann, 1938 ss
  -One More River. Hutchinson, 1929
  -Red Herrings Ltd. Cassell, 1940
  Rings on her Finger. Heinemann, 1936; Doubleday, 1936
  -Treasure on Earth. Heinemann, 1937
  Whispering Tongues. Heinemann, 1934; Doubleday, 1934

KIRK, LYDIA
  The Cuernavaca Question. Doubleday, 1974
  The Embassy Madonna. Doubleday, 1971
  The Man on the Raffles Verandah. Doubleday, 1969

KIRK, MICHAEL. Pseudonym of Bill Knox, 1928-   , q.v. Other pseudonyms: Robert MacLeod, q.v., Noah Webster.

KIRK, RUSSELL (AMOS). 1918-   .
  Lost Lake; see The Surly Sullen Bell
  Old House of Fear. Fleet, 1961; Gollancz, 1962
  The Surly Sullen Bell. Fleet, 1962. Also published as: Lost Lake. Paperback Library, 1966 ss

KIRKBRIDE, RONALD (DE LEVINGTON). 1912-   .
  A Girl Named Tamiko; see Tamiko
  -Jenny Wren. Angus, 1957
  Katrina. Allen, 1970
  -Only the Unafraid. Barker, 1953
  The Secret Journey. Barker, 1965
  The Short Night. Barker, 1968

  -Song of the Undersea. Cassell, 1964; Astor-Honor, 1967
  -Tamiko. Cassell, 1959. U.S. title: A Girl Named Tamiko. Fell, 1959
  -Yuki. Barker, 1967

KIRKWOOD, JAMES
  P.S. Your Cat is Dead. Stein, 1972; Quartet, 1974
  Some Kind of Hero. Crowell, 1975

KIRSCH, ROBERT R. 1922-   . Pseudonym: Robert Dundee, q.v.

KIRST, HANS HELLMUT. 1914-   . Series character: Supt. Konstantin Keller = KK.
  The Adventures of Private Faust; see Who's in Charge Here?
  Brothers in Arms. Collins, 1965; Harper, 1967. (Translation of Kameraden. Munich, 1961.)
  Camp 7 Last Stop. Collins, 1969. U.S. title: Last Stop Camp 7. Coward, 1969. (Translation of Letzte Station Camp 7. Munich, 1966.)
  Damned to Success; see A Time for Scandal
  Death Plays the Last Card. Fontana, 1968. U.S. title: The Last Card. Pyramid, 1967. (Translation of Die Letzte Karte Spielt der Tod. Munich, 1955.)
  -The Fox of Maulen. Collins, 1968. U.S. title: The Wolves. Coward, 1968. (Translation of Die Wolfe. Munich, 1967.)
  Hero in the Tower. Collins, 1972; Coward, 1972. (Translation of Held im Turm. Munich, 1970.)
  The Last Card; see Death Plays the Last Card
  Last Stop Camp 7; see Camp 7 Last Stop
  -The Lieutenant Must be Mad. Harrap, 1951. (Translation of Wir Nannten Ihn Galgenstrick. Munich, 1950.)
  The Night of the Generals. Collins, 1963; Harper, 1963. (Translation of Die Nacht der Generale. Munich, 1962.)
  No Fatherland; see Undercover Man
  The Officer Factory. Collins, 1962; Doubleday, 1963. (Translation of Fabrik der Offiziere. Munich, 1960.)
  Soldiers' Revolt; see The 20th of July
  A Time for Scandal. Collins, 1973. U.S. title: Damned to Success. Coward, 1973. (Translation of Verdammt zum Erfolg. Munich, 1971.) KK
  A Time for Truth. Collins, 1974; Coward, 1974. (Translation of Verurteilt zur Wahrheit. Munich, 1972.) KK
  -The 20th of July. Collins, 1966. U.S. title: Soldiers' Revolt. Harper, 1966. (Translation of Aufstand der Soldaten. Munich, 1965.)
  Undercover Man. Collins, 1970. U.S. title: No Fatherland. Coward, 1970. (Translation of Kein Vaterland. Munich, 1968.)
  -Who's in Charge Here? Collins, 1971. U.S. title: The Adventures of Private Faust. Coward, 1971. (Translation of Faustrecht. Munich, 1969.)

KISTLER, MARY
  The Night of the Tiger. Lancer, 1972

KITCHIN, C(LIFFORD) H(ENRY) B(ENN). 1895-1967. Series character: Malcolm Warren, in all titles.
  The Cornish Fox. Secker, 1949

  Crime at Christmas. Woolf, 1934; Harcourt, 1935
  Death of his Uncle. Constable, 1939
  Death of my Aunt. Woolf, 1929; Harcourt, 1935

KITCHIN, FREDERICK HARCOURT. 1867-1932. Pseudonym: Bennet Copplestone, q.v.
  Dead Men's Tales. Blackwood, 1926; Houghton, 1926, as by Bennet Copplestone ss

KLAINER, ALBERT S. Joint pseudonym with Joann Klainer: L. T. Peters, q.v.

KLAINER, JOANN. Joint pseudonym with Albert S. Klainer: L. T. Peters, q.v.

KLEIN, ERNST. 1876-   .
  The Blackmailer. Avon, 1952
  The Stolen Bride. Nisbet, 1930

KLEIN, KATE
  Plain Unvarnished Murder, with Roslyn S. Hastings, q.v. Arcadia, 1959
  The Seaway Tombstone. Arcadia, 1961

KLEIN, NORMAN
  The Destroying Angel. Farrar, 1933
  No! No! the Woman! Farrar, 1932
  Terror by Night. Farrar, 1935

KLINGER, HENRY. Series character: Lt. Shomri Shomar, in all titles.
  Essence of Murder. Perma, 1963
  Lust for Murder. Trident, 1966
  Murder Off Broadway. Perma, 1962
  Wanton for Murder. Perma, 1961

KLINGSBERG, HARRY (M.)
  Doowinkle, D.A. Dial, 1940 ss

KLOP, THOMAS
  Harmattan. Bobbs, 1975

KLOSE, KEVIN, 1940-   , and PHILIP A(LGIE) McCOMBS, 1944-   .
  The Typhoon Shipments. Norton, 1974

KNAPP, G(EORGE) L(EONARD). 1872-   .
  The Face of Air. Lane (New York & London), 1912
  The Scales of Justice. Lippincott, 1910

KNAPP, GREGORY C(ROMWELL)
  Stranglehold. Little, 1973

KNEBEL, FLETCHER. 1911-   .
  The Bottom Line. Doubleday, 1974; Hodder, 1975
  Convention, with Charles W. Bailey II, 1929-   . Harper, 1964; Weidenfeld, 1964
  Dark Horse. Doubleday, 1972; Hodder, 1973
  Night of Camp David. Harper, 1965; Weidenfeld, 1965
  Seven Days in May, with Charles W. Bailey II, 1929-   . Harper, 1962; Weidenfeld, 1962
  Trespass. Doubleday, 1969; Allen, 1969
  Vanished. Doubleday, 1968; Allen, 1968
  The Zinzin Road. Harper, 1966; Allen, 1967

KNEVELS, GERTRUDE. 1881-1962.
  By Candle-Light. Appleton, 1926
  Death on the Clock. Doubleday, 1940
  The Diamond Rose Mystery. Appleton, 1928
  Octagon House. Appleton, 1925
  Out of the Dark. Penn, 1932

KNIGHT, ADAM. Pseudonym of Lawrence Lariar, 1908-   , q.v. Other pseudonyms: Michael Lawrence, Michael Stark, qq.v. Series character: Steve

Conacher, in at least those marked SC.
Girl Running. Signet, 1956 SC
I'll Kill You Next! Appleton, 1954 SC
Kiss and Kill. Crown, 1953 SC
Knife at my Back. Crown, 1952 SC
Murder for Madame. Crown, 1951 SC
Stone Cold Blonde. Crown, 1951 SC
Sugar Shannon. Belmont, 1960
The Sunburned Corpse. Crown, 1952 SC
Triple Slay. Signet, 1959 SC

KNIGHT, ALANNA
Castle Clodha. Avon, 1972
Lament for Lost Lovers. Avon, 1973
Legend of the Loch. Lancer, 1970
October Witch. Lancer, 1971
The White Rose. Avon, 1974

KNIGHT, BERNARD. 1931-   . Pseudonym: Bernard Picton, q.v.

KNIGHT, CLIFFORD (REYNOLDS). 1886-   .
Series character: Huntoon Rogers = HR.
The Affair at Palm Springs. Dodd, 1938 HR
The Affair in Death Valley. Dodd, 1940 HR
The Affair of the Black Sombrero. Dodd, 1939 HR
The Affair of the Circus Queen. Dodd, 1940 HR
The Affair of the Corpse Escort. McKay, 1946 HR
The Affair of the Crimson Gull. Dodd, 1941 HR
The Affair of the Dead Stranger. Dodd, 1944 HR
The Affair of the Fainting Butler. Dodd, 1943 HR
The Affair of the Ginger Lei. Dodd, 1938 HR
The Affair of the Golden Buzzard. McKay, 1946 HR
The Affair of the Heavenly Voice. Dodd, 1937; Hale, 1938 HR
The Affair of the Jade Monkey. Dodd, 1943 HR
The Affair of the Limping Sailor. Dodd, 1942 HR
The Affair of the Scarlet Crab. Dodd, 1937; Gollancz, 1937 HR
The Affair of the Sixth Button. McKay, 1947 HR
The Affair of the Skiing Clown. Dodd, 1941 HR
The Affair of the Splintered Heart. Dodd, 1942 HR
The Affair on the Painted Desert. Dodd, 1939 HR
Dark Abyss. Dutton, 1949
The Dark Road. Dutton, 1951
Death and Little Brother. Dutton, 1952
Death of a Big Shot. Dutton, 1951
Hangman's Choice. Dutton, 1949
The Yellow Cat. Dutton, 1950

KNIGHT, DAVID. Pseudonym of Richard S(cott) Prather, 1921-   , q.v.
Other pseudonyms: Douglas Ring, q.v.
Series character: Shell Scott = SS (continued under the Prather byline).
Case No. 561: Dragnet; see Dragnet: Case No. 561
Dragnet: Case No. 561. PB, 1956. British title: Case No. 561: Dragnet. WDL, 1957. (Novelization of the TV series.)
Pattern for Murder. Graphic, 1952. Also published as: The Scrambled Yeggs, as by Richard S. Prather. GM, 1958; Muller pb, 1961 SS
The Scrambled Yeggs; see Pattern for Murder

KNIGHT, EDWARD FREDERICK. 1852-1925.
A Desperate Voyage. Milne, 1898
-Save Me from my Friends. Longmans, 1891
The Threatening Eye. Vizetelly, 1885

KNIGHT, ERIC MOWBRAY. 1897-1943. Pseudonym: Richard Hallas, q.v.

KNIGHT, FRANK [FRANCIS EDGAR KNIGHT]. 1905-   .
-Captains of the "Calabar". Ward, 1961
-Pekoe Reef. Ward, 1962
-The Sea's Fool. Ward, 1960

KNIGHT, H.
The Mystery of Stephen Claverton & Co. Routledge, 1894

KNIGHT, KATHLEEN MOORE. Pseudonym: Alan Amos, q.v. Series characters: Margot Blair = MB; Elisha Macomber = EM.
Acts of Black Night. Doubleday, 1938 EM
Akin to Murder. Doubleday, 1953; Hammond, 1955 EM
Bait for Murder. Doubleday, 1948; Hammond, 1952 EM
The Bass Derby Murder. Doubleday, 1949; Hammond, 1953 EM
Beauty is a Beast. Doubleday, 1959; Hammond, 1960 EM
Bells for the Dead. Doubleday, 1942; Cherry Tree, 1943 EM
Birds of Ill Omen. Doubleday, 1948; Hammond, 1951
The Blue Horse of Taxco. Doubleday, 1947; Hammond, 1950
The Case of the Tainted Token; see The Tainted Token
The Clue of the Poor Man's Shilling. Doubleday, 1936. British title: The Poor Man's Shilling. Hammond, 1947 EM
A Cry in the Jungle. Hammond, 1958. (U.S. title?)
Death Blew Out the Match. Doubleday, 1935; Heinemann, 1935 EM
Death Came Dancing. Doubleday, 1940; Cherry Tree, 1946 EM
Death Goes to a Reunion. Doubleday, 1952; Hammond, 1954 EM
Design in Diamonds. Doubleday, 1944; Hammond, 1945 MB
Dying Echo. Doubleday, 1949; Hammond, 1952
Exit a Star. Doubleday, 1941; Cherry Tree, 1943 MB
Footbridge to Death. Doubleday, 1947; Hammond, 1949 EM
High Rendezvous. Doubleday, 1954; Hammond, 1956
Intrigue for Empire. Doubleday, 1944; Hammond, 1946. Also published as: Murder for Empire. Thriller Novel Classic, 194? (abridged)
Invitation to Vengeance. Doubleday, 1960; Hammond, 1961
Murder for Empire; see Intrigue for Empire
Murder Greets Jean Holton; see The Wheel That Turned
The Poor Man's Shilling; see The Clue of the Poor Man's Shilling
Port of Seven Strangers. Doubleday, 1945; Hammond, 1948
Rendezvous with the Past. Doubleday, 1940; Cherry Tree, 1951 MB
The Robineau Look. Doubleday, 1955. British title: The Robineau Murders. Hammond, 1956
The Robineau Murders; see The Robineau Look
Seven were Suspect; see Seven were Veiled
Seven were Veiled. Doubleday, 1937. British title: Seven were Suspect. Cherry Tree, 1942 EM

The Silent Partner. Doubleday, 1950; Hammond, 1953
Stream Sinister. Doubleday, 1945; Hammond, 1948
The Tainted Token. Doubleday, 1938; Cherry Tree, 1942. Also published as: The Case of the Tainted Token. Mystery Novel Classic, 1943 EM
Terror by Twilight. Doubleday, 1942; Cherry Tree, 1943 EM
They're Going to Kill Me. Doubleday, 1955; Hammond, 1957
Three of Diamonds. Doubleday, 1953; Hammond, 1955 EM
Trademark of a Traitor. Doubleday, 1943; Hammond, 1945
The Trouble at Turkey Hill. Doubleday, 1946; Hammond, 1949 EM
Valse Macabre. Doubleday, 1952; Hammond, 1955 EM
The Wheel That Turned. Doubleday, 1936. Also published as: Murder Greets Jean Holton. Thriller Novel Classic, 194? EM

KNIGHT, LEONARD A(LFRED). 1895-   .
Series character: Jerry Scant, in at least those marked JS.
The Astounding Dr. Yell. Low, 1950
The Brazen Head. Low, 1948
Close the Frontier. Low, 1939
Conqueror's Road. Low, 1945
Contraband. Low, 1949
The Creaking Tree Mystery. Low, 1931 JS
The Creeping Death. Low, 1933 JS
The Dancing Stones. Low, 1946
Dangerous Knowledge. Low, 1950
Deadman's Bay. Low, 1930 JS
Death Stands Near. Low, 1936
High Treason. Gryphon, 1954
Judgment Rock. Low, 1947
Man Hunt. Low, 1930
The Morlo. Gryphon, 1956
Murder by Experiment. Low, 1935 JS
Night Express Murder. Low, 1936
One Way Only. Gryphon, 1956
The Pawn. Low, 1931
The Paying Guest. Low, 1951
Redbeard. Low, 1935
The Riddle of Nap's Hollow. Low, 1932
Rider in the Sky. Gryphon, 1953
The S. S. Mystery. Low, 1938
The Solander Box Mystery. Low, 1940 JS
Spanish Cove. Low, 1945
Spring Cruise. Low, 1934
Super-Cinema Murder. Low, 1937
The Valley of Green Shadows. Gryphon, 1955
The Viking Feast Mystery. Low, 1951

KNIGHT, MALCOLM
Kiss of Death. Merit (Chicago), 1960

KNIGHT, MAXWELL
Crime Cargo. Allan, 1934
Gunman's Holiday. Allan, 1935

KNIPE, EMILIE BENSON. 1870-1958. Pseudonym: Therese Benson, q.v.

KNIPSCHEER, JAMES M. W. Pseudonym: James M. Fox, q.v.

KNOBLOCK, K(ENNETH) T(HOMAS). 1898-   .
Murder in the Mind. Harper, 1932
Take Up the Bodies. Harper, 1935
There's Been Murder Done. Harper, 1931; Selwyn, 1931

KNOTT, FREDERICK (M. P.). 1918-   .
Dial "M" for Murder. Random, 1953; French (London), 1955. (A play.)
Wait Until Dark. Dramatists Play Service, 1967; French (London), 1968. (A play.)

Write Me a Murder. Dramatists Play Service, 1962; French (London), 1963. (A play.)

KNOTTS, RAYMOND. Pseudonym of Gordon Volk, 1885-   , q.v.
Meeting by Moonlight. Doubleday, 1946. (British title?)

KNOWLAND, HELEN (DAVIS HERRICK)
Madame Baltimore. Dodd, 1949. Also published as: Baltimore Madame. Mercury, 1954

KNOWLER, JOHN. 1932-   .
Divinitas. Cape, 1969. Also published as: Seeds of Corruption. Corgi, 1971
Seeds of Corruption; see Divinitas
The Singing Lizard. Cape, 1967; Farrar, 1967
The Trap. Cape, 1964; Knopf, 1965

KNOWLES, MABEL WINIFRED. Pseudonym: Lester Lurgan, q.v.

KNOWLTON, EDWARD ROGERS. 1909-   . Pseudonym: Kerk Rogers, q.v.
The Codfish Watch. Lenox, 1970

KNOWLTON, ROBERT A(LMY). 1914-   .
Court of Crows. Gollancz, 1961; Harper, 1961

KNOWLTON, WINTHROP. See: GEORGE (J. W.) GOODMAN, 1930-   .

KNOX, BILL [WILLIAM KNOX]. 1928-   .
Pseudonyms: Robert MacLeod, q.v., Michael Kirk, Noah Webster. Series characters: Colin Thane & Phil Moss = T&M; Webb Carrick = WC.
Blacklight. Long, 1967; Doubleday, 1967 WC
Blueback. Long, 1969; Doubleday, 1969 WC
Children of the Mist. Long, 1970. U.S. title: Who Shot the Bull? Doubleday, 1970 T&M
The Cockatoo Crime. Long, 1958
Deadline for a Dream. Long, 1957. U.S. title: In at the Kill. Doubleday, 1961 T&M
Death Calls the Shots. Long, 1961
Death Department. Long, 1959 T&M
The Deep Fall. Long, 1966. U.S. title: The Ghost Car. Doubleday, 1966 T&M
Devilweed. Long, 1966; Doubleday, 1966 WC
Die for Big Betsy. Long, 1961
Draw Batons! Long, 1973; Doubleday, 1973 T&M
Figurehead; see The Klondyker
The Ghost Car; see The Deep Fall
In at the Kill; see Deadline for a Dream
Justice on the Rocks. Long, 1967; Doubleday, 1967 T&M
The Killing Game; see The Man in the Bottle
The Klondyker. Long, 1968. U.S. title: Figurehead. Doubleday, 1968 WC
Leave It to the Hangman. Long, 1960; Doubleday, 1960 T&M
Little Drops of Blood. Long, 1962; Doubleday, 1962 T&M
The Man in the Bottle. Long, 1963. U.S. title: The Killing Game. Doubleday, 1963 T&M
Rally to Kill. Long, 1975; Doubleday, 1975 T&M
Sanctuary Isle. Long, 1962. U.S. title: The Grey Sentinels. Doubleday, 1963 T&M
The Scavengers. Long, 1964; Doubleday, 1964 WC
Seafire. Long, 1970; Doubleday, 1971 WC
Stormtide. Long, 1972; Doubleday, 1973 WC

The Tallyman. Long, 1969; Doubleday, 1969 T&M
The Taste of Proof. Long, 1965; Doubleday, 1965 T&M
To Kill a Witch. Long, 1971; Doubleday, 1972 T&M
The View from Daniel Pike, with Edward Boyd, q.v. Hutchinson, 1974; St. Martin's, 1974 ss
Whitewater. Long, 1974; Doubleday, 1974 WC
Who Shot the Bull?; see Children of the Mist

KNOX, RONALD A(RBUTHNOTT). 1888-1957. Series character: Miles Bredon = MB.
The Body in the Silo. Hodder, 1933. U.S. title: Settled Out of Court. Dutton, 1934 MB
Double Cross Purposes. Hodder, 1937 MB
The Footsteps at the Lock. Methuen, 1928 MB
Settled Out of Court; see The Body in the Silo
Still Dead. Hodder, 1934; Dutton, 1934 MB
The Three Taps. Methuen, 1927; Simon, 1927 MB
The Viaduct Murder. Methuen, 1925; Simon, 1926

KNOX, TIMOTHY
Death in the State House. Houghton, 1934

KNYE, CASSANDRA
The Castle and the Key. Paperback Library, 1967
The House That Fear Built. Paperback Library, 1966

KOEHLER, ROBERT PORTNER. 1905-   . Series characters: Avery Gregg and Tony Ellis = G&E; Pecos Appleby = PA; Al Branson = AB.
The Blue Parakeet Murders. Phoenix, 1948 G&E
The Case of the Dead Cadet. Phoenix, 1938
Corpse in the Wind. Phoenix, 1944
The Doctor's Murder Case. Phoenix, 1939
Here Come the Dead. Phoenix, 1942 PA
The Hooded Vulture Murders. Phoenix, 1947 G&E
Murder Expert. Phoenix, 1945 AB
Murder in the Green Sedan. Phoenix, 1942 PA
Puppets of Chance. Sears, 1933
The Road House Murders. Phoenix, 1946; Boardman, 1948 G&E
Salute to Murder. Phoenix, 1944
Sing a Song of Murder. Phoenix, 1941 PA
Some Try Murder. Phoenix, 1943 PA
Steps to Murder. Phoenix, 1943; Boardman, 1944 AB
Tread Gently, Death. Phoenix, 1945 AB

KOENIG, LAIRD (P.). See also: PETER L(EE) DIXON, 1932-   .
The Little Girl Who Lives Down the Lane. Coward, 1974; Souvenir, 1974

KOESTLER, ARTHUR. 1905-   .
Darkness at Noon. Cape, 1940; Macmillan, 1941. Play version: see Sidney Kingsley, 1906-   .

KOLB, KEN(NETH). 1926-   .
The Couch Trip. Random, 1970
Night Crossing. Playboy Press, 1974

KOLBE, JOHN A.
The Riddle of the Keys. Fiction House, 1937
Vampires of Vengeance. Fiction House, 1935

KONING, HANS
The Petersburg-Cannes Express. Harcourt, 1975; H. Hamilton, 1975

KONVITZ, JEFFREY. 1944-   .
The Sentinel. Simon, 1974; Secker, 1974

KOONCE, CHARLES
The Weeping Willow Murders. Burton, 1934

KOONTZ, DEAN R(AY). 1945-   . Pseudonyms: Brian Coffey, K. R. Dwyer, qq.v.
After the Last Race. Atheneum, 1974
-A Werewolf Among Us. Ballantine, 1973

KOOTZ, (SAMUEL MELVIN). 1898-   . Series character: Jason Emory, in both titles.
Puzzle in Paint. Crown, 1943
Puzzle in Petticoats. Crown, 1944

KORNBLUTH, C(YRIL) M. 1923-1958. Pseudonyms: Simon Eisner, Jordan Park, qq.v.
The Syndic. Doubleday, 1953; Sphere, 1968
Takeoff. Doubleday, 1952

KOROTKIN, JUDITH. 1931-   .
Spotlight. Popular Library, 1974

KOSINSKI, JERZY (NIKODEM). 1933-   .
Cockpit. Houghton, 1975; Hutchinson, 1975

KOSKI, DOMINIC. See: VIRGIL (JOSEPH) SCOTT, 1914-   .

KOSTA, VICTOR. Pseudonym of Georges Simenon, 1903-   , q.v.

KOVALSKY, J. B.
The Early Days of August. Caravelle, 1967
The Runner is Red. Caravelle, 1967

KOZHEVNIKOV, VADIM
Shield and Sword. MacGibbon, 1971. (Translation of Shchit i Mech. Moscow, 1966.)

KRAMER, KARL. Pseudonym of Edward A. Morris.
-Action Along the Humboldt. Ace, 1956
Deadly September. Monarch, 1960
-Fair Game. Popular Library, 1955
A Flame Too Hot. Monarch, 1964
Kiss Me Quick. Monarch, 1959
Not for a Curse. Monarch, 1959

KRASLOW, DAVID, 1926-   , and R(OBERT) S. BOYD, 1928-   .
A Certain Evil. Little, 1965; Barker, 1966

KRASNER, WILLIAM. 1917-   . Series character: Sam Birge, in all titles.
The Gambler. Harper, 1950; Corgi, 1952
North of Welfare. Harper, 1954; Constable, 1955
The Stag Party. Harper, 1957
Walk the Dark Streets. Harper, 1949; Corgi, 1952

KRASNEY, SAMUEL A. 1922-   . Series character: Lt. Abe Larson, in at least those marked AL.
Death Cries in the Street. Rinehart, 1955; Muller, 1956 AL
Design for Dying. Ace, 1958 AL

Homicide Call. Morrow, 1962; Allen, 1963 AL
Homicide West. Morrow, 1961; Allen, 1962 AL
A Mania for Blondes. Ace, 1961
Morals Squad. Ace, 1959; WDL, 1960
The Rapist. Ace, 1959

KREPPS, ROBERT W(ILSON). 1919-   .
-Gamble My Last Game. Macmillan, 1958; Panther, 1961

KROLL, HARRY HARRISON. 1888-   .
The Ghosts of Slave Driver's Bend. Bobbs, 1937; Lane, 1938

KRONEMILLER, HILDA. Pseudonym: Hilda Lawrence, q.v.

KROPP, LLOYD
Who is Mary Stark? Doubleday, 1974

KRUGER, PAUL. Pseudonym of Elizabeth Roberta Sebenthal, 1917-   . Other pseudonym: Harry Davis, q.v. Series character: Phil Kramer = PK.
The Bronze Claws. Simon, 1972 PK
A Bullet for a Blonde. Dell, 1958
The Cold Ones. Simon, 1972 PK
Dig Her a Grave. Ace, 1960
The Finish Line. Simon, 1968; Hale, 1971
If the Shroud Fits. Simon, 1969; Hale, 1971 PK
Message from Marise. GM, 1963; Muller pb, 1964
Weave a Wicked Web. Simon, 1967; Hale, 1971 PK
Weep for Willow Green. Simon, 1966; Hale, 1970 PK

KRUGER, (CHARLES) RAYNE
The Even Keel. Longmans, 1955
Ferguson. Longmans, 1956; Appleton, 1957
My Name is Celia. Longmans, 1954; Macmillan, 1955
The Spectacle. Longmans, 1953; Macmillan, 1954
Tanker. Longmans, 1952
Young Villain with Wings. Longmans, 1953

KRULL, FELIX. Pseudonym of Stanley White, 1913-   . Other pseudonym: James Dillon White, q.v.
The Village Pub Murders. Ward, 1962

KRUMGOLD, JOSEPH (QUINCY). 1908-   .
Thanks to Murder. Vanguard, 1935; Gollancz, 1935

KUETHER, EDITH LYMAN. 1915-   . Pseudonym: Margaret Malcolm, q.v.

KUHN, GEORGE R.
Comic Tragedy. Vantage, 1968

KUHNS, WILLIAM. 1943-   .
The Reunion. Morrow, 1973; Cassell, 1973

KUMMER, FREDERIC ARNOLD. 1873-1943. Pseudonym: Arnold Fredericks, q.v. Series character: Judge Henry Tyson = HT.
-The Brute. Watt, 1912
Death at Eight Bells. Lothrop, 1937; Hutchinson, 1937
Design for Murder. Lothrop, 1936; Hutchinson, 1936
-Forbidden Wine. Sears, 1931; Hutchinson, 1931
-Gentlemen in Hades. Sears, 1930; Long, 1932

The Green God. Watt, 1911
-Ladies in Hades. Sears, 1928; Hamilton, 1928
-A Lost Paradise. Watt, 1914
Manhattan Masquerade. Sears, 1934
-The Painted Woman. Watt, 1917
-Plaster Saints. Macaulay, 1922
The Road to Fortune. Doran, 1925; Hodder, 1926
The Scarecrow Murders. Dodd, 1938; Hutchinson, 1938 HT
-A Song of Sixpence. Watt, 1913
The Twisted Face. Dodd, 1938; Hutchinson, 1938 HT
The Web. Century, 1919

KUNICZAK, W(IESLAW) S(TANISLAW). 1930-   .
The Sempinski Affair. Doubleday, 1969; Hart-Davis, 1970

KUNST, EARLE
The Mystery of Evangeline Fairfax. Metropolitan, 1910

KURLAND, MICHAEL (J.). 1938-   . Pseudonym: Jennifer Plum, q.v.
Mission: Police Action. Pyramid, 1969
Mission: Tank War. Pyramid, 1968
Mission: Third Force. Pyramid, 1967
A Plague of Spies. Pyramid, 1969

KURNITZ, HARRY. 1907-1968. Pseudonym: Marco Page, q.v.
Invasion of Privacy. Random, 1955; Eyre, 1956
Reclining Figure. Random, 1955. (Play based on the author's novel of the same title published as by Marco Page, q.v.)
A Shot in the Dark. Random, 1962. (Play based on L'Idiote by Marcel Achard.)

KUTAK, ROSEMARY. 1908-   . Series character: Dr. Marc Castleman, in both titles.
Darkness of Slumber. Lippincott, 1944
I am the Cat. Farrar, 1948

KUTCH, ARCHIE
Young Sleuth's Victory; or, A Detective's Adventure. Ogilvie, 1885

KUTCHIN, VICTOR. 1851-1939.
The Strange Case of John R. Graham. Dean, 1929

KUTTNER, HENRY. 1914-1958. Pseudonym: Lewis Padgett, q.v. Series character: Dr. Michael Gray = MG.
Man Drowning. Harper, 1952; Four Square, 1961
Murder of a Mistress. Permabooks, 1957 MG
Murder of a Wife. Permabooks, 1958 MG
The Murder of Ann Avery. Permabooks, 1956 MG
The Murder of Eleanor Pope. Permabooks, 1956 MG

KYD, THOMAS. Pseudonym of Alfred Bennett Harbage, 1901-1976. Series character: Sam Phelan = SP.
Blood is a Beggar. Lippincott, 1946; Hammond, 1949 SP
Blood of Vintage. Lippincott, 1947; Hammond, 1950 SP
Blood on the Bosom Devine. Lippincott, 1948 SP
Cover his Face. Lippincott, 1949

KYLE, DUNCAN. Pseudonym of John Franklin Broxholme, 1930-   .
A Cage of Ice. Collins, 1970; St. Martin's, 1971
Flight into Fear. Collins, 1972; St. Martin's, 1972

A Raft of Swords. Collins, 1974. U.S. title: The Suvarov Adventure. St. Martin's, 1974
The Suvarov Adventure; see A Raft of Swords
Terror's Cradle. Collins, 1975; St. Martin's, 1974

KYLE, ELISABETH. Pseudonym of Agnes Mary Robertson Dunlop.
-Broken Glass. Davies, 1940
-But We are Exiles. Davies, 1942
-Carolina House. Davies, 1955
-Carp Country. Davies, 1946
-Conor Sands. Davies, 1952
-Douce. Davies, 1950
-Down the Water. Davies, 1975
-Free as Air. Davies, 1974
-The Heron Tree. Davies, 1973
-High Season. Davies, 1968
-Lost Karim. Davies, 1948
-Love is for the Living. Davies, 1966; Holt, 1967
Mally Lee. Davies, 1947; Doubleday, 1947
-A Man of Talent. Davies, 1948
Mirror Dance. Davies, 1970; Holt, 1971
-The Other Miss Evans. Davies, 1958
-The Pleasure Dome. Davies, 1958
Queen's Evidence. Davies, 1969
-The Regent's Candlesticks. Davies, 1954
Return to the Alcazar. Davies, 1962
The Scent of Danger. Davies, 1971; Holt, 1972
-The Silver Pineapple. Davies, 1972
-The Skater's Waltz. Davies, 1944
-The "Tontine Bell." Davies, 1951
-The White Lady. Davies, 1941

KYLE, ELLA JANE
Old Gumber's Mill. Ben Hur Press, 1928

KYLE, ROBERT. Series character: Ben Gates = BG.
Ben Gates is Hot. Dell, 1964 BG
Blackmail, Inc. Dell, 1958 BG
The Crooked City. Dell, 1954
The Golden Urge. Dell, 1954
Kill Now, Pay Later. Dell, 1960 BG
Model for Murder. Dell, 1959 BG
Nice Guys Finish Last. Dell, 1955
Some Like It Cool. Dell, 1962 BG
A Tiger in the Night. Dell, 1955

KYLE, SEFTON. Pseudonym of Roy Vickers, 1888-1965, q.v. Other pseudonyms: David Durham, John Spencer, qq.v. Series character: Det. Insp. Rason, in at least those titles marked R (also appears in books as by David Durham and Roy Vickers, qq.v.)
The Bloomsbury Treasure. Jenkins, 1932
The Body in the Safe. Jenkins, 1937 R
Dead Man's Dower. Jenkins, 1925
The Durand Case. Jenkins, 1936
During his Majesty's Pleasure. Jenkins, 1938 R
The Girl Known as D 13. Jenkins, 1940
Guilty, But——. Jenkins, 1927
The Hawk. Jenkins, 1930; Dial, 1930, as by Roy Vickers
The Judge's Dilemma. Jenkins, 1939
The Life He Stole. Jenkins, 1934 R
Love was Married. Jenkins, 1943
The Man in the Shadow. Jenkins, 1924 R
The Man Without a Name. Jenkins, 1935
-Miss X. Jenkins, 1939
Missing! Jenkins, 1938
The Notorious Miss Walters. Jenkins, 1937
Number Seventy-Three. Jenkins, 1936
The Price of Silence. Jenkins, 1942
Red Hair. Jenkins, 1933 R
The Shadow over Fairholme. Jenkins, 1940
Silence. Jenkins, 1935
The Vengeance of Mrs. Danvers. Jenkins, 1932

L

LA BERN, ARTHUR (JOSEPH)
-The Big Money-Box. Kimber, 1960
Brighton Belle. Allen, 1963
Frenzy; see Goodbye Piccadilly, Farewell Leicester Square
Goodbye Piccadilly, Farewell Leicester Square. Allen, 1966; Stein, 1967. Also published as: Frenzy. Pan, 1972; Stein, 1972
-It Always Rains on Sunday. Nicholson, 1945
-It was Christmas Every Day. Jarrolds, 1952
It will be Warmer When It Snows. Allen, 1966
A Nice Class of People. Allen, 1969
-Night Darkens the Streets. Nicholson, 1947
Nightmare. Allen, 1975
-Pennygreen Street. Jarrolds, 1950

LABORDE, JEAN. 1918- .
The Dominici Affair. Morrow, 1974; Collins, 1974. (Translation of Un Matin d'ete a Lurs. Paris, 1952.) (Fictionalized true crime.)
A Fair Trial. Doubleday, 1962. British title: The Falcon and the Dove. Bodley Head, 1962. (Translation of Les Bonnes Causes. Paris, 1954.)
The Falcon and the Dove; see A Fair Trial
A Privileged Character. Doubleday, 1963. (Probably translation of Un Homme a Part Entiere. Paris, 1961.)

LA COSTE, GUY ROBERT. Joint pseudonym with Eadfrid A. Bingham: Guy Berton, q.v.

LACROIX, JEAN PAUL. 1914- .
The Innocent Gunman. Elek, 1957. (Translation of Le Gangster aux Etoiles. Paris, 1954.)

LACROIX, RAMON. Pseudonym of Ernest L(ionel) McKeag, 1896- . Other pseudonyms: Griff, Mark Grimshaw, qq.v.
-Danger for Love. Modern Fiction, 1947
-Hotel for Scandal. Modern Fiction, 1947
-Illicit Cargo. Modern Fiction, 1947
Murder at Le Touquet. Modern Fiction, 1947

LACRUZ, MARIO
The Suspect. Methuen, 1956. (Translation of El Inocente. Barcelona, 1953.)

LACY, ED. Pseudonym of Leonard S. Zinberg, 1911-1968. Series characters: Lee Hayes = LH; Toussaint M. Moore = TM; Dave Wintino = DW.
Be Careful How You Live. Harper, 1959; Boardman, 1959. Also published as: Dead End. Pyramid, 1960
The Best That Ever Did It. Harper, 1955; Hutchinson, 1957. Also published as: Visa to Death. Perma, 1956
The Big Bust. Pyramid, 1969; New English Library pb, 1970
The Big Fix. Pyramid, 1960; Boardman, 1961
Blonde Bait. Zenith, 1959
Breathe No More, My Lady. Avon, 1958
Bugged for Murder. Avon, 1961
Dead End; see Be Careful How You Live
A Deadly Affair. Hillman, 1960
Death in Passing; see Sin in Their Blood
Devil for the Witch. Boardman, 1958. (U.S. title?)
Double Trouble. Lancer, 1967; Boardman, 1965 DW
Enter Without Desire. Avon, 1954
The Freeloaders. Berkley, 1961; Boardman, 1962
Go for the Body. Avon, 1954; Boardman, 1959
Harlem Underground. Pyramid, 1965 LH
In Black & Whitey. Lancer, 1967 LH
Lead with Your Left. Harper, 1957; Boardman, 1957 DW
The Men from the Boys. Harper, 1956; Boardman, 1960
Moment of Untruth. Lancer, 1964; Boardman, 1965 TM
The Napalm Bugle. Pyramid, 1968
Pity the Honest. Macfadden, 1965; Boardman, 1964
Room to Swing. Harper, 1957; Boardman, 1958 TM
The Sex Castle. Paperback Library, 1963; Digit, 1965. Also published as: Shoot It Again. Paperback Library, 1969
Shakedown for Murder. Avon, 1958
Shoot It Again; see The Sex Castle
Sin in Their Blood. Eton, 1952. British title: Death in Passing. Boardman, 1959
South Pacific Affair. Belmont, 1961
Strip for Violence. Eton, 1953
Two Hot to Handle. Paperback Library, 1963; Digit, 1966
Visa to Death; see The Best That Ever Did It
The Woman Aroused. Avon, 1951; Hale, 1969

LADLINE, ROBERT. Series character: J. A. (Rem) Remington, in at least those marked JR.
A Devil in Downing Street. Jenkins, 1937 JR
The Man Who Made a King. Jenkins, 1936
The Quest of the Vanishing Star. Jenkins, 1932
The Shoe Fits. Jenkins, 1936
Sinister Craft. Jenkins, 1939 JR
The Sky's the Limit. Jenkins, 1937 JR
Stop That Man! Jenkins, 1940 JR
They Stuck at Nothing. Jenkins, 1935
When Fools Endanger Us. Jenkins, 1938 JR
When the Police Failed. Jenkins, 1933
The Wolf Swept Down. Jenkins, 1935

LADOUX, GEORGES (EMILE). 1875-1933.
The Kaiser's Blonde Spy. Hutchinson, 1934

LADY, FREDERICK
The City of Fear. Wright, 1933
The Master of Money. Jarrolds, 1931
A Million Pounds Reward. Jarrolds, 1929

LAFFEATY, CHRISTINA. 1932- .
The Reluctant Bride. Hale, 1966. U.S. title: Mistress of Tara. Paperback Library, 1967

LAFFIN, JOHN (ALFRED CHARLES). 1922- . Pseudonyms: Carl Dekker, Mark Napier, Dirk Sabre, qq.v.
Crime on my Hands. Horwitz, 1958
The Dancer of San Jose. Horwitz, 1958
Death by Ballot. King, 1954
Death has my Number. Horwitz, 1957
The Devil's Emissary. Horwitz, 1958
-Devil's Goad. Dent, 1970
I'll Die Tonight. Horwitz, 1957
Jungle Manhunt. Horwitz, 1955
Murder in Paradise. Horwitz, 1958
Murder on Flight 354. King, 1956
My Brother's Executioner. Horwitz, 1957
Temptress on Trial. Horwitz, 1958
They Voted Me to Die. Horwitz, 1957
-The Walking Wounded. Amalgamated, 1963

LAFLIN, JACK. Series character: Gregory Hiller, in at least those marked GH.
The Flaw. Belmont, 1964
The Reluctant Spy. Belmont, 1966
A Silent Kind of War. Belmont, 1965; Digit, 1966 GH
The Spy in White Gloves. Belmont, 1965 GH
The Spy Who Didn't. Belmont, 1966 GH
The Spy Who Loved America. Belmont, 1964 GH
The Temple at Ilumquh. Award, 1970

LA FORCE, BEATRICE
The Sound of Hasty Footsteps. Bouregy, 1963

LAFORE, LAURENCE (DAVIS). 1917- .
Nine Seven Juliet. Doubleday, 1968

LAFOREST, SERGE
The Intruder. International, 1969

LA FOUNTAINE, GEORGE. 1934- .
Two Minute Warning. Coward, 1975

LA FRANCE, MARSTON. 1927?- .
Miami Murder-Go-Round. World, 1951

LA GARDE, HENRY
Tide Waits for No Man. Robertson, 1952

LAING, ALEXANDER (KINNAN). 1903-1976. Series character: Doctor Scarlett = S. See also: THOMAS PAINTER.
The Cadaver of Gideon Wyck. Farrar, 1934; Butterworth, 1934
Dr. Scarlett. Farrar, 1936; Rich, 1937 S
The Methods of Dr. Scarlett. Farrar, 1937; Cassell, 1938 S

LAING, JANET
Before the Wind. Dent, 1918; Dutton, 1918
-The Borderlanders. Dent, 1904
-The Honeycombers. Hodder, 1922
-The Moment More. Hodder, 1924
The Villa Jane. Hodder, 1929; Century, 1929
-The Wizard's Aunt. Dent, 1903

LAING, KENNETH. Pseudonym of Kenneth (Joseph Robb) Langmaid, q.v. Series character: "Rolling" Stone, in at least those marked RS.
The House of Darkness. Diamond, 1927
The Malignant Snowman. Jenkins, 1950 RS
The Midnight Walkers. Jenkins, 1951 RS
No Man's Laughter. Jenkins, 1950
The Pay Off. Jenkins, 1951
The Red Horsemen. Jenkins, 1930
The Shadow People. Jenkins, 1952; Roy, 1956 RS

LAING, PATRICK. Pseudonym of Amelia Reynolds Long, 1904-1978, q.v. Other pseudonyms: Adrian Reynolds, Peter Reynolds, qq.v. Joint pseudonym with Edna McHugh: Kathleen Buddington Coxe, q.v. Series character: Patrick Laing, in all titles.
A Brief Case of Murder. Phoenix, 1949
If I Should Murder. Phoenix, 1945
The Lady is Dead. Phoenix, 1951
Murder from the Mind. Phoenix, 1946
The Shadow of Murder. Phoenix, 1947
Stone Dead. Phoenix, 1945; Wells Gardner, 1947

LAIT, JACK [JAQUIN L. LAIT]. 1882-1954.
Series character: Polack Annie = PA.
  The Beast of the City. Grosset, 1932.
    (Novelization of the movie.)
  The Big House. Grosset, 1930. (Noveli-
    zation of the movie.)
  Gangster Girl. Grosset, 1930 PA
  Put on the Spot. Grosset, 1930 PA

LAIT, ROBERT. 1921-   .
  A Chance to Kill. Macmillan (London),
    1968
  Switched Out. MacGibbon, 1970

LAKE, JAMES (THOMAS)
  The Day They Hijacked Death. Boardman,
    1963
  Down Among the Dead Men. Boardman, 1961

LAKE, JOE BARRY. Pseudonym: Joe Barry,
  q.v.

LAKER, ROSALIND
  The Smuggler's Bride. Doubleday, 1975;
    Hale, 1976

LAKIN, RICHARD
  Angel Take Care. Hodder, 1947
  The Body Fell on Berlin. Hodder, 1943;
    Putnam, 1943

LAMARRE, JOSEPH
  -The Passion of the Beast. Stratford,
    1928

LA MASTER, SLATER. 1890-   .
  The Phantom in the Rainbow. McClurg,
    1929; H. Hamilton, 1931

LAMB, ANTONIA. 1943-   .
  The Greenhouse. Pyramid, 1966
  Greystones. Pyramid, 1966
  Lady in Shadows. Lancer, 1968
  Remember the Summer We Lived at the
    Pad. Lancer, 1973

LAMB, LYNTON. 1907-   . Series charac-
  ters: Supt. Quill and Inspector Glo-
  ver, in at least those marked Q&G.
  Death of a Dissenter. Gollancz, 1969
    Q&G
  Man in a Mist. Gollancz, 1974 Q&G
  Picture Frame. Gollancz, 1972
  Worse Than Death. Gollancz, 1971

LAMBERT, DEREK (WILLIAM). 1929-   .
  Pseudonym: Richard Falkirk, q.v.
  Angels in the Snow. Joseph, 1969; Cow-
    ard, 1969
  The Red House. Joseph, 1972; Coward,
    1972
  Touch the Lion's Paw. Arlington, 1975;
    Saturday Review Press, 1975
  The Yermakov Transfer. Arlington, 1974;
    Saturday Review Press, 1974

LAMBERT, DUDLEY. See: ROSA LAMBERT.

LAMBERT, ELISABETH
  The Sleeping House Party. Coward, 1951;
    Joseph, 1951

LAMBERT, ERIC. 1918-1966.
  -Ballarat. Muller, 1962
  -The Dark Backward. Muller, 1958
   Diggers Die Hard. Fleetway, 1958
  -Dolphin. Muller, 1963
  -The Drip Dry Man. Muller, 1963
  -Glory Thrown In. Muller, 1959
   Hiroshima Reef. Muller, 1967; Norton,
     1967
  -Kelly. Muller, 1964
  -The Long White Night. Muller, 1965
   The Rehabilitated Man. Muller, 1960
  -A Short Walk to the Stars. Muller, 1964
  -The Tender Conspiracy. Muller, 1965

  -The Twenty Thousand Thieves. Muller,
    1952
  -The Veterans. Muller, 1954
  -Waterman. Muller, 1956

LAMBERT, GERALD B(ARNES). 1886-1967.
  Murder in Newport. Scribner, 1938

LAMBERT, HUBERT STEEL. 1899-   . Pseudonym: T. B. Marle, q.v.

LAMBERT, LESLIE HARRISON.   -1940.
  Pseudonym: A. J. Alan, q.v.

LAMBERT, R. F.
  The Crooked Men Came. Pendulum, 1946

LAMBERT, ROBERT. 1930-   .
  A Piece of the Moon. Saturday Review
    Press, 1975

LAMBERT, ROSA and DUDLEY. Series charac-
  ter: Glyn Morgan, in at least those
  marked GM.
  Crime in Quarantine. Nelson, 1938
  Death Goes to Brussels; see Monsieur
    Faux-Pas
  The Mediterranean Murder. Wishart, 1930
    GM
  Monsieur Faux-Pas. Wishart, 1928. Also
    published as: Death Goes to Brussels.
    Nelson, 1937 GM
  The Mystery of the Golden Wings. Nel-
    son, 1935; Macaulay, 1936 GM

LAMBOT, ISOBEL (MARY). 1926-   . Pseudo-
  nym: Daniel Ingham, q.v.
  Come Back and Die. Hale, 1972
  Danger Merchant. Hale, 1968
  Dangerous Refuge. Hale, 1966
  Deadly Return. Hale, 1966
  Grip of Fear. Hale, 1974
  Killer's Laughter. Hale, 1968
  Let the Witness Die. Hale, 1969
  Point of Death. Hale, 1969
  The Queen Dies First. Hale, 1968
  Shroud of Canvas. Hale, 1967
  Taste of Murder. Hale, 1966; Ace, 1972
  Watcher on the Shore. Hale, 1972

LAMENSDURF, LEONARD
  In the Blood. Dell, 1974
  The Paper Coffin. Dell, 1973

LAMPEN, C(HARLES) DUDLEY
  The Dead Prior. Stock, 1896

LAMSON, DAVID (ALBERT)
  Whirlpool. Scribner, 1937

LANCASTER, PAUL
  The Disappearance of Norman Langdale.
    Paul, 1929
  The Executioner's Axe. Paul, 1930
  The Jolly Roger Mystery. Paul, 1930

LAND, MYRICK (EBBEN). 1922-   .
  Last Flight. Norton, 1975
  Quicksand. Harper, 1969; Gollancz, 1970
  Search the Dark Woods. Funk, 1955

LANDAU, MARK ALEKSANDROVICH. 1886-1957.
  Pseudonym: Mark Aldanov, q.v.

LANDELS, D. H. Pseudonym of Donald (Lan-
  dels) Henderson, 1905-   , q.v.
  The Announcer. Hurst, 1944. U.S. title:
    A Voice Like Velvet, as by Donald
    Henderson. Random, 1948
  The Headmaster. Hurst, 1947
  His Lordship the Judge. Paul, 1936
  -A Man of Character. Hurst, 1944

  Teddington Tragedy. Paul, 1935
  -Uncle Xavier. Hurst, 1947
  -The Understudy. Hurst, 1945
  A Voice Like Velvet; see The Announcer

LANDON, CHRISTOPHER (GUY). 1911-   .
  Dead Men Rise Up Never. Heinemann,
    1963; Sloane, 1963
  A Flag in the City. Heinemann, 1953;
    Macmillan, 1954
  Hornets' Nest. Heinemann, 1956
  Ice-Cold in Alex. Heinemann, 1957;
    Sloane, 1957
  The Mirror Room. Heinemann, 1960; White
    Lion, 1972
  The Shadow of Time. Heinemann, 1957.
    U.S. title: Unseen Enemy. Doubleday,
    1957
  Stone Cold Dead in the Market. Heine-
    mann, 1955
  Unseen Enemy; see The Shadow of Time

LANDON, EDWIN J.
  Suspicion. Long, 1931

LANDON, HERMAN. 1882-1960. Series charac-
  ters: The Gray Phantom = GP; The Pic-
  aroon = P. (Note that Gray in all
  U.S. titles is spelled Grey in Bri-
  tish titles.) Most of the Picaroon
  books are collections of long short
  stories or novelets.
  The Back-Seat Murder. Liveright, 1931;
    Jarrolds, 1931
  Buy My Silence! Cassell, 1929 P
  Death on the Air. Liveright, 1929; Jar-
    rolds, 1929
  The Elusive Picaroon. Cassell, 1932 P
  The Forbidden Door. Dial, 1927; Hutch-
    inson, 1927
  Gray Magic. Watt, 1925. British title:
    The Grey Phantom's Triumph. Hutchin-
    son, 1927 GP
  The Gray Phantom. Watt, 1921; Long,
    1923 GP
  The Gray Phantom's Return. Watt, 1922;
    Long, 1926 GP
  The Grey Phantom's Triumph; see Gray
    Magic
  Gray Terror. Watt, 1923; Long, 1925 GP
  The Green Shadow. Dial, 1928; Cassell,
    1927 P
  Hands Unseen. Watt, 1924; Hutchinson,
    1926 GP
  Haunting Fingers. Jarrolds, 1930
  Murder Mansion. Liveright, 1928. Bri-
    tish title: Mystery Mansion. Cassell,
    1928
  Mystery Mansion; see Murder Mansion
  The Owl's Warning. Liveright, 1932;
    Jarrolds, 1932
  The Picaroon Does Justice. Cassell,
    1928 P
  The Picaroon in Pursuit. Cassell, 1932
    P
  The Picaroon: Knight Errant. Cassell,
    1933 P
  The Picaroon Resumes Practice. Cassell,
    1931 P
  The Room Under the Stairs. Watt, 1923;
    Hutchinson, 1925
  The Silver Chest. Jarrolds, 1932
  Three Brass Elephants. Liveright, 1930.
    British title: Whispering Shadows.
    Jarrolds, 1930
  The Trailing of the Picaroon. Cassell,
    1930 P
  The Voice in the Closet. Liveright,
    1930
  Whispering Shadows; see Three Brass
    Elephants

LANDON, HILARY. Series character: Timothy
  Drewer, in at least those marked TD.
  Circle Round a Corpse. Gifford, 1948 TD
  Exit Sir Toby Belch. Gifford, 1950
  Murder at Morning Prayers. Gifford,
    1947 TD

LANDON, LOUISE. Pseudonym of Louise Platt Hauck, 1883-1943, q.v. Other pseudonym: Lane Archer, q.v.
The Green Light. Penn, 1931; Paul, 1931
The Strange Death of a Doctor. Penn, 1933; Paul, 1933

LANE, GRANT. Pseudonym of Stephen Gould Fisher, 1912-   . See also: Steve Fisher. Other pseudonym: Stephen Gould, q.v.
Spend the Night. Phoenix, 1935

LANE, GRET. Series characters: John Barrin, in at least those marked JB; Inspector Hook, in at least those marked H; Kate Marsh, in at least those marked KM.
The Cancelled Score Mystery. Jenkins, 1929
The Curlew Coombe Mystery. Jenkins, 1930
Death in Mermaid Lane. Jenkins, 1940 KM
Death Prowls the Cove. Jenkins, 1942 JB
Death Visits the Summer-House. Jenkins, 1939 JB
Found on the Road. Jenkins, 1926
The Guest with the Scythe. Jenkins, 1943
The Hotel Cremona Mystery. Jenkins, 1932 JB
The Lantern House Affair. Jenkins, 1931 KM
The Red Mirror Mystery. Jenkins, 1938 H
The Stolen Scar. Jenkins, 1925
Three Died That Night. Jenkins, 1937 H
The Unknown Enemy. Jenkins, 1933 JB

LANE, J(OHN) RUSSELL
-The House Between the Trees. Clark, 1909

LANE, JEREMY. 1893-1963. Series character: Whitney Wheat, in at least those marked WW.
Death to Drumbeat. Phoenix, 1944
Kill Him Tonight. Phoenix, 1946 WW
The Left Hand of God. Washburn, 1929
Like a Man. Washburn, 1928; Allan, 1936
Murder Menagerie. Phoenix, 1946 WW
Murder Spoils Everything. Phoenix, 1949 WW

LANE, KENDALL
Gambit. GM, 1966. (Novelization of the movie.)

LANE, KENNETH WESTMACOTT. 1893-   .
Pseudonym: Keith West, q.v.

LANG, ANDREW. 1844-1912. Pseudonym: A. Huge Longway, q.v.
The Disentanglers. Longmans, 1902 ss
The Mark of Cain. Scribner, 1886; Arrowsmith, 1886

LANG, ANTHONY. Pseudonym of John (George) Hazlette Vahey, 1881-   , q.v. Other pseudonyms: Henrietta Clandon, John Haslette, Vernon Loder, John Mowbray, Walter Proudfoot, qq.v.
The Case with Three Threads. Melrose, 1928
The Crime. Melrose, 1927
The Daring Diana. Melrose, 1929
Evidence. Melrose, 1930
Fly Country. Melrose, 1928

LANG, BRAD
Crockett on the Loose. Leisure, 1975

LANG, HARRY
The Corpse on the Hearth. Macrae Smith, 1946; Boardman, 1946

LANG, HILARY
-The House of Mystery. Mellifont, 1947

LANG, JACK
The Biter. Mayflower, 1968. U.S. title: The Photo Game. Belmont, 1971

LANG, JOHN. 1817-1864.
Botany Bay. Tegg, 1859. Also published as: Clever Criminals; or, Recollections of Botany Bay. Ward, 1878 ss
Clever Criminals; see Botany Bay
The Secret Police; or, Plot and Passion. Ward, 1859 ss

LANG, MARIA. Pseudonym of Dagmar Lange, 1914-   . Series character: Christer Wick, in all titles.
Death Awaits Thee. Hodder, 1967. (Translation of Se, Doden pa dig Vantar. Stockholm, 1955.)
No More Murders. Hodder, 1967. (Translation of Inte Flera Mord. Stockholm, 1951.)
A Wreath for the Bride. Hodder, 1966; Regnery, 1968. (Translation of Kung Liljekonvalj av Dungen. Stockholm, 1957.)

LANG, THEO. Pseudonym of Theo Langbehn. Other pseudonym: Peter Piper, q.v.
The House in Gowderdale. Macdonald, 1947

LANGBEHN, THEO. Pseudonyms: Theo Lang, Peter Piper, qq.v.

LANGDON, GEE. 1907-   .
Clue from the Past. Hale, 1973

LANGDON, JOHN (FRANKLIN COASTEN). 1913-   . Pseudonym: John Gannold, q.v.
Vicious Circuit. Macmillan, 1953

LANGE, JOHN. Pseudonym of Michael Crichton, 1942-   , q.v. Other pseudonym: Jeffery Hudson, q.v.
Binary. Knopf, 1972; Heinemann, 1972
Drug of Choice. Signet, 1970. British title: Overkill. Sphere, 1972
Easy Go. Signet, 1968; Sphere, 1972
Grave Descend. Signet, 1970
Odds On. Signet, 1966
Overkill; see Drug of Choice
Scratch One. Signet, 1967
The Venom Business. World, 1969
Zero Cool. Signet, 1969; Sphere, 1972

LANGE, OLIVER
Incident at La Junta. Stein, 1973

LANGELAAN, GEORGE. 1908-   .
Turncoat. Hale, 1967

LANGHAM, JAMES R. Series character: Samuel G. Abbott, in both titles.
A Pocket Full of Clues. Simon, 1941; Hale, 1943, as A Pocketful of Clues
Sing a Song of Homicide. Simon, 1940. British title: Sing a Song of Murder. Hale, 1942
Sing a Song of Murder; see Sing a Song of Homicide

LANGLEY, FREDERIC. Joint pseudonym with Ronald D. Ellik, 1938-1968: Frederic Davies, q.v.

LANGLEY, LEE. Pseudonym of Sarah Langley, 1927-   .
Dead Center. Doubleday, 1968; Hale, 1969
Osiris Died in Autumn. Doubleday, 1964. British title: Twilight of Death. Hale, 1965
Twilight of Death; see Osiris Died in Autumn

LANGLEY, NOEL. 1911-   .
Tales of Mystery and Revenge. Barker, 1950 ss

LANGLEY, SARAH. 1927-   . Pseudonym: Lee Langley, q.v.

LANGMAID, KENNETH (JOSEPH ROBB). Pseudonym: Kenneth Laing, q.v.
Mystery Cruise. Hale, 1958

LANGSLOW, JANE. See: MARGARET R(IVERS) LARMINIE, 1885-   .

LANGTON, JANE (GILLSON). 1922-   . Series character: Homer Kelly, in both titles.
Dark Nantucket Moon. Harper, 1975
The Minuteman Murder; see The Transcendental Murder
The Transcendental Murder. Harper, 1964. Also published as: The Minuteman Murder. Dell, 1976

LANHAM, EDWIN (MOULTRIE). 1904-   . Series characters: Lt. Gray, in at least those marked G; Lt. Madigan, in at least those marked M.
The Case of the Missing Corpse; see Death of a Corinthian
Death in the Wind. Harcourt, 1956; Boardman, 1957 G
Death of a Corinthian. Harcourt, 1953; Boardman, 1954. Also published as: The Case of the Missing Corpse. Bestseller, 1955 G
Double Jeopardy. Harcourt, 1959; Gollancz, 1959
Headline for Murder; see Slug It Slay
Headlined for Murder; see Slug It Slay
It Shouldn't Happen to a Dog. Boardman, 1947
Monkey on a Chain. Harcourt, 1963; Gollancz, 1963
Murder on my Street. Harcourt, 1958; Gollancz, 1958
No Hiding Place. Harcourt, 1962; Gollancz, 1962
One Murder Too Many. Harcourt, 1952; Boardman, 1953 M
Passage to Danger. Harcourt, 1962; Gollancz, 1962
Politics is Murder. Harcourt, 1947 M
Six Black Camels. Harcourt, 1961; Gollancz, 1961
Slug It Slay. Harcourt, 1946; Boardman, 1948. Also published as: Headlined for Murder. Bantam, 1948. And as: Headline for Murder. Boardman, 1950 M

LANNING, GEORGE (WILLIAM, JR.) 1925-   .
The Pedestal. Harper, 1966; Joseph, 1967

LANSDALE, NINA
The White Island. Arbor, 1975

LANZA, CLARA and JAMES C. HARVEY. For Lanza, see also: (DR.) WILLIAM A(LEXANDER) HAMMOND, 1828-1900.
Scarabaeus. Lovell, 1892

LAPATINE, KENNETH A.
The Trials and Tribulations of Aaron Amsted. Walker, 1974

LARANY, DANIEL
The Big Red Sun. Prentice-Hall, 1971. (Translation of Le Grand Soleil Rouge. Paris, 1969.)

LARBALESTIER, P(HILIP) G(EORGE). Series character: Det.-Insp. Michael Farrant, in at least those marked MF.
Black Shrouds the Bride. Gifford, 1951 MF

Darling, Don't Be Dumb. Gifford, 1950 MF
Death Casts No Shadow. Gifford, 1951 MF
Officer, That's Your Man. Gifford, 1947 ss
The Singing Sword. Gifford, 1954
The Yellow Card Mystery. Gifford, 1950

LARIAR, LAWRENCE. 1908-   . Pseudonyms: Adam Knight, Michael Lawrence, Michael Stark, qq.v. Series character: Homer Bull = HB.
The Day I Died. Appleton, 1952
Death is Confidential. Hillman, 1959
Death is the Host; see Death Paints the Picture
Death Paints the Picture. Phoenix, 1943. Also published as: Death is the Host. Crime Novel Selection, 1943 HB
Friday for Death. Crown, 1949; Boardman, 1950
The Girl with the Frightened Eyes. Dodd, 1945; Cassell, 1950 HB
He Died Laughing. Phoenix, 1943; Boardman, 1946 HB
The Man with the Lumpy Nose. Dodd, 1944 HB
Win, Place and Die! Appleton, 1953
You Can't Catch Me. Crown, 1951

LARKIN, R(OCHELLE) T. 1935-   . Series character: The Donna, in all titles.
For Godmother and Country. Lancer, 1972
The Godmother. Lancer, 1971
Honor Thy Godmother. Lancer, 1972

LARKING, CUTHBERT. 1842-1910.
-Of the Deepest Dye. Hurst, 1897

LARMINIE, MARGARET R(IVERS), 1885- and JANE LANGSLOW
Gory Knight. Longmans, 1937

LARNER, CELIA
-Miranda. Milton House, 1973
Summer's Lease. Milton House, 1974

LA ROCHE, K. ALISON
Dear Dead Professor. Phoenix, 1944

LARSON, CHARLES. 1922-   . Series character: Nils-Frederik Blixen, in both titles.
Matthew's Hand. Doubleday, 1974; Gollancz, 1978
Someone's Death. Lippincott, 1973

LARSON, RUSSELL W. 1908?-   .
Death Stalks a Marriage. Bellevue Books, 1956

LARTEGUY, JEAN. 1920-   .
Presumed Dead. Allen, 1974. (Translation of Enquete sur un Crucifie. Paris, 1973.)

LASCELLES, ESME
The Italian Maze. Milton House, 1973

LA SPINA, (FANNY) GREYE (BRAGG). 1880-
-Invaders from the Dark. Arkham, 1960. Also published as: Shadow of Evil. Paperback Library, 1966

LATHAM, ALISON. Joint pseudonym with Esther Latham: Murray Latham, q.v.

LATHAM, EDYTHE
-The Seasons of God. Doubleday, 1963

LATHAM, ESTHER. Joint pseudonym with Alison Latham: Murray Latham, q.v.

LATHAM, LORRAINE. 1948-   .
Identity Crisis. Morrow, 1975

LATHAM, MURRAY. Joint pseudonym of Alison Latham and Esther Latham.
Enjoy Such Liberty. Hutchinson, 1943
Even from the Law. Hutchinson, 1946
Flight Without Wings. Hutchinson, 1950
River in the Dark. Hutchinson, 1945
Some Names are Dangerous. Hutchinson, 1948

LATHEN, EMMA. Joint pseudonym of Mary J. Latsis and Martha Hennissart. Other joint pseudonym: R. B. Dominic, q.v. Series character: John Putnam Thatcher, in all titles.
Accounting for Murder. Macmillan, 1964; Gollancz, 1965
Ashes to Ashes. Simon, 1971; Gollancz, 1971
Banking on Death. Macmillan, 1961; Gollancz, 1962
By Hook or By Crook. Simon, 1975; Gollancz, 1975
Come to Dust. Simon, 1968; Gollancz, 1969
Death Shall Overcome. Macmillan, 1966; Gollancz, 1967
The Longer the Thread. Simon, 1971; Gollancz, 1972
Murder Against the Grain. Macmillan, 1967; Gollancz, 1967
Murder Makes the Wheels Go Round. Macmillan, 1966; Gollancz, 1966
Murder to Go. Simon, 1969; Gollancz, 1970
Murder Without Icing. Simon, 1972; Gollancz, 1973
Pick Up Sticks. Simon, 1970; Gollancz, 1971
A Place for Murder. Macmillan, 1963; Gollancz, 1963
A Stitch in Time. Macmillan, 1968; Gollancz, 1968
Sweet and Low. Simon, 1974; Gollancz, 1974
When in Greece. Simon, 1969; Gollancz, 1969

LATHROP, GEORGE PARSONS. 1851-1898.
Would You Kill Him? Harper, 1890; Douglas, 1889

LATIMER, JOHN. 1937-   .
Border of Darkness. Doubleday, 1972; Milton House, 1973

LATIMER, JONATHAN (WYATT). 1906-   .
Pseudonym: Peter Coffin, q.v. Series character: Bill Crane = BC.
Black is the Fashion for Dying. Random, 1959. British title: The Mink-Lined Coffin, Methuen, 1960
The Dead Don't Care. Doubleday, 1938; Methuen, 1938 BC
The Fifth Grave. Popular Library, 1950. British title: Solomon's Vineyard. Methuen, 1941
Headed for a Hearse. Doubleday, 1935; Methuen, 1936 BC
The Lady in the Morgue. Doubleday, 1936; Methuen, 1937 BC
The Mink-Lined Coffin; see Black is the Fashion for Dying
Murder in the Madhouse. Doubleday, 1935; Hurst, 1935 BC
Red Gardenias. Doubleday, 1939; Methuen, 1939. Also published as: Some Dames are Deadly. Jonathan, 1955 BC
Sinners and Shrouds. Simon, 1955; Methuen, 1956
Solomon's Vineyard; see The Fifth Grave
Some Dames are Deadly; see Red Gardenias

LATIMER, RUPERT. Pseudonym of Algernon Victor Mills, 1905-   .
Death in Real Life. Macdonald, 1943
Murder After Christmas. Macdonald, 1944

LA TOURRETTE, JACQUELINE. 1926-   .
-The Joseph Stone. Leisure, 1971
-The Madonna Creek Witch. Dell, 1973
-A Matter of Sixpence. Dell, 1972
The Pompeii Scroll. Delacorte, 1975
The Previous Lady. Dell, 1974

LATSIS, MARY J. Joint pseudonyms with Martha Hennissart: R. B. Dominic, Emma Lathen, qq.v.

LATTA, GORDON. 1904-   . Series character: Arnholt, in all titles.
Arnholt Makes His Bow. Benn, 1931. U.S. title: The Toni Diamonds. Dial, 1931
Exit Arnholt. Bles, 1935
Re-Enter Arnholt. Benn, 1932
The Toni Diamonds; see Arnholt makes His Bow

LATTER, SIMON. Both titles are novelizations of The Girl from UNCLE TV series.
The Global Globules Affair. Souvenir pb, 1967
The Golden Boats of Taradata Affair. Souvenir pb, 1967

LAUBEN, PHILIP
Boogie was a Gent. Hale, 1975

LAUFERTY, LILIAN. 1887-1958.
The Crimson Thread. Simon, 1942; Jarrolds, 1943
The Hungry House. Simon, 1943; Jarrolds, 1944

LAUMER, (JOHN) KEITH. 1925-   . Novelizations of The Avengers TV series = A.
The Afrit Affair. Berkley, 1968 A
Deadfall. Doubleday, 1971; Hale, 1974. Also published as: Fat Chance. PB, 1975; New English Library pb, 1975
The Drowned Queen. Berkley, 1968 A
Fat Chance; see Deadfall
The Gold Bomb. Berkley, 1968 A

LAUNAY, DROO [ANDREW JOSEPH LAUNAY]. 1930-   . Series character: Adam Flute, in all titles.
A Corpse in Camera. Boardman, 1963
Death and Still Life. Boardman, 1964
The New Shining White Murder. Boardman, 1962
The Scream. Boardman, 1965
She Modelled her Coffin. Boardman, 1961
The Two-Way Mirror. Boardman, 1964

LAURENCE, JOHN. Pseudonym of John Laurence Pritchard, 1885-   .
The Double Cross Inn. Long, 1929
The Fanshawe Court Mystery. Hodder, 1925
The Gold Treasure Mystery. Low, 1938
The Great Aeroplane Mystery. Low, 1935
The Honeymoon Mystery. Long, 1929
The Linkram Jewels. Jenkins, 1924
Murder in the Stratosphere. Low, 1938
The Mysteries of Ryeburn Manor. Long, 1930
Mystery from the Air. Low, 1934
Mystery Money. Long, 1930
The Perfect Alibi. Jenkins, 1926
The Pursuing Shadow. Hodder, 1927
The Riddle of Wraye. Low, 1936
The Secret of Sheen. Long, 1927; International Fiction Library, 1929
The Whiteoakes Murder. Low, 1937

LAURENCE, ROSS
The Fast Buck. Ace, 1953

LAURENS, MARSHALL
The Z Effect. PB, 1974

LAURENSON, R(OBERT) M(ARK). Series character: Marc Jordan, in at least those marked MJ.
Better Off Dead. Arcadia, 1955; Foulsham, 1956
The Case of the Six Bullets. Phoenix, 1949; Foulsham, 1950 MJ
The Railroad Murder Case. Phoenix, 1948; Foulsham, 1950 MJ

LAURENT-CELY, JACQUES. 1919-   . Pseudonym: Cecil Saint-Laurent, q.v.

LAURISTON, VICTOR. 1881-   .
The Twenty-First Burr. Doran, 1922

LAVERY, EMMET (GODFREY). 1902-   .
Murder in a Nunnery. French, 1944. (Play based on the novel by Eric Shepherd, 1892-   , q.v.)

LAW, MARJORIE J. Pseudonym of Marjorie Jean Liddelow.
Death in the Spring. Cassell, 1965

LAWLESS, ANTHONY. Pseudonym of Philip MacDonald, 1899-   . Other pseudonym: Martin Porlock, q.v. Joint pseudonym with Ronald MacDonald, 1860-1933: Oliver Fleming, q.v.

LAWRENCE, ALFRED
Cade's County. Popular Library, 1972. (Novelization of the TV series.)
Columbo. Popular Library, 1972. (Novelization of the TV series.)
The Dean's Death. Popular Library, 1975; Wingate, 1977. (Novelization of the Columbo TV series.)

LAWRENCE, DAVID. Pseudonym of David Henry St. Lawrence Morris, 1920-   . Series character: Danny Leather, in both titles.
Dead Orchid. Ward, 1958
Death has Two Hands. Ward, 1958

LAWRENCE, GIL. Pseudonym of Gilbert L. Geis.
Fury with Legs. Pyramid, 1958
The Woman Racket. Pyramid, 1959

LAWRENCE, H(ENRY) L(IONEL). 1908-   .
The Children of Light. Macdonald, 1960
The Sparta Medallion. Macdonald, 1961

LAWRENCE, HADLEY
The Intruder. Micron, 1961

LAWRENCE, HILDA. Pseudonym of Hilda Kronemiller. Series character: Mark East = ME.
The Bleeding House; see Duet of Death
Blood Upon the Snow. Simon, 1944; Chapman, 1946 ME
Composition for Four Hands; see Duet of Death
Death has Four Hands; see Duet of Death
Death of a Doll. Simon, 1947; Chapman, 1948 ME
Duet in Death; see Duet of Death
Duet of Death. Simon, 1949; Chapman, 1949. Also published as: Duet in Death. Ace, 1963. (Two novelets, Composition for Four Hands and The House. The former was reprinted separately as: Death has Four Hands. Bestseller, 1950. The latter was reprinted separately as: The Bleeding House. Bestseller, 1950.)
The Pavilion. Simon, 1946; Chapman, 1948
A Time to Die. Simon, 1945; Chapman, 1947 ME

LAWRENCE, JAMES D. Series character: Angela Harpe, in all titles.
The Dream Girl Caper. Pyramid, 1975
The Emerald Oil Caper. Pyramid, 1975
The Gilded Snatch Caper. Pyramid, 1975
The Godmother Caper. Pyramid, 1975

LAWRENCE, JOSEPH I(VERS)
Tower of Terror. Macaulay, 1933

LAWRENCE, MARGERY (H.)
-Autumn Rose. Hale, 1971
-Bride of Darkness. Hale, 1967
-The Bridge of Wonder. Hale, 1939
-Cardboard Castle. Hale, 1951
-The Crooked Smile. Jarrolds, 1935
-Dead End. Hale, 1964
-Drums of Youth. Hurst, 1929
-Emma of Alkistan. Hale, 1953
-Evil Harvest. Hale, 1954
-The Floating Cafe, and other stories. Jarrolds, 1936 ss
-The Gilded Jar. Hale, 1948
-Green Archer. Hale, 1962
The Green Bough. Hale, 1968
Madame Holle. Jarrolds, 1934
The Madonna of the Seven Moons. Hurst, 1931; Bobbs, 1933
-Master of Shadows. Hale, 1959 ss
Miss Brandt: Adventuress. Hutchinson, 1923
-Nights of the Round Table. Hutchinson, 1926 ss
Number Seven Queer Street. Hale, 1945; Mycroft, 1969 ss
-Over My Shoulder. Hale, 1968
-Snapdragon. Hurst, 1931 ss
-Spanish Interlude. Hale, 1959
-Step Light, Lady. Hale, 1942
-Strange Caravan. Hale, 1941
-The Unforgetting Heart. Hale, 1963
-The Yellow Triangle. Hale, 1965

LAWRENCE, MARY MARGARET
Seven Thunders. Dell, 1974

LAWRENCE, MICHAEL. Pseudonym of Lawrence Lariar, 1908-   , q.v. Other pseudonyms: Adam Knight, Michael Stark, qq.v. Series character: Johnny Amsterdam, in both titles.
I Like It Cool. Popular Library, 1960
Naked and Alone. Popular Library, 1959

LAWRENCE, ROBERT JACKSON
Murder in Mayfair. Comet, 1958

LAWS, GERALDINE. See: LEONARD (REGINALD) GRIBBLE, 1908-   .

LAWSON, W. B. Series characters: The Dalton Boys = DB; Jesse James = JJ.
Bob Ford, the Slayer of Jesse James; or, The Dramatic Life and Death of a Noted Desperado. Street, 1898 JJ
The Dalton Boys and the M.K. and T. Robbery. Street, 1899 DB
The Dalton Boys in California; or, A Bold Hold-Up at Ceres. Street, 1893 DB
Frank James in St. Louis; or, The Mysteries of a Great City. Street, 1898
The Hatfield-McCoy Feud. Street, 1898
Jesse James at Coney Island; or, The Wall Street Banker's Secret. Street, 1898 JJ
Jesse James' Double; or, The Man from Missouri. Street, 1898 JJ
Jesse James in New York; or, A Plot Against a Millionaire. Street, 1898 JJ
Jesse James' Oath; or, Tracked to Death. Street, 1898 JJ
The Red Canyon Mystery. Street, 1902

LAYARD, G(EORGE) S(OMES). 1857-1925.
The Amateur Criminal. Allan, 1925 ss

LAYHEW, JANE
Rx for Murder. Lippincott, 1946

LAYLAND-BARRATT, FRANCES
Lycanthia. Jenkins, 1935

LAYTON, FRANK GEORGE. 1872-1941.
"Hanged by the Neck." Nicholson, 1935

LEA, G(EORGE) F(RANCIS) PERCIVALE. 1907-   .
A Detective Unawares. Hurst, 1928

LEA, HUGH
The Ghosts of Perranprah. Hodder, 1937
The Mine of Ill Omen. Hodder, 1939

LEACH, CHRISTOPHER. 1925-   .
The Send-Off. Chatto, 1973; Scribner, 1974

LEACH, DOUGLAS
The Big Boys. Hale, 1969
The Man on the Marsh. Hale, 1969
Three for a Killing. Hale, 1971

LEACOCK, STEPHEN. 1869-1944.
Frenzied Fiction. Lane (New York), 1918 ss, at least one criminous
Further Foolishness. Lane (New York), 1916 ss, at least one criminous
Nonsense Novels. Lane (New York), 1911 ss, at least one criminous

LEADER, CHARLES. Pseudonym of Robert Charles Smith, 1938-   . Other pseudonym: Robert Charles, q.v.
The Angry Darkness. Hale, 1968
Cargo to Saigon. Hale, 1969
Death of a Marine. Hale, 1970
The Double M Man. Hale, 1969
The Dragon Roars. Hale, 1970
Frontiers of Violence. Hale, 1966
The Golden Lure. Hale, 1967
Murder in Marrakech. Hale, 1966
Nightmare on the Nile. Hale, 1967
Salesman of Death. Hale, 1971
-Scavengers at War. Hale, 1974
Strangler's Moon. Hale, 1968
A Wreath from Bangkok. Hale, 1975
A Wreath of Poppies. Hale, 1975

LEADER, MARY
Triad. Coward, 1973; Hodder, 1973

LEADERMAN, GEORGE. Pseudonym of Richard Blundell Robinson, 1905-   .
Death in Pursuit. Hurst, 1935
The Door was Violence. Hurst, 1935

LEAHY, W(ILLIAM) A(UGUSTINE). 1867-   .
The Incendiary. Rand, 1897

LEAMAN, ADELE
The Green Bag. Skeffington, 1932

LEAN, FLORENCE MARRYAT CHURCH. 1837-1899. Pseudonym: Florence Marryat, q.v.

LEARMONTH, DAVID
-After the Battle. Hutchinson, 1933
-The Empty Glass. Hutchinson, 1931
-Galloping Gold. Hutchinson, 1926
Red Mammon. Hutchinson, 1928
-Tainted Turf. Hutchinson, 1927
-Tic-Tac. Hutchinson, 1930

LEAROYD, C(YRIL) G(EORGE)
Physicians' Fare. Arnold, 1939; Longmans, 1939 ss, some criminous

LEARY, FRANCIS (W.)
This Dark Monarchy. Dutton, 1949; Evans, 1950

LEASOR, (THOMAS) JAMES. 1923-   . Series characters: Dr. Jason Love = JL; the owner of Aristo Autos = AA.

The Chinese Widow. Heinemann, 1975
Host of Extras. Heinemann, 1973 JL
Love-All. Heinemann, 1971 JL
Never Had a Spanner on Her. Heinemann, 1970 AA
Passport for a Pilgrim. Heinemann, 1968; Doubleday, 1969 JL
Passport in Suspense. Heinemann, 1967. U.S. title: The Yang Meridian. Putnam, 1968 JL
Passport to Oblivion. Heinemann, 1964; Lippincott, 1965. Also published as: Where the Spies Are. Signet, 1965; Pan, 1965 JL
Passport to Peril. Heinemann, 1966. U.S. title: Spylight. Lippincott, 1966 JL
Spylight; see Passport to Peril
They Don't Make Them Like That Any More. Heinemann, 1969; Doubleday, 1970 AA
A Week of Love. Heinemann, 1969 JL ss
Where the Spies Are; see Passport to Oblivion
The Yang Meridian; see Passport in Suspense

LE BAILLY, PIERRE
Watch of Evil. Exposition, 1964; Hodder, 1967. (Translation of Les Bons Sentiments. Paris, 1958.)

LE BAS, MARY
Castle Walk. Nelson, 1934
-Second Thoughts. Nelson, 1935

LEBHAR, BERTRAM
The Black Eye Snapshot. Street, 1912
The Snapshot Chap. Street, 1910

LEBHERZ, RICHARD
The Altars of the Heart. Barrie, 1957; Grove, 1957
The Man in the White Raincoat. Hogarth, 1961; London House, 1961
The Nazi Overcoat. Panther, 1967

LEBLANC, MAURICE (MARIE EMILE). 1864-1941. Series character: Arsene Lupin = AL (see also: Edgar Jepson, 1863-1938).
The Arrest of Arsene Lupin; see Arsene Lupin versus Holmlock Shears
Arsene Lupin, Gentleman Burglar; see The Exploits of Arsene Lupin
Arsene Lupin Intervenes; see Jim Barnett Intervenes
Arsene Lupin, Super Sleuth; see The Girl with the Green Eyes
Arsene Lupin versus Herlock Sholmes; see Arsene Lupin versus Holmlock Shears
Arsene Lupin versus Holmlock Shears. Richards, 1909. U.S. title: The Blonde Lady. Doubleday, 1910. Also published as: Arsene Lupin versus Herlock Sholmes. Donohue, 1910. And as: The Arrest of Arsene Lupin. Nash, 1911. And as: Sherlock Holmes versus Arsene Lupin: The Case of the Golden Blonde. Atomic, 1946. And as: The Fair-Haired Lady. (Translation of Arsene Lupin contre Herlock Sholmes. Paris, 1908.) AL ss
The Blonde Lady; see Arsene Lupin versus Holmlock Shears
The Bomb-Shell. Hurst, 1916. U.S. title: The Woman of Mystery. Macaulay, 1916. (Translation of L'Eclat d'Obus. Paris, 1916.) AL
The Candlestick with Seven Branches. Hurst, 1925. U.S. title: Memoirs of Arsene Lupin. Macaulay, 1925. (Translation of La Comtesse de Cagliostro. Paris, 1924.) AL

Coffin Island. Hurst, 1920. U.S. title: The Secret of Sarek. Macaulay, 1920. (Translation of L'Ile aux Trents Cercueils. Paris, 1920.) AL
The Confessions of Arsene Lupin. Mills, 1912; Doubleday, 1913. (Translation of Les Confidences d'Arsene Lupin. Paris, 1913.) AL ss
The Crystal Stopper. Hurst, 1913; Doubleday, 1913. (Translation of Le Bouchon de Cristal. Paris, 1912.) AL
Dorothy the Rope Dancer. Hurst, 1923. U.S. title: The Secret Tomb. Macaulay, 1923. (Translation of Dorothee, Danseuse de Corde. Paris, 1923.)
The Double Smile. Skeffington, 1933. U.S. title: The Woman with Two Smiles. Macaulay, 1933. (Translation of La Femme aux Deux Sourires. Paris, 1933.) AL
The Eight Strokes of the Clock. Cassell, 1922; Macaulay, 1922. (Translation of Les Huits Coups de l'Horloge. Paris, 1922.) AL ss
813. Mills, 1910; Doubleday, 1910. (Translation of 813. Paris, 1910.) AL
The Exploits of Arsene Lupin. Cassell, 1909; Harper, 1907. Also published as: The Seven of Hearts. Cassell, 1908. And as: (The Extraordinary Adventures of) Arsene Lupin, Gentleman Burglar. Donohue, 1910. (Translation of Arsene Lupin, Gentleman-Cambrioleur. Paris, 1907.) AL ss
The Extraordinary Adventures of Arsene Lupin, Gentleman Burglar; see The Exploits of Arsene Lupin
The Fair-Haired Lady; see Arsene Lupin versus Holmlock Shears
From Midnight to Morning. Hurst, 1933; Macaulay, 1933. (Translation of De Minuit a Sept Heures. Paris, 1922.)
The Frontier. Mills, 1912; Doran, 1912. (Translation of La Frontiere. Paris, 1911.)
The Girl with the Green Eyes. Hurst, 1927. U.S. title: Arsene Lupin, Super-Sleuth. Macaulay, 1927. (Translation of La Demoiselle aux Yeux Verts. Paris, 1927.) AL
The Golden Triangle. Hurst, 1917; Macaulay, 1917. (Translation of La Triangle d'Or. Paris, 1918.) AL
The Hollow Needle. Nash, 1911; Doubleday, 1910. (Translation of L'Aiguille Creuse. Paris, 1909.) AL
Jim Barnett Intervenes. Mills, 1928. U.S. title: Arsene Lupin Intervenes. Macaulay, 1929. (Translation of L'Agence Barnett et Cie. Paris, 1928.) AL ss
Man of Miracles. Skeffington, 1932; Macaulay, 1931. (Translation of Le Prince de Jericho. Paris, 1930.)
The Melamare Mystery. Mills, 1929; Macaulay, 1930. (Translation of La Demeure Mysterieuse. Paris, 1929.) AL
Memoirs of Arsene Lupin; see The Candlestick with Seven Branches
The Return of Arsene Lupin. Skeffington, 1933; Macaulay, 1933. (Translation of Victor, de la Brigade Mondaine. Paris, 1933.) AL
The Secret of Sarek; see Coffin Island
The Secret Tomb; see Dorothy the Rope Dancer
The Seven of Hearts; see The Exploits of Arsene Lupin
Sherlock Holmes versus Arsene Lupin: The Case of the Golden Blonde; see Arsene Lupin versus Holmlock Shears
The Teeth of the Tiger. Hurst, 1915; Doubleday, 1914. (Translation of Les Dents du Tigre. Paris, 1921.) AL
-The Tremendous Event. Hurst, 1924; Macaulay, 1922. (Translation of Le Formidable Evenement. Paris, 1921.)

-Wanton Venus. Long, 1935; Macaulay, 1935. (Translation of L'Image de la Femme Nue. Paris, 1934.)
The Woman of Mystery; see The Bomb-Shell
The Woman with Two Smiles; see The Double Smile

LE BRETON, AUGUSTE. 1913- .
The Law of the Streets Collins, 1957. (Translation of Le Loi des Rues. Paris, 1955.)
Rififi in New York. Stein, 1968. (Translation of Du Rififi a New York. Paris, 1967.)

LECALE, ERROL. Pseudonym of Wilfred (Glassford) McNeilly, 1921- , q.v. Other pseudonyms: W(illiam) Howard Baker, William A. Ballinger, Desmond Reid, qq.v.
Castledoom. New English Library pb, 1974
The Death Box. New English Library pb, 1974
The Severed Hand. New English Library pb, 1974
The Tigerman of Terrahpur. New English Library pb, 1973
Zombie. New English Library pb, 1975

LE CARRE, JOHN. Pseudonym of David John Moore Cornwell, 1931- . Series character: George Smiley = GS.
Call for the Dead. Gollancz, 1961; Walker, 1962. Also published as: The Deadly Affair. Penguin, 1968; Signet, 1968 GS
The Deadly Affair; see Call for the Dead
The Looking Glass War. Heinemann, 1965; Coward, 1965 GS
A Murder of Quality. Gollancz, 1962; Walker, 1963 GS
A Small Town in Germany. Heinemann, 1968; Coward, 1968
The Spy Who Came in from the Cold. Gollancz, 1963; Coward, 1964 GS
Tinker, Tailor, Soldier, Spy. Hodder, 1974; Knopf, 1974 GS

LECHMERE, DAVID
In Deadly Peril. Ouseley, 1908

LECOMBER, BRIAN
Turn Killer. Hodder, 1975; Stein, 1975

LEDERER, NORBERT (LEWIS). 1888-1955. See: LILLIAN DAY, 1893- .

LEDIG, ALMA. See: ERNESTINE MALAN.

LEDIG, GERT. 1921- .
The Brutal Years. Weidenfeld, 1959. (Translation of Faustrecht. Munich, 1957.)

LEE, AUSTIN. 1904-1965. Pseudonyms: John Austwick, Julian Callender, qq.v. Series character: Miss Hogg, in all titles.
Call in Miss Hogg. Cape, 1956
Miss Hogg and the Bronte Murders. Cape, 1956
Miss Hogg and the Covent Garden Murders. Cape, 1960
Miss Hogg and the Dead Dean. Cape, 1958
Miss Hogg and the Missing Sisters. Cape, 1961
Miss Hogg and the Squash Club Murder. Cape, 1957
Miss Hogg Flies High. Cape, 1958
Miss Hogg's Last Case. Cape, 1963
Sheep's Clothing. Cape, 1955

LEE, BABS. Pseudonym of Marion van der Veer Lee, 1914- . Series character: Argus Steele, in all titles.

Measured for Murder, with Clare Castler Saunders, q.v. Scribner, 1944; Muller, 1945
A Model is Murdered. Scribner, 1942
Passport to Oblivion. Scribner, 1943

LEE, BRETON
The Pit of Death. Fiction House, 1935

LEE, DORIAN
-The Bad Companions. Long, 1955
-The Captive Years. Long, 1951
-Crooked Paths. Swan, 1943
-Cut the Cards, Lady. Long, 1952
-Dark Star Rising. Long, 1947
-The Fledgeling. Long, 1952
-Green Bracken. Long, 1953
-Home to Our Valley. Long, 1956
-Lover Come Home. Long, 1950
-Luke's Summer. Long, 1951
-Prisoner Go Free. Long, 1954
Sandover Goes Gay. Swan, 1946
-Snakes have Fangs. Long, 1946
-Strange Partner. Long, 1948
-Uncertain Treasure. Swan, 1947
-Wild Apple Orchard. Long, 1954

LEE, EDWARD. Pseudonym of Edward Lee Fouts, 1902- . Series character: Red Blake, in both titles.
Death Goes Fishing; see A Fish for Murder
A Fish for Murder. Doubleday, 1944; Hurst, 1947. Also published as: Death Goes Fishing. Thriller Novel Classic, 1944 (abridged). And as: Lust to Kill. Jonathan, 1955
Lust to Kill; see A Fish for Murder
The Needle's Eye. Doubleday, 1941

LEE, ELSIE. Pseudonym of Elsie Lee Sheridan. Series character: Sam Benedict (who also appears in books by Howard L. Oleck, 1911- , and Brad Williams, 1918- , qq.v.) = SB.
Barrow Sinister. Dell, 1969. British title: Romantic Assignment. Hale, 1974
The Blood Red Oscar. Lancer, 1962
Clouds over Vellanti. Lancer, 1965; Hale, 1972
A Comedy of Terrors. Lancer, 1964. (Novelization of the movie.)
The Curse of Carranca. Lancer, 1966
Dark Moon, Lost Lady. Lancer, 1965; Hale, 1973
Diplomatic Lover. Dell, 1971
Doctor's Office. Lancer, 1968
The Drifting Sands. Lancer, 1966
An Eligible Connection. Dell, 1975; Chivers, 1974
Fulfillment. Lancer, 1969
Mansion of the Golden Windows. Lancer, 1966
The Masque of the Red Death. Lancer, 1964. (Novelization of the movie.)
Muscle Beach Party. Lancer, 1964. (Novelization of the movie.)
Mystery Castle. Lancer, 1969; Hale, 1973
The Passions of Medora Graeme. Arbor, 1972
Prior Betrothal. Arbor, 1973
Romance on the Rhine. Lancer, 1967; Hale, 1974
Romantic Assignment; see Barrow Sinister
Sam Benedict: Cast the First Stone. Lancer, 1963. (Novelization of the TV series; the cover of the book attributes it to Norman Daniels, q.v.) SB
Satan's Coast. Lancer, 1969
Season of Evil. Lancer, 1965
The Second Romance. (U.S.), 1966; Hale, 1974
The Second Season. Dell, 1973
Silence is Golden. Dell, 1971

Sinister Abbey. Lancer, 1967
The Spy at the Villa Miranda. Lancer, 1967
Star-Crossed Love. Dell, 1972
Star of Danger. Dell, 1971
The Unhappy Parting. (U.S.), 1967; Hale, 1973
The Wicked Guardian. Dell, 1973
Winegarden. Arbor, 1971

LEE, FLEMING. See: LESLIE CHARTERIS, 1907- .

LEE, GERALD
Murder and Music. Talbot, 1943

LEE, GYPSY ROSE. Stage name of Rose Louise Hovick, 1914-1970. The books signed by her were actually written by Craig Rice, 1908-1957, q.v. Series character: Gypsy Rose Lee, in both titles.
The G-String Murders. Simon, 1941. British title: The Strip-Tease Murders. Lane, 1943. Also published as: Lady of Burlesque. Tower, 1942
Lady of Burlesque; see The G-String Murders
Mother Finds a Body. Simon, 1942; Lane, 1944
The Strip-Tease Murders; see The G-String Murders

LEE, H. FLETCHER. See: OLIVE LETHBRIDGE.

LEE, H. H.
-Fun Fair. Swan, 1942
Racket Busters, Incorporated. Swan, 1946
Snappy Vendetta. Swan, 1944

LEE, HERBERT PATRICK
Hell's Harbour. Melrose, 1936

LEE, JENNETTE (BARBOUR PERRY). 1860-1951. Series character: Millicent Newberry, in all titles.
Dead Right. Scribner, 1925; Hurst, 1925
The Green Jacket. Scribner, 1917; Skeffington, 1918
The Mysterious Office. Scribner, 1922; Hurst, 1922

LEE, JOHN (DARRELL). 1931- . Series character: Brian Douglas, in both titles.
Assignment in Algeria. Walker, 1971. British title: The Killing Wind. Long, 1972
Caught in the Act. Morrow, 1968; Long, 1969
The Killing Wind; see Assignment in Algeria

LEE, JOHN W.
Background to Death. Pictorial Art, 1945
Death by the Radio. Mitre, 1946
One from Five. Halle, 1946

LEE, LEONARD
The Twisted Mirror. Ziff-Davis, 1947

LEE, MANFRED BENNINGTON. 1905-1971. Joint pseudonyms with Frederic Dannay, 1905- : Ellery Queen, Barnaby Ross, qq.v.

LEE, MARION BEVERIDGE
The Man with the Rake. Abbey, 1901

LEE, MARION VAN DER VEER. 1914- . Pseudonym: Babs Lee, q.v.

LEE, NOEL
Danger in Numbers. Wright, 1944
Fear Without End. Wright, 1949
Papers Mean Peril. Wright, 1942

LEE, NORMA. Series character: Norma "Nicky" Lee (The Beautiful Gunner), in all titles.
Another Woman's Man. Laurie, 1954
The Beautiful Gunner. Laurie, 1953
The Broadway Jungle. Laurie, 1954
Lover—Say It with Mink! Laurie, 1953

LEE, NORMAN
The "Four Winds" Mystery. Mitre, 1946
Peril at Journey's End. Foster, 1947

LEE, NORMAN. 1905-1962. Pseudonyms: Raymond Armstrong, Mark Corrigan, Robertson Hobart, qq.v.

LEE, SUSAN RICHMOND. Pseudonym: Curtis Yorke, q.v.

LEE, THORNE. Pseudonym of Thornton Shiveley.
The Monster of Lazy Hook. Duell, 1949
Summer Shock. Abelard, 1956

LEECH, AUDREY
Pawn of Evil. Pyramid, 1971
Terror of Stormcastle. Paperback Library, 1973
The Witches of Omen. Pyramid, 1971

LEES, DAN. 1927- . Series character: Jeff Plummer, in all titles.
Elizabeth R.I.P. Constable, 1974; St. Martin's, 1975
The Rainbow Conspiracy. Constable, 1971; Walker, 1972
Rape of a Quiet Town. Constable, 1973; Walker, 1973
Zodiac. Constable, 1972; Walker, 1973

LEES, HANNAH. Pseudonym of Elizabeth Head Fetter, 1904-1973.
The Dark Device. Harper, 1947; Murray, 1949
Death in the Doll's House, with Lawrence P(aul) Bachmann, 1912- , q.v. Random, 1943; Murray, 1944
Prescription for Murder. Random, 1941; Murray, 1943

LEES, HAROLD P(ERCY)
Ten Thousand Passports to Hell. Hale, 1968
This Way to Evil. Hale, 1971
The Violence of Hate. Hale, 1970

LE FANU, JOSEPH SHERIDAN. 1814-1873.
All in the Dark. Bentley, 1866; Harper, 1862
Checkmate. Hurst, 1871; Evans, 1871
-Chronicles of Golden Friars. Bentley, 1871
The Evil Guest. Downey, 1894
Ghost Stories and Mysteries. Dover, 1975 ss, taken from earlier collections
Guy Deverell. Bentley, 1865; Harper, 1866
Haunted Lives. Tinsley, 1868
The House by the Church-Yard. Bentley, 1863
In a Glass Darkly. Bentley, 1872 ss
A Lost Name. Bentley, 1868
Madam Crowl's Ghost, and other tales of mystery. Bell, 1923 ss
-The Rose and the Key. Chapman, 1871
-The Tenants of Malory. Tinsley, 1867; Harper, 1867
Uncle Silas. Bentley, 1864; Munro, 1878
-The Watcher and other weird stories. Downey, 1894 ss
Willing to Die. Hurst, 1873
Wylder's Hand. Bentley, 1864; Carleton, 1865
The Wyvern Mystery. Tinsley, 1869

LEFEVRE, C.
Murder in Marseilles. Brown Watson, 1953

LEFEVRE, EDWIN. 1871-1943.
The Plunderers. Harper, 1916 ss

LEFFINGWELL, ALBERT. 1895-1946. Pseudonyms: Dana Chambers, Giles Jackson, qq.v.
Nine Against New York. Holt, 1941

LEFFINGWELL, ALSOP
The Mystery of Bar Harbor. Dillingham, 1887

LEFFLAND, ELLA. 1931-   .
-Mrs. Munck. Houghton, 1970; H. Hamilton, 1971

LEGARET, JEAN. 1913-1976.
Tightrope. Little, 1970. (Translation of Le Conde. Paris, 1967.)

LEGGETT, H. W.
-The Man Who Came Back. Gramol, 1935
-The Second Mrs. Savenage. Gramol, 1936
Under Suspicion. Hamilton, 1935

LEHMAN, R(UDOLF) C(HAMBERS). 1856-1929.
The Adventures of Picklock Holes. Bradbury Agnew, 1901; Aspen, 1975 ss

LE HURAY, C. P.
Death for a Holiday. Big Ben, 1946

LEIGH, HILARY
Greystones. Pyramid, 1966

LEIGH, LOIS (E.) AUSTEN. See: LOIS (E.) AUSTEN-LEIGH.

LEIGH, SUSANNAH
Dark Labyrinth. GM, 1975

LEIGHTON, FLORENCE. Pseudonym of Florence Leighton Pfalzgraf, 1902-   .
As Strange a Maze. Archer, 1935

LEIGHTON, MARIE (FLORA BARBARA) CONNOR. 18??-1941.
The Amazing Verdict. Richards, 1904
-Beauty's Queen. White, 1884
Black Silence. Ward, 1913
-The Bride of Dutton Market. Ward, 1911
Builders of Ships. Ward, 1911
Convict 413L. Ward, 1910
Convict 99, with Robert Leighton, 1859-1933. Richards, 1898
Convict 100. Ward, 1920
Dark Peril. Hodder, 1916
Deep Waters. Ward, 1909
-The Duchess Grace. Ward, 1918
Ducks and Drakes. Ward, 1913
Every Man has his Price. Ward, 1917
An Eye for an Eye. Ward, 1909
-The Fires of Love. Ward, 1915
-For Love or Money. Ward, 1922
The Gates of Sorrow. Ward, 1915
Geraldine Walton—Woman! Ward, 1914
The Girl of the Yellow Diamonds. Pearson, 1920
Greed. Ward, 1911
Guilty or Innocent? Ward, 1918
The Hand of the Unseen. Ward, 1918
The Harvest of Sin. Bowden, 1898
Her Convict Husband. Ward, 1913
-Her Fate and His. Ward, 1921
-Her Heart's Awakening. Chapman, 1893
-Her Ladyship's Silence. Cassell, 1907
-Her Marriage Lines. Ward, 1912
Hidden Hands. Newnes, 1918
Human Nature. Ward, 1916
-Husband and Wife. White, 1888
In God's Good Time. Richards, 1903
In the Grip of a Lie. Long, 1916
In the Plotter's Web. Mellifont, 1937
In the Shadow of Guilt, with Robert Leighton, 1859-1933. Richards, 1901; Brentano's, 1901
Joan Mar, Detective. Ward, 1910
Justice! Ward, 1910
-The Lady of Balmerino. Trischler, 1891
Lucile Dar, Detective. Ward, 1919
The Man Who Knew All. Long, 1916
A Marked Woman. Hodder, 1916
Michael Dred, Detective; with Robert Leighton, 1859-1933. Richards, 1899; Brentano's, 1899
The Missing Miss Randolph. Ward, 1912
"Money." Ward, 1909
The Money Spider. Mellifont, 1936
-A Morganatic Marriage. White, 1885
The Mystery of the Three Fingers. Long, 1916
-A Napoleon of the Press. Hodder, 1900
The Opal Heart. Ward, 1920
Put Yourself in her Place. Ward, 1908
Red Gold. Ward, 1919
The Red Painted Box. Macqueen, 1897
Sealed Lips. Ward, 1906
-The Shame of Silence. Long, 1917
-The Silence of Dr. Duveen. Mellifont, 1937
The Silent Clue. Ward, 1921
The Silver Stair. Ward, 1914
-The Stolen Honeymoon. Odhams, 1921
The Story of a Great Sin. Ward, 1916
-The Triangle. Ward, 1912
-The Triumph of Manhood. Chapman, 1889
Two Black Pearls. White, 1886
-Under the Broad Arrow. Hodder, 1914
Vengeance is Mine. Ward, 1917
-Was She Worth It? Aldine, 1922
The Way of Sinners. Ward, 1914
Who Killed Lord Luxmore?, with Robert Leighton, 1859-1933. Pearson, 1929
-The Woman Bars the Way. Gramol, 1933

LEIGHTON, ROBERT. 1859-1933. See: MARIE (FLORA BARBARA) CONNOR LEIGHTON, 18??-1941.

LEIGHTON, WING
-Whistle Me over the Water. Hurst, 1944

LEINSTER, MURRAY. Pseudonym of Will(iam) F(itzgerald) Jenkins, 1896-1975, q.v.
Guns for Achin. Wright, 1936
Murder in the Family. Hamilton, 1935
Murder Madness. Brewer, 1931
Murder Will Out. Hamilton, 1932
No Clues. Wright, 1935
Scalps. Brewer, 1930. British title: Wings of Chance. Hamilton, 1935
Wanted Dead or Alive! Wright, 1950
Wings of Chance; see Scalps

LEITE, GEORGE THURSTON. 1920-   . Joint pseudonym with Jody Scott, 1923-   : Thurston Scott, q.v.

LEITFRED, ROBERT H. Series character: Simon Crole, in all titles.
The Corpse That Spoke. Green Circle, 1936; Harrap, 1937
Death Cancels the Evidence. Green Circle, 1938. Also published as: Murder is my Racket. Tech Mysteries, 194?
The Man Who was Murdered Twice. Green Circle, 1937
Murder is my Racket; see Death Cancels the Evidence

LE JEMLYS. Pseudonym of Symmes W. Jelley.
Lawyer Manton of Chicago. Eagle, 1888
The Scarlet Handkerchief. Laird, 1889
Shadowed to Europe. Belford, 1885

LEJEUNE, ANTHONY. Pseudonym of Edward Anthony Thompson. Series character: Adam Gifford, in at least those marked AG.
Crowded and Dangerous. Macdonald, 1959
The Dark Trade. Macdonald, 1965; Doubleday, 1966. Also published as: Death of a Pornographer. Lancer, 1967 AG
Death of a Pornographer; see The Dark Trade
Duel in the Shadows. Macdonald, 1962 AG
Glint of Spears. Macdonald, 1963
Mr. Diabolo. Macdonald, 1960
News of Murder. Macdonald, 1961 AG

LEM, STANISLAW. 1921-   .
The Investigation. Seabury, 1974. (Translation of Sledztwo. Krakow, 1959.)

LEMARCHAND, ELIZABETH (WHARTON). 1906-   . Series character: Det.-Insp. Pollard, in all titles.
The Affacombe Affair. Hart-Davis, 1968
Alibi for a Corpse. Hart-Davis, 1969
Buried in the Past. Hart-Davis, 1974; Walker, 1975
Cyanide with Compliments. MacGibbon, 1972; Walker, 1973
Death of an Old Girl. Hart-Davis, 1967; Award, 1970
Death on Doomsday. Hart-Davis, 1971; Walker, 1973
Let or Hindrance. Hart-Davis, 1973. U.S. title: No Vacation from Murder. Walker, 1974
No Vacation from Murder; see Let or Hindrance

LE MAY, ALAN. 1899-   .
One of Us is a Murderer. Doubleday, 1930; Jarrolds, 1930

LEMIEUX, KENNETH. 1923-   . Pseudonym: Kenneth Orvis, q.v.

LEMMON, LAURA ELIZABETH. 1917-   . Pseudonym: Lee Wilson, q.v.

LENEHAN, J(OHN) C(HRISTOPHER). Series characters: Inspector Kilby, in at least those marked K; Charlie Ryan, in at least those marked CR.
Boston Belle Meets Murder. Jenkins, 1935 CR
Carnival of Death. Jenkins, 1934
Deadly Decree. Jenkins, 1936
Death Dances Thrice. Jenkins, 1933 CR
Driven to Death. Jenkins, 1944 CR
Guilty But Not Insane. Jenkins, 1938 CR
The Joyful Jays. Jenkins, 1941
The Mansfield Mystery. Jenkins, 1932 K
The Marked Pistol. Jenkins, 1929
The Masked Blackmailer. Jenkins, 1933 CR
One Murder Too Many. Jenkins, 1943
The Silecroft Case. Jenkins, 1931 K
The Tunnel Mystery. Jenkins, 1929; Mystery League, 1931 K

LENNOX, GILBERT
X14. Nelson, 1931

LENNOX, JOHN
The Paper Doll. Quality, 1949

LENOTRE, G. Pseudonym of Louis Leon Theodore Gosselin, 1857-1925.
-The Woman Without a Name. Collins, 1923. (Translation of La Femme sans Nom. Paris, 1922.)

LENTON, ANTHONY
Murder Beat. Hale, 1971
Murder City. Hale, 1972

LENTON, DUDLEY
 The Blue Mandarin. Modern, 1938
 Crooks of Paris. Modern, 1938
 The Desert Trail. Modern, 193?
 In Lands of Terror. Modern, 193?
 The League of Five. Modern, 1935
 The Mystery of the Ironworks. Modern, 193?
 The Spy in the Navy. Modern, 193?
 The Tiger of Karan. Modern, 1938

LEON, HENRY CECIL. 1902-1976. Pseudonym: Henry Cecil, q.v.

LEONARD, A. B. Pseudonym of Earl Augustus Aldrich, 1886-   .
 The Judson Murder Case. Clode, 1933; Butterworth, 1933

LEONARD, CHARLES L. Pseudonym of M(ary) V(iolet) Heberden, 1906-   , q.v. Series character: Paul Kilgerrin, in all titles.
 Assignment to Death; see The Fanatic of Fez
 Deadline for Destruction. Doubleday, 1942
 Expert in Murder. Doubleday, 1945
 The Fanatic of Fez. Doubleday, 1943. Also published as: Assignment to Death. Thriller Novel Classic, 194? (abridged)
 The Fourth Funeral. Doubleday, 1948; Museum, 1951
 Pursuit in Peru. Doubleday, 1946; Museum, 1948
 Search for a Scientist. Doubleday, 1947; Museum, 1950
 The Secret of the Spa. Doubleday, 1944
 Secrets for Sale. Doubleday, 1950
 Sinister Shelter. Doubleday, 1949; Museum, 1951
 The Stolen Squadron. Doubleday, 1942
 Treachery in Trieste. Doubleday, 1951

LEONARD, CONSTANCE (BRINK). 1923-   .
 The Other Maritha. Dodd, 1972; Milton House, 1974
 Steps to Nowhere. Dodd, 1974; Milton House, 1974

LEONARD, ELMORE. 1925-   .
 The Big Bounce. Hale, 1969. (U.S. title?)
 Fifty-Two Pickup. Delacorte, 1974; Secker, 1974
 The Moonshine War. Doubleday, 1969; Hale, 1970
 Mr. Majestyk. Dell, 1974. (Novelization of the movie.)
 -Valdez is Coming. GM, 1970; Hale, 1969

LEONARD, FRANK (G.). 1935?-1974.
 Box 100. Harper, 1972

LEONARD, GEORGE (BURR). 1923-   .
 Beyond Control. Macmillan, 1975

LEONARD, PHYLLIS G(RUBBS). 1924-   .
 Prey of the Eagle. McKay, 1974

L'EPINE, CHARLES. Pseudonym.
 The Devil in a Domino. Greening, 1897
 The Lady of the Leopard. Greening, 1899

LEQUEUX, WILLIAM (TUFNELL). 1864-1927.
 The Amazing Count. Ward, 1929
 Annette of the Argonne. Hurst, 1916
 As We Forgave Them. White, 1904
 At the Sign of the Sword. Jack, 1915
 Behind the Bronze Door; see The Bronze Face
 Behind the German Lines. London Mail, 1917
 Behind the Throne. Methuen, 1905
 Beryl of the Biplane. Pearson, 1917 ss
 The Black Owl. Ward, 1926
 Blackmailed. Nash, 1927
 Bleke, the Butler. Jarrolds, 1924 ss
 The Blue Bungalow. Hurst, 1925
 Bolo the Super-Spy. Odhams, 1918
 The Bomb-Makers. Jarrolds, 1917 ss
 The Bond of Black. White, 1899; Dillingham, 1899
 The Breath of Suspicion. Long, 1917
 The Broadcast Mystery. Holden, 1925
 The Broken Thread. Ward, 1916
 The Bronze Face. Ward, 1923. U.S. title: Behind the Bronze Door. Macaulay, 1923
 The Catspaw. Lloyds, 1918
 The Chameleon. Hodder, 1927. U.S. title: Poison Shadows. Macaulay, 1927
 "Cinders" of Harley Street. Ward, 1916 ss
 Cipher Six. Hodder, 1919
 The Closed Book. Methuen, 1904; Smart Set, 1904
 Concerning This Woman. Newnes, 1928
 Confessions of a Ladies' Man. Hutchinson, 1905 ss
 The Count's Chauffeur. Nash, 1907 ss
 The Court of Honour. White, 1901
 The Crime Code; see Double Nought
 The Crimes Club. Nash, 1927 ss
 The Crinkled Crown. Ward, 1929; Macaulay, 1929
 The Crooked Way. Methuen, 1908
 The Crystal Claw. Hodder, 1924; Macaulay, 1924
 The Czar's Spy. Hodder, 1905; Smart Set, 1905
 The Dangerous Game; see Hidden Hands
 The Day of Temptation. White, 1899; Dillingham, 1899
 The Death-Doctor. Hurst, 1912
 The Devil's Carnival. Hurst, 1917
 Devil's Dice. White, 1897; Rand, 1897
 The Doctor of Pimlico. Cassell, 1919; Macaulay, 1920
 Donovan of Whitehall. Pearson, 1917 ss
 Double Nought. Hodder, 1927. U.S. title: The Crime Code. Macaulay, 1928
 The Double Shadow. Hodder, 1915
 The Elusive Four. Cassell, 1921 ss
 England's Peril. White, 1899
 An Eye for an Eye. White, 1900
 The Factotum and other stories. Ward, 1931 ss
 The Fatal Face. Hurst, 1926
 Fatal Fingers. Cassell, 1912
 Fatal Thirteen. Paul, 1909
 The Fifth Finger. Paul, 1921; Moffat, 1921
 Fine Feathers. Paul, 1924
 The Forbidden Word. Odhams, 1919
 The Four Faces. Paul, 1914; Brentano's, 1914
 Further Secrets of Potsdam. London Mail, 1917 ss
 The Gamblers. Hutchinson, 1901
 The Gay Triangle. Jarrolds, 1922 ss
 The German Spy. Newnes, 1914 ss
 -The German Spy System from Within. Hodder, 1915
 The Golden Face. Cassell, 1922; Macaulay, 1922
 The Golden Three. Ward, 1930; Fiction League, 1931
 The Great Court Scandal. White, 1907
 The Great God Gold. Badger, 1910. (British title?)
 The Great Plot. Hodder, 1907
 The Green Ray; see The Mystery of the Green Ray
 Guilty Bonds. Routledge, 1891; Fenno, 1895
 The Hand of Allah. Cassell, 1914. Also published as: The Riddle of the Ring. Federation Press, 1927
 The Heart of a Princess. Ward, 1920
 Her Majesty's Minister. Hodder, 1901; Dodd, 1901
 Her Royal Highness. Hodder, 1914
 Hidden Hands. Hodder, 1926. U.S. title: The Dangerous Game. Macaulay, 1926
 The Hotel X. Ward, 1919 ss
 The House of Evil. Ward, 1927
 The House of the Wicked. Hurst, 1906
 The House of Whispers. Nash, 1909; Brentano's, 1910
 The Hunchback of Westminster. Methuen, 1904
 Hushed Up! Nash, 1911
 Hushed Up at German Headquarters. London Mail, 1917 ss
 The Idol of the Town. White, 1904
 If Sinners Entice Thee. White, 1898; Dillingham, 1899
 In Secret. Odhams, 1921 ss
 In White Raiment. White, 1900
 The Indiscretions of a Lady's Maid. Nash, 1911 ss
 The Intriguers. Hodder, 1920; Macaulay, 1921
 The King's Incognito. Odhams, 1919
 The Lady in the Car. Nash, 1908; Lippincott, 1908 ss
 The Lady-in-Waiting. Ward, 1921
 -Landru: His Secret Love Affairs. Paul, 1922
 The Lawless Hand. Hurst, 1927; Macaulay, 1928
 The Letter E. Cassell, 1926. U.S. title: The Tattoo Mystery. Macaulay, 1927
 The Little Blue Goddess. Ward, 1918
 The Looker-On. White, 1908
 The Lost Million. Nash, 1913
 The Luck of the Secret Service. Pearson, 1921 ss
 The Lure of Love. Ward, 1919
 Lying Lips. Paul, 1910
 Mademoiselle of Monte Carlo. Cassell, 1921; Macaulay, 1921
 A Madonna of the Music Halls. White, 1897. Also published as: A Secret Sin; or, The Madonna of the Music Halls. Gardner, 1913
 The Maker of Secrets. Ward, 1914
 The Man About Town. Long, 1916
 The Man from Downing Street. Hurst, 1904
 The Marked Man. Ward, 1925
 The Mask. Long, 1905
 The Minister of Evil. Cassell, 1918
 The Money-Spider. Cassell, 1911; Badger, 1911
 More Mysteries of a Great City; see Mysteries of a Great City
 More Secrets of Potsdam. London Mail, 1917 ss
 Mysteries. Ward, 1913 ss
 Mysteries of a Great City. Hodder, 1920. Reprinted in paperback in two volumes: Mysteries of a Great City, and More Mysteries of a Great City, both Mellifont, 1934 ss
 The Mysterious Mr. Miller. Hodder, 1906
 The Mysterious Three. Ward, 1915
 The Mystery of a Motor-Car. Hodder, 1906
 The Mystery of Mademoiselle. Hodder, 1926
 The Mystery of Nine. Nash, 1912
 The Mystery of the Green Ray. Hodder, 1915. Also published as: The Green Ray. Hodder, 1916
 No Greater Love. Ward, 1917
 No. 7, Saville Square. Ward, 1920
 Number 70, Berlin. Hodder, 1916
 Of Royal Blood. Hutchinson, 1900
 The Office Secret. Ward, 1927
 The Open Verdict. Hodder, 1921
 The Pauper of Park Lane. Cassell, 1908; Cupples, 1908
 The Peril of Helen Marklove and other stories. Jarrolds, 1928 ss

The Place of the Dragons. Ward, 1916
Poison Shadows; see The Chameleon
The Power of the Borgias. Odhams, 1921. (Novelization of the movie.)
The Price of Power. Hurst, 1913
The Rainbow Mystery. Hodder, 1917 ss
Rasputin the Rascal Monk. Hurst, 1917
Rasputinism in London. Cassell, 1919
The Rat Trap. Ward, 1928; Macaulay, 1930
The Red Hat. London Daily Mail, 1904
The Red Room. Cassell, 1909; Little, 1911
The Red Widow; or, The Death-Dealers of London. Cassell, 1920
Revelations of the Secret Service. White, 1911 ss
The Riddle of the Ring; see The Hand of Allah
The Room of Secrets. Ward, 1913
Sant of the Secret Service. Odhams, 1918
The Scandal-Monger. Ward, 1917 ss
The Scarlet Sign. Ward, 1926
The Secret Formula. Ward, 1928
The Secret Life of the Ex-Tsaritza. Odhams, 1918
The Secret of the Square. White, 1907
A Secret Service; see Strange Tales of a Nihilist
The Secret Shame of the Kaiser. Hurst, 1919
A Secret Sin; or, A Madonna of the Music Halls; see A Madonna of the Music Halls
The Secret Telephone. Jarrolds, 1921; McCann, 1920 ss
Secrets of Monte Carlo. White, 1899; Dillingham, 1900 ss
The Secrets of Potsdam. London Daily Mail, 1917 ss
Secrets of the Foreign Office. Hutchinson, 1903 ss
Secrets of the White Tsar. Odhams, 1919
The Seven Secrets. Hutchinson, 1903
The Sign of Silence. Ward, 1915
The Sign of the Seven Sins. Lippincott, 1901. (British title?)
The Sign of the Stranger. White, 1904
Sins of the City. White, 1905
The Sister Disciple. Hurst, 1918
Society Intrigues I Have Known. Odhams, 1920 ss
Sons of Satan. White, 1914
The Spider's Eye. Cassell, 1905
Spies of the Kaiser. Hurst, 1909 ss
The Spy Hunter. Pearson, 1916
The Sting. Hodder, 1928; Macaulay, 1928
Stolen Souls. Tower, 1895; Stokes, 1895 ss
The Stolen Statesman. Skeffington, 1918
Stolen Sweets. Nash, 1908
Strange Tales of a Nihilist. Ward, 1892; Cassell (New York), 1892. Also published as: A Secret Service; Being Strange Tales of a Nihilist. Ward, 1896 ss
The Stretton Street Affair. Cassell, 1924; Macaulay, 1922
The Tattoo Mystery; see The Letter E
The Temptress. Tower, 1895; Stokes, 1895
The Terror of the Air. Lloyds, 1920
This House to Let. Hodder, 1921
Three Glass Eyes. Treherne, 1903
Three Knots. Ward, 1922
The Tickencote Treasure. Newnes, 1903
Tracked by Wireless. Paul, 1922; Moffat, 1922 ss
Twice Tried. Hurst, 1928
Two in a Tangle. Hodder, 1917
The Under-Secretary. Hutchinson, 1902
The Unknown Tomorrow. White, 1910
The Unnamed. Hodder, 1902
The Valley of the Shadow. Methuen, 1905
The Valrose Mystery. Ward, 1925
The Veiled Man. White, 1899

The Voice from the Void. Cassell, 1922; Macaulay, 1923
The Way to Win. Marshall, 1916
Whatsoever a Man Soweth. White, 1906
Where the Desert Ends. Cassell, 1923
The White Glove. Nash, 1915
The White Lie. Ward, 1914
Whither Thou Goest. Lloyds, 1920
Who Giveth This Woman? Hodder, 1905
Whoso Findeth a Wife. White, 1897; Rand, 1898
Whosoever Loveth: Being the Secret of a Lady's Maid. Hutchinson, 1907
Wiles of the Wicked. White, 1900
Without Trace. Nash, 1912
The Woman at Kensington. Cassell, 1906
The Woman in the Way. Nash, 1908
A Woman's Debt. Ward, 1924
The Yellow Ribbon. Hodder, 1918
The Young Archduchess. Ward, 1922; Moffat, 1922
The Zeppelin Destroyer. Hodder, 1916
-Zoraida. Tower, 1895; Stokes, 1895

LERMINA, JULES (HYPPOLYTE). 1839-1915.
The Chase. Nimmo, 1880
Three Exploits of M. Parent. Osgood, 1894. (Three novelets.)

LEROUX, ETIENNE. 1922- .
One for the Devil. Allen, 1969; Houghton, 1968. (Translation of Een vir Azazel. Cape Town, 1964.)
The Third Eye. Allen, 1969; Houghton, 1969. (Translation of Die Derde Oog. Cape Town, 1966.)

LEROUX, GASTON. 1868-1927. Series characters: Cheri-Bibi, in at least those marked CB; Joseph Rouletabille, in at least those marked JR.
The Adventures of a Coquette. Laurie, 1926
The Amazing Adventures of Carolus Herbert. Mills, 1922. (Translation of Le Capitaine Hyx. Paris, 1920.)
Balaoo. Hurst, 1913. (Translation of Balaoo. Paris, 1912.)
The Bride of the Sun. Hodder, 1916; McBride Nast, 1915. (Translation of L'Epouse du Soleil. Paris, 1913.)
The Burgled Heart. Long, 1925. U.S. title: The New Terror. Macaulay, 1926. (Translation of Le Coeur Cambriole. Paris, 1922.)
Cheri-Bibi and Cecily. Laurie, 1923. U.S. title: Missing Men. Macaulay, 1923. (Translation of Cheri-Bibi et Cecily. Paris, 1921.) CB
Cheri-Bibi, Mystery Man. Long, 1924. U.S. title: The Dark Road. Macaulay, 1924. (Translation of Fatalitas. Paris, 1921.) CB
The Dancing Girl. Long, 1924. U.S. title: Nomads of the Night. Macaulay, 1925 CB
The Dark Road; see Cheri-Bibi, Mystery Man
The Double Life. Laurie, 1916; Kearney, 1909
The Floating Prison. Laurie, 1922. U.S. title: Wolves of the Sea. Macaulay, 1923. (Translation of Les Cages Flottantes. Paris, 1921.)
The Haunted Chair. Dutton, 1931. (Translation of Le Lauteril Nante. Paris, 1911.)
The Kiss That Killed. Macaulay, 1934. (Translation of La Poupee Sangiante. Paris, 1924.)
Lady Helena; or, The Mysterious Lady. Laurie, 1931; Dutton, 1931. (Translation of Lady Helena. Paris, 1929.)

The Machine to Kill. Macaulay, 1935. (Translation of La Machine a Assassiner. Paris, 1923.)
The Man of a Hundred Faces; see The Man of a Hundred Masks
The Man of a Hundred Masks. Cassell, 1930. U.S. title: The Man of a Hundred Faces. Macaulay, 1930. (Translation of Mister Flow. Paris, 1927.)
The Man Who Came Back from the Dead. Nash, 1916. (Translation of L'Homme qui Revient de Loin. Paris, 1917.)
The Man with the Black Feather. Hurst, 1912; Small, 1912
The Masked Man. Long, 1927; Macaulay, 1929
The Midnight Lady. Long, 1930
The Missing Archduke. Long, 1931
Missing Men; see Cheri-Bibi and Cecily
Murder in the Bedroom; see The Mystery of the Yellow Room
The Mystery of the Yellow Room. London Daily Mail, 1908; Brentano's, 1908. Also published as: Murder in the Bedroom. Brussel, 1945. (Translation of Le Mystere de la Chambre Jaune. Paris, 1908.) JR
The New Idol. Long, 1928; Macaulay, 1929. (Translation of Le Coup d'etat de Cheri-Bibi. Paris, 1925.) CB
The New Terror; see The Burgled Heart
Nomads of the Night; see The Dancing Girl
The Octopus of Paris; see The Sleuth Hounds
The Perfume of the Lady in Black. London Daily Mail, 1909; Brentano's, 1909. (Translation of Le Parfum de la Dame en Noir. Paris, 1909.) JR
The Phantom Clue; see The Slave Bangle
The Phantom of the Opera. Mills, 1911; Bobbs, 1911. (Translation of Le Fantome de L'Opera. Paris, 1911.)
The Secret of the Night. Nash, 1914; Macaulay, 1914 JR
The Slave Bangle. Long, 1925. U.S. title: The Phantom Clue. Macaulay, 1926 JR
The Sleuth Hound. Long, 1926. U.S. title: The Octopus of Paris. Macaulay, 1927 JR
The Son of Three Fathers. Long, 1927; Macaulay, 1928. (Translation of Le Fils de Trois Peres. Paris, 1926.)
The Veiled Prisoner. Mills, 1923
Wolves of the Sea; see The Floating Prison

LEROY, AMELIE CLAIRE. 1851- . Pseudonym: Esme Stuart, q.v.

LESLIE, ALEEN
The Windfall. World, 1970

LESLIE, DESMOND. 1921- .
The Amazing Mr. Lutterworth. Wingate, 1958
Angels Weep! Laurie, 1948
-Careless Lives. Macdonald, 1945
Hold Back the Night. Owen, 1956
-Pardon my Return. Macdonald, 1946

LESLIE, EDWARD. Pseudonym of Leslie Edward Sellicks, 1902- .
The Red Slayer. Jenkins, 1929
The Seventh Entanglement. Jenkins, 1930
-White Man's Prestige. Warne, 1939

LESLIE, F. ANDREW
The Haunting of Hill House. Dramatists Play Service, 1964. (3-act play based on the novel by Shirley Jackson, 1920-1965, q.v.)

LESLIE, FRANCIS. Series character: Jimmy Langry, in at least those marked JL.

The Second Stroke. Hurst, 1949
Study of Death. Hurst, 1943 JL
Who Keeps the Keys? Hurst, 1948 JL

LESLIE, JEAN. Series character: Peter
    Ponsonby = PP.
  Blood on my Shoes; see Shoes for my
    Love
  The Darling Sin. Doubleday, 1951; Hodder, 1952
  A Hair of the Dog. Doubleday, 1947
  The Intimate Journal of Warren Winslow.
    Doubleday, 1952; Hodder, 1953
  The Man Who Held Five Aces. Doubleday,
    1949; Hodder, 1950
  One Cried Murder. Doubleday, 1945;
    Edwards, 1946 PP
  Shoes for my Love. Doubleday, 1948.
    Also published as: Blood on my Shoe.
    Bestseller, 1951
  Three-Cornered Murder. Doubleday, 1947;
    Hodder, 1948 PP
  Two Faced Murder. Doubleday, 1946; Edwards, 1946 PP

LESLIE, JOSEPHINE
  The Devil and Mrs. Devine. PB, 1974;
    Millington, 1975

LESLIE, MIRIAM
  Cavanaugh Keep. Lancer, 1963

LESLIE, NORMAN
  Death Comes by Air. Nelson, 1937
  Death Comes to Kenya. Ward, 1948
  How Bad Can They Be? Barker, 1955
  The Kiwi Club. Ward, 1939
  The Man with the Glass Eye. Ward, 1948
  Prelude to Murder. Barker, 1954
  Raid over England. Ward, 1938
  Shadow over Europe. Ward, 1947
  Widows can be Dangerous. Barker, 1958
  Winged Victory. Nelson, 1931

LESLIE, PETER
  The Autumn Accelerator. Four Square,
    1969. (Novelization of The Invaders
    TV series.)
  -The Bastard Brigade. New English Library pb, 1970
  -The Bitter Enders. New English Library
    pb, 1972. (Novelization of the
    movie.)
  -The Bombers. New English Library pb,
    1972
  The Cornish Pixie Affair. Four Square,
    1967. (Novelization of Girl from
    UNCLE TV series.)
  The Diving Dames Affair. Four Square,
    1967; Ace, 1967. (Novelization of Man
    from UNCLE TV series.)
  -The Extremists. New English Library pb,
    1970
  -The Fakers. New English Library pb,
    1971
  The Finger in the Sky Affair. Four
    Square, 1966; Ace, 1970. (Novelization of Man from UNCLE TV series.)
  -The Four Letter Crowd. New English Library pb, 1971
  The Frighteners. Four Square, 1968.
    (Novelization of the Daktari TV
    series.)
  The Gay Deceiver. MacGibbon, 1967;
    Stein, 1967
  Hell for Tomorrow. Consul, 1965; Macfadden, 1965. (Novelization of the
    Secret Agent TV series.)
  -Killer Corps. New English Library pb,
    1971
  The Mogul Men. Corgi, 1967
  The Night of the Tribolites. Four
    Square, 1968. (Novelization of The
    Invaders TV series.)
  -The Plastic Magicians. New English Library pb, 1970

  The Radioactive Camel Affair. Four
    Square, 1966; Ace, 1966. (Novelization of Man from UNCLE TV series.)
  The Splintered Sunglasses Affair. Four
    Square, 1968; Ace, 1968. (Novelization of Man from UNCLE TV series.)
  The Stone-Cold-Dead in the Market
    Affair. Four Square, 1966; Ace, 1970.
    (Novelization of Man from UNCLE TV
    series.)
  -Storm Squad. New English Library pb,
    1971
  The Unfair Fare Affair. Four Square,
    1968; Ace, 1968. (Novelization of Man
    from UNCLE TV series.)

LESLIE, THANE
  Yu-Malu, the Dragon Princess. Wright,
    1967

LESLIE-MELVILLE, BETTY
  That Nairobi Affair. Doubleday, 1975

LESSER, MILTON. 1928-   . Pseudonyms:
    Andrew Frazer, Stephen Marlowe, Jason
    Ridgway, C. H. Thames, qq.v. See
    also: RICHARD S(COTT) PRATHER,
    1921-

LESTER, E(DWARD) C(ASTELLAIN). Series
    character: Nathaniel Moody, in both
    titles.
  The Guy Fawkes Murder. Long, 1936
  The Murder of Martin Fotherill. Long,
    1937

LESTER, FRANK. Pseudonym of Frank (Hugh)
    Usher, 1909-   , q.v. Other pseudonym: Charles Franklin, q.v. Series
    character: Geoffrey Slade, in at
    least those marked GS.
  The Bamboo Girl. Hale, 1961
  The Corpse Wore Rubies. Hale, 1958 GS
  Death and the South Wind. Hale, 1958
  Death in Sunlight. Hale, 1965
  Death of a Frightened Traveller. Hale,
    1959
  Death of a Pale Man. Hale, 1960
  Finch Takes to Crime. Hale, 1963
  Fly Me a Killer. Hale, 1962
  The Golden Murder. Hale, 1959 GS
  Hide My Body. Hale, 1961
  Lead Me to the Gallows. Hale, 1962

LESTER, VINCENT
  Crook's Crossing. Butterworth, 1935
  Justice by Accident. Butterworth, 1936

LETHBRIDGE, OLIVE
  The Black Parrot. Hurst, 1931. (Novelization of the play by H. Fletcher
    Lee.)

LETHBRIDGE, SYBIL CAMPBELL
  -The Crime of Jane Dacre. Methuen, 1926

LETHERBY, JACK
  Murder Lays the Odds. Ward, 1953
  The Outsider. Ward, 1953

LETT, GORDON
  The Many-Headed Monster. Hodder, 1957
  Rossano. Hodder, 1955

LETTON, JENNETTE (DOWLING)
  Allegra's Child. Macrae Smith, 1969
  The Brass Bound Book. Milton House,
    1975. (U.S. title?)
  Cragsmoor. Macrae Smith, 1966
  Don't Cry Little Sister. Macrae Smith,
    1971
  The Haunting of Cliffside. Walker, 1975
  Hilltop; see Jenny and I

  Incident at Hendon. Macrae Smith, 1967
  Jenny and I. Macrae Smith, 1963; Hale,
    1964. Also published as: Hilltop.
    Paperback Library, 1968

LEVEL, MAURICE. 1875-1926.
  Crises: Tales of Mystery and Horror.
    Erskine Macdonald, 1920. U.S. title:
    Tales of Mystery and Horror. McBride,
    1920. Also published as: Grand
    Guignol Stories. Philpot, 1922 ss
  Grand Guignol Stories; see Crises:
    Tales of Mystery and Horror
  The Grip of Fear. Richards, 1909; Kennerley, 1909
  The Shadow. Philpot, 1923. U.S. title:
    Those Who Return. McBride, 1923.
    (Translation of L'Ombre. Paris,
    1921.)
  Tales of Mystery and Horror; see Crises: Tales of Mystery and Horror
  Those Who Return; see The Shadow

LEVENE, PHILIP. 1926-   . Series character: Ambrose West = AW.
  Ambrose in London. Hale, 1959 AW
  Ambrose in Paris. Hale, 1960 AW
  Kill Two Birds. French (London), 1963.
    (3-act play.)
  Murder When Necessary. Evans, 1958.
    (3-act play.)

LEVERAGE, (CARL) HENRY. 1885-   .
  -The Ice Pilot. Doubleday, 1921
  The Phantom Alibi. Chelsea, 1926
  The Purple Limited. Chelsea, 1927
  Where Dead Men Walk. Moffat, 1920
  Whispering Wires. Moffat, 1918
  The White Cipher. Moffat, 1919

LEVEY, ROBERT A.
  Dictators Die Hard. Mystery House, 1959
  Murder in Lima. Avon, 1957

LEVICK, J. D.
  Tangled Web. Jarrolds, 1946

LEVIEN, MARION
  Odds on Murder. Dorrance, 1974

LEVIN, IRA. 1929-   .
  A Kiss Before Dying. Simon, 1953;
    Joseph, 1954
  -Rosemary's Baby. Random, 1967; Joseph,
    1967
  The Stepford Wives. Random, 1972;
    Joseph, 1972
  Veronica's Room. Random, 1974; Joseph,
    1975. (Play.)

LEVIN, MEYER. 1905-   .
  Compulsion. Simon, 1956; Muller, 1957

LEVINE, WILLIAM. 1881-   . Pseudonym:
    Will Levinrew, q.v.

LEVINREW, WILL. Pseudonym of William
    Levine, 1881-   . Series character:
    Prof. Herman Brierly = HB.
  Death Points a Finger. Mystery League,
    1933 HB
  For Sale—Murder. Mystery League, 1932
  Murder from the Grave. McBride, 1930;
    Cassell, 1931 HB
  Murder on the Palisades. McBride, 1930;
    Gollancz, 1930. Also published as:
    The Wheelchair Corpse. Bart, 1945 HB
  The Poison Plague. McBride, 1929; Cassell, 1930 HB
  The Wheelchair Corpse; see Murder on
    the Palisades

LEVINSON, RICHARD. See: WILLIAM LINK.

LEVINSON, SAUL
  Murder is Dangerous. Phoenix, 1949
  Red-Hot Murder. Phoenix, 1949

LEVISON, ERIC. Series character: Dr. Edward Lester, in all titles.
Ashes of Evidence. Bobbs, 1921
The Eye Witness. Bobbs, 1921; Page (London), 1921
Hidden Eyes. Bobbs, 1920

LE VOLEUR. Pseudonym of Rosa Nouchette Carey, 1840-1909, q.v.
By Order of the Brotherhood. Jarrolds, 1895; Macmillan, 1895
The Champington Mystery. Digby, 1900
-For Love of a Bedouin Maid. Hutchinson, 1897; Rand, 1897
-In the Tsar's Dominions. Hutchinson, 1899

LEVON, FRED. Pseudonym of L. Fred Ayvazian, 1919- .
The Manx Cat. World, 1970; Hale, 1972
Much Ado about Murder. Dodd, 1955; Boardman, 1957

LEVY, BARBARA
The Missing Matisse. Doubleday, 1969
Place of Judgment. Doubleday, 1965
The Shining Mischief. Putnam, 1971

LEVY, JOSE. See: C(YRIL ARTHUR EDWARD) RANGER GULL, 1876-1923.

LEWELLEN, T(HEODORE) C(HARLES). 1940- .
The Billikin Courier. Random, 1968

LEWIN, ALBERT
The Unaltered Cat. Scribner, 1967; Harvill, 1967

LEWIN, MICHAEL. 1885-1961. Pseudonym: Douglas Furber, q.v.

LEWIN, MICHAEL Z. 1943- . Series character: Albert Samson, in all titles.
Ask the Right Question. Putnam, 1971; H. Hamilton, 1972
The Enemies Within. Knopf, 1974; H. Hamilton, 1974
The Way We Die Now. Putnam, 1973; H. Hamilton, 1974

LEWIS, ALFRED HENRY. 1857-1914.
The Apaches of New York. Dillingham, 1912 ss
The Boss, and How He Came to Rule New York. Barnes, 1903
Confessions of a Detective. Barnes, 1906 ss

LEWIS, ARTHUR H. 1906- .
Children's Party. Trident, 1972
Copper Beeches. Trident, 1971

LEWIS, CECIL DAY. 1904-1972. Pseudonym: Nicholas Blake, q.v.

LEWIS, FLORENCE JAY
The Climax. Books Inc., 1944. (Novelization of the movie.)

LEWIS, FREDERICK. Pseudonym of Frederick Lewis Collins, 1882- .
The Strange Case of Mary Page. Clode, 1916

LEWIS, GITA. See: HENRIETTA MARTIN.

LEWIS, H.
The Mystery of Lady Chetwynd's Spectre. Henderson

LEWIS, MRS. HARRIET
The Hampton Mystery. Henderson

LEWIS, H. H.
-Pearls and Perjury. Coker, 1950

LEWIS, HERSHELL G.
Two Thousand Maniacs! Novel Books, 1964. (Novelization of the movie.)

LEWIS, HILDA (WINIFRED). 1896-1974.
The Case of the Little Doctor; see Said Dr. Spendlove
Said Dr. Spendlove. Jarrolds, 1940. U.S. title: The Case of the Little Doctor. Random, 1949
Strange Story. Jarrolds, 1945; Random, 1947

LEWIS, JACK. Pseudonyms: Stephen Hood, Lewis Jackson, qq.v. All titles feature Sexton Blake and were published by Amalgamated Press.
The Affair of the Oriental Doctor. 1920
The Affair of the World's Champion. 1920
The Case of the Bendigo Heirlooms. 1922
The Case of the Transatlantic Flyers. 1919
The Chink in the Armour. 1919
The Fallen Star. 1922
The False Alibi. 1920
The House of Fear. 1923
The Jewels of Wu Ling. 1920
The Kestrel Syndicate. 1919
The Kestrel's Claw. 1920
Kestrel's Conspiracy. 1921
The Lady of Ravensedge. 1921
The Mystery of XO4. 1920
The Red Heart of the Incas. 1919

LEWIS, JACK
A Night for Evil. Challenge, 1967

LEWIS, JAMES
The Canary That Died. JMC Publications, 1975

LEWIS, JANET [JANET LEWIS WINTERS]. 1899- .
The Trial of Soren Qvist. Doubleday, 1947; Gollancz, 1947

LEWIS, JULIUS WARREN. 1833-1920. Pseudonym: Leon Lewis, q.v.

LEWIS, JUNE R(OSEMARIE)
The Witch's Mark. Hale, 1975

LEWIS, KEN
Look Out Behind You. Ace, 1957

LEWIS, LANGE. Pseudonym of Jane Beynon, 1915- , q.v. Series character: Richard Tuck, in all titles.
The Birthday Murder. Bobbs, 1945; Bodley Head, 1951
Death Among Friends; see Murder Among Friends
Juliet Dies Twice. Bobbs, 1943; Bodley Head, 1948
Meat for Murder. Bobbs, 1943; Bodley Head, 1950
Murder Among Friends. Bobbs, 1942. British title: Death Among Friends. Bodley Head, 1950
The Passionate Victims. Bobbs, 1952; Bodley Head, 1953

LEWIS, LEON. Pseudonym of Julius Warren Lewis, 1833-1920.
-The Diamond Seeker of Brazil. Bonner's, 1891
The Man of Mystery; or, Where is Ben Stobie? Weeks, 1894

LEWIS, MARY CHRISTIANNA MILNE. 1907- .
Pseudonyms: Christianna Brand, China Thompson, qq.v.

LEWIS, MATTHEW GREGORY. 1775-1818.
Adelgitha; or, The Fruits of a Single Error. Hughes, 1806; Longworth, 1808. (5-act play.)
Ambrosio; or, The Monk; see The Monk
The Monk. Bell, 1796; Moore, 1845. Also published as: Ambrosio; or, The Monk. Bell, 1798
-Rosario, the Female Monk. Laird, 1891. (Original title?)

LEWIS, MERVYN
Death of Gold. Hale, 1970

LEWIS, MICHAEL (ARTHUR). 1890-1970.
The Brand of the Beast. Allen, 1925; Dial, 1925
The Crime of Herbert Wratislaus. Jenkins, 1931
The Island of Disaster. Allen, 1926
Roman Gold. Allen, 1927; Houghton, 1928
The Three Amateurs. Allen, 1929; Houghton, 1929

LEWIS, NORMAN. 1903- .
Darkness Visible. Cape, 1960; Pantheon, 1960
The Day of the Fox. Cape, 1955; Rinehart, 1955
Dragon Tree Island; see The Tenth Year of the Ship
Every Man's Brother. Heinemann, 1967; Morrow, 1968
Flight from a Dark Equator. Collins, 1972; Putnam, 1972
-Samara. Cape, 1949
The Sicilian Specialist. Collins, 1975; Random, 1974
-A Single Pilgrim. Cape, 1953; Rinehart, 1954
A Small War Made to Order. Collins, 1966; Harcourt, 1966
-The Tenth Year of the Ship. Collins, 1962; Harcourt, 1962. Also published as: Dragon Tree Island. Fontana, 1964
-The Volcanoes Above Us. Cape, 1957; Pantheon, 1957
-Within the Labyrinth. Cape, 1950

LEWIS, (ERNEST MICHAEL) ROY. 1933- .
Series character: Inspector Crow, in at least those marked C.
Blood Money. Collins, 1973 C
Double Take. Collins, 1975
Error of Judgment. Collins, 1971 C
The Fenokee Project. Collins, 1971
A Fool for a Client. Collins, 1972
A Lover Too Many. Collins, 1969; World, 1971 C
Of Singular Purpose. Collins, 1973
A Part of Virtue. Collins, 1975 C
A Question of Degree. Collins, 1974 C
A Secret Singing. Collins, 1972 C
A Wolf by the Ears. Collins, 1970; World, 1972

LEWIS, TED. 1940- . Series character: Jack Carter = JC.
All the Way Home and All the Night Through. New Authors, 1965
Billy Rags. Joseph, 1973
Get Carter; see Jack's Return Home
Jack Carter and the Law; see Jack Carter's Law
Jack Carter's Law. Joseph, 1974. U.S. title: Jack Carter and the Law. Knopf, 1975 JC
Jack's Return Home. Joseph, 1970; Doubleday, 1970. Also published as: Get Carter. Pan, 1971; Popular Library, 1971 JC
Plender. Joseph, 1971

LEWIS, W(ALTER) R(EGINALD) SUNDERLAND.
  1861- .
  Cubwood. Lane, 1924; Boni, 1926

LEY, ALICE CHETWYND. 1915- .
  Letters for a Spy. Hale, 1970

LEY, ARTHUR. Pseudonym: Ray Luther, q.v.

LEYFORD, HENRY. Pseudonym.
  Murder Moon. Macaulay, 1933

LEYS, JOHN K(IRKWOOD). 1846-1909.
  At the Sign of the Golden Horn. Newnes, 1898
  The Black Terror. Low, 1899; Page, 1900
  A Broken Fetter. Digby, 1905
  Children of Mammon. Digby, 1908
  A Desperate Game. Digby, 1906
  Held in the Toils. Ward, 1904
  The House-Boat Mystery. Ward, 1905
  The Lawyer's Secret. Warne, 1897
  The Missing Bridegroom. Digby, 1908
  The Prisoner's Secret. Ward, 1904
  A Sore Temptation. Chatto, 1901
  A Suburban Vendetta. Pearson, 1900
  Under a Mask. Bentley, 1897
  Underground. Greening, 1909
  A Wolf in Sheep's Clothing. Ward, 1905

LEYTON, PATRICK
  The Barronwell Mystery. Paul, 1929
  By Foul Means. Paul, 1928; International Fiction, 1929
  The Crime at Grandison Hall. Paul, 1929
  The Crime with Ten Solutions. Jenkins, 1935
  The Dalmayne Mystery. Jenkins, 1928
  Exit Silas Danvers. Jenkins, 1932
  Foul Play at Lentwood. Jenkins, 1935
  Gentlemen of the Jury, with Arthur Compton-Rickett, 1869-1937, q.v. Jenkins, 1927
  Grim Inheritance. Jenkins, 1941
  Harvest of Hate. Jenkins, 1948
  Haunted Abbey. Jenkins, 1936
  The Inevitable Crime. Jenkins, 1926
  The Island of Atonement. Selwyn, 1928
  The Man Who Knew. Jenkins, 1925; Small, 1926
  Murder Will Out. Jenkins, 1930
  The Ordeal of Mark Bannister, with Arthur Compton-Rickett, 1869-1937, q.v. Jenkins, 1930
  Outside the Law. Jenkins, 1927
  Silent Death. Jenkins, 1940
  Treasure at Greyladies. Jenkins, 1934
  Within Twenty-Four Hours. Jenkins, 1931

LIBBEY, LAURA JEAN. 1862-1924.
  Aleta's Terrible Secret; or, The Strange Mystery of a Wedding Eve. Westbrook, 190?
  The Crime of Hallowe'en; or, The Heiress of Graystone Hall. Munro, 1891
  Little Rosebud's Lovers; or, A Cruel Revenge. Munro, 1888
  Parted by Fate; or, The Mystery of Black-Tor Lighthouse. Bonner, 1890

LIBBY, ALFRED F.
  The Long Fast Ride. Vantage, 1966

LICHFIELD, RICHARD
  Diana K.C. Henry Walker, 1930

LIDDELOW, MARJORIE JEAN. Pseudonym: Marjorie J. Law, q.v.

LIDDON, E(LOISE) S. 1897- . Series character: Peggy Fairfield, in both titles.
  The Riddle of the Florentine Folio. Doubleday, 1935
  The Riddle of the Russian Princess. Doubleday, 1934

LIE, JONAS. 1899-1945.
  The Devil's Birthday. Cassirer, 1940. (Translation of Natten dil Frandens Geburtsdag. Oslo, 1934.)

LIEBELER, JEAN MAYER
  You, the Jury. Farrar, 1944; Skeffington, 1946, as by Virginia Mather

LIEBERMAN, HERBERT (HENRY). 1933- .
  Crawlspace. McKay, 1971; Hutchinson, 1972
  The Eighth Square. McKay, 1973; Hutchinson, 1973

LIEBLING, HOWARD
  The Trial of Billy Jack. B. J. Enterprises, 1974. (Novelization of the movie.)

LIGGETT, HUNTER. Pseudonym of Lauran Bosworth Paine, 1916- . Other pseudonyms: John Armour, Reg Batcheor, Kenneth Bedford, Frank Bosworth, Mark Carrel, Robert Clarke, Richard Dana, J. F. Drexler, Troy Howard, Jared Ingersol, John Kilgore, J. K. Lucas, John Morgan, qq.v.
  Murder for Money. Hale, 1969
  The Murder Maze. Hale, 1969
  The Victim Died Twice. Hale, 1969
  The Unknown Murderer. Hale, 1975

LILIENTHAL, DAVID ELI, JR. 1927- .
  Pseudonym: David Ely, q.v.

LILLEY, PETER. Joint pseudonym with Anthony Stansfeld: Bruce Buckingham, q.v.

LILLEY, TOM [THOMAS WILLIAM LILLEY]. 1924- . Series character: Ralph Carter, in both titles.
  The K Section. Macmillan (London), 1972
  The Officer from Special Branch; see The Projects Section
  The Projects Section. Macmillan (London), 1970. U.S. title: The Officer from Special Branch. Doubleday, 1971

LILLIE, ARTHUR
  The Cobra Diamond. Ward, 1890
  -An Indian Wizard. Simpkin, 1887

LILLIE, HELEN. 1915-
  Call Down the Sky. Hurst, 1973
  The Listening Silence. Hurst, 1970; Hawthorn, 1974

LILLINGSTON, CLAUDE. 1881- .
  His Patients Died. Blackwood, 1936

LILLY, JEAN. Series character: Bruce Perkins = BP.
  Death in B-Minor. Dutton, 1934; Cassell, 1935 BP
  Death Thumbs a Ride. Dutton, 1940 BP
  False Face. Dutton, 1929 BP
  The Seven Sisters. Dutton, 1928; Dent, 1929

LIMNELIUS, GEORGE. Pseudonym of Lewis (George) Robinson, 1886- , q.v.
  The Medbury Fort Murder. Benn, 1929; Doubleday, 1929
  Tell No Tales. Bles, 1931

LINAKIS, STEVEN. 1923- .
  The Killing Ground. McKay, 1970

LINCOLN, FREEMAN. See: JOSEPH C(ROSBY) LINCOLN, 1870-1944.

LINCOLN, JOSEPH C(ROSBY). 1870-1944.
  Blair's Attic, with Freeman Lincoln. Coward, 1929; Cassell, 1930
  Extricating Obadiah. Appleton, 1917
  Out of the Fog. Appleton, 1940
  The Ownley Inn, with Freeman Lincoln. Coward, 1939; Cassell, 1940
  Storm Girl. Appleton, 1937

LINCOLN, NATALIE SUMNER. 1881-1935. Series character: Det. Insp. Mitchell, in at least those marked M.
  The Blue Car Mystery. Appleton, 1926 M
  C.O.D. Appleton, 1915
  The Cat's Paw. Appleton, 1922 M
  The Dancing Silhouette. Appleton, 1927 M
  The Fifth Latchkey. Appleton, 1929
  I Spy. Appleton, 1916 M
  The Lost Despatch. Appleton, 1913
  The Man Inside. Appleton, 1914
  Marked "Cancelled." Appleton, 1930
  The Meredith Mystery. Appleton, 1923 M
  The Missing Initial. Appleton, 1925 M
  The Moving Finger. Appleton, 1918 M
  The Nameless Man. Appleton, 1917 M
  The Official Chaperon. Appleton, 1915
  P.P.C. Appleton, 1927 M
  The Red Seal. Appleton, 1920
  The Secret of Mohawk Pond. Appleton, 1928
  13 Thirteenth Street. Appleton, 1932
  The Thirteenth Letter. Appleton, 1924
  The Three Strings. Appleton, 1918 M
  The Trevor Case. Appleton, 1912
  The Unseen Ear. Appleton, 1921

LINCOLN, VICTORIA. 1904- .
  The Swan Island Murders. Farrar, 1930; Cassell, 1931

LINDALL, EDWARD. Pseudonym of Edward Ernest Smith, 1915- .
  A Day for Angels. Constable, 1975
  Death and the Maiden. Constable, 1973
  -The Fires of Kiwai. Heinemann, 1968
  A Gathering of Eagles. Collins, 1970
  -The Killers of Karawala. Hutchinson, 1961; Morrow, 1962
  -A Kind of Justice. Hutchinson, 1964; Morrow, 1964
  A Lively Form of Death. Constable, 1972
  No Place to Hide. Hutchinson, 1959. U.S. title: The Paper Ghost. Morrow, 1961
  -Northward the Coast. Heinemann, 1966
  The Paper Ghost; see No Place to Hide
  Search for Tomorrow. Constable, 1974
  Springs of Violence. Hutchinson, 1963; Morrow, 1963
  -Stranger Among Friends. Hutchinson, 1956
  -A Time Too Soon. Heinemann, 1967; Morrow, 1967

LINDAU, RUDOLPH. 1829-1900.
  Liquidated and The Seer. Appleton, 1878. (Two stories.)

LINDHOLM, ANNA CHANDLER. 1870- . Pseudonym: Dorothy Fay, q.v.

LINDLEY, ERICA. See: AILEEN QUIGLEY.

LINDOP, AUDREY ERSKINE. 1920- .
  Details of Jeremy Stratton; see The Outer Ring
  I Start Counting. Doubleday, 1966; Collins, 1966
  I Thank a Fool; see Mist over Talla
  Journey into Stone. Doubleday, 1972; Macmillan (London), 1973
  Mist over Talla. Doubleday, 1957. British title: I Thank a Fool. Collins, 1958

-Nicola. Doubleday, 1959; Collins, 1964
-The Outer Ring. Appleton, 1955. British title: Details of Jeremy Stratton. Heinemann, 1955
The Self-Appointed Saint. Doubleday, 1975; Macmillan (London), 1975
Sight Unseen. Doubleday, 1969; Collins, 1969
The Tall Headlines. Macmillan, 1950; Heinemann, 1950

LINDSAY, C(HARLES) McDONALD
Betrayed!; or, What Might Come to Pass. Drane, 1928
Murder at Constantia. Jenkins, 1932

LINDSAY, DAVID T. Series character: Inspector Jackson, in at least those marked J.
-Air Bandits. Jenkins, 1937
Another Case for Inspector Jackson. Hamilton, 1937 J
The Black Fetish. Hamilton, 1937
-The Flying Armada. Hamilton, 1938
-The Flying Crusader. Hamilton, 1937
-The Green Ray. Hamilton, 1937
Inspector Jackson Goes North. Hamilton, 1939 J
Inspector Jackson Investigates. Hamilton, 1936 J
The Man Nobody Knew. Hamilton, 1938 J
Masked Judgment. Hamilton, 1937
Mystery of the Tumbling V. Hamilton, 1940
-The Ninth Plague. Hamilton, 1936
Stranglehold. Hamilton, 1939
The Temple of the Flaming God. Hamilton, 1938
The Two Red Capsules. Hamilton, 1936
Wings over Africa. Hamilton, 1936
Wings over the Amazon. Hamilton, 1937

LINDSAY, HOWARD. 1889-   . See: DAMON RUNYON, 1880-1946.

LINDSAY, KATHLEEN. 1903-   .
-After the Wedding. Jenkins, 1943
-Another Woman's Love. Jenkins, 1950
-Beware of the Dawn. Hurst, 1959
-Brave Heart of Youth. Jenkins, 1944
-Danger Zone. Jenkins, 1936
-Dangerous Madonna. Jenkins, 1938
-Dangerous to Know. Hutchinson, 1956
-Dark Destiny. Hutchinson, 1955
-The Devil's Dominion. Hutchinson, 1956
-Enchantress of the Nile. Hurst, 1965
-Fair Intruder. Jenkins, 1942
-For Ever You'll be Mine. Hurst, 1958
-Glamour Girl. Jenkins, 1942
-The Glorious Masquerade. Jenkins, 1937
The Green Domino. Alexander-Ouseley, 1928
-Harvest of Deceit. Long, 1934
-He Should have been King. Hutchinson, 1954
-Heaven will be Ours. Jenkins, 1948
-Here in Eden. Hutchinson, 1951
His Crooked Highness. Jenkins, 1938
-If Love be Ours. Jenkins, 1948
-Incomparable Doll. Hurst, 1967
-Into Temptation. Jenkins, 1949
-It Happened at the Cape. Jenkins, 1931
-A Lady for Botany Bay. Hurst, 1961
-Lady Make-Believe. Jenkins, 1941
-Less Than the Dust. Hurst, 1963
-Lilli Marlene. Jenkins, 1950
-Love Not Denied. Jenkins, 1946
-Love's Atonement. Hurst, 1963
-Loyal Lady. Hurst, 1965
-Madonna of Hell. Hutchinson, 1954
-The Moonlight Path. Jenkins, 1940
-My Dear Heart. Hurst, 1970
The Mystery at Greystones. Jenkins, 1932
-'Neath the Southern Cross. Jenkins, 1931
-Paulette. Hurst, 1962

-Queen of the Mirage. Hurst, 1966
Rebel Lady. Jenkins, 1939
-Render Unto Caesar. Hurst, 1969
-The Road to Ballarat. Hurst, 1958
-Rustle of Spring. Hurst, 1967
-She was my Beloved. Hurst, 1968
-So Near to Love. Hutchinson, 1951
-Song of the Dawn. Hurst, 1965
-The Splendour Falls. Hutchinson, 1952
Storm Maiden. Jenkins, 1939
-Stormy Paradise. Hurst, 1957
Suspense. Jenkins, 1940
-Take This my Heart. Jenkins, 1947
-Theodora. Hurst, 1964
-There is no Yesterday. Hurst, 1962
-This Man is Mine. Jenkins, 1947
-Tomorrow We Die. Hutchinson, 1955
-Treachery. Jenkins, 1937
-Unbroken Barriers. Jenkins, 1940
-Virginia. Hurst, 1969
-Wind of Desire. Long, 1933
-Winsome Lass. Hurst, 1960

LINDSAY, R(OBERT) HOWARD. 1910-   .
Fowl Murder. Little, 1941

LINEBARGER, PAUL MYRON ANTHONY. 1913-1966. Pseudonym: Carmichael Smith, q.v.

LINGO, ADA E.
Murder in Texas. Houghton, 1935

LININGTON, (BARBARA) ELIZABETH. 1921-   .
Pseudonyms: Anne Blaisdell, Lesley Egan, Dell Shannon, qq.v. (Note: Several novels published in the U.S. as by Dell Shannon have appeared in England as by Barbara Elizabeth Linington.) Series character: Ivor Maddox, in all titles, which are published in England as by Anne Blaisdell.
Crime by Chance. Lippincott, 1973; Gollancz, 1974
Date with Death. Harper, 1966; Gollancz, 1966
Greenmask! Harper, 1964; Gollancz, 1965
No Evil Angel. Harper, 1964; Gollancz, 1965
Policeman's Lot. Harper, 1968; Gollancz, 1969
Practice to Deceive. Harper, 1971; Gollancz, 1971
Something Wrong. Harper, 1967; Gollancz, 1968

LINK, WILLIAM and RICHARD LEVINSON
Prescription: Murder. French (New York), 1963. (Play.)

LINKLATER, ERIC (ROBERT RUSSELL). 1899-1974.
Mr. Byculla. Hart-Davis, 1950; Harcourt, 1951

LINKLATER, JOSEPH LANE. Pseudonym of Alex Watkins. Series character: Silas Booth, in at least those marked SB. (Note: The usual byline on these books is J. Lane Linklater, but a few are as by Joseph Linklater.)
And She had a Little Knife. Mill, 1948. British title: She had a Little Knife. Foulsham, 1950 SB
The Bishop's Cap. Mill, 1948. British title: The "Bishop's Cap" Murder. Foulsham, 1949 SB
The "Bishop's Cap" Murder; see The Bishop's Cap
Black Opal. Mill, 1947; Boardman, 1949 SB

The Green Glove. Mystery House, 1959; Ward, 1960
Odd Woman Out. Bouregy, 1956; Ward, 1959 SB
Shadow for a Lady. Mill, 1947; Boardman, 1948 SB
She had a Little Knife; see And She had a Little Knife
A Tisket, a Casket. Mystery House, 1959 SB

LINN, EDWARD
The Adversaries. Saturday Review Press, 1973

LINNELL, GERTRUDE.   -1933.
The Black Ghost of the Highway. Longmans, 1931

LINTON, ADELIN SUMNER BRIGGS. 1899-   .
Pseudonym: Aldin Vinton, q.v.

LINTON, DUKE
Big-Time Racketeer. Scion, 1951
Bury Me Deep. Scion, 1950
Call Me Al. Scion, 1952
Crazy to Kill. Scion, 1950
Dames Die Too. Scion, 1950
The Dark Brings Death. Scion, 1951
Daughter of the Sidewalk. Scion, 1953
Deadline. Scion, 1954
Enough Rope. Scion, 1950
Give Me the Lowdown. Scion, 1953
Hold Everything. Scion, 1953
How Dead Can You Be? Scion, 1952
Keep Moving, Bud. Scion, 1952
Kill and Desire. Scion, 1950
Killer Bait. Scion, 1953
Lend Me a Rod. Scion, 1951
Sinner. Scion, 1953
Sin's Half Mile. Scion, 1953
So Dead, So Sweet. Scion, 1953
Strip Tease Angel. Scion, 1953
The Swinging Corpse. Scion, 1954
That Dame Sal. Scion, 1952
They've Got Me Again. Scion, 1952
Too Late for Death. Scion, 1950
Too Many Yesterdays. Scion, 1951
Was She Poison? Scion, 1953
What Do I Care? Scion, 1952
Who's Sorry Now? Scion, 1953

LION, LEON M. See: MARIAN BOWER.

LIPKE, KAY [KATHERINE BELLOWS LIPKE]
Rain on the Roof. Dial, 1931; Methuen, 1932

LIPMAN, CLAYRE and MICHEL
House of Evil. Lion, 1954; Banner, 1959

LIPMAN, MICHEL. See: CLAYRE LIPMAN.

LIPMAN, WILLIAM (R.)
Yonder Grow the Daisies. Washburn, 1929

LIPPINCOTT, DAVID (McCORD). 1925-   .
E Pluribus Bang! Viking, 1970; Joseph, 1971
The Voice of Armageddon. Putnam, 1974; Hodder, 1975

LIPPINCOTT, NORMAN
Murder at Glen Athol. Doubleday, 1935; World's Work, 1935

LIPSKY, ELEAZAR
Day of Judgment; see Lincoln McKeever
The Devil's Daughter. Meredith, 1969
The Hoodlum. Lion, 1953. (Retitled reprint of ?)
The Kiss of Death. Penguin (New York), 1947; Penguin (London), 1949
Lincoln McKeever. Appleton, 1953; Deutsch, 1954. Also published as: Day of Judgment. Corgi, 1955

Murder One. Doubleday, 1948
The People Against O'Hara. Doubleday, 1950; Wingate, 1951
The Scientists. Appleton, 1959; Longmans, 1959

LISTER, STEPHEN. Pseudonym.
Delorme in Deep Water. Davies, 1958

LITCHFIELD, CECIL
Bags of Blackmail. Pawling, 1934

LITSEY, EDWIN CARLILE. 1874-   .
The Beast. Mystery House, 1959

LITTELL, BLAINE
The Dolorosa Deal. Saturday Review, 1973; Collins, 1973

LITTELL, ROBERT. 1935-   .
The Defection of A. J. Lewinter. Houghton, 1973; Hodder, 1973
-The October Circle. Houghton, 1975; Hodder, 1976
Sweet Reason. Houghton, 1974; Hodder, 1974

LITTLE, CLARKE
"Outlaws" or "When the Devil Drives". Ward, 1902 ss

LITTLE, CONSTANCE and GWENYTH. (NOTE: The byline on all English titles is Conyth Little, except for the starred ones, which are signed in England as in the U.S.)
The Black Coat. Doubleday, 1948; Collins, 1949
Black Corridors. Doubleday, 1940; Collins, 1941
The Black Curl. Doubleday, 1953
The Black Dream. Doubleday, 1952; Collins, 1953
The Black Express; see Great Black Kanba
The Black Eye. Doubleday, 1945; Collins, 1946
The Black Gloves. Doubleday, 1939; Collins, 1940
The Black Goatee. Doubleday, 1947; Collins, 1947
The Black-Headed Pins. Doubleday, 1938; Davies, 1939 *
The Black Honeymoon. Doubleday, 1944; Collins, 1944
The Black House. Doubleday, 1950; Collins, 1950
The Black Iris. Doubleday, 1953; Collins, 1953
The Black Lady; see The Black Rustle
The Black Paw. Doubleday, 1941; Collins, 1941
The Black Piano. Doubleday, 1948; Collins, 1948
The Black Rustle. Doubleday, 1943. British title: The Black Lady. Collins, 1944
The Black Shrouds. Doubleday, 1941; Collins, 1942
The Black Smith. Doubleday, 1950; Collins, 1951
The Black Stocking. Doubleday, 1946; Collins, 1947
The Black Thumb. Doubleday, 1942; Collins, 1943
The Blackout. Doubleday, 1951; Collins, 1952
Great Black Kanba. Doubleday, 1944. British title: The Black Express. Collins, 1945
The Grey Mist Murders. Doubleday, 1938

LITTLE, CONYTH. See: CONSTANCE and GWENYTH LITTLE.

LITTLE, GWENYTH. See: CONSTANCE LITTLE, 1915-   .

LITTLE, PAUL H. Pseudonyms: Paula Minton, Hugo Paul, qq.v.

LITTLE, PHILIP
Who was He? Street (Magnet #367)

LITTLECHILD, JOHN GEORGE
The Reminiscences of Chief-Inspector Littlechild. Leadenhall, 1894 ss

LITTLEFIELD, ANNE
Which Mrs. Bennett? Doubleday, 1959

LITVINOFF, IVY. 1889?-1977.
His Master's Voice: A Detective Story. Heinemann, 1930. U.S. title: Moscow Mystery. Coward, 1943. Revised edition: Gollancz, 1973

LITWAK, LEO (EZRA). 1924-   .
Waiting for the News. Doubleday, 1969; MacGibbon, 1971

LIVINGSTON, ARMSTRONG. 1885-   . Series characters: Jimmy Treynor, in at least those marked JT; Peter Creighton, in at least those marked PC.
The Case of the Walking Corpse. Lucom, 1945
The Double Cross. Henkle, 1929; Skeffington, 1929 JT
The Guilty Accuser. Chelsea, 1928; Jarrolds, 1928 PC
In Cold Blood. Bobbs, 1931; Skeffington, 1932 JT
The Ju-Ju Man, with Thomas H. Griffiths. Siebel, 1926; Paul, 1924
Light Fingered Ladies. Chelsea, 1927; Jarrolds, 1928 PC
Magic for Murder. Cavalcade, 1945; Skeffington, 1936
The Monk of Hambleton. Henkle, 1928 PC
The Monster in the Pool. Bobbs, 1929; Skeffington, 1930 JT
Murder is Easy! Speller, 1936; Skeffington, 1933
The Murder Trap. Bobbs, 1930; Skeffington, 1932 JT
The Mystery of the Twin Rubies. Moffat, 1922; Paul, 1923
Night of Crime. Sovereign House, 1938 JT
On the Right Wrists. Chelsea, 1925; Jarrolds, 1927 PC
Trackless Death. Bobbs, 1930; Skeffington, 1930 PC

LIVINGSTON, KENNETH. Pseudonym of Kenneth Livingston Stewart, 1894-   .
The Cloze Papers. Rich, 1936
The Dodd Cases. Methuen, 1933; Doubleday, 1934 ss

LIVINGSTON, WALTER. 1895-   .
The Mystery of Burnleigh Manor. Mystery League, 1930
The Mystery of Villa Sineste. Mystery League, 1931

LIVINGSTONE, ALICE
A Sealed Book. Sunday Circle, 1904; Fenno, 1906

LLEWELLYN, RICHARD. Pseudonym of Richard David Vivian Llewellyn Lloyd, 1906-   . Series character: Edmund Trothe, in all titles.
But We Didn't Get the Fox. Joseph, 1970; Doubleday, 1969
The End of the Rug. Joseph, 1969; Doubleday, 1968
The Night is a Child. Joseph, 1974; Doubleday, 1972

White Horse to Banbury Cross. Joseph, 1972; Doubleday, 1970

LLOYD, HERBERT
-Children of Chance. Andrews, 1893
A Lawyer's Secret. Andrews, 1896 ss

LLOYD, JACK (BATES)
The Key Without a Lock. Vantage, 1964

LLOYD, JOHN. See also: ELWYN JONES, 1923-   .
Death at Roman Farm. Hale, 1968
Until They are Dead. Hale, 1967

LLOYD, LAVENDER. 1924-   .
The Linton Memorial. Longmans, 1957

LLOYD, NELSON (McALLISTER). 1873-   .
The Robberies Co., Ltd. Scribner, 1906

LLOYD, RICHARD DAVID VIVIAN LLEWELLYN. 1906-   . Pseudonym: Richard Llewellyn, q.v.

LLOYD, STEPHANIE. Pseudonym of Morton Jay Golding, 1925-   . Other pseudonym: Patricia Morton, q.v.
Graveswood. Paperback Library, 1966

LLOYD, TOM
Champion and Crook. Aldine, 1929
'Gainst Chink and Gunman. Aldine, 1931
Samson's Surrender. Aldine, 1927

LLOYD, VICTOR (HENRY)
Don't Tie Me Down. Angus (Sydney), 1961; Angus (London), 1962
-The Hidden Enemy. Angus (London), 1957

LLOYD, WALLACE. Pseudonym of James Algie.
Bergen Worth. Unwin, 1901
-Houses of Glass. Dillingham, 1898

LOBAN, ETHEL H.
The Calloused Eye. Doubleday, 1931
Signed in Yellow. Doubleday, 1930

LOBAUGH, ELMA K. 1907-   . Pseudonym: Kenneth Lowe, q.v.
I am Afraid. Doubleday, 1949
Shadows in Succession. Doubleday, 1946
She Never Reached the Top. Doubleday, 1945

LOBELL, G(RISELDA) G. See: N(ATHAN) D(AVID) LOBELL.

LOBELL, N(ATHAN) D(AVID) and G(RISELDA) G. LOBELL
The Shadow and the Blot. Harper, 1949

LOCK, ARNOLD CHARLES COOPER. Pseudonym: Charles Cooper, q.v.

LOCK, SANFORD
Mail for McNair. Hutchinson, 1940

LOCKE, DOUGLAS
The House of Two Wives. Lancer, 1967. Also published as: Death Lives in the Mansion. Lancer, 1969

LOCKE, EDWARD. See: GEORGE C(HARLES) JENKS, 1850-1929.

LOCKE, G(LADYS) E(DSON). 1887-   .
Series character: Detective-Inspector Burton, in at least those marked B.
The Fenwood Murders. Long, 1931
The Golden Lotus. Page, 1927; Harrap, 1927
Grey Gables. Long, 1929

The House on the Downs. Page, 1925 B
The Purple Mist. Page, 1924 B
The Ravensdale Mystery. Page, 1935
The Red Cavalier. Page, 1922
The Redmaynes. Page, 1928; Long, 1929
-Ronald o' the Moors. Four Seas, 1919
The Scarlet Macaw. Page, 1923 B
That Affair at Portstead Manor. French, 1914

LOCKE, MARTIN. Pseudonym of W(illiam) Murdoch Duncan, 1909-1975, q.v. Other pseudonyms: John Cassells, John Dallas, Neill Graham, Peter Malloch, Lovat Marshall, qq.v.
The Vengeance of Mortimer Daly. Ward, 1961

LOCKE, ROBERT DONALD
A Taste of Brass. Dell, 1957

LOCKE, W(ILLIAM) J(OHN). 1863-1930.
The Joyous Adventures of Aristide Pujol. Lane (London & New York), 1912 ss

LOCKHART, JOHN G(ILBERT). 1891- .
East All the Way. Benn, 1928; Appleton, 1928
That Followed After. Benn, 1929

LOCKRIDGE, FRANCES (LOUISE DAVIS), 1896-1963, and RICHARD (ORSON), 1898- .
See also: RICHARD LOCKRIDGE; and RICHARD and FRANCES LOCKRIDGE. British byline on those titles below marked FR: Francis Richards. Series characters: Mr. & Mrs. (Pam & Jerry) North = N (see also: Owen Davis); Bill Weigand = BW (BW also appears in every N novel except Murder by the Book); Nathan Shapiro = NS (see also the Richard Lockridge entry); Bernard Simmons = BS (see also the Richard Lockridge entry); Paul Lane = PL; Captain/Inspector Merton Heimrich = ML (see also the Richard Lockridge entry, and the Richard and Frances Lockridge entry).
And Left for Dead. Lippincott, 1962; Hutchinson, 1962 BS
Call It Coincidence; see Murder and Blueberry Pie
Case of the Murdered Redhead; see The Faceless Adversary
Catch as Catch Can. Lippincott, 1958; Long, 1960, by FR
Curtain for a Jester. Lippincott, 1953 N
Dead as a Dinosaur. Lippincott, 1952; Hutchinson, 1956 N
Death has a Small Voice. Lippincott, 1953; Hutchinson, 1954 N
Death of a Tall Man. Lippincott, 1946; Hutchinson, 1949 N, MH
Death of an Angel. Lippincott, 1955; Hutchinson, 1957. Also published as: Mr. & Mrs. North and the Poisoned Playboy. Avon, 1957 N
Death on the Aisle. Lippincott, 1942; Hutchinson, 1948 N
Death Takes a Bow. Lippincott, 1943; Hutchinson, 1945 N
The Devious Ones. Lippincott, 1964. British title: Four Hours to Fear. Long, 1965, by FR BS
The Dishonest Murderer. Lippincott, 1949; Hutchinson, 1951 N
The Drill is Death. Lippincott, 1961; Long, 1963, by FR NS
The Faceless Adversary. Lippincott, 1956. Also published as: Case of the Murdered Redhead. Avon, 1957 NS
Four Hours to Fear; see The Devious Ones
The Golden Man. Lippincott, 1960; Hutchinson, 1961

Hanged for a Sheep. Lippincott, 1942; Hutchinson, 1944 N
The Innocent House. Lippincott, 1959; Long, 1961, by FR
The Judge is Reversed. Lippincott, 1960; Hutchinson, 1961 N
A Key to Death. Lippincott, 1954 N
Killing the Goose. Lippincott, 1944; Hutchinson, 1947 N
The Long Skeleton. Lippincott, 1958; Hutchinson, 1960 N
Mr. & Mrs. North and the Poisoned Playboy; see Death of an Angel
Mr. & Mrs. North Meet Murder; see The Norths Meet Murder
Murder and Blueberry Pie. Lippincott, 1959. British title: Call It Coincidence. Long, 1962, by FR NS
Murder by the Book. Lippincott, 1963; Hutchinson, 1964 N
Murder Comes First. Lippincott, 1951 N
Murder has Its Points. Lippincott, 1961; Hutchinson, 1962 N
Murder in a Hurry. Lippincott, 1950; Hutchinson, 1952 N
Murder is Served. Lippincott, 1948; Hutchinson, 1950 N
Murder is Suggested. Lippincott, 1959; Hutchinson, 1961 N
Murder Out of Turn. Stokes, 1941; Joseph, 1941 N
Murder Within Murder. Lippincott, 1946; Hutchinson, 1949 N
Night of Shadows. Lippincott, 1962; Long, 1964, by FR PL
The Norths Meet Murder. Stokes, 1940; Joseph, 1940. Also published as: Mr. & Mrs. North Meet Murder. Avon, 1952 N
Payoff for the Banker. Lippincott, 1945; Hutchinson, 1948 N
A Pinch of Poison. Stokes, 1941; Hutchinson, 1948 N
Quest for the Bogeyman. Lippincott, 1964; Hutchinson, 1965 PL
The Tangled Cord. Lippincott, 1957; Hutchinson, 1959 BW
The Ticking Clock. Lippincott, 1962; Hutchinson, 1963
Untidy Murder. Lippincott, 1947 N
Voyage into Violence. Lippincott, 1956; Hutchinson, 1959 N

LOCKRIDGE, RICHARD (ORSON). 1898- .
See also: FRANCES and RICHARD LOCKRIDGE; and RICHARD and FRANCES LOCKRIDGE. Series characters: Captain/Inspector Merton Heimrich = MH (see also FRANCES and RICHARD LOCKRIDGE, and RICHARD and FRANCES LOCKRIDGE); Bernard Simmons = BS (see also FRANCES and RICHARD LOCKRIDGE); Nathan Shapiro = NS (see also FRANCES and RICHARD LOCKRIDGE).
Death in a Sunny Place. Lippincott, 1971; Long, 1973
Death in the Mind, with G(eorge) H. Estabrooks, 1896?-1973. Dutton, 1945
Death on the Hour. Lippincott, 1974; Long, 1975 BS
Die Laughing. Lippincott, 1969; Long, 1970, by Francis Richards NS
Inspector's Holiday. Lippincott, 1971; Long, 1972 MH
A Matter of Taste. Lippincott, 1949; Hutchinson, 1951
Murder Can't Wait. Lippincott, 1964; Long, 1965, by Francis Richards MH & NS
Murder for Art's Sake. Lippincott, 1967; Long, 1968, by Francis Richards NS
Murder in False-Face. Lippincott, 1968; Hutchinson, 1969
Murder Roundabout. Lippincott, 1966;

Long, 1967, by Francis Richards MH
Not I, Said the Sparrow. Lippincott, 1973; Long, 1974 MH
Or was He Pushed? Lippincott, 1975; Long, 1976 NS
A Plate of Red Herrings. Lippincott, 1968; Long, 1969, by Francis Richards BS
Preach No More. Lippincott, 1971; Long, 1972 NS
A Risky Way to Kill. Lippincott, 1969; Long, 1970, by Francis Richards MH
Something Up a Sleeve. Lippincott, 1972; Long, 1973 BS
Squire of Death. Lippincott, 1965; Long, 1966, by Francis Richards BS
Troubled Journey. Lippincott, 1970; Hutchinson, 1971
Twice Retired. Lippincott, 1970; Long, 1971 BS
With Option to Die. Lippincott, 1967; Long, 1968, by Francis Richards MH
Write Murder Down. Lippincott, 1972; Long, 1974 NS

LOCKRIDGE, RICHARD (ORSON), 1898- , and FRANCES, 1896-1963. See also: FRANCES and RICHARD LOCKRIDGE; and RICHARD LOCKRIDGE. Series character: Captain/Inspector Merton Heimrich, in all titles (see also FRANCES and RICHARD LOCKRIDGE, and RICHARD LOCKRIDGE). British byline on all titles marked FR: Francis Richards.
Accent on Murder. Lippincott, 1958; Long, 1960, by FR
Burnt Offering. Lippincott, 1955; Hutchinson, 1957, by FR
A Client is Cancelled. Lippincott, 1951; Hutchinson, 1955
Death and the Gentle Bull. Lippincott, 1954; Hutchinson, 1956. Also published as: Killer in the Straw. Mercury, 1955
Death by Association. Lippincott, 1952; Hutchinson, 1957. Also published as: Trial by Terror. Mercury, 1954
The Distant Clue. Lippincott, 1963; Long, 1964, by FR
First Come, First Kill. Lippincott, 1962; Long, 1963, by FR
Foggy, Foggy Death. Lippincott, 1950; Hutchinson, 1953
I Want to Go Home. Lippincott, 1948
Killer in the Straw; see Death and the Gentle Bull
Let Dead Enough Alone. Lippincott, 1956; Hutchinson, 1958, by FR
No Dignity in Death; see —With One Stone
Practice to Deceive. Lippincott, 1957; Hutchinson, 1959, by FR
Show Red for Danger. Lippincott, 1960; Long, 1961, by FR
Spin Your Web, Lady! Lippincott, 1949; Hutchinson, 1952
Stand Up and Die. Lippincott, 1953; Hutchinson, 1955
Think of Death. Lippincott, 1947
Trial by Terror; see Death by Association
—With One Stone. Lippincott, 1961. British title: No Dignity in Death. Long, 1962, by FR

LOCKWOOD, DAVID
Death has Scarlet Candles. Hodder, 1949
Night & Green Ginger. Hodder, 1951

LOCKWOOD, ETHEL
The Haunted Hammock. Lenox Hill, 1973; Remploy, 1973

LOCKWOOD, MARY. 1934- .
-The Accessory. Random, 1968; Macdonald, 1969

LOCKWOOD, P(HILIP) H.
A Modern Man-Hunt. Stock, 1904 ss

LODER, VERNON. Pseudonym of John (George) Hazlette Vahey, 1881- , q.v. Other pseudonyms: Henrietta Clandon, John Haslette, Anthony Lang, John Mowbray, Walter Proudfoot, qq.v. Series characters: Inspector Brews = B; Inspector Chace = C; Donald Cairn = DC.
Between Twelve and One; see Whose Hand?
The Button in the Plate. Collins, 1938
The Case of the Dead Doctor. Collins, 1935
Choose Your Weapon. Collins, 1937
The Deaf-Mute Murders. Collins, 1936
Death at the Horse Show. Collins, 1935 C
Death at the Wheel. Collins, 1933
Death in the Thicket. Collins, 1932
Death of an Editor. Collins, 1931; Morrow, 1931 B
The Death Pool; see The Essex Murders
The Essex Murders. Collins, 1930. U.S. title: The Death Pool. Morrow, 1931 B
Kill in the Ring. Collins, 1938
The Little Man Murders. Collins, 1936
The Men with the Double Faces. Collins, 1937 DC
Murder from Three Angles. Collins, 1934 C
The Mystery at Stowe. Collins, 1928
Red Stain. Collins, 1931; Morrow, 1932
Ship of Secrets. Collins, 1936
The Shop Window Murders. Collins, 1930; Morrow, 1930
Suspicion. Collins, 1933
Two Dead. Collins, 1934
The Vase Mystery. Collins, 1929
Whose Hand? Collins, 1929. U.S. title: Between Twelve and One. Morrow, 1929
A Wolf in the Fold. Collins, 1938 DC

LODGE, MRS.
-The Daringfords. Digby, 1900
-George Elvaston. Tinsley, 1883
-Lady Ottoline. Tinsley, 1881
The Mystery of Bloomsbury Crescent. Digby, 1896
The Mystery of Monkswood. Digby, 1899
-A Son of the Gods. Digby, 1898
-Under a Ban. Munro, 1884. (British title?)

LODWICK, JOHN. 1916-1959.
Brother Death. Heinemann, 1948; Duell, 1951
The Destroyer; see Peal of Ordnance
First Steps Inside the Zoo. Heinemann, 1950. U.S. title: The Man Dormant. Duell, 1950
-Just a Song at Twilight. Heinemann, 1949
-Love Bade Me Welcome. Heinemann, 1952; Roy, 1953
The Man Dormant; see First Steps Inside the Zoo
-Peal of Ordnance. Methuen, 1947. Also published as: The Destroyer. Digit, 1958
-Something in the Heart. Heinemann, 1948
Somewhere a Voice is Calling. Heinemann, 1953; Roy, 1953
-Stamp Me Mortal. Heinemann, 1950
-Twenty East of Greenwich. Heinemann, 1947

LOEWENGARD, HEIDI HUBERTA FREYBE. 1914- . Pseudonym: Martha Albrand, q.v.

LOFTS, NORAH (ROBINSON). 1904- . Pseudonym: Peter Curtis, q.v.
Charlotte. Hodder, 1972
Checkmate. Corgi, 1975; Crest, 1978
The Golden Fleece; see Michael and All Angels
Michael and All Angels. Joseph, 1943. U.S. title: The Golden Fleece. Knopf, 1944

LOGAN, CAROLYNNE and MALCOLM
One of These Seven. Mystery House, 1946; Quality, 1948

LOGAN, DON
The Rapist. PB, 1975

LOGAN, GUY H. B.
The Eternal Moment. Paul, 1932

LOGAN, MALCOLM. See: CAROLYNNE LOGAN.

LOMAS, JOHN
The Man with the Scar. Heinemann, 1926; Houghton, 1926

LOMAX, W(ILLIAM) J(OSEPH). 1863- .
-The Ambassador's Kiss. Nash, 1925
The Riddle of the Book-Mark. Nash, 1926

LOMBARD, LOUIS. 1861-1927.
-The Vicious Virtuoso. Neely, 1898

LOMBARD, NAP. Joint pseudonym of Pamela Hansford Johnson, 1912- , and Neil Stewart.
The Grinning Pig; see Murder's a Swine
Murder's a Swine. Hutchinson, 1943. U.S. title: The Grinning Pig. Simon, 1943
Tidy Death. Cassell, 1940

LONDON, JACK. 1876-1916.
The Assassination Bureau, Ltd. McGraw-Hill, 1963; Deutsch, 1963. (Completed by Robert L. Fish, 1912- , q.v.)

LONG, AMELIA REYNOLDS. 1904-1978. Pseudonyms: Patrick Laing, Adrian Reynolds, Peter Reynolds, qq.v. Joint pseudonym with Edna McHugh: Kathleen Buddington Coxe, q.v. Series characters: "Peter" Piper, in at least those marked PP; Steve Carter, in at least those marked SC; Edward Trelawny, in at least those marked ET.
The Carter Kidnapping Case; see Invitation to Death
The Corpse at the Quill Club. Phoenix, 1940; Grafton, 1945 PP
The Corpse Came Back. Phoenix, 1949
Death has a Will. Phoenix, 1944; Swan, 1950 SC
Death Looks Down. Ziff-Davis, 1945 ET
Death Wears a Scarab. Phoenix, 1943; Quality, 1946 SC
Four Feet in the Grave. Phoenix, 1941 PP
The House with Green Shutters. Phoenix, 1950 SC
Invitation to Death. Phoenix, 1940. British title (?): The Carter Kidnapping Case. Pemberton, 1944 ET
It's Death, My Darling! Mystery House, 1948 PP
The Lady Saw Red. Phoenix, 1951
Murder by Magic. Phoenix, 1947; Grafton, 1946 SC
Murder by Scripture. Phoenix, 1942 PP
Murder by Treason. Phoenix, 1944; Pemberton, 1948 SC
Murder Goes South. Phoenix, 1942 PP
Murder Times Three. Phoenix, 1940; Foulsham, 1950 ET
Murder to Type. Phoenix, 1943 SC
Once Acquitted. Phoenix, 1945; Quality, 1947 SC
The Shakespeare Murders. Phoenix, 1939; Grafton, 1945 ET
Symphony in Murder. Ziff-Davis, 1944; Quality, 1953 ET
The Triple Cross Murders. Ziff-Davis, 1943; Gardner, 1947 ET

LONG, DEREK. Both titles below were published by Amalgamated Press and feature Sexton Blake.
The Case of Lord Greyburn's Son. 1946
The Mystery of the Italian Ruins. 1950

LONG, ERNEST LAURIE. 1886- . Series character: Captain Flynn, in at least those marked F. At least many of the books are probably more sea adventure than crime fiction.
Abaft 'Midships. Ward, 1949
Anchor's Aweigh. Ward, 1940
As They Rise. Ward, 1934
The Blindness of Flynn. Ward, 1959 F
Buoyed Cables. Ward, 1941
Cabine de Luxe. Ward, 1961
Captain Flynn. Ward, 1939 F
Captain Flynn Ret'd. Ward, 1950 F
Captain Flynn, Sheriff. Ward, 1962 F
Carried Away. Ward, 1945
A Chief in Embryo. Ward, 1953
Clear Round. Ward, 1946
Coolie Tramp. Ward, 1956
The Crew of L.C. 454. Ward, 1947
Crime Cruise. Ward, 1957
A Cumsha Cruise. Ward, 1937
A Curtailed Voyage. Ward, 1957
Deep Channels. Ward, 1943
Dope Ship. Ward, 1954
Double Banked. Ward, 1940
Flat Aback. Ward, 1954
Flynn, A.B. Ward, 1936 F
Flynn of the "Martagon." Eldon, 1934 F
Flynn's Sampler. Ward, 1945 F
The Fortunes of Flynn. Ward, 1938 F
Foul Hawsers. Ward, 1935
Four in a Fairlead. Ward, 1950
The Gabbart Destiny. Ward, 1956
The Galleys of St. John. Ward, 1945
Gauges Steady. Ward, 1946
The Ghost of the Dunsany. Ward, 1941
Gold Ballast. Ward, 1952
The Good Ship Rajah. Ward, 1961
The Haven of St. Garth. Ward, 1951
High Noon to High Noon. Ward, 1959
Hunslett's Yard. Ward, 1962
In Full Commission. Ward, 1964
Lieutenant Flynn, R.N. Ward, 1948 F
Live Lumber. Ward, 1937
Loot Curran, R.N. Ward, 1963
The Lugger Audace. Ward, 1956
Lumber Ship. Ward, 1949
Madam Captain. Ward, 1958
The Masters of Kaolina. Ward, 1959
On Schedule. Ward, 1935
Open Roadsteads. Ward, 1963
Opium Clipper. Ward, 1942
Ould Flynn. Ward, 1953 F
Port of Destination. Eldon, 1933
Purser's Mate. Ward, 1938
River Passage. Ward, 1956
A Saga of the Cliffs. Ward, 1944
The Sailor and the Widow. Ward, 1957
The Schooner "Sybil." Ward, 1936
Sea Dust. Ward, 1938
Sea Range. Ward, 1939
Seconds and Thirds. Ward, 1936
Son of Flynn. Ward, 1940
Storm Canvas. Ward, 1939
The Strong Room of the Sutro. Ward, 1948
Surgeons Adrift. Ward, 1960
Trawl Adrift. Ward, 1958
The Trials of the Phideas. Ward, 1944
Two Little Ships. Ward, 1935
Unhappy Ship. Ward, 1951
The Vengeance of Flynn. Ward, 1942 F
'Way Aloft. Ward, 1947

Young Flynn. Ward, 1937

LONG, FRANK BELKNAP. 1903- .
John Carstairs, Space Detective. Fell, 1949; Cherry Tree, 1951 ss

LONG, FRANK CARLETON
-The Duke of Arcanum. Laird, 1894
-The Lady of the Lens. Crandall, 1891

LONG, GABRIELLE MARGARET VERE CAMPBELL. 1886-1952. Pseudonyms: Marjorie Bowen, George R. Preedy, Joseph Shearing, qq.v., Margaret Campbell.

LONG, GEORGE
Fortune's Wheel. Greening, 1905
Hand and Land. Drane, 1906
-In the Days of Marlborough. Greening, 1908
A Just Fate. Greening, 1907
-Two Lives in Parenthesis. Drane, 1906
-Valhalla. Drane, 1906

LONG, HARMAN. Series character: Franklyn Keen, in at least those marked FK.
The Corpse Can't Walk. Rich, 1950
The Golden Cat. Rich, 1947 FK
Master of Evil. Rich, 1946
Seven to Die. Rich, 1946 FK
Silverface. Rich, 1948
Silverface Surrenders. Rich, 1949

LONG, JULIUS
Keep the Coffins Coming. Messner, 1947. Also published as: Murder in her Big Blue Eyes. Avon, 1950

LONG, LILY AUGUSTA. -1927. Pseudonym: Roman Doubleday, q.v.

LONG, LYDIA BELKNAP
Crucible of Evil. Avon, 1974
The Deadly Nightshade. Beagle, 1972
Fire of the Witches. Popular Library, 1972
Legacy of Evil. Beagle, 1973
Shape of Fear. Beagle, 1971
To the Dark Tower. Lancer, 1969
The Witch Tree. Lancer, 1971

LONG, MANNING. 1906- . Series character: Liz Parrott, in at least those marked LP.
Bury the Hatchet. Duell, 1944; Hammond, 1949 LP
Dull Thud. Duell, 1947; Hammond, 1950 LP
False Alarm. Duell, 1943. Also published as: Invitation to Murder. Arrow, 194? LP
Here's Blood in Your Eye. Duell, 1941; Hammond, 1946
Invitation to Murder; see False Alarm
Modeled in Murder. Best Novel Selection, 1943. (Retitled reprint of ?)
Savage Breast. Duell, 1948; Hammond, 1951 LP
Short Shrift. Duell, 1945; Hammond, 1949 LP
Vicious Circle. Duell, 1942; Hammond, 1946 LP

LONG, MAX (FREEDOM). 1890- . Series character: Komako Koa, in all titles.
Death Goes Native. Lippincott, 1941
The Lava Flow Murders. Lippincott, 1940
Murder Between Dark and Dark. Lippincott, 1939; Hutchinson, 1940

LONG, PATRICK. Series character: Martyn Cale, in both titles.
Eagle Six. Everest, 1975
Heil Britannia. Everest, 1973

LONG, WILLIAM. 1922- . Pseudonyms: Will Creed, Peter Yates, qq.v.

LONGBAUGH, HARRY. Pseudonym of William (W.) Goldman, 1931- , q.v.
No Way to Treat a Lady. GM, 1964; Muller pb, 1964. Reprinted as by William Goldman: Harcourt, 1968; Coronet, 1968

LONGMAN, M. E.
I was Murdered. Wright, 1936
The Phantom Millionaire. Wright, 1935
Terror Island. Wright, 1934; Godwin, 1934

LONGMATE, NORMAN (RICHARD). 1925- . Series characters: Insp./Supt. Bradbury and Sgt. Raymond, in all titles.
Death in Office. Hale, 1961
Death Won't Wash. Cassell, 1957
A Head for Death. Cassell, 1958
Strip Death Naked. Cassell, 1959
Vote for Death. Cassell, 1960

LONGRIGG, ROGER (ERSKINE). 1929- .
Pseudonym (?): Ivor Drummond, q.v.
-The Desperate Criminals. Macmillan (London), 1971

LONGSTREET, STEPHEN. 1907- . Pseudonyms: Paul Haggard, Henri Weiner, qq.v.
The Crime. Simon, 1959

LONGSTRETH, T(HOMAS) MORRIS. 1886- .
In Scarlet and Plain Clothes. Macmillan, 1933
Murder at Belle Butte, with Henry Vernon. Century, 1931 ss
-The Silent Five. Century, 1924
Sons of the Mounted Police. Century, 1928 ss
-Trial by Wilderness. Appleton, 1940

LONGWAY, A. HUGE. Pseudonym of Andrew Lang, 1844-1912, q.v.
Much Darker Days. Longmans, 1884. (Parody of Hugh Conway's novel, Dark Days, q.v.)

LONSDALE, FREDERICK. See: DENYS G. HERRIOT.

LOOKABEE, EMMITT. Pseudonym.
A Twist of Yarn. Pageant, 1966

LOOMIS, NOEL (MILLER). 1905-1969.
Murder Goes to Press. Phoenix, 1937

LORAC, E. C. R. Pseudonym of Edith Caroline Rivett, 1894-1958. Other pseudonym: Carol Carnac, q.v. Series character" Insp./Supt. MacDonald, in at least those marked M.
Accident by Design. Collins, 1950; Doubleday, 1951 M
The Affair on Thor's Head. Low, 1932 M
And Then Put Out the Light; see Policemen in the Precinct
Ask a Policeman. Collins, 1955 M
Bats in the Belfry. Collins, 1937; Macaulay, 1937 M
Black Beadle. Collins, 1939
Case in the Clinic. Collins, 1941 M
The Case of Colonel Marchand. Low, 1933; Macaulay, 1933 M
Checkmate to Murder. Collins, 1944; Arcadia, 1944 M
Crime Counter Crime. Collins, 1936 M
Crook o' Lune. Collins, 1953. U.S. title: Shepherd's Crook. Doubleday, 1953 M
Dangerous Domicile. Collins, 1957 M
Death at Dyke's Corner. Collins, 1940 M

Death Before Dinner. Collins, 1948. U.S. title: A Screen for Murder. Doubleday, 1948 M
Death Came Softly. Collins, 1943; Mystery House, 1943
Death in Triplicate. Collins, 1958. U.S. title: People Will Talk. Doubleday, 1958 M
Death of an Author. Low, 1935; Macaulay, 1937
Death on the Oxford Road. Low, 1933 M
The Devil and the C.I.D. Collins, 1938 M
Dishonour Among Thieves. Collins, 1959. U.S. title: The Last Escape. Doubleday, 1959 M
The Dog It was That Died. Collins, 1952; Doubleday, 1952 M
Fell Murder. Collins, 1944 M
Fire in the Thatch. Collins, 1946; Mystery House, 1946 M
The Greenwell Mystery. Low, 1932; Macaulay, 1934 M
I Could Murder Her; see Murder of a Martinet
John Brown's Body. Collins, 1939 M
The Last Escape; se Dishonour Among Thieves
Let Well Alone. Collins, 1954 M
Murder by Matchlight. Collins, 1945; Mystery House, 1946 M
Murder in Chelsea. Low, 1934; Macaulay, 1935 M
Murder in St. John's Wood. Low, 1934; Macaulay, 1934 M
Murder in the Mill-Race. Collins, 1952. U.S. title: Speak Justly of the Dead. Doubleday, 1953 M
Murder in Vienna. Collins, 1956 M
Murder of a Martinet. Collins, 1951. U.S. title: I Could Murder Her. Doubleday, 1951 M
Murder on a Monument. Collins, 1958 M
The Murder on the Burrows. Low, 1931; Macaulay, 1932 M
Murderer's Mistake; see The Theft of the Iron Dogs
The Organ Speaks. Low, 1935 M
A Pall for a Painter. Collins, 1936 M
Part for a Poisoner. Collins, 1948. U.S. title: Place for a Poisoner. Doubleday, 1949 M
People Will Talk; see Death in Triplicate
Picture of Death. Collins, 1957 M
Place for a Poisoner; see Part for a Poisoner
Policemen in the Precinct. Collins, 1949. U.S. title: And Then Put Out the Light. Doubleday, 1950 M
Post After Post-Mortem. Collins, 1936 M
Relative to Poison. Collins, 1947; Doubleday, 1948 M
Rope's End—Rogue's End. Collins, 1942 M
A Screen for Murder; see Death Before Dinner
Shepherd's Crook; see Crook o' Lune
Shroud of Darkness. Collins, 1954; Doubleday, 1954 M
The Sixteenth Stair. Collins, 1942 M
Slippery Staircase. Collins, 1938 M
Speak Justly of the Dead; see Murder in the Mill-Race
Still Waters. Collins, 1949 M
The Theft of the Iron Dogs. Collins, 1946. U.S. title: Murderer's Mistake. Mystery House, 1947
These Names Make Clues. Collins, 1937 M
Tryst for a Tragedy. Collins, 1940 M

LORAINE, PHILIP. Pseudonym of Robin Estridge.
And to my Beloved Husband——; see White Lie the Dead

The Angel of Death. Hodder, 1961; Mill, 1961
Ask the Rattlesnake. Collins, 1975. U.S. title: Wrong Man in the Mirror. Random, 1975
The Break in the Circle. Hodder, 1951; Mill, 1951. Also published as: Outside the Law. PB, 1953
Day of the Arrow. Collins, 1964; Mill, 1964. Also published as: The Eye of the Devil. Fontana, 1966. And as: 13. Lancer, 1966
The Dead Men of Sestos. Collins, 1968; Random, 1968
The Dublin Nightmare. Hodder, 1952. U.S. title: Nightmare in Dublin. Mill, 1952
Exit with Intent. Hodder, 1950
The Eye of the Devil; see Day of the Arrow
A Mafia Kiss. Collins, 1968; Random, 1969
Nightmare in Dublin; see The Dublin Nightmare
Outside the Law; see The Break in the Circle
Photographs have been Sent to Your Wife. Collins, 1971; Random, 1971
13; see Day of the Arrow
Voices in an Empty Room. Collins, 1973; Random, 1974
White Lie the Dead. Hodder, 1950. U.S. title: And to my Beloved Husband——. Mill, 1950
W.I.L. One to Curtis. Collins, 1967; Random, 1967
Wrong Man in the Mirror; see Ask the Rattlesnake

LORD, DANIEL A(LOYSIUS). 1888-1955.
-Murder in the Sacristy. Queen's Work, 1941

LORD, GARLAND. Joint pseudonym of (Mary) Isabel Garland, 1903-   , q.v., and Mindret Lord.
Murder, Plain and Fancy. Doubleday, 1943
Murder with Love. Morrow, 1943
Murder's Little Helper. Doubleday, 1941
She Never Grew Old. Doubleday, 1942

LORD, GRACE VIRGINIA.   -1885. Pseudonym: Virginia Champlin, q.v.

LORD, GRAHAM. 1943-   .
Marshmallow Pie. Macmillan (London), 1970; Coward, 1970
The Spider and the Fly. H. Hamilton, 1974; Viking, 1975

LORD, JEREMY. Pseudonym of Ben Ray Redman, 1896-1961. Series character: Colonel Winston Creevy, in both titles.
The Bannerman Case. Doubleday, 1935; Hurst, 1936
Sixty-Nine Diamonds. Doubleday, 1940; Hurst, 1940

LORD, MINDRET. Joint pseudonym with (Mary) Isabel Garland, 1903-   , q.v.: Garland Lord, q.v.

LORE, PHILLIPS. Pseudonym of Terence Lore Smith, q.v.
Who Killed the Pie Man? Saturday Review Press, 1975

LORENZ, FREDERICK. Pseudonym of Lorenz Heller, q.v. Other pseudonyms: Larry Heller, Larry Holden, qq.v.
Hot. Lion, 1956
Night Never Ends. Lion, 1954
A Party Every Night. Lion, 1956
A Rage at Sea. Lion, 1953
Ruby. Lion, 1956
The Savage Chase. Lion, 1954

LORIMER, GEORGE C(LAUDE). 1838-1904.
-The Master of Millions. Revell, 1903

LORIMER, GEORGE HORACE. 1868-1937.
The False Gods. Appleton, 1906

LORIMER, GRAEME and SARAH
Acquittal. Little, 1938; Cape, 1938

LORIMER, NORMA (OCTAVIA). 1864-   .
A Mender of Images. Hutchinson, 1920; Brentano's, 1921

LORIMER, SARAH. See: GRAEME LORIMER.

LORING, ANN
The Mark of Satan. Award, 1969
The 13th Doll. Award, 1970

LORING, PETER. Pseudonym of Samuel Shellabarger, 1888-1954. Other pseudonym: John Esteven, q.v.
-Miss Rolling Stone. Macrae Smith, 1939. British title: He Travels Alone. Hodder, 1939

LORIOT, NOELLE. Pseudonym: Laurence Oriol, q.v.

LORRAINE, JOHN. Pseudonym.
Men of Career. Crown, 1960

LORRIMER, CLAIRE
Relentless Storm. Avon, 1975
The Shadow Falls. Avon, 1974
A Voice in the Dark. Souvenir, 1967; Bantam, 1977

LORY, ROBERT. 1936-   .
The Curse of Leo. Pinnacle, 1974
Gemini Smile, Gemini Kill. Pinnacle, 1975
The Green Flames of Aries. Pinnacle, 1974
The Revenge of Taurus. Pinnacle, 1974

LOTT, S(TANLEY) MAKEPEACE. Series character: Stephen Ringway, in both titles.
The Judge will Call It Murder. Rich, 1951
Twopence for a Rat's Tail. Rich, 1947

LOTTMAN, EILEEN. 1927-   . Pseudonym: Maud Willis, q.v.
The Hemlock Tree. Popular Library, 1975

LOUGHEAD, FLORA HAINES (APPONYI). 1855-   .
-The Abandoned Claim. Houghton, 1891; Watt, 1891
-The Black Curtain. Houghton, 1898; Duckworth, 1899
The Man Who was Guilty. Houghton, 1886

LOUIS, EDWARD
His Lordship the Crook. Skeffington, 1932

LOVATT, WILLIAM F.
The Curse of Kama. Houghton (London), 1932

LOVELL, B. E. 1920-   .
...And Incidentally, Murder! Bouregy, 1952
A Rage to Kill. Ace, 1957

LOVELL, MARC. Pseudonym of Mark McShane, 1930-   , q.v.
Dreamers in a Haunted House. Doubleday, 1975; Hale, 1976
An Enquiry into the Existence of Vampires. Doubleday, 1974. British title: Vampire in the Shadows. Hale, 1976

The Ghost of Megan. Doubleday, 1968. Also published as: Memory of Megan. Ace, 1970
The Imitation Thieves. Doubleday, 1971
Memory of Megan; see The Ghost of Megan
A Presence in the House. Doubleday, 1972
Vampire in the Shadows; see An Enquiry into the Existence of Vampires

LOVESEY, PETER. 1936-   . Series characters: Sgt. Cribb and Constable Thackeray, in all titles.
Abracadaver. Macmillan (London), 1972; Dodd, 1972
A Case of Spirits. Macmillan (London), 1975; Dodd, 1975
The Detective Wore Silk Drawers. Macmillan (London), 1971; Dodd, 1971
Invitation to a Dynamite Party. Macmillan (London), 1974. U.S. title: The Tick of Death. Dodd, 1974
Mad Hatter's Holiday. Macmillan (London), 1973; Dodd, 1973
The Tick of Death; see Invitation to a Dynamite Party
Wobble to Death. Macmillan (London), 1970; Dodd, 1970

LOW, DOROTHY MACKIE. Pseudonym of Lois Dorothea Low, 1916-   . Other pseudonym: Lois Paxton, q.v.
-Dear Liar. Hurst, 1963
-A House in the Country. Hurst, 1968
-The Intruder. Hurst, 1965
Isle for a Stranger. Hurst, 1962; Ace, 1968
-A Ripple on the Water. Hurst, 1964
To Burgundy and Back. Hurst, 1970; Ace, 1972

LOW, GARDNER. Pseudonym of (Percival) Charles Rodda, 1891-   , q.v. Other pseudonym: Gavin Holt, q.v. Joint pseudonym with Eric Ambler, 1909-   , q.v.: Eliot Reed, q.v.
Invitation to Kill. Gollancz, 1937; Putnam, 1937

LOW, LOIS DOROTHEA. 1916-   . Pseudonyms: Dorothy Mackie Low, Lois Paxton, qq.v.

LOW, WERNER A.
Peace Bridge. Vantage, 1975

LOWDEN, DESMOND. 1937-   .
Bandersnatch. Eyre, 1969; Holt, 1969
Bellman and True. Eyre, 1975; Holt, 1975
The Boondocks. Eyre, 1972; Holt, 1973

LOWE, F(REDERICK) J(AMES)
Blood Money. Stockwell, 1957
The Killer from the Grave. Stockwell, 1959

LOWE, KENNETH. Pseudonym of Elma K. Lobaugh, 1907-   , q.v.
The Catalyst. Doubleday, 1958; Boardman, 1959
Haze of Evil. Doubleday, 1953
No Tears for Shirley Minton. Doubleday, 1955; Boardman, 1957

LOWE, MARJORIE G(RIFFITHS). 1909-   .
Jess. Macdonald, 1961. U.S. title: The Sudden Lady. Putnam, 1961
Raking for the Moon. Macmillan (London), 1963
The Sudden Lady; see Jess

LOWELL, J. R.
Daughter of Darkness. Delacorte, 1972; Souvenir, 1973

LOWING, ANNE. Pseudonym of Christine Geach, 1930-   .
  Black Midnight. Hale, 1968
  The Captain's Pawn. Hale, 1975
  The Denbigh Affair. Hale, 1967
  The Gossamer Thread. Hale, 1972
  The Masked Ball. Hale, 1967
  Melyonen. Hale, 1973
  The Napoleon Ring. Hale, 1975
  Shadow on the Wind. Hale, 1960
  Yasmin. Hale, 1969

LOWIS, CECIL CHAMPAIN. 1866-1948.
  The Ava Mining Syndicate. Greening, 1908
  The District Bungalow. Cape, 1927; Doubleday, 1928
  -The Dripping Tamarinds. Laurie, 1933
  Four Blind Mice. Lane (London & New York), 1920
  -The Grass Spinster. Cape, 1925
  Green Sandals. Cape, 1926; Doran, 1927
  The Green Tunnel. Dickson, 1935
  -The Huntress. Cape, 1929
  -In the Hag's Hands. Laurie, 1931
  -The Machinations of the Myo-ok. Methuen, 1903
  -The Penal Settlement. Cape, 1928
  -Prodigal's Portion. Dickson, 1936
  -The Runagate. Cape, 1924
  -Snags and Shallows. Lane (London), 1922
  -The Treasury-Officer's Wooing. Macmillan (London), 1899

LOWNDES, MARIE BELLOC. 1868-1947.
  Afterwards. Doubleday, 1925. (British title?)
  And Call It Accident. Hutchinson, 1939; Longmans, 1936
  Another Man's Wife. Heinemann, 1934; Longmans, 1934
  Before the Storm. Longmans, 1941. (British title?)
  -Bread of Deceit. Hutchinson, 1925
  The Chianti Flask. Heinemann, 1935; Longmans, 1934
  The Chink in the Armour. Methuen, 1912; Scribner, 1912. Also published as: The House of Peril. Readers Library, 1935
  The Christine Diamond. Hutchinson, 1940; Longmans, 1940
  Cressida: No Mystery. Heinemann, 1928; Knopf, 1930
  -The Empress Eugenie. Longmans, 1938. (3-act play.)
  The End of her Honeymoon. Methuen, 1914; Scribner, 1913
  The Fortune of Bridget Malone; see The Marriage-Broker
  From Out the Vasty Deep; see From the Vasty Deep
  From the Vasty Deep. Hutchinson, 1920. U.S. title: From Out the Vasty Deep. Doran, 1921
  The Gentleman Anonymous; see Out of the War?
  Good Old Anna. Hutchinson, 1915; Doran, 1916
  -The Heart of Penelope. Heinemann, 1904
  The House by the Sea. Hutchinson, 1937. U.S. title: Vanderlyn's Adventure. Cape & Smith, 1931
  The House of Peril; see The Chink in the Armour
  The Injured Lover. Hutchinson, 1939
  Jenny Newstead. Heinemann, 1932; Putnam, 1932
  -The Key. Benn, 1930. (3-act play.)
  -A Labour of Hercules. Todd, 1943 (16 pp. pamphlet.)
  Letty Lynton. Heinemann, 1931; Cape & Smith, 1931
  Lizzie Borden: A Study in Conjecture. Hutchinson, 1940; Longmans, 1939
  The Lodger. Methuen, 1913; Scribner, 1913
  The Lonely House. Hutchinson, 1920; Doran, 1920
  Love and Hatred. Chapman, 1917; Doran, 1917
  -Love is a Flame. Benn, 1932
  -Love's Revenge. Readers Library, 1909
  The Marriage-Broker. Heinemann, 1937. U.S. title: The Fortune of Bridget Malone. Longmans, 1937
  Motive. Hutchinson, 1938. U.S. title (?): Why It Happened. Longmans, 1938
  One of Those Ways. Heinemann, 1929; Knopf, 1929
  -Out of the War? Chapman, 1918. Also published as: The Gentleman Anonymous. Allan, 1934
  -The Philosophy of the Marquise. Richards, 1899
  -The Price of Admiralty. Newnes, 1915
  -The Reason Why. Benn, 1932
  Reckless Angel. Longmans, 1939. (British title?)
  The Second Key. Longmans, 1936. (British title?)
  -Some Men and Women. Hutchinson, 1925; Doubleday, 1928 ss
  The Story of Ivy. Heinemann, 1927; Doubleday, 1928
  The Terriford Mystery. Hutchinson, 1924; Doubleday, 1924
  "Thou Shalt Not Kill." Hutchinson, 1927
  The Uttermost Farthing. Heinemann, 1908; Kennerley, 1910
  Vanderlyn's Adventure; see The House by the Sea
  What Really Happened. Hutchinson, 1926; Doubleday, 1926. Play version: Benn, 1932
  What Timmy Did. Hutchinson, 1921; Doran, 1922
  When No Man Pursueth. Heinemann, 1910; Kennerley, 1911
  Who Rides on a Tiger. Heinemann, 1936; Longmans, 1935
  -Why be Lonely?, with F. S. Lowndes. Benn, 1931. (Play.)
  Why It Happened; see Motive
  -Why They Married. Heinemann, 1923
  -With All John's Love. Benn, 1930. (3-act play.)

LOWRY, BRIDGET
  Burden's End. Methuen, 1930

LUARD, NICHOLAS (LAMBERT). 1937-   .
  The Robespierre Serial. Weidenfeld, 1975; Harcourt, 1975
  Traveling Horseman. Weidenfeld, 1975
  The Warm and Golden War. Secker, 1967; Pantheon, 1968

LUCAS, (JOHN) CARY
  Unfinished Business. Simon, 1947

LUCAS, J. K. Pseudonym of Lauran Bosworth Paine, 1916-   . Other pseudonyms: John Armour, Reg Batchelor, Kenneth Bedford, Frank Bosworth, Mark Carrel, Robert Clarke, Richard Dana, J. F. Drexler, Troy Howard, Jared Ingersol, John Kilgore, Hunter Liggett, John Morgan, qq.v.
  The Born Survivor. Hale, 1975
  Haight is the Killer. Hale, 1969

LUCAS, NETLEY (EVELYN). 1903-   .
  The Red Stranger. Paul, 1927

LUCAS, NORMAN. Series character: Supt. Bill Rowlands, in all titles.
  Corner in Crime. Jenkins, 1952; Roy, 1957

The Red Dice. Jenkins, 1952
Situations Vacant. Jenkins, 1956
Testament of Death. Jenkins, 1953

LUCENTINI, FRANCO. See: C(ARLO) FRUTTERO.

LUCK, PETER
  Crime Legitimate. Jenkins, 1937
  Infallible Witness. Jenkins, 1932
  The Killing of Ezra Burgoyne. Jenkins, 1929
  Terror by Night. Jenkins, 1934
  The Transome Murder Mystery. Jenkins, 1930
  Two Shots. Jenkins, 1931
  Under the Fourth—? Jenkins, 1927
  Who Killed Robin Cockland? Jenkins, 1933
  The Wingrave Case. Jenkins, 1935
  The Wrong Number. Jenkins, 1926

LUDDECKE, WERNER J(ORG). 1911-   .
  Morituri. GM, 1965
  Thursday at Dawn. Doubleday, 1965; Allen, 1966

LUDERS-KNEGTMANS, ANNEKE. Pseudonym: Adrienne Mans, q.v.

LUDLAM, HARRY
  The Coming of Jonathan Smith. Long, 1964

LUDLUM, JEAN KATE
  Under a Cloud. Bonner, 1891

LUDLUM, ROBERT. 1927-   . Pseudonym: Jonathan Ryder, q.v.
  The Matlock Paper. Dial, 1973; Hart-Davis, 1973
  The Osterman Weekend. World, 1972; Hart-Davis, 1972
  The Rhinemann Exchange. Dial, 1974; Hart-Davis, 1975
  The Scarlatti Inheritance. World, 1971; Hart-Davis, 1971

LUEHRMANN, ADELE
  The Curious Case of Marie Dupont. Century, 1916
  The Other Brown. Century, 1917
  The Triple Mystery. Dodd, 1920

LUGER, HANS
  Appointment with Desire. Scion, 1953
  The Bigger They Are. Scion, 1952
  Black Fedora. Scion, 1952
  Come Out with Your Hands Up. Scion, 1952
  Double or Quits. Scion, 1952
  Handle with Care. Scion, 1952
  Harvest for Harpies. Scion, 1953
  Killers End. Scion, 1952
  Lady—This is It! Scion, 1950
  Leave It to Me. Scion, 1952
  Line Up. Scion, 1953
  The Marble Heart. Scion, 1954
  Midnight Sister. Scion, 1953
  One-Way Ticket. Scion, 1952
  Prelude to Passion. Scion, 1954
  Six Foot Deep. Scion, 1950
  This Side Up. Scion, 1952
  You Don't Say! Scion, 1951

LUHRS, VICTOR. 1912-   .
  The Longbow Murder. Norton, 1941

LUKENS, JOHN
  -Adders Abounding. Hodder, 1954
  -The Bright Promise. Hodder, 1958
  -Mine is the Power. Hodder, 1951

LUND, T. Series character: Dick Weston, in at least those marked DW.

The Murder of Dave Brandon. Laurie, 1931 DW
Robbery at Portage Bend. Laurie, 1933; Kendall, 1933 DW
-Steele Bey's Revenge. Laurie, 1934
-Up North. Laurie, 1929
The Vanished Prospector. Laurie, 1937
Weston of the North-West Mounted Police; see Weston of the Royal North-West Mounted Police
Weston of the Royal North-West Mounted Police. Laurie, 1928. Also published as: Weston of the North-West Mounted Police. Mellifont, 1938 DW

LUNN-ROCKLIFFE, PAUL
The Fake. Stockwell, 1973

LUPTON, LEONARD
Murder Without Tears. Graphic, 1957

LURGAN, LESTER. Pseudonym of Mabel Winifred Knowles.
The League of the Triangle. Greening, 1911

LUSKA, SIDNEY. Pseudonym of Henry Harland.
-As It was Written. Cassell (London & New York), 1885

LUSTGARTEN, EDGAR (MARCUS). 1907- .
Blondie Iscariot. Museum, 1949; Scribner, 1948
A Case to Answer. Eyre, 1947. U.S. title: One More Unfortunate. Scribner, 1947
Game for Three Losers. Museum, 1952; Scribner, 1952
I'll Never Leave You. Hart-Davis, 1971
One More Unfortunate; see A Case to Answer

LUTHER, MARK LEE and LILLIAN C. FORD
Series character: Arthur Raneleigh, in both titles.
Card 13. Bobbs, 1930
The Saranoff Murder. Bobbs, 1930

LUTHER, RAY. Pseudonym of Arthur Ley.
Intermind. Banner, 1967

LUTZ, JOHN (THOMAS). 1939- .
The Truth of the Matter. PB, 1971

LYALL, GAVIN (TUDOR). 1932- .
Blame the Dead. Hodder, 1972; Viking, 1973
Judas Country. Hodder, 1975; Viking, 1975
Midnight Plus One. Hodder, 1965; Scribner, 1965
The Most Dangerous Game. Hodder, 1964; Scribner, 1963
Shooting Script. Hodder, 1966; Scribner, 1966
Venus with Pistol. Hodder, 1969; Scribner, 1969
The Wrong Side of the Sky. Hodder, 1961; Scribner, 1961

LYDECKER, J. J.
Half Moon Street. Muller, 1975

LYDSTON, G(EORGE) FRANK. 1858-1923.
Poker Jim, Gentleman and other tales and sketches. Monarch, 1907 ss

LYELL, WILLIAM DARLING. 1860- .
In the Eye of the Law. Hodge, 1898
The House in Queen Anne Square. Blackwood, 1920; Putnam, 1921
The Justice-Clerk. Hodge, 1923

LYLE-SMYTHE, ALLAN. 1914- . Pseudonym: Alan Caillou, q.v.

LYMINGTON, JOHN. Pseudonym of John Newton Chance, 1911- , q.v. Other pseudonym: J. Drummond, q.v.
-Give Daddy the Knife, Darling. Hodder, 1969
-The Nowhere Place. Hodder, 1969

LYNCH, DAN
Four-Time Loser. GM, 1962

LYNCH, FRANCES. Pseudonym of D(avid) G(uy) Compton, 1930- , q.v. By-line also: (David) Guy Compton, q.v.
Twice Ten Thousand Miles. Souvenir, 1974; St. Martin's, 1974. Also published as: Candle at Midnight. Dell, 1977

LYNCH, LAWRENCE L. Pseudonym of Emma Murdoch Van Deventer. Titles published in England under author's real name are starred. Series character: Francis Ferrars, in at least those marked FF.
Against Odds. Rand, 1894; Ward, 1894 *
A Blind Lead. Laird, 1912; Ward, 1912 *
The Danger Line. Ward, 1903. (U.S. title?)
Dangerous Ground; or, The Rival Detectives. Loyd, 1885. British title: The Rival Detectives; or, Dangerous Ground. Ward, 1887
A Dead Man's Step. Rand, 1893; Ward, 1893 *
The Detective's Daughter; or, Madeline Payne; see Madeline Payne, the Detective's Daughter
The Diamond Coterie. Loyd, 1882; Routledge, 1887
The Doverfields Diamonds. Ward, 1907 * (U.S. title?)
High Stakes. Laird, 1899; Ward, 1901
The Last Stroke. Laird, 1896; Ward, 1897 FF
The Lost Witness; or, The Mystery of Leah Paget. Laird, 1890; Ward, 1890
Madeline Payne, the Detective's Daughter. Loyd, 1884. British title: The Detective's Daughter; or, Madeline Payne. Ward, 1887 *
Man and Master. Laird, 1908; Ward, 1909
Moina; see Moina; or, Against the Mighty
Moina; or, Against the Mighty. Laird, 1891. British title: Moina. Ward, 1891
A Mountain Mystery; or, The Outlaws of the Rockies. Loyd, 1886
No Proof. Rand, 1895; Ward, 1895 *
Out of the Labyrinth. Loyd, 1885; Ward, 1887
The Rival Detectives; or, Dangerous Ground; see Dangerous Ground
A Sealed Verdict. Long, 1910 * (U.S. title?)
Shadowed by Three. Donnelly, 1879; Ward, 1884 FF
A Slender Clue; or, The Mystery of Mardi Graz. Laird, 1891; Ward, 1891 *
Under Fate's Wheel. Laird, 1900; Ward, 1900 *
The Unseen Hand. Ward, 1896 * (U.S. title?)
The Woman Who Dared. Ward, 1902. (U.S. title?)
A Woman's Tragedy; or, The Detective's Trick. Ward, 1904 * (U.S. title?)

LYNCH, MIRIAM. Pseudonym of Mary Wallace, q.v.
Amber Twilight. Belmont, 1967
Bells of Widows Bay. Pinnacle, 1971
Blacktower. Paperback Library, 1966; New English Library pb, 1967
The Brides of Lucifer. Lancer, 1973
Creighton's Castle. Ballantine, 1975
A Crime for Christmas. Arcadia, 1959
Daughters of Cain. Lancer, 1970
Deadly Rose. Belmont, 1969
The Devil's Mirror. PB, 1973
Doctor Garrett's Girl. Dell, 1970
The Doomsday Bells. Lancer, 1968
From Secret Places. PB, 1973
Gateway to the Grave. Arcadia, 1958
Graymists. Paperback Library, 1967
Grow Cold Along with Me. Arcadia, 1958
Hate Thy Neighbor. PB, 1973
A Heritage of Danger. Bouregy, 1964
House of Evil. Bouregy, 1966
House of Yesteryear. Beagle, 1974
Journey into Twilight. Lancer, 1970
The Light in the Tower. Curtis, 1973
A Meeting with Murder. Arcadia, 1956
Moon of Darkness. Belmont, 1969
The Night of the Moonrose. Paperback Library, 1966
The Nightmare Dance. Popular Library, 1972
Nightmare's Morning. Pinnacle, 1971
Pale Hand of Danger. Bouregy, 1962
Poor Roger is Dead. Arcadia, 1957
Riverwood. Lancer, 1971
The Road to Midnight. Paperback Library, 1966
The Secret of Lucifer's Island. Paperback Library, 1967
The Silken Web. Bouregy, 1961
A Summer for Witches. Bouregy, 1962
Unwilling Rebel. Pyramid, 1975
Where Evil Waits. Beagle, 1974
Where Shadows Lie. Pinnacle, 1972
The Witches of Windlake. Popular Library, 1971
The Witch's Song. Lancer, 1972
Witches' Holiday. Lancer, 1971
Your Casket Awaits, Madame. Arcadia, 1957

LYNCH, W. WARE. See: IRENE KING, 1943- .

LYNDE, FRANCIS. 1856-1930.
Blind Man's Buff. Scribner, 1928
The Grafters. Bobbs, 1904
The Price. Scribner, 1911
Scientific Sprague. Scribner, 1912 ss
Stranded in Arcady. Scribner, 1917
-The Wreckers. Scribner, 1920
Young Blood. Scribner, 1929

LYNDS, DENNIS. 1924- . Pseudonyms: William Arden, Michael Collins, John Crowe, Carl Dekker, Maxwell Grant, Mark Sadler, qq.v.
Charlie Chan Returns. Bantam (New York & London), 1974. (Featuring the character created by Earl Derr Biggers, 1884-1933, q.v.)
Crossfire. PB, 1975. (Novelization of the SWAT TV series.)

LYNN, DAVID
Death of an Undertaker. Kangaroo, 1943
-The Misadventures of Mr. Larkin. Staples, 1942
Murder in the Bazaar. Kangaroo, 1945
Zombie. Kangaroo, 1945 ss

LYNN, ERNEST
The Yellow Stub. White House, 1926

LYNN, JACK. 1927- .
The Professor. Allison, 1971

LYNN, KAY
Dark Shadows. Hutchinson, 1935
Laughing Mountains. Hutchinson, 1934; Dutton, 1936

LYNN, MARGARET. Pseudonym of Gladys Starkey Battye, 1915- .
A Light in the Window. Hodder, 1967; Doubleday, 1968
Mrs. Maitland's Affair; see Stranger by Night
Stranger by Night. Hodder, 1963. U.S. title: Mrs. Maitland's Affair. Doubleday, 1963
Sunday Evening. Hodder, 1969; Doubleday, 1971
Sweet Epitaph. Hodder, 1971; Doubleday, 1972
To See a Stranger. Hodder, 1961; Doubleday, 1962
Whisper of Darkness. Hodder, 1965; Paperback Library, 1966

LYNRAVN, N(ORMAN) S(OREN). See: L(INCOLN) W(ILLIAM) MARTIN.

LYNWOOD, LESLIE J.
Lester Grayling, K.C. Bale, 1921 ss

LYNX, J. J.
The Prince of Thieves. Cassell, 1963; Atheneum, 1964

LYON, (MABEL) DANA. 1897- . Series character: Hilda Trenton = HT.
The Bathtub Murder, with Josephine Hugheston. Williams, 1933
The Frightened Child. Harper, 1948. Also published as: House on Telegraph Hill. Mercury, 1951
House on Telegraph Hill; see The Frightened Child
I'll be Glad When You're Dead. Royce, 1945
It's my Own Funeral. Farrar, 1944; Hammond, 1948
The Lost One. Harper, 1958; Gollancz, 1958
Spin the Web Tight. Ace, 1963 HT
The Tentacles. Harper, 1950 HT
The Trusting Victim. Ace, 1964

LYON, EDNA WRIGHT
The Unfinished Murder. Humphries, 1935

LYON, HARRIS MERTON. -1916.
Graphics. Reed, 1913 ss, some criminous

LYON, WINSTON. Series character: Batman = B (in novelizations of the TV series).
Batman vs. the Fearsome Foursome. Signet, 1966 B
Batman vs. Three Villains of Doom. Signet, 1966; Four Square, 1966 B
Criminal Court. PB, 1966

LYONS, ARTHUR (JR.). 1946- . Series character: Jacob Ashe, in both titles.
All God's Children. Mason/Charter, 1975; Robson, 1977
The Dead are Discreet. Mason/Charter, 1974; Robson, 1977

LYONS, AUGUSTA WALLACE
Season of Doubt. Signet, 1961

LYONS, DELPHINE
The Depths of Yesterday. Lancer, 1966
Flower of Evil. Pyramid, 1965
House of Four Widows. Lancer, 1965
Phantom at Lost Lake. Lancer, 1970
Valley of Shadows. Lancer, 1968

LYONS, SOPHIE [SOPHIE VAN ELKAN LYONS BURKE].
The Amazing Adventures of Sophie Lyons. Ogilvie, 1913

LYS, CHRISTIAN. Pseudonym of Percy (James) Brebner, 1864-1922, q.v.
-The Black Card. Lawrence, 1899
-The Doctor's Idol. Warne, 1893
-The Dunthorpes of Westleigh. Downey, 1896
-The Fortress of Yadasara. Warne, 1899. Also published as: The Knight of the Silver Star, as by Percy Brebner. Warne, 1925
The Hepsworth Millions. Warne, 1898
The Knight of the Silver Star; see The Fortress of Yadasara
-A London Cobweb. Trischler, 1892
The Mystery of Ladyplace. Warne, 1900
-Suspicion. Ward, 1889

LYSAGHT, ELIZABETH J.
-The Gold of Ophir. Ward, 1890
-Sealed Orders. Bentley, 1886
-The Veiled Picture; or, The Wizard's Legacy. Simpkin, 1890

LYTTLE, ANDREW. 1902- .
The Long Night. Bobbs, 1936; Eyre, 1937
A Name for Evil. Bobbs, 1947

M

McAFEE, PAUL K.
Discord in Harmony. Lenox Hill, 1973

MacALISTER, IAN
Driscoll's Diamonds. GM, 1973; Coronet, 1974
Skylark Mission. GM, 1973; Coronet, 1974
Strike Force 7. GM, 1974; Coronet, 1975
Valley of the Assassins. GM, 1975; Coronet, 1976

McALLISTER, ALISTER. 1877-1943. Pseudonym: Lynn Brock, q.v.

MacANALLY, G(EORGE) H. See: M(ARGUERITE) BRYANT.

MACARDLE, DOROTHY. 1889- .
-Dark Enchantment. Davies, 1953; Doubleday, 1953
-Earth-Bound. Harrigan, 1924 ss
-Fantastic Summer. Davies, 1946. U.S. title: The Unforeseen. Doubleday, 1946
-The Seed was Kind. Davies, 1944
-Uneasy Freehold. Davies, 1941. U.S. title: The Uninvited. Doubleday, 1942
The Unforeseen; see Fantastic Summer
The Uninvited; see Uneasy Freehold

MacARTHUR, D(AVID) WILSON. 1903- .
Pseudonym: David Wilson, q.v.
Convict Captain. Collins, 1939
Death at Slack Water. Ward, 1962
Harry Hogbin. Ward, 1961
Landfall. Melrose, 1933
-Lola of the Isles. Cassell, 1926
The Mystery of the "David M". Melrose, 1932
The Past Dies Hard. Ward, 1965
The Quest of the "Stormalong". Melrose, 1934
A Rhino in the Kitchen. Ward, 1964
-The Road from Chilanga. Jarrolds, 1957
-Simba Bwana. Hurst, 1956
-Yellow Stockings. Cassell, 1925
-The Young Chevalier. Collins, 1946

MACAULAY, MILDRED. Joint pseudonym with Richard Macaulay: Carter Cullen, q.v.

MACAULAY, RICHARD. Joint pseudonym with Mildred Macaulay: Carter Cullen, q.v.

MACAULAY, ROSE. 1881-1958.
Mystery at Geneva. Collins, 1922; Boni, 1923

McAULIFFE, FRANK. Series character: Augustus Mandrell, in all titles, each containing four novelets.
For Murder I Charge More. Ballantine, 1971
Of All the Bloody Cheek. Ballantine, 1965; New English Library, 1971
Rather a Vicious Gentleman. Ballantine, 1968

McBAIN, ED. Pseudonym of Evan Hunter, 1926- , q.v. Other pseudonyms: Curt Cannon, Hunt Collins, Ezra Hannon, Richard Marsten, qq.v. Series characters: the men of the 87th Precinct = P.
Ax. Simon, 1964; H. Hamilton, 1964 P
Blood Relatives. Random, 1975; H. Hamilton, 1976 P
Bread. Random, 1974; H. Hamilton, 1974 P
The Con Man. Perma, 1957; Boardman, 1960 P
Cop Hater. Perma, 1956; Boardman, 1958 P
Doll. Delacorte, 1965; H. Hamilton, 1966 P
Eighty Million Eyes. Delacorte, 1966; H. Hamilton, 1966 (3 P novelets.)
The Empty Hours. Simon, 1962; Boardman, 1963. (3 P novelets.)
Fuzz. Doubleday, 1968; H. Hamilton, 1968 P
Give the Boys a Great Big Hand. Simon, 1960; Boardman, 1962 P
Hail, Hail, the Gang's All Here! Doubleday, 1971; H. Hamilton, 1971 P
Hail to the Chief. Random, 1973; H. Hamilton, 1973 P
He Who Hesitates. Delacorte, 1965; H. Hamilton, 1965 P
The Heckler. Simon, 1960; Boardman, 1962 P
Jigsaw. Doubleday, 1970; H. Hamilton, 1970 P
Killer's Choice. Perma, 1958; Boardman, 1960 P
Killer's Payoff. Perma, 1958; Boardman, 1960 P
Killer's Wedge. Simon, 1959; Boardman, 1961 P
King's Ransom. Simon, 1959; Boardman, 1961 P
Lady Killer. Perma, 1958; Boardman, 1961 P
Lady, Lady, I Did It! Simon, 1961; Boardman, 1963 P
Let's Hear It for the Deaf Man. Doubleday, 1973; H. Hamilton, 1973 P
Like Love. Simon, 1962; H. Hamilton, 1964 P
The Mugger. Perma, 1956; Boardman, 1959 P
The Pusher. Perma, 1956; Boardman, 1959 P
Sadie When She Died. Doubleday, 1972; H. Hamilton, 1972 P
See Them Die. Simon, 1960; Boardman, 1963 P
The Sentries. Simon, 1965; H. Hamilton, 1965
Shotgun. Doubleday, 1969; H. Hamilton, 1969 P
Ten Plus One. Simon, 1963; H. Hamilton, 1964 P
'Til Death. Simon, 1959; Boardman, 1961 P
Where There's Smoke. Random, 1975; H. Hamilton, 1975

MacBETH, GEORGE (MANN). 1932- .
 The Samurai. Harcourt, 1975; Quartet, 1976

McCABE, CAMERON. Pseudonym of Ernest (William Julius) Borneman, 1915- , q.v.
 The Face on the Cutting Room Floor. Gollancz, 1937

McCAGUE, JAMES (P.). 1909- .
 -The Big Ivy. Crown, 1955
 -The Fortune Road. Harper, 1965
 -To be a Hero. Crown, 1962

McCAIN, GEORGE NOX. 1856-1934.
 The Crimson Dice. Jordan, 1903; Isbister, 1903

McCALL, ANTHONY. Pseudonym of Henry Kane, 1918- , q.v.
 Holocaust. Trident, 1967
 Operation Delta. Trident, 1966; Joseph, 1967

McCALL, JOHN J.
 Downbeat on a Debutante. Consul, 1964

McCALL, K. T.
 Angel Hold Fire. Atlas, 1958
 Babes Up in Arms. Atlas, 1958
 Black Lace Blackmail. Atlas, 1958
 Caviar to Kill. Atlas, 1958
 Dame on the Make. Atlas, 1958
 Dance with Me Deadly. Horwitz, 1957
 Deadly but Delectable. Horwitz, 1957
 The Lady's a Decoy. Horwitz, 1957
 M'amselle It's Murder. Horwitz, 1957
 Million Dollar Mayhem. Atlas, 1958
 A Redhead for Free. Horwitz, 1957

McCALL, VINCENT. Pseudonym of Nigel Morland, 1905- , q.v. Other pseudonyms: Mary Dane, John Donavan, Norman Forrest, Roger Garnett, Neal Shepherd, qq.v.
 Eleven Thrilling Mysteries. Martin, 1945 ss
 Smash and Grab. Martin, 1946

McCALLUM, NEIL. 1916- .
 A Scream in the Sky. Cassell, 1964

McCANN, THOMAS
 Come Out, Come Out, Whoever You Are. Collins, 1971

MacCARGO, J. T. All titles novelizations of the Mannix TV series.
 The Faces of Murder. Belmont, 1975
 A Fine Day for Dying. Belmont, 1975
 Round Trip to Nowhere. Belmont, 1975
 A Walk on the Blind Side. Belmont, 1975

McCARRY, CHARLES. 1929- .
 The Miernik Dossier. Saturday Review Press, 1973; Hutchinson, 1974
 The Tears of Autumn. Saturday Review Press, 1975; Hutchinson, 1975

McCARTHY, DAVID (EDGAR). 1925- .
 Killing at the Big Tree. Doubleday, 1960; Heinemann, 1961

McCARTHY, EDWARD V., JR.
 The Pied Piper of Helfenstein. Doubleday, 1975; Hale, 1976

McCARTHY, JAMES REMINGTON. 1900- .
 Special Agent. Bobbs, 1938

McCARTHY, JUSTIN. 1830-1912.
 -The Dictator. Chatto, 1883; Harper, 1893

McCARTHY, JUSTIN HUNTLY. 1860-1936.
 Doom! Chatto, 1886; Harper, 1886
 Red Diamonds. Chatto, 1893; Appleton, 1894

McCARTHY, SHAUN LLOYD. 1928- . Pseudonyms: Theo Callas, Desmond Cory, qq.v.

McCARTHY, WILSON. 1930- .
 The Detail. Hutchinson, 1973
 The Fourth Man. Hutchinson, 1975

McCARTNEY, P.
 Who Sups with the Devil? New English Library pb, 1975

McCARY, REED
 Kiss and Kill. Avon, 1957

McCHESNEY, MARY F. Pseudonym: Joe Rayter, q.v.

McCLEAN, J. SLOAN
 The Aerie. Nash, 1975

McCLINTOCK, ALLERDYCE. Pseudonym.
 The Case of the Three Broken Necks. Jenkins, 1965

McCLOY, HELEN (WORRELL CLARKSON). 1904- . Series characters: Basil Willing = BW; Miguel Urizar = MU.
 Alias Basil Willing. Random, 1951; Gollancz, 1951 BW
 Before I Die. Dodd, 1963; Gollancz, 1963
 Better Off Dead. Dell 10¢ pb, 1951
 A Change of Heart. Dodd, 1973; Gollancz, 1973
 Cue for Murder. Morrow, 1942 BW
 Dance of Death. Morrow, 1938. British title: Design for Dying. Heinemann, 1938 BW
 The Deadly Truth. Morrow, 1941; H. Hamilton, 1942 BW
 Design for Dying; see Dance of Death
 Do Not Disturb. Morrow, 1943
 The Further Side of Fear. Dodd, 1967; Gollancz, 1967
 The Goblin Market. Morrow, 1943; Hale, 1951 MU
 He Never Came Back; see Unfinished Crime
 The Long Body. Random, 1955; Gollancz, 1955 BW
 The Man in the Moonlight. Morrow, 1940; H. Hamilton, 1940 BW
 Minotaur Country. Dodd, 1975; Gollancz, 1975
 Mr. Splitfoot. Dodd, 1968; Gollancz, 1969 BW
 The One That Got Away. Morrow, 1945; Gollancz, 1954 BW
 Panic. Morrow, 1944; Gollancz, 1972
 A Question of Time. Dodd, 1971; Gollancz, 1971
 She Walks Alone. Random, 1948; Coker, 1950. Also published as: Wish You were Dead. Bestseller, 1958 MU
 The Singing Diamonds. Dodd, 1965. British title: Surprise, Surprise. Gollancz, 1965 ss, 2 about BW
 The Slayer and the Slain. Random, 1957; Gollancz, 1958
 The Sleepwalker. Dodd, 1974; Gollancz, 1974
 Surprise, Surprise; see The Singing Diamonds
 Through a Glass, Darkly. Random, 1950; Gollancz, 1951 BW
 Two-Thirds of a Ghost. Random, 1956; Gollancz, 1957 BW
 Unfinished Crime. Random, 1954. British title: He Never Came Back. Gollancz, 1954
 Who's Calling? Morrow, 1942; Nicholson, 1948 BW
 Wish You were Dead; see She Walks Alone

McCLURE, JAMES (HOWE). 1939- . Series characters: Lt. Kramer and Sgt. Zondi = K&Z.
 The Caterpillar Cop. Gollancz, 1972; Harper, 1973 K&Z
 Four and Twenty Virgins. Gollancz, 1973
 The Gooseberry Fool. Gollancz, 1974; Harper, 1974 K&Z
 Snake. Gollancz, 1975; Harper, 1976 K&Z
 The Steam Pig. Gollancz, 1971; Harper, 1972 K&Z

MacCLURE, VICTOR. 1887-1963. Pseudonym: Peter Craig, q.v. Series character: Archie Burford = AB.
 The Clue of the Dead Goldfish. Harrap, 1933; Lippincott, 1934 AB
 The Counterfeit Murders. Harrap, 1932 AB
 The "Crying Pig" Murder. Harrap, 1929; Morrow, 1930
 Death Behind the Door. Harrap, 1933; Houghton, 1933 AB
 Death on the Set. Harrap, 1934; Lippincott, 1935 AB
 The Diva's Emeralds. Harrap, 1937 AB
 Hi-Spy-Kick-the-Can. Harrap, 1936 AB
 The House of Dearth. Hodder, 1937
 -If They Fall—. Harrap, 1935
 -Nicolette of the Quarter. Unwin, 1923

McCOMB, KATHERINE (WOODS). 1895- .
 A Day for Murder. Bouregy, 1963
 Death in a Downpour. Arcadia, 1960

McCOMBS, PHILIP A(LGIE). 1944- . See: KEVIN KLOSE, 1940- .

McCOMBS, R. L. F.
 Clue in Two Flats. Mystery House, 1940; Eldon, 1942

McCONAUGHY, J. W.
 -The Boss, with Edward Sheldon. Fly, 1911; Palmer, 1913
 The Typhoon. Fly, 1912

McCONNAUGHEY, JAMES. 1908- .
 Three for the Money. Sloane, 1954; Hammond, 1955

McCONNELL, JAMES DOUGLAS RUTHERFORD. 1915- . Pseudonym: Douglas Rutherford, q.v. Joint pseudonym with Francis Durbridge, 1912- , q.v.: Paul Temple, q.v.

McCONNOR, VINCENT
 The French Doll. Hill & Wang, 1965; Gollancz, 1966

MacCORMICK, PAT
 -The Grave Gives Up. Exposition, 1964 ss

McCORMICK, VICTORIA. 1914- . Pseudonym: Janet Green, q.v.

McCOY, HORACE. 1897-1959.
 Corruption City. Dell, 1959; WDL, 1961
 I Should Have Stayed Home. Barker, 1938
 Kiss Tomorrow Goodbye. Random, 1948; Barker, 1949
 No Pockets in a Shroud. Signet, 1948; Barker, 1937
 -Scalpel. Appleton, 1952; Barker, 1953
 They Shoot Horses, Don't They? Simon, 1935; Barker, 1935. New edition, including screenplay of movie version: Avon, 1969

McCOY, TRENT
 I'll Come Quietly. Cooper, 1952
 Order a Coffin Now. Hamilton Stafford, 1951

Quinton Clyde, Private Investigator. Baker, 1952
Wake the Sleeping Wolf. Hamilton Stafford, 1952

McCRACKEN, MIKE
Black Death. Hamilton Stafford, 1952
The Black Hammer. Hamilton Stafford, 1952
Killer in Canvas Jeans. Hamilton Stafford, 1952
-The Spahis. Hamilton Stafford, 1953

McCRAE, ELIZABETH
House of the Whispering Winds. Signet, 1966
The Intrusion. Signet, 1967
Sudden Darkness. Signet, 1968
A Well-Furnished Life. Signet, 1967

McCREADY, JACK. Pseudonym of Talmage Powell, 1920-   , q.v.
The Raper. Monarch, 1962

McCUE, LILLIAN BUENO. 1902-   . Pseudonym: Lillian de la Torre, q.v.

McCULLEY, JOHNSTON. 1883-1958. Series characters: The Avenging Twins = AT; Black Star = BS; The Crimson Clown = CC; The Spider (John Warwick) = S; The Thunderbolt = T.
Alias the Thunderbolt. Chelsea, 1927; Cassell, 1930 T
The Avenging Twins. Chelsea, 1927; Hutchinson, 1927 AT
The Avenging Twins Collect. Chelsea, 1927 AT
-Black Grandee. Hale, 1955
The Black Star. Chelsea, 1921; Hutchinson, 1924 BS
Black Star Again; see Black Star's Revenge
Black Star's Campaign. Chelsea, 1924; Hutchinson, 1925 BS
Black Star's Return. Chelsea, 1926; Hutchinson, 1927 BS
Black Star's Revenge. Chelsea, 19??. British title: Black Star Again. Hutchinson, 1934 BS
-The Blocked Trail. Watt, 1932; Hutchinson, 1933
Broadway Bab. Watt, 1919; Hutchinson, 1926
The Crimson Clown. Chelsea, 1928; Cassell, 1927. (4 CC novelets.)
The Crimson Clown Again. Chelsea, 192?; Cassell, 1928 CC
The Demon. Chelsea, 1925
-The Devil's Doubloons. Hutchinson, 1955
The Masked Woman. Watt, 1920; Jenkins, 1925
The Rollicking Rogue. Arcadia, 1941; Hutchinson, 1939
The Scarlet Scourge. Chelsea, 1925
The Spider's Debt. Chelsea, 1930; Hutchinson, 1930 S
The Spider's Den. Chelsea, 1925 S
The Spider's Fury. Chelsea, 1930; Hutchinson, 1931 S
The Thunderbolt Collects. Lloyd, 1921 T
The Thunderbolt's Jest. Chelsea, 1927 T
A White Man's Chance. Watt, 1927; Hutchinson, 1927

McCULLOUGH, ESTHER MORGAN
The Five Devils of Kilmainham. Taylor, 1955; Hodder, 1957

McCULLOUGH, ROSE
A Basket of Summer Fruit. Vantage, 1970

McCULLY, (ETHEL) WALBRIDGE. Series character: District Attorney Galbreath = G.
Blood on Nassau's Moon. Doubleday, 1945
Death Rides Tandem. Doubleday, 1942 G
Doctors Beware! Doubleday, 1943 G

McCURTIN, PETER. Series characters: The Assassin = A; The Marksman = M (see also: Frank Scarpetta).
Boston Bust Out. Dell, 1973; Mayflower, 1975 A
Cosa Nostra. Belmont, 1971; New English Library pb, 1972
Death Hunt. Belmont, 1973 M
-Escape from Devil's Island. Belmont, 1972
Mafioso. Belmont, 1970; New English Library pb, 1971
Manhattan Massacre. Dell, 1973; Mayflower, 1975 A
New Orleans Holocaust. Dell, 1973; Mayflower, 1975 A
Omerta. Leisure, 1972
-The Pleasure Principle. Leisure, 1974
The Sun Dance Murders. Belmont, 1970
The Syndicate. Belmont, 1972
Vendetta. Belmont, 1973 M

McCUTCHAN, PHILIP (DONALD). 1920-   . Series characters: Commander Esmonde Shaw, in at least those marked ES; Simon Shard = SS.
The All-Purpose Bodies. Harrap, 1969; Day, 1970 ES
Bluebolt One. Harrap, 1962; Berkley, 1965 ES
-Bowering's Breakwater. Harrap, 1964
The Bright Red Business Men. Harrap, 1969; Day, 1969 ES
Call for Simon Shard. Harrap, 1974 SS
Coach North. Harrap, 1974; Walker, 1975
The Day of the Coastwatch. Harrap, 1968
The Dead Line. Harrap, 1966; Berkley, 1966 ES
-The German Helmet. Harrap, 1972
Gibralter Road. Harrap, 1960; Berkley, 1965 ES
Half a Bag of Stringer. Harrap, 1970
Hartinger's Mouse. Harrap, 1970 ES
Hopkinson and the Devil of Hate. Harrap, 1961
-The Kid. Harrap, 1958
Leave the Dead Behind Us. Harrap, 1962
The Man from Moscow. Harrap, 1963; Day, 1965 ES
-Man, Let's Go On. Harrap, 1970
-Marley's Empire. Harrap, 1963
Moscow Coach. Harrap, 1964; Day, 1966 ES
The Oil Bastards. Harrap, 1972
-Poulter's Passage. Harrap, 1967
Redcap. Harrap, 1961; Berkley, 1965 ES
The Screaming Dead Balloons. Harrap, 1968; Day, 1968 ES
Skyprobe. Harrap, 1966; Day, 1967 ES
Sladd's Evil. Harrap, 1965; Day, 1967
-Storm South. Harrap, 1959
This Drakotny—. Harrap, 1971 ES
A Time for Survival. Harrap, 1966
A Very Big Bang. Hodder, 1975 SS
Warmaster. Harrap, 1963; Day, 1964 ES
-Whistle and I'll Come. Harrap, 1957

McCUTCHEON, GEORGE BARR. 1866-1928. Series character: Anderson Crow, in both titles.
Anderson Crow, Detective. Dodd, 1920 ss
The Daughter of Anderson Crow. Dodd, 1907; Hodder, 1907

McCUTCHEON, HUGH (DAVIE-MARTIN). 1909-   . Series characters: Jimmy Carroll, in at least those marked JC; Anthony Howard, in at least those marked AH; Richard Logan, in at least those marked RL.
And the Moon was Full; see Killer's Moon
The Angel of Light. Rich, 1951. U.S. title: Murder at the Angel. Dutton, 1952 AH
The Black Attendant. Long, 1966 JC
Brand for the Burning. Long, 1969
Comes the Blind Fury. Long, 1959
Cover Her Face. Rich, 1954 AH
The Deadly One. Long, 1962
A Hot Wind from Hell. Long, 1968
Instrument of Vengeance. Long, 1975
Killer's Moon. Long, 1966. U.S. title: And the Moon was Full. Doubleday, 1967
The Long Night Through. Rich, 1956 AH
Murder at the Angel; see The Angel of Light
None Shall Sleep Tonight. Rich, 1953; Dutton, 1953
Prey for the Nightingale. Rich, 1953
Red Sky at Night. Long, 1972; Walker, 1972
The Scorpion's Nest. Long, 1967
Something Wicked. Long, 1970
Suddenly, in Vienna. Long, 1963 RL
To Dusty Death. Long, 1960 RL
Treasure of the Sun. Long, 1964 JC
Yet She Must Die. Long, 1962; Doubleday, 1962

MacDANIEL, CHARLES. Pseudonym of Charles M. Garrison.
Murder on the Moon. Vantage, 1968

McDANIEL, DAVID (EDWARD). 1939-1977. Starred titles are novelizations of The Man from UNCLE TV series.
The Dagger Affair. Ace, 1965; Four Square, 1966 *
The Hollow Crown Affair. Ace, 1969 *
The Monster Wheel Affair. Ace, 1967; Four Square, 1967 *
The Prisoner #2. Ace, 1969. (Novelization of the TV series.)
The Rainbow Affair. Ace, 1967 *
The Utopia Affair. Ace, 1968 *
The Vampire Affair. Ace, 1966; Four Square, 1966 *

McDERMID, FINLAY
Ghost Wanted. Simon, 1943. Also published as: Kiss the Blonde Goodbye. Bestseller, 1948
Kiss the Blonde Goodbye; see Ghost Wanted
See No Evil. Simon, 1959; Boardman, 1959

MacDERMOTT, P. L.
Julius Vernon; or, A Strange Case of Circumstantial Evidence. Ward, 1892
The Last King of Yewle. Ward, 1893; Cassell (New York), 1893

MacDONALD, DONALD. Series character: Briggs, in at least those marked B.
Briggs Investigates. Hale, 1968 B
No Judges' Rules. Hale, 1969
The Organizer. Hale, 1970
The Ryan Affair. Hale, 1970
Two Bullets for Briggs. Hale, 1971 B
Two Kinds of Murder. Hale, 1971

MacDONALD, GEORGE A(LEXANDER)
The Light Side of the Law. Cassell, 1910 ss

McDONALD, GREGORY. 1937-   .
Fletch. Bobbs, 1974; Gollancz, 1976
-Running Scared. Obolensky, 1964; Gollancz, 1977

MacDONALD, HAZEL CHRISTIE
Death Walks Softly. Phoenix, 1950

McDONALD, HUGH C.
The Grey Mask Murders. DeVoras, 1941

McDONALD, HUGH C(HISHOLM). 1913- .
  The Auditorium Affair. Hale, 1973

MACDONALD, JOHN. Pseudonym of Kenneth Millar, 1915- , q.v. Other pseudonyms: John Ross Macdonald, Ross Macdonald, qq.v. Series character: Lew Archer, in the title below and continued under the JRM and RM bylines.
  The Moving Target. Knopf, 1949; Cassell, 1951. Also published as: Harper, as by Ross Macdonald. PB, 1966

MacDONALD, JOHN D(ANN). 1916- . Series character: Travis McGee = TM.
  All These Condemned. GM, 1954
  April Evil. Dell, 1956; Hale, 1957
  Area of Suspicion. Dell, 1954; Hale, 1956. Revised edition: GM, 1961
  The Beach Girls. GM, 1959; Muller, 1964
  Border Town Girl. Popular Library, 1956. British title: Five Star Fugitive. Hale, 1970 (Two novelets.)
  The Brass Cupcake. GM, 1950; Muller, 1955
  Bright Orange for the Shroud. GM, 1965; Hale, 1967 TM
  A Bullet for Cinderella. Dell, 1955; Hale, 1960. Also published as: On the Make. Dell, 1960
  Cape Fear; see The Executioners
  Clemmie. GM, 1958
  The Crossroads. Simon, 1959; Hale, 1961
  Cry Hard, Cry Fast. Popular Library, 1955; Hale, 1969
  The Damned. GM, 1952; Muller, 1964
  Darker Than Amber. GM, 1966; Hale, 1968 TM
  Dead Low Tide. GM, 1953; Fawcett (London), 1955
  A Deadly Shade of Gold. GM, 1965; Hale, 1967 TM
  Deadly Welcome. Dell, 1959; Hale, 1961
  Death Trap. Dell, 1957; Hale, 1958
  The Deceivers. GM, 1958
  The Deep Blue Good-By. GM, 1964; Hale, 1965 TM
  The Dreadful Lemon Sky. Lippincott, 1974; Hale, 1976 TM
  Dress Her in Indigo. GM, 1969; Hale, 1971 TM
  The Drowner. GM, 1963; Hale, 1964
  The Empty Trap. Popular Library, 1957
  The End of the Night. Simon, 1960; Hale, 1964
  End of the Tiger and other stories. GM, 1966; Hale, 1967 ss
  The Executioners. Simon, 1958; Hale, 1959. Also published as: Cape Fear. Crest, 1962
  Five Star Fugitive; see Border Town Girl
  A Flash of Green. Simon, 1962; Hale, 1971
  The Girl in the Plain Brown Wrapper. GM, 1968; Hale, 1969 TM
  The Girl, the Gold Watch & Everything. GM, 1962; Coronet, 1968
  Hurricane; see Murder in the Wind
  Judge Me Not. GM, 1951; Muller, 1964
  A Key to the Suite. GM, 1962; Hale, 1968
  The Last One Left. Doubleday, 1967; Hale, 1968
  The Long Lavender Look. GM, 1970; Fawcett (London), 1970 TM
  A Man of Affairs. Dell, 1957; Hale, 1959
  Man-Trap; see Soft Touch
  Murder for the Bride. GM, 1951; Fawcett (London), 1954
  Murder in the Wind. Dell, 1956. British title: Hurricane. Hale, 1957
  The Neon Jungle. GM, 1953; Fawcett (London), 1954
  Nightmare in Pink. GM, 1964; Hale, 1966 TM
  On the Make; see A Bullet for Cinderella
  On the Run. GM, 1963; Hale, 1965
  One Fearful Yellow Eye. GM, 1966; Hale, 1968 TM
  One Monday We Killed Them All. GM, 1961; Hale, 1963
  The Only Girl in the Game. GM, 1960; Hale, 1962
  Pale Gray for Guilt. GM, 1968; Hale, 1969 TM
  The Price of Murder. Dell, 1957; Hale, 1958
  A Purple Place for Dying. GM, 1964; Hale, 1966 TM
  The Quick Red Fox. GM, 1964; Hale, 1966 TM
  The Scarlet Ruse. GM, 1973; Hale, 1975 TM
  Slam the Big Door. GM, 1960; Hale, 1961
  Soft Touch. Dell, 1958; Hale, 1960. Also published as: Man-Trap. Pan, 1961
  A Tan and Sandy Silence. GM, 1972; Hale, 1973 TM
  The Turquoise Lament. Lippincott, 1973; Hale, 1975 TM
  Weep for Me. GM, 1951; Muller, 1964
  Where is Janice Gantry? GM, 1961; Hale, 1963
  You Kill Me; see You Live Once
  You Live Once. Popular Library, 1956; Hale, 1976. Also published as: You Kill Me. GM, 1961

MACDONALD, JOHN ROSS. Pseudonym of Kenneth Millar, 1915- , q.v. Other pseudonyms: John Macdonald, Ross Macdonald, qq.v. Series character: Lew Archer = LA (originated under the John Macdonald byline, continued as by John Ross Macdonald and finally as Ross Macdonald).
  The Drowning Pool. Knopf, 1950; Cassell, 1952, as by John Macdonald LA
  Experience with Evil; see Meet Me at the Morgue
  Find a Victim. Knopf, 1954; Cassell, 1955 LA
  The Ivory Grin. Knopf, 1952; Cassell, 1953. Also published as: Marked for Murder. PB, 1953 LA
  Marked for Murder; see The Ivory Grin
  Meet Me at the Morgue. Knopf, 1953. British title: Experience with Evil. Cassell, 1954
  The Name is Archer. Bantam, 1955 LA ss
  The Way Some People Die. Knopf, 1951; Cassell, 1953 LA

MacDONALD, PHILIP. 1899- . Pseudonym: Martin Porlock, q.v. Joint pseudonym with Ronald MacDonald, 1860-1933: Oliver Fleming, q.v. Series character: Colonel Anthony Gethryn = AG.
  The Choice. Collins, 1931. U.S. title: The Polferry Riddle. Doubleday, 1931. Also published as: The Polferry Mystery. Collins, 1932 AG
  The Crime Conductor. Collins, 1932; Doubleday, 1931 AG
  The Dark Wheel, with A. Boyd Correll, q.v. Collins, 1948; Morrow, 1948. Also published as: Sweet and Deadly. Zenith, 1959
  Death and Chicanery. Jenkins, 1963; Doubleday, 1962 ss
  Death on my Left. Collins, 1933; Doubleday, 1933
  Fingers of Fear. Collins, 1953. U.S. title: Something to Hide. Doubleday, 1952 ss
  Guest in the House. Jenkins, 1956; Doubleday, 1955. Also published as: No Time for Terror. Bestseller, 1956
  Harbour. Collins, 1931; Doubleday, 1931, as by Anthony Lawless
  The Link. Collins, 1930; Doubleday, 1930 AG
  The List of Adrian Messenger. Jenkins, 1960; Doubleday, 1959 AG
  The Man out of the Rain. Jenkins, 1957; Doubleday, 1955 ss
  The Maze. Collins, 1932. U.S. title: Persons Unknown. Doubleday, 1931 AG
  Menace; see R.I.P.
  Murder Gone Mad. Collins, 1931; Doubleday, 1931
  No Time for Terror; see Guest in the House
  The Noose. Collins, 1930; Dial, 1930 AG
  The Nursemaid Who Disappeared. Collins, 1938. U.S. title: Warrant for X. Doubleday, 1938 AG
  Persons Unknown; see The Maze
  The Polferry Mystery; see The Choice
  The Polferry Riddle; see The Choice
  The Rasp. Collins, 1924; Dial, 1925 AG
  R.I.P. Collins, 1933. U.S. title: Menace. Doubleday, 1933
  Rope to Spare. Collins, 1932; Doubleday, 1932 AG
  Rynox. Collins, 1930. U.S. title: The Rynox Murder Mystery. Doubleday, 1931. Also published as: The Rynox Mystery. Collins, 1933
  The Rynox Murder Mystery; see Rynox
  The Rynox Mystery; see Rynox
  Something to Hide; see Fingers of Fear
  Sweet and Deadly; see The Dark Wheel
  Warrant for X; see The Nursemaid Who Disappeared
  The White Crow. Collins, 1928; Dial, 1928 AG
  The Wraith. Collins, 1931; Doubleday, 1931 AG

MacDONALD, RONALD. 1860-1933. Joint pseudonym with Philip MacDonald, 1899- , q.v.: Oliver Fleming, q.v.

MACDONALD, ROSS. Pseudonym of Kenneth Millar, 1915- , q.v. Other pseudonyms: John Macdonald, John Ross Macdonald, qq.v. Series character: Lew Archer (begun under the John Macdonald byline and continued as by John Ross Macdonald and finally as Ross Macdonald) = LA. Titles marked * were published in Britain as by John Ross Macdonald. All titles are presently published as by Ross Macdonald, as are reprints of all earlier titles.
  The Barbarous Coast. Knopf, 1956; Cassell, 1957 * LA
  Black Money. Knopf, 1966; Collins, 1966 LA
  The Chill. Knopf, 1964; Collins, 1964 LA
  The Doomsters. Knopf, 1958; Collins, 1958 * LA
  The Far Side of the Dollar. Knopf, 1965; Collins, 1965 LA
  The Ferguson Affair. Knopf, 1960; Collins, 1961
  The Galton Case. Knopf, 1959; Cassell, 1960 * LA
  The Goodbye Look. Knopf, 1969; Collins, 1969 LA
  The Instant Enemy. Knopf, 1968; Collins, 1968 LA
  Sleeping Beauty. Knopf, 1973; Collins, 1973 LA
  The Underground Man. Knopf, 1971; Collins, 1971 LA
  The Wycherly Woman. Knopf, 1961; Collins, 1962

The Zebra-Striped Hearse. Knopf, 1962; Collins, 1963 LA

MacDONALD, (ALLEN) WILLIAM COLT. 1891- . Series character: Gregory Quist (in western detective stories) = GQ.
Action at Arcanum. Lippincott, 1958; Hodder, 1961 GQ
Blind Cartridges. Doubleday, 1951; Hodder, 1954
The Comanche Scalp. Lippincott, 1955; Hodder, 1958 GQ
Destination Danger. Lippincott, 1955; Hodder, 1957 GQ
The Devil's Drum. Lippincott, 1956; Hodder, 1962 GQ
The Gloved Saskia. Avalon, 1964; Hodder, 1965 GQ
Law and Order, Unlimited. Doubleday, 1953; Hodder, 1955 GQ
Mascarada Pass. Doubleday, 1954; Hodder, 1957 GQ
The Osage Bow. Hodder, 1964 (U.S. title?) GQ
Tombstone for a Troubleshooter. Lippincott, 1960; Hodder, 1961 GQ

MACDONELL, ARCHIBALD GORDON. 1895-1941. Pseudonyms: John Cameron, Neil Gordon, qq.v.

McDONELL, GORDON. 1905- .
Burning Secret. Hart-Davis, 1959
The Clocktower. Harrap, 1952; Little, 1951
Intruder from the Sea. Harrap, 1953; Little, 1953
Jump for Glory. Harrap, 1936; Green Circle, 1937
My Sister, Good Night. Harrap, 1948; Little, 1948
The Reprieve of Roger Maine. Chatto, 1962; Prentice-Hall, 1961
Silver Bugle. Harrap, 1938
They Won't Believe Me. Harrap, 1947
Wind Without Rain. Chatto, 1963

McDONELL, MARGARET
Althea. Doubleday, 1951

McDONNELL, H. KEVIN
The Terror of Toynham Hall. Modern, 193?
The Vanishing Clue. Modern, 1938
The Vengeance of Five. Modern, 1938

McDOUGALD, ROMAN. 1907?-1960. Series character: Philip Cabot = PC.
The Blushing Monkey. Simon, 1953; Boardman, 1953 PC
The Deaths of Lora Karen. Simon, 1944 PC
Lady Without Mercy. Simon, 1948; Boardman, 1955
Purgatory Street. Simon, 1946
The Whistling Legs. Simon, 1945 PC
The Woman Under the Mountain. Simon, 1950; Boardman, 1951

MacDOUGALL, (SAMUEL) MICHAEL. 1906- .
Danger in the Cards. Ziff-Davis, 1943

McDOUGALL, MURDOCH C(HRISTIE)
Chase the Snowman. Boardman, 1957
Soft as Silk. Boardman, 1957

MacDOUGALL, RUTH DOAN
The Cost of Living. PB, 1971
One Minus One. Avon, 1972

McDOWELL, (ROBERT) EMMETT. -1976. Byline also: Robert Emmett McDowell, q.v. Series character: Jonathan Knox, in at least those marked JK.
Bloodline to Murder. Ace, 1960 JK
In at the Kill. Ace, 1960 JK
Stamped for Death. Ace, 1958 JK
Switcheroo. Ace, 1954
Three for the Gallows. Ace, 1958. (Three novelets.) JK

McDOWELL, ROBERT EMMETT. -1976. Byline also: (Robert) Emmett McDowell, q.v.
The Hound's Tooth. Mill, 1965; Cassell, 1967
Portrait of a Victim. Bouregy, 1964

MacDUFF, DAVID. 1905- .
Murder Strikes Three. Modern Age, 1937

McDUFF, E. M.
Murder in the Theatre. Lothian (Adelaide), 1947

McELFRESH, (ELIZABETH) ADELINE. 1918- . Pseudonym: John Cleveland, q.v.
-Charlotte Wade. Arcadia, 1952
Keep Back the Dark. Phoenix, 1950
Murder with Roses. Phoenix, 1950; Foulsham, 1953
My Heart went Dead. Phoenix, 1949
Shattered Halo. Avalon, 1956; Ward, 1960

McELROY, HUGH (FRANCIS). Series character: Insp. William Brewer, in at least those marked WB.
The Curtain of the Dark. Chapman, 1944 WB
The House of Malory. Chapman, 1948
The Silver Venus. Chapman, 1942
Unkindly Cup. Chapman, 1946 WB

McELROY, JOSEPH
Lookout Cartridge. Knopf, 1974

MacELWAIN, MIRANDA
The Penguin Island Murders. Quality, 1954

McENERY, JOHN
-A Black Inheritance. Greening, 1909
The Vision of the Foam. Greening, 1907

McEVOY, HUGH
Jones, A., Finds the Body. Gifford, 1946

McEVOY, MARJORIE (HARTE)
-Brazilian Stardust. Arcadia, 1967
Castle Doom. Beagle, 1973
-Dusky Cactus. Jenkins, 1968
The Grenfell Legacy. Jenkins, 1968; Pyramid, 1971
-Moon over the Danube. Jenkins, 1966
-No Castle of Dreams. Jenkins, 1960
Peril at Polvellyn. Beagle, 1973
The Queen of Spades. Ballantine, 1975
Ravensmount. Beagle, 1974
-A Red, Red Rose. Jenkins, 1960
Softly Treads Danger. Jenkins, 1963
-The White Castello. Jenkins, 1969
Who Walks by Moonlight? Lancer, 1973
The Wych Stone. Beagle, 1974

McFADDEN, G(ERTRUDE) V(IOLET)
-The Bridegroom. Lane (London), 1928
The Honest Lawyer. Lane (London & New York), 1916
-Maumbury Rings. Hodder, 1920; Doran, 1921
-Narcissus in the Way. Lane (London), 1922
The Preventive Man. Lane (London & New York), 1920
-The Roman Way. Lane (London) 1925
Sheriff's Deputy. Lane (London), 1924
-So Speed We. Lane (London), 1926
The Trusty Servant. Lane (London & New York), 1920
The Turning Sword. Lane (London), 1923

MacFADYEN, VIRGINIA
Bittern Point. Boni, 1924
-Windows Facing West. Boni, 1924; Paul, 1925

MacFALL, (CHAMBERS) HALDANE (COOKE), 1860-1928, and DION (WILLIAM PALGRAVE) CLAYTON CALTHROP, 1878-1937, q.v.
Rouge. Brown, 1906

McFARLANE, ARTHUR E(MERSON). 1876- .
Behind the Bolted Door? Dodd, 1916; Nash, 1916

McFARLANE, LESLIE. Series character: Michael Brent, in both titles.
The Murder Tree. Dutton, 1931; Paul, 1932
Streets of Shadow. Dutton, 1930; Paul, 1931

MacFARLANE, PETER CLARK. 1871-1924.
-The Centurion's Story. Revell, 1910
-The Crack in the Bell. Doubleday, 1918
-The Quest of the Yellow Pearl. Revell, 1909
-Those Who Have Come Back. Little, 1914 ss

McFATHER, NELLE. 1936- .
The Red Jaguar. Ace, 1974
Whispering Island. Ace, 1974

McFERRAN, JOYCE
Death Takes Over. Hale, 1967

McGAUGHY, DUDLEY DEAN. Pseudonyms: Dudley Dean, Owen Dudley, qq.v.

McGAW, J. W.
For Gain Not Glory. Hale, 1970

McGERR, PATRICIA. 1917- . Series character: Selena Mead = SM.
Catch Me If You Can. Doubleday, 1948; Collins, 1949
Dangerous Landing. Dell, 1975
Daughter of Darkness. Popular Library, 1974
Death in a Million Living Rooms. Doubleday, 1951. British title: Die Laughing. Collins, 1952
Die Laughing; see Death in a Million Living Rooms
Fatal in my Fashion. Doubleday, 1954; Collins, 1955
Follow, as the Night. Doubleday, 1950. British title: Your Loving Victim. Collins, 1951
For Richer, For Poorer, Till Death. Luce, 1969; Hale, 1971
Is There a Traitor in the House? Doubleday, 1964; Collins, 1965 SM
Legacy of Danger. Luce, 1970 SM
Murder is Absurd. Doubleday, 1967; Gollancz, 1967
Pick Your Victim. Doubleday, 1946; Collins, 1947
Save the Witness. Doubleday, 1949; Collins, 1950
The Seven Deadly Sisters. Doubleday, 1947; Collins, 1948
Stranger with my Face. Luce, 1968; Hale, 1970
Your Loving Victim; see Follow, as the Night

McGHEE, BILL
Cut and Run. Hammond, 1962

McGIBENY, DONALD
 Slag. Bobbs, 1922
 .32 Caliber. Bobbs, 1920

McGINNIS, E. L.
 The Strasburg Collection. Belmont, 1969

McGIRR, EDMUND. Pseudonym of Kenneth Giles, 1922-1972, q.v. Other pseudonym: Charles Drummond, q.v. Series character: Piron, in at least those marked P.
 Bardel's Murder. Gollancz, 1973; Walker, 1974 P
 Death Pays the Wages. Gollancz, 1970
 An Entry of Death. Gollancz, 1969; Walker, 1969 P
 The Funeral was in Spain. Gollancz, 1966 P
 A Hearse with Horses. Gollancz, 1967 P
 Here Lies My Wife. Gollancz, 1967
 The Lead-Lined Coffin. Gollancz, 1968
 A Murderous Journey. Gollancz, 1974; Walker, 1975 P
 No Better Fiend. Gollancz, 1971; Walker, 1971 P

McGIVERN, WILLIAM P(ETER). 1924-   .
 Pseudonym: Bill Peters, q.v.
 The Big Heat. Dodd, 1952; H. Hamilton, 1953
 But Death Runs Faster. Dodd, 1948; Boardman, 1949. Also published as: The Whispering Corpse. PB, 1950
 The Caper of the Golden Bulls. Dodd, 1966; Collins, 1967
 Caprifoil. Dodd, 1972; Collins, 1973
 Chicago-7; see The Seven File
 A Choice of Assassins. Dodd, 1963; Collins, 1964
 The Crooked Frame. Dodd, 1952
 The Darkest Hour. Dodd, 1955; Collins, 1956. Also published as: Waterfront Cop. PB, 1956
 Heaven Ran Last. Dodd, 1949; Digit, 1958
 Killer on the Turnpike. PB, 1961 ss
 Lie Down, I Want to Talk to You. Dodd, 1967; Collins, 1968
 Margin of Terror. Dodd, 1953; Collins, 1955
 Night Extra. Dodd, 1957; Collins, 1958
 Night of the Juggler. Putnam, 1975; Collins, 1975
 Odds Against Tomorrow. Dodd, 1957; Collins, 1958
 A Pride of Place. Dodd, 1962
 Reprisal. Dodd, 1973; Collins, 1974
 The Road to the Snail. Dodd, 1961
 Rogue Cop. Dodd, 1954; Collins, 1955
 Savage Streets. Dodd, 1959; Collins, 1960
 The Seven File. Dodd, 1956; Collins, 1957. Also published as: Chicago-7. Sphere, 1970
 Seven Lies South. Dodd, 1960; Collins, 1961
 Shield for Murder. Dodd, 1951
 Very Cold for May. Dodd, 1950
 Waterfront Cop; see The Darkest Hour
 The Whispering Corpse; see But Death Runs Faster

McGLOIN, JOSEPH THADDEUS. 1917-   .
 Pseudonym: Thaddeus O'Finn, q.v.

M'GOVAN, JAMES. Pseudonym of William C. Honeyman.
 Brought to Bay; or, Experiences of a City Detective. Menzies, 1878 ss
 Criminals Caught; or, Records of a City Detective. Jenkins, 1921 ss
 Hunted Down; or, Recollections of a City Detective. Menzies, 1878 ss
 The Invisible Pickpocket; or, Records of a City Detective. Jenkins, 1922 ss
 Solved Mysteries; or, Revelations of a City Detective. Menzies, 1888 ss
 Strange Clues; or, Chronicles of a City Detective. Menzies, 1881 ss
 Traced and Tracked; or, Memoirs of a City Detective. Menzies, 1884 ss

McGOVERN, JAMES. 1923-
 The Berlin Couriers. Abelard, 1960
 Fraulein. Crown, 1956; Calder, 1957
 No Ruined Castles. Putnam, 1957; Calder, 1958

MacGOWAN, ALICE, 1858-   , and PERRY NEWBERRY, 1870-1938. Series character: Jerry Boyne, in all titles.
 The Million Dollar Suitcase. Stokes, 1922; Hutchinson, 1922
 The Mystery Woman. Stokes, 1924; Hutchinson, 1924
 The Seventh Passenger. Stokes, 1926; Hutchinson, 1928
 Shaken Down. Stokes, 1925; Hutchinson, 1925
 Who is This Man? Stokes, 1927; Hutchinson, 1927

McGRADY, MIKE. See: HARVEY ARONSON.

MacGRATH, HAROLD. 1871-1932.
 -The Adventures of Kathlyn. Bobbs, 1914
 -The Best Man. Bobbs, 1907 ss
 The Blue Rajah Murder. Doubleday, 1930; Long, 1930
 -Captain Wardlaw's Kitbags. Garden City, 1923
 The Carpet from Bagdad. Bobbs, 1911
 -The Cellini Plaque. Doubleday, 1925; Curtis Brown, 1925
 The Changing Road. Doubleday, 1928; Long, 1928
 Deuces Wild. Bobbs, 1914
 The Drums of Jeopardy. Doubleday, 1920; Hodder, 1923
 -The Enchanted Hat. Bobbs, 1908
 -Enchantment. Bobbs, 1905 ss
 The Girl in his House. Harper, 1918
 The Green Complex. Doubleday, 1930; Long, 1930
 The Green Stone. Doubleday, 1924; Curtis Brown, 1924
 -The Luck of the Irish. Bobbs, 1917
 -The Man on the Box. Bobbs, 1904; Hodder, 1914
 The Man with Three Names. Doubleday, 1920; Hutchinson, 1920
 The Million Dollar Mystery. Grosset, 1915. (Novelization of the movie.)
 The Pagan Madonna. Doubleday, 1921
 Pidgin Island. Bobbs, 1914
 The Private Wire to Washington. Harper, 1919
 The Voice in the Fog. Bobbs, 1915
 The Wolves of Chaos. Doubleday, 1929; Long, 1929
 The World Outside. Doubleday, 1923; Long, 1923
 The Yellow Typhoon. Harper, 1919; Hodder, 1923

McGRATH, MANDA
 East of Singapore. Wright, 1935
 -Footlights. Wright, 1935
 The Girl from Scotland Yard. Wright, 1935
 -The Last Ditch. Wright, 1934
 Outside the Law. Wright, 1935
 -Wise Virgin. Wright, 1934

MacGREGOR, JAMES MURDOCH. 1925-   .
 Pseudonym: J. T. McIntosh, q.v.

McGREW, FENN. Joint pseudonym of Julia McGrew and Caroline K. Fenn. Series character: Lt. Charles Hillary = CH.
 Made for Murder. Rinehart, 1954 CH
 Murder by Mail. Rinehart, 1951
 Taste of Death. Rinehart, 1953 CH

McGREW, JULIA. Joint pseudonym with Caroline K. Fenn: Fenn McGrew, q.v.

McGUIRE, ATHA
 Homicide Hussy. GM, 1955

McGUIRE, FRANCES MARGARET (CHEADLE)
 -September Comes In. Heinemann, 1961
 Time in the End. Heinemann, 1963

McGUIRE, NICHOLAS. Pseudonym of Nicholas Melides, 1912-   , q.v.
 Mosquito Serenade. Paladin, 1950

McGUIRE, PATRICK O. Pseudonym.
 Fiesta for Murder. Hammond, 1962
 A Time for Murder. Hammond, 1955

McGUIRE, (DOMINIC) PAUL. 1905-   .
 Series characters: Inspector/Superintendent Fillinger, in at least those marked F; Chief Insp. Cummings, in at least those marked C.
 The Black Rose Murder; see Murder in Bostall
 Born to be Hanged. Skeffington, 1935
 Burial Service. Heinemann, 1938. U.S. title: A Funeral in Eden. Morrow, 1938
 Cry Aloud for Murder. Heinemann, 1937
 Daylight Murder. Skeffington, 1934. U.S. title: Murder at High Noon. Doubleday, 1935 C, F
 Death Fugue. Skeffington, 1933 F
 Death Tolls the Bell; see The Tower Mystery
 Enter Three Witches; see The Spanish Steps
 A Funeral in Eden; see Burial Service
 Murder at High Noon; see Daylight Murder
 Murder by the Law. Skeffington, 1932 F
 Murder in Bostall. Skeffington, 1931. U.S. title: The Black Rose Murder. Brentano's, 1932 C
 Murder in Haste. Skeffington, 1934 C, F
 Prologue to the Gallows. Skeffington, 1936
 7.30 Victoria. Skeffington, 1935 C
 The Spanish Steps. Heinemann, 1940. U.S. title: Enter Three Witches. Morrow, 1940
 There Sits Death. Skeffington, 1935 F
 Three Dead Men. Skeffington, 1931; Brentano's, 1932 F
 Threepence to Marble Arch. Skeffington, 1936
 The Tower Mystery. Skeffington, 1932. U.S. title: Death Tolls the Bell. Coward, 1933 F
 W.1. Heinemann, 1937

McGURK, SLATER. Pseudonym of Arthur Joseph Roth, 1925-   .
 The Big Dig. Macmillan, 1968; Hale, 1968
 The Copenhagen Affair; see The Denmark Bus
 The Denmark Bus. Walker, 1966. Also published as: The Copenhagen Affair. Lancer, 1968
 The Grand Central Murders. Macmillan, 1964; Hammond, 1965

MacHARG, WILLIAM (BRIGGS). 1872-1951.
 The Affairs of O'Malley. Dial, 1940. Also published as: Smart Guy. Popular Library, 1951 ss
 The Blind Man's Eyes, with Edwin Balmer, 1883-1959, q.v. Little, 1916; Nash, 1916
 The Indian Drum, with Edwin Balmer, 1883-1959, q.v. Little, 1917; Paul, 1919

The Surakarta, with Edwin Balmer, 1883-1959, q.v. Small, 1913

McHUGH, AUGUSTIN. See: BARTON (WOOD) CURRIE, 1878- .

McHUGH, EDNA. Joint pseudonym with Amelia Reynolds Long, 1904-1978, q.v.: Kathleen Buddington Coxe, q.v.

McHUGH, FRANCES Y(OULIN)
Bluethorne. Arcadia, 1966
The China Shepherdess. Arcadia, 1966
The Dropped Living Room. Lenox Hill, 1972
Emerald Mountain. Lenox Hill, 1970
The Frightened Bowerbird. Arcadia, 1968
The Ghost Wore Black. Lenox Hill, 1970
High on a Hill. Arcadia, 1967
The Hyacinth Spell. Lenox Hill, 1972
Love Like an Arrow. Lenox Hill, 1972; Remploy, 1973
The Missing Grandfather. Arcadia, 1968
The Pale Pink House. Arcadia, 1967
The Rocking Chair. Arcadia, 1969
Saratoga Lady. Lenox Hill, 1970
Shadow Acres. Arcadia, 1967
Shadow over Mount Sharon. Belmont, 1973
Summer Velvet. Lenox Hill, 1972
Vow of Love. Lenox Hill, 1972
Window on the Seine. Arcadia, 1969

MacILWAIN, DAVID. Pseudonym: Richard Rayner, q.v.

MacINNES, HELEN. 1907- .
Above Suspicion. Little, 1941; Harrap, 1941
Assignment in Brittany. Little, 1942; Harrap, 1942
Decision at Delphi. Harcourt, 1960; Collins, 1961
The Double Image. Harcourt, 1966; Collins, 1967
Horizon. Little, 1946; Harrap, 1945
I and My True Love. Harcourt, 1953; Collins, 1953
Message from Malaga. Harcourt, 1971; Collins, 1972
Neither Five nor Three. Harcourt, 1951; Collins, 1951
North from Rome. Harcourt, 1958; Collins, 1958
Pray for a Brave Heart. Harcourt, 1955; Collins, 1955
The Salzburg Connection. Harcourt, 1968; Collins, 1969
The Snare of the Hunter. Harcourt, 1974; Collins, 1974
The Unconquerable; see While Still We Live
The Venetian Affair. Harcourt, 1963; Collins, 1964
While Still We Live. Little, 1944. British title: The Unconquerable. Harrap, 1944

McINTIRE, MARGUERITE (GERTRUDE PEARMAN)
Old-Fashioned Murder. Farrar, 1941

McINTIRE, WEBB KYLE
-Cider Row. Exposition, 1961

McINTOSH, J. T. Pseudonym of James Murdoch MacGregor, 1925- . Series characters: Ambrose and Dominique Frayne, in both titles.
A Coat of Blackmail. Muller, 1970; Doubleday, 1971
Take a Pair of Private Eyes. Muller, 1968; Doubleday, 1968. (Novelization of a TV play by Peter O'Donnell, 1920- , q.v.)

McINTOSH, KINN HAMILTON. 1930- .
Pseudonym: Catherine Aird, q.v.

MacINTYRE, JOHN T(HOMAS). 1871-1951.
Pseudonym: Kerry O'Neil, q.v. Series character: Ashton Kirk = AK.
Ashton-Kirk: Criminologist. Penn, 1918; Robinson, 1921 AK
Ashton-Kirk: Investigator. Penn, 1910; Robinson, 1921 AK
Ashton-Kirk: Secret Agent. Penn, 1912; Palmer, 1916. Also published as: Secret Agent: Ashton-Kirk. Robinson, 1921 AK
Ashton-Kirk: Special Detective. Penn, 1912. British title: Special Detective: Ashton-Kirk. Robinson, 1922 AK
In the Dead of Night. Lippincott, 1908; Ward, 1909
In the Toils. Penn, 1898. (5-act play.)
The Museum Murder. Doubleday, 1929; Bles, 1930
-The Ragged Edge. McClure, 1902
Secret Agent: Ashton-Kirk; see Ashton-Kirk: Secret Agent
-Signing Off. Farrar, 1938
"Slag." Scribner, 1927
Special Detective: Ashton-Kirk; see Ashton-Kirk: Special Detective
Steps Going Down. Farrar, 1936
-The Street Singer. Penn, 1908

MacISAAC, FRED(ERICK JOHN). 1886-1940.
The Dealer of Death. Methuen, 1938
Death Rides the Deep. Methuen, 1938
Don't Let Him Burn! Methuen, 1938
False-Face. Methuen, 1939
The Hole in the Wall. Waterson, 1927
Hot Gold. Methuen, 1938
The Mental Marvel. McClurg, 1930
Millions for Murder. Methuen, 1938
The Murder Special. Methuen, 1938
Tin Hats. Chelsea, 1926
The Vanishing Professor. Waterson, 1927; Methuen, 1939
The Wild Man of Cape Cod. Methuen, 1938
The Winged Murderer. Methuen, 1939
The Yellow Shop. Hurst, 1928

MacIVERS, SARAH
Cry of the Wind. Belmont, 1974
The Curse of Ravenswood. Macfadden, 1973
Night Without End. Belmont, 1975

MACKAIL, DENIS (GEORGE). 1892- .
-According to Gibson. Heinemann, 1923; Houghton, 1923 ss
The "Majestic" Mystery. Heinemann, 1924; Houghton, 1924

McKAY, HERBERT. 1881- .
A Camouflage Revolution. Wells Gardner, 1929. Also published as: The Mystery of White Fell Gill. James, 1947

MACKAY, HUGH LEWIS. 1897-1963. Pseudonym: Hugh Matheson, q.v.

McKAY, KELVIN
Murder at Barclay House. Phoenix, 1937

McKAY, RANDLE and R. J. GERRARD. For McKay, see also: LASSITER WREN.
The "Intelligence" Game of Secret Service Cases and Problems. McBride, 1935 puzzle ss

McKEAG, ERNEST L(IONEL). 1896- .
Pseudonyms: Griff, Mark Grimshaw, Ramon Lacroix, qq.v.
Green Eyes are Dangerous. Jonathan (London), 1947
The Sign of the Spider. Fiction House, 1939
A Traitor in the Fleet. Wright, 1939

McKECHNIE, N(EIL) K(ENNETH)
The Saddleroom Murder. Penn, 1937

McKELWAY, ST. CLAIR. 1905- .
The Edinburgh Caper. Holt, 1962; Gollancz, 1963

McKENNA, MARTHE. 1892-1969. Series character: Clive Granville, in at least those marked CG.
Arms and the Spy. Jarrolds, 1942
Double Spy. Jarrolds, 1938
Drums Never Beat. Jarrolds, 1936
Hunt the Spy. Jarrolds, 1939
Lancer Spy. Jarrolds, 1937 CG
Nightfighter Spy. Jarrolds, 1943
Set a Spy. Jarrolds, 1937
The Spy in Khaki. Jarrolds, 1941 CG
A Spy was Born. Jarrolds, 1935; McBride, 1935
Spying Blind. Jarrolds, 1939
Three Spies for Glory. Jarrolds, 1950
Watch Across the Channel. Jarrolds, 1944
What's Past is Prologue. Jarrolds, 1951

McKENNA, STEPHEN. 1888-1967.
The Datchley Inheritance. Ward, 1929; Dodd, 1929
Tales of Intrigue and Revenge. Hutchinson, 1924; Little, 1925 ss
While of Sound Mind. Hutchinson, 1936

McKENZIE, A(DELBERT) R(OLAND). 1907- .
Death Gets a Head. Phoenix, 1942

MacKENZIE, ANDREW (CARR). Series character: Supt. Brannigan, in the titles marked B, and others.
Always Fight Back. Boardman, 1955
A Grave is Waiting. Boardman, 1957
The House at the Estuary. Ward, 1948
A Man from the Past. Boardman, 1958
The Man Who Wanted to Die. Ward, 1951 B
The Missile. Boardman, 1959
Point of a Gun. Ward, 1951
The Reaching Hand. Boardman, 1957
Search in the Dark. Ward, 1948
Shadow of a Spy. Boardman, 1958
Shadows on the River. Ward, 1949
Splash of Red. Ward, 1949
Three Hours to Hang. Boardman, 1955
Voice from the Cell. Hale, 1961
Week of Suspense. Hale, 1962
Whisper If You Dare! Ward, 1950 B

MacKENZIE, (ANTHONY EDWARD MONTAGU) COMPTON. 1883-1973. Series character: Commander Roger Waterlow = RW.
Extremes Meet. Cassell, 1928; Doubleday, 1928 RW
The Three Couriers. Cassell, 1929; Doubleday, 1929 RW
Water on the Brain. Cassell, 1933; Doubleday, 1933

MacKENZIE, DONALD. 1908- . Series characters: Harry Chalice and Crying Eddie = C&E.
The Chalice Caper; see Sleep is for the Rich
Cool Sleeps Balaban. Collins, 1964; Houghton, 1964
Dangerous Silence. Collins, 1960; Houghton, 1960
Dead Straight. Hodder, 1969; Houghton, 1969
Death is a Friend. Hodder, 1967; Houghton, 1967 C&E
Double Exposure. Collins, 1963; Houghton, 1963. Also published as: I, Spy. Avon, 1964
The Genial Stranger. Collins, 1962; Houghton, 1962
I, Spy; see Double Exposure
The Juryman. Elek, 1957; Houghton, 1958
Knife Edge. Houghton, 1961

MacKENZIE, Donald

The Kyle Contract. Hodder, 1971; Houghton, 1970
The Lonely Side of the River. Hodder, 1965; Houghton, 1965
Manhunt; see Nowhere to Go
Moment of Danger; see Scent of Danger
Night Boat from Puerto Vedra. Hodder, 1970; Houghton, 1970
Nowhere to Go. Elek, 1956. U.S. title: Manhunt. Houghton, 1957
Postscript to a Dead Letter. Macmillan (London), 1973; Houghton, 1973
The Quiet Killer; see Three Minus Two
Salute from a Dead Man. Hodder, 1966; Houghton, 1966 C&E
Scent of Danger. Collins, 1958; Houghton, 1958. Also published as: Moment of Danger. Pan, 1959; Dell, 1959
Sleep is for the Rich. Macmillan (London), 1971; Houghton, 1971. Also published as: The Chalice Caper. Mayflower, 1974 C&E
The Spreewald Collection. Macmillan (London), 1975; Houghton, 1975
Three Minus Two. Hodder, 1968. U.S. title: The Quiet Killer. Houghton, 1968
Zaleski's Percentage. Macmillan (London), 1974; Houghton, 1974

McKENZIE, DONALD J.

Detective Against Detective. Street (Magnet)
Face to Face. Street (Magnet)
A Past Master of Crime; or, Detective Bush's Clever Work. Street (Magnet), 1899
The Reporter Detective. Street (Magnet), 1900
Under his Thumb. Street, 1889
The Wall Street Wonder. Street (Magnet)
The Working Man Detective; or, A Crime Against the Poor. Street (Magnet), 1899

MacKENZIE, JEANNE

-All for the Apple. Hutchinson, 1948
The Deadly Game. Hutchinson, 1939
-The Homeward Tide. Hutchinson, 1935
-Linda Walked Alone. Hutchinson, 1944
-The Wayward Heart. Hutchinson, 1951

MacKENZIE, NIGEL. Series character: Det. Insp. Charles Tremayne, in at least those marked CT.

Bandit's Moon. Wright, 1952
Blood on the Snow. Wright, 1966
The Case of the Glass Slipper. Wright, 1962
Consider Your Verdict. Wright, 1952
Could It be Murder? Wright, 1948
The Dark Night. Wright, 1950
The Dark Road. Wright, 1961
Day of Judgment. Wright, 1956
Death for a Traitor. Wright, 1948
Death Holds his Court. Wright, 1960
Death in the Smog. Wright, 1963
Death Takes a Holiday. Wright, 1966
Fear Stalks the City. Wright, 1965
Footprints of Death. Wright, 1957
The Ghost Walks. Wright, 1949
The Horror in the Dark. Wright, 1962
The House of Horror. Wright, 1959
In Great Danger. Wright, 1959
Killer at Large. Wright, 1961 CT
Killing's No Murder. Wright, 1968
Missing—A Lady. Wright, 1964
Missing, Believed Dead. Wright, 1968
Murder for Two. Wright, 1951
The Murder in Cardigan Square. Wright, 1954
Murder in the Rain Forest. Wright, 1952
Murder over Karmak. Wright, 1949
Murder Round the Corner. Wright, 1968
Night of Fear. Wright, 1964 CT
No Escape from Murder. Wright, 1964
Pyramid of Death. Wright, 1953
Queue Here for Murder. Wright, 1961
Race Toward Death. Wright, 1963 CT
The Red Light. Wright, 1950
Seven Days to Death. Wright, 1959
Strange Happening. Wright, 1967
Three Steps to Murder. Wright, 1965

MACKENZIE, SCOBIE. 1906-

Doctor Fram. Eyre, 1933; Dutton, 1933
Three Dead, One Hurt. Eyre, 1934

MacKENZIE, SUSAN

Death has Many Doors. Lancer, 1968

MacKENZIE, W(ILLIAM) A(NDREW). 1870- . Series character: Sir Nigel Lacaita, in at least those marked NL.

The Bite of the Leech. Holden, 1914 NL
The Black Butterfly. Ward, 1907 NL
The Drexel Dream. Chatto, 1904 NL
-Flower o' the Peach. Ward, 1916
-The Glittering Road. Ward, 1903
His Majesty's Peacock. Richards, 1904 NL
-In the House of the Eye. Ward, 1907
-The Red Star of Night. Constable, 1911

McKEOWN, NORMAN ROBERT. Pseudonym: Norman Giles, q.v.

MacKERSEY, IAN

-Long Night's Journey. Hale, 1974

MACKIE, JOHN. 1862-1939.

-The Bush Mystery; or, The Lost Explorer. Nisbet, 1912
-The Man Who Forgot. Jarrolds, 1901

McKIMMEY, JAMES

Blue Mascara Tears. Ballantine, 1965; Boardman, 1966
A Circle in the Water. Morrow, 1965; Muller, 1966
Cornered! Dell, 1960; Boardman, 1965
The Hot Fire. Hale, 1969
The Long Ride. Dell, 1961; Boardman, 1963
The Man with the Gloved Hand. Random, 1972; Hale, 1974
Never be Caught. Boardman, 1966. (Three novelets.)
The Perfect Victim. Dell, 1958; Boardman, 1965
Run If You're Guilty. Lippincott, 1963; Boardman, 1964
The Satyr. Monarch, 196?
Squeeze Play. Dell, 1962; Boardman, 1965
24 Hours to Kill. Dell, 1961; Boardman, 1963
Winner Take All. Dell, 1959; Boardman, 1963
The Wrong Ones. Dell, 1961; Boardman, 1964

MACKIN, MRS. MARIE

The Mystery of the Marbletons. Abbey, 1900

MacKINLAY, (MALCOLM) STERLING. 1876- .

The Enemy Agent. Long, 1932

McKINLEY, F(RANCES) BURKS. 1907- .

Death Sails the Nile. Stratford, 1933

MacKINNON, ALLAN. Series characters: Mike Darroch = MD; Det. Insp. Duncan MacCallum = DM; Don Kendrick = DK.

Assignment in Iraq. Collins, 1960; Doubleday, 1960 MD
Cormorant's Isle. Long, 1962; Doubleday, 1962
Danger by my Side. Collins, 1950
Dead on Departure. Long, 1964. U.S. title: Report from Argyll. Doubleday, 1964 DK
House of Darkness. Collins, 1947; Doubleday, 1947 DM
Man Overboard; see No Wreath from Manuela
Map of Mistrust. Collins, 1948; Doubleday, 1948
Money on the Black; see Nine Days' Murder
Murder, Repeat Murder. Collins, 1952; Doubleday, 1952
Nine Days' Murder. Collins, 1945. U.S. title: Money on the Black. Doubleday, 1946 DM
No Wreath from Manuela. Long, 1965. U.S. title: Man Overboard. Doubleday, 1965 DK
Red-Winged Angel. Collins, 1958. U.S. title: Summons from Baghdad. Doubleday, 1958 MD
Report from Argyll; see Dead on Departure
Summons from Baghdad; see Red-Winged Angel

MACKINNON, CHARLES ROY. 1924- . Pseudonym: Graham Montrose, q.v.

MacKINNON, CLARK K.

The Flame Lily. Dakers, 1954
Leopard Valley. Long, 1963
Lost Hyena. Long, 1962

MacKINTOSH, ELIZABETH. 1896-1952. Pseudonyms: Gordon Daviot, Josephine Tey, qq.v.

MacKINTOSH, IAN

The Brave Cannot Yield. Hale, 1970
Count Not the Cost. Hale, 1968
A Drug Called Power. Hale, 1968
The Man from Destiny. Hale, 1969
A Slaying in September. Hale, 1967

MacKINTOSH, MAY. Series characters: Laurie Grant and Stewart Noble, in at least those marked G&N.

Appointment in Andalusia. Collins, 1972; Delacorte, 1972 G&N
Assignment in Andorra; see A King and Two Queens
The Double Dealers. Collins, 1975. U.S. title: Highland Fling. Delacorte, 1975
Highland Fling; see The Double Dealers
A King and Two Queens. Collins, 1973. U.S. title: Assignment in Andorra. Delacorte, 1973 G&N
The Sicilian Affair. Collins, 1974; Delacorte, 1974 G&N

McKNIGHT, BOB. 1906- .

The Bikini Bombshell. Ace, 1959
Downwind. Ace, 1957
Drop Dead, Please. Ace, 1961
The Flying Eye. Ace, 1961
Homicide Handicap. Ace, 1963
Kiss the Babe Goodbye. Ace, 1960
Murder Mutuel. Ace, 1958
Running Scared. Ace, 1960
A Slice of Death. Ace, 1960
A Stone Around her Neck. Ace, 1962
Swamp Sanctuary. Ace, 1959

MacKNUTT, M. G.

Death on the Cuff. Phoenix, 1951

McLACHLAN, ALEX(ANDER). See: R(OBERT) J(AMES) FLETCHER, 1877- .

McLACHLIN, DONALD

No Case for the Crown. Sidgwick, 1972

McLAREN, CHRISTABEL

-The Divine Gift. Longmans, 1929

McLAREN, JACK. 1887- .
 The Crystal Skull. Allan, 1936
 -The Devil of the Depths. Allan, 1935
 -A Diver Went Down. Mandrake, 1929
 -Stories of Fear. Pendulum, 1947 ss

McLAREN, MORAY
 -A Dinner with the Dead. Serif, 1947 ss
 -Escape and Return. Chapman, 1947
 The Pursuit. Jarrolds, 1959

MacLAREN-ROSS, J(ULIAN)
 -Better Than a Kick in the Pants. Lawson, 1945 ss
 -Bitten by the Tarantula. Wingate, 1945
 The Doomsday Book. H. Hamilton, 1961; Obolensky, 1961
 -The Funny Bone. Elek, 1956
 -My Name is Love. Times Press, 1964
 -The Nine Men of Soho. Wingate, 1946 ss
 -Of Love and Hunger. Wingate, 1947
 -The Stuff to Give the Troops. Cape, 1944 ss
 Until the Day She Dies. H. Hamilton, 1960

McLARTY, NANCY
 Chain of Death. Doubleday, 1962

McLAUGHLIN, ROBERT, 1925-   , and PHIL FORAN
 Nothing to Report. Little, 1975

McLAUGHLIN, ROBERT J.
 A Horsehair Santa Claus and other stories. Christopher, 1931 ss

McLAUGHLIN, W(ILLIAM) R(AFFAN) D(AVIDSON). 1908- .
 Syndicate of Evil. Hale, 1965

MacLEAN, ALISTAIR (STUART). 1923- .
 Pseudonym: Ian Stuart, q.v.
 Bear Island. Collins, 1971; Doubleday, 1971
 Breakheart Pass. Collins, 1974; Doubleday, 1974
 Caravan to Vaccares. Collins, 1970; Doubleday, 1970
 Circus. Collins, 1975; Doubleday, 1975
 Fear is the Key. Collins, 1961; Doubleday, 1961
 Force 10 from Navarone. Collins, 1968; Doubleday, 1968
 The Golden Rendezvous. Collins, 1962; Doubleday, 1962
 The Guns of Navarone. Collins, 1957; Doubleday, 1957
 Ice Station Zebra. Collins, 1963; Doubleday, 1963
 The Last Frontier. Collins, 1959. U.S. title: The Secret Ways. Doubleday, 1959
 Night Without End. Collins, 1960; Doubleday, 1960
 Puppet on a Chain. Collins, 1969; Doubleday, 1969
 The Secret Ways; see The Last Frontier
 South by Java Head. Collins, 1958; Doubleday, 1958
 The Way to Dusty Death. Collins, 1973; Doubleday, 1973
 When Eight Bells Toll. Collins, 1966; Doubleday, 1966
 Where Eagles Dare. Collins, 1967; Doubleday, 1967

McLEAN, ALLAN CAMPBELL. 1922-   . Series character: Insp. Neil MacLeod, in at least those marked NM.
 The Carpet-Slipper Murder. Ward, 1956; Washburn, 1957 NM
 Deadly Honeymoon. Ward, 1958
 Death on All Hallows. Ward, 1958; Washburn, 1958 NM
 Murder by Invitation. Ward, 1959 NM
 Stand-In for Murder. Ward, 1960

MacLEAN, ARTHUR (GEORGE). Pseudonym: Arthur Kirby, q.v. All titles below feature Sexton Blake and, where not otherwise indicated, were published by Amalgamated Press.
 Bargain in Blood. 1962
 Broken Toy. 1956
 Canvas Jungle. 1956
 Dark Frontier. 1956
 Deadline for Danger. 1957
 Fatal Curtain. 1958
 Find Me a Killer! 1957. Also published as: Slaying on the 16th Floor. Mayflower, 1965
 The House on the Bay. 1958
 The Man Who Killed Me; see Redhead for Danger
 Mask of Fury. 1957
 Mission to Mexico. 1960
 Night Beat. 1956
 Pursuit to Algeria. 1961
 Redhead for Danger. 1958. Also published as: The Man Who Killed Me. 1962
 The Savage Squeeze. Mayflower, 1965
 Slaying on the 16th Floor; see Find Me a Killer!
 Touch of Evil. 1959

MacLEAN, KATHERINE. 1925- .
 The Man in the Bird Cage. Ace, 1970

MacLEAN, ROBINSON
 The Baited Blonde. Mill, 1949; Barker, 1950

McLEAVE, HUGH (GEORGE). 1923- .
 Only Gentlemen Can Play. Barker, 1975; Harcourt, 1974
 A Question of Negligence. Collins, 1973; Harcourt, 1974
 The Steel Balloon. Muller, 1964
 The Sword and the Scales. Davies, 1967; World, 1968
 Vodka on Ice. Harcourt, 1969

McLEISH, DOUGAL
 The Traitor Game. Houghton, 1968
 The Valentine Victim. Houghton, 1968

MacLEOD, ADAM GORDON. Series character: Sir William Burrill = WB.
 The Case of Matthew Crake. Harrap, 1932; Dial, 1933 WB
 The Cathra Mystery. Harrap, 1926; Dial, 1926
 Death Stalked the Fells. Harrap, 1937 WB
 The Marloe Mansions Murder. Harrap, 1928; Dial, 1928 WB

MacLEOD, ANGUS. 1925- .
 Blessed Above Women. Dobson, 1965; Roy, 1967
 The Eighth Seal. Dobson, 1962; Roy, 1962
 The Tough and the Tender. Dobson, 1960; Roy, 1960

MacLEOD, CHARLOTTE (MATILDA HUGHES). 1922- .
 Mystery of the White Knight. Avalon, 1964
 Next Door to Danger. Avalon, 1965

McLEOD, K.
 Body for a Blonde. Harlequin, 1954

MacLEOD, ROBERT. Pseudonym of Bill Knox, 1928-   , q.v. Other pseudonyms: Michael Kirk, Noah Webster. Series characters: Talos Cord = TC; Jonathan Gaunt = JG.
 All Other Perils. Long, 1974; Doubleday, 1975, as by Michael Kirk
 A Burial in Portugal. Long, 1973; Doubleday, 1973, as by Noah Webster JG
 Cave of Bats. Long, 1964; Holt, 1966 TC
 Drum of Power. Long, 1964. U.S. title: The Drum of Ungara, as by Bill Knox. Doubleday, 1963
 The Drum of Ungara; see Drum of Power
 Flickering Death; see A Property in Cyprus
 The Iron Sanctuary; see Lake of Fury
 Isle of Dragons. Long, 1967 TC
 A Killing in Malta. Long, 1972; Doubleday, 1972, as by Noah Webster JG
 Lake of Fury. Long, 1966. U.S. title: The Iron Sanctuary. Holt, 1968 TC
 Nest of Vultures. Long, 1973 TC
 Path of Ghosts. Long, 1971; McCall, 1971 TC
 Place of Mists. Long, 1969; McCall, 1970 TC
 A Property in Cyprus. Long, 1970. U.S. title: Flickering Death, as by Noah Webster. Doubleday, 1970 JG
 A Witchdance in Bavaria. Long, 1975; Doubleday, 1976, as by Noah Webster JG

MacLEOD, RUTH
 Hawks of Glenaerie. Manor, 1974
 Murder on Vacation. Avalon, 1962

M'LEVY, JAMES
 At War with Society; or, Tales of the Outcasts. Cameron, 1870 ss
 Casebook of a Victorian Detective. Canongate, 1975 ss, taken from The Sliding Scale of Life and from Curiosities of Crime in Edinburgh, qq.v.
 Curiosities of Crime in Edinburgh. Kay, 1861; Nimmo, 1861; Vickers, 1861 ss (All three British firms seem to have issued the book in the same year.)
 The Mysteries of the City; or, Under the Surface of Society. Cameron, 186? ss
 Romances of Crime; or, The Disclosures of a Detective. Griffin, 1869 ss
 The Sliding Scale of Life; or, Thirty Years' Observations of Falling Men and Women in Edinburgh. Houlston, 1861 ss

McLOUGHLIN, ROY
 The Yank in Fleet Street. Methuen, 1939

McMAHON, BRIAN PATRICK. See: THOMAS PATRICK McMAHON.

McMAHON, ROBERT. See: LEO BERGSON.

McMAHON, THOMAS PATRICK
 Cornered at Six, with Brian Patrick McMahon. Simon, 1972
 The Hubschmann Effect. Simon, 1973. British title: The Little Victims. Constable, 1974
 The Issue of the Bishop's Blood. Doubleday, 1972; Collins, 1973
 Jink. Simon, 1971
 The Little Victims; see The Hubschmann Effect
 Mayday, with Brian Patrick McMahon. Simon, 1973

McMANIS, J. ALLEN
 The Hooded Asp. Wetzel, 1928

McMANUS, CHRIS
 -The Deep-Sea Tow. Harrap, 1954
 -The "Hades Belle." Harrap, 1955
 -Whisky Johnny. Harrap, 1956

McMIKLE, BARBARA
   The Secret of the Weeping Monk. Bantam, 1975

MacMILLAN, GEORGETTE
   The Woman in Mauve. Chelsea, 1925

McMORROW, THOMAS. 1886-   .
   The Sandalwood Fan. Sears, 1928
   The Strange History of Ambrose Hinkle. Sears, 1929

McMULLEN, MARY. 1920-   .
   A Country Kind of Death. Doubleday, 1975; Hale, 1977
   Death of Miss X; see Strangle Hold
   The Doom Campaign. Doubleday, 1974; Hale, 1976
   Strangle Hold. Harper, 1951. British title: Death of Miss X. Collins, 1952

McMURDIE, ANNIE LAURIE. Pseudonym of Bruce (Bingham) Cassiday, 1920-   , q.v. Other pseudonyms: Carson Bingham, Mary Anne Drew, Michael Stratford, qq.v.
   Nightmare Hall. Lancer, 1973

McNALTY, A(RTHUR) SALISBURY. 1880-1969.
   The Mystery of Captain Burnaby. Pawling, 1934

McNAMARA, ED. 1911-   .
   Once Over Deadly. Abelard (New York & London), 1958

McNAMARA, LENA B(ROOKE). 1891-   . Pseudonym: Evalina Mack, q.v.
   The Penance was Death. Bruce, 1964
   Pilgrim's End. Ace, 1967

MacNAUGHT, THOMAS P.
   The Recollections of a Glasgow Detective Officer. Simpkin, 1887 ss
   Thrilling Detective Stories. Simpkin, 1891 ss

MACNAUGHTAN, RICHARD
   The Preparatory School Murder. Fenland, 1934

MacNEE, PATRICK
   Dead Duck. Hodder, 1966. (Based on The Avengers TV series.)
   Deadline. Hodder, 1965

MacNEIL, NEIL. Pseudonym of W(illis) T(odhunter) Ballard, 1903-   , q.v. Other pseudonyms: P. D. Ballard, John Shepherd, qq.v. Joint pseudonym with Norbert Davis, q.v.: Harrison Hunt, q.v. Series characters: Tony Costaine and Bert McCall, in all titles.
   The Death Ride. GM, 1960; Muller pb, 1962
   Death Takes an Option. GM, 1958; Fawcett (London), 1960
   Hot Dam. GM, 1960; Muller pb, 1960
   Mexican Slay Ride. GM, 1961; Muller pb, 1963
   The Spy Catchers. GM, 1963
   Third on a Seesaw. GM, 1959; Muller pb, 1961
   Two Guns for Hire. GM, 1959; Muller pb, 1960

McNEILE, H(ERMAN) C(YRIL). 1888-1937.
   This author's works have appeared as by H. C. McNeile and/or Sapper, and are collectively listed here. Note that a number of McNeile ss were published separately in booklet form in the U.S.; these are listed separately at the end of this entry. Series characters: Hugh "Bulldog" Drummond = BD (see also: Gerard Fairlie, 1899-   ; and: Henry Reymond); Ronald Standish = RS.
   Ask for Ronald Standish. Hodder, 1936 RS ss
   The Black Gang. Hodder, 1922; Doran, 1922 BD
   Bulldog Drummond. Hodder, 1920; Doran, 1920. Four-act play version, with Gerald Du Maurier: French (London & New York), 1925 BD
   Bulldog Drummond and the Female of the Species; see The Female of the Species
   Bulldog Drummond at Bay. Hodder, 1935; Doubleday, 1935 BD, RS
   Bulldog Drummond Meets a Murderess; see The Female of the Species
   Bulldog Drummond Returns; see The Return of Bulldog Drummond
   Bulldog Drummond Strikes Back; see Knock-Out
   Bulldog Drummond's Third Round; see The Third Round
   Challenge. Hodder, 1937; Doubleday, 1937 BD
   The Dinner Club. Hodder, 1923; Doran, 1923 ss
   The Female of the Species. Hodder, 1928; Doubleday, 1928. Also published as: Bulldog Drummond and the Female of the Species. Sun Dial, 1943. And as: Bulldog Drummond Meets a Murderess. Thriller Novel Classic, 194? BD
   The Final Count. Hodder, 1926; Doran, 1926 BD
   The Finger of Fate. Hodder, 1930; Doubleday, 1931 ss
   Guardians of the Treasure; see The Island of Terror
   -The Human Touch. Hodder, 1918; Doran, 1918 ss
   The Island of Terror. Hodder, 1931. U.S. title: Guardians of the Treasure. Doubleday, 1931
   -Jim Brent. Hodder, 1926
   Jim Maitland. Hodder, 1923; Doran, 1924
   Knock-Out. Hodder, 1933. U.S. title: Bulldog Drummond Strikes Back. Doubleday, 1933 BD
   -The Lieutenant and Others. Hodder, 1915 ss
   The Man in Ratcatcher, and other stories. Hodder, 1921; Doran, 1921 ss
   Men, Women and Guns. Hodder, 1916; Doran, 1916 ss, one criminous
   Michael Cassidy, Sergeant; see Sergeant Michael Cassidy, R.E.
   -Mufti. Hodder, 1919; Doran, 1919 ss
   -No Man's Land. Hodder, 1917; Doran, 1917 ss
   -Out of the Blue. Hodder, 1925; Doran, 1925 ss
   The Return of Bulldog Drummond. Hodder, 1932. U.S. title: Bulldog Drummond Returns. Doubleday, 1932 BD
   Ronald Standish. Hodder, 1933 RS
   -The Saving Clause. Hodder, 1927 ss
   -Sergeant Michael Cassidy, R.E. Hodder, 1915. U.S. title: Michael Cassidy, Sergeant. Doran, 1916 ss
   -Shorty Bill. Hodder, 1926 ss, taken from No Man's Land, and The Human Touch, qq.v.
   Temple Tower. Hodder, 1929; Doubleday, 1929 BD
   The Third Round. Hodder, 1924. U.S. title: Bulldog Drummond's Third Round. Doran, 1924 BD
   Tiny Carteret. Hodder, 1930; Doubleday, 1930
   -When Carruthers Laughed. Hodder, 1934 ss
   -Word of Honour. Hodder, 1926; Doran, 1926 ss

   The criminous nature of these short stories has not been confirmed:
   An Act of Providence. Doran, 1927
   Billie Finds the Answer. Doran, 1927
   The Brides of Mertonbridge Hall. Doubleday, 1932
   Bulton's Revenge. Doran, 1924
   The Diamond Hair Slide. Doran, 1927
   Dilemma. Doran, 1927
   The Ducking of Herbert Polton, and Coincidence. Doran, 1924
   The Eleventh Hour. Doran, 1926
   The Fatal Second. Doran, 1916
   The Great Magor Diamond, and The Creaking Door. Doubleday, 1931
   The Haunted Rectory. Doubleday, 1931
   The Hidden Witness. Doubleday, 1929
   A Hundred Per Cent. Doran, 1927
   The Loyalty of Peter Drayton, and Mrs. Peter Skeffington's Revenge. Doran, 1926
   The Man in Yellow, and The Empty House. Doubleday, 1933
   Mark Danver's Sin, and The Madman of Coral Reef Lighthouse. Doran, 1923
   A Matter of Tar. Doubleday, 1932
   The Message. Doran, 1926
   The Missing Chauffeur. Doubleday, 1931
   Molly's Aunt at Angmering. Doran, 1923
   The Motor-Gun. Doran, 1916
   A Native Superstition. Doran, 1925
   Once Bit, Twice Hit. Doran, 1927
   The Other Side of the Wall. Doran, 1925
   Peter Cornish's Revenge. Doran, 1923
   The Professor's Christmas Party, and A Student of the Obvious. Doran, 1925
   A Question of Identity. Doran, 1925
   A Question of Mud. Doubleday, 1929
   Relative Values. Doran, 1927
   The Rout of the Oliver Samuelsons. Doran, 1926
   The Rubber Stamp, and A Matter of Voice. Doran, 1926
   The Saving Clause. Doran, 1926
   A Scrap of Paper. Doran, 1924
   The Taming of Sydney Marsham. Doran, 1926
   That Bullet Hole has a History! Doran, 1924
   Three of a Kind, and The Haunting of Jack Burnham. Doran, 1926
   The Truce of the Bear. Doran, 1918
   Uncle James's Golf Match. Hodder, 1932
   The Undoing of Mrs. Cransby. Doubleday, 1928
   The Valley of the Shadow. Doran, 1924
   When Carruthers Laughed. Doran, 1927
   Who was This Woman?, Two Photographs, and The King of Hearts. Doran, 1925
   Word of Honour. Doran, 1926

McNEILLY, WILFRED (GLASSFORD). 1921-   .
   Pseudonyms: W(illiam) Howard Baker, William A. Ballinger, Errol Lecale, Desmond Reid, qq.v. Series character (with many other authors): Sexton Blake = SB.
   The Break Out. Mayflower, 1965 SB
   The Case of the Muckrakers. Mayflower, 1966; Macfadden, 1967 SB
   The Case of the Stag at Bay. Mayflower, 1965 SB
   Come Dark, Come Evil. Amalgamated, 1962 SB
   Death in the Top Twenty. Mayflower, 1965 SB
   Killer Pack. Amalgamated, 1962 SB
   Land of the Free. Mayflower, 1966
   No Way Out. Consul, 1966; Macfadden, 1966. (Novelization of the Secret Agent TV series.)

Terror Loch. Amalgamated, 1962 SB
Wanted for Questioning. Mayflower, 1965 SB
The War Runners. New English Library, 1970

MACOMBER, DARIA. Joint pseudonym of Ferdinan Stevenson and Patricia Robinson.
Bury Her Deep; see A Clearing in the Fog
A Clearing in the Fog. World, 1970. British title (?): Bury Her Deep. Hale, 1971
Hunter, Hunter, Get Your Gun; see Return to Octavia
Return to Octavia. NAL, 1967. British title: Hunter, Hunter, Get Your Gun. Hodder, 1966

MACONECHY, J(OANNA)
Four Extra Daughters. Chatto, 1932
James Ballingray, Murderer. Collins, 1925
The Secret Journal of Charles Dunbar. Collins, 1923
Vanishing Shadows. Chatto, 1930

McPARTLAND, JOHN. 1911-195?
Affair in Tokyo. GM, 1954
Big Red's Daughter. GM, 1953
Danger for Breakfast. GM, 1956; Fawcett (London), 1957
The Face of Evil. GM, 1954; Fawcett (London), 1955
I'll See You in Hell. GM, 1956; Red Seal, 1958
The Kingdom of Johnny Cool. GM, 1959; Muller pb, 1960
The Last Night. GM, 1959; Muller pb, 1960
Love Me Now. GM, 1952; Muller, 1957
No Down Payment. Simon, 1957; Macdonald, 1958
Ripe Fruit. GM, 1958; Fawcett (London), 1959
Tokyo Doll. GM, 1953; Fawcett (London), 1954
The Wild Party. GM, 1956; Red Seal, 1959

MacPHAIL, JAMES A. Joint pseudonym with Cornelia Warriner: James Crockett, q.v.

McPHELLAMY, STEPHEN
Murder Without Alibis. Quality, 1947

MACPHERSON, JOHN F.
-A Yankee Napoleon. Long, 1907
-Yetta the Magnificent. Long, 1908

MacQUADE, MIKE
Who's for Dying? Hale, 1961

MacQUEEN, JAMES WILLIAM. 1900- .
Pseudonym: James G. Edwards, q.v.

McRAE, G. R(OY)
The Passing of Mr. Quinn. London Book Co., 1929. (Novelization of the film based on an Agatha Christie ss.)

MACRAE, TRAVIS. Pseudonym of Anita MacRae Feagles, 1926- . Series characters: Jim and Kate Harris = H.
Death in View. Holt, 1960; Hammond, 1961 H
Multiple Murder; see Twenty Per Cent
Trial by Slander. Rinehart, 1960; Hammond, 1960
Twenty Per Cent. Holt, 1961. British title: Multiple Murder. Hammond, 1962 H

McREAY, ERNEST L.
Murder at Eight Bells. Columbine, 1939

MacROSS, ROSS. Joint pseudonym of James Reach, 1909?-1970, q.v., and Tom Taggart. Other Reach pseudonyms, used for plays: Hilda Manning, John Reed, qq.v.
The Beautiful and Dead. GM, 1954

McROYD, ALLAN. Series character: Inspector Franklin Brady, in all titles.
Death in Costume. Greystone, 1940
The Double Shadow Murders. Greystone, 1939
The Golden Goose Murders. Greystone, 1938

McSHANE, MARK. 1930- . Pseudonym: Marc Lovell, q.v. Series characters: Det. Sgt. Norman Pink, in at least those marked NP; Myra Savage = MS.
The Crimson Madness of Little Doom. Hale, 1967; Doubleday, 1966
The Girl Nobody Knows. Hale, 1966; Doubleday, 1965 NP
Ill Met by a Fish Shop on George Street. Hodder, 1969; Doubleday, 1968
The Man Who Left Well Enough. McCall, 1971
Night's Evil. Hale, 1966; Doubleday, 1966 NP
The Passing of Evil. Cassell, 1961
Seance; see Seance on a Wet Afternoon
Seance for Two. Hale, 1974; Doubleday, 1972 MS
Seance on a Wet Afternoon. Cassell, 1961. U.S. title: Seance. Doubleday, 1962 MS
The Singular Case of the Multiple Dead. Hodder, 1970; Putnam, 1969
The Straight and Crooked. Long, 1960
Untimely Ripped. Cassell, 1962; Doubleday, 1963
The Way to Nowhere. Hale, 1967 NP

MacSWAN, NORMAN
-The Inn with the Wooden Door. Cassell, 1958

MacTYRE, PAUL. Pseudonym of Robert James Adams.
-Bar Sinister. Hodder, 1964
-Fish on a Hook. Hodder, 1963
-Midge. Hodder, 1962

MacVEAN, PHYLLIS. 1892- . Pseudonyms: Phyllis Hambledon, Philippa Vane, qq.v.

MacVEIGH, SUE. Pseudonym of Elizabeth Custer Nearing, 1898- . Series characters: Capt. Andy MacVeigh and his wife Sue, in all titles.
The Corpse and the Three Ex-Husbands. Houghton, 1941
Grand Central Murder. Houghton, 1939
Murder Under Construction. Houghton, 1939
Streamlined Murder. Houghton, 1940

MacVICAR, ANGUS. 1908- . Starred titles are 1-act plays.
The Canisbay Conspiracy. Long, 1966
The Cavern. Paul, 1936
Crime's Masquerader. Paul, 1938
The Crooked Finger. Paul, 1937
The Crouching Spy. Paul, 1941
The Dancing Horse. Long, 1961
Death by the Mistletoe. Paul, 1934
Death on the Machar. Paul, 1947
Duel in Glenfinnan. Long, 1969
11 for Danger. Paul, 1939
Escort to Adventure. Paul, 1952
-Final Proof. Brown, 1958 *

Flowering Death. Paul, 1937
Fugitive's Road. Paul, 1949
The Golden Venus Affair. Long, 1972
The Grey Shepherds. Long, 1964
Greybreek. Long, 1947
The Hammers of Fingal. Long, 1963
The Killings on Kersivay. Long, 1962
Maniac. Long, 1969
-Mercy Flight. Brown, 1959 *
Murder at the Open. Long, 1965
Night on the Killer Reef. Long, 1967
-The Other Man. Pemberton, 1947
The Painted Doll Affair. Long, 1973
The Purple Rock. Paul, 1933
The Screaming Gull. Paul, 1935
The Singing Spider. Paul, 1938
-Storm Tide. Brown, 1960 *
-Stranger at Christmas. Brown, 1964 *
Strangers from the Sea. Paul, 1939
The Temple Falls. Paul, 1935
The Ten Green Brothers. Paul, 1936
-Under Suspicion. Brown, 1962 *

McWATTERS, GEORGE S.
Detectives of Europe and America; or, Life in the Secret Service; see Knots Untied; or, Ways and Byways in the Hidden Life of American Detectives
Forgers and Confidence Men; or, The Secrets of the Detective Service Revealed. Laird, 1892 ss
The Gambler's Wax Finger and other startling detective experiences. Laird, 1892 ss
Knots Untied; or, Ways and Byways in the Hidden Life of American Detectives. Burr, 1871. Also published as: Detectives in Europe and America; or, Life in the Secret Service. Burr, 1877 ss

M—, Mr. Pseudonym of Charles Welch Mason, 1866- .
The Chest of Opium. Beeman, 1896
The Shen's Pigtail, and Other Cues of Anglo-China Life. Unwin, 1894 ss

MAARTENS, MAARTEN. Pseudonym of Joost Marius Williem van der Poorten Schwartz, 1858-1915. See also: ANONYMOUS (The Black Box Murder).
-The Sin of Joost Avelingh. Remington, 1889; Lovell, 1890

MAASS, EDGAR. 1896- .
A Lady at Bay. Scribner, 1953

MAASS, JOACHIM. 1901-1972.
Gabrielle; see The Gouffe Case
The Gouffe Case. Barrie, 1960; Harper, 1960. Also published as: Gabrielle. Corgi, 1964. (Translation of Der Fall Gouffe. Vienna, 1958.)
The Magic Year. Barrie, 1964. (Translation of Der Magische Jahr. Vienna, 1957.)

MACAO, MARSHALL
Kak-Abdullah Conspiracy. Tandem, 1974
The Rape of Sun Lee Fong. Tandem, 1974
Red Plague in Bolivia. Tandem, 1974
Return of the Opium Wars. Tandem, 1974
Son of the Flying Tiger. Tandem, 1974

MACE, GUSTAVE. 1835-1904.
My First Crime. Vizetelly, 1886. (Translation of Mon Premier Crime. Paris, 1885.) See also: R. Millar.

MACE, HELEN
And Death Came Too. Hammond, 1961
Death of a Golden Goose. Hammond, 1965
House of Hate. Hammond, 1958
Murder Among Those Present. Hammond, 1957

MACE, MERLDA
  Blondes Don't Cry. Messner, 1945
  Headlong for Murder. Messner, 1943
  Motto for Murder. Messner, 1943

MACHARD, ALFRED. 1887- .
  The Wolf Man. Clode, 1925; Butterworth, 1925

MACHEN, ARTHUR. 1863-1947.
  The Three Impostors. Lane, 1895; Roberts, 1895

MACHRAY, ROBERT. 1857- .
  The Ambassador's Glove. Long, 1904
  A Blow Over the Heart. Chatto, 1902
  The Disappearance of Lady Diana. Everett, 1909
  -Grace O'Malley, Princess and Pirate. Cassell, 1898; Stokes, 1898
  Her Honour. Chatto, 1907
  Her Secret Life. White, 1913
  The Mystery of Lincoln's Inn. Chatto, 1903; Munro, 1903
  The Mystery of the Middle Temple. Everett, 1908
  The Private Detective. Chatto, 1906
  Sentenced to Death. Chatto, 1910
  -Sir Hector. Constable, 1901
  The Stanhope Gate Mystery. White, 1915
  The Woman Wins. Chatto, 1911

MACIAS, GABRIEL
  Detective Reynold's Hardest Case; or, An Ocean Chase. Street (Magnet), 1900

MACK, EVALINA. Pseudonym of Lena B(rooke) McNamara, 1891- .
  Corpse in the Cove. Arcadia, 1955
  Death Among the Sands. Arcadia, 1957
  Death of a Portrait. Arcadia, 1952
  Murder in Miniature. Arcadia, 1959

MACK, JOHNNY
  Body in the Boathouse. Paget, 1949
  Fall Guy. Paget, 1949
  Faust of the F.B.I. Hamilton Stafford, 1953
  Payoff. Paget, 1949
  Shakedown. Paget, 1949
  Shamus. Paget, 1949

MACK, THOMAS
  The Spectre Bullet. Gernsback, 1932

MACK, W. GAZLEY
  The Kidnapper, and Railway Line Murder. Stockwell, 1944

MACK, W(ALTER) H(AWLEY). 1906- .
  -Mr. Birdsall Breezes Through. Hillman-Curl, 1937

MACK, WILLARD. 1878-1934.
  Kick-In. French, 1925. (A play.) (For novelization, see D. Torbett.)

MACKLIN, MARK
  The Thin Edge of Mania. Ace, 1956

MACKWORTH, JOHN (DOLBEN). 1887- .
  The Axe is Laid. Longmans (London & New York), 1925
  Broadcast. Longmans (London & New York), 1925

MADDEN, CECIL. See: MACGREGOR URQUHART.

MADDEN, E(DWARD) S(TANISLAUS)
  Craig's Spur. Heinemann, 1961; Vanguard, 1961

MADDEROM, GARY. 1937- .
  The Four Chambered Villain. Macmillan, 1971
  The Jewels That Got Away. Curtis, 1973

MADDOCK, LARRY. Pseudonym of Jack Owen Jardine, 1931- . Series characters: Hannibal Fortune and Webley, in all titles.
  The Emerald Elephant Gambit. Ace, 1967
  The Flying Saucer Gambit. Ace, 1966
  The Golden Goddess Gambit. Ace, 1967

MADDOCK, LUCIE (LACOSTE)
  Fantine Avenel. Cornhill, 1922

MADDOCK, STEPHEN. Pseudonym of J(ames) M(organ) Walsh, 1897-1952, q.v. Other pseudonym: H. Haverstock Hill, q.v. Series characters: Inspector Slane, in at least those marked S; Timothy Terrel, in at least those marked TT.
  Close Shave. Collins, 1952
  Conspirators at Large. Collins, 1937 TT
  Conspirators in Capri. Collins, 1935 TT
  Conspirators Three. Collins, 1936 TT
  Danger After Dark. Collins, 1934 TT
  Date with a Spy. Collins, 1941
  Doorway to Danger. Collins, 1938 TT
  Drums Beat at Dusk. Collins, 1943
  East of Piccadilly. Collins, 1948 S
  Exit Only. Collins, 1947 S
  The Eye at the Keyhole. Collins, 1935 TT
  Forbidden Frontiers. Collins, 1936 TT
  Gentlemen of the Night. Collins, 1934 TT
  I'll Never Like Friday Again. Collins, 1945
  Keep Your Fingers Crossed. Collins, 1949
  Lamp-Post 592. Collins, 1938 TT
  Overture to Trouble. Collins, 1946
  Private Line. Collins, 1950 S
  Public Mischief. Collins, 1951
  Something on the Stairs. Collins, 1944
  Spades at Midnight. Collins, 1940
  Spies Along the Severn. Collins, 1939
  Step Aside to Death. Collins, 1942
  The White Siren. Collins, 1934 TT
  A Woman of Destiny. Collins, 1933 TT

MADDUX, BERTON J.
  The Veil Withdrawn. Dillingham, 1910

MADELEY, JOAN
  The Shining Head. Hale, 1955

MADISON, RICK
  Hit the Jackpot. Spencer, 1952
  The Lady Gets Wise. Spencer, 1952
  Save Your Tears. Spencer, 1953
  Set Up for Danger. Spencer, 1952
  Star Witness. Spencer, 1953
  Stranger Beware. Spencer, 1952
  Terror Rides the West Wind. Spencer, 1951

MADREYHIJO, L.
  A Phonographic Mystery. Remington, 1890

MADSEN, AXEL. 1930- .
  Borderlines. Macmillan, 1975

MAGARSHACK, DAVID. 1899- . Series character: Supt. Mooney, in all titles.
  Big Ben Strikes Eleven. Constable, 1934
  Death Cuts a Caper. Constable, 1935; Holt, 1935
  Three Dead. Constable, 1937

MAGEE, BRYAN (EDGAR). 1930- .
  To Live in Danger. Hutchinson, 1960

MAGGIO, JOE. 1938- .
  Company Man. Putnam, 1972

MAGGS, DEREK
  Reporting Murder. Fiction House, 1945

MAGILL, MARCUS. Pseudonym of Brian Merrikin Hill, 1896- .
  Death-in-the-Box. Knopf (London), 1929; Lippincott, 1930
  I Like a Good Murder. Knopf (London), 1930; Lippincott, 1930
  Murder in Full Flight. Hutchinson, 1932; Lippincott, 1933
  Murder Out of Tune. Hutchinson, 1931; Lippincott, 1931
  Who Shall Hang? Knopf (London), 1929; Lippincott, 1929

MAGNAY, SIR WILLIAM. 1855-1917.
  -The Amazing Duke. Unwin, 1907
  The Black Lake. Paul, 1915
  The Cloak of Darkness. Ward, 1915
  Count Zarka. Ward, 1903; Page, 1903
  The Duke's Dilemma. Long, 1906
  The Fall of a Star. Macmillan (London), 1897
  -Fauconberg. Ward, 1905
  The Fruit of Indiscretion. Paul, 1913
  The Heiress of the Season. Smith, Elder, 1899; Appleton, 1899
  The Hunt Ball Mystery. Ward, 1918; Brentano's, 1918
  The Long Hand. Paul, 1912
  -The Man of the Hour. Ward, 1902
  The Man-Trap. Smith, Elder, 1900
  The Master Spirit. Ward, 1906; Little, 1906
  The Mystery of the Unicorn. Ward, 1907
  Paul Burdon. Paul, 1912
  The Pitfall. Ward, 1908
  The Players. Hodder, 1913
  -A Poached Peerage. Ward, 1909
  The Powers of Mischief. Ward, 1909
  The Price of Delusion. Paul, 1914
  The Pride of Life. Smith, Elder, 1899
  -A Prince of Lovers. Ward, 1905; Little, 1905
  The Red Chancellor. Ward, 1901; Brentano's, 1901
  The Red Stain. Ward, 1908
  Rogues in Arcady. Ward, 1912

MAGNUS, GEORGE G.
  -Two in the Dark. Ouseley, 1908

MAGOON, CAREY. Joint pseudonym of Elizabeth Carey and Marian Austin Waite Magoon, 1885- .
  I Smell the Devil. Farrar, 1943; Cassell, 1949

MAGOON, MARIAN AUSTIN WAITE. 1885- . Joint pseudonym with Elizabeth Carey: Carey Magoon, q.v.

MAGOWAN, RONALD
  Barracuda. Hale, 1972
  Fox in the Sea. Hale, 1975
  Funeral for a Commissar. Hale, 1970; Roy, 1970
  Monopoly to Murder. Hale, 1968

MAGUIRE, MICHAEL. Series character: Simon Drake in both titles.
  Shot Silk. Wingate, 1975
  Slaughter Horse. Wingate, 1975

MAGUIRE, P. P.
  A Certain Dr. Mellor. Browne & Nolan, 1946

MAHANNAH, FLOYD
  The Broken Angel. Macrae Smith, 1957; Boardman, 1959
  The Broken Body; see The Golden Goose
  The Golden Goose. Duell, 1951; Boardman, 1952. Also published as: The Broken Body. Signet, 1952

The Golden Widow. Macrae Smith, 1956; Boardman, 1957
No Luck for a Lady; see The Yellow Hearse
Stopover for Murder. Macrae Smith, 1953; Boardman, 1954
The Yellow Hearse. Duell, 1950; Boardman, 1951. Also published as: No Luck for a Lady. Signet, 1951

MAHNER-MONS, HANS. Pseudonym: Hans Possendorf, q.v.

MAIBAUM, RICHARD. See: CYRIL HUME, 1900- .

MAINWARING, DANIEL (GEOFFREY HOMES). 1902-1977. Pseudonym: Geoffrey Homes, q.v.
One Against the Earth. Long & Smith, 1933

MAINWARING, MARION
Murder at Midyears. Macmillan, 1953; Gollancz, 1954
Murder in Pastiche. Macmillan, 1954; Gollancz, 1955

MAINWARING, MICHAEL
The Emissary. Allison, 1974

MAIR, ALISTAIR. 1924- .
The Douglas Affair. Heinemann, 1966; Morrow, 1966
Where the East Wind Blows. Heinemann, 1972

MAIR, GEORGE B(ROWN). 1914- . Series character: David Grant = DG.
Black Champagne. Jarrolds, 1968; Berkley, 1969 DG
Crimson Jade. Jarrolds, 1971 DG
The Day Khrushchev Panicked. Cassell, 1961; Random, 1962
Death's Foot Forward. Jarrolds, 1963; Random, 1964 DG
The Girl from Peking. Jarrolds, 1967; Berkley, 1968 DG
Goddesses Never Die. Jarrolds, 1969 DG
The Jade Cat. Pyramid, 1974
Kisses from Satan. Jarrolds, 1966; Berkley, 1968 DG
Live, Love, and Cry. Jarrolds, 1965; Berkley, 1968 DG
Miss Turquoise. Jarrolds, 1964; Random, 1965 DG
Paradise Spells Danger. Jarrolds, 1973 DG
A Wreath of Camellias. Jarrolds, 1970 DG

MAIR, JOHN
Never Come Back. Gollancz, 1941; Little, 1941

MAIS, S(TUART) P(ETRE) B(RODIE). 1885-1975.
Black Spider. Hutchinson, 1941
-Caper Sauce. Hutchinson, 1948
-Colour Blind. Richards, 1920
Come Love, Come Death. Hutchinson, 1951
-Interlude. Chapman, 1917
Men in Blue Glasses. Hutchinson, 1940
-Old King Cole. Cassell, 1938
Quest Sinister. Richards, 1922
-Rebellion. Richards, 1917
The Three-Coloured Pencil. Eyre, 1937
Who Dies? Hutchinson, 1949

MAITLAND, JAMES A.
The Lawyer's Story; or, The Orphan's Wrongs. Pearson, 1853
-Sartoroe: A Tale of Norway. Peterson, 1858

MAITLAND, OSCAR
The Society Detective. Street, 1889

MAKIN, WILLIAM J(AMES). 1894- , Series characters: Det. Insp. Evans, in at least those marked E; Det. Insp. Graves, in at least those marked G.
The Adventure of Red Head of the Red Sea. Jarrolds, 1933. Also published as: Red Head of the Red Sea. Newnes, 1937
The Covent Garden Murder; see Murder at Covent Garden
The Exploits of Jonathan Jow. Pearson, 1936
The Four Brains. Eldon, 1934
Gipsy in Evening Dress. Eldon, 1935 G
Murder at Covent Garden. Jarrolds, 1930. Also published as: The Covent Garden Murder. Newnes, 1938 E
Murder at Full Moon. Eldon, 1937 G
The Price of Exile. First Novel Library, 1922
Queer Mr. Quell. Hodder, 1937; McBride, 1938
Red Head of the Red Sea; see The Adventures of Red Head of the Red Sea
Red Mask. Hamilton, 1935 E
Red Sea Spy. Jarrolds, 1936
Syncopated Love. Jarrolds, 1930

MAKRIS, JOHN N.
Nightshade. Ace, 1953

MALAN, ERNESTINE and ALMA K. LEDIG
Cobwebs and Clues. Dorrance, 1944

MALCOLM, DAVID
A Fiend Incarnate. Tait, 1895
Fifty Thousand Dollars Ransom. Tait, 1896

MALCOLM, JEAN (EILEEN)
Discourse with Shadows. Doubleday, 1958; Gollancz, 1958

MALCOLM, MARGARET. Pseudonym of Edith Lyman Kuether, 1915- .
Headless Beings. Doubleday, 1973

MALCOLM-SMITH, GEORGE. 1901- .
Come Out, Come Out. Doubleday, 1965. British title: Dividend of Death. Hale, 1966
Dividend of Death; see Come Out, Come Out
If a Body Meet a Body. Doubleday, 1959; Hale, 1961
The Lady Finger. Doubleday, 1962
Mugs, Molls and Dr. Harvey; see The Square Peg
The Square Peg. Doubleday, 1952. Also published as: Mugs, Molls and Dr. Harvey. Graphic, 1955
The Trouble with Fidelity. Doubleday, 1957; Hale, 1959

MALIM, BARBARA. Series character: Simon Chard, in at least those marked SC.
By That Sin. Archer, 1935
Death by Misadventure. Murray, 1934; Macmillan, 1934
Missing from Monte Carlo. Walker, 1929
Murder on Holiday. Murray, 1937 SC
Seven Looked On. Butterworth, 1939 SC
"To This End". Walker, 1927

MALINA, FRED
Murder Over Broadway. Phoenix, 1948
Some Like 'Em Shot. Mill, 1949

MALING, ARTHUR (GORDON), 1923- .
Bent Man. Harper, 1975; Prior, 1976
Decoy. Harper, 1969; Joseph, 1971
Dingdong. Harper, 1974

Go-Between. Harper, 1970. British title: Lambert's Son. Joseph, 1972
Lambert's Son; see Go-Between
Loophole. Harper, 1971
The Snowman. Harper, 1973

MALLARY, AMOS
The Eight Penny Spy. Hale, 1971

MALLESON, LUCY BEATRICE. 1899-1973. Pseudonyms: Anthony Gilbert, J. Kilmeny Keith, Anne Meredith, qq.v.

MALLET, JACQUELINE
They Can't Hang Me! Comyns, 1947; Harper, 1974

MALLETT, RICHARD
Watson's Revenge. Aspen, 1974 ss

MALLETTE, GERTRUDE E(THEL). 1887- .
Mystery in Blue. Doubleday, 1945

MALLEY, LOUIS
Horns of the Devil. Appleton, 1951. Also published as: Shadow of the Mafia. Monarch, 1958
Shadow of the Mafia; see Horns of the Devil
Stool Pigeon. Avon, 1953
Tiger in the Streets. Ace, 1957

MALLOCH, PETER. Pseudonym of W(illiam) Murdoch Duncan, 1909-1975, q.v. Other pseudonyms: John Cassells, John Dallas, Neill Graham, Martin Locke, Lovat Marshall, qq.v.
The Adjuster. Long, 1970
Anchor Island. Long, 1962
Backwash. Long, 1969
The Big Killing. Long, 1974
The Big Steal. Long, 1966
Blood Money. Long, 1962
Blood on Pale Fingers. Long, 1969
Break-Through. Long, 1963
Cop-Lover. Long, 1964
Death Whispers Softly. Long, 1968
The Delinquents. Long, 1974
Die, My Beloved. Long, 1967
11.20 Glasgow Central. Rich, 1955
Fly Away Death. Long, 1958
Fugitive's Road. Long, 1963
The Grab. Long, 1970
Hardiman's Landing. Long, 1960
Johnny Blood. Long, 1967
Kickback. Long, 1973
Killer's Blade. Long, 1975
Lady of No Compassion. Long, 1966
Murder of a Student. Long, 1968
Murder of the Man Next Door. Long, 1966
My Shadow. Long, 1959
The Nicholas Snatch. Long, 1964
The Slugger. Long, 1971
The Sniper. Long, 1965
Sweet Lady Death. Rich, 1956
Tread Softly, Death. Rich, 1957
Two with a Gun. Long, 1971
Walk In, Death. Rich, 1957
Write-Off. Long, 1972

MALLORY, ARTHUR. Series character: Dr. Kirke Montgomery = KM.
Apperson's Folly. Chelsea, 1930 KM
The Black Valley Murders. Chelsea, 1930 KM
Doctor Krook. Chelsea, 1929
The Fiery Serpent. Chelsea, 1929
The House of Carson. Chelsea, 1927
Mysteries of Black Valley. Chelsea, 1930 KM

MALLORY, DREW. Pseudonym of Brian (Francis Wynne) Garfield, 1939- , q.v. Other pseudonym: Frank O'Brian, q.v. See also: DONALD E(DWIN) WESTLAKE, 1934- .
 Target Manhattan. Putnam, 1975

MALLORY, ROOSEVELT. Series character: Radcliff, in all titles.
 Double Trouble. Holloway, 1975
 Harlem Hit. Holloway, 1974
 San Francisco Vendetta. Holloway, 1974

MALM, DOROTHEA. 1915- .
 Claire: Memoirs of a Governess. Putnam, 1956; Davies, 1957
 Every Third Thought. Doubleday, 1962; Davies, 1962
 On a Fated Night. Doubleday, 1965; Davies, 1966
 The Paper Mistress. Coward, 1959; Davies, 1960
 To the Castle. Appleton, 1957; Davies, 1955
 The Woman Question. Appleton, 1957; Davies, 1957

MALMAR, McKNIGHT
 Fog is a Shroud. Hurst, 1950
 Never Say Die. Hurst, 1944; Coward, 1943
 The Past Won't Die. Hurst, 1948

MALO, VINCENT GASPARD
 And Why Not? Barker, 1958; Abelard, 1959
 Murder on the Mistral. Barker, 1957; Abelard, 1958

MALONEY, RALPH (LISTON). 1927-1973.
 The Nixon Recession Caper. Norton, 1972

MALOT, HECTOR (HENRI). 1830-1907.
 -Baccarat; or, The Gambler's Career. Fox, 1891
 -Doctor Claude. Vizetelly, 1880. (Translation of Le Docteur Claude. Paris, 1879.)
 -The Woman in the Case. Laird, 1899

MALZBERG, BARRY N. 1939- . Pseudonym: Mike Barry, q.v.

MANCERON, GENEVIEVE
 The Deadlier Sex. Dell, 1961

MANCHESTER, IVY
 Pinecastle. Curtis, 1973

MANCHESTER, WILLIAM (RAYMOND). 1922- .
 Beard the Lion. Mill, 1958; Cassell, 1959. Also published as: Cairo Intrigue. PB, 1959
 Cairo Intrigue; see Beard the Lion
 The City of Anger. Ballantine, 1953
 Shadow of the Monsoon. Doubleday, 1956; Cassell, 1956

MANCINI, ANTHONY
 Minnie Santangelo's Mortal Sin. Coward, 1975

MANDEL, PAUL and SHEILA
 The Black Ship. Popular Library, 1968

MANDEL, SHEILA. See: PAUL MANDEL.

MANDEVILLE, D. E.
 Hot Line—Capricorn. Hale, 1972

MANER, WILLIAM
 Die of a Rose. Doubleday, 1970
 The Image Killer. Doubleday, 1968; Hale, 1970
 There Goes the Bride. Hale, 1973

MANGAT RAI, EDWARD NIRMAL
 The Lairu Murders. Hind Pocket Books, 1973

MANGIONE, JERRE (GERLANDO). 1909- .
 Night Search. Crown, 1965. British title: To Walk the Night. Muller, 1967

MANKIEWICZ, DON M(ARTIN). 1922- .
 It Only Hurts a Minute. Putnam, 1966; Deutsch, 1968
 See How They Run. Knopf, 1951
 Trial. Harper, 1955; Deutsch, 1955

MANLY, A(NGIE) S(TEWART)
 Secrets of a Dark Plot in New York Society. Rhodes, 1893. Also published as: Kidnapped; or, Secrets of a Great Mystery. Rhodes, 1899

MANLY, MARLINE. Pseudonym of St. George (Henry) Rathborne, 1854-1938, q.v. Other pseudonym: Doctor Mark Merrick, q.v.
 Old Specie, the Treasury Detective; or, The Harbor Lights of New York. Street (Magnet), 189?
 The Poker King; or, A Cool Million at Stake. Street, 1890
 Rube Burrows League; or, The Swamp Angels of Alabama. Street, 1891
 The Vestibule Limited Mystery. Street (Magnet), 189?

MANN, ABBY
 Kojak. PB, 1974. (Novelization of the TV series.)

MANN, ABEL. Pseudonym of John Creasey, 1908-1973, q.v. Other pseudonyms: Gordon Ashe, M. E. Cooke, Norman Deane, Robert Caine Frazer, Patrick Gill, Michael Halliday, Charles Hogarth, Brian Hope, Colin Hughes, Kyle Hunt, Peter Manton, J. J. Marric, Richard Martin, Rodney Mattheson, Anthony Morton, Jeremy York, qq.v.
 Danger Woman. PB, 1966

MANN, (FRANCIS) ANTHONY. 1914- .
 Tiara. Bodley Head, 1973

MANN, E(RNEST) L.
 The Chislehurst Mystery. Eyre, 1938

MANN, EDWARD ANDREW
 The Portals. Simon, 1974

MANN, JACK. Pseudonym of E(velyn) Charles (H.) Vivian, 1882-1947, q.v. Other pseudonym: Charles Cannell, q.v. Series characters: Rex Coulson = RC; Gregory George Gordon Green = Gs.
 Coulson Alone. Wright, 1936 RC
 Coulson Goes South. Wright, 1933 RC
 The Dead Man's Chest. Wright, 1934; Godwin, 1935 RC
 Detective Coulson. Wright, 1936 RC
 Egyptian Nights. Wright, 1934 RC
 Gees' First Case. Wright, 1936; Bookfinger, 1970 Gs
 The Glass Too Many. Wright, 1940; Bookfinger, 1973 Gs
 Grey Shapes. Wright, 1937; Bookfinger, 1970 Gs
 Her Ways are Death. Wright, 1939 Gs
 The Kleinert Case. Wright, 1938 Gs
 Maker of Shadows. Wright, 1938 Gs
 Nightmare Farm. Wright, 1937; Bookfinger, 1975 Gs
 The Ninth Life. Wright, 1939; Bookfinger, 1970 Gs

 Reckless Coulson. Wright, 1933 RC

MANN, JESSICA
 Captive Audience. Macmillan (London), 1975; McKay, 1975
 A Charitable End. Collins, 1971; McKay, 1971
 Mrs. Knox's Profession. Macmillan (London), 1972; McKay, 1972
 The Only Security. Macmillan (London), 1973. U.S. title: Troublecross. McKay, 1973
 The Sticking Place. Macmillan (London), 1974; McKay, 1974
 Troublecross; see The Only Security

MANN, JOSEPHINE
 A Place with Two Faces. PB, 1974

MANN, LEONARD. 1895- .
 A Murder in Sydney. Cape, 1937; Doubleday, 1937

MANN, PATRICK. Pseudonym of Leslie Waller, 1923- , q.v. Other pseudonym: C. S. Cody, q.v.
 Dog Day Afternoon. Delacorte, 1973; Hart-Davis, 1975
 -The Vacancy. Putnam, 1973; Hart-Davis, 1975

MANN, RODERICK
 Nothing to Declare. Jenkins, 1957

MANNERS, ALEXANDRA. Pseudonym of Anne Rundle, q.v. Other pseudonym: Joanne Marshall, q.v.
 Candles in the Wood. Millington, 1975; Putnam, 1974
 The Singing Swans. Putnam, 1975
 The Stone Maiden. Millington, 1974; Putnam, 1973

MANNERS, DAVID X. 1912- .
 Dead to the World. McKay, 1947
 Memory of a Scream. Mystery House, 1946

MANNERS, GORDON
 Murders at the Crab Apple Cafe. Jenkins, 1933

MANNIN, ETHEL (EDITH). 1900- .
 Mission to Beirut. Hutchinson, 1973

MANNING, ADELAIDE FRANCES OKE. 1891-1959. Joint pseudonyms with Cyril Henry Coles, 1898-1965: Manning Coles, Francis Gaite, qq.v.

MANNING, ARTHUR
 -The Short Madness. Hale, 1960
 Tainted Money. Hale, 1963
 -We Never Die in the Winter. Jenkins, 1958

MANNING, BRUCE. See: GWEN BRISTOW, 1903- .

MANNING, HILDA. Pseudonym of James Reach, 1909?-1970, q.v. Other pseudonym: John Rand, q.v. Joint pseudonym with Tom Taggart: Ross MacRoss, q.v.
 Dangerous Ladies. French, 1942. (3-act play.)
 Detective in Spite of Himself. French, 1950. (3-act play.)

MANNING, JAMES C.
 Blue Invective. Bobbs, 1973

MANNINGHAM, BASIL. Pseudonym of B(asil) H(enry) Homersham, 1902- , q.v.
 Motive for Murder. Hale, 1939

MANNON, M. M. Joint pseudonym of Martha Mannon and Mary Ellen Mannon. Series character: Sheriff George White, in at least those marked GW.

The Corpse in the Elevator. Arcadia, 1956
Here Lies Blood. Bobbs, 1942 GW
Murder on the Program. Bobbs, 1944 GW

MANNON, MARTHA. Joint pseudonym with Mary Ellen Mannon: M. M. Mannon, q.v.

MANNON, MARY ELLEN. Joint pseudonym with Martha Mannon: M. M. Mannon, q.v.

MANOR, JASON. Pseudonym of Oakley M(axwell) Hall, 1920- , q.v. Series character: Steve Summers = SS.
The Girl in the Red Jaguar; see The Red Jaguar
No Halo for Me; see The Pawns of Fear
The Pawns of Fear. Viking, 1955; Secker, 1955. Also published as: No Halo for Me. Popular Library, 1956 SS
The Red Jaguar. Viking, 1955; Secker, 1955. Also published as: The Girl in the Red Jaguar. Popular Library, 1955 SS
Too Dead to Run. Viking, 1953; Secker, 1954
The Tramplers. Viking, 1956; Secker, 1956

MANOUSSI, JEAN. See: LOUISE JORDAN MILN, 1864-1933.

MANS, ADRIENNE. Pseudonym of Anneke Luders-Knegtmans.
On the Shores of Night. Walker, 1967; Harrap, 1968. (Translation of An den Ufern der Nacht.)

MANSFIELD, PAUL H. 1922- .
Final Exposure. Collins, 1957; Macmillan, 1958

MANSON, WILL. Series character: Black, in at least those marked B.
The Chinese Conundrum. Caravelle, 1967 B
The Dangerous One. Caravelle, 1968 B
The Deadly Game. Caravelle, 1967
The Duke. Caravelle, 1968
The Mathematician. Caravelle, 1967
A Man Called Black. Caravelle, 1967 B
A Talent for Violence. Tower, 1970
A Very Black Deed. Caravelle, 1968 B

MANTINBAND, JAMES M. Pseudonym: Oliver Keystone, q.v.

MANTLE, BEATRICE
In the House of Another. Century, 1920

MANTON, PETER. Pseudonym of John Creasey, 1908-1973, q.v. Other pseudonyms: Gordon Ashe, M. E. Cooke, Norman Deane, Robert Caine Frazer, Patrick Gill, Michael Halliday, Charles Hogarth, Brian Hope, Colin Hughes, Kyle Hunt, Abel Mann, J. J. Marric, Richard Martin, Rodney Mattheson, Anthony Morton, Jeremy York, qq.v.
The Charity Murders. Wright, 1954
The Circle of Justice. Wright, 1938
The Crime Syndicate. Wright, 1939
The Crooked Killer. Wright, 1954
Death Looks On. Wright, 1939
The Greyvale School Mystery. Low, 1937
The Midget Marvel. Mellifont, 1940
Murder in the Highlands. Wright, 1939
Murder Manor. Wright, 1937
No Escape from Murder. Wright, 1952
Policeman's Triumph. Wright, 1948
Stand By for Danger. Wright, 1937
Thief in the Night. Wright, 1950
Three Days Terror. Wright, 1938

MANTZ, LEW
Hijacker's Morgue. Hamilton Stafford, 1952
The Snatch. Hamilton Stafford, 1952
Trapped. Hamilton Stafford, 1952

MANVELL, (ARNOLD) ROGER. 1909- .
The Dreamers. Gollancz, 1958; Simon, 1958
The Passion. Heinemann, 1960

MAPPLE, NELSON
-Bye-Bye, Blackbeard! Hurst, 1937
-The Haunted Suit. Hurst, 1939
High Explosive. Hurst, 1938
-Midsummer Mischief. Hurst, 1937

MARA, BERNARD
A Bullet for my Lady. GM, 1955; Fawcett (London), 1956
French for Murder. GM, 1954
This Gun for Gloria. GM, 1956

MARAIS, MARC
Duel for a Dark Lady. New English Library pb, 1975

MARASCO, ROBERT
Burnt Offerings. Delacorte, 1973; Hodder, 1973

MARBLE, DANA
Sail into Silence. Mystery House, 1958

MARBLE, M(ARGARET) S(HARP). 1913- .
Die by Night. Rinehart, 1947; Barker, 1948
Everybody Makes Mistakes. Rinehart, 1946; Barker, 1947
The Lady Forgot. Harper, 1947

MARCH, JERMYN. Pseudonym of Dorothy Anna Webb.
The Dago. Hurst, 1928. U.S. title: The Scarlet Thumb. Henkle, 1929
Dear Traitor. Hurst, 1925
The Man Behind the Face. Hurst, 1927
Rust of Murder. Hurst, 1924; Watt, 1925
The Scarlet Thumb; see The Dago

MARCH, LINDSAY
These Cliffs are Dangerous. Simon, 1973; H. Hamilton, 1973

MARCH, MAXWELL
The Man of Dangerous Secrets; see Other Man's Danger
Other Man's Danger. Collins, 1933. U.S. title: The Man of Dangerous Secrets. Doubleday, 1933
Rogue's Holiday. Collins, 1935; Doubleday, 1935
The Shadow in the House. Collins, 1936; Doubleday, 1936

MARCH, WILLIAM. Pseudonym of William Edward March Campbell, 1894-1954.
The Bad Seed. Rinehart, 1954; H. Hamilton, 1954

MARCHANT, BESSIE. 1862-1941.
-A Dangerous Mission. Blackie, 1918
-From the Scourge of the Tongue. Melrose, 1901
-The Gold-Marked Charm. Blackie, 1918
-Joyce Harrington's Trust. Blackie, 1916
-A Mysterious Inheritance. Blackie, 1915
-The Mystery of the Silver Run. Wells Gardner, 1907
-The Secret of the Everglades. Blackie, 1902; Mershon, 1915

MARCHANT, CATHERINE. Pseudonym of Catherine (Ann McMullen) Cookson, 1906- , q.v.

The Fen Tiger. Macdonald, 1963. U.S. title: The House on the Fens. Lancer, 1965
Heritage of Folly. Macdonald, 1962; Lancer, 1965
House of Men. Macdonald, 1963; Lancer, 1965
The House on the Fens; see The Fen Tiger
-Miss Martha Mary Crawford. Heinemann, 1975; Morrow, 1976

MARCHETTI, VICTOR
The Rope-Dancer. Grosset, 1971; Allen, 1972

MARCHMONT, ARTHUR W(ILLIAM). 1852-1923.
-At the Call of Honour. Cassell, 1910
-Because of Misella. Cassell, 1916
By Hand Unseen. Ward, 1922
-By Right of Sword. Hutchinson, 1897; Grosset, 1897
-By Snare of Love. Ward, 1904; Stokes, 1903
By Wit of Woman. Ward, 1906; Stokes, 1906
The Case of Lady Broadstone. Hodder, 1910; Empire Book Co., 1908
-A Courier of Fortune. Ward, 1905; Stokes, 1904
-A Dash for a Throne. Hutchinson, 1899; New Amsterdam, 1899
Dorothy Marlow; or, A Heritage of Peril. Rand, 1900. Also published as: The Heritage of Peril. New Amsterdam, 1901. (British title?)
The Eagrave Square Mystery. Hodder, 1912
-Elfa. Hodder, 1911
Face to Face with Death. Ogilvie, 1905. (British title?)
-The Faith-Healer. Hurst, 1924
-For Love or Crown. Hutchinson, 1901; Stokes, 1901
-The Greatest Gift. Hutchinson, 1899; Buckles, 1900
-The Heir to the Throne. Ward, 1914
-Her Sentinel. Cassell, 1916
The Heritage of Peril; see Dorothy Marlow; or, A Heritage of Peril
-"His Majesty." Skeffington, 1920
-An Imperial Marriage. Ward, 1909; Dodge, 1909
In the Cause of Freedom. Ward, 1907; Stokes, 1907
-In the Name of a Woman. Longmans, 1901; Stokes, 1900
-In the Name of the People. Ward, 1911
-Isa. London Daily Mail, 1911
-The Lady Passenger. Hodder, 1915
The Little Anarchist. Ward, 1907
Madeline Power. Oliphant Anderson, 1891
The Man Who was Dead. Cassell, 1907; Stokes, 1908
A Man Without a Memory. Ward, 1919
-A Millionaire Girl. Cassell, 1908
A Millionaire Mystery. Ward, 1924
Miser Hoadley's Secret. Methuen, 1904; New Amsterdam, 1902
A Moment's Error; or, The Mystery of Mortimer Strange. Methuen, 1904; Rand, 1898. Also published as: The Mystery of Mortimer Strange; or, A Moment's Error. Rand, 1907
-My Lady of the Yellow Domino. Hodder, 1914
My Lost Self. Cassell, 1908; Cupples, 1908
The Mystery of Mortimer Strange; see A Moment's Error; or, The Mystery of Mortimer Strange
The Old Mill Mystery. Taylor, 1892. (British title?)
Parson Thring's Secret. London Daily Mail, 1910; Cassell (New York), 1895
-The Price of Freedom; or, In the Grip of Hate. New Amsterdam, 1903. (British title?)

Prince Punnie. Ward, 1923
-The Queen's Advocate. Ward, 1904; Stokes, 1904
-The Ruby Heart of Kishgar. Hodder, 1912
-Sarita, the Carlist. Hutchinson, 1902; Stokes, 1902
Sir Gregory's Silence. Cassell, 1909
-Sir Jaffray's Wife. Warne, 1895; Rand, 1898
A Tight Corner. Cassell, 1915
-Under the Black Eagle. Ward, 1913
-The Unguarded Hour. Cassell, 1918
-When I was Czar. Ward, 1903; Stokes, 1903
-When Love Called. Hodder, 1913
-When the Empire Crashed. Ward, 1920
-Who? London Daily Mail, 1911

MARCIN, MAX. 1879-1948.
Are You My Wife? Moffat, 1910. British title: The Wife He Never Saw. Nash, 1911
-Cheating Cheaters. French, 1932. (4-act play.)
-The Nightcap, with Guy Bolton, 1884-   . French, 1929. (3-act play.)
-The Substitute Prisoner. Moffat, 1911
The Wife He Never Saw; see Are You My Wife?

MARCOTT, JAMES. Pseudonym of Duane R. Schermerhorn.
Hard to Kill. GM, 1975

MARCUS, A(RTHUR) A. Series character: Pete Hunter = PH.
Make Way for Murder. Graphic, 1955
Post-Mark Homicide; see The Widow Gay
Walk the Bloody Boulevard. Graphic, 1951 PH
The Widow Gay. McKay, 1948. Also published as: Post-Mark Homicide. Graphic, 1953 PH

MARCUS, CARL
Mark Castle—Cable Address: Roma. Publishers Export Co., 1966

MARDER, IRVING
The Paris Bit. Collins, 1967; Dodd, 1968

MAREAN, BEATRICE
The Tragedies of Oak Hurst. Donohue, 1891

MARFIELD, DWIGHT. Series characters: Gail McGurk = GM; Dudley Brent = DB; Major Krim = K; Inspector Skane = S.
The Ghost on the Balcony. Dutton, 1939 K
The Man with a Paper Skull. Dutton, 1932 S, GM and DB
The Mandarin's Sapphire. Dutton, 1938 S
Mystery of King Cobra. Dutton, 1933 DB, S & K
Mystery of the East Wind. Dutton, 1930 DB, GM & S
The Sword in the Pool. Dutton, 1932 DB, GM & S

MARIE, JEANNE. Pseudonym of Marie Beatrice Wilson, 1922-   .
Arrow of Terror. Lenox Hill, 1973; Remploy, 1974
Black for a Bride. Lenox Hill, 1973; Remploy, 1974
Wait for Me, Wendy. Lenox Hill, 1974; Remploy, 1974

MARIN, A. C. Pseudonym of Alfred Coppel, 1921-   , q.v.
The Clash of Distant Thunder. Harcourt, 1968; Heinemann, 1969
Rise with the Wind. Harcourt, 1969; Heinemann, 1969

A Storm of Spears. Harcourt, 1971; Hale, 1973

MARIN, MUNA LEE DE MUNOZ. Joint pseudonym with Maurice C. Guiness: Newton Gayle, q.v.

MARINER, DAVID. Pseudonym of David MacLeod Smith, 1920-   .
The Beaufort Dossier. Hale, 1973; Zebra, 1974
The Chatham Rats. Hale, 1969. U.S. title: Operation Scorpio. Pinnacle, 1975
Countdown 1000; see A Shackleton Called Sheila
Devil's Bread. Hale, 1969. U.S. title: The Yaroslav Incident. Zebra, 1974
The Last Bridge; see A White Lie and No Glory
Operation Scorpio; see The Chatham Rats
A Shackleton Called Sheila. Hale, 1970. U.S. title: Countdown 1000. Pinnacle, 1974
Symbol of Vengeance. Hale, 1975
A White Lie and No Glory. Hale, 1971. U.S. title: The Last Bridge. Pinnacle, 1974
The Yaroslav Incident; see Devil's Bread

MARINER-SCARRITT, ELIZABETH
Quid Est. Abbey, 1902

MARINO, NICK. Pseudonym of Will(iam Charles) Oursler, 1913-   , q.v. Joint pseudonym with Margaret Scott: Gale Gallagher, q.v. Series character: Mike Macauley, in both titles.
City Limits. Pyramid, 1958; Digit, 1958. (Written by Richard Deming, 1915-   , q.v., from an outline by Oursler.)
One Way Street. Holt, 1952

MARIO, QUEENA. 1896-1951.
Death Drops Delilah. Dutton, 1944
Murder in the Opera House. Dutton, 1934
Murder Meets Mephisto. Dutton, 1942

MARION, ELIZABETH. 1916-   .
The Keys to the House. Crowell, 1944; Hale, 1948

MARION, FRANCES. 1886-1973.
The Secret Six. Grosset, 1931. (Novelization of the movie.)

MARK, GEOFFREY
The Veils of Fear. Long, 1960

MARKHAM, ROBERT. Pseudonym of Kingsley (William) Amis, 1922-   , q.v. Series character: James Bond (continuation of the character created by Ian Fleming, 1908-1964, q.v.) = JB.
Colonel Sun. Cape, 1968; Harper, 1968 JB

MARKHAM, VIRGIL. 1899-   .
The Black Door; see Shock!
The Dead are Prowling. Collins, 1934
The Deadly Jest. Collins, 1935
Death in the Dusk. Knopf (London & New York), 1928
The Devil Drives. Collins, 1932; Knopf, 1932
Inspector Rusby's Finale. Collins, 1933; Farrar, 1933
Red Warning; see Song of Doom
Shock! Collins, 1930. U.S. title: The Black Door. Knopf, 1930

Snatch. Collins, 1936
Song of Doom. Collins, 1932. U.S. title: Red Warning. Farrar, 1933

MARKO, ZEKIAL
Scratch a Thief. GM, 1961. Also published as: Once a Thief. GM, 1965

MARKS, PERCY. 1891-   .
Knave of Diamonds. Reynal, 1943

MARKS, PETER
Collector's Choice. Random, 1972

MARKSMAN, H. CARSON
The Lust of Treasure. Allan, 1934

MARKSON, DAVID (MERRILL). 1927-   . Series character: Harry Fannin, in all titles.
Epitaph for a Dead Beat. Dell, 1961
Epitaph for a Tramp. Dell, 1959. Also published as: Fannin. Belmont, 1971
Fannin; see Epitaph for a Tramp
Miss Doll, Go Home. Dell, 1965

MARKSTEIN, GEORGE
The Cooler. Souvenir, 1974; Doubleday, 1974

MARLE, T. B. Pseudonym of Hubert Steel Lambert, 1899-   .
-Candid Escort. Barker, 1936
Cleopatra's Nose. Barker, 1937
-The Croatian. Shirt, 1936
-It Happened in Vienna. Butterworth, 1934

MARLETT, MELBA. 1909-   . Series character: Sarah O'Brien = SO.
Another Day Toward Dying. Doubleday, 1943 SO
Death has a Thousand Doors. Doubleday, 1941 SO
Death is in the Garden. Doubleday, 1951
The Devil Builds a Chapel. Doubleday, 1942
Escape While I Can. Doubleday, 1944
The Frightened Ones. Doubleday, 1956 ss
Tomorrow will be Monday. Doubleday, 1946
Witness in Peril. Cherry Tree, 1948. (U.S. title?)

MARLOW, EDWINA
Danger at Dahlkari. Putnam, 1975
Falconridge. Ace, 1969
The Lady at Lyon House. Ace, 1970
The Master of Phoenix Hall. Ace, 1968
Midnight at Mallyncourt. Berkley/Putnam, 1975
When Emmalyn Remembers. Ace, 1970

MARLOW, SIDNEY. Pseudonym of Paschal Heston Coggins, 1852-1917.
-Harry Ambler; or, The Stolen Deed. Penn, 1890. Also published as: Harry Ambler and How He Saved the Homestead. Penn, 1893
Harry Ambler and How He Saved the Homestead; see Harry Ambler
-The Moncasket Mystery and How Tom Hardy Solved It. Penn, 1912

MARLOWE, CHARLES. Pseudonym of Harriett Jay, 1857-1932. See: ROBERT (WILLIAM) BUCHANAN, 1841-1901.

MARLOWE, DAN J(AMES). 1914-   . Series characters: Earl Drake = ED; Johnny Killain = JK.
Backfire. Berkley, 1961
Death Deep Down. GM, 1965
Doom Service. Avon, 1960 JK
Doorway to Death. Avon, 1959; Digit, 1959 JK

The Fatal Frails. Avon, 1960 JK
Flashpoint. GM, 1970. Also published as: Operation Flashpoint. GM, 1972; Coronet, 1972 ED
Four for the Money. GM, 1966
Killer with a Key. Avon, 1959 JK
The Name of the Game is Death. GM, 1962; Muller pb, 1963. Also published as: Operation Overkill. Coronet, 1973 ED
Never Live Twice. GM, 1964
One Endless Hour. GM, 1969; Gold Lion, 1973. Also published as: Operation Endless Hour. Coronet, 1975 ED
Operation Breakthrough. GM, 1971; Coronet, 1972 ED
Operation Checkmate. GM, 1972; Coronet, 1973 ED
Operation Deathmaker. GM, 1975; Coronet, 1977 ED
Operation Drumfire. GM, 1972; Coronet, 1972 ED
Operation Endless Hour; see One Endless Hour
Operation Fireball. GM, 1969; Coronet, 1972 ED
Operation Flashpoint; see Flashpoint
Operation Hammerlock. GM, 1974; Coronet, 1975 ED
Operation Overkill; see The Name of the Game is Death
Operation Stranglehold. GM, 1973; Coronet, 1974 ED
Operation Whiplash. GM, 1973; Coronet, 1974 ED
The Raven is a Blood Red Bird, with William Odell. GM, 1967
Route of the Red Gold. GM, 1967
Shake a Crooked Town. Avon, 1961 JK
Strongarm. GM, 1963
The Vengeance Man. GM, 1966

MARLOWE, DEREK. 1938- .
A Dandy in Aspic. Gollancz, 1966; Putnam, 1966. (U.S. and British texts differ considerably.)
The Disappearance; see Echoes of Celandine
Do You Remember England? Cape, 1972; Viking, 1972
Echoes of Celandine. Cape, 1970; Viking, 1970. Also published as: The Disappearance. Penguin, 1977
Nightshade. Cape, 1975; Viking, 1976
Somebody's Sister. Cape, 1974; Viking, 1974

MARLOWE, FRANCIS. Series character: "Doc" Summers, in at least those marked DS.
Adventure Mysterious. Gray, 1934
-The Brig Jane May. Jarrolds, 1911
The Crime of Philip Garrison. Gray, 1935 DS
Crooked Business. Gramol, 1933
Crooked Company. Gramol, 1933
The Hatton Garden Mystery. Gray, 1934 DS
In Pursuit of a Million. Gray, 1936 DS
The Man Who Lost an Hour. Aldine, 1926
The Secret of the Sandhills. Low, 1907
Seven Red-Headed Men. Gramol, 1934
The Son-in-Law Syndicate. Gramol, 1934
-The Sunset Express. Nelson, 1925

MARLOWE, GREG. Series character: Greg Marlowe, in all titles.
Behind the Enemy. Hamilton Stafford, 1952
Burma Battle. Hamilton Stafford, 1953
Death-Mask of War. Hamilton Stafford, 1952
Espionage! Hamilton Stafford, 1953

MARLOWE, HUGH. Pseudonym of Henry Patterson, 1929- . Other pseudonyms: Martin Fallon, James Graham, Jack Higgins, Harry Patterson, qq.v.
A Candle for the Dead. Abelard (London & New York), 1966. Also published as: The Violent Enemy, as by Jack Higgins. Hodder pb, 1969
Passage by Night. Abelard (London & New York), 1964. Reprinted as by Jack Higgins: GM, 1977
Seven Pillars to Hell. Abelard (London & New York), 1963
The Violent Enemy (as by Jack Higgins); see A Candle for the Dead

MARLOWE, PIERS. Series characters: Supt. Frank Drury and Insp. Bill Hazard, in at least those marked D&H.
Cash My Chips, Croupier. Hale, 1969
The Dead Don't Scare. Gifford, 1963 D&H
Demon in the Blood. Paul, 1955
The Double Thirteen. Low, 1947
Hire Me a Hearse. Hale, 1968 D&H
Killer in the Shade. Hale, 1973
A Knife for Your Heart. Gifford, 1966 D&H
Loaded Dice. Low, 1949
The Men in her Death. Gifford, 1964 D&H
Promise to Kill. Gifford, 1965 D&H

MARLOWE, R.
All or Nothing. Spencer, 1953
Big Time Girl. Spencer, 1952
Bullets Speak Louder. Spencer, 1950
Homicide Dragnet. Spencer, 1952
Identity Unknown. Spencer, 1952
Perilous Assignment. Spencer, 1952
Vengeance is Mine. Spencer, 1953

MARLOWE, STEPHEN. Pseudonym of Milton Lesser, 1928- . Other pseudonyms: Andrew Frazer, Jason Ridgway, C. H. Thames, qq.v. See also: RICHARD S(COTT) PRATHER, 1921- . Series character: Chester Drum = CD.
Blonde Bait. Avon, 1959
Catch the Brass Ring. Ace, 1954
The Cawthorn Journals. Prentice-Hall, 1975; Allen, 1976. Also published as: Too Many Chiefs. New English Library pb, 1977
Come Over, Red Rover. Macmillan, 1968
Danger is my Line. GM, 1960; Muller pb, 1961 CD
Dead on Arrival. Ace, 1956
Death is my Comrade. GM, 1960; Muller pb, 1961 CD
Drum Beat—Berlin. GM, 1964 CD
Drum Beat—Dominique. GM, 1965 CD
Drum Beat—Erica. GM, 1967 CD
Drum Beat—Madrid. GM, 1966 CD
Drum Beat—Marianne. GM, 1968 CD
Francesca. GM, 1963; Muller pb, 1963 CD
Homicide is my Game. GM, 1959; Muller pb, 1962 CD
Jeopardy is my Job. GM, 1962; Muller pb, 1963 CD
Killers are my Meat. GM, 1957; Fawcett (London), 1958 CD
The Man with No Shadow. Prentice-Hall, 1974; Allen, 1974
Manhunt is my Mission. GM, 1961; Muller pb, 1962 CD
Mecca for Murder. GM, 1956; Fawcett (London), 1957 CD
Model for Murder. Graphic, 1955
Murder is my Dish. GM, 1957 CD
Passport to Peril. Crest, 1959
Peril is my Pay. GM, 1960; Muller pb, 1961 CD
The Search for Bruno Heidler. Macmillan, 1966; Boardman, 1967
The Second Longest Night. GM, 1955; Fawcett (London), 1958 CD
The Summit. Geis, 1970
Terror is my Trade. GM, 1958; Muller pb, 1960 CD
Too Many Chiefs; see The Cawthorn Journals
Trouble is my Name. GM, 1957; Fawcett (London), 1958 CD
Turn Left for Murder. Ace, 1955
Violence is my Business. GM, 1958; Fawcett (London), 1959 CD

MARNAN, BASIL
-A Daughter of the Veldt. Heinemann, 1901; Holt, 1901
A Fair Freebooter. Cassell, 1902
-The Resident Magistrate. Hurst, 1902

MARQUAND, JOHN P(HILLIPS). 1893-1960. Series character: Mr. Moto = M.
Don't Ask Questions. Hale, 1941
It's Loaded, Mr. Bauer. Hale, 1949
Last Laugh, Mr. Moto. Little, 1942; Hale, 1943 M
The Last of Mr. Moto; see Stopover: Tokyo
-Ming Yellow. Little, 1935; Dickson, 1935
Mr. Moto is So Sorry. Little, 1938; Hale, 1939 M
Mr. Moto Takes a Hand; see No Hero
No Hero. Little, 1935. British title: Mr. Moto Takes a Hand. Hale, 1940. Also published as: Your Turn, Mr. Moto. Berkley, 1963 M
Right You Are, Mr. Moto; see Stopover: Tokyo
Stopover: Tokyo. Little, 1957; Collins, 1957. Also published as: The Last of Mr. Moto. Berkley, 1963. And as: Right You Are, Mr. Moto. Popular Library, 1977 M
Thank You, Mr. Moto. Little, 1936; Jenkins, 1937 M
Think Fast, Mr. Moto. Little, 1937; Hale, 1938 M
Your Turn, Mr. Moto; see No Hero

MARQUIS, DON(ALD R. P.). 1878-1937.
The Cruise of the Jasper B. Appleton (New York & London), 1916

MARR, R.
Death at Salterton Court. Everybody's, 1945

MARR, RICHARD. Pseudonym: "Burmar," q.v.

MARRIC, J. J. Pseudonym of John Creasey, 1908-1973. Other pseudonyms: Gordon Ashe, M. E. Cooke, Norman Deane, Robert Caine Frazer, Patrick Gill, Michael Halliday, Charles Hogarth, Brian Hope, Colin Hughes, Kyle Hunt, Abel Mann, Peter Manton, Richard Martin, Rodney Mattheson, Anthony Morton, Jeremy York, qq.v. Series character: Commander George Gideon, in all titles.
Gideon of Scotland Yard; see Gideon's Day
Gideon's Art. Hodder, 1971; Harper, 1971
Gideon's Badge. Hodder, 1966; Harper, 1965
Gideon's Day. Hodder, 1955; Harper, 1955. Also published as: Gideon of Scotland Yard. Berkley, 1958
Gideon's Fear. Evans, 1966. (Play based on Gideon's Week, q.v.)
Gideon's Fire. Hodder, 1961; Harper, 1961
Gideon's Fog. Hodder, 1975; Harper, 1975
Gideon's Lot. Hodder, 1965; Harper, 1964
Gideon's March. Hodder, 1962; Harper, 1962
Gideon's Men. Hodder, 1972; Harper, 1972
Gideon's Month. Hodder, 1958; Harper, 1958

Gideon's Night. Hodder, 1957; Harper, 1957
Gideon's Power. Hodder, 1969; Harper, 1969
Gideon's Press. Hodder, 1973; Harper, 1973
Gideon's Ride. Hodder, 1963; Harper, 1963
Gideon's Risk. Hodder, 1960; Harper, 1960
Gideon's River. Hodder, 1968; Harper, 1968
Gideon's Sport. Hodder, 1970; Harper, 1970
Gideon's Staff. Hodder, 1959; Harper, 1959
Gideon's Vote. Hodder, 1964; Harper, 1964
Gideon's Week. Hodder, 1956; Harper, 1956. Also published as: Seven Days to Death. Pyramid, 1958
Gideon's Wrath. Hodder, 1967; Harper, 1967
Seven Days to Death; see Gideon's Week

MARRINER, BRIAN
A Splinter of Ice. Hale, 1975

MARRIOTT, CRITTENDEN. 1867-1932.
Via Berlin. Shores, 1917

MARRIOTT, JAMES WILLIAM. 1884-
Pseudonym: Roger Wray, q.v.

MARRIOTT, TAM. See: ADELE BLOOD.

MARRIOTT-WATSON, H(ENRY) B(RERETON).
See: H(ENRY) B(RERETON) MARRIOTT WATSON, 1863-1921.

MARRYAT, FLORENCE. Pseudonym of Mrs. Florence Marryat Church Lean, 1837-1899.
Blindfold. White, 1890; Lovell, 1890
-The Blood of the Vampire. Hutchinson, 1897
-Driven to Bay. White, 1887; Munro, 1887
-A Fatal Silence. Farran, 1891; Hovenden, 1891
The Hampstead Mystery. White, 1894
-In the Name of Liberty. Digby, 1897
-Iris the Avenger. Hutchinson, 1899
-The Lost Diamonds, with Charles Ogilvie. Ludgate Monthly, 1891
On Circumstantial Evidence. White, 1889; Lovell, 1889
-The Poison of Asps. Appleton, 1871. (British title?)
-The Root of All Evil. Tinsley, 1880; Munro, 1891
-A Scarlet Sin. Blackett, 1890; Lovell, 1890

MARS, ALASTAIR. 1915-
Arctic Submarine. Elek, 1955
Atomic Submarine. Elek, 1957. U.S. title: Fire in Anger. Mill, 1958
Fire in Anger; see Atomic Submarine
Submarine at Bay. Elek, 1956

MARSDEN, ANTONY. Pseudonym of Graham Sutton. Series characters: Inspector Buck, in at least those marked B; Jim Beverley, in at least those marked JB.
Death on the Downs. Jarrolds, 1929 B
Death Strikes from the Rear. Low, 1934 B
The Man in the Sandhills. Jarrolds, 1927; Boni, 1927 JB
The Mercenary. Jarrolds, 1931
The Moonstone Mystery. Jarrolds, 1928 JB
The Mycroft Murder Case. Low, 1935
Salter's Folly. Jarrolds, 1927
The Six-Hour Mystery. Jarrolds, 1929
Swooning Venus. Low, 1932
Thieves' Justice. Jarrolds, 1929

MARSDEN, JOHN PENNINGTON
Job Lot Sketches and Stories. Hallowell, 1892 ss, one criminous

MARSH, ANNE
Room 12a. Pearson, 1939

MARSH, CHARLES L(EONARD). 1854?-1930.
A Gentleman Juror. Rand, 1899

MARSH, JAMES J.
The Peking Switch. McKay, 1972

MARSH, JEAN. Pseudonym of Evelyn Marshall, 1897- .
Death Among the Stars. Long, 1955
Death at Peak Hour. Long, 1957
Death Stalks the Bride. Long, 1943
Death Visits the Circus. Long, 1953
Identity Unwanted. Long, 1951
Murder Next Door. Long, 1933
The Pattern is Murder. Long, 1953
The Shore House Mystery. Hamilton, 1929

MARSH, JOHN. 1907- . Joint pseudonym with Florence Shepherd: Harrington Hastings, q.v. Series character: Ray Felton, in at least those marked RF.
-Body Made Alive: A Study in the Macabre. Stanley Smith, 1936
The Brain of Paul Menoloff. Robertson, 1953
By the World Condemned. Amalgamated, 1949
City of Fear. Gifford, 1958 RF
The Cruise of the Carefree. Ward, 1955
Girl in a Net. Hale, 1962
-A Glimpse of Paradise. Boardman, 1944
The Golden Teddybear. Boardman, 1965
Hate Thy Neighbor. Hale, 1969
The Hidden Answer. Gifford, 1956
House of Echoes. Gifford, 1956
-Lonely Pathway. Paul, 1933
-Maiden Armour. Paul, 1932
-Many Parts. Swan, 1946
Master of High Beck. Hale, 1969
Monk's Hollow. Gifford, 1968
Murderer's Maze. Gifford, 1957 RF
Not My Murder. Gifford, 1967
Operation Snatch. Gifford, 1958 RF
The Reluctant Executioner. Hale, 1959
-Return They Must. Paul, 1933
The Secret of the Seven Sisters. Ward, 1950
Shipwrecked Schoolship. Swan, 1949
Small and Deadly. Hale, 1960
Two Mrs. Farrells. Boardman, 1946
-The Wrong That Was Done. Leng, 1935

MARSH, (EDITH) NGAIO. 1899- . Series character: Insp./Supt. Roderick Alleyn, in all titles.
Artists in Crime. Bles, 1938; Furman, 1938
Black as He's Painted. Collins, 1974; Little, 1974
The Bride of Death; see Spinsters in Jeopardy
Clutch of Constables. Collins, 1968; Little, 1969
Colour Scheme. Collins, 1943; Little, 1943
Dead Water. Collins, 1964; Little, 1963
Death and the Dancing Footman. Collins, 1942; Little, 1941
Death at the Bar. Collins, 1940; Little, 1940
Death at the Dolphin. Collins, 1967. U.S. title: Killer Dolphin. Little, 1966
Death in a White Tie. Bles, 1938; Furman, 1938
Death in Ecstasy. Bles, 1936; Sheridan, 1941
Death of a Fool; see Off with His Head
Death of a Peer; see Surfeit of Lampreys
Died in the Wool. Collins, 1945; Little, 1945
Enter a Murderer. Bles, 1935; PB, 1941
False Scent. Collins, 1960; Little, 1959
Final Curtain. Collins, 1947; Little, 1947
Hand in Glove. Collins, 1962; Little, 1962
Killer Dolphin; see Death at the Dolphin
A Man Lay Dead. Bles, 1934; Sheridan, 1942
Night at the Vulcan; see Opening Night
The Nursing-Home Murder, with Dr. H(enry) Jellett (1872-1948). Bles, 1935; Sheridan, 1941
Off with His Head. Collins, 1957. U.S. title: Death of a Fool. Little, 1956
Opening Night. Collins, 1951. U.S. title: Night at the Vulcan. Little, 1951
Overture to Death. Collins, 1939; Furman, 1939
Scales of Justice. Collins, 1955; Little, 1955
Singing in the Shrouds. Collins, 1959; Little, 1958
Spinsters in Jeopardy. Collins, 1954; Little, 1953. Also published as: The Bride of Death. Mercury, 1955
Surfeit of Lampreys. Collins, 1941. U.S. title: Death of a Peer. Little, 1940
Swing, Brother, Swing. Collins, 1949. U.S. title: A Wreath for Rivera. Little, 1949
Tied Up in Tinsel. Collins, 1972; Little, 1972
Vintage Murder. Bles, 1937; Sheridan, 1940
When in Rome. Collins, 1970; Little, 1971
A Wreath for Rivera; see Swing, Brother, Swing

MARSH, PATRICK. Pseudonym of Leslie Hiscock, 1902- .
Breakdown. Longmans (London), 1952; Longmans (New York), 1953

MARSH, REBECCA. Pseudonym of William Arthur Neubauer, 1916- .
Lady Detective. Arcadia, 1960

MARSH, RICHARD. 1867-1915. Series characters: Augustus Champnell, in at least those marked AC; Judith Lee, in at least those marked JL.
-Ada Vernham, Actress. Long, 1900; Page, 1900
The Adventures of Judith Lee. Methuen, 1916 ss JL
Amusement Only. Hurst, 1901 ss
The Ape and the Diamond; see The Devil's Diamond
-Apron-Strings. Long, 1920
An Aristocratic Detective. Bell, 1900 AC
The Beetle. Skeffington, 1897; Brentano's, 1915 AC
Between the Dark and the Daylight. Long, 1902
Both Sides of the Veil. Methuen, 1901
A Case of Identity; see The Twickenham Peerage
The Chase of the Ruby. Skeffington, 1900
-Coming of Age. Long, 1916
The Coward Behind the Curtain. Methuen, 1908
The Crime and the Criminal. Ward, 1897
Curios: Some Strange Adventures of Two Bachelors. Long, 1898 ss

Cuthbert Grahame's Will; see A Duel
The Dagger of Fate. Westbrook, 1922. (British title?)
The Datchet Diamonds. Ward, 1898
-The Deacon's Daughter. Long, 1917
The Death Whistle. Treherne, 1903. U.S. title: The Whistle of Fate. Street, 1906
The Devil's Diamond. Henry, 1893. U.S. title: The Ape and the Diamond. Street, ca.1928
-A Drama of the Telephone and other tales. Digby Long, 1911 ss
A Duel. Methuen, 1904. Also published as: Cuthbert Grahame's Will. Pearson, 1930
-The Flying Girl. Ward, 1915
Frivolities. Bowden, 1899. Also published as: The Purse Which was Found and other stories. Pearson, 1918 ss
The Garden of Mystery. Long, 1906
Garnered. Methuen, 1904 ss, one criminous
The Girl and the Miracle. Methuen, 1907
The Girl in the Blue Dress. Long, 1909 ss
The Goddess: A Demon. White, 1900
The Great Temptation. Unwin, 1916; Brentano's, 1916
-A Hero of Romance. Ward, 1900
-His Love or His Life. Chatto, 1915
The House of Mystery. White, 1898
-If It Please You. Methuen, 1913
In Full Cry. White, 1899; Street, 1928
In the Service of Love. Methuen, 1906
The Interrupted Kiss. Cassell, 1909
-The Joss: A Reversion. White, 1901
Judith Lee: Some Pages from her Life. Methuen, 1912 ss JL
Justice—Suspended. Chatto, 1913
Live Men's Shoes. Methuen, 1910
-Love in Fetters. Cassell, 1914
The Lovely Mrs. Blake. Cassell, 1910
-The Magnetic Girl. Long, 1903
-The Mahatma's Pupil. Henry, 1893
A Man with Nine Lives. Ward, 1915
Margot—and her Judges. Chatto, 1914
The Marquis of Putney. Methuen, 1905
Marvels and Mysteries. Methuen, 1900 ss
A Master of Deception. Cassell, 1913
-A Metamorphosis. Methuen, 1903
-Miss Arnott's Marriage. Long, 1904
-Molly's Husband. Cassell, 1914
Mrs. Musgrave—and her Husband. Pioneer, 1894; Appleton, 1895
The Mystery of Philip Bennion's Death. Ward, 1897. Also published as: Philip Bennion's Death. Ward, 1899
On the Jury. Methuen, 1918
Outwitted. Long, 1919
Philip Bennion's Death; see The Mystery of Philip Bennion's Death
The Purse Which was Found and other stories; see Frivolities
-The Romance of a Maid of Honour. Long, 1907
A Royal Indiscretion. Methuen, 1909
The Seen and the Unseen. Methuen, 1900; New Amsterdam, 1900 AC
A Spoiler of Men. Chatto, 1905
A Strange Wooing; see The Strange Wooing of Mary Bowler
The Strange Wooing of Mary Bowler. Pearson, 1895. U.S. title: A Strange Wooing. Street, 1929
-The Surprising Husband. Methuen, 1908
Tom Ossington's Ghost. Bowden, 1898
The Twickenham Peerage. Methuen, 1902; Street, 19??
-Twin Sisters. Cassell, 1911
-Violet Forster's Lover. Cassell, 1912
Who Killed Lady Poynder? Appleton, 1907. (British title?)
The Whistle of Fate; see The Death Whistle

The Woman in the Car. Unwin, 1914
The Woman with One Hand, and Mr. Ely's Engagement. Bowden, 1899. (Two novelets.)

MARSHALL, ARCHIBALD. Pseudonym of Arthur Hammond Marshall, 1866-1934. See also: Horace Annesley Vachell, 1861-1955.
The House of Merrilees. Rivers, 1905; Turner, 1905
The Mystery of Redmarsh Farm. Paul, 1911; Dodd, 1925
Nothing Hid. Collins, 1934; Houghton, 1935
The Terrors and other stories. Methuen, 1913 ss, some criminous

MARSHALL, ARTHUR HAMMOND. 1866-1934. Pseudonym: Archibald Marshall, q.v.

MARSHALL, BRUCE. 1899-   .
The Accounting. Houghton, 1958
The Month of the Falling Leaves. Constable, 1963; Doubleday, 1963
-Operation Iscariot. Constable, 1974

MARSHALL, CHARLES HUNT. Joint pseudonym with George Worthing Yates, q.v.: Peter Hunt, q.v.

MARSHALL, EDISON (TESLA). 1894-1967.
The Death Bell. Garden City, 1924

MARSHALL, (DAVID) EDWARD. 1870-1933.
-The Middle Wall. Dillingham, 1904

MARSHALL, EVELYN. 1897-   . Pseudonym: Jean Marsh, q.v.

MARSHALL, MRS. FRANCIS BRIDGES. Pseudonym: Alan St. Aubyn, q.v.

MARSHALL, HURST
Enter Two Murderers. Longmans, 1937

MARSHALL, IAN
The Strange Case of Vintrix Polbarton. Nelson, 1929
The Vengeance of Kali. Nelson, 1930

MARSHALL, JOANNE. Pseudonym of Anne Rundle, q.v. Other pseudonym: Alexandra Manners, q.v.
Follow a Shadow. Collins, 1974; Putnam, 1974

MARSHALL, LOVAT. Pseudonym of W(illiam) Murdoch Duncan, 1909-1975, q.v. Other pseudonyms: John Cassells, John Dallas, Neill Graham, Martin Locke, Peter Malloch, qq.v. Series character: Sugar Kane, in all titles.
Blood on the Blotter. Hale, 1968
Date with Murder. Hale, 1973
The Dead are Dangerous. Hale, 1966
The Dead are Silent. Hale, 1966
Death Casts a Shadow. Hale, 1972
Death is For Ever. Hale, 1969
Death Strikes in Darkness. Hale, 1965
Key to Murder. Hale, 1975
Ladies can be Dangerous. Hale, 1964
Loose Lady Death. Hale, 1973
Moment for Murder. Hale, 1972
Money Means Murder. Hale, 1968
Murder in Triplicate. Hale, 1963
Murder is the Reason. Hale, 1964
Murder of a Lady. Hale, 1967
Murder to Order. Hale, 1975
Murder Town. Hale, 1974
Murder's Just for Cops. Hale, 1971
Murder's Out of Season. Hale, 1970
The Strangler. Hale, 1974
Sugar Cuts the Corners. Long, 1957
Sugar for the Lady. Hurst, 1955
Sugar on the Carpet. Hurst, 1956
Sugar on the Cuff. Hale, 1960
Sugar on the Kill. Hale, 1961
Sugar on the Loose. Hale, 1962

Sugar on the Prowl. Hale, 1962
Sugar on the Target. Long, 1958

MARSHALL, MARGUERITE MOOERS. 1887-   .
Murder Without Morals. Clifford Lewis, 1947

MARSHALL, RAYMOND. Pseudonym of Rene Brabazon Raymond, 1906-   . Other pseudonyms: James Hadley Chase, James L. Docherty, Ambrose Grant, qq.v. Most of the titles below were subsequently reprinted as by James Hadley Chase. Series characters: "Brick Top" Corridon = C; Don Micklem = DM.
Blondes' Requiem. Jarrolds, 1945; Crown, 1946
But a Short Time to Live. Jarrolds, 1951
Hit and Run. Hale, 1958
In a Vain Shadow. Jarrolds, 1951
Just the Way It Is. Jarrolds, 1944
Lady, Here's Your Wreath. Jarrolds, 1940
Make the Corpse Walk. Jarrolds, 1946
Mallory. Jarrolds, 1950 C
Mission to Siena. Hale, 1955 DM
Mission to Venice. Hale, 1954 DM
No Business of Mine. Jarrolds, 1947
The Paw in the Bottle. Jarrolds, 1949
The Sucker Punch. Jarrolds, 1954
The Things Men Do. Jarrolds, 1953
Trusted Like the Fox. Jarrolds, 1948
The Wary Transgressor. Jarrolds, 1952
Why Pick on Me? Jarrolds, 1951 C
You Find Him—I'll Fix Him. Hale, 1956

MARSHALL, SIDNEY
Some Like It Hot. Morrow, 1941

MARSHALL, WILLIAM LEONARD. 1944-   .
-The Age of Death. Macmillan (London), 1970; Viking, 1971
-The Fire Circle. Macmillan (London), 1969
-The Middle Kingdom. Macmillan (London), 1971
Yellowthread Street. H. Hamilton, 1975; Holt, 1976

MARSON, G(ERALD) F(RANCIS)
Ghosts, Ghouls and Gallows. Rider, 1946

MARSTEN, RICHARD. Pseudonym of Evan Hunter, 1926-   , q.v. Other pseudonyms: Curt Cannon, Hunt Collins, Ezra Hannon, Ed McBain, qq.v.
Big Man. PB, 1959
Death of a Nurse; see Murder in the Navy
Even the Wicked. Permabooks, 1958
Murder in the Navy. GM, 1955. Also published as: Death of a Nurse, as by Ed McBain. PB, 1968; Coronet, 1972
Runaway Black. GM, 1954; Red Seal, 1957. Reprinted as by Ed McBain: PB, 1968; Coronet, 1971
The Spiked Heel. Holt, 1956; Constable, 1957
Vanishing Ladies. Permabooks, 1957; Boardman, 1961

MARTEL, CHARLES. Pseudonym of Thomas Delf, 1810-1865.
The Detective's Note-Book. Ward, 1860 ss
Diary of an Ex-Detective. Ward, 1860 ss

MARTEN, JON C(HISHOLM). See: CORNELIUS CONYN.

MARTENS, PAUL. Pseudonym of Stephen Southwold, 1887-1964, q.v. Other pseudonym: Neil Bell, q.v.
-Death Rocks the Cradle. Collins, 1933

The Truth About My Father. Collins, 1934. Reprinted as by Neil Bell: Collins, 1936

MARTIN, A(RCHIBALD) E(DWARD). 1885- .
The Bridal Bed Murders. Simon, 1954. British title: The Chinese Bed Mysteries. Reinhardt, 1955
The Chinese Bed Mysteries; see The Bridal Bed Murders
The Curious Crime. Doubleday, 1952; Muller, 1953
Death in the Limelight. Simon, 1946; Reinhardt, 1956
The Outsiders. Simon, 1945; Nimmo, 1948
Sinners Never Die. Simon, 1944; Nimmo, 1947

MARTIN, A. RICHARD. Series character: Branders Noble, in both titles.
The Cassiodore Case. Methuen, 1927; McBride, 1928
The Death of the Claimant. Methuen, 1929; McBride, 1929

MARTIN, ABSALOM
Kastle Krags. Duffield, 1922

MARTIN, AYLWIN LEE. Series character: Matt Hughes, in at least those marked MH.
-Black Blood. Low, 1929
The Crimson Frame. GM, 1952
Death for a Hussy. Graphic, 1952 MH
Death on a Ferris Wheel. GM, 1951; Fawcett (London), 1954 MH
Fear Comes Calling. GM, 1952
-Mad Interlude. Low, 1930

MARTIN, CARL (L.). 1892- .
Delta Deputies. Greenwich, 1959 ss

MARTIN, CAROLINE
The Blue Ridge Mystery. Weed, 1897

MARTIN, DESMOND
Death When You Want It. Hale, 1974
No Hero. Boardman, 1957
Prescription for Death. Hale, 1972
Wine, Women, and Murder. Boardman, 1955

MARTIN, DON
"Shed No Tears." Murray & Gee, 1948

MARTIN, DOROTHEA. Pseudonym of Kathleen (Douglas) Hewitt, 1893- , q.v.
Black Sunshine. Mathews, 1933

MARTIN, ED
To Hell with the Law. Columbine, 1939

MARTIN, FRANCIS
Ace in the Hole. Hamilton Stafford, 1954
Blood on the Sand. Hamilton Stafford, 1954

MARTIN, H(ECTOR) D(AULIN)
Encore to Murder. Skeffington, 1939
Time for Murder. Skeffington, 1938

MARTIN, HELEN R(IEMENSNYDER). 1868-1939.
The House on the Marsh. Dodd, 1936

MARTIN, HENRIETTA and GITA LEWIS
The Naked Eye. Greenberg, 1950; Jarrolds, 1951

MARTIN, IAN KENNEDY. Series character: Jack Regan, in both titles.
The Manhattan File; see Regan and the Manhattan File
Regan. Barker, 1975; Holt, 1975. Also published as: The Sweeney. Futura, 1975
Regan and the Manhattan File. Barker, 1975. U.S. title: The Manhattan File. Holt, 1976
The Sweeney; see Regan

MARTIN, JAMES E. 1936- .
The 95 File. Simon, 1973; Collins, 1973

MARTIN, KAY
Vanessa. Putnam, 1974

MARTIN, L(INCOLN) W(ILLIAM) and N(ORMAN) S(OREN) LYNRAVN
Murder on Mount Capita. Angus (Sydney), 1944; Quality (London), 1946

MARTIN, LANE
Bait. C. Warren, 1951
Chicago Rod. C. Warren, 1951
Verdict. C. Warren, 1951

MARTIN, NELL COLUMBIA BOYER. 1890- .
Pseudonym: Columbia Boyer, q.v.

MARTIN, OLIVER. Pseudonym of Ernest Davies, 1873- , q.v. Series character: Timothy Cullinan, in at least those marked TC.
The Iron Door. Hodder, 1923 TC
The Mermaid. Faber, 1926 TC
-Middle Distance. Benn, 1929

MARTIN, RALPH
The Man Who Haunted Himself. Award, 1970; Tandem, 1970. (Novelization of the movie, adapted from The Case of Mr. Pelham, by Anthony Armstrong, q.v.)

MARTIN, RICHARD. Pseudonym of John Creasey, 1908-1973, q.v. Other pseudonyms: Gordon Ashe, M. E. Cooke, Norman Deane, Robert Caine Frazer, Patrick Gill, Michael Halliday, Charles Hogarth, Brian Hope, Colin Hughes, Kyle Hunt, Abel Mann, Peter Manton, J. J. Marric, Rodney Mattheson, Anthony Morton, Jeremy York, qq.v.
Adrian and Jonathan. Hodder, 1954
Keys to Crime. Earl, 1947
Vote for Murder. Earl, 1948

MARTIN, ROBERT (LEE). 1908-1976. Pseudonym: Lee Roberts, q.v. Series character: Jim Bennett, in at least those marked JB.
Bargain for Death. Curtis, 1972; Hale, 1964 JB
Catch a Killer. Dodd, 1956; Hale, 1958 JB
A Coffin for Two. Curtis, 1972; Hale, 1962 JB
Dark Dream. Dodd, 1951; Muller, 1954
The Echoing Shore. Dodd, 1955; Muller, 1956. Also published as: The Tough Die Hard. Bantam, 1957
Hand-Picked for Murder. Dodd, 1957; Hale, 1958 JB
Just a Corpse at Twilight. Dodd, 1955; Muller, 1957
A Key to the Morgue. Dodd, 1959; Hale, 1960 JB
Killer Among Us. Dodd, 1958; Hale, 1959 JB
Sleep, My Love. Dodd, 1953; Muller, 1955 JB
She, Me, and Murder. Curtis, 1971; Hale, 1962 JB
Tears for the Bride. Dodd, 1954; Muller, 1955 JB
To Have and To Kill. Dodd, 1960; Hale, 1961 JB
The Tough Die Hard; see The Echoing Shore

The Widow and the Web. Dodd, 1954; Muller, 1956 JB

MARTIN, ROBERT BERNARD. 1918- . Pseudonym: Robert Bernard, q.v.

MARTIN, SHANE. Pseudonym of George H(enry) Johnston, 1912-1970, q.v. Series character: Professor Challis, in all titles.
The Man Made of Tin. Collins, 1958
Mourner's Voyage; see A Wake for Mourning
The Myth is Murder. Collins, 1959. U.S. title: The Third Statue. Morrow, 1959
The Saracen Shadow. Collins, 1957
The Third Statue; see The Myth is Murder
Twelve Girls in the Garden. Collins, 1957; Morrow, 1957
A Wake for Mourning. Collins, 1962. U.S. title: Mourner's Voyage. Doubleday, 1963

MARTIN, STUART. 1882- .
-Babe Jardine. Selwyn, 1927
Capital Punishment. Hutchinson, 1931
The Fifteen Cells. Selwyn, 1927; Harper, 1928 ss
The Green Ghost. Selwyn, 1928
The Hangman's Guests. Hutchinson, 1931; Harper, 1931 ss
-Inheritance. Ouseley, 1912
The Mystery of Clough Mills. Mascot, 1920
Only Seven were Hanged. Harper, 1929. (British title?)
-Pirates of the Main. Pearson, 1924
-Princess of Paradise. Selwyn, 1928
-The Surf Queen. Hurst, 1925
The Trial of Scotland Yard. Hutchinson, 1930; Harper, 1930 ss

MARTIN, THOMAS HECTOR. 1913- . Pseudonym: Martin Thomas, q.v.

MARTIN, TROY KENNEDY and KEN(NETH) WLASCHIN, q.v.
The Italian Job. Sphere, 1969; Signet, 1969. (Novelization of the movie.)

MARTING, RUTH LENORE. 1907- . Pseudonym: Hilea Bailey, q.v.

MARTON, GEORGE. 1900- .
Catch Me a Spy, with Tibor Meray. Allen, 1971; Harper, 1969
The Obelisk Conspiracy, with Michael Burren. Allen, 1975; Stuart, 1976
The Raven Never More, with Tibor Meray. Spearman, 1966
Three-Cornered Cover, with Christopher Felix. Allen, 1973; Holt, 1972

MARTYN, DON. Pseudonym of Barbara Martyn Borbolla.
House of Shadows. Hale, 1969
Nightmare Fiesta. Hale, 1967
No Guest at the Villa. Hale, 1971
Only at Sunset. Hale, 1970
Operation Castanets. Hale, 1966
Sinister Legacy. Hale, 1968
Treachery at Guadamonte. Hale, 1965

MARTYN, FREDERIC
A Burglar in Baulk. Pearson, 1910
A Holiday in Gaol. Methuen, 1911; Macmillan, 1911
The Reminiscences of a Rogue. Routledge, 1908

MARTYN, OLIVER. Pseudonym of Herbert Oliver White, 1885- .
The Body in the Pound. Eldon, 1933. U.S. title: The Man They Couldn't Hang. Morrow, 1933

MARTYN, WYNDHAM. 1875- . Series characters: Christopher Bond = CB; Anthony Trent = AT.
-All the World to Nothing. Low, 1913; Little, 1912
Anthony Trent: Avenger. Jenkins, 1928 AT
Anthony Trent, Master Criminal. Jenkins, 1922; Moffat, 1918 AT
The Bathurst Complex. Jenkins, 1924. U.S. title: The Murder in Beacon Street. McBride, 1930
The Blue Ridge Crime. Jenkins, 1937 AT
Cairo Crisis. Jenkins, 1945 CB
Capture. Jenkins, 1940 CB
Christopher Bond, Adventurer. Jenkins, 1933 CB
The Chromium Cat. Jenkins, 1952 CB
Criminals All. Jenkins, 1935 AT
Death by the Lake. Jenkins, 1934 AT
The Death Fear. Jenkins, 1929; McBride, 1929 AT
The Denmede Mystery. Jenkins, 1936 CB
The Ghost City Killings. Jenkins, 1940 AT
The Great Ling Plot. Jenkins, 1933 AT
The Headland House Affair. Jenkins, 1941 AT
The House of Secrets. Jenkins, 1936 AT
The Last Scourge. Jenkins, 1946 AT
The Man Outside. Dodd, 1910
Manhunt in Murder. Jenkins, 1950; Roy, 1958 AT
The Marrowby Myth. Jenkins, 1938 CB
Men Without Faces. Jenkins, 1943 AT
The Murder in Beacon Street; see The Bathurst Complex
Murder Island. Jenkins, 1929; McBride, 1929 AT
Murder Walks the Deck. Jenkins, 1938 AT
The Mysterious Mr. Garland. Jenkins, 1923 AT
Nightmare Castle. Jenkins, 1935 AT
Noonday Devils. Jenkins, 1939 CB
The Old Manor Crime. Jenkins, 1937 AT
The Recluse of Fifth Avenue. Jenkins, 1925; McBride, 1929
The Return of Anthony Trent. Jenkins, 1923; Barse, 1925 AT
The Scarlett Murder. Jenkins, 1931 AT
The Secret of the Silver Car. Jenkins, 1922; Moffat, 1920 AT
Shadow Agent. Jenkins, 1941 CB
The Social Storming. Jenkins, 1930
The Spies of Peace. Jenkins, 1934 CB
Stones of Enchantment. Jenkins, 1948 AT
Trent Fights Again. Jenkins, 1939 AT
Trent of the Lone Hand. Jenkins, 1927 AT
The Trent Trail. Jenkins, 1930; McBride, 1930 AT
The Triumphant Prodigal. Jenkins, 1928
Under Cover. Jarrolds, 1914; Little, 1914. (Novelization of the play by Roi Cooper Megrue, 1883-1927, q.v.)

MARVELL, HOLT. Pseudonym of Eric Maschwitz, 1901- , q.v. See also: VAL (HENRY) GIELGUD, 1900- .

MARVIN, DWIGHT EDWARDS. 1851-1940.
-Prof. Slagg of London. Broadway, 1908

MARVIN, SUSAN
The Secret of the Villa Como. Lancer, 1966

MARY, JULES. 1851-1922.
The Mendon Mystery. Vizetelly, 1888

MASCHWITZ, ERIC. 1901- . Pseudonym: Holt Marvell. See: VAL (HENRY) GIELGUD, 1900- .
Little Red Monkey, with Bevis Winter, 1918- , q.v. Jenkins, 1953. (Novelization of Maschwitz's TV play.)

MASCOTT, TRINA
The Wife Who Ran Away. Dell, 1975

MASH, MAURICE H. B. Joint pseudonym with Willan George Bosworth, 1904- : Maurice Worth, q.v.

MASKE, JOHN. Series characters: Duncan Cainsforth = DC; Jeremy Flack = JF; Clarence E. Hemingway = CH.
The Cherbourg Mystery. Rich, 1934 JF & CH
The Dinard Mystery. Rich, 1933 DC
Ghost of a Cardinal. Rich, 1935 JF & CH
The Saint-Malo Mystery. Rich, 1933 JF & DC

MASON, A(LFRED) E(DWARD) W(OODLEY). 1865-1948. Series character: Inspector Hanaud = H.
The Affair at the Semiramis Hotel; see The Four Corners of the World
At the Villa Rose. Hodder, 1910; Scribner, 1910. 4-act play version: Hodder, 1928 H
Blanche de Maletroit. Capper, 1894. (1-act play based on the story "The Sire de Maletroit's Door" by Robert Louis Stevenson.)
The Clock; see The Four Corners of the World
Dilemmas. Hodder, 1934; Doubleday, 1935 ss
Ensign Knightley and other stories. Constable, 1901; Stokes, 1901 ss, some criminous
The Four Corners of the World. Hodder, 1917; Scribner, 1917 ss (Two stories in this collection were also published separately as little books: The Affair at the Semiramis Hotel. Scribner, 1917, 77 pp., is an H story; The Clock, Paget, 1910, 12 pp, is not.)
The House in Lordship Lane. Hodder, 1946; Dodd, 1946 H
The House of the Arrow. Hodder, 1924; Doran, 1924 H
No Other Tiger. Hodder, 1927; Doran, 1927
The Prisoner in the Opal. Hodder, 1928; Doubleday, 1928 H
-Running Water. Hodder, 1907; Century, 1907
The Sapphire. Hodder, 1933; Doubleday, 1933
The Secret Fear. Doubleday, 1940 (22 pp.)
The Summons. Hodder, 1920; Doran, 1920
They Wouldn't be Chessmen. Hodder, 1935; Doubleday, 1935 H
-The Watchers. Arrowsmith, 1899; Stokes, 1899
The Winding Stair. Hodder, 1923; Doran, 1923
The Witness for the Defence. Hodder, 1913; Scribner, 1914. 4-act play version: French, 1913.

MASON, ARTHUR CHARLES. 1879- . Pseudonym: Mason Scrope, q.v.

MASON, BENJAMIN FRANKLIN. 1852-1927.
Through War to Peace. Pacific Press, 1891. (Sequel to title below.)
The Village Mystery; or, The Spectres of St. Argyle. Whiting, 1887

MASON, BURNHAM F.
The Stroke of a Knife. Street (Magnet)

MASON, CAROLINE ATWATER. 1853-1939.
-The Mystery of Miss Motte. Page, 1909

MASON, CHARLES. Pseudonym: S. C. Mason, q.v.

MASON, (SYDNEY) CHARLES. 1911- .
Death in Regatta Week. Long, 1960

MASON, CHARLES WELCH. 1866- . Pseudonym: Mr. M—., q.v.

MASON, COLIN. 1926- .
Hostage. Macmillan (London), 1973; Walker, 1973

MASON, EDITH HELEN. 1895- . Pseudonym: Hilary Mason, q.v.

MASON, GREGORY. Joint pseudonym of Doris Meek and Adrienne Jone Other joint pseudonym: Mason Gregory, q.v.
With Soul So Dead. Arcadia, 1956

MASON, HILARY. Pseudonym of Edith Helen Mason, 1895- .
Tread Warily. Paul, 1937

MASON, HOWARD. Pseudonym of Jennifer Ramage.
Body Below. Joseph, 1955
Fit as a Filly; see Photo Finish
Photo Finish. Joseph, 1954. U.S. title: Fit as a Filly. Morrow, 1954
Proud Adversary. Joseph, 1951
The Red Bishop. Joseph, 1953; Mill, 1954

MASON, JOHN WILLIAM
Hot Blood—Cold Blood. Hale, 1958
Jail Bait. Hale, 1959
The Saboteurs. Muller, 1955
The Tiger's Back. Hale, 1957

MASON, LEONIE
Murder by Accident. Temple, 1947

MASON, MICHAEL. 1939- .
71 Hours. Coward, 1972

MASON, PAULE
The Dark Mirror. Collins, 1967. U.S. title: Here Lies Georgia Linz. World, 1968
Here Lies Georgia Linz; see The Dark Mirror
The Man in the Garden; see The Shadow
The Shadow. Collins, 1969. U.S. title: The Man in the Garden. McKay, 1969

MASON, PHILIP. 1906- . Pseudonym: Philip Woodruff, q.v.

MASON, RAYMOND [CLARENCE RAY MASON].
And Two Shall Meet. GM, 1954; Red Seal, 1958
Forever is Today. GM, 1955; Fawcett (London), 1958
-Love After Five. GM, 1956
Someone and Felicia Warwick. GM, 1962; Muller pb, 1963

MASON, ROBERT
And the Shouting Dies. Hurst, 1940
Arab Agent. Hurst, 1944
-Cairo Communique. Hurst, 1942 ss
Courage for Sale. Hurst, 1939
-More News from Middle East. Hurst, 1943
Murder to Measure. Pawling, 1934
-No Easy Way Out. Jarrolds, 1952
The Slaying Squad. Hurst, 1934
-Tandra. Hurst, 1945
-The Tender Leaves. Jarrolds, 1950
-There is a Green Hill. Hurst, 1946
Three Cheers for Treason! Hurst, 1940

MASON, S. C. Pseudonym of Charles Mason.
   Series character: Derek Glover = DG.
   'Bloody Murder'. Bell, 1937
   -The Gold of Gabria. Warne, 1950
   The Man on the Spot. Bles, 1938 DG
   Murder at Bador. Bell, 1938 DG
   Murder on Manoeuvres. Bell, 1937

MASON, SARA ELIZABETH. Series character:
   Sheriff Bill Davies = BD.
   The Crimson Feather. Doubleday, 1945;
      Gordon Martin, 1946 BD
   The House That Hate Built. Doubleday,
      1944
   Murder Rents a Room. Doubleday, 1943 BD
   The Whip. Morrow, 1948; Corgi, 1952

MASON, TALLY. Pseudonym of August Derleth, 1909-1971, q.v.
   Consider Your Verdict. Stackpole, 1937
      ss, in quiz form

MASON, (FRANCIS) VAN WYCK. 1897-   .
   Pseudonym: Geoffrey Coffin, q.v.
   Series character: Capt./Maj./Col.
      Hugh North = HN.
   The Branded Spy Murders. Doubleday,
      1932; Eldon, 1936 HN
   The Bucharest Ballerina Murders.
      Stokes, 1940; Jarrolds, 1941 HN
   The Budapest Parade Murders. Doubleday,
      1935; Eldon, 1935 HN
   The Cairo Garter Murders. Doubleday,
      1938; Jarrolds, 1938 HN
   The Castle Island Case. Reynal, 1937;
      Jarrolds, 1938. Revised edition, with
      HN added: The Multi-Million-Dollar
      Murders. Cardinal, 1960; Hale, 1963
   The China Sea Murders; see The Shanghai
      Bund Murders
   Dardanelles Derelict. Doubleday, 1949;
      Barker, 1950 HN
   The Deadly Orbit Mission. Doubleday,
      1968; Hale, 1968 HN
   The Fort Terror Murders. Doubleday,
      1931; Eldon, 1936 HN
   The Gracious Lily Affair. Doubleday,
      1957; Hale, 1958 HN
   Himalayan Assignment. Doubleday, 1952;
      Hale, 1953 HN
   The Hong Kong Airbase Murders. Double-
      day, 1937; Jarrolds, 1940 HN
   Maracaibo Mission. Doubleday, 1965;
      Hale, 1966 HN
   The Multi-Million-Dollar Murders; see
      The Castle Island Case
   The Rio Casino Intrigue. Reynal, 1941;
      Jarrolds, 1942 HN
   Saigon Singer. Doubleday, 1946; Barker,
      1948 HN
   Secret Mission to Bangkok. Doubleday,
      1960; Hale, 1961 HN
   Seeds of Murder. Doubleday, 1930;
      Eldon, 1937 HN
   The Seven Seas Murders. Doubleday,
      1936; Eldon, 1937 (4 NH novelets)
   The Shanghai Bund Murders. Doubleday,
      1933; Eldon, 1934. Revised edition:
      The China Sea Murders. PB, 1959; Con-
      sul, 1961 HN
   The Singapore Exile Murders. Doubleday,
      1939; Jarrolds, 1939 HN
   Spider House. Mystery League, 1932;
      Hale, 1959
   The Sulu Sea Murders. Doubleday, 1933;
      Eldon, 1936. Revised edition: PB,
      1958 HN
   Trouble in Burma. Doubleday, 1962;
      Hale, 1963 HN
   Two Tickets to Tangier. Doubleday,
      1955; Hale, 1956 HN
   The Vesper Service Murders. Doubleday,
      1931; Eldon, 1935 HN
   The Washington Legation Murders.
      Doubleday, 1935; Eldon, 1937 HN
   The Yellow Arrow Murders. Doubleday,
      1932; Eldon, 1935 HN

   Zanzibar Intrigue. Doubleday, 1963;
      Hale, 1964 HN

MASSEY, CHARLOTTE
   Polmarran Tower. Macdonald, 1975

MASSEY, MORRELL. Series character: Thorn-
   ton Zane, in both titles.
   Left Hand Left. Penn, 1932; Hutchinson,
      1932
   Through the Lens. Penn, 1933

MASSEY, RUTH
   The Crime in the Boulevard Raspail.
      Nelson, 1932. U.S. title: Death in
      the Wind. Nelson (New York), 1932

MASSIE, CHRIS
   -The Confessions of a Vagabond. Low,
      1931
   -Corridor of Mirrors. Faber, 1941
   Death Goes Hunting. Faber, 1953
   -Escape from Julia. Faber, 1947
   -Esther Vanner. Low, 1937
   Falcon Road; see Hallelujah Chorus
   Farewell, Pretty Ladies. Random, 1942.
      (British title?)
   -Flood Light. Low, 1932
   The Green Circle; see The Green Orb
   The Green Orb. Faber, 1943. U.S. title:
      The Green Circle. Random, 1943
   -The Incredible Truth. Random, 1958.
      (British title?)
   -Lady. Heinemann, 1925
   The Love Letters. Random, 1944. (Bri-
      tish title?)
   -My Love is Stone. Faber, 1949
   -The Other House. Secker, 1938
   -Peccavi. Chapman, 1929
   -Penny Whipp. Secker, 1939
   -Pity My Simplicity. Faber, 1944
   -Portrait of a Beautiful Woman. Low,
      1944
   -They Being Dead Yet Speak. Chapman,
      1929
   -The Undivided Light. Faber, 1952
   -When My Ship Comes Home. Faber, 1959

MASSON, RENE. 1922-   .
   The Bottle Organ. Wingate, 1962.
      (Translation of L'Orgue a Bouteilles.
      Paris, 1950.)
   Cage of Darkness; see Sicily Street
   Green Oranges. Knopf, 1953. (Transla-
      tion of Oranges Vertes. Paris, 1953.)
   Landru; see Number One
   Number One. Hutchinson, 1964. U.S.
      title: Landru. Doubleday, 1965.
      (Translation of Les Roses de Gambais.
      Paris, 1962.)
   Sicily Street. Wingate, 1961. U.S.
      title: Cage of Darkness. Knopf, 1951.
      (Translation of Les Gamins du Roidu
      Sicile. Paris, 1950.)

MASTERMAN, J(OHN) C(ECIL). 1891-1977.
   Series character: Ernest Brendel =
   EB.
   Bits and Pieces. Hodder, 1961. (ss, in-
      cluding a Sherlock Holmes pastiche
      and 2 about EB.)
   The Case of the Four Friends. Hodder,
      1957 EB
   An Oxford Tragedy. Gollancz, 1933 EB

MASTERMAN, MARGARET. 1910-   .
   Death of a Friend. Nicholson, 1938
   -Gentleman's Daughters. Nicholson, 1931
   -The Grandmother. Nicholson, 1934

MASTERMAN, WALTER S(IDNEY). 1876-   .
   See also: L. Patrick Greene. Series
      characters: Sir Arthur Sinclair, in
      at least those marked AS; Dick Sel-
      don, in at least those marked DS.

   The Avenger Strikes. Jarrolds, 1936;
      Dutton, 1937 AS
   Back from the Grave. Jarrolds, 1940 AS
   The Baddington Horror. Jarrolds, 1934;
      Dutton, 1934 AS
   Blood on the Floor; see 2 L.O.
   The Bloodhounds Bay. Jarrolds, 1936;
      Dutton, 1936 DS
   The Border Line. Jarrolds, 1936; Dut-
      ton, 1937 DS
   The Crime of the Reckaviles; see The
      Curse of the Reckaviles
   The Curse of Cantire. Jarrolds, 1939 AS
   The Curse of the Reckaviles. Methuen,
      1927; Dutton, 1927. Also published
      as: The Crime of the Reckaviles.
      Methuen, 1934 AS
   The Death Coins. Jarrolds, 1940
   Death Turns Traitor. Methuen, 1935;
      Dutton, 1936 AS
   The Flying Beast. Jarrolds, 1932; Dut-
      ton, 1932 AS
   The Green Toad. Gollancz, 1928; Dutton,
      1929
   The Hooded Monster. Jarrolds, 1939
   The Hunted Man. Jarrolds, 1938; Dutton,
      1938 AS
   The Man Without a Head. Jarrolds, 1942
   The Mystery of Fifty-Two. Jarrolds,
      1931; Dutton, 1931 AS
   The Nameless Crime. Jarrolds, 1932;
      Dutton, 1932 AS
   The Perjured Alibi. Methuen, 1935; Dut-
      ton, 1935
   The Rose of Death. Methuen, 1934; Dut-
      ton, 1936 AS
   The Secret of the Downs. Jarrolds,
      1938; Dutton, 1939 AS
   The Silver Leopard. Jarrolds, 1941 AS
   The Tangle. Jarrolds, 1931
   2 L.O. Gollancz, 1928; Dutton, 1928.
      Also published as: Blood on the
      Floor. Newnes, 1935 AS
   The Wrong Letter. Methuen, 1926; Dut-
      ton, 1926 AS
   The Wrong Verdict. Jarrolds, 1937; Dut-
      ton, 1938 AS
   The Yellow Mistletoe. Jarrolds, 1930;
      Dutton, 1930 AS

MASTERS, ANTHONY. 1940-   . Pseudonym:
   Richard Tate, q.v.
   The Syndicate. Joseph, 1971

MASTERS, JOHN. 1914-   .
   The Breaking Strain. Joseph, 1967;
      Delacorte, 1967

MASTERS, W. W.
   Murder in the Mirror. Longmans, 1931

MASTERSON, WHIT. Joint pseudonym of
   Robert Wade, 1920-   , q.v., and
   Bill Miller, 1920-1961. This byline
   continued by Wade alone after Mil-
   ler's death. Other joint pseudonyms:
   Will Daemer, Wade Miller, Dale Wil-
   mer, qq.v. See also: BOB WADE.
   All through the Night. Dodd, 1955;
      Allen, 1956. Also published as: A Cry
      in the Night. Bantam, 1956; Corgi,
      1958
   Badge of Evil. Dodd, 1956; Allen, 1956.
      Also published as: Touch of Evil.
      Bantam, 1958
   A Cry in the Night; see All Through the
      Night
   The Dark Fantastic. Dodd, 1959; Allen,
      1960
   Dead, She was Beautiful. Dodd, 1955;
      Allen, 1955
   The Death of Me Yet. Dodd, 1970; Hale,
      1972

Evil Come, Evil Go. Dodd, 1961; Allen, 1961
The Gravy Train. Dodd, 1971; Hale, 1972. Also published as: The Great Train Hijack. Pinnacle, 1976
The Great Train Hijack; see The Gravy Train
A Hammer in his Hand. Dodd, 1960; Allen, 1960
Killer with a Badge; see 711—Officer Needs Help
The Last One Kills. Dodd, 1969; Hale, 1972
The Man on a Nylon String. Dodd, 1963; Allen, 1963
The Man with Two Clocks. Dodd, 1974; Hale, 1975
Play Like You're Dead. Dodd, 1967; Hale, 1969
711—Officer Needs Help. Dodd, 1965. British title: Killer with a Badge. Allen, 1966. Also published as: Warning Shot. Popular Library, 1967
A Shadow in the Wild. Dodd, 1957; Allen, 1957
Touch of Evil; see Badge of Evil
The Undertaker Wind. Dodd, 1973; Hale, 1974
Warning Shot; see 711—Officer Needs Help
Why She Cries, I Do Not Know. Dodd, 1972; Hale, 1974

MASUR, HAROLD Q. 1912- . See also: HELEN TRAUBEL. Series character: Scott Jordan = SJ.
The Attorney. Random, 1973; Souvenir, 1974
The Big Money. Simon, 1954; Boardman, 1955 SJ
Bury Me Deep. Simon, 1947; Boardman, 1961 SJ
The Last Breath; see The Last Gamble
The Last Gamble. Simon, 1958; British title: The Last Breath. Boardman, 1958. Also published as: Murder on Broadway. Dell, 1959 SJ
The Legacy Lenders. Random, 1967; Boardman, 1967 SJ
Make a Killing. Random, 1964; Boardman, 1964 SJ
Murder on Broadway; see The Last Gamble
The Name is Jordan. Pyramid, 1962 SJ ss
Send Another Hearse. Random, 1960; Boardman, 1960 SJ
So Rich, So Lovely, and So Dead. Simon, 1952; Boardman, 1953 SJ
Suddenly a Corpse. Simon, 1949; Boardman, 1950 SJ
Tall, Dark, and Deadly. Simon, 1956; Boardman, 1957 SJ
You Can't Live Forever. Simon, 1951; Boardman, 1951

MATCHA, JACK. 1919- .
Ask for Lois. Monarch, 1962
-Gambler's Girl. Athena, 1961
Prowler in the Night. GM, 1959; Digit, 1959

MATHER, BERKELY. Pseudonym of John Evan Weston Davies. Series character: Peter Feltham = PF.
The Achilles Affair. Collins, 1959; Scribner, 1959 PF
The Break; see The Break in the Line
The Break in the Line. Collins, 1970. U.S. title: The Break. Scribner, 1970
Geth Straker. Fontana, 1962. (Based on the TV series.) ss
The Gold of Malabar. Collins, 1966; Scribner, 1967
The Pass Beyond Kashmir. Collins, 1960; Scribner, 1960
The Road and the Star. Collins, 1965; Scribner, 1965
Snowline. Collins, 1973; Scribner, 1973
The Springers. Collins, 1968. U.S. title: A Spy for a Spy. Scribner, 1968
A Spy for a Spy; see The Springers
The Terminators. Collins, 1971; Scribner, 1971
With Extreme Prejudice. Collins, 1975; Scribner, 1976 PF

MATHER, VIRGINIA. Pseudonym of Jean Mayer Liebeler, q.v.

MATHERS, HELEN B(UCKINGHAM). 1853-1920.
Blind Justice. Ward, 1890. U.S. title: Hedri; or, Blind Justice. Lovell, 1889
-Eyre's Acquittal. Bentley, 1884; Lovell, 1883
-Found Out. Warne, 1885; Munro, 1885
Hedri; see Blind Justice
-The Juggler and the Soul. Skeffington, 1896
-Land o' the Leal. Bentley, 1878; Munro, 1878
Love, the Thief. Paul, 1909
Murder or Manslaughter. Routledge, 1885; Munro, 1885
The Mystery of No. 13. White, 1891; U.S. Book Co., 1890
-Story of a Sin. Routledge, 1882; Munro, 1883

MATHESON, HUGH. Pseudonym of Hugh Lewis Mackay, 1897-1963
The Balance of Fear. Gibbs, 1961
The Third Force. Wingate, 1959; Washburn, 1960

MATHESON, JEAN (CHISHOLM)
-The Cistern and the Fountain. Collins, 1951
-The Day of the Fair. Collins, 1955
The Dire Departed. Hodder, 1958
-The Island. Collins, 1952
So Difficult to Die. Collins, 1957
-The Visit. Collins, 1954

MATHESON, RICHARD (BURTON). 1926- .
Fury on Sunday. Lion, 1953
Hell House. Viking, 1971; Corgi, 1973
Ride the Nightmare. Ballantine, 1959; Consul, 1961
Someone is Bleeding. Lion, 1953
A Stir of Echoes. Lippincott, 1958; Cassell, 1958

MATHESON, SYLVIA ANNE. Pseudonym: Max Mundy, q.v.

MATHEWS, D(ONNA) L(ORRAINE). 1922- .
The Fatal Amateur. Rinehart, 1959; Jenkins, 1960
The Late Unlamented; see A Very Welcome Death
The Reach of Fear. Rinehart, 1958; Jenkins, 1959
A Very Welcome Death. Holt, 1961. British title: The Late Unlamented. Jenkins, 1961

MATHEWS, FRANCES AYMAR
The Flame Dancer. Dillingham, 1908; Unwin, 1908
A Little Tragedy at Tien-Tsin. Cooke, 1904 ss
The Staircase of Surprise. Appleton, 1905

MATHEWS, FRANCES (H. SHORTT). See: VERE (DAWSON) SHORTT, 1872-1915.

MATHEWS, NIEVES (M.). 1917- .
She Died Without Lights. Hodder, 1956

MATHIESON, THEODORE. 1913- .
The Devil and Ben Franklin. Simon, 1961
The Great "Detectives". Simon, 1960 ss

MATSCHAT, CECILE HULSE. 1895?-1976.
Series characters: Andrea Reid (Ramsay) and David Ramsay, in both titles.
Murder at the Black Crook. Farrar, 1943; Cassell, 1945
Murder in Okefenokee. Farrar, 1941

MATSUMOTO, SEICHO. 1909- .
Points and Lines. Kodansha (U.S.), 1970; Kodansha (U.K.), 1978. (Translation of Ten to Sen. Tokyo, 1957.)

MATTHESON, RODNEY. Pseudonym of John Creasey, 1908-1973, q.v. Other pseudonyms: Gordon Ashe, M. E. Cooke, Norman Deane, Robert Caine Frazer, Patrick Gill, Michael Halliday, Charles Hogarth, Brian Hope, Colin Hughes, Kyle Hunt, Abel Mann, Peter Manton, J. J. Marric, Richard Martin, Anthony Morton, Jeremy York, qq.vv.
The Dark Shadow. Fiction House, 193?
The Secret of Ferrars. Fiction House, 193?

MATTHEW, CHARLES
Bazi Bazoum; or, A Strange Detective; See Mabel Seymour; or, A Strange Detective
The Inspector's Puzzle; or, Trapped at the Last Turn. Street (Magnet), 1899
Mabel Seymour; or, A Strange Detective. Street 1891. British title (?): Bazi Bazoum; or, A Strange Detective. Ward, 1889

MATTHEWS, ANTHONY. Pseudonym of Dudley Barker, 1910- . Used as byline on some titles published in England as by another Barker pseudonym: Lionel Black, q.v.

MATTHEWS, (JAMES) BRANDER. 1852-1929.
-His Father's Son. Harper, 1895; Longmans, 1895
The Last Meeting. Scribner, 1885; Unwin, 1885
-A Tale of Twenty-Five Hours, with George H. Jessop. Appleton, 1892
Tales of Fantasy and Fact. Harper, 1896 ss
With My Friends. Longmans, 1891 ss, some criminous

MATTHEWS, CLAYTON (HARTLEY). 1918- . Joint pseudonym with Patricia Matthews, 1927- : Patty Brisco, q.v. See also: ARTHUR MOORE.
The Big Score. Brandon, 1973
Dive into Death. Sherbourne, 1969
Hagar's Castle. Powell, 1969 ss
The Mendoza File. Powell, 1970
The Negotiator. Pyramid, 1975
Nylon Nightmare. Powell, 1970

MATTHEWS, PATRICIA. 1927- . Joint pseudonym with Clayton (Hartley) Matthews, 1918- , q.v.: Patty Brisco, q.v.

MATTHEWS, T(HOMAS) S(TANLEY). 1901- .
To the Gallows I Must Go. Knopf, 1931; H. Hamilton, 1931

MATURIN, CHARLES ROBERT. 1780-1824. Pseudonym: Dennis Jasper Murphy, q.v.
Melmoth: The Wanderer. Constable, 1820; Wells, 1821

MAUGHAM, ROBERT CECIL ROMER. 1916- .
Pseudonym: Robin Maugham, q.v.

MAUGHAM, ROBIN. Pseudonym of Robert Cecil
    Romer Maugham, 1916-   .
-The Barrier. Allen, 1973
  The Intruder; see Line on Ginger
-Line on Ginger. Chapman, 1949; Harcourt, 1950. Also published as: The
    Intruder. New English Library, 1968
  The Link: A Victorian Mystery. Heinemann, 1969; McGraw, 1969
  The Man with Two Shadows. Longmans,
    1958; Harper, 1959
-The 1946 MS. War Facts Press, 1943
-November Reef. Longmans, 1962
-Testament: Cairo, 1898. DeHarrington,
    1972. (31-page ss.)

MAUGHAM, W(ILLIAM) SOMERSET. 1874-1965.
    Ashenden; or, The British Agent. Heinemann, 1928; Doubleday, 1928 ss

MAURICE, ARTHUR B(ARTLETT). 1873-1946.
    The Riddle of the Rovers. Dodd, 1942

MAURICE, MICHAEL. Pseudonym of Conrad
    Arthur Skinner, 1889-   .
    The Final Sentence. Chapman, 1926
-Frail Ghost. Low, 1935
-The Last House. Low, 1933
    The Long Way Round. Unwin, 1925. U.S.
    title (?): The Permanent Eclipse.
    Frank-Maurice, 1926
-Luther Wing. Low, 1930
-Marooned. Low, 1932
    The Permanent Eclipse; see The Long Way
    Round

MAVITY, NANCY BARR. 1890-   . Series
    character: Peter Piper = PP.
    The Body on the Floor. Doubleday, 1929;
      Collins, 1930 PP
    The Case of the Missing Sandals.
      Doubleday, 1930; Collins, 1931 PP
    The Fate of Jane McKenzie. Doubleday,
      1933; Collins, 1933
    He Didn't Mind Hanging; see The Man Who
      Didn't Mind Hanging
    The Man Who Didn't Mind Hanging.
      Doubleday, 1932. British title: He
      Didn't Mind Hanging. Collins, 1932 PP
    The Other Bullet. Doubleday, 1930; Collins, 1931 PP
    The State vs. Elna Jepson. Doubleday,
      1937
    The Tule Marsh Murder. Doubleday, 1929;
      Collins, 1930 PP

MAXFIELD, HENRY S.
    Another Spring. Little, 1974
    Legacy of a Spy. Harper, 1958; Heinemann, 1958

MAXON, P. B.
    The Waltz of Death. Mystery House,
      1941

MAXWELL, ALLAN. Pseudonym of William
    J(ohn) Bayfield, 1871-1958, q.v.
    Other pseudonym: Allan Blair, q.v.
    The Priest's Secret. Amalgamated, 1936
      (Sexton Blake.)

MAXWELL, BRIGID. 1916-   .
    The Case of the Six Mistresses. Harrap,
      1955

MAXWELL, C. F.
    Plan 79. Gifford, 1947

MAXWELL, GERALD. 1862-   .
-The Fear of Life. Blackwell, 1908
    The Last Lord Avanley. Mills, 1909

MAXWELL, HELEN K.
    The Girl in a Mask. Little, 1971

MAXWELL, HERBERT
-The Quest of the Crooked. Digby Long,
    1907
    The Three Judges. Digby Long, 1908
    ss, mostly criminous
    The Unclaimed Million. Ward, 1904

MAXWELL, PATRICIA. 1942-   .
    The Bewitching Grace. Popular Library,
      1974
    Bride of a Stranger. GM, 1974
    Court of the Thorn Tree. Popular Library, 1974
    Dark Masquerade. GM, 1974
    Plantation Inn. GM, 1971
    The Secret of Mirror House. GM, 1970
    The Stranger at Plantation Inn. GM,
      1971

MAXWELL, RICHARD
    The Minus Man. Putnam, 1975

MAXWELL, VICKY. Pseudonym of Anne(tte
    Isobel) Worboys, q.v.
    Chosen Child. Collins, 1973
    Flight to the Villa Mistra. Collins,
      1973
    The Way of the Tamarisk. Collins, 1974;
      Delacorte, 1975, as by Anne Worboys

MAXWELL, W(ILLIAM) B(ABINGTON). 1866-1938.
    Jacob's Ladder, and other stories.
      Hutchinson, 1937 ss, some criminous
    Like Shadows on the Wall. Hutchinson,
      1929 ss

MAY, GEOFFREY. Joint pseudonym with Ethel
    M. Dolbey: E. M. D. Hawthorn, q.v.

MAY, HENRY BAK
    The Doctor Didn't Prescribe Murder.
      Exposition, 1957

MAY, ROBERT HAROLD
    7 Murders. Macaulay, 1932

MAYBURY, ANNE. Pseudonym of Anne Buxton.
    Other pseudonym: Katherine Troy, q.v.
    The titles below were mostly published in the U.S. as gothics, but
    apparently in England as romances.
    Beloved Enemy. Collins, 1957
    The Brides of Bellenmore; see My Dearest Elizabeth
    Bridge to the Moon. Collins, 1960
    Dear Lost Love. Collins, 1957
    Enchanter's Nightshade. Also published
      as: Winds of Night. Ace, 1967.
      (British title?)
    The Falcon's Shadow. Ace, 1967. (British title?)
    Follow Your Heart. Collins, 1955
    Forbidden. Collins, 1956
    The Gay of Heart. Collins, 1959
    Green Fire. Collins, 1963; Ace, 1966
    The House of Fand. Ace, 1966. (British
      title?)
    I am Gabriella! Collins, 1962; Ace,
      1966
    Jessamy Court. Collins, 1975; Random,
      1974
    Jessica. Collins, 1965
    The Midnight Dancers. Collins, 1974;
      Random, 1973
    The Minerva Stone. Hodder, 1968; Holt,
      1968
    The Moonlit Door. Hodder, 1967; Holt,
      1967
    My Dearest Elizabeth. Collins, 1964.
      U.S. title: The Brides of Bellenmore.
      Ace, 1964
    My Love has a Secret. Collins, 1958
    The Night My Enemy. Collins, 1962; Ace,
      1967
    The Other Juliet. Collins, 1955
    The Pavilion at Monkshood. Collins,
      1966; Ace, 1966
    The Rebel Heart. Collins, 1959
    Ride a White Dolphin. Hodder, 1971;
      Random, 1971
    Shadow of a Stranger. Collins, 1960;
      Ace, 1966
    Someone Waiting. Ace, 1966. (British
      title?)
    The Stars Cannot Tell. Collins, 1958
    Stay Until Tomorrow. Collins, 1961;
      Ace, 1967
    The Terracotta Palace. Hodder, 1971;
      Random, 1970
    Walk in the Paradise Garden. Collins,
      1973; Random, 1972
    Whisper in the Dark. Ace, 1966. (British title?)
    Winds of Night; see Enchanter's Nightshade

MAYDWELL, W. D.
    Convict International. Mellifont, 1941
    The Dart Board Mystery. Mellifont, 1940
    Death in the Tote Box. Mellifont, 1941
    The Football Pools Mystery. Mellifont,
      1940
    The Football Racket. Mellifont, 1940
    The Greyhound Murder Mystery. Mellifont, 1940
    The Soccer League Scandal. Mellifont,
      1941

MAYFAIR, FRANKLIN. Pseudonym of Felix
    Mendelsohn, Jr., 1906-   .
    Over My Dead Body. Book Co., 1965

MAYFIELD, SERENA
    The Lonely Terror. PB, 1973
    Stranger in the House. PB, 1972

MAYHEW, G. A.
    Murder at Daybreak. Vantage, 1975

MAYLON, B. J.
    The Corpse with Knee Action. Phoenix,
      1940

MAYNARD, LAWRENCE M.
    The Pig is Fat. Farrar, 1930; Gollancz,
      1930

MAYNE, CLARICE and R. THURSTON HOPKINS
    The Amber Girl. Palmer, 1923

MAYNE, ETHEL COLBURN. 187?-1941.
-Blindman. Chapman, 1919
-The Clearer Vision. Unwin, 1898 ss
-Come In. Chapman, 1917
-The Fourth Ship. Chapman, 1908
-Inner Circle. Constable, 1925 ss
-Jessie Vandeleur. Allen, 1902
-Nine of Hearts. Constable, 1923 ss
-One of our Grandmothers. Chapman, 1916
-Things That No One Tells. Chapman, 1910
    ss

MAYNE, WILLIAM (JAMES CARTER). 1928-   .
-Ravensgill. Dutton, 1970

MAYO, GAEL
    It's Locked In with You. Hutchinson,
      1968

MAYO, ISABELLA FYVIE. 1843-1914.
    The Mystery of Allan Grale. Bentley,
      1885; Harper, 1886

MAYO, JAMES. Pseudonym of Stephen Coulter, 1913-   , q.v. Series character: Charles Hood, in at least those
    marked CH.
    Asking for It. Heinemann, 1971
    Hammerhead. Heinemann, 1964; Morrow,
      1964 CH
    Let Sleeping Girls Lie. Heinemann,
      1965; Morrow, 1966 CH

The Man Above Suspicion. Heinemann,
  1969 CH
Once in a Lifetime. Heinemann, 1968.
  U.S. title: Sergeant Death. Morrow,
  1968 CH
The Quickness of the Hand. Deutsch,
  1952
Rebound. Heinemann, 1961
A Season of Nerves. Heinemann, 1962
Sergeant Death; see Once in a Lifetime
Shamelady. Heinemann, 1966; Morrow,
  1966 CH

MAYO, KATHERINE. 1868?-1940.
  Mounted Justice. Houghton, 1922.
    (ss; fictionalized true crime.)
  The Standard-Bearers. Houghton, 1918 ss

MAYOR, DOROTHY
  It's an Ill Wind. Mill, 1947
  Last Call for Lissa. Mill, 1948

MAYOR, F(LORA) M(acDONALD). 1872- .
  The Room Opposite, and other tales of
    mystery and imagination. Longmans,
    1935 ss

MAYSE, ARTHUR
  The Desperate Search. Morrow, 1952;
    Harrap, 1953
  Morgan's Mountain. Morrow, 1960; Har-
    rap, 1961
  Perilous Passage. Morrow, 1949; Muller,
    1952

MAYSON, WALTER H(ENRY). 1835-1904.
  The Stolen Fiddle. Warne, 1897

MAZ. Pseudonym of Alfred Leonardus
  Mazure.
  -The Adventures of Dick Boss. Literary
    Press, 1948
  -Cash on Destruction. Spearman, 1962
  -Pigeon Parade. Spearman, 1961
  -Priscilla Darling. Muller, 1963

MAZURE, ALFRED LEONARDUS. Pseudonym:
  Maz, q.v.

MEAD, MATT
  Star Crossed. Macfadden, 1969. (Sexton
    Blake.)

MEAD, (EDWARD) SHEPHERD. 1914- .
  How to Succeed at Business Spying by
    Trying. Simon, 1968; Harrap, 1969

MEADE, DOROTHY COLE
  Death over her Shoulder. Scribner, 1939
  Fatal Shadows. Long & Smith, 1933
  The Shadow of a Hair. Hamilton, 1939

MEADE, L(ILLIE) T(HOMAS). Pseudonym of
  Elizabeth Thomasina Meade Smith,
  1854-1914. Note: Robert Eustace, co-
  author of some titles below, is the
  pseudonym of either Robert Eustace
  Barton, 1868-1943, or Eustace Raw-
  lins, 1854- .
  -The Blue Diamond. Chatto, 1901
  The Brotherhood of the Seven Kings,
    with Robert Eustace. Ward, 1899 ss
  The Chateau of Mystery. Everett, 1907
  -The Cleverest Woman in England. Nisbet,
    1898
  Confessions of a Court Milner. Long,
    1902
  A Double Revenge. Digby, 1902
  -Dr. Rumsey's Patient, with Clifford
    Halifax. Chatto, 1896; International
    News, 1896
  -The Fountain of Beauty. Long, 1909
  From the Hand of the Hunter. Long, 1906
  The Gold Star Line, with Robert Eu-
    stace. Ward, 1899 ss
  A Golden Shadow. Ward, 1906
  -Her Happy Face. Ward, 1914
  -The Home of Silence. Sisley's, 1907
  The House of Black Magic. White, 1912
  -In an Iron Grip. Chatto, 1894
  The Lost Square, with Robert Eustace.
    Ward, 1902 ss
  -The Maid Indomitable. Ward, 1916
  -A Maid of Mystery. White, 1904
  A Master of Mysteries, with Robert Eu-
    stace. Ward, 1898 ss
  -The Medicine Lady. Cassell (London &
    New York), 1892
  Micah Faraday, Adventurer. Ward, 1910
    ss
  The Necklace of Parmona. Ward, 1909
  On the Brink of a Chasm. Chatto, 1898;
    Buckles, 1899
  The Oracle of Maddox Street. Ward, 1904
    ss
  A Race with the Sun, with Clifford
    Halifax. Ward, 1901 ss
  The Sanctuary Club, with Robert Eu-
    stace. Ward, 1900 ss
  The Secret of the Dead. White, 1901
  Silenced. Ward, 1904 ss
  A Son of Ishmael. White, 1896; New Am-
    sterdam, 1896
  The Sorceress of the Strand. Ward, 1903
    ss
  Stories from the Diary of a Doctor,
    with Clifford Halifax. Newnes, 1894;
    Lippincott, 1895 ss
  Stories from the Diary of a Doctor:
    Second Series, with Clifford Halifax.
    Sands, 1896 ss
  This Troublesome World, with Clifford
    Halifax. Chatto, 1893
  Twenty-Four Hours. White, 1911
  Under the Dragon Throne, with Robert
    K(ennaway) Douglas. Gardner, 1897 ss
  The Voice of the Charmer. Chatto, 1895
  Where the Shoe Pinches, with Clifford
    Halifax. Chambers, 1900 ss

MEADE, RICHARD. Pseudonym of Ben(jamin
  Leopold) Haas, 1926- , q.v. Series
  character: John Allison, in both
  titles.
  Beyond the Danube; see The Danube Runs
    Red
  The Danube Runs Red. Random, 1968. Bri-
    tish title: Beyond the Danube.
    Davies, 1967
  The Lost Fraulein. Random, 1970. Bri-
    tish title: A Score of Arms. Davies,
    1969
  A Score of Arms; see The Lost Fraulein

MEADOW, HERB
  Uncertain Glory. Grosset, 1944. (Novel-
    ization of the movie.)

MEADOWS, ALICE MAUD. -1913.
  Blind Man's Buff. Everett, 1907
  -Cut by Society. Digby, 1906
  Days of Doubt. Ward, 1901
  -The Dukedom of Portsea. Laurie, 1909
  The Extreme Penalty. Digby, 1906
  The Eye of Fate. Ward, 1899
  -A Ghost from the Past. Laurie, 1911
  -Her Soul's Desire. Laurie, 1910
  -The House at the Corner. Laurie, 1908
  I Charge You Both. Digby, 1905
  -The Infatuation of Marcella. Digby,
    1909
  -An Innocent Sinner. Digby, 1910
  A Million of Money. Sisley, 1907; Bren-
    tano's, 1907
  -The Moth and the Flame. Milne, 1908
  The Odd Trick. Long, 1908
  -One Life Between. Ward, 1901
  Out from the Night. Ward, 1899
  -The Romance of a Madhouse. Arrowsmith,
    1891
  -Three Lovers and One Lass. Digby, 1908
  -A Ticket-of-Leave Girl. Digby, 1911
  -When the Heart is Young. Digby, 1895
  -The Wicked World. Laurie, 1910

MEADOWS, CATHERINE
  Doctor Moon; see Henbane
  Friday Market. Gollancz, 1938; Macmil-
    lan, 1938
  Henbane. Gollancz, 1934. U.S. title:
    Doctor Moon. Putnam, 1935

MEADOWS, FELTON
  The Death Dealers. Mellifont, 1939

MEAGHER, GEORGE E(DWARD). 1895- .
  Tomorrow's Horizon. Dorrance, 1947

MEAGHER, JOSEPH W(ILLIAM)
  Miss Bantling is Missing. Macdonald,
    1958

MEAKER, MARIJANE. Pseudonym: Vin Packer,
  q.v.

MEANS, MARY. Joint pseudonym with Theodore Saunders: Denis Scott, q.v.

MEARSON, LYON. 1888-1966.
  Footsteps in the Dark. Macaulay, 1927;
    Hutchinson, 1928
  Phantom Fingers. Macaulay, 1927; Hutch-
    inson, 1929
  The Whisper on the Stair. Macaulay,
    1924; Hutchinson, 1924

MECHEM, KIRKE. 1889- .
  A Frame for Murder. Doubleday, 1936

MECHEM, PHILIP. 1892-1969.
  And Not for Love. Duell, 1942. Also
    published as: Murders I've Seen.
    Croydon, 1945, abridged
  The Columbine Cabin Murders. Scribner,
    1932
  Murders I've Seen; see And Not for Love

MEDUSA, K.
  I Spy. Scion, 1951
  Lowdown on G Men. Scion, 1951
  They Kill by Night. Scion, 1952

MEE, HUAN. Pseudonym.
  -A Beauty Spot. Gale, 1894 ss
  A Diplomatic Woman. Sands, 1900; Har-
    per, 1900 ss
  The Jewel of Death. Ward, 1902
  Weaving the Web. Ward, 1902
  -Wheels Within Wheels. Ward, 1901

MEEK, DORIS. Joint pseudonyms with Adrienne Jones: Mason Gregory, Gregory
  Mason, qq.v.

MEEKER, ARTHUR, JR. 1902- .
  -Strange Capers. Covici, 1931; Paul,
    1931

MEGAW, ARTHUR STANLEY. 1872- . Pseudonym: Arthur Stanley, q.v.

MEGGS, BROWN (MOORE). 1930- .
  The Matter of Paradise. Random, 1975;
    Collins, 1976
  Saturday Games. Random, 1974; Collins,
    1975

MEGRUE, ROI COOPER. 1883-1927. See also:
  RICHARD PARKER.
  Under Cover. French, 1918; Bickers,
    1914. (4 act play; for novelization
    see: Wyndham Martyn, 1875- .)

MEIK, VIVIAN. 1895- .
  The Curse of Red Shiva. Philip Allan,
    1936; Hillman-Curl, 1938
  Devils' Drums. Philip Allan, 1933 ss
  Veils of Fear. Philip Allan, 1934

MEIRING, DESMOND
The President Plan. Constable, 1974

MEISELS, ANDREW
Six Other Days. Pyramid, 1973

MEISSNER, HANS (OTTO). 1909-   .
Duel in the Snow. Davies, 1970; Morrow, 1972. (Translation of Alatna. Gutersloh, 1964.)

MELCHIOR, IB (JORGEN). 1917-   .
Order of Battle. Harper, 1972; Souvenir, 1973
Sleeper Agent. Harper, 1975; Souvenir, 1976

MELDRUM, JAMES. Pseudonym of James (William) Mitchell, 1926-   , q.v. Other pseudonym: James Munro, q.v.
The Semonov Impulse. Weidenfeld, 1975; St. Martin's, 1976

MELIDES, NICHOLAS. 1912-   . Pseudonym: Nicholas McGuire, q.v.
-Buns from the Gutter. Paladin, 1951

MELTON, WILLIAM. 1920-   .
Nine Lives to Pompeii. McKay, 1974; Weidenfeld, 1974

MELVILLE, ALAN. Pseudonym of William Melville Caverhill, 1910-   .
The Danube Flows Red. Skeffington, 1937
Death of Anton. Skeffington, 1936
Quick Curtain. Skeffington, 1934
The Vicar in Hell. Skeffington, 1935
Warning to Critics. Skeffington, 1936
Week-End at Thrackley. Skeffington, 1934

MELVILLE, ANNABELLE (McCONNELL). 1910-   .
Rue the Reservoir. Bruce, 1956

MELVILLE, JENNIE. Pseudonym of Gwendoline (Williams) Butler, 1922-   , q.v. Series character: Charmian Daniels, in at least those marked CD.
Burning is a Substitute for Loving. Joseph, 1963; London House, 1964 CD
Come Home and Be Killed. Joseph, 1962; London House, 1964 CD
A Different Kind of Summer. Hodder, 1967
The Hunter in the Shadows. Hodder, 1969; McKay, 1970
Ironwood. Hodder, 1972; McKay, 1972
Murderers' Houses. Joseph, 1964 CD
Nell Alone. Joseph, 1966
A New Kind of Killer; see A New Kind of Killer, an Old Kind of Death
A New Kind of Killer, an Old Kind of Death. Hodder, 1970. U.S. title: A New Kind of Killer. McKay, 1971
Nun's Castle. Hodder, 1974; McKay, 1973
Raven's Forge. Macmillan (London), 1975; McKay, 1975
The Summer Assassin. Hodder, 1971
There Lies Your Love. Joseph, 1965 CD

MENDELSOHN, FELIX, JR. 1906-   . Pseudonym: Franklin Mayfair, q.v.

MENDES, CATULLE. 1841-1909.
Number 56, and other stories. Laurie, 1928. (Translation of Rue des Filles-Dieu, 56. Paris, 1895.) 4 ss, of which the first is criminous

MERAY, TIBOR. See: GEORGE MARTON, 1900-   .

MERCER, CECIL WILLIAM. 1885-1960. Pseudonym: Dornford Yates, q.v.

MERCER, IAN
Curs in Clover. Earl, 1948
Epitaph for a Blonde. Boardman, 1959
The Green Windmill. Crowther, 1945
Journey into Darkness. Boardman, 1958
A Man Gets into his Tomb. Earl, 1948
Mission to Majorca. Boardman, 1958

MEREDITH, ANNE. Pseudonym of Lucy Beatrice Malleson, 1899-1973. Other pseudonyms: Anthony Gilbert, J. Kilmeny Keith, qq.v.
Home is the Heart; see There's Always Tomorrow
Portrait of a Murderer. Gollancz, 1933; Reynal, 1934
There's Always Tomorrow. Faber, 1941. U.S. title: Home is the Heart. Howell Soskin, 1942

MEREDITH, DAVID WILLIAM. Pseudonym of Earl Schenck Miers, 1910-1972.
The Christmas Card Murders. Knopf, 1951

MEREDITH, K(ENNETH) LINCOLN
The Golden Chalice. Boardman, 1958

MEREDITH, PETER. Pseudonym of Brian Arthur Worthington-Stuart. Other pseudonym: Brian Stuart, q.v.
Checkmate. Ward, 1950
-The City of Shadows. Warne, 1952
The Crocodile Man. Ward, 1951
The Denzil Emeralds. Ward, 1954
Floodwater. Ward, 1950
Invitation to a Ball. Ward, 1949
Oasis. Ward, 1951
Sands of the Desert. Ward, 1953

MERITON, PETER. Pseudonym of (Alfred) John Hunter, 1891-1961, q.v. Other pseudonyms: John Addiscombe, L. H. Brenning, Anthony Dax, Anthony Drummond, qq.v. Series character: Bill Langley, in at least those marked BL.
The Affair of the Fraternizing Soldier. Amalgamated, 1946. (Sexton Blake.)
After Darvray Died. Hurst, 1938 BL
Captain Dack. Hurst, 1939
Conspiracy. Hurst, 1945
The Man from Madrid. Amalgamated, 1943. (Sexton Blake.)
Plunder. Hurst, 1948
Three Die at Midnight. Hurst, 1937; Dutton, 1937, as by John Hunter BL

MERITT, PAUL.   -1895.
The Golden Plough. French (London & New York), 1878? (4-act play.)
-The Hidden Million. Munro, 1883

MERIVALE, BERNARD. 1882-1939. See: ARNOLD RIDLEY, 1896-   . And also: RUTH ALEXANDER.

MERLAND, OLIVER
All titles below feature Sexton Blake and were published by Amalgamated Press.
The Branded Spy. 1919
The Case of Larachi the Lascar. 1924
The Case of the Man in Black. 1923
The Case of the Nameless Man. 1920
The Face in the Film. 1923

MERLE, ROBERT. 1908-   .
The Day of the Dolphin. Simon, 1969; Weidenfeld, 1969. (Translation of Un Animal doue de Raison. Paris, 1967.)

MERRETT, CHARLES H(ENRY)
Hidden Lives. Long, 1929
Sacrifice. Garamond, 1935. (1-act play.)

MERRICK, CHARLES
The Stolen Heiress. Hodder, 1938

MERRICK, GORDON. 1916-   .
Between Darkness and Day; see The Vallency Tradition
The Eye of One; see The Hot Season
The Hot Season. Morrow, 1958. British title: The Eye of One. Hale, 1959
-The Vallency Tradition. Messner, 1955. British title: Between Darkness and Day. Hale, 1957

MERRICK, LEONARD. 1864-1939.
The Call from the Past, and other stories. Nelson, 1910 ss, some criminous
Mr. Bazalgette's Agent. Routledge, 1888

MERRICK, DOCTOR MARK. Pseudonym of St. George (Henry) Rathborne, 1854-1938, q.v. Other pseudonym: Marline Manly, q.v.
The Great Travers Case. Street, 1890

MERRICK, MOLLIE. Series character: Red Hanlon, in both titles.
Mysterious Mr. Frame. Washburn, 1938
Upper Case. Washburn, 1936

MERRICK, WILLIAM. 1916-1969.
-No One of That Name. Holt, 1964
The Packard Case. Random, 1961; Gollancz, 1961

MERRILEES, FRANCIS
The Pit. Macdonald, 1945

MERRILL, JAMES MILFORD. 1847-1936. Pseudonym: Morris Redwing, q.v.

MERRILL, P. J. Pseudonym of Holly Roth, 1916-1964, q.v. Other pseudonym: K. G. Ballard, q.v.
The Slender Thread. Harcourt, 1959; Macdonald, 1960

MERRITT, A(BRAHAM). 1884-1943.
Burn, Witch, Burn! Liveright, 1933; Methuen, 1934
Creep, Shadow! Doubleday, 1934. British title: Creep, Shadow, Creep! Methuen, 1935
Creep, Shadow, Creep!; see Creep, Shadow!
Seven Footprints to Satan. Boni, 1928; Richards, 1928

MERSEREAU, JOHN. 1898-   .
The Corpse Comes Ashore. Lippincott, 1941
Murder Loves Company. Lippincott, 1940

MERTZ, BARBARA GROSS. 1927-   . Pseudonyms: Barbara Michaels, Elizabeth Peters, qq.v.

MERWIN, BANNISTER
The Girl and the Bill. Dodd, 1909

MERWIN, SAM(UEL KIMBALL), JR. 1910-   . Series character: Amy Brewster = AB.
The Big Frame. Handi-Books, 1943
The Creeping Shadow. GM, 1952
Death in the Sunday Supplement. Gateway, 1942
Killer to Come. Abelard (New York), 1953; Abelard (London), 1959
Knife in my Back. Mystery House, 1945; Quality, 1947 AB
A Matter of Policy. Mystery House, 1946; Quality, 1952 AB
Message from a Corpse. Mystery House, 1945; Quality, 1947 AB
Murder in Miniatures. Doubleday, 1940

MERWIN, SAMUEL. 1874-1936.
Lady Can Do. Houghton, 1929

MESERVEY, RUSS
Masquerade into Madness. GM, 1953; Red Seal, 1957

MESSENGER, ELIZABETH (MARGERY ESSON). 1908- .
Dive Deep for Death. Hale, 1959
Golden Dawns the Sun. Hale, 1962
Growing Evil. Hale, 1964
A Heap of Trouble. Hale, 1963
Light on Murder. Hale, 1960
Material Witness. Hale, 1959
Murder Stalks the Bay. Hale, 1958
Publicity for Murder. Hale, 1961
The Tail of the 'Dozing Cat'. Hale, 1965
Uncertain Quest. Hale, 1965
The Wrong Way to Die. Hale, 1961
You Won't Need a Coat. Hale, 1964

MESSER, MONA (NAOMI ANNE). 189?- .
Pseudonym: Anne Hocking, q.v.
Mouse Trap. Jarrolds, 1931; Putnam, 1931

MESSMANN, JON. Series characters: Jefferson Boone (The Handyman) = JB; Ben Martin (The Revenger) = BM.
A Bullet for the Bride. Pyramid, 1972
City for Sale. Signet, 1975 BM
Fire in the Streets. Signet, 1974 BM
The Inheritors. Pyramid, 1975 JB
Jefferson Boone, Handyman. Pyramid, 1974 JB
Killers at Sea. Belmont, 1970
The Moneta Papers. Pyramid, 1973; New English Library pb, 1977 JB
Murder Today, Money Tomorrow. Pyramid, 1973 JB
A Promise for Death. Signet, 1975 BM
Ransom! Pyramid, 1975 JB
The Revenger. Signet, 1973 BM
The Stiletto Signature. Signet, 1974 BM
The Swiss Secret. Pyramid, 1974 JB
The Vendetta Contract. Signet, 1975 BM

METCALFE, EDITH
-The Handle of Sin. Ward, 1917
Pyramids of Snow. Ward, 1903

METCALFE, HERBERT
The Amazing Dr. Khan. Church, 1966
The Packet of Death. Church, 1967

METCALFE, JOHN. 1891- .
The Smoking Leg and other stories. Jarrolds, 1925; Doubleday, 1926 ss
Spring Darkness. Constable, 1928

METCALFE, WHITAKER
Two Weeks Before Murder. Arcadia, 1959

METHLEY, VIOLET M(ARY)
The Last Enemy. Blackie, 1936

METHOLD, KENNETH (WALTER). 1931- .
Pseudonym: Alexander Cade, q.v.
All Suspect. Macdonald, 1960
The Man on his Shoulder. Macdonald, 1962

MEYER, BILL
Ultimatum. Signet, 1966

MEYER, CHARLES
The Power of Gold. Warne, 1895
Shadows of Life. Warne, 1894 ss

MEYER, LYNN
Paperback Thriller. Random, 1975; Deutsch, 1976

MEYER, NICHOLAS. 1945- .
The Seven-Per-Cent Solution. Dutton, 1974; Hodder, 1975. (A Sherlock Holmes pastiche.)
Target Practice. Harcourt, 1974; Hodder, 1975

MEYERS, ALFRED. 1906-1963.
Murder Ends the Song. Reynal, 1941; Rich, 1941

MEYERS, MARTIN
Kiss and Kill. Popular Library, 1975

MEYERS, ROY LETHBRIDGE
The Man They Couldn't Kill. Blackfriars, 1944

MEYERSTEIN, E(DWARD) H(ARRY) W(ILLIAM). 1889-1952.
The Pageant, and other stories. Sidney Press, 1934 ss, some criminous

MEYNELL, LAURENCE (WALTER). 1899- .
Series characters: George Stanhope Berkley, in at least those marked GB; Hooky Heffern(m)an, in at least those marked HH.
The Abandoned Doll. Collins, 1960
And be a Villain. Nicholson, 1939
Asking for Trouble. Ward, 1931
Bluefeather. Harrap, 1928; Appleton, 1928 GB
-Break for Summer. H. Hamilton, 1965
The Breaking Point. Collins, 1957
The Bright Face of Danger. Collins, 1948
Camouflage. Harrap, 1930. U.S. title: The Mystery at Newton Ferry. Lippincott, 1930
-Consummate Rose. Hutchinson, 1931
The Creaking Chair. Collins, 1941
The Curious Crime of Miss Julia Blossom. Macmillan (London), 1970
-The Dancers in the Reeds. H. Hamilton, 1963
The Dandy. Nicholson, 1938
Danger Round the Corner. Collins, 1952 HH
The Dark Square. Collins, 1941
Death by Arrangement. Macmillan (London), 1972; McKay, 1972
Death of a Philanderer. Collins, 1968; Doubleday, 1969
Death's Eye. Harrap, 1929. U.S. title: The Shadow and the Stone. Appleton, 1929
Die by the Book. Collins, 1966
Don't Stop for Hooky Hefferman. Macmillan (London), 1975; Stein, 1977 HH
The Door in the Wall. Nicholson, 1937; Harper, 1937
Double Fault. Collins, 1965
The Echo in the Cave. Collins, 1949
-The Empty Saddle. H. Hamilton, 1965
-The End of the Long Hot Summer. Hale, 1972
The Evil Hour. Collins, 1947
The Fairly Innocent Little Man. Macmillan (London), 1974; Stein, 1978 HH
The Fatal Flaw. Macmillan (London), 1973; Stein, 1978
-The Footpath. Hale, 1975
-The Fortunate Miss East. Hale, 1973
The Frightened Man. Collins, 1952 HH
The Gentlemen Go By; see Watch the Wall
Give Me the Knife. Collins, 1954
His Aunt Came Late. Nicholson, 1939
Hooky and the Crock of Gold. Macmillan (London), 1975 HH
The House in Marsh Road. Collins, 1960
The House in the Hills. Nicholson, 1937; Harper, 1938
The House on the Cliff. Hutchinson, 1932; Lippincott, 1932
The Hut. Nicholson, 1938
The Lady on Platform One. Collins, 1950
A Little Matter of Arson. Macmillan (London), 1972
The Man No One Knew. Collins, 1951
The Mauve Front Door. Collins, 1967
More Deadly Than the Male. Collins, 1964
The Mystery of Newton Ferry; see Camouflage
Odds on Bluefeather. Harrap, 1934; Lippincott, 1935 GB
Of Malicious Intent. Collins, 1969
"On the Night of the 18th..." Nicholson, 1936; Harper, 1936
One Step from Murder. Collins, 1958
Paid in Full. Harrap, 1933. U.S. title: So Many Doors. Lippincott, 1933
Party of Eight. Collins, 1950
The Pit in the Garden. Collins, 1961
Saturday Out. Collins, 1956; Walker, 1962
-Scoop. H. Hamilton, 1964
The Shadow and the Stone; see Death's Eye
-Shadow in the Sun. H. Hamilton, 1966
-The Shelter. Hale, 1970
Sleep of the Unjust. Collins, 1963
So Many Doors; see Paid in Full
Storm Against the Wall. Hutchinson, 1931; Lippincott, 1931
Strange Landing. Collins, 1946
-The Suspect Scientist. H. Hamilton, 1966
Third Time Unlucky! Harrap, 1935
The Thirteen Trumpeters. Macmillan (London), 1973; Stein, 1978 HH
Too Clever by Half. Collins, 1953 HH
-A View from the Terrace. Hale, 1972
Virgin Luck. Collins, 1963; Simon, 1964
Watch the Wall. Harrap, 1933. U.S. title: The Gentlemen Go By. Lippincott, 1934
Where is She Now? Collins, 1955
The Woman in Number Five. Hale, 1974

MEYNELL, MARY
Week-End at Green Trees. Bles, 1955

MEYRICK, GORDON
Body on the Pavement. Eldon, 1942; Mystery House, 1945
Danger at my Heels. Crowther, 1943
The Ghost Hunters. Crowther, 1947 ss
The Green Phantom. Eldon, 1941
Pennyworth of Murder. Eldon, 1943

MIALL, DERWENT
Disclosures of a Press Agent. Greening, 1912 ss
The Powers of Darkness. Ward, 1905
Solving a Mystery. Henderson, 1906
The Strange Case of Vincent Hume. Everett, 1906
A Threefold Threat. Ward, 1917

MIALL, ROBERT. Series character: Jason King = JK.
The Adventurer. Pan, 1973
Jason King. Pan, 1972 JK
Kill Jason King. Pan, 1972 JK
The Protectors. Pan, 1973

MICHAELS, BARBARA. Pseudonym of Barbara Gross Mertz, 1927- . Other pseudonym: Elizabeth Peters, q.v.
Ammie, Come Home. Meredith, 1968; Jenkins, 1969
The Crying Child. Dodd, 1971; Souvenir, 1971
The Dark on the Other Side. Dodd, 1970; Souvenir, 1973
Greygallows. Dodd, 1972; Souvenir, 1974

House of Many Shadows. Dodd, 1974; Souvenir, 1976
The Jackal's Head. Meredith, 1968
The Master of Blacktower. Appleton, 1966; Jenkins, 1967
Mystery on the Moors. Paperback Library, 1972
Prince of Darkness. Meredith, 1969; Coronet, 1971
The Sea King's Daughter. Dodd, 1975; Souvenir, 1977
Sons of the Wolf. Meredith, 1967; Jenkins, 1968
Witch. Dodd, 1973; Souvenir, 1975

MICHAELS, STEVE. Pseudonym of Michael (Angelo) Avallone (Jr.), 1924- , q.v. Other pseudonyms: Priscilla Dalton, Mark Dane, Jean-Anne de Pre, Dora Highland, Dorothea Nile, Edwina Noone, Sidney Stuart, Max Walker, qq.v.
The Main Attraction. Belmont, 1963

MICHEAUX, OSCAR. 1884- .
-The Case of Mrs. Wingate. Book Supply, 1944
-The Forged Note. Western Book Supply, 1915
-The Story of Dorothy Stanfield. Book Supply, 1946
-The Wind from Nowhere. Book Supply, 1941

MICHEL, M(ILTON) SCOTT. 1916- . Series character: Wood Jaxon, in at least those marked WJ.
The Black Key. Mystery House, 1946
House in Harlem. Harlequin, 1950. (U.S. title?)
Murder in the Consulting Room; see The Psychiatric Murders
The Murder of Me. Fell, 1961. (3-act play.)
The Psychiatric Murders. Mystery House, 1946. British title: Murder in the Consulting Room. Hammond, 1954
Sinister Warning; see The X-Ray Murders
Sweet Murder. Coward, 1943; Hammond, 1945 WJ
The X-Ray Murders. Coward, 1942; Hammond, 1945. Canadian title: Sinister Warning. Harlequin, 1950 WJ

MICHELSON, MIRIAM. 1870- .
A Yellow Journalist. Appleton, 1905 ss

MIDDLEMASS, JEAN
-At the Altar Steps. Digby, 1910
-Baiting the Trap. Chapman, 1874
-Blanche Coningham's Surrender. White, 1898
-By Fair Means. White, 1884
-Count Remeny. Long, 1905
-Dandy. Tinsley, 1881
-An Evil Angel. Digby, 1908
-The Falkners of Greenhurst. Digby, 1904
-Fallen from Favour. Digby, 1902
-A Felon's Daughter. Digby, 1906
-Four in Hand. Tinsley, 1881
-A Girl in a Thousand. Chapman, 1885
-His Lawful Wife. Digby, 1901
-How I Became Eminent. Eden, 1892
Hush Money. Digby, 1895
-In Storm and Strife. Digby, 1899
-Innocence at Play. Tinsley, 1880
-Lady Muriel's Secret. Munro, 1884. (British title?)
-Lil. Hurst, 1872
-The Loadstone of Love. White, 1886
-Loves Old and New. Digby, 1908
-Mignon's Peril. Digby, 1909
-Mr. Dorillon. Chatto, 1876
-The Mysterious Mrs. Nutford. Aldine, 1896
The Mystery of Clement Dunraven. Digby, 1894
-Nelly Jocelyn, Widow. White, 1887
-Patty's Partner. Tinsley, 1882
-Poisoned Arrows. White, 1884
The Queen Wasp. Digby, 1900
-Ruth Anstey. Digby, 1904
-Sackcloth and Broadcloth. Tinsley, 1880
-Sealed by a Kiss. Tinsley, 1880
-She's Fooling Thee! Aldine, 1895
-Silvermead. Munro, 1884. (British title?)
-Touch and Go. Chatto, 1877
-Two False Moves. White, 1890
-Vaia's Lord. Sonnenschein, 1888
-A Veneered Scamp. Long, 1906
-Vengeance is Mine. Aldine, 1895
-A Wheel of Fire. Digby, 1901
-Wild Georgie. Chapman, 1873
-A Woman's Calvary. Digby, 1903
-The Yellow Badge. Digby, 1899

MIDDLETON, ELIZABETH. Pseudonym: Elizabeth Antill, q.v.

MIDDLETON, J(ESSE) E(DGAR). 1872-1960.
The Clever Ones. Nelson, 1936
-Green Plush. Methuen, 1932

MIDDLETON, TED
Operation Tokyo. Avon, 1956; Boardman, 1958

MIDGLEY, JOHN. 1931- .
Donovan. Chivers, 1974

MIERS, EARL SCHENCK. 1910-1972. Pseudonym: David William Meredith, q.v.

MIKES, GEORGE. 1912- .
The Spy Who Died of Boredom. Deutsch, 1973; Harper, 1974

MILBROOK, JOHN
A Bridgeport Dagger. Lane, 1930

MILES, DAVID. Pseudonym of Brendan Leo Cronin, 1907- . Other pseudonym: Michael Cronin, q.v.
Inside Out. Hale, 1960
Nice and Easy. Hale, 1961
Over the Edge. Hale, 1964
Split Down the Middle. Hale, 1962

MILES, DENNIS. 1927- .
-Pattern of Chalk. New Authors, 1966

MILES, JOHN. Pseudonym of John Miles Bickham.
The Blackmailer. Bobbs, 1974
Dally with a Deadly Doll. Ace, 1961
The Night Hunters. Bobbs, 1973; Hale, 1975
Operation Nightfall, with Tom Morris. Bobbs, 1975; Souvenir, 1976
The Silver Bullet Gang. Bobbs, 1974; Hale, 1976

MILES, RICHARD. 1939- .
-Angel Loves Nobody. Pyramid, 1974
-The Moonbathers, Pyramid, 1974
-That Cold Day in the Park. Pyramid, 1974

MILES, STELLA
Murder at the Arab Stud. Jenkins, 1951
Murder Knows No Master. Jenkins, 1952
Prescription for Murder. Jenkins, 1954
Saddled with Murder. Jenkins, 1953

MILFORD, FRED C.
In Crime's Disguise. Trischler, 1890
55 Guineas Reward. Field, 1886
-Lost! A Day. Field, 1886

MILLAR, FLORENCE N. Series character: Chief-Inspector Douglas Grant, in at least those marked DG.
Fishing is Dangerous. Gifford, 1946 DG
Grant's Overture. Gifford, 1946 DG
-The Lone Kiwi. Dawson, 1948

MILLAR, KENNETH. 1915- . Pseudonyms: John Macdonald, John Ross Macdonald, Ross Macdonald, qq.v. All titles are presently published as by Ross Macdonald. Series character (in subordinate roles): Chet Gordon = CG.
Blue City. Knopf, 1947; Cassell, 1949
The Dark Tunnel. Dodd, 1944. Also published as: I Die Slowly. Lion, 1955 CG
I Die Slowly; see The Dark Tunnel
Night Train; see Trouble Follows Me
The Three Roads. Knopf, 1948; Cassell, 1950
Trouble Follows Me. Dodd, 1946. Also published as: Night Train. Lion, 1955 CG

MILLAR, MARGARET (ELLIS STURM). 1915- . Series characters: Dr. Paul Prye = PP; Inspector Sands = S.
An Air That Kills. Random, 1957. British title: The Soft Talkers. Gollancz, 1957
Beast in View. Random, 1955; Gollancz, 1955
Beyond This Point are Monsters. Random, 1970; Gollancz, 1971
-The Cannibal Heart. Random, 1949; H. Hamilton, 1950
The Devil Loves Me. Doubleday, 1942 PP
Do Evil in Return. Random, 1950; Museum, 1952
-Experiment in Springtime. Random, 1947
The Fiend. Random, 1964; Gollancz, 1964
Fire will Freeze. Random, 1944
How Like an Angel. Random, 1962; Gollancz, 1962
The Invisible Worm. Doubleday, 1941; Long, 1943 PP
The Iron Gates. Random, 1945. British title: Taste of Fears. Hale, 1950 S
The Listening Walls. Random, 1959; Gollancz, 1959
The Lively Corpse; see Rose's Last Summer
Rose's Last Summer. Random, 1952; Museum, 1954. Also published as: The Lively Corpse. Dell, 1956
The Soft Talkers; see An Air That Kills
A Stranger in My Grave. Random, 1960; Gollancz, 1960
Taste of Fears; see The Iron Gates
Vanish in an Instant. Random, 1952; Museum, 1953
Wall of Eyes. Random, 1943 S
The Weak-Eyed Bat. Doubleday, 1942 PP

MILLAR, R.
Half a Corpse. Eyre, 1935. (Based on My First Crime by Gustave Mace, 1835-1904, q.v.)

MILLARD, JOE [JOSEPH JOHN MILLARD]. 1908- .
The Hunted. Award, 1974. (Novelization of the Hec Ramsey TV series.)
The Hunting Party. Award, 1971; Tandem, 1971. (Novelization of the movie.)
Mansion of Evil. GM, 1950
The Million Dollar Bloodhound. Award, 1973
Thunderbolt and Lightfoot. Award, 1974; Tandem, 1974. (Novelization of the movie.)
The Wickedest Man. GM, 1954; Muller pb, 1960

MILLARD, OSCAR (E.)
A Missing Person. McKay, 1972

MILLER, AGNES
   The Colfax Book-Plate. Century, 1926; Benn, 1927
   The Obole of Paradise. Hutchinson, 1930

MILLER, MRS. ALEX McVEIGH
   -The Bride of the Tomb. Lovell, 1888
   -Countess Vera; or, The Oath of Vengeance. Munro, 1883
   The Mystery of Suicide Place. Westbrook, 19??
   -Nina's Peril. U.S. Book Co., 1891
   -Queenie's Terrible Secret; or, A Young Girl's Strange Fate. Munro, 1883
   -Sworn to Silence; or, Aline Rodney's Secret. Munro, 1890

MILLER, ALICE DUER. 1874-1942.
   Death Sentence. Dodd, 1935; Allan, 1936
   Manslaughter. Dodd, 1921; Parsons, 1922

MILLER, BEN E.
   Death Deal. Powell, 1969
   The Set-Up. Powell, 1969

MILLER, BILL. 1920-1961. Joint pseudonyms with Robert Wade, 1920-   , q.v.: Will Daemer, Whit Masterson, Wade Miller, Dale Wilmer, qq.v. See also: BOB WADE.

MILLER, D(OROTHY) B(LANCHE)
   The Unpardonable Crime. Houghton (London), 1935

MILLER, DENIS
   The Chinese Jade Affair. Milton House, 1973

MILLER, ELIZABETH YORK
   The Blue Paroquet. Brentano's (London), 1928
   The Macowen Murder. Gramol, 1935
   Marked Dangerous. Wright, 1935
   The Mark of Yekel. Bles, 1927

MILLER, FLOYD C. 1912-   .
   The Savage Streets. Popular Library, 1956

MILLER, G. W.
   Fettered by Fate. Digby, 1899

MILLER, HELEN TOPPING. 1884-   .
   Who is This Girl? Appleton, 1941

MILLER, HUGH. 1937-   .
   -Ambulance. New English Library, 1975; St. Martin's, 1975
   The Drop Out. New English Library pb, 1973
   Double Deal. New English Library pb, 1974
   Feedback. New English Library pb, 1974
   -King Pin. New English Library, 1974
   The Open City. New English Library, 1973
   Short Circuit. New English Library pb, 1974

MILLER, JOHN. Pseudonym of Joseph Samachson, 1906-   .
   Murder of a Professor. Putnam, 1937; Hale, 1937

MILLER, LANORA. 1932-   .
   The Devil's Due. Ace, 1975
   Quickthorn. Ace, 1975

MILLER, LAURITZ
   Operation Godiva. Tuttle, 1971

MILLER, MARC. Pseudonym of Marc(eil Genee Kolstad) Baker, 1911-   , q.v.
   Death at the Easel. Arcadia, 1956
   Death is a Liar. Arcadia, 1959
   The Plaid Shroud. Arcadia, 1957

MILLER, MERLE. 1919-   .
   A Secret Understanding. Viking, 1956; Heinemann, 1957

MILLER, NATHAN
   X's Page. Exposition, 1952

MILLER, ORMAN L. 1893-   .
   The Mystery of the Horse with the Wrong Harness. Vantage, 1975

MILLER, R. S. 1936-   . Pseudonym: Fran Huston, q.v.

MILLER, SIGMUND (STEPHEN). 1917-   .
   -One Bright Day. Dramatists Play Service, 1952. (3-act play.)
   The Snow Leopard. GM, 1961; Ward, 1959
   -That's the Way the Money Goes. Crown, 1962

MILLER, VICTOR B. All titles are novelizations of the Kojak TV series.
   Death is not a Passing Grade. PB, 1975. British title: Marked for Murder. Star, 1976
   Girl in the River. PB, 1975; Star, 1975
   Gun Business. PB, 1975; Wingate, 1978
   Marked for Murder; see Death is not a Passing Grade
   Requiem for a Cop. PB, 1974; Wingate, 1976
   Siege. PB, 1974
   Take-Over. PB, 1975
   Therapy in Dynamite. PB, 1975
   The Trade-Off. PB, 1975
   A Very Deadly Game. PB, 1975

MILLER, WADE. Joint pseudonym of Robert Wade, 1920-   , q.v., and Bill Miller, 1920-1961. Other joint pseudonyms: Will Daemer, Whit Masterson, Dale Wilmer, qq.v. See also: BOB WADE. Series character: Max Thursday = MT.
   The Big Guy. GM, 1953; Red Seal, 1958
   Branded Woman. GM, 1952; Fawcett (London), 1954
   Calamity Fair. Farrar, 1950 MT
   Deadly Weapon. Farrar, 1946; Low, 1947
   Devil May Care. GM, 1950; Fawcett (London), 1957
   Devil on Two Sticks. Farrar, 1949. Also published as: Killer's Choice. Signet, 1950
   Fatal Step. Farrar, 1948; Low, 1949 MT
   The Girl from Midnight. GM, 1962
   Guilty Bystander. Farrar, 1947; Low, 1948 MT
   The Killer. GM, 1951; Fawcett (London), 1957
   Killer's Choice; see Devil on Two Sticks
   Kiss Her Goodbye. Lion, 1956; Allen, 1957
   Kitten with a Whip. GM, 1959; Muller, 1960
   Mad Baxter. GM, 1955; Fawcett (London), 1956
   Murder Charge. Farrar, 1950 MT
   Nightmare Cruise. Ace, 1961. British title: The Sargasso People. Allen, 1961
   The Sargasso People; see Nightmare Cruise
   Shoot to Kill. Farrar, 1951; Allen, 1953 MT
   Sinner Take All. GM, 1960; Muller pb, 1961
   South of the Sun. GM, 1953; Red Seal, 1953
   Stolen Woman. GM, 1950; Fawcett (London), 1958
   The Tiger's Wife. GM, 1951; Red Seal, 1958
   Uneasy Street. Farrar, 1948; Low, 1949 MT

MILLER, WALTER A.
   Scum in the Pot. Comet, 1958

MILLER, WARREN
   The Banker's Millions. Street (Magnet)
   The Confession of a Thug. Street (Magnet)
   The Crimson Glove. Street (Magnet)
   The Deed of a Night. Street (Magnet)
   In Terror's Grasp. Street (Magnet)
   The Man Who Made Diamonds. Street (Magnet)
   A Midnight Vigil. Street (Magnet)
   The Missing Bullet. Street (Magnet)
   The Power of a Villain. Street (Magnet)
   The Price of Protection. Street (Magnet)
   The Sleepless Eye. Street (Magnet)
   An Unfortunate Rogue. Street (Magnet)

MILLET, F(RANCIS) D(AVIS). 1846-1912.
   A Capillary Crime and other stories. Harper, 1892 ss

MILLHAUSER, BERTRAM
   Whatever Goes Up. Doubleday, 1945

MILLHISER, MARLYS (JOY). 1938-   .
   Michael's Wife. Putnam, 1972
   Nella Waits. Putnam, 1974

MILLIN, SARAH GERTRUDE. 1889-   .
   Three Men Die. Chatto, 1934; Harper, 1934

MILLINGTON, FRANCES (RYAN). 1899-1977.
   The Crime Across the Way. Phoenix, 1937

MILLS, ALGERNON VICTOR. 1905-   . Pseudonym: Rupert Latimer, q.v.

MILLS, ARTHUR (HOBART). 1887-   .
   -The Ant Heap. Hutchinson, 1934
   The Apache Girl. Collins, 1930
   Black Royalty. Collins, 1933
   The Blue Spider. Collins, 1929
   Brighton Alibi. Collins, 1936
   The Broken Sword. Collins, 1938
   Cafe in Montparnasse. Collins, 1936
   The Danger Game. Hutchinson, 1926
   Don't Touch the Body. Collins, 1947
   Escapade. Collins, 1931
   French Girl. Collins, 1937
   Gentleman of Rio. Collins, 1933
   The Gold Cat. Hutchinson, 1925
   Intrigue Island. Collins, 1930
   Jewel Thief. Collins, 1939
   The Jockey Died First. Staples, 1953
   Judgment of Death. Collins, 1932
   Last Seen Alive. Evans, 1951
   Live Bait. Hutchinson, 1927
   The Maliday Mystery. Staples, 1954
   Modern Cameos. Hutchinson, 1928 ss
   One Man's Secret. Collins, 1932
   Paris Agent. Collins, 1935
   -Pillars of Salt. Duckworth, 1922
   -The Primrose Path. Duckworth, 1923 ss
   Pursued. Collins, 1929
   Shroud of Snow. Evans, 1950
   Stowaway. Collins, 1931
   -Ursula Vanet. Bale, 1921
   White Negro. Collins, 1940
   -White Snake. Hutchinson, 1928
   The Yellow Dragon. Hutchinson, 1924
   Your Number is Up. Evans, 1952

MILLS, CARLEY. 1897-   .
   A Nearness of Evil. Coward, 1961

MILLS, HARRY
   A Daughter of Satan. Katahdin, 1896

His Downward Path. Ogilvie, 1895
The Mossbank Murder. Ogilvie, 1896
The Woman Stealer. Katahdin, 1896

MILLS, HUGH (TRAVERS). Pseudonym: Hugh Travers, q.v.
-The Early Doors. Cresset, 1966
-The House by the Lake. Evans, 1956. (A play.)
In Pursuit of Evil. Triton, 1966; Lippincott, 1967

MILLS, JAMES. 1932- .
One Just Man. Simon, 1974; Sphere, 1976
The Panic in Needle Park. Farrar, 1966; Sphere, 1971
The Prosecutor. Farrar, 1969; Allen, 1970
Report to the Commissioner. Farrar, 1972; Barrie, 1972

MILLS, JOHN. 1930- .
The October Men. Oberon (Ottawa), 1973

MILLS, (WILLIAM) MERVYN. 1906- .
The Long Haul. Macmillan (London), 1956; St. Martin's, 1956

MILLS, OSMINGTON. Pseudonym of Vivian Collin Brooks, 1922- . Series characters: Chief Inspector Baker, in at least those marked B; Patrick C. Shirley and Insp. Rip Irving, in at least those marked S&I.
At One Fell Swoop. Bles, 1963; Roy, 1965 B
The Case of the Flying Fifteen. Bles, 1956 B
Death Enters the Lists. Bles, 1967; Roy, 1967 S&I
Dusty Death. Bles, 1965; Roy, 1966 S&I
Enemies of the Bride. Bles, 1966; Roy, 1967 S&I
Ghost of a Clue. Bles, 1970
Headlines Make Murder. Bles, 1962
Many a Slip. Bles, 1969 S&I
The Misguided Missile. Bles, 1958 B
No Match for the Law. Bles, 1957
Stairway to Murder. Bles, 1959 B
Sundry Fell Designs. Bles, 1968; Roy, 1968
Traitor Betrayed. Bles, 1964; Roy, 1966 B
Trial by Ordeal. Bles, 1961; Roy, 1961 B
Unlucky Break. Bles, 1955; Roy, 1957 B

MILLS, (HARRY ROLAND) WOOSNAM. Series character: John Melrose, in at least those marked JM.
Biting Fortune. Nelson, 1939 JM
Blind Reckoning. Hodder, 1951
Dark Encounter. Nelson, 1938 JM
Dusty Coinage. Hodder, 1953
French Hazard. Hodder, 1942
Grim Chancery. Nelson, 1937 JM
Knaves Rampant. Nelson, 1938 JM
Phantom Scarlet. Hodder, 1940
Shadow Crusade. Hodder, 1941
Tarnished Gold. Hodder, 1951

MILLSON, JULIE
The Face of the Foe. Hale, 1970
The Night has Red Eyes. Hale, 1970

MILLWARD, EDWARD J. Series character: Insp. Gil Flicker = GF.
The Aero Clubs Mystery. Harrap, 1939 GF
The Body Lies. Harrap, 1936 GF
The Copper Bottle. Methuen, 1929; Dutton, 1929
The House of Wraith. Harrap, 1935; Houghton, 1935

MILN, H. CRICHTON. -1957.
The Case of the Rival Race Gangs. Amalgamated Press, 1924. (Sexton Blake.)

MILN, LOUISE JORDAN. 1864-1933.
The Invisible Foe. Jarrolds, 1918; Stokes, 1920. (Novelization of the play by Walter Hackett.)
Mr. Wu. Cassell, 1918; Stokes, 1920. (Adapted from the play by Harry M. Vernon, 1878- , and Harold Owens, 1872- .)
The Purple Mask. Hodder, 1918; Stokes, 1918. (Adapted from the play Le Chevalier au Masque by Paul Armont and Jean Manoussi.)

MILNE, A(LAN) A(LEXANDER). 1882-1956.
Four Days' Wonder. Methuen, 1933; Dutton, 1933
The Fourth Wall. French (London), 1929. U.S. title: The Perfect Alibi. French (New York), 1929. (A play.)
The Perfect Alibi; see The Fourth Wall
The Red House Mystery. Methuen, 1922; Dutton, 1922
A Table Near the Band, and other stories. Methuen, 1950; Dutton, 1950 ss, two criminous

MILNE, SHIRLEY. Series character: Det.-Sgt. Steytler = S.
Beware the Lurking Scorpion. Hale, 1966; London House, 1967
False Witness. Hale, 1964 S
The Hammer of Justice. Hale, 1963 S
Stiff Silk. Hale, 1962 S

MILNER, GEORGE. Pseudonym of George Hardinge.
The Crime Against Marcella. Hodder, 1963
A Dying Fall. H. Hamilton, 1957
A Leavetaking. Hodder, 1966; Dodd, 1966
-The Scarlet Fountains. Collins, 1956
Shark Among Herrings. Collins, 1954
Stately Homicide. Collins, 1953
Your Money and Your Life. H. Hamilton, 1957

MILTON, DAVID SCOTT. 1934- .
Paradise Road. Atheneum, 1974; Ellis, 1974

MILTON, GLADYS ALEXANDRA. Pseudonym: Anthony Carlyle, q.v.

MILTON, JOSEPH. Series character: Bart Gould, in all titles.
Assignment: Assassination. Lancer, 1964. Also published as: The Running Spy. Lancer, 1967
Baron Sinister. Lancer, 1965
The Big Blue Death. Lancer, 1965
The Death Makers. Lancer, 1966
The Man Who Bombed the World. Lancer, 1966
Operation: World War Three. Lancer, 1966
President's Agent. Lancer, 1963
The Running Spy; see Assignment: Assassination
Worldbreaker. Lancer, 1964

MINCHIN, DEVON (GEORGE). 1919- .
The Money Movers. Angus (Sydney), 1972

MINICK, MICHAEL
The Kung Fu Avengers. Bantam (New York & London), 1975

MINNEY, R. J. See: JULIET (EVANGELINE CLYN) RHYS-WILLIAMS, 1898- .

MINOT, GEORGE E(VANS). 1898- .
Murder Will Out. Marshall Jones, 1928. (Somewhat "novelized" true crime accounts.)

MINTON, PAULA. Pseudonym of Paul H. Little. Other pseudonym: Hugo Paul, q.v.
The Dark of Memory. Lancer, 1967
Engraved in Evil. Lancer, 1964
Fog Hides the Fury. Lancer, 1966
The Girl from Nowhere. Major, 1975
Hand of the Imposter. Lancer, 1965
Loom of Terror. Lancer, 1968
The Mask of Medusa. Major, 1975
Orphan of the Shadows. Lancer, 1965
Portrait of Terror. Belmont, 1967
Secret Melody. Lancer, 1964
Shadow of a Witch. Belmont, 1967
Thunder over the Reefs. Lancer, 1967

MIRON, CHARLES
Airport Cop. Manor, 1974

MITCHAM, GILROY. Pseudonym of William Simpson Newton, 1923- . Series character: Nick Marshall = NM.
The Dead Reckoning. Dobson, 1960; Roy, 1960 NM
The Full Stop. Dobson, 1957; Roy, 1957 NM
The Man from Bar Harbour. Dobson, 1958; Roy, 1958 NM
Uncertain Judgement. Dobson, 1961; Roy, 1962

MITCHELL, EDMUND. 1861-1917.
-The Despoilers. Cassell, 1904
Plotters of Paris. Hutchinson, 1900
-The Temple of Death. Hutchinson, 1894

MITCHELL, GLADYS (MAUDE WINIFRED). 1901- . Pseudonym: Malcolm Torrie, q.v. Series character: Mrs. Adela Beatrice Lestrange Bradley, in all titles.
Adders on the Heath. Joseph, 1963; London House, 1963
Brazen Tongue. Joseph, 1940
Come Away, Death. Joseph, 1937
Convent on Styx. Joseph, 1975
The Croaking Raven. Joseph, 1966
Dance to Your Daddy. Joseph, 1969
The Dancing Druids. Joseph, 1948
Dead Men's Morris. Joseph, 1936
Death and the Maiden. Joseph, 1947
Death at the Opera. Grayson, 1934. U.S. title: Death in the Wet. Macrae-Smith, 1934
Death in the Wet; see Death at the Opera
Death of a Delft Blue. Joseph, 1964; London House, 1964
The Devil at Saxon Wall. Grayson, 1935
The Devil's Elbow. Joseph, 1951
The Echoing Strangers. Joseph, 1952
Faintley Speaking. Joseph, 1954
Gory Dew. Joseph, 1970
Groaning Spinney. Joseph, 1950
Hangman's Curfew. Joseph, 1941
A Hearse in May-Day. Joseph, 1972
Here Comes a Chopper. Joseph, 1946
A Javelin for Jonah. Joseph, 1974
Lament for Leto. Joseph, 1971
Laurels are Poison. Joseph, 1942
The Longer Bodies. Gollancz, 1930
The Man Who Grew Tomatoes. Joseph, 1959; London House, 1959
Merlin's Furlong. Joseph, 1953
The Murder of Busy Lizzie. Joseph, 1973
My Bones will Keep. Joseph, 1962; British Book Centre, 1962
My Father Sleeps. Joseph, 1944
The Mystery of a Butcher's Shop. Gollancz, 1929; Dial, 1930
The Nodding Canaries. Joseph, 1961
Pageant of Murder. Joseph, 1965; London House, 1965
Printer's Error. Joseph, 1939
The Rising of the Moon. Joseph, 1945
St. Peter's Finger. Joseph, 1938
The Saltmarsh Murders. Gollancz, 1932; Macrae-Smith, 1933

Say It with Flowers. Joseph, 1960; London House, 1960
Skeleton Island. Joseph, 1967
Speedy Death. Gollancz, 1929; Dial, 1929
Spotted Hemlock. Joseph, 1958; British Book Centre, 1958
Sunset over Soho. Joseph, 1943
Three Quick and Five Dead. Joseph, 1968
Tom Brown's Body. Joseph, 1949
Twelve Horses and the Hangman's Noose. Joseph, 1956; British Book Centre, 1958
The Twenty-Third Man. Joseph, 1957
Watson's Choice. Joseph, 1955; McKay, 1976
When Last I Died. Joseph, 1941; Knopf, 1942
Winking at the Brim. Joseph, 1974; McKay, 1977
The Worsted Viper. Joseph, 1943

MITCHELL, HUTTON
The Deviations of Diana. Philpot, 1923
The Fourth Man. Selwyn, 1931

MITCHELL, JAMES (WILLIAM). 1926- .
Pseudonyms: James Meldrum, James Munro, qq.v. Series character: David Callan, in at least those marked DC.
-Among Arabian Sands. Davies, 1963
Callan; see A Magnum for Schneider
Death and Bright Water. H. Hamilton, 1974; Morrow, 1974 DC
Here's a Villain! Davies, 1957. U.S. title: The Lady is Waiting. Morrow, 1958
-Ilion Like a Mist. Cassell, 1969. Also published as: Venus in Plastic. Corgi, 1970
The Lady is Waiting; see Here's a Villain!
A Magnum for Schneider. Jenkins, 1969. U.S. title: A Red File for Callan. Simon, 1971. Also published as: Callan. Corgi, 1974 DC
A Red File for Callan; see A Magnum for Schneider
Russian Roulette. H. Hamilton, 1973; Morrow, 1973 DC
Smear Job. H. Hamilton, 1975; Putnam, 1977 DC
-Steady, Boys, Steady. Davies, 1960
Venus in Plastic; see Ilion Like a Mist
A Way Back. Davies, 1959; Morrow, 1960, as The Way Back
-The Winners. Cassell, 1970

MITCHELL, LEBBEUS. 1879- .
The Parachute Murder. Macaulay, 1933

MITCHELL, NORMA. See: WILBUR DANIEL STEELE, 1886-1970.

MITCHELL, S(ILAS) WEIR. 1829-1914.
The Adventures of Francois. Century, 1898; Macmillan (London), 1898
The Autobiography of a Quack, and The Case of George Dedlow. Century, 1900
-A Diplomatic Adventure. Century, 1906

MITCHELL, SCOTT. Pseudonym of Lionel Robert Holcombe Godfrey, 1932- . Other pseudonym: Elliot Kennedy, q.v. Series character: Brock Devlin, in at least those marked BD.
Come, Sweet Death. Hammond, 1967 BD
Dead on Arrival. Hale, 1974
Deadly Persuasion. Hammond, 1964 BD
Death's Busy Crossroads. Hale, 1975
Double Bluff. Jenkins, 1968
The Girl in the Wet-Look Bikini. Hale, 1973
A Haven for the Damned. Hale, 1971
A Knife-Edged Thing. Cassell, 1969
The Lonely Shroud. Hammond, 1964 BD
Nice Guys Don't Win. Hale, 1974 BD
Over My Dead Body. Hale, 1974
Rage in Babylon. Hale, 1972
Sables Spell Trouble. Hammond, 1963
Some Dames Play Rough. Hammond, 1963 BD
You'll Never Get to Heaven. Hale, 1972

MITCHELL, WILL
The Goldfish Murders. GM, 1950; Red Seal, 1958

MITFORD, BERTRAM. 1855-1914.
-Aletta. White, 1900
-Averno. Ward, 1913
-A Border Scourge. Long, 1910
The Curse of Clement Waynflete. Ward, 1894
-Dorrien of Cranston. Hurst, 1903
-A Duel Resurrection. Ward, 1910
-The Expiation of Wynne Palliser. Ward, 1896
-The Fire Trumpet. Blackett, 1889
Fordham's Feud. Ward, 1897
-Forging the Blades. Nash, 1908
A Frontier Mystery. White, 1905
-Golden Face. Trischler, 1892
-The Gun-Runner. Chatto, 1899; Fenno, 1898
-Harley Greenoak's Charge. Chatto, 1906
-Haviland's Chum. Chatto, 1903
The Heath Hover Mystery. Ward, 1911
-In the Whirl of the Rising. Methuen, 1904
-The Induna's Wife. White, 1898
-An Island of Eden. Ward, 1913
-John Ames, Native Commissioner. White, 1900
-The King's Assegai. Chatto, 1894; Fenno, 1894
-A Legacy of the Granite Hills. Long, 1909
-The Luck of Gerard Ridgeley. Chatto, 1894
-Ravenshaw of Rietholine. Ward, 1910
-The Red Derelict. Methuen, 1904
-Renshaw Fanning's Quest. Chatto, 1894
-The River of Unrest. Ward, 1912
-The Ruby Sword. White, 1899
-Seaford's Snake. Ward, 1912
-A Secret of the Lebombo. Hurst, 1905
-Selmin of Selmingfold. Ward, 1912
The Sign of the Spider. Methuen, 1896; Dodd, 1896
-The Sirdar's Oath. White, 1904
-The Triumph of Hilary Blackland. Chatto, 1901
-Tween Snow and Fire. Heinemann, 1892; Cassell (New York), 1892
A Veldt Official. Ward, 1895
A Veldt Vendetta. Ward, 1903
-The Weird of Deadly Hollow. Sutton, 1891
-The White Hand and the Black. Long, 1907
-The White Shield. Cassell, 1895; Stokes, 1895
-The Word of the Sorceress. Hutchinson, 1902

MITFORD, C. GUISE
The Dual Identity. Long, 1915
The Hidden Mask. Greening, 1914
-His Dainty Whim. Hutchinson, 1902
-In Camera. Long, 1916
-Izelle of the Dunes. Long, 1907
-Love in Lilac-Land. Long, 1910
The Paxton Plot. Long, 1908
-The Spell of the Snow. Pearson, 1900
-The Wooing of Martha. Nash, 1911

MITTON, G(ERALDINE) E(DITH)
The Judge's Daughters. Nash, 1921

MIZZEN, MATT. Pseudonym of Henry Llewellyn Williams, 1842- .
Binnacle Jack; or, The Cavern of Death. De Witt, 18??
Delaware Dick; or, The Chase of the Whip. De Witt, 18??
The Flying Arrow; or, The Pirate's Revenge. De Witt, 18??

MOBERLY, L(UCY) G(ERTRUDE). 1860- .
-Fingers of Fate. Ward, 1929
-In a Fair Ground. Ward, 1931
-A Leap in the Dark. Mills, 1925
-A Mystery Chain. Ward, 1932
-A Tangled Web. Ward, 1908

MOCKLER, GRETCHEN
Roanleigh. Signet, 1966

MODELL, MERRIAM. 1908- . Pseudonym: Evelyn Piper, q.v.

MOFFAT, GWEN. 1928- .
The Corpse Road. Gollancz, 1974
Deviant Death. Gollancz, 1973
Hard Option. Gollancz, 1975
Lady with a Cool Eye. Gollancz, 1973
Miss Pink at the Edge of the World. Gollancz, 1975; Scribner, 1975

MOFFATT, JAMES. Series characters: Silas Manners, in at least those marked SM; Johnny Canuck, in at least those marked JC.
Blood is a Personal Thing. Compact, 1965
Blue Line Murder. Compact, 1965; Leisure, 1970 JC
Course of Villainy. Compact, 1966
-The Courtyard. New English Library pb, 1970
Curtain of Hate. Compact, 1966
The Eighth Veil. Compact, 1965
The Girl from H.A.R.D. New English Library, 1973
Justice for a Dead Spy. New English Library pb, 1971 SM
The Naked Light. New English Library pb, 1970
Perfect Assignment. New English Library pb, 1975. (Girl from H.A.R.D. series)
The Sleeping Bomb. New English Library pb, 1970 SM
Terror-Go-Round. Compact, 1966
Time for Sleeping. Compact, 1965; Leisure, 1970 JC
The Twisted Thread. Compact, 1966
Virginia Box and the "Unsatisfied". New English Library pb, 1974. (Girl from H.A.R.D. series.)

MOFFETT, CLEVELAND. 1863-1926.
The Bishop's Purse, with Oliver Herford, 1863- . Appleton, 1913
The Master Mind. Appleton, 1927
The Mysterious Card. Small, 1912
Possessed. McCann, 1920
The Seine Mystery. Dodd, 1925; Melrose, 1924
Through the Wall. Appleton, 1909; Melrose, 1910
True Detective Stories from the Archives of the Pinkertons. Doubleday, 1897 ss

MOISEIWITSCH, MAURICE
-Bring Me my Bow. Muller, 1942
-Comrade Souvarin. Muller, 1945
-Mr. Penny. Muller, 1938
-Mr. Penny at War. Angus, 1942
-Mr. Penny Comes Down Heads. Argus, 1945 ss
Post-Mortem. Marlowe, 1947
She, the Accused. Heinemann, 1956
-A Sky-Blue Life. Heinemann, 1956
-The Sleeping Tiger. Heinemann, 1955
Woolf Sarason, Special Agent. Muller, 1941

-Yesterday's Enemy. Corgi, 1959. (Novelization of the play by Peter N. Newman.)

MOLE, WILLIAM. Pseudonym of William Antony Younger, 1917-1962. Series character: Casson Duker = CD.
Goodbye is not Worthwhile. Eyre, 1956 CD
The Hammersmith Maggot. Eyre, 1955. U.S. title: Small Venom. Dodd, 1956. Also published as: Shadow of a Killer. Dell, 1959 CD
The Lobster Guerillas. Eyre, 1953
Shadow of a Killer; see The Hammersmith Maggot
Skin Trap. Eyre, 1957. U.S. title: You Pay for Pity. Dodd, 1958 CD
Small Venom; see The Hammersmith Maggot
-Trample an Empire. Eyre, 1952
You Pay for Pity; see Skin Trap

MOLL, ELICK. 1907- .
Night Without Sleep. Little, 1950; Davies, 1951

MOLLOY, J(OSEPH) FITZGERALD. 1858-1908.
An Excellent Knave. Hutchinson, 1893; Lovell, 1892
His Wife's Soul. Hutchinson, 1893. U.S. title: Sweet is Revenge. Taylor, 1891. Also published in England as: Sweet is Revenge; or, His Wife's Soul. Hutchinson, 1895
How Came He Dead? Lovell, 1890. (British title?)
-It is no Wonder. Hurst, 1882
-A Justified Sinner. Downey, 1897
-Merely Players. Tinsley, 1881
-A Modern Magician. Ward, 1887; Lovell, 1888
Sweet is Revenge; see His Wife's Soul
-That Villain, Romeo! Ward, 1886
-What Hast Thou Done? Hurst, 1883; Harper, 1883

MOLNAR, LOUIS. See: CHARLES SAXBY.

MOLYNEAUX, C. B.
Death Called Twice. Pemberton, 1949
Murder in a Madhouse. Pemberton, 1946
The Poison Cocktail Murders. Pemberton, 1944

MONAHAN, JOHN. Pseudonym of W(illiam) R(iley) Burnett, 1899- , q.v.
Big Stan. GM, 1953; Fawcett (London), 1955

MONIG, CHRISTOPHER. Pseudonym of Kendell Foster Crossen, 1910- , q.v. Other pseudonyms: Bennett Barlay, M. E. Chaber, Richard Foster, Clay Richards, qq.v. Series character: Brian Brett, in all titles.
Abra-Cadaver. Dutton, 1958; Boardman, 1958
The Burned Man. Dutton, 1956; Boardman, 1957. Also published as: Don't Count the Corpses. Dell, 1958
Don't Count the Corpses; see The Burned Man
The Lonely Graves. Dutton, 1960; Boardman, 1961
Once Upon a Crime. Dutton, 1959; Boardman, 1960

MONIGLE, MARTHA
The Doll Castle. Ballantine, 1975

MONK, ELLIOT. See: BEATRICE BASKERVILLE.

MONKSHOOD, G. F. Pseudonym of William James Clarke, 1872- .
My Lady Ruby and John Basileon, Chief of Police. Greening, 1899. (2 stories.)

MONMOUTH, JACK. Pseudonym of William Leonard Pember. Series character: Tom Langley, in at least those marked TL.
The Donovan Case. Jarrolds, 1955 TL
Lightning over Mayfair. Hale, 1958 TL
Lonely, Lovely Lady. Jarrolds, 1956 TL
Not Ready to Die. Hale, 1960
Sleepy-Eyed Blonde. Hale, 1957 TL

MONNOW, PETER. Pseudonym of Glynn Croudace, 1917- , q.v.
Fire Opal. Jenkins, 1968
The Hooded Skull. Hale, 1972
The Killing of Alquin Judd. Jenkins, 1969

MONRO, GAVIN. Pseudonym of Gertrude Monro-Higgs.
A Bent for Blackmail. Hale, 1967
Marked with a Cross. Hale, 1968
Trip to Eternity. Hale, 1970
Who Killed Amanda? Hale, 1967

MONRO-HIGGS, GERTRUDE. Pseudonym: Gavin Monro, q.v.

MONROE, ROY. Pseudonym. 1913- .
The Judge Speaks. Exposition, 1958

MONSARRAT, NICHOLAS (JOHN TURNEY). 1910- .
Castle Garac. Pan, 1968; Knopf, 1955
The Nylon Pirates. Cassell, 1960; Sloane, 1960
The Ship That Died of Shame, and other stories. Cassell, 1959; Sloane, 1959 ss
Smith & Jones. Cassell, 1963; Sloane, 1963
Something to Hide. Cassell, 1965; Morrow, 1966
-The Time Before This. Cassell, 1962; Sloane, 1962

MONSKY, MARK. 1941- .
Looking Out for #1. Simon, 1975

MONTAGU, IRVING
Absolutely True. Allen, 1893

MONTAGUE, CHARLES HOWARD
The Countess Muta. Belford, 1889; Routledge, 1890
-The Doctor's Mistake; or, What Myrta Saw, with Clement Milton Hammond. T. Downey, 1888
The Face of Rosenfel. Burt, 1888
-The Romance of Lilies. Harris, 1886
Two Strokes of the Bell. Harris, 1886
Written in Red, with C. W. Dyar. Cassell (New York), 1890

MONTAGUE, JEFFREY. Series character: John Jeremy, in both titles.
John Jeremy—Cracksman. Allan, 1936
The Mandarin's Pearl. Quality, 1942

MONTAGUE, JOSEPH
Whose Millions? Chelsea, 1925

MONTANDON, PAT
The Intruders. Coward, 1975

MONTANYE, C(ARLETON) S(TEVENS). 1892-1948.
Moons in Gold. Lippincott, 1936; Harrap, 1937

MONTEILHET, HUBERT. 1928- .
Andromache; or, The Inadvertent Murder. Simon, 1970; Hodder, 1971. (Translation of Andromac ou le Meurtre par Inadvertance. Paris, 1968.)
Cupid's Executioners. Simon, 1967; Hodder, 1967. (Translation of Les Bourreaux de Cupidon. Paris, 1966.)
The Cupidevil. Simon, 1970; Hodder, 1970. (Translation of Le Cupidiable. Paris, 1967.)
Murder at Leisure. Simon, 1971; Hodder, 1972. (Translation of Meurtre a Loisir. Paris, 1969.)
A Perfect Crime, or Two. Simon, 1971. (Translation of De Quelques Crimes Parfaits. Paris, 1969.)
Phoenix from the Ashes; see Return from the Ashes
Praying Mantis; see The Praying Mantises
The Praying Mantises. Simon, 1962. British title: Praying Mantis. H. Hamilton, 1962. (Translation of Les Mantes Religieuses. Paris, 1960.)
The Prisoner of Love. Simon, 1965; Chapman, 1966. (Translation of Le Forcat de l'Amour. Paris, 1965.)
Return from the Ashes. Simon, 1963. British title: Phoenix from the Ashes. H. Hamilton, 1963. (Translation of Le Retour des Cendres. Paris, 1961.)
The Road to Hell. Simon, 1964; Chapman, 1965. (Translation of Les Paves du Diable. Paris, 1963.)

MONTGOMERIE, JAMES
Implosion. Baker, 1974

MONTGOMERY, IONE. Series character: Christopher Gibson, in both titles.
Death Won a Prize. Doubleday, 1941; Cherry Tree (abridged), 1944
The Golden Dress. Doubleday, 1940; Boardman, 1944

MONTGOMERY, MARY. -1975.
Somebody Knew. Arcadia, 1961

MONTGOMERY, ROBERT BRUCE. 1921- .
Pseudonym: Edmund Crispin, q.v.

MONTROSE, DAVID. Series character: Russell Teed, in at least those marked RT.
The Body on Mount Royal. Harlequin, 1953
The Crime on Cote des Neiges. Collins pb (Toronto), 1951 RT
-Gambling with Fire. Hale, 1969
Murder over Dorval. Collins pb (Toronto), 1952 RT

MONTROSE, GRAHAM. Pseudonym of Charles Roy Mackinnon, 1924- . Series character: Angel Brown, in all titles.
Angel Abroad. Hale, 1969
Angel and the Nero. Hale, 1971
Angel and the Red Admiral. Hale, 1972
Angel at Arms. Hale, 1971
Angel in Paradise. Hale, 1970
Angel of Death. Hale, 1968
Angel of no Mercy. Hale, 1968
Angel of Vengeance. Hale, 1970
Ask an Angel. Hale, 1970
Fanfare for Angel. Hale, 1971
A Matter of Motive. Hale, 1969
Send for Angel. Hale, 1970
Where Angel Treads. Hale, 1969

MONTROSS, DAVID. Pseudonym of Jean Louise Backus, 1914- . Series character: Remsen, in all titles.
Fellow-Traveler. Doubleday, 1965; Hale, 1966
Traitor's Wife. Doubleday, 1962; Gollancz, 1962

Troika. Doubleday, 1963; Gollancz, 1963. Also published as: Who is Elissa Sheldon? Paperback Library, 1967
Who is Elissa Sheldon?; see Troika

MOODEY, MARTHA LIVINGSTON
-Alan Thorne. Lothrop, 1889
The Tragedy of Brinkwater. Cassell (New York), 1887; Cassell (London), 1888

MOODIE, EDWIN
The Great Shakes. Museum, 1956

MOODY, ALAN B. 1900-1944.
The House in Ralston Place. Gem, 1926

MOODY, LAURENCE. 1907- .
Some Must Die. Hale, 1964

MOONEY, JAMES. See also: John W. Postgate.
A Millionaire's Folly; or, The Beautiful Unknown. Ogilvie, 1888
The Trail of the Barrow; or, The Brother's Revenge. Ogilvie, 1888

MOOR, EMILY. Pseudonym of Richard Deming, 1915- , q.v. Other pseudonym: Max Franklin, q.v. See also: NICK MARINO.
The Shadowed Porch. Beagle, 1972

MOORCOCK, MICHAEL (JOHN). 1939- .
Series character: Jerry Cornelius = JC.
The Chinese Agent. Hutchinson, 1970; Macmillan, 1970
A Cure for Cancer. Allison, 1970; Holt, 1971 JC
The English Assassin. Allison, 1972; Harper, 1974 JC

MOORE, ANDREW
The Serbian Assignment. Apollo, 1971

MOORE, ARTHUR and CLAYTON (HARTLEY) MATTHEWS, 1918- , q.v. For Moore, see also: DON HOYT. Joint pseudonyms of Arthur Moore and Marilyn Granbeck: Adam Hamilton, Van Saxon, qq.v. Joint pseudonym of Arthur Moore and Alfred Harris, 1928- , q.v.: Gwen Addison, q.v. Joint pseudonym of Clayton Matthews and Patricia Matthews, 1927- : Patty Brisco, q.v.
Las Vegas. PB, 1974; Futura, 1975

MOORE, AUSTIN. Pseudonym of (Charles) Augustus (Carlow) Muir, 1892- , q.v.
Birds of the Night. Hodder, 1930; Smith, 1931. Reprinted as by Augustus Muir: Methuen, 1937
The House of Lies. Hodder, 1932; Doubleday, 1932. Revised and published as by Augustus Muir: Methuen, 1939

MOORE, BRIAN. 1921- .
The Revolution Script. Holt, 1971; Cape, 1971

MOORE, CARLYLE. 1875- . See also: GEORGE C(HARLES) JENKS, 1850-1929.
Listening In. French (New York & London), 1928. (Play.)
Stop Thief! French, 1917. (Play.)

MOORE, CHARLES K.
A Case of Blackmail. Arrowsmith, 1900

MOORE, CLAYTON. Pseudonym of Marilyn Granbeck. Other pseudonym: Ben Grant, q.v. Joint pseudonyms with Arthur Moore, q.v.: Adam Hamilton, Van Saxon, qq.v.

The Corrupters. Berkley, 1974
End of Reckoning. Berkley, 1974

MOORE, DONALD. 1923- .
Highway of Fear. Hodder, 1961

MOORE, DORINNE
The Caverns of Falkenhorst. Berkley, 1973
Flight from Eden Key. Berkley, 1974
The Legend of Monk's Court. Beagle, 1974
Masquerade at Monfalcone. Berkley, 1974
Miranda's Curse. Berkley, 1973

MOORE, DORIS LANGLEY. 1903- .
-All Done by Kindness. Cassell, 1951

MOORE, EMMA
Shallow Runs the River. Belmont, 1967

MOORE, F(RANK) FRANKFORT. 1855-1931.
-"I Forbid the Banns". Hutchinson, 1893; Street, 1901

MOORE, FREDERICK FERDINAND. 1877- .
The Devil's Admiral. Doubleday, 1913; Richards, 1913

MOORE, H(ARRY) F. S.
Death at 7:10. Doubleday, 1943
Murder Goes Rolling Along. Doubleday, 1942
Shed a Bitter Tear. Doubleday, 1944

MOORE, IRVING. See: LILLIAN BERGQUIST.

MOORE, MARY GALBRAITH. 1930- . Pseudonym: Helena Osborne, q.v.

MOORE, PHILIPS
Death Drives the Lead Car. Arcadia, 1961
Once Upon a Friday. Tower, 1965. Also published as: The Psycho. Tower, 1969
The Psycho; see Once Upon a Friday

MOORE, ROBERT LOWELL, JR. 1925- .
Pseudonym: Robin Moore, q.v.

MOORE, ROBIN. Pseudonym of Robert Lowell Moore, Jr., 1925- .
Court-Martial, with Henry Rothblatt. Doubleday, 1971; Harrap, 1972
The Family Man, with Milt Machlin. Pyramid, 1974; Panther, 1977
The Fifth Estate. Doubleday, 1973; Allen, 1973
French Connection II, with Milt Machlin. Dell, 1975; Futura, 1975. (Novelization of the movie.)
The Italian Connection, with Al Dempsey. Pinnacle, 1975
The Khaki Mafia, with June Collins. Crown, 1971
The London Switch, with Al Dempsey. Pinnacle, 1974
Phase of Darkness, with Al Dempsey. Third Press, 1974; New English Library, 1975
The Set-Up, with Milt Machlin. Pyramid, 1975; Coronet, 1977

MOORE, RUTH. 1903- .
-Lizzie and Caroline. Morrow, 1972

MOORE, WINNIE FIELDS
Wings of Destiny. Wetzel, 1930 ss

MOORHOUSE, HERBERT JOSEPH. 1882- .
Pseudonym: Hopkins Moorhouse, q.v.

MOORHOUSE, HOPKINS. Pseudonym of Herbert Joseph Moorhouse, 1882- . Series character: Addison Kent = AK.
-Every Man for Himself. Hodder, 1920
The Gauntlet of Alceste. Musson (Toronto), 1921; Hodder, 1922; McCann, 1922 AK
The Golden Scarab. Hodder, 1926 AK

MORAN, MIKE. Pseudonym of William (Thomas) Ard, 1922-1960, q.v. Other pseudonyms: Ben Kerr, Thomas Wills, q.v.
Double Cross. Popular Library, 1953

MORAND, PAUL. 1888- .
East India and Company. Boni, 1927
ss, some criminous

MORDEN, T. R.
Steps in Mystery. Smith, 1935

MOREL, DIGHTON. Pseudonym of Kenneth Lewis Warner, 1918- .
Moonlight Red. Secker, 1960

MORELLA, JANE
Dark Memories. Lancer, 1971

MORELLI, SPIKE
Coffin for a Cutie. Harborough, 1952
Deal Me Out. Harborough, 1952
Give It to Me Straight. Harborough, 1953
More Than Kisses, Baby. Harborough, 1952
No Place for Me. Harborough, 1953
Take It and Like It. Archer, 1951
This Way for Hell. Leisure Library, 195?. (British title?)
You'll Never Get Me. Archer, 1950

MORETTE, EDGAR
The Sturgis Wager. Stokes, 1899

MORGAN, ALLAN. Series character: Blood, in all titles.
Blood. Award, 1974; Tandem, 1974
The Cat Cay Warrant. Award, 1974
The Spandau Warrant. Award, 1974; Tandem, 1974

MORGAN, BRYAN (STANFORD). 1923-1976.
The Business at Blanche Capel. H. Hamilton, 1953; Little, 1953

MORGAN, CLARINDA
Devil's Cavern. Lancer, 1969

MORGAN, DAN. 1925- .
The Richest Corpse in Show Business. Compact, 1966

MORGAN, DEAN. Series characters: Rogue Ransome, in at least those marked RR; Rostron Outfit, in at least those marked RO.
Assassin Trail. Hamilton Stafford, 1952
Assignment to Sante Fe. Hamilton Stafford, 1952
Contract for a Homicide. Hamilton Stafford, 1952
Desperate Justice. Hamilton Stafford, 1952
Four Guns to Carson City. Hamilton Stafford, 1952
Four of a Kind. Hamilton Stafford, 1951
Green Hell Rampage. Hamilton Stafford, 1952
Murder on Coney Island. Hamilton Stafford, 1952
Nevada Alibi. Hamilton Stafford, 1952
Rogue Ransome—Manhunter. Hamilton Stafford, 1952 RR
Rogue Ransome—Racket Buster. Hamilton Stafford, 1952 RR
Rogue Ransome—Triggerman. Hamilton Stafford, 1952 RR

The Rostron Outfit. Hamilton Stafford, 1951 RO
Rostron Outfit in Chicago. Hamilton Stafford, 1952 RO
Rostron Outfit in Mexico. Hamilton Stafford, 1952 RO
Rostron Outfit in Rio. Hamilton Stafford, 1952 RO
Rostron Outfit to Texas. Hamilton Stafford, 1952 RO
Rostron Outfit—Undercover Agents. Hamilton Stafford, 1952 RO

MORGAN, GEOFFREY. 1916- . Series character: Ricky Straight, in at least those marked RS.
Heavenly Body. Robertson, 1953 RS
Murderer's Moon. Jenkins, 1942
No Crest for the Wicked. Robertson, 1952 RS

MORGAN, JASON
Death is a Swinger. Lancer, 1971

MORGAN, JOHN. Pseudonym of Lauran Bosworth Paine, 1916- . Other pseudonyms: John Armour, Reg Batchelor, Kenneth Bedford, Frank Bosworth, Mark Carrel, Robert Clarke, Richard Dana, J. F. Drexler, Troy Howard, Jared Ingersol, John Kilgore, Hunter Liggett, J. K. Lucas, qq.v.
Death to Comrade X. Hale, 1969
The Ivory Penguin. Hale, 1974
The Killer's Manual. Hale, 1972
The Midnight Murder. Hale, 1971
Murderers Don't Smile. Hale, 1969
The Nicest Corpse. Hale, 1970
The Perfect Frame. Hale, 1970
Spy in the Tunnel. Hale, 1969
To Kill a Hero. Hale, 1969

MORGAN, JOHNNY [JOHN GLANFIL MORGAN]
-Involved. Heinemann, 1967
-Nothing Barred. Secker, 1965

MORGAN, LORNA NICHOLL
Another Little Murder. Macdonald, 1947
The Death Box. Macdonald, 1946
Murder in Devil's Hollow. World's Work, 1944
Talking of Murder. Harrap, 1945

MORGAN, MICHAEL. Joint pseudonym of C. E. Carle and Dean M. Dorn.
The Blonde Body; see Nine More Lives
Decoy. Ace, 1953
-His Kind of Woman. Pyramid, 1954
Nine More Lives. Random, 1947. Also published as: The Blonde Body. Lion, 1949

MORGAN, MURRAY C(ROMWELL). 1916- . Pseudonym: Cromwell Murray, q.v.
The Viewless Winds. Dutton, 1949

MORGAN, PATRICK. Series character: Bill Cartwright (Operation Hang Ten series), in all titles.
Beach Queen Blowout. Macfadden, 1971
Cute and Deadly Surf Twins. Macfadden, 1970
Deadly Group Down Under. Macfadden, 1970
Death Car Surfside. Macfadden, 1972
Freaked Out Stranger. Manor, 1973
The Girl in the Telltale Bikini. Macfadden, 1971
Hang Dead Hawaiian Style. Macfadden, 1969
Scarlet Surf at Makaha. Macfadden, 1970
Too Mini Murders. Macfadden, 1969
Topless Dancer Hangup. Macfadden, 1971

MORGAN, THOMAS CHRISTOPHER. Pseudonym: John Muir, q.v.

MORICE, ANNE. Pseudonym of Felicity Shaw, 1918- . Series character: Tessa Crichton, in all titles
Death and the Dutiful Daughter. Macmillan (London), 1973; St. Martin's, 1974
Death in the Grand Manor. Macmillan (London), 1970
Death of a Gay Dog. Macmillan (London), 1971
Death of a Heavenly Twin. Macmillan (London), 1974; St. Martin's, 1974
Killing with Kindness. Macmillan (London), 1974; St. Martin's, 1975
Murder in Married Life. Macmillan (London), 1971
Murder on French Leave. Macmillan (London), 1972
Nursery Tea and Poison. Macmillan (London), 1975; St. Martin's, 1975

MORLAND, CATHERINE
Castle Black. Beagle, 1972

MORLAND, NIGEL. 1905- . Pseudonyms: Mary Dane, John Donavan, Norman Forrest, Roger Garnett, Vincent McCall, Neil Shepherd, qq.v. Series characters: Det. Insp. Rory Luccan = RL; Mrs. Palmyra Pym = PP; Chief Inspector Andy McMurdo = AM; Steven Malone = SM.
The Big Killing. Foster, 1946 (63 pp.)
Blood on the Stars. Low, 1951 AM
A Bullet for Midas. Cassell, 1958 PP
Call Him Early for the Murder. Cassell, 1952 PP
The Careless Hangman; see The Clue of the Careless Hangman
The Case of the Innocent Wife. Arrow, 1947 (31 pp.)
The Case Without a Clue. Cassell, 1938; Farrar, 1938 PP
The Clue in the Mirror. Cassell, 1937; Farrar, 1938 PP
The Clue of the Bricklayer's Aunt. Cassell, 1936; Farrar, 1937 PP
The Clue of the Careless Hangman. Cassell, 1940. U.S. title: The Careless Hangman. Farrar, 1941 PP
A Coffin for the Body. Cassell, 1943 PP
The Concrete Maze. Cassell, 1960 PP
Corpse in the Circus. Vallancey, 1945 (16 pp.)
Corpse in the Circus and other stories. Polybooks, 1946 (62 pp.) ss
The Corpse on the Flying Trapeze. Cassell, 1941; Farrar, 1941 PP
The Corpse was No Lady. Low, 1950 AM
The Dear, Dead Girls. Cassell, 1961 PP
Death and the Golden Boy. Cassell, 1958 PP
Death for Sale. Hale, 1957 AM
Death Takes a Star. Todd, 1943 (16 pp.)
Death Takes an Editor. Aldor, 1949 SM
Death to the Ladies. Hale, 1959 AM?
Death When She Wakes. Evans, 1951 RL
Death's Sweet Music; see Exit to Music and other stories
Dressed to Kill. Cassell, 1947 PP
Dumb Alibi. M B Books, 194?
Exit to Music and other stories. Bonde, 1947. Also published as: Death's Sweet Music. Century, 1947, abr. ss
-Fish are So Trusting. Century, 1948
A Girl Died Singing. Evans, 1952 RL
A Gun for a God. Cassell, 1940. U.S. title: Murder in Wardour Street. Farrar, 1940 PP
The Hatchet Murders. Arrow, 1947
He Hanged his Mother on Monday. Low, 1951 AM

How Many Coupons for a Shroud? Laird, 1946 (34 pp.) ss
A Knife for the Killer. Cassell, 1939. U.S. title: Murder at Radio City. Farrar, 1939 PP
The Laboratory Murder and other stories. Polybooks, 1944 (16 pp.) ss
The Lady had a Gun. Cassell, 1951 PP
Look in Any Doorway. Cassell, 1957 PP
Mrs. Pym of Scotland Yard. Vallancey, 1946 PP ss
The Moon Murders. Cassell, 1935 PP
The Moon was Made for Murder. Low, 1953 AM
Murder at Radio City; see A Knife for the Killer
Murder in Wardour Street; see A Gun for a God
Murder Runs Wild. Halle, 1946
No Coupons for a Shroud. Low, 1949 AM
The Phantom Gunman. Cassell, 1935 PP
A Rope for the Hanging. Cassell, 1938; Farrar, 1939 PP
She Didn't Like Dying. Low, 1948 AM
Sing a Song of Cyanide. Cassell, 1953 PP
So Quiet a Death. Cassell, 1960 PP
The Sooper's Cases. Todd, 1943 (16 pp.)
Strangely She Died. Jenkins, 1946 SM
The Street of the Leopard. Cassell, 1936 PP
26 Three-Minute Thrillers. Arrow, 1947. (32 pp.) ss
Two Dead Charwomen. Low, 1949 AM

MORLEY, CHARLES
The Confessions of an Old Burglar. Newnes, 1900 ss

MORLEY, CHRISTOPHER (DARLINGTON). 1890-1957.
The Haunted Bookshop. Doubleday, 1919; Chapman, 1920
Tales from a Rolltop Desk. Doubleday, 1921; Curtis Brown, 1921 ss

MORLEY, F(RANK) V(IGOR). 1899- . Dwelly Lane. Eyre, 1952. U.S. title: Death in Dwelly Lane. Harper, 1952

MORNINGSTAR, LILLIAN
Hour of Death. Phoenix, 1950

MOROSO, JOHN A(NTONIO). 1874-1957.
The City of Silent Men; see The Quarry
The Listening Man. Appleton, 1924 ss
The People Against Nancy Preston. Holt, 1921; Methuen, 1922
The Quarry. Little, 1913. British title: The City of Silent Men. Low, 1922

MORRAH, DERMOT (MICHAEL MacGREGOR). 1896-1974.
The Mummy Case. Faber, 1933. U.S. title: The Mummy Case Mystery. Harper, 1933

MORRELL, DAVID. 1943- .
First Blood. Evans, 1972; Barrie, 1972
Testament. Evans, 1975; Chatto, 1976

MORRIS, ANTHONY P(ASCHEL). 1849-1921. Series character: Mark Magic, in at least those marked MM.
Burnt Powder; or, The Young Army Detective. Novelist Publishing, 1883
The Cipher Detective; or, Mark Magic on a New Trail. Westbrook, 19?? MM
Electro Pete, the Man of Fire; or, The Wharf Rats of Locust Point. Westbrook, 19??
The Head Hunter; or, Mark Magic in the Mines. Westbrook, 19?? MM
Mark Magic, the Detective; or, A Story of a Beautiful Woman's Strange Career. Westbrook, 19?? MM

MORRIS, ARTHUR
    The Dealer in Death and other stories.
      Cotton, 1897 ss

MORRIS, BESSIE C. Joint pseudonym with
    Anne B. Spear: Forfex et Hesta, q.v.

MORRIS, CHARLES (SMITH). 1833-1922. Pseu-
    donym: C. E. Tripp, q.v.
    Cap Colt, the Quaker Detective. West-
      brook, 19??
    The Detective's Crime; or, The Van
      Peltz Diamonds. Rand, 1887
    The Pinkerton Ferret; or, Three Against
      One. Westbrook, 19??
    The Stolen Letter; or, Frank Sharp, the
      Washington Detective. Rand, 1887

MORRIS, DAVID HENRY ST. LAWRENCE.
    1920-   . Pseudonym: David Lawrence,
    q.v.

MORRIS, EDWARD
    The Five Fowlers. Bles, 1953
    The Plume of Smoke. Bles, 1952
    The Small Hotel. Bles, 1953

MORRIS, EDWARD A. Pseudonym: Karl
    Kramer, q.v.

MORRIS, GOODALL VARNE
    Gold of Vala. Fontana, 1970

MORRIS, GWENDOLEN SUTHERLAND. Pseudonym:
    Morris Sutherland, q.v

MORRIS, IRA
    Kidnap. Dobson, 1974

MORRIS, JEAN. 1924-   . Pseudonym:
    Kenneth O'Hara, q.v.
    Man and Two Gods. Cassell, 1953;
      Viking, 1954

MORRIS, JOE ALEX. 1904-   .
    The Bird Watcher. McKay, 1966; Cassell,
      1968

MORRIS, JOHN. Joint pseudonym of John
    Hearne and Morris Cargill, 1914-   .
    Series character: Robin McKay, in
    all titles.
    The Candywine Development. Collins,
      1970; Citadel, 1971
    The Checkerboard Caper. Citadel, 1975
    Fever Grass. Collins, 1969; Putnam,
      1969

MORRIS, R. A. V.
    The Lyttleton Case. Collins, 1922

MORRIS, T(HOMAS) B(ADEN). 1900-   .
    Series character: Inspector Headley,
    in at least those marked H.
    Blind Bargain. Hale, 1957
    Crash into Murder. Hale, 1961
    The Crime of Mildred Bentham. French,
      1955. (A play.)
    The Crooked Tree. Deane, 1963; Baker,
      1963. (A play.)
    Death Among the Orchids. Hale, 1959
    Deserted Night. Evans, 1961. (A play.)
    The Horns of Truth. Hale, 1972
    Mandrakes in the Cupboard. Hale, 1960
    Mine Enemy My Friend. Miller, 1960. (A
      play.)
    The Muddy Leaf Mystery. Hale, 1971
    Murder on the Loire. Hale, 1964
    Murder Without Men. French, 1948. (A
      play.)
    Nightmare Chessboard. French, 1959. (A
      play.)
    Orchids with Murder. Hale, 1966 H
    The Papyrus Murder. Hale, 1958 H
    Return to a Traitor. Hale, 1962
    Shadows on Abu Simbel. Hale, 1967
    Simple Justice. French, 1949. (A play.)
    So Many Dangers. Hale, 1960
    Storm in the Sand. Hale, 1965
    Third Time Unlucky. Hale, 1973
    Two Aunts and a Grandmother. French,
      1946. (A play.)
    Undying Serpent. Hale, 1970
    Wild Justice. Hale, 1965
    -The Woman and the Wheel. Muller, 1953

MORRIS, TOM. See: JOHN MILES.

MORRIS, W(ALTER) F(REDERICK). 1892-   .
    Bretherton: Khaki or Field Grey? Bles,
      1929. U.S. title: "G.B." Dodd, 1929
    The Channel Mystery. Joseph, 1939
    "G.B."; see Bretherton
    The Hold-Up. Bles, 1933
    No Turning Back. Joseph, 1937
    -Pagan. Bles, 1931
    Something to his Advantage. Bles, 1935

MORRISON, ALEXANDER
    The Crookshaven Murder. Houghton, 1927

MORRISON, ARTHUR. 1863-1945. Series char-
    acter: Martin Hewitt = MH.
    Adventures of Martin Hewitt. Ward,
      1896 MH ss
    Chronicles of Martin Hewitt. Ward,
      1895; Appleton, 1896 MH ss
    The Dorrington Deed-Box. Ward, 1897 ss
    The Green Diamond; see The Green Eye of
      Goona
    The Green Eye of Goona. Nash, 1904.
      U.S. title: The Green Diamond. Page,
      1904 ss
    The Hole in the Wall. Methuen, 1902;
      McClure, 1902
    Martin Hewitt, Investigator. Ward,
      1894; Harper, 1894 MH ss
    The Red Triangle. Nash, 1903; Page,
      1903 MH ss

MORRISON, EMMELINE
    -A Tale Untold. Hutchinson, 1956

MORRISON, HUGO
    The Low Road. Methuen, 1930

MORRISON, JAMES W. R.
    Operation Steal. Hale, 1972

MORRISON, ROBERTA. Pseudonym of Jean
    Francis Webb, 1910-   , q.v.
    Tree of Evil. Paperback Library, 1966

MORRISON, THOMAS JAMES. 1906-   . Pseu-
    donym: Alan Muir, q.v.

MORRISON, (JAMES) WOODS
    Road End. Putnam, 1927

MORRISSEY, J(AMES) L(AWRENCE)
    Design for Blackmail. Hutchinson, 1935
    The Double Problem. Burns, 1932
    High Doom. Hutchinson, 1933
    Necktie for Norman. Gifford, 1949
    Off with his Head. Gifford, 1947
    Poison is Queen. Gifford, 1949

MORROW, SUSAN.   -1975.
    Dancing with a Tiger. Doubleday, 1968;
      Hale, 1969
    The Insiders. Doubleday, 1967; Hale,
      1967
    The Moonlighters. Doubleday, 1966;
      Hale, 1967
    Murder may Follow. Doubleday, 1959;
      Collins, 1960
    The Rules of the Game. Doubleday, 1964;
      Hale, 1964
    A Season of Evil. Doubleday, 1969

MORROW, WILLIAM C(HAMBERS). 1853-1923.
    The Ape, the Idiot and Other People.
      Lippincott, 1897; Richards, 1898
      ss, some criminous

    Blood-Money. Walker, 1882
    -A Man; his Mark. Lippincott, 1900;
      Richards, 1900

MORSE, ANNE CHRISTENSON. 1915-   . Pseu-
    donym: Ann Head, q.v.

MORSE, ELIZABETH
    The Emerald Buddha. Dutton, 1935

MORSE, F(LORENCE) V(OLPE). 1887-   .
    Black Eagles are Flying. Doubleday,
      1943

MORTIMER, PETER. Pseudonym (?) of Dorothy
    James Roberts, 1903-   .
    If a Body Kill a Body. Mystery House,
      1946

MORTLOCK, BILL. Pseudonym.
    A Planned Coincidence. Gollancz, 1963;
      Macmillan, 1964

MORTON, ANTHONY. Pseudonym of John Crea-
    sey, 1908-1973, q.v. Other pseudo-
    nyms: Gordon Ashe, M. E. Cooke, Nor-
    man Deane, Robert Caine Frazer, Pat-
    rick Gill, Michael Halliday, Charles
    Hogarth, Brian Hope, Colin Hughes,
    Kyle Hunt, Abel Mann, Peter Manton,
    J. J. Marric, Richard Martin, Rodney
    Mattheson, Jeremy York, qq.v. Series
    character: John Mannering (The Baron)
    = JM.
    Affair for the Baron. Hodder, 1967;
      Walker, 1968 JM
    Alias Blue Mask; see Alias the Baron
    Alias the Baron. Low, 1939. U.S. title:
      Alias Blue Mask. Lippincott, 1939 JM
    Attack the Baron. Low, 1951 JM
    Bad for the Baron. Hodder, 1962. U.S.
      title: The Baron and the Stolen
      Legacy. Scribner, 1967 JM
    The Baron Again. Low, 1938. U.S. title:
      Salute Blue Bask. Lippincott, 1938 JM
    The Baron and the Arrogant Artist. Hod-
      der, 1972; Walker, 1973 JM
    The Baron and the Beggar. Low, 1947;
      Duell, 1950 JM
    The Baron and the Chinese Puzzle. Hod-
      der, 1965; Scribner, 1966 JM
    The Baron and the Missing Old Masters.
      Hodder, 1968; Walker, 1969 JM
    The Baron and the Mogul Swords; see A
      Sword for the Baron
    The Baron and the Stolen Legacy; see
      Bad for the Baron
    The Baron and the Unfinished Portrait.
      Hodder, 1969; Walker, 1970 JM
    The Baron at Bay. Low, 1938. U.S.
      title: Blue Mask at Bay. Lippincott,
      1938 JM
    The Baron at Large. Low, 1939. U.S.
      title: Challenge Blue Mask! Lippin-
      cott, 1939. Reprinted under the Bri-
      tish title: Walker, 1975 JM
    The Baron Branches Out; see A Branch
      for the Baron
    The Baron Comes Back. Low, 1943 JM
    The Baron Goes A-Buying. Hodder, 1971;
      Walker, 1972 JM
    The Baron Goes East. Low, 1953 JM
    The Baron Goes Fast. Hodder, 1954;
      Walker, 1972 JM
    The Baron in France. Hodder, 1953;
      Walker, 1976 JM
    The Baron—King Maker. Hodder, 1975;
      Walker, 1975 JM
    The Baron on Board. Hodder, 1964;
      Walker, 1968 JM
    The Baron Returns. Harrap, 1937. U.S.
      title: The Return of Blue Mask. Lip-
      pincott, 1937 JM

Black for the Baron. Hodder, 1959. U.S. title: If Anything Happens to Hester. Doubleday, 1962 JM
Blame the Baron. Low, 1949; Duell, 1951 JM
Blood Red; see Red Eye for the Baron
Blue Mask at Bay; see The Baron at Bay
Blue Mask Strikes Again; see Versus the Baron
Blue Mask Victorious; see Call for the Baron
Books for the Baron. Low, 1949; Duell, 1952 JM
A Branch for the Baron. Hodder, 1961. U.S. title: The Baron Branches Out. Scribner, 1967 JM
Burgle the Baron. Hodder, 1973; Walker, 1974 JM
Call for the Baron. Low, 1940. U.S. title: Blue Mask Victorious. Lippincott, 1940. Reprinted under the British title: Walker, 1976 JM
Career for the Baron. Low, 1946; Duell, 1950 JM
A Case for the Baron. Low, 1945; Duell, 1949 JM
Challenge Blue Mask!; see The Baron at Large
Cry for the Baron. Low, 1950; Walker, 1970 JM
Danger for the Baron. Hodder, 1953; Walker, 1974 JM
Deaf, Dumb and Blonde; see Nest-Egg for the Baron
The Double Frame; see Frame the Baron
Frame the Baron. Hodder, 1957. U.S. title: The Double Frame. Doubleday, 1961 JM
Help from the Baron. Hodder, 1955; Walker, 1977 JM
Hide the Baron. Hodder, 1956; Walker, 1978 JM
If Anything Happens to Hester; see Black for the Baron
Introducing Mr. Brandon. Low, 1944
Last Laugh for the Baron. Hodder, 1970; Walker, 1971 JM
The Man in the Blue Mask; see Meet the Baron
Meet the Baron. Harrap, 1937. U.S. title: The Man in the Blue Mask. Lippincott, 1937 JM
Mr. Quentin Investigates. Low, 1943
Nest-Egg for the Baron. Hodder, 1954. U.S. title: Deaf, Dumb and Blonde. Doubleday, 1961 JM
Red Eye for the Baron. Hodder, 1958. U.S. title: Blood Red. Doubleday, 1960 JM
The Return of Blue Mask; see The Baron Returns
Reward for the Baron. Low, 1945 JM
A Rope for the Baron. Low, 1948; Duell, 1949 JM
Salute Blue Mask; see The Baron Again
Salute for the Baron. Hodder, 1960; Walker, 1973 JM
Shadow the Baron. Low, 1951 JM
Sport for the Baron. Hodder, 1966; Walker, 1969 JM
A Sword for the Baron. Hodder, 1963. U.S. title: The Baron and the Mogul Swords. Scribner, 1966 JM
Trap the Baron. Low, 1950; Walker, 1971 JM
Versus the Baron. Low, 1940. U.S. title: Blue Mask Strikes Again. Lippincott, 1940 JM
Warn the Baron. Low, 1952 JM

MORTON, GUY (MAINWARING). 1896- . Pseudonym: Peter Traill, q.v. Series character: Konrad Roque, in at least those marked KR.
Ashes of Murder. Skeffington, 1935; Greenberg, 1936
Black Gold. Brentano's (London), 1924; Small, 1924
The Black Robe. Hodder, 1927; Minton, 1927
The Burleigh Murders. Skeffington, 1936
The Forbidden Road. Hodder, 1928
King of the World; or, The Pommeray Case. Hodder, 1927
Mystery at Hardacres. Skeffington, 1936
The Mystery at Hermit's End. Skeffington, 1932
The Perrin Murder Case. Skeffington, 1930; Greenberg, 1934 KR
The Ragged Robin Murders. Skeffington, 1935; Greenberg, 1937 KR
The Scarlet Thumb Print. Skeffington, 1931 KR
The Silver-Voiced Murder. Skeffington, 1933
The 3-7-9 Murder. Skeffington, 1934
Zola's Thirteen. Skeffington, 1929

MORTON, MICHAEL. 1864-1931. See: VICTORIA MORTON.

MORTON, PATRICIA. Pseudonym of Morton Jay Golding, 1925- . Other pseudonyms: Stephanie Lloyd, q.v.
Caves of Fear. Lancer, 1968
A Child of Value. Lancer, 1966
Destiny's Child. Belmont, 1967
A Gathering of Moondust. Lancer, 1965
Province of Darkness. Banner, 1967

MORTON, T. C. ST. C. and LADBROKE (LIONEL DAY) BLACK, 1877-1940, q.v.
All Square with Fate. Nicholson, 1932

MORTON, VICTORIA
The Whirlpool. Dutton, 1916
The Yellow Ticket. Fly, 1914. (Novelization of the play by Michael Morton, 1864-1931.)

MORTON, WILLIAM. Pseudonym of W(illiam) B(lair) M(orton) Ferguson, 1882- , q.v. Series character: "Biff" Corrigan, in at least those marked BC.
The Case of Casper Gault. Hurst, 1932
Little Lost Lady. Hurst, 1931. U.S. title: The Murder of Christine Wilmerding, as by W(illiam) B(lair) M(orton) Ferguson. Liveright, 1932
Masquerade. Nelson, 1928; Chelsea, 1927 BC
The Murder of Christine Wilmerding; see Little Lost Lady
The Murderer. Hurst, 1932. U.S. title: The Pilditch Puzzle, as by W(illiam) B(lair) M(orton) Ferguson. Liveright, 1932
The Mystery of the Human Bookcase. Hurst, 1931; Mason, 1931 BC
The Pilditch Puzzle; see The Murderer

MOSCO, MAISIE. See: BRIAN COMFORT.

MOSELEY, DANA
Dead of Summer. Abelard, 1953; Bodley Head, 1955

MOSER, MAURICE and CHARLES F. RIDEAL
Stories from Scotland Yard. Routledge, 1890. U.S. title: True Detective Stories. Lovell, 1890 ss

MOSHER, J(OHN) S.
Liar Dice. Simon, 1939

MOSLEY, LEONARD O(SWALD). 1911- .
So I Killed Her. Joseph, 1936; Doubleday, 1937

MOSLEY, NICHOLAS. 1923- .
Assassins. Hodder, 1966; Coward, 1967

MOSS, (IVAN) WILLIAM STANLEY. 1921- .
-Bats with Baby Faces. Boardman, 1951

MOTT, MARIE MURPHY
The Cape Jasmine Murder. Vantage, 1963

MOTTA, LUIGI. 1881- .
Flames on the Bosphorus. Odhams, 1920. (Translation of Fiamme sul Bosforo. Milan, 1913.)

MOTTE, PETER. Pseudonym of Richard (Motte) Harrison, 1901- , q.v. See also: Reginald (Wilfrid) Campbell, 1894-1950.
A Dog's Death, with Reginald W(ilfrid) Campbell, 1894-1950. Cassell, 1953
Fall of the Curtain. Cassell, 1958
Fell Clutch. Cassell, 1956
The House at Hag's Curtain. Cassell, 1958
Phoenix from the Gutter. Cassell, 1956
The Village Called Death. Cassell, 1955

MOTTRAM, R(ALPH) H(ALE). 1883-1971.
The Headless Hound and other stories. Chatto, 1931 ss, some criminous

MOULTON, H(UGH LAURENCE) FLETCHER. 1876- .
-A Certain Liveliness. Arrowsmith, 1928
-The Girl He Left Behind Him. Arrowsmith, 1927
-The Man in the Turkish Bath. Longmans, 1941
-The Unofficial Executor. Cassell, 1934
Urgent Private Affairs. Arrowsmith, 1930
-Without the Law. Arrowsmith, 1926

MOUNCE, DAVID R.
Operation Cuttlefish. Pyramid, 1972
The Shield Project. Pyramid, 1971

MOUNTENEY-JEPHSON, R(ICHARD). 1842- .
Blackmail. Routledge, 1885

MOUNTJOY, HENRY
The Minister of Police. Bobbs, 1912

MOWATT, IAN. 1948- .
Just Sheaffer, or Storms in the Troubled Heir. Harcourt, 1973; Hutchinson, 1974

MOWBRAY, JOHN. Pseudonym of John (George) Haslette Vahey, 1881- , q.v. Other pseudonyms: Henrietta Clandon, John Haslette, Anthony Lang, Vernon Loder, Walter Proudfoot, qq.v.
Call the Yard. Skeffington, 1931
The Frontier Mystery. Collins, 1940
The Megeve Mystery. Collins, 1941
On Secret Service. Collins, 1939
The Radio Mystery. Collins, 1941
-The Way of the Weasel. Partridge, 1922

MOWERY, WILLIAM BYRON. 1899- .
The Black Automatic. Little, 1937
The Long Arm of the Mounted. Whittlesey, 1948 ss
The Phantom Canoe. Little, 1935
Sagas of the Mounted Police. Bouregy, 1953. Also published as: Tales of the Mounted Police. Airmont, 1962 ss
Tales of the Mounted Police; see Sagas of the Mounted Police

MOYES, PATRICIA. 1923- . Series characters: Henry and Emmy Tibbett, in all titles.
Black Widower. Collins, 1975; Holt, 1975
The Curious Affair of the Third Dog. Collins, 1973; Holt, 1973
Dead Men Don't Ski. Collins, 1959; Holt, 1960

Death and the Dutch Uncle. Collins, 1968; Holt, 1968
Death on the Agenda. Collins, 1962; Holt, 1962
Down Among the Dead Men; see The Sunken Sailor
Falling Star. Collins, 1964; Holt, 1964
Johnny Under Ground. Collins, 1965; Holt, 1966
Many Deadly Returns; see Who Saw Her Die?
Murder a la Mode. Collins, 1963; Holt, 1963
Murder Fantastical. Collins, 1967; Holt, 1967
Season of Snows and Sins. Collins, 1971; Holt, 1971
The Sunken Sailor. Collins, 1961. U.S. title: Down Among the Dead Men. Holt, 1961
Who Saw Her Die? Collins, 1970. U.S. title: Many Deadly Returns. Holt, 1970

MOYZISCH, L(UDWIG) C(ARL)
Operation Cicero. Coward, 1950; Wingate, 1950. (Translation of Der Fall Cicero. Frankfurt, 1950.)

MUAT, PAGAN
Murder's No Picnic. Gifford, 1947

MUDDOCK, J(OYCE) E(MMERSON PRESTON). 1843-1934. Pseudonym: Dick Donovan, q.v.
-From the Bosom of the Deep. Swan, 1886
Whose was the Hand? Digby, 1901

MUGGERIDGE, MALCOLM. 1903- .
Affairs of the Heart. H. Hamilton, 1949; Walker, 1961

MUIR, ALAN. Pseudonym of Thomas James Morrison, 1906- .
Death Comes on Derby Day. Jarrolds, 1939

MUIR, (CHARLES) AUGUSTUS (CARLOW). 1892- . Pseudonym: Austin Moore, q.v.
The Ace of Danger; see The Black Pavilion
Beginning the Adventure. Methuen, 1932. U.S. title: The Dark Adventure. Putnam, 1933
The Black Pavilion. Methuen, 1926. U.S. title: The Ace of Danger. Bobbs, 1927
The Blue Bonnet. Methuen, 1926; Bobbs, 1926
The Bronze Door. Methuen, 1936
-Candlelight in Avalon. Bles, 1954
Castles in the Air. Methuen, 1938
The Crimson Crescent. Methuen, 1935
The Dark Adventure; see Beginning the Adventure
The Green Lantern. Methuen, 1933
The Man Who Stole the Crown Jewels. Methuen, 1937
Raphael, M.D. Methuen, 1935 ss
The Red Carnation. Methuen, 1937
The Riddle of Garth. Methuen, 1933
The Sands of Fear. Methuen, 1940
Satyr Mask. Methuen, 1936
The Shadow on the Left. Methuen, 1928; Bobbs, 1928
The Silent Partner. Methuen, 1929; Bobbs, 1930
The Third Warning. Methuen, 1925; Bobbs, 1925

MUIR, D(OROTHY) ERSKINE (SHEEPSHANKS). 1889- .
Five to Five. Blackie, 1934
In Muffled Night. Methuen, 1933

MUIR, DENIS
Death Defies the Doctor. Phoenix, 1944

MUIR, DEXTER. Pseudonym of Leonard (Reginald) Gribble, 1908- , q.v. Other pseudonyms: Sterry Browning, Leo Grex, Louis Grey, qq.v. See also: JANET GREEN.
The Pilgrims Meet Murder. Jenkins, 1948
Rosemary for Death. Jenkins, 1952
The Speckled Swan. Jenkins, 1949

MUIR, JEAN. 1906-1973.
The Smiling Medusa. Dodd, 1969; Hale, 1971
Stranger, Tread Light. Dodd, 1971; Hale, 1973

MUIR, JOHN. Pseudonym of Thomas Christopher Morgan.
Creatures of Satan. Hutchinson, 1956
Crook's Turning. Hutchinson, 1958
The Devil's Post Office. Hutchinson, 1955

MUIR, P. P. and E(DWARD) D(EVEREUX) H(AMILTON) TOLLEMACHE
Green Wounds. Boardman, 1947
-Mirage. Boardman, 1945

MUIR, THOMAS. Series character: Roger Crammond, in at least those marked RC.
Death Below Zero. Hutchinson, 1950
Death in Reserve. Hutchinson, 1948
Death in Soundings. Hutchinson, 1955 RC
Death in the Loch. Hutchinson, 1949 RC
Death on the Agenda. Hutchinson, 1953
Death on the Trooper. Hutchinson, 1948
Death Under Virgo. Hutchinson, 1952 RC
Death Without Question. Hutchinson, 1951 RC
Trouble Aboard. Hutchinson, 1957

MUKERJI, DHAN GOPAL. 1890-1936.
The Secret Listeners of the East. Dutton, 1926

MULHOLLAND, JOHN. 1898-1970. See: CORTLAND FITZSIMMONS, 1893-1949.

MULHOLLAND, P. H.
The Calypso Murders. Avon, 1957

MULKEEN, THOMAS P. Series character: Clem Talbot, in both titles.
Honor Thy Godfather. Stein, 1973
My Killer Doesn't Understand Me. Stein, 1973

MULLALLY, FREDERIC. 1920- . Series character: Bob Sullivan, in at least those marked BS.
The Assassins. Barker, 1964; Walker, 1965
-Clancy. Hart-Davis, 1971
Danse Macabre. Secker, 1959. U.S. title: Marianne. Viking, 1960 BS
-Hitler has Won. Macmillan (London), 1975
The Malta Conspiracy. Hart-Davis, 1972 BS
Man with Tin Trumpet. Barker, 1961
Marianne; see Danse Macabre
The Munich Involvement. Barker, 1968 BS
No Other Hunger. Barker, 1966; McKay, 1966
-Oh, Wicked Wanda. Sphere, 1970
-The Prizewinner. Barker, 1967
Split Scene. Barker, 1963
-Venus Afflicted. Hart-Davis, 1973

MULLEN, CLARENCE. 1907- . Series characters: Tony Lantz and Eddie Wright, in both titles.
A Good Place for Murder. Phoenix, 1948
Thereby Hangs a Corpse. Mystery House, 1946

MULLER, MARY
Flagdown. Souvenir, 1974

MULLER, PAUL. 1924- . Series character: Paul Muller, in all titles.
Danger—Dame at Work. Hale, 1968; Roy, 1968
Don't Push Your Luck. Hale, 1970
Finders, Losers—. Hale, 1968
The Friendly Fiends. Hale, 1972
Goodbye, Shirley. Hale, 1969
The Hasty Heiress. Hale, 1968; Roy, 1969
The Lady is Lethal. Hale, 1968; Roy, 1968
Make Mine Mayhem. Hale, 1967
Slay Time. Hale, 1968; Roy, 1969
Some Dames Don't. Hale, 1970
This is Murder. Hale, 1971
A Viper in her Bosom. Hale, 1975
Why Pick on Me? Hale, 1969
The Wistful Wanton. Hale, 1971
You Kill Me! Hale, 1967

MULVIHILL, WILLIAM. 1923- .
The Mantrackers. Signet, 1960

MUMFORD, ETHEL WATTS. 1878-1940.
All in the Night's Work, with George (Fitzalan) Bronson-Howard, 1883-1922, q.v. Garden City, 1924
-Dupes. Putnam, 1901
Out of the Ashes. Moffat, 1913

MUNDY, MAX. Pseudonym of Sylvia Anne Matheson. Series character: Russell Jones = RJ.
Death Cries Ole. Long, 1966 RJ
Death is a Tiger. Long, 1960
Dig for a Corpse. Long, 1962 RJ
Pagan Pagoda. Long, 1965 RJ

MUNDY, TALBOT. Pseudonym of William Lancaster Gribbon, 1879-1940. Series characters: Jimgrim (James Schuyler Grim) = J; Chullunder Ghose, in at least those marked CG; Cotswold Ommony, in at least those marked CO; Athelstan King, in at least those marked AK.
-Black Light. Hutchinson, 1930; Bobbs, 1930
C.I.D. Hutchinson, 1932; Century, 1932 CG
-Caesar Dies. Hutchinson, 1934
Caves of Terror. Hutchinson, 1932 AK
Cock o' the North; see Gup Bahadur
The Devil's Guard; see Ramsden
Diamonds See in the Dark. Hutchinson, 1937
East and West. Appleton, 1937. (British title?)
-The Eye of Zeitoon. Hutchinson, 1920; Bobbs, 1920
Full Moon; see There was a Door
The Gungu Sahib. Hutchinson, 1933; Appleton, 1934 CG
-Guns of the Gods. Hutchinson, 1921; Bobbs, 1921
-Gup Bahadur. Hutchinson, 1929. U.S. title: Cock o' the North. Bobbs, 1929
-Her Reputation, with Bradley King. Bobbs, 1923. (British title?)
The Hundred Days. Hutchinson, 1930; Century, 1931 J
-The Ivory Trail. Constable, 1920; Bobbs, 1919
Jimgrim. Hutchinson, 1931; Century, 1931 J, CG
Jimgrim and Allah's Peace. Hutchinson, 1933; Appleton, 1936 J
Jungle Jest. Hutchinson, 1931; Century, 1932 CO
The King in Check. Hutchinson, 1933; Appleton, 1934 J

302/ Mundy, Talbot

-King of the Khyber Rifles. Constable, 1917; Bobbs, 1916 AK
The Lion of Petra. Hutchinson, 1932; Appleton, 1933 J
The Lost Trooper. Hutchinson, 1931 J
The Marriage of Meldrum Strange. Hutchinson, 1930
The Mystery of Khufu's Tomb. Hutchinson, 1933; Appleton, 1935 J
The Nine Unknown. Hutchinson, 1924; Bobbs, 1924 J, AK, CG
Old Ugly Face. Hutchinson, 1939; Appleton, 1940 J
Om. The Secret of Ahbor Valley. Hutchinson, 1924; Bobbs, 1924 CO
Ramsden. Hutchinson, 1926. U.S. title: The Devil's Guard. Bobbs, 1926 J
The Red Flame of Erinpura. Hutchinson, 1934 CG
The Seventeen Thieves of El-Kabil. Hutchinson, 1935 J
There was a Door. Hutchinson, 1935. U.S. title: Full Moon. Appleton, 1935
The Thunder Dragon Gate. Hutchinson, 1937; Appleton, 1937 J
-Told in the East. Bobbs, 1920. (British title?) (Three novelets.)
-The Valiant View. Hutchinson, 1939 ss
-When Trails were New. Hutchinson, 1932
-The Winds of the World. Cassell, 1916; Bobbs, 1917
The Woman Ayisha. Hutchinson, 1930 J

MUNRO, DENNIS
Death Defies the Doctor. Green Dragon, 194?

MUNRO, HUGH. Series character: Clutha = C.
A Clue for Clutha. Macdonald, 1960 C
Clutha and the Lady. Hale, 1973 C
Clutha Plays a Hunch. Macdonald, 1959; Washburn, 1959 C
Get Clutha. Hale, 1974 C
-Tribal Town. Macdonald, 1964
Who Told Clutha. Macdonald, 1958; Washburn, 1958 C

MUNRO, JAMES. Pseudonym of James (William) Mitchell, 1926-   , q.v. Other pseudonym: James Meldrum, q.v. Series character: John Craig, in all titles.
Die Rich, Die Happy. Hammond, 1965; Knopf, 1966
The Innocent Bystanders. Jenkins, 1969; Knopf, 1970
The Man Who Sold Death. Hammond, 1964; Knopf, 1965
The Money That Money Can't Buy. Hammond, 1967; Knopf, 1968

MUNRO, NEIL. 1864-1930.
The Lost Pibroch. Blackwood, 1896 ss, some criminous

MUNSLOW, BRUCE (JAMES)
Deep Sand. Hodder, 1955
Joker Takes Queen. Long, 1965; Holt, 1966
No Safe Road. Long, 1959; Walker, 1962
The Secret of the Little Flea. World's Work, 1951
Spider Run Alive. Long, 1961

MURFI, LIDIE
The Magnolia Curse. PB, 1973

MURFREE, MARY NOAILLES. 1850-1922. Pseudonym: Charles Egbert Craddock, q.v.

MURIEL, JOHN ST. CLAIR. 1909-   . Pseudonym: Simon Dewes, q.v.

MURPHY, D(AVID) J(OHN). 1905-   .
Inspector Malone Sails In. Selwyn, 1947

MURPHY, DENNIS JASPER. Pseudonym of Charles Robert Maturin, 1780-1824, q.v.
Fatal Revenge; or, The Family of Montorio. Longmans, 1807

MURPHY, JOHN. Pseudonym of Ronan Calistus Grady, Jr., 1921-   .
The El Greco Puzzle. Scribner, 1974
The Gunrunners. Macmillan, 1966; H. Hamilton, 1966
The Long Reconnaissance. Doubleday, 1970
Pay on the Way Out. Scribner, 1975; Hale, 1977

MURPHY, KEN. 1935-   .
The Wind in his Fists. Chatto, 1969

MURPHY, MARGUERITE
Borrowed Alibi. Avalon, 1961
Dangerous Legacy. Avalon, 1962

MURPHY, ROBERT (WILLIAM). 1902-1971. See also: HELEN (NEWINGTON) WILLS, 1906-   .
Murder in Waiting. Scribner, 1938

MURPHY, W(ARREN) B. 1933-   . See also: RICHARD SAPIR, 1936-   . Series characters: Ed Razoni and William Jackson = R&J.
City in Heat. Pinnacle, 1973 R&J
Dead End Street. Pinnacle, 1973 R&J
Down and Dirty. Pinnacle, 1974 R&J
Lynch Town. Pinnacle, 1974 R&J
On the Dead Run. Pinnacle, 1975 R&J
One Night Stand. Pinnacle, 1973 R&J
Subways are for Killing. Pinnacle, 1973

MURRAY, ANDREW. 1880-1929. All titles feature Sexton Blake and were published by Amalgamated Press.
Across the Divide. 1919
The Admiral's Secret. 1920
The Adventure of the Speed Mad Camden. 1928
Ambergris! 1921
The Barrier Reef Mystery. 1917
The Bathchair Mystery. 1919
The Beachcomber. 1920
Beyond the Law. 1922
The Black Bat. 1917
The Black Chrysanthemum. 1916
The Black Opal Mine. 1921
Blood-Brotherhood. 1920
The Broken Trail. 1919
The Case of the Amber Crown. 1923
The Case of the Burmese Dagger. 1919
The Case of the Cinema Star. 1921
The Case of the Cotton Beetle. 1923
The Case of the Master Organizer. 1923
The Case of the Mystery Millionaire. 1921
The Case of the Paralyzed Man. 1922
The Case of the Seaside Crooks. 1919
The Case of the Two Brothers. 1918
The Case of the Uncut Gems. 1922
The Case of the Undischarged Bankrupt. 1921
The Case of the Un-Named Film. 1922
The Case of the Woman in Black. 1922
The Catspaw. 1917
The Changeling. 1920
The City of Apes. 1921
A Convict by Proxy. 1919
The Crook's Double. 1923
The Ex-Soldier Employment Swindle. 1919
The Fatal Fortune. 1939 (Reprint of unidentified earlier title.)
The First-Born Son. 1919
The Golden Belts. 1916
The Great Explosion. 1922
The Half-Caste. 1917
The Head Hunter's Secret. 1920
The Hidden Message. 1921
His Excellency's Secret. 1916
Ill Gotten Gains. 1915
In the Midnight Express. 1920
Loot! 1919
The Luck of the Darrells. 1918
The Man Behind the Curtain. 1923
The Mandarin's Seal. 1919
The Man from Kura-Kura. 1920
The Man in the Grey Cowl. 1921
Marooned! 1921
The Missing Ships. 1918
The Mosque of the Mahdi. 1918
The Motor Coach Mystery. 1922
The Mystery of the Clock. 1922
The Mystery of the Hundred Chests. 1921
The Mystery of the Thousand Peaks. 1920
"North of 55°". 1923
Outcasts. 1919
The Oyster-Bed Mystery. 1923
The Palzer Experiment. 1920
The Prisoner of the Kremlin. 1922
The Rajah's Revenge. 1915
The Red Crescent. 1919
The Secret of Draker's Folly. 1917
The Secret of the Glacier. 1920
The Secret of the Green Lagoon. 1928
The Secret of the Hulk. 1918
The Secret of the Hunger Desert. 1920
Settler or Slaver. 1919
The Sheikh's Son. 1920
The Station Master's Secret. 1919
Tinker's Lone Hand. 1921
Vengeance. 1919
Victims of Villainy. 1916

MURRAY, ANDREW
The Lady of the Guns. Murray, 1920

MURRAY, AUDREY ALISON
The Blanket. Deutsch, 1957; Vanguard, 1958

MURRAY, BEATRICE. Pseudonym of Richard Posner, 1944-   , q.v. Other pseudonyms: Iris Foster, Paul Todd, qq.v.
The Dark Sonata. Dell, 1971

MURRAY, CHARLES T(HEODORE). 1843-   .
Sub Rosa. Carleton, 1880

MURRAY, CROMWELL. Pseudonym of Murray C(romwell) Morgan, 1916-   , q.v.
Day of the Dead. McKay, 1946

MURRAY, DAVID CHRISTIE. 1847-1907.
-The Bishop's Amazement. Downey, 1896
-The Bishop's Bible, with Henry Herman (1832-1894, q.v.). Chatto, 1890; Lovell, 1890
-A Bit of Human Nature; and, The "Lively Fanny." Chatto, 1885 ss
-Bob Martin's Little Girl. Chatto, 1892; Taylor, 1892
The Brangwyn Mystery. Long, 1906
-By the Gate of the Sea. Chatto, 1883; Harper, 1883
-A Capful o'Nails. Chatto, 1896
-The Church of Humanity. Chatto, 1901
-Coals of Fire and other stories. Chatto, 1882; Munro, 1883 ss
-Cynic Fortune. Chatto, 1886; Harper, 1886
A Dangerous Catspaw, with Henry Murray. Longmans, 1889; Harper, 1889
-Despair's Last Journey. Chatto, 1901
-First Person Singular. Chatto, 1886; Harper, 1885
He Fell Among Thieves, with Henry Herman (1832-1894, q.v.). Macmillan (London), 1891; Lovell, 1891
-Hearts. Chatto, 1883; Harper, 1883
-His Father's Honour. Ward, 1909
-His Own Ghost. Chatto, 1902
In Direst Peril. Chatto, 1894; Harper, 1894

In His Grip. Long, 1907
The Investigations of John Pym. White, 1895 ss
-John Vale's Guardian. Macmillan (London), 1890
-Joseph's Coat. Chatto, 1881; Munro, 1881
-A Life's Atonement. Griffith, 1880; Harper, 1881
-The Martyred Fool. Smith, 1895; Harper, 1895
-A Model Father. Grant, 1883; Harper, 1882
-Mount Despair, and other stories. Chatto, 1895 ss
-Old Blazer's Hero. Chatto, 1887; Lovell, 1888
-One Traveller Returns, with Henry Herman (1832-1894, q.v.). Chatto, 1887; Lovell, 1888
-Only a Shadow, with Henry Herman (1832-1894, q.v.). Griffith, 1891
Paul Jones's Alias, with Henry Herman (1832-1894, q.v.). Chatto, 1894 ss
-The Penniless Millionaire. Long, 1907
-The Queen's Scarf. Blackett, 1889
A Race for Millions. Chatto, 1898
-Rainbow Gold. Smith, 1885; Munro, 1885
-A Rising Star. Hutchinson, 1894; Collier, 1894
A Rogue's Conscience. Downey, 1897; Buckles, 1899
-Schwartz. Macmillan (London), 1889 ss
-Sweetbriar in Town, and other tales, with Henry Herman (1832-1894, q.v.). Munro, 1889. (British title?)
-Tales in Prose and Verse. Chatto, 1898 ss
-This Little World. Chatto, 1897; Appleton, 1898
Time's Revenges. Chatto, 1893; Harper, 1892
-V.C. Chatto, 1904
-Val Strange. Chatto, 1883; Harper, 1882
-Verona's Father. Chatto, 1903
A Wasted Crime. Chatto, 1893; Harper, 1893
-The Way of the World. Chatto, 1884; Harper, 1884
-The Weaker Vessel. Macmillan (London), 1888; Harper, 1889
-Wild Darrie, with Henry Herman (1832-1894, q.v.). Longmans, 1889; Munro, 1889
-A Woman in Armour. Long, 1908
-Young Mrs. Barter's Repentence. Munro, 1888. (British title?)

MURRAY, EDGAR JOYCE. 1878- . Pseudonym: Sidney Drew, q.v. All titles feature Sexton Blake and were published by Amalgamated Press.
The Affair of the Phantom Car. 1925
The Calcroft Case. 1926
The Case of the Crimson Wizard. 1922
The Case of the Lone Plantation. 1926
The City of Masks. 1926
The Great Circus Mystery. 1924
The Legacy of Doom. 1925
The Mansion of Shadows. 1923
The Menace of the Silent Death. 1926
The Palace of Terror. 1927
The Pride of the Stable. 1921
The Riddle of the Golden Fingers. 1927
The Tangle of Terror. 1926

MURRAY, EDWARD
The Four Liars. Butterworth, 1940

MURRAY, EUSTACE CLARE GRENVILLE. 1824-1881. Pseudonym: Mark Hope, q.v.

MURRAY, FIONA
Invitation to Danger. Hale, 1965
A Nice Day for Murder. Hale, 1971

MURRAY, INSPECTOR. Pseudonym of Alexander Duke Bailie.
Joseph Prickett, the Scotland Yard Detective. Laird, 1888
The League of Guilt; or, A Great Detective's Greatest Case. Ogilvie, 1892

MURRAY, LIEUTENANT M. M.
The Arkansas Ranger; or, The Story of a Dark Crime. Donohue
The Dog Detective and his Young Master. Street, 1888
Held for Ransom. Street, 1889
Life for a Life. Laird, 1887
Masked Lady; or, The Fortunes of a Dragoon. Street, 1889
Mezzoni, the Brigand; or, The King of the Mountains. Street, 1889

MURRAY, MAX. 1901-1956.
Breakfast with a Corpse. Joseph, 1956. U.S. title: A Corpse for Breakfast. Washburn, 1957
A Corpse for Breakfast; see Breakfast with a Corpse
The Doctor and the Corpse. Joseph, 1953; Farrar, 1952
Good Luck to the Corpse. Joseph, 1953; Farrar, 1951
The King and the Corpse. Joseph, 1949; Farrar, 1948
The Neat Little Corpse. Joseph, 1951; Farrar, 1950
No Duty on a Corpse. Joseph, 1950. U.S. title: The Queen and the Corpse. Farrar, 1949
The Queen and the Corpse; see No Duty on a Corpse
The Right Honourable Corpse. Joseph, 1952; Farrar, 1951
Royal Bed for a Corpse. Joseph, 1955; Washburn, 1955
The Sunshine Corpse. Joseph, 1954
Twilight at Dawn. Joseph, 1957
The Voice of the Corpse. Joseph, 1948; Farrar, 1947
Wait for the Corpse. Joseph, 1957; Washburn, 1957

MURRAY, PATRICIA (HAGAN). See: FLORENCE STEVENSON.

MURRAY, PAUL (COOPER). 1920- .
The Free Agent. Holt, 1952

MURRAY, RICHARD. 1910-1957. Pseudonym: Richard English, q.v.

MURRAY, SINCLAIR. Pseudonym of (Edward) Alan Sullivan, 1868-1947, q.v.
-Antidote. Murray, 1932
-The Broken Marriage. Murray, 1928; Dutton, 1929
-Cornish Interlude. Murray, 1932
The Crucible. Bles, 1925
-Double Lives. Murray, 1929
-The Golden Foundling. Murray, 1931
-The Money Spinners. Low, 1936
-The Obstinate Virgin. Low, 1934
-Queer Partners. Murray, 1930
-What Fools Men Are! Low, 1933
Whispering Lodge. Murray, 1927
-With Love from Rachel. Low, 1937

MURRAY, W(ILLIAM) H(UTCHINSON). 1913- .
Appointment in Tibet; see Five Frontiers
Dark Rose the Phoenix. Secker, 1965; McKay, 1965
Five Frontiers. Dent, 1959. U.S. title: Appointment in Tibet. Putnam, 1959
Maelstrom. Secker, 1962
-The Spurs of Troodos. Dent, 1960

MURRAY, WILLIAM. 1926- .
The Killing Touch. Dutton, 1974

MUSSI, MARY. 1907- . Pseudonym: Josephine Edgar, q.v.

MUSTO, BARRY. 1930- .
Codename—Bastille. Hale, 1972
The Fatal Flaw. Hale, 1970
The Lawrence Barclay File. Hale, 1969
No Way Out. Hale, 1973
Storm Centre. Hale, 1970
The Weighted Scales. Hale, 1973

MUZZEY, VIRGINIA REYNOLDS
A Quiet Murder. Dorrance, 1973

MUZZY, ALICE M.
-Three Fair Philanthropists. Abbey, 1901

MYERS, GEORGE L.
Aboard "The American Duchess". Putnam, 1900. (Plagiarization of Headon Hill's The Queen of Night, q.v.)

MYERS, ISABEL BRIGGS. Series character: Peter Jerningham, in both titles.
Give Me Death. Stokes, 1934; Gollancz, 1935
Murder Yet to Come. Stokes, 1930; Gollancz, 1930

MYGATT, GERALD. 1887- .
Nightmare. Penn, 1929

MYLES, SYMON. Pseudonym of Ken Follett, 1949- , q.v. Series character: "Apples" Carstairs, in both titles.
The Big Apple; see The Big Needle
The Big Black. Everest, 1974
The Big Needle. Everest, 1974. U.S. title: The Big Apple. Zebra, 1975

MYRER, ANTON
The Intruder. Little, 1965; Heinemann, 1966

NABARRO, DERRICK
-The Chariot of Desire. Cassell, 1956
-North from Singapore. Cassell, 1956
The Rod of Anger. Cassell, 1953; Sloane, 1953
-The Seeds of Destruction. Cassell, 1954

NABOKOFF-SIRIN, VLADIMIR (VLADIMIROVICH). Also known as: VLADIMIR NABOKOV. 1899-1977.
Despair. Long, 1937. Reprinted as by Vladimir Nabokov: Weidenfeld, 1966; Putnam, 1966

NAHUM, LUCIEN
Shadow 81. Doubleday, 1975

NAKAGAWA, KARL S.
The Rendezvous of Mysteries. Dorrance, 1928

NAPIER, GEOFFREY. Pseudonym of Bernard Glemser, 1908- .
A Dear Hungarian Friend. Macdonald, 1966. U.S. title: A Very Special Agent. Funk, 1967
A Very Special Agent; see A Dear Hungarian Friend
The Wrong Box. Dell, 1966. (Novelization of the movie based on Robert Louis Stevenson's novel, q.v.)

NAPIER, MARK. Pseudonym of John (Alfred Charles) Laffin, 1922- , q.v. Other pseudonyms: Carl Dekker, Dirk Sabre, qq.v.
Doorways to Danger. Abelard, 1966

NAPIER, MELISSA
    Castle of Dark Evil. Avon, 1972
    Child of Satan. PB, 1973
    Haunted Woman. Popular Library, 1971
    The House by the Bridge. Avon, 1972
    House in White Mist. Avon, 1972
    House of Dark Laughter. Avon, 1972
    House of Rising Water. Avon, 1972
    Mermaid of Dark Mountain. Avon, 1972
    The Possession of Elizabeth Calder. PB, 1973

NARCEJAC, THOMAS. 1908-   . See: PIERRE (PROSPER) BOILEAU, 1906-   .

NASH, ANNE. 1890-   . Series character: Mark Tudor = MT.
    Cabbages and Crime. Doubleday, 1945; Hammond, 1948
    Death by Design. Doubleday, 1944; Hammond, 1954 MT
    Said with Flowers. Doubleday, 1943; Hammond, 1953 MT
    Unhappy Rendezvous. Doubleday, 1946; Hammond, 1950

NASH, CHANDLER. Pseudonym of Katherine Chandler Hunt.
    Murder is my Shadow. Macmillan, 1959; Hale, 1960

NASH, FRANK. 1912-   .
    The House Cried Murder. Phoenix, 1952

NASH, N. RICHARD. Pseudonym: N. Richard Nusbaum, q.v.

NASH, SIMON. Pseudonym of Raymond Chapman, 1924-   . Series characters: Inspector Montero and Adam Ludlow, in all titles.
    Dead of a Counterplot. Bles, 1962
    Dead Woman's Ditch. Bles, 1964; Roy, 1966
    Death over Deep Water. Bles, 1963; Roy, 1965
    Killed by Scandal. Bles, 1962; Roy, 1964
    Unhallowed Murder. Bles, 1966; Roy, 1966

NASIELSKI, ADAM
    The Ace of Spades. Macdonald, 1939

NASON, LEONARD H(ASTINGS). 1895-   .
    Contact Mercury. Doubleday, 1946
    The Man in the White Slicker. Doubleday, 1929

NAUGHTON, EDMUND. 1926-   .
    A Case in Madrid. Curtis, 1973
    The Maximum Game. Warner, 1975
    McCabe. Macmillan, 1959; Deutsch, 1960. Also published as: McCabe and Mrs. Miller. Fontana, 1971
    McCabe and Mrs. Miller; see McCabe

NAZEL, JOSEPH. Series characters: Black = B; Iceman (Henry Highland West) = I.
    Billion Dollar Death. Holloway, 1974 I
    The Black Exorcist. Holloway, 1974 I
    Black is Black. Pinnacle, 1974 B
    Canadian Kill. Holloway, 1974 I
    Iceman No. 7. Holloway, 1975 I
    My Name is Black! Pinnacle, 1973 B
    Slick Revenge. Holloway, 1974 I
    Spinning Target. Holloway, 1974 I
    Sunday Fix. Holloway, 1974 I

NEAL, ADELINE PHYLLIS. 1894-1977. Pseudonym: A. F. Grey, q.v.

NEARING, ELIZABETH CUSTER. 1898-   .
    Pseudonym: Sue MacVeigh, q.v.

NEBEL, (LOUIS) FREDERICK
    Fifty Roads to Town. Little, 1936; Cape, 1936
    Six Deadly Dames. Avon, 1950 ss
    Sleepers East. Little, 1933; Collins, 1934

NED, NEVADA. Pseudonym of E. O. Tilburn. Other pseudonym: Dr. N. T. Oliver, q.v.
    Convict 72. Eagle, 1888
    The Great Bank Mystery. Laird, 1901
    The King of Gold; or, The Mystery of the Lost Mine. Eagle, 1888
    Mexican Bill, the Cowboy Detective. Laird, 1889
    The Mystery of Dagget's Bank. Laird, 1896

NEELEY, DETA P(ETERSON). 1902-   .
    A Candidate for Hell. Meador, 1939
    Murder at Sunset Rock. Meador, 1944
    Through Devil's Gate, with Nathan Glen Neeley. Meador, 1941

NEELEY, NATHAN GLEN. See: DETA P(ETERSON) NEELEY, 1902-   .

NEELY, RICHARD
    The Damned Innocents. Ace, 1971. Also published as: Dirty Hands. Signet, 1976
    Death to my Beloved. Signet, 1969
    Dirty Hands; see The Damned Innocents
    The Japanese Mistress. Saturday Review Press, 1972
    The Plastic Nightmare. Ace, 1969; Hale, 1971
    The Ridgway Women. Crowell, 1975; Constable, 1976
    The Sexton Women. Putnam, 1972; Barker, 1974
    The Smith Conspiracy. Signet, 1972
    The Walter Syndrome. McCall, 1970; Souvenir, 1971
    While Love Lay Sleeping. Ace, 1969; Hale, 1970

NEGULESCO, BRIAN. Pseudonym.
    The Woman from A.U.N.T. Exposition, 1970

NEIDIG, WILLIAM J(ONATHAN). 1870-   .
    The Fire Flingers. Dodd, 1919

NEIL, JOHN
    -The Eye of the Gods. Gramol, 1933
    Lord of the Gallows. Mowl, 1934
    The Man of Mystery. Gray, 193?

NELMS, HENNING. 1900-   . Pseudonym: Hake Talbot, q.v.

NELSON, C(HOLMONDELEY) M. 1903-   .
    Barren Harvest. Doubleday, 1949

NELSON, COUTTS
    What Old Father Thames Said. Tinsley, 1876

NELSON, HUGH LAWRENCE. 1907-   . Series characters: Jim Dunn = JD; Steve Johnson = SJ.
    The Copper Lady. Rinehart, 1947; Barker, 1949 SJ
    Dark Echo. Rinehart, 1949; Barker, 1949 SJ
    Dead Giveaway. Rinehart, 1950; Barker, 1951 SJ
    The Fence. Rinehart, 1953 JD
    Fountain of Death. Rinehart, 1948; Barker, 1949 SJ
    Gold in Every Grave. Rinehart, 1951; Barker, 1953 JD
    Island of Escape. Rinehart, 1948
    Kill with Care. Rinehart, 1953 JD
    Murder Comes High. Rinehart, 1950; Barker, 1952 JD
    Ring the Bell at Zero. Rinehart, 1949; Barker, 1950 JD
    The Season for Murder. Rinehart, 1952; Benn, 1956 JD
    The Sleep is Deep. Rinehart, 1952; Benn, 1955 JD
    Suspect. Rinehart, 1954 JD
    The Title is Murder. Rinehart, 1947; Barker, 1947 SJ

NELSON, JACK A.
    The Parajacker. Paperback Library, 1974

NELSON, MICHAEL HARRINGTON. 1921-   .
    Pseudonym: Henry Stratton, q.v.

NELSON, MILDRED
    The Dark Stone. Pyramid, 1972
    The Island. PB, 1973

NELSON, MOLLY
    Terror in Exton. Modern Fiction, 1946

NEPEAN, EDITH (BELLIS)
    -Dangerous Diversion! Paul, 1932
    -Midnight Surrender. Paul, 1953
    -Moonlight Madness. Paul, 1926
    -Perilous Waters. Paul, 1943
    Secret Lover. Paul, 1937

NESBIT, E(DITH) [EDITH NESBIT BLAND]. 1858-1924.
    Dormant. Methuen, 1911
    -Fear. Paul, 1910
    -Grim Tales. Innes, 1893 ss
    The House with No Address. Newnes, 1914; Doubleday, 1909
    -The Red House. Methuen, 1902; Harper, 1902
    -The Secret of Kyriels. Hurst, 1899
    Something Wrong. Innes, 1893 ss
    To the Adventurous. Hutchinson, 1923 ss, some criminous

NESS, TOM T. Pseudonym of Thomas L. Thienes.
    Short of Murder. Phoenix, 1948

NESTORIEN, ARTHUR. Pseudonym.
    In Sin or Folly? Digby, 1893

NETTELL, RICHARD (GEOFFREY)
    Girl in Blue Pants. Hodder, 1967

NETTLETON, ARTHUR. Pseudonym of Arthur Nettleton Gaunt.
    Sinister Secret. Fiction House, 1937

NETTON, BUDLEIGH. Series character: Derek Carrington, in at least the one marked DC and one other.
    Death Rides the Range. Low, 1938
    Desert Shadows. Low, 1939 DC
    Guns in the Desert. Low, 1937

NETTSON, KLAUS. U.S. byline of Klaus Netzen, q.v.

NETZEN, KLAUS. Byline on U.S. editions: Klaus Nettson. Series characters: The Killers = K.
    The Churchill Mission; see The Winston Churchill Murder
    The Fatal Friends. Mayflower, 1975; Pinnacle, 1974 K
    Mission into Auschwitz; see Night and Fog
    Night and Fog. Mayflower, 1974. U.S. title: Mission into Auschwitz. Pinnacle, 1974 K
    Pearl of Blood. Mayflower, 1975; Pinnacle, 1975 K
    To Win and To Lose. Mayflower, 1974; Pinnacle, 1974
    The Winston Churchill Murder. Mayflower, 1974. U.S. title: The Churchill Mission. Zebra, 1974

NEUBAUER, WILLIAM ARTHUR. 1916- .
    Pseudonym: Rebecca Marsh, q.v.

NEUMANN, ROBERT. 1897-1975.
    The Inquest. Hutchinson, 1944; Dutton, 1945

NEVILLE, BARBARA ALISON BOODSON. 1925- . Pseudonym: Edward Candy, q.v.

NEVILLE, MARGOT. Joint pseudonym of Margot Goyder, 1903- , and Aune Neville Goyder Joske, 1893- . Series character: Inspector Grogan, in at least those marked G.
    Come See Me Die. Bles, 1963 G
    Come, Thick Night. Bles, 1951. U.S. title: Divining Rod for Murder. Doubleday, 1952
    Confession of Murder. Bles, 1960 G
    Divining Rod for Murder; see Come, Thick Night
    Drop Dead. Bles, 1962 G
    The Flame of Murder. Bles, 1958 G
    The Hateful Voyage. Bles, 1956
    Head on the Sill. Bles, 1966 G
    Ladies in the Dark. Bles, 1965 G
    Lena Hates Men; see Murder in Rockwater
    Murder and Gardenias. Bles, 1946 G
    Murder and Poor Jenny. Bles, 1954 G
    Murder Before Marriage. Bles, 1951; Doubleday, 1951 G
    Murder Beyond the Pale. Bles, 1961 G
    Murder in a Blue Moon. Bles, 1948; Doubleday, 1949 G
    Murder in Rockwater. Bles, 1944. U.S. title: Lena Hates Men. Arcadia, 1953 G
    Murder of a Nymph. Bles, 1949; Doubleday, 1950 G
    Murder of Olympia. Bles, 1956 G
    Murder of the Well-Beloved. Bles, 1953; Doubleday, 1953 G
    Murder to Welcome Her. Bles, 1957 G
    My Bad Boy. Bles, 1964 G
    The Seagull Said Murder. Bles, 1952 G
    Sweet Night for Murder. Bles, 1959 G

NEVINS, FRANCIS M(ICHAEL), JR. 1943- .
    Publish and Perish. Putnam, 1975; Hale, 1977

NEW, CLARENCE HERBERT. 1862-1933.
    The Unseen Hand. Doubleday, 1918 ss

NEWBERRY, PERRY. 1870-1938. See: ALICE MacGOWAN, 1858- .

NEWCOME, L(OUIS) A.
    Capture of the Paddy Ryan Gang of Burglars. Newcome, 1887
    The Post Office Burglars of the Shawangunk Mountains. Newcome, 1886

NEWELL, AUDREY
    Murder is not Mute. Macrae-Smith, 1940
    Who Killed Cavelotti? Century, 1930

NEWELL, ROBERT HENRY. 1836-1901. Pseudonym: Orpheus C. Kerr, q.v.

NEWHAFER, RICHARD (L.). 1922- . See: GILBERT A(LEXANDER) RALSTON, 1912- .

NEWHALL, MRS. LAURA EUGENIA. Pseudonym: Ada L. Halstead, q.v.

NEWKIRK, CLYDE C. 1870-1938. Pseudonym: Newton Newkirk, q.v.

NEWKIRK, NEWTON. Pseudonym of Clyde C. Newkirk, 1870-1938.
    Stealthy Steve, the Six-Eyed Sleuth: His Quest of the Big Blue Diamond. Luce, 1904

NEWLAND, N. M.
    Walk to Your Grave. Phoenix, 1951

NEWMAN, BERNARD (CHARLES). 1897-1968.
    Pseudonym: Don Betteridge, q.v.
    Series character: Papa Pontivy, in at least those marked P.
    -Armed Doves. Jarrolds, 1931
    Black Market. Gollancz, 1942 P
    Centre Court Murder. Gollancz, 1951
    Cup Final Murder. Gollancz, 1950
    -The Dangerous Age. Hale, 1967
    Dead Man Murder. Gollancz, 1946
    Death at Lord's. Gollancz, 1952
    Death of a Harlot. Laurie, 1934; Godwin, 1935
    Death to the Fifth Column. Gollancz, 1941 P
    Death to the Spy. Gollancz, 1939 P
    Death Under Gibraltar. Gollancz, 1938
    Double Menace. Hale, 1954 P
    Draw the Dragon's Teeth. Hale, 1967
    Evil Phoenix. Hale, 1966
    German Spy. Gollancz, 1936; Hillman-Curl, 1936
    The Jail-Breakers. Hale, 1968
    Lady Doctor—Woman Spy. Hutchinson, 1937
    Maginot Line Murder. Gollancz, 1939. U.S. title: Papa Pontivy and the Maginot Murder. Holt, 1940 P
    Moscow Murder. Gollancz, 1948 P
    The Mussolini Murder Plot. Hutchinson, 1936; Hillman-Curl, 1939
    Operation Barbarossa. Hale, 1956 P
    The Otan Plot. Hale, 1957 P
    Papa Pontivy and the Maginot Murder; see Maginot Line Murder
    The Red Spider Web. Latimer House, 1947
    Second Front—First Spy. Gollancz, 1944 P
    Secret Servant. Gollancz, 1935; Hillman-Curl, 1936
    Secret Weapon. Gollancz, 1941
    Shoot! Gollancz, 1949
    Siegfried Spy. Gollancz, 1940
    Silver Greyhound. Hale, 1960
    The Spy at No. 10. Hale, 1965 P
    Spy Catchers. Gollancz, 1945 P in 4 of 31 ss
    The Spy in the Brown Derby. Gollancz, 1945 P
    Taken at the Flood. Hale, 1958
    This is Your Life. Hale, 1963 P
    The Travelling Executioners. Hale, 1964
    The Wishful Think. Hale, 1954

NEWMAN, G(ORDON) F. Series character: Terry Sneed, in at least those marked TS.
    -The Abduction. New English Library, 1972
    -The Player and the Guest. New English Library, 1972
    The Price. New English Library, 1974
    Sir, You Bastard. Allen, 1970; Simon, 1971 TS
    The Split. New English Library, 1972
    -3 Professional Ladies. New English Library, 1973
    You Nice Bastard. New English Library, 1972 TS

NEWMAN, MARGARET (EDITH). 1926- .
    Pseudonym: Anne Betteridge, q.v.
    Murder to Music. Long, 1959

NEWMAN, PETER N. See: MAURICE MOISEIWITSCH.

NEWMAN, ROBERT (HOWARD). 1909- .
    -The Enchanter. Houghton, 1962

NEWMAN, RONALD M.
    The Man with the Million Pounds. Hutchinson, 1923

NEWMAN, TERENCE [TERRY NEWMAN]. 1927- .
    Aftermath of Murder. Blackfriars, 1947
    -Along for the Ride. Cassell, 1961
    -From a High Tower. Cassell, 1965
    -"The Independent." Cassell, 1959
    -No More a Brother. Cassell, 1958
    The Raphael "Resurrection". Eyre, 1954

NEWNHAM-DAVIS, LT. COL. N(ATHANIEL). 1854-1917.
    "Baby" Wilkinson's V.C. and other stories. Downey, 1899 ss
    -Jadoo. Downey, 1898
    -Three Men and a God, and other stories. Downey, 1896 ss

NEWTON, (WILFRID) DOUGLAS. 1884-1951.
    -The Beggar, and other stories. Washbourne, 1933 ss
    -Black Finger. Mellifont, 1940
    -The Brute. Cassell, 1928; Appleton, 1924
    The Crime Specialist. Mellifont, 1942
    Dark Pathway. Cassell, 1938
    Double Crossed. Appleton (London & New York), 1922
    -Dr. Odin. Cassell, 1933
    -Eyes of Men. Cassell, 1928
    Falcon of the Foreign Office. Mellifont, 1940
    -The Golden Cat. Cassell, 1930
    -I, Savaran! Cassell, 1937
    -Infinite Morning. Cassell, 1938
    The Jade-Green Garter. Cassell, 1929
    Laughing Gangster. Pemberton, 1948
    -The Lover Who Lost Himself. Gramol, 1933
    -Marie Vee. Cassell, 1924
    Marked Woman. Eldon, 1949
    Of Six Suspects. Mitre, 1944
    -Over the Top. Pearson, 1917 ss
    -Phillip and the Flappers. Pearson, 1918
    -Phillip in Particular. Simpkin, 1916
    The Red Judas. Cassell, 1934
    -Savaran and the Great Sand. Cassell, 1939
    -The Sixth Director. Fiction House, 1943
    Sookey. Cassell, 1925; Dodd, 1926
    -The Witch of Nun. Cassell, 1936

NEWTON, ELIZABETH. Pseudonym: Gillan Vase, q.v.

NEWTON, WATSON JAMES
    Cupid and the Creeds. Neale, 1900

NEWTON, WILLIAM SIMPSON. 1923- . Pseudonym: Gilroy Mitcham, q.v.

NGAGOYEANES, NICHOLAS. 1939- . Pseudonym: Nicholas Gage, q.v.

NIALL, MICHAEL. Pseudonym of Howard Breslin.
    Bad Day at Black Rock. GM, 1954; Fawcett (London), 1955
    Run Like a Thief. Mill, 1962; Boardman, 1963

NICHOLAS, J. W.
    -At Midnight's Chime. Arrowsmith, 1889
    The House of Mystery. Arrowsmith, 1891
    -The Household of Hertz. Arrowsmith, 1903
    -The Story of Clovelly's Wife. Arrowsmith, 1893 ss
    -The Two Crosses. Arrowsmith, 1887
    -The White Bird, and other stories. Stockwell, 1923 ss

NICHOLAS, JEROME
  The Asbestos Mask. Hodder, 1948
  Deirdre. Hodder, 1952
  Salute to Tomorrow. Hodder, 1949
  Whispering Steel. Hodder, 1949
  The Widow's Peak. Hodder, 1946

NICHOLAS, ROBERT
  The White Shroud. Collins, 1961

NICHOLS, (JOHN) BEVERLEY. 1899- .
  Series character: Horatio Green, in all titles.
  Death to Slow Music. Hutchinson, 1956; Dutton, 1956
  The Moonflower. Hutchinson, 1955. U.S. title: The Moonflower Murder. Dutton, 1955
  The Moonflower Murder; see The Moonflower
  Murder by Request. Hutchinson, 1960; Dutton, 1960
  No Man's Street. Hutchinson, 1954; Dutton, 1954
  The Rich Die Hard. Hutchinson, 1957; Dutton, 1958

NICHOLS, FAN. Pseudonym of Frances Nichols Hanna.
  -Angel Face. Popular Library, 1955
  -Ask for Linda. Popular Library, 1953
  Be Silent, Love. Simon, 1960; Boardman, 1961. Also published as: The Girl in the Death Seat. Ace, 196?
  The Caged. GM, 1952; Fawcett (London), 1959
  Count Me In. Popular Library, 1953
  -Deadline for Lovers. Godwin, 1938
  -Devil Take Her. Popular Library, 1954
  The Girl in the Death Seat; see Be Silent, Love
  He Walks by Night. Popular Library, 1957
  Hideaway. Berkley, 1959
  -I Know My Love. Popular Library, 1958
  -I'll Never Let You Go. Popular Library, 1955
  The Loner. Simon, 1956; Boardman, 1957
  -Love Me Now. Monarch, 1958
  One by One. Arco, 1951
  -Pawn. Godwin, 1938
  Possess Me Not. Fell, 1946; Allen, 1948
  -Scandal. Godwin, 1937

NICHOLS, PETER. Pseudonym.
  Patchwork of Death. Holt, 1965; Hale, 1967

NICHOLS, SARAH
  The Clouded Moon. Popular Library, 1975
  Grave's Company. Popular Library, 1975
  House of Rancour. Popular Library, 1974
  Satan's Spring. Popular Library, 1974
  That Dark Inn. Curtis, 1973
  The Very Dead of Winter. Popular Library, 1974
  Widow's Walk. Curtis, 1972

NICHOLSON, JOHN. Pseudonym of Norman Howe Parcell.
  Costello—Psychic Investigator. Stockwell, 1954 ss

NICHOLSON, KATE. Pseudonym of Judith Fay.
  Hook, Line and Sinker. Bles, 1966

NICHOLSON, MARGARET BEDA LARMINIE. 1924- . Pseudonym: Margaret Yorke, q.v.

NICHOLSON, MEREDITH. 1866-1947.
  The House of a Thousand Candles. Bobbs, 1905; Daily Mail, 1908
  The Port of Missing Men. Bobbs, 1907; Gay & Bird, 1907
  The Siege of the Seven Suitors. Houghton, 1910; Constable, 1910

NICHOLSON, RENTON. 1809-1861.
  Dombey and Daughter. Farris, 1847

NICOLAI, CHARLES. Series character: John Nolan, in all titles.
  Death at Chestnut Hill. Hammond, 1955
  A Killer is Loose. Hammond, 1954
  Murder in the Fine Arts. Hammond, 1964

NICOLAS, F. R. E. Pseudonym of Nicolas Freeling, 1927- , q.v.
  Valparaiso. Gollancz, 1964; Harper, 1965, as by Nicolas Freeling

NICOLE, CHRISTOPHER ROBIN. 1930- . Pseudonyms: Robin Cade, Andrew York, qq.v.

NICOLE, CLAUDE
  The Cliffs of Death. Belmont, 1973

NICOLE, CLAUDETTE
  Bloodroots Manor. GM, 1970
  The Chinese Letter. Popular Library, 1973
  Circle of Secrets. GM, 1972
  The Dark Mill. GM, 1970
  Dark Whispers. Pyramid, 1975
  The Haunted Heart. Pyramid, 1972
  The Haunting of Drumroe. GM, 1971; Gold Lion, 1973
  House at Hawk's End. GM, 1971; Gold Lion, 1974
  The Mistress of Orion Hall. GM, 1970; Coronet, 1971
  The Secret of Harbor House. Pyramid, 1975

NICOLE, CLAUDIA
  Moonwater. Paperback Library, 1971

NICOLET, C(HARLES) C(ATHCART). 1900- .
  Death of a Bridge Expert. Simon, 1932; Gollancz, 1933

NICOLL, HENRY MAURICE DUNLOP. 1884-1953. Pseudonym: Martin Swayne, q.v.

NICOLSON, J(OHN) U(RBAN). 1885- .
  Fingers of Fear. Covici, 1937

NIELSEN, HELEN (BERNICE). 1918- .
  After Midnight. Morrow, 1966; Gollancz, 1967
  Borrow the Night. Morrow, 1956; Gollancz, 1956. Also published as: Seven Days Before Dying. Dell, 1958
  The Crime is Murder. Morrow, 1956; Gollancz, 1957
  The Darkest Hour. Morrow, 1969; Gollancz, 1969
  Dead on the Level; see Gold Coast Nocturne
  Detour. Washburn, 1953. Also published as: Detour to Death. Dell, 1955
  Detour to Death; see Detour
  False Witness. Ballantine, 1959
  The Fifth Caller. Morrow, 1959; Gollancz, 1959
  Gold Coast Nocturne. Washburn, 1951. British title: Murder by Proxy. Gollancz, 1952. Also published as: Dead on the Level. Dell, 1954
  A Killer in the Street. Morrow, 1967; Gollancz, 1967
  The Kind Man. Washburn, 1951; Gollancz, 1952
  Murder by Proxy; see Gold Coast Nocturne
  Obit Delayed. Washburn, 1952; Gollancz, 1953
  Seven Days Before Dying; see Borrow the Night
  The Severed Key. Gollancz, 1973
  Shot on Location. Morrow, 1971; Gollancz, 1971
  Sing Me a Murder. Morrow, 1960; Gollancz, 1961
  Stranger in the Dark. Washburn, 1955; Gollancz, 1956
  Verdict Suspended. Morrow, 1964; Gollancz, 1965
  Woman Missing and other stories. Ace, 1961 ss
  The Woman on the Roof. Washburn, 1954; Gollancz, 1955

NIELSEN, VIRGINIA [VIRGINIA NIELSEN McCALL]. 1909- .
  Dangerous Dream. Avalon, 1961
  The Mystery of Fyfe House. Avalon, 1962

NIGHTINGALE, URSULA
  Bitters Wood. Popular Library, 1973
  Dawn Comes Soon. Curtis, 1973
  Deviltower. Popular Library, 1971

NILE, DOROTHEA. Pseudonym of Michael (Angelo) Avallone (Jr.), 1924- , q.v. Other pseudonyms: Priscilla Dalton, Mark Dane, Jean-Anne de Pre, Dora Highland, Steve Michaels, Edwina Noone, Sidney Stuart, Max Walker, qq.v.
  The Evil Men Do. Tower, 1966
  Mistress of Farrondale. Tower, 1966
  Terror at Deepcliff. Tower, 1966
  The Third Shadow. Avon, 1973
  The Vampire Cameo. Lancer, 1968

NISBET. HUME. 1849-1921?
  -Ashes. Author's Cooperative, 1890. Also published as: Wasted Fires. Methuen, 1902
  -"Bail Up!" Chatto, 1890
  -The Black Drop. Trischler, 1891
  Children of Hermes. Hurst, 1901
  -A Colonial King. White, 1905
  Comrades of the Black Cross. White, 1899
  -A Crafty Foe. White, 1901
  -A Desert Bride. White, 1894
  -The Divers. Black, 1892
  -Doctor Bernard St. Vincent. Ward, 1889
  -A Dream of Freedom. White, 1902
  -The Empire Makers. White, 1900
  -For Liberty. White, 1898
  -The Great Secret. White, 1895
  -The Haunted Station, and other stories. White, 1894 ss
  -Her Loving Slave. Digby, 1894
  -Hunting for Gold; or, Adventures in the Klondyke. White, 1897
  -In Sheep's Clothing. White, 1900
  -A Losing Game. White, 1901
  -My Love Noel. White, 1896
  -Paths of the Dead. Long, 1899
  -The Queen's Desire. White, 1893
  -The Rebel Chief. White, 1896
  The Revenge of Valerie. White, 1900
  A Singular Crime. White, 1894
  -Stories Weird and Wonderful. White, 1900 ss
  -The Swampers. White, 1897
  -A Sweet Sinner. White, 1897
  Wasted Fires; see Ashes

NISOT, E. H. See: (MAVIS) ELIZABETH (HOCKING) NISOT, 1893- .

NISOT, (MAVIS) ELIZABETH (HOCKING). 1893- . Pseudonym: William Penmare, q.v. Series character: Commissaire Payran, in at least those marked P.
  Alixe Derring. Paul, 1934
  Extenuating Circumstances. Paul, 1937
  False Witness. Paul, 1938 P

Hazardous Holiday. Paul, 1936 P
Shortly After Midnight. Paul, 1934
The Sleepless Men. Doubleday, 1959, as
  by E. H. Nisot
Twelve to Dine. Paul, 1935 P
Unnatural Deeds. Paul, 1939 P

NISTLER, ERWIN N. and GERRY P. BRODERICK
  Roadside Night. Pyramid, 1963

NITSUA, BENJAMIN. Pseudonym of Benjamin
  Fish Austin, 1850-1932.
  The Mystery of Ashton Hall. Austin,
  1910

NIXON, ALAN. 1937-   . Series character:
  Lawrence Maver, in both titles.
  The Attack on Vienna. Bodley Head,
  1971; St. Martin's, 1972
  Item 7. Bodley Head, 1970; Simon, 1971

NIXON, ALLAN. 1918-   . Series charac-
  ter: Garrity = G.
  Garrity; see Get Garrity
  Get Garrity. Avon, 1969. British title:
  Garrity. New English Library pb, 1970
  G
  Go for Garrity. Avon, 1970 G
  Goodnight, Garrity. Avon, 1969; New
  English Library pb, 1971 G
  The Scavengers. Avon, 1969; New English
  Library pb, 1970

NOBLE, EDWARD
  Fisherman's Gat. Blackwood, 1906. U.S.
  title: The Issue. Doubleday, 1907
  The Issue; see Fisherman's Gat
  Shadows from the Thames. Pearson, 1900
  ss

NOEL, L. Pseudonym of Leonard Noel Bar-
  ker, 1882-   .
  -Bars of Steel. Paul, 1929
  -The Cardboard Hero. Paul, 1930
  -Crescent Moon. Paul, 1947
  -Flame of Folly. Paul, 1933
  -Forbidden Frontiers. Paul, 1937
  -Isle of Innocence. Paul, 1928
  Lady All Alone. Paul, 1936
  Mystery Street. Paul, 1930
  -One Last Chance. Paul, 1933
  -The Silver Shadow. Paul, 1944
  -Star of Evil. Paul, 1931
  -Uneasy Years. Paul, 1931
  -The Veil of Islam. Paul, 1927

NOEL, STERLING. 1903-   .
  Chain of Death; see Hydra-Head
  Death Do Us Part. Boardman, 1959. (U.S.
  title?)
  Empire of Evil. Avon, 1961
  Few Die Well. Farrar, 1953; Hale, 1954
  House of Secrets. Deutsch, 1956. (U.S.
  title?)
  Hydra-Head. Boardman, 1955. Also pub-
  lished as: Chain of Death. Corgi,
  1958. (U.S. title?)
  I Killed Stalin. Farrar, 1951; Hale,
  1952
  I See Red. Ace, 1955
  Intrigue in Paris; see Storm over Paris
  Prelude to Murder. Avon, 1959
  Run for Your Life! Avon, 1958
  Storm over Paris. Farrar, 1955. Also
  published as: Intrigue in Paris.
  Avon, 1957
  We Who Survived. Avon, 1959

NOLAN, FREDERICK (W.). 1931-   .
  The Algonquin Project; see The Oshawa
  Project
  Kill Petrosino! Barker, 1975
  No Place to be a Cop. Barker, 1974
  The Oshawa Project. Barker, 1974. U.S.
  title: The Algonquin Project. Morrow,
  1974
  The Ritter Double-Cross. Barker, 1974;
  Morrow, 1975

NOLAN, JAMES VINCENT
  Meet Mike Desmond. Grafton, 1946
  Murder Strikes Twice. Grafton, 1945
  Murder Walks Alone. Grafton, 1945

NOLAN, JEANNETTE COVERT. 1896-   .
  Series character: Lace White, in at
  least those marked LW.
  A Fearful Way to Die. Washburn, 1956;
  Muller, 1957 LW
  Final Appearance. Duell, 1943 LW
  "I Can't Die Here." Messner, 1945 LW
  Murder Will Out; see Profile in Gilt
  Profile in Gilt. Funk, 1941. Also pub-
  lished as: Murder Will Out. Detective
  Novel Classics, 194?
  Sudden Squall. Washburn, 1955; Muller,
  1956 LW
  Where Secrecy Begins. Long, 1938

NOLAN, WILLIAM F(RANCIS). 1928-   .
  Series character: Bart Challis = BC.
  Death is for Losers. Sherbourne, 1968
  BC
  Impact-20. Paperback Library, 1963
  ss, some criminous
  Space for Hire. Lancer, 1971
  The White Cad Cross-Up. Sherbourne,
  1969 BC

NONWEILER, ARVILLE
  Murder on the Pike. Phoenix, 1944

NOONE, EDWINA. Pseudonym of Michael (An-
  gelo) Avallone (Jr.), 1924-   , q.v.
  Other pseudonyms: Priscilla Dalton,
  Mark Dane, Jean-Anne de Pre, Dora
  Highland, Steve Michaels, Dorothea
  Nile, Sidney Stuart, Max Walker,
  qq.v.
  The Cloisonne Vase. Curtis, 1970
  The Craghold Creatures. Beagle, 1972
  The Craghold Crypt. Curtis, 1973
  The Craghold Curse. Beagle, 1972
  The Craghold Legacy. Beagle, 1971
  Corridor of Whispers. Ace, 1965
  Dark Cypress. Ace, 1965
  Daughter of Darkness. Signet, 1966
  Heirloom of Tragedy. Lancer, 1965
  Seacliffe. Signet, 1968
  The Second Secret. Belmont, 1966
  The Victorian Crown. Belmont, 1966

NOONE, JOHN
  The Man with the Chocolate Egg. H. Hamilton, 1966; Grove, 1967

NORDEN, ERIC
  The Ultimate Solution. Paperback Library, 1973

NORHAM, GERALD
  Dead Branch. Hale, 1975
  The Exporters. Hale, 1972
  Gallows March. Hale, 1971
  A Question of Coercion. Hale, 1972

NORMAN, BARRY. Series character: Paul
  Baker, in both titles.
  The Hounds of Sparta. Allen, 1968
  The Matter of Mandrake. Allen, 1967;
  Walker, 1968

NORMAN, BRUCE. Series character: James
  Mallaby, in at least those marked JM.
  The Black Pawn. Arrowsmith, 1927; Dial,
  1927 JM
  -"Late of London Wall..." Arrowsmith,
  1931
  -The Luck of Jocelyn Pinner, R.N. Arrow-
  smith, 1931
  The Thousand Hands. Arrowsmith, 1926;
  Dial, 1927 JM

NORMAN, EARL. Series character: Burns
  Bannion, in all titles.
  Kill Me in Atami. Berkley, 1962
  Kill Me in Shimbashi. Berkley, 1959
  Kill Me in Shinjuku. Berkley, 1961
  Kill Me in Tokyo. Berkley, 1958
  Kill Me in Yokohama. Berkley, 1960
  Kill Me in Yoshiwara. Berkley, 1961
  Kill Me on the Ginza. Berkley, 1962

NORMAN, JAMES. Pseudonym of James Norman
  Schmidt, 1912-   . Series character:
  Gimiendo Hernandez Quinto, in at
  least those marked GQ.
  An Inch of Time. Morrow, 1944; Joseph,
  1945 GQ
  Murder, Chop Chop. Morrow, 1942;
  Joseph, 1943 GQ
  The Nightwalkers. Ziff-Davis, 1946;
  Joseph, 1948

NORMAN, JOHN
  The Case of the Four Pages. Swan, 1946
  The Concert Party Murders. Swan, 1945
  The Express Train Murder. Swan, 1946
  The Mystery of the Aztec Chain. Swan,
  1946

NORO, FRED
  Do No Evil. International, 1969

NORRIS, KATHLEEN (THOMPSON). 1880-1966.
  The Black Flemings. Doubleday, 1926;
  Murray, 1926. Also published as:
  Gabrielle. Paperback Library, 1965
  Gabrielle; see The Black Flemings
  Mystery House. Doubleday, 1939
  The Mystery of Pine Point. Murray, 1936
  (U.S. title?)
  Romance at Hillyard House; see The
  Secrets of Hillyard House
  The Secret of the Marshbanks. Double-
  day, 1940; Murray, 1940
  The Secrets of Hillyard House. Double-
  day, 1947. British title: Romance at
  Hillyard House. Murray, 1948

NORRIS, STANLEY
  For his Friend's Honor. Street, 1900

NORRIS, W(ILLIAM) E(DWARD). 1847-1925.
  -The Baffled Conspirators. Blackett,
  1890; Lovell, 1890
  -Jack's Father, and other stories.
  Methuen, 1891; Lovell, 1891. (The
  U.S. edition contains only 3 of the
  7 ss in the British edition; the
  others are in: Mysterious Mrs. Wil-
  kinson and other stories. Lovell,
  1891.) ss
  Mysterious Mrs. Wilkinson and other
  stories; see Jack's Father, and other
  stories
  Not Guilty. Constable, 1910; Bren-
  tano's, 1910
  -The Rogue. Bentley, 1888; Holt, 1888
  -Troubled Tranton. Constable, 1915;
  Brentano's, 1916

NORSWORTHY, GEORGE
  Casino. Low, 1934
  Crime at the Villa Gloria. Low, 1936;
  Greenberg, 1936
  Dames-Errant. Low, 1935
  -The Hartness Millions. Low, 1936
  A House-Party Mystery. Low, 1935
  Murder at Mulberry Cottage. Low, 1937
  Murder in Sussex. Hutchinson, 1940

NORTH, ANTHONY
  Strike Deep. Dial, 1974

NORTH, BARCLAY. Pseudonym of W(illiam)
  C(adwalader) Hudson, 1843-1915, q.v.
  The Diamond Button: Whose was It? Cassell (New York), 1889; Cassell (London), 1890

N

NORTH, BARCLAY (continued)
520%; or, The Great Franklin Syndicate. Street, 1900
Linked to Crime. Street (Magnet)
The Stevedore Mystery. Street (Magnet), 1900

NORTH, CHARLES
Beware of the Dog! Morrow, 1939. British title: Out of the Dog House. Cassell, 1940

NORTH, ERIC. Pseudonym of Bernard Charles Cronin, 1884- . Other pseudonym: Dennis Adair, q.v.
A Chip on my Shoulder. Dobson, 1955; Roy, 1956
The Name is Smith. Dobson, 1957; Roy, 1957
Nobody Stops Me. Dobson, 1960; Roy, 1960

NORTH, GIL. Pseudonym of Geoffrey Horne, 1916- , q.v. Series character: Sgt. Cluff, in all titles.
The Confounding of Sergeant Cluff. Chapman, 1966
The Methods of Sergeant Cluff. Chapman, 1961
More Deaths for Sergeant Cluff. Chapman, 1963
No Choice for Sergeant Cluff. Eyre, 1971
The Procrastination of Sergeant Cluff. Eyre, 1969
Sergeant Cluff and the Day of Reckoning. Chapman, 1967
Sergeant Cluff and the Madmen. Chapman, 1964
Sergeant Cluff and the Price of Pity. Chapman, 1965
Sergeant Cluff Goes Fishing. Chapman, 1962
Sergeant Cluff Rings True. Eyre, 1972
Sergeant Cluff Stands Firm. Chapman, 1960

NORTH, JESSICA
The High Valley. Random, 1973; Heinemann, 1974
River Rising. Random, 1975

NORTH, WILLIAM. 1869- . Pseudonym: Ralph Rodd, q.v.

NORTON, ALICE MARY. 1912?- . Pseudonym: Andre Norton, q.v. Joint pseudonym with Grace Allen Hogarth, 1905- : Allen Weston, q.v.

NORTON, ANDRE. Pseudonym of Alice Mary Norton, 1912?- . Joint pseudonym with Grace Allen Hogarth, 1905- : Allen Weston, q.v.
The White Jade Fox. Dutton, 1975

NORTON, (FRANK R.) BROWNING, 1909- , and CHARLES A. LANDOLF
1 Prefer Murder. Graphic, 1956

NORTON, OLIVE (MARION CLAYDON). 1913- .
The Corpse-Bird Cries. Cassell, 1971
Dead on Prediction. Cassell, 1970
Now Lying Dead. Cassell, 1967
A School for Liars. Cassell, 1966
The Speight Street Angle. Corgi, 1968

NORWAY, G(EORGE)
-Adventures of Johnnie Pascoe. Nisbet, 1889
-Bessie Kitson. National Society's Depository, 1896
-The Brand of Cain. Ward, 1888
-A Dangerous Conspirator. Jarrold, 1897
Falsely Accused. Digby, 1900
In False Attire. Digby, 1902
-Mignonette. National Society Depository, 1903
-Riverslea. National Society Depository, 1900
-Tregarthen. Hurst, 1896

NORWAY, NEVIL SHUTE. 1899-1960. Pseudonym: Nevil Shute, q.v.

NORWOOD, ELLIOTT
Audit in Death. Hale, 1970
Bullets in the Bush. Hale, 1969

NORWOOD, HAYDEN
Death Down East. Phoenix, 1941
-They Met at Mrs. Bloxom's. Rodale, 1938

NORWOOD, JOHN. Pseudonym of Delbert Raymond Stark.
No Time to Laugh. Ward, 1956

NORWOOD, JOSEPH
Breaking the Shell. Burke, 1923

NORWOOD, VICTOR (GEORGE CHARLES). 1920- . Pseudonyms: Johnny Dark, Mark Hampton, Hank Janson, Nat Karta, qq.v.
The Caves of Death. Scion, 1951
Cry of the Beast. Scion, 1952
Hell's Wenches. (U.S.), 1963
The Island of Creeping Death. Scion, 1952
The Long Way Home. 1968
Night of the Black Horror.
The Skull of Kanaima. Scion, 1952
The Temple of the Dead. Scion, 1951
The Untamed. Scion, 1951
Valley of the Damned. 1968

NOTLEY, F(RANCES) E(LIZA) M(ILLETT). 1820- .
Beneath the Wheels. Tinsley, 1870

NOTLEY, JOHN (FRANKE). 1911- .
Corruption in Cantock. Jarrolds, 1941
-Hotel Geneva. Jarrolds, 1942
Murder has an Echo. Mystery House, 1945

NOTTINGHAM, POPPY
Hatred's Web. Ace, 1974
Shadow of a Cat. Ace, 1974
Without a Grave. Ace, 1975

NOVAK, ROBERT. Series character: Joe Blaze, in all titles.
The Big Payoff. Belmont, 1974
The Concrete Cage. Belmont, 1974
Thrill Killers. Belmont, 1974

NOVELLO, IVOR. See: PHYLLIS BOTTOME, 1884-1963.

NOY, JOHN. Series character: Rufus Deville, in at least those marked RD.
Gangsters of the Air. Hamilton, 1938 RD
The Great Airways Plot. Hamilton, 1938 RD
The Mystery of the Crested Falcon. Hamilton, 1939 RD
The Pirate Airship. Hamilton, 1932
Red Devil of the Air Police. Hamilton, 1937 RD

NOYES, STANLEY. 1924- .
Shadowbox. Macmillan, 1970

NUETZEL, CHARLES (ALEXANDER). 1934- .
Murder Times 4. Powell, 1969
Softly as I Kill You. Powell, 1969

NULL, GARY. 1945- . Both titles are in the Secret Circle series.
Cuban Expedition. Pyramid, 1974
Operation Royal Family. Pyramid, 1975

NUSBAUM, N. RICHARD. Pseudonym of N. Richard Nash.
Incognito. French (New York), 1941. (Play.)

NUTTALL, ANTHONY
The Chinese Doll Affair. Hale, 1973
The Hot End of the Stick. Hale, 1971
It Adds Up to Trouble. Hale, 1972
A Pistol at my Head. Hale, 1972
The Ventilated Head. Hale, 1974

NUTTALL, JEFF. 1933- .
Snipe's Spinster. Calder, 1975

NYLAND, GENTRY
Mr. South Burned his Mouth. Morrow, 1941. British title: Run for Your Money. Long, 1941. Also published as: Hot Bullets for Love. Double Action Detective Novel, 1943

NYSON, J. E.
Death Calls at Scotland Yard. Blackfriars, 1946

O

OAKES, PHILIP (BARLOW). 1928- .
Experiment at Proto. Deutsch, 1973; Coward, 1973

OAKLEY, JOHN. See also: NANCY OAKLEY.
The Blackmailer. Ward, 1902
The Great Craneboro' Conspiracy. Ward, 1907
That Wilmslow Girl! Aldine, 1895

OAKLEY, NANCY and JOHN. See also: JOHN OAKLEY.
The Clevedon Case. Jenkins, 1923; Lippincott, 1924
The Lint House Mystery. Jenkins, 1925

OAKROYD, SIMON
Maybe He's Dead. Belmont, 1971

O'BRIAN, FRANK. Pseudonym of Brian (Francis Wynne) Garfield, 1939- , q.v. Other pseudonym: Drew Mallory, q.v.
The Rimfire Murders. Bouregy, 1962

O'BRIEN, FITZ-JAMES. 1828-1862.
What was It? and other stories. Ward, 1889

O'BRIEN, FLANN. Pseudonym of Brian O'Nolan, 1911-1966.
The Third Policeman. MacGibbon, 1967; Walker, 1967

O'BRIEN, HOWARD VINCENT. 1888-1947.
Four-and-Twenty Blackbirds. Doubleday, 1928; Hodder, 1928

O'BRIEN, LEE
Sweet William is Dead. Popular Library, 1975

O'BRIEN, MORROUGH
The League of the Ring and Torn Apart. Ireland's Own Library, 1914 ss

O'BRIEN, ROBERT C. Pseudonym of Robert L. Conly, 1918-1973.
A Report from Group 17. Atheneum, 1972; Gollancz, 1973

O'BRIEN, SALIEE
Beelfontaine. Berkley, 1974
The Bride of Gaylord Hall. Berkley, 1972
Heiress to Evil. Beagle, 1974
Shadow of the Caravan. Berkley, 1974

O'BRINE, (PADRAIC) MANNING. 1915-   .
    Series character: Michael the
    O'Kelly, in at least those marked MO.
  Corpse to Cairo. Hammond, 1952
  Crambo. Joseph, 1970
  Dagger Before Me. Hammond, 1957
  Dead as a Dodo; see Dodos Don't Duck
  Deadly Interlude. Hammond, 1954 MO
  Dodos Don't Duck. Hammond, 1953. Also
    published as: Dead as a Dodo. Corgi,
    1954 MO
  The Hungry Killer. Hammond, 1955 MO
  Killers Must Eat. Hammond, 1951 MO
  Mills. Jenkins, 1969; Lippincott, 1969
  No Earth for Foxes. Barrie, 1974; Delacorte, 1975
  Passport to Treason. Hammond, 1955 MO

O'CALLAGHAN, DMITRI
  The Scavengers. Paperback Library,
    1963. (Novelization of the movie.)

OCKLEY, G. T.
  The Devil on Board. Heath Cranston,
    1937
  -The Man Under the Window. Houghton
    (London), 1935
  -The Tempestuous Wooer. Houghton (London), 1936

O'CONNELL, FREDERICK WILLIAM. 1876-1929.
    Pseudonym: Cearnach Conall, q.v.

O'CONNELL, T. J.
  Dead Man's Hoard. Mitre, 1946
  The Tyson Murder Case. Mitre, 1946

O'CONNOR, DERMOT
  The Eye of the Eagle. Long, 1971
  The Restless Quiet. Long, 1971
  The Slender Chance. Long, 1973

O'CONNOR, JOHN M(ARSHALL). 1909-   .
  Anonymous Footsteps. Cheshire, 1932

O'CONNOR, MICHAEL P(ATRICK). See:
    G(RANVILLE) P(RATT) WILLIS.

O'CONNOR, RAMONCITA SAYER
  Murder Won't Wait. Arcadia, 1953

O'CONNOR, RICHARD. 1915-1975. Pseudonyms:
    Frank Archer, Patrick Wayland, qq.v.

ODELL, WILLIAM. See: DAN J(AMES) MARLOWE,
    1914-   .

ODLUM, JEROME. 1905-1954.
  Each Dawn I Die. Bobbs, 1938
  The Mirabilis Diamond. Scribner, 1945
  The Morgue is Always Open. Scribner,
    1944
  Night and No Moon. Howell Soskin, 1942
  Nine Lives are Not Enough. Sheridan,
    1940; Boardman, 1944

O'DONNELL, ELLIOT. 1872-1965.
  -The Dead Riders. Rider, 1952
  The Devil in the Pulpit. Archer, 1932
  -Jennie Barlowe, Adventuress. Greening,
    1906
  Murder at Hide and Seek. Eldon, 1945

O'DONNELL, LILLIAN. Series character:
    Norah Mulcahaney = NM.
  Babes in the Woods. Abelard (New York
    & London), 1965
  The Baby Merchants. Putnam, 1975; Bantam (London), 1976 NM
  Death Blanks the Screen. Arcadia, 1961
  Death of a Player. Abelard (New York &
    London), 1964
  Death on the Grass. Arcadia, 1960
  Death Schuss. Abelard (New York & London), 1963
  Dial 577 R-A-P-E. Putnam, 1974; Barker,
    1974 NM

  Dive into Darkness. Abelard (New York &
    London), 1971
  Don't Wear Your Wedding Ring. Putnam,
    1973; Barker, 1974 NM
  The Face of the Crime. Abelard (New
    York & London), 1968
  Murder Under the Sun. Abelard (New York
    & London), 1964
  The Phone Calls. Putnam, 1972; Hodder,
    1972
  The Sleeping Beauty Murders. Abelard
    (New York & London), 1967
  The Tachi Tree. Abelard (New York &
    London), 1968

O'DONNELL, PETER. 1920-   . See also:
    J. T. McINTOSH. Series character:
    Modesty Blaise, in all titles.
  I, Lucifer. Souvenir, 1967; Doubleday,
    1967
  The Impossible Virgin. Souvenir, 1971;
    Doubleday, 1971
  Modesty Blaise. Souvenir, 1965; Doubleday, 1965
  Pieces of Modesty. Pan, 1972 ss
  Sabre-Tooth. Souvenir, 1966; Doubleday,
    1966
  The Silver Mistress. Souvenir, 1973
  A Taste for Death. Souvenir, 1969;
    Doubleday, 1969

O'DONNELL, CAPTAIN SIMON
  The Great Diamond Robbery. Ogilvie,
    1895
  The Runaway Wife; or, Love and Vengeance. Laird, 1889

O'DRISCOLL, MICHAEL
  Flood's First Case. Mitre, 1946

O'DUFFY, EIMAR (ULTAN). 1893-1935.
  The Bird Cage. Bles, 1932; Kinsey, 1933
  Head of a Girl. Bles, 1935
  The Secret Enemy. Bles, 1932

OELLRICHS, INEZ (HILDEGARD). 1907-   .
    Series character: Matt Winters, in at
    least those marked MW.
  And Die She Did. Doubleday, 1945; Hammond, 1953 MW
  Death in a Chilly Corner. Hammond, 1964
  Death of a White Witch. Doubleday,
    1949; Hammond, 1953 MW
  The Kettel Mill Mystery. Doubleday,
    1939; Davies, 1940 MW
  The Man Who Didn't Answer. Doubleday,
    1939; Davies, 1939 MW
  Murder Comes at Night. Doubleday, 1940;
    Hammond, 1951 MW
  Murder Helps. McKay, 1947 MW
  Murder Makes Us Gay. Doubleday, 1941;
    Hammond, 1952

OEMLER, MARIE CONWAY. 1879-1932.
  A Woman Named Smith. Century, 1919;
    Heinemann, 1920

O'FARRELL, BRIAN
  Mystery on the River. Blackwell, 1936

O'FARRELL, WILLIAM. 1904-1962. Pseudonym:
    William Grew, q.v.
  Brandy for a Hero. Duell, 1948
  Causeway to the Past. Duell, 1950;
    Corgi, 1954
  The Devil His Due. Doubleday, 1955;
    Hale, 1955
  The Golden Key. Lancer, 1962
  Grow Young and Die. Doubleday, 1952;
    Dakers, 1954
  Gypsy, Go Home. GM, 1961
  Harpoon of Death; see The Snakes of St.
    Cyr

  Lovely in Death; see The Snakes of St.
    Cyr
  Repeat Performance. Houghton, 1942;
    Allen, 1948
  The Secret Fear; see Walk the Dark
    Bridge
  The Snakes of St. Cyr. Duell, 1951.
    British title: Harpoon of Death.
    Dakers, 1953. Also published as:
    Lovely in Death. Bestseller, 1955
  These Arrows Point to Death. Duell,
    1951; Foulsham, 1952
  Thin Edge of Violence. Duell, 1949
  The Ugly Woman. Duell, 1948
  Walk the Dark Bridge. Doubleday, 1952.
    British title: The Secret Fear.
    Corgi, 1954
  Wetback. Dell, 1956

OFFORD, LENORE GLEN. 1905-   . Series
    characters: Bill & Coco Hastings = H;
    Todd McKinnon = TM.
  And Turned to Clay; see My True Love
    Lies
  Clues to Burn. Duell, 1942; Grayson,
    1943 H
  The Glass Mask. Duell, 1944; Jarrolds,
    1946 TM
  Murder Before Breakfast; see Murder on
    Russian Hill
  Murder on Russian Hill. Macrae Smith,
    1938. British title: Murder Before
    Breakfast. Jarrolds, 1938 H
  My True Love Lies. Duell, 1947. British
    title: And Turned to Clay. Jarrolds,
    1950
  The 9 Dark Hours. Duell, 1941; Eldon,
    1941
  Skeleton Key. Duell, 1943; Eldon, 1944
    TM
  The Smiling Tiger. Duell, 1949; Jarrolds, 1951 TM
  Walking Shadow. Simon, 1959; Ward, 1961
    TM

OFFUTT, ANDREW (JEFFERSON). 1934-   .
  Operation: Super Ms. Berkley, 1974

O'FINN, THADDEUS. Pseudonym of Joseph
    Thaddeus McGloin, 1917-   .
  Happy Holiday! Rinehart, 1950

O'FLAHERTY, LIAM. 1896-   .
  The Assassin. Cape, 1928; Harcourt,
    1928
  The Informer. Cape, 1925; Knopf, 1925

O'FLAHERTY, LOUISE. 1920-   .
  The House of the Lost Woman. Pyramid,
    1974

O'FLANAGAN, DENIS
  Everything Happens to Joe. Nimmo, 1947

O'FRANCIS, MARY. Pseudonym: Margaret
    Blount, q.v.

OGBURN, DOROTHY (STEVENS). 1890-   .
  Death on the Mountain. Little, 1931
  Ra-Ta-Plan—! Little, 1930; Nash, 1931
  The Will and the Deed. Dodd, 1935

OGILVIE, ELISABETH (MAY). 1917-   .
  Bellwood. McGraw-Hill, 1969
  The Face of Innocence. McGraw-Hill,
    1970
  The Witch Door. McGraw-Hill, 1959;
    Allen, 1961

OGILVIE, FRANCES
  Green Bondage. Farrar, 1931; Nicholson,
    1932

OGNALL, LEOPOLD HORACE. 1908-   . Pseudonyms: Harry Carmichael, Hartley
    Howard, qq.v.

O'GRADY, ROHAN. Pseudonym of June O'Grady Skinner, 1922- .
Bleak November. Dial, 1970; Joseph, 1971
Let's Kill Uncle. Macmillan, 1963; Longmans, 1964
The Master of Montrolfe Hall; see Pippin's Journal
Pippin's Journal. Macmillan, 1962; Gollancz, 1962. Also published as: The Master of Montrolfe Hall. Ace, 1965

O'HANLON, JAMES D. Series character: Jason Cordry, in all titles.
As Good as Murdered. Random, 1940; Cherry Tree, 1941
Murder at Coney Island. Phoenix, 1939
Murder at Horsethief. Phoenix, 1941; Boardman, 1943
Murder at Malibu. Phoenix, 1937
Murder at 300 to 1. Phoenix, 1938; Long, 1939

O'HARA, BORIS
The St. Valentine's Day Massacre. Dell, 1967. (Novelization of the movie.)

O'HARA, KENNETH. Pseudonym of Jean Morris, 1924- , q.v. Series character: Dr. Alun Barry, in at least those marked AB.
The Bird-Cage. Gollancz, 1968; Random, 1969
The Company of St. George. Gollancz, 1972
Double Cross Purposes. Cassell, 1962
Sleeping Dogs Lying. Cassell, 1960; Macmillan, 1962 AB
Underhandover. Cassell, 1961; Macmillan, 1963
Unknown Man, Seen in Profile. Gollancz, 1967
A View to a Death. Cassell, 1958 AB

O'HARA, KEVIN. Pseudonym of Marten Cumberland, 1892- , q.v. Series character: Chico Brett, in all titles.
Always Tell the Sleuth. Hurst, 1953
And Here is the Noose! Long, 1959
The Customer's Always Wrong. Hurst, 1951
Danger: Women at Work! Long, 1958
Don't Neglect the Body. Long, 1964
Don't Tell the Police. Long, 1963
Exit and Curtain. Hurst, 1952
If Anything Should Happen. Long, 1962
It Leaves Them Cold. Hurst, 1954
It's Your Funeral. Long, 1966
Keep Your Fingers Crossed. Hurst, 1955
The Pace That Kills. Hurst, 1955
Sing, Clubman, Sing! Hurst, 1952
Taking Life Easy. Long, 1961
Well, I'll be Hanged! Long, 1958
Women Like to Know. Jarrolds, 1957

O'HARA FAMILY, THE. Pseudonym of John and Michael Banim.
The Ghost-Hunter and His Family. Carey, 1833

O'HIGGINS, HARVEY J(ERROLD). 1876-1929. See also: HARRIET FORD; and: ARTHUR HORNBLOW, 1865- .
The Adventures of Detective Barney. Century, 1915 ss
Detective Duff Unravels It. Liveright, 1929 ss
The Dummy, with Harriet Ford. French, 1925. (4-act play.)

OHNET, GEORGES. Pseudonym of Georges Henot, 1848-1918.
Antoinette; or, The Marl-Pit Mystery; see The Great Marl-Pit
A Debt of Hatred. Cassell (New York), 1891

-Doctor Rameau. Chatto, 1889; Rand, 1889. (Translation of Le Docteur Rameau. Paris, 1889.)
The Great Marl-Pit. Remington, 1886. U.S. title: Antoinette; or, The Marl-Pit Mystery. Lippincott, 1889. Also published as: The Marl-Pit Mystery. Vizetelly, 1889. (Translation of Le Grande Marniere. Paris, 1885.)
-In Deep Abyss. Greening, 1904; Funk, 1901. (Translation of Au Fond du Gouffre. Paris, 1899.)
The Marl-Pit Mystery; see The Great Marl-Pit
The Poison Dealer. Laurie, 1906
-A Weird Gift. Chatto, 1890; Munro, 1890. (Translation of L'Ame de Pierre. Paris, 1890.)
The Woman of Mystery. Chatto, 1903

O'KEEFE, BOB
Diamonds can be Dangerous. Spearhead (Pretoria), 1953
Gold Without Glitter. Central News Agency (South Africa), 1957

OLAY, LIONEL
The Dark Corners of the Night. Signet, 1960

OLD HUTCH. Pseudonym of O. S. Adams.
The Detective's Clew; or, The Tragedy of Elm Grove. Street, 1888

OLD SLEUTH. Pseudonym of Harlan Page Halsey, 1839?-1898, q.v. Other pseudonyms: Tony Pastor, Judson R. Taylor, qq.v. Series character: Old Sleuth, in at least those marked OS.
Aggravating Joe, the Prince of Mischief. Ogilvie, 1894
Allie Baird, the Settler's Son. Parlor Car, 1897
Almon Mitchell's Double. Royal, ca.1897
An Amazing Wizard. Ogilvie, 1898
The American Detective in Russia. Munro, 1892
The American Monte Cristo. Royal, ca.1897
The American Thug. Munro, 1897
Amzi, the Detective. Ogilvie, 1896
Archie the Tumbler. Ogilvie, 1895
Arkie, the Runaway. Ogilvie, 1895
Arlie Bright. Ogilvie, 1896
The Autobiography of a Bottle of Bourbon. Munro, ca.1891
The Bank Robbers. Royal, ca.1897
A Beautiful Blackmailer. Royal, ca.1908
A Beautiful Fugitive. Parlor Car, 1898
Bertie Bland, the Detective. Ogilvie, 1895
The Bicycle Detective; see Bicycle Jim
Bicycle Jim. Ogilvie, 1895. Also published as: The Bicycle Detective. Ogilvie
Billy Mischief, a Regular Trained Detective. Royal, ca.1908
Billy Preston. Parlor Car, 1897
Billy, the Tramp. Ogilvie, 1895
Black Jess, the Outlaw. Royal, ca.1908
The Boy Detective. Munro, 1894
A Boy Fugitive. Ogilvie, 1896
Breezy Frank. Ogilvie, 1897
Bruce Angelo, the City Detective. Street, 1887
Cad Metti, the Female Detective. Ogilvie, 1895
Carroll Moore. Ogilvie, 1897
The Central Park Mystery. Ogilvie, 1898
The Chief of the Counterfeiters. Westbrook, 1920's
A Clever Detective. Ogilvie, 1894

Clew by Clew. Munro, 1894
A Close Call. Parlor Car, 1897
Clyde, the Resolute Detective. Parlor Car, 1897
Coal Tom. Ogilvie, 1894
The Confessions of an Imp. Munro, ca.1892
The Cowboy Detective. Ogilvie, 1895
Creco the Swordsman. Ogilvie, 1897
Creston, the Detective. Parlor Car, 1897
Criminals Run Down. Royal, ca.1897
Crusoe Harry. Ogilvie, 1896
A Cute Boy Detective. Ogilvie, 1895
A Daring Conspiracy. Royal, ca.1897
Daring Maddie. Ogilvie, 1898
A Dashing Fugitive. Parlor Car, 1897
Days and Nights of Peril. Ogilvie, 1897
Dead Straight. Parlor Car, 1897
Desmond Dare. Parlor Car, 1897
A Desperate Chance. Parlor Car, 1897
Detective Archie. Munro, 1895
Detective Dale. Parlor Car, 1898
Detective Gay. Ogilvie, 1896
Detective Hanley. Ogilvie, 1896
Detective Kennedy. Ogilvie, 1896
Detective Murdock, the Silent. Royal, ca.1908
Detective Payne. Ogilvie, 1899
Detective Payne's Shadow. Ogilvie
Detective Thrash. Royal, ca.1908
The Detective Trio. Ogilvie, 1895
A Detective's Daughter. Ogilvie, 1898
A Detective's Enigma. Ogilvie, 1897
Dick, the Boy Detective. Ogilvie
The "Dock Rats" of New York. Westbrook, 1908
The Doom of the Demon Band. Westbrook, 1908
A Double Crime. Munro, 1897
Dudie Dunne. Ogilvie, 1895
The Duke of Omaha. Ogilvie, 1895
An Eastern Vendetta. Royal, ca.1897
The Ex-Pugilist Detective. Ogilvie, 1895
A Famous Boy. Parlor Car, 1897
The Fastest Boy in New York. Munro, 1892
The Female Detective. Ogilvie, 1905
A Female Ventriloquist. Ogilvie, 1896
Fighting for a Fortune. Royal, ca.1897
Fighting his Way. Royal, ca.1897
A Final Triumph. Ogilvie
Fire-Bomb Jack. Ogilvie, 1898
The Floating Head. Westbrook, 1920's
Flyaway Ned. Ogilvie, 1895
From Death to Life. Royal, ca.1897
Funny Bob. Ogilvie, 1894
Gentleman Thorne. Royal, ca.1908
The Giant Athlete. Munro, 1896
The Giant Detective Among the Cowboys. Westbrook, 1908
The Giant Detective Among the Italian Brigands. Royal, ca.1897
The Giant Detective in France. Munro, 1892
Gipsy Reno, the Detective. Ogilvie, 1896
Gipsy Rose, the Female Detective. Ogilvie, 1898
The Girl Champion. Royal, ca.1897
A Golden Legacy. Ogilvie, 1896
Grant McKenzie. Ogilvie, 1897
The Great Bank Robbery. Royal, ca.1908
Great Billy. Ogilvie, 1894
A Great Boy. Ogilvie, 1897
A Great Capture. Parlor Car, 1897
The Great Indian Scout Detective. Royal, ca.1897
The Great River Mystery. Westbrook, 1909
The Gypsy Detective. Munro, 1892
The Haunting Shadow. Royal, ca.1897
The Headless Mystery. Royal, ca.1897
Headless Girl of the North River. Westbrook, 1920's
Henry Broch, Old Sleuth's Assistant. Royal, ca.1908 OS

His Greatest "Shadow". Ogilvie, 1896
In the Russian Secret Service. Westbrook, 1909
The Irish Detective. Munro, 1892
Iron Burgess, the Government Detective. Royal, ca.1908
The Italian Bandit. Royal, ca.1897
Jack and Jill. Parlor Car, 1898
Jack Breakaway. Ogilvie, 1896
Jack the Juggler. Ogilvie, 1895
Jack the Juggler's Ordeal. Ogilvie
Jack the Juggler's Trial. Ogilvie, 1896
Jolly Jess. Ogilvie, 1896
Kefton, the Detective. Ogilvie, 1895
The Kidnapped Heiress. Royal, ca.1908
The King of Fun. Ogilvie, 1896
The King of the Detectives. Munro, 1891
The King's Detective. Parlor Car, 1898
Kingsley the Detective. Ogilvie, 1897
The Lady Detective. Munro, 1892
A Lady Shadower. Parlor Car, 1897
The League of Counterfeiters. Westbrook, 1908
A League of Three. Ogilvie
Life in New York. Ogilvie, 1897
The Little Colonel. Ogilvie, 1895
A Little Cowboy. Ogilvie, 1895
A Little Cowboy in New York. Ogilvie
Little Dead-Sure. Ogilvie, 1895
A Little Giant. Ogilvie, 1895
The Little Miner. Ogilvie, 1896
Lively Luke. Parlor Car, 1897
The Lone House by the Sea. Westbrook, 1920's
Lorie. Ogilvie, 1896
Lure of the Black Pool. Westbrook, 1912
Magic Dick, a Boy Detective. Ogilvie, 1894
Malcolm the Wonder. Ogilvie, 1896
A Man of Mystery. Ogilvie
The Man Who Vanished. Ottenheimer, 189?
The Manordale Mystery. Ogilvie, 1898
The Man-Trapper. Munro, 1894
Marie, the Dancing Girl. Parlor Car, 1897
A Marvelous Escape. Ogilvie, 1898
The Mechanic's Son. Ogilvie, 1896
A Midnight Quest. Westbrook, 1908
A Million in Diamonds. Westbrook, 1920's
A Million in Jewels. Munro, 1896
Mura, the Western Detective. Munro, 1891
Murray, the Detective. Ogilvie
The Mysteries of New York. Royal, ca. 1897
The Mysterious Yankee. Royal, ca.1908
The Mystery of New York Bay. Royal, ca.1897
A Mystery of One Night. Ogilvie, 1898
The New York Detective. Munro, 1892
Night and Morning. Ogilvie
Nimble Ike, the Detective. Ogilvie
Nimble Ike, the Trick Ventriloquist. Ogilvie, 1894
Nimble Ike's Mystery. Ogilvie, 1896
Nimble Ike's Romance. Ogilvie
Norval, the Detective. Ogilvie, 1895
Old Electricity, the Lightning Detective. Munro, 1892
Old Ironsides Among the Italian Brigands. Royal, ca.1908
The Old Miser's Mystery. Royal, ca.1897
The Old Miser's Ward. Ogilvie
Old Sleuth, the Avenger. Westbrook, 1920's OS
Old Sleuth, the Detective. Munro, 1891 OS
Old Sleuth to the Rescue. Westbrook, 1920's OS
Old Sleuth's Greatest Case. Westbrook, 1920's OS
Old Sleuth's Triumph. Munro, 1892 OS
Old Sleuth's Winning Hand. Westbrook, 1920's OS
Old Sleuth's Wonderful Revelation. Royal, ca.1908 OS
Old Terrible. Royal, ca.1908

The Omnipotent Avenger. Royal, ca.1897
On the Wing. Ogilvie, 1897
On Their Track. Royal, ca.1897
A One Night Mystery. Ogilvie, 1898 ss
Only a Photograph. Ogilvie, 1899
Oscar. Parlor Car, 1897
Pawnee Tom. Ogilvie, 1896
The Phantom of Meadow Creek. Westbrook, 1920's
The Phantom Wreck. Munro, 1899
Plot and Counterplot. Royal, ca.1897
Plucky Bob. Ogilvie, 1896
A Plucky Girl. Ogilvie, 1897
Preston Jayne. Ogilvie
The Prince of Ventriloquists. Ogilvie, 1895
A Puzzling Shadow. Ogilvie, 1895
Queen of the Highway. Ogilvie, 1905
Ramsey, the Detective. Parlor Car, 1898
Ray's Adventure. Royal, ca.1908
Red Cecil, the Detective. Ogilvie, 1898
A Remarkable Feat. Parlor Car, 1898
A Remarkable "Shadow". Parlor Car, 1897
Resolute Jack. Ogilvie, 1895
The River Detective and the Wharf Rat's Game. Westbrook, 1920's
The River Tragedy. Westbrook, 1920's
Romance of a Salvation Army Girl. Ogilvie, 1894
The Runaway. Ogilvie
Seth Bond. Parlor Car, 1898
The Shadow Detective. Munro, 1891
Shadowed by 2. Westbrook, 1908
Shadowed to his Doom. Westbrook, 1908
The Sheik's Capture. Royal, ca.1897
A Single Clue. Ogilvie
Snap and Jenny. Ogilvie
A Startling Discovery. Royal, ca.1908
A Straight Clue. Ogilvie, 1897
A Straight-Out Detective. Ogilvie, 1894
"Straight to the Mark". Ogilvie, 1897
A Struggle to Win. Parlor Car, 1898
A Successful "Shadow". Parlor Car, 1898
The Surprise of his Life. Royal, ca. 1897
A Ten Day Mystery. Ogilvie, 1897
A Terrible Youth. Ogilvie, 1896
The Terror in the Night. Westbrook, 1920's
The Three Boy Detectives. Parlor Car, 1895
Three Little Tramps. Ogilvie, 1894
Thrifty Abe. Parlor Car, 1898
A Thrilling Mystery. Munro, 1895
Tom, the Young Explorer. Parlor Car, 1898
Tracked by a Female Detective. Westbrook, 1920's
Tracked by a Woman. Munro, 1904
Tracked on a Wheel. Ogilvie, 1896
A Tragic Mystery. Royal, ca.1897
A Tragic Quest. Ogilvie, 1899
Tragedy and Strategy. Royal, ca.1897
Trapped by a Female Detective. Westbrook, 1920's
Trapping the Moonshiners. Westbrook, 1920's
Tricks and Triumphs. Ogilvie, 1896
True Blue, the Detective. Ogilvie, 1894
The Twin Athletes. Parlor Car, 1898
The Twin Ventriloquists. Ogilvie, 1895
The Two Conspirators. Ogilvie, 1896
Two Wonderful Detectives. Ogilvie, 1898
The Ubiquitous Yank. Munro, 1891
Under a Veil. Ogilvie, 1897
Under Sentence of Death. Royal, ca.1897
Variety Jack. Royal, ca.1908
Vavel, the Wonderful Treasure Seeker. Ogilvie, 1894
The "Veiled Beauty". Westbrook, 1920's

The Ventriloquist Detective. Ogilvie
Weaver Webb. Ogilvie, 1896
A Weird Courtship. Ogilvie
A Weird Sea Mystery. Ogilvie
The West Point Lieutenant. Ogilvie
The West Shore Mystery. Munro, 1891
Winning a Princess. Ogilvie
Witch of Manhattan. Ogilvie
The Wizard Detective. Royal, ca.1908
The Wizard Tramp. Parlor Car, 1897
The Woman of Death. Westbrook, 1908
Wonder Jack. Ogilvie, 1894
A Wonderful Detective. Ogilvie, 1895
Woodchuck Jerry, the Country Detective. Ogilvie
Woodchuck Jerry. Ogilvie, 1894
Yankey Rue, the Ex-Pugilist Detective. Ogilvie, 1894
A Young Alladin. Ogilvie, 1898
Young Chauncey. Ogilvie, 1898
Young Dash. Ogilvie, 1897
The Young Engineer. Ogilvie, 1896
Young Gingers. Ogilvie, 1895
Young Harold. Ogilvie, 1898
The Young Magician. Royal, 1905
Young Vigilance. Ogilvie, 1897
Zantelli. Ogilvie, 1897

OLD SPICER. Pseudonym.
A Dead Witness. Street (Magnet)
A Desperate Game. Street (Magnet)
A High Class Swindler. Street (Magnet)
In the Shadow. Street (Magnet)
A Matter of Thousands. Street (Magnet)
The Palace of Chance. Street (Magnet)
On the Brink of Ruin. Street (Magnet)
A Question of Evidence. Street (Magnet)
The Shadow of Guilt. Street (Magnet)
The Sport of Fate. Street (Magnet)
The Stolen Jewels. Street (Magnet)
The Tattooed Wrist. Street (Magnet), 1896
The Three Finger Marks. Street (Magnet)
Tightening of the Coils. Street (Magnet)

OLDE, NICHOLAS
The Incredible Adventures of Rowland Hern. Heinemann, 1928 ss

OLDEN, MARC. Series character: Robert Sand = RS.
Black Samurai. Signet, 1974 RS
Cocaine. Signet, 1975
The Deadly Pearl. Signet, 1974 RS
The Golden Kill. Signet, 1974
The Inquisition. Signet, 1974
The Katana. Signet, 1975
Killer Warrior. Signet, 1974
Sword of Allah. Signet, 1975
The Warlock. Signet, 1975

OLDFELD, PETER. Joint pseudonym of Per Jacobsson, 1894-1963, and Vernon Bartlett, 1894-   .
The Alchemy Murder. Washburn, 1929; Constable, 1929
The Death of a Diplomat. Washburn, 1928; Constable, 1928

OLDFIELD, CLAUDE HOUGHTON. 1889-   .
Pseudonym: Claude Houghton, q.v.

OLDSEY, BERNARD (STANLEY). 1924-   .
The Spanish Season. Harcourt, 1970

OLECK, HOWARD L(EONER). 1911-   .
Series character: Sam Benedict, who also appears in books by Elsie Lee and Brad Williams, 1918-   , qq.v.
A Singular Fury. World, 1968

OLESKER, HARRY. 1923?-1969.
Exit Dying. Random, 1959; Boardman, 1961
Impact. Random, 1961; Boardman, 1961

Now Will You Try for Murder? Simon, 1958; Boardman, 1959

OLIPHANT, MRS. MARGARET (OLIPHANT WILSON). 1828-1997.
-The Duke's Daughters, and, The Fugitives. Blackwood, 1890
Mystery of Blencarrow; see The Mystery of Mrs. Blencarrow
The Mystery of Mrs. Blencarrow. Blackett, 1890. U.S. title: Mystery of Blencarrow. Donohue, 1894
-Stories of the Seen and the Unseen. Blackwood, 1902; Roberts, 1889 ss

OLIVER, EDWIN. 1867-
A Rogue's Progress. Treherne, 1903

OLIVER, GAIL. Pseudonym of Marian Gallagher Scott, 1892-   . Other pseudonym: Katherine Wolffe, q.v.
The Moon Saw Murder. Macmillan, 1937; Bles, 1938

OLIVER, GEORGE. 1873-1961. Pseudonym: Oliver Onions, q.v.

OLIVER, JOHN
Detection in a Topper. Herbert Joseph, 1936

OLIVER, LIONEL
-Mexican Adventure. Eldon, 1935
Mongolian Interlude. Eldon, 1936

OLIVER, DR. N. T. Pseudonym of E. O. Tilburn. Other pseudonym: Nevada Ned, q.v.
-Almeda. Rand, 1889
The Confession of Lorraine Herschel. Laird, 1896. Also published as: A Desperate Deed. Laird, 1900
A Desperate Deed; see The Confession of Lorraine Herschel
-Dr. Wilbur's Note Book. Rand, 1889
-The Fateful Hand; or, Saved by Lightning. Laird, 1896
An Unconscious Crime. Laird, 1891
The Whitechapel Mystery. Eagle, 1889
-A Woman of Nerve. Laird, 1900

OLIVY, D. J.
Never Ask a Policeman. Gollancz, 1970; Coward, 1970

OLMSTEAD, EDWIN
-Nightly She Sings. Knopf, 1937. British title: Clip-Joint. Constable, 1938

OLMSTED, HOWARD J.
The Hot Diary. Ace, 1960

OLMSTEAD, LORENA ANN. 1890-   .
Cover of Darkness. Avalon, 1961
Death Walked In. Avalon, 1960
Footsteps of the Cat. Avalon, 1963
Setup for Murder. Avalon, 1962
To Love a Stranger. Avalon, 1964

OLSEN, D. B. Pseudonym of (Julia Clara Catherine) Dolores B(irk Olsen) Hitchens, 1907-1972, q.v. Other pseudonyms: Dolan Birkley, Noel Burke, qq.v. Series characters: Rachel and Jennifer Murdock = M; Lt. Stephen Mayhew = SM; Professor A. Pennyfeather = P.
The Alarm of the Black Cat. Doubleday, 1942 M
Bring the Bride a Shroud. Doubleday, 1945; Aldor, 1945 P
The Cat and Capricorn. Doubleday, 1951 M
The Cat Saw Murder. Doubleday, 1939; Heinemann, 1940 M & SM
The Cat Walk. Doubleday, 1953 M
The Cat Wears a Mask. Doubleday, 1949 M
The Cat Wears a Noose. Doubleday, 1944 M & SM
Cat's Claw. Doubleday, 1943 M & SM
Cat's Don't Need Coffins. Doubleday, 1946; Aldor, 1946 M & SM
Cats Don't Smile. Doubleday, 1945; Aldor, 1948 M
Cats Have Tall Shadows. Ziff-Davis, 1948 M
Catspaw for Murder. Doubleday, 1943 M & SM
The Clue in the Clay. Phoenix, 1938 SM
Dead Babes in the Wood; see Enrollment Cancelled
Death Cuts a Silhouette. Doubleday, 1939
Death Walks on Cat Feet. Doubleday, 1956 M
Death Wears Cat's Eyes. Doubleday, 1950 M
Devious Design. Doubleday, 1948 P
Enrollment Cancelled. Doubleday, 1952. Also published as: Dead Babes in the Wood. Dell, 1954 P
Gallows for the Groom. Doubleday, 1947 P
Love Me in Death. Doubleday, 1951 P
Night of the Bowstring. Hale, 1963. (U.S. title?)
Something About Midnight. Doubleday, 1950 P
The Ticking Heart. Doubleday, 1940 SM
Widows Ought to Weep. Ziff-Davis, 1947

O'MAHONEY, CHARLES KINGSTON. Pseudonym: Charles Kingston, q.v.

O'MALLEY, FRANK. Pseudonym of Frank O'Rourke, 1916-   , q.v.
The Best Go First. Random, 1950; Benn, 1955

O'MALLEY, LADY MARY DOLLING SAUNDERS. 1889-1974. Pseudonym: Ann Bridge, q.v.

O'MALLEY, PATRICK. Series characters: Harrigan & Hoeffler, in all titles.
The Affair of Chief Strongheart. Mill, 1964
The Affair of John Donne. Mill, 1964
The Affair of Jolie Madame. Mill, 1963; Hale, 1965
The Affair of Swan Lake. Mill, 1962
The Affair of the Blue Pig. Mill, 1965
The Affair of the Bumbling Briton. Mill, 1965
The Affair of the Red Mosaic. Mill, 1961

O'MANT, HEDLEY. Pseudonym: Hedley Scott, q.v.

O'MEARA, WALTER (ANDREW). 1897-   .
Minnesota Gothic. Holt, 1956. Also published as: Castle Danger. Macfadden, 1966

O'NAIR, MAIRI. Pseudonym of Constance May Evans, 1890-   .
Beautiful Crook. Mills, 1937
Dangerous Lady. Mills, 1934
The Girl with the X-Ray Eyes. Mills, 1935 ss
Jennifer Disappears. Mills, 1935
Judy Ashbane, Police Decoy. Mills, 1944
Mystery at Butlin's. Mills, 1960

O'NEIL, KERRY. Pseudonym of John T(homas) MacIntyre, 1871-1951, q.v. Series character: Jerry Mooney = JM.
Death at Dakar. Doubleday, 1942

Death Strikes at Heron House. Farrar, 1944 JM
Mooney Moves Around. Reynal, 1939 JM
Ninth Floor: Middle City Tower. Farrar, 1943 JM

O'NEIL, RUSSELL
The Alcatraz Incident. McKay, 1971

O'NEILL, ARCHIE. Series character: Jeff Pride, in all titles.
The Da Vinci Rose. Bantam, 1973
The Duplicate Stiff. Bantam, 1974
The Ginzberg Circle. Bantam, 1974
High Bid for Murder. Bantam, 1974

O'NEILL, DESMOND
Life has No Price. Gollancz, 1959; Dodd, 1960

O'NEILL, EDWARD A.
The Rotterdam Delivery. Coward, 1975; Gollancz, 1976

O'NEILL, JAMES
Garrison Tales from Tonquin. Copeland, 1895 ss, some criminous

O'NEILL, JAMES
The Molly Maguires. GM, 1969. (Novelization of the movie.)

O'NEILL, JOHN. 1869-   .
Souls in Hell. Brown, 1924. British title: As We Sow. Methuen, 1926

O'NEILL-BARNA, ANNE
Wentworth Hall. Popular Library, 1974

ONIONS, OLIVER. Pseudonym of George Oliver, 1873-1961.
A Case in Camera. Arrowsmith, 1920; Macmillan, 1921
In Accordance with the Evidence. Secker, 1912; Luce, 1913

O'NOLAN, BRIAN. 1911-1966. Pseudonym: Flann O'Brien, q.v.

OPERATOR 1384. Pseudonym of John Henry Harvey. Other pseudonym: John H. Barrington, q.v.
The Black Arab. Rich, 1937
The Catacombs of Death. Hutchinson, 1936
The Devil's Diplomats. Hutchinson, 1935
Jackals of the Secret Service. Rich, 1938
-Queen of the Riffs. Lane, 1937
The Scourge of the Desert. Rich, 1936
-Spies and Rebels. Rich, 1939
-The White Tuareg. Rich, 1936

OPPENHEIM, E(DWARD) PHILLIPS. 1866-1946. Pseudonym: Anthony Partridge, q.v. Series character: Peter Ruff = PR.
Aaron Rodd, Diviner. Hodder, 1920; Little, 1927 ss
The Adventures of Mr. Joseph P. Cray. Hodder, 1925; Little, 1927 ss
Advice Limited. Hodder, 1935; Little, 1936 ss
The Amazing Judgment. Downey, 1897
The Amazing Partnership. Cassell, 1914; Little, 1932, in the omnibus Shudders and Thrills ss
The Amazing Quest of Mr. Ernest Bliss. Hodder, 1922. U.S. title: The Curious Quest. Little, 1919
Ambrose Lavendale, Diplomat. Hodder, 1920 ss
An Amiable Charlatan; see The Game of Liberty
And Still I Cheat the Gallows. Hodder, 1938 ss

Anna, the Adventuress. Ward, 1904; Little, 1904
As a Man Lives. Ward, 1898; Little, 1908. Also published as: The Yellow House. Doscher, 1908
Ask Miss Mott. Hodder, 1936; Little, 1937 ss
The Avenger; see Conspirators
The Bank Manager. Hodder, 1934. U.S. title: The Man Without Nerves. Little, 1934
The Battle of Basinghall Street. Hodder, 1935; Little, 1935
Berenice. Ward, 1910; Little, 1907
The Betrayal. Ward, 1904; Dodd, 1904
The Bird of Paradise. Hodder, 1936. U.S. title: Floating Peril. Little, 1936
The Black Box. Hodder, 1917; Grosset, 1915. (Novelization of the movie.)
Blackman's Wood. Readers Library, 1929. (With Underdog by Agatha Christie, 1890-1976, q.v.)
The Box with Broken Seals; see The Strange Case of Mr. Jocelyn Thew
Burglars Must Dine. Todd, 1943. (From Ask Miss Mott, q.v.)
The Channay Syndicate. Hodder, 1927; Little, 1927 ss
Chronicles of Melhampton. Hodder, 1928 ss
The Cinema Murder; see The Other Romilly
The Colossus of Arcadia. Hodder, 1938; Little, 1938
Conspirators. Ward, 1907. U.S. title: The Avenger. Little, 1908
The Court of St. Simon (by Anthony Partridge); see Seeing Life
Crooks in the Sunshine. Hodder, 1932; Little, 1933 ss
Curious Happenings to the Rooke Legatees. Hodder, 1937; Little, 1938 ss
The Curious Quest; see The Amazing Quest of Mr. Ernest Bliss
A Daughter of Astrea. Arrowsmith, 1898; Doscher, 1909
A Daughter of the Marionis. Ward, 1895. U.S. title: To Win the Love He Sought. Doscher, 1910. Reprinted under the British title: Little, 1920
The Devil's Paw. Hodder, 1921; Little, 1920
The Double Four. Cassell, 1911. U.S. title: Peter Ruff and the Double Four. Little, 1912 ss PR
The Double Life of Mr. Alfred Burton. Methuen, 1914; Little, 1913
The Double Traitor. Hodder, 1918; Little, 1915
The Dumb Gods Speak. Hodder, 1937; Little, 1937
Enoch Strone; see Master of Men
Envoy Extraordinary. Hodder, 1937; Little, 1937
The Evil Shepherd. Hodder, 1923; Little, 1922
The Ex-Detective. Hodder, 1933; Little, 1933 ss
The Ex-Duke. Hodder, 1927. U.S. title: The Interloper. Little, 1927
Exit a Dictator. Hodder, 1939; Little, 1939
Expiation. Maxwell, 1887
The Exploits of Pudgy Pete & Co. Hodder, 1928 ss
The Falling Star. Hodder, 1911. U.S. title: The Moving Finger. Little, 1911
False Evidence. Ward (London), 1896; Ward (New York), 1897
Floating Peril; see The Bird of Paradise
For the Queen. Ward, 1912; Little, 1913 ss
The Fortunate Wayfarer. Hodder, 1928; Little, 1928

Gabriel Samara. Hodder, 1925. U.S. title: Gabriel Samara, Peacemaker. Little, 1925
Gabriel Samara, Peacemaker; see Gabriel Samara
The Gallows of Chance. Hodder, 1934; Little, 1934
The Game of Liberty. Cassell, 1915. U.S. title: An Amiable Charlatan. Little, 1916 ss
Gangsters' Glory; see Inspector Dickins Retires
General Besserley's Puzzle Box. Hodder, 1935; Little, 1935 ss
General Besserley's Second Puzzle Box. Hodder, 1939; Little, 1940 ss
The Glenlitten Murder. Hodder, 1929; Little, 1929
The Golden Beast. Hodder, 1926; Little, 1926
The Golden Web; see The Plunderers
The Governors. Ward, 1908; Little, 1909
The Grassleyes Mystery. Hodder, 1940; Little, 1940
The Great Awakening. Ward, 1902. U.S. title: A Sleeping Memory. Dillingham, 1902
The Great Bear. Todd, 1943. (16 pp.)
The Great Impersonation. Hodder, 1920; Little, 1920
The Great Prince Shan. Hodder, 1922; Little, 1922
The Great Secret; see The Secret
Harvey Garrard's Crime. Hodder, 1927; Little, 1926
Havoc. Hodder, 1912; Little, 1911
The Hillman. Methuen, 1917; Little, 1917
His Father's Crime; see The Mystery of Mr. Bernard Brown
The Honourable Algernon Knox, Detective. Hodder, 1920 ss
The Human Chase. Hodder, 1929; Little, 1932, in the omnibus Shudders and Thrills ss
The Illustrious Prince. Hodder, 1910; Little, 1910
The Inevitable Millionaires. Hodder, 1923; Little, 1925
Inspector Dickins Retires. Hodder, 1931. U.S. title: Gangsters' Glory. Little, 1931 ss
The Interloper; see The Ex-Duke
Jacob's Ladder. Hodder, 1921; Little, 1921
Jeanne of the Marshes. Ward, 1909; Little, 1909
Jennerton & Co. Hodder, 1929; Little, 1931, in the omnibus Clowns and Criminals ss
Jeremiah and the Princess. Hodder, 1933; Little, 1933
Judy of Bunter's Buildings. Hodder, 1936. U.S. title: The Magnificent Hoax. Little, 1936
The Kingdom of the Blind. Hodder, 1917; Little, 1916
Last Train Out. Hodder, 1941; Little, 1940
The Light Beyond. Hodder, 1928; Little, 1928
The Lighted Way. Hodder, 1912; Little, 1912
The Lion and the Lamb. Hodder, 1930; Little, 1930
The Little Gentleman from Okehampstead. Hodder, 1926 ss
The Long Arm. Ward, 1909. U.S. title: The Long Arm of Mannister. Little, 1908 ss
The Long Arm of Mannister; see The Long Arm

The Lost Ambassador; see The Missing Delora
A Lost Leader. Ward, 1906; Little, 1906
Madame. Hodder, 1927. U.S. title: Madame and Her Twelve Virgins. Little, 1927 ss
Madame and Her Twelve Virgins; see Madame
The Magnificent Hoax; see Judy of Bunter's Buildings
A Maker of History. Ward, 1905; Little, 1906
The Malefactor; see Mr. Wingrave, Millionaire
The Man and His Kingdom. Ward, 1899; Lippincott, 1900
The Man from Sing Sing; see Moran Chambers Smiled
The Man Who Changed His Plea. Hodder, 1942; Little, 1942
The Man Who Thought He was a Pauper. Polybooks, 1943. (16 pp.)
The Man Without Nerves; see The Bank Manager
The Master Mummer. Ward, 1905; Little, 1904
Master of Men. Methuen, 1901. U.S. title: Enoch Strone. Dillingham, 1902
Matorni's Vineyard. Hodder, 1929; Little, 1928
The Mayor on Horseback. Little, 1937
Michael's Evil Deeds. Hodder, 1924; Little, 1923 ss
The Milan Grill Room. Hodder, 1940; Little, 1941 ss
The Million Pound Deposit. Hodder, 1930; Little, 1930
A Millionaire of Yesterday. Ward, 1900; Lippincott, 1900
The Mischief-Maker. Hodder, 1913; Little, 1912
Miss Brown of X.Y.O. Hodder, 1927; Little, 1927
The Missing Delora. Methuen, 1910. U.S. title: The Lost Ambassador. Little, 1910
The Missioner. Ward, 1908; Little, 1907
Mr. Billingham, the Marquis and Madelon. Hodder, 1927; Little, 1929 ss
Mr. Grex of Monte Carlo. Methuen, 1915; Little, 1915
Mr. Laxworthy's Adventures. Cassell, 1913 ss
Mr. Lessingham Goes Home. Hodder, 1919. U.S. title: The Zeppelin's Passenger. Little, 1918
Mr. Marx's Secret. Ward, 1909; Westbrook, 1912
Mr. Mirakel. Hodder, 1943; Little, 1943
Mr. Wingrave, Millionaire. Ward, 1906. U.S. title: The Malefactor. Little, 1907
The Modern Prometheus. Unwin, 1896; Neely, 1897
A Monk of Cruta. Beeton's Christmas Annual, 1894; Neely, 1894. Also published as: The Tragedy of Andrea. Ogilvie, 1906
Moran Chambers Smiled. Hodder, 1932. U.S. title: The Man from Sing Sing. Little, 1932
The Moving Finger; see The Falling Star
Murder at Monte Carlo. Hodder, 1933; Little, 1933
Mysteries of the Riviera. Cassell, 1916 ss
Mysterious Mr. Sabin. Ward, 1898; Little, 1905
The Mystery of Mr. Bernard Brown. Bentley, 1896; Little, 1910. Also published as: The New Tenant. Collier, 1912. And as: His Father's Crime. Street, 1929
The Mystery Road. Hodder, 1924; Little, 1923

The New Tenant; see The Mystery of Mr.
   Bernard Brown
Nicholas Goade, Detective. Hodder,
   1927; Little, 1929 ss
Nobody's Man. Hodder, 1922; Little,
   1921
The Ostrekoff Jewels. Hodder, 1932;
   Little, 1932
The Other Romilly. Hodder, 1918. U.S.
   title: The Cinema Murder. Little,
   1917
The Passionate Quest. Hodder, 1924;
   Little, 1924
The Pawns Count. Hodder, 1918; Little,
   1918
The Peer and the Woman. Ward, 1895;
   Taylor, 1892
A People's Man. Methuen, 1915; Little,
   1914
Peter Ruff. Hodder, 1912. U.S. title
   (?): Recalled by the Double-Four.
   Little, 1931, in the omnibus Clowns
   and Criminals ss
Peter Ruff and the Double-Four; see The
   Double Four
The Plunderers. Hodder, 1912. U.S.
   title: The Golden Web. Little, 1910,
   as by Anthony Partridge. Reprinted in
   Britain under the U.S. title: Lloyds,
   1918
The Postmaster of Market Deignton.
   Routledge, 1897
A Prince of Sinners. Ward, 1903; Lit-
   tle, 1903
Prodigals of Monte Carlo. Hodder, 1926;
   Little, 1926
The Profiteers. Hodder, 1921; Little,
   1921
A Pulpit in the Grill Room. Hodder,
   1938; Little, 1939 ss
Recalled by the Double-Four; see Peter
   Ruff
The Secret. Ward, 1907. U.S. title: The
   Great Secret. Little, 1908
Seeing Life. Lloyd's, 1919. U.S. title:
   The Court of St. Simon, as by Anthony
   Partridge. Little, 1912
The Seven Conundrums. Hodder, 1924;
   Little, 1923 ss
The Shy Plutocrat. Hodder, 1941; Lit-
   tle, 1941
Simple Peter Cradd. Hodder, 1931; Lit-
   tle, 1931
Sinners Beware. Hodder, 1932; Little,
   1932 ss
Sir Adam Disappeared. Hodder, 1939;
   Little, 1939
Slane's Long Shots. Hodder, 1930; Lit-
   tle, 1930 ss
A Sleeping Memory; see The Great Awak-
   ening
The Spy Paramount. Hodder, 1935; Lit-
   tle, 1935
The Spymaster. Hodder, 1938; Little,
   1938
Stolen Idols. Hodder, 1925; Little,
   1925
The Strange Boarders of Palace Cres-
   cent. Hodder, 1935; Little, 1934
The Strange Case of Mr. Jocelyn Thew.
   Hodder, 1919. U.S. title: The Box
   with the Broken Seals. Little, 1919
The Stranger's Gate. Hodder, 1940;
   Little, 1939
The Survivor. Ward, 1901; Brentano's,
   1901
The Temptation of Tavernake. Hodder,
   1913. U.S. title: The Tempting of
   Tavernake. Little, 1912
The Tempting of Tavernake; see The
   Temptation of Tavernake
The Terrible Hobby of Sir Joseph Londe,
   Bt. Hodder, 1924; Little, 1927 ss
Those Other Days. Ward, 1912; Little,
   1913 ss
To Win the Love He Sought; see A
   Daughter of the Marionis

The Tragedy of Andrea; see A Monk of
   Cruta
The Traitors. Ward, 1902; Dodd, 1903
The Treasure House of Martin Hews. Hod-
   der, 1929; Little, 1929
Up the Ladder of Gold. Hodder, 1931;
   Little, 1931
The Vanished Messenger. Methuen, 1916;
   Little, 1914
The Vindicator. Little, 1907. (British
   title?)
The Way of These Women. Methuen, 1914;
   Little, 1913
What Happened to Forester. Hodder,
   1929; Little, 1930 ss
The Wicked Marquis. Hodder, 1919; Lit-
   tle, 1919
The World's Great Snare. Ward, 1896;
   Lippincott, 1896
The Wrath to Come. Hodder, 1925; Lit-
   tle, 1924
The Yellow Crayon. Ward, 1903; Dodd,
   1903
The Yellow House; see As a Man Lives
The Zeppelin's Passenger; see Mr. Les-
   singham Goes Home

ORAM, JOHN. Both titles are novelizations
of Man from U.N.C.L.E. TV series.
   The Copenhagen Affair. Ace, 1965; Four
   Square, 1966
   The Stone-Cold Dead in the Market
   Affair. Ace, 1970; Four Square, 1966

ORBISON, KECK. Joint pseudonym of Maud
Keck, q.v., and Olive Orbison.
   The Key to the Case. Washburn, 1929.
   British title: The Crested Key.
   Long, 1929

ORBISON, OLIVE. Joint pseudonym with Maud
Keck, q.v.: Keck Orbison, q.v.

ORCUTT, WILLIAM DANA. 1870-1953.
   -The Balance. Stokes, 1922

ORCZY, BARONESS (EMMUSKA) [EMMA MAGDALENA
ROSALIA MARIA JOSIFA BARBARA, BARO-
NESS ORCZY]. 1865-1947. Series char-
acter: The Old Man in the Corner =
OM.
   The Case of Miss Elliott. Unwin, 1905
   ss
   Castles in the Air. Cassell, 1921;
   Doran, 1922 ss
   Lady Molly of Scotland Yard. Cassell,
   1910; Arno, 1976 ss
   The Man in Gray. Cassell, 1918; Doran,
   1918 ss
   The Man in the Corner; see The Old Man
   in the Corner
   The Old Man in the Corner. Greening,
   1909. U.S. title: The Man in the Cor-
   ner. Dodd, 1909 ss Arno, 1975
   The Old Man in the Corner Unravels the
   Mystery of the Fulton Gardens Mys-
   tery, and The Moorland Tragedy.
   Doran, 1925 ss OM
   The Old Man in the Corner Unravels the
   Mystery of the Khaki Tunic. Doran,
   1923 OM
   The Old Man in the Corner Unravels the
   Mystery of the Pearl Necklace, and
   The Tragedy in Bishop's Road. Doran,
   1924 ss OM
   The Old Man in the Corner Unravels the
   Mystery of the Russian Prince, and of
   Dog's Tooth Cliff. Doran, 1924 ss OM
   The Old Man in the Corner Unravels the
   Mystery of the White Carnation, and
   The Montmartre Hat. Doran, 1925 ss OM
   Skin o' My Tooth. Hodder, 1928; Double-
   day, 1928 ss

Unraveled Knots. Hutchinson, 1925;
   Doran, 1926 OM ss (9 of the 13 ss
   in this volume were previously published in the U.S. in the 5 Doran
   booklets identified above.)

ORDE-POWLETT, NIGEL (AMYAS). 1900-   .
Series character: Anthony Rillington,
in both titles.
   The Cast of Death. Benn, 1932; Hough-
   ton, 1932
   Driven Death. Benn, 1933

ORDWAY, PETER. 1916-   .
   Conspiracy of Vipers. Davies, 1961;
   British Book Service, 1961
   The Face in the Shadows. Wyn, 1953
   High Kill; see The Teak Forest
   Night of Reckoning. Hale, 1967; Simon,
   1965
   The Teak Forest. Boardman, 1958. Also
   published as: High Kill. World Dis-
   tributors, 1960

O'REILLY, MARY BOYLE. 1873-   .
   The Black Fan. Reilly, 1928

ORFORD, ELLEN
   The Bride of Raven Island. Curtis, 1974
   The Maze. Curtis, 1973
   The Sutter House. Popular Library, 1975

ORGAN, PERRY
   The House on Cheyne Walk. Heinemann,
   1975; Coward, 1975

ORGILL, DOUGLAS (WILLIAM). 1922-   .
Series character: William Mallett =
WM.
   The Astrid Factor. Davies, 1968;
   Walker, 1968
   The Cautious Assassin; see Ride a Tiger
   The Days of Darkness. Davies, 1965.
   U.S. title: Man in the Dark. Morrow,
   1965
   The Death Bringers. Davies, 1962. U.S.
   title: Journey into Violence. Morrow,
   1963 WM
   The Jasius Pursuit. Macmillan (London),
   1973; St. Martin's, 1973
   Journey into Violence; see The Death
   Bringers
   Man in the Dark; see The Days of Dark-
   ness
   Ride a Tiger. Davies, 1963. U.S. title:
   The Cautious Assassin. Morrow, 1964.
   Reprinted in Britain under the U.S.
   title: Corgi, 1965 WM

ORIOL, LAURENCE. Pseudonym of Noelle
Loriot.
   A Murder to Make You Grow Up Little
   Girl. Macdonald, 1968; World, 1972.
   (Translation of Un Meurte, ca fait
   Grandir. Paris, 1967.)
   Short Circuit. Macdonald, 1967; World,
   1968. (Translation of L'Interne de
   Service. Paris, 1966.)

ORMEROD, ROGER
   Full Fury. Hale, 1975
   The Silence of the Night. Hale, 1974
   A Spoonful of Luger. Hale, 1975
   Time to Kill. Hale, 1974

ORMOND, FREDERIC. Pseudonym of Frederick
Merrill Van Rensselaer Dey, 1861-
1922. Other pseudonyms: Marmaduke
Dey, Varick Vanardy, qq.v.
   The Three Keys. Watt, 1909

ORNSTIEN, ALFRED
   The Secret of the Ashes. Hutchinson,
   1926

O'ROURKE, FRANK. 1916-   . Pseudonym:
    Frank O'Malley, q.v.
  The Abduction of Virginia Lee. Lippincott, 1970
  High Dive. Random, 1954
  Latigo. Random, 1953; Panther, 1960
  The Man Who Found his Way. Morrow, 1957; Panther, 1960
  A Private Anger, and Flight and Pursuit. Morrow, 1963
  P's Progress. Morrow, 1966
  Window in the Dark. Morrow, 1960

ORPET, FRED. Pseudonym of Fred East, 1895-   .
  Murder's No Accident. Arcadia, 1954

ORR, CLIFFORD. 1899-1951.
  The Dartmouth Murders. Farrar, 1929; Hamilton, 1931
  The Wailing Rock Murders. Farrar, 1932; Cassell, 1933

ORR, MARY
  The Tejera Secrets. Dial, 1974

ORR, MYRON DAVID
  White Gold. Capper, 1936

ORUM, POUL. 1919-   .
  The Whipping Boy. Gollancz, 1975. U.S. title: Scapegoat. Pantheon, 1975. (Translation of Syndebuk. Copenhagen, 1972.)

ORVIS, KENNETH. Pseudonym of Kenneth Lemieux, 1923-   . Series character: Adam Breck, in at least those marked AB.
  -Cry Hallelujah! Dobson, 1970
  The Damned and the Destroyed. Dobson, 1962
  The Disinherited. Hale, 1974
  The Doomsday List. Hale, 1974 AB
  Into a Dark Mirror. Dobson, 1971
  Night Without Darkness. Chatto, 1965; Coward, 1966 AB

OSBORN, DAVID. 1923-   .
  -The Glass Tower. Hodder, 1971
  Open Season. Heinemann, 1974; Dial, 1974

OSBORNE, GEOFFREY. 1930-   . Series characters: James Dingle and Glyn Jones, in at least those marked D&J.
  Balance of Fear. Hale, 1968 D&J
  Checkmate for China. Hale, 1969
  Death's No Antidote. Hale, 1971
  The Power Bug. Hale, 1968
  A Time for Vengeance. Hale, 1974
  Traitor's Gate. Hale, 1969 D&J

OSBORNE, HELENA. Pseudonym of Mary Galbraith Moore, 1930-   .
  The Arcadian Affair. Hodder, 1969. U.S. title: The Yellow Gold of Tiryns. Coward, 1969
  My Enemy's Friend; see Pay-Day
  Pay-Day. Hodder, 1972. U.S. title: My Enemy's Friend. Coward, 1972
  The Yellow Gold of Tiryns; see The Arcadian Affair

OSBORNE, MARK. Pseudonym of John William Bobin,   -1935, q.v. Other pseudonym: John Ascott, q.v. All titles feature Sexton Blake, and were published by Amalgamated Press.
  The Boarding House Mystery. 1931
  The Case of the Crook Iron Master. 1934
  The Consulting Room Crime. 1932. Revised and reprinted as: The Consulting Room Mystery. 1940.
  The Consulting Room Mystery; see The Consulting Room Crime
  Dead Man's Bay. 1932
  The Dog Track Murder. 1934
  The Great Art-Gallery Crime. 1934
  The Kennels Crime. 1932
  The Mystery of the Lost Legionnaire. 1933
  The Stables Crime. 1933

OSBORNE, WILLIAM HAMILTON. 1873-   .
  Series character: William Murgatroyd = WM.
  The Blue Buckle. McBride, 1914; Hodder, 1915
  The Boomerang. McBride, 1915
  The Catspaw. Dodd, 1911; Hodder, 1916
  -The Girl of Lost Island. Hodder, 1916. (U.S. title?)
  The Red Mouse. Dodd, 1909; Hodder, 1916 WM
  The Running Fight. Dodd, 1910 WM

OSBOURNE, LLOYD. 1868-1947. See also: ROBERT LOUIS STEVENSON, 1850-1894.
  The Grierson Mystery. Heinemann, 1928. U.S. title: Not to be Opened. Cosmopolitan, 1928
  -The Kingdoms of the World. Methuen, 1911. U.S. title: A Person of Some Importance. Bobbs, 1911
  Not to be Opened; see The Grierson Mystery
  Peril. Heinemann, 1929; Doubleday, 1929
  A Person of Some Importance; see The Kingdoms of the World
  The Under-World. Appleton, 1907. (Play.)

OSGOOD, LUCIAN AUSTIN
  Murder in the Tomb. Unique Mystery Novels, 1937

OSLER, ERIC RICHARD. 1900-   . Pseudonym: T. Dick, q.v.

OSMOND, ANDREW. 1938-   . See also: DOUGLAS (RICHARD) HURD, 1930-   .
  -Saladin! Hutchinson, 1975

OSTLERE, GORDON. 1921-   . Pseudonym: Richard Gordon, q.v.

OSTRANDER, ISABEL (EGENTON). 1883-1924. See also: William J. Burns, 1861-1932. Pseudonyms: Robert Orr Chipperfield, David Fox, Douglas Grant, qq.v. Series character: Timothy McCarty = TM.
  Annihilation. McBride, 1924; Hurst, 1923 TM
  Ashes to Ashes. McBride, 1919; Hurst, 1921
  At One-Thirty. Watt, 1915; Simpkin, 1916
  The Black Joker. McBride, 1925; Hurst, 1926
  The Braddigan Murder; see The Sleeping Cop
  The Clue in the Air. Watt, 1917; Skeffington, 1920 TM
  The Crimson Blotter. McBride, 1921; Hurst, 1921
  Dust to Dust. McBride, 1924; Hurst, 1924
  The Heritage of Cain. Watt, 1916; Hurst, 1922
  How Many Cards? McBride, 1920; Hurst, 1922 TM
  Impulse; see Liberation
  Island of Intrigue. McBride, 1918; Hurst, 1919
  Liberation. McBride, 1924. British title: Impulse. Hurst, 1925
  McCarty, Incog. McBride, 1922; Hurst, 1923 TM
  The Mathematics of Guilt. McBride, 1926; Hurst, 1927
  The Neglected Clue. McBride, 1925; Hurst, 1925
  The Sleeping Cat. McBride, 1926; Hurst, 1926
  The Sleeping Cop, with Christopher (B.) Booth, q.v. Chelsea, 1927. British title: The Braddigan Murder. Hutchinson, 1928
  Suspense. McBride, 1918; Skeffington, 1919
  The Tattooed Arm. McBride, 1922; Hurst, 1922
  The Twenty-Six Clues. Watt, 1919; Hurst, 1921 TM

OSTRANDER, KATE
  The Doom of Glendour. Saturday Review Press, 1975
  Foxfire Cove. Berkley, 1975
  The Ghosts of Ballyduff. Popular Library, 1972
  The Image Seller. Popular Library, 1974
  Ring of Darkness. Berkley, 1974
  Sea Tower. Popular Library, 1974
  The Specter of the Dunes. Popular Library, 1974

O'SULLIVAN, J(AMES) B(RENDAN). 1919-   . Series character: Steve Silk, in at least those marked SS.
  Backlash. Ward, 1960 SS
  Casket of Death. Grafton, 1946 ss
  Cherry in the Wine Glass. Grafton, 1945
  Choke Chain. Ward, 1958 SS
  Cold Chisel. Ward, 1960
  Death Came Late. Pillar, 1945 SS
  The Death Card. Pillar, 1945 SS
  Death on Ice. Pillar, 1946 SS
  The Death Seat. Ward, 1957
  Death Stalks the Stadium. Pillar, 1946 SS
  Disordered Death. Ward, 1957
  Don't Hang Me Too High. Laurie, 1954; Mill, 1954 SS
  Double Negative. Ward, 1962
  Gate Fever. Ward, 1959 SS
  Guilt Edged. Ward, 1959
  Hue and Cry. Ward, 1961
  I Die Possessed. Laurie, 1953; Mill, 1953
  It Could Happen to You. Pillar, 1946
  The Long Spoon. Ward, 1956 SS
  Lunge Wire. Ward, 1965
  Make My Coffin Big. Ward, 1964 SS
  Murder Proof. Ward, 1968
  Nerve Beat. Laurie, 1953 SS
  Pick Up. Ward, 1964
  Raid. Ward, 1958 SS
  Someone Walked over My Grave. Laurie, 1954 SS
  The Stuffed Man. Laurie, 1955 SS
  There is One S.O.S. Ward, 1961
  The Third Horseman. Mellifont, 1946

O'SULLIVAN, VINCENT. 1872-1940.
  A Book of Bargains. Smithers, 1896 ss
  Sentiment, and other stories. Duckworth, 1913 ss, some criminous

OTIS, G. H.
  Bourbon Street. Lion, 1953
  Hot Cargo. Lion, 1953

O'TOOLE, GEORGE
  An Agent on the Other Side. McKay, 1973; Barker, 1974

OTT, E. HARRISON. Pseudonym of Richard Hill Wilkinson, 1904-   , q.v. Other pseudonyms: Eugene Hayford, Paul Pray, qq.v.
  Mystery of "Crazy Canyon" Ranch. Drama Guild, 1940. (Play.)

OTTOLENGUI, RODRIGUES. 1861?-1937. Series
characters: John Barnes = JB; Robert
Leroy Mitchell = RM.
An Artist in Crime. Putnam, 1892
JB & RM
A Conflict of Evidence. Putnam, 1893;
Ward, 1904 JB
The Crime of the Century. Putnam, 1896
JB & RM
Final Proof; or, The Value of Evidence.
Putnam, 1898 ss JB & RM
A Modern Wizard. Putnam, 1894

OURSLER, (CHARLES) FULTON. 1893-1952.
Pseudonym: Anthony Abbot, q.v. See
also: ANONYMOUS (Dark Masquerade);
and: GRACE (PERKINS) OURSLER,
1900-   .
The Spider, with Lowell Brentano
(1895-1950). French, 1926. (Play.)
The Wager, and The House at Fernwood.
Pony, 1946. (Two novelets.)

OURSLER, GRACE (PERKINS). 1900-   .
The Spider. Grosset, 1929. (Novelization of the play by Fulton Oursler,
1893-1952, q.v., and Lowell Brentano, 1895-1950.)

OURSLER, WILL(IAM CHARLES). 1913-   .
Pseudonym: Nick Marino, q.v. Joint
pseudonym with Margaret Scott: Gale
Gallagher, q.v. Series characters:
Philip Strong & James Matthews = S&M.
Bullets for a Blonde; see Departure De-
layed
Departure Delayed. Simon, 1947. Also
published as: Bullets for a Blonde.
Bestseller, 1949
Folio on Florence White. Simon, 1942;
Art & Educational Publishers, 1947
S&M
Murder Memo to the Commissioner: The
Carl Houston Case. Simon, 1950
The Trial of Vincent Doon. Simon, 1941;
Museum, 1943 S&M

OUSELEY, JOHN MULVY. See: SIDNEY WARWICK.

OVALOV, LEV S(ERGEYEVICH). 1905-   .
Comrade Spy. Award, 1965

OVERHOLSER, STEPHEN
Molly and the Confidence Man. Doubleday, 1975

OVERTON, ROBERT
A Chase Round the World. Warne, 1900
-Dangerous Days. Routledge, 1905
-Decoyed Across the Seas. Warne, 1907

OWEN, DEAN. Pseudonym of Dudley Dean
McGaughy.
Hec Ramsey. Award, 1973. (Novelization
of the TV series.)
A Killer's Bargain. Manor, 1973

OWEN, ERIC R.
Dr. Zollinoff's Revenge. Modern, 193?

OWEN, GEORGE W(ASHINGTON).   -1916.
-The Leech Club; or, The Mysteries of
the Catskills. Lee, 1874

OWEN, H(ARRY) COLLINSON. 1882-1956.
The Adventures of Antoine. Hodder, 1919
ss
-Hector Duval. Cassell, 1929
The Riverton Wagers. Cassell, 1931
The Rockingham Diamond. Hodder, 1923

OWEN, HANS C.
Ways of Death. Green Circle, 1937

OWEN, HAROLD. 1872-   . See: LOUISE JOR-
DAN MILN, 1864-1933.

OWEN, J(OHN) L(AWTON)
The Great Jekyll Diamond. Roxburghe,
1897

OWEN, JAMES
Deferred Payment. Rivers, 1930
-Forty Years On. Rivers, 1928

OWEN, RAY
Date with Doom. Hale, 1971
End of the Road. Hale, 1972
The Fall Guy. Hale, 1969
Find Tracey George. Hale, 1968
Flight from Fear. Hale, 1969
Mask of Shadows. Hale, 1972
Seek and Destroy. Hale, 1970
So Deadly a Web. Hale, 1971
Who Cries for a Loser? Hale, 1969

OWEN, WENDY
-There Goes Davey Cohen. Hutchinson,
1966
Whatever Happened to Ruby? Owen, 1968

OXFORD, JANE
Die for Love. Ward, 1961

OZAKI, MILTON K. 1913-   . Pseudonym:
Robert O. Saber, q.v. Series charac-
ters: Prof. Caldwell & Lt. Phelan, in
at least those marked C&P.
Case of the Cop's Wife. GM, 1958; Faw-
cett (London), 1960
Case of the Deadly Kiss. GM, 1957
The Cuckoo Clock. Ziff-Davis, 1946.
Also published as: Too Many Women.
Handi-Books, 1950 C&P
The Deadly Pickup. Graphic, 1952
Dressed to Kill. Graphic, 1954
The Dummy Murder Case. Graphic, 1951
C&P
A Fiend in Need. Ziff-Davis, 1947 C&P
Inquest. GM, 1960; Muller pb, 1961
Maid for Murder. Ace, 1955
Murder Doll. Berkley, 1959
Never Say Die. Ace, 1956
Too Many Women; see The Cuckoo Clock
Wake Up and Scream. GM, 1959; Muller
pb, 1961

P

PACE, ERIC. 1936-   .
Any War will Do. Random, 1973; Deutsch,
1974
Saberlegs. World, 1970; Deutsch, 1971

PACE, TOM. Series character: Ben Garden
= BG.
Afternoon of a Loser. Harper, 1969;
Gollancz, 1970
Fisherman's Luck. Harper, 1971; White
Lion, 1973 BG
The Treasure Hunt. Harper, 1970 BG

PACKARD, FRANK (LUCIUS). 1877-1942.
Series character: Jimmie Dale = JD.
The Adventures of Jimmie Dale. Doran,
1917; Cassell, 1918 JD
The Big Shot. Doubleday, 1929; Hodder,
1929
Broken Waters. Doran, 1925; Hodder,
1927
The Devil's Mantle. Doran, 1927; Hod-
der, 1928
Doors of the Night. Doran, 1922; Hod-
der, 1922
The Dragon's Jaws. Doubleday, 1937;
Hodder, 1937
The Four Stragglers. Doran, 1923; Hod-
der, 1923
From Now On. Doran, 1919
The Further Adventures of Jimmie Dale.
Doran, 1919; Hodder, 1926 JD
The Gold Skull Murders. Doubleday,
1931; Hodder, 1931
The Hidden Door. Doubleday, 1933; Hod-
der, 1933
Jimmie Dale and the Blue Envelope Mur-
der. Doubleday, 1930; Hodder, 1930 JD
Jimmie Dale and the Missing Hour.
Doubleday, 1935; Hodder, 1935 JD
Jimmie Dale and the Phantom Clue.
Doran, 1922; Hodder, 1923 JD
The Locked Book. Doran, 1924; Hodder,
1924
The Miracle Man. Doran, 1914; Hodder,
1914
More Knaves Than One. Doubleday, 1938;
Hodder, 1938 ss
-The Night Operator. Doran, 1919 ss
Pawned. Doran, 1921; Hodder, 1921
The Purple Ball. Doubleday, 1933; Hod-
der, 1934
The Red Ledger. Doran, 1926; Hodder,
1926
-Running Special. Doran, 1925; Hodder,
1926 ss
Shanghai Jim. Doubleday, 1928; Hodder,
1928. (Four stories.)
The Sin That was His. Doran, 1917; Hod-
der, 1926
The Slave Junk; see Two Stolen Idols
Tiger Claws. Doubleday, 1928; Hodder,
1929
Two Stolen Idols. Doran, 1927. British
title (?): The Slave Junk. Hodder,
1927
The White Moll. Doran, 1920; Hodder,
1920
The Wire Devils. Doran, 1918

PACKER, BERNARD J(ULES). 1934-   .
Caro. Dutton, 1975. British title:
Doctor Caro. Heinemann, 1977

PACKER, JOY (PETERSON). 1905-1977.
The Man in the Mews. Eyre, 1964; Dutton, 1965

PACKER, PETER
-The Love Thieves. Holt, 1962; Barker,
1962

PACKER, VIN. Pseudonym of Marijane
Meaker.
Alone at Night. GM, 1963; Muller pb,
1963
Come Destroy Me. GM, 1954; Digit, 1958
The Damnation of Adam Blessing. GM,
1960; Muller pb, 1962
Dark Don't Catch Me. GM, 1956
Dark Intruder. GM, 1952; Red Seal, 1958
Don't Rely on Gemini. Delacorte, 1969;
Macmillan (London), 1970
The Evil Friendship. GM, 1958
5:45 to Suburbia. GM, 1958; Red Seal,
1959
The Girl on the Best Seller List. GM,
1960; Muller pb, 1961
The Hare in March. Signet, 1966
Intimate Victims. GM, 1962; Muller pb,
1963
Look Back to Love. GM, 1953; Red Seal,
1958
Something in the Shadows. GM, 1961;
Muller pb, 1962
-Spring Fire. GM, 1952; Sphere, 1969
3-Day Terror. GM, 1957
The Thrill Kids. GM, 1955
The Twisted Ones. GM, 1959; Red Seal,
1959
Whisper His Sin. GM, 1954; Red Seal,
1959
The Young and Violent. GM, 1956

PADDON, (WILLIAM) WREFORD. 1917-   .
A Corpse in the Coupe. Hammond, 1951
Solo for No Voices. Boardman, 1955

PADGET, MEG
 House of Strangers. Lancer, 1965

PADGETT, LEWIS. Pseudonym of Henry Kuttner, 1914-1958, q.v.
 The Brass Ring. Duell, 1946; Low, 1947
 The Day He Died. Duell, 1947

PAEON, DR. JUPITER. Pseudonym.
 The Dead Man's Secret; or, The Adventures of a Medical Student. Munro, 1885

PAGANO, JO. 1906-   .
 The Condemned. Prentice-Hall, 1947
 Die Screaming. Zenith, 1958

PAGE, ALAIN
 So Late, Monsieur Calone. International, 1969

PAGE, EMMA
 Element of Chance. Collins, 1975
 Family and Friends. Collins, 1972
 A Fortnight by the Sea. Collins, 1973
 In Loving Memory. Collins, 1970

PAGE, EVELYN. 1902-   . Joint pseudonym with Dorothy Blair, 1903-   : Roger Scarlett, q.v.

PAGE, MARCO. Pseudonym of Harry Kurnitz, 1907-1968, q.v.
 Fast Company. Dodd, 1938; Heinemann, 1938
 Reclining Figure. Random, 1952; Eyre, 1952
 The Shadowy Third. Dodd, 1946. British title: Suspects All. Cherry Tree, 1948. Reprinted as by Harry Kurnitz: Paperback Library, 1964
 Suspects All; see The Shadowy Third

PAGE, MICHAEL F(ITZGERALD). 1922-   .
 The Innocent Bystander. Hale, 1957
 Spare the Vanquished. Hale, 1952

PAGE, NORVELL W. Pseudonym: Grant Stockbridge, q.v.

PAGE, STANLEY HART. Series character: Christopher Hand, in all titles.
 Fool's Gold. Knopf, 1933; Paul, 1934
 Murder Flies the Atlantic. King, 1933
 The Resurrection Murder Case. Knopf, 1932; Paul, 1933
 Sinister Cargo. Knopf, 1932; Paul, 1933
 The Tragic Curtain. Dial, 1935

PAHLOW, GERTRUDE (CURTIS BROWN). 1881-   .
 Somebody Shot the Captain. Skeffington, 1930. U.S. title: Murder in the Morning. Clode, 1931

PAIGE, LESLIE
 A House Possessed. Belmont, 1974
 Queen of Hearts. Belmont, 1974
 She Walks in Shadow. Belmont, 1974

PAIN, BARRY (ERIC ODELL). 1864-1928.
 -Collected Tales. Secker, 1916; Stokes, 1916 ss
 -Confessions of Alphonse. Laurie, 1917
 Deals. Hodder, 1904 ss
 The Death of Maurice. Skeffington, 1920
 The Luck of Norman Dale, with James Blyth, 1864-1915, q.v. Nash, 1908
 The Memoirs of Constantine Dix. Unwin, 1905 ss
 One Kind and Another. Secker, 1914; Stokes, 1915 ss
 The Problem Club. Collins, 1919 ss
 The Shadow of the Unseen, with James Blyth, 1864-1915, q.v. Chapman, 1907
 -Stories and Interludes. Henry, 1892; Harper, 1892 ss
 -Stories in Grey. Laurie, 1911 ss
 -Stories in the Dark. Richards, 1901 ss

PAIN, MARGARET CAMERON
 The de Marigny Affair. Stockwell, 1974

PAINE, ALBERT B(IGELOW). 1861-1937.
 The Mystery of Evelin Delorme. Arena, 1894

PAINE, LAURAN BOSWORTH. 1916-   . Pseudonyms: John Armour, Reg Batchelor, Kenneth Bedford, Frank Bosworth, Mark Carrel, Robert Clarke, Richard Dana, J. F. Drexler, Troy Howard, Jared Ingersol, John Kilgore, Hunter Liggett, J. K. Lucas, John Morgan, qq.v.

PAINTER, THOMAS and ALEXANDER (KINNAN) LAING, 1903-1976, q.v.
 The Motives of Nicholas Holtz. Farrar, 1936. British title: The Glass Centipede. Butterworth, 1936

PALERMO, ANTHONY J(AMES)
 Who? Vantage, 1964

PALESCANDOLO, FRANK. Pseudonym: Frank Paley, q.v.

PALEY, FRANK. Pseudonym of Frank Palescandolo.
 Rumble on the Docks. Crown, 1953

PALLEN, CONDE B(ENOIST). 1858-1929.
 -Crucible Island. Manhattanville, 1919; Harding, 1920
 Ghost House. Manhattanville, 1928; Harding, 1929
 The King's Coil. Manhattanville, 1928

PALMER, BRUCE (HAMILTON). 1932-   .
 Blind Man's Mark. Simon, 1959. Also published as: The Shattered Affair. Avon, 1960
 Flesh and Blood. Simon, 1960
 -Hecatomb. Simon, 1965
 The Shattered Affair; see Blind Man's Mark

PALMER, EVA PEARL
 Rival Claimants. Day Library, 1895

PALMER, GRETTA. See: EVELYN (DAVIES) JOHNSON, 1904-   .

PALMER, JOHN
 The Haunted Cavern. Gomez, 1796

PALMER, JOHN. Pseudonym of Edgar John Palmer Watts, 1904-   .
 Above and Below. Hodder, 1967
 The Caves of Claro. Hodder, 1964
 Cretan Cipher. Hodder, 1965
 So Much for Gennaro. Hodder, 1968

PALMER, JOHN (LESLIE). 1885-1944. Pseudonym: Christopher Haddon, q.v. Joint pseudonym with Hilary (Aiden) St. George Saunders, 1898-1951, q.v.: Francis Beeding, q.v.
 Mandragora. Gollancz, 1940. U.S. title: The Man with Two Names. Dodd, 1940

PALMER, LUCILE
 Cat-Eye. Sargent, 1949

PALMER, MADELYN. 1910-   . Pseudonym: Geoffrey Peters, q.v.
 Dead Fellah. Cape, 1961

PALMER, P. K. Series character: Jedediah Killinger III, in both titles.
 The Rainbow/Seagreen Case. Pinnacle, 1974
 The Turquoise/Yellow Case. Pinnacle, 1974

PALMER, PAUL. Pseudonym of Gloria Goddard, 1897-   .
 Murder from Heaven. Phoenix, 1939

PALMER, (CHARLES) STUART. 1905-1968. Pseudonym: Jay Stewart, q.v. Series characters: Hildegarde Withers = HW; Howie Rook = HR.
 Ace of Jades. Mohawk, 1931
 The Adventure of the Marked Man and one other. Aspen, 1973   2 ss
 At One Fell Swoop; see The Green Ace
 Cold Poison. Mill, 1954. British title: Exit Laughing. Collins, 1954 HW
 Death in Grease Paint; see Unhappy Hooligan
 Exit Laughing; see Cold Poison
 Four Lost Ladies. Mill, 1949; Collins, 1950 HW
 The Green Ace. Mill, 1950. British title: At One Fell Swoop. Collins, 1951 HW
 Hildegarde Withers Makes the Scene, with Fletcher Flora, 1914-1969, q.v. Random, 1969 HW
 Miss Withers Regrets. Doubleday, 1947; Collins, 1948 HW
 The Monkey Murder, and other Hildegarde Withers stories. Bestseller, 1950 HW ss
 Murder on the Blackboard. Brentano's, 1932; Eldon, 1934 HW
 Murder on Wheels. Brentano's, 1932; Long, 1932 HW
 Nipped in the Bud. Mill, 1951; Collins, 1952. Also published as: Trap for a Redhead. Bestseller, 1955 HW
 No Flowers by Request; see Omit Flowers
 Omit Flowers. Doubleday, 1937. British title: No Flowers by Request. Collins, 1937
 The Penguin Pool Murder. Brentano's, 1931; Long, 1932 HW
 People vs. Withers and Malone, with Craig Rice, 1908-1957, q.v. Simon, 1963 HW (Also features Craig Rice's series character John J. Malone.) ss
 The Puzzle of the Blue Banderilla. Doubleday, 1937; Collins, 1937 HW
 The Puzzle of the Briar Pipe; see The Puzzle of the Red Stallion
 The Puzzle of the Happy Hooligan. Doubleday, 1941; Collins, 1941 HW
 The Puzzle of the Pepper Tree. Doubleday, 1933; Jarrolds, 1934 HW
 The Puzzle of the Red Stallion. Doubleday, 1936. British title: The Puzzle of the Briar Pipe. Collins, 1936 HW
 The Puzzle of the Silver Persian. Doubleday, 1934; Collins, 1935 HW
 The Riddles of Hildegarde Withers. Jonathan Press, 1947 HW ss
 Rook Takes Knight. Random, 1968 HR
 Trap for a Redhead; see Nipped in the Bud
 Unhappy Hooligan. Harper, 1956. British title: Death in Grease Paint. Collins, 1956 HR

PALMTAG, DINAH
 Starling Street. Dell, 1973

PAMELY, C(ARL) D(OUGLAS)
 Tales of Mystery and Terror. Stockwell, 1926

PANBOURNE, OLIVER. Pseudonym of Howard Rockey, 1886-1934.
 The Varanoff Tradition. Macrae Smith, 1926

PANCOAST, CHALMERS L(OWELL). 1880- .
-Cub. Devin-Adair, 1928
Pass the Aspirin. Pancoast, 1945 ss, some criminous

PANGBORN, EDGAR. 1909-1976.
The Trial of Callista Blake. St. Martin's, 1962; Davies, 1962

PANGBORN, FREDERIC W(ERDEN). 1855- .
-Alice; or, The Wages of Sin. Dillingham, 1883
-Perdida; A Round Unvarnished Tale Truthfully Delivered. Wright, 1889

PAPE, RICHARD (BERNARD). 1916- .
No Time to Die. Elek, 1962

PARADISE, LUKE
The Corpse Wore Nylon. Scion, 1950
Scar on a Corpse. Scion, 1950

PARADISE, MARY. Pseudonym of Dorothy Eden, 1912- , q.v.
Face of an Angel. Hale, 1961; Ace, 1966
Shadow of a Witch. Hale, 1962; Ace, 1966

PARADISE, VIOLA (ISABEL). 1887- .
A Girl Died Laughing. Harper, 1935; Heinemann, 1935

PARCELL, NORMAN HOWE. Pseudonym: John Nicholson, q.v.

PARGETER, EDITH (MARY). 1913- . Pseudonym: Ellis Peters, q.v. Series characters: the Felse family = F (continued in books under the Ellis Peters byline).
The Assize of the Dying. Heinemann, 1958; Doubleday, 1958 ss
Fallen into the Pit. Heinemann, 1951 F

PARIS, MATTHEW
Mystery. Avon, 1973

PARISH, DAVID MONROE
The House of Rhinestad. Pageant, 1965

PARK, HUGH
Death Flies Low. Stockwell, 1942

PARK, J. A.
Strange Occupation. Fortune, 1933. U.S. title: Dangerous Escapade. Greenberg, 1935

PARK, JACQUELINE
Charlie's Back in Town. Popular Library, 1975

PARK, JORDAN. Pseudonym of C(yril) M. Kornbluth, 1923-1958, q.v. Other pseudonym: Simon Eisner, q.v.
The Man of Cold Rages. Pyramid, 1958

PARK, MALCOLM
The Honest Rogue. Macdonald, 1947

PARKE, F. G. Pseudonym.
First Night Murder. Dial, 1931; Paul, 1932

PARKER, BEATRICE. Pseudonym of Tom Huff.
Betrayal at Blackcrest. Dell, 1971
Come to Castlemoor. Dell, 1970
Jamintha. Dell, 1975
Stranger by the Lake. Dell, 1971
Wherever Lynn Goes. Dell, 1975

PARKER, BOB
Crooked Cop. Manor, 1973

PARKER, CLAIRE
The Rookies. Bantam, 1973. (Novelization of the TV series.)

PARKER, GAY
Dead in the Eye of the Law. Warne, 1892
Mr. Perkins of New Jersey; or, The Stolen Bonds. Routledge, 1888; Ogilvie, 1888

PARKER, HERBERT
-The Cuckoo Woman. Anglo-Eastern, 1922
The Midnight Lady. Anglo-Eastern, 1922

PARKER, (PERMELIA) JANE MARSH. 1836-1913.
The Midnight Cry. Dodd, 1886

PARKER, KEN(NETH FULLER)
There's Always a Murder. French, 1951. (3-act play.)

PARKER, LEE. Series character: Donovan, in all titles.
The Assassination is Set for July 4. Award, 1974
Blue Print for Execution. Award, 1974
The Guns of Mazatlan. Award, 1975

PARKER, M. M.
Big Phil's Kid. Meredith, 1969

PARKER, MAUDE. 189?-1959. Series character: Jim Little, in at least those marked JL.
Along Came a Spider. Hodder, 1957
Blood Will Tell; see The Intriguer
Death Do Us Part. Hodder, 1960
Death Makes a Deal. Hodder, 1961
Final Crossroads. Hodder, 1955. (= Murder in Jackson Hole?)
The Intriguer. Rinehart, 1952. British title: Blood Will Tell. Hodder, 1952 JL
Invisible Red. Rinehart, 1953; Hodder, 1954
Murder in Jackson Hole. Rinehart, 1955 JL
Which Mrs. Torr? Rinehart, 1951; Hodder, 1952 JL

PARKER, NORMAN
Don't Cry, Little Girl. Whitmore, 1970

PARKER, PERCY SPURLARK. 1940- .
Good Girls Don't Get Murdered. Scribner, 1974

PARKER, RICHARD. 1915- .
Boy on a Chain. Davies, 1964. U.S. title: Killer. Doubleday, 1964
-Draughts in the Sun. Collins, 1955
-Fiddler's Place. Davies, 1961
The Gingerbread Man. Collins, 1953; Scribner, 1954
Harm Intended. Secker, 1957; Scribner, 1956
Killer; see Boy on a Chain
A Kind of Misfortune. Collins, 1954; Scribner, 1955
Only Some had Guns. Collins, 1952
-The Sword of Ganelon. Collins, 1957

PARKER, RICHARD
Three Knots. Macaulay, 1924
-Under Fire. Macaulay, 1916. (Novelization of the play by Roi Cooper Megrue, 1883-1927, q.v.)
-The Whip. Macaulay, 1913. (Novelization of the play by Cecil Raleigh, q.v.)

PARKER, ROBERT (BOGARDUS). 1906-1955.
Headquarters Budapest. Farrar, 1944
Passport to Peril. Rinehart, 1951; Hodder, 1952
Ticket to Oblivion. Rinehart, 1950; Macmillan (London), 1951

PARKER, ROBERT B(ROWN). 1932- . Series character: Spenser, in all titles.
God Save the Child. Houghton, 1974; Deutsch, 1975
The Godwulf Manuscript. Houghton, 1974; Deutsch, 1975
Mortal Stakes. Houghton, 1975; Deutsch, 1976

PARKES, (GRAHAM) ROGER. 1933- . See also: EDWARD BOYD.
Death-Mask. Constable, 1970
The Guardians. Constable, 1973; St. Martin's, 1974
Line of Fire. Constable, 1971

PARKMAN, SYDNEY M(ULLER). 1895- .
The Accidental Adventurer. Hodder, 1931
Account Closed. Hodder, 1932
The Acting Second Mate. Hodder, 1935. U.S. title: Out from Shanghai. Harper, 1935
Captain Bowker. Hodder, 1946
The Cuban Legacy. Hodder, 1940
East of Singapore. Hodder, 1931; Macrae Smith, 1932
The Facts About Floyd. Hodder, 1938
The Island Feud. Hodder, 1937
Night-Action! Hodder, 1936; Harper, 1936
Out from Shanghai; see The Acting Second Mate
The Passing of Tony Blount. Hodder, 1939
Plunder Bar. Hodder, 1934
-The Reef Pearlers. U. of London Press, 1937
Seven Days' Hard. Hodder, 1938
-Ship Ashore. Hodder, 1936; Harper, 1937
Sunk Without Trace. Hodder, 1933
The Tide Watchers. Hodder, 1937
-The Trail of the Shadow. U. of London Press, 1937
Uncharted. Hodder, 1935. U.S. title: The Uncharted Island. Harper, 1936
The Uncharted Island; see Uncharted

PARMER, CHARLES (B.)
Murder at the Kentucky Derby. Doubleday, 1942

PARMER, ENRIQUE
Maple Hall Mystery: A Romance. Author's Publishing, 1880

PARRISH, RANDALL. 1858-1923.
The Air Pilot. McClurg, 1913
The Case and the Girl. Knopf, 1922; Paul, 1923
-Comrades of Peril. McClurg, 1919
-"Contraband." McClurg, 1916; Curtis Brown, 1916
Gift of the Desert. McClurg, 1922; Unwin, 1923
The Mystery of the Silver Dagger. Doran, 1920; Hodder, 1920
The Strange Case of Cavendish. Doran, 1918; Hodder, 1919

PARRY, HUGH JONES. 1916- . Pseudonym: James Cross, q.v.

PARSONS, ANTHONY. 1893-1963. All those titles listed without publisher were published by Amalgamated Press and feature Sexton Blake.
The Affair of the Missing Parachutist. 1947
The "Allah's Eye" Conspiracy. 1938
The Bad Man of Cairo. 1951
The Blackmailed Refugee. 1945
Calling Whitehall 1212. 1943
The Car Park Mystery. 1954
The Case of the Banned Film. 1952
The Case of the Blackmailed Prince. 1952

The Case of the Crook Rajah. 1939
The Case of the Dangra Millions. 1949
The Case of the Frightened Man. 1955
The Case of the Indian Dancer. 1951
The Case of the Indian Millionaire.
  1944
The Case of the Indian Watcher. 1955
The Case of the Japanese Contract. 1952
The Case of the Missing D.F.C. 1943
The Case of the Missing G.I. Bride.
  1946
The Case of the Missing Major. 1940
The Case of the Missing Scientist. 1952
The Case of the Missing Surgeon. 1949
The Case of the Nameless Millionaire.
  1953
The Case of the Prince's Diary. 1953
The Case of the Prince's Prisoners.
  1946
The Case of the Renegade Naval Officer.
  1944
The Case of the Second Crime. 1954
The Case of the Secret Road. 1943
The Case of the Sinister Farm. 1954
The Case of the Six O'Clock Scream.
  1955
The Case of the Spanish Legatee. 1945
The Case of the Spiv's Secret. 1950
The Case of the Stolen Evidence. 1945
The Case of the Swindler's "Stooge".
  1946
The Case of the Unknown Heir. 1953
The Case of the Wicked Three. 1954
The Clue of the Stolen Rupees. 1941
The Crime of the Cashiered Major. 1943
Crook's Deputy. 1953
The Crooks of Tunis. 1955
Death by the Nile. Wright, 1955
Death of a Governor. Wright, 1954
Death on the Mall. Wright, 1947
The Euston Road Mystery. 1947
The Great Dollar Fraud. 1950
The Harem Mystery. 1939
Hotel Homicide. 1956
The House with Steel Shutters. 1942
The Income Tax Conspiracy. 1948
Living in Fear. 1950
The Loot of France. 1945
The Loot of Pakistan. 1948
The Man from China. 1940
The Man from Kenya. 1947
The Man from Maybrick Road. 1954
The Man from Occupied France. 1941
The Man Who Backed Out! 1948
The Man Who had to Quit. 1946
The Man Without a Passport. 1952
The Millionaire's Nest Egg. 1951
Murder at the Red Cockatoo. Wright,
  1955
Murder at the Stadium. Pyramid (London),
The Mystery of Avenue Road. 1948
The Mystery of the Bankrupt Estate.
  1946
The Mystery of the Blitzed Tower. 1951
The Mystery of the Bombed Monastery.
  1944
The Mystery of the Cairo Express. 1944
The Mystery of the Crooked Gift. 1951
The Mystery of the Free Frenchmen. 1940
The Mystery of the Girl in Green. 1951
The Mystery of the Indian Relic. 1944
The Mystery of the Mason's Arms. 1952
The Mystery of the One-Day Alibi. 1948
The Mystery of the Red Cockatoo. 1948
The Mystery of the Stolen Despatches.
  1942
The Mystery of the 250,000 Rupees. 1946
The Mystery of the Whitehall Bomb. 1947
No Alibi for Murder. Wright, 1951
On the Stroke of Nine. 1941
The Plot of the Yellow Emperor. 1942
The Prisoner in the Hold. 1955
Retired from the Yard. 1951
The Riddle of Big Ben. 1938
The Riddle of Cubicle 7. 1943
The Riddle of the Burmese Curse. 1947
The Riddle of the Captured Quisling.
  1942
The Riddle of the Disguised Greek. 1943
The Riddle of the Escaped P.O.W. 1947
The Riddle of the Gambling Den. 1945
The Riddle of the Indian Alibi. 1946
The Riddle of the Prince's Stooge. 1950
The Riddle of the Rajah's Curios. 1949
The Riddle of the Russian Bride. 1948
The Secret of Oil Creek. 1940
The Secret of the Burma Road. 1942
The Secret of the Castle Ruins. 1954
The Secret of the Golden Horse. 1939
The Secret of the Indian Lawyer. 1953
The Secret of the Moroccan Bazaar. 1954
The Secret of the Roman Temple. 1955
The Secret of the Ten Bales. 1937
The Stowaway of the S. S. Wanderer.
  1942
Terror at Tree Tops. 1948
Those on the List. 1950
The Trail of the Missing Scientist.
  1955

PARSONS, CORNELIA MITCHELL
  A Secret of the Sea. Ogilvie, 1896

PARSONS, LUKE
  Clough Plays Murder. Jarrolds, 1942

PARTRIDGE, ANTHONY. Pseudonym of E(dward)
  Phillips Oppenheim, 1866-1946, q.v.
  The Black Watcher; see The Kingdom of
    Earth
  The Distributors; see The Ghosts of
    Society
  The Ghosts of Society. Hodder, 1908.
    U.S. title: The Distributors.
    McClure, 1908
  The Kingdom of Earth. Mills, 1909;
    Little, 1909. Also published as: The
    Black Watcher, as by E. Phillips
    Oppenheim. Hodder, 1912
  Passers-By. Ward, 1911; Little, 1910

PASSINGHAM, W(ILLIAM) J(OHN). 1897-   .
  Series character (with many other
    authors): Sexton Blake = SB
  Angels in Aldgate. Long, 1933
  The Case of the Ace Accomplice. Amalgamated, 1953 SB
  The Mystery of Theyne Manor. Mellifont,
    1937
  The World Championship Mystery. Amalgamated, 1953 SB

PASTOR, TONY. Pseudonym of Harlan Page
  Halsey, 1839?-1898, q.v. Other pseudonyms: Old Sleuth, Judson R. Taylor,
  qq.v.
  Fritz, the German Detective. Ogilvie,
    1882
  -Night Scenes in New York. American
    News, 1876
  O'Neil McDarragh, the Detective. American News, 1877
  The Swordsman of Warsaw; or, Ralpho of
    the Iron Arm. Street, 1889
  Tom and Jerry; or, The Double Detectives. Street, 1889

PATCH, DAN E. L. 1886-   .
  -Aamon Always. Bica, 1940
  -Behind the Veil. Zondervan, 1947
  The Hour Struck. Zondervan, 1945
  -Moon over Willow Run. Zondervan, 1943
  Past Finding Out. Bica, 1939

PATERNOSTER, (GEORGE) SIDNEY. 1866-   .
  -Children of Earth. Long, 1905
  The Cruise of the Conqueror. Page,
    1906. (British title?)
  -The Folly of the Wise. Long, 1907
  -The Great Gift. Lane, 1917
  -Gutter Tragedies. Treherne, 1903 ss
  The Hand of the Spoiler. Hodder, 1908
  The Lady of the Blue Motor. Long, 1907;
    Page, 1907
  The Master Criminal. Empire, 1907.
    (British title?)
  The Motor Pirate. Chatto, 1903; Page,
    1904
  -The Orphan-Monger. Milne, 1908

PATERSON, (JAMES EDMUND) NEIL. 1916-
  Man on the Tight Rope. Hodder, 1953;
    Random, 1953

PATON, RAYMOND
  The Autobiography of a Blackguard.
    Hutchinson, 1923; Houghton, 1924

PATRICK, CHANN
  The House of Retrogression. Jacobsen,
    1932

PATRICK, KEATS. Pseudonym of Walter
  Karig, 1898-1956.
  Death is a Tory. Bobbs, 1935; Melrose,
    1936. Also published as: The Pool of
    Death. Select Publications, 1942
    (abridged)

PATRICK, Q. Pseudonym of Richard Wilson
  Webb, 1901-   , with Mary Louise
  (White) Aswell, q.v., with Martha
  Mott Kelley, alone, and with Hugh
  Callingham Wheeler, 1913-   . Other
  joint pseudonyms of Webb and Wheeler:
  Patrick Quentin, Jonathan Stagge,
  qq.v. Unless otherwise specified below, titles are by Wheeler and Webb.
  Series character: Timothy Trant = TT.
  Cottage Sinister. Swain, 1931; Longmans, 1932. (Written by Webb and
    Kelley.)
  Danger Next Door. Cassell, 1951
  Darker Grows the Valley; see The
    Grindle Nightmare
  Death and the Maiden. Simon, 1939; Cassell, 1939 TT
  Death for Dear Clara. Simon, 1937; Cassell, 1937 TT
  Death Goes to School. Smith & Haas,
    1936; Cassell, 1936
  Death in Bermuda; see Return to the
    Scene
  Death in the Dovecote; see Murder in
    the Woman's City Club
  File on Claudia Cragge. Morrow, 1938;
    Jarrolds, 1938. (Crime File #4.)
  File on Fenton and Farr. Morrow, 1937;
    Jarrolds, 1938. (Crime File #3.)
  The Grindle Nightmare. Hartney, 1935.
    British title: Darker Grows the
    Valley. Cassell, 1935. (Written by
    Webb and Aswell.)
  Murder at Cambridge. Farrar, 1933. British title: Murder at the 'Varsity.
    Longmans, 1933. (Written by Webb alone.)
  Murder at the 'Varsity; see Murder at
    Cambridge
  Murder at the Women's City Club. Swain,
    1932. British title: Death in the
    Dovecote. Cassell, 1934. (Written by
    Webb and Kelley.)
  Return to the Scene. Simon, 1941. British title: Death in Bermuda. Cassell, 1941
  S. S. Murder. Farrar, 1933; Cassell,
    1933. (Written by Webb and Aswell.)

PATRICK, VICTOR
  Three to Make Murder. Mystery House,
    1947

PATTEE, FRED LEWIS. 1863-1950.
  -The House of the Black Ring. Holt, 1905

PATTEN, BRIAN. 1946-   .
  Mr. Moon's Last Case. Allen, 1975

PATTEN, GILBERT. 1866-1945. Pseudonym: Burt L. Standish, q.v.

PATTERSON, ARTHUR M. [ARTHUR WILLIS PATTERSON]. 1888- .
The Heaviest Pipe. Jacobs, 1921

PATTERSON, HARRY. Pseudonym of Henry Patterson, 1929- . Other pseudonyms: Martin Fallon, James Graham, Jack Higgins, Hugh Marlowe, qq.v. Series character: Nick Miller, in at least those marked NM.
Brought in Dead. Long, 1967 NM
Comes the Dark Stranger. Long, 1962
Cry of the Hunter. Long, 1960
The Dark Side of the Island. Long, 1963; GM, 1977, as by Jack Higgins
The Graveyard Shift. Long, 1965 NM
Hell is Always Today. Long, 1968. Reprinted as by Jack Higgins: Arrow, 1977
Hell is Too Crowded. Long, 1962; GM, 1976, as by Jack Higgins. Reprinted in Britain as by Jack Higgins: Coronet, 1977
The Iron Tiger. Long, 1966; GM, 1974, as by Jack Higgins. Reprinted in Britain as by Jack Higgins: Coronet, 1973
Pay the Devil. Barrie, 1963
A Phoenix in the Blood. Barrie, 1964
Sad Wind from the Sea. Long, 1959
The Thousand Faces of Night. Long, 1961
Thunder at Noon. Long, 1964
Toll for the Brave. Long, 1971; GM, 1976, as by Jack Higgins. Reprinted in Britain as by Jack Higgins: Arrow, 1977
Wrath of the Lion. Long, 1964; GM, 1977, as by Jack Higgins. Reprinted in Britain as by Jack Higgins: Coronet, 1976

PATTERSON, HENRY. 1929- . Pseudonyms: Martin Fallon, James Graham, Jack Higgins, Hugh Marlowe, Harry Patterson, qq.v.

PATTERSON, (ISABELLA) INNIS. Series character: Sebald Craft, in both titles.
The Eppworth Case. Farrar, 1930
The Standish Gaunt Case. Farrar, 1931

PATTERSON, J. T.
What Next?; or, The Honest Thief. Transylvania, 1899

PATTERSON, JOHN M(cREADY)
Doubly Dead. Doubleday, 1969; Hale, 1969

PATTERSON, ROBERT
Gold is the Color of Blood. Ballantine pb, 1960; Muller, 1961
-Man with a Past. Muller, 1963

PATTINSON, JAMES. 1915- . Series character: Harvey Landon, in at least those marked HL.
Across the Narrow Seas. Harrap, 1960
The Angry Island. Hale, 1968
Away with Murder. Hale, 1972
Contact Mr. Delgado. Harrap, 1959 HL
Cordley's Castle. Hale, 1974
Crusader's Cross. Hale, 1975
The Deadly Shore. Hale, 1970
Feast of the Scorpion. Hale, 1975
Find the Diamonds. Hale, 1973
A Fortune in the Sky. Hale, 1973
Freedman. Hale, 1975
The Golden Reef. Hale, 1969
The Haunted Sea. Hale, 1974
The Last Stronghold. Hale, 1968 HL
The Liberators. Harrap, 1961 HL
The Marakano Formula. Hale, 1973
The Murmansk Assignment. Hale, 1971
The Mystery of the Gregory Kotovsky. Harrap, 1958. U.S. title: The Silent Voyage. McDowell, 1959
Ocean Prize. Hale, 1972
On Desperate Seas. Harrap, 1961
The Petronov Plan. Hale, 1974
The Plague Makers. Hale, 1969
The Rodriguez Affair. Hale, 1970
Sea Fury. Hale, 1971
Search Warrant. Hale, 1973
The Silent Voyage; see The Mystery of the Gregory Kotovsky
The Sinister Stars. Hale, 1971
Three Hundred Grand. Hale, 1970
Watching Brief. Hale, 1971
Weed. Hale, 1972
Whispering Death. Hale, 1969
Wild Justice. Harrap, 1960

PATTISON, RUTH. Pseudonym of Ruth Abbey, q.v.
The Shadow Between. Hale, 1970; Ace, 1974, as by Ruth Abbey

PATTON, DAVID KNOX
Murder on the Pacific. Dodd, 1940

PAUL, BARBARA
The Seventeenth Stair. Macdonald, 1975; St. Martin's, 1975

PAUL, ELLIOT (HAROLD). 1891-1958. Pseudonym: Brett Rutledge, q.v. Series character: Homer Evans, in all titles.
The Black and the Red. Random, 1956
The Black Gardenia. Random, 1952
Fracas in the Foothills. Random, 1940
Hugger-Mugger in the Louvre. Random, 1940; Nicholson, 1949
I'll Hate Myself in the Morning, and Summer in December. Random, 1945; Nicholson, 1949. (2 short novels, one about HE.)
Mayhem in B-Flat. Random, 1940; Corgi, 1951
Murder on the Left Bank. Random, 1951; Corgi, 1951
The Mysterious Mickey Finn; or, Murder at the Cafe du Dome. Modern Age, 1939; Penguin, 1953
Waylaid in Boston. Random, 1953

PAUL, ERNEST. Series character: George Barclay, in at least those marked GB.
Curtains for Komespi. Hale, 1968 GB
The Golden Fleece. Hale, 1969
Jewels in Jeopardy. Hale, 1967 GB
The Komespi Affair. Hale, 1968 GB
The Reluctant Cloak and Dagger Man. Hale, 1971
The Silent Murders. Hale, 1969

PAUL, GENE
The Big Make. Lion, 1957
Little Killer. Lion, 1952
Naked in the Dark. Lion, 1953

PAUL, HUGO. Pseudonym of Paul H. Little. Other pseudonym: Paula Minton, q.v.
Rich, Hip and Deadly. Lancer, 1966
The Smashers. Lancer, 1964

PAUL, JOHN
Murder by Appointment. Skeffington, 1952
Oil by Murder. Skeffington, 1953

PAUL, PHYLLIS
-A Cage for the Nightingale. Heinemann, 1957
-Camilla. Heinemann, 1949
-Constancy. Heinemann, 1951
Echo of Guilt; see Pulled Down
An Invisible Darkness. Heinemann, 1967
-The Lion of Cooling Bay. Heinemann, 1953
A Little Treachery. Heinemann, 1962; Norton, 1962
Pulled Down. Heinemann, 1964; Norton, 1965. Also published as: Echo of Guilt. Lancer, 1966
-Rox Hall Illuminated. Heinemann, 1956
Twice Lost. Heinemann, 1960; Norton, 1960

PAULEY, BARBARA ANNE
Blood Kin. Doubleday, 1972

PAULL, H(ARRY) M(AJOR). 1854-1934.
Bluff! Hodder, 1928

PAULL, JESSYCA. Joint pseudonym of Julia Perceval and Rosaylmer Burger. Pseudonym of Rosaylmer Burger: C. H. Wallace, q.v. Series characters: Tracy Larrimore and Mike Thompson, in all titles.
Destination: Terror. Award, 1968
Passport to Danger. Award, 1968
Rendezvous with Death. Award, 1969

PAVEY, L(EONARD) A(RTHUR). 1888- .
-Forward from Youth. Grayson, 1936

PAWLEY, E.
Death was her Escort. Streamlined, 1947

PAXTON, LOIS. Pseudonym of Lois Dorothea Low. Other pseudonym: Dorothy Mackie Low, q.v.
The Man Who Died Twice. Hurst, 1968
The Quiet Sound of Fear. Hurst, 1971; Hawthorn, 1971
Who Goes There? Hurst, 1972; Ace, 1974

PAYES, RACHEL (RUTH) C(OSGROVE). 1922- . Pseudonym: E. L. Arch, q.v.
Curiosity Killed Kitty. Avalon, 1962
Death Sleeps Lightly. Avalon, 1960
Forsythia Finds Murder. Avalon, 1960
Memoirs of Murder. Avalon, 1964
The Mystery of Echo Caverns. Avalon, 1966
O Charitable Death. Doubleday, 1968; Hale, 1968
Shadow of Fear. Avalon, 1961
The Silent Place. Ace, 1969

PAYN, JAMES. 1830-1898.
-Another's Burden. Downey, 1897
-At Her Mercy. Chapman, 1872; Harper, 1874
-The Bateman Household. Hall, 1860
A Beggar on Horseback; or, A County Family; see A County Family
-Bentinck's Tutor. Low, 1868
-The Best of Husbands. Bentley, 1874; Harper, 1874
-A Bitter Reckoning. Munro, 1885. (British title?)
-Blondel Parva. Bradbury, 1868
-Bred in the Bone. Harper, 1871. (British title?)
-The Burnt Million. Chatto, 1890; Lovell, 1889
By Proxy. Chatto, 1878; Harper, 1878
-The Canon's Ward. Chatto, 1884; Harper, 1884
-Carlyon's Year. Bradbury, 1868; Harper, 1867
-Cecil's Tryst. Tinsley, 1872; Harper, 1872
-The Clyffards of Clyffe. Hurst, 1866; Peterson, 1871?
A Confidential Agent. Chatto, 1880; Harper, 1880

-A County Family. Tinsley, 1869. U.S. title: A Beggar on Horseback; or, A County Family. Harper, 1869
The Disappearance of George Driffell. Smith, 1896
-The Eavesdropper. Smith, 1888; Harper, 1888
-Fallen Fortunes. Tinsley, 1876; Appleton, 1876
The Family Scapegrace; see Richard Arbour; or, The Family Scapegrace
-For Cash Only. Chatto, 1882; Harper, 1882
Found Dead. Tinsley, 1869; Harper, 1869
-From Exile. Chatto, 1881; Harper, 1881
-Glow-Worm Tales. Chatto, 1887; Harper, 1887 ss
-A Grape from a Thorn. Smith, 1881; Harper, 1881
-Gwendoline's Harvest. Tinsley, 1870; Harper, 1870
-Halves, a novel (and other tales). Tinsley, 1876; Harper, 1876 ss
-The Heir of the Ages. Smith, 1886; Harper, 1886
-In Market Overt. Cox, 1895; Lippincott, 1895
-Kit. Chatto, 1883; Harper, 1882
-Less Black Than We're Painted. Chatto, 1878; Harper, 1878
-Like Father, Like Son. Tinsley, 1871
Lost Sir Massingberd. Low, 1864; Peterson, 1870
-The Luck of the Darrells. Longmans, 1885; Harper, 1885
-A Marine Residence, and other stories. Chapman, 1871 ss
-Married Beneath Him. Macmillan (London), 1864; Peterson, 187?
-Maxims by a Man of the World. Tinsley, 1869
-Mirk Abbey. Hurst, 1866
-A Modern Dick Whittington; or, A Patron of Letters. Cassell, 1892; Taylor, 1892
-Murphy's Master, and other stories. Tinsley, 1873; Harper, 1873 ss
The Mystery of Mirbridge. Chatto, 1888; Harper, 1888
-Not Wooed, But Won. Chapman, 1871
-One of the Family. Harper, 1868. (British title?)
-A Perfect Treasure. Tinsley, 1869
-A Prince of the Blood. Ward, 1888; Harper, 1888
-Richard Arbour, or, The Family Scapegrace. Edmonston, 1861. Also published as: The Family Scapegrace; or, Richard Arbour. Chapman, 1869
-Stories and Sketches. Smith, 1857 ss
-A Stumble on the Threshold. Cox, 1892; Appleton, 1892
-Sunny Stories, and some shady ones. Chatto, 1891; Lovell, 1891 ss, some criminous
-The Talk of the Town. Smith, 1885; Harper, 1884
-Thicker Than Water. Longmans (London), 1883; Harper, 1883
-A Trying Patient. Chatto, 1893 ss
Two Hundred Pounds Reward, and other tales. Chapman, 1879 ss, some criminous
-Under One Roof. Chatto, 1879; Harper, 1879
-Walter's Word. Tinsley, 1875; Harper, 1875
-What He Cost Her. Chatto, 1877; Harper, 1877
A Woman's Vengeance. Bentley, 1872; Harper, 1872
-The Word and the Will. Chatto, 1890; Lovell, 1890

PAYNE, ALAN. Pseudonym of John (William) Jakes, 1932- , q.v. Other pseudonym: Jay Scotland, q.v.
This'll Slay You. Ace, 1958

PAYNE, DONALD GORDON. 1924- . Pseudonym: Donald Gordon, q.v.

PAYNE, EVELYN
Held Open for Death. Arcadia, 1958

PAYNE, GEORGE
Oonah; or, The Story of a Crime. Ward, 1884

PAYNE, HAROLD. Pseudonym of George C. Kelly, -1895.
The Gilded Fly. Price, 1892

PAYNE, LAURENCE. 1919- . Series character: Chief Inspector Sam Birkett, in at least those marked SB.
Birds in the Belfry. Hodder, 1966; Lippincott, 1967
Deep and Crisp and Even. Hodder, 1964 SB
The First Body; see The Nose on my Face
The Nose on my Face. Hodder, 1961; Macmillan, 1962. Also published as: The First Body. Avon, 1964 SB
Spy for Sale. Hodder, 1969; Doubleday, 1970
Too Small for his Shoes. Hodder, 1962; Macmillan, 1963 SB

PAYNE, RACHEL ANN
Ghostwind. Paperback Library, 1966

PAYNE, RONALD CHARLES. Joint pseudonym with John William Garrod: John Castle, q.v.

PAYNE, WILL. 1865-1954.
-The Losing Game. Dillingham, 1910
Overlook House. Dodd, 1921
The Scarred Chin. Dodd, 1920

PAYNTER, T(HOMAS) C(AMBORNE). 1901- .
-Cannon Law. Longmans, 1928
They Sailed on a Friday. Longmans, 1928

PEACOCK, DENNIS (MAX CORNELIUS WOODRUFFE). 1899- .
The Perilous Secret. Hutchinson, 1929
The Secret of the Mere. Hutchinson, 1931
A Thief by Night. Hutchinson, 1929

PEACOCK, THOMAS LOVE. 1785-1866.
Crotchet Castle. Hookham, 1831
Nightmare Abbey. Hookham, 1818; Carey, 1819

PEARCE, CHARLES E. Pseudonym: Detective Dunn, q.v.
-The Ball of Fortune. Blackie, 1883
The Bungalow Under the Lake. Paul, 1910
-Corinthian Jack. Paul, 1920
-The Crimson Mascot. Paul, 1914
The Eyes of Alicia. Paul, 1913
-A Foe in the Shadow. Aldine, 1919
-The Last of the Darrells. Aldine, 1925
-Love Besieged. Paul, 1909; McClurg, 1911
-Madame Flirt. Paul, 1922
The Mystery of Judith. Lloyd, 1923
The Mystery of the Furlined Cloak. Lloyd, 1921
-Red Revenge. Paul, 1911
The Secret of Room No. 13. Lloyd, 1922
-The Soul of a Shop Girl. Aldine, 1915
-A Star of the East. Paul, 1912
The Tanglewood Mystery. Aldine, 1926

PEARCE, DICK [RICHARD ELMO PEARCE]. 1909- .
The Darby Trial. Lippincott, 1954

PEARL, JACK [JACQUES BAIN PEARL]. 1923- .
The Cops. Pinnacle, 1972
A Jury of his Peers. Prentice-Hall, 1975
Lepke. PB, 1975. (Novelization of the movie.)
Our Man Flint. PB, 1965. (Novelization of the movie.)
The Plot to Kill the President. Pinnacle, 1972
Robin and the 7 Hoods. PB, 1964. (Novelization of the movie.)
A Time to Kill...A Time to Die. Norton, 1971; Hale, 1974
Victims. Trident, 1973; Hale, 1976

PEARLMAN, GILBERT
The Adventures of Sherlock Holmes' Smarter Brother. Ballantine, 1975. (Novelization of the movie.)

PEARSON, D(AVID) A. G.
The Golden Stone. Methuen, 1929; Dutton, 1929

PEARSON, DIANE
Bride of Tancred. Bantam, 1967

PEARSON, EDMUND (LESTER). 1880-1937.
The Adventure of the Lost Manuscripts. Aspen, 1974

PEARSON, PETER. 1913- .
Postscript for Malpas. Macmillan (London), 1975

PEARSON, ROBERT E.
The Fat Boy Must Die. Vega, 1963

PEARSON, SHEPHERD. Pseudonym of John Edward Gunby Hadath, -1954.
The Second Count. Gifford, 1944

PEARSON, WILLIAM. 1922- .
The Beautiful Frame. Simon, 1953; Reinhardt, 1954
Hunt the Man; see Hunt the Man Down
Hunt the Man Down. Simon, 1956. British title: Hunt the Man. Ward, 1957

PEART, JANE
Night of the Darkest Moon. Lancer, 1973

PEATTIE, ELIA W(ILKINSON). 1862-1935.
The Judge. Rand, 1891

PECHEY, ARCHIBALD THOMAS. 1876-1961.
Pseudonyms: Mark Cross, Valentine, qq.v.

PECK, LEONARD. 1906- . Pseudonym: Leonard Brain, q.v.
Touch Pitch. Long, 1967

PECK, (LADY) WINIFRED (FRANCES KNOX)
Arrest the Bishop? Faber, 1949
The Warrielaw Jewel. Faber, 1933; Dutton, 1933

PECKHAM, RICHARD. Pseudonym of Raymond P(eckham) Holden, 1894- , q.v.
Murder in Strange Houses. Minton, 1929; Eyre, 1930

PEDDIE, JAMES
Dangerous Dilemmas. Crown, 18?? ss
Secrets of a Private Enquiry Office. Clarke, 1881 ss

PEDLER, JOHN BRANFROST SIMPSON. Pseudonym: Dominic Torr, q.v.

PEDRICK, GALE
Meet the Rev. Low, 1947

PEEBLES, NILES N. Series character: Ross McKellar, in both titles.
  Blood Brother, Blood Brother. Pyramid, 1969
  See the Red Blood Run. Pyramid, 1968

PEEL, COLIN D(UDLEY)
  Adapted to Stress. Hale, 1973
  Bitter Autumn. Hale, 1973
  Cold Route to Freedom. Hale, 1975
  On a Still Night. Hale, 1975
  One Sword Less. Hale, 1973

PEEL, FREDERICK. 1888-   . Joint pseudonym with Charles Siddle, 1892-   : Rufus Slingsby, q.v.

PEI, MARIO (ANDREW). 1901-   .
  -The Sparrows of Paris. Philosophical, 1958

PELL, FRANKLYN. Pseudonym of Frank E. Pelligrin.
  Hangman's Hill. Dodd, 1946

PELLEY, WILLIAM DUDLEY. 1890-1965.
  The Blue Lamp. Fiction League, 1931

PELLIGRIN, FRANK E. Pseudonym: Franklyn Pell, q.v.

PEMBER, WILLIAM LEONARD. Pseudonym: Jack Monmouth, q.v.

PEMBER-HILLER, GUY
  Run Corpse, Run. Double Action Detective Novel, 1943; Swan, 1946

PEMBERTON, MARGARET
  Rendezvous with Danger. Macdonald, 1974

PEMBERTON, MAX. 1863-1950. Series character: Capt. Black, in at least those marked B.
  -The Adventures of Captain Jack. Mills, 1909
  Aladdin in London; see The Lodestar
  A Bagman in Jewels. Skeffington, 1919
  Behind the Curtain. Nash, 1916
  Captain Black. Cassell, 1911; Doran, 1911 B
  -A Daughter of the States. Dodd, 1904. (British title?)
  The Diamond Ship. Cassell, 1907; Appleton, 1907
  The Diary of a Scoundrel. Ward, 1891
  -Doctor Xavier. Hodder, 1903; Appleton, 1903
  Dolores and Some Others. Mills, 1931 ss, some criminous
  -Feo. Hodder, 1900; Dodd, 1900
  -The Fortunate Prisoner. Hodder, 1909; Dillingham, 1909
  -The Garden of Swords. Cassell, 1899; Dodd, 1899
  A Gentleman's Gentleman. Innes, 1896; Harper, 1896
  The Giant's Gate. Cassell, 1901; Stokes, 1901
  -The Gold Wolf. Ward, 1903; Dodd, 1903
  -The Great White Army. Cassell, 1915
  -Her Wedding Night. Jenkins, 1918 ss
  -The House of Fortune. Nash, 1912
  -The Hundred Days. Cassell, 1905; Appleton, 1905
  -I Crown Thee King. Methuen, 1902
  -The Impregnable City. Cassell, 1895; Dodd, 1895
  The Iron Pirate. Cassell, 1893; Rand, 1897 B
  Jewel Mysteries from a Dealer's Notebook; see Jewel Mysteries I Have Known
  Jewel Mysteries I Have Known. Ward, 1894. U.S. title: Jewel Mysteries from a Dealer's Notebook. Fenno, 1904 ss
  John Dighton, Mystery Millionaire. Cassell, 1923
  -Kronstadt. Cassell, 1898; Appleton, 1898
  -The Lady Evelyn. Hodder, 1906; Authors & Newspapers, 1906
  -Leila and her Lover. Ward, 1913
  -The Lodestar. Ward, 1907; Authors & Newspapers, 1907. Also published as: Aladdin of London; or, Lodestar. Empire, 1907
  -Love the Harvester. Methuen, 1908; Dodd, 1900
  -Lucienne, with Isabelle & Horizon of God. Mills, 1925
  -The Man of Silver Mount. Cassell, 1918
  The Man Who Drove the Car. Nash, 1910
  -Mid the Thick Arrows. Hodder, 1905
  -Millionaire's Island. Cassell, 1913
  The Mystery of the Green Heart. Methuen, 1910; Dodd, 1910
  -Night Lights. Mills, 1929 ss
  The Phantom Army. Pearson, 1898; Appleton, 1898
  -Pro Patria. Ward, 1901; Dodd, 1901
  -A Puritan's Wife. Cassell, 1895; Dodd, 1896
  -Queen of the Jesters. Pearson, 1897; Dodd, 1897
  -Red Morn. Cassell, 1904
  -The Sea Wolves. Cassell, 1894; Harper, 1894
  -The Shadow on the Sea. Westbrook, 1907. (British title?)
  -The Show Girl. Cassell, 1909; Winston, 1909
  -The Summer Book. Mills, 1911 ss
  Swords Reluctant; see War and the Woman
  Two Women. Methuen, 1914
  -War and the Woman. Cassell, 1912. U.S. title: Swords Reluctant. Dillingham, 1912
  Wheels of Anarchy. Cassell, 1908
  White Motley. Cassell, 1913; Sturgis, 1911
  -White Walls. Ward, 1910
  -A Woman of Kronstadt. Readers Library, 1941
  -A Woman Who Knew. Hutchinson, 1922 ss

PEMBERTON, MAX JOSEPH
  -An Adventurer from the West. Mills, 1925
  -The Bottles of Scented Sweets. Mills, 1926
  -Hindoo Khan. Mills, 1922
  Kidnapper of Women. Mills, 1927
  The Mystery of a Millionaire. Mills, 1924
  -Under the Red Flag. Mills, 1923

PEMBROKE, THOMAS. See: MILESON HORTON.

PENDLETON, DON(ALD EUGENE). 1927-   .
Series character: Mack Bolan (The Executioner), in all titles (see also: JIM PETERSON).
  Assault on Soho. Pinnacle, 1971; Corgi, 1973
  Battle Mask. Pinnacle, 1970; Sphere, 1973
  Boston Blitz. Pinnacle, 1972; Corgi, 1974
  California Hit. Pinnacle, 1972; Corgi, 1974
  Canadian Crisis. Pinnacle, 1975; Corgi, 1977
  Caribbean Kill. Pinnacle, 1972; Corgi, 1973
  Chicago Wipeout. Pinnacle, 1971; Corgi, 1973
  Continental Contract. Pinnacle, 1971; Sphere, 1973
  Death Squad. Pinnacle, 1969; Sphere, 1973
  Detroit Deathwatch. Pinnacle, 1974; Corgi, 1976
  Firebase Seattle. Pinnacle, 1975; Corgi, 1976
  Hawaiian Hellground. Pinnacle, 1975; Corgi, 1976
  Jersey Guns. Pinnacle, 1974; Corgi, 1975
  Miami Massacre. Pinnacle, 1970; Corgi, 1973
  New Orleans Knockout. Pinnacle, 1974; Corgi, 1976
  Nightmare in New York. Pinnacle, 1971; Corgi, 1973
  Panic in Philly. Pinnacle, 1973; Corgi, 1975
  St. Louis Showdown. Pinnacle, 1975; Corgi, 1977
  San Diego Siege. Pinnacle, 1972; Corgi, 1974
  Texas Storm. Pinnacle, 1974; Corgi, 1975
  Vegas Vendetta. Pinnacle, 1971; Corgi, 1973
  War Against the Mafia. Pinnacle, 1969; Sphere, 1973
  Washington IOU. Pinnacle, 1972; Corgi, 1974

PENDLETON, TOM. Pseudonym of Edmund van Zandt.
  Hodak. McGraw, 1969; Joseph, 1970

PENDOWER, JACQUES. 1899-1976. Pseudonym: T. C. H. Jacobs, q.v. Series character: Slade McGinty, in at least those marked SM.
  Anxious Lady. Hale, 1960
  Betrayed; see The Widow from Spain
  Cause for Alarm. Hale, 1971
  The Dark Avenue. Hale, 1955
  Date with Fear. Hale, 1974
  Death on the Moor. Hale, 1962
  Diamonds for Danger. Hale, 1970
  Double Diamond. Hale, 1959
  The Golden Statuette. Hale, 1969
  Hunted Woman. Ward, 1955
  The Long Shadow. Hale, 1959
  Master Spy. Hale, 1964 SM
  Mission in Tunis. Hale, 1958; Paperback Library, 1967
  Operation Carlo. Hale, 1963 SM
  Out of this World. Hale, 1966
  The Perfect Wife. Hale, 1962 SM
  She Came by Night. Hale, 1971
  Sinister Talent. Hale, 1964 SM
  Spy Business. Hale, 1965
  Traitor's Island. Hale, 1967 SM
  A Trap for Fools. Hale, 1968
  Try Anything Once. Hale, 1967
  The Widow from Spain. Hale, 1961. U.S. title: Betrayed. Paperback Library, 1967

PENFIELD, CORNELIA. 1892-1938.
  After the Deacon was Murdered. Putnam, 1933
  After the Widow Changed her Mind. Putnam, 1933

PENLEY, NORMAN
  -The Girl in the Green Beret. Modern, 1935
  -The Loveless Isle. Modern, 1935
  Miss Melbourn's Million. Modern, 193?

PENMARE, WILLIAM. Pseudonym of (Mavis) Elizabeth (Hocking) Nisot, 1893-   , q.v.
  The Black Swan. Hodder, 1928
  The Man Who Could Stop War. Hodder, 1929
  The Scorpion. Hodder, 1929

PENNY, F(ANNY) E(MILY FARR). -1939.
-Chowra's Revenge. Hutchinson, 1937
-Dark Corners. Chatto, 1908
 The Elusive Bachelor. Hutchinson, 1935
-The Familiar Stranger. Hutchinson, 1936
-A Forest Officer. Methuen, 1900
-The Inevitable Law. Chatto, 1907
-Jackals and Others. Mills, 1939
-The Lady of the Rifle. Hodder, 1932
-Living Dangerously. Hodder, 1925
 Magic in the Air. Hodder, 1933
 The Malabar Magician. Chatto, 1912
-Missing! Chatto, 1917
 Pulling the Strings. Hodder, 1927
-A Spell of the Devil. Hutchinson, 1935
-The Swami's Curse. Hodder, 1922

PENNY, RUPERT. Pseudonym of Ernest Basil
 Charles Thornett. Series character:
 Inspector Edward Beale, in all
 titles.
 The Lucky Policeman. Collins, 1938
 Policeman in Armour. Collins, 1937
 Policeman's Evidence. Collins, 1938
 Policeman's Holiday. Collins, 1937
 Sealed-Room Murder. Collins, 1941
 She had to have Gas. Collins, 1939
 Sweet Poison. Collins, 1940
 The Talkative Policeman. Collins, 1936

PENOYRE, MARY
 Breach of Security. Barker, 1974
 Let Him Go, Let Him Tarry. Barker, 1975

PENROSE, MARGARET
 Death on the Files. Long, 1961
 The Fatal Fifth. Long, 1963

PENTECOST, HUGH. Pseudonym of Judson
 (Pentecost) Philips, 1903-   , q.v.
 Series characters: Luke Bradley = LB;
 Pierre Chambrun = PC; George Crowder
 = GC; John Jericho = JJ; Lt. Pascal =
 P; Julian Quist = JQ; Grant Simon =
 GS; Dr. John Smith = JS.
 Around Dark Corners. Dodd, 1970 GC ss
 The Assassins. Dodd, 1955
 Bargain with Death. Dodd, 1974; Hale,
 1976 PC
 The Beautiful Dead. Dodd, 1973; Hale,
 1975 JQ
 Birthday, Deathday. Dodd, 1972; Hale,
 1975 PC
 The Brass Chills. Dodd, 1943; Hale,
 1944 LB
 Cancelled in Red. Dodd, 1939; Heine-
 mann, 1939 LB
 The Cannibal Who Overate. Dodd, 1962;
 Boardman, 1963 PC
 Cat and Mouse. Royce, 1945
 The Champagne Killer. Dodd, 1972; Hale,
 1974 JQ
 Chinese Nightmare. Dell 10¢ pb, 1951
 Choice of Violence. Dodd, 1961; Board-
 man, 1962 GC
 The Creeping Hours. Dodd, 1966; Board-
 man, 1967 JJ
 The Dead Man's Tale. Royce, 1945
 Dead Woman of the Year. Dodd, 1967;
 Macdonald, 1968 JJ
 The Deadly Friend. Dodd, 1961; Board-
 man, 1962
 The Deadly Joke. Dodd, 1971; Hale, 1972
 PC
 Death Wears a Copper Tie and other sto-
 ries. Edwards, 1946 ss
 Don't Drop Dead Tomorrow. Dodd, 1971;
 Hale, 1973 JQ
 The Evil That Men Do. Dodd, 1966;
 Boardman, 1966 PC
 The Gilded Nightmare. Dodd, 1968; Gol-
 lancz, 1969 PC
 Girl Watcher's Funeral. Dodd, 1969;
 Gollancz, 1970 PC
 The Girl with Six Fingers. Dodd, 1969;
 Gollancz, 1970 JJ
 The Golden Trap. Dodd, 1967; Macdonald,
 1968 PC
 Hide Her from Every Eye. Dodd, 1966;
 Boardman, 1966 JJ
 Honeymoon with Death. Dodd, 1975; Hale,
 1976 JQ
 I'll Sing at Your Funeral. Dodd, 1942;
 Hale, 1945 LB
 The Judas Freak. Dodd, 1974; Hale, 1976
 JQ
 The Kingdom of Death. Dodd, 1960;
 Boardman, 1961
 Lt. Pascal's Tastes in Homicide. Dodd,
 1954; Boardman, 1955. (Three novel-
 ets.) P
 The Lonely Target. Dodd, 1959; Board-
 man, 1960 GS
 Memory of Murder. Ziff-Davis, 1947.
 (3 novelets.) JS
 The Obituary Club. Dodd, 1958; Board-
 man, 1959 GS
 Only the Rich Die Young. Dodd, 1964;
 Boardman, 1964 P
 A Plague of Violence. Dodd, 1970; Hale,
 1972 JJ
 Secret Corridors. Century, 1945 ss, at
 least one about LB
 Shadow of Madness. Dodd, 1950 JS
 The Shape of Fear. Dodd, 1964; Board-
 man, 1964 PC
 Sniper. Dodd, 1965; Boardman, 1966 JJ
 The Tarnished Angel. Dodd, 1963; Board-
 man, 1963
 Time of Terror. Dodd, 1975 PC
 The 24th Horse. Dodd, 1940; Hale, 1951
 LB
 Walking Dead Man. Dodd, 1973; Hale,
 1975 PC
 Where the Snow was Red. Dodd, 1949;
 Hale, 1951 JS

PENTELOW, JOHN NIX. 1872-1931. Titles be-
 low were published by Amalgamated
 Press and feature Sexton Blake.
 The Cleopatra Needle Mystery. 1927
 Missing in Mexico. 1925
 The Three Masked Men. 1927

PEOPLE, GRANVILLE CHURCH. Pseudonym:
 Granville Church, q.v.

PERCEVAL, JULIA. Joint pseudonym with
 Rosaylmer Burger: Jessyca Paull, q.v.

PERCY, CATHERINE. Pseudonym.
 Death is Skin Deep. Abelard, 1953

PERCY, EDWARD. Pseudonym of Edward Percy
 Smith, 1891-   .
 Ladies in Retirement, with Reginald
 Denham, 1894-   . English Theatre
 Guild, 1940; Century, 1940. (3-act
 play.)
 The Lost Hat. Year Book Press, 1936;
 Baker, 1936. (1-act play.)
 Play with Fire. English Theatre Guild,
 1942. Also published as: The Shop at
 Sly Corner. English Theatre Guild,
 1946; Dramatists Play Service, 1949.
 (3-act play.)
 The Shop at Sly Corner; see Play with
 Fire
 Suspect, with Reginald Denham,
 1894-   . Secker, 1937; Dramatists
 Play Service, 1940. (3-act play.)
 Trunk Crime, with Reginald Denham,
 1894-   . Dramatists Play Service,
 1940

PERDUE, VIRGINIA. 1899-1945. Series char-
 acter: Eleanora Burke = EB.
 Alarum and Excursion. Doubleday, 1944;
 Jarrolds, 1947
 The Case of the Foster Father. Double-
 day, 1942; Jarrolds, 1946 EB
 The Case of the Grieving Monkey.
 Doubleday, 1941 EB
 He Fell Down Dead. Doubleday, 1943;
 Jarrolds, 1944
 The Singing Clock. Doubleday, 1941;
 Jarrolds, 1945

PEREIRA, MICHAEL (NICHOLAS O'DONNELL).
 1928-
 An Angel Came Down. Bles, 1966
 Brought to Bay. Bles, 1974
 An Echo from Silence. Bles, 1968
 Equal Antagonism. Collins, 1975
 The Fifth Answer. Bles, 1969
 Masquerade. Collins, 1973
 Pigeon's Blood. Bles, 1970
-A River Grown Deep. Hutchinson, 1959
 Second Cousin Twice Removed. Collins,
 1974
 The Singing Millionaire. Collins, 1972
 Stranger in the Land. Bles, 1967
 When One Door Shuts. Bles, 1969

PERELLI, M.
 Blind Murder. Scion, 1952
 Blonde for Danger. Scion, 1952
 Body Ran Home. Locker, 1950
 A Dame Doles Death. Scion, 1953
 Nothing to Hide. Scion, 1952
 She Sure Slipped. Scion, 1952
 Some Dames Don't. Scion, 1952
 Take It Easy. Milestone, 1953
 Two Dames Too Many. Scion, 1952

PERELMAN, S(IDNEY) J(OSEPH). 1904-   .
 The Ill-Tempered Clavicord. Simon,
 1952; Reinhardt, 1953 ss, some
 criminous
 Keep It Crisp. Random, 1946; Heinemann,
 1947 ss, some criminous

PERKINS, FREDERICK B(EECHER). 1828-1899.
 Scrope; or, The Lost Library. Roberts,
 1874

PERKINS, KENNETH. 1890-1951.
-Gold. Stokes, 1929; Hutchinson, 1930
 The Horror of the Juvenal Manse; see
 Voodoo'd
 The Mark of the Moccasin; see The Moc-
 casin Murders
 The Moccasin Murders. King, 1931. Bri-
 tish title: The Mark of the Moccasin.
 Paul, 1929
-Queen of the Night. McClurg, 1925
 Voodoo'd. Harper, 1931. British title:
 The Horror of the Juvenal Manse.
 Hutchinson, 1931

PEROWNE, BARRY. Pseudonym of Philip
 Atkey, 1908-   , q.v. Series charac-
 ter (following E. W. Hornung, q.v.):
 A. J. Raffles = AR.
 All Exits Blocked; see Gibraltar Pri-
 soner
 The A.R.P. Mystery. Amalgamated, 1939
 AR
 Arrest These Men! Cassell, 1932
 Ask No Mercy. Cassell, 1937
 Blonde Without Escort. Cassell, 1940
 Enemy of Women. Cassell, 1934
 Gibraltar Prisoner. Cassell, 1942. U.S.
 title: All Exits Blocked. Mystery
 House, 1942
 The Girl on Zero. Cassell, 1939
 I'm No Murderer. Cassell, 1938; Hill-
 man-Curl, 1939
 Ladies in Retreat. Cassell, 1935
 Raffles After Dark. Cassell, 1933. U.S.
 title: The Return of Raffles. Day,
 1933 AR
 Raffles and the Key Man. Lippincott,
 1940 AR
 Raffles' Crime in Gibraltar. Amalgama-
 ted, 1937 AR
 Raffles in Pursuit. Cassell, 1934 AR
 Raffles Revisited. Harper, 1974; H.

Hamilton, 1975 AR ss
Raffles Under Sentence. Cassell, 1936 AR ss
Raffles vs. Sexton Blake. Amalgamated, 1937 AR
The Return of Raffles; see Raffles After Dark
Rogues' Island; see The Tilted Moon
She Married Raffles. Cassell, 1936 AR
A Singular Conspiracy. Bobbs, 1974
Ten Words of Poison; see The Whispering Cracksman
They Hang Them in Gibraltar. Hillman-Curl, 1939. (British title?) AR
The Tilted Moon. Cassell, 1949. U.S. title: Rogues' Island. Mill, 1950
The Whispering Cracksman. Cassell, 1940. U.S. title: Ten Words of Poison. Arcadia, 1941

PERRAULT, E(RNEST) G.
Spoil! Doubleday, 1975; Collins, 1976
The Twelfth Mile. Doubleday, 1972; Collins, 1973

PERRAULT, GILLES
Dossier 51. Weidenfeld, 1971; Morrow, 1971. (Translation of Le Dossier 51. Paris, 1969.)

PERRELLI, NICK
At Dead of Night. Milestone, 1954
Dead on Time. Milestone, 1954
Rita Takes a Ride. Tempest, 1950
Sweet and Low. Milestone, 1954
Terror in Tokyo. Tempest, 1950
Virgin's Vendetta. Tempest, 1950
Virgins Die Lonely. Tempest, 1949

PERRETT, GEOFFREY. 1940-   .
Executive Privilege. Coward, 1974

PERRING, DOUGLAS
The Apostles of Violence. Hale, 1957

PERROT, IRENE
Freedom from Fear. Stockwell, 1975

PERRY, CHARLES E.
The Gables Mystery. Modern, 193?
In Satan's Bonds. Modern, 1935

PERRY, FRANK
The Mystery of the Girl in Blue. Dodge, 1938

PERRY, GEORGE SESSIONS. 1910-1956. See: DOROTHY CAMERON DISNEY.

PERRY, JAMES D(eWOLFF). 1895-   .
Murder Walks the Corridors. Macmillan, 1937. British title: Corridors of Fear. Constable, 1937

PERRY, PATRICIA
Deadly Memorial. Hale, 1973

PERRY, RITCHIE (JOHN ALLEN). 1942-   .
Series character: Philis, in all titles.
The Fall Guy. Collins, 1972; Houghton, 1972
A Hard Man to Kill; see Nowhere Man
Holiday with a Vengeance. Collins, 1974; Houghton, 1975
Nowhere Man. Collins, 1973. U.S. title: A Hard Man to Kill. Houghton, 1973
Ticket to Ride. Collins, 1973; Houghton, 1974
Your Money and Your Wife. Collins, 1975; Houghton, 1976

PERRY, ROBIN. 1917-   .
Welcome for a Hero. Livingston, 1975

PERRY, TYLINE
The Never Summer Mystery. King, 1932
The Owner Lies Dead. Covici, 1930; Gollancz, 1930

PERRY, WILL
Death of an Informer. Pyramid, 1973

PERTWEE, MICHAEL (H. R.). 1916-   .
Deadly Poison, with Roland Pertwee, 1885-1963, q.v. French, 1955. (Play.)

PERTWEE, ROLAND. 1885-1963. See also: MICHAEL (H. R.) PERTWEE, 1916-   .
-The Camelion's Dish. Davies, 1940
A Chalk Stream Killing. Jenkins, 1939
Death in a Domino. Houghton, 1932. (British title?)
Dirty Work. English Theatre Guild, 1954. (A play.)
-The Eagle and the Wren. Cassell, 1923
Expert Evidence. English Theatre Guild, 1946. (A play.)
Four Winds. Nicholson, 1935; Little, 1935
Gentlemen March; see The Romance of Nikko Cheyne
Hell's Loose; see The Million Pound Cipher
Interference. Cassell, 1927; Houghton, 1927. As a play: French, 1929
-It Means Mischief, with John Hastings Turner. Heinemann, 1932
-May We Come Through? and other stories. Davies, 1940 ss
Men of Affairs. Knopf, 1922. (British title?)
The Million Pound Cipher. Heinemann, 1929. U.S. title: Hell's Loose. Houghton, 1929. Also published as: MW-XX.3. Heinemann, 1929
-Morosco. Nicholson, 1934
MW-XX.3; see The Million Pound Cipher
-No Such Word. Nicholson, 1934
-A Prince of Romance. Heinemann, 1932
-Pursuit. Heinemann, 1930; Houghton, 1930
-Rivers to Cross. Cassell, 1926; Houghton, 1927
-The Romance of Nikko Cheyne. Cassell, 1927. U.S. title: Gentlemen March. Houghton, 1927
-Royal Heritage. Houghton, 1931. (British title?)
-A South Sea Bubble. Cassell, 1924. U.S. title: Treasure Trail. Knopf, 1924
Such an Enmity. Nicholson, 1936; Little, 1936
To Kill a Cat, with Harold Dearden. English Theatre Guild, 1939; Century, 1939. (3-act play.)
The Transactions of Lord Louis Lewis. Murray, 1917; Dodd, 1918 ss
Treasure Trail; see A South Sea Bubble

PERUTZ, LEO. 1884-1957.
From Nine to Nine. Viking, 1926; Lane, 1927. (Translation of Vom Neun bis Neun.)
The Master of the Day of Judgment. Boni, 1930; Mathews, 1929. (Translation of Der Meister des Jungsten Tages. Munich, 1923.)

PESKETT, S. JOHN. 1906-   .
Murders at Turbot Towers. Butterworth, 1937

PETER, JOHN (DESMOND)
Runaway. Doubleday, 1969

PETERS, ALAN
-By Their Deeds. Heath, 1946
The Secret Formula. Heath, 1932
Who Killed the Doctors? Heath, 1933; Loring, 1934

PETERS, BILL. Pseudonym of William P(eter) McGivern, 1924-   , q.v.
Blondes Die Young. Dodd, 1952; Foulsham, 1956

PETERS, BRYAN. Pseudonym of Peter (Bryan) George, 1924-1966, q.v. Other pseudonym: Peter Bryant, q.v.
The Big H. Boardman, 1961; Holt, 1963
Cool Murder. Mayflower, 1965
Hong Kong Kill. Boardman, 1958; Washburn, 1959
-Sons of Nippon. Digit, 1961
-Starbuck. Digit, 1957

PETERS, BRYAN. Pseudonym of Peter (Bryan) George, 1924-1966, q.v. Other pseudonym: Peter Bryant, q.v. Series character: Anthony Brandon, in at least those marked AB.
The Big H. Boardman, 1961; Holt, 1963 AB
Hong Kong Kill. Boardman, 1958; Washburn, 1959 AB
-Sons of Nippon. Digit, 1961
-Starbuck. Digit, 1957

PETERS, ELIZABETH. Pseudonym of Barbara Gross Mertz, 1927-   . Other pseudonym: Barbara Michaels, q.v. Series character: Jacqueline Kirby = JK.
Borrower of the Night. Dodd, 1973; Cassell, 1974
The Camelot Caper. Meredith, 1969; Cassell, 1976
Crocodile on the Sandbank. Dodd, 1975; Cassell, 1976
The Dead Sea Cipher. Dodd, 1970; Cassell, 1975
The Jackal's Head. Meredith, 1968; Jenkins, 1969
The Murders of Richard III. Dodd, 1974 JK
The Night of Four Hundred Rabbits. Dodd, 1971. British title: Shadows in the Moonlight. Coronet, 1975
The Seventh Sinner. Dodd, 1972; Coronet, 1975 JK
Shadows in the Moonlight; see The Night of Four Hundred Rabbits

PETERS, ELLIS. Pseudonym of Edith (Mary) Pargeter, 1913-   , q.v. Series characters: one or more members of the Felse family: Inspector George Felse, wife Bunty, son Dominic = F (see also Edith Pargeter entry).
Black is the Colour of my True Love's Heart. Collins, 1967; Morrow, 1967 F
City of Gold and Shadows. Macmillan (London), 1973; Morrow, 1974 F
Death and the Joyful Woman. Collins, 1961; Doubleday, 1961 F
Death Mask. Collins, 1959; Doubleday, 1960
Death to the Landlords! Macmillan (London), 1972; Morrow, 1972 F
Flight of a Witch. Collins, 1964 F
Funeral of Figaro. Collins, 1962; Morrow, 1964
The Grass-Widow's Tale. Collins, 1968; Morrow, 1968 F
The Horn of Roland. Macmillan (London), 1974; Morrow, 1974
The House of Green Turf. Collins, 1969; Morrow, 1969 F
The Knocker on Death's Door. Macmillan (London), 1970; Morrow, 1971 F
Mourning Raga. Macmillan (London), 1969; Morrow, 1970 F
A Nice Derangement of Epitaphs. Collins, 1965. U.S. title: Who Lies Here? Morrow, 1965 F
The Piper on the Mountain. Collins, 1966; Morrow, 1966 F
Where There's a Will; see The Will and the Deed

Who Lies Here?; see A Nice Derangement of Epitaphs
The Will and the Deed. Collins, 1960. U.S. title: Where There's a Will. Doubleday, 1960. Reprinted in the U.S. under the British title: Avon, 1966

PETERS, GEOFFREY. Pseudonym of Madelyn Palmer, 1910-   , q.v.
The Chill of a Corpse. Ward, 1968
The Claw of a Cat. Ward, 1964
The Eye of a Serpent. Ward, 1964
The Flick of a Fin. Ward, 1967
The Mark of a Buoy. Ward, 1967
The Twist of a Stick. Ward, 1966
The Whirl of a Bird. Ward, 1965

PETERS, L. T. Joint pseudonym of Albert S. Klainer and Joann Klainer.
The Eleventh Plague. Simon, 1973; Secker, 1974

PETERS, LUDOVIC. Pseudonym of Peter (Ludwig) Brent, 1931-   , q.v. Series character: Ian Firth, in at least those marked IF.
Cry Vengeance. Abelard (London & New York), 1961
Double Take. Hodder, 1968
Fall of Terror. Hodder, 1968
The Killing Game. Hodder, 1969
Out by the River. Hodder, 1964; Walker, 1965 IF
Riot '71. Hodder, 1967; Walker, 1967 IF
A Snatch of Music. Abelard (London & New York), 1962 IF
Tarakian. Abelard (London), 1963; Abelard (New York), 1964 IF
Two After Malic. Hodder, 1965; Walker, 1966 IF
Two Sets to Murder. Hodder, 1963; Coward, 1964 IF

PETERS, MAUREEN. 1935-   . Pseudonym: Veronica Black, q.v.

PETERS, RON. Series character: Stash Koval, in both titles.
The Big Stash. Curtis, 1972
Stash Spots a Murder. Curtis, 1973

PETERSEN, HERMAN. 1893-   . Series character: Doc Miller = M.
The D.A.'s Daughter. Duell, 1943
Murder in the Making. McBride, 1940 M
Murder R.F.D. Duell, 1942 M
Old Bones. Duell, 1943; Swan, 1950 M

PETERSEN, JAN. 1907-   .
Gestapo Trial. Gollancz, 1939

PETERSON, JAMES
Arrivederci, Baby! Dell, 1966. (Novelization of the movie.)

PETERSON, JIM. Series character: Mack Bolan (The Executioner), in the title below and those by Don(ald Eugene) Pendleton, 1927-   , q.v.
Sicilian Slaughter. Pinnacle, 1973; Corgi, 1973

PETERSON, MARGARET (ANN). 1883-1933. Pseudonym: Glint Green, q.v.
-Adventurous Youth. Hurst, 1925
-Blind Eyes. Melrose, 1914
-Butterfly Wings. Hurst, 1916
Deadly Nightshade. Hurst, 1924
-Dear, Lovely One! Benn, 1930
The Death Drum. Hurst, 1919
Death in Goblin Waters. Hutchinson, 1934
Every Cloud; see Poor Delights
The Eye of Isis. Hutchinson, 1931
Fatal Shadows. Hutchinson, 1931
-Fate and the Watcher. Hurst, 1917
Fear Shadowed. Hutchinson, 1927
The Feet of Death. Hutchinson, 1927
-The First Stone. Hurst, 1923
-Flame of the Forest. Benn, 1930
Green Stones of Evil. Melrose, 1921
Guilty, My Lord. Hutchinson, 1928
-Life—and a Fortnight. Benn, 1929
-Like a Rose. Benn, 1928
-Love is Enough. Hurst, 1921
-Love's Burden. Hurst, 1918
-Love's Service. Hutchinson, 1932
Moonflowers. Hutchinson, 1926
-Ninon. Cassell, 1922
-Pamela and her Lion Man. Hutchinson, 1926
-Passionate Particles. Benn, 1927
-The Pitiful Rebellion. Hurst, 1925
The Question. Benn, 1928
-Scarlet Blossoms. Hutchinson, 1927
-The Scent of the Rose. Cassell, 1923
-The Sword-Points of Love. Hurst, 1919
-Twice Broken. Hutchinson, 1933
-Twinkleface, the Merry Elf. Hutchinson, 1926
The Unknown Hand. Hurst, 1924

PETRIE, GLEN
The Branch Bearers. Macmillan (London), 1973; Stein, 1973
-The Coming Out Party. Macmillan (London), 1972
-A Form of Release. Macmillan (London), 1971

PETRIE, RHONA. Pseudonym of Eileen-Marie Duell, 1922-   . Series character: Inspector Marcus MacLurg, in at least those marked MM.
Come Hell and High Water. Gollancz, 1970 ss
Dead Loss. Gollancz, 1966
Death in Deakins Wood. Gollancz, 1963; Dodd, 1964 MM
Despatch of a Dove. Gollancz, 1969
Foreign Bodies. Gollancz, 1967
MacLurg Goes West. Gollancz, 1968 MM
Murder by Precedent. Gollancz, 1964 MM
Running Deep. Gollancz, 1965 MM
Thorne in the Flesh. Gollancz, 1971

PETTEE, F(LORENCE) M(AE). 1888-   .
The Palgrave Mummy. Payson, 1929; Skeffington, 1929
White Dominoes. Reilly, 1921

PETTERSSON, JULIUS. 1889-1925. Pseudonym: Julius Regis, q.v.

PETTIT, PAUL. 1911-   .
The Drug-Run. Barker, 1960
The Spaniard. Valentine, 1953; Harper, 1954

PEVERETT, ALLAN
Death Stalks in Kenya. Stockwell, 1957
The Lurking Terror. Stockwell, 1960

PEYRE, JOSEPH. 1892-1968.
A Matador Dies. Bles, 1937. (Translation of Sang et Lumieres. Paris, 1935.)

PEYROU, MANUEL
Thunder of the Roses. Herder, 1972. (Translation of El Estruendo de las Rosas.)

PFALZGRAF, FLORENCE LEIGHTON. 1902-   . Pseudonym: Florence Leighton, q.v.

PFLAUM, MELANIE (LOWENTHAL). 1909-   .
-Bolero. Heinemann, 1956; St. Martin's, 1957
The Insiders. Cassell, 1963
-Windfall. Cassell, 1962

PHELAN, JIM [JAMES LEO PHELAN]. 1895-   .
Lifer. Davies, 1938
Murder by Numbers. Methuen, 1941

PHILIP, ALEX(ANDER) J(OHN). 1879-   .
Complete Change. Collins, 1926

PHILIP, J. C.
Memoirs of an Aberdeen Detective. Rosemont, 1903 ss

PHILIPS, (JOHN) AUSTIN (DRURY). 1875-1947.
-The Boy at the Bank. Mills, 1928
-The Girl Out in Corsica. Hutchinson, 1927
The Man in the Night Mail Train. Hutchinson, 1927
The Real Thing. Paul, 1933
-Somewhere in Sark. Selwyn, 1935
The Unknown Goddess. Hutchinson, 1929
-Were They Justified? Hutchinson, 1925

PHILIPS, GEORGE NORMAN. 1888?-   . Pseudonym: Anthony Skene, q.v. All titles were published by Amalgamated Press and feature Sexton Blake.
The Affair of the Seven Warnings. 1926
The Albino's Double. 1922
The Amazing Affair of the Renegade Prince. 1925
The Case of the Crook M.P. 1929
The Case of the Rejuvenated Millionaire. 1928. Reprinted in 1939 as by Anthony Skene.
The Gangster's Revenge. 1930
The Giant City Swindle. 1927. Reprinted in 1938 as by Anthony Skene.
The Man Who Squealed. 1929
The Mystery of the Shot P.C. 1928. Reprinted in 1940 as by Anthony Skene.
The Mystery of the Swanley Viaduct. 1925. Reprinted in 1937 as by Anthony Skene.
The Radium Profiteer. 1929
The Riddle of the Three Marked Men. 1930
The Roumanian Envoy. 1921
Victim of the Waterway. 1929

PHILIPS, JUDSON (PENTECOST). 1903-   . Pseudonym: Hugh Pentecost, q.v. Series characters: Coyle & Donovan = C&D; Carole Trevor and Max Blythe = T&B; Peter Styles = PS.
The Black Glass City. Dodd, 1965; Gollancz, 1965 PS
The Dead Can't Love. Dodd, 1963; Gollancz, 1963
A Dead Ending. Dodd, 1962; Gollancz, 1963
Death Delivers a Postcard. Washburn, 1939; Hurst, 1940 T&B
The Death Syndicate. Washburn, 1938; Hurst, 1939 T&B
Escape a Killer. Dodd, 1971; Gollancz, 1972 PS
The Fourteenth Trump. Dodd, 1942; Hale, 1951 C&D
Hot Summer Killing. Dodd, 1968; Gollancz, 1969 PS
Killer on the Catwalk. Dodd, 1959; Gollancz, 1960
The Larkspur Conspiracy. Dodd, 1973; Gollancz, 1974 PS
The Laughter Trap. Dodd, 1964; Gollancz, 1965 PS
Murder Clear, Track Fast. Dodd, 1961; Gollancz, 1962
Murder in Marble. Dodd, 1940; Hale, 1949
Nightmare at Dawn. Dodd, 1970; Gollancz, 1971 PS
Odds on the Hot Seat. Dodd, 1941; Hale, 1946 C&D
The Power Killers. Dodd, 1974; Gollancz, 1975 PS

PHILIPS, JUDSON
Red War, with T(homas) M(arvin) Johnson (1889-). Doubleday, 1936
Thursday's Folly. Dodd, 1967; Gollancz, 1968 PS
The Twisted People. Dodd, 1965; Gollancz, 1965 PS
The Vanishing Senator. Dodd, 1972; Gollancz, 1973 PS
Walk a Crooked Mile. Dodd, 1975; Gollancz, 1976 PS
Whisper Town. Dodd, 1960; Gollancz, 1961
The Wings of Madness. Dodd, 1966; Gollancz, 1967 PS

PHILIPS, PAGE
At Bay. Macaulay, 1914; Hodder, 1916. (Novelization of the play by George Scarborough, q.v.)

PHILLIFENT, JOHN T(HOMAS). 1916-1976.
Starred titles are novelizations of Man from U.N.C.L.E. TV series.
The Corfu Affair. Four Square, 1967; Ace, 1969 *
The Lonely Man. Boardman, 1965
The Mad Scientist Affair. Four Square, 1966; Ace, 1966 *
The Power Cube Affair. Four Square, 1968; Ace, 1968 *

PHILLIPS, CONRAD
Alone in the Grass. Barker, 1954
The Barber's Wife. Barker, 1953
Cry of the Dingo. Barker, 1956 ss
Dolls with Sad Faces. Barker, 1957; Roy, 1957
The Empty Cot. Barker, 1958
Shadow Play. Barker, 1954
Sunny Draper. Barker, 1956
The Unrepentant. Barker, 1958; Roy, 1958
Walk in the Dark. Barker, 1955

PHILLIPS, DAVID GRAHAM. 1867-1911.
The Master Rogue. McClure, 1903; Richards, 1904

PHILLIPS, DENNIS (JOHN ANDREW). 1924- .
Pseudonyms: Peter Chambers, Peter Chester, qq.v. See also: W(ILLIAM ARTHUR) HOWARD BAKER, 1925- .
Revenge Incorporated. Hale, 1970

PHILLIPS, DERYCK. 1914- .
Design for Destruction. Whiting, 1966

PHILLIPS, GERALD WILLIAM. 1884- .
Pseudonym: John Huntingdon, q.v.

PHILLIPS, GORDON
High Explosive. Nisbet, 1925; Dodd, 1926

PHILLIPS, H(ENRY) LAWRENCE. 1868- .
The Detective's Dilemma. Nelson, 1932
-A Friendless Millionaire. Nelson, 1928
The House of Secrets. Nelson, 1931
The Moor Barn Mystery. Butterworth, 1935
The Park Mystery. Nelson, 1933
The Tangle. Nelson, 1931

PHILLIPS, JAMES ATLEE. 1915- . Pseudonym: Philip Atlee, q.v.
The Case of the Shivering Chorus Girls. Coward, 1942; Bodley Head, 1950
The Deadly Mermaid. Dell, 1954
Pagoda. Macmillan, 1951; Bodley Head, 1953
Suitable for Framing. Macmillan, 1949; Bodley Head, 1952

PHILLIPS, JEAN
Green Wood. Lancer, 1965

PHILLIPS, LEON. Pseudonym of Noel B(ertram) Gerson, 1914- , q.v. Other pseudonym: Samuel Edwards, q.v.
Split Bamboo. Doubleday, 1966

PHILLIPS, MARK. Joint pseudonym of Larry M(ark) Harris, 1933- , q.v., and Randall (Phillips) Garrett, q.v. Other pseudonym of Larry M(ark) Harris: Laurence M. Janifer, q.v. Series character: Kenneth Malone, in all titles.
Brain Twister. Pyramid, 1962
The Impossibles. Pyramid, 1963
Supermind. Pyramid, 1963

PHILLIPS, RUSSELL R.
Death Smiles. Macaulay, 1936

PHILLIPS, STELLA. 1927- . Series character: Insp. Matthew Furnival, in at least those marked MF.
Dear Brother, Here Departed. Hale, 1975
Death in Arcady. Hale, 1969 MF
Death in Sheep's Clothing. Hale, 1971
Death Makes the Scene. Hale, 1970
Down to Death. Hale, 1967 MF
The Hidden Wrath. Hale, 1968 MF
Yet She Must Die. Hale, 1973

PHILLIPS, WATTS. 1825-1874.
The Hooded Snake: A Story of the Secret Police. Ward, 1860
Not Guilty. DeWitt, 187?. (A 4-act play.)
On the Jury. DeWitt, 187?. (A 4-act play.)
The Wentworth Mystery. Dicks, 18??

PHILLPOTTS, EDEN. 1862-1960. Pseudonym: Harrington Hext, q.v. Series character: Avis Bryden = AB.
Address Unknown. Hutchinson, 1949
-The American Prisoner. Methuen, 1904; Macmillan, 1903
The Anniversary Murder; see Physician, Heal Thyself
Awake Deborah! Methuen, 1940; Macmillan, 1941
Black, White, and Brindled. Richards, 1923; Macmillan, 1923 ss
Bred in the Bone. Hutchinson, 1932; Macmillan, 1933 AB
-The Bronze Venus. Richards, 1921
The Captain's Curio. Hutchinson, 1933; Macmillan, 1933
The Changeling. Hutchinson, 1944
A Close Call. Hutchinson, 1936; Macmillan, 1936
A Clue from the Stars. Hutchinson, 1932; Macmillan, 1932
A Deal with the Devil. Bliss, 1895
A Deed Without a Name. Hutchinson, 1941; Macmillan, 1942
Dilemma. Hutchinson, 1949
Doubloons; see The Sinews of War
The End of a Life. Arrowsmith, 1891
The End of Count Rollo. Todd, 1943. (From Peacock House and other mysteries, q.v.)
The End of Count Rollo and other stories. Polybooks, 1946. (ss, extracted from Peacock House and other mysteries, q.v.
-A Fight to a Finish. Cassell, 1911
Flower of the Gods. Hutchinson, 1942; Macmillan, 1943
"Found Drowned." Hutchinson, 1931; Macmillan, 1931
George and Georgina. Hutchinson, 1952
Ghostwater. Methuen, 1941; Macmillan, 1941
The Grey Room. Hurst, 1921; Macmillan, 1921
The Hidden Hand. Hutchinson, 1952
-His Brother's Keeper. Hutchinson, 1952
Jig-Saw; see The Marylebone Miser
The Judge's Chair. Murray, 1914 ss
The Jury. Hutchinson, 1927; Macmillan, 1927
Lycanthrope, the Mystery of Sir William Wolf. Butterworth, 1937; Macmillan, 1938
The Marylebone Miser. Hutchinson, 1926. U.S. title: Jig-Saw. Macmillan, 1926
The Master of Merripit. Ward, 1914
Miser's Money. Heinemann, 1920; Macmillan, 1920
Mr. Digweed & Mr. Lumb. Hutchinson, 1933; Macmillan, 1934
Monkshood. Methuen, 1939; Macmillan, 1939
My Adventure in the Flying Scotsman. Hogg, 1888; Aspen, 1976
-Once Upon a Time. Hutchinson, 1936 ss
Peacock House and other mysteries. Hutchinson, 1926; Macmillan, 1927 ss
Physician, Heal Thyself. Hutchinson, 1935. U.S. title: The Anniversary Murder. Dutton, 1936
Portrait of a Scoundrel. Murray, 1938; Macmillan, 1938
-Quartet. Hutchinson, 1946
The Red Redmaynes. Hutchinson, 1923; Macmillan, 1922
A Shadow Passes. Hutchinson, 1933; Macmillan, 1934 AB
The Sinews of War, with (Enoch) Arnold Bennett, 1867-1931, q.v. Laurie, 1906. U.S. title: The Doubloons. McClure, 1906
The Statue, with (Enoch) Arnold Bennett, 1867-1931, q.v. Cassell, 1908; Moffat Yard, 1908
There was an Old Man. Hutchinson, 1959
There was an Old Woman. Hutchinson, 1947
They were Seven. Hutchinson, 1944; Macmillan, 1945
The Three Knaves. Macmillan (London), 1912
-Through a Glass Darkly. Hutchinson, 1951
A Tiger's Cub. Arrowsmith, 1892
The Transit of the Red Dragon, and other tales. Arrowsmith, 1903 (Three novelets.)
The Unlucky Number. Newnes, 1906 ss
A Voice from the Dark. Hutchinson, 1925; Macmillan, 1925
The Wife of Elias. Hutchinson, 1935; Dutton, 1937
Witch's Cauldron. Hutchinson, 1933; Macmillan, 1933 AB

PHILMORE, R. Pseudonym of Herbert Edmund Howard, 1900- . Series characters: Inspector Garnett = G; Swan = S.
Death in Arms. Collins, 1939 G
The Good Books. Gollancz, 1936 S
Journey Downstairs. Gollancz, 1934; Doubleday, 1934 S
No Mourning in the Family. Collins, 1937 S
Procession of Two. Collins, 1940 G
Riot Act. Gollancz, 1935 S
Short List. Collins, 1938 S

PHIPPS, SARAH E.
The Old House by the Sea. Neely, 1901

PHRAILE, LORIMER
I am Being Poisoned. Swan, 1947

PICARD, SAM. Series character: John Scott = JS.
Dead Man Running. Award, 1971
The Man Who Never Was. Award, 1971 JS
The Notebooks. Award, 1969; Tandem, 1970 JS

PICKERING, EDITH
Murder of a Headmistress. Longmans, 1937

PICKERING, R(OBERT) E(ASTON). 1934-   .
  Himself Again. Gollancz, 1966. U.S.
  title: The Uncommitted Man. Farrar,
  1967

PICKERING, YORKE
  -The Dancing Water. Gifford, 1944
  -No Sweet Aspersion. Gifford, 1946
  A Shadow Passes. Gifford, 1949

PICTON, BERNARD. Pseudonym of Bernard
  Knight, 1931-   .
  The Lately Deceased. Jenkins, 1963
  Mistress Murder. Hale, 1966
  Policeman's Progress. Hale, 1969
  Russian Roulette. Hale, 1968
  The Thread of Evidence. Hale, 1965
  Tiger at Bay. Hale, 1970

PIDGIN, CHARLES FELTON. 1844-1923. Series
  character: Quincy Adams Sawyer = QS.
  The Chronicles of Quincy Adams Sawyer,
  Detective, with J(ohn) M. Taylor,
  1888-   . Page, 1912 QS ss
  The Further Adventures of Quincy Adams
  Sawyer. Page, 1909 QS
  The Hidden Man. Mayhew, 1906

PIERCE, GILBERT A(SHVILLE). 1841-1901.
  A Dangerous Woman. Donnelly, 1884

PIERCE, JOHN LEONARD, JR. 1921-   .
  Pseudonym: John Bramlett, q.v.

PIERCE, NOEL. 1907-   .
  Messenger from Munich. Coward, 1973

PIERCE, RICHARD
  Run, Traitor, Run. Lancer, 1968

PIERSON, ELEANOR. 1903-   .
  The Defense Rests. Howell Soskin, 1942
  The Good Neighbor Murder. Howell Soskin, 1941

PIERSON, ERNEST DeLANCEY
  -A Bargain in Souls. Laird, 1892. Also
  published as: An Uncle from India.
  Laird, 1897
  -The Black Ball. Belford, 1889
  A Dangerous Quest. Street (Magnet)
  A Hidden Clue. Street (Magnet)
  The Lady of the Lilacs. Street (Magnet)
  The Missing Cashier. Street (Magnet)
  The Portland Place Mystery. Street
  (Magnet)
  The Secret of the Diamond. Street (Magnet)
  The Secret of the Marionettes. National
  Book Co., 1892
  -The Shadow of the Bars. Belford, 1888
  -A Slave of Circumstances. Belford, 1888
  Stairs of Sand. Street (Magnet)
  An Uncle from India; see A Bargain in
  Souls
  -A Vagabond's Honor. Belford, 1889

PIFER, DRURY L.
  Circle of Women. Doubleday, 1970;
  Secker, 1970

PIGGOTT, WILLIAM. Pseudonym: Hubert
  Wales, q.v.

PIKE, ROBERT L. Pseudonym of Robert
  L(loyd) Fish, 1912-   , q.v. See
  also: JACK LONDON, 1876-1916. Series
  characters: Lt. Clancy = C; Lt. Jim
  Reardon = JR.
  Bank Job. Doubleday, 1974; Hale, 1975
  JR
  Bullitt; see Mute Witness
  The Gremlin's Grampa. Doubleday, 1972
  JR
  Mute Witness. Doubleday, 1963; Deutsch,
  1965. Also published as: Bullitt.
  Avon, 1968; Penguin, 1969 C

  Police Blotter. Doubleday, 1965;
  Deutsch, 1966 C
  The Quarry. Doubleday, 1964 C
  Reardon. Doubleday, 1970 JR

PILGRIM, CHAD
  The Silent Slain. Abelard (New York &
  London), 1958

PIM, SHEILA. 1909-   .
  A Brush with Death. Hodder, 1950
  Common or Garden Crime. Hodder, 1945
  Creeping Venom. Hodder, 1946
  -The Flowering Shamrock. Hodder, 1949
  A Hive of Suspects. Hodder, 1952; British Book Centre, 1953
  -Other People's Business. Hodder, 1957
  -The Sheltered Garden. Hodder, 1964

PINCHER, (HENRY) CHAPMAN. 1914-   .
  The Giantkiller. Weidenfeld, 1967
  Not with a Bang. Weidenfeld, 1965
  The Penthouse Conspirators. Joseph,
  1970
  The Skeleton at the Villa Wolkonsky.
  Joseph, 1975

PINCHOT, ANN
  The Twisted Cross. Paperback Library,
  1964

PINE, WILLIAM. Pseudonym of Terry Harknett, 1936-   , q.v. Other pseudonyms: Joseph Hedges, Thomas H. Stone,
  William Terry, qq.v.
  The Protectors. Constable, 1967

PINGET, ROBERT. 1919-   .
  The Inquisitory. Calder, 1966; Grove,
  1967. (Translation of L'Inquisitoire.
  Paris, 1962.)
  Recurrent Melody. Calder, 1975. (Translation of Passacaille. Paris, 1969.)

PINK, HAL. Series character: Sgt./Insp.
  Docker, in at least those marked D.
  The Black Sombrero Mystery. Hutchinson,
  1940
  The Cossack Mystery. Mellifont, 1934
  The Fellowship of the Feather. Mellifont, 1933
  The Gas Mask Gang. Mellifont, 1933
  The Green Triangle Mystery. Hutchinson,
  1938 D
  -The Heritage of Kid McCleod. Mellifont,
  1932
  -Jean of the Lazy J Ranch. Mellifont,
  1932
  The Masked Terror. Mellifont, 1933
  -The Rattlesnake. Mellifont, 1934
  The Rodeo Murder Mystery. Hutchinson,
  1941 D
  The Secret Service Mystery. Mellifont,
  1936
  The Strelsen Castle Mystery. Hutchinson, 1939
  The Test Match Mystery. Hutchinson,
  1940 D

PINKERTON, A. FRANK. Byline sometimes:
  Frank Pinkerton. Pseudonym: Detective
  Patrick Ryan, q.v.
  Cornered at Last; see Five Thousand
  Dollars Reward
  The Crime of the Midnight Express; see
  Dyke Darrel, the Railroad Detective
  Dyke Darrel, the Railroad Detective;
  or, The Crime of the Midnight Express. Laird, 1886. British title:
  The Crime of the Midnight Express.
  Routledge, 1887. Also published as:
  A Race for Life. Laird, 1898

  Five Thousand Dollars Reward; or, Cornered at Last. Laird, 1886. British
  title: Cornered at Last. Routledge,
  1887
  The Great Adams Express Robbery; see
  Jim Cummings
  Jim Cummings; or, The Great Adams Express Robbery. Laird, 1887. British
  title: The Great Adams Express Robbery. Routledge, 1887
  Marked for Life; or, The Gambler's
  Fate. Laird, 1887
  A Race for Life; see Dyke Darrel, the
  Railroad Detective
  Saved at the Scaffold; or, Nic Brown,
  the Chicago Detective. Laird, 1888
  The Whitechapel Murders; or, An American Detective in London. Laird, 1889

PINKERTON, ALLAN. 1819-1884.
  Bank-Robbers and the Detectives. Carleton, 1883
  Bucholz and the Detectives. Carleton,
  1880
  The Burglar's Fate and the Detectives.
  Carleton, 1883
  Claude Melnotte as a Detective, and
  other stories. Keen, 1875 ss
  Criminal Reminiscences and Detective
  Sketches. Carleton, 1879 ss
  The Detective and the Somnambulist.
  Keen, 1875. Also published as: The
  Somnambulist and the Detective.
  Carleton, 1884
  A Double Life and the Detectives.
  Carleton, 1884
  The Expressman and the Detective. Keen,
  1874
  The Gypsies and the Detectives. Carleton, 1879
  Mississippi Outlaws and the Detectives.
  Carleton, 1879. (3 stories.)
  The Model Town and the Detectives.
  Carleton, 1876
  The Molly Maguires and the Detectives.
  Carleton, 1877
  Professional Thieves and the Detective.
  Carleton, 1881
  The Rail-Road Forger and the Detectives. Carleton, 1881
  The Somnambulist and the Detective; see
  The Detective and the Somnambulist
  The Spiritualists and the Detectives.
  Carleton, 1877
  Strikers, Communists, Tramps and Detectives. Carleton, 1878

PINKERTON, FRANK. See: A. FRANK PINKERTON.

PINKERTON, MYRON
  The Creole's Crime; see A Woman's Revenge
  The Rokewood Tragedy; see The Stolen
  Will
  The Stolen Will; or, The Rokewood Tragedy. Laird, 1887. British title: The
  Rokewood Tragedy. Routledge, 1887
  A Woman's Revenge; or, The Creole's
  Crime. Laird, 1887. British title:
  The Creole's Crime. Routledge, 1887

PINSENT, ELLEN F(RANCES PARKER).
  1866-   .
  Jenny's Case. Swan, 1892

PIPER, EVELYN. Pseudonym of Merriam
  Modell, 1908-   .
  Bunny Lake is Missing. Harper, 1957;
  Secker, 1958
  Death of a Nymph; see The Motive
  Hanno's Doll. Atheneum, 1961; Secker,
  1962
  The Innocent. Simon, 1949; Boardman,
  1951

Piper, Evelyn
- The Lady and Her Doctor. Doubleday, 1956
- The Motive. Simon, 1950; Boardman, 1951. Also published as: Death of a Nymph. Mercury, 1951
- The Naked Murderer. Atheneum, 1962
- The Nanny. Atheneum, 1964; Secker, 1965
- The Plot. Simon, 1951; Boardman, 1952
- The Stand-In. Washburn, 1970

PIPER, H. BEAM. 1904-1964.
- Murder in the Gunroom. Knopf, 1953

PIPER, PETER. Pseudonym of Theo Langbehn. Other pseudonym: Theo Lang, q.v. Series character: Inspector Gray, in at least those marked G.
- The Corpse That Came Back; see Death in the Canongate
- Death Came in Straw. Hurst, 1945
- Death in the Canongate. Hodder, 1952. U.S. title: The Corpse That Came Back. Random, 1954 G
- Margot Leck. Hurst, 1947
- Murder After the Blitz. Hurst, 1943 G
- The Woman Delia. Hodder, 1957

PIRKIS, C(ATHERINE) L(OUISA).   -1910.
- A Dateless Bargain. Hurst, 1887; Appleton, 1887
- The Experiences of Loveday Brooke, Lady Detective. Hutchinson, 1894 ss

PITCAIRN, JOHN JAMES. 1860-1936. Joint pseudonym with R(ichard) Austin Freeman, 1862-1943, q.v.: Clifford Ashdown, q.v.

PITMAN, WILLIAM DENT
- The Quincunx Case. Turner, 1904; Richards, 1904

PITT, FRANKLIN
- Brothers of the Thin Wire. Street, 1915

PITTS, DENIS. 1930-   .
- This City is Ours. Mason/Charter, 1975. British title: Target Manhattan. Hodder, 1976

PLAGEMANN, BENTZ. 1913-   .
- The Boxwood Maze. Saturday Review Press, 1972
- Wolfe's Cloister. Saturday Review Press, 1974

PLAIN, JOSEPHINE. Series character: Colin Anstruther, in all titles.
- The Pazenger Problem. Butterworth, 1936
- The Secret of the Sandbanks. Butterworth, 1934
- The Secret of the Snows. Butterworth, 1935

PLANTZ, DONALD
- Marked for Death. Monarch, 1964

PLATT, CHARLES. See: LILIAN BAMBURG.

PLATT, EDWARD. Pseudonym: Paul Trent, q.v.

PLATT, KIN. 1911-   . Series character: Max Roper = MR.
- Dead as They Come. Random, 1972; Hale, 1974
- The Giant Kill. Random, 1974; Hale, 1975 MR
- The Kissing Gourami. Random, 1970; Hale, 1973 MR
- Match Point for Murder. Random, 1975 MR
- A Pride of Women; see The Princess Stakes Murder
- The Princess Stakes Murder. Random, 1973. British title: A Pride of Women. Hale, 1974. Reprinted in Britain under the U.S. title: Hale, 1977 MR
- The Pushbutton Butterfly. Random, 1970; Hale, 1971 MR

PLATT, ROBERT. 1894-   .
- The Swaying Corpse. Phoenix, 1941

PLAYER, ROBERT. Pseudonym of Robert Furneaux Jordan, 1905-   .
- The Homicidal Colonel. Gollancz, 1970
- The Ingenious Mr. Stone. Gollancz, 1945; Rinehart, 1946
- Let's Talk of Graves, of Worms, and Epitaphs. Gollancz, 1975
- Oh! Where are Bloody Mary's Earrings? Gollancz, 1972; Harper, 1973

PLAYFAIR, JOCELYN
- Murder without Mystery. Hodder, 1939

PLEASANTS, W. SHEPARD
- The Stingaree Murders. Mystery League, 1932

PLEYDELL, GEORGE. Pseudonym of George Pleydell Bancroft, 1868-   .
- The Ware Case. Doran, 1913; Methuen, 1913

PLOMER, WILLIAM (CHARLES FRANKLYN). 1903-1973.
- The Case is Altered. Woolf, 1932; Farrar, 1932

PLUM, JOSEPHINE. Pseudonym of Michael (J.) Kurland, 1938-   , q.v.
- The Secret of Benjamin Square. Lancer, 1972

PLUM, MARY. Series character: John Smith = JS.
- The Broken Vase Mystery; see Murder at the World's Fair
- Dead Man's Secret. Harper, 1931; Eyre, 1931 JS
- The Killing of Judge MacFarlane. Harper, 1930; Eyre, 1930 JS
- Murder at the Hunting Club. Harper, 1932; Eyre, 1932 JS
- Murder at the World's Fair. Harper, 1933. British title: The Broken Vase Mystery. Eyre, 1933 JS
- Murder of a Redhaired Man. Arcadia, 1952; Eyre, 1951
- State Department Cat. Doubleday, 1945; Eyre, 1946
- Susanna, Don't You Cry! Doubleday, 1946

PLUMMER, T(HOMAS) ARTHUR. Pseudonym: Michael Sarne, q.v. Series character: Detective Inspector Andrew Frampton, in at least those marked AF.
- The Ace of Death. Paul, 1930
- Alias—The Crimson Snake. Paul, 1933
- The Barush Mystery. Paul, 1946 AF
- The Black Rat. Paul, 1955 AF
- The Black Ribbon Murders. Paul, 1940 AF
- The Bonfire Murder; see Was the Mayor Murdered?
- "Brent"—of Bleak House. Paul, 1948
- The Broken Trust. Thomson, 1929
- Condemned to Live. Paul, 1957 AF
- Cornered. Leng, 1938
- Creaking Gallows. Paul, 1934
- Crime at Crooked Gables. Paul, 1941 AF
- Death Haunts the Repertory. Paul, 1950
- The Death Letter. Paul, 1951
- Death on Danger Hill. Paul, 1931
- The Death Symbol. Paul, 1937 AF
- Death Takes a Hand. Paul, 1934
- The Devil's Tea-Party. Paul, 1942 AF
- The Dumb Witness. Paul, 1936; Macaulay, 1936 AF
- The Elusive Killer. Long, 1958 AF
- Five were Murdered! Paul, 1938 AF
- The Fool of the 'Yard'. Paul, 1942 AF
- Frampton—of "the Yard"! Paul, 1935; Macaulay, 1935 AF
- Frampton Sees Red. Paul, 1953 AF
- -The Girl in a Hurry. Thomson, 1932
- Haunting Lights. Paul, 1932
- -Her Own Affair. Leng, 1939
- The Hospital Thief. Long, 1959 AF
- The House in Sinister Lane. Paul, 1931
- Hunted! Paul, 1948 AF
- The "J for Jennie" Murders. Paul, 1945 AF
- Lonely Hollow Mystery. Paul, 1933
- -Lying Lips. Leng, 1938
- The Man They Feared. Paul, 1937 AF
- The Man They Put Away. Paul, 1938 AF
- The Man Who Changed His Face. Paul, 1943 AF
- The Man with the Crooked Arm. Paul, 1945 AF
- -Margaret Benson's Vow. Leng, 1934
- Melody of Death. Paul, 1940 AF
- Murder at Brownhill. Long, 1962 AF
- Murder at Lantern Corner. Long, 1957 AF
- Murder at Marlington. Paul, 1951
- Murder—by an Idiot. Paul, 1944 AF
- The Murder House. Paul, 1930
- Murder in the Surgery. Paul, 1955 AF
- Murder in the Village. Paul, 1945 AF
- Murder in Windy Coppice. Paul, 1954 AF
- Murder Limps By. Paul, 1943 AF
- The Murder of Doctor Grey. Paul, 1950 AF
- Murder Through Room 45. Paul, 1952 AF
- The Muse Theatre Murder. Paul, 1939 AF
- Pagan Joe. Paul, 1956 AF
- The Pierced Ear Murders. Paul, 1947 AF
- A Scream at Midnight. Paul, 1954 AF
- Shadowed by the C.I.D. Paul, 1932 AF
- Shot at Night. Paul, 1934 AF
- The Silent Four. Paul, 1947 AF
- Simon takes 'the Rap'. Paul, 1944 AF
- The Spider Man. Long, 1961 AF
- Staring Eyes! Paul, 1935
- The Starry Eyed Murder. Paul, 1952
- The Strangler. Paul, 1945 AF
- Strychnine for One. Paul, 1949 AF
- Two Men from the East. Paul, 1939 AF
- The Vestry Murder. Long, 1959 AF
- Was the Mayor Murdered? Paul, 1936. U.S. title: The Bonfire Murder. Macaulay, 1937 AF
- The Westlade Murders. Paul, 1953 AF
- Where was Trail Murdered? Paul, 1956 AF
- Who Fired the Factory? Paul, 1947 AF
- The Yellow Disc Murders. Paul, 1950 AF

PLYMPTON, A(LMIRA) G(EORGE). 1852-   .
- A Willing Transgressor, and other stories. Roberts, 1897 ss

POATE, ERNEST M. Series character: Dr. Bentiron = B.
- Behind Locked Doors. Chelsea, 1923 B
- Doctor Bentiron: Detective. Chelsea, 1930 B (Three novelets.)
- Murder on the Brain. Chelsea, 1930
- Pledged to the Dead. Chelsea, 1925
- The Trouble at Pinelands. Chelsea, 1922

POCOCK, ROGER (S.). 1865-   .
- The Cheerful Blackguard; see The Splendid Blackguard
- The Dragon Slayer. Chapman, 1896. Also published as: Sword and Dragon. Hodder, 1909
- The Splendid Blackguard. Murray, 1915. U.S. title: The Cheerful Blackguard. Bobbs, 1915
- Sword and Dragon; see The Dragon Slayer

POE, EDGAR A(LLAN). 1809-1849. Series character: C. Auguste Dupin = D (see also Michael Harrison, 1907-   ).

The Prose Romances of Edgar A. Poe. Graham, 1843. (Contains only "The Murders in the Rue Morgue", D, in its first book appearance.)
Tales. Wiley and Putnam (New York & London), 1845. (Contains, in addition to "Rue Morgue", first book appearances of the other two D stories, "The Mystery of Marie Roget" and "The Purloined Letter".)
The Works of the Late Edgar Allan Poe. Volume II. Redfield, 1850. (Contains the first book appearance of "Thou Art the Man".)

POE, EDGAR ALLAN, JR. 1896- .
The House Party Murders. Lippincott, 1940

POHL, FREDERIK. 1919- .
Edge of the City. Ballantine, 1957. (Novelization of the movie.)

POLK, DORA (BEALE). 1923- .
The House on the Black Moor. Beagle, 1972
The Linnet Estate. McKay, 1973
Tower of the Crow. McKay, 1975

POLLAND, MADELEINE (ANGELA CAHILL). 1918- .
The Little Spot of Bother. Hutchinson, 1967. U.S. title: Minutes of a Murder. Holt, 1967
Minutes of a Murder; see The Little Spot of Bother
Package to Spain. Hutchinson, 1971; Walker, 1971
-Random Army. Hutchinson, 1969
Thicker Than Water. Hutchinson, 1967; Holt, 1965

POLLARD, CAPTAIN A(LFRED) O(LIVER). 1893- .
A.R.P. Spy. Hutchinson, 1940
Air Reprisal. Hutchinson, 1938
Black Out. Hutchinson, 1938
Blood Hunt. Hutchinson, 1946
The Cipher Five. Hutchinson, 1932
Counterfeit Spy. Hutchinson, 1952
Criminal Airman. Hutchinson, 1953
Dead Man's Secret. Hutchinson, 1949
A Deal in Death. Hutchinson, 1947
The Death Curse. Hutchinson, 1948
The Death Flight. Hutchinson, 1932
The Death Game. Hutchinson, 1936
Death Intervened. Hutchinson, 1951
The Death Parade. Hutchinson, 1951
The Death Squadron. Hutchinson, 1943
Double-Cross. Hutchinson, 1946
The Fifth Freedom. Hutchinson, 1945
Flanders Spy. Hutchinson, 1938
Forged Evidence. Long, 1962
Gestapo Fugitive. Hutchinson, 1944
The Havenhurst Affair. Hutchinson, 1933
Hidden Cipher. Hutchinson, 1937
Homicidal Spy. Hutchinson, 1954
Invitation to Death. Hutchinson, 1944
The Iron Curtain. Hutchinson, 1947
The Murder Germ. Hutchinson, 1937
Murder Hide-and-Seek. Hutchinson, 1931
Murder in the Air. Hutchinson, 1935
Murder of a Diplomat. Hutchinson, 1939
The Phantom 'Plane. Hutchinson, 1934
-Pirdale Island. Hutchinson, 1930
Red Hazard. Hutchinson, 1950
The Riddle of Loch Lemman. Hutchinson, 1933
Rum Alley. Hutchinson, 1931
The Secret Formula. Hutchinson, 1939
The Secret of Castle Voxzel. Hutchinson, 1935

The Secret Pact. Hutchinson, 1940
The Secret Vendetta. Hutchinson, 1949
The Secret Weapon. Hutchinson, 1941
Sinister Secret. Hutchinson, 1956
Smuggler's Buoy. Hutchinson, 1958
Unofficial Spy. Hutchinson, 1936
Wanted by the Gestapo. Hutchinson, 1942
Wrong Verdict. Long, 1960

POLLARD, PERCIVAL. 1869-1911.
Lingo Dan. Neale, 1903 ss

POLLITZ, EDWARD A., JR. 1937- .
The Forty-First Thief. Delacorte, 1975; Hart-Davis, 1976
-The 200% Rule. Bobbs, 1974; New English Library, 1975

POLLOCK, CHANNING. 1880-1946.
Synthetic Gentleman. Farrar, 1934

POLLOCK, COURTENAY (EDWARD MAXWELL). 1877-1943.
The Mystery of Rapallo. Methuen, 1919

POLLOCK, G(UY) C(AMERON) and ANNE (WETZELL) ARMSTRONG
To See Ourselves. Hutchinson, 1936

POLLOCK, ROBERT. 1930- .
Loophole, or "How to Rob a Bank". Hodder, 1972; Dutton, 1973

POLLOCK, WALTER HERRIES. 1850-1926.
A Nine Men's Morrice. Longmans, 1889 ss, some criminous

POLONSKY, ABRAHAM. Joint pseudonym with Mitchell A. Wilson, 1913-1973, q.v.: Emmett Hogarth, q.v.

POLSKY, THOMAS. Series character: L. F. "Scoop" Griddle = SG.
The Cudgel. Dutton, 1950; Boardman, 1952
Curtains for the Copper. Dutton, 1941 SG
Curtains for the Editor. Dutton, 1939 SG
Curtains for the Judge. Dutton, 1939 SG

POND, E. J.
The Ince Murder Case. Heritage, 1934

POND, RUTH POWER
The Oaks of Bashan. Dorrance, 1969

PONDER, ZITA INEZ
The Bandaged Face. Selwyn, 1927; Macaulay, 1929

PONS, MAURICE. 1927- .
Mademoiselle B. St. Martin's, 1974. (Translation of Mademoiselle B. Paris, 1973.)

PONTHIER, FRANCOIS
Assignment Basra. Cassell, 1969; McKay, 1969. (Translation of Le Rendevous de Bassora. Paris, 1966.)
The Harpoon. Cassell, 1969; McKay, 1970. (Translation of Le Harpon. Paris, 1966.)

POOLE, HELEN LEE
The House of Clouds. Lancer, 1966

POOLE, MICHAEL. Pseudonym of Reginald Heber Poole, 1885- , q.v. See also: F(rederick) H(aydn) Dimmock, 1895- . Series characters: Freddie Browne and Jim Fanshaw = B&F.
-Browne Fights the Fifth Column. Oxford, 1942 B&F

-Browne Follows the Clue. Oxford, 1936 B&F
-Browne of the Secret Service. Oxford, 1940 B&F
-Browne's £50,000 Mystery. Oxford, 1937 B&F
-Browne's First Case. Oxford, 1935 B&F
Death Follows the Trail. Melrose, 1935
Gang's Orders. Amalgamated Press, 1930. (Sexton Blake.)
-The Gwythyn Clay Mystery. Oxford, 1940 B&F
Let Justice be Done! Mellifont, 1946
-The Missing Bank Manager. Oxford, 1938 B&F
-Mystery at Merrilees. Oxford, 1939 B&F
The Roll Film Mystery. Crowther, 1941
-The Vanished Stamps Mystery. Oxford, 1941
-The Wagoner's Halt Mystery. Blackie, 1940

POOLE, REGINALD HEBER. 1885- . Pseudonym: Michael Poole, q.v. See also: F(REDERICK) H(AYDN) DIMMOCK, 1895- . Series character (with many other authors): Sexton Blake, in those titles without publisher below, which were issued by Amalgamated Press.
The Case of the Russian Crown Jewels. 1921
The Davenham Heritage. Long, 1928
The Great Trunk Mystery. 1927. Reprinted in 1939 as by H. Gregory.
John Quinton's Secret. Aldine, 1926
The King's Secret. 1920
The Prison Breakers. 1920
The Trail Under the Sea. 1920
Unjustly Branded. 1919

POPE, LEO
Malachi Breen Times Two. Caravelle, 1967

POPKIN, ZELDA. 1898- . Series character: Mary Carner = MC.
Dead Man's Gift. Lippincott, 1941; Hutchinson, 1948 MC
A Death of Innocence. Lippincott, 1971; Allen, 1972
Death Wears a White Gardenia. Lippincott, 1938; Hutchinson, 1939 MC
Murder in the Mist. Lippincott, 1940; Hutchinson, 1941 MC
No Crime for a Lady. Lippincott, 1942 MC
So Much Blood. Lippincott, 1944; Hutchinson, 1946
Time Off for Murder. Lippincott, 1940; Hutchinson, 1940 MC

POPPLEWELL, JACK
Dead on Nine. French (London), 1956. (3-act play.)

PORCELAIN, SIDNEY E. Series character: Stephen Clay, in both titles.
The Crimson Cat Murders. Phoenix, 1946
The Purple Pony Murders. Phoenix, 1944; Partridge, 1948

PORLOCK, MARTIN. Pseudonym of Philip MacDonald, 1899- , q.v. Joint pseudonym with Ronald MacDonald, 1860-1933: Oliver Fleming, q.v.
Escape; see Mystery in Kensington Gore
Mystery at Friar's Pardon. Collins, 1931; Doubleday, 1932, as by Philip MacDonald
Mystery in Kensington Gore. Collins, 1932. U.S. title: Escape, as by Philip MacDonald. Doubleday, 1932
The Mystery of Mr. X; see X v. Rex
Mystery of the Dead Police; see X v. Rex

330/ Porlock, Martin

X v. Rex. Collins, 1933. U.S. title: Mystery of the Dead Police, as by Philip MacDonald. Doubleday, 1933. Also published as: The Mystery of Mr. X. Literary Press, 1934

PORTER, ADMIRAL (DAVID DIXON). 1813-1891.
Allan Dare and Robert le Diable. Appleton, 1884

PORTER, HAROLD EVERETT. 1887-1936. Pseudonym: Holworthy Hall, q.v.

PORTER, JOYCE. 1924- . Series characters: Insp. Wilfred Dover = WD; Edmund Brown = EB; Constance Morrison-Burke = CM.
The Chinks in the Curtain. Cape, 1967; Scribner, 1968 EB
Dover and the Unkindest Cut of All. Cape, 1967; Scribner, 1967 WD
Dover Goes to Pott. Cape, 1968; Scribner, 1968 WD
Dover One. Cape, 1964; Scribner, 1964 WD
Dover Strikes Again. Weidenfeld, 1970; McKay, 1973 WD
Dover Three. Cape, 1965; Scribner, 1966 WD
Dover Two. Cape, 1965; Scribner, 1965 WD
It's Murder with Dover. Weidenfeld, 1973; McKay, 1973 WD
A Meddler and Her Murder. Weidenfeld, 1972; McKay, 1973 CM
Neither a Candle nor a Pitchfork. Weidenfeld, 1969; McCall, 1970 EB
Only with a Bargepole. Weidenfeld, 1971; McKay, 1974 EB
The Package Included Murder. Weidenfeld, 1975; Bobbs, 1976 CM
Rather a Common Sort of Crime. Weidenfeld, 1970; McCall, 1970 CM
Sour Cream with Everything. Cape, 1966; Scribner, 1966 EB

PORTER, LINN BOYD. 1851-1916. Pseudonym: Albert Ross, q.v.

PORTER, MONICA E.
The Mercy of the Court. Norton, 1955

PORTER, REBECCA N(EWMAN). 1883- .
The Rest Hollow Mystery. Century, 1922; Long, 1924

PORTER, WILLIAM SYDNEY. 1862-1910. Pseudonym: O. Henry, q.v.

PORTWAY, CHRISTOPHER (JOHN). 1923- .
All Exits Barred. Hale, 1971; Pinnacle, 1974
Lost Vengeance. Hale, 1973
The Tirana Assignment. Hale, 1974; Pinnacle, 1975

PORTWINE, E. T.
-Death Swamp, and other adventure stories. Vawser, 1946 ss
The Limping Wolf. Featherstone, 1946
The Zero Ray Terrors. Vawser, 1946

POSNER, JACOB D. 1883- . Pseudonym: Gregory Dean, q.v.

POSNER, RICHARD. 1944- . Pseudonyms: Iris Foster, Beatrice Murray, Paul Todd, qq.v.
The Mafia Man. GM, 1973; Gold Lion, 1973
The Seven-Ups. GM, 1973; Futura, 1974. (Novelization of the movie.)
The Trigger Man. GM, 1974

POSSENDORF, HANS. Pseudonym of Hans Mahner-Mons.
The 77th Day. Hutchinson, 1937. (Translation of Gerbergasse 7. Munich, 1933.)

POST, MELVILLE DAVISSON. 1871-1930. Series characters: Uncle Abner = A; Sir Henry Marquis = HM; Randolph Mason = RM.
The Bradmoor Murder. Sears, 1929. British title (with contents rearranged): The Garden in Asia. Brentano's (London), 1929 HM ss
The Corrector of Destinies. Clode, 1908. Also published as: Randolph Mason, Corrector of Destinies. Putnam, 1923 RM ss
The Garden in Asia; see The Bradmoor Murder
The Man of Last Resort; or, The Clients of Randolph Mason. Putnam, 1897. Also published as: Randolph Mason: The Clients. Putnam, 1923 RM ss
The Methods of Uncle Abner. Aspen, 1974 A ss
Monsieur Jonquelle, Prefect of Police. Appleton, 1923 ss
The Mystery at the Blue Villa. Appleton, 1919 ss
The Nameless Thing. Appleton, 1912 ss
Randolph Mason: The Clients; see The Man of Last Resort
Randolph Mason, Corrector of Destinies; see The Corrector of Destinies
Randolph Mason: The Strange Schemes; see The Strange Schemes of Randolph Mason
The Silent Witness. Farrar, 1930 ss
The Sleuth of St. James's Square. Appleton, 1920 HM ss
The Strange Schemes of Randolph Mason. Putnam, 1896. Also published as: Randolph Mason: The Strange Schemes. Putnam, 1922 RM ss
Uncle Abner, Master of Mysteries. Appleton, 1918; Stacey, 1972 A ss
Walker of the Secret Service. Appleton, 1924 ss

POST, MORTIMER
Candidate for Murder. Doubleday, 1936

POSTGATE, JOHN W(ILLIAM). 1851-1921.
The Mystery of Paul Chadwick. Laird, 1896
Private Detective No. 39; or, The Mysterious Client. Ogilvie, 1892
The Stolen Laces. Laird, 1889. (Byline given as John T. Postgate.)
The Strange Case of Henry Toplass and Capt. Shiers. Homewood, 1893
Two Women in Black. Belford, 1886. Also published as by James Mooney: Donohue, 1894
A Woman's Devotion; or, The Mixed Marriage. Rand, 1887

POSTGATE, RAYMOND (WILLIAM). 1896-1971.
The Ledger is Kept. Joseph, 1953
Somebody at the Door. Joseph, 1943; Knopf, 1943
Verdict of Twelve. Collins, 1940; Doubleday, 1940

POTTER, DAN
The Way of an Eagle. Stein, 1970; Secker, 1970

POTTER, GEORGE WILLIAM, JR. 1930- .
Pseudonym: E. L. Withers, q.v.

POTTER, J. L. Series character: Jeff Tyler, in all titles.
Kill, Sweet Charity, Kill. Chicago Paperback House, 1962
—Or Murder for Free. Chicago Paperback House, 1962
Room at the Bottom. Chicago Paperback House, 1962

POTTER, JEREMY. 1922- . Series character: Sgt./Insp. Hiscock, in at least those marked H.
The Dance of Death. Constable, 1968; Walker, 1969 H
Death in Office. Constable, 1965 H
Disgrace and Favour. Constable, 1975
Foul Play. Constable, 1967
Going West. Constable, 1972
Hazard Chase. Constable, 1964
A Trail of Blood. Constable, 1970; McCall, 1971

POTTS, JEAN. 1910- .
An Affair of the Heart. Scribner, 1970; Gollancz, 1970
Blood will Tell; see Lightning Strikes Twice
Death of a Stray Cat. Scribner, 1955; Gollancz, 1955
The Diehard. Scribner, 1956; Gollancz, 1956
The Evil Wish. Scribner, 1962; Gollancz, 1962
The Footsteps on the Stairs. Scribner, 1966; Gollancz, 1967
Go, Lovely Rose. Scribner, 1954; Gollancz, 1955
Home is the Prisoner. Scribner, 1960; Gollancz, 1960
Lightning Strikes Twice. Scribner, 1958. British title: Blood will Tell. Gollancz, 1959
The Little Lie. Scribner, 1968; Gollancz, 1969
The Man with the Cane. Scribner, 1957; Gollancz, 1958
My Brother's Killer. Scribner, 1975; Gollancz, 1976
The Only Good Secretary. Scribner, 1965; Gollancz, 1966
The Trash Stealer. Scribner, 1967; Gollancz, 1968
The Troublemaker. Scribner, 1972; Gollancz, 1973

POU, GENEVIEVE LONG. 1919- . Pseudonym: Genevieve Holden, q.v.

POURNELLE, JERRY E. Pseudonym: Wade Curtis, q.v.

POWELL, FRANCES. Pseudonym of Frances Powell Case.
-The By-Ways of Braithe. Scribner, 1904; Harper (London), 1904
The House on the Hudson. Scribner, 1903; Harper (London), 1903
An Old Maid's Vengeance. Scribner, 1911
Old Mr. Davenant's Money. Scribner, 1908
The Prisoner of Ornith Farm. Scribner, 1906

POWELL, ISABELLA BAYNE. See: ISABELLA BAYNE-POWELL.

POWELL, LESTER. 1912- . Series character: Philip Odell, in at least those marked PO.
The Big M. Hale, 1973
The Black Casket. Collins, 1953 PO
A Count of Six. Collins, 1948
Shadow Play. Collins, 1949 PO
Spot the Lady. Collins, 1950 PO
Still of Night. Collins, 1952 PO

POWELL, MICHAEL. 1905- .
A Waiting Game. Joseph, 1975; St. Martin's, 1976

POWELL, P(ERCIVAL) H(ENRY). Series characaction: Supt. Gaden, in at least those marked G.
Death of an Expert Witness. Hale, 1957
Fatal Mistake. Hale, 1956
Murder Premeditated. Jenkins, 1951; Roy, 1958
-No Moonlight. Nimmo, 1948
Now Lying Dead. Jenkins, 1953 G
Only Three Died. Low, 1951
The Police Murders. Hale, 1955
Why Kill a Butler? Jenkins, 1952; Roy, 1957 G

POWELL, RICHARD (PITTS). 1908- .
Series characters: Arab & Andy Blake = B.
All Over But the Shooting. Simon, 1944; Hodder, 1949 B
And Hope to Die. Simon, 1947; Hodder, 1950 B
The Case of the Curious Chair; see Don't Catch Me
Death Talks Out of Turn. U.S. Government Printing Office, 1944
Don't Catch Me. Simon, 1943; Hodder, 1949. Also published as: The Case of the Curious Chair. Handi-Books, 1944 B
False Colors. Simon, 1955; Hodder, 1956. Also published as: Masterpiece in Murder. Dell, 1956
Lay That Pistol Down. Simon, 1945; Hodder, 1950 B
Leave Murder to Me; see A Shot in the Dark
Masterpiece in Murder; see False Colors
On the Hook; see Shark River
Say It with Bullets. Simon, 1953; Hodder, 1955
Shark River. Simon, 1950; Hodder, 1951. Also published as: On the Hook. Ace, 1954
Shell Game. Simon, 1950; Hodder, 1952
Shoot If You Must. Simon, 1946; Hodder, 1949 B
A Shot in the Dark. Simon, 1952. British title: Leave Murder to Me. Hodder, 1952

POWELL, ROSAMUND BAYNE. 1879-   . See: ROSAMUND BAYNE-POWELL.

POWELL, TALMAGE. 1920- . Pseudonym: Jack McCready, q.v. Series character: Ed Rivers = ER.
Corpus Delectable. PB, 1964 ER
The Girl Who Killed Things. Zenith, 1960
The Girl's Number Doesn't Answer. PB, 1960 ER
The Killer is Mine. PB, 1959 ER
Man-Killer. Ace, 1960
The Smasher. Macmillan, 1959
Start Screaming Murder. Permabooks, 1962 ER
With a Madman Behind Me. Permabooks, 1962 ER

POWER, PATRICIA
The Face of the Foe. Doubleday, 1973; Hale, 1974
This Deadly Grief. Doubleday, 1972; Hale, 1973

POWERS, J.
Big Slam. World Distributors, 1953
Front Page Murder. World Distributors, 1954

POWLETT, NIGEL AMYAS ORDE. 1900- .
See: NIGEL (AMYAS) ORDE-POWLETT.

POWLEY, JEAN. Pseudonym: Ann Cardwell, q.v.

POYER, JOE [JOSEPH JOHN POYER]. 1939- .
The Balkan Assignment. Doubleday, 1971; Gollancz, 1972
The Chinese Agenda. Doubleday, 1972; Gollancz, 1973
North Cape. Doubleday, 1969; Gollancz, 1970
Operation Malacca. Doubleday, 1968; Sphere, 1976
The Shooting of the Green. Doubleday, 1973; Barker, 1974

POYNTER, BEULAH
The Disappearance of Mary Amber. Greengerg, 1934
-Lost Rapture. Greenberg, 1934
Murder on 47th Street. Doubleday, 1931
The Murillo Mystery. Altemus, 1927

PRAED, MRS. CAMPBELL [ROSA CAROLINE MURRAY-PRIOR PRAED]. 1851-1925.
The Brother of the Shadow. Routledge, 1886
The Mystery Woman. Cassell, 1913
Outlaw and Lawmaker. Chatto, 1893; Appleton, 1894

PRATHER, RICHARD S(COTT). 1921- .
Pseudonyms: David Knight, Douglas Ring, qq.v. Series character: Shell Scott = SS (see also David Knight entry).
Always Leave 'Em Dying. GM, 1954; Fawcett (London), 1957 SS
Bodies in Bedlam. GM, 1951; Fawcett (London), 1957 SS
Case of the Vanishing Beauty. GM, 1950; Fawcett (London), 1957 SS
The Cheim Manuscript. PB, 1969 SS
The Cockeyed Corpse. GM, 1964 SS
Dagger of Flesh. Falcon, 1952; Panther, 1961
Dance with the Dead. GM, 1960; Muller pb, 1962 SS
Darling, It's Death. GM, 1952; Fawcett (London), 1957 SS
Dead-Bang. PB, 1971 SS
Dead Heat. PB, 1963 SS
Dead Man's Walk. PB, 1965; Four Square, 1968 SS
Dig That Crazy Grave. GM, 1961; Muller pb, 1962 SS
Double in Trouble, with Stephen Marlowe, q.v. PB, 1959 SS, plus Marlowe's series character Chester Drum
Everybody had a Gun. GM, 1951; Muller, 1953 SS
Find This Woman. GM, 1951; Fawcett (London), 1959 SS
Gat Heat. Trident, 1967; Four Square, 1968 SS
Have Gat—Will Travel. GM, 1957; Fawcett (London), 1958 SS ss
Joker in the Deck. GM, 1964; Muller pb, 1965 SS
Kill Him Twice. PB, 1965 SS
Kill Me Tomorrow. PB, 1969 SS
Kill the Clown. GM, 1962; Muller pb, 1963 SS
The Kubla Khan Caper. Trident, 1966 SS
Lie Down, Killer. Lion, 1952; Fawcett (London), 1958
The Meandering Corpse. Trident, 1965; Four Square, 1967 SS
Over Her Dear Body. GM, 1959; Panther, 1960 SS
Pattern for Panic. Abelard, 1954. Revised version, with SS: GM, 1961; Muller pb, 1962

Ride a High Horse. GM, 1953. Also published as: Too Many Crooks. GM, 1956; Fawcett (London), 1957 SS
The Shell Scott Sampler. PB, 1969 ss SS
Shell Scott's Seven Slaughters. GM, 1961; Muller pb, 1962 SS ss
Slab Happy. GM, 1958 SS
Strip for Murder. GM, 1955; Fawcett (London), 1957 SS
The Sure Thing. PB, 1975 SS
The Sweet Ride. PB, 1972 SS
Take a Murder, Darling. GM, 1958; Muller pb, 1961 SS
Three's a Shroud. GM, 1957; Gold Lion, 1973. (Three novelets.) SS
Too Many Crooks; see Ride a High Horse
The Trojan Hearse. PB, 1964; Four Square, 1967 SS
The Wailing Frail. GM, 1956; Fawcett (London), 1957 SS
Way of a Wanton. GM, 1952; Fawcett (London), 1958 SS

PRATT, AMBROSE. 1874-1944.
The Counterstroke. Ward, 1906; Fenno, 1907
The Great "Push" Experiment. Richards, 1902
-Her Assigned Husband. Simpkin, 1916
King of the Rocks. Hutchinson, 1900
The Leather Mask. Ward, 1907
The Living Mummy. Ward, 1910; Stokes, 1910
-Vigorous Daunt, Billionaire. Ward, 1905; Fenno, 1908

PRATT, CORNELIA ATWOOD. See: RICHARD SLEE.

PRATT, ELEANOR BLAKE ATKINSON COX. 1899-   . Pseudonym: Eleanor Blake, q.v.

PRATT, (MURRAY) FLETCHER. 1897-1956.
The Cunning Mulatto and Other Cases of Ellis Parker, American Detective. Smith & Haas, 1935. British title: Detective No. 1. Methuen, 1936 ss

PRATT, GRACE TYLER
The Bainbridge Mystery. Sherman, 1911

PRATT, THEODORE. 1901-1969. Pseudonym: Timothy Brace, q.v.

PRAVIEL, ARMAND. 1875-   .
The Murder of Monsieur Fualdes. Collins, 1923; Seltzer, 1924. (Translation of L'Assassinat de Monsieur Fualdes. Paris, 1922.)

PRAY, PAUL. Pseudonym of Richard Hill Wilkinson, 1904-   , q.v. Other pseudonyms: Eugene Hayford, E. Harrison Ott, qq.v.
The Ghost in the Belfry. Drama Guild, 1941. (3-act play.)

PREBBLE, MARJORIE MARY CURTIS. 1921-   .
Pseudonym: Marjorie Curtis, q.v.

PREEDY, GEORGE R. Pseudonym of Gabrielle Margaret Vere Campbell Long, 1886-1952. Other pseudonyms: Marjorie Bowen, Joseph Shearing, qq.v., Margaret Campbell.
-Beneath the Passion Flower. McBride, 1932. (British title?)
-Black Man—White Maiden. Hodder, 1941
The Devil Snard. Benn, 1932
-Dove in the Mulberry Tree. Jenkins, 1939
-Dr. Chaos and the Devil Snard. Cassell, 1933
The Fair Young Widow. Jenkins, 1939
-Findernes' Flowers. Hodder, 1941

-The Fourth Chamber. Hodder, 1944
-General Crack. Lane, 1928
-Julia Ballantyne. Hodder, 1952
-Lady in a Veil. Hodder, 1943
-Laurell'd Captains. Hutchinson, 1935
-Lyndley Waters. Hodder, 1942
 My Tattered Loving. Jenkins, 1937
-Nightcap and Plume. Hodder, 1945
-No Way Home. Hodder, 1947
 Painted Angel. Jenkins, 1938
-The Pavilion of Honour. Lane, 1932
 The Poisoners. Hutchinson, 1936
-Primula. Hodder, 1940
 The Prince's Darling; see The Rocklitz
-The Rocklitz. Lane, 1930. U.S. title: The Prince's Darling. Dodd, 1930
-The Sacked City. Hodder, 1949
-Tumult in the North. Lane, 1931; Dodd, 1931
-Violante. Cassell, 1932

PRENTIS, JOHN H(ARCOURT). 1878- .
 The Case of Doctor Horace. Baker, 1907

PRESCOT, JULIAN. Pseudonym of John Budd. Series character: Julian Prescot, in all titles.
 Both Sides of the Case. Barker, 1958
 The Case Continued. Barker, 1959
 Case for Court. Barker, 1964
 Case for Hearing. Barker, 1963
 Case for the Accused. Barker, 1961
 Case for Trial. Barker, 1962
 Case Proceeding. Barker, 1960
 The Case Re-Opened. Barker, 1965
 The Krakatao Cult. Barker, 1966

PRESCOTT, H(ILDA) F(RANCES) M(ARGARET). 1896- .
 Dead and Not Buried. Constable, 1938; Dodd, 1938

PRESCOTT, S. C.
 The Amber Gods. Ticknor, 1863 ss
 The Bauer Murder; or, The Last of his Race. Elliott, 1863

PRESNELL, FRANK G. 1906- . Series characters: John and Anne Webb = W.
 No Mourners Present. Morrow, 1940; Nicholson, 1943 W
 Send Another Coffin. Morrow, 1939; Heinemann, 1939 W
 Too Hot to Handle. Mill, 1951

PRESS, SYLVIA
-The Care of Devils. Beacon, 1958; Constable, 1958

PREST, THOMAS PECKET. 1810-1879. Many of the following were published anonymously and without dates. The publisher in most instances was Edward Lloyd.
 Adventures by Night. 1846
 Agnes the Unknown; or, The Beggar's Secret. 1849
 Almira's Curse; or, The Black Tower of Bransdorf. 1842
 Angelina; or, The Mystery of St. Mark's Abbey. 1841
 The Apparition. 1846
 The Black Mantle; or, The Murder at the Old Ferry. 1851
 The Black Monk; or, The Secret of the Grey Turret. 1844
 Blanche Heriot; or, The Chertsey Curfew. 1851
 Blanche; or, The Mystery of the Doomed House. 1847
 The Blighted Heart; or, The Murder in the Old Priory Ruins. 1851
 The Brigand; or, The Mountain Chief. 1851
 The Child of Two Fathers; or, The Mysteries of the Days of Old. 1848
 The Convict. 1846
 Crime; or, The Gamester's Daughter. 1843?
 The Death Grasp; or, A Father's Curse. 1842
 The Death Ship; or, The Pirate's Bride and the Maniac of the Deep. 1846
 The Divorce; or, The Mystery of the Wreck. 1847
 Don Caesar de Bazan. 1845
 Ela the Outcast; or, The Gipsy of Rosemary Dell. 1841
 Emily Fitzormond. 1841
 Emily Percy. 1842
 Ernestine de Lacy; or, The Robber's Foundling. 1842
 Ethelinde; or, The Fatal Vow. 1848
 Evelina, the Pauper's Child; or, Poverty, Crime and Sorrow. 1851
 Fatherless Fanny; or, The Mysterious Orphan. 1841
 The First False Step; or, The Path of Crime. 1846
 Gallant Tom. 1841
 Geraldine; or, The Secret Assassins of the Old Stone Cross. 1844
 Gertrude of the Rock. 1842
 The Gipsy Boy. 1847
 Grace Walter. 1853
 The Hebrew Maiden; or, The Lost Diamond. 1841
 The Harvest Home. 1852
 Jack Junk; or, The Tar for all Weathers. 1851
 Jane Shore; or, London in the Reign of Edward the Fourth. 1846
 Jonathan Bradford; or, The Murder at the Roadside Inn. 1846
 Kathleen; or, The Secret Marriage. 1842
 The Lone Cottage; or, Who's the Stranger? 1845
 The Love Child. 1847
 The Maniac Father; or, The Victim of Seduction.
 Manuscripts from the Diary of a Physician. Two Series. 1844
 Mariette; or, The Forger's Wife and the Child of Destiny. 1845
 Martha Willis; or, The Maid, the Profligate, and the Felon. 1844
 Mary Clifford; or, The Foundling Apprentice Girl. 1841
 May Grayson; or, Love and Treachery. 1842
 Mazeppa; or, The Wild Horse of the Ukraine. 1850
 The Miller and his Men; or, The Secret Robbers of Bohemia. 1852
 The Miller's Maid. 1847
 The Miser of Shoreditch; or, The Curse of Avarice. 1849
 My Poll and My Partner Joe. 1849
 Newgate. 1847
 The Old House of West Street; or, London in the Last Century. 1846
 Paul Clifford. 1844
 Pedlar's Acre; or, The Murderess of Seven Husbands. 1848
 Phoebe, the Miller's Daughter. 1842
 Ranger of the Tomb; or, The Gipsy's Prophecy. 1847
 Retribution; or, The Murder at the Old Dyke. 1849
 Richard Parker; or, The Mutiny at the Nore. 1851
 The Rivals; or, The Spectre at the Hall. 1847
 Rosalie; or, The Vagrant's Daughter. 1848
 The Royal Twins; or, The Sisters of Mystery. 1848
 Sawney Bean, the Man Eater of Midlothian. 1851
 Schamyl, the Sultan, Warrior and Prophet of the Caucasus. 1854
 The Skeleton's Clutch; or, The Goblet of Gore. 1842
 The String of Pearls; or, The Sailor's Gift. 1849
 Theresa; or, The Orphan of Geneva. 1844
 Varney the Vampire; or, The Feast of Blood. 1847; Dover, 1972
 Vice and Its Victim; or, Phoebe, the Peasant's Daughter. 1854
 Widow Mortimer; or, The Marriage in the Dark. 1850
 The Wife's Dream; or, A Profligate's Lesson. 1843?

PRESTON, ELLIOTT
-An American Venus. Drane, 1900

PRESTON, JACK. Pseudonym of John Preston Buschlen, 1888- .
 Heil! Hollywood. Reilly, 1939

PRESTON, JAMES. 1913- . Series character: Det. Sgt. Bob Christie, in at least those marked BC.
 Axes of Hate. Long, 1963 BC
 Breakdown. Long, 1965
 Bushfire. Long, 1969
 Crashout. Long, 1968
 Death Takes Revenge. Long, 1970
 The Empty Years. Cresset, 1962
 Gaol in Conflict. Long, 1966
 The Killer Came Riding. Long, 1963
 Murder at Sundown. Long, 1968
 Power Failure. Long, 1971
 Prison Feud. Long, 1962
 Racing Axes. Long, 1966
 Shattered Steel. Long, 1964 BC
 Valley of No Escape. Long, 1961

PRESTON, T. See: JACK GRATUS.

PRICE, ANTHONY. 1928- . Series character: Dr. David Audley, in all titles.
 The Alamut Ambush. Gollancz, 1971; Doubleday, 1972
 Colonel Butler's Wolf. Gollancz, 1972; Doubleday, 1973
 The Labyrinth Makers. Gollancz, 1970; Doubleday, 1971
 October Men. Gollancz, 1973; Doubleday, 1974
 Other Paths to Glory. Gollancz, 1974; Doubleday, 1975
 Our Man in Camelot. Gollancz, 1975; Doubleday, 1976

PRICE, EVADNE. Pseudonym of Helen Zenna Smith, 1896- .
 Diary of a Red-Haired Girl. Long, 1932
 The Haunted Light. Long, 1933
 Once a Crook, with Kenneth Attiwell. French, 1943. (A 3-act play.)
-The Phantom Light. French, 1949. (A play.)
-Probationer! Hurst, 1934
 Red for Danger! Long, 1936

PRICE, FRANK J(OHN), JR.
 Mind Wreckers, Limited, and Other Adventures of Barrow—Ace Insurance Detective. Spectator, 1933 ss

PRICE, J. L. See: ARTHUR W(ILLIAM) UPFIELD, 1888-1964.

PRICE, WESLEY
 Death is a Stowaway. Godwin, 1933; Wright, 1935

PRICHARD, (VERNON) HESKETH. 1876-1922. See also: K(ATHERINE O'BRIEN) PRICHARD.

November Joe, the Detective of the Woods. Hodder, 1913; Houghton, 1913 ss

PRICHARD, K(ATHERINE O'BRIEN) and (VERNON) HESKETH PRICHARD, 1876-1922, q.v. Series character: Don Q = Q.
The Cahusac Mystery. Heinemann, 1912; Sturgis, 1912
The Chronicles of Don Q. Chapman, 1904; Lippincott, 1904 ss Q
Don Q in the Sierra; see The New Chronicles of Don Q
Don Q's Love Story. Greening, 1909; Grosset, 1925 Q
Ghosts. Pearson, 1899 ss
-Karadac, Count of Gerzy. Constable, 1901; Stokes, 1901
-A Modern Mercenary. Smith Elder, 1899; Doubleday, 1899
The New Chronicles of Don Q. Unwin, 1906. U.S. title: Don Q in the Sierra. Lippincott, 1906 ss Q
-Roving Hearts. Smith Elder, 1903 ss

PRICKETT, (ALEXANDER THOMAS) STEPHEN. 1939- .
Do It Yourself Doom. Gollancz, 1962

PRIDHAM, SYLVIA SANDYS
Case of the Poisoned Pup. Arcadia, 1961

PRIESTLEY, CLIVE RYLAND. 1892- . Pseudonym: Clive Ryland, q.v.

PRIESTLEY, J(OHN) B(OYNTON). 1894- .
See also: RUTH HOLLAND.
Benighted. Heinemann, 1927. U.S. title: The Old Dark House. Harper, 1928
Black-Out in Gretley. Heinemann, 1942; Harper, 1942
Bright Shadow. French (London), 1950. (3-act play.)
Dangerous Corner. Heinemann, 1932. (3-act play.)
The Doomsday Men. Heinemann, 1938; Harper, 1938
I'll Tell You Everything, with Gerald (William) Bullett, 1894-1958, q.v. Heinemann, 1933; Macmillan, 1932
An Inspector Calls. Heinemann, 1947; Dramatists Play Service, 1948. (3-act play.)
Mystery at Greenfingers. French (London), 1937. (Play.)
The Old Dark House; see Benighted
Salt is Leaving. Pan, 1966; Harper, 1975
Saturn Over the Water. Heinemann, 1961; Doubleday, 1961
The Shapes of Sleep. Heinemann, 1962; Doubleday, 1962

PRIESTLEY, LEE (SHORE). 1904- .
Murder Takes the Baths. Arcadia, 1952

PRINCE, PETER. 1942- .
Dogcatcher. Gollancz, 1974

PRIOR, ALLAN. 1922- .
-The Contract. Cassell, 1970; Simon, 1971
-A Flame in the Air. Joseph, 1951
The Interrogators. Cassell, 1965; Simon, 1965
-The Joy Ride. Joseph, 1952
-The Loving Cup. Cassell, 1968; Simon, 1969
One Away. Eyre, 1961
The Operators. Cassell, 1966; Simon, 1967
Paradiso. Cassell, 1972; Simon, 1973
Z Cars Again. Trust Books, 1963. (Novelization of the TV series.)

PRITCHARD, JOHN LAURENCE. 1885- .
Pseudonym: John Laurence, q.v.

PRITCHETT, ARIADNE
Ghosts of Kings. GM, 1972
Karamour. GM, 1968
Legacy of Evil. GM, 1973
Mill Reef Hall. GM, 1968

PRIWIN, H(ANS) W(OLFGANG)
Inspector Hornleigh Investigates. Hodder, 1939

PROCTER, ARTHUR (WYMAN). 1889-1961.
Murder in Manhattan. Morrow, 1930

PROCTER, MAURICE. 1906-1973. Series characters: Insp. Martineau, in at least those marked M; Supt. Philip Hunter, in at least those marked PH.
A Body to Spare. Hutchinson, 1962; Harper, 1962 M
The Chief Inspector's Statement. Hutchinson, 1951. U.S. title: The Pennycross Murders. Harper, 1953 PH
Death has a Shadow. Hutchinson, 1965. U.S. title: Homicide Blonde. Harper, 1965 M
Devil in Moonlight. Hutchinson, 1962
The Devil was Handsome. Hutchinson, 1961; Harper, 1961 M
Devil's Due. Hutchinson, 1960; Harper, 1960 M
The Dog Man. Hutchinson, 1969
Each Man's Destiny. Longmans, 1947
The End of the Street. Longmans, 1949
Exercise Hoodwink. Hutchinson, 1967; Harper, 1967 M
The Graveyard Rolls; see Moonlight Flitting
Hell is a City. Hutchinson, 1954. U.S. title: Somewhere in This City. Harper, 1954. Also published as: Murder, Somewhere in This City. Avon, 1956 M
Hideaway. Hutchinson, 1968; Harper, 1968 M
His Weight in Gold. Hutchinson, 1966; Harper, 1966 M
Homicide Blonde; see Death has a Shadow
Hurry the Darkness. Hutchinson, 1952; Harper, 1951
I Will Speak Daggers. Hutchinson, 1956. U.S. title: The Ripper. Harper, 1956. Also published as: The Ripper Murders. Avon, 1957 PH
Killer at Large. Hutchinson, 1959; Harper, 1959 M
Man in Ambush. Hutchinson, 1958; Harper, 1959 M
The Midnight Plumber. Hutchinson, 1957; Harper, 1958 M
Moonlight Flitting. Hutchinson, 1963. U.S. title: The Graveyard Rolls. Harper, 1964 M
Murder, Somewhere in This City; see Hell is a City
No Proud Chivalry. Longmans, 1947
The Pennycross Murders; see The Chief Inspector's Statement
The Pub Crawler. Hutchinson, 1956; Harper, 1957
Rich is the Treasure. Hutchinson, 1952
The Ripper; see I Will Speak Daggers
The Ripper Murders; see I Will Speak Daggers
Rogue Running. Hutchinson, 1967; Harper, 1966 M
Somewhere in This City; see Hell is a City
The Spearhead Death. Hutchinson, 1960
Three at the Angel. Hutchinson, 1958; Harper, 1958
Two Men in Twenty. Hutchinson, 1964; Harper, 1964 M

PROCTOR, FRED J.
Timothy Twill's Secret. Tarstow, 1891

PROKOSCH, FREDERIC. 1908- .
The Conspirators. Harper, 1943; Chatto, 1943
A Tale for Midnight. Little, 1955; Secker, 1956

PRONZINI, BILL. 1943- . Pseudonyms: Jack Foxx, Alex Saxon, qq.v. Series character: unnamed private eye = PE.
Panic! Random, 1972; Hale, 1974
The Snatch. Random, 1971; Hale, 1974 PE
Snowbound. Putnam, 1974; Weidenfeld, 1975
The Stalker. Random, 1971; Hale, 1974
Undercurrent. Random, 1973; Hale, 1975 PE
The Vanished. Random, 1973; Hale, 1974 PE

PROPPER, MILTON (MORRIS). 1906-1962. Series character: Tommy Rankin, in all titles.
And Then Silence; see The Boudoir Murder
The Blood Transfusion Murders. Harper, 1943. British title: Murders in Sequence. Jenkins, 1947
The Boudoir Murder. Harper, 1931. British title: And Then Silence. Faber, 1931
The Case of the Cheating Bride. Harper, 1938; Harrap, 1939
The Divorce Court Murder. Harper, 1934; Faber, 1934
The Election Booth Murder. Harper, 1935. British title: Murder at the Polls. Harrap, 1936
The Family Burial Murders. Harper, 1934; Harrap, 1935
The Great Insurance Murders. Harper, 1937; Harrap, 1938
The Handwriting on the Wall. Harper, 1941. British title: You Can't Gag the Dead. Jenkins, 1949
Hide the Body! Harper, 1939; Harrap, 1940
Murder at the Polls; see The Election Booth Murder
Murder of an Initiate; see The Student Fraternity Murder
Murders in Sequence; see The Blood Transfusion Murders
One Murdered, Two Dead. Harper, 1936; Harrap, 1937
The Station Wagon Murder. Harper, 1940
The Strange Disappearance of Mary Young. Harper, 1929; Harrap, 1929
The Student Fraternity Murder. Bobbs, 1932. British title: Murder of an Initiate. Faber, 1933
The Ticker-Tape Murder. Harper, 1930; Faber, 1930
You Can't Gag the Dead; see The Handwriting on the Wall

PROSPER, JOHN. Joint pseudonym of John Chipman Farrar, 1896-1974, and Prosper Buranelli, 1890-1960, q.v.
Gold-Killer. Doran, 1922

PROUDFOOT, WALTER. Pseudonym of John (George) Hazlette Vahey, 1881- , q.v. Other pseudonyms: Henrietta Clandon, John Haslette, Anthony Lang, Vernon Loder, John Mowbray, qq.v. Series character: Inspector Bill Vallance, in at least those marked BV.
Arrest. Hutchinson, 1933 BV
Conspiracy. Hutchinson, 1933 BV
Crime in the Arcade. Hutchinson, 1931
The Trail of the Ruby. Hutchinson, 1932

PROUT, GEOFFREY. 1894- .
The Mystery of the Marshes. Lloyd's, 1923

PRUITT, ALAN. Pseudonym of Alvin Emanuel Rose. Series character: Don Carson, in both titles.
The Restless Corpse. Ziff-Davis, 1947
Typed for a Corpse. Handi-Books, 1951

PRYCE, LARRY
Black Gunn. Tandem, 1974

PRYCE, RICHARD. 1864-1942.
-The Quiet Mrs. Fleming. Methuen, 1891

PRYCE-JONES, DAVID. 1936-   .
The England Commune. Quartet, 1975

PRYDE, ANTHONY and R(OSE) K(IRKPATRICK) WEEKES, 1874-   , q.v. Anthony Pryde is the pseudonym of A(gnes) R(ussell) Weekes, q.v.
The Purple Pearl. Allen, 1923; Dodd, 1922

PUCCETTI, ROLAND
The Death of the Fuhrer. Hutchinson, 1972; St. Martin's, 1972
The Trial of John and Henry Norton. Hutchinson, 1973

PUDNEY, JOHN (SLEIGH). 1909-1977.
-The Accomplice. Bodley Head, 1950
Hero of a Summer's Day. Lane, 1951
The Net. Joseph, 1952
-A Ring for Luck. Joseph, 1953
Thin Air. Joseph, 1961
-Trespass in the Sun. Joseph, 1957

PUGH, EDWIN (WILLIAM), 1874-1930, and CHARLES GLEIG, 1862-   , q.v.
The Rogues' Paradise. Bowden, 1898

PUGH, MARSHALL
A Dream of Treason. Deutsch, 1974; Coward, 1974
Last Place Left. Deutsch, 1969; Harper, 1969
A Murmur of Mutiny. Deutsch, 1972; Harper, 1972

PUISSESSEAU, RENE
Someone Will Die Tonight in the Caribbean. Knopf, 1958; Allen, 1959. (Translation of Quelqu'un Mourra ce Soir aux Caraibes. Paris, 1957.)

PULLEIN-THOMPSON, JOANNA MAXWELL CANNAN. 1898-   . Pseudonym: Joanna Cannan, q.v.

PULLEIN-THOMPSON, JOSEPHINE (MARY WEDDERBURN). Series character: Insp. James Flecker, in all titles.
Gin and Murder. Hammond, 1959
Murder Strikes Pink. Hammond, 1963
They Died in the Spring. Hammond, 1960

PULSFORD, NORMAN GEORGE. 1902-   . Pseudonym: A. C. Trevor, q.v.

PUNNETT, IVOR MACAULAY. Joint pseudonym with Margaret Punnett, 1932-   : Roger Simons, q.v.

PUNNETT, MARGARET. 1932-   . Joint pseudonym with Ivor Macaulay Punnett: Roger Simons, q.v.

PUNSHON, E(RNEST) R(OBERTSON). 1872-   . Series characters: Carter & Bell = C&B; Bobby Owen = BO.
Arrows of Chance. Ward, 1917
The Attending Truth. Gollancz, 1952 C&B
The Bath Mysteries. Gollancz, 1936; Hillman-Curl, 1938 BO
The Bittermeads Mystery. Knopf, 1922
The Blue John Diamond. Cherry Tree (abridged), 1946; Clode, 1929
Brought to Light. Gollancz, 1954 BO
Comes a Stranger. Gollancz, 1938 BO
The Conqueror Inn. Gollancz, 1943; Macmillan, 1944 BO
The Cottage Murder. Benn, 1931; Houghton, 1932 C&B
The Crossword Murder; see Crossword Mystery
Crossword Mystery. Gollancz, 1934. U.S. title: The Crossword Murder. Knopf, 1934 BO
The Dark Garden. Gollancz, 1941 BO
Dark is the Clue. Gollancz, 1955 BO
Death Among the Sunbathers. Benn, 1934 BO
Death Comes to Cambers. Gollancz, 1935 BO
Death in the Chalkpit. Mystery Novel of the Month, 194? (British title?)
Death of a Beauty Queen. Gollancz, 1935 BO
Death of a Tyrant; see Dictator's Way
Diabolic Candelabra. Gollancz, 1942 BO
Dictator's Way. Gollancz, 1938. U.S. title: Death of a Tyrant. Hillman-Curl, 1938 BO
Dunslow. Ward, 1922
The Dusky Hour. Gollancz, 1937; Hillman-Curl, 1938 BO
Everybody Always Tells. Gollancz, 1950 BO
Four Strange Women. Gollancz, 1940 BO
Genius in Murder. Benn, 1932; Houghton, 1933 C&B
The Glittering Desire. Ward, 1910
The Golden Dagger. Gollancz, 1951 BO
Helen Passes By. Gollancz, 1947 BO
Hidden Lives. Ward, 1913
The House of Godwinsson. Gollancz, 1948 BO
Information Received. Benn, 1933; Houghton, 1934 BO
It Might Lead Anywhere. Gollancz, 1946; Macmillan, 1947 BO
Murder Abroad. Gollancz, 1939 BO
Music Tells All. Gollancz, 1948 BO
The Mystery of Lady Isobel. Hurst, 1907
Mystery of Mr. Jessop. Gollancz, 1937; Hillman-Curl, 1937 BO
Mystery Villa. Gollancz, 1934 BO
Night's Cloak. Gollancz, 1944; Macmillan, 1944 BO
Proof, Counter Proof. Benn, 1931 C&B
The Secret Search. Gollancz, 1951 BO
Secrets Can't Be Kept. Gollancz, 1944; Macmillan, 1946 BO
Six were Present. Gollancz, 1956 BO
So Many Doors. Gollancz, 1949; Macmillan, 1950 BO
The Solitary House. Ward, 1919; Knopf, 1918
The Spin of the Coin. Hurst, 1908
Strange Ending. Gollancz, 1953 BO
Suspects—Nine. Gollancz, 1939 BO
Ten Star Clues. Gollancz, 1941 BO
There's a Reason for Everything. Gollancz, 1945; Macmillan, 1946 BO
Triple Quest. Gollancz, 1955
Truth Came Out. Benn, 1932; Houghton, 1934 C&B
The Unexpected Legacy. Benn, 1929 C&B
The Woman's Footprint. Hodder, 1919

PURCELL, MARY. 1906-   .
The Pilgrim Came Late. Clanmore, 1947

PURDY, CLAIRE LEE. See: BENSON WHEELER.

PURDY, JENNIE BOUTON. Pseudonym: Shubael, q.v.

PURLEY, JOHN. Pseudonym of Reginald George Thomas, 1899-   . Series character (with many other authors): Sexton Blake.
The Mansion on the Moor. Amalgamated, 1943

PURSER, PHILIP. 1925-   .
Four Days to the Fireworks. Hodder, 1964; Walker, 1965
Holy Father's Navy. Hodder, 1971
Night of Glass. Hodder, 1968
Peregrination 22. Cape, 1962
The Twentymen. Hodder, 1967; Walker, 1967

PURTELL, JOSEPH
The Tiffany Caper. Coward, 1974; Cassell, 1975
To a Blindfold Lady. Reynal, 1942

PUTNAM, FRANK
The Raid on the Mint. Street, ca.1900

PUTNAM, XENO
Crystal Tower. Shores, 1917

PUZEY, F. G.
Cupid Among the Clues. Hartley, 1931

PUZO, MARIO. 1920-   . Pseudonym: Mario Cleri, q.v.
The Godfather. Putnam, 1969; Heinemann, 1969

PYKE, RIVINGTON
The Fellow Passengers. Greening, 1898
The Man Who Disappeared. Bentley, 1896

Q

"Q". Pseudonym of Sir Arthur T(homas) Quiller-Couch, 1863-1944, q.v.
Dead Man's Rock. Cassell (London & New York), 1887
I Saw Three Ships, and other winter's tales. Cassell (London & New York), 1892 ss

Q, JOHN. Pseudonym of (Everette) Howard Hunt, 1918-   , q.v. Other pseudonyms: Gordon Davis, Robert Dietrich, David St. John, qq.v. At least some of the titles below were reprinted as by John Quirk. Series character: Peter Trees, in all titles.
The Bunnies. Avon, 1965
The Survivor. Avon, 1965
The Tournament. Signet, 1966

QUARRY, NICK. Pseudonym of Marvin (H.) Albert, q.v. Other pseudonym: Anthony Rome, q.v. Series character: Jake Barrow = JB.
The Don is Dead. GM, 1972; Coronet, 1972
The Girl with No Place to Hide. GM, 1959; Muller pb, 1961 JB
The Hoods Come Calling. GM, 1958; Fawcett (London), 1959 JB
No Chance in Hell. GM, 1960; Muller pb, 1962 JB
Some Die Hard. GM, 1961; Muller pb, 1963 JB
Till It Hurts. GM, 1960; Muller pb, 1962 JB
Trail of a Tramp. GM, 1958; Muller pb, 1960 JB
The Vendetta. GM, 1973

QUARTERMAIN, H. J.
Death Before Launching. H. Hamilton, 1964

QUARTERMAIN, JAMES. Pseudonym. Series character: Carbo, in all titles.
The Diamond Hook. Constable, 1970; Doubleday, 1970
The Diamond Hostage. Constable, 1975
The Man Who Walked on Diamonds. Constable, 1971; Doubleday, 1972
Rock of Diamond. Constable, 1972; Doubleday, 1972

QUEEN, ELLERY. Joint pseudonym of Frederic Dannay, 1905- , and Manfred Bennington Lee, 1905-1971. Other joint pseudonym: Barnaby Ross, q.v. Series characters: Ellery and Inspector Richard Queen = Q (see also: next entry).
The Adventures of Ellery Queen. Stokes, 1934; Gollancz, 1935 ss Q
The American Gun Mystery. Stokes, 1933; Gollancz, 1933. Also published as: Death at the Rodeo. Mercury, 1951 Q
And On the Eighth Day. Random, 1964; Gollancz, 1964 Q
Calamity Town. Little, 1942; Gollancz, 1942 Q
Calendar of Crime. Little, 1952; Gollancz, 1952 ss Q
The Case Book of Ellery Queen. Bestseller, 1945. (A paperback collection of ss reprinted from The Adventures, and The New Adventures, qq.v., along with three Queen radio plays uncollected elsewhere.) ss Q
The Case of the Seven Murders; see Double, Double
Cat of Many Tails. Little, 1949; Gollancz, 1949 Q
The Chinese Orange Mystery. Stokes, 1934; Gollancz, 1934 Q
Cop Out. World, 1969; Gollancz, 1969
Death at the Rodeo; see The American Gun Mystery
The Devil to Pay. Stokes, 1938; Gollancz, 1938 Q
The Door Between. Stokes, 1937; Gollancz, 1937 Q
Double, Double. Little, 1950; Gollancz, 1950. Also published as: The Case of the Seven Murders. PB, 1958 Q
The Dragon's Teeth. Stokes, 1939; Gollancz, 1939. Also published as: The Virgin Heiresses. PB, 1954 Q
The Dutch Shoe Mystery. Stokes, 1931; Gollancz, 1931 Q
The Egyptian Cross Mystery. Stokes, 1932; Gollancz, 1932 Q
Face to Face. New American Library, 1967; Gollancz, 1967 Q
A Fine and Private Place. World, 1971; Gollancz, 1971 Q
The Finishing Stroke. Simon, 1958; Gollancz, 1958 Q
The Four of Hearts. Stokes, 1938; Gollancz, 1939 Q
The Fourth Side of the Triangle. Random, 1965; Gollancz, 1965 Q
The French Powder Mystery. Stokes, 1930; Gollancz, 1930 Q
The Glass Village. Little, 1954; Gollancz, 1954
The Greek Coffin Mystery. Stokes, 1932; Gollancz, 1932 Q
Halfway House. Stokes, 1936; Gollancz, 1936 Q
The House of Brass. New American Library, 1968; Gollancz, 1968 Q
Inspector Queen's Own Case. Simon, 1956; Gollancz, 1956 Q
The King is Dead. Little, 1952; Gollancz, 1952
The Lamp of God. Dell 10¢ pb, 1951. (A novelet originally appearing in The New Adventures of Ellery Queen, q.v.)
The Last Woman in His Life. World, 1970; Gollancz, 1970 Q
More Adventures of Ellery Queen. Bestseller, 1940. (A paperback collection of ss reprinted from The Adventures, and The New Adventures, qq.v.) ss Q
The Murderer is a Fox. Little, 1945; Gollancz, 1945 Q
The New Adventures of Ellery Queen. Stokes, 1940; Gollancz, 1940 ss Q
The Origin of Evil. Little, 1951; Gollancz, 1951 Q

The Player on the Other Side. Random, 1963; Gollancz, 1963 Q
QBI: Queen's Bureau of Investigation. Little, 1954; Gollancz, 1955 ss Q
QED: Queen's Experiments in Detection. New American Library, 1968; Gollancz, 1969 ss Q
Queens Full. Random, 1965; Gollancz, 1966 ss Q
The Quick and the Dead; see There was an Old Woman
The Roman Hat Mystery. Stokes, 1929; Gollancz, 1929 Q
The Scarlet Letters. Little, 1953; Gollancz, 1953 Q
Sherlock Holmes vs. Jack the Ripper; see A Study in Terror
The Siamese Twin Mystery. Stokes, 1933; Gollancz, 1934 Q
The Spanish Cape Mystery. Stokes, 1935; Gollancz, 1935 Q
A Study in Terror. Lancer, 1966. British title: Sherlock Holmes vs. Jack the Ripper. Gollancz, 1967. (Novelization of the movie, with Ellery added as a character in the "framing story".) Q
Ten Days' Wonder. Little, 1948; Gollancz, 1948 Q
There was an Old Woman. Little, 1943; Gollancz, 1944. Also published as: The Quick and the Dead. PB, 1956 Q
The Virgin Heiresses; see The Dragon's Teeth

QUEEN, ELLERY. Pseudonym. Series characters: Tim Corrigan = TC; Mike McCall = MM; Ellery Queen = EQ (see also: previous entry). See also: WILLIAM RAND.
Beware the Young Stranger. PB, 1965
The Black Hearts Murder. Lancer, 1970 MM
Blow Hot, Blow Cold. PB, 1964
The Blue Movie Murders. Lancer, 1972; Gollancz, 1973 MM
The Campus Murders. Lancer, 1969 MM
The Copper Frame. PB, 1965; Four Square, 1968
Dead Man's Tale. PB, 1961; Four Square, 1967
Death Spins the Platter. PB, 1962; Gollancz, 1975
The Devil's Cook. PB, 1966
Ellery Queen, Master Detective. Grosset, 1941. Also published as: The Vanishing Corpse. Pyramid, 1968. (Novelization of the movie.) EQ
The Four Johns. PB, 1964. British title: Four Men Called John. Gollancz, 1964
Four Men Called John; see The Four Johns
The Golden Goose. PB, 1964; Four Square, 1967
Guess Who's Coming to Kill You? Lancer, 1968
How Goes the Murder? Popular Library, 1967 TC
Kill as Directed. PB, 1963
The Killer Touch. PB, 1965
Kiss and Kill. Dell, 1969
The Last Man Club. Whitman, 1940. ("Novelettization" of the radio play.) EQ
The Last Man Club. Pyramid, 1968. (Reprint edition combining the earlier "novelettizations" The Last Man Club and The Murdered Millionaire, qq.v.)
The Last Score. PB, 1964
Losers, Weepers. Dell, 1966
The Madman Theory. PB, 1966

Murder with a Past. PB, 1963
The Murdered Millionaire. Whitman, 1942. ("Novelettization" of the radio play.) EQ
The Penthouse Mystery. Grosset, 1941. (Novelization of the movie.) EQ
The Perfect Crime. Grosset, 1942. (Novelization of the movie.) EQ
A Room to Die In. PB, 1965
Shoot the Scene. Dell, 1966
The Vanishing Corpse; see Ellery Queen, Master Detective
What's in the Dark? Popular Library, 1968. British title: When Fell the Night. Gollancz, 1970 TC
When Fell the Night; see What's in the Dark?
Where is Bianca? Popular Library, 1966; Four Square, 1966 TC
Which Way to Die? Popular Library, 1967 TC
Who Spies, Who Kills? Popular Library, 1966; Four Square, 1967 TC
Why So Dead? Popular Library, 1966; Four Square, 1966 TC
Wife or Death. PB, 1963; Four Square, 1963

QUENTIN, DOROTHY
-The Cottage in the Woods. Ward, 1964
-Dangerous Affair. Ward, 1962
-The Dark Castle. Ward, 1963
-Duel Across the Water. Ward, 1966
-House of Illusion. Ward, 1966
-Perilous Voyage. Ward, 1964
-The Prisoner in the Square. Ward, 1961
-What News of Kitty? Ward, 1967

QUENTIN, PATRICK. Joint pseudonym of Hugh Callingham Wheeler, 1913- , and Richard Wilson Webb, 1901- . Other pseudonyms: Q. Patrick, Jonathan Stagge, qq.v. Series character: Peter Duluth = PD.
Black Widow. Simon, 1952. British title: Fatal Woman. Gollancz, 1953 PD
Family Skeletons. Random, 1965; Gollancz, 1965
Fatal Woman; see Black Widow
The Fate of the Immodest Blonde; see Puzzle for Pilgrims
The Follower. Simon, 1950; Gollancz, 1950
The Green-Eyed Monster. Random, 1960; Gollancz, 1960
Love is a Deadly Weapon; see Puzzle for Fiends
The Man in the Net. Simon, 1956; Gollancz, 1956
The Man with Two Wives. Simon, 1955; Gollancz, 1955
My Son, the Murderer. Simon, 1954. British title: The Wife of Ronald Sheldon. Gollancz, 1954 PD
The Ordeal of Mrs. Snow. Random, 1962; Gollancz, 1961 ss
Puzzle for Fiends. Simon, 1946; Gollancz, 1947. Also published as: Love is a Deadly Weapon. PB, 1949 PD
A Puzzle for Fools. Simon, 1936; Gollancz, 1936 PD
Puzzle for Pilgrims. Simon, 1947; Gollancz, 1948. Also published as: The Fate of the Immodest Blonde. PB, 1950 PD
Puzzle for Players. Simon, 1938; Gollancz, 1939 PD
Puzzle for Puppets. Simon, 1944; Gollancz, 1944 PD
Puzzle for Wantons. Simon, 1945; Gollancz, 1946. Also published as: Slay the Loose Ladies. PB, 1948 PD
Run to Death. Simon, 1948; Gollancz, 1948 PD

Shadow of Guilt. Random, 1959; Gollancz, 1959
Slay the Loose Ladies; see Puzzle for Wantons
Suspicious Circumstances. Simon, 1957; Gollancz, 1957
The Wife of Ronald Sheldon; see My Son, the Murderer

QUEST, RODNEY. 1897-   . Series character: Peter Quentin = PQ.
The Cerebus Murders. Harrap, 1969; McCall, 1970 PQ
Countdown to Doomsday. Harrap, 1966
Death of a Sinner. Harrap, 1971 PQ
The Fenton Affair. Harrap, 1967
Just Off Bond Street. Hutchinson, 1963
Murder with a Vengeance. Harrap, 1971 PQ
Secret Establishment. Hutchinson, 1961
The Venus of Samos. Hutchinson, 1962

QUICK, DOROTHY. 1900-   .
The Cry in the Night. Arcadia, 1957; Cherry Tree, 1950
The Doctor Looks at Murder. Arcadia, 1959
The Fifth Dagger. Scribner, 1947
Peril at Dune's Edge. Cherry Tree, 1945
Something Evil. Arcadia, 1958
Too Strange a Hand. Arcadia, 1959

QUIGLEY, AILEEN
The Brackenroyds Inheritance. Signet, 1975. Also published as by Erica Lindley: Signet, 1977

QUIGLEY, JOHN. 1927-   .
The Last Checkpoint. Collins, 1971; McCall, 1971
The Secret Soldier. Hutchinson, 1966; New American Library, 1966

QUILLER-COUCH, SIR ARTHUR T(HOMAS). 1863-1944. Pseudonym: "Q", q.v.
Castle Dor, with Daphne du Maurier, 1907-   , q.v. Dent, 1962; Doubleday, 1962
Foe-Farrell. Collins, 1918; Macmillan, 1918
Old Fires and Profitable Ghosts. Cassell, 1900; Scribner, 1900 ss
Poison Island. Smith, Elder, 1907; Scribner, 1906
Q's Mystery Stories. Dent, 1937 ss

QUILTY, RAFE
The Tenth Session. Cape, 1972

QUIN, ANN (MARIE). 1936-1973.
-Berg. Calder, 1964; Scribner, 1965

QUIN, B(ASIL) G(ODFREY). Series character: Clarkson-Parry, in at least those marked CP.
The Death Box. Hutchinson, 1929; Greenberg, 1932 CP
Mistigris. Hutchinson, 1932 CP
The Murder Rehearsal. Hutchinson, 1931; Greenberg, 1932 CP
The Mystery of the Black Gate. Hutchinson, 1930
The Phantom Murderer. Hutchinson, 1932

QUINCE, JAMES
Casual Slaughters. Nicholson, 1935
Notice to Quit. Hodder, 1932
The Tin Tree. Hodder, 1930

QUINN, E(LEANOR) BAKER. Series character: James Strange, in at least those marked JS.
The Dead Harm No One. Heinemann, 1938
Death is a Restless Sleeper. Heinemann, 1940; Mystery House, 1941 JS
One Man's Muddle. Heinemann, 1936; Macmillan, 1937 JS

QUINN, JAKE. Series character: Patrick Shannon, in both titles.
The Mindbenders. Leisure, 1975
Shallow Grave. Leisure, 1974

QUINN, OLGA
Spies Go Running. Hale, 1971
Spies on the Roof. Hale, 1969

QUINN, PATRICK
The Barbed-Wire Hurdlers. Hale, 1969
The Big Game. Hale, 1970
The Fatal Complaint. Hale, 1970
Once Upon a Private Eye. Hale, 1968
Thrice Upon a Killing Spree. Hale, 1970
Twice Upon a Crime. Hale, 1969

QUINN, SEABURY (GRANDIN). 1889-1969.
The Phantom-Fighter. Mycroft, 1966 ss

QUINN, SIMON. Pseudonym of Martin (Cruz) Smith, 1942-   , q.v. Series character: The Inquisitor, in at least those marked I.
The Devil in Kansas. Dell, 1974 I
His Eminence, Death. Dell, 1974 I
The Human Factor. Dell, 1975; Futura, 1975. (Novelization of the movie.)
Last Rites for the Vulture. Dell, 1975
The Last Time I Saw Hell. Dell, 1974 I
The Midas Coffin. Dell, 1975
Nuplex Red. Dell, 1974

QUINTANO, DOROTHY G.
Weekend at the Villa. Doubleday, 1974

QUIRK, JOHN. See: JOHN Q.

QUIRK, LESLIE (W.), 1882-   . See: HORATIO (GATES) WINSLOW, 1882-   .

QUIROULE, PIERRE. Pseudonym of W(alter) W(illiam) Sayer, 1892-   . Those titles listed below without publisher feature Sexton Blake and were published by Amalgamated Press. Note: Many Sexton Blake titles originally published as by W. W. Sayer were reprinted with new titles as by Pierre Quiroule; see the W. W. Sayer listing. See also: R. C. ARMOUR.
The Case of the Bismarck Memoirs. Mayflower, 1966. (Sexton Blake.)
The Circle of Death. Mellifont, 1936
The Golf Links Mystery. Mellifont, 1935
The Hated Eight. 1938
The Hour of Recognition. Mellifont, 1932
The Man with Two Souls. Amalgamated, 1935
The Mystery of the Missing Envoy. 1939
The Mystery of No. 7 Bitton Court. 1938
The Mystery of No. 13 Cavendish Square. 1936
The Painted Death. Nelson, 1935
The Riddle of the Evil Eye. 1939
The Riddle of the Ugly Face. 1939
The Secret of the Armaments King. 1935
Secret of the Circle. Mellifont, 1934
The Secret of the Woods. 1934
The Silhouette Symbol. Mellifont, 1935
The Slaver's Secret. 1934
The Three Lepers' Heads. 1937

RABE, PETER. Series characters: Daniel Port = DP; Manny DeWitt = MD.
Agreement to Kill. GM, 1957; Fawcett (London), 1958
Anatomy of a Killer. Abelard (New York & London), 1960
Benny Muscles In. GM, 1955; Fawcett (London), 1958
Black Mafia. GM, 1974
Blood on the Desert. GM, 1958; Muller pb, 1960
The Box. GM, 1962; Muller pb, 1963
Bring Me Another Corpse. GM, 1959; Muller pb, 1960 DP
Code Name Gadget. GM, 1967 MD
The Cut of the Whip. Ace, 1958
Dig My Grave Deep. GM, 1956; Fawcett (London), 1957
Girl in a Big Brass Bed. GM, 1965 MD
A House in Naples. GM, 1956; Fawcett (London), 1958
It's My Funeral. GM, 1957; Fawcett (London), 1959 DP
Journey into Terror. GM, 1957; Fawcett (London), 1959
Kill the Boss Good-By. GM, 1956; Fawcett (London), 1957
Mission for Vengeance. GM, 1958
Murder Me for Nickels. GM, 1960; Muller pb, 1961
My Lovely Executioner. GM, 1960; Jenkins, 1967
The Out is Death. GM, 1957; Fawcett (London), 1959 DP
A Shroud for Jesso. GM, 1955; Fawcett (London), 1956
The Spy Who was Three Feet Tall. GM, 1966 MD
Stop This Man! GM, 1955; Fawcett (London), 1957
Time Enough to Die. GM, 1959; Muller pb, 1961 DP
War of the Dons. GM, 1972; Coronet, 1973

RABON, WALTER
Spider on the Belly. Vantage, 1967

RABOU, CHARLES (FELIX HENRI). 1803-1870.
The Widow's Walk; or, The Mystery of Crime. Appleyard, 18??. (Translation of L'Allee des Veuves.)

RACE, PHILIP
Johnny Come Deadly. Hillman, 1961
Killer Take All. GM, 1959; Muller pb, 1961
Self-Made Widow. GM, 1958; Fawcett (London), 1960

RADANO, GENE
Stories Cops Only Tell Each Other. Stein, 1974 ss

RADCLIFFE, ANN (WARD). 1764-1823.
The Castles of Athlin and Dunbayne. Hookham, 1789; Bradford, 1796, as by Anne Rattcliffe
The Confessional of the Black Penitents; see The Italian
The Italian; or, The Confessional of the Black Penitents. Wogan, 1797; Magill, 1797. Also published as: The Confessional of the Black Penitents. Folio Society, 1956
The Mysteries of Udolpho. Wogan, 1794; White, 1795
The Romance of the Forest. Hookham, 1791; Etheridge, 1795
A Sicilian Romance. Hookham, 1790; Rice, 1795

RADCLIFFE, (HENRY) GARNETT. 1899-   .
The Flower Gang. Butterworth, 1929; Houghton, 1930
Forgotten of Allah. Butterworth, 1936
The Great Orme Terror. Butterworth, 1934
In the Grip of the Brute. Butterworth, 1937
The Prisoners in the Wall. Butterworth, 1933
-The Return of the Ceteosaurus, and other tales. Drane's, 1926 ss

The Sky Wolves. Butterworth, 1938
The Straight Road. Butterworth, 1935
The 13th Mummy. Butterworth, 1936
Top Floor Back. Macdonald, 1943

RADCLIFFE, JANETTE. Pseudonym of Janet
   Louis Roberts, 1925-   , q.v. Other
   pseudonyms: Louisa Bronte, Rebecca
   Danton, qq.v.
-The Blue-Eyed Gypsy. Dell, 1974
-The Gentleman Pirate. Dell, 1975
-The Moonlight Gondola. Dell, 1975

RADCLIFFE, JOCELYN
   Blackwood. Curtis, 1974

RADFORD, E(DWIN ISAAC), 1891-   , and
   M(ONA) A(UGUSTA MANGAN). Series char-
   acter: Doctor Manson, in at least
   those marked M.
A Cosy Little Murder. Hale, 1963 M
Crime Pays No Dividends. Melrose, 1945
   M
Dead Water. Hale, 1971 M
Death and the Professor. Hale, 1961
Death at the Chateau Noir. Hale, 1960 M
Death has Two Faces. Hale, 1972
Death of an Ancient Saxon. Hale, 1969 M
Death of a Frightened Editor. Hale,
   1959 M
Death of a "Gentleman". Hale, 1966 M
Death of a Peculiar Rabbit. Hale, 1969
   M
Death on the Broads. Long, 1957 M
Death Takes the Wheel. Hale, 1962 M
Death's Inheritance. Hale, 1961 M
From Information Received. Hale, 1962 M
The Greedy Killers. Hale, 1971 M
The Heel of Achilles. Melrose, 1950 M
The Hungry Killer. Hale, 1964 M
Inspector Manson's Success. Melrose,
   1944 M
It's Murder to Live. Melrose, 1947 M
John Kyleing Died. Melrose, 1949 M
Jones's Little Murders. Hale, 1967 M
Look In at Murder. Long, 1956 M
Married to Murder. Hale, 1959
Mask of Murder. Hale, 1965 M
The Middlefold Murders. Hale, 1967 M
Murder is Ruby Red. Hale, 1970
Murder Isn't Cricket. Melrose, 1946 M
Murder Jigsaw. Melrose, 1944 M
Murder Magnified. Hale, 1965 M
Murder of Three Ghosts. Hale, 1963 M
Murder on My Conscience. Hale, 1960 M
Murder Speaks. Hale, 1970 M
No Reason for Murder. Hale, 1967 M
The Safety First Murders. Hale, 1968 M
The Six Men. Hale, 1958
Trunk Call to Murder. Hale, 1968 M
Two Ways to Murder. Hale, 1969 M
Who Killed Dick Whittington? Melrose,
   1947 M

RADFORD, JOHN P. Series character: Joe
   Maguire, in all titles.
All of Our Aircraft are Missing. Can-
   yon, 1974
The Game Show Girls. Canyon, 1975
The Most Happy Con Man. Canyon, 1974
The Parisian Pigeon Drop. Canyon, 1974

RADFORD, M(ONA) A(UGUSTA MANGAN). See:
   RADFORD, E(DWIN ISAAC), 1891-   .

RADFORD, RUBY L(ORRAINE). 1891-   .
   Crime and Judy. Avalon, 1960

RAE, HUGH C(RAUFORD). 1935-   . Pseudo-
   nym: Robert Crawford, q.v.
A Few Small Bones. Blond, 1968. U.S.
   title: The House at Balnesmoor.
   Coward, 1969
The House at Balnesmoor; see A Few
   Small Bones
The Interview. Blond, 1969; Coward,
   1969

The Marksman. Constable, 1971; Coward,
   1971
Night Pillow. Blond, 1967; Viking, 1967
The Rock Harvest. Constable, 1973
The Rookery. Constable, 1974; St. Mar-
   tin's, 1975
The Saturday Epic. Blond, 1970; Coward,
   1970
The Shooting Gallery. Constable, 1972;
   Coward, 1972
Skinner. Blond, 1965; Viking, 1965

RAE-BROWN, CAMPBELL
   The Avenging Kiss. Digby, 1912
   The Devil's Shilling. Drane, 1897
   The Great Newmarket Mystery. Long, 1909
   -The Resurrection of His Grace. Green-
      ing, 1899
   -Very Long Odds and a Strange Finish.
      Routledge, 1893 ss

RAGG, THOMAS MURRAY. 1897-   . Pseudonym: Murray Thomas, q.v.

RAGOSTA, MILLIE J.
   Lorena Veiled. Ballantine, 1974
   Taverna in Terrazzo. Ballantine, 1975

RAGSDALE, LULAH
   The Crime of Philip Guthrie. Morrill,
      1892
   -A Shadow's Shadow. Lippincott, 1893

RAINE, RICHARD. Pseudonym of Raymond H.
   Sawkins, 1923-   , q.v. Other pseu-
   donyms: Jay Bernard, Colin Forbes,
   qq.v. Series character: David Mar-
   tini, in all titles.
Bombshell. Dent, 1970; Harcourt, 1970
The Corder Index; see A Wreath for
   America
Night of the Hawk. Heinemann, 1968;
   Harcourt, 1968
A Wreath for America. Heinemann, 1967.
   U.S. title: The Corder Index. Har-
   court, 1967

RAINE, WILLIAM MacLEOD. 1871-1954.
   Cry Murder. Phoenix, 1947. British
      title: Cry Murder in the Market
      Place. Hodder, 1941
   Cry Murder in the Market Place; see Cry
      Murder
   Tangled Trails. Houghton, 1921; Hodder,
      1921

RAINHAM, THOMAS
   Too Late to Mend. Hurst, 1957

RAINIER, PAUL J.
   Scared Stiff. Merit, 1954

RAISON, MILTON M(ICHAEL). 1903-   .
   Series character: Tony Woolrich = TW.
   The Gay Mortician. Murray, 1946;
      Archer, 1947 TW
   Murder in a Lighter Vein. Murray, 1947
      TW
   No Weeds for the Widow. Murray, 1946;
      Kelly, 1951 TW
   Nobody Loves a Dead Man. Murray, 1945;
      Archer, 1946 TW
   The Phantom of Forty-Second Street,
      with Jack Harvey. Macaulay, 1936 TW
   Tunnel 13. Murray, 1948

RALEIGH, ALAN. Pseudonym of Elijah Brown,
   1867-   .
   The Man in the Car. Long, 1913

RALEIGH, CECIL. Pseudonym of Cecil Rowlands, 1856-1914. See also: RICHARD
   PARKER.

The Sins of Society. Paul, 1909; Dillingham, 1910. (Novelization of the
   play by Cecil Raleigh and Henry Hamilton, 1853?-1918.)

RALEIGH, H(ILARY) M(ASON). 1893-   .
-The Chronicles of Slyme Court. Bles,
   1935
Excess Baggage. Methuen, 1932; Dutton,
   1932
The Machinations of Dr. Grue. Bles,
   1938
-The Merry Mug. Bles, 1936
-Royal Exchange. Methuen, 1932
-Sheikh Stuff. Bles, 1937

RALPH, JULIAN. 1853-1903.
   The Millionairess. Lothrop, 1902;
      Methuen, 1902

RALSTON, GILBERT A(LEXANDER). 1912-   .
   Series character: Dakota = D.
   Ben. Bantam, 1972. (Novelization of the
      movie.)
   Chain Reaction. Pinnacle, 1975 D
   Cat Trap. Pinnacle, 1974 D
   Dakota Warpath. Pinnacle, 1973 D
   The Deadly, Deadly Art. Pinnacle, 1974
   The Frightful Sin of Cisco Newman, with
      Richard (L.) Newhafer, 1922-   .
      Prentice-Hall, 1972
   Murder's Money. Pinnacle, 1975 D
   Red Revenge. Pinnacle, 1974 D

RAMAGE, JENNIFER. Pseudonym: Howard
   Mason, q.v.

RAME, DAVID. Pseudonym of A(rthur) D(urham) Divine, 1904-   , q.v. Other
   pseudonym: David Divine, q.v.

RAMPO, EDOGAWA. Pseudonym of Taro Hirai,
   1894-   .
   Japanese Tales of Mystery and Imagina-
      tion. Tuttle, 1956 ss

RAMSAY, DIANA. Pseudonym of Rhoda
   Brandes. Series character: Lt. Mere-
   dith = M.
The Dark Descends; see Descent into the
   Dark
Deadly Discretion. Collins, 1973 M
Descent into the Dark. Collins, 1975.
   U.S. title: The Dark Descends. Har-
   per, 1975
A Little Murder Music. Collins, 1972 M
No Cause to Kill. Collins, 1974 M

RAMSAY, R(INA)
   The Step in the House. Hurst, 1926

RAMSDALE, FRED
   The Brand of the Crook. Mellifont, 1942
   Poison on the Menu. Grafton, 1945

RAMSEY, GUY (HAYLETT WALKER)
   Stop Press Murder. Dakers, 1953

RAND, JOHN. Pseudonym of James Reach,
   1909?-1970. Other pseudonym: Hilda
   Manning, q.v. Joint pseudonym with
   Tom Taggart: Ross MacRoss, q.v.
   Cruise of Death. French, 1947. (3-act
      play.)
   Murder at the DeSoto. French, 1938.
      (1-act play.)

RAND, LOU
   The Gay Detective. Paperback Library,
      1965. Also published as: Rough Trade.
      Paperback Library, 1965

RAND, REX
   Desperation. Modern Fiction, 1956
   -Playing for Time. Modern Fiction, 1956

R

-She Wanted a Guy. Modern Fiction, 1955
-Surrendered. Modern Fiction, 1955

RAND, STEVE. Pseudonym of Jay Bennett, 1912- , q.v.
All Her Vices. Monarch, 1961

RAND, WILLIAM. Pseudonym of William Roos, 1911- . See also: AUDREY (KELLEY) ROOS, 1912- . Joint pseudonym with Audrey (Kelley) Roos, 1912- : Kelley Roos, q.v.
Ellery Queen's The Four of Hearts Mystery. Dramatic Publishing Co., 1949. (Dramatization of the novel by and about Ellery Queen, q.v.)

RANDALL, ANTHONY A(SHETON). Series character: Roger Patten, in at least those marked RP.
Flashpoint. Hale, 1966 RP
Ride a Tiger. Hale, 1965 RP
Suicide Passage. Hale, 1967
To Catch a Spy. Hale, 1965

RANDALL, FLORENCE ENGEL. 1917- .
Haldane Station. Harcourt, 1973; Millington, 1975
Hedgerow. Harcourt, 1967
The Place of Sapphires. Harcourt, 1969; Millington, 1974

RANDALL, ROGER
The Scarlet Death. Modern, 193?

RANDALL, RONA. Pseudonym of Rona Green Shambrook. These titles are at least mostly published in England as romances and in the U.S. as gothics.
The Arrogant Duke. Collins, 1966; Ace, 1972
Bright Morning. Collins, 1952
Broken Tapestry. Hurst, 1969; Ace, 1973
The Cedar Tree. Collins, 1957
Dancing Cinderella. Collins, 1959
Delayed Harvest. Collins, 1950
Desert Flower. Collins, 1955
The Doctor Falls in Love. Collins, 1958
Dragonmede. Collins, 1974; Simon, 1974
Enchanted Eden. Collins, 1960
Faith, Hope and Charity. Collins, 1954
The Fleeting Hour. Collins, 1947
A Girl Called Ann. Collins, 1956; Ace, 1973
Girl in Love. Collins, 1961
Girls in White. Collins, 1952
Glenrannoch. Collins, 1973
Hotel de Luxe. Collins, 1961; Ace, 1967
House Surgeon at Luke's. Collins, 1962
The Howards of Saxondale. Collins, 1946
I Married a Doctor. Collins, 1947
The Island Doctor. Collins, 1951
Journey to Love. Collins, 1953; Ace, 1972
Knight's Keep. Collins, 1967; Ace, 1967
The Late Mrs. Lane. Collins, 1945
Leap in the Dark. Collins, 1956; Ace, 1967
Love and Dr. Maynard. Collins, 1959
Lyonhurst; see Walk into my Parlour
The Merry Andrews. Collins, 1954
The Midnight Walker. Ace, 1973. (British title?)
The Moon Returns. Collins, 1942
Mountain of Fear. Ace, 1972. (British title?)
Murmuring Willow; see The Willow Herb
Nurse Stacey Comes Aboard. Collins, 1958
Rebel Wife. Collins, 1944
Runaway from Love. Collins, 1956
Seven Days from Midnight. Collins, 1965; Ace, 1967
Shadows on the Sand. Collins, 1949; Ace, 1973
Silent Thunder. Hurst, 1971
The Silver Cord. Ace, 1968. (British title?)
Sister at Sea. Collins, 1960
The Street of the Singing Fountain. Collins, 1948
Time Remembered, Time Lost. Ace, 1973. (British title?)
Walk into my Parlour. Collins, 1962; Ace, 1967. Revised edition: Lyonhurst. Fontana, 1977; Ballantine, 1977
The Watchman's Stone. Collins, 1975; Simon, 1975
The Willow Herb. Collins, 1965. U.S. title: Murmuring Willow. Ace, 1967
The Witching Hour. Hurst, 1970; Ace, 1970

RANDALL, WILLIAM. Pseudonym of William R. Gwinn.
Deadly the Daring. Mystery House, 1958

RANDALL, WILLIAM R.
The Crystal Eye. Regent, 1935
The Syndicate Murders. Greenberg, 1935

RANDAU, CARL (ALBERT), 1893-1969, and LEANE ZUGSMITH, 1903- . See also: KENNETH WHITE, 1905-1953.
The Visitor. Random, 1944; Gollancz, 1945

RANDELL, CHRISTINE
Black Candle. Paperback Library, 1968
Curse of Deepwater. Paperback Library, 1974
Mallory Grange. Paperback Library, 1971
The Secret of Tarn-End House. Paperback Library, 1969
The Weeping Tower. Paperback Library, 1967
Whisper of Fear. Paperback Library, 1966
A Woman Possessed. Paperback Library, 1966

RANDOLPH, ELLEN. Pseudonym of W(illiam) E(dward) D(aniel) Ross, 1912- , q.v. Other pseudonyms: Rose Dana, Jan Daniels, Clarissa Ross, Dan Ross, Dana Ross, Marilyn Ross, qq.v.
The Castle on the Hill. Bouregy, 1964
Paris in September. Bouregy, 1965
Rendezvous in Amsterdam. Bouregy, 1965
The Secret of Graytowers. Bouregy, 1968
-Threads of Love. Avalon, 1969

RANDOLPH, MARION. Pseudonym of Marie Fried Rodell, 1912-1975.
Breathe No More. Holt, 1940; Heinemann, 1940
Grim Grow the Lilacs. Holt, 1941; Museum, 1943
This'll Kill You. Holt, 1940; Museum, 1944

RANDOLPH, VANCE, 1892- , and NANCY CLEMENS, pseudonym.
The Camp-Meeting Murders. Vanguard, 1936; Cassell, 1937

RANIER, PAUL J.
Scared Stiff. Merit, 1954

RANK, MARY O. 1922- .
A Dream of Falling. Houghton, 1959. British title: Dream of Death. Hale, 1960

RANSOME, STEPHEN. Pseudonym of Frederick C(lyde) Davis, 1902-1977, q.v. Other pseudonym: Murdo Coombs, q.v. Series characters: Steve Ransome = SR; Detective Lt. Lee Barcello = LB.
Alias His Wife. Dodd, 1965; Gollancz, 1965 LB
Death Checks In. Doubleday, 1939. British title: Whose Corpse? Davies, 1939
False Bounty. Doubleday, 1948; Gollancz, 1949. Also published as: I, the Executioner. Ace, 1953
The Frazer Acquittal. Doubleday, 1955; Gollancz, 1955
Hear No Evil. Doubleday, 1953; Gollancz, 1954 SR
Hearses Don't Hurry. Doubleday, 1941
The Hidden Hour. Dodd, 1966; Gollancz, 1966 LB
I, the Executioner; see False Bounty
I'll Die for You. Doubleday, 1959; Gollancz, 1959
Meet in Darkness. Dodd, 1964; Gollancz, 1964
The Men in her Death. Doubleday, 1956; Gollancz, 1957
The Night, the Woman. Dodd, 1963; Gollancz, 1963
One-Man Jury. Dodd, 1964; Gollancz, 1965 LB
A Shroud for Shylock. Doubleday, 1939
The Shroud Off Her Back. Doubleday, 1953; Gollancz, 1953 SR
The Sin File. Dodd, 1965; Gollancz, 1966 LB
So Deadly My Love. Doubleday, 1957; Gollancz, 1958
Some Must Watch. Doubleday, 1961; Gollancz, 1961
Trap #6. Doubleday, 1971; Gollancz, 1972 LB
The Unspeakable. Doubleday, 1960; Gollancz, 1960
Warning Bell. Doubleday, 1960; Gollancz, 1960
Whose Corpse?; see Death Checks In
Without a Trace. Doubleday, 1962; Gollancz, 1962

RAPHAEL, CHAIM. 1908- . Pseudonym: Jocelyn Davey, q.v.

RAPHAEL, FREDERIC (MICHAEL). 1931- .
Who were You with Last Night? Cape, 1971

RAPHAEL, JOHN N(ATHANIEL). 1868-1917.
The Mystery of the Rue de Babylone. Grafton, 1916

RAPHAEL, MRS. L.
-The Double Mystery. Drane, 1924

RAPIER, JOHN
The Secret Mission of Colonel Death. Alliance, 1946

RATH, E. J. Joint pseudonym of J. Chauncey Corey Brainerd and Edith Rathbone Jacobs Brainerd.
Too Many Crooks. Watt, 1918

RATH, VIRGINIA (ANNE). 1905- . Series characters: Rocky Allan = RA; Michael Dundas = MD.
The Anger of the Bells. Doubleday, 1937 RA
The Dark Cavalier. Doubleday, 1938 MD
Death at Dayton's Folly. Doubleday, 1935 RA
Death Breaks the Ring. Doubleday, 1941 MD
Death of a Lucky Lady. Doubleday, 1940 MD
A Dirge for Her. Ziff-Davis, 1947 MD
Epitaph for Lydia. Doubleday, 1942 MD
An Excellent Night for a Murder. Doubleday, 1937 RA
Ferryman, Take Him Across! Doubleday, 1936 RA
Murder on the Day of Judgment. Doubleday, 1936 RA

Murder with a Theme Song. Doubleday, 1939 RA, MD
Posted for Murder. Doubleday, 1942 MD
A Shroud for Rowena. Ziff-Davis, 1947 MD

RATHBONE, CORNELIA KANE
Darkened Windows. Appleton, 1924
Jeremy Takes a Hand. Appleton, 1927

RATHBONE, EDWARD
-The Brass Knocker. Cape, 1934; Appleton, 1934

RATHBONE, JULIAN. 1935-   . Series character: Nur Bey, in at least those marked NB.
Bloody Marvelous. Joseph, 1975; St. Martin's, 1976
Diamonds Bid. Joseph, 1967; Walker, 1967 NB
Hand Out. Joseph, 1968; Walker, 1968 NB
Kill Cure. Joseph, 1975; St. Martin's, 1975
Trip Trap. Joseph, 1972; St. Martin's, 1972 NB
With My Knives I Know I'm Good. Joseph, 1969; Putnam, 1970

RATHBONE, RICHARD A(DAMS)
Death in the Drawing Room. Comet, 1954

RATHBORNE, ST. GEORGE (HENRY). 1854-1938. Pseudonyms: Marline Manly, Doctor Mark Merrick, qq.v.
A Bar Sinister. Hobart, 1897. British title: A Cruel Case; or, The Bar Sinister. Aldine, 1897
Baron Sam. American News, 1893; Aldine, 1894
The Carteret Affair. Laird, 1891; Aldine, 1894. Also published as: Witch or Wife. Laird, 1895
A Cruel Case; see A Bar Sinister
The Detective and the Poisoner. Laird, 1892; Aldine, 1894
Masked in Mystery. Hobart, 1897; Henderson, 1897. Also published as: Under Egyptian Skies; or, Masked in Mystery. Street, 1900
Miss Pauline of New York. American News, 1893; Aldine, 1894
-The Spider's Web. Street, 1898
Under Egyptian Skies; see Masked in Mystery
Witch or Wife; see The Carteret Affair

RATHBUN, F. P.
Suspected: A Story of Mystery. Henderson, 1894

RATHBURNE, FAY P.
Cruel Suspicion. Street (Magnet)
A Woman in the Case; or, Debtor to the Devil. Ogilvie, 1891

RATTCLIFFE, ANNE. See: ANN (WARD) RADCLIFFE, 1764-1823.

RATTRAY, SIMON. Pseudonym of Elleston Trevor, 1920-   , q.v. Name originally: Trevor Dudley Smith, q.v. Other pseudonyms: Mansell Black, Adam Hall, Warwick Scott, Caesar Smith, qq.v. Series character: Hugo Bishop, in all titles.
Bishop in Check. Boardman, 1953; Mill, 1961. Reprinted as by Adam Hall: Remploy, 1972; Pyramid, 1971
Dead Circuit. Boardman, 1955. U.S. title: Rook's Gambit, as by Adam Hall. Pyramid, 1972. Reprinted under the U.S. title as by Adam Hall: Remploy, 1972

Dead Sequence. Boardman, 1957
Dead Silence. Boardman, 1954. U.S. title: Pawn in Jeopardy, as by Adam Hall. Pyramid, 1971. Reprinted in Britain under the U.S. title: Remploy, 1972, as by Adam Hall
Knight Sinister. Boardman, 1951; Pyramid, 1971, as by Adam Hall. Reprinted in Britain as by Adam Hall: Remploy, 1972
Pawn in Jeopardy; see Dead Silence
Queen in Danger. Boardman, 1952; Pyramid, 1971, as by Adam Hall. Reprinted in Britain as by Adam Hall: Remploy, 1972
Rook's Gambit; see Dead Circuit

RAUCH, CONSTANCE. 1937-   .
The Landlady. Putnam, 1975

RAVEN, SIMON (ARTHUR NOEL). 1927-   .
-Boys will be Boys. Blond, 1963
Brother Cain. Blond, 1959; Simon, 1960
-Close of Play. Blond, 1962
Doctors Wear Scarlet. Blond, 1960; Simon, 1961
The Sabre Squadron. Blond, 1966; Harper, 1967

RAWLENCE, GUY. 1888-   .
The Highwayman. Watt, 1911. British title (?): The Romantic Road. Unwin, 1910

RAWLINGS, FRANK
The Lisping Man. Gateway, 1942

RAWLINS, EUSTACE. 1854-   . Pseudonym (?): Robert Eustace. See: DOROTHY L(EIGH) SAYERS, 1893-1957; L(ILLIE) T(HOMAS) MEADE; GERTRUDE WARDEN.

RAWSON, CLAYTON. 1906-1971. Pseudonym: Stuart Towne, q.v. Series character: The Great Merlini, in all titles.
Death from a Top Hat. Putnam, 1938; Collins, 1938
The Footprints on the Ceiling. Putnam, 1939; Collins, 1939
The Headless Lady. Putnam, 1940; Collins, 1942
No Coffin for the Corpse. Little, 1942; Stacey, 1972

RAWSON, TABOR
I Want to Live! Signet, 1958. (Novelization of the movie.)

RAY, DAVID
All in a Day's Work. Panther, 1966. (Novelization of the TV series.)

RAY, JEAN. Pseudonym of Jean Raymond de Kremer, 1887-1964.
Ghouls in my Grave. Berkley, 1965

RAY, RENE
-A Man Named Seraphin. Eyre, 1952
Wraxton Marne. Green, 1946

RAYMOND, CLIFFORD S(AMUEL). 1875-   .
Four Corners. Doran, 1921
The Men on the Dead Man's Chest. Bobbs, 1930
The Mystery of Hartley House. Doran, 1917
One of Three. Doran, 1919
-Our Very Best People. Bobbs, 1931

RAYMOND, DIANA
-The Five Days. Cassell, 1959
Incident on a Summer's Day. Cassell, 1974

RAYMOND, ERNEST. 1888-   .
-A Chorus Ending. Cassell, 1951
-The Marsh. Cassell, 1937
-The Tree of Heaven. Cassell, 1965
We, the Accused. Cassell, 1935; Stokes, 1935

RAYMOND, RENE BRABAZON. 1906-   . Pseudonyms: James Hadley Chase, James L. Docherty, Ambrose Grant, Raymond Marshall, qq.v.

RAYNE, GODFREY
Earmarked for Murder. Hale, 1968
Headline—Murder! Hale, 1967

RAYNER, AUGUSTUS ALFRED. 1894-   . Pseudonym: Whyte Hall, q.v.

RAYNER, CLAIRE (BERENICE). 1931-   .
Death on the Table. Corgi, 1969
The House on the Fen. Corgi, 1967; Bantam, 1967
-Lady Mislaid. Corgi, 1968
-The Meddlers. Cassell, 1970

RAYNER, RICHARD. Pseudonym of David MacIlwain.
Darling Daughter. Hale, 1961
Dig Deep for Julie. Hale, 1963
Stand-In for Danger. Hale, 1963
The Trouble with Ruth. Hale, 1960

RAYTER, JOE. Pseudonym of Mary F. McChesney. Series character: Johnny Powers = JP.
Asking for Trouble. Mill, 1955; Ward, 1957 JP
Stab in the Dark. Mill, 1955; Ward, 1958
The Victim was Important. Scribner, 1954; Reinhardt, 1954 JP

REA, M(ARGARET LUCILE) P(AINE). Series character: Lt. Powledge = P.
Blackout at Rehearsal. Doubleday, 1943
Compare These Dead! Doubleday, 1941 P
A Curtain for Crime. Doubleday, 1941 P
Death of an Angel. Doubleday, 1943 P
Death Walks the Dry Tortugas. Doubleday, 1942

REACH, ANGUS BETHUNE. 1821-1856.
Clement Lorimer; or, The Book with the Iron Clasp. Bogue, 1849

REACH, JAMES. 1909?-1970. Joint pseudonym with Tom Taggart: Ross MacRoss, q.v. Pseudonyms for plays: John Rand, Hilda Manning, qq.v. The first four titles below are novels; the remainder are plays, published by Samuel French (New York) unless otherwise indicated. The number of acts is given in parenthesis.
Blind Gambit. Coward, 1954; Foulsham, 1956
The Innocent One. Coward, 1953; Foulsham, 1956. Play version (3 acts): French, 1965
Late Last Night. Morrow, 1949; Heinemann, 1950
Sunset Strip. Popular Library, 1957

Afraid of the Dark. 1953 (3)
Bear Witness. 1970 (2)
The Black Hawk. 1952 (3)
The Blackout Mystery. 1942 (1)
The Case of the Laughing Dwarf. 1938 (3)
The Case of the Squealing Cat. 1937 (3)
The Clock Struck Twelve. 1949 (3)
Danger—Girls Working! 1938 (?)
Dark Doings. 1951 (3)
Dead of the Night. 1952 (3)
Dragnet. 1956 (3) (Dramatization of the TV series.)
For the Defense. 1967 (3)

Fright. 1937 (1)
The Girl in the Rain. 1953 (3)
The Green Ghost. 1935 (3)
House of Horrors. 1937 (3)
The House on the Lake. 1949 (3)
It Happened at Midnight. 1941 (3)
It Walks at Midnight. Baker, 1956 (3)
Lunatics at Large. 1936 (3)
The Missing Witness. 1936 (3)
Mr. Snoop is Murdered. 1941 (1)
Murder is my Business. 1958 (3) (Dramatization of the novel by Brett Halliday, q.v.)
Murder Takes the Stage. 1957 (3)
The Night was Dark. 1940 (3)
The Old Man's Money. 1950 (3)
Once Upon a Midnight. 1948 (3)
One Mad Night. 1935 (3)
Shadows in the Night. 1942 (3)
Storm over Hollywood. 1946 (3)
The Tennis Club Mystery. 1941 (1)
Welcome, Danger! 1937 (3)
We're All Guilty. 1962 (?)
The Window. 1936 (1)
Women in White. 1953 (3)
You, the Jury. 1958 (3)

READ, OPIE (PERCIVAL). 1852-1939.
The Mystery of Margaret. Wessels, 1907

READ, PIERS PAUL. 1941-   .
The Upstart. Alison, 1973; Lippincott, 1973

READE, BILL
A Bomb for Atuna. Barker, 1975
I Wonder What Happened to Tom? Corgi, 1968
The Ibeza Syndicate. Barker, 1975; St. Martin's, 1976
What Have They Done to You, Ben? Corgi, 1967; Bantam, 1968

READE, CHARLES. 1814-1884.
Foul Play, with Dion(ysius Lardner) Boucicault, 1820-1890. Ticknor, 1868
The Jilt. Chatto, 1884 ss, at least one criminous

READE, HAMISH. Pseudonym of Simon James Halliday Gray, 1936-   .
A Comeback for Stark. Faber, 1968; Putnam, 1968

REAGAN, THOMAS (JAMES) B(UTLER). 1916-   . Pseudonym: Jim Thomas, q.v.
Bank Job. Torquil/Dodd Mead, 1964; Hale, 1966
The Big Fall. Hammond, 1967
Blood Money. Putnam, 1970; Long, 1971
The Caper. Putnam, 1969; Long, 1970
The Inside-Out Heist. Putnam, 1970; Hale, 1972
An Unkindness of Ravens. Hammond, 1967

REDD, REBECCA FERGUS
The Brierfield Tragedy. Lovell, 1884

REDDOCH, JENNIFER
A Chair for Death. Popular Library, 1973
The Legacy of Mendoubia. Popular Library, 1973
Night of the Hellebore. Popular Library, 1974

REDFERN, JOHN
The Victim Needs a Nurse. Jarrolds, 1940

REDFIELD, MALISSA
Games of Chance with Strangers. Doubleday, 1971

REDGATE, JOHN. Pseudonym of Adam Kennedy, q.v.
The Killing Season. Trident, 1967; Cape, 1968

REDGRAVE, MICHAEL
The Aspern Papers. Heinemann, 1959. (Play based on the story by Henry James, 1843-1916, q.v.)

REDMAN, BEN RAY. 1896-1961. Pseudonym: Jeremy Lord, q.v.

REDMOND, A(NTON) E(DWARD)
Cancelled Out. Hale, 1972
Dead is Forever. Hale, 1973
No Exit. Hale, 1973

REDMOND, LIAM
Death is So Kind. Devin-Adair, 1959

REDMOND-HOWARD, L(OUIS) G. 1884-   .
The Dilemma of Death. Modern, 1935
Murder was Never Bolder. Grafton, 1946
The Mystery of Beacon Hill. Modern, 193?
Radio Blackmail. Mellifont, 1936
The Siege of Scotland Yard. Brentano's (London), 1929

REDNOUR, HAROLD P.
The Oblong Circle. French (New York), 1954. (Play.)

REDWING, MORRIS. Pseudonym of James Milford Merrill, 1847-1936.
Detective Against Detective; or, A Great Conspiracy. Laird, 1888
Forced Apart; or, Exiled by Fate. Laird, 1886
The Great Trunk Tragedy; or, Shadowed to Australia. Laird, 1888
Tracked to Death; or, Eagle Gray, the Western Detective. Laird, 1886

REDWOOD, ALEC
The Lady is Not Fooling. Hale, 1974

REED, BLAIR. Pseudonym: Adam Ring, q.v.
Pass Key to Murder. Phoenix, 1948

REED, DAVID V. Pseudonym of David Vern, 1924-   .
I Thought I'd Die. Green Dragon, 194?
Murder in Space. Galaxy, 1954

REED, EDWARD CHARLES. 1891-   .
Boothroyd's Mill. Long, 1929
-Clowning Through. Long, 1928
The Dream Murder. Long, 1929
-The Free Heart. Long, 1927
-History of Edward Brown. Long, 1932
The Mirror. Long, 1925
The Padgate Mystery. Long, 1930
-Passionate Youth. Long, 1926
The Strangler. Long, 1929
-The Tents of Shame. Long, 1927
-Venus Besieged. Long, 1927
-A Wise Fool. Long, 1924

REED, EDWARD J(AMES). 1830-1906.
Fort Minster, M.P. Arrowsmith, 1885

REED, ELIOT. Joint pseudonym of Eric Ambler, 1909-   , q.v., and (Percival) Charles Rodda, 1891-   , q.v. Other pseudonyms of Charles Rodda: Gardner Low, Gavin Holt, qq.v.
Charter to Danger. Collins, 1954
The Maras Affair. Collins, 1953; Doubleday, 1953
Passport to Panic. Collins, 1958
Skytip. Hodder, 1951; Doubleday, 1950
Tender to Danger; see Tender to Moonlight
Tender to Moonlight. Hodder, 1952. U.S. title: Tender to Danger. Doubleday, 1951

REED, HARLAN. Series character: Dan Jordan, in both titles.
The Case of the Crawling Cockroach. Dutton, 1937
The Swing Music Murder. Dutton, 1938

REED, HARRY
A Piece of Something Big. Lancer, 1972

REED, ISHMAEL. 1938-   .
The Last Days of Louisiana Red. Random, 1974
Mumbo Jumbo. Doubleday, 1972

REED, LANGFORD. See: FRANCES EVELYN.

REED, WALLACE. Series character: Lt. Bill Lloyd, in at least those marked BL.
Marked for Murder. Phoenix, 1941 BL
Motive for Murder. Arcadia, 1957
No Sign of Murder. Phoenix, 1940 BL
Time to Kill. Phoenix, 1940 BL

REES, ARTHUR J(OHN). 1872-1942. See also: JOHN R(EAY) WATSON, 1872-   . Series characters: Insp. Luckraft = L; Colwin Grey = CG.
Aldringham's Last Chance. Lane, 1933; Dodd, 1933 L
The Brink. Lane, 1931. U.S. title: The Swaying Rock. Dodd, 1931
The Corpse That Traveled. Dodd, 1938 L (British title?)
Cup of Silence. Lane, 1924; Dodd, 1925
-The Flying Argosy. Jarrolds, 1934
Greymarsh. Jarrolds, 1927; Dodd, 1927 CG
The Hand in the Dark. Lane (London & New York), 1920
Investigations of Colwin Grey. Jarrolds, 1932 CG ss
Island of Destiny. Lane, 1923; Dodd, 1923 L
The Moon Rock. Lane, 1922; Dodd, 1922
Mystery at Peak House; see Peak House
The Pavilion by the Lake. Lane, 1930; Dodd, 1930 L
Peak House. Jarrolds, 1933. U.S. title: Mystery at Peak House. Dodd, 1933
The River Mystery. Jarrolds, 1932; Dodd, 1932 L
The Shrieking Pit. Lane (London & New York), 1919
Simon of Hangletree. Hutchinson, 1926. U.S. title: The Unquenchable Flame. Dodd, 1926 CG (with L in a walk-on role)
The Swaying Rock; see The Brink
The Threshold of Fear. Hutchinson, 1925; Dodd, 1925 CG
Tragedy at Twelvetrees. Lane, 1931; Dodd, 1931 L
The Unquenchable Flame; see Simon of Hangletree

REES, DILWYN. Pseudonym of Glyn (Edmund) Daniel, 1914-   , q.v. Series character: Sir Richard Cherington, in title below and that under Glyn Daniel byline.
The Cambridge Murders. Gollancz, 1945

REES, GEORGE. Titles below were published by Amalgamated Press and feature Sexton Blake.
The Secret of the Jungle. 1953
The Secret of the Suez Canal. 1954

REES, OLWEN
Death of Virginia. Gifford, 1945
There's No One in the Village. Gifford, 1949

REESE, JOHN (HENRY)
  The Looters. Random, 1968; Hale, 1969
  Pity Us All. Random, 1969; Hale, 1970
  Weapon Heavy. Doubleday, 1973; Milton House, 1975

REESE, SAMMY [SAMUEL PHARR REESE]. 1930- .
  I'm Waiting. Doubleday, 1974

REEVE, ARTHUR B(ENJAMIN). 1880-1936.
  Series character: Craig Kennedy = CK.
  The Adventuress. Harper, 1917; Collins, 1918 CK
  Atavar, the Dream Dancer. Harper, 1924 CK
  The Black Hand; see The Silent Bullet
  The Boy Scout's Craig Kennedy. Harper, 1925 CK ss
  The Clutching Hand. Reilly, 1934 CK
  Constance Dunlap, Woman Detective. Hearst's, 1916; Hodder, 1916 ss
  Craig Kennedy, Detective; see The War Terror
  Craig Kennedy Listens In. Harper, 1923; Hodder, 1924 CK ss
  Craig Kennedy on the Farm. Harper, 1925 CK ss
  The Diamond Queen; see The Social Gangster
  The Dream Doctor. Hearst's, 1914; Hodder, 1916 CK ss
  The Ear in the Wall. Hearst's, 1916; Hodder, 1917 CK
  Enter Craig Kennedy. Macaulay, 1935. (4 connected novelets.)
  The Exploits of Elaine. Hearst's, 1915; Hodder, 1915 CK ss
  The Film Mystery. Harper, 1921; Hodder, 1922 CK
  The Fourteen Points. Harper, 1925 CK ss
  Gold of the Gods. Hearst's, 1915; Hodder, 1916 CK ss
  Guy Garrick. Hearst's, 1914; Hodder, 1916
  The Kidnap Club. Macaulay, 1932 CK
  The Master Mystery. Grosset, 1919. (Novelization of the movie.)
  The Mystery Mind. Grosset, 1921. (Novelization of the movie.)
  The Panama Plot. Harper, 1918; Collins, 1920 CK ss
  Pandora. Harper, 1926 CK
  The Poisoned Pen. Harper, 1911; Hodder, 1916 CK ss
  The Radio Detective. Grosset, 1926 CK (Novelization of the movie.)
  The Romance of Elaine. Hearst's, 1916; Hodder, 1916 CK ss (The U.S. edition combines the text of the British edition with part of The Triumph of Elaine, q.v.)
  The Silent Bullet. Dodd, 1912. British title: The Black Hand. Nash, 1912 CK ss
  The Social Gangster. Hearst's, 1916. British title: The Diamond Queen. Hodder, 1917 CK ss
  The Soul Scar. Harper, 1919 CK
  The Stars Scream Murder. Appleton, 1936 CK
  The Treasure Train. Harper, 1917; Collins, 1920 CK ss
  The Triumph of Elaine. Hodder, 1916 CK ss (Part of this is included in the U.S. edition of The Romance of Elaine, q.v.)
  The War Terror. Hearst's, 1915. British title: Craig Kennedy, Detective. Simpkin, 1916 CK ss

REEVE, CHRISTOPHER
  The Emerald Kiss. Jarrolds, 1932; Morrow, 1931
  The Ginger Cat. Collins, 1929; Morrow, 1929
  The House That Waited. Ward, 1944
  Hunter's Way. Jarrolds, 1934
  Lady, Be Careful. Ward, 1948; Mill, 1950
  Murder Steps Out. Ward, 1942; Mill, 1951
  The Toasted Blonde. Collins, 1930; Morrow, 1930

REEVE, CLARA
  The Champion of Virtue. Keymer, 1777. Also published as: The Old English Baron. Dilly, 1778; Stewart, 1797

REEVES, ROBERT. Series character: Cellini Smith, in all titles.
  Cellini Smith, Detective. Houghton, 1943
  Come Out Killing; see No Love Lost
  Dead and Done For. Knopf, 1939; Cassell, 1940
  No Love Lost. Holt, 1941. Also published as: Come Out Killing. Mercury, 1953 (abridged)

REEVES, RUTH (ELIZABETH TRAUGHBER). 1902- .
  Lament for a Lonesome Corpse. Phoenix, 1951

REGESTER, SEELEY. Pseudonym of Mrs. M(eta) V(ictoria Fuller) Victor, 1831-1886, q.v.
  The Dead Letter. Beadle, 1867
  The Figure Eight; or, The Mystery of Meredith Place. Beadle, 1869

REGIS, JULIUS. Pseudonym of Julius Pettersson, 1889-1925. Series character: Maurice Wallion, in both titles.
  The Copper House. Holt, 1923; Hodder, 1923. (Translation of Kopparhuset. Stockholm, 1918.)
  No. 13 Toroni. Holt, 1922; Hodder, 1922. (Translation of Nr. 13 Toroni. Stockholm, 1919.)

REID, C. LESTOCK
  -The Greatest Game. Long, 1930
  -Masque of Mutiny. Temple, 1947
  -Peter's Profession. Long, 1927
  Revenge with a Vengeance. Robertson, 1952

REID, DESMOND. House name, used by Wilfred (Glassford) McNeilly, 1921- , q.v., and others. Other McNeilly pseudonyms: W. Howard Baker, W. A. Ballinger, Errol Lecale, qq.vv. Series character (with many other authors): Sexton Blake, in at least those marked SB.
  The Abductors. Mayflower, 1968 SB
  Anger at World's End. Amalgamated, 1963 SB
  The Babcock Boys. Mayflower, 1966
  Beat on an Orange Drum. Mayflower, 1965
  Bullets are Trumps. Amalgamated, 1961 SB
  Caribbean Crisis. Amalgamated, 1962 SB
  The Case of the Renegade Agent. Mayflower, 1968 SB
  Conflict Within. Amalgamated, 1960 SB
  Contract for a Killer. Amalgamated, 1960 SB
  The Corpse Came Too. Amalgamated, 1961 SB
  Cult of Darkness. Amalgamated, 1963 SB
  Dead on Cue. Amalgamated, 1962 SB
  Dead Respectable. Mayflower, 1967 SB
  The Deadlier of the Species. Mayflower, 1966 SB
  Deadly Persuasion. Amalgamated, 1961 SB
  Death in Dockland. Amalgamated, 1962 SB
  Death on a High Note. Amalgamated, 1962 SB
  Death on the Spike. Mayflower, 1966 SB
  Death Waits in Tucson. Mayflower, 1966
  Flashpoint for Treason. Amalgamated, 1957 SB
  Frenzy in the Flesh. Mayflower, 1966; Macfadden, 1968 SB
  The Girl Who Saw Too Much. Amalgamated, 1963 SB
  High Heels and Homicide. Amalgamated, 1958 SB
  Homicide Blues. Amalgamated, 1957 SB
  Hunt the Lady! Amalgamated, 1961 SB
  Let My People Be. Mayflower, 1965 SB
  The Man from Pecos. Mayflower, 1966
  Murder by Moonlight. Amalgamated, 1961 SB
  Murder Comes Calling! Amalgamated, 1960 SB
  Murder Made Easy. Amalgamated, 1960 SB
  Murder's Rock. Amalgamated, 1961 SB
  Roadhouse Girl. Amalgamated, 1957 SB
  Showdown in Sydney. Amalgamated, 1959 SB
  The Slave Brain. Mayflower, 1967 SB
  The Slaver. Mayflower, 1969
  The Snowman Cometh. Mayflower, 1966 SB
  Something to Kill About. Amalgamated, 1961 SB
  Stand-In for Murder. Amalgamated, 1957 SB
  State of Fear. Amalgamated, 1961 SB
  Victim Unknown. Amalgamated, 1957 SB
  Witch-Hunt! Amalgamated, 1960 SB
  The World-Shakers. Amalgamated, 1960 SB

REID, PHILIP. Joint pseudonym of Richard Ingrams and Andrew Osmond, 1938- , q.v. See also: DOUGLAS (RICHARD) HURD, 1930- .
  Harris in Wonderland. Cape, 1973. U.S. title: The Fun House. Houghton, 1974

REID, WALTER
  Off Lands End. Griffin, 1866 ss, two criminous

REILLY, HELEN. 1891-1962. Pseudonym: Kieran Abbey, q.v. Series character: Inspector McKee = M.
  All Concerned Notified. Doubleday, 1939; Heinemann, 1939 M
  The Canvas Dagger. Random, 1956; Hale, 1957 M
  Certain Sleep. Random, 1961; Hale, 1962 M
  Compartment K. Random, 1955. British title: Murder Rides the Express. Hale, 1956 M
  The Day She Died. Random, 1962; Hale, 1963 M
  The Dead Can Tell. Random, 1940 M
  Dead for a Ducat. Doubleday, 1939; Heinemann, 1939 M
  Dead Man Control. Doubleday, 1936; Heinemann, 1937 M
  Death Demands an Audience. Doubleday, 1940 M
  The Diamond Feather. Doubleday, 1930 M
  Ding Dong Bell. Random, 1958; Hale, 1959 M
  The Doll's Trunk Murder. Farrar, 1932; Hutchinson, 1933
  The Double Man. Random, 1952; Museum, 1954 M
  The Farmhouse. Random, 1947; Hammond, 1950 M
  File on Rufus Ray. Morrow, 1937; Jarrolds, 1937
  Follow Me. Random, 1960; Hale, 1961 M
  Lament for the Bride. Random, 1951; Museum, 1954 M
  The Line-Up. Doubleday, 1934; Cassell, 1935 M
  McKee of Centre Street. Doubleday, 1934 M

Man with the Painted Head. Farrar, 1931
Mr. Smith's Hat. Doubleday, 1936; Cassell, 1936 M
Mourned on Sunday. Random, 1941 M
Murder at Arroways. Random, 1950; Museum, 1952 M
Murder in Shinbone Alley. Doubleday, 1940 M
Murder in the Mews. Doubleday, 1931 M
Murder on Angler's Island. Random, 1945; Hammond, 1948 M
Murder Rides the Express; see Compartment K
Name Your Poison. Random, 1942 M
Not Me, Inspector. Random, 1959; Hale, 1960 M
The Opening Door. Random, 1944 M
The Silver Leopard. Random, 1946; Hammond, 1949 M
Staircase 4. Random, 1949; Hammond, 1950 M
Tell Her It's Murder. Random, 1954; Museum, 1955 M
The Thirty-First Bullfinch. Doubleday, 1930
Three Women in Black. Random, 1941 M
The Velvet Hand. Random, 1953; Museum, 1955 M

REISNER, MARY
Black Hazard. Belmont, 1966
Bride of Death. Belmont, 1968
Death Hall. Belmont, 1968
The Four Witnesses. Dodd, 1947; Hammond, 1948. Also published as: Web of Fear. Belmont, 1967
The House of Cobwebs. Dodd, 1944; Methuen, 1948
The Hunted. Belmont, 1967
Katherine and the Dark Angel. Dodd, 1948; Hammond, 1949
Mirror of Delusion. Dodd, 1946; Hammond, 1947
Shadows on the Wall. Dodd, 1943. British title: Twelve Steps at Miramar. Methuen, 1946
Twelve Steps at Miramar; see Shadows on the Wall
Web of Fear; see The Four Witnesses

REIZENSTEIN, ELMER L. 1892-1967. See: ELMER L. RICE; D. TORBETT.
On Trial. French, 1919. (Play.)

REMENHAM, JOHN. Pseudonym of John Alexander Vlasto, 1877-1958. Other pseudonym: John Alexander, q.v. Series character: Inspector Bliss, in at least those marked B.
Arsenic. Skeffington, 1930 B
The Canal Mystery. Skeffington, 1928 B
The Crooked Bough. Macdonald, 1948
The Dump. Skeffington, 1931 B
Fog. Skeffington, 1929
The Loom. Skeffington, 1933
The Lurking Shadow. Macdonald, 1946
-The Peacemaker. Macdonald, 1947
Righteous Abel. Macdonald, 1943
Sea Gold. Skeffington, 1931
Seed of Envy. Macdonald, 1944
-Tregear's Treasure. Skeffington, 1932

REMNANT, RICHARD
At the Back o' Beyond. Chambers, 1930 ss, a few criminous

REMY, JACQUES. 1911- .
Race for Life. Lane, 1957. (Translation of Si Tous les Gars du Monde. Paris, 1956.)

RENARD, MAURICE. 1875-1939.
Blind Circle, with (Marie Joseph) Albert Jean, 1892- . Dutton, 1928; Gollancz, 1929
The Hands of Orlac. Dutton, 1929. (Translation of Les Mains d'Orlac. Paris, 192?.)

New Bodies for Old. Macaulay, 1923
The Snake of Luvercy. Dutton, 1930. (Translation of Lui? Paris, 1927.)

RENDALL, VERNON (HORACE). 1869- .
The London Nights of Belsize. Lane (London & New York), 1917 ss

RENDELL, RUTH. 1930- . Series character: Chief Inspector Wexford = W.
The Best Man to Die. Long, 1969; Doubleday, 1970 W
The Face of Trespass. Hutchinson, 1974; Doubleday, 1974
From Doon with Death. Long, 1964; Doubleday, 1965 W
A Guilty Thing Surprised. Hutchinson, 1970; Doubleday, 1970 W
In Sickness and in Health; see Vanity Dies Hard
Murder Being Once Done. Hutchinson, 1972; Doubleday, 1972 W
A New Lease of Death. Long, 1967; Doubleday, 1967. Also published as: Sins of the Fathers. Ballantine, 1970 W
No More Dying Then. Hutchinson, 1971; Doubleday, 1972 W
One Across, Two Down. Hutchinson, 1971; Doubleday, 1971
The Secret House of Death. Long, 1968; Doubleday, 1969
Shake Hands for Ever. Hutchinson, 1975; Doubleday, 1975 W
Sins of the Fathers; see A New Lease of Death
Some Lie and Some Die. Hutchinson, 1973; Doubleday, 1973 W
To Fear a Painted Devil. Long, 1965; Doubleday, 1965
Vanity Dies Hard. Long, 1966. U.S. title: In Sickness and in Health. Doubleday, 1966. Reprinted under British title: Beagle, 1970
Wolf to the Slaughter. Long, 1967; Doubleday, 1968 W

RENEK, MORRIS
Las Vegas Strip. Knopf, 1975; Secker, 1975

RENFROE, MARTHA KAY. 1938- . Pseudonym: M. K. Wren, q.v.

RENNERT, MAGGIE. 1922- . Series character: Guy Silvestri, in both titles.
Circle of Death. Prentice-Hall, 1974
Operation Alcestis. Prentice-Hall, 1975

RENNIE, J(AMES) ALAN. 1899-1969.
-Aces Run Wild. Quality, 1950
The Riddle of Rainbow Mountain. Muller, 1938

RENNIE, NEVILLE
Strange Instrument. Aldor, 1948

RENWICK, PETER
Black Hogan Strikes Again. Low, 1937
Leatherface Lonergan Stakes a Claim. Low, 1936
Red Saunders Bites the Dust. Low, 1937

RESSICH, JOHN SELLAR MATHISON. 1877- .
Joint pseudonym with Eric de Banzie, 1894- : Gregory Baxter, q.v.

REVELL, LOUISA. Series character: Julia Tyler, in all titles.
The Bus Station Murders. Macmillan, 1947; Boardman, 1949
The Kindest Use a Knife. Macmillan, 1952; Boardman, 1953

The Men with Three Eyes. Macmillan, 1955
No Pockets in Shrouds. Macmillan, 1948; Boardman, 1949
A Party for the Shooting. Macmillan, 1960
See Rome and Die. Macmillan, 1957; Gollancz, 1958
A Silver Spade. Macmillan, 1950; Boardman, 1950

REVELLI, GEORGE. Series character: Amanda Nightingale, in all titles.
Amanda's Castle. Bantam, 1972; Mayflower, 1973
Commander Amanda Nightingale. Grove, 1968; New English Library, 1969
Resort to War. Grove, 1971; New English Library, 1971

REYBOLD, MALCOLM
The Inspector's Opinion. Saturday Review Press, 1975

REYBURN, WALLACE (MacDONALD). 1913- .
Follow a Shadow. Cassell, 1956
Good and Evil. Cassell, 1962
Port of Call. Cassell, 1957
The Street That Died. Cassell, 1960
Three Women. Cassell, 1960

REYMOND, HENRY
Deadlier Than the Male. Hodder pb, 1966; Signet, 1967. (Novelization of the Bulldog Drummond movie.) (Bulldog Drummond also appears in books by H. C. McNeile, 1888-1937, his creator, and by Gerard Fairlie, 1899- , qq.v.)

REYNAUD-FOURTON, ALAIN
The Reluctant Assassin. Collins, 1964; Coward, 1964

REYNOLDS, ADRIAN. Pseudonym of Amelia Reynolds Long, 1904-1978, q.v. Other pseudonyms: Patrick Laing, Peter Reynolds, qq.v. Joint pseudonym with Edna McHugh: Kathleen Buddington Coxe, q.v. Series character: Prof. Dennis Barrie, in all titles.
Formula for Murder. Phoenix, 1947
The Leprechaun Murders. Phoenix, 1950
The Round Table Murders. Phoenix, 1952

REYNOLDS, MRS. BAILLIE [GERTRUDE M. ROBINS REYNOLDS]
Accessory After the Fact. Hodder, 1928. U.S. title: The Innocent Accomplice. Doubleday, 1928
The Affair at the Chateau. Hodder, 1929; Doubleday, 1929
-Beware of the Dog. Mills, 1910; Brentano's, 1911
Black Light. Hodder, 1937; Doubleday, 1938
-Brother Wolf. Wright, 1931
A Castle to Let. Cassell, 1917; Doran, 1917
-Confession Corner, and other stories. Hurst, 1922 ss
-The Court Favourite. Mills, 1915
-The Flight of the Duchess, and other stories. Wright, 1935 ss
-The Gift of the Gauntlet. Hodder, 1927; Doran, 1927
The Innocent Accomplice; see Accessory After the Fact
The Intrusive Tourist. Hodder, 1935; Doubleday, 1935
It is Not Safe to Know. Hodder, 1939; Doubleday, 1939
-The Kingdom and the Wall, and other tales. Mills, 1916 ss
-The Lonely Stronghold. Cassell, 1918; Doran, 1918

The Lost Discovery. Hodder, 1923; Doran, 1923
The Missing Two. Hodder, 1932; Doubleday, 1932
The Nameless Stranger and What Happened at Flaunce. Wright, 1933
The Notorious Miss Lisle. Hodder, 1911; Doran, 1911
-"Open, Sesame!" Skeffington, 1919; Doran, 1918
-Out of the Night. Hodder, 1910; Doran, 1910
The Prisoner of the Garret. Partridge, 1915
-The Queen's Hand. Mills, 1911 ss
-The Sheikh Touch, and other stories. Hurst, 1931 ss
-The Spell of Sarnia. Hodder, 1925; Doran, 1925
The Stranglehold. Doubleday, 1930. (British title?)
-The Swashbuckler, and other tales. Mills, 1913 ss
-The Terrible Baron, and other stories. Wright, 1933 ss
Trouble at Glaye. Hodder, 1936; Doubleday, 1936
Very Private Secretary. Hodder, 1933; Doubleday, 1933
-A Wayward Girl. Partridge, 1913
Whereabouts Unknown. Hutchinson, 1931; Doubleday, 1931

REYNOLDS, BONNIE JONES
-The Truth About Unicorns. Stein, 1972; Garnstone, 1974

REYNOLDS, GEORGE
Victor Maury, the French Detective. Ogilvie, 1882

REYNOLDS, GEORGE WILLIAM MacARTHUR. 1814-1879. Dates and publishers for this author are very uncertain, and many U.S. titles remain uncorrelated with British counterparts. No judgment on the relative criminous content of the titles has been made.
Agnes (Evelyn); or, Beauty and Pleasure. 1855
Alfred (de Rosaun); or, The Adventures of a French Gentleman. 1840. Also published as: Life in Paris; or, The Adventures of Alfred de Rosaun in the French Metropolis
The Banker's Daughter; or, The Lost Witness.
The Bronze Statue; or, The Virgin's Kiss. 1849
Canonbury House; or, The Queen's Prophecy. 1858
Caroline of Brunswick.
Catherine Volmar; or, A Father's Revenge.
Ciprini; or, The Secrets of the Picture Gallery. Peterson, 18??. (British title?)
The Coral Island; or, The Hereditary Curse. 1849
Count Christoval.
The Countess of Lascelles; or, Self-Sacrifice.
The Days of Hogarth; or, The Mysteries of Old London. Dicks, 1884
The Drunkard's Progress. Henderson, 1841
Edgar Montrose; or, The Mysterious Penetent.
Ellen Monroe.
Ellen Percy; or, The Memoirs of an Actress. 1855
The Empress Eugenie's Boudoir; or, Mysteries of the Court of France. 1857. Also published as: The Mysteries of the Court of France.
Esther de Medina; or, The Crimes of London.
Eustace Quentin.
Faust. 1847
The Fortunes of the Ashtons.
The French Self-Instructor. 1846
The Gipsey Chief; or, The Haunted Oak.
Grace Darling; or, The Heroine of the Fern Islands. 1839
Gretna Green; or, All for Love.
Imogen Hartland; or, The Star of the Circus?
Isabella Vincent.
Joseph Wilmot; or, The Memoirs of a Manservant. 1853
Karaman, the Bandit Chief.
Kenneth. 1851
Lady Saxondale's Crimes.
Leila; or, The Star of Mingrelia.
Life in London.
Life in Paris; or, The Adventures of Alfred de Rosaun in the French Metropolis; see Alfred (de Rosaun)
Lord Saxondale; or, Life Among the London Aristocracy
The Loves of the Harem. 1855
Margaret; or, The Discarded Queen.
Mary Middleton; or, The History of a Fortune.
Mary Price; or, The Memoirs of a Servant Girl. 1853
Mary Stuart, Queen of Scots. Dicks, 1884
The Massacre of Glencoe. 1853
Master Timothy's Bookcase; or, The Magic Lanthorn of the World. Emans, 1842
Mrs. Fitzherbert.
The Mysteries of London (8 volumes). 1845-1850
The Mysteries of the Court of France; see The Empress Eugenie's Boudoir
The Mysteries of the Court of London (8 volumes). 1848-1856.
Mysteries of the Court of Naples.
The Mysteries of the Marchmonts. Munro, 18??. (British title?)
The Necromancer; or, The Mysteries of the Court of Henry the Eighth.
Omar Pasha; or, The Vizier's Daughter.
The Parricide; or, A Youth's Career of Crime.
Pickwick Abroad; or, Tour in France. 1839
Pope Joan; or, The Female Pontiff.
The Reformed Highwayman.
Robert Bruce, the Hero King of Scotland.
Robert Macaire in England. 1839
Rosa Lambert; or, The Memoirs of an Unfortunate Woman. 1854
Rose Foster.
The Rye House Plot; or, Ruth, the Conspirator's Daughter. 1854
The Seamstress; or, The White Slave of England.
A Sequel to Don Juan. 1843
The Slave Women of England.
The Soldier's Wife. 1853
The Steam Packet. 1850
Venetian Trelawney.
Vivian Bertram.
Wallace, the Hero of Scotland.
The White Lady.
The Young Duchess; or, Memoirs of a Lady of Quality
The Youthful Imposter. 1835

REYNOLDS, LOUISE (CLARISSA)
The Walton Mystery. Ward, 1872

REYNOLDS, MACK [DALLAS McCORD REYNOLDS]. 1917- .
The Case of the Little Green Men. Phoenix, 1951

REYNOLDS, MINNIE JOSEPHINE. 1865- .
The Crayon Clue. Kennerley, 1915

REYNOLDS, PETER. Pseudonym of Amelia Reynolds Long, 1904-1978, q.v. Other pseudonyms: Patrick Laing, Adrian Reynolds, qq.v. Joint pseudonym with Edna McHugh: Kathleen Buddington Coxe, q.v.
Behind the Evidence. Visionary Pub. Co., 1936

REYNOLDS, QUENTIN (JAMES). 1902-1965.
The Man Who Wouldn't Talk. Random, 1953

REYNOLDS, W(ARWICK)
The Mawpeth Millions. Amalgamated, 1946. (Sexton Blake.)

REYWALL, JOHN. Pseudonym.
The Trial of Alvin Boaker. Random, 1948

RHOADES, KNIGHT
She Died on the Stairway. Arcadia, 1947

RHODE, JOHN. Pseudonym of Cecil John Charles Street, 1884-1964. Other pseudonym: Miles Burton, q.v. Series character: Dr. Priestley = P.
A.S.F.: The Story of a Great Conspiracy. Bles, 1924. U.S. title: The White Menace. McBride, 1926
The Affair of the Substitute Doctor; see Dr. Goodwood's Locum
The Alarm. Bles, 1925
An Artist Dies. Bles, 1956. U.S. title: Death of an Artist. Dodd, 1956 P
Blackthorn House. Bles, 1949; Dodd, 1949 P
The Bloody Tower. Collins, 1938. U.S. title: The Tower of Evil. Dodd, 1938 P
Body Unidentified; see Proceed with Caution
The Bricklayer's Arms. Collins, 1945. U.S. title: Shadow of a Crime. Dodd, 1945 P
By Registered Post. Bles, 1953. U.S. title: The Mysterious Suspect. Dodd, 1953 P
The Case of the Forty Thieves; see Death at the Inn
The Claverton Affair; see The Claverton Mystery
The Claverton Mystery. Collins, 1933. U.S. title: The Claverton Affair. Dodd, 1933 P
The Corpse in the Car. Collins, 1935; Dodd, 1935 P
The Davidson Case. Bles, 1929. U.S. title: Murder at Bratton Grange. Dodd, 1929 P
Dead Men at the Folly. Collins, 1932; Dodd, 1932 P
Dead of the Night; see Night Exercise
Dead on the Track. Collins, 1943; Dodd, 1943 P
Death at Breakfast. Collins, 1936; Dodd, 1936 P
Death at the Dance. Bles, 1952; Dodd, 1952 P
Death at the Helm. Collins, 1941; Dodd, 1941 P
Death at the Inn. Bles, 1953. U.S. title: The Case of the Forty Thieves. Dodd, 1954 P
Death in Harley Street. Bles, 1946; Dodd, 1946 P
Death in the Hop Fields. Collins, 1937. U.S. title: The Harvest Murder. Dodd, 1937 P
Death in Wellington Road. Bles, 1952; Dodd, 1952 P
Death Invades the Meeting. Collins, 1944; Dodd, 1944 P
Death of a Bridegroom. Bles, 1957; Dodd, 1958 P
Death of a Godmother. Bles, 1955. U.S. title: Delayed Payment. Dodd, 1956 P
Death of an Artist; see An Artist Dies

Death of an Author. Bles, 1947; Dodd, 1948 P
Death on Sunday. Collins, 1939. U.S. title: The Elm Tree Murder. Dodd, 1939 P
Death on the Board. Collins, 1937. U.S. title: Death Sits on the Board. Dodd, 1937 P
Death on the Boat Train. Collins, 1940; Dodd, 1940 P
Death on the Lawn. Bles, 1954; Dodd, 1955 P
Death Pays a Dividend. Collins, 1939; Dodd, 1939 P
Death Sits on the Board; see Death on the Board
Death Takes a Partner. Bles, 1958; Dodd, 1958 P
Delayed Payment; see Death of a Godmother
Dr. Goodwood's Locum. Bles, 1951. U.S. title: The Affair of the Substitute Doctor. Dodd, 1951 P
Dr. Priestley Investigates; see Pinehurst
Dr. Priestley Lays a Trap; see The Motor Rally Mystery
Dr. Priestley's Quest. Bles, 1926 P
The Domestic Agency. Bles, 1955. U.S. title: Grave Matters. Dodd, 1955 P
The Double Florin. Bles, 1924
Double Identities; see The Two Graphs
The Dovebury Murders. Bles, 1954; Dodd, 1954 P
Drop to his Death, with Carter Dickson, q.v. (pseudonym of John Dickson Carr, 1905-1977, q.v.). Heinemann, 1939. U.S. title: Fatal Descent. Dodd, 1939
The Ellerby Case. Bles, 1927; Dodd, 1927 P
The Elm Tree Murder; see Death on Sunday
Experiment in Crime; see Nothing But the Truth
Family Affairs. Bles, 1950. U.S. title: The Last Suspect. Dodd, 1951 P
Fatal Descent; see Drop to his Death
The Fatal Garden; see Up the Garden Path
The Fatal Pool. Bles, 1960; Dodd, 1961 P
The Fire at Greycombe Farm; see Mystery at Greycombe Farm
The Fourth Bomb. Collins, 1942; Dodd, 1942 P
Grave Matters; see The Domestic Agency
The Hanging Woman. Collins, 1931; Dodd, 1931 P
The Harvest Murder; see Death in the Hop Fields
Hendon's First Case. Collins, 1935; Dodd, 1935 P
The House on Tollard Ridge. Bles, 1929; Dodd, 1929 P
In Face of the Verdict. Collins, 1936. U.S. title: In the Face of the Verdict. Dodd, 1940 P
In the Face of the Verdict; see In Face of the Verdict
Invisible Weapons. Collins, 1938; Dodd, 1938 P
The Lake House. Bles, 1946. U.S. title: Secret of the Lake House. Dodd, 1946 P
The Last Suspect; see Family Affairs
Licensed for Murder. Bles, 1958; Dodd, 1958 P
The Links in the Chain; see The Paper Bag
Mademoiselle from Armentieres. Bles, 1927
Men Die at Cyprus Lodge. Collins, 1943; Dodd, 1944 P
The Motor Rally Mystery. Collins, 1933. U.S. title: Dr. Priestley Lays a Trap. Dodd, 1933 P
Murder at Bratton Grange; see The Davidson Case
Murder at Derivale. Bles, 1958; Dodd, 1958 P
Murder at Lilac Cottage. Collins, 1940; Dodd, 1940 P
Murder at the Motor Show; see Mystery at Olympia
The Murders in Praed Street. Bles, 1928; Dodd, 1928 P
The Mysterious Suspect; see By Registered Post
Mystery at Greycombe Farm. Collins, 1932. U.S. title: The Fire at Greycombe Farm. Dodd, 1932 P
Mystery at Olympia. Collins, 1935. U.S. title: Murder at the Motor Show. Dodd, 1936 P
Night Exercise. Collins, 1942. U.S. title: Dead of the Night. Dodd, 1942
Nothing But the Truth. Bles, 1947. U.S. title: Experiment in Crime. Dodd, 1947 P
Open Verdict. Bles, 1956; Dodd, 1957 P
The Paddington Mystery. Bles, 1925 P
The Paper Bag. Bles, 1948. U.S. title: The Links in the Chain. Dodd, 1948 P
Peril at Cranbury Hall. Bles, 1930; Dodd, 1930 P
Pinehurst. Bles, 1930. U.S. title: Dr. Priestley Investigates. Dodd, 1930 P
Poison for One. Collins, 1934; Dodd, 1934 P
Proceed with Caution. Collins, 1937. U.S. title: Body Unidentified. Dodd, 1938 P
Robbery with Violence. Bles, 1957; Dodd, 1957 P
The Robthorne Mystery. Collins, 1934; Dodd, 1934 P
The Secret Meeting. Bles, 1951; Dodd, 1951 P
Secret of the Lake House; see The Lake House
Shadow of a Crime; see The Bricklayer's Arms
Shadow of an Alibi; see The Telephone Call
Shot at Dawn. Collins, 1934; Dodd, 1935 P
Signal for Death; see They Watched by Night
The Telephone Call. Bles, 1948. U.S. title: Shadow of an Alibi. Dodd, 1948 P
They Watched by Night. Collins, 1941. U.S. title: Signal for Death. Dodd, 1941 P
Three Cousins Die. Bles, 1959; Dodd, 1960 P
Too Many Suspects; see Vegetable Duck
The Tower of Evil; see The Bloody Tower
Tragedy at the Unicorn. Bles, 1928; Dodd, 1928 P
Tragedy on the Line. Collins, 1931; Dodd, 1931 P
Twice Dead. Bles, 1960; Dodd, 1960 P
The Two Graphs. Bles, 1950. U.S. title: Double Identities. Dodd, 1950 P
Up the Garden Path. Bles, 1949. U.S. title: The Fatal Garden. Dodd, 1949 P
The Vanishing Diary. Bles, 1961; Dodd, 1961 P
Vegetable Duck. Collins, 1944. U.S. title: Too Many Suspects. Dodd, 1945 P
The Venner Crime. Odhams, 1933; Dodd, 1934 P
The White Menace; see A.S.F.: The Story of a Great Conspiracy

RHODES, DENYS
Flyaway Peter. Richards, 1952

RHODES, EVAN H. 1929- .
-The Carrion Eaters. Stein, 1974; Allen, 1975

RHODES, KATHLYN
Crime on a Cruise. Hutchinson, 1935
-In Search of Stephanie. Hutchinson, 1941
-It Happened in Cairo. Hutchinson, 1944
The Lady was Warned. Hutchinson, 1936
-Strange Quartet. Hutchinson, 1938

RHYS-WILLIAMS, JULIET (EVANGELINE GLYN). 1898- .
Forty-Nine Chances. Rich, 1947. (Novelization of the play They had his Number, by R. J. Minney and Juliet Rhys-Williams.)

RICE, CRAIG. 1908-1957. Pseudonyms: Daphne Sanders, Michael Venning, q.v. See also: GYPSY ROSE LEE; (CHARLES) STUART PALMER, 1905-1968. Series characters: John J. Malone and the Justuses = M&J (see also: Larry M. Harris); Bingo Riggs and Handsome Kusak = R&K.
The April Robin Murders, with Ed McBain, q.v. Random, 1958; Hammond, 1959 R&K
The Big Midget Murders. Simon, 1942 M&J
But the Doctor Died. Lancer, 1967 M&J
The Corpse Steps Out. Simon, 1940; Eyre, 1940 M&J
Death at Three; see Eight Faces at Three
The Double Frame; see Knocked for a Loop
Eight Faces at Three. Simon, 1939; Eyre, 1939. Also published as: Death at Three. Cherry Tree, 1941 M&J
The Fourth Postman. Simon, 1948; Hammond, 1951 M&J
Having Wonderful Crime. Simon, 1943; Nicholson, 1944 M&J
Home Sweet Homicide. Simon, 1944
Innocent Bystander. Simon, 1949; Hammond, 1958
Knocked for a Loop. Simon, 1957. British title: The Double Frame. Hammond, 1958 M&J
The Lucky Stiff. Simon, 1945 M&J
My Kingdom for a Hearse. Simon, 1957; Hammond, 1959 M&J
The Name is Malone. Pyramid, 1958; Hammond, 1960 M ss
The Right Murder. Simon, 1941; Eyre, 1948 M&J
The Sunday Pigeon Murders. Simon, 1942; Nicholson, 1948 R&K
Telefair. Bobbs, 1942. Also published as: Yesterday's Murder. Popular Library, 1950
The Thursday Turkey Murders. Simon, 1943; Nicholson, 1946 R&K
Trial by Fury. Simon, 1941; Hammond, 1950 M&J
The Wrong Murder. Simon, 1940; Eyre, 1942 M&J
Yesterday's Murder; see Telefair

RICE, ELMER L. 1892-1967. Name originally: Elmer L. Reizenstein, q.v. See also: D. TORBETT.
Cock Robin, with Philip Barry, 1896- . French, 1929. (Play.)

RICE, JEFF. Series character: Carl Kolchak, in both titles.
The Night Stalker. PB, 1973
The Night Strangler. PB, 1973. (Novelization of the TV movie.)

RICE, LAVERNE
Well-Dressed for Murder. Doubleday, 1938

RICE, LOUISE (GUEST). 1880- .
By Whose Hand? Macaulay, 1930

RICH, ARTHUR T.
   The Curate Finds the Corpse. Bear, 1945

RICH, KATHLEEN
   The Deadly Rose; see Jacqueminot
   Jacqueminot. Tower, 1967. Also published as: The Deadly Rose. Belmont, 1972
   The Lucifer Mask. Tower, 1967

RICH, NICHOLAS
   The Blane Document. Hale, 1972
   The Seajet Spies. Hale, 1973
   Spy Now, Pay Later. Hale, 1972

RICH, WILLARD. Pseudonym.
   Brain-Waves and Death. Scribner, 1940

RICHARD, SUSAN
   Ashley Hall. Paperback Library, 1967
   Chateau Saxony. Paperback Library, 1971
   Intruder at Maison Benedict. Paperback Library, 1967
   The Secret of Chateau Kendall. Paperback Library, 1967
   Terror at Nelson Woods. Paperback Library, 1973

RICHARDS, ALLEN. Pseudonym of Richard A. Rosenthal, 1925- .
   To Market, to Market. Macmillan, 1961. British title: The Merchandise Murders. Hammond, 1964

RICHARDS, CLAY. Pseudonym of Kendell Foster Crossen, 1910- , q.v. Other pseudonyms: Bennett Barlay, M. E. Chaber, Richard Foster, Christopher Monig, qq.v. Series characters: Grant Kirby = GK; Kim Locke = KL (begun under the Kendell Foster Crossen byline).
   Death of an Angel. Bobbs, 1963 GK
   The Gentle Assassin. Bobbs, 1964; Boardman, 1965 KL
   The Marble Jungle. Obolensky, 1961; Cassell, 1963 GK
   Who Steals my Name. Bobbs, 1964; Boardman, 1965

RICHARDS, DAVID. Pseudonym of Richard (Leslie) Townshend Bickers, 1917- , q.v.
   Double Game. Digit, 1958

RICHARDS, FRANCIS. See: FRANCES (LOUISE DAVIS) LOCKRIDGE, 1896-1963; and RICHARD (ORSON) LOCKRIDGE, 1898- .

RICHARDS, HEDLEY
   The Beautiful Suspect. Fiction House, 1937
   The Deputy Avenger. Aldine, 1920
   The Meshes of Fear; or, The Curse of the Blue Diamonds. Henderson
   The Ossington Mystery. Henderson

RICHARDS, JAMES BRINSLEY. 1846-1892.
   The Alderman's Children. Bentley, 1891

RICHARDS, LESLIE
   Pursue the Wind. Manor, 1975

RICHARDS, MARK
   Vengeance is Mine. Columbine, 1940

RICHARDS, MARSDEN
   -A Brace for the Law. Digby, 1892

RICHARDS, PAUL
   Moscow at Noon is the Target. Award, 1973
   Our Spacecraft is Missing! Award, 1970
   The President has been Kidnapped! Award, 1971

RICHARDS, ROBIN
   Cold Blood. Hutchinson, 1920

RICHARDS, RONALD CHARLES WILLIAM. 1923- . Pseudonym: K. Allen Sadler, q.v.

RICHARDS, ROSS
   The Death Seekers. Hale, 1964
   Murder on the Monte. Mayflower, 1966. (Sexton Blake.)

RICHARDS, WILLIAM
   Dead Man's Tide. Graphic, 1953

RICHARDSON, ANTHONY (THOMAS STEWART CURRIE). 1899- .
   The Rose of Kantara. Odhams, 1951

RICHARDSON, CARL
   Effigy of a Spy. Hale, 1971
   Jump the High Wall. Hale, 1969
   The Name of the Game is Death. Hale, 1971

RICHARDSON, FRANK (COLLINS). 1870-1917.
   The Secret Kingdom. Duckworth, 1905
   2835 Mayfair. Laurie, 1907; Kennerley, 1907. Also published as: The Mayfair Mystery. Collins, 1929

RICHARDSON, H(ENRY) M(ARRIOTT). 1876- .
   The Rock of Justice. Hutchinson, 1928
   The Temple Murder. Hutchinson, 1926

RICHARDSON, LEANDER P(EASE). 1856-1918.
   The Prairie Detective. Street, 1889

RICHARDSON, MOZELLE (GRONER). 1914- .
   A Candle in the Wind. Morrow, 1973
   The Curse of Kalispoint. Paperback Library, 1971
   The Masks of Thespis. Warner, 1973
   Portrait of Fear. Paperback Library, 1971
   The Song of India. Morrow, 1975

RICHART, MARY
   Murder in the Town. Farrar, 1947

RICHBERG, DONALD (RANDALL). 1881-1960.
   -In the Dark. Forbes, 1912
   The Shadow Men. Forbes, 1911

RICHMOND, D.
   The Film Star Vanishes. Bear, 1945

RICHMOND, MARY
   -All That Glitters. Wright, 1954
   -Barbed Wire. Hale, 1941
   -Be My Love. Wright, 1967
   -Beloved Enemy. Wright, 1965
   -Brides of Doom. Wright, 1946
   -Cabin Nineteen. Wright, 1953
   -The Clock Strikes Ten. Wright, 1944
   Concealed Identity. Wright, 1938
   Danger Ahead. Wright, 1937
   -The Dark Countess. Wright, 1958
   Dark Horizon. Wright, 1937
   -The Devil Laughed. Wright, 1950
   Disciples of Satan. Wright, 1936
   -Enchanted Wooing. Wright, 1946
   -Evening in Paris. Wright, 1949
   -Feast of Lanterns. Wright, 1968
   -Fettered Love. Wright, 1955
   -Flight from a Throne. Wright, 1951
   -Flower in the Desert. Wright, 1943
   Footprints in the Sand. Wright, 1939
   -For Ever Beloved. Wright, 1968
   -For Those in Peril. Wright, 1957
   -Garden of Memories. Wright, 1947
   -Good-Time Girl. Wright, 1956
   -The Grim Tomorrow. Wright, 1953
   -Hearts in Turmoil. Wright, 1946
   -Hell Hath No Fury. Wright, 1956
   The Hidden Horror. Wright, 1937
   Hounded! Wright, 1936
   -Hour of Destiny. Wright, 1954
   -If I Should Lose You. Wright, 1959
   -I'll Always Remember. Wright, 1964
   In Deep Water. Wright, 1934
   In Fear of the Hangman. Wright, 1938
   In the Grip of the Dragon. Wright, 1939
   -Incredible Adventure. Wright, 1969
   -Indian Love Lyrics. Wright, 1958
   -Indian Lullaby. Wright, 1964
   Insurgent Love. Wright, 1940
   -I've Found My Love. Wright, 1955
   Jewels of Death. Wright, 1938
   -Journey to Happiness. Wright, 1963
   Judgment of Death. Wright, 1942
   -Justice for Julia. Wright, 1955
   -Kashmiri Love Song. Wright, 1967
   Lady in Distress. Wright, 1936
   -Lady of the Night. Wright, 1950
   -A Leap in the Dark. Wright, 1949
   -Look to the Dawn. Wright, 1946
   -Love Without Honour. Wright, 1956
   -Love's the Only Guide. Wright, 1964
   -Magnet for Danger. Wright, 1943
   -Maid of Athens. Wright, 1948
   -The Mandarin's Bride. Wright, 1945
   The Mark of the Dragon. Wright, 1935
   -Market of Venus. Hale, 1941
   -Marry in May. Wright, 1963
   The Masked Terror. Wright, 1934; Godwin, 1935
   -The Memory of You. Wright, 1950
   Murder by a Maniac. Wright, 1937
   -No Escape. Wright, 1952
   -Oasis of Tears. Wright, 1952
   -One Enchanted Evening. Wright, 1965
   -One Fine Day. Wright, 1966
   -One Glorious Spring. Wright, 1968
   -Only a Love Song. Wright, 1965
   -Paradise for Two. Wright, 1954
   -The Passionate Atonement. Wright, 1960
   Passport to Danger. Wright, 1938
   -Perilous Adventure. Wright, 1962
   Pirate Love. Wright, 1937
   The Pointing Finger. Wright, 1940
   Poison Weed. Wright, 1940
   -Prisoner of Love. Wright, 1962
   -Put Back the Clock. Wright, 1952
   -Queen of my Heart. Wright, 1963
   Red Claws. Wright, 1940
   -Red Dawning. Wright, 1946
   -The Reluctant Duchess. Wright, 1957
   -Reluctant Rebel. Wright, 1967
   -Risk All for Love. Wright, 1959
   -The Secret Hour. Wright, 1949
   The Secret of the Marshes. Wright, 1940
   The Secret of the Priory. Wright, 1935
   The Seven Bloodhounds. Wright, 1937
   Shadow of the Gallows. Wright, 1940
   -Shadow of the Past. Wright, 1960
   -A Star is Falling. Wright, 1960
   -The Steadfast Heart. Wright, 1961
   Stealthy Death. Wright, 1935
   Strange Cargo. Wright, 1933
   Suspicious Company. Wright, 1938
   -Tempest at Dawn. Wright, 1944
   Terror by Night. Wright, 1939
   Terror Stalks Abroad. Wright, 1935
   -That Fatal Night. Wright, 1949
   -Thin Ice. Wright, 1950
   -This Man Belongs to Me. Wright, 1951
   -This Road is Dangerous. Wright, 1950
   To Have and To Hold. Wright, 1961
   To Make You Mine. Wright, 1963
   Tomorrow's Harvest. Wright, 1947
   -Tragedy at Blue Aloes. Wright, 1958
   -Traitor's Harvest. Wright, 1942
   -Troubled Heritage. Wright, 1942
   -Unnatural Death. Wright, 1952
   -Unwelcome Rapture. Wright, 1961
   -Unwilling to Wed. Wright, 1959
   -The Valley of Doom. Wright, 1947
   -The Valley of the Shadow. Wright, 1947
   -Waltz of my Heart. Wright, 1968
   -Web of Enchantment. Wright, 1962
   -Wild Reckoning. Wright, 1953
   The Woman Cain. Wright, 1936

RICKARD, JESSIE LOUISA (MOORE). 1879-   .
   Byline sometimes: Mrs. Victor Rickard.
  -Ascendancy House. Jarrolds, 1944
   The Baccarat Club; see The Mystery of Vincent Dane
  -A Bird of Strange Plumage. Hodder, 1927
  -Blindfold. Cape, 1922
  -Cathy Rossiter. Hodder, 1919; Doran, 1920
  -The Dark Stranger. Hodder, 1930
  -Dregs. Rivers, 1914
   The Empty Villa. Hodder, 1929; Liveright, 1929
  -The Frantic Boast. Duckworth, 1917
  -The Guests of Chance. Hodder, 1928
   The Light Above the Crossroads. Duckworth, 1916; Dodd, 1918
   The Light That Lies. Hodder, 1927
   Murder by Night. Jarrolds, 1936
   The Mystery of Tara Heston. Jarrolds, 1938
   The Mystery of Vincent Dane. Hodder, 1930. U.S. title: The Baccarat Club. Liveright, 1929
   Not Sufficient Evidence. Constable, 1926
  -Old Sins have Long Shadows. Constable, 1924; Houghton, 1924
  -The Passionate City. Hodder, 1928
  -A Perilous Elopement. Hodder, 1928
  -Sensation at Blue Harbour. Jarrolds, 1934
  -Shandon Hall. Jarrolds, 1950
   Upstairs. Constable, 1925; Doubleday, 1926
  -White Satin. Jarrolds, 1945
  -Without Justification. Cape, 1923
  -Yesterday's Love. Hodder, 1931
  -The Young Man in Question. Jarrolds, 1933
  -Young Mr. Gibbs. Nash, 1911
  -Young Mrs. Henniker. Jarrolds, 1931

RICKARD, MRS. VICTOR. 1879-   . Byline usually: JESSIE LOUISA (MOORE) RICKARD, q.v.

RICKETT, FRANCES
   The Prowler. Simon, 1963; Hale, 1964
   Tread Softly. Simon, 1964; Hale, 1964

RICO, DON. Series characters: Burgess (Buzz) Cardigan, in at least those marked BC; Casey Grant, in at least those marked CG.
   The Daisy Dilemma. Lancer, 1967 BC
   Lorelei. Belmont, 1966
   The Man from Pansy. Lancer, 1967 BC
   Nightmare of Eyes. Lancer, 1967
   Passion Flower Puzzle. Lancer, 1969
   The Ring-a-Ding Girl. Paperback Library, 1969 CG
   So Sweet, So Deadly. Paperback Library, 1970 CG
   The Swinging Virgin. Paperback Library, 1969 CG

RIDDELL, FLORENCE
   The Valley of Suspicion. Bles, 1930. U.S. title: Suspicion. Lippincott, 1931

RIDDELL, GILBERT
   Murder with Music. Alliance, 1935

RIDDELL, MRS. J. H. [CHARLOTTE ELIZA LAWSON COWAN RIDDELL]. 1832-1906.
   Above Suspicion. Tinsley, 1876; Estes, 1876
  -Alaric Spenceley; or, A High Ideal. Skeet, 1881
  -Austin Friars. Tinsley, 1870
  -The Banshee's Warning, and other tales. Remington, 1894 ss
  -Daisies and Buttercups. Bentley, 1882; Harper, 1882
  -Did He Deserve It? Downey, 1897
   The Disappearance of Mr. Jeremiah Redworth. Routledge, 1879; Munro, 1878
  -The Earl's Promise. Tinsley, 1873
  -Far Above Rubies. Tinsley, 1867; Lippincott, 1867
  -The Footfall of Fate. White, 1900
  -Frank Sinclair's Wife, and other stories. Tinsley, 1874 ss
  -The Government Official. Bentley, 1887
  -Handsome Phil, and other stories. White, 1899 ss
  -The Head of the Firm. Heinemann, 1892; Lovell, 1891
  -Her Mother's Darling. Tinsley, 1877; Munro, 1880
  -Home, Sweet Home. Tinsley, 1873
  -Idle Tales. Ward, 1888 ss
  -A Life's Assize. Tinsley, 1871; Harper, 1871
  -Miss Gascoigne. Ward, 1887; Appleton, 1887
  -Mitre Court. Bentley, 1885
  -Mortmorley's Estate. Tinsley, 1874
  -My First Love. Hutchinson, 1891; Lovell, 1891
   The Nun's Curse. Ward, 1888; Munro, 1888
  -Poor Fellow! White, 1902; Dick, 1858
  -The Prince of Wales's Garden-Party, and other stories. Chatto, 1882; Munro, 1882 ss
  -Princess Sunshine, and other stories. Ward, 1889; Lovel, 1890 ss
  -The Race for Wealth. Tinsley, 1886; Harper, 1866
  -The Rich Husband. Tinsley, 1867; Peterson, 1867
  -A Rich Man's Daughter. White, 1897; International News, 1895
  -The Rusty Sword; or, Thereby Hangs a Tale. Christian Knowledge Society, 1893
  -The Senior Partner. Bentley, 1881; Harper, 1882
   A Silent Tragedy. White, 1893
  -A Struggle for Fame. Bentley, 1883; Harper, 1883
  -Susan Drummond. Bentley, 1884; Harper, 1884
  -The Uninhabited House. Routledge, 1866
  -Weird Stories. Hogg, 1884 ss

RIDDELL, JOHN. Pseudonym of Corey Ford, 1902-1969.
   The John Riddell Murder Case: A Philo Vance Parody. Scribner (New York & London), 1930

RIDEAL, CHARLES F. See: MAURICE MOSER.

RIDEAUX, CHARLES DE BALZAC. 1900-1971. Pseudonym: John Chancellor, q.v.

RIDEOUT, HENRY MILNER. 1877-1927.
  -Admiral's Light. Houghton, 1907
   Dulcarnon. Duffield, 1925; Hurst, 1926
   Fern Seed. Duffield, 1921; Hurst, 1922
  -Man Eater. Duffield, 1924; Hurst, 1927
   No Man's Money; see Tin Cowrie Dass
  -Tin Cowrie Dass. Duffield, 1918. British title: No Man's Money. Jarrolds, 1919
   The Twisted Foot. Houghton, 1910; Constable, 1910

RIDER, ANNE. 1924-   .
   The Bad Samaritan. Bodley Head, 1965
   A Safe Place. Bobbs, 1974

RIDER, SARAH
   The Misplaced Corpse. Houghton, 1940

RIDGE, W(ILLIAM) PETT.   -1930.
   A Breaker of Laws. Harper (London), 1900; Macmillan, 1900
   By Order of the Magistrate; see Mord Em'ly
   Mord Em'ly. Pearson, 1898. U.S. title: By Order of the Magistrate. Harper, 1898. Also published as: "Mordemly"; or, By Order of the Magistrate. Harper, 1898

RIDGEWAY, PHILIP and COLIN FRASER
   The Switch. Compact, 1964

RIDGWAY, JASON. Pseudonym of Milton Lesser, 1928-   . Other pseudonyms: Andrew Frazer, Stephen Marlowe, C. H. Thames, qq.v. See also: RICHARD S(COTT) PRATHER, 1921-   . Series character: Brian Guy = BG.
   Adam's Fall. Permabooks, 1960 BG
   Hardly a Man is Now Alive. Permabooks, 1962 BG
   People in Glass House. Permabooks, 1961 BG
   The Treasure of the Cosa Nostra. PB, 1966 BG
   West Side Jungle. Signet, 1958

RIDLEY, ARNOLD. 1896-   . See also: RUTH ALEXANDER.
   The Ghost Train. French (London), 1930; French (New York), 1931. (3-act play.)
   Murder Happens. French (London), 1951. (3-act play.)
   Peril at End House. French (London), 1945. (3-act play based on the Agatha Christie novel, q.v.)
   Recipe for Murder. Deane, 1936; Baker, 1936. (A play.)
   The Wrecker, with Bernard Merivale, 1882-1939. French (London), 1930. (3-act play.)

RIDLEY, NAT, JR. House name. Series character: Nat Ridley, in all titles.
   The Crime on the Limited; or, Nat Ridley in the Follies. Garden City, 1926
   A Daring Abduction; or, Nat Ridley's Biggest Fight. Garden City, 1926
   The Double Dagger; or, Nat Ridley's Mexican Trail. Garden City, 1926
   The Great Circus Mystery; or, Nat Ridley on a Crooked Trail. Garden City, 1926
   Guilty or Not Guilty? or, Nat Ridley's Great Race Track Case. Garden City, 1926
   In the Grip of the Kidnappers. Garden City, 1926
   In the Nick of Time; or, Nat Ridley Saving a Life. Garden City, 1926
   The Mountain Inn Mystery; or, Nat Ridley with the Forest Rangers. Garden City, 1927
   The Race Track Crooks; or, Nat Ridley's Queerest Puzzle. Garden City, 1926
   A Scream in the Dark; or, Nat Ridley's Crimson Clue. Garden City, 1926
   A Secret of the Stage; or, Nat Ridley and the Bouquet of Death. Garden City, 1926
   The Stolen Liberty Bonds. Garden City, 1926
   The Stolen Nugget of Gold; or, Nat Ridley on the Yukon. Garden City, 1926
   Tracked to the West; or, Nat Ridley at the Magnet Mine. Garden City, 1926
   The Western Express Robbery; or, Nat Ridley and the Mail Thieves. Garden City, 1927

RIEFE, ALAN. 1925-   . Series character: Huntington Cage, in all titles.
   The Black Widower. Popular Library, 1975
   The Bullet-Proof Man. Popular Library, 1975

The Conspirators. Popular Library, 1975; New English Library pb, 1977
The Killer with a Golden Touch. Popular Library, 1975
The Lady Killers. Popular Library, 1975; New English Library pb, 1976
The Silver Puma. Popular Library, 1975

RIEMAN, (MILDRED) TERRY
Vamp Till Ready. Harper, 1954; Gollancz, 1955

RIENITS, REX. 1909-1971.
Assassin for Hire. Muller, 1952

RIESENBERG, FELIX. 1879-1939.
The Left-Handed Passenger. Doubleday, 1935; Nicholson, 1935

RIESS, CURT. 1902- .
High Stakes. Putnam, 1942

RIFKIN, SHEPARD. 1918- .
Ladyfingers. GM, 1969; Coronet, 1969
McQuaid. Putnam, 1974; Hale, 1975
The Murderer Vine. Dodd, 1970; Hale, 1973

RIGONI, ORLANDO JOSEPH. 1897- .
Pseudonym: Leslie Ames, q.v.

RIGSBY, HOWARD. 1909- . Pseudonym: Vechel Howard, q.v.
As a Man Falls. GM, 1954; Muller, 1960
The Avenger. Crowell, 1957. Also published as: Naked to my Pride. Popular Library, 1958
Calliope Reef. Doubleday, 1967
Clash of Shadows. Lippincott, 1959; Hale, 1961
Kill and Tell. Morrow, 1951; Muller, 1954
Lucinda. GM, 1954; Fawcett (London), 1955
Murder for the Holidays. Morrow, 1951; Muller, 1952
Naked to my Pride; see The Avenger
-A Time for Passion. Dell, 1960
The Tulip Tree. Doubleday, 1963

RILEY, FRANK
Jesus II. Sherbourne, 1972
The Kocska Formula. Sherbourne, 1971

RILLA, WOLF (PETER)
The Dispensable Man. Allen, 1973; Day, 1974

RIMEL, DUANE W(ELDON). 1915- .
The Curse of Cain. McKay, 1945
The Jury is Out. Cherry Tree, 1947
Motive for Murder. Cherry Tree, 1945

RIMMER, ROBERT H. 1917- .
The Zolotov Affair. Sherbourne, 1967; New English Library pb, 1969

RINEHART, MARY ROBERTS. 1876-1958. Series character: Hilda Adams = HA.
The After House. Houghton, 1914; Simpkin, 1915
The Album. Farrar, 1933; Cassell, 1933
Alibi for Isabel. Farrar, 1944; Cassell, 1946. Title story published separately: Dell 10¢ pb, 1951 ss
The Amazing Adventures of Letitia Carberry. Bobbs, 1911; Hodder, 1919 ss
The Bat, with Avery Hopwood, 1884-1928. French (New York & London), 1932. (A play based on Rinehart's novel The Circular Staircase, q.v.)
The Bat, with Avery Hopwood, 1884-1928. Doran, 1926; Cassell, 1926. (Novelization of the play.)
The Buckled Bag; see Mary Roberts Rinehart's Crime Book
The Case of Elinor Norton; see The State vs. Elinor Norton
The Case of Jennie Brice. Bobbs, 1913; Hodder, 1919
The Circular Staircase. Bobbs, 1908; Cassell, 1909
The Curve of the Catenary. Royce, 1945
Dangerous Days. Doran, 1919; Hodder, 1919
The Door. Farrar, 1930; Hodder, 1930
The Double Alibi; see Miss Pinkerton
Episode of the Wandering Knife. Rinehart, 1950. British title: The Wandering Knife. Cassell, 1951. (Three novelets.)
The Frightened Wife. Rinehart, 1953; Cassell, 1954 ss
The Great Mistake. Farrar, 1940; Cassell, 1941
Haunted Lady. Farrar, 1942; Cassell, 1942 HA
Locked Doors; see Mary Roberts Rinehart's Crime Book
The Man in Lower Ten. Bobbs, 1909; Cassell, 1909
Mary Roberts Rinehart's Crime Book. Farrar, 1933. (Includes two otherwise uncollected Hilda Adams novelets, The Buckled Bag and Locked Doors, of which the latter was later published separately: Dell 10¢ pb, 1951.)
Miss Pinkerton. Farrar, 1932. British title: The Double Alibi. Cassell, 1932 HA
The Mystery Lamp; see The Red Lamp
The Pool; see The Swimming Pool
The Red Lamp. Doran, 1925. British title: The Mystery Lamp. Hodder, 1925
Sight Unseen, and The Confession. Doran, 1921; Hodder, 1921. (Two novelets.)
The State vs. Elinor Norton. Farrar, 1934. British title: The Case of Elinor Norton. Cassell, 1934
The Swimming Pool. Rinehart, 1952. British title: The Pool. Cassell, 1952
Two Flights Up. Doubleday, 1928; Hodder, 1928
The Wall. Farrar, 1938; Cassell, 1938
The Wandering Knife; see Episode of the Wandering Knife
Where There's a Will. Bobbs, 1912
The Window at the White Cat. Bobbs, 1910; Nash, 1911
The Yellow Room. Farrar, 1945; Cassell, 1949

RING, ADAM. Pseudonym of Blair Reed, q.v.
Killers Play Rough. Crown, 1946

RING, DOUGLAS. Pseudonym of Richard S(cott) Prather, 1921- , q.v. Other pseudonym: David Knight, q.v.
The Peddler. Lion, 1952. Reprinted as by Prather: GM, 1963; Muller pb 1963

RIOTI, R.
Scarlet Widow. Milestone, 1953

RIPLEY, (HAROLD) AUSTIN. 1896- .
How Good a Detective are You? Stokes, 1934; Foulsham, 1939 ss in quiz form
Minute Mysteries. Houghton, 1932 ss in quiz form
Minute Mysteries. PB, 1949 ss in quiz form (A pb original, not a reprint of the above volume.)
Mystery Puzzles. Stokes, 1937 ss in quiz form

RIPLEY, CLEMENTS. 1892-1954.
Murder Walks Alone. Messner, 1935; Eldon, 1935

RIPLEY, JACK. Pseudonym of John (William) Wainwright, 1921- , q.v. Series character: John George Davis, in all titles.
Davis Doesn't Live Here Any More. H. Hamilton, 1971; Doubleday, 1972
My God How the Money Rolls In. H. Hamilton, 1972
My Word You Should Have Seen Us. H. Hamilton, 1972
The Pig That Got Up and Slowly Walked Away. H. Hamilton, 1971

RIPPON, MARION (EDITH). 1921- .
Behold, the Druid Weeps. Doubleday, 1970; Hale, 1972
The Hand of Solange. Doubleday, 1969
The Ninth Tentacle. Doubleday, 1974

RISCO, M.
Corpse at College. Scion, 1952
Over My Dead Body. Milestone, 1953
Ramona. Milestone, 1953
Visa for Violence. Milestone, 1954

RISING, LAWRENCE
She Who was Helena Cass. Doran, 1920; Hodder, 1920

RITA. Pseudonym of Eliza Margaret J. Gollan Humphreys, 1860-1938.
-The Doctor's Secret. White, 1890; Lovell, 1890
-Grim Justice. Newnes, 1907
The Mystery of a Turkish Bath. White, 1888; Lovell, 1888
-An Old Rogue's Tragedy. Hutchinson, 1899
The Philanthropic Burglar. Modern, 193?
-The Pointing Finger. Nash, 1907

RITCHIE, HETTY
Death Runs on Skis. Methuen, 1935

RITCHIE, JACK
A New Leaf, and other stories. Dell, 1971 ss

RITCHIE, ROBERT WELLES. See also: EARL DERR BIGGERS, 1844-1933.
Deep Furrows. Crowell, 1927; Bles, 1927

RITNER, PETER. 1927- .
Red Carpet for the Shah. Morrow, 1975; Weidenfeld, 1976

RITSON, JOHN. Pseudonym of Douglas Gordon Baber, 1918- .
Beneath the Precipice. Boardman, 1962
The Deadly Blunder. Boardman, 1964
Death of a Mind. Boardman, 1962
The Desperate Venture. Boardman, 1963

RITTENBERG, MAX. 1880- .
-Every Man his Price. Methuen, 1914; Dillingham, 1914
-Gold and Thorns. Ward, 1915
-The Mind Reader. Appleton (London & New York), 1913
-Swirling Waters. Methuen, 1913; Dillingham, 1913

RIVERS, ANNE
Payment for Silence. Hurst, 1974; Walker, 1975

RIVERS, RONALD
"The Coniackers"; or, The Driggs-Guyon Gang of Notorious Counterfeiters. Laird, 1889

RIVES, ANNE
The Incident. Dutton, 1962. British title: Over the Tunnel. Harvill, 1962. (Translation of L'Incident. Paris, 1961.)

RIVES, HALLIE ERMINIE. 1876-1956.
   The Magic Man. Dodd, 1927; Hutchinson, 1928

RIVETT, EDITH CAROLINE. 1894-1958. Pseudonyms: Carol Carnac, E. C. R. Lorac, qq.v.

ROAN, TOM
   The Dragon Strikes Back. Melrose, 1936; Messner, 1936
   Greedy Fingers. Mellifont, 1953

ROBB, JOHN
   -Advance South. Hamilton Stafford, 1955
   -American Legionnaire. Hamilton Stafford, 1952
   -Broken Ramparts. Hamilton Stafford, 1951
   Four Corpses in a Million. Big Ben, 1942
   I Shall Avenge. Hamilton Stafford, 1954
   -The Last Deserter. Hamilton Stafford, 1952
   -The Lost Garrison. Hamilton Stafford, 1952
   -March of the Legion. Hamilton Stafford, 1951
   Mission of Mercy. Hamilton Stafford, 1954
   -Patrol to Zaruse. Hamilton Stafford, 1952
   Punitive Action. Hamilton Stafford, 1954
   -Revolt in the Desert. Hamilton Stafford, 1952
   -Space Beam. Hamilton Stafford, 1951
   -State of Emergency. Hamilton Stafford, 1955
   Storm Evil. Hamilton Stafford, 1954
   We, the Condemned. Hamilton Stafford, 1954
   Zone Zero. Hamilton Stafford, 1954

ROBBE-GRILLET, ALAIN. 1922-   .
   The Erasers. Calder, 1963; Grove, 1964. (Translation of Les Gommes. Paris, 1962.)
   -In the Labyrinth. Grove, 1960. (Translation of Dans le Labyrinthe. Paris, 1959.)
   -Jealousy. Calder, 1960; Grove, 1959. (Translation of La Jalousie. Paris, 1957.)
   -Last Year at Marienbad. Calder, 1962; Grove, 1962. (Translation of L'Annee Derniere a Marienbad. Paris, 1961.)
   The Voyeur. Calder, 1959; Grove, 1958. (Translation of Le Voyeur. Paris, 1959.)

ROBBINS, CLARENCE AARON. 1888-1949. Pseudonym: Tod Robbins, q.v.

ROBBINS, CLIFTON. 1890-   . Series characters: Clay Harrison = CH; Staveley = S.
   Death Forms Threes. Rich, 1940 S
   Death on the Highway. Benn, 1933 CH
   Dusty Death. Benn, 1931; Appleton, 1932 CH
   The Man Without a Face. Benn, 1932. U.S. title: The Mystery of Mr. Cross. Appleton, 1933 CH
   Methylated Murder. Butterworth, 1935 CH
   Murder by Twenty-Five. Butterworth, 1936
   The Mystery of Mr. Cross; see The Man Without a Face
   Six Sign-Post Murder. Rich, 1939 S
   Smash and Grab. Benn, 1934; Appleton, 1934 CH

ROBBINS, TOD. Pseudonym of Clarence Aaron Robbins, 1888-1949.
   The Master of Murder. Allan, 1933
   -Mysterious Martin. Ogilvie, 1912
   The Three Freaks; see The Unholy Three
   The Unholy Three. Lane, 1917. Also published as: The Three Freaks. Allan, 1934

ROBERTS, ANTHONY. Pseudonym of John B(asil) Watney, 1915-   , q.v.
   Scheme for One. Gifford, 1945

ROBERTS, ARTHUR GUY. 1903-   . Pseudonym: Guy Clifford, q.v.

ROBERTS, BEN. See: IVAN GOFF.

ROBERTS, CARL ERIC BECHHOFER. 1894-1949. Pseudonym: Ephesian, q.v. See also: GEORGE GOODCHILD, 1888-   , and (CARL ERIC) BECHHOFER ROBERTS.

ROBERTS, DAVID. 1924-   .
   Journey from Baghdad. Doubleday, 1969

ROBERTS, DOROTHY JAMES. 1903-   . Pseudonym (?): Peter Mortimer, q.v.

ROBERTS, DORRIS
   Beginning of a Crime. Dorrance, 1958

ROBERTS, JAMES HALL. Pseudonym of Robert L(ipscomb) Duncan, 1927-   , q.v.
   -The Burning Sky. Morrow, 1966
   The February Plan. Morrow, 1967; Deutsch, 1967
   The Q Document. Morrow, 1964; Cape, 1965

ROBERTS, JAN
   The Judas Sheep. Souvenir, 1974; Saturday Review Press, 1975

ROBERTS, JANET LOUISE. 1925-   . Pseudonyms: Louisa Bronte, Rebecca Danton, Janette Radcliffe, qq.v. Some of the titles below are more straight romance than gothic.
   The Cardross Luck. Dell, 1974
   Castlereagh. PB, 1975
   The Curse of Kenton. Avon, 1972
   The Dancing Doll. Dell, 1973
   Dark Rose. Lancer, 1971
   The Devil's Own. Avon, 1972
   The Dornstein Ikon. Avon, 1973
   The First Waltz. Dell, 1974
   The Golden Thistle. Dell, 1973
   Isle of the Dolphins. Avon, 1973
   Jewels of Terror. Lancer, 1970
   La Casa Dorada. Dell, 1973
   Love Song. Pinnacle, 1971
   A Marriage of Inconvenience. Dell, 1972
   My Lady Mischief. Dell, 1973
   Ravenswood. Avon, 1971
   Rivertown. Avon, 1972
   The Weeping Lady. Lancer, 1971

ROBERTS, KATHERINE. 1895-   .
   Center of the Web. Doubleday, 1942
   Private Report. Doubleday, 1943

ROBERTS, LEE. Pseudonym of Robert (Lee) Martin, 1908-1976, q.v. Series character: Dr. Clinton Shannon, in at least those marked CS.
   The Case of the Missing Lovers. Dodd, 1957; Foulsham, 1958
   Death of a Ladies' Man. GM, 1960; Muller pb, 1960. Reprinted in Britain as by Robert Martin: Hale, 1969 CS
   If the Shoe Fits. Dodd, 1959; Hale, 1960 CS
   Judas Journey. Dodd, 1956. British title: Mahogany Murder. Foulsham, 1957
   Little Sister. GM, 1952
   Mahogany Murder; see Judas Journey
   Once a Widow. Dodd, 1957; Hale, 1961
   The Pale Door. Dodd, 1955; Foulsham, 1956
   Suspicion. Curtis, 1971; Hale, 1964 CS

ROBERTS, LILLIAN
   Rafferty and the Gold Dust Twins. Paperback Library, 1975. (Novelization of the movie.)

ROBERTS, MARION. Series characters: Anne and David Layton, in at least those marked L.
   A Mask for Crime. Eldon, 1935 L
   Red Greed. Eldon, 1934 L
   The Yellow Robed Wago. Eldon, 1936

ROBERTS, MARY CARTER
   Little Brother Fate. Farrar, 1957; Gollancz, 1958

ROBERTS, MORLEY. 1857-1942.
   -The Adventure of the Broad Arrow. Hutchinson, 1897
   -The Degradation of Geoffrey Alwith. Downey, 1895; Sergel, 1895
   -The Descent of the Duchess. Sands, 1900
   The Fugitives; see Taken by Assault; or, The Fugitives
   -The Grinder's Wheel. Nelson, 1907
   -Midsummer Madness. Nash, 1909 ss
   -The Plunderers. Methuen, 1900
   -The Prey of the Strongest. Hurst, 1906
   The Scent of Death. Nash, 1931
   -Taken by Assault; or, The Fugitives. Sands, 1901. U.S. title: The Fugitives. McClure, 1900

ROBERTS, R(ICHARD) ELLIS. 1879-1953.
   -The Other End. Palmer, 1923 ss

ROBERTS, ROY. Pseudonym of Alexander Brinchmann, 1888-   .
   The Crayfish Club. Hodder, 1931

ROBERTS, SUZANNE
   House of Cain. Dell, 1975
   Terror at Tansey Hill. Dell, 1975
   To Kill a House. Lancer, 1973

ROBERTS, THOMAS A. 1947-   .
   The Heart of the Dog. Random, 1972

ROBERTS, W(ALTER) ADOLPHE. 1886-1962. Pseudonym: Stephen Endicott, q.v.
   The Haunting Hand. Macaulay, 1926; Hutchinson, 1927
   The Mind Reader. Macaulay, 1929
   The Top-Floor Killer. Nicholson, 1935

ROBERTS, WILLO DAVIS. 1928-   .
   Becca's Child. Lancer, 1972
   Dangerous Legacy. Lancer, 1972
   Devil Boy. Signet, 1970
   Didn't Anybody Know My Wife? Putnam, 1974
   The Evil Children. Lancer, 1973
   The Face of Danger. Lancer, 1972
   The Gates of Montrain. Lancer, 1971
   The Ghosts of Harrel. Lancer, 1971
   The Girl Who Wasn't There. Arcadia, 1957
   The Gods in Green. Lancer, 1973
   The House at Fern Canyon. Lancer, 1970
   Inherit the Darkness. Lancer, 1972
   Invitation to Evil. Lancer, 1970
   Key Witness. Putnam, 1975
   King's Pawn. Lancer, 1971
   Murder at Grand Bay. Arcadia, 1955
   Murder is so Easy. Vega, 1961
   Return to Darkness. Lancer, 1969
   Shadow of a Past Love. Lancer, 1970
   Shroud of Fog. Ace, 1970
   Sing a Dark Song. Lancer, 1972

Sinister Gardens. Lancer, 1972
The Suspected Four. Vega, 1962
The Tarot Spell. Lancer, 1970
The Terror Trap. Lancer, 1971
The Waiting Darkness. Lancer, 1970
The Watchers. Lancer, 1971
White Jade. Doubleday, 1975

ROBERTSHAW, JAMES
-Merivale; or, Phases of Southern Life. Dillingham, 1898

ROBERTSON, ALEXANDER
-Irish Monte Cristo Abroad; or, The Secrets of the Catacombs. Street, 1889
-Irish Monte Cristo's Search; or, The Bonanza King in New York. Street, 1889
-Irish Monte Cristo's Trail; or, Hunted from the Pyramids to Berlin. Street, 1890
-Joe Leslie's Wife; or, A Skeleton in the Closet. Smith, 1892
Old Specie, the Treasury Detective; or, The Harbor Lights of New York. Street, 1890
The Vestibule Limited Mystery. Street, 1891

ROBERTSON, ANDREW
The Kidnapped Squatter and other Australian tales. Longmans, 1891 ss

ROBERTSON, COLIN. 1906- . Series characters: Peter Grayleigh = PG; Supt. Bradley = B; Inspector John Martin, in at least those marked JM; Vicky McBain = VM; Edward North = EN; Insp. Robert Strong, in at least those marked RS; Alan Steel = AS.
Alibi in Black. Ward, 1944 PG
The Amazing Corpse. Ward, 1942 PG
The Black Onyx Ring. Mellifont, 1936
Calling Peter Grayleigh. Ward, 1948 PG
Clash of Steel. Hale, 1965 AS
Conflict of Shadows. Hale, 1963 B
The Dark Knight. Ward, 1946 PG
Dark Money. Hale, 1962
Dead on Time. Hale, 1964 B
Death Wears Red Shoes. Ward, 1949 PG
Demon's Moon. Ward, 1951
Devil or Saint? Ward, 1936
The Devil's Cloak. Hale, 1969 B
The Devil's Lady. Ward, 1947 PG
Double Take. Hale, 1967 B
Dusky Limelight. Ward, 1950 EN
The Eastlake Affair. Long, 1957 VM
Explosion! Ward, 1945 PG
The Fake. Ward, 1937 JM
The Frightened Widow. Hale, 1963 B
Ghost Fingers. Ward, 1941
The Golden Triangle. Hale, 1959 VM
The Green Diamonds. Hale, 1970 B
House of Intrigue. Ward, 1937
The Judas Spies. Hale, 1966 AS
Killer's Mask. Hale, 1966 B
Knaves' Castle. Ward, 1948 PG
Lady, Take Care. Allen, 1952 EN
A Lonely Place to Die. Hale, 1969 PG
The Marble Tomb Mystery. Ward, 1936 RS
Murder in the Morning. Long, 1957 B
Murder Sits Pretty. Hale, 1961 VM
Night Shadows. Ward, 1935 JM
Night Trap. Hale, 1960
No Trial—No Error. Allen, 1953 EN
North for Danger. Allen, 1952 EN
Painted Faces. Ward, 1935 RS
Peter Grayleigh Flies High. Ward, 1951 PG
Project X. Hale, 1968 AS
Sinister Moonlight. Hale, 1965 B
Smugglers' Moon. Ward, 1954 PG
Soho Spy. Ward, 1940 RS

The Stalking Stranger. Ward, 1939 JM
Sweet Justice. Ward, 1949
The Temple of Dawn. Ward, 1939 PG
The Threatening Shadows. Hale, 1959 VM
The Tiger's Claws. Ward, 1951 VM
Time to Kill. Hale, 1961 B
Twice Dead. Hale, 1968 B
Two Must Die. Ward, 1946 PG
Venetian Mask. Ward, 1956 VM
White Menace. Ward, 1938 RS
Who Rides a Tiger? Long, 1958 VM
Without Motive. Pendulum, 1946 ss
The Yellow Strangler. Ward, 1934; Hillman-Curl, 1938
You Can Keep the Corpse. Ward, 1955 VM
Zero Hour. Ward, 1942 PG

ROBERTSON, CONSTANCE NOYES. 1897- .
Pseudonym: Dana Scott, q.v.

ROBERTSON, HELEN. Pseudonym of Helen (Jean Mary) Edmiston, 1913- , q.v. Series character: Insp. Lathom Dynes, in at least those marked LD.
The Chinese Goose. Macdonald, 1960. U.S. title: Swan Song. Doubleday, 1960 LD
The Crystal-Gazers. Macdonald, 1957; Doubleday, 1958 LD
Swan Song; see The Chinese Goose
Venice of the Black Sea. Macdonald, 1956 LD
The Winged Witnesses. Macdonald, 1955

ROBERTSON, JOHN
Death Goes to Sea. Foster, 1947

ROBERTSON, KEITH CARLTON. 1914- .
Pseudonym: Carlton Keith, q.v.

ROBERTSON, L(ILIAN) M.
-Due to the Lion Tamer. Joseph, 1964
Frederika and the Convict; see Mr. Cooper's Frederika
Mr. Cooper's Frederika. Hodder, 1965. U.S. title: Frederika and the Convict. Doubleday, 1965

ROBERTSON, LILIAN MAY. Pseudonym: Glen Steuart, q.v.

ROBERTSON, MANNING K. Series character: Steve Carradine, in at least those marked SC.
Blueprint for Destruction. Badger, 196? SC
Night Passage to Kano. Badger, 196? SC
-Rosaria. Badger, 1961
The Secret Enemy. Badger, 196?
Seek and Destroy. Badger, 1965 SC

ROBERTSON, MUIRHEAD. Pseudonym of Henry Johnson.
A Lombard Street Mystery. Bartholomew, 1888

ROBERTSON, WILFRID. 1892- .
-The House on the Broads. Quality, 1954

ROBERTSON, WILLIAM
Morris Hume, Detective. Hodge, 1905 ss

ROBESON, KENNETH. House name. The first series listed below is all Doc Savage stories, reprinted from the pulps; the second series is all Avenger stories, reprinted from the pulps through #24, thereafter new stories by Ron(ald Joseph) Goulart, 1933- , q.v., under the Kenneth Robeson byline. The Doc Savage stories were all written by Lester Dent, 1905-1959, q.v., except where indicated. Authorship of The Avenger series is indicated by Paul Ernst (1886- , q.v.) = PE (#1-24) and Ron Goulart = RG (#25-36). The series number is given in parenthesis for both series. Ex-

cept where indicated, Doc Savage titles were first published in book form by Bantam; all Avenger titles were published by Warner Paperback Library.
The Annihilist. 1968; Bantam (London), 1969 (31)
The Black Spot. 1974 (76) (By Laurence Donovan.)
Brand of the Werewolf. 1965; Bantam (London), 1965 (5)
Cold Death. 1968; Bantam (London), 1968 (21) (By Laurence Donovan.)
The Crimson Serpent. 1974 (78)
The Czar of Fear. 1968; Bantam (London), 1968 (22)
The Dagger in the Sky. 1969 (40)
The Deadly Dwarf. 1968; Bantam (London), 1968 (28)
Death in Silver. 1968; Bantam (London), 1968 (26)
The Derrick Devil. 1973 (74)
The Devil Ghengis. 1974 (79)
Devil on the Moon. 1970 (50)
The Devil's Playground. 1968; Bantam (London), 1968 (25) (By Alan Hathaway.)
Dust of Death. 1969; Bantam (London), 1969 (35)
The Fantastic Island. 1966; Bantam (London), 1967 (14)
Fear Cay. 1966; Bantam (London), 1966 (11)
The Feathered Octopus. 1970 (48)
The Flaming Falcons. 1968; Bantam (London), 1969 (30)
Fortress of Solitude. 1968; Bantam (London), 1968 (23)
The Freckled Shark. 1972 (67)
The Giggling Ghosts. 1971 (56)
The Golden Peril. 1970 (55)
The Gold Ogre. 1969 (42)
The Green Death. 1971 (65)
The Green Eagle. 1968; Bantam (London), 1968 (24)
Haunted Ocean. 1970 (51) (By Laurence Donovan.)
He Could Stop the World. 1970 (54)
Hex. 1969; Bantam (London), 1968 (37)
The King Maker. 1975 (80)
Land of Always-Night. 1966 (13)
Land of Fear. 1973 (75)
Land of Long Juju. 1970 (47) (By Laurence Donovan.)
The Land of Terror. 1965; Tandem, 1965 (8)
The Living Fire Menace. 1971 (61)
The Lost Oasis. 1965; Bantam (London), 1965 (6)
Mad Eyes. 1969; Bantam (London), 1969 (33)
Mad Mesa. 1972 (66)
The Majii. 1971 (60)
The Man of Bronze. Street, 1933; Bantam (London), 1964 (1)
The Man Who Shook the Earth. 1969 (43)
The Man Who Smiled No More. 1970 (45) (By Laurence Donovan.)
The Mental Wizard. 1970 (53)
Merchants of Disaster. 1969 (41)
The Metal Monster. 1973 (72)
Meteor Menace. 1964; Bantam (London), 1964 (3)
The Midas Man. 1970 (46)
The Monsters. 1965; Bantam (London), 1965 (4)
The Motion Menace. 1971 (64)
The Munitions Master. 1971 (58)
Murder Melody. 1967 (15) (By Laurence Donovan.)
Murder Mirage. 1972 (71) (By Laurence Donovan.)
The Mystery of the Snow. 1972 (69)
The Mystery Under the Sea. 1968; Bantam (London), 1969 (27)

The Mystic Mullah. 1965; Bantam (London), 1966 (9)
The Other World. 1968; Bantam (London), 1969 (29)
The Phantom City. 1966; Bantam (London), 1966 (10)
Pirate of the Pacific. 1967; Bantam (London), 1967 (19)
The Pirate's Ghost. 1971 (62)
Poison Island. 1971 (57)
The Polar Treasure. 1965; Bantam (London), 1965 (4)
Quest of Qui. 1966; Bantam (London), 1965 (12)
Quest of the Spider. Street, 1933 (68)
The Red Skull. 1967; Bantam (London), 1967 (17)
Red Snow. 1969 (38)
Resurrection Day. 1969; Bantam (London), 1969 (36)
The Sargasso Ogre. 1967; Bantam (London), 1967 (18)
The Sea Angel. 1970 (49)
The Sea Magician. 1970 (44)
The Secret of the Sky. 1967; Bantam (London), 1968 (20)
The Seven Agate Devils. 1973 (73)
The South Pole Terror. 1974 (77)
Spook Hole. 1972 (70)
The Spook Legion. 1967; Bantam (London), 1967 (16)
The Squeaking Goblin. 1969; Bantam (London), 1969 (32)
The Submarine Mystery. 1971 (63)
The Terror in the Navy. 1969; Bantam (London), 1969 (34)
The Thousand-Headed Man. 1964; Bantam (London), 1964 (2)
The Vanisher. 1970 (52)
World's Fair Goblin. 1969 (39)
The Yellow Cloud. 1971 (59)
The Black Chariots. 1974 (30) (RG)
The Black Death. 1974 (22) (PE)
The Blood Countess. 1975 (33) (RG)
The Blood Ring. 1972 (6) (PE)
The Cartoon Crimes. 1974 (31) (RG)
Death in Slow Motion. 1973 (18) (PE)
The Death Machine. 1975 (32) (RG)
Demon Island. 1975 (36) (RG)
The Devil's Horns. 1972 (4) (PE)
Dr. Time. 1974 (28) (RG)
The Flame Breathers. 1973 (12) (PE)
The Frosted Death. 1972 (5) (PE)
The Glass Man. 1975 (34) (RG)
The Glass Mountain. 1973 (8) (PE)
The Green Killer. 1974 (20) (PE)
The Happy Killers. 1974 (21) (PE)
The Hate Master. 1973 (16) (PE)
House of Death. 1973 (15) (PE)
The Iron Skull. 1975 (35) (RG)
Justice, Inc. 1972 (1) (PE)
The Man from Atlantis. 1974 (25) (RG)
Midnight Murder. 1974 (24) (PE)
Murder on Wheels. 1973 (13) (PE)
Nevlo. 1973 (17) (PE)
The Nightwitch Devil. 1974 (29) (RG)
Pictures of Death. 1973 (19) (PE)
The Purple Zombie. 1974 (27) (RG)
Red Moon. 1974 (26) (RG)
River of Ice. 1973 (11) (PE)
The Sky Walker. 1972 (3) (PE)
The Smiling Dogs. 1973 (10) (PE)
Stockholders in Death. 1972 (7) (PE)
Three Gold Coins. 1973 (14) (PE)
Tuned for Murder. 1973 (9) (PE)
The Wilder Curse. 1974 (23) (PE)
The Yellow Hoard. 1972 (2) (PE)

ROBEY, GEORGE. 1869- .
Bits and Pieces. Jarrolds, 1928 ss, some criminous

ROBINS, ELIZABETH. 1862-1952.
The Messenger. Century, 1919; Hodder, 1919
The Secret That was Kept. Harper, 1926; Hutchinson, 1926

ROBINS, RAYMOND. 1900- .
Murder at Bayside. Crowell, 1933; Hutchinson, 1934

ROBINSON, B(ERTRAM) FLETCHER
The Chronicles of Addington Peace. Harper (London), 1905 ss
The Trail of the Dead, with J. Malcolm Fraser. Langton (Toronto), 1904; Ward, 1904

ROBINSON, DAVID. 1915- .
The Confession of Andrew Clare. McKay, 1968
The Confessions of Alma Quartier. Signet, 1962

ROBINSON, DEREK. 1932- .
Rotten with Honour. Barrie, 1973; Viking, 1973

ROBINSON, E(THELBERT) M(cKENNON)
Death Designs a Dress. Hammond, 1958
The Secret of the Swinging Room. Hammond, 1957

ROBINSON, EDWARD L(OUIS). 1921- .
Sloth and Heathen Folly. Macmillan, 1972

ROBINSON, ELIOT H(ARLOW). 1884- .
Dee Dee. Small, 1925; Hutchinson, 1926
The Scarred Hand. Page, 1931

ROBINSON, ERNEST H(ERBERT). 1880- .
The Disappearance of "Straight Left" Smith. Lloyd's, 1921
Dr. Quick, the Masked Detective. Aldine
Gold for the Bank of England. Lloyd's, 1921
The Will on the Watch. Lloyd's, 1922
The Yellow Claws of Wong. Lloyd's, 1922

ROBINSON, F(REDERICK) W(ILLIAM). 1830-1901.
-The Hands of Justice. Chatto, 1883; Harper, 1883
The Keeper of the Keys. Hurst, 1890; Lovell, 1890
Lazarus in London. Hurst, 1885; Harper, 1885
Memoirs of Jane Cameron, Female Convict. Hurst, 1864
99, Dark Street. Maxwell, 1887; Harper, 1887
-The Woman in the Dark. Chatto, 1895
-A Woman's Ransom. Hurst, 1963; Burnham, 1964
-The Wrong That was Done. Hurst, 1892; Lovell, 1891

ROBINSON, FRANK M(ALCOLM). 1926- .
The Power. Lippincott, 1956; Eyre, 1957

ROBINSON, (DR.) J(OHN) H(OVEY). 1825- .
-The Boston Conspiracy; or, The Royal Police. Dow, 1847
-Cepherine; or, The Secret Cabal. Brady, 1862
The House of Silence. Street, 1890
-Nightshade; or, The Masked Robber of Hounslow Heath. Brady, 1861
-Sibylla; or, The Mystery of the Brown-Stone House. Brady, 1864
-The Uncle's Crime; or, The Doctor's Beautiful Ward. Starr, 1870

ROBINSON, JIM
Together Brothers. Award, 1974; Tandem, 1974. (Novelization of the movie.)

ROBINSON, L(EONARD) W(ALLACE). 1912- .
The Assassin. World, 1968; Macdonald, 1969

ROBINSON, LEWIS (GEORGE). 1886- .
Pseudonym: George Limnelius, q.v.
The General Goes Too Far. Nicholson, 1935; Putnam, 1936
-The Inward Glance. Chapman, 1940
The Manuscript Murder. Barker, 1933; Doubleday, 1934, as by George Limnelius
No More Ancestors. Nicholson, 1938

ROBINSON, PATRICIA. Joint pseudonym with Ferdinan Stevenson: Daria Macomber, q.v.

ROBINSON, PHILIP (BEDFORD). 1926- .
-Masque of a Savage Mandarin. Macdonald, 1969
The Pakistani Agent. Hart-Davis, 1965

ROBINSON, RICHARD BLUNDELL. 1905- .
Pseudonym: George Leaderman, q.v.

ROBINSON, ROBERT (HENRY). 1927- .
-The Conspiracy. Hodder, 1968
Landscape with Dead Dons. Gollancz, 1956; Rinehart, 1956

ROBINSON, TIMOTHY. 1934- .
When Scholars Fall. Hutchinson, 1961

ROBISON, HAROLD (R.)
Rat Alley. Monarch, 1965

ROBY, ADELAIDE Q.
Sea Urchin. Milton House, 1974

ROBY, MARY LINN. 1930- .
Afraid of the Dark. Dodd, 1965
All Your Lovely Words are Spoken. Ace, 1970
And Die Remembering. Signet, 1972
Before I Die. Hale, 1966
The Broken Key. Hawthorn, 1973; Milton House, 1974
Cat and Mouse. Hale, 1967
The Cry of the Peacock; see The White Peacock
Dig a Narrow Grave. Signet, 1971
The House at Kilgallen. Signet, 1973
If She Should Die. Signet, 1972
In the Dead of the Night. Signet, 1969
Lie Quiet in Your Grave. Signet, 1970
Marsh House. Hawthorn, 1974; Milton House, 1975
Pennies on her Eyes. Signet, 1969
Reap the Whirlwind. Signet, 1972
Shadow over Grove House. Signet, 1973
The Silent Walls. Signet, 1974
Some Die in Their Beds. Signet, 1970
Speak No Evil of the Dead. Signet, 1973
Still as the Grave. Dodd, 1964; Collins, 1965
That Fatal Touch. Signet, 1970
This Land Turns Evil Slowly. Signet, 1971
The Tower Room. Hawthorn, 1974; Milton House, 1975
When the Witch is Dead. Signet, 1972
The White Peacock. Hawthorn, 1972. British title: The Cry of the Peacock. Milton House, 1974

ROCCO, A.
Build Me a Blonde. Milestone, 1953

ROCHE, ARTHUR SOMERS. 1883-1935.
Among Those Present. Sears, 1930
Callingham's Girl, with Ethel P(ettit) Roche. Dodd, 1937
The Case Against Mrs. Ames. Dodd, 1934; Archer, 1935
Conspiracy. Sears, 1934
Death was a Wedding Guest. Cherry Tree, 1942. (U.S. title?)
-Devil-May-Care. Century, 1926
The Eyes of the Blind. Doran, 1919
Find the Woman. Cosmopolitan, 1921; Hodder, 1921

The Great Abduction. Sears, 1933
Hard to Get. Dodd, 1937; Cherry Tree, 1940
Honest Crook. Cherry Tree, 1941. (U.S. title?)
In the Money. Dodd, 1936
A Lady of Resource. Dodd, 1938
Loot. Bobbs, 1916
-Marriage for Two. Sears, 1929
No Stockings. Boston American, 1928
Penthouse. Dodd, 1935
The Pleasure Buyers. Macmillan, 1925
Plunder. Bobbs, 1917
Ransom! Doran, 1918
Shadow of Doubt. Dodd, 1935
Slander. Sears, 1933
The Sport of Kings. Bobbs, 1917
The Star of Midnight. Dodd, 1936; Cherry Tree, 1940
Uneasy Street. Cosmopolitan, 1920
-The Wrong Wife. Sears, 1932

ROCHE, ETHEL P(ETTIT). See: ARTHUR SOMERS ROCHE, 1883-1935.

ROCHE, KAY
-The Game and the Candle. Hurst, 1951
The Shuttered House. Hurst, 1950

ROCHE, PETER
Dean of Clonbury. Wright, 1957

ROCHE, REGINA MARIA. 1764?-1845.
The Children of the Abbey. Lane, 1796; Davis, 1798

ROCHESTER, DEVEREAUX
Forever Timeless. Vantage, 1969

ROCHESTER, GEO(RGE) E(RNEST). Pseudonym: Jeffrey Gaunt, q.v.
Adventures at Greystones. Popular Library (London), 1936
The Air Ranger. Hamilton, 1936
The Air Trail. Popular Library (London), 1936
The Black Bat Rides the Sky. Daniels, 1948
The Black Chateau. Amalgamated, 1935
The Black Hawk. Hamilton, 1936
The Black Mole. Popular Library (London), 1936
-The Black Octopus. Warne, 1954
The Bulldog Breed. Hamilton, 1936
Buzzard's Roost. Hutchinson, 1955
The Crimson Threat. Amalgamated, 1934
Dead Man's Gold. Amalgamated, 1935
-Drums of War. Warne, 1957
The Flying Beetle. Hamilton, 1935
The Flying Cowboys. Hamilton, 1936
The Freak of St. Freda's! Popular Library (London), 1936
Grey Shadow. Hamilton, 1936
Lair of the Vampire. Daniels, 1948
The Mystery of Flying V Ranch. Hamilton, 1936
North Sea Patrol. Hamilton, 1938
Porson's Flying Service. Popular Library (London), 1936
The Return of Grey Shadow. Eldon, 1949
The Scarlet Squadron. Ace (London), 1938
Secret Pilot. Epworth, 1954
The Secret Squadron in German. Hamilton, 1938
The Shadow of the Guillotine. Popular Library (London), 1936
The Sky Bandits. Ace (London), 1938
Sons of the Legion. Daniels, 1948
The Squadron Without a Number. Hamilton, 1937
Traitor's Rock. Eldon, 1933
The Vultures of Desolate Island. Ace (London), 1938
Wings of Doom. Hamilton, 1936
The Worst Squadron in France. Eldon, 1949

ROCK, GILBERT
The Crime of Golden Gully. Street (Magnet)

ROCK, PHILIP. 1927-   .
-The Dead in Guanajuato. Meredith, 1968
Dirty Harry. Bantam (New York & London), 1971. (Novelization of the movie.)
-The Extraordinary Seaman. Meredith, 1967; Souvenir, 1967
Hickey and Boggs. Popular Library, 1972. (Novelization of the movie.)
Tick...Tick...Tick. Popular Library, 1970. (Novelization of the movie.)

ROCKEY, HOWARD. 1886-1934. Pseudonym: Oliver Panbourne, q.v.

ROCKWOOD, HARRY. Pseudonym of Ernest A. Young, q.v.
Abner Ferret, the Lawyer Detective. Ogilvie, 1883
Allan Keene, the War Detective. Ogilvie, 1884
Clarice Dyke, the Female Detective. Ogilvie, 1883
The Dexter Bank Robbery. Street (Magnet)
Donald Dyke, the Yankee Detective. Ogilvie, 1882
Dyke and Burr, the Rival Detectives. Ogilvie, 1883. Also published as: The Rival Detectives. Ogilvie, 1883
Fred Danford, the Skillful Detective; or, The Watertown Mystery. Ogilvie, 1885. Also published as: The Watertown Mystery. Street (Magnet)
The Handkerchief Clue. Street (Magnet)
Harry Pinkurten, the King of Detectives. Ogilvie, 1882
Harry Sharpe, the New York Detective. Ogilvie, 1893
Luke Leighton, the Government Detective. Ogilvie, 1884
The Man and the Crime. Street (Magnet)
Mrs. Donald Dyke, Detective. Street, 1900
Nat Foster, the Boston Detective. Ogilvie, 1883
Neil Nelson, the Veteran Detective; or, Tracking Mail Robbers. Ogilvie, 1885
The Railway Detective. Street (Magnet), 1900
The Rival Detectives; see Dyke and Burr, the Rival Detectives
The Secret of the Missing Checks. Street (Magnet)
Tales of Romance and Mystery. General Publishing, 1891 ss
Walt Wheeler, the Scout Detective. Ogilvie, 1884
The Watertown Mystery; see Fred Danford, the Skillful Detective

RODD, RALPH. Pseudonym of William North, 1869-   .
Blind Man's Bluff. Collins, 1929
The Claverton Case. Mellifont, 1940
-From the House of Bondage. Collins, 1924
-Madame Knits. Cassell, 1936
-A Man Beguiled. Collins, 1929
-Maureen Versus Fate. Collins, 1925
Midnight Murder. Collins, 1931
The Secret of the Flames. Collins, 1924; Dial, 1929
Sleuth o' the World. Collins, 1933
-The Story of Joan Courage. Cassell, 1932
-The Whipping Girl. Collins, 1923
Without Judge or Jury. Collins, 1928; Dial, 1929

RODDA, (PERCIVAL) CHARLES. 1891-   .
Pseudonyms: Gardner Low, Gavin Holt, qq.v. Joint pseudonym with Eric Ambler, 1909-   , q.v.: Eliot Reed, q.v.
-Golden Corn. Hodder, 1945
-The House Upstairs. Barrie, 1949
-Pilgrim Come Home. Hodder, 1945
-Providence Hall. Hodder, 1943
The Scarlet Mask. Nelson, 1926
-South Sea Gold. Nelson, 1926
-Tango. Benn, 1928

RODELL, MARIE FRIED. 1912-1975. Pseudonym: Marion Randolph, q.v.

RODELL, VIC
Free-Lance Murder. Mystery House, 1957

RODEN, H(ENRY) W(ISDOM). 1895-1963. Series character: Sid Ames, in all titles.
One Angel Less. Morrow, 1945; Hammond, 1949
Too Busy to Die. Morrow, 1944; Hammond, 1947
Wake for a Lady. Morrow, 1946; Hammond, 1950
You Only Hang Once. Morrow, 1944; Hammond, 1946

RODNEY, BRYAN. Series character: Francis Villiers, in all titles.
The Owl Flies Home. Wright, 1952
The Owl Hoots. Wright, 1945
The Owl Meets the Devil. Wright, 1949

ROE, IVAN. 1917-   . Pseudonym: Richard Savage, q.v.

ROE, KIM
The Gang Buster. Hale, 1961

ROE, WILLIAM JAMES. 1843-   . Pseudonym: G. I. Cervius, q.v.

ROEBURT, JOHN. 1908?-1972. Series characters: Johnny Devereaux = JD; Jigger Moran = JM.
Al Capone. Pyramid, 1959. (Novelization of the movie.)
Case of the Hypnotized Virgin; see Corpse on the Town
Case of the Tearless Widow; see Jigger Moran
The Climate of Hell. Abelard (New York & London), 1958. Also published as: The Long Nightmare. Crest, 1958; Digit, 1959
Corpse on the Town. Graphic, 1950. Revised edition: Case of the Hypnotized Virgin. Avon, 1956 JM
Did You Kill Mona Leeds?; see The Lunatic Time
The Hollow Man. Simon, 1954; Jarrolds, 1955 JD
Jigger Moran. Greenberg, 1944; Wells Gardner, 1948. Also published as: Case of the Tearless Widow. Handi-Books, 1946. And as: Wine, Women and Murder. Avon, 1958 JM
The Lady and the Prowler; see The Unholy Wife
The Long Nightmare; see The Climate of Hell
The Lunatic Time. Simon, 1956. Also published as: Did You Kill Mona Leeds? Crest, 1958
The Mobster. Pyramid, 1960
Murder in Manhattan; see There are Dead Men in Manhattan
Seneca, U.S.A. Curl, 1947
Sing Out, Sweet Homicide. Dell, 1961. (Novelization of Roaring Twenties TV series.)
Ruby Maclaine. Hillman, 196?

Roeburt, John (continued)
- There are Dead Men in Manhattan. Mystery House, 1946. Also published as: Murder in Manhattan. Avon, 1957. And as: Triple Cross. Belmont, 1962 JM
- They Who Sin. Avon, 1959
- Tough Cop. Simon, 1949 JD
- Triple Cross; see There are Dead Men in Manhattan
- The Unholy Wife. Avon, 1957. British title: The Lady and the Prowler. (Novelization of the movie.)
- Wine, Women and Murder; see Jigger Moran

ROFFEY, JACK
- Hostile Witness. Evans, 1966; Arrow, 1968

ROFFMAN, JAN. Pseudonym of Margaret Summerton, q.v.
- Ashes in an Urn. Doubleday, 1966. (British title?)
- A Bad Conscience. Doubleday, 1972. (British title?)
- A Daze of Fears. Doubleday, 1968. (British title?)
- A Dying in the Night. Macdonald, 1975; Doubleday, 1974
- Death of a Fox; see Winter of the Fox
- Grave of Green Water. Long, 1968; Doubleday, 1968
- The Hanging Woman. Bles, 1965
- Likely to Die. Bles, 1964
- Mask of Words; see A Penny for the Guy
- A Penny for the Guy. Bles, 1965; Doubleday, 1965. Also published as: Mask of Words. Ace, 1973
- Reflection of Evil; see Winter of the Fox
- Seeds of Suspicion. Long, 1968
- A Walk in the Dark. Long, 1969; Doubleday, 1970
- Winter of the Fox. Bles, 1964. U.S. title: Death of a Fox. Doubleday, 1964. Also published as: Reflection of Evil. Ace, 1967
- With Murder in Mind. Doubleday, 1963. (British title?)

ROGERS, BEN
- The Murder at the Coffee Stall. Modern, 193?
- Murder Pays a Call. Modern, 1938
- The Vengeance of the Tong. Modern, 193?

ROGERS, GARET. Pseudonym.
- -Scandal in Eden. Dial, 1963; Putnam (London), 1964

ROGERS, JOEL TOWNSLEY
- Lady with the Dice. Handi-Books, 1946
- Never Leave my Bed; see The Stopped Clock
- Once in a Red Moon. Brentano's (New York & London), 1923
- The Red Right Hand. Simon, 1945
- The Stopped Clock. Simon, 1958. Also published as: Never Leave my Bed. Beacon, 1960

ROGERS, KERK. Pseudonym of Edward Rogers Knowlton, 1909- , q.v.
- -Beach Patrol. Mill, 1943
- -Too Many Yesterdays. Mill, 1942
- Vantage Point. Mystery House, 1959
- With Intent to Destroy. Mill, 1944; Hammond, 1946

ROGERS, MILTON
- Born Reckless. Avon, 1959. (Novelization of the movie.)

ROGERS, RAY MOUNT
- The Negotiator. McKay, 1975

ROGERS, RUTH. 1890- . Pseudonym: Ruth Alexander, q.v.

ROGERS, SAMUEL (GREENE ARNOLD). 1894- . Series character: Professor Hatfield = H.
- Don't Look Behind You! Harper, 1944
- Murder is Grim; see You'll Be Sorry!
- You Leave Me Cold! Harper, 1946 H
- You'll Be Sorry! Harper, 1945. British title: Murder is Grim. Hammond, 1955 H

ROGGER, L(OUIS) L(UCIEN)
- The Faceless Corpse Murders. Longmans, 1937

ROHDE, ROBERT H.
- Hunted Down. Chelsea, 1928
- Sucker Money. Chelsea, 1927

ROHDE, WILLIAM L(AURENCE)
- -Give Me a Little Something. Pyramid, 1956
- -The Gun-Crasher. Pyramid, 1957
- The Heel. Pyramid, 1953
- Help Wanted--for Murder. GM, 1950; Fawcett (London), 1953
- High Red for Dead. GM, 1951; Fawcett (London), 1953. Also published as: Murder on the Line. GM, 1957
- Murder on the Line; see High Red for Dead
- Uneasy Lies the Head. Ace, 1957
- -V.I.P. Pyramid, 1957

ROHMER, ELIZABETH SAX. Pseudonym of Rose Elizabeth Knox Ward, 1886- .
- Bianca in Black. Mystery House, 1958

ROHMER, RICHARD
- Ultimatum. PB, 1973

ROHMER, SAX. Pseudonym of Arthur Henry Sarsfield Ward, 1883-1959. Other pseudonym: Michael Furey, q.v. Series characters: Fu Manchu (and Nayland Smith) = FM; Nayland Smith alone = NS; Paul Harley = PH; Daniel "Red" Kerry = DK; Gaston Max = GM; Sumuru = S.
- The Bat Flies Low. Cassell, 1935; Doubleday, 1935
- Bat-Wing. Cassell, 1921; Doubleday, 1921 PH
- Bimbashi Baruk of Egypt; see Egyptian Nights
- The Bride of Fu Manchu. Cassell, 1933. U.S. title: Fu Manchu's Bride. Doubleday, 1933. Reprinted under the British title: Pyramid, 1962 FM
- Brood of the Witch-Queen. Pearson, 1918; Doubleday, 1924
- Daughter of Fu Manchu. Cassell, 1931; Doubleday, 1931 FM
- The Day the World Ended. Cassell, 1930; Doubleday, 1930 GM
- The Devil Doctor. Methuen, 1916. U.S. title: The Return of Fu-Manchu. McBride, 1916 FM
- Dope. Cassell, 1919; McBride, 1919 DK
- The Dream-Detective. Jarrolds, 1920; Doubleday, 1925 ss
- The Drums of Fu Manchu. Cassell, 1939; Doubleday, 1939 FM
- Egyptian Nights. Hale, 1944. U.S. title: Bimbashi Baruk of Egypt. McBride, 1944. (British edition presented as a novel; U.S. edition as a collection of ss.)
- Emperor Fu Manchu. Jenkins, 1959; GM, 1959 FM
- The Emperor of America. Cassell, 1929; Doubleday, 1929
- The Exploits of Captain O'Hagan. Jarrolds, 1916; Bookfinger, 1968 ss
- The Fire Goddess; see Virgin in Flames
- Fire-Tongue. Cassell, 1921; Doubleday, 1922 PH
- Fu Manchu's Bride; see The Bride of Fu Manchu
- The Golden Scorpion. Methuen, 1919; McBride, 1920 GM, FM
- The Green Eyes of Bast. Cassell, 1920; McBride, 1920
- Grey Face. Cassell, 1924; Doubleday, 1924
- The Hand of Fu-Manchu; see The Si-Fan Mysteries
- Hangover House. Jenkins, 1950; Random, 1949
- The Haunting of Low Fennel. Pearson, 1920 ss, including one about NS (All but one story appear in the U.S. edition of Tales of East and West, q.v.)
- The Insidious Dr. Fu-Manchu; see The Mystery of Dr. Fu-Manchu
- The Island of Fu Manchu. Cassell, 1941; Doubleday, 1941 FM
- The Mask of Fu Manchu. Cassell, 1933; Doubleday, 1932 FM
- The Moon is Red. Jenkins, 1954
- Moon of Madness. Cassell, 1927; Doubleday, 1927
- The Mystery of Dr. Fu-Manchu. Methuen, 1913. U.S. title: The Insidious Dr. Fu-Manchu. McBride, 1913 FM
- Nude in Mink; see Sins of Sumuru
- -The Orchard of Tears. Methuen, 1918; Bookfinger, 1970
- President Fu Manchu. Cassell, 1936; Doubleday, 1936 FM
- The Quest of the Sacred Slipper. Pearson, 1919; Doubleday, 1919
- Re-Enter Dr. Fu-Manchu. Jenkins, 1957. U.S. title: Re-Enter Fu Manchu. GM, 1957 FM
- Re-Enter Fu Manchu; see Re-Enter Dr. Fu Manchu
- The Return of Dr. Fu-Manchu; see The Devil Doctor
- Return of Sumuru; see Sand and Satin
- Salute to Bazarada and other stories. Cassell, 1939; Bookfinger, 1971 ss, including three about PH
- Sand and Satin. Jenkins, 1955. U.S. title: Return of Sumuru. GM, 1954 S
- The Secret of Holm Peel and other strange stories. Ace, 1970 ss, including one about FM
- Seven Sins. Cassell, 1944; McBride, 1943 PH
- Shadow of Fu Manchu. Jenkins, 1949; Doubleday, 1948 FM
- She Who Sleeps. Cassell, 1928; Doubleday, 1928
- The Si-Fan Mysteries. Methuen, 1917. U.S. title: The Hand of Fu-Manchu. McBride, 1917 FM
- Sinister Madonna. Jenkins, 1956; GM, 1956 S
- The Sins of Severac Bablon. Cassell, 1914; Bookfinger, 1967
- Sins of Sumuru. Jenkins, 1950; GM, 1950 S
- Slaves of Sumuru. Jenkins, 1952. U.S. title: Sumuru. GM, 1951 S
- Sumuru; see Slaves of Sumuru
- Tales of Chinatown. Cassell, 1922; Doubleday, 1922 ss, including PH, DK
- Tales of East and West. Cassell, 1932; Doubleday, 1933. (The British edition contains 10 ss, including PH, NS; the U.S. edition includes 6 of the 7 ss from The Haunting of Low Fennel, q.v., and 5 of the 10 ss from the British edition of Tales of East and West.)
- Tales of Secret Egypt. Methuen, 1918; McBride, 1919 ss
- The Trail of Fu Manchu. Cassell, 1934; Doubleday, 1934 FM
- Virgin in Flames. Jenkins, 1953. U.S. title: The Fire Goddess. GM, 1952 S

White Velvet. Cassell, 1936; Doubleday, 1936
The Wrath of Fu Manchu and other stories. Stacey, 1973; Daw, 1976 ss, including 4 about FM
The Yellow Claw. Methuen, 1915; McBride, 1915 GM
Yellow Shadows. Cassell, 1925; Doubleday, 1926 RK
Yu'an Hee See Laughs. Cassell, 1932; Doubleday, 1932

ROLFE, EDWIN, 1909-1954, and LESTER FULLER, 1908- .
The Glass Room. Rinehart, 1946; Low, 1948

ROLFE, MARO O(RLANDO). 1852-1925.
The Band of Mystery. Street (Magnet)
The Branded Hand. Street (Magnet)
-Clyde, the Trailer; or, The Brothers of Death. Beadle, 1872
The Cross of the Dust. Street (Magnet)
An Eye for an Eye. Street (Magnet)
The Man Who Knew. Street (Magnet)
-The Man-Hunter; or, The Counterfeiters of the Border. Beadle, 1873
On the Stroke of Midnight. Street (Magnet)
A Queen of Blackmailers. Street (Magnet)
A Rascal's Nerve. Street (Magnet)
A Secret Suspicion. Street (Magnet)
A Transatlantic Puzzle. Street (Magnet)
The Two Conspirators. Street (Magnet)

ROLLINS, ALICE (MARLAND) WELLINGTON. 1847-1897.
The Finding of the Gentian. [Author, New York], 1895 5ss, 2 criminous

ROLLINS, KATHLEEN. Joint pseudonym with Davis Dresser, 1904-1977, q.v.: Hal Debrett, q.v.

ROLLINS, WILLIAM, JR. 1897- . Pseudonym: O'Connor Stacy, q.v.
Midnight Treasure. Coward, 1929
The Ring and the Lamp. Simon, 1947
The Shadow Before. McBride, 1934
-The Wall of Men. Modern Age, 1938

ROLLS, ANTHONY. Pseudonym of C(olwyn) E(dward) Vulliamy, 1886- , q.v.
Clerical Error; see The Vicar's Experiments
Family Matters. Bles, 1933
Lobelia Grove. Bles, 1932
Scarweather. Bles, 1934
The Vicar's Experiments. Bles, 1932. U.S. title: Clerical Error. Little, 1932

ROMAINE, DALLAS
The Malicious Madonna. Berkley, 1975

ROMAN, ERIC. 1926- .
After the Trial. Citadel, 1968

ROMAN, HOWARD
Pitfall in August. Harper, 1960; Allen, 1961

ROMANES, NORMAN HUGH
Young Lord Folliot. Jenkins, 1931. Also published as: The Case of Young Lord Folliot. Athenaeum, 1943

ROMANO, DEANE (LOUIS). 1927- .
Banacek. Bantam, 1973. (Novelization of the TV series.)

ROMANO, DON. All titles in a Mafia series.
Operation Cocaine. Pyramid, 1974
Operation Hijack. Pyramid, 1974
Operation Hit Man. Pyramid, 1974
Operation Loan Shark. Pyramid, 1974
Operation Porno. Pyramid, 1973

ROMANOFF, ALEXANDER NICHOLAYEVITCH. 1881-1945. Pseudonym: Achmed Abdullah, q.v.

ROME, ANTHONY. Pseudonym of Marvin (H.) Albert, q.v. Other pseudonym: Nick Quarry, q.v. Series character: Tony Rome, in all titles.
The Lady in Cement. PB, 1961; Hale, 1962
Miami Mayhem. PB, 1960; Hale, 1961. Also published as: Tony Rome. Dell, 1967, as by Marvin H. Albert
My Kind of Game. Dell, 1962
Tony Rome; see Miami Mayhem

ROME, TONY
God's Gift to All Women. New English Library pb, 1971

ROMER, ISABELLA F(RANCES). -1852.
-Sturmer. Lea, 1842; Bentley, 1841

ROMSEY, PETER
The Lidless Eye. Jenkins, 1950; Roy, 1957

RONALD, E. B. Pseudonym of Ronald (Ernest) Barker, 1920-1976, q.v. Series character: Rupert "Brad" Bradley, in all titles.
The Cat and Fiddle Murders. Gollancz, 1954; Rinehart, 1954
Death by Proxy. Boardman, 1956
A Sort of Madness. Boardman, 1958; Abelard, 1959

RONALD, JAMES. 1905- . Pseudonym: Kirk Wales. Series character: Julian Mendoza, in at least those marked JM.
Counsel for the Defense. Gramol, 1932
Cross Marks the Spot. Hodder, 1933 JM
The Dark Angel; see Six were to Die
Death Croons the Blues. Hodder, 1934; Phoenix, 1940 JM
Diamonds of Death. Gramol, 1934
The Green Ghost Murder. Gramol, 1936
Hanging's Too Good. Rich, 1938
-Lord Peter Goes A-Wooing. Gramol, 1933
The Man Who Made Monsters. Gramol, 1935
The Monocled Man. Gramol, 1933
Murder for Cash. Rich, 1938
The Murder in Gay Ladies; see Murder in the Family
Murder in the Family. Lane, 1936; Lippincott, 1940. Also published as: The Murder in Gay Ladies. Mercury, 1952
She Got What She Asked For. Lippincott, 1941. (British title?)
Six were to Die. Hodder, 1932; Mystery House, 1941, as by Kirk Wales
-Star Dust. Gramol, 1932
The Sundial Drug Mystery. Gramol, 1934
They Can't Hang Me! Rich, 1938; Doubleday, 1938
This Way Out. Rich, 1940; Lippincott, 1939
The Unholy Trio. Gramol, 1933

RONNS, EDWARD. Pseudonym of Edward S(idney) Aarons, 1916-1975, q.v. Other pseudonym: Paul Ayres, q.v.
The Art Studio Murders. Handi-Books, 1950. Reprinted as by Aarons: Macfadden, 1964
The Big Bedroom. Pyramid, 1959
The Black Orchid. Pyramid, 1959. (Novelization of the movie.)
But Not for Me. Pyramid, 1959; World Distributors, 1960. (Novelization of the movie.)
Catspaw Ordeal. GM, 1950; Gaywood, 1953. Reprinted as by Aarons: GM, 1966
The Corpse Hangs High. Phoenix, 1939
The Cowl of Doom; see Death in a Lighthouse
Dark Destiny. Graphic, 1953. Reprinted as by Aarons: Macfadden, 1968
Dark Memory. Handi-Books, 1950
Death in a Lighthouse. Phoenix, 1938. Also published as: The Cowl of Doom. Hangman's House, 1946
Death is my Shadow. Mystery House, 1957. Reprinted as by Aarons: Macfadden, 1965
The Decoy. GM, 1951. Reprinted as by Aarons: GM, 1966
Don't Cry, Beloved. GM, 1952. Reprinted as by Aarons: GM, 1966
Gang Rumble. Avon, 1958
Gift of Death. McKay, 1948. Reprinted as by Aarons: Macfadden, 1964
The Glass Cage. Pyramid, 1962
I Can't Stop Running. GM, 1951. Reprinted as by Aarons: GM, 196?
The Lady Takes a Flyer. Avon, 1958. (Novelization of the movie.)
Lady, the Guy is Dead; see No Place to Live
Million Dollar Murder. GM, 1950; Fawcett (London), 1952. Reprinted as by Aarons: GM, 196?
Murder Money. Phoenix, 1938. Also published as: $1,000,000 in Corpses. Best Detective Selections, 1943
The Net. Graphic, 1953. Reprinted as by Aarons: Macfadden, 1969
No Place to Live. McKay, 1947; Boardman, 1950. Also published as: Lady, the Guy is Dead. Avon, 1950 (abridged). Reprinted under original title as by Aarons: Macfadden, 1964
$1,000,000 in Corpses; see Murder Money
Passage to Terror. GM, 1952. Reprinted as by Aarons: GM, 1966
Pickup Alley. Avon, 1957. (Novelization of the movie.)
Point of Peril. Mystery House, 1956. Reprinted as by Aarons: Macfadden, 1965
Say It with Murder. Graphic, 1954; Red Seal, 1960. Reprinted as by Aarons: Macfadden, 196?
State Department Murders. GM, 1950; Fawcett (London), 1957. Reprinted as by Aarons: GM, 196?; Coronet, 1974
Terror in the Town. McKay, 1947. Reprinted as by Aarons: Macfadden, 1964
They All Ran Away. Graphic, 1955. Reprinted as by Aarons: Macfadden, 1970

RONZONE, BENJAMIN ANTHONY. 1848- .
Pseudonym: Baron, q.v.

ROOF, KATHERINE METCALF
Murder on the Salem Road. Houghton, 1931

ROOK, CLARENCE. -1915.
The Hooligan Nights. Richards, 1899; Holt, 1899

ROOK, TONY. 1932- .
Strange Mansion. Milton House, 1974

ROOS, AUDREY (KELLEY), 1912- , and WILLIAM ROOS, 1911- . Joint pseudonym: Kelley Roos, q.v. Pseudonym of William Roos: William Rand, q.v.
A Few Days in Madrid. Scribner, 1965; Deutsch, 1966
Speaking of Murder. Random, 1957; French (London), 1959. (Play.)

ROOS, KELLEY. Joint pseudonym of Audrey (Kelley) Roos, 1912-   , q.v., and William Roos, 1911-   . Pseudonym of William Roos: William Rand, q.v. Series characters: Jeff and Haila Troy = T.
Bad Trip. Dodd, 1971
Beauty Marks the Spot; see Triple Threat
The Blonde Died Dancing. Dodd, 1956. British title: She Died Dancing. Eyre, 1957
Cry in the Night. Dodd, 1966
Dangerous Blondes; see If the Shroud Fits
The Frightened Stiff. Dodd, 1942; Hale, 1951 T
Ghost of a Chance. Wyn, 1947 T
Grave Danger. Dodd, 1965; Eyre, 1966
If the Shroud Fits. Dodd, 1941. Also published as: Dangerous Blondes. Jonathan, 1951 T
Made Up for Murder; see Made Up to Kill
Made Up to Kill. Dodd, 1940. British title: Made Up for Murder. Jarrolds, 1941 T
Murder in Any Language. Wyn, 1948 T
Murder Noon and Night; see Requiem for a Blonde
Necessary Evil. Dodd, 1965; Eyre, 1965
One False Move. Dodd, 1966 T
Requiem for a Blonde. Dodd, 1958. British title (?): Murder Noon and Night. Eyre, 1959
Sailor, Take Warning! Dodd, 1944; Hale, 1952 T
Scent of Mystery. Dell, 1959. (Novelization of the movie.)
She Died Dancing; see The Blonde Died Dancing
Suddenly One Night. Dodd, 1970
There was a Crooked Man. Dodd, 1945; Hale, 1953 T
To Save his Life. Dodd, 1968; Cassell, 1969
Triple Threat. Wyn, 1949. (Three novelets, of which one was published separately as: Beauty Marks the Spot. Dell 10¢ pb, 1951.) T
What did Hattie See? Dodd, 1970; Cassell, 1970
Who Saw Maggie Brown? Dodd, 1967

ROOS, WILLIAM. 1911-   . Pseudonym: William Rand, q.v. Joint pseudonym with Audrey (Kelley) Roos, 1912-   , q.v.: Kelley Roos, q.v.

ROOSEVELT, FRANKLIN D(ELANO). 1882-1945.
The President's Mystery Story. Farrar, 1935; Lane, 1936. Revised edition: Prentice-Hall, 1967. (A mystery novel suggested by Roosevelt and written, a chapter each, by 7 mystery writers.)

ROOT, GROSVENOR T., M.D.
Bird in the Hand. Carlton, 1972

ROOT, PAT
The Devil on the Stairs. Simon, 1956
Evil Became Them. Simon, 1952; Redman, 1953

ROOTE, MIKE
Badge 373. Award, 1973. (Novelization of the movie.)
Born to Win. Award, 1971. (Novelization of the movie.)
CC and Company. Award, 1970. (Novelization of the movie.)
Enter the Dragon. Award, 1973; Tandem, 1974. (Novelization of the movie.)
Prime Cut. Award, 1973. (Novelization of the movie.)
Scorpio. Award, 1973; Tandem, 1973. (Novelization of the movie.)

ROPER, L. V.
Death—as in Matador. Popular Library, 1975
Rage. Curtis, 1973. (Novelization of the movie.)

ROSAIRE, FORREST. 1902-   .
White Night. Lippincott, 1956; Cape, 1954

ROSCOE, JOHN. 1921-   . Joint pseudonym with Michael Ruso: Mike Roscoe, q.v.

ROSCOE, MIKE. Joint pseudonym of John Roscoe, 1921-   , and Michael Ruso. Series character: Johnny April = JA.
Death is a Round Black Ball. Crown, 1952; Foulsham, 1954 JA
The Midnight Eye. Ace, 1958
One Tear for my Grave. Crown, 1955; Foulsham, 1956 JA
Riddle Me This. Crown, 1952; Foulsham, 1955 JA
Slice of Hell. Crown, 1954; Foulsham, 1955 JA

ROSCOE, THEODORE
A Grave Must be Deep. Popular (London), 1947. (U.S. title?)
I'll Grind Their Bones. Dodge, 1936; Harrap, 1937
Murder on the Way! Dodge, 1935
Only in New England. Scribner, 1959
Seven Men. Handi-Books, 1942
To Live and Die in Dixie. Scribner, 1961

ROSE, ALVIN EMANUEL. Pseudonym: Alan Pruitt, q.v.

ROSE, ELIZABETH
Grand Jury. Avon, 1974

ROSE, F(REDERICK) HORACE (VINCENT). 1876-   .
-Bride of the Kalahari. Duckworth, 1940
-The Four Kings in the Street of Gold. Duckworth, 1942
-The Harp of Life. Duckworth, 1946
-Hell's Acre. Duckworth, 1941
-Kruger's Wagon. Duckworth, 1943
-The Maniac's Dream. Duckworth, 1946
-The Night of the World. Duckworth, 1944
-Palace and Prison. Duckworth, 1946
-Pharoah's Crown. Duckworth, 1943
-The Prodigal Soldier. Duckworth, 1942
-Rock of Ages. Duckworth, 1944

ROSE, GEOFFREY. 1932-   .
The Bright Adventure. Macmillan (London), 1975; St. Martin's, 1976
A Clear Road to Archangel. Macmillan (London), 1973; St. Martin's, 1976
Nobody on the Road. Macmillan (London), 1972; St. Martin's, 1976

ROSE, GEORGE. 1817-1882. Pseudonym: Arthur Sketchley, q.v.

ROSEN, NORMA STAHL. 1925-   .
Touching Evil. Harcourt, 1969

ROSEN, VICTOR
Dark Plunder. Lion, 1955
A Gun in his Hand. GM, 1951; Red Seal, 1958

ROSENBACH, A(BRAHAM) S(IMON) W(OLF). 1876-1952.
The Unpublishable Memoirs. Kennerley, 1917; Castle, 1924 ss

ROSENBERG, ELIZABETH. See: JOHN ROSENBERG, 1931-   .

ROSENBERG, JOHN. 1931-   .
-A Company of Strangers. Hogarth, 1959
-The Desperate Art. Longmans, 1955
Fanfare for a Murderer, with Elizabeth Rosenberg. Hogarth, 1960
-Mirror and Knife. Hogarth, 1961
Out Brief Candle, with Elizabeth Rosenberg. Hogarth, 1959

ROSENBERG, PHILIP. 1942-   .
Contract on Cherry Street. Crowell, 1975; Secker, 1976

ROSENBERGER, JOSEPH. Series characters: Richard Carnellion (The Death Merchant) = RC; Murder Master = MM.
The Albanian Connection. Pinnacle, 1973 RC
The Billionaire Mission. Pinnacle, 1974 RC
The Caribbean Caper. Manor, 1974 MM
The Castro File. Pinnacle, 1974 RC
The Chinese Conspiracy. Pinnacle, 1973 RC
Death Merchant. Pinnacle, 1972 RC
Death Trap. Manor, 1973 MM
The Hooker-Smash Operation. Manor, 1974 MM
The KGB Frame. Pinnacle, 1975 RC
The Laser War. Pinnacle, 1974 RC
The Mainline Plot. Pinnacle, 1974 RC
Manhattan Wipeout. Pinnacle, 1975 RC
The Mato Grosso Horror. Pinnacle, 1975 RC
Operation Overkill. Pinnacle, 1972 RC
The Psychotron Plot. Pinnacle, 1972 RC
Satan Strike. Pinnacle, 1972 RC

ROSENBLUM, ROBERT (J.). 1938-   .
The Good Thief. Doubleday, 1974; Hart-Davis, 1975
The Mushroom Cave. Doubleday, 1973; Gollancz, 1974

ROSENHAYN, PAUL. 1877-1929. Series character: Joe Jenkins, in both titles.
Joe Jenkins' Case Book. Heinemann, 1930 ss
Joe Jenkins: Detective. Heinemann, 1929; Doubleday, 1930 ss

ROSENKRANTZ, BARON PALLE (ADAM VILHELM). 1867-1941.
The Magistrate's Own Case. Methuen, 1908; McClure, 1908
The Man in the Basement. Empire, 1907

ROSENTHAL, NORMAN C.
Silenced Witnesses. Ace, 1955

ROSENTHAL, RICHARD A. 1925-   . Pseudonym: Allen Richards, q.v.

ROSENWALD, FRANCIS
A Big Man in Saludas. Ballantine, 1962

ROSER, VAL
Murder in the Wind. Long, 1947

ROSMANITH, OLGA L.
-Don't Say No. Popular Library, 1956
-The Long Thrill. Lion, 1952
-Passenger List. Murray, 1940
Signature to a Crime. Cassell, 1938
-Storm Cloud Over Vienna. Murray, 1940
-Unholy Flame. GM, 1952

ROSMER, JEAN. Pseudonym of Jeanne Ichord Alcanter de Brahm, 1890-   .
In Secret Service. Lippincott, 1937. (Translation of Napoleone. Paris, 1929.)

ROSNER, JOSEPH. 1922-   .
The Habits of Command. Harcourt, 1975

ROSS, ALBERT. Pseudonym of Linn Boyd Porter, 1851-1916.
His Foster Sister. Dillingham, 1896

ROSS, ALBERT. Pseudonym of Arthur D. Goldstein, q.v.
If I Knew What I was Doing... Random, 1974

ROSS, ANGUS. 1927-   . Series character: Marcus Aurelius Farrow, in all titles.
The Amsterdam Diversion. Long, 1974
The Bradford Business. Long, 1974
The Dunfermline Affair. Long, 1973
The Edinburgh Exercise. Long, 1975
The Huddersfield Job. Long, 1971
The Manchester Thing. Long, 1970
The Leeds Fiasco. Long, 1975
The London Assignment. Long, 1972

ROSS, BARNABY. Joint pseudonym of Frederic Dannay, 1905-   , and Manfred Bennington Lee, 1905-1971. Other joint pseudonym: Ellery Queen, q.v. Series character: Drury Lane, in all titles.
Drury Lane's Last Case. Viking, 1933; Cassell, 1933. Reprinted as by Ellery Queen: Little, 1946
The Tragedy of X. Viking, 1932; Cassell, 1932. Reprinted as by Ellery Queen: Stokes, 1940
The Tragedy of Y. Viking, 1932; Cassell, 1932. Reprinted as by Ellery Queen: Stokes, 1941
The Tragedy of Z. Viking, 1933; Cassell, 1933. Reprinted as by Ellery Queen: Little, 1942

ROSS, CARLTON. Pseudonym of Edwy Searles Brooks, 1889-1965, q.v. Other pseudonyms: Berkeley Gray, Victor Gunn, qq.v.
The Black Skull Murders. Swan, 1942
Racketeers of the Turf. Swan, 1947

ROSS, CHARLES H(ENRY). 1842?-1897.
Hot and Cold. Routledge, 1872
A Private Enquiry. Tinsley, 1870

ROSS, CLARISSA. Pseudonym of W(illiam) E(dward) D(aniel) Ross, 1912-   , q.v. Other pseudonyms: Rose Dana, Jan Daniels, Ellen Randolph, Dan Ross, Dana Ross, Marilyn Ross, qq.v.
Beware the Kindly Stranger. Lancer, 1970
China Shadow. Avon, 1974
The Corridors of Fear. Avon, 1971
Dark Harbor Hunting. Avon, 1975
Drifthaven. Avon, 1974
Durrell Towers. Pyramid, 1966
Evil of Dark Harbor. Avon, 1975
Face in the Pond. Avon, 1969
Fogbound. Arcadia, 1967
Gemini in Darkness. Lancer, 1970
Ghost of Dark Harbor. Avon, 1974
The Ghosts of Grantmeer. Avon, 1972
Glimpse into Terror. Lancer, 1971
The Haunting of Villa Gabriel. Paperback Library, 1971
A Hearse of Dark Harbor. Avon, 1974
It Comes by Night. Lancer, 1972
Jennifer by Moonlight. Bantam, 1973
A Love to Cherish. Bantam, 1973
Mistress of Ravenswood. Arcadia, 1966
Mists of Dark Harbor. Avon, 1974
Out of the Fog. Lancer, 1970
Phantom of Dark Harbor. Avon, 1972
Phantom of Glencourt. Lancer, 1972
Secret of Mallet Castle. Arcadia, 1966
Secret of the Pale Lover. Lancer, 1970
Shadow on Capricorn. Bantam, 1972
Shadow over the Garden. Belmont, 1975
The Spectral Mist. Hale, 1968
Terror at Dark Harbor. Avon, 1975
Voice from the Grave. Lancer, 1971
Whisper of Danger. Bantam, 1974
Whispers in the Night. Bantam, 1971

ROSS, DAN. Pseudonym of W(illiam) E(dward) D(aniel) Ross, 1912-   , q.v. Other pseudonyms: Rose Dana, Jan Daniels, Ellen Randolph, Clarissa Ross, Dana Ross, Marilyn Ross, qq.v. Several titles published as by W. E. D. Ross were reprinted in paperback as by Dan Ross.
The Castle on the Cliff. Avalon, 1967
Cliffhaven. Avalon, 1966
Murder at City Hall. Avalon, 1965
The Mystery of Fury Castle. Avalon, 1965
Out of the Night. Avalon, 1963

ROSS, DANA. Pseudonym of W(illiam) E(dward) D(aniel) Ross, 1912-   , q.v. Other pseudonyms: Rose Dana, Jan Daniels, Ellen Randolph, Clarissa Ross, Dan Ross, Marilyn Ross, qq.v.
Demon of the Darkness. PB, 1975
The Figure in the Shadows. Popular Library, 1972
The Haunting of Clifton Court. Popular Library, 1972
Lodge Sinister. PB, 1975
Night of the Dead. Popular Library, 1973
This Shrouded Night. PB, 1975

ROSS, DONALD
Dead Men Do Tell Tales. Methuen, 1938
The Devil was Kind. Whitman, 1938. (British title?)
Five Keys to Mystery. Methuen, 1938
House of Horror. Methuen, 1939
M.D.—Doctor of Murder. Methuen, 1938
Murder C.O.D. Methuen, 1938

ROSS, GENE
Corpse in the Boudoir. Harborough, 1953
"Lady, Throw Me a Curve." Archer, 1950
Step Up, Sucker. Harborough, 1953
This Way for Hell. Archer, 1950
Two Smart Dames. Archer, 1949
You're Dead, My Lovely. Archer, 1950

ROSS, GEORGE. See: JOHN (FREDERICK) BURKE, 1922-   ; and: JOSEPH (ARNOLD) HAYES, 1918-   .

ROSS, HAL. 1941-   .
The Fleur de Lys Affair. Doubleday, 1975; New English Library, 1976

ROSS, HELEN HALYBURTON
-Dark Gethryn. Jenkins, 1932
-The House of the Talisman. Butterworth, 1927
-The Lost Oasis. Hutchinson, 1933
-A Man with his Back to the East. Butterworth, 1926
The Mystery of the Lotus Queen. Jenkins, 1931
-Peel Rocke—Black Sheep. Jenkins, 1932
The Scarab Clue. Hutchinson, 1935
-The Sea of Death. Jenkins, 1931
-The Shadow of Egypt. Butterworth, 1928
-The Silence of Jeremy Langton. Hutchinson, 1934
-Sin and Sand. Butterworth, 1929

ROSS, IVAN T. Pseudonym of Robert Rossner, 1932-   , q.v. Series character: Ben Gordon = BG.
The Man Who Would Do Anything. Doubleday, 1963; Heinemann, 1964
Murder Out of School. Simon, 1960; Heinemann, 1960 BG
Old Students Never Die. Doubleday, 1962; Heinemann, 1963 BG

Requiem for a Schoolgirl. Simon, 1961; Heinemann, 1961 BG
Teacher's Blood. Doubleday, 1964; Hale, 1966 BG

ROSS, JAMES. 1911-   .
They Don't Dance Much. Houghton, 1940; Jarrolds, 1940

ROSS, JEROME. See: DOROTHY SALISBURY DAVIS, 1916-   .

ROSS, JOHN. Series character: The Major (Major Seary), in at least those marked M.
The Black Spot. Hodder, 1936
Bless the Wasp. Hodder, 1938
The Drone-Man. Hodder, 1937
Federal Agent. Collins, 1941
The Major. Hodder, 1938 M
The Major Steps Out. Hodder, 1939 M
The Man from the Chamber of Horrors. Hodder, 1939
The Moccasin Men. Hodder, 1936 M
The Tall Man. Collins, 1940

ROSS, JONATHAN. Pseudonym of John Rossiter, 1916-   , q.v. Series character: Inspector George Rogers, in at least those marked GR.
The Blood Running Cold. Cassell, 1968 GR
The Burning of Billy Toober. Constable, 1974; Walker, 1976 GR
Dead at First Hand. Cassell, 1969 GR
The Deadest Thing You Ever Saw. Cassell, 1969; McCall, 1970 GR
Diminished by Death. Cassell, 1968 GR
Here Lies Nancy Frail. Constable, 1972; Saturday Review Press, 1972

ROSS, LEONARD. Pseudonym of Leo (Calvin) Rosten, 1908-   , q.v.
-Adventure in Washington. Harcourt, 1940
Balkan Express; see Dateline: Europe
The Dark Corner. Century, 1945; Edwards, 1946, as by L. C. Rosten
-Dateline: Europe. Harcourt, 1939. British title: Balkan Express. Heinemann, 1939

ROSS, MANDER
The Sorting Van Murder. Melrose, 1935

ROSS, MARILYN. Pseudonym of W(illiam) E(dward) D(aniel) Ross, 1912-   , q.v. Other pseudonyms: Rose Dana, Jan Daniels, Ellen Randolph, Clarissa Ross, Dan Ross, Dana Ross, qq.v. Novelizations of the Dark Shadows TV series = DS (published by Paperback Library).
The Amethyst Tears. Beagle, 1974
The Aquarius Curse. Paperback Library, 1970
Assignment: Danger. Paperback Library, 1967
Barnabas Collins. 1968 DS
Barnabas Collins and Quentin's Demon. 1970 DS
Barnabas Collins and the Gypsy Witch. 1970 DS
Barnabas Collins and the Mysterious Ghost. 1970 DS
Barnabas Collins vs. the Warlock. 1969 DS
Barnabas, Quentin and Dr. Jekyll's Son. 1971 DS
Barnabas, Quentin and the Avenging Ghost. 1970 DS
Barnabas, Quentin and the Body Snatchers. 1971 DS
Barnabas, Quentin and the Crystal Coffin. 1970 DS
Barnabas, Quentin and the Frightened Bride. 1970 DS

Ross, Marilyn

Barnabas, Quentin and the Grave Robbers. 1971 DS
Barnabas, Quentin and the Haunted Cave. 1970 DS
Barnabas, Quentin and the Hidden Tomb. 1971 DS
Barnabas, Quentin and the Mad Magician. 1971 DS
Barnabas, Quentin and the Magic Potion. 1971 DS
Barnabas, Quentin and the Mummy's Curse. 1970 DS
Barnabas, Quentin and the Nightmare Assassin. 1970 DS
Barnabas, Quentin and the Scorpio Curse. 1970 DS
Barnabas, Quentin and the Sea Ghost. 1971 DS
Barnabas, Quentin and the Serpent. 1970 DS
Barnabas, Quentin and the Vampire Beauty. 1972 DS
Barnabas, Quentin and the Witch's Curse. 1970 DS
Behind the Purple Veil. Paperback Library, 1973
Beware, My Love. Paperback Library, 1965
The Brides of Saturn. Berkley, 1975
Cameron Castle. Paperback Library, 1967
The Curse of Collinwood. 1968 DS
Dark Legend. Paperback Library, 1966
Dark Shadows. 1966 DS
Dark Stars over Seacrest. Paperback Library, 1972
Dark Towers of Fog Island. Popular Library, 1975
The Demon of Barnabas Collins, 1969 DS
Desperate Heiress. Paperback Library, 1966
The Devil's Daughter. Paperback Library, 1973
Don't Look Behind You. Paperback Library, 1973
Face in the Fog. Curtis, 1973
Face in the Shadows. Paperback Library, 1973
The Foe of Barnabas Collins. 1969 DS
Fog Island. Paperback Library, 1965
Fog Island Secret. Popular Library, 1975
A Garden of Ghosts. Popular Library, 1974
A Gathering of Evil. Paperback Library, 1966
The Ghost and the Garnet. Beagle, 1975
Ghost Comes Knocking. Paperback Library, 1971
Ghost Ship of Fog Island. Popular Library, 1975
Haunting of Fog Island. Curtis, 1973
House of Dark Shadows. Paperback Library, 1970. (Novelization of the movie.)
House of Ghosts. Paperback Library, 1973
The Light in the Tower. Paperback Library, 1965
Loch Sinister. Popular Library, 1974
The Locked Corridor. Paperback Library, 1965
The Long Night of Fear. Paperback Library, 1972
Marta. Paperback Library, 1973
Memory of Evil. Paperback Library, 1966
Message from a Ghost. Paperback Library, 1972
Mistress of Moorwood Manor. Paperback Library, 1972
Mistress of Ravenswood. Paperback Library, 1967
The Mystery at Collinwood. 1967 DS
The Mystery of Fury Castle. Paperback Library, 1967
Night of the Phantom. Paperback Library, 1972
The Peril of Barnabas Collins. 1969 DS
The Phantom and Barnabas Collins, 1969 DS
Phantom Manor. Paperback Library, 1966
The Phantom of Belle Acres. Curtis, 1973
Phantom of Fog Island. Paperback Library, 1971
Phantom of the Swamp. Paperback Library, 1972
Phantom of the Thirteenth Floor. Popular Library, 1975
Ravenhurst. Popular Library, 1975
Satan's Island. Warner, 1975
Satan's Rock. Paperback Library, 1966
The Secret of Barnabas Collins. 1969 DS
Secrets of Sedbury Manor. Curtis, 1973
Shadow over Emerald Castle. Ballantine, 1975
Shorecliff. Paperback Library, 1968
The Sinister Garden. Paperback Library, 1972
Step into Terror. Paperback Library, 1973
Strangers at Collins House. 1967 DS
Tread Softly, Nurse Scott. Paperback Library, 1966
The Vampire Contessa. Pinnacle, 1975
Victoria Winters. 1967 DS
The Witch of Bralhaven. Paperback Library, 1973
Witches' Cove. Paperback Library, 1971

ROSS, MARK
Ace High. Warren, 1951
Alibi. Warren, 1951
Blackmail. Warren, 1951
Crisis for Two. Warren, 1952
Last Card. Warren, 1952
Manhunt. Warren, 1951
Night Ride. Warren, 1952
Noon Jury. Warren, 1952
Operator X. Warren, 1951
Quiet City. Warren, 1952
Strange Money. Warren, 1951
This Woman is Dangerous. Warren, 1952

ROSS, PAUL. Pseudonym. Series character: Terry Bunker (Chopper Cop) = TB.
The Assassin. Manor, 1974
Dynamite Monster Boogie Concert. Popular Library, 1975 TB
Freebie and the Bean. Warner, 1975; Futura, 1975. (Novelization of the movie.)
The Hitchhike Killer. Popular Library, 1972 TB
Valley of Death. Popular Library, 1972 TB

ROSS, PHYLLIS (FREEDMAN). 1926-1970.
Miranda Clair. PB, 1965

ROSS, REGINA
Falls the Shadow. Delacorte, 1974; Barker, 1974

ROSS, SAM. 1912- .
Hang-Up. Coward, 1968; Hale, 1969
The Hustlers. Popular Library, 1956
He Ran All the Way. Farrar, 1947
The Keepers; see Ready for the Tiger
Ready for the Tiger. Farrar, 1964; Barrie, 1965. Also published as: The Keepers. New English Library pb, 1969
The Tight Corner. Farrar, 1956; Boardman, 1957
-You Belong to Me. Popular Library, 1955

ROSS, SHEILA
-Five Days Till Noon. Collins, 1973
The Foam on the River. Collins, 1975
-A Log Across the Road. Collins, 1971. Reprinted in two volumes: A State of Emergency. Fontana, 1973; and: Wars Within Wars. Fontana, 1973
-The Perfect Carrier. Collins, 1972
A State of Emergency; see A Log Across the Road
-The Tower of Monte Rado. Collins, 1974
Wars Within Wars; see A Log Across the Road

ROSS, W(ILLIAM) E(DWARD) D(ANIEL). 1912- . Pseudonyms: Rose Dana, Jan Daniels, Ellen Randolph, Clarissa Ross, Dan Ross, Dana Ross, Marilyn Ross, qq.v. At least some of the titles below are gothics.
An Act of Love. Avalon, 1970
Behind Locked Shutters. Arcadia, 1968
Castle on the Hill. Hale, 1968
Christopher's Mansion. Bouregy, 1969
Dark is my Shadow. Arcadia, 1969
Dark Mansion. Avalon, 1973
Dark of the Moon. Arcadia, 1968
Dark Villa of Capri. Arcadia, 1968
Destination Terror. Paperback Library, 1968
The Enchanted Voyage. Hale, 1968
The Forbidden Castle. Lenox, 1972. British title: Rendezvous in Australia. Hale, 1967
The Ghost of Oaklands. Arcadia, 1967
The Haunted Garden. Paperback Library, 1970
The House on Mount Vernon Street. Lenox, 1972
Magic Valley. Hale, 1970
Mansion on the Moors. Avalon, 1971
The Music Room. Dell, 1971
Nightmare Abbey. Berkley, 1975
One Louisburg Square. Lenox, 1974; Remploy, 1975
Our Share of Love. Hale, 1969
Rendezvous in Australia; see The Forbidden Castle
Reunion in Renfrew. Avalon, 1972; Hale, 1974
The Room Without a Key. Lenox, 1971
Rothhaven. Avalon, 1972
Sable in the Rain. Lenox, 1970
The Third Spectre. Arcadia, 1967
This Man I Love. Hale, 1970
The Twilight Web. Arcadia, 1968. Reprinted as by Dan Ross: Macfadden, 1970
The Web of Love. Hale, 1970
The Whispering Gallery. Lenox, 1970
Whispers in the Night. Lenox, 1970
Wind over the Citadel. Lenox, 1971
Witch of Goblin's Acres. Lenox, 1974; Remploy, 1974
The Yesteryear Phantom. Lenox, 1971

ROSS, WILLIAM
Bamboo Terror. Tuttle, 1969

ROSS, Z(OLA) H(ELEN GIRDEY). 1912- . Pseudonyms: Helen Arre, Bert Iles, qq.v. Series characters: Beau Smith and Pogy Rogers = S&R.
One Corpse Missing. Bobbs, 1948 S&R
Overdue for Death. Bobbs, 1947
Three Down Vulnerable. Bobbs, 1946 S&R

ROSSI, BRUNO. Series character: Johnny Rock (The Sharpshooter), in all titles.
Blood Bath. Leisure, 1974
Blood Oath. Leisure, 1974
A Dirty Way to Die. Leisure, 1975
Head Crusher. Leisure, 1974
Hit Man. Leisure, 1974
The Killing Machine. Leisure, 1973
Las Vegas Vengeance. Leisure, 1975
Mafia Death Watch. Leisure, 1975
Muzzle Blast. Leisure, 1974
Night of the Assassins. Leisure, 1974

No Quarter Given. Leisure, 1974
Savage Slaughter. Leisure, 1975
Scarfaced Killer. Leisure, 1975
Stiletto. Leisure, 1975
Triggerman. Leisure, 1975
The Worst Way to Die. Leisure, 1974

ROSSI, JEAN BAPTISTE. 1931-   . Pseudonym: Sebastien Japrisot, q.v.

ROSSITER, JOHN. 1916-   . Pseudonym: Jonathan Ross, q.v. Series character: Roger Tallis, in at least those marked RT.
The Deadly Gold; see The Golden Virgin
The Deadly Green. Cassell, 1970; Walker, 1971 RT
The Golden Virgin. Constable, 1975. U.S. title: The Deadly Gold. Walker, 1975 RT
The Manipulators. Cassell, 1973; Simon, 1974
The Murder Makers. Cassell, 1970; Walker, 1977
A Rope for General Dietz. Constable, 1972; Walker, 1972 RT
The Victims. Cassell, 1971
The Villains. Cassell, 1974; Walker, 1976

ROSSMANN, JOHN F. Series character: Britt St. Vincent, in all titles.
The Door. Signet, 1975
The Mind-Masters. Signet, 1974
Shamballah. Signet, 1975

ROSSNER, ROBERT. 1932-   . Pseudonym: Ivan T. Ross, q.v.
The End of Someone Else's Rainbow. Saturday Review Press, 1974

ROSTAND, ROBERT. Pseudonym of Robert (S.) Hopkins, q.v. Series character: Mike Locken, in at least those marked ML.
The Killer Elite. Delacorte, 1973; Hodder, 1974 ML
The Vengeance Run. Berkley, 1972; Arrow, 1976
Viper's Game. Delacorte, 1974; Hodder, 1975 ML

ROSTEN, LEO (CALVIN). 1908-   . Pseudonym: Leonard Ross, q.v.
A Most Private Intrigue. Atheneum, 1967; Gollancz, 1967

ROTH, ARTHUR JOSEPH. 1925-   . Pseudonym: Slater McGurk, q.v.

ROTH, HOLLY. 1916-1964. Pseudonyms: K. G. Ballard, P. J. Merrill, qq.v. Series character: Inspector Medford = M.
Button, Button. Harcourt, 1966; H. Hamilton, 1967
The Content Assignment. Simon, 1954; H. Hamilton, 1954. Also published as: The Shocking Secret. Dell, 1955
The Crimson in the Purple. Simon, 1956; H. Hamilton, 1957
The Mask of Glass. Vanguard, 1954; H. Hamilton, 1955
Operation Doctors; see Too Many Doctors
Shadow of a Lady. Simon, 1957; H. Hamilton, 1957 M
The Shocking Secret; see The Content Assignment
The Sleeper. Simon, 1955; H. Hamilton, 1955
Too Many Doctors. Random, 1962. British title: Operation Doctors. H. Hamilton, 1962 M
The Van Dreisen Affair. Random, 1960; H. Hamilton, 1960

ROTHBERG, ABRAHAM. 1922-   .
The Heirs of Cain. Putnam, 1966
The Stalking Horse. Saturday Review Press, 1972
The Thousand Doors. Holt, 1965; Heinemann, 1965

ROTHMAN, JUDITH
With Murder in Mind. Hale, 1975

ROTHWELL, H(ENRY) T(ALBOT). Series character: Mike Brooks, in at least those marked MB.
Dive Deep for Danger. Hale, 1966; Roy, 1966 MB
Duet for Three Spies. Hale, 1967; Roy, 1967 MB
Exit a Spy. Hale, 1966 MB
No Honour Amongst Spies. Hale, 1969; Roy, 1969 MB
No Kisses from the Kremlin. Hale, 1969

ROTHWELL, UNA
Death on the Run. Hale, 1965
Murder is Lonely. Hale, 1964

ROUDYBUSH, ALEXANDRA (BROWN). 1911-   .
Before the Ball was Over. Doubleday, 1965. British title: A Season for Death. Hale, 1966
A Capital Crime. Doubleday, 1969
Death of a Moral Person. Doubleday, 1967; Hale, 1968
A Gastronomic Murder. Doubleday, 1973; New English Library, 1974
The House of the Cat. Doubleday, 1970; New English Library, 1975
A Season for Death; see Before the Ball was Over
Suddenly in Paris. Doubleday, 1975
A Sybaritic Death. Doubleday, 1972; New English Library, 1972

ROUECHE, BERTON. 1911-   .
Black Weather. Reynal, 1945
The Cats; see Feral
Feral. Harper, 1974. British title: The Cats. Gollancz, 1975
The Last Enemy. Dell, 1956; Gollancz, 1956
-Rooming House. Lion, 1953

ROUGVIE, CAMERON. Series character: Robert Belcourt, in all titles.
The Gredos Reckoning. Barker, 1966
Medal from Pamplona. Barker, 1964; Ballantine, 1964
Tangier Assignment. Barker, 1965; Ballantine, 1965
When Johnny Died. Barker, 1967

ROURKE, JAMES F. 1922-   . Joint pseudonym with Hollis Spurgeon Summers, 1915-   : Jim Hollis, q.v.

ROURKE, THOMAS. Pseudonym of Daniel Joseph Clinton, 1900-   .
The Scarlet Flower. Farrar, 1933; Nicholson, 1934

ROUVEROL, JEAN
Storm Wind Rising. GM, 1974

ROVIN, JEFF. Series character: Roger Garrison, in both titles.
Hollywood Detective: Garrison. Manor, 1975
Hollywood Detective: The Wolf. Manor, 1975

ROWAN, DEIRDRE. Pseudonym of Jeanne Williams, 1930-   . Other pseudonym: Jeanne Crecy, q.v.
Dragon's Mount. GM, 1973
Shadow of the Volcano. GM, 1975
Silver Wood. GM, 1974

ROWDEN, DICK
Bright Like Blood. Pyramid, 1969

ROWE, ANNE (VON MEIBOM). Series characters: Inspector Barry = B: Inspector Pettengill = P.
Cobra Venom; see Too Much Poison
Curiosity Killed a Cat. Morrow, 1941; Gifford, 1945
Deadly Intent. Mill, 1946. British title (?): The Painted Monster. Gifford, 1945 B
Fatal Purchase. Mill, 1945; Gifford, 1946
The Little Dog Barked. Morrow, 1942; Gifford, 1944 P
-Men are Strange Lovers. King, 1935
The Painted Monster; see Deadly Intent
Too Much Poison. Mill, 1944. British title: Cobra Venom. Gifford, 1946 B
The Turn of a Wheel. Macaulay, 1930
Up to the Hilt. Mill, 1945; Nimmo, 1947 B

ROWE, JOHN G(ABRIEL). 1874-   .
The Cartsley Mystery. Modern, 193?
The Death Flash; or, The Horror of Monkstone Wood. Modern, 193?
The Fighting Lieutenant. Modern, 1935
Gentleman George. Modern, 1935
The Man with the Seared Hand; see The Seared Hand
The Mystery of the Derelict. Modern, 1935; Cupples, 1927
The Seared Hand. Step, 1925. Also published as (?): The Man with the Seared Hand. Modern, 193?
The Secret of the Old Lighthouse. Crowther, 1945
Spies of the Secret Police. Modern, 193?
Struck Down. Modern, 193?

ROWLAND, HENRY C(OTTRELL). 1874-1933.
-The Apple of Discord. Dodd, 1913
The Closing Net. Dodd, 1912; Hurst, 1913
Duds. Harper, 1920
Mile High. Harper, 1921
-The Mountains of Fears. Barnes, 1905 ss
-Pearl Island. Watt, 1919; Collins, 1921
The Peddler. Harper, 1920
The Return of Frank Clamart. Harper, 1923
-Sea Scamps. McClure, 1903 ss
-The Sultana. Dodd, 1914
-To Windward. Barnes, 1904; Nutt, 1905

ROWLAND, JOHN (HERBERT SHELLEY). 1907-   . Series character: Insp. Shelley, in at least those marked S.
Bloodshed in Bayswater. Jenkins, 1935 S
Calamity in Kent. Jenkins, 1950 S
The Cornish Riviera Mystery. Jenkins, 1939 S
The Crooked House. Jenkins, 1940 S
Dangerous Company. Jenkins, 1937
Death Beneath the River. Jenkins, 1943 S
The Death of Nevill Norway. Jenkins, 1942
Death on Dartmoor. Jenkins, 1936 S
The Devil Comes to Devon. Jenkins, 1938 S
Grim Souvenir. Jenkins, 1944
Gunpowder Alley. Jenkins, 1941 S
Murder—By Persons Unknown. Mellifont, 1941
Murder in the Museum. Jenkins, 1938 S
The Orange-Tree Mystery. Jenkins, 1949 S
The Professor Dies. Jenkins, 1936 S
Puzzle in Pyrotechnics. Jenkins, 1947 S
Sinister Creek. Fiction House, 1946
Slow Poison. Jenkins, 1939
The Spy with the Scar. Jenkins, 1940
Suicide Alibi. Jenkins, 1937 S
Time for Killing. Jenkins, 1950

ROWLANDS, CECIL. 1856-1914. Pseudonym: Cecil Raleigh, q.v. See also: RICHARD PARKER.

ROWLEY, J. DE LA MARE
The Passage in Park Lane. Butterworth, 1928

ROWSELL, E. P.
Recollections of a Relieving Officer. Ward, 1861. Also published as by Francis W. Rowsell: Maxwell, 1886

ROWSELL, FRANCIS W. See: E. P. ROWSELL.

ROY, ARCHIE (EDMISTON). 1924- .
All Evil Shed Away. Long, 1970; World, 1972
The Curtained Sleep. Long, 1969; World, 1971
Deadlight. Long, 1968
Sable Night. Long, 1973

ROY, IAN
Lord Lynmore's Life. Nisbet, 1917

ROYCE, KENNETH. 1920- . Pseudonym: Oliver Jacks, q.v. Series character: Spider Scott = SS.
The Angry Island. Cassell, 1963
Bones in the Sand. Cassell, 1967
The Concrete Boot. Hodder, 1971; McKay, 1971 SS
The Day the Wind Dropped. Cassell, 1964
The Long Corridor. Cassell, 1960
The Masterpiece Affair; see Spider Underground
The Miniatures Frame. Hodder, 1972; Simon, 1972 SS
My Turn to Die. Barker, 1958
The Night Seekers. Cassell, 1962
No Paradise. Cassell, 1961
A Peck of Salt. Cassell, 1968
A Single to Hong Kong. Hodder, 1969
The Soft-Footed Moor. Barker, 1959
Spider Underground. Hodder, 1973. U.S. title: The Masterpiece Affair. Simon, 1973 SS
Trap Spider. Hodder, 1974 SS
The Woodcutter Operation. Hodder, 1975; Simon, 1975
The XYY Man. Hodder, 1970; McKay, 1970 SS

ROYDE-SMITH, NAOMI (GWLADYS)
All Star Cast. Macmillan (London & New York), 1936
The Altar-Piece. Macmillan (London), 1939
John Fanning's Legacy. Constable, 1927
Madam Julia's Tale and other queer stories. Gollancz, 1932 ss
-The Tortoiseshell Cat. Constable, 1925; Boni, 1925
-The Younger Venus. Macmillan (London), 1938; Macmillan (New York), 1939

ROYER, LOUIS-CHARLES
-African Mistress. Pyramid, 1953
-French Doctor. Pyramid, 1951
-The Harem. Dell, 1952
-Love Camp. Pyramid, 1953
-The Man from Paris. Pyramid, 1956
The Redhead from Chicago. Pyramid, 1954
-Savage Triangle. Pyramid, 1954
-Unrepentant Sinners. Pyramid, 1957

ROYS, WILLIS E.
Flame Eternal and The Maharajah's Son. Osberg, 1936. (2 stories, the second criminous.)

RUBEL, JAMES L(YON). 1894- .
No Business for a Lady. GM, 1950; Fawcett (London), 1952

RUBENSTEIN, SAMUEL LEONARD. 1922- . Joint pseudonym with Robert G. Weaver: Rubin Weber, q.v.

RUBENSTEIN, STANLEY (JACK)
Merry Murder. Jarrolds, 1949

RUBINSTEIN, PAUL. 1935- . See: PETER (JOSEPH) TANOUS, 1938- .

RUCK, BERTA [AMY ROBERTA RUCK OLIVER]. 1878- .
The Pearl Thief. Dodd, 1926; Hodder, 1926

RUD, ANTHONY M(ELVILLE). 1893-1942. Series character: J. C. K. ("Jiggers") Masters = JM.
The Devil's Heirloom. Garden City, 1924
House of the Damned. Macaulay, 1934 JM
The Rose Bath Riddle. Macaulay, 1934 JM
-The Sentence of the Six-Gun. Garden City, 1926
The Stuffed Men. Macaulay, 1935; Newnes, 1936 JM

RUDD, COLIN
The Red Flowers of Death. Hale, 1970
The Violent Dawn. Hale, 1971

RUDORFF, RAYMOND
The Dracula Archives. PB, 1972

RUEGG, JUDGE (ALFRED HENRY). 1854-1941. Series character: Rosie Bright = RB.
David Betterton. Daniel, 1931 RB
Flash. Daniel, 1928
John Clutterbuck. Daniel, 1923 RB
A Staffordshire Knot; or, The Two Houses. Daniel, 1926

RUELL, PATRICK. Pseudonym of Reginald (Charles) Hill, 1936- , q.v.
The Castle of the Demon. Long, 1971
Death Takes the Low Road. Hutchinson, 1974
Red Christmas. Long, 1972
Urn Burial. Hutchinson, 1975

RUNDLE, ANNE. Pseudonyms: Alexandra Manners, Joanne Marshall, qq.v.
Amberwood. Hale, 1973; Bantam, 1974
-Forest of Fear. Hurst, 1969
Heronbrook. Hale, 1975; Bantam, 1975
-Lost Lotus. Hale, 1972
-The Moon Marriage. Hurst, 1967
-Rakehell. Hurst, 1970
-Swordlight. Hurst, 1968

RUNYON, CHARLES (W.). 1928- .
Anatomy of Violence. Ace, 1963
The Black Moth. GM, 1967
Bloody Jungle. Ace, 1966
Color Him Dead. GM, 1963; Muller pb, 1964
The Death Cycle. GM, 1963; New English Library, 1969
No Place to Hide. GM, 1970
Power Kill. GM, 1972
The Prettiest Girl I Ever Killed. GM, 1965
Something Wicked. Lancer, 1973

RUNYON, DAMON, 1880-1946, and HOWARD LINDSAY, 1889- .
A Slight Case of Murder. Dramatists Play Service, 1940. (2-act play.)

RUNYON, POKE
Commando X. Pyramid, 1967
Night Jump—Cuba. Pyramid, 1967

RUSE, GARY ALAN. 1946- .
Houndstooth. Prentice-Hall, 1975

RUSHTON, CHARLES. Pseudonym of Charles Rushton Shortt, 1904- . Series characters: Insp. Cadman, in at least those marked C; James O'Hannay and Floyd East, in at least those marked O&E.
Another Crime. Jenkins, 1934
Black Destiny. Jenkins, 1929
Bloody with Spurring. Jenkins, 1939
Crime Looks Up. Jenkins, 1947
Danger in the Deed. Jenkins, 1933
Dark Amid the Blaze. Jenkins, 1950
The Dead Men. Jenkins, 1935
Death in the Wood. Jenkins, 1936
Devil's Power. Jenkins, 1952; Roy, 1956 C
The Doctor from Devil's Island. Jenkins, 1935
Furnace for a Foe. Jenkins, 1951; Roy, 1957 C
Madman's Manor. Jenkins, 1932
The Master of Fear. Jenkins, 1930 O&E
Murder in Bavaria. Jenkins, 1937
The Murder Market. Jenkins, 1934
Murder on Trust. Jenkins, 1943 C
Murder Out of Tune. Jenkins, 1939
Night of Murder. Jenkins, 1937
No Beast So Fierce. Jenkins, 1950; Roy, 1958 C
No Second Stroke. Jenkins, 1938
Terror Tower. Jenkins, 1933
The Trail of Blood. Jenkins, 1929 O&E

RUSO, MICHAEL. Joint pseudonym with John Roscoe, 1921- : Mike Roscoe, q.v.

RUSSELL, A(NDREW) J(OSEPH)
The Devalino Caper. Random, 1975

RUSSELL, AGNES
A Flame in the Heather. Hale, 1974
Hill of the Wild Cat. Hale, 1975
-A Red Rose for Annabel. Hale, 1973

RUSSELL, ARTHUR
The Croaker. Mellifont, 1936
The Mystery of the Luminous Ray. Mellifont, 1935
Tragedy at Cumberland Park. Fenland, 1933

RUSSELL, MAJOR C(HARLES) E(DMUND). 1878- .
Adventures of the D.C.I. Doubleday, 1924; Curtis Brown, 1924 ss
True Adventures of the Secret Service. Doubleday, 1923; Hurst, 1924 ss

RUSSELL, CHARLOTTE
Dark Music. Lancer, 1972

RUSSELL, CHARLOTTE MURRAY. Series characters: Jane Amanda Edwards = JE; Homer Fitzgerald = HF.
The Bad Neighbor Murder. Doubleday, 1946 JE
Between Us and Evil. Doubleday, 1950 HF
The Careless Mrs. Christian. Doubleday, 1949 HF
The Case of the Topaz Flower. Doubleday, 1939
The Clue of the Naked Eye. Doubleday, 1939 JE
Cook Up a Crime. Doubleday, 1951 JE
Death of an Eloquent Man. Doubleday, 1936 JE
Dreadful Reckoning. Doubleday, 1941
Hand Me a Crime. Doubleday, 1949; Cherry Tree, 1950 JE
I Heard the Death Bell. Doubleday, 1940 JE
Ill Met in Mexico. Doubleday, 1948 JE
June, Moon, and Murder. Doubleday, 1952 HF
Lament for William. Doubleday, 1947 HF
Market for Murder. Doubleday, 1953
The Message of the Mute Dog. Doubleday, 1942 JE

Murder at the Old Stone House. Doubleday, 1935 JE
Murder Steps In. Doubleday, 1942
Night on the Devil's Pathway; see Night on the Pathway
Night on the Pathway. Doubleday, 1938. British title: Night on the Devil's Pathway. World's Work, 1938 JE
No Time for Crime. Doubleday, 1945 JE
The Tiny Diamond. Doubleday, 1937; World's Work, 1937 JE

RUSSELL, DONN
A Difference in Death. Faber, 1957

RUSSELL, DORA
-Betrayed. White, 1885
The Broken Seal. Hurst, 1887; Lovell, 1886
-An Evil Reputation. Griffith, 1892
-A Fatal Past. Simpkin, 1896; Lovell, 1891
-Footprints in the Snow. Tinsley, 1877
-A Hidden Chain. Digby, 1894; Rand, 1896
-The Last Signal. White, 1893; Taylor, 1892
-The Secret of the River. Hurst, 1891
-The Silent Watchers. Digby, 1903
-A Strange Message. Low, 1889; Lovell, 1888
-A Torn-Out Page. Digby, 1899; Rand, 1897

RUSSELL, E(NID) S. Series character: Ben Louis = BL.
The Fortunate Island. Doubleday, 1973
Nice Enough to Murder. Doubleday, 1971 BL
She Should Have Cried on Monday. Doubleday, 1968; Hale, 1969 BL

RUSSELL, FOX
The Escapades of Mr. Alfred Dimmock. Everett, 1906 ss, some criminous
-In the Wrong Box. Everett, 1904
The Phantom Spy. Nelson, 1904

RUSSELL, JACK GOLDEN. See: GEORGE CLAYTON JOHNSON.

RUSSELL, JOHN. 1885-1956.
Cops 'n Robbers. Norton, 1930; Butterworth, 1930 ss
-Far Wandering Men. Norton, 1929; Butterworth, 1929 ss
-In Dark Places. Knopf, 1923; Butterworth, 1923 ss
The Red Mark, and other stories. Knopf, 1919. British title: Where the Pavement Ends. Butterworth, 1921. Reprinted in the U.S. under the British title: Knopf, 1921 ss
Where the Pavement Ends; see The Red Mark

RUSSELL, MARTIN (JAMES). 1934- .
Series character: Jim Larkin = JL.
Advisory Service. Collins, 1971
The Client. Collins, 1975
Concrete Evidence. Collins, 1972 JL
Crime Wave. Collins, 1974 JL
Danger Money. Collins, 1968
Deadline. Collins, 1971 JL
Double Hit. Collins, 1973
Hunt to Kill. Collins, 1969
Murder by the Mile. Collins, 1975
No Return Ticket. Collins, 1966
No Through Road. Collins, 1965; Coward, 1966
Phantom Holiday. Collins, 1974

RUSSELL, RAY. 1924- .
The Case Against Satan. Obolensky, 1962; Souvenir, 1963

RUSSELL, VICTOR
People of the Night. Harlequin, 1955

RUSSELL, W(ILLIAM) CLARK. 1844-1911.
Alone on a Wide, Wide Sea. Chatto, 1892; Taylor, 1892
-The Convict Ship. Chatto, 1895; Cassell (New York), 1893
The Copsford Mystery; see Is He the Man?
-The Death Ship. Hurst, 1888; Munro, 1888. Also published as: The Flying Dutchman; or, The Death Ship. Lovell, 1888
The Flying Dutchman; see The Death Ship
The Frozen Pirate. Low, 1887; Harper, 1887
-The Hunchback's Charge. Low, 1867
-In the Middle Watch. Chatto, 1885; Harper, 1885
Is He the Man? Tinsley, 1876. U.S. title: The Copsford Mystery; or, Is He the Man? New Amsterdam, 1896
-An Ocean Tragedy. Chatto, 1890; Harper, 1889
-The Phantom Death, and other stories. Chatto, 1895; Stokes, 1895 ss
The Tragedy of Ida Noble. Hutchinson, 1893; Appleton, 1891

RUSSELL, WILLIAM. Pseudonyms: Inspector F, Waters, qq.v.

RUSSO, JOHN
The Night of the Living Dead. Paperback Library, 1974. (Novelization of the movie.)

RUTHERFORD, (SAMUEL) ANWORTH. 1877- .
-The Bottle of Dust. Caxton, 1940
-Hidden Island. Little, 1927
-Sandlappers. Caxton, 1935
-Squaberry Canyon. Caxton, 1932

RUTHERFORD, CECILE
Desperate Encounter. Hale, 1971

RUTHERFORD, CONSTANCE
-The Blazing Star. Macdonald, 1914
The Door Without a Key. Hale, 1948
Double Entry. Heinemann, 1939
The Forgotten Terror. Heinemann, 1939
-The Lily Field. Hodder, 1933
-The Straight Furrow. Melrose, 1920

RUTHERFORD, DOUGLAS. Pseudonym of James Douglas Rutherford McConnell, 1915- . Joint pseudonym with Francis Durbridge, 1912- , q.v.: Paul Temple, q.v.
The Black Leather Murders. Collins, 1966; Walker, 1966
Clear the Fast Lane. Collins, 1971; Holt, 1972
Comes the Blind Fury. Faber, 1950
The Creeping Flesh. Collins, 1963; Walker, 1965
Flight into Peril; see Telling of Murder
The Gilt-Edged Cockpit. Collins, 1969; Doubleday, 1971
Grand Prix Murders. Collins, 1955
-The Gunshot Grand Prix. Collins, 1972
Kick Start. Collins, 1973; Walker, 1974
-Killer on the Track. Collins, 1973
The Long Echo. Collins, 1957; Abelard, 1958
Meet a Body. Faber, 1951
Murder is Incidental. Collins, 1961
Mystery Tour. Collins, 1975; Walker, 1976
On the Track of Death; see A Shriek of Tyres
The Perilous Sky. Collins, 1956
-Race Against the Sun. Collins, 1975
-Rally to the Death. Collins, 1974
A Shriek of Tyres. Collins, 1958. U.S. title: On the Track of Death. Abelard, 1959

Skin for Skin. Collins, 1968; Walker, 1968
Telling of Murder. Faber, 1952. U.S. title: Flight into Peril. Dodd, 1952

RUTHERFORD, WARD
The Gallows Set. Bles, 1969
Great Big Laughing Hannah. Bles, 1970

RUTLAND, HARRIET. Series character: Mr. Winkley = W.
Bleeding Hooks. Skeffington, 1940. U.S. title: The Poison Fly Murder. Harrison-Hilton, 1940 W
Blue Murder. Skeffington, 1950; Smith & Durrell, 1942
Knock, Murderer, Knock! Skeffington, 1938; Harrison-Hilton, 1939 W
The Poison Fly Murder; see Bleeding Hooks

RUTLAND, LYNN
The Death Ray Mystery. Northwestern, 1940. (3-act play.)
The Jeweled Cat. Northwestern, 1940. (3-act play.)

RUTLEDGE, ARTHUR
Object of Jealousy. Barker, 1961; Tower, 1965

RUTLEDGE, BRETT. Pseudonym of Elliot (Harold) Paul, 1891-1958, q.v.
The Death of Lord Haw Haw. Random, 1940; Laurie, 1941

RUTLEDGE, MARYSE. Pseudonym of Mrs. Marice Rutledge Gibson Hale, 1884- .
-The Sad Adventurers. Stokes, 1924; Constable, 1924
The Silver Peril. Fiction League, 1931

RUTLEDGE, NANCY. Pseudonym: Leigh Bryson, q.v.
Beware the Hoot Owl. Farrar, 1944; Boardman, 1946
Blood on the Cat. Farrar, 1945; Boardman, 1946
Cry Murder. Dutton, 1954; Muller, 1955
Easy to Murder. Doubleday, 1951; Boardman, 1952
Emily Will Know. Doubleday, 1949. British title: Murder for Millions. Harrap, 1950. Reprinted in the U.S. under the British title: Bestseller, 1951
Escape into Danger. Hale, 1960
The Frightened Murderer. Random, 1957; Hale, 1959
Murder for Millions; see Emily Will Know
Murder on the Mountain. Muller, 1957
The Preying Mantis. Doubleday, 1947; Boardman, 1949
Wanted for Murder. Random, 1956; Muller, 1956

RUTTER, AMANDA
Murder at Eastover. Arcadia, 1958
Murder is Where You Find It. Arcadia, 1959

RUTTER, OWEN. 1889-1944.
The Monster of Mu. Benn, 1932

RUUTH, MARIANNE. 1933- .
Game of Shadows. Ace, 1974
Tapestry of Terror. Ace, 1975

RYAN, FLOYD CURTISS
Murder on the Ranch. Nicholson, 1935; Empire, 1935

R

RYAN, J. M.
Mother's Day. GM, 1969; Allen, 1970

RYAN, JESSICA (CADWALADER). 1914?-1972. Series characters: Gregory (Grischa) Pavlov and O'Shaunnessey, in both books.
Clue of the Frightening Coin; see The Man Who Asked Why
Exit Harlequin. Doubleday, 1947
The Man Who Asked Why. Doubleday, 1945. Also published as: Clue of the Frightening Coin. Novel Selections, 194?

RYAN, JIM
The Bludgeon. Hale, 1973
The Vengeance Business. Hale, 1973

RYAN, DETECTIVE PATRICK. Pseudonym of A. Frank Pinkerton, q.v.
A Daring Horse Thief. Laird, 1890

RYAN, PAUL WILLIAM. 1906-1947. Pseudonym: Robert Finnegan, q.v.

RYAN, R(ACHEL) R.
Death of a Sadist. Jenkins, 1937
Devil's Shelter. Jenkins, 1937
Echo of a Curse. Jenkins, 1939
Freak Museum. Jenkins, 1938
No Escape. Jenkins, 1940
The Right to Kill. Jenkins, 1936
The Subjugated Beast. Jenkins, 1938

RYAN, STELLA
Death Never Weeps. Coward, 1946

RYCK, FRANCIS
Account Rendered. Collins, 1975. U.S. title: The Sern Charter. Coward, 1976. (Translation of Le Prix des Choses. Paris, 1973.)
Green Light, Red Catch. Collins, 1972; Stein, 1973. (Translation of Feu Vert pour Poissons Rouge. Paris, 1967.)
Loaded Gun. Collins, 1971; Stein, 1971. (Translation of Drole de Pistolet. Paris, 1969.)
Sacrificial Pawn. Collins, 1973; Stein, 1974. (Translation of L'Incroyant. Paris, 1970.)
The Sern Charter; see Account Rendered
Undesirable Company. Collins, 1974; Stein, 1974. (Translation of Le Compagnon Indesirable. Paris, 1972.)
Woman Hunt. Collins, 1972; Stein, 1972. (Translation of Le Peau de Torpedo. Paris, 1968.)

RYDELL, FORBES. Joint pseudonym of (DeLoris Florine) Stanton Forbes, 1923-   , q.v., and Helen B. Rydell. Other Forbes pseudonym: Tobias Wells, q.v.
Annalisa. Dodd, 1959; Gollancz, 1960
If She Should Die. Doubleday, 1961; Gollancz, 1961
No Questions Asked. Doubleday, 1963; Gollancz, 1963
They're Not Home Yet. Doubleday, 1962; Gollancz, 1962

RYDELL, HELEN B. Joint pseudonym with (DeLoris Florine) Stanton Forbes, 1923-   , q.v.: Forbes Rydell, q.v.

RYDER, JONATHAN. Pseudonym of Robert Ludlum, 1927-   , q.v.
The Cry of the Halidon. Delacorte, 1974; Weidenfeld, 1974
Trevayne. Delacorte, 1973; Weidenfeld, 1974

RYDER, SABIN
Three on the Road. Avalon, 1963

RYERSON, FLORENCE, 1894-   , and COLIN (CAMPBELL) CLEMENTS, 1894-   . Series character: Jimmy Lane = JL.
Blind Man's Buff. Long & Smith, 1933. British title: Sleep No More. Grayson, 1933 JL
The Borgia Blade. Appleton, 1937
Fear of Fear. Appleton, 1931; Skeffington, 1931 JL
Seven Suspects. Appleton, 1930; Skeffington, 1930 JL
Shadows. Appleton, 1934 JL
Sleep No More; see Blind Man's Buff
Stick 'Em Up! Penn, 1929. (1-act play.)
Through the Night. French, 1940. (Play.)

RYLAND, CLIVE. Pseudonym of Clive Ryland Priestley, 1892-   . Series characters: Chief Insp. Bassett, in at least those marked B; Supt. Shannon, in at least those marked S.
The Blind Beggar Murder. Hutchinson, 1935
The Case Against Alder. Hutchinson, 1941
The Case of the Back Seat Girl. Hutchinson, 1952 B
The Case of the Brown-Eyed Housemaid. Hutchinson, 1951
The Dark Lady Murders. Hutchinson, 1940
Death at Screaming Pool. Hutchinson, 1937
Death Serves a Fault. Hutchinson, 1936
In Walks Murder. Hutchinson, 1951 B
The Lone Crook Murders. Hutchinson, 1938
Monday Never Came. Hutchinson, 1947
Murder in Queer Street. Hutchinson, 1941 B
Murder of Margaret. Hutchinson, 1949
Murder on Bag Hill. Hutchinson, 1945 S
Murder on the Cliff. Grayson, 1934
Murder on the Common. Hutchinson, 1939 S
The Murders at the Manor. Grayson, 1933
The Notting Hill Murder. Grayson, 1932
The Selminster Murders. Hutchinson, 1952
So Death Came. Hutchinson, 1938
Three Died for Morson. Hutchinson, 1950
The Twelfth Night Murders. Hutchinson, 1939
Visitors for Venning. Hutchinson, 1948

RYLAND, JOHN KNOX. Series character: Inspector Rodway, in all titles.
Death Meets the Coroner. Paul, 1936
The Easter Guests Mystery. Paul, 1935
The Tragedy Near Tring. Paul, 1934

RYLEY, ELIZABETH
Homicide with Charm. Swan, 1946

S

S., I. Pseudonym of Isidor Schneider, 1896-   .
-Doctor Transit. Boni, 1925

SABATINI, RAFAEL. 1875-1950.
Turbulent Tales. Hutchinson, 1946 ss

SABER, ROBERT O. Pseudonym of Milton K. Ozaki, 1913-   , q.v. Series characters: Carl Good, in at least those marked CG; Max Keene, in at least those marked MK.
The Affair of the Frigid Blonde. Handi-Books, 1950
The Black Dark Murders. Handi-Books, 1949
Chicago Woman; see The Dove
City of Sin. Original Novels, 1952
A Dame Called Murder. Graphic, 1955 MK
The Deadly Lover. Phantom, 1951
The Dove. Handi-Books, 1951. Also published as: Chicago Woman. Pyramid, 1953 CG
Murder Doll. Phantom, 1952 CG
No Way Out. Phantom, 1952; Comyns, 1952
Out of the Night. Harlequin, 1954. (U.S. title?)
The Scented Flesh. Handi-Books, 1951 CG
Sucker Bait. Graphic, 1955 CG
A Time for Murder. Graphic, 1956 MK
Too Young to Die. Graphic, 1954 CG

SABRE, DIRK. Pseudonym of John (Alfred Charles) Laffin, 1922-   , q.v. Other pseudonyms: Cark Dekker, Mark Napier, qq.v.
Murder by Bamboo. Hammond, 1958

SACHS, EMANIE (LOUISE) N(AHM)
The Octangle. Cape & Smith, 1930; Eyre, 1932

SACKVILLE, ORME
The Curse of Amen-Tah. Modern, 193?
The Island of Ghosts. Modern, 1935
The Jungle Goddess. Modern, 193?
McLoon of the South Seas. Modern, 1935
The Valley of Skulls. Modern, 1935

SADDLER, K. ALLEN. Pseudonym of Ronald Charles William Richards, 1923-   . Series character: Dave Stevens, in all titles.
Gilt Edge. Elek, 1966
The Great Brain Robbery. Elek, 1965
Talking Turkey. Joseph, 1968

SADE, MARK. See: ROGER BLAKE.

SADLER, MARK. Pseudonym of Dennis Lynds, 1924-   , q.v. Other pseudonyms: William Arden, Michael Collins, John Crowe, Carl Dekker, Maxwell Grant, qq.v. Series character: Paul Shaw, in all titles.
Circle of Fire. Random, 1973
The Falling Man. Random, 1970
Here to Die. Random, 1971
Mirror Image. Random, 1972

SADLIER, ANNA T(HERESA). 1854-   .
Phileas Fox, Attorney. Ave Maria, 1909

SAFONOV, MADELEINE. See: ALICE M. DODGE.

SAGE, DANA
The Moon was Red. Simon, 1944
The 22 Brothers. Simon, 1950

SAGER, GORDON
The Formula. Lippincott, 1952. British title: The Rape of Europa. Chapman, 1952

ST. AUBYN, ALAN. Pseudonym of Mrs. Frances Bridges Marshall.
-A Fair Imposter. White, 1898
A Fellow of Trinity, with Walt Wheeler. Chatto, 1890; Rand, 1890
-Mrs. Dunbar's Secret. Chatto, 1899
-The Red Van. Digby, 1906
-The Scarlet Lady. White, 1902
The Tremlett Diamonds. Chatto, 1895

ST. CLAIR, DEXTER. Pseudonym of Prentice Winchell, 1895-   . Other pseudonyms: Spencer Dean, Jay de Bekker, Stewart Sterling, Dexter St. Clare, qq.v.
The Lady's Not for Living. GM, 1963; Muller pb, 1964

ST. CLAIR, EILEEN ADAMS
Murder Unplanned. Quality, 1949
Murdered Man's Derby. Gramol, 1935

ST. CLAIR, ELIZABETH
  Secret of the Locket. Signet, 1975

ST. CLAIR, IAN
  Bled White. Stockwell, 1938

ST. CLAIR, JEANANNE
  The House on Vickers' Island. Lenox, 1974; Remploy, 1975

ST. CLAIR, KATHERINE
  Room Beneath the Stairs. Bobbs, 1975

ST. CLAIR, LEONARD
  The Emerald Trap. Putnam, 1974; Constable, 1975
  A Fortune in Death. GM, 1972; Constable, 1976

ST. CLAIR, MIKE
  Daddy's Gone a'Hunting. Bantam, 1969. (Novelization of the movie.)

ST. CLAIR, ROBERT (R.). 1898-   . All titles are plays, in three acts except where otherwise indicated.
  Black Cat. Hardin, 1935
  The Curse of Siva. Banner, 1940
  The Curse of the Crystal Ball. Eldridge, 1938
  The Death Bird. Northwestern, 1938
  "The Fire-Bug." Northwestern, 1938
  The Fury Within. Northwestern, 1951
  The Ghost City. Penn, 1933
  The Ghost House. (Cedar Rapids), 1946
  "The Ghost in the Glass." Northwestern, 1934
  The Ghost in the Wall. Bugbee, 1941
  "Ghost of the Air." Northwestern, 1932
  Ghostly Quarantine. Heuer, 1941
  The Green Light. Northwestern, 1938
  The High School Mystery. Northwestern, 1939
  "The House of Greed." Northwestern, 1938
  The House of Vengeance. Denison, 1949
  Hurricane House. Penn, 1932
  Kigi Sets a Trap. Denison, 1952
  Margie and the Wolf Man. Eldridge, 1950
  Mark Twain's A Double Barrelled Detective Story. Peterson, 1955. (Based on the Mark Twain novel, q.v.)
  The Mountain House Mystery. Heuer, 1942
  Murder with Magic. Wetmore, 1941
  The Mysterious Cane of Dr. Chang. Penn, 1934
  Mystery in Hawaii. Denison, 1954
  Perilous Voyage. Northwestern, 1954. (Two acts.)
  The Phantom Bells. Bugbee, 1935
  The Phantom Bus. Dramatic, 1932
  "The Phantom Dirigible." Northwestern, 1932
  The Phantom Miner. Bugbee, 1940
  "The Phantom Tiger." Northwestern, 1933
  Queen from Mars. Northwestern, 1952
  The Secret Door. Northwestern, 1939
  The Singing Ghost. Northwestern, 1942
  Sinister Station. Bugbee, 1936
  "The Sixth Key." Northwestern, 1932
  The Television Mystery. Denison, 1949
  Tiger House. Northwestern, 1949
  The Tiger's Necklace. Northwestern, 1937
  The Tower Room Mystery. Northwestern, 1932
  The Trailer Mystery. Northwestern, 1954
  The Vampire Bat. Peterson, 1940
  Who Killed Ann Gage? Eldridge, 1943
  The Woman in Red. Penn, 1941
  The Zombie. Northwestern, 1941

ST. CLARE, DEXTER. Pseudonym of Prentice Winchell, 1895-   . Other pseudonyms: Spencer Dean, Jay de Bekker, Stewart Sterling, Dexter St. Clair, qq.v.
  Saratoga Mantrap. GM, 1951

ST. CLOUD, RUPERT. See: J(OHN FREEMAN) FAIRFAX-BLAKEBOROUGH, 1883-   .

ST. DAVID, JOHN. Pseudonym of David John Walsh, 1859-   .
  The Vanishing of Ira Bouck. [Author], 1936

ST. DENNIS, MADELON
  The Death Kiss. Fiction League, 1932
  The Perfumed Lure. Clode, 1932

ST. GEORGE, GEOFFREY
  The Proteus Pact. Little, 1975; Gollancz, 1976

ST. GEORGE, JOSEPH
  The Dangerous Impersonation. Hamilton, 1938

ST. JOHN, DARBY
  The Westgate Mystery. Random, 1941. Also published as: The Bride Brings Death. Mystery Novel Classic, 1943

ST. JOHN, DAVID. Pseudonym of (Everette) Howard Hunt, 1918-   , q.v. Other pseudonyms: Gordon Davis, Robert Dietrich, John Q, qq.v. Series character: Peter Ward, in all titles.
  The Coven. Weybright, 1971
  Diabolus. Weybright, 1971
  Festival for Spies. Signet, 1966. Reprinted as by E. Howard Hunt: Signet, 1973
  Hazardous Duty; see On Hazardous Duty
  The Mongol Mask. Weybright, 1968; Hale, 1969
  On Hazardous Duty. Signet, 1965. British title: Hazardous Duty. Muller, 1966. Reprinted as by E. Howard Hunt: Signet, 1972
  One of Our Agents is Missing. Signet, 1967. Reprinted as by E. Howard Hunt: Signet, 1973
  Return from Vorkuta. Signet, 1965; Muller, 1967. Reprinted as by E. Howard Hunt: Signet, 1974
  The Sorcerers. Weybright, 1969
  The Towers of Silence. Signet, 1966. Reprinted as by E. Howard Hunt: Signet, 1974
  The Venus Probe. Signet, 1966. Reprinted as by E. Howard Hunt: Signet, 1974

ST. JOHN, GENEVIEVE
  The Dark Watch. Belmont, 1966
  Daughter of Evil. Belmont, 1967
  Death in the Desert. Belmont, 1966
  Ghost of Channing House. Lancer, 1969
  Night of Evil. Belmont, 1967
  The Secret of Dresden Farm. Belmont, 1971
  The Secret of Kensington Manor. Belmont, 1965
  The Shadow on Spanish Swamp. Belmont, 1966
  Sinister Voice. Belmont, 1967
  Strangers in the Night. Paperback Library, 1967

ST. JOHN, NICOLE. Pseudonym of Norma Johnston.
  The Medici Ring. Random, 1975; Collins, 1976

ST. JOHN, PERCY B(OLINGBROKE). 1821-1899.
  The Blue Dwarf. Hogarth, ca.1870

SAINT-LAURENT, CECIL. Pseudonym of Jacques Laurent-Cely, 1919-   .
  The Cautious Maiden. Crown, 1955. (Translation of Une Sacree Salade. Paris, 1954.)

ST. LEGER, WARHAM. See: HENRY POTTINGER STEPHENS.

ST. MARS, F. 1883-   .
  Off the Beaten Track. Chambers, 1920
  ss, some criminous

ST. MICHAELS, DONELLA
  The Prisoner. Lancer, 1966

ST. MOORE, A.
  Angel Face Tatters the Kimono. International, 1969

ST. THOMAS, HAROLD
  Night of the Long Shadows. Harrap, 1967

SAKS, ELMER ELIOT. Pseudonym of F(rank) Dubrez Fawcett, 1891-1968, q.v. Other pseudonyms: Spike Gordon (?), Griff, Ben Sarto, qq.v.
  The Case of the Indiana Torturer. Bear, 1945
  -Innocents on Broadway. Bear, 1944

SALAS, FLOYD
  What Now My Love. Grove, 1969

SALAWAY, RALPH. Pseudonym: Al Fray, q.v.

SALCROFT, ARTHUR
  John Traile: Smuggler. Hutchinson, 1929
  The Mystery of the Walled Garden. Hutchinson, 1928
  The Twisted Grin. Hutchinson, 1929

SALE, RICHARD (BERNARD). 1911-   .
  Benefit Performance. Simon, 1946
  Cardinal Rock. Cassell, 1940
  Death at Sea. Popular Library, 1948. British title: Destination Unknown. World's Work, 1943
  Death Looks In; see Lazarus #7
  Destination Unknown; see Death at Sea
  For the President's Eyes Only. Simon, 1971. British title: The Man Who Raised Hell. Cassell, 1971
  Home is the Hangman. Popular Library, 1949. (Two novelets, one published separately in England as: Sailor, Take Warning. Big Ben, 1942.)
  Lazarus Murder Seven; see Lazarus #7
  Lazarus #7. Simon, 1942. British title: Death Looks In. Cassell, 1943. Also published as: Lazarus Murder Seven. Handi-Books, 1943
  The Man Who Raised Hell; see For the President's Eyes Only
  Murder at Midnight. Popular Library, 1950. (Two novelets.)
  Not Too Narrow—Not Too Deep. Simon, 1936; Cassell, 1936
  Passing Strange. Simon, 1942
  Sailor, Take Warning; see Home is the Hangman

SALINGER, PIERRE (EMILE GEORGE). 1925-   .
  On the Instructions of My Government. Doubleday, 1971. British title: For the Eyes of the President Only. Collins, 1971

SALISBURY, CAROLA. Pseudonym of Michael Butterworth, 1924-   , q.v.
  Dark Inheritance. Collins, 1976; Doubleday, 1975
  Mallion's Pride. Collins, 1975. U.S. title: The Pride of the Trevallions. Doubleday, 1975
  The Pride of the Trevallions; see Mallion's Pride

SALKELD, MICHAEL
    Missing from the Shelf. Bles, 1936

SALMON, GERALDINE GORDON. 1897- .
    Pseudonym: J. G. Sarasin, q.v.

SALT, SARAH. Pseudonym of Coralie von
    Werner Hobson, 1891- .
    Murder for Love. Davies, 1937. (Two
        stories.)

SALTER, ELIZABETH (FULTON). 1918- .
    Series character: Insp. Michael
    Hornsley, in at least those marked
    MH.
    Death in a Mist. Bles, 1957; Ace, 1968
        MH
    Once Upon a Tombstone. Hutchinson,
        1965; Ace, 1967 MH
    There was a Witness. Bles, 1960; Ace,
        1963 MH
    The Voice of the Peacock. Bles, 1962 MH
    Will to Survive. Bles, 1958; Ace, 1968

SALTER, MARION (ARMOUR)
    The Cat's-Paw. Rinehart, 1952

SALTMARSH, MAX
    The Clouded Moon. Joseph, 1937; Knopf,
        1938
    Highly Inflammable. Joseph, 1936;
        Little, 1936
    Highly Unsafe. Joseph, 1936
    Indigo Death. Joseph, 1938

SALTUS, EDGAR (EVERTSON). 1855-1921.
    -The Monster. Pulitzer, 1912
    The Pace That Kills. Belford, 1889
    The Paliser Case. Boni, 1919
    A Transient Guest, and Other Episodes.
        Belford, 1889 ss, some criminous

SALVATO, SHARON ANNE
    Briarcliff Manor. Stein, 1974
    The Meredith Legacy. Stein, 1975
    Scarborough House. Stein, 1975; Col-
        lins, 1976

SALWEY, REGINALD E(RNEST)
    -The Hand on the Web. Heath, 1925
    -A Peerage in Peril. Rivers, 1928
    -The Secret of Providence Lodge. Wes-
        tern Gazette, 1923 ss
    Wildwater Terrace. Digby, 1890

SAMACHSON, JOSEPH. 1906- . Pseudonym:
    John Miller, q.v.

SAMARAKIS, ANTONIS
    The Flaw. Weybright, 1969; Heinemann,
        1969

SAMPSON, GEORGE (RICHARD). 1916- .
    A Drug on the Market. Hale, 1967
    Playing with Fire. Hale, 1968

SAMPSON, RICHARD HENRY. 1896- . Pseu-
    donym: Richard Hull, q.v.

SAMPSON, VICTOR. 1855-1940. Series char-
    acters: Insp. Downes and Sgt. Hop-
    kins, in both titles.
    The Komani Mystery. Jenkins, 1930
    The Murder of Paul Rougier. Jenkins,
        1928

SAMUEL, JOSEPH
    The Murdered Cliche. Quality, 1947

SAN ANTONIO. Pseudonym of F(rederic)
    Dard, q.v. Series character: San An-
    tonio, in all titles.
    Alien Archipelago. Joseph, 1971.
        (Translation of L'Archipel des Malo-
        trus. Paris, 1969.)
    Crooks' Hill. Sphere, 1969; Paperback
        Library, 1969. (Translation of Le
        Gala des Emplumes. Paris, 1963.)
        Title on inside of British edition
        reads: Puck of Crooks' Hill.)
    From A to Z. Duckworth, 1968; Paperback
        Library, 1970. (Translation of De l'A
        jusqu'a Z. Paris, 1961.)
    The Hatchet Man. Paperback Library,
        1970
    Knights of Arabia. Duckworth, 1969;
        Paperback Library, 1970. (Translation
        of Berurier au Serail. Paris, 1964.)
    Puck of Crooks' Hill; see Crook's Hill
    Stone Dead. Sphere, 1969; Paperback Li-
        brary, 1970. (Translation of C'Est
        Mort et ca ne Sait Pas. Paris, 1954.)
    The Strangler. Duckworth, 1968; Paper-
        back Library, 1970. (Translation of
        La Fin des Haricots. Paris, 1961.)
    The Sub Killers. Joseph, 1971. (Trans-
        lation of La Rate au Court Bouillon.
        Paris, 1958.)
    Thugs and Bottles. Sphere, 1969; Paper-
        back Library, 1970. (Translation of
        Du Brut Pour les Brutes. Paris,
        1960.)
    Tough Justice. Duckworth, 1967; Norton,
        1969. (Translation of Messieurs les
        Hommes. Paris, 1955.)

SANBORN, B. X. Pseudonym of Bill S(an-
    born) Ballinger, 1912-   , q.v.
    Other pseudonym: Frederic Freyer,
    q.v.
    The Doom-Maker. Dutton, 1959; Boardman,
        1959. Also published as: The Blonde
        on Borrowed Time. Zenith, 1960

SANBORN, RUTH BURR. 1894- . Series
    character: Angeline Tredennick, in
    both titles.
    Murder by Jury. Little, 1932; Jarrolds,
        1933
    Murder on the Aphrodite. Macmillan,
        1935; Jarrolds, 1936

SANDBERG, H. W.
    The Crazy Quilt Murders. Phoenix, 1938

SANDBERG, PETER LARS. 1934- .
    Wolf Mountain. Playboy, 1975

SANDERS, BRUCE. Series character: Howard
    Digburn, in at least those marked HD.
    Blonde Blackmail. Jenkins, 1945
    Code of Dishonour. Jenkins, 1964
    Deadly Jade. Jenkins, 1947
    Feminine for Spy. Jenkins, 1967
    Kiss for a Killer. Jenkins, 1953; Roy,
        1956
    Madame Bluebeard. Jenkins, 1951; Roy,
        1957
    Midnight Hazard. Jenkins, 1955
    Pink Silk Alibi. Jenkins, 1946
    The Scarlet Widow. Jenkins, 1943
    Secret Dragnet. Jenkins, 1956; Roy,
        1957 HD
    Tawny Menace. Jenkins, 1948
    To Catch a Spy. Jenkins, 1958; Roy,
        1958 HD

SANDERS, CHARLES WESLEY
    The Memory Man. Lloyd's, 1921
    Murder in the North-West. Collins, 1931
    Murder Trail. Collins, 1929
    Poison Lockspur. Collins, 1930

SANDERS, DAPHNE. Pseudonym of Craig Rice,
    1908-1957, q.v. Other pseudonym:
    Michael Venning, q.v. See also: GYPSY
    ROSE LEE; GEORGE SANDERS, 1906-1972.
    To Catch a Thief. Dial, 1943

SANDERS, GEORGE. 1906-1972.
    Crime on My Hands. Simon, 1944; Ed-
        wards, 1948. (Ghost-written by Craig
        Rice, 1908-1957, q.v., and Cleve
        Cartmill, 1908-1964, q.v.)
    Stranger at Home. Simon, 1946; Pilot,
        1947. (Ghost-written by Leigh Brack-
        ett, 1915-1978, q.v.)

SANDERS, JOHN (EDWARD). 1930- . Series
    character: Nicholas Pym, in at least
    those marked NP.
    -Cromwell's Cavalier. Hale, 1968
    A Firework for Oliver. Heinemann, 1964;
        Walker, 1965 NP
    The Hat of Authority. Heinemann, 1965
        NP
    -Without Trumpet or Drum. Heinemann,
        1966

SANDERS, LAWRENCE. 1920- .
    The Anderson Tapes. Putnam, 1970;
        Allen, 1970
    The First Deadly Sin. Putnam, 1973;
        Allen, 1974

SANDERS, MARIAN K.,   -1977, and MOR-
    TIMER S. EDELSTEIN
    The Bride Laughed Once. Farrar, 1943

SANDERS, W. FRANKLIN
    The Whip Hand. GM, 1961

SANDERSON, AVERIL D.
    Long Shadows. Constable, 1935

SANDERSON, (RONALD) DOUGLAS. 1922- .
    Pseudonyms: Martin Brett, Malcolm
    Douglas, qq.v.
    Black Reprieve. Hale, 1965
    Catch a Fallen Starlet. Avon, 1960.
        (British title?)
    Cry Wolfram. Secker, 1959. U.S. title:
        Mark It for Murder. Avon, 1959
    Dark Passions Subdue. Avon, 1953. (Bri-
        tish title?)
    A Dead Bullfighter. Hale, 1975
    The Final Run. Secker, 1956
    Lam to Slaughter. Hale, 1964
    Mark it for Murder; see Cry Wolfram
    Night of the Horns. Secker, 1958
    No Charge for Framing. Hale, 1969

SANDFORD, KEN(NETH LESLIE). 1915- .
    Series character: Max Hale, in both
    titles.
    Dead Reckoning. Hutchinson, 1955
    Dead Secret. Long, 1957

SANDS, CHRISTOPHER NICHOLSON JOHNSTON.
    1857-1934. Pseudonym: Christopher
    N(icholson) Johnston, q.v.

SANDS, LESLIE
    Intent to Murder. English Theatre
        Guild, 1953. (Play.)
    Something to Hide. English Theatre
        Guild, 1953. (3-act play.) Novel
        based on this play: Muller, 1965

SANDS, MARTIN. Pseudonym of John (Fred-
    erick) Burke, 1922-   , q.v. Other
    pseudonyms: Jonathan Burke, Harriet
    Esmond, qq.v. Joint pseudonym with
    George Theiner, 1927-   : Jonathan
    George, q.v.
    The Jokers. Pan, 1967. (Novelization
        of the movie.)
    Maroc 7. Pan, 1967. (Novelization of
        the movie.)

SANDULESCU, JACQUES and ANNIE GOTTLIEB
    The Carpathian Caper. Putnam, 1975

SANDYS, JAMES. Series character: Mr.
    Springfield, in at least those marked
    S.
    And So We Die. Paul, 1941

Darkest Under the Lamp. Paul, 1949 S
The Death Echo. Paul, 1948
Death Finds the Gloves. Paul, 1939
Death is Merciful. Paul, 1948
From Laughter to Death. Paul, 1945
Green Eye of Death. Paul, 1943
The Hand Without Mercy. Paul, 1940
Harlequin of Doom. Paul, 1939
The Lodestar of Death. Paul, 1946
The Lone Commando. Paul, 1944
The Man Who Wasn't There. Paul, 1953 S
The Silken Shroud. Paul, 1947
A Stripe for a Stripe. Paul, 1938
Thicker Than Water. Paul, 1941 S
This is Death Calling. Paul, 1943
The Vengeance Due. Paul, 1938
Voices of the Storm. Paul, 1940

SANDYS, MILES
Michael Carmichael. Laird, 1902

SANFORD, URSULA
The Poisoned Anemones. PB, 1974

SANGER, JOAN
The Case of the Missing Corpse. Green Circle, 1936

SANGSTER, JIMMY. 1927-   . Series characters: Katy Touchfeather = KT; John Smith = JS.
Foreign Exchange. Triton, 1968; Norton, 1968 JS
The Man Who Could Cheat Death, with Barre Lyndon. Avon, 1959
Private I. Triton, 1967; Norton, 1967 JS
The Terror of the Tongs. Digit, 1962. (Novelization of the movie.)
Touchfeather. Triton, 1968; Norton, 1968 KT
Touchfeather, Too. Triton, 1970; Norton, 1970 KT
Your Friendly Neighborhood Death Pedlar. Triton, 1971; Dodd, 1972

SANTIAGO, V. J. Pseudonym. Series character: Joseph Madden (The Vigilante), in both titles.
Detour to a Funeral. Pinnacle, 1975
An Eye for an Eye. Pinnacle, 1975

SAPIR, RICHARD. 1936-   . See also: next entry.
Bressio. Random, 1975

SAPIR, RICHARD, 1936-   , and WARREN (B.) MURPHY, 1933-   , q.v. See also: previous entry. Series character: Remo Williams (The Destroyer), in all titles.
Acid Rock. Pinnacle, 1973; Corgi, 1975
Assassin's Playoff. Pinnacle, 1975; Corgi, 1978
Chinese Puzzle. Pinnacle, 1972; Corgi, 1973
Created: The Destroyer. Pinnacle, 1971; Corgi, 1973
Deadly Seeds. Pinnacle, 1975; Corgi, 1978
Death Check. Pinnacle, 1972; Corgi, 1973
Death Therapy. Pinnacle, 1972; Corgi, 1974
Dr. Quake. Pinnacle, 1972; Corgi, 1974
Funny Money. Pinnacle, 1975; Corgi, 1977
Holy Terror. Pinnacle, 1975; Corgi, 1978
Judgment Day. Pinnacle, 1974; Corgi, 1976
Kill or Cure. Pinnacle, 1973; COrgi, 1975
Last War Dance. Pinnacle, 1974; Corgi, 1977
Mafia Fix. Pinnacle, 1972; Corgi, 1974
Murder Ward. Pinnacle, 1974; Corgi, 1976
Murder's Shield. Pinnacle, 1973; Corgi, 1975
Oil Slick. Pinnacle, 1974; Corgi, 1977
Slave Safari. Pinnacle, 1973; Corgi, 1976
Summit Chase. Pinnacle, 1973; Corgi, 1975
Terror Squad. Pinnacle, 1973; Corgi, 1975
Union Bust. Pinnacle, 1973; Corgi, 1974

SAPPER. Pseudonym of H(erman) C(yril) McNeile, 1888-1937, q.v. This author's works have variously appeared under his own name and/or under his pseudonym, and are all collectively listed under his real name herein.

SARASIN, J. G. Pseudonym of Geraldine Gordon Salmon, 1897-   .
-Across the Border. Hutchinson, 1933
-The Ambush. Hutchinson, 1940
The Black Glove. Hutchinson, 1925; Doran, 1926
-The Cargo of Gold. Hutchinson, 1933
-The Caspian Song. Hutchinson, 1935
-Chronicles of a Cavalier. Hutchinson, 1924
-City of Refuge. Hutchinson, 1928
-The Corsair. Hutchinson, 1951
-The Court of Dusty Feet. Hutchinson, 1942
-The Dark Turnpike. Hutchinson, 1943
-The Drums of War. Hutchinson, 1956
-The Eighth Wonder. Hutchinson, 1952
Fleur de Lys. Hutchinson, 1929; Doubleday, 1929
Flittermouse. Hutchinson, 1931
-The Flying Palatine, and other stories. Hutchinson, 1935 ss
-The House of the Winds. Hutchinson, 1941
-Invasion Coast. Hutchinson, 1948
-The Iron Mask. Hutchinson, 1928
-The Island of Unrest. Hutchinson, 1955
-Lady and Leader. Hutchinson, 1931
-The Lost Duchess. Hutchinson, 1927
-The Lost Kingdom. Hutchinson, 1954
-The Lovers of Astrea. Hutchinson, 1930
-The Magpie on the Gallows. Hutchinson, 1953
-The Man from Troy. Hutchinson, 1937
The Mystery of Martin Guerre. Hutchinson, 1934
-No Land Without Liberty. Hutchinson, 1962
-A Phoenix in Castile. Hutchinson, 1950
-The Pirate's Pack. Hutchinson, 1934
-Quest of Youth. Hutchinson, 1923
-Remember! Hutchinson, 1946
-Six Ropes for Glory. Hutchinson, 1937
-Southern Fires. Hutchinson, 1929
-Star Above Paris. Hutchinson, 1938
-The State Torch. Hutchinson, 1944
-Storm-Bound. Hutchinson, 1930
-Thunderbolt. Hutchinson, 1958
-Tiger-Heart. Hutchinson, 1936
-Wings Without Freedom. Hutchinson, 1951

SARDOU, VICTORIEN. 1831-1908.
The Black Pearl. Brentano's, 1888

SARGEANT, ADELINE. Variant spelling sometimes encountered on the U.S. editions of works by (Emily Frances) Adeline Sergeant, 1851-1904, q.v.

SARIOLA, MAURI. Series character: Osmo Kilpi, in both titles.
The Helsinki Affair. Cassell, 1970; Walker, 1971. (Translation of Lavaen tien Laki. Finland, 1970.)
The Torvick Affair. Walker, 1972

SARL, ARTHUR J.
The Mystery of Flat 60. Aldine, 1921
Racing Ramp. Hutchinson, 1939

SARMIENTO, DOROTHY
Roles and Relations. Chapman, 1956

SARNE, MICHAEL. Pseudonym of T(homas) Arthur Plummer, q.v.
-The Scarlet Saint. Paul, 1932

SAROYAN, WILLIAM. 1908-   . See: HENRY CECIL.

SARSFIELD, MAUREEN. Series character: Insp. Lane Parry, in at least those marked LP.
Dinner for None. Nicholson, 1948. U.S. title: A Party for Lawty. Coward, 1948 LP
-Gloriana. Nicholson, 1946
Green December Fills the Graveyard. Pilot, 1945; Coward, 1946 LP
A Party for Lawty; see Dinner for None

SARTO, BEN. Pseudonym. Many of these were written by F(rank) Dubrez Fawcett, 1891-1968, q.v. Other Fawcett pseudonyms: Spike Gordon (?), Griff, Elmer Eliot Saks, qq.v. Series character: Miss Otis, in at least those marked O.
Baby Moll. Modern Fiction, 1957
Beech of the Boulevard. Modern Fiction, 1952
Blonde Horror. Modern Fiction, 1956
Blood and Blondes. Modern Fiction, 1954
Bodies Fetch Good Prices. Beacon, 1954
Bowery Birdie. Modern Fiction, 1947
Call Me Shameless. Beacon, 1954
Chain-Gang Queenie. Beacon, 1955
Chicago Dames. Modern Fiction, 1949
City of Sin. Modern Fiction, 1952
Claws for a Cutie. Modern Fiction, 1955
Corpse in the Cabin. Modern Fiction, 1954
Corrupted Women. Modern Fiction, 1952
Crooked Lady. Modern Fiction, 1956
Dames for Hire. Beacon, 1953
Dangerous Blonde. Modern Fiction, 1957
The Dead Don't Cry. Modern Fiction, 1956
Dead Reckoning. Modern Fiction, 1955
Death by the Seine. Modern Fiction, 1956
Death for a Dumb-Bell. Modern Fiction, 1957
Death Rides the Train. Modern Fiction, 1954
Decoy Babes. Beacon, 1956
Diamonds for a Blonde. Modern Fiction, 1958
Disillusioned. Modern Fiction, 1955
Down-River Dolls. Modern Fiction, 1957
Dread. Modern Fiction, 1955
Duchess of Dope. Modern Fiction, 1948
Dynamite. Modern Fiction, 1956
Dynamite Doll. Beacon, 1954
Eastside Exposure. Modern Fiction, 1955
Elsa the Terrible. Modern Fiction, 1954
Espionage. Modern Fiction, 1957
Fear. Modern Fiction, 1955
Floozie Takes Lawman. Modern Fiction, 1952
Gangster Lady. Modern Fiction, 1953
Gorilla Moll. Modern Fiction, 1953
Grand Graft Hotel. Modern Fiction, 1947
Hi-Jacker's Lady. Modern Fiction, 1949
Hire Me a Rope. Modern Fiction, 1958
Hot Dames Die Cold. Modern Fiction, 1958
House of Sin. Modern Fiction, 1956
I Kill 'Em Inch by Inch. Modern Fiction, 1949
I'll Get By. Modern Fiction, 1948
"Jews" Pellegrini. Modern Fiction, 1947 O

Killer in Love. Modern Fiction, 1948
Kiss Me, Kill Me. Modern Fiction, 1953
Lady Bites. Milestone, 1953
Lidy Takes Plenty. Modern Fiction, 1952
Manhattan Terrors. Modern Fiction, 1952
Miami for Murder. Modern Fiction, 1954
Micky's Hide. Modern Fiction, 1956
Million Dollar Murder. Modern Fiction, 1957
Miss Otis Blows Town. Milestone, 1953 O
Miss Otis Comes to Piccadilly. Modern Fiction, 1949 O
Miss Otis Desires. Milestone, 1954 O
Miss Otis Gets Fresh. Milestone, 1954 O
Miss Otis Goes French. Milestone, 1953 O
Miss Otis Goes Up. Modern Fiction, 1949 O
Miss Otis has a Daughter. Modern Fiction, 1948 O
Miss Otis Hits Back. Milestone, 1953 O
Miss Otis Makes a Date. Milestone, 1953 O
Miss Otis Makes Hay. Milestone, 1954 O
Miss Otis Moves In. Milestone, 1953 O
Miss Otis Plays Ball. Milestone, 1954 O
Miss Otis Plays Eve. Milestone, 1953 O
Miss Otis Relents. Milestone, 1954 O
Miss Otis Says Yes. Milestone, 1953 O
Miss Otis Takes the Rap. Modern Fiction, 1953 O
Miss Otis Throws a Come-Back. Modern Fiction, 1947 O
The Oldest Profession. Modern Fiction, 1952
The Pace Grows Hotter. Modern Fiction, 1956
Pinday and the "White Slaver". Modern Fiction, 1947
Pleasure Girl. Modern Fiction, 1957
Queen of Crook's Harem. Modern Fiction, 1949
Rebecca of the Snatch Racket. Modern Fiction, 194?
Riviera Nights. Modern Fiction, 1958
Rope for a Lady. Modern Fiction, 1954
Satan is Blonde. Modern Fiction, 1957
She Ruled with a Rod. Modern Fiction, 1947
Sidewalk Floozie. Modern Fiction, 194?
Sinister Wooing. Modern Fiction, 1954
Snake Hips. Modern Fiction, 1954
Soho Spiv. Modern Fiction, 1948
Stay Out of Menchis. Modern Fiction, 1958
Susie Comes to Soho. Beacon, 1953
Swamp Fever. Modern Fiction, 1957
Take Over, Angel. Modern Fiction, 1955
Take What's Coming. Modern Fiction, 1952
There's Always a Dame. Modern Fiction, 1949
They Burn for Me. Modern Fiction, 1954
Tigress of Brazil. Modern Fiction, 1952
Tombstones are Free to Quitters. Modern Fiction, 1947
Vice City. Modern Fiction, 1957
Vice Volcano. Modern Fiction, 1956
The Vicious Breed. Modern Fiction, 1957
Viper's Brood. Modern Fiction, 1954
Where You Throw Blood. Modern Fiction, 1957
The Wolf Shows his Teeth. Modern Fiction, 1952
You Die in Valpaso. Modern Fiction, 1957

SATCHELL, WILLIAM
The Greenstone Door. Sidgwick, 1914

SAUL, OSCAR
The Dark Side of Love. Harper, 1974; Cassell, 1975

SAUNDERS, ALLAN
The Big Cough. French, 1939. (1-act play.)
Three Taps at Twelve. French, 1933. (3-act play.)

SAUNDERS, CLARE CASTLER. See also: BABS LEE.
Design for Treachery. Scribner, 1947

SAUNDERS, DAVID. Pseudonym of Daniel Sontup, 1922- .
M-Squad. Belmont, 1962. (Novelization of the TV series.)

SAUNDERS, HILARY (AIDEN) ST. GEORGE. 1898-1951. Joint pseudonym with John (Leslie) Palmer, 1885-1944, q.v.: Francis Beeding, q.v. Joint pseudonym with Geoffrey Dennis: Barum Browne, q.v.
The Sleeping Bacchus. Joseph, 1951

SAUNDERS, LAWRENCE. Joint pseudonym of Burton Davis, 1893- , and Clare Ogden Davis, 1892- . Series characters: Wylie King and Nels Lundberg, in at least those marked K&L.
The Columnist Murder. Farrar, 1931 K&L
The Devil's Den. Covici, 1933 K&L
-Six Weeks. Covici, 1932
Smoke Screen. Sears, 1930

SAUNDERS, MONTAGU
-The Mystery in the Drood Family. Cambridge University Press, 1914

SAUNDERS, THEODORE. Joint pseudonym with Mary Means: Denis Scott, q.v.

SAVAGE, DAVID. Pseudonym (?) of Harry Hossent, 1916- , q.v.
The Spy Who Got Off at Las Vegas. Jenkins, 1969

SAVAGE, JOHN
A Shady Place to Die. Dell, 1957

SAVAGE, RICHARD. Pseudonym of Ivan Roe, 1913- . Series character: Dr. Ferenc, in at least those marked F.
The Horrible Hat. Jarrolds, 1948 F
The Innocents. Museum, 1958; Washburn, 1959
The Lightning's Eye. Museum, 1957
Murder for Fun. Jarrolds, 1947 F
Murder Goes to School. Jarrolds, 1946
The Poison and the Root. Jarrolds, 1950
Stranger's Meeting. Museum, 1957
When the Moon Died. Ward, 1955

SAVAGE, RICHARD HENRY. 1846-1903.
-After Many Years. Neely, 1895
-The Anarchist. Neely, 1894; Routledge, 1894. Also published as: Storm Signals. Rand, 1897
Brought to Bay. Home, 1900; White, 1900
Captain Landon. Rand, 1899; White, 1899
-A Captive Princess. Home, 1898; Routledge, 1898
Checked Through, Missing Trunk No. 17580. Rand, 1896; Routledge, 1896
Commander Leigh; see Special Orders for Commander Leigh
A Daughter of Judas. Neely, 1894; Routledge, 1895
-Delilah of Harlem. American News, 1893; Routledge, 1894
-An Egyptian Tragedy, and other stories. Digby, 1902. (U.S. title?) ss
-An Exile from London. Home, 1896; Routledge, 1897
-A Fascinating Traitor. Home, 1897; Routledge, 1897
-For a Young Queen's Bright Eyes. Home, 1902; White, 1902
-For Her Life. Rand, 1897; Routledge, 1897
-For Life and Love. Neely, 1893; Routledge, 1894
-The Golden Rapids of High Life. Home, 1902; French, 1903
-The Hacienda on the Hill. Home, 1899; Routledge, 1899
-Her Foreign Conquest. Home, 1896; Routledge, 1897
-His Cuban Sweetheart. Home, 1895; Routledge, 1896, with Mrs. Archibald Clavering Gunter
-In the Emperor's Villa. Ward, 1906. (U.S. title?)
-In the Esbekieyeh Gardens, and other stories. Routledge, 1901 ss (U.S. title?)
-In the Old Chateau. Neely, 1895; Routledge, 1895
-In the Shadow of the Pyramids. Rand, 1898; Routledge, 1898
-In the Swim. Rand, 1898; Routledge, 1898
The King's Secret. Home, 1900; White, 1901
The Last Traitor of Long Island. Home, 1903; French, 1903
The Little Lady of Lagunitas. American News, 1892; Routledge, 1892
Lost Countess Falka. Rand, 1896; Routledge, 1897
The Masked Venus. American News, 1893; Routledge, 1893
-The Midnight Passenger. Home, 1900; White, 1901
-Miss Devereux of the Mariquita. Routledge, 1895. (U.S. title?)
A Modern Corsair. Rand, 1897; Routledge, 1897
-A Monte Cristo in Khaki. Home, 1903; French, 1903
My Official Wife. Home, 1891; Routledge, 1891
The Mystery of a Shipyard. Home, 1901; White, 1902
Our Mysterious Passenger, and other stories. Street, 1899; Henderson, 1899 ss
-The Passing Show. Neely, 1893; Routledge, 1907. Also published as: The Spider of Truxillo. Neely, 1895
-Prince Schamyl's Wooing. Routledge, 1892. (U.S. title?)
-The Princess of Alaska. Neely, 1894; Routledge, 1894
-The Shield of his Honor. Home, 1900; White, 1900
-Special Orders for Commander Leigh. Home, 1902. British title: Commander Leigh. White, 1903
The Spider of Truxillo; see The Passing Show
Storm Signals; see The Anarchist
-Tales of Adventure. Home, 1900 ss
-The White Lady of Khaminavatka. Rand, 1898; Routledge, 1899

SAVAGE, WALLACE
A Bait of Perjury. Dorke House, 1970

SAVI, GERALD B(ARTON)
-Alive or Dead. Hodder, 1938
The Last Lap. Wright, 1935
-The Misfit. Wright, 1936
-The Mosquito Net. Wright, 1933
Raw Material. Wright, 1934

SAVILE, FRANK (MACKENZIE)
The Pursuit. Arnold, 1910; Little, 1910

SAWKINS, RAYMOND H. 1923- . Pseudonyms: Jay Bernard, Colin Forbes, Richard Raine, qq.v. Series character: Supt. John Snow, in all titles.
Snow Along the Border. Heinemann, 1968; Harcourt, 1968

Snow in Paradise. Heinemann, 1967; Harcourt, 1967
Snow on High Ground. Heinemann, 1966; Harcourt, 1967

SAWYER, EUGENE T. 1846-1924.
The Coleraine Tragedy. Street (Magnet), 1901
The Los Huecos Mystery. Street, 1900
The Maltese Cross; or, The Detective's Quest. Street, 1888
Old Quartz, the Nevada Detective. Street (Magnet), 1900; Henderson, 1890
The Prince of Fraud. Rose (Toronto), 1891
A Strike of Millions. Street (Magnet), 1907
The Tiger's Head Mystery. Street (Magnet), 1901

SAWYER, JOHN. Joint pseudonym with Nancy Sawyer: Nancy Buckingham, q.v.

SAWYER, NANCY. Joint pseudonym with John Sawyer: Nancy Buckingham, q.v.

SAXBY, CHARLES
Death Cuts the Film. Dutton, 1939
Death in the Sun. Dutton, 1940; Hale, 1941
Death Joins the Woman's Club. Dutton, 1940
Death over Hollywood, with Louis Molnar. Dutton, 1937
Death Wore Roses. Dutton, 1942
Even Bishops Die. Dutton, 1942
Murder at the Mike. Dutton, 1938
Out of It All. Dutton, 1941

SAXE, R. B. Series character: John Dobbs (The Ghost), in at least those marked JD.
The Ghost Does a Richard III. Long, 1943 JD
The Ghost Knows his Greengages. Constable, 1940 JD
The Ghost Pulls the Jackpot. Long, 1945 JD
What Can You Lose? Long, 1947

SAXON, ALEX. Pseudonym of Bill Pronzini, 1943-   , q.v. Other pseudonym: Jack Foxx, q.v.
A Run in Diamonds. PB, 1973

SAXON, JOHN A. 1886?-1947. Series character: Sam Welpton, in both titles.
Half-Past Mortem. Mill, 1947; Foulsham, 1951. (Ghost-written by Robert Leslie Bellem, q.v.)
Liability Limited. Mill, 1947. British title: This was No Accident. Foulsham, 1949
This was No Accident; see Liability Limited

SAXON, PETER. Pseudonym used by W(illiam Arthur) Howard Baker, 1925-   , q.v., and probably others. Other Baker pseudonyms: W. A. Ballinger, William Arthur, Richard Williams, qq.v. Series character (with many other authors): Sexton Blake, in at least those marked SB.
Act of Violence. Amalgamated, 1957 SB
Black Honey. Mayflower, 1968 SB
Corruption. Sphere, 1968
A Cry in the Night. Amalgamated, 1957 SB
The Curse of Rathlaw. Baker, 1969
Danger Ahead. Amalgamated, 1956 SB
Dark Ways to Death. Baker, 1968
The Darkest Night. Mayflower, 1966 SB
Decoy for Murder. Amalgamated, 1956 SB
The Disoriented Man. Mayflower, 1966 SB
-The Enemy Sky. Corgi, 1969
Flight into Fear. Amalgamated, 1956 SB
Front Page Woman. Amalgamated, 1956 SB
The Haunting of Alan Mais. Mayflower, 1970
The Killing Bone. Baker, 1970
The Last Days of Berlin. Amalgamated, 1957 SB
Lovely—But Lethal! Amalgamated, 1961 SB
The Naked Blade. Amalgamated, 1958 SB
Satan's Child. Mayflower, 1967 SB
The Sea Tigers. Amalgamated, 1958 SB
This Spy Must Die. Mayflower, 1967 SB
Through the Dark Curtain. Baker, 1968
-The Torturer. Mayflower, 1967
-The Unfeeling Sky. Corgi, 1968
The Vampires of Finistere. Baker, 1970
Vengeance is Ours! Mayflower, 1965 SB
The Violent Hours. Amalgamated, 1957 SB
The Violent Ones. Amalgamated, 1959 SB
The Voodoo Drum. Amalgamated, 1948 SB
-The Warring Sky. Corgi, 1970
White Mercenary. Amalgamated, 1962 SB
Woman of Saigon. Amalgamated, 1956 SB

SAXON, VAN. Joint pseudonym of Marilyn Granbeck and Arthur Moore, q.v. Other joint pseudonym: Adam Hamilton, q.v. Pseudonyms of Marilyn Granbeck: Ben Grant, Clayton Moore, qq.v. For Arthur Moore, see also: DON HOYT.
Hollywood Hitman. Zebra, 1975

SAXTON, MARK. 1914-   .
The Broken Circle. Farrar, 1941
Danger Road. Farrar, 1939; Heinemann, 1940
-Paper Chase. Bobbs, 1964
The Year of August. Farrar, 1943

SAYER, W(ALTER) W(ILLIAM). 1892-   .
Pseudonym: Pierre Quiroule, q.v. All titles without publisher feature Sexton Blake and were published by Amalgamated Press. Many of the books were reprinted (and retitled) and published as by a Sayer pseudonym, P. Quiro(u)le, as indicated.
The Adventure of the Albanian Avenger. 1925. Reprinted as: The Mystery of the Albanian Avenger. 1936
The Black Limousine. 1926. Reprinted as: The £100,000 Insurance Swindle. 1936
The Case of the Cabaret Girl. 1923
The Case of the Five Dummy Books. 1923. Reprinted: 1934
The Case of the King's Spy. 1920. Reprinted as: The Missing Spy. 1934
The Case of the Strange Wireless Message. 1920
The Crimson Domino. 1922. Reprinted as: The Red Domino. 1934
The Ethiopian's Secret. 1926. Reprinted 1936.
The Forest of Fortune. 1924. Reprinted: 1935.
The Havana Mystery; see The Mystery of the Lost Battle-Ship
The Living Shadow; see The Mystery of the Living Shadow
The Lost Expedition. 1923. Reprinted: 1936
The Man with the Black Wallet; see The Secret of the Black Wallet
Mine Sinister Host. Wright, 1948
The Missing Spy; see The Case of the King's Spy
The Mystery Box. 1920. Reprinted: 1934
The Mystery of the Albanian Avenger; see The Adventure of the Albanian Avenger
The Mystery of the Living Shadow. 1920. Reprinted as: The Living Shadow. 1934
The Mystery of the Lost Battle-Ship. 1924. Reprinted as: The Havana Mystery. 1935
The Mystery of the Missing Aviator; see The Secret of the Six Black Dots
The Mystery of the Platinum Nugget! 1925. Reprinted as: The Soho Cafe Crime. 1935
The Mystery of the Turkish Agreement. 1920
The Nemesis Club. Wright, 1946
The £100,000 Insurance Swindle; see The Black Limousine
The Outlaws of Yugo-Slavia. 1923. Reprinted: 1934
The Phantom of the Pacific. 1922. Reprinted: 1934
The Red Domino; see The Crimson Domino
The Red Mountain; see The Secret of the Red Mountain
The Riders of the Sands. 1922. Reprinted: 1934
The Sacred City. 1921. Reprinted: 1934
The Secret of the Black Wallet. 1924. Reprinted as: The Man with the Black Wallet. 1935
The Secret of the Frozen North. 1921
The Secret of the Oblong Chest. 1922
The Secret of the Red Mountain. 1921. Reprinted as: The Red Mountain. 1934
The Secret of the Six Black Dots. 1921. Reprinted as: The Mystery of the Missing Aviator. 1937
The Secret of Thirty Years! 1925
Sellers of Death. Wright, 1940
The Soho Cafe Crime; see The Mystery of the Platinum Nugget!
The Vanished Million. 1924. Reprinted: 1935

SAYERS, DOROTHY L(EIGH). 1893-1957.
Series characters: Lord Peter Wimsey = PW; Montague Egg = ME.
Busman's Honeymoon. Gollancz, 1937; Harcourt, 1937 PW
Clouds of Witness. Unwin, 1926; Dial, 1927 PW
The Dawson Pedigree; see Unnatural Death
The Documents in the Case, with Robert Eustace (pseudonym of either Eustace Rawlins, 1854-   , or Robert Eustace Barton, 1868-1943). Benn, 1930; Brewer, 1930
The Five Red Herrings. Gollancz, 1931. U.S. title: Suspicious Characters. Brewer, 1931 PW
Gaudy Night. Gollancz, 1935; Harcourt, 1936 PW
Hangman's Holiday. Gollancz, 1933; Harcourt, 1933. (12 ss: 4 about PW, 6 about ME, 2 non-series.)
Have His Carcase. Gollancz, 1932; Brewer, 1932 PW
The Image in the Mirror. Todd, 1943. (16 pp booklet containing a ss from Hangman's Holiday, q.v.)
In the Teeth of the Evidence. Gollancz, 1939; Harcourt, 1940. (17 ss: 2 about PW, 5 about ME, 10 non-series.)
The Incredible Elopement of Lord Peter Wimsey. Todd, 1943. (16 pp booklet containing a ss from Hangman's Holiday, q.v.)
Lord Peter. Harper, 1972. (All 21 PW ss, complete under one cover in the second edition, including the 3 ss uncollected in Sayers' lifetime.)
Lord Peter Views the Body. Gollancz, 1928; Brewer, 1929. (12 ss about PW.)
The Man with No Face. Todd, 1943. (16 pp booklet containing a ss from Lord Peter Views the Body, q.v.)
Murder Must Advertise. Gollancz, 1933; Harcourt, 1933 PW
The Nine Tailors. Gollancz, 1934; Harcourt, 1934 PW
Striding Folly. New English Library, 1972. (The 3 PW ss uncollected in Sayers' lifetime.)

Strong Poison. Gollancz, 1930; Brewer, 1930 PW
Suspicious Characters; see The Five Red Herrings
Unnatural Death. Benn, 1927. U.S. title: The Dawson Pedigree. Dial, 1928 PW
The Unpleasantness at the Bellona Club. Benn, 1928; Payson, 1928 PW
Whose Body? Unwin, 1923; Boni, 1923 PW

SCANLON, D.
Big Shot. World Distributors, 1953
School for Murder. World Distributors, 1953
Snatch. World Distributors, 1952

SCANLON, NOEL. Series character: Quinn, in both titles.
Quinn. Murray, 1973
Quinn and the Desert Oil. Murray, 1975

SCANNELL, VERNON. 1922-   .
The Big Chance. Long, 1960
-The Big Time. Longmans, 1965
-The Dividing Night. Putnam (London), 1962
-The Face of the Enemy. Putnam (London), 1961
-The Fight. Nevill, 1953
The Shadowed Place. Long, 1961
-The Wound and the Scar. Nevill, 1953

SCARBOROUGH, GEORGE. See also: PAGE PHILIPS.
The Lure. Dillingham, 1914

SCARLETT, ROGER. Pseudonym of Dorothy Blair, 1903-   , and Evelyn Page, 1902-   . Series character: Inspector Kane, in all titles.
The Back Bay Murders. Doubleday, 1930; Selwyn, 1931
The Beacon Hill Murders. Doubleday, 1930; Heinemann, 1930
Cat's Paw. Doubleday, 1931
In the First Degree. Doubleday, 1933
Murder Among the Angells. Doubleday, 1932

SCARLETT, SUSAN
-The Man in the Dark. Hodder, 1940
Murder While You Work. Hodder, 1944

SCARPETTA, FRANK. Series character: Philip Magellan (The Marksman), in all titles (see also: Peter McCurtin).
Body Count. Belmont, 1974
Counterattack. Belmont, 1974
Death to the Mafia. Belmont, 1973
Die, Killer, Die. Belmont, 1975
Headhunter. Belmont, 1973
Icepick in the Spine. Belmont, 1975
Kill! Belmont, 1974
Killer on the Prowl. Belmont, 1975
Kill Them All. Belmont, 1973
Mafia Massacre. Belmont, 1974
Mafia Wipe-Out. Belmont, 1973
The Murder Machine. Belmont, 1975
Open Contract. Belmont, 1974
Slaughterhouse. Belmont, 1973
Stone Killer. Belmont, 1974
This Animal Must Die. Belmont, 1975
The Torture Contract. Belmont, 1975

SCERBANENCO, GIORGIO. 1911-   .
Duca and the Milan Murders. Cassell, 1970; Walker, 1970. (Translation of Traditori di Tutti. Milan, 1966.)

SCHABELITZ, R(UDOLPH) F(REDERICK). 1884-1959. See: WILLETTA ANN BARBER, 1911-   .

SCHERE, MONROE. Pseudonym: Abigail Winter, q.v.

SCHERF, MARGARET. 1908-   . Series characters: Emily & Henry Bryce = B; Rev. Martin Buell = MB; Grace Severance = GS.
Always Murder a Friend. Doubleday, 1948; Low, 1949 MB
The Banker's Bones. Doubleday, 1968; Hale, 1969 GS
The Beautiful Birthday Cake. Doubleday, 1971 GS
The Case of the Hated Senator; see Dead: Senate Office Building
The Case of the Kippered Corpse. Putnam, 1941
The Cautious Overshoes. Doubleday, 1956 MB
The Corpse Grows a Beard. Putnam, 1940; Partridge, 1946
The Corpse in the Flannel Nightgown. Doubleday, 1965; Hale, 1966 MB
The Corpse with One Shoe; see The Green Plaid Pants
The Curious Custard Pie. Doubleday, 1950. Also published as: Divine and Deadly. Bestseller, 1953 MB
Dead: Senate Office Building. Doubleday, 1953. Also published as: The Case of the Hated Senator. Ace, 1954
Death of the Diplomat; see The Diplomat and the Gold Piano
The Diplomat and the Gold Piano. Doubleday, 1963. British title: Death of the Diplomat. Hale, 1964 B
Divine and Deadly; see The Curious Custard Pie
The Elk and the Evidence. Doubleday, 1952 MB
For the Love of Murder; see Gilbert's Last Toothache
Gilbert's Last Toothache. Doubleday, 1949. Also published as: For the Love of Murder. Bestseller, 1950 MB
Glass on the Stairs. Doubleday, 1954; Barker, 1955 B
The Green Plaid Pants. Doubleday, 1951. Also published as: The Corpse with One Shoe. Detective Book Club, 1951 B
The Gun in Daniel Webster's Bust. Doubleday, 1949 B
If You Want a Murder Well Done. Doubleday, 1974
Judicial Body. Doubleday, 1957
Murder Makes Me Nervous. Doubleday, 1948; Low, 1952
Never Turn Your Back. Doubleday, 1959 MB
The Owl in the Cellar. Doubleday, 1945; Nimmo, 1947
They Came to Kill. Putnam, 1942
To Cache a Millionaire. Doubleday, 1972 GS

SCHERMERHORN, DUANE R. Pseudonym: James Marcott, q.v.

SCHINKE, NORMA S.
The Devil Wolf. Small, 1924; Unwin, 1924

SCHISGALL, OSCAR. 1901-   .
Baron Ixell, Crime Breaker. Longmans (New York & London), 1929 ss
The Devil's Daughter. Fiction League, 1932

SCHLEIFER, GERRY
Five Million Francs. Joseph, 1973

SCHLEY, STURGES MASON. Series character: Dr. Quentin Toby = QT.
Deepening Blue. Doubleday, 1935
Dr. Toby Finds Murder. Random, 1941 QT
Dream Sinister. Morrow, 1950. British title: The Starry-Eyed Chipmunk. Gollancz, 1951 QT
The Starry-Eyed Chipmunk; see Dream Sinister
Vengeance Pulls the Trigger; see Who'd Shoot a Genius?
Who'd Shoot a Genius? Random, 1940. Also published as: Vengeance Pulls The Trigger. Death House, 1944 QT

SCHMIDT, JAMES NORMAN. 1912-   . Pseudonym: James Norman, q.v.

SCHMITT, LEO F(RANCIS). 1891-   .
The Shyster Lawyer. Schmitt, 1929 ss

SCHNURR, WILLIAM
Johnny Death. PB, 1974

SCHOENFELD, HOWARD
Let Them Eat Bullets. GM, 1954; Fawcett (London), 1955

SCHOFIELD, WILLIAM G(REENOUGH). 1909-   .
The Cat in the Convoy. Macrae, 1946
Payoff in Black. Macrae, 1947; Cherry Tree, 1948

SCHOLEY, ERIC
Answer in the Negative. Ward, 1952

SCHOLEY, JEAN
The Dead Past. Heinemann, 1961; Macmillan, 1962

SCHRADER, LEONARD
The Yakuza. Futura, 1975. (Novelization of the movie.)

SCHURMACHER, EMILE C. 1903-1976.
Assignment X: Top Secret. Paperback Library, 1965

SCHURR, CATHLEEN
Dark Encounter. Rinehart, 1955. British title: Dark Death. Foulsham, 1957

SCHWARTZ, ALVIN. 1916-   .
The Blowtop. Dial, 1948

SCHWARTZ, JOOST MARIUS WILLIEM VAN DER POORTEN. 1858-1915. Pseudonym: Maarten Maartens, q.v. See also: ANONYMOUS (The Black Box Murder).

SCHWEITZER, GERTRUDE
The Ledge. Delacorte, 1972; Macdonald, 1973

SCIASCIA, LEONARDO. 1921-   .
Equal Danger. Harper, 1973; Cape, 1974. (Translation of Il Contesto. Turin, 1971.)
Mafia Vendetta. Knopf, 1964; Cape, 1963. (Translation of Il Giorno della Avetta. Turin, 1961.)
A Man's Blessing. Harper, 1968; Cape, 1969. (Translation of A Ciascuno il Suo. Turin, 1966.)

SCOBIE, ALASTAIR. 1918-   .
The Cape Town Affair. Cassell, 1952
Kangaroo Shoots Man. Cassell, 1949
Murder a la Mozambique. Cassell, 1950

SCOFIELD, CHARLES J(OSIAH). 1853-   .
A Subtle Adversary. Scofield, 1891

SCOTLAND, JAY. Pseudonym of John (William) Jakes, 1932-   , q.v. Other pseudonym: Alan Payne, q.v.
The Seventh Man. Mystery House, 1958

SCOTT, LADY A(IMEE BYNG HALL)
-Another Man's Wife. Nash, 1925
-The Blue Vase. Holden, 1922
-The Open Prison. Eldon, 1934
-The Painted Window. Eldon, 1934
The Sealed Envelope. Hutchinson, 1927
-The Unknown Path. Hutchinson, 1926

SCOTT, A. W.
    Life Experiences of a Detective. Detective's Museum Pub. Co., 1878 ss

SCOTT, ANTONIA
    Falcon's Island. PB, 1973

SCOTT, BARBARA MONTAGU
    -And, Which, the Knave? Hutchinson, 1946
    -The Devil Within. Hutchinson, 1956
    -The Road Back. Hutchinson, 1952
    The Wolf Troubleth Not. Hurst, 1943

SCOTT, DANA. Pseudonym of Constance Noyes Robertson, 1897- .
    Five Fatal Letters. Farrar, 1937

SCOTT, DENIS. Joint pseudonym of Mary Means and Theodore Saunders. Series character: Mike James, in both titles.
    The Beckoning Shadow. Bobbs, 1946; Hammond, 1956
    Murder Makes a Villain. Bobbs, 1944; Hammond, 1955

SCOTT, EVELYN. 1893- . Pseudonym: Ernest Souza, q.v.

SCOTT, G. FIRTH
    -At Friendly Point. Bowden, 1898 ss
    Possessed. Rider, 1912
    The Rider of Waroona. Long, 1912
    -The Track of Midnight. Low, 1897
    The Twillford Mystery. Everett, 1904

SCOTT, GENEVIEVE
    The Water Horse. Gollancz, 1974

SCOTT, SIR (JAMES) GEORGE. 1851-1935.
    Why Not? Arnold, 1929

SCOTT, HEDLEY. Pseudonym of Hedley O'Mant. Series character (with many other authors): Sexton Blake, in both titles.
    The Mystery of the Missing Refugee. Amalgamated, 1939
    The Suspected Six. Amalgamated, 1938

SCOTT, J(AMES) M(AURICE). 1906- .
    -The Black Joke. Hodder, 1950
    -The Bright Eyes of Danger. Hodder, 1950
    -Cap Across the River. Hodder, 1949
    -Dingo. Heinemann, 1966; Chilton, 1967
    I Keep My Word. Heinemann, 1957
    -In a Beautiful Pea-Green Boat. Bles, 1968; Chilton, 1969
    -The Land of Seals. Hodder, 1938
    -Michael Anonymous. Chilton, 1971. (British title?)
    The Other Half of the Orange. Heinemann, 1955; Dutton, 1955
    -The Other Side of the Moon. Hodder, 1946
    -The Pole of Inaccessibility. Hodder, 1947
    Sea-Wyf; see Sea-Wyf and Biscuit
    Sea-Wyf and Biscuit. Heinemann, 1955. U.S. title: Sea-Wyf. Dutton, 1956. Also published as: Seawife. Crest, 1957
    Seawife; see Sea-Wyf
    -The Silver Land. Hodder, 1937
    -Snowstone. Hodder, 1936
    The Touch of the Nettle. Hodder, 1951
    -Unknown River. Hodder, 1939
    -Where the River Bends. Heinemann, 1962
    -The Will and the Way. Hodder, 1949; Dutton, 1949

SCOTT, JACK DENTON. 1915- . See also: ANNE DAMER.
    Spargo. World, 1972

SCOTT, JEFFRY
    Trust Them and Die. Hale, 1969

SCOTT, JODY. 1923- . Joint pseudonym with George Thurston Leite, 1920- : Thurston Scott, q.v.

SCOTT, JOHN REED. 1869- .
    The Cab of the Sleeping Horse. Putnam (New York & London), 1916
    -In Her Own Right. Lippincott (New York & London), 1911
    The Man in Evening Clothes. Putnam (New York & London), 1917
    -The Red Emerald. Lippincott (New York & London), 1914
    The Woman in Question. Lippincott (New York & London), 1909

SCOTT, JUNE (MEINDL)
    Bitter Honeycomb. Dorrance, 1972

SCOTT, JUSTIN (BLAZER). Pseudonym: J. S. Blazer, q.v.
    Many Happy Returns. McKay, 1973
    Treasure for Treasure. McKay, 1974; Barker, 1974

SCOTT, LEROY. 1875-1929. Series character: Bob Clifford, in at least those marked BC.
    Children of the Whirlwind. Houghton, 1921
    Cordelia the Magnificent. Holt, 1923
    Counsel for the Defense. Doubleday, 1912; Newnes, 1914
    -A Daughter of Two Worlds. Houghton, 1919
    Folly's Gold. Houghton, 1926 BC
    The Living Dead Man. Washburn, 1929; Nash, 1929
    Mary Regan. Houghton, 1918 BC
    No. 13 Washington Square. Houghton, 1914
    Partners of the Night. Century, 1916; Nash, 1917 ss
    -The Shears of Destiny. Doubleday, 1910; Hodder, 1910

SCOTT, LILY K.
    A House of Women. Pyramid, 1966

SCOTT, MANSFIELD. Series characters: Kendall "Dizzy" McArthur = KM; Malcome Steele = MS.
    Behind Red Curtains. Small, 1919; Nash, 1920 MS
    The Black Circle. Clode, 1928; Lane, 1929 MS
    The Phantom Passenger. Clode, 1927; Lane, 1928
    The Spider's Web. Clode, 1929 KM
    The Sportsman-Detective. Clode, 1930 KM

SCOTT, MARGARET. Joint pseudonym with Will(iam Charles) Oursler, 1913- , q.v.: Gale Gallagher, q.v.

SCOTT, MARGERIE
    Mrs. Tenterden. Milton House, 1975

SCOTT, MARIAN
    Dead Hands Reaching. Macmillan, 1932

SCOTT, MARY (EDITH CLARKE), 1888- , and JOYCE (TARLTON) WEST
    The Mangrove Murder. Angus, 1964
    No Red Herrings. Angus, 1964
    -Such Nice People. Angus, 1962
    -Who Put It There? Angus, 1965

SCOTT, MARY SEMPLE
    Crime Hound. Scribner, 1940

SCOTT, MAURICE
    -In the Thraldom of Fear. Stevens, 1936
    The Mark of the Broad Arrow. Henderson
    -A Modern Circe. Stevens, 1937

SCOTT, MILTON
    Dear, Dead Harry. Phoenix, 1949

SCOTT, R(EGINALD) T(HOMAS) M(AITLAND). 1882- . Series characters: Aurelius Smith = AS; Richard Wentworth (The Spider; stories reprinted from pulp magazines; see also: Grant Stockbridge) = RW.
    The Agony Column Murders. Dutton, 1946 AS
    Ann's Crime. Dutton, 1926; Heinemann, 1927. Also published as: Smith of the Secret Service (with no author given). Amalgamated, 1929 AS
    Aurelius Smith—Detective. Dutton, 1927; Heinemann, 1928 AS ss
    The Black Magician. Dutton, 1925; Heinemann, 1926 AS
    The Mad Monk. Kendall, 1931; Rich, 1933
    Murder Stalks the Mayor. Dutton, 1936; Rich, 1935 AS
    The Nameless Ones. Dutton, 1947 AS
    Secret Service Smith. Dutton, 1923; Hodder, 1924 AS ss
    Smith of the Secret Service; see Ann's Crime
    The Spider Strikes! Berkley, 1969 RW
    The Wheel of Death. Berkley, 1969 RW

SCOTT, RONEY
    Shakedown. Ace, 1953

SCOTT, STEVE
    The Cop-Killers. Manor, 1972

SCOTT, SUTHERLAND. Series character: Dr. Septimus Dodds, in at least those marked SD.
    The A.R.P. Murder. Paul, 1939 SD
    Capital Punishment. Paul, 1949
    Crazy Murder Show. Paul, 1937; Hillman-Curl, 1937. Also published as: Murder on Stage. Mystery Novel of the Month, 1941 SD
    Diagnosis—Murder. Paul, 1954 SD
    Doctor Dodds' Experiment. Paul, 1956 SD
    Escape to Murder. Paul, 1946
    The Influenza Mystery. Paul, 1938 SD
    The Mass Radiography Murders. Paul, 1947
    Murder in the Mobile Unit. Paul, 1940 SD
    Murder is Infectious. Paul, 1936 SD
    Murder on Stage; see Crazy Murder Show
    Murder Without Mourners. Paul, 1936 SD
    The Night Air is Dangerous. Paul, 1943
    Operation Urgent. Paul, 1947
    Tincture of Murder. Paul, 1951

SCOTT, TARN
    Don't Let Her Die. GM, 1957

SCOTT, THURSTON. Joint pseudonym of George Thurston Leite, 1920- , and Jody Scott, 1923- .
    Cure It with Honey. Harper, 1951. Also published as (?): I'll Get Mine. Popular Library, 1952

SCOTT, VIRGIL (JOSEPH). 1914- .
    The Dead Tree Gives No Shelter. Swallow, 1947; Archer, 1950
    The Kreutzman Formula, with Dominic Koski. Simon, 1974
    -The Savage Affair. Harcourt, 1958; Methuen, 1958

SCOTT, WARWICK. Pseudonym of Elleston Trevor, 1920- , q.v. Name originally: Trevor Dudley Smith, q.v. Other pseudonyms: Mansell Black, Adam Hall, Simon Rattray, Caesar Smith, qq.v.

Cockpit; see Image in the Dust
Doomsday; see The Domesday Story
The Domesday Story. Davies, 1952. U.S. title: Doomsday. Lion, 1953. Reprinted as by Elleston Trevor: Mayflower, 1966
Image in the Dust. Davies, 1951. U.S. title: Cockpit. Lion, 1953. Reprinted as by Elleston Trevor: Mayflower, 1967
Naked Canvas. Davies, 1954; Popular Library, 1955. Reprinted as by Elleston Trevor: Mayflower, 1965

SCOTT, WILL. Series character: Disher = D.
The Black Stamp; see Disher-Detective
Disher-Detective. Cassell, 1925. U.S. title: The Black Stamp. Macrae-Smith, 1926 D
Giglamps. Cassell, 1924 ss
The Man. Paul, 1930. U.S. title: The Mask. Macrae-Smith, 1929 D
The Mask; see The Man
Shadows. Cassell, 1928; Macrae-Smith, 1928 D

SCOTT, WILLIAM
Getting the Boy. Elek, 1966

SCOTT, WILLIAM R. Pseudonym: Weldon Hill, q.v.

SCOTT-HERON, GIL. 1949- .
The Vulture. World, 1970

SCOTT-MONCRIEFF, DAVID
The Vaivaisukko's Bride. Scots Digest, 1949

SCOWCROFT, RICHARD (PINGREE). 1916- .
Back to Fire Mountain. Little, 1973

SCRIBNER, FRANK K(IMBALL). 1866-1935.
The Secret of Frontellac. Small, 1912; Gay, 1912

SCRIBNER, HARVEY. 1850- .
My Mysterious Clients. Clarke, 1900 ss, some criminous

SCROPE, MASON. Pseudonym of Arthur Charles Mason, 1879- .
The Man with the Big Head. Wells Gardner, 1929

SCUDDER, ANTOINETTE (QUINBY). 1898- .
-The Grey Studio. Ruth Hill, 1934

SEABROOKE, JOHN PAUL
The Eyewitness. Chelsea, 1925; Jarrolds, 1926
Four Knocks on the Door. Chelsea, 1925; Jarrolds, 1927
The Green Bag. Chelsea, 1926
Shadow Hall. Chelsea, 1926; Jarrolds, 1927
The Woman in 919. Chelsea, 1926

SEAFARER. Pseudonym of C(larence) Hedley Barker, q.v. Other pseudonym: Frank Hedley, q.v. Series character: Captain Firebrace, in at least those marked F.
Bold Buccaneer. Ward, 1953
Captain Firebrace. Ward, 1958 F
Captain Firebrace and the Java Queen. Ward, 1958 F
Crook's Cruise. Ward, 1960
Firebrace and Father Kelly. Ward, 1959 F
The Haunted Ship. Ward, 1956
Make Way for a Sailor. Ward, 1947
The Sailor and the Widow. Ward, 1957
Santa Maria. Ward, 1955
Smuggler's Pay for Firebrace. Ward, 1959 F
Voyage into Peril. Ward, 1954

SEAFORTH. Pseudonym of George C(ecil) Foster, 1893- , q.v.
Misprision of Felony. Jenkins, 1941

SEA-LION. Pseudonym of Geoffrey Martin Bennett, 1909- . Series character: Desmond Drake, in at least those marked DD.
Cargo for Crooks. Collins, 1948
Damn Desmond Drake. Hutchinson, 1953 DD
Death in Russian Habit. Long, 1958
Death in the Dog Watches. Long, 1962
Desmond Drake Goes West. Hutchinson, 1956 DD
The Diamond Rock. Hutchinson, 1952
Down Among the Dead Men. Long, 1961
The Invisible Ships. Hutchinson, 1950
Meet Desmond Drake. Hutchinson, 1952 DD
Operation Fireball. Long, 1959
Phantom Fleet. Collins, 1946
-The Quest of John Clare. Hutchinson, 1951
Sea of Troubles. Collins, 1947
Sink Me the Ship. Collins, 1946
The Stolen Cipher. Hutchinson, 1955
This Creeping Evil. Hutchinson, 1950
When Danger Threatens. Collins, 1949

SEALIS, HATHERLY. Pseudonym of Charles Freeman Foster, 1830- .
The Veiled Lady. Broadway, 1905

SEAMAN, DONALD (PETER). 1922- .
The Bomb That Could Lip-Read. H. Hamilton, 1974; Stein, 1974
The Chameleon Course; see The Defector
The Defector. H. Hamilton, 1975. U.S. title: The Chameleon Course. Coward, 1976
Island of Death. Muller, 1956

SEAMARK, Pseudonym of Austin J. Small, -1929, q.v.
The Avenging Ray. Hodder, 1930; Doubleday, 1930, as by Austin J. Small
Down River. Hodder, 1929. U.S. title: The Needle's Kiss. Doubleday, 1929, as by Austin J. Small
The Master Mystery. Hodder, 1928; Doubleday, 1928, as by Austin J. Small
The Mystery Maker. Hodder, 1929; Doubleday, 1930, as by Austin J. Small
The Needle's Kiss; see Down River
Out of the Dark. Hodder, 1931 ss
Pawns and Kings. Hodder, 1931 ss
The Silent Six. Hodder, 1926
The Vantine Diamonds. Hodder, 1930; Doubleday, 1930, as by Austin J. Small
The Web of Destiny. Hodder, 1929. U.S. title: The Web of Murder. Doubleday, 1929, as by Austin J. Small
The Web of Murder; see The Web of Destiny

SEARLE, WESTON
The Honeyfall. Regency, 1972

SEARLS, HANK [HENRY HUNT SEARLS]. 1922- .
Pentagon. Geis, 1971

SEARS, RUTH McCARTHY
The Gift of the Sea. Lenox, 1973; Remploy, 1973
The Golden Sentinals. Lenox, 1974; Remploy, 1974
The Grangerfjord Monks. Lenox, 1974; Remploy, 1975
Heir of Grangerfjord Castle. Lenox, 1974; Remploy, 1975
In the Shadow of the Tower. Lenox, 1972; Remploy, 1973
A Lonely Place; see The Phantom Empire

The Phantom Empire. Lenox, 1974. Also published as: A Lonely Place. Leisure, 1976
Port of No Return. Lenox, 1973; Remploy, 1974
St. George Manor. Lenox, 1973; Remploy, 1973
The Spirit of Cove Island. Leisure, 1975
-Three Silver Birches. Dell, 1975
Wind in the Cypress. Leisure, 1975

SEA-WRACK. Pseudonym of Edward Horace Crebbin.
McInnes of the N.I.D. Rich, 1941 ss

SEATON, STUART
Cage of Fear. Long, 1960
Don't Take It to Heart. Boardman, 1955
Dust in Your Eyes. Boardman, 1957

SEBASTIAN, PAUL
The Black Shadow. Fiction House, 1937
The Red Boulders Mystery. Fiction House, 1937
Secret Service. Fiction House, 1937
The Spy Gang. Fiction House, 1941

SEBENTHAL, ELIZABETH ROBERTA. 1917- .
Pseudonyms: Harry Davis, Paul Kruger, qq.v.

SECRIST, KELLIHER. Joint pseudonym of Dan T. Kelliher and W. G. Secrist. Series character: Sham Payne, in both titles.
Murder Makes By-Lines. Mystery House, 1941
Murder Melody. Phoenix, 1939. Also published as: She Screamed Blue Murder. Ideal, 1946
She Screamed Blue Murder; see Murder Melody

SECRIST, W. G. Joint pseudonym with Dan T. Kelliher: Kelliher Secrist, q.v.

SEDERBERG, ARELO (CHARLES). 1930- .
60 Hours of Darkness. Sherbourne, 1974

SEE, INGRAM
No Scars to See. Bouregy, 1965

SEELEY, CLINTON. 1921- .
Storm Fear. Holt, 1954; Ward, 1957

SEELEY, MABEL (HODNEFIELD). 1903- .
The Beckoning Door. Doubleday, 1950; Collins, 1950
The Blonde with the Deadly Past; see The Whistling Shadow
The Chuckling Fingers. Doubleday, 1941; Collins, 1942
The Crying Sisters. Doubleday, 1939; Collins, 1940
Eleven Came Back. Doubleday, 1943; Collins, 1943
The Listening House. Doubleday, 1938; Collins, 1939
The Whispering Cup. Doubleday, 1940; Collins, 1941
The Whistling Shadow. Doubleday, 1954; Jenkins, 1958. Also published as: The Blonde with the Deadly Past. Mercury, 1955

SEIBERT, ELIZABETH G.
-The Abrus Necklace. Macrae-Smith, 1956
Death Follows the Flower Show. Arcadia, 1958

SEIFERT, ADELE. See also: SHIRLEY (LOUISE) SEIFERT, 1889- . Series character: Gregory Trent, in all titles.
Deeds Ill Done. Mill, 1939. British title (?): Kill Your Own Snakes. Boardman, 1947 GT

Kill Your Own Snakes; see Deeds Ill
    Done
Shadows Tonight. Mill, 1939; Boardman,
    1943
3 Blind Mice. Mill, 1942; Boardman,
    1945

SEIFERT, SHIRLEY (LOUISE), 1889-   , and
    ADELE SEIFERT, q.v.
Death Stops at the Old Stone Inn.
    Hillman-Curl, 1938

SEIGNOLLE, CLAUDE
-The Accursed. Coward, 1967; Allen,
    1967. (Translation of Les Maledic-
    tions. Paris, 1963.) (Two stories.)

SEILAZ, AILEEN
The Veil of Silence. Ace, 1965

SELA, OWEN. Series character: Nicholas
    Maasten = NM.
The Bearer Plot. Hodder, 1972; Pan-
    theon, 1973 NM
The Bengali Inheritance. Hodder, 1975;
    Pantheon, 1975
The Kiriov Tapes. Hodder, 1973; Pan-
    theon, 1974 NM
The Portuguese Fragment. Hodder, 1974;
    Pantheon, 1973 NM

SELBORNE, JOHN
-The House of the Siren. Everett, 1911
The Thousand Secrets. Everett, 1911;
    Kennerley, 1915

SELDEN, CATHARINE
Villa Nova; or, The Ruined Castle.
    Lane, 1805

SELDES, GILBERT VIVIAN. 1893-1970. Pseu-
    donym: Foster Johns, q.v.

SELLARS, ELEANORE KELLY
Murder a la Mode. Dodd, 1941; Muller,
    1943

SELLERS, MARY
The Cry of the Cat. Warner, 1975
The House on Black Bayou. Warner, 1975

SELLICKS, LESLIE EDWARD. 1902-   . Pseu-
    donym: Edward Leslie, q.v.

SELMAN, ROBERT
Once Upon a Crime. Morrow, 1947; Foul-
    sham, 1949

SELMARK, GEORGE. Pseudonym of (Leslie)
    Seldon Truss, 1892-   , q.v.
Murder in Silence. Cassell, 1939;
    Doubleday, 1940

SELTZER, CHARLES ALDEN. 1875-1942.
Parade of the Empty Boots. Doubleday,
    1937; Hodder, 1938

SELVER, (PERCY) PAUL. 1888-1970.
Private Life. Jarrolds, 1929; Harper,
    1930

SELWYN. Pseudonym of Selwyn Victor Wat-
    son.
Operation Ballerina. Hodder, 1953

SELWYN, FRANCIS. Series character: Sgt.
    Verity, in both titles.
Cracksman on Velvet. Deutsch, 1974;
    Stein, 1974. Also published as: Ser-
    geant Verity and the Cracksman.
    Futura, 1975
Sergeant Verity and the Cracksman; see
    Cracksman on Velvet
Sergeant Verity and the Imperial Dia-
    mond. Deutsch, 1975; Stein, 1976

SEMPRUN, JORGE
The Second Death of Ramon Mercader.
    Weidenfeld, 1973; Grove, 1973.
    (Translation of La Deuxieme Mort de
    Ramon Mercader. Paris, 1969.)

SEMYONOV, JULIAN (SEMENOVICH). 1931-   .
Petrovka 38. MacGibbon, 1965; Stein,
    1965. (Translation of Petrovka 38.
    Moscow, 1964.)

SENNOCKE, T. J. R. Series character:
    Sgt. Mallory, in at least those
    marked M.
Inquest on a Lady. Rudkin, 1941
Inquest on a Mistress. Rudkin, 1943 M
Inquest Betraying. Rudkin, 1943 M
Inquests by Jury. Rudkin, 1944
Inquests on the Deceased. Rudkin, 1944
What is Your Verdict? Eyre, 1936.
    (Problems in detection, with solu-
    tions.)

SERENY, GITTA
The Medallion. Gollancz, 1957

SERGE, VICTOR. 1890-1947.
The Case of Comrade Tulayev. Doubleday,
    1950; H. Hamilton, 1951. (Translation
    of L'Affaire Toulaev. Paris, 1949.)

SERGEANT, (EMILY FRANCES) ADELINE. 1851-
    1904. U.S. byline sometimes: Adeline
    Sargeant.
-Accused and Accuser. Methuen, 1904
-Beneath the Veil. Long, 1903
-A Broken Idol. Hurst, 1893
-A Deadly Foe. Hutchinson, 1895
-Deveril's Diamond. Hurst, 1889
-Dr. Endicott's Experiment. Chatto,
    1894; Cassell (New York), 1895
An East London Mystery. Hurst, 1892
The Great Mill Street Mystery. Lovell,
    1890. Also published as: The Mill
    Street Mystery. Westbrook, ca.1920.
    (British title?)
-The House in the Crescent. Long, 1907
-A Life Sentence. Hurst, 1891; Lovell,
    1889
-The Master of Beechwood. Methuen, 1902;
    Burt, 1902
The Mill Street Mystery; see The Great
    Mill Street Mystery
-Miss Betty's Mistake. Hurst, 1898
-The Missing Elizabeth. Chatto, 1905
Mrs. Lygon's Husband. Methuen, 1905
My Lady's Diamonds. Ward, 1901;
    Buckles, 1901
The Mystery of the Moat. Methuen, 1905
-An Open Foe. Bentley, 1884
The Progress of Rachel. Methuen, 1904
The Quest of Geoffrey Darrell. Methuen,
    1907
-The Sin of Laban Routh. Digby, 1905
Sir Anthony. Hurst, 1892. U.S. title:
    Sir Anthony's Secret; or, A False Po-
    sition. Taylor, 1891
Sir Anthony's Secret; see Sir Anthony
-This Body of Death. Hurst, 1901
-The Treasure of Captain Scarlett.
    Hutchinson, 1901
-Under False Pretences. Ward, 1892;
    Lovell, 1889
Under Suspicion. Methuen, 1904
The Yellow Diamond. Methuen, 1904

SERLING, ROBERT J(EROME). 1918-   .
The President's Plane is Missing.
    Doubleday, 1967; Cassell, 1968

SERNER, MARTIN GUNNAR. 1886-1947. Pseudo-
    nym: Frank Heller, q.v.

SERRESTER, LEONARD
The Frog Murders. Dorrance, 1955

SERVICE, ROBERT W(ILLIAM). 1876-1958.
The House of Fear. Dodd, 1927; Unwin,
    1927
The Master of the Microbe. Barse, 1926;
    Unwin, 1927
The Poisoned Paradise. Dodd, 1922

SETH, RONALD (SYDNEY)
-The Patriot. Owen, 1954
Spy in the Nude. Hale, 1962

SETON, GRAHAM. Pseudonym of Graham Seton
    Hutchison, 1890-1946. Series charac-
    ter: Col. Duncan Grant = DG.
According to Plan. Rich, 1938 DG
Blood Money. Hutchinson, 1934
Colonel Grant's Tomorrow. Butterworth,
    1931; Farrar, 1932 DG
Eye for an Eye. Hutchinson, 1932; Far-
    rar, 1933
The Governor of Kattowitz. Butterworth,
    1930. U.S. title: The Sign of Arnim.
    Cosmopolitan, 1931
The K Code Plan. Rich, 1938 DG
Minos Magnificent. Hutchinson, 1935
The Red Colonel. Hutchinson, 1947 DG
Scar 77. Rich, 1936 DG
The Sign of Arnim; see The Governor of
    Kattowitz
Tiger's Cub. Rich, 1940
The V Plan. Eyre, 1941; Smith & Dur-
    rell, 1941 DG
The Viper of Luxor. Hutchinson, 1933
The W Plan. Butterworth, 1929; Cosmo-
    politan, 1930 DG

SEUFFERT, MUIR. Series character: Mike
    Hubbard, in all titles.
Devil at the Door. Hale, 1972
Hand of a Killer. Hale, 1967
Trespassers will Die. Hale, 1968

SEVERN, RICHARD
An Array of Eagles. Hale, 1971
Blood and Gold. Hale, 1964
The Desperate Rendezvous. Hale, 1966
The Forest and the Damned. Hale, 1965
A Game for Hawks. Hale, 1968
The Killing Match. Hale, 1970
Quest to Kill. Hale, 1974
Stalk a Long Shadow. Hale, 1967

SEVERNE, FLORENCE
In the Meshes. Osgood, 1894

SEVERY, MELVIN (LINWOOD). 1863-   .
    Series character: George Maitland, in
    all titles.
The Darrow Enigma. Dodd, 1904; Rich-
    ards, 1904
Maitland's Master Mystery. Ball, 1912
The Mystery of June 13. Dodd, 1905;
    Stevens, 1905

SEVILLE, MARJORIE
The Quest of the Emerald. Hutchinson,
    1927

SEWARD, JACK [JOHN NEIL SEWARD].
    1924-   . Series character: Curt
    Stone, in all titles.
Assignment: Find Cherry. Tower, 1969
The Cave of the Chinese Skeletons.
    Tuttle, 1964
The Chinese Pleasure Girl. Tower, 1969
The Frogman Assassination. Tower, 1969
The Eurasian Virgins. Tower, 1969

SEWARD, WILLIAM WARD. 1913-   .
Skirts of the Dead Night. Bookman, 1950

SEYMOUR, ARTHUR
The Fall of the Mighty. Odhams, 1919

SEYMOUR, GERALD
Harry's Game. Collins, 1975; Random, 1975

SEYMOUR, H(ENRY). Pseudonym of Helmut Hartmann.
Appointment with Murder. Gifford, 1962
The Big Steal. Hale, 1972
The Bristol Affair. Gifford, 1960
Cold Wind of Death. Hale, 1972
Hot Ice. Gifford, 1966
In the Still of the Night. Gifford, 1966
Infernal Idol. Gifford, 1967
Intrigue in Tangier. Gifford, 1958
The Paperchase Murder. Gifford, 1961
Run for Your Money. Gifford, 1959

SHAFER, ROBERT (JONES). 1920-   .
-The Conquered Place. Putnam (New York), 1954; Putnam (London), 1955

SHAFFER, A(NTHONY JOSHUA), 1926-   , and P(ETER LEVIN) SHAFFER, 1926-   . Joint pseudonym: Peter Antony, q.v. See also: next entry.
Withered Murder. Gollancz, 1955; Macmillan, 1956

SHAFFER, ANTHONY (JOSHUA). 1926-   .
Joint pseudonym with Peter (Levin) Shaffer, 1926-   : Peter Antony, q.v. See also: previous entry.
Sleuth. Calder, 1971; Dodd, 1970. (A play.)

SHAFFER, ERVIN ADAM
Major Washington. Hobson, 1947

SHAFFER, JACK
Sweet Revenge. Vantage, 1965

SHAGAN, STEVE. 1927-   .
City of Angels. Putnam, 1975; Joseph, 1975. Also published as: Hustle. Signet, 1975; Star, 1976

SHAKESPEARE, BRIAN. See: JOHN DE ST. JORRE, 1936-   .

SHALLIT, JOSEPH. Series character: Dan Morrison, in all titles.
The Billion Dollar Body. Lippincott, 1947; Hammond, 1952. Also published as: The Case of the Billion Dollar Body. Avon, 1954
The Case of the Billion Dollar Body; see The Billion Dollar Body
Juvenile Hoods; see Kiss the Killer
Kiss the Killer. Lippincott, 1952; Hammond, 1954. Also published as: Juvenile Hoods. Avon, 1957
Lady, Don't Die on My Doorstep. Lippincott, 1951; Hammond, 1952
Yell Bloody Murder. Lippincott, 1951. British title: Yell Ruddy Murder. Hammond, 1953
Yell Ruddy Murder; see Yell Bloody Murder

SHAMBROOK, RONA GREEN. Pseudonym: Rona Randall, q.v.

SHAND, WILLIAM. Series character: Bill Tempest, in all titles.
A Man Called Tempest. Jenkins, 1957
Tempest in a Tea-Cup. Jenkins, 1958; Roy, 1959
Tempest Weaves a Shroud. Jenkins, 1957

SHANE, MARK. Pseudonym of Victor (George Charles) Norwood, 1920-   , q.v. Other pseudonyms: Johnny Dark, Mark Hampton, Hank Janson, Nat Karta, qq.v.
Borrowed Time. Comyns, 1952
Death at her Fingers. Comyns, 1953
Honey Ain't So Sweet. Comyns, 1953
Jail and Farewell. Comyns, 1953
The Lady Bites the Dust. Comyns, 1952
Obsession to Kill. Comyns, 1953

SHANE, SUSANNAH. Pseudonym of H(arriette Cora) Ashbrook, 1898-1946, q.v. Series character: Christopher Saxe, in at least those marked CS.
The Baby in the Ash Can. Dodd, 1944; Nicholson, 1947 CS
Diamonds in the Dumplings. Doubleday, 1946 CS
Lady in a Million. Dodd, 1943; Nicholson, 1948 CS
Lady in a Wedding Dress. Dodd, 1943
Lady in Danger. Dodd, 1942; Nicholson, 1948 CS
Lady in Lilac. Dodd, 1941

SHANKS, EDWARD (BUXTON). 1892-1953.
The Dark Green Circle; see Old King Cole
Old King Cole. Macmillan (London), 1936. U.S. title: The Dark Green Circle. Bobbs, 1936
The Richest Man. Collins, 1923; Knopf, 1924

SHANN, B. V. See: MARTEN CUMBERLAND, 1892-   .

SHANNON, ALASTAIR
The Black Scorpion. Bles, 1926

SHANNON, BRAD. Series character: Lefty O'Connor, in at least those marked O.
The Big Snatch. Scion, 1950
Blues for my Baby. Scion, 1950
The Body was Lonely. Scion, 1952
Bury the Guy! Scion, 1951 O
Cons on the Run. Scion, 1951
The Countless Steps. Scion, 1952
The Dead Don't Cry. Scion, 1951
Death Pulls No Punches. Scion, 1951
Don't Mention It. Scion, 1951
Fall Guy. Scion, 1950
Heads You Lose. Scion, 1952
I Wake Screaming. Scion, 1953
The Lady's for Killing. Scion, 1950
Lefty Cuts Loose. Scion, 1951 O
Lefty Hands It Out. Scion, 1951 O
Lefty O'Connor Moves In. Scion, 1950 O
Lefty Takes Over. Scion, 1952 O
Murder!—So What? Scion, 1951
Rubberneck. Scion, 1952
Sadie Swings the Blues. Scion, 1953
Some Get It. Scion, 1953
"Stir" Crazy. Scion, 1950
They Say I'm Bad. Scion, 1953
You Talk Too Much. Scion, 1951

SHANNON, CARL. Pseudonym of Wilbur Owings Hogue, 1910?-1952.
Fatal Footsteps. Phoenix, 1948; Boardman, 1951
Lady, That's My Skull. Phoenix, 1947; Boardman, 1948
Murder Me Never. Boardman, 1951

SHANNON, DELL. Pseudonym of (Barbara) Elizabeth Linington, 1921-   , q.v. Other pseudonyms: Anne Blaisdell, Lesley Egan, qq.v. Series character: Lt. Luis Mendoza, in all titles.
The Ace of Spades. Morrow, 1961; Oldbourne, 1963, as by Barbara Elizabeth Linington
Case Pending. Harper, 1960; Gollancz, 1960
Chance to Kill. Morrow, 1967; Gollancz, 1968
Coffin Corner. Morrow, 1966; Gollancz, 1967
Crime File. Morrow, 1974; Gollancz, 1975
Crime on Their Hands. Morrow, 1969; Gollancz, 1970
Death by Inches. Morrow, 1965; Gollancz, 1967
The Death-Bringers. Morrow, 1965; Gollancz, 1966
Death of a Busybody. Morrow, 1963; Oldbourne, 1963, as by Barbara Elizabeth Linington. Reprinted as by Dell Shannon: Gollancz, 1978
Deuces Wild. Morrow, 1975; Gollancz, 1975
Double Bluff. Morrow, 1963; Oldbourne, 1964, as by Barbara Elizabeth Linington. Reprinted as by Dell Shannon: Gollancz, 1978
Extra Kill. Morrow, 1962; Oldbourne, 1962, as by Barbara Elizabeth Linington
Kill with Kindness. Morrow, 1968; Gollancz, 1969
Knave of Hearts. Morrow, 1962; Oldbourne, 1963, as by Barbara Elizabeth Linington
Mark of Murder. Morrow, 1964; Gollancz, 1965
Murder with Love. Morrow, 1972; Gollancz, 1972
No Holiday for Crime. Morrow, 1973; Gollancz, 1974
Rain with Violence. Morrow, 1967; Gollancz, 1969
The Ringer. Morrow, 1971; Gollancz, 1972
Root of All Evil. Morrow, 1964; Gollancz, 1966
Schooled to Kill. Morrow, 1969; Gollancz, 1970
Spring of Violence. Morrow, 1973; Gollancz, 1974
Unexpected Death. Morrow, 1970; Gollancz, 1971
Whim to Kill. Morrow, 1971; Gollancz, 1971
With a Vengeance. Morrow, 1966; Gollancz, 1968
With Intent to Kill. Morrow, 1972; Gollancz, 1973

SHANNON, J(OHN) C.
Who Shall Condemn? and other stories. Robinson, 1894 ss, some criminous

SHANNON, JIMMY
The Devil's Passkey. Appleton, 1952

SHAPIRO, LIONEL (SEBASTIAN BERK). 1908-   .
The Sealed Verdict. Doubleday, 1947; Jarrolds, 1950
Torch for a Dark Journey. Doubleday, 1950; Jarrolds, 1951

SHAPLEIGH, MARY YALE
-Johnny Counterfeit. Hopkins, 1938

SHARD, JOHN
I am Maud Latimer. Laurie, 1941

SHARKEY, MRS. EMMA AUGUSTA BROWN. 1858-   . Pseudonym: Mrs. E. Burke Collins, q.v.

SHARKEY, JACK [JOHN MICHAEL SHARKEY]. 1931-   . Series character: George Herbert Henry, in both titles.
Death for Auld Lang Syne. Holt, 1962; Joseph, 1963
Murder, Maestro, Please. Abelard (New York & London), 1960

SHARLAND, MICHAEL
Nervestorm. Ellis, 1975

SHARMAN, MIRIAM. Pseudonym of Maisie
  Sharman Bolton, 1915- . Other
  pseudonym: Stratford Davis, q.v.
  Death Pays All Debts. Gollancz, 1965
  The Face of Danger. Gollancz, 1967
  Law of Probability. Macdonald, 1971
  Seeds of Violence. Gollancz, 1966

SHARP, ALAN. 1934- .
  Night Moves. Paperback Library, 1975;
    Corgi, 1975. (Novelization of the
    movie.)

SHARP, DAVID. Series character: Professor
  Henry Arthur Fielding, in at least
  those marked HF.
  The Code-Letter Mystery; see None of my
    Business
  Disputed Quarry. Jenkins, 1938 HF
  Elderly Gentleman Shot. Jenkins, 1939
  Everybody Suspect. Jenkins, 1939 HF
  Exit Second Murderer. Jenkins, 1940
  The Frightened Sailor. Jenkins, 1939 HF
  I, the Criminal. Benn, 1932; Houghton,
    1933 HF
  The Inconvenient Corpse. Benn, 1933 HF
  Marriage and Murder. Benn, 1934 HF
  My Particular Murder. Benn, 1931;
    Houghton, 1931 HF
  None of my Business. Benn, 1931. U.S.
    title: The Code-Letter Mystery.
    Houghton, 1932 HF
  When No Man Pursueth. Benn, 1930 HF

SHARP, GUSTAVUS
  The Confessions of an Attorney. Cor-
    nish, 1852 ss

SHARP, JACK
  The Telltale Tattoo. Street (Magnet)
  The Wall Street Swindlers. Street (Mag-
    net)

SHARP, LUKE. Pseudonym of Robert Barr,
  1850-1912, q.v.

SHARP, ROBERT (GEORGE)
  The Blonde Gangster. Fiction House,
    1935
  The Cry from the Ether. Fiction House,
    1935
  Death Comes to Rehearsal. Hutchinson,
    1951
  Death in the Headlines. Hutchinson,
    1950
  Death Rides the Rail. Fiction House,
    1947
  Horror Castle. Gray, 1936
  In the Hands of the Enemy. Fiction
    House, 1935
  -Love is King. Fiction House, 1938
  The Racketeers. Fiction House, 1948

SHARP, WILLOUGHBY
  Murder in Bermuda. Kendall, 1933; Eyre,
    1935
  Murder of the Honest Broker. Kendall,
    1934

SHATTUCK, DORA (RICHARDS). Pseudonym:
  Richard Shattuck, q.v.
  The Wailing Woman. Paperback Library,
    1973

SHATTUCK, RICHARD. Pseudonym of Dora
  (Richards) Shattuck, q.v.
  The Body In the Bridal Bed; see The
    Wedding Guest Sat on a Stone
  The Half-Haunted Saloon. Simon, 1945
  Said the Spider to the Fly. Simon, 1944
  The Snark was a Boojum. Morrow, 1941;
    Hale, 1941. Also published as: With
    Blood and Kisses. Mercury, 1954
  The Wedding Guest Sat on a Stone. Mor-
    row, 1940; Hale, 1941. Also published
    as: The Body in the Bridal Bed. Mer-
    cury, 1953

With Blood and Kisses; see The Snark
  was a Boojum

SHAW, BYNUM (GILLETTE). 1923- .
  The Nazi Hunter. Norton, 1968

SHAW, CHARLES. 1900- . Pseudonym: Bant
  Singer, q.v.

SHAW, D. B.
  Ten True Secret Service Stories. Ogil-
    vie ss

SHAW, DAVID. 1943- .
  -The Levy Caper. Macmillan, 1974

SHAW, FELICITY. 1918- . Pseudonym:
  Anne Morice, q.v.

SHAW, FRANK H(UBERT). 1878- .
  Atlantic Murder. Mathews, 1932;
    McBride, 1933

SHAW, HERBERT. See also: ANTHONY ARM-
  STRONG.
  The Man Who Lived Twice. Columbine,
    1939

SHAW, JOSEPH T(HOMPSON). 1874-1952.
  Blood on the Curb. Dodge, 1936
  Danger Ahead. Mohawk, 1932
  Derelict. Knopf, 1930
  It Happened at the Lake. Dodd, 1937

SHAW, ROBIN. 1936- .
  Running. Putnam, 1973; Gollancz, 1974

SHAW, STANLEY GORDON. 1884-1938?
  The Secret of the Monastery. Amalgama-
    ted, 1928. (Sexton Blake.)

SHAW, STOCKER
  "Eblis." Hornsey Journal, 1933

SHAW, W. J.
  Old Anthony's Secret. [Author], 1888
  Solomon's Story. Thomson, 1880

SHAW, WILENE
  -The Fear and the Guilt. Ace, 1954
  -Heat Lightning. Ace, 1954
  -The Mating Call. Ace, 1954
  -Out for Kicks. Ace, 1959
  -See How They Run. Ace, 1957

SHAY, FRANK. 1888-1954. Series character:
  Dan (DeeDee) Doner, in both titles.
  The Charming Murder. Macaulay, 1930
  Murder on Cape Cod. Macaulay, 1931

SHAYNE, GORDON. Pseudonym of Bevis Winter, 1918- , q.v. Other pseudonyms: Al Bocca, Peter Cagney, qq.v.
  And So to Death. Jasmit, 1952
  Ticket to Eternity. Jasmit, 1954

SHEA, JOHN D.
  A Private Detective: The Marvelous
    Career of a Notorious Criminal.
    Laird, 1889

SHEAHAN, K. M.
  -An Artist in Crime. Jenkins, 1936
  Dangerous Men. Jenkins, 1935
  The Stormberg Jewel Case. Jenkins, 1931

SHEARING, JOSEPH. Pseudonym of Gabrielle
  Margaret Vere Campbell Long, 1886-
  1952. Other pseudonyms: Marjorie
  Bowen, George R. Preedy, qq.v., Mar-
  garet Campbell.
  The Abode of Love. Hutchinson, 1945
  Airing in a Closed Carriage. Hutchin-
    son, 1943; Harper, 1943

Album Leaf. Heinemann, 1933. U.S.
  title: The Spider in the Cup. Smith,
  1934. Reprinted in the U.S. as by
  Margaret Campbell: Signet, 1975
Aunt Beardie. Hutchinson, 1940; Har-
  rison-Hilton, 1940
Blanche Fury; or, Fury's Ape. Heine-
  mann, 1939; Harrison-Hilton, 1939
The Crime of Laura Sarelle; see Laura
  Sarelle
The Fetch. Hutchinson, 1942. U.S.
  title: The Spectral Bride. Smith,
  1942. Reprinted in the U.S. under the
  British title as by Margaret Camp-
  bell: Signet, 1975
For Her to See. Hutchinson, 1947. U.S.
  title: So Evil My Love. Harper, 1947
Forget-Me-Not. Heinemann, 1932. U.S.
  title: Lucile Clery. Harper, 1932.
  Reprinted as: The Strange Case of
  Lucile Clery. World, 1944
The Golden Violet. Heinemann, 1936;
  Smith, 1941
The Heiress of Frascati; see Within the
  Bubble
The Lady and the Arsenic. Heinemann,
  1937; Smith, 1944
Laura Sarelle. Hutchinson, 1940. U.S.
  title: The Crime of Laura Sarelle.
  Smith, 1941
Lucile Clery; see Forget-Me-Not
Mignonette. Heinemann, 1949; Harper,
  1948
Moss Rose. Heinemann, 1934; Smith &
  Haas, 1935
Night's Dark Secret, as by Margaret
  Campbell. Signet, 1975. (Original
  title? Original byline?)
Orange Blossoms. Heinemann, 1938
So Evil My Love; see For Her to See
The Spectral Bride; see The Fetch
The Spider in the Cup; see Album Leaf
The Strange Case of Lucile Clery; see
  Forget-Me-Not
To Bed at Noon. Heinemann, 1951
Within the Bubble. Heinemann, 1950.
  U.S. title: The Heiress of Frascati.
  Berkley, 1966

SHECKLEY, ROBERT. 1928- . Series char-
  acter: Stephen Dain = SD.
  Calibre .50. Bantam, 1961 SD
  Dead Run. Bantam, 1961 SD
  The Game of X. Delacorte, 1965; Cape,
    1966
  Live Gold. Bantam, 1962 SD
  The Man in the Water. Regency, 1962
  The Tenth Victim. Ballantine, 1965;
    Mayflower, 1966. (Novelization of the
    movie.)
  Time Limit. Bantam, 1967; New English
    Library pb, 1967 SD
  White Death. Bantam, 1963 SD

SHEDD, GEORGE C(LIFFORD). 1877-1937.
  Gangster War on Bar "G". Swan, 1949
  -In the Shadow of the Hills. Macaulay,
    1919
  The Invisible Enemy. Macaulay, 1918
  The Isle of Strife. Small, 1912
  The Lady of Mystery House. Macaulay,
    1917; Gardner, 1920
  -The Passport Invisible. Doran, 1918
  -Those Who Walk in Darkness. Doran, 1917

SHEDD, MARGARET (COCHRAN). 1900- .
  Run. Doubleday, 1956; Gollancz, 1956

SHEEHAN, PERLEY POORE. 1875-1943.
  The House with a Bad Name. Boni, 1920;
    Brentano's (London), 1923
  Three Sevens. Chelsea, 1927
  The Whispering Chorus. Watt, 1927;
    Benn, 1928

SHEEN, GEORGE
  Assignment Greece. Digit, 1958
  -Extermination Camp. Digit, 1958

-Malayan Story. Digit, 1958
The Traitor. Digit, 1958

SHEERS, JAMES C.
The Counterfeit Courier. Dell, 1961

SHEFLER, HARRY F.
Devil Take the Hindmost. Exposition, 1955

SHELDON, MRS. GEORGIE. Pseudonym of Sarah Elizabeth Forbush Downs, 1843-   .
Max. Street, 1892
The Shadow of a Crime; see Trixy
Trixy; or, The Shadow of a Crime. Burt, 1888. British title: The Shadow of a Crime. Aldine, 1897
The Welfleet Mystery. Red Lion, 1901. (U.S. title?)

SHELDON, GILBERT. 1870-   . Pseudonym: James Colwall, q.v.

SHELDON, RICHARD
Harsh Evidence. Hutchinson, 1950
Poor Prisoner's Defense. Hutchinson, 1949; Simon, 1949

SHELDON, SIDNEY. 1917-   .
The Naked Face. Morrow, 1970; Hodder, 1971
The Other Side of Midnight. Morrow, 1974; Hodder, 1974

SHELDON, WALTER J. 1917-   .
The Blue Kimono Kill. GM, 1965
Devil's Box. Lancer, 1968
Gold Bait. GM, 1973
The House of Happy Mayhem. Banner, 1967
The Man Who Paid His Way. Lippincott, 1955; Corgi, 1957
The Red Flower Kill. GM, 1971
The Yellow Music Kill. GM, 1974

SHELLABARGER, SAMUEL. 1888-1954. Pseudonyms: John Esteven, Peter Loring, qq.v.

SHELLEY, M(ARY) W(OLLSTONECRAFT GODWIN). 1797-1851.
Frankenstein. Lackington, 1818; Daggers, 1845

SHELLEY, SIDNEY (JOSEPH). 1921-   .
-The Bay of Deception. Gibbs, 1964
Bowmanville Break. Delacorte, 1968. Also published as: The Mackenzie Break. Dell, 1971; Sphere, 1971
Francine. Belmont, 1963
The Mackenzie Break; see Bowmanville Break

SHENKIN, ELIZABETH (SHOEMAKER).   -1975.
Brownstone Gothic. Holt, 1961
Midsummer's Nightmare. Rinehart, 1960; Ward, 1961

SHEPHERD, DONALD LEE. 1932-   . Pseudonym: Barbara Keverne, q.v.

SHEPHERD, ERIC. 1892-   . Series characters: The Nuns and others of Harrington Convent, in both titles.
More Murder in a Nunnery. Sheed, 1954
Murder in a Nunnery. Sheed, 1940

SHEPHERD, FLORENCE. Joint pseudonym with John Marsh, 1907-   , q.v.: Harrington Hastings, q.v.

SHEPHERD, JOAN. Pseudonym of B. J. Buchanan.
The Girl on the Left Bank. Washburn, 1953
Tender is the Knife. Washburn, 1956

SHEPHERD, JOHN. Pseudonym of W(illis) T(odhunter) Ballard, 1903-   , q.v. Other pseudonyms: P. D. Ballard, Neil MacNeil, qq.v. Joint pseudonym with Norbert Davis, q.v.: Harrison Hunt, q.v. Series character (continued from the W. T. Ballard byline): Bill Lennox = BL.
Lights, Camera, Murder. Belmont, 1960 BL

SHEPHERD, L. P.
Cape House. Dell, 1974

SHEPHERD, MICHAEL. Pseudonym.
The Road to Gandolfo. Dial, 1975; Hart-Davis, 1976

SHEPHERD, NEAL. Pseudonym of Nigel Morland, 1905-   , q.v. Other pseudonyms: Mary Dane, John Donavan, Norman Forrest, Roger Garnett, Vincent McCall, qq.v. Series character: Chief Inspector Michael "Napper" Tandy, in all titles.
Death Flies Low. Constable, 1938
Death Rides Swiftly. Constable, 1939
Death Walks Softly. Constable, 1938
Exit to Music. Constable, 1940

SHER, JACK
The Cold Companion. Rinehart, 1948

SHERARD, R(OBERT) H(ARBOROUGH). 1861-   .
-After the Fault. Sisley's, 1906
Agatha's Quest. Trischler, 1890; Minerva, 1890
-The American Marquis. Simpkin, 1888
-A Bartered Honour. Remington, 1883
By Right Not Law. Cassell (London & New York), 1891
-The Ghost's Revenge, and other stories of modern Paris. Digby, 1902 ss
-The Iron Cross. Pearson, 1897
-Jacob Niemand. Ward, 1895
-Rogues. Chatto, 1889
-The Typewritten Letter. Trischler, 1891
An Underground Mystery. Digby, 1903

SHERATON, NEIL. Pseudonym of Norman Edward Mace Smith, 1914-   .
Cairo Ring. Hale, 1958

SHERIDAN, ELSIE LEE. Pseudonym: Elsie Lee, q.v.

SHERIDAN, JUANITA. See also: (HELEN) DOROTHY DUDLEY, 1895-   . Series characters: Lily Wu and Janice Cameron, in all titles.
The Chinese Chop. Doubleday, 1949; Barker, 1951
The Kahuna Killer. Doubleday, 1951; Heinemann, 1955
The Mamo Murders. Doubleday, 1952. British title: While the Coffin Waited. Heinemann, 1953
The Waikiki Widow. Doubleday, 1953
While the Coffin Waited; see The Mamo Murders

SHERIDAN, LEE
The Pit and the Pendulum. Lancer, 1961. (Novelization of the movie.)

SHERIDAN, SOL(OMON) N(EIL). 1859-   .
The Typhoon's Secret. Doubleday, 1920

SHERIDAN, WILFRED
The Five Brains. Jarrolds, 1924
Tommy Weston, Adventuress. Jarrolds, 1925

SHERLOCK, A. B.
-Galleon Treasure. Sheldon, 1929
Red Darkness. Hurst, 1940
-The Sea Raiders. Sheldon, 1927
The Yellow Beetle. Sheldon, 1931

SHERLOCK, JOHN. 1932-   .
The Ordeal of Major Grigsby. Morrow, 1964; Hutchinson, 1964

SHERMAN, CHARLOTTE A. Pseudonym of Jory Tecumseh Sherman, 1932-   .
The Shuttered Room. Major, 1975

SHERMAN, JORY TECUMSEH. 1932-   . Pseudonym: Charlotte A. Sherman, q.v.

SHERMAN, ROBIN
Jigsaw. Pinnacle, 1973

SHERMAN, ROGER
Beware of the Cat. Apollo, 1972

SHERRIFF, R(OBERT) C(EDRIC). 1896-   .
Home at Seven. Gollancz, 1951. (3-act play.)
Shred of Evidence. French (London), 1961. (3-act play.)

SHERRING, A(LBERT) W(ILLIAM HENRY)
The Big Haul. Hale, 1962
Double Exposure. Hale, 1965
Night of Vengeance. Hale, 1960
The Pay Off. Hale, 1961
The Tip Off. Hale, 1959

SHERRY, EDNA.   -1967. See also: MILTON HERBERT GROPPER, 1897-1955.
Backfire. Dodd, 1956; Hodder, 1957. Also published as: Murder at Nightfall. Dell, 1957
Call the Witness. Dodd, 1961; Hodder, 1962
The Defense Does Not Rest. Dodd, 1959; Hodder, 1960
Girl Missing. Dodd, 1962; Hodder, 1963
Murder at Nightfall; see Backfire
No Questions Asked. Dodd, 1949; Hodder, 1950
She Asked for Murder; see Tears for Jessie Hewitt
Strictly a Loser. Dodd, 1965; Hodder, 1966
Sudden Fear. Dodd, 1948; Hodder, 1949
The Survival of the Fittest. Dodd, 1960; Hodder, 1961
Tears for Jessie Hewitt. Dodd, 1958; Hodder, 1959. Also published as: She Asked for Murder. Dell, 1959

SHERRY, JOHN
The Loring Affair. PB, 1964

SHERWOOD, EVELYN
A Candidate for Danger. Melrose, 1910

SHERWOOD, JOHN (HERMAN MULSO). 1913-   . Series character: Charles Blessington, in at least those marked CB.
Ambush for Anatol. Hodder, 1952; Doubleday, 1952. Also published as: Murder of a Mistress. Mercury, 1954 CB
Disappearance of Dr. Bruderstein. Hodder, 1949. U.S. title: Dr. Bruderstein Vanishes. Doubleday, 1949 CB
Dr. Bruderstein Vanishes; see Disappearance of Dr. Bruderstein
The Half Hunter. Gollancz, 1961. U.S. title: The Sleuth and the Liar. Doubleday, 1961
Mr. Blessington's Imperialist Plot; see Mr. Blessington's Plot
Mr. Blessington's Plot. Hodder, 1951. U.S. title: Mr. Blessington's Imperialist Plot. Doubleday, 1951 CB
Murder of a Mistress; see Ambush for Anatol
The Sleuth and the Liar; see The Half Hunter

Two Died in Singapore. Hodder, 1954 CB
Undiplomatic Exit. Hodder, 1958;
  Doubleday, 1958
Vote Against Poison. Hodder, 1956 CB

SHIEL, M(ATTHEW) P(HIPPS). 1865-1947.
  Sometime joint pseudonym with Louis
  Tracy, 1863-1928, q.v.: Gordon
  Holmes, q.v.
The Best Short Stories of M. P. Shiel.
  Gollancz, 1948 ss
The Black Box. Richards, 1931; Vanguard, 1930
Dr. Krasinski's Secret. Jarrolds, 1930;
  Vanguard, 1929
-The Dragon. Richards, 1913; Clode,
  1941. Revised edition: The Yellow
  Peril. Gollancz, 1929
-The Evil That Men Do. Ward, 1904
-Here Comes the Lady. Richards, 1928 ss
How the Old Woman Got Home. Richards,
  1927; Vanguard, 1928
-The Last Miracle. Laurie, 1906
-The Lost Viol. Clode, 1905; Ward, 1908
-The Pale Ape. Laurie, 1911 ss
Prince Zaleski. Lane, 1895; Roberts,
  1895 ss
The Rajah's Sapphire. Ward, 1896
-Shapes in the Fire. Lane, 1896;
  Roberts, 1896 ss
Unto the Third Generation. Chatto, 1903
The Weird o' It. Richards, 1902
-Xelucha and Others. Arkham, 1975 ss
-The Yellow Danger. Richards, 1898;
  Fenno, 1899
The Yellow Peril; see The Dragon

SHILL, J.
Murder in Paradise. Blackfriars, 1946

SHIMER, R(UTH) H.
The Correspondent. Popular Library,
  1974
The Cricket Cage. Harper, 1975; Prior,
  1977
Squaw Point. Harper, 1972

SHIPPEY, LEE. 1884- .
The Girl Who Wanted Experience. Houghton, 1937
Where Nothing Ever Happens. Houghton,
  1935 ss, some criminous

SHIPWAY, GEORGE. 1908- .
The Chilean Club. Davies, 1971. U.S.
  title: The Yellow Room. Doubleday,
  1971

SHIVELEY, THORNTON. Pseudonym: Thorne
  Lee, q.v.

SHIVELLEY, ANGELA
Dread of Night. Paperback Library, 1966

SHOLL, ANNA McCLURE
The Mystery of Lostland Academy. Federation, 1925
This Way Out. Hearst's, 1915 ss
The Unclaimed Letter. Dorrance, 1921

SHORE, JULIAN
Rattle His Bones. Morrow, 1941

SHORE, NORMAN
Hong Kong Nightstop. Hale, 1973

SHORE, P. R.
The Bolt. Methuen, 1929; Dutton, 1929
The Death Film. Methuen, 1932

SHORE, VIOLA BROTHERS. 1895- . Series
  characters: Colin Keats and Gwynn
  Leith, in both titles.
The Beauty-Mask Murder. Smith, 1930.
  British title: The Beauty-Mask Mystery. Hamilton, 1932
The Beauty-Mask Mystery; see The
  Beauty-Mask Murder

Murder on the Glass Floor. Smith, 1932;
  Harrap, 1933

SHORT, (CHARLES) CHRISTOPHER (DUDLEY)
The Big Cat. Chapman, 1962; Dodd, 1965
The Black Room. Cape, 1964; Dodd, 1966
The Blue-Eyed Boy. Stacey, 1972; Dodd,
  1966
Dark Lantern. Chapman, 1962; Scribner,
  1961. Also published as: The Swastika
  Rises. New English Library pb, 1968
The Naked Skier. Stacey, 1972
The Swastika Rises; see Dark Lantern

SHORT, ERNEST (HENRY), 1875-1959, and
  ARTHUR COMPTON-RICKETT, 1869-1937,
  q.v. For Compton-Rickett, see also:
  PATRICK LEYTON.
The Hope Strange Mystery. Jenkins, 1927

SHORT, LUKE. Pseudonym of Frederick Dilley Glidden, 1908-1975.
Barren Land Murders. GM, 1951; Muller,
  1954. Also published as: Barren Land
  Showdown. GM, 1957

SHORTELL, L(ESLIE) T.
French for Trouble. Rich, 1947
The Hounds are Restless Tonight. Rich,
  1949
-People Apart. Rich, 1944

SHORTT, CHARLES RUSHTON. 1904- . Pseudonym: Charles Rushton, q.v.

SHORTT, VERE (DAWSON), 1872-1915, and
  FRANCES (H. SHORTT) MATHEWS
-The Rod of the Snake. Lane (London &
  New York), 1917

SHOUBRIDGE, DONALD
-The Stories of Donald Shoubridge. Pendulum, 1945 ss
Yard Lengths. Pendulum, 1946 ss

SHRIBER, IONE SANDBERG. 1911- . Series
  character: Bill Grady = BG.
As Long as I Live. Rinehart, 1947
A Body for Bill. Farrar, 1942; Nicholson, 1946 BG
The Dark Arbor. Farrar, 1940; Nicholson, 1945 BG
Family Affair. Farrar, 1941 BG
Head Over Heels in Murder. Farrar, 1940
  BG
Invitation to Murder. Farrar, 1943;
  Nicholson, 1946 BG
The Last Straw. Rinehart, 1946 BG
Murder Well Done. Farrar, 1941 BG
Never Say Die. Rinehart, 1950
Pattern for Murder. Farrar, 1944 BG
Ready or Not. Rinehart, 1953; Boardman,
  1954

SHROYER, FREDERICK (BENJAMIN). 1916- .
It Happened in Wayland; see Wayland 13
There None Embrace. Ward, 1966; Nash,
  1974
Tower of Hate; see Wayland 13
Wayland 13. Quadriga, 1962. U.S. title:
  It Happened in Wayland. Reynal, 1963.
  Also published as: Tower of Hate.
  Corgi, 1963. Revised edition: Welcome
  back to Wayland. Major, 1978
Welcome Back to Wayland; see Wayland 13

SHUB, JOYCE L.
Moscow by Nightmare. Coward, 1973; Collins, 1973

SHUBAEL. Pseudonym of Jennie Bouton
  Purdy.
The Dark Stain. Abbey, 1903

SHUBIN, SEYMOUR. 1921- .
-Anyone's My Name. Simon, 1953. British
  title: A Stranger to Myself. Benn,
  1954

SHULMAN, IRVING. 1913- .
The Amboy Dukes. Doubleday, 1947
The Big Brokers. Dial, 1951
-Calibre. Popular Library, 1957
Children of the Dark. Holt, 1956
Cry Tough. Dial, 1949
The Notorious Landlady. GM, 1962. (Novelization of the movie.)
Platinum High School. Bantam, 1960.
  (Novelization of the movie.)
-The Roots of Fury, with Peggy Bristol.
  Doubleday, 1961; Mayflower, 1967
-The Short End of the Stick, and other
  stories. Doubleday, 1959 ss

SHULMAN, MILTON. 1913- .
Kill 3. Random, 1967; Collins, 1967

SHULMAN, SANDRA (DAWN). 1944- .
The Bride of Devil's Leap. Paperback
  Library, 1968
Castlecliff. Paperback Library, 1967
The Daughters of Astaroth. Paperback
  Library, 1968
The Lady of Arlac. Paperback Library,
  1969
The Menacing Darkness. Paperback Library, 1966
The Prisoner of Garve. Paperback Library, 1970
The Temptress. Paperback Library, 1972

SHURA, MARY FRANCIS. Pseudonym: Mary
  Craig, q.v.

SHURMAN, IDA
Death Beats the Band. Phoenix, 1943

SHUTE, NEVIL. Pseudonym of Nevil Shute
  Norway. 1899-1960.
So Disdained. Cassell, 1928. U.S.
  title: The Mysterious Aviator.
  Houghton, 1928

SHUTE, WALTER.   -ca.1940. Pseudonym:
  Walter Edwards, q.v. All titles were
  published by Amalgamated Press and
  feature Sexton Blake.
The Affair of the Rival Cinema Kings.
  1928
The Case of the Discharged P.C. 1929
The Fatal Number. 1929
The Mystery of Merlyn Mansions. 1929
The Mystery of the Uninvited Guest.
  1929
The "Talkie" Murder Mystery. 1930

SIBLEY, CELESTINE
The Malignant Heart. Doubleday, 1958;
  Gollancz, 1958

SIBLEY, PATRICIA
High Walk to Wandlemere. Hodder, 1973;
  Dell, 1974

SIBLY, JOHN. 1920- .
Girl on the Run. Cape, 1958

SIDDALL, ROGER B(EARD). 1896- .
Travers, A Mystery Story. Beard, 1952

SIDDLE, CHARLES. 1892- . Joint pseudonym with Frederick Peel, 1888- :
  Rufus Slingsby, q.v.

SIDEMAN, ABNER
Murder on Both Sides. Charlton, 1945

SIEGAL, BENJAMIN. 1914- .
The Jurors. Delacorte, 1973; Hale, 1975

374 / Siegel, Doris

SIEGEL, DORIS. Pseudonym: Susan Wells, q.v.
How Still My Love. Mill, 1957; Gollancz, 1958

SIEGEL, JACK [JACOB]. 1913- .
Dawn at Kahlenberg. Pyramid, 1966
The Ruby. Pyramid, 1972

SIEVEKING, LANCE(LOT DE GIBERNE). 1896- .
Stampede. Cayme, 1924; Brentano's, 1928
A Tomb with a View. Faber, 1950
The Ultimate Island. Routledge, 1925

SIGEL, EFREM
The Kermanshah Transfer. Macmillan, 1973

SILBERRAD, UNA L(UCY). 1872- .
-The Escape of Andrew Cole. Hutchinson, 1941
-The Lyndwood Affair. Hutchinson, 1918
The Mystery of Barnard Hanson. Hutchinson, 1915
-The Strange Story in The Falconer Papers. Hutchinson, 1934

SILBERSTANG, EDWIN. 1930- .
Losers, Weepers. Doubleday, 1975
Rapt in Glory. PB, 1964

SILLER, VAN. Pseudonym of Hilda van Siller. Series characters: Richard Massey, in at least those marked RM; Allan Stewart, in at least those marked AS.
Bermuda Murder. Hammond, 1956
The Biltmore Call. Ward, 1967 AS
A Complete Stranger. Doubleday, 1965; Ward, 1966 AS
The Curtain Between. Doubleday, 1947; Jarrolds, 1949. Also published as: Fatal Bride. Mercury, 1948 RM
Deception of Death; see The Old Friend
Echo of a Bomb. Doubleday, 1943; Jarrolds, 1944 RM
Fatal Bride; see The Curtain Between
Fatal Lover; see The Last Resort
Good Night, Ladies. Doubleday, 1943; Jarrolds, 1945
The Hell with Elaine. Doubleday, 1974; Hale, 1975
It had to be You. Doubleday, 1970. British title (?): Whisper of Death. Hale, 1971
The Last Resort. Lippincott, 1951; Hammond, 1954. Also published as: Fatal Lover. Bestseller, 1953
The Lonely Breeze. Doubleday, 1965. British title: The Murders at Hibiscus Key. Hammond, 1965
The Mood for Murder. Doubleday, 1966; Ward, 1967 AS
Murder is my Business. Hammond, 1957
The Murders at Hibiscus Key; see The Lonely Breeze
The Old Friend. Doubleday, 1973. British title (?): Deception of Death. Hale, 1974
One Alone. Doubleday, 1946; Jarrolds, 1948
Paul's Apartment. Doubleday, 1948; Hammond, 1953
The Red Geranium. Hammond, 1966
The Road. Hammond, 1960
Somber Memory. Doubleday, 1945; Jarrolds, 1946
Sudden Storm. Jenkins, 1968
Under a Cloud. Doubleday, 1944; Jarrolds, 1946
The Watchers. Doubleday, 1969; Hale, 1969
Whisper of Death; see It had to be You
The Widower. Doubleday, 1958; Hammond, 1959

SILLIMAN, VERA
Haunted Wood Hollow. Commercial, 1928

SILLIPHANT, STIRLING. See also: CHARLES EINSTEIN.
The Slender Thread. Signet, 1966. (Novelization of the movie.)

SILVER, R. NORMAN
A Daughter of Mystery. Jarrolds, 1901; Page, 1901
A Double Mask. Jarrolds, 1918
The Golden Dwarf. Jarrolds, 1903; Page, 1903
Hate, the Destroyer. Ward, 1900
-Held Apart. Ward, 1905

SILVERMAN, MARGUERITE R(UTH). Series character: Inspector Christopher Adrian, in at least those marked CA.
9 had No Alibi. Nicholson, 1951 CA
The Vet It was That Died. Nicholson, 1945 CA
Who Should Have Died? Nicholson, 1948

SILVERWOOD, ROGER. 1932- .
Deadly Daffodils. Hale, 1970
Dying for a Drink. Hale, 1971
The Illegitimate Spy. Hale, 1972

SIMENON. GEORGES. 1903- . Pseudonym: Victor Kosta. This entry is in two parts: the first, the Jules Maigret series; the second, the non-series novels, many if not all of which are criminous.
At the Gai-Moulin. (Included in the twosome Maigret Abroad, q.v.) Routledge, 1940; Harcourt, 1940. (Translation of La Danseuse du Gai-Moulin. Paris, 1931.)
A Battle of Nerves. (Included in the twosome The Patience of Maigret, q.v.) Routledge, 1939; Harcourt, 1940. (Translation of La Tete d'un Homme. Paris, 1931.)
The Crime at Lock 14. (Included in Britain in the twosome Triumph of Inspector Maigret, q.v. In the U.S., published in a twosome with The Shadow in the Courtyard, q.v.) Hurst, 1934; Covici, 1934. Also published as: Maigret Meets a Milord. Penguin, 1963. (Translation of Le Charretier de la 'Providence'. Paris, 1931.)
A Crime in Holland. (Included in the twosome Maigret Abroad, q.v.) Routledge, 1940; Harcourt, 1940. (Translation of Un Crime en Hollande. Paris, 1931.)
The Crime of Inspector Maigret. (Included in Britain in the twosome Introducing Inspector Maigret, q.v.; published as a separate volume in the U.S.) Hurst, 1933; Covici, 1932. Also published as: Maigret and the Hundred Gibbets. Penguin, 1963. (Translation of Le Pendu de St.-Pholien. Paris, 1931.)
The Crossroad Murders. (Included in Britain in the twosome Inspector Maigret Investigates, q.v.; published as a separate volume in the U.S.) Hurst, 1933; Covici, 1933. Also published as: Maigret at the Crossroads. Penguin, 1963. (Translation of La Nuit du Carrefour. Paris, 1931.)
Death of a Harbourmaster. (Included in the twosome Maigret and Monsieur Labbe, q.v.) Routledge, 1941; Harcourt, 1942. (Translation of Le Port des Brumes. Paris, 1932.)

The Death of Monsieur Gallet. (Included in Britain in the twosome Introducing Inspector Maigret, q.v.; published as a separate volume in the U.S.) Hurst, 1933; Covici, 1932. Also published as: Maigret Stonewalled. Penguin, 1963. (Translation of M. Gallet Decede. Paris, 1931.)
A Face for a Clue. (Included in the twosome The Patience of Maigret, q.v.) Routledge, 1939; Harcourt, 1940. (Translation of Le Chien Jaune. Paris, 1931.)
Five Times Maigret; see A Maigret Omnibus
The Flemish Shop. (Included in the twosome Maigret to the Rescue, q.v.) Routledge, 1940; Harcourt, 1941. (Translation of Chez les Flamands. Paris, 1932.)
The Guinguette by the Seine. (Included in the twosome Maigret to the Rescue, q.v.) Routledge, 1940; Harcourt, 1941. (Translation of La Guinguette a Deux Sous. Paris, 1932.)
Inspector Maigret and the Burglar's Wife; see Maigret and the Burglar's Wife
Inspector Maigret and the Dead Girl; see Maigret and the Dead Girl
Inspector Maigret and the Killers; see Maigret and the Gangsters
Inspector Maigret and the Strangled Stripper; see Maigret in Montmartre
Inspector Maigret in New York's Underworld; see Maigret in New York's Underworld
Inspector Maigret Investigates. Hurst, 1933. (A twosome consisting of The Crossroad Murders and The Strange Case of Peter the Lett, qq.v.)
Introducing Inspector Maigret. Hurst, 1933. (A twosome consisting of The Death of Monsieur Gallet and The Crime of Inspector Maigret, qq.v.)
Liberty Bar. (Included in the twosome Maigret Travels South, q.v.) Routledge, 1940; Harcourt, 1940. (Translation of Liberty Bar. Paris, 1932.)
The Lock at Charenton. (Included in the twosome Maigret Sits It Out, q.v.) Routledge, 1941; Harcourt, 1941. (Translation of L'Ecluse No. 1. Paris, 1933.)
Madame Maigret's Friend. H. Hamilton, 1960. U.S. title: Madame Maigret's Own Case. Doubleday, 1959. (Translation of L'Amie de Mme. Maigret. Paris, 1950.)
Madame Maigret's Own Case; see Madame Maigret's Friend
The Madman of Bergerac. (Included in the twosome Maigret Travels South, q.v.) Routledge, 1940; Harcourt, 1940. (Translation of Le Fou de Bergerac. Paris, 1932.)
Maigret Abroad. Routledge, 1940; Harcourt, 1940. (A twosome consisting of A Crime in Holland and At the Gai-Moulin, qq.v.)
Maigret Afraid. H. Hamilton, 1961. (Translation of Maigret a Peur. Paris, 1953.)
Maigret and Monsieur Charles. H. Hamilton, 1973. (Translation of Maigret et Monsieur Charles. Paris, 1972.)
Maigret and Monsieur Labbe. Routledge, 1941; Harcourt, 1942. (A twosome consisting of Death of a Harbourmaster, q.v., and The Man from Everywhere, a non-Maigret story listed in Part II hereof.)
Maigret and the Bum; see Maigret and the Dosser

Maigret and the Burglar's Wife. H. Hamilton, 1955. U.S. title: Inspector Maigret and the Burglar's Wife. Doubleday, 1956. (Translation of Maigret et la Grande Perche. Paris, 1951.)

Maigret and the Calame Report; see Maigret and the Minister

Maigret and the Dead Girl. H. Hamilton, 1955. U.S. title: Inspector Maigret and the Dead Girl. Doubleday, 1955. Also published as: Maigret and the Young Girl, in: The Second Maigret Omnibus. H. Hamilton, 1964; Harcourt, 1965, as Maigret Cinq. (Translation of Maigret et la Jeune Morte. Paris, 1954.)

Maigret and the Dosser. H. Hamilton, 1973. U.S. title: Maigret and the Bum. Harcourt, 1974. (Translation of Maigret et le Clochard. Paris, 1963.)

Maigret and the Enigmatic Lett; see The Strange Case of Peter the Lett

Maigret and the Flea. H. Hamilton, 1972. U.S. title: Maigret and the Informer. Harcourt, 1973. (Translation of Maigret et l'Indicateur. Paris, 1971.)

Maigret and the Gangsters. H. Hamilton, 1974. U.S. title: Inspector Maigret and the Killers. Doubleday, 1954. (Translation of Maigret, Lognon et les Gangsters. Paris, 1952.)

Maigret and the Headless Corpse. H. Hamilton, 1967; Harcourt, 1968. (Translation of Maigret et le Corps sans Tete. Paris, 1955.)

Maigret and the Hundred Gibbets; see The Crime of Inspector Maigret

Maigret and the Informer; see Maigret and the Flea

Maigret and the Killer. H. Hamilton, 1971; Harcourt, 1971. (Translation of Maigret et le Tueur. Paris, 1969.)

Maigret and the Lazy Burglar. (Published as a separate volume in Britain; included in the U.S. in the collection A Maigret Trio, q.v.) H. Hamilton, 1963; Harcourt, 1973. (Translation of Maigret et le Voleur Paresseux. Paris, 1961.)

Maigret and the Loner. H. Hamilton, 1975; Harcourt, 1975. (Translation of Maigret et l'Homme Tout Seul. Paris, 1971.)

Maigret and the Madwoman. H. Hamilton, 1972; Harcourt, 1972. (Translation of La Folle de Maigret. Paris, 1970.)

Maigret and the Man on the Bench; see Maigret and the Man on the Boulevard

Maigret and the Man on the Boulevard. H. Hamilton, 1975. U.S. title: Maigret and the Man on the Bench. Harcourt, 1975. (Translation of Maigret et l'Homme du Banc. Paris, 1953.)

Maigret and the Millionaires. H. Hamilton, 1974; Harcourt, 1974. (Translation of Maigret Voyage. Paris, 1958.)

Maigret and the Minister. H. Hamilton, 1969. U.S. title: Maigret and the Calame Report. Harcourt, 1969. (Translation of Maigret chez le Ministre. Paris, 1955.)

Maigret and the Nahour Case. H. Hamilton, 1967. (Translation of Maigret et l'Affaire Nahour. Paris, 1967.)

Maigret and the Old Lady. (Published as a separate volume in Britain; included in the U.S. in the collection Maigret Cinq, q.v.) H. Hamilton, 1958; Harcourt, 1965. (Translation of Maigret et la Vieille Dame. Paris, 1950.)

Maigret and the Reluctant Witnesses. (Published as a separate volume in Britain; included in the U.S. in the twosome Versus Inspector Maigret, q.v.) H. Hamilton, 1959; Doubleday, 1960. (Translation of Maigret et la Temoins Recalcitrants. Paris, 1959.)

Maigret and the Saturday Caller. H. Hamilton, 1964; White Lion, 1975. (Translation of Maigret et le Client du Samedi. Paris, 1962.)

Maigret and the Wine Merchant. H. Hamilton, 1971; Harcourt, 1971. (Translation of Maigret et le Marchand de Vin. Paris, 1970.)

Maigret and the Young Girl; see Maigret and the Dead Girl

Maigret at the Crossroads; see The Crossroad Murders

Maigret Cinq; see The Second Maigret Omnibus

Maigret Goes Home; see The Saint-Fiacre Affair

Maigret Goes to School. (Published as a separate volume in Britain; included in the U.S. in the collection Five Times Maigret, q.v.) H. Hamilton, 1957; Harcourt, 1964. (Translation of Maigret a l'Ecole. Paris, 1954.)

Maigret has Doubts. H. Hamilton, 1968. (Translation of Une Confidence de Maigret. Paris, 1959.)

Maigret has Scruples. (Published as a separate volume in Britain; included in the U.S. in the twosome Versus Inspector Maigret, q.v.) H. Hamilton, 1959; Doubleday, 1960. (Translation of Les Scrupules de Maigret. Paris, 1958.)

Maigret Hesitates. H. Hamilton, 1970; Harcourt, 1970. (Translation of Maigret Hesite. Paris, 1968.)

Maigret in Court. H. Hamilton, 1961. (Translation of Maigret aux Assises. Paris, 1960.)

Maigret in Montmartre. (Included in Britain in the twosome Maigret Right and Wrong, q.v.) H. Hamilton, 1954. U.S. title: Inspector Maigret and the Strangled Stripper. Doubleday, 1954. (Translation of Maigret au 'Picratt's'. Paris, 1951.)

Maigret in New York's Underworld. Doubleday, 1955. Also published as: Inspector Maigret in New York's Underworld. Signet, 1956. (Translation of Maigret a New-York. Paris, 1947.)

Maigret in Society. (Published as a separate volume in Britain; included in the U.S. in the collection A Maigret Trio, q.v.) H. Hamilton, 1962; Harcourt, 1973. (Translation of Maigret et les Vieillards. Paris, 1960.)

Maigret in Vichy; see Maigret Takes the Waters

Maigret Keeps a Rendezvous. Routledge, 1940; Harcourt, 1941. (A twosome consisting of The Sailors' Rendezvous and The Saint-Fiacre Affair, qq.v.)

Maigret Loses His Temper. H. Hamilton, 1965; Harcourt, 1974. (Translation of La Colere de Maigret. Paris, 1963.)

Maigret Meets a Milord; see The Crime at Lock 14

Maigret Mystified; see The Shadow in the Courtyard

A Maigret Omnibus. H. Hamilton, 1962. U.S. title: Five Times Maigret. Harcourt, 1964. (A collection of five Maigret novels, of which the underlined titles were first U.S. appearances: Maigret in Montmartre; Maigret's Mistake; Maigret has Scruples; Maigret and the Reluctant Witnesses; Maigret Goes to School.)

Maigret on Holiday. Routledge, 1950. (A twosome consisting of A Summer Holiday and To Any Lengths, qq.v.)

Maigret on the Defensive. H. Hamilton, 1966. (Translation of Maigret se Defend. Paris, 1964.)

A Maigret Quartet. H. Hamilton, 1972. U.S. title: A Maigret Trio. Harcourt, 1973. (A collection of four Maigret novels, of which the last-named was omitted from the U.S. edition: Maigret's Failure; Maigret in Society; Maigret and the Lazy Burglar; Maigret's Special Murder. All three included in the U.S. edition are first U.S. appearances.)

Maigret Rents a Room; see Maigret Takes a Room

Maigret Returns. (Included in the twosome Maigret Sits It Out.) Routledge, 1941; Harcourt, 1941. (Translation of Maigret. Paris, 1934.)

Maigret Right and Wrong. H. Hamilton, 1954. (A twosome consisting of Maigret in Montmartre and Maigret's Mistake, qq.v.)

Maigret Sets a Trap. H. Hamilton, 1965; Harcourt, 1972. (Translation of Maigret Tend un Piege. Paris, 1955.)

Maigret Sits It Out. Routledge, 1941; Harcourt, 1941. (A twosome consisting of The Lock at Charenton and Maigret Returns, qq.v.)

Maigret Stonewalled; see The Death of Monsieur Gallet

Maigret Takes a Room. H. Hamilton, 1960. U.S. title: Maigret Rents a Room. Doubleday, 1961. (Translation of Maigret en Meuble. Paris, 1951.)

Maigret Takes the Waters. H. Hamilton, 1969. U.S. title: Maigret in Vichy. Harcourt, 1969. (Translation of Maigret a Vichy. Paris, 1968.)

Maigret to the Rescue. Routledge, 1940; Harcourt, 1941. (A twosome consisting of The Flemish Shop and The Guinguette by the Seine, qq.v.)

Maigret Travels South. Routledge, 1940; Harcourt, 1940. (A twosome consisting of Liberty Bar and The Madman of Bergerac, qq.v.)

A Maigret Trio; see A Maigret Quartet

Maigret's Boyhood Friend. H. Hamilton, 1970; Harcourt, 1970. (Translation of L'Ami d'Enfance de Maigret. Paris, 1968.)

Maigret's Dead Man; see Maigret's Special Murder

Maigret's Failure. (Published as a separate volume in Britain; included in the U.S. in the collection A Maigret Trio, q.v.) H. Hamilton, 1962; Harcourt, 1973. (Translation of Un Echec de Maigret. Paris, 1956.)

Maigret's First Case. (Published as a separate volume in Britain; included in the U.S. in the collection Maigret Cinq, q.v.) H. Hamilton, 1958; Harcourt, 1965. (Translation of La Premier Enquete de Maigret. Paris, 1949.)

Maigret's Little Joke. H. Hamilton, 1957. U.S. title: None of Maigret's Business. Doubleday, 1958. (Translation of Maigret s'Amuse. Paris, 1957.)

Maigret's Memoirs. H. Hamilton, 1963; White Lion, 1974. (Translation of Les Memoires de Maigret. Paris, 1951.)

Maigret's Mistake. (Included in Britain in the twosome Maigret Right and Wrong, q.v., and in the U.S. in the collection Five Times Maigret, q.v.) H. Hamilton, 1954; Harcourt, 1964. (Translation of Maigret Se Trompe. Paris, 1953.)

Maigret's Pickpocket. H. Hamilton, 1968; Harcourt, 1968. (Translation of Le Voleur de Maigret. Paris, 1967.)
Maigret's Revolver. H. Hamilton, 1956. (Translation of Le Revolver de Maigret. Paris, 1952.)
Maigret's Special Murder. H. Hamilton, 1964. U.S. title: Maigret's Dead Man. Doubleday, 1964. (Translation of Maigret et son Mort. Paris, 1948.)
The Methods of Maigret; see My Friend Maigret
My Friend Maigret. H. Hamilton, 1956. U.S. title: The Methods of Maigret. Doubleday, 1957. (Translation of Mon Ami Maigret. Paris, 1949.)
No Vacation for Maigret; see A Summer Holiday
None of Maigret's Business; see Maigret's Little Joke
The Patience of Maigret. Routledge, 1939; Harcourt, 1940. (A twosome consisting of A Battle of Nerves and A Face for a Clue, qq.v.)
The Patience of Maigret. H. Hamilton, 1966. (Translation of La Patience de Maigret. Paris, 1965.)
The Sailor's Rendezvous. (Included in the twosome Maigret Keeps a Rendezvous, q.v.) Routledge, 1940; Harcourt, 1941. (Translation of Au Rendez-Vous des Terre-Neuvas. Paris, 1931.)
The Saint-Fiacre Affair. (Included in the twosome Maigret Keeps a Rendezvous, q.v.) Routledge, 1940; Harcourt, 1941. Also published as: Maigret Goes Home. Penguin, 1967. (Translation of L'Affaire Saint-Fiacre. Paris, 1932.)
The Second Maigret Omnibus. H. Hamilton, 1964. U.S. title: Maigret Cinq. Harcourt, 1965. (A collection of five Maigret novels, of which the underlined titles were first U.S. appearances: Maigret and the Young Girl; Maigret's Little Joke; Maigret and the Old Lady; Maigret's First Case; Maigret Takes a Room.)
The Shadow in the Courtyard. (Included in Britain in the twosome Triumph of Inspector Maigret, q.v. In the U.S., published in a twosome with The Crime at Lock 14, q.v.) Hurst, 1934; Covici, 1934. Also published as: Maigret Mystified. Penguin, 1964. (Translation of L'Ombre Chinoise. Paris, 1932.)
The Short Cases of Inspector Maigret. Doubleday, 1959. (Five stories taken from various collections of Maigret short cases published in France.) ss
The Strange Case of Peter the Lett. (Included in Britain in the twosome Inspector Maigret Investigates, q.v. Published in the U.S. as a separate volume.) Hurst, 1933; Covici, 1933. Also published as: Maigret and the Enigmatic Lett. Penguin, 1963. (Translation of Pietr-le-Letton. Paris, 1931.)
A Summer Holiday. (Included in Britain in the twosome Maigret on Holiday, q.v.) Routledge, 1950. U.S. title: No Vacation for Maigret. Doubleday, 1953. (Translation of Les Vacances de Maigret. Paris, 1948.)
To Any Lengths. (Included in Britain in the twosome Maigret on Holiday, q.v.) Routledge, 1950. (Translation of Signe Picpus. Paris, 1944.)
Triumph of Inspector Maigret. Hurst, 1934. (A twosome consisting of The Shadow in the Courtyard and The Crime at Lock 14, qq.v.)

Versus Inspector Maigret. Doubleday, 1960. (A twosome consisting of Maigret and the Reluctant Witnesses and Maigret has Scruples, qq.v.)

II.

The Accomplices. H. Hamilton, 1966; Harcourt, 1964. (U.S. edition is a twosome with The Blue Room, q.v.) (Translation of Les Complices. Paris, 1955.)
Account Unsettled. H. Hamilton, 1962. U.S. title: The Fugitive. Doubleday, 1955. (Translation of Crime Impuni. Paris, 1954.)
Across the Street. Routledge, 1954. (Translation of La Fenetre des Rouet. Paris, 1945.)
Act of Passion. Routledge, 1953; Prentice-Hall, 1952. (Translation of Lettre a Mon Juge. Paris, 1947.)
Affairs of Destiny. Routledge, 1952; Harcourt, 1945. (A twosome consisting of Newhaven-Dieppe and The Woman of the Grey House, qq.v.)
Aunt Jeanne. Routledge, 1953. (Translation of Tante Jeanne. Paris, 1951.)
Banana Tourist. (Included in the twosome Lost Moorings, q.v.) Routledge, 1946. (Translation of Touriste de Bananes. Paris, 1938.)
Belle. (Included in Britain in the twosome Violent Ends, q.v., and in the U.S. in the collection Tidal Wave, q.v.) H. Hamilton, 1954; Doubleday, 1954. (Translation of Le Mort de Belle. Paris, 1952.)
The Bells of Bicetre; see The Patient
Betty. H. Hamilton, 1975; Harcourt, 1975. (Translation of Betty. Paris, 1961.)
Big Bob. H. Hamilton, 1969. (Translation of Le Grand Bob. Paris, 1954.)
Black Rain. (Included in Britain in the twosome Black Rain, q.v.; published in the U.S. as a separate volume.) Routledge, 1949; Reynal, 1947. (Translation of Il Pleut, Bergere. Paris, 1941.)
Black Rain. Routledge, 1949. (A twosome consisting of The Survivors and Black Rain, qq.v.)
Blind Alley; see Blind Path
Blind Path. (Included in Britain in the twosome Lost Moorings, q.v.; published in the U.S. as a separate volume.) Routledge, 1946. U.S. title: Blind Alley. Reynal, 1946. (Translation of Chemin sans Issue. Paris, 1938.)
The Blue Room. H. Hamilton, 1965; Harcourt, 1964. (U.S. edition in a twosome with The Accomplices, q.v.) (Translation of Le Chambre Bleue. Paris, 1964.)
The Bottom of the Bottle. (Included in the U.S. in the collection Tidal Wave, q.v. Published as a separate volume in Britain.) H. Hamilton, 1977; Doubleday, 1954. (Translation of La Fond de la Bouteille. Paris, 1949.)
The Breton Sisters. (Included in the twosome Havoc by Accident, q.v.) Routledge, 1943; Harcourt, 1943. (Translation of Les Demoiselles de Concarneau. Paris, 1936.)
The Brothers Rico. (Included in Britain in the twosome Violent Ends, q.v., and in the U.S. in the collection Tidal Wave, q.v.) H. Hamilton, 1954; Doubleday, 1954. (Translation of Les Freres Rico. Paris, 1952.)
The Burgomaster of Furnes. Routledge, 1952. (Translation of Le Bourgmestre de Furnes. Paris, 1939.)
The Burial of M. Bouvet; see Inquest on Bouvet

The Cat. H. Hamilton, 1972; Harcourt, 1967. (Translation of Le Chat. Paris, 1967.)
Chez Krull. (Included in Britain in the twosome A Sense of Guilt, q.v.; published in the U.S. as a separate volume.) H. Hamilton, 1955; White Lion, 1974. (Translation of Chez Krull. Paris, 1939.)
Chit of a Girl. (Included in the twosome Chit of a Girl, q.v.) Routledge, 1949. Also published as: Girl in Waiting, in the twosome Girl in Waiting. Pan, 1957. (Translation of La Marie du Port. Paris, 1938.)
Chit of a Girl. Routledge, 1949. Also published as: Girl in Waiting. Pan, 1957. (A twosome consisting of Chit of a Girl and Justice, qq.v.)
The Clockmaker; see The Watchmaker of Everton
The Confessional. H. Hamilton, 1967; Harcourt, 1968. (Translation of Le Confessional. Paris, 1966.)
Danger Ahead. H. Hamilton, 1955. (A twosome consisting of Red Lights and The Watchmaker of Everton, qq.v.)
Danger Ashore; see The Window over the Way
Danger at Sea; see The Mystery of the 'Polarlys'
Destinations. Doubleday, 1955. (A twosome consisting of The Hitchhiker and The Burial of M. Bouvet, qq.v.)
The Disappearance of Odile. H. Hamilton, 1972; Harcourt, 1972. (Translation of La Disparition d'Odile. Paris, 1971.)
The Disintegration of J.P.G. Routledge, 1937. (Translation of L'Evade. Paris, 1936.)
The Door. H. Hamilton, 1964. (Translation of La Porte. Paris, 1962.)
Escape in Vain. Routledge, 1943; Harcourt, 1944. (A twosome consisting of The Lodger and One Way Out, qq.v.)
The Fate of the Malous. H. Hamilton, 1962. (Translation of La Destin des Malou. Paris, 1947.)
The First-Born; see Magnet of Doom
Four Days in a Lifetime. (Included in the U.S. in the twosome Satan's Children, q.v.; published as a separate volume in Britain.) H. Hamilton, 1977; Prentice-Hall, 1953. (Translation of Les Quatre Jours du Pauvre Homme. Paris, 1949.)
The Fugitive; see Account Unsettled
The Gendarme's Report. (Included in a twosome with The Window over the Way, q.v.) Routledge, 1951. (Translation of Le Rapport du Gendarme. Paris, 1944.)
The Girl in his Past. H. Hamilton, 1976; Prentice-Hall, 1953. (Translation of Le Temps d'Anais. Paris, 1951.)
Girl in Waiting; see Chit of a Girl
The Glass Cage. H. Hamilton, 1973; Harcourt, 1973. (Translation of La Cage de Verre. Paris, 1971.)
The Green Thermos. (Included in the twosome On the Danger Line, q.v.) Routledge, 1944; Harcourt, 1944. (Translation of Le Suspect. Paris, 1938.)
The Hatter's Ghosts. (Included in the twosome The Judge and the Hatter, q.v.) H. Hamilton, 1956. U.S. title: The Hatter's Phantoms. Harcourt, 1976. (Translation of Les Fantomes du Chapelier. Paris, 1949.)
The Hatter's Phantoms; see The Hatter's Ghosts

Havoc by Accident. Routledge, 1943; Harcourt, 1943. (A twosome consisting of Talatala and The Breton Sisters, qq.v.)
The Heart of a Man. (Included in Britain in the twosome A Sense of Guilt, q.v.; published in the U.S. as a separate volume) H. Hamilton, 1955; Prentice-Hall, 1951. (Translation of Les Volets Verts. Paris, 1950.)
The Hitchhiker; see Red Lights
Home Town. (Included in the twosome On the Danger Line, q.v.) Routledge, 1944; Harcourt, 1944. (Translation of Faubourg. Paris, 1937.)
The House by the Canal. (Included in a twosome with The Ostenders, q.v.) Routledge, 1952. (Translation of La Maison du Canal. Paris, 1933.)
The House on Quai Notre Dame; see The Others
I Take This Woman; see The Trial of Bebe Donge
In Case of Emergency. H. Hamilton, 1960; Doubleday, 1958. (Translation of En Cas de Malheur. Paris, 1956.)
In Two Latitudes. Routledge, 1942. (A twosome consisting of The Mystery of the 'Polarlys' and Tropic Moon, qq.v.)
The Innocents. H. Hamilton, 1973; Harcourt, 1974. (Translation of Les Innocents. Paris, 1972.)
Inquest on Bouvet. H. Hamilton, 1958. U.S. title: The Burial of M. Bouvet. (Included in the twosome Destinations, q.v.) Doubleday, 1955. (Translation of L'Enterrement de M. Bouvet. Paris, 1950.)
The Iron Staircase. H. Hamilton, 1963; Harcourt, 1977. (Translation of L'Escalier de Fer. Paris, 1953.)
The Judge and the Hatter. H. Hamilton, 1956. (A twosome consisting of The Witnesses and The Hatter's Ghosts, qq.v.)
Justice. (Included in the twosome Chit of a Girl, q.v.) Routledge, 1949. (Translation of Cour d'Assises. Paris, 1941.)
The Little Man from Archangel. (Published as a separate volume in Britain; published in the U.S. in a twosome with Sunday, q.v.) H. Hamilton, 1957; Harcourt, 1966. (Translation of Le Petit Homme d'Archangelsk. Paris, 1956.)
The Little Saint. H. Hamilton, 1966; Harcourt, 1965. (Translation of Le Petit Saint. Paris, 1965.)
The Lodger. (Included in the twosome Escape in Vain, q.v.) Routledge, 1943; Harcourt, 1944. (Translation of Le Locataire. Paris, 1934.)
Lost Moorings. Routledge, 1946. (A twosome consisting of Blind Path and Banana Tourist, qq.v.)
The Magician. (Published as a separate volume in Britain; included in the U.S. in the twosome The Magician and the Widow, q.v.) H. Hamilton, 1974; Doubleday, 1955. (Translation of Antoine et Julie. Paris, 1953.)
The Magician and the Widow. Doubleday, 1955. (A twosome consisting of The Magician and The Widow, qq.v.)
Magnet of Doom. Routledge, 1948. U.S. title: The First-Born. Reynal, 1947. (Translation of L'Aine des Ferchaux. Paris, 1945.)
Maigret and Monsieur Labbe. Routledge, 1941; Harcourt, 1942. (A twosome consisting of Death of a Harbourmaster, a Maigret novel listed in Part I hereof, and The Man from Everywhere, q.v.)

The Man from Everywhere. (Included in the twosome Maigret and Monsieur Labbe.) Routledge, 1941; Harcourt, 1942. (Translation of Le Relais d'Alsace. Paris, 1931.)
The Man on the Bench in the Barn. H. Hamilton, 1970; Harcourt, 1969. (Translation of La Main. Paris, 1968.)
The Man Who Watched the Trains Go By. Routledge, 1942; Reynal, 1946. (Translation of L'Homme Qui Regardait Passer les Trains. Paris, 1938.)
The Man with the Little Dog. H. Hamilton, 1965. (Translation of L'Homme au Petit Chien. Paris, 1964.)
Monsieur la Souris. (Included in the twosome Poisoned Relations, q.v.) Routledge, 1950. (Translation of Monsieur la Souris. Paris, 1938.)
Monsieur Monde Vanishes. H. Hamilton, 1967; Harcourt, 1977. (Translation of La Fuite de M. Monde. Paris, 1945.)
The Move; see The Neighbors
Mr. Hire's Engagement. (Included in the twosome Sacrifice, q.v.) H. Hamilton, 1956. (Translation of Les Fiancailles de M. Hire. Paris, 1933.)
The Murderer. (Included in a twosome with A Wife at Sea, q.v.) Routledge, 1949. (Translation of L'Assassin. Paris, 1937.)
The Mystery of the 'Polarlys'. (Included in Britain in the twosome In Two Latitudes, q.v., and in the U.S. in the twosome On Land and Sea, under the byline Victor Kosta.) Routledge, 1942; Hanover House, 1954. (Translation of Le Passager du 'Polarlys'. Paris, 1932.)
The Negro. H. Hamilton, 1959. (Translation of Le Negre. Paris, 1957.)
The Neighbors. H. Hamilton, 1968. U.S. title: The Move. Harcourt, 1968. (Translation of Le Demenagement. Paris, 1967.)
A New Lease of Life. H. Hamilton, 1963. U.S. title: A New Lease on Life. Doubleday, 1963. (Translation of Une Vie comme Neuve. Paris, 1951.)
A New Lease on Life; see A New Lease of Life
Newhaven-Dieppe. (Included in the twosome Affairs of Destiny, q.v.) Routledge, 1942; Harcourt, 1945. (Translation of L'Homme de Londres. Paris, 1934.)
November. H. Hamilton, 1970; Harcourt, 1970. (Translation of Novembre. Paris, 1969.)
The Old Man Dies. H. Hamilton, 1968; Harcourt, 1967. (Translation of La Mort d'Auguste. Paris, 1966.)
On Land and Sea (as by Victor Kosta). Hanover House, 1954. (A twosome consisting of Danger Ashore and Danger at Sea, qq.v.)
On the Danger Line. Routledge, 1944; Harcourt, 1944. (A twosome consisting of Home Town and The Green Thermos, qq.v.)
One Way Out. (Included in the twosome Escape in Vain, q.v.) Routledge, 1943; Harcourt, 1944. (Translation of Les Suicides. Paris, 1934.)
The Ostenders. (Included in a twosome with The House by the Canal, q.v.) Routledge, 1952. (Translation of Le Clan des Ostendais. Paris, 1947.)
The Others. H. Hamilton, 1975. U.S. title: The House on Quai Notre Dame. Harcourt, 1975. (Translation of Les Autres. Paris, 1962.)
The Patient. H. Hamilton, 1963. U.S. title: The Bells of Bicetre. Harcourt, 1964. (Translation of Les Anneaux de Bicetre. Paris, 1963.)

Pedigree. H. Hamilton, 1962; London House, 1963. (Translation of Pedigree. Paris, 1948.)
Poisoned Relations. (Included in the twosome Poisoned Relations, q.v.) Routledge, 1950. (Translation of Les Soeurs Lacroix. Paris, 1938.)
Poisoned Relations. Routledge, 1950. (A twosome consisting of Monsieur la Souris and Poisoned Relations, qq.v.)
The Premier. (Published as a separate volume in Britain; included in the U.S. in a twosome with The Train, q.v.) H. Hamilton, 1961; Harcourt, 1966. (Translation of Le President. Paris, 1958.)
The Prison. H. Hamilton, 1969; Harcourt, 1969. (Translation of La Prison. Paris, 1968.)
Red Lights. (Included in Britain in the twosome Danger Ahead, q.v., and in the U.S. in the twosome Destinations, q.v.) H. Hamilton, 1955. U.S. title: The Hitchhiker. Doubleday, 1955. (Translation of Feux Rouges. Paris, 1953.)
The Rich Man. H. Hamilton, 1971; Harcourt, 1971. (Translation of Le Riche Homme. Paris, 1970.)
Sacrifice. H. Hamilton, 1956. (A twosome consisting of Mr. Hire's Engagement and Young Cardinaud, qq.v.)
Satan's Children. Prentice-Hall, 1953. (A twosome consisting of I Take This Woman and Four Days in a Lifetime, qq.v.)
A Sense of Guilt. H. Hamilton, 1955. (A twosome consisting of Chez Krull and The Heart of a Man, qq.v.)
The Shadow Falls. Routledge, 1945; Harcourt, 1945. (Translation of Le Testament Donadieu. Paris, 1937.)
The Snow was Black; see The Stain on the Snow
The Son. H. Hamilton, 1958. (Translation of Le Fils. Paris, 1957.)
The Stain on the Snow. Routledge, 1953. U.S. title: The Snow was Black. Prentice-Hall, 1950. (Translation of La Neige Etait Sale. Paris, 1948.)
The Stowaway. H. Hamilton, 1957. (Translation of Le Passager Clandestin. Paris, 1947.)
Strange Inheritance. Routledge, 1950. (Translation of Le Voyageur de la Toussaint. Paris, 1941.)
Strangers in the House. Routledge, 1951; Doubleday, 1954. (Translation of Les Inconnus dans la Maison. Paris, 1940.)
Striptease. H. Hamilton, 1959. (Translation of Strip-Tease. Paris, 1958.)
Sunday. (Published as a separate volume in Britain; included in the U.S. in a twosome with The Little Man from Archangel, q.v.) H. Hamilton, 1960; Harcourt, 1966. (Translation of Dimanche. Paris, 1958.)
The Survivors. (Included in the twosome Black Rain, q.v.) Routledge, 1949. (Translation of Les Rescapes du Telemaque. Paris, 1938.)
Talatala. (Included in the twosome Havoc by Accident, q.v.) Routledge, 1943; Harcourt, 1943. (Translation of Le Blanc a Lunettes. Paris, 1937.)
Teddy Bear. H. Hamilton, 1971; Harcourt, 1972. (Translation of L'Ours en Peluche. Paris, 1960.)
Three Beds in Manhattan. H. Hamilton, 1976; Doubleday, 1964. (Translation of Trois Chambres a Manhattan. Paris, 1946.)
Ticket of Leave. Routledge, 1954. U.S. title: The Widow. (Included in the twosome The Magician and the Widow, q.v.) Doubleday, 1955. (Translation of La Veuve Couderc. Paris, 1942.)

Tidal Wave. Doubleday, 1954. (A collection consisting of Belle, The Bottom of the Bottle, and The Brothers Rico, qq.v.)
The Train. (Published as a separate volume in Britain; included in the U.S. in a twosome with The Premier, q.v.) H. Hamilton, 1964; Harcourt, 1966. (Translation of Le Train. Paris, 1961.)
The Trial of Bebe Donge. (Published as a separate volume in Britain; included in the U.S. in the twosome Satan's Children, q.v.) Routledge, 1952. U.S. title: I Take This Woman. Prentice-Hall, 1953. (Translation of La Verite sur Bebe Donge. Paris, 1942.)
Tropic Moon. (Included in Britain in the twosome In Two Latitudes, q.v.; published in the U.S. as a separate volume.) Routledge, 1942; Harcourt, 1943. (Translation of Le Coup de Lune. Paris, 1933.)
The Venice Train. H. Hamilton, 1974; Harcourt, 1974. (Translation of Le Train de Venise. Paris, 1965.)
Violent Ends. H. Hamilton, 1954. (A twosome consisting of Belle and The Brothers Rico, qq.v.)
The Watchmaker; see The Watchmaker of Everton
The Watchmaker of Everton. (Included in Britain in the twosome Danger Ahead, q.v., and in the U.S. in the twosome The Witnesses and the Watchmaker, q.v.) H. Hamilton, 1955. U.S. title: The Watchmaker. Doubleday, 1956. Also published as: The Clockmaker. Jove, 1977. (Translation of L'Horloger d'Everton. Paris, 1954.)
The Widow; see Ticket of Leave
The Widower. H. Hamilton, 1961. (Translation of Le Veuf. Paris, 1959.)
A Wife at Sea. (Included in a twosome with The Murderer, q.v.) Routledge, 1949. (Translation of Les Pitard. Paris, 1935.)
The Window over the Way. (Included in Britain in a twosome with The Gendarme's Report, q.v., and in the U.S. in the twosome On Land and Sea, q.v.) Routledge, 1951. U.S. title: Danger Ashore. Hanover House, 1954. (Translation of Les Gens d'en Face. Paris, 1933.)
The Witnesses. (Included in Britain in the twosome The Judge and the Hatter, q.v., and in the U.S. in the twosome The Witnesses and The Watchmaker, q.v.) H. Hamilton, 1956; Doubleday, 1956. (Translation of Les Temoins. Paris, 1954.)
The Witnesses and the Watchmaker. Doubleday, 1956. (A twosome consisting of The Witnesses and The Watchmaker, qq.v.)
The Woman of the Grey House. (Included in the twosome Affairs of Destiny, q.v.) Routledge, 1942; Harcourt, 1945. (Translation of Le Haut Mal. Paris, 1933.)
Young Cardinaud. (Included in the twosome Sacrifice, q.v.) H. Hamilton, 1956. (Translation of Le Fils Cardinaud. Paris, 1942.)

SIMMAT, RUDOLPH
Murder on Mitcham Common. Newnes, 1936

SIMMEL, JOHANNES MARIO. 1924- .
The Berlin Connection; see To the Bitter End
The Cain Conspiracy; see Cain '67

Cain '67. McGraw, 1971. Also published as: The Cain Conspiracy. Popular Library, 1976. (Translation of Alle Menschen werden Bruder. Munich, 1967.)
Dear Fatherland. Random, 1969; Deutsch, 1969. Also published as: Double Agent—Triple Cross. Popular Library, 1977. (Translation of Lieb Vaterland, Magst Ruhig Sein. Munich, 1965.)
Double Agent—Triple Cross; see Dear Fatherland
It Can't Always be Caviar. Doubleday, 1965; Blond, 1965. Also published as: The Monte Cristo Cover-Up. Popular Library, 1977. (Translation of Es Muss Nicht Immer Kaviar Sein. Munich, 1960.)
Love is Just a Word. McGraw, 1969. (Translation of Liebe ist Nur ein Wort. Munich, 1962.)
The Monte Cristo Cover-Up; see It Can't Always be Caviar
To the Bitter End. McGraw, 1970. Also published as: The Berlin Connection. Popular Library, 1977. (Translation of Bis Zur Bitteren Neige. Munich, 1962.)

SIMMONS, ADDISON. 1902- .
Dead Weight. Phoenix, 1946
Death on the Campus. Crowell, 1935

SIMMONS, DENIS
The Stolen Laces. Laird, 1889

SIMMONS, MARY KAY
Cameron Hill. Dell, 1972
The Captain's House. Dell, 1970
Diamonds of Alcazar. Dell, 1972
Flight from Riversedge. Dell, 1975
The Girl with the Key. Dell, 1974
The Gypsy Grove. Dell, 1974
Haggard's Cove. Dell, 1975
The Hermitage. Dell, 1970
Megan. Dell, 1971
Saracen Gardens. Dell, 1973
The Willow Pond. Dell, 1972
The Year of the Rooster. Delacorte, 1971

SIMMS, WILLIAM GILMORE. 1806-1870.
Martin Faber, The Story of a Criminal. Harper, 1833

SIMON. Joint pseudonym of Roger d'Este Burford, 1904- , and Oswell Blakeston, 1907- , q.v. Pseudonym of Burford alone: Roger East, q.v.
The Cat with the Mustache. Wishart, 1935. Also published as: The Mystery of the Hypnotic Room. Curtis Warren, 1950
Death on the Swim. Wishart, 1934
Murder Among Friends. Wishart, 1933
The Mystery of the Hypnotic Room; see The Cat with the Mustache

SIMON, C. E.
-The Second Tablet. Fiction House, 1947
Sleeping Draught. Houghton (London), 1934

SIMON, ROBERT A(LFRED). 1897- .
The Weekend Mystery. Watt, 1926; Collins, 1927

SIMON, ROGER L(ICHTENBERG). 1943- .
Series character: Moses Wine, in both titles.
The Big Fix. Straight Arrow, 1973; Deutsch, 1974
Wild Turkey. Straight Arrow, 1975; Deutsch, 1976

SIMON, RUTH (CORABEL SHIMER). 1918- .
-A Castle for Tess. Follett, 1967

SIMON, S. J. Pseudonym of Simon Jasha Skidelsky. See: CARYL BRAHMS (pseudonym of Doris Caroline Abrahams, 1901-).

SIMONDS, PETER. 1906- . Pseudonym: Richard Greaves, q.v.

SIMONS, ROGER. Joint pseudonym of Margaret Punnett, 1932- , and Ivor Macaulay Punnett. Series character: Inspector Fadiman Wace, in at least those marked FW.
Arrangement for Murder. Bles, 1961; Roy, 1963 FW
Bullet for a Beast. Bles, 1964; Roy, 1965 FW
Dead Reckoning. Bles, 1965
Death on Display. Bles, 1968; Roy, 1969 FW
A Frame for Murder. Bles, 1960 FW
Gamble with Death. Bles, 1961; Roy, 1963 FW
The Houseboat Killings. Bles, 1959 FW
The Killing Chase. Bles, 1962 FW
Murder by Design. Hale, 1974
Murder First Class. Bles, 1969; Roy, 1970 FW
Murder Joins the Chorus. Bles, 1960 FW
Picture of Death. Hale, 1973
Reel of Death. Bles, 1970 FW
Silver and Death. Bles, 1963 FW
Taxed to Death. Bles, 1967 FW
The Veil of Death. Bles, 1966; Roy, 1967 FW

SIMPSON, ALAN (FRANCIS). 1929- . See: RAY(MOND PERCY) GALTON.

SIMPSON, CHARLES H.
Life in the Far West; or, A Detective's Adventures Among the Indians and Outlaws of Montana. Rhodes, 1896
Life in the Mines; or, Crime Avenged. Rhodes, 1896

SIMPSON, HELEN (DE GUERRY). 1897-1940. See also: CLEMENCE DANE.
Vantage Striker. Heinemann, 1931. U.S. title (?): The Prime Minister is Dead. Doubleday, 1931

SIMPSON, HOWARD R. 1925- .
Assignment for a Mercenary. Harper, 1965
Rendezvous Off Newport. Curtis, 1973; Hale, 1974
The Three Day Alliance. Doubleday, 1971; Hale, 1973

SIMPSON, M. E.
And One for the Pot. Hale, 1973

SIMPSON, MARGARET. 1913- .
The Chrome Connection. Deutsch, 1975
Sorry Wrong Number. Deutsch, 1973

SIMPSON, ROBERT
The Gray Charteris. Hodder, 1922; McCann, 1922
Welcome Danger. London Book Co., 1930

SIMPSON, RONALD
End of a Diplomat. Monarch, 1964
Make Every Kiss Count. Monarch, 1961
The Return of Colonel Pho. Monarch, 1965

SIMPSON, SPENCER
Crooks in Cabaret. Nicholson, 1935
The Four Dead Men. Methuen, 1936; Macaulay, 1937

SIMS, DOROTHY RICE. See: (GEORGE) VALENTINE WILLIAMS, 1883-1946.

SIMS, GEORGE. 1923- .
Deadhand. Gollancz, 1971

Hunters Point. Gollancz, 1973; Penguin, 1977
The Last Best Friend. Gollancz, 1967; Stein, 1968
The Sand Dollar. Gollancz, 1969
Sleep No More. Gollancz, 1966; Harcourt, 1966
The Terrible Door. Bodley Head, 1964; Horizon, 1964

SIMS, GEORGE. 1902-1966. Pseudonym: Paul Cain, q.v.

SIMS, GEORGE R(OBERT). 1847-1922. Series character: Dorcas Dene = DD.
Anna of the Underworld. Chatto, 1916
As It was in the Beginning. White, 1896 ss, some criminous
Behind the Veil. Greening, 1913 ss
Biographs of Babylon. Chatto, 1902 ss, at least one criminous
The Black Stain. Jarrolds, 1907
A Blind Marriage, and other stories. Chatto, 1901 ss
-A Cabinet Minister's Wife and other tales. Paul, 1910 ss
The Case of George Candlemas. Chatto, 1890
The Coachman's Club; or, Tales Told Out of School. White, 1897 ss
The Death Gamble. Paul, 1909 ss
Detective Inspector Chance. Ferret Fantasy, 1974 ss
The Devil in London. Paul, 1909; Dodge, 1909
Dorcas Dene, Detective. White, 1897 ss DD
Dorcas Dene, Detective. Second Series. White, 1898 ss DD
Dramas of Life. Chatto, 1890; U.S. Book Co., 1890 ss
For Life and After. Chatto, 1906
His Wife's Revenge. Chatto, 1907
In London's Heart. Chatto, 1900; Buckles, 1900
-Joyce Pleasantry and other stories. Chatto, 1908 ss
-Li Ting of London and other stories. Chatto, 1905 ss
-The Life We Live. Chatto, 1904 ss
Mary Jane Married. Chatto, 1888 ss
-Memoirs of a Landlady. Chatto, 1894 ss
A Missing Husband and other tales. Chatto, 1890 ss
-My Two Wives and other stories. Chatto, 1894 ss
The Mysteries of Modern London. Pearson, 1906
The Mystery of Mary Anne and other stories. Chatto, 1907 ss
-Off the Track in London. Jarrolds, 1911
-Once Upon a Christmas Time. Chatto, 1898 ss
-The Ring o' Bells. Chatto, 1886 ss
Rogues and Vagabonds. Chatto, 1885; Munro, 1886
-Scenes from the Show. Chatto, 1895 ss
-The Small-Part Lady, and other stories. Chatto, 1900 ss
The Social Kaleidoscope. First Series. Francis, 1879 ss, some criminous
The Social Kaleidoscope. Second Series. Francis, 1881 ss, some criminous
-Stories in Black and White. Fuller, 1885 ss
Tales of Today. Chatto, 1889; Munro, 1887 ss
The Ten Commandments. Chatto, 1896 ss, some criminous
-The Theatre of Life. Fuller, 1881 ss
-Three Brass Balls. Fuller, 1882
Tinkletop's Crime and other tales. Chatto, 1891; Ogilvie, (?)
-Two London Fairies. Greening, 1906
-Watches of the Night. Greening, 1907
-Young Mrs. Caudle. Chatto, 1904
-Zeph and other stories. Fuller, 1882 ss

SIMSON, CICELY DEVENISH FRASER. See; CICELY (DEVENISH) FRASER-SIMSON.

SIMSON, ERIC ANDREW. 1895- . Pseudonym: Laurence Kirk, q.v.

SINCLAIR, CLAUDE EDWARD ROBERT
-The House at Ballyslane. Witherby, 1949
-Problem Island. Witherby, 1950

SINCLAIR, DENNIS
The Temple Dogs Guard My Fate. Signet, 1969

SINCLAIR, FIONA. Series character: Inspector Paul Grainger, in at least those marked PG.
But the Patient Died; see Dead of a Physician
Dead of a Physician. Bles, 1961. U.S. title: But the Patient Died. Doubleday, 1962 PG
Meddle with the Mafia. Bles, 1963 PG
Most Unnatural Murder. Bles, 1965
Scandalize My Name. Bles, 1960 PG
Three Slips to a Noose. Bles, 1964 PG

SINCLAIR, FREDRIC
Drop One, Carry Four. Doubleday, 1947

SINCLAIR, MAY. 1865?-1946.
Uncanny Stories. Hutchinson, 1923; Macmillan, 1923 ss

SINCLAIR, MICHAEL
How to Steal a Million. Signet, 1966; New English Library pb, 1966. (Novelization of the movie.)

SINCLAIR, MICHAEL. Pseudonym.
The Dollar Covenant. Gollancz, 1973; Norton, 1973
Folio Forty-One; see Norslag
A Long Time Sleeping. Gollancz, 1975
Norslag. Gollancz, 1972. U.S. title: Folio Forty-One. Putnam, 1972
Sonntag. Gollancz, 1971; Putnam, 1971

SINCLAIR, OLGA. 1923- .
Bitter Sweet Summer. Hale, 1970; Simon, 1972
-Hearts by the Tower. Hale, 1968. U.S. title (?): Night of the Black Tower. Lancer, 1968
-The Man at the Manor. Gresham, 1967; Dell, 1972
-Man of the River. Hale, 1968
Night of the Black Tower; see Hearts by the Tower
-Wild Dreams. Hale, 1973

SINCLAIR, ROBERT B(RUCE). 1905- .
The Eleventh Hour. Mill, 1951; Cassell, 1951
It Couldn't Be Murder. Mill, 1954; Boardman, 1955

SINCLAIR, SALLY
Muted Murder. Arcadia, 1953

SINGER, BANT. Pseudonym of Charles Shaw, 1900- . Series character: Delaney, in all titles.
Blind Alley; see You're Wrong, Delaney
Don't Slip, Delaney. Collins, 1954
Have Patience, Delaney! Collins, 1954
Your Move, Delaney! Collins, 1956
You're Wrong, Delaney. Collins, 1953; Crown, 1953. Also published as: Blind Alley. Pyramid, 1954

SINGER, CAMPBELL. See: JOHN (FREDERICK) BURKE, 1927- ; and: JOSEPH (ARNOLD) HAYES, 1918- .

SINGER, LOREN
The Parallax View. Doubleday, 1970; New English Library, 1970
That's the House, There. Doubleday, 1973; New English Library, 1974

SINGER, NORMAN
The Shakedown Kid. Manor, 1975

SINGER, SALLY M.
For Dying You Always Have Time. Putnam, 1971

SINGLETON, FRANK
-A Change of Sky. Chatto, 1953
Independent Means. Chatto, 1948; Macmillan, 1948

SINSTADT, GERALD. Series character: Geoffrey Landon, in both titles.
The Fidelio Score. Long, 1965; Lancer, 1967
Ship of Spies; see Whisper in a Lonely Place
Whisper in a Lonely Place. Long, 1966. U.S. title: Ship of Spies. Lancer, 1967

SIODMAK, CURT. 1902- .
Donovan's Brain. Knopf, 1942; Chapman, 1944
Hauser's Memory. Putnam, 1968; Jenkins, 1969
The Third Ear. Putnam, 1971

SIRENGO, CHARLES A.
A Cowboy Detective. Ogilvie, 189?
Further Adventures of a Cowboy Detective. Ogilvie, 189?

SITWELL, S(YDNEY) M(ARY)
-A Great Revenge. Christian Knowledge Society, 1885

SJOWALL, MAJ, 1935- , and PER WAHLOO, 1926-1975, q.v. Series character: Martin Beck, in all titles.
The Abominable Man. Pantheon, 1972; Gollancz, 1973. (Translation of Den Vedervardige Mannen fran Saffle. Stockholm, 1971.)
Cop Killer. Pantheon, 1975; Gollancz, 1975. (Translation of Polismordaren. Stockholm, 1974.)
The Fire Engine That Disappeared. Pantheon, 1971; Gollancz, 1972. (Translation of Brandbilen som Forsvann. Stockholm, 1969.)
The Laughing Policeman. Pantheon, 1970; Gollancz, 1971. (Translation of Den Skrattande Polisen. Stockholm, 1968.)
The Locked Room. Pantheon, 1973; Gollancz, 1974. (Translation of Det Slutna Rummet. Stockholm, 1972.)
The Man on the Balcony. Pantheon, 1968; Gollancz, 1969. (Translation of Mannen pa Balkongen. Stockholm, 1967.)
The Man Who Went Up in Smoke. Pantheon, 1969; Gollancz, 1970. (Translation of Mannen som Gick Upp in Rok. Stockholm, 1966.)
Murder at the Savoy. Pantheon, 1971; Gollancz, 1972. (Translation of Polis, Polis, Potatismos! Stockholm, 1970.)
Roseanna. Pantheon, 1967; Gollancz, 1968. (Translation of Roseanna. Stockholm, 1965.)

SKALLAND, HARLEY L.
The Wrong Slant of Red. Dorrance, 1967

SKENE, ANTHONY. Pseudonym of George Norman Philips, 1888?- . Series character (with many other authors): Sexton Blake, in those titles listed without publisher (which was Amalgamated Press).

Skene, Anthony

The Affair of the Bronzed Basilisk. 1943
The Circus Crime. 1933
The Crook's Accomplice. 1930
Crook Town. 1932
The Death Gang. 1931; Red Mask, 194?
The Death of Four. 1931
The Death Trap. 1930
Derelict House. 1933
The Fatal Mascot. 1932
Five Dead Men. Paul, 1932
Gallows Alley. Paul, 1934
Green Mask. 1932
The Haunted Hotel Mystery. 1941
The Legacy of Fear. 1931
The Man Who Lost his Memory. 1947
The Masks. Paul, 1933
Missing Men. 1934
Monsieur Zenith. Paul, 1936
The Mystery of the Bombed Hotel. 1942
The Nameless Five. 1931
The Night-Club Crime. 1931
The Night Raiders. 1930
The £1,000,000 Plot. 1933
The Red Stilleto. 1932
The Ripper Returns. Pemberton, 1948
The Riverside Club Murder. 1934
The Road House Murder. 1933
The Rush Hour Crime. 1935
The Silent Menace. 1933
The Silver Circle. Amalgamated, 1934
The Terror of the Tenements. 1937
The Vault of Doom. 1931

SKETCHLEY, ARTHUR. Pseudonym of George Rose, 1817-1882.
Mrs. Brown on the Tichborne Case. Routledge, 1872

SKIDELSKY, SIMON JASHA. Pseudonym: S. J. Simon. See: CARYL BRAHMS.

SKINNER, CONRAD ARTHUR. 1889- . Pseudonym: Michael Maurice, q.v.

SKINNER, JOHN
Murder in the Village. Methuen, 1930

SKINNER, JUNE O'GRADY. 1922- . Pseudonym: Rohan O'Grady, q.v.

SKIRROW, DESMOND. Series character: John Brock, in at least those marked JB.
I was Following This Girl. Bodley Head, 1967; Doubleday, 1968 JB
I'm Trying to Give It Up. Bodley Head, 1968; Doubleday, 1969 JB
It Won't Get You Anywhere. Bodley Head, 1966; Lippincott, 1966 JB
-Poor Quail. Bodley Head, 1969

SKOTTOWE, B(RITIFFE) C(ONSTABLE). 1857- .
Sudden Death; or, My Lady the Wolf. Sonnenschein, 1886

SKVORECKY, JOSEF (VOLCAV). 1924- .
Miss Silver's Past. Grove, 1975; Bodley Head, 1976. (Translation of Lvice. Prague, 1969.)
The Mournful Demeanour of Lieutenant Boruvka. Gollancz, 1973 ss (Translation of Smutek Porucika Boruvky. Prague, 1966.)

SLADE, H(ERBERT). See: W(ALTER) B(URTON) BALDRY, 1888- .

SLADEK, JOHN. 1937- . Joint pseudonym with Thomas M(ichael) Disch, 1940- , q.v.: Thom Demijohn, q.v.
Black Aura. Cape, 1974

SLANEY, GEORGE WILSON. 1884- . Pseudonym: George Woden, q.v.

SLATE, JOHN. Pseudonym of John Russell Fearn, 1908-1960. Other pseudonym: Hugo Blayn, q.v. Series character: Black Maria = BM.
Black Maria, M.A. Rich, 1944 BM
Death in Silhouette. Rich, 1950 BM
Framed in Guilt. Rich, 1948
Maria Marches On. Rich, 1945 BM
One Remained Seated. Rich, 1946 BM
Thy Arm Alone. Rich, 1947 BM

SLATER, HUMPHREY. 1906- .
Calypso. Longmans, 1953
The Conspirator. Lehmann, 1948; Harcourt, 1948
-Three Among Mountains. Wingate, 1959

SLATER, MONTAGUE. 1902- . Pseudonym: Richard Johns, q.v.

SLATER, WILL
The Adventures of D'Arcy Dewpond, Detective. Drane, 1927 ss
-The Bells of Palmdale, and other stories. Drane, 1925 ss
"Land of the Free." Drane, 1928

SLAVITT, DAVID R(YTMAN). 1935- .
-ABCD. Doubleday, 1972; H. Hamilton, 1974
-Killing of the King. Doubleday, 1974; Allen, 1974

SLEATH, FREDERICK
-A Breaker of Ships. Hutchinson, 1922
-The Gold of the Sunset. Hutchinson, 1924
Green Swallows. Hutchinson, 1930
-The Hill of the Crows. Jenkins, 1921
-The Red Vulture. Hutchinson, 1923; Houghton, 1923
-The Seventh Vial. Jenkins, 1920
-Sniper Jackson. Jenkins, 1919

SLEE, RICHARD and CORNELIA ATWOOD PRATT
-Dr. Berkeley's Discovery. Putnam, 1899

SLESAR, HENRY. 1927- .
A Bouquet of Clean Crimes and Neat Murders. Avon, 1960 ss
The Bridge of Lions. Macmillan, 1963; Gollancz, 1964
A Crime for Mothers and others. Avon, 1962 ss
Enter Murderers. Random, 1960; Gollancz, 1961
The Gray Flannel Shroud. Random, 1959; Deutsch, 1960
The Seventh Mask. Ace, 1969. (Novelization of the Edge of Night TV series.)
The Thing at the Door. Random, 1974; H. Hamilton, 1975

SLIGH, NIGEL
-The Beast with Two Backs. Laurie, 1951
-The Fugitives. Laurie, 1947
-The Loved and the Loving. Laurie, 1953
-The Overlords. Laurie, 1955
-The Time and the Torture. Laurie, 1950
-Tomorrow and Yesterday. Laurie, 1954
-Traitor's Bridge. Laurie, 1952

SLIMAN, DAVID
Manhunting. Maclaren ss

SLINGSBY, RUFUS. Pseudonym of Charles Siddle, 1892- , and Frederick Peel, 1888- .
The Murders at Highbridge. Long, 1929

SLOAN, SARAH
Image of Stephanie. Lenox, 1972; Remploy, 1973
Raventree. Lenox, 1972; Remploy, 1974

SLOANE, WILLIAM (MILLIGAN). 1906-1974.
The Edge of Running Water. Farrar, 1939; Methuen, 1940. Also published as: The Unquiet Corpse. Dell, 1956
To Walk the Night. Farrar, 1937; Barker, 1938
The Unquiet Corpse; see The Edge of Running Water

SMALL, AUSTIN J. -1929. Pseudonym: Seamark, q.v.
The Death Maker; see Master Vorst
Frozen Gold. Heinemann, 1924. U.S. title: The Frozen Trail. Houghton, 1924. Reprinted as by Seamark: Hodder, 1935
Love's Enemy. Hodder, 1929
The Man They Couldn't Arrest. Hodder, 1927; Doran, 1927
Master Vorst. Hodder, 1926. U.S. title: The Death Maker. Doran, 1926
Pearls of Desire. Heinemann, 1924; Houghton, 1925

SMALLEY, DAVE E.
Stumbling. Barse, 1929

SMART, HAWLEY. 1833-1893.
At Fault. Chapman, 1883; Munro, 1883
-Bad to Beat. White, 1886; Rand, 1886
-Beatrice and Benedick. White, 1891; Taylor, 1891
-Belles and Ringers. Chapman, 1880; Munro, 1881
Bit and Bridal; see Bitter is the Rind
-Bitter is the Rind. Bentley, 1870. Also published as: Bit and Bridal. Everett, 1909
-A Black Business. White, 1890
-Bound to Win. Chapman, 1877
-Broken Bonds. Hurst, 1874
-Cecile; or, Modern Idolators. Bentley, 1871
-Cleverly Won. White, 1887
False Cards. Hurst, 1873
-A Family Failing. U.S. Book Co., 1891. (British title?)
-From Post to Finish. Chapman, 1884; Harper, 1884
The Great Tontine. Chapman, 1881; Munro, 1884
-Hard Lines. Chapman, 1883
-The Last Coup. White, 1889
-Lightly Lost. White, 1885
-Long Odds. White, 1889; Lovell, 1889
-The Master of Rathkelly. White, 1888
-A Member of Tattersall's. White, 1892; Lovell, 1892
-The Outsider. White, 1886; Munro, 1887
-Play or Pay. Chapman, 1878
-Plucked. Diprose, 1886
"The Plunger." White, 1891; Lippincott, 1891
-The Pride of the Paddock. White, 1888; Lovell, 1888
-A Race for a Wife. Bentley, 1870; Munro, 1882
-A Racing Rubber. White, 1895
-Saddle and Sabre. Chapman, 1888
-Salvage. Ward, 1884 ss
-Social Sinners. Chapman, 1880
Struck Down. Warne, 1885; Munro, 1885
-Sunshine and Snow. Chapman, 1878
-Thrice Past the Post. White, 1891
Tie and Trick. Chapman, 1885; Harper, 1885
-Two Kisses. Bentley, 1875; Loring, 1877
-Vanity's Daughter. White, 1893; Taylor, 1892
Without Love or Licence. Chatto, 1890

SMITH, ARTHUR. 1896- .
-Against All Odds. Stockwell, 1973
Cloggy Dick. Stockwell, 1974

SMITH, ADAM. Joint pseudonym of George (J. W.) Goodman, 1920- , q.v., and Winthrop Knowlton.

SMITH, ANN T.
Death in the Cards. Phoenix, 1946

SMITH, ANNIE L. [MRS. LYDIA ANNIE JOCELYN SMITH]. 1836- .
The Black Mask; or, Bonnie Orielle's Lovers. Neely, 1898

SMITH, ANTHONY HECKSTALL. 1904- . See: ANTHONY HECKSTALL-SMITH.

SMITH, C.I.D. 1894- . Series character: Insp. Barlowe, in both titles.
No Epitaph for Mr. Zarke. Jenkins, 1941
Thy Guilt is Great. Jenkins, 1939

SMITH, CAESAR. Pseudonym of Elleston Trevor, 1920- , q.v. Name originally: Trevor Dudley Smith, q.v. Other pseudonyms: Mansell Black, Adam Hall, Simon Rattray, Warwick Scott, qq.v.
Heatwave. Wingate, 1957; Ballantine, 1958. Reprinted as by Elleston Trevor: White Lion, 1972

SMITH, CARMICHAEL. Pseudonym of Paul Myron Anthony Linebarger, 1913-1966.
Atomsk. Duell, 1949

SMITH, CHARLES MERRILL
Reverend Randollph and the Wages of Sin. Putnam, 1974; Barker, 1975

SMITH, CHARLOTTE (TURNER). 1749-1806.
The Old Manor House. Bell, 1793

SMITH, CHESTER ALFRED. 1920- .
The Web of Deceit. Comet, 1957

SMITH, (ALEXANDER) CLARK. 1919- .
Series character: Nicky Mahoun, in all titles.
The Case of Torches. Hammond, 1957
The Deadly Reaper. Hammond, 1956
The Speaking Eye. Hammond, 1955

SMITH, DAVID MacLEOD. 1920- . Pseudonym: David Mariner, q.v.

SMITH, DEREK
Whistle Up the Devil. Gifford, 1953

SMITH, DON(ALD TAYLOR). 1909- . Series characters: Tim Parnell = TP; Phil Sherman = PS.
China Coaster. Holt, 1953
Corsican Takeover. GM, 1974; Coronet, 1974 TP
Death Stalk in Spain. Award, 1972 PS
Haitian Vendetta. Award, 1973 PS
The Libyan Contract. Award, 1974 PS
The Man Who Played Thief. GM, 1969; Hale, 1971 TP
The Marseilles Enforcer. Award, 1972 PS
Night of the Assassin. Award, 1972 PS
The Padrone. GM, 1971; Coronet, 1971 TP
The Payoff. GM, 1973; Coronet, 1974 TP
The Peking Connection. Award, 1975 PS
Perilous Holiday. Holt, 1951
Secret Mission: Angola. Award, 1970 PS
Secret Mission: Athens. Award, 1971 PS
Secret Mission: Cairo. Award, 1970 PS
Secret Mission: Corsica. Award, 1968; Tandem, 1968 PS
Secret Mission: Istanbul. Award, 1969; Tandem, 1971 PS
Secret Mission: Morocco. Award, 1968; Tandem, 1968 PS
Secret Mission: Munich. Award, 1970 PS
Secret Mission: North Korea. Award, 1970 PS
Secret Mission: Peking. Award, 1968; Tandem, 1971 PS
Secret Mission: Prague. Award, 1968; Tandem, 1971 PS

Secret Mission: The Kremlin Plot. Award, 1971 PS
Secret Mission: Tibet. Award, 1969; Tandem, 1971 PS

SMITH, EDGAR (HERBERT). 1934- .
A Reasonable Doubt. Coward, 1970

SMITH, EDWARD ERNEST. 1915- . Pseudonym: Edward Lindall, q.v.

SMITH, EDWARD PERCY. 1891- . Pseudonym: Edward Percy, q.v.

SMITH, ERNEST BRAMAH. 1868-1942. Pseudonym: Ernest Bramah, q.v.

SMITH, ESSEX. Pseudonym of Frances Essex Theodora Hope.
The Wye Valley Mystery. Hutchinson, 1929

SMITH, FRANK A(LLAN). 1927- . Series character: Supt. Pepper, in at least those marked P.
Corpse in Handcuffs. Hale, 1969 P
Defectors are Dead Men. Hale, 1971 P
The Traitor Mask. Hale, 1974

SMITH, FRANK E. 1919- . Pseudonym: Jonathan Craig, q.v.

SMITH, (DAVID) FRED(ERICK). 1888-1976.
The Broadcast Murders. Day, 1931

SMITH, FREDERICK E(SCREET). 1922- .
Pseudonym: David Farrell, q.v.
The Devil Behind Me. Hodder, 1962
The Grotto of Tiberius. Hodder, 1961
A Killing for the Hawks. Harrap, 1966; McKay, 1967
Laws be Their Enemy. Hutchinson, 1955
Lydia Trendennis. Hutchinson, 1957; Paperback Library, 1964
Of Masks and Minds. Hutchinson, 1954
The Persuaders Again!; see The Persuaders #2
The Persuaders #1. Pan, 1972; Ballantine, 1972. (Two novelettizations of the TV series.)
The Persuaders #2. Pan, 1972; Ballantine, 1972. Also published as: The Persuaders Again! Ian Henry, 1976. (Two novelettizations of the TV series.)
The Persuaders #3. Pan, 1973. (Three novelettizations of the TV series.)
-Saffron's War. Futura, 1975
The Sin and the Sinners. Jarrolds, 1958
633 Squadron. Hutchinson, 1956; Signet, 1964
633 Squadron, Operation Rhine Maiden. Cassell, 1975
-The Storm Knight. Harrap, 1966
-The Tormented. Cassell, 1974
-Waterloo. Baker, 1970; Award, 1971. (Novelization of the movie.)
-The Wider Sea of Love. Harrap, 1969

SMITH, FREDERICK M(ILLER). 1870- .
The Stolen Signet. Duffield, 1909

SMITH, FREDERIKA SHUMWAY
The House and the Tower. Christopher, 1951

SMITH, GARRET
I Did It! Chelsea, 1928

SMITH, GEORGE MALCOLM. 1901- . See: GEORGE MALCOLM-SMITH.

SMITH, GODFREY. 1926- .
-The Business of Loving. Gollancz, 1961; Stein, 1968
The Flaw in the Crystal. Gollancz, 1954; Putnam, 1954

-The Friends. Gollancz, 1957; Stein, 1968
-The Network. Hodder, 1965

SMITH, GUY N(EWMAN)
The Slime Beast. New English Library pb, 1975
The Sucking Pit. New English Library pb, 1975
Werewolf by Moonlight. New English Library pb, 1974

SMITH, H(ERBERT) MAYNARD. 1869-1949. Series character: Inspector Frost, in all titles.
Inspector Frost and Lady Brassingham. Benn, 1930
Inspector Frost and the Waverdale Fire. Benn, 1931
Inspector Frost and the Whitbourne Murder. Benn, 1939
Inspector Frost in Crevenna Cove. Benn, 1933; Minton, 1933
Inspector Frost in the Background. Faber, 1941
Inspector Frost in the City. Benn, 1930; Doubleday, 1930
Inspector Frost's Jigsaw. Benn, 1929; Doubleday, 1929

SMITH, HELEN ZENNA. 1896- . Pseudonym: Evadne Price, q.v.

SMITH, HORACE (HERBERT). 1868-1936.
Crooks of the Waldorf. Macaulay, 1929; Long, 1930. (Fictionalized true crime.)

SMITH, J(OHN) F(REDERICK)
Woman and her Master. Bradley, 1897

SMITH, JACK NICKLE
-The Black Troopers. Hale, 1972
-Is He Dead, Miss Ffinch? Tallis, 1969

SMITH, JOHN TALBOT. 1855-1923. ·
The Art of Disappearing. Young, 1902. Also published as: The Man Who Vanished. Benziger, 1922

SMITH, JOHNSTON
Murder in the Square. Archer, 1933

SMITH, LAURA
-Cuckoo in the Nest. Hale, 1970
Friarsmead. Hale, 1969
From this Day Forth. Hale, 1970
-The Maitland Inheritance. Hale, 1969

SMITH, LAURENCE DWIGHT. Series character: Dick Whelan = DW.
The Corpse with the Listening Ear. Mystery House, 1940 DW
Death is Thy Neighbor. Lippincott, 1938
Follow This Fair Corpse. Mystery House, 1941 DW
Girl Hunt. Lippincott, 1937

SMITH, LOU
Fear and the Dead Man. Collins, 1968
Psycho in Focus. Macmillan (London), 1969
The Secret of MI6. Hale, 1975; St. Martin's, 1978

SMITH, MARK. 1935- .
The Death of the Detective. Knopf, 1974; Secker, 1975
Toyland. Little, 1965

SMITH, MARTIN (CRUZ). 1942- . Pseudonym: Simon Quinn, q.v. Series character: Roman Grey = RG.

Smith, Martin

The Analog Bullet. Belmont, 1972
Canto for a Gypsy. Putnam, 1972; Barker, 1975 RG
Gypsy in Amber. Putnam, 1971; Barker, 1975 RG

SMITH, NAOMI GWLADYS ROYDE. See: NAOMI (GWLADYS) ROYDE-SMITH.

SMITH, NEVILLE
Gumshoe. Fontana, 1971; Ballantine, 1972. (Novelization of the movie.)

SMITH, NORMAN EDWARD MACE. 1914- .
Pseudonym: Neil Sheraton, q.v.

SMITH, PAULINE C(OGGESHALL). 1908- .
Nothing But Blood. Chicago Paperback House, 1962

SMITH, RICHARD N. 1937- .
Death Be Nimble. Signet, 1967

SMITH, ROBERT CHARLES. 1938- . Pseudonyms: Robert Charles, Charles Leader, qq.v.

SMITH, ROBERT KIMMEL. 1930- .
Ransom. McKay, 1971; Constable, 1972

SMITH, SHELLEY. Pseudonym of Nancy Hermione Bodington, 1912- . Series character: Jacob Chaos, in at least those marked JC.
An Afternoon to Kill. Collins, 1953; Harper, 1954
Background for Murder. Swan, 1942 JC
The Ballad of the Running Man. H. Hamilton, 1961; Harper, 1962
The Cellar at No. 5; see The Party at No. 5
Come and Be Killed! Collins, 1946; Harper, 1947
The Crooked Man; see Man Alone
Death Stalks a Lady. Swan, 1945
A Grave Affair. H. Hamilton, 1971; Doubleday, 1973
He Died of Murder! Collins, 1947; Harper, 1948 JC
The Lord Have Mercy. H. Hamilton, 1956; Harper, 1956. Also published as: The Shrew is Dead. Dell, 1959
Man Alone. Collins, 1952. U.S. title: The Crooked Man. Harper, 1952
Man with a Calico Face. Collins, 1951; Harper, 1950
The Party at No. 5. Collins, 1954. U.S. title: The Cellar at No. 5. Harper, 1954
Rachel Weeping. H. Hamilton, 1957; Harper, 1957. (Three novelets.)
The Shrew is Dead; see The Lord Have Mercy
This is the House. Collins, 1945
The Woman in the Sea. Collins, 1948; Harper, 1948

SMITH, SPENSER
The Dead Don't Matter. Long, 1960

SMITH, SURREY. Pseudonym of William Dinner, q.v.
The Astonished Guardsman. Boardman, 1965
No Tears for Teddy. Boardman, 1964

SMITH, TERRENCE LORE. Pseudonym: Phillips Lore, q.v. Series character: Webster Daniels, in both titles.
The Devil and Webster Daniels. Doubleday, 1975
The Thief Who Came to Dinner. Doubleday, 1971

SMITH, (JAMES) THORNE. 1893-1934.
Did She Fall? Cosmopolitan, 1930; Barker, 1936

SMITH, TREVOR DUDLEY. Original name of Elleston Trevor, 1920- , q.v. Pseudonyms: Mansell Black, Trevor Burgess, Adam Hall, Simon Rattray, Warwick Scott, Caesar Smith, qq.v.
Double Who Double Crossed. Swan, 1944
Escape to Fear. Swan, 1948
Now Try the Morgue. Swan, 1948
Over the Wall. Swan, 1943

SMITH, VERN E.
The Jones Men. Regnery, 1974; Weidenfeld, 1975

SMITH, WALLACE
-The Happy Alienist. Smith & Haas, 1936; Heinemann, 1936

SMITH, WILBUR
-The Train from Katanga. Heinemann, 1965. U.S. title: The Dark of the Sun. Dell, 1977

SMITH, WILLARD K. Series character: Inspector Dan Carr, in both titles.
Bowery Murder. Doubleday, 1929; Collins, 1930
The Sultan's Skull. Archer, 1933

SMITH, WILLIAM DALE. 1929- . Pseudonym: David Anthony, q.v.

SMITH, YORK
The Banana Murders. Macdonald, 1958
Night of Wrath. Macdonald, 1959

SMITH, Z. Z. Pseudonym of David Westheimer, 1917- , q.v.
A Very Private Island. Signet, 1963

SMITHIES, MURIEL. Pseudonym: Muriel Howe, q.v.

SMITHIES, RICHARD H(UGO) R(IPMAN). 1936- . Series character: Inspector McAlpin, in at least those marked M.
An Academic Question. Horizon, 1965. Also published as: Death Gets an A. Signet, 1968 M
Death Gets an A; see An Academic Question
Death Takes a Gamble; see Disposing Mind
Disposing Mind. Horizon, 1966. Also published as: Death Takes a Gamble. Signet, 1968 M
Fern Dead. Barrie, 1971. (U.S. title?)
The Shoplifter. Horizon, 1968; Jenkins, 1969
The Tease. Signet, 1975

SMYLES, L. E.
A Millionaire's Folly; or, The Beautiful Unknown. Street (Magnet), 1900

SMYTHE, ALAN LYLE. 1914- . Pseudonym: Alan Caillou, q.v.

SMYTHIES, MRS. G. [HARRIET MARIA GORDON SMYTHIES]
Guilty or Not Guilty. Ward, 1864

SNAITH, J(OHN) C(OLLIS). 1876-1936.
-Broke of Covenden. Constable, 1904; Turner, 1905
The Council of Seven. Collins, 1921; Appleton, 1921
The Crime of Constable Kelly. Nelson, 1924
Curiouser and Curiouser. Hutchinson, 1935. U.S. title: Lord Cobleigh Disappears. Appleton, 1936

Henry Northcote. Constable, 1906; Turner, 1906
Lord Cobleigh Disappears; see Curiouser and Curiouser
-Mistress Dorothy Marvin. Ward, 1900
-One of the Ones. Hutchinson, 1937
Thus Far. Hodder, 1925; Appleton, 1925
The Unforeseen. Hodder, 1930; Appleton, 1930
-William Jordan Junior. Long, 1925

SNEDDON, ROBERT W(ILLIAM). 1880- .
-The Galleon's Gold. Methuen, 1925
Monsieur X. Methuen, 1926; Dial, 1928

SNELL, EDMUND. 1889- . Series characters: Reggie Faulkner, in at least those marked RF; Peter Pennington, in at least those marked PP.
And Then...One Dark Night. Skeffington, 1933
Anti-Crime Ltd. Mellifont, 1939
Back from the Dead. Mellifont, 1940
Blue Murder. Unwin, 1927; Lippincott, 1933
Calling All Cars. Mellifont, 1938
-Corrigan's Way. Unwin, 1924
The Crimson Butterfly. Unwin, 1924
The Crimson Swastika. Mellifont, 1938
Crooks Limited. Skeffington, 1934
The Dope Dealer. Mellifont, 1941
Emerald of Death. Everybody's, 1944
The Finger of Destiny and other stories. Quality, 1938 ss
Grid Murder. Mellifont, 1937
-Kontrol. Benn, 1928; Lippincott, 1928
Murder at the Miramar. Skeffington, 1936
Murder in Switzerland. Hale, 1938; Hillman-Curl, 1938 RF
-The Purple Shadow. Unwin, 1927
The Red Spinner. Hale, 1937; Hillman-Curl, 1938 RF
The Sign of the Scorpion. Skeffington, 1935
-The Sound Machine. Skeffington, 1932
Suicide House. Mellifont, 1941
The White Owl. Hodder, 1930; Lippincott, 1930
Yellow Jacket. Skeffington, 1936 PP
The Yellow Seven. Unwin, 1923; Century, 1923 PP
The Yu-Chi Stone. Unwin, 1925; Macaulay, 1926
The "Z" Ray. Skeffington, 1932; Lippincott, 1932 RF

SNELLING, LAURENCE. 1933- .
The Heresy. H. Hamilton, 1973; Norton, 1973

SNODGRESS, G. M.
The Crestwood Traps. Papillon, 1974

SNOW, C(HARLES) P(ERCY). 1905- .
Death Under Sail. Heinemann, 1932; Doubleday, 1932
The Sleep of Reason. Macmillan (London), 1968; Scribner, 1969

SNOW, CHARLES H(ORACE). 1877- . Pseudonym: Charles Ballew, q.v. Series character: Tommy Thorne, in at least those marked TT.
The Bonanza Murder Case. Wright, 1934 TT
The Brush Creek Murders. Wright, 1937
The Buckhorn Murder Case. Wright, 1952
The Desert Castle Mystery. Wright, 1936
The Highgrade Murder. Wright, 1949
Hollow Stump Mystery. Wright, 1934
The Lakeside Murder. Wright, 1933 TT
The Mountain Murder Case. Wright, 1951
Murder on the Cattle Ranch. Wright, 1935
The Mysterious Missile. Wright, 1950
The Mystery of Devil's Canyon. Wright, 1941

The Sign of the Death Circle. Wright, 1935 TT
The Silent Shot. Wright, 1932
Twice Murdered. Wright, 1954

SNOW, LYNDON. Pseudonym of Dorothy Phoebe Ansle. Other pseudonyms: Laura Conway, Hebe Elsna, qq.v. Titles under this byline were apparently published in Britain as romances; those also published in the U.S. as gothics are listed below.
Francesca. Collins, 1970; Saturday Review Press, 1973, as by Laura Conway
Moment of Truth. Collins, 1968; Saturday Review Press, 1975, as by Laura Conway

SNOW, WALTER. 1907-1973.
The Golden Nightmare. Austin-Phelps, 1952

SNOWDEN, (JAMES) KEIGHLEY. 1860- .
-Hate of Evil. Hutchinson, 1907
-Jack the Outlaw. Simpkin, 1926
The Plunder Pit. Methuen, 1898

SNYDER, CHARLES M(cCOY). 1859- .
The Flaw in the Sapphire. Metropolitan, 1909

SOHL, JERRY [GERALD ALLAN SOHL]. 1913- .
-The Altered Ego. Rinehart, 1954
The Odious Ones. Rinehart, 1959; Consul, 1961
Prelude to Peril. Rinehart, 1957

SOMERS, CHRISTOPHER. See: J(OHN FREEMAN) FAIRFAX-BLAKEBOROUGH, 1883- .

SOMERS, JOHN
The Brethren of the Axe. Murray, 1926; Dutton, 1927

SOMERS, MARK
Merely Michael. Hutchinson, 1922. U.S. title: The Haunted House of Marley. Moffat, 1923

SOMERS, PAUL. Pseudonym of Paul Winterton, 1908- . Other pseudonyms: Roger Bax, Andrew Garve, qq.v. Series character: Hugh Curtis = HC.
Beginner's Luck. Collins, 1958; Harper, 1958 HC
The Broken Jigsaw. Collins, 1961; Harper, 1961
Operation Piracy. Collins, 1958; Harper, 1959 HC
The Shivering Mountain. Collins, 1959; Harper, 1959 HC

SOMERS, SUZANNE
The House on Thunder Hill. Curtis, 1973
The Mists of Mourning. Tower, 1966
The Romany Curse. Belmont, 1971
Until Death. Curtis, 1973

SOMERVILLE, CHARLES (CECIL LEE D'MONTRAL). 1876?-1931.
An Artist in Crime. Curtiss, 1928; Paul, 1929
The Master Rogue. Lippincott, 1935

SOMERVILLE, HENRY
Black Triangle. Modern, 1938
The Leland Case. Modern, 193?

SOMERVILLE, IVAN
Scattered Death. Alexandrian, 1931

SOMERVILLE-LARGE, PETER. 1928- .
Couch of Earth. Gollancz, 1975

SONIN, RAY. 1907- .
The Dance Band Mystery. Quality, 1940
The Death Pack. Fenland, 1933
Murder in Print. Jenkins, 1953; Roy, 1956
The Mystery of the Tailor's Dummy. Harrap, 1935
Twice Times Murder. Jenkins, 1954

SONTUP, DANIEL. 1922- . Pseudonym: David Saunders, q.v.

SOUTAR, ANDREW. 1879- . Series characters: Phineas Spinnet, in at least those marked PS; Kharduni, in at least those marked K.
Back from the Dead. Hodder, 1920
-Back to Eden. Hutchinson, 1927
-Battling Barker. Hutchinson, 1923
-A Beggar in Purple. Hodder, 1918
The Black Spot Mystery. Hutchinson, 1938 PS
-Broken Ladders. Cassell, 1912
-Butterflies in the Rain. Hutchinson, 1926
Chain Murder. Hutchinson, 1939 PS
The Chosen of the Gods. Harper (London), 1910
Consider Your Verdict. Hutchinson, 1928
-Corinthian Days. Hutchinson, 1923
-Cowards' Castle. Hutchinson, 1934
-Dear Fools. Hutchinson, 1927
-Delilah of Mayfair. Hutchinson, 1926
-The Devil's Triangle. Hutchinson, 1931
Eight Three Five. Hutchinson, 1935 PS
-Equality Island. Hodder, 1919
Facing East. Hutchinson, 1936 PS
The Great Conspiracy. Hutchinson, 1934
-The Green Orchard. Cassell, 1916
-Hagar, Called Hannah. Hutchinson, 1933
The Hanging Sword! Hutchinson, 1933 PS
-Hornets Nest. Murray, 1922
-The Imperfect Lover. Hodder, 1919
-In the Blood. Jarrolds, 1928
-The Island of Test. Harper (London), 1910
Justice is Done. Hutchinson, 1936 K
Kharduni. Hutchinson, 1933; Macaulay, 1934 K
The Leopard's Spots. Hutchinson, 1928
-Magpie House. Cassell, 1913
-The Marquis. Hodder, 1919
The Master Key. Federation, 1926
The Money Spinners and other stories. Hutchinson, 1934 ss
Motive for the Crime. Hutchinson, 1941
-Mr. Nobody of England. Hutchinson, 1942
The Museum Mystery. Hutchinson, 1936 PS
Neither do I Condemn Thee. Hutchinson, 1924
Night of Horror. Hutchinson, 1934 PS
"Not Mentioned..." Hutchinson, 1930
One Page Missing. Hutchinson, 1938 PS
Opportunity. Hutchinson, 1932
-Ostrich Man. Hutchinson, 1937
-Other Men's Shoes. Hodder, 1918
-Pagans. Hutchinson, 1928
-The Perverted Village. Hutchinson, 1936
The Phantom in the House. Hutchinson, 1928
-The Prodigal, and other stories. Hodder, 1919 ss
Public Ghost Number One. Hutchinson, 1941
Pursuit. Hutchinson, 1927
-Rainbow Nights, and other stories. Hodder, 1919 ss
-The Road to Romance. Murray, 1921
Secret Ways. Hutchinson, 1932; Kendall, 1934
Silence! Hutchinson, 1930
Silent Accuser. Hutchinson, 1938 PS
Sinister River. Hutchinson, 1936
-Snow in the Desert. Hodder, 1919
"The Stars I'd Give—". Hutchinson, 1937
The Strange Case of Sir Merton Quest. Hutchinson, 1940 PS

A Stranger Came to Dinner. Hutchinson, 1939 PS
Study in Suspense. Hutchinson, 1941 PS
Thirty Pieces of Silver. Hutchinson, 1931
The White Lie Company, and The Woman with the Green Eyes. Hodder, 1927
The Wolves and the Lamb. Hutchinson, 1940 PS
-Worldly Goods. Hutchinson, 1928

SOUTH, MARSHALL
The Curse of the Sightless Fish. World's Work, 1948

SOUTHCOTT, AUDLEY
The Black General. Macdonald, 1969; Morrow, 1969

SOUTHNEY, LYN
Deadly Fresco. Moray, 1939

SOUTHWICK, ALBERT P(LYMPTON). 1855-1929.
The Catherwood Mystery. Taylor, 1892

SOUTHWOLD, STEPHEN. 1887-1964. Pseudonyms: Neil Bell, Paul Martens, qq.v.

SOUTHWORTH, MRS. E(MMA) D(OROTHY) E(LIZA) N(EVITTE). 1819-1899. At least some of these titles contain significant crime/gothic elements. Considerable bibliographic confusion exists for this author, most of which has resisted removal, as will be evident below.
Allworth Abbey. Peterson, 1865
The Artist's Love. Peterson, 1872
Astrea; or, The Bridal Day. (London), 1862. (U.S. title?)
Beatrice; The Forsaken Daughter. 1872
Brandon Coyle's Wife. Bonner's, 1893
The Bridal Eve. Peterson, 1864; Milner, 1878
The Bride of an Evening; see The Gipsy's Prophecy
The Bride of Llewellyn. Peterson, 1866
The Bride's Fate. Milner, 1878. (U.S. title?)
The Broken Engagement; or, Speaking the Truth for a Day. Peterson, 1862
Broken Pledges. Peterson, 1891
Captain Rock's Pet. 1863
The Changed Brides. Peterson, 1869; Milner, 1878
The Christmas Guest. Peterson, 1870
The Coral Lady; or, The Bronzed Beauty of Paris. Alexander, 1867
Cruel as the Grave. Peterson, 1871
The Curse of Clifton; or, The Widowed Bride. Hart, 1853; Clarke, 1853
David Lindsay. Bonner's, 1893
The Deserted Wife. Appleton, 1851; Clarke, 1856
The Discarded Daughter; or, The Children of the Isle. Peterson, 1875
"Em." Bonner's, 1892
Em's Husband. Bonner's, 1892
An Exile's Bride. 1887
Fair Play; or, The Test of the Lone Island. 1868
Fallen Pride; or, The Mountain Girl's Love. Peterson, 1868
The Family Doom; or, The Sin of a Countess. Peterson, 1888
The Fatal Marriage. Peterson, 1863; Milner, 1878
The Fatal Secret. Peterson, 1877
For Woman's Love. Bonner's, 1890
The Fortune Seeker. Peterson, 1866; Milner, 1878
Gertrude Haddon. Bonner's, 1894

Southworth, Mrs. E. D. E. N.

The Gipsy's Prophecy; or, The Bride of an Evening. Peterson, 1861. British title: The Bride of an Evening; or, The Gipsy's Prophecy. Milner, 18??
Gloria. Bonner's, 1891
Hagar; or, The Deserted Wife. Milner, 18??. (U.S. title?)
The Haunted Homestead. Peterson, 1860 ss
Hester Strong's Life Work. (Boston), 1869
Hickory Hall; or, The Outcast. Peterson, 1861
The Hidden Hand. (U.S.), 18??; Ward, 1859
How He Won Her. Peterson, 1869; (London), 1869
India. Peterson, 1856
Ishmael; or, In the Depths. (U.S.), 1884
The Island Princess; or, The Double Marriage. Bryce, 1857
The Lady of the Isle. Peterson, 1859
A Leap in the Dark. Bonner's, 1890
Lilith. Bonner's, 1891
Little Ned's Engagement. Street, 1908
The Lost Bride. Lea, 1858. (U.S. title?)
The Lost Heir of Linlithgow. Peterson, 1872
The Lost Heiress. (Philadelphia), 1855; Ward, 1855
Love's Labor Won. Peterson, 1862
The Maiden Widow. Peterson, 1870
Mark Sutherland; or, Power and Principle. Cassell, 1853. (U.S. title?)
The Missing Bride; or, Miriam the Avenger. 1872
The Mother-in-law; or, The Isle of Rays. Clarke, 1853. (U.S. title?)
Mother's Secret. (London), 1883. (U.S. title?)
The Mysterious Marriage. Street, 1908
The Mystery of Dark Hollow. Peterson, 1875
Nearest and Dearest. Bonner's, 1889
A Noble Lord. Peterson, 1872
Only a Girl's Heart. Bonner's, 1893; Modern, 1935
The Phantom Wedding; or, The Fall of the House of Flint. Peterson, 1878
The Prince of Darkness. Peterson, 1869
The Red Hill Tragedy. Peterson, 1877
The Rejected Bride. Bonner's, 1894
Retribution. (New York), 1849; Lea, 1858
Self-Made. 1861
Self-Raised; or, From the Depths. Peterson, 1876; Milner, 18??
Shannondale. (New York), 1851. British title: Winny Darling; or, Three Beauties of Shannondale. Clarke, 1856
A Skeleton in the Closet. Bonner's, 1893
The Spectre Lover. Peterson, 1875
Sybil Brotherton. Peterson, 1879
The Test of Love; see The Trail of the Serpent
A Tortured Heart; see The Trail of the Serpent
The Trail of the Serpent. (U.S.), 1879. Also published as: The Test of Love, plus: A Tortured Heart. Street, 1907
Tried for Her Life. Philadelphia, 1871
The Two Sisters; or, Virginia and Magdalene; see Virginia and Magdalene
The Unknown. 1874
Unknown; or, The Mystery of Raven Rocks. Bonner's, 1889
The Unloved Wife. Bonner's, 1891
Virginia and Magdalene; or, The Foster Sisters. Peterson, 1852. Also published as: The Two Sisters; or, Virginia and Magdalene. Peterson, 1875. British title: The Two Sisters. Lea, 1859
Vivia; or, The Secret of Power. Peterson, 1875
The Widow's Son. Peterson, 1867
The Wife's Victory. Peterson, 1854 ss
Winny Darling; see Shannondale
Woman's Fate. Modern, 1935. (U.S. title?)

SOUTHWORTH, LOUIS. Pseudonym of Thomas Gridley.
Corpse on London Bridge. Hale, 1969
Felon in Disguise. Hale, 1966

SOUVESTRE, PIERRE, 1874-1914, and MARCEL ALLAIN, 1885- . Series character: Fantomas, in all titles; series continued by Allain, q.v.
The Exploits of Juve. Paul, 1916; Brentano's, 1917
Fantomas. Paul, 1915; Brentano's, 1915
A Limb of Satan. Paul, 1924. U.S. title: The Long Arm of Fantomas. Macaulay, 1924
The Long Arm of Fantomas; see A Limb of Satan
Messengers of Evil. Paul, 1917; Brentano's, 1917
A Nest of Spies. Paul, 1917; Brentano's, 1917
A Royal Prisoner. Paul, 1919; Brentano's, 1918
Slippery as Sin. Paul, 1920; Moffat, 1923

SOUZA, ERNEST. Pseudonym of Evelyn Scott, 1893- .
Blue Rum. Cape & Smith, 1930; Cape, 1930

SOWMAN, GORDON
Expendable Agent. Church, 1968

SPADE, DANNY. Pseudonym of Dail Ambler, q.v.
The Dame Plays Rough. Scion, 1950
'Frisco Rock. Scion, 1951
A Gun for Sale. Scion, 1952
Kiss Me as You Go. Milestone, 1953
Lady Likes to Sin. Milestone, 1953
Nothing to Hide. Milestone, 1953
Silk and Cordite. Scion, 1951
Story of a Killer. Milestone, 1953
That's All I Need. Milestone, 1954
Twice as Dead. Scion, 1952
You Slay Me. Scion, 1950
You'll Play This My Way. Scion, 1951

SPAIN, JOHN. Pseudonym of Cleve F(ranklin) Adams, 1895-1949, q.v. Joint pseudonym with Robert Leslie Bellem, q.v.: Franklin Charles, q.v. Series character: Bill Rye = BR.
Death is Like That. Dutton, 1943 BR
Dig Me a Grave. Dutton, 1942 BR
The Evil Star. Dutton, 1944

SPAIN, NANCY. 1917- . Series characters: Miriam Birdseye = MB; Johnny DuVivien = JD.
Cinderella Goes to the Morgue. Hutchinson, 1950 MB
Death Before Wicket. Hutchinson, 1946 JD
Death Goes on Skis. Hutchinson, 1949 MB
The Kat Strikes. Hutchinson, 1955
Murder, Bless It! Hutchinson, 1948 JD
Not Wanted on Voyage. Hutchinson, 1951 MB
Out, Damned Tot! Hutchinson, 1952 MB
Poison for Teacher. Hutchinson, 1949 MB
Poison in Play. Hutchinson, 1946 JD
R in the Month. Hutchinson, 1950 MB

SPAIN, RICHARD
The Strange Citadel. Jenkins, 1931

SPAIN, TERRY
Time to Kill. Popular Library, 1953

SPANN, WELDON (OMA). 1924- .
Discharge to Danger. Hale, 1969
Hunter for Hire. Hale, 1970
Plunge into Peril. Hale, 1970
Return to Violence. Hale, 1969
The Stink of Murder. Hale, 1969
Wall of Jeopardy. Hale, 1970

SPARK, MURIEL (SARAH). 1918- .
The Comforters. Macmillan (London), 1957; Lippincott, 1957
Robinson. Macmillan (London), 1958; Lippincott, 1958

SPARKES, BOYDEN. See: CLAIRE CARVALHO.

SPARKIA, ROY B(ENARD). 1914- .
-Boss Man. Lion, 1954
Build My Gallows High. GM, 1956; Fawcett (London), 1957
The Vanishing Vixen. Crest, 1959; Muller, 1960

SPARROY, MASSICKS. Pseudonym.
The Leper's Bell. Collins, 1921; Putnam, 1921
The Listening Woman. Faber, 1932; Little, 1932

SPATZ, H. DONALD. 1913- .
Death on the Nose. Phoenix, 1942
Murder with Long Hair. Phoenix, 1940
3 Girls and a Killer. Crime Novel Selection, 194? (Retitled reprint?)

SPEAR, ANNE B. Joint pseudonym with Bessie C. Morris: Forfex et Hesta, q.v.

SPEARMAN, FRANK H(AMILTON). 1859-1937.
The Nerve of Foley, and other railroad stories. Harper, 1900 ss, some criminous

SPEARS, RAYMOND S(MILEY). 1876- .
Diamond Tolls. Doubleday, 1920

SPEIGHT, T(HOMAS) W(ILKINSON). 1830-1915.
As It was Written. Chatto, 1902
-Back to Life. Taylor, 1891. (British title?)
-A Barren Title. Chatto, 1886; Harper, 1885
A Bootless Crime. Digby, 1909
-Brought to Light. Wood, 1867; Hilton, 1967
-Burgo's Romance. Chatto, 1894
-By Fate's Caprice. Digby, 1904
-By Fortune's Whim. Digby, 1903
The Celestial Ruby. Digby, 1904
The Chains of Circumstance. Digby, 1900
The Crime in the Wood. Long, 1899
The Doom of Siva. Chatto, 1899
The Fate of the Hara Diamond. Greening, 1907
Foiled. Digby, 1911
-Foolish Margaret. Wood, 1867
-For Himself Alone. Munro, 1884. (British title?)
The Grey Monk. Chatto, 1895
The Heart of a Mystery. Jarrolds, 1896; Fenno, 1896
-Her Ladyship. Chatto, 1903
In the Dead of Night. Bentley, 1874
-Juggling Fortune. Long, 1900
-A Late Repentance. Digby, 1901
The Loudwater Tragedy. Chatto, 1892
The Master of Trenance. Chatto, 1896
A Minion of the Moon. Chatto, 1897; New Amsterdam, 1896
-Mr. Spenyard's Two Experiments. Digby, 1908
The Mysteries of Heron Dyke. Bentley, 1880; Harper, 1881
-On the Fringe. Digby, 1912

The Plotters. Digby, 1905
The Price of a Secret. Digby, 1908
Quittance in Full. Chatto, 18??
The Sandycroft Mystery. Chatto, 1890
-Second Love. Digby, 1900
A Secret of the Sea. Bentley, 1876
The Secret of Wyvern Towers. Chatto, 1898
The Sport of Chance. Digby, 1903
-Stepping Blindfold. Chatto, 1903
-The Strange Experiences of Mr. Verschoyle. Chatto, 1901
-Tangled Lives. Jarrolds, 1910
-Time Bargains. Digby, 1907
-Under a Cloud. Digby, 1906
Under Lock and Key. Tinsley, 1869; Turner, 1869
Ursula Lenorme: Lady Companion. Digby, 1909 ss
The Web of Fate. Chatto, 1900
-Wife or No Wife?, and A Close Shave. Chatto, 1887. (Two stories.)

SPENCE, EDWARD F(ORDHAM). 1860- .
The Crime of Sybil Cresswell. Benn, 1929
-A Freak of Fate. White, 1886

SPENCE, (JAMES) LEWIS (THOMAS CHALMERS). 1874-1955.
The Archer in the Arras, and other tales of mystery. Grant, 1932 ss

SPENCE, RALPH
The Gorilla. French, 1950. (3-act play.)

SPENCE, WILL. All titles below are plays, with the number of acts given in parentheses.
The Dark House. Dramatists Play Service, 1939 (3)
The Full Moon. French, 1935 (1)
"Ghostly Fingers." Northwestern, 1932 (3)
"The Green Phantom." Northwestern, 1935 (3)
"The House of Fear." Northwestern, 1937 (3)
The Sign of the Four. Northwestern, 1940 (3) (Suggested by the story by A. Conan Doyle, 1859-1930, q.v.)
Whispering Walls. French, 1935 (3)
Wits' End. French, 1935 (1)
The Woman in Black. Northwestern, 1938 (3)

SPENCER, MRS. BELLA Z(ILFA). 1840-1867.
Right and Wrong; or, She Told the Truth at Last, with other stories. Holland, 1870 ss, title story criminous

SPENCER, CLAIRE
-Gallows Orchard. Cape & Smith, 1930; Cape, 1930

SPENCER, ERLE
The Death of Captain Shand. Hodder, 1930
The Four Lost Ships. Hodder, 1931
The King of Spain's Daughter. Hodder, 1934
Or Give Me Death! Harrap, 1936
The Piccadilly Ghost. Hodder, 1929; Macmillan, 1930
Stop, Press! Hodder, 1932

SPENCER, GEOFFREY. Pseudonym of Alexander (Douglas Chesney) Wilson, 1893- , q.v.
-Confessions of a Scoundrel. Laurie, 1933

SPENCER, HANK
Bad-Luck Cutie. Modern Fiction, 1953
Dumb Babes Don't Die. Modern Fiction, 1954
The Flesh Game. Modern Fiction, 1954
The Gallows are High. Modern Fiction, 1953
Gentleman's Relish. Modern Fiction, 1954
Neck of Sinners. Modern Fiction, 1954
No Face for a Killer. Modern Fiction, 1953
Vice Squad. Modern Fiction, 1954

SPENCER, JOHN. Pseudonym of Roy Vickers, 1888-1965, q.v. Other pseudonyms: David Durham, Sefton Kyle, qq.v.
Swell Garrick. Hodder, 1933. Reprinted as by Vickers: Newnes, 1935
The Whispering Death. Hodder, 1932. Reprinted as by Vickers: Newnes, 1935. U.S. edition, as by Vickers: Jefferson House, 1947

SPENCER, LEE
The Furtive Men. Jarrolds, 1951

SPENCER, PHILIP (HERBERT). 1924- .
Full Term. Faber, 1961

SPENDER, J(EAN) M(AUDE)
The Charge is Murder! Eyre, 1934
Death Comes in the Night. Eyre, 1938
Death Renders Account. Hale, 1960
Full Moon for Murder. Evans, 1948
Murder on the Prowl. Hale, 1960
Seven Days for Hanging. Hale, 1958

SPENSER, JAMES. Pseudonym of Francis Harold Guest, 1901- .
-The Awkward Marine. Longmans, 1948
Crime Against Society. Longmans, 1938
The Five Mutineers. Longmans, 1935
-Limey. Longmans, 1933
-Limey Breaks In. Longmans, 1934
-The Wheels. Longmans, 1938

SPERDUTI, DOMINICK ROCKE
For You, I Commit Murder. Christopher, 1956
That Night at Nine. William-Frederick, 1958

SPEWACK, SAMUEL. 1899-1971.
Murder in the Gilded Cage. Simon, 1929
The Skyscraper Murder. Macaulay, 1928

SPICER, BART. 1918- . Joint pseudonym with Betty Coe Spicer: Jay Barbette, q.v. Series character: Carney Wilde = CW.
Act of Anger. Atheneum, 1962; Barker, 1963
The Adversary. Putnam, 1974; Hart-Davis, 1974
Black Sheep, Run. Dodd, 1951; Collins, 1952 CW
Blues for the Prince. Dodd, 1950; Collins, 1951 CW
The Burned Man. Atheneum, 1966; Hale, 1967
The Dark Light. Dodd, 1949; Collins, 1950 CW
The Day of the Dead. Dodd, 1955; Hodder, 1956
Exit, Running. Dodd, 1959; Hodder, 1960 CW
The Golden Door. Dodd, 1951; Collins, 1951 CW
Kellogg Junction. Atheneum, 1969; Hodder, 1970
The Long Green. Dodd, 1952. British title: Shadow of Fear. Collins, 1953 CW
Shadow of Fear; see The Long Green
The Taming of Carney Wilde. Dodd, 1954; Hodder, 1955 CW

SPICER, BETTY COE. Joint pseudonym with Bart Spicer, 1918- , q.v.: Jay Barbette, q.v.

SPICER, DOROTHY (GLADYS)
The Crystal Ball. Ballantine, 1975
Desert Adventure. Bouregy, 1968; Gold Lion, 1973
Eye of the Cat. Lancer, 1973
The Humming Top. Phillips, 1968
The Tower Room. Avon, 1973; Remploy, 1973
The Witch's Web. Ballantine, 1975

SPIESS, JAN
The Amber Bead. Cassell, 1961

SPILLANE, MICKEY [FRANK MORRISON SPILLANE]. 1918- . Series characters: Mike Hammer = MH; Tiger Mann = TM.
The Big Kill. Dutton, 1951; Barker, 1952 MH
Bloody Sunrise. Dutton, 1965; Barker, 1965 TM
The Body Lovers. Dutton, 1967; Barker, 1967 MH
The By-Pass Control. Dutton, 1966; Barker, 1967 TM
Day of the Guns. Dutton, 1964; Barker, 1965 TM
The Death Dealers. Dutton, 1965; Barker, 1966 TM
The Deep. Dutton, 1961; Barker, 1961
The Delta Factor. Dutton, 1967; Corgi, 1969
The Erection Set. Dutton, 1972; Allen, 1972
The Flier. Corgi, 1964. (Two novelets.)
The Girl Hunters. Dutton, 1962; Barker, 1962 MH
I, the Jury. Dutton, 1947; Barker, 1952 MH
Killer Mine. Signet, 1968; Corgi, 1965. (Two novelets.)
Kiss Me, Deadly. Dutton, 1952; Barker, 1953 MH
The Last Cop Out. Dutton, 1973; Allen, 1973
The Long Wait. Dutton, 1951; Barker, 1953
Me, Hood! Corgi, 1963. (Three novelets.)
Me, Hood! Signet, 1969. (Two novelets, only one from the British collection of the same name.)
My Gun is Quick. Dutton, 1950; Barker, 1951 MH
One Lonely Night. Dutton, 1951; Barker, 1952 MH
Return of the Hood. Corgi, 1964. (Two novelets.)
The Snake. Dutton, 1964; Barker, 1964 MH
Survival Zero. Dutton, 1970; Corgi, 1970 MH
The Tough Guys. Signet, 1969. (Three novelets from various British collections of Spillane's novelets.)
The Twisted Thing. Dutton, 1966; Barker, 1966 MH
Vengeance is Mine! Dutton, 1950; Barker, 1951 MH

SPILLER, ANDREW. Series character: Detective Inspector "Duck" Mallard, in at least those marked M.
Alias Mr. Orson. Paul, 1951 M
And Thereby Hangs—. Paul, 1948
As They Shall Sow. Paul, 1952 M
Birds of a Feather. Paul, 1950
Black Cap for Murder. Paul, 1956
Brains Trust for Murder. Paul, 1956 M
Brief Candle. Paul, 1949
Crooked Highway. Archer, 1947
Curtain Call for Murder. Long, 1957 M
The Evil That Men Do. Paul, 1953 M
If Murder Interferes with Business. Archer, 1945

Spiller, Andrew

It's in the Bag. Paul, 1955
Kiss the Book. Paul, 1952
The Man Who Caught the 4:15. Paul, 1950
The Man Who Dressed to Kill. Long, 1960
Murder has Three Dimensions. Archer, 1948
Murder is a Shady Business. Paul, 1954
Murder on a Shoestring. Long, 1958
Murder Without Malice. Paul, 1954 M
Phantom Circus. Paul, 1950
Queue Up to Listen. Archer, 1946 M
Ring Twice for Murder. Paul, 1955
Rope for Breakfast. Archer, 1945
Sing a Song of Murder. Long, 1959
They Tell No Tales. Paul, 1953
What's in a Name? Archer, 1947 M
When Crook Meets Crook. Archer, 1947
Who Plays with Sin. Paul, 1951
Whom Nobody Owns. Archer, 1945
You Can't Get Away with Murder! Archer, 1948

SPINELLI, MARCOS. 1904-1970.
Assignment Without Glory. Lippincott, 1945; Davies, 1945

SPOFFORD, HARRIET (ELIZABETH PRESCOTT). 1835-1921.
The Amber Gods and other stories. Ticknor, 1963 ss, at least one criminous
-A Lost Jewel. Lee, 1891

SPOONER, JOHN D. 1937-   .
The King of Terrors. Little, 1975; Arrow, 1976

SPRAGUE, JOYCE CLAYPOOL
Dynasty of Fear. Lenox, 1973; Remploy, 1974

SPRIGG, C(HRISTOPHER) ST. JOHN. 1907-1937. Series character: Charles Venables = CV.
The Corpse with the Sunburnt Face. Nelson, 1935; Doubleday, 1935
Crime in Kensington. Eldon, 1933. U.S. title: Pass the Body. Dial, 1933
Death of an Airman. Hutchinson, 1934; Doubleday, 1935
Death of a Queen. Nelson, 1935 CV
Fatality in Fleet Street. Eldon, 1933 CV
Pass the Body; see Crime in Kensington
The Perfect Alibi. Eldon, 1934; Doubleday, 1934 CV
The Six Queer Things. Jenkins, 1937; Doubleday, 1937

SPRIGGE, S(AMUEL) SQUIRE. 1860-1937.
Odd Issues. Smithers, 1899 ss, some criminous

SPRING, GERALD MAX. 1897-   . Pseudonym: Richard Bodwell, q.v.

SPRINGER, BOB. See: CHARLOTTE SPRINGER.

SPRINGER, CHARLOTTE and BOB
Smugglers' Moon. Exposition, 1954

SPRINGER, NORMAN
-The Blood Ship. Watt, 1922; Unwin, 1923

SPRISSLER, ALFRED
The Avenging Note. Gernsback, 1932

SPROTT, HELEN
The Fake. [Author], 1936

SPROUL, KATHLEEN. Series character: Dick Wilson = DW.
The Birthday Murder. Dutton, 1932 DW
Death Among the Professors; see Death and the Professors
Death and the Professors. Dutton, 1933. British title: Death Among the Professors. Eyre, 1934 DW
Death Listened In. Phoenix, 1946
Murder Off Key. Dutton, 1934 DW
The Mystery of the Closed Car. Dutton, 1935 DW

SPROULE, WESLEY (R.)
Freeway to Murder. Hale, 1967
Hell in the Afternoon. Hale, 1967
Killer Waiting. Hale, 1967
Violent Death. Hale, 1967
Walk Softly. Hale, 1968

SPRY, THEODORE JAMES. 1898-   . Pseudonym: Palmer White, q.v.

SPURGEON, DOUGLAS W.
The Ippletree Manor Mystery. Ward, 1925
The Missing Witness. Ward, 1927
The Wheel of Circumstance. Ward, 1926

SQUERENT, WILL
Your Golden Jugular. Macmillan, 1970; Hale, 1971

STABLES, (WILLIAM) GORDON. 1840-1910.
The Mystery of a Millionaire's Grave. Remington, 1890
The Rose of Allandale. Digby, 1896

STACEY, BARNARD
Satan's Secret. Ward, 1956

STACKELBERG, GENE
Double Agent. Popular Library, 1959

STACPOOLE, H(ENRY) DeVERE. 1863-1951. Pseudonym: Tyler De Saix, q.v. See also: MARGARET (ROBSON) STACPOOLE.
The Cottage on the Fells. Laurie, 1908. Also published as: Murder on the Fell. Cherry Tree, 1937
-Golden Ballast. Hutchinson, 1924; Dodd, 1924
-Green Coral. Hutchinson, 1935 ss
The House of Crimson Shadows. Hutchinson, 1925; Small, 1926
Men, Women, and Beasts. Hutchinson, 1922 ss, some criminous
Murder on the Fell; see The Cottage on the Fell
The Mystery of Uncle Ballard. Cassell, 1927; Doubleday, 1928
Stories of East and West. Hutchinson, 1926 ss, some criminous
The Tales of Mynheer Amayat. Newnes, 1930 ss
The Vengeance of Mynheer Van Lok and other stories. Hutchinson, 1934 ss

STACPOOLE, MARGARET (ROBSON)
-London, 1913. Hutchinson, 1914; Duffield, 1914
The Man Who Found Himself; see Uncle Simon
Uncle Simon, with H(enry) DeVere Stacpoole, 1863-1951, q.v. Hutchinson, 1920. U.S. title: The Man Who Found Himself. Lane, 1920

STACTON, DAVID. Pseudonym: Bud Clifton, q.v.

STACY, O'CONNOR. Pseudonym of William Rollins, Jr., 1897-   , q.v.
Murder at Cypress Hall. Macaulay, 1933

STADLEY, PAT
Autumn of a Hunter. Random, 1970; Collins, 1971. Also published as: The Murder Hunt. Major, 1977
The Black Leather Barbarians. Signet, 1965
-Daddy-O. Signet, 1960
The Murder Hunt; see Autumn of a Hunter

STAFFORD, CAROLINE
The House by Exmoor. Simon, 1975; Millington, 1976

STAFFORD, EARL FRANKLIN
A Kiss for a Killer. Jarrolds, 1941

STAFFORD, JOHN K.
Back from the Grave. Street (Magnet)
The Broken Pen. Street (Magnet)
Cheating Justice. Street (Magnet)
The Convent Mystery. Street (Magnet)
The Crime of Bohemia. Steet (New Magnet)
A Daring Express Messenger. Street (Magnet)
The Death Demon. Street (Magnet)
The Divided Trail. Street (New Magnet)
Forging the Links. Street (New Magnet)
In After Years. Street (New Magnet)
In the Clutch of the Law. Street (New Magnet)
Into his Own Trap. Street (New Magnet)
King Among Crooks. Street (Magnet)
Millionaire's Crime. Street (Magnet)
Morgan the Dauntless. Street (New Magnet)
The Nameless Dread. Street (New Magnet)
An Oath of Vengeance. Street (Magnet)
On a Blind Trail. Street (New Magnet)
Only a Bullet. Street (Magnet)
Piece by Piece. Street (New Magnet)
Shadowed Round the World. Street (Magnet)
Shot from Above. Street (Magnet)
A Skein Well Tangled. Street (New Magnet)
Smugglers at Odds. Street (Magnet)
The Spurious Note Maker. Street (Magnet)
Tracked to his Doom. Street (New Magnet)
The Trail to the End. Street (New Magnet)
The Triple Cross. Street (New Magnet)
Under the Surface. Street (Magnet)
An Unknown Foe. Street (New Magnet)
When Thieves Fall Out. Street (Magnet)
When Threads Get Tangled. Street (New Magnet)
When Trails Cross. Street (New Magnet)
With Bullet and Steel. Street (New Magnet)

STAFFORD, MARJORIE
Death Plays the Gramophone. Macmillan, 1953

STAFFORD, MURIEL. 1903-   .
X Marks the Dot. Duell, 1943

STAGG, CLINTON H(OLLAND). 1890-1916. Series character: Thornley Colton, in at least those marked TC.
High Speed. Watt, 1916; Richards, 1920
Silver Sandals. Watt, 1916. British title (?): Thornley Colton, Blind Reader of Hearts. Simpkin, 1915 TC
Thornley Colton, Blind Detective. Watt, 1923 ss TC
Thornley Colton, Blind Reader of Hearts; see Silver Sandals

STAGG, JAMES. Pseudonym of Gilbert Johns, q.v. All titles below feature Sexton Blake and were published by Amalgamated Press.
Assignment in Beirut. 1956
Crime of Violence. 1958
Desert Intrigue. 1960
Murder Down Below. 1958
Nightmare in Naples. 1957
Panic in the Night. 1957
Passport to Danger. 1957
Time for Murder. 1959

STAGGE, JONATHAN. Joint pseudonym of Richard Wilson Webb and Hugh Callingham Wheeler, 1913- . Other joint pseudonyms: Q. Patrick, Patrick Quentin, qq.v. Series character: Dr. Hugh Westlake, in all titles.
Call a Hearse; see The Yellow Taxi
Death and the Dear Girls; see Death, My Darling Daughters
Death, My Darling Daughters. Doubleday, 1945. British title: Death and the Dear Girls. Joseph, 1946
Death's Old Sweet Song. Doubleday, 1946; Joseph, 1947
The Dogs Do Bark. Doubleday, 1937; British title: Murder Gone to Earth. Joseph, 1936
Funeral for Five; see Turn of the Table
Light from a Lantern; see The Scarlet Circle
Murder by Prescription. Doubleday, 1938. British title: Murder or Mercy. Joseph, 1937
Murder Gone to Earth; see The Dogs Do Bark
Murder in the Stars; see The Stars Spell Death
Murder or Mercy; see Murder by Prescription
The Scarlet Circle. Doubleday, 1943. British title: Light from a Lantern. Joseph, 1943
The Stars Spell Death. Doubleday, 1939. British title: Murder in the Stars. Joseph, 1940
The Three Fears. Doubleday, 1949; Joseph, 1949
Turn of the Table. Doubleday, 1940. British title: Funeral for Five. Joseph, 1940
The Yellow Taxi. Doubleday, 1942. British title: Call a Hearse. Joseph, 1942

STAHL, RAY
Death Stalks "The Wild Goose". Hamilton Stafford, 1952
No Answer from a Corpse. Hamilton Stafford, 1953

STALLWORTH, LYN
Pot Shot. Walker, 1968

STAMPER, JOSEPH. 1886- .
The Shipyard Menace. Amalgamated, 1943. (Sexton Blake.)

STAND, MARGUERITE. Series characters: Bill Rice, in at least those marked BR; Police Constable Robins, in at least those marked R.
Death Came in Lucerne. Hale, 1966 BR
Death Came in the Studio. Hale, 1969
Death Came to "Lighthouse Steps". Hale, 1968 BR
Death Came Too Soon. Hale, 1970
Death Came with Darkness. Hale, 1965 BR
Death Came with Diamonds. Hale, 1966 BR
Death Came with Flowers. Hale, 1966
Diana is Dead. Hale, 1967 R
Escape from Murder. Hale, 1964 BR
L for Murder. Hale, 1968
Murder at Cloud Hospital. Hale, 1969
Murder in the Camp. Hale, 1964 R

STANDISH, BURT L. Pseudonym of Gilbert Patten, 1866-1945.
Dick Merriwell's Detective Work. Street, 1911
Dick Merriwell's Mystery; or, Working for Right. Street, 1903
The Motor Wizard's Mystery. Street, 1914

STANDISH, ROBERT. Pseudonym of Digby George Gerahty.
Private Enterprise, and other stories. Davies, 1954 ss, some criminous
The Window Hack. Davies, 1966

STANFORD, ALFRED (BOLLER). 1900- .
The Mission in Sparrow Brush Lane. Morrow, 1965

STANFORD, DON(ALD KENT). 1918- . Series character: Dallas Webster = DW.
Bargain in Blood. GM, 1951; Muller, 1958 DW
Mulligan's Pirates. PB, 1966; Deutsch, 1967
The Slaughtered Lovelies. GM, 1950; Red Seal, 1957 DW

STANLEY, ARTHUR. Pseudonym of Arthur Stanley Megaw, 1872- .
The Monkhurst Case. Macdonald, 1946

STANLEY, BENNETT. Pseudonym of S(tanley) B(ennett) Hough, 1917- , q.v.
The Alscott Experiment. Hodder, 1954
Government Contract. Hodder, 1956

STANLEY, FAY GRISSOM
Murder Leaves a Ring. Rinehart, 1950

STANLEY, GEORGE. Series character: Black Pilgrim, in at least those marked BP.
The Adventures of the Black Pilgrim. Modern Fiction, 1945 BP ss
The Blue Light. Blackie, 1935
The Brotherhood of Death. Mitre, 1946
Case of the Seven Keys. Modern Fiction, 1945
Further Adventures of the Black Pilgrim. Modern Fiction, 1945 BP
Gangsters All. Mitre, 1945
Gangsters Parade. Mitre, 1945
The League of Twelve. Mellifont, 1940
Men of the Mist. Martin & Reid, 1947
The Missing Million. Gifford, 1938
Rubberface. Modern Fiction, 1945
The Secret of the Seven Spiders. Fenland, 1932
The Seven Saints. Swan, 1945
The Seven Shadows. Blackie, 1935
The Sign of Seven. Coker, 1950
Silver Slave. Regency, 1945
Sinister Valley. Bear, 1946

STANLEY, JACKSON
The Florentine Ring. Doubleday, 1962

STANLEY, OLIN
Legal Fire. Vantage, 1959

STANLEY, RAY
The Hippy Cult Murders. Macfadden, 1970

STANLEY, SANDRA
Rogue's Castle. PB, 1974

STANLEY, WILLIAM
Mr. Holroyd Takes a Holiday. Abelard (London & New York), 1966

STANNARD, HENRIETTA ELIZA VAUGHAN PALMER. 1856-1911. Pseudonym: John Strange Winter, q.v.

STANNERS, H(AROLD) H. 1894- . Series character: Professor Harding, in all titles.
At the Tenth Clue. Eyre, 1937
The Crowning Murder. Eyre, 1938
Murder at Markendon Court. Eyre, 1936

STANSFELD, ANTHONY. Joint pseudonym with Peter Lilley: Bruce Buckingham, q.v.

STANTON, CORALIE. Pseudonym of Alice Cecil Seymour Hosken.
The Adventuress; see Miriam Lemaire, Money Lender
The Amateur Adventuress. Thomson, 1930
Called to Judgment, with (Ernest Charles) Heath Hosken. Paul, 1913
The Dog Star, with (Ernest Charles) Heath Hosken. Cassell, 1913
-Her Fugitive. Thomson, 1929
Ironmouth. Paul, 1916
The Love That Kills, with (Ernest Charles) Heath Hosken. Milne, 1909
The Man Made Law, with (Ernest Charles) Heath Hosken. Everett, 1908
Miriam Lemaire, Money Lender, with (Ernest Charles) Heath Hosken. Cassell, 1906. U.S. title: The Adventuress. McBride, 1907 ss
The Muzzled Ox, with (Ernest Charles) Heath Hosken. Paul, 1911
The Second Best, with (Ernest Charles) Heath Hosken. Long, 1907
The Sinners' Syndicate, with (Ernest Charles) Heath Hosken. Hurst, 1907
-The Way of Escape. Leng, 1932
The White Horseman, with (Ernest Charles) Heath Hosken. Nash, 1924

STANTON, KEN. Series character: William Martin (Tiger Shark), in all titles.
Cold Blue Death. Macfadden, 1970
Evil Cargo. Manor, 1973
Operation Deep Sea. Manor, 1972
Operation Mermaid. Manor, 1974
Operation Sea Monster. Manor, 1974
Operation Steelfish. Manor, 1973
Sargasso Secret. Macfadden, 1971
Seek, Strike and Destroy. Macfadden, 1971
Stalkers of the Sea. Macfadden, 1972
Ten Seconds to Zero. Macfadden, 1970
Whirlwind Beneath the Sea. Manor, 1972

STANTON, PAUL. Pseudonym of (Arthur) David Beaty, 1919- , q.v.
-Call Me Captain. Joseph, 1959; Mill, 1960
-The Gun Garden. Joseph, 1965; Mill, 1965
-Village of Stars. Joseph, 1960; Mill, 1960

STANTON-HOPE, WILLIAM E(DWARD). 1889-1961. See also: (WILLIAM EDWARD) STANTON HOPE.
Dead Man's Sands. Amalgamated, 1929. (Sexton Blake.)

STAPLETON, A.
The Limping Death. Gnome, 1945

STAPLETON, D. (AND D.). Joint pseudonym of Douglas Stapleton, 1904- , q.v., and Dorothy Stapleton.
Corpse and Robbers. Arcadia, 1954
The Crime, the Place, and the Girl. Arcadia, 1955
Late for the Funeral. Arcadia, 1953

STAPLETON, DOROTHY. Joint pseudonym with Douglas Stapleton, 1904- , q.v.: D. (and D.) Stapleton, q.v.

STAPLETON, DOUGLAS. 1904- . Joint pseudonym with Dorothy Stapleton: D. (and D.) Stapleton, q.v.
The Corpse is Indignant, with Helen A. Carey. Five Star, 1946

STAPP, ROBERT
A More Perfect Union. Harper's Magazine Press, 1970

STARK, INSPECTOR
At Death's Call. Street (New Magnet)
The Call of the Deep. Street (New Magnet)

The Cost of a Clue. Street (New Magnet)
The Crimson Clue. Street (New Magnet)
A Deed of Darkness. Street (Magnet)
A Demand for Justice. Street (New Magnet)
Eye of Gold. Street (Magnet)
The Great Green Diamond. Street (New Magnet)
The Hand in Red. Street (Magnet)
Hunted and Haunted. Street (New Magnet)
In League with Satan. Street (New Magnet)
Kentucky Moonshiner. Street (Magnet)
A Life at Stake. Street (New Magnet)
A Long Baffled Capture. Street (New Magnet)
The Mafia's Victim. Street (Magnet)
The Missing Bracelet. Street (Magnet)
A Modern Sorceress. Street (Magnet)
The Nitroglycerine League. Street (Magnet)
Out of the Underworld. Street (New Magnet)
Revealed by Lightning. Street (Magnet)
Ring of Iron. Street (Magnet)
The Root of All Evil. Street (Magnet)
The Secret of the Dead. Street (New Magnet)
Shadow of an Assassin. Street (Magnet)
The Shadow of the Rope. Street (New Magnet)
A Telegraph Clue. Street (Magnet)
Tricked and Trapped. Street (New Magnet)
The Unseen Hand. Street (New Magnet)
A Victim of the Occult. Street (New Magnet)
The Victor's Spoils. Street (New Magnet)
The Water Trail. Street (Magnet)
The Western Ferret. Street (Magnet)
When the Quarry Turns. Street (New Magnet)
Where the Clue Leads. Street (New Magnet)
With Chains of Brass. Street (New Magnet)

STARK, DELBERT RAYMOND. Pseudonym: John Norwood, q.v.

STARK, ERNEST
Ed. Somers, the Pinkerton Detective; or, The Murdered Man. Ogilvie, 1886

STARK, JAMES. Pseudonym of Robert Conroy Goldston, 1927-   .
The Greek Virgin. Avon, 1962

STARK, MICHAEL. Pseudonym of Lawrence Lariar, 1908-   , q.v. Other pseudonyms: Adam Knight, Michael Lawrence, qq.v.
Run for Your Life! Crown, 1946; Boardman, 1948. Also published as: Kill-Box. Ace, 1954

STARK, RICHARD. Pseudonym of Donald E(dwin) Westlake, 1933-   , q.v. Other pseudonyms: Tucker Coe, Timothy J. Culver, qq.v. Series characters: Parker = P; Alan Grofield = AG.
The Black Ice Score. GM, 1968; Coronet, 1969 P
The Blackbird. Macmillan, 1969; Hodder, 1970 AG
Butcher's Moon. Random, 1974; Coronet, 1977 P, AG
The Dame. Macmillan, 1969; Hodder, 1969 AG
The Damsel. Macmillan, 1967; Hodder, 1968 AG
Deadly Edge. Random, 1971; Coronet, 1972 P
The Green Eagle Score. GM, 1967; Coronet, 1968 P
The Handle. PB, 1966. British title: Run Lethal. Coronet, 1972 P, AG
The Hunter. PB, 1962. British title: Point Blank. Coronet, 1967 P
The Jugger. PB, 1965; Coronet, 1971 P
Killtown; see The Score
Lemons Never Lie. World, 1971 AG
The Man with the Getaway Face. PB, 1963. British title: The Steel Hit. Coronet, 1971 P
The Mourner. PB, 1963; Coronet, 1971 P
The Outfit. PB, 1963; Coronet, 1971 P
Plunder Squad. Random, 1972; Coronet, 1974 P
Point Blank; see The Hunter
The Rare Coin Score. GM, 1967; Coronet, 1968 P
Run Lethal; see The Handle
The Score. PB, 1964. British title: Killtown. Coronet, 1971 P & AG
The Seventh. PB, 1966. British title: The Split. Coronet, 1969 P
Slayground. Random, 1971; Coronet, 1973 P
The Sour Lemon Score. GM, 1969; Coronet, 1969 P
The Split; see The Seventh
The Steel Hit; see The Man with the Getaway Face

STARK, SHELDON. 1919-   .
Too Many Sinners. Ace, 1954

STARNES, RICHARD. 1922-   . Series characters: Barney Forge & Dr. St. George Peachy = F&P.
And When She was Bad She was Murdered. Lippincott, 1950; Muller, 1953 F&P
Another Mug for the Bier. Lippincott, 1950; Muller, 1952 F&P
The Flypaper War. Trident, 1969; Hutchinson, 1970
The Other Body in Grant's Tomb. Lippincott, 1951; Muller, 1954 F&P
Requiem in Utopia. Trident, 1967

STARR, JIMMY. 1904-   . Series character: Joe Medford, in all titles.
The Corpse Came C.O.D. Murray, 1944; Coker, 1951
Heads You Lose. Fell, 1950
Three Short Biers. Murray, 1945

STARR, JONATHAN
Crook. Cape & Smith, 1930
Grapevine. Liveright, 1930

STARR, JULIAN
The Disagreeable Woman. Dillingham, 1895

STARR, RICHARD (HENRY). 1878-   . Pseudonym: Richard Essex, q.v.
-Gangster's Girl. Jenkins, 1935
-Married to a Spy. Hurst, 1915
-Mary Elizabeth—Adventuress. Low, 1932

STARRETT, (CHARLES) VINCENT (EMERSON). 1886-1974. Series characters: Riley Blackwood = RL; Walter Ghost = WG; Jimmie Lavender = JL.
The Blue Door. Doubleday, 1930 ss, JL in two of them
The Case Book of Jimmie Lavender. Gold Label, 1944 JL ss
Coffins for Two. Covici, 1924 ss
Dead Man Inside. Doubleday, 1931; World's Work, 1935 WG
The End of Mr. Garment. Doubleday, 1932 WG
The Great Hotel Murder. Doubleday, 1935; Nicholson, 1935 RB
The Laughing Buddha. Magna, 1937. (A digest-size paperback, whose publisher scattered his own additions to the text throughout the book. Restored to its original condition, it was published as: Murder in Peking. Lantern, 1946; Edwards, 1947.)
Midnight and Percy Jones. Covici, 1936; Nicholson, 1938 RB
Murder in Peking; see The Laughing Buddha
Murder on "B" Deck. Doubleday, 1929; World's Work, 1936 WG
-The Quick and the Dead. Arkham, 1965 ss
The Unique Hamlet. (Chicago), 1920

STAUFFER, FRANK H. [FRANCIS HENRY STAUFFER]. 1832-1895.
Darke Darrell, the Boy Detective. Street, 1888

STAYTON, FRANK. 1874-   .
-The Passionate Adventure. Nash, 1924; Century, 1924

STEAD, C(HRISTIAN) K(ARLSON), 1932-   .
Smith's Dream. Longman Paul (Auckland), 1971; Longmans, 1932

STEAD, PHILIP JOHN
-The Charlatan. Macdonald, 1948
-Fausta. Macdonald, 1950
In the Street of the Angel. Art & Educ. Publishers, 1947

STEAD, ROBERT J(OHN) C(AMPBELL). 1880-   .
The Bail Jumper. Unwin, 1914
The Copper Disc. Doubleday, 1931

STEARN, JESS
The Reporter. Doubleday, 1970

STEARNS, EDGAR FRANKLIN. 1879-   . Pseudonym: Edgar Franklin, q.v.

STEBEL, S(IDNEY) L(EO). 1924-   . Pseudonym: Leo Bergson, q.v.
The Vorovich Affair. Viking, 1975. British title: Narc. Constable, 1976. Reprinted in Britain under the U.S. title: Penguin, 1977

STED, RICHARD
They All Bleed Red. Simon, 1954; Boardman, 1955

STEEGMULLER, FRANCIS. 1906-   . Pseudonym: David Keith, q.v.

STEEL, DAVID
Beauty is Found in a Grave. Comyns, 1952
Death is a Dame. Comyns, 1953
Lovely But Lethal. Comyns, 1952
Too Tough for Death. Comyns, 1953
You'll Have to Talk. Comyns, 1953

STEEL, KURT. Pseudonym of Rudolf Hornaday Kagey, 1904-1946. Series character: Hank Hyer = HH.
Ambush House. Harcourt, 1943 HH
Crooked Shadow. Little, 1939; Swan, 1945 HH
Dead of Night. Little, 1940; Swan, 1944 HH
The Imposter. Harcourt, 1942; Gifford, 1945
Judas, Incorporated. Little, 1939 HH
Madman's Buff. Little, 1941; Swan, 1945 HH
Murder for What? Bobbs, 1936 HH
Murder Goes to College. Bobbs, 1936 HH

Murder in G-Sharp. Bobbs, 1937. Also published as: Strangler's Holiday. Select, 1942 (abridged) HH
Murder of a Dead Man. Bobbs, 1935. Also published as: The Traveling Corpses. Crime Novel Selection, 1942 (abridged) HH
Strangler's Holiday; see Murder in G-Sharp
The Traveling Corpses; see Murder of a Dead Man

STEELE, CHESTER K. Series character: Colonel Robert Lee Ashley = RA.
The Crime at Red Towers. Clode, 1927
The Diamond Cross Mystery. Sully, 1918; Jenkins, 1920 RA
The Golf Course Mystery. Sully, 1919 RA
The Great Radio Mystery. Chelsea, 1928
The House of Disappearances. Chelsea, 1927
The Mansion of Mystery. Cupples, 1911

STEELE, CURTIS. House name. Series character: James Christopher (Operator 5), in all titles.
The Army of the Dead. Corinth, 1966
Blood Reign of the Dictator. Corinth, 1966
Hosts of the Flaming Death. Corinth, 1966
Invasion of the Yellow Warlords. Corinth, 1966
The Invisible Empire. Corinth, 1966
Legions of the Death Master. Corinth, 1966
March of the Flame Marauders. Corinth, 1966
The Masked Invasion. Freeway, 1974
Master of Broken Men. Corinth, 1966
The Yellow Scourge. Freeway, 1974

STEELE, DeFOREST C.
Glitter-Gold Mountain. Christopher, 1951

STEELE, DERWENT
The Avenger. Modern, 1935
The Black Gangster. Modern, 193?
The Phantom Slayer. Modern, 1935
The Poison Gang. Modern, 193?
The Purple Plague. Modern, 1935

STEELE, FRANCESCA MARIA. Pseudonym: Darley Dale, q.v.

STEELE, JACK
The House of Iron Men. FitzGerald, 1911

STEELE, JACLEN
The Forbidden Room. GM, 1952

STEELE, TEDD
Artists, Models and Murder. Crown (Canada), 1946

STEELE, TOM
Cunning Against Force. Signet (Magnet)

STEELE, V. M. Series character: Chief-Inspector Saunders, in at least those marked S.
Beloved of Ishmael. Paul, 1937
Hunters of Humans. Paul, 1936 S
The Scarred Wrists. Paul, 1935 S

STEELE, WILBUR DANIEL. 1886-1970.
Full Cargo. Doubleday, 1952 ss, some criminous
Land's End, and other stories. Harper, 1918 ss, some criminous
The Man Who Saw Through Heaven. Harper, 1927 ss, some criminous
The Post Road, with Norma Mitchell. French (New York), 1935. (2-act play.)

The Shame Dance, and other stories. Harper, 1923; Unwin, 1924 ss, some criminous
-The Sound of Rowlocks. Harper, 1938
-The Way to Gold. Doubleday, 1955

STEEMAN, (STANISLAUS) ANDRE. 1895- . Series character: Wenceslas Vorobeitchik, in both titles.
The Night of the 12th-13th. Lippincott, 1933. (Translation of La Nuit du 12 au 13. Paris, 1931.)
Six Dead Men. Farrar, 1932; Hurst, 1933. (Translation of Six Hommes Morts. Paris, 1931.)

STEERS, HELEN. Pseudonym of Helen Steers Burgess.
Death will Find Me. Dodd, 1947

STEEVES, HARRISON R. 1881- .
Good Night, Sheriff. Random, 1941; Rich, 1942

STEFAN, ILLY
Guilty, My Lord. Opium Books, 1968

STEIN, AARON MARC. 1906- . Pseudonyms: George Bagby, Hampton Stone, qq.v. Series characters: Tim Mulligan & Elsie Mae Hunt = M&H; Matt Erridge = ME.
Alp Murder. Doubleday, 1970; Hale, 1971 ME
...and High Water. Doubleday, 1946 M&H
Blood on the Stars. Doubleday, 1964; Hale, 1964 ME
The Case of the Absent-Minded Professor. Doubleday, 1943 M&H
The Cradle and the Grave. Doubleday, 1948 M&H
Days of Misfortune. Doubleday, 1949 M&H
The Dead Thing in the Pool. Doubleday, 1952 M&H
Deadly Delight. Doubleday, 1967; Hale, 1969 ME
Death Meets 400 Rabbits. Doubleday, 1953 M&H
Death Takes a Paying Guest. Doubleday, 1947 M&H
Executioner's Rest; see I Fear the Greeks
Faces of Death; see Snare Andalucian
The Finger. Doubleday, 1973; Hale, 1974 ME
Frightened Amazon. Doubleday, 1950 M&H
Home and Murder. Doubleday, 1962 ME
I Fear the Greeks. Doubleday, 1966. British title: Executioner's Rest. Hale, 1967 ME
Kill is a Four-Letter Word. Doubleday, 1968; Hale, 1969 ME
Lock and Key. Doubleday, 1973
Mask for Murder. Doubleday, 1952 M&H
Moonmilk and Murder. Doubleday, 1955; Macdonald, 1956 M&H
Never Need an Enemy. Doubleday, 1959; Boardman, 1960 ME
Only the Guilty. Doubleday, 1942 M&H
Pistols for Two. Doubleday, 1951 M&H
The Second Burial. Doubleday, 1949 M&H
Shoot Me Dacent. Doubleday, 1951; Macdonald, 1957 M&H
Sitting Up Dead. Doubleday, 1958; Macdonald, 1959 ME
Snare Andalucian. Doubleday, 1968. British title: Faces of Death. Hale, 1968 ME
The Sun is a Witness. Doubleday, 1940 M&H
Three—with Blood. Doubleday, 1950 M&H
Up to No Good. Doubleday, 1941 M&H
We Saw Him Die. Doubleday, 1947 M&H

STEIN, GERTRUDE. 1874-1946.
Blood on the Dining Room Floor. Banyan, 1948

STEIRMAN, HY. 1921- .
Cry of the Hawk. Paperback Library, 1970
Strike Terror. Paperback Library, 1968

STELLIER, KILSYTH. Pseudonym of A. Welbourne Summers.
Taken by Force. Gale, 1893

STEPHENS, DeVERE ASHMORE
Echoes from Castor Hills. Comet, 1959

STEPHENS, EDWARD (CARL). 1924- .
The Submariner. Doubleday, 1973

STEPHENS, HENRY POTTINGER and WARHAM ST. LEGER
The Basilisk. Sonnenschein, 1886. U.S. title: From Darkness to Light; or, The Basilisk's Love. Donnelley, 1886

STEPHENS, RICCARDO
The Cruciform Mark. Chatto, 1896
-The Eddy. Blackwood, 1907
-Mr. Peters. Bliss, 1897; Harper, 1897
The Mummy. Nash, 1912
-The Prince and the Undertaker, and What They Undertook. Sands, 1898
-The Wooing of Grey Eyes, and other stories. Murray, 1901 ss

STEPHENS, ROBERT NEILSON. 1867-1906.
The Mystery of Murray Davenport. Page, 1903; Nash, 1903

STEPHENSON, H(UMPHREY) M(EIGH). 1882- .
Death on the Deep; see Yo-Ho, and a Bottle of Rum!
A Killer and his Star. Hutchinson, 1935
The Missing Partner. Hutchinson, 1932
On the Highest Hill. Long, 1927
Yo-Ho, and a Bottle of Rum! Hutchinson, 1930. U.S. title (?): Death on the Deep. Doubleday, 1931

STEPHENSON, (WILLIAM) RALPH (EWING). 1910- .
Body in my Arms. Gifford, 1963
Darkest Death. Gifford, 1964
Down Among the Dead Men. Gifford, 1966
Festival Death. Gifford, 1966
Spies in Concert. Gifford, 1965

STERLING, STEWART. Pseudonym of Prentice Winchell, 1895- . Other pseudonyms: Jay de Bekker, Spencer Dean, Dexter St. Clair, Dexter St. Clare, qq.v. Series characters: Ben Pedley = BP; Gil Vine = GV.
Alarm in the Night. Dutton, 1949 BP
Alibi Baby. Ives Washburn, 1955; Boardman, 1955 GV
The Big Ear. Dutton, 1953; Boardman, 1955
The Blonde in Suite 14; see Dead to the World
The Body in the Bed. Lippincott, 1959; Boardman, 1960 GV
Candle for a Corpse. Lippincott, 1957; Boardman, 1958. Also published as: Too Hot to Kill. Avon, 1958 BP
Dead Certain. Ace, 1960 GV
Dead of Night. Dutton, 1950 GV
Dead Right. Lippincott, 1956; Boardman, 1957. Also published as: The Hotel Murders. Avon, 1957 GV
Dead Sure. Dutton, 1949; Hennel Locke, 1951 GV
Dead to the World. Lippincott, 1958; Boardman, 1959. Also published as: The Blonde in Suite 14. Avon, 1959 GV
Dead Wrong. Lippincott, 1947 GV
Down Among the Dead Men. Putnam, 1943; Wells Gardner, 1949
Dying Room Only. Ace, 1960 BP
Fire on Fear Street. Lippincott, 1958; Boardman, 1959 BP
Five Alarm Funeral. Putnam, 1942 BP

The Hinges of Hell. Ives Washburn, 1955; Boardman, 1956 BP
The Hotel Murders; see Dead Right
Nightmare at Noon. Dutton, 1951 BP
Too Hot to Handle. Random, 1961; Boardman, 1962 BP
Too Hot to Kill; see Candle for a Corpse
Where There's Smoke. Lippincott, 1946 BP

STERLING, THOMAS. 1921- .
The Evil of the Day. Simon, 1955; Gollancz, 1955. Also published as: Murder in Venice. Dell, 1959
The House Without a Door. Simon, 1950; Boardman, 1951
Murder in Venice; see The Evil of the Day
The Silent Siren. Simon, 1958; Gollancz, 1958
Strangers and Afraid. Simon, 1952; Boardman, 1952

STERN, DANIEL. 1928- .
The Suicide Academy. McGraw, 1968; Allen, 1969

STERN, DAVID. 1909- . Pseudonym: Peter Stirling, q.v.

STERN, G(LADYS) B(RONWYN). 1890- .
The Shortest Night. Heinemann, 1931; Knopf, 1931

STERN, PHILIP VAN DOREN. 1900- . Pseudonym: Peter Storme, q.v.
Love is the One with Wings. Farrar, 1951. British title (?): It's Always Too Late to Mend. Jarrolds, 1952

STERN, RICHARD G. 1928- .
In Any Case. McGraw, 1962; MacGibbon, 1963

STERN, RICHARD MARTIN. 1915- . Series character: Johnny Ortiz = JO.
The Bright Road to Fear. Ballantine, 1958; Secker, 1959
Cry Havoc. Scribner, 1963; Cassell, 1964
Death in the Snow. Scribner, 1973; Hale, 1974 JO
High Hazard. Scribner, 1962
I Hide, We Seek. Scribner, 1965; Deutsch, 1966
The Kessler Legacy. Scribner, 1967; Cassell, 1968
Manuscript for Murder. Scribner, 1970; Hale, 1973
Merry Go Round. Scribner, 1969; Cassell, 1970
Murder in the Walls. Scribner, 1971; Hale, 1973 JO
Power. McKay, 1975; Secker, 1975
Quidnunc County; see These Unlucky Deeds
Right Hand Opposite. Scribner, 1964
The Search for Tabitha Carr. Scribner, 1960; Secker, 1960
Suspense. Ballantine, 1959. (Four novelets.)
These Unlucky Deeds. Scribner, 1960. British title: Quidnunc County. Eyre, 1961
-The Tower. McKay, 1973; Secker, 1973
You Don't Need an Enemy. Scribner, 1972; Hale, 1973 JO

STERNE, JULIAN. Pseudonym of Nosta H. Webster.
The Secret of the Zodiac. Boswell, 1933

STERREY, CHARLES E(RNEST)
-In the Grip of Destiny. Allen, 1913
The Voice from the Night. Allen, 1912

STEUART, GLEN. Pseudonym of Lilian May Robertson.
The Evil That Men Do. Long, 1937
The Glass Fish. Long, 1935

STEVEN, E. E.
Kat and Copy-Cat. Patten, 1929

STEVENS, CURTIS
The Gravy Train Hit. Joseph, 1975

STEVENS, FRANCES MOYER ROSS. 1895-1948. Pseudonym: Christopher Hale, q.v.

STEVENS, FRANK (EDMUND). 1909- .
She Left a Silver Slipper. Mill, 1954; Foulsham, 1955

STEVENS, FRANKLIN. 1933- . Pseudonym: Steve Franklin, q.v.

STEVENS, JAMES. 1936- .
In Shadows of Desire. Exposition, 1964

STEVENS, JON
Deadly Matrimony. Hale, 1972
The Nightmare Kick. Hale, 1971

STEVENS, K. M.
Panic in the Solomons. Bles, 1951

STEVENS, LUCILE VERNON. 1899- .
-Crepe Myrtle Tree. Avalon, 1970
Death Wore Gold Shoes. Avalon, 1966
-Dowry of Diamonds. Avalon, 1968
-Green Shadows. Avalon, 1973
-Home to Cypresswood. Avalon, 1972
-Love in a Mist. Avalon, 1967
-The Red Tower. Avalon, 1968
-The Redbird Affair. Avalon, 1974
Search Through the Mist. Avalon, 1971
-Threads of Gold. Avalon, 1968

STEVENS, SHANE. 1941- .
Dead City. Holt, 1973; Barrie, 1974
Go Down Dead. Morrow, 1967
Rat Pack. Seabury, 1974

STEVENSON, ANNE (KATHERINE). 1933- .
-Flash of Splendour. Collins, 1968
The French Inheritance. Collins, 1974; Putnam, 1974
A Game of Statues. Collins, 1972; Putnam, 1972
A Relative Stranger. Collins, 1970; Putnam, 1970

STEVENSON, BURTON E(GBERT). 1872-1962. Series character: Jim Godfrey = JG.
Affairs of State. Holt, 1906; Chatto, 1907
The Clue of the Red Carnation; see The Red Carnation
Death Wears a Carnation; see The Red Carnation
The Destroyer. Dodd, 1913; Nash, 1913
The Girl from Alsace; see Little Comrade
The Gloved Hand. Dodd, 1912; Nash, 1920 JG
The Holladay Case. Holt, 1903; Heinemann, 1903 JG
The House Next Door. Dodd, 1932; Hutchinson, 1932 JG
A King in Babylon. Small, 1917; Hutchinson, 1918
The Kingmakers. Dodd, 1922; Hutchinson, 1922
Little Comrade. Holt, 1915; Hutchinson, 1915. Also published as: The Girl from Alsace. Grosset, 1919
The Marathon Mystery. Holt, 1904 JG
The Mystery of the Boule Cabinet. Dodd, 1912; Nash, 1915 JG
The Mystery of Villa Aurelia; see Villa Aurelia
The Red Carnation. Dodd, 1939. British title: Death Wears a Carnation. Cassell, 1940. Also published as: The Clue of the Red Carnation. Mystery Novel of the Month, 1942
The Storm Center. Dodd, 1924; Hutchinson, 1924
That Affair at Elizabeth. Holt, 1907 JG
Villa Aurelia. Dodd, 1932. British title: The Mystery of Villa Aurelia. Rich, 1933

STEVENSON, D(OROTHY) E(MILY). 1892-1973.
Crooked Adam. Farrar, 1942; Collins, 1969

STEVENSON, FERDINAN. Joint pseudonym with Patricia Robinson: Daria Macomber, q.v.

STEVENSON, FLORENCE. Series character: Kitty Telefair = KT.
Altar of Evil. Award, 1973 KT
Bianca, with Patricia (Hagen) Murray. Signet, 1973
The Curse of the Concullens. Signet, 1970
Dark Odyssey. Signet, 1974
Feast of Eggshells. Signet, 1970
The Ides of November. Signet, 1975
Kilmeny in the Dark Wood. Signet, 1973
The Mistress of Devil's Manor. Award, 1973 KT
Ophelia. Signet, 1969
A Shadow on the House. Signet, 1975
The Silent Watcher. Award, 1975 KT
The Sorcerer of the Castle. Award, 1974 KT
Where Satan Dwells. Award, 1971 KT
The Witching Hour. Award, 1971 KT
Witch's Crossing. Signet, 1975

STEVENSON, LOUIS LACY
Big Game. Brentano's, 1924

STEVENSON, ROBERT LOUIS. 1850-1894.
The Body Snatcher. Merriam, 1895
The Dynamiter. Longmans, 1885; Munro, 1886
The Merry Men and other tales. Chatto, 1887; Harper, 1887 ss
New Arabian Nights. Chatto, 1882; Holt, 1882. (ss; a selection of which were published separately as: The Pavilion on the Links. Chatto, 1913.)
The Pavilion on the Links; see New Arabian Nights
The Strange Case of Dr. Jekyll and Mr. Hyde, with other fables. Longmans, 1896; Munro, 1886 ss
The Suicide Club. Scribner, 1896
The Wrecker. Cassell, 1892; Scribner, 1892
The Wrong Box, with Lloyd Osbourne (1868-1947), q.v. Longmans, 1889; Scribner, 1889

STEVENSON, TRAILL
The Diamond in the Hoof. Cassell, 1926
The Island Murder. Jenkins, 1936
Murder at the Bar. Jenkins, 1936
The Nudist Murder. Jenkins, 1937
The Silver Arrow Murder. Jenkins, 1939

STEWARD, DWIGHT
The Acupuncture Murders. Harper, 1973; Barker, 1973

STEWARD, PAULL. Series character: Everhard, in all titles.
Dangerous Men. Harrap, 1926
Gaboreau. Harrap, 1927
Gaboreau the Terrible. Harrap, 1927

STEWART, ALFRED WALTER. 1880-1947. Pseudonym: J. J. Connington, q.v.

STEWART, ANDREW. Pseudonym of Andrew Herbert Dakers, 1887- .
  Circumstantial Evidence. Bodley Head, 1928
  -"Once I was Blind." Cassell, 1926

STEWART, ANITA (MARIE). 1901- .
  The Devil's Toy. Dutton, 1935

STEWART, DICK
  The Belrox Mystery. Street (Magnet)
  The Brotherhood of Freedom. Street (Magnet)
  Casting the Net. Street (New Magnet)
  Checkmating a Countess. Street (Magnet)
  A Clique of Knaves. Street (New Magnet)
  Closing the Circle. Street (New Magnet)
  Confederate Rogues. Street (Magnet)
  A Crime Without a Name. Street (Magnet)
  The Downward Path. Street (Magnet)
  An Expert in Craft. Street (New Magnet)
  A Game of Draw. Street (Magnet)
  The Green Goods Speculator. Street (Magnet)
  The Human Cat. Street (Magnet)
  The Human Question Mark. Street (New Magnet)
  In the Name of the Law. Street (New Magnet)
  The King of Scamps. Street (Magnet)
  The "L" Mystery. Street (Magnet)
  The Lure of Mammon. Street (New Magnet)
  The Man Who Hid. Street (Magnet)
  On Death's Trail. Street (New Magnet)
  Only a Headless Nail. Street (Magnet)
  A Political Plotter. Street (Magnet)
  A Queen of Chance. Street (New Magnet)
  A Race with Death. Street (Magnet)
  The Scamp Hunter. Street (New Magnet)
  The Scarlet Spot. Street (New Magnet)
  Search for a Motive. Street (Magnet)
  The Sign of the Crescent. Street (New Magnet)
  The Skeleton Clew. Street (Magnet)
  The Strength of the Weak. Street (New Magnet)
  The Unbidden Guests. Street (New Magnet)
  An Unheeded Warning. Street (Magnet)
  Villain's Work. Street (Magnet)
  Welding the Chain. Street (New Magnet)
  When the Clews Point Wrong. Street (New Magnet)
  Without a Name. Street (New Magnet)

STEWART, EDWARD. 1938- .
  Heads. Macmillan, 1969; Deutsch, 1970
  Rock Rude. Simon, 1970; Joseph, 1972
  They've Shot the President's Daughter. Doubleday, 1973; Allen Lane, 1973

STEWART, FLORA
  Blood Relations. Jenkins, 1967
  Deadly Nightcap. Jenkins, 1966

STEWART, FRED MUSTARD. 1936- .
  The Mephisto Waltz. Coward, 1969; Joseph, 1969
  -The Methuselah Enzyme. Arbor, 1970; Joseph, 1971

STEWART, FRED S.
  The Crippled Hand. Street (Magnet)

STEWART, IAN. 1928- .
  The Peking Payoff. Macmillan, 1975

STEWART, J(OHN) I(NNES) M(ACKINTOSH). 1906- . Pseudonym: Michael Innes, q.v.

STEWART, JAMES
  Danger from Grassen. Black, 1946
  Escape to Crime. Black, 1946
  Spies Over France. Nelson, 1941

STEWART, JAMES E.
  The Mail Robber; or, The Clever Capture of a Dishonest Postal Clerk. Laird, 1889

STEWART, JAY. Pseudonym of (Charles) Stuart Palmer, 1905-1968, q.v.
  Before It's Too Late. Mill, 1950. Reprinted as by Stuart Palmer: Dell, 1952

STEWART, KENNETH LIVINGSTON. 1894- .
  Pseudonym: Kenneth Livingston, q.v.

STEWART, MARY (FLORENCE ELINOR). 1916- .
  Airs Above the Ground. Hodder, 1965; Mill, 1965
  The Gabriel Hounds. Hodder, 1967; Mill, 1967
  The Ivy Tree. Hodder, 1961; Mill, 1961
  Madam, Will You Talk? Hodder, 1955; Mill, 1956
  The Moon-Spinners. Hodder, 1962; Mill, 1963
  My Brother Michael. Hodder, 1960; Mill, 1960
  Nine Coaches Waiting. Hodder, 1958; Mill, 1959
  This Rough Magic. Hodder, 1964; Mill, 1964
  Thunder on the Right. Hodder, 1957; Mill, 1958
  Wildfire at Midnight. Hodder, 1956; Appleton, 1956

STEWART, NEIL. Joint pseudonym with Pamela Hansford Johnson, 1912- : Nap Lombard, q.v.

STEWART, RAMONA. 1922- .
  The Apparition. Little, 1973; Deutsch, 1974
  The Possession of Joel Delaney. Little, 1970; Deutsch, 1971

STICKNEY, F. L.
  The Rubber Mask. Chelsea, 1937

STILES, W(ILLIAM) C(URTIS). 1851-1911.
  Double Jeopardy. Home, 1898

STILGEBAUER, EDWARD. 1868- .
  The Star of Hollywood. Paul, 1927; World, 1929

STILSON, CHARLES B(ILLINGS)
  The Seven Blue Diamonds. Watt, 1927; Hutchinson, 1927

STIMSON, MARY (DRAKE STURDIVANT). 1897- .
  Marijuana Murder. Dorrance, 1940

STIMSON, ROBERT G. and JAMES BELLAH
  The Avenger Tapes. Pinnacle, 1971

STINE, HANK [HENRY EUGENE STINE]. 1945- .
  The Prisoner #3: A Day in the Life. Ace, 1970. (Novelization of The Prisoner TV series.)

STINSON, HUNTER
  Fingerprints. Holt, 1925

STIRLING, PETER. Pseudonym of David Stern, 1909- .
  Stop Press—Murder! Phoenix, 1947

STITT, DAVID E.
  The Stars of Evil. Pageant, 1967

STIVENS, DAL(LAS GEORGE). 1911- .
  The Wide Arch. Angus (Sydney), 1958

STOCKBRIDGE, GRANT. Pseudonym of Norvell W. Page. Series character: Richard Wentworth (The Spider), in all titles (see also: R. T. M. Scott, 1882-).
  The City Destroyer. PB, 1975; New English Library pb, 1976
  City of Flaming Shadows. Berkley, 1970
  Death and the Spider. PB, 1975; New English Library pb, 1976
  Death Reign of the Vampire King. PB, 1975; New English Library pb, 1976
  Hordes of the Red Butcher. PB, 1975; New English Library pb, 1976
  Wings of the Black Death. Berkley, 1970

STOCKTON, FRANK R(ICHARD). 1834-1902.
  The Lady, or the Tiger, and other stories. Scribner, 1884; Douglas, 1884 ss
  The Stories of Three Burglars. Dodd, 1889; Low, 1890

STOCKWELL, GAIL. Series character: Kingsley Toplitt = KT.
  The Candy Killings. Greystone, 1940
  Death by Invitation. Macmillan, 1937 KT
  The Embarrassed Murderer. Macmillan, 1938; Lane, 1938 KT

STODDARD, CHARLES. Pseudonym of Charles Stanley Strong, 1906- . Series character: Mallory, in at least those marked M.
  The Caribou Patrol. Foulsham, 1957 M (U.S. title?)
  Death Rides the Rails. Foulsham, 1955 M (U.S. title?)
  -Devil's Portage. Gateway, 1942; Cassell, 1940
  The Golden Arrow. Foulsham, 1956 M (U.S. title?)
  The Killer of Fort Norman. Arcadia, 1944 M
  The Killer of Sheep River. Arcadia, 1946 M
  Mallory of the Royal Mounted. Arcadia, 1944; Wells Gardner, 1946 M
  -North of the Stars. Dodge, 1937; Cassell, 1938
  -Northwest Trouble. Phoenix, 1948
  -Prairie Peril. Arcadia, 1946; Wright, 1949
  Timber Beasts. Arcadia, 1945 M
  The Trapper of Rat River. Arcadia, 1941; Wells Gardner, 1943 M
  Trooper MacLean. Caslon, 1936; Cassell, 1938
  Tundra Trail. Arcadia, 1947; Wells Gardner, 1948 M
  The Wilderness Patrol. Dodge, 1938; Cassell, 1938

STOKER, ALAN. Pseudonym: Alan Evans, q.v.

STOKER, BRAM [ABRAHAM STOKER]. 1847-1912.
  Dracula. Constable, 1897; Doubleday, 1899
  Dracula's Guest. Routledge, 1914; Hillman-Curl, 1937 ss
  The Garden of Evil; see The Lair of the White Worm
  The Jewel of Seven Stars. Heinemann, 1903; Harper, 1904
  The Lady of the Shroud. Heinemann, 1909; Paperback Library, 1966
  The Lair of the White Worm. Rider, 1911. U.S. title: The Garden of Evil. Paperback Library, 1966
  The Man. Heinemann, 1905
  The Mystery of the Sea. Heinemann, 1902; Doubleday, 1902
  The Snake's Pass. Low, 1891; Harper, 1890
  Under the Sunset. Low, 1882

STOKES, CEDRIC. Pseudonym of George Beardmore, 1908- , q.v. Other pseudonym: George Wolfenden, q.v.
    The Staffordshire Assassins. Macdonald, 1945

STOKES, DONALD (HUBERT). 1913-
    Appointment with Fear. Coward, 1950
    Captive in the Night. Coward, 1951

STOKES, FRANCIS WILLIAM. 1883- . Pseudonym: Francis Everton, q.v.

STOKES, MANNING LEE. Series characters: Christopher Fenn, in at least those marked CF; Barnaby Jones, in at least those marked BJ.
    The Case of the Judas Spoon. Arcadia, 1957 CF
    The Case of the Presidents' Heads. Arcadia, 1956 CF
    The Case of the Winking Buddha. St. John, 1950
    The Crooked Circle. Graphic, 1951. Also published as: Too Many Murderers. Graphic, 1955
    The Dying Room. Phoenix, 1947
    The Grave's in the Meadow. Arcadia, 1959
    Green for a Grave. Phoenix, 1946 BJ
    Hang the Hangman. Arcadia, 1956
    The Iron Tiger. Arcadia, 1958
    The Lady Lost Her Head. Pheonix, 1950
    Murder Can't Wait. Graphic, 1955
    Too Many Murderers; see The Crooked Circle
    Under Cover of Night. Dell, 1958
    The Wolf Howls Murder. Phoenix, 1945 BJ

STONE, A.
    American Pep. Shores, 1918
    Fighting Byng. Britton, 1919

STONE, ANDREW L.
    Cry Terror. Signet, 1958. (Novelization of the movie.)
    The Decks Ran Red. Signet, 1958. (Novelization of the movie.)
    Julie. Signet, 1956; Panther, 1957. (Novelization of the movie.)

STONE, AUSTIN
    Blood Stays Red. Gifford, 1949
    Deadly Night-Blade. Gifford, 1950
    Death Throws a Party. Gifford, 1949
    The Headsman. Eldon, 1936
    Murders in the Mortuary. Eldon, 1935; Putnam, 1936

STONE, CLARA
    Death in Cranford. Hutchinson, 1959

STONE, DAVID (ANTHONY). 1929- .
    The Tired Spy. Putnam, 1961; Davies, 1961

STONE, EDMUND
    Dawn for Danger. Consul, 1965

STONE, ELINORE COWAN
    Fear Rides the Fog. Appleton, 1937

STONE, ELIZABET M. Series character: Maggie Slone, in both titles.
    Murder at the Mardi Gras. Sheridan, 1947
    Poison, Poker and Pistols. Sheridan, 1946

STONE, ELNA
    Dark Masquerade. Lancer, 1973
    Ghost at the Wedding. Belmont, 1971
    Secret of the Willows. Belmont, 1971
    Whisper of Fear. Beagle, 1973

STONE, GRACE ZARING. 1891- . Pseudonym: Ethel Vance, q.v.
    Dear Deadly Cara. Random, 1968

STONE, HAMPTON. Pseudonym of Aaron Marc Stein, 1906- , q.v. Other pseudonym: George Bagby, q.v. Series characters: Gibson and Mac, in all titles.
    The Babe with the Twistable Arm. Simon, 1962; Hale, 1964
    The Corpse in the Corner Saloon. Simon, 1948
    The Corpse That Refused to Stay Dead. Simon, 1952; Dobson, 1954
    The Corpse was No Bargain at All. Simon, 1968; Hale, 1969
    The Corpse Who had Too Many Friends. Simon, 1953; Foulsham, 1954
    The Funniest Killer in Town. Simon, 1967
    The Girl Who Kept Knocking Them Dead. Simon, 1957; Foulsham, 1957
    The Girl with the Hole in her Head. Simon, 1949; Boardman, 1958
    The Kid was Last Seen Hanging Ten. Simon, 1966
    The Kid Who Came Home with a Corpse. Simon, 1972
    The Man Who had Too Much to Lose. Simon, 1955; Foulsham, 1955
    The Man Who Looked Death in the Eye. Simon, 1961
    The Man Who was Three Jumps Ahead. Simon, 1959; Boardman, 1960
    The Murder That Wouldn't Stay Solved. Simon, 1951
    The Needle That Wouldn't Hold Still. Simon, 1950; Boardman, 1958
    The Real Serendipitous Kill. Simon, 1964
    The Strangler; see The Strangler Who Couldn't Let Go
    The Strangler Who Couldn't Let Go. Simon, 1956. British title: The Strangler. Foulsham, 1957
    The Swinger Who Swung by the Neck. Simon, 1970

STONE, HARRIET
    Heiress of Bayou Vache. Lancer, 1965

STONE, PETER (H.). 1930- .
    Charade. GM, 1963; Fontana, 1964. (Novelization of the movie.)

STONE, SCOTT C(LINTON) S(TUART). 1932- .
    The Dragon's Eye. GM, 1969

STONE, SIMON. Pseudonym of Howard Barrington, 1906- . Series character: Sir Brian Dinsmore Conway, in at least those marked BC.
    Bookmaker's Body. Hutchinson, 1947 BC
    Conway, K.C. Hutchinson, 1945 BC
    Demi-Paradise Regained. Hutchinson, 1945
    I, Spy. Hutchinson, 1941
    Knight Missing. Hutchinson, 1944; Macmillan, 1945 BC
    Murder Conc Mad. Hutchinson, 1951
    The Price of Admiralty. Hutchinson, 1942

STONE, THOMAS H. Pseudonym of Terry Harknett, 1936- , q.v. Other pseudonyms: Joseph Hedges, William Pine, William Terry, qq.v.
    Black Death. New English Library pb, 1973
    Dead Set. New English Library pb, 1972
    One Horse Race. New English Library pb, 1972
    Squeeze Play. New English Library pb, 1973
    Stopover for Murder. New English Library pb, 1973

STONEHAM, C(HARLES) THURLEY. 1895- . Pseudonym: Norgrove Thurley, q.v.
    -Adventure for Wealth. Long, 1957
    Kenya Mystery. Museum, 1954
    The Man in the Pig Mask. Hutchinson, 1929
    The Prowling Terror. Long, 1957
    Rogues in the Forest. Long, 1958

STORER, MARIA LONGWORTH. 1849- .
    The Borodino Mystery. Herder, 1916
    -Probation. Herder, 1916
    -Sir Christopher Leighton; or, The Marquis de Vaudreuil's Story. Herder, 1915
    -The Villa Rossignol; or, The Advance of Islam. Herder, 1918

STOREY, ANTHONY. 1928- .
    -Brothers Keepers. Boyars, 1975
    -The Centre Holds. Calder, 1973
    Platinum Ass. Allen, 1975
    Platinum Jag. Calder, 1972

STOREY, MICHAEL. 1941- .
    Soft in the Middle. Knopf, 1972; Cape, 1972

STORM, JOAN. Series character: Sarah Vanessa, in all titles.
    Bitter Rubies. Hammond, 1952
    Dark Emerald. Hammond, 1951
    Deadly Diamond. Hammond, 1953

STORM, LESLEY. Pseudonym of Mabel Margaret Cowie Clark.
    Gallows-Bird. Hutchinson, 1937

STORM, MICHAEL
    Baby Don't Love Hoodlums. Harborough, 1953
    Baby Don't Say Goodbye. Harborough, 1953
    Chicago Terror. Harborough, 1952
    The Devil has a Racket. Harborough, 1954
    Dragons Come Expensive. Harborough, 1953
    Elvira Digs a Grave. Harborough, 1952
    The Grey Messengers. Blackie, 1940
    Hot Dames on Cold Slabs. Archer, 1950
    Kiss the Corpse Goodbye. Harborough, 1952
    Lovelies are Never Lonely. Harborough, 1952
    Make Mine a Corpse. Archer, 1950
    Make Mine a Harlot. Archer, 1949
    Make Mine a Redhead. Harborough, 1952
    Make Mine a Virgin. Archer, 1949
    Make Mine Beautiful. Archer, 1949
    Make Mine Dangerous. Archer, 1949
    Me and My Ghoul. Harborough, 1953
    Satan Buys a Wreath. Archer, 1951
    Stella Buys a Shroud. Harborough, 1952
    "Sucker for a Red-Head." Archer, 1950
    Sweetheart with a Wreath. Harborough, 1953
    Tiptoe thro' a Graveyard. Harborough, 1953
    A Woman's Friend. Curtis Warren, 1950
    You'll be Better Off Dead. Harborough, 1953

STORM, MICHAEL
    China Cane. Mystery House, 1959
    Cry, Tiger! Mystery House, 1958
    Edge of Danger. Mystery House, 1957

STORME, PETER. Pseudonym of Philip Van Doren Stern, 1900- , q.v.
    The Thing in the Brook. Simon, 1937; Hale, 1937

STORRS, LEWIS AUSTIN. 1866- .
    Koheleth. Dillingham, 1897

STORY, JACK TREVOR. 1918-   . Series character (with many other authors): Sexton Blake = SB.
  Assault and Pepper. Fleetway, 1961 SB
  The Big Steal! Fleetway, 1960 SB
  The Blonde and the Boodle. Amalgamated, 1957 SB
  Collapse of Stout Party. Amalgamated, 1958 SB
  Company of Bandits. Mayflower, 1965 SB
  Courier for Crime. Amalgamated, 1959 SB
  -Crying Makes Your Nose Run. Bruce, 1974
  Danger on the Flip Side. Amalgamated, 1960 SB
  Danger's Child. Fleetway, 1961 SB
  -Dishonourable Member. Secker, 1969
  The Frightened People. Amalgamated, 1958 SB
  -Green to Pagan Street. Harrap, 1952
  -Hitler Needs You. Allison, 1971
  Home Sweet Homicide. Amalgamated, 1959 SB
  Invitation to a Murder! Amalgamated, 1959 SB
  -I Sit in Hanger Lane. Secker, 1968
  -Little Dog's Day. Allison, 1971
  -Live Now, Pay Later. Secker, 1963
  -Man Pinches Bottom. Allen, 1962
  Mix Me a Person. Allen, 1959; Macmillan, 1960
  -The Money Goes Round and Round. Redman, 1958
  Murder in the Sun. Amalgamated, 1958 SB
  Murder—with Love. Amalgamated, 1956 SB
  Nine O'Clock Shadow. Amalgamated, 1958 SB
  -One Last Mad Embrace. Allison, 1970
  Protection for a Lady. Laurie, 1950
  Rogue's Harbour. Fleetway, 1961 SB
  The Season of the Skylark. Amalgamated, 1957 SB
  She Ain't Got No Body. Amalgamated, 1958 SB
  -Something for Nothing. Secker, 1963
  Story on Crime. Baker, 1975
  Suddenly It's Murder. Fleetway, 1961 SB
  The Trouble with Harry. Boardman, 1949; Macmillan, 1950
  -The Urban District Lover. Secker, 1964
  Vacation with Fear. Amalgamated, 1957 SB
  Violence in Quiet Places. Amalgamated, 1960 SB
  -The Wind in the Snottygobble Tree. Allison, 1971

STOUT, REX. 1886-1975. Series characters: Nero Wolfe & Archie Goodwin = W&G; Inspector Cramer (also in the W&G stories) = C; Tecumseh Fox = TF; Dol Bonner (also in some of the W&G stories) = DB. See also: ANONYMOUS (The President Vanishes).
  Alphabet Hicks. Farrar, 1941; Collins, 1942. Also published as: The Sound of Murder. Pyramid, 1965
  And be a Villain. Viking, 1948. British title: More Deaths Than One. Collins, 1949 W&G
  And Four to Go. Viking, 1958. British title: Crime and Again. Collins, 1959. (4 W&G novelets.)
  Bad for Business. Farrar, 1940 (in the omnibus The Second Mystery Book); Collins, 1945 TF
  Before Midnight. Viking, 1955; Collins, 1956 W&G
  The Black Mountain. Viking, 1954; Collins, 1955 W&G
  Black Orchids. Farrar, 1942; Collins, 1943. Also published as: The Case of the Black Orchids. Avon, 1950. (Two W&G novelets. Some paperback editions contain only the first of these, the title story. The second novelet has been reprinted separately as: Cordially Invited to Meet Death. Jonathan, 194?. And as: Invitation to Murder. Avon, 1956.)
  The Broken Vase. Farrar, 1941; Collins, 1942 TF
  The Case of the Black Orchids; see Black Orchids
  Case of the Red Box; see The Red Box
  Champagne for One. Viking, 1958; Collins, 1959 W&G
  Cordially Invited to Meet Death; see Black Orchids
  Crime and Again; see And Four to Go
  Crime on her Hands; see The Hand in the Glove
  Curtains for Three. Viking, 1951; Collins, 1951. (3 W&G novelets.)
  Death of a Doxy. Viking, 1966; Collins, 1967 W&G
  Death of a Dude. Viking, 1969; Collins, 1970 W&G
  Door to Death; see Three Doors to Death
  The Doorbell Rang. Viking, 1965; Collins, 1966 W&G
  Double for Death. Farrar, 1939; Collins, 1940 TF
  Even in the Best Families; see In the Best Families
  A Family Affair. Viking, 1975; Collins, 1976 W&G
  The Father Hunt. Viking, 1968; Collins, 1969 W&G
  Fer-de-Lance. Farrar, 1934; Cassell, 1935. Also published as: Meet Nero Wolfe. Mercury, 19?? W&G
  The Final Deduction. Viking, 1961; Collins, 1962 W&G
  Gambit. Viking, 1962; Collins, 1963 W&G
  The Golden Spiders. Viking, 1953; Collins, 1954 W&G
  The Hand in the Glove. Farrar, 1937. British title: Crime on her Hands. Collins, 1939 DB
  Homicide Trinity. Viking, 1962; Collins, 1963. (3 W&G novelets.)
  If Death Ever Slept. Viking, 1957; Collins, 1958 W&G
  In the Best Families. Viking, 1950. British title: Even in the Best Families. Collins, 1951 W&G
  Invitation to Murder; see Black Orchids
  The League of Frightened Men. Farrar, 1935; Cassell, 1935 W&G
  Meet Nero Wolfe; see Fer-de-Lance
  Might as Well be Dead. Viking, 1956; Collins, 1957 W&G
  More Deaths Than One; see And be a Villain
  The Mother Hunt. Viking, 1963; Collins, 1964 W&G
  Mountain Cat. Farrar, 1939; Collins, 1940. Also published as: The Mountain Cat Murders. Dell, 1943
  The Mountain Cat Murders; see Mountain Cat
  Murder by the Book. Viking, 1951; Collins, 1952 W&G
  Murder in Style; see Plot It Yourself
  Not Quite Dead Enough. Farrar, 1944. (2 W&G novelets.)
  Out Goes She; see Prisoner's Base
  Over My Dead Body. Farrar, 1940; Collins, 1940 W&G
  Please Pass the Guilt. Viking, 1973; Collins, 1974 W&G
  Plot It Yourself. Viking, 1959. British title: Murder in Style. Collins, 1960 W&G
  Prisoner's Base. Viking, 1952. British title: Out Goes She. Collins, 1953 W&G
  The Red Box. Farrar, 1937; Cassell, 1937. Also published as: Case of the Red Box. Avon, 1958 W&G
  The Red Bull; see Some Buried Caesar
  Red Threads. Farrar, 1939 (in the omnibus The Mystery Book); Collins, 1941 C
  A Right to Die. Viking, 1964; Collins, 1965 W&G
  The Rubber Band. Farrar, 1936; Cassell, 1936. Also published as: To Kill Again. Hillman, 1960 W&G
  The Second Confession. Viking, 1949; Collins, 1950 W&G
  The Silent Speaker. Viking, 1946; Collins, 1947 W&G
  Some Buried Caesar. Farrar, 1939; Collins, 1939. Also published as: The Red Bull. Dell, 1945 W&G
  The Sound of Murder; see Alphabet Hicks
  Three at Wolfe's Door. Viking, 1960; Collins, 1961. (3 W&G novelets.)
  Three Doors to Death. Viking, 1950; Collins, 1950. (3 W&G novelets, of which one was reprinted separately as: Door to Death. Dell 10¢ pb, 1951.)
  Three for the Chair. Viking, 1957; Collins, 1958. (3 W&G novelets.)
  Three Men Out. Viking, 1954; Collins, 1955. (3 W&G novelets.)
  Three Witnesses. Viking, 1956; Collins, 1956. (3 W&G novelets.)
  To Kill Again; see The Rubber Band
  Too Many Clients. Viking, 1960; Collins, 1961 W&G
  Too Many Cooks. Farrar, 1938; Collins, 1938 W&G
  Too Many Women. Viking, 1947; Collins, 1948 W&G
  Trio for Blunt Instruments. Viking, 1964; Collins, 1965. (3 W&G novelets.)
  Triple Jeopardy. Viking, 1951; Collins, 1952. (3 W&G novelets.)
  Trouble in Triplicate. Viking, 1949; Collins, 1949. (3 W&G novelets.)
  Where There's a Will. Farrar, 1940; Collins, 1941 W&G

STOWELL, WILLIAM AVERILL. 1882-1950.
  The Marston Murder Case. Appleton, 1930
  The Mystery of the Singing Walls. Appleton, 1925
  The Wake of the Setting Sun. Appleton, 1923

STRACHAN, T(ONY) S(IMPSON). 1920-   .
  Fire Escape. Laurie, 1950
  Key Major. Heinemann, 1954
  No Law in Illyria. Heinemann, 1957
  No One to Worry Us. Laurie, 1949
  The Short Weekend. Hammond, 1953

STRAHAN, KAY CLEAVER. 1888-   . Series character: Lynn MacDonald = LM.
  Death Traps. Doubleday, 1930; Gollancz, 1930
  The Desert Lake Mystery. Bobbs, 1936; Methuen, 1937 LM
  The Desert Moon Mystery. Doubleday, 1928; Gollancz, 1928 LM
  Footprints. Doubleday, 1929; Gollancz, 1929 LM
  The Hobgoblin Murder. Bobbs, 1934; Methuen, 1935 LM
  The Meriweather Mystery. Doubleday, 1932 LM
  October House. Doubleday, 1932; Gollancz, 1931 LM

STRAKER, J(OHN) F(OSTER). 1904-   . Series characters: Johnny Inch, in at least those marked JI; Inspector Pitt, in at least those marked P.
  A Coil of Rope. Harrap, 1962
  Death of a Good Woman. Harrap, 1961 P
  Final Witness. Harrap, 1963
  The Ginger Horse. Harrap, 1956 P

The Goat. Harrap, 1972 JI
Goodbye, Aunt Charlotte! Harrap, 1958 P
A Gun to Play With. Harrap, 1956
Hell is Empty. Harrap, 1958
A Letter for Obi. Harrap, 1971 JI
A Man Who Cannot Kill. Harrap, 1969
Miscarriage of Murder. Harrap, 1967
Murder for Missemily. Harrap, 1961 P
Pick Up the Pieces. Harrap, 1955 P
Postman's Knock. Harrap, 1954 P
Ricochet. Harrap, 1965
The Shape of Murder. Harrap, 1964
Sin and Johnny Inch. Harrap, 1968 JI
Tight Circle. Harrap, 1970 JI

STRANGE, CARLTON
The Beechcourt Mystery. Newnes, 1894

STRANGE, DOROTHY. See: ARTHUR W(ILLIAM) UPFIELD, 1888-1964.

STRANGE, JOHN STEPHEN. Pseudonym of Dorothy Stockbridge Tillett, 1896- . Series characters: Barney Gantt = BG; Lt./Capt. George Honegger = GH; Van Dusen Ormsberry = VO.
All Men are Liars. Doubleday, 1948. British title: Come to Judgment. Collins, 1949 GH
The Ballot Box Murders; see Rope Enough
The Bell in the Fog. Doubleday, 1936; Collins, 1937 BG
Black Hawthorn. Doubleday, 1933. British title: The Chinese Jar Mystery. Collins, 1934
Catch the Gold Ring. Doubleday, 1955. British title: A Handful of Silver. Collins, 1955
The Chinese Jar Mystery; see Black Hawthorn
The Clue of the Second Murder. Doubleday, 1929; Collins, 1929 VO
Come to Judgment; see All Men are Liars
The Corpse and the Lady; see Silent Witnesses
Dead End; see Let the Dead Past—
Deadly Beloved. Doubleday, 1952; Collins, 1952 BG
Eye Witness. Doubleday, 1961; Collins, 1962 GH
The Fair and the Dead; see Reasonable Doubt
For the Hangman. Doubleday, 1934; Collins, 1935
A Handful of Silver; see Catch the Gold Ring
Let the Dead Past—. Doubleday, 1953. British title: Dead End. Collins, 1953
Look Your Last. Doubleday, 1943; Collins, 1944 BG
Make My Bed Soon. Doubleday, 1948; Collins, 1948 BG
The Man Who Killed Fortescue. Doubleday, 1928; Collins, 1929 VO
Murder at World's End; see The Strangler Fig
Murder Game; see Murder on the Ten-Yard Line
Murder Gives a Lovely Light. Doubleday, 1941; Collins, 1942 GH
Murder on the Ten-Yard Line. Doubleday, 1931. British title: Murder Game. Collins, 1931 VO
Night of Reckoning. Doubleday, 1958; Collins, 1959
A Picture of the Victim. Doubleday, 1940; Collins, 1940 BG
Reasonable Doubt. Doubleday, 1951; Collins, 1951. Also published as: The Fair and the Dead. Bestseller, 1953
Rope Enough. Doubleday, 1938; Collins, 1939. Also published as: The Ballot Box Murders. Mystery Novel Classic, 1943 BG
Silent Witnesses. Doubleday, 1938. British title: The Corpse and the Lady. Collins, 1938 BG

The Strangler Fig. Doubleday, 1930; Collins, 1931. Also published as: Murder at World's End. Mystery Novel Classic, 1943
Uneasy is the Grave; see Unquiet Grave
Unquiet Grave. Doubleday, 1949. British title: Uneasy is the Grave. Collins, 1950

STRANGE, MARK. Pseudonym.
Midnight. Faber, 1927

STRANGER, L. D.
-The Great Snake Murder. Richmond, 1915
-The Odd One Out. Nelson, 1936

STRATEMEYER, EDWARD. 1862-1930.
Reuben Stone's Discovery; or, The Young Miller of Torrent Bend. Merriam, 1895

STRATENUS, LOUISE
Suspected. Chapman, 1892. (Translation of Gewroken. Arnheim, 1890.)

STRATFORD, MICHAEL. Pseudonym of Bruce (Bingham) Cassiday, 1920- , q.v. Other pseudonyms: Carson Bingham, Mary Anne Drew, Annie Laurie McMurdie, qq.v.
The Sniper. Award, 1974; Tandem, 1974. (Novelization of the Adam 12 TV series.)

STRATTON, CHRIS
Change of Mind. Pyramid, 1969. (Novelization of the movie.)
Dead on Arrival. Award, 1972. (Novelization of the Adam 12 TV series.)
A Fine Pair. Popular Library, 1969. (Novelization of the movie.)
The Hostages. Award, 1974; Tandem, 1974. (Novelization of the Adam 12 TV series.)
Rock! Pyramid, 1970. (Novelization of the Then Came Bronson TV series.)
The Runaway. Award, 1974. (Novelization of the Adam 12 TV series.)
The Ticket. Pyramid, 1970; New English Library pb, 1970. (Novelization of the Then Came Bronson TV series.)
Underground. Popular Library, 1970. (Novelization of the movie.)

STRATTON, HENRY. Pseudonym of Michael Harrington Nelson, 1921- .
Blanket. Macdonald, 1959

STRATTON, ROY (OLIN). Series characters: Scott Gregory and Justin Bassett, in both titles.
The Decorated Corpse. Mill, 1962; Boardman, 1963
One Among None. Mill, 1965; Boardman, 1965

STRATTON, TED [JOHN THEODORE STRATTON]. 1902- .
Tourist Trap. Putnam, 1975; Hale, 1977

STRATTON, THOMAS. Joint pseudonym of (Thomas Eu)Gene DeWeese, 1934- , q.v., and Robert Stratton Coulson, 1918- . Other pseudonym of DeWeese: Jean DeWeese, q.v.
The Invisibility Affair. Ace, 1967. (Novelization of Man from U.N.C.L.E. TV series.)
The Mind-Twisters Affair. Ace, 1967. (Novelization of Man from U.N.C.L.E. TV series.)

STRAUB, PETER
Julia. Coward, 1975; Cape, 1976

STRAUS, RALPH. 1882- . Pseudonym: Robert Erstone Forbes, q.v.
Five Men Go to Prison. Chapman, 1935
Pengard Awake. Methuen, 1920; Appleton, 1920

STRAUSS, THEODORE. 1912- .
Black Caesar; see Night at Hogwallow
Dark Hunger; see Moonrise
Moonrise. Viking, 1946; H. Hamilton, 1947. Also published as: Dark Hunger. Bantam, 1951
Night at Hogwallow. Little, 1937; British title: Black Caesar. Heinemann, 1937

STREET, A(RTHUR) G(EORGE). 1892- .
A Crook in the Furrow. Faber, 1940

STREET, BRADFORD
For Pete's Sake. Avon, 1974. (Novelization of the movie.)
The Glass Bottom Boat. Dell, 1966. (Novelization of the movie.)
In Like Flint. Dell, 1966. (Novelization of the movie.)
Primus. Bantam, 1971. (Novelization of the TV series.)

STREET, CECIL JOHN CHARLES. 1884-1961. Pseudonyms: Miles Burton, John Rhode, qq.v.

STREET, JAMES
Carbon Monoxide. Low, 1937
Death in an Armchair. Jenkins, 1936
A Wastrel Goes West. Low, 1937

STREET, PENNY
The Chinese Bottle. Pocket Editions, 1945
Murder in a Barge. Pocket Editions, 1946
The Sign of Blood. Pictorial Art, 1946

STREVENS, ROBERT
Murder in Manuscript. Rich, 1948

STRIBLING, T(HOMAS) S(IGISMUND). 1881-1965. Series character: Prof. Henry Poggioli, in both titles.
Best Dr. Poggioli Detective Stories. Dover (New York), 1975; Dover (London), 1976 ss
Clues of the Caribbees. Doubleday, 1929; Heinemann, 1930 ss

STRINGER, ARTHUR (JOHN ARBUTHNOTT). 1874-1950.
The City of Peril. Knopf, 1923
The Diamond Thieves. Bobbs, 1923; Hodder, 1925 ss
The Door of Dread. Bobbs, 1916; Amalgamated, 1925
-Empty Hands. Bobbs, 1924; Hodder, 1924
The Ghost Plane. Bobbs, 1940
The Gun-Runner. Dodge, 1909
The Hand of Peril. Macmillan, 1915
The House of Intrigue. Bobbs, 1918
In Bad with Sinbad. Bobbs, 1926
The Man Who Couldn't Sleep. Bobbs, 1919 ss
-Manhandled, with Russell Holman. Grosset, 1924. (Novelization of the movie.)
-Marriage by Capture. Bobbs, 1933; Methuen, 1934
Never-Fail Blake; see The Shadow
Night Hawk. McClure, 1908
Phantom Wires. Little, 1907; Daily Mail, 1909
The Shadow. Century, 1913. Also published as: Never-Fail Blake. Burt, 1924
-Shadowed Victory. Bobbs, 1943; Hodder, 1944

-The Silver Poppy. Appleton, 1903; Methuen, 1904
-Star in a Mist. Bobbs, 1943
-The Story Without a Name, with Russell Holman. Grosset, 1924. (Novelization of the movie.)
-Twin Tales. Bobbs, 1921. (2 novelets.)
The Under Groove. McClure, 1908 ss
The Wire Tappers. Little, 1906
-The Wolf Woman. Bobbs, 1928; Paul, 1929

STROBEL, MARIAN. 1895-   . Series character: A. Lincoln Lacy, in both titles.
Ice Before Killing. Scribner, 1943
Kiss and Kill. Scribner, 1946

STRONG, BEN. Joint pseudonym of Emeric Hulme-Beaman, q.v., and William Senior Ellis. Series character: Prof. Adrian Criddle = AC.
The Secret of Gnome Head. Hodder, 1928 AC
The Shadow on the Course. Hamilton, 1926
The Studdingly Stables Mystery. Hodder, 1926
The Track of the Slayer. Hodder, 1925 AC

STRONG, CHARLES STANLEY. 1906-   . Pseudonym: Charles Stoddard, q.v.

STRONG, EDMUND C.
Manacle and Bracelet; or, The Dead Man's Secret. Laird, 1888

STRONG, HARRINGTON
The Brand of Silence. Chelsea, 1924
The Hooded Stranger. Hutchinson, 1926
Legal Settlement. Lloyd, 1922
The Scarlet Scourge. Hutchinson, 1927
The Spider's Den. Hutchinson, 1926
Who Killed William Drew? Chelsea, 1925; Skeffington, 1926

STRONG, HERO. Pseudonym of Clara Augusta Jones. Other pseudonym: Clara Augusta, q.v.
A Beautiful Woman's Sin; or, The Scarred Arm. Street, 1890
-Born to Command; or, The Mistress of Hillmere. Street, 1890
Found Dead; or, The Charles Street Mystery. Street, 1892

STRONG, L(EONARD) A(LFRED) G(EORGE). 1896-1958. Series character: Insp. Ellis McKay = EM.
All Fall Down. Collins, 1944; Doubleday, 1944 EM
Murder Plays an Ugly Scene; see Othello's Occupation
Odd Man In. Pitman, 1938 ss
Othello's Occupation. Collins, 1945. U.S. title: Murder Plays an Ugly Scene. Doubleday, 1945 EM
Slocombe Dies. Collins, 1942
Treason in the Egg. Collins, 1958 EM
Which I Never. Collins, 1950; Macmillan, 1952 EM

STROUP, WILLIAM
The Mark of Pak San Ri. Book Company of America, 1965

STRUTTON, BILL
The Carpaccio Caper; see A Glut of Virgins
A Glut of Virgins. Macdonald, 1974. U.S. title: The Carpaccio Caper. Coward, 1973
A Jury of Angels. Hodder, 1957

STUART, ALAN
The Unwilling Angel. Ward, 1955

STUART, BRIAN. Pseudonym of Brian Arthur Worthington-Stuart. Other pseudonym: Peter Meredith, q.v. Series character: Knock-Out Kavanagh, in at least those marked KK.
The Affair at Sidi Brahim. Ward, 1948 KK
Beth Takes Charge. Ward, 1954
The Case is Altered. Ward, 1955
Diamond Cut Diamond. Ward, 1955
Knock-Out Kavanagh. Ward, 1948 KK
Mysterious Monsieur Moray. Ward, 1950
The Serpent's Fang. Ward, 1951
The Silver Phantom Murder. Ward, 1950 KK

STUART, DONALD. 1927-   . Pseudonym: Gerald Verner, q.v. Those titles listed below without publisher were published by Amalgamated Press and feature Sexton Blake. Other series character: Lionel Crane, in at least those marked LC.
The Bells of Doom. 1936
The Burmese Dagger. 1939
The Case of the Missing Estate Agent. 1932
The Cottage of Terror. 1935
Danger at Westway's. 1938
Dead Man's Secret. 1932
The Death Road. 1930
The Embankment Crime. 1932
The Empty House Murder. 1933
The Fence's Victim. 1930
The Garden City Crime. 1931
Guilty, But Insane. 1933
The Hidden Menace. 1939
The Hooded Raider. 1931
The Man in the Dark. Wright, 1935
The Man Outside. Wright, 1934
Midnight Murder. Wright, 1935 LC
The Motor Bus Murder. 1934
The Next Victim. 1931
The £1,000,000 Film Murder. 1933
The Riddle of the Sunken Garden. 1937
The Secret of Moor House. 1938
The Secret of Seven. 1932
The Secret of the Hulk. 1940
The Secret of the Sealed Room. 1935
The Shadow. Wright, 1934
The Squealer's Secret. 1932
The Terror of Lonely Tor. 1931
The Third Victim. 1939
The Three Who Paid. 1938
The Time of the Crime. 1938
The Truth About Lord Tench. 1935
Twenty Years of Hate. 1940
The Unknown Menace. 1937
The Valley of Terror. Wright, 1935
The Village of Fear. 1934
The White Friar. Wright, 1934; Godwin, 1935 LC

STUART, ELIZABETH
Shaking Shadow. Signet, 1967

STUART, ESME. Pseudonym of Amelie Claire Leroy, 1851-   .
Arrested. White, 1896; Appleton, 1897

STUART, IAN. Pseudonym of Alistair (Stuart) MacLean, 1922-   , q.v.
The Black Shrike; see The Dark Crusader
The Dark Crusader. Collins, 1961. U.S. title: The Black Shrike. Scribner, 1961
The Satan Bug. Collins, 1962; Scribner, 1962
The Snow on the Ben. Ward, 1961

STUART, ILIAN
The Man in the Rolls-Royce. Heinemann, 1958

STUART, JANE. 1942-   .
Passerman's Hollow. McGraw, 1974

STUART, JOHN
Ashes to Ashes. International Publishers, 1969

STUART, MIRANDA. Pseudonym of Muriel Lillah Stuart Thompson, 1902-   .
Dead Men Sing No Songs. Hodder, 1939

STUART, ROBERT
Duncan Ross—Detective-Sergeant. Blackie, 1935

STUART, SIDNEY. Pseudonym of Michael (Angelo) Avallone (Jr.), 1924-   , q.v. Other pseudonyms: Mark Dane, Jean-Anne de Pre, Priscilla Dalton, Dora Highland, Steve Michaels, Dorothea Nile, Edwina Noone, Max Walker, qq.v.
The Beast with the Red Hands. Popular Library, 1973
The Night Walker. Award, 1964. (Novelization of the movie.)
Young Dillinger. Belmont, 1965. (Novelization of the movie.)

STUART, WILLIAM L(ISLE). 1915-   .
Dead Ahead; see The Dead Lie Still
The Dead Lie Still. Farrar, 1945. Also published as: Dead Ahead. Ace, 1953
Night Cry. Dial, 1948; Boardman, 1951

STUBBS, JEAN. 1926-   . Series character: Inspector Lintott, in both titles.
Dear Laura. Macmillan (London), 1973; Stein, 1973
The Painted Face. Macmillan (London), 1974; Stein, 1974

STURGEON, THEODORE (HAMILTON). 1918-   . Name originally: Edward Hamilton Waldo.
Some of Your Blood. Ballantine, 1961; Sphere, 1967
Sturgeon's West, with Don Ward. Doubleday, 1973 ss

STURROCK, JEREMY. U.S. byline: J. G. Jeffreys. Pseudonyms of Ben(jamin James) Healey, 1908-   , q.v. Series character: Jeremy Sturrock, in all titles.
The Thief Taker; see The Village of Rogues
The Village of Rogues. Macmillan (London), 1972. U.S. title: The Thief Taker. Walker, 1972
A Wicked Way to Die. Macmillan (London), 1973; Walker, 1973
The Wilful Lady. Macmillan (London), 1975; Walker, 1975

STURT, E. M. LEADER
A Detective's Memoirs and other stories. Drane, 1921 ss

STUTLEY, S. J. and A. E. COPP
The Melbourne Mystery. Bodley Head, 1929
The Poisoned Glass. Bodley Head, 1930

STUYVESANT, ALICE. Pseudonym of Alice M(uriel Livingston) Williamson, 1869-1933, q.v. Other pseudonym: Dona Teresa de Savallo, q.v. See also: C(HARLES) N(ORRIS) WILLIAMSON, 1859-1920.

STYLES, (FRANK) SHOWELL. 1908-   . Pseudonym: Glyn Carr, q.v. Series character: Abercrombie Lewker, in at least those marked AL (also in those under the Glyn Carr byline).
Dark Hazard. Selwyn, 1948
-The Frigate Captain. Faber, 1954

-Gentleman Johnny. Faber, 1962
Hammer Island. Selwyn, 1947 AL
Kidnap Castle. Selwyn, 1947
-Land from the Sea. Faber, 1952
-Mr. Nelson's Ladies. Faber, 1953
-Path to Glory. Faber, 1951
-Quinn of the "Fury". Faber, 1958
The Rising of the Lark. Selwyn, 1948
-The Sea Officer. Faber, 1961
-Shadow Buttress. Faber, 1959
-Sir Devil. Selwyn, 1949
-A Sword for Mr. Fitton. Faber, 1975
Traitor's Mountain. Selwyn, 1945; Macmillan, 1946 AL

SUDAK, EUNICE
The Icepick in Ollie Birk. Lancer, 1966
The Raven. Lancer, 1963. (Novelization of the movie.)
Tales of Terror. Lancer, 1962. (Novelization of the movie.)
-X. Lancer, 1963. (Novelization of the movie.)

SUE, (MARIE JOSEPH) EUGENE. 1804-1857.
The Female Bluebeard; or, The Adventurer. (London), 1845; Winchester, 1844
The Mysteries of Paris. Wiley, 1843; Winchester, 1844. (Translation of Les Mysteres de Paris. Paris, 1843-4.)

SUGAR, ANDREW. Series characters: Alex Jason (The Enforcer) = AJ; Israeli Commandos = IC.
The Alps Assignment. Manor, 1975 IC
The Aswan Assignment. Manor, 1974 IC
Calling Dr. Kill. Lancer, 1973 AJ
Caribbean Kill. Manor, 1975 AJ
The Enforcer. Lancer, 1973 AJ
The Fireball Assignment. Manor, 1974 IC
The Kamikaze Assignment. Manor, 1975 IC
Kill City. Lancer, 1973 AJ
-Yank. Manor, 1975

SULLIVAN, (EDWARD) ALAN. 1868-1947. Pseudonym: Sinclair Murray, q.v.
The Jade God. Bles, 1924; Century, 1925

SULLIVAN, SEAN MEI
Super Man Chu. Ballantine, 1974. (Novelization of the movie.)

SULLIVAN, VIRGINIA
Permanent Wave. Macrae Smith, 1929

SULLY, KATHLEEN (M.). 1910-   .
-Merrily to the Grave. Davies, 1958
-Through the Wall. Davies, 1957

SULZBERGER, C(YRUS) L(EO). 1912-   .
The Tooth Merchant. Quadrangle, 1973; Collins, 1973

SUMMERS, A. WELBOURNE. Pseudonym: Kilsyth Stellier, q.v.

SUMMERS, HOLLIS SPURGEON. 1915-   .
Joint pseudonym with James F. Rourke, 1922-   : Jim Hollis, q.v.

SUMMERS, KEITH
Design for Death. Boardman, 1957

SUMMERTON, MARGARET. Pseudonym: Jan Roffman, q.v.
The Ghost Flowers. Collins, 1973; Doubleday, 1973
A Memory of Darkness. Hodder, 1967; Dutton, 1967
Nightingale at Noon. Hodder, 1963; Dutton, 1963
Quin's Hide. Hodder, 1964; Dutton, 1965
The Red Pavilion. Hodder, 1968
Ring of Mischief. Hodder, 1965; Dutton, 1965
The Saffron Summer. Collins, 1975; Doubleday, 1975

The Sand Rose. Collins, 1969; Doubleday, 1969
The Sea House. Hodder, 1961; Holt, 1961
A Small Wilderness. Hodder, 1959
The Sunset Hour. Hodder, 1957
Sweetcrab. Collins, 1971; Doubleday, 1971
Theft in Kind. Hodder, 1962

SUMNER, CID RICKETTS. 1890-1970.
Withdraw Thy Foot. Coward, 1964; Hale, 1966

SUMNER, E. E. Pseudonym.
Chance Encounter. Hale, 1967
The Juryman. Hale, 1968
Second-Hand Death. Hale, 1966

SUNDERLAND, KAYE
Late Harvest. Paul, 1933

SUNDMAN, PER OLOF. 1922-
Two Days, Two Nights. Pantheon, 1969. (Translation of Tva Dagar, Tva Natter. Stockholm, 1965.)

SUNMAN, WILLIAM R.
The Mystery of Wolverston Grange. Crombie, 1889

SUTCLIFFE, HALLIWELL. 1870-1932.
Persons Unknown. Long, 1928

SUTHERLAND, MORRIS. Pseudonym of Gwendolen Sutherland Morris.
-The Hunting Ground. Rich, 1934
-Mountain Fires. Rich, 1937
The Perilous Errand. Rich, 1935
-Second Storm. Butterworth, 1930
-Send Danger. Rich, 1934

SUTHERLAND, NEIL PULSFORD
The Pawn. Heinemann, 1952

SUTHERLAND, WILLIAM. Pseudonym of John Murray Cooper, 1908-   .
Behind the Head-Lines. Arrowsmith, 1933
Death Rides the Air Line. Arrowsmith, 1934; Kendall, 1934
The Proverbial Murder Case. Arrowsmith, 1935

SUTPHEN, (WILLIAM GILBERT) VAN TASSEL. 1861-   .
The Cardinal's Rose. Harper (New York), 1900; Harper (London), 1901
The Gates of Chance. Harper, 1904; Ward, 1908 ss
In Jeopardy. Harper, 1922

SUTTON, ELIZABETH
Dead Fingers. Fly, 1918

SUTTON, GRAHAM. Pseudonym: Antony Marsden, q.v.

SWAIN, VIRGINIA. 1899-   .
-The Hollow Skin. Farrar, 1938

SWAN, ANNIE S. [MRS. ANNIE S. SWAN BURDETT-SMITH]. 1859-
-The Curse of Cowden. Hutchinson, 1897
-The Dark House. Leng, 1941
-A Mask of Gold. Hodder, 1906
The Maclure Mystery. Leng, 1932
-The Secret of Skye. Leng, 1940
-The Secret Panel. Oliphant, 1888

SWANN, FRANCIS. 1913-   .
Angelica. Lancer, 1973
The Brass Key. Simon, 1964; Gollancz, 1965
Day of Dark Memory. Avon, 1970
Greenwood. Lancer, 1965

Hacienda Triste. Lancer, 1968
Hellgate Plantation. Lancer, 1973
Hermit Island. Lancer, 1967
House of Terror. Lancer, 1968
Royal Street. Lancer, 1966
You'll Hang, My Love; with Lucille Emerick. Lancer, 1967

SWARTWOUT, R(OBERT) E(GERTON)
The Boat Race Murder. Grayson, 1933

SWATRIDGE, CHARLES. Joint pseudonym with Irene Maude Mossop Swatridge: Theresa Charles, q.v. Pseudonym of Irene Maude Mossop Swatridge alone: Jan Tempest, q.v.

SWATRIDGE, IRENE MAUDE MOSSOP. Pseudonym: Jan Tempest, q.v. Joint pseudonym with Charles Swatridge: Theresa Charles, q.v.

SWAYNE, MARTIN. Pseudonym of Henry Maurice Dunlop Nicoll, 1884-1953.
-The Blue Germ. Hodder, 1918; Doran, 1918

SWEENEY, W. A.
Murder by Legacy. Modern Fiction, 1945

SWEM, CHARLES LEE
Werewolf. Doubleday, 1928; Hutchinson, 1929

SWIFT, ANTHONY. Pseudonym of J(oseph) Jefferson Farjeon, 1883-1955, q.v.
Interrupted Honeymoon. Hale, 1945
Murder at a Police Station. Hale, 1943; Bobbs, 1943, as by J. Jefferson Farjeon
November 9th at Kersea. Hale, 1944

SWIFT, BENJAMIN. Pseudonym of William Romaine Paterson, 1871-   .
The Death Man. Chapman, 1908
-The Destroyer. Unwin, 1898; Stokes, 1898
-Lady of the Night. Nash, 1913
-Ludus Amoris. Wellby, 1902
-The Tormenter. Unwin, 1897; Scribner, 1897
-What Lies Beneath. Chapman, 1917

SWIFT, IKE
Sketches of Gotham. Fox, 1906 ss, some criminous

SWIGGETT, HOWARD. 1891-1957.
The Corpse in the Derby Hat. Little, 1937. British title: The Stairs Lead Nowhere. Heinemann, 1937
The Hidden and the Hunted. Morrow, 1950; Heinemann, 1951
Most Secret...Most Immediate. Houghton, 1944
The Stairs Lead Nowhere; see The Corpse in the Derby Hat
The Strongbox. Houghton, 1955; Hodder, 1956

SWINGLER, J. H.
Circumstantial Evidence. Digby Long, 1897

SWINNERTON, FRANK (ARTHUR). 1884-   .
On the Shady Side. Hutchinson, 1970; Doubleday, 1971

SWINSON, ARTHUR. 1915-1970. Series character: Sergeant Cork, in both titles.
Sergeant Cork's Casebook. Arrow, 1965 ss
Sergeant Cork's Second Casebook. Arrow, 1966 ss

SWITZER, ROBERT
I was Going Anyway. Macmillan, 1961

SWORD, JOHN, SENIOR. 1877- .
 The Bullitzer Baby Case. Jarrolds, 1925

SYDNEY, GEORGE. House name.
 Countdown for Murder. Amalgamated, 1962. (Sexton Blake.)

SYKES, CHRISTOPHER (HUGH). 1907- .
 High-Minded Murder. Home, 1944

SYKES, CLAUDE W(ALTER). 1883- .
 The Nine Pointed Star. Hamilton, 1926
 The Strange Adventures of Handel Archimedes. Hamilton, 1929

SYKES, W(ILLIAM) STANLEY. 1894- .
 Series character: Inspector Drury, in at least those marked D.
 The Harness of Death. Lane, 1932; Dodd, 1932 D
 The Man Who was Dead; see The Missing Money-Lender
 The Missing Money-Lender. Lane, 1931. U.S. title: The Man Who was Dead. Dodd, 1931 D
 The Ray of Doom. Hodder, 1935

SYLVESTER, JOHN. Pseudonym of Hector Hawton, 1901- , q.v.
 The Phantom. Lunn, 1946
 The Terror of Tregarwith. Amalgamated, 1943. (Sexton Blake.)

SYLVESTER, ROBERT (McPHIERSON). 1907-1975
 The Big Boodle. Random, 1954; Hammond, 1957. Also published as: Night in Havana. Corgi, 1958

SYMONDS, F(RANCIS) ADDINGTON. 1893- .
 Those titles listed below without publisher feature Sexton Blake and were published by Amalgamated Press. Other series character: Insp./Supt. Maxwell Quayne, in at least those marked MQ.
 By Order of the Soviet. 1925
 The Case of the Golden Stool. 1925
 The Case of the Hold-Up King. 1927
 The Case of the Twisted Trail. 1922
 Death Goes Window Shopping. Ward, 1961 MQ
 The Golden Casket. 1921
 The Iron Claw. 1921
 The Man from Australia. 1928
 Murder of Me. Wells Gardner, 1946
 Out of the Fog. 1926
 Portrait of the Accused. Boardman, 1952
 The Red Dwarf. 1922
 Smile and Murder. Boardman, 1954
 Spotlight on Murder. Ward, 1962 MQ
 Stone Dead. Ward, 1961 MQ
 The Valley of Fear. 1921

SYMONS, BERYL (MARY ELIZABETH TAUBMAN).
 Series characters: Jane Carberry, in at least those marked JC; Insp. Henry Doight, in at least those marked HD.
 Blind Justice. Jenkins, 1933
 By Whose Hand? Jenkins, 1936
 The Devine Court Mystery. Jenkins, 1928 HD
 Haunted Hollow. Jenkins, 1934
 Jane Carberry and the Laughing Fountain. Jenkins, 1943 JC
 Jane Carberry: Detective. Jenkins, 1940 JC
 Jane Carberry Investigates. Jenkins, 1940 JC
 Jane Carberry's Week-End. Jenkins, 1947 JC
 The Leering House. Jenkins, 1929 HD
 Magnet for Murder. Jenkins, 1941 JC
 The Opal Murder Case. Jenkins, 1932 HD
 Strange Witness. Jenkins, 1934
 Through a Glass Darkly. Jenkins, 1938

SYMONS, JULIAN (GUSTAVE). 1912- .
 Series characters: Insp. Bland = B; Francis Quarles = FQ.
 The Belting Inheritance. Collins, 1965; Harper, 1965
 Bland Beginning. Gollancz, 1949; Harper, 1949 B
 Bogue's Fortune; see The Paper Chase
 The Broken Penny. Gollancz, 1953; Harper, 1953
 The Colour of Murder. Collins, 1957; Harper, 1958
 The End of Solomon Grundy. Collins, 1964; Harper, 1964
 Francis Quarles Investigates. Panther, 1965 ss FQ
 The Gigantic Shadow. Collins, 1958. U.S. title: The Pipe Dream. Harper, 1959
 The Immaterial Murder Case. Gollancz, 1945; Macmillan, 1957 B
 The Killing of Francie Lake. Collins, 1962. U.S. title: The Plain Man. Harper, 1962
 A Man Called Jones. Gollancz, 1947 B
 The Man Who Killed Himself. Collins, 1967; Harper, 1967
 The Man Who Lost His Wife. Collins, 1970; Harper, 1971
 The Man Whose Dreams Came True. Collins, 1968; Harper, 1969
 Murder! Murder! Fontana, 1961 ss FQ
 The Narrowing Circle. Gollancz, 1954; Harper, 1955
 The Paper Chase. Collins, 1956. U.S. title: Bogue's Fortune. Harper, 1957
 The Pipe Dream; see The Gigantic Shadow
 The Plain Man; see The Killing of Francie Lake
 The Players and the Game. Collins, 1972; Harper, 1972
 The Plot Against Roger Rider. Collins, 1973; Harper, 1973
 The Progress of a Crime. Collins, 1960; Harper, 1960
 The Thirty-First of February. Gollancz, 1950; Harper, 1951
 A Three-Pipe Problem. Collins, 1975; Harper, 1975

SYMONS, MAURICE. Series character: George Roberts, in all titles.
 The Girl in Ocean View. Boardman, 1961
 Lot 41—Dead Auctioneer. Boardman, 1964
 Pattern of Murder. Boardman, 1962

T

TABOR, PAUL. 1908-1974. Pseudonym: Paul Tabori, q.v.

TABORI, GEORGE
 The Good One. Permabooks, 1960

TABORI, PAUL. Pseudonym of Paul Tabor, 1908-1974. Series characters: The Hunters = H.
 -Bricks Upon Dust. Hodder, 1945
 Diana Meets Murder. Progressive Press, 1949
 The Doomsday Brain. Tandem, 1968; Pyramid, 1967 H
 -The Frontier. Low, 1950
 -Hazard Island. New English Library, 1973
 He Never Came Back; see The Leaf of a Lime Tree
 -Heritage of Mercy. Low, 1949
 The Invisible Eye. Tandem, 1969; Pyramid, 1967 H
 -Japanese Jeopardy. Hodder, 1943
 The Leaf of a Lime Tree. Hodder, 1945. U.S. title: He Never Came Back. Dutton, 1947
 -Lily Dale. New English Library, 1972
 Murder in Majorca. Consul, 1961
 Perdita's End. Cassell, 1952
 -The Pleasure House. New English Library, 1974
 -Salvatore. Cassell, 1951
 Sneeze on a Monday. Hodder, 1941
 -Song of the Scorpions. New English Library, 1971
 They Came to London. Hodder, 1943; Macmillan, 1943
 The Torture Machine. Pyramid, 1969

TACK, ALFRED. 1906- . Series character: John Harley, in at least those marked JH.
 The Big Kidnap. Long, 1969
 Death Kicks a Pebble. Jenkins, 1951
 Death Takes a Dive. Jenkins, 1950; Roy, 1957 JH
 Forecast—Murder. Long, 1967
 The Great Hijack. Long, 1970; Doubleday, 1970
 Interviewing's Killing. Jenkins, 1947 JH
 Killing Business. Jenkins, 1949
 A Murder is Staged. Jenkins, 1949
 Murder Takes Over. Long, 1966
 P.A. to Murder. Long, 1966
 The Prospect's Dead. Jenkins, 1948 JH
 Return of the Assassin. Barker, 1975; Putnam, 1974
 Selling's Murder! Jenkins, 1946
 The Spy Who Wasn't Exchanged. Long, 1968; Doubleday, 1969
 The Test Match Murder. Jenkins, 1948
 The Top Steal. Long, 1968; Doubleday, 1968

TAFFRAIL. Pseudonym of Henry Taprell Dorling, 1883-1968, under which byline some of these titles may have appeared.
 -Arctic Convoy. Hodder, 1956
 -Chenies. Hodder, 1943
 Cypher K. Hodder, 1932
 Dover—Ostend. Hodder, 1933
 -Euridice. Hodder, 1953
 -Fred Travis, A.B. Hodder, 1939
 -H.M.S. Anonymous. Jenkins, 1920
 -The Jade Lizard. Hodder, 1951
 -Kerrell. Hodder, 1931
 The Lonely Bungalow. Hodder, 1930
 The Man from Scapa Flow. Hodder, 1933
 -Michael Bray. Hodder, 1925
 -Mid-Atlantic. Hodder, 1936
 -Minor Operation. Pearson, 1917 ss
 Mystery of Milford Haven. Hodder, 1936
 Mystery Cruise. Hodder, 1937
 -The Navy in Action. Hodder, 1940
 -The New Moon. Hodder, 1952
 -Off Shore. Pearson, 1917 ss
 -"Oh, Joshua." Hodder, 1920
 Operation 'M.O.'. Hodder, 1938
 -Pincher Martin, O.D. Chambers, 1916
 -Pirates. Hodder, 1929
 -Sea, Spray and Spindrift. Pearson, 1917 ss
 Second Officer. Hodder, 1935
 Seventy North—70°N. Hodder, 1934
 The Shetland Plan. Hodder, 1939
 -Stand By! Pearson, 1916 ss
 -The Sub. Hodder, 1917
 -Toby Shad. Hodder, 1949
 -The Watch Below. Pearson, 1918 ss

TAFT, WILLIAM NELSON. 1889- .
 On Secret Service. Harper, 1921 ss

TAGGART, DONALD
 Dial M for Money. GM, 1972

TAGGART, TOM. Joint pseudonym with James Reach, 1909?-1970, q.v.: Ross MacRoss, q.v.

TAIN, ISABEL
  The Cherrycake Death. Long, 1967

TAIT, EUPHEMIA MARGARET. Pseudonym: John Ironside, q.v.

TAIT, JAMES SELWIN. 1846-1917.
  My Friend Pasquale and other stories. Tait, 1892 ss, some criminous
  -Who is the Man? Tait, 1892; Chapman, 1890

TAIT, WILLIAM
  Tip and Run. Hutchinson, 1940

TAKAGI, AKIMITSU. 1920- .
  The Informer. Anthos, 1965

TALBOT, CARL. Pseudonym of Charles Hammond Hipkins, 1893- .
  The Cameron Mystery. Eldon, 1935
  Love in Danger. Eldon, 1934
  The White Badger. Eldon, 1935

TALBOT, HAKE. Pseudonym of Henning Nelms, 1900- . Series character: Rogan Kincaid, in both titles.
  The Hangman's Handyman. Simon, 1942
  Rim of the Pit. Simon, 1944

TALBOT, HENRY
  Catch Me a Traitor. Hale, 1966
  Cold Line to Moscow. Hale, 1968
  A Spy in the Hand. Hale, 1966

TANJONG
  The Scarlet Bee. Hutchinson, 1919

TANNOCK, MALCOLM
  The Humming Cliff. Ward, 1950
  Uneasy Money. Ward, 1951

TANOUS, PETER (JOSEPH), 1938- , and PAUL RUBINSTEIN, 1935- .
  The Petrodollar Takeover. Putnam, 1975; Deutsch, 1976

TARG, WILLIAM, 1907- , and LOUIS HERMAN, 1905- .
  The Case of Mr. Cassidy. Phoenix, 1939

TARMEY, MARTIN
  Murphy's Game; see Outrage
  Outrage. Barrie, 1970. U.S. title: Murphy's Game. Harcourt, 1971
  Skinman. Barrie, 1970; Harcourt, 1970

TARNE, ROSINA
  You Murdered Me. Crowther, 1946

TARPEY, J(ESSE TOLER) KINGSLEY
  The Bulldog Murder. Butterworth, 1930

TARRANT, C. A. Pseudonym.
  The Cat Climbs. Secker, 1936; Lippincott, 1937

TARRANT, NOELINE
  Dead on Noon. Hale, 1965

TASHKENT, RENN
  The Ambiguous Man. Tallis, 1969
  Wreath for a Spy. Tallis, 1967

TATE, PETER
  -Country Love and Poison Rain. Doubleday, 1973

TATE, RICHARD. Pseudonym of Anthony Masters, 1940- , q.v.
  Birds of a Bloodied Feather. Constable, 1974
  The Dead Travel Fast. Constable, 1971
  The Donor. Constable, 1970
  The Emperor on Ice. Constable, 1973

TATE, SYLVIA. 1919- .
  Never by Chance. Harper, 1947

TATE, VELMA. 1913- . Pseudonym: Francine Davenport, q.v.

TATTERSALL, IVAN. Pseudonym of Ivan Tattersall Hodgkinson, 1891- .
  The Society of Nobles. Chapman, 1928. U.S. title: The Avenging Brotherhood. McBride, 1929

TATTERSALL, (HONOR) JILL. 1931- .
  Enchanter's Castle. Collins, 1966
  Lady Ingram's Retreat. Collins, 1970. U.S. title: Lady Ingram's Room. Morrow, 1971
  Lady Ingram's Room; see Lady Ingram's Retreat
  Lyonesse Abbey. Collins, 1968; Morrow, 1968
  The Midnight Oak. Collins, 1967
  Midsummer Masque. Collins, 1972; Morrow, 1972
  A Summer's Cloud. Collins, 1965
  A Time at Tarragon. Collins, 1969
  The Wild Hunt. Hodder, 1974; Morrow, 1974
  The Witches of All Saints. Hodder, 1975; Morrow, 1975

TAUB, HAROLD J.
  The Takers. Pyramid, 1968

TAUBE, LESTER S. 1920- .
  The Cossack Cowboy. Allen, 1971
  The Diamond Boomerang; see The Grabbers
  The Grabbers. Allen, 1969. U.S. title: The Diamond Boomerang. PB, 1970
  Myer for Hire. Allen, 1970
  Peter Krimsov. Allen, 1969

TAUBES, FRANK
  Run...Run...Run. Crowell, 1955; Muller, 1955

TAUBMAN-GOLDIE, VALENTINE FRANCIS
  The Case of Sir Edward Talbot. Heinemann, 1922; Dutton, 1922

TAUNTON, H(AROLD) R(OBY). 1880- .
  Death in Diamonds. Hurst, 1936
  It Prowls at Dark. Hurst, 1937
  The Red Club. Hurst, 1926
  The Second Wager. Hurst, 1927
  Six Foot of Rope. Hurst, 1938

TAVIS, ALEC. Pseudonym of Alastair MacTavish Dunnett, 1908- .
  The Duke's Day. H. Hamilton, 1970; Houghton, 1970

TAYLOR, A. FRANK
  How I Made a Million Dollars. Pageant, 1960

TAYLOR, BERT L(ESTON), 1866-1921, and ALVIN V. THOITS
  Under Three Flags. Rand, 1896

TAYLOR, C(ONSTANCE) LINDSAY. 1907- .
  Pseudonym: Guy Cullingford, q.v.
  Murder with Relish. Skeffington, 1948

TAYLOR, EDITH. 1913- .
  The Serpent Under It. Norton, 1973; Barker, 1973

TAYLOR, ELSPETH
  Second Thursday. Bles, 1967

TAYLOR, FRANK
  House of the Hunter. Chicago Paperback House, 1962

TAYLOR, GEORGIA ELIZABETH
  The Death of Jason Darby. World, 1970

TAYLOR, GRIFFIN
  Mortlake. Houghton, 1960; H. Hamilton, 1961

TAYLOR, H. BALDWIN. Pseudonym of Hillary (Baldwin) Waugh, 1920- , q.v. Other pseudonym: Harry Walker, q.v. Series character: David Halliday = DH.
  The Duplicate. Doubleday, 1964; Heinemann, 1965 DH
  The Missing Tycoon; see The Trouble with Tycoons
  The Triumvirate. Doubleday, 1966; Heinemann, 1966 DH
  The Trouble with Tycoons. Doubleday, 1967. British title: The Missing Tycoon. Hale, 1967

TAYLOR, HENDERSON
  Counterpoise of Death. Modern, 193?
  Phantom Killer. Modern, 1938

TAYLOR, JACK. Pseudonym: Jonathan Gray, q.v.

TAYLOR, JUDSON R. Pseudonym of Harlan Page Halsey, 1837-1898, q.v. Other pseudonyms: Old Sleuth, Tony Pastor, qq.v.
  Abner Ferret, the Lawyer Detective. Published in an omnibus by Ogilvie under the Judson R. Taylor byline, but originally published as by Harry Rockwood, q.v.
  Gipsy Blair, the Western Detective. Ogilvie, 1882
  Macon Moore, the Southern Detective. Ogilvie, 1882
  The Man from the South. Street (Magnet)
  Old Stonewall, the Colorado Detective. Street, 1888
  Phil Scott, the Indian Detective. Ogilvie, 1882

TAYLOR, KATHARINE HAVILAND
  The Secret of the Little Gods. Hodder, 1927

TAYLOR, MARY
  Murder on Tuesday. Hale, 1972

TAYLOR, MARY ANN
  The Serpent Heart. Pyramid, 1971

TAYLOR, MARY IMLEY. -1938.
  The Man Who Awoke. Chelsea, 1927; Nelson, 1929

TAYLOR, MATT
  The Famous McGarry Stories. Detective Book Club, 1958 ss

TAYLOR, CAPTAIN (PHILIP) MEADOWS. 1808-1876.
  Confessions of a Thug. Bentley, 1839

TAYLOR, P(HILIP NEVILLE) WALKER. 1903- . Series character: Commander Wraithlea, in all titles.
  Murder in the Flagship. Butterworth, 1936; Mill, 1937
  Murder in the Game Reserve. Butterworth, 1937; Mill, 1938
  Murder in the Suez Canal. Butterworth, 1937
  Murder in the Taj Mahal. Butterworth, 1938

TAYLOR, PHOEBE ATWOOD. 1909-1976. Pseudonym: Alice Tilton, q.v. Series character: Asey Mayo, in all titles.
  The Annulet of Guilt. Norton, 1938; Collins, 1939
  The Asey Mayo Trio. Messner, 1946; Collins, 1946. (3 novelets.)

Banbury Bog. Norton, 1938; Collins, 1939
The Cape Cod Mystery. Bobbs, 1931
The Criminal C.O.D. Norton, 1940; Collins, 1940
The Crimson Patch. Norton, 1936; Gollancz, 1936
The Deadly Sunshade. Norton, 1940; Collins, 1941
Death Lights a Candle. Bobbs, 1932
Deathblow Hill. Norton, 1935; Gollancz, 1936
Diplomatic Corpse. Little, 1951; Collins, 1951
Figure Away. Norton, 1937; Collins, 1938
Going, Going, Gone. Norton, 1943; Collins, 1944
The Mystery of the Cape Cod Players. Norton, 1933; Eyre, 1934
The Mystery of the Cape Cod Tavern. Norton, 1934; Eyre, 1935
Octagon House. Norton, 1937; Collins, 1938
Out of Order. Norton, 1936; Gollancz, 1937
The Perennial Boarder. Norton, 1941; Collins, 1942
Proof of the Pudding. Norton, 1945; Collins, 1945
Punch with Care. Farrar, 1946; Collins, 1947
Sandbar Sinister. Norton, 1934; Gollancz, 1936
The Six Iron Spiders. Norton, 1942; Collins, 1943
Spring Harrowing. Norton, 1939; Collins, 1939
Three Plots for Asey Mayo. Norton, 1942. (3 novelets.)
The Tinkling Symbol. Norton, 1935; Gollancz, 1935

TAYLOR, R. M.
Detective Bob Bridger; or, The Man from Scotland Yard. Street, 1890

TAYLOR, R. W.
Whiplash. Gold Star, 1964

TAYLOR, RAY WARD. 1908- .
Doomsday Square. Dutton, 1966; Gollancz, 1967

TAYLOR, SAM S. Series character: Neal Cotten, in all titles.
No Head for her Pillow. Dutton, 1952; Foulsham, 1954
Sleep No More. Dutton, 1949; Boardman, 1951
So Cold, My Bed. Dutton, 1953; Foulsham, 1955

TAYLOR, SAMUEL W(OOLLEY). 1907- .
The Grinning Gismo. Wyn, 1951; Hodder, 1952
The Man with My Face. Wyn, 1948; Hodder, 1949

TAYLOR, SELMAN
The Marshmead Murders. Hale, 1967
Murder Grows Roots. Hale, 1970

TAYLOR, THEODORE
The Body Trade. GM, 1968

TAYLOR, TOM. 1817-1880. See also: H. C. Williams.
The Ticket-of-Leave Man. Lacy's, 1863; French, 186?. (4-act play.)

TAYLOR, WALKER
The Admiral's a Spy. Hodder, 1941
Spylight. Eyre, 1943
Spyrocket. Eyre, 1944

TEAGLE, MIKE
Death over San Silvestro. Hillman-Curl, 1936
Murders in Silk. Hillman-Curl, 1938; Long, 1939

TEAGUE, JOHN JESSOP. 1856-1929. Pseudonym: Morice Gerard, q.v.

TEAGUE, RUTH (TOWNSEND MILLS), 1896- , and WALTER (DORWIN) TEAGUE, 1883-1960.
You Can't Ignore Murder. Putnam, 1942

TEAGUE, WALTER (DORWIN). 1883-1960. See: RUTH (TOWNSEND MILLS) TEAGUE, 1896- .

TEBBETTS-TAYLOR, ELIZABETH
Now I Lay Me Down to Die. Arcadia, 1955

TEDESCHI, FRANK L. See: BARBARA NINDE BYFIELD.

TEED, G(EORGE) H(AMILTON). 1878-1939. By-line sometimes: Hamilton Teed. Those titles below listed without publisher feature Sexton Blake and were published by Amalgamated Press.
The Adventure of the Bogus Sheik. 1928
The Adventure of the Voodoo Queen. 1928
The Bailiff's Secret. 1938
The Black Eagle. 1925
The Black Emperor. 1926
Bottom of Suez. Columbine, 1939
The Cabaret Crime. 1929
The Case of the Bogus Monk. 1928
The Case of the Chinese Pearls. 1925
The Case of the Clairvoyant's Ruse. 1924
The Case of the Courtlandt Jewels. 1922
The Case of the Disguised Apache. 1927
The Case of the Jade-Handled Knife. 1924
The Case of the Mummified Hand. 1926
The Case of the Portuguese Giantess. 1928
The Case of the Ten Diamonds. 1925
Cassidy the Con Man. 1930
The China Town Mystery. 1932
The Clue of the Four Wigs. 1925
The Crime of the Catacombs. 1931
The Crime on Gallows Hill. 1931
The Crimson Belt. 1923
The Crook of Canada. 1930
The Crook of Costa Blanca. 1931
The Crook of Marsden Manor. 1930
The Crook of Monte Carlo. 1932
The Crook of Paris. 1930
The Crook of Shanghai. 1932
The Crook's Decoy. 1933
Crooks in Clover. 1928
Crooks' Vendetta. Columbine, 1939
The Cross-Channel Crime. 1931
The Diamond Dragon. 1922
The Diamond Sunburst. 1917
The Dictator's Secret. 1936
The Eighth Millionaire. 1928
The Eight-Pointed Star. 1923
The Fatal Amulet. 1934
Five in Fear. Smith, 1936
Gang War. 1931
The Great Canal Plot. 1925
The Great Ivory Swindle. 1924
The Gunners. 1929
The Hand of Vengeance. Mellifont, 1935
The House of Cellars. 1932
The House of Curtains. 1931
The House of Silence. 1930
The Island of the Guilty. 1926
The Isle of Horror. 1933
The Ivory Screen. 1922
Killer Aboard. Amalgamated, 1934
The Martello Tower Mystery. 1935
The Masked Killer. 1930
Missing at Lloyds. Mellifont, 1935
The Mitcham Murder Mystery. Mellifont, 1935
Murder in Manchuria. 1934
Murder Ship. Smith, 1935
The Mystery of Cell 13. 1934
The Mystery of the Cashiered Officer. 1935
The Mystery of the Film City. 1927
The Mystery of the Man from Rio. 1929
The Mystery of the Old Age Pensioner. 1933
The Mystery of the Seine. 1925
Mystery on the Broads. Mellifont, 1935
The Night-Club Mystery. 1927
The Orloff Diamond. 1923
The Pearls of Doom. 1929
The Phantom of the Creek. 1932
Prisoner of the Chateau. 1929
The Riddle of the Russian Gold. 1926
Rogues of Ransom. 1933
The Rogues' Republic. 1927
The Rubber Smugglers. 1928
The Secret Emerald Mines. 1923
The Secret of the Coconut Groves. 1925
The Secret of the President's Daughter. 1929
The Secret of the Strong Room. 1930
The Secret of the Thieves' Kitchen. 1930
The Shadow Crook. Smith, 1936
Spies Ltd. Wright, 1938
The Spirit Smugglers. 1922
The Terror of Gold-Digger Creek. 1928
The Terror of Tangier. 1927
The Tiger of Canton. 1927
The Two Mysteries. 1916
Under the Eagle's Wing. 1925
The Victim of Black Magic. 1928
The Victim of the Gang. 1930
Voodoo Island. Columbine, 1939
The Yellow Skull. 1931
The Yellow Tiger! 1915

TEED, HAMILTON. See: G(EORGE) H(AMILTON) TEED, 1878-1939.

TEILHET, DARWIN L. 1904-1964. See also: HILDEGARDE TOLMAN TEILHET, 1908- . Series characters: Jean Henri St. Amand = JS; Baron von Kaz = K.
The Big Runaround. Coward, 1964; Gollancz, 1964. Also published as: Dangerous Encounter. Paperback Library, 1965
The Broken Face Murders, with Hildegarde Tolman Teilhet. Doubleday, 1940; Gollancz, 1940 K
The Crimson Hair Murders, with Hildegarde Tolman Teilhet. Doubleday, 1936; Gollancz, 1937 K
Dangerous Encounter; see The Big Runaround
Death Flies High. Morrow, 1931; Long, 1932 JS
The Fear Makers. Appleton, 1945; Gollancz, 1946
The Feather Cloak Murders, with Hildegarde Tolman Teilhet. Doubleday, 1936; Gollancz, 1937 K
Murder in the Air. Morrow, 1931 JS
Odd Man Pays. Little, 1944
The Talking Sparrow Murders. Morrow, 1934; Gollancz, 1934
The Ticking Terror Murders. Doubleday, 1935; Methuen, 1936 K

TEILHET, HILDEGARDE TOLMAN. 1908- . Pseudonym: Hildegarde Tolman, q.v. See also: DARWIN L. TEILHET, 1904-1964. Series character: Sam Hook = SH.
The Assassins. Doubleday, 1946; Gollancz, 1947 SH
The Double Agent. Doubleday, 1945; Gollancz, 1946, as by Darwin L. and Hildegarde Tolman Teilhet SH
A Private Undertaking. Coward, 1952; Macdonald, 1953. Also published as: The Screaming Bride. Mercury, 1954

The Rim of Terror. Coward, 1950; Gollancz, 1950, as by Darwin L. and Hildegarde Tolman Teilhet
The Screaming Bride; see A Private Undertaking
The Terrified Society. Doubleday, 1947

TELFAIR, RICHARD. Series character: Monty Nash = MN.
The Bloody Medallion. GM, 1959; Muller pb, 1960 MN
The Corpse That Talked. GM, 1959; Muller pb, 1960 MN
Good Luck, Sucker. GM, 1961; Muller pb, 1962 MN
Scream Bloody Murder. GM, 1960; Muller pb, 1961 MN
The Slavers. GM, 1961; Muller pb, 1962 MN
Target for Tonight. Dell, 1962. (Novelization of the Danger Man TV series.)

TELFER, DARIEL
The Corrupters. Simon, 1964; Muller, 1964
The Guilty Ones. Simon, 1961; Muller, 1961
Love is for Hating. Muller, 1963

TEMPEST, BURTON
Murder by Dart. Mitre, 1946

TEMPEST, JAN. Pseudonym of Irene Maude Mossop Swatridge. Joint pseudonym with Charles Swatridge: Theresa Charles, q.v.
House of the Pines. Mills, 1946; Ace, 1968

TEMPEST, SARAH
A Winter of Fear. Hurst, 1967

TEMPLE, PAUL. Joint pseudonym of Francis Durbridge, 1912-   , q.v., and James Douglas Rutherford McConnell, 1915-   . Other McConnell pseudonym: Douglas Rutherford, q.v. Series character: Paul Temple (see also Francis Durbridge entry), in both titles.
East of Algiers. Hodder, 1959. Reprinted as by Francis Durbridge: Hodder pb, 1962
The Tyler Mystery. Hodder, 1957. Reprinted as by Francis Durbridge: Hodder pb, 1960

TEMPLE, RICHARD
The Schulsinger Affair. Hale, 1971
Spy is a Dirty Word. Hale, 1970

TEMPLE, ROBIN. Pseudonym of (Samuel) Andrew Wood, 1890-   , q.v.
-Cuckoo Fair. Ward, 1932
-The Dark Man. Jenkins, 1939
-Escape If You Can. Ward, 1934
-The Golden Stranger. Mellifont, 1953
-Hoodwink. Ward, 1933
-It Always Happens. Ward, 1934
-Little White Hen. Jenkins, 1938
-London Lights were Shining. Jenkins, 1941
-Maureen of the Island. Jenkins, 1938
-Spaniard's House. Macdonald, 1946
-Street Paved with Water. Jenkins, 1939. Reprinted as by Samuel Andrew Wood: Cherry Tree, 1946
-The Sweet Enemy. Jenkins, 1940
-Tide Rip. Ward, 1933. Reprinted as by Samuel Andrew Wood: Mellifont, 1951
-Till Doomsday. Ward, 1932

TEMPLE, WILLIAM F(REDERICK). 1914-   .
Shoot at the Moon. Simon, 1966; Whiting, 1966

TEMPLE-ELLIS, N. A. Pseudonym of Neville Aldridge Holdaway, 1894-   . Series character: Montrose Arbuthnot, in at least those titles marked MA.
A Case in Hand. Hodder, 1933
The Cauldron Bubbles. Methuen, 1930
Dead in No Time. Hodder, 1935. U.S. title: Murder in the Ruins. Dial, 1936 MA
Death of a Decent Fellow. Hodder, 1914
The Hollow Land. Hodder, 1934
The Inconsistent Villains. Methuen, 1929; Dutton, 1929 MA
The Man Who was There. Methuen, 1930; Dutton, 1930 MA
Murder in the Ruins; see Dead in No Time
Quest. Methuen, 1931
Six Lines. Hodder, 1932
Three Went In. Hodder, 1934

TEMPLETON, CHARLES
The Kidnapping of the President. McClelland (Toronto), 1974; Simon, 1975; Quartet, 1976

TEMPLETON, JESSE. Pseudonym of George Goodchild, 1888-   , q.v. Other pseudonym: Alan Dare, q.v.
-Between the Tides. Ward, 1929. Reprinted as by George Goodchild: Ward, 1936
-The Bitter Test. Ward, 1930
The Call of the North (as by George Goodchild); see Jake Canuke
-Clay-Face. Ward, 1930
Dead or Alive. Ward, 1929. Reprinted as by George Goodchild: Ward, 1937
-The Eternal Conflict. Hurst, 1925. Reprinted as by George Goodchild: Archer, 1950
-The Feud. Hurst, 1925. Reprinted as by George Goodchild: Hodder, 1935
Inch of the C.I.D. Ward, 1932. Reprinted as by George Goodchild: Ward, 1936
-Jake Canuke. Hurst, 1924. Reprinted as by George Goodchild: Hodder, 1932. Also published as: The Call of the North, as by George Goodchild. Newnes, 1938
-Love's Challenge. Mellifont, 1932
-Ten Fathoms Deep. Ward, 1931. Reprinted as by George Goodchild: Ward, 1938
-The Timber Wolf. Hurst, 1927
-Virginia's Quest. Mellifont, 1934
-Winning Through. Ward, 1932. Reprinted as by George Goodchild: Ward, 1935
The Woman Accused. Mellifont, 1934
The Yellow Hibiscus. Ward, 1931

TENNANT, EMMA. 1937-   .
The Last of the Country House Murders. Cape, 1974

TERAMOND, EDMOND GAUTIER. 1869-   .
Pseudonym: Guy de Teramond, q.v.

TERHUNE, ALBERT PAYSON. 1872-1942.
The Amateur Inn. Doran, 1923; Hodder, 1924
Black Caesar's Clan. Doran, 1922; Hodder, 1924
Black Gold. Doran, 1922; Hodder, 1922
Blundell's Last Guest. Chelsea, 1927
Grudge Mountain. Harper, 1939. British title: The Mystery of Grudge Mountain. Chapman, 1939
Letters of Marque. Harper, 1934
Loot! Harper, 1940
The Man in the Dark. Dutton, 1921
The Mystery of Grudge Mountain; see Grudge Mountain
The Pest. Dutton, 1923
The Runaway Bag. Doran, 1925
The Secret of Sea-Dream House. Harper, 1929; Butterworth, 1929

The Tiger's Claw. Doran, 1924; Hodder, 1925
Unseen! Harper, 1937

TERRALL, ROBERT
A Killer is Loose Among Us. Duell, 1948
Madam is Dead. Duell, 1947
They Deal in Death. Simon, 1943

TERRELL, THOMAS. 1852-1928.
The City of the Just. Trischler, 1892

TERRIS, E. WILMOT
The Hidden Death. Modern, 1938
Mystery of the Purple Cloak. Modern, 193?

TERROT, CHARLES (HUGH). 1917-   .
The Chelsea Rainbow. Collins, 1955. U.S. title: The Neon Rainbow. Dutton, 1956

TERRY, J. E. HAROLD. See: BEAMISH TINKER.

TERRY, WILLIAM. Pseudonym of Terry Harknett, 1936-   , q.v. Other pseudonyms: Joseph Hedges, William Pine, Thomas H. Stone, qq.v.
Once a Copper. Hammond, 1965

TESSIER, ERNEST MAURICE. 1885-1973. Pseudonym: Maurice Dekobra, q.v.

TEY, JOSEPHINE. Pseudonym of Elizabeth MacKintosh, 1896-1952. Other pseudonym: Gordon Daviot, q.v. Series character: Insp. Alan Grant (see also Gordon Daviot entry) = AG.
Brat Farrar. Davies, 1949; Macmillan, 1950. Also published as: Come and Kill Me. PB, 1951
Come and Kill Me; see Brat Farrar
The Daughter of Time. Davies, 1951; Macmillan, 1952 AG
The Franchise Affair. Davies, 1948; Macmillan, 1948 AG
Miss Pym Disposes. Davies, 1946; Macmillan, 1948
A Shilling for Candles. Methuen, 1936; Macmillan, 1954 AG
The Singing Sands. Davies, 1952; Macmillan, 1953 AG
To Love and Be Wise. Davies, 1950; Macmillan, 1951 AG

THACKERAY, ALEC
One Way Ticket. Hutchinson, 1975

THAMES, C. H. Pseudonym of Milton Lesser, 1928-   . Other pseudonyms: Andrew Frazer, Stephen Marlowe, Jason Ridgway, qq.v. See also: RICHARD S(COTT) PRATHER, 1921-   .
Blood of my Brother. Permabooks, 1963
Violence is Golden. Bouregy, 1956

THANET, OCTAVE. Pseudonym of Alice French, 1850-1934.
The Lion's Share. Bobbs, 1907

THAYER, CHARLES W(HEELER). 1910-   .
Checkpoint. Harper, 1964
Moscow Interlude. Harper, 1962. British title: Natasha. Joseph, 1962
Natasha; see Moscow Interlude

THAYER, GERALDINE
The Dark Rider. Avalon, 1961

THAYER, (EMMA REDINGTON) LEE. 1874-1973. Series character: Peter Clancy, in all titles except Doctor S.O.S.
Accessory After the Fact. Dodd, 1943; Hurst, 1944
Accident, Manslaughter or Murder? Dodd, 1945; Hurst, 1946
Alias Dr. Ely. Doubleday, 1927; Hurst, 1927

And One Cried Murder. Dodd, 1961; Long, 1962
Blood on the Knight. Dodd, 1952; Hurst, 1953
Clancy's Secret Mission; see Do Not Disturb
A Clue for Clancy; see Pig in a Poke
Counterfeit. Sears, 1933. British title: The Counterfeit Bill. Hurst, 1934
The Counterfeit Bill; see Counterfeit
Dark of the Moon. Dodd, 1936. British title: Death in the Gorge. Hurst, 1937
The Darkest Spot. Sears, 1928; Hurst, 1928
Dead End Street. Dodd, 1936. British title: Murder in the Mirror. Hurst, 1936
Dead Men's Shoes. Sears, 1929; Hurst, 1929
Dead on Arrival. Dodd, 1960; Long, 1962
Dead Reckoning. Dodd, 1954. British title: Murder on the Pacific. Hurst, 1955
Dead Storage. Dodd, 1935. British title: The Death Weed. Hurst, 1935
Death in the Gorge; see Dark of the Moon
Death Walks in Shadow; see Dusty Death
The Death Weed; see Dead Storage
Death Within the Vault; see Within the Vault
Do Not Disturb. Dodd, 1951. British title: Clancy's Secret Mission. Hurst, 1952
Doctor S.O.S. Doubleday, 1925; Hurst, 1925
Dusty Death. Dodd, 1966. British title: Death Walks in Shadow. Long, 1966
Evil Root. Dodd, 1949; Hurst, 1951
Fatal Alibi; see Who Benefits?
Five Bullets. Dodd, 1944; Hurst, 1947
The Glass Knife. Sears, 1932; Hurst, 1932
Guilt Edged. Dodd, 1951. British title: Guilt-Edged Murder. Hurst, 1953
Guilt-Edged Murder; see Guilt Edged
Guilt is Where You Find It. Dodd, 1957; Long, 1958
Guilty! Dodd, 1940; Hurst, 1941
A Hair's Breadth. Dodd, 1946; Hurst, 1947
Hallowe'en Homicide. Dodd, 1941; Hurst, 1942
Hanging's Too Good. Dodd, 1943; Hurst, 1945
Hell-Gate Tides. Sears, 1933; Hurst, 1933
The Jaws of Death. Dodd, 1946; Hurst, 1948
The Key. Doubleday, 1924; Hurst, 1924
The Last Shot. Sears, 1931; Hurst, 1931
Last Trump. Dodd, 1937; Hurst, 1937
Lightning Strikes Twice. Dodd, 1939; Hurst, 1939
A Man's Enemies. Dodd, 1937. British title: This Man's Doom. Hurst, 1938
Murder in the Mirror; see Dead End Street
Murder is Out. Dodd, 1942; Hurst, 1943
Murder on Location. Dodd, 1942; Hurst, 1944
Murder on the Pacific; see Dead Reckoning
Murder Stalks the Circle. Dodd, 1947; Hurst, 1949
The Mystery of the 13th Floor. Century, 1919
No Holiday for Death. Dodd, 1954; Hurst, 1955
Out, Brief Candle! Dodd, 1948; Hurst, 1950
Persons Unknown. Dodd, 1941; Hurst, 1942
Pig in a Poke. Dodd, 1948. British title: A Clue for Clancy. Hurst, 1950
A Plain Case of Murder. Dodd, 1944; Hurst, 1945
Poison. Doubleday, 1926; Heinemann, 1926
The Prisoner Pleads "Not Guilty." Dodd, 1953; Hurst, 1954
The Puzzle; see Q.E.D.
Q.E.D. Doubleday, 1922. British title: The Puzzle. Hurst, 1923
Ransom Racket. Dodd, 1938; Hurst, 1938
Red-Handed; see Sudden Death
The Scrimshaw Millions. Sears, 1932; Hurst, 1933
The Second Bullet. Sears, 1934. British title: The Second Shot. Hurst, 1935
The Second Shot; see The Second Bullet
Set a Thief. Sears, 1931. British title: To Catch a Thief. Hurst, 1932
The Sinister Mark. Doubleday, 1923; Hurst, 1923
Stark Murder. Dodd, 1939; Hurst, 1940
Still No Answer. Dodd, 1958. British title: Web of Hate. Long, 1959
The Strange Sylvester Affair; see That Strange Sylvester Affair
Sudden Death. Dodd, 1935. British title: Red-Handed. Hurst, 1936
That Affair at the Cedars. Doubleday, 1921; Hurst, 1924
That Strange Sylvester Affair. Dodd, 1938. British title: The Strange Sylvester Affair. Hurst, 1939
They Tell No Tales. Sears, 1930; Hurst, 1930
This Man's Doom; see A Man's Enemies
To Catch a Thief; see Set a Thief
Too Long Endured. Dodd, 1950; Hurst, 1952
Two Ways to Die. Dodd, 1959; Long, 1961
The Unlatched Door. Century, 1920
Web of Hate; see Still No Answer
Who Benefits? Dodd, 1955. British title: Fatal Alibi. Hurst, 1956
Within the Vault. Dodd, 1950. British title: Death Within the Vault. Hurst, 1951
X Marks the Spot. Dodd, 1940; Hurst, 1941

THAYER, TIFFANY (ELLSWORTH). 1902-1959. Pseudonym: John Doe, q.v.
The Illustrious Corpse. Fiction League, 1930
Thirteen Men. Kendall, 1930; Long, 1938

THEINER, GEORGE. 1927- . Joint pseudonym with John (Frederick) Burke, 1922- , q.v.: Jonathan George, q.v.

THEMERSON, STEFAN. 1910- .
Tom Harris. Gaberbocchus, 1967; Knopf, 1968

THEROUX, PAUL. 1941- .
Murder in Mount Holly. Ross, 1969

THIELEN, BERNARD
A Charm of Finches. Mystery House, 1959
Open Season. Mystery House, 1958

THIENES, THOMAS L. Pseudonym: Tom T. Ness, q.v.

THIERRY, JAMES FRANCIS
The Adventure of the Eleven Cuff-Buttons. Neale, 1918

THIESSEN, VAL
My Brother, Cain. Monarch, 1964

THOITS, ALVIN T. See: BERT L(ESTON) TAYLOR, 1866-1921.

THOM, ROBERT. 1929- .
Bloody Mama. Paperback Library, 1970; New English Library pb, 1970. (Novelization of the movie.)

THOMAS, A(LBERT) E(LLSWORTH). 1872- .
The Double Cross. Dodd, 1924; Methuen, 1925

THOMAS, ALAN (ERNEST WENTWORTH). 1896- . Series character: Inspector Widgeon, in at least those marked W.
-The Calvertson Story. Gollancz, 1970
Daggers Drawn. Benn, 1930; Brewer, 1930
The Death of Laurence Vining. Benn, 1928; Lippincott, 1929 W
Death of the Home Secretary. Benn, 1933 W
-The Director. Gollancz, 1958
The Fugitives. Gollancz, 1953
-The Governor. Gollancz, 1961
-The Judge. Gollancz, 1966
-The Lonely Years. Benn, 1930
The Mask and the Man. Gollancz, 1951
-The Professor. Gollancz, 1969
The Stolen Cellini. Benn, 1931; Holt, 1932
Summer Adventure. Benn, 1933
-The Surgeon. Gollancz, 1964
-That We Might Live. Harrap, 1935
The Tremayne Case. Benn, 1929; Lippincott, 1930

THOMAS, ANNIE [ANNIE HALL THOMAS CUDLIP]. 1838-1918.
A Dangerous Secret. Low, 1864
-False Colours. Tinsley, 1869; Harper, 1869
-False Pretenses. Digby, 1895
Four Women in the Case. White, 1896
A Mystery and other stories. Munro, 1892 ss (British title?)
-A Narrow Escape. Chapman, 1875; Gill, 1876
-The Sloan Square Scandal and other stories. Swan, 1890; U.S. Book Co., 1890 ss

THOMAS, CAROLYN. Pseudonym of Actea Caroline Duncan, 1913- .
The Cactus Shroud. Lippincott, 1957; Boardman, 1957
The Hearse Horse Snickered. Lippincott, 1954; Boardman, 1955
Narrow Gauge to Murder. Lippincott, 1953; Boardman, 1956
Prominent Among the Mourners. Lippincott, 1946; Cherry Tree, 1949

THOMAS, CURTIS. Pseudonym: Thomas Kinney, q.v.

THOMAS, DYLAN (MARLAIS). 1914-1953.
The Doctor and the Devils. Dent, 1953; New Directions, 1953

THOMAS, EUGENE. 1894- . Series character: Mrs. Caywood Weston = CW.
The Dancing Dead. Sears, 1933 CW
Death Rides the Dragon. Sears, 1932 CW
The Intimate Stranger. Sears, 1932; Smith, 1936
Shadow of Chu-Sheng. Sears, 1933
Yellow Magic. Sears, 1934

THOMAS, H(ENRY) W(ILTON). 1867- .
The Long Shadow. Methuen, 1927

THOMAS, JACK
The Fear Dealers. Bantam, 1975

THOMAS, JACQUES
Machine Gun Murder. Fiction House, 1935

THOMAS, JIM. Pseudonym of Thomas (James) B(utler) Reagan, 1916- , q.v.
Cross Purposes. McCall, 1971

THOMAS, LESLIE. 1931- .
Orange Wednesday. Constable, 1967; Delacorte, 1968

THOMAS, LOUIS (C.). 1921- .
Good Children Don't Kill. Frewin, 1967; Dodd, 1968. (Translation of Les Mauvaises Frequentations. Paris, 1964.)

THOMAS, MARTIN. Pseudonym of Thomas Hector Martin, 1913- . All titles without publisher below feature Sexton Blake (= SB) and were published by Amalgamated Press, Fleetway, or Mayflower.
Assignment Doomsday. 1961
Brainwashed. 1968
Bred to Kill. 1960
Catch a Tiger. 1959
A Cold Night for Murder. 1959
The Copy-Cat Killings. 1957
Date with Danger! 1960
Dead Man's Destiny. 1960
Death and a Dark Horse. Mayflower, 1967
Death in Small Doses. 1963
Design for Vengeance. 1960
An Event Called Murder. 1967
The Evil Eye. 1958
Fear is my Shadow. 1959
The Hands of Cain. Mayflower, 1966; Lancer, 1967
Lady in Distress. 1958
Laird of Evil. 1965
The Mind Killers. 1965
The Mini-Skirt Murders. Baker, 1969 SB
Shadow of a Gun. 1959
Sorcerers of Set. 1966
The Sound of Murder. 1963
Spotlight on Murder. 1962
Such Men are Dangerous. 1965

THOMAS, MAUD M(AY)
Wait Long, Wait Still. Arcadia, 1954

THOMAS, MURRAY. Pseudonym of Thomas Murray Ragg, 1897- . Series character: Inspector Wilkins, in all titles.
Buzzards Pick the Bones. Longmans, 1932
Inspector Wilkins Reads the Proofs. Jenkins, 1935
Inspector Wilkins Sees Red. Jenkins, 1934

THOMAS, OWEN
Rope Fodder. Rivers, 1932

THOMAS, PAUL
Code Name: Rubble. Tower, 1967
The Defector; see The Spy
The Spy. Tower, 1965. Also published as: The Defector. Tower, 1966

THOMAS, REGINALD GEORGE. 1899- .
Pseudonym: John Purley, q.v.

THOMAS, RICHARD H. 1854-1904.
-Penelve; or, Among the Quakers. Headley, 1898; Winston, 1898

THOMAS, ROBERT
Dead Ringer. GM, 1964. (Novelization of the movie.)

THOMAS, RONALD WILLS. 1910- . Pseudonyms: Jeff Bogar, Ronald Wills, qq.v.

THOMAS, ROSS. 1926- . Pseudonym: Oliver Bleeck, q.v. Series characters: McCorkle & Padillo = M&P.
The Backup Men. Morrow, 1971; Hodder, 1971 M&P
Cast a Yellow Shadow. Morrow, 1967; Hodder, 1968 M&P
The Cold War Swap. Morrow, 1966. British title: Spy in the Vodka. Hodder, 1967 M&P
The Fools in Town are on Our Side. Morrow, 1971; Hodder, 1970
If You Can't be Good. Morrow, 1973; H. Hamilton, 1974
The Money Harvest. Morrow, 1975; H. Hamilton, 1975
The Porkchoppers. Morrow, 1972; H. Hamilton, 1974
The Seersucker Whipsaw. Morrow, 1967; Hodder, 1968
The Singapore Wink. Morrow, 1969; Hodder, 1969
Spy in the Vodka; see The Cold War Swap

THOMAS, TAMMY
Wild is My Heart. Exposition, 1965

THOMAS-STANFORD, CHARLES. 1858-1932.
The Ace of Hearts. Methuen, 1912

THOMES, WILLIAM H(ENRY). 1824-1895.
-The Belle of Australia; or, Who am I? DeWolfe, 1883; Henderson, 1890
The Bushrangers. Lee, 1865
-The Gold-Hunters' Adventures; or, Life in Australia. Loyd, 1883. British title (?): A Gold-Hunter's Adventures Between Melbourne and Ballarat. Ward, 1885
A Gold-Hunter's Adventures Between Melbourne and Ballarat; see The Gold-Hunters' Adventures
-The Gold-Hunters in Europe; or, The Dead Alive. Lee, 1869
Running the Blockade; or, U.S. Secret Service Adventures. Lee, 1875

THOMEY, TEDD. 1920- .
And Dream of Evil. Abelard, 1954
Flight to Takla-Ma. Monarch, 1962
I Want Out. Ace, 1959
Killer in White. GM, 1956; Fawcett (London), 1958

THOMPSON, ANNE ARMSTRONG
Message from Absalom. Simon, 1975; Hodder, 1976
The Swiss Legacy. Simon, 1974

THOMPSON, ARTHUR
The Starved. Belmont, 1965

THOMPSON, ARTHUR LEONARD BELL. 1917-1975. Pseudonym: Francis Clifford, q.v.

THOMPSON, CHARLES MINER. 1864-1941.
The Calico Cat. Houghton, 1908
The Nimble Dollar, with other stories. Houghton, 1895 ss

THOMPSON, CHINA. Pseudonym of Mary Christianna Milne Lewis, 1907- . Other pseudonym: Christianna Brand, q.v.
-Starrbelow. Hutchinson, 1958; Scribner, 1958

THOMPSON, D(ANIEL) P(IERCE). 1795-1868.
Centeola; and other tales. Carleton, 1864 ss

THOMPSON, EDWARD ANTHONY. Pseudonym: Anthony Lejeune, q.v.

THOMPSON, ESTELLE
The Edge of Nowhere. Hodder, 1965
Find a Crooked Sixpence. Hodder, 1970; Walker, 1977
The Glass Houses. Hodder, 1967
The Lawyer and the Carpenter. Hodder, 1963; Washburn, 1964
-The Meadows of Tallon. Hale, 1974
-A Mischief Past. Hale, 1971
-Three Women in the House. Hale, 1973
A Twig is Bent. Abelard (London & New York), 1961
The Wrong Saturday. Hodder, 1968

THOMPSON, FRANK
The Transgressor. Badger, 1920

THOMPSON, GRACE E. Pseudonym: Camilla Hope, q.v.

THOMPSON, J. LEE
Murder Without Crime. French (London), 1943; French (New York), 1944. (3-act play.)

THOMPSON, JIM. 1906-1977.
After Dark, My Sweet. Popular Library, 1955
The Alcoholics. Lion, 1953
Bad Boy. Lion, 1953
Child of Rage. Lancer, 1972
The Criminal. Lion, 1953
Cropper's Cabin. Lion, 1952
The Getaway. Signet, 1959; Allen, 1972
The Golden Gizmo. Lion, 1954
The Grifters. Regency, 1963
Heed the Thunder. Greenberg, 1946
A Hell of a Woman. Lion, 1954
Ironside. Popular Library, 1967. (Novelization of the TV series.)
The Kill-Off. Lion, 1957
The Killer Inside Me. Lion, 1952; Sphere, 1973
King Blood. Sphere, 1973. (Published in the U.S. in 1954—title?)
Nothing But a Man. Popular Library, 1970. (Novelization of the movie.)
The Nothing Man. Dell, 1954
Nothing More Than Murder. Harper, 1949
-Now and on Earth. Modern Age, 1942
Pop. 1280. GM, 1964
Recoil. Lion, 1953
Roughneck. Lion, 1954
Savage Night. Lion, 1953
South of Heaven. GM, 1967
A Swell-Looking Babe. Lion, 1954
Texas by the Tail. GM, 1965
The Transgressors. Signet, 1961
The Undefeated. Popular Library, 1969. (Novelization of the movie.)
Wild Town. Signet, 1957

THOMPSON, KENNETH (PUGH). 1909- .
Member's Lobby. Joseph, 1966; London House, 1967
Pattern of Conquest. Joseph, 1967

THOMPSON, LLOYD S.
Death Stops the Show. Crown, 1946
Hear Not My Steps. Abelard, 1953

THOMPSON, MURIEL LILLAH STUART. 1902- . Pseudonym: Miranda Stuart, q.v.

THOMPSON, VANCE. 1863-1925. Series character: Mr. Guelpa = G.
Diplomatic Mysteries. Lippincott, 1905 ss
The Green Ray. Bobbs, 1924; Hutchinson, 1925
Mr. Guelpa. Bobbs, 1925; Hutchinson, 1926 G
The Pointed Tower. Bobbs, 1922; Hutchinson, 1923 G
The Scarlet Iris. Bobbs, 1924. British title: The Tarnished Woman. Hutchinson, 1924
Spinners of Life. Lippincott, 1903; Methuen, 1904
The Tarnished Woman; see The Scarlet Iris

THOMPSON, W. CRAWFORD
A Suitcase Full of Money. Curtis, 1973

THOMSON, A(RTHUR) A(LEXANDER MALCOLM). 1894- .
An Air for Murder, with Philip King. French, 1958. (A play.)

But Once a Year, with (Thomas) F(alkland) L(itton) Cary, q.v. Jenkins, 1951
Danger Inside, with Ivan Butler. French, 1960. (Play.)
The Late Lamented. French, 1949. (Play.)
Murder at the Ministry, with (Thomas) F(alkland) L(itton) Cary, q.v. Jenkins, 1947
The Proof of the Poison, with Philip Weathers. French, 1963. (Play.)
The Shadow Witness, with Philip Weathers. French, 1961. (Play.)

THOMSON, BASIL (HOME). 1861-1939. Series character: P. C. (Supt.) Richardson = R.
Carfax Abbey. Methuen, 1928
The Case of Naomi Clynes; see Inspector Richardson C.I.D.
The Case of the Dead Diplomat; see Richardson Goes Abroad
A Court Intrigue. Heinemann, 1896
The Dartmoor Enigma; see Richardson Solves a Dartmoor Mystery
Death in the Bathroom. Eldon, 1936. U.S. title: Who Killed Stella Pomeroy? Doubleday, 1936 R
Inspector Richardson C.I.D. Eldon, 1934. U.S. title: The Case of Naomi Clynes. Doubleday, 1934 R
The Kidnappers. Eldon, 1933
The Metal Flask. Methuen, 1929
Milliner's Hat Mystery. Eldon, 1937. U.S. title: The Mystery of the French Milliner. Doubleday, 1937 R
Mr. Pepper, Investigator. Castle, 1925 ss
A Murder Arranged. Eldon, 1937. U.S. title: When Thieves Fall Out. Doubleday, 1937 R
The Mystery of the French Milliner; see Milliner's Hat Mystery
P. C. Richardson's First Case. Eldon, 1933; Doubleday, 1933 R
The Prince from Overseas. Chapman, 1930
Richardson Goes Abroad. Eldon, 1935. U.S. title: The Case of the Dead Diplomat. Doubleday, 1935 R
Richardson Scores Again. Eldon, 1934. U.S. title: Richardson's Second Case. Doubleday, 1934 R
Richardson Solves a Dartmoor Mystery. Eldon, 1935. U.S. title: The Dartmoor Enigma. Doubleday, 1936 R
Richardson's Second Case; see Richardson Scores Again
When Thieves Fall Out; see A Murder Arranged
Who Killed Stella Pomeroy?; see Death in the Bathroom

THOMSON, DAVID LANDSBOROUGH. 1901-1964. Pseudonym: T. L. Davidson, q.v.

THOMSON, EDWARD
The Adventures of Burnaby Lee; or, The Struggle of a Son and Heir. Tegg, 1852

THOMSON, JUNE. Series character: Inspector Finch, in all titles (but called Insp. Rudd in the U.S. Doubleday editions).
Death Cap. Constable, 1973; Doubleday, 1977
The Long Revenge. Constable, 1974; Doubleday, 1975
Not One of Us. Constable, 1972; Harper, 1971

THORBURN, C. H.
The Mysterious Stranger. Derby, 1890

THORMANBY. Pseudonym of W(illmott) Willmott Dixon, 1843-   , q.v.
The Black Bean. Heath, 1913
-Romances of the Road. Everett, 1901

THORN, RONALD SCOTT. Pseudonym of Ronald Wilkinson, 1920-
The Dark Shadow; see Second Opinion
-Experiment with Eros. Hale, 1967
-The Full Treatment. Heinemann, 1959
Second Opinion. Heinemann, 1961; Macmillan, 1961. Also published as: The Dark Shadow. Macfadden, 1964
The Twin Serpents. Heinemann, 1965; Macmillan, 1965
-Upstairs and Downstairs. Spearman, 1957; Greenberg, 1958

THORNBURG, NEWTON (KENDALL). 1930-   .
Knockover. GM, 1968; Coronet, 1968
To Die in California. Little, 1973

THORNBURY, ETHEL (M.). 1894-   .
We've been Waiting for You. Bobbs, 1947

THORNDIKE, (ARTHUR) RUSSELL. 1885-1972. Series character: Dr. Syn = S.
The Amazing Quest of Doctor Syn. Rich, 1938 S
The Courageous Exploits of Doctor Syn. Rich, 1939 S
The Devil in the Belfry; see Herod's Peal
Doctor Syn. Nelson, 1915; Doubleday, 1915 S
Doctor Syn on the High Seas. Rich, 1936 S
Doctor Syn Returns. Rich, 1935. U.S. title: The Scarecrow Rides. Dial, 1935 S
-The First Englishman. Rich, 1949
The Forbidden Room. Dial, 1933. (British title?)
The Further Adventures of Doctor Syn. Rich, 1936 S
Herod's Peal. Butterworth, 1931. U.S. title: The Devil in the Belfry. Dial, 1932
-The House of Jeffreys. Rich, 1943
-Jet and Ivory. Rich, 1934
The Master of the Macabre. Rich, 1947
The Scarecrow Rides; see Doctor Syn Returns
The Shadow of Doctor Syn. Rich, 1944 S
-Show House—Sold. Rich, 1941
The Slype. Holden, 1927; Dial, 1928
The Vandekkers. Butterworth, 1929; Appleton, 1930
-The Water Witch. Butterworth, 1932

THORNE, (ERIC) ANTHONY
So Long at the Fair. Heinemann, 1947; Random, 1947

THORNE, E(RNEST) P(OLLETT). Series characters: Major "Brains" Cunningham, in at least those marked C; Quentin Eady, in at least those marked QE; Geoff Fennell, in at least those marked GF.
The Angel Steps In. Wright, 1960
Assignment Haiti. Wright, 1963 GF
The Bengal Spider Plan. Wright, 1961 C
The Black Sadhu. Wright, 1935
Black Sunset. Wright, 1963
The Caribbean Affair. Wright, 1966 C
Chinese Poker. Wright, 1964 C
Code Word "Proton". Wright, 1968
Date with the Departed. Wright, 1955 C
The Death Rust. Wright, 1965
The Devil's Chapel. Wright, 1957 QE
Die Wearing a Rose. Wright, 1959 QE
Evil in the Cup. Wright, 1958 QE
Expect No Mercy. Wright, 1962 QE
The Face of Inspector Britt. Wright, 1947 C
Gallows Inn. Wright, 1958 QE
Ganges Mud. Wright, 1936
The House of the Fragrant Lotus. Wright, 1962 C
The Jungle Hut. Wright, 1966
Justice is Mine. Wright, 1950 C
Lady with a Gun. Wright, 1955 C
The Moon Dance. Wright, 1953 C
The Moscow File. Wright, 1967
Operation Dragnet. Wright, 1966 C
Red Bamboo. Wright, 1954 C
Seven Red Herrings. Wright, 1956 QE
The Shadow of Dr. Ferrari. Wright, 1950 C
Sinister Sanctuary. Wright, 1949 C
The Smile of Cheng Su. Wright, 1946 C
They Never Come Back. Wright, 1961 GF
Three Silent Men. Wright, 1939
White Arab. Wright, 1936
Yoga Mist. Wright, 1937
Zero Minus Nine. Wright, 1964 C

THORNE, EMILY
Aaron's Serpent. Avalon, 1962
The House on Sixteenth Street. Avalon, 1966
The Mystery of Knickerbocker Towers. Avalon, 1960
Nothing to Pretend. Avalon, 1963

THORNE, GUY. Pseudonym of C(yril Arthur Edward) Ranger Gull, 1876-1923, q.v.
-And It Came to Pass. Jarrolds, 1916
-Back to Lilac Land. Dillingham, 1920. (British title?)
-A Butterfly on the Wheel. Readers Library, 1928
-Chance in Chains. Laurie, 1913; Sturgis, 1914
-The Charioteer. Ward, 1907
-The Cruiser on Wheels. Jack, 1915
-The Dark Dominion. Ward, 1923
-Divorce. Greening, 1911
-Doris Moore. Ward, 1919
-The Drunkard. Greening, 1912; Sturgis, 1912
-The Eyes of Pharaoh. Ward, 1924
-False Gods. Ward, 1923
The Fanshawe Murder. In An Omnibus Thriller of Murder and Mystery (four novels by different authors). Laurie, 1931
-First It was Ordained. Ward, 1906
-Fishport. Ward, 1922
The Gentleman from Nowhere. Modern, 193?
-The Hammers of Hate. Skeffington, 1919
-Harder Than Steel. Laurie, 1919
The House of Danger. Ward, 1920
-The Lapse of the Bishop. Ward, 1920
-The Lone Hater. Ward, 1921
Lucky Mr. Loder. Ward, 1918
-Muriel Wins Through. Long, 1923
The Mystery of St. Michael's. Jenkins, 1924
-An Officer and a Gentleman? and other stories. White, 1909 ss
The Oven. Greening, 1902
-The Polluted City. Ward, 1917
Rescuing Rupert. Long, 1917
-The Secret Monitor. Skeffington, 1918
-The Secret Sea-Plane. Hodder, 1915
The Secret Service Submarine. Jack, 1915; Sully, 1915
-Sweetheart Submarine. Greening, 1911
-The Tears of Hate. Ward, 1921
-The Voiceless Victims. Laurie, 1922
-When It was Dark. Greening, 1903; Putnam, 1904
-When the Wicked Man. Allen, 1916
-When the World Reeled. Ward, 1924
-A Year and a Day. Ward, 1922

THORNE, JIM
The White Hand of Athene. Pinnacle, 1974

THORNE, MABEL. See: PAUL THORNE.

THORNE, PAUL
　Murder in the Fog. Penn, 1929
　The Secret Toll, with Mabel Thorne. Dodd, 1922
　The Sheridan Road Mystery, with Mabel Thorne. Dodd, 1921
　Spiderweb Clues. Penn, 1928
　That Evening in Shanghai. Penn, 1931

THORNER, WILLIAM E.
　The Cat of Bast and other stories of mystery. Regency, 1958　ss

THORNETT, ERNEST BASIL CHARLES. Pseudonym: Rupert Penny, q.v.

THORNTON, CHARLES
　The Story of the Fast Mail. Continental, 1891. Also published as: The Fast Mail. Donohue, 189?

THORP, RODERICK (MAYNE, JR.). 1936-　.
　The Detective. Dial, 1966; Barker, 1967

THORPE, EDWARD
　The Night I Caught the Santa Fe Chief. Joseph, 1972; St. Martin's, 1973

THORSON, DELOS RUSSELL. 1906-　. Joint pseudonym with Sara Winfree Thorson, 1906-　: Kit Christian, q.v.

THORSON, SARA WINFREE. 1906-　. Joint pseudonym with Delos Russell Thorson, 1906-　: Kit Christian, q.v.

THRELFALL, T. R.
　The Strange Adventures of a Magistrate. Everett, 1903

THUM, MARCELLA
　Fernwood. Doubleday, 1973. British title: The Haunting Cavalier. Milton House, 1974

THURLEY, NORGROVE. Pseudonym of C(harles) Thurley Stoneham, 1895-　, q.v.
　Bamboo Elephants. Paul, 1956
　Death for Dollars. Paul, 1951
　The Devil's Steps. Paul, 1947
　Giants of Darkness. Paul, 1957
　Grow Grey with Fear. Paul, 1952
　Lonely Water. Paul, 1948
　Murder Strikes North. Paul, 1951
　The Trail of the Ghosts. Paul, 1955
　The Treacherous Border. Long, 1958
　The Woman in the Case. Long, 1959

THURMAN, CARYL. 1938-　. See: IRENE KING, 1943-　.

THURMAN, STEVE. Pseudonym of Frank Castle, q.v.
　"Mad Dog" Coll. Monarch, 1961. (Novelization of the movie.)
　Night After Night. Monarch, 1959

THURSTON, KATHERINE CECIL.　-1911.
　-The Masquerader. Harper, 1904

THURSTON, (ERNEST) TEMPLE. 1879-1933.
　The Diamond Pendant. Doubleday, 1932. (British title?)
　John Boddy: Leaves from a Constable's Notebook. Ward, 1931　ss
　Man in a Black Hat. Cassell, 1930; Doubleday, 1931
　Portrait of a Spy. Putnam (London), 1928; Doubleday, 1929

THURSTON, WESLEY S.　-1966.
　The Trumpets of November. Geis, 1966

THWAITES, FREDERICK J(OSEPH)
　-The Dark Abyss. Harcourt (London), 1955
　The Mad Doctor. Quality, 1938
　The Mad Doctor in Harley Street. Quality, 1939

THYNNE, ALEXANDER
　The Carry-Cot. Allen, 1972. Also published as: Blue Blood. Star, 1974

THYNNE, MOLLY. Series character: Dr. Constantine = C.
　The Case of Sir Adam Braid. Nelson, 1930
　The Crime at the "Noah's Ark". Nelson, 1931　C
　The Draycott Murder Mystery; see The Red Dwarf
　He Dies and Makes No Sign. Hutchinson, 1933　C
　Murder in the Dentist Chair. Hutchinson, 1932; Covici, 1932　C
　The Murder on the "Enriqueta". Nelson, 1929. U.S. title: The Strangler. Minton, 1929
　The Red Dwarf. Nelson, 1928. U.S. title: The Draycott Murder Mystery. Stokes, 1928
　The Strangler; see The Murder on the "Enriqueta"

TIBBITTS, GEORGE F(RANKLIN). 1864-　.
　The Mystery of Kun-Ja-Muck Cave. Brieger, 1924

TICKELL, JERRARD. 1905-1966.
　Appointment with Venus. Hodder, 1951. U.S. title: Island Rescue. Doubleday, 1952
　-At Dusk All Cats are Grey. Chapman, 1940
　-Dark Adventure. Mellifont, 1953
　High Water at Four. Hodder, 1965; Doubleday, 1966
　The Hunt for Richard Thorpe; see Whither Do You Wander?
　Island Rescue; see Appointment with Venus
　Jill Fell Down. Heinemann, 1938; Morrow, 1939
　-Silk Purse. Heinemann, 1937
　-Soldier from the Wars Returning. Chapman, 1942
　Villa Mimosa. Hodder, 1960; Doubleday, 1961
　Whither Do You Wander? Hodder, 1959. U.S. title: The Hunt for Richard Thorpe. Doubleday, 1960
　Yolan; see Yolan of the Plains
　Yolan of the Plains. Richards, 1928. U.S. title: Yolan. Putnam, 1929

TICKNER, F. C.　All titles are 16-32 page booklets.
　The Dance of Death. Danceland, 1946
　Death at the Towers. Danceland, 1946
　Line-Up for Murder. Beverley, 1944
　Murder Makes a Call. Danceland, 1946
　Murderers Three. Danceland, 1946
　Three Were to Die. Danceland, 1946

TIDYMAN, ERNEST. 1928-　. Series character: John Shaft = JS.
　Goodbye, Mr. Shaft. Dial, 1973; Weidenfeld, 1974　JS
　The Last Shaft. Weidenfeld, 1975　JS
　Line of Duty. Little, 1974; Allen, 1974
　Shaft. Macmillan, 1970; Joseph, 1971　JS
　Shaft Among the Jews. Dial, 1972; Weidenfeld, 1973　JS
　Shaft has a Ball. Bantam, 1973; Corgi, 1973　JS
　Shaft's Big Score. Bantam, 1972; Corgi, 1972　JS
　Shaft's Carnival of Killers. Bantam, 1974; Bantam (London), 1974　JS
　Starstruck. Allen, 1975

TIGER, JOHN. Pseudonym of Walter (Herman) Wager, 1924-　, q.v. Other pseudonym: Walter Hermann, q.v. Series designations: novelizations of the I Spy TV series = IS; novelizations of the Mission Impossible TV series = MI.
　Code Name: Little Ivan. Popular Library, 1969　MI
　Countertrap. Popular Library, 1967　IS
　Death Hits the Jackpot. Avon, 1954
　Death-Twist. Popular Library, 1968　IS
　Doomdate. Popular Library, 1967　IS
　I Spy. Popular Library, 1965　IS
　Masterstroke. Popular Library, 1966　IS
　Mission Impossible. Popular Library, 1967　MI
　Superkill. Popular Library, 1967　IS
　Wipeout. Popular Library, 1967　IS

TIGHE, HARRY. 1877-　.
　The Man in the Fog. Heath, 1916

TILBURN, E. O. Pseudonyms: Nevada Ned, Dr. N. T. Oliver, qq.v.

TILDEN, FREEMAN. 1883-　.
　The Spanish Prisoner. Doubleday, 1928

TILLETT, DOROTHY STOCKBRIDGE. 1896-　.
　Pseudonym: John Stephen Strange, q.v.

TILTON, ALICE. Pseudonym of Phoebe Atwood Taylor, 1909-1976, q.v. Series character: Leonidas Witherall, in all titles.
　Beginning with a Bash. Norton, 1972; Collins, 1937
　Cold Steal. Norton, 1939; Collins, 1940
　The Cut Direct. Norton, 1938; Collins, 1938
　Dead Ernest. Norton, 1944; Collins, 1945
　File for Record. Norton, 1943; Collins, 1944
　The Hollow Chest. Norton, 1941; Collins, 1942
　The Iron Clew. Farrar, 1947. British title: The Iron Hand. Collins, 1947
　The Iron Hand; see The Iron Clew
　The Left Leg. Norton, 1940; Collins, 1941

TIMINS, DOUGLAS
　A Double Quest. Methuen, 1930
　The Extra Passenger. Hutchinson, 1928
　The Phantom Train. Hutchinson, 1926

TINAYRE, (MARGUERITE SUZANNE) MARCELLE (CHASTEAU). 1877-　.
　Death at the Chateau. Jarrolds, 1934. (Translation of Chateau en Limousin. Paris, 1934.)

TINKER, BEAMISH. Pseudonym of F(ryniwyd) Tennyson Jesse, 1889?-1958, q.v.
　The Man Who Stayed at Home. Mills, 1915. (Novelization of the play by Lechmere Worrall and J. E. Harold Terry.)

TIPPETTE, GILES. 1936-　.
　The Bank Robber. Macmillan, 1970
　The Trojan Cow. Macmillan, 1971

TITTERTON, J.
　Death Ray Dictator. Organ, 1946

TOBIAS, KATHERINE. Pseudonym of Theodore Mark Gottfried, 1928-　. Other pseudonym: Harry Gregory, q.v.
　The Lady in the Lightning. Lancer, 1966

TODD, PAUL. Pseudonym of Richard Posner, 1944- , q.v. Other pseudonyms: Iris Foster, Beatrice Murray, qq.v.
Blood All Over. Warner, 1975

TODD, ROBERT HENRY
The Solver of Mysteries and other stories. Charters, 1930 ss

TODD, RUTHVEN. 1914- . Pseudonym: R. T. Campbell, q.v.

TOEPFER, RAY GRANT. 1923- .
Endplay. GM, 1975; Coronet, 1976
The Witness. Muller, 1966

TOLER, BUCK. Pseudonym of Harold Ernest Kelly, 1899- . Other pseudonyms: Darcy Glinto, Gordon Holt, qq.v.
The Bronsville Massacre. Mitre, 1943
It's Only Saps That Die. Everybody's, 1944
Killer on the Run. Everybody's, 1946
Tough on the Wops. Robin Hood, 1947

TOLLEMACHE, E(DWARD) D(EVEREUX) H(AMILTON). See: P. P. MUIR.

TOLMAN, HILDEGARDE. Pseudonym of Hildegarde Tolman Teilhet, 1908- , q.v. See also: DARWIN L. TEILHET, 1904-1964.
Hero by Proxy. Little, 1942; Gollancz, 1943, as by Darwin L. Teilhet

TOMA, DAVID and JACK PEARL, q.v.
The Airport Affair. Dell, 1975

TOMERLIN, JOHN (E.). 1930- . Joint pseudonym with Charles Beaumont, 1929-1967, q.v.: Keith Grantland, q.v.
Comeback. Paperback Library, 1969
Return to Vikki. GM, 1959; Consul, 1961

TOM-GALLON, NELLIE and CALDER WILSON
He Who Walked in Scarlet. Unwin, 1924
Monsieur Zero. Unwin, 1923 ss

TOMS, BERNARD. 1931- .
The Strange Affair. Constable, 1966

TOOMBS, JANE JENKE
Point of Lost Souls. Avon, 1975
A Topaz for My Lady Fair. Ballantine, 1975

TOPOR, ROLAND. 1938- .
The Tenant. Allen, 1966; Doubleday, 1966. (Translation of Le Locataire Chemerique. Paris, 1964.)

TOPOR, TOM. 1938- .
Tightrope Minor. Doubleday, 1971

TORBETT, D.
Kick-In. Clode, 1915. (Novelization of the play by Willard Mack, 1878-1934, q.v.)
On Trial. Dodd, 1915. (Novelization of the play by Elmer L. Reizenstein, 1892-1967, q.v.)
-Sinners. Clode, 1915. (Novelization of the play by Owen Davis, q.v.)

TORDAY, URSULA. Pseudonyms: Paula Allardyce, Charity Blackstock, qq.v., Lee Blackstock.

TORGERSON, EDWIN DEAL. Series character: Pierre Montigny, in both titles.
The Cold Finger Curse. Falcon, 1933
The Murderer Returns. Lane, 1931; Smith, 1930

TORR, DOMINIC. Pseudonym of John Branfrost Simpson Pedler.
Diplomatic Cover. Barker, 1965; Harcourt, 1966
A Mission of Mercy. Hodder, 1969; Stein, 1969
The Treason Line. Cape, 1968; Stein, 1968

TORRES, EDWIN
Carlito's Way. Saturday Review Press, 1975

TORREY, ROGER
42 Days for Murder. Hillman-Curl, 1938

TORREY, WARE. 1905-1967. Pseudonym: Lee Crosby, q.v.

TORRIE, MALCOLM. Pseudonym of Gladys (Maude Winifred) Mitchell, 1901- , q.v. Series character: Timothy Herring, in all titles.
Bismarck Herrings. Joseph, 1971
Churchyard Salad. Joseph, 1969
Heavy as Lead. Joseph, 1966
Late and Cold. Joseph, 1967
Shade of Darkness. Joseph, 1970
Your Secret Friend. Joseph, 1968

TORRIO, VINCENTE
Bootlegger. New English Library pb, 1975
The Executioner. New English Library pb, 1975

TOURGEE, ALBION (WINEGAR). 1838-1905.
With Gauge and Swallow, Attorneys. Lippincott, 1889 ss

TOUSSAINT-SAMAT, JEAN. 1865- .
The Dead Man at the Window. Lippincott, 1934. (Translation of Le Mort a la Fenetre. Paris, 1933.)
Ships Aflame! Lippincott, 1935
Shoes That had Walked Twice. Lippincott, 1933. (Translation of L'Horrible Mort de Miss Gildchrist. Paris, 1932.)

TOWER, DIANA
Dark Diamond. Ballantine, 1975
A Gleam of Sapphire. Ballantine, 1975
Red Lion. Ballantine, 1974

TOWER, STELLA (MARY HODGSON). 1891- .
Pseudonym: Faith Wolseley, q.v.
Dumb Vengeance. Hutchinson, 1933
Yesterday's Bones. Hutchinson, 1934

TOWNE, STUART. Pseudonym of Clayton Rawson, 1906-1971, q.v. Series character: Don Diavolo, in both titles.
Death from Nowhere. Yogi, 194?. (Two DD novelets disguised as a novel.)
Death Out of Thin Air. Coward, 1941; Cassell, 1947. (Two DD novelets.)

TOWNEND, PAUL. 1925- .
Died o' Wednesday. Collins, 1959; Walker, 1962
The Man on the End of the Rope. Collins, 1960; Dutton, 1960
The Road to El Saida. Collins, 1961

TOWNEND, PETER (ROBERT GASCOIGNE). 1935- . Pseudonym: Peter Gascoigne, q.v. Series character: Philip Quest, in both titles.
Out of Focus. Heinemann, 1971; St. Martin's, 1972
Zoom! Heinemann, 1972; St. Martin's, 1972

TOWNER, (JAMES) AUSBURN. 1836-1909.
-The House Terrible. Collier, 1893
-Seven Days in a Pullman Car. Ogilvie, 1883 ss

TOWNLEY, HOUGHTON
-The Bishop's Emeralds. Greening, 1907; Watt, 1908
The Case of the Human Mole. Amalgamated Press, 1927. (Sexton Blake.)
-Dazzled. Trischler, 1891
-The Gay Lord Waring. Greening, 1910; Watt, 1910
His Own Accuser. Ward, 1894
-The Scarlet Feather. Watt, 1909. (British title?)
The Secret of the Raft. Greening, 1909
-The Sin of the Duchess. Greening, 1909
-The Splendid Coward. Greening, 1908

TOWNSEND, CHARLES. 1857-1914.
The Mahoney Million. New Amsterdam, 1903

TOWNSEND, EDWARD W(ATERMAN). 1855- .
-Lees and Leaven. McClure, 1903

TOY, BARBARA. See: MOIE CHARLES.

TOYE, NINA
The Shadow of Fear. Heinemann, 1921
The Twice Murdered Man. Eyre, 1935

TOYE, STANLEY (PERCIVAL). Series character: Anthony Read, in at least those marked AR.
Cyanide! Nelson, 1940 AR
The Laughing Cat. Melrose, 1950
The Line Between. Melrose, 1948
Murder in the Lady Chapel. Melrose, 1944
Prelude to Peril. Melrose, 1946 AR
Sinners in Clover. Melrose, 1945 AR

TOZER, BASIL (JOHN JOSEPH). 1872- .
A Daughter of Belial. Redman, 1908
A Dealer in Antiques. Ward, 1923
The Elusive Lord Bagtor. Laurie, 1939
The Riddle of the Forest. Laurie, 1931
Secret Traffic. Laurie, 1935
Vengeance. Ward, 1916

TRACEY, GRANT
Call It Murder. Hale, 1972
The Paradise Conspiracy. Hale, 1972
The Take-Away Girl. Hale, 1973

TRACY, DON(ALD FISKE). 1905- . Pseudonym: Roger Fuller, q.v. Series character: Giff Speer = GS.
The Big Blackout. Detective Book Club, 1959
The Big Brass Ring. Trident, 1963
The Black Amulet. PB, 1968
A Corpse can Sure Louse Up a Weekend! PB, 1973
Criss-Cross. Vanguard, 1934; Constable, 1935
Deadly to Bed. PB, 1960 GS
The Editor. PB, 1973
Flats Fixed—Among Other Things. PB, 1974 GS
Fun and Deadly Games. PB, 1968 GS
The Hated One. Simon, 1963; Cassell, 1963
How Sleeps the Beast. Mill, 1938; Constable, 1937
-Last Year's Snow. Mill, 1937; Constable, 1937
Look Down on Her Dying. PB, 1968 GS
Naked She Died. PB, 1962 GS
-No Trespassing. Lippincott, 1961
Pot of Trouble. PB, 1971 GS
Round Trip. Vanguard, 1934; Constable, 1935

TRACY, HUGH
Career with Death. Hale, 1970
Death in Disguise. Hale, 1969

TRACY, LOUIS. 1863-1928. Pseudonym, jointly in part with M(atthew) P(hipps) Shiel, 1865-1947, q.v.: Gordon Holmes, q.v. Series characters: Inspector Furneaux, in at least those marked F (also in titles under the Gordon Holmes byline); Reginald Brett, in at least those marked RB.
The Albert Gate Affair. Ward, 1904. U.S. title: The Albert Gate Mystery. Fenno, 1904 RB
The Albert Gate Mystery; see The Albert Gate Affair
An American Emperor. Pearson, 1897; Putnam, 1897
-At the Court of the Maharaja. American News, 1906. (British title?)
The Bartlett Mystery. Clode, 1919. (British title?)
The Black Cat. Hodder, 1925; Clode, 1925 F
-The Captain of the Kansas. Jarrolds, 1931; Clode, 1907
The Case of Mortimer Fenley. Cassell, 1915. U.S. title: The Strange Case of Mortimer Fenley. Clode, 1919 F
-Cynthia's Chauffeur. Clode, 1910. (= Sylvia's Chauffeur?)
-A Dangerous Situation. Clode, 1932. (British title?)
-The Darkest Hour. Digby, 1903; Westbrook, 1920?
-The Day of Wrath. Chambers, 1916; Clode, 1916
Diana of the Moorland; see Diana of the Moors
Diana of the Moors. Cassell, 1914. U.S. title: Diana of the Moorland. Clode, 1918
A Fatal Legacy. Ward, 1903
Fennell's Tower. Ward, 1908
The Final War. Pearson, 1896; Putnam, 1896
-Flower of the Gorse. Cassell, 1916; Clode, 1915
The Gleave Mystery. Hodder, 1926; Clode, 1926 F
-The Great Mogul. Clode, 1905. (British title?)
-Heart's Delight. Ward, 1906
-His Unknown Wife. Cassell, 1915; Clode, 1916
The House of Peril. Clode, 1922. (British title?) F
The House of Silence; see The Silent House
-The Invaders. Pearson, 1901
A Japanese Revenge. Westbrook, ca.1920. (British title?)
Karl Grier. Hodder, 1906; Clode, 1906. Also published as: The Man with the Sixth Sense. Odhams, 1921
The King of Diamonds. White, 1904; Clode, 1904
-The King's Messenger. White, 1905
The Lastingham Murder; see The Third Miracle
The Law of the Talon. Hodder, 1926; Clode, 1926 F
The Lost Provinces. Pearson, 1898; Putnam, 1898
The Manning-Burke Murder; see The One Girl in a Million
The Man with the Sixth Sense; see Karl Grier
The Message. Ward, 1909; Clode, 1908
-Minkie. Ward, 1910; Clode, 1907
-Mirabil's Island. Ward, 1912; Clode, 1912
-A Morganatic Wife. White, 1904
A Mysterious Disappearance. Hodder, 1928; Clode, 1905, as by Gordon Holmes
No Other Way. Ward, 1913; Clode, 1912, as by Gordon Holmes
Number Seventeen. Cassell, 1916; Clode, 1915 F
The One Girl in a Million. Hodder, 1928. U.S. title: The Manning-Burke Murder. Clode, 1930 F
-One Wonderful Night. Ward, 1913; Clode, 1913
The Park Lane Mystery. Hodder, 1924
The Passing of Charles Lanson. Hodder, 1925; Clode, 1924 F
The Pelham Affair. Clode, 1923. (British title?)
The Pillar of Light. Ward, 1905; Clode, 1904. Also published as: The Wreck of the Chinook. Clode, 1930
The Postmaster's Daughter. Cassell, 1917; Clode, 1916 F
-Princess Kate. White, 1903
-Rainbow Island. Ward, 1903
The Revellers. White, 1904; Clode, 1917
The Sandling Case; see What Would You have Done?
-The Second Baronet. Hodder, 1923
The Silent Barrier. Ward, 1909; Clode, 1911
The Silent House. Nash, 1911. U.S. title: The House of Silence. Clode, 1911, as by Gordon Holmes
-A Son of the Immortals. Ward, 1912; Clode, 1909
-Souls on Fire. Clode, 1904. (British title?)
-The Stowaway. Ward, 1910; Clode, 1909. Also published as: The Stowaway Girl. Clode, 1912
The Stowaway Girl; see The Stowaway
The Stowmarket Mystery. Ward, 1904; Fenno, 1904 RB
The Strange Case of Mortimer Fenley; see The Case of Mortimer Fenley
The Strange Disappearance of Lady Delia. Pearson, 1901
Sylvia's Chauffeur. Ward, 1911. (= Cynthia's Chauffeur?)
The Terms of Surrender. Cassell, 1914; Clode, 1913
The Third Miracle. Hodder, 1927. U.S. title: The Lastingham Murder. Clode, 1929 F
The Token. Hodder, 1924; Clode, 1924 F
The Turning Point. Hodder, 1924; Clode, 1923
-Waifs of Circumstance. Hodder, 1906
What Would You have Done? Hodder, 1928. U.S. title: The Sandling Case. Clode, 1931 F
The Wheel o' Fortune. Ward, 1908; Clode, 1907
-The Wings of the Morning. Clode, 1903. (British title?)
-The Winning of Winifred. White, 1906
The Woman in the Case. Hodder, 1927; Clode, 1928 F
-The Wooing of Esther Gray. Pearson, 1902
The Wreck of the Chinook; see The Pillar of Light

TRACY, VIRGINIA
The Moment After. Doubleday, 1930; Mathews, 1931
Personal Appearance of a Lioness. Lippincott, 1937
"Persons Unknown." Century, 1914

TRAFTON, EDWIN H.
"Cell 13." Ogilvie, 1888

TRAIL, ARMITAGE. Pseudonym of Maurice Coons.
Scarface. Clode, 1930; Long, 1931
The Thirteenth Guest. Whitman, 1929

TRAILL, PETER. Pseudonym of Guy (Mainwaring) Morton, 1896-   , q.v.
-The Angel. Grayson, 1934
-Carry Me Home. Grayson, 1934
The Deceiving Mirror. Jenkins, 1947
-The Divine Spark. Faber, 1926
-Golden Oriole. Methuen, 1940
-Great Dust. Grayson, 1932
-Half Mast. Grayson, 1936
-The Life Fashionable. Brentano's (London), 1929
-Mutation Mink. Jenkins, 1950
Not Proven. Barker, 1938
The Portly Peregrine. Jenkins, 1948
-Red, Green and Amber. Grayson, 1935 ss
-The Rope of Sand. Jenkins, 1951
-Six of One. Barker, 1938 ss
-The Sleeve of Night. Grayson, 1937
-So Sits the Turtle. Jenkins, 1948
-Some Take a Lover. Faber, 1928
-Under the Cherry Tree. Faber, 1926
-The White Hen. Faber, 1927
-Wings of Tomorrow. Jenkins, 1950

TRAIN, ARTHUR. 1875-1945. Series character: Mr. Tutt = T.
The Adventures of Ephraim Tutt. Scribner, 1930 T
The Blind Goddess. Scribner, 1926
By Advice of Counsel. Scribner, 1921 T ss
The Confessions of Artemas Quibble. Scribner, 1911
"C.Q."; or, In the Wireless House. Century, 1912
The Hermit of Turkey Hollow. Scribner, 1921 T
McAllister and his Double. Scribner, 1905; Newnes, 1905 ss
Manhattan Murder. Scribner, 1936
Mortmain. Appleton, 1907 ss
Mr. Tutt Comes Home. Scribner, 1941 T ss
Mr. Tutt Finds a Way. Scribner, 1945 T ss
Mr. Tutt Takes the Stand. Scribner, 1936 T ss
Mr. Tutt's Case Book. Scribner, 1936 T
Murderers' Medicine. Constable, 1937. (U.S. title?)
Old Man Tutt. Scribner, 1938 T ss
Page Mr. Tutt. Scribner, 1926 T ss
Tut, Tut! Mr. Tutt. Scribner, 1923; Nash, 1924 T
Tutt and Mr. Tutt. Scribner, 1920 T ss
Tutt for Tutt. Scribner, 1934 T ss
When Tutt Meets Tutt. Scribner, 1927 T ss
Yankee Lawyer—Autobiography of Ephraim Tutt. Scribner, 1943 T

TRALINS, (STANLEY) ROBERT. 1926-   . Series character: Lee Crosley = LC.
The Chic Chick Spy. Belmont, 1966 LC
Dragnet '67. Popular Library, 1967. (Novelization of the TV series.)
The Miss from S.I.S. Belmont, 1966 LC
The Ring-a-Ding UFOs. Belmont, 1967 LC

TRANTER, NIGEL (GODWIN). Pseudonym of Nye Tredgold, 1909-   .
-Balefire. Hodder, 1958
-Bridal Path. Ward, 1952
Cable from Kabul. Hodder, 1968
-Cheviot Chase. Ward, 1952
-The Chosen Course. Ward, 1949
-Colours Flying. Ward, 1948
-Delayed Action. Ward, 1944
-Drug on the Market. Hodder, 1962
-Ducks and Drakes. Ward, 1953
-Eagle's Feathers. Ward, 1941
-The Enduring Flame. Hodder, 1957
-Fair Game. Ward, 1950
-Fast and Loose. Ward, 1951
-Flight of Dutchmen. Ward, 1947

-The Flockmasters. Hodder, 1960
-The Freebooters. Ward, 1950
-The Gilded Fleece. Ward, 1942
-Gold for Prince Charlie. Hodder, 1962
-Harsh Heritage. Ward, 1939
-High Spirits. Collins, 1950
-Island Twilight. Ward, 1947
-Kettle of Fish. Hodder, 1961
-The Long Coffin. Ward, 1956
-Mammon's Daughter. Ward, 1939
The Man Behind the Curtain. Hodder, 1959
-Man's Estate. Ward, 1946
-The Night Riders. Ward, 1954
-The Queen's Grace. Ward, 1953
-Rio d'Oro. Ward, 1955
-Root and Branch. Ward, 1948
-Rum Week. Ward, 1954
-Spanish Galleon. Hodder, 1960
The Stone. Hodder, 1958; Putnam, 1959
-There are Worse Jungles. Ward, 1955
-Tidewrack. Ward, 1951
-Tinker's Pride. Ward, 1945
-Trespass. Moray, 1937
-Watershed. Ward, 1941

TRASK, KEITH
Captain King Investigates; see Murder Incidental
Dead Men Do Tell. Farrar, 1931
Murder Incidental. Farrar, 1931. British title: Captain King Investigates. Butterworth, 1932

TRASK, MERRILL. Pseudonym of Hal Braham, q.v. Other pseudonym: Mel Colton, q.v.
Murder in Brief. Mystery House, 1956

TRAUBEL, HELEN
The Metropolitan Opera Murders. Simon, 1951. (Ghost-written by Harold Q. Masur, 1912-   , q.v.)

TRAVER, ROBERT. Pseudonym of John Donaldson Voelker, 1903-   . See also: ELIHU WINER.
Anatomy of a Murder. St. Martin's, 1958; Faber, 1958
-Laughing Whitefish. McGraw, 1965; Allen, 1967
Small-Town D.A. Dutton, 1954; Faber, 1959

TRAVERS, HUGH. Pseudonym of Hugh (Travers) Mills, q.v. Series character: Madame Aubry, in both titles.
Madame Aubry and the Police. Elek, 1966; Harper, 1967
Madame Aubry Dines with Death. Elek, 1967; Harper, 1967

TRAVERS, ROBERT (JOHN). 1911?-1974.
The Apartment on K Street. Little, 1972

TRAVIS, GERRY. Pseudonym of Louis (Preston) Trimble, 1917-   , q.v. Other pseudonym: Stuart Brock, q.v.
The Big Bite. Mystery House, 1957
A Lovely Mask for Murder. Mystery House, 1956
-Tarnished Love. Phoenix, 1942

TRAVIS, GRETCHEN
The Cottage. Putnam, 1973; Franklin, 1974
Holiday of Fear. Signet, 1968
She Fell Among Thieves. Doubleday, 1963; Hale, 1964
Too Old to Die. Putnam, 1968; Hale, 1969
2 Spruce Lane. Putnam, 1975

TREAT, LAWRENCE. 1903-   . Name originally: Lawrence Arthur Goldstone, q.v. Series characters: Bill Decker = BD; Jub Freeman = JF; Mitch Taylor = MT; Carl Wayward = CW.

B as in Banshee. Duell, 1940. Also published as: Wail for the Corpses. Best Detective Selection, 1943 CW
Big Shot. Harper, 1951; Boardman, 1952 MT, BD, JF
D as in Dead. Duell, 1941 CW
F as in Flight. Morrow, 1948; Boardman, 1949 JF, BD
H as in Hangman. Duell, 1942 CW
H as in Hunted. Duell, 1946; Boardman, 1950 JF
Lady, Drop Dead. Abelard (New York & London), 1960 MT, JF
The Leather Man. Duell, 1944; Rich, 1947
O as in Omen. Duell, 1943 CW
Over the Edge. Morrow, 1948; Boardman, 1958 JF, BD
P as in Police. Davis, 1970 MT, JF ss
Q as in Quicksand. Duell, 1947. British title: Step into Quicksand. Boardman, 1959 MT, JF
Step into Quicksand; see Q as in Quicksand
T as in Trapped. Morrow, 1947 MT, JF
Trial and Terror. Morrow, 1949; Boardman, 1958
V as in Victim. Duell, 1945; Rich, 1950 MT, JF
Venus Unarmed. Doubleday, 1961
Wail for the Corpses; see B as in Banshee
Weep for a Wanton. Ace, 1956; Boardman, 1957 MT, JF

TREBOR, SNIVIG C. Pseudonym of Robert C. Givins.
The Millionaire Tramp. Cook County Review, 1886. Also published as by Robert C. Givins: Around the World Publishing Co., 1913

TREDGOLD, NYE. 1909-   . Pseudonym: Nigel (Godwin) Tranter, q.v.

TREE, GREGORY. Pseudonym of John Franklin Bardin, 1916-   , q.v. Other pseudonym: Douglas Ashe, q.v. Series characters: Bill Bradley and Noel Mayberry = B&M.
The Case Against Butterfly. Scribner, 1951 B&M
The Case Against Myself. Scribner, 1950; Gollancz, 1951 B&M
So Young to Die. Scribner, 1953; Gollancz, 1953

TREECE, HENRY. 1911-1966.
Ask for King Billy. Faber, 1955
Bang, You're Dead! Faber, 1966
Desperate Journey. Faber, 1954
Don't Expect Any Mercy. Faber, 1958
Hunter Hunted. Faber, 1957
Killer in Dark Glasses. Faber, 1965

TREETON, ERNEST A.
The Crooked Finger. Lloyd's, 1921
The Entombed Convict. Lloyd's, 1921
The Instigator. Chatto, 1903
A New Jack Sheppard. Routledge, 1907
The Saving of Christian Sergison. Hodder, 1903

TREGARRON, YATE
Murderers' Island. Methuen, 1925

TREGASKIS, RICHARD (WILLIAM). 1916-1973.
China Bomb. Washburn, 1967

TREIBICH, S(TEPHEN) J(OHN). 1936-1972.
Haelstrom Manor. Lancer, 1967

TREMAYNE, RAYMOND
Some Rogues and Daphne. Low, 1924

TREMBATH, HAROLD
Double Dealing. Cole, 1942
Murder in Berlin. Cole, 1942

TREMBATH, HEDLEY
The Fighting Cartoonist Detective. Swan, 1946

TRENCH, JOHN. 1920-   . Series character: Martin Cotterell = MC.
Beyond the Atlas. Macdonald, 1963; Macmillan, 1963
Dishonoured Bones. Macdonald, 1953; Macmillan, 1955 MC
Docken Dead. Macdonald, 1953; Macmillan, 1954 MC
What Rough Beast. Macdonald, 1957; Macmillan, 1957 MC

TRENT, ILONA
Too Many Crooks. Vantage, 1968

TRENT, LAWRENCE
Girl Stalker. Greenleaf, 1972

TRENT, LEE
A Bird in the Hand. Hale, 1972

TRENT, PAUL. Pseudonym of Edward Platt. Series character: Peter Quayle, in at least those marked PQ.
-Adair and Son. Ward, 1940
-Adam. Ward, 1917
The Air Bandits. Ward, 1935
-Andrew Reforms. Ward, 1946
-At the World's Mercy. Ward, 1924
-A Battle of Giants. Ward, 1931
-Baxter's Son. Ward, 1929
-Bentley's Conscience. Ward, 1916
-The Best of Three. Ward, 1942
The Blackguard. Hayes, 1923
The Blackmailer. Ward, 1914
-"Blue Peter." Odhams, 1919
-The Broken Way. Ward, 1933
-Brotherhood. Odhams, 1922
-Brotherly Love. Ward, 1930
-The Bush King. Ward, 1926
-Celia. Hayes, 1921
-Celia's Career. Ward, 1928
-Churstons. Ward, 1920
-Clubs and Hearts. Ward, 1933
-The Counterbalance. Ward, 1918
The Craven Mystery. Ward, 1929
The Crooked Samaritan. Ward, 1933
-Delilah. Hayes, 1920
-The Devil in Her. Ward, 1944
-Ethel Norman's Secret. Ward, 1915
-Eve. Hayes, 1919
-Falkland's Choice. Ward, 1930
-Family Property. Ward, 1940
-Fettered. Ward, 1924
-A Final Chance. Ward, 1932
-The First-Born. Ward, 1943
-Flying Peter. Wright, 1938
-The Foundling. Ward, 1913
-From Father to Son. Ward, 1939
-Gentlemen of the Sea. Ward, 1915
-Gold Poison. Ward, 1942
-The Golden Rat. Ward, 1932
-The Great Autumn Double. Wright, 1934
-The Heart Specialist. Odhams, 1921
-Her Month of Freedom. Ward, 1932
-Her Wild Oats. Ward, 1930
-The Honour of the Family. Ward, 1941
-In the Toils. Long, 1925
-The Ironmaster's Daughter. Ward, 1939
The Island Murder. Ward, 1934
-It Might have Been. Ward, 1933
-Ivor's Chance. Ward, 1936
-Jane Ventures. Ward, 1944
-John and Son. Ward, 1946
-The Judgment of Ann. Ward, 1931

Trent, Paul

-The Lady of Longbourne. Ward, 1915
A Legacy of Vengeance. Ward, 1923
-A Long Lane. Ward, 1943
-The Lost Generation. Ward, 1938
-Love Cruisers. Ward, 1935
-The Maid of Mansfield. Ward, 1915
-The Man Who Made Good. Odhams, 1920
-The Man Who Stood Alone. Ward, 1926
-Mark Ryder's Vow. Ward, 1922
The Master of the Skies. Odhams, 1920
-Max Logan. Ward, 1914
-Maxine. Ward, 1937
-Michael Durrant. Ward, 1925
-The Million Heiress. Ward, 1941
A Modern Portia. Ward, 1938
-The Money Sense. Ward, 1928
-Mortgaged Lives. Wright, 1935
Mr. Justice Philbank. Ward, 1934
-Natalie Limited. Ward, 1936
-A Naval Adventuress. Ward, 1919
Nesbit's Compact. Ward, 1915
-Nurse to Dives. Ward, 1937
-The Pathway to Fame. Ward, 1931
-The Peacemaker. Ward, 1927
-Peter Hyde, M.P. Ward, 1920
-The Price of a Soul. Mills, 1916
-Private and Confidential. Ward, 1940
Quayle of the Yard. Ward, 1935 PQ
Quayle's First Case. Ward, 1936 PQ
-Red Mirage. Wright, 1937
-The Red Streak. Ward, 1930
-The Ruling Vice. Ward, 1917
-The Sacrifice. Ward, 1928
-The Second Chance. Ward, 1913
Shattered. Ward, 1934
-A Soviet Marriage. Laurie, 1930
-Stephen Vale. Ward, 1918
-The Strange Inheritance. Ward, 1921
-The Strong Right Arm. Odhams, 1922
-The Supplanter. Ward, 1914
-Tainted Gold. Ward, 1918
-The Unexpected Daughter. Ward, 1930
The Vow. Hodder, 1911; Stokes, 1911
-Wheat and Tares. Ward, 1914
-When Greek Meets Greek. Ward, 1916
-A Wife by Purchase. Milne, 1909
-Wilton's Silence. Ward, 1921
-Wings Behind Bars. Wright, 1940
-Wings of Love. Wright, 1935
-A Woman of Action. Ward, 1919
-Workers All. Ward, 1923
-The Years Between. Ward, 1939

TRENT, TIMOTHY
-All Dames are Dynamite. Godwin, 1935
Fall Guy. Godwin, 1936
-Night Boat. Godwin, 1934

TREVANIAN. Pseudonym. Series character: Jonathan Hemlock, in both titles.
The Eiger Sanction. Crown, 1972; Heinemann, 1973
The Loo Sanction. Crown, 1973; Heinemann, 1974

TREVOR, A. C. Pseudonym of Norman George Pulsford, 1902- .
Death Haunts the Lounge. Harrap, 1936

TREVOR, ELLESTON. 1920- . Name originally: Trevor Dudley Smith, q.v. Pseudonyms: Mansell Black, Trevor Burgess, Adam Hall, Simon Rattray, Warwick Scott, Caesar Smith, qq.v.
-The Billboard Madonna. Heinemann, 1960; Morrow, 1961
A Blaze of Roses. Heinemann, 1952; Harper, 1952. Also published as: The Fire Raiser. New English Library pb, 1970
-The Burning Shore. Heinemann, 1961. U.S. title: The Pasang Run. Harper, 1962
-Bury Him Among Kings. Heinemann, 1970; Doubleday, 1970
-Chorus of Echoes. Boardman, 1950
-Dream of Death. Digit, 1958
The Fire-Raiser; see A Blaze of Roses
-The Flight of the Phoenix. Heinemann, 1964; Harper, 1964
The Immortal Error. Swan, 1946
-The Mind of Max Duvine. Swan, 1960; Wehman, 1960
Night Stop. Doubleday, 1975. (British title?)
-The Paragon. New English Library, 1975
The Pasang Run; see The Burning Shore
-The Passion and the Pity. Heinemann, 1953
A Place for the Wicked. Heinemann, 1968; Doubleday, 1968
-Redfern's Miracle. Boardman, 1951
-The Second Chance. Digit, 1965
-Secret Arena. Jenkins, 1951
-The Shoot. Heinemann, 1966; Doubleday, 1966
-Silhouette. Swan, 1959
-Tiger Street. Boardman, 1951; Lion, 1954
-Touch of Purple. French (London & New York), 1973. (A play.)
The V.I.P. Heinemann, 1959; Morrow, 1960
-Weave a Rope of Sand. Consul, 1965

TREVOR, G. S. and M. E.
The Bloodhound of the Law. Sea-Side Times Print, 1908

TREVOR, GLEN. Pseudonym of James Hilton, 1900-1954.
Murder at School. Benn, 1931. U.S. title: Was It Murder? Harper, 1933. Reprinted as by James Hilton.

TREVOR, JAMES. Series character: John Savage, in both titles.
The Savage Game. Award, 1967
The Savage Height. Award, 1969

TREVOR, LESLIE. All titles are novelizations of the Policewoman TV series.
Code 1013: Assassin. Award, 1975
Death of a Call Girl. Award, 1975
The Rape. Award, 1975; Tandem, 1975

TREVOR, M. E. See: G. S. Trevor.

TREVOR, RALPH. Pseudonym of J(ames) R(eginald) Wilmot, 1897- , q.v.
The Ace of Clubs Murder. Wright, 1939
Behind the Green Mask. Wright, 1940
The Corpse in the Caravan. Wright, 1939
Death Burns the Candle. Wright, 1938
Death Comes Too Late. Wright, 1938
Death in the Surgery. Wright, 1937
The Deputy Avenger. Wright, 1938
Easy for the Crook. Wright, 1939
The Eyes Through the Mask. Wright, 1935
Front Page Murder. Wright, 1942
The Ghost Counts Ten. Wright, 1938
The Girl in the Crimson Cloak. Wright, 1940
High Spy. Wright, 1942
The House of Silence. Wright, 1935
Invitation to Murder. Wright, 1936
Meet Doctor Death. Wright, 1940
The Monday Night Murder. Wright, 1935
The Moorcroft Manor Mystery. Wright, 1935
Murder for Two Pins. Wright, 1939
A Murder has been Arranged. Wright, 1942
Murder in Silk. Wright, 1937
Murder in the Fifth Column. Wright, 1940
Murder Without Regret. Wright, 1937
On the Night of the Ninth. Wright, 1935
The Phantom Raider. Wright, 1941
Red Stands for Danger. Wright, 1941
Sky-High Terror. Wright, 1940
Some Persons Unknown. Wright, 1935
Under Suspicion. Wright, 1936
Viper's Vengeance. Wright, 1938
Who Killed the Crooner? Wright, 1941

TREW, ANTONY (FRANCIS). 1906- .
The Zhukov Briefing. Collins, 1975; St. Martin's, 1976

TREYNOR, ALBERT M.
The Long Patrol. Dodd, 1926; Hutchinson, 1927
-Rogues of the North. Chelsea, 1922; Hutchinson, 1924
Snow Blind. Dodd, 1929; Hamilton, 1930
The Trail from Devil's Country. Dodd, 1926; Hutchinson, 1926

TREYNOR, BLAIR
If You Should Ever Need Me; see She Ate Her Cake
She Ate Her Cake. Morrow, 1946. British title: If You Should Ever Need Me. Nimmo, 1948
Silver Doll. Holt, 1952
Widow's Pique. Mill, 1956; Ward, 1958

TRICE, BOROUGH. Pseudonym of Arthur Bruce Allen, 1903-1975.
'Orrible Murder. Big Ben, 1942

TRIEM, PAUL ELLSWORTH. 1882- .
Alias John Doe. Chelsea, 1930; Hamilton, 1931

TRIESCHMAN, CHARLES
Two. Dell, 1974. (Novelization of the movie.)

TRIMBLE, LOUIS (PRESTON). 1917- .
Pseudonyms: Stuart Brock, Gerry Travis, qq.v.
Blondes are Skin Deep. Lion, 1951
Cargo for the Styx. Ace, 1959
The Case of the Blank Cartridge. Phoenix, 1949
The Corpse Without a Country. Ace, 1959
Date for Murder. Phoenix, 1942
The Dead and the Deadly. Ace, 1963
Design for Dying. Phoenix, 1945
The Duchess of Skid Row. Ace, 1960
Fit to Kill. Phoenix, 1941
Girl on a Slay Ride. Avon, 1960
Give Up the Body. Superior, 1946
Love Me and Die. Ace, 1960
Murder Trouble. Phoenix, 1945; Wells Gardner, 1949
Nothing to Lose But My Life. Ace, 1957
Obit Deferred. Ace, 1959
The Smell of Trouble. Ace, 1958
Stab in the Dark. Ace, 1956
The Surfside Caper. Ace, 1961
The Tide Can't Wait. Mystery House, 1957; Wright, 1959
Till Death Do Us Part. Ace, 1959
Tragedy in Turquoise. Phoenix, 1942
You Can't Kill a Corpse. Phoenix, 1946

TRINIAN, JOHN
The Big Grab. Pyramid, 1963
House of Evil. Pyramid, 1962
North Beach Girl. Muller pb, 1961. (Original U.S. title?) Also published as: Strange Lovers. Macfadden, 1967
The Savage Breast. Muller pb, 1962. (U.S. title?)
Scratch a Thief. Ace, 1961
Strange Lovers; see North Beach Girl

TRIPP, C. E. Pseudonym of Charles (Smith) Morris, 1833-1922, q.v.
Ace High, the 'Frisco Detective. Book Club of California, 1948

TRIPP, MILES (BARTON). 1923- . Pseudonyms: John Michael Brett, Michael Brett, qq.v.

-The Chicken. Macmillan (London), 1966.
    Also included in: The Chicken and
    Zella. Pan, 1968
The Chicken and Zella; see The Chicken
The Claws of God. Macmillan (London),
    1972
-The Eighth Passenger. Heinemann, 1969
-The Fifth Point of the Compass. Macmillan (London), 1967
Five Minutes with a Stranger. Macmillan (London), 1971
-A Glass of Red Wine. Macdonald, 1960
-The Image of Man. Finlayson, 1955
Kilo Forty. Macmillan (London), 1963;
    Holt, 1964
Malice and the Maternal Instinct. Macmillan (London), 1969
A Man Without Friends. Macmillan (London), 1970
Obsession. Macmillan (London), 1973
A Quartet of Three. Macmillan (London), 1965
-One is One. Macmillan (London), 1968
-The Skin Dealer. Macmillan (London), 1964; Holt, 1965
Woman at Risk. Macmillan (London), 1974

TROLLOPE, ANTHONY. 1815-1882.
    The Eustace Diamonds. Chapman, 1873;
    Harper, 1872

TROLLOPE, T(HOMAS) ADOLPHUS. 1810-1892.
    A Siren. Smith & Elder, 1870; Arno, 1976

TROTT, NICHOLAS
    Monkey Boat. Macmillan, 1932

TROTTA, GERI [GERALDINE TROTTA]
    Dead as Diamonds. Boardman, 1956
    Veronica Died Monday. Dodd, 1952;
    Boardman, 1953

TROUBETZKOY, PRINCESS PAUL
    -The Clock Strikes. Rich, 1943
    Gallows Seed. Grayson, 1934; Kendall, 1935
    -Spider Spinning. Hale, 1936
    -Storm Tarn. Grayson, 1933

TROWN, ROBERT C(OOPER)
    Battle Without Glory. Hutchinson, 1947

TROY, KATHERINE. Pseudonym of Anne Buxton. Other pseudonym: Anne Maybury, q.v.
    -Enchanter's Nightshade. Collins, 1963
    -Falcon's Shadow. Collins, 1964
    -The House of Fand. Collins, 1966
    The Night of the Enchantress. Hodder, 1967
    Roseheath; see Storm over Roseheath
    -Someone Waiting. Collins, 1961
    Storm over Roseheath. Hodder, 1969.
    U.S. title: Roseheath. McKay, 1969
    -Whisper in the Dark. Collins, 1961

TROY, SIMON. Pseudonym of Thurman Warriner, q.v. Series character: Inspector Smith, in at least those marked S.
    Blind Man's Garden. Gollancz, 1970 S
    Cease Upon the Midnight. Gollancz, 1964; Macmillan, 1965 S
    Don't Play with the Rough Boys. Gollancz, 1963; Macmillan, 1964 S
    Drunkard's End. Gollancz, 1960;
        Walker, 1961
    Half-Way to Murder. Gollancz, 1955
    No More A-Roving. Gollancz, 1965 S
    Road to Rhuine. Collins, 1952; Dodd, 1952 S
    Second Cousin Removed. Gollancz, 1961;
        Macmillan, 1962 S
    Sup with the Devil. Gollancz, 1967 S
    Swift to its Close. Gollancz, 1969;
        Stein, 1969 S

Tonight and Tomorrow. Gollancz, 1967
Waiting for Oliver. Gollancz, 1962;
    Macmillan, 1963

TRUAX, RHODA. 1891-   .
    The Accident Ward Mystery. Little, 1937

TRUESDELL, JUNE
    Be Still, My Love. Dodd, 1947; Boardman, 1948
    Burden of Proof. Boardman, 1951
    The Morgue the Merrier. Dodd, 1945;
        Boardman, 1947

TRUMAN, MAJOR BEN(JAMIN) C(UMMINGS). 1835-1916.
    Occidental Sketches. San Francisco
    News, 1881 ss, at least one criminous

TRUMAN, MARCUS GEORGE. 1890-   . Pseudonym: Mark Beckett, q.v.

TRUSS, (LESLIE) SELDON. 1892-   . Pseudonym: George Selmark, q.v. Series characters: Chief Inspector Gidleigh = G; Det. Insp. Shane = S; Inspector Bass = B.
    Always Ask a Policeman. Hodder, 1953;
        Doubleday, 1952 G
    The Barberton Intrigue. Hodder, 1956.
        U.S. title: A Store of Wrath. Doubleday, 1956 G
    The Bride That Got Away. Hale, 1967;
        Doubleday, 1967, as by George Selmark
    The Coroner Presides; see Mr. Coroner Presides
    The Corpse That Got Away. Hale, 1969
    The Crooks' Shepherd; see Draw the Blinds
    The Daughters of Belial. Jarrolds, 1934
    Deadline for a Diplomat; see Rooksmiths
    Death was No Lady. Hodder, 1952;
        Doubleday, 1952 G
    The Disappearance of Julie Hintz. Hodder, 1940 G
    The Doctor was a Dame; see Put Out the Light
    Draw the Blinds. Hodder, 1936. U.S.
        title: The Crooks' Shepherd. Lothrop, 1936 G
    Escort to Danger. Hodder, 1935 S
    Eyes at the Window. Hale, 1966;
        Doubleday, 1966, as by George Selmark
    False Face; see The Long Night
    Footsteps Behind Them. Hodder, 1937 G
    Foreign Bodies. Hodder, 1938 B
    Gallows Bait. Butterworth, 1928. U.S.
        title: The Living Alibi. Coward, 1929 S
    The Hands of the Shadow. Hale, 1968
    The Hidden Men. Hodder, 1959. U.S.
        title: A Man to Match the Hour.
        Doubleday, 1959 G
    The High Wall. Hodder, 1954. U.S.
        title: The Other Side of the Wall.
        Doubleday, 1955 G
    The Hunterstone Outrage. Butterworth, 1931; Mystery League, 1931
    In Secret Places. Hodder, 1958; Doubleday, 1958 G
    Ladies Always Talk. Hodder, 1950. U.S.
        title: Why Slug a Postman. Doubleday, 1950 G
    The Living Alibi; see Gallows Bait
    The Long Night. Hodder, 1956. U.S.
        title: False Face. Doubleday, 1955 G
    A Man to Match the Hour; see The Hidden Men
    The Man Who Played Patience. Hodder, 1937
    The Man Without Pity. Butterworth, 1930. U.S. title: Number Nought.
        Dodd, 1930 S
    Mr. Coroner Presides. Harrap, 1932.
        U.S. title: The Coroner Presides.
        Minton, 1932 S
    Murder Paves the Way. Hodder, 1936 S

Never Fight a Lady. Hodder, 1951;
    Doubleday, 1950 G
Number Nought; see The Man Without Pity
One Man's Death. Hale, 1960. U.S.
    title: One Man's Enemies. Doubleday, 1960 G
One Man's Enemies; see One Man's Death
The Other Side of the Wall; see The High Wall
Put Out the Light. Hodder, 1954. U.S.
    title: The Doctor was a Dame. Doubleday, 1953 G
Rooksmiths. Hodder, 1936 B (Also published as: Deadline for a Diplomat.
    Merit, 1954, with series character changed from Bass to Gidleigh.)
Seven Years Dead. Hale, 1961; Doubleday, 1961 G
She Could Take Care. Hodder pb, 1937
The Stolen Millionaire. Butterworth, 1929; Coward, 1929
A Store of Wrath; see The Barberton Intrigue
Sweeter for his Going. Hodder, 1950 G
Technique for Treachery. Hale, 1963;
    Doubleday, 1963 G
They Came by Night. Jarrolds, 1933
A Time to Hate. Hale, 1962; Doubleday, 1962 G
The Town That Went Sick. Hale, 1965 G
The Truth About Claire Veryan. Hodder, 1957; Doubleday, 1957 G
Turmoil at Brede. Harrap, 1932; Mystery League, 1931
Walk a Crooked Mile. Hale, 1964 G
Where's Mr. Chumley? Hodder, 1949;
    Doubleday, 1948 G
Why Slug a Postman?; see Ladies Always Talk

TRYON, THOMAS. 1926-   .
    The Other. Knopf, 1971; Cape, 1971

TUCKER, ALLAN JAMES. 1929-   . Pseudonym: David Craig, q.v.

TUCKER, (ARTHUR) WILSON. 1914-   .
    Series character: Charles Horne = CH.
    The Chinese Doll. Rinehart, 1946; Cassell, 1948 CH
    The Dove. Rinehart, 1948; Cassell, 1950 CH
    The Hired Target. Ace, 1957
    Last Stop. Doubleday, 1963; Hale, 1965
    The Man in My Grave. Rinehart, 1956;
        Macdonald, 1958
    A Procession of the Damned. Doubleday, 1965; Hale, 1967
    Red Herring. Rinehart, 1951; Cassell, 1953 CH
    The Stalking Man. Rinehart, 1949; Cassell, 1950 CH
    This Witch. Doubleday, 1971; Gollancz, 1972
    Time Bomb. Rinehart, 1955. Also published as: Tomorrow Plus X. Avon, 1957
    To Keep or Kill. Rinehart, 1947; Cassell, 1950 CH
    To the Tombaugh Station. Ace, 1960
    Tomorrow Plus X; see Time Bomb
    The Warlock. Doubleday, 1967; Hale, 1968

TUDOR, ANTHONY
    The Case of Paul Breen. Page, 1911

TUITE, HUGH (GEORGE SPENCER)
    -Mr. Dovecourt's Decoy. Collins, 1926
    The Secret of the Blue Vase. Jenkins, 1924

TULLY, ANDREW (FREDERICK JR.). 1914-   .
    The Brahmin Arrangement. Coward, 1974

TUPPER, EDITH SESSIONS
By a Hair's Breadth. Street (Magnet), 1900
By Whose Hand? Fracher, 1889

TUPPER, MARTIN FARQUHAR. 1810-1889.
The Crock of Gold. Bentley, 1844

TURNBULL, AGNES SLIGH. 1888-   .
The Flowering. Houghton, 1972; Collins, 1972
The Richlands. Houghton, 1974; Collins, 1975
The Wedding Bargain. Houghton, 1966; Collins, 1967

TURNBULL, DORA AMY DILLON. 1878-1961.
Pseudonym: Patricia Wentworth, q.v.

TURNBULL, MARGARET.   -1942. Series character: Juliet Jackson, in at least those marked JJ.
The Bride's Mirror; see In the Bride's Mirror
-The Close-Up. Harper, 1918
The Coast Road Murder. Lippincott, 1934 JJ
-In the Bride's Mirror. Lippincott, 1934. British title: The Bride's Mirror. Ward, 1934
Madame Judas. Lippincott, 1926; Jenkins, 1926 JJ
The Return of Jenny Weaver. Lippincott, 1932; Ward, 1932
Rogues' March. Lippincott, 1928 JJ

TURNER, BESSIE (A.).
Circumstantial Evidence. Munro, 1884
A Woman in the Case. Carleton, 1875

TURNER, BILL. 1927-   . U.S. byline is sometimes the author's full name: William Price Turner.
Another Little Death. Constable, 1970; Walker, 1971
Bound to Die. Constable, 1967; Walker, 1967
Circle of Squares. Constable, 1969; Walker, 1969
Hot-Foot. Constable, 1973
Sex Trap. Constable, 1968
Solden's Women. Constable, 1972

TURNER, CHARLES (CYRIL). 1870-   .
Unlawful. Paul, 1927

TURNER, EDGAR
-The Armada Gold, with (William) Reginald Hodder (q.v.). Richards, 1908
-The Lady and the Burglar. Ward, 1904
The Purloined Prince, with (William) Reginald Hodder (q.v.). Caxton, 1905
-The Submarine Girl. Paul, 1909

TURNER, J(OHN) V(ICTOR). 1900-1945. Pseudonyms: Nicholas Brady, David Hume, qq.v. Series character: Amos Petrie, in all titles.
Amos Petrie's Puzzle. Bles, 1933
Below the Clock. Collins, 1936; Appleton, 1936
Death Joins the Party. Bles, 1935
Death must have Laughed. Putnam (London), 1932. U.S. title: First Round Murder. Holt, 1932
First Round Murder; see Death must have Laughed
Homicide Haven. Collins, 1935; Appleton, 1936
Murder—Nine and Out. Bles, 1934
Who Spoke Last? Putnam (London), 1932; Holt, 1933

TURNER, JAMES (ERNEST). 1909-   . Series character: Rampion Savage, in at least those marked RS.
The Blue Mirror. Cassell, 1965 RS
The Crystal Wave. Cassell, 1957 RS
The Dark Index. Cassell, 1959 RS
A Death by the Sea. Cassell, 1955
The Deeper Malady. Cassell, 1959
The Frontiers of Death. Cassell, 1957; British Book Centre, 1959 RS
The Glass Interval. Cassell, 1961 RS
Mass of Death. Fortune, 1937 RS
Murder at Landred Hall. Cassell, 1954 RS
The Nettle Shade. Cassell, 1963 RS
Requiem for Two Sisters. Cassell, 1968 RS
The Slate Landscape. Cassell, 1964 RS
The Stone Dormitory. Cassell, 1971 RS
The Strange Little Snakes. Cassell, 1956
Staircase to the Sea. Kimber, 1974 ss

TURNER, JOHN HASTINGS. See: ROLAND PERTWEE, 1885-1963.

TURNER, PHILIP. Pseudonym: Stephen Chance, q.v.

TURNER, RAY
Arson by Proxy. Hale, 1971

TURNER, ROBERT (HARRY). 1915-   . Pseudonym: Mercer B. Cook, q.v.
The Girl in the Cop's Pocket. Ace, 1956
The Night is for Screaming. Pyramid, 1960
Shroud 9. Powell, 1970 ss
The Tobacco Auction Murders. Ace, 1954

TURNER, RUSSELL
The Short Night. Hillman-Curl, 1957

TURNER, WILLIAM PRICE. 1927-   . See: BILL TURNER.

TURNEY, CATHERINE
The Other One. Holt, 1952

TURNGREN, ANNETTE. 1902-   . Pseudonym: A. T. Hopkins, q.v.

TUTE, WARREN (STANLEY). 1914-   .
A Matter of Diplomacy. Dent, 1969; Coward, 1970
Next Saturday in Milan. Constable, 1975
The Powder Train. Dent, 1970; Ballantine, 1975
The Resident. Constable, 1973; Ballantine, 1975
The Tarnham Connection. Dent, 1971; Ballantine, 1974

TUTTIETT, MARY GLEED.   -1923. Pseudonym: Maxwell Grey, q.v.

TUTTLE, GENE
Slade, Range Detective. Avalon, 1973; Hale, 1975

TUTTLE, W(ILBUR) C(OLEMAN). 1883-   . An American author of mostly westerns, many of which have strong detective elements. Note that some uncorrelated title changes likely persist in the following list, and that many of Tuttle's books were apparently published only in Britain. Series character: Hashknife Hartley, in at least those marked HH.
Arizona Drifters. Collins, 1964
Bluffer's Luck. Houghton, 1937; Collins, 1932
Buckshot Range. Collins, 1966
Danger Trail. Collins, 1958
The Dead-Line. Collins, 1927
The Deputy. Avalon, 1959
The Devil's Payday. World's Work, 1929
Diamond Hitch. Collins, 1962
Double-Crossers of Ghost Tree. Collins, 1965
Double Trouble. Collins, 1964
Dynamite Days. Collins, 1960
The Flood of Fate. Collins, 1926
Galloping Gold. Collins, 1961
Ghost Guns. Collins, 1957
Ghost Trails. Houghton, 1940; Collins, 1926
Gold at K-BAR-T. Collins, 1961
Gun Feud. Popular Library, 1951
Hashknife of Stormy River. Houghton, 1935; Collins, 1931 HH
Hashknife of the Canyon Trail. Collins, 1928 HH
Hashknife of the Double Bar 8. Houghton, 1936; Collins, 1927 HH
Henry the Sheriff. Houghton, 1936
Hidden Blood. Houghton, 1943; Collins, 1929
Horse-Shoe Luck. Collins, 1934
The House of the Hawk. Collins, 1963
The Keeper of Red Horse Pass. Houghton, 1937; Collins, 1930
The King of Dancing Valley. Collins, 1958
The Lone Wolf. Collins, 1967
Loot of the Lazy F. Collins, 1933
Lucky Partners. Collins, 1967
Me and Rudolph. Avalon, 1958
Medicine Maker. Collins, 1967
The Medicine-Man. Houghton, 1939; Collins, 1925 HH
Mission River Justice. Avalon, 1955; Collins, 1956
Montana Man. Avalon, 1966
The Morgan Trail. Houghton, 1928 HH
Mystery at the JHC Ranch. Houghton, 1932
The Mystery of the Red Triangle. Houghton, 1942; Collins, 1929 HH
Outlaw Empire. Avalon, 1960
Passengers for Painted Rock. Collins, 1962
The Payroll of Fate. Collins, 1966
Piperock Tales. Avalon, 1963
Reddy Brant, His Adventures. Century, 1920
The Redhead from Sun Dog. Houghton, 1930; Collins, 1930
Renegade Sheriff. Avalon, 1953; Collins, 1954
Rifled Gold. Houghton, 1934; Collins, 1934 HH
The Rim Rider. Collins, 1959
Road to the Moon. Collins, 1965
Rocky Rhodes. Collins, 1936
Rustlers' Roost. Collins, 1927
Sad Sontag Plays his Hunch. Garden City, 1926. British title (?): Sontag of Sundown. World's Work, 1929
Salt for the Tiger. Avalon, 1952; Collins, 1954
The Santa Dolores Stage. Houghton, 1934; Collins, 1935 HH
The Shadow Shooter. Collins, 1955
The Shame of Arizona. Collins, 1957
Shotgun Gold. Houghton, 1940; Collins, 1941 HH
The Silver Bar Mystery. Houghton, 1933; Collins, 1932
Silver Buckshot. Collins, 1959
The Singing Kid. World's Work, 1953
Singing River. Houghton, 1939; Collins, 1931
Sontag of Sundown; see Sad Sontag Plays his Hunch
Spawn of the Desert. World's Work, 1929
Spooky Riders. Collins, 1930
Stockade. Collins, 1965
Straight Shooting. Garden City, 1926
Straws in the Wind. Houghton, 1948; Collins, 1948
Sun Dog Loot. Collins, 1926
Thicker Than Water. Houghton, 1927 HH

Thunderbird Range. Avalon, 1954; Collins, 1955
The Tin God of Twisted River. Houghton, 1941; Collins, 1942
The Trail of Deceit. Houghton, 1951
The Trail to Kingdom Come. Collins, 1960
Trouble at the JHC. Hillman, 1950
The Trouble Trailer. Houghton, 1946; Collins, 1946
Tumbling River Range. Houghton, 1935; Collins, 1929
The Turquoise Trail. Collins, 1935
Twisted Trails. Popular Library, 1950
Valley of Suspicion. Collins, 1964
The Valley of Twisted Trails. Houghton, 1931; Collins, 1932 HH
The Valley of Vanishing Herds. Houghton, 1942 HH
Wandering Dogies. Houghton, 1938; Collins, 1939
West of Aztec Pass. Collins, 1963
Wild Horse Valley. Houghton, 1938; Collins, 1939
Wolf Creek Valley; see The Wolf Pack of Lobo Butte
The Wolf Pack of Lobo Butte. Houghton, 1945. British title: Wolf Creek Valley. Collins, 1946

TUTTON, BARBARA (IVY CURTIS). 1914-   .
Black Widow. Hale, 1963
Plague Spot. Hale, 1965
Rich to Die. Hale, 1962
Take Me Alive. Hale, 1961

TWAIN, MARK. Pseudonym of Samuel Langhorne Clemens, 1835-1910.
A Double-Barrelled Detective Story. Harper, 1902; Chatto, 1902
A Murder, A Mystery, and A Marriage. Manuscript House, 1945
Simon Wheeler, Detective. New York Public Library, 1963
The Stolen White Elephant. Osgood, 1882; Chatto, 1882
Tom Sawyer, Detective, and other stories. Harper, 1896; Chatto, 1897 ss

TWEEDALE, VIOLET (CHAMBERS)
The Beautiful Mrs. Davenant. Jenkins, 1920; Stokes, 1920
Unsolved Mysteries. Digby, 1895 ss

TYLER, CHARLES W(ALLER). 1841-   .
Blue Jean Billy. Chelsea, 1926; Lloyd's, 1921
Quality Bill's Girl. Chelsea, 1925; Hutchinson, 1926

TYLER, ESTHER
Murder on the Bluff. Simon, 1936. British title: The Family Skeleton. Bell, 1937

TYLER, FROOM
Gallows Parade. Dickson, 1933 ss

TYLER, ROBERT LEE
Lawyer Bell from Boston. Street, 1893

TYNAN, KATHARINE [KATHARINE TYNAN HINKSON]. 1861-1931.
The Rattlesnake. Ward, 1917

TYNDALL, JOHN. Series character: Roger Turnbull, in both titles.
Death in Lebanon. Bles, 1971
Death in the Jordan. Bles, 1970

TYNER, PAUL. 1939-   .
Shoot It. Little, 1968; Heinemann, 1969

TYRE, NEDRA
Death is a Lover; see Mouse in Eternity
Death of an Intruder. Knopf, 1953; Collins, 1954

Everyone Suspect. Macmillan, 1964; Gollancz, 1965
Hall of Death. Simon, 1960. Also published as: Reformatory Girls. Ace, 1962
Journey to Nowhere. Knopf, 1954; Collins, 1954
Mouse in Eternity. Knopf, 1952; Macdonald, 1953. Also published as: Death is a Lover. Mercury, 1953
Reformatory Girls; see Hall of Death
Twice So Fair. Random, 1971

TYRELL, PATRICK
The Robber King. Laird, 1889

TYRER, WALTER. 1900-   . Those titles listed without publisher feature Sexton Blake and were published by Amalgamated Press or Fleetway.
The Affair of Danny the "Dip". 1950
The Affair of the Hollywood Contract. 1949
The Case Against Dr. Ripon. 1948
The Case of the Bogus Baron. 1952
The Case of the Conscript Miner. 1944
The Case of the Cottage Crime. 1950
The Case of the Council Swindle. 1954
The Case of the Forbidden Island. 1955
The Case of the Missing Nazi. 1953
The Case of the Naval Defaulter. 1950
The Case of the Naval Stores Bucket. 1953
The Case of the Returning Soldier. 1955
The Case of the Swindled Guarantor. 1954
The Case of the Two Crooked Baronets. 1951
The Clue of the Pin-Up Girl. 1956
The Crime in Room 27. 1954
The Crime on the Moors. 1946
The Crimes at Fenton Towers. 1951
The Curse of the Carrington's. 1943
Daughter of the Scaffold. Amalgamated, 1935
The Dilemma of Dr. Hiley. 1952
Ellen Morgan. Columbine, 1939
The Evil Spell. 1950
The Hangman's Daughter. Amalgamated, 1936
The Hire-Purchase Fraud. 1952
The Holiday Camp Mystery. 1947
Jane the Ripper. Columbine, 1939
The Motor Coach Mystery. 1948
The Mystery of Squadron X. 1943
The Mystery of the Mad Millionaires. 1955
The Mystery of the Missing Angler. 1949
The Mystery of the Rio Star. 1950
The Mystery of the Swindler's Stooge. 1953
The Mystery of the Three Demobbed Men. 1956
The Mystery of the Woman Overboard. 1948
One of the Eleven. 1949
The Riddle of the French Alibi. 1954
The Scrap-Metal Mystery. 1952
The Secret of the Sands. 1945
The Secret of the Snows. 1953
She Sent her Mother to the Scaffold. Amalgamated, 1936
The Strange Affair of the Shot Gun Sniper. 1955
Such Friends are Dangerous. Staples, 1954
Trunk Crime Number Three. Columbine, 1939

TYRRELL, MABEL L(OUISE)
-The Forgotten Hills. Hodder, 1936
-Mysterious Journey. Hodder, 1940
-The Noble Error. Hodder, 1930

-Patchwork Palace. Hodder, 1933
-Pull the House Down. Hodder, 1938
-The Street of Fortune. Hodder, 1939
-That's Mark Avery. Hodder, 1942
-The Thief. Hodder, 1953
-Thirteen Moons. Hodder, 1937
-The Toledo Sword. Hodder, 1957

TYRRELL, ROSS
The Pathway of Adventure. Knopf, 1920

TYSON, J(OHN) AUBREY. 1870-   .
The Barge of Haunted Lives. Macmillan, 1923; Mills, 1924
The Rhododendron Man. Dutton, 1930; Mills, 1930
The Scarlet Tanager. Macmillan, 1922; Mills, 1922
-The Stirrup Cup. Appleton, 1903

TYTLER, SARAH. Pseudonym of Henrietta Keddie, 1827-1914.
The Blackhall Ghosts. Chatto, 1888; Rand, 1888

U

UHNAK, DOROTHY. Series character: Christie Opara = CO.
The Bait. Simon, 1968; Hodder, 1968 CO
Law and Order. Simon, 1973; Hodder, 1973
The Ledger. Simon, 1970; Hodder, 1971 CO
The Witness. Simon, 1969; Hodder, 1970 CO

ULLMAN, ALBERT E(DWARD)
The Kidnappers. Amour, 1932

ULLMAN, ALLAN
The Naked Spur, with Rolfe Bloom. Random, 1953; Corgi, 1955. (Novelization of the movie.)
Night Man, with Lucille Fletcher, 1912-   (q.v.). Random, 1951; Gollancz, 1951. (Novelization of the screenplay by Lucille Fletcher.)
Sorry, Wrong Number, with Lucille Fletcher, 1912-   (q.v.). Random, 1948; Gollancz, 1948. (Novelization of the play by Lucille Fletcher.)

ULLMAN, JAMES MICHAEL
Full Coverage; see Good Night, Irene
Good Night, Irene. Simon, 1965. British title: Full Coverage. Cassell, 1966
House of Cards; see The Venus Trap
Lady on Fire. Simon, 1968; Cassell, 1969
The Neon Haystack. Simon, 1963; Cassell, 1964
The Venus Trap. Simon, 1966. British title: House of Cards. Cassell, 1967

ULLMANN, RICHARD (EDWIN)
A Taste of Poison. Laurie, 1954

ULRICH, MAX
Bank Robbery. Constable, 1967. (Translation of Raub in der Munchner Lombard-Bank. Munich, 1965.)

ULSH, WAYNE C.
Rip-Off. Pyramid, 1975

UMBSTAETTER, H(ERMAN) D(ANIEL). 1851-1913.
The Red Hot Dollar and other stories from The Black Cat. Page, 1911 ss

UNDERHILL, G(EORGE) F(REDERICK)
-The Hand of Vengeance. Trischler, 1890
-In at the Death. Swan, 1888
-A Nasty Cropper. Trischler, 1889
-The Rogues of Society, and The Doctor of Duddlestone. Diprose, 1899

UNDERWOOD, MICHAEL. Pseudonym of John Michael Evelyn, 1916-   . Series character: Insp./Supt. Simon Manton, in at least those marked SM.
Adam's Case. Hammond, 1961; Doubleday, 1961 SM
The Anxious Conspirator. Macdonald, 1965; Doubleday, 1965 SM
Arm of the Law. Hammond, 1959 SM
The Case Against Philip Quest. Macdonald, 1962 SM
Cause of Death. Hammond, 1960 SM
A Crime Apart. Macdonald, 1966
The Crime of Colin Wise. Macdonald, 1964; Doubleday, 1964 SM
Death by Misadventure. Hammond, 1960 SM
Death on Remand. Hammond, 1956 SM
False Witness. Hammond, 1957; Walker, 1961 SM
Girl Found Dead. Macdonald, 1963 SM
The Juror. Macmillan (London), 1975; St. Martin's, 1975
Lawful Pursuit. Hammond, 1958; Doubleday, 1958 SM
The Man Who Died on Friday. Macdonald, 1967
The Man Who Killed Too Soon. Macdonald, 1968
Murder Made Absolute. Hammond, 1955; Washburn, 1957 SM
Murder on Trial. Hammond, 1954; Washburn, 1958 SM
A Pinch of Snuff. Macmillan (London), 1974; St. Martin's, 1974
Reward for a Defector. Macmillan (London), 1973; St. Martin's, 1973
The Shadow Game. Macdonald, 1969 SM
Shem's Demise. Macmillan (London), 1970
The Silent Liars. Macmillan (London), 1970; Doubleday, 1970
A Trout in the Milk. Macmillan (London), 1971; Walker, 1972
The Unprofessional Spy. Macdonald, 1964; Doubleday, 1964 SM

UNDERWOOD, REGINALD
Secret Fear. Fortune, 1943

UNEKIS, RICHARD
The Chase. Walker, 1962; Gollancz, 1963. Also published as: Pursuit. Signet, 1964

UNTERMEYER, WALTER, JR. 1915-   .
Dark the Summer Dies. Lion, 1953
Evil Roots. Lion, 1954

UPFIELD, ARTHUR W(ILLIAM). 1888-1964.
Series character: Insp. Napoleon Bonaparte = NB.
An Author Bites the Dust. Angus, 1948; Doubleday, 1948 NB
The Bachelors of Broken Hill. Heinemann, 1958; Doubleday, 1950 NB
The Barrakee Mystery. Hutchinson, 1929. U.S. title: The Lure of the Bush. Doubleday, 1965 NB
The Battling Prophet. Heinemann, 1956 NB
The Beach of Atonement. Hutchinson, 1930
The Body at Madman's Bend; see Madman's Bend
The Bone is Pointed. Angus, 1938; Doubleday, 1947 NB
Bony and the Black Virgin. Heinemann, 1959; Collier pb, 1965 NB
Bony and the Kelly Gang. Heinemann, 1960. U.S. title: Valley of Smugglers. Doubleday, 1960 NB
Bony and the Mouse. Heinemann, 1959. U.S. title: Journey to the Hangman. Doubleday, 1959 NB
Bony and the White Savage. Heinemann, 1961. U.S. title: The White Savage. Doubleday, 1961 NB
Bony Buys a Woman. Heinemann, 1957. U.S. title: The Bushman Who Came Back. Doubleday, 1957 NB
The Bushman Who Came Back; see Bony Buys a Woman
Bushranger of the Skies. Angus, 1940. U.S. title: No Footprints in the Bush. Doubleday, 1944 NB
Cake in the Hat Box. Heinemann, 1955. U.S. title: Sinister Stones. Doubleday, 1954 NB
The Clue of the New Shoe; see The New Shoe
Death of a Lake. Heinemann, 1954; Doubleday, 1954 NB
Death of a Swagman. Aldor, 1946; Doubleday, 1945 NB
The Devil's Steps. Aldor, 1948; Doubleday, 1946 NB
Gripped by Drought. Hutchinson, 1932
The House of Cain. Hutchinson, 1928; Dorrance, 1929
Journey to the Hangman; see Bony and the Mouse
The Lake Frome Monster. Heinemann, 1966. (Completed by J. L. Price and Dorothy Strange.) NB
The Lure of the Bush; see The Barrakee Mystery
Madman's Bend. Heinemann, 1963. U.S. title: The Body at Madman's Bend. Doubleday, 1964 NB
The Man of Two Tribes. Heinemann, 1956; Doubleday, 1956 NB
Mr. Jelly's Business. Angus, 1937. U.S. title: Murder Down Under. Doubleday, 1943 NB
The Mountains have a Secret. Heinemann, 1952; Doubleday, 1948 NB
Murder Down Under; see Mr. Jelly's Business
Murder Must Wait. Heinemann, 1953; Doubleday, 1953 NB
The Mystery of Swordfish Reef. Angus, 1939; Doubleday, 1943 NB
The New Shoe. Heinemann, 1952; Doubleday, 1951. Also published as: The Clue of the New Shoe. Thorpe, 1974 NB
No Footprints in the Bush; see Bushranger of the Skies
A Royal Abduction. Hutchinson, 1932
The Sands of Windee. Hutchinson, 1931; British Book Centre, 1959 NB
Sinister Stones; see Cake in the Hat Box
Valley of Smugglers; see Bony and the Kelly Gang
Venom House. Heinemann, 1953; Doubleday, 1952 NB
The White Savage; see Bony and the White Savage
The Widows of Broome. Heinemann, 1951; Doubleday, 1950 NB
The Will of the Tribe. Heinemann, 1962; Doubleday, 1962 NB
Winds of Evil. Angus, 1937; Doubleday, 1944 NB
Winged Mystery; see Wings Above the Diamantina
Wings Above the Claypan; see Wings Above the Diamantina
Wings Above the Diamantina. Angus, 1936. U.S. title: Wings Above the Claypan. Doubleday, 1943. Also published as: Winged Mystery. Hamilton, 1937 NB

UPHILL, THOMAS
Strange Heritage. Hutchinson, 1926

UPSHAW, HELEN
The Return of Jennifer. Dodd, 1964; Redman, 1965

UPWARD, ALLEN. 1863-1926.
The Accused Princess. Pearson, 1900
The Ambassador's Adventure. Cassell, 1901
-Athelstane Ford. Pearson, 1899
A Bride's Madness. Arrowsmith, 1897
The Club of Masks; see The Domino Club
A Crown of Straw. Chatto, 1896; Dodd, 1896
A Day's Tragedy: A Novel in Rhyme. Chapman, 1897
The Domino Club. Faber, 1926. U.S. title: The Club of Masks. Lippincott, 1926
-God Save the Queen! Chatto, 1897
High Treason. Primrose, 1903
The House of Sin. Faber, 1926; Lippincott, 1927
The International Spy; see The Phantom Torpedo-Boats
-Lord Alistair's Rebellion. Rivers, 1909
On Her Majesty's Service. Primrose, 1904
-One of God's Dilemmas. Heinemann, 1896; Arnold, 1896
-The Ordeal by Fire. Digby, 1904
The Phantom Torpedo-Boats. Chatto, 1905. U.S. title: The International Spy. Dillingham, 1905
The Prince of Balkistan. Chatto, 1895; Lippincott, 1895
The Queen Against Owen. Chatto, 1894
Romance of Politics. Tyndale, 1904
Secret History of Today. Chapman, 1904 ss
Secrets of the Courts of Europe. Arrowsmith, 1897 ss
The Venetian Key. Faber, 1927; Lippincott, 1927
The Wonderful Career of Ebenezer Lobb. Hurst, 1900 ss
The Wrongdoer. Arrowsmith, 1900
The Yellow Hand. Digby, 1904

URELL, WILLIAM FRANCIS. Pseudonym: William Francis, q.v.

URIS, LEON (MARCUS). 1924-   .
Topaz. McGraw, 1967; Kimber, 1968

URNER, NATHAN D(ANE). 1839-1893. Pseudonym: Burke Brentford, q.v.
The Detective's Secret. Laird, 1888
Link by Link; or, The Chain of Evidence. Laird, 1888

URQUHART, MACGREGOR. Series character: Chief Inspector Smarles, in at least those marked S.
-Alamein. Digit, 1958
The Bitter Lemon Mob. Boardman, 1966 S
The Bluebottle. Boardman, 1964 S
-Breakthrough. Digit, 1958
Contact Lens. Boardman, 1964 S
Dig the Missing. Boardman, 1963 S
-First Stop to Hell. Digit, 1962
-Foxhole. Digit, 1958
Frail on North Circular. Boardman, 1962 S
Girl on the Waterfront. Boardman, 1962 S
The Grey Man. Boardman, 1965 S
-Hungary Fights. Digit, 1957
Investigation, with Cecil Madden. Evans, 1958. (3-act play.)
The Open Mouth. Boardman, 1967 S
-Partisan. Digit, 1958
-Private Death. Digit, 1958
-Speedo! Digit, 1958
-Through the Bamboo Curtain. Digit, 1960

URQUHART, PAUL. Pseudonym of Ladbroke (Lionel Day) Black, 1877-1940, q.v. See also: T. C. St. C. Morton. Those titles below without publisher feature Sexton Blake and were published by Amalgamated Press.
  The Boro Council Ramp. 1937
  The Brooklands Mystery. 1932
  The Building Estate Murder. 1934
  The Bungalow Crime. 1932
  The Crime at the Crossroads. 1934
  The Crime of Count Dureen. 1935
  The Double Cross. 1933
  The Exploits of a Dead Man. Amalgamated, 1934
  Found in Possession. Amalgamated, 1935
  Gun Rule. 1931
  The Man on the Dole. 1938
  Mr. Kilmer Sees Red. 1933
  Murder by Mistake. 1934
  The Mystery of the Lorry Driver. 1939
  The Mystery of the Rajah's Jewels. 1932
  The Mystery of the Thirteenth Chest. 1931
  Presumed Dead. 1932
  The Secret of the Dead Man. 1938
  The Secret of the Evacuee. 1940
  -The Shadow. Ward, 1908
  The Victims of Devil's Alley. 1933
  -The Web. Ward, 1907
  Yellow Vengeance. 1933

USHER, FRANK (HUGH). 1909- . Pseudonyms: Charles Franklin, Frank Lester, qq.v. Series character: Daye Smith, in at least those marked DS.
  Body in Velvet. Hale, 1963
  The Boston Crab. Hale, 1970
  Deadly Legacy. Hale, 1971
  Death in Error. Hale, 1959 DS
  Death is Waiting. Long, 1958 DS
  Die, My Darling. Hale, 1960 DS
  The Faceless Stranger. Hale, 1961 DS
  Fall into my Grave. Hale, 1962 DS
  First to Kill. Long, 1959 DS
  Ghost of a Chance. Long, 1956 DS
  The Lonely Cage. Long, 1965 DS
  The Man from Moscow. Hale, 1965
  No Flowers in Brazlov. Hale, 1968
  Portrait of Fear. Long, 1957 DS
  The Price of Death. Long, 1957 DS
  Shot in the Dark. Hale, 1961 DS
  Stairway to Murder. Hale, 1964 DS
  Who Killed Rosa Gray? Hale, 1962 DS

USHER, GRAY. 1903- . Series character: Supt. Michael Drexel, in at least those marked MD.
  A Dame to Discover. Scion, 1952
  Death Goes Caving. Long, 1959
  Death in the Bag. Long, 1958 MD
  Death in the Straw. Long, 1955 MD
  Death Sped the Plough. Long, 1956 MD
  Death Takes a Teacher. Long, 1957 MD
  Don't Crowd Me. Scion, 1952
  Double Snatch. Scion, 1951
  Flames Burn High. Baker, 1954
  For Pete's Sake! Scion, 1951
  I was a Spy in Britain. Baker, 1952
  Intrigue. Scion, 1951
  Sleep If You Dare. Milestone, 1953
  Triggerman! Scion, 1951

USHER, JACK
  Brothers and Sisters Have I None. Mill, 1958; Heinemann, 1959. Also published as: Reason for Murder. PB, 1960
  The Fix. Mill, 1959. British title: The Girl in the White Mercedes. Heinemann, 1960
  The Girl in the White Mercedes; see The Fix
  Reason for Murder; see Brothers and Sisters Have I None

USHER, WILFRID
  Creeping Shadows. Paul, 1929
  The Great Hold-Up Mystery. Paul, 1928; International Fiction Library, 1929
  The Mystery of the Seven. Paul, 1930

V

VACHA, ROBERT
  Phantoms over Potsdam. Everest, 1975
  Spy for Churchill. Everest, 1974

VACHELL, HORACE ANNESLEY. 1861-1955.
  The Disappearance of Martha Penny. Hodder, 1934
  The Enchanted Garden and other stories. Cassell, 1929 ss
  Experiences of a Bond Street Jeweler. Cassell, 1912 ss
  An Impending Sword. Murray, 1909
  Loot from the Temple of Fortune. Murray, 1913; Doran, 1914 ss, some criminous
  The Mote House Mystery; see Mr. Allen
  Mr. Allen, with Archibald Marshall (q.v.; pseudonym of Arthur Hammond Marshall, 1866-1934). Hodder, 1926. U.S. title: The Mote House Mystery, as by Archibald Marshall and H. A. Vachell. Dodd, 1926
  Quinneys'. Murray, 1914; Doran, 1914
  Quinney's Adventures. Murray, 1924; Doran, 1924 ss

VACHETTE, EUGENE. 1827-1902. Pseudonym: Eugene Chavette, q.v.

VACULIK, LUDVIK. 1926- .
  The Guinea Pigs. Third Press, 1973; London Magazine Editions, 1974. (Translation of Morcata.)

VACZEK, LOUIS CHARLES. 1913- . Pseudonym: Peter Hardin, q.v.

VAHEY, JOHN (GEORGE) HASLETTE. 1881- . Pseudonyms: Henrietta Clandon, John Haslette, Anthony Lang, Vernon Loder, John Mowbray, Walter Proudfoot, qq.v.
  Death by the Gaff. Skeffington, 1932
  -Down River. Ward, 1925
  -Fiddlestrings. Ward, 1925
  Mr. Nemesis. Ward, 1930
  -The Money Barons. Ward, 1928
  Mystery at the Inn. Ward, 1931
  -Payment Down. Ward, 1927
  Secrets for Sale. Eyre, 1935
  -Solitude Limited. Ward, 1928
  Spies in Ambush. Eyre, 1934
  The Storm Lady. Ward, 1926
  Tragic Lesson. Hutchinson, 1933
  -Up North. Ward, 1926
  Witness in Support. Skeffington, 1932

VAIL, LAURENCE. 1891- .
  Murder! Murder! Davies, 1931

VAILE, WILLIAM N(EWELL). 1876- .
  The Mystery of the Golconda. Doubleday, 1925; Heinemann, 1925

VAIZEY, GEORGE (DE HORNE)
  -The Chairman. Harrap, 1941
  -The Failure. Harrap, 1947
  -Give Me Yesterday. Harrap, 1964
  Guile Wears a Coronet. Harrap, 1939
  -Inherit the Wind. Harrap, 1952
  Into Thin Air. Harrap, 1939
  -The Mirror Lies. Harrap, 1943
  -Or By Default. Harrap, 1957
  -The Road Home. Harrap, 1954
  -Sister Theatre. Harrap, 1950
  Tangled Web. Faith, 1974
  -Through Another Gate. Harrap, 1945

VALBECK, MICHAEL
  Headlong from Heaven. Unie-Volkspers (Cape Town), 1947; Mill, 1947

VALE, G. B.
  The Mystery of the Papyrus. Methuen, 1929

VALE, RENA M.
  The House on Rainbow Leap. PB, 1973

VALENTINE. Pseudonym of Archibald Thomas Pechey, 1876-1961. Other pseudonym: Mark Cross, q.v. Series characters: Daphne Wrayne and the Four Adjusters = DW (see also the Mark Cross entry).
  The Adjusters. Anglo-Eastern, 1930 DW (3 novelets.)
  A Flight to a Finish. Ward, 1929
  Strange Experiment. Ward, 1937
  The Unseen Hand. Jarrolds, 1924

VALENTINE, DOUGLAS. Pseudonym of (George) Valentine Williams, 1893-1946, q.v. Series character: Dr. Adolph Grundt (Clubfoot) = AG (see also Valentine Williams entry).
  The Man with the Clubfoot. Jenkins, 1918; McBride, 1918, as by Valentine Williams AG
  Okewood of the Secret Service; see The Secret Hand
  The Secret Hand. Jenkins, 1919. U.S. title: Okewood of the Secret Service, as by Valentine Williams. McBride, 1919

VALENTINE, JO. Pseudonym of Charlotte Armstrong, 1905-1969, q.v.
  The Trouble in Thor. Coward, 1953; Davies, 1953. Also published as: And Sometimes Death. PB, 1955

VALLANCE, DOUGLAS
  The Kildallon Affair. Hale, 1969
  Man in the Lubianka. Hale, 1971
  A Prize of Traitors. Hale, 1970
  A Safe Job. Hale, 1969

VALLEY, MEL
  Magnum Force. Paperback Library, 1974; Star, 1977. (Novelization of the movie.)

VALLINGS, GABRIELLE (FRANCESCA LILLIAN MAY)
  Jury of Four. Hutchinson, 1938

VALLS-RUSSELL, JOSEPH LAWRENCE. Pseudonym: Ray Alan, q.v.

VANARDY, VARICK. Pseudonym of Frederick Merrill Van Rensselaer Dey, 1861-1922. Other pseudonyms: Marmaduke Dey, Frederic Ormond, qq.v. Series characters: Bingham Harvard = BH; Crewe (Birge Moreau) = C.
  Alias the Night Wind. Dillingham, 1913 BH
  The Girl by the Roadside. Macaulay, 1917; Jarrolds, 1923
  The Lady of the Night Wind. Macaulay, 1919; Skeffington, 1926 BH
  The Night Wind's Promise. Dillingham, 1914 BH
  The Return of the Night Wind. Dillingham, 1914 BH
  Something Doing. Macaulay, 1919 C
  The Two-Faced Man. Macaulay, 1918; Jarrolds, 1920 C
  Up Against It. Macaulay, 1920

VAN ARSDALE, WIRT. Pseudonym of Martha Wirt Davis.
  The Professor Knits a Shroud. Doubleday, 1951

VAN ATTA, WINFRED (LOWELL). 1910- .
A Good Place to Work and Die. Doubleday, 1970; Hale, 1971
Hatchet Man. Doubleday, 1962; Boardman, 1964
Shock Treatment. Doubleday, 1961; Boardman, 1964

VAN BEEVER, ROBERT F. Joint pseudonym with Fred(erick) G(ordon) Jarvis, (Jr.), 1930- , q.v.: Fritz Gordon, q.v.

VANCE, ETHEL. Pseudonym of Grace Zaring Stone, 1891- , q.v.
Escape. Little, 1939; Collins, 1939
Reprisal. Little, 1942; Collins, 1943
The Secret Thread. Harper, 1948; Collins, 1948

VANCE, JACK. 1916- . Byline also: John Holbrook Vance, q.v. Pseudonyms: Peter Held, Alan Wade, qq.v.
The Many Worlds of Magnus Ridolph. Ace, 1966
Marune: Alastor 933. Ballantine, 1975

VANCE, JOHN HOLBROOK. 1916- . Byline also: Jack Vance, q.v. Pseudonyms: Peter Held, Alan Wade, qq.v. Series character: Sheriff Joe Bain = JB.
Bad Ronald. Ballantine, 1973
The Deadly Isles. Bobbs, 1969; Hale, 1970
The Fox Valley Murders. Bobbs, 1966; Hale, 1967 JB
The Man in the Cage. Random, 1960; Boardman, 1960
The Pleasant Grove Murders. Bobbs, 1967; Hale, 1968 JB

VANCE, LOUIS JOSEPH. 1879-1933. Series character: Michael Lanyard (The Lone Wolf) = ML.
Alias the Lone Wolf. Doubleday, 1921; Hodder, 1921 ML
The Bandbox. Little, 1912; Richards, 1912
Baroque. Dutton, 1923; Hodder, 1923
-Beau Revel. Nash, 1920. (U.S. title?)
The Black Bag. Bobbs, 1908; Richards, 1908
The Brass Bowl. Bobbs, 1907; Richards, 1907
The Bronze Bell. Dodd, 1909; Richards, 1909
Cynthia-of-the-Minute. Dodd, 1911; Richards, 1911
The Dark Mirror. Doubleday, 1920; Hurst, 1921
The Dark Power. Bles, 1925. (U.S. title?)
The Dead Ride Hard. Lippincott, 1926; Bles, 1927
The Destroying Angel. Little, 1912; Richards, 1913
Detective. Lippincott, 1932; Jarrolds, 1933
Encore the Lone Wolf. Lippincott, 1933; Jarrolds, 1934 ML
The False Faces. Doubleday, 1918; Skeffington, 1920 ML
-Lip-Service. Bles, 1928. (U.S. title?)
The Lone Wolf. Little, 1914; Nash, 1915 ML
The Lone Wolf Returns. Dutton, 1923; Hodder, 1924 ML
The Lone Wolf's Last Prowl. Lippincott, 1934; Jarrolds, 1935 ML
The Lone Wolf's Son. Lippincott, 1931; Jarrolds, 1932 ML
No Man's Land. Dodd, 1910; Stevens, 1910
Nobody. Doran, 1915; Hodder, 1916
The Pool of Flame. Dodd, 1909; Richards, 1910
Red Masquerade. Doubleday, 1921; Hodder, 1921 ML

Sheep's Clothing. Little, 1915
The Street of Strange Faces. Lippincott, 1934; Jarrolds, 1934
-Terence O'Rourke, Gentleman Adventurer. Wessels, 1905; Richards, 1906
The Trembling Flame. Lippincott, 1931; Jarrolds, 1932
The Woman in the Shadow. Lippincott, 1930; Jarrolds, 1931

VANCE, WILLIAM
Homicide Lost. Graphic, 1956

VANDAM, ALBERT D(RESDEN). 1843-1903.
A Court Tragedy. Chatto, 1900
Masterpieces of Crime. Remington, 1892 ss
The Mystery of the Patrician Club. Chapman, 1894; Lippincott, 1894

VANDEBURG, MILLIE BIRD
The Clean Hand. Cassell, 1928
The Door to the Moor. Cassell, 1927; Dorrance, 1925

VANDERCOOK, JOHN W(OMACK). 1902-1963. Series characters: Bertram Lynch and Robert Deane, in all titles.
Murder in Fiji. Doubleday, 1936; Heinemann, 1936
Murder in Haiti. Macmillan, 1956; Eyre, 1956. Also published as: Out for a Killing. Avon, 1958
Murder in New Guinea. Macmillan, 1959; Allen, 1960
Murder in Trinidad. Doubleday, 1933; Heinemann, 1934
Out for a Killing; see Murder in Haiti

VAN DER ELST, VIOLET. 1882-1966.
The Brain Master. Modern Fiction, 1946 ss
Death of the Vampire Baroness. Modern Fiction, 1945 ss
The Mummy Comes to Life. Modern Fiction, 1946 ss
The Satanic Power. Van Der Elst Press, 1945 ss
The Secret Power. Van Der Elst Press, 1945 ss
The Strange Doctor and other mystic stories. Van Der Elst Press, 1945 ss
The Torture Chamber and other stories. Doge, 1937 ss

VANDERGRIFF, AOLA
The Bell Tower of Wyndspelle. Warner, 1975
House of the Dancing Dead. Warner, 1974
Sisters of Sorrow. Warner, 1974
Wyndspelle. Warner, 1975

VANDERPUIJE, NII AKRAMPAHENE. 1925- .
The Counterfeit Corpse. Comet, 1956

VANDERVEER, STEWART
Death for the Lady. Phoenix, 1939

VAN DER ZEE, JOHN. 1936- .
Blood Brotherhood. Harcourt, 1970

VAN DEUSEN, DELIA
The Garden Club Murders. Bobbs, 1941; Selwyn, 1943
Many a Murder; see Murder Bicarb
Murder Bicarb. Bobbs, 1940; Selwyn, 1943. Also published as: Many a Murder. Croydon (abridged), 1944

VAN DEVENTER, EMMA MURDOCH. Pseudonym: Lawrence L. Lynch, q.v.

VAN DE WATER, FREDERIC F(RANKLYN). 1890-1968. Series character: John Tarleton = JT.
Alibi. Doubleday, 1930

The Eye of Lucifer. Appleton, 1927
Havoc. Doubleday, 1931; Skeffington, 1931
Hidden Ways. Bobbs, 1935; Jenkins, 1937
Horsemen of the Law. Appleton, 1926 ss
Hurrying Feet. Appleton, 1928
Plunder. Doubleday, 1933 JT
Still Waters. Doubleday, 1929; Skeffington, 1932 JT

VAN DE WETERING, JANWILLEM. 1931- .
Outsider in Amsterdam. Houghton, 1975; Heinemann, 1976

VAN DINE, S. S. Pseudonym of Willard Huntington Wright, 1888-1939. Series character: Philo Vance, in all titles.
The Benson Murder Case. Scribner, 1926; Benn, 1926
The Bishop Murder Case. Scribner, 1929; Cassell, 1929
The Canary Murder Case. Scribner, 1927; Benn, 1927
The Casino Murder Case. Scribner, 1934; Cassell, 1934
The Dragon Murder Case. Scribner, 1933; Cassell, 1934
The Garden Murder Case. Scribner, 1935; Cassell, 1935
The Gracie Allen Murder Case. Scribner, 1938; Cassell, 1938. Also published as: The Smell of Murder. Bantam, 1950
The Greene Murder Case. Scribner, 1928; Benn, 1928
The Kennel Murder Case. Scribner, 1933; Cassell, 1933
The Kidnap Murder Case. Scribner, 1936; Cassell, 1936
The Scarab Murder Case. Scribner, 1930; Cassell, 1930
The Smell of Murder; see The Gracie Allen Murder Case
The Winter Murder Case. Scribner, 1939; Cassell, 1939

VAN DYCKE, TOM and BEN KERNER
Not with my Neck. Messner, 1947

VAN DYKE, HENRY. 1928- .
-Blood of Strawberries. Farrar, 1969
Dead Piano. Farrar, 1971

VAN DYKE, JULIUS. Pseudonym of Frederick Anthony Edwards, 1896- . Other pseudonym: Charman Edwards, q.v.
The Black Market Murders. Fore, 1945

VANE, DEREK. Pseudonym of Mrs. B. Eaton-Back.
Dancer's End. Eldon, 1934
The Ferrybridge Mystery. Moffat, 1920. (British title?)
£500 Reward. Eldon, 1933
Intrigue and Matrimony. Hurst, 1928
-Lady Varley. Paul, 1914
The Mystery of the Moat House. Cosmopolitan (London), 1901
-The Paradise of Fools. Everett, 1913
The Scar. Bles, 1924; Clode, 1925
The Secret Door. Everett, 1907
The Sign of the Snake. Hurst, 1927; Macrae Smith, 1928
-The Sin and the Woman. Remington, 1893
-The Soul of a Man. Holden, 1913
-The Three Daughters of Night. Hutchinson, 1897
The Trump Card. Hurst, 1925
-The Unguarded Hour. Thomson, 1929
-What Fools Women Are! Nash, 1928
The White Panthers. Nash, 1930; Macmillan, 1930
Who Goes There? Eldon, 1933

VANE, NIGEL. Series characters: Li-Sin = L; Philip Quest, in at least those marked PQ.
The Devil's Dozen. Modern, 1935
The Menace of Li-Sin. Modern, 193? L
The Midnight Men. Smith, 1936
The Vanishing Death. Modern, 193? PQ
The Veils of Death. Modern, 1935 PQ
The Vengeance of Li-Sin. Modern, 1935 L

VANE, PHILIPPA. Pseudonym of Phyllis Mac-Vean, 1892-   . Other pseudonym: Phyllis Hambledon, q.v.
Here is the Evidence. Hammond, 1950
Priority for Death. Hammond, 1948

VANGE, NORMAN
A Spy in Damascus. Low, 1940

VAN GREENAWAY, PETER. 1929-   .
Doppelganger. Gollancz, 1975
Judas! Gollancz, 1972. U.S. title: The Judas Gospel. Atheneum, 1972
The Judas Gospel; see Judas!
The Man Who Held the Queen to Ransom and Sent Parliament Packing. Weidenfeld, 1968; Atheneum, 1969
The Medusa Touch. Gollancz, 1973; Stein, 1973
-Take the War to Washington. Gollancz, 1974; St. Martin's, 1975

VAN GULIK, ROBERT (HANS). 1910-1967. Series character: Judge Dee, in all titles.
The Chinese Bell Murders. Joseph, 1958; Harper, 1959. (3 novelets.)
The Chinese Gold Murders. Joseph, 1959; Harper, 1961. (3 novelets.)
The Chinese Lake Murders. Joseph, 1960; Harper, 1960. (3 novelets.)
The Chinese Maze Murders. Joseph, 1962. (3 novelets.)
The Chinese Nail Murders. Joseph, 1961; Harper, 1962. (3 novelets.)
Dee Goong An (translated by Robert Van Gulik). [Author], 1949; Arno, 1976. (3 novelets.)
The Emperor's Pearl. Heinemann, 1963; Scribner, 1964. (3 novelets.)
The Fox-Magic Murders; see Poets and Murder
The Haunted Monastery. Heinemann, 1963; Scribner, 1969. (3 novelets.)
Judge Dee at Work. Heinemann, 1967; Scribner, 1973 ss
The Lacquer Screen. Heinemann, 1964; Scribner, 1970. (3 novelets.)
The Monkey and the Tiger. Heinemann, 1965; Scribner, 1966. (2 novelets.)
Murder in Canton. Heinemann, 1966; Scribner, 1967
Necklace and Calabash. Heinemann, 1967; Scribner, 1971
New Year's Eve in Lan-Fang. (Beirut), 1958. (32 pp.)
The Phantom of the Temple. Heinemann, 1966; Scribner, 1966
Poets and Murder. Heinemann, 1968; Scribner, 1972. Also published as: The Fox-Magic Murders. Panther, 1973
The Red Pavilion. Heinemann, 1964; Scribner, 1968. (3 novelets.)
The Willow Pattern. Heinemann, 1965; Scribner, 1965. (3 novelets.)

VAN HAZINGA, CYNTHIA
Ghost River Inn. Popular Library, 1973
The House on Gannet's Point. Popular Library, 1974

VAN HEARN, J.
Don't Betray Me. Belmont, 1962

VAN HORN, CHARLES
The Quest of Krang. Hutchinson, 1938

VAN LHIN, ERIK. Pseudonym of Lester del Rey, 1915-   .
Police Your Planet. Avalon, 1956

VAN LOON, MRS. ELIZABETH
The Mystery of Allanwold. Peterson, 1880
The Shadow of Hampton Mead. Peterson, 1878
-Under the Willows; or, The Three Countesses. Peterson, 1879

VAN ORSDELL, JOHN
Ragland. World, 1972

VAN RAALTE, JOSEPH
The Vice Squad. Vanguard, 1931
The Walls are High. Vanguard, 1931

VAN RENSBURG, HELEN and LOUWRENS
Death in a Dark Pool. Joseph, 1954
The Man with Two Ties. Joseph, 1955

VAN RENSBURG, LOUWRENS. See: HELEN VAN RENSBURG.

VAN SICKLE, V. A. Pseudonym of Arthur Hawthorne Carhart, 1892-   .
The Wrong Body. Knopf, 1937

VAN SILLER, HILDA. Pseudonym: Van Siller, q.v.

VAN URK, VIRGINIA (NELLIS). Series character: Tom Craig, in both titles.
Grounds for Murder. Arcadia, 1958
Speaking of Murder. Phoenix, 1951

VAN VOGT, A(LFRED) E(LTON). 1912-   .
The House That Stood Still. Greenberg, 1950. Revised edition: The Mating Cry. Beacon, 1960

VAN ZANDT, EDMUND. Pseudonym of Tom Pendleton, q.v.

VAN ZILE, EDWARD S(IMS). 1863-1931.
Defending the Bank. Lothrop, 1903
-Kings in Adversity. Neely, 1897
The Last of the Van Slacks. Neely, 1894

VAN ZYL, P. R.
The Prosecutor. Putnam, 1974

VARDRE, LESLIE. Pseudonym of L(eslie) P(urnell) Davies, 1914-   , q.v.
A Grave Matter (as by L. P. Davies); see The Nameless Ones
The Nameless Ones. Long, 1967. U.S. title: A Grave Matter, as by L. P. Davies. Doubleday, 1968
The Reluctant Medium (as by L. P. Davies); see Tell It to the Dead
Tell It to the Dead. Long, 1966. U.S. title: The Reluctant Medium, as by L. P. Davies. Doubleday, 1967

VARLEY, HENRY
The R.O.F. Murders. Mitre, 1945

VARNADO, DONALD (ROBERT)
Washington Woman. Vantage, 1956

VARNAM, JOHN
Beware of the Dog. Hodder, 1954
Death Rehearses. Hodder, 1950
Travelling Deadman. Hodder, 1951

VARNEY, GEORGE
The Bungalow of Dead Birds. Nelson, 1929
The Missing Link. Jarrolds, 1927

VASE, GILLAN. Pseudonym of Elizabeth Newton.
A Great Mystery Solved. Remington, 1878; McBride, 1914

VAUGHAN, JULIAN
Jamo and the Bent Playboy. Hale, 1973

VAUGHAN, ROBERT. 1937-   .
The Valkyrie Mandate. Simon, 1974; New English Library, 1975

VAUGHN, JASON
Trailer Park. Vantage, 1975

VEDDER, JOHN K. Pseudonym of Frank Gruber, 1904-1969, q.v. Other pseudonyms: Stephen Acre, Charles K. Boston, qq.v.
The Last Doorbell. Holt, 1941. Also published as: Kiss the Boss Goodbye, as by Frank Gruber. Mercury, 1954

VEIGA, JOSE J(ACINTO DA). 1915-   .
The Three Trials of Manirema. Knopf, 1970. (Translation of A Hora dos Ruminentes. Rio de Janeiro, 1969.)

VEILLER, BAYARD. 1869-1943. See also: Marvin Dana, 1867-   .
Bait for a Tiger. Reynal, 1941
The Thirteenth Chair. French, 1922. (3-act play.)
The Trial of Mary Dugan. French, 1928. (3-act play.)
Within the Law. Fly, 1913. Also as a 4-act play: French, 1917

VEITCH, JAMES
Crime and the Curator. Fiction House, 1946
Wait for Death. Blackfriars, 1944

VENABLES, TERRY. See: GORDON M(acLEAN) WILLIAMS, 1934-   . Joint pseudonym with Gordon M(acLean) Williams: P. B. Yuill, q.v.

VENNING, MICHAEL. Pseudonym of Craig Rice, 1908-1957, q.v. Other pseudonym: Daphne Sanders, q.v. See also: GYPSY ROSE LEE; (CHARLES) STUART PALMER, 1905-1968. Series character: Melville Fairr, in all titles.
Jethro Hammer. Coward, 1944; Nicholson, 1947
The Man Who Slept All Day. Coward, 1942
Murder Through the Looking Glass. Coward, 1943; Nicholson, 1947

VERALDI, GABRIEL. 1926-   .
Spies of Good Intent. Atheneum, 1969; Deutsch, 1969. (Translation of Les Espions de Bonne Volonte. Paris, 1969.)

VERCORS. Pseudonym of Jean Marcel Bruller, 1902-   , q.v.
You Shall Know Them. Little, 1953. British title: Borderline. Macmillan (London), 1954. Also published as: The Murder of the Missing Link. PB, 1955. (Translation of Les Animaux Denatures. Paris, 1952.)

VERMANDEL, JANET GREGORY
The Claverse Affair. Dodd, 1974; Milton House, 1975
Dine with the Devil. Dodd, 1970; Hale, 1972
Last Seen in Samarra. Dodd, 1972; Milton House, 1975

416/ Vermandel, Janet Gregory

Murder Most Fair; see So Long at the Fair
Of Midnight Honor. Dodd, 1972
Scratch a Lover. Dodd, 1969; Hale, 1970
So Long at the Fair. Dodd, 1968. British title: Murder Most Fair. Jenkins, 1968

VERN, DAVID. 1924-   . Pseudonym: David V. Reed, q.v.

VERNEDE, R(OBERT) E(RNEST). 1875-1917.
The Flight of Faviel; see The Pursuit of Mr. Faviel
The Port Allington Stories and others. Heinemann, 1921. U.S. title: Port Allington Stories. Doran, 1920 ss
The Pursuit of Mr. Faviel. Rivers, 1905. U.S. title (somewhat revised): The Flight of Faviel. Holt, 1912

VERNER, GERALD. Pseudonym of Donald Stuart, 1897-   , q.v. Series characters: Sexton Blake (with many other authors), in those titles given without publisher (which was Amalgamated Press); Supt. Robert Budd, in at least those marked RB; Trevor Lowe, in at least those marked TL; Simon Gale, in at least those marked SG; Peter Chard, in at least those marked PC; Felix Heron, in at least those marked FH; Michael Dene, in at least those marked MD.
Alias the Ghost. Wright, 1933
The Angel. Wright, 1939
The Black Hunchback. Wright, 1933
Black Skull. Wright, 1933
The Black Skull. 1929
The Box of Doom. 1928
The Case of Mr. Budd; see The Cleverness of Mr. Budd
The Cleverness of Mr. Budd. Wright, 1935. U.S. title: The Case of Mr. Budd. Macaulay, 1938 RB (3 novelets.)
The Clue of the Green Candle. Wright, 1938 TL
The Clue of the Second Tooth. 1927
The Con Man. Wright, 1934
The Coupon Crimes. Mellifont, 1946
The Crime of Four. 1930
The Crimson Ramblers. Wright, 1960. (Novelization of the TV play.)
The Crooked Circle. Wright, 1935; Macaulay, 1937 RB
Dead Secret. Wright, 1967 FH
The Death Play. Wright, 1933
Death Set in Diamonds. Wright, 1965 TL
Dene of the Secret Service. Wright, 1941 MD, TL
The Embankment Murder. Wright, 1933
The Faceless Ones. Wright, 1964
The Fatal Manuscript. 1929
The Football Pool Murders. Wright, 1939 RB
The Frightened Man. Wright, 1937
Ghost House. Wright, 1961
The Ghost Man. Wright, 1936; Macaulay, 1936
The Ghost Squad. Wright, 1963
The Glass Arrow. Wright, 1937 TL
Green Mask. Wright, 1934 RB
Grim Death. Wright, 1960
The Grim Joker. Wright, 1936 RB
The Hand of Fear. Wright, 1936
The Hangman. Wright, 1934; Godwin, 1935 TL
The Heel of Achilles. Wright, 1945 MD
The Huntsman. Wright, 1940
I am Death. Wright, 1963

The Jockey. Wright, 1937 RB
The Lady of Doom. Wright, 1934 TL
The Last Warning. Wright, 1962 RB
Meet Mr. Callaghan. French (London), 1953. (Play based on The Urgent Hangman by Peter Cheyney, 1896-1951, q.v.)
Mister Big. Wright, 1966 RB
Mr. Budd Again. Wright, 1939 RB
Mr. Budd Investigates. Wright, 1940 RB (3 novelets.)
Mr. Midnight. Wright, 1933 RB
Mr. Whipple Explains. Wright, 1936. (3 novelets.)
The Moor House Murders. Wright, 1964
Murder in Manuscript. Wright, 1963 RB
The Mystery of Sherwood Towers. 1928. Reprinted in 1940 as by Donald Stuart
The Mystery of the Phantom Blackmailer. 1928
The Next to Die. Wright, 1934 TL
Noose for a Lady. Wright, 1952 SG
The Nursery Rhyme Murders. Wright, 1960 RB
Phantom Hollow. Wright, 1933 TL
The Poisoner. Wright, 1940
The "Q" Squad. Wright, 1935; Macaulay, 1938
Queer Face. Wright, 1935
The Red Tape Murders. Wright, 1962 RB
The Return of Mr. Budd. Wright, 1938 RB
The Riddle of the Phantom Plague. 1928
The River House Mystery. Wright, 1938 TL
The River Men. Wright, 1936
The Royal Flush Murders. Wright, 1948 RB
The Secret of the Vault. 1930
The Seven Clues. Wright, 1936 MD
The Seven Lamps. Wright, 1947 RB
The Shadow Men. Wright, 1961 TL
The Show Must Go On. Wright, 1950. (Novelization of the radio play.)
The Silent Slayer. 1929
The Silver Horseshoe. Wright, 1935 RB
Sinister House. Wright, 1934 RB (Three novelets.)
Six Men Died. Wright, 1964 RB
Sorcerer's House. Hutchinson, 1956 SG
The Squealer. Wright, 1934
Terror Tower. Wright, 1935 TL
They Walk in Darkness. Wright, 1947 PC
The Third Key. Wright, 1961
Thirsty Evil. Westhouse, 1945 PC
The Three Gnomes. Wright, 1937 TL
The Tipster. Wright, 1949 RB
The Token. Wright, 1937 TL
Towards Zero. French (London), 1957; Dramatists Play Service, 1957. (Play based on the novel by Agatha Christie, 1890-1976, q.v.)
The Tudor Garden Mystery. Wright, 1966 FH
The Twelve Apostles. Wright, 1946 RB
The Vampire Man. Wright, 1941
The Watcher. Wright, 1936 TL
The Whispering Woman. Wright, 1949 RB
White Wig. Wright, 1935
The Witches' Moon. Wright, 1938 RB

VERNEY, F(RANK) E(DWIN)
The Man with the Black Patch. Hutchinson, 1931

VERNON, HARRY M. 1878-   . See: LOUISE JORDAN MILN, 1864-1933.

Bibliography of Crime Fiction

VERNON-HARCOURT, F. C. 1845-   . See: F(rederick) C. Vernon Harcourt.

VERRON, ROBERT
The Country Club Murder. Wright, 1948
The Curse at Craig's End. Wright, 1953
The Day of the Dust. Wright, 1964
Death Waits Outside. Wright, 1953
The Fifth Must Die! Wright, 1949
Freak Island Murders. Wright, 1947
Moon Killer. Wright, 1962
Murder Calls the Tune. Wright, 1958
Murder Indicted. Wright, 1957
Murder Lands the Odds. Wright, 1963
Murder Lifts the Veil. Wright, 1955
Murder Most Black. Wright, 1954
Murder Most Monstrous. Wright, 1958
Murder of No Consequence. Wright, 1960
Murder on Demand. Wright, 1961
Murder Points East. Wright, 1956
Murder with Impatience. Wright, 1944
Party to Murder. Wright, 1960
Return a Gain for Murder. Wright, 1961
Right Turn for Murder. Wright, 1952

VESEY, ARTHUR H(ENRY). 1869-   . Byline also: Arthur Henry Veysey, q.v.
The Castle of Lies. Appleton, 1906
The Clock and the Key. Appleton, 1905; Sidney Appleton, 1905

VESTAL, STANLEY. Pseudonym of Walter Stanley Campbell, 1887-   .
The Wine Room Murder. Little, 1935

VEXIN, NOEL
Murder on Montmartre. Dell, 1960

VEYSEY, ARTHUR HENRY. 1869-   . Byline also: Arthur H(enry) Vesey, q.v.
A Cheque for Three Thousand. Dillingham, 1897; Arrowsmith, 1905, as by Arthur Henry Vesey
-Hats Off! Dillingham, 1899
-A Pedigree in Pawn. Dillingham, 1898
The Stateroom Opposite. Dillingham, 1900
-The Two White Elephants. Dillingham, 1899

VICARY, JEAN
Castle at Glencarris. Avon, 1972
The Ice Maiden. Avon, 1972
Saverstall. Ace, 1967

VICAS, VICTOR and VICTOR HAIM
The Impromptu Impostor. Abelard, 1971. (Translation of L'Inconnu de la Mer Mort. Paris, 1969.)

VICKERS, RALPH
The Confrontation. Hale, 1970
Enticement to Danger. Hale, 1969

VICKERS, ROY. 1888-1965. Pseudonyms: David Durham, Sefton Kyle, John Spencer, qq.v. Series characters: Insp. Rason, in at least those marked R (see also David Durham and Sefton Kyle); Department of Dead Ends, in at least those marked DDE; Hugh Stanton, in at least those marked HS.
Bardelow's Heir. Jenkins, 1933 R
Best Detective Stories of Roy Vickers. Faber, 1965 ss R DDE
Brenda Gets Married. Jenkins, 1941
A Date with Danger. Jenkins, 1942; Vanguard, 1944
The Department of Dead Ends. Bestseller, 1947 ss R DDE
The Department of Dead Ends. Faber, 1949; Detective Book Club, 1949. (A different collection from the above.) ss R DDE

The Deputy for Cain. Jenkins, 1931
Double Image and other stories. Jenkins, 1955; Detective Book Club, 1955 ss
Eight Murders in the Suburbs. Jenkins, 1954. U.S. title: Six Murders in the Suburbs. Detective Book Club, 1958. (Two stories omitted from the U.S. edition.)
The Enemy Within. Jenkins, 1938
Find the Innocent. Jenkins, 1959
Four Past Four. Jenkins, 1925; Jefferson House, 1945
The Girl in the News. Jenkins, 1937
A Girl of These Days. Jenkins, 1929
Gold and Wine. Jenkins, 1949; Walker, 1961 HS
The Gold Game. Jenkins, 1930
Hide Those Diamonds! Newnes, 1935
His Other Wife. Jenkins, 1926
I'll Never Tell. Jenkins, 1937
Ishmael's Wife. Jenkins, 1924
Kidnap Island. Newnes, 1935 R
The Life Between. Jenkins, 1938
Maid to Murder; see Murdering Mr. Velfrage
The Man in the Red Mask. Newnes, 1935
The Marriage for the Defence. Jenkins, 1932
Money Buys Everything. Jenkins, 1934 R
A Murder for a Million. Jenkins, 1924
Murder in Two Flats. Jenkins, 1951; Mill, 1952 HS
Murder of a Snob. Jenkins, 1949; British Book Centre, 1958
Murder Will Out. Faber, 1950; Detective Book Club, 1954 ss R DDE
Murdering Mr. Velfrage. Faber, 1950. U.S. title: Maid to Murder. Mill, 1950
The Mystery of the Scented Death. Jenkins, 1922 R
Playgirl Wanted. Jenkins, 1940
The Radingham Mystery. Jenkins, 1928
The Rose in the Dark. Jenkins, 1930
Seven Chose Murder. Jenkins, 1959; Detective Book Club, 1959 ss R DDE
She Walked in Fear. Jenkins, 1940 R
Six Came to Dinner. Jenkins, 1948 HS
Six Murders in the Suburbs; see Eight Murders in the Suburbs
The Sole Survivor and The Kynsard Affair. Gollancz, 1952; Detective Book Club, 1951. (Two novelets.)
Terror of Tongues. Jenkins, 1937 R
They Can't Hang Caroline. Jenkins, 1950 HS
The Unforbidden Sin. Jenkins, 1926
The Vengeance of Henry Jarroman. Jenkins, 1923
War Bride. Jenkins, 1942
The White Raven. Jenkins, 1927

VICKERY, WILLIAM P(AUL)
The Racketeer's Will. Amalgamated, 1932. (Sexton Blake.)

VICTOR, H(AROLD) L(AUDER). 1897- .
Deceptions. Paul, 1935
Fate and Four Sinners. Paul, 1934
Murder in Duplicate. Low, 1935

VICTOR, MRS. M(ETTA) V(ICTORIA FULLER). 1831-1886. Pseudonym: Seeley Regester, q.v.
-Born to Betray; or, A Game Well Played. Street, 1890; Aldine, 1895
-The Brown Princess. Street, 1888
Dora Elmyr's Worst Enemy; or, Guilty, or Not Guilty. Street, 1878. Also published as: Guilty or Not Guilty; or, Dora Elmyr's Worst Enemy. Street, 1890
-The Gay Captain. Street, 1891; Aldine, 1896
Guilty or Not Guilty; see Dora Elmyr's Worst Enemy
-The Phantom Wife. Street, 1888
-Who Owned the Jewels? or, The Heiress of the Sandalwood Chest. Street, 1891
-Who was He? Beadle, 1866

VIDAL, EUGENE GORE. 1925- . Pseudonym: Edgar Box, q.v.

VIDOCQ, (EUGENE FRANCOIS). 1775-1857.
Memoirs of Vidocq. Carey & Hart, 18??; Hunt and Clarke, 18??. Also published as: Vidocq, the Police Spy. Routledge, 1866. (Translation of Memoires de Vidocq. Paris, 1828-9.) ss

VIELE, HERMAN KNICKERBOCKER. 1856-1908.
On the Lightship. Duffield, 1909 ss, some criminous

VIGILANT. Pseudonym. Series character: Barry Link (Lynx), in at least those marked BL.
Fighting the Red Shadow. Hamilton, 1932
Lynx, Counter Spy. Hamilton, 1937 BL
Lynx, Spyflyer. Hamilton, 1936 BL
Lynx, V.C. Hamilton, 1936 BL
Lynx, V.C., Flies Again. Crowther, 1944 BL

VIGNANT, JEAN FRANCOIS
The Alpine Affair. Chelsea, 1970. (Translation of Meurtre a l'Alpe d'Heuz. Paris, 1968.)

VILLER, FREDRIK. Pseudonym of Christian Sparre, 1859- .
The Black Tortoise. Doubleday, 1901; Heinemann, 1901

VILLIERS, DAVID HUGH. Pseudonym: David Buckingham, q.v.

VINCE, HENRY SCOTT
Two Pardons. Ward, 1889

VINCENT, CLAIRE
Garden of Satan. Lancer, 1970
Spellbound. Tower, 1966
Unholy Spell. Belmont, 1972

VINCENT, DWIGHT. See: DAY KEENE.

VINCENT, LADY KITTY (EDITH BLANCHE). 1887- . Series character: Gyp Kidnadze, in at least those marked GK.
"No. 3." Jenkins, 1924 GK
The Ruby Cup. Jenkins, 1928 GK
These Within. Jenkins, 1943
An Untold Tale. Jenkins, 1934 GK

VINCENT, (A.) LOUIS. 1876- .
Youth at Bay. Hutchinson, 1934

VINCENT, RICHARD
Portrait in Black. Bantam, 1960. (Novelization of the movie.)

VINING, KEITH
Too Hot for Hell. Ace, 1952

VINN, WALGER
Suddenly He Knew. Greenwich, 1957

VINTER, MICHAEL. 1927- .
All This Shall Perish. Hale, 1970
Colour of Dried Blood. Hale, 1967
Die Here a Stranger. Hale, 1968
A Place of Execution. Hale, 1969
Rat in a Trap. Hale, 1971
A Vintage So Evil. Hale, 1968
The Wounds of Treason. Hale, 1972

VINTON, ALDIN. Pseudonym of Adelin Sumner Briggs Linton, 1899- .

Mystery in Green. Phoenix, 1937. Also published as: Corpse in the Cab. Hangman's House, 1942

VINTON, ARTHUR DUDLEY. 1852-1906.
The Pomfret Mystery. Ogilvie, 1886
The Unpardonable Sin. Ogilvie, 1889

VIPOND, DON (HARRY). 1932- .
Night of the Shooting Star. Bobbs, 1975

VIRDEN, KATHARINE
The Crooked Eye. Doubleday, 1930; Chapman, 1930
The Thing in the Night. Doubleday, 1930

VISIAK, E(DWARD) H(AROLD). 1878- .
Medusa. Gollancz, 1929

VIVIAN, E(VELYN) CHARLES (H.). 1882-1947. Pseudonyms: Charles Cannell, Jack Mann, qq.v. Series character: Inspector Head, in at least those marked H.
Accessory After. Ward, 1934 H
And Then There were None. Ward, 1941
Arrested. Hale, 1949
The Barking Dog Murder Case; see Tramp's Evidence
The Capsule Mystery. Ward, 1935
Cigar for Inspector Head. Ward, 1935 H
Curses Come Home. Hale, 1942
Dangerous Guide. Hale, 1943
Delicate Fiend. Ward, 1930
Double or Quit. Ward, 1930
Evidence in Blue. Ward, 1938. U.S. title: The Man in Gray. Hillman-Curl, 1938 H
False Truth. Ward, 1932
Following Feet. Melrose, 1911
The Forbidden Door. Ward, 1927
Girl in the Dark. Ward, 1933
House for Sale. Amalgamated, 1934
The Impossible Crime. Ward, 1940
Infamous Fame. Ward, 1932
Innocent Guilt. Ward, 1931
Jewels Go Back. Ward, 1934
The Keys of the Flat. Ward, 1933
Ladies in the Case. Ward, 1933
-Lone Isle. Ward, 1932
Man Alone. Ward, 1928
The Man in Gray; see Evidence in Blue
The Man with a Scar. Ward, 1940
Nine Days. Ward, 1928
One Tropic Night. Ward, 1930
Other Gods. Hale, 1945
Problem by Rail. Ward, 1939 H
The Rainbow Puzzle. Ward, 1938 H
Samson. Hale, 1944
Seventeen Cards. Ward, 1935 H
Shadow on the House. Ward, 1934 H
She Who Will Not—. Hale, 1945
The Tale of Fleur. Ward, 1929
.38 Automatic. Ward, 1937 H
Touch and Go. Ward, 1939 H
Tramp's Evidence. Ward, 1937. U.S. title: The Barking Dog Murder Case. Hillman-Curl, 1937 H
Unwashed Gods. Ward, 1931
Vain Escape. Hale, 1952
Who Killed Gatton? Ward, 1936 H
With Intent to Kill. Ward, 1936 H

VIVIAN, FRANCIS. Pseudonym of Arthur Ernest Ashley, 1906- . Series character: Supt. Gordon Knollis, in at least those marked GK; Insp. John Burnell, in at least those marked JB.
The Arrow of Death. Jenkins, 1938
Black Alibi. Jenkins, 1938 JB
Dark Moon. Jenkins, 1939
Darkling Death. Jenkins, 1956; Roy, 1957 GK
Dead Opposite the Church. Jenkins, 1959
Death at the Salutation. Jenkins, 1937 JB

The Death of Mr. Lomas. Jenkins, 1941
  GK
The Elusive Bowman. Hodder, 1951
The Frog was Yellow. Jenkins, 1940
The Ladies of Locksley. Jenkins, 1953;
  Roy, 1957 GK
The Laughing Dog. Hodder, 1949
Murder in Angel Yard. Fiction House,
  1946
The Ninth Enemy. Hodder, 1948 GK
Sable Messenger. Jenkins, 1947 GK
The Singing Masons. Hodder, 1950
The Sleeping Island. Hodder, 1951
The Three Short Men. Jenkins, 1939 GK
The Threefold Cord. Jenkins, 1947 GK

VLASTO, JOHN ALEXANDER. 1877-1958. Pseudonyms: John Alexander, John Remenham, qq.v.

VOELKER, JOHN DONALDSON. 1903-   . Pseudonym: Robert Traver, q.v.

VOGAN, ARTHUR JAMES
  The Black Police. Hutchinson, 1891

VOGEL, HARRY B(ENJAMIN)
  -Gentleman Garnet. Smith, 1902
  -The Tragedy of a Flirtation. Greening, 1909
  Two Million. Unwin, 1925

VOLK, GORDON. 1885-   . Pseudonym: Raymond Knotts, q.v.
  And the Deep Blue Sea. Paul, 1944; Farrar, 1944, as by Raymond Knotts
  -Bamboo Bay. Skeffington, 1934
  The Cliff Mill Mystery. Skeffington, 19
  Cliffs of Sark. Skeffington, 1936
  -Cornish Cruise. Paul, 1947
  -The Devil's Whirlpool. Skeffington, 1928
  -Fifty-Fifty. Skeffington, 1935
  -Galleon Rock. Hale, 1939
  -Gold Out of China. Paul, 1946
  -The Green Ship. Skeffington, 1931
  -In Brighton Waters. Skeffington, 1936
  -Island Schooner. Paul, 1950
  -The Isle of Men. Skeffington, 1932
  The Lighthouse Mystery. Skeffington, 1930
  -The Lobster Pot. Paul, 1949
  -The Lonely Shore. Skeffington, 1937
  -The "Maid of Sussex". Paul, 1948
  -The Sea Case. Skeffington, 1929
  -South of the Line. Skeffington, 1934
  -Thunder Island. Skeffington, 1933
  -The Tideless Sea. Skeffington, 1932
  -The Zoo Ship. Skeffington, 1938

VOLTAIRE, (FRANCOIS MARIE AROUET DE). 1694-1778.
  Zadig; or, The Book of Fate. Brindley (London), 1749

VON BLOCK, BELA
  The World Rapers. Hart-Davis, 1974

VON DEGAN. Pseudonym of Baroness Ann Crawford von Rabe, 1846-
  The Mystery of the Campagna, and A Shadow on a Wave. Cassell, 1891; Unwin, 1891

VON DODERER, HEIMITO. 1896-1966.
  Every Man a Murderer. Knopf, 1964. (Translation of Ein Mord den Jeder Begeht. Munich, 1938.)

VON ELSNER, DON (BYRON). 1909-   .
  Series characters: David Danning = DD; Jake Winkman = JW.
  The Ace of Spies. Award, 1966; Tandem, 1968 JW
  A Bullet for Your Dreams. Lancer, 1968 DD
  Countdown for a Spy. Signet, 1966 DD

Don't Just Stand There, Do Someone. Signet, 1962 DD
How to Succeed at Murder Without Really Trying. Signet, 1963. Also published as: The Jake of Diamonds. Award, 1967; Tandem, 1967 JW
The Jack of Hearts. Award, 1968 JW
The Jake of Diamonds; see How to Succeed at Murder Without Really Trying
Just Not Making Mayhem Like They Used To. Signet, 1961 DD
Pour a Swindle Through a Loophole. Belmont, 1964 DD
Those Who Prey Together Slay Together. Signet, 1961; New English Library pb, 1962 DD
Who Says a Corpse has to be Dull. Signet, 1963 DD
You Can't Do Business with Murder. Signet, 1962 DD

VON HARBOU, THEA. 1888-   .
  The Spy. Readers Library, 1928. U.S. title: Spies. Putnam, 1928. (Translation of Spione. Berlin, 1928.)

VON HINDEBURG, AGNES BLANCHE MARIE. 1873-   . Pseudonym: Marie Hay, q.v.

VON HUTTEN, BARONESS [BETTINA RIDDLE FREIFRAU VON HUTTEN ZUM STOLZENBERG]. 1874-   .
  Cowardly Custard. Hutchinson, 1936. U.S. title: Gentleman's Agreement. Dutton, 1936
  Die She Must. Hutchinson, 1934; Dutton, 1936
  -The Elgin Marble. Hutchinson, 1937. U.S. title: Youth Without Glory. Dutton, 1938
  Gentleman's Agreement; see Cowardly Custard
  Monkey-Puzzle. Long, 1932
  What Happened is This. Hutchinson, 1938; Dutton, 1939
  Youth Without Glory; see The Elgin Marble

VON LINSINGEN, F(REDERICK) W(ILLIAM) B(ERRY). 1901-   .
  The Pressure-Gauge Murder. Methuen, 1929; Dutton, 1930

VONNEGUT, KURT, JR. 1922-   .
  Mother Night. GM, 1961; Cape, 1968

VON RABE, BARONESS ANN CRAWFORD. 1846-   . Pseudonym: Von Degan, q.v.

VON RIMANOCZY, CHARLES ADOLPH. 1906-   . Pseudonym: Charles Eland, q.v.

VOSPER, FRANK. 1899-   .
  Love from a Stranger. Collins, 1936. (3-act play based on the Agatha Christie ss "Philomel Cottage".)
  Murder on the Second Floor. Putnam, 1929. (Play.) Novelization of the play: Readers Library, 1929

VOSPER, G. VENNING
  -The Squire of Landrewn. Paul, 1946
  Who Killed the Chauffeur? Paul, 1941

VOSS BARK, CONRAD. See: BARK, CONRAD VOSS.

VOUTE, EMILE
  The Passport. Kennerley, 1915

VOWELL, DAVID
  The Assassinator. Bantam (New York), 1974; Bantam (London), 1975
  Dragnet 1968. Popular Library, 1967. (Novelization of the TV series.)

VREELAND, (WILLIAM CANTWELL) FRANK (THORPE). 1891-   .
  Dishonored. Grosset, 1931. (Novelization of the movie.)
  June 13. Longmans, 1940. (3-act play, from the movie, The Night of June 13, based on a Vera Caspary story.)

VROOMAN, H(ENRY) WELLINGTON
  Half a Million Insurance; or, Dr. Lauterback's Strange Patient. American News, 1888

VULLIAMY, C(OLWYN) E(DWARD). 1886-   .
  Pseudonym: Anthony Rolls, q.v.
  Body in the Boudoir. Joseph, 1956
  Cakes for Your Birthday. Joseph, 1959; British Book Centre, 1959
  Don Among the Dead Men. Joseph, 1952
  Floral Tribute. Joseph, 1963
  Justice for Judy. Joseph, 1960
  Tea at the Abbey. Joseph, 1961

VULPIUS, C(HRISTIAN) A(UGUST). 1762-1827.
  Rinaldo Rinaldini, Captain of Banditti. Maiden, 1801

W

W. W. Pseudonym of Mrs. Fortune.
  The Detective's Album: Tales of the Australian Police. Clarson (Melbourne), 1871 ss

WADDELL, C. C.
  You're My Man! Queensway, 1936

WADDELL, C(HARLES) C(AREY). 1868-1930. Pseudonym: Charles Carey, q.v.
  The Girl of the Guard Line. Moffat, 1915
  Juror No. 17. Long, 1931
  Midnight to High Noon. Whitman, 1929

WADDELL, E(LEANOR) LEE
  Murder at Drake's Anchorage. Dutton, 1949

WADDELL, MARTIN. Series character: Otley = O.
  -Come Back When I'm Sober. Hodder, 1969
  Otley. Hodder, 1966; Stein, 1966 O
  Otley Forever. Hodder, 1968; Stein, 1968 O
  Otley Pursued. Hodder, 1967; Stein, 1967 O
  Otley Victorious. Hodder, 1969; Stein, 1969 O

WADE, ALAN. Pseudonym of John Holbrook Vance, 1916-   , q.v. Byline also: Jack Vance, q.v. Other pseudonym: Peter Held, q.v.
  Isle of Peril. Mystery House, 1957

WADE, BOB [ROBERT WADE], 1920-   , and BILL MILLER, 1920-1961. Joint pseudonyms: Will Daemer, Whit Masterson, Wade Miller, Dale Wilmer, qq.v. See also: ROBERT WADE, 1920-   .
  Pop Goes the Queen. Farrar, 1947. British title: Murder—Queen High. Allen, 1958, as by Wade Miller

WADE, GARRISON. Pseudonym.
  Alias John Smith. Vantage, 1966

WADE, HARRISON
  So Lovely to Kill. Graphic, 1956

WADE, HENRY. Pseudonym of Henry Lancelot Aubrey-Fletcher, 1887-1969. Series characters: Constable John Bragg = JB; Chief Insp. Poole = P.
  Be Kind to the Killer. Constable, 1952

Bury Him Darkly. Constable, 1936 P
Constable, Guard Thyself! Constable, 1934; Houghton, 1935 P
Diplomat's Folly. Constable, 1951; Macmillan, 1952
The Duke of York's Steps. Constable, 1929; Payson, 1929 P
The Dying Alderman. Constable, 1930; Brewer, 1930
A Dying Fall. Constable, 1955; Macmillan, 1955
Gold was Our Grave. Constable, 1954; Macmillan, 1954 P
The Hanging Captain. Constable, 1932; Harcourt, 1933
Heir Presumptive. Constable, 1935; Macmillan, 1953
Here Comes the Copper. Constable, 1938 JB ss
The High Sheriff. Constable, 1937
The Litmore Snatch. Constable, 1957; Macmillan, 1957
Lonely Magdalen. Constable, 1940. Revised edition: Constable, 1946 P
The Missing Partners. Constable, 1928; Payson, 1928
Mist on the Saltings. Constable, 1933
New Graves at Great Norne. Constable, 1947
No Friendly Drop. Constable, 1931; Brewer, 1932 P
Policeman's Lot. Constable, 1933 P ss
Released for Death. Constable, 1938 JB
Too Soon to Die. Constable, 1953; Macmillan, 1954 P
The Verdict of You All. Constable, 1926; Payson, 1927

WADE, JONATHAN
Back to Life. Collins, 1961; Pantheon, 1962
The Boy with the Sling. Collins, 1965
Running Sand. Collins, 1962; Random, 1963

WADE, KATHLEEN
Act of Violence. Hutchinson, 1954
A Cloak for Malice. Hutchinson, 1949
Crime at Gargoyles. Hutchinson, 1947
The Dark Moment. Hutchinson, 1951
Death at Aranshore. Gifford, 1942
Death on "Calamity". Gifford, 1945

WADE, ROBERT. 1920- . Joint pseudonyms with Bill Miller, 1920-1961: Will Daemer, Whit Masterson, Wade Miller, Dale Wilmer, qq.v. See also: BOB WADE, 1920- .
Knave of Eagles. Random, 1969; Hale, 1970
The Stroke of Seven. Morrow, 1965; Heinemann, 1966

WADELTON, MAGGIE-OWEN
Sarah Mandrake. Paperback Library, 1966

WADHAM, RUTH
Weekend in Baghdad. Gollancz, 1958; Macmillan, 1959

WAER, JACK
Murder in Las Vegas. Avon, 1955
-Sweet and Low-Down. Popular Library, 1955
17 and Black. Viking, 1954

WAGER, WALTER (HERMAN). 1924- . Pseudonyms: Walter Hermann, John Tiger, qq.v.
Sledgehammer. Macmillan, 1970; Hodder, 1971
Swap. Macmillan, 1972; Futura, 1977
Telefon. Macmillan, 1975; Barker, 1975
Viper Three. Macmillan, 1971

WAGNER, CONSTANCE. 1903- .
The Major has Seven Guests. Stokes, 1940; Hale, 1941

WAGNER, ELAINE. 1939- .
A Case of Bottled Murder. Doubleday, 1973

WAGNER, GEOFFREY (ATHELING). 1927- .
-Born of the Sun. Falcon, 1949; Popular Library, 1954
-The Dispossessed. Ward, 1957; Devin-Adair, 1956
-The Lake Lovers. Quadriga, 1962; Macmillan, 1963
The Passionate Land. Ward, 1956; Simon, 1953
The Passionate Strangers. Popular Library, 1964. (British title?)
Season of Assassins. Quadriga, 1961; GM, 1961
-A Summer Stranger. Redman, 1959
Venables. Murray, 1952; Simon, 1952

WAGNER, SHARON (B.). 1936- .
Circle of Evil. Lancer, 1971
Colors of Death. Beagle, 1974
Country of the Wolf. Lancer, 1970
The Cove in Darkness, with Bernard L. Casey. Lancer, 1973
Cry of the Cat. Belmont, 1973
Curse of Still Valley. Lancer, 1969
Dark Side of Paradise. Ballantine, 1975
Dark Waters of Death. Ballantine, 1975
Haitian Legacy. Avon, 1974
Havenhurst. Ballantine, 1975
Legacy of Loneliness. Avon, 1974
Maridu. Lancer, 1971
Moonwind. Lancer, 1972
Satan's Acres. Ace, 1974
Shades of Evil. Beagle, 1974
Shadow of the Sun. Lancer, 1973
The Turquoise Talisman. Ballantine, 1975

WAGONER, DAVID (RUSSELL). 1926- .
The Man in the Middle. Harcourt, 1954; Gollancz, 1955

WAHL, ALBERTA (ELIZABETH) HUGHES. 1904- .
Handsome, But Dead. Howell, 1942; Boardman, 1946

WAHLOO, PER [PETER]. 1926-1975. See also: MAJ SJOWALL. Series character: Chief Insp. Peter Jensen = PJ.
The Assignment. Joseph, 1965; Knopf, 1966. (Translation of Uppdraget. Stockholm, 1963.)
The Generals. Joseph, 1974; Pantheon, 1974. (Translation of Generalerna. Stockholm, 1965.)
The Lorry. Joseph, 1968. U.S. title: A Necessary Action. Pantheon, 1969. (Translation of Lastbilen. Stockholm, 1962.)
Murder on the Thirty-First Floor. Joseph, 1966. U.S. title: The Thirty-First Floor. Knopf, 1967. (Translation of Mord pa 31: a Vaningen. Stockholm, 1966.) PJ
A Necessary Action; see The Lorry
The Steel Spring. Joseph, 1970; Delacorte, 1970. (Translation of Stalspranget. Stockholm, 1968.)
The Thirty-First Floor; see Murder on the Thirty-First Floor

WAINWRIGHT, JOHN (WILLIAM). 1921- .
Pseudonym: Jack Ripley, q.v. Series characters: Chief Insp. Lennox, in at least those marked L; Supt. Gilliant, in at least those marked G; Supt. Charles Ripley, in at least those marked CR.
The Big Tickle. Macmillan (London), 1969
Cause for a Killing. Macmillan (London), 1974

Coppers Don't Cry. Macmillan (London), 1975
The Crystallised Carbon Pig. Collins, 1966; Walker, 1967 G
The Darkening Glass. Collins, 1968
Death in a Sleeping City. Collins, 1965
Death of a Big Man. Macmillan (London), 1975; St. Martin's, 1975 G
The Devil You Don't. Macmillan (London), 1973
Dig the Grave and Let Him Die. Macmillan (London), 1971
Edge of Extinction. Collins, 1968
The Evidence I Shall Give. Macmillan (London), 1974 L
Evil Intent. Collins, 1966 CR
Freeze Thy Blood Less Coldly. Macmillan (London), 1970 L
The Hard Hit. Macmillan (London), 1974; St. Martin's, 1975 CR
High-Class Kill. Macmillan (London), 1973
Kill the Girls and Make Them Cry. Macmillan (London), 1974
Landscape with Violence. Macmillan (London), 1975; St. Martin's, 1976 G
The Last Buccaneer. Macmillan (London), 1971
Night is a Time to Die. Macmillan (London), 1972
A Pride of Pigs. Macmillan (London), 1973
Prynter's Devil. Macmillan (London), 1970
Requiem for a Loser. Macmillan (London), 1972 G
Square Dance. Macmillan (London), 1975; St. Martin's, 1975 L
The Take-Over Man. Collins, 1969
Talent for Murder. Collins, 1967; Walker, 1967
Ten Steps to the Gallows. Collins, 1967
A Touch of Malice. Macmillan (London), 1973 CR
Web of Silence. Collins, 1968
The Worms Must Wait. Collins, 1967 CR

WAINWRIGHT, RICHARD A.
Hunted Down. Street (Magnet)
A Kidnapped Millionaire. Street (Magnet)

WAITT, ISABEL (WOODMAN)
Death a la King. Phoenix, 1943. British title: It's Murder, Miss King. Morris, 1946
It's Murder, Miss King; see Death a la King
Murder at Pirate's Head. Edwards, 1946

WAKE, EDITH
Death and Mrs. Lovely. Wells Gardner, 1947

WAKEFIELD, H(ERBERT) RUSSELL. 1888-1965.
Belt of Suspicion. Collins, 1936
Hearken to the Evidence. Bles, 1933; Doubleday, 1934
Hostess to Death. Collins, 1938
Imagine a Man in a Box. Allan, 1931; Appleton, 1931 ss, at least one criminous

WAKEFIELD, JOHN. 1921- .
Death the Sure Physician. Constable, 1965; Dodd, 1966

WAKEFIELD, R. I. Pseudonym of Gertrude M. White.
You Will Die Today! Dodd, 1953

WAKEVAINEN, CLARA A. Pseudonym: Carol West, q.v.

WALCOTT, EARLE ASHLEY. 1859- .
Blindfolded. Bobbs, 1906
The Open Door. Dodd, 1910

WALDRON, SIMON
Caught in the Middle. Hale, 1972
The Grayson Affair. Hale, 1975
Hot Ice. Hale, 1969
Leap Before You Look. Hale, 1968
Time to Run. Hale, 1968

WALES, HUBERT. Pseudonym of William Piggott.
-Blue Flames. Long, 1918
The Brocklebank Riddle. Century, 1914. British title: The Thirty Days. Cassell, 1915
The Thirty Days; see The Brocklebank Riddle

WALES, KIRK. Pseudonym of James Ronald, 1905- , q.v.

WALK, CHARLES EDMONDS
The Crimson Cross. McClurg, 1913; Cazenove, 1913
The Green Seal. McClurg, 1914
The Paternoster Ruby. McClurg, 1910
The Silver Blade. McClurg, 1908
The Time Lock. McClurg, 1912
The Yellow Circle. McClurg, 1909

WALKER, CHARLES M(AURICE)
Death of a Jazz King. Paul, 1936

WALKER, DAVID (ESDAILE). 1907- .
Diamonds for Danger; see Diamonds for Moscow
Diamonds for Moscow. Chapman, 1953. U.S. title: Diamonds for Danger. Harper, 1954
-The Rigoville Match. Chapman, 1955

WALKER, DAVID (HARRY). 1911- .
Black Dougal. Collins, 1973; Houghton, 1974
CAB-Intersec; see Devil's Plunge
Devil's Plunge. Collins, 1968. U.S. title: CAB-Intersec. Houghton, 1968
Mallabec. Collins, 1965; Houghton, 1965
The Storm and the Silence. Cape, 1950; Houghton, 1949
Winter of Madness. Collins, 1964; Houghton, 1964

WALKER, G. LEITCH. See: R(ICHARD) ANDRE.

WALKER, GERALD. 1928- .
Cruising. Stein, 1970; Allen, 1971

WALKER, GERTRUDE
Diamonds Don't Burn. Jenkins, 1955
So Deadly Fair. Putnam, 1948

WALKER, HARRY. Pseudonym of Hillary (Baldwin) Waugh, 1920- , q.v. Other pseudonym: H. Baldwin Taylor, q.v.
The Case of the Missing Gardener. Arcadia, 1954

WALKER, IRA. Pseudonym of Irma (Ruth Roden) Walker, 1921- , q.v. Series character: Steve Rhoden, in both titles.
The Man in the Driver's Seat. Abelard (New York & London), 1964
Someone's Stolen Nellie Grey. Abelard (New York & London), 1963

WALKER, IRMA (RUTH RODEN). 1921- .
Pseudonym: Ira Walker, q.v.
The Murdoch Legacy. Bobbs, 1975

WALKER, JERRY. Series character: Lawrence Marley, in at least those marked LM.
The Crimson Trail. Cosmos, 1949
A Date with Destiny. Cosmos, 1949 LM
Mission Accomplished. Cosmos, 1947; Mitre, 1948 LM

WALKER, KEITH. 1927- .
The Escape. Vantage, 1970

WALKER, MAX
Code Name: Judas. Popular Library, 1968. (Novelization of the Mission Impossible TV series.)
Code Name: Rapier. Popular Library, 1968. (Novelization of the Mission Impossible TV series.)
The Last Escape. Popular Library, 1970. (Novelization of the movie. Although signed by Walker, this book was in fact written by Michael Avallone, 1924- , q.v.)

WALKER, PETER N(ORMAN). 1936- . Pseudonyms: Christopher Coram, Tom Ferris, qq.v. Series character: Carnaby, in at least those titles containing his name.
Carnaby and the Assassins. Hale, 1968
Carnaby and the Conspirators. Hale, 1969
Carnaby and the Demonstrators. Hale, 1972
Carnaby and the Eliminators. Hale, 1971
Carnaby and the Gaolbreakers. Hale, 1968
Carnaby and the Hijackers. Hale, 1967
Carnaby and the Infiltrators. Hale, 1974
Carnaby and the Saboteurs. Hale, 1970
The Dovingsby Death. Hale, 1975
Fatal Accident. Hale, 1970
Identification Parade. Hale, 1972
Major Incident. Hale, 1974
Panda One Investigates. Hale, 1973
Panda One on Duty. Hale, 1971
Special Duty. Hale, 1971

WALKER, ROWLAND. 1876- . Series character: Deville McKeene, in at least those marked DM.
Captain McBlaid of the Air Police. Partridge, 1932
Covenant with Death. Blackie, 1939
Death Flies High. Low, 1936
Deville McKeene, the British Ace. Partridge, 1919 DM
The Exploits of Capt. McKeene. Aldine, 1926 DM
-The Fifth Form Detective. Partridge, 1924
-The Phantom Airman. Partridge, 1920
-Phantom Island. Ward, 1925
When Spy Meets Spy. Blackie, 1935
The Woman in Whitehall. Low, 1937

WALKER, T. MIKE. 1937- .
Voices from the Bottom of the World. Grove, 1970

WALKER, THOMAS
Felonry of New South Wales. Dymock (Sydney), 1891 ss

WALL, JOHN
Guardian Angel in the Underworld. Vantage, 1958

WALL, WILLIAM
Wake Up Dead. Papillon, 1974

WALLACE, ARTHUR
Passion Pulls the Trigger. Valhalla, 1936

WALLACE, BRYAN EDGAR. 1904- . Series character: Bill Tern = BT.
Death Packs a Suitcase. Hodder, 1961 BT
The Device. Hodder, 1962 BT
The Man Who Would Not Swim. Hodder, 1963
Murder in Touraine. Hodder, 1966
Murder is not Enough. Hodder, 1964
Murder on the Night Ferry. Hodder, 1965

WALLACE, C. H. Pseudonym of Rosaylmer Burger. Joint pseudonym with Julia Perceval: Jessyca Paull, q.v. Series character: Steve Ramsay, in all titles.
Crashlanding in the Congo. Belmont, 1965
E.T.A. for Death. Belmont, 1967
Highflight to Hell. Belmont, 1966
Tailwind to Danger. Belmont, 1966

WALLACE, C. S.
Westbound Murder. Farrar, 1941

WALLACE, CARLTON. Series character: Edmund Bendilow, in at least those marked EB.
Death at No. 47. Mellifont, 1937
Death in the Kettle. Long, 1938 EB
Death of a Libertine. Long, 1936 EB
Death of a Wife. Long, 1938
The Devil Breathes But Once. Long, 1937 EB
Mr. Death; see Mr. Death Walks Abroad
Mr. Death Walks Abroad. Long, 1933. U.S. title: Mr. Death. Doubleday, 1934 EB
Sinister Alibi. Long, 1934; Doubleday, 1934 EB

WALLACE, (RICHARD HORATIO) EDGAR. 1875-1932. See also: Robert (G.) Curtis. Series characters: J. G. Reeder = JR; Four Just Men = JM; Educated Evans = EE; Det. Sgt./Insp. Elk = E; The Ringer = R; Sanders = S (continued in books by Francis Gerard, 1905- , q.v.); Supt. Minter = M; T. B. Smith = TS.
The Admirable Carfew. Ward, 1914 ss, some criminous TS
The Adventures of Heine. Ward, 1919 ss
The African Millionaire. Davis-Poynter, 1972. (A play.)
Again Sanders. Hodder, 1928; Doubleday, 1929 ss S
Again the Ringer. Hodder, 1929. U.S. title: The Ringer Returns. Doubleday, 1931 R
Again the Three; see Again the Three Just Men
Again the Three Just Men. Hodder, 1928. U.S. title: The Law of the Three Just Men. Doubleday, 1931. Also published as: Again the Three. Pan, 1968 ss JM
Again the Three Just Men (U.S. edition); see The Law of the Four Just Men
Angel Esquire. Arrowsmith, 1908; Holt, 1908
The Angel of Terror. Hodder, 1922; Small, 1922. Also published as: The Destroying Angel. Pan, 1959
The Arranways Mystery; see The Coat of Arms
The Avenger. Long, 1926. U.S. title: The Hairy Arm. Small, 1925
Barbara on her Own. Newnes, 1926
Big Foot. Long, 1927 M
The Big Four. Readers Library, 1929 ss
The Black. Readers Library, 1929 ss (Not to be confused with the title below.)
The Black; see The Man from Morocco
The Black Abbot. Hodder, 1926; Doubleday, 1927
Blue Hand. Ward, 1925; Small, 1926
Bones. Ward, 1915 ss S
Bones in London. Ward, 1921 ss, S in some of them
Bones of the River. Newnes, 1923 ss S
The Book of All Power. Ward, 1923
Bosambo of the River. Ward, 1914 ss S

The Brigand. Hodder, 1927 ss
The Calendar. Collins, 1930; Doubleday, 1931
Captains of Souls. Long, 1923; Small, 1922
Captain Tatham of Tatham Island. Gale & Polden, 1909. Revised edition: The Island of Galloping Gold. Newnes, 1916. Also published as: Eve's Island. Newnes, 1926
The Case of the Frightened Lady. French (London), 1932. U.S. title: Criminal at Large. French, 1934. (A play, based on The Frightened Lady, q.v.)
The Cat Burglar; see Forty-Eight Short Stories
Chick. Ward, 1923
Circumstantial Evidence; see Forty-Eight Short Stories
The Clever One; see The Forger
The Clue of the New Pin. Hodder, 1923; Small, 1923
The Clue of the Silver Key. Hodder, 1930. U.S. title: The Silver Key. Doubleday, 1930
The Clue of the Twisted Candle. Newnes, 1917; Small, 1916
The Coat of Arms. Hutchinson, 1931. U.S. title: The Arranways Mystery. Doubleday, 1932
The Colossus; see The Joker
The Council of Justice. Ward, 1908. (See also the U.S. edition of The Four Just Men.) JM
Criminal at Large; see The Case of the Frightened Lady
The Crimson Circle. Hodder, 1922; Doubleday, 1929
The Daffodil Murder; see The Daffodil Mystery
The Daffodil Mystery. Ward, 1920. U.S. title: The Daffodil Murder. Small, 1921
The Dark Eyes of London. Ward, 1924; Doubleday, 1929
The Daughters of the Night. Newnes, 1925
The Day of Uniting. Hodder, 1926; Mystery League, 1930
A Debt Discharged. Ward, 1916
The Destroying Angel; see The Angel of Terror
The Devil Man. Collins, 1931; Doubleday, 1931
Diana of Kara-Kara; see Double Dan
The Door with Seven Locks. Hodder, 1926; Doubleday, 1926
The Double. Hodder, 1928; Doubleday, 1928
Double Dan. Hodder, 1924. U.S. title: Diana of Kara-Kara. Small, 1924
Down Under Donovan. Ward, 1918
The Duke in the Suburbs. Ward, 1909
The Edgar Wallace Reader. World, 1943. (ss, reassembled from earlier collections.)
Educated Evans. Webster, 1924 ss EE
The Educated Man; see Good Evans!
Elegant Edward. Readers Library, 1928 ss
Eve's Island; see Captain Tatham of Tatham Island
The Face in the Night. Long, 1924; Doubleday, 1929
The Feathered Serpent. Hodder, 1927; Doubleday, 1928
The Fellowship of the Frog. Ward, 1925; Doubleday, 1928 E
Fighting Snub Reilly; see Forty-Eight Short Stories
Flat 2. Long, 1927; Garden City, 1924
The Flying Fifty-Five. Hutchinson, 1922
The Flying Squad. Hodder, 1928; Doubleday, 1929
The Forger. Hodder, 1927. U.S. title: The Clever One. Doubleday, 1928

For Information Received. Newnes, 1929 ss
Forty-Eight Short Stories. Newnes, 1929. ss This collection precedes by one month six separate collections assembled from this title, as follows: The Cat Burglar. Newnes, 1929 (8 ss). Circumstantial Evidence. Newnes, 1929; World, 1934 (8 ss). Fighting Snub Reilly. Newnes, 1929; World, 1934 (8 ss in British edition; U.S. edition has 11 ss from Forty-Eight Short Stories and For Information Received, q.v.). The Governor of Chi-Foo. Newnes, 1929; World, 1933 (8 ss in British edition; U.S. edition contains 13 ss). The Little Green Man. Newnes, 1929 (8 ss). The Prison Breakers. Newnes, 1929 (8 ss).
The Four Just Men. Tallis, 1905; Tallis, 1906 (with solution to mystery); Newnes, 1911 (with complete final chapter); Small, 1920. (The U.S. edition includes The Council of Justice, abridged, q.v.)
Four Square Jane. Readers Library, 1929; World Wide, 19??
The Fourth Plague. Ward, 1913; Doubleday, 1930
The Frightened Lady. Hodder, 1933. U.S. title: The Mystery of the Frightened Lady. Doubleday, 1933. (For play version see: The Case of the Frightened Lady.)
The Gaol Breaker; see We Shall See
The Gaunt Stranger. Hodder, 1925. U.S. title: The Ringer. Doubleday, 1926. (See also: the play and the British novel titled The Ringer.)
The Ghost of Down Hill. Readers Library, 1929; World Wide, 19??. (2 novelets.)
The Girl from Scotland Yard; see The Square Emerald
The Golden Hades. Collins, 1929
Good Evans! Webster, 1926. Also published as: The Educated Man. Readers Library, 1929 ss EE
The Governor of Chi-Foo; see Forty-Eight Short Stories
The Green Archer. Hodder, 1923; Small, 1924
The Green Pack. French (London), 1933. (Play.)
The Green Ribbon. Hutchinson, 1929; Doubleday, 1930
Green Rust. Ward, 1919; Small, 1920
Grey Timothy. Ward, 1913. Also published as: Pallard the Punter. Ward, 1914
Gunman's Bluff; see The Gunner
The Gunner. Long, 1928. U.S. title: Gunman's Bluff. Doubleday, 1929
The Guv'nor; see The Guv'nor and other stories
The Guv'nor and other stories. Collins, 1932. U.S. title: Mr. Reeder Returns. Doubleday, 1932. (4 novelets, also published in two volumes: The Guv'nor. Collins, 1933; and: Mr. J. G. Reeder Returns. Collins, 1934.) JR
The Hairy Arm; see The Avenger
The Hand of Power. Long, 1926; Mystery League, 1930
The India-Rubber Men. Hodder, 1929; Doubleday, 1930
The Iron Grip. Readers Library, 1930 ss
The Island of Galloping Gold; see Captain Tatham of Tatham Island
Jack o' Judgment. Ward, 1920; Small, 1921
The Joker. Hodder, 1926. U.S. title: The Colossus. Doubleday, 1932 E
The Just Men of Cordova. Ward, 1917 JM

Kate, Plus Ten. Ward, 1919; Small, 1917 TS
The Keepers of the King's Peace. Ward, 1917 ss S
Killer Kay. Newnes, 1930 ss
A King by Night. Long, 1925; Doubleday, 1926
The Lady Called Nita. Newnes, 1930 ss
The Lady of Ascot. Hutchinson, 1930
The Lady of Little Hell. Newnes, 1929 ss
The Last Adventure. Hutchinson, 1934 ss
The Law of the Four Just Men. Hodder, 1921. U.S. title: Again the Three Just Men. Doubleday, 1933 ss JM
The Law of the Three Just Men; see Again the Three Just Men
Lieutenant Bones. Ward, 1918 ss S
The Little Green Man; see Forty-Eight Short Stories
The Lone House Mystery. Collins, 1929. (1 novelet and 3 ss.) SM
The Man at the Carlton. Hodder, 1931; Doubleday, 1932
The Man from Morocco. Long, 1925. U.S. title: The Black. Doubleday, 1930
The Man Who Bought London. Ward, 1915
The Man Who Changed His Name. Hodder, 1929. (A play.)
The Man Who Knew. Newnes, 1919; Small, 1918
The Man Who was Nobody. Ward, 1927
The Melody of Death. Arrowsmith, 1915; Dial, 1927
The Million Dollar Story. Newnes, 1926
The Mind of Mr. J. G. Reeder. Hodder, 1925. U.S. title: The Murder Book of Mr. J. G. Reeder. Doubleday, 1929 ss JR
The Missing Million. Long, 1923. U.S. title: The Missing Millions. Small, 1925
Mr. Commissioner Sanders; see Sanders
Mr. J. G. Reeder Returns; see The Guv'nor and other stories
Mr. Justice Maxell. Ward, 1922
Mr. Reeder Returns; see The Guv'nor and other stories
The Mixer. Long, 1927 ss
More Educated Evans. Webster, 1927 ss EE
The Mystery of the Frightened Lady; see The Frightened Lady
Nig-Nog. World, 1934 ss
The Nine Bears. Ward, 1910. U.S. title: The Other Man. Dodd, 1911. Revised editions: The Secret House, and Silinski, Master Criminal, qq.v. TS
The Northing Tramp. Hodder, 1926; Doubleday, 1929. Also published as: The Tramp. Pan, 1965
Number Six. Newnes, 1922
On the Spot. Long, 1931; Doubleday, 1931
The Orator. Hutchinson, 1928 ss
The Other Man; see The Nine Bears
Pallard the Punter; see Grey Timothy
Penelope of the Polyantha. Hodder, 1926
The People of the River. Ward, 1912 ss S
Planetoid 127 and The Sweizer Pump. Readers Library, 1929. (Two novelets.)
The Prison Breakers; see Forty-Eight Short Stories
Red Aces. Hodder, 1929; Doubleday, 1930. (Three novelets about JR.)
The Reporter. Readers Library, 1929 ss
The Ringer. Hodder, 1929; French, 1929. (Play based on The Gaunt Stranger, q.v.) Novelization of the play: The Ringer. Hodder, 1927

Wallace, Edgar

The Ringer Returns; see Again the Ringer
The River of Stars. Ward, 1913. (Brief appearance by S.)
Room 13. Long, 1924 JR
Sanders. Hodder, 1926. U.S. title: Mr. Commissioner Sanders. Doubleday, 1930 S ss
Sanders of the River. Ward, 1911; Doubleday, 1930 S ss
Sandi, the King Maker. Ward, 1922 S
The Secret House. Ward, 1917; Small, 1919. (Revised edition of The Nine Bears, q.v.) TS
Sergeant Sir Peter. Chapman, 1932; Doubleday, 1933 ss
Silinski, Master Criminal. World, 1930. (Revision of The Nine Bears, q.v.)
The Silver Key; see The Clue of the Silver Key
The Sinister Man. Hodder, 1924; Small, 1925
The Square Emerald. Hodder, 1926. U.S. title: The Girl from Scotland Yard. Doubleday, 1927
The Squeaker. Hodder, 1927. U.S. title: The Squealer. Doubleday, 1928
The Squealer; see The Squeaker
The Steward. Collins, 1932 ss
The Strange Countess. Hodder, 1925; Small, 1926
The Stretelli Case and other mystery stories. World, 1930 ss, from earlier collections
The Terrible People. Hodder, 1926; Doubleday, 1926
The Terror. Hodder, 1929. (A play.) Novelization: Collins, 1929
Terror Keep. Hodder, 1927; Doubleday, 1927 JR
The Thief in the Night. Readers Library, 1928; World Wide, 19??
The Three Just Men. Hodder, 1926; Doubleday, 1930 JM
The Three Oak Mystery. Ward, 1924
The Tomb of T'sin. Ward, 1916. Abridged edition: Hutchinson, 1973
The Traitor's Gate. Hodder, 1927; Doubleday, 1927
The Tramp; see The Northing Tramp
The Twister. Long, 1928; Doubleday, 1929
The Undisclosed Client. Digit, 1963 ss, some from earlier collections
The Valley of Ghosts. Odhams, 1922; Small, 1923
We Shall See. Hodder, 1926. U.S. title: The Gaol Breaker. Doubleday, 1931
When the Gangs Came to London. Long, 1932; Doubleday, 1932
White Face. Hodder, 1930; Doubleday, 1931 E
The Woman from the East. Hutchinson, 1934 ss
The Yellow Snake. Hodder, 1926

WALLACE, F(LOYD) L.
Three Times a Victim. Ace, 1957
Wired for Scandal. Ace, 1959

WALLACE, FRANCIS
Front Man. Rinehart, 1952
Little Hercules. Mill, 1939; Cherry Tree, 1941

WALLACE, IAN. Pseudonym. Series character: Claudine St. Cyr = CS.
Croyd. Putnam, 1967
Deathstar Voyage. Putnam, 1969; Dobson, 1972 CS
The Purloined Prince. McCall, 1971 CS

WALLACE, IRVING. 1916- .
The Plot. Simon, 1967; Cassell, 1967

WALLACE, JOHN
Invasion. Popular Publications, 193?
Millionaire Gangster. Long, 1937
The Sedan Murder Mystery. Windsor, 1938
Vengeance of ?. Popular Publications, 193?

WALLACE, MARY. Pseudonym: Miriam Lynch, q.v.
From this Death Forward. Arcadia, 1959

WALLACE, PAT
House of Scorpio. Avon, 1975

WALLACE, ROBERT
The Body on the Beach. Watt, 1932
The Jig-Saw Murder Case. Gabriel, 1933
Seven Men are Murdered. Fiction League, 1930

WALLACE, ROBERT. House name. Series character: Richard Curtis Van Loan (The Phantom Detective), in all titles.
The Beast-King Murders. Regency, 1965
The Broadway Murders. Regency, 1965
The Corpse Parade. Regency, 1966
The Curio Murders. Regency, 1966
The Daggers of Kali. Regency, 1965
The Dancing Doll Murders. Regency, 1965
Death Glow. Regency, 1966
Death Under Contract. Regency, 1966
Fangs of Murder. Regency, 1966
The Forty Thieves. Regency, 1966
The Green Glare Murders. Regency, 1966
The Melody Murders. Regency, 1966
Murder Money. Regency, 1966
Murder Stalks a Billion. Regency, 1966
Murder Trail. Regency, 1966
Murder Under the Big Top. Regency, 1965
Stones of Satan. Corinth, 1966
The Trail to Death. Regency, 1965
Tycoon of Crime. Regency, 1965
The Uniformed Killers. Corinth, 1966
The Vampire Murders. Regency, 1965
Yellow Shadows of Death. Regency, 1965

WALLACE, TREVOR
The Air Cavalier. Wright, 1937
Bandits Aloft. Wright, 1936
The Battling Skyman. Wright, 1938
Cargo for Death. Wright, 1938
The Curse of the Silver Wings. Wright, 1938
The Flying Headhunter. Wright, 1939
Galahad of the Air. Wright, 1937
The Mystery of DS 24. Wright, 1937
Raiders of the Southern Seas. Wright, 1936
The Skyriders. Wright, 1937
Tail Spin Morgan. Wright, 1938
Two Gun Hedgehopper. Wright, 1938

WALLACE, WILLIAM
Tales of Mystery and Crime. Edmund Ward, 1948 ss

WALLENSTEIN, MARCEL (H.)
Merlin's Forest. Constable, 1965

WALLER, BRUCE
The Crime Squadron. Columbine, 1939

WALLER, LESLIE. 1923- . Pseudonyms: C. S. Cody, Patrick Mann, qq.v.
Assignment K; see "K"
The Coast of Fear. Doubleday, 1974; Allen, 1975
"K". GM, 1963. British title: Assignment K. Mayflower, 1976

WALLING, R(OBERT) A(LFRED) J(OHN). 1869-1949. Series characters: Garstang = G; Philip Tolefree = PT.
The Bachelor Flat Mystery; see VIII to IX
Behind the Yellow Blind. Hodder, 1932. U.S. title: Murder at Midnight. Morrow, 1932 G
Bury Him Deeper. Hodder, 1937. U.S. title: Marooned with Murder. Morrow, 1937 PT
By Hook or By Crook. Hodder, 1941. U.S. title: By Hook or Crook. Morrow, 1941 PT
By Hook or Crook; see By Hook or By Crook
Castle-Dinas. Hodder, 1942. U.S. title: The Corpse with the Eerie Eye. Morrow, 1942 PT
The Cat and the Corpse. Hodder, 1935. U.S. title: The Corpse in the Green Pajamas. Morrow, 1935 PT
The Coroner Doubts. Hodder, 1938. U.S. title: The Corpse with the Blue Cravat. Morrow, 1938 PT
A Corpse by Any Other Name; see The Doodled Asterisk
The Corpse in the Coppice; see Mr. Tolefree's Reluctant Witnesses
The Corpse in the Crimson Slippers. Hodder, 1936; Morrow, 1936 PT
The Corpse in the Green Pajamas; see The Cat and the Corpse
The Corpse with the Blistered Hand; see Dust in the Vault
The Corpse with the Blue Cravat; see The Coroner Doubts
The Corpse with the Dirty Face. Hodder, 1936; Morrow, 1936. Also published as: The Crime in Cumberland Court. Hodder, 1938 PT
The Corpse with the Eerie Eye; see Castle-Dinas
The Corpse with the Floating Foot; see The Mystery of Mr. Mock
The Corpse with the Grimy Glove; see More Than One Serpent
The Corpse with the Missing Watch. Morrow, 1949 PT
The Corpse with the Red-Headed Friend; see They Liked Entwhistle
The Corpse Without a Clue. Hodder, 1944; Morrow, 1944 PT
The Crime in Cumberland Court; see The Corpse with the Dirty Face
The Dinner-Party at Bardolph's. Jarrolds, 1927. U.S. title: That Dinner at Bardolph's. Morrow, 1928
The Doodled Asterisk. Hodder, 1943. U.S. title: A Corpse by Any Other Name. Morrow, 1943 PT
Dust in the Vault. Hodder, 1939. U.S. title: The Corpse with the Blistered Hand. Morrow, 1939 PT
VIII to IX. Hodder, 1934. U.S. title: The Bachelor Flat Mystery. Morrow, 1934 PT
The Fatal Five Minutes. Hodder, 1932; Morrow, 1932 PT
The Five Suspects. Hodder, 1935. U.S. title: Legacy of Death. Morrow, 1934 PT
Follow the Blue Car. Hodder, 1933. U.S. title: In Time for Murder. Morrow, 1933 PT
In Time for Murder; see Follow the Blue Car
The Late Unlamented. Hodder, 1948; Morrow, 1948 PT
Legacy of Death; see The Five Suspects
The Man with the Squeaky Voice. Methuen, 1930; Morrow, 1930
Marooned with Murder; see Bury Him Deeper
More Than one Serpent. Hodder, 1938. U.S. title: The Corpse with the Grimy Glove. Morrow, 1938 PT
Mr. Tolefree's Reluctant Witnesses. Hodder, 1936. U.S. title: The Corpse in the Coppice. Morrow, 1935 PT
Murder at Midnight; see Behind the Yellow Blind
Murder at the Keyhole. Methuen, 1929; Morrow, 1929

The Mystery of Mr. Mock. Hodder, 1937.
U.S. title: The Corpse with the
Floating Foot. Morrow, 1936 PT
Prove It, Mr. Tolefree; see The Tolliver Case
The Spider and the Fly; see Why Did Trethewy Die?
Stroke of One. Methuen, 1931; Morrow, 1931 G
The Strong Room. Jarrolds, 1927
That Dinner at Bardolph's; see The Dinner-Party at Bardolph's
They Liked Entwhistle. Hodder, 1939.
U.S. title: The Corpse with the Red-Headed Friend. Morrow, 1939 PT
The Tolliver Case. Hodder, 1934. U.S. title: Prove It, Mr. Tolefree. Morrow, 1933 PT
Why Did Trethewy Die? Hodder, 1940.
U.S. title: The Spider and the Fly. Morrow, 1940 PT

WALLIS, A(RTHUR) J(AMES) and CHARLES F. BLAIR, JR.
Thunder Above. Holt, 1956; Jarrolds, 1959

WALLIS, HENRY MARRIAGE. Pseudonym: Ashton Hilliers, q.v.

WALLIS, J(AMES) H(AROLD). 1885-1958.
Series character: Inspector Wilton Jacks = WJ.
The Capital City Mystery. Dutton, 1932; Jarrolds, 1933 WJ
Cries in the Night. Dutton, 1933; Jarrolds, 1935 WJ
House of Murder; see Murder Mansion
Murder by Formula. Dutton, 1931; Jarrolds, 1932 WJ
Murder Mansion. Dutton, 1934. British title: House of Murder. Jarrolds, 1934 WJ
The Mystery of Vaucluse. Dutton, 1933; Jarrolds, 1934 WJ
The Niece of Abraham Pein. Dutton, 1943; Jarrolds, 1944
Once Off Guard. Dutton, 1942; Jarrolds, 1943. Also published as: The Woman in the Window. World, 1944
The Servant of Death. Dutton, 1932; Jarrolds, 1933 WJ
The Synthetic Philanthropist. Dutton, 1943; Jarrolds, 1945
The Woman He Chose. Dutton, 1934
The Woman in the Window; see Once Off Guard

WALLIS, RUTH (OTIS) SAWTELL. 1895-1978.
Series character: Eric Lund = EL.
Blood from a Stone. Dodd, 1945; Hammond, 1955
Cold Bed in the Clay. Dodd, 1947 EL
Forget My Fate. Dodd, 1950 EL
No Bones About It. Dodd, 1944; Hammond, 1950 EL
Too Many Bones. Dodd, 1943; Hammond, 1947

WALLMANN, JEFFREY M.
Judas Cross. Random, 1974; Barrie, 1974
The Spiral Web. Signet, 1969

WALPOLE, HORACE. 1717-1797.
The Castle of Otranto. Lownds, 1765; Longworth, 1801

WALPOLE, HUGH (SEYMOUR). 1884-1941. See also: EDWARD CHODOROV, 1904-   .
Above the Dark Circus. Macmillan (London), 1931. U.S. title: Above the Dark Tumult. Doubleday, 1931
Above the Dark Tumult; see Above the Dark Circus
All Souls' Night. Macmillan (London), 1933; Doubleday, 1933 ss
The Killer and the Slain. Macmillan (London), 1942; Doubleday, 1942

Portrait of a Man with Red Hair. Macmillan (London), 1925; Doran, 1925

WALSH, DAVID JOHN. 1859-   . Pseudonym: John St. David, q.v.

WALSH, GEO(RGE) E(THELBERT). 1865-   .
The Mysterious Burglar. Buckles, 1901; Ward, 1903

WALSH, GOODWIN
The Voice of the Murderer. Putnam, 1926

WALSH, J(AMES) M(ORGAN). 1897-1952. Pseudonyms: H. Haverstock Hill, Stephen Maddock, George M. White, qq.v.
Series characters: Bromley Kay, in at least those marked BK; Oliver Keene, in at least those marked OK; Colonel Ormiston, in at least those marked O; Mike Harman, in at least those marked MH; Inspector Quaile, in at least those marked Q; Inspector Storm, in at least those marked S.
The Bandits of the Night. Hamilton, 1932
The Black Cross. Hamilton, 1928
Black Dragon. Collins, 1938 OK
The Black Ghost. Hamilton, 1930; Brewer, 1931
The Brethren of the Compass, with E. J. Blythe. Jarrolds, 1925
Bullets for Breakfast. Collins, 1939
Chalk-Face. Hodder, 1937
The Company of Shadows. Hamilton, 1926; Brewer, 1931
The Crimes of Cleopatra's Needle. Hamilton, 1928
Danger Zone. Collins, 1942 OK
Death at his Elbow. Collins, 1941 OK
Dial 999. Collins, 1938 OK
Exit Simeon Hex. Hamilton, 1930; Brewer, 1931
Express Delivery. Collins, 1946 MH
Face Value. Collins, 1944 OK
A Girl of the Islands. Hamilton, 1932
The Hairpin Mystery. Hamilton, 1926
The Half Ace. Collins, 1936 O
The Hand of Doom. Hamilton, 1927 Q
The Images of Han. Hamilton, 1927 BK
Island Alert. Collins, 1943 OK
Island of Spies. Collins, 1937 OK
King of Tiger Bay. Collins, 1952
King's Enemies. Collins, 1939 OK
King's Messenger. Collins, 1933
Lady Incognito. Collins, 1932 Q
The League of Missing Men. Hamilton, 1932 BK
The Man Behind the Curtain. Hamilton, 1931 BK
The Man from Whitehall. Collins, 1934 CO
The Man Who Grew Bulbs. Vallancey, 1945
Mutton Dressed as Lamb, and Live Bait. Polybooks, 1944. (2 stories.)
Mystery House. Hamilton, 1931
The Mystery Man. Hamilton, 1929
The Mystery of the Green Caterpillars. Hamilton, 1929
Next, Please. Collins, 1951
Once on Tiger Bay. Collins, 1947
The Purple Stain. Hamilton, 1928
Return to Tiger Bay. Collins, 1950
The Secret Service Girl. Collins, 1933 O
Secret Weapons. Collins, 1940 OK
The Silent Man. Collins, 1935 O
The Silver Greyhound. Hamilton, 1928 S
Spies are Abroad. Collins, 1933 O
Spies from the Skies. Collins, 1941 OK
Spies in Pursuit. Collins, 1934 O
Spies in Spain. Collins, 1937 O
Spies Never Return. Collins, 1935 O
Spies' Vendetta. Collins, 1936
The Tempania Mystery. Hamilton, 1929 Q

Tiger in the Night. Collins, 1935 O
Time to Kill. Collins, 1949 MH
Walking Shadow. Collins, 1948 MH
The Week-End Crime Book, with Audrey Baldwin. Hamilton, 1929 quiz ss
The Whisperer. Hamilton, 1931 S
Whispers in the Dark. Collins, 1945 OK
The White Mask. Hamilton, 1925; Doran, 1927

WALSH, MAURICE. 1879-   .
Danger Under the Moon. Chambers, 1956; Lippincott, 1957
The Man in Brown. Chambers, 1945. U.S. title: Nine Strings to Your Bow. Lippincott, 1945
Nine Strings to Your Bow; see The Man in Brown

WALSH, PAUL E.
KKK. Avon, 1956
Murder in Baraoca. Avon, 1958
The Murder Room. Avon, 1957

WALSH, PERCY
Chin-Chin-Chinaman. French, 1929. (1-act play.)
The Clueless Trail. Eldon, 1933

WALSH, ROBERT
Violent Hours. Signet, 1958

WALSH, THOMAS. 1908-   .
The Action of the Tiger. Simon, 1968; Hale, 1969
Dangerous Passenger. Little, 1959
The Dark Window. Little, 1956; H. Hamilton, 1956
The Eye of the Needle. Simon, 1961; Cassell, 1962
The Face of the Enemy. Simon, 1966; Cassell, 1968
The Night Watch. Little, 1952; H. Hamilton, 1952
Nightmare in Manhattan. Little, 1950; H. Hamilton, 1951
The Resurrection Man. Simon, 1966; Cassell, 1967
The Tenth Point. Simon, 1965; Cassell, 1965
A Thief in the Night. Simon, 1962; Cassell, 1963
To Hide a Rogue. Simon, 1964; Cassell, 1965

WALSH, WILLIAM THOMAS. 1891-1949.
Out of the Whirlwind. McBride, 1935. British title: A Murder Makes a Man. Longmans, 1935

WALSHE, DOUGLAS. 1880-   .
-Close-Up. Wright, 1934
-Dancing Cheat. Gramol, 1935
-Duty Be Damned! Hutchinson, 1932
Fairly Caught. Leng, 1937
Find the Lady! Hutchinson, 1929
Guilty! Gramol, 1935
-Hartington's Luck. Mowl, 1935
-Her Lips Betrayed. Gramol, 1935
-His First Affair. Leng, 1931
The Man Behind the Curtain. Hutchinson, 1929
-Siren in Satin. Gramol, 1935
The Smoke-Screen. Hutchinson, 1928
-Spider Girls. Hutchinson, 1930
-Their Wife. Wright, 1934
-Two for a Pair. Wright, 1936

WALTER, A(LEXIA) E. and H(UBERT) C(ONRAD) WALTER. Series character: Sir Edgar Ewart, in both titles.
Betrayal. Methuen, 1929; Dutton, 1930
The Patriot. Methuen, 1928; Dutton, 1928

WALTER, ELIZABETH
  Snowfall and Other Chilling Events.
  Harvill, 1965; Stein, 1966 ss

WALTER, H(UBERT) C(ONRAD). See: A(LEXIA)
  E. WALTER.

WALTER, HUGH
  A Bullet for Charles. Macdonald, 1955

WALTERMIRE, BEECHER W(ESLEY). 1858-   .
  The Adventures of a Skeleton. Ogilvie,
  1890

WALTERS, SHELLY. Pseudonym.
  The Dunes. McKay, 1974

WALTHEW, NICHOLAS
  Murder at the "Black Swan". Hutchinson,
  1939

WALTMORE, IAIN
  No Doubts After Friday. Cassell, 1961

WALTON, FRANCIS. Pseudonym of Alfred Hodder, 1866-1907. See: JOSIAH FLYNT.

WALTON, GEORGE LINCOLN. 1854-   .
  Oscar Montague—Paranoiac. Lippincott,
  1919

WALTON, MARION. 1928-   .
  Cardinal Error. Hale, 1973
  The Paduan Conspiracy. Hale, 1973

WALTON, THOMAS
  -Married or Trapped. Stockwell, 1936
  The Sins of the Fathers; or, The Wye
  Valley Mystery. Stock, 1908

WALWORTH, JEANNETTE (RITCHIE) H(ADERMANN). 1837-1918.
  The Silent Witness. Cassell, 1888

WALWORTH, MANSFIELD TRACY. 1830-1873.
  -Beverly; or, The White Mask. Carleton,
  1872
  -Delaplaine; or, The Sacrifice of Irene.
  Carleton, 1871
  -Hotspur. Carleton, 1864
  Lulu. Carleton, 1863
  -Married in Mask. Burt, 1888
  The Mission of Death. Sadlier, 186?
  -Stormcliff. Carlton, 1866
  -Warwick. Carleton, 1869
  -Zahara; or, A Leap for Empire. Dillingham, 1888

WALZ, AUDREY. Pseudonym: Francis Bonnamy,
  q.v.

WAMBAUGH, JOSEPH. 1937-   .
  The Blue Knight. Little, 1972; Joseph,
  1973
  The Choirboys. Delacorte, 1975; Weidenfeld, 1976
  The New Centurions. Little, 1970;
  Joseph, 1971
  The Onion Field. Delacorte, 1973;
  Weidenfeld, 1974

WARBY, MARJORIE
  More Than All. Collins, 1975

WARD, ARTHUR HENRY SARSFIELD. 1883-1959.
  Pseudonyms: Michael Furey, Sax Rohmer, qq.v.

WARD, B. E. M.
  Black Cat Murders. Regency, 1945
  Hellmouth Horrors. Regency, 1945
  Murder at the Playhouse. Mitre, 1945
  -A Night of Love. Regency, 1946
  -School on Lone Island. Regency, 1945
  She was No Angel. Regency, 1945
  Viper's Vengeance. Regency, 1945

WARD, CHRISTOPHER (LONGSTRETH). 1868-
  1943.
  Twisted Tales. Holt, 1924 ss, including 2 detective/mystery parodies

WARD, COLIN
  House Party Murder. Collins, 1933; Morrow, 1934

WARD, (DOROTHY) DEWEY
  The Curse of Seabrea; see The Unsheltered
  The House in Paris. Dell, 1971
  The Unsheltered. Random, 1963. British
  title: The Curse of Seabrea. Muller,
  1964

WARD, DON. See: THEODORE (HAMILTON)
  STURGEON, 1918-   .

WARD, ELIZABETH C. 1936-   . Pseudonym:
  E. C. Allen, q.v.

WARD, ERNEST
  Five for Bridge. Crowell, 1940

WARD, GERALD
  Time to Kill. Jarrolds, 1957

WARD, HAROLD. Pseudonym: Zorro, q.v.
  Series character: The Vulture = V.
  The Blood of Buddha. Melrose, 1934
  Murder of a Painted Lady. Melrose, 1937
  The Vulture. Pearson, 1936   V
  "The Vulture" Strikes. Pearson, 1936   V

WARD, HENRY (L.). 1913-   .
  The Green Suns. Sidgwick, 1961. (Translation of Les Soleils Verts. Paris,
  1956.)
  Hell's Above Us. Sidgwick, 1960.
  (Translation of L'Enfer est dans le
  Ciel. Paris, 1960.)

WARD, HERBERT D(ICKINSON). 1861-   .
  The Burglar Who Moved Paradise. Houghton, 1897
  The White Crown and other stories.
  Houghton, 1894   ss, some criminous

WARD, MRS. HUMPHREY [MARY AUGUSTA ARNOLD
  WARD]. 1851-1920.
  The Case of Richard Meynell. Smith
  Elder, 1911; Doubleday, 1911

WARD, I(RENE) E(LLEN)
  Death Came Too Soon. Hale, 1975

WARD, JULIAN. 1908-   .
  The Compass Points to Fear. Hodder,
  1949
  Death Sleeps in Kensington. Hodder,
  1951
  Death Without a Funeral. Hutchinson,
  1957
  No Medal If I Die. Hutchinson, 1956
  We Died in Bond Street. Hodder, 1952

WARD, ROSE ELIZABETH KNOX. 1886-   .
  Pseudonym: Elizabeth Sax Rohmer, q.v.

WARD, STEVE
  Odds Against Linda. Ace, 1960

WARD, WILLIAM. House name. See also:
  H(ARRY) F(REEMAN) WOOD; ANONYMOUS
  (The Black Box Murder). Series character: Jeff Clayton, in all titles.
  Jeff Clayton and the Outlaws. Westbrook, 1911
  Jeff Clayton in the Heart of Trouble.
  Westbrook, 1910
  Jeff Clayton's Blind Trail. Westbrook,
  1910
  Jeff Clayton's Brigand Foe. Westbrook,
  1911
  Jeff Clayton's Dancing Bubble. Westbrook, 1911
  Jeff Clayton's Daring Leap. Westbrook,
  1911
  Jeff Clayton's Deal with Death. Westbrook, 1911
  Jeff Clayton's Decoy. Westbrook, 1911
  Jeff Clayton's Demon Pursuer. Westbrook, 1911
  Jeff Clayton's Discovery. Westbrook,
  1911
  Jeff Clayton's Fatal Shot. Westbrook,
  1911
  Jeff Clayton's Golden Ladder. Westbrook, 1911
  Jeff Clayton's Last Bullet. Westbrook,
  1911
  Jeff Clayton's Last Ship. Westbrook,
  1911
  Jeff Clayton's Long Chase. Westbrook,
  1911
  Jeff Clayton's Lost Clue. Westbrook,
  1910
  Jeff Clayton's Man-Trap. Westbrook,
  1910
  Jeff Clayton's Master Stroke. Westbrook, 1910
  Jeff Clayton's Mexican Plot. Westbrook,
  1912
  Jeff Clayton's Pursuit. Westbrook, 1911
  Jeff Clayton's Puzzle. Westbrook, 1911
  Jeff Clayton's Red Mystery. Westbrook,
  1911
  Jeff Clayton's Riddle. Westbrook, 1910
  Jeff Clayton's Strange Quest. Westbrook, 1910
  Jeff Clayton's Surprise. Westbrook,
  1910
  Jeff Clayton's Thunder Bolt. Westbrook,
  1910
  Jeff Clayton's Triumph. Westbrook, 1910
  Jeff Clayton's White Mission. Westbrook, 1910
  Jeff Clayton's Winged Flight. Westbrook, 1911

WARD-THOMAS, EVELYN BRIDGET PATRICIA
  STEPHENS. 1928-   . Pseudonym:
  Evelyn Anthony, q.v.

WARDEN, FLORENCE. Pseudonym of Florence
  Alice Price James, 1857-1929.
  -Abbot's Moat. White, 1913
  -Adela's Ordeal. Stevens, 1894; International News, 1893
  The Adventures of a Pretty Woman. Paul,
  1909
  -At the World's Mercy. Stevens, 1884;
  Munro, 1884
  The Bad Lord Lockington. Long, 1912
  -The Baronet's Wife. Unwin, 1908
  Beatrice Foyle's Crime. Pearson, 1903
  -The Beauty Doctor. Greening, 1911
  -The Beauty of the Family. White, 1910
  -Blindman's Marriage. Laurie, 1907
  -The Bohemian Girls. White, 1899
  The Case for the Lady. Greening, 1910
  The Case of Sir Geoffrey. Long, 1908
  -City and Suburban. White, 1890; Lovell,
  1890
  -Cliff's End Farm and other stories.
  White, 1905   ss
  The Colonel's Past. Ward, 1910
  Cross-Fires. Cassell, 1915
  The Dazzling Miss Davison. Unwin, 1908;
  Fly, 1910
  Deldee; or, The Iron Hand; see A Dog
  with a Bad Name
  Deldee, the Ward of Warington; see A
  Dog with a Bad Name
  A Desperate Game. Burt, 1902. (British
  title?)
  A Devil's Bargain. Long, 1908
  The Disappearance of Nigel Blair. Ward,
  1911

-Doctor Darch's Wife. White, 1896; Collier, 1896
-A Dog with a Bad Name. Bentley, 1885. U.S. title: The Iron Hand; or, Deldee, the Ward of Warington. Munro, 1884. Also published as: Deldee, the Ward of Warington. Appleton, 1885. And as: Deldee; or, The Iron Hand. Lovell, 1887
-Dolly the Romp. White, 1897
-Doris's Fortune. Stevens, 1886; Appleton, 1886
The Empress of the Andes. Laurie, 1909
The Face in the Flashlight. Long, 1905
-The Farm in the Hills. Sands, 1899
-The Fight for a Soul. Digby, 1912
A Fight to a Finish. Chatto, 1901
-The Financier's Wife. Laurie, 1906
-The Fog Princes. Ward, 1889; Lovell, 1889
-Forge and Furnace. New Amsterdam, 1896. (British title?)
-A Girl with Money. Ward, 1917
The Girl with the Haunting Eyes. Ward, 1920
-The Girls at the Grange. White, 1897
-Girls will be Girls. White, 1898
-The Good Ship "Dove". Ward, 1919
-Grave Lady Jane. White, 1893; Taylor, 1892
-The Grey Moth. Ward, 1920
-The Half-Smart Set. Milne, 1908
The Harlingham Case. Ward, 1918
-The Heart of a Girl. Chatto, 1903
-Heiress of Densley Wold. Cassell, 1907
-"Highest References." Railway and General Automatic Library, 1892; Lovell, 1891
-A Hole and Corner Marriage. Pearson, 1902
-The House by the River. Unwin, 1905; Ogilvie, 1905
-A House in the Hills. Fenno, 1899. (British title?)
The House on the Marsh. Stevens, 1877; Munro, 1883
-A House with a History. White, 1901
-An Impossible Husband. Long, 1904
The Inn by the Shore. Jarrolds, 1897. U.S. title: The Mystery of the Inn by the Shore. Bonner's, 1895
The Iron Hand; or, Deldee, the Ward of Waringham; see A Dog with a Bad Name
-Joan, the Curate. Chatto, 1898; Buckles, 1899
-Kitty's Engagement. White, 1895; Appleton, 1895
-Lady Anne's Trustee, and other stories. White, 1908 ss
A Lady in Black. White, 1896
-The Lady in Furs. Ward, 1922
-Lady Joan's Companion. Digby, 1902
-Lady Lee. Laurie, 1908
-Lady Rodway's Ordeal. Ward, 1909
Lady Ursula's Husband. Ward, 1914
-Laidlaw's Wife. Long, 1911
Law Not Justice. Hurst, 1906
A Life's Arrears. Cassell, 1908
-The Light in the Upper Storey. Ward, 1917
-Lilith. Ward, 1923
-The Little Grey Mouse. White, 1915
Little Miss Prim. White, 1898
-Lord Penworth's Daughter. Ward, 1913
-Lord Quare's Visitor. Long, 1915
-Love and Lordship. Chatto, 1906
-The Love That Lasts. Ward, 1900; Street, 1899
-Love's Sentinel. Long, 1913
-The Lovely Mrs. Pemberton. Long, 1901; Buckles, 1901
-A Lowly Lover. White, 1900
-Mad Sir Geoffrey. Everett, 1907
-The Major. White, 1913
The Man with the Amber Eyes. Long, 1907
-The Marriage Broker. Laurie, 1907
-Married by Stealth. Ward, 1918
-The Master-Key. Pearson, 1898

-The Matheson Money. Long, 1910
The Mill House Mystery. Jarrolds, 1911
-The Millionaire's Son. Ward, 1908
The Mis-Rule of Three. Unwin, 1903; Wycil, 1903
Miss Ferriby's Clients. Laurie, 1910
Missing—A Young Girl. U.S. Book Co., 1890. (British title?)
-Mollie the Handful. White, 1912
-Morals and Millions. White, 1901
-My Child and I. White, 1894; Lippincott, 1894
-My Lady of Whims. Chatto, 1907
The Mystery of Dudley Horne. White, 1897
The Mystery of Fourways. Fenno, 1900. (British title?)
The Mystery of the Inn by the Shore; see The Inn by the Shore
A Mystery of the Thames. Ward, 1913
A Night Surprise. Ward, 1919
-No. 3 the Square. Long, 1903
-Nurse Revel's Mistake. Simpkin, 1889; Lovell, 1899
The Old House at the Corner. Chatto, 1906
-Once Too Often. Long, 1901
-Our Widow. White, 1896; International News, 1895. Also published as: Three Wayward Girls. International News, 1895
-An Outsider's Year. Long, 1903
A Passage Through Bohemia. Ward, 1893; Hovendon, 1893
-A Patched-Up Affair. Pearson, 1901
-A Perfect Fool. White, 1894; International News, 1894
-The Plain Miss Cray. White, 1900; Buckles, 1900
Playing the Knave. Laurie, 1905
The Precipice. Ward, 1923
-Pretty Miss Smith. Heinemann, 1891; U.S. Book Co., 1891
-The Price of Silence. Ward, 1916
A Prince of Darkness. Ward, 1886; Appleton, 1885
-Ralph Ryder of Brent. Bentley, 1892; National Book Co., 1892. Also published as: A Young Wife's Trial; or, Ralph Ryder of Brent. White, 1893
-The Real Mrs. Daybrook. Long, 1906
Rogues Fall Out. Ward, 1908
Room Nineteen. Ward, 1915
St. Cuthbert's Tower. Cassell, 1889; Lovell, 1889
-A Scarborough Romance. Ward, 1894
-Scheherazade. Ward, 1887; Appleton, 1887
The Secret of Lynndale. White, 1899
-Seamew Abbey. Heinemann, 1892; Lovell, 1891
A Sensational Case. Ward, 1898; International News, 1894
Serle's Secret. Everett, 1909
-A Shock to Society. White, 1892; Lovell, 1892
Sir Julian's Crime. Ward, 1921
-Sir Morecambe's Marriage. Ward, 1909
-Sir Penywern's Wife. Ward, 1915
-The Socialism of Lady Jim. Digby, 1908
A Society Scare. Hurst, 1909
-Something in the City. Long, 1902; Buckles, 1902
-A Spoilt Girl. White, 1895; Lippincott, 1895
-A Sporting Offer. Ward, 1918
-A Terrible Family. Stevens, 1893; International News, 1893
-The Things That Women Do. White, 1912
-Those Westerton Girls. Bentley, 1891; Lovell, 1891
Three Wayward Girls; see Our Widow
-Tom Dawson. Chatto, 1904
-Town Lady and Country Lass. White, 1900
-Two Lads and a Lass, and other stories. White, 1896 ss

-A Vagrant Wife. Stevens, 1885; Appleton, 1885
The Veiled Lady. Long, 1909
-A Very Rough Diamond. Nisbet, 1899
-Wedded But Not a Wife. White, 1911
-What She Ought to Be. Chatto, 1904
-When the Devil Drives. Ward, 1910
The White Countess. Long, 1907
The White Witch. Bentley, 1884
Who was Lady Thurne? Long, 1905
-Why She Left Him. Long, 1914
-A Wild Wooing. White, 1893
-The Wiles of Wilhelmina. White, 1913
-A Wilful Ward. White, 1891
-A Witch of the Hills. Bentley, 1888; Lovell, 1888
-The Wolf at the Door. Digby, 1909; Roberts, 1877
The Woman with the Diamonds. White, 1895
A Woman's Face; or, A Lakeland Mystery. Ward, 1888; Appleton, 1888
-Woman's Story. Everett, 1895
-The Wraith of Olverstone. Ward, 1916
-The Youngest Miss Brown. Chatto, 1905
A Young Wife's Trial; see Ralph Ryder of Brent

WARDEN, GERTRUDE
-An Actress's Husband. White, 1909
An Angel of Evil. Stevens, 1897
As a Bird to the Snare. Arrowsmith, 1888
-Beauty in Distress. Digby, 1903
Beyond the Law. Ward, 1902
The Crime in the Alps. White, 1908
-The Dancing Leaves. Ward, 1908
-The Dark Arches. Dicks, 189?
-Diana of Dartmoor. Digby, 1913
-Five Old Maids. Stevens, 1895
-The Game of Love. Digby, 1904
-The Grey Wolf's Daughter. International News, 1894. (British title?)
-Haunted. Ward, 1911
-The Haunted House at Kew. Stevens, 1893
-A Heart of Stone. Digby, 1905
-Her Fairy Prince. Stevens, 1896; Lippincott, 1895
-Her Faithful Knight. Street, 1899. (British title?)
-Merely Man. White, 1909
-The Millionaire and the Lady. Long, 1907
The Moth and the Footlights. Digby, 1906
-Nobody's Widow. Digby, 1903
The Nut-Browne Mayd: A Riviera Mystery. White, 1907
-The Path of Virtue. White, 1912
Robert the Devil. Digby, 1906
-Scoundrel or Saint? Digby, 1902
A Secret Foe. International News, 1896. (British title?)
The Secret of a Letter. International News, 1894. (British title?)
-The Sentimental Sex. Lane, 1896; Appleton, 1896
Set to Partners. Digby, 1902
-The Severn Affair. Long, 1909
-Stand and Deliver. White, 1910
The Stolen Pearl, with Robert Eustace. Ward, 1903
A Syndicate of Sinners. Digby, 1901
-Two Girls and a Saint. White, 1915
Whose was the Crime? Street, 1899. (British title?)
-A Wise and Foolish Virgin. White, 1904
-The Woman Who Tempted. Ward, 1912
-The Wooing of a Fairy. Hurst, 1897

WARDEN, LEWIS (CHRISTOPHER). 1913-
Murder on Wheels. Avalon, 1964

WARE, JUDITH
  Detour to Denmark. Paperback Library, 1967
  The Faxon Secret. Paperback Library, 1966
  The Fear Place. Paperback Library, 1967
  Quarry House. Paperback Library, 1965
  Thorne House. Paperback Library, 1965
  A Touch of Fear. Signet, 1969

WARE, WALLACE
  The Charka Memorial. Doubleday, 1954

WARING, D. GAINSBOROUGH
  -Against My Fire. Long, 1941
  -And If I Laugh... Long, 1940
  Deep Malice. Long, 1939
  Fortune Must Follow. Long, 1937
  Hated Therewith. Long, 1942
  -Not Quite So Black. Hale, 1948
  -Nothing Irredeemable. Long, 1936
  The Oldest Road. Long, 1938
  Out of Evil. Long, 1937
  This Day's Madness. Long, 1939
  -This New Corn. Long, 1940

WARING, J(AMES) H(ENRY)
  Murder on the Camp. Stockwell, 1973
  Was It Murder? Stockwell, 1969 ss

WARING, MAIN. Pseudonym of William Thomas Mainwaring Hughes, 1893- .
  Clinging Shadows. Melrose, 1936

WARMAN, CY. 1855-1914.
  The Express Messenger and other tales of the rail. Scribner, 1897; Chatto, 1897 ss, some criminous

WARMAN, (WILLIAM) ERIK. 1904- . Series character: Insp. John Isidore Bloom, in at least those marked JB.
  Incident. Grasshopper Press, 1943
  No Place for the Young. Fortune, 1934
  Pattern for Murder. Harrap, 1943 JB
  Relative to Murder. Harrap, 1940 JB
  Soft at the Centre. Dakers, 1953

WARNEFORD, LIEUTENANT (ROBERT)
  Tales of the Coast Guard. Brown, 1856 ss

WARNER, DOUGLAS
  Death of a Bogey. Cassell, 1962
  Death of a Dreamer. Cassell, 1964; Walker, 1965
  Death of a Nude. Cassell, 1964
  Death of a Snout. Cassell, 1961; Walker, 1962
  Death of a Tom. Cassell, 1963; Macmillan, 1964
  Death on a Warm Wind. Rapp, 1968; Doubleday, 1968

WARNER, KENNETH LEWIS. 1918- . Pseudonym: Dighton Morel, q.v.

WARNER, OLIVER (MARTIN WILSON). 1903-1976.
  A Secret of the Marsh. Chatto, 1927; Dutton, 1927

WARNER, PETER. 1942- .
  Loose Ends. McGraw, 1972

WARNER, WARREN. Pseudonym of Samuel Warren, 1807-1877, q.v.
  The Experiences of a Barrister. Brown (anonymously), 1856; Cornish Lamport (with an excerpt from Charles Dickins' Household Words), 1852. Also published in (with 11 ss added): The Experiences of a Barrister and Confessions of an Attorney (as by Samuel Warren). Estes, 1884. And as: The Lawyer-Detective; or, Twenty-Two Celebrated Criminal Cases Unraveled. Loyd, 1887 ss

WARREN, C. DELVES
  Some Cases of Sherwood Lang, Detective. Drane's, 1923 ss

WARREN, CHARLES MARQUIS. 1912- .
  Deadhead. Coward, 1949; Boardman, 1950

WARREN, DOUG(LAS). 1935- .
  A Case of Rape. Pyramid, 1975. (Novelization of the TV movie.)
  Scarlet Starlet. Ace, 1959
  Walking Tall. Pinnacle, 1973. (Novelization of the movie.)

WARREN, GEORGE
  -The Bike Bastards. Brandon, 1975
  Body for the Widow. Brandon, 1973
  The Laughing Widow. Brandon, 1974

WARREN, J(OHN) RUSSELL. 1886- . Pseudonym: Gilbert Coverack, q.v. Series character: Inspector M'Guire, in at least those marked M (see also Gilbert Coverack byline).
  A Bride for Bombay. Ward, 1931
  Castle Enigma. Ward, 1930
  Gas-Mask Murder. Heinemann, 1939. U.S. title: Murder in the Blackout. Sheridan, 1940 M
  Half a Clue. Ward, 1930
  Missing from his Home. Melrose, 1950
  Murder from Three Angles. Heinemann, 1939; Furman, 1939 M
  Murder in the Blackout; see Gas-Mask Murder
  "Princess Proxy." Ward, 1932
  Snow Upon the Desert. Ward, 1932
  This Inward Horror; see This Mortal Coil
  This Mortal Coil. Melrose, 1947. U.S. title: This Inward Horror. Dutton, 1948

WARREN, JAMES. Series characters: James Warren, in at least those marked W; James Weston, in at least those marked JW.
  Brush of Death. Collins, 1958 JW
  Cold Steel. Collins, 1957 JW
  The Disappearing Corpse; see The Runaway Corpse
  The Gold Pistol. Collins, 1956
  The Lady was Disturbed. Collins, 1956 W
  No Sleep at All. Collins, 1941; Alliance, 1941 JW
  Prowl No More, Lady. Collins, 1942
  The Runaway Corpse. Collins, 1957. U.S. title: The Disappearing Corpse. Washburn, 1958 W
  She Fell Among Actors. Collins, 1944; Doubleday, 1944 JW

WARREN, MARY DOUGLAS. Pseudonym of Maysie Greig, 1902- , q.v. Other pseudonym: Jennifer Ames, q.v.

WARREN, PAULETTE
  Brooding Mansion. Lancer, 1973
  Dark Shadow at Bitterhill. Lancer, 1970
  Ghost at Ravenkill Manor. Lancer, 1969
  Hazard House. Popular Library, 1972
  Horror House. Lancer, 1973
  Night Falls at Bitterhill. Lancer, 1969
  Nurse at Brooding Mansion. Lancer, 1969
  Ravenkill. Lancer, 1965
  Some Beckoning Wraith. Lancer, 1965
  Storm over Bitterhill. Lancer, 1969

WARREN, ROBERT PENN. 1905- .
  Meet Me in the Green Glen. Random, 1971; Secker, 1972

WARREN, SAMUEL. 1807-1877. Pseudonym: Warren Warner, q.v.
  Passages from the Diary of a Late Physician. (London), 1832-8 (three volumes); Harper, 1845 ss

WARREN, VERNON. Pseudonym of George Warren Vernon Chapman, 1925- . Series character: Mark Brandon = MB.
  Appointment in Hell. Gifford, 1956
  Backlash. Gifford, 1960
  The Blue Mauritius. Gifford, 1954 MB
  Brandon in New York. Gifford, 1953 MB
  Brandon Returns. Gifford, 1954 MB
  Brandon Takes Over. Gifford, 1953 MB
  Bullets for Brandon. Gifford, 1955 MB
  By Fair Means or Foul. Gifford, 1956
  Farewell by Death. Gifford, 1961
  Invitation to Kill. Gifford, 1963
  Mister Violence. Gifford, 1961
  No Bouquets for Brandon. Gifford, 1955 MB
  Runaround. Gifford, 1958 MB
  Stop-Over Danger. Gifford, 1959
  Three Steps to Hell. Gifford, 1957

WARRICK, MILLIGAN
  The Bandit Trust. Moray, 1934
  Granite Shadows. Moray, 1937
  The Yawning Lion. Grant, 1932

WARRINER, CORNELIA. Joint pseudonym with James A. MacPhail: James Crockett, q.v.

WARRINER, THURMAN. Pseudonym: Simon Troy, q.v. Series character: Mr. Scotter = S.
  Death's Bright Angel. Hodder, 1956 S
  Death's Dateless Night. Hodder, 1952 S
  The Doors of Sleep. Hodder, 1955 S
  Ducats in her Coffin. Hodder, 1951 S
  The Golden Lantern. Hodder, 1958
  Heavenly Bodies. Hodder, 1960 S
  Method in his Murder. Hodder, 1950; Macmillan, 1951 S
  She Died, Of Course. Hodder, 1958 S

WARWICK, CHESTER
  My Pal, the Killer. Ace, 1961

WARWICK, FREDERICK
  The Shadow Behind. Modern, 1938

WARWICK, JAMES
  Blind Alley. French (New York), 1936. (Play.)

WARWICK, PAULINE. Pseudonym of Betty Evelyn Davies.
  Death of a Sinner. Cassell, 1944

WARWICK, SIDNEY
  -Cat's Eyes. Newnes, 1911
  -Conscience Money. Greening, 1914
  -Dreams to Sell. Hodder, 1923
  -A Girl's Temptation. Thomson, 1928
  -The Great Temptation. Thomson, 1923
  A Guilty Silence, with John Mulvy Ouseley. Gay, 1907
  Harvest of Guilt. Newnes, 1911
  -A House of Lies. Cassell, 1909
  In a Bad Man's Grip. Thomson, 1921
  -An Irregular Marriage. Greening, 1911
  Justice Astray. Hodder, 1924
  -The Lone Hand. Hodder, 1922
  The Night of Secrets. Newnes, 1919
  Night of the Thirteenth. Mellifont, 1937
  The River House Mystery. Newnes, 1910
  -The Road Back. Cassell, 1910
  The Silver Basilisk. Hodder, 1924
  -A Slip of a Girl. Hodder, 1923
  -That American Girl. Leng, 1934
  -The Woman Pays. Newnes, 1915

WASHBURN, ROBERT COLLYER
  The Jury of Death. Doubleday, 1930; Paul, 1931

WASSERMAN, (CARL) JACOB. 1873-1934.
    The Maurizius Case. Liveright, 1929;
    Allen, 1930. (Translation of Der Fall
    Maurizius. Berlin, 1928.)

WATEN, JUDAH L(EON)
    Shares in Murder. Australasian Book
    Society, 1957

WATERBURY, JENNIE BULLARD
    -A New Race Diplomatist. Lippincott,
    1900

WATERS. Pseudonym of William Russell.
    Other pseudonym: Inspector F, q.v.
    Autobiography of a London Detective;
    see Autobiography of an English De-
    tective
    Autobiography of an English Detective.
    Maxwell, 1863. U.S. title: Autobio-
    graphy of a London Detective. Dick,
    1864 ss
    The Detective Officer; see The Recol-
    lections of a Policeman
    Diary of a Detective Police Officer;
    see The Recollections of a Policeman
    The Experiences of a French Detective
    Officer. Clarke, 1861; Arno, 1976 ss
    The Game of Life. Ward, 1857. Also pub-
    lished as: Leonard Harlowe; or, The
    Game of Life. Ward, 1862
    The Heir-at-law, and other tales. Lea,
    1861 ss
    -Kirke Webbe, the Privateer Captain.
    Knight, 1858. Also published as: The
    Privateer Captain. Clarke, 1861
    Leaves from the Diary of a Law Clerk.
    Brown, 1857 ss
    Leaves from the Journal of a Custom-
    House Officer. (London), 1868 ss
    Leonard Harlowe; see The Game of Life
    The Privateer Captain; see Kirke Webbe,
    the Privateer Captain
    Recollections of a Detective; see Re-
    collections of a Detective Police-
    Officer
    Recollections of a Detective Police-
    Officer. Brown, 1856. U.S. title: The
    Recollections of a Policeman. Cornish
    Lamport, 1852. Also published as:
    Diary of a Detective Police Officer.
    Dick, 1864. And as: The Detective Of-
    ficer and other tales (with 3 ss
    added). Chambers, 1878. And as: The
    Recollections of a Detective. Loyd,
    1887 ss
    Recollections of a Detective Police-
    Officer. Second Series. Kent, 1859 ss
    (A volume of this main title, Ward,
    1875, contains both first and second
    series.)
    The Recollections of a Policeman; see
    Recollections of a Detective Police-
    Officer
    Recollections of a Sheriff's Officer.
    Aldine Chambers, 1860 ss
    -The Romance of a Common Life. Clarke,
    1861
    A Skeleton in Every House. Clarke,
    1860; Dick, 18?? ss
    Strange Stories of a Detective; or,
    Curiosities of Crime. Dick, 1863 ss
    (British title?)
    Undiscovered Crimes. Ward, 1862 ss
    The Valazy Family and other narratives.
    Ward, 1869 ss

WATERS, THOMAS A. 1938-   .
    Blackwood Cult. Lancer, 1969
    Bow Street Terror. Lancer, 1970
    -Centerforce. Dell, 1974
    In the Halls of Evil. Lancer, 1967
    The Lost Victim. Random, 1973
    Love That Spy. Lancer, 1968
    The Psychedelic Spy. Lancer, 1967

WATKINS, ALAN
    Till the Dying Day. Horwitz, 1965

WATKINS, ALEX. Pseudonym: Joseph Lane
    Linklater, q.v.

WATKINS, ARTHUR THOMAS LEVY. Pseudonym:
    Arthur Watkyn, q.v.

WATKINS, RICHARD HOWELLS
    The Air Murders. Doubleday, 1929;
    Selwyn, 1929
    Half a Clew. Clode, 1927
    The Master of Revels. Doubleday, 1928

WATKINS, RON
    Death Draws the Curtain. Hale, 1973
    A Paper Chase. Hale, 1972

WATKINSON, VALERIE [VALERIE MAE WATKINSON
    ELLISTON]. 1929-   .
    The Sped Arrow. Scribner, 1964

WATKYN, ARTHUR. Pseudonym of Arthur
    Thomas Levy Watkins.
    Amber for Anna. French (London), 1965.
    (3-act play.)
    Not in the Book. French (London), 1958.
    (Play.)

WATNEY, JOHN B(ASIL). 1915-   . Pseudo-
    nym: Anthony Roberts, q.v.
    -Common Love. Putnam, 1954
    -The Glass Facade. Cape, 1963
    Leopard with a Thin Skin. Cape, 1959
    The Quarrelling Room. Cape, 1960
    The Unexpected Angel. Collins, 1949

WATSON, COLIN. 1920-   . Series charac-
    ter: Inspector Purbright, in at least
    those marked P.
    Broomsticks over Flaxborough. Eyre,
    1972. U.S. title: Kissing Covens.
    Putnam, 1972 P
    Bump in the Night. Eyre, 1960; Walker,
    1961
    Charity Ends at Home. Eyre, 1968; Put-
    nam, 1968 P
    Coffin, Scarcely Used. Eyre, 1958; Put-
    nam, 1967 P
    The Flaxborough Crab. Eyre, 1969. U.S.
    title: Just What the Doctor Ordered.
    Putnam, 1969 P
    Hopjoy was Here. Eyre, 1962; Walker,
    1963 P
    Just What the Doctor Ordered; see The
    Flaxborough Crab
    Kissing Covens; see Broomsticks over
    Flaxborough
    Lonelyheart 4122. Eyre, 1967; Putnam,
    1967 P
    The Naked Nuns. Eyre, 1975. U.S. title:
    Six Nuns and a Shotgun. Putnam, 1975
    P
    The Puritan. Eyre, 1966
    Six Nuns and a Shotgun; see The Naked
    Nuns

WATSON, H(ENRY) B(RERETON) MARRIOTT.
    1863-1921. Series character: Dick
    Ryder = DR.
    The Adventurers. Harper (London), 1898;
    Harper (New York), 1899
    Aftermath. Chapman, 1919 ss, some cri-
    minous
    Alise of Astra. Methuen, 1910; Little,
    1911
    At a Venture. Methuen, 1911 ss, some
    criminous
    The Castle by the Sea. Methuen, 1909;
    Little, 1909
    Chapman's Wares. Mills, 1915 ss, some
    criminous
    Diogenes of London and other fantasies
    and sketches. Methuen, 1893 ss, some
    criminous
    The Excelsior. Methuen, 1918
    Galloping Dick. Lane, 1896; Stone, 1896
    DR

The Golden Precipice. Cassell, 1908
The High Toby. Methuen, 1906 DR
The King's Highway. Mills, 1910 DR
The Pester Finger. Skeffington, 1919
The Privateers. Methuen, 1907; Double-
    day, 1907
Romances at Random. Hutchinson, 1909
The Web of the Spider. Hutchinson, 1891

WATSON, JOHN. 1921-   .
    The File of the Golden Goose. Sphere,
    1969. (Novelization of the movie.)

WATSON, JOHN R(EAY), 1872-   , and
    ARTHUR J(OHN) REES, 1872-1942, q.v.
    Series character: Crewe, in both
    titles.
    The Hampstead Mystery. Lane (London &
    New York), 1916
    The Mystery of the Downs. Lane, 1918

WATSON, LEWIS H. Pseudonym: Lewis Har-
    rison, q.v.

WATSON, MARJORIE
    Heir to Polventon. Collins, 1973; Sat-
    urday Review Press, 1974

WATSON, MAURICE
    Reclining Nude. Cassell, 1960

WATSON, ROBERT (PATRICK)
    Louisa Reignier: The Communion of Crime
    and Criminals. Smith, 1895

WATSON, SELWYN VICTOR. Pseudonym: Selwyn,
    q.v.

WATT, LAUCHLIN MacLEAN. 1867-   .
    The Advocate's Wig. Jenkins, 1932

WATTERS, (EUGENE) RUTHERFORD
    Murder in Three Moves. Figgis (Dublin),
    1960

WATTS, EDGAR JOHN PALMER. 1904-   .
    Pseudonym: John Palmer, q.v.

WAUGH, HILLARY (BALDWIN). 1920-   .
    Pseudonyms: H. Baldwin Taylor, Harry
    Walker, qq.v. Series characters:
    Chief Fred Fellows = FF; Frank Ses-
    sions = FS; Sheridan Wesley = SW.
    Born Victim. Doubleday, 1962; Gollancz,
    1963 FF
    A Bride for Hampton House. Doubleday,
    1975; Gollancz, 1976
    Case of the Brunette Bombshell; see
    Rich Man, Dead Man
    The Con Game. Doubleday, 1968; Gol-
    lancz, 1968 FF
    Death and Circumstance. Doubleday,
    1963; Gollancz, 1963 FF
    Doctor on Trial; see Parrish for the
    Defense
    The Eighth Mrs. Bluebeard. Doubleday,
    1958; Foulsham, 1959
    End of a Party. Doubleday, 1965; Gol-
    lancz, 1965 FF
    Finish Me Off. Doubleday, 1970; Gol-
    lancz, 1971 FS
    Girl on the Run. Doubleday, 1965; Gol-
    lancz, 1966
    The Girl Who Cried Wolf. Doubleday,
    1958; Foulsham, 1960
    Hope to Die. Coward, 1948; Boardman,
    1949 SW
    If I Live to Dine; see Madam Will Not
    Dine Tonight
    Jigsaw; see Sleep Long, My Love
    Last Seen Wearing—. Doubleday, 1952;
    Gollancz, 1953

The Late Mrs. D. Doubleday, 1962; Gollancz, 1962 FF
Madam Will Not Dine Tonight. Coward, 1947; Boardman, 1949. Also published as: If I Live to Dine. Graphic, 1949 SW
The Missing Man. Doubleday, 1964; Gollancz, 1964 FF
Murder on the Terrace. Foulsham, 1961
The Odds Run Out. Coward, 1949; Boardman, 1950 SW
Parrish for the Defense. Doubleday, 1974; Gollancz, 1975. Also published as: Doctor on Trial. Dell, 1977
Prisoner's Plea. Doubleday, 1963; Gollancz, 1964 FF
Pure Poison. Doubleday, 1966; Gollancz, 1967 FF
A Rag and a Bone. Doubleday, 1954; Foulsham, 1955
Rich Man, Dead Man. Doubleday, 1956. British title: Rich Man, Murder. Foulsham, 1956. Also published as: Case of the Brunette Bombshell. Crest, 1957
Rich Man, Murder; see Rich Man, Dead Man
Road Block. Doubleday, 1960; Gollancz, 1961 FF
Run When I Say Go. Doubleday, 1969; Gollancz, 1969
The Shadow Guest. Doubleday, 1971; Gollancz, 1971
Sleep Long, My Love. Doubleday, 1959; Gollancz, 1960. Also published as: Jigsaw. Pan, 1962 FF
That Night It Rained. Doubleday, 1961; Gollancz, 1961 FF
"30" Manhattan East. Doubleday, 1968; Gollancz, 1969 FS
The Young Prey. Doubleday, 1969; Gollancz, 1970 FS

WAY, ISABEL STEWART
Bell, Book and Candleflame. Beagle, 1971
Fleur Macabre. Tower, 1967
The House on Sky High Road. Belmont, 1970

WAYDE, BERNARD
An Anarchist's Oath. Street, ca.1900
The Belt of Diamonds. Street, ca.1900
A Compact of Crime. Street, ca.1900
The Coiner's League. Street, ca.1900
The Crooked Inspector. Street, ca.1900
A Custom House Fraud. Street, ca.1900
A False Claim. Street, ca.1900
A Golden Clue. Street, ca.1900
A Government Trust. Street, ca.1900
The Hand on the Window Sill. Street, ca.1900
In the Secret Vault. Street, ca.1900
The King of Anarchists. Street, ca.1900
The Man from Texas. Street, ca.1900
The Man Who Made Money. Street, ca.1900
The Money Jugglers. Street, ca.1900
A Privateer's Defiance. Street, 1903
A Question of Policy. Street, ca.1900
The Smuggler's Ally. Street, ca.1900
The Tracker Tracked. Street, ca.1900
The Treasury's Millions. Street, ca.1900
The Untaxed Whiskey. Street, ca.1900

WAYE, CECIL. Series character: Christopher Perrin, in all titles.
The End of the Chase. Hodder, 1932
The Figure of Eight. Hodder, 1931; Kinsey, 1933
Murder at Monk's Barn. Hodder, 1931
The Prime Minister's Pencil. Hodder, 1933; Kinsey, 1933

WAYLAND, PATRICK. Pseudonym of Richard O'Connor, 1915-1975. Other pseudonym: Frank Archer, q.v. Series character: Lloyd Nicolson, in all titles.
Counterstroke. Doubleday, 1964; Hale, 1965
Double Defector. Doubleday, 1964; Hale, 1966
The Waiting Game. Doubleday, 1965; Hale, 1967

WAYNAR, CHRIS
Fire on the Cliffs. Ace, 1975

WAYNE, CHARLES STOKES. 1858- . Pseudonym: Horace Hazeltine, q.v.

WAYNE, HILARY
Tickletoby. Jenkins, 1949

WEAR-GIFFORD, J.
-Lure of Contraband. Jarrolds, 1920
The Riddle of the River. Jarrolds, 1923

WEATHERHEAD, JOHN
A Force of Innocence. Harrap, 1966
-The Sacred Shaft. Harrap, 1967
-Transplant. Harrap, 1969

WEATHERLY, (JOHN) MAX. 1921- .
The Mantis and the Moth. Houghton, 1964; Gollancz, 1965

WEATHERS, PHILIP. See: A(RTHUR) A(LEXANDER MALCOLM) THOMSON, 1894- ; and: (THOMAS) FALKLAND L(ITTON) CARY.

WEAVER, NICKY
Love, Blood and Tears. Kozy, 1963

WEAVER, ROBERT G. Joint pseudonym with Samuel Leonard Rubenstein, 1922- : Rubin Weber, q.v.

WEBB, ANTHONY. Pseudonym of Norman Scarlyn Wilson, 1901- . Series character: Mr. Pendlebury, in at least those marked P.
Bill Blunders Through. Jenkins, 1944
Mr. Pendlebury and the Suicide Club. Harrap, 1941 P
Mr. Pendlebury Makes a Catch. Harrap, 1939 P
Mr. Pendlebury's Hat Trick. Harrap, 1938 P
Mr. Pendlebury's Second Case. Harrap, 1938 P
Murder in Reverse. Harrap, 1945 P
One Man Saw Them Die. Harrap, 1940 P
Pass Along, Madam! Harrap, 1940
A Queer Bag of Bodies. Harrap, 1947 P
Thank You, Mr. Pendlebury. Harrap, 1939 P
Verdict Without Jury. Harrap, 1937 P

WEBB, DOROTHY ANNA. Pseudonym: Jermyn March, q.v.

WEBB, FORREST. Pseudonym of Richard Forrest-Webb, 1929- . Other pseudonym: David Forrest, q.v.
-Brannington's Leopard. Hodder, 1973; Doubleday, 1974
The Caviar Cruise. Hodder, 1975; Doubleday, 1977
-The Snowboys. Hodder, 1973; Doubleday, 1973

WEBB, JACK. 1920- . Pseudonym: John Farr, q.v. Series characters: Father Joseph Shanley and Sammy Golden = S&G.
The Bad Blonde. Rinehart, 1956; Boardman, 1957 S&G
The Big Sin. Rinehart, 1952; Boardman, 1953 S&G
The Brass Halo. Rinehart, 1957; Boardman, 1958 S&G
The Broken Doll. Rinehart, 1955; Boardman, 1956 S&G
The Damned Lovely. Rinehart, 1954; Boardman, 1955 S&G
The Deadly Sex. Rinehart, 1959; Boardman, 1960 S&G
The Delicate Darling. Rinehart, 1959; Boardman, 1960 S&G
The Gilded Witch. Regency, 1963; Boardman, 1963 S&G
Make My Bed Soon. Holt, 1963; Boardman, 1964
The Naked Angel. Rinehart, 1953. British title: Such Women are Dangerous. Boardman, 1954 S&G
One for My Dame. Holt, 1961; Boardman, 1962
Such Women are Dangerous; see The Naked Angel

WEBB, JEAN FRANCIS. 1910- . Pseudonym: Roberta Morrison, q.v.
The Bride of Cairngore. McKay, 1974
Carnavaron's Castle. Meredith, 1969
The Craigshaw Curse. Meredith, 1968
No Match for Murder. Macmillan, 1942
Roses from a Haunted Garden. McKay, 1971
Somewhere Within This House. McKay, 1973

WEBB, L. J. Pseudonym.
Walking the Dusk. Coward, 1932

WEBB, MARTHA T(OOKE)
The Will and the Willful. Dorrance, 1969

WEBB, RICHARD WILSON. 1901- . Joint pseudonym with Mary Louise Aswell; Martha Mott Kelley; and Hugh Callingham Wheeler, 1913- ; as well as solo pseudonym: Q. Patrick, q.v. Joint pseudonyms with Hugh Callingham Wheeler: Patrick Quentin, Jonathan Stagge, qq.v.

WEBB, SIDNEY HASTINGS
The Painted Honeymoon. Low, 1925

WEBBER, F. SIDNEY
A Baltic Mystery. Nelson, 1926

WEBER, RUBIN. Joint pseudonym of Robert G. Weaver and Samuel Leonard Rubinstein, 1922- .
The Grave-Maker's House. Harper, 1964

WEBLING, PEGGY
Strange Enchantment. Hutchinson, 1929

WEBSTER, F(REDERICK) A(NNESLEY) M(ICHAEL). 1886- . Series character: Ebbie Entwhistle = EE.
-The Adventures of Husky Hillier. Mellifont, 1937
All is Not Gold. Thames, ss
Beneath the Mask. Skeffington, 1948
-Beyond All Fear. Wright, 1934
-Beyond the Frontier. Shaw, 1931 ss
-The Black Shadow. Nisbet, 1922; Moffat, 1923
-By Peak and Pass. Shaw, 1931
The Crime Scientist. Warne, 1930 EE ss
Dark Trails Go East. Wright, 1932
East of Kashgar. Skeffington, 1940
Echoing Footsteps. Thames, ss
Gathering Storm. Wright, 1933
-Gold and Glory. Shaw, 1932 ss
-The Hill of Riches. Hutchinson, 1923
The Islands of the Condemned. Wright, 1933
-The Ivory Talisman. Warne, 1930
Killing No Murder. Thames, ss

-Lost City of Light. Warne, 1934
The Man in the Portrait. Thames, ss
The Man Who Knew. Selwyn, 1927
-M'Sango, the Witch Doctor. Shaw, 1927
Old Ebbie: Detective Up-to-Date. Chapman, 1923 EE ss
Old Ebbie Returns. Chapman, 1925 EE ss
On Government Service. Thames, ss
-Stirring Adventures. Shaw, 1931
To Meet the Law. Thames, ss
-The White Nigger. Mellifont, 1937

WEBSTER, H. M.
The Ballycronin Mystery. Hurst, 1947
The Secret of Baron's Folly. Hurst, 1949
The Tontine Treasure. Hurst, 1951

WEBSTER, HENRY KITCHELL. 1875-1932.
The Alleged Great-Aunt, with Janet Ayer Fairbank and Margaret Ayer Barnes. Bobbs, 1935; Paul, 1935
The Butterfly. Appleton, 1914
The Clock Strikes Two. Bobbs, 1928; Hamilton, 1928
The Corbin Necklace. Bobbs, 1926. British title: The Mystery of the Corbin Necklace. Hamilton, 1929
The Ghost Girl. Appleton, 1913
The Man with the Scarred Hand. Bobbs, 1930
The Mystery of the Corbin Necklace; see The Corbin Necklace
Philopena. Bobbs, 1927; Nash, 1927
The Quartz Eye. Bobbs, 1928; Hodder, 1929
The Sealed Trunk. Bobbs, 1929; Paul, 1929
The Whispering Man. Appleton, 1908; Nash, 1908
Who is the Next? Bobbs, 1931; Garland (London), 1976

WEBSTER, (ALICE) JEAN (CHANDLER). 1876-1916.
The Four-Pools Mystery. Century, 1908; Hodder, 1916

WEBSTER, NOAH. Pseudonym of Bill Knox, 1928- , q.v. Other pseudonyms: Robert McLeod, q.v., Michael Kirk.

WEBSTER, NOSTA H. Pseudonym: Julian Sterne, q.v.

WEDLAKE, GEORGE E. C.
Looted Gold. Jenkins, 1934
The Wrecking Ray. Jenkins, 1935

WEEKES, A(GNES) R(USSELL). See also: next entry. Pseudonym: Anthony Pryde, q.v.
The Story of Leland Gay. Constable, 1932; Dodd, 1932, as by Anthony Pryde

WEEKES, A(GNES) R(USSELL) and R(OSE) K(IRKPATRICK) WEEKES, 1894- , q.v. Pseudonym of Agnes Russell Weekes: Anthony Pryde, q.v. See also: preceding entry.
Affair at the "Vere Arms". Ward, 1935
Alda Abducted. Ward, 1942
-The Duke of Cameron Avenue. Macmillan, 1904. (British title?)
The Emerald Necklace. Ward, 1931; Dodd, 1931, as by Anthony Pryde and R. K. Weekes
The Figure on the Terrace. Ward, 1933
The Girl in the Other Seat. Appleton, 1911. (British title?)
-The Green Cross. Ward, 1937
Ninety in the Shade. Ward, 1937
-Real Life. Bobbs, 1921. (British title?)
-Traitor and Loyalist. Macmillan, 1904. (British title?)

WEEKES, R(OSE) K(IRKPATRICK). 1894- .
See also: A(GNES) R(USSELL) WEEKES.
B14. Allen, 1920. U.S. title: Convict B 14. Brentano's, 1920

WEEKS, JACK
The Grey Affair. Dell, 1961. British title (?): A Time to Kill. Cassell, 1961
The Limbo Touch. GM, 1968
A Time to Kill; see The Grey Affair

WEEKS, WILLIAM E.
All in the Racket. Boni, 1930

WEEKS, WILLIAM RAWLE. 1920- .
Knock and Wait a While. Houghton, 1957; Muller, 1957

WEES, FRANCES SHELLEY. 1902- .
The Country of the Strangers. Doubleday, 1960. British title: Dangerous Deadline. Ward, 1961
Dangerous Deadline; see The Country of the Strangers
Detectives, Ltd.; see The Maestro Murders
Faceless Enemy. Doubleday, 1966; Cassell, 1967
The Keys of my Prison. Doubleday, 1956; Jenkins, 1956
The Last Concubine. Abelard, 1970
The Maestro Murders. Mystery League, 1931. British title: Detectives, Ltd. Eyre, 1933
M'Lord, I am Not Guilty. Doubleday, 1954; Jenkins, 1954
The Mystery of the Creeping Man. Macrae Smith, 1931; Eyre, 1934
This Unnecessary Murder. Jenkins, 1957
Under the Quiet Water. Macrae Smith, 1949; Hurst, 1951
Where is Jenny Now? Doubleday, 1958; Jenkins, 1958

WEIDMAN, JEROME
"I, and I Alone." Pockettes, 1972

WEIGALL, ARTHUR (EDWARD PEARSE BROME). 1880-1934.
The King Who Preferred Moonlight. Hutchinson, 1928

WEIL, BARRY
Dossier IX. H. Hamilton, 1969; Bobbs, 1969

WEIL, JERRY. 1928- .
The Spy Who Came Home to Die. Five Star, 1967

WEILL, GUS. 1933- .
A Woman's Eyes. Dial, 1975; Constable, 1976

WEINER, HENRI. Pseudonym of Stephen Longstreet, 1907- . Other pseudonym: Paul Haggard, q.v.
Crime on the Cuff. Morrow, 1936. Also published as: The Case of the Severed Skull. Mystery Novel of the Month, 1940

WEINER, JACK B. 1929- .
The Morning After. Delacorte, 1973; Hart-Davis, 1974

WEINER, MORRIS COLBY
The Price of Silence. Vantage, 1967

WEINSTEIN, SOL. 1928- . Series character: Oy-Oy-7, in all titles.
Loxfinger. PB, 1965
Matzohball. PB, 1966
On the Secret Service of His Majesty, the Queen. PB, 1966
You Only Live Until You Die. Trident, 1968

WEINTRAUB, SIDNEY. 1922- .
Mexican Slay Ride. Hale, 1962; Abelard, 1962
The Siamese Coup Affair. Boardman, 1963

WEIR, DONALD
-Balkan Saga. Oliver, 1937
-Black Lobster. Wright, 1951
-The Death Stone. Wright, 1939
-The Hot Seat. Wright, 1940
-Red Flows the Barada. Wright, 1948

WEIR, HUGH C(OSGRO). 1884- .
Miss Madelyn Mack, Detective. Page, 1914 ss

WEIR, MARIPOSA
A Chase Round the World; or, A Detective by Chance. Street, 1890

WEISMAN, JOHN, 1942- , and BRIAN (D.) BOYER, 1939- . Series characters: The Headhunters, in all titles.
Heroin Triple Cross. Pinnacle, 1974
Quadraphone Homicide. Pinnacle, 1975
The Starlight Motel Incident. Pinnacle, 1974
Three Faces of Death. Pinnacle, 1974

WEISMILLER, EDWARD (RONALD). 1915- .
The Serpent Sleeping. Putnam, 1962

WEISS, DAVID. 1909- .
The Assassination of Mozart. Hodder, 1970; Morrow, 1971

WEISS, MARTIN L.
Death Hitches a Ride. Ace, 1954
Hate Alley. Ace, 1957

WEISSL, AUGUST
The Mystery of the Green Car. Nelson, 1913. (Translation of Der Grune Auto.)

WELCOME, JOHN. Pseudonym of John Needham Huggard Brennan, 1914- . Series character: Richard Graham, in at least those marked RG.
Beware of Midnight. Faber, 1961; Knopf, 1961
Go for Broke. Faber, 1972; Walker, 1972 RG
Hard to Handle. Faber, 1964 RG
Hell is Where You Find It. Faber, 1968 RG
Mr. Merston's Money. Constable, 1951
On the Stretch. Faber, 1969
Red Coats Galloping. Constable, 1949
Run for Cover. Faber, 1958; Knopf, 1959 RG
Stop at Nothing. Faber, 1959; Knopf, 1960
Wanted for Killing. Faber, 1965; Holt, 1967 RG

WELDEN, ELLIS
Sudden Death of the M.F.H. Heath Cranston, 1938

WELFORD, MAURICE
Queen of Crookdom. Modern, 193?
The Secret Guest Mystery. Modern, 1938
Thameside Gold. Modern, 1938

WELLARD, JAMES (HOWARD). 1909- .
Action of the Tiger. St. Martin's, 1955; Macmillan (London), 1955
A Moment in Time. Dodd, 1947. British title: Spotlight on Murder. Foulsham, 1949
The Snake in the Grass. Dodd, 1942; United Authors, 1946

Wellard, James

Spotlight on Murder; see A Moment in Time

WELLER, MARY ELIZABETH PHYLLIS. Joint pseudonym with Agnes Rosemary Cooper: Ramsay Bell, q.v.

WELLES, (GEORGE) ORSON. 1915- .
Mr. Arkadin. Crowell, 1956; Allen, 1956

WELLMAN, MANLY WADE. 1905- .
A Double Life. Century, 1947. (Novelization of the movie.)
Find My Killer. Farrar, 1947; Low, 1948
Sherlock Holmes's War of the Worlds, with Wade Wellman, 1939- . Warner, 1975

WELLMAN, WADE. 1939- . See: MANLY WADE WELLMAN, 1905- .

WELLS, A(RTHUR) W(ALTER). 1894- .
All This is Ended. Melrose, 1936 ss, two criminous

WELLS, ANNA MARY. 1906- .
Fear of Death. Wingate, 1951
Murderer's Choice. Knopf, 1943; Hammond, 1950
The Night of May Third. Doubleday, 1956; Foulsham, 1957
Sin of Angels. Simon, 1948; Hammond, 1951
A Talent for Murder. Knopf, 1942; Hammond, 1948

WELLS, CAROLYN. 1870-1942. Pseudonym: Rowland Wright, q.v. Series characters: Kenneth Carlisle = KC; Alan Ford = AF; Lorimer Lane = LL; Fleming Stone = FS; Pennington Wise = PW.
The Affair at Flower Acres. Doran, 1923 PW
All at Sea. Lippincott (Philadelphia & London), 1927; Thomson, 1929 FS
Anybody But Anne. Lippincott (Philadelphia & London), 1914 FS
Anything But the Truth. Lippincott (Philadelphia & London), 1925 FS
The Beautiful Derelict. Lippincott (Philadelphia & London), 1935 FS
The Black Night Murders. Lippincott, 1941 FS
The Bride of a Moment. Doran, 1916; Hodder, 1920 AF
The Broken O. Lippincott (Philadelphia & London), 1933 FS
The Bronze Hand. Lippincott (Philadelphia & London), 1926 FS
Calling All Suspects. Lippincott, 1939 FS
A Chain of Evidence. Lippincott, 1912 FS
The Clue. Lippincott, 1909; Hodder, 1920 FS
The Clue of the Eyelash. Lippincott (Philadelphia & London), 1933 FS
The Come-Back. Doran, 1921; Hodder, 1921 PW
Crime Incarnate. Lippincott, 1940 FS
The Crime in the Crypt. Lippincott (Philadelphia & London), 1928 FS
Crime Tears On. Lippincott, 1939 FS
The Curved Blades. Lippincott (Philadelphia & London), 1916 FS
The Daughter of the House. Lippincott (Philadelphia & London), 1925 FS
Deep-Lake Mystery. Doubleday, 1928
Devil's Work. Lippincott, 1940 FS
The Diamond Pin. Lippincott (Philadelphia & London), 1919 FS
The Doomed Five. Lippincott (Philadelphia & London), 1930 FS

The Doorstep Murders. Doubleday, 1930 KC
The Elusive Vicky Van; see Vicky Van
Eyes in the Wall. Lippincott (Philadelphia & London), 1934 FS
Face Cards. Putnam (New York & London), 1925
Faulkner's Folly. Doran, 1917 AF
Feathers Left Around. Lippincott (Philadelphia & London), 1923 FS
For Goodness' Sake. Lippincott (Philadelphia & London), 1935 FS
The Fourteenth Key. Putnam (New York & London), 1924 LL
Fuller's Earth. Lippincott (Philadelphia & London), 1932 FS
The Furthest Fury. Lippincott (Philadelphia & London), 1924 FS
The Ghosts' High Noon. Lippincott (Philadelphia & London), 1930 FS
Gilt-Edged Guilt. Lippincott, 1938 FS
The Gold Bag. Lippincott (Philadelphia & London), 1911 FS
Horror House. Lippincott (Philadelphia & London), 1931 FS
The Huddle. Lippincott (Philadelphia & London), 1936 FS
The Importance of Being Murdered. Lippincott, 1939 FS
In the Onyx Lobby. Doran, 1920; Hodder, 1920 PW
In the Tiger's Cage. Lippincott (Philadelphia & London), 1934 FS
The Killer. Lippincott, 1938 FS
The Luminous Face. Doran, 1921 PW
The Man Who Fell Through the Earth. Doran, 1919; Harrap, 1924 PW
The Mark of Cain. Lippincott (Philadelphia & London), 1917 FS
The Master Murderer. Lippincott (Philadelphia & London), 1933 FS
The Maxwell Mystery. Lippincott (Philadelphia & London), 1913 FS
The Missing Link. Lippincott, 1938 FS
Money Musk. Lippincott (Philadelphia & London), 1936 FS
More Lives Than One. Boni, 1923; Hutchinson, 1924 LL
The Moss Mystery. Garden City, 1924
Murder at the Casino. Lippincott, 1941 FS
Murder in the Bookshop. Lippincott (Philadelphia & London), 1936 FS
Murder on Parade. Lippincott, 1940 FS
Murder Plus. Lippincott, 1940 FS
Murder Will In. Lippincott, 1942 FS
The Mystery Girl. Lippincott (Philadelphia & London), 1922 FS
The Mystery of the Sycamore. Lippincott (Philadelphia & London), 1921 FS
The Mystery of the Tarn. Lippincott (Philadelphia & London), 1937 FS
Prillilgirl. Lippincott (Philadelphia & London), 1924 FS
The Radio Studio Murder. Lippincott (Philadelphia & London), 1937 FS
Raspberry Jam. Lippincott (Philadelphia & London), 1920 FS
The Red-Haired Girl. Lippincott (Philadelphia & London), 1926 FS
The Roll-Top Desk Mystery. Lippincott (Philadelphia & London), 1932 FS
The Room with the Tassels. Doran, 1918 AF
The Sixth Commandment. Doran, 1927
The Skeleton at the Feast. Doubleday, 1931 KC
Sleeping Dogs. Doubleday, 1929 KC
Spooky Hollow. Lippincott (Philadelphia & London), 1923 FS
The Tannahill Tangle. Lippincott (Philadelphia & London), 1928 FS
The Tapestry Room Murder. Lippincott (Philadelphia & London), 1929 FS
Triple Murder. Lippincott (Philadelphia & London), 1929 FS
The Umbrella Murder. Lippincott (Philadelphia & London), 1931 FS

The Vanishing of Betty Varian. Doran, 1922; Collins, 1924 PW
The Vanity Case. Putnam (New York & London), 1926
Vicky Van. Lippincott (Philadelphia & London), 1918. Also published as: The Elusive Vicky Van. Mellifont, 1934 FS
The Visiting Villain. Lippincott (Philadelphia & London), 1934 FS
Wheels Within Wheels. Doran, 1923 PW
Where's Emily. Lippincott (Philadelphia & London), 1927 FS
The White Alley. Lippincott (Philadelphia & London), 1915 FS
Who Killed Caldwell? Lippincott, 1942 FS
The Wooden Indian. Lippincott (Philadelphia & London), 1935 FS

WELLS, CHARLIE [CHARLES HARDING WELLS]
The Last Kill. Signet, 1955
Let the Night Cry. Abelard (New York), 1953; Abelard (London), 1959

WELLS, H(ERBERT) G(EORGE). 1866-1946.
The Stolen Bacillus, and other incidents. Methuen, 1895 ss, at least one criminous

WELLS, MICHAEL
The Doublecrossers. Hale, 1961

WELLS, ROBERT M.
The Finger of Smoke. Street (New Magnet)
A Fortune in Peril. Street (New Magnet)
On Fortune's Wheel. Street (New Magnet)
Out of Chaos. Street (New Magnet)
A Woman of Nerve. Street (New Magnet)

WELLS, SUSAN. Pseudonym of Doris Siegel, q.v. Series character: Anthony Ware, in all titles.
Death is my Name. Scribner, 1942; Cherry Tree, 1943
Footsteps in the Air. Simon, 1940; Cassell, 1941
Murder is not Enough. Simon, 1939; Cassell, 1939
The Witches' Pond. Doubleday, 1947

WELLS, TOBIAS. Pseudonym of De Loris Florine Stanton Forbes, 1923- . Other pseudonyms: Stanton Forbes, Forbes Rydell, qq.v. Series character: Knute Severson, in all titles.
Brenda's Murder. Doubleday, 1973; Hale, 1974
Dead by the Light of the Moon. Doubleday, 1967; Gollancz, 1968
A Die in the Country. Doubleday, 1972; Hale, 1974
Die Quickly, Dear Mother. Doubleday, 1969; Hale, 1969
Dinky Died. Doubleday, 1970; Hale, 1970
The Foo Dog. Doubleday, 1971. British title: The Lotus Affair. Hale, 1973
Hark, Hark, the Watchdogs Bark. Doubleday, 1975; Hale, 1976
Have Mercy Upon Us. Doubleday, 1974; Hale, 1975
How to Kill a Man. Doubleday, 1972; Hale, 1973
The Lotus Affair; see The Foo Dog
A Matter of Love and Death. Doubleday, 1966; Gollancz, 1966
Murder Most Fouled Up. Doubleday, 1968; Hale, 1969
What Should You Know of Dying? Doubleday, 1967; Gollancz, 1967
What to Do Until the Undertaker Comes. Doubleday, 1971; Hale, 1973
The Young Can Die Protesting. Doubleday, 1969; Hale, 1970

WELLSLEY, JULIE
   Castle on the Mountain. Dell, 1972
   Climb the Dark Mountain. Lancer, 1970
   House Malign. Lancer, 1969
   Stranger in a Dark Land. Lancer, 1969
   Two Faces of Fear. Lancer, 1971
   The Wine of Vengeance. Lancer, 1969

WELTON, ARTHUR D(ORMAN). 1867-   .
   The 27th Ride. Sears, 1932

WEMPE, IRENE
   Come to my Funeral. Ballantine, 1967

WENLOCK, ARTHUR
   The Countermine. Rivers, 1904

WENTWORTH, PATRICIA. Pseudonym of Nora Amy Dillon Turnbull, 1878-1961.
   Series character: Maud Silver = MS.
   Account Rendered; see Who Pays the Piper?
   The Alington Inheritance. Hodder, 1960; Lippincott, 1958 MS
   The Amazing Chance. Hodder, 1926; Lippincott, 1927
   Anna, Where are You? Hodder, 1953; Lippincott, 1951. Also published as: Death at Deep End. Pyramid, 1963 MS
   The Annam Jewel. Melrose, 1924; Small, 1925
   Anne Belinda. Hodder, 1927; Lippincott, 1928
   The Astonishing Adventure of Jane Smith. Melrose, 1923; Small, 1923
   Beggar's Choice. Hodder, 1930; Lippincott, 1931
   The Benevent Treasure. Hodder, 1956; Lippincott, 1954 MS
   The Black Cabinet. Hodder, 1925; Small, 1926
   The Blind Side. Hodder, 1939; Lippincott, 1939
   Blindfold. Hodder, 1935; Lippincott, 1935
   The Brading Collection. Hodder, 1952; Lippincott, 1950 MS
   The Case is Closed. Hodder, 1937; Lippincott, 1937 MS
   The Case of William Smith. Hodder, 1950; Lippincott, 1948 MS
   The Catherine Wheel. Hodder, 1951; Lippincott, 1949 MS
   The Chinese Shawl. Hodder, 1943; Lippincott, 1943 MS
   The Clock Strikes Twelve. Hodder, 1945; Lippincott, 1944 MS
   The Coldstone. Hodder, 1930; Lippincott, 1930
   Danger Calling. Hodder, 1931; Lippincott, 1931
   Danger Point. Hodder, 1942. U.S. title: In the Balance. Lippincott, 1941 MS
   Dark Threat; see Pilgrim's Rest
   Dead or Alive. Hodder, 1936; Lippincott, 1936
   Death at Deep End; see Anna, Where are You?
   Devil-in-the-Dark. Hodder, 1934. U.S. title: Touch and Go. Lippincott, 1934
   The Dower House Mystery. Hodder, 1925; Small, 1925
   Down Under. Hodder, 1937; Lippincott, 1937
   Eternity Ring. Hodder, 1950; Lippincott, 1948 MS
   Fear by Night. Hodder, 1934; Lippincott, 1934
   The Fingerprint. Hodder, 1959; Lippincott, 1956 MS
   Fool Errant. Hodder, 1927; Lippincott, 1929
   The Gazebo. Hodder, 1958; Lippincott, 1956. Also published as: The Summerhouse. Pyramid, 1967 MS
   The Girl in the Cellar. Hodder, 1961 MS
   Grey Mask. Hodder, 1928; Lippincott, 1929 MS
   Hole and Corner. Hodder, 1936; Lippincott, 1936
   Hue and Cry. Hodder, 1927; Lippincott, 1927
   In the Balance; see Danger Point
   The Ivory Dagger. Hodder, 1953; Lippincott, 1951 MS
   The Key. Hodder, 1946; Lippincott, 1944 MS
   Kingdom Lost. Hodder, 1931; Lippincott, 1930
   Ladies' Bane. Hodder, 1954; Lippincott, 1952 MS
   Latter End. Hodder, 1949; Lippincott, 1947 MS
   The Listening Eye. Hodder, 1957; Lippincott, 1955 MS
   Lonesome Road. Hodder, 1939; Lippincott, 1939 MS
   Miss Silver Comes to Stay. Hodder, 1951; Lippincott, 1949 MS
   Miss Silver Deals with Death; see Miss Silver Intervenes
   Miss Silver Intervenes. Hodder, 1944. U.S. title: Miss Silver Deals with Death. Lippincott, 1943 MS
   Mr. Zero. Hodder, 1938; Lippincott, 1938
   Nothing Venture. Cassell, 1932; Lippincott, 1932
   Out of the Past. Hodder, 1955; Lippincott, 1953 MS
   Outrageous Fortune; see Seven Green Stones
   Pilgrim's Rest. Hodder, 1948; Lippincott, 1946. Also published as: Dark Threat. Popular Library, 1951 MS
   Poison in the Pen. Hodder, 1957; Lippincott, 1955 MS
   Pursuit of a Parcel. Hodder, 1942; Lippincott, 1942
   Red Danger. Cassell, 1932. U.S. title: Red Shadow. Lippincott, 1932
   The Red Lacquer Case. Melrose, 1924; Small, 1925
   Red Shadow; see Red Danger
   Red Stefan. Hodder, 1935; Lippincott, 1935
   Rolling Stone. Hodder, 1940; Lippincott, 1940
   Run! Hodder, 1938; Lippincott, 1938
   Seven Green Stones. Cassell, 1933. U.S. title: Outrageous Fortune. Lippincott, 1933
   She Came Back; see The Traveller Returns
   Silence in Court. Hodder, 1947; Lippincott, 1945
   The Silent Pool. Hodder, 1956; Lippincott, 1954 MS
   Spotlight. Hodder, 1949. U.S. title: Wicked Uncle. Lippincott, 1947 MS
   The Summerhouse; see The Gazebo
   Through the Wall. Hodder, 1952; Lippincott, 1950 MS
   Touch and Go; see Devil-in-the-Dark
   The Traveller Returns. Hodder, 1948. U.S. title: She Came Back. Lippincott, 1945 MS
   Unlawful Occasions. Hodder, 1941. U.S. title: Weekend with Death. Lippincott, 1941
   Vanishing Point. Hodder, 1955; Lippincott, 1953 MS
   Walk with Care. Cassell, 1933; Lippincott, 1933
   The Watersplash. Hodder, 1953; Lippincott, 1951 MS
   Weekend with Death; see Unlawful Occasions
   Who Pays the Piper? Hodder, 1940. U.S. title: Account Rendered. Lippincott, 1940
   Wicked Uncle; see Spotlight
   Will-o'-the-Wisp. Hodder, 1928; Lippincott, 1928

WENZELL, ISABEL d'ESTE
   Dragon's Lair. Lancer, 1967

WERNER, GEORGE
   One Helluva Blow. Gold Star, 1964

WERRY, RICHARD R. 1916-   .
   Hammer Me Home. Dodd, 1955

WESLEY, MARY. 1912-   .
   The Sixth Seal. Macdonald, 1969; Stein, 1971

WESLEY, ROBERT
   The Rogue with a Past. Street (Magnet)

WEST, ALROY
   The Baying Hound. Wright, 1934
   The Beach of Skulls. Wright, 1937
   The Black Matador. Wright, 1937
   The Crouching Men. Wright, 1933
   Hate Island. Wright, 1934; Godwin, 1935
   The Knife Terror. Wright, 1935
   The Man Who Didn't Exist. Wright, 1935
   The Messengers of Death. Wright, 1935

WEST, CAROL. Pseudonym of Clara A. Wakevainen.
   Laughing Malefactor. Vantage, 1965

WEST, DAVID. Pseudonym of David Derek Stacton.
   Wish Me Dead. Eyre, 1960

WEST, EDWARD (CHARLES) SACKVILLE
   The Ruin. Heinemann, 1926

WEST, ELLIOT. 1924-   .
   Man Running. Little, 1959; Weidenfeld, 1959
   The Night is a Time for Listening. Random, 1966; Gollancz, 1966
   These Lonely Victories. Putnam, 1972; Gollancz, 1973

WEST, GEOFFREY PHILIP
   How Did Elmer Die? Longmans, 1938

WEST, JOHN B. Series character: Rocky Steele, in all titles.
   Bullets are my Business. Signet, 1960
   Cobra Venom. Signet, 1959
   Death on the Rocks. Signet, 1961
   An Eye for an Eye. Signet, 1959
   Never Kill a Cop. Signet, 1961
   A Taste for Blood. Signet, 1960

WEST, JOYCE (TARLTON). See: MARY (EDITH CLARKE) SCOTT, 1888-   .

WEST, KEITH. Pseudonym of Kenneth Westmacott Lane, 1893-   .
   -Bamboo. Jarrolds, 1931
   Hanging Waters. Lovat Dickson, 1933; Putnam, 1933
   -The Hollow Hub. Hale, 1951
   The House That Chak Built. Jenkins, 1935
   -The Widows of the Magistrate. Hale, 1949

WEST, LYN
   Corpse Without a Jacket. Everybody's, 1946
   The Lost House Mystery. Mitre, 1944

WEST, MORRIS L(ANGLO). 1916-   . Pseudonym: Michael East, q.v.
   The Ambassador. Heinemann, 1965; Morrow, 1965
   Backlash; see The Second Victory
   The Big Story. Heinemann, 1957. U.S. title: The Crooked Road. Morrow, 1957
   The Crooked Road; see The Big Story
   -Daughter of Silence. Heinemann, 1961; Morrow, 1961. 3-act play based on this novel: Morrow, 1962

Harlequin. Collins, 1974; Morrow, 1974
-The Heretic. Heinemann, 1970; Morrow, 1969. (Play.)
-Kundu. Angus, 1957; Dell, 1956
The Salamander. Heinemann, 1973; Morrow, 1973
The Second Victory. Heinemann, 1958. U.S. title: Backlash. Morrow, 1958
Summer of the Red Wolf. Heinemann, 1971; Morrow, 1971
The Tower of Babel. Heinemann, 1968; Morrow, 1968

WEST, NICHOLSON
-Gold Island. Cassell, 1904
The Mysterious Millionaire. Greening, 1906

WEST, PAUL. See: WILLIAM (ANDREW) JOHNSTON, 1871-1929.

WESTALL, SHEILA
The Galmart Affair. Hale, 1975

WESTALL, WILLIAM (BURY). 1835-1903.
-As a Man Sows. Ward, 1894
-As Luck Would Have It. Chatto, 1900
-Back to Africa. Ward, 1891
-Ben Clough and other stories. Ward, 1892; Lovell, 1891 ss
-Birch Dene. Ward, 1889; Harper, 1889
Dr. Wynne's Revenge. Chatto, 1904
-Don or Devil? Pearson, 1901
-A Fair Crusader. Hurst, 1888; Harper, 1887
-For Honour and Life. Osgood, 1894; Harper, 1894
Her Ladyship's Secret. Chatto, 1901
-Her Two Millions. Ward, 1887; Harper, 1887
John Brown & Larry Lohengrin; see Larry Lohengrin
-Larry Lohengrin. Tinsley, 1881. Also published as: John Brown & Larry Lohengrin. Ward, 1889
Mr. Fortescue; see Nigel Fortescue
-Nigel Fortescue. Ward, 1888. U.S. title: Mr. Fortescue. Lovell, 1888
The Old Bank. Chatto, 1902
-The Old Factory. Tinsley, 1881
-The Princes of Peele. Lovell, 1892. (British title?)
-A Queer Race. Cassell (London & New York), 1887
-Ralph Norbreck's Trust. Tinsley, 1883
-A Red Bridal. Chatto, 1899
-Red Rivington. Hurst, 1882
-Roy of Roy's Court. Ward, 1892
The Sacred Crescents. Chatto, 1902
-Sons of Belial. Chatto, 1895; Cassell, 1895
Strange Crimes. Ward, 1890; Lovell, 1890 ss
-Trust-Money. Chatto, 1892
-Two Pinches of Snuff. Ward, 1886; Harper, 1886
A Very Queer Business, and other stories. Chatto, 1904 ss
-A Woman Tempted Him. Chatto, 1898

WESTBIE, CONSTANCE LOVEALL
The Birdcage Murders. Bouregy, 1964

WESTBROOK, PERRY D(ICKIE). 1916- .
Series character: Dr. Samuel Cutting = SC.
Happy Deathday. Phoenix, 1947 SC
Infra Blood. Phoenix, 1950 SC
It Boils Down to Murder. Arcadia, 1953
The Red Herring Murder. Phoenix, 1949 SC
The Sting of Death. Arcadia, 1955

WESTERHAM, S. C. Pseudonym of Cyril A(rgentine) Alington, 1872-1955, q.v.
Mixed Bags. Christopher, 1929; McBride, 1929

WESTHEIMER, DAVID. 1917- . Pseudonym: Z. Z. Smith, q.v.
The Avila Gold. Putnam, 1974; Joseph, 1975
Going Public. Mason, 1973; Joseph, 1973
The Olmec Head. Little, 1974; Joseph, 1974
Over the Edge. Little, 1972; Joseph, 1974

WESTLAKE, DONALD E(DWIN). 1933- .
Pseudonyms: Tucker Coe, Timothy J. Culver, Richard Stark, qq.v. Series character: Dortmunder = D.
Bank Shot. Simon, 1972; Hodder, 1972 D
-Brothers Keepers. Evans, 1975; Hodder, 1977
The Busy Body. Random, 1966; Boardman, 1966
Cops and Robbers. Evans, 1972; Hodder, 1973
The Curious Facts Preceding My Execution. Random, 1968 ss
The Fugitive Pigeon. Random, 1965; Boardman, 1966
Gangway!, with Brian (Francis Wynne) Garfield, 1939- , q.v. Evans, 1973; Barker, 1974
God Save the Mark. Random, 1967; Joseph, 1968
Help I am Being Held Prisoner. Evans, 1974; Hodder, 1975
The Hot Rock. Simon, 1970; Hodder, 1971 D
I Gave at the Office. Simon, 1971; Hodder, 1972
Jimmy the Kid. Evans, 1974; Hodder, 1975 D
Killing Time. Random, 1961; Boardman, 1962. Also published as: The Operator. Dell, 1964
Killy. Random, 1963; Boardman, 1964
The Mercenaries. Random, 1960; Boardman, 1961. Also published as: The Smashers. Dell, 1962; Four Square, 1963
The Operator; see Killing Time
Pity Him Afterwards. Random, 1964; Boardman, 1965
The Smashers; see The Mercenaries
Somebody Owes Me Money. Random, 1969; Hodder, 1970
The Spy in the Ointment. Random, 1966; Boardman, 1967
361. Random, 1962; Boardman, 1962
Two Much! Evans, 1975; Hodder, 1976
Who Stole Sassi Manoon? Random, 1969; Hodder, 1971

WESTON, ALLEN. Joint pseudonym of Alice Mary Norton, 1912?- , and Grace Allen Hogarth, 1905- . Other Norton pseudonym: Andre Norton, q.v.
Murders for Sale. Hammond, 1954

WESTON, CAROLYN. Series characters: Casey Kellogg and Al Krug = K&K.
Danju Gig. Random, 1969. British title: Spy in Black. Hale, 1972
Poor, Poor Ophelia. Random, 1972; Gollancz, 1973 K&K
Spy in Black; see Danju Gig
Susannah Screaming. Random, 1975; Gollancz, 1976 K&K
Tormented. Berkley, 1958

WESTON, GARNETT (JAMES). Series character: Highway = H.
Citizens—to Arms!; see The Man with the Monocle
Dead Men are Dangerous. Stokes, 1937; Hutchinson, 1937 H
Death Never Forgets; see Murder in Haste

The Hidden Portal. Doubleday, 1946
Legacy of Fear. Mill, 1950
The Man with the Monocle. Doubleday, 1943. British title (?): Citizens—to Arms! Cassell, 1943
Murder in Haste. Stokes, 1935. British title: Death Never Forgets. Hutchinson, 1935 H
Murder on Shadow Island. Farrar, 1933; Hutchinson, 1933
Poldrate Street. Messner, 1944
The Undertaker Dies. Hutchinson, 1940

WESTON, GEORGE. 1880- .
Queen of the World. Dodd, 1923
Wings of Destiny. Dodd, 1929
The Wondering Moon. Dodd, 1926

WESTON, HELEN GRAY
House of False Faces. Paperback Library, 1967
Mystic Manor. Paperback Library, 1966

WESTON, JOHN (HARRISON), 1932- .
The Walled Parrot. McGraw, 1975

WEST-WATSON, KEITH CAMPBELL. Pseudonym: Keith Campbell, q.v.

WESTWOOD, A(NNE) M(cDOUGALL). 1887- .
The Flying Firs. Hurst, 1930

WETHERELL, JUNE
The Cottage at Avalanche. Popular Library, 1972
Her Stepfather's House. Lancer, 1973
House by the Bay. Dell, 1971
The House on Cabra. Belmont, 1966
Legacy of the Lost. Lancer, 1970
Opal Street. Lancer, 1967
Thirteen Winston Street. Popular Library, 1971
Touch of the Witch. Lancer, 1969
Willoughby Manor. Ballantine, 1974

WEVERKA, ROBERT. 1926- .
Griff. Bantam, 1973. (Novelization of the TV movie.)
Moonrock. Bantam (New York), 1973; Bantam (London), 1975. (Novelization of the Search TV series.)
One Minute to Eternity. Morrow, 1969
Search. Bantam, 1973. (Novelization of the TV series.)
The Sting. Bantam, 1973; Corgi, 1973. (Novelization of the movie.)

WEYMAN, STANLEY J(OHN). 1855-1928.
The Man in Black. Cassell (London & New York), 1894

WEYMOUTH, ANTHONY. Pseudonym of Ivo Geikie Cobb, 1887- . Series character: Inspector Treadgold, in at least those marked T.
Cornish Crime. Hodder pb, 1937
The Doctors are Doubtful. Barker, 1935 T
Frozen Death. Barker, 1934 T
Hard Liver. Barker, 1936 T
Inspector Treadgold Investigates. Rich, 1941 ss T
No, Sir Jeremy. Barker, 1935 T
Tempt Me Not. Rich, 1937

WHALEY, F(RANCIS) J(OHN) 1897-1977.
Challenge to Murder. Skeffington, 1937
Death at Datchets. Hale, 1941
Enter a Spy. Hale, 1941
The Mystery of Number Five. Hale, 1940
Reduction of Staff. Skeffington, 1936
Southern Electric Murder. Skeffington, 1938
Swift Solution. Hale, 1939
This Path is Dangerous. Hale, 1938
Trouble in College. Skeffington, 1936

WHARTON, ALTHEA
　The White Ghost of Fenwick Hall. PB, 1974

WHEATLEY, CHRIS
　Baby, Don't Get Rough. Gray, 1953
　Dames, Diamonds and Death! Grayling, 1951
　Date for a Dame. Gray, 1951
　Dizzy Dames Die Fast. Gray, 1951
　Hot Dames—Cold Lead. Grayling, 1951
　Murder at the Blue Garter. Gray, 1951
　Never Trust a Dame. Gray, 1956
　This Dame Spells Death. Grayling, 1950

WHEATLEY, DENNIS (YATES). 1897-1977.
　Series characters; Roger Brook, in at least those marked RB; Julian Day, in at least those marked JD; Duke de Richleau, in at least those marked DR; Gregory Sallust, in at least those marked GS.
　Bill for the Use of a Body. Hutchinson, 1964　JD
　Black August. Hutchinson, 1934; Dutton, 1934　GS
　The Black Baroness. Hutchinson, 1940; Macmillan, 1942　GS
　Code Word—Golden Fleece. Hutchinson, 1946　DR
　Come into my Parlour. Hutchinson, 1946　GS
　Contraband. Hutchinson, 1936　GS
　Curtain of Fear. Hutchinson, 1953
　Dangerous Inheritance. Hutchinson, 1965　DR
　The Dark Secret of Josephine. Hutchinson, 1955　RB
　Desperate Measures. Hutchinson, 1974　RB
　The Devil Rides Out. Hutchinson, 1935; Hutchinson (U.S.), 1978　DR
　The Eunuch of Stamboul. Hutchinson, 1935; Little, 1935
　Evil in a Mask. Hutchinson, 1969
　The Fabulous Valley. Hutchinson, 1934
　Faked Passports. Hutchinson, 1940; Macmillan, 1943　GS
　File on Bolitho Blane; see Murder Off Miami
　File on Robert Prentice; see Who Killed Robert Prentice?
　The Forbidden Territory. Hutchinson, 1933; Dutton, 1933　DR
　Gateway to Hell. Hutchinson, 1970; Ballantine, 1973
　The Golden Spaniard. Hutchinson, 1938　DR
　Gunmen, Gallants, and Ghosts. Hutchinson, 1943　ss
　The Haunting of Toby Jugg. Hutchinson, 1948; Hutchinson (U.S.), 1978
　Herewith the Clues! Hutchinson, 1939
　The Irish Witch. Hutchinson, 1973
　The Island Where Time Stands Still. Hutchinson, 1954　GS
　The Ka of Gifford Hillary. Hutchinson, 1956; Hutchinson (U.S.), 1978
　The Launching of Roger Brook. Hutchinson, 1947　RB
　The Malinsay Massacre. Hutchinson, 1938
　The Man Who Killed the King. Hutchinson, 1951; Putnam, 1965　RB
　The Man Who Missed the War. Hutchinson, 1945
　Mayhem in Greece. Hutchinson, 1962
　Mediterranean Nights. Hutchinson, 1942　ss
　Murder Off Miami. Hutchinson, 1936. U.S. title: File on Bolitho Blane. Morrow, 1936
　The Prisoner in the Mask. Hutchinson, 1957　DR
　The Quest of Julian Day. Hutchinson, 1939　JD
　The Rape of Venice. Hutchinson, 1959　RB
　The Ravishing of Lady Mary Ware. Hutchinson, 1971
　The Rising Storm. Hutchinson, 1949　RB
　The Satanist. Hutchinson, 1960; Ballantine, 1974
　The Scarlet Impostor. Hutchinson, 1940; Macmillan, 1942　GS
　The Second Seal. Hutchinson, 1950　DR
　The Secret War. Hutchinson, 1937
　The Shadow of Tyburn Tree. Hutchinson, 1948; Ballantine, 1973　RB
　Sixty Days to Live. Hutchinson, 1939
　Star of Ill-Omen. Hutchinson, 1952
　Strange Conflict. Hutchinson, 1941　DR
　The Strange Story of Linda Lee. Hutchinson, 1972
　Such Power is Dangerous. Hutchinson, 1933
　The Sultan's Daughter. Hutchinson, 1963　RB
　The Sword of Fate. Hutchinson, 1941; Macmillan, 1944　JD
　They Found Atlantis. Hutchinson, 1936; Lippincott, 1936
　They Used Dark Forces. Hutchinson, 1964　GS
　Three Inquisitive People. Hutchinson, 1940　DR
　To the Devil—a Daughter. Hutchinson, 1953; Hutchinson (U.S.), 1978
　Traitor's Gate. Hutchinson, 1958　GS
　Uncharted Seas. Hutchinson, 1938
　Unholy Crusade. Hutchinson, 1967
　"V" for Vengeance. Hutchinson, 1942; Macmillan, 1942　GS
　Vendetta in Spain. Hutchinson, 1961　DR
　The Wanton Princess. Hutchinson, 1966　RB
　The White Witch of the South Seas. Hutchinson, 1968　GS
　Who Killed Robert Prentice? Hutchinson, 1937. U.S. title: File on Robert Prentice. Greenberg, 1937

WHEELER, BENSON and CLAIRE LEE PURDY
　The Riddle of the Eighth Guest. Speller, 1936

WHEELER, EDW(ARD) L(YTTON). 1854?-1885.
　Deadwood Dick's Last Shot. Ogilvie, 1902
　Fritz, the Bound Boy Detective. Westbrook, ca.1920
　Fritz to the Front. Westbrook, ca.1920
　The Frontier Detective. Westbrook, ca.1920
　The Heart of Oak Detective. Westbrook, ca.1920

WHEELER, FRANCIS
　Sylvanian Adventure. Hurst, 1939

WHEELER, GORDON
　Easy Come. Random, 1974

WHEELER, H. E. Series characters: Kendal Graydon, in at least those marked KG; Stephen Rant, in at least those marked SR.
　Dead Men Turn Green. Jenkins, 1939　KG
　Death Calls the Jester. Jenkins, 1936　KG
　Death Takes a Ride. Jenkins, 1942　SR
　No Crime is Perfect. Jenkins, 1935
　The Syndicate of Death. Jenkins, 1937
　The Third Attempt. Jenkins, 1946　SR

WHEELER, HUGH CALLINGHAM. 1913-　　.
　Joint pseudonyms with Richard Wilson Webb, 1901-　: Q. Patrick, Patrick Quentin, Jonathan Stagge, qq.v.

WHEELER, KEITH. 1911-　　.
　Epitaph for Mister Wynn. Putnam, 1971; Hodder, 1972
　The Last Mayday. Doubleday, 1968; Hodder, 1969

WHEELER, PAUL. 1934-　　.
　And the Bullets were Made of Lead. Hutchinson, 1968; Doubleday, 1969
　Ransom. Fontana, 1975; Ballantine, 1974

WHEELER, SAMUEL WATSON
　Count de Mornay; or, Back from the Dead. [Author], 1894

WHEELER-NICHOLSON, MALCOLM. 1890-　　.
　Death Over London. Gateway, 1940

WHEELOCK, DOROTHY
　Dead Giveaway. Phoenix, 1942
　Murder at Montauk. Phoenix, 1940

WHELTON, PAUL. Series character: Garry Dean, in all titles.
　Angels are Painted Fair. Lippincott, 1947; Foulsham, 1951. Also published as (?): Lures of Death. Graphic, 1950
　Call the Lady Indiscreet. Lippincott, 1946; Aldor, 1946
　Death and the Devil. Lippincott, 1944. Also published as: Flash—Hold for Murder. Graphic, 1949
　Flash—Hold for Murder; see Death and the Devil
　In Comes Death. Lippincott, 1951; Gifford, 1952
　Lures of Death; see Angels are Painted Fair
　Pardon My Blood. Lippincott, 1950; Gifford, 1951
　Uninvited Corpse; see Women are Skin Deep
　Women are Skin Deep. Lippincott, 1948; Foulsham, 1951. Also published as (?): Uninvited Corpse. Graphic, 1950

WHIPPLE, KENNETH. 1894-　　.
　The Fires at Fitch's Folly. Crowell, 1935
　The Killings in Carter Cave. King, 1934
　The Murders at Loon Lake. King, 1933

WHISHAW, FRED(ERICK J.)
　-The Adventures of a Stowaway. Griffith, 1897
　-The Brothers of the People. Pearson, 1898
　-Called Back to Tsarland. Jarrold, 1899
　-The Caxborough Scandal. White, 1910
　-Clutterbuck's Treasure. Griffith, 1898
　-Countess Ida. Long, 1904
　-The Degenerate. Everett, 1909
　　The Diamond of Evil. Long, 1902
　-A Fool with Women. Long, 1904
　-The Great Green God. White, 1906
　-The Heart of Noel. Everett, 1910
　-Her Highness. Long, 1906
　　The Informer. Long, 1905
　-Lost Sir Brian. Wells Gardner, 1903
　-Lovers at Fault. White, 1904
　-The Madness of Gloria. Digby, 1907
　-Mazeppa. Chatto, 1902
　-My Terrible Twin. Arrowsmith, 1896
　-Mystery Island. Shaw, 1904
　-The Patriots. Digby, 1906
　-The Persecuted. Laurie, 1907
　-A Race for Life. Griffith, 1898
　-The Revolt of Beatrix. Long, 1908
　-The Romance of the Woods. Longmans, 1895
　-A Royal Hoax. Everett, 1908
　-A Russian Coward. Laurie, 1906
　-A Russian Judas. White, 1911
　-A Secret of Berry Pomeroy. Griffith, 1902
　-The Secret Syndicate. Long, 1907
　-A Splendid Imposter. Chatto, 1903
　-A Village Temptress. Everett, 1909
　-The Vortex. Paul, 1909
　-The White Witch of the Matabele. Griffith, 1897
　　The Yellow Satchel. Routledge, 1903; Dutton, 1903

WHITAKER, BERYL (SALISBURY). 1916-   .
Series character: John Abbot, in all titles.
The Chained Crocodile. Hale, 1967
The Man Who Wasn't There. Hale, 1968
A Matter of Blood. Hale, 1967
Of Mice and Murder. Hale, 1967

WHITAKER, C(UTHBERT) W(ILFRID)
The Gift of Hermes. Blackwood, 1924
-The House of Lyes. Blackwood, 1923

WHITAKER, H(ERMAN). 1867-1919.
The Mystery of the Barranca. Harper (New York & London), 1913
-Over the Border. Harper, 1917; Collins, 1924
-The Planter. Harper (New York & London), 1909

WHITAKER, LEO
Return to Hawkeston Hall. Major, 1975

WHITE, ALAN. 1924-   . Pseudonyms: James Fraser, Alec Whitney, qq.v. Series character: Det. Insp. Armstrong, in at least those marked A.
Armstrong. Barrie, 1973; Doubleday, 1977, as by Alec Whitney A
Climate of Revolt. Barrie, 1971
Death Finds the Day; see The Long Day's Dying
Death in Darkness. Barrie, 1975; Doubleday, 1977, as by Alec Whitney A
Death in Duplicate. Barrie, 1974 A
-Kibbutz. Barrie, 1970. U.S. title: Possess the Land. Harcourt, 1970
The Long Day's Dying. Hodder, 1965. U.S. title: Death Finds the Day. Harcourt, 1965
The Long Drop. Jenkins, 1969; Harcourt, 1970
The Long Fuse. Barrie, 1973; Harcourt, 1974
The Long Midnight. Barrie, 1972; Harcourt, 1974
The Long Night's Walk. Hodder, 1968; Harcourt, 1969
The Long Summer. Barrie, 1974; Harcourt, 1975
The Long Watch. Barrie, 1971; Harcourt, 1971
Possess the Land; see Kibbutz
-The Wheel. Hodder, 1966; Harcourt, 1967

WHITE, ALICEN
Nor Spell nor Charm. Lancer, 1971

WHITE, ARED. Series character: Captain Fox Elton = FE.
Agent B-7. Houghton, 1934; Eyre, 1935 FE
Seven Tickets to Singapore. Houghton, 1939; Rich, 1941
The Spy Net. Houghton, 1931; Eyre, 1931 FE

WHITE, EDWARD LUCAS. 1866-1934.
Lukundoo, and other stories. Doran, 1927; Benn, 1927 ss

WHITE, ETHEL LINA. 1887-1944.
The Elephant Never Forgets. Collins, 1937; Harper, 1938
The Eternal Journey. Ward, 1930
Fear Stalks the Village. Ward, 1932; Harper, 1942
The First Time He Died. Collins, 1935
Her Heart in her Throat; see Midnight House
The Lady Vanishes; see The Wheel Spins
The Man Who Loved Lions. Collins, 1943. U.S. title: The Man Who Was Not There. Harper, 1943
The Man Who Was Not There; see The Man Who Loved Lions
Midnight House. Collins, 1942. U.S. title: Her Heart in her Throat. Harper, 1942. Also published as: The Unseen. Paperback Library, 1966
Put Out the Light. Ward, 1931; Harper, 1933. Also published as: Sinister Light. Paperback Library, 1966
She Faded into Air. Collins, 1941; Harper, 1941
Sinister Light; see Put Out the Light
Some Must Watch. Ward, 1933; Harper, 1941. Also published as: The Spiral Staircase. World, 1946
The Spiral Staircase; see Some Must Watch
Step in the Dark. Collins, 1938; Harper, 1939
They See in Darkness. Collins, 1944
The Third Eye. Collins, 1937; Harper, 1937
'Twill Soon be Dark. Ward, 1929
The Unseen; see Midnight House
Wax. Collins, 1935; Doubleday, 1935
The Wheel Spins. Collins, 1936; Harper, 1936. Also published as: The Lady Vanishes. Paperback Library, 1966
While She Sleeps. Collins, 1940; Harper, 1940
The Wish-Bone. Ward, 1927

WHITE, FRED(ERICK) M(ERRICK). 1859-   .
Ambition's Slave. Ward, 1916
The Argus Eye. Ward, 1919
Blackmail! Ward, 1918
The Brand of Silence. Ward, 1911
A Broken Memory. Long, 1930
The Cardinal Moth. Ward, 1905; Street, 19??
The Case for the Crown. Ward, 1919
Claxton's Mill. Ward, 1912
A Clue in Wax. Ward, 1930
The Corner House. Ward, 1906; Fenno, 1906
The Councillors of Falconhoe. Ward, 1924
Craven Fortune. Ward, 1908
A Crime on Canvas. Ward, 1909; Fenno, 1909
The Crimson Blind. Ward, 1905; Fenno, 1905. Also published as: The Mystery of the Crimson Blind. Westbrook, ca. 1911
A Deal in Letters. Long, 1923
The Devil's Advocate. Long, 1930
Dropped from the Fast Express; or, A Daughter's Sacrifice. Laird, 1911. (British title?)
The Edge of the Sword. Ward, 1908
The Ends of Justice. Ward, 1916
A Fatal Dose. Ward, 1907
The Fight for the Child. Long, 1925
The Five Knots. Ward, 1910; Little, 1908
The Four Fingers. Ward, 1911. U.S. title: The Mystery of the Four Fingers. Watt, 1908
A Front of Brass. Ward, 1912
The Garden o' Dreams. Ward, 1909
The Golden Bat. Shoe Lane, 19??
The Golden Rose. Ward, 1913
The Green Bungalow. Long, 1930
The Grey Woman. Ward, 1928
The Happy Exile. Skeffington, 1920
A Harbour of Refuge. Ward, 1918
Hard Pressed. Ward, 1913; Fenno, 1910
The Honour of his House. Ward, 1921
The House of Mammon. Ward, 1914
A House of Sorrows. Ward, 1911
Jim Crowshaw's Mary. Ward, 1913
The King Diamond. Ward, 1927
Lady Clara. Ward, 1913
The Lady in Blue. Ward, 1918
The Law of the Land. Ward, 1908
The Leopard's Spots. Ward, 1920
The Lord of the Manor. Ward, 1908
Love, the Foe. Ward, 1910
The Man Called Gillray. Ward, 1912
The Man Who was Two. Ward, 1922
The Man with the Vandyk Beard. Long, 1925
A Matter of Millions. Ward, 1909
The Midnight Guest. Cassell, 1907; McBride, 1907
My Lady Bountiful. Ward, 1915
The Mystery of the Crimson Blind; see The Crimson Blind
The Mystery of the Four Fingers; see The Four Fingers
The Mystery of the Ravenspurs. Ward, 1912; Ogilvie, 1911
The Nether Millstone. Little, 1907. (British title?)
Netta. Ward, 1909
Number 13. Ward, 1914
On the Night Express. Long, 1930
The Open Door. Ward, 1912
Paul Quentin. Ward, 1915
Paul, the Sage. Ward, 1910
The Phantom Car. Ward, 1929
Powers of Darkness. Ward, 1915
The Psalm Stone. Ward, 1915
A Queen of the Stage. Ward, 1911
The Riddle of the Rail. Ward, 1926
The Robe of Lucifer. Innes, 1896
A Royal Wrong. Ward, 1913
The Salt of the Earth. Ward, 1916
The Scales of Justice. Ward, 1909; Kearney, 1909
The Secret of the Sands. Ward, 1912
The Seed of Empire. Ward, 1916
The Sentence of the Court. Ward, 1917
A Shadowed Love. Ward, 1914
The Slave of Silence. Ward, 1907; Little, 1906
A Society Jezebel. Ward, 1917
The Sundial. Ward, 1910; Dodge, 1908
Tregarthen's Wife. Newnes, 1901
The Turn of the Tide. Ward, 1923
The Weight of the Cross. Ward, 1906; Fenno, 1906
The White Bride. Ward, 1910
The White Glove. Ward, 1919
The Wings of Victory. Ward, 1921
The Yellow Face. White, 1906; Fenno, 1907

WHITE, GEORGE M. Pseudonym of J(ames) M(organ) Walsh, 1897-1952, q.v. Other pseudonyms: H. Haverstock Hill, Stephen Maddock, qq.v.
The Mystery of the Crystal Skull. Hamilton, 1926. Reprinted as by J. M. Walsh: Hamilton, 1929

WHITE, GERTRUDE M. Pseudonym: R. I. Wakefield, q.v.

WHITE, GRACE MILLER
-The Confessions of a Wife. Ogilvie, 1905
Convict 999. Ogilvie, 1907
-Dangers of Working Girls. Ogilvie, 1904
-Fast Life in New York. Ogilvie, 1905
-From the Valley of the Missing. Watt, 1911; Hutchinson, 1912
-The Ghost of Glen George. Macaulay, 1925; Hodder, 1926
The Great Express Robbery. Ogilvie, 1907
The House of Mystery. Ogilvie, 1905
Kidnapped for Revenge. Ogilvie
The King of the Opium Ring. Ogilvie, 1901
The Life That Kills. Ogilvie
Lured from Home. Ogilvie, 1906
-A Marked Woman. Ogilvie, 1907
-New York by Night. Ogilvie
-Prisoner of War. Ogilvie, 1904

The Queen of the White Slaves. Ogilvie, 1904
-Ruled Off the Turf. Ogilvie, 1906
Secrets of the Police. Ogilvie, 1906. (A play.)
-The Secret of the Storm County. Fly, 1917; Hodder, 1924
The Square Mark, with H(ilda) L. Deakin, q.v. Dutton, 1930; Methuen, 1929
-The Warning Bell. Ogilvie, 1905. (A play.)
-When Tragedy Grins. Watt, 1912; Palmer, 1916

WHITE, HERBERT OLIVER. 1885- . Pseudonym: Oliver Martyn, q.v.

WHITE, JAMES DILLON. Pseudonym of Stanley White, 1913- . Other pseudonym: Felix Krull, q.v.
-The Edge of the Forest. Heinemann, 1952
-Flamingo Lake. Heinemann, 1954
-The Hound of Heaven. Hutchinson, 1966
The Leipzig Affair. Hutchinson, 1974
-Lords of Human Kind. Hutchinson, 1971
Night on the Bare Mountain. Heinemann, 1957
-The Princess of Persia. Hutchinson, 1961
-The Quiet River. Heinemann, 1953
-The Running Lions. Hutchinson, 1972
-The Spoletta Story. Heinemann, 1952
-A Spread of Sail. Hutchinson, 1975
-A Stranger in Town. Heinemann, 1953
Sweet Evil. Hutchinson, 1968

WHITE, JON (EWBANK) MANCHIP. 1924- .
The Garden Game. Chatto, 1973; Bobbs, 1974
The Game of Troy. Chatto, 1971; McKay, 1971
Nightclimber. Chatto, 1968; Morrow, 1968

WHITE, KENNETH. 1905-1953.
The Visitor. Dramatic Publishing Co., 1945. (A play based on the novel by Carl Randau, 1893-1969, q.v., and Leane Zugsmith, 1903- .

WHITE, LESLIE T(URNER). 1903- .
5,000 Trojan Horses. World's Work, 1943
Harness Bull. Harcourt, 1937; Hamilton, 1938. Also published as: Vice Squad. Bestseller, 1954
Homicide. Harcourt, 1937; Hamilton, 1938
Me, Detective. Harcourt, 1936
River of Fear; see The River of No Return
The River of No Return. Macrae Smith, 1941; World's Work, 1947. Also published as: River of Fear. Adventure Novel Classic, 194?
Six Weeks South of Texas. World's Work, 1948
Vice Squad; see Harness Bull

WHITE, LIONEL
Before I Die; see To Find a Killer
The Big Caper. GM, 1955; Fawcett (London), 1956
Clean Break. Dutton, 1955; Boardman, 1955. Also published as: The Killing. Tower, 1964
Coffin for a Hood. GM, 1958; Fawcett (London), 1959
The Crimshaw Memorandum. Dutton, 1967; Macdonald, 1968
A Death at Sea. Dutton, 1961; Boardman, 1962
Death of a City. Bobbs, 1970; Hale, 1972
Death Takes the Bus. GM, 1957; Fawcett (London), 1958
Flight into Terror. Dutton, 1955; Boardman, 1957

A Grave Undertaking. Dutton, 1961; Boardman, 1962
Hijack. Macfadden, 1969; Hale, 1970
Hostage for a Hood. GM, 1957; Fawcett (London), 1958
The House Next Door. Dutton, 1956; Boardman, 1958
The House on K Street. Dutton, 1965; Boardman, 1966
Invitation to Violence. Dutton, 1958; Boardman, 1958
The Killing; see Clean Break
Lament for a Virgin. GM, 1960; Muller, 1960
Love Trap. Signet, 1955
Marilyn K. Monarch, 1960
The Merriweather File. Dutton, 1959; Boardman, 1960
The Mexico Run. GM, 1974
The Money Trap. Dutton, 1963; Boardman, 1964
The Night of the Rape. Dutton, 1967; Hale, 1969
Obsession. Dutton, 1962; Boardman, 1963
Operation—Murder. GM, 1956; Fawcett (London), 1958
A Party to Murder. GM, 1966; Jenkins, 1968
Rafferty. Dutton, 1959; Boardman, 1960
The Ransomed Madonna. Dutton, 1964; Boardman, 1965
A Rich and Dangerous Game. McKay, 1974
Right for Murder. Boardman, 1957. (U.S. title?)
Run, Killer, Run. Avon, 1959
The Snatchers. GM, 1953; Red Seal, 1958
Steal Big. GM, 1960; Muller, 1961
The Time of Terror. Dutton, 1960; Boardman, 1961
To Find a Killer. Dutton, 1954; Boardman, 1956. Also published as: Before I Die. Tower, 1964
Too Young to Die. GM, 1958; Fawcett (London), 1959

WHITE, MARION. 1901- .
Out of the Night. Mill, 1938

WHITE, PALMER. Pseudonym of Theodore James Spry, 1898-
-The Circle of Confusion. Chapman, 1930
-Mystery Island. Chapman, 1930

WHITE, PERCY. 1852- .
-Corruption. Heinemann, 1895; Appleton, 1895
-The Grip of the Bookmaker. Hutchinson, 1901
-The Heart of the Dancer. Hutchinson, 1900
-The House of Intrigue. Hurst, 1909

WHITE, R.
Corollary to Murder. Stockwell, 1942

WHITE, R(EGINALD) J(AMES)
A Second-Hand Tomb. Macmillan (London), 1971; Harper, 1971
The Smartest Grave. Collins, 1961; Harper, 1961
The Women of Peasenhall. Macmillan (London), 1969; Harper, 1969

WHITE, SAMUEL ALEXANDER. 1885- .
Morgan of the Mounted. Phoenix, 1939; Coker, 1949
Nighthawk of the Northwest. Phoenix, 1938; Foulsham, 1944
North of the Law. Doubleday, 1920
Northwest Law. Phoenix, 1942. British title: Northwest Patrol. Coker, 1949
Northwest Patrol; see Northwest Law
-Secret Harbour. Doubleday, 1926; Hodder, 1926

WHITE, STANLEY. 1913- . Pseudonyms: Felix Krull, James Dillon White, qq.v.

WHITE, STEWART EDWARD. 1873-1946.
The Mystery, with Samuel Hopkins Adams, 1871-1958, q.v. McClure, 1907; Hodder, 1907
The Sign at Six. Bobbs, 1912; Hodder, 1912

WHITE, T(ERENCE) H(ANBURY). 1906-1964.
Darkness at Pemberley. Gollancz, 1932; Century, 1933
-Gone to Ground. Collins, 1935

WHITE, TRENTWELL MASON. 1901- .
The Thing in the Road. Marshall Jones, 1930

WHITE, VALERIE
Case. Barker, 1954
Case for Treachery. Barker, 1955
Lost Person. Heinemann, 1957

WHITE, W(ILLIAM) J(OHN). 1920- .
The Devil You Know. Cape, 1962
The Hard Man. Cape, 1958
One for the Road. Cape, 1956

WHITE, W(ILLIAM EDWARD BRADDON) HOLT. 1878- . See: W(ILLIAM EDWARD BRADDON) HOLT-WHITE, 1878- .

WHITE, WILLIAM ANTHONY PARKER. 1911-1968.
Pseudonyms: Anthony Boucher, H. H. Holmes, qq.v. See also: THEO DURRANT.

WHITE, WILLIAM PATTERSON. 1884- .
Cloudy in the West. Little, 1928; Hodder, 1928

WHITECHURCH, VICTOR L(ORENZO). 1868-1933.
The Adventures of Captain Ivan Koravitch. Blackwood, 1925 ss
-The Course of Justice. Isbister, 1903
The Crime at Diana's Pool. Unwin, 1927; Duffield, 1927
Murder at Exbridge; see Murder at the College
Murder at the College. Collins, 1932. U.S. title: Murder at Exbridge. Dodd, 1932
Murder at the Pageant. Collins, 1930; Duffield, 1931
The Robbery at Rudwick House. Duffield, 1929
Shot on the Downs. Unwin, 1927; Duffield, 1928
Stories of the Railway; see Thrilling Stories of the Railway
The Templeton Case. Long, 1924; Clode, 1924
Thrilling Stories of the Railway. Pearson, 1912. Also published as: Stories of the Railway. Routledge, 1977 ss

WHITEHOUSE, ARCHIBALD
Crime on a Convoy Carrier. World's Work, 1943
-Wings of Adventure. Hamilton, 1936

WHITEHOUSE, WESLEY L(EONARD)
Confidential Mission. Robertson, 1951
The Man from Australia. Robertson, 1953

WHITELAW, DAVID
The Big Picture. Bles, 1936
Black Out. Hutchinson, 1928
Black-Out Murder. Bles, 1943
Blackmail de Luxe. Bles, 1939
A Castle in Bohemia. Hodder, 1914
The Face. Bles, 1937
The Feud. Bles, 1937
A Flutter in Kings. Hodder, 1916
For Conduct Unbefitting. Holden, 1925

Frame-Up. Bles, 1939
The Gang. Greening, 1908
Garments of Repentance. Macdonald, 1948
Girl Friday. Bles, 1940
The Girl from the East. Greening, 1912
A Hair of the Dog. Holden, 1925
Horace Steps Out. Bles, 1941
Horror on the Loch. Bles, 1938
Hotel Sinister. Bles, 1935
The House in Cavendish Square. Macdonald, 1950
I Could a Tale Unfold. Jenkins, 1957; Roy, 1959
The Impostor. Hodder, 1915
-The Island of Romance. Holden, 1926
The Jackal. Bles, 1940
-The League of St. Louis. Hodder, 1913
Legacy in Green. Macdonald, 1954
The Lexicon Murders. Macdonald, 1945
-The Little Hour of Peter Wells. Hodder, 1913
-Little Lady of Arrock. Chapman, 1921
Lovers in Waiting. Macdonald, 1947
-MacStodger's Affinity. Greening, 1906
Madcap Betty. Hutchinson, 1927
The Madgwick Affair. Ward, 1918
The Man from Mexico City. Hutchinson, 1927
The Man on the Dover Road. Hodder, 1919
The Man with the Red Beard. Greening, 1911
The Master of Merlains. Ward, 1918
-Moon of Valleys. Greening, 1909
The Moor. Macdonald, 1949
Murder Besieged. Macdonald, 1953
Murder Calling. Bles, 1934; Kendall, 1934
Murder in Motley. Bles, 1935
Mystery at Furze Acres. Nash, 1929
The Mystery of Enid Belairs. Hodder, 1915. Also published as: The Odean Theatre Mystery. Shoe Lane, 19??
Number Fifteen. Nash, 1931
The Odean Theatre Mystery; see The Mystery of Enid Belairs
-Pirates' Gold. Hodder, 1920
Presumed Dead. Macdonald, 1952
The Princess Galva. Greening, 1910
The Roof. Bles, 1933
The Secret of Chauville. Greening, 1911
Spanish Heels. Grayson, 1932
-The Stones of Khor. Hutchinson, 1924
-The Valley of Bells. Jarrolds, 1918
The Villa Petroff. Hutchinson, 1926
Wolf's Crag. Bles, 1936
The Yellow Door. Macdonald, 1951

WHITELOCK, LOUISE CLARKSON. 1865-   .
   Pseudonym: L. Clarkson, q.v.

WHITFIELD, RAOUL. 1898-1945.
   Death in a Bowl. Knopf, 1931
   Green Ice. Knopf, 1930. Also published as: The Green Ice Murders. Avon, 1947
   The Green Ice Murders; see Green Ice
   The Virgin Kills. Knopf, 1932

WHITMAN, CHARLES. 1916-   .
   Death Out of Focus. Cassell, 1970
   Death Suspended. Cassell, 1971
   Doctor Death. Cassell, 1970

WHITMAN, H(ENRY) E(SMOND) O(RAM). 1900-   .
   The Pirate of Pittsburgh. Houghton, 1925. British title: The High Jacker. Hodder, 1925

WHITNEY, ALEC. Pseudonym of Alan White, 1924-   , q.v. Other pseudonym: James Fraser, q.v.
   Every Man has his Price. Allen, 1968
   -The Triple Zero. Allen, 1971

WHITNEY, E. G.
   The Sleeping Cupid. Daily Mirror, 1967. (Novelization of Man in a Suitcase TV series.)

WHITNEY, J. L. H.
   The Whisper of Shadows. Ace, 1965

WHITNEY, PHYLLIS A(YAME). 1903-   .
   Black Amber. Appleton, 1964; Hale, 1965
   Blue Fire. Appleton, 1961; Hodder, 1962
   Columbella. Doubleday, 1966; Hale, 1967
   Hunter's Green. Doubleday, 1968; Heinemann, 1969
   Listen for the Whisperer. Doubleday, 1972; Heinemann, 1972
   Lost Island. Doubleday, 1970; Heinemann, 1971
   The Mask and the Moonflower; see The Moonflower
   The Moonflower. Appleton, 1958. British title: The Mask and the Moonflower. Hurst, 1960
   The Quicksilver Pool. Appleton, 1955; Coronet, 1973
   Red Carnelian; see Red is for Murder
   Red is for Murder. Ziff-Davis, 1943. Also published as: Red Carnelian. Paperback Library, 1968; Coronet, 1976
   Sea Jade. Appleton, 1964; Hale, 1966
   Seven Tears for Apollo. Appleton, 1963; Coronet, 1969
   Silverhill. Doubleday, 1967; Heinemann, 1968
   Skye Cameron. Appleton, 1957; Hurst, 1959
   Snowfire. Doubleday, 1973; Heinemann, 1973
   Spindrift. Doubleday, 1975; Heinemann, 1975
   Thunder Heights. Appleton, 1960; Coronet, 1973
   The Trembling Hills. Appleton, 1956; Coronet, 1974
   The Turquoise Mask. Doubleday, 1974; Heinemann, 1975
   Window on the Square. Appleton, 1962; Coronet, 1969
   The Winter People. Doubleday, 1969; Heinemann, 1970

WHITSON, JOHN H(ARVEY). 1854-   .
   -The Castle of Doubt. Little, 1907

WHITTAKER, CAPT. FREDERICK. 1838-   .
   The Red Rajah. Westbrook, ca.1920
   -Transgressing the Law. Bonner's, 1893

WHITTEN, LESLIE H(UNTER). 1928-   .
   Death of a Nurse; see Moon of the Wolf
   Moon of the Wolf. Doubleday, 1967. British title: Death of a Nurse. Hale, 1969
   Progeny of the Adder. Doubleday, 1965; Hodder, 1966

WHITTINGTON, HARRY. 1915-   . Pseudonym: Whit Harrison, q.v.
   -Across That River. Ace, 1957
   Backwoods Tramp. GM, 1959; Muller pb, 1961
   The Brass Monkey. Handi-Books, 1951
   Brute in Brass. GM, 1956; Red Seal, 1958
   Burden's Mission. Avon, 1968
   Call Me Killer. Graphic, 1951
   Connolly's Woman. GM, 1960; Muller pb, 1962
   -Desert Stake-Out. GM, 1961; Muller pb, 1963
   Desire in the Dust. GM, 1956; Fawcett (London), 1957
   The Devil Wears Wings. Abelard (New York & London), 1960
   Die, Lover; see Vengeful Sinner
   Don't Speak to Strange Girls. GM, 1963; Muller pb, 1963
   The Doomsday Affair. Ace, 1965; Four Square, 1965. (Novelization of The Man from U.N.C.L.E. TV series.)
   -Doomsday Mission. Banner, 1967
   Drawn to Evil. Ace, 1952
   Fires That Destroy. GM, 1951
   God's Back was Turned. GM, 1961; Muller pb, 1962
   Guerrilla Girls. Pyramid, 1960; New English Library pb, 1970
   Halfway to Hell. Avon, 1959
   A Haven for the Damned. GM, 1962; Muller pb, 1963
   Heat of Night. GM, 1960; Muller pb, 1961
   Hell Can Wait. GM, 1960; Muller pb, 1962
   Hot as Fire, Cold as Ice. Belmont, 1962
   The Humming Box. Ace, 1956
   Journey into Violence. Pyramid, 1961
   The Lady was a Tramp. Handi-Books, 1951
   Man in the Shadow. Avon, 1957. (Novelization of the movie.)
   Married to Murder. Phantom, 1951
   Mourn the Hangman. Graphic, 1952
   Murder is my Mistress. Graphic, 1951
   The Naked Jungle. Ace, 1955
   A Night for Screaming. Ace, 1960
   Nita's Place. Pyramid, 1960
   One Deadly Dawn. Ace, 1957
   One Got Away. Ace, 1955
   Play for Keeps. Abelard (New York & London), 1957
   Rebel Woman. Avon, 1960
   -Saddle the Storm. GM, 1954; Fawcett (London), 1955
   Satan's Widow. Phantom, 1952
   Saturday Night Town. Crest, 1956; Fawcett (London), 1958
   69 Babylon Park. Avon, 1962
   Slay Ride for a Lady. Handi-Books, 1950
   So Dead My Love! Ace, 1953
   Strange Bargain. Avon, 1959
   Strangers on Friday. Abelard (New York & London), 1959
   Teen-Age Jungle. Avon, 1958
   Temptations of Valerie. Avon, 1957. (Novelization of the movie.)
   A Ticket to Hell. GM, 1959; Muller pb, 1960
   -Trouble Rides Tall. Abelard (New York & London), 1958
   -Vengeance is the Spur. Abelard (New York & London), 1960
   Vengeful Sinner. Croydon, 1953. Also published as: Die, Lover. Avon, 1960, abridged
   Web of Murder. GM, 1958; Fawcett (London), 1959
   A Woman on the Place. Ace, 1956; Red Seal, 1960
   You'll Die Next! Ace, 1954; Red Seal, 1959

WHITTON, CHARLES
   The Judas Way. Long, 1923
   The Purple Trident. Long, 1924

WIBBERLEY, LEONARD PATRICK O'CONNOR. 1915-   . Pseudonym: Leonard Holton, q.v.

WICK, CARTER. Pseudonym of Collin Wilcox, 1924-   , q.v.
   The Faceless Man. Saturday Review Press, 1975; H. Hamilton, 1976

WICK, STUART MARY. Pseudonym of Kathleen Freeman, 1897-1959, q.v. Other pseudonym: Mary Fitt, q.v.
   And Where's Mr. Bellamy? Hutchinson, 1948
   -The Statue and the Lady. Hodder, 1950

WICKER, TOM [THOMAS GREY WICKER]. 1926-   . Pseudonym: Paul Connolly, q.v.
   The Devil Must. Harper, 1957
   -The Judgment. Sloane, 1961; Cassell, 1962

WICKES, MARTHA
The Mystery of Sun Dial Court. Penn, 1926

WICKHAM, HARVEY. 1872-1930. Series character: Ferris McClue, in at least those marked FM.
The Boncoeur Affair. Clode, 1923; Skeffington, 1925 FM
The Clue of the Primrose Petal. Clode, 1921; Brentano's (London), 1923 FM
Jungle Terror. Doubleday, 1920
The Scarlet X. Clode, 1922; Brentano's (London), 1923 FM
The Trail of the Squid. Clode, 1924 FM

WICKING, G(EORGE) W(ALTER)
Bales of Trouble. Wright, 1937
Boom-Time Gold. Angus, 1936
The Glory Box Mystery. Angus, 1937
The Mysterious Valley. Angus, 1938

WICKS, FREDERICK. 1840-1910.
Golden Lives. Blackwood, 1891. Also published as: A Woman's Courage. Remington, 1892
The Infant. Remington, 1895
My Undiscovered Crimes. Blackwood, 1909 ss
The Stories of the Broadmoor Patient, and the Poor Clerk. Remington, 1893
The Veiled Hand. Remington, 1892; Harper, 1893
A Woman's Courage; see Golden Lives

WICKWARE, FRANCIS SILL
Dangerous Ground. Doubleday, 1946

WIDDEMER, MARGARET. 1897- .
The Red Castle Women. Doubleday, 1968; Jenkins, 1969

WIEGAND, WILLIAM (GEORGE). 1928- .
At Last, Mr. Tolliver. Rinehart, 1950; Hodder, 1951

WIENER, WILLARD. 1900- .
Four Boys and a Gun. Dial, 1944

WIGHT, NATALIE
Death in the Inner Office. Phoenix, 1938

WIGNALL, TREVOR C. 1883-1958. Both titles were published by Amalgamated Press and feature Sexton Blake.
The Case of the Japanese Detective. 1920
The House with the Red Blinds. 1920

WILCOX, COLLIN, 1924- . Pseudonym: Carter Wick, q.v. Series characters: Lt. Frank Hastings = FH; Stephen Drake = SD; McCloud (novelizations of the TV series) = M.
Aftershock. Random, 1975; Hale, 1976 FH
The Black Door. Dodd, 1967; Cassell, 1968 SD
Dead Aim. Random, 1971; Hale, 1973 FH
The Disappearance. Random, 1970; Hale, 1971 FH
Hiding Place. Random, 1973; Hale, 1974 FH
The Lonely Hunter. Random, 1969; Hale, 1971 FH
Long Way Down. Random, 1974; Hale, 1975 FH
McCloud. Award, 1974 M
The New Mexico Connection. Award, 1974; Tandem, 1974 M
The Third Figure. Dodd, 1968; Hale, 1969 SD

WILCOX, HARRY. Pseudonym: Mark Derby, q.v.

WILCOX, HENRY S. 1855- .
A Strange Flaw. Thompson, 1906

WILCOX, JESS. Pseudonym of Morris Hershman, 1920- , q.v. Other pseudonym: Evelyn Bond, q.v.
Kill Me, Sweet. Monarch, 1960

WILDE, OSCAR (FINGAL O'FLAHERTIE WILLS). 1854-1900.
Lord Arthur Savile's Crime, and other stories. Osgood, 1891; Dodd, 1891 ss, one criminous

WILDE, PERCIVAL. 1887-1953.
Design for Murder. Random, 1941; Gollancz, 1942
Inquest. Random, 1940; Gollancz, 1939
Mystery Week-End. Harcourt, 1938; Gollancz, 1938
P. Moran, Operative. Random, 1947; Gollancz, 1947 ss
Rogues in Clover. Appleton, 1929 ss
Tinsley's Bones. Random, 1942; Gollancz, 1943

WILDER, ROBERT (INGERSOLL). 1901- .
An Affair of Honor. Putnam, 1969; Allen, 1970
Fruit of the Poppy. Putnam, 1965; Allen, 1965
Walk with Evil. Crest, 1957; Allen, 1958

WILEY, HUGH. 1884- .
The Copper Mask, and other stories. Knopf, 1932 ss
Jade, and other stories. Knopf, 1921; Heinemann, 1922 ss
Manchu Blood. Knopf, 1927 ss
Murder by the Dozen. Popular Library, 1951 ss

WILKES-HUNTER, R(ICHARD). Pseudonyms: Marc Brody, Tod Conrad, Alex Crane, qq.v. All data below refer to Australian editions, the relative criminous content of which has not been ascertained.
Badge for a Gunfighter. Leisure, 1954
Bank Robbery Hostage. Leisure, 1956
Borneo Patrol. Webster, 1958
Commando. Webster, 1958
Commandos are Expendable. Cleveland Publishing, 1954
Crusade into Crime. Australian Publishing, 1948
The Day I Stopped Running. Leisure, 1953
Death Date. Leisure, 1957
Deserters Don't Come Back. Leisure, 1955
Fast with a Gun. Cleveland Publishing, 1955
Fighter Pilot. Leisure, 1955
Five Came to Kill. Leisure, 1954
Five Days to Kill. Horwitz, 1956
Fool from Down Under. Cleveland Publishing, 1954
Gunsmoke Haze. Cleveland Publishing, 1955
Heritage of the Horned Steer. Leisure, 1954
Hostage. Cleveland Publishing, 1955
Kid with a Gun. Cleveland Publishing, 1955
Kokoda Trail. Webster, 1958
Partisans Die Alone. Leisure, 1954
Patient is the Hunter. Leisure, 1953
Range Justice. Cleveland Publishing, 1955
Ride West of the Law. Leisure, 1953
Run with the Weasel. Leisure, 1953
Six Gun Empire. Cleveland Publishing, 1954
Take This Gun. Cleveland Publishing, 1954
Task Demolition. Leisure, 1954
A Tomb for Mr. Lee. Leisure, 1957
Trail of the Hunted. Leisure, 1954
Train a Fast Gun. Leisure, 1955
Violent Holiday. Leisure, 1954
White Trails over London. Leisure, 1953

WILHELM, KATE [KATE WILHELM KNIGHT]. 1928- .
City of Cain. Little, 1974; Gollancz, 1975
More Bitter Than Death. Simon, 1963; Hale, 1965
-The Nevermore Affair. Doubleday, 1966

WILK, MAX. 1920- .
Eliminate the Middle Man. Norton, 1974

WILKES, ALLENE TUPPER
The Creaking Chair. French (New York & London), 1926. (Play.)

WILKINS, W. A.
The Cleverdale Mystery; or, The Machine and Its Wheels. Fords Howard, 1882

WILKINSON, (JOHN) BURKE. 1913- .
Series character: Geoffrey Mildmay = GM.
Last Clear Chance. Little, 1954; Hodder, 1954 GM
Night of the Short Knives. Scribner, 1964; Hodder, 1965
Proceed at Will. Little, 1948; Hodder, 1949 GM
Run, Mongoose. Little, 1950; Hodder, 1951 GM

WILKINSON, ELLEN (CICELY). 1891- .
-Clash. Harrap, 1929
The Division Bell Mystery. Harrap, 1932

WILKINSON, G(EOFFREY) K(EDINGTON). 1907- .
Nick the Click. Cassell, 1968; Putnam, 1968

WILKINSON, RICHARD HILL. 1904- . Pseudonyms: Eugene Hayford, E. Harrison Ott, Paul Pray, qq.v.
The Ghost of Grand Canyon. Baker, 1936. (3-act play.)
Mad Murder. Meador, 1931
Murder on the High Seas. Drama Guild, 1938. (3-act play.)
Night of Terror. Baker, 1936. (3-act play.)
The Pennington Case. Drama Guild, 1937. (3-act play.)
Tea at Four. Drama Guild, 1934. (1-act play.)

WILKINSON, (WILLIAM) RODERICK. 1917- .
The Big Still. Long, 1958; British Book Centre, 1959
Everything Goes Dead. Hale, 1967
Murder Belongs to Me! Museum, 1956
The Network. Hale, 1969
The Pressure Man. Hale, 1967

WILKINSON, RONALD. 1920- . Pseudonym: Ronald Scott Thorn, q.v.

WILLARD, JOHN. 1885- .
The Cat and the Canary. Readers Library, 1927. U.S. title: The Cat Creeps. Jacobson, 1930. The play: French (London), 1927

WILLARD, JOSHUA
The Thorne Theatre Mystery. Phoenix, 1937

WILLARD, JOSIAH FLYNT. 1869-1907. Pseudonym: Josiah Flynt, q.v.

WILLARDS, E(RNST) S(EYMOUR)
My Mother was Hanged. Heinemann, 1958. (Translation of Mijn Moeder werd Opgehangen. Amsterdam, 1956.)

WILLEFORD, CHARLES. Pseudonym: Will Charles, q.v.

WILLETS, GILSON. 1869- .
Anita, the Cuban Spy. Neely, 1898
The Double Cross. Dillingham, 1910; Unwin, 1910
The First Law. Dillingham, 1911; Unwin, 1911

WILLETT, E(RNEST) NODALL
The Sitting Emperor. Gardner, 1930

WILLETT, HILDA. 1878- .
Accident in Piccadilly. Paul, 1935
-April, May and June. Paul, 1931
Bucket in a Well. Paul, 1932
Diamonds of Death. Longmans, 1930
Found Shot. Paul, 1934
It's Quiet in the Country. Gifford, 1946
Murder at the Party. Paul, 1931
Mystery on the Centre Court. Paul, 1933
Peril in Darkness. Paul, 1935
-So It Goes On. Paul, 1930
Tragedy in Pewsey Chart. Longmans, 1929

WILLIAM, PETER
The Affair at Abu Mina. Macrae Smith, 1944. Also published as: Death at Abu Mina. Thriller Novel Classic, 194? (abridged)

WILLIAMS, ALAN. 1890- .
Room Service. Godwin, 1936

WILLIAMS, ALAN (EMLYN). 1935- .
Barbouze. Blond, 1964. U.S. title: The False Beards. Harper, 1965
The Beria Papers. Blond, 1973; Simon, 1973
The Brotherhood. Blond, 1968. U.S. title: The Purity League. Putnam, 1969
The False Beards; see Barbouze
Gentleman Traitor. Blond, 1974; Harcourt, 1975
Long Run South. Blond, 1962; Little, 1962
The Purity League; see The Brotherhood
Snake Water. Blond, 1965; Harper, 1965
The Tale of the Lazy Dog. Blond, 1970; Simon, 1970

WILLIAMS, ALEXANDER (HAZARD). 1894-1952.
Pseudonym: Forrester Hazard, q.v.
Series character: Det. Sgt. Pietro Tonelli, in all titles.
Death over Newark. Payson, 1933
The Jinx Theatre Murder. Payson, 1933
Murder in the WPA. McBride, 1937

WILLIAMS, BEN AMES. 1889-1953. Series character: Inspector Tope, in at least those marked T.
Audacity. Dutton, 1924
The Bellmer Mystery; see Death on Scurvy Street
Crucible. Dutton, 1937
Death on Scurvy Street. Dutton, 1929. British title: The Bellmer Mystery. Paul, 1930 T
The Dreadful Night. Dutton, 1928; Paul, 1929
An End to Mirth. Dutton, 1931
Hostile Valley. Dutton, 1934

A Killer Among Us. Lion, 1957. (Retitled reprint of ?)
Lady in Peril; see Money Musk
-Leave Her to Heaven. Houghton, 1944; Hale, 1946
Mischief. Dutton, 1933
Money Musk. Dutton, 1932. Also published as: Lady in Peril. Popular Library, 1948 T
Pascal's Mill. Dutton, 1943
Pirate's Purchase. Dutton, 1931
The Silver Forest. Dutton, 1926; Mills, 1927

WILLIAMS, BRAD. 1918- . Series character: Sam Benedict = SB (who also appears in books by Elsie Lee and Howard L. Olack, 1911- , qq.v.).
A Borderline Case. Mill, 1960. British title: Death Lies in Waiting. Jenkins, 1961
A Conflict of Interest, with J. W. Ehrlich. Holt, 1971 SB
Death Lies in Waiting; see A Borderline Case
Make a Killing. Mill, 1961; Jenkins, 1962
A Matter of Confidence, with J. W. Ehrlich. Holt, 1973 SB
A Stranger to Herself. Doubleday, 1964; Gollancz, 1965
Tumulto. Avon, 1974
The Well-Dressed Skeleton. Mill, 1962; Jenkins, 1963

WILLIAMS, CHARLES
A Master of Crime. Odhams, 1919

WILLIAMS, CHARLES. 1909- .
Aground. Viking, 1960; Cassell, 1961
All the Way. Dell, 1958. British title: The Concrete Flamingo. Cassell, 1960
And the Deep Blue Sea. Signet, 1971; Cassell, 1972
The Big Bite. Dell, 1956; Cassell, 1957
Big City Girl. GM, 1951; Fawcett (London), 1953
The Catfish Tangle. Cassell, 1963. (U.S. title?)
The Concrete Flamingo; see All the Way
Dead Calm. Viking, 1963; Cassell, 1964
The Diamond Bikini. GM, 1956; Consul, 1962
Don't Just Stand There; see The Wrong Venus
Girl Out Back. Dell, 1958
Go Home, Stranger. GM, 1954; Red Seal, 1957
Gulf Coast Girl; see Scorpion Reef
Hell Hath No Fury. GM, 1953; Red Seal, 1958. Also published as: The Hot Spot. Cassell, 1965
Hill Girl. GM, 1951; Red Seal, 1958
The Hot Spot; see Hell Hath No Fury
The Long Saturday Night. GM, 1962; Cassell, 1964
Man in Motion; see Man on the Run
Man on a Leash. Putnam, 1973; Cassell, 1974
Man on the Run. GM, 1958. British title: Man in Motion. Cassell, 1959
Mix Yourself a Redhead; see A Touch of Death
Nothing in her Way. GM, 1953; Fawcett (London), 1954
Nude on Thin Ice. Avon, 1961
Operator. Cassell, 1958. (U.S. title?)
River Girl. GM, 1951
The Sailcloth Shroud. Viking, 1960; Cassell, 1960
Scorpion Reef. Macmillan, 1955; Cassell, 1956. Also published as: Gulf Coast Girl. Dell, 1956
Stain of Suspicion; see Talk of the Town

Talk of the Town. Dell, 1958. British title: Stain of Suspicion. Cassell, 1959. Reprinted in the U.S. under the British title: PB, 1973
A Touch of Death. GM, 1954; Fawcett (London), 1955. Also published as: Mix Yourself a Redhead. Cassell, 1965
Uncle Sagamore and his Girls. GM, 1959
The Wrong Venus. New American Library, 1966. British title: Don't Just Stand There. Cassell, 1967

WILLIAMS, DAVID (FFRANCON). 1909- .
Agent from the West. Cape, 1956

WILLIAMS, EDWIN ALFRED. Pseudonym: Edwin De Caire, q.v.

WILLIAMS, ELIOT CRAWSHAY. 1879- .
-No Apparent Motive. Long, 1948
-Stay of Execution. Jarrolds, 1933
-The Stroud Case. Long, 1953

WILLIAMS, ELMA M(ARY)
Escape to Death. Ward, 1961
Strange Legacy. Ward, 1961
Tomorrow a Stranger. Ward, 1962

WILLIAMS, (GEORGE) EMLYN. 1905- .
A Murder has been Arranged. Collins, 1930; French (New York), 1931. (3-act play.)
Night Must Fall. Gollancz, 1935; Random, 1936. (3-act play.)

WILLIAMS, ERIC (ERNEST). 1911- .
Series characters: Roger and Kate Starte, in both titles.
The Borders of Barbarism. Heinemann, 1961; Coward, 1962
Dragoman Pass. Collins, 1959; Coward, 1959

WILLIAMS, F(RANK) CHENHALLS. 1880- .
-The Inner Number. Longmans, 1927

WILLIAMS, G. MOUNTFORD
Silk Rope. Duckworth, 1947

WILLIAMS, GILBERT M. 1917- . Pseudonym: Michael Wolfe, q.v.

WILLIAMS, GORDON M(acLEAN). 1934- .
Joint pseudonym with Terry Venables: P. B. Yuill, q.v.
Big Morning Blues. Hodder, 1974
-The Camp. Secker, 1966; Stein, 1966
-From Scenes Like These. Secker, 1968; Morrow, 1969
The Last Day of Lincoln Charles. Secker, 1965; Stein, 1965
The Siege of Trencher's Farm. Secker, 1969; Morrow, 1969
-They Used to Play on Grass, with Terry Venables. Hodder, 1971

WILLIAMS, H. C.
The Ticket-of-Leave Man. (London), 1875. (Novelization of the play by Tom Taylor, 1817-1880, q.v.)

WILLIAMS, H(UGH) NOEL. 1870-1925.
Tainted Gold. Paul, 1915

WILLIAMS, HAROLD. 1853- . Pseudonym: George Afterem, q.v.

WILLIAMS, HARPER
The Thing in the Woods. McBride, 1924

WILLIAMS, HENRY
How to Murder Your Wife. Dell, 1965. (Novelization of the movie.)

WILLIAMS, HENRY LLEWELLYN. 1842- .
Pseudonym: Matt Mizzen, q.v.

WILLIAMS, HENRY SMITH. 1863-1943.
The Witness of the Sun. Doubleday, 1920

WILLIAMS, J. ARTHUR
The Clue of the Cone. Hutchinson, 1946

WILLIAMS, J(OHN) ELLIS
Murder at the Eisteddfod. Gomer, 1973

WILLIAMS, JAY. 1914-1978. Pseudonym:
Michael Delving, q.v.

WILLIAMS, JEANNE. 1930- . Pseudonyms:
Jeanne Crecy, Deirdre Rowan, qq.v.

WILLIAMS, JOHN (STANLEY). 1925- .
-Death is a Lizard. Hutchinson, 1963
-The God-Seeker. Hutchinson, 1966
-On the Way Out. New Authors, 1962
The Spinsters. Hutchinson, 1967

WILLIAMS, JOHN B., M.D.
The Baronet's Crime. Westbrook, 1912
Dead Yet Living; or, The Baltimore Bank
Robbery. Westbrook, 1912
Leaves from the Note-Book of a New York
Detective. Dick, 1865 ss
The Secret Compact; or, The Lone House
by the River. Westbrook, 1912
Under a Mask. Westbrook, 1912
The Vial with the White Powder; or,
Deadly Foes to the Grave. Westbrook,
1912

WILLIAMS, KIRBY. Pseudonym. Series character: Dr. Thackeray Place, in both
titles.
The C.V.C. Murders. Doubleday, 1929;
Hutchinson, 1929
The Opera Murders. Scribner, 1933

WILLIAMS, LAWRENCE. 1915- .
-The Fiery Furnace. Simon, 1960; Muller,
1960
-The Smoke-Filled Boudoir. Simon, 1965

WILLIAMS, LYNN
Lake of the Wind. Dell, 1971
Once Upon a Nightmare. Dell, 1971
Picture Her Missing. Dell, 1973
Rendezvous with Danger. Dell, 1973
The Secret of Hedges Hall. Dell, 1973
Shadows over Seascape. Dell, 1972
Threads of Intrigue. Dell, 1973
Where is Jane? Dell, 1972

WILLIAMS, MARGARET WETHERBY. Pseudonym:
Margaret Erskine, q.v.

WILLIAMS, MOUNTFORD
Hound Island. Nelson, 1940

WILLIAMS, NATHAN WINSLOW. 1860-1924.
Pseudonym: Richard Dallas, q.v.

WILLIAMS, NEIL
Also Ran. New English Library pb, 1974
-Scorch. New English Library pb, 1975

WILLIAMS, NEIL WYNN
The Electric Theft. Greening, 1906;
Small, 1906

WILLIAMS, OSCAR
The Dance of Death and other stories.
Morris, 1946 ss
The Dawn Must Come. Morris, 1948
Death Stalks the River. Pan, 1945
Devil's Luck. Mellifont, 1934
Harringay's Last Gamble. Morris, 1946
ss
Justice Never Sleeps. Morris, 1945
Reparation. Mellifont, 1934
The Sign of the Tiger. Morris, 1945
The Vengeance of Sheevra. Morris, 1945

WILLIAMS, P(HILIP) C(LAXTON). Series
character: Mr. Hoyland, in at least
those marked H.
Hoyland Intervenes. Atlas, 1944 H
Hoyland Steps Out. Pictorial Art, 1946
H
Mr. Hoyland Looks Round. Bale, 1941 H
ss
Murder will Out. Pictorial Art, 194? H
Time for Crime. Pocket Editions, 1945

WILLIAMS, RICHARD. House name, used by
W(illiam Arthur) Howard Baker,
1925- , q.v., and others. Other
Baker pseudonyms: William Arthur, W.
A. Ballinger, qq.v. Series character
(with many other authors): Sexton
Blake, in all titles.
Hurricane Warning! Amalgamated, 1960
Large Type Killer. Amalgamated, 1960
The Man with the Iron Chest. Mayflower,
1965
Murder by Proxy. Amalgamated, 1963
The Slaying of Julian Summers. Amalgamated, 1963
The Sniper. Mayflower, 1965
Somebody Wants Me Dead. Amalgamated,
1962
Speak Ill of the Dead. Amalgamated,
1963
Torment was a Redhead. Amalgamated,
1962
Vendetta! Amalgamated, 1961

WILLIAMS, RUTH
Cry Rape. Award, 1974. (Novelization of
the TV movie.)

WILLIAMS, SIDNEY (CLARK). 1878-1949.
Series character: Jabez Twombley =
JT.
The Aconite Murders. Dodd, 1936 JT
The Body in the Blue Room. Penn, 1922;
Hurst, 1924
The Drury Club Case. Penn, 1927
In the Tenth Moon. Penn, 1923; Hurst,
1924
The Murder of Miss Betty Sloan. Appleton, 1935 JT
Mystery in Red. Penn, 1925; Hurst, 1925

WILLIAMS, STEPHEN DANIEL
The Adventures of Shylar Homes. Carlton, 1966 ss

WILLIAMS, (GEORGE) VALENTINE. 1883-1946.
Pseudonym: Douglas Valentine, q.v.
Series characters: Sgt. Trevor Dene =
TD; Mr. Treadgold = T; Dr. Adolph
Grundt (Clubfoot) = AG (see also Douglas Valentine).
The Clock Ticks On. Hodder, 1933;
Houghton, 1933 TD
Clubfoot the Avenger. Jenkins, 1924;
Houghton, 1924 AG
The Clue of the Rising Moon. Hodder,
1935; Houghton, 1935 TD
Courier to Marrakesh. Hodder, 1944;
Houghton, 1946 AG
The Crouching Beast. Hodder, 1928;
Houghton, 1928 AG
The Curiosity of Mr. Treadgold; see Mr.
Treadgold Cuts In
Dead Man Manor. Hodder, 1936; Houghton,
1936 T
Death Answers the Bell. Hodder, 1931;
Houghton, 1932 TD
The Eye in Attendance. Hodder, 1927;
Houghton, 1927 TD
Fog, with Dorothy Rice Sims. Hodder,
1933; Houghton, 1933
The Fox Prowls. Hodder, 1939; Houghton,
1939
The Gold Comfit Box. Hodder, 1932. U.S.
title: The Mystery of the Gold Box.
Houghton, 1932 AG
Island Gold; see The Return of Clubfoot
The Key Man; see The Pigeon House

The Knife Behind the Curtain. Hodder,
1930; Houghton, 1930 ss
Mannequin. Hodder, 1930. U.S. title:
The Mysterious Miss Morrisot. Houghton, 1930
Masks Off at Midnight. Hodder, 1934;
Houghton, 1934 TD
Mr. Ramosi. Hodder, 1926; Houghton,
1926
Mr. Treadgold Cuts In. Hodder, 1937.
U.S. title: The Curiosity of Mr.
Treadgold. Houghton, 1937 T ss
The Mysterious Miss Morrisot; see
Mannequin
The Mystery of the Gold Box; see The
Gold Comfit Box
The Orange Divan. Jenkins, 1923;
Houghton, 1923
The Pigeon House. Hodder, 1926. U.S.
title: The Key Man. Houghton, 1926
The Portcullis Room. Hodder, 1934;
Houghton, 1934
The Red Mass. Hodder, 1925; Houghton,
1925
The Return of Clubfoot. Jenkins, 1923.
U.S. title: Island Gold. Houghton,
1923 AG
Skeleton Out of the Cupboard. Hodder,
1946
The Spider's Touch. Hodder, 1936;
Houghton, 1936 AG
The Three of Clubs. Hodder, 1924;
Houghton, 1924
The Yellow Streak. Jenkins, 1922;
Houghton, 1922

WILLIAMSON, ALICE M(URIEL LIVINGSTON).
[MRS. C. N. WILLIAMSON]. 1869-1933.
See also: C(HARLES) N(ORRIS) WILLIAMSON, 1859-1920. Pseudonym: Dona Teresa de Savallo, q.v.
-The Barn Stormers. Hutchinson, 1897;
Stokes, 1897, as by Mrs. Harcourt
Williamson
-Bewitched. Wright, 1934
-A Bid for a Coronet. Routledge, 1901
-Black Sleeves. Chapman, 1928
-The Castle of Shadows. Methuen, 1905;
Hudson, 1909
-Children of the Zodiac. Chapman, 1929
-The Flower Forbidden. Hodder, 1911
-Fortune's Sport. Pearson, 1898
-Frozen Slippers. Chapman, 1930
-The Girl in the Secret. Wright, 1934
-The Girl of the Passion Play. Hodder,
1911
The Girl Who Had Nothing. Ward, 1905
-The Golden Carpet. Chapman, 1931
-Hollywood Love. Chapman, 1928
-Honeymoon Hate. Chapman, 1931
The House by the Lock. Bowden, 1899;
Dodge, 1906
-The Indian Princess. Mills, 1924 ss
-Keep This Door Shut. Benn, 1933
-Lady Mary of the Dark House. Bowden,
1898
-Last Year's Wife. Benn, 1932
-The Lightning Conductor Comes Back.
Chapman, 1933
-The Little White Nun. White, 1903
-The Man Himself. Philpot, 1925
-My Lady Cinderella. Routledge, 1900;
Dodge, 1906
-Name the Woman. Methuen, 1924
-The Newspaper Girl. Pearson, 1899
-Ordered South. Routledge, 1900
-Papa. Methuen, 1902
-Princess Mary's Locked Book. Cassell
(London), 1912; Cassell (New York),
1913
-Publicity for Anne. Mills, 1926
-Queen Sweetheart. White, 1901
-The Sea Could Tell. Methuen, 1904

Secret Gold. Methuen, 1925; Doubleday, 1925
-Sheikh Bill. Mills, 1927
-The Silent Battle. Hurst, 1902
Told at Monte Carlo. Mills, 1926 ss
The Turnstile of Night. Hurst, 1904
-'Twixt Devil and Deep Sea. Pearson, 1901
-The Underground Syndicate. Hodder, 1910
The Vanity Box. Hodder, 1913; Doubleday, 1911, as by Alice Stuyvesant
A Woman in Grey. Routledge, 1898; Burt, (date?)
-The Woman Who Dared. Methuen, 1903

WILLIAMSON, C(HARLES) N(ORRIS), 1859-1920, and A(LICE) M(URIEL) LIVINGSTON), 1869-1933, q.v. Pseudonym of A(lice) M(uriel) Livingston) Williamson: Dona Teresa de Savallo, q.v.
Alias Richard Power. Hodder, 1921
-Berry Goes to Monte Carlo. Mills, 1921 ss
-Briar Rose. Odhams, 1919
-Champion. Cassell, 1913
-The Cowboy Countess. Methuen, 1917
-The Demon. Methuen, 1912
-The Fortune Hunters and others. Mills, 1923 ss
The Great Pearl Secret. Methuen, 1921; Doubleday, 1921
The House of Silence. Hodder, 1921
-The Lady from the Air. Hodder, 1922; Doubleday, 1923
The Lion's Mouse. Methuen, 1919; Doubleday, 1919
-Lord John in New York. Methuen, 1918
-Love and the Spy. Leng, 1908
-The Marquis of Loveland. McClure, 1908. (British title?)
-The Minx Goes to the Front. Mills, 1919 ss
The Night of the Wedding. Hodder, 1921; Doran, 1923
-The Powers and Maxine. Empire, 1907. (British title?)
-Scarlet Runner. Methuen, 1908 ss
The Second Latchkey. Doubleday, 1920. (British title?)
-The Shop-Girl. Methuen, 1916; Grosset, 1916
-A Soldier of the Legion. Nelson, 1915
-This Woman to this Man. Methuen, 1917
-Tiger Lily. Mills, 1917
-The Wedding Day. Methuen, 1914

WILLIAMSON, MRS. HARCOURT. Pseudonym of A(lice) M(uriel) Livingston) Williamson, 1869-1933, q.v.

WILLIAMSON, HUGH ROSS. 1901-1978.
A Wicked Pack of Cards. Joseph, 1961; Guild, 1965

WILLIAMSON, MARGARET
The White Feather Mystery. Regency, 1945

WILLIAMSON, S(AMUEL) C(HARLES)
The Compost Heap Corpses. Regency, 1966

WILLIS, G(RANVILLE) P(RATT)
Escape at Dawn, with Michael P(atrick) O'Connor. Hale, 1961
It Began in Singapore, with Michael P(atrick) O'Connor. Hale, 1958
Somebody Killed Milner. Hale, 1968

WILLIS, GEORGE ANTHONY ARMSTRONG. 1897-1976. Pseudonym: Anthony Armstrong, q.v.

WILLIS, M(ABEL) AUDREY
Flowers of Vengeance. Jarrolds, 1925

WILLIS, MAUD. Pseudonym of Eileen Lottman, 1927- , q.v.
The Devil's Rain. Dell, 1975. (Novelization of the movie.)

WILLIS, TED [EDWARD HENRY WILLIS]. 1918- . See also: HENRY CECIL. Series character: George Dixon, in at least those marked GD.
The Blue Lamp. Convoy, 1950 GD
Death May Surprise Us. Macmillan (London), 1974. U.S. title: Westminster One. Putnam, 1975
The Devil's Churchyard. Parrish, 1957
Dixon of Dock Green, with Charles Hatton. Kimber, 1960 GD
The Left-Handed Sleeper. Macmillan (London), 1975; Putnam, 1976
Westminster One; see Death May Surprise Us

WILLIS, W. G. and MRS. GREEN
Whose Hand? or, The Mystery of No Man's Heath. Rand, 1890

WILLOCK, COLIN (DENNISTOUN). 1919- . Series character: Nathaniel Goss, in all titles.
Death at Flight. Heinemann, 1956
Death at the Strike. Heinemann, 1957
Death in Covert. Heinemann, 1961

WILLOCK, RUTH. 1904- .
I, Victoria Strange. Hawthorn, 1975; Collins, 1975
The Moonlit Trap. Hawthorn, 1973; Collins, 1974
The Night of the Visitor. Ace, 1965; Hodder, 1966
The Street of the Small Steps. Hawthorn, 1972; Collins, 1973

WILLOUGHBY, JOHN
Crimsoned Millions. Clode, 1927

WILLS, C(HARLES) J(AMES). 1842-1912.
The Pit Town Coronet. Ward, 1888

WILLS, (MAITLAND) CECIL M(ELVILLE). 1891- . Series characters: Roger Ellerdine = RE; Geoffrey Boscobell = GB; Sylvester Horatio Pinkney = SP.
Author in Distress. Heritage, 1934. Also published as: Number 19. Bodley Head, 1934 GB
A Body in the Dawn. Hodder, 1938 GB
The Case of the Calabar Bean. Hodder, 1939 GB
The Case of the Empty Beehive. Hale, 1959 SP
The Case of the R.E. Pipe. Hodder, 1940 GB, RE
The Chamois Murder. Heritage, 1935 GB
The Clue of the Golden Ear-Ring. Hodder, 1950 RE, GB
The Clue of the Lost Hour. Hodder, 1949 GB, RE
The Colonel's Foxhound. Hale, 1960 SP
The Dead Voice. Hodder, 1952 RE
Death at the Pelican. Heritage, 1934 GB
Death in the Dark. Hutchinson, 1955 RE
Death of a Best Seller. Hale, 1959 SP
Death on the Line. Hutchinson, 1954
"Death Treads—". Heritage, 1935 GB
Defeat of a Detective. Hodder, 1936 GB
Fatal Accident. Hodder, 1936 GB
It Pays to Die. Hodder, 1953 RE
Justice in Jeopardy. Hale, 1961 RE
Mere Murder. Hale, 1958 RE
Midsummer Murder. Hutchinson, 1956
Number 18; see Author in Distress
On the Night in Question. Hodder, 1937 GB
Then Came the Police. Heritage, 1935 GB
The Tiger Strikes Again. Hutchinson, 1957 RE

What Say the Jury? Hodder, 1952 RE
Who Killed Brother Treasurer? Hodder, 1951 RE

WILLS, HELEN (NEWINGTON), 1906- , and ROBERT W(ILLIAM) MURPHY, 1902-1971, q.v.
Death Serves an Ace. Scribner, 1939; Hutchinson, 1939

WILLS, RONALD. Pseudonym of Ronald Wills Thomas, 1910- . Other pseudonym: Jeff Bogar, q.v.
The Big Fish. Wingate, 1951; Roy, 1954
The Black Weever. Wingate, 1952; Roy, 1955
Food for Fishes. Dakers, 1954
Live Bait. Wingate, 1950

WILLS, THOMAS. Pseudonym of William (Thomas) Ard, 1922-1960, q.v. Other pseudonyms: Ben Kerr, Mike Moran, qq.v.
Mine to Avenge. GM, 1955; Fawcett (London), 1956
You'll Get Yours. Lion, 1952

WILLSDON, ANDREW
Murder Breeds Murder. Hale, 1971
The One-Off Job. Hale, 1970

WILMER, DALE. Joint pseudonym of Robert Wade, 1920- , q.v., and Bill Miller, 1920-1961. Other joint pseudonyms: Will Daemer, Wade Miller, Whit Masterson, qq.v. See also: BOB WADE.
Dead Fall. Bouregy, 1954
Jungle Heat. Pyramid, 1954; Panther, 1962
Memo for Murder. Graphic, 1951

WILMOT, EILEEN
Dangerous Search. Wright, 1958
Holiday with Danger. Wright, 1959
Homicide at Saxondale. Progressive, 1949
The Lurking Terror. Mellifont, 1956
Murder Insoluble. Progressive, 1950
Murder Will. Coker, 1951
Not a Nice Murder! Brown Watson, 1949
Poison for One. Fiction House, 1947
Voodoo Drums. Fiction House, 1947

WILMOT, J(AMES) R(EGINALD). 1897- . Pseudonym: Ralph Trevor, q.v.
Death in the Stalls. Nicholson, 1934. U.S. title: Death in the Theatre. Kendall, 1934
Death in the Theatre; see Death in the Stalls
Night Tide. Nicholson, 1936
-A Young Girl's Bondage. Newnes, 1935

WILMOT, ROBERT PATRICK. Series character: Steve Considine, in all titles.
Blood in Your Eye. Lippincott, 1952; Boardman, 1954
Death Rides a Painted Horse. Lippincott, 1954; Boardman, 1955
Murder on Monday. Lippincott, 1953; Boardman, 1954

WILSON, A. G. Pseudonym of W. G. A. Harrison.
Come Away Death. Hurst, 1936
Spider Ballet. Hurst, 1938

WILSON, ALEXANDER (DOUGLAS CHESNEY). 1893- . Pseudonym: Geoffrey Spencer, q.v. Series character: Sir Leonard Wallace, in at least those marked LW.
Chronicles of the Secret Service. Jenkins, 1940 ss LW
The Crimson Dacoit. Jenkins, 1933
The Death of Dr. Whitelaw. Longmans (London & New York), 1930

The Devil's Cocktail. Longmans (London & New York), 1928
Double Events. Jenkins, 1937
Double Masquerade. Jenkins, 1940
Get Wallace! Jenkins, 1934 LW
His Excellency, Governor Wallace. Jenkins, 1936 LW
The Magnificent Hobo. Jenkins, 1935
Microbes of Power. Jenkins, 1937 LW
Mr. Justice. Jenkins, 1937
Murder Mansion. Longmans (London & New York), 1929
The Mystery of Tunnel 51. Longmans (London & New York), 1928 LW
Scapegoats for Murder. Jenkins, 1939
The Sentimental Crook. Jenkins, 1934
Wallace at Bay. Jenkins, 1938 LW
Wallace Intervenes. Jenkins, 1939 LW
Wallace of the Secret Service. Jenkins, 1933 ss LW

WILSON, ALEXANDER. 1893- . See: RUTH WILSON.

WILSON, CALDER. See: NELLIE TOM-GALLON.

WILSON, CAROLYN. 1938- .
The Scent of Lilacs. Ace, 1966

WILSON, CHRISTOPHER
For a Woman's Honour. Paul, 1911
-The Heart of Delilah. Blackwood, 1912
The Missing Millionaire. Blackwood, 1911
-The Wings of Destiny. Daily Mail, 1909

WILSON, COLIN (HENRY). 1931- .
The Black Room. Weidenfeld, 1971
The Glass Cage. Barker, 1966; Random, 1967
-The God of the Labyrinth. Hart-Davis, 1970
The Killer. New English Library, 1970. U.S. title: Lingard. Crown, 1970
Lingard; see The Killer
Necessary Doubt. Barker, 1964; Trident, 1964
The Philosopher's Stone. Barker, 1969; Crown, 1971
Ritual in the Dark. Gollancz, 1960; Houghton, 1960
The Schoolgirl Murder Case. Hart-Davis, 1974; Crown, 1974
The Violent World of Hugh Greene; see The World of Violence
The World of Violence. Gollancz, 1963. U.S. title: The Violent World of Hugh Greene. Houghton, 1963

WILSON, DANA
Make with the Brains, Pierre. Messner, 1946. British title: Scenario for Murder. Foulsham, 1949. Also published as: Uneasy Virtue. Avon, 1948

WILSON, DAVID. Pseudonym of D(avid) Wilson MacArthur, 1903- , q.v.
Murder in Mozambique. Jenkins, 1963
The Search for Geoffrey Goring. Jenkins, 1962

WILSON, DAVID. Series character: McCloud, in all titles (which are novelizations of the TV series.)
The Corpse Maker. Award, 1974; Tandem, 1974
A Dangerous Place to Die. Award, 1975; Tandem, 1975
The Killing. Award, 1974; Tandem, 1974
Park Avenue Executioner. Award, 1975; Tandem, 1975

WILSON, E. LEA
The Vanishing Hand. [Author], 1893. (Three stories.)

WILSON, G(ERTRUDE) M(ARY BRYANT). 1899- . Series character: Inspector Lovick, in at least those marked L.
Bury That Poker. Hale, 1957 L
The Bus Ran Late. Hale, 1971
Cake for Caroline. Hale, 1967
A Deal of Death Caps. Hale, 1970 L
Death is Buttercups. Hale, 1969
The Devil's Skull. Hale, 1965 L
Do Not Sleep. Hale, 1968 L
Gipsies Don't Have Them. Hale, 1974
The Headless Man. Hale, 1967
I was Murdered. Hale, 1957; Walker, 1961 L
It Rained That Friday. Hale, 1960
Murder on Monday. Hale, 1963 L
Nightmare Cottage. Hale, 1963
Roberta Died. Hale, 1962 L
Shadows on the Landing. Hale, 1959 L
She Kept on Dying. Hale, 1972
She Sees Things. Hale, 1975
Shot at Dawn. Hale, 1964 L
Thirteen Stannergate. Hale, 1958
Three Fingered Death. Hale, 1961
Witchwater. Hale, 1961 L

WILSON, GREGORY
The Boxing Mystery. Modern, 1938
The Factory Mystery. Modern, 1938

WILSON, GROVE. 1883-1954.
The Monster of Snowdon Hall. Washburn, 1932; Skeffington, 1933
The Mysterious Wife. Frank-Maurice, 1927
Sport of the Gods. Frank-Maurice, 1926

WILSON, IVOR (ARTHUR). 1924- . Series character: Greg Flamm, in at least those marked GF.
But Not for Love. Collins, 1962 GF
Empty Tigers. Collins, 1965 GF
Lilies That Fester. Collins, 1964
That Feeds on Men. Collins, 1963 GF

WILSON, JACK [JOHN AITKEN WILSON]. 1937-
-Adam Grey. Muller, 1964. Also published as: The Night Comer. Corgi, 1966
The Night Comer; see Adam Grey
-The Tomorrow Country. Muller, 1967
-The Wild Summer. Muller, 1963

WILSON, JACQUELINE. 1945- .
Hide and Seek. Macmillan (London), 1972; Doubleday, 1973
Snap. Macmillan (London), 1974
Truth or Dare. Macmillan (London), 1973; Doubleday, 1974

WILSON, JEANNE (PATRICIA PAULINE). 1920- .
Model for Murder. Ward, 1968
No Medicine for Murder. Ward, 1967

WILSON, JOHN ANTHONY BURGESS. 1917- . Pseudonym: Anthony Burgess, q.v.

WILSON, JOS(EPH) N(ATHANIEL PUBLICOVER). 1894- .
-Hell's Harvest. Meador, 1940

WILSON, LEE. Pseudonym of Laura Elizabeth Lemmon, 1917- .
This Deadly Dark. Dodd, 1946

WILSON, MARIE BEATRICE. 1922- .
Pseudonym: Jeanne Marie, q.v.

WILSON, MITCHELL A. 1913-1973. Joint pseudonym with Abraham Polonsky: Emmett Hogarth, q.v.
Footsteps Behind Her. Simon, 1941
The Huntress. Doubleday, 1966; Secker, 1966

None So Blind. Simon, 1945; Allen, 1947
The Panic-Stricken. Simon, 1946
Stalk the Hunter. Simon, 1943

WILSON, NORMAN SCARLYN. 1901- . Pseudonym: Anthony Webb, q.v.

WILSON, P(HILIP) W(HITWELL). 1875-1956. Series character: Sir Julian Morthoe, in all titles.
Black Tarn. Farrar, 1945; Boardman, 1948
Bride's Castle. Farrar, 1944; Boardman, 1946
The Old Mill. Rinehart, 1946; Boardman, 1948

WILSON, ROBERT McNAIR. 1882- . Pseudonym: Anthony Wynne, q.v.

WILSON, RUTH and ALEXANDER, 1893- .
The Town is Full of Rumors. Simon, 1941

WILSON, STANLEY KIDDER. 1879- .
The Scream of the Doll. Duffield, 1931

WILSON, T(REVOR) E(DWARD)
Fugitive from Fear. Hale, 1972
Knock Softly on Death's Door. Hale, 1971
-The Parasites. Hale, 1973

WILSON, WILLIAM. 1935- .
Detour. Putnam, 1974

WILSON-BARRETT, ALFRED. 1871- . See: ALFRED WILSON BARRETT, 1871- .

WILSTACH, JOHN
-The Fate of Fay Delray. Macaulay, 1933
Under Cover Man. Morrow, 1931

WIMHURST, CECIL GORDON EUGENE. Pseudonym: Nigel Brent, q.v.

WINCH, EDGAR
The Hunting of Hillary. Skeffington, 1929
-The Mountain of Gold. Hurst, 1928
-When the Tide Runs Out. Hurst, 1930

WINCHELL, PRENTICE. 1895- . Pseudonyms: Spencer Dean, Jay de Bekker, Dexter St. Clair, Dexter St. Clare, Stewart Sterling, qq.v.

WINCHESTER, CLARENCE (ARTHUR CHARLES). 1892- .
City of Lies. Collins, 1942
-The Devil Rides High. Collins, 1933
-Three Men in a Plane. Collins, 1941

WINCHESTER, STANLEY
Ten Per Cent of Your Life. Allen, 1973

WINCOR, RICHARD
The St. Ives Murders. Oceana, 1958
Sherlock Holmes in Tibet. Weybright, 1968

WINDSOR, GEORGE
Nelson Lord—One of our Agents. Stockwell, 1974

WINDSOR, HUGH
Dead Man's Shoes. Gifford, 1964
Lead Him to Death. Gifford, 1963
The Source of Death. Gifford, 1964

WINDSOR-RICHARDS, A(RTHUR BEDLINGTON). 1904- .
Of Hidden Depths. Gifford, 1966

WINDUST, CHARLES
    Some Crime Stories. Weekly Dispatch, 1899 ss

WINER, ELIHU
    Anatony of a Murder. French (New York), 1966. (3-act play based on the novel by Robert Traver, q.v.)

WINGARD, ALAN
    The Graffiti Gambit. Paperback Library, 1974

WINN, PATRICK. 1906- . Series character: Inspector Lyon, in at least those marked L.
    Colour of Murder. Hale, 1965
    Dead Innocent. Hale, 1966 L
    Dusty Sunset. Hale, 1962
    Fact X. Hale, 1966 L
    Invisible Evidence. Hale, 1963
    Postscript to Murder. Hale, 1964 L

WINNER, PERCY. 1899-1974.
    Scene in the Ice-Blue Eyes. Harcourt, 1947

WINNINGTON, ALAN
    Berlin Epitaph; see Berlin Halt
    Berlin Halt. Hale, 1973. U.S. title: Berlin Epitaph. Pinnacle, 1974
    Catseyes. Cassell, 1967
    The Fairfax Millions. Hale, 1974

WINSLOW, HORATIO (GATES), 1882- , and LESLIE (W.) QUIRK, 1882- .
    Into Thin Air. Doubleday, 1929; Gollancz, 1928

WINSLOW, JOAN
    Griffin Towers. Ace, 1966

WINSLOW, PAULINE GLEN
    Death of an Angel. Macmillan (London), 1975; St. Martin's, 1975
    Gallows Child; see The Strawberry Marten
    The Strawberry Marten. Macmillan (London), 1973. U.S. title: Gallows Child. St. Martin's, 1978

WINSOR, DIANA. 1946- . Series character: Tavy Martin, in both titles.
    The Death Convention. Macmillan (London), 1974; Stein, 1978
    Red on Wight. Macmillan (London), 1972; Stein, 1978

WINSOR, G(EORGE) McLEOD
    The Mysterious Disappearances. Faber, 1926. U.S. title: Vanishing Men. Morrow, 1927
    -Once Bitten, and What Ensued. Jenkins, 1930
    -Station X. Jenkins, 1919
    Vanishing Men; see The Mysterious Disappearances

WINSOR, ROY. 1912- .
    The Corpse That Walked. GM, 1974

WINSTANLEY, L(ILIAN). 1875- .
    The Double Disappearance. Hutchinson, 1925
    The Face on the Stair. Hutchinson, 1927

WINSTON, DAOMA. 1922- .
    The Carnaby Curse. Belmont, 1967
    The Castle of Closing Doors. Belmont, 1967
    Death Watch. Ace, 1975
    Dennison Hill. Paperback Library, 1970
    The Devil's Daughter. Lancer, 1971
    Devil's Princess. Lancer, 1971
    Emerald Station. Avon, 1974; Futura, 1977
    Flight of a Fallen Angel. Lancer, 1971
    The Golden Valley. Simon, 1975
    The Haversham Legacy. Simon, 1974; Futura, 1977
    House of Mirror Images. Lancer, 1970
    The Inheritance. Avon, 1972
    Kingdom's Castle. Berkley, 1972
    The Long and Living Shadow. Belmont, 1968
    The Love of Lucifer. Lancer, 1971
    The Mansion of Smiling Masks. Signet, 1967
    Moorhaven. Avon, 1974
    Pity My Love. Belmont, 1967
    The Return. Avon, 1972
    The Secrets of Cromwell Crossing. Lancer, 1965
    Seminar in Evil. Lancer, 1972
    Shadow of an Unknown Woman. Lancer, 1967
    Shadow on Mercer Mountain. Lancer, 1967
    Sinister Stone. Paperback Library, 1966
    The Trap. Popular Library, 1973
    The Trificante Treasure. Lancer, 1968
    The Unforgotten. Berkley, 1973
    The Vampire Curse. Paperback Library, 1971
    The Victim. Popular Library, 1972
    The Wakefield Witches. Award, 1966
    Walk Around the Square. Ace, 1975

WINSTON, PETER. Series characters: The Adjusters, in all titles (novelizations of the TV series).
    The ABC Affair. Award, 1967; Tandem, 1967
    Assignment to Bahrein. Award, 1967; Tandem, 1967
    Doomsday Vendetta. Award, 1968
    The Glass Cipher. Award, 1968; Tandem, 1968

WINTER, ABIGAIL. Pseudonym of Monroe Schere.
    Whispering Caverns. Simon, 1974

WINTER, BEVIS. 1918- . Pseudonyms: Al Bocca, Peter Cagney, Gordon Shayne, qq.v. See also: ERIC MASCHWITZ, 1901- . Series character: Steve Craig, in at least those marked SC.
    Blondes End up Dead. Jenkins, 1959 SC
    The Dark and Deadly. Jenkins, 1961 SC
    Darker Grows the Street. Jenkins, 1955 SC
    The Dead Sleep for Keeps. Jenkins, 1955 SC
    Let the Lady Die. Jenkins, 1957 SC
    Make Mine Murder. Warren, 1949
    Next Stop—the Morgue. Jenkins, 1956 SC
    The Night was Made for Murder. Jenkins, 1957 SC
    A Noose of Emeralds. Mystery House, 1956. (British title?) SC
    Redheads are Poison. Hamilton & Co., 1948
    Redheads Cool Fast. Jenkins, 1954 SC

WINTER, JOHN STRANGE. Pseudonym of Henrietta Eliza Vaughan Palmer Stannard, 1856-1911.
    A Mystery of Mayfair. White, 1908

WINTERBOTHAM, RUSSELL ROBERT. 1904-1971. Pseudonym: J. Harvey Bond, q.v.

WINTERTON, PAUL. 1908- . Pseudonyms: Roger Bax, Andrew Garve, Paul Somers, qq.v.

WINTHROP, WILMA
    Hostage of Evil. Lancer, 1966
    Island of the Accursed. Lancer, 1966
    Tryst with Terror. Lancer, 1965

WINTLE, ALFRED DANIEL. Pseudonym: Michael Cobb, q.v.

WINTLE, GILBERT
    -The Gentleman Tramp. Ward, 1907
    -Gold of Cathay. Ward, 1908
    -Meshes of Mischance. Ward, 1906
    Strange Partners. Ward, 1905

WINTLE, HAROLD
    -The Great Betrayal. Ouseley, 1911

WINTLE, W(ILLIAM) J(AMES)
    Nights with an Old Lag. Ouseley, 1911 ss

WINWARD, WALTER
    Fives Wild. Weidenfeld, 1975; Atheneum, 1976

WIRE, H(AROLD) C(HANNING)
    Marked Man. Appleton, 1934; World's Work, 1950
    Mountain Man. Crowell, 1929; Skeffington, 1930
    -The Witness Tree. Crowell, 1930

WISE, ARDATH
    Dark Waters. Lenox, 1974; Remploy, 1974
    The Gold Door. Lenox, 1972
    Tiger Hill. Lenox, 1975

WISE, ARTHUR. 1923- .
    The Death's-Head. Cassell, 1962
    Leatherjacket. Weidenfeld, 1970
    The Little Fishes. Gollancz, 1961
    The Naughty Girls. Allen, 1972
    Who Killed Enoch Powell? Weidenfeld, 1970; Harper, 1971

WISEMAN, RICHARD
    First Person Plural. Macmillan (London), 1975

WISHART, GERTRUDE
    Madame Lies Murdered. Long, 1940

WISSMANN, RUTH (H.). 1914- .
    Claws of the Crow. Paperback Library, 1974
    Desert of Darkness. Paperback Library, 1972
    Fear Waits on Cypress Road. Doubleday, 1975; Hale, 1976
    The Shadow of Sheila Ann. Paperback Library, 1974
    To Hang a Witch. Paperback Library, 1974

WITHERS, E. L. Pseudonym of George William Potter, Jr., 1930- .
    The Birthday. Doubleday, 1962
    Diminishing Returns. Rinehart, 1960; Harrap, 1961
    Heir Apparent. Doubleday, 1961; Harrap, 1962
    The House on the Beach. Rinehart, 1957; Harrap, 1958
    The Salazar Grant. Rinehart, 1959; Harrap, 1960

WITHERS, JULIA
    Caprice. Dell, 1967. (Novelization of the movie.)
    Echo in a Dark Wind. Signet, 1966
    The Shuttered Room. Dell, 1967; Mayflower, 1967. (Novelization of the movie.)

WITLEY, A. F. Pseudonym of Sandor Forbat, 1890- .
    Dangerously Blonde. Pallas, 1938

WITNEY, FREDERIC C.
    Grand Guignol. Constable, 1947. (1-act plays.)

WITTING, CLIFFORD. 1907-   . Series
    characters: Inspector Charlton = C;
    Sergeant/Insp. Peter Bradford = PB.
  A Bullet for Rhino. Hodder, 1950 C
  The Case of the Busy Bees. Hodder, 1952
    C, PB
  The Case of the Michaelmas Goose. Hod-
    der, 1938 C
  Catt Out of the Bag. Hodder, 1939 C
  Crime in Whispers. Hodder, 1964 PB
  Dead on Time. Hodder, 1948 C, PB
  Driven to Kill. Hodder, 1961 PB
  Let X be the Murderer. Hodder, 1947
    C, PB
  Measure for Murder. Hodder, 1941 C
  Midsummer Murder. Hodder, 1937 C
  Mischief in the Offing. Hodder, 1958
  Murder in Blue. Hodder, 1937; Scribner,
    1937 C
  Silence After Dinner. Hodder, 1953
    PB, C
  Subject—Murder. Hodder, 1945 C, PB
  There was a Crooked Man. Hodder, 1960;
    British Book Centre, 1962 PB
  Villainous Saltpetre. Hodder, 1962

WITTMAN, GEORGE
  A Matter of Intelligence. Macmillan,
    1975

WLASCHIN, KEN(NETH). See also: TROY KEN-
    NEDY MARTIN.
  To Kill the Pope. New English Library
    pb, 1971

WODEHOUSE, P(ELHAM) G(RENVILLE). 1881-
    1975.
  The Crime Wave at Blandings. Double-
    day, 1937. (British title?) ss
  Do Butlers Burgle Banks? Jenkins, 1968;
    Simon, 1968
  The Little Nugget. Methuen, 1913; Watt,
    1914
 -The Old Reliable. Jenkins, 1951;
    Doubleday, 1951
  Ukridge. Jenkins, 1924 ss

WODEN, GEORGE. Pseudonym of George Wilson
    Slaney, 1884-   .
  The Cathkin Mystery. Hutchinson, 1937
 -Mungo. Hutchinson, 1932
  The Mystery of the Amorous Music Mas-
    ter. Hutchinson, 1951
  The Puzzled Policeman. Hutchinson, 1949
 -The Queer Folk Next Door. Hutchinson,
    1942
  The Wrenfield Mystery. Parsons, 1923

WOGAN, CHARLES
  Cyanide for the Chorister. Long, 1950
  The Hangman's Hands. Long, 1947
  The Horror at Wardens Hall. Long, 1948

WOHL, BURTON
 -High Encounter. Bantam (New York & Lon-
    don), 1975
  The Ten Tola Bars. Delacorte, 1975;
    Hamlyn, 1978

WOLF, JACK (CLIFFORD). 1922-   . Series
    character: Timothy Rourke = TR.
  Death Rides a Camel. Hammond, 1960
  Payoff on Fever Street. Hammond, 1962
    TR
  Two Shadows for Death. Hammond, 1961 TR

WOLF, MARI. 1927-   .
  The Golden Frame. Permabooks, 1961

WOLFE, MICHAEL. Pseudonym of Gilbert M.
    Williams, 1917-   . Series charac-
    ter: Michael Keefe, in both titles.
  Man on a String. Harper, 1973
  The Two-Star Pigeon. Harper, 1975

WOLFE, WINIFRED (HARRIET)
  Never Step on a Rainbow. Harper, 1965;
    Gollancz, 1966

WOLFENDEN, GEORGE. Pseudonym of George
    Beardmore, 1908-   , q.v. Other
    pseudonym: Cedric Stokes, q.v.
  The House in Spitalfields. Hurst, 1937
 -The Little Doves of Destruction. Hurst,
    1942
  The Spy Who Died in Bed. Hurst, 1941

WOLFF, WILLIAM ALMON. 1885-   . Series
    character: Lieutenant Mitchell = M.
  Manhattan Night. Minton, 1930 M
  Murder at Endor. Minton, 1933; Putnam
    (London), 1933 M
  The Trial of Mary Dugan. Doubleday,
    1928; Heinemann, 1928

WOLFFE, KATHERINE. Pseudonym of Marian
    Gallagher Scott, 1892-   . Other
    pseudonym: Gail Oliver, q.v.
  The Attic Room. Morrow, 1942
  Bride of Death; see Tall Man Walking
  Death's Long Shadow. Five Star, 1946
  Tall Man Walking. Doubleday, 1936. Bri-
    tish title: Bride of Death. Bell,
    1937

WOLFSON, P(INCUS) J(ACOB). 1903-   .
  Bodies are Dust. Vanguard, 1931

WOLFSON, VI
  Nothing Happens to Children in Beverly
    Hills. Putnam, 1975; Hale, 1976

WOLFSON, VICTOR. 1910-   . Pseudonym:
    Langdon Dodge, q.v.
  The Lonely Steeple. Simon, 1945

WOLK, GEORGE
 -Jeremiah Painter. Dell, 1973; New Eng-
    lish Library, 1976
  The Leopold Contract. Random, 1969
  The Man Who Dealt in Blood. Warner,
    1974

WOLSELEY, FAITH. Pseudonym of Stella
    (Mary Hodgson) Tower, 1891-   , q.v.
 -Old Mrs. Warren. Crisp, 1945
  Screened. Murray, 1937
  Which Way Came Death? Murray, 1936

WOOD, (SAMUEL) ANDREW. 1890-   . Byline
    sometimes: S. Andrew Wood, but all
    works are listed here. Pseudonym:
    Robin Temple, q.v. Series characters:
    Magnus Keeble, in at least those
    marked MK; Sasha, in at least those
    marked S; Koregorvsky, in at least
    those marked K.
  Big Ben Struck Twelve. Hurst, 1948 MK
  Blind Man's Buff. Jenkins, 1939
  Bright Angel. Ward, 1933; Dutton, 1933
    K
  Castle Dangerous. Cherry Tree, 1941
 -Cinderella All Alone. Jenkins, 1926
  Deep Flows the River. Mellifont, 1950
  Eros is No Hangman. Hurst, 1949 MK
 -The Flower of Desire. Dutton, 1927.
    (British title?)
  The Four Pitiful People. Hurst, 1947
  Hangman's Child. Hodder, 1936
  Hell for Leather. Jarrolds, 1930
 -Her Second Self. Thomson, 1933
  I'll Blackmail the World. Hodder, 1935
 -The Isle of Enchantment. Jenkins, 1925
  It's Easy to Kill. Hodder, 1938
  Judgement Castle. Dragon, 1955
  King Vagabond. Hodder, 1936 S
  The Little Widow Murder. Fiction House,
    1949
  The Man Who Came Back. Cherry Tree,
    1942
  The Midnight Road. Mellifont, 1943
 -The Misleading Lady. Cassell, 1926
  Murder at the Wishing Well. Mellifont,
    1944
  Murder by the Minute. Dragon, 1955 MK
  Not Proven Castle. Hodder, 1936
 -Odds Against Her. Leng, 1929
 -Phantom Railway. Muller, 1954
  Port of Little Ships. Hurst, 1947
  The Prom Concert Murders. Hurst, 1948
    MK
  Red-Handed They Came. Mellifont, 1945
  Red Square. Ward, 1934; Dutton, 1934
    K, S
  Release the Prisoner. Hodder, 1937
  The River Will Hide Me. Cherry Tree,
    1949
  Serenade for Murder. Cherry Tree, 1944
  Sinister Island. Cherry Tree, 1945
  Sinners' Castle. Jenkins, 1941; Swift,
    1941
  Stick at Nothing. Jenkins, 1939
  Ten Peacocks. Ward, 1934
  There is No Ogpu. Jenkins, 1940
 -Volcano Island. Venturebooks, 1950
 -Wed for Wealth. Thomson, 1931
  White Sin. Ward, 1933

WOOD, BARI. 1936-   .
  The Killing Gift. Putnam, 1975; Heine-
    mann, 1976

WOOD, CLEMENT. 1888-1950. Series charac-
    ters: Skelton Keyne = SK; Lal Reed =
    LR.
  The Corpse in the Guest Room. Arcadia,
    1945 SK
  Death in Ankara. Mystery House, 1944 LR
  Death on the Pampas. Mystery House,
    1944 LR
  Double Jeopardy. Arcadia, 1947 SK
  The Shadow from the Bogue. Dutton, 1928
  The Tabloid Murders. Macaulay, 1930

WOOD, ELLEN PRICE. 1814-1887. See: MRS.
    HENRY WOOD.

WOOD, ERIC. Series characters: Arnold
    Keene and Bernard Young = K&Y.
  Death in the Mews. Hamilton, 1937 K&Y
  Death of an Oddfellow. Hamilton, 1938
    K&Y
  Hands of Death. Hamilton, 1937 K&Y
  Murder from the Grave. Hamilton, 1938
  The Mystery of Maybury Manor. Cassell,
    1920

WOOD, ERNEST
  Feloniously and Wilfully. Long, 1947

WOOD, H(ARRY) F(REEMAN)
 -Avenged on Society. Heinemann, 1893;
    Lovell, 1892
  The Englishman of the Rue Cain. Chatto,
    1889; Rand, 1889
  The Night Mail; see The Passenger from
    Scotland Yard
  The Night of the 3rd Ult. Lovell, 1890
  The Passenger from Scotland Yard. Chat-
    to, 1888; Munro, 1888. Also published
    as: The Night Mail; or, The Passenger
    from Scotland Yard. Munro, 1894. Also
    published as by William Ward: Economy
    Book League, 1933
 -Under Masks. Sisley's, 1908

WOOD, MRS. HENRY [ELLEN PRICE WOOD].
    1814-1887. Here listed is the book
    fiction attributed to this British
    author. No attempt has been made to
    distinguish among her works on the
    basis of criminous content. Note that
    a number of U.S. titles remain uncor-
    related with their British originals.
  About Ourselves. Nisbet, 1883
  Adam Grainger. Bentley, 1876. U.S.
    title: Adam Grainger and other sto-
    ries. Macmillan, 18?? ss

Wood, Mrs. Henry

Anne Hereford. Tinsley, 1868. U.S. title: The Mystery; or, Anne Hereford. Peterson, 1862
Ashley, and other stories. Bentley, 1897 ss
Barren Honor. Dick, 1868. (British title?)
Bessy Rane. Bentley, 1870; Peterson, 1870
Bessy Wells. Daldy, 1875
Castle Wafer; or, The Plain Gold Ring. Dick, 1868. (British title?)
Castle's Heir; see Lady Adelaide's Oath
The Channings. Bentley, 1862; Peterson, 1862
Clara Lake's Dream. Peterson, ca.1873. (British title?)
Count Netherleigh. Bentley, 1881; Munro, 1881
Cyrilla Maude's First Love. Peterson, ca.1873. (British title?)
Danesbury House. Scottish Temperance League, 1860; Harper, 18??
Dene Hollow. Bentley, 1871; Peterson, 1871
The Diamond Bracelet; see The Lost Will
Doctor's Daughter. Ogilvie, 1881. (British title?)
East Lynne. Bentley, 1861; Dick, 1861
Edina. Bentley, 1876; Peterson, 1876
Elster's Folly. Tinsley, 1866; Peterson, 1866
Featherstone's Story. Bentley, 1889
Final Ending of It. Ogilvie, 1881. (British title?)
Five Thousand a Year. Peterson, ca. 1873. (British title?)
The Foggy Night at Offord. Nisbet, 1863; Peterson, 1863
Frances Hildyard. Peterson, ca.1873. (British title?)
George Canterbury's Will. Tinsley, 1870; Peterson, 1870
Gervase Castonel; or, The Six Grey Powders. Dick, 1863. (British title?)
Great Feast. Ogilvie, 1881. (British title?)
The Haunted Tower. Peterson, 1864. (British title?)
The Heir to Ashly. Dick, 1862. (British title?)
Helen Whitney's Edding, and other stories. Munro, 1885 ss (British title?)
The House of Halliwell. Bentley, 1890; U.S. Book Co., 1890
Johnny Ludlow. Bentley, 1874; Munro, 1881 ss, some reprinted as: Under the Rose. Carleton, 1878
Johnny Ludlow. Second Series. Bentley, 1880 ss
Johnny Ludlow. Third Series. Bentley, 1885; Macmillan, 18?? ss
Johnny Ludlow. Fourth Series. Bentley, 1890 ss
Johnny Ludlow. Fifth Series. Bentley, 1890; Macmillan, 189? ss
Johnny Ludlow. Sixth Series. Bentley, 1899; Macmillan, 1901 ss
Lady Adelaide's Oath. Bentley, 1867. U.S. title: Castle's Heir; or, Lady Adelaide's Oath. Peterson, ca.1871
Lady Grace and other stories. Bentley, 1887; Lovell, 1887 ss
A Life's Secret. Wood, 1867; Peterson, ca.1873
Light and a Dark Christmas. Peterson, 1866. (British title?)
Lord Oakburn's Daughters. Bradbury, 1864; Peterson, 1865
The Lost Bank Note. Peterson, 1863. (British title?)
Lost in the Post, and other tales. Munro, 1881 ss (British title?)
The Lost Will. Peterson, 1865. Also published as: The Diamond Bracelet. Peterson, ca.1873. (British title?)
Marrying Beneath Your Station. Peterson, ca.1873. (British title?)
Martyn Ware's Temptation. Peterson, ca.1873. (British title?)
The Master of Graylands. Bentley, 1873; Peterson, 1873
Mildred Arkell. Peterson, 1865. (British title?)
Mrs. Halliburton's Troubles. Bentley, 1862; Dick, 1863
Missing Letter. Ogilvie, 1882. (British title?)
My Cousin Caroline's Wedding. Peterson, ca.1873. (British title?)
My Husband's First Love. Peterson, ca.1873. (British title?)
The Mystery; see Anne Hereford
The Mystery of Jessie Page, and other stories. Munro, 1885 ss (British title?)
The Nobleman's Wife. Peterson, ca.1873. (British title?)
Orville College. Tinsley, 1867; Peterson, ca.1873
Oswald Gray. Black, 1864; Peterson, 1864
Out of the Deep; or, Cast Up by the Sea. Gill, 1875. (British title?)
Parkwater. Bentley, 1876; Peterson, ca.1873
Pomeroy Abbey. Bentley, 1878; Munro, 1878
The Red Court Farm. Tinsley, 1868; Peterson, 1865
Robert Ashton's Wedding Day, and other stories. Munro, 1881 ss (British title?)
Roland Yorke. Bentley, 1869; Peterson, 1869
Rose Lodge. Munro, 1881 ss (British title?)
The Runaway Match. Peterson, 1863. (British title?)
Rupert Hall. Peterson, 1876. (British title?)
St. Martin's Eve. Tinsley, 1866; Peterson, 1866
Self-Convicted. Peterson, ca.1873. (British title?)
The Shadow of Ashlydyat. Bentley, 1863; Peterson, 1863
Smuggler's Ghost. Peterson, ca.1873. (British title?)
Squire Trevlyn's Heir; see Trevlyn Hold
The Story of Charles Strange. Bentley, 1888; Laird, 1889
The Story of Dorothy Grape, and other tales. Munro, 1885 ss (British title?)
A Tale of Sin, and other tales. Munro, 1881 ss (British title?)
Told in the Twilight. Bentley, 1875
Trevlyn Hold; or, Squire Trevlyn's Heir. Tinsley, 1864. U.S. title: Squire Trevlyn's Heir; or, Trevlyn Hold. Peterson, 1863
Under the Rose; see Johnny Ludlow
The Unholy Wish, and other stories. Bentley, 1890; Munro, 1885 ss
Verner's Pride. Bradbury, 1863; Peterson, 1863
Was He Severe? Ogilvie, 1881. (British title?)
Will He Betray Her? Ogilvie, 1882. (British title?)
William Allair; or, Running Away to Sea. Griffith, 1864; Peterson, 1864
Within the Maze. Bentley, 1872; Peterson, 1872

WOOD, JAMES (ALEXANDER FRASER). 1918- .
Bay of Seals. Hutchinson, 1964
Be Thou My Judge. Hutchinson, 1966. U.S. title: Voyage into Nowhere. Vanguard, 1967
A Black Horse Running. Hutchinson, 1972
Cry of the Kestrel. Hutchinson, 1962
Fire Rock. Hutchinson, 1965; Vanguard, 1966
The Friday Run. Hutchinson, 1967; Vanguard, 1971
Highland Gathering. Hutchinson, 1970
The Lisa Bastian. Hutchinson, 1960; Vanguard, 1961
North Beat. Hutchinson, 1973
Northern Mission. Duckworth, 1954
North Kill. Hutchinson, 1975
The Rain Islands. Duckworth, 1957
Road to Canossa. Hutchinson, 1971
The Sealer. Hutchinson, 1959; Vanguard, 1960
The Seine Fishers. Duckworth, 1965
The Shop in Loch Street. Hutchinson, 1958
Three Blind Mice. Hutchinson, 1969; Vanguard, 1973
The Uist Project. Hutchinson, 1973
Voyage into Nowhere; see Be Thou My Judge

WOOD, LESLIE
Hardship Our Garment. Hutchinson, 1947

WOOD, S(AMUEL) ANDREW. 1890- . See: (SAMUEL) ANDREW WOOD.

WOOD, SALLY (CALKINS). 1897- .
Death in Lord Byron's Room. Morrow, 1948
Murder of a Novelist. Simon, 1941; Swan, 1946

WOOD, WALTER. 1866- .
-The Lord of the Dyke. Cassell, 1907
-Margaret the Peacemaker. Cassell, 1910
The Revenge of Gilbert Strange. Cassell, 1908
The Secret Paper. Cassell, 1909

WOODBRIDGE, H. HORATIO
Dig: Two Heads Wanted. Price, 1876

WOODBURY, DAVID O(AKES). 1896- .
Series character: George Riam, in both titles.
Five Days to Oblivion. Devin-Adair, 1963
Mr. Faraday's Formula. Devin-Adair, 1965

WOODFIN, HENRY
Virginia's Thing. Harper, 1968

WOODFORD, JACK. Pseudonym of Josiah Pitt Woolfolk, 1894-1971.
Find the Motive. Long & Smith, 1932; Paul, 1933
Five Fatal Days. Carlyle, 1933

WOODGATE, M(ILDRED) V(IOLET). 1904- .
The Mystery of Pauline's Lady; see Pauline's Lady
Pauline's Lady. Hurst, 1931. Also published as (abridged): The Mystery of Pauline's Lady. Mellifont, 1945
The Secret of the Sapphire Ring. Hurst, 1930
The Silver Mirror. Bles, 1935
The Two Houses on the Cliff. Hurst, 1931

WOODHALL, EDWIN THOMAS. 1886- .
The Atlantic Murders. Mellifont, 1939
Eleven Men Died. Mellifont, 1937
The Greyhound Stadium Plot. Mellifont, 1940
The Kidnap Murders. Mellifont, 1939
-The Mystery Flier. Mellifont, 1940
-Nazi Speedway Plot. Mellifont, 1940

WOOD-HILL, H.
  The Reluctant Spy. Gifford, 1946

WOODHOUSE, MARTIN. 1932- . Series character: Giles Yeoman = GY.
  Blue Bone. Heinemann, 1973; Coward, 1973 GY
  Bush Baby; see Rock Baby
  Mama Doll. Heinemann, 1972; Coward, 1972 GY
  Phil and Me. Heinemann, 1970; Coward, 1970
  Rock Baby. Heinemann, 1968. U.S. title: Bush Baby. Coward, 1968 GY
  Tree Frog. Heinemann, 1966; Coward, 1966 GY

WOODIWISS, JOHN C(ECIL). Series character: Insp. Hopton, in at least those marked H.
  Death's Visiting Card. Melrose, 1936 H
  The Ebony Torso. Gifford, 1939 H
  Mouseback. Melrose, 1937

WOODMAN, MICHAEL
  Bullion. Sphere, 1971
  The Medusa Kiss. Sphere, 1970; Beagle, 1971

WOODROW, MRS. WILSON [NANCY MANN WADDEL WOODROW]. 1875?-1935.
  Burned Evidence. Putnam (New York), 1925; Putnam (London), 1926
  -Come Alone. Macaulay, 1929
  The Hornet's Nest. Little, 1917
  The Moonhill Mystery. Macaulay, 1930
  Pawns of Murder. Smith, 1932; Paul, 1933
  -The Second Chance. Watt, 1925; Collins, 1925
  The Silver Butterfly. Bobbs, 1908
  -Swallowed Up. Brentano's (New York), 1922; Brentano's (London), 1923

WOODRUFF, PHILIP. Pseudonym of Philip Mason, 1906- .
  Call the Next Witness. Cape, 1945; Harcourt, 1946
  Whatever Dies. Cape, 1948 ss

WOODS, KATHERINE
  Murder in a Walled Town. Houghton, 1934; Eyre, 1936

WOODS, SARA. Pseudonym of Sara Hutton Bowen-Judd, 1922- . Series character: Antony Maitland, in all titles.
  And Shame the Devil. Collins, 1967; Holt, 1972
  Bloody Instructions. Collins, 1962; Harper, 1962
  The Case is Altered. Collins, 1967; Harper, 1967
  Done to Death. Macmillan (London), 1974; Holt, 1975
  Enter Certain Murderers. Collins, 1966; Harper, 1966
  Enter the Corpse. Macmillan (London), 1973; Holt, 1974
  Error of the Moon. Collins, 1963
  An Improbable Fiction. Collins, 1970; Holt, 1971
  The Knavish Crows. Collins, 1971
  Knives have Edges. Collins, 1968; Holt, 1970
  Let's Choose Executors. Collins, 1966; Harper, 1967
  Malice Domestic. Collins, 1962
  Past Praying For. Collins, 1968; Harper, 1968
  Serpent's Tooth. Collins, 1971; Holt, 1973
  A Show of Violence. Macmillan (London), 1975; McKay, 1975
  Tarry and be Hanged. Collins, 1969; Holt, 1971
  The Taste of Fears. Collins, 1963. U.S. title: The Third Encounter. Harper, 1963
  They Love Not Poison. Macmillan (London), 1972; Holt, 1972
  The Third Encounter; see The Taste of Fears
  This Little Measure. Collins, 1964
  Though I Know She Lies. Collins, 1965; Holt, 1972
  Trusted Like the Fox. Collins, 1964; Harper, 1965
  The Windy Side of the Law. Collins, 1965; Harper, 1965
  Yet She Must Die. Macmillan (London), 1973; Holt, 1974

WOODS, WILLIAM B.
  Lancaster Triple Thousand. Exposition, 1956

WOODTHORPE, R(ALPH) C(ARTER). 1886- . Series characters: Matilda Perks = MP; Nicholas Slade = NS.
  A Dagger in Fleet Street. Nicholson, 1934
  Death in a Little Town. Nicholson, 1935; Doubleday, 1935 MP
  Death Wears a Purple Shirt; see Silence of a Purple Shirt
  The Necessary Corpse. Nicholson, 1939 Doubleday, 1939 NS
  The Public School Murder. Nicholson, 1932
  Rope for a Convict. Nicholson, 1939; Doubleday, 1940
  The Shadow on the Downs. Nicholson, 1935; Doubleday, 1935 MP
  Silence of a Purple Shirt. Nicholson, 1934. U.S. title: Death Wears a Purple Shirt. Doubleday, 1934 NS

WOODWARD, EDWARD (EMBERLIN)
  Bill Marshall, Turf Sleuth. Mellifont, 1942
  Black Sheep. Unwin, 1926
  -Blizzard. Hutchinson, 1932
  Dead Man's Plaything. Kemsley, 1950
  -Dear Delusion. Long, 1947
  Death Amidst Satin. Long, 1940
  -Dr. Greenfingers. Long, 1933
  Each Night We Die. Hutchinson, 1936
  -False Colours. Mellifont, 1941
  -Fingers Before Forks. Selwyn, 1931
  -The Gamblers. Unwin, 1925
  -Gentlemen at Large. Long, 1948
  -A Hive of Glass. Long, 1950
  The House of Terror. Selwyn, 1929; Mystery League, 1930
  -A Lady Fell in Love. Long, 1945
  Love is a Fiend. Long, 1945
  -"Midas" Monkhouse, M.F.H. Hutchinson, 1932
  -Noughts and Crosses. Mellifont, 1943
  -Panther Face. Mellifont, 1942
  -The Pigeon Wins. Unwin, 1924
  -Promise for Tomorrow. Long, 1949
  -Race Gang. Cherry Tree, 1940
  -Shake Hands for Ever. Long, 1947
  -The Sky's the Limit. Cherry Tree, 1940
  -So This is Love! Long, 1943
  -There are Giants. Hutchinson, 1934
  -Tiger Tooth. Cherry Tree, 1944
  -Troubled Harvest. Long, 1951
  The Turf Bandits. Mellifont, 1941
  Winter Wheat. Hutchinson, 1932
  -Women are Like That. Long, 1942

WOODWARD, HELEN (ROSEN). 1882- .
  The Bowling Green Murders, with Frances Amherst. Random, 1940; Hale, 1942
  Money to Burn. McKay, 1945

WOODWARD, R(OBERT) PITCHER
  Trains That Met in the Blizzard. Salmagundi, 1896. Also published as: Frozen Humor. Dillingham, 1896 ss, some criminous

WOODWARD, S(HERMAN) M(ELVILLE). 1871-1953.
  Shot in the Pulpit. Quality, 1939

WOODY, WILLIAM
  Mistress of Horror House. Ace, 1959

WOOLF, PHILIP, M.D. 1848-1903.
  Who is Guilty? Cassell, 1886; Maxwell, 1886

WOOLFOLK, JOSIAH PITT. 1894-1971. Pseudonym: Jack Woodford, q.v.

WOOLFOLK, WILLIAM
  Blacker Than Murder; see The Naked Hunter
  -My Name is Morgan. Doubleday, 1963; Allen, 1963
  The Naked Hunter. Popular Library, 1954. British title (?): Blacker Than Murder. Hale, 1958
  The Overlords. Doubleday, 1973; Allen, 1973
  The President's Doctor. Playboy, 1975; Allen, 1976
  Run While You Can. Popular Library, 1956; Hale, 1958
  Way of the Wicked. Monarch, 1959

WOOLL, EDWARD. 1878- .
  Libel. Heinemann, 1934. (Play.) Novel based on this play: Blackie, 1935; Macrae Smith, 1936
  -The Lodestar. Heinemann, 1935
  -The Nettle. Macdonald, 1947
  -There is a Tide—. Blackie, 1934

WOOLRICH, CORNELL (GEORGE HOPLEY). 1903-1968. Pseudonyms: George Hopley, William Irish, qq.v.
  Beware the Lady; see The Bride Wore Black
  Beyond the Night. Avon, 1959 ss
  Black Alibi. Simon, 1942; Hale, 1951
  The Black Angel. Doubleday, 1943; Hale, 1949
  The Black Curtain. Simon, 1941
  The Black Path of Fear. Doubleday, 1944
  The Bride Wore Black. Simon, 1940; Hale, 1942. Also published as: Beware the Lady. Pyramid, 1953
  The Dark Side of Love. Walker, 1965 ss
  Death is my Dancing Partner. Pyramid, 1959
  The Doom Stone. Avon, 1960
  Hotel Room. Random, 1958 ss, some with criminous elements
  Manhattan Love Song. Godwin, 1932
  Nightmare. Dodd, 1956 ss
  Nightwebs. Harper, 1971; Gollancz, 1973. (Four ss and the complete Woolrich bibliography omitted from the British edition.) ss
  Rendezvous in Black. Rinehart, 1948; Hale, 1950
  Savage Bride. GM, 1950
  The Ten Faces of Cornell Woolrich. Simon, 1965; Boardman, 1966 ss
  Violence. Dodd, 1958 ss

WORBOYS, ANNE(TTE ISOBEL). Pseudonym: Vicky Maxwell, q.v.
  The Lion of Delos. Hodder, 1975; Delacorte, 1974

WORKMAN, JAMES
  -The Apologetic Tiger. Hodder, 1958
  Contrabandits. Horwitz, 1968
  -Face of Fortune. Hodder, 1961
  -Lucifer at Ponsfordville. Hodder, 1959

WORMSER, RICHARD (EDWARD). 1908-1977.
Pseudonym: Ed Friend, q.v.
The Body Looks Familiar. Dell, 1958
The Communist's Corpse. Smith & Haas, 1935; Gollancz, 1935
Drive East on 66. GM, 1961; Muller, 1962
The Hanging Heiress. Mill, 1949. Also published as: The Widow Wore Red. Crest, 1958
The Invader. GM, 1972
The Late Mrs. Five. GM, 1960
The Man with the Wax Face. Smith & Haas, 1934
A Nice Girl Like You. GM, 1963; Muller, 1963
Perfect Pigeon. GM, 1962
The Takeover. GM, 1971; Coronet, 1972
Torn Curtain. Dell, 1966; Mayflower, 1966. (Novelization of the movie.)
The Widow Wore Red; see The Hanging Heiress

WORRALL, LECHMERE. See: BEAMISH TINKER.

WORSLEY, T(HOMAS) C(UTHBERT)
Five Minutes, Sir Matthew. Ross, 1969

WORSLEY-GOUGH, BARBARA
Alibi Innings. Joseph, 1954
Lantern Hill. Joseph, 1957

WORTH, CEDRIC. 1900-   . Series character: Inspector Sevrel, in both titles.
The Corpse That Knew Everybody. Dutton, 1941
The Trail of the Serpent. Dutton, 1940

WORTH, MAURICE. Joint pseudonym of Maurice H. B. Mash and Willan George Bosworth, 1904-   . Other pseudonym of Willan George Bosworth: Willan G. Borth, q.v.
The Golden Pheasant Mystery. Hutchinson, 1927
The Pagoda Mystery. Hutchinson, 1928
The Plaza Mystery. Hutchinson, 1928

WORTH, NIGEL. Pseudonym of Noel Wright, 1890-   .
-The Arms of Phaedra. Mills, 1924
-The Man in the Box. Mills, 1923
Roger Sinclair's Treasure. Hutchinson, 1927
The Wise Man of Welby. Mills, 1924

WORTH, RICHARD
The Amateur Boxer. Modern, 1938
The Coup That Failed. Lloyd's, 1921
The Murder in the Fog. Aldine, 1927

WORTHINGTON-STUART, BRIAN ARTHUR. Pseudonyms: Peter Meredith, Brian Stuart, qq.v.

WORTS, GEORGE F(RANK). 1892-   . Pseudonym: Loring Brent, q.v.
The Blue Lacquer Box. Kinsey, 1939; Hurst, 1940. Also published as: The Case of the Blue Lacquered Box. Mystery Novel Classic, 1942
The Case of the Blue Lacquered Box; see The Blue Lacquer Box
Dangerous Young Man. Kinsey, 1940; Hurst, 1940
Five Who Vanished. McBride, 1945
The Greenfield Mystery. Whitman, 1929
The House of Creeping Horror. King, 1934
Laughing Girl. Kinsey, 1941. Also published as: Murder and the Secret Weapon. Thriller Novel Classic, 194?
The Monster of the Lagoon. Popular Publications (London), 1947. (U.S. title?)
Murder and the Secret Weapon; see Laughing Girl

Overboard. Kinsey, 1943
Peter the Brazen. Lippincott (Philadelphia & London), 1919
The Phantom President. Cape & Ballou, 1932
Red Darkness. Harper Allen, 1928
The Silver Fang. McClurg, 1930
Where Some Men are Men. Wright, 1937. (U.S. title?)

WOUK, HERMAN. 1915-   .
The Traitor. French (New York), 1949. (2-act play.)

WRAY, G. W.
Death on the Roads. Bale, 1938

WRAY, I. Pseudonym.
Murder—and Ariadne. Methuen, 1931
The Vye Murder. Methuen, 1930

WRAY, J(AMES) JACKSON
-Jonas Haggerley. Shaw, 1887
-The Secret of the Mere; or, Under the Surface. Nisbet, 1885

WRAY, NICHOLAS
Dale of the Secret Service. Mellifont, 1940
Death Deals a Diamond. Mellifont, 1942
The Fortune Cheats. Mellifont, 1943
The Lightship Murders. Mellifont, 1940
Who was the Killer? Mellifont, 1942

WRAY, ROGER. Pseudonym of James William Marriott, 1884-   .
The Rayner Case. Jarrolds, 1925

WREN, LASSITER and RANDLE McKAY, q.v.
The Baffle Book. Doubleday, 1928; Heinemann, 1930 puzzle ss
The Mystery Puzzle Book. Crowell, 1933; Hurst, 1934 puzzle ss
The Second Baffle Book. Doubleday, 1929 puzzle ss
The Third Baffle Book. Doubleday, 1930 puzzle ss

WREN, M. K. Pseudonym of Martha Kay Renfroe, 1938-   . Series character: Conan Flagg, in both titles.
Curiosity Didn't Kill the Cat. Doubleday, 1973; Hale, 1975
A Multitude of Sins. Doubleday, 1975; Hale, 1976

WREN, P(ERCIVAL) C(HRISTOPHER). 1885-1941.
Bubble Reputation. Murray, 1936. U.S. title: The Cortenay Treasure. Houghton, 1936
Cardboard Castle. Murray, 1938; Houghton, 1938
The Cortenay Treasure; see Bubble Reputation
Mammon; see The Mammon of Righteousness
The Mammon of Righteousness. Murray, 1930. U.S. title: Mammon. Stokes, 1930
The Man the Devil Didn't Want; see Paper Prison
Mysterious Waye. Murray, 1930; Stokes, 1930
-Odd—But Even So. Murray, 1941; Macrae Smith, 1942 ss
Paper Prison. Murray, 1939. U.S. title: The Man the Devil Didn't Want. Macrae Smith, 1940
Two Feet from Heaven. Murray, 1940

WRENN, HAROLD A(LBERT). 1909-   . Series character: William Mitchell, in at least those marked WM.
The Clue of the Stone. French, 1964. (1-act play.)

Due to Expire. Hale, 1958 WM
Infamous Conduct. Hale, 1961. As a 1-act play: French, 1963
The Lady Prefers Murder. Hammond, 1954 WM
Tangle. Hammond, 1953 WM
The Toby Jug Murders. Hammond, 1955 WM
Unguarded Moment. Hale, 1959 WM

WRIGHT, ARTHUR
-A Colt from the Country. Newnes, 1922
A Crooked Game. Newnes, 1928
-Fettered by Fate. Newnes, 1921
-Gambler's Gold. Newnes, 1923
-Gaming for Gold. Newnes, 1929
-A Good Recovery. Newnes, 1928
-Keane of Kalgoorlie. Newnes, 1907
A Rogue's Luck. Newnes, 1923
-A Rough Passage. Newnes, 1920
Rung In. Newnes, 1924

WRIGHT, ELSIE N. 1907-   .
Strange Murders at Greystones. International Fiction Library, 1931

WRIGHT, JOHN. Pseudonym: Wade Wright, q.v.

WRIGHT, JUNE
The Devil's Caress. Hutchinson, 1952
Faculty of Murder. Long, 1961
Make-Up for Murder. Long, 1966
Murder in the Telephone Exchange. Hutchinson, 1948
Reservation for Murder. Long, 1958
So Bad a Death. Hutchinson, 1949

WRIGHT, MASON
The Army Post Murders. Farrar, 1931
Murder on Polopel, with William R(eno) Kane, 1885-   . Doubleday, 1929

WRIGHT, NOEL. 1890-   . Pseudonym: Nigel Worth, q.v.

WRIGHT, OLIVER
The Riverport Mail. Nash, 1912

WRIGHT, ROWLAND. Pseudonym of Carolyn Wells, 1870-1942, q.v.
The Disappearance of Kimball Webb. Dodd, 1920

WRIGHT, S(YDNEY) FOWLER. 1874-1965. Pseudonym: Sydney Fowler, q.v.

WRIGHT, THOMAS. 1859-1936.
The Mystery of St. Dunstans. Low, 1892

WRIGHT, WADE. Pseudonym of John Wright.
Blonde Target. Hale, 1966
Blood in the Ashes. Hale, 1964
Don't Come Back! Hale, 1973
The Hades Hello. Hale, 1973
A Hearse Waiting. Hale, 1965
No Haloes in Hell. Hale, 1969
Shadows Don't Bleed. Hale, 1967
The Sharp Edge. Hale, 1968
Suddenly You're Dead. Hale, 1964
Two Faces of Death. Hale, 1970
Until She Dies. Hale, 1965

WRIGHT, WILLARD HUNTINGTON. 1888-1939.
Pseudonym: S. S. Van Dine, q.v.

WUORIO, EVA-LIS. 1918-   .
Explosion; see Midsummer Lokki
Midsummer Lokki. Dobson, 1967; Holt, 1967. Also published as: Explosion. Lancer, 1968
The Terror Factor; see Z for Zaborra
The Woman with the Portuguese Basket. Dobson, 1963; Holt, 1964
Z for Zaborra. Dobson, 1965; Holt, 1966. Also published as: The Terror Factor. Lancer, 1970

WURR, H. J.
  The Giant Hunchback. Rich, 1939
  Hunt in the Highlands. Bell, 1937
  Who Dies Next? Rich, 1939

WYKES, ALAN. 1914-   .
  -The Pen-Friend. Duckworth, 1950
  Pursuit Till Morning. Duckworth, 1948; Random, 1947

WYLIE, I(DA) A(LEXA) R(OSS). 1885-   .
  Rogues and Company. Lane, 1921; Mills, 1921

WYLIE, NOEL
  Dumb Witness. Hammond, 1958
  Saddle a Killer. Hammond, 1960

WYLIE, PHILIP (GORDON). 1902-1971. See also: EDWIN BALMER, 1883-1959; and: ANONYMOUS (The Smiling Corpse).
  Corpses at Indian Stones. Farrar, 1943
  Danger Mansion. Bantam (Los Angeles), 1940
  Experiment in Crime; see Three to be Read
  The Murderer Invisible. Farrar, 1931
  The Savage Gentleman. Farrar, 1932
  The Smuggled Atom Bomb; see Three to be Read
  The Spy Who Spoke Porpoise. Doubleday, 1969
  Three to be Read. Rinehart, 1951. (Contains: Experiment in Crime, The Smuggled Atom Bomb, and Sporting Blood, of which the first two were each published separately by Avon in 1956.)

WYLLIE, JOHN (VECTIS CAREW). 1914-   . Series character: Dr. Quarshie, in both titles.
  The Butterfly Flood. Doubleday, 1975; Barrie, 1977
  Skull Still Bone. Doubleday, 1975; Barrie, 1975

WYMARK, EDWARD. 1933-   .
  As Good as Gold. Coward, 1967; Longmans, 1967

WYND, OSWALD (MORRIS). 1913-   . Pseudonym: Gavin Black, q.v.
  Death the Red Flower. Cassell, 1965; Harcourt, 1965
  -The Forty Days. Collins, 1972; Harcourt, 1973
  -Stars in the Heather. Blackwood, 1956
  Sumatra Seven Zero. Cassell, 1968; Harcourt, 1968
  Walk Softly, Men Praying. Cassell, 1967; Harcourt, 1967
  -A Wall in the Long Dark Night. Cassell, 1962
  -When Ape is King. Home & Van Thal, 1949

WYNNE, ANTHONY. Pseudonym of Robert McNair Wilson, 1882-   . Series character: Dr. Eustace Hailey, in all titles.
  The Blue Vesuvius. Hutchinson, 1930; Lippincott, 1931
  The Case of the Gold Coins. Hutchinson, 1933; Lippincott, 1934
  The Case of the Green Knife. Hutchinson, 1932. U.S. title: The Green Knife. Lippincott, 1932
  The Case of the Red-Haired Girl. Hutchinson, 1932. U.S. title: The Cotswold Case. Lippincott, 1933
  The Cotswold Case; see The Case of the Red-Haired Girl
  The Dagger. Hutchinson, 1928; Lippincott, 1929
  Death of a Banker. Hutchinson, 1934; Lippincott, 1934
  Death of a Golfer. Hutchinson, 1937; Lippincott, 1937. Also published as: Murder in the Morning. Detective Novel Classic, 194?
  Death of a King. Hutchinson, 1938. U.S. title: Murder Calls Dr. Hailey. Lippincott, 1938
  Death of a Shadow. Hutchinson, 1950
  Death Out of the Night; see The Loving Cup
  Door Nails Never Die. Hutchinson, 1939; Lippincott, 1939
  The Double Mystery; see The Double-Thirteen Mystery
  The Double-Thirteen Mystery. Hutchinson, 1926. U.S. title: The Double Thirteen. Lippincott, 1926
  Emergency Exit. Hutchinson, 1941; Messner, 1944
  The Fourth Finger. Hutchinson, 1929; Lippincott, 1929
  The Green Knife; see The Case of the Green Knife
  The Holbein Mystery. Hutchinson, 1935. U.S. title: The Red Lady. Lippincott, 1935
  The Horseman of Death. Hutchinson, 1927; Lippincott, 1928
  The House on the Hard. Hutchinson, 1940
  The Loving Cup. Hutchinson, 1933. U.S. title: Death Out of the Night. Lippincott, 1933
  Murder Calls Dr. Hailey; see Death of a King
  Murder in a Church. Hutchinson, 1942
  Murder in the Morning; see Death of a Golfer
  Murder in Thin Air. Hutchinson, 1936; Lippincott, 1936
  Murder of a Lady. Hutchinson, 1931. U.S. title: The Silver Scale Mystery. Lippincott, 1931
  The Mystery of the Ashes. Hutchinson, 1927; Lippincott, 1927
  The Mystery of the Evil Eye. Hutchinson, 1925. U.S. title: The Sign of Evil. Lippincott, 1925
  The Red Lady; see The Holbein Mystery
  Red Scar. Hutchinson, 1928; Lippincott, 1928
  The Room with the Iron Shutters. Hutchinson, 1929; Lippincott, 1929
  The Sign of Evil; see The Mystery of the Evil Eye
  The Silver Arrow. Hutchinson, 1931. U.S. title: The White Arrow. Lippincott, 1932
  The Silver Scale Mystery; see Murder of a Lady
  Sinners Go Secretly. Hutchinson, 1927; Lippincott, 1927 ss
  The Toll-House Murder. Hutchinson, 1935; Lippincott, 1935
  The White Arrow; see The Silver Arrow
  The Yellow Crystal. Hutchinson, 1930; Lippincott, 1930

WYNNE, BARRY
  -The Day Gibraltar Fell. Macdonald, 1969
  -The Sniper. Macdonald, 1968
  The Spies Within. Jenkins, 1964

WYNNE, FRED(ERICK) E(DWARD). 1870-   .
  -Digby's Miracle. Jenkins, 1924
  -Faith Unfaithful. Brown, 1908
  -Fortune's Fool. Brown, 1907
  A Mediterranean Mystery. Jenkins, 1923; Duffield, 1923

WYNNTON, PATRICK
  The Agent Outside. Longmans, 1931
  The Black Turret. Hodder, 1925; Bobbs, 1925

  The Honourable Pursuit. Hodder, 1930. U.S. title: Strange Pursuit. Lippincott, 1930
  The Lady Zia; see Zia
  The Lost Mark. Hodder, 1929; Lippincott, 1929
  Spider's Parlour. Longmans, 1933
  Strange Pursuit; see The Honourable Pursuit
  The Ten Jewels. Hodder, 1931; Lippincott, 1931
  The Third Messenger. Hodder, 1926; Doran, 1927
  Zia. Hodder, 1928. U.S. title: The Lady Zia. Doubleday, 1928

XV 8
  Narcissus Murders. Libra, 1945

XANTIPPE. Pseudonym.
  Death Catches Up with Mr. Kluck. Doubleday, 1935

YAFFE, JAMES. 1927-   .
  The Deadly Game. Dramatists Play Service, 1960. (2-act play adapted from the novel A Dangerous Game by Friedrich Duerrenmatt, 1921-   , q.v.)
  Nothing But the Night. Little, 1957; Cape, 1958

YARDLEY, HERBERT O(SBORN). 1889-   .
  The Blonde Countess. Longmans, 1934; Faber, 1934
  Crows are Black Everywhere, with Carl Grabo. Putnam, 1945
  Red Sun of Nippon. Longmans, 1934

YARDLEY, JAMES. Series character: Kiss Darling, in both titles.
  A Kiss a Day Keeps the Corpses Away. Joseph, 1971; Signet, 1971
  Kiss the Boys and Make Them Die. Joseph, 1970; Signet, 1970

YARNELL, DUANE
  Mantrap. Crest, 1957
  Murder Bait. Crest, 1958

YARROW, ARNOLD. 1920-   .
  Softly, Softly Casebook. Pan, 1973. (Novelets adapted from scripts for the British TV series Softly, Softly.)

YATES, ALAN GEOFFREY. 1923-   . Pseudonyms: Carter Brown, Caroline Farr, qq.v.
  The Cold Dark Hours. Horwitz, 1958

YATES, BROCK (WENDEL). 1933-   .
  Dead in the Water. Farrar, 1975

YATES, DORNFORD. Pseudonym of Cecil William Mercer, 1885-1960. Series characters: Chandos = C; Jonah Mansel = JM; Bertram Pleydell = BP; Supt. Falcon = F. (Characters overlap series in Yates' work, and most books about BP are not criminous.)
  Adele & Co. Hodder, 1932; Minton, 1931 BP, JM
  Blind Corner. Hodder, 1927; Minton, 1927 C, JM
  Blood Royal. Hodder, 1929; Minton, 1930 C
  By Royal Command; see Fire Below
  Cost Price. Ward, 1949. U.S. title: The Laughing Bacchante. Putnam, 1949 C, JM

448/ Yates, Dornford

An Eye for a Tooth. Ward, 1943; Putnam, 1944 C, JM
Fire Below. Hodder, 1930. U.S. title: By Royal Command. Minton, 1931 C
Gale Warning. Ward, 1939; Putnam, 1940 C, JM
The House That Berry Built. Ward, 1945; Putnam, 1945 BP, JM, F
The Laughing Bacchante; see Cost Price
Ne'er-Do-Well. Ward, 1954 C, JM, F
Period Stuff. Ward, 1942 ss, some criminous F
Perishable Goods. Hodder, 1928; Minton, 1928 C, JM, BP
Red in the Morning. Ward, 1946. U.S. title: Were Death Denied. Putnam, 1946 C, JM
Safe Custody. Hodder, 1932; Minton, 1932
She Fell Among Thieves. Hodder, 1935; Minton, 1935 C, JM
She Painted Her Face. Ward, 1937; Putnam, 1937
Shoal Water. Ward, 1940; Putnam, 1941 JM
Storm Music. Hodder, 1934; Minton, 1934
Were Death Denied; see Red in the Morning

YATES, EDMUND (HODGSON). 1831-1894.
-After Office-Hours. Ward, 1861
-Black Sheep. Tinsley, 1867; Harper, 1867
-Broken to Harness. Bentley, 1864; Loring, 1866
-Cast Away. Chapman, 1872
A Dangerous Game; see The Impending Sword
-Dr. Wainwright's Patient. Chapman, 1871
-The Forlorn Hope. Tinsley, 1867; Loring, 1867
Going to the Bad. Gill, 1876. (British title?)
The Impending Sword. Tinsley, 1874. U.S. title: A Dangerous Game. Gill, 1874
-Kissing the Rod. Tinsley, 1866; Harper, 1866
-Land at Last. Chapman, 1866; Harper, 1866
-Nobody's Fortune. Chapman, 1872; Estes, 187?
-A Righted Wrong. Tinsley, 1870
-The Rock Ahead. Tinsley, 1868
-Running the Gauntlet. Chapman, 1865; Loring, 1866
A Silent Witness. Tinsley, 1875; Gill, 1875
-Two by Tricks. Routledge, 1874
-Wages of Sin. Gill, 1875. (British title?)
-A Waiting Race. Tinsley, 1872; Appleton, 187?
-Wrecked in Port. Chapman, 1869; Harper, 1869
-The Yellow Flag. Tinsley, 1872; Estes, 187?

YATES, GEORGE WORTHING. Joint pseudonym with Charles Hunt Marshall: Peter Hunt, q.v. Series character: Hazlitt Woar = HW.
The Body That Came by Post. Morrow, 1937; Dickson & Davies, 1937 HW
The Body That Wasn't Uncle. Morrow, 1939; Davies, 1939 HW
If a Body. Morrow, 1941 HW
There was a Crooked Man. Morrow, 1936; Dickson & Davies, 1936

YATES, LIONEL (PEEL) and HONOR (MAHON) GOODHART
The Eclipse of James Trent, D.I. Murray, 1924

YATES, MARGARET (POLK), 1915-   , and PAULA BRAMLETTE, 1917-   .
Death Casts a Vote. Dutton, 1948
The Widow's Walk. Dutton, 1945

YATES, MARGARET (EVELYN) TAYLER. 1887-1952. Series character: Anne Davenport McLean (Davvie), in all titles.
Death Sends a Cable. Macmillan, 1938; Davies, 1939
The Hush-Hush Murders. Macmillan, 1937; Dickson, 1938
Midway to Murder. Macmillan, 1941
Murder by the Yard. Macmillan, 1942

YATES, PETER. Pseudonym of William Long, 1922-   . Other pseudonym: Will Creed, q.v. Series characters: the Thatcher family, in at least those marked T.
Curtain Call for Murder. Five Star, 1945 T
Death Comes to Dinner. Five Star, 1945 T
Death in the Hands of Talent. Five Star, 1945
The Dress Circle Murders. Five Star, 1945

YORCK, RUTH L(ANDSHOFF). 1909-1966.
So Cold the Night. Harper, 1948

YORK, ANDREW. Pseudonym of Christopher Robin Nicole, 1930-   . Other pseudonym: Robin Cade, q.v. Series character: Jonas Wilde, in all titles.
The Captivator. Hutchinson, 1973; Doubleday, 1974
The Co-Ordinator. Hutchinson, 1967; Lippincott, 1967
The Deviator. Hutchinson, 1969; Lippincott, 1969
The Dominator. Hutchinson, 1969
The Eliminator. Hutchinson, 1966; Lippincott, 1967
The Expurgator. Hutchinson, 1972; Doubleday, 1973
The Fascinator. Hutchinson, 1975; Doubleday, 1975
The Infiltrator. Hutchinson, 1971; Doubleday, 1971
The Predator. Hutchinson, 1968; Lippincott, 1968

YORK, ELIZABETH
The Medea Legend. PB, 1975

YORK, HELEN. 1918-   .
Malverne Manor. Doubleday, 1974

YORK, JEREMY. Pseudonym of John Creasey, 1908-1973, q.v. Other pseudonyms: Gordon Ashe, M. E. Cooke, Norman Deane, Robert Caine Frazer, Michael Halliday, Patrick Gill, Charles Hogarth, Brian Hope, Colin Hughes, Kyle Hunt, Abel Mann, Peter Manton, J. J. Marric, Richard Martin, Rodney Mattheson, Anthony Morton, qq.v. Series character (in revised editions of books that originally lacked such a character): Supt. Folly = F. Some titles published in the U.S. as by Jeremy York were originally published in England as by Michael Halliday, and are listed in that entry herein.
By Persons Unknown. Bles, 1941
Close the Door on Murder. Melrose, 1948; McKay, 1973, F
Death to my Killer. Melrose, 1950; Macmillan, 1966
Find the Body. Melrose, 1945; Macmillan, 1967, F
The Gallows are Waiting. Melrose, 1949; McKay, 1973
Hide and Kill. Long, 1959; Scribner, 1960

Let's Kill Uncle Lionel. Melrose, 1947; McKay, 1976
Murder Came Late. Melrose, 1946; Macmillan, 1969, F
Murder in the Family. Melrose, 1944; McKay, 1976, as by John Creasey
Murder Unseen. Bles, 1942
My Brother's Killer. Long, 1958; Scribner, 1959
No Alibi. Melrose, 1943
Run Away to Murder. Melrose, 1947; Macmillan, 1970
Safari with Fear. Melrose, 1953
Seeds of Murder. Paul, 1956; Scribner, 1958
Sentence of Death. Melrose, 1950; Macmillan, 1964
Sight of Death. Paul, 1956; Scribner, 1958
So Soon to Die. Paul, 1955; Scribner, 1957
To Kill or Die; see To Kill or to Die
To Kill or to Die. Long, 1960. U.S. title: To Kill or Die. Macmillan, 1965
Voyage with Murder. Melrose, 1952
Wilful Murder. McNaughton, 1946. (British title? Byline?)
Yesterday's Murder. Melrose, 1945

YORKE, CLIFTON
The Swift Hand of Vengeance. Modern, 1938
The Voice from the Grave. Modern, 193?

YORKE, CURTIS. Pseudonym of Susan Richmond Lee.
The Brown Portmanteau and other stories. Jarrolds, 1889
The Mystery of Belgrave Square. White, 1889

YORKE, MARGARET. Pseudonym of Margaret Beda Larminie Nicholson, 1924-   . Series character: Patrick Grant = PG.
Dead in the Morning. Bles, 1970 PG
Grave Matters. Bles, 1973 PG
Mortal Remains. Bles, 1974 PG
No Medals for the Major. Bles, 1974 PG
Silent Witness. Bles, 1972; Walker, 1975 PG
The Small Hours of the Morning. Bles, 1975; Walker, 1975

YORKE, PRESTON
The Case of the Strangled Seven. Everybody's, 1943
The Case of the Swinging Spider. Everybody's, 1944
Death on Priority! Mitre, 1945
The Gamma Ray Murders. Everybody's, 1943

YORKE, VICTORIA
-Five of Hearts. Long, 1927
-Sealed Lips. Long, 1928
-Suppressed Evidence. Long, 1931

YOUD, (CHRISTOPHER) SAMUEL. 1922-   . Pseudonym: John Christopher, q.v.
Holly Ash. Cassell, 1955. U.S. title: The Opportunist. Harper, 1957

YOUNG, COLLIER. 1908-   .
The Todd Dossier. Delacorte, 1969; Macmillan (London), 1969. (Ghost-written by Robert Bloch, 1917-   , q.v.)

YOUNG, EDWARD (PRESTON)
The Fifth Passenger. Cassell, 1963; Harper, 1963

YOUNG, ERIC BRETT
The Dancing Beggars. Hutchinson, 1929; Lippincott, 1929
The Murder at Fleet. Hutchinson, 1927; Lippincott, 1928

YOUNG, ERNEST A. Pseudonym: Harry Rockwood, q.v.
-Barbara's Rival; or, Only a Woman's Heart. Lovell, 1885
A Criminal Queen; or, The Fatal Shot. Laird, 1888
Defending a Home. Ogilvie, 1891
File No. 114. Ogilvie, 1886. (A Sequel to File No. 113 by Emile Gaboriau, 1883-1873, and possibly published as by Gaboriau.)
-Fugitives of Pearl Hill. Ogilvie, 1891
Luke Darby, the "World" Detective; or, Romance of the Dexter, Maine, Bank Robbery and Murder. Ogilvie, 1887
-A Wife's Honor. Ogilvie, 1885. Also published as: A Woman's Honor. Lovell, 1886
A Woman's Honor; see A Wife's Honor

YOUNG, FRANCIS BRETT. 1884-1954.
The Case Bird and other stories. Heinemann, 1933; Harper, 1933 ss, at least one criminous

YOUNG, G. H. R.
The Talking Skull and other selected short stories grave and gay. Wells Gardner, 1947 ss

YOUNG, GEORGE. 1919- .
Code-Name Caruso. Hutchinson, 1961
The Man Called Lenz. Hutchinson, 1954; Coward, 1955

YOUNG, GORDON (RAY). 1886-1948.
Crooked Shadows. Garden City, 1924
The Devil's Passport. Century, 1933; Cassell, 1934
Hurricane Williams' Vengeance; see The Vengeance of Hurricane Williams
The Vengeance of Hurricane Williams. Doran, 1925. British title: Hurricane Williams' Vengeance. Unwin, 1925

YOUNG, HOWARD IRVING
Not Herbert. French (New York), 1926. (4-act play.)

YOUNG, KENDAL. Pseudonym of Phyllis Brett Young, q.v.
The Ravine. Allen, 1961

YOUNG, PHYLLIS BRETT. Pseudonym: Kendal Young, q.v.
A Question of Judgment. Allen, 1970; Putnam, 1969
Undine. Longmans, 1964; Putnam, 1964

YOUNG, R(OSE) E(MMET). 1869- .
Murder at Manson's. Day, 1927

YOUNGER, ELIZABETH HELY. Pseudonym: Elizabeth Hely, q.v.

YOUNGER, WILLIAM ANTONY. 1917-1962. Pseudonym: William Mole, q.v.

YUDKOFF, ALVIN
Circumstances Beyond Control. Rinehart, 1955. Also published as: Network of Fear. Bestseller, 1956 (abridged)

YUILL, P. B. Pseudonym of Gordon M(acLean) Williams, 1934- , q.v., and Terry Venables. Series character: James Hazell = JH.
The Bornless Keeper. Macmillan (London), 1974; Walker, 1975
Hazell and the Three Card Trick. Macmillan (London), 1975; Walker, 1976 JH
Hazell Plays Solomon. Macmillan (London), 1974; Walker, 1975 JH

Z

Z. Z. Pseudonym of Louis Zangwill, 1869- .
A Nineteenth Century Miracle. Chatto, 1897

ZANE, LEHI
Brenda. GM, 1952; Red Seal, 1957

ZANGWILL, ISRAEL. 1864-1926.
The Big Bow Mystery. Henry, 1892; Rand, 1895

ZANGWILL, LOUIS. 1869- . Pseudonym: Z. Z., q.v.

ZARUBICA, MLADIN
Scutari. Farrar, 1967
-The Year of the Rat. Harcourt, 1964; Collins, 1965

ZENO. Pseudonym.
Grab. Macmillan (London), 1970; Stein, 1970

ZHDANOV, ALEKSANDR IVANOVICH. Pseudonym.
Shadow of Peril. Doubleday, 1963

ZINBERG, LEONARD S. 1911-1968. Pseudonym: Ed Lacy, q.v.

ZIREN, GOLAND
The Don. Pyramid, 1972

ZORE, H.
Alibi Off Broadway. Scion, 1954
Black Orchid. Muir Watson, 1950
Blue Orchid. Scion, 1953
Carnival of Death. Scion, 1953
Cover That Corpse. Scion, 1953
Flame. Scion, 1953
It's a Sin. Scion, 1953
The Lady is a Tramp. Scion, 1953
Savage Siren. Scion, 1953
Shadow of a Sin. Scion, 1953
This was a Woman. Scion, 1953
What's Ya Problem? Scion, 1953

ZORRO. Pseudonym of Harold Ward, q.v. Series character: Dr. Death, in all titles.
The Gray Creatures. Corinth, 1966
The Shriveling Murders. Corinth, 1966
12 Must Die. Corinth, 1966

ZUCKERMAN, ALBERT
Tiger Kittens. Doubleday, 1973

ZUCKMAYER, CARL. 1896- .
Carnival Confession. Methuen, 1961. (Translation of Die Fastnachtsbeichte. Frankfurt, 1959.)

ZUGSMITH, LEANE. 1903- . See: CARL (ALBERT) RANDAU, 1893-1969; and: KENNETH WHITE, 1905-1953.

ZUKAS, EDGAR V.
A Handful of Stars. Vantage, 1964

ZUMWALT, EVA. 1936- .
Masquerade of Evil. Ace, 1975

Title Index

The following index is an alphabetical listing of all titles identified in the Author Index. Following each title is the byline under which the book is entered in the Author Index. All initial articles (A, An, and The) have been omitted from titles to facilitate scanning of the index; all titles are rendered in full in the Author Index. The bylines are given in abbreviated form—initials and last name only—except when to do so would produce ambiguity. In addition, although many books were issued by two authors under a joint byline, only the first author is given here, since it is under that name that the book is described in the Author Index.

Title Index

A

ABC Affair. P. Winston
ABCD. D. R. Slavitt
A.B.C. Investigates. Ephesian
ABC Murders. A. Christie
A.B.C. Solves Five. Ephesian
A.B.C.'s Test Case. Ephesian
A. J. Alan's Second Book. A. J. Alan
A-100. Bruce Harrison
A.R.P. Murder. Sutherland Scott
A.R.P. Mystery. B. Perowne
A.R.P. Spy. A. O. Pollard
A.S.F. J. Rhode
ATS Mystery. G. Coverack
Aamon Always. D. E. L. Patch
Aardvark Affair. G. Brandner
Aaron Rodd, Diviner. E. P. Oppenheim
Aaron's Serpent. E. Thorne
Abaft 'Midships. E. L. Long
Abandon Hope. I. Garland
Abandoned Car Crime. Gwyn Evans
Abandoned Claim. F. H. Loughead
Abandoned Doll. L. Meynell
Abandoned Power. J. Fores
Abandoned Room. W. Camp
Abbey Court Murder. A. Haynes
Abbey Murder. J. Hatton
Abbey Mystery. R. M. Gilchrist
Abbot's Cup. C. A. Alington
Abbot's House. L. Conway
Abbot's Moat. F. Warden
Abduction. T. Burke
Abduction. S. Cohen
Abduction. G. F. Newman
Abduction of Princess Chriemhild. L. F. Griffin
Abduction of Virginia Lee. F. O'Rourke
Abductor. D. Hitchens
Abductors. D. Reid
Abel Coincidence. J. N. Chance
Abimelech Pott, the Don Quixote of the Bar. H. W. Jessup
Abner Crane's Vengeance. A. G. Hales
Abner Ferret, the Lawyer Detective. H. Rockwood
Abner Ferret, the Lawyer Detective. J. R. Taylor
Aboard the American Duchess. H. Hill
Aboard "The American Duchess." G. L. Myers
Abode of Love. J. Shearing
Abolition of Death. James Anderson
Abominable Man. M. Sjowall
Abominable Twilight. Reginald Campbell
Abomination. H. Janson
About Doctor Ferrel. D. Keene
About Face. F. Kane
About Ourselves. H. Wood
About the Murder of a Man Afraid of Women. A. Abbot
About the Murder of a Startled Lady. A. Abbot
About the Murder of Geraldine Foster. A. Abbot
About the Murder of the Circus Queen. A. Abbot
About the Murder of the Clergyman's Mistress. A. Abbot
About the Murder of the Night Club Lady. A. Abbot
About Two A.M. C. F. Coe
Above and Below. J. Palmer
Above Suspicion. R. O. Chipperfield
Above Suspicion. H. MacInnes
Above Suspicion. J. H. Riddell
Above the Dark Circus. H. Walpole
Above the Dark Tumult. H. Walpole
Above the Law. J. A. Goodwin
Abra-Cadaver. C. Monig
Abracadaver. P. Lovesey

Abrus Necklace. E. G. Seibert
Absense. M. Eyre
Absent Friends. C. J. C. Hyne
Absolutely True. I. Montagu
Abyssinian Mystery. G. Chester
Academic Question. R. H. R. Smithies
Accent on Murder. R. Lockridge
Accessory. M. Lockwood
Accessory After. E. C. Vivian
Accessory After the Fact. W. A. Hobday
Accessory After the Fact. B. Reynolds
Accessory After the Fact. L. Thayer
Accessory to Murder. P. Barrington
Accident by Design. E. C. R. Lorac
Accident for Inspector West. J. Creasey
Accident in Piccadilly. H. Willett
Accident, Manslaughter or Murder? L. Thayer
Accident or Murder? N. Carter
Accident to Adeline. E. Burgess
Accident Ward Mystery. R. Traux
Accidental Accomplice. W. A. Johnston
Accidental Adventurer. S. M. Parkman
Accidental Clue. B. Graeme
Accidental Don Juan. E. Jepson
Accidental Murder. C. F. Gregg
Accidental Password. N. Carter
Accidents Do Happen. M. Burton
Accidents Will Happen. V. Bridges
Accomplice. J. Bland
Accomplice. M. Head
Accomplice. F. T. Hill
Accomplice. J. Pudney
Accomplices. Leonard Cooper
Accomplices. G. Simenon
According to Gibson. D. MacKail
According to Orders. F. B. Austin
According to Plan. L. Jackson
According to Plan. G. Seton
According to the Evidence. H. Cecil
Account Closed. S. M. Parkman
Account Paid. C. Brooks
Account Rendered. P. Barrington
Account Rendered. P. Cheyney
Account Rendered. F. Ryck
Account Rendered. P. Wentworth
Account to Render. S. Coulter
Account Unsettled. G. Simenon
Accounting. B. Marshall
Accounting for Murder. E. Lathen
Accursed. C. Seignolle
Accuse the Toff. J. Creasey
Accused. H. R. Daniels
Accused and Accuser. A. Sergeant
Accused Princess. A. Upward
Ace High. G. Goodchild
Ace High. Mark Ross
Ace High, the 'Frisco Detective. C. E. Tripp
Ace in the Hole. F. Martin
Ace-in-the-Hole Haggerty. R. M. Hankins
Ace of Clubs Murder. R. Trevor
Ace of Danger. L. Grex
Ace of Danger. Augustus Muir
Ace of Death. T. A. Plummer
Ace of Hearts. F. Du Boisgobey
Ace of Hearts. C. Thomas-Stanford
Ace of Jades. S. Palmer
Ace of Knaves. L. Charteris
Ace of Spades. R. Andre
Ace of Spades. H. Holt
Ace of Spades. A. Nasielski
Ace of Spades. D. Shannon
Ace of Spades Murder. H. S. Keeler
Ace of Spies. D. Von Elsner
Ace Up My Sleeve. J. H. Chase
Aces & Eights. P. Garlington
Aces, Eights, and Murder. M. V. Heberden
Aces of the White Death. R. J. Hogan
Aces Run Wild. J. A. Rennie
Achievements of John Carruthers. E. C. Cox
Achilles Affair. B. Mather
Achilles' Isle. R. Batchelor
Achilles Mandate. M. Fogarty
Acid. H. Imbert-Terry
Acid Drop. S. George
Acid Rock. R. Sapir
Aconite Murders. S. Williams

Acquainted with Murder. F. Hurt
Acquittal. G. Lorimer
Acquitted! M. Frazer
Acrefield Mystery. F. Grierson
Across 110th. W. Ferris
Across That River. H. Whittington
Across the Border. J. G. Sarasin
Across the Common. E. Berridge
Across the Divide. A. Murray
Across the Footlights. F. Hume
Across the Frontiers. H. Edmonds
Across the Narrow Seas. J. Pattinson
Across the Pacific. C. E. Blaney
Across the Street. G. Simenon
Across the World for a Wife. G. Boothby
Act of Anger. B. Spicer
Act of Darkness. P. Hastings
Act of Fear. Michael Collins
Act of Love. W. E. D. Ross
Act of Mercy. F. Clifford
Act of Passion. Wenzell Brown
Act of Passion. G. Simenon
Act of Providence. H. C. McNeile
Act of Silence. Anthony Graham
Act of Violence. E. Fadiman
Act of Violence. B. Heatter
Act of Violence. P. Saxon
Act of Violence. K. Wade
Acting Second Mate. S. M. Parkman
Action Along the Humboldt. K. Kramer
Action at Arcanum. W. C. MacDonald
Action at World's End. W. Chambers
Action for the Picaroon. J. Cassells
Action in Diamonds. C. R. Cooper
Action Man. J. Flynn
Action of the Tiger. A. Kent
Action of the Tiger. T. Walsh
Action of the Tiger. J. Wellard
Actor Manager. A. Askew
Actor's Blood. B. Hecht
Actor's Knife. Howel Evans
Actor's Secret. H. E. Hill
Actress. A. Applin
Actress Detective. Anonymous
Actress's Daughter. M. A. Fleming
Actress's Husband. G. Warden
Acts of Black Night. K. M. Knight
Acupuncture Murders. D. Steward
Ada Vernham, Actress. R. Marsh
Adair and Son. P. Trent
Adam. P. Trent
Adam and Evelina. P. Allardyce
Adam Grainger. H. Wood
Adam Grey. Jack Wilson
Adam's Case. M. Underwood
Adam's Fall. J. Ridgway
Adam's Rib. P. Allardyce
Adam's Tale. G. Honeycombe
Adapted to Stress. C. D. Peel
Adders Abounding. J. Lukens
Adder's Brood. N. Carter
Adders on the Heath. G. Mitchell
Addicted to Murder. T. S. Drachman
Address Unknown. E. Phillpotts
Adela's Ordeal. F. Warden
Adele & Co. D. Yates
Adelgitha. Mathew Gregory Lewis
Adjuster. P. Malloch
Adjusters. Valentine
Adjustments. I. R. G. Hart
Admirable Carfew. E. Wallace
Admirable Lady Biddy Fane. F. Barrett
Admiral Teach. C. J. C. Hyne
Admiral's a Spy. W. Taylor
Admiral's Light. H. M. Rideout
Admiral's Million. A. D. Divine
Admiral's Secret. A. Murray
Admiralty Murders. M. Adam
Admiralty Regrets--. Reginald Campbell
Admiralty's Secret. C. Dawe
Adopted. A. L. Halstead
Adopted Face. A. S. Carter
Adopters. W. Hegner
Adrian and Jonathan. Richard Martin

Adriana. G. Dyer
Adrienne de Portalis. A. C. Gunter
Adrift with a Vengeance. K. Cornwallis
Advance Agent. J. August
Advance South. J. Robb
Advancement of Learning. R. Hill
Adventure at Eighty. J. J. Farjeon
Adventure Calling! S. Horler
Adventure for Nine. J. J. Farjeon
Adventure for Two. A. Applin
Adventure for Wealth. C. T. Stoneham
Adventure in the Night. W. Dawson
Adventure in Washington. L. Ross
Adventure Isle. G. A. England
Adventure Mysterious. F. Marlowe
Adventure of Red Head of the Red Sea. W. J. Makin
Adventure of the Albanian Avenger. W. W. Sayer
Adventure of the Annamese Prince. W. M. Graydon
Adventure of the Blue Room. S. Fowler
Adventure of the Bogus Sheik. G. H. Teed
Adventure of the Broad Arrow. Morley Roberts
Adventure of the Christmas Pudding. A. Christie
Adventure of the Egyptian Student. R. C. Armour
Adventure of the Eleven Cuff-Buttons. J. F. Thierry
Adventure of the Lost Manuscript. E. Pearson
Adventure of the Man "On Bail." W. J. Bayfield
Adventure of the Marked Man and One Other. S. Palmer
Adventure of the Oil Pirates. R. C. Armour
Adventure of the Orient Express. A. Derleth
Adventure of the Peerless Peer. P. J. Farmer
Adventure of the Red-Headed Man. W. J. Bayfield
Adventure of the Rogue's Apprentice. W. M. Graydon
Adventure of the Silk Smugglers. R. C. Armour
Adventure of the Speed Mad Camden. A. Murray
Adventure of the Unique Dickensians. A. Derleth
Adventure of the Voodoo Queen. G. H. Teed
Adventure Trail. D. B. Hobart
Adventure with Crime. J. Bell
Adventurer. R. Miall
Adventurer from the West. M. J. Pemberton
Adventurer of the Bay. O. Binns
Adventurers. J. A. Hodge
Adventurers. H. B. M. Watson
Adventurers of the Night. G. A. Birmingham
Adventures at Greystones. G. E. Rochester
Adventures by Night. T. P. Prest
Adventure's End. J. Harris
Adventures of a Bashful Bachelor. C. Augusta
Adventures of a Chemist. F. A. Fawcett
Adventures of a Chemist. F. A. Hawkes
Adventures of a Coquette. G. Leroux
Adventures of a Journalist. H. Cadett
Adventures of a Lady Detective. Mrs. G. Corbett
Adventures of a Lady Pearl Broker. B. Heron-Maxwell
Adventures of a Nice Young Man. Aix
Adventures of a Pretty Woman. F. Warden
Adventures of a Skeleton. B. W. Waltermire
Adventures of a Social Detective. C. Bramley
Adventures of a Solicitor. W. Chesney
Adventures of a Stowaway. F. Whishaw
Adventures of a Turf Detective. F. D. A. C. De L'Isle
Adventures of Ah Foo, the Chinese Sherlock Holmes. C. Bishop
Adventures of Alonzo MacTavish. P. Cheyney
Adventures of an Attorney in Search of Practice. Anonymous
Adventures of an Engineer. W. Chesney
Adventures of an Equerry. M. Gerard
Adventures of an Ugly Girl. Mrs. G. Corbett
Adventures of Antoine. H. Collinson Owen
Adventures of Archer Dawe, Sleuth-Hound. J. S. Fletcher
Adventures of Blackshirt. B. Graeme
Adventures of Burnaby Lee. E. Thomson
Adventures of Caleb Williams. W. Godwin
Adventures of Captain Ivan Koravitch. V. L. Whitechurch
Adventures of Captain Jack. M. Pemberton
Adventures of Captain Kettle. C. J. C. Hyne
Adventures of Captain Mounsell. W. W. Dixon
Adventures of D'Arcy Dewpond, Detective. W. Slater
Adventures of Detective Barney. H. J. O'Higgins
Adventures of Dick Boss. Maz
Adventures of Doc Lavington
Adventures of Dr. Burton. A. C. Gunter
Adventures of Dr. Thorndyke. R. A. Freeman
Adventures of Ellery Queen. E. Queen
Adventures of Ephraim Tutt. A. Train
Adventures of Felix Boyd. S. Campbell
Adventures of Francois. S. W. Mitchell
Adventures of Harrison Keith, Detective. N. Carter
Adventures of Heine. E. Wallace
Adventures of Hiram Holliday. P. Gallico
Adventures of Husky Hillier. F. A. M. Webster
Adventures of Jimmie Dale. F. Packard
Adventures of Jimmy Strange. E. Dudley
Adventures of John Johns. F. Carrell
Adventures of Johnnie Pascoe. G. Norway
Adventures of Judith Lee. R. Marsh
Adventures of Julia. P. Cheyney
Adventures of Julia and Two Other Spy Stories. P. Cheyney
Adventures of Kathlyn. H. MacGrath
Adventures of Latimer Field, Curate. S. Hocking
Adventures of Louis Dural. Marguerite Bryant
Adventures of Marmaduke Clegg. M. Gerard
Adventures of Martin Hewitt. Arthur Morrison
Adventures of Miss Gregory. P. Gibbon
Adventures of Mr. Topham, Comedian. C. R. Gull
Adventures of Mr. Joseph P. Cray. E. P. Oppenheim
Adventures of M. D'Haricot. J. S. Clouston
Adventures of Napoleon Prince. M. Edginton
Adventures of Picklock Holes. R. C. Lehman
Adventures of Police Constable Vane, M.A. A. Askew
Adventures of Private Faust. H. H. Kirst
Adventures of Romney Pringle. C. Ashdown
Adventures of Sam Spade and other stories. D. Hammett
Adventures of Scout Grey. R. L. Bellamy
Adventures of Sherlock Holmes. A. C. Doyle
Adventures of Sherlock Holmes' Smarter Brother. G. Pearlman
Adventures of Shylar Homes. S. D. Williams
Adventures of Solar Pons. A. Derleth
Adventures of the Black Pilgrim. G. Stanley
Adventures of the D.C.I. C. E. Russell
Adventures of the Infallible Godahl. F. I. Anderson
Adventures of Tyler Tatlock, Private Detective. D. Donovan
Adventures with a Goat. R. T. Campbell
Adventuress. A. B. Reeve
Adventuress. C. Stanton
Adventuress of France. E. Gaboriau
Adventurous Annie. E. Everett-Green
Adventurous Exploits of the Younger Brothers. H. Dale
Adventurous Youth. M. Peterson
Adversaries. E. Linn
Adversary. B. Spicer
Advice Limited. E. P. Oppenheim
Advisory Service. M. Russell
Advocate's Wig. L. M. Watt
Aerial Burglars. J. Blyth
Aerie. J. S. McClean
Aero Clubs Mystery. E. J. Millward
Aeroplane Mystery. D. T. Hughes
Affacombe Affair. E. Lemarchand
Affair at Abu Mina. P. William
Affair at Aliquid. G. D. H. Cole
Affair at Alkali. V. Coffman
Affair at Dead End. J. N. Chance
Affair at Falconers. M. Howe
Affair at Flower Acres. C. Wells
Affair at Helen's Court. C. Carnac
Affair at Little Todsham. G. Greenaway
Affair at Little Wokeham. F. W. Crofts
Affair at Lover's Leap. R. G. Dean
Affair at Palm Springs. C. Knight
Affair at Pine Court. N. R. Gilbert
Affair at Quala. T. Helmore
Affair at Ritos Bay. Muriel Bradley
Affair at Royalties. G. Baxt
Affair at Sidi Brahim. B. Stuart
Affair at the Boat Landing. A. B. Cunningham
Affair at the Chateau. B. Reynolds
Affair at the Grotto. E. H. Fonseca
Affair at the Semiramis Hotel. A. E. W. Mason
Affair at the "Vere Arms." A. R. Weekes
Affair at Tideways. E. A. Heath
Affair for the Baron. A. Morton
Affair in Death Valley. C. Knight
Affair in Duplex 9B. W. A. Johnston
Affair in Hong Kong. D. Daniels
Affair in Marakesh. D. Daniels
Affair in Tokyo. J. McPartland
Affair of Chief Strongheart. P. O'Malley
Affair of Danny the "Dip." W. Tyrer
Affair of Honor. R. Wilder
Affair of John Donne. P. O'Malley
Affair of Jolie Madame. P. O'Malley
Affair of State. P. Frank
Affair of Strangers. J. Crosby
Affair of Swan Lake. P. O'Malley
Affair of the Atlantic Mail Robbery. R. C. Armour
Affair of the Black Sombrero. C. Knight
Affair of the Blackfriars Financier. L. H. Brooks
Affair of the Blood-stained Egg-cosy. James Anderson
Affair of the Blue Pig. P. O'Malley
Affair of the Bronzed Basilisk. A. Skene
Affair of the Bumbling Briton. P. O'Malley
Affair of the Circus Queen. C. Knight
Affair of the Corpse Escort. C. Knight
Affair of the Country Club. H. H. C. Gibbons
Affair of the Crimson Gull. C. Knight
Affair of the Crook Explorer. R. C. Armour
Affair of the Cross-Roads. H. H. C. Gibbons

Title Index

Affair of the Dead Stranger. C. Knight
Affair of the Demobilized Soldier. W. J. Bayfield
Affair of the Diamond Star. H. H. C. Gibbons
Affair of the Exotic Dancer. B. Benson
Affair of the Fainting Butler. C. Knight
Affair of the Family Diamonds. W. J. Bayfield
Affair of the Fraternizing Soldier. P. Meriton
Affair of the Frigid Blonde. R. O. Saber
Affair of the Gallows Tree. S. Chalmers
Affair of the Ginger Lei. C. Knight
Affair of the Golden Buzzard. C. Knight
Affair of the Heart. J. Potts
Affair of the Heavenly Voice. C. Knight
Affair of the Hollywood Contract. W. Tyrer
Affair of the Jade Monkey. C. Knight
Affair of the Kidnapped Crook. H. H. C. Gibbons
Affair of the Limping Sailor. C. Knight
Affair of the Malacca Stick. C. Andrews
Affair of the Missing Parachutist. A. Parsons
Affair of the Missing Witness. W. M. Graydon
Affair of the Oriental Doctor. Jack Lewis
Affair of the Phantom Car. E. J. Murray
Affair of the Red Mosaic. P. O'Malley
Affair of the Rival Cinema Kings. W. Shute
Affair of the Scarlet Crab. C. Knight
Affair of the Seven Mummy Cases. W. J. Bayfield
Affair of the Seven Warnings. G. N. Philips
Affair of the Sixth Button. C. Knight
Affair of the Skiing Clown. C. Knight
Affair of the Smuggled Millions. M. B. Dix
Affair of the Spiv's Secret. J. Hunter
Affair of the Splintered Heart. C. Knight
Affair of the Substitute Doctor. J. Rhode
Affair of the Syrian Dagger. C. Andrews
Affair of the Three Gunmen. W. M. Graydon
Affair of the Trade Rivals. R. C. Armour
Affair of the World's Champion. Jack Lewis
Affair on the Painted Desert. C. Knight
Affair on Thor's Head. E. C. R. Lorac
Affair Ravel. J. Courage
Affair with a Rich Girl. J. N. Chance
Affairs of Death. N. Fitzgerald
Affairs of Destiny. G. Simenon
Affairs of O'Malley. W. MacHarg
Affairs of Paula. H. Janson
Affairs of State. B. E. Stevenson
Affairs of the Heart. M. Muggeridge
Afraid in the Dark. M. Derby
Afraid of the Dark. J. Reach
Afraid of the Dark. M. L. Roby
African Contract. S. Jason
African Gold. W. M. Graydon
African Millionaire. G. Allen
African Millionaire. E. Wallace
African Mistress. L. Royer
African Poison Murders. E. Huxley
Afrit Affair. K. Laumer
After Dark. W. Collins
After-Dark. Ron Fraser
After Dark, My Sweet. J. Thompson
After Darvray Died. P. Meriton
After-Dinner Story. W. Irish
After House. M. R. Rinehart
After Innocence. I. Gordon
After Many Days. C. Dawe
After Many Years. R. H. Savage
After Midnight. M. Albrand
After Midnight. W. F. Fauley
After Midnight. H. Nielsen
After Office-Hours. E. Yates
After Rome, Africa. B. Glanville
After Sundown. W. W. Fenn
After the Act. Winston Graham
After the Battle. D. Learmonth
After the Bribe Takers. Lieut. Carlton
After the Deacon Was Murdered. C. Penfield
After the Deed. J. S. Clouston
After the Execution. T. Hyde
After the Fact. A. Brock
After the Fault. R. H. Sherard
After the Fine Weather. M. Gilbert
After the First Death. Lawrence Block
After the Funeral. A. Christie
After the Island. H. Bourne
After the Lady. P. Allardyce
After the Last Race. D. Koontz
After the Night Has Passed. A. L. Halstead
After the Trial. E. Roman
After the Verdict. N. Carter
After the Verdict. Anthony Gilbert
After the Verdict. R. Hichens
After the Verdict. E. Jordan
After the Wedding. K. Lindsay
After the Widow Changed Her Mind. C. Penfield
Aftermath. H. B. M. Watson
Aftermath of Murder. M. Fitt
Aftermath of Murder. R. Harrison
Aftermath of Murder. T. Newman
Afternoon at the Seaside. A. Christie
Afternoon for Lizards. D. Eden
Afternoon of a Loser. T. Pace
Afternoon of Violence. C. Barling
Afternoon to Kill. Shelley Smith
Afternoon Walk. D. Eden
Aftershock. C. Wilcox
Afterwards. M. B. Lowndes
Again Inspector Flagg. J. Cassells
Again McLean. G. Goodchild
Again, Mr. Sandyman. Neill Graham
Again Sanders. E. Wallace
Again the Dreamer. W. M. Duncan
Again the Remover. Roland Daniel
Again the Ringer. E. Wallace
Again the Three. E. Wallace
Again the Three Just Men. E. Wallace
Against All Odds. Arthur Smith
Against Desperate Odds. N. Carter
Against My Fire. D. G. Waring
Against Odds. L. L. Lynch
Against the Evidence. L. Egan
Against the F.B.I. R. Carni
Against the Law. D. Durham
Against the Public Interest. R. Gaines
Against the Stream. J. Hatton
Agatha Webb. A. K. Green
Agatha's Quest. R. H. Sherard
Age of Death. W. L. Marshall
Age of the Junkman. P. D. Ballard
Agency. P. Gottlieb
Agent. T. Hinde
Agent B-7. Ared White
Agent Counter Agent. N. Carter
Agent Extraordinary. S. Bayne
Agent from the West. D. Williams
Agent Intervenes. M. Annesley
Agent No. 5. J. Corbett
Agent of Death. N. De Mille
Agent of the Devil. H. Habe
Agent of the Id. B. Byers
Agent on the Other Side. G. O'Toole
Agent Outside. P. Wynnton
Agents of the League. C. Davy
Aggravating Joe, the Prince of Mischief. Old Sleuth
Agnes. G. W. M. Reynolds
Agnes the Unknown. T. P. Prest
Agony Column. E. D. Biggers
Agony Column Murders. R. T. M. Scott
Agony Terrace. A. Griffiths
Agreement to Kill. P. Rabe
Aground. C. Williams
Ahead of the Game. N. Carter
Aim to Kill. R. Gatenby
Ainceworth Mystery. G. Baxter
Air Apparent. J. Gardner
Air Bandits. D. T. Lindsay
Air Bandits. P. Trent
Air Bridge. H. Innes
Air Cavalier. T. Wallace
Air Devil. B. Beverley
Air Disaster. H. Innes
Air for Murder. A. A. Thomson
Air Gold. Colin Hope
Air Killer. J. Corbett
Air Ministry, Room 28. G. Frankau
Air Murders. R. H. Watkins
Air Peril. Colin Hope
Air Pilot. R. Parrish
Air Pirate. C. R. Gull
Air Ranger. G. E. Rochester
Air Reprisal. A. O. Pollard
Air-Ship. J. S. Fletcher
Air Sleuth. J. Bolton
Air Smugglers. J. Bolton
Air That Kills. Francis King
Air That Kills. M. Millar
Air Trail. G. E. Rochester
Airing in a Closed Carriage. J. Shearing
Airline Pirates. J. Gardner
Airport Affair. D. Toma
Airport Cop. C. Miron
Airs Above the Ground. M. Stewart
Airtight Alibi. C. F. Gregg
Akin to Murder. K. M. Knight
Al Capone. J. Roeburt
Aladdin in London. F. Hume
Aladdin in London. M. Pemberton
Alain of Halfdene. A. Burr
Alamein. M. Urquhart
Alamut Ambush. A. Price
Alan Thorne. M. L. Moodey
Alaric Spenceley. J. H. Riddell
Alarm. J. Rhode
Alarm at Black Brake. J. N. Chance
Alarm in the Night. S. Sterling
Alarm of the Black Cat. D. B. Olsen
Alarming Clock. M. Avallone
Alarum and Excursion. V. Perdue
Alas, Poor Father. J. Fleming
Alaskan. G. Goodchild
Albanian Connection. J. Rosenberger
Albatross. C. Armstrong
Albatross Murders. I. Jones
Albert Gate Affair. L. Tracy
Albert Gate Mystery. L. Tracy
Albino's Double. G. N. Philips
Albion Case. D. Craig
Album. M. R. Rinehart
Album Leaf. J. Shearing
Alcatraz Incident. R. O'Neil
Alchemy Murder. P. Oldfeld
Alcoholics. J. Thompson
Alda Abducted. A. R. Weekes
Aldeburg Cezanne. J. A. Graham
Alden Case. R. Bridges
Alderman's Children. J. B. Richards
Aldringham's Last Chance. A. J. Rees
Aleta's Terrible Secret. L. J. Libbey
Aletta. B. Mitford
Aleutian Blue Mink. J. M. Fox
Alexandrovitch Is Missing! Anne Edwards
Alfred. G. W. M. Reynolds
Algonquin Project. F. Nolan
Alias. F. Andreas
Alias Basil Willing. H. McCloy
Alias Ben Alibi. I. S. Cobb
Alias Blackshirt. B. Graeme
Alias Blue Mask. A. Morton
Alias Dr. Ely. L. Thayer
Alias His Wife. S. Ransome
Alias John Doe. P. E. Triem
Alias John Smith. G. Wade
Alias Man. D. Craig
Alias Mr. Death. G. W. Jones
Alias Mr. Orson. A. Spiller
Alias Norman Conquest. B. Gray
Alias Red Ryan. C. N. Buck
Alias Richard Power. W. Allison
Alias Richard Power. C. N. Williamson
Alias the Baron. A. Morton

Alias--The Crimson Snake. T. A. Plummer
Alias the Dead. G. H. Coxe
Alias the Eagle. M. Harvey
Alias the Ghost. G. Verner
Alias the Hangman. V. Gunn
Alias the Lone Wolf. L. J. Vance
Alias the Night Wind. V. Vanardy
Alias the Saint. L. Charteris
Alias the Thunderbolt. J. McCulley
Alias the Victim. L. Gribble
Alias Uncle Hugo. M. Coles
Alibi. H. Carmichael
Alibi. J. Creasey
Alibi. G. A. England
Alibi. Mark Ross
Alibi. F. F. Van De Water
Alibi and Dr. Morelle. E. Dudley
Alibi at Dusk. B. Benson
Alibi Baby. S. Sterling
Alibi for a Corpse. E. Lemarchand
Alibi for a Judge. H. Cecil
Alibi for a Witch. E. Ferrars
Alibi for Isabel. M. R. Rinehart
Alibi for Murder. C. Armstrong
Alibi in Black. C. Robertson
Alibi Innings. B. Worsley-Gough
Alibi Off Broadway. H. Zore
Alibi Too Much. H. Kaner
Alice. E. Bulwer-Lytton
Alice. E. V. Cunningham
Alice. F. W. Pangborn
Alice and Me. W. Judson
Alice Devine. E. Jepson
Alice Dies Twice. K. Carr
Alice Dies Twice. B. Grant
Alice, Where Art Thou? E. Cadell
Alien. J. Bell
Alien Archipelago. San Antonio
Alien Minds. E. E. Evans
Alien Souls. A. Abdullah
Alien Virus. A. Caillou
Alington Inheritance. P. Wentworth
Alise of Astra. H. B. M. Watson
Alive and Dead. E. Ferrars
Alive or Dead. G. B. Savi
Alixe Derring. E. Nisot
All Along the River. M. E. Braddon
All at Sea. C. Wells
All Brides Are Beautiful. M. Corrigan
All Cats Are Grey. C. G. Givens
All Change for Murder. V. Gunn
All Change, Humanity! C. Houghton
All Concerned Notified. H. Reilly
All Dames Are Dynamite. T. Trent
All Done by Kindness. Doris Langley Moore
All England at Home. John Gloag
All Evil Shed Away. A. Roy
All Exits Barred. C. Portway
All Exits Blocked. B. Perowne
All Fall Down. A. Kennington
All Fall Down. L. A. G. Strong
All for a Woman. J. J. Dratler
All for Him. Anonymous
All for One and One for Death. S. Forbes
All for the Apple. J. MacKenzie
All for the Love of a Lady. L. Ford
All God's Children. A. Lyons
All Grass Isn't Green. A. A. Fair
All Her Vices. S. Rand
All Honorable Men. D. Karp
All I Can Get. W. Ard
All in a Day's Work. D. Ray
All in Good Crime. M. Hervey
All in the Dark. J. S. Le Fanu
All in the Night's Work. E. W. Mumford
All in the Racket. W. E. Weeks
All Is Discovered. J. Cannan
All Is Not Gold. F. A. M. Webster
All Is Vanity. J. Bell
All Leads Negative. P. Alding
All Men Are Liars. J. S. Strange
All Men Are Lonely Now. F. Clifford
All Men Are Murderers. C. Blackstock
All My Dead Men. B. Byers
All My Enemies. S. Baron
All My Enemies. Rosemary Harris
All My Pretty Chickens. A. Hocking
All Night at Mr. Stanyhurst's. H. Edwards
All of Our Aircraft Are Missing. J. P. Radford
All on a Summer's Day. J. Garden
All or Nothing. A. Bocca
All or Nothing. M. Catto
All or Nothing. P. Marlowe
All Other Perils. Robert MacLeod
All over but the Shooting. R. Powell
All-Purpose Bodies. P. McCutchan
All Roads Lead to Friday. H. Innes
All Shot Up. C. Himes
All Souls' Night. H. Walpole
All Square with Fate. T. C. St. C. Morton
All Star Cast. N. Royde-Smith
All Stations to Malta. G. Hackforth-Jones
All Suspect. K. Methold
All Suspected. W. J. Bayfield
All That Glitters. M. Coles
All That Glitters. N. B. Gerson
All That Glitters. M. Richmond
All the Silent Voices. Roger Fuller
All the Skeletons in All the Closets. K. Fowler
All the Way. C. Williams
All the Way Down. M. E. Chaber
All the Way Home and All the Night Through. T. Lewis
All the World to Nothing. W. Martyn
All These Condemned. J. D. MacDonald
All This Is Ended. A. W. Wells
All This Shall Perish. M. Vinter
All Through the Night. W. Masterson
All Thugs Are Dangerous. Roland Daniel
All Very Irregular. V. Bridges
All Your Lovely Words Are Spoken M. L. Roby
"Allah's Eye." A. Parsons
Allan Dare and Robert le Diable. A. Porter
Allan Keene, the War Detective. H. Rockwood
Alleged Great-Aunt. H. K. Webster
Allegra's Child. J. Letton
Alley Girl. Jonathan Craig
Alley Kids. B. Appel
Allie Baird, the Settler's Son. Old Sleuth
Alligator. I*n Fl*m*ng
Allingham Case-Book. M. Allingham
Allingham Minibus. M. Allingham
All's Fair on Lake Garda. A. J. Evans
Allworth Abbey. E. Southworth
Almack, the Detective. E. H. Cragg
Almeda. N. T. Oliver
Almira's Curse. T. P. Prest
Almon Mitchell's Double. Old Sleuth
Almost Dead. W. Herber
Almost Midnight. M. Caidin
Almost Perfect Murder. H. Footner
Almost Without Murder. B. Graeme
Aloha Means Goodbye. N. A. Hintze
Alone at Night. V. Packer
Alone in the Grass. C. Phillips
Alone on a Wide, Wide Sea. W. C. Russell
Along a Dark Path. V. Johnston
Along Came a Spider. E. Davis
Along Came a Spider. M. Parker
Along for the Ride. T. Newman
Along the Road. A. Hodges
Alonzo MacTavish Again. P. Cheyney
Alp Murder. A. M. Stein
Alpha List. James Anderson
Alpha Trip. G. Billing
Alphabet Hicks. R. Stout
Alphabet Murders. A. Christie
Alphonsine. A. Belot
Alpine Affair. J. F. Vignant
Alpine Crack-Up. J. W. Hornby
Alps Assignment. A. Sugar
Alscott Experiment. B. Stanley
Also Ran. N. Williams
Alster Case. J. R. Gillies
Altar of Evil. F. Stevenson
Altar-Piece. N. Royde-Smith
Altars of the Heart. R. Lebherz
Altered Ego. J. Sohl
Alternate Case. J. F. Dinneen
Althea. M. McDonell
Althea's Falcon. D. M. Carlisle
Aluminum Turtle. B. Kendrick
Alvarez Journal. R. Burns
Always Ask a Policeman. S. Truss
Always Expect the Unexpected. B. Graeme
Always Fight Back. A. MacKenzie
Always in August. A. Head
Always Kill a Stranger. R. L. Fish
Always Leave 'Em Dying. R. S. Prather
Always Murder a Friend. M. Scherf
Always Say Die. E. Ferrars
Always Take the Big Ones. Peter Chambers
Always Tell the Sleuth. Kevin O'Hara
Always the Wolf. N. Easton
Amanda's Castle. G. Revelli
Amaranth Club. J. S. Fletcher
Amateur Adventuress. C. Stanton
Amateur Agent. Christopher Adams
Amateur Boxer. R. Worth
Amateur Cracksman. E. W. Hornung
Amateur Crime. A. B. Cox
Amateur Criminal. G. S. Layard
Amateur Crook. H. Clevely
Amateur Detectives. C. B. Booth
Amateur Emigrants. T. Cobb
Amateur Gentleman. J. Farnol
Amateur Governess. M. A. Gibbs
Amateur in Crime. W. M. Graydon
Amateur in Violence. M. Gilbert
Amateur Inn. A. P. Terhune
Amateur Murderer. C. J. Daly
Amateurs. W. Cook
Amazing Adventures of Carolus Herbert. G. Leroux
Amazing Adventures of Letitia Carberry. M. R. Rinehart
Amazing Adventures of Mr. Henry Button. L. Despard
Amazing Adventures of Sophie Lyons. S. Lyons
Amazing Affair of the Renegade Prince. G. N. Philips
Amazing Affair of the Shipyard Sabotage. S. Hope
Amazing Chance. P. Wentworth
Amazing Corpse. C. Robertson.
Amazing Count. W. LeQueux
Amazing Dr. Khan. H. Metcalfe
Amazing Duke. W. Magnay
Amazing Judgment. E. P. Oppenheim
Amazing Mr. Blackshirt. R. Graeme
Amazing Mr. Bunn. B. Atkey
Amazing Mr. Lutterworth. D. Leslie
Amazing Mr. Sandyman. Neill Graham
Amazing Mrs. Pollifax. D. Gilman
Amazing Partnership. E. P. Oppenheim
Amazing Quest of Doctor Syn. R. Thorndike
Amazing Quest of Mr. Ernest Bliss. E. P. Oppenheim
Amazing Scoundrel. N. Carter
Amazing Test Match Crime. A. Alington
Amazing Verdict. M. Leighton
Amazing Web. H. S. Keeler
Amazing Wizard. Old Sleuth
Amazon. N. Carter
Ambart Trial. K. Ingram
Ambassador. M. L. West
Ambassador of Death. J. F. Fishter
Ambassador's Adventure. A. Upward
Ambassador's Glove. R. Machray
Ambassador's Kiss. W. J. Lomax
Ambassador's Plot. S. D. Frances

Ambassador's Trunk. G. Barton
Ambassador's Wife. P. Gibbs
Amber and Jade. A. Griffin
Amber Bead. J. Spiess
Amber Eyes. F. Crane
Amber Eyes. Roland Daniel
Amber Eyes of the Lion. S. Dembo
Amber for Anna. A. Watkyn
Amber Girl. C. Mayne
Amber Gods. S. C. Prescott
Amber Gods and Other Stories. H. Spofford
Amber Junk. M. E. Hanshew
Amber Nine. J. Gardner
Amber to Red. V. Hill
Amber Twilight. M. Lynch
Ambergris! A. Murray
Amberleigh. M. E. Edward
Amberwood. A. Rundle
Ambiguous Man. R. Tashkent
Ambition's Slave. F. M. White
Ambitious Lady. J. S. Fletcher
Amblers. B. L. Farjeon
Amboy Dukes. I. Shulman
Ambrose in London. P. Levene
Ambrose in Paris. P. Levene
Ambrose Lavendale, Diplomat. E. P. Oppenheim
Ambrosio. M. G. Lewis
Ambrotox and Limping Dick. O. Fleming
Ambulance. H. Miller
Ambush. W. Edwards
Ambush. J. G. Sarasin
Ambush for Anatol. J. Sherwood
Ambush for the Hunter. F. L. Green
Ambush House. K. Steel
Ambushers. D. Hamilton
American Baron. J. De Mille
American Cavalier. W. C. Hudson
American Detective in Russia. Old Sleuth
American Emperor. L. Tracy
American Gothic. R. Bloch
American Gun Mystery. E. Queen
American Legionnaire. J. Robb
American Marquis. N. Carter
American Marquis. R. H. Sherard
American Monte Cristo. J. Hawthorne
American Monte Cristo. Old Sleuth
American Penman. J. Hawthorne
American Pep. A. Stone
American Prisoner. E. Phillpotts
American Thug. Old Sleuth
American Tragedy. T. Dreiser
American Venus. E. Preston
Amethyst Box. A. K. Green
Amethyst Button. B. Baskerville
Amethyst Cross. F. Hume
Amethyst Spectacles. F. Crane
Amethyst Tears. Marilyn Ross
Amiable Charlatan. E. P. Oppenheim
Amiable Crimes of Dirk Memling. Rupert Hughes
Amigo, Amigo. F. Clifford
Ammie, Come Home. B. Michaels
Among Arabian Sands. J. Mitchell
Among the Brigands. J. De Mille
Among the Counterfeiters. N. Carter
Among the Nihilists. N. Carter
Among the Ruins and Other Stories. M. C. Hay
Among Thieves. G. Cuomo
Among Those Absent. M. Coles
Among Those Present. P. Barrington
Among Those Present. A. S. Roche
Amongst Those Missing. P. Capon
Amoret. C. Gibbon
Amorous Captive. H. Janson
Amos Petrie's Puzzle. J. V. Turner
Amphitheatre Plot. N. Carter
Amphorae Pirates. L. Cameron
Amsterdam. N. Carter
Amsterdam Diversion. Angus Ross
Amusement Only. R. Marsh
Amy. K. W. Eyre
Amyas Egerton, Cavalier. M. H. Hervey
Amzi, the Detective. Old Sleuth
Analog Bullet. Martin Smith
Anarchist. R. H. Savage

Anarchist's Oath. B. Wayde
Anatomy Lesson. M. Goldberg
Anatomy of a Crime. J. F. Dinneen
Anatomy of a Killer. P. Rabe
Anatomy of a Murder. R. Traver
Anatomy of a Murder. E. Winer
Anatomy of Violence. C. Runyon
Ancestor. R. Carol
Anchor Island. P. Malloch
Anchor's Aweigh. E. L. Long
Ancient Pond. Courtney Browne
Ancora Scipio. T. Gates
And a Bottle of Rum. B. Graeme
And All That Beauty--. R. Bridges
And Be a Villain. J. Cannan
And Be a Villain. L. Maynell
And Be a Villain. R. Stout
And Be My Love. L. Baker
And Being Dead. M. Erskine
And Billy Disappeared. W. B. Hare
And Call It Accident. M. B. Lowndes
And Cauldron Bubble. B. Flynn
And Dangerous to Know. E. Daly
And Death Came Too. Anthony Gilbert
And Death Came Too. R. Hull
And Death Came Too. H. Mace
And Death Drove On. Robert Fleming
And Die Remembering. M. L. Roby
And Die She Did. I. Oellrichs
And Died So? V. Gielgud
And Dream of Evil. T. Thomey
And Four to Go. R. Stout
...And Hang Him. K. P. Arbuthnot
And Here Is the Noose! Kevin O'Hara
...and High Water. A. M. Stein
And Home Came Ted. W. B. Hare
And Hope to Die. L. Charbonneau
And Hope to Die. R. Powell
And If I Laugh. D. G. Waring
...And Incidentally, Murder! B. E. Lovell
And It Came to Pass. G. Thorne
And Kill Once More. A. Fray
And Left for Dead. F. Lockridge
And Let the Coffin Pass. K. Abbey
And Loving It! W. Johnston
And Murder Came Too. G. Compton
And Murder Won. H. C. Davis
And No One Wept. A. Hocking
And Not for Love. P. Mechem
And Now the Screaming Starts. D. Case
And on the Eighth Day. E. Queen
And One Cried Murder. L. Thayer
And One for the Dead. P. Audemars
And One for the Pot. M. E. Simpson
And One Must Die. R. Henneker
And Only Man. A. Dick
...And Presumed Dead. L. Fletcher
"And Shall Trelawney Die?" J. Hocking
And Shame the Devil. S. Woods
And She Had a Little Knife. J. L. Linklater
And So He Had to Die. D. C. Cameron
And So to Bed. W. Ard
And So to Death. W. Irish
And So to Death. G. Shayne
And So to Eternity. Whitney Brown
And So to Murder. Carter Dickson
And So We Die. J. Sandys
And Sometimes Death. J. Valentine
And Still I Cheat the Gallows. E. P. Oppenheim
And Sudden Death. C. F. Adams
And Sudden Death. J. S. Fletcher
And the Body Came Too. L. Boden
And the Bullets Were Made of Lead. P. Wheeler
And the Deep Blue Sea. G. Volk
And the Deep Blue Sea. C. Williams
And the Devil. C. Cannell
And the Girl Screamed. G. Brewer
And the Moon Was Full. H. McCutcheon
And the Shouting Dies. Robert Mason

And the Undead Sing. Carter Brown
And the Winds Blew. H. J. Heinecke
And Then Came Fear. M. Cumberland
And Then Look Down. M. Garratt
And Then Murder. J. Fast
And Then...One Dark Night. E. Snell
And Then Put Out the Light. E. C. R. Lorac
And Then Silence. M. Propper
And Then the Screaming Started. O. Blakeston
And Then There Was Georgia. J. Blackmore
And Then There Were Nine. W. H. L. Crauford
And Then There Were None. A. Christie
And Then There Were None. E. C. Vivian
And Thereby Hangs--. A. Spiller
And to My Beloved Husband--. P. Loraine
And Turned to Clay. L. G. Offord
And Two Shall Meet. Raymond Mason
And When She Was Bad She Was Murdered. R. Starnes
And Where She Stops. T. B. Dewey
And Where's Mr. Bellamy? S. M. Wick
And, Which, the Knave? B. M. Scott
And Why Not? V. G. Malo
And Worms Have Eaten Them. M. Cumberland
"And Worms Have Eaten Them..." W. J. Elliott
Andean Murders. L. Hazard
Anderson Crow, Detective. G. B. McCutcheon
Anderson Tapes. L. Sanders
Andra Fiasco. W. Garner
Andre Cornelis. P. Bourget
Andrew and His Wife. T. Cobb
Andrew Reforms. P. Trent
Andrewlina. J. S. Fletcher
Andrew's Wife. K. Booton
Andromache. H. Monteilhet
Angel. G. Brewer
Angel! C. Brown
Angel. P. Traill
Angel. G. Verner
Angel Abroad. G. Montrose
Angel Among Witches. A. Gale
Angel and the Cuckoo. G. Kersh
Angel and the Nero. G. Montrose
Angel and the Red Admiral. G. Montrose
Angel, Angel, Down We Go. W. Johnston
Angel Astray. H. Janson
Angel at Arms. G. Montrose
An Angel Came Down. M. Pereira
Angel Esquire. E. Wallace
Angel Eyes. R. Dietrich
Angel Face. F. Nichols
Angel Face Tatters the Kimono. A. St. Moore
Angel Hold Fire. K. T. McCall
Angel in Paradise. G. Montrose
Angel in the Case. E. Elder
Angel Loves Nobody. R. Miles
Angel of Death. P. D. Ballard
Angel of Death. N. Carter
Angel of Death. P. Loraine
Angel of Death. G. Montrose
Angel of Evil. G. Warden
Angel of Light. H. McCutcheon
Angel of No Mercy. G. Montrose
Angel of Terror. E. Wallace
Angel of the Bells. F. Du Boisgobey
Angel of the Chimes. F. Du Boisgobey
Angel of the Covenant. J. M. Cobban
Angel of Vengeance. G. De Villiers
Angel of Vengeance. G. Montrose
Angel, Shoot to Kill. H. Janson
Angel Steps In. E. P. Thorne
Angel Street. P. Hamilton
Angel Take Care. R. Lakin
Angel with Dirty Wings. J. E. Hasty
Angelic Avengers. P. Andrezel
Angelica. F. Swann
Angelina. T. P. Prest
Angell, Pearl and Little God. Winston Graham

Angels Are Cowards. D. Garth
Angels Are Painted Fair. P. Whelton
Angels Fell. B. Fischer
Angel's Flight. L. Cameron
Angels in Aldgate. W. J. Passingham
Angels in the Gutter. J. Hilton
Angels in the Snow. Derek Lambert
Angels of Doom. L. Charteris
Angel's Ransom. D. Dodge
Angel's Tear. J. Blackmore
Angels Weep! D. Leslie
Anger at World's End. D. Reid
Anger of Olivia. T. Cobb
Anger of the Bells. V. Rath
Angry Amazons. C. Brown
Angry Darkness. C. Leader
Angry Dream. G. Brewer
Angry Heart. L. Edgley
Angry Island. J. Pattinson
Angry Island. K. Royce
Angry Millionaire. S. Jepson
Angry Mountains. H. Innes
Angry Night. W. H. Baker
Angry Ocean. G. Johnston
Angry Scar. D. Daniels
Angry Silence. John Burke
Angry Wind. L. Ames
Animal-Lover's Book of Beastly Murder. P. Highsmith
Anita, the Cuban Spy. G. Willets
Ann Turns Detective. Roland Daniel
Anna of the Plains. A. Askew
Anna of the Underworld. G. R. Sims
Anna, the Adventuress. E. P. Oppenheim
Anna, Where Are You? P. Wentworth
Annalisa. F. Rydell
Annam Jewel. P. Wentworth
Anna's. C. N. Boyle
Anne Belinda. P. Wentworth
Anne Hereford. H. Wood
Anne of Destiny House. Wilma Forrest
Anne of the Flying Gap. H. H. Hill
Annette of the Argonne. W. LeQueux
Annexation Society. J. S. Fletcher
Annie Deane. R. H. Adelman
Annie Wallace. H. P. Halsey
Annihilation. I. Ostrander
Annihilist. K. Robeson
Anniversary Murder. E. Phillpotts
Announcer. D. H. Landels
Ann's Crime. R. T. M. Scott
Annulet of Guilt. P. A. Taylor
Anonymous Assassin. J. F. Drexler
Anonymous Footsteps. J. M. O'Connor
Another Case for Inspector Jackson. D. T. Lindsay
Another Chorus. John Burke
Another Crime. C. Rushton
Another Day. J. Farnol
Another Day--Another Death. G. Bagby
Another Day, Another Stiff. Michael Brett
Another Day Toward Dying. M. Marlette
Another Little Death. Bill Turner
Another Little Drink. P. Cheyney
Another Little Murder. L. N. Morgan
Another Man's Life. M. Head
Another Man's Murder. M. G. Eberhart
Another Man's Poison. H. Holman
Another Man's Shadow. J. Bude
Another Man's Shoes. V. Bridges
Another Man's Wife. J. Chancellor
Another Man's Wife. M. B. Lowndes
Another Man's Wife. Lady A. Scott
Another Morgue Heard From. F. C. Davis
Another Mug for the Bier. R. Starnes
Another Mystery in Suva. F. Arthur
Another Night, Another Day. D. F. Gardiner
Another Spring. H. S. Maxfield
Another Way of Dying. F. Clifford
Another Way to Die. J. Crowe
Another Woman's House. M. G. Eberhart

Another Woman's Love. K. Lindsay
Another Woman's Man. Norma Lee
Another Woman's Poison. W. H. L. Crauford
Another Woman's Shoes. F. Durbridge
Another's Burden. J. Payn
Another's Crime. J. Hawthorne
Answer in the Negative. H. Hamilton
Answer in the Negative. E. Scholey
Answer That Bell! M. Baillie-Saunders
Answer to Heaven. P. Gallagher
Answered. F. Hume
Ant Heap. A. Mills
Antagonists. O. Cameron
Antagonists. W. Haggard
Anthill. D. Gilles
Anthony Ravenhill, Crime Merchant. R. Francis Foster
Anthony Trent: Avenger. W. Martyn
Anthony Trent, Master Criminal. W. Martyn
Anti-Crime Ltd. E. Snell
Anti-Death League. K. Amis
Antidote. S. Murray
Antidote to Venom. F. W. Crofts
Antoinette. G. Ohnet
Anxious Conspirator. M. Underwood
Anxious Lady. J. Pendower
Any Kind of Danger. E. G. Cousins
Any Man's Girl. B. Heatter
Any Minute Now. A. Bocca
Any Number Can Play. D. Bloodworth
Any Number Can Play. E. H. Heth
Any Old Port in a Storm. H. Clement
Any Shape or Form. E. Daly
Any War Will Do. E. Pace
Anybody but Anne. C. Wells
Anybody's Pearls. H. Footner
Anyone's Grief. R. Drayton
Anyone's My Name. S. Shubin
Anything but Saintly. R. Deming
Anything but the Truth. C. Wells
Anything Can Happen. G. F. Gibbs
Anything for a Quite Life. A. A. Avery
Anything for Kicks. Morton Cooper
Anything Might Happen. H. Balfour
Anything Once. D. Grant
Anything to Declare? F. W. Crofts
Anytime, Anywhere. M. Caidin
Apache. A. Askew
Apache Girl. A. Mills
Apaches of New York. Alfred H. Lewis
Apartment Next Door. W. A. Johnston
Apartment on K Street. R. Travers
Ape, a Dog, and a Serpent. G. Kersh
Ape and the Diamond. Richard Marsh
Ape in Velvet. R. Foley
Ape Man. H. T. Johnson
Ape-Man's Offering. H. Kaner
Ape of London. T. Crisp
Ape, the Idiot and Other People. W. C. Morrow
Aphrodite Means Death. J. Appleby
Apollo Fountain. D. Daniels
Apollo Legacy. A. Barker
Apollo Wore a Wig. R. T. Campbell
Apologetic Tiger. J. Workman
Apostles of Violence. M. G. Braun
Apostles of Violence. D. Perring
Apparition. T. P. Prest
Apparition. R. Stewart
Apperson's Folly. A. Mallory
Apple a Day. H. Brinton
Apple of Discord. H. C. Rowland
Apple Tree. D. Du Maurier
Appleby at Allington. M. Innes
Appleby File. M. Innes
Appleby on Ararat. M. Innes
Appleby Plays Chicken. M. Innes
Appleby Talking. M. Innes
Appleby Talks Again. M. Innes
Appleby's Answer. M. Innes
Appleby's End. M. Innes
Appleby's Other Story. M. Innes
Applegreen Cat. F. Crane
Apples of Sin. C. Kernahan
Appleshaw. C. Damien
Applewood Mystery. F. Burleigh
Appointed Date. J. J. Farjeon

Appointment at Eight. H. Desmond
Appointment at Nine. D. M. Disney
Appointment in Adalusia. M. MacKintosh
Appointment in Cairo. G. Brewer
Appointment in Hell. G. Brewer
Appointment in Hell. V. Warren
Appointment in Manila. Elinor Chamberlain
Appointment in New Orleans. T. Claymore
Appointment in Tenerife. R. Harding
Appointment in Tibet. W. H. Murray
Appointment in Vienna. S. Gainham
Appointment in Zahrein. Michael Barrett
Appointment with Danger. W. H. Baker
Appointment with Danger. D. Garth
Appointment with Death. C. Barling
Appointment with Death. A. Christie
Appointment with Death. P. Frankau
Appointment with Death. M. Hervey
Appointment with Desire. H. Luger
Appointment with Dishonor. W. H. Gage
Appointment with Fear. D. Stokes
Appointment with Murder. H. Seymour
Appointment with My Lady. F. Griffin
Appointment with the Hangman. T. C. H. Jacobs
Appointment with Venus. J. Tickell
Appointment with Yesterday. C. Fremlin
Apprehensive Dog. H. C. Bailey
Apprentice to Fear. H. Brinton
April Evil. J. D. MacDonald
April, May and June. H. Willett
April Robin Murders. C. Rice
April Shroud. R. Hill
April's Grave. S. Howatch
Apron-Strings. R. Marsh
Aquanauts. D. Bard
Aquarius Angel. L. Bullock
Aquarius Curse. Marilyn Ross
Aquarius, My Evil. J. De Pre
Arab Agent. Robert Mason
Arab Plague. N. Carter
Arabesque. G. Household
Arabian Nights Murder. J. D. Carr
Araby's Husband. A. Askew
Arafat Is Next! Lionel Black
Araminta and the River. Alan Graham
Araway Oath. H. Adams
Arch-Criminal. Roland Daniel
Archdeacons Afloat. C. A. Alington
Archdeacons Ashore. C. A. Alington
Archer in the Arras, and other tales of mystery. L. Spence
Archer Plus Twenty. H. Clevely
Archibald Malmaison. J. Hawthorne
Archie the Tumbler. Old Sleuth
Architect's Secret. W. J. Bayfield
Arctic Assignment. R. Charles
Arctic Convoy. Taffrail
Arctic Submarine. A. Mars
Arctic Trail. W. M. Graydon
Arden Mystery. M. Harvey
Are You My Wife? M. Marcin
Area of Suspicion. J. D. MacDonald
Arena. W. Haggard
Argus Eye. F. M. White
Argus Pheasant. J. C. Beecham
Argyle Case. A. Hornblow
Arigato. R. Condon
Arising from an Accident. P. Dewdney
Aristocratic Detective. R. Marsh
Arizona Drifters. W. C. Tuttle
Arkansas Ranger. M. M. Murray
Arkie, the Runaway. Old Sleuth
Arlie Bright. Old Sleuth
Arm of Mrs. Egan and other strange stories. W. F. Harvey
Arm of the Law. Lieut. Carlton
Arm of the Law. M. Underwood
Armada Gold. E. Turner
Armadale. W. Collins
Armchair in Hell. H. Kane
Armed...Dangerous... B. Halliday
Armed Doves. B. Newman
Armed with a New Terror. T. Du Bois
Armitage Case. Michael Kent
Armitage Secret. H. Howard
Armorer of Tyre. S. Cobb

Arms and the Spy. M. McKenna
Arms for Adonis. C. Jay
Arms for Oblivion. J. Hedges
Arms for the Love of Allah. Anthony Harding
Arms of Phaedra. N. Worth
Arms of Venus. J. Appleby
Armstrong. Alan White
Army DeFaulter's Secret. L. C. Douthwaite
Army Doctor's Romance. G. Allen
Army of the Dead. C. Steele
Army Post Murders. M. Wright
Arncliffe Puzzle. Gordon Holmes
Arnholt Makes His Bow. G. Latta
Around Dark Corners. H. Pentecost
Arrangement for Murder. R. Simons
Arranways Mystery. E. Wallace
Array of Eagles. R. Severn
Arrest. W. Proudfoot
Arrest and Trial. N. Daniels
Arrest of Arsene Lupin. M. Leblanc
Arrest the Bishop? W. Peck
Arrest the Saint. L. Charteris
Arrest These Men! B. Perowne
Arrested. Esme Stuart
Arrested. E. C. Vivian
Arrested for Murder. Roland Daniel
Arresting Delia. S. Fowler
Arrival in Suspicion. S. Harvester
Arrivederci, Baby! James Peterson
Arrogant Alibi. C. D. King
Arrogant Duke. Rona Randall
Arrow of Death. Roland Daniel
Arrow of Death. F. Vivian
Arrow of Terror. J. Marie
Arrow Pointing Nowhere. E. Daly
Arrow Points to Murder. F. De Laguna
Arrows of Chance. E. R. Punshon
Arsenal Stadium Mystery. L. Gribble
Arsene Lupin. E. Jepson
Arsene Lupin, Gentleman Burglar. M. Leblanc
Arsene Lupin Intervenes. M. Leblanc
Arsene Lupin, Super-Sleuth. M. Leblanc
Arsene Lupin versus Herlock Sholmes. M. Leblanc
Arsene Lupin versus Holmlock Shears. M. Leblanc
Arsenic. J. Remenham
Arsenic and Gold. B. Atkey
Arsenic and Old Lace. J. Kesselring
Arsenic for the Teacher. O. Keystone
Arsenic in Richmond. D. Frome
Arsenic on the Menu. B. H. Homersham
Arson and Old Lace. S. Angus
Arson by Proxy. Ray Turner
Art of Disappearing. J. T. Smith
Art School Murders. M. Dalton
Art Studio Murders. E. Ronns
Art Thou the Man? G. Berton
Art Treasure Murders. J. L. Benton
Arterial Road Murder. A. Blair
Artful Schemer. N. Carter
Arthur. J. A. Graham
Arthur Mervyn. C. B. Brown
Article 92: Murder-Rape. W. Beech
Artifex Intervenes. R. Keverne
Artificial Fate. C. Boutelle
Artificial Girl. R. W. Cole
Artificial Man. L. P. Davies
Artist and Model. R. de Pont-Jest
Artist Detective. Anonymous
Artist Dies. J. Rhode
Artist in Crime. R. Ottolengui
Artist in Crime. K. M. Sheahan
Artist in Crime. C. Somerville
Artists in Crime. N. Marsh
Artist's Love. E. Southworth
Artist's Model. Mrs. C. Kernahan
Artists, Models and Murder. Tedd Steele
Artist's Murder. F. L. Cary
Artless Heiress. C. B. Kelland
Arundel Motto. M. C. Hay
As a Bird to the Snare. G. Warden
As a Crook Sows. N. Carter
As a Man Falls. H. Rigsby
As a Man Lives. E. P. Oppenheim

As a Man Sows. W. Westall
As a Thief in the Night. R. A. Freeman
As Bad as I Am. W. Ard
As Darker Crows the Night. E. Giles
As Deadly Does. J. Corby
As Empty as Hate. M. Halliday
As for the Woman. F. Iles
As Good as a Mile. E. Albert
As Good as Dead. T. B. Dewey
As Good as Gold. E. Wymark
As Good as Murdered. J. D. O'Hanlon
As I Was Goint to St. Ives. A. Hocking
As If She Were Mine. Alex Hamilton
As It Was in the Beginning. G. R. Sims
As It Was Written. S. Luska
As It Was Written. T. W. Speight
As Lonely as the Damned. M. Halliday
As Long as I live. I. S. Shriber
As Luck Would Have It. W. Westall
As Merry as Hell. M. Halliday
As Old as Cain. M. E. Chaber
As Strange a Maze. F. Leighton
As the Devil Burned. H. Kemp
As the Stars Fade. B. Hector
As They Rise. E. L. Long
As They Shall Sow. A. Spiller
As We Forgave Them. W. LeQueux
As We Sow. John O'Neill
Asbestos Mask. J. Nicholas
Ascendancy House. J. L. Rickard
Ascent of D-13. A. Garve
Aseptic Murders. C. Brown
Asey Mayo Trio. P. O. Taylor
Ash. C. Cannell
Ashenden. W. S. Maugham
Ashes. C. F. Coe
Ashes. H. Nisbet
Ashes and Diamonds. J. Andrzeyevski
Ashes for the Living. N. Cromarty
Ashes in an Urn. J. Roffman
Ashes in the Cellar. T. C. H. Jacobs
Ashes of Evidence. E. Levison
Ashes of Falconwyck. Angela Gray
Ashes of Loda. A. Garve
Ashes of Murder. G. Morton
Ashes to Ashes. E. Lathen
Ashes to Ashes. I. Ostrander
Ashes to Ashes. John Stuart
Ashiel Mystery. C. Bryce
Ashley, and other stories. H. Wood
Ashley Hall. S. Richard
Ashton-Kirk: Criminologist. J. T. MacIntyre
Ashton-Kirk: Investigator. J. T. MacIntyre
Ashton-Kirk: Secret Agent. J. T. MacIntyre
Ashton-Kirk: Special Detective. J. T. MacIntyre
Asimov's Mysteries. I. Asimov
Ask a Policeman. E. C. R. Lorac
Ask Agamemnon. Jenni Hall
Ask an Angel. G. Montrose
Ask for King Billy. H. Treece
Ask for Linda. F. Nichols
Ask for Lois. J. Matcha
Ask for Ronald Standish. H. C. McNeile
Ask for Trouble. M. Cronin
Ask Miss Mott. E. P. Oppenheim
Ask No Mercy. B. Perowne
Ask No Question. M. Hocking
Ask No Questions. L. Dean
Ask No Questions. B. Duff
Ask the Rattlesnake. P. Loraine
Ask the Right Question. M. Z. Lewin
Asking for It. J. Mayo
Asking for Trouble. L. Meynell
Asking for Trouble. J. Rayter
Asking Price. H. Cecil
Aspern Papers. M. Redgrave
Asphalt Jungle. W. R. Burnett
Asphodel. M. E. Braddon

Assassin. James Anderson
Assassin. Evelyn Anthony
Assassin. E. M. Harper
Assassin. S. Jepson
Assassin. Liam O'Flaherty
Assassin. L. W. Robinson
Assassin. Paul Ross
Assassin--Code Name Vulture. N. Carter
Assassin for Hire. R. Rienits
Assassin Trail. Dan Morgan
Assassin Who Gave Up His Gun. E. V. Cunningham
Assassination. B. Abro
Assassination Affair. J. H. Hunter
Assassination Brigade. N. Carter
Assassination Bureau, Ltd. J. London
Assassination File. J. Gardner
Assassination Is Set for July 4. L. Parker
Assassination of Mozart. D. Weiss
Assassinator. D. Vowell
Assassins. N. Mosley
Assassins. F. Mullally
Assassins. H. Pentecost
Assassins. H. T. Teilhet
Assassins and Victims. C. Black
Assassins Don't Die in Bed. M. Avallone
Assassins for Peace. R. Charles
Assassins Have Starry Eyes. D. Hamilton
Assassin's Playoff. R. Sapir
Assassins Road. S. Harvester
Assault and Pepper. J. T. Story
Assault on a Queen. J. Finney
Assault on Agathon. A. Caillou
Assault on Aimata. A. Caillou
Assault on England. N. Carter
Assault on Fellawi. A. Caillou
Assault on Kolchak. A. Caillou
Assault on Loveless. A. Caillou
Assault on Ming. A. Caillou
Assault on Soho. D. Pendleton
Assignment. P. Wahloo
Assignment Abacus. L. P. Davies
Assignment--Amazon Queen. E. S. Aarons
Assignment--Andalusia. R. C. Galway
Assignment--Angelina. E. S. Aarons
Assignment--Ankara. E. S. Aarons
Assignment Argentina. R. C. Galway
Assignment: Assassination. J. Milton
Assignment--Bangkok. E. S. Aarons
Assignment Basra. F. Ponthier
Assignment--Black Gold. E. S. Aarons
Assignment--Black Viking. E. S. Aarons
Assignment--Budapest. E. S. Aarons
Assignment--Burma Girl. E. S. Aarons
Assignment--Carlotta Cortez. E. S. Aarons
Assignment--Ceylon. E. S. Aarons
Assignment--Cong Hai Kill. E. S. Aarons
Assignment: Danger. Marilyn Ross
Assignment Death Squad. R. C. Galway
Assignment Doomsday. Martin Thomas
Assignment Fenland. R. C. Galway
Assignment: Find Cherry. J. Seward
Assignment for a Mercenary. Howard R. Simpson
Assignment for Trouble. M. Carrel
Assignment Gaolbreak. R. C. Galway
Assignment--Golden Girl. E. S. Aarons
Assignment Greece. G. Sheen
Assignment Haiti. E. P. Thorne
Assignment--Helene. E. S. Aarons
Assignment Hong Kong. J. Dark
Assignment in Algeria. John Lee
Assignment in Andorra. M. MacKintosh
Assignment in Beirut. J. Stagg
Assignment in Brittany. H. MacInnes
Assignment in Guiana. G. H. Coxe
Assignment in Iraq. A. MacKinnon
Assignment in the Islands. J. Blair
Assignment in Tokyo. J. T. Elton
Assignment: Israel. N. Carter
Assignment K. H. Howard
Assignment K. L. Waller
Assignment--Karachi. E. S. Aarons

Assignment—Lili Lamaris. E. S. Aarons
Assignment London. R. C. Galway
Assignment—Lowlands. E. S. Aarons
Assignment—Madeleine. E. S. Aarons
Assignment Malta. R. C. Galway
Assignment—Maltese Maiden. E. S. Aarons
Assignment—Manchurian Doll. E. S. Aarons
Assignment—Mara Tirana. E. S. Aarons
Assignment—Moon Girl. E. S. Aarons
Assignment, Murder. Neill Graham
Assignment: Murder. D. Hamilton
Assignment New York. R. C. Galway
Assignment—Nuclear Nude. E. S. Aarons
Assignment—Palermo. E. S. Aarons
Assignment—Peking. E. S. Aarons
Assignment—Quayle Question. E. S. Aarons
Assignment—School for Spies. E. S. Aarons
Assignment Sea Bed. R. C. Galway
Assignment—Silver Scorpion. E. S. Aarons
Assignment—Sorrento Siren. E. S. Aarons
Assignment—Star Stealers. E. S. Aarons
Assignment—Stella Marni. E. S. Aarons
Assignment—Suicide. E. S. Aarons
Assignment—Sulu Sea. E. S. Aarons
Assignment—Sumatra. E. S. Aarons
Assignment Sydney. R. C. Galway
Assignment Tahiti. A. Gardner
Assignment—The Cairo Dancers. E. S. Aarons
Assignment—The Girl in the Gondola. E. S. Aarons
Assignment to Bahrein. P. Winston
Assignment to Death. C. L. Leonard
Assignment to Disaster. E. S. Aarons
Assignment to Santa Fe. Dan Morgan
Assignment to Vengeance. B. Cleeve
Assignment—Tokyo. E. S. Aarons
Assignment Tokyo. J. Dark
Assignment—Treason. E. S. Aarons
Assignment—White Rajah. E. S. Aarons
Assignment Without Glory. M. Spinelli
Assignment X. E. C. Schurmacher
Assignment—Zoraya. E. S. Aarons
Assisted by Lessinger. R. Essex
Assisted by Sadie. W. B. Hare
Assize of the Dying. E. Pargeter
Assurance Double Sure. J. Esteven
Astonished Guardsman. Surrey Smith
Astonishing Adventure of Jane Smith. P. Wentworth
Astounding Crime on Torrington Road. W. Gillette
Astounding Dr. Yell. L. A. Knight
Astrea. E. Southworth
Astrid Factor. D. Orgill
Astronaut. J. Baumgarten
Aswan Assignment. A. Sugar
Asylum. W. Johnston
At a Farthing's Rate. H. Gibbs
At a Venture. H. B. M. Watson
At Bay. Mrs. Alexander
At Bay. G. Greenfield
At Day. P. Philips
At Bertram's Hotel. A. Christie
At Dawn I Die. J. Corbett
At Dead of Night. N. Perrelli
At Death's Call. I. Stark
At Death's Door. L. Bruce
At Dusk All Cats Are Grey. J. Tickell
At Face Value. N. Carter
At Fault. H. Smart
At Friendly Point. G. F. Scott
At Large. E. W. Hornung
At Last, Mr. Tolliver. W. Wiegand
At Her Mercy. J. Payn
At Market Value. G. Allen
At Midnight and Other Stories. A. Cambridge
At Midnight's Chime. W. J. Newton
At Mystery's Threshold. N. Carter
At Night to Die. H. Hamilton
At Nine Bells. S. Emery
At 9:45. Owen Davis

At Odds with Scotland Yard. N. Carter
At One Fell Swoop. O. Mills
At One Fell Swoop. S. Palmer
At One-Thirty. I. Ostrander
At Sixty Miles Per Hour. J. Drummond
At Some Forgotten Door. D. M. Disney
At Ten Paces. C. G. Booth
At the Altar Steps. J. Middlemass
At the Back o' Beyond. R. Remnant
At the Bar. C. A. Collins
At the Blue Gates. R. Keverne
At the Call of Honour. A. W. Marchmont
At "The Cedars." A. Hocking
At the Court of the Maharaja. L. Tracy
At the End of a Road. C. Houghton
At the Foot of the Rainbow. J. B. Hendryx
At the Gai-Moulin. G. Simenon
At the Green Dragon. J. J. Farjeon
At the House of Dree. G. Gardiner
At the House of the Priest. J. Adye
At the Knife's Point. N. Carter
At the Point of a .38. B. Halliday
At the Shrine of the Buddha. W. M. Graydon
At the Sign of the Clove and Hoof. Z. Johnson
At the Sign of the Golden Horn. J. K. Leys
At the Sign of the Sword. W. LeQueux
At the Silver Butterfly. Roland Daniel
At the Tenth Clue. H. H. Stanners
At the Time Appointed. A. M. Barbour
At the Villa Rose. A. E. W. Mason
At the World's Mercy. P. Trent
At the World's Mercy. F. Warden
At Thompson's Ranch. N. Carter
At War with Society. J. M'Levy
At War with the Unknown. C. Frisbie
At What Cost, and Other Stories. H. Conway
Atavar, the Dream Dancer. A. B. Reeve
Athelstane Ford. A. Upward
Atlanta Deathwatch. R. Dennis
Atlantic City Murder Mystery. N. Goldsmith
Atlantic Fury. H. Innes
Atlantic Murder. F. H. Shaw
Atlantic Murders! E. T. Woodhall
Atom at Spithead. D. Divine
Atom-Busters. P. Graham
Atom of Doubt. B. George
Atomic Murder. L. Gribble
Atomic Submarine. A. Mars
Atoms and Evil. R. Bloch
Atomsk. Carmichael Smith
Attack Alarm. H. Innes
Attack on Vienna. Alan Nixon
Attack the Baron. A. Morton
Attending Truth. E. R. Punshon
Attention! Saturnin Dax. M. Cumberland
Attic Murder. S. Fowler
Attic Room. K. Wolffe
Attic Rope. D. Daniels
Attorney. Anonymous
Attorney. H. Q. Masur
Auber File. M. Home
Auctioned. H. Janson
Audacious Picaroon. J. Cassells
Audacity. B. A. Williams
Audit in Death. E. Norwood
Auditorium Affair. Hugh C. McDonald
Audrey Rose. F. De Felitta
August Incident. A. Dean
Aunt Beardie. J. Shearing
Aunt Ivy Diddit. E. G. Gless
Aunt Jeanne. G. Simenon
Aunt Miranda's Murder. J. N. Chance
Aunt Phipps. T. Gallon
Aunt Sunday Sees It Through. J. J. Farjeon
Aunt Sunday Takes Command. J. J. Farjeon

Aunt What's-Her-Name! W. B. Hare
Aupres de ma Blonde. N. Freeling
Aurelius Smith—Detective. R. T. M. Scott
Aurora Floyd. M. E. Braddon
Austin Friars. J. H. Riddell
Australian Bush Track. D. Hennessey
Author Bites the Dust. A. W. Upfield
Author in Distress. C. M. Wills
Author Unknown. C. Dane
Author's Choice. M. Kantor
Autobiography of a Blackguard. R. Paton
Autobiography of a Bottle of Bourbon. Old Sleuth
Autobiography of a French Detective. M. Canler
Autobiography of a London Detective. Waters
Autobiography of a Quack, and The Case of George Dedlow. S. W. Mitchell
Autobiography of an English Detective. Waters
Autobiography of an Italian Detective. Anonymous
Autopsy. J. R. Feegel
Autumn Accelerator. P. Leslie
Autumn of a Hunter. P. Stadley
Autumn Rose. Margery Lawrence
Ava Mining Syndicate. C. C. Lowis
Avalanche. G. Atherton
Avalanche. K. Boyle
Avenged on Society. H. F. Wood
Avenger. M. Blood
Avenger. R. Gar
Avenger. J. Goodwin
Avenger. Samuel Gordon
Avenger. H. Kane
Avenger. E. P. Oppenheim
Avenger. H. Rigsby
Avenger. D. Steele
Avenger. E. Wallace
Avenger of Blood. J. M. Cobban
Avenger Strikes. W. S. Masterman
Avenger Tapes. R. G. Stimson
Avengers. D. Enefer
Avengers. H. Hill
Avenging Brotherhood. I. Tattersall
Avenging Eagle. T. P. Hurley
Avenging Ikon. C. Barry
Avenging Kiss. C. Rae-Brown
Avenging Note. A. Sprissler
Avenging Nymph. H. Janson
Avenging of Ruthanna. Mrs. C. Kernahan
Avenging Parrot. Anne Austin
Avenging Picaroon. J. Cassells
Avenging Ray. Seamark
Avenging Saint. L. Charteris
Avenging Seven. L. H. Brooks
Avenging Twins. J. McCulley
Avenging Twins Collect. J. McCulley
Avenham Mystery. B. Bolt
Average Jones. S. H. Adams
Average Man. A. C. Fox-Davies
Averno. B. Mitford
Avery's Fortune. W. M. Green
Avila Gold. D. Westheimer
Avima Affair. N. Calmer
Awake and Die. R. Ames
Awake Deborah! E. Phillpotts
Awakening Dream. K. Cameron
Awakening of Theodore Wrenn. M. Crombie
Award of Justice. A. M. Barbour
Away Went the Little Fish. M. Bennett
Away with Murder. J. Pattinson
Awkward Lie. M. Innes
Awkward Marine. J. Spenser
Ax. E. McBain
Ax of Atlantis. L. Grimes
Axe for the Rani. R. Bond
Axe Is Laid. J. Mackworth
Axe to Grind. A. A. Fair
Axes of Hate. James Preston
Aynsley's Case. G. M. Fenn
Aztec Avenger. N. Carter
Azure Rose. R. W. Kauffman

Title Index

B

B as in Banshee. L. Treat
B14. R. K. Weekes
Babbington Case. N. Carter
Babcock Boys. D. Reid
Babe in the Woods. W. Ard
Babe Jardine. Stuart Martin
Babe with the Twistable Arm. Hampton Stone
Babes in the Woods. L. O'Donnell
Babes Up in Arms. K. T. McCall
Babiole, the Pretty Milliner. F. Du Boisgobey
Baboon's Paw. R. C. Armour
Baby Doll Murders. J. O. Causey
Baby, Don't Dare Squeal. H. Janson
Baby, Don't Get Rough. C. Wheatley
Baby Don't Love Hoodlums. M. Storm
Baby Don't Say Goodbye. M. Storm
Baby Face. M. Corrigan
Baby Face. D. Gray
Baby Grand and other stories. S. Aumonier
Baby in the Ash Can. S. Shane
Baby Merchants. L. O'Donnell
Baby Moll. S. Brackeen
Baby Moll. B. Sarto
Baby Sitter. R. Boyle
Baby-Snatcher. C. Kendall
Baby, the Rain Must Fall. H. Foote
"Baby" Wilkinson's V.C. and other stories. N. Newham-Davis
Baby, Your Type's Murder. M. Brody
Baby, You're Guilt-Edged. C. Brown
Babylon. G. Allen
Babysitter. John Fraser
Baccarat. H. Malot
Baccarat Club. J. L. Rickard
Bach Festival Murders. B. Bloch
Bachelor Flat Mystery. R. A. J. Walling
Bachelors Get Lonely. A. A. Fair
Bachelors of Broken Hill. A. W. Upfield
Bachelor's Widow. M. Dekobra
Back-Alley Blond. Griff
Back Bay Murders. R. Scarlett
Back Country. W. Fuller
Back Door to Death. R. Foley
Back from the Dead. E. Snell
Back from the Dead. A. Soutar
Back from the Grave. W. S. Masterman
Back from the Grave. J. K. Stafford
Back Home. I. S. Cobb
Back in Daylight. E. H. Clements
Back Number. E. Everett-Green
Back Room Girl. F. Durbridge
Back-Seat Murder. Herman Landon
Back to Africa. W. Westall
Back to Eden. A. Soutar
Back to Fire Mountain. R. Scowcroft
Back to Life. T. W. Speight
Back to Lilac Land. G. Thorne
Back to the Old Home. M. C. Hay
Back to the Wall. R. P. Hansen
Back to Victoria. J. J. Farjeon
Backfire. D. J. Marlowe
Backfire. E. Sherry
Background for Murder. Shelley Smith
Background to Danger. E. Ambler
Background to Death. J. W. Lee
Background to Murder, and other stories. T. S. Denham
Backing Winds. J. Bell
Backlash. P. Durst
Backlash. J. B. O'Sullivan
Backlash. V. Warren
Backlash. M. L. West
Backlash of Infamy. H. Janson
Backslider. G. Allen
Backstage Mystery. O. R. Cohen
Backup Men. Ross Thomas
Backwash. P. Malloch
Backwaters. M. S. Boyd
Backwoods Princess. H. Footner
Backwoods Teaser. G. Brewer
Backwoods Tramp. H. Whittington
Backyard. J. Femling
Bad Blonde. J. Webb

Bad Boy. S. D. Frances
Bad Boy. J. Thompson
Bad Companions. D. Lee
Bad Conscience. J. Roffman
Bad Day at Black Rock. M. Niall
Bad Day for a Black Brother. B. B. Johnson
Bad Die Young. Peter Chambers
Bad Dream. M. Gair
Bad Dream of Death. J. N. Chance
Bad End Valley. W. B. Bannerman
Bad for Business. R. Stout
Bad for the Baron. A. Morton
Bad Girl. H. Janson
Bad Girls. B. Clifton
Bad Investment. L. Cassels
Bad Lord Lockington. F. Warden
Bad-Luck Cutie. H. Spencer
Bad Man of Cairo. A. Parsons
Bad Men Make Good Wives. M. Hayes
Bad Neighbor Murder. C. M. Russell
Bad Night's Work. O. J. Currington
Bad Ronald. J. H. Vance
Bad Samaritan. A. Rider
Bad Seed. Maxwell Anderson
Bad Seed. W. March
Bad Step. M. Derby
Bad Summer. J. Appleby
Bad to Beat. H. Smart
Bad Trip. K. Roos
Baddington Horror. W. S. Masterman
Badge. B. Bolt
Badge for a Gunfighter. R. Wilkes-Hunter
Badge of Evil. W. Masterson
Badge of Honor. D. Barnes
Badge of Honor. D. Brennan
Badge of Infamy. P. Durst
Badge 373. M. Roote
Badger in the Dusk. N. Brent
Badger's Daughter. R. Crawford
Badmen on Halfaday Creek. J. B. Hendryx
Raffle Book. L. Wren
Baffled, But Not Beaten. N. Carter
Baffled Conspirators. W. E. Norris
Baffled Imposter. S. W. Hopkins
Baffled Oath. N. Carter
Baffling Quest. R. Dowling
Bag and Baggage. B. Capes
Bag of Diamonds. G. M. Fenn
Bagful of Bones. A. Kennington
Baghdad Defections. B. Keller
Bagman in Jewels. M. Pemberton
Bags of Blackmail. C. Litchfield
Bagshot Mystery. O. Gray
Bahamas Murder Case. L. Ford
Bail Jumper. R. J. C. Stead
"Bail Up!" H. Nisbet
Bailiff's Secret. G. H. Teed
Bainbridge Murder. C. Fitzsimmons
Bainbridge Mystery. G. T. Pratt
Bait. Lionel Black
Bait. M. Carroll
Bait. L. Martin
Bait. D. Uhnak
Bait for a Killer. G. Bagby
Bait for a Tiger. B. Veiller
Bait for Murder. K. M. Knight
Bait Money. Max Collins
Bait of Perjury. W. Savage
Baited Blonde. R. MacLean
Baiting the Trap. J. Middlemass
Baja Bandidos. L. Derrick
Baker Street. J. Coopersmith
Balance. W. D. Orcutt
Balance of Fear. H. Matheson
Balance of Fear. G. Osborne
Balaoo. G. Leroux
Balcony. F. Cowen
Balcony. D. C. Disney
Baldragon. J. B. Harris-Burland
Balefire. N. Tranter

Bales of Trouble. G. W. Wicking
Bali Ballet Murder. C. Conyn
Balkan Assignment. J. Poyer
Balkan Express. L. Ross
Balkan Saga. D. Weir
Balkan Spy. D. Betteridge
Ball of Fortune. C. E. Pearce
Ballad of Loving Jenny. C. Brown
Ballad of the Running Man. Shelley Smith
Ballarat. Eric Lambert
Balloon Man. C. Armstrong
Ballot Box Murders. J. S. Strange
Ballot Box Mystery. H. H. C. Gibbons
Ballycronin Mystery. H. M. Webster
Ballyho Bey. A. C. Gunter
Baltic Mystery. F. S. Webber
Baltimore Madame. H. Knowland
Bamboo. K. West
Bamboo Bay. G. Volk
Bamboo Blonde. D. B. Hughes
Bamboo Bomb. J. Dark
Bamboo Elephants. N. Thurley
Bamboo Girl. F. Lester
Bamboo Prison. H. Gibbs
Bamboo Screen. S. Harvester
Bamboo Terror. W. Ross
Bamboo Whistle. C. V. Frost
Banacek. Deane Romano
Banana Murders. Y. Smith
Banana Tourist. G. Simenon
Banbury Bog. P. A. Taylor
Bancaster Mystery. A. N. Hodges
Bancock Murder Case. A. B. Cunningham
Band of Mystery. M. O. Rolfe
Band Played Murder. E. Howie
Bandaged Face. Z. I. Ponder
Bandaged Nude. R. Finnegan
Bandar-Log Murder. C. Comstock
Bandbox. L. J. Vance
Bandersnatch. D. Lowden
Bandit. L. Charteris
Bandit of Syracuse. S. Cobb
Bandit Trust. M. Warrick
Bandits Aloft. T. Wallace
Bandit's Moon. N. MacKenzie
Bandits of the Air. N. Carter
Bandits of the Night. J. M. Walsh
Bang! Bang! G. Ade
Bang Bang Birds. A. Diment
Bang! Bang! You're Dead! June Drummond
Bang, You're Dead! H. Treece
Bangkok Murders. Reginald Campbell
Banishment of Jessop Blythe. J. Hatton
Bank Draft Puzzle. N. Carter
Bank Job. R. L. Pike
Bank Job. T. B. Reagan
Bank Manager. E. P. Oppenheim
Bank Note Plates. Lieut. Carlton
Bank Robber. G. Tippette
Bank Robbers. A. Griffiths
Bank Robbers. Old Sleuth
Bank-Robbers and the Detectives. A. Pinkerton
Bank Robbery. M. Ulrich
Bank Robbery Hostage. R. Wilkes-Hunter
Bank Shot. D. E. Westlake
Bank Tragedy. M. R. Hatch
Bank Vault Mystery. L. F. Booth
Bank with the Bamboo Door. D. Hitchens
Banker's Bones. M. Scherf
Banker's Daughter. G. W. M. Reynolds
Banker's Millions. Warren Miller
Banker's Trust. J. W. Bobin
Banker's Victim. O. Bradbury
Banking on Death. E. Lathen
Bannantyne Sapphires. F. Hird
Banner for Pegasus. J. Bonett
Bannerman Case. J. Lord
Banners of Blood. J. H. Hunter
Banners Yellow. J. E. Gordon
Bannon. A. Evans
Banquet Ceases. M. Fitt
Banshee's Warning, and Other Tales. J. H. Riddell
Banyon. W. Johnston

Baptist Ring. W. Chesney
Bar Sinister. K. G. Ballard
Bar Sinister. C. A. Collins
Bar Sinister. P. MacTyre
Bar Sinister. S. Rathbone
Barbara. M. E. Braddon
Barbara Heathcote's Trial. R. N. Carey
Barbara on Her Own. E. Wallace
Barbara's Rival. E. A. Young
Barbarous Coast. R. Macdonald
Barbary Freight. R. Burke
Barbary Hoard. J. Appleby
Barbary Kate. F. Hay
Barbed Wire. E. Everett-Green
Barbed Wire. M. Richmond
Barbed-Wire Hurdlers. P. Quinn
Barber of Littlewick. M. Drewe
Barber's Shop Crime. W. Edwards
Barber's Wife. C. Phillips
Barberton Intrigue. S. Truss
Barbouze. Alan Williams
Barca. L. Cameron
Barclay Place. R. Foley
Bardelow's Heir. Roy Vickers
Bardel's Murder. E. McGirr
Bare Bodkin. F. Gerard
Bare Trap. F. Kane
Barefoot Witch. M. Clare
Barely Seen. F. Kane
Bargain. M. Gilbert
Bargain for Death. Robert Martin
Bargain in Blood. Arthur MacLean
Bargain in Blood. D. Stanford
Bargain in Crime. N. Carter
Bargain in Souls. E. D. Pierson
Bargain with Death. H. Pentecost
Barge Girl. C. Clements
Barge of Haunted Lives. J. A. Tyson
Barker Case. G. Barrett
Barker's Drift. C. Cannell
Barking Clock. H. S. Keeler
Barking Dog Murder Case. E. C. Vivian
Barlow Casebook. Elwyn Jones
Barlow Comes to Judgment. Elwyn Jones
Barlow in Charge. Elwyn Jones
Barn Stormers. A. M. Williamson
Barnabas Collins. Marilyn Ross
Barnabas Collins and Quentin's Doom.
 Marilyn Ross
Barnabas Collins and the Gypsy Witch.
 Marilyn Ross
Barnabas Collins and the Mysterious
 Ghost. Marilyn Ross
Barnabas Collins vs. the Warlock.
 Marilyn Ross
Barnabas, Quentin and Dr. Jekyll's Son.
 Marilyn Ross
Barnabas, Quentin and the Avenging Ghost.
 Marilyn Ross
Barnabas, Quentin and the Body Snatchers.
 Marilyn Ross
Barnabas, Quentin and the Crystal Coffin.
 Marilyn Ross
Barnabas, Quentin and the Frightened
 Bride. Marilyn Ross
Barnabas, Quentin and the Grave Robbers.
 Marilyn Ross
Barnabas, Quentin and the Haunted Cave.
 Marilyn Ross
Barnabas, Quentin and the Hidden Tomb.
 Marilyn Ross
Barnabas, Quentin and the Mad Magician.
 Marilyn Ross
Barnabas, Quentin and the Magic Potion.
 Marilyn Ross
Barnabas, Quentin and the Mummy's Curse.
 Marilyn Ross
Barnabas, Quentin and the Nightmare
 Assassin. Marilyn Ross
Barnabas, Quentin and the Scorpio Curse.
 Marilyn Ross
Barnabas, Quentin and the Sea Ghost.
 Marilyn Ross
Barnabas, Quentin and the Serpent.
 Marilyn Ross
Barnabas, Quentin and the Vampire Beauty.
 Marilyn Ross
Barnabas, Quentin and the Witch's Curse.
 Marilyn Ross
Barney. W. Johnston
Baron Again. A. Morton
Baron and the Arrogant Artist. A. Morton
Baron and the Beggar. A. Morton
Baron and the Chinese Puzzle. A. Morton
Baron and the Missing Old Masters.
 A. Morton
Baron and the Mogul Swords. A. Morton
Baron and the Stolen Legacy. A. Morton
Baron and the Unfinished Portrait.
 A. Morton
Baron at Bay. A. Morton
Baron at Large. A. Morton
Baron Branches Out. A. Morton
Baron Comes Back. A. Morton
Baron Goes A-Buying. A. Morton
Baron Goes East. A. Morton
Baron Goes Fast. A. Morton
Baron in France. A. Morton
Baron Ixell, Crime Breaker. O. Schisgall
Baron--King Maker. A. Morton
Baron Montez of Panama and Paris.
 A. C. Gunter
Baron of Hong Kong. N. Daniels
Baron on Board. A. Morton
Baron Returns. A. Morton
Baron Sam. St. George Rathborne
Baron Sinister. J. Milton
Baron Trigault's Vengeance. E. Gaboriau
Baronet Rag-Picker. C. S. Coom
Baronet's Bride. M. A. Fleming
Baronet's Crime. J. B. Williams
Baronet's Wife. F. Warden
Baroni. A. Harris
Baron's Mission to Peking. N. Daniels
Baroque. L. J. Vance
Barotique Mystery. G. H. Coxe
Barracuda. R. Magowan
Barradine Detects. E. Jepson
Barrakee Mystery. A. W. Upfield
Barred from the West End. J. Hunter
Barrel Mystery. N. Carter
Barrel Mystery. W. J. Flynn
Barren Harvest. C. M. Nelson
Barren Heritage. L. R. Davis
Barren Honor. H. Wood
Barren Land Murders. L. Short
Barren Land Showdown. L. Short
Barren Title. T. W. Speight
Barrier. R. Maugham
Barrier Reef Mystery. A. Murray
Barrington Mystery. L. Brock
Barronwell Mystery. H. Leyford
Barrow Sinister. Elsie Lee
Bars of Gold. G. Ellinger
Bars of Steel. L. Noel
Bartenstein Case. J. S. Fletcher
Bartenstein Mystery. J. S. Fletcher
Bartered Honour. R. H. Sherard
Bartlett Mystery. L. Tracy
Barton Manor Mystery. Gwyn Evans
Barton Mystery. G. Goodchild
Barush Mystery. T. A. Plummer
Basement Room and other stories. G.
 Greene
Basil. W. Collins
Basil and Annette. B. L. Farjeon
Basilisk. H. P. Stephens
Basket of Summer Fruit. R. McCullough
Basle Express. M. Coles
Bass Derby Murder. K. M. Knight
Bastard Brigade. P. Leslie
Bastard Verdict. Winifred Duke
Bastion of the Damned. J. Cassells
Bat. M. R. Rinehart
Bat Flies Low. S. Rohmer
Bat of the Battery. Anonymous
Bat Out of Hell. F. Durbridge
Bat Staffel. R. J. Hogan
Bat that Flits. N. Collins
Bat-Wing. S. Rohmer
Bat Woman. C. Gibbons
Bateman Household. J. Payn
Bath Mysteries. E. R. Punshon
Bath of Acid. C. Franklin
Bathchair Mystery. A. Murray
Bathing Pool Mystery. A. Blair
Bathtub Murder. D. Lyon
Bathurst Complex. W. Martyn
Batman. B. Kane
Batman vs. the Fearsome Foursome.
 W. Lyon
Batman vs. Three Villains of Doom.
 W. Lyon
Bats Fly at Dusk. A. A. Fair
Bats Fly Up for Inspector Ghote.
 H. R. F. Keating
Bats in the Belfry. E. C. R. Lorac
Bats with Baby Faces. W. S. Moss
Battered Caravanserai. P. Capon
Battle for Inspector West. J. Creasey
Battle for the Cup. P. Gill
Battle for the Right. N. Carter
Battle Mask. D. Pendleton
Battle of Basinghall Street. E. P.
 Oppenheim
Battle of Giants. P. Trent
Battle of Hate. N. Buntline
Battle of Nerves. G. Simenon
Battle of the April Storm. L. Forrester
Battle of the Singing Men. G. Kersh
Battle of Wits. S. Campbell
Battle Road. S. Harvester
Battle Song. W. H. Baker
Battle Without Glory. R. C. Trown
Battling Barker. A. Soutar
Battling Prophet. A. W. Upfield
Battling Skyman. T. Wallace
Bauer Murder. S. C. Prescott
Bawlerout. F. Halsey
Baxter Family. A. Askew
Baxter Letters. D. Hitchens
Baxter's Second Death. I. Greig
Baxter's Son. P. Trent
Bay of Deception. S. Shelley
Bay of Seals. J. Wood
Bay of the Damned. W. Carrier
Bay Prowler. M. Barry
Baying Hound. A. West
Bazi Bazoum. C. Matthew
Be a Good Boy. J. Fleming
Be Absolute for Death. R. Chance
Be Careful How You Live. E. Lacy
Be Home by Eleven. A. Dean
Be Kind to the Killer. Henry Wade
Be My Ghost. R. Chapman
Be My Love. M. Richmond
Be My Victim. R. Dietrich
Be Shot for Sixpence. M. Gilbert
Be Silent, Love. F. Nichols
Be Still, My Love. J. Truesdell
Be Thou My Judge. J. Wood
Beach Girls. J. D. MacDonald
Beach House. V. Coffman
Beach of Atonement. A. W. Upfield
Beach of Skulls. A. West
Beach of Terror, and other stories.
 B. Crimshaw
Beach Patrol. K. Rogers
Beach Queen Blowout. P. Morgan
Beachcomber. A. Murray
Beachy Head Murder. A. Gask
Beacon Fires. M. Gerard
Beacon Hill Murders. R. Scarlett
Beacon in the Night. B. S. Ballinger
Beacons of Death. M. B. Dix
Beads of Silence. L. Bamburg
Beagle Scented Murder. F. Gruber
Beak of Death. L. Bennet-Thompson
Beam of Black Light. O. John
Beam of Malice. Alex Hamilton
Bear Island. Alistair MacLean
Bear Witness. J. Reach

Title Index

Beard the Lion. W. Manchester
Bearer Plot. O. Sela
Beast. E. C. Litsey
Beast in View. M. Millar
Beast-King Murders. R. Wallace
Beast Must Die. N. Blake
Beast of the City. J. Lait
Beast with Five Fingers. W. F. Harvey
Beast with the Red Hands. S. Stuart
Beast with Two Backs. N. Sligh
Beastmark the Spy. J. S. Clouston
Beasts of Brahm. M. Hansom
Beat Back the Tide. D. Hitchens
Beat Not the Bones. C. Jay
Beat on an Orange Drum. D. Reid
Beat the Devil. J. Helvick
Beaten at the Post. B. Delannoy
Beating the Nobblers. J. Fairfax-Blakeborough
Beatrice. E. Southworth
Beatrice and Benedick. H. Smart
Beatrice Foyle's Crime. F. Warden
Beatrix Randolph. J. Hawthorne
Beau Blackstone. R. Falkirk
Beau Revel. L. J. Vance
Beaufort Dossier. D. Mariner
Beaumaroy Home from the Wars. Anthony Hope
Beaumont Tradition. D. Daniels
Beaurand Mystery. H. Greville
Beautiful Alien. S. Hocking
Beautiful and Dead. R. MacRoss
Beautiful Birthday Cake. M. Scherf
Beautiful Blackmailer. Old Sleuth
Beautiful But Bad. R. Colby
Beautiful but Dangerous. T. W. Hanshew
Beautiful Crook. M. O'Nair
Beautiful Dead. H. Pentecost
Beautiful Derelict. C. Wells
Beautiful Devil. Detective Dunn
Beautiful Frame. W. Pearson
Beautiful Friend. R. Collier
Beautiful Fugitive. Old Sleuth
Beautiful Gunner. Norma Lee
Beautiful Jack, the Double-Edged Detective. Anonymous
Beautiful Mrs. Davenant. V. Tweedale
Beautiful Murder. J. Ingersol
Beautiful Savage. Mrs. C. Kernahan
Beautiful Schemer. D. T. Hughes
Beautiful Scourge. E. Gaboriau
Beautiful Stranger. Bernice Carey
Beautiful Suspect. H. Richards
Beautiful Trap. B. S. Ballinger
Beautiful White Devil. G. Boothby
Beautiful Woman's Sin. Hero Strong
Beauty--A Snare. Glint Green
Beauty and the Beat. H. Janson
Beauty and the Policeman and Other Stories. S. Horler
Beauty Doctor. F. Warden
Beauty for Inspector West. J. Creasey
Beauty in Distress. G. Warden
Beauty Is a Beast. K. M. Knight
Beauty Is Found in a Grave. D. Steel
Beauty Kill. R. Hawkes
Beauty-Killer. B. Fleming
Beauty Marks the Spot. K. Roos
Beauty-Mask Murder. V. B. Shore
Beauty-Mask Mystery. V. B. Shore
Beauty of the Family. F. Warden
Beauty Parlor Murder. G. Chester
Beauty Queen Killer. J. Creasey
Beauty Sleep. R. Darby
Beauty Spot. H. Mee
Beauty That Must Die. Barbara James
Beauty Vanishes. D. Brande
Beauty's Queen. M. Leighton
Because of Misella. A. W. Marchmont
Because of the Cats. N. Freeling
Because of the Woman. C. H. Bullivant
Becca's Child. W. D. Roberts
Beckoning. V. Coffman
Beckoning Door. M. Seeley
Beckoning Dream. E. Berckman
Beckoning Finger. H. Harding
Beckoning Hand and other stories. G. Allen

Beckoning Lady. M. Allingham
Beckoning Shadow. Denis Scott
Becky. H. Janson
Bed Disturbed. E. Ford
Bed of Ashes. D. Daniels
Bedelia. V. Caspray
Bedeviled. Libbie Block
Bedford Row Mystery. J. S. Fletcher
Bedroom Bang Bang. D. Davis
Bedroom Bolero. M. Avallone
Bedrooms Have Windows. A. A. Fair
Bedside Corpse. S. Friedman
Bee Sting Deal. G. Beare
Beech of the Boulevard. B. Sarto
Beechcourt Mystery. C. Strange
Beelfontaine. S. O'Brien
Beelzebub Business. G. Brandner
Beer for Psyche. D. Gardiner
Beetle. R. Marsh
Before I Die. G. Joseph
Before I Die. H. McCloy
Before I Die. M. L. Roby
Before I Die. L. White
Before I Wake. H. Debrett
Before I Wake. M. Echard
Before It's Too Late. L. Cameron
Before It's Too Late. Jay Stewart
Before Midnight. R. Stout
Before the Ball Was Over. A. Roudybush
Before the British Raj. A. Griffiths
Before the Cock Crowed. W. E. Hayes
Before the Crossing. S. Jameson
Before the Fact. F. Iles
Before the Storm. M. B. Lowndes
Before the Wind. E. F. Charles
Before the Wind. J. Laing
Beg Pardon, Sir! R. W. Kauffman
Beggar, and Other Stories. D. Newton
Beggar in Purple. A. Soutar
Beggar on Horseback. J. Payn
Beggars All. K. N. Burt
Beggar's Choice. H. C. Branson
Beggar's Choice. P. Wentworth
Beggar's Manor. R. M. Gilchrist
Begin, Murderer! D. Cory
Begin with a Gun. M. Cronin
Beginner's Luck. P. Somers.
Beginning of a Crime. Dorris Roberts
Beginning the Adventure. Augustus Muir
Beginning with a Bash. A. Tilton
Beginnings of Mr. P. J. Davenant. F. S. Hamilton
Begins with Murder. W. Collison
Begonia Walk. Gavin Holt
Begotten Murder. M. Carroll
Beguiling Shore. D. F. Gardiner
Begumbagh. Anonymous
Behind a Mask. L. M. Alcott
Behind a Mask. N. Carter
Behind a Mask. T. Douglas
Behind a Mask. J. Hatton
Behind a Throne. N. Carter
Behind Closed Doors. N. Carter
Behind Closed Doors. A. K. Green
Behind Locked Doors. E. M. Poate
Behind Locked Shutters. W. E. D. Ross
Behind Red Curtains. Mansfield Scott
Behind Shuttered Windows. A. Askew
Behind That Curtain. E. D. Biggers
Behind That Door. G. Goodchild
Behind That Mask. H. S. Keeler
Behind the Arras. Anthony Graham
Behind the Black Mask. N. Carter
Behind the Bolted Door? A. E. McFarlane
Behind the Bronze Door. W. LeQueux
Behind the Crimson Blind. Carter Dickson
Behind the Curtain. H. R. Addison
Behind the Curtain. M. Pemberton
Behind the Devil Screen. M. Keck
Behind the Door. E. J. Anders
Behind the Enemy. G. Marlowe

Behind the Evidence. L. Blackledge
Behind the Evidence. P. Reynolds
Behind the First Wall. P. Graham
Behind the Fog. H. H. Bashford
Behind the German Lines. W. LeQueux
Behind the Granite Gateway. W. S. King
Behind the Green Mask. R. Trevor
Behind the Head-Lines. W. Sutherland
Behind the Headlines. R. Chapman
Behind the Monocle. J. S. Fletcher
Behind the Panel. J. S. Fletcher
Behind the Picture. M. M. Bodkin
Behind the Purple Mask. J. H. Chase
Behind the Purple Veil. Marilyn Ross
Behind the Ranges. O. Binns
Behind the Scarlet Door. L. Cameron
Behind the Screen. D. Doubtfire
Behind the Throne. W. LeQueux
Behind the Veil. D. E. L. Patch
Behind the Veil. George R. Sims
Behind the Walls. W. M. Graydon
Behind the Wire Fence. L. Allan
Behind the Yellow Blind. R. A. J. Walling
Behold a Fair Woman. F. Duncan
Behold, Here's Poison! G. Heyer
Behold the Body! O. Cecil
Behold the City. R. W. Howe
Behold, the Druid Weeps. M. Rippon
Behold! The Executioner! E. Harding
Behold the Fire. M. Blankfort
Behold the Judge. J. Brophy
Behold This Woman. D. Goodis
Beholder. P. Freund
Beirut Incident. N. Carter
Belfry Murder. M. Dalton
Belgrade Case. C. Bradley
Belgrave Manor Crime. M. Dalton
Believe This...You'll Believe Anything. J. H. Chase
Believed Violent. J. H. Chase
Bell. D. Daniels
Bell, Book and Candleflame. I. S. Way
Bell in the Fog. J. S. Strange
Bell Is Answered. R. East
Bell of Death. Anthony Gilbert
Bell on Lonely. M. P. Hood
Bell Street Murders. S. Fowler
Bell Tower of Wyndspelle. A. Vandergriff
Bella. D. Eden
Bella Donna Was Poisoned. C. Brown
Bella on the Roof. H. Ford
Bellamy Case. J. Hay
Bellamy Trial. F. N. Hart
Belle. G. Simenon
Belle of Australia. W. H. Thomes
Belle of the Ballet. A. Applin
Belle of Toorak. E. W. Hornung
Belle Starr, the Bandit Queen. Anonymous
Belles and Ringers. H. Smart
Bellman and True. D. Lowden
Bellmer Mystery. B. A. Williams
Bellringer. L. Kamarck
Bells at Old Bailey. D. Bowers
Bells for the Dead. K. M. Knight
Bells of Bicetre. G. Simenon
Bells of Doom. D. Stuart
Bells of Old Bailey. D. Bowers
Bells of Palmdale, and Other Stories. W. Slater
Bells of Penraven. B. L. Farjeon
Bells of Widows Bay. M. Lynch
Bellwood. E. Ogilvie
Beloved Enemy. P. Allardyce
Beloved Enemy. M. K. Douglas
Beloved Enemy. A. Maybury
Beloved Enemy. M. Richmond
Beloved Lady. B. Jefferis
Beloved of Ishmael. V. M. Steele
Beloved Stranger. J. Blackmore
Beloved Traitor. E. Bond
Beloved Traitor. H. Janson
Below Bridge. R. Dowling
Below Suspicion. J. D. Carr
Below the Belt. David Hume

Below the Clock. J. V. Turner
Below the Dead-Line. S. Campbell
Below the Surface. E. K. Chatterton
Belrox Mystery. D. Stewart
Belt of Diamonds. B. Wayde
Belt of Suspicion. H. R. Wakefield
Beltane the Smith. J. Farnol
Belting Inheritance. J. Symons
Ben. G. A. Ralston
Ben Bradley's Puzzle. W. G. Forbes
Ben Bradley's Weirdest Case. W. G. Forbes
Ben Clough and Other Stories. W. Westall
Ben Gates Is Hot. R. Kyle
Ben Hassan's Secret. W. V. Cook
Ben on the Job. J. J. Farjeon
Ben Sees It Through. J. J. Farjeon
Beneath the Mask. F. A. M. Webster
Beneath the Passion Flower. G. R. Preedy
Beneath the Precipice. J. Ritson
Beneath the Sea. G. M. Fenn
Beneath the Wheels. F. E. M. Notley
Beneath the Veil. A. Sergeant
Beneath Your Very Boots. C. J. C. Hyne
Benefactors' Club. A. Abdullah
Benefit Performance. R. Sale
Benefits of Death. R. Jeffries
Benevent Treasure. P. Wentworth
Benevolent Blackmail. W. R. M. Churcher
Benevolent Blackmailer. T. Harknett
Benevolent Picaroon. J. Cassells
Bengal Fire. L. G. Blochman
Bengal Spider Plan. E. P. Thorne
Bengali Inheritance. O. Sela
Benighted. J. B. Priestley
Benjamin Butts Junr. Anonymous
Benjamin Seven. M. Kerr
Benny Muscles In. P. Rabe
Benny Went First. V. Kathrens
Benson Murder Case. S. S. Van Dine
Bent Copper. J. Ashford
Bent for Blackmail. G. Monro
Bent Man. A. Maling
Bent, Not Broken. G. M. Fenn
Bentinck's Tutor. J. Payn
Bentley's Conscience. P. Trent
Benton of the Royal Mounted. R. S. Kendall
Benwell Mystery. Hawkshaw
Berenice. E. P. Oppenheim
Berg. A. Quin
Berg Case. J. Bentley
Bergen Worth. W. Lloyd
Bergman's Blitz. T. Barling
Beria Papers. Alan Williams
Berkeley Street Mystery. M. R. Hatch
Berkshire Mystery. G. D. H. Cole
Berlin. N. Carter
Berlin at Midnight. R. Joseph
Berlin Couriers. J. McGovern
Berlin Ending. Howard Hunt
Berlin Epitaph. A. Winnington
Berlin Halt. A. Winnington
Berlin Indictment. E. Fischer
Berlin Memorandum. Adam Hall
Berlin Spy Trap. Geoffrey Davison
Bermuda Burial. C. D. King
Bermuda Calling. D. Garth
Bermuda Murder. V. Siller
Bernan Affair. J. Kessel
Bernard Treve's Boots. L. Clarke
Berry Goes to Monte Carlo. C. N. Williamson
Berry Green. E. H. Clements
Bertha's Secret. F. Du Boisgobey
Bertie Bland, the Detective. Old Sleuth
Beryl of the Biplane. W. LeQueux
Besides the Wench Is Dead. M. Erskine
Besieged. L. Cullinan
Bess of Bentley's. A. Askew
Bessy Rane. H. Wood
Bessy Wells. H. Wood
Best Detective Stories of Cyril Hare. C. Hare
Best Detective Stories of Roy Vickers. Roy Vickers
Best Dr. Poggioli Detective Stories. T. S. Stribling
Best Go First. F. O'Malley
Best Laid Plans. A. Hocking
Best-Laid Schemes. Mark Cross
Bessie Kitson. G. Norway
Best Man. H. MacGrath
Best Man to Die. R. Rendell
Best of Her Sex. F. Hume
Best of Husbands. J. Payn
Best of Mr. Fortune. H. C. Bailey
Best of Three. P. Trent
Best Short Stories of M. P. Shiel. M. P. Shiel
Best Stories of Peter Cheyney. P. Cheyney
Best Story Ever. J. S. Clouston
Best That Ever Did It. E. Lacy
Best Thinking Machine Detective Stories. J. Futrelle
Best Will Always Do. E. Clarke
Betencourt Five. S. F. Griffin
Beth Takes Charge. B. Stuart
Betray Me--If You Dare. P. Carlon
Betrayal. E. P. Oppenheim
Betrayal. A. E. Walter
Betrayal and other stories. H. Acton
Betrayal at Blackcrest. Beatrice Parker
Betrayal into Darkness. R. S. S. Hall
Betrayal of John Fordham. B. L. Farjeon
Betrayed. D. Essex
Betrayed!! C. M. Lindsay
Betrayed. J. Pendower
Betrayed. Dora Russell
Betrayers. D. Hamilton
Better Corpses. C. J. Daly
Better Dead. J. M. Barrie
Better Dead. J. Bonett
Better Luck Next Crime. M. Hervey
Better Off Dead. R. M. Laurenson
Better Off Dead. H. McCloy
Better Part of Valor. B. Heatter
Better Than a Kick in the Pants. J. MacLaren-Ross
Better Than Dying. R. Faherty
Better Than Weapons. L. Christie
Better to Eat You. C. Armstrong
Better Wed than Dead. H. Kane
Betty. G. Simenon
Between Darkness and Day. G. Merrick
Between Life and Death. F. Barrett
Between Midnight and Dawn. I. L. Cassilis
Between Murders. S. King
Between the Dark and the Daylight. R. Marsh
Between the Lines. B. Delannoy
Between the Tides. J. Templeton
Between Twelve and One. V. Loder
Between Us and Evil. C. M. Russell
Beverly. M. T. Walworth
Beware, My Love. Marilyn Ross
Beware of Johnny Washington. F. Durbridge
Beward of Midnight. J. Welcome
Beware of the Boquet. Joan Aiken
Beware of the Cat. Roger Sherman
Beware of the Dawn. K. Lindsay
Beware of the Dog! C. North
Beware of the Dog. B. Reynolds
Beware of the Dog. J. Varnam
Beware of the Trains. E. Crispin
Beware the Bog. M. Kingsbury
Beware the Crimson Cord. B. Edmunds
Beware the Curves. A. A. Fair
Beware the Hoot Owl. N. Rutledge
Beware the Kindly Stranger. Clarissa Ross
Beware the Lady. C. Woolrich
Beware the Lurking Scorpion. S. Milne
Beware the Night. J. Blackmore
Beware the Pale Horse. B. Benson
Beware! The Picaroon. J. Cassells
Beware the Shadows. J. Carrick
Beware the Young Stranger. E. Queen
Beware Your Neighbor. M. Burton
Bewitched. R. Gilmour
Bewitched. A. M. Williamson
Bewitching Grace. P. Maxwell
Beyond a Reasonable Doubt. C. W. Grafton
Beyond All Fear. F. A. M. Webster
Beyond Baker Street. M. Jaffee
Beyond Compare. C. Gibbon
Beyond Control. G. Leonard
Beyond Desire. R. Himmel
Beyond Dover. V. Gielgud
Beyond Mombasa. J. Hilton
Beyond Pursuit. N. Carter
Beyond Reasonable Doubt. R. Hull
Beyond Recall. Dorothy Fletcher
Beyond the Atlas. J. Trench
Beyond the Danube. R. Meade
Beyond the Dark. K. Abbey
Beyond the End. C. Boutelle
Beyond the Fourth Door. J. J. Deegan
Beyond the Frontier. F. A. M. Webster
Beyond the Frontiers. L. Cargill
Beyond the Law. E. Dalton
Beyond the Law. A. Murray
Beyond the Law. G. Warden
Beyond the Locked Door. L. Allan
Beyond the Night. C. Woolrich
Beyond the Outposts. J. B. Hendryx
Beyond the Skyline. R. Aitken
Beyond the Skyline. R. Hardinge
Beyond These Voices. M. E. Braddon
Beyond This Place. A. J. Cronin
Beyond This Point Are Monsters. M. Millar
Beyond Tolerance. Hank Hobson
Bianca. F. Stevenson
Bianca in Black. E. S. Rohmer
Bicycle Detective. Old Sleuth
Bicycle Highwayman. F. M. Bicknell
Bicycle Jim. Old Sleuth
Bid for a Coronet. A. M. Williamson
Bid for Beauty. H. Janson
Bid for Empire. A. Griffiths
Bid for Fortune. G. Boothby
Bid for Freedom. G. Boothby
Bid for Life. S. Campbell
Bid Me Discourse. M. C. Hay
Bid the Babe Bye-Bye. C. Brown
Bier for a Chaser. R. Foster
Bier for a Hussy. A. Holt
Big Apple. S. Myles
Big Bedroom. E. Ronns
Big Ben Alibi. N. Gordon
Big Ben Looks On! J. Guildford
Big Ben Strikes Eleven. D. Magarshack
Big Ben Struck Twelve. A. Wood
Big Bet. E. H. Heth
Big Bite. Gerry Travis
Big Bite. C. Williams
Big Black. S. Myles
Big Blackmail. Frank King
Big Blackout. D. Tracy
Big Blue Death. J. Milton
Big Bob. G. Simenon
Big Boodle. R. Sylvester
Big Boss. R. Gar
Big Bounce. E. Leonard
Big Bow Mystery. I. Zangwill
Big Boys. D. Leach
Big Boys Don't Cry. M. Corrigan
Big Brain. B. Gray
Big Brass Ring. D. Tracy
Big Brokers. I. Shulman
Big Bruiser. A. Eichler
Big Business Murder. G. D. H. Cole
Big Bust. E. Lacy
Big C. M. Cronin
Big Call. G. Ashe
Big Caper. L. White
Big Cat. C. Short
Big Chance. V. Scannell
Big Chill. B. Copper
Big Circus Mystery. H. King
Big City. J. G. Brandon
Big City Girl. C. Williams
Big Clock. K. Fearing
Big Cough. A. Saunders
Big Dano. R. Arana
Big Deal. E. Ellison

Big Deal. A. Evans
Big Dig. S. McGurk
Big Dive. K. F. Crossen
Big Dream. S. Fisher
Big Ear. S. Sterling
Big Easy. J. Conaway
Big Enough Wreath. W. Garner
Big Fall. T. B. Reagan
Big Fear. T. Durrant
Big Feeling. D. Karp
Big Fish. F. Beeding
Big Fish. R. Charles
Big Fish. R. Wills
Big Fix. A. Barker
Big Fix. M. Colton
Big Fix. Spike Gordon
Big Fix. E. Hunter
Big Fix. E. Jarvis
Big Fix. E. Lacy
Big Fix. R. L. Simon
Big Foot. E. Wallace
Big Four. A. Christie
Big Four. E. Wallace
Big Frame. J. K. Baxter
Big Frame. The Gordons
Big Frame. Sam Merwin
Big Gamble. G. H. Coxe
Big Game. M. Brand
Big Game. P. Quinn
Big Game. L. L. Stevenson
Big Gold Dream. C. Himes
Big Goodbye. Peter Chambers
Big Grab. J. Trinian
Big Greed. K. Giles
Big Guy. Wade Miller
Big H. H. Janson
Big H. Bryan Peters
Big Hand for the Corpse. G. Bagby
Big Haul. A. W. Sherring
Big Heart. J. G. Brandon
Big Heat. W. P. McGivern
Big Heist. H. C. Davis
Big House. J. Lait
Big Ivy. J. McCague
Big Job. J. Boland
Big Kidnap. A. Tack
Big Kill. M. Spillane
Big Killing. P. Malloch
Big Killing. N. Morland
Big Kiss-Off. D. Keene
Big Kiss-Off of 1944. A. Bergman
Big Knockover. D. Hammett
Big Loser. E. Kennedy
Big M. L. Powell
Big Make. G. Paul
Big Man. Edward Brown
Big Man. R. Marsten
Big Man, a Fast Man. B. Appel
Big Man in Saludas. F. Rosenwald
Big Midget Murders. C. Rice
Big Money. H. Q. Masur
Big Money-Box. A. La Bern
Big Morning Blues. Gordon M. Williams
Big Needle. S. Myles
Big Nick. P. Buranelli
Big Night. S. Ellin
Big Payoff. R. Novak
Big Phil's Kid. M. M. Parker
Big Picture. D. Whitelaw
Big Racket. Roland Daniel
Big Radium Mystery. M. E. Cooke
Big Red Sun. D. Larany
Big Red's Daughter. J. McPartland
Big Rumble. Wenzell Brown
Big Runaround. D. L. Teilhet
Big Score. C. Matthews
Big Secret Suzuki. J. P. Conty
Big Shot. Roland Daniel
Big Shot. F. Packard
Big Shot. D. Scanlon
Big Shot. L. Treat
Big Sin. J. Webb
Big Slam. J. Powers
Big Sleep. R. Chandler
Big Smear. W. H. Baker
Big Snatch. A. Ferguson
Big Snatch. H. Howard
Big Snatch. B. Shannon

Big Squeal. Roland Daniel
Big Squeeze. B. Arthur
Big Squeeze. M. Corrigan
Big Stake. R. Jocelyn
Big Stan. J. Monahan
Big Stash. R. Peters
Big Steal. W. H. Baker
Big Steal. E. Basinsky
Big Steal. P. Malloch
Big Steal. H. Seymour
Big Steal! J. T. Story
Big Still. Roderic Wilkinson
Big Story. M. L. West
Big, Strong Man! C. Edwards
Big Success. I. Gordon
Big Take. W. B. M. Ferguson
Big Tickle. M. Cronin
Big Tickle. J. Wainwright
Big Time. V. Scannell
Big Time Girl. R. Marlowe
Big-Time Racketeer. D. Linton
Big Timer. W. M. Duncan
Big-Timer. P. A. Toxall
Big Tomorrow. D. Bateson
Big Top Dame. N. Karta
Big Trail. C. Houghton
Big Twist. Hank Hobson
Big Water. M. Derby
Big Wind for Summer. G. Black
Big Woman. M. Colton
Bigamist. J. J. Chichester
Bigger They Are. J. Ditton
Bigger They Are. H. Luger
Bigger They Come. A. A. Fair
Biggest Holdup. J. F. Dinneen
Bijoux. F. Des Ligneris
Bike Bastards. G. Warren
Bikini Bombshell. B. McKnight
Bill Blunders Through. A. Webb
Bill for Damages. N. Easton
Bill for the Use of a Body. D. Wheatley
Bill Marshall, Turf Sleuth. E. Woodward
Billboard Madonna. E. Trevor
Billiard-Room Mystery. B. Flynn
Billie Finds the Answer. H. C. McNeile
Billikin Courier. T. C. Lewellen
Billion Dollar Body. J. Shallit
Billion Dollar Brain. L. Deighton
Billion Dollar Death. J. Nazel
Billion-Dollar Hold-Up. M. Calland
Billion Dollar Killing. P. E. Erdman
Billion Dollar Sure Thing. P. E. Erdman
Billionaire Mission. J. Rosenberger
Billy Binks, Hero, and Other Stories. G. Boothby
Billy Hamilton. A. C. Gunter
Billy Mischief, a Regular Trained Detective. Old Sleuth
Billy Preston. Old Sleuth
Billy Rags. T. Lewis
Billy, the Tramp. Old Sleuth
Billy's Bargain. E. Everett-Green
Biltmore Call. V. Siller
Bimbashi Baruk of Egypt. S. Rohmer
Bimini Run. Howard Hunt
Binary. J. Lange
Bind. S. Ellin
Binnacle Jack. Anonymous
Binnacle Jack. M. Mizzen
Biographs of Babylon. G. R. Sims
Birch Dene. W. Westall
Birchwood. J. Banville
Bird. T. Hinde
Bird Cage. E. O'Duffy
Bird-Cage. Kenneth O'Hara
Bird in a Guilt-Edged Cage. C. Brown
Bird in Last Year's Nest. S. Herron
Bird in the Chimney. D. Eden
Bird in the Hand. G. T. Root
Bird in the Hand. Lee Trench
Bird of Paradise. E. P. Oppenheim
Bird of Prey. V. Canning
Bird of Prey. M. Cumberland
Bird of Strange Plumage. J. L. Rickard

Bird Walking Weather. G. Bagby
Bird Watcher. J. A. Morris
Birdcage Murders. C. L. Westbie
Birds and other stories. D. Du Maurier
Birds in the Belfry. L. Payne
Bird's Nest. S. Jackson
Birds of a Bloodied Feather. R. Tate
Birds of a Feather. A. Spiller
Birds of a Feather Affair. M. Avallone
Birds of Ill Omen. K. M. Knight
Birds of Prey. M. E. Braddon
Birds of Prey. G. Bronson-Howard
Birds of Prey. A. C. Brown
Birds of Prey. N. Carter
Birds of Prey. I. Fairlie
Birds of the Night. Austin Moore
Birdwatcher. E. Gordon
Birdwatcher's Quarry. M. Coles
Birth of a Dark Soul. B. Cleeve
Birthday. E. L. Withers
Birthday, Deathday. H. Pentecost
Birthday Gifts and other stories. G. D. H. Cole
Birthday Murder. Lange Lewis
Birthday Murder. K. Sproul
Birthmark. C. Houghton
Bishop in Check. S. Rattray
Bishop Murder Case. S. S. Van Dine
Bishop Must Move. K. Bird
Bishop of Hell. M. Bowen
Bishop Pendle. F. Hume
Bishop's Amazement. D. C. Murray
Bishop's Bible. D. C. Murray
Bishop's Cap. J. L. Linklater
"Bishop's Cap" Murder. J. L. Linklater
Bishop's Crime. H. C. Bailey
Bishop's Emeralds. H. Townley
Bishop's Gambit. T. Cobb
Bishop's Move. L. Hiscott
Bishop's Palace. Jan Alexander
Bishop's Park Mystery. D. Dike
Bishop's Purse. C. Moffett
Bishop's Scapegoat. T. B. Clegg
Bishop's Secret. F. Hume
Bishop's Sword. N. Berrow
Bismarck Herrings. M. Torrie
Bit and Bridal. H. Smart
Bit of a Shunt Up the River. D. Cory
Bit of Human Nature. D. C. Murray
Bit of Red May. O. Dale
Bitch. G. Brewer
Bite. E. Corder
Bite of an Apple, and other stories. N. Carter
Bite of the Leech. W. A. MacKenzie
Bite the Hand. R. Fenisong
Biter. Jack Lang
Biting Fortune. W. Mills
Bits and Pieces. J. C. Masterman
Bits and Pieces. G. Robey
Bitten by the Tarantula. J. MacLaren-Ross
Bitter Autumn. C. D. Peel
Bitter Conquest. C. Blackstock
Bitter Enders. P. Leslie
Bitter Ending. A. Irving
Bitter Fortune. J. Boland
Bitter Harvest. W. Haggard
Bitter Honey. J. Blackmore
Bitter Honeycomb. June Scott
Bitter Is the Fruit. C. J. Collins
Bitter Is the Harvest. T. Craig
Bitter Is the Rind. H. Smart
Bitter Justice. S. Cowan
Bitter Lemon Mob. M. Urquhart
Bitter Love. J. Blackmore
Bitter Love. E. Woodward
Bitter Reason. F. Cowen
Bitter Reckoning. J. Payn
Bitter Rubies. J. Storm
Bitter Springs. Clifford King
Bitter Sweet Summer. O. Sinclair
Bitter Tea. G. Black
Bitter Test. J. Templeton
Bittermeads Mystery. E. R. Punshon
Bittern Point. V. MacFadyen
Bitters Wood. U. Nightingale

Black. E. Wallace
Black Abbot. E. Wallace
Black Abolitionist. J. F. Bradley
Black Account. D. Jordan
Black Ace. G. Dilnot
Black Agent. B. Flynn
Black Alibi. F. Vivian
Black Alibi. C. Woolrich
Black Alice. T. Demijohn
Black Amber. P. A. Whitney
Black Amulet. D. Tracy
Black and the Red. Elliot Paul
Black Angel. B. Kingsley
Black Angel. C. Woolrich
Black Arab. J. Halstead
Black Arab. Operator 1384
Black Arrows. F. Beeding
Black as He's Painted. N. Marsh
Black Asp. J. L. Hamilton
Black Attendant. H. McCutcheon
Black August. D. Wheatley
Black Aura. J. Sladek
Black Automatic. W. B. Mowery
Black Autumn. E. Evans
Black Bag. L. J. Vance
Black Ball. E. D. Pierson
Black Band. Anonymous
Black Band. M. E. Braddon
Black Bar. G. M. Fenn
Black Baroness. D. Wheatley
Black Bartlemy's Treasure. J. Farnol
Black Bat. A. Murray
Black Bat Rides the Sky. G. E. Rochester
Black Beadle. E. C. R. Lorac
Black Bean. Thormanby
Black Beret. P. Fry
Black Bird. Alexander Edwards
Black, Black Hearse. F. Freyer
Black Blood. G. M. Fenn
Black Blood. A. L. Martin
Black Book. G. Bronson-Howard
Black Bottle. R. S. L. Harding
Black Box. T. C. H. Jacobs
Black Box. E. P. Oppenheim
Black Box. M. P. Shiel
Black Box Murder. Anonymous
Black Bread. W. B. M. Ferguson
Black Buck. L. C. Hopkins
Black Bullets. Gavin Holt
Black Burying. H. Carstairs
Black Business. H. Smart
Black Butterfly. W. A. MacKenzie
Black Cabinet. P. Wentworth
Black Caesar. T. Strauss
Black Caesar's Clan. A. P. Terhune
Black Camel. E. D. Biggers
Black Camels. R. Johnston
Black Camels of Qashran. R. Johnston
Black Candle. C. Randell
Black Cap. Gwyn Evans
Black Cap for Murder. A. Spiller
Black Cap Murder. V. Gunn
Black Card. P. Brebner
Black Card. C. Lys
Black Cargo. W. M. Graydon
Black Carnation. F. Hume
Black Casket. L. Powell
Black Castle. J. J. Farjeon
Black Cat. R. St. Clair
Black Cat. L. Tracy
Black Cats Are Lucky. A. Fielding
Black Chalice. C. Goodall
Black Champagne. G. B. Mair
Black Chariots. K. Robeson
Black Chateau. G. E. Rochester
Black Chronicle. W. E. Hayes
Black Chrysanthemum. A. Murray
Black Circle. C. Baines
Black Circle. Mansfield Scott
Black Cloak Murders. C. Buchanan
Black Coat. Constance Little
Black Coffee. A. Christie
Black Company. W. B. M. Ferguson
Black Corridors. Constance Little
Black Cotton Gloves. P. Fry
Black Cripple. R. Keverne
Black Cross. J. M. Walsh
Black Curl. Constance Little

Black Curtain. F. H. Loughead
Black Curtain. C. Woolrich
Black Cypress. F. Crane
Black Dagger. E. S. Brooks
Black Dark Murders. R. O. Saber
Black Death. H. Adams
Black Death. N. Carter
Black Death. M. Dalton
Black Death. Anthony Gilbert
Black Death. M. McCracken
Black Death. K. Robeson
Black Death. T. H. Stone
Black Destiny. C. Rushton
Black Devil. T. C. H. Jacobs
Black Doctor and other tales of terror and mystery. A. C. Doyle
Black Doll. W. E. Hayes
Black Door. C. F. Adams
Black Door. V. Markham
Black Door. C. Wilcox
Black Dougal. D. Walker
Black Dragon. J. M. Walsh
Black Dream. Constance Little
Black Drop. H. Nisbet
Black Dudley Murder. M. Allingham
Black Eagle. Roland Daniel
Black Eagle. G. H. Teed
Black Eagle Mystery. G. Bonner
Black Eagles Are Flying. F. V. Morse
Black Edged. B. Flynn
Black Emperor. F. Gerard
Black Emperor. S. Jason
Black Emperor. G. H. Teed
Black Envelope. D. Frome
Black Exorcist. J. Nazel
Black Express. Constance Little
Black Eye. Constance Little
Black Eye Snapshot. B. Lebhar
Black-Eyed Stranger. C. Armstrong
Black Fame. J. C. Ellis
Black Fan. M. B. O'Reilly
Black Fear. J. Halstead
Black Feather. B. Atlee
Black Fedora. H. Luger
Black Fetish. D. T. Lindsay
Black Finger. D. Newton
Black Fire. L. Goldman
Black Flame. J. Halstead
Black Flamingo. V. Canning
Black Flemings. K. Norris
Black Fog. C. J. Dutton
Black for a Bride. J. Marie
Black for the Baron. A. Morton
Black Friday. D. Goodis
Black Gang. H. C. McNeile
Black Gangster. D. Goines
Black Gangster. D. Steele
Black Garden. C. Arnothy
Black Gardenia. Elliot Paul
Black General. A. Southcott
Black Ghost. J. M. Walsh
Black Ghost of the Highway. G. Linnell
Black Girl Lost. D. Goines
Black-Girl, White-Lady. A. Hyder
Black Glass City. J. Philips
Black Glove. J. G. Sarasin
Black Gloves. Constance Little
Black Goatee. Constance Little
Black Gold. G. Morton
Black Gold. A. P. Terhune
Black Gold Murders. J. B. Ethan
Black Gold of Malverde. R. L. Graves
Black Grandee. J. McCulley
Black Gull Rock. M. Gerard
Black Gunn. L. Pryce
Black Hammer. M. McCracken
Black Hand. W. C. Blakeman
Black Hand. A. B. Reeve
Black Hate. J. Halstead
Black Hawk. J. Reach
Black Hawk. G. E. Rochester
Black Hawthorn. J. S. Strange

Black Hazard. M. Reisner
Black-Headed Pins. Constance Little
Black Heart. M. E. Cooke
Black Heart. S. Horler
Black Hearts Murder. E. Queen
Black Heather. V. Coffman
Black Hercules. S. Jason
Black Highway. J. N. Chance
Black-Hill Murder Case. R. Hardinge
Black Hogan Strikes Again. P. Renwick
Black Honey. C. R. Gull
Black Honey. P. Saxon
Black Honeymoon. Constance Little
Black Horse Running. J. Wood
Black Horse Tavern. R. Danton
Black House. R. Bridges
Black House. Constance Little
Black House in Harley Street. J. S. Fletcher
Black Hunchback. G. Verner
Black Ice Score. R. Stark
Black Image. F. Hume
Black Inheritance. J. McEnery
Black Ink Mystery. Gareth H. Browning
Black Iris. Constance Little
Black Is Beautiful. B. B. Johnson
Black Is Black. J. Nazel
Black Is the Colour of My True Love's Heart. Ellis Peters
Black Is the Fashion for Dying. Jonathan Latimer
Black Italian. S. Jepson
Black Jess, the Outlaw. Old Sleuth
Black John of Halfaday Creek. J. B. Hendryx
Black Joke. J. M. Scott
Black Joker. I. Ostrander
Black Joss. J. G. Brandon
Black Key. M. S. Michel
Black Lace Blackmail. K. T. McCall
Black Lace Hangover. C. Brown
Black Lady. Constance Little
Black Lake. W. Magnay
Black Land, White Land. H. C. Bailey
Black Leather Barbarians. P. Stadley
Black Leather Case. M. Cronin
Black Leather Murders. D. Rutherford
Black Light. T. Howard
Black Light. G. Kinnell
Black Light. T. Mundy
Black Light. B. Reynolds
Black Limousine. W. W. Sayer
Black Lobster. D. Weir
Black Look. M. Butterworth
Black Lord. S. Jason
Black Mafia. P. Rabe
Black Magic. "Capstan"
Black Magic. T. S. King
Black Magician. R. T. M. Scott
Black Mail. D. M. Disney
Black Mamba. A. Broome
Black Man--White Maiden. G. R. Preedy
Black Man, White Man, Dead Man. M. J. Kingsley
Black Mantle. T. P. Prest
Black Maria, M.A. J. Slate
"Black Maria" Mystery. W. J. Bayfield
Black Market. Roland Daniel
Black Market. B. Newman
Black Market Murders. H. Keyworth
Black Market Murders. J. Van Dyke
Black Mask. J. Cournos
Black Mask. E. W. Hornung
Black Mask. A. L. Smith
Black Mass. F. Breton
Black Master. M. Grant
Black Master. S. Jason
Black Matador. A. West
Black Midnight. A. Lowing
Black Mirror. B. Benson
Black Mirror. Winifred Duke
Black Mitre. W. M. Duncan
Black Mole. G. E. Rochester
Black Money. R. Macdonald

Black Monk. Anonymous
Black Monk. T. P. Prest
Black Morning. A. Bocca
Black Moth. C. Runyon
Black Motor-Car. J. B. Harris-Burland
Black Mountain. R. Stout
Black Nail. A. Applin
Black Nat. J. Halstead
Black Night Murders. C. Wells
Black Octopus. G. E. Rochester
Black Onyx Ring. C. Robertson
Black Opal. L. Allan
Black Opal. J. L. Linklater
Black Opal Mine. A. Murray
Black Orchid. G. Goodchild
Black Orchid. E. Ronns
Black Orchid. H. Zore
Black Orchids. R. Stout
Black Out. A. O. Pollard
Black Out. D. Whitelaw
Black-Out Crime. G. Chester
Black-Out in Gretley. J. B. Priestley
Black-Out Murder. D. Whitelaw
Black-Out Murders. L. Grex
Black Owl. W. LeQueux
Black Panther. D. Barton
Black Parrot. H. Hervey
Black Parrot. O. Lethbridge
Black Patch. F. Hume
Black Path of Fear. C. Woolrich
Black Pavilion. Augustus Muir
Black Paw. Constance Little
Black Pawn. Bruce Norman
Black Pearl. V. Sardou
Black Pearl Murders. M. S. Buchanan
Black Pearl of Passion. D. Fay
Black Piano. Constance Little
Black Pigeon. Anne Austin
Black Plumes. M. Allingham
Black Police. A. J. Vogan
Black Prince. S. Jason
Black Rain. G. Simenon
Black Rat. T. A. Plummer
Black Raven. Roland Daniel
Black Reprieve. D. Sanderson
Black Ribbon Murders. T. A. Plummer
Black Robe. W. Collins
Black Robe. G. Morton
Black Room. C. Short
Black Room. Colin Wilson
Black Rose. G. Croudace
Black Rose Murder. P. McGuire
Black Royalty. A. Mills
Black Rustle. Constance Little
Black Sadhu. E. P. Thorne
Black Sambo Affair. V. Gielgud
Black Samurai. M. Olden
Black Satchel. H. S. Keeler
Black Scorpion. A. Shannon
Black Seven. C. Kendall
Black Shadow. P. Sebastian
Black Shadow. F. A. M. Webster
Black Shadows. G. M. Fenn
Black Sheep. S. P. Hyatt
Black Sheep. B. Spicer
Black Sheep. E. Woodward
Black Sheep. E. Yates
Black Sheep, White Lamb. D. S. Davis
Black Ship. P. Mandel
Black Shrike. I. Stuart
Black Shrouds. Constance Little
Black Shrouds the Bride. P. G. Larbalester
Black Silence. M. Leighton
Black Sister. D. Edgvist
Black Skull. G. Verner
Black Skull Murders. Carlton Ross
Black Sleeves. A. M. Williamson
Black Smith. Constance Little
Black Sombrero Mystery. H. Pink
Black Spectacles. J. D. Carr
Black Spider. Mark Cross
Black Spider. C. Dawe
Black Spider. S. P. B. Mais
Black Spiders. J. Creasey
Black Spot. K. Robeson
Black Spot. John Ross

Black Spot Mystery. A. Soutar
Black Stage. Anthony Gilbert
Black Stain. G. R. Sims
Black Stamp. Will Scott
Black Star. J. McCulley
Black Star Again. J. McCulley
Black Star's Campaign. J. McCulley
Black Star's Return. J. McCulley
Black Star's Revenge. J. McCulley
Black Stocking. Constance Little
Black Stone. G. F. Gibbs
Black Streak. W. M. Graydon
Black Sunday. Thomas Harris
Black Sunday. A. Kent
Black Sunset. E. P. Thorne
Black Sunshine. Dorothea Martin
Black Swan. Nancy Graham
Black Swan. W. Penmare
Black Swastika. J. G. Brandon
Black Tarn. P. W. Wilson
Black Templar. J. Halstead
Black Terrace. K. Kendall
Black Terror. C. Bishop
Black Terror. F. W. Irwin
Black Terror. J. K. Leys
Black Thumb. Constance Little
Black Tide Rising. L. P. Greene
Black Tortoise. F. Viller
Black Tower. P. D. James
Black Triangle. H. Somerville
Black Trinity. T. C. H. Jacobs
Black Troopers. J. N. Smith
Black Troopers and Other Stories. Anonymous
Black Turret. P. Wynnton
Black Unicorn. June Drummond
Black Valley Murders. A. Mallory
Black Vanguard. E. Atiyah
Black Velvet. C. B. Dignan
Black Vendetta. M. Gattzden
Black Venus Contract. P. Atlee
Black Vintage. M. Gerard
Black Vulture. G. Ashcroft
Black Watcher. A. Partridge
Black Weather. B. Roueche
Black Weever. R. Wills
Black Welcome. N. Fitzgerald
Black, White, and Brindled. E. Phillpotts
Black Widow. R. Harrison
Black Widow. P. Quentin
Black Widow. B. Tutton
Black Widow Weeps. C. Brown
Black Widower. P. Moyes
Black Widower. A. Riefe
Black Windmill. C. Egleton
Black Wings. M. Dalton
Black Wings Has My Angel. E. Chaze
Black Wolf Mystery. R. J. Diven
Blackadder. G. Croudace
Blackbird. R. Stark
Blackbird Sings of Murder. W. M. Duncan
Blackbirder. D. B. Hughes
Blackboard Jungle. E. Hunter
Blackdrop Hall. H. Carstairs
Blacker Than Murder. W. Woolfolk
Blackfingers. J. Cassells
Blackgable Inn. M. Eyre
Blackguard. P. Trent
Blackhall Ghosts. S. Tytler
Blackladies. E. Everett-Green
Blacklash. J. Brunner
Blacklight. B. Knox
Blackmail. Ruth Alexander
Blackmail. W. T. Call
Blackmail. V. Chute
Blackmail. J. Goodwin
Blackmail. H. I. Hancock
Blackmail. J. Ironside
Blackmail. R. Mounteney-Jephson
Blackmail. Mark Ross

Blackmail! F. M. White
Blackmail de Luxe. D. Whitelaw
Blackmail Gang. C. Bishop
Blackmail in Blankshire. C. A. Alington
Blackmail in Red. F. Grierson
Blackmail, Inc. R. Kyle
Blackmail Is Murder. Craig Cooper
Blackmailed. A. Applin
Blackmailed. W. LeQueux
Blackmailed Baronet. H. E. Hill
Blackmailed Refugee. A. Parsons
Blackmailer. G. Axelrod
Blackmailer. Roland Daniel
Blackmailer. R. C. Elliott
Blackmailer. R. Fenisong
Blackmailer. E. Klein
Blackmailer. J. Miles
Blackmailer. J. Oakley
Blackmailer. P. Trent
Blackmailer and the Blonde. Leslie Carroll
Blackmailers. H. Cecil
Blackmailers. E. Gaboriau
Blackmailers & Co. J. C. Ellis
Blackmailer's Bluff. N. Carter
Blackman's Wood. E. P. Oppenheim
Blackout. Constance Little
Blackout at Rehearsal. M. P. Rea
Blackout Mystery. J. Reach
Blackshirt. B. Graeme
Blackshirt Again. B. Graeme
Blackshirt at Large. R. Graeme
Blackshirt, Counter-Spy. B. Graeme
Blackshirt Finds Trouble. R. Graeme
Blackshirt Helps Himself. R. Graeme
Blackshirt in Peril. R. Graeme
Blackshirt Interferes. B. Graeme
Blackshirt Meets the Lady. R. Graeme
Blackshirt Mystery. W. M. Graydon
Blackshirt on the Spot. R. Graeme
Blackshirt Passes By. R. Graeme
Blackshirt Saves the Day. R. Graeme
Blackshirt Sees It Through. R. Graeme
Blackshirt Sets the Pace. R. Graeme
Blackshirt Stirs Things Up. R. Graeme
Blackshirt Strikes Back. B. Graeme
Blackshirt Takes a Hand. B. Graeme
Blackshirt Takes the Trail. R. Graeme
Blackshirt the Adventurer. B. Graeme
Blackshirt the Audacious. B. Graeme
Blackshirt Wins the Trick. R. Graeme
Blackstone. R. Falkirk
Blackstone and the Scourge of Europe. R. Falkirk
Blackstone's Fancy. R. Falkirk
Blackthorn. D. Daniels
Blackthorn House. J. Rhode
Blacktower. M. Lynch
Blackwell's Ghost. Angela Gray
Blackwood. J. Radcliffe
Blackwood Cult. T. A. Waters
Blade Is Bright. S. Horler
Blade of Castlemayne. A. Esler
Blade-o'-Grass. B. L. Farjeon
Blade of Light. D. Carpenter
"Blairmount?" Blinkhoolie
Blair's Attic. J. C. Lincoln
Blame the Baron. A. Morton
Blame the Dead. G. Lyall
Blanche. T. P. Prest
Blanche Coningham's Surrender. J. Middlemass
Blanche de Maletroit. A. E. W. Mason
Blanche Fury. J. Shearing
Blanche Heriot. T. P. Prest
Blanco Case. S. Horler
Bland Beginning. J. Symons
Blane Document. N. Rich
Blank Cheque. Richard Brown
Blank Cheque for Murder. O. Beeby
Blank Page. K. C. Constantine
Blank Wall. E. S. Holding
Blanket. A. A. Murray
Blanket. H. Stratton

B

Blast of Trumpets. G. Ashe
Blasted Acre. G. Ellinger
Blatchington Tangle. G. D. H. Cole
Blaze at Noon. M. Clare
Blaze of Roses. E. Trevor
Blazing Affair. M. Avallone
Blazing Garage Crime. A. Blair
Blazing Launch Murder. R. Hardinge
Blazing Star. Constance Rutherford
Blazing Trails. F. W. Hilton
Bleak House. C. Dickens
Bleak November. R. O'Grady
Bleak Strand. G. K. Hohn
Bled White. I. St. Clair
Bleeding Hooks. H. Rutland
Bleeding House. Hilda Lawrence
Bleeding Scissors. B. Fischer
Bleke, the Butler. W. LeQueux
Bless the Wasp. John Ross
Blessed Above Women. A. MacLeod
Blessing Way. T. Hillerman
Blessington Method, and other strange tales. S. Ellin
Bleston Mystery. R. M. Kennedy
Blight. J. Creasey
Blighted Heart. T. P. Prest
Blind Alley. G. Simenon
Blind Alley. B. Singer
Blind Alley. J. Warwick
Blind Allies. B. Kendrick
Blind Barber. J. D. Carr
Blind Bargain. T. B. Morris
Blind Beak. E. Dudley
Blind Beggar Murder. C. Ryland
Blind Beggar of Bethnal Green and Bessy. Anonymous
Blind Cartridges. W. C. MacDonald
Blind Cave. L. Katcher
Blind Chance. B. Kingsley
Blind Circle. M. Renard
Blind Corner. D. Yates
Blind Date. Leigh Howard
Blind Date for a Private Eye. B. Graeme
Blind Drifts. C. B. Clason
Blind Eyes. M. Peterson
Blind Frog. F. Grierson
Blind Fury. S. Gluck
Blind Gambit. J. Reach
Blind Geese. Winifred Duke
Blind Girl's Buff. E. Berckman
Blind Goddess. A. Train
Blind Justice. I. L. Cassilis
Blind Justice. H. B. Mathers
Blind Justice. B. Symons
Blind Lead. L. L. Lynch
Blind Love. W. Collins
Blind Man. R. W. Kauffman
Blind Man with a Pistol. C. Himes
Blind Man's Bluff. B. Kendrick
Blind Man's Bluff. R. Rodd
Blind Man's Buff. J. Futrelle
Blind Man's Buff. F. Lynde
Blind Man's Buff. A. M. Meadows
Blind Man's Buff. F. Ryerson
Blind Man's Buff. A. Wood
Blind Man's Daughter. N. Carter
Blind Man's Eyes. W. MacHarg
Blind Man's Garden. S. Troy
Blind Man's Mark. B. Palmer
Blind Man's Night. J. Esteven
Blind Man's Secret. C. Brisbane
Blind Marriage, and other stories. G. R. Sims
Blind Miller. C. A. Cookson
Blind Murder. M. Perelli
Blind Path. G. Simenon
Blind Policy. G. M. Fenn
Blind Quest. W. Dainton
Blind Reckoning. W. Mills
Blind Saw Murder. H. C. Huston
Blind Side. F. Clifford
Blind Side. N. Cromarty
Blind Side. P. Wentworth
Blind Spot. J. Creasey
Blind Spot. J. Harrington
Blind Terror. W. Hughes
Blind Villain. E. Berckman

Blindfold. L. Fletcher
Blindfold. F. Marryat
Blindfold. J. L. Rickard
Blindfold. P. Wentworth
Blindfold Mystery. N. Carter
Blindfolded. E. A. Walcott
Blinding Light. C. Collins
Blindman. E. C. Mayne
Blindman's Marriage. F. Warden
Blindness of Flynn. E. L. Long
Blinkey Morgan, the Detective's Foe. Hawkshaw
Blizzard. W. Woodward
Blockade Runners. W. M. Graydon
Blocked Trail. J. McCulley
Blonde. C. Brown
Blonde and Beautiful. R. Foster
Blonde and Johnny Malloy. B. Kerr
Blonde and the Boodle. J. T. Story
Blonde at Bay. M. Brody
Blonde, Bad and Beautiful. C. Brown
Blonde Baggage. M. Holland
Blonde Bait. E. Lacy
Blonde Bait. S. Marlowe
Blonde, Beautiful and--BLAM! C. Brown
Blonde Betrayer. J. Godey
Blonde Blackmail. B. Sanders
Blonde Body. M. Morgan
Blonde Bombshell. D. Foster
Blonde Countess. H. O. Yardley
Blonde Cried Murder. J. Creighton
Blonde Cried Murder. B. Halliday
Blonde Died Dancing. K. Roos
Blonde Died First. D. Chambers
Blonde Dynamite. A. Bocca
Blonde for Danger. B. Gray
Blonde for Danger. M. Perelli
Blonde for Murder. W. B. Gibson
Blonde Gangster. R. Sharp
Blonde Genius. J. T. Edson
Blonde Horror. B. Sarto
Blonde in Black. B. Benson
Blonde in Suite 14. S. Sterling
Blonde Is Dead. J. Dow
Blonde Lady. M. Leblanc
Blonde Madonna. H. D. Dearden
Blonde Murder Case. Roland Daniel
Blonde on a Broomstick. C. Brown
Blonde on Borrowed Time. B. X. Sanborn
Blonde on the Rocks. C. Brown
Blonde on the Spot. H. Janson
Blonde on the Street Corner. D. Goodis
Blonde Target. W. Wright
Blonde, the Gangster and the Private Eye. Dale Clark
Blonde Verdict. C. Brown
Blonde with the Deadly Past. M. Seeley
Blonde Without Escort. B. Perowne
Blonde Wore Black. Peter Chambers
Blondel Parva. J. Payn
Blondes Are My Trouble. Martin Brett
Blondes Are Skin Deep. L. Trimble
Blondes Die Young. Bill Peters
Blondes Don't Cry. M. Mace
Blondes End Up Dead. B. Winter
Blondes' Requiem. R. Marshall
Blondie Iscariot. E. Lustgarten
Blood. A. Morgan
Blood All Over. P. Todd
Blood and Blondes. B. Sarto
Blood and Caviare. M. Dekobra
Blood and Gold. R. Severn
Blood and Honey. G. G. Fickling
Blood and Judgment. M. Gilbert
Blood and Sun-Tan. T. C. H. Jacobs
Blood and Thirsty. F. Bonnamy
Blood and Thunder. H. Clevely
Blood and Water. P. De Polnay
Blood Bargain. Michael Bradley
Blood Bath. H. Janson
Blood Bath. B. Rossi
Blood Beast. D. Ballenger

Blood Bond. H. Curties
Blood Brother, Blood Brother. N. N. Peebles
Blood-Brotherhood. A. Murray
Blood Brotherhood. J. Van Der Zee
Blood Countess. K. Robeson
Blood Cries for Vengeance. H. Desmond
Blood Debt. S. Jason
Blood Eagle, and other mystery tales. P. H. Emerson
Blood Emerald. V. Blake
Blood Fix. D. Ballenger
Blood for Breakfast. D. Ballenger
Blood from a Stone. R. S. Wallis
Blood Hunt. A. O. Pollard
Blood in the Ashes. W. Wright
Blood in the Bank. N. Brent
Blood in Your Eye. R. P. Wilmot
Blood Is a Beggar. T. Kyd
Blood Is a Personal Thing. J. Moffatt
Blood Kin. B. A. Pauley
Blood, M'Lud. H. Carstairs
Blood Money. C. H. Bullivant
Blood Money. Max Collins
Blood Money. A. Drummond
Blood Money. J. Goodwin
Blood Money. D. Hammett
Blood Money. R. Lewis
Blood Money. F. J. Lowe
Blood Money. P. Malloch
Blood-Money. W. C. Morrow
Blood Money. T. B. Reagan
Blood Money. G. Seton
Blood Money, and other stories. C. Gibbon
Blood Moon. Jan Alexander
Blood Oath. B. Rossi
Blood of Angels. A. Barker
Blood of Buddha. Harold Ward
Blood of My Brother. C. H. Thames
Blood of Strawberries. H. Van Dyke
Blood of the North. J. B. Hendryx
Blood of the Vampire. F. Marryat
Blood of Vintage. T. Kyd
Blood on a Harvest Moon. D. Anthony
Blood on a Window's Cross. James Fraser
Blood on Baker Street. A. Boucher
Blood on Biscayne Bay. B. Halliday
Blood on Her Shoe. Medora Field
Blood on His Hands! M. Afford
Blood on Lake Louisa. B. Kendrick
Blood on My Rug. E. L. Cushing
Blood on My Shoes. Jean Leslie
Blood on Nassau's Moon. W. McCully
Blood on Pale Fingers. P. Malloch
Blood on the Beach. H. Holley
Blood on the Black Market. B. Halliday
Blood on the Blonde. G. Jackson
Blood on the Blotter. L. Marshall
Blood on the Boards. W. C. Gault
Blood on the Bosom Devine. T. Kyd
Blood on the Cat. N. Rutledge
Blood on the Common. A. Fuller
Blood on the Curb. J. T. Shaw
Blood on the Desert. P. Rabe
Blood on the Dining Room Floor. G. Stein
Blood on the Floor. W. S. Masterman
Blood on the Heather. S. Chalmers
Blood on the Ivy. H. Ellson
Blood on the Knight. L. Thayer
Blood on the Lake. R. Hobart
Blood on the Pavement. Neill Graham
Blood on the River. W. L. Heath
Blood on the Sand. F. Martin
Blood on the Shrine. J. G. Brenter
Blood on the Snow. N. MacKenzie
Blood on the Stars. B. Halliday
Blood on the Stars. N. Morland
Blood on the Stars. A. M. Stein
Blood on the Strip. L. Derrick
Blood on the Yukon Trail. J. B. Hendryx
Blood Pearls of Sulu. D. Del Mar
Blood Pit. M. Carrel

Blood Red. A. Morton
Blood-Red Badge. N. Carter
Blood Red Death. M. Bardon
Blood Red Leaf. W. M. Duncan
Blood Red Oscar. Elsie Lee
Blood Reign of the Dictator. C. Steele
Blood Relations. F. Stewart
Blood Relatives. E. McBain
Blood Ring. K. Robeson
Blood Risk. B. Coffey
Blood Royal. G. Allen
Blood Royal. D. Yates
Blood Ruby. Jan Alexander
Blood Running Cold. Jonathan Ross
Blood Runs Cold. R. Bloch
Blood Runs Cold. A. B. Cunningham
Blood Runs Cold. L. Eby
Blood Ship. N. Springer
Blood Sport. V. Cross
Blood Sport. D. Francis
Blood Stays Red. Austin Stone
Blood Tells. T. Armour
Blood Trail. W. H. Baker
Blood Transfusion Murders. M. Propper
Blood Upon the Snow. Hilda Lawrence
Blood Velvet. A. Kennington
Blood Vengeance. M. Carroll
Blood Vengeance. S. Jason
Blood White Rose. B. L. Farjeon
Blood Will Out. M. Carr
Blood Will Tell. G. Bagby
Blood Will Tell. N. Carter
Blood Will Tell. A. Christie
Blood Will Tell. M. Parker
Blood Will Tell. J. Potts
Bloodhound of the Law. G. S. Trevor
Bloodhounds Bay. W. S. Masterman
Bloodhound's Revenge. W. M. Graydon
Bloodhouse. K. Cook
Bloodline to Murder. E. McDowell
Bloodroots Manor. Claudette Nicole
Bloodshed in Bayswater. J. Rowland
Bloodstain. David Alexander
Bloodstained Bokhara. W. C. Gault
Bloodstained Toy. A. Campbell
Bloodstone. L. Benedict
Bloodstone Terror. N. Carter
Bloodwater. J. Crowe
Bloody Benders. R. H. Adleman
Bloody Bokhara. W. C. Gault
Bloody Chasm. J. W. De Forrest
Bloody Hand. M. Braun
Bloody Instructions. S. Woods
Bloody Jungle. D. Runyon
Bloody Mama. R. Thom
Bloody Marvelous. J. Rathbone
Bloody Medallion. R. Telfair
Bloody Monday Conspiracy. Ralph Hayes
Bloody Moonlight. F. Brown
'Bloody Murder.' S. C. Mason
Bloody Passage. J. Graham
Bloody Precinct. B. Douglas
Bloody Spur. C. Einstein
Bloody Success. M. Culpan
Bloody Sun at Noon. G. Beare
Bloody Sunrise. M. Spillane
Bloody Tower. J. Rhode
Bloody Vengeance. J. Ehrlich
Bloody Wig Murders. G. Bagby
Bloody with Spurring. C. Rushton
Bloody Wood. M. Innes
Bloomsbury Treasure. S. Kyle
Bloomsbury Wonder. T. Burke
Blotting Book. E. F. Benson
Blow-Down. L. G. Blochman
Blow for Vengeance. N. Carter
Blow Hot, Blow Cold. Gerald Butler
Blow Hot, Blow Cold. E. Queen
Blow of a Hammer and other stories. N. Carter
Blow Out My Torch. J. A. Howard
Blow Over the Heart. R. Machray
Blow the House Down. J. Blackburn
Blowtop. A. Schwartz
Bludgeon. Jim Ryan
Blue Bed. Glyn Jones
Blue Blood. A. Thynne

Blue Blood Flows East. D. Glinto
Blue Blood Runs Red. W. E. Johns
Blue Blood Will Out. T. Heald
Blue Bone. M. Woodhouse
Blue Bonnet. Augustus Muir
Blue Bucket Mystery. F. Grierson
Blue Buckle. W. H. Osborne
Blue Bungalow. W. LeQueux
Blue Car Mystery. N. S. Lincoln
Blue Circle. E. Jordan
Blue City. K. Millar
Blue Days and Fair. H. Gibbs
Blue Death. Michael Collins
Blue Devil Suite. D. Daniels
Blue Diamond. A. Askew
Blue Diamond. P. Costello
Blue Diamond. A. Haynes
Blue Diamond. R. W. Keene
Blue Diamond. Mrs. C. Kernahan
Blue Diamond. L. T. Meade
Blue Door. V. Starrett
Blue Dwarf. P. B. St. John
Blue Envelope. S. Kerr
Blue-Eyed Boy. C. Short
Blue-Eyed Gypsy. Janette Radcliffe
Blue-Eyed Manchu. A. Abdullah
Blue Eyes. J. Charyn
Blue Fire. P. A. Whitney
Blue Flames. H. Wales
Blue Flower Mystery. N. Cassera
Blue Geranium. D. Birkley
Blue Germ. M. Swayne
Blue Hand. M. E. Braddon
Blue Hand. E. Wallace
Blue Harpsichord. D. Keith
Blue Horse of Taxco. K. M. Knight
Blue Hour. J. Godey
Blue Ice. H. Innes
Blue Invective. J. C. Manning
Blue Jean Billy. C. W. Tyler
Blue John Diamond. E. R. Punshon
Blue Kimono Kill. W. J. Sheldon
Blue Knight. J. Wambaugh
Blue Lacquer Box. G. F. Worts
Blue Lamp. W. D. Pelley
Blue Lamp. T. Willis
Blue Lenses and other stories. D. Du Maurier
Blue Light. G. Stanley
Blue Lightning. G. Baxter
Blue Lights. A. Fredericks
Blue Line Murder. J. Moffatt
Blue Macaw. C. Edwards
Blue Mandarin. D. Lenton
Blue Mascara Tears. J. McKimmey
Blue Mask. J. Cassells
Blue Mask at Bay. A. Morton
Blue Mask Strikes Again. A. Morton
Blue Mask Victorious. A. Morton
Blue Mauritius. V. Warren
Blue Mirror. J. Turner
Blue Mist and Mystery. E. Everett-Green
Blue Mountains Murderer. F. P. Clune
Blue Movie Murders. E. Queen
Blue Murder. R. L. Bellem
Blue Murder. E. Hale
Blue Murder. B. Halliday
Blue Murder. H. Rutland
Blue Murder. E. Snell
Blue Octavo. J. Blackburn
Blue Orchid. H. Zore
Blue Parakeet Murders. R. P. Koehler
Blue Paroquet. E. Y. Miller
Blue Parrot. M. Dekobra
Blue Pavilion. W. Buchan
Blue Pete. L. Allan
Blue Pete: Detective. L. Allan
"Blue Peter." P. Trent
Blue Pheasant. J. Boswell
Blue Poppy. C. Baines
Blue Print for Execution. L. Parker
Blue Print Murders. J. G. Brandon

Blue Rajah Murder. H. MacGrath
Blue Ribbon. W. Irish
Blue Ridge Crime. W. Martyn
Blue Ridge Mystery. Caroline Martin
Blue Room. G. Simenon
Blue Rum. E. Souza
Blue Santo Murder Mystery. M. Armstrong
Blue Sash. O. Binns
Blue Scarab. D. G. Adee
Blue Scarab. R. A. Freeman
Blue Sea & Yellow Sun. R. Batchelor
Blue Shadow Mystery. J. H. Chase
Blue Silver. V. Bridges
Blue Spectacles. H. S. Keeler
Blue Spider. A. Mills
Blue Talisman. F. Hume
Blue Taper. Gimone Hall
Blue Taxi. A. W. Barrett
Blue Vase. Lady A. Scott
Blue Veil. F. Du Boisgobey
Blue Vesuvius. A. Wynne
Blue Wall. R. W. Child
Blue Water. C. H. Barker
Blue Water Murder. P. Atkey
Blue Wolf. L. Allan
Blueback. B. Knox
Bluebeard's Keys. Gwyn Evans
Bluebeard's Seventh Wife. W. Irish
Bluebeard's Wife. H. Desmond
Bluebolt One. P. McCutchan
Bluebottle. M. Urquhart
Bluefeather. L. Meynell
Blueprint for Destruction. M. K. Robertson
Blueprint for Larceny. P. Chester
Blueprint for Murder. R. Bax
Blueprint to Kill. K. Evans
Blueprints for a Blonde. M. Brody
Blues for a Black Sister. B. B. Johnson
Blues for My Baby. B. Shannon
Blues for the Prince. B. Spicer
Bluethorne. F. Y. McHugh
Bluff. H. Adams
Bluff! H. M. Paull
Bluffer's Luck. W. C. Tuttle
Bluffing of Gaston Leroux. W. Dinner
Blundell's Last Guest. A. P. Terhune
Blunderer. P. Highsmith
Blunt Instrument. G. Heyer
Blunted Sword. D. Divine
Blushing Monkey. R. McDougald
Board Stiff. Robert James
Boarding-House Mystery. E. S. Brooks
Boarding House Mystery. M. Osborne
Boat-House Riddle. J. J. Connington
Boat Race Murder. R. E. Swartwout
Boat Train Mystery. C. Barry
Bob Bridger, Detective. Anonymous
Bob Covington. A. C. Gunter
Bob Ford, the Slayer of Jesse James. W. B. Lawson
Bob Hits the Headlines. J. J. Farjeon
Bob Martin's Little Girl. D. C. Murray
Bob Younger's Fate. Anonymous
Bob Younger's Fate. E. S. Deane
Boden's Boy. T. Gallon
Bodies Are Dust. P. J. Wolfson
Bodies Are Where You Find Them. B. Halliday
Bodies Fetch Good Prices. B. Sarto
Bodies in a Bookshop. R. T. Campbell
Bodies in a Cupboard. H. Desmond
Bodies in Bedlam. R. S. Prather
Body. C. Brown
Body and Soul. A. Dare
Body at Busman's Hollow. F. Hurt
Body at Madman's Bend. A. W. Upfield
Body Beautiful. B. S. Ballinger
Body Behind the Bar. C. F. Gregg
Body Behind the Curtain. E. G. Cousins
Body Below. Howard Mason
Body Beneath a Mandarin Tree. F. Crane
Body Blow. K. Hopkins
Body Came Back. B. Halliday

Body Count. F. Scarpetta
Body Drank Coffee. N. Hill
Body Fell on Berlin. R. Lakin
Body for a Blonde. K. McLeod
Body for Bill. I. S. Shriber
Body for McHugh. J. Flynn
Body for Sale. R. Deming
Body for the Bride. G. Bagby
Body for the Widow. G. Warren
Body Found Stabbed. J. Cameron
Body Goes Round and Round. T. Du Bois
Body in Bedford Square. J. Frome
Body in My Arms. R. Stephenson
Body in the Barrage Balloon. C. Curzon
Body in the Basket. G. Bagby
Body in the Beck. J. Cannan
Body in the Bed. B. S. Ballinger
Body in the Bed. S. Sterling
Body in the Blue Room. S. Williams
Body in the Boathouse. J. Mack
Body in the Bonfire. C. Bush
Body in the Boot. V. Gunn
Body in the Boudoir. C. E. Vulliamy
Body in the Bridal Bed. R. Shattuck
Body in the Bungalow. J. Corbett
Body in the Bunker. H. Adams
Body in the Car. A. Hodges
Body in the Dawn. C. M. Wills
Body in the Drum Mystery. M. Hervey
Body in the Dumb River. G. Bellairs
Body in the Library. A. Christie
Body in the Pound. O. Martyn
Body in the Road. M. Dalton
Body in the Safe. C. F. Gregg
Body in the Safe. S. Kyle
Body in the Shaft. R. Francis Foster
Body in the Silo. R. A. Knox
Body in the Trawl. A. Glanville
Body in the Turl. D. Frome
Body in Velvet. F. Usher
Body Lies. E. J. Millward
Body Looks Familiar. R. Wormser
Body Lovers. M. Spillane
Body Made Alive. John Marsh
Body Missed the Boat. J. Iams
Body Next Door. E. K. Goldthwaite
Body of a Girl. M. Gilbert
Body of the Crime. L. Heller
Body on Mount Royal. D. Montrose
Body on Page One. D. Ames
Body on the Beach. S. Brackeen
Body on the Beach. J. Decrest
Body on the Beach. R. Hardinge
Body on the Beach. R. Wallace
Body on the Beam. Anthony Gilbert
Body on the Bench. D. B. Hughes
Body on the Bus. L. Hollingsworth
Body on the Floor. N. B. Mavity
Body on the Line. Mary Archer
Body on the Pavement. G. Meyrick
Body on the Sidewalk. Bernice Carey
Body Ran Home. M. Perelli
Body Rolled Downstairs. I. H. Irwin
Body Snatcher. R. L. Stevenson
Body Snatchers. C. Brooks
Body That Came by Post. G. W. Yates
Body That Wasn't Uncle. G. W. Yates
Body to Spare. M. Procter
Body Trade. Theodore Taylor
Body Unidentified. J. Rhode
Body Unknown. B. Graeme
Body Vanishes. V. Gunn
Body Was Lonely. B. Shannon
Body Was of No Account. J. C. Cooper
Body Was Quite Cold. R. G. Dean
Bodyguard Man. Philip Evans
Body's Name Was Jones. P. Jaye
Bogey Men. R. Bloch
Bogue's Fortune. J. Symons
Bogus Clew. N. Carter
Bogus Tourist-Agency. W. M. Graydon
Boheme Combination. R. Close
Bohemian Girls. F. Warden
Boiled Alive. B. Buckingham
Boka Lives! H. Calvin
Bold Buccaneer. Seafarer
Bold House Murders. Eugene Franklin
Bolero. M. Pflaum

Bolero Murders. M. Avallone
Bolo the Super-Spy. W. LeQueux
Bolt. P. R. Shore
Bolt from the Blue. Scott Graham
Bolthole. D. Craig
Bolts and Bars. F. C. V. Harcourt
Bolts from Blue Skies. N. Carter
Bomb for Atuna. B. Reade
Bomb Job. H. Kane
Bomb-Makers. W. LeQueux
Bomb-Shell. M. Leblanc
Bomb That Could Lip Read. D. Seaman
Bombers. P. Leslie
Bombay Mail. L. G. Blochman
Bombs Burst Once. G. Church
Bombs from the Murder Wolves. R. J. Hogan
Bombshell. C. Brown
Bombshell. G. G. Fickling
Bombshell. R. Raine
Bonanza Murder Case. C. H. Snow
Boncoeur Affair. H. Wickham
Bond Grayson Murdered! N. S. Bortner
Bond of Black. W. LeQueux
Bond of Hate. J. Carrick
Bond Street Murder. J. G. Brandon
Bond Street Raiders. J. G. Brandon
Bondage of Brandon. B. Hemyng
Bonded Dead. M. E. Chaber
Bonded Villain. N. Carter
Bone and a Hank of Hair. L. Bruce
Bone House. W. Butler
Bone Is Pointed. A. W. Upfield
Bone of the Dinosaur. G. D. H. Cole
Bonecrack. D. Francis
Bones. E. Wallace
Bones Don't Lie. C. T. Gardner
Bones in London. E. Wallace
Bones in the Barrow. J. Bell
Bones in the Brickfield. M. Burton
Bones in the Sand. K. Royce
Bones in the Wilderness. G. Bellairs
Bones of Contention. E. Candy
Bones of Contention. R. Foley
Bones of Contention. N. Gage
Bones of Napoleon. J. W. Bellah
Bones of the River. E. Wallace
Bonfire Murder. T. A. Plummer
Bonnie. H. Barron
Bonnie and Clyde. B. Hirschfeld
Bonus for Murder. J. G. Brandon
Bony and the Black Virgin. A. W. Upfield
Bony and the Kelly Gang. A. W. Upfield
Bony and the Mouse. A. W. Upfield
Bony and the White Savage. A. W. Upfield
Bony Buys a Woman. A. W. Upfield
Boodle. L. Charteris
Boogie Was a Gent. P. Lauben
Book for Banning. N. Easton
Book Her for Murder. M. Brody
Book of All Power. E. Wallace
Book of Bargains. V. O'Sullivan
Book of Master Crimes. M. Hervey
Book of Murder. F. I. Anderson
Book of Strange Sins. C. Kernahan
Book of the Crime. E. Daly
Book of the Dead. E. Daly
Book of the Lion. E. Daly
Book with the Orange Leaves. H. S. Keeler
Booked for Death. M. Cumberland
Bookmaker's Body. S. Stone
Bookmaker's Crime. A. Steffens Hardy
Books for the Baron. A. Morton
Bookshop Mystery. J. S. Childers
Boom-Time Gold. G. W. Wicking
Boomerang. A. Garve
Boomerang. B. Graeme
Boomerang. W. H. Osborne
Boomerang Clue. A. Christie
Boomerang Murder. F. Grierson
Boon Companions. June Drummond
Boondocks. D. Lowden
Boothroyd's Mill. E. C. Reed

Bootlaces for Bastion. R. Harrison
Bootlegger. V. Torrio
Bootlegger's Victim. R. C. Armour
Bootless Crime. T. W. Speight
Booty. D. Grant
Booty for a Babe. C. Brown
Border Line. W. S. Masterman
Border of Darkness. John Latimer
Border Scourge. B. Mitford
Border Town Girl. J. D. MacDonald
Borderlanders. J. Laing
Borderline. Vercors
Borderline Case. B. Williams
Borderline Cases. C. F. Adams
Borderline Murder. M. Amos
Borderlines. A. Madsen
Borders of Barbarism. Eric Williams
Bored to Death. M. Delving
Borgia Blade. F. Ryerson
Borgia Cabinet. J. S. Fletcher
Borgia Head Mystery. V. Gunn
Borgia Testament. N. Balchin
Bormann Brief. C. Egleton
Born Bad. Anonymous
Born Beautiful. Keith Campbell
Born Innocent. B. J. Hurwood
Born Loser. C. Brown
Born of the Son. G. Wagner
Born Reckless. M. Rogers
Born Survivor. J. K. Lucas
Born to Be Hanged. M. E. Chaber
Born to Be Hanged. P. McGuire
Born to Be Murdered. D. Allan
Born to Betray. M. V. Victor
Born to Command. Hero Strong
Born to Die. K. David
Born to Sin. H. L. Gates
Born to Win. M. Roote
Born Victim. H. Waugh
Borneo Patrol. R. Wilkes-Hunter
Bornless Keeper. P. B. Yuill
Boro Council Ramp. P. Urquhart
Borodino Mystery. M. L. Storer
Borough Council Murders. J. Austwick
Borough Treasurer. J. S. Fletcher
Borrow the Night. H. Nielsen
Borrowdale Tragedy. W. J. Dawson
Borrowed Alibi. L. Egan
Borrowed Alibi. M. Murphy
Borrowed Cottage. A. Campbell
Borrowed Crime. W. Irish
The Borrowed Liner. L. Clarke
Borrowed Shield. R. E. Enright
Borrowed Time. M. Shane
Borrower of the Night. Elizabeth Peters
Bosambo of the River. E. Wallace
Boss. J. W. McConaughy
Boss, and How He Came to Rule New York. Alfred Henry Lewis
Boss Man. R. B. Sparkia
Boss of Taroomba. E. W. Hornung
Boss of the Skeletons. W. B. M. Ferguson
Boston Avenger. M. Barry
Boston Belle Meets Murder. J. C. Lenehan
Boston Blackie. J. Boyle
Boston Blitz. D. Pendleton
Boston Bust Out. P. McCurtin
Boston Conspiracy. J. H. Robinson
Boston Crab. F. Usher
Botany Bay. John Lang
Both Sides of the Case. J. Prescot
Both Sides of the Veil. R. Marsh
Bottle. Anonymous
Bottle of Dust. A. Rutherford
Bottle Organ. R. Masson
Bottle with the Black Label. N. Carter
Bottle with the Green Wax Seal. H. S. Keeler
Bottles of Scented Sweets. M. J. Pemberton
Bottletop Affair. G. Cotler
Bottom Line. F. Knebel
Bottom of Suez. G. H. Teed
Bottom of the Bottle. G. Simenon

Bottom of the Matter. A. Burr
Bottom of the Well. F. U. Adams
Boudoir Murder. M. Propper
Boulevard. L. H. Brennan
Boulevard Mutes. N. Carter
Bound by a Spell. H. Conway
Bound to Die. Bill Turner
Bound to John Company. M. E. Braddon
Bound to Kill. J. Blackburn
Bound to Win. H. Smart
Bound Together. H. Conway
Bouquet of Clean Crimes and Neat Murders. H. Slesar
Bourbon Street. G. H. Otis
Bournewick Murders. L. Blow
Bout with the Mildew Gang. S. Fowler
Bow Street Terror. T. A. Waters
Bowerings' Breakwater. P. McCutchan
Bowery Birdie. B. Sarto
Bowery Murder. W. K. Smith
Bowling Green Murders. H. Woodward
Bowman at a Venture. H. Howard
Bowman on Broadway. H. Howard
Bowman Strikes Again. H. Howard
Bowman Touch. H. Howard
Bowmanville Break. S. Shelley
Bowsham Puzzle. J. Habberton
Bowstring Murders. Carr Dickson
Box. P. Rabe
Box for a Long Journey. E. E. Cameron
Box from Japan. H. S. Keeler
Box Hill Murder. J. S. Fletcher
Box of Doom. G. Verner
Box of Secrets. M. Crossley
Box Office Murders. F. W. Crofts
Box 100. F. Leonard
Box with Broken Seals. E. P. Oppenheim
Boxing Mystery. Gregory Wilson
Boxwood Maze. B. Plagemann
Boy at the Bank. A. Philips
Boy Behind the Gun. C. E. Blaney
Boy Detective. C. E. Blaney
Boy Detective. Old Sleuth
Boy Fugitive. Old Sleuth
Boy in the Pool. C. R. Bittle
Boy on a Chain. R. Parker
Boy on a Dolphin. D. Divine
Boy Scout's Craig Kennedy. A. B. Reeve
Boy Who Invented the Bubble Gum. P. Gallico
Boy with the Sling. J. Wade
Boy Without a Memory. J. W. Bobin
Boys of Red House. E. Everett-Green
Boys Will Be Boys. S. Raven
Brace for the Law. Marsden Richards
Brace of Rogues. N. Islay
Brackenroyds Inheritance. A. Quigley
Bracknell's Law. W. Hildick
Brad Dolan's Blonde Cargo. W. Fuller
Brad Dolan's Miami Manhunt. W. Fuller
Braddigan Murder. I. Ostrander
Bradford Business. Angus Ross
Brading Collection. P. Wentworth
Bradmoor Murder. M. D. Post
Braes of Yarrow. C. Gibbon
Brahmin Arrangement. A. Tully
Brain and Ten Fingers. G. Kersh
Brain Guy. B. Appel
Brain Master. V. Van Der Elst
Brain of Paul Menoloff. John Marsh
Brain Trust Murder. Diplomat
Brain Twister. M. Phillips
Brain-Waves and Death. W. Rich
Brains Trust for Murder. A. Spiller
Brainstorm. Reginald Campbell
Brainwashed. Martin Thomas
Bramble Bush. D. Duncan
Branch Bearers. G. Petrie
Branch for the Baron. A. Morton
Branches of Evil. M. J. Kingsley
Brand for the Burning. H. McCutcheon
Brand Image. H. Janson
Brand Inheritance. Dorothy Fletcher
Brand of Cain. G. Norway

Brand of Silence. Harrington Strong
Brand of Silence. F. M. White
Brand of the Beast. Michael Lewis
Brand of the Broad Arrow. A. Griffiths
Brand of the Crook. F. Ramsdale
Brand of the Werewolf. K. Robeson
Brand X. C. Brand
Branded. G. Biss
Branded Hand. M. O. Rolfe
Branded Prince. W. Chesney
Branded Spy. O. Merland
Branded Spy Murders. V. W. Mason
Branded Woman. Wade Miller
Brandon Case. J. J. Connington
Brandon Coyle's Wife. E. Southworth
Brandon in New York. V. Warren
Brandon Is Missing. D. Allan
Brandon Returns. V. Warren
Brandon Takes Over. V. Warren
Brandy for a Hero. W. O'Farrell
Brandy for the Parson. R. Foxall
Brandy on the Rocks. Maryl James
Brandy Pole. J. N. Chance
Brangwyn Mystery. D. C. Murray
Brannington's Leopard. F. Webb
Brant Adams, the Emperor of Detectives. Anonymous
Brass Bed. F. Flora
Brass Bound Book. J. Letton
Brass Bowl. L. J. Vance
Brass Chills. H. Pentecost
Brass Cupcake. J. D. MacDonald
Brass Go-Between. O. Bleeck
Brass Gong Tree. J. W. Bellah
Brass Halo. J. Webb
Brass Key. F. Swann
Brass Knocker. E. Rathbone
Brass Knuckle. L. Grex
Brass Knuckles. F. Gruber
Brass Monkey. H. Whittington
Brass Rainbow. Michael Collins
Brass Ring. L. Padgett
Brass Shroud. B. Cassiday
Brassbound. M. D. Bickel
Brat. G. Brewer
Brat Farrar. J. Tey
Brave, Bad Girls. T. B. Dewey
Brave Cannot Yield. I. MacKintosh
Brave Heart of Youth. K. Lindsay
Brave Interlude. G. Goodchild
Brave Little Woman. M. A. Denison
Bravo 9. W. B. Day
Bravo of London. E. Bramah
Braydon Mystery. E. Healey
Brazen. C. Brown
Brazen Bull. G. Kersh
Brazen Confession. C. F. Gregg
Brazen Head. L. A. Knight
Brazen Seductress. H. Janson
Brazen Tongue. G. Mitchell
Brazilian Sleigh Ride. R. L. Fish
Brazilian Stardust. M. McEvoy
Breach of Reason. E. H. John
Breach of Security. M. Penoyre
Breach of Trust. W. M. Graydon
Bread. E. McBain
Bread for the Dead. B. Carson
Bread of Deceit. M. B. Lowndes
Break. J. Giovanni
Break. B. Mather
Break for a Lovely. H. Janson
Break for Summer. L. Meynell
Break in the Circle. P. Loraine
Break in the Line. B. Mather
Break of Day. B. King
Break Out. W. McNeilly
Break the Toff. J. Creasey
Break-Through. P. Malloch
Breakaway. Lionel Black
Breakaway. E. Cannon
Breakdown. J. Boland
Breakdown. P. Marsh
Breakdown. James Preston
Breaker of Laws. W. P. Ridge
Breaker of Ships. F. Sleath
Breakers Ahead. A. M. Barbour
Breakfast for Three. Marguerite Bryant
Breakfast with a Corpse. M. Murray

Breakheart Pass. Alistair MacLean
Breaking Point. B. Copper
Breaking Point. D. Du Maurier
Breaking Point. A. A. Flint
Breaking Point. W. Hewlett
Breaking Point. L. Meynell
Breaking Strain. J. Masters
Breaking the Shackles. F. Barrett
Breaking the Shell. Joseph Norwood
Breakthrough. M. Urquhart
Breastplate for Aaron. S. Harvester
Breath of Murder. W. M. Duncan
Breath of Scandal. E. Balmer
Breath of Suspicion. H. Desmond
Breath of Suspicion. E. Ferrars
Breath of Suspicion. W. LeQueux
Breathe No More. C. Franklin
Breathe No More. M. Randolph
Breathe No More, My Lady. H. Bailey
Breathe No More, My Lady. E. Lacy
Breckenridge Enigma. L. Geoghegan
Bred in the Bone. J. Payn
Bred in the Bone. E. Phillpotts
Bred to Kill. Martin Thomas
Breed of the Beverleys. S. Horler
Breezy Frank. Old Sleuth
Bren Hardy Again. W. J. Elliott
Bren Hardy, Tough Dame. W. J. Elliott
Brenda. L. Zane
Brenda Gets Married. Roy Vickers
Brenda Yorke, and other tales. M. C. Hay
Brenda's Murder. T. Wells
"Brent"--of Bleak House. T. A. Plummer
Bressant. J. Hawthorne
Bressio. R. Sapir
Bretherton. W. F. Morris
Brethren of the Axe. J. Somers
Brethren of the Compass. J. M. Walsh
Breton Sisters. G. Simenon
Briar Patch. C. Blackstock
Briar Rose. C. N. Williamson
Briarcliff Manor. S. A. Salvato
Bribe Was Beautiful. C. Brown
Brickbats for Bastion. R. Harrison
Bricklayer's Arms. J. Rhode
Bricks upon Dust. P. Tabori
Bridal Bed Murders. A. E. Martin
Bridal Eve. E. Southworth
Bridal Path. N. Tranter
Bride Brings Death. Darby St. John
Bride by Candlelight. D. Eden
Bride Dined Alone. V. Kelsey
Bride for Arundel. Jan Daniels
Bride for Bombay. J. R. Warren
Bride for Hampton House. H. Waugh
Bride from the Bush. E. W. Hornung
Bride from the Desert. G. Allen
Bride from the Sea. G. Boothby
Bride in Black. A. Askew
Bride Laughed Once. M. K. Sanders
Bride of a Day. F. Du Boisgobey
Bride of a Moment. C. Wells
Bride of a Stranger. P. Maxwell
Bride of an Evening. E. Southworth
Bride of Cairngore. J. F. Webb
Bride of Chance. V. Blake
Bride of Darkness. Margery Lawrence
Bride of Death. N. Marsh
Bride of Death. M. Reisner
Bride of Death. K. Wolffe
Bride of Devil's Leap. S. Shulman
Bride of Donnybrook. L. Ames
Bride of Dutton Market. M. Leighton
Bride of Fu Manchu. S. Rohmer
Bride of Gaylord Hall. S. O'Brien
Bride of Infelice. A. L. Halstead
Bride of Lenore. C. Kavanaugh
Bride of Llewellyn. E. Southworth
Bride of Menace. A. Barron
Bride of Misfortune. V. Blake
Bride of Moat House. P. Curtis

Bride of Newgate. J. D. Carr
Bride of Pendorric. V. Holt
Bride of Raven Island. E. Orford
Bride of Tancred. D. Pearson
Bride of Terror. E. Bond
Bride of the Kalahari. F. H. Rose
Bride of the Shadows. L. M. Jansen
Bride of the Sun. G. Leroux
Bride of the Tomb. A. M. Miller
Bride of the Unliving. L. Churchill
Bride of the Wolf. W. E. Groves
Bride Regrets. M. Carleton
Bride That Got Away. S. Truss
Bride Wears Black. W. H. L. Crauford
Bride Wore Black. C. Woolrich
Bride Wore Weeds. H. Janson
Bridegroom. G. V. McFadden
Bride's Castle. P. W. Wilson
Bride's Fate. E. Southworth
Bride's Madness. A. Upward
Bride's Mirror. M. Turnbull
Brides of Bellenmore. A. Maybury
Brides of Doom. M. Richmond
Brides of Lucifer. M. Lynch
Brides of Mertonbridge Hall. H. C. McNeile
Brides of Solomon and other stories. G. Household
Bridge House. L. Crosby
Bridge of Asses. J. Gautier
Bridge of Fear. D. Eden
Bridge of Lions. H. Slesar
Bridge of Magpies. G. Jenkins
Bridge of Sand. F. Gruber
Bridge of Strange Music. J. Blackmore
Bridge of Wonder. Margery Lawrence
Bridge Players. C. R. Gull
Bridge That Went Nowhere. R. L. Fish
Bridge to the Moon. A. Maybury
Bridge to Vengeance. Winston Graham
Bridgeport Dagger. J. Milbrook
Brief Candle. A. Spiller
Brief Candles. F. Gaite
Brief Case of Murder. P. Laing
Brief for O'Leary, and two other episodes in his career. B. Graeme
Brief Return. M. G. Eberhart
Brief Tales from the Bench. H. Cecil
Brierfield Tragedy. R. F. Redd
Brig Jane May. F. Marlowe
Brigand. T. P. Prest
Brigand. E. Wallace
Brigand's Secret. W. M. Graydon
Briggs Investigates. D. MacDonald
Bright Adventure. G. Rose
Bright Angel. A. Wood
Bright as a Diamond. A. Allyson
Bright Blue Death. N. Carter
Bright Cantonese. A. Cordell
Bright Corner. J. B. Priestley
Bright Danger. H. M. Kahler
Bright Day. M. Hocking
Bright Deadly Summer. Barbara James
Bright Eyes of Danger. J. M. Scott
Bright Face of Danger. J. Fast
Bright Face of Danger. L. Meynell
Bright Green Waistcoat. P. Fry
Bright Lights. R. O. Chipperfield
Bright Like Blood. D. Rowden
Bright Morning. Rona Randall
Bright Nemesis. J. Gunther
Bright Orange for the Shroud. J. D. MacDonald
Bright Promise. J. Lukens
Bright Red Business Men. P. McCutchan
Bright Road to Fear. R. M. Stern
Bright Serpent. J. M. Fox
Bright Star of Danger. W. Chambers
Brighter Buccaneer. L. Charteris
Brighton Alibi. A. Mills
Brighton Beach Mystery. C. Kingston
Brighton Belle. A. La Bern
Brighton Belle and other stories. Francis King
Brighton Monster and others. G. Kersh
Brighton Murder Trial. B. Hamilton
Brighton Mystery. B. Hemyng
Brighton Rock. G. Greene

Brighton Tragedy. G. Boothby
Brimstone Bed. D. Keene
Bring Back Her Body. S. Brock
Bring 'Em Back Dead! David Hume
Bring Him Back Dead. D. Keene
Bring Me Another Corpse. P. Rabe
Bring Me Another Murder. W. Chambers
Bring Me My Bow. M. Moiseiwitsch
Bring the Bride a Shroud. D. B. Olsen
Brink. A. J. Rees
Brink of Disaster. G. Cullingford
Brink of Silence. G. M. Jay
Bristol Affair. H. Seymour
British Museum Mystery. W. Jardine
Brittle Thread. D. Hall
Britz of Headquarters. M. Barber
Brixham Manor Mystery. E. S. Brooks
Broad Highway. J. Farnol
Broadcast. J. Mackworth
Broadcast Murder. "Capstan"
Broadcast Murders. F. Smith
Broadcast Mystery. W. LeQueux
Broads Don't Scare Easy. H. Janson
Broadway Bab. J. McCulley
Broadway Bob, the Bounder Detective. Anonymous
Broadway Butterfly Murders. T. Bliss
Broadway Cross. N. Carter
Broadway Jungle. Norma Lee
Broadway Murders. E. J. Doherty
Broadway Murders. R. Wallace
Broadway Virgin. L. Bull
Brock. G. Kersh
Brocken Spectre. Karen Campbell
Brocklebank Riddle. H. Wales
Broke of Covenden. J. C. Snaith
Broken Alibi. T. C. H. Jacobs
Broken Angel. F. Mahannah
Broken Bars. N. Carter
Broken Blossoms. T. Burke
Broken Body. F. Mahannah
Broken Bond. N. Carter
Broken Bonds. H. Smart
Broken Boy. J. Blackburn
Broken Branch. Keith Campbell
Broken Circle. R. Goyne
Broken Circle. M. Saxton
Broken Doll. A. Kent
Broken Doll. J. Webb
Broken Engagement. E. Southworth
Broken Face Murders. D. L. Teilhet
Broken Faith. I. D. Hardy
Broken Fang. U. Key
Broken Fetter. J. K. Leys
Broken Glass. E. Kyle
Broken Heart. Mary Bennett
Broken Honeymoon. C. H. Bullivant
Broken Idol. A. Sergeant
Broken Jigsaw. P. Somers
Broken Key. M. L. Roby
Broken Knife. T. C. H. Jacobs
Broken Ladders. A. Soutar
Broken Law. J. B. Harris-Burland
Broken Marriage. S. Murray
Broken Memory. F. M. White
Broken Men. V. Gielgud
Broken Necks and other stories. B. Hecht
Broken Net. H. Bindloss
Broken O. C. Wells
Broken on Crime's Wheel. N. Carter
Broken Pen. J. K. Stafford
Broken Penny. J. Symons
Broken Pledges. E. Southworth
Broken Ramparts. J. Robb
Broken River. J. Hawkins
Broken Rosary. G. Johnson
Broken Seal. H. Hill
Broken Seal. Dora Russell
Broken Shield. B. Benson
Broken Sphinx. K. Kimbrough
Broken Stirrup-Leather. C. Granville
Broken Sword. M. Gerard

Broken Sword. A. Mills
Broken Tapestry. Rona Randall
Broken Thread. W. LeQueux
Broken Three. K. Detzer
Broken to Harness. E. Yates
Broken Toy. Arthur MacLean
Broken Trail. H. Bindloss
Broken Trail. N. Carter
Broken Trail. A. Murray
Broken Trust. T. A. Plummer
Broken Vase. R. Stout
Broken Vase Mystery. M. Plum
Broken Waters. F. Packard
Broken Way. P. Trent
Broken Window. E. Booth
Broker's End. L. F. Booth
Bronkurst Case. T. C. H. Jacobs
Bronsville Massacre. B. Toler
Bronze Bell. L. J. Vance
Bronze Buddha. C. L. Daniels
Bronze Claws. P. Kruger
Bronze Door. Augustus Muir
Bronze Face. W. LeQueux
Bronze Hand. C. Wells
Bronze Mermaid. P. Ernst
Bronze Perseus. S. B. Hough
Bronze Statue. G. W. M. Reynolds
Brood of Folly. M. Erskine
Brood of the Witch-Queen. S. Rohmer
Brooding House. A. Brennan
Brooding Lake. D. Eden
Brooding Mansion. P. Warren
Brooding Mist. Rose Dana
Brooding Wild. R. Cullum
Brookham Mystery. E. De Wil
Brooklands Mystery. W. B. Baldry
Brooklands Mystery. P. Urquhart
Brooklyn Angel. M. Hervey
Brooklyn Moll Shoots Bedmate. Griff
Brooklyn Murders. G. D. H. Cole
Broomstick. I. Karlova
Broomstick in the Hall. J. Blackmore
Broomsticks over Flaxborough. C. Watson
Brother Berserk. J. W. Hanson
Brother Cain. P. Capon
Brother Cain. S. Raven
Brother Death. J. Lodwick
Brother for Hugh. M. Coles
Brother of the Shadow. C. Praed
Brother Orchid. L. Brady
Brother Rat. N. Karta
Brother Rogue and Brother Saint. T. Gallon
Brother Sinister. C. Bramwell
Brother Spy. T. C. H. Jacobs
Brother Wolf. B. Reynolds
Brotherhood. L. J. Carlino
Brotherhood. P. Trent
Brotherhood. Alan Williams
Brotherhood of Death. N. Carter
Brotherhood of Death. G. Stanley
Brotherhood of Freedom. D. Stewart
Brotherhood of Satan. L. Q. Jones
Brotherhood of the Seven Kings. L. T. Meade
Brotherhood of Velvet. D. Karp
Brotherly Love. P. Trent
Brothers and Sisters Have I None. J. Usher
Brothers Brannigan. H. E. Helseth
Brothers in Arms. H. H. Kirst
Brothers in Blood. P. D. Ballard
Brothers in Law. H. Cecil
Brothers Keepers. A. Storey
Brothers Keepers. D. E. Westlake
Brothers of Benevolence. J. Cassells
Brothers of Judgment. W. M. Duncan
Brothers of Silence. F. Gruber
Brothers of the Chain. George Griffith
Brothers of the People. F. Whishaw
Brothers of the Thin Wire. F. Pitt
Brothers Rico. G. Simenon
Brothers Sackville. G. D. H. Cole
Brought in Dead. Harry Patterson

Title Index

Brought to Bay. N. Carter
Brought to Bay. J. M'Govan
Brought to Bay. M. Pereira
Brought to Bay. R. H. Savage
Brought to Light. E. R. Punshon
Brought to Light. T. W. Speight
Brought to the Mark. N. Carter
Brown Book. J. B. Harris-Burland
Brown Mask. P. Brebner
Brown Murder Case. Roland Daniel
Brown Paper Twice. C. Davy
Brown Portmanteau and other stories. Curtis Yorke
Brown Princess. M. V. Victor
Brown Suede Jacket. P. Fry
Browne Fights the Fifth Column. M. Poole
Browne Follows the Clue. M. Poole
Browne of the Secret Service. M. Poole
Browne's 450,000 Mystery. M. Poole
Browne's First Case. M. Poole
Brownie's Plot. T. Cobb
Browns of the Yard. A. Brock
Brownstone Gothic. E. Shenkin
Brownstone House. R. Foley
Brownsville Murders. B. S. Keirstead
Bruce Angelo. Anonymous
Bruce Angelo, the City Detective. Old Sleuth
Bruce Douglas, A Man of the People. R. A. Gunn
Brumblingham Hall. J. Blyth
Brunettes Are Dangerous. Roland Daniel
Brunettes Are No Better. S. Coburn
Brush Creek Murders. C. H. Snow
Brush of Death. J. Warren
Brush with Death. S. Pim
Brush with Fate. C. Dawe
Brussels Dossier. W. H. Baker
Brutal Kook. M. Avallone
Brutal Question. O. W. Bayer
Brutal Years. G. Ledig
Brute. G. Des Cars
Brute. F. A. Kummer
Brute. D. Newton
Brute in Brass. H. Whittington
Bubble Moon. R. Bridges
Bubble Reputation. P. C. Wren
Bubbles. M. Foster
Bubbles We Buy. A. Jones
Buccaneer in Spats. A. Abdullah
Buccaneer's Parrot. J. Courage
Buccaneer's Pride. B. Bolt
Buchanan of "The Press." S. Bent
Bucharest Ballerina Murders. V. W. Mason
Bucholz and the Detectives. A. Pinkerton
Bucket in a Well. H. Willett
Buckhorn Murder Case. C. H. Snow
Buckled Bag. M. R. Rinehart
Buckshot Range. W. C. Tuttle
Budapest Parade Murders. V. W. Mason
Budapest Tradeoff. R. Carroll
Buddha of Fleet Street. F. Grierson
Buddha's Secret. Roland Daniel
Buffalo Box. F. Gruber
Buffalo Hook. R. Butler
Bugged for Murder. E. Lacy
Bugles Blowing. N. Freeling
Build Me a Blonde. A. Rocco
Build My Gallows High. G. Homes
Build My Gallows High. R. B. Sparkia
Builders of Ships. M. Leighton
Building Estate Murder. P. Urquhart
Built for Trouble. H. Fray
Bull Moose. R. Cullum
Bulldog and Rats. M. Allain
Bulldog Breed. G. E. Rochester
Bulldog Drummond. H. C. McNeile
Bulldog Drummond and the Female of the Species. H. C. McNeile
Bulldog Drummond at Bay. H. C. McNeile
Bulldog Drummond Attacks. G. Fairlie
Bulldog Drummond Meets a Murderess. H. C. McNeile
Bulldog Drummond on Dartmoor. G. Fairlie
Bulldog Drummond Returns. H. C. McNeile
Bulldog Drummond Stands Fast. G. Fairlie
Bulldog Drummond Strikes Back. H. C. McNeile
Bulldog Drummond's Third Round. H. C. McNeile
Bulldog Has the Key. F. W. Bronson
Bulldog Murder. J. K. Tarpey
Bullet for a Beast. R. Simons
Bullet for a Blonde. P. Kruger
Bullet for Charles. H. Walter
Bullet for Cinderella. J. D. MacDonald
Bullet for Midas. N. Morland
Bullet for My Baby. C. Brown
Bullet for My Lady. B. Mara
Bullet for My Love. O. R. Cohen
Bullet for Pretty Boy. M. Avallone
Bullet for Rhino. C. Witting
Bullet for the Bride. J. Messmann
Bullet for the Countess. S. Horler
Bullet for Your Dreams. D. Von Elsner
Bullet in His Cap. Robert Fleming
Bullet in the Ballet. C. Brahms
Bullet in the Cornice. M. Beckett
Bullet Proof. R. Angel
Bullet Proof. A. Dean
Bullet Proof. F. Kane
Bullet-Proof Man. A. Riefe
Bullet-Proof Martyr. J. A. Howard
Bullets and Brown Eyes. M. Corrigan
Bullets Are Final. E. Kennedy
Bullets Are My Business. J. B. West
Bullets Are Trumps. D. Reid
Bullets Bite Deep. David Hume
Bullets for a Blonde. W. Oursler
Bullets for Brandon. V. Warren
Bullets for Breakfast. J. M. Walsh
Bullets for Snoopers. Griff
Bullets for the Bridegroom. D. Dodge
Bullets in the Bush. E. Norwood
Bullets Make Holes. J. Bentley
Bullets Speak Louder. R. Marlowe
Bullets to Baghdad. Philip Chambers
Bullion. M. Woodman
Bullion Mystery. N. Carter
Bullitt. R. L. Pike
Bullitzer Baby Case. J. Sword
Bull's Eye. M. Kennedy
Bulls Like Death. M. Fitt
Bulton's Revenge. H. C. McNeile
Bump and Grind Murders. C. Brown
Bump in the Night. C. Watson
Bunch of Crooks. Roland Daniel
Bundle for the Toff. J. Creasey
Bundle of Clews. N. Carter
Bungalow Crime. P. Urquhart
Bungalow Mystery. A. Haynes
Bungalow of Dead Birds. G. Varney
Bungalow on the Roof. A. Abdullah
Bungalow Tragedy. W. J. Bayfield
Bungalow Under the Lake. C. E. Pearce
Bunker at the 5th. M. Dods
Bunnies. J. Quirk
Bunny Lake Is Missing. E. Piper
Buns from the Gutter. N. Melides
Buoyed Cables. E. L. Long
Burden of Guilt. C. Brown
Burden of Guilt. I. Gordon
Burden of Isabel. J. M. Cobban
Burden of Proof. J. Ashford
Burden of Proof. J. Barlow
Burden of Proof. V. Canning
Burden of Proof. N. Carter
Burden of Proof. J. Truesdell
Burden's End. B. Lowry
Burden's Mission. H. Whittington
Burdock. A. L. Elsworthy
Burglar. D. Goodis
Burglar and the Lady. O. Harper
Burglar in Baulk. F. Martyn
Burglar of White Birches. W. M. Graydon
Burglar Who Moved Paradise. H. D. Ward
Burglar's Accomplice. Beechwood
Burglars' Club. H. A. Hering
Burglar's Fate and the Detectives. A. Pinkerton
Burglars in Bucks. G. D. H. Cole
Burglars Must Dine. E. P. Oppenheim
Burgle the Baron. A. Morton
Burgled Heart. G. Leroux
Burglings of Tutt. R. Andom
Burgomaster of Furnes. G. Simenon
Burgo's Romance. T. W. Speight
Burial in Portugal. Robert MacLeod
Burial of M. Bouvet. G. Simenon
Burial Service. P. McGuire
Buried for Pleasure. E. Crispin
Buried in the Past. E. Lemarchand
Buried Motive. B. Cassiday
Buried Once. M. Dalman
Buried Rubies. E. Jepson
Buried Secret. N. Carter
Burke's Law. Roger Fuller
Burleigh Murders. G. Morton
Burma Battle. G. Marlowe
Burma Ruby. J. S. Fletcher
Burmese Dagger. D. Stuart
Burn. N. Gant
Burn Forever. L. Ford
Burn, Killer, Burn. P. Crump
Burn, Witch, Burn! A. Merritt
Burned Evidence. W. Woodrow
Burned Man. C. Monig
Burned Man. B. Spicer
Burning Beacon. T. Charles
Burning Conscience. C. Kingston
Burning Court. J. D. Carr
Burning Eye. V. Canning
Burning Fuse. B. Benson
Burning Fuse. Jay Bernard
Burning Gold. F. L. Cary
Burning Is a Substitute for Loving. J. Melville
Burning Man. T. J. Kelly
Burning of Billy Toober. Jonathan Ross
Burning of Troy. M. Gair
Burning Question. C. Carnac
Burning Sappho. G. Baxt
Burning Secret. G. McDonell
Burning Shore. E. Trevor
Burning Sky. J. H. Roberts
Burnt Bones Mystery. M. Dalman
Burnt Caravan. B. Bolt
Burnt Earth. W. F. Fauley
Burn Million. J. Payn
Burnt Offering. R. Lockridge
Burnt Offerings. R. Marasco
Burnt-Out Case. G. Greene
Burnt Powder. A. P. Morris
Burqa. H. Campbell
Bury Her Deep. D. Macomber
Bury Him Among Kings. E. Trevor
Bury Him Darkly. J. Blackburn
Bury Him Darkly. Henry Wade
Bury Him Deeper. R. A. J. Walling
Bury in Haste. A. Eichler
Bury Me Deep. H. L. Ingham
Bury Me Deep. D. Linton
Bury Me Deep. H. Q. Masur
Bury Me in Gold Lame. S. Forbes
Bury Me in Lead. I. Goodwin
Bury Me Not. W. Francis
Bury Me Not at Sea. M. Eyre
Bury That Poker. G. M. Wilson
Bury the Guy! B. Shannon
Bury the Hatchet. Manning Long
Bury Their Dead. Alex Fraser
Bus Ran Late. G. M. Wilson
Bus Station Murders. L. Revell
Bus That Vanished. L. Groc
Bush Baby. M. Woodhouse
Bush King. P. Trent
Bush Mystery. J. Mackie
Bush Track. D. Hennessey
Bushfire. James Preston
Bushigrams. G. Boothby

Bushman. A. Crane
Bushman Who Came Back. A. W. Upfield
Bushmaster. B. Bolt
Bushranger of the Skies. A. W. Upfield
Bushrangers. W. H. Thomes
Business at Blanche Capel. B. Morgan
Business of Bodies. S. Forbes
Business of Loving. Godfrey Smith
Busman's Honeymoon. D. L. Sayers
Busy Body. E. Ferrars
Busy Body. D. E. Westlake
Busy Whisper. T. Cobb
But a Short Time to Live. R. Marshall
But Death Runs Faster. W. P. McGivern
But I Wouldn't Want to Die There. S. Forbes
But Ill He Lived. B. Jones
But Not for Love. I. Wilson
But Not for Me. E. Ronns
But Not Forgotten. R. Fenisong
But Not Yet Slain. B. Appel
But Once a Year. A. A. Thomson
But Soft--We Are Observed. H. Belloc
But the Doctor Died. C. Rice
But the Patient Died. J. G. Edwards
But the Patient Died. Fiona Sinclair
But We Are Exiles. E. Kyle
But We Didn't Get the Fox. R. Llewellyn
Butcher of Belgrade. N. Carter
Butcher of Bruton Street. A. Applin
Butcherknife Killings. S. Harkins
Butcher's Moon. R. Stark
Butcher's Wife. O. Cameron
Butler Died in Brooklyn. R. Fenisong
Buttercup Case. F. Crane
Butterflies in the Rain. A. Soutar
Butterfly. J. M. Cain
Butterfly. H. K. Webster
Butterfly Flood. J. Wyllie
Butterfly Murder. C. Andrews
Butterfly of Paris. L. H. Brennan
Butterfly on the Wheel. G. Thorne
Butterfly Picnic. Joan Aiken
Butterfly Plague. T. Findley
Butterfly Revolution. W. Butler
Butterfly Wings. M. Peterson
Butterscotch Prince. Richard Hall
Button, Button. M. Bramhall
Button, Button. H. Roth
Button in the Plate. V. Loder
Buy My Silence! Herman Landon
Buzzards Pick the Bones. Murray Thomas
Buzzard's Roost. G. E. Rochester
By a Hair's Breadth. H. Hill
By a Hair's Breadth. E. S. Tupper
By a Vanished Hand. A. Feeny
By Advice of Counsel. A. Train
By an Unseen Hand. N. Carter
By Birth a Lady. G. M. Fenn
By Bitter Experience. Scott Graham
By Blood Alone. F. Corey
By Breathless Ways. B. Bolt
By Candle-Light. G. Knevels
By Dawn's Early Light. H. Clement
By Demons Possessed. E. Grayson
By Fair Means. J. Middlemas
By Fair Means or Foul. V. Warren
By Fate's Caprice. T. W. Speight
By Force of Circumstances. Gordon Holmes
By Fortune's Whim. T. W. Speight
By Foul Means. H. Leyford
By Hand Unseen. A. W. Marchmont
By Her Own Hand. F. Bonham
By His Own Hand. M. Cronin
By Hook or by Crook. Anthony Gilbert
By Hook or By Crook. E. Lathen
By Hook or By Crook. R. A. J. Walling
By Hook or Crook. R. A. J. Walling
By Horror Haunted. C. Fremlin
By-Line for Murder. A. Garve
By Mead and Stream. C. Gibbon
By Misadventure. F. Barrett
By Misadventure. A. Brock
By Misadventure. R. J. Fletcher
By Night. R. Clay
By Night at Dinsmore. J. Esteven
By Order of the Brotherhood. Le Voleur
By Order of the Czar. J. Hatton
By Order of the Dead. W. V. Cook
By Order of the Five. H. Adams
By Order of the King. A. Askew
By Order of the King! W. M. Graydon
By Order of the Magistrate. W. P. Ridge
By Order of the Soviet. F. A. Symonds
By Order of the Tong. J. G. Brandon
By Papuan Waters. O. Binns
By-Pass Control. M. Spillane
By-Pass Murder. D. Frome
By Peak and Pass. F. A. M. Webster
By Persons Unknown. J. York
By Proxy. J. Payn
By Registered Post. J. Rhode
By Right Not Law. R. H. Sherard
By Right of Sword. A. W. Marchmont
By Royal Command. D. Yates
By Saturday. S. Fowler
By Snare of Love. A. W. Marchmont
By Some Person Unknown. P. Barrington
By Telegraph. J. M. Cobban
By That Sin. B. Malim
By the Gate of the Sea. D. C. Murray
By the North Door. M. E. Atkins
By the Pricking of My Thumbs. A. Christie
By the Skin of His Teeth. R. C. Armour
By the Terms of the Will. W. M. Graydon
By the Watchman's Clock. L. Ford
By the World Condemned. John Marsh
By Their Deeds. A. Peters
By Third Degree. H. S. Keeler
By Way of Confession. R. Gore-Browne
By-Ways of Braithe. F. Powell
By Whose Hand? B. Baskerville
By Whose Hand. F. Crisp
By Whose Hand? R. Hardinge
By Whose Hand? Louise Rice
By Whose Hand? B. Symons
By Whose Hand? E. S. Tupper
By Wit of Woman. A. W. Marchmont
Bye, Baby Bunting. D. Keene
Bye, Bye, Baby! J. H. Bond
Bye-Bye, Blackbeard! N. Mapple

C

CAB-Intersec. D. Walker
CC and Company. M. Roote
C.I.D. T. Mundy
C.I.D. of Dexter Drake. E. Barker
C.I.D. Room. P. Alding
C.O.D. N. S. Lincoln
"C.Q." A. Train
C.V.C. Murders. K. Williams
Cab Driver's Secret. N. Carter
Cab No. 44. Richard F. Foster
Cab of the Sleeping Horse. J. R. Scott
Cabana Murders. J. Y. Dane
Cabaret. L. H. Brennan
Cabaret Crime. F. Grierson
Cabaret Crime. G. H. Teed
Cabbages and Crime. A. Nash
Cabbages and Kings. O. Henry
Cabin of Fear. D. Hitchens
Cabin Nineteen. M. Richmond
Cabinda Affair. M. Head
Cabine de Luxe. E.L. Long
Cabinet Minister Resigns. A. Duncan
Cabinet Minister's Wife and other stories. G. R. Sims
Cabinet Secret. G. Boothby
Cable-Car. June Drummond
Cable from Kabul. N. Tranter
Cable-Man. W. Chesney
Cactus. C. Chadwick
Cactus Shroud. C. Thomas
Cad Metti, the Female Detective. Old Sleuth
Cadaver of Gideon Wyck. A. Laing
Cade. J. H. Chase
Cade's County. A. Lawrence
Caesar Dies. T. Mundy
Cafe in Montparnasse. A. Mills
Cage. S. Horler
Cage Five Is Going to Break. E. R. Johnson
Cage for the Nightingale. P. Paul
Cage of Corruption. Griff
Cage of Darkness. R. Masson
Cage of Fear. S. Seaton
Cage of Ice. D. Kyle
Cage of Shadows. A. Hill
Cage Until Tame. L. Henderson
Cage Without Bars. P. Barrington
Caged. C. R. Cooper
Caged! H. Hill
Caged. F. Nichols
Cahusac Mystery. K. Prichard
Cain '67. J. M. Simmel
Cain's Girl Friend. W. Grote
Cain's Hundred. E. L. Heyman
Cain's Woman. O. G. Benson
Cairo Communique. Robert Mason
Cairo Crisis. W. Martyn
Cairo Garter Murders. V. W. Mason
Cairo Intrigue. W. Manchester
Cairo Mafia. N. Carter
Cairo Ring. N. Sheraton
Cake for Caroline. G. M. Wilson
Cakes for Your Birthday. C. E. Vulliamy
Cakes to Kill. H. C. Beck
Calamity at Harwood. G. Bellairs
Calamity Comes of Age. G. Baxter
Calamity Comes to Flenton. C. Ashton
Calamity Conquest. B. Gray
Calamity Fair. Wade Miller
Calamity House. M. Billett
Calamity in Kent. J. Rowland
Calamity Town. E. Queen
Calcroft Case. E. J. Murray
Calculated Risk. R. Foley
Calculated Risk. J. Hayes
Calderwood. M. Heath
Caldwell Shadow. D. Daniels
Caleb, Who Is Hotter Than a $2 Pistol. S. Ashley
Caleb Williams. W. Godwin
Calendar. E. Wallace
Calendar of Crime. E. Queen
Calibre. I Shulman
Calibre .50. R. Sheckley
Calico Cat. C. M. Thompson
California Detective. Anonymous
California Hit. D. Pendleton
Calina. L. Gardner
Call a Hearse. J. Stagge
Call After Midnight. M. G. Eberhart
Call Back to Crime. P. Alding
Call-Box Murder. G. Barnett
Call-Box Mystery. J. Ironside
Call Conquest for Danger. B. Gray
Call Down the Sky. H. Lillie
Call for Blackshirt. R. Graeme
Call for Michael Shayne. B. Halliday
Call for Simon Shard. P. McCutchan
Call for Superintendent Flagg. J. Cassells
Call for the Baron. A. Morton
Call for the Dead. J. Le Carre
Call for the Saint. L. Charteris
Call from Austria. M. Albrand
Call from the Past, and other stories. L. Merrick
Call Girl Murders. J. G. Brandon
Call Girls for Murder. J. B. Ethan
Call Her Savage. J. Grecco
Call Him Early for the Murder. N. Morland
Call in Miss Hogg. A. Lee
Call in the Feds. "G-Man"
Call in the Night. N. Carter
Call in the Night. S. Howatch
"Call in the Yard." M. A. Clune
Call in the Yard. David Hume
Call It Accident. R. Foley
Call It Coincidence. F. Lockridge

Title Index

Call It Murder. G. Tracey
Call It Rhodesia. W. A. Ballinger
Call It Treason. G. Howe
Call McLean. G. Goodchild
Call Me Al. D. Linton
Call Me Captain. P. Stanton
Call Me Deadly. H. Braham
Call Me Duke. H. Grey
Call Me Killer. H. Whittington
Call Me Pandora. A. Dean
Call Me Shameless. B. Sarto
Call Me Sometime. R. Angel
Call Mr. Fortune. H. C. Bailey
Call of Death. T. S. King
Call of Glengarron. N. Buckingham
Call of the Blood. K. Kellow
Call of the Deep. I. Stark
Call of the Flesh. V. Coffman
Call of the North. J. Templeton
Call of the People. L. Clarke
Call of the World. C. H. Bullivant
Call Off the Corpse. J. Bentley
Call on Kuprin. M. Edelman
Call on the Phone. N. Carter
Call Out the Flying Squad! H. Holt
Call the Lady Indiscreet. P. Whelton
Call the Next Witness. P. Woodruff
Call the Toff. J. Creasey
Call the Witness. E. Sherry
Call the Yard! H. Clevely
Call the Yard. J. Mowbray
Call to Danger. C. Coram
Call to Die. C. Coram
Callaghan. P. Cheyney
Callaghan Meets His Fate. M. Chesney
Callaghan of Intelligence. M. Chesney
Callan. J. Mitchell
Callao Clue. R. Howes
Called Back. H. Conway
Called Back to Tsarland.
Called to Account. N. Carter
Called to Judgment. C. Stanton
Called to the Bar. B. Hemyng
Callers for Dr. Morelle. E. Dudley
Calling Alan Fraser. H. Desmond
Calling All Cars. H. Holt
Calling All Cars. E. Snell
Calling All Suspects. C. Wells
Calling Bulldog Drummond. G. Fairlie
Calling Dr. Kill. A. Sugar
Calling Lord Blackshirt. B. Graeme
Calling Mr. Callaghan. P. Cheyney
Calling Peter Grayleigh. C. Robertson
Calling Scotland Yard. H. Holt
Calling Whitehall 1212. H. Clevely
Calling Whitehall 1212. A. Parsons
Callingham's Girl. A. S. Roche
Calliope Reef. H. Rigsby
Calloused Eye. E. H. Loban
Calverston Story. Alan Thomas
Calypso. H. Slater
Calypso Murders. P. H. Mulholland
Cambodia. N. Carter
Cambodian Quest. R. J. Casey
Cambridge Murders. A. Broome
Cambridge Murders. D. Rees
Camden Ruby Murder. A. Bliss
Came the Dawn. R. Bax
Camel. L. Berners
Camelion's Dish. R. Pertwee
Camelot Caper. Elizabeth Peters
Camels Are Coming. W. E. Johns
Cameos. O. R. Cohen
Camera Clue. G. H. Coxe
Camera Fiend. E. W. Hornung
Cameron Castle. Marilyn Ross
Cameron Hill. M. Flavin
Cameron Hill. M. K. Simmons
Cameron Mystery. C. Talbot
Camerton Slope. R. F. Bishop
Camilla. P. Paul
Camouflage! E. W. Alais
Camouflage. L. Meynell
Camouflage Revolution. H. McKay
Camp. Gordon M. Williams
Camp-Meeting Murders. V. Randolph
Camp of Fear. L. H. Gordon
Camp 7 Last Stop. H. H. Kirst

Campaign Train. The Gordons
Campanile Murders. W. Chambers
Campbell's Kingdom. H. Innes
Campden Hill Mystery. Elliot Bailey
Campus Corpse. K. Hopkins
Campus Murders. E. Queen
Can a Mermaid Kill? T. B. Dewey
Can Death Be Sleep? H. Brinton
Can Ladies Kill? P. Cheyney
Canadian Bomber Contract. P. Atlee
Canadian Crisis. D. Pendleton
Canadian Kill. J. Nazel
Canal Mystery. J. Remenham
Canaries Also Sing. E. Allen
Canaries Sometimes Croak. J. Cooper
Canary Murder Case. S. S. Van Dine
Canary That Died. James Lewis
Canary Yellow. E. Cadell
Canceled Czech. Lawrence Block
Cancelled Accounts. H. Greene
Cancelled in Red. H. Pentecost
Cancelled Out. A. E. Redmond
Cancelled Score Mystery. Gret Lane
Cancelled Will. E. A. Dupuy
Candid Escort. T. B. Marle
Candid Impostor. G. H. Coxe
Candidate. R. Alonso
Candidate for a Coffin. J. G. Brandon
Candidate for a Coffin. Neill Graham
Candidate for Danger. E. Sherwood
Candidate for Hell. D. P. Neeley
Candidate for Lilies. R. East
Candidate for Murder. M. Post
Candidates for Glory. J. Fores
Candidates for Murder. A. Hocking
Candidates for Murder. Frank King
Candidate's Wife. V. Coffman
Candle. L. C. Hopkins
Candle at Midnight. F. Lynch
Candle for a Corpse. S. Sterling
Candle for the Dead. H. Marlowe
Candle-Holders. V. Gielgud
Candle in the Sun. D. Daniels
Candle in the Wind. M. Richardson
Candle of the Night. M. Clare
Candle of the Wicked. E. Balmer
Candle of the Wicked. Elizabeth Brown
Candlelight in Avalon. Augustus Muir
Candles Are All Out. N. Fitzgerald
Candles for the Dead. H. Carmichael
Candles in the Night. A. Carr
Candles in the Wood. A. Manners
Candleshoe. M. Innes
Candlestick with Seven Branches. M. Leblanc
Candy Kid. D. B. Hughes
Candy Killings. G. Stockwell
Candy Man. R. Cullum
Candyleg. O. Demaris
Candywine Development. John Morris
Cane-Patch Mystery. A. B. Cunningham
Canisbay Conspiracy. A. MacVicar
Cankerworm. G. M. Fenn
Cannibal. N. De Mille
Cannibal Heart. M. Millar
Cannibal Who Overate. H. Pentecost
Cannon Law. T. C. Paynter
Cannon, the Falling Blonde. P. Denver
Cannonball. J. Chamier
Canonbury House. G. W. M. Reynolds
Canon's Ward. J. Payn
Canterbury Kilgrims. J. N. Chance
Canterbury Mystery. J. S. Fletcher
Canter's Chase. Margaret Archer
Canto for a Gypsy. Martin Smith
Canvas Coffin. W. C. Gault
Canvas Dagger. H. Reilly
Canvas Jungle. Arthur MacLean
Cap Across the River. J. M. Scott
Cap and Gown for a Shroud. E. N. Gilla
Cap Colt, the Quaker Detective. C. Morris
Capac Legacy. S. Gianetta
Cape. M. Caidin
Cape Cod Mystery. P. A. Taylor

Cape Fear. J. D. MacDonald
Cape House. L. P. Shepherd
Cape Jasmine Murder. M. M. Mott
Cape of Shadows. H. Gibbs
Cape Town Affair. A. Scobie
Caper. T. B. Reagan
Caper of the Golden Bulls. W. P. McGivern
Caper Sauce. S. P. B. Mais
Capful o' Nails. D. C. Murray
Capillary Crime and other stories. F. D. Millet
Capital City Mystery. J. H. Wallis
Capital Crime. L. Ford
Capital Crime. A. Roudybush
Capital Murder. J. Z. Alner
Capital Punishment. Stuart Martin
Capital Punishment. Sutherland Scott
Capitol Hell. L. Derrick
Capitol Hill Affair. L. James
Capitol Offense. J. Davey
Caprice. J. Withers
Caprifoil. W. P. McGivern
Caprimulgus. W. F. Harvey
Capsule Mystery. E. C. Vivian
Captain Black. M. Pemberton
Captain Bowker. S. M. Parkman
Captain Bulldog Drummond. G. Fairlie
Captain Castle. C. Dawe
Captain Christine. Basil Carey
Captain Clew, the Flying Detective. Anonymous
Captain Crash. G. Goodchild
Captain Cut-Throat. J. D. Carr
Captain Dack. P. Meriton
Captain Firebrace. Seafarer
Captain Firebrace and the Java Queen. Seafarer
Captain Flynn. E. L. Long
Captain Flynn Ret'd. E. L. Long
Captain Flynn, Sheriff. E. L. Long
Captain Gardiner of the International Police. R. Allen
Captain Gault. W. H. Hodgson
Captain Kettle, Ambassador. C. J. C. Hyne
Captain Kettle, K.C.B. C. J. C. Hyne
Captain Kettle on the War-Path. C. J. C. Hyne
Captain Kettle's Bit. C. J. C. Hyne
Captain King Investigates. K. Trask
Captain Landon. R. H. Savage
Captain Lucifer. B. Bolt
Cap'n Luke, Filibuster. "Capstan"
Captain Marraday's Marriage. T. Cobb
Captain McBlaid of the Air Police. R. Walker
Captain Millett's Island. K. N. Burt
Captain Must Die. R. Colby
Captain Nice. W. Johnston
Captain of the Guard. C. Houghton
Captain of the Kansas. L. Tracy
Captain of the Polestar, and other stories. A. C. Doyle
Captain of the Vulture. M. E. Braddon
Captain Overboard. F. Andreas
Captain Rock's Pet. E. Southworth
Captain Samson, A.B. Gavin Douglas
Captain Sentimental and other stories. E. Jepson
Captain Shannon. C. Kernahan
Cap'n Sue. H. Footner
Captain Shannon. C. Kernahan
Captain Sinister. G. Goodchild
Captain Sparkle, Pirate. N. Carter
Captain Tatham of Tatham Island. E. Wallace
Captain Wardlaw's Kitbags. H. MacGrath
Captain's Curio. E. Phillpotts
Captain's House. M. K. Simmons
Captains of Souls. E. Wallace
Captains of the "Calabar." F. Knight

C

Captain's Pawn. A. Lowing
Captive in the Land. J. Aldridge
Captivator. A. York
Captive. N. Daniels
Captive. The Gordons
Captive. B. Kingsley
Captive Audience. Jessica Mann
Captive City. J. Appleby
Captive in the Land. J. Aldridge
Captive in the Night. D. Stokes
Captive Princess. R. H. Savage
Captive Years. D. Lee
Captives of Mora Island. V. Canning
Captors. J. Farris
Capture. W. Martyn
Capture of Paul Beck. M. M. Bodkin
Capture of the Paddy Ryan Gang of Burglars. L. A. Newcome
Captured by Cannibals. J. Hatton
Captured Cruiser. C. J. C. Hyne
Car Park Mystery. A. Parsons
Caracol Reef. M. Andrews
Carambola. D. Dodge
Caravan Adventure. J. J. Farjeon
Caravan Crime. G. Chester
Caravan Mystery. F. Hume
Caravan of Night. M. Erskine
Caravan to Vaccares. Alistair MacLean
Caravanners. J. Dering
Caravans by Night. H. Hervey
Carbon Monoxide. J. Street
Carbuncle Clue. F. Hume
Carcellini Emerald, with other tales. Mrs. B. Harrison
Card 13. M. L. Luther
Cardboard Castle. Margery Lawrence
Cardboard Castle. P. C. Wren
Cardboard Hero. L. Noel
Cardinal Error. M. Walton
Cardinal Moth. F. M. White
Cardinal Rock. R. Sale
Cardinal Sin. H. Conway
Cardinalli Contract. E. R. Johnson
Cardinal's Rose. V. Sutphen
Cardross Luck. J. L. Roberts
Cards of the Gambler. B. Kiely
Cards on the Table. A. Christie
Cardyce for the Defence. B. Graeme
Care of Devils. S. Press
Care of the Commander. R. L. Dearden
Career for the Baron. A. Morton
Career in C. Major and other stories. J. M. Cain
Career with Death. H. Tracy
Careful, He Might Hear You. S. L. Elliott
Careful Man. R. Deming
Careless Corpse. B. Halliday
Careless Corpse. C. D. King
Careless Hangman. N. Morland
Careless Lives. D. Leslie
Careless Mrs. Christian. C. M. Russell
Caress Before Killing. C. Brown
Caress of Conquest. S. D. Frances
Caretaker. F. Hume
Carfax Abbey. B. Thomson
Carfax Baines. W. M. Graydon
Cargo for Crooks. Sea Lion
Cargo for Death. T. Wallace
Cargo for the Styx. L. Trimble
Cargo of Eagles. M. Allingham
Cargo of Fear. J. L. Currier
Cargo of Gold. J. G. Sarasin
Cargo of Spent Evil. J. M. Brett
Cargo to Saigon. C. Leader
Caribbean Affair. E. P. Thorne
Caribbean Caper. J. Rosenberger
Caribbean Conspiracy. B. Conrad
Caribbean Crisis. D. E. Bingley
Caribbean Crisis. D. Reid
Caribbean Cutie. Griff
Caribbean Kidnap. M. Cronin
Caribbean Kill. D. Pendleton
Caribbean Kill. A. Sugar
Caribbean Mystery. A. Christie
Caribou Patrol. C. Stoddard
Carlent Manor Crime. L. Grex
Carleton Case. E. H. Clark

Carlito's Way. E. Torres
Carlyon's Year. J. Payn
Carmen's Messenger. H. Bindloss
Carnaby and the Assassins. P. N. Walker
Carnaby and the Conspirators. P. N. Walker
Carnaby and the Demonstrators. P. N. Walker
Carnaby and the Eliminators. P. N. Walker
Carnaby and the Gaolbreakers. P. N. Walker
Carnaby and the Hijackers. P. N. Walker
Carnaby and the Infiltrators. P. N. Walker
Carnaby and the Saboteurs. P. N. Walker
Carnaby Curse. D. Winston
Carnacki, the Ghost Finder. W. H. Hodgson
Carnacki, the Ghost Finder, and a Poem. W. H. Hodgson
Carnavaron's Castle. J. F. Webb
Carnelian Cat. J. Deweese
Carnellian Circle. H. John
Carnival Confession. C. Zuckmayer
Carnival for Killing. N. Carter
Carnival Girl. R. Glendinning
Carnival Murder. N. Brady
Carnival of Crime. N. Carter
Carnival of Death. A. Eadie
Carnival of Death. D. Keene
Carnival of Death. D. Kirby
Carnival of Death. J. C. Lenehan
Carnival of Death. H. Zore
Carny Kill. R. E. Alter
Caro. B. J. Packer
Carolina House. E. Kyle
Caroline Affair. C. H. Gibbs-Smith
Caroline of Brunswick. G. W. M. Reynolds
Caroline Ormesby's Crime. H. Adams
Carp Country. E. Kyle
Carpaccio Caper. B. Strutton
Carpathian Caper. J. Sandulescu
Carpet Courtship. T. Cobb
Carpet from Bagdad. H. MacGrath
Carpet-Slipper Murder. A. C. MacLean
Carr of Dimscaur. T. Douglas
Carriage 7 Seat 15. C. Aveline
Carried Away. E. L. Long
Carriers of Death. J. Creasey
Carrington Assignment. R. Child
Carrington's Cases. J. S. Clouston
Carrion Crows. D. Bennett
Carrion Eaters. W. A. Ballinger
Carrion Eaters. E. H. Rhodes
Carrismore Ruby. J. S. Fletcher
Carriston's Gift and other stories. F. J. Fargus
Carroll Moore. Old Sleuth
Carry-Cot. A. Thynne
Carry Me Home. P. Traill
Carry My Coffin Slowly. L. Herrington
Carson Inheritance. D. Daniels
Carson Loan Mystery. A. De Brune
Carter Kidnapping Case. A. R. Long
Carteret Affair. S. Rathbone
Carteret Hotel Mystery. J. Corbett
Carteret's Cure. R. Keverne
Cartoon Crimes. K. Robeson
Cartsley Mystery. J. G. Rowe
Cartwright Gardens Murder. J. S. Fletcher
Cartwright Is Dead, Sir! H. Baker
Caruthers Affair. W. N. Harben
Carven Ball. J. Haslette
Carver. P. Barker
Carver of the Swamp. "Capstan"
Casbah Killers. N. Carter
Case. V. White
Case Against Alder. C. Ryland
Case Against Andrew Fane. Anthony Gilbert

Case Against Butterfly. G. Tree
Case Against Dr. Ripon. W. Tyrer
Case Against Love. D. Decoin
Case Against Mrs. Ames. A. S. Roche
Case Against Myself. G. Tree
Case Against Paul Raeburn. J. Creasey
Case Against Philip Quest. M. Underwood
Case Against Satan. R. Russell
Case and Exceptions. F. T. Hill
Case and the Girl. R. Parrish
Case Bird and other stories. F. B. Young
Case-Book of Anthony Slade. L. Gribble
Case Book of Ellery Queen. E. Queen
Case Book of Jimmie Lavender. V. Starrett
Case Book of Mr. Campion. M. Allingham
Case-Book of Sherlock Holmes. A. C. Doyle
Case Books of X 37. A. J. Dawson
Case Continued. J. Prescot
Case Dead and Buried. C. Barry
Case File: FBI. The Gordons
Case for Appeal. L. Egan
Case for Court. J. Prescot
Case for Equity. K. Hill
Case for Hearing. J. Prescot
Case for Inspector Flagg. J. Cassells
Case for Inspector West. J. Creasey
Case for M.I.5. W. Jardine
Case for Mr. Crook. Anthony Gilbert
Case for Mr. Fortune. H. C. Bailey
Case for Mr. Paul Savoy. J. Gregory
Case for Mrs. Heydon. R. Bridges
Case for Punishment. H. Hunter
Case for Sergeant Beef. L. Bruce
Case for Solomon. B. Graeme
Case for the Accused. J. Prescot
Case for the Baron. A. Morton
Case for the C.I.D. P. C. De Crespigny
Case for the Courts. Mrs. C. Kernahan
Case for the Crown. F. M. White
Case for the Defence. M. Fitt
Case for the Defendent. H. Aufricht-Ruda
Case for the Dreamer. W. M. Duncan
Case for the Lady. F. Warden
Case for the Prosecution. W. M. Graydon
Case for Three Detectives. L. Bruce
Case for Treachery. V. White
Case for Tressider. C. Barry
Case for Trial. J. Prescot
Case in Camera. O. Onions
Case in Hand. N. A. Temple-Ellis
Case in Madrid. E. Naughton
Case in Nullity. E. Berckman
Case in the Clinic. E. C. R. Lorac
Case Is Altered. H. L. Jones
Case Is Altered. W. Plomer
Case Is Altered. B. Stuart
Case Is Altered. S. Woods
Case Is Closed. P. Wentworth
Case Load--Maximum. E. R. Johnson
Case No. 561. D. Knight
Case of Ailsa Gray. G. M. Fenn
Case of Alan Copeland. M. Dalton
Case of Anne Bickerton. S. Fowler
Case of Blackmail. E. W. Alais
Case of Blackmail. C. K. Moore
Case of Books. B. Graeme
Case of Bottled Murder. E. Wagner
Case of Caroline Animus. D. Chambers
Case of Casper Gault. W. Morton
Case of Colonel Marchand. E. C. R. Lorac
Case of Comrade Tulayev. V. Serge
Case of Constable Shields. R. Greaves
Case of Dan Morris. C. Jude
Case of Doctor Horace. J. H. Prentis
Case of Dr. Morel. K. Bramson
Case of Doctor Plemen. R. De Pont-Jest
Case of Doctor Tracey. R. A. Here
Case of Elinor Norton. M. R. Rinehart
Case of Elymas the Sorcerer. B. Flynn
Case of George Candlemas. G. R. Sims
Case of Identity. L. Brain
Case of Identity. R. Marsh

Title Index

Case of Jennie Brice. M. R. Rinehart
Case of John Muir of Merchant Navy. L. Jackson
Case of Joshua Locke. R. G. Dean
Case of L.A.C. Dickson. J. Drummond
Case of Lady Broadstone. A. W. Marchmont
Case of Larachi the Lascar. O. Merland
Case of Libel. J. Bingham
Case of Lord Greyburn's Son. D. Long
Case of Many Clues. N. Carter
Case of Marie Corwin. G. Dean
Case of Mary Fielding. M. Erskine
Case of Matthew Crake. A. G. MacLeod
Case of Miss Dunstable. J. Hocking
Case of Miss Elliott. B. Orczy
Case of Mr. Budd. G. Verner
Case of Mr. Cassidy. W. Targ
Case of Mrs. Wingate. O. Micheaux
Case of Mortimer Fenley. L. Tracy
Case of Naomi Clynes. B. Thomson
Case of Need. J. Hudson
Case of Paul Breen. A. Tudor
Case of Rape. D. Warren
Case of Reuben Malachi. H. Sutherland Edwards
Case of Richard Eden. Mark Allerton
Case of Richard Meynell. Mrs. H. Ward
Case of Robert Quarry. A. Garve
Case of Robert Robertson. S. Elvestad
Case of Sir Adam Braid. M. Thynne
Case of Sir Edward Talbot. V. F. Taubman-Goldie
Case of Sir Geoffrey. F. Warden
Case of Sonia Wayward. M. Innes
Case of Spirits. P. Lovesey
Case of the Abominable Snowman. N. Blake
Case of the Absent-Minded Professor. A. M. Stein
Case of the Ace Accomplice. W. J. Passingham
Case of the Acid Throwers. J. Creasey
Case of the Adopted Daughter. W. M. Graydon
Case of the Advertised Murder. M. Bardon
Case of the African Emigrant. R. Hardinge
Case of the African Hoodoo. R. Hardinge
Case of the African Trader. R. Hardinge
Case of the Amateur Actor. C. Bush
Case of the Amber Crown. A. Murray
Case of the American Tourists. J. Hunter
Case of the Amorous Aunt. E. S. Gardner
Case of the Angels' Trumpets. Michael Burt
Case of the Angry Mourner. E. S. Gardner
Case of the April Fools. C. Bush
Case of the Back Seat Girl. C. Ryland
Case of the Backward Mule. E. S. Gardner
Case of the Baited Hook. E. S. Gardner
Case of the Baker Street Irregulars. A. Boucher
Case of the Banned Film. A. Parsons
Case of the Barking Clock. H. S. Keeler
Case of the Baronet's Memoirs. Richard Grant
Case of the Beautiful Beggar. E. S. Gardner
Case of the Beautiful Body. Jonathan Craig
Case of the Beckoning Dead. J. Donavan
Case of the Bendigo Heirlooms. Jack Lewis
Case of the Benevolent Bookie. C. Bush
Case of the Berlin Spy. D. Betteridge
Case of the Bigamous Spouse. E. S. Gardner
Case of the Billion Dollar Body. J. Shallit
Case of the Biscay Pirate. L. Jackson
Case of the Bismarck Memoirs. P. Quiroule
Case of the Black-Eyed Blonde. E. S. Gardner
Case of the Black Magician. R. Hardinge
Case of the Black Orchids. R. Stout
Case of the Black Sheep. S. Finley
Case of the Black Twenty-Two. B. Flynn
Case of the Blackmailed Banker. A. Blair
Case of the Blackmailed King. Roland Daniel
Case of the Blackmailed Prince. A. Parsons
Case of the Blank Cartridge. L. Trimble
Case of the Blind Mouse. M. J. Freeman
Case of the Blonde Bonanza. E. S. Gardner
Case of the Blood-Stained Dime. M. Bardon
Case of the Bludgeoned Teacher. J. Hollis
Case of the Blue Lacquered Box. G. F. Worts
Case of the Blue Orchid. H. Desmond
Case of the Bogus Baron. W. Tyrer
Case of the Bogus Bride! H. H. C. Gibbons
Case of the Bogus Ingots. W. J. Bayfield
Case of the Bogus Laird. J. W. Bobin
Case of the Bogus Monk. G. H. Teed
Case of the Bogus Prince. G. Chester
Case of the Bogus Treasure Hunt. W. M. Graydon
Case of the Bonfire Body. C. Bush
Case of the Bookmaker Baronet. J. W. Bobin
Case of the Borrowed Brunette. E. S. Gardner
Case of the Bouncing Betty. M. Avallone
Case of the Brass-Bound Chest. G. Chester
Case of the Brazen Beauty. Jonathan Craig
Case of the Bronze Statue. J. Hunter
Case of the Brooklyn Mobsters. L. Dexter
Case of the Brown-Eyed Housemaid. C. Ryland
Case of the Brunette Bombshell. H. Waugh
Case of the Buried Clock. E. S. Gardner
Case of the Burmese Dagger. A. Murray
Case of the Burnt Bohemian. C. Bush
Case of the Busy Bees. C. Witting
Case of the Cabaret Girl. W. W. Sayer
Case of the Calabar Bean. C. M. Wills
Case of the Calendar Girl. E. S. Gardner
Case of the Canny Killer. H. S. Keeler
Case of the Careless Cupid. E. S. Gardner
Case of the Careless Kitten. E. S. Gardner
Case of the Careless Thief. C. Bush
Case of the Caretaker's Cat. E. S. Gardner
Case of the Cashiered Officer. W. M. Graydon
Case of the Cautious Coquette. E. S. Gardner
Case of the Chased and the Unchaste. T. B. Dewey
Case of the Cheating Bride. M. Propper
Case of the Chinese Courier. R. Hardinge
Case of the Chinese Gong. C. Bush
Case of the Chinese Pearls. G. H. Teed
Case of the Cinema Star. A. Murray
Case of the Clairvoyant's Ruse. G. H. Teed
Case of the Climbing Corpse. Gwyn Evans
Case of the Climbing Rat. C. Bush
Case of the Cold Coquette. Jonathan Craig
Case of the Coloured Wind. J. Donavan
Case of the Conscript Miner. W. Tyrer
Case of the Constant God. R. King
Case of the Constant Suicides. J. D. Carr
Case of the Cop's Wife. M. K. Ozaki
Case of the Copy-Hook Killing. R. Howes
Case of the Corner Cottage. C. Bush
Case of the Corporal's Leave. C. Bush
Case of the Cottage Crime. W. Tyrer
Case of the Cotton Beetle. A. Murray
Case of the Council Swindle. W. Tyrer
Case of the Counterfeit Colonel. C. Bush
Case of the Counterfeit Eye. E. S. Gardner
Case of the Courtlandt Jewels. G. H. Teed
Case of the Crawling Cockroach. Harlan Reed
Case of the Crazy Atom. H. Hawton
Case of the Crazy Pilot. P. Conde
Case of the Crime Reporter. R. Hardinge
Case of the Criminal's Daughter. H. Clevely
Case of the Crimson Conjuror. Gwyn Evans
Case of the Crimson Kiss. E. S. Gardner
Case of the Crimson Wizard. E. J. Murray
Case of the Crook Banker. Ladbroke Black
Case of the Crook Councilor. A. Blair
Case of the Crook Iron Master. M. Osborne
Case of the Crook M.P. G. N. Philips
Case of the Crook Rajah. A. Parsons
Case of the Crooked Candle. E. S. Gardner
Case of the Crooked Skipper. J. Hunter
Case of the Crumpled Knave. A. Boucher
Case of the Crying Swallow. E. S. Gardner
Case of the Cultured Pearls. J. W. Bobin
Case of the Curious Bride. E. S. Gardner
Case of the Curious Chair. R. Powell
Case of the Curious Client. C. Bush
Case of the Curious Heel. K. F. Crossen
Case of the Dancing Sandwiches. F. Brown
Case of the Dangerous Dowager. E. S. Gardner
Case of the Dangra Millions. A. Parsons
Case of the Daring Decoy. E. S. Gardner
Case of the Daring Divorcee. E. S. Gardner
Case of the Dark Hero. P. Cheyney
Case of the Dark Stranger. M. Dalton
Case of the Dark Wanton. P. Cheyney
Case of the Dead Cadet. R. P. Koehler
Case of the Dead Diplomat. B. Thomson
Case of the Dead Divorcee. W. Holder
Case of the Dead Doctor. V. Loder
Case of the Dead Grandmother. M. Bardon
Case of the Dead Man Gone. C. Bush
Case of the Dead Shepherd. C. Bush
Case of the "Dead" Spy. J. Drummond
Case of the Deadly Diamonds. C. Bush
Case of the Deadly Diary. William Du Bois
Case of the Deadly Drops. G. Benedict
Case of the Deadly Kiss. M. K. Ozaki
Case of the Deadly Toy. E. S. Gardner
Case of the Death Computer. J. N. Chance
Case of the Defaulting Sailor. J. Hunter
Case of the Demented Spiv. G. Bellairs
Case of the Demure Defendant. E. S. Gardner
Case of the Deported Aliens. W. J. Bayfield
Case of the Deportee. G. Chester
Case of the Deserted War Bride. J. Hunter
Case of the Deserted Wife. W. J. Bayfield
Case of the Dictator's Double. A. Blair
Case of the Discharged P.C. W. Shute
Case of the Discharged Policeman. L. Jackson
Case of the Disguised Apache. G. H. Teed
Case of the Dope Dealers. M. Frazer
Case of the Doped Favourite. J. Hunter
Case of the Doped Heavyweight. L. Jackson

C

Case of the Double Event. J. Hunter
Case of the Double Tangle. W. J. Bayfield
Case of the Dowager's Etchings. R. King
Case of the Drowning Duck. E. S. Gardner
Case of the Drowsy Mosquito. E. S. Gardner
Case of the Dubious Bridegroom. E. S. Gardner
Case of the Duplicate Daughter. E. S. Gardner
Case of the Ebony Queen. C. Adkins
Case of the Eccentric Will. R. C. Armour
Case of the Eight Brothers. M. V. Heberden
Case of the Eighteenth Ostrich. C. Curzon
Case of the Empty Beehive. C. M. Wills
Case of the Empty Tin. E. S. Gardner
Case of the Extra Grave. C. Bush
Case of the Extra Man. C. Bush
Case of the Fabulous Fake. E. S. Gardner
Case of the Faithful Heart. B. Flynn
Case of the Famished Parson. G. Bellairs
Case of the Fan-Dancer's Horse. E. S. Gardner
Case of the Fast Young Lady. Michael Burt
Case of the Fatal Film. J. Hunter
Case of the Fatal Souvenir. L. Jackson
Case of the Fatal Taxi Cab. W. M. Graydon
Case of the Fear Makers. J. N. Chance
Case of the Fenced-In Woman. E. S. Gardner
Case of the Fiery Fingers. E. S. Gardner
Case of the Fifth Key. G. Dean
Case of the Fighting Padre. L. Jackson
Case of the Fighting Soldier. C. Bush
Case of the First-Class Carriage. C. Carnac
Case of the Five Dummy Books. W. W. Sayer
Case of the Five Fugitives. L. Jackson
Case of the Five Merchants. W. M. Graydon
Case of the Five Red Herrings. L. Jackson
Case of the Flowery Corpse. C. Bush
Case of the Flying Ass. C. Bush
Case of the Flying Fifteen. O. Mills
Case of the Foot-Loose Doll. E. S. Gardner
Case of the Forbidden Island. W. Tyrer
Case of the Forty Thieves. J. Rhode
Case of the Foster Father. V. Perdue
Case of the Four Barons. W. M. Graydon
Case of the Four Friends. J. C. Masterman
Case of the Four Pages. John Norman
Case of the Fourth Detective. C. Bush
Case of the Frantic Ladies. L. Floyd
Case of the French Raiders. J. Hunter
Case of the Frightened Brother. Frank King
Case of the Frightened Fish. William Du Bois
Case of the Frightened Girl. R. Hardinge
Case of the Frightened Lady. E. Wallace
Case of the Frightened Man. A. Parsons
Case of the Frightened Mannequin. C. Bush
Case of the Fugitive Nurse. E. S. Gardner
Case of the Gambler's Corpse. R. Clarke
Case of the Gangster's Moll. J. G. Brandon
Case of the Giant Killer. H. C. Branson
Case of the Gilded Fly. E. Crispin
Case of the Gilded Lily. E. S. Gardner
Case of the Girl on Remand. J. Hunter
Case of the Girl Reporter. J. W. Bobin
Case of the Glamorous Ghost. E. S. Gardner
Case of the Glass Slipper. N. MacKenzie
Case of the Gloating Landlord. R. Fenisong
Case of the Gold Coins. A. Wynne

Case of the Gold-Digger's Purse. E. S. Gardner
Case of the Golden Stool. F. A. Symonds
Case of the Good Employer. C. Bush
Case of the Grand Alliance. C. Bush
Case of the Greedy Rainmaker. George Douglas
Case of the Green Caravan. R. Hardinge
Case of the Green-Eyed Sister. E. S. Gardner
Case of the Green Felt Hat. C. Bush
Case of the Green Knife. A. Wynne
Case of the Grieving Monkey. V. Perdue
Case of the Grinning Gorilla. E. S. Gardner
Case of the Half-Wakened Wife. E. S. Gardner
Case of the Hanging Lady. N. Jones
Case of the Hanging Rope. C. Bush
Case of the Happy Medium. C. Bush
Case of the Happy Warrior. C. Bush
Case of the Hated Senator. M. Scherf
Case of the Haunted Brides. William Du Bois
Case of the Haunted Husband. E. S. Gardner
Case of the Haven Hotel. C. Bush
Case of the Head Dispenser. J. W. Bobin
Case of the Headless Corpse. D. Allan
Case of the Headless Jesuit. G. Bellairs
Case of the Heavenly Twin. C. Bush
Case of the Hesitant Hostess. E. S. Gardner
Case of the Hold-Up King. F. A. Symonds
Case of the Hollow Man. M. Carrel
Case of the Horrified Heirs. E. S. Gardner
Case of the Housekeeper's Hair. C. Bush
Case of the Howling Dog. E. S. Gardner
Case of the Hula Clock. D. Gardiner
Case of the Human Ape. W. M. Graydon
Case of the Human Mole. H. Townley
Case of the Hypnotized Virgin. J. Roebert
Case of the Ice-Cold Hands. E. S. Gardner
Case of the Income-Tax Frauds. W. J. Bayfield
Case of the Indian Dancer. A. Parsons
Case of the Indian Millionaire. A. Parsons
Case of the Indian Watcher. A. Parsons
Case of the Indiana Torturer. E. E. Saks
Case of the Innocent Victims. J. Creasey
Case of the Innocent Wife. N. Morland
Case of the Innocent Witness. M. Carrel
Case of the International Adventurer. J. W. Bobin
Case of the Irate Witness. E. S. Gardner
Case of the Island Princess. R. C. Armour
Case of the Island Trader. J. W. Bobin
Case of the Ivory Arrow. H. S. Keeler
Case of the Jack of Clubs. Gwyn Evans
Case of the Jade-Handled Knife. G. H. Teed
Case of the Japanese Contract. A. Parsons
Case of the Japanese Detective. T. C. Wignall
Case of the Jeweled Ragpicker. H. S. Keeler
Case of the Journeying Boy. M. Innes
Case of the Judas Spoon. M. L. Stokes
Case of the Jumbo Sandwich. C. Bush
Case of the Kidnapped Colonel. C. Bush
Case of the Kidnapped Legatee. R. C. Armour
Case of the Kidnapped Prisoner. A. Blair

Case of the Kidnapped Specialist. R. Hardinge
Case of the King of Montavia. Roland Daniel
Case of the King's Spy. W. W. Sayer
Case of the Kippered Corpse. M. Scherf
Case of the Lame Canary. E. S. Gardner
Case of the Late Pig. M. Allingham
Case of the Laughing Dwarf. J. Reach
Case of the Laughing Jesuit. Michael Burt
Case of the Laughing Virgin. Jonathan Craig
Case of the Lavendar Gripsack. H. S. Keeler
Case of the Lazy Lover. E. S. Gardner
Case of the Leaning Man. C. Bush
Case of the Legion Deserter. H. Clevely
Case of the Little Doctor. Hilda Lewis
Case of the Little Green Men. M. Reynolds
Case of the Lone Plantation. E. J. Murray
Case of the Lonely Heiress. E. S. Gardner
Case of the Lonely Lovers. W. Daemer
Case of the Long-Firm Frauds. J. W. Bobin
Case of the Long-Legged Models. E. S. Gardner
Case of the Lucky Legs. E. S. Gardner
Case of the Lucky Loser. E. S. Gardner
Case of the Mad Inventor. J. Creasey
Case of the Magic Mirror. C. Bush
Case of the Malevolent Twin. L. Eby
Case of the Malverne Diamonds. L. Gribble
Case of the Man in Black. O. Merland
Case of the Man on Leave. G. Chester
Case of the Man Who Never Slept. Gwyn Evans
Case of the Man with No Name. J. Drummond
Case of the Marsden Rubies. L. Gribble
Case of the Master Organizer. A. Murray
Case of the Mexican Knife. G. Homes
Case of the Michaelmas Goose. C. Witting
Case of the Mill Owner's Son. W. M. Graydon
Case of the Millionaire Newspaper Owner. R. C. Armour
Case of the Millionaire's Blackmail. W. J. Bayfield
Case of the Mischievous Doll. E. S. Gardner
Case of the Missing Airmen. G. Elliott
Case of the Missing Bridegroom. G. Dilnot
Case of the Missing Bullion. P. Gordon
Case of the Missing Co-Ed. W. Hardy
Case of the Missing Corpse. E. Lanham
Case of the Missing Corpse. J. Sanger
Case of the Missing D.F.C. A. Parsons
Case of the Missing Diary. A. Fielding
Case of the Missing Estate Agent. D. Stuart
Case of the Missing G.I. Bride. A. Parsons
Case of the Missing Gardener. H. Walker
Case of the Missing Hand. M. Hervey
Case of the Missing Lovers. Lee Roberts
Case of the Missing Major. A. Parsons
Case of the Missing Men. C. Bush
Case of the Missing Minutes. C. Bush
Case of the Missing Musician. R. Hardinge
Case of the Missing Nazi. W. Tyrer
Case of the Missing Sandals. N. B. Mavity
Case of the Missing Scientist. A. Parsons
Case of the Missing Ships. S. Hope
Case of the Missing Stoker. L. Jackson
Case of the Missing Surgeon. A. Parsons
Case of the Monday Murders. C. Bush
Case of the Monta Grandee Diamonds. S. Hope
Case of the Moth-Eaten Mink. E. S. Gardner
Case of the Moving Finger. A. Christie
Case of the Muckrakers. W. McNeilly

Case of the Mummified Hand. G. H. Teed
Case of the Murdered Caretaker. C. Gates
Case of the Murdered Commissionaire. J. G. Brandon
Case of the Murdered Financier. J. Creasey
Case of the Murdered Madame. H. Kane
Case of the Murdered Mahout. W. M. Graydon
Case of the Murdered Major. C. Bush
Case of the Murdered Model. T. B. Dewey
Case of the Murdered Pawn Broker. W. Edwards
Case of the Murdered Postman. R. Hardinge
Case of the Murdered Redhead. F. Lockridge
Case of the Murdered Taxi Driver. A. Blair
Case of the Murdered Wedding Guest. W. Jardine
Case of the Murderer's Bride. E. S. Gardner
Case of the Musical Cow. E. S. Gardner
Case of the Mysterious Germs. R. C. Armour
Case of the Mysterious Jockey. W. M. Graydon
Case of the Mysterious Moll. H. S. Keeler
Case of the Mystery Champion. A. Steffens Hardy
Case of the Mystery Millionaire. A. Murray
Case of the Mythical Monkeys. E. S. Gardner
Case of the Nabob's Son. W. M. Graydon
Case of the Nameless Corpse. C. B. Kelland
Case of the Nameless Man. O. Merland
Case of the Nameless Millionaire. A. Parsons
Case of the Naval Defaulter. W. Tyrer
Case of the Naval Stores Bucket. W. Tyrer
Case of the Negligent Nymph. E. S. Gardner
Case of the Nervous Accomplice. E. S. Gardner
Case of the Nervous Nude. Jonathan Craig
Case of the Night Club Queen. J. G. Brandon
Case of the Night Lorry Driver. L. Jackson
Case of the Old Oak Chest. H. H. C. Gibbons
Case of the One-Eyed Witness. E. S. Gardner
Case of the 100% Alibis. C. Bush
Case of the Open Drawer. L. Allan
Case of the Painted Girl. Frank King
Case of the Painted Ladies. B. Flynn
Case of the Paralyzed Man. A. Murray
Case of the Perfect Alibi. M. Carrel
Case of the Perfumed Mouse. T. Du Bois
Case of the Perjured Parrot. E. S. Gardner
Case of the Petticoat Murder. Jonathan Craig
Case of the Phantom Fingerprints. K. F. Crossen
Case of the Phantom Fortune. E. S. Gardner
Case of the Plastic Man. J. Donavan
Case of the Plastic Mask. J. Donavan
Case of the Platinum Blonde. C. Bush
Case of the Poisoned Cocktails. O. Boyd
Case of the Poisoned Pen. Gwyn Evans
Case of the Poisoned Pup. S. S. Pridham
Case of the Pornographic Photos. Lawrence Block
Case of the Portuguese Giantess. G. H. Teed
Case of the Postponed Murder. E. S. Gardner
Case of the Praying Evangelist. D. W. F. Hardie
Case of the President's Heads. M. L. Stokes
Case of the Press Photographer. W. J. Bayfield
Case of the Prince's Diary. A. Parsons
Case of the Prince's Prisoners. A. Parsons
Case of the Prodigal Daughter. C. Bush
Case of the Purloined Picture. C. Bush
Case of the Purple Calf. B. Flynn
Case of the Queenly Contestant. E. S. Gardner
Case of the R. E. Pipe. C. M. Wills
Case of the Radioactive Redhead. G. G. Fickling
Case of the Rajah's Son. H. E. Hill
Case of the Red Box. R. Stout
Case of the Red Brunette. C. Bush
Case of the Red Crimona's. H. H. C. Gibbons
Case of the Red-Haired Girl. A. Wynne
Case of the Redoubled Cross. R. King
Case of the Rejuvenated Millionaire. G. N. Philips
Case of the Reluctant Model. E. S. Gardner
Case of the Renegade Agent. D. Reid
Case of the Renegade Naval Officer. A. Parsons
Case of the Repatriated Prisoner. G. Chester
Case of the Restless Redhead. E. S. Gardner
Case of the Returning Soldier. W. Tyrer
Case of the Rival Race Gangs. H. C. Miln
Case of the River Smugglers. D. T. Hughes
Case of the Rolling Bones. E. S. Gardner
Case of the Runaway Corpse. E. S. Gardner
Case of the Running Man. C. Bush
Case of the Running Mouse. C. Bush
Case of the Russian Cross. C. Bush
Case of the Russian Crown Jewels. R. H. Poole
Case of the Rusted Room. J. Donavan
Case of the Sapphire Brooch. C. Bush
Case of the Scared Rabbits. G. Bellairs
Case of the Screaming Woman. E. S. Gardner
Case of the Seaside Crooks. A. Murray
Case of the Second Chance. C. Bush
Case of the Second Crime. A. Parsons
Case of the Secret Agent. R. Hardinge
Case of the Secret Plans. C. H. Barker
Case of the Secret Road. A. Parsons
Case of the Seven Bells. C. Bush
Case of the Seven Keys. G. Stanley
Case of the Seven Murders. E. Queen
Case of the Seven of Calvary. A. Boucher
Case of the Seven Sneezes. A. Boucher
Case of the Seven Whistlers. G. Bellairs
Case of the Severed Skull. H. Weiner
Case of the Shapely Shadow. E. S. Gardner
Case of the Shaven Blonde. R. Hobart
Case of the Shivering Chorus Girls. J. A. Phillips
Case of the Shoplifter's Shoe. E. S. Gardner
Case of the Shot Looter. M. Frazer
Case of the Silent Partner. E. S. Gardner
Case of the Silent Safe-Cutters. H. H. C. Gibbons
Case of the Silent Stranger. Jonathan Craig
Case of the Silken Petticoat. C. Bush
Case of the Singing Skirt. E. S. Gardner
Case of the Sinister Farm. A. Parsons
Case of the Six Bullets. R. M. Laurenson
Case of the Six Mistresses. B. Maxwell
Case of the Six O'Clock Scream. A. Parsons
Case of the 16 Beans. H. S. Keeler
Case of the Sleeping Partner. E. S. Brooks
Case of the Sleepwalker's Niece. E. S. Gardner
Case of the Smoking Chimney. E. S. Gardner
Case of the Smuggled Currency. H. Clevely
Case of the Society Blackmailer. W. M. Graydon
Case of the Solid Key. A. Boucher
Case of the Spanish Legatee. A. Parsons
Case of the Spiv's Secret. A. Parsons
Case of the Spurious Spinster. E. S. Gardner
Case of the Squealing Cat. J. Reach
Case of the Stag at Bay. W. McNeilly
Case of the Stepdaughter's Secret. E. S. Gardner
Case of the Stolen Bridegroom. H. Adams
Case of the Stolen Evidence. A. Parsons
Case of the Stolen Mine. R. Hardinge
Case of the Stolen Police Dossier. A. Blair
Case of the Stolen Ransome. J. Hunter
Case of the Stranded Touring Company. L. Carlton
Case of the Strange Beauties. Frank King
Case of the Strange Wireless Message. W. W. Sayer
Case of the Strangled Seven. P. Yorke
Case of the Strangled Starlet. J. H. Chase
Case of the Straw Man. D. M. Disney
Case of the Stuttering Bishop. E. S. Gardner
Case of the Substitute Face. E. S. Gardner
Case of the Sulky Girl. E. S. Gardner
Case of the Sun Bather's Diary. E. S. Gardner
Case of the Suppressed Will. W. M. Graydon
Case of the "Suspect" Watchmaker. L. Jackson
Case of the Swindled Guarantor. W. Tyrer
Case of the Swindler's "Stooge." A. Parsons
Case of the Swinging Spider. P. Yorke
Case of the Tainted Token. K. M. Knight
Case of the Talking Bug. The Gordons
Case of the Talking Dust. J. Donavan
Case of the Tea-Cosy's Aunt. Anthony Gilbert
Case of the Tearless Widow. J. Roeburt
Case of the Ten Diamonds. G. H. Teed
Case of the Terrified Typist. E. S. Gardner
Case of the Theatrical Profiteer. W. M. Graydon
Case of the 13th Coach. E. G. Bartlett
Case of the Three Absconding Swindlers. C. Brisbane
Case of the Three Broken Necks. A. McClintock
Case of the Three Lost Letters. C. Bush
Case of the Three-Ring Puzzle. C. Bush
Case of the Three Strange Faces. C. Bush
Case of the Three Survivors. H. Clevely
Case of the Topaz Flower. C. M. Russell
Case of the Trade Secret. J. W. Bobin
Case of the Transatlantic Flyers. Jack Lewis
Case of the Transposed Legs. H. S. Keeler
Case of the Treble Twist. C. Bush
Case of the Triple Twist. C. Bush
Case of the Troubled Trustee. E. S. Gardner
Case of the Tudor Queen. C. Bush
Case of the Turning Tide. E. S. Gardner
Case of the Twin Detectives. E. S. Brooks
Case of the Twisted Scarf. F. Durbridge
Case of the Twisted Trail. F. A. Symonds
Case of the Two Bankers. J. W. Bobin
Case of the Two Brothers. A. Murray
Case of the Two Crooked Baronets. W. Tyrer

Case of the Two Doctors. N. Carter
Case of the Two-Faced Swindler. J. Drummond
Case of the Two Guardians. W. M. Graydon
Case of the Two Pearl Necklaces. A. Fielding
Case of the Two Scapegraces. W. M. Graydon
Case of the Two Strange Ladies. H. S. Keeler
Case of the Unconquered Sisters. T. Downing
Case of the Uncut Gems. A. Murray
Case of the Undischarged Bankrupt. A. Murray
Case of the Unfortunate Village. C. Bush
Case of the Unhappy Angels. G. Homes
Case of the Unknown Heir. A. Parsons
Case of the Un-Named Film. A. Murray
Case of the Vagabond Virgin. E. S. Gardner
Case of the Vanished Husband. W. J. Bayfield
Case of the Vanishing Artist. Frank King
Case of the Vanishing Beauty. R. S. Prather
Case of the Vanishing Women. R. Archer
Case of the Velvet Claws. E. S. Gardner
Case of the Village Tramp. Jonathan Craig
Case of the Violent Virgin. M. Avallone
Case of the Violet Smoke. J. Donavan
Case of the Walking Corpse. A. Livingston
Case of the Walking Corpse. B. Halliday
Case of the Waylaid Wolf. E. S. Gardner
Case of the Weird Sisters. C. Armstrong
Case of the Wicked Three. A. Parsons
Case of the Winking Buddha. M. L. Stokes
Case of the Withered Hand. J. G. Brandon
Case of the Woman in Black. A. Murray
Case of the Worried Waitress. E. S. Gardner
Case of the Would-Be Widow. J. G. Brandon
Case of the Wounded Mastiff. N. Harman
Case of Torches. Clark Smith
Case of William Smith. P. Wentworth
Case of Young Lord Folliot. N. H. Romanes
Case on Cloud Nine. L. Freeman
Case Pending. D. Shannon
Case Proceeding. J. Prescot
Case Re-Opened. J. Prescot
Case to Answer. E. Lustgarten
Case 29. J. Cassells
Case with Four Clowns. L. Bruce
Case with Nine Solutions. J. J. Connington
Case with No Conclusion. L. Bruce
Case with Ropes and Rings. L. Bruce
Case with Three Husbands. M. Erskine
Case with Three Threads. Anthony Lang
Case Without a Clue. N. Carter
Case Without a Clue. N. Morland
Case Without a Corpse. L. Bruce
Casebook of a Victorian Detective. J. M'Levy
Casebook of Crime. A. Brock
Casebook of Lucius Leffing. J. P. Brennan
Casebook of Solar Pons. A. Derleth
Cases of Susan Dare. M. G. Eberhart
Cash My Chips, Croupier. M. G. Eberhart
Cash on Delivery. F. Du Boisgobey
Cashelmara. S. Howatch
Cash on Destruction. Maz
Cashier's Secret. N. Carter
Casino. G. Norsworthy
Casino for Sale. C. Brahms
Casino Murder Case. S. S. Van Dine
Casino Mystery. M. E. Cooke
Casino Mystery. Elaine Hamilton
Casino Royale. I. Fleming
Casinopoly. H. Janson
Cask. F. W. Crofts
Casket of Death. J. B. O'Sullivan
Caspian Song. J. G. Sarasin

Cassidy the Con Man. G. H. Teed
Cassidy's Girl. D. Goodis
Cassie. M. Conte
Cassiodore Case. A. R. Martin
Cast a Green Shadow. M. V. Hunt
Cast a Yellow Shadow. Ross Thomas
Cast Away. E. Yates
Cast, in Order of Disappearance. S. Brett
Cast Iron Alibi. D. Betteridge
Cast of Death. N. Orde-Powlette
Cast Out. M. Gerard
Casting of the Shadows. J. Dory
Casting the Net. D. Stewart
Castle and the Key. C. Knye
Castle at Glencarris. J. Vicary
Castle at Witch's Coven. V. Coffman
Castle Barra. V. Coffman
Castle Black. C. Morland
Castle by the Sea. H. B. M. Watson
Castle Clodha. Alanna Knight
Castle Conquest. B. Gray
Castle Danger. W. O'Meara
Castle Dangerous. V. Gunn
Castle Dangerous. A. Wood
Castle-Dinas. R. A. J. Walling
Castle Doom. M. McEvoy
Castle Dor. A. T. Quiller-Couch
Castle Enigma. J. R. Warren
Castle Fell. D. Duff
Castle Foam. H. W. French
Castle for Tess. R. Simon
Castle Garac. N. Monsarrat
Castle Gay. J. Buchan
Castle in Bohemia. D. Whitelaw
Castle in Canada. C. Farr
Castle in Spain. J. De Mille
Castle in Spain. C. Farr
Castle Island Case. V. W. Mason
Castle Malindine. H. Ford
Castle Mandragora. M. Durham
Castle Minerva. V. Canning
Castle Mirage. A. Brennan
Castle Morvant. D. Daniels
Castle of Closing Doors. D. Winston
Castle of Dark Evil. Melissa Napier
Castle of Doubt. J. H. Whitson
Castle of Eagles. C. Heaven
Castle of Evil. S. Abbott
Castle of Fear. S. Abbott
Castle of Fear. J. J. Farjeon
Castle of Fear. R. S. L. Harding
Castle of Lies. A. H. Vesey
Castle of Lugas. A. Fernandez
Castle of Otranto. H. Walpole
Castle of Shadows. A. M. Williamson
Castle of Sin. J. Cassells
Castle of Terror. C. Farr
Castle of the Demon. P. Ruell
Castle of Vengeance. M. Hastings
Castle on the Cliff. Dan Ross
Castle on the Hill. E. Randolph
Castle on the Hill. W. E. D. Ross
Castle on the Island. L. Ames
Castle on the Mountain. J. Wellsley
Castle Perilous. V. Johnston
Castle Rock Mystery. G. F. Gibbs
Castle Sinister. Gwyn Evans
Castle Skull. J. D. Carr
Castle Terror. M. Z. Bradley
Castle to Let. B. Reynolds
Castle Ugly. Marianne Barrett
Castle Wafer. H. Wood
Castle Walk. M. Le Bas
Castlecliff. S. Shulman
Castlecourt Diamond Case. G. Bonner
Castledoom. E. Lecale
Castleford Conundrum. J. J. Connington
Castlereagh. J. L. Roberts
Castle's Heir. H. Wood
Castles in the Air. Augustus Muir
Castles in the Air. B. Orczy

Castles of Athlin and Dunbayne. A. Radcliffe
Castro File. J. Rosenberger
Casual Murderer. H. Footner
Casual Slaughters. V. Hanson
Casual Slaughters. J. Quince
Cat. V. Gielgud
Cat. G. Simenon
Cat Among the Pigeons. A. Christie
Cat and Capricorn. D. B. Olsen
Cat and Feather. D. Basil
Cat and Fiddle Murders. E. B. Ronald
Cat and Mouse. C. Brand
Cat and Mouse. E. K. Goldthwaite
Cat and Mouse. M. Halliday
Cat and Mouse. H. Pentecost
Cat and Mouse. M. L. Roby
Cat and Mouse Murder. E. K. Goldthwaite
Cat and the Canary. John Willard
Cat and the Clock. C. G. Booth
Cat and the Corpse. R. A. J. Walling
Cat and the Fiddle. P. Costello
Cat Burglar. E. Wallace
Cat Cay Warrant. A. Morgan
Cat Climbs. C. A. Tarrant
Cat Creeps. John Willard
Cat Dies First. W. H. L. Crauford
Cat-Eye. L. Palmer
Cat Got Your Tongue? C. Carpenter
Cat in Gloves. D. Delaney
Cat in the Convoy. W. G. Schofield
Cat in the Hat Box. A. W. Upfield
Cat Jumps. M. Burton
Cat O' Nine Tails. P. J. Gillette
Cat of Bast and other stories of mystery. W. E. Thorner
Cat of Many Tails. E. Queen
Cat Saw Murder. D. B. Olsen
Cat Screams. T. Downing
Cat Trap. G. A. Ralston
Cat Walk. D. B. Olsen
Cat Watchers. J. N. Chance
Cat Wears a Mask. D. B. Olsen
Cat Wears a Noose. D. B. Olsen
Cat Who Ate Danish Modern. L. J. Braun
Cat Who Could Read Backwards. L. J. Braun
Cat Who Turned On and Off. L. J. Braun
Cat Will Mew. Fredrick Jackson
Cat with the Mustache. Simon
Catacombs. Jay Bennett
Catacombs of Death. Operator 1384
Catalyst. J. Bell
Catalyst. K. Lowe
Catalyst Club. G. Dyer
Catastrophe. E. Gaboriau
Catastrophe at Cliff Haven. T. K. Cook
Catastrophe Club. Frank King
Catastrophe in Bohemia and other stories. H. S. Brooks
Catch. J. Boland
Catch a Fallen Starlet. D. Sanderson
Catch a Falling Spy. N. Benchley
Catch a Killer. U. Curtiss
Catch a Killer. Robert Martin
Catch a Tiger. O. Cameron
Catch a Tiger. Martin Thomas
Catch and Kill. N. Blake
Catch and Squeeze. Craig Cooper
Catch-as-Catch-Can. C. Armstrong
Catch as Catch Can. F. Lockridge
Catch-'Em-Alive-O! Michael Burt
Catch Me a Phoenix! C. Brown
Catch Me a Renegade. H. Janson
Catch Me a Spy. G. Marton
Catch Me a Traitor. Henry Talbot
Catch Me--If You Can. B. Cobb
Catch Me If You Can. P. McGerr
Catch the Brass Ring. S. Marlowe
Catch the Gold Ring. J. S. Strange
Catch the Saint. L. Charteris
Catching a Tartar. G. W. Appleton
Caterpillar Cop. J. McClure
Catfish Tangle. C. Williams
Catherine Volmar. G. W. M. Reynolds
Catherine Wheel. P. Wentworth
Catherwood Mystery. A. P. Southwick
Cathkin Mystery. G. Woden
Cathra Mystery. A. G. MacLeod

Title Index

Cathy Rossiter. J. L. Rickard
Catmur's Caves. R. Dowling
Catnapped. The Gordons
Cats. B. Roueche
Cat's Claw. D. B. Olsen
Cat's Cradle. P. Flower
Cat's Cradle. S. Harvester
Cat's Cradle Murder. Jerome Barry
Cat's Don't Need Coffins. D. B. Olsen
Cats Don't Smile. D. B. Olsen
Cat's Eye. C. Aveline
Cat's Eye. R. A. Freeman
Cat's-Eye Ring. F. Du Boisgobey
Cat's Eyes. S. Warwick
Cats Have Tall Shadows. D. B. Olsen
Cats in Crime...and others. A. L.
   Germeshausen
Cat's Paw. A. Hocking
Cat's Paw. C. B. Kelland
Cat's Paw. N. S. Lincoln
Cat's-Paw. M. Salter
Cat's Paw. R. Scarlett
Cat's Prey. D. Eden
Cats Prowl at Night. A. A. Fair
Cat's Whisker. H. C. Bailey
Catseyes. A. Winnington
Catspaw. W. LeQueux
Catspaw. A. Murray
Catspaw. W. H. Osborne
Catspaw for Murder. D. B. Olsen
Catspaw Ordeal. E. Ronns
Catspaws. C. Brooks
Catt Among the Pigeons. C. Connell
Catt Out of the Bag. C. Witting
Caught at Last! D. Donovan
Caught Dead. B. Halliday
Caught in a Trap. J. C. Hutcheson
Caught in a Whirlpool. N. Carter
Caught in Mid-Ocean. Anonymous
Caught in Mid-Ocean. O. Harper
Caught in Terror. M. Bardsley
Caught in the Act. John Lee
Caught in the Machine. C. Campbell
Caught in the Middle. S. Waldron
Caught in the Net. E. Gaboriau
Caught in the Toils. N. Carter
Cauldron Bubble. G. Goodchild
Cauldron Bubbles. N. A. Temple-Ellis
Cause for a Killing. J. Wainwright
Cause for Alarm. E. Ambler
Cause for Alarm. J. Pendower
Cause for Malice. F. Hurt
Cause for Suspicion. T. C. H. Jacobs
Cause of Death. M. Underwood
Cause of the Crime. L. Frank
Cause of the Screaming. D. Elias
Cause Unknown. J. J. Farjeon
Causeway to the Past. W. O'Farrell
Cautious Assassin. D. Orgill
Cautious Maiden. C. Saint-Laurent
Cautious Overshoes. M. Scherf
Cautley Conundrum. A. Fielding
Cautley Mystery. A. Fielding
Cavalier Conquest. B. Gray
Cavalier of Chance. S. Horler
Cavalier of Crime. F. Hedley
Cavalier of the Night. R. Armstrong
Cavalier's Corpse. T. Du Bois
Cavalier's Cup. Carter Dickson
Cavaliers of Death. R. Forbes
Cavanaugh Keep. M. Leslie
Cave and the Beast. I. Garrick
Cave of Bats. Robert MacLeod
Cave of the Chinese Skeletons. J. Seward
Cave with Two Exits. H. H. Cooper
Cavern. A. MacVicar
Caverns of Falkenhorst. Dorinne Moore
Caves of Blackscar. Haydon Dean
Caves of Claro. J. Palmer
Caves of Death. V. Norwood
Caves of Fear. P. Morton

Caves of Guernica. Samuel Edwards
Caves of Night. J. Christopher
Caves of Shend. D. Hennessey
Caves of Steel. I. Asimov
Caves of Terror. T. Mundy
Caviar Cruise. F. Webb
Caviar to Kill. K. T. McCall
Cawthorn Journals. S. Marlowe
Caxborough Scandal. F. Whishaw
Cease upon the Midnight. S. Troy
Cecile. H. Smart
Cecile's Fortune. F. Du Boisgobey
Cecile's Tryst. J. Payn
Cedar Tree. Rona Randall
Celebate's Wife. H. Flowerdew
Celebrated Cases of Dick Tracy, 1931-1951.
   C. Gould
Celebrated Detective. Anonymous
Celestial Ruby. T. W. Speight
Celia. P. Trent
Celia's Career. P. Trent
Cell. D. Case
Cell Car 54. J. M. Fox
Cell Murder Mystery. D. B. Hobart
"Cell 13." E. H. Trafton
Cellar at No. 5. Shelley Smith
Cellar Boys. W. H. Baker
Cellini Plaque. H. MacGrath
Cellini Smith, Detective. Robert Reeves
Cemetery First Stop! David Hume
Censor. J. Gardner
Centeola; and other tales. D. P. Thompson
Center of the Web. K. Roberts
Centerforce. T. A. Waters
Centipede. B. Boothby
Central Park Murder. B. Duff
Central Park Mystery. Old Sleuth
Centre Court Murder. B. Newman
Centre Holds. A. Storey
Centurion's Story. P. C. MacFarlane
Cepherine. J. H. Robinson
Cerebus Murders. R. Quest
Certain Dr. Mellor. P. P. Maguire
Certain Dr. Thorndyke. R. A. Freeman
Certain Evil. D. Kraslow
Certain Liveliness. H. F. Moulton
Certain Sleep. H. Reilly
Certified Check. N. Carter
Certified Insane. R. C. Armour
Chain-Gang Queenie. B. Sarto
Chain Invisible. C. R. Gull
Chain Murder. A. Soutar
Chain of Clues. N. Carter
Chain of Command. I. R. Blacker
Chain of Command. D. Buttenshaw
Chain of Darkness. K. Cook
Chain of Death. N. McLarty
Chain of Death. S. Noel
Chain of Evidence. N. Carter
Chain of Evidence. C. Wells
Chain of Infamy. G. Beare
Chain Reaction. C. Hodder-Williams
Chain Reaction. G. A. Ralston
Chained. F. Hird
Chained Crocodile. B. Whitaker
Chains of Circumstance. T. W. Speight
Chair for Death. J. Reddoch
Chair for Martin Rome. H. E. Helseth
Chair-Lift. E. H. Clements
Chairman. G. Vaizey
Chalet Diabolique. V. Coffman
Chalice Caper. D. MacKenzie
Chalk Face. W. Frank
Chalk-Face. J. M. Walsh
Chalk Garden. E. Bagnold
Chalk Stream Killing. R. Pertwee
Challenge. H. C. McNeile
Challenge at Le Mans. L. Kenyon
Challenge Blue Mask! A. Morton
Challenge for the Dreamer. W. M. Duncan
Challenge for the Picaroon. J. Cassells
Challenge for Three. D. Garth
Challenge of the Bush. C. R. Cooper
Challenge to Murder. F. J. Whaley
Challenge to the Four. Mark Cross
Chamber of Horrors. R. Bloch
Chambered Tomb. Charlotte Hunt
Chameleon. H. S. Keeler

Chameleon. W. LeQueux
Chameleon Course. D. Seaman
Chameleon File. L. James
Chamois Murder. C. M. Wills
Champagne for One. R. Stout
Champagne Killer. H. Pentecost
Champagne Mystery. G. Garston
Champdoce Mystery. E. Gaboriau
Champington Mystery. Le Voleur
Champion. C. N. Williamson
Champion and Crook. T. Lloyd
Champion Clue-Finder. Anonymous
Champion from Far Away. B. Hecht
Champion of Virtue. Clara Reeve
Championship Crime. J. G. Brandon
Chance Child. Mrs. C. Kernahan
Chance Discovery. N. Carter
Chance Elson. W. T. Ballard
Chance Encounter. E. E. Sumner
Chance in Chains. G. Thorne
Chance Marriage. E. Gaboriau
Chance Meeting. Leigh Howard
Chance to Die. Lionel Black
Chance to Kill. R. Lait
Chance to Kill. D. Shannon
Chance to Poison. G. Bromley
Chancer. J. Brown
Chandler Policy. D. M. Disney
Chandu Men. F. Crisp
Change for Heaven. A. Hillgarth
Change Here for Babylon. N. Bawden
Change of Heart. H. McCloy
Change of Heir. M. Innes
Change of Mind. C. Stratton
Change of Pace. T. Cobb
Change of Sky. F. Singleton
Changed Brides. E. Southworth
Changed Face. T. Craig
Changeling. M. Higgins
Changeling. A. Murray
Changeling. E. Phillpotts
Changing Heart. P. Barrington
Changing Pulse of Madame Touraine.
   A. C. Gunter
Changing Road. H. MacGrath
Channay Syndicate. E. P. Oppenheim
Channel Million. G. Collins
Channel Mystery. L. H. Brennan
Channel Mystery. W. F. Morris
Channel Tunnel Mystery. S. G. Hedges
Channing Affair. R. Dark
Channings. H. Wood
Chant of Jimmie Blacksmith. T. Keneally
Chantal. G. Des Cars
Chantic Bird. D. Ireland
Chanticleer's Muffled Crow. A. Dean
Chaperone. E. Gordon
Chaplain's Craze. G. M. Fenn
Chapman's Wares. H. B. M. Watson
Charabanc Mystery. M. Burton
Charade. P. Stone
Charge from the Grave. S. Gibney
Charge Is Murder. M. Cumberland
Charge Is Murder! J. M. Spender
Charge Is Treason. W. H. Baker
Charing Cross Mystery. J. S. Fletcher
Chariot of Desire. D. Nabarro
Chariot of the Sun. M. Clare
Charioteer. G. Thorne
Charitable End. Jessica Mann
Charity Ends at Home. C. Watson
Charity Fund Mystery. G. Chester
Charity Ghost. T. Gallon
Charity Murders. P. Manton
Charka Memorial. W. Ware
Charlatan. S. Horler
Charlatan. P. J. Stead
Charleston Knife's in Town. Ralph Dennis
Charley Hunter. Anonymous
Charlie Chan Carries On. E. D. Biggers
Charlie Chan Returns. D. Lynds
Charlie Finds a Corpse. R. Denton
Charlie Sent Me! C. Brown
Charlie's Back in Town. Jacqueline Park
Charlotte. N. Lofts

C

C

Charlotte Wade. A. McElfresh
Charlotte's Inheritance. M. E. Braddon
Charm of Finches. B. Thielen
Charmer Chased. C. Brown
Charmian, Lady Vibart. J. Farnol
Charming Murder. F. Shay
Charred Witness. G. H. Coxe
Charter Lane Mystery. G. C. Keech
Charter to Danger. E. Reed
Charteris Mystery. A. Fielding
Chase. N. Daniels
Chase. K. R. Dwyer
Chase. H. Foote
Chase. R. M. Gilchrist
Chase. R. G. Hubler
Chase. J. Lermina
Chase. R. Unekis
Chase Around the World. Anonymous
Chase for Millions. N. Carter
Chase in the Dark. N. Carter
Chase of the Golden Plate. J. Futrelle
Chase of the Linda Belle. H. Footner
Chase of the Ruby. R. Marsh
Chase Round the World. R. Overton
Chase Round the World. M. Weir
Chase the Snowman. M. C. McDougall
Chased by Fire. N. Gould
Chasm. V. Canning
Chasm. R. W. Kauffman
Chastity House. John Burke
Chateau Chaumond. A. Delmonico
Chateau d'Or. M. J. Holmes
Chateau of Mystery. L. T. Meade
Chateau of Shadows. M. Heath
Chateau Saxony. S. Richard
Chatham Rats. D. Mariner
Chattering Gods. R. Crawley
Chatterton Mystery. E. Everett-Green
Chautauqua. D. Keene
Cheat. R. Dietrich
Cheat the Hangman. E. Ferrars
Cheaters. L. Baker
Cheating Cheaters. M. Marcin
Cheating Justice. J. K. Stafford
Check No. 777. N. Carter
Check to the King. M. Gerard
Checked Through, Missing Trunk No. 17580. R. H. Savage
Checkerboard Caper. John Morris
Checkmate. S. Horler
Checkmate. J. S. Le Fanu
Checkmate. N. Lofts
Checkmate. P. Meredith
Checkmate and Deathmate. M. Ashley
Checkmate by the Colonel. G. Griswold
Checkmate for China. G. Osborne
Checkmate in Rio. N. Carter
Checkmate to Murder. E. C. R. Lorac
Checkmated Scoundrel. N. Carter
Checkmating a Countess. D. Stewart
Checkpoint. C. W. Thayer
Checkpoint Charlie. G. De Villiers
Cheer for the Dead. E. Colter
Cheerful Blackguard. R. Pocock
Cheerful Knave. Keble Howard
Cheese from a Mousetrap. J. M. Fox
Cheim Manuscript. R. S. Prather
Chekhov Proposal. Constance Carey
Chelsea Mystery. Elaine Hamilton
Chelsea Rainbow. C. Terrot
Cheltenham Square Murder. J. Bude
Chemes. Taffrail
Cheng Ling Mystery. Elliot Bailey
Cheque for Three Thousand. A. H. Veysey
Cherbourg Mystery. J. Maske
Cherchez la Femme. B. Graeme
Cheri-Bibi and Cecily. G. Leroux
Cheri-Bibi, Mystery Man. G. Leroux
Cherry-Fair. Winifred Duke
Cherry Harvest. E. H. Clements
Cherry in the Wine Glass. J. B. O'Sullivan
Cherrycake Death. I. Tain
Cherry's Choice. L. Cargill
Chess Murders. Means Davis
Chessboard Spies. Geoffrey Davison
Chest of Opium. Mr. M--
Chestermarke Instinct. J. S. Fletcher

Cheung, Detective. H. S. Keeler
Chevalier Casse-Cou. F. Du Boisgobey
Cheviot Chase. N. Tranter
Cheyne Mystery. F. W. Crofts
Chez Krull. G. Simenon
Chianti Flask. M. B. Lowndes
Chic Chick Spy. R. Tralins
Chicago Chick. H. Janson
Chicago Dames. B. Sarto
Chicago 11. D. Keene
Chicago Payoff. A. Capelli
Chicago Princess. R. Barr
Chicago Rod. L. Martin
Chicago-7. W. P. McGivern
Chicago Slaughter. M. Barry
Chicago Terror. M. Storm
Chicago Winter's Tale. A. B. Crunden
Chicago Wipeout. D. Pendleton
Chicago Woman. R. O. Saber
Chichester Intrigue. T. Cobb
Chick. E. Wallace
Chicken. M. Tripp
Chicken and Zella. M. Tripp
Chickens in the Airshaft. S. Franklin
Chief. C. Dawe
Chief Constable. V. Brown
Chief Constable. C. F. Gregg
Chief Counsel. A. L. Furman
Chief in Embryo. E. L. Long
Chief Inspector McLean. G. Goodchild
Chief Inspector's Statement. M. Procter
Chief Legatee. A. K. Green
Chief of the Counterfeiters. Old Sleuth
Chief Witness. H. Adams
Chiffon Scarf. M. G. Eberhart
Child at the Window. W. Hewlett
Child Divided. H. Cecil
Child Killer. E. T. Hamill
Child of Darkness. D. Daniels
Child of Evil. O. R. Cohen
Child of Mystery. H. M. Jones
Child of Night. Anne Edwards
Child of Rage. J. Thompson
Child of Satan. Melissa Napier
Child of the North. R. Cullum
Child of the Regiment. C. E. Blaney
Child of Two Fathers. T. P. Prest
Child of Value. P. Morton
Child Slaves of New York. C. E. Blaney
Child Witness. H. C. Davis
Child Witness. H. N. Halsey
Childerbridge Mystery. G. Boothby
Children Are Gone. A. Cavanaugh
Children Are Watching. P. L. Dixon
Children of Chance. A. Carlyle
Children of Chance. H. Lloyd
Children of Despair. J. Creasey
Children of Earth. S. Paternoster
Children of Hate. J. Creasey
Children of Hermes. H. Nisbet
Children of Houndstooth. K. Kimbrough
Children of Light. Robert (G.) Curtis
Children of Light. H. L. Lawrence
Children of Mammon. J. K. Leys
Children of the Abbey. R. M. Roche
Children of the Dark. I. Shulman
Children of the Griffin. E. Giles
Children of the Gutter. A. Applin
Children of the Mist. B. Knox
Children of the Night. J. Blackburn
Children of the Storm. D. Dwyer
Children of the Whirlwind. L. Scott
Children of the Zodiac. A. M. Williamson
Children's Overture. H. Gibbs
Children's Party. Arthur H. Lewis
Child's Garden of Death. R. Forrest
Child's Play. A. Campbell
Child's Play. K. Christie
Child's Play. U. Curtiss
Chilean Club. G. Shipway
Chill. E. C. Bentley

Chill. R. Macdonald
Chill and the Kill. J. Fleming
Chill Factor. R. Falkirk
Chill of a Corpse. G. Peters
Chillers and Thrillers. Anonymous
Chillery Court Mystery. R. Francis Foster
Chimney Murder. E. M. Channon
Chin-Chin-Chinaman. P. Walsh
Chin Chin, the Chinese Detective. A. W. Aiken
China Bomb. R. Tregaskis
China Cane. M. Storm
China Coaster. Don Smith
China Doll. N. Carter
China Governess. M. Allingham
China Kill. S. Hamill
China Rose. L. Crichton
China Roundabout. J. Bell
China Sea Murders. V. W. Mason
China Shadow. Clarissa Ross
China Shepherdess. F. Y. McHugh
China Town Mystery. G. H. Teed
Chinatown Stories. C. B. Fernald
Chinatown Trunk Mystery. O. Harper
Chinese Agenda. J. Poyer
Chinese Agent. M. Moorcock
Chinese Bed Mysteries. A. E. Martin
Chinese Bell Murders. R. Van Gulik
Chinese Blake. James Bennett
Chinese Bottle. P. Street
Chinese Box. K. W. Eyre
Chinese Brown of Scotland Yard. C. Bishop
Chinese Cabinet. A. Applin
Chinese Cabinet. "Capstan"
Chinese Chanty. V. Clemow
Chinese Chop. J. Sheridan
Chinese Coats. F. Heller
Chinese Coffin. J. Hedges
Chinese Connection. William Crawford
Chinese Conspiracy. J. Rosenberger
Chinese Conundrum. W. Manson
Chinese Crimson. A. S. Fleischman
Chinese Doll. W. Tucker
Chinese Doll Affair. A. Nuttall
Chinese Door. V. Coffman
Chinese Executioner. P. Boulle
Chinese Fish. J. Bommart
Chinese Gold Murders. R. Van Gulik
Chinese Goose. H. Robertson
Chinese Hammer. S. Harvester
Chinese Jade Affair. D. Miller
Chinese Jar. F. Hume
Chinese Jar Mystery. J. S. Strange
Chinese Keyhole. R. Himmel
Chinese Label. J. F. Davis
Chinese Lake Murders. R. Van Gulik
Chinese Letter. Claudette Nicole
Chinese Mask. B. S. Ballinger
Chinese Maze Murders. R. Van Gulik
Chinese Nail Murders. R. Van Gulik
Chinese Nightmare. H. Pentecost
Chinese Orange Mystery. E. Queen
Chinese Parrot. E. D. Biggers
Chinese Paymaster. N. Carter
Chinese Pleasure Girl. J. Seward
Chinese Poison. C. Hackforth-Jones
Chinese Poker. E. P. Thorne
Chinese Puzzle. M. Bower
Chinese Puzzle. M. Burton
Chinese Puzzle. M. Dekobra
Chinese Puzzle. R. Sapir
Chinese Red. R. Burke
Chinese Red. G. Collins
Chinese Shawl. P. Wentworth
Chinese Visitor. J. Eastwood
Chinese White. H. B. Drake
Chinese Widow. J. Leasor
Ching Ching on the Trail. E. H. Burrage
Chink in the Armour. Jack Lewis
Chink in the Armour. M. B. Lowndes
Chinks in the Curtain. J. Porter
Chink's Victim. J. G. Brandon

Title Index

Chip on My Shoulder. E. North
Chipstead of the Lone Hand. S. Horler
Chiselers. Albert Conroy
Chiseller. Duff Johnson
Chislehurst Mystery. E. L. Mann
Chit of a Girl. G. Simenon
Chivalry and the Gibbet. G. Curtis
Chocolate Charlie. T. Fitzgerald
Chocolate Cobweb. C. Armstrong
Chocolate Mousse Murders. F. Halliday
Choice. M. Brandel
Choice. P. MacDonald
Choice Cuts. P. Boileau
Choice of Angels. H. Arvonen
Choice of Assassins. W. P. McGivern
Choice of Enemies. T. Allbeury
Choice of Evils. Mrs. Alexander
Choice of Theodora. T. Cobb
Choice of Two Women. Gerald Butler
Choice of Violence. H. Pentecost
Choirboys. J. Wambaugh
Choirine Makes a Killing. C. Brown
Choke Chain. J. B. O'Sullivan
Choose Your Weapon. V. Loder
Chord in Crimson. G. Gallagher
Chorus Ending. E. Raymond
Chorus of Echoes. E. Trevor
Chosen Child. V. Maxwell
Chosen Course. N. Tranter
Chosen Girl. J. Buell
Chosen Instrument. H. Calvin
Chosen Man. Anonymous
Chosen Man. H. P. Halsey
Chosen of the Gods. A. Soutar
Chosen Sparrow. V. Caspary
Chowra's Revenge. F. E. Penny
Chris: A Love Story. J. Ironside
Christabel's Room. A. Clement
Christine Diamond. M. B. Lowndes
Christmas at Candleshoe. M. Innes
Christmas at Poverty Castle. T. Gallon
Christmas Card Murders. D. W. Meredith
Christmas Egg. M. Kelly
Christmas Guest. E. Southworth
Christmas Hirelings. M. E. Braddon
Christmas Murder. C. Hare
Christmas Spy. J. Howlett
Christmas Tree Murders. J. Y. Dane
Christmas Without Roddy. W. Fennerton
Christopher Bond, Adventurer. W. Martyn
Christopher Henrick. J. Hatton
Christopher Quarles, College Professor and Master Detective. P. Brebner
Christopher's Mansion. W. E. D. Ross
Chrome Connection. M. Simpson
Chromium Cat. W. Martyn
Chronicles of a Cavalier. J. G. Sarasin
Chronicles of Addington Peace. B. F. Robinson
Chronicles of Cardewe Manor. L. Farmer
Chronicles of Dennis Chetwynd. H. J. Fidler
Chronicles of Don Q. K. Prichard
Chronicles of Golden Friars. J. S. Le Fanu
Chronicles of Martin Hewitt. Arthur Morrison
Chronicles of Melhampton. E. P. Oppenheim
Chronicles of Michael Danevitch of the Russian Secret Service. D. Donovan
Chronicles of Quincy Adams Sawyer, Detective. C. F. Pidgin
Chronicles of Slyme Court. H. M. Raleigh
Chronicles of Solar Pons. A. Derleth
Chronicles of the Bow Street Police-Office. P. Fitzgerald
Chronicles of the Imp. J. Farnol
Chronicles of the Secret Service. A. Wilson
Chuckling Fingers. M. Seeley
Church of Humanity. D. C. Murray
Churchill Mission. K. Netzen
Churchyard Salad. M. Torrie
Churstons. P. Trent
Cider Row. W. K. McIntire
Cigar for Inspector Head. E. C. Vivian
Cigarette Clew. N. Carter

Cinderella All Alone. A. Wood
Cinderella Goes to the Morgue. N. Spain
"Cinders" of Harley Street. W. LeQueux
Cinema City. C. R. Gull
Cinema Crime. R. Goyne
Cinema Crimes. J. Creasey
Cinema Murder. E. P. Oppenheim
Cinnabar Shroud. K. Ashley
Cinnamon Murder. F. Crane
Cintra Story. M. Clare
Cipher. Alex Gordon
Cipher Detective. A. P. Morris
Cipher Five. A. O. Pollard
Cipher of Death. F. L. Gregory
Cipher Six. W. LeQueux
Cipher Stories Puzzle Book. K. S. Cooper
Ciprini. G. W. M. Reynolds
Circe Complex. D. Cory
Circle in the Water. J. McKimmey
Circle of Confusion. Palmer White
Circle of Danger. P. Alding
Circle of Death. H. Arvonen
Circle of Death. C. J. Dutton
Circle of Death. Richard Grant
Circle of Death. P. Quiroule
Circle of Death. M. Rennert
Circle of Dust. J. Cassells
Circle of Evil. V. Johnston
Circle of Evil. S. Wagner
Circle of Fear. P. Carlon
Circle of Fire. M. Sadler
Circle of Freedom. Mark Cross
Circle of Guilt. C. Kingston
Circle of Justice. P. Manton
Circle of Secrets. Claudette Nicole
Circle of Shadows. D. Holt
Circle of Squares. Bill Turner
Circle of Vengeance. N. Jorgenson
Circle of Von Boden. R. Harrison
Circle of Women. D. L. Pifer
Circle Round a Corpse. Hilary Landon
Circular Staircase. M. R. Rinehart
Circular Study. A. K. Green
Circumstances Beyond Control. A. Yudkoff
Circumstantial Evidence. A. I. Abbott
Circumstantial Evidence. N. Carter
Circumstantial Evidence. F. W. Crofts
Circumstantial Evidence. F. J. Fargus
Circumstantial Evidence. Andrew Stewart
Circumstantial Evidence. J. H. Swingler
Circumstantial Evidence. Bessie Turner
Circumstantial Evidence. E. Wallace
Circus. Alistair MacLean
Circus Crime. A. Skene
Circus Detective. Anonymous
Cire Perdue. J. Butler
Cistern and the Fountain. J. Matheson
Citadel of the Bats. M. Hastings
Citizens--to Arms! Garnett Weston
City and Suburban. F. Warden
City Beyond. L. Emerick
City Destroyer. G. Stockbridge
City for Sale. J. Messmann
City in Heat. W. B. Murphy
City Limit Blonde. A. Bocca
City Limits. N. Marino
City of Angels. S. Shagan
City of Anger. W. Manchester
City of Apes. A. Murray
City of Brass, and other Simon Ark stories. E. D. Hoch
City of Cain. K. Wilhelm
City of Crooks. S. Blake
City of Fear. F. Lady
City of Fear. John Marsh
City of Flaming Shadows. G. Stockbridge
City of Forever. B. Blackburn
City of Gold and Shadows. Ellis Peters
City of Horrors. W. J. Bayfield
City of Kites. T. Callas
City of Lies. C. Winchester

City of Lost Women. Griff
City of Masks. E. J. Murray
City of Mystery. A. C. Gunter
City of Peril. A. Stringer
City of Purple Dreams. Anonymous
City of Refuge. J. G. Sarasin
City of Shadows. P. Meredith
City of Silent Men. J. A. Moroso
City of Sin. R. O. Saber
City of Sin. B. Sarto
City of the Golden Gate. E. Everett-Green
City of the Just. T. Terrell
City of the Living Dead. B. House
City of the Soul. M. Home
Claim of the Fleshless Corpse. G. Bruce
Claimant. W. Chesney
Claire. D. Malm
Clairvoyant Countess. D. Gilman
Clairvoyante. B. L. Farjeon
Clancy. F. Mullally
Clancy of the Mounted Police. O. Binns
Clancy's Secret Mission. L. Thayer
Clang on the Anvil. H. C. Danby
Clap Hands If You Believe in Faries. John Fraser
Clara Lake's Dream. H. Wood
Clare of Claresmede. C. Gibbon
Claret, Sandwiches and Sin. M. Donne
Clarice Dyke, the Female Detective. H. Rockwood
Clark Gifford's Body. K. Fearing
Clash. E. Wilkinson
Clash by Night. R. Croft-Cooke
Clash of Distant Thunder. A. C. Marin
Clash of Hawks. R. Charles
Clash of Shadows. H. Rigsby
Clash of Steel. C. Robertson
Claud the Charmer. E. Everett-Green
Claude Duval of Ninety-Five. F. Hume
Claude Melnotte as a Detective, and other stories. A. Pinkerton
Claudia Pole. C. Dawe
Clause in the Will. W. M. Graydon
Claustrophobia. R. Child
Claverse Affair. J. G. Vermandel
Claverton Affair. J. Rhode
Claverton Case. R. Rodd
Claverton Mystery. J. Rhode
Claw of a Cat. G. Peters
Claws for a Cutie. B. Sarto
Claws of Fate. D. Dayle
Claws of God. M. Tripp
Claws of Mercy. J. Harris
Claws of the Cougar. N. Berrow
Claws of the Crow. P. Wissmann
Claws of the Red Dragon. C. Bishop
Claws of the Tiger. N. Carter
Claxton's Mill. F. M. White
Clay. H. Imbert-Terry
Clay Assassin. J. Godey
Clay-Face. J. Templeton
Clay Hand. D. S. Davis
Clean Break. L. White
Clean, Bright, and Slightly Oiled. G. Kersh
Clean Hand. M. B. Vandeburg
Clean Kill. M. Gilbert
Clean Up. Joe Barry
Clean-Up. L. C. Douthwaite
Clear and Present Danger. B. Kendrick
Clear Case of Murder. H. Desmond
Clear Road to Archangel. G. Rose
Clear Round. E.L. Long
Clear the Fast Lane. D. Rutherford
Clearer Vision. E. C. Mayne
Clearing in the Fog. D. Macomber
Cleek of Scotland Yard. T. W. Hanshew
Cleek, the Man of the Forty Faces. T. W. Hanshew
Cleek, the Master Detective. T. W. Hanshew
Cleek's Government Cases. T. W. Hanshew
Cleek's Greatest Riddles. T. W. Hanshew
Cleft of Stars. G. Jenkins

Clement Lorimer. A. B. Reach
Clemmie. J. D. MacDonald
Cleopatra Jones. R. Goulart
Cleopatra Jones and the Casino of Gold. R. Goulart
Cleopatra Needle Mystery. J. N. Pentelow
Cleopatra's Nose. T. B. Marle
Cleopatra's Tears. H. S. Keeler
Clerical Error. A. Rolls
Clerk of Portwick. G. M. Fenn
Clerycastle. M. Heath
Clevedon Case. N. Oakley
Clever Celestial. N. Carter
Clever Criminals. John Lang
Clever Detective. Old Sleuth
Clever One. E. Wallace
Clever Ones. J. E. Middleton
Cleverdale Mystery. W. A. Wilkes
Cleverest Woman in England. L. T. Meade
Cleverly Won. H. Smart
Cleverness of Mr. Budd. G. Verner
Clew Against Clew. N. Carter
Clew by Clew. N. Carter
Clew by Clew. Old Sleuth
Clew of the Forgotten Murder. C. Kendrake
Click of the Gate. A. Campbell
Client. M. Russell
Client Is Cancelled. R. Lockridge
Clients of Omega. D. Bloodworth
Cliff Face. D. Buckingham
Cliff Mill Mystery. G. Volk
Cliff Mystery. H. Aide
Cliff-Path Mystery. H. Hill
Cliffhaven. Dan Ross
Clifford Affair. A. Fielding
Clifford Mystery. A. Fielding
Cliff's End Farm and other stories. F. Warden
Cliff's Head. D. Kamm
Cliffs of Death. Claude Nicole
Cliffs of Dread. V. Coffman
Cliffs of Night. B. Brandon
Cliffs of Sark. G. Volk
Cliffside Castle. D. Daniels
Climate for Conspiracy. P. Harcourt
Climate of Courage. J. Cleary
Climate of Hell. J. Roeburt
Climate of Revolt. Alan White
Climax. G. C. Jenks
Climax. N. Karta
Climax. F. J. Lewis
Climax at the Falls. G. Baxter
Climb the Dark Mountain. J. Wellsley
Climb the Wall. M. Cronin
Climbing Corpse. A. Brede
Cling of the Clay. M. Hayes
Clinging Shadows. M. Waring
Clinic of Dr. Aicadre. Muriel Harris
Clip-Joint. E. Olmstead
Clipped Hedges. F. Hird
Clique of Gold. E. Gaboriau
Clique of Knaves. D. Stewart
Clive Lorimer's Marriage. E. Everett-Green
Cloak and Dagger Lover. M. Greig
Cloak for Malice. K. Wade
Cloak of Darkness. W. Magnay
Cloak of Guilt. N. Carter
Cloakroom Murder. W. Jardine
Clock. R. Goyne
Clock. A. E. W. Mason
Clock and Bell. S. Claudia
Clock and the Key. A. H. Vesey
Clock in the Hatbox. Anthony Gilbert
Clock Strikes. P. Troubetzkoy
Clock Strikes Ten. M. Richmond
Clock Strikes Thirteen. H. Brean
Clock Strikes Twelve. P. Wentworth
Clock Strikes Two. H. K. Webster
Clock Struck One. F. Hume
Clock Struck Seven. G. Goodchild
Clock Struck Twelve. J. Reach
Clock That Wouldn't Stop. E. Ferrars
Clock Ticks. C. Houghton
Clock Ticks On. V. Williams
Clock Without Hands. G. Kersh
Clockmaker. G. Simenon
Clockmaker of Heidelberg. H. Edmonds

Clocks. A. Christie
Clocktower. G. McDonell
Clockwork Orange. A. Burgess
Cloggy Dick. Arthur Smith
Cloisonne Vase. E. Noone
Close Call. J. L. Berry
Close Call. Old Sleuth
Close Call. E. Phillpotts
Close Doesn't Count. John Craig
Close Her Pale Blue Eyes. H. Hull
Close His Eyes. O. Dwight
Close of Play. S. Raven
Close Quarters. M. Gilbert
Close Shave. S. Maddock
Close the Door on Murder. J. York
Close the Frontier. L. A. Knight
Close to the Wind. J. Harris
Close-Up. M. Turnbull
Close-Up. D. Walshe
Close-Up of a Killing. R. M. Douglas
Closed Book. W. LeQueux
Closed Circuit. W. Haggard
Closed Door. R. M. Douglas
Closed Door. F. Du Boisgobey
Closed Door. S. Horler
Closely Confined. E. Burgess
Closing Circle. L. Cameron
Closing Door. J. Blackmore
Closing Net. H. C. Rowland
Closing the Circle. D. Stewart
Clotherstones. B. Goldie
Cloud. R. Bridges
Cloud over Malverton. N. Buckingham
Cloud the Smiter. A. Gask
Clouded in Mystery. M. A. A. B.
Clouded Mirror. E. Bond
Clouded Moon. S. Nichols
Clouded Moon. M. Saltmarsh
Clouds in the Wind. F. L. Green
Clouds of Fear. R. Bryant
Clouds of War. Ralph Hayes
Clouds of Witness. D. L. Sayers
Clouds over Vellanti. Elsie Lee
Cloudy in the West. W. P. White
Clough Plays Murder. L. Parsons
Clove Crest. I. A. Greenfield
Cloven Foot. M. E. Braddon
Cloven Foot. O. C. Kerr
Cloven-Footed Angel. M. Dekobra
Cloverdale Skeleton. C. L. Hooper
Clown. C. Brown
Clowning Through. E. C. Reed
Cloze Papers. K. Livingston
Club Car Mystery. G. I. Colbron
Club of Masks. A. Upward
Club of Queer Trades. G. K. Chesterton
Club of Skulls. Wilfred Barclay
Club 17. B. Kerr
Clubbable Woman. R. Hill
Clubfoot the Avenger. V. Williams
Clubs and Hearts. P. Trent
Clue. A. V. Arnold
Clue. C. Wells
Clue for Clancy. L. Thayer
Clue for Clutha. H. Munro
Clue for Mr. Fortune. H. C. Bailey
Clue for Murder. R. Barker
Clue from the Past. G. Langdon
Clue from the Stars. E. Phillpotts
Clue from the Unknown. N. Carter
Clue in the Air. I. Ostrander
Clue in the Clay. D. B. Olsen
Clue in the Glass. W. B. M. Ferguson
Clue in the Mirror. N. Morland
Clue in Two Flats. R. L. F. McCombs
Clue in Wax. F. M. White
Clue of the Artificial Eye. J. S. Fletcher
Clue of the Bricklayer's Aunt. N. Morland
Clue of the Careless Hangman. N. Morland
Clue of the Charred Diary. W. J. Bayfield
Clue of the Cloakroom Ticket. R. C. Armour
Clue of the Clock. M. Harvey
Clue of the Clot. C. Barry

Clue of the Cone. J. Arthur Williams
Clue of the Curious Cat. R. Brode
Clue of the Dead Goldfish. V. MacClure
Clue of the Eyelash. C. Wells
Clue of the Four Wigs. G. H. Teed
Clue of the Fourteen Keys. M. Burton
Clue of the Frightening Coin. Jessica Ryan
Clue of the Golden Ear-Ring. C. M. Wills
Clue of the Golden Tooth. J. Brooke
Clue of the Green Candle. G. Verner
Clue of the Green-Eyed Girl. N. Burnaby
Clue of the Hungry Corpse. I. Jones
Clue of the Ivory Claw. F. H. Dimmock
Clue of the Judas Tree. L. Ford
Clue of the Leather Noose. D. B. Hobart
Clue of the Lost Hour. C. M. Wills
Clue of the Missing Link. Gwyn Evans
Clue of the Naked Eye. C. M. Russell
Clue of the New Pin. E. Wallace
Clue of the New Shoe. A. W. Upfield
Clue of the Pin-Up Girl. W. Tyrer
Clue of the Poor Man's Shilling. K. M. Knight
Clue of the Postage Stamp. A. Bray
Clue of the Primrose Petal. H. Wickham
Clue of the Purple Asters. J. Cassells
Clue of the Rising Moon. V. Williams
Clue of the Second Murder. J. S. Strange
Clue of the Second Tooth. G. Verner
Clue of the Silver Brush. M. Burton
Clue of the Silver Cellar. M. Burton
Clue of the Silver Key. E. Wallace
Clue of the Six Kissing Girls. C. Herbert
Clue of the Stolen Rupees. A. Parsons
Clue of the Stone. H. A. Wrenn
Clue of the Tattooed Man. J. G. Brandon
Clue of the Twisted Candle. E. Wallace
Clue Sinister. C. Carnac
Clue to Danger. A. Furness
Clue to the Labyrinth. C. B. Clason
Clueless Trail. P. Walsh
Clues. W. Henderson
Clues for Dr. Coffee. L. G. Blochman
Clues from a Detective's Camera. H. Hill
Clues of the Caribbees. T. S. Stribling
Clues to Burn. L. G. Offord
Clues to Christabel. M. Fitt
Clunk's Claimant. H. C. Bailey
Cluny Problem. A. Fielding
Cluster of Gems. R. Carr
Cluster of Separate Sparks. Joan Aiken
Clutch of Circumstance. J. Barnes
Clutch of Circumstance. M. B. Cooke
Clutch of Constables. N. Marsh
Clutch of Coppers. G. Ashe
Clutch of Dread. N. Carter
Clutching Claw. R. Kettering
Clutching Hand. C. J. Dutton
Clutching Hand. A. B. Reeve
Clutha and the Lady. H. Munro
Clutha Plays a Hunch. H. Munro
Clutterbuck's Treasure. F. Whishaw
Clyde, the Resolute Detective. Old Sleuth
Clyde, the Trailer. M. O. Rolfe
Clyffards of Clyffe. J. Payn
Clytie. J. Hatton
Coach North. P. McCutchan
Coachman's Club. George R. Sims
Coal Tom. Old Sleuth
Coals of Fire and other stories. D. C. Murray
Coast of Adventure. H. Bindloss
Coast of Chance. Esther Chamberlain
Coast of Fear. K. G. Ballard
Coast of Fear. L. Waller
Coast of Intrigue. W. Chambers
Coast of No Return. M. Hastings
Coast Road Murder. M. Turnbull
Coat of Arms. E. Wallace
Coat of Blackmail. J. T. McIntosh

Coatine Case. A. J. Colton
Cobalt 60. R. L. Graves
Cobra Candlestick. E. Barker
Cobra Diamond. A. Lillie
Cobra Kill. N. Carter
Cobra Venom. A. Rowe
Cobra Venom. J. B. West
Cobweb. P. Flower
Cobweb Castle. J. S. Fletcher
Cobweb House. E. H. Holloway
Cobwebs and Clues. E. Malan
Cocaine. D. Forde
Cocaine. M. Olden
Cocaine Connection. R. L. Brent
Cock o' the North. T. Mundy
Cock-Pit of Roses. James Fraser
Cock Robin. E. L. Rice
Cockatoo Crime. B. Knox
Cockeyed Corpse. R. S. Prather
Cockleburr. R. Crawford
Cockney Cavalcade. G. Ingram
Cockpit. J. Kosinski
Cockpit. Warwick Scott
Cockroach Sings. A. Campbell
Cock's Tail Murder. H. Austin
Cocksure Dame. J. Cairo
Cocktail for Cupid and other stories.
  P. Cheyney
Cocktail Party and other stories.
  P. Cheyney
Cocktails and the Killer. P. Cheyney
Cocktails with a Stranger. C. Franklin
Coconut Wireless. F. Kauffman
Code. N. Carter
Code-Letter Mystery. D. Sharp
Code-Name Caruso. George Young
Code Name Gadget. P. Rabe
Code Name "Icy." L. Agniel
Code Name: Judas. M. Walker
Code Name: Little Ivan. J. Tiger
Code Name: Rapier. M. Walker
Code Name: Rubble. P. Thomas
Code Name Sebastian. J. L. Johnson
Code Name: Werewolf. N. Carter
Code of Conduct. Elliott Arnold
Code of Dishonour. B. Sanders
Code 1013: Assassin. L. Trevor
Code Three. J. M. Fox
Code Word--Golden Fleece. D. Wheatley
Code Word "Proton." E. P. Thorne
Codename--Bastille. B. Musto
Codfish Watch. E. R. Knowlton
Coffee for None. A. B. Caldwell
Coffee for One. E. Hale
Coffee in the Morning. G. Greenaway
Coffin Bird. C. Brown
Coffin Corner. G. Bagby
Coffin Corner. D. Shannon
Coffin Fits. A. Bocca
Coffin Following. Gwendoline Butler
Coffin for a Cutie. S. Morelli
Coffin for a Hood. L. White
Coffin for a Murderer. Reginald Campbell
Coffin for Baby. Gwendoline Butler
Coffin for Christopher. D. Ames
Coffin for Dimitrios. E. Ambler
Coffin for One. F. Beeding
Coffin for Pandora. Gwendoline Butler
Coffin for the Body. N. Morland
Coffin for the Canary. Gwendoline Butler
Coffin for Two. Robert Martin
Coffin from Hong Kong. J. H. Chase
Coffin from the Past. Gwendoline Butler
Coffin in Malta. Gwendoline Butler
Coffin in Oxford. Gwendoline Butler
Coffin Island. M. Leblanc
Coffin, Scarcely Used. C. Watson
Coffin Things. M. Avallone
Coffin Waiting. Gwendoline Butler
Coffin's Dark Number. Gwendoline Butler
Coffins for Three. F. C. Davis
Coffins for Two. Gwyn Evans
Coffins for Two. V. Starrett
Coffy. P. W. Fairman
Cogan's Trade. G. V. Higgins
Co-Heiresses. E. Everett-Green
Coil of Mystery. B. Bolt
Coil of Rope. J. F. Straker

Coin of Edward VII. F. Hume
Coiner's League. B. Wayde
Cold and Unhonoured. F. Hurt
Cold Bed in the Clay. R. S. Wallis
Cold Blood. L. Bruce
Cold Blood. Robin Richards
Cold-Blooded Murder. F. W. Crofts
Cold Blue Death. K. Stanton
Cold Chisel. J. B. O'Sullivan
Cold Coming. M. Kelly
Cold Companion. J. Sher
Cold Cream. A. Applin
Cold Dark Hours. A. G. Yates
Cold Dark Night. S. Gainham
Cold Dead Coed. H. Janson
Cold Death. K. Robeson
Cold Evil. B. Flynn
Cold Eyes. J. F. Dwyer
Cold Finger Curse. E. D. Torgerson
Cold Front. B. Everitt
Cold Jungle. G. Black
Cold Line to Moscow. Henry Talbot
Cold Night for Murder. Martin Thomas
Cold Night's Death. Barbara Harrison
Cold Ones. P. Kruger
Cold Poison. S. Palmer
Cold Route to Freedom. C. D. Peel
Cold Spell. J. Bruce
Cold Steal. A. Tilton
Cold Steel. J. Warren
Cold Terror. R. Chetwynd-Hayes
Cold War in a Country Garden. L.
  Gutteridge
Cold War Swap. Ross Thomas
Cold Waters. P. M. Hubbard
Cold Wind of Death. H. Seymour
Coldharbour. M. Cobb
Coldstone. P. Wentworth
Cole of Spyglass Mountain. A. P. Hankins
Coleraine Tragedy. E. T. Sawyer
Coleville Skeleton. R. C. Finney
Colfax Book-Plate. A. Miller
Collapse of Stout Party. J. T. Story
Collar for the Killer. H. Brean
Collected Stories of Ben Hecht. B. Hecht
Collected Tales. B. Pain
Collection of Strangers. D. Hitchens
Collector. J. Fowles
Collector's Choice. Peter Marks
Collector's Item. A. Dean
Collision Ahead. R. Johnston
Collusion. T. Cobb
Collusion. T. D. Irwin
Colonel and the Corpse. Tod Conrad
Colonel Blessington. P. Frankau
Colonel Bogus. J. Blackburn
Colonel Butler's Wolf. A. Price
Colonel Dam. J. S. Clouston
Colonel Gore's Second Case. L. Brock
Colonel Gore's Third Case. L. Brock
Colonel Grant's Tomorrow. G. Seton
Colonel Paternoster. R. Inchbald
Col. Ross of Piedmont. J. E. Cooke
Colonel Sun. R. Markham
Colonel Thorndyke's Secret. G. A.
  Henty
Colonel's Foxhound. C. M. Wills
Colonel's Past. F. Warden
Colonial King. H. Nisbet
Color Him Dead. C. Runyon
Color of Hate. J. L. Hensley
Colorado Jim. G. Goodchild
Colors of Death. S. Wagner
Colossus. E. Wallace
Colossus of Arcadia. E. P. Oppenheim
Colour Blind. C. A. Cookson
Colour Blind. S. P. B. Mais
Colour of Darkness. A. Dipper
Colour of Dried Blood. M. Vinter
Colour of Murder. J. Symons
Colour of Murder. P. Winn

Colour of Violence. J. Ashford
Colour Scheme. N. Marsh
Coloured Glass. I. R. G. Hart
Colours Flying. N. Tranter
Colt from the Country. A. Wright
Columbella. P. A. Whitney
Columbia. Anonymous
Columbine Cabin Murders. P. Mechem
Columbo. A. Lawrence
Columnist Murder. L. Saunders
Colwyn Dane--the Outlawed Detective.
  M. Grimshaw
Comanche Scalp. W. C. MacDonald
Combination-Lock Mystery. Anonymous
Come Alone. W. Woodrow
Come Along with Me. S. Jackson
Come and Be Killed. D. Bennett
Come and Be Killed! Shelley Smith
Come and Get Me. Griff
Come and Go. F. Gaite
Come and Kill Me. S. Gluck
Come and Kill Me. J. Tey
Come Away, Death. G. Mitchell
Come Away Death. A. G. Wilson
Come Back. Duff Johnson
Come-Back. C. Wells
Come Back and Die. I. Lambot
Come Back, Charleston Blue. C. Himes
Come Back for More. A. Fray
Come Back for the Body. David Hume
Come Back, My Love. E. S. Aarons
Come Back to Murder. S. H. Courtier
Come Back When I'm Sober. M. Waddell
Come Blonde, Came Murder. P. George
Come Dark, Come Evil. W. McNeilly
Come Destroy Me. V. Packer
Come Die with Me. J. Dark
Come Die with Me. J. Eastwood
Come Die with Me. W. C. Gault
Come Feed on Me. Morton Cooper
Come Hell and High Water. R. Petrie
Come Here and Die. M. Halliday
Come Home and Be Killed. J. Melville
Come Home to Crime. N. Deane
Come Home to Death. G. Ashe
Come In. E. C. Mayne
Come In Number One, Your Time Is Up.
  D. Jewell
Come into My Parlour. D. Wheatley
Come Kill with Me. H. Kane
Come Like a Storm. E. G. Cousins
Come Love, Come Death. S. P. B. Mais
Come Murder Me. J. Kieran
Come Night, Come Evil. Jonathan Craig
Come-On. W. Chambers
Come-On Girl. S. Friedman
Come Out, Come Out. G. Malcolm-Smith
Come Out, Come Out, Whoever You Are.
  T. McCann
Come Out Fighting. Duff Johnson
Come Out Killing. Robert Reeves
Come Out with Your Hands Up. H. Luger
Come Over, Red Rover. S. Marlowe
Come Quickly, Honey. H. Janson
Come See Me Die. M. Neville
Come See Them Die. H. Hadley
Come Sweet Death. M. S. Curry
Come, Sweet Death. S. Mitchell
Come, Thick Night. M. Neville
Come to Castlemoor. Beatrice Parker
Come to Dust. E. Lathen
Come to Judgment. J. S. Strange
Come to My Funeral. I. Wempe
Come-Uppance of Arthur Hearne. Angus Hall
Come Watch Him Die. S. Jason
Comeback. J. Tomerlin
Comeback for Stark. H. Reade
Comedian. K. Hewitt
Comedians. G. Greene
Comedy of Terrors. A. Carr
Comedy of Terrors. J. De Mille
Comedy of Terrors. M. Innes
Comedy of Terrors. Elsie Lee
Comedy of the Unexpected. G. W. Appleton

C

Comes a Stranger. E. R. Punshon
Comes the Blind Fury. H. McCutcheon
Comes the Blind Fury. D. Rutherford
Comes the Dark Stranger. Harry Patterson
Comethup. T. Gallon
Comets Have Long Tails. M. Johnston
Comet's Tail. A. Dick
Comforters. M. Spark
Comic Tragedy. G. R. Kuhn
Coming Back of Laurence Averil. M. Drake
Coming Home to Roost. G. M. Fenn
Coming of Age. R. Marsh
Coming of Aurora. P. C. De Crespigny
Coming of Carew. B. Graeme
Coming of Cosgrove. L. Y. Erskine
Coming of Jonathan Smith. H. Ludlam
Coming of the Monster. O. F. Dudley
Coming-Out Party. R. Frede
Coming Out Party. G. Petrie
Comlyn Alibi. H. Hill
Commander Amanda Nightingale. G. Revelli
Commander Leigh. R. H. Savage
Commander-1. P. George
Commandments Six and Eight. A. Griffin
Commando. R. Wilkes-Hunter
Commando Escape. Stagg Green
Commando X. P. Runyon
Commandos are Expendable. R. Wilkes-Hunter
Commemorations. H. Herlin
Commencement Day Murders. L. M. Floyd
Commerce Patrol. I. F. Anderson
Commission for Disaster. J. N. Chance
Commissioner. R. Dougherty
Committal Chamber. R. Braddon
Commodore Junk. G. M. Fenn
Common Love. J. B. Watney
Common or Garden Crime. S. Pim
Common Sense Is All You Need. J. J. Connington
Communicating Door. W. Camp
Communist's Corpse. R. Wormser
Compact. R. Cullum
Compact of Crime. B. Wayde
Companion to Evil. M. Farnsworth
Companion to Sirius. G. Goodchild
Company Man. J. Maggio
Company of Bandits. J. T. Story
Company of St. George. Kenneth O'Hara
Company of Shadows. J. M. Walsh
Company of Sinners. W. M. Duncan
Company of Strangers. J. Rosenberg
Compare These Dead! M. P. Rea
Compartment K. H. Reilly
Compass Points to Fear. J. Ward
Compassionate Crook. P. Goulden
Compassionate Rogue. G. Goodchild
Complete Change. A. J. Philip
Complete State of Death. J. Gardner
Complete Steel. C. Aird
Complete Stranger. V. Siller
Complete Werewolf and other tales of fantasy and science fiction. A. Boucher
Compliments of a Fiend. F. Brown
Composite Lady. T. Cobb
Composition for Four Hands. Hilda Lawrence
Compost Heap Corpses. S. C. Williamson
Compound for Death. D. M. Disney
Compulsion. M. Levin
Computer Kill. R. E. Banks
Comrade Jill. H. Adams
Comrade Souvarin. M. Moiseiwitsch
Comrade Spy. L. S. Ovalov
Comrades of Peril. R. Parrish
Comrades of the Black Cross. H. Nisbet
Comrades of the Right Hand. N. Carter
Con Game. M. Cronin
Con Game. H. Waugh
Con Man. E. McBain
Con Man. G. Verner
Conant. W. R. Burnett
Conceal and Disguise. H. Kane
Concealed Identity. M. Richmond
Concerning a Woman of Sin and other stories. B. Hecht
Concerning Blackshirt. R. Graeme
Concerning Miss Duncan. Mary Archer
Concerning Peter Jackson and others. G. Fraukau
Concerning the Saint. L. Charteris
Concerning This Woman. W. LeQueux
Concert Party Murders. John Norman
Concerto. P. Austin
Concerto for Fear. N. W. Firth
Concerto of Death. G. J. Barrett
Concrete Boot. K. Royce
Concrete Cage. R. Novak
Concrete Castle. F. Gerard
Concrete Castle Murders. F. Gerard
Concrete Crime. M. Coles
Concrete Curtain. J. Bogar
Concrete Evidence. M. Russell
Concrete Flamingo. C. Williams
Concrete Kimono. J. P. Carstairs
Concrete Maze. N. Morland
Concrete Nymph. N. Karta
Concubine. M. East
Condamine Case. M. Dalton
Condemned. H. Carmichael
Condemned. H. Desmond
Condemned. J. Pagano
Condemned as a Nihilist. G. A. Henty
Condemned Door. F. Du Boisgobey
Condemned to Death. J. R. Eyre
Condemned to Live. T. A. Plummer
Condition Green. N. Goble
Conditional Sentence. H. Fleetwood
Conduct of a Member. V. Gielgud
Cone of Silence. D. Beaty
Confederate. H. Fielding
Confederate Rogues. D. Stewart
Confederate Spy. T. N. Conrad
Confess to Dr. Morelle. E. Dudley
Confession. H. Carmichael
Confession. R. Francis Foster
Confession Corner, and other stories. B. Reynolds
Confession of a Thug. Warren Miller
Confession of Andrew Clare. David Robinson
Confession of Hercule. P. Audemars
Confession of Lorraine Herschel. N. T. Oliver
Confession of Murder. C. Barling
Confession of Murder. M. Neville
Confession to Murder. F. Arthur
Confessional. G. Simenon
Confessional of the Black Penitents. A. Radcliffe
Confessions of a Con Man. Will Irwin
Confessions of a Convict. P. A. Foxall
Confessions of a Convict. J. Hawthorne
Confessions of a Court Milner. L. T. Meade
Confessions of a Currency Girl. C. Dawe
Confessions of a Detective. Alfred H. Lewis
Confessions of a Ladies' Man. W. LeQueux
Confessions of a Scoundrel. G. Spencer
Confessions of a Thug. Meadows Taylor
Confessions of a Vagabond. C. Massie
Confessions of a Wife. Grace M. White
Confessions of Alma Quartier. David Robinson
Confessions of Alphonse. B. Pain
Confessions of an Attorney. G. Sharp
Confessions of an Imp. Old Sleuth
Confessions of an Old Burglar. Charles Morley
Confessions of Arsene Lupin. M. Leblanc
Confessions of Artemas Quibble. A. Train
Confessions of Cleodora. C. Dawe
Confessor. J. Donahue
Confetti Can Be Red. M. Cumberland
Confetti for a Killing. C. Edwards
Confidence King. N. Carter
Confidence Man. L. V. Erskine
Confident Morning. V. Gielgud
Confidential. D. H. Clarke
Confidential Agent. G. Greene
Confidential Agent. J. Payn
Confidential Mission. W. L. Whitehouse
Conflict. M. E. Braddon
Conflict. H. Janson
Conflict. C. B. Kelland
Conflict of Evidence. R. Ottolengui
Conflict of Interest. B. Williams
Conflict of Shadows. C. Robertson
Conflict of Women. E. Darby
Conflict Within. D. Reid
Confounding of Sergeant Cluff. G. North
Confrontation. N. Garbo
Confrontation. Ralph Vickers
Confucius in a Tail-Coat. M. Dekobra
Confusion at Campden Trig. V. B. Harris
Congo. W. A. Ballinger
Congo Venus. M. Head
"Coniackers." R. Rivers
Conjure Man Dies. Rudolph Fisher
Conjufer's Coffin. G. Cullingford
Conjurers. Marilyn Harris
Connecting Link. N. Carter
Connecting Rooms. W. Hughes
Connie Burt. G. Boothby
Connie Morgan Hits the Trail. J. B. Hendryx
Connie Morgan in Alaska. J. B. Hendryx
Connie Morgan in Barren Lands. J. B. Hendryx
Connie Morgan in the Arctic. J. B. Hendryx
Connie Morgan in the Cattle Country. J. B. Hendryx
Connie Morgan in the Fur Country. J. B. Hendryx
Connie Morgan in the Lumber Camps. J. B. Hendryx
Connie Morgan, Prospector. J. B. Hendryx
Connie Morgan with the Forest Rangers. J. B. Hendryx
Connie Morgan with the Mounted. J. B. Hendryx
Connoisseur's Case. M. Innes
Connolly's Woman. H. Whittington
Conor Sands. E. Kyle
Conover's Folly. D. Daniels
Conquered Place. R. Shafer
Conqueror Inn. E. R. Punshon
Conqueror's Road. L. A. Knight
Conquest After Midnight. B. Gray
Conquest Before Autumn. M. Eden
Conquest Calls the Tune. B. Gray
Conquest Goes Home. B. Gray
Conquest Goes West. B. Gray
Conquest in California. B. Gray
Conquest in Command. B. Gray
Conquest in Ireland. B. Gray
Conquest in Scotland. B. Gray
Conquest in the Underworld. B. Gray
Conquest Likes It Hot. B. Gray
Conquest Marches On. B. Gray
Conquest of Fortune. George Griffith
Conquest on the Run. B. Gray
Conquest Overboard. B. Gray
Conquest Takes All. B. Gray
Conquest Touch. B. Gray
Cons on the Run. B. Shannon
Conscience. A. Griffin
Conscience Makes Heroes. G. Abrahams
Conscience Money. S. Warwick
Conscience of a King. A. C. Gunter
Consequences of a Duel. F. Du Boisgobey
Conservatory. P. Hastings
Consider the Evidence. J. Ashford
Consider the Lilies. H. Ainsworth
Consider Your Verdict. R. Hardinge
Consider Your Verdict. N. MacKenzie
Consider Your Verdict. T. Mason
Consider Your Verdict. A. Soutar
Conspiracy. R. Baker
Conspiracy. P. Meriton
Conspiracy. W. Proudfoot

Conspiracy. R. Robinson
Conspiracy. A. S. Roche
Conspiracy at Angel. B. Flynn
Conspiracy Island. Peter Craig
Conspiracy of Love. L. Hoffman
Conspiracy of Rumors. N. Carter
Conspiracy of Silence. M. Blizard
Conspiracy of Silence. E. Butler
Conspiracy of Vipers. P. Ordway
Conspirator. H. Slater
Conspirator of Cordova. S. Cobb
Conspirators. W. Haggard
Conspirators. F. Kane
Conspirators. E. P. Oppenheim
Conspirators. F. Prokosch
Conspirators. A. Riefe
Conspirators at Large. S. Maddock
Conspirators in Capri. S. Maddock
Conspirators Three. S. Maddock
Constable and the Lady. J. Bude
Constable 42Z. E. A. B. D.
Constable, Guard Thyself! Henry Wade
Constables Don't Count. Alex Fraser
Constance, and Calbot's Rival. J. Hawthorne
Constance Dunlap, Woman Detective. A. B. Reeve
Consulting Room Crime. M. Osborne
Consulting Room Mystery. M. Osborne
Consummate Rose. L. Meynell
Consummate Scoundrel. G. Boothby
Contact and other stories. F. N. Hart
Contact Lens. M. Urquhart
Contact Lost. D. Craig
Contact Man. R. Betteridge
Contact Mercury. L. H. Nason
Contact Mr. Delgado. J. Pattinson
Contango Day. B. Jefferis
Content Assignment. H. Roth
Contents of the Coffin. J. S. Fletcher
Contessa Came Too. J. Bryan
Contesting the County, and other tales. B. Hemyng
Continental Conspiracy. F. W. Irwin
Continental Contract. D. Pendleton
Continental Op. D. Hammett
Contraband. C. F. Adams
Contraband. H. Janson
Contraband. C. B. Kelland
Contraband. L. A. Knight
"Contraband." R. Parrish
Contraband. D. Wheatley
Contraband Coast. W. Chambers
Contraband Cruises. Will Allen
Contrabandits. J. Workman
Contrabando. K. Detzer
Contract. H. Carlisle
Contract. O. Demaris
Contract. A. Prior
Contract for a Homicide. Dan Morgan
Contract for a Killer. D. Reid
Contract for a Killing. R. L. Brent
Contract for Death. D. Ingham
Contract on Cherry Street. P. Rosenberg
Contract on the President. J. Crosby
Contract with a Killer. H. Jobson
Convent Mystery. J. K. Stafford
Convent on Styx. G. Mitchell
Convention. F. Knebel
Conversation with a Corpse. R. C. Dennis
Convertible Hearse. W. C. Gault
Convict. N. Buntline
Convict. T. P. Prest
Convict B 14. R. K. Weekes
Convict by Proxy. A. Murray
Convict Captain. D. W. MacArthur
Convict Colonel. F. Du Boisgobey
Convict 413L. M. Leighton
Convict Has Escaped. J. Budd
Convict International. W. D. Maydwell
Convict 999. Grace M. White
Convict 99. M. Leighton
Convict 100. M. Leighton
Convict 1066. B. Gray
Convict 72. N. Ned

Convict Ship. W. C. Russell
Convict's Hoard. M. G. Hugi
Convict's Marriage. A. Bouvier
Convict's Sweetheart. Anonymous
Convict's Sweetheart. O. Harper
Conway, K.C. S. Stone
Cook General. J. Cashman
Cook Up a Crime. C. M. Russell
Cool Cottontail. J. Ball
Cool Day for Killing. W. Haggard
Cool Man. W. R. Burnett
Cool Murder. P. George
Cool Sleeps Balaban. D. MacKenzie
Cool Sugar. H. Janson
Cooler. G. Markstein
Coolie Tramp. E. L. Long
Coomsberrow Mystery. J. Colwall
Co-Ordinator. A. York
Cop. J. Karney
Cop Hater. E. McBain
Cop in a Tight Frame. Neill Graham
Cop-Kill. William Crawford
Cop Killer. G. Bagby
Cop Killer. M. Sjowall
Cop-Killers. Steve Scott
Cop-Lover. P. Malloch
Cop Out. E. Queen
Copenhagen Affair. S. McGurk
Copenhagen Affair. J. Oram
Copper at Sea. G. Fairlie
Copper Beeches. Arthur H. Lewis
Copper Bottle. E. J. Millward
Copper Box. J. S. Fletcher
Copper Butterfly. S. Harvester
Copper Disc. R. J. C. Stead
Copper Frame. E. Queen
Copper House. J. Regis
Copper Lady. H. L. Nelson
Copper Mask, and other stories. H. Wiley
Copperhead. J. Henderson
Coppers and Gold. H. Brinton
Coppers Don't Cry. J. Wainwright
Coppersmith. R. J. Griffin
Coppersmith's Dolls. R. J. Griffin
Cops. J. Pearl
Cops and Robbers. O. Henry
Cops and Robbers. D. E. Westlake
Cops 'n Robbers. J. Russell
Copsford Mystery. W. C. Russell
Copy-Cat Killings. Martin Thomas
Copy for Crime. C. Carnac
Coral Island. G. W. M. Reynolds
Coral Lady. E. Southworth
Coral Pin. F. Du Boisgobey
Coral Princess Murders. F. Crane
Corbin Necklace. H. K. Webster
Cord and Cheese. J. De Mille
Cord for a Killer. W. M. Duncan
Cordelia the Magnificent. L. Scott
Corder Index. R. Raine
Cordially Invited to Meet Death. R. Stout
Cordley's Castle. J. Pattinson
Cords of Vanity. D. Hennessey
Co-Respondent. G. W. Appleton
Corfu Affair. J. T. Phillifent
Corinthian Days. A. Soutar
Corinthian Jack. E. Pearce
Corioli Affair. M. Deasy
Cork and the Serpent. Macdonald Hastings
Cork in Bottle. Macdonald Hastings
Cork in the Doghouse. Macdonald Hastings
Cork on Location. Macdonald Hastings
Cork on the Telly. Macdonald Hastings
Cork on the Water. Macdonald Hastings
Cork Street Crime. J. G. Brandon
Cormorant Crag. G. M. Fenn
Cormorant's Isle. A. MacKinnon
Corner House. F. M. White
Corner in Coffee. C. T. Brady
Corner in Corpses. A. Bocca
Corner in Crime. Norman Lucas

Corner in Diamonds. M. Gerard
Corner Men. J. Gardner
Corner of the Playground. S. Harvester
Cornered. L. King
Cornered! J. McKimmey
Cornered. T. A. Plummer
Cornered at Last. N. Carter
Cornered at Last. A. F. Pinkerton
Cornered at Six. T. P. McMahon
Cornish Coast Conspiracy. D. Ames
Cornish Coast Murder. J. Bude
Cornish Crime. A. Weymouth
Cornish Cruise. G. Volk
Cornish Fox. C. H. B. Kitchin
Cornish Interlude. S. Murray
Cornish Mystery. M. Durham
Cornish Penny. C. T. Cade
Cornish Pixie Affair. P. Leslie
Cornish Riviera Mystery. J. Rowland
Corollary to Murder. R. White
Coronation Mysteries and other stories. H. Hill
Coronation Mystery. G. Chester
Coroner Doubts. R. A. J. Walling
Coroner Presides. S. Truss
Coroner's Pidgin. M. Allingham
Coroner's Verdict. R. Keverne
Corporal Cameron. R. Connor
Corporal Cameron of the North West Mounted Police. R. Connor
Corporal Died in Bed. B. Graeme
Corporal Downey Takes the Trail. J. B. Hendryx
Corpse. C. Brown
Corpse and Robbers. D. Stapleton
Corpse and the Lady. J. S. Strange
Corpse and the Three Ex-Husbands. P. MacTyre
Corpse at Camp Two. G. Carr
Corpse at Casablanca. B. Cobb
Corpse at College. M. Risco
Corpse at Least. S. H. Courtier
Corpse at the Carnival. G. Bellairs
Corpse at the Quill Club. A. R. Long
Corpse Awaits. O. F. Jerome
Corpse-Bird Cries. O. Norton
Corpse by Any Other Name. R. A. J. Walling
Corpse by the River. H. Arre
Corpse Came Back. A. R. Long
Corpse Came C.O.D. Jimmy Starr
Corpse Came Calling. G. C. Bestor
Corpse Came Calling. B. Halliday
Corpse Came Too. D. Reid
Corpse Can Sure Louse Up a Weekend! D. Tracy
Corpse Candle. G. Bagby
Corpse Can't Walk. H. Long
Corpse Comes Ashore. J. Mersereau
Corpse de Ballet. L. Cores
Corpse Died Twice. B. Frost
Corpse Diplomatique. D. Ames
Corpse Errant. M. Durham
Corpse for a Client. H. W. Gabriel
Corpse for Breakfast. M. Murray
Corpse for Charlie. J. Courage
Corpse for Charybdis. S. Gilruth
Corpse for Christmas. W. A. Ballinger
Corpse for Christmas. C. Brown
Corpse for Christmas. H. Kane
Corpse from "The City." J. G. Brandon
Corpse from the Sky. J. M. Crouch
Corpse Grows a Beard. M. Scherf
Corpse Guards Parade. M. Kennedy
Corpse Had Red Hair. A. Campbell
Corpse Hangs High. E. Ronns
Corpse in Camera. D. Launay
Corpse in Canonicals. G. D. H. Cole
Corpse in Cold Storage. M. Kennedy
Corpse in Community. D. Fisher
Corpse in Company K. R. Avery
Corpse in Diplomacy. M. Borgenicht
Corpse in Handcuffs. F. A. Smith
Corpse in My Bed. David Alexander
Corpse in the Boudoir. G. Ross
Corpse in the Cab. Aldin Vinton
Corpse in the Cabin. B. Sarto
Corpse in the Car. J. Rhode

Corpse in the Caravan. R. Trevor
Corpse in the Cargo. B. Cobb
Corpse in the Church. T. F. W. Hickey
Corpse in the Circus. N. Morland
Corpse in the Circus and other stories. N. Morland
Corpse in the Clouds. P. Conde
Corpse in the Constable's Garden. G. D. H. Cole
Corpse in the Coppice. R. A. J. Walling
Corpse in the Corner Saloon. Hampton Stone
Corpse in the Coupe. W. Paddon
Corpse in the Cove. E. Mack
Corpse in the Crevasse. G. Carr
Corpse in the Crimson Slippers. R. A. J. Walling
Corpse in the Derby Hat. H. Swiggett
Corpse in the Elevator. M. Mannon
Corpse in the Flannel Nightgown. M. Scherf
Corpse in the Green Pajamas. R. A. J. Walling
Corpse in the Guest Room. C. Wood
Corpse in the Picture Window. B. Cassiday
Corpse in the Snowman. N. Blake
Corpse in the Waxworks. J. D. Carr
Corpse in the Wind. R. P. Koehler
Corpse Incognito. B. Cobb
Corpse Is Indignant. Douglas Stapleton
Corpse Maker. David Wilson
Corpse Moved Upstairs. F. Gruber
Corpse Next Door. J. Farris
Corpse of the Old School. J. Iams
Corpse on Ice. J. Hedges
Corpse on London Bridge. L. Southworth
Corpse on the Bridge. C. Barry
Corpse on the Flying Trapeze. N. Morland
Corpse on the Hearth. Harry Lang
Corpse on the Mat. M. Kennedy
Corpse on the Town. J. Roeburt
Corpse on the White House Lawn. Diplomat
Corpse Parade. M. Hervey
Corpse Parade. R. Wallace
Corpse Road. G. Moffat
Corpse Rode On. J. G. Brandon
Corpse Said No. B. Frost
Corpse Steps Out. C. Rice
Corpse That Came Back. P. Piper
Corpse That Got Away. S. Truss
Corpse That Knew Everybody. C. Worth
Corpse That Never Was. B. Halliday
Corpse That Refused to Stay Dead. Hampton Stone
Corpse That Spoke. R. H. Leitfred
Corpse That Talked. R. Telfair
Corpse That Traveled. A. J. Rees
Corpse That Walked. O. R. Cohen
Corpse That Walked. R. Winsor
Corpse to Bury. J. B. Fearnley
Corpse to Cairo. M. O'Brine
Corpse to Copenhagen. Jonathan Burke
Corpse to Cuba. A. Kent
Corpse Too Many. J. Callender
Corpse Was a Blonde. H. Brown
Corpse Was No Bargain at All. Hampton Stone
Corpse Was No Lady. N. Morland
Corpse Who had Too Many Friends. Hampton Stone
Corpse Who Wouldn't Die. E. J. Doherty
Corpse with Knee Action. B. J. Maylon
Corpse with One Shoe. M. Scherf
Corpse with the Blistered Hand. R. A. J. Walling
Corpse with the Blue Cravat. R. A. J. Walling
Corpse with the Dirty Face. R. A. J. Walling
Corpse with the Eerie Eye. R. A. J. Walling
Corpse with the Floating Foot. R. A. J. Walling
Corpse with the Grimy Glove. R. A. J. Walling
Corpse with the Listening Ear. L. D. Smith
Corpse with the Missing Watch. R. A. J. Walling
Corpse with the Purple Thighs. G. Bagby
Corpse with the Red-Headed Friend. R. A. J. Walling
Corpse with the Sticky Fingers. G. Bagby
Corpse with the Sunburnt Face. C. S. Sprigg
Corpse Without a Clue. R. A. J. Walling
Corpse Without a Country. L. Trimble
Corpse Without a Jacket. L. West
Corpse Without Boots. L. Hill
Corpse Without Flesh. G. Bruce
Corpse Won't Sing. S. H. Courtier
Corpse Wore a Wig. G. Bagby
Corpse Wore Nylon. L. Paradise
Corpse Wore Rubies. F. Lester
Corpses at Enderby. G. Bellairs
Corpses at Indian Stones. P. Wylie
Corpses Can't Walk. Robert (G.) Curtis
Corpses Don't Care. E. Ellison
Corpses Galore. J. Bruce
Corpses Never Argue. David Hume
Corpus Delectable. T. Powell
Corrector of Destinies. M. D. Post
Correspondent. R. H. Shimer
Corridor of Death. Lieut. Carlton
Corridor of Mirrors. A. Hill
Corridor of Mirrors. C. Massie
Corridor of Venus. N. Bell
Corridor of Whispers. E. Noone
Corridors of Fear. S. Horler
Corridors of Fear. J. D. Perry
Corridors of Fear. Clarissa Ross
Corrie Who? M. Foster
Corrigan's Way. E. Snell
Corrupt City. E. Ellison
Corrupt Ones. J. C. Barton
Corrupted Women. B. Sarto
Corrupter. H. Barron
Corrupters. Clayton Moore
Corrupters. D. Telfer
Corruption. R. Curle
Corruption. P. Saxon
Corruption. Percy White
Corruption City. H. McCoy
Corruption in Cantock. J. Notley
Corruption's Tutor. J. Cello
Corruptors. W. Francis
Corsair. J. G. Sarasin
Corsican. B. S. Ballinger
Corsican Contract. E. Clark
Corsican Cross. Michael Bradley
Corsican Death. R. Hawkes
Corsican Takeover. Don Smith
Cortenay Treasure. P. C. Wren
Cosa Nostra. P. McCurtin
Cosa Nostra Circus. G. Corbin
Cosgrove: Detective. M. M. Innes
Cossack Cowboy. L. S. Taube
Cossack Mystery. H. Pink
Cost of a Clue. I. Stark
Cost of Living. R. D. MacDougall
Cost Price. D. Yates
Costello--Psychic Investigator. J. Nicholson
Cosy Little Murder. E. Radford
Cotfold Conundrums. D. G. Browne
Cotswold Case. A. Wynne
Cottage. Gretchen Travis
Cottage at Avalanche. J. Wetherell
Cottage at Chapelyard. F. Keinzley
Cottage in the Chine. H. Hill
Cottage in the Woods. D. Quentin
Cottage Murder. E. R. Punshon
Cottage of Terror. D. Stuart
Cottage on the Fells. H. D. Stacpoole
Cottage Sinister. Q. Patrick
Cotton Comes to Harlem. C. Himes
Couch. R. Bloch
Couch of Earth. P. Somerville-Large
Couch Trip. K. Kolb
Could It Be Murder? N. MacKenzie
Coulson Alone. Jack Mann
Coulson Goes South. Jack Mann
Council of Comforters. W. M. Duncan
Council of Crooks. W. J. Bayfield
Council of Death. N. Carter
Council of Justice. E. Wallace
Council of Seven. J. C. Snaith
Council of Ten. S. Cobb
Council of the Rat. J. Cassells
Councillors of Falconhoe. F. M. White
Counsel for the Defense. J. Ashford
Counsel for the Defense. J. Ronald
Counsel for the Defense. L. Scott
Counsel for the Killer. M. Carrel
Counsellor. J. J. Connington
Count Backwards to Zero. B. Halliday
Count Bruga. B. Hecht
Count Bunker. J. S. Clouston
Count Christoval. G. W. M. Reynolds
Count de Mornav. S. W. Wheeler
Count-Down. H. Howard
Count Down for Conquest. B. Gray
Count in Kensington. C. A. Alington
Count Me In. F. Nichols
Count Netherleigh. H. Wood
Count Not the Cost. I. MacKintosh
Count of Nine. A. A. Fair
Count of Six. L. Powell
Count Philip. P. Benoit
Count Remeny. J. Middlemass
Count the Cost. E. Ferrars
Count the Hours. C. Fraser-Simson
Count the Ways. D. M. Disney
Count Zarka. W. Magnay
Countdown at Monaco. L. Kenyon
Countdown for a Spy. D. Von Elsner
Countdown for Murder. G. Sydney
Countdown 1000. D. Mariner
Countdown to Crisis. M. Eden
Countdown to Doomsday. R. Quest
Countdown to Murder. H. D. Kastle
Counter Currents. E. Janis
Counter-Feat. H. Janson
Counter Paradise. N. Fleming
Counter Plot. E. Z. Frank
Counter-Spy. G. Dilnot
Counterattack. F. Scarpetta
Counterbalance. P. Trent
Counterfeit. H. Howard
Counterfeit. L. Thayer
Counterfeit Agent. N. Carter
Counterfeit Bill. L. Thayer
Counterfeit Bridegroom. L. M. Borden
Counterfeit Corpse. F. Findley
Counterfeit Corpse. N. A. Vanderpuije
Counterfeit Courier. J. C. Sheers
Counterfeit Gentleman. C. B. Kelland
Counterfeit Kill. Gordon Davis
Counterfeit Murder. W. Bannister
Counterfeit Murders. V. MacClure
Counterfeit Spy. A. O. Pollard
Counterfeit Wife. B. Halliday
Counterfeiter's Roguery. E. C. Derby
Counterfeiter's Wake. Lieut. Carlton
Countermine. A. Wenlock
Counterpoint Murder. G. D. H. Cole
Counterpoise of Death. H. Taylor
Counterpol. J. Boland
Counterpol in Paris. J. Boland
Counterspy. B. Cleeve
Counterspy Express. A. S. Fleischman
Counterspy Murders. P. Cheyney
Counterstroke. A. Pratt
Counterstroke. P. Wayland
Countertrap. J. Tiger
Counterweight. D. Brown
Countess and the Spy. G. De Villiers
Countess Ida. F. Whishaw
Countess Londa. G. Boothby
Countess Muta. C. H. Montague
Countess of Lascelles. G. W. M. Reynolds
Countess of Lowndes Square. E. F. Benson
Countess of Zelle. M. Gerard
Countess Vera. A. M. Miller
Countless Steps. B. Shannon

Country Club Murder. R. Verron
Country Coffins. Dale Clark
Country Family. J. S. Clouston
Country-House Burglar. M. Gilbert
Country Kind of Death. M. McMullen
Country Love and Poison Rain. P. Tate
Country of Again. P. M. Hubbard
Country of the Kind. S. Jennifer
Country of the Strangers. F. S. Wees
Country of the Wolf. S. Wagner
Country Squire. G. M. Fenn
Country Tragedy. F. C. Hall
Count's Chauffeur. W. LeQueux
Count's Millions. F. Du Boisgobey
Count's Millions. E. Gaboriau
Count's Secret. E. Gaboriau
County Affairs. R. Armfelt
County Family. J. Payn
County Kill. W. C. Gault
County Library Murders. J. Austwick
Coup That Failed. R. Worth
Coupon Crimes. G. Verner
Coupons for Death. N. Brady
Courage for Sale. Robert Mason
Courage of the North. J. B. Hendryx
Courageous Exploits of Doctor Syn. R. Thorndike
Courier for Crime. J. T. Story
Courier of Fortune. A. W. Marchmont
Courier to Marrakesh. V. Williams
Courier to Peking. J. Goodfield
Course in Murder. L. Chaytor
Course of Justice. V. L. Whitechurch
Course of Villainy. J. Moffatt
Court Favorite. B. Reynolds
Court Intrigue. B. Thomson
Court Martial. J. Ehrlich
Court-Martial. Robin Moore
Court of Crows. R. A. Knowlton
Court of Dusty Feet. J. G. Sarasin
Court of Honor. W. LeQueux
Court of Last Resort. L. H. Hart
Court of St. Simon. E. P. Oppenheim
Court of Shadows. G. Jackson
Court of the Thorn Tree. P. Maxwell
Court Short. J. Balfour
Court Tragedy. A. D. Vandam
Courtesy Dame. R. M. Gilchrist
Courtesy of Death. G. Household
Courthouse. J. N. Iannuzzi
Courtier to Death. Anthony Gilbert
Courtland's Crime. A. M. Burrage
Courtney Entry. J. Harris
Courts of Morning. J. Buchan
Courtway Case. R. Goyne
Courtyard. J. Moffatt
Cousin to Terror. C. Bramwell
Cove in Darkness. S. Wagner
Coven. C. Brown
Coven. David St. John
Coven Gibbet. J. N. Chance
Covenant with Death. S. Becker
Covenant with Death. F. Grierson
Covenant with Death. J. Harris
Covenant with Death. R. Walker
Covent Garden Murder. W. J. Makin
Covent Garden Mystery. W. J. Bayfield
Cover Girls. P. W. Fairman
Cover Her Face. P. D. James
Cover Her Face. H. McCutcheon
Cover Her with Roses. R. Anderson
Cover His Face. T. Kyd
Cover of Darkness. L. A. Olmsted
Cover That Corpse. H. Zore
Cover-Up Story. M. Babson
Coward Behind the Curtain. R. Marsh
Cowardly Custard. B. Von Hutten
Cowards' Castle. A. Soutar
Coward's Club. F. Grierson
Cowboy Countess. C. N. Williamson
Cowboy Detective. Old Sleuth
Cowboy Detective. C. A. Sirengo
Cowl of Doom. E. Ronns
Cowled Menace. W. E. Hawkins
Crabtree Affair. M. Innes
Crabtree House. Howel Evans
Crack in the Bell. P. C. MacFarlane
Crack in the Mirror. M. Haedrich

Crack in the Teacup. M. Gilbert
Crack of Dawn. L. Ford
Crack of Doom. L. Bruce
Crack of Doom. R. Cromie
Crack of Doom. G. Hackforth-Jones
Crack-Up. H. Atkinson
Crackerjack. W. B. M. Ferguson
Crackshot Detective. Anonymous
Cracksman All. G. C. Foster
Cracksman on Velvet. F. Selwyn
Crackswoman. Roland Daniel
Crackswoman. C. Dawe
Cradle and the Grave. A. M. Stein
Cradled in Fear. A. Boutell
Cradled in Murder. Rudd Fleming
Cradle's Revenge. Eric Bailey
Craft and Cunning. W. M. Graydon
Crafty Foe. H. Nisbet
Crag Island. W. M. Graydon
Craghold Creatures. E. Noone
Craghold Crypt. E. Noone
Craghold Curse. E. Noone
Craghold Legacy. E. Noone
Cragsmoor. J. Letton
Craig and the Jaguar. K. Benton
Craig and the Midas Touch. K. Benton
Craig and the Tunisian Tangle. K. Benton
Craig Kennedy, Detective. A. B. Reeve
Craig Kennedy Listens In. A. B. Reeve
Craig Kennedy on the Farm. A. B. Reeve
Craig Poisoning Mystery. A. Fielding
Craigallen Castle. Mrs. Gore
Craig's Spur. E. S. Madden
Craigshaw Curse. J. F. Webb
Craine's First Case. E. P. Healey
Crambo. M. O'Brine
Cranes of Ibycus. M. Craig
Crank in the Corner. C. Bush
Crash! A. Applin
Crash. H. Franklin
Crash and Carry. S. Christie
Crash into Murder. T. B. Morris
Crash Programme. J. R. Daniels
Crashlanding in the Congo. C. H. Wallace
Crashout. James Preston
Crater. R. Gore-Browne
Crater's Gold. P. E. Curtiss
Crave Pity from the Wind. B. Freestone
Craven Castle. L. Churchill
Craven Fortune. F. M. White
Craven Mystery. P. Trent
Crawlspace. H. Lieberman
Crawshay Jewel Mystery. Roland Daniel
Crayfish Club. R. Roberts
Crayfish Dinner. C. Keith
Crayon Clue. M. J. Reynolds
Crazy Joe. M. Barone
Crazy Kill. C. Hamblett
Crazy Kill. C. Himes
Crazy Mixed-Up Corpse. M. Avallone
Crazy Mixed-Up Nude. G. G. Fickling
Crazy Murder Show. Sutherland Scott
Crazy-Quilt. F. Hume
Crazy Quilt Murders. H. W. Sandberg
Crazy to Kill. A. Cardwell
Crazy to Kill. D. Linton
Creaking Chair. L. Meynell
Creaking Chair. A. T. Wilkes
Creaking Gallows. T. A. Plummer
Creaking Gate. V. Bridges
Creaking Tree Mystery. L. A. Knight
Cream and Cider. H. Gibbs
Created: The Destroyer. R. Sapir
Creative Murders. C. Brown
Creature of the Night. F. Hume
Creatures of Satan. John Muir
Creco the Swordsman. Old Sleuth
Credit for a Murder. S. Dean
Creep, Shadow! A. Merritt
Creep, Shadow, Creep! A. Merritt
Creepers. J. Creasey

Creeping Death. L. A. Knight
Creeping Flesh. D. Rutherford
Creeping Hours. H. Pentecost
Creeping Jenny Mystery. B. Flynn
Creeping Shadow. Sam Merwin
Creeping Shadows. W. Usher
Creeping Siamese. D. Hammett
Creeping Venom. S. Pim
Creeping Vicar. I. Hamilton
Creeps. A. Abbot
Creeps Medley. M. Hervey
Creggan Peerage. C. R. Gull
Creighton's Castle. M. Lynch
Crenland Castle. M. Gerard
Creole Slave's Revenge. O. Harper
Creole's Crime. M. Pinkerton
Crepe Myrtle Tree. L. V. Stevens
Crescent Brotherhood. N. Carter
Crescent Moon. L. Noel
Cresselly Inheritance. J. Blackmore
Cressida. M. B. Lowndes
Crested Key. K. Orbison
Creston, the Detective. Old Sleuth
Crestwood Traps. G. M. Snodgress
Cretan. E. Ayrton
Cretan Cipher. J. Palmer
Cretan Counterfeit. K. Farrer
Crevice. W. J. Burns
Crew of L.C. 454. E. L. Long
Cricket Cage. R. H. Shimer
Cries in the Night. J. H. Wallis
Crilly Court Mystery. H. S. Keeler
Crime. G. Bernanos
Crime. Anthony Lang
Crime. S. Longstreet
Crime. T. P. Prest
Crime a la Carte. M. Hervey
Crime Across the Way. F. Millington
Crime Against Judy Bishop. C. Barling
Crime Against Marcella. G. Milner
Crime Against Society. J. Spenser
Crime and a Clock. Whyte Hall
Crime and Again. R. Stout
Crime and Co. S. Fowler
Crime and Judy. R. L. Radford
Crime and Punishment. R. Ackland
Crime and Punishment. F. M. Dostoevski
Crime and the Casket. J. Ironside
Crime and the Confessor. H. G. Hutchinson
Crime and the Criminal. R. Marsh
Crime and the Curator. J. Veitch
Crime and the Motive. N. Carter
Crime and the Underworld. C. Bishop
Crime Apart. M. Underwood
Crime at Black Dudley. M. Allingham
Crime at Cape Folly. S. Browning
Crime at Christmas. C. H. B. Kitchin
Crime at Cloysters. R. Bayne-Powell
Crime at Cobb's House. H. Corey
Crime at Crooked Gables. T. A. Plummer
Crime at Crown Inn. M. Frazer
Crime at Diana's Pool. V. L. Whitechurch
Crime at Gargoyles. K. Wade
Crime at Grandison Hall. H. Leyford
Crime at Guildford. F. W. Crofts
Crime at Halfpenny Bridge. G. Bellairs
Crime at Honotassa. M. G. Eberhart
Crime at Keeper's. T. Cobb
Crime at Lock 14. G. Simenon
Crime at Nornes. F. W. Crofts
Crime at Orcival. E. Gaboriau
Crime at Porches Hill. R. Bayne-Powell
Crime at Red Towers. C. K. Steele
Crime at Tattenham Corner. A. Haynes
Crime at the Conquistador. S. Callaway
Crime at the Crossroads. P. Urquhart
Crime at the Crossways. B. Flynn
Crime at the Fair. H. King
Crime at the "Noah's Ark." M. Thynne
Crime at the Quay. A. Blair
Crime at the Quay Inn. E. Aldhouse
Crime at the Seaside Hotel. A. Blair
Crime at the Villa Gloria. G. Norsworthy
Crime at 3 a.m. H. Clevely
Crime Beat Crisis. H. Janson

C

Crime by Chance. E. Linington
Crime Cargo. M. Knight
Crime Club. Anonymous
Crime Club. F. Froest
Crime Club. W. Holt-White
Crime Coast. E. Gill
Crime Code. W. LeQueux
Crime Combine. David Hume
Crime Conductor. P. MacDonald
Crime Confessions. J. W. Firth
Crime Cop. L. Holden
Crime Counter Crime. E. C. R. Lorac
Crime Cruise. E. L. Long
Crime Cult. M. Grant
Crime de Luxe. E. Gill
Crime Doctor. E. W. Hornung
Crime File. D. Shannon
Crime for Christmas. M. Lynch
Crime for Mothers and others. H. Slesar
Crime Gang. M. E. Cooke
Crime, Gentlemen, Please. D. Ames
Crime Haters. G. Ashe
Crime Hound. M. S. Scott
Crime in a Big Way. C. Bishop
Crime in Cabin 66. A. Christie
Crime in Car 13. S. Chalmers
Crime in Carson's Shack. R. Hardinge
Crime in Concrete. M. Coles
Crime in Corn-Weather. M. M. Atwater
Crime in Crystal. H. R. Campbell
Crime in Cumberland Court. R. A. J. Walling
Crime in Holland. G. Simenon
Crime in Ink. C. Carvalho
Crime in Kensington. C. S. Sprigg
Crime in Lepers' Hollow. G. Bellairs
Crime in Paradise. N. Carter
Crime in Park Lane. W. Jardine
Crime in Quarantine. Rosa Lambert
Crime in Reverse. J. D. Kennedy
Crime in Room 27. W. Tyrer
Crime in the Alps. G. Warden
Crime in the Arcade. W. Proudfoot
Crime in the Boulevard Raspail. R. Massey
Crime in the Close. A. Dick
Crime in the Crypt. F. W. Gumley
Crime in the Crypt. C. Wells
Crime in the Crystal. R. Hare
Crime in the Dutch Garden. H. Adams
Crime in the Kiosk. J. G. Brandon
Crime in the Wood. W. M. Graydon
Crime in the Wood. T. W. Speight
Crime in Threadneedle Street. George Davis
Crime in Time. M. Burton
Crime in Washington Mews. H. Crooken
Crime in Whispers. C. Witting
Crime Inc. J. S. Endicott
Crime Incarnate. C. Wells
Crime Insoluble. M. Durham
Crime Is Murder. H. Nielsen
Crime Is My Business. W. H. Baker
Crime Is of the Essence. J. Csida
Crime Legitimate. P. Luck
Crime Limited. L. C. Douthwaite
Crime Looks Up. C. Rushton
Crime Maker. B. Fleming
Crime Master. W. M. Duncan
Crime Medley. M. Hervey
Crime Most Foul. George Douglas
Crime of a Christmas Toy. H. Herman
Crime of a Countess. N. Carter
Crime of Bohemia. J. K. Stafford
Crime of Colin Wise. M. Underwood
Crime of Constable Kelly. J. C. Snaith
Crime of Convict 13. W. M. Graydon
Crime of Corporal Sherwood. G. Chester
Crime of Count Dureen. P. Urquhart
Crime of Four. G. Verner
Crime of Golden Gully. G. Rock
Crime of Gunga Dass. C. Brisbane
Crime of Hallowe'en. L. J. Libbey
Crime of Herbert Wratislaus. Michael Lewis
Crime of his Life. C. Conrad
Crime of Honor. G. Arpino
Crime of Inspector Maigret. G. Simenon
Crime of Jane Dacre. S. C. Lethbridge
Crime of Julian Masters. E. Atiyah

Crime of Keziah Keene. V. Campbell
Crime of Laura Sarelle. J. Shearing
Crime of Maunsell Grange. F. Breton
Crime of Mildred Bentham. T. B. Morris
Crime of Monte Carlo. Anonymous
Crime of One's Own. E. Grierson
Crime of Peter Ropner. H. Heslop
Crime of Philip Garrison. F. Marlowe
Crime of Philip Guthrie. L. Ragsdale
Crime of Silence. P. Carlon
Crime of Sybil Cresswell. E. F. Spence
Crime of the Boulevard. J. Claretie
Crime of the Camera. N. Carter
Crime of the Cashiered Major. A. Parsons
Crime of the Catacombs. G. H. Teed
Crime of the Century. A. Abbot
Crime of the Century. N. Carter
Crime of the Century. D. Donovan
Crime of the Century. R. Ottolengui
Crime of the Chromium Bowl. E. B. Black
Crime of the Crossword. J. Garland
Crime of the Crystal. F. Hume
Crime of the French Cafe and other stories. N. Carter
Crime of the 'Liza Jane. F. Hume
Crime of the Midnight Express. A. F. Pinkerton
Crime of the Opera House. F. Du Boisgobey
Crime of the Reckaviles. W. S. Masterman
Crime of the Under-Seas. G. Boothby
Crime of Their Life. F. Kane
Crime of Vera Seymour. B. Heygate
Crime of Violence. R. King
Crime of Violence. J. Stagg
Crime of Wilfred Hanson. Alfred James Alderson
Crime on a Convoy Carrier. A. Whitehouse
Crime on a Cruise. K. Rhodes
Crime on Canvas. F. M. White
Crime on Cote des Neiges. D. Montrose
Crime on Gallows Hill. G. H. Teed
Crime on her Hands. R. Stout
Crime on Her Hands. R. Stout
Crime on My Hands. R. Chapman
Crime on My Hands. R. Chapman
Crime on My Hands. R. Drayton
Crime on My Hands. C. G. Hodges
Crime on My Hands. H. Janson
Crime on My Hands. J. Laffin
Crime on My Hands. G. Sanders
Crime on the Cliff. L. Jackson
Crime on the Clyde. G. Chester
Crime on the Cuff. H. Weiner
Crime on the French Frontier. J. Hunter
Crime on the Heath. C. V. Frost
Crime on the Kennet. C. A. Alington
Crime on the Limited. N. Ridley
Crime on the Moor. T. C. Bridges
Crime on the Moors. W. Tyrer
Crime on the Promenade. J. Hunter
Crime on the Solent. F. W. Crofts
Crime on Their Hands. D. Shannon
Crime or Folly? B. M. Clay
Crime Oracle. M. Grant
Crime Out of Mind. D. Ames
Crime Pays No Dividends. E. Radford
Crime Philosopher. R. Goyne
Crime Reporter's Secret. G. Dilnot
Crime School. M. Cumberland
Crime Scientist. F. A. M. Webster
Crime Specialist. D. Newton
Crime Squadron. B. Waller
Crime Syndicate. P. Manton
Crime Takes the Count. Elliott Dane
Crime Takes Wings. J. S. Dawe
Crime Tears On. C. Wells
Crime, the Place, and the Girl. D. Stapleton
Crime to Music. P. Drax
Crime Unlimited. David Hume
Crime Upon Crime. A. Gask
Crime Wave. M. Russell

Crime Wave at Blandings. P. G. Wodehouse
Crime Wave at Little Cornford. H. Adams
Crime Wind. M. Holbrook
Crime with Many Voices. M. Halliday
Crime with Ten Solutions. H. Leyford
Crime Within Crime. P. Drax
Crime Without a Clue. T. Cobb
Crime Without a Flaw. L. Despard
Crime Without a Name. D. Stewart
Crime Without Reason. George Douglas
Crimes at Fenton Towers. W. Tyrer
Crimes at Rillington Place. J. N. Chance
Crimes Club. W. LeQueux
Crime's Masquerader. A. MacVicar
Crimes of Cleopatra's Needle. J. M. Walsh
Criminal. J. Thompson
Criminal Airman. A. O. Pollard
Criminal at Large. E. Wallace
Criminal C.O.D. P. A. Taylor
Criminal Conversation. N. Freeling
Criminal Court. W. Lyon
Criminal Croesus. George Griffith
Criminal Link. N. Carter
Criminal Queen. E. A. Young
Criminal Reminiscences and Detective Sketches. A. Pinkerton
Criminal Square. H. Hastings
Criminal Tendencies. J. Goodman
Criminal Yarns. T. C. Bridges
Criminals All. W. Martyn
Criminals Caught. J. M'Govan
Criminals I Have Known. A. Griffiths
Criminals Run Down. Old Sleuth
Crimshaw Memorandum. L. White
Crimson Alibi. O. R. Cohen
Crimson Belt. G. H. Teed
Crimson Blade. M. S. Buchanan
Crimson Blind. F. M. White
Crimson Blotter. I. Ostrander
Crimson Box. H. S. Keeler
Crimson Butterfly. E. Snell
Crimson Candle. E. Bond
Crimson Cat. F. Grierson
Crimson Cat Murders. S. E. Porcelain
Crimson Chair, and other stories. R. Dowling
Crimson Circle. E. Wallace
Crimson Claw. W. Hewlett
Crimson Clown. J. McCulley
Crimson Clown Again. J. McCulley
Crimson Clue. G. H. Coxe
Crimson Clue. I. Stark
Crimson Crescent. Augustus Muir
Crimson Crime. G. M. Fenn
Crimson Cross. C. E. Walk
Crimson Cryptogram. F. Hume
Crimson Dacoit. A. Wilson
Crimson Dice. G. N. McCain
Crimson Domino. G. Goodchild
Crimson Domino. W. W. Sayer
Crimson Feather. M. Crossley
Crimson Feather. S. E. Mason
Crimson Flash. N. Carter
Crimson Frame. A. L. Martin
Crimson Friday. D. C. Disney
Crimson Glove. Warren Miller
Crimson Goddess. E. S. Carrington
Crimson Hair Murders. D. L. Teilhet
Crimson Hairs. Whiddon Graham
Crimson Hand. R. C. Finney
Crimson Honeymoon. H. Hill
Crimson Ice. C. Fitzsimmons
Crimson in the Purple. H. Roth
Crimson Jade. G. B. Mair
Crimson Madness of Little Doom. M. McShane
Crimson Mascot. C. E. Pearce
Crimson Mask. W. H. L. Crauford
Crimson Mask. A. Steffens Hardy
Crimson Moon. I. Foster
Crimson Pall. W. Dawson
Crimson Patch. P. A. Taylor
Crimson Paw. M. G. Eberhart
Crimson Poppies. M. Benson

Title Index

Crimson Query. A. Eadie
Crimson Quest. D. Barr
Crimson Ramblers. G. Verner
Crimson Rope. H. Asbury
Crimson Serpent. K. Robeson
Crimson Shadow. Roland Daniel
Crimson Stain. A. Bradshaw
Crimson Swastika. E. Snell
Crimson Thread. L. Lauferty
Crimson Threat. G. E. Rochester
Crimson Trail. J. Walker
Crimsoned Millions. J. Willoughby
Crinkled Crown. W. LeQueux
Crippled Canary. V. Gunn
Crippled Hand. F. S. Stewart
Crises. M. Level
Crisis. J. Cello
Crisis. D. E. Fisher
Crisis Comes to Mister Smith. Richard Fisher
Crisis for Two. Mark Ross
Criss-Cross. D. Tracy
Criton Hunt Mystery. R. Jocelyn
Croaked the Raven. B. Fischer
Croaker. G. Ashe
Croaker. R. Garnett
Croaker. Arthur Russell
Croaking Raven. G. Mitchell
Croation. T. B. Marle
Crock of Gold. M. F. Tupper
Crockett on the Loose. B. Lang
Crockett's Woman. E. Hatch
Crocodile Club. A. Broome
Crocodile Down the River. G. C. Foster
Crocodile Man. P. Meredith
Crocodile on the Sankbank. Elizabeth Peters
Cromwell's Cavalier. J. Sanders
Cronin Mystery. John Arthur Fraser
Crook. Jonathan Starr
Crook Bait. L. C. Douthwaite
Crook Cargo. J. Hunter
Crook from Chicago. S. Hood
Crook in the Furrow. A. G. Street
Crook of Canada. G. H. Teed
Crook of Chinatown. W. M. Graydon
Crook of Costa Blanca. G. H. Teed
Crook of Crauford Court. L. Essex
Crook of Fleet Street. Gwyn Evans
Crook o' Lune. E. C. R. Lorac
Crook of Marsden Manor. G. H. Teed
Crook of Mayfair. H. H. C. Gibbons
Crook of Monte Carlo. G. H. Teed
Crook of Newmarket. A. Steffens Hardy
Crook of Paris. G. H. Teed
Crook of Shanghai. G. H. Teed
Crook Ship. M. Frazer
Crook Stuff. R. Keverne
Crook Town. A. Skene
Crooked. M. Foster
Crooked Adam. D. E. Stevenson
Crooked Alley. Irene Alexander
Crooked Bough. J. Remenham
Crooked Business. F. Marlowe
Crooked Circle. M. L. Stokes
Crooked Circle. G. Verner
Crooked City. R. Kyle
Crooked Coffins. Griff
Crooked Company. F. Marlowe
Crooked Cop. Bob Parker
Crooked Coronet. M. Arlen
Crooked Cross. C. J. Dutton
Crooked Eye. K. Virden
Crooked Finger. A. MacVicar
Crooked Finger. E. A. Treeton
Crooked Five! J. G. Brandon
Crooked Frame. W. P. McGivern
Crooked Furrow. J. Farnol
Crooked Gambler. R. Hardinge
Crooked Game. A. Wright
Crooked Highway. A. Spiller
Crooked Hinge. J. D. Carr
Crooked House. A. Christie
Crooked House. B. Fleming
Crooked House. J. Rowland
Crooked Inn. E. Dudley
Crooked Inspector. B. Wayde
Crooked Jacket. D. Dayle

Crooked Killer. P. Manton
Crooked Lady. B. Sarto
Crooked Lane. F. N. Hart
Crooked Lanes. R. S. Holland
Crooked Lip. H. Adams
Crooked Man. Shelley Smith
Crooked Men Came. R. F. Lambert
Crooked Mile. N. Fagan
Crooked Money. J. E. Day
Crooked Paths. D. Lee
Crooked Phoenix. B. Jones
Crooked Road. M. L. West
Crooked Samaritan. P. Trent
Crooked Shadow. K. Steel
Crooked Shadows. J. Crowe
Crooked Shadows. Gordon Young
Crooked Shamrock. C. B. Gilford
Crooked Sign. B. Bolt
Crooked Sixpence. L. Grex
Crooked Staircase. V. Gunn
Crooked Straight. E. Dudley
Crooked Tree. T. B. Morris
Crooked Way. W. LeQueux
Crooked Wreath. C. Brand
Crookedshaws. Winifred Duke
Crookery Inn. M. Crossley
Crooking Finger. C. F. Adams
Crook's Accomplice. A. Skene
Crooks and Vagabonds. R. Keverne
Crook's Blind. N. Carter
Crooks' Caravan. Frank King
Crook's Cargo. J. G. Brandon
Crooks' Castle. B. Atkey
Crook's Castle. G. Dilnot
Crooks Convoy. A. Blair
Crooks' Cross. Frank King
Crook's Crossing. V. Lester
Crook's Cruise. Seafarer
Crook's Decoy. G. H. Teed
Crook's Deputy. G. H. Teed
Crook's Double. W. J. Bayfield
Crook's Double. N. Carter
Crook's Double. A. Murray
Crooks' Game. G. Dilnot
Crooks' Hill. San Antonio
Crooks in Cabaret. S. Simpson
Crooks in Clover. G. H. Teed
Crooks in the Sunshine. E. P. Oppenheim
Crooks Ltd. L. Bidston
Crook's Loot. W. Jardine
Crooks of Paris. D. Lenton
Crooks of the Waldorf. Horace Smith
Crooks of Tunis. A. Parsons
Crook's Shadow. J. J. Farjeon
Crooks' Shepherd. S. Truss
Crook's Turning. John Muir
Crooks' Vendetta. G. H. Teed
Crookshaven Murder. Alexander Morrison
Crooner's Swan Song. L. Grex
Cropper's Cabin. J. Thompson
Cross-Channel Crime. G. H. Teed
Cross-Country. H. D. Kastle
Cross Cut. C. R. Cooper
Cross-Eyed Bear. D. B. Hughes
Cross-Eyed Bear Murders. D. B. Hughes
Cross-Fires. F. Warden
Cross for Tomorrow. M. Farnsworth
Cross Marks the Spot. J. Ronald
Cross of Gold Affair. F. Davies
Cross of Lazzaro. J. Harris
Cross of Murder. Carter Dickson
Cross of the Dust. M. O. Rolfe
Cross Over Nine. W. C. Butler
Cross Purposes. A. Dick
Cross Purposes. Jim Thomas
Crossbow Murder. Carter Dickson
Crossed Needles. N. Carter
Crossed Path. W. Collins
Crossed Skis. C. Carnac
Crossed Wires. N. Carter

Crossfire. D. Lynds
Crossing of Clues. E. C. Derby
Crossroad Murders. G. Simenon
Crossroads. J. D. MacDonald
Crossword Murder. E. R. Punshon
Crossword Mystery. E. R. Punshon
Crotchet Castle. T. L. Peacock
Crouching at the Door. D. K. Broster
Crouching Beast. V. Williams
Crouching Men. A. West
Crouching Spy. A. MacVicar
Crow and the Cat. P. De Polnay
Crow Hollow. D. Eden
Crowded and Dangerous. A. Lejeune
Crowing Hen. R. Davis
Crown: Bamboo Shoot-Out. T. Harknett
Crown Colony. N. Harman
Crown Diamond. N. Carter
Crown: Macao Mayhem. T. Harknett
Crown of India. S. Fuller
Crown of Night. P. Audemars
Crown of Straw. A. Upward
Crown Swindle. M. L. Eades
Crown: The Sweet and Sour Kill. T. Harknett
Crowned Skull. F. Hume
Crowner's Quest. A. Broome
Crowning Murder. H. H. Stanners
Crowning of Esther. M. Gerard
Crowns Can Kill. H. Janson
Crows Are Black Everywhere. H. O. Yardley
Crows Can't Count. A. A. Fair
Crow's Inn Tragedy. A. Haynes
Croyd. Ian Wallace
Crucible. S. Murray
Crucible. B. A. Williams
Crucible Island. C. B. Pallen
Crucible of Circumstance. P. Brebner
Crucible of Evil. Lydia Belknap Long
Cruciform Mark. R. Stephens
Cruel as a Cat. M. Halliday
Cruel as the Grave. I. Bayne
Cruel as the Grave. E. Southworth
Cruel Case. S. Rathbone
Cruel Dart. H. Carstairs
Cruel Deadline. R. Gaines
Cruel Fire. E. Atiyah
Cruel Is the Night. Howard Hunt
Cruel Lady. M. Corrigan
Cruel Legacy. L. H. Hudson
Cruel London. J. Hatton
Cruel Secret. Anonymous
Cruel Suspicion. F. P. Rathburne
Cruise of Death. J. Rand
Cruise of Terror. S. Hope
Cruise of the Albatross. G. Allen
Cruise of the Carefree. John Marsh
Cruise of the Conqueror. S. Paternoster
Cruise of the Jasper B. Appleton. D. Marquis
Cruise with Death. F. Draco
Cruiser in Action. Reginald Campbell
Cruiser on Wheels. G. Thorne
Cruising. Gerald Walker
Crumblerock Crime! W. J. Bayfield
Crumpled Cup. H. Kane
Crumpled Leaf. Mrs. Alexander
Crumpled Lilies. C. Dawe
Crusade into Crime. R. Wilkes-Hunter
Crusader's Cross. J. Pattinson
Crusoe Harry. Old Sleuth
Cry Aloud for Murder. P. McGuire
Cry at Dusk. L. Dent
Cry, Baby, Cry! J. Ehrlich
Cry Baby Killer. J. Hilton
Cry Blood. H. V. Dixon
Cry, Brother, Cry. J. Karney
Cry Flesh. D. Karp
Cry Flood! E. J. Fredericks
Cry for Help. N. Carter
Cry for Help. D. M. Disney
Cry for My Lovely. S. D. Frances
Cry for the Baron. A. Morton
Cry for the Lost. G. Dessart
Cry from the Dark. W. H. Baker
Cry from the Ether. R. Sharp

Cry Hallelujah! K. Orvis
Cry Hard, Cry Fast. J. C. MacDonald
Cry Havoc. R. M. Stern
Cry Hold! P. Harris
Cry in Absence. M. Jones
Cry in the Jungle. K. M. Knight
Cry in the Night. A. Golsworthy
Cry in the Night. W. Masterson
Cry in the Night. D. Quick
Cry in the Night. K. Roos
Cry in the Night. P. Saxon
Cry in the Valley. G. K. Cowan
Cry Kill. Wenzell Brown
Cry Killer! K. Fearing
Cry Me a Killer. Garrity
Cry Murder. E. Howie
Cry Murder. W. M. Raine
Cry Murder. N. Rutledge
Cry Murder in the Market Place. W. M. Raine
Cry of Blood. F. Du Boisgobey
Cry of the Beast. V. Norwood
Cry of the Cat. M. Sellers
Cry of the Cat. S. Wagner
Cry of the Dingo. C. Phillips
Cry of the Flesh. R. Himmel
Cry of the Halidon. J. Ryder
Cry of the Hawk. H. Steirman
Cry of the Hunter. Harry Patterson
Cry of the Kestrel. J. Wood
Cry of the Owl. P. Highsmith
Cry of the Peacock. M. L. Roby
Cry of the Wind. S. MacIvers
Cry of Whiteness. T. J. Fleming
Cry on My Shoulder. H. Howard
Cry on the Wind. W. H. Boore
Cry Passion. R. Jessup
Cry Plague! T. S. Drachman
Cry Rape. Ruth Williams
Cry Revenge! A. C. Clark
Cry Scandal. W. Ard
Cry Shadow. M. Grant
Cry the Soft Rain. A. Dwyer-Joyce
Cry Terror. A. L. Stone
Cry, Tiger! M. Storm
Cry Tough. I. Shulman
Cry Uncle! Michael Brett
Cry Vengeance. L. Peters
Cry Witch. N. A. Hintze
Cry Wolf. M. Carleton
Cry Wolfram. D. Sanderson
Crying Child. B. Michaels
Crying Makes Your Nose Run. J. T. Story
"Crying Pig" Murder. V. MacClure
Crying Sisters. M. Seeley
Cryptogram. J. De Mille
Cryptogram. W. M. Graydon
Crystal Ball. D. Spicer
Crystal Beads Murder. A. Haynes
Crystal Cell. Gwyn Evans
Crystal Claw. W. LeQueux
Crystal Clear. E. Cadell
Crystal Crow. Joan Aiken
Crystal Eye. W. R. Randall
Crystal-Gazers. H. Robertson
Crystal Mouse. B. H. Deal
Crystal Mystery. N. Carter
Crystal Skull. Warren Hill
Crystal Skull. J. McLaren
Crystal Stopper. W. Leblanc
Crystal Tower. X. Putnam
Crystal Wave. J. Turner
Crystal Window. P. Brisco
Crystallized Carbon Pig. J. Wainwright
Cub. C. L. Pancoast
Cuban Expedition. G. Null
Cuban Heel. B. Carson
Cuban Heel. P. Jefferson
Cuban Legacy. S. M. Parkman
Cuban Treasure Island. W. P. Kelly
Cubwood. W. R. S. Lewis
Cuckoo Clock. M. K. Ozaki
Cuckoo Fair. Robin Temple
Cuckoo in Harley Street. S. Fairway
Cuckoo in the Nest. Laura Smith
Cuckoo Line Affair. A. Garve
Cuckoo Woman. H. Parker
Cuckoos on the Hearth. P. Fennelly

Cudgel. T. Polsky
Cue for Murder. Matt Bryant
Cue for Murder. H. McCloy
Cuernavaca Question. Lydia Kirk
Cuirass of Diamonds. E. Jepson
Cul-de-Sac. S. Dewes
Cult of Darkness. D. Reid
Cult of the Queer People. W. M. Duncan
Cummings Report. J. Brogan
Cumsha Cruise. E. L. Long
Cunning Against Force. Tom Steele
Cunning and the Haunted. R. Jessup
Cunning as a Fox. M. Halliday
Cunning Enemy. V. Hill
Cunning Mulatto and Other Cases of Ellis Parker, American Detective. F. Pratt
Cup and the Lip. E. Ferrars
Cup Final Crime. L. Bidston
Cup Final Murder. B. Newman
Cup Final Mystery. A. Edgar
Cup of Cold Poison. J. Fleming
Cup of Silence. A. J. Rees
Cup of Thanatos. Charlotte Hunt
Cup That Kills. G. J. Barrett
Cup, the Blade or the Gun. M. Eberhart
Cup-Tie Mystery. F. W. Irwin
Cupid Among the Clues. F. G. Puzey
Cupid and the Creeds. W. J. Newton
Cupidevil. H. Monteilhet
Cupid's Executioners. H. Monteilhet
Curate Finds the Corpse. A. T. Rich
Curate's Crime. A. Dick
Cure for Cancer. M. Moorcock
Cure It with Honey. Thurston Scott
Cure of Souls. J. M. Cobban
Curio Murders. R. Wallace
Curios. R. Marsh
Curiosities of Crime in Edinburgh. J. M'Levy
Curiosities of Detection. Robert Curtis
Curiosity Didn't Kill the Cat. M. K. Wren
Curiosity Killed a Cat. A. Rowe
Curiosity Killed Kitty. R. C. Payes
Curiosity Killed the Cat. J. Cockin
Curiosity of Etienne MacGregor. P. Cheyney
Curiosity of Mr. Treadgold. V. Williams
Curious Affair of the Third Dog. P. Moyes
Curious Case of Gen. Delaney Smythe. W. H. Gardner
Curious Case of Marie Dupont. A. Luehrmann
Curious Case of the Crook's Memoirs. W. M. Graydon
Curious Crime. A. E. Martin
Curious Crime of Miss Julia Blossom. L. Meynell
Curious Crimes. B. Hemyng
Curious Custard Pie. M. Scherf
Curious Facts Preceding My Execution. D. E. Westlake
Curious Happenings to the Rooke Legatees. E. P. Oppenheim
Curious Mr. Tarrant. C. D. King
Curious Quest. E. P. Oppenheim
Curious Were Killed. D. Bennett
Curiouser and Curiouser. J. C. Snaith
Curiously Planned. Camilla Hope
Curlew Coombe Mystery. Gret Lane
Currie, Curtis & Co., Crammers. C. J. C. Hyne
Curs in Clover. I. Mercer
Curse! N. Buntline
Curse. F. Hume
Curse at Craig's End. R. Verron
Curse in the Colophon. E. Goodspeed
Curse of Amen-Tah. O. Sackville
Curse of Cain. D. W. Rimel
Curse of Cantire. W. S. Masterman
Curse of Carlyon. E. Everett-Green
Curse of Carne's Hold. G. A. Henty

Curse of Carranca. Elsie Lee
Curse of Clement Waynflete. B. Mitford
Curse of Clifton. E. Southworth
Curse of Cloud. J. B. Harris-Burland
Curse of Collinwood. Marilyn Ross
Curse of Cowden. A. S. Swan
Curse of Deepwater. C. Randell
Curse of Doone. S. Horler
Curse of Kali. A. Greening
Curse of Kali. H. E. Hill
Curse of Kalispoint. M. Richardson
Curse of Kama. W. F. Lovatt
Curse of Kenton. J. L. Roberts
Curse of Khatra. T. C. H. Jacobs
Curse of Leo. R. Lory
Curse of Mallory Hall. D. Daniels
Curse of Rathlaw. P. Saxon
Curse of Ravenswood. S. MacIvers
Curse of Red Shiva. V. Meik
Curse of Scotland. Gordon Bligh
Curse of Seabrea. Dewey Ward
Curse of Siva. R. St. Clair
Curse of Still Valley. S. Wagner
Curse of the Bronze Lamp. Carter Dickson
Curse of the Carrington's. W. Tyrer
Curse of the Casa Del Monte. E. E. Cameron
Curse of the Clodaghs. F. Cowen
Curse of the Concullens. F. Stevenson
Curse of the Crystal Ball. R. St. Clair
Curse of the Island Pool. V. Coffman
Curse of the Kings. V. Holt
Curse of the Mandarin's Fan. B. House
Curse of the Moors. F. Hurd
Curse of the Reckaviles. W. S. Masterman
Curse of the Santyres. Gwyn Evans
Curse of the Sightless Fish. M. South
Curse of the Silver Wings. T. Wallace
Curse of the Snake. G. Boothby
Curse of the Track. J. Hunter
Curse of the Wolfskin. J. Crecy
Cursed Be the Treasure. H. B. Drake
Curses Come Home. E. C. Vivian
Cursing Stones Murder. G. Bellairs
Curtailed Voyage. E. L. Long
Curtain. A. Christie
Curtain at Eight. O. R. Cohen
Curtain Between. V. Siller
Curtain Call. M. Cronin
Curtain Call. R. Foley
Curtain Call for a Corpse. J. Bell
Curtain Call for Murder. A. Spiller
Curtain Call for Murder. P. Yates
Curtain for a Jester. F. Lockridge
Curtain for Crime. M. P. Rea
Curtain Has Lace Fringes. G. Joseph
Curtain of Fear. D. Wheatley
Curtain of Glass. D. Ambler
Curtain of Hate. J. Moffatt
Curtain of Strom. J. Gollomb
Curtain of the Dark. H. McElroy
Curtained Sleep. A. Roy
Curtains for a Chorine. C. Brown
Curtains for a Lover. R. Dietrich
Curtains for Carrie. D. Glinto
Curtains for Conquest? B. Gray
Curtains for Komespi. Ernest Paul
Curtains for the Copper. T. Polsky
Curtains for the Editor. T. Polsky
Curtains for the Judge. T. Polsky
Curtains for Three. R. Stout
Curve of the Catenary. M. R. Rinehart
Curved Blades. C. Wells
Curves Can Cast Shadows. Griff
Curves for a Coroner. C. Brown
Curves for Danger. A. Bocca
Curzon. F. Durbridge
Custom House. Francis King
Custom House Fraud. B. Wayde
Custom of the Country. P. M. Hubbard
Customer's Always Wrong. Kevin O'Hara
Cut and Run. B. McGhee
Cut by Society. A. M. Meadows
Cut by the County. M. E. Braddon
Cut Direct. A. Tilton

Title Index

Cut for Partners. E. K. Goldthwaite
Cut Me In. H. Collins
Cut Me In. J. Karney
Cut of the Whip. P. Rabe
Cut Price Murder. M. Hervey
Cut the Cards, Lady. D. Lee
Cut Thin to Win. A. A. Fair
Cut Throat. C. Bush
Cute and Deadly Surf Twins. P. Morgan
Cute Boy Detective. Old Sleuth
Cuthbert Grahame's Will. R. Marsh
Cutie Cashed His Chips. C. Brown
Cutie on Call. H. Janson
Cutie Takes the Count. C. Brown
Cutie Wins a Corpse. C. Brown
Cutting Edge. K. Jackson
Cyanide! S. Toye
Cyanide for the Chorister. C. Wogan
Cyanide with Compliments. E. Lemarchand
Cyborg. M. Caidin
Cyborg IV. M. Caidin
Cynic Fortune. D. C. Murray
Cynic's Desperate Mission. H. Kaner
Cynthia. E. V. Cunningham
Cynthia-of-the Minute. L. J. Vance
Cynthia Wakeham's Money. A. K. Green
Cynthia's Chauffeur. L. Tracy
Cypher 8. I. F. Anderson
Cypher K. Taffrail
Cypress Chest. G. Cumberland
Cypress Man. Jane Beynon
Cypress Road. M. Home
Cyrilla Maude's First Love. H. Wood
Czar of Fear. K. Robeson
Czar of Halfaday Creek. J. B. Hendryx
Czar's Spy. W. LeQueux
Czech Point. N. Fleming

D

D.A. Breaks a Seal. E. S. Gardner
D.A. Breaks an Egg. E. S. Gardner
D.A. Calls a Turn. E. S. Gardner
D.A. Calls It Murder. E. S. Gardner
D.A. Cooks a Goose. E. S. Gardner
D.A. Draws a Circle. E. S. Gardner
D.A. Goes to Trial. E. S. Gardner
D.A. Holds a Candle. E. S. Gardner
D.A. Takes a Chance. E. S. Gardner
D.A.'s Daughter. H. Petersen
D.E.Q. L. Gorell
D.I. J. Ashford
D.N.A. Business. H. Calvin
D as in Dead. L. Treat
D for Delinquent. B. Clifton
"D" Notice. B. Graeme
Da Vinci Rose. A. O'Neill
Dacobra. J. B. Harris-Burland
Daddy Cool. D. Goines
Daddy-O. P. Stadley
Daddy's Gone a'Hunting. M. St. Clair
Daffodil Affair. M. Innes
Daffodil Blonde. F. Crane
Daffodil Murder. E. Wallace
Daffodil Mystery. E. Wallace
Dagger. A. Wynne
Dagger Affair. D. McDaniel
Dagger and Cord. A. De Brune
Dagger and the Cross. J. Hatton
Dagger Before Me. M. O'Brine
Dagger Drawn. L. Hill
Dagger in Fleet Street. R. C. Woodthorpe
Dagger in the Dark. W. F. Eberhardt
Dagger in the Sky. K. Robeson
Dagger of Fate. R. Marsh
Dagger of Flesh. R. S. Prather
Dagger of the Mind. K. Fearing
Daggers Drawn. Alan Thomas
Daggers of Kali. R. Wallace

Dago. J. March
Dagwort Coombe Murder. L. Brock
Dahlia. B. Goldie
Dain Curse. D. Hammett
Dainty Was a Jane. D. Glinto
Daisy Canfield. B. Haas
Daisy-Chain for Satan. J. Fleming
Daisy Dilemma. D. Rico
Dakota Project. J. Beeching
Dakota Warpath. G. A. Ralston
Dale of the Secret Service. N. Wray
Dalehouse Murder. F. Everton
Dally with a Deadly Doll. J. Miles
Dalmayne Mystery. H. Leyford
Dalton Boys and the M.K. and T. Robbery.
  W. B. Lawson
Dalton Boys in California. W. B. Lawson
Dame. C. Brown
Dame. R. Stark
Dame Ain't Safe. A. Bocca
Dame Between Two. D. Glinto
Dame Called Murder. R. O. Saber
Dame Came Late. R. Angel
Dame Doles Death. M. Perelli
Dame in Danger. T. B. Dewey
Dame in Distress. Craig Cooper
Dame Is Snatched. R. Commorde
Dame on a Death Round. M. Brody
Dame on the Lam. J. Dark
Dame on the Make. K. T. McCall
Dame Plays Rough. D. Spade
Dame to Discover. G. Usher
Dame Trouble There. R. Angel
"Dames Are Out." D. Glinto
Dames Can Be Deadly. Peter Chambers
Dames, Diamonds and Death! C. Wheatley
Dames Die Too. D. Linton
Dames Don't Care. P. Cheyney
Dames Don't Dictate. R. Angel
Dames Don't Forget. Griff
Dames-Errant. G. Norsworthy
Dames for Danger. J. Cairo
Dames for Hire. B. Sarto
Dames Play Rough. N. W. Firth
Dames Spell Trouble. M. Hervey
Dame's the Game. A. Fray
Damn Desmond Drake. Sea Lion
Damnation of Adam Blessing. V. Packer
Damned. J. D. MacDonald
Damned and the Destroyed. K. Orvis
Damned Are the Meek. S. Friedman
Damned If He Does. B. Kerr
Damned Innocents. R. Neely
Damned Lovely. J. Webb
Damned One. G. Des Cars
Damned Spot. H. Adams
Damned to Success. H. H. Kirst
Damning Trifles. M. C. Johnson
Damosel Croft. R. M. Gilchrist
Damsel. R. Stark
Dan Gunn, the Man from Mauston, A
  Countryman Who Did Up the Town. L.
  Armstrong
Dan, the Detective. H. Alger
Dance Band Mystery. R. Sonin
Dance for a Dead Uncle. C. Ashton
Dance Hall of the Dead. T. Hillerman
Dance in Darkness. D. Daniels
Dance of Death. C. Brown
Dance of Death. H. McCloy
Dance of Death. J. Potter
Dance of Death. F. C. Tickner
Dance of Death and other stories.
  O. Williams
Dance of Love. D. B. Dodson
Dance of the Dwarfs. G. Household
Dance on a Hornet's Nest. J. Blackmore
Dance to Your Daddy. G. Mitchell
Dance with Me Deadly. K. T. McCall
Dance with the Dead. R. S. Prather
Dance with the Devil. D. Dwyer
Dance Without Music. P. Cheyney
Dancer and the King, with J. S. Dawley.
  C. E. Blaney
Dancer of San Jose. J. Laffin
Dancer's Daughter. J. Edgar
Dancer's End. D. Vane
Dancers in Mourning. M. Allingham

Dancers in the Reeds. L. Meynell
Dancing Beggars. E. B. Young
Dancing Cheat. D. Walshe
Dancing Cinderella. Rona Randall
Dancing Dead. E. Thomas
Dancing Death. C. Bush
Dancing Detective. W. Irish
Dancing Doll. F. Condon
Dancing Doll. J. L. Roberts
Dancing Doll Murders. R. Wallace
Dancing Druids. G. Mitchell
Dancing Floor. J. Buchan
Dancing Girl. G. Leroux
Dancing Horse. A. MacVicar
Dancing Leaves. G. Warden
Dancing Man. P. M. Hubbard
Dancing of the Fox. Winifred Duke
Dancing Silhouette. N. S. Lincoln
Dancing Star. Captain Ingrham
Dancing Stones. L. A. Knight
Dancing Water. Y. Pickering
Dancing with a Tiger. S. Morrow
Dancing with Death. J. Coggin
Dancing with Death. J. Corbett
Dandy. L. Meynell
Dandy. J. Middlemass
Dandy in Aspic. D. Marlowe
Danes Abbey. M. Gerard
Danesbury House. H. Wood
Danger Aft. N. Ashe
Danger After Dark. S. Maddock
Danger Ahead. M. Richmond
Danger Ahead. P. Saxon
Danger Ahead. J. T. Shaw
Danger Ahead. G. Simenon
Danger! and other stories. A. C. Doyle
Danger Ashore. G. Simenon
Danger at Bravo Key. Ronald Johnston
Danger at Cliff House. C. F. Gregg
Danger at Dahlkari. E. Marlow
Danger at Midnight. F. Griffin
Danger at my Heels. G. Meyrick
Danger at Olduvai. J. Blair
Danger at Ringside. H. R. Cleaver
Danger at Sea. G. Simenon
Danger at Westway's. D. Stuart
Danger Below. G. Goodchild
Danger Below. G. Hackforth-Jones
Danger by My Side. A. MacKinnon
Danger Calling. P. Wentworth
Danger--Dame at Work. P. Muller
Danger--Death at Work. R. Garnett
Danger Follows. C. Fraser-Simson
Danger for Blackshirt. R. Graeme
Danger for Breakfast. J. McPartland
Danger for Love. R. Lacroix
Danger for the Baron. A. Morton
Danger from Grassen. James Stewart
Danger Game. E. Hunt
Danger Game. A. Mills
Danger--Girls Working! J. Reach
Danger: Hospital Zone. U. Curtiss
Danger in Diamonds. G. J. Barrett
Danger in Eden. J. Ames
Danger in My Blood. S. Brackeen
Danger in Numbers. Noel Lee
Danger in Paradise. O. R. Cohen
Danger in Paradise. A. S. Fleischman
Danger in Suburbia. R. Goyne
Danger in the Cards. M. MacDougall
Danger in the Dark. P. Carlon
Danger in the Dark. A. M. Chase
Danger in the Dark. M. G. Eberhart
Danger in the Dark. C. F. Gregg
Danger in the Deed. C. Rushton
Danger Inside. A. A. Thomson
Danger Is My Line. S. Marlowe
Danger Key. N. Carter
Danger Line. G. Goodchild
Danger Line. L. L. Lynch
Danger Mansion. D. Daniels
Danger Mansion. P. Wylie
Danger Merchant. I. Lambot
Danger Money. M. G. Eberhart
Danger Money. T. C. H. Jacobs

Danger Money. M. Russell
Danger Next Door. Q. Patrick
Danger of Folly. N. Carter
Danger on the Flip Side. J. T. Story
Danger on the Map. A. Aldous
Danger Point. P. Wentworth
Danger Preferred. S. Horler
Danger Road. M. Saxton
Danger Round the Corner. L. Meynell
Danger Signal. P. Bottome
Danger Signal and other tales. B. Hemyng
Danger Trail. W. C. Tuttle
Danger Under the Moon. M. Walsh
Danger Wakes My Heart. J. Ames
Danger Within. M. Gilbert
Danger Woman. Abel Mann
Danger: Women at Work! Kevin O'Hara
Danger Zone. K. Lindsay
Danger Zone. J. M. Walsh
Dangerfield Talisman. J. J. Connington
Dangerous Affair. D. Quentin
Dangerous Age. A. J. Baker
Dangerous Age. B. Newman
Dangerous American. A. E. Hotchner
Dangerous Angel. C. B. Kelland
Dangerous Assignment. J. Blair
Dangerous Beauty. J. J. Farjeon
Dangerous Blonde. B. Sarto
Dangerous Blondes. K. Roos
Dangerous Brute. R. Jocelyn
Dangerous Business. E. Balmer
Dangerous by Nature. M. Coles
Dangerous Cargo. H. Footner
Dangerous Cargoes. R. Hobart
Dangerous Catspaw. D. C. Murray
Dangerous Child. F. Cowen
Dangerous Company. J. Rowland
Dangerous Connections. C. Gibbon
Dangerous Conspirator. G. Norway
Dangerous Corner. Ruth Holland
Dangerous Course. M. K. Douglas
Dangerous Cross-Roads. Laurence Kirk
Dangerous Curves. P. Cheyney
Dangerous Days. R. Overton
Dangerous Days. M. R. Rinehart
Dangerous Dead. W. Brandon
Dangerous Deadline. F. S. Wees
Dangerous Design. L. Goldman
Dangerous Dilemmas. J. Peddie
Dangerous Diversion! E. Nepean
Dangerous Domicile. E. C. R. Lorac
Dangerous Dream. V. Nielsen
Dangerous Edge. E. L. Hewitt
Dangerous Enchantment. M. Garratt
Dangerous Encounter. D. L. Teilhet
Dangerous Escapade. J. A. Park
Dangerous Exchange. M. Eden
Dangerous Fortune. T. C. H. Jacobs
Dangerous Game. A. Applin
Dangerous Game. F. Duerrenmatt
Dangerous Game. W. LeQueux
Dangerous Game. E. Yates
Dangerous Ground. L. L. Lynch
Dangerous Ground. F. S. Wickware
Dangerous Guide. E. C. Vivian
Dangerous Harbour. W. E. Huntsberry
Dangerous Haven. G. Bettany
Dangerous Homecoming. V. F. Freethy
Dangerous Honeymoon. A. Kielland
Dangerous House. J. Herbrand
Dangerous Impersonation. J. St. George
Dangerous Inheritance. G. Ferrand
Dangerous Inheritance. I. L. Forrester
Dangerous Inheritance. D. Wheatley
Dangerous Islands. A. Bridge
Dangerous Isles. Basil Carey
Dangerous Journey. N. Deane
Dangerous Knowledge. K. Bennett
Dangerous Knowledge. L. A. Knight
Dangerous Ladies. H. Manning
Dangerous Lady. O. R. Cohen
Dangerous Lady. M. Cronin
Dangerous Lady. M. O'Nair
Dangerous Landing. P. McGerr
Dangerous Legacy. G. H. Coxe
Dangerous Legacy. M. Murphy
Dangerous Legacy. W. D. Roberts
Dangerous Limelight. R. Armstrong
Dangerous Love. J. Blackmore
Dangerous Love. D. Dayle
Dangerous Lovers. A. Applin
Dangerous Madonna. K. Lindsay
Dangerous Men. K. M. Sheahan
Dangerous Men. P. Steward
Dangerous Mission. Roland Daniel
Dangerous Mission. B. Marchant
Dangerous Mr. Dell. David Hume
Dangerous Mr. X. F. Duncan
Dangerous Moment. Roland Daniel
Dangerous Money. R. Hardinge
Dangerous Nan McGrew. G. Batson
Dangerous Oasis. M. Hastings
Dangerous One. R. Ames.
Dangerous One. W. Manson
Dangerous Ones. C. Franklin
Dangerous Passenger. T. Walsh
Dangerous Paths. H. S. Cooper
Dangerous Pawn. Winston Graham
Dangerous Place to Die. David Wilson
Dangerous Playmate. Philip Chambers
Dangerous Promise. R. Bell
Dangerous Quest. J. Creasey
Dangerous Quest. E. D. Pierson
Dangerous Refuge. I. Lambot
Dangerous Search. E. Wilmot
Dangerous Secret. Annie Thomas
Dangerous Shadow. J. B. Priestley
Dangerous Silence. D. MacKenzie
Dangerous Situation. L. Tracy
Dangerous Stable. N. Gould
Dangerous Sunlight. J. Bude
Dangerous to Know. J. P. Duff
Dangerous to Know. K. Lindsay
Dangerous to Lean Out. K. Fitzgerald
Dangerous to Me. R. Foley
Dangerous Trade. G. Hackforth-Jones
Dangerous Twin. H. C. Davis
Dangerous Twins. E. Jepson
Dangerous Visit. F. Hurt
Dangerous Water. W. Chambers
Dangerous Waters. J. Bentley
Dangerous Waters. M. Frazer
Dangerous Woman. M. Blount
Dangerous Woman. G. A. Pierce
Dangerous Young Man. G. F. Worts
Dangerously Blonde. A. F. Witley
Danger's Bright Eyes. S. Horler
Danger's Child. J. T. Story
Danger's Green Eyes. M. Corrigan
Dangers of Working Girls. Grace M. White
Dangerville Inheritance. A. C. Fox-Davies
Dangling Carrot. D. Keene
Dangling Man. H. Kane
Daniel P. Wack, "Dumb-Bell." H. M. Kohler
Danju Gig. C. Weston
Danny Spade Sees Red. D. Ambler
Danny Spade Spells Danger. D. Ambler
Danish Gambit. W. Butler
Danse Macabre. K. Kellow
Danube Flows Red. A. Melville
Danube Runs Red. R. Meade
Danvers Jewels. M. Cholmondeley
Danziger Transcript. C. Fick
D'Arblay Mystery. R. A. Freeman
Darby Trial. D. Pearce
Dardanelles Derelict. V. W. Mason
Dare-Devil Conquest. B. Gray
Dare Lorimer's Heritage. E. Everett-Green
Dared by a Dame. Griff
Daredevil. L. Charteris
Daring Abduction. N. Ridley
Daring Anna Alcott. A. Applin
Daring Conspiracy. Old Sleuth
Daring Diana. Anthony Lang
Daring Experiment and other stories. L. D. Blake
Daring Express Messenger. J. K. Stafford
Daring Horse Thief. P. Ryan
Daring Maddie. Old Sleuth
Daringfords. Mrs. Lodge
Dark. M. Derby
Dark Abyss. C. Knight
Dark Abyss. F. J. Thwaites
Dark Adventure. Augustus Muir
Dark Adventure. J. Tickell
Dark Amid the Blaze. C. Rushton
Dark and Deadly. B. Winter
Dark and Deadly Love. E. Evans
Dark and Light Stories. M. Hope
Dark Angel. L. Della
Dark Angel. J. Ronald
Dark Arbor. I. S. Shriber
Dark Arches. G. Warden
Dark Avenue. F. Hume
Dark Avenue. J. Pendower
Dark Backward. Eric Lambert
Dark Bahama. P. Cheyney
Dark Before Dawn. T. Dick
Dark Below. M. T. Hinkemeyer
Dark Beneath the Pines. A. Eliot
Dark Between the Stars. J. Blackmore
Dark Beyond Moura. V. Coffman
Dark Blood, Dark Terror. B. Cleeve
Dark Brings Death. D. Linton
Dark Bureau. E. Dudley
Dark Carnival. J. Ames
Dark Castle. D. Quentin
Dark Cavalier. V. Rath
Dark Chamber. L. Cline
Dark Circle. G. Ashe
Dark Citadel. C. Farr
Dark Cliffs. D. Farrell
Dark Corner. M. Blizard
Dark Corner. C. Dale
Dark Corner. L. Ross
Dark Corners. F. E. Penny
Dark Corners of the Night. L. Olay
Dark Corsican. J. Appleby
Dark Countess. M. Richmond
Dark Crusade. J. M. Fox
Dark Crusader. I. Stuart
Dark Cypress. E. Noone
Dark Dame. W. Collison
Dark Danger. S. Horler
Dark Days. F. J. Fargus
Dark Dealing. A. C. Brown
Dark Death. Anthony Gilbert
Dark Death. C. Schurr
Dark Deeds. H. Desmond
Dark Deeds. D. Donovan
Dark Descends. D. Ramsay
Dark Design. F. Hurt
Dark Destiny. K. Lindsay
Dark Destiny. E. Ronns
Dark Device. H. Lees
Dark Diamond. D. Tower
Dark Disguise. J. Bentley
Dark Doings. J. Reach
Dark Dominion. G. Thorne
Dark Don't Catch Me. V. Packer
Dark Door. M. Collis
Dark Dream. Robert Martin
Dark Duet. P. Cheyney
Dark Echo. H. L. Nelson
Dark Eden. B. Kevern
Dark Edge of Violence. M. Carrel
Dark Emerald. J. Storm
Dark Enchantment. D. Macardle
Dark Encounter. Howard Hunt
Dark Encounter. W. Mills
Dark Encounter. C. Schurr
Dark Eyes and Danger. H. Clevely
Dark Eyes of London. E. Wallace
Dark Fantastic. M. Echard
Dark Fantastic. W. Masterson
Dark Forest. R. Foxall
Dark Frontier. E. Ambler
Dark Frontier. Arthur MacLean
Dark Garden. M. G. Eberhart
Dark Garden. E. R. Punshon
Dark Geraldine. J. Ferguson
Dark Gethryn. H. H. Ross
Dark God. J. Chancellor
Dark Gondola. V. Coffman

Title Index

Dark Green Circle. E. Shanks
Dark Guardian. V. Blake
Dark Harbor Hunting. Clarissa Ross
Dark Harvest. J. Creasey
Dark Harvest. C. Kenyon
Dark Hazard. W. R. Burnett
Dark Hazard. S. Styles
Dark Heritage. John Foster
Dark Hero. P. Cheyney
Dark Highway. A. Gask
Dark Hill. R. Foley
Dark Hollow. A. K. Green
Dark Horizon. M. Richmond
Dark Horse. N. Gould
Dark Horse. F. Knebel
Dark Horseman. J. Budd
Dark Hostess. S. Horler
Dark House. M. Cumberland
Dark House. M. K. Douglas
Dark House. G. M. Fenn
Dark House. W. Spence
Dark House. A. S. Swan
Dark House in Florissant. R. W. Kauffman
Dark Hunger. D. James
Dark Hunger. T. Strauss
Dark Index. J. Turner
Dark Inheritance. M. C. Hay
Dark Inheritance. C. Salisbury
Dark Intent. R. Foley
Dark Interlude. P. Cheyney
Dark Interval. Joan Aiken
Dark Intruder. R. Dowling
Dark Intruder. V. Packer
Dark Is My Destiny. H. S. Hurst
Dark Is My Shadow. W. E. D. Ross
Dark Is the Clue. E. R. Punshon
Dark Is the Tunnel. M. Burton
Dark Island. R. Barr
Dark Island. D. Daniels
Dark Journey. F. W. Crofts
Dark Journey. Julien Green
Dark Journey. S. Horler
Dark Kiss. D. Enefer
Dark Knight. C. Robertson
Dark Labyrinth. L. Barth
Dark Labyrinth. S. Leigh
Dark Lady. D. M. Disney
Dark Lady. J. J. Farjeon
Dark Lady. Gavin Holt
Dark Lady Murders. C. Ryland
Dark Lantern. C. Short
Dark Legacy. M. Alan
Dark Legacy. T. Charles
Dark Legend. L. Hayes
Dark Legend. Marilyn Ross
Dark Light. B. Spicer
Dark Love, Dark Magic. O. T. Jackson
Dark Mambo. W. H. Baker
Dark Man. R. Chetwynd-Hayes
Dark Man. Robin Temple
Dark Mansion. C. Farr
Dark Mansion. H. R. Kaye
Dark Mansion. W. E. D. Ross
Dark Masquerade. Anonymous
Dark Masquerade. P. Maxwell
Dark Masquerade. Elna Stone
Dark Memories. J. Morella
Dark Memory. E. Ronns
Dark Menace. C. Birkin
Dark Messenger. C. L. Cooper
Dark Mill. Claudette Nicole
Dark Mill Stream. A. Gask
Dark Mind. R. Goyne
Dark Mirror. B. Copper
Dark Mirror. P. Mason
Dark Mirror. L. J. Vance
Dark Moment. K. Wade
Dark Money. C. Robertson
Dark Moon. A. D. Divine
Dark Moon. F. Vivian
Dark Moon, Lost Lady. Elsie Lee
Dark Mosaic. C. Brooker
Dark Music. C. Russell
Dark Mystery. G. Ashe
Dark Nantucket Moon. J. Langton
Dark Night. R. Francis Foster
Dark Night. S. Horler
Dark Night. N. MacKenzie
Dark Night of Love. C. Clements
Dark Nights. T. Burke
Dark Number. E. Boyd
Dark Odyssey. F. Stevenson
Dark of Memory. P. Minton
Dark of Summer. D. Dwyer
Dark of the Moon. J. D. Carr
Dark of the Moon. W. E. D. Ross
Dark of the Moon. L. Thayer
Dark of the Sun. Wilbur Smith
Dark on the Other Side. B. Michaels
Dark Page. N. Bell
Dark Page. S. Fuller
Dark Palazzo. V. Coffman
Dark Passage. D. Goodis
Dark Passions Subdue. D. Sanderson
Dark Pathway. D. Newton
Dark Peril. J. Creasey
Dark Peril. M. Leighton
Dark Place. Mildred Davis
Dark Places. C. Allen
Dark Places. Alex Fraser
Dark Places. P. Gibbon
Dark Plot. S. Cobb
Dark Plunder. V. Rosen
Dark Power. W. Arden
Dark Power. E. S. Holding
Dark Power. L. J. Vance
Dark Prophecy. M. Alan
Dark Purpose. Doris Hume
Dark Rainbow. Gerald Butler
Dark Returners. J. P. Brennan
Dark Rider. G. Thayer
Dark River. P. Clark
Dark Road. J. Cross
Dark Road. D. M. Disney
Dark Road. C. Knight
Dark Road. G. Leroux
Dark Road. N. MacKenzie
Dark Road of Danger. C. H. Barker
Dark Roots of Fear. B. Gaston
Dark Rose. J. L. Roberts
Dark Rose the Phoenix. W. H. Murray
Dark Saviour. R. Harling
Dark Sea. P. C. De Crespigny
Dark Secret. E. C. Clapp
Dark Secret. M. A. Fleming
Dark Secret of Josephine. D. Wheatley
Dark Secrets. W. M. Graydon
Dark Shadow. H. Desmond
Dark Shadow. E. Mattheson
Dark Shadow. R. S. Thorn
Dark Shadow at Bitterhill. P. Warren
Dark Shadows. K. Lynn
Dark Shadows. Marilyn Ross
Dark Ships. H. Footner
Dark Shore. S. Howatch
Dark Side Also. P. Conway
Dark Side of Love. O. Saul
Dark Side of Love. C. Woolrich
Dark Side of Magic. R. Aspinall
Dark Side of Paradise. S. Wagner
Dark Side of the Island. M. Hebden
Dark Side of the Island. Harry Patterson
Dark Side of the Street. M. Fallon
Dark Sonata. E. Bond
Dark Sonata. R. Murray
Dark Spot. L. Allan
Dark Square. L. Meynell
Dark Stage. D. Daniels
Dark Stain. B. Appel
Dark Stain. Shubael
Dark Star. R. W. Chambers
Dark Star Rising. D. Lee
Dark Stars over Seacrest. Marilyn Ross
Dark Stone. Mildred Nelson
Dark Stranger. J. L. Rickard
Dark Street. P. Cheyney
Dark Street. Gavin Holt
Dark Street Murders. P. Cheyney
Dark Summer. N. Buckingham
Dark Sun, Pale Shadows. N. Grey
Dark Symmetry. L. Conway
Dark the Summer Dies. W. Untermeyer
Dark Threat. P. Wentworth
Dark Tide. G. Croudace
Dark Tower. J. Edgar
Dark Towers of Fog Island. Marilyn Ross
Dark Trade. A. Lejeune
Dark Trails Go East. F. A. M. Webster
Dark Tunnel. K. Millar
Dark Turnpike. J. G. Sarasin
Dark Understudy. E. Greenwood
Dark Vendetta. R. Charles
Dark Vengeance. A. Barron
Dark Villa. D. Daniels
Dark Villa of Capri. W. E. D. Ross
Dark Voyage. H. Addis
Dark Wanton. P. Cheyney
Dark Watch. G. St. John
Dark Waterfront. M. Hervey
Dark Waters. F. Cockrell
Dark Waters. W. Corcoran
Dark Waters. Ardath Wise
Dark Waters of Death. S. Wagner
Dark Ways to Death. P. Saxon
Dark Wheel. P. MacDonald
Dark Whispers. Claudette Nicole
Dark Window. T. Walsh
Darke Darrell, the Boy Detective. F. H. Stauffer
Darken the Moon. F. B. Clark
Darkened Room. A. Clarke
Darkened Room. R. Goyne
Darkened Room. M. Harrison
Darkened Windows. C. K. Rathbone
Darkening Door. B. S. Ballinger
Darkening Glass. J. Wainwright
Darkening Night. J. Elliott
Darekning Willows. P. Dalton
Darker Grows the Street. B. Winter
Darker Grows the Valley. Q. Patrick
Darker Heritage. G. A. Cerra
Darker Than Amber. J. D. MacDonald
Darker the Night. H. Brean
Darker Traffic. Martin Brett
Darkest Death. R. Stephenson
Darkest Hour. W. P. McGivern
Darkest Hour. H. Nielsen
Darkest Hour. L. Tracy
Darkest Night. P. Saxon
Darkest Room. G. Corren
Darkest Spot. L. Thayer
Darkest Under the Lamp. J. Sandys
Darkhaven. D. Daniels
Darkling Death. F. Vivian
Darkness as a Bride. M. Cumberland
Darkness at Mantia. I. Barry
Darkness at Noon. S. Kingsley
Darkness at Noon. A. Koestler
Darkness at Pemberley. T. H. White
Darkness Falling. B. Kevern
Darkness Falls from the Air. N. Balchin
Darkness I Leave You. N. W. Hooke
Darkness of Slumber. R. Kutak
Darkness over Hycroft. F. A. Chittenden
Darkness Visible. N. Lewis
Darkwater. Jan Alexander
Darkwater. D. Eden
Darling Clementine. D. Eden
Darling Daughter. R. Rayner
Darling Delinquent. H. Janson
Darling, Don't. Keith Campbell
Darling, Don't Be Dumb. P. G. Larbalestier
Darling, It's Death. R. S. Prather
Darling Murderess. C. Franklin
Darling Sin. Jean Leslie
Darling, This Is Death. D. Chambers
Darling You're Doomed. C. Brown
Darrell Markham. M. E. Braddon
Darrow Enigma. M. Severy
Darrow Enigma. M. Severy
Darsham's Folly. H. Esmond
Darsham's Tower. H. Esmond

D

Dart Board Mystery. W. D. Maydwell
Dartmoor. M. H. Hervey
Dartmoor Enigma. B. Thomson
Dartmoor Mystery. M. B. Dix
Dartmouth Murders. C. Orr
Darwich Castle. B. Kingsley
Dash for a Throne. A. W. Marchmont
Dashiell Hammett Omnibus. D. Hammett
Dashiell Hammett Story Omnibus. D. Hammett
Dashing Dick's Daughter. E. Everett-Green
Dashing Fugitive. Old Sleuth
Dastard "Dr." Anonymous
Datchet Diamonds. R. Marsh
Datchley Inheritance. S. McKenna
Date After Dark and other stories. P. Cheyney
Date for a Dame. C. Wheatley
Date for Homicide. R. Carni
Date for Murder. L. Trimble
Date with a Dead Man. B. Halliday
Date with a Spy. S. Maddock
Date with Danger. J. Ames
Date with Danger. G. Chester
Date with Danger! Martin Thomas
Date with Danger. Roy Vickers
Date with Darkness. D. Hamilton
Date with Death. W. H. L. Crauford
Date with Death. L. Ford
Date with Death. E. K. Goldthwaite
Date with Death. E. Linington
Date with Destiny. J. Walker
Date with Doom. R. Owen
Date with Fear. J. Pendower
Date with Murder. L. Marshall
Date with the Departed. E. P. Thorne
Dateless Bargain. C. L. Pirkis
Dateline Darlene. H. Janson
Dateline Debbie. H. Janson
Dateline Diane. H. Janson
Dateline: Europe. L. Ross
Daughter Fair. P. Graaf
Daughter of Allah. C. H. Bullivant
Daughter of Anderson Crow. G. B. McCutcheon
Daughter of Astrea. E. P. Oppenheim
Daughter of Belial. B. Tozer
Daughter of Bonnie & Clyde. L. W. Brent
Daughter of Darkness. R. Goyne
Daughter of Darkness. J. R. Lowell
Daughter of Darkness. P. McGerr
Daughter of Darkness. E. Noone
Daughter of Evil. G. St. John
Daughter of France. J. Hatton
Daughter of Fu Manchu. S. Rohmer
Daughter of Illusion. J. Budd
Daughter of Judas. R. H. Savage
Daughter of Kings. G. W. Gough
Daughter of Mystery. R. N. Silver
Daughter of Satan. Harry Mills
Daughter of Shame. H. Janson
Daughter of Silence. M. L. West
Daughter of the House. C. Wells
Daughter of the Marionis. E. P. Oppenheim
Daughter of the Pangaran. D. Divine
Daughter of the Scaffold. W. Tyrer
Daughter of the Sidewalk. D. Linton
Daughter of the Stars and other tales. H. Conway
Daughter of the States. M. Pemberton
Daughter of the Veldt. B. Marnan
Daughter of Time. J. Tey
Daughter of Two Worlds. L. Scott
Daughters in Law. H. Cecil
Daughters of Ardmore Hall. D. Eden
Daughters of Astaroth. S. Shulman
Daughters of Belial. S. Truss
Daughters of Cain. M. Lynch
Daughters of the Night. E. Wallace
Davenham Heritage. R. H. Poole
David Betterton. J. Ruegg
David Dimsdale, M.D. M. H. Hervey
David Lindsay. E. Southworth
David Poindexter's Disappearance, and other tales. J. Hawthorne
Davidian Report. D. B. Hughes
Davidson Case. J. Rhode

Davis Doesn't Live Here Any More. J. Ripley
Davy Jones. A. Hillgarth
Dawn at Kahlenberg. J. Siegal
Dawn Comes Soon. U. Nightingale
Dawn for Danger. Edmund Stone
Dawn Must Come. O. Williams
Dawn of Darkness. J. Creasey
Dawson Pedigree. D. L. Sayers
Day and Night Stories. A. Blackwood
Day Before Tomorrow. D. Helwig
Day for Angels. E. Lindall
Day for Murder. K. McComb
Day Gibralter Fell. B. Wynne
Day He Died. L. Padgett
Day I Died. L. Lariar
Day I Stopped Running. R. Wilkes-Hunter
Day in Monte Carlo. M. Albrand
Day It Rained Diamonds. M. E. Chaber
Day Khrushchev Panicked. G. B. Mair
Day Miss Bessie Lewis Disappeared. D. M. Disney
Day of Dark Memory. F. Swann
Day of Disaster. J. Creasey
Day of Dwarfs. P. Everett
Day of Fear. G. Ashe
Day of Judgment. E. Lipsky
Day of Judgment. N. MacKenzie
Day of Reckoning. N. Carter
Day of Reckoning. F. Du Boisgobey
Day of Reckoning. J. Garden
Day of Temptation. W. LeQueux
Day of Terror. M. E. Cooke
Day of the Adder. N. Fitzgerald
Day of the Arrow. P. Loraine
Day of the Coastwatch. P. McCutchan
Day of the Dead. C. Murray
Day of the Dead. B. Spicer
Day of the Dolphin. R. Merle
Day of the Dust. R. Verron
Day of the Fair. J. Matheson
Day of the Fox. N. Lewis
Day of the Guns. M. Spillane
Day of the Jackal. F. Forsyth
Day of the Monkey. D. Karp
Day of the Ram. W. C. Gault
Day of Uniting. E. Wallace
Day of Vengeance. D. Dayle
Day of Wrath. L. Tracy
Day She Died. H. Reilly
Day the Bookies Took a Bath. A. P. Hagan
Day the Call Came. T. Hinde
Day the Fish Came Out. K. Cicellis
Day the Sun Fell. R. L. Duncan
Day the Wind Dropped. K. Royce
Day the World Ended. S. Rohmer
Day They Hijacked Death. J. Lake
Day They Kidnapped Queen Victoria. H. K. Fleming
Day They Robbed the Bank of England. J. Brophy
Day Will Come. M. E. Braddon
Daybreak at Deest. R. Gaines
Daylight Fear. F. Cowen
Daylight Murder. P. McGuire
Daylight Robbery. J. W. Bobin
Days Among the Dead. I. Baker
Days Are Long. R. Barker
Days of Danger. J. Creasey
Days of Darkness. D. Orgill
Days of Doubt. A. M. Meadows
Days of Hogarth. G. W. M. Reynolds
Days of Misfortune. A. M. Stein
Days of Vengeance. D. Enefer
Day's Tragedy. A. Upward
Daze of Fears. J. Roffman
Dazzled. H. Townley
Dazzling Miss Davison. F. Warden
De Bercy Affair. Gordon Holmes
De Marigny Affair. M. C. Pain

Deacon and Actress. A. C. Gunter
Deacon Brodie. D. Donovan
Deacon's Daughter. R. Marsh
Deacon's Second Wind. A. C. Gunter
Dead Accomplice. N. Carter
Dead Account. G. Burnett
Dead Against My Principles. K. Hopkins
Dead Against the Lawyers. R. Jefferies
Dead Ahead. W. L. Stuart
Dead Aim. C. Wilcox
Dead and Alive. H. Innes
Dead and Done For. Robert Reeves
Dead, and Done With. M. Cronin
Dead and Dumb. E. Crispin
Dead and Gone. B. Bird
Dead and Kicking. F. Castle
Dead and Not Buried. H. F. M. Prescott
Dead and the Damned. W. H. Baker
Dead and the Deadly. L. Trimble
Dead Angel. J. Dolph
Dead Are Blind. M. Afford
Dead Are Dangerous. L. Marshall
Dead Are Discreet. A. Lyons
Dead Are Prowling. V. Markham
Dead Are Silent. L. Marshall
Dead as a Dinosaur. F. Lockridge
Dead as a Dodo. M. O'Brine
Dead as a Dummy. G. Homes
Dead as Diamonds. G. Trotta
Dead as They Come. K. Platt
Dead at First Hand. Jonathan Ross
Dead at the Take-Off. L. Dent
Dead Babes in the Wood. D. B. Olsen
Dead-Bang. R. S. Prather
Dead Beat. R. Bloch
Dead Before Midnight. R. Charles
Dead Branch. G. Norham
Dead Bullfighter. D. Sanderson
Dead by Now. M. Erskine
Dead by the Light of the Moon. T. Wells
Dead Calm. C. Williams
Dead Can Tell. H. Reilly
Dead Can't Love. J. Philips
Dead Center. Mary Collins
Dead Center. L. Langley
Dead Cert. D. Francis
Dead Certain. S. Sterling
Dead Certainty. N. Gould
Dead Certainty. H. Janson
Dead Circuit. S. Rattray
Dead City. S. Stevens
Dead City Round Up. E. Z. Frank
Dead Corse. M. Kelly
Dead Darling. Jonathan Craig
Dead Do Talk. J. Bentley
Dead Dogs Bite. E. M. Curtiss
Dead Dolls Don't Talk. D. Keene
Dead Don't Bite. D. G. Browne
Dead Don't Care. Jonathan Latimer
Dead Don't Cry. B. Sarto
Dead Don't Cry. B. Shannon
Dead Don't Matter. Spencer Smith
Dead Don't Rise. Duff Johnson
Dead Don't Scare. P. Marlowe
Dead Don't Speak. M. Erskine
Dead Drunk. G. Bagby
Dead Drunk. H. Howard
Dead Duck. P. MacNee
Dead Easy. R. Angel
Dead End. E. Lacy
Dead End. Margery Lawrence
Dead End. J. S. Strange
Dead End Street. W. B. Murphy
Dead End Street. L. Thayer
Dead Ending. J. Philips
Dead Ernest. A. Tilton
Dead Fall. D. Wilmer
Dead Fellah. M. Palmer
Dead File. B. Copper
Dead Fingers. E. Sutton
Dead for a Ducat. L. Bruce
Dead for a Ducat. H. Reilly
Dead Game. M. Avallone
Dead Girl's Shoes. B. Cobb
Dead Give Away. D. Gray

Title Index

Dead Giveaway. D. Blunt
Dead Giveaway. H. L. Nelson
Dead Giveaway. D. Wheelock
Dead Hand. I. R. G. Hart
Dead Hands Reaching. Marion Scott
Dead Harm no One. E. B. Quinn
Dead Have no Friends. J. Donavan
Dead Have no Mouths. C. Barry
Dead Heart. C. Gibbon
Deat Heat. P. Ayres
Dead Heat. B. Hemyng
Dead Heat. R. S. Prather
Dead Heat on a Merry-Go-Round. E. L. Heyman
Dead Hero. W. C. Gault
Dead If I Remember. S. H. Courtier
Dead in a Ditch. V. Gunn
Dead in a Row. Gwendoline Butler
Dead in Bed. H. Kane
Dead in Bed. D. Keene
Dead in Guanajuato. P. Rock
Dead in No Time. N. A. Temple-Ellis
Dead in the Eye of the Law. G. Parker
Dead in the Morning. M. Yorke
Dead in the Water. B. Yates
Dead in Transit. M. Cronin
Dead Indeed. M. R. Hodgkin
Dead Ingleby. T. Gallon
Dead Innocent. P. Winn
Dead Is Forever. A. E. Redmond
Dead Is the Door-Nail. P. Haggard
Dead Letter. M. Ehrlich
Dead Letter. S. Regester
Dead Letters. J. George
Dead Level. Russell Gordon
Dead Liberty. D. Craig
Dead Lie Still. W. L. Stuart
Dead Line. P. McCutchan
Dead-Line. W. C. Tuttle
Dead Lion. J. Bonett
Dead Little Rich Girl. N. Davis
Dead Little Rich Girl. T. Harknett
Dead Look Down. S. Esmond
Dead Loss. M. Cronin
Dead Loss. R. Petrie
Dead Love Has Chains. M. E. Braddon
Dead Low Tide. J. D. MacDonald
Dead Man at the Window. J. Toussaint-Samat
Dead Man Blues. W. Irish
Dead Man Calling. G. Black
Dead Man Control. H. Reilly
Dead, Man, Dead. David Alexander
Dead Man Falling. D. Cory
Dead Man Friday. J. F. Hutton
Dead Man Inside. V. Starrett
Dead Man Laughs. V. Gunn
Dead Man Manor. V. Williams
Dead Man Murder. B. Newman
Dead Man Running. J. Blackburn
Dead Man Running. S. Picard
Dead Man Sings. Roland Daniel
Dead Man Talks Too Much. W. Dickinson
Dead Man Twice. C. Bush
Dead Man's Alibi. L. Hollingsworth
Dead Man's Bay. C. Arley
Dead Man's Bay. M. Osborne
Dead Man's Bluff. R. Jeffries
Dead Man's Booty. O. Bradshaw
Dead Man's Chest. P. Capon
Dead Man's Chest. Jack Mann
Dead Man's Corner. Roland Daniel
Dead Man's Court. M. H. Hervey
Dead Man's Cross. H. C. Davis
Dead Man's Destiny. Martin Thomas
Dead Man's Diary. B. Halliday
Dead Man's Diary. C. Kernahan
Dead Man's Dower. S. Kyle
Dead Man's Effects. H. C. Bailey
Dead Man's Evidence. J. G. Brandon
Dead Man's Face. F. J. Fargus
Dead Man's Float. A. Dean
Dead Man's Folly. A. Christie
Dead Man's Gate. J. Hunter
Dead Man's Gift. Z. Popkin
Dead Man's Gold. R. Bridges
Dead Man's Gold. J. A. Dunn
Dead Man's Gold. G. E. Rochester
Dead Man's Grip. N. Carter
Dead Man's Hat. H. Footner
Dead Man's Heath. J. J. Farjeon
Dead Man's Hoard. T. J. O'Connell
Dead Man's Island. J. Hunter
Dead Man's Knock. J. D. Carr
Dead Man's Knock. J. N. Chance
Dead Man's Love. T. Gallon
Dead Man's Mirror. A. Christie
Dead Man's Money. J. S. Fletcher
Dead Man's Music. C. Bush
Dead Man's Peak. C. Brisbane
Dead Man's Plaything. E. Woodward
Dead Man's Quarry. I. Jerrold
Dead Man's Riddle. M. Kelly
Dead Man's Rock. Q
Dead Man's Rooms. B. Delannoy
Dead Man's Sands. W. E. Stanton-Hope
Dead Man's Secret. J. Paeon
Dead Man's Secret. M. Plum
Dead Man's Secret. A. O. Pollard
Dead Man's Secret. D. Stuart
Dead Man's Shadow. Basil Carey
Dead Man's Shoes. R. C. Armour
Dead Man's Shoes. H. C. Bailey
Dead Man's Shoes. L. Bruce
Dead Man's Shoes. E. Cameron
Dead Man's Shoes. J. N. Chance
Dead Man's Shoes. M. Innes
Dead Man's Shoes. H. Windsor
Dead Man's Step. L. L. Lynch
Dead Man's Story, and other tales. H. Herman
Dead Man's Tale. H. Pentecost
Dead Man's Tale. E. Queen
Dead Man's Tide. W. Richards
Dead Man's Treasure. M. Brand
Dead Man's Treasure. J. Goodwin
Dead Man's Vengeance. Roland Daniel
Dead Man's Walk. R. S. Prather
Dead Man's Warning. V. Gunn
Dead Man's Watch. G. D. H. Cole
Dead March for Penelope. G. Bellairs
Dead March for Penelope Blow. G. Bellairs
Dead March in Three Keys. P. Curtis
Dead Men. C. Rushton
Dead Men Alive. D. Cory
Dead Men Are Dangerous. Garnett Weston
Dead Men at the Folly. J. Rhode
Dead Men Do Tell. K. Trask
Dead Men Do Tell Tales. Donald Ross
Dead Men Don't Answer. T. Claymore
Dead Men Don't Ski. P. Moyes
Dead Men Grin. B. Fischer
Dead Men Leave No Fingerprints. W. Chambers
Dead Men of Eden. V. M. Grayland
Dead Men of Sestos. P. Loraine
Dead Men Rise Up Never. C. Landon
Dead Men Sing No Songs. M. Stuart
Dead Men Tell... R. Dark
Dead Men Tell No Tales. E. W. Hornung
Dead Men Turn Green. H. E. Wheeler
Dead Men's Bells. V. Gunn
Dead Men's Fingers. P. Helm
Dead Men's Morris. G. Mitchell
Dead Men's Plans. M. G. Eberhart
Dead Men's Shoes. M. E. Braddon
Dead Men's Shoes. L. Thayer
Dead Men's Tales. F. H. Kitchin
Dead Mrs. Stratton. A. Berkeley
Dead Mouse. A. Allen
Dead Needle. Alex Hamilton
Dead of a Counterplot. S. Nash
Dead of a Physician. Fiona Sinclair
Dead of Night. K. Steel
Dead of Night. S. Sterling
Dead of Summer. Josephine Gill
Dead of Summer. M. Kelly
Dead of Summer. D. Moseley
Dead of the Night. H. Carmichael
Dead of the Night. J. Reach
Dead of the Night. J. Rhode
Dead of Winter. C. Cornish
Dead of Winter. C. Hale
Dead of Winter. W. H. Hallahan
Dead on Arrival. G. Bagby
Dead on Arrival. H. Gordon
Dead on Arrival. S. Marlowe
Dead on Arrival. S. Mitchell
Dead on Arrival. C. Stratton
Dead on Arrival. L. Thayer
Dead on Course. M. Black
Dead on Cue. G. Compton
Dead on Cue. D. Reid
Dead on Delivery. A. Bocca
Dead on Departure. A. MacKinnon
Dead on Nine. J. Popplewell
Dead on Noon. N. Tarrant
Dead on Prediction. O. Norton
Dead on the Dot. George Douglas
Dead on the Level. H. Nielsen
Dead on the Stone. R. Amberley
Dead on the Track. J. Rhode
Dead on Time. A. Bocca
Dead on Time. C. F. Gregg
Dead on Time. O. John
Dead on Time. N. Perrelli
Dead on Time. C. Robertson
Dead on Time. C. Witting
Dead Ones Don't Talk. R. Gar
Dead Opposite the Church. F. Vivian
Dead or Alive. Anonymous
Dead or Alive. J. Creasey
Dead or Alive. J. Templeton
Dead or Alive. P. Wentworth
Dead Orchid. D. Lawrence
Dead Parrot. M. Keyes
Dead Past. J. Scholey
Dead Piano. H. Van Dyke
Dead Pigeon. J. M. Fox
Dead Pigeon. R. P. Hansen
Dead Pigeon on Beethoven Street. S. Fuller
Dead Pigs at Hungry Farm. B. Graeme
Dead Prior. C. D. Lampen
Dead Reckoning. J. E. Bloundelle-Burton
Dead Reckoning. F. Bonnamy
Dead Reckoning. P. Conde
Dead Reckoning. George Douglas
Dead Reckoning. B. Hamilton
Dead Reckoning. G. Mitcham
Dead Reckoning. K. Sandford
Dead Reckoning. B. Sarto
Dead Reckoning. R. Simons
Dead Reckoning. L. Thayer
Dead Regimental. B. Bavin
Dead Respectable. D. Reid
Dead Return. W. Carter
Dead Ride Hard. L. J. Vance
Dead Riders. E. O'Donnell
Dead Right. Jennette Lee
Dead Right. S. Sterling
Dead Ringer. F. Brown
Dead Ringer. J. H. Chase
Dead Ringer. F. Findley
Dead Ringer. Robert Thomas
Dead Rite. F. Kane
Dead Run. J. Foxx
Dead Run. H. Holley
Dead Run. R. Sheckley
Dead Say No. Max Gordon
Dead Sea Cipher. Elizabeth Peters
Dead Sea Fruit. M. E. Braddon
Dead Secret. R. Ackland
Dead Secret. W. Collins
Dead Secret. K. Sandford
Dead Secret. G. Verner
Dead: Senate Office Building. M. Scherf
Dead Sequence. S. Rattray
Dead Set. T. H. Stone
Dead Shall Be Raised. G. Bellairs
Dead, She Was Beautiful. W. Masterson
Dead Silence. J. Bruce
Dead Silence. S. Rattray
Dead Skip. J. Gores
Dead Sleep for Keeps. B. Winter

D

Dead Sleep Late. E. Kennedy
Dead Snakes' Venom. H. Kemp
Dead So Soon. Richard Grayson
Dead Stay Dumb. J. H. Chase
Dead Stop. M. Burton
Dead Stop. D. M. Disney
Dead Storage. G. Bagby
Dead Storage. L. Thayer
Dead Straight. D. MacKenzie
Dead Straight. Old Sleuth
Dead Stranger. N. Carter
Dead Sure. H. Brean
Dead Sure. S. Sterling
Dead Take No Bows. R. Burke
Dead Tale-Tellers. J. N. Chance
Dead Thing in the Pool. A. M. Stein
Dead to Rights. D. Allan
Dead to the World. N. Baker
Dead to the World. F. Durbridge
Dead to the World. D. X. Manners
Dead to the World. S. Sterling
Dead Travel Fast. R. Tate
Dead Tree Gives No Shelter. V. Scott
Dead Trouble. M. Carroll
Dead Trouble. D. Devine
Dead, Upstairs in the Tub. Michael Brett
Dead Voice. C. M. Wills
Dead Walk. G. Collins
Dead Water. N. Marsh
Dead Water. E. Radford
Dead Weight. R. Fenisong
Dead Weight. F. Kane
Dead Weight. A. Simmons
Dead Were Strangers. M. Clinten
Dead with Sorrow. P. Andemars
Dead Witness. Old Spicer
Dead Woman of the Year. H. Pentecost
Dead Woman's Ditch. S. Nash
Dead Wrong. G. Bagby
Dead Wrong. R. S. Hastings
Dead Wrong. L. Holden
Dead Wrong. S. Sterling
Dead Yellow Women. D. Hammett
Dead Yesterday. R. Fenisong
Dead Yet Living. J. B. Williams
Deadest Thing You Ever Saw. Jonathan Ross
Deadfall. D. Cory
Deadfall. K. Laumer
Deadhand. G. Sims
Deadhead. C. Carpenter
Deadhead. C. M. Warren
Deadlier of the Species. D. Reid
Deadlier Sex. B. S. Ballinger
Deadlier Sex. G. Manceron
Deadlier Than the Male. James Gunn
Deadlier Than the Male. G. Holden
Deadlier Than the Male. H. Reymond
Deadlight. A. Roy
Deadline. P. Brickhill
Deadline. T. B. Dewey
Deadline. J. Eastwood
Deadline. H. Howard
Deadline. T. Heald
Deadline. A. Irving
Deadline. D. Linton
Deadline. P. MacNee
Deadline. M. Russell
Deadline at Dawn. W. Irish
Deadline Dolly. D. Enefer
Deadline for a Diplomat. S. Truss
Deadline for a Dream. B. Knox
Deadline for Danger. Arthur MacLean
Deadline for Destruction. C. L. Leonard
Deadline for Lovers. E. M. Clare
Deadline for Lovers. F. Nichols
Deadline for Macall. G. Fairlie
Deadlock. R. Busby
Deadlock. R. Fenisong
Deadlocked! L. P. Kelley
Deadly Affair. E. Lacy
Deadly Affair. J. Le Carre
Deadly Alliance. William Crawford
Deadly Bedfellows. F. C. Davis
Deadly Beloved. W. Ard
Deadly Beloved. J. S. Strange
Deadly Blunder. J. Ritson
Deadly Boodle. J. M. Flynn
Deadly but Delectable. K. T. McCall

Deadly Chase. Carter Cullen
Deadly Chase. J. M. Eshleman
Deadly Climate. U. Curtiss
Deadly Combo. J. Farr
Deadly Company. G. Kent
Deadly Contact. A. Dean
Deadly Cyborgs. P. Edwards
Deadly Daffodils. R. Silverwood
Deadly Dames. M. Douglas
Deadly, Deadly Art. G. A. Ralston
Deadly Deal. S. Jason
Deadly Deceit. E. Burgess
Deadly Decree. J. C. Lenehan
Deadly Delight. A. M. Stein
Deadly Desire. R. Colby
Deadly Diamond. J. Storm
Deadly Diary. William Du Bois
Deadly Discretion. D. Ramsay
Deadly Ditto. C. Hale
Deadly Doctor. S. Jason
Deadly Doll. J. Barbette
Deadly Doll. H. Kane
Deadly Dove. R. King
Deadly Dowager. E. Greenwood
Deadly Downbeat. Jonathan Burke
Deadly Duo. M. Allingham
Deadly Duo. R. Jessup
Deadly Dwarf. K. Robeson
Deadly Edge. R. Stark
Deadly Ernest. A. Bocca
Deadly Ernest. J. Cockin
Deadly Errand. M. Hillary
Deadly Eurasian. A. Cordell
Deadly Finger. H. Kane
Deadly Foe. A. Sergeant
Deadly Fresco. L. Southney
Deadly Friend. H. Pentecost
Deadly Game. N. Daniels
Deadly Game. Graham Hastings
Deadly Game. J. MacKenzie
Deadly Game. W. Manson
Deadly Game. J. Yaffe
Deadly Gold. J. Rossiter
Deadly Green. J. Rossiter
Deadly Group Down Under. P. Morgan
Deadly Hall. J. D. Carr
Deadly Homecoming. T. George
Deadly Honeymoon. Lawrence Block
Deadly Honeymoon. A. C. MacLean
Deadly Image. G. H. Coxe
Deadly Intent. A. Rowe
Deadly Interlude. M. O'Brine
Deadly Is the Diamond. M. G. Eberhart
Deadly Is the Evil Tongue. A. Hocking
Deadly Isles. J. H. Vance
Deadly Jade. B. Sanders
Deadly Jest. V. Markham
Deadly Jigsaw. R. Bay
Deadly Joke. H. Pentecost
Deadly Joker. N. Blake
Deadly Kind of Lonely. S. Forbes
Deadly Kitten. C. Brown
Deadly Lampshade. D. Gray
Deadly Legacy. W. Arden
Deadly Legacy. F. Usher
Deadly Lover. R. O. Saber
Deadly Lovers. Anthony Graham
Deadly Lure. W. Chambers
Deadly Marriage. R. Jeffries
Deadly Matrimony. Jon Stevens
Deadly Meeting. R. Bernard
Deadly Memorial. P. Perry
Deadly Mermaid. J. A. Phillips
Deadly Miss. C. Brown
Deadly Miss Ashley. F. C. Davis
Deadly Mission. Roland Daniel
Deadly Mission. H. Janson
Deadly Night-Blade. Austin Stone
Deadly Night Call. W. Irish
Deadly Night-Cap. H. Carmichael
Deadly Nightcap. H. Hawton

Deadly Nightcap. F. Stewart
Deadly Nightshade. K. Cameron
Deadly Nightshade. E. Daly
Deadly Nightshade. James Fraser
Deadly Nightshade. Jean Fraser
Deadly Nightshade. Lydia Belknap Long
Deadly Nightshade. M. Peterson
Deadly Noose. R. Foley
Deadly One. H. McCutcheon
Deadly Orbit Mission. V. W. Mason
Deadly Pattern. Douglas Clark
Deadly Pay-Off. W. H. Duhart
Deadly Pearl. M. Olden
Deadly Percheron. J. F. Bardin
Deadly Persuasion. S. Mitchell
Deadly Persuasion. D. Reid
Deadly Pickup. M. K. Ozaki
Deadly Poison. M. Pertwee
Deadly Prey. Ralph Hayes
Deadly Purpose. R. P. Hansen
Deadly Quiet. D. Enefer
Deadly Race. T. C. H. Jacobs
Deadly Reaper. Clark Smith
Deadly Record. N. W. Hooke
Deadly Relations. R. Gatenby
Deadly Return. I. Lambot
Deadly Reunion. W. L. Harter
Deadly Revenge. A. Askew
Deadly Rose. M. Lynch
Deadly Rose. K. Rich
Deadly Scarab. N. Carter
Deadly Sea, Deadly Sand. I. Foster
Deadly Secret. A. Abbot
Deadly Seeds. R. Sapir
Deadly September. K. Kramer
Deadly Sex. J. Webb
Deadly Shade of Gold. J. D. MacDonald
Deadly Shore. J. Pattinson
Deadly Streets. H. Ellison
Deadly Summer. G. M. Barnes
Deadly Sunshade. P. A. Taylor
Deadly the Daring. W. Randall
Deadly to Bed. D. Tracy
Deadly Trade. B. Jones
Deadly Travelers. T. Eden
Deadly Truth. H. McCloy
Deadly Weapon. Wade Miller
Deadly Welcome. J. D. MacDonald
Deadman's Bay. L. A. Knight
Deadwood Dick's Last Shot. E. L. Wheeler
Deaf, Dumb and Blonde. A. Morton
Deaf-Mute Murders. V. Loder
Deal in Death. A. O. Pollard
Deal in Diamonds. N. Carter
Deal in Letters. F. M. White
Deal in Violence. W. Arden
Deal Me Out. J. S. Blazer
Deal Me Out. S. Morelli
Deal of Death Caps. G. M. Wilson
Deal with the Devil. E. Phillpotts
Dealer in Antiques. B. Tozer
Dealer in Death and other stories.
   Arthur Morris
Dealer of Death. F. MacIsaac
Dealing Out Death. W. T. Ballard
Deals. B. Pain
Dean Dunham. H. Alger
Dean of Clonbury. P. Roche
Dean's Daughters. H. Adams
Dean's Death. A. Lawrence
Dear Angel. A. Dick
Dear Brother, Here Departed. S. Phillips
Dear Conspirator. G. Goodchild
Dear Daughter Dead. S. B. Hough
Dear, Dead Days. J. Barbette
Dear, Dead Girls. N. Morland
Dear, Dead Harry. Milton Scott
Dear Dead Mother-in-Law. K. Hill
Dear Dead Professor. K. A. LaRoche
Dear Dead Woman. Anthony Gilbert
Dear, Dead Women. D. Chambers
Dear, Deadly Beloved. J. Flagg
Dear Deadly Cara. G. Z. Stone
Dear Delusion. E. Woodward
Dear Fatherland. J. M. Simmel

Title Index

Dear Fools. A. Soutar
Dear Hungarian Friend. G. Napier
Dear Laura. J. Stubbs
Dear Liar. D. M. Low
Dear Life. H. E. Bates
Dear Lost Love. A. Maybury
Dearly Beloved Wives. W. H. L. Crauford
Dear Old Gentleman. G. Goodchild
Dear Traitor. J. March
Death a la King. I. Waitt
Death About Face. F. Kane
Death Across the Tamagash. M. Hastings
Death After Dark. F. Griffin
Death After Evensong. Douglas Clark
Death After Lunch. R. D. Abrahams
Death After School. A. Holden
Death Against the Clock. Anthony Gilbert
Death Against Venus. D. Chambers
Death Ain't Commercial. G. Bagby
Death Amidst Satin. E. Woodward
Death Among Doctors. J. G. Edwards
Death Among Friends. H. Ainsworth
Death Among Friends. Lange Lewis
Death Among the Orchids. T. B. Morris
Death Among the Professors. K. Sproul
Death Among the Sands. E. Mack
Death Among the Stars. K. Giles
Death Among the Stars. Jean Marsh
Death Among the Sunbathers. E. R. Punshon
Death Among the Tulips. A. Hocking
Death Among the Writers. E. De Caire
Death and a Dark Horse. Martin Thomas
Death and Benedict. I. Bayne
Death and Bitters. K. Christian
Death and Bright Water. J. Mitchell
Death and Chicanery. P. MacDonald
Death and Circumstance. H. Waugh
Death and Daisy Bland. N. Blake
Death and Festivals. Richard Blum
Death and His Brother. M. Bidwell
Death and His Sweetheart. Winifred Duke
Death and Letters. E. Daly
Death and Lilacs. F. Bayard
Death and Little Brother. C. Knight
Death and Little Girl Blue. V. J. Hanson
Death and Mary Dazill. M. Fitt
Death and Mr. Gilly. W. M. Duncan
Death and Mr. Potter. R. Foley
Death and Mr. Prettyman. K. Giles
Death and Mrs. Lovely. E. Wake
Death and Still Life. D. Launay
Death and Taxes. T. B. Dewey
Death and Then. D. Dodge
Death and the Archdeacon. N. Harman
Death and the Bridegroom. F. Hurt
Death and the Bright Day. M. Fitt
Death and the Dancing Footman. N. Marsh
Death and the Dark Daughter. F. Hurt
Death and the Dear Girls. J. Stagge
Death and the Devil. P. Whelton
Death and the Durlings. V. Fletcher
Death and the Dutch Uncle. P. Moyes
Death and the Dutiful Daughter. A. Morice
Death and the Gentle Bull. R. Lockridge
Death and the Gilded Man. Carter Dickson
Death and the Golden Boy. N. Morland
Death and the Golden Image. Whyte Hall
Death and the Joyful Woman. Ellis Peters
Death and the Leaping Ladies. C. Drummond
Death and the Maiden. E. Lindall
Death and the Maiden. G. Mitchell
Death and the Maiden. Q. Patrick
Death and the Naked Lady. J. Flagg
Death and the Night Watches. V. Bell
Death and the Pleasant Voices. M. Fitt
Death and the Professor. E. Radford
Death and the Professors. K. Sproul
Death and the Shortest Day. M. Fitt
Death and the Sky Above. A. Garve
Death and the South Wind. F. Lester
Death and the Spider. G. Stockbridge
Death and the Visiting Fireman. H. R. F. Keating
Death and the Women. A. Golsworthy

Death Angel. C. B. Clason
Death Answers the Bell. V. Williams
Death--as in Matador. L. V. Roper
Death at a Masquerade. M. E. Corne
Death at Abu Mina. P. William
Death at Aranshore. K. Wade
Death at Ash House. M. Burton
Death at Breakfast. J. Rhode
Death at Broadcasting House. V. Gielgud
Death at Chestnut Hill. C. Nicolai
Death at Court Lady. S. Horler
Death at Crane's Court. E. Dillon
Death at Dakar. K. O'Neil
Death at Dale's End. J. Brooke
Death at Dancing Stones. M. Fitt
Death at Datchets. F. J. Whaley
Death at Dayton's Folly. V. Rath
Death at Deep End. P. Wentworth
Death at Devil-Fish Point. D. Boyle
Death at Dusk. P. Ketchum
Death at Dyke's Corner. E. C. R. Lorac
Death at Eight Bells. F. A. Kummer
Death at Flight. C. Willock
Death at Flood Tide. L. A. Brennan
Death at Four Corners. Anthony Gilbert
Death at Half-Term. J. Bell
Death at Hallows End. L. Bruce
Death at Heel. F. Andreas
Death at Her Elbow. D. C. Cameron
Death at Her Fingers. M. Shane
Death at His Elbow. J. M. Walsh
Death at Lord's. B. Newman
Death at Lover's Leap. R. G. Dean
Death at Low Tide. M. Burton
Death at My Elbow. H. Desmond
Death at My Heels. D. Kirby
Death at My Heels, and other stories. M. Hervey
Death at No. 47. C. Wallace
Death at One Below. H. Hamilton
Death at Peak Hour. Jean Marsh
Death at Pyford Hall. D. Fisher
Death at Roman Farm. John Lloyd
Death at St. Asprey's School. L. Bruce
Death at Salterton Court. R. Marr
Death at Screaming Pool. C. Ryland
Death at Sea. R. Sale
Death at Sea. L. White
Death at 7:10. H. F. S. Moore
Death at Shinglestrand. P. Capon
Death at Slack Water. D. W. MacArthur
Death at Springtime. D. C. Andrews
Death at Swaythling Court. J. J. Connington
Death at the Bank. B. Francis
Death at the Bar. C. Drummond
Death at the Bar. N. Marsh
Death at "The Bottoms." A. B. Cunningham
Death at the Cascades. B. J. Farmer
Death at the Chase. M. Innes
Death at the Chateau. M. Tinayre
Death at the Chateau Noir. E. Radford
Death at the Club. M. Burton
Death at the Crossroads. M. Burton
Death at the Dam. C. F. Adams
Death at the Dance. J. Rhode
Death at the Depot. D. G. Hastings
Death at the Dog. J. Cannan
Death at the Dolphin. N. Marsh
Death at the Door. Anthony Gilbert
Death at the Dowager. B. Huber
Death at the Drome. W. R. Hutton
Death at the Easel. M. Baker
Death at the Feast. N. Carter
Death at the Furlong Post. C. Drummond
Death at the Golden Cockerel. W. R. Hutton
Death at the Golden Crown. A. Dick
Death at the Helm. J. Rhode
Death at the Horse Show. V. Loder
Death at the Inn. R. A. Freeman
Death at the Inn. J. Rhode
Death at the Isthmus. G. H. Coxe
Death at the Manor. M. E. Corne
Death at the Medical Board. J. Bell
Death at the Mike. A. Eichler
Death at the Opera. G. Mitchell
Death at the Pelican. C. M. Wills

Death at the President's Lodging. M. Innes
Death at the Rodeo. E. Queen
Death at the Salutation. F. Vivian
Death at the Strike. C. Willock
Death at the Towers. F. C. Tickner
Death at the Villa. M. Dalton
Death at the Wedding. A. Hocking
Death at the Wheel. V. Loder
Death at Three. C. Rice
Death at Traitor's Gate. V. Gunn
Death at Windward Hill. H. J. Hultman
Death Awaits Thee. M. Lang
Death Be Nimble. R. N. Smith
Death Beats the Band. I. Shurman
Death Beckons Quietly. W. M. Duncan
Death Before Bedtime. E. Box
Death Before Breakfast. C. F. Adams
Death Before Breakfast. G. Bellairs
Death Before Breakfast. D. Fearon
Death Before Day. M. Dalman
Death Before Dinner. E. C. R. Lorac
Death Before Honour. David Hume
Death Before Launching. H. J. Quartermain
Death Before Wicket. N. Spain
Death Begs the Question. L. Eby
Death Behind the Door. F. W. Gumley
Death Behind the Door. V. MacClure
Death Bell. Edison Marshall
Death Below the Dam. E. H. Fonseca
Death Below Zero. H. S. Head
Death Below Zero. T. Muir
Death Beneath Jerusalem. R. Bax
Death Beneath the River. J. Rowland
Death Beyond the Go-Thru. B. Kendrick
Death Bids for Corners. A. Dickson
Death Bird. R. St. Clair
Death Bird Contract. P. Atlee
Death Blanks the Screen. L. O'Donnell
Death Blew Out the Match. K. M. Knight
Death Boards the Lazy Lady. R. Darby
Death Box. E. Lecale
Death Box. L. N. Morgan
Death Box. B. G. Quin
Death Breaks the Ring. V. Rath
Death Bringers. D. Orgill
Death-Bringers. D. Shannon
Death Brings a Storke. A. Boutell
Death Brings in the New Year. G. Bellairs
Death Brokers. P. D. Ballard
Death Burns the Candle. R. Trevor
Death Business. Anthony Graham
Death by Apparition. Reginald Campbell
Death by Appointment. F. Bonnamy
Death--by Appointment. J. Corbett
Death by Appointment. C. Goodall
Death by Arrangement. L. Meynell
Death by Association. R. Lockridge
Death by Ballot. John Laffin
Death by Bequest. F. Hurt
Death by Chalk Face. J. Gale
Death by Clue. H. C. Beck
Death by Computer. D. M. Disney
Death by Demonstration. P. Carlon
Death by Design. A. Derleth
Death by Design. A. Nash
Death by Desire. R. Goyne
Death by Drowning. Robin Daniel
Death by Dynamite. J. L. Bonney
Death by Hoax. Lionel Black
Death by Inches. D. Shannon
Death by Invitation. G. Stockwell
Death by Marriage. E. G. Cousins
Death by Misadventure. B. Malim
Death by Misadventure. M. Underwood
Death by Moonlight. M. Innes
Death by Night. J. Creasey
Death by Order. W. Byford-Jones
Death by Proxy. J. Crosby
Death by Proxy. E. B. Ronald
Death by Remote Control. E. Hogarth

Death by Request. R. John
Death by the Day. Lawrence Fisher
Death by the Gaff. J. H. Vahey
Death by the Lake. L. Bruce
Death by the Lake. Roland Daniel
Death by the Lake. W. Martyn
Death by the Mistletoe. A. MacVicar
Death by the Nile. A. Parsons
Death by the Radio. J. W. Lee
Death by the Sea. J. Turner
Death by the Seine. B. Sarto
Death by Treble Chance. E. G. Cousins
Death by Two Hands. P. Drax
Death by Water. M. Innes
Death Called China. R. Carni
Death Called Twice. C. B. Molyneaux
Death Calls at Scotland Yard. J. E. Nyson
Death Calls the Jester. H. E. Wheeler
Death Calls the Shots. B. Knox
Death Calls the Tune. F. W. Gumley
Death Calls Three Times. G. Barnett
Death Came Back. E. Hale
Death Came Back. C. Kingston
Death Came by Night. G. Bligh
Death Came Dancing. K. M. Knight
Death Came in Lucerne. M. Stand
Death Came in Straw. P. Piper
Death Came in the Studio. M. Stand
Death Came Late. J. B. O'Sullivan
Death Came Smiling. E. Dewhurst
Death Came Softly. E. C. R. Lorac
Death Came to Lighthouse Steps. M. Stand
Death Came Too Soon. M. Stand
Death Came Too Soon. I. E. Ward
Death Came Uninvited. E. Backhouse
Death Came with Darkness. M. Stand
Death Came with Diamonds. M. Stand
Death Came with Flowers. M. Stand
Death Can Wait. G. W. Cooke
Death Cancels the Evidence. R. H. Leitfred
Death Cap. S. Brydon
Death Cap. R. T. Campbell
Death Cap. J. Thomson
Death Car Surfside. P. Morgan
Death Card. J. B. O'Sullivan
Death Carries a Cane. S. King
Death Casts a Long Shadow. Anthony Gilbert
Death Casts a Lure. M. Johnston
Death Casts a Shadow. L. Marshall
Death Casts a Vote. M. Yates
Death Casts No Shadow. P. G. Larbalestier
Death Catches Up with Mr. Kluck. Xantippe
Death Changes His Mind. Frank King
Death Charter. E. L. Adams
Death Check. R. Sapir
Death Checks In. S. Ransome
Death Chime. L. Gribble
Death Circle. N. Carter
Death Claims. J. Hansen
Death Climbs a Hill. E. Backhouse
Death Coins. W. S. Masterman
Death Collection. M. Arrighi
Death Comes as the End. A. Christie
Death Comes Ashore. E. F. Charles
Death Comes at Night. K. Ingram
Death Comes by Air. N. Leslie
Death Comes by Post. J. Carr
Death Comes Courting. I. Garland
Death Comes Early. W. R. Cox
Death Comes Easy. B. Feltner
Death Comes Grinning. W. Creed
Death Comes in the Night. J. M. Spender
Death Comes Laughing. V. Gunn
Death Comes Like a Thief. V. Ellis
Death Comes on Derby Day. Alan Muir
Death Comes on Friday. L. Day
Death Comes Swiftly. J. G. Brandon
Death Comes to Cambers. E. R. Punshon
Death Comes to Casanova. H. G. Coulter
Death Comes to Dinner. A. Colin
Death Comes to Dinner. S. Gluck
Death Comes to Dinner. P. Yates
Death Comes to Fanshawe. J. Corbett
Death Comes to Kenya. N. Leslie
Death Comes to Lady's Steps. W. M. Duncan
Death Comes to Perigord. J. Ferguson
Death Comes to Rehearsal. R. Sharp
Death Comes to Tea. T. Du Bois
Death Comes to the Hermit. J. Harrell
Death Comes Too Late. R. Trevor
Death Comes Wholesale. R. Drayton
Death Commits Bigamy. J. M. Fox
Death Conducts a Tour. R. Darby
Death Convention. D. Winsor
Death Counts Five. H. L. Gates
Death Counts Three. H. Carmichael
Death Cracks a Bottle. K. Giles
Death Crag. B. Gaston
Death Cries in the Street. S. A. Krasney
Death Cries Ole. M. Mundy
Death Croons the Blues. J. Ronald
Death Crosses the Line. E. F. Charles
Death Cruises South. R. Denbie
Death Cry. D. Hauck
Death Cues the Pageant. E. Ainsworth
Death Curse. A. O. Pollard
Death Cuts a Caper. D. Magarshack
Death Cuts a Silhouette. D. B. Olsen
Death Cuts the Deck. R. L. Fish
Death Cuts the Film. C. Saxby
Death Cycle. C. Runyon
Death Dams the Tide. J. Guildford
Death Dances Thrice. J. C. Lenehan
Death Darkens Council. V. Bell
Death Date. R. Wilkes-Hunter
Death Dates a Dame. J. Death
Death Deal. Anonymous
Death Deal. B. E. Miller
Death Dealers. I. Asimov
Death Dealers. B. Gaston
Death Dealers. F. Meadows
Death Dealers. M. Spillane
Death Deals a Diamond. N. Wray
Death Deals a Double. J. Bude
Death Deals in Diamonds. B. Jones
Death Dealt the Cards. E. Hale
Death Deep Down. D. J. Marlowe
Death Defies the Doctor. B. Cobb
Death Defies the Doctor. Denis Muir
Death Defies the Doctor. D. Munro
Death Delivers a Postcard. J. Philips
Death Demands an Audience. H. Reilly
Death Demon. J. K. Stafford
Death Department. B. Knox
Death Designs a Dress. E. M. Robinson
Death Devils. P. Edwards
Death Dines Out. T. Du Bois
Death Disposes. M. Dalmon
Death Disturbs Mr. Jefferson. A. Hocking
Death Dives Deep. M. Avallone
Death Do Us Part. S. Noel
Death Do Us Part. M. Parker
Death-Doctor. W. LeQueux
Death Doubles Death. G. Braddon
Death Down East. E. Blake
Death Down East. H. Norwood
Death Draws the Curtain. R. Watkins
Death Draws the Line. J. Iams
Death Drive. M. E. Cooke
Death Drives the Lead Car. P. Moore
Death Drops Delilah. Q. Mario
Death Drops the Pilot. G. Bellairs
Death Drum. M. Peterson
Death Duel. A. Hocking
Death Dupes a Lady. R. Howes
Death Duty Swindle. W. J. Bayfield
Death Echo. J. Sandys
Death Elects a Mayor. J. G. Edwards
Death Enters the Lists. O. Mills
Death Enters the Ward. I. Bayne-Powell
Death Express. A. Eadie
Death Fear. W. Martyn
Death Files for Congress. T. O. Henle
Death Filled the Glass. C. Armstrong
Death Film. P. R. Shore
Death Finds a Foothold. G. Carr
Death Finds a Target. M. Fitt
Death Finds the Day. Alan White
Death Finds the Gloves. J. Sandys
Death Fire. L. Bennet-Thompson
Death Flash. J. G. Rowe
Death Flies High. J. R. Holden
Death Flies High. D. L. Teilhet
Death Flies High. R. Walker
Death Flies Low. H. Park
Death Flies Low. N. Shepherd
Death Flies West. J. F. Bonnell
Death Flight. A. O. Pollard
Death Follows a Formula. N. Gayle
Death Follows the Flower Show. E. G. Seibert
Death Follows the Trail. M. Poole
Death for a Dropout. P. Bloxham
Death for a Dumb-Bell. B. Sarto
Death for a Holiday. D. P. Le Huray
Death for a Hussy. A. Holt
Death for a Hussy. A. L. Martin
Death for a Playmate. J. Ball
Death for a Traitor. N. MacKenzie
Death for Auld Lang Syne. J. Sharkey
Death for Dear Clara. Q. Patrick
Death for Dollars. N. Thurley
Death for Madame. R. T. Campbell
Death for Mr. Big. J. Gonzales
Death for My Beloved. D. M. Disney
Death for My Neighbor. Muriel Bradley
Death for Safe Custody. B. Francis
Death for Safety. E. Dennis
Death for Sale. H. Kane
Death for Sale. N. Morland
Death for Short. J. Gale
Death for the Lady. S. Vanderveer
Death for the Surgeon. G. Eldredge
Death for Two. C. Ashton
Death Forms Threes. C. Robbins
Death Framed in Silver. A. Campbell
Death from a Top Hat. C. Rawson
Death from Below. G. Ashe
Death from Nowhere. S. Towne
Death from the Air. P. Conde
Death Fugue. P. McGuire
Death Fungus. W. Allen
Death Gamble. J. A. Dunn
Death Gamble. G. R. Sims
Death Game. A. O. Pollard
Death Gang. D. Dell
Death Gang. A. Skene
Death Gets a Head. A. R. McKenzie
Death Gets a Place. J. Brown
Death Gets an A. R. H. R. Smithies
Death Glides In. A. L. Elsworthy
Death Glow. R. Wallace
Death Goes Ashore. A. Glanville
Death Goes by Bus. L. Cargill
Death Goes Caving. G. Usher
Death Goes Fishing. Edward Lee
Death Goes Hunting. C. Massie
Death Goes Native. Max Long
Death Goes on Skis. N. Spain
Death Goes to a Party. M. Jaffe
Death Goes to a Reunion. K. M. Knight
Death Goes to Brussels. Rosa Lambert
Death Goes to School. Q. Patrick
Death Goes to Sea. J. Robertson
Death Goes to the Fair. J. Courage
Death Goes Touring. F. W. Gumley
Death Goes Window Shopping. F. A. Symonds
Death Gong. S. Jepson
Death Grasp. T. P. Prest
Death Greets a Guest. C. Ashton
Death Grip. Al Conroy
Death Hall. M. Reisner
Death Has a Double. Frank King
Death Has a Past. A. Boutell
Death Has a Shadow. M. Procter
Death Has a Small Voice. F. Lockridge
Death Has a Thousand Doors. M. Marlette
Death Has a Thousand Entrances. P. Helm
Death Has a Will. A. R. Long
Death Has Deep Roots. M. Gilbert
Death Has Four Hands. Hilda Lawrence

Title Index

Death Has Green Eyes! N. Carter
Death Has Green Fingers. Lionel Black
Death Has Many Doors. F. Brown
Death Has Many Doors. S. MacKenzie
Death Has My Number. J. Laffin
Death Has No Tongue. J. Cowdroy
Death Has Scarlet Candles. D. Lockwood
Death Has Seven Faces. H. Austin
Death Has Ten Thousand Doors. B. Chetwynd
Death Has Three Lives. B. Halliday
Death Has Two Doors. V. Bell
Death Has Two Faces. N. Herries
Death Has Two Faces. E. Radford
Death Has Two Hands. D. Lawrence
Death Haunts the Charnel Estate. Jackson Evans
Death Haunts the Dark Lane. A. B. Cunningham
Death Haunts the Lounge. A. C. Trevor
Death Haunts the Repertory. T. A. Plummer
Death Heads North. J. B. Hendryx
Death Her Destination. W. Jardine
Death Hides a Mask. M. E. Corne
Death Hitches a Ride. M. L. Weiss
Death Hits the Jackpot. J. Tiger
Death Holds His Court. N. MacKenzie
Death House. C. Brisbane
Death House. Roland Daniel
Death House Doll. D. Keene
Death Hunch. R. Humphreys
Death Hunt. P. McCurtin
Death in a Bowl. R. Whitfield
Death in a Chilly Corner. I. Oellrichs
Death in a Dark Pool. H. Van Rensburg
Death in a Deck-Chair. M. Kennedy
Death in a Domino. R. Pertwee
Death in a Downpour. K. McComb
Death in a Duffle Coat. M. Burton
Death in a Hurry. G. Ashe
Death in a Lighthouse. E. Ronns
Death in a Little Town. R. C. Woodthorpe
Death in a Million Living Rooms. P. McGerr
Death in a Mist. E. Salter
Death in a Pheasant's Eye. James Fraser
Death in a Quiet Place. E. G. Cousins
Death in a Salubrious Place. W. J. Burley
Death in a Sleeping City. J. Wainwright
Death in a Sunny Place. R. Lockridge
Death in a White Tie. N. Marsh
Death in Aberration. J. C. Cooper
Death in Act IV. B. Francis
Death in Albert Park. L. Bruce
Death in Ambush. J. Bude
Death in Ambush. S. Gilruth
Death in Amsterdam. N. Freeling
Death in an Armchair. J. Street
Death in Ankara. C. Wood
Death in Arcady. S. Phillips
Death in Arms. R. Philmore
Death in B-Minor. J. Lilly
Death in Bermuda. Q. Patrick
Death in Botanist's Bay. E. Ferrars
Death in Budapest. V. Gielgud
Death in Captivity. M. Gilbert
Death in Clairvoyance. J. Bell
Death in Cold Print. J. Creasey
Death in Cold Storage. E. Healey
Death in Costume. A. McRoyd
Death in Covert. C. Willock
Death in Cranford. C. Stone
Death in "D" Division. J. G. Brandon
Death in Dark Glasses. G. Bellairs
Death in Darkness. C. Barry
Death in Darkness. George Douglas
Death in Darkness. Alan White
Death in Deakins Wood. R. Petrie
Death in Deep Green. M. Hastings
Death in Desolation. G. Bellairs
Death in Despair. G. Bellairs
Death in Diamonds. G. Ashe

Death in Diamonds. K. Giles
Death in Diamonds. H. R. Taunton
Death in Disguise. H. Tracy
Death in Dockland. D. Reid
Death in Don Mills. H. Garner
Death in Downing Street. J. G. Brandon
Death in Dream Time. S. H. Courtier
Death in Duplicate. J. G. Brandon
Death in Duplicate. George Douglas
Death in Duplicate. Alan White
Death in Dwelly Lane. F. V. Morley
Death in Ecstasy. N. Marsh
Death in Error. F. Usher
Death in Fancy Dress. J. J. Farjeon
Death in Fancy Dress. Anthony Gilbert
Death in Five Boxes. Carter Dickson
Death in Flames. G. Ashe
Death in Four Colors. B. Bird
Death in Four Letters. F. Beeding
Death in Gelly Wood. H. Keyworth
Death in Goblin Waters. M. Peterson
Death in Grease Paint. S. Palmer
Death in Harbour. R. Goyne
Death in Harley Street. J. Rhode
Death in High Heels. C. Brand
Death in High Places. G. Ashe
Death in High Provence. G. Bellairs
Death in Jermyn Street. J. G. Brandon
Death in Lebanon. J. Tyndall
Death in Life. N. Carter
Death in Lilac Time. F. Crane
Death in Lord Byron's Room. S. Wood
Death in Melting. Richard Grayson
Death in Mermaid Lane. Gret Lane
Death in Midwinter. J. B. Hilton
Death in Office. N. Longmate
Death in Office. J. Potter
Death in 1-2-3. R. D. Abrahams
Death in Our Wake. A. Glanville
Death in Passing. E. Lacy
Death in Perpetuity. D. G. Browne
Death in Piccadilly. Elliot Bailey
Death in Piccadilly. R. Garnett
Death in Ptarmigan Forest. C. Coram
Death in Pursuit. G. Leaderman
Death in Quiet Places. Elliot Bailey
Death in Real Life. R. Latimer
Death in Regatta Week. Charles Mason
Death in Reserve. T. Muir
Death in Retirement. J. Bell
Death in Room Five. G. Bellairs
Death in Russian Habit. Sea Lion
Death in Sanctuary. I. Baker
Death in Seven Hours. S. Davis
Death in Seven Volumes. D. G. Browne
Death in Shallow Water. M. Burton
Death in Sheep's Clothing. S. Phillips
Death in Silhouette. J. Slate
Death in Silver. K. Robeson
Death in Slow Motion. K. Robeson
Death in Small Doses. Martin Thomas
Death in Soundings. T. Muir
Death in Stanley Street. W. J. Burley
Death in Sunlight. F. Lester
Death in Ten Point Bold. E. Bruton
Death in the A.R.P. G. Davison
Death in the Air. A. Christie
Death in the Back Seat. D. C. Disney
Death in the Bag. G. Usher
Death in the Bathroom. B. Thomson
Death in the Blackout. Anthony Gilbert
Death in the Blue Hour. F. Crane
Death in the Blue Lake. B. Borge
Death-in-the-Box. M. Magill
Death in the Canongate. P. Piper
Death in the Cards. A. T. Smith
Death in the Castle. P. S. Buck
Death in the Chalkpit. E. R. Punshon
Death in the Church. K. Giles
Death in the Clouds. A. Christie
Death in the Copse. A. G. E. Cromwell
Death in the Coverts. R. Jeffries
Death in the Crease. Richard Curtis
Death in the Cup. M. Dalton
Death in the Dark. Stacey Bishop
Death in the Dark. M. Dalton
Death in the Dark. C. M. Wills
Death in the Deep South. W. Greene

Death in the Desert. G. St. John
Death in the Dimness. I. B. Colley
Death in the Ditch. J. G. Brandon
Death in the Diving Pool. C. Carnac
Death in the Dog Watches. Sea Lion
Death in the Doll's House. H. Lees
Death in the Dormitory. M. Brucker
Death in the Dovecote. Q. Patrick
Death in the Drawing Room. R. A. Rathbone
Death in the Dunes. P. H. Dobbins
Death in the Dusk. V. Markham
Death in the East. C. Franklin
Death in the Fearful Night. G. Bellairs
Death in the Fens. Colin Hope
Death in the Fifth Position. E. Box
Death in the Fog. M. G. Eberhard
Death in the Forest. N. Brand
Death in the Forest. M. Dalton
Death in the Glass. N. Gayle
Death in the Gorge. L. Thayer
Death in the Grand Manor. A. Morice
Death in the Green Fields. J. Atholl
Death in the Hands of Talent. P. Yates
Death in the Headlines. R. Sharp
Death in the Hop Fields. J. Rhode
Death in the House. A. Berkeley
Death in the Inkwell. J. J. Farjeon
Death in the Inner Office. N. Wight
Death in the Jordan. J. Tyndall
Death in the Jungle. Gwyn Evans
Death in the Kettle. C. Wallace
Death in the Library. J. Greenfield
Death in the Library. P. Ketchum
Death in the Life Department. C. P. Cleary
Death in the Limelight. A. Applin
Death in the Limelight. A. E. Martin
Death in the Loch. T. Muir
Death in the Mews. T. C. H. Jacobs
Death in the Mews. Eric Wood
Death in the Middle Watch. L. Bruce
Death in the Mind. R. Lockridge
Death in the Mist. R. C. Finney
Death in the Mist. F. Hurt
Death in the Night. P. Ketchum
Death in the Night Watches. G. Bellairs
Death in the North Sea. J. R. L. Anderson
Death in the Picture. G. Braddon
Death in the Quadrangle. E. Dillon
Death in the Quarry. J. G. Brandon
Death in the Quarry. G. D. H. Cole
Death in the Ring. R. Gilmour
Death in the Rising Sun. J. Creasey
Death in the Scillies. H. C. Davis
Death in the Senate. Diplomat
Death in the Shingle. H. Desmond
Death in the Signal Box. H. Keyworth
Death in the Silver Ring. J. Brown
Death in the Smog. N. MacKenzie
Death in the Snow. R. M. Stern
Death in the Spanish Sun. N. Deane
Death in the Spring. M. J. Law
Death in the Stalls. J. R. Wilmot
Death in the State House. T. Knox
Death in the Stocks. G. Heyer
Death in the Straw. G. Usher
Death in the Sun. G. D. H. Cole
Death in the Sun. S. Coulter
Death in the Sun. C. Saxby
Death in the Sunday Supplement. Sam Merwin
Death in the Surgery. R. Trevor
Death in the Tankard. G. D. H. Cole
Death in the Thames. J. R. L. Anderson
Death in the Theatre. D. Dayle
Death in the Theatre. J. R. Wilmot
Death in the Thicket. V. Loder
Death in the 13th Dose. B. Cobb
Death in the Top Twenty. W. McNeilly
Death in the Tote Box. W. D. Maydwell
Death in the Trees. G. Ashe
Death in the Tunnel. M. Burton
Death in the Village. J. Garden
Death in the Virgins. R. H. Barbour
Death in the Wasteland. G. Bellairs

Death in the Wet. G. Mitchell
Death in the Wheelbarrow. W. Gore
Death in the Wind. J. A. Jordan
Death in the Wind. E. Lanham
Death in the Wind. R. Massey
Death in the Wood. C. Rushton
Death in the Wrong Bed. S. Farrar
Death in the Wrong Room. Anthony Gilbert
Death in the Yew Alley. M. Ervin
Death in Three Masks. B. Healey
Death in Tiger Valley. Reginald Campbell
Death in Triplicate. E. C. R. Lorac
Death in View. T. Macrae
Death in Waiting. J. Bland
Death in Wellington Road. J. Rhode
Death in White Pajamas. J. Bude
Death in Willow Pattern. W. J. Burley
Death Intervened. A. O. Pollard
Death Invades the Meeting. J. Rhode
Death Is a Black Camel. H. B. Kaye
Death Is a Cold, Keen Edge. E. Basinsky
Death Is a Dame. D. Steel
Death Is a Dark Man. D. Highland
Death Is a Drag. D. Hoyt
Death Is a Friend. D. MacKenzie
Death Is a Gold Coin. R. Fenisong
Death Is a Liar. Marc Miller
Death Is a Lizard. John Williams
Death Is a Lovely Dame. M. Blood
Death Is a Lovely Lady. R. Fenisong
Death Is a Lover. N. Tyre
Death Is a Red Rose. D. Eden
Death Is a Restless Sleeper. E. B. Quinn
Death Is a Round Black Ball. M. Roscoe
Death Is a Silent Room. Jay Bennett
Death Is a Stowaway. W. Price
Death Is a Swinger. Jason Morgan
Death Is a Tiger. M. Mundy
Death Is a Tory. K. Patrick
Death Is an Artist. S. Gardiner
Death Is an Early Riser. J. M. Bigelow
Death Is Buttercups. G. M. Wilson
Death Is Confidential. L. Lariar
Death Is for Ever. L. Marshall
Death Is for Losers. W. F. Nolan
Death Is in the Garden. M. Marlette
Death Is Late to Lunch. T. Du Bois
Death Is Like That. J. Spain
Death Is Merciful. J. Sandys
Death Is My Bridegroom. D. M. Devine
Death Is My Comrade. S. Marlowe
Death Is My Dancing Partner. C. Woolrich
Death Is My Lover. S. Brock
Death Is My Name. S. Wells
Death Is My Shadow. J. Corbett
Death Is My Shadow. L. Ronns
Death Is No Lady. M. E. Corne
Death Is No Sportsman. C. Hare
Death Is not a Passing Grade. V. B. Miller
Death Is Skin Deep. C. Percy
Death Is So Final. Alex Fraser
Death Is So Kind. L. Redmond
Death Is So Lonely. L. Amino
Death Is the End. G. W. Cooke
Death Is the Host. L. Lariar
Death Is the Last Lover. H. Kane
Death Is the Pay-Off. S. Burke
Death Is Thy Neighbor. L. D. Smith
Death Is Too Good for You. M. Alexander
Death Is Waiting. F. Usher
Death Is Where You Meet It. Max James
Death Joins the Party. R. Boyd
Death Joins the Party. J. V. Turner
Death Joins the Woman's Club. C. Saxby
Death Keeps a Secret. C. B. Kelland
Death Kicks a Pebble. A. Tack
Death Kiss. M. St. Dennis
Death Knell. B. Kendrick
Death Knocks Three Times. Anthony Gilbert
Death Knows No Calendar. J. Bude
Death Laughs Aloft. P. Conde
Death Leaves a Diary. H. Carmichael
Death Leaves No Card. M. Burton
Death Leaves Us Naked. L. Hollingsworth
Death Let Loose. H. Desmond
Death Letter. T. A. Plummer
Death Lies Deep. W. Guinn

Death Lies in Waiting. B. Williams
Death Lifts the Latch. Anthony Gilbert
Death Light. Richard Grant
Death Lights a Candle. P. A. Taylor
Death Like Thunder. H. Holman
Death Likes It Hot. E. Box
Death List. A. C. Clark
Death List. R. Hawkes
Death Listened In. K. Sproul
Death Lives in the Mansion. D. Locke
Death Lives Next Door. Gwendoline Butler
Death Looks Down. A. R. Long
Death Looks In. R. Sale
Death Looks On. P. Manton
Death Loop. P. Conde
Death Lottery. E. Hyams
Death Loves a Shining Mark. A. Hocking
Death Machine. K. Robeson
Death Maker. A. J. Small
Death Makers. Ralph Hayes
Death Makers. J. Milton
Death Makes a Claim. Hank Hobson
Death Makes a Date. J. Corbett
Death Makes a Date. F. W. Irwin
Death Makes a Deal. M. Parker
Death Makes a Prophet. J. Bude
Death Makes the Scene. S. Phillips
Death Man. D. Kirby
Death Man. B. Swift
Death Mask. A. Applin
Death-Mask. R. Parkes
Death Mask. Ellis Peters
Death-Mask of War. G. Marlowe
Death-Masque. K. Hayles
Death Master. B. Appel
Death May Surprise Us. T. Willis
Death Meets 400 Rabbits. A. M. Stein
Death Meets the Coroner. J. K. Ryland
Death Meets the Deadline. D. R. George
Death Meets the King's Messenger. G. Collins
Death Merchant. J. Rosenberger
Death Miser. J. Creasey
Death Must Have Laughed. J. V. Turner
Death Must Wait. D. Kingery
Death, My Darling Daughters. J. Stagge
Death, My Lover. P. Allardyce
Death-Mystery. N. Buntline
Death Near the River. Monte Cooper
Death Never Forgets. Garnett Weston
Death Never Weeps. S. Ryan
Death Occurred. N. Hoult
Death of a Banker. A. Wynne
Death of a Barrow Boy. Charles Harris
Death of a Beauty Queen. E. R. Punshon
Death of a Best Seller. C. M. Wills
Death of a Big Man. J. Wainwright
Death of a Big Shot. C. Knight
Death of a Blue-Eyed Soul Brother. B. B. Johnson
Death of a Bogey. D. Warner
Death of a Bookseller. B. J. Farmer
Death of a Bovver Boy. L. Bruce
Death of a Bride. G. D. H. Cole
Death of a Bridegroom. J. Rhode
Death of a Bridge Expert. C. C. Nicolet
Death of a Bullionaire. A. B. Cunningham
Death of a Busybody. G. Bellairs
Death of a Busybody. D. Shannon
Death of a Cad. J. Bude
Death of a Call Girl. L. Trevor
Death of a Canary. Neill Graham
Death of a Celebrity. H. Footner
Death of a Cheat. J. M. Eshleman
Death of a Citizen. D. Hamilton
Death of a City. L. White
Death of a Cloven Hoof. Frank King
Death of a Clown. E. Backhouse
Death of a Commuter. L. Bruce
Death of a Con Man. J. Bell
Death of a Convict. T. Herd
Death of a Corinthian. E. Lanham
Death of a Courier. R. Hawkes
Death of a Curate. K. H. Ashley

Death of a Dastard. H. Kane
Death of a Decent Fellow. N. A. Temple-Ellis
Death of a Delft Blue. G. Mitchell
Death of a Designer. N. Brand
Death of a Detective. L. W. Brent
Death of a Diplomat. P. Oldfeld
Death of a Dissenter. L. Lamb
Death of a Doctor. J. Armour
Death of a Dog. L. Eyles
Death of a Doll. C. Brown
Death of a Doll. Hilda Lawrence
Death of a Doxy. R. Stout
Death of a Dreamer. D. Warner
Death of a Dude. R. Stout
Death of a Dwarf. H. Kemp
Death of a Fashion Writer. M. Charlton
Death of a Fat God. H. R. F. Keating
Death of a Fellow Traveller. D. Ames
Death of a Fire-Raiser. George Davis
Death of a First Mate. C. Barry
Death of a Flack. H. Kane
Death of a Flower Child. R. Clarke
Death of a Fool. N. Marsh
Death of a Fox. J. Roffman
Death of a Friend. M. Masterman
Death of a Frightened Editor. E. Radford
Death of a Frightened Traveller. F. Lester
Death of a Gay Dog. A. Morice
Death of a Gentleman. J. Courage
Death of a "Gentleman." E. Radford
Death of a Ghost. M. Allingham
Death of a Goblin. G. Hythe
Death of a Godmother. J. Rhode
Death of a Golden Goose. H. Mace
Death of a Golfer. A. Wynne
Death of a Good Woman. J. F. Straker
Death of a Governor. A. Parsons
Death of a Greek. J. G. Brandon
Death of a Halo. Frank King
Death of a Harbourmaster. G. Simenon
Death of a Harlot. B. Newman
Death of a Heavenly Twin. A. Morice
Death of a Hippie. Michael Brett
Death of a Hittite. S. Angus
Death of a Holy Murderer. M. Duke
Death of a Hooker. H. Kane
Death of a Jazz King. C. M. Walker
Death of a King. A. Wynne
Death of a Ladies' Man. Lee Roberts
Death of a Lady Killer. C. Carnac
Death of a Lake. A. W. Upfield
Death of a Libertine. C. Wallace
Death of a Love. R. Hobart
Death of a Low-Handicap Man. B. Ball
Death of a Lucky Lady. V. Rath
Death of a Marine. C. Leader
Death of a Merchant of Death. N. S. Bortner
Death of a Mermaid. G. Brandon
Death of a Millionaire. G. D. H. Cole
Death of a Millionaire. R. Dana
Death of a Mind. J. Ritson
Death of a Moral Person. A. Roudybush
Death of a Nude. D. Warner
Death of a Nurse. R. Marsten
Death of a Nurse. L. H. Whitten
Death of a Nymph. E. Piper
Death of a Painted Lady. B. Cleeve
Death of a Pale Man. F. Lester
Death of a Peculiar Rabbit. E. Radford
Death of a Peeping Tom. B. Cobb
Death of a Peer. N. Marsh
Death of a Philanderer. L. Meynell
Death of a Player. L. O'Donnell
Death of a Poison-Tongue. J. Bell
Death of a Pornographer. A. Lejeune
Death of a Portrait. E. Mack
Death of a Postman. J. Creasey
Death of a Puppet. G. Hythe

Death of a Puppeteer. W. G. Beyer
Death of a Pusher. R. Deming
Death of a Queen. C. S. Sprigg
Death of a Racehorse. J. Creasey
Death of a Revolutionist. J. Dall
Death of a Saboteur. H. Footner
Death of a Sadist. R. R. Ryan
Death of a Sardine. J. Fleming
Death of a Scapegoat. G. Hythe
Death of a Scoundrel. T. C. H. Jacobs
Death of a Shadow. G. Bellairs
Death of a Shadow. A. Wynne
Death of a Shrew. C. Barling
Death of a Shrew. A. Kennington
Death of a Sinner. R. Arnold
Death of a Sinner. R. Quest
Death of a Sinner. P. Warwick
Death of a Skin-Diver. S. Jay
Death of a Snout. D. Warner
Death of a Socialite. J. G. Brandon
Death of a Spinster. M. Dalton
Death of a Spinster. F. Duncombe
Death of a Spinster. Dorothy Johnson
Death of a Spy. S. Horler
Death of a Star. G. D. H. Cole
Death of a Stranger. M. Halliday
Death of a Stray Cat. J. Potts
Death of a Swagman. A. W. Upfield
Death of a Tall Man. F. Lockridge
Death of a Tax Inspector. S. Chance
Death of a Tin God. G. Bellairs
Death of a Tom. D. Warner
Death of a Train. F. W. Crofts
Death of a Tyrant. E. R. Punshon
Death of a Viewer. H. Adams
Death of a Village. J. Courage
Death of a Weirdy. G. Carr
Death of a White Witch. I. Oellrichs
Death of a Wicked Servant. B. Cleeve
Death of a Wide-Boy. W. R. Hutton
Death of a Wife. C. Wallace
Death of a Wild Bird. J. N. Chance
Death of a Witch. H. Hawton
Death of a World. J. J. Farjeon
Death of a Worldly Woman. A. B. Cunningham
Death of an Ad Man. A. Eichler
Death of an Admiral. G. Hackforth-Jones
Death of an Airman. C. S. Sprigg
Death of an Alderman. J. B. Hilton
Death of an Ambassador. M. Coles
Death of an Ancient Saxon. E. Radford
Death of an Angel. F. Lockridge
Death of an Angel. M. P. Rea
Death of an Angel. C. Richards
Death of an Angel. P. G. Winslow
Death of an Artist. A. Eichler
Death of an Artist. J. Rhode
Death of an Aryan. E. Huxley
Death of an Assassin. J. Creasey
Death of an Aunt. G. Harknett
Death of an Author. E. C. R. Lorac
Death of an Author. J. Rhode
Death of an Editor. V. Loder
Death of an Eloquent Man. C. M. Russell
Death of an Expert Witness. P. H. Powell
Death of an Extra. V. Gielgud
Death of an Informer. W. Perry
Death of an Innocent. J. N. Chance
Death of an Intruder. N. Tyre
Death of an Oddfellow. Eric Wood
Death of an Old Girl. E. Lemarchand
Death of an Old Goat. R. Barnard
Death of an Old Sinner. D. S. Davis
Death of an Uncle. P. Hambledon
Death of an Undertaker. D. Lynn
Death of Anton. A. Melville
Death of Captain Shand. E. Spencer
Death of Cecelia. H. Hartley
Death of Cold. L. Bruce
Death of Cosmo Revere. C. Bush
Death of Daddy-O. David Alexander
Death of Dr. Whitelaw. A. Wilson
Death of Duboyne. W. J. Bayfield
Death of Four. A. Skene

Death of Gold. Mervyn Lewis
Death of Henrietta. L. M. Armistead
Death of His Uncle. C. H. B. Kitchin
Death of Humpty-Dumpty. David Alexander
Death of Innocence. Z. Popkin
Death of Jason Darby. G. E. Taylor
Death of Jezebel. C. Brand
Death of John Tait. A. Fielding
Death of Kyralessa. C. V. Gheorghiu
Death of Laura. H. C. Davis
Death of Laurence Vining. Alan Thomas
Death of Lord Haw Haw. B. Rutledge
Death of Maurice. B. Pain
Death of Me Yet. W. Masterson
Death of Miss Cunningham. J. Cousseau
Death of Miss X. M. McMullen
Death of Mr. Balishberger. B. Hrabel
Death of Mr. Dodsley. J. Ferguson
Death of Mr. Gantley. M. Burton
Death of Mr. Lomas. F. Vivian
Death of Mrs. Preedy. L. Jackson
Death of Monsieur Gallet. G. Simenon
Death of My Aunt. C. H. B. Kitchin
Death of Nevill Norway. J. Rowland
Death of Our Dear One. M. Erskine
Death of the Claimant. A. R. Martin
Death of the Deputy. F. Didelot
Death of the Detective. Mark Smith
Death of the Diplomat. M. Scherf
Death of the Doctor's Wife. Whyte Hall
Death of the Falcon. N. Carter
Death of the Fuhrer. R. Puccetti
Death of the Home Secretary. Alan Thomas
Death of the Party. R. Fenisong
Death of the Vampire Baroness. V. Van Der Elst
Death of Two Brothers. M. Burton
Death of Virginia. O. Rees
Death Off the Fairway. H. Adams
Death on a Back Bench. F. Hobson
Death on a Dude Ranch. F. Bonnamy
Death on a Ferris Wheel. A. L. Martin
Death on a High Note. D. Reid
Death on a Pale Horse. B. Jones
Death on a Quiet Beach. S. Challis
Death on a Quiet Day. M. Innes
Death on a Smokeboat. R. Graham
Death on a Summer Day. E. Booth
Death on a Warm Wind. D. Warner
Death on a Wet Sunday. P. Capon
Death on All Hallows. A. C. MacLean
Death on Allhallowe'en. L. Bruce
Death on Bodmin Moor. V. Gunn
Death on "Calamity." K. Wade
Death on Danger Hill. T. A. Plummer
Death on Dartmoor. J. Rowland
Death on Delivery. E. Allen
Death on Delivery. J. G. Brandon
Death on Delivery. H. Gore-Browne
Death on Delivery. F. W. Gumley
Death on Demand. G. Ashe
Death on Deposit. F. Grierson
Death on Display. R. Simons
Death on Doomsday. E. Lemarchand
Death on Herons' Mere. M. Fitt
Death on Ice. J. B. O'Sullivan
Death on Jerusalem Road. D. Angus
Death on Location. W. R. Cox
Death on May Morning. M. Dalman
Death on Milestone Buttress. G. Carr
Death on My Left. P. MacDonald
Death on My Shoulder. C. Franklin
Death on Paper. J. Bude
Death on Priority! P. Yorke
Death on Raven's Scar. Albert Harding
Death on Remand. M. Underwood
Death on Romney Marsh. L. Bruce
Death on Scurvy Street. B. A. Williams
Death on Shivering Sand. V. Gunn
Death on Sunday. J. Rhode
Death on the Agenda. M. Bidwell
Death on the Agenda. P. Moyes
Death on the Agenda. T. Muir
Death on the Air. Herman Landon
Death on the Aisle. F. Lockridge
Death on the Atoll. B. Francis
Death on the Barrier Reef. E. Antill
Death on the Beach. P. Broad

Death on the Black Sands. L. Bruce
Death on the Board. J. Rhode
Death on the Boat Train. J. Rhode
Death on the Border. R. P. Holden
Death on the Borough Council. J. Bell
Death on the Bridge. R. Howes
Death on the Broads. E. Radford
Death on the Campus. A. Simmons
Death on the Centre Court. G. Goodchild
Death on the Champs-Elysees. F. Didelot
Death on the Cherwell. M. D. Hay
Death on the Cliff. T. Cobb
Death on the Clock. G. Knevels
Death on the Cuff. M. G. MacKnutt
Death on the Deep. H. M. Stephenson
Death on the Diamond. C. Fitzsimmons
Death on the Door Mat. M. V. Heberden
Death on the Doorstep. George Douglas
Death on the Double. H. Kane
Death on the Down Beat. S. Farr
Death on the Downbeat. C. Brown
Death on the Downs. A. Marsden
Death on the Files. M. Penrose
Death on the First Tee. H. Adams
Death on the Grass. L. O'Donnell
Death on the Highway. C. Robbins
Death on the Hit Parade. B. Gray
Death on the Hour. R. Lockridge
Death on the Last Train. G. Bellairs
Death on the Lawn. J. Rhode
Death on the Limited. R. Denbie
Death on the Line. C. M. Wills
Death on the Machar. A. MacVicar
Death on the Mall. A. Parsons
Death on the Moor. J. Pendower
Death on the Motorway. C. Coram
Death on the Mountain. D. Ogburn
Death on the Move. G. Ashe
Death on the Nile. A. Christie
Death on the Nose. H. D. Spatz
Death on the Outer Shoal. A. Fuller
Death on the Oxford Road. E. C. R. Lorac
Death on the Pack Road. H. Andover
Death on the Pampas. C. Wood
Death on the Piazza. Jean Fraser
Death on the Reserve. J. Bell
Death on the River Kwai. G. De Villiers
Death on the Riviera. J. Bude
Death on the Roads. G. W. Wray
Death on the Rocks. J. R. L. Anderson
Death on the Rocks. J. B. West
Death on the Roof. B. Francis
Death on the Run. J. M. Hickman
Death on the Run. U. Rothwell
Death on the Set. V. MacClure
Death on the Sixth Day. H. Farrell
Death on the Spike. D. Reid
Death on the Swim. Simon
Death on the Table. C. Rayner
Death on the Trooper. T. Muir
Death on the Waterfront. R. Archer
Death on the Way. F. W. Crofts
Death on Tiptoe. R. C. Ashby
Death on Tour. J. Courage
Death Opens the Ball. J. R. Benson
Death Out of Darkness. M. Halliday
Death Out of Focus. W. C. Gault
Death Out of Focus. C. Whitman
Death Out of the Night. A. Wynne
Death Out of Thin Air. S. Towne
Death over Deep Water. S. Nash
Death over Her Shoulder. D. C. Meade
Death over Hollywood. C. Saxby
Death over London. M. Wheeler-Nicholson
Death over Newark. Alexander Williams
Death over San Dilvestro. M. Teagle
Death over Sunday. J. F. Bonnell
Death Overseas. C. Barry
Death Pack. R. Sonin
Death Packs a Suitcase. B. E. Wallace
Death Paints a Picture. M. Burton

D

Death Paints a Portrait. W. Herber
Death Paints the Picture. L. Lariar
Death Parade. H. Desmond
Death Parade. A. O. Pollard
Death Pays a Dividend. J. Rhode
Death Pays All Debts. M. Sharman
Death Pays Dividends. J. W. Hornby
Death Pays the Piper. L. Gribble
Death Pays the Wages. E. McGirr
Death Penalty. A. Draper
Death Play. G. Verner
Death Plays Solitaire. R. L. Goldman
Death Plays the Gramophone. Marjorie Stafford
Death Plays the Last Card. H. H. Kirst
Death Plot. L. H. Brenning
Death Points a Finger. W. Levinrew
Death Pool. J. Corbett
Death Pool. V. Loder
Death Prowls the Cove. Gret Lane
Death Pulls a Doublecross. Lawrence Block
Death Pulls No Punches. B. Shannon
Death Race. S. Jason
Death Rattle. A. B. Caldwell
Death Ray Dictator. J. Titterton
Death Ray Mystery. L. Rutland
Death Registers at the Eagle Arms. K. Frost
Death Rehearses. J. Varnam
Death Reign of the Vampire King. G. Stockbridge
Death Renders Account. J. M. Spender
Death Requests the Pleasure. M. Dekobra
Death Ride. N. MacNeil
Death-Riders. C. Cofyn
Death Rides a Black Steed. L. Churchill
Death Rides a Camel. J. Wolf
Death Rides a Hobby. R. Howes
Death Rides a Painted Horse. R. P. Wilmot
Death Rides a Sorrel Horse. A. B. Cunningham
Death Rides Swiftly. N. Shepherd
Death Rides Tandem. W. McCully
Death Rides the Air Line. W. Sutherland
Death Rides the Deep. F. MacIsaac
Death Rides the Desert. D. Adair
Death Rides the Dragon. E. Thomas
Death Rides the Forest. Rupert Grayson
Death Rides the Rail. R. Sharp
Death Rides the Rails. C. Stoddard
Death Rides the Range. B. Netton
Death Rides the Speedway. D. Forde
Death Rides the Storm. K. Kendall
Death Rides the Train. B. Sarto
Death Ring. E. S. Drewry
Death Rings a Bell. C. Fitzsimmons
Death Rings No Bell. G. Braddon
Death Road. D. Stuart
Death Rocks the Cradle. P. Martens
Death Rope Island. P. Goulden
Death Round the Corner. J. Creasey
Death Runs on Skis. H. Ritchie
Death Rust. E. P. Thorne
Death Sails in a High Wind. T. Du Bois
Death Sails the Nile. F. B. McKinley
Death Schuss. L. O'Donnell
Death Seance. F. W. Gumley
Death Seat. J. B. O'Sullivan
Death Seekers. Ross Richards
Death Sends a Cable. M. T. Yates
Death Sends for the Doctor. G. Bellairs
Death Sentence. B. Garfield
Death Sentence. A. D. Miller
Death Serves a Fault. C. Ryland
Death Serves an Ace. H. Wills
Death Set in Diamonds. G. Verner
Death Sets the Pace. L. Cargill
Death Shall Overcome. E. Lathen
Death Ship. A. Blair
Death Ship. H. Edmonds
Death Ship. S. Hope
Death Ship. T. P. Prest
Death Ship. W. C. Russell
Death Sign. Gwyn Evans
Death Singer. J. A. Jordan
Death Sits In. C. Glick
Death Sits In. H. A. Keller
Death Sits on the Board. J. Rhode
Death Slams the Door. P. Cade
Death Sleeps in Kensington. J. Ward
Death Sleeps Lightly. R. C. Payes
Death Smiles. R. R. Phillips
Death Song. R. Hawkes
Death Speaking. Gwyn Evans
Death Sped the Plough. G. Usher
Death Spins the Platter. E. Queen
Death Spins the Wheel. G. Bellairs
Death Spoke Sweetly. R. Garnett
Death Springs the Trap. E. K. Goldthwaite
Death Squad. D. Pendleton
Death Squadron. A. O. Pollard
Death Stalk in Spain. Don Smith
Death Stalked the Fells. A. G. MacLeod
Death Stalks a Lady. Shelley Smith
Death Stalks a Marriage. R. W. Larson
Death Stalks in Kenya. A. Peverett
Death Stalks in Soho. J. G. Brandon
Death Stalks the Bride. Jean Marsh
Death Stalks the Cobbled Square. J. N. Chance
Death Stalks the Fleet. H. Cope
Death Stalks the River. O. Williams
Death Stalks the Stadium. J. B. O'Sullivan
Death Stalks the Wakely Family. A. Derleth
Death Stalks the Waterway. S. Dewes
Death Stalks "The Wild Goose." R. Stahl
Death Stands By. J. Creasey
Death Stands Near. A. Knight
Death Stands Round the Corner. W. M. Duncan
Death Starts a Rumour. M. Fitt
Death Steals the Show. J. Bude
Death Stills the Brush. F. W. Gumley
Death Stone. D. Weir
Death Stops at the Old Stone Inn. S. Seifert
Death Stops the Bells. R. M. Baker
Death Stops the Frolic. G. Bellairs
Death Stops the Manuscript. R. M. Baker
Death Stops the Rehearsal. R. M. Baker
Death Stops the Show. L. S. Thompson
Death Strain. N. Carter
Death Strikes at Dawn. H. Desmond
Death Strikes at Heron House. K. O'Neil
Death Strikes at Six Bells. G. Baxter
Death Strikes from the Rear. A. Marsden
Death Strikes Home. M. W. Glidden
Death Strikes in Darkness. L. Marshall
Death Strikes Out. G. Finley
Death Suspended. C. Whitman
Death Swamp, and other adventure stories. E. T. Portwine
Death Symbol. T. A. Plummer
Death Syndicate. J. Philips
Death Takes a Bow. F. Lockridge
Death Takes a Detour. M. Burton
Death Takes a Dive. G. W. Cooke
Death Takes a Dive. E. Heath
Death Takes a Dive. A. Tack
Death Takes a Flat. M. Burton
Death Takes a Gamble. R. H. R. Smithies
Death Takes a Hand. F. Griffin
Death Takes a Hand. T. A. Plummer
Death Takes a Holiday. N. MacKenzie
Death Takes a Partner. J. Rhode
Death Takes a Paying Guest. A. M. Stein
Death Takes a Redhead. Anthony Gilbert
Death Takes a Ride. R. C. Finney
Death Takes a Ride. H. E. Wheeler
Death Takes a Sabbatical. R. Bernard
Death Takes a Star. N. Morland
Death Takes a Teacher. G. Usher
Death Takes a Wife. Anthony Gilbert
Death Takes an Editor. N. Morland
Death Takes an Option. N. MacNeil
Death Takes Over. J. McFerran
Death Takes Revenge. James Preston
Death Takes Small Bites. G. H. Johnston
Death Takes the Bus. L. White
Death Takes the Joystick. P. Conde
Death Takes the Last Train. R. Bernard
Death Takes the Living. M. Burton
Death Takes the Low Road. P. Ruell
Death Takes the Stage. Gavin Holt
Death Takes the Stump. E. H. Duthoit
Death Takes the Wheel. E. Radford
Death Talks Out of Turn. R. Powell
Death Talks Shop. P. Haggard
Death Tears a Comic Strip. T. Du Bois
Death That Lurks Unseen. J. S. Fletcher
Death the Red Flower. O. Wynd
Death the Showman. John Fraser
Death the Sure Physician. J. Wakefield
Death Therapy. R. Sapir
Death Throws a Party. Austin Stone
Death Thumbs a Ride. J. Lilly
Death to Comrade X. John Morgan
Death to Drumbeat. J. Lane
Death to My Beloved. R. Neely
Death to My Killer. J. York
Death to Slow Music. B. Nichols
Death to the Fifth Column. B. Newman
Death to the Killer. C. F. Caunter
Death to the Ladies. N. Morland
Death to the Landlords! Ellis Peters
Death to the Mafia. F. Scarpetta
Death to the Rescue. M. Kennedy
Death to the Spy. D. Dayle
Death to the Spy. B. Newman
Death to Windward. H. Brinton
Death Tolls the Bell. M. Hervey
Death Tolls the Bell. P. McGuire
Death Tolls the Gong. J. G. Brandon
Death Took a Greek God. N. Forrest
Death Took a Publisher. N. Forrest
Death-Torch Terror. B. House
Death Tower. M. Grant
Death Trap. H. Carmichael
Death Trap. R. W. Cole
Death Trap. P. H. Dobbins
Death Trap. E. P. Green
Death Trap. J. D. MacDonald
Death Trap. J. Rosenberger
Death Trap. A. Skene
Death Traps. K. C. Strahan
Death Traps the Killer. Mary Dane
"Death Treads--." C. M. Wills
Death Treads Softly. G. Bellairs
Death Trick. J. F. Burke
Death Trust. Anonymous
Death Trust. A. L. Halstead
Death Turns Right. T. B. Dewey
Death Turns the Tables. J. D. Carr
Death Turns Traitor. W. S. Masterman
Death-Twist. J. Tiger
Death Under Contract. R. Wallace
Death Under Desolate. J. N. Chance
Death Under Gibraltar. B. Newman
Death Under Sail. C. P. Snow
Death Under Snowdon. G. Carr
Death Under the Moonflower. T. Downing
Death Under the Stars. V. Bell
Death Under the Table. P. Godfrey
Death Under Virgo. T. Muir
Death Unheralded. George Douglas
Death Visits Downspring. M. Burton
Death Visits the Apple Hole. A. B. Cunningham
Death Visits the Cinema. F. W. Irwin
Death Visits the Circus. Jean Marsh
Death Visits the Parish. F. W. Gumley
Death Visits the Summer-House. Gret Lane
Death Waits in Tucson. D. Reid
Death Waits Outside. R. Verron
Death Walked In. L. A. Olmsted
Death Walked in Berlin. M. M. Kaye
Death Walked in Cyprus. M. M. Kaye
Death Walked in Kashmir. M. M. Kaye
Death Walks by the River. V. Bell
Death Walks In. G. Chester
Death Walks in Eastrepps. F. Beeding

Death Walks in Marble Halls. L. G. Blochman
Death Walks in Scarlet. L. Cargill
Death Walks in Shadow. L. Thayer
Death Walks on Cat Feet. P. Haggard
Death Walks on Cat Feet. D. B. Olsen
Death Walks Softly. Hazel C. MacDonald
Death Walks Softly. N. Shepherd
Death Walks the Dry Tortugas. M. P. Rea
Death Walks the Post. V. Hanson
Death Walks the Woods. C. Hare
Death Warmed Over. Mary Collins
Death Was a Wedding Guest. A. S. Roche
Death Was Her Escort. E. Pawley
Death Was No Lady. S. Truss
Death Was the Echo. R. Dana
Death-Watch. J. D. Carr
Death Watch. J. Hawkins
Death Watch. D. Winston
Death Wears a Carnation. B. E. Stevenson
Death Wears a Copper Tie and other stories. H. Pentecost
Death Wears a Green Hat. W. Creed
Death Wears a Mask. Therese Benson
Death Wears a Mask. D. G. Browne
Death Wears a Mask. Anthony Gilbert
Death Wears a Purple Shirt. R. C. Woodthorpe
Death Wears a Scarab. A. R. Long
Death Wears a Silk Stocking. W. M. Duncan
Death Wears a White Coat. T. Du Bois
Death Wears a White Gardenia. Z. Popkin
Death Wears Cat's Eyes. D. B. Olsen
Death Wears Pink Shoes. Robert James
Death Wears Red Shoes. C. Robertson
Death Weed. L. Thayer
Death Went Hunting. George Douglas
Death When She Wakes. N. Morland
Death When You Want It. Desmond Martin
Death Whispers. J. B. Carr
Death Whispers Softly. P. Malloch
Death Whistle. R. Marsh
Death Will Find Me. H. Steers
Death Wish. V. Caspray
Death Wish. B. Garfield
Death Wish. E. S. Holding
Death-Wish Green. F. Crane
Death with a Difference. B. Cobb
Death With Blue Ribbon. L. Bruce
Death Within the Vault. L. Thayer
Death Without a Funeral. J. Ward
Death Without Question. T. Muir
Death Woman. J. N. Chance
Death Won a Prize. I. Montgomery
Death Won't Wait. Anthony Gilbert
Death Won't Wash. N. Longmate
Death Wore a Petticoat. H. Janson
Death Wore Fins. Dale Clark
Death Wore Gold Shoes. L. V. Stevens
Death Wore Roses. C. Saxby
Death Writes an Ed. M. Holbrook
Deathblow Hill. P. A. Taylor
Deathmaster. W. M. Duncan
Death's Bright Angel. T. Warriner
Death's Bright Dart. V. C. Clinton-Baddeley
Death's Busy Crossroads. S. Mitchell
Death's Counterfeit. H. Clevely
Death's Dateless Night. T. Warriner
Death's Doorway. V. Gunn
Death's Duet. H. Carstairs
Death's Eye. L. Meynell
Death's Foot Forward. G. B. Mair
Death's Head. C. Black
Death's-Head. Arthur Wise
Death's Head Conspiracy. N. Carter
Death's Inheritance. E. Radford
Death's Juggler. C. J. Daly
Death's Long Shadow. J. Barbette
Death's Long Shadow. K. Wolffe
Death's Lovely Mask. J. Flagg

Death's Mannikins. M. Afford
Death's No Antidote. G. Osborne
Deaths of Lora Karen. R. McDougald
Death's Old Sweet Song. J. Stagge
Death's Second Self. J. F. Drabble
Death's Sweet Music. N. Morland
Death's Sweet Song. Clifton Adams
Death's Treasure Hunt. W. C. Harvey
Death's Visiting Card. J. C. Woodiwiss
Deathstar Voyage. Ian Wallace
Deathstone. E. L. Arch
Deathwishers. T. Journet
Deaves Affair. H. Footner
Debt. O. Hogstrand
Debt Discharged. E. Wallace
Debt of Hatred. G. Ohnet
Debt of Vengeance. Mrs. E. B. Collins
Debt to Dishonour. A. Furness
Decayed Gentlewoman. E. Ferrars
Deceivers. R. Goldhurst
Deceivers. J. D. MacDonald
Deceiver's Door. C. B. Booth
Deceiving Mirror. P. Traill
Deception. C. Kavanaugh
Deception of Death. V. Siller
Deception of Ursula. T. Cobb
Deceptions. H. L. Victor
Decision. E. Chodorov
Decision. H. Kane
Decision at Dawn. A. Calin
Decision at Delphi. H. MacInnes
Decision before Dawn. G. Howe
Deck with Flowers. E. Cadell
Decker. W. Graeme-Holder
Decks Ran Red. A. L. Stone
Decorated Corpse. R. Stratton
Decoration. K. Hewitt
Decoy. C. F. Adams
Decoy. J. D. Beresford
Decoy. Francis Dana
Decoy. A. Maling
Decoy. M. Morgan
Decoy. E. Ronns
Decoy Babes. B. Sarto
Decoy Detective. Anonymous
Decoy for Murder. P. Saxon
Decoy in Diamonds. N. Gates
Decoy Murders. A. Douglas
Decoyed Across the Seas. R. Overton
Deductions of Colonel Gore. L. Brock
Dee Dee. E. H. Robinson
Dee Goong An. R. Van Gulik
Deed Is Drawn. W. A. Barber
Deed of a Night. Warren Miller
Deed of Darkness. I. Stark
Deed of Innocence. J. Blackmore
Deed Without a Name. D. Bowers
Deed Without a Name. E. Phillpotts
Deeds Ill Done. A. Seifert
Deeds of Dr. Deadcert. J. Fleming
Deep. M. Spillane
Deep Among the Dead Men. J. Blackburn
Deep and Crisp and Even. L. Payne
Deep as the Grave. O. Keystone
Deep Blue Good-By. J. D. MacDonald
Deep Channels. E. L. Long
Deep Cold Green. C. Brown
Deep Cover. B. Garfield
Deep Currents. A. Fielding
Deep, Deep Freeze. W. Garner
Deep End. F. Brown
Deep End. O. Dudley
Deep End. J. Hayes
Deep Fall. B. Knox
Deep Flows the River. A. Wood
Deep Freeze. J. Bruce
Deep Furrows. R. W. Ritchie
Deep Green Death. B. Gaston
Deep in Dark Country. P. Drew
Deep Is My Desire. I. Gordon
Deep Is My Grave. J. Death
Deep Is the Blue. M. Ehrlich
Deep Is the Lake. M. Clare
Deep Is the Pit. H. V. Dixon
Deep Kill. D. Da Cruz
Deep-Lake Mystery. C. Wells
Deep Lay the Dead. F. C. Davis
Deep Malice. D. G. Waring

Deep Moat Grange. S. R. Crockett
Deep Pool. J. Blackmore
Deep Sand. B. Munslow
Deep-Sea Tow. C. McManus
Deep Secret. R. Chapman
Deep Six. J. M. Flynn
Deep Valley. W. Anthony
Deep Water. P. Highsmith
Deep Waters. M. Leighton
Deepening Blue. S. M. Schley
Deeper Game. N. Carter
Deeper Malady. J. Turner
Deeper Scar. S. Gluck
Deeper Stain. F. Hird
Defeat of a Detective. C. M. Wills
Defection of A. J. Lewinter. R. Littell
Defector. N. Carter
Defector. C. Collingwood
Defector. D. Seaman
Defector. P. Thomas
Defectors Are Dead Men. F. A. Smith
"Defend the Rock." P. Groom
Defenders. E. S. Aarons
Defending a Home. E. A. Young
Defending the Bank. E. S. Van Zile
Defense Does Not Rest. E. Sherry
Defense Rests. E. Pierson
Deferred Payment. J. Owen
Definite Object. J. Farnol
Defrauded Yeggman. H. S. Keeler
Defy the Tempest. S. Dannett
Degenerate. F. Whishaw
Degradation of Geoffrey Alwith. Morley Roberts
Deirdre. J. Nicholas
Delacott Mystery. C. Kingston
Delafield Affair. F. F. Kelly
Delaplaine. M. T. Walworth
Delaware Dick. M. Mizzen
Delay in Danger. S. Harvester
Delay of Doom. P. Capon
Delayed Action. R. W. Hatch
Delayed Action. N. Tranter
Delayed Harvest. Rona Randall
Delayed Payment. J. Rhode
Deldee. F. Warden
Deldee, the Ward of Warington. F. Warden
Delfina. S. Brackeen
Delgado Killings. R. Hawkes
Delicate Ape. D. B. Hughes
Delicate Case of Murder. S. Gluck
Delicate Darling. J. Webb
Delicate Dust of Death. P. Audemars
Delicate Fiend. E. C. Vivian
Delicious Danger. H. Janson
Delilah. P. Trent
Delilah of Harlem. R. H. Savage
Delilah of Mayfair. A. Soutar
Delilah Was Deadly. C. Brown
Delinquent! Morton Cooper
Delinquents. A. Bloomfield
Delinquents. P. Malloch
Deliver Me From Eva. P. Bailey
Deliver Us from Evil. H. Desmond
Deliver Us from Wolves. L. Holton
Deliver Us to Evil. J. L. Hensley
Delivery of Furies. V. Canning
Delorme in Deep Water. S. Lister
Delta Deputies. Carl Martin
Delta Factor. M. Spillane
Demagogue. C. Dawe
Demand for Justice. I. Stark
Demarest Inheritance. M. Carleton
Demi-Paradise Regained. S. Stone
Demise of a Louse. W. T. Ballard
Democrat Dies. P. Frankau
Demolished Man. A. Bester
Demon. J. McCulley
Demon. C. N. Williams
Demon Again. E. M. Keate
Demon Barber of Broadway. Griff
Demon Child. D. Dwyer
Demon Detective. Anonymous
Demon in the Blood. P. Marlowe
Demon Island. K. Robeson

Demon Jockey. B. Hemyng
Demon of Barnabas Collins. Marilyn Ross
Demon of Desire. W. J. Elliott
Demon of Hong Kong. R. S. L. Harding
Demon of the Air. E. M. Keate
Demon of the Darkness. Dana Ross
Demon Stirs. O. Cameron
Demon Tower. V. Coffman
Demon Within. B. Hastings
Demoniacs. J. D. Carr
Demon's Eye. N. Carter
Demon's Moon. C. Robertson
Demons of the Night. N. Carter
Dempsey Diamonds. A. Arnot
Den of Savage Men. B. Jones
Denbigh Affair. A. Lowing
Dene Hollow. H. Wood
Dene of the Secret Service. G. Verner
Denis Dent. E. W. Hornung
Denmark Bus. S. McGurk
Denmede Mystery. W. Martyn
Dennisdale Tragedy. H. Andover
Dennison Hill. D. Winston
Denver Lil. F. Foden
Denver's Double. George Griffith
Denzil Emeralds. P. Meredith
Denzil's Device. B. Delannoy
Depart This Life. E. Ferrars
Department K. H. Howard
Department of Dead Ends. Roy Vickers
Department of Death. J. Creasey
Department of Queer Complaints. Carter Dickson
Departure Deferred. W. H. Baker
Departure Delayed. W. Oursler
Departure of Mr. Gaudette. D. M. Disney
Deposit Vault Puzzle. N. Carter
Depository Mystery. G. Chester
Depths. J. Creasey
Depths of Yesterday. D. Lyons
Deputy. W. C. Tuttle
Deputy Avenger. H. Richards
Deputy Avenger. R. Trevor
Deputy for Cain. Roy Vickers
Derelict. C. J. C. Hyne
Derelict. J. T. Shaw
Derelict House. A. Skene
Derelicts. W. M. Graydon
Derision. C. Edwards
Derrick Devil. K. Robeson
Derring-Do. H. Craigie
Derry Down Death. A. Curry
Deruga Trial. R. Huch
Desborough Mystery. A. M. Diehl
Descent into the Dark. D. Ramsay
Desert Adventure. D. Spicer
Desert Bride. H. Nisbet
Desert Castle Mystery. C. H. Snow
Desert Convoy. M. Hastings
Desert Crime. Roland Daniel
Desert Desire. J. Chancellor
Desert Episode. G. Greenfield
Desert Flower. Rona Randall
Desert Flyer. J. Bolton
Desert Fury. H. Janson
Desert Intrigue. E. Ellison
Desert Intrigue. J. Stagg
Desert Lake Mystery. K. C. Strahan
Desert Moon Mystery. K. C. Strahan
Desert Night. W. E. Johns
Desert of Darkness. P. Wissmann
Desert of Doom. W. M. Graydon
Desert of Salt. K. R. Butler
Desert Shadows. B. Netton
Desert Squadron. J. R. Holden
Desert Stake-Out. H. Whittington
Desert Stalker. M. Barry
Desert Trail. R. C. Armour
Desert Trail. D. Lenton
Desert Wooing. C. H. Bullivant
Deserted by the Devil. T. Irving-James
Deserted Night. T. B. Morris
Deserted Wife. E. Southworth
Deserter of the Foreign Legion. W. M. Graydon
Deserters. G. C. Jenks
Deserters Don't Come Back. R. Wilkes-Hunter
Design for an Accident. D. Egerton
Design for Blackmail. J. L. Morrissey
Design for Danger. E. Ellison
Design for Death. J. Day
Design for Death. K. Summers
Design for Destruction. Deryck Phillips
Design for Dupes. H. Janson
Design for Dying. A. Jeffers
Design for Dying. S. A. Krasney
Design for Dying. H. McCloy
Design for Dying. L. Trimble
Design for Murder. G. Batson
Design for Murder. F. Durbridge
Design for Murder. F. A. Kummer
Design for Murder. P. Wilde
Design for Murder, and five other stories. L. H. Fox
Design for Treachery. C. C. Saunders
Design for Treason. G. Dickson
Design for Vengeance. Martin Thomas
Design in Diamonds. K. M. Knight
Design in Evil. R. King
Desirable Alien. A. Kennington
Desirable Dictator. J. Fores
Desirable Woman. C. Dawe
Desire in the Dust. H. Whittington
Desire of the Eyes and other stories. G. Allen
Desire to Kill. A. Campbell
Desired. C. Brown
Desmond Dare. Old Sleuth
Desmond Drake Goes West. Sea Lion
Desmond Rourke, Irishman. J. Haslette
Despair. V. Nabokoff-Sirin
Despair and Delight. R. Arnold
Despair's Last Journey. D. C. Murray
Despatch of a Dove. R. Petrie
Desperado. J. Hunter
Desperate Art. J. Rosenberg
Desperate Asylum. F. Flora
Desperate Chance. N. Carter
Desperate Chance. O. Harper
Desperate Chance. J. D. J. Kelley
Desperate Chance. Old Sleuth
Desperate Conspiracy. G. Boothby
Desperate Criminals. R. Longrigg
Desperate Cure. R. Fenisong
Desperate Deed. N. T. Oliver
Desperate Dilemma. H. Danvers
Desperate Encounter. Cecile Rutherford
Desperate Expedient. C. N. Boyle
Desperate Gamble. H. Desmond
Desperate Game. J. K. Leys
Desperate Game. Old Spicer
Desperate Game. F. Warden
Desperate Games. P. Boulle
Desperate Heiress. Marilyn Ross
Desperate Holiday. F. Cowen
Desperate Hours. J. Hayes
Desperate Journey. H. Treece
Desperate Justice. Dan Morgan
Desperate Love. C. Dawe
Desperate Measures. D. Wheatley
Desperate Moment. M. Albrand
Desperate Night. H. C. Davis
Desperate People. F. Durbridge
Desperate Remedy. B. Bolt
Desperate Rendezvous. R. Severn
Desperate Search. C. Eland
Desperate Search. A. Mayse
Desperate Steps. Mark Cross
Desperate Venture. J. Ritson
Desperate Voyage. E. F. Knight
Desperate Witch. Anthony Graham
Desperation. R. Rand
Despite the Evidence. P. Alding
Despoilers. E. Mitchell
Destination Dames. H. Janson
Destination Danger. W. C. MacDonald
Destination--Death. H. Desmond
Destination Dieppe. W. H. Baker
Destination: Terror. J. Paull
Destination Terror. W. E. D. Ross
Destination Unknown. A. Christie
Destination Unknown. R. Goyne
Destination Unknown. J. Hunter
Destination Unknown. R. Sale
Destinations. G. Simenon
Destiny. A. Askew
Destiny Is My Name. David Hume
Destiny on Demand. M. Butcher
Destiny's Child. P. Morton
Destiny's Daughter. C. H. Bullivant
Destroy the U.S.A. W. F. Jenkins
Destroyer. C. Goodall
Destroyer. J. Lodwick
Destroyer. B. E. Stevenson
Destroyer. B. Swift
Destroyer and the Red-Haired Death. S. Horler
Destroying Angel. J. Creighton
Destroying Angel. N. Klein
Destroying Angel. L. J. Vance
Destroying Angel. E. Wallace
Destruction Committee. W. J. Coughlin
Destructors. M. Franklin
Detail. W. McCarthy
Detail for the Dreamer. W. M. Duncan
Details of Jeremy Stratton. A. E. Lindop
Detection in a Topper. J. Oliver
Detection Unlimited. G. Heyer
Detections of Dr. Sam: Johnson. L. De La Torre
Detective. R. Thorp
Detective. L. J. Vance
Detective Against Detective. D. J. MacKenzie
Detective Against Detective. M. Redwing
Detective and the Poisoner. S. Rathbone
Detective and the Somnambulist. A. Pinkerton
Detective Archie. Old Sleuth
Detective Ben. J. J. Farjeon
Detective Bob Bridger. R. M. Taylor
Detective Burr's Seven Clues. Anonymous
Detective Coulson. Jack Mann
Detective Crime Stories. L. Dexter
Detective Dale. Old Sleuth
Detective Duff Unravels It. H. J. O'Higgins
Detective Fleet of London. Anonymous
Detective for Vengeance. Anonymous
Detective Gay. Old Sleuth
Detective Gordon's Grip. Anonymous
Detective Hanley. Old Sleuth
Detective in Distress. B. Cobb
Detective in Italy. H. Forbes
Detective in Spite of Himself. H. Manning
Detective Inspector Chance. G. R. Sims
Detective Johnson of New Orleans. H. I. Hancock
Detective Kennedy. Old Sleuth
Detective Murdock, the Silent. Old Sleuth
Detective No. 1. F. Pratt
Detective Officer. Waters
Detective Payne. Old Sleuth
Detective Payne's Shadow. Old Sleuth
Detective Reynold's Hardest Case. G. Macias
Detective Sketches. Anonymous
Detective Stories. Anonymous
Detective Stories. W. Henderson
Detective Story. S. Kingsley
Detective Sylvia Shale. S. Groom
Detective Thrash. Old Sleuth
Detective Trio. Old Sleuth
Detective Unawares. G. F. P. Lea
Detective Wore Silk Drawers. P. Lovesey
Detectives. N. Daniels
Detective's Album. W. W.
Detective's Clew. Old Hutch
Detective's Crime. F. Du Boisgobey
Detective's Crime. C. Morris
Detective's Daughter. L. L. Lynch
Detective's Daughter. Old Sleuth

Title Index

Detective's Dilemma. F. Du Boisgobey
Detective's Dilemma. H. L. Phillips
Detective's Due. L. Egan
Detective's Enigma. Old Sleuth
Detective's Eye. F. Du Boisgobey
Detective's Holiday. C. Barry
Detective's Honeymoon. M. Danvers
Detectives in Gum Boots. R. East
Detectives, Ltd. F. S. Wees
Detective's Memoirs and other stories. E. M. L. Sturt
Detective's Note-Book. C. Martel
Detective's Notebook. Anonymous
Detectives of Europe and America. G. S. McWatters
Detective's Pretty Neighbor and other stories. N. Carter
Detective's Secret. N. D. Urner
Detective's Theory. N. Carter
Detective's Triumph. F. Du Boisgobey
Detective's Triumphs. D. Donovan
Detective's Victory. Anonymous
Dethroned Heiress. E. A. Dupuy
Detour. M. E. Goldsmith
Detour. H. Nielsen
Detour. W. Wilson
Detour at Night. G. Endore
Detour Through Devon. G. Endore
Detour to a Funeral. V. J. Santiago
Detour to Death. H. Nielsen
Detour to Denmark. J. Ware
Detour to Oblivion. F. C. Davis
Detours. O. R. Cohen
Detroit Deathwatch. D. Pendleton
Detroit Massacre. M. Barry
Deuces Wild. H. MacGrath
Deuces Wild. D. Shannon
Devalino Caper. A. J. Russell
Devastation. Mrs. C. Kernahan
Devastators. D. Hamilton
Devereux Court Mystery. M. Burton
Deveril's Diamond. A. Sergeant
Deviant Death. G. Moffat
Deviations of Diana. H. Mitchell
Deviator. A. York
Device. B. E. Wallace
Devil and Ben Franklin. T. Mathieson
Devil and Destiny. T. Du Bois
Devil and Mary Ann. C. Cookson
Devil and Miss Thrace, and other stories. M. Hervey
Devil and Mrs. Devine. Josephine Leslie
Devil and the C.I.D. E. C. R. Lorac
The Devil and the Crusader. A. Askew
Devil and the Deep. S. Horler
Devil and the Deep. H. Janson
Devil and the Deep Blue Sea. E. Jordan
Devil and Webster Daniels. T. L. Smith
Devil and X.Y.Z. B. Browne
Devil at Saxon Wall. G. Mitchell
Devil at the Door. M. Seuffert
Devil at Your Elbow. D. M. Devine
Devil Behind Me. F. E. Smith
Devil Boy. W. D. Roberts
Devil Breathes But Once. C. Wallace
Devil Builds a Chapel. M. Marlette
Devil by the Sea. N. Bawden
Devil Child. P. J. Cooper
Devil Comes to Bolobyn. S. Horler
Devil Comes to Devon. J. Rowland
Devil Daddy. J. Blackburn
Devil, Devil. M. Avallone
Devil Doctor. S. Rohmer
Devil Drives. R. Ames
Devil Drives. J. N. Chance
Devil Drives. V. Markham
Devil Finds Work. M. Delving
Devil Fish. P. Groom
Devil for the Witch. E. Lacy
Devil Ghengis. K. Robeson
Devil Has a Racket. M. Storm
Devil Has Four Faces. J. Jakes
Devil Has the Best Tunes. H. L. V. Fletcher
Devil Has Wings. P. Conde
Devil Held the Aces. P. Doncaster
Devil His Due. W. O'Farrell
Devil in a Domino. C. L'Epine

Devil in Broad Daylight. J. Bramlett
Devil in Davos. G. Brewer
Devil in Downing Street. R. Ladline
Devil in Dungarees. Albert Conroy
Devil in Greenlands. J. N. Chance
Devil in Harbour. C. Gavin
Devil in Her. H. Duval
Devil in Her. P. Trent
Devil in Kansas. Simon Quinn
Devil in London. G. R. Sims
Devil in Moonlight. M. Procter
Devil in the Belfry. R. Thorndike
Devil in the Bush. M. Head
Devil-in-the-Dark. P. Wentworth
Devil in the Maze. V. Gunn
Devil in the Pines. L. Cameron
Devil in the Pulpit. E. O'Donnell
Devil in the Sky. Muriel Bradley
Devil in the Wind. G. Greenaway
Devil in Velvet. J. D. Carr
Devil Kinsmere. R. Fairbairn
Devil Laughed. M. Richmond
Devil Loves Me. M. Millar
Devil Man. E. Wallace
Devil May Care. Wade Miller
Devil-May-Care. A. S. Roche
Devil Must. T. Wicker
Devil of Aske. P. Hill
Devil of Danehurst. J. Hunter
Devil of Pei-Ling. H. Asbury
Devil of the Depths. J. McLaren
Devil on Board. G. T. Ockley
Devil on His Trail. J. Hawkins
Devil on Lammas Night. S. Howatch
Devil on the Moon. K. Robeson
Devil on the Stairs. P. Root
Devil on Two Sticks. Wade Miller
Devil or Man? P. Beare
Devil or Saint? C. Robertson
Devil Rides Out. D. H. Wheatley
Devil Snard. G. R. Preedy
Devil Spider. Glint Green
Devil-Stick. F. Hume
Devil Take All. A. Brennan
Devil Take All. M. Caidin
Devil Take Her. F. Nichols
Devil Take the Blue-Tail Fly. J. F. Bardin
Devil Take the Foremost. T. Kinney
Devil Take the Hindmost. H. F. Shefler
Devil Takes a Hill Town. C. G. Givens
Devil That Slumbers. W. Allen
Devil Threw Dice. A. Dean
Devil Thumbs a Ride. R. C. Du Soe
Devil to Pay. R. Dolphin
Devil to Pay. George Douglas
Devil to Pay. F. N. Greene
Devil to Pay. H. Kane
Devil to Pay. E. Queen
Devil to Play. L. Holton
Devil Was a Woman. B. Graeme
Devil Was Handsome. M. Procter
Devil Was Kind. Donald Ross
Devil Was Sick. M. Durham
Devil Wears Wings. H. Whittington
Devil Within. B. M. Scott
Devil Within Us. D. Basinger
Devil Wolf. N. S. Schinke
Devil Woman. Roland Daniel
Devil Wore Scarlet. D. Gray
Devil You Don't. J. Wainwright
Devil You Know. W. J. White
Devilday. Angus Hall
Deville McKeene, the British Ace. R. Walker
Devil's Ace. F. Hume
Devil's Admiral. F. F. Moore
Devil's Advocate. H. T. Johnson
Devil's Advocate. F. M. White
Devil's Agent. H. Habe
Devil's Apprentice. G. Davison

Devil's Bargain. F. Warden
Devil's Behind You. H. E. Helseth
Devil's Birthday. J. Lie
Devil's Box. W. J. Sheldon
Devil's Bread. D. Mariner
Devil's Bridge. M. Deasy
Devil's Brood. C. H. Barker
Devils Burn Too. Clay Henry
Devil's Cameo. W. H. Dye
Devil's Can-Can. W. H. Baker
Devil's Caress. J. Wright
Devil's Carnival. W. LeQueux
Devil's Cavern. C. Morgan
Devil's Chapel. E. P. Thorne
Devil's Chaplain. G. Bronson-Howard
Devil's Church. F. Draco
Devil's Churchyard. T. Willis
Devil's Cloak. C. Robertson
Devils' Cockpit. N. Carter
Devil's Cocktail. A. Wilson
Devil's Coffin. H. Gordon
Devil's Cook. E. Queen
Devil's Current. K. Bennett
Devil's Dagger. M. G. Kiddy
Devil's Daughter. Griff
Devil's Daughter. E. Lipsky
Devil's Daughter. Marilyn Ross
Devil's Daughter. O. Schisgall
Devil's Daughter. D. Winston
Devil's Den. L. Saunders
Devil's Derelicts. F. C. V. Harcourt
Devil's Diamond. R. Marsh
Devil's Diamonds. G. Davison
Devil's Dice. W. LeQueux
Devil's Die. G. Allen
Devil's Diplomats. Operator 1384
Devil's Dominion. K. Lindsay
Devil's Door. L. Halliday
Devil's Doorstep. D. Kamm
Devil's Double. C. H. Bullivant
Devil's Doubloons. J. McCulley
Devil's Dozen. N. Carter
Devil's Dozen. N. Vane
Devil's Dreamer. A. Brennan
Devil's Dress. M. M. Fletcher
Devil's Drive. A. W. Allan
Devil's Drum. L. Gorell
Devil's Drum. W. C. MacDonald
Devils' Drums. V. Meik
Devil's Due. Lanora Miller
Devil's Due. M. Procter
Devil's Edge. J. N. Chance
Devil's Elbow. G. Mitchell
Devil's Emissary. J. Laffin
Devil's Eye. J. A. Jordan
Devil's Footprints. E. Bond
Devil's Goad. J. Laffin
Devil's Gold. J. B. Hendryx
Devil's Guard. T. Mundy
Devil's Heirloom. A. M. Rud
Devil's Highway. H. Janson
Devil's Hole. P. Ainsworth
Devil's Horns. K. Robeson
Devil's Innocents. J. Edgar
Devil's Instrument. M. M. Fletcher
Devil's Island Death Camp. P. Edwards
Devil's Keg. R. Cullum
Devils' Kloof. L. P. Greene
Devil's Lady. H. L. Gates
Devil's Lady. C. Robertson
Devil's Laughter. L. H. Brenning
Devil's Lieutenant. M. Fagyas
Devil's Lighter. J. Ballem
Devil's Luck. O. Williams
Devil's Mansion. R. Jardin
Devil's Mantle. F. Packard
Devil's Mirror. M. Lynch
Devil's Mistress. J. W. Brodie-Innes
Devil's Mistress. V. Coffman
Devil's Nest. H. H. Harper
Devil's Own. G. Bowman
Devil's Own. P. Curtis
Devil's Own. J. L. Roberts
Devil's Passkey. J. Shannon
Devil's Passport. Gordon Young
Devil's Paw. E. P. Oppenheim

D

Devil's Pawn. E. Bruton
Devil's Payday. W. C. Tuttle
Devil's Playground. K. Robeson
Devil's Plunge. D. Walker
Devil's Portage. C. Stoddard
Devil's Post Office. John Muir
Devil's Power. C. Rushton
Devil's Princess. D. Winston
Devil's Punchbowl. D. Decker
Devil's Rain. M. Willis
Devil's Reckoning. M. Burton
Devil's Ring. L. Kenyon
Devil's Shelter. R. R. Ryan
Devil's Shilling. C. Rae-Brown
Devil's Signpost. A. Drummond
Devil's Skull. G. M. Wilson
Devil's Smile. R. Foxall
Devil's Snare. M. Cumberland
Devil's Son. N. Carter
Devil's Spawn. C. Birkin
Devil's Spawn. R. Foxall
Devil's Steps. N. Thurley
Devil's Steps. A. W. Upfield
Devil's Stronghold. L. Ford
Devil's Tea-Party. T. A. Plummer
Devils' Tears. E. Hale
Devil's Torch. G. Dickson
Devil's Toy. Anita Stewart
Devil's Triangle. A. Soutar
Devil's Vicar. V. Coffman
Devil's Vineyard. B. Kevern
Devil's Virgin. V. Coffman
Devil's Whirlpool. G. Volk
Devil's Whisper. R. Barnett
Devil's Whisper. L. Borden
Devil's Work. C. Wells
Deviltower. U. Nightingale
Devilweed. B. Knox
Devine Court Mystery. B. Symons
Devious Design. D. B. Olsen
Devious Murder. G. Bellairs
Devious Ones. F. Lockridge
Devious Ways. P. Freund
Devlin the Barber. B. L. Farjeon
Devon Maze. J. D. Fitz
Devouring Fire. L. Gorell
Dew in the Morning. M. Curtis
Dewey Death. C. Blackstock
Dexter Bank Robbery. H. Rockwood
Diablo Manor. D. Daniels
Diabolic Candelabra. E. R. Punshon
Diabolist. M. A. Drew
Diabolus. David St. John
Diagnosis: Homicide. L. G. Blochman
Diagnosis: Murder. R. King
Diagnosis--Murder. Sutherland Scott
Dial 577 R-A-P-E. L. O'Donnell
Dial M for Money. D. Taggart
Dial "M" for Murder. F. Knott
Dial 999. J. M. Walsh
Diamond and the Lady. J. Blyth
Diamond Beach. L. Forrester
Diamond Bikini. C. Williams
Diamond Boomerang. L. S. Taube
Diamond Bracelet. H. Wood
Diamond Bubble. R. L. Fish
Diamond-Buckled Shoe. B. Bolt
Diamond Button. B. North
Diamond Coterie. L. L. Lynch
Diamond Crime Detective. Benett Hill
Diamond Cross Mystery. C. K. Steele
Diamond Cut Diamond. J. Bunker
Diamond Cut Diamond. N. Carter
Diamond Cut Diamond. B. Stuart
Diamond Dragon. G. H. Teed
Diamond Dress. O. John
Diamond Duel. S. G. Hedges
Diamond Feather. H. Reilly
Diamond Fingers. J. Ingersol
Diamond Flood. R. C. Armour
Diamond Hair Slide. H. C. McNeile
Diamond Hitch. W. C. Tuttle
Diamond Hook. J. Quartermain
Diamond Hostage. J. Quartermain
Diamond in the Hoof. T. Stevenson
Diamond Master. J. Futrelle
Diamond Mine Case. N. Carter
Diamond Mountain. T. Keeping

Diamond Murders. J. S. Fletcher
Diamond Necklace. Frederick Jackson
Diamond of Evil. F. Whishaw
Diamond of Ti Lingo. J. G. Brandon
Diamond Pendant. T. Thurston
Diamond Pin. C. Wells
Diamond Queen. M. Dekobra
Diamond Queen. A. B. Reeve
Diamond Racket. N. Anthony
Diamond Ransom Murders. N. Child
Diamond Rock. Sea Lion
Diamond Rose Mystery. G. Knevels
Diamond Seeker of Brazil. Leon Lewis
Diamond Ship. M. Pemberton
Diamond-Studded Typewriter. C. Keith
Diamond Sunburst. G. H. Teed
Diamond Thieves. A. Stringer
Diamond Tolls. R. S. Spears
Diamond Trail. O. Binns
Diamond Trail. N. Carter
Diamond Trail. T. Gallon
Diamond Trip. Jenni Hall
Diamonds. J. S. Fletcher
Diamonds and Hearts. J. C. Goodwin
Diamonds Are Deadly. J. Eastwood
Diamonds Are Forever. I. Fleming
Diamonds Are Trumps. H. Adams
Diamonds Bid. J. Rathbone
Diamonds Can Be Dangerous. B. O'Keefe
Diamonds Can Be Trouble. E. Harrison
Diamonds Don't Burn. Gertrude Walker
Diamonds for a Blonde. B. Sarto
Diamonds for Danger. J. Pendower
Diamonds for Danger. D. Walker
Diamonds for Moscow. D. Walker
Diamonds Going and Coming. H. G. Dyar
Diamonds in the Dumplings. S. Shane
Diamonds of Alcazar. M. K. Simmons
Diamonds of Death. B. Chase
Diamonds of Death. W. Jackson
Diamonds of Death. J. Ronald
Diamonds of Death. H. Willett
Diamonds See in the Dark. T. Mundy
Diamonds Spell Death. L. Edgley
Diamonds to Amsterdam. M. Coles
Diamonds Worth a Death or Two. P. Campion
Diana Defiant. A. Applin
Diana Is Dead. M. Stand
Diana K.C. R. Lichfield
Diana Meets Murder. P. Tabori
Diana of Dartmoor. G. Warden
Diana of Kara Kara. W. Wallace
Diana of the Moorland. L. Tracy
Diana of the Moors. L. Tracy
Diana of the Woods. L. C. Douthwaite
Diana's Luck. A. Applin
Diane and Her Friends. A. Sherburne Hardy
Diane Game. S. Cohen
Diane of the Islands. B. Bolt
Diary. W. Ard
Diary of a Detective Police Officer. Waters
Diary of a Great French Detective. Anonymous
Diary of a Judge. H. R. Addison
Diary of a Police Surgeon. G. Graham
Diary of a Red-Haired Girl. E. Price
Diary of a Scoundrel. M. Pemberton
Diary of an Ex-Detective. C. Martel
Diary of Death. W. Collison
Diary of Death. F. W. Gumley
Diary of Evil. N. Hawthorne
Diavolo. M. E. Braddon
Dibchick. Richard Dark
Dice Are Dark. B. Flynn
Dice Spelled Murder. A. Fray
Dice Were Loaded. M. Cumberland
Dick. B. J. Friedman
Dick Merriwell's Detective Work. B. L. Standish
Dick Merriwell's Mystery. B. L. Standish

Dick, the Boy Detective. Old Sleuth
Dick Tracy. W. Johnston
Dick Tracy and the Woo Woo Sisters. C. Gould
Dicker in Souls, and other stories. W. S. Gidley
Dictator. Justin McCarthy
Dictator of Death. Frank King
Dictator's Daughter. E. Jepson
Dictator's Destiny. D. Betteridge
Dictators Die Hard. R. A. Levey
Dictator's Secret. G. H. Teed
Dictator's Way. E. R. Punshon
Dictatorship of the Dove. F. Gerard
Did He Deserve It? J. H. Riddell
Did She Fall? T. Smith
Did She Fall or Was She Pushed? D. M. Disney
Did You Kill Mona Leeds? J. Roeburt
Didn't Anybody Know My Wife? W. D. Roberts
Die a Little Every Day. Lawrence Fisher
Die All, Die Merrily. L. Bruce
Die Anytime, After Tuesday! C. Brown
Die--As in Murder. L. Grex
Die by Night. M. S. Marble
Die by the Book. L. Meynell
Die, Damn You! P. Durst
Die, Darling, Die. E. Bruton
Die for Big Betsy. B. Knox
Die for Love. J. Oxford
Die Here a Stranger. M. Vinter
Die in the Country. T. Wells
Die in the Dark. Anthony Gilbert
Die, Jessica, Die. J. De Pre
Die, Killer, Die. F. Scarpetta
Die Laughing. R. Lockridge
Die Laughing. P. McGerr
Die Like a Dog. F. Gruber
Die Like a Dog. B. Halliday
Die Like a Man. M. Delving
Die, Little Goose. David Alexander
Die, Lover. H. Whittington
Die, My Beloved. P. Malloch
Die, My Darling. F. Usher
Die Now, Live Later. B. Copper
Die of a Rose. W. Maner
Die on Easy Street. J. A. Howard
Die Quickly, Brother. J. W. Hornby
Die Quickly, Dear Mother. T. Wells
Die Rich Die Happy. J. Munro
Die Screaming. J. Pagano
Die She Must. B. Von Hutten
Die to a Distant Drum. W. Arden
Die Wearing a Rose. E. P. Thorne
Die with Me, Lady. R. Cocking
Diecast. Michael Brett
Died in the Grass. C. Franklin
Died in the Red. D. Gray
Died in the Wool. N. Marsh
Died o'Wednesday. S. Carver
Died o' Wednesday. Paul Townend
Died on a Rainy Sunday. Joan Aiken
Diehard. J. Potts
Difference in Death. Donn Russell
Difference to Me. J. Bryan
Different Kind of Summer. J. Melville
Different Night. O. Hesky
Difficult Problem and other stories. A. K. Green
Dig a Dead Doll. G. G. Fickling
Dig a Narrow Grave. M. L. Roby
Dig Another Grave. D. C. Cameron
Dig Deep for Julie. R. Rayner
Dig for a Corpse. M. Mundy
Dig Her a Grave. P. Kruger
Dig Me a Grave. J. Spain
Dig Me Later. M. Hagen
Dig My Grave Deep. P. Rabe
Dig That Crazy Grave. R. S. Prather
Dig the Grave and Let Him Die. J. Wainwright
Dig the Grave Deep. N. Brent
Dig the Missing. M. Urquhart
Dig Those Heels. H. Janson
Dig: Two Heads Wanted. H. H. Woodbridge

Title Index

Digby's Miracle. F. E. Wynne
Digger of the Pit. M. Hastings
Diggers Die Hard. Eric Lambert
Digger's Game. G. V. Higgins
Dignity and Purity. I. Jefferies
Dilemma. J. Brampton
Dilemma. N. Edwards
Dilemma. H. C. McNeile
Dilemma. E. Phillpotts
Dilemma for Dax. M. Cumberland
Dilemma of Commander Brett. W. Chesney
Dilemma of Death. L. G. Redmond-Howard
Dilemma of Dr. Riley. W. Tyrer
Dilemma of the Dead Lady. W. Irish
Dilemmas. A. E. W. Mason
Dillinger. H. Clement
Dimbleby's. L. C. Douthwaite
Diminished by Death. Jonathan Ross
Diminishing Returns. E. L. Withers
Dinah for Danger. J. Bogar
Dinard Mystery. J. Maske
Dine and Be Dead. Gwendoline Butler
Dine with Murder. M. Halliday
Dine with the Devil. J. G. Vermandel
Ding Dong Bell. H. Reilly
Dingdong. A. Maling
Dingo. J. M. Scott
Dinky Died. T. Wells
Dinner After Death. T. Irving-James
Dinner at Antoine's. F. P. Keyes
Dinner at Dupre's. B. Halliday
Dinner Club. H. C. McNeile
Dinner for None. M. Sarsfield
Dinner in New York. S. Fowler
Dinner-Party at Bardolph's. R. A. J. Walling
Dinner with the Dead. M. McLaren
Dinosaur. L. Kamarck
Diogenes of London and other fantasies and sketches. H. B. M. Watson
Dion O'Dare. C. E. Blaney
Diplomat. J. Aldridge
Diplomat and the Gold Piano. M. Scherf
Diplomat Dies. L. Gribble
Diplomatic Adventure. S. W. Mitchell
Diplomatic Corpse. P. A. Taylor
Diplomatic Cover. D. Torr
Diplomatic Death. C. Forsyte
Diplomatic Incident. J. Kelly
Diplomatic Lover. Elsie Lee
Diplomatic Mysteries. V. Thompson
Diplomatic Woman. H. Mee
Diplomat's Diary. Julien Gordon
Diplomat's Folly. Henry Wade
Dire Departed. J. Matheson
Director. Alan Thomas
Directors' Corridor. C. Francis
Dirge for a Dead Witch. Winifred Duke
Dirge for a Dog. Jennifer Jones
Dirge for Her. V. Rath
Dirty Business. L. Edgley
Dirty Butter for Servants. J. Fleming
Dirty Game. W. H. Baker
Dirty Gertie. H. Kane
Dirty Hands. R. Neely
Dirty Harry. P. Rock
Dirty Pool. G. Bagby
Dirty Scenario. J. Ballem
Dirty Story. E. Ambler
Dirty Way to Die. G. Bagby
Dirty Way to Die. B. Rossi
Dirty Work. R. Pertwee
Disagreeable Woman. Julian Starr
Disappearance. R. Carroll
Disappearance. J. Cowdroy
Disappearance. Derek Marlowe
Disappearance. C. Wilcox
Disappearance of a Niece. K. Field
Disappearance of Archibald Forsyth. Ian Alexander
Disappearance of Cropton. J. Fairfax-Blakeborough
Disappearance of Dr. Bruderstein. J. Sherwood
Disappearance of George Driffell. J. Payn
Disappearance of Julie Hintz. S. Truss
Disappearance of Kimball Webb. R. Wright
Disappearance of Lady Diana. R. Machray
Disappearance of Martha Penny. H. A. Vachell
Disappearance of Mary Amber. B. Poynter
Disappearance of Mr. Derwent. T. Cobb
Disappearance of Mr. Jeremiah Redworth. J. H. Riddell
Disappearance of Nicholson. C. Ainsworth
Disappearance of Nigel Blair. F. Warden
Disappearance of Norman Langdale. P. Lancaster
Disappearance of Odile. G. Simenon
Disappearance of Roger Tremayne. B. Graeme
Disappearance of "Straight Left" Smith. Ernest H. Robinson
Disappearance of the Duke. Mrs. C. Kernahan
Disappearance of Uncle David. J. J. Farjeon
Disappearing Bridegroom. M. Erskine
Disappearing Bullets. G. J. Brenn
Disappearing Corpse. J. Warren
Disappearing Eye. F. Hume
Disappearing Island. G. Jenkins
Disappearing Parson. M. Burton
Disappearing Princess. N. Carter
Disaster at Dungeness. R. Johnston
Disc. J. B. Harris-Burland
Discarded Daughter. E. Southworth
Discharge to Danger. W. Spann
Disciple of Satan. N. Carter
Disciples of Satan. M. Richmond
Discipline of Christine. B. Goldie
Disclosures of a Press Agent. D. Miall
Discord in Harmony. P. K. McAfee
Discord in the Air. E. H. Clements
Discords of the Deep. L. A. Cunningham
Discourse with Shadows. J. Malcolm
Disentanglers. Andrew Lang
Disgrace and Favour. J. Potter
Disgrace to the College. G. D. H. Cole
Disguise for a Dead Gentleman. G. Compton
Disher-Detective. Will Scott
Dishonest Murderer. F. Lockridge
Dishonor Among Thieves. S. Dean
Dishonored. F. Vreeland
Dishonour Among Thieves. David Hume
Dishonour Among Thieves. E. C. R. Lorac
Dis-Honourable. D. Hennessey
Dishonourable Member. J. T. Story
Dishonoured Bones. J. Trench
Disillusioned. B. Sarto
Disinformer. O. John
Disinherited. K. Orvis
Disintegration of J.P.G. G. Simenon
Disordered Death. J. B. O'Sullivan
Disoriented Man. P. Saxon
Dispatch and Secrecy. G. Grison
Dispensable Man. W. Rilla
Disposal Unit. J. Boland
Disposing Mind. R. H. R. Smithies
Disposing of Henry. R. Bax
Dispossessed. G. Wagner
Disputed Barricade. H. Gibbs
Disputed Quarry. D. Sharp
Disqualified. F. Johnston
Dissemblers. T. Cobb
Dissemblers. J. Creasey
Distant Clue. R. Lockridge
Distracting Guest. R. Jocelyn
Distributors. A. Partridge
District Bungalow. C. C. Lewis
Disturbance on Berry Hill. E. Fenwick
Disturbing Affair of Noel Blake. N. Bell
Ditto, Brother Rat! W. Garner
Diva's Emeralds. V. MacClure
Dive Deep for Danger. H. T. Rothwell
Dive Deep for Death. E. Messenger
Dive into Danger. C. Forsyte
Dive into Darkness. L. O'Donnell
Dive into Death. C. Matthews
Diver Went Down. J. McLaren
Divers. H. Nisbet
Divers Diamonds. A. Dekker
Diversions of Dawson. B. Copplestone
Dives and Son. E. Davies
Divide by Seven. R. Chambers
Divide the Night. D. Honig
Divided Trail. J. K. Stafford
Divided We Fall. E. Burgess
Dividend of Death. G. Malcolm-Smith
Dividend on Death. B. Halliday
Dividend Was Death. W. J. Coughlin
Dividing Night. V. Scannell
Divinations of Kala Persad and other stories. H. Hill
Divine and Deadly. M. Scherf
Divine Gift. C. McLaren
Divine Spark. P. Traill
Diving Dames Affair. P. Leslie
Diving Death. C. Forsyte
Divining Rod for Murder. M. Neville
Divinitas. J. Knowler
Division Bell Mystery. E. Wilkinson
Divorce. T. P. Prest
Divorce. G. Thorne
Divorce Court Murder. M. Propper
Divorced Princess. R. de Pont-Jest
Dixon Hawke, Secret Agent. J. Creasey
Dixon Hawke's Case Book. Anonymous
Dixon of Dock Green. T. Willis
Dizzy Dames Die Fast. C. Wheatley
Do Butlers Burgle Banks? P. G. Wodehouse
Do Evil in Return. M. Millar
Do It Yourself Doom. S. Prickett
Do No Evil. F. Noro
Do Not Disturb. H. McCloy
Do Not Disturb. L. Thayer
Do Not Fold, Spindle or Mutilate. D. M. Disney
Do Not Murder Before Christmas. J. Iams
Do Not Sleep. G. M. Wilson
Do Unto Others. D. M. Disney
Do You Deal in Murder? A. Allyson
Do You Know This Voice? E. Berckman
Do You Like Tahiti? E. Clerk
Do You Remember England? Derek Marlowe
Doc Churston. O. Binns
Doc Grip, the Sporting Detective. Anonymous
Dock Brief. D. Barr
"Dock Rats" of New York. Old Sleuth
Dock Walloper. B. Appel
Docken Dead. J. Trench
Dockyard Mystery. S. Hope
Doctor and the Corpse. M. Murray
Doctor and the Devil. C. W. Gardner
Doctor and the Devils. D. Thomas
Doctor Artz. R. Hichens
Doctor Baxter's Invention. W. P. Kelly
Doctor Bentiron: Detective. E. M. Poate
Dr. Berkeley's Discovery. R. Slee
Doctor Bernard St. Vincent. H. Nisbet
Dr. Bruderstein Vanishes. J. Sherwood
Doctor Burton. A. C. Gunter
Doctor Burton's Success. A. C. Gunter
Doctor Claude. H. Malot
Doctor Caro. B. J. Packer
Dr. Chaos and the Devil Snard. G. R. Preedy
Doctor Cobb's Game. R. V. Cassill
Doctor Cockaigne. N. E. Davies
Dr. Cunliffe--Investigator. H. Frankish
Doctor Dale's Dilemma. G. W. Appleton
Doctor Darch's Wife. F. Warden
Doctor Deals with Murder. W. M. Duncan
Doctor Death. N. Carter
Doctor Death. J. Hartenfels
Doctor Death. C. Whitman
Doctor Detective. P. Graham
Doctor Didn't Prescribe Murder. H. B. May
Doctor Died at Dusk. G. Homes
Doctor Disappears. M. Dalman
Doctor Dodds' Experiment. Sutherland Scott
Dr. Duvene's Crime. G. Chester

D

Dr. Endicott's Experiment. A. Sergeant
Dr. Falke of Harley Street. S. Fairway
Doctor Falls in Love. Rona Randall
Dr. Fell, Detective, and other stories. J. D. Carr
Dr. Ferraro's Frame-Up. C. Brisbane
Doctor Fix. H. Janson
Doctor for the Dead. M. Higgins
Doctor Fram. S. Mackenzie
Doctor Frigo. E. Ambler
Doctor from Devil's Island. C. Rushton
Doctor Garrett's Girl. M. Lynch
Dr. Gatskill's Blue Shoes. P. Conant
Dr. Glazebrook's Revenge. A. C. Brown
Doctor Glennie's Daughter. B. L. Farjeon
Dr. Goodwood's Locum. J. Rhode
Dr. Greenfingers. E. Woodward
Dr. Grimshawe's Secret. N. Hawthorne
Doctor Havelock's Wife. Rona Randall
Doctor, His Wife, and the Clock. A. K. Green
Doctor Is Sick. A. Burgess
Doctor Izard. A. K. Green
Dr. Krasinski's Secret. M. P. Shiel
Doctor Krook. A. Mallory
Doctor Looks at Murder. D. Quick
Dr. Mabuse, Master of Mystery. N. Jacques
Dr. Manton. M. Gerard
Doctor Mephisto. J. Joseph-Renaud
Doctor Moon. C. Meadows
Dr. Morel. K. Bramson
Dr. Morelle. E. Dudley
Dr. Morelle and Destiny. E. Dudley
Dr. Morelle and the Doll. E. Dudley
Dr. Morelle and the Drummer Girl. E. Dudley
Dr. Morelle at Midnight. E. Dudley
Dr. Morelle Meets Murder and other new adventures. E. Dudley
Dr. Morelle Takes a Bow. E. Dudley
Dr. Nicholas Stone. E. S. De Puy
Doctor Nikola. G. Boothby
Dr. Nikola's Experiment. G. Boothby
Doctor No. I. Fleming
Doctor of Pimlico. W. LeQueux
Dr. Palliser's Patient. G. Allen
Doctor Paradise. J. J. Dratler
Dr. Phibes. W. Goldstein
Dr. Phibes Rises Again. W. Goldstein
Dr. Priestley Investigates. J. Rhode
Dr. Priestley Lays a Trap. J. Rhode
Dr. Priestley's Quest. J. Rhode
Dr. Quake. R. Sapir
Doctor Quartz, Magician. N. Carter
Doctor Quartz's Quick Move. N. Carter
Dr. Quick, the Masked Detective. Ernest H. Robinson
Dr. Ricardo. W. Garrett
Dr. Rumsey's Patient. L. T. Meade
Doctor S.O.S. L. Thayer
Dr. Sam: Johnson, Detector. L. De La Torre
Doctor Samovar, Crook. Spike Gordon
Dr. Scarlett. A. Laing
Doctor Severin's Secret. S. Fairway
Doctor Sinister. G. Chester
Dr. Sinister. Gwyn Evans
Dr. Somerville's Crime. M. H. Hervey
Dr. Strangelove. P. Bryant
Doctor Syn. R. Thorndike
Doctor Syn on the High Seas. R. Thorndike
Doctor Syn Returns. R. Thorndike
Dr. Tancred Begins. G. D. H. Cole
Doctor--There's Danger. F. L. Cary
Dr. Thorndyke Intervenes. R. A. Freeman
Dr. Thorndyke Investigates. R. A. Freeman
Dr. Thorndyke Omnibus. R. A. Freeman
Dr. Thorndyke's Case-Book. R. A. Freeman
Dr. Thorndyke's Cases. R. A. Freeman
Dr. Thorndyke's Dilemma. J. H. Dirckx
Dr. Thorndyke's Discovery. R. A. Freeman
Dr. Time. K. Robeson
Dr. Toby Finds Murder. S. M. Schley
Doctor Transit. I. S.
Doctor Vandyke. J. E. Cooke
Doctor Villagos. F. Du Boisgobey
Dr. Wainwright's Patient. E. Yates
Doctor Was a Dame. S. Truss

Doctor Who Held Hands. H. Footner
Doctor Who Wouldn't Tell. W. M. Graydon
Dr. Wilbur's Note Book. N. T. Oliver
Dr. Wynne's Revenge. W. Westall
Doctor Xavier. M. Pemberton
Dr. Zollinoff's Revenge. E. R. Owen
Doctors Also Die. D. M. Devine
Doctors Are Doubtful. A. Weymouth
Doctors Beware! W. McCully
Doctor's Crime. M. Danvers
Doctor's Daughter. P. Allardyce
Doctor's Daughter. H. Wood
Doctor's Defence. S. Fairway
Doctor's Double. E. W. Alais
Doctor's Double. N. Gould
Doctor's First Murder. R. Hare
Doctor's Idol. C. Lys
Doctor's Mistake. C. H. Montague
Doctor's Murder Case. R. P. Koehler
Doctor's Office. Elsie Lee
Doctor's Secret. W. J. Bayfield
Doctor's Secret. S. Campbell
Doctor's Secret. Rita
Doctor's Strategem. N. Carter
Doctors Wear Scarlet. S. Raven
Doctor's Wife. M. E. Braddon
Documentary Evidence. R. Halket
Documents in the Case. D. L. Sayers
Documents Marked "Secret." John Gloag
Documents of Death. J. Creasey
Documents of Murder. T. C. H. Jacobs
Dodd Cases. K. Livingston
Dodge City Bombers. L. Derrick
Dodging the Law. N. Carter
Dodos Don't Duck. M. O'Brine
Dog and Duck Mystery. H. Bogue
Dog Day Afternoon. P. Mann
Dog Detective. Anonymous
Dog Detective and His Young Master. M. M. Murray
Dog Eat Dog. W. Chambers
Dog Eat Dog. Mary Collins
Dog-Face. J. Easton
Dog Fight with Death. G. Davison
Dog Fog. W. B. M. Ferguson
Dog It Was. R. Harrison
Dog It Was That Died. G. Braddon
Dog It Was That Died. H. R. F. Keating
Dog It Was That Died. E. C. R. Lorac
Dog Man. M. Procter
Dog Star. C. Stanton
Dog Track Murder. M. Osborne
Dog with a Bad Name. F. Warden
Dogcatcher. P. Prince
Dog's Death. P. Motte
Dogs Do Bark. J. Stagge
Dogs of War. W. H. Baker
Dogs of War. F. Forsyth
Dog's Ransom. P. Highsmith
Dogwatch. C. Coffin
Doings of Raffles Haw. A. C. Doyle
Doll. E. McBain
Doll Baby. H. Barron
Doll Castle. M. Monigle
Doll for the Big House. C. Brown
Doll for the Toff. J. Creasey
Dollar Covenant. Michael Sinclair
Dolls and Dollars. J. Dekker
Dolls Are Deadly. B. Halliday
Dolls Are Murder. H. Q. Masur
Doll's Bad News. J. H. Chase
Doll's Done Dancing. B. Flynn
Doll's Trunk Murder. H. Reilly
Dolls with Sad Faces. C. Phillips
Dolly and the Cookie Bird. D. Halliday
Dolly and the Doctor Bird. D. Halliday
Dolly and the Singing Bird. D. Halliday
Dolly and the Starry Bird. D. Halliday
Dolly Dolly Spy. A. Diment
Dolly the Romp. F. Warden
Dolly's Walk. C. Edwards
Dolomite Cavern. W. P. Kelly
Dolores. G. Kelton
Dolores and Some Others. M. Pemberton

Dolores Divine, Guilty or Innocent? K. M. Ellis
Dolorosa Deal. B. Littell
Dolphin. Eric Lambert
Dolphin Mystery. J. P. Hutton
Dombey and Daughter. R. Nicholson
Domes of Silence. O. J. Friend
Domesday Story. Warwick Scott
Domestic Agency. J. Rhode
Domestic Animal. Francis King
Dominant Third. E. Hely
Dominator. A. York
Dominici Affair. J. Laborde
Domino Club. A. Upward
Domino Plan. E. Granville
Domino Principle. A. Kennedy
Don. G. Ziren
Don Among the Dead Men. C. E. Vulliamy
Don Belasco of Key West. A. C. Gunter
Don Caesar de Bazan. T. P. Prest
Don is Dead. N. Quarry
Don or Devil? W. Westall
Don Q in the Sierra. K. Prichard
Don Q's Love Story. K. Prichard
Donald Dyke, the Yankee Detective. H. Rockwood
Donavan. C. Brown
Donavan's Day. C. Brown
Done in the Dark. N. Carter
Done to Death. S. Woods
Donkey from the Mountains. E. Atiyah
Donna. R. T. Larkin
Donna Died Laughing. C. Brown
Donor. R. Tate
Donovan. J. Midgley
Donovan Affair. Owen Davis
Donovan Case. J. Monmouth
Donovan of Whitehall. W. LeQueux
Donovan's Brain. C. Siodmak
Don't Argue with Death. L. Gribble
Don't Ask Questions. J. P. Marquand
Don't Be Afraid of the Dark. P. Henneker
Don't Bet on Living, Alice. K. Carr
Don't Betray Me. J. Berry
Don't Betray Me. J. Van Hearn
Don't Bleed on Me. B. Copper
Don't Bother to Knock. Peter Chambers
Don't Bother to Knock. C. Dekker
Don't Break the Seal. A. M. Burrage
Don't Call Me Madame. H. Kane
Don't Call Tonight. W. C. Gault
Don't Catch Me. R. Powell
Don't Come Back! W. Wright
Don't Come Crying to Me. W. Ard
Don't Count the Corpses. C. Monig
Don't Crowd Me. E. Hunter
Don't Crowd Me. G. Usher
Don't Cry, Beloved. E. Ronns
Don't Cry for Long. T. B. Dewey
Don't Cry for Me. W. C. Gault
Don't Cry, Little Girl. N. Parker
Don't Cry Little Sister. J. Letton
Don't Dare Me, Sugar. H. Janson
Don't Dig Deeper. W. Francis
Don't Drop Dead Tomorrow. H. Pentecost
Don't Embarrass the Bureau. B. F. Connors
Don't Ever Love Me. O. R. Cohen
Don't Expect Any Mercy. H. Treece
Don't Feed the Animals. J. Farr
Don't Get Caught. M. E. Chaber
Don't Get Caught. Carter Cullen
Don't Get Me Wrong. P. Cheyney
Don't Go Away Dead. H. Kane
Don't Go Away Mad. J. Hayes
Don't Go in Alone. G. Holden
Don't Go into the Woods Today. D. M. Disney
Don't Go Out After Dark. N. Berrow
Don't Go to Ceuta. H. Franklin
Don't Go to Sleep in the Dark. C. Fremlin
Don't Hang Me Too High. J. B. O'Sullivan

Title Index

Don't Jump, Mr. Boland! N. Berrow
Don't Just Stand There. C. Williams
Don't Just Stand There, Do Someone. D. Von Elsner
Don't Kill, My Love. R. Foley
Don't Let Her Die. Tarn Scott
Don't Let Him Burn! F. MacIsaac
Don't Let Him Kill. G. Ashe
Don't Lie to Me. T. Coe
Don't Lie to the Police. B. Cobb
Don't Look Back. M. Borgenicht
Don't Look Behind You. M. Erskine
Don't Look Behind You! S. Rogers
Don't Look Behind You. Marilyn Ross
Don't Look Down. V. Katcha
Don't Look Now. D. Du Maurier
Don't Make Me Kill. M. Clinten
Don't Mention It. B. Shannon
Don't Mention My Name. E. K. Goldthwaite
Don't Mess with Murder. A. Allyson
Don't Monkey with Murder. E. Ferrars
Don't Mourn for Me. E. Ellison
Don't Mourn Me, Toots. H. Janson
Don't Neglect the Body. Kevin O'Hara
Don't Open the Door. U. Curtiss
Don't Open the Door! Anthony Gilbert
Don't Play with the Rough Boys. S. Troy
Don't Point that Thing at Me. K. Bonfiglioli
Don't Push Me Around. E. Gilbert
Don't Push Your Luck. P. Muller
Don't Rely on Gemini. V. Packer
Don't Say No. O. L. Rosmanith
Don't Scare Easy. H. Janson
Don't Scare Me, Sister. D. Foster
Don't Shoot, Darling. H. Holt
Don't Slip, Delaney. B. Singer
Don't Speak to Strange Girls. H. Whittington
Don't Stop for Hooky Hefferman. L. Meynell
Don't Take It to Heart. S. Seaton
Don't Tell the Police. Kevin O'Hara
Don't Tempt Me. S. Coburn
Don't Tempt the Hangman. Spike Gordon
Don't Tie Me Down. V. Lloyd
Don't Touch Me. Spike Gordon
Don't Touch the Body. A. Mills
Don't Try Anything Funny. J. M. Fox
Don't Wear Your Wedding Ring. L. O'Donnell
Doodled Asterisk. R. A. J. Walling
Doom. H. Imbert-Terry
Doom! Justin Huntly McCarthy
Doom Campaign. M. McMullen
Doom Candle. Richard Grant
Doom Dealer. D. Fox
Doom in the Midnight Sun. E. M. Boyd
Doom-Maker. B. X. Sanborn
Doom of Glendour. K. Ostrander
Doom of Siva. T. W. Speight
Doom of the Demon Band. Old Sleuth
Doom of the Reds. N. Carter
Doom Service. D. J. Marlowe
Doom Stone. C. Woolrich
Doom Window. M. Drake
Doomdate. J. Tiger
Doomed Five. C. Wells
Doomed Flight. J. R. Holden
Doomed Men. W. Jardine
Doomed Oasis. H. Innes
Doomed to Failure. N. Carter
Doom's Caravan. G. Household
Doomsday. Warwick Scott
Doomsday Affair. H. Whittington
Doomsday Bag. M. Avallone
Doomsday Bells. M. Lynch
Doomsday Book. J. MacLaren-Ross
Doomsday Brain. P. Tabori
Doomsday Committee. R. Gallagher
Doomsday Conspiracy. Ralph Hayes
Doomsday England. M. Cooney
Doomsday Formula. N. Carter
Doomsday List. K. Orvis
Doomsday Men. J. B. Priestley

Doomsday Mission. H. Whittington
Doomsday Squad. Clark Howard
Doomsday Square. R. W. Taylor
Doomsday Vendetta. P. Winston
Doomsters. R. Macdonald
Doomway. E. Bond
Door. M. R. Rinehart
Door. J. F. Rossmann
Door. G. Simenon
Door Between. E. Queen
Door Closed Softly. A. Campbell
Door Fell Shut. M. Albrand
Door in the Wall. L. Meynell
Door into Terror. J. Coulson
Door Nails Never Die. A. Wynne
Door of Death. J. Esteven
Door of Doubt. N. Carter
Door of Dread. A. Stringer
Door of the Unreal. G. Biss
Door to Death. R. Stout
Door to the Moor. M. B. Vandeburg
Door to the Tower. S. Dannett
Door Was Violence. G. Leaderman
Door with Seven Locks. E. Wallace
Door Without a Key. Constance Rutherford
Doorbell Rang. R. Stout
Doors. E. Hannon
Doors of Sleep. T. Warriner
Doors of the Night. F. Packard
Doors Open. M. Gilbert
Doors to Death. L. Crosby
Doorstep Murders. C. Wells
Doorway to Danger. S. Maddock
Doorway to Death. H. Arvonen
Doorway to Death. J. Creasey
Doorway to Death. H. Desmond
Doorway to Death. D. J. Marlowe
Doorways to Danger. Mark Napier
Doowinkle, D. A. A. H. Klingsberg
Dope. S. Rohmer
Dope-Darling. L. Burke
Dope Dealer. E. Snell
Dope Dealers. L. Cross
Dope Devils. W. J. Elliott
Dope is for Dopes. Griff
Dope Ring. J. Hill
Dope Runners. G. Grantham
Dope Ship. E. L. Long
Dope Specialist. F. Johnston
Doped and the Damned. Griff
Dopefiend. D. Goines
Doppelganger. H. Innes
Doppelganger. P. Van Greenway
Dora Elmyr's Worst Enemy. M. V. Victor
Dora Myrl, the Lady Detective. M. M. Bodkin
Dora's Device. G. P. Cather
Dorcas Dene, Detective. G. R. Sims
Doris. Dorothy Johnson
Doris Moore. G. Thorne
Doris's Fortune. F. Warden
Dormant. E. Nesbit
Dormitory Women. R. V. Cassill
Dormouse Has Nine Lives. Frank King
Dormouse--Peacemaker. Frank King
Dormouse--Undertaker. Frank King
Dornstein Ikon. J. L. Roberts
Dorothy Marlow. A. W. Marchmont
Dorothy the Rope Dancer. M. Leblanc
Dorothy's Double. G. A. Henty
Dorothy's Venture. M. C. Hay
Dorrien of Cranston. B. Mitford
Dorrington Deed-Box. Arthur Morrison
Dossier Closed. C. Eland
Dossier 51. G. Perrault
Dossier IX. B. Weil
Dossier No. 113. E. Gaboriau
Dossier on a Mantis. W. R. Bennett
Double. E. Wallace
Double Acrostic. G. Goodchild
Double Agent. J. Bingham

Double Agent. G. Stackelberg
Double Agent. H. T. Teilhet
Double Alibi. M. R. Rinehart
Double Banked. E. L. Long
Double Barrel. N. Freeling
Double-Barrelled Detective Story. M. Twain
Double Blackmail. G. D. H. Cole
Double Bluff. S. Mitchell
Double Bluff. D. Shannon
Double Chance. J. S. Fletcher
Double Crime. J. J. Farjeon
Double Crime. Old Sleuth
Double Cross. A. Capelli
Double Cross. A. Livingston
Double Cross. M. Moran
Double-Cross. A. O. Pollard
Double Cross. A. E. Thomas
Double Cross. P. Urquhart
Double Cross. G. Willets
Double Cross Inn. J. Laurence
Double-Cross Murder. R. Gilmour
Double Cross Purposes. R. A. Knox
Double Cross Purposes. Kenneth O'Hara
Double Crossed. D. Newton
Double-Crosser. J. Cassells
Double-Crossers of Ghost Tree. W. C. Tuttle
Double-Crossing Traitor. Roland Daniel
Double Cunning. G. M. Fenn
Double Dagger. N. Ridley
Double Dan. E. Wallace
Double Darkness. E. Fenton
Double Deal. H. Miller
Double Dealers. M. MacKintosh
Double Dealing. F. P. Jordan
Double Dealing. Harold Trembath
Double Death. J. N. Chance
Double Death. F. W. Crofts
Double Death. C. Forsyte
Double Death Mystery. L. Geoghegan
Double Death of Frederic Belot. C. Aveline
Double Defector. P. Wayland
Double Detection. B. Cobb
Double Diamond. J. Pendower
Double Disappearance. L. Winstanley
Double Doom. J. Bell
Double, Double. E. Queen
Double Duel. S. Cobb
Double Entry. Constance Rutherford
Double Events. A. Wilson
Double Exposure. D. MacKenzie
Double Exposure. A. W. Sherring
Double Fault. L. Meynell
Double Feature. A. Fowles
Double Finesse. H. Howard
Double Florin. J. Rhode
Double for Blackshirt. R. Graeme
Double for Death. G. Ashe
Double for Death. N. Deane
Double for Death. R. Stout
Double for Detection. C. Carnac
Double for the Toff. J. Creasey
Double Fortune. B. L. Hoskins
Double Four. E. P. Oppenheim
Double Frame. A. Morton
Double Frame. C. Rice
Double Game. D. Richards
Double-Handed Game. N. Carter
Double Hit. M. Russell
Double House. E. Dejeans
Double Identities. J. Rhode
Double Identity. N. Carter
Double Identity. G. H. Coxe
Double Image. I. R. G. Hart
Double Image. H. MacInnes
Double Image and other stories. Roy Vickers
Double in Trouble. R. S. Prather
Double Indemnity. J. M. Cain
Double Jeopardy. M. M. Goldsmith
Double Jeopardy. E. Lanham
Double Jeopardy. W. C. Stiles
Double Jeopardy. C. Wood
Double Kill. D. Bogard
Double Kill. D. Da Cruz
Double Knot. G. M. Fenn

Double Life. O. F. Jerome
Double Life. G. Leroux
Double Life. M. W. Wellman
Double Life and the Detectives. A. Pinkerton
Double Life of Mr. Alfred Burton. E. P. Oppenheim
Double Lives. S. Murray
Double M Man. C. Leader
Double Man. H. Reilly
Double Mask. R. N. Silver
Double Masquerade. A. Wilson
Double Menace. B. Newman
Double Motive. J. Creasey
Double Mystery. N. Carter
Double Mystery. L. Raphael
Double Mystery. A. Wynne
Double Negative. J. B. O'Sullivan
Double Nought. W. LeQueux
Double or Quit. E. C. Vivian
Double or Quits. M. Dekobra
Double or Quits. A. A. Fair
Double or Quits. H. Luger
Double Plot. N. Carter
Double Problem. J. L. Morrissey
Double Quest. D. Timins
Double Revenge. L. T. Meade
Double Run. J. Ashford
Double Scoop. B. Cable
Double Shadow. W. LeQueux
Double Shadow Murders. A. McRoyd
Double Shuffle. J. H. Chase
Double Shuffle. D. B. Hobart
Double Shuffle Club. N. Carter
Double Sin and other stories. A. Christie
Double Smile. M. Leblanc
Double Snare. Rosemary Harris
Double Snatch. G. Usher
Double Solution. C. F. Gregg
Double Spy. M. McKenna
Double Take. J. Bruce
Double Take. M. Colton
Double Take. D. Craig
Double Take. R. Huggins
Double Take. H. Janson
Double Take. R. Lewis
Double Take. L. Peters
Double Take. C. Robertson
Double the Bluff. G. Fairlie
Double Thirteen. P. Marlowe
Double-Thirteen Mystery. A. Wynne
Double Thumb. F. Grierson
Double Tragedy. Anonymous
Double Tragedy. F. W. Crofts
Double Traitor. E. P. Oppenheim
Double Treasure. C. B. Kelland
Double Trouble. A. Bocca
Double Trouble. E. Lacy
Double Trouble. R. Mallory
Double Trouble. W. C. Tuttle
Double Turn. C. Carnac
Double Who Double Crossed. T. D. Smith
Double Z. M. Grant
Doublecross of Death. J. Creasey
Doublecrosser. Roland Daniel
Doublecrossers. M. Wells
Doubled in Diamonds. V. Canning
Doubles in Death. W. Grew
Doubling of Joseph Brereton. R. Hodder
Doubloons. E. Phillpotts
Doubly Dead. R. Cobb
Doubly Dead. E. Ferrars
Doubly Dead. J. M. Patterson
Doubtful Disciple. W. Haggard
Douce. E. Kyle
Dough for the Dormouse. Frank King
Douglas Affair. A. Mair
Dove. R. O. Saber
Dove. W. Tucker
Dove in the Mulberry Tree. G. R. Preedy
Dovebury Murders. J. Rhode
Dover and the Unkindest Cut of All. J. Porter
Dover Goes to Pott. J. Porter
Dover One. J. Porter
Dover-Ostend. Taffrail

Dover Strikes Again. J. Porter
Dover Three. J. Porter
Dover Train Mystery. Anthony Gilbert
Dover Two. J. Porter
Doverfields' Diamonds. L. L. Lynch
Dovingsby Death. P. N. Walker
Dower Chest. A. Dean
Dower House Mystery. M. Beckett
Dower House Mystery. P. Wentworth
Down. W. Grove
Down Among the Ad Men. W. A. Ballinger
Down Among the Dead Men. J. Lake
Down Among the Dead Men. P. Moyes
Down Among the Dead Men. Sea Lion
Down Among the Dead Men. R. Stephenson
Down Among the Dead Men. S. Sterling
Down Among the Jocks. R. Dennis
Down and Dirty. W. B. Murphy
Down and Out. W. J. Bayfield
Down and Out. N. Carter
Down-Beat Kill. Peter Chambers
Down East. W. M. Graydon
Down East! L. Jackson
Down Express. G. W. Appleton
Down I Go. B. Kerr
Down Payment on Death. J. Eldridge
Down "Plug Street" Way, and other stories. G. Goodchild
Down River. Seamark
Down River. J. H. Vahey
Down-River Dolls. B. Sarto
Down the Green Stairs and other stories. J. J. Farjeon
Down the Water. E. Kyle
Down There. D. Goodis
Down Through the Night. J. Fast
Down to Death. S. Phillips
Down Under. P. Wentworth
Down Under Donovan. E. Wallace
Down Yonder with Judge Priest. I. S. Cobb
Downbeat for a Dirge. B. Bird
Downbeat on a Debutante. J. J. McCall
Downe Reserve. M. Blount
Downey of the Mounted. J. B. Hendryx
Downing Street Discovery. J. G. Brandon
Downtown Doll. H. Janson
Downward Path. R. Chapman
Downward Path. E. Gaboriau
Downward Path. D. Stewart
Downwind. B. McKnight
Dowry of Diamonds. L. V. Stevens
Dracula. B. Stoker
Dracula Archives. R. Rudorff
Dracula's Guest. B. Stoker
Drag the Dark. F. C. Davis
Dragnet. J. G. Brandon
Dragnet. J. Reach
Dragnet: Case No. 561. D. Knight
Dragnet 1968. D. Vowell
Dragnet '67. R. Tralins
Dragnet: The Case of the Courteous Killer. R. Deming
Dragnet: The Case of the Crime King. R. Deming
Dragoman Pass. Eric Williams
Dragon. Jack Bennett
Dragon. M. P. Shiel
Dragon Flame. N. Carter
Dragon for Christmas. G. Black
Dragon Hunt. Garrity
Dragon in Harness. S. Gluck
Dragon in Spring. A. Barker
Dragon Island. M. Hastings
Dragon Keepers. Rodney Hughes
Dragon Murder Case. S. S. Van Dine
Dragon of Lung Wang. M. Harvey
Dragon Road. S. Harvester
Dragon Roars. C. Leader
Dragon Slayer. R. Pocock
Dragon Strikes Back. T. Roan
Dragon Tree. V. Canning
Dragon Tree Island. N. Lewis
Dragon Under the Hill. G. Honeycombe
Dragonfly. K. R. Dwyer
Dragonhead Deal. R. J. Harper
Dragonmede. Rona Randall

Dragons at the Gate. R. L. Duncan
Dragon's Cave. C. B. Clason
Dragon's Claw. Roland Daniel
Dragon's Claw. J. A. Dunn
Dragons Come Expensive. M. Storm
Dragons Drive You. E. Balmer
Dragon's Eye. S. C. S. Stone
Dragon's Jaws. F. Packard
Dragon's Lair. I. D. Wenzell
Dragon's Mount. D. Rowan
Dragon's Silk. P. Herring
Dragon's Spine. L. Cameron
Dragon's Teeth. E. Queen
Dragons to Slay. Bok
Drakmere Must Die. W. H. L. Cranford
Dram of Poison. C. Armstrong
Dram of Poison. M. Jackson
Drama of Mr. Dilly. C. Edwards
Drama of Mount Street. H. Flatau
Drama of the Rue de la Paix. A. Belot
Drama of the Telephone and other tales. R. Marsh
Dramas of Life. G. R. Sims
Dramatic Murder. Elizabeth Anthony
Draughts in the Sun. R. Parker
Draw Batons! B. Knox
Draw the Blinds. S. Truss
Draw the Curtain Close. T. B. Dewey
Draw the Dragon's Teeth. B. Newman
Drawback to Murder. W. A. Barber
Drawn Blanc. R. Gadney
Drawn Blank. R. Jocelyn
Drawn Conclusion. W. A. Barber
Drawn to Evil. H. Whittington
Draycott Murder Mystery. M. Thynne
Dread. B. Sarto
Dread Cave. J. Courage
Dread Journey. D. B. Hughes
Dread of Night. A. Shivelley
Dread the Sunset. M. Carleton
Dreadful Hollow. N. Blake
Dreadful Hollow. I. Karlova
Dreadful Lemon Sky. J. D. MacDonald
Dreadful Night. B. A. Williams
Dreadful Reckoning. C. M. Russell
Dreadful Summit. S. Ellin
Dream. L. Freeman
Dream and a Forgetting. J. Hawthorne
Dream and the Dead. P. Audemars
Dream--and the Woman. T. Gallon
Dream Before Dying. M. Alexander
Dream Daughter. A. Askew
Dream-Detective. S. Rohmer
Dream Doctor. A. B. Reeve
Dream Girl Caper. J. D. Lawrence
Dream Is Deadly. C. Brown
Dream Murder. A. Broome
Dream Murder. E. C. Reed
Dream of a Woman. J. J. Dratler
Dream of Death. M. O. Bank
Dream of Death. E. Trevor
Dream of Fair Woman. C. Armstrong
Dream of Falling. M. O. Rank
Dream of Freedom. H. Nisbet
Dream of Raven. Anonymous
Dream of Treason. M. Edelman
Dream of Treason. M. Pugh
Dream Sinister. S. M. Schley
Dream Walker. C. Armstrong
Dreamer at Large. W. M. Duncan
Dreamer Deals with Murder. W. M. Duncan
Dreamer Intervenes. W. M. Duncan
Dreamers. R. Manvell
Dreamers: A Club. J. K. Bangs
Dreamers in a Haunted House. M. Lovell
Dreaming God. Basil Carey
Dream's Fulfillment. H. C. Bentley
Dreams to Sell. S. Warwick
Dreamwalker. J. Fitzpatrick
Dregs. J. L. Rickard
Dresden Green. N. Freeling
Dress Circle Murders. P. Yates
Dress Her in Indigo. J. D. MacDonald
Dress Up and Die. D. Elias
Dressed to Kill. A. Bocca
Dressed to Kill. B. Channing
Dressed to Kill. P. Cheyney
Dressed to Kill. E. L. Fetta

Dressed to Kill. D. H. Hyde
Dressed to Kill. N. Morland
Dressed to Kill. M. K. Ozaki
Dressed Up to Kill. E. G. Cousins
Dressing of Diamond. N. Freeling
Dressing-Room Murder. J. S. Fletcher
Drexel Dream. W. A. MacKenzie
Drifthaven. Clarissa Ross
Drifting Death. H. Carstairs
Drifting Death. B. Gaston
Drifting Sands. Elsie Lee
Drill Is Death. F. Lockridge
Drink Alone and Die. B. Cobb
Drink for Mr. Cherry. D. Gardiner
Drink No Deeper. C. Edwards
Drink the Green Water. H. Austin
Drink to Yesterday. M. Coles
Drink with the Dead. J. M. Flynn
Drinks on the Victim. M. V. Heberden
Drip Dry Man. Eric Lambert
Dripping Tamarinds. C. C. Lowis
Driscoll's Diamonds. I. MacAlister
Drive East on 66. R. Wormser
Driven. R. Gehman
Driven Death. N. Orde-Powlett
Driven Flesh. L. Easton
Driven from Cover. N. Carter
Driven to Bay. F. Marryat
Driven to Death. J. C. Lenehan
Driven to Desperation. N. Carter
Driven to Kill. D. M. Disney
Driven to Kill. R. Dolphin
Driven to Kill. C. Witting
Driven to the Wall. S. Campbell
Drone-Man. John Ross
Droonin' Watter. J. S. Fletcher
Drop Dead. G. Ashe
Drop Dead. G. Bagby
Drop Dead. June Drummond
Drop Dead. B. McKnight
Drop Dead. M. Neville
Drop Detective. Anonymous
Drop of a Hat. R. Fenisong
Drop One, Carry Four. Fredric Sinclair
Drop Out. H. Miller
Drop That Gun. R. Angel
Drop to His Death. J. Rhode
Dropped from the Fast Express. F. M. White
Dropped Living Room. F. Y. McHugh
Drought. J. Creasey
Drove Road. Winifred Duke
Drown Her Remembrance. S. Gilruth
Drown Him Deep. Barbara Cooper
Drown the Wind. M. P. Hood
Drowned Queen. K. Laumer
Drowned Rat. E. Ferrars
Drowner. J. D. MacDonald
Drowning. J. Ehrlich
Drowning Pool. J. R. MacDonald
Drowning Stone. H. Fosburgh
Drowning Wire. M. Claire
Drug Called Power. I. MacKintosh
Drug in the Market. C. Baines
Drug of Choice. J. Lange
Drug on the Market. H. Brinton
Drug on the Market. D. Dodge
Drug on the Market. G. Sampson
Drug on the Market. N. Tranter
Drug Run. William Crawford
Drug-Run. P. Pettit
Drum Beat--Berlin. S. Marlowe
Drum Beat--Dominique. S. Marlowe
Drum Beat--Erica. S. Marlowe
Drum Beat--Madrid. S. Marlowe
Drum Beat--Marianne. S. Marlowe
Drum Madness. The Edingtons
Drum of Power. Robert MacLeod
Drum of Ungara. Robert MacLeod
Drums Beat at Dusk. S. Maddock
Drums Beat at Night. Gavin Holt
Drums Beat Red. D. Graeme
Drums Call the Major. L. P. Greene
Drums Never Beat. M. McKenna
Drums of Death. J. Addiscombe
Drums of Doom. O. Binns
Drums of Fu Manchu. S. Rohmer
Drums of Jeopardy. H. MacGrath
Drums of Sacrifice. W. R. Foran
Drums of the Dark Gods. W. A. Ballinger
Drums of War. G. E. Rochester
Drums of War. J. G. Sarasin
Drums of Youth. Margery Lawrence
Drunkard. G. Thorne
Drunkard's End. S. Troy
Drunkard's Progress. G. W. M. Reynolds
Drury Lane's Last Case. B. Ross
Drury Club Case. S. Williams
Dry Spell. J. Creasey
Dry Taste of Fear. Dorothea Bennett
Dry Tortugas. W. Chambers
Dual Identity. C. G. Mitford
Duane and the Art Murders. J. L. Benton
Duane of the FBI. J. L. Benton
Duane of the G-Men. J. L. Benton
Dublin Nightmare. P. Loraine
Duca and the Milan Murders. G. Scerbanenco
Ducats in her Coffin. T. Warriner
Duchess Grace. M. Leighton
Duchess in Difficulties. A. Griffiths
Duchess of Dope. B. Sarto
Duchess of Pontifex Square. G. W. Appleton
Duchess of Powysland. G. Allen
Duchess of Skid Row. L. Trimble
Ducking of Herbert Polton, and Coincidence. H. C. McNeile
Ducks and Drakes. M. Leighton
Ducks and Drakes. N. Tranter
Ducks in Thunder. J. J. Dratler
Duckworth's Diamonds. E. Everett-Green
Dude Ranch Murders. M. F. Ford
Dudie Dunne. Old Sleuth
Dudley Carleon. M. E. Braddon
Duds. H. C. Rowland
Due or Die. F. Kane
Due to a Death. M. Kelly
Due to Expire. H. A. Wrenn
Due to the Lion Tamer. L. M. Robertson
Duel. R. Marsh
Duel Across the Water. D. Quentin
Duel for a Dark Lady. M. Marais
Duel in Glenfinnan. A. MacVicar
Duel in the Shadows. A. Lejeune
Duel in the Snow. H. Meissner
Duel Murder. B. Gray
Duel of Brains. N. Carter
Duel Resurrection. B. Mitford
Duenna to a Murder. R. King
Duet. D. Daniels
Duet for Death. M. Cronin
Duet for Three Spies. H. T. Rothwell
Duet for Two Guns. D. Ambler
Duet for Two Hands. M. H. Bell
Duet in Death. Hilda Lawrence
Duet of Death. Hilda Lawrence
Duet to Corruption. J. Cello
Duffy. H. J. Brown
Dugdale Millions. W. C. Hudson
Duke. J. S. Clouston
Duke. H. Ellson
Duke. W. Manson
Duke Decides. H. Hill
Duke in the Suburbs. E. Wallace
Duke of Arcanum. F. C. Long
Duke of Cameron Avenue. A. R. Weekes
Duke of Omaha. Old Sleuth
Duke of York's Last Trick. C. F. Gregg
Dukedom of Portsea. A. M. Meadows
Duke's Daughters, and The Fugitives. M. Oliphant
Duke's Day. A. Tavis
Duke's Dilemma. W. Magnay
Duke's Last Trick. C. F. Gregg
Dulcarnon. H. M. Rideout
Dull Dead. Gwendoline Butler
Dull Thud. Manning Long
Dull Tree. H. Canelstein
Dum-Dum for the President. Martin Brett
Dumaresq's Daughter. G. Allen
Dumb Alibi. N. Morland
Dumb as They Come. M. Corrigan
Dumb Babes Don't Die. H. Spencer
Dumb Detective. Anonymous
Dumb Gods Speak. E. P. Oppenheim
Dumb Vengeance. S. Tower
Dumb Witness. A. Christie
Dumb Witness. M. Hervey
Dumb Witness. T. A. Plummer
Dumb Witness. N. Wylie
Dumb Witness and other stories. N. Carter
Dumbo Dossier. E. Cannon
Dumdum Murder. C. Brown
Dummy. H. J. O'Higgins
Dummy Murder Case. M. K. Ozaki
Dummy Robberies. M. E. Cooke
Dump. J. Remenham
Dumpling. C. Kernahan
Duncan Dynasty. D. Daniels
Duncan Ross--Detective-Sergeant. R. Stuart
Duncraig. M. Heath
Dunes. S. Walters
Dunfermline Affair. Angus Ross
Dungeon. M. L. Falcon
Dunleary. M. Heath
Dunslow. E. R. Punshon
Dunthorpes of Westleigh. C. Lys
Duo. C. Armstrong
Dupe. G. Biss
Dupe Negative. A. Fowles
Dupes. E. W. Mumford
Duplicate. H. B. Taylor
Duplicate Death. A. C. Fox-Davies
Duplicate Death. G. Heyer
Duplicate Duke. H. Hill
Duplicate Stiff. A. O'Neill
Durand Case. S. Kyle
During Her Majesty's Pleasure. M. E. Braddon
During His Majesty's Pleasure. S. Kyle
Durrell Towers. Clarissa Ross
Dusk at Penarder. Gavin Holt
Dusk to Dawn. C. Graves
Dusky Cactus. S. McEvoy
Dusky Death. R. Garnett
Dusky Hour. E. R. Punshon
Dusky Limelight. C. Robertson
Dusky Night. V. Bridges
Dust. J. Hawthorne
Dust and the Curious Boy. P. Graaf
Dust and the Heat. M. Gilbert
Dust in My Throat. J. Farrimond
Dust in the Sun. J. Cleary
Dust in the Vault. R. A. J. Walling
Dust in Your Eyes. S. Seaton
Dust of Death. K. Robeson
Dust to Dust. I. Ostrander
Dusty Coinage. W. Mills
Dusty Death. M. Burning
Dusty Death. O. Mills
Dusty Death. C. Robbins
Dusty Death. L. Thayer
Dusty Sunset. P. Winn
Dutch Detective. W. B. Hare
Dutch Shoe Mystery. E. Queen
Dutch the Diver. G. M. Fenn
Duty Be Damned! D. Walshe
Duty Free. F. Gaite
Dwarf's Chamber and other stories. F. Hume
Dwelling Place. C. Cookson
Dwelly Lane. F. V. Morley
Dying Alderman. Henry Wade
Dying Business. E. Dewar
Dying Echo. K. M. Knight
Dying Fall. H. Dolson
Dying Fall. G. Milner
Dying Fall. Henry Wade
Dying for a Drink. R. Silverwood
Dying High. A. Curry
Dying in the Night. J. Roffman
Dying Room. M. L. Stokes

Dying Room Only. S. Sterling
Dying to Live and other stories. S. Horler
Dying Ukranian. P. Howarth
Dying Witnesses. M. Halliday
Dyke and Burr, the Rival Detectives. H. Rockwood
Dyke Darrel, the Railroad Detective. A. F. Pinkerton
Dynamite! R. P. Connolly
Dynamite. B. Sarto
Dynamite Days. W. C. Tuttle
Dynamite Doll. B. Sarto
Dynamite Drury. L. P. Greene
Dynamite Drury Again. L. P. Greene
Dynamite Drury Patrols. L. P. Greene
Dynamite Monster Boogie Concert. Paul Ross
Dynamite on Wheels. Duff Johnson
Dynamite Trap. N. Carter
Dynamiter. R. L. Stevenson
Dynasty of Doom. P. A. Foxall
Dynasty of Fear. J. C. Sprague

E

E Pluribus Bang! D. Lippincott
E.T.A. for Death. C. H. Wallace
Each Dawn I Die. J. Odlum
Each Life to Live. R. Gehman
Each Man's Destiny. M. Procter
Each Night We Die. E. Woodward
Eagle and the Wren. R. Pertwee
Eagle Flies from England. E. Atiyah
Eagle Has Landed. J. Higgins
Eagle Six. P. Long
Eagle's Eye. W. J. Flynn
Eagle's Feathers. N. Tranter
Eagle's Nest. D. Daniels
Eagrave Square Mystery. A. W. Marchmont
Eames-Erskine Case. A. Fielding
Ear for Murder. Michael Brett
Ear in the Wall. A. B. Reeve
Ear to the Ground. J. H. Chase
Earl Derr Biggers Tells Ten Stories. E. D. Biggers
Earl Without an Earldom. Scott Graham
Earl's End. L. Gorell
Earl's Promise. J. H. Riddell
Earl's Return. W. M. Graydon
Earl's Ward. S. Cobb
Early Boyd. C. Brown
Early Days of August. J. B. Kovalsky
Early Doors. Hugh Mills
Early Morning Murder. M. Burton
Early Morning Poison. B. Cobb
Earmarked for Murder. G. Rayne
Ears of the Jungle. P. Boulle
Earth-Bound. D. Macardle
Earth to Ashes. A. Brock
Earthly Purgatory. L. Dougall
Earthquake. W. Holt-White
East All the Way. J. G. Lockhart
East and West. T. Mundy
East Coast Mystery. H. Edmonds
East India and Company. P. Morand
East London Mystery. A. Sergeant
East Lynne. H. Wood
East of Algiers. P. Temple
East of Broadway. O. R. Cohen
East of Desolation. J. Higgins
East of Kashgar. F. A. M. Webster
East of Mansion House. T. Burke
East of Piccadilly. S. Maddock
East of Singapore. G. Goodchild
East of Singapore. M. McGrath
East of Singapore. S. M. Parkman
East Side Assignment. R. Kirby
East Side Detective. Anonymous
Easter Dinner. D. Downes
Easter Guests Mystery. J. K. Ryland
Eastern Men--Chicago Women. Griff
Eastern Vendetta. Old Sleuth
Eastlake Affair. C. Robertson
Eastside Exposure. B. Sarto
Eastward in Eden. D. Garth
Easy Come. G. Wheeler

Easy Come, Easy Go. A. Bocca
Easy for the Crook. R. Trevor
Easy Go. J. Lange
Easy Money. B. Atkey
Easy Money. F. Johnston
Easy Prey. J. Bell
Easy to Kill. A. Christie
Easy to Kill. H. Footner
Easy to Murder. N. Rutledge
Easy Victim. L. Farago
Easy Way to Go. G. H. Coxe
Eat Me If You Must. N. Karta
Eavesdropper. J. Payn
Eavesdropping on Death. C. C. Estes
Ebenezer Investigates. N. Brady
"Eblis." S. Shaw
Ebony Bed Murder. J. R. Gillies
Ebony Box. J. S. Fletcher
Ebony Mirror. F. A. Gallimore
Ebony Stag. B. Flynn
Ebony Torso. J. C. Woodiwiss
Echo Answers Murder. N. Fitzgerald
Echo from Silence. M. Pereira
Echo in a Dark Wind. J. Withers
Echo in the Cave. L. Meynell
Echo My Tears. Jan Foster
Echo of a Bomb. M. Derby
Echo of a Bomb. V. Siller
Echo of a Curse. R. R. Ryan
Echo of Barbara. Jonathan Burke
Echo of Guilt. P. Paul
Echo of Treason. Jonathan Burke
Echoes from Castor Hills. D. A. Stephens
Echoes of Celandine. D. Marlowe
Echoing Footsteps. F. A. M. Webster
Echoing Shore. Robert Martin
Echoing Strangers. G. Mitchell
Echoing Wave. D. Giberson
Eclipse of James Trent, D.I. L. Yates
Ecstacy. H. Janson
Ecstatic Thief. G. K. Chesterton
Ed Noon in London. M. Avallone
Ed. Somers, the Pinkerton Detective. E. Stark
Eddy. R. Stephens
Edgar Huntley. C. B. Brown
Edgar Montrose. G. W. M. Reynolds
Edgar Wallace Reader. E. Wallace
Edge of Beauty. B. Ferm
Edge of Beyond. J. B. Hendryx
Edge of Danger. M. Storm
Edge of Doom. J. Brady
Edge of Doom. M. Dalton
Edge of Extinction. J. Wainwright
Edge of Glass. C. Gaskin
Edge of Hazard. G. Horton
Edge of Honesty. C. Gleig
Edge of Horror. H. Desmond
Edge of Nowhere. E. Thompson
Edge of Panic. H. Kane
Edge of Running Water. W. Sloan
Edge of Terror. F. Cowen
Edge of Terror. B. Flynn
Edge of Terror. M. Halliday
Edge of the City. F. Pohl
Edge of the Forest. R. Barr
Edge of the Forest. J. D. White
Edge of the Law. R. Deming
Edge of the Sword. F. M. White
Edina. H. Wood
Edinburgh Caper. S. McKelway
Edinburgh Exercise. Angus Ross
Editor. D. Tracy
Educated Evans. E. Wallace
Educated Man. E. Wallace
Education of Mr. P. J. Davenant. F. S. Hamilton
Eel Pie Murders. D. Frome
Eel Pie Mystery. D. Frome
Eenie, Meenie, Minie--Murder! W. G. Beyer
Effigy of a Spy. C. Richardson

Efford Tangle. G. Goodchild
Egg-Shaped Thing. C. Hodder-Williams
Egremont Mystery. L. Elmont
Egyptian Cross Mystery. E. Queen
Egyptian Nights. Jack Mann
Egyptian Nights. S. Rohmer
Egyptian Tragedy and other stories. R. H. Savage
Egypt's Choice. D. Broun
Eiger Sanction. Trevanian
Eight Crooked Trenches. F. Beeding
Eight Faces at Three. C. Rice
Eight Murders in the Suburbs. Roy Vickers
Eight O'Clock Alibi. C. Bush
Eight of Diamonds. H. G. Hutchinson
Eight of Swords. J. D. Carr
Eight Penny Spy. A. Mallary
Eight-Pointed Star. G. H. Teed
Eight Strokes of the Clock. M. Leblanc
813. M. Leblanc
Eight Three Five. A. Soutar
VIII to IX. R. A. J. Walling
Eight Went Cruising. C. H. Barker
Eighth Circle. S. Ellin
Eighth Millionaire. G. H. Teed
Eighth Mrs. Bluebeard. H. Waugh
Eighth Passenger. M. Tripp
Eighth Seal. A. MacLeod
Eighth Square. H. Lieberman
Eighth Veil. J. Moffatt
Eighth Wonder. J. G. Sarasin
Eighty Dollars to Stamford. L. Fletcher
Eighty Million Eyes. E. McBain
Eileen the Spy. Anonymous
El Dorado. R. Cromie
El Greco Puzzle. J. Murphy
El Rancho Rio. M. G. Eberhart
Ela the Outcast. T. P. Prest
Elderly Gentleman Shot. D. Sharp
Eldorado Red. D. Goines
Eldrida, the Red Rover's Daughter. N. Buntline
Eleanor's Victory. M. E. Braddon
Election Booth Murder. M. Propper
Election by Murder. A. Eichler
Electric Theft. N. W. Williams
Electric Train. D. Beaty
Electro Pete, the Man of Fire. A. P. Morris
Elegant Edward. E. Wallace
Elegy for a Revolutionary. C. J. Driver
Element of Chance. Emma Page
Element of Risk. E. Cannon
Element of Risk. M. Derby
Elemental. R. Chetwynd-Hayes
Elementary, My Dear Freddie. W. H. L. Craurford
Elephant. G. Goodchild
Elephant God. G. Casserly
Elephant Murders. E. S. Brown
Elephant Never Forgets. Ethel L. White
Elephant Valley. F. Farr
Elephants Can Remember. A. Christie
Elephant's Work. E. C. Bentley
Elevated Railroad Mystery and other stories. N. Carter
Eleven. P. Highsmith
Eleven Bullets for Mohammed. H. Arvay
Eleven Came Back. M. Seeley
11 for Danger. A. MacVicar
11 Harrowhouse. G. A. Browne
Eleven Men Died. E. T. Woodhall
Eleven of Diamonds. B. Kendrick
Eleven-Thirty Till Twelve. R. Greene
Eleven Thrilling Mysteries. V. McCall
11.20 Glasgow Central. P. Malloch
Eleven Were Brave. F. Beeding
Eleventh Hour. A. Armstrong
Eleventh Hour. J. S. Fletcher
Eleventh Hour. Donald Forbes
Eleventh Hour. H. C. McNeile
Eleventh Hour. R. B. Sinclair
Eleventh Plague. N. Berrow
Eleventh Plague. L. T. Peters
Elfa. A. W. Marchment
Elgin Marble. B. Von Hutten

Title Index

Eligible Connection. Elsie Lee
Eliminate the Middle Man. M. Wilk
Elimination Syndicate. J. A. Dunn
Eliminator. A. York
Eliza Grimwood. Anonymous
Elizabeth is Missing. L. De La Torre
Elizabeth R.I.P. D. Lee
Elk and the Evidence. M. Scherf
Ellen Monroe. G. W. M. Reynolds
Ellen Morgan. W. Tyrer
Ellen Percy. G. W. M. Reynolds
Ellerby Case. J. Rhode
Ellery Queen, Master Detective. E. Queen
Ellery Queen's The Four of Hearts Mystery. W. Rand
Ellice Quentin, and other stories. J. Hawthorne
Elm Tree Murder. J. Rhode
Elope to Death. G. Ashe
Elsa the Terrible. B. Sarto
Elster's Folly. H. Wood
Elusive Bachelor. F. E. Penny
Elusive Bowman. F. Vivian
Elusive Corpse. N. Karta
Elusive Criminal. R. Broemel
Elusive Epicure. C. Keith
Elusive Four. W. LeQueux
Elusive Isabel. J. Futrelle
Elusive Killer. T. A. Plummer
Elusive Knave. N. Carter
Elusive Lady. M. Cronin
Elusive Lord Bagtor. B. Tozer
Elusive Mr. Drago. T. C. H. Jacobs
Elusive Mrs. Pollifax. D. Gilman
Elusive Nephew. M. Dalman
Elusive Picaroon. J. Cassells
Elusive Picaroon. Herman Landon
Elusive Quest. F. Cowen
Elusive Vicky Van. C. Wells
Elusive Witness. D. E. Bingley
Elvin Court Mystery. A. I. Etheridge
Elvira Digs a Grave. M. Storm
"Em." E. Southworth
Emancipation of Ambrose. M. Cobb
Embankment Crime. D. Stuart
Embankment Murder. G. Verner
Embarrassed Murderer. G. Stockwell
Embarrassing Death. R. Jeffries
Embarrassment of Riches. M. Fischer
Embassy. V. Brome
Embassy. S. Coulter
Embassy Ball. V. R. Coxe
Embassy Case. H. Hill
Embassy Detective. W. M. Graydon
Embassy Madonna. Lydia Kirk
Embassy Murder. A. Hodges
Embers of Hate. B. Jones
Embezzler. J. M. Cain
Embrace of Death. C. C. Estes
Embroidered Sunset. Joan Aiken
Emerald Buddha. J. B. Ames
Emerald Buddha. E. Morse
Emerald Clasp. F. Beeding
Emerald Elephant Gambit. L. Maddock
Emerald Embassy. F. Gerard
Emerald Heart. M. Carrel
Emerald Hill. D. Daniels
Emerald Kiss. C. Reeve
Emerald Mountain. F. Y. McHugh
Emerald Murder Case. Dennis Dean
Emerald Murder Trap. J. Gregory
Emerald Necklace. E. Fraser
Emerald Necklace. A. R. Weekes
Emerald of Catherine the Great. H. Belloc
Emerald of Death. E. Snell
Emerald Oil Caper. J. D. Lawrence
Emerald Spider. Gavin Holt
Emerald Station. D. Winston
Emerald Tiger. E. Jepson
Emerald Trap. L. St. Clair
Emergency Exit. H. Carmichael
Emergency Exit. M. Cronin

Emergency Exit. A. Wynne
Emergency in the Pyrenees. A. Bridge
Emergency Procedure. M. Frederics
Emergency Room. J. Kerr
Emigrants de Luxe. M. Dekobra
Emily. C. F. Barrington
Emily Coulton Dies. M. B. Dix
Emily Fitzormond. T. P. Prest
Emily Moreland. H. M. Jones
Emily Percy. T. P. Prest
Emily Will Know. N. Rutledge
Emissary. Michael Mainwaring
Emma of Alkistan. Margery Lawrence
"Emma Slasky." J. Grecco
Emperor Fu Manchu. S. Rohmer
Emperor of America. S. Rohmer
Emperor of Detectives. Anonymous
Emperor of Evil. C. J. Daly
Emperor of Hallelujah Island. G. Goodchild
Emperor on Ice. R. Tate
Emperor's Old Clothes. F. Heller
Emperor's Pearl. R. Van Gulik
Emperor's Snuff-Box. J. D. Carr
Empire Makers. H. Nisbet
Empire of Crime. N. Carter
Empire of Evil. S. Noel
Empire on Arumac. M. Hale
Empress Eugenie. M. B. Lowndes
Empress Eugenie's Boudoir. G. W. M. Reynolds
Empress of the Andes. F. Warden
Empty Bed. H. Adams
Empty Cot. C. Phillips
Empty Flat. Frank King
Empty Glass. D. Learmonth
Empty Hands. A. Stringer
Empty Hills. A. Holden
Empty Hotel. A. C. Gunter
Empty Hours. E. McBain
Empty House. F. Grierson
Empty House. I. Karlova
Empty House Murder. D. Stuart
Empty House Mystery. B. Bolt
Empty Mail Bags. E. C. Derby
Empty Man. M. Heimer
Empty Quarter. L. Cameron
Empty Saddle. L. Meynell
Empty Tigers. I. Wilson
Empty Trap. J. D. MacDonald
Empty Villa. J. L. Rickard
Empty Years. James Preston
Em's Husband. E. Southworth
Emu's Head. C. Dawe
Enchanted Circle. A. Grace
Enchanted Eden. Rona Randall
Enchanted Garden and other stories. H. A. Vachell
Enchanted Hat. H. MacGrath
Enchanted Ship. R. Andom
Enchanted Type-Writer. J. K. Bangs
Enchanted Voyage. W. E. D. Ross
Enchanted Wooing. M. Richmond
Enchanter. R. Newman
Enchanter's Castle. J. Tattersall
Enchanter's Nightshade. A. Maybury
Enchanter's Nightshade. K. Troy
Enchantment. H. MacGrath
Enchantress. G. Bolton
Enchantress. C. H. Bullivant
Enchantress of the Nile. K. Lindsay
Encore Allain! B. Graeme
Encore the Lone Wolf. L. J. Vance
Encore to Murder. H. P. Martin
Encounter Darkness. S. Forbes
Encounter with Evil. A. Dean
End in Sight. Clifford King
End is Known. G. H. Hall
End of a Big Wheel. C. Fox
End of a Call Girl. W. C. Gault
End of a Cigarette. E. Gellibrand
End of a Diplomat. Ronald Simpson
End of a JD. J. Gonzales
End of a Life. E. Phillpotts
End of a Millionaire. P. D. Ballard
End of a Party. H. Waugh
End of a Shadow. A. Clarke
End of a Stripper. R. Dietrich

End of an Ancient Mariner. G. D. H. Cole
End of an Author. J. J. Farjeon
End of Andrew Harrison. F. W. Crofts
End of Chapter. N. Blake
End of Count Rollo. E. Phillpotts
End of Count Rollo and other stories. E. Phillpotts
End of Her Honeymoon. M. B. Lowndes
End of It All. J. Danvers
End of Mr. Garment. V. Starrett
End of Reckoning. Clayton Moore
End of Solomon Grundy. J. Symons
End of Someone Else's Rainbow. R. Rossner
End of Steel. C. R. Cooper
End of the Affair. G. Greene
End of the Chase. C. Waye
End of the Game. F. Duerrenmatt
End of the Line. S. Baron
End of the Line. Graham Fisher
End of the Line. B. Hitchens
End of the Long Hot Summer. L. Meynell
End of the Mildew Gang. S. Fowler
End of the Night. J. D. MacDonald
End of the Road. A. Armstrong
End of the Road. R. Owen
End of the Rug. R. Llewellyn
End of the Running. A. Evans
End of the Street. M. Procter
End of the Tiger and other stories. J. D. MacDonald
End of the Track. A. Garve
End of the Trail. L. Allan
End of Violence. B. Benson
End Play. R. Braddon
End to Mirth. B. A. Williams
Endgame. H. Ardman
Endless Chain. N. Bell
Endless Colonnade. R. Harling
Endless Night. A. Christie
Endplay. R. G. Toepfer
Ends of Justice. F. M. White
Endure No Longer. M. Albrand
Enduring Flame. N. Tranter
Enduring Old Charms. D. M. Disney
Enemies of England. C. R. Gull
Enemies of the Bride. O. Mills
Enemies Within. M. Z. Lewin
Enemy Agent. S. MacKinlay
Enemy and Brother. D. S. Davis
Enemy in the House. M. G. Eberhart
Enemy of Women. B. Perowne
Enemy Sky. P. Saxon
Enemy to Society. G. Bronson-Howard
Enemy Unseen. F. W. Crofts
Enemy Within. J. Creasey
Enemy Within. Roy Vickers
Enemy Within the Gates. S. Horler
Enforcer. B. Appel
Enforcer. J. Cassells
Enforcer. O. Demaris
Enforcer. A. Sugar
Engaged to Murder. M. V. Heberden
Engagement with Death. G. Ashe
Engaging Picaroon. J. Cassells
England Commune. D. Pryce-Jones
England Made Me. G. Greene
England's Peril. W. LeQueux
English Assassin. M. Moorcock
English Murder. C. Hare
English Wife. C. Blackstock
Englishman of the Rue Cain. H. F. Wood
Englishwoman. A. Askew
Engraved in Evil. P. Minton
Enigma of Conrad Stone. C. Houghton
Enjoy Such Liberty. M. Latham
Enoch Strone. E. P. Oppenheim
Enormous Shadow. R. Harling
Enough Rope. D. Linton
Enough to Kill a Horse. E. Ferrars
Enquiries are Continuing. J. Ashford
Enquiry. D. Francis
Enquiry into the Existence of Vampires. M. Lovell
Enrollment Cancelled. D. B. Olsen

E

Ensign Knightley and other stories. A. E. W. Mason
Enter a Murderer. N. Marsh
Enter a Spy. F. J. Whaley
Enter Bridget. T. Cobb
Enter Certain Murderers. S. Woods
Enter Craig Kennedy. A. B. Reeve
Enter Dr. Nikola. G. Boothby
Enter Murderers. H. Slesar
Enter Sir John. C. Dane
Enter Sleeping. D. Karp
Enter Superintendent Flagg. J. Cassells
Enter the Ace. S. Horler
Enter the Corpse. S. Woods
Enter the Dormouse. Frank King
Enter the Dragon. M. Roote
Enter the Picaroon. J. Cassells
Enter the Saint. L. Charteris
Enter Three Witches. P. McGuire
Enter Two Murderers. H. Marshall
Enter Without Desire. E. Lacy
Enterprising Burglar. H. Balfour
Enterprising Picaroon. J. Cassells
Entertaining Murder. F. Grierson
Enticement to Danger. Ralph Vickers
Entombed Convict. E. A. Treeton
Entrapped. F. G. Bissagar
Entrapped. A. M. Diehl
Entry of Death. E. McGirr
Envious Casca. G. Heyer
Envoy Extraordinary. E. P. Oppenheim
Envoy of the Emperor. F. Gerard
Envoy on Excursion. C. Brahms
Epilogue. B. Graeme
Episode at Toledo. A. Bridge
Episode of the Stolen Voice. R. C. Armour
Episode of the Wandering Knife. M. R. Rinehart
Epitaph for a Blonde. I. Mercer
Epitaph for a Dead Actor. D. Gray
Epitaph for a Dead Beat. D. Markson
Epitaph for a Lobbyist. R. B. Dominic
Epitaph for a Nurse. A. Hocking
Epitaph for a Spy. E. Ambler
Epitaph for a Teddy Bear. L. Barth
Epitaph for a Tramp. D. Markson
Epitaph for Joanna. H. Howard
Epitaph for Lemmings. S. Harvester
Epitaph for Love. H. Clewes
Epitaph for Lydia. V. Rath
Epitaph for Meredith. N. Cromarty
Epitaph for Mister Wynn. K. Wheeler
Epitaph to a Bad Cop. J. Fredman
Epitaph to Treason. W. A. Ballinger
Eppworth Case. I. Patterson
Epsom Mystery. H. Hill
Equal Antagonism. M. Pereira
Equal Danger. L. Sciascia
Equal Partners. H. Fielding
Equality Island. A. Soutar
Erase My Name. J. Donahue
Erasers. A. Robbe-Grillet
Erection Set. M. Spillane
Eric Allen's Broadcast Stories. Eric Allen
Eric Hearle, Detective. A. Joscelyn
Eric the Archer. M. H. Hervey
Ermine. M. A. Fleming
Ernest Maltravers. E. Bulwer-Lytton
Ernestine de Lacy. T. P. Prest
Eros Is No Hangman. A. Wood
Errant Knights. M. Hebden
Erring Under-Secretary. F. Beeding
Error in Judgment. A. Corliss
Error of Her Ways. F. Barrett
Error of Judgment. G. H. Coxe
Error of Judgment. R. Lewis
Error of the Moon. S. Woods
Escalation. H. Janson
Escalator. A. Gardner
Escapade. A. Mills
Escapades of Mr. Alfred Dimmock. F. Russell
Escape. M. Aldanov
Escape. Royal Brown
Escape. H. Desmond
Escape. C. Franklin
Escape. H. Janson
Escape. M. Porlock
Escape. E. Vance
Escape. K. Walker
Escape a Killer. J. Philips
Escape Agents. C. J. C. Hyne
Escape and Be Secret. C. H. Gibbs-Smith
Escape and Return. M. McLaren
Escape at Dawn. G. P. Willis
Escape at Sunrise. M. Cronin
Escape for Sandra. P. Cheyney
Escape from Dartmoor. M. Beckett
Escape from Devil's Island. P. McCurtin
Escape from Julia. C. Massie
Escape from Liberty. L. P. Greene
Escape from Murder. M. Stand
Escape from Prague. B. Cleeve
Escape from Spain. A. D. Divine
Escape from Zahrein. Michael Barrett
Escape If You Can. Robin Temple
Escape in Vain. G. Simenon
Escape into Danger. N. Rutledge
Escape into Murder. M. Jackson
Escape of Andrew Cole. U. L. Silberrad
Escape of General Gerard. D. Betteridge
Escape of Mr. Trimm. I. S. Cobb
Escape of the Notorious Sir William Heans, and The Mystery of Mr. Daunt. W. Hay
Escape on Monday. D. Doubtfire
Escape the Night. M. G. Eberhart
Escape to Crime. James Stewart
Escape to Danger. P. Conway
Escape to Death. C. Franklin
Escape to Death. E. M. Williams
Escape to Eternity. W. B. M. Ferguson
Escape to Fear. T. D. Smith
Escape to Love. E. S. Aarons
Escape to Murder. Sutherland Scott
Escape to Nowhere. D. Karp
Escape to Quebec. M. Kennedy
Escape While I Can. M. Marlette
Escape with Gun Cotton. Rupert Grayson
Escaped from Sing Sing. Hawkshaw
Escapemanship. J. Ditton
Escaping Club. A. J. Evans
Escort Job. H. Kane
Escort to Adventure. A. MacVicar
Escort to Danger. S. Truss
Espionage! G. Marlowe
Espionage. B. Sarto
Espionage for a Lady. T. Ferris
Espionage Killings. J. G. Brandon
Esprit de Corpse. F. Kane
Essence of Murder. H. Klinger
Essex Murders. V. Loder
Essex Road Crime. J. Drummond
Establishment of Innocence. H. Aronson
Estate of the Beckoning Lady. M. Allingham
Esther de Medina. G. W. M. Reynolds
Esther Lawes. E. Jepson
Esther Vanner. C. Massie
Etched in Murder. K. Jones
Etched in Violence. M. Cumberland
Eternal Conflict. J. Templeton
Eternal Instinct. A. Applin
Eternal Journey. Ethel L. White
Eternal Moment. G. H. B. Logan
Eternity, Here I Come! David Hume
Eternity Ring. P. Wentworth
Ethel Norman's Secret. P. Trent
Ethel Opens the Door. D. Fox
Ethelinde. T. P. Prest
Ethiopian's Secret. W. W. Sayer
Etonian. A. Askew
Etruscan Bull. F. Gruber
Etruscan Net. M. Gilbert
Eugene Aram. E. Bulwer-Lytton
Eugene Vidocq: Soldier, Thief, Spy, Detective. D. Donovan
Eugenia. Anonymous
Eugenia. A. Hurlba
Eulalie. M. A. Earl
Eulalie. W. S. Hayward
Eunuch of Stamboul. D. Wheatley
Eurasian Virgins. J. Seward
Euridice. Taffrail
Euryale in London. C. Dane
Eustace Diamonds. A. Trollope
Eustace Quentin. G. W. M. Reynolds
Euston Road Mystery. A. Parsons
Euthanasia. Anonymous
Eve. J. H. Chase
Eve. P. Trent
Eve--And the Law. A. Askew
Eve Finds the Killer. R. Garnett
Eve--It's Extortion. C. Brown
Eve of His Dying. C. Brown
Eve of Judgment. Roger Fuller
Eve Was No Lady. R. Drayton
Evelina, the Pauper's Child. T. P. Prest
Evelyn. A. Askew
Even Bishops Die. C. Saxby
Even Doctors Die. L. Anson
Even from the Law. M. Latham
Even If You Run. D. Cory
Even in Death. S. Devine
Even in the Best Families. R. Stout
Even Jericho. Warner Hall
Even Keel. R. Kruger
Even More Nightmares. R. Bloch
Even the Rich Girl. H. L. Gates
Even the Wicked. R. Marsten
Evening in Paris. M. Richmond
Event Called Murder. Martin Thomas
Eventide. B. Ferm
Events of that Week. N. Bentley
Ever-Loving Blues. C. Brown
Ever Mohun. F. T. Jane
Ever Singing Die Oh! Die. O. Blakeston
Evergreen Death. James Fraser
Every Bet's a Sure Thing. T. B. Dewey
Every Cloud. M. Peterson
Every Little Crook and Nanny. E. Hunter
Every Man a Murderer. H. Von Doderer
Every Man an Enemy. W. H. Baker
Every Man for Himself. H. Moorhouse
Every Man Has His Price. M. Leighton
Every Man Has His Price. A. Whitney
Every Man His Price. M. Rittenberg
Every Man's Brother. N. Lewis
Every Night About Half Past Eight, and other stories. L. J. Beeston
Every Third Thought. D. Malm
Everybody Adored Cara. A. Head
Everybody Always Tells. E. R. Punshon
Everybody Had a Gun. R. S. Prather
Everybody Makes Mistakes. M. S. Marble
Everybody Suspect. D. Sharp
Everybody's Ready to Die. J. Fredericks
Everyone Suspect. N. Tyre
Everything Goes Dead. Roderic Wilkinson
Everything Happens to Hector. D. Batchelor
Everything Happens to Joe. D. O'Flanagan
Everything He Touched. M. Cumberland
Everything Is Thunder. J. L. Hardy
Eve's Island. E. Wallace
Evidence. Anthony Lang
Evidence Before Gabriel. Conrad Frost
Evidence by Telephone. N. Carter
Evidence I Shall Give. J. Wainwright
Evidence in Blue. E. C. Vivian
Evidence Most Blind. D. Keene
Evidence of the Accused. R. Jeffries
Evidence of Things Seen. E. Daly
Evidence Unseen. L. R. Davis
Evidence You Will Hear. H. Jobson
Evidently Murdered. Jay Hall
Evil Among Us. J. Crecy

Evil Angel. J. Middlemass
Evil at Nunnery Manor. R. Abbey
Evil at Queen's Priory. V. Coffman
Evil at Roger's Cross. C. Cookson
Evil Became Them. P. Root
Evil Cargo. K. Stanton
Evil Chateau. S. Horler
Evil Children. W. D. Roberts
Evil Come, Evil Go. W. Masterson
Evil Cross. S. Esmond
Evil Damp. K. R. Butler
Evil Days. B. Fischer
Evil Eye. P. Boileau
Evil Eye. Martin Thomas
Evil Eyes. Roland Daniel
Evil Formula. N. Carter
Evil Friendship. V. Packer
Evil Genius. G. Bagby
Evil Genius. W. Collins
Evil Guest. J. S. Le Fanu
Evil Harvest. Margery Lawrence
Evil Hour. L. Meynell
Evil in a Mask. D. Wheatley
Evil in the Cup. E. P. Thorne
Evil in the Family. G. Corren
Evil in the House. E. Bond
Evil in the House. E. Ford
Evil Intent. J. Wainwright
Evil Is as Evil Does. R. Gatenby
Evil Is the Night. J. Creighton
Evil Island. J. Blair
Evil Men Do. C. Fitzsimmons
Evil Men Do. D. Nile
Evil Messenger. S. Horler
Evil Money. T. Harknett
Evil of Dark Harbor. Clarissa Ross
Evil of the Day. T. Sterling
Evil of Time. E. Berckman
Evil Ones. G. J. Barrett
Evil Phoenix. B. Newman
Evil Reputation. Dora Russell
Evil Root. L. Thayer
Evil Roots. W. Untermeyer
Evil Shadows. Roland Daniel
Evil Shepherd. E. P. Oppenheim
Evil Spell. W. Tyrer
Evil Star. J. Spain
Evil That Men Do. E. Fawcett
Evil That Men Do. A. Hocking
Evil That Men Do. H. Pentecost
Evil That Men Do. M. P. Shiel
Evil That Men Do. A. Spiller
Evil That Men Do. G. Steuart
Evil That Waited. M. Farnsworth
Evil Under the Sun. A. Christie
Evil Vanguard. M. Hay
Evil Wish. J. Potts
Evvie. V. Caspray
Ewe Lamb. M. Erskine
Ex-Con. S. Friedman
Ex-Detective. E. P. Oppenheim
Ex-Duke. E. P. Oppenheim
Ex-Gangster. C. F. Caunter
Ex Officio. T. J. Culver
Ex-Pugilist Detective. Old Sleuth
Ex-Serviceman's Secret. R. Hardinge
Ex-Soldier Employment Swindle. A. Murray
Excavator's Secret. H. H. C. Gibbons
Excellent Intentions. R. Hull
Excellent Knave. J. F. Molloy
Excellent Mystery. C. D. Jones
Excellent Night for a Murder. V. Rath
Excelsior. H. B. M. Watson
Except for One Thing. H. Blayn
Excess Baggage. H. M. Raleigh
Exchanged Identity. F. Du Boisgobey
Exclusive. H. Janson
Excuse My Gun. R. Angel
Execution of Diamond Deutsch. C. F. Gregg
Executioner. P. Boulle
Executioner. V. Torrio
Executioners. N. Carter

Executioners. J. Creasey
Executioners. J. D. MacDonald
Executioner's Axe. P. Lancaster
Executioner's Rest. A. M. Stein
Executive Privilege. G. Perrett
Executive Wife. R. Colby
Exercise Hoodwink. M. Procter
Exhibit No. Thirteen. R. Jeffries
Exhumed! A. Blair
Exile From London. R. H. Savage
Exiled to Siberia. W. M. Graydon
Exiles. J. M. Fox
Exile's Bride. E. Southworth
Exit a Dictator. E. P. Oppenheim
Exit a Spy. H. T. Rothwell
Exit a Star. K. M. Knight
Exit an Admiral. A. W. Allen
Exit and Curtain. Kevin O'Hara
Exit Arnholt. G. Latta
Exit Charlie. A. Atkinson
Exit Dying. H. Olesker
Exit for a Dame. R. Ellington
Exit from Prague. C. Cleeve
Exit Harlequin. C. F. Gregg
Exit Harlequin. Jessica Ryan
Exit in Green. Martin Brett
Exit John Horton. J. J. Farjeon
Exit Laughing. S. Palmer
Exit Mr. Brent. G. Davison
Exit Mr. Marlowe. V. Bridges
Exit Mr. Shane. J. Cassells
Exit Only. S. Maddock
Exit Pretty Poll. E. Burgess
Exit, Running. B. Spicer
Exit Screaming. H. Dalmas
Exit Screaming. C. Hale
Exit Second Murderer. D. Sharp
Exit Silas Danvers. H. Leyford
Exit Simeon Hex. J. M. Walsh
Exit Sir John. B. Flynn
Exit Sir Toby Belch. Hilary Landon
Exit the Disguiser. S. Horler
Exit the Skeleton. H. Adams
Exit This Way. M. V. Heberden
Exit to Music. N. Shepherd
Exit to Music and other stories. N. Morland
Exit with Intent. P. Loraine
Exit Without Permit. C. Franklin
Exodus: 20. O. B. Davis
Exorcism. C. Blackstock
Exorcism of Jenny Slade. D. Daniels
Exotic. C. Brown
Exotic Seductress. H. Janson
Expect No Mercy. E. P. Thorne
Expectant Nymph. H. Janson
Expected Death. M. Fitt
Expendable Agent. G. Sowman
Expendable Man. D. B. Hughes
Expendable Spy. J. D. Hunter
Expensive Place to Die. L. Deighton
Experience with Evil. J. R. Macdonald
Experiences of a Barrister. W. Warner
Experiences of a Bond Street Jeweler. H. A. Vachell
Experiences of a French Detective Officer. Waters
Experiences of a Lady Detective. Anonymous
Experiences of a Real Detective. Inspector F
Experiences of an American Detective. Anonymous
Experiences of Loveday Brooke, Lady Detective. C. L. Pirkis
Experiment. W. Butler
Experiment at Proto. P. Oakes
Experiment in Crime. J. Rhode
Experiment in Crime. P. Wylie
Experiment in Springtime. M. Millar
Experiment in Terror. The Gordons
Experiment of Doctor Nevill. E. Hulme-Beaman
Experiment Perilous. M. Carpenter
Experiment with Eros. R. S. Thorn

Experiments in Crime. G. Frankau
Expert Evidence. C. F. Gregg
Expert Evidence. R. Pertwee
Expert in Craft. D. Stewart
Expert in Murder. C. L. Leonard
Expert Witness. P. Conway
Expiation. E. P. Oppenheim
Expiation of Wynne Palliser. B. Mitford
Exploiters. Samuel Edwards
Exploits of a Dead Man. P. Urquhart
Exploits of a Physician Detective. George Butler
Exploits of a Private Detective. S. Campbell
Exploits of a Race-Course Detective. N. Gould
Exploits of Arsene Lupin. M. Leblanc
Exploits of Asaf Khan. Afghan
Exploits of Black Thumb. W. Bouchier
Exploits of Capt. McKeene. R. Walker
Exploits of Captain O'Hagan. S. Rohmer
Exploits of Danby Croker. R. A. Freeman
Exploits of Elaine. A. B. Reeve
Exploits of Fidelity Dove. D. Durham
Exploits of Jo Salis, a British Spy. W. O. Greener
Exploits of Jonathan Jow. W. J. Makin
Exploits of Juve. P. Souvestre
Exploits of Kesho Naik, Dacoit. E. C. Cox
Exploits of Pudgy Pete & Co. E. P. Oppenheim
Exploits of Sherlock Holmes. Adrian C. Doyle
Exploits of the Chevalier Dupin. M. Harrison
Explosion. D. C. Disney
Explosion! C. Robertson
Explosion. E. Wuorio
Explosive Situation. G. Hackforth-Jones
Expo 80. John Burke
Exporters. G. Norham
Express Delivery. J. M. Walsh
Express Messenger and other tales of the rail. C. Warman
Express Train Murder. John Norman
Expressman and the Detective. A. Pinkerton
Expresso Jungle. W. H. Baker
Expropriators. J. Blythe
Expurgator. A. York
Exquisite Corpse. Alfred Chester
Exquisite Lady. G. Fairlie
Extenuating Circumstances. E. Nisot
Exterior to the Evidence. J. S. Fletcher
Extermination Camp. G. Sheen
Extinction Bomber. S. B. Hough
Extortion. H. Howard
Extortion Incorporated. J. Cooper
Extortioners. J. Creasey
Extortioners. O. Demaris
Extortionists. B. Bavin
Extra Kill. D. Shannon
Extra Passenger. D. Timins
Extraordinary Adventures of Arsene Lupin, Gentleman Burglar. M. Leblanc
Extraordinary Case of Mr. Bell. W. Jackson
Extraordinary Experience. L. Bryce
Extraordinary Seaman. P. Rock
Extreme License. Jerome Barry
Extreme Penalty. A. M. Meadows
Extreme Remedies. M. Borgenicht
Extremes Meet. C. MacKenzie
Extremists. P. Leslie
Extricating Obadiah. J. C. Lincoln
Eye at the Keyhole. S. Maddock
Eye for a Tooth. D. Yates
Eye for an Eye. O. W. Bayer
Eye for an Eye. L. Brackett
Eye for an Eye. F. Hickok
Eye for an Eye. M. Leighton
Eye for an Eye. W. LeQueux
Eye for an Eye. M. O. Rolfe
Eye for an Eye. V. J. Santiago
Eye for an Eye. G. Seton
Eye for an Eye. J. B. West
Eye in Attendance. J. N. Chance

Eye in Attendance. V. Williams
Eye in the Museum. J. J. Connington
Eye of a Serpent. G. Peters
Eye of Abu. A. Dare
Eye of Fate. A. M. Meadows
Eye of Gold. I. Stark
Eye of Isis. M. Peterson
Eye of Jinas and other stories. T. A. Fraser
Eye of Kali. E. R. Brayshaw
Eye of Lucifer. F. F. Van De Water
Eye of Nemesis. P. C. De Crespigny
Eye of One. G. Merrick
Eye of Osiris. R. A. Freeman
Eye of Shiva. L. Grimes
Eye of the Cat. D. Spicer
Eye of the Devil. P. Loraine
Eye of the Eagle. D. O'Connor
Eye of the Gods. J. Neil
Eye of the Hurricane. H. Howard
Eye of the Needle. Ronald Johnston
Eye of the Needle. T. Walsh
Eye of the Peacock. A. M. Dodge
Eye of the Peacock. O. Goff
Eye of the Sun. E. S. Ellis
Eye of Zeitoon. T. Mundy
Eye Spy. M. Finch
Eye Stones. H. Esmond
Eye with Mascara. M. Finch
Eye Witness. G. H. Coxe
Eye-Witness! J. Doe
Eye Witness. E. Levison
Eye Witness. J. S. Strange
Eyes Around Me. G. Black
Eyes at the Window. O. S. Cornelius
Eyes at the Window. S. Truss
Eyes in the Night. Gavin Holt
Eyes in the Night. C. M. Howarth
Eyes in the Night. B. Kendrick
Eyes in the Wall. C. Wells
Eyes of Alicia. C. E. Pearce
Eyes of Death. J. Bentley
Eyes of Desire. C. H. Bullivant
Eyes of Green. N. Bawden
Eyes of Max Carrados. E. Bramah
Eyes of Men. D. Newton
Eyes of Omar. L. C. Douthwaite
Eyes of Pharaoh. G. Thorne
Eyes of St. Emlyn. A. Feist
Eyes of the Blind. A. S. Roche
Eyes of the Shadow. M. Grant
Eyes of the Tiger. N. Carter
Eyes That Watch You. W. Irish
Eyes Through the Mask. R. Trevor
Eyes Through the Tree. M. C. Keator
Eyewitness. M. Hebden
Eyewitness. J. P. Seabrooke
Eyre's Acquittal. H. B. Mathers
Eyrie of an Eagle. A. Delmonico
Eyrie of the Fox. M. Eyre

F

F as in Flight. L. Treat
F.B.I. Showdown. "G-Man"
F.B.I. Special Agent. "G-Man"
FBI Story. The Gordons
"F" Cipher. J. G. Bethune
F Corridor. J. G. Edwards
F.E.U.D. H. Janson
F.O.B. Murder. B. Hitchens
Fabulists. B. Capes
Fabulous. C. Brown
Fabulous Clipjoint. F. Brown
Fabulous Finn. D. Cushman
Fabulous Valley. D. Wheatley
Fabulous Wink. K. Bennett
Face. D. Whitelaw
Face and the Mask. R. Barr
Face Cards. C. Wells
Face for a Clue. G. Simenon
Face in the Film. O. Merland
Face in the Flashlight. F. Warden
Face in the Fog. Marilyn Ross
Face in the Mirror. G. F. Bradby
Face in the Mirror. A. Furness

Face in the Night. E. Wallace
Face in the Pond. Clarissa Ross
Face in the Shadow. N. Carter
Face in the Shadows. V. Johnson
Face in the Shadows. P. Ordway
Face in the Shadows. Marilyn Ross
Face Me When You Walk Away. B. Freemantle
Face of a Hero. P. Boulle
Face of Air. G. L. Knapp
Face of an Angel. M. Paradise
Face of Danger. Graham Fisher
Face of Danger. W. D. Roberts
Face of Danger. M. Sharman
Face of Death. M. Gault
Face of Evil. J. McPartland
Face of Fear. L. Crump
Face of Fortune. J. Workman
Face of Hate. T. Du Bois
Face of Innocence. E. Ogilvie
Face of Inspector Britt. E. P. Thorne
Face of Jalanath. Ronald Hardy
Face of Night. B. Brunner
Face of Rosenfel. C. H. Montagne
Face of Stone. S. Horler
Face of the Crime. L. O'Donnell
Face of the Enemy. V. Scannell
Face of the Enemy. T. Walsh
Face of the Foe. J. Millson
Face of the Foe. P. Power
Face of the Man from Saturn. H. S. Keeler
Face of the Tiger. U. Curtiss
Face of Trespass. R. Rendell
Face on the Cutting Room Floor. C. McCabe
Face on the Stair. L. Winstanley
Face the Music. C. Franklin
Face to Face. D. J. MacKenzie
Face to Face. E. Queen
Face to Face with Death. A. W. Marchmont
Face Value. L. P. Greene
Face Value. J. M. Walsh
Faceless Adversary. F. Lockridge
Faceless Corpse Murders. L. L. Rogger
Faceless Enemy. F. S. Wees
Faceless Fugitive. R. Charles
Faceless Man. C. Wick
Faceless Men. O. Beeby
Faceless Ones. L. Hardy
Faceless Ones. G. Verner
Faceless Stranger. F. Usher
Faces in the Dark. P. Boileau
Faces of a Bad Girl. J. N. Chance
Faces of Danger. R. King
Faces of Death. A. M. Stein
Faces of Murder. J. T. MacCargo
Facets. I. R. G. Hart
Facing Death. J. J. Farjeon
Facing East. A. Soutar
Fact X. P. Winn
Factor's Wife. C. Blackstock
Factory Girl. C. E. Blaney
Factory Girl. M. E. Braddon
Factory Mystery. Gregory Wilson
Factory on the Cliff. N. Gordon
Factotum and other stories. W. LeQueux
Facts About Floyd. S. M. Parkman
Faculty of Murder. S. Wright
Fade into Murder. S. Holmes
Fade out the Stars. M. Cumberland
Fadeout. J. Hansen
Failure. G. Vaizey
Fainting Lady. M. Frazer
Faintley Speaking. G. Mitchell
Fair Affair. P. Champagne
Fair and the Dead. J. S. Strange
Fair Brigand. G. Horton
Fair Criminal. N. Carter
Fair Crusader. W. Westall
Fair Devil. E. Greenwood
Fair Exchange. E. Colles
Fair Exchange. P. Harcourt
Fair Freebooter. B. Marnan

Fair Freelance. G. Campbell
Fair Game. G. Bartram
Fair Game. K. Kramer
Fair Game. N. Tranter
Fair-Haired Lady. M. Leblanc
Fair Imposter. A. St. Aubyn
Fair Insurgent. E. Horton
Fair Intruder. K. Lindsay
Fair-Isle Jumper Mystery. Hallam James
Fair Maids Missing. P. Audemars
Fair Murder. N. Brady
Fair Mystery. Anonymous
Fair Mystery. B. M. Clay
Fair Play. E. Southworth
Fair Prey. Will Duke
Fair Prisoner. M. Gerard
Fair Quakeress. O. Bradbury
Fair Refugee. M. Gerard
Fair Sinner. Mrs. C. Kernahan
Fair Trial. J. Laborde
Fair Warning. M. G. Eberhart
Fair Young Widow. G. R. Preedy
Fairbairn Case. J. Bentley
Fairer Than She. T. Charles
Fairfax Millions. A. Winnington
Fairfax Mystery. J. Keating
Fairly Caught. D. Walshe
Fairly Dangerous Thing. R. Hill
Fairly Innocent Little Man. L. Meynell
Fairway Island. H. G. Hutchinson
Fairways and Foul. J. Carrick
Fairy of the Film. H. T. Johnson
Faith Has No Country. R. V. Beste
Faith-Healer. A. W. Marchmont
Faith, Hope and Charity. I. S. Cobb
Faith, Hope and Charity. Rona Randall
Faith That Kills. E. Hulme-Beaman
Faith Unfaithful. F. E. Wynne
Faithful Achates. A. Gould
Fake. P. Lunn-Rockliffe
Fake. C. Robertson
Fake. H. Sprott
Faked Passports. D. Wheatley
Fakers. P. Leslie
Faking It. Gerald Green
Fakir's Curse. K. Bruce
Falcon and the Dove. J. Laborde
Falcon Cuts In. D. Drake
Falcon Meets a Lady. D. Drake
Falcon Mystery. S. Guise
Falcon of the Foreign Office. D. Newton
Falcon Road. C. Massie
Falconlough. M. Heath
Falconridge. E. Marlow
Falcon's Island. Antonia Scott
Falcon's Prey. D. Drake
Falcon's Shadow. A. Maybury
Falcon's Shadow. K. Troy
Falkland's Choice. P. Trent
Falkner's of Greenhurst. J. Middlemass
Fall Girl. R. Deming
Fall Guy. Jerome Barry
Fall Guy. Joe Barry
Fall Guy. H. Howard
Fall Guy. J. Mack
Fall Guy. R. Owen
Fall Guy. Ritchie Perry
Fall Guy. B. Shannon
Fall Guy. T. Trent
Fall Guy for a Killer. S. Acre
Fall Guy for Murder. L. Goldman
Fall into My Grave. F. Usher
Fall of a Dictator. A. Gask
Fall of a Sparrow. V. Gielgud
Fall of a Star. W. Magnay
Fall of an Eagle. J. Cleary
Fall of Marty Moon. A. Frazer
Fall of Midas. J. Astley
Fall of Rock. K. R. Butler
Fall of Terror. L. Peters
Fall of the Curtain. P. Motte
Fall of the Mighty. A. Seymour
Fall of the Sparrow. N. Balchin
Fall Over Cliff. J. Bell
Fallen Among Thieves. A. W. A'Beckett

Fallen Among Thieves. A. Applin
Fallen Among Thieves. S. P. Hyatt
Fallen Angel. M. Avallone
Fallen Angel. W. Ericson
Fallen Angel. M. Holland
Fallen Eagles. Geoffrey Davison
Fallen Fortunes. J. Payn
Fallen From Favour. J. Middlemass
Fallen into the Pit. E. Pargeter
Fallen Leaves. W. Collins
Fallen Pride. E. Southworth
Fallen Sparrow. D. B. Hughes
Fallen Star. Jack Lewis
Falling Man. W. Forma
Falling Man. M. Sadler
Falling Star. P. Moyes
Falling Star. E. P. Oppenheim
Fallout for a Spy. R. L. Hershatter
Falls the Shadow. R. Ross
Falmont Claiments. A. Bercovici
False. G. Fleming
False Alarm. Manning Long
False Alibi. J. G. Brandon
False Alibi. Jack Lewis
False Beards. Alan Williams
False Bounty. S. Ransome
False Cards. H. Smart
False Claim. B. Wayde
False Claimant. N. Carter
False Colors. R. Powell
False Colours. Annie Thomas
False Colours. E. Woodward
False Combination. N. Carter
False Evidence. E. P. Oppenheim
False Face. V. Caspray
False Face. L. Edgley
False-Face. S. Horler
False Face. J. Lilly
False-Face. F. MacIsaac
False Face. S. Truss
False Faces. L. J. Vance
False Finger Tip. S. Kearney
False Freedom. L. Emsley
False Gods. G. H. Lorimer
False Gods. G. Thorne
False Idols. B. Ferm
False Intruder. G. Goodchild
False Joanna. J. Fredman
False Pretenses. T. Cobb
False Pretenses. W. J. Elliott
False Pretenses. Annie Thomas
False Purple. S. Horler
False Scent. Mrs. Alexander
False Scent. J. S. Fletcher
False Scent. I. Greig
False Scent. N. Marsh
False Scents. W. J. Bayfield
False to any Man. L. Ford
False Truth. E. C. Vivian
False Witness. Mark Allerton
False Witness. Mary Cross
False Witness. S. Milne
False Witness. H. Nielsen
False Witness. E. Nisot
False Witness. M. Underwood
Falsely Accused. G. Norway
Families Repaired. J. S. Fletcher
Family Affair. H. Conway
Family Affair. M. Innes
Family Affair. I. S. Shriber
Family Affair. R. Stout
Family Affairs. J. Rhode
Family and Friends. Emma Page
Family at Tammerton. M. Erskine
Family Burial Murders. M. Propper
Family Doom. E. Southworth
Family Failing. H. Smart
Family Man. Robin Moore
Family Matter. F. Gaite
Family Matters. A. Rolls
Family Plot. V. Canning
Family Property. P. Trent
Family Scapegrace. J. Payn
Family Skeleton. D. M. Disney
Family Skeleton. J. Hawk
Family Skeleton. E. Tyler
Family Skeletons. P. Quentin
Familiar Stranger. F. E. Penny
Family Tomb. M. Gilbert
Famine. J. Creasey
Famous Boy. Old Sleuth
Famous Burdick Case. Anonymous
Famous Cases of Dr. Thorndyke. R. A. Freeman
Famous McGarry Stories. Matt Taylor
Fan Fare. H. Janson
Fanatic of Fez. C. L. Leonard
Fancies and Goodnights. J. Collier
Fancy Dress Ball. J. J. Farjeon
Fancy Free and other stories. C. Gibbon
Fancy's Knell. B. H. Deal
Fanfare for a Murderer. J. Rosenberg
Fanfare for Angel. G. Montrose
Fanfare for Murder. H. Desmond
Fanfare for Shadows. P. Capon
Fangs of Murder. R. Wallace
Fangs of the Serpent. G. R. Fox
Fangs of the Sky Leopard. R. J. Hogan
Fannin. D. Markson
Fanny. H. Janson
Fanny McBride. C. Cookson
Fanny White and Her Friend Jack Rawlings. Anonymous
Fanshaw Case. G. K. Cowan
Fanshawe Court Mystery. J. Laurence
Fanshawe Murder. G. Thorne
Fantastic Island. K. Robeson
Fantastic Summer. D. Macardle
Fantasy and Fugue. Roy Fuller
Fantine Avenel. L. Maddock
Fantoccini. F. Barrett
Fantomas. P. Souvestre
Fantomas Captured. M. Allain
Far Above Rubies. J. H. Riddell
Far and Away. A. Boucher
Far Better Dead! M. Cumberland
Far Cry. F. Brown
Far Place. B. Fuller
Far Pursuit. O. Binns
Far Sands. A. Garve
Far Side of the Dollar. R. Macdonald
Far to Go. M. Aswell
Far Traveller. F. Gaite
Far Wandering Men. J. Russell
Far West Detective. Anonymous
Fare Prey. Laine Fisher
Farewell by Death. V. Warren
Farewell Crown and Goodbye King. M. Bennett
Farewell, My Lovely. R. Chandler
Farewell Nikola. G. Boothby
Farewell Party. June Drummond
Farewell, Pretty Ladies. C. Massie
Farewell to Passion. D. Keene
Farewell to the Admiral. P. Cheyney
Farewell to the Castle. J. Corby
Farewell to Vienna. Forothy Fletcher
Farm at Paranao. Laurence Kirk
Farm at Santa Fe. Laurence Kirk
Farm in the Hills. F. Warden
Farm Villains. J. N. Chance
Farmhouse. H. Reilly
Farrowshot Park Affair. W. J. Bayfield
Farther Off From England. L. Chancellor
Fascinating Traitor. R. H. Savage
Fascinator. A. York
Fashion in Shrouds. M. Allingham
Fashioned for Murder. G. H. Coxe
Fast and Loose. L. Della
Fast and Loose. A. Griffiths
Fast and Loose. N. Tranter
Fast Buck. J. H. Chase
Fast Buck. B. Fischer
Fast Buck. H. Janson
Fast Buck. R. Laurence
Fast Company. M. Page
Fast Exit. M. Cronin
Fast Life in New York. Grace M. White
Fast Mail. C. Thornton
Fast Man with a Dollar. R. Avery
Fast Money. E. A. Clancy
Fast One. P. Cain
Fast Shuffle. T. Herd
Fast with a Gun. R. Wilkes-Hunter
Fast Work. P. Cheyney
Fast Work and other stories. P. Cheyney
Faster She Runs. R. Colby
Faster We Live. B. Brennan
Fastest Boy in New York. Old Sleuth
Fat Boy Must Die. R. E. Pearson
Fat Chance. K. Laumer
Fat Death. M. Avallone
Fat Man's Agony. G. Carr
Fatal Accident. P. N. Walker
Fatal Accident. C. M. Wills
Fatal Ace. A. Applin
Fatal Affinity. S. L. Cumberland
Fatal Alibi. G. Bellairs
Fatal Alibi. L. Bidston
Fatal Alibi. L. Thayer
Fatal Amateur. D. L. Mathews
Fatal Amulet. G. H. Teed
Fatal Bargain. N. Carter
Fatal Beauty. G. D. H. Cole
Fatal Bonds. R. Dowling
Fatal Bride. V. Siller
Fatal Call. A. Dorrington
Fatal Car. R. Hardinge
Fatal Cast. C. T. Gardner
Fatal Chair. Hawkshaw
Fatal Choice. D. M. Disney
Fatal Complaint. P. Quinn
Fatal Curtain. Arthur MacLean
Fatal Descent. J. Rhode
Fatal Diamonds. E. C. Donnelly
Fatal Dose. B. Cobb
Fatal Dose. F. M. White
Fatal Element. E. C. Clark
Fatal Entrance. R. Barratt
Fatal Error. J. Boland
Fatal Error. C. F. Gregg
Fatal Face. W. LeQueux
Fatal Falsehood. N. Carter
Fatal Fascination. J. N. Chance
Fatal Fifth. M. Penrose
Fatal Finale. P. H. Dobbins
Fatal Finger Mark, Rose Courtenay's First Case. M. Danvers
Fatal Fingers. W. LeQueux
Fatal Five Minutes. R. A. J. Walling
Fatal Flaw. L. Meynell
Fatal Flaw. B. Musto
Fatal Flirt. D. Hitchens
Fatal Flower. L. Benedict
Fatal Footsteps. C. Shannon
Fatal Forgery. J. G. Brandon
Fatal Fortune. F. Hurt
Fatal Fortune. A. Murray
Fatal Foursome. F. Kane
Fatal Frails. D. J. Marlowe
Fatal Friday. F. Gerard
Fatal Friends. K. Netzen
Fatal Friendship. Gwyn Evans
Fatal Garden. J. Rhode
Fatal Glove. C. Augusta
Fatal Harvest. A. Amos
Fatal Holiday. B. Cobb
Fatal Hour. N. Carter
Fatal Hour. E. Harrison
Fatal Image. T. S. King
Fatal in Furs. J. M. Fox
Fatal in My Fashion. P. McGerr
Fatal Kiss Mystery. R. King
Fatal Lady. R. Foley
Fatal Legacy. L. Tracy
Fatal Lover. V. Siller
Fatal Manuscript. G. Verner
Fatal Marriage. M. E. Braddon
Fatal Marriage. E. Southworth
Fatal Mascot. A. Skene

Fatal Memoirs. W. Edwards
Fatal Mistake. P. H. Powell
Fatal Move, and other stories. C. Conall
Fatal Nugget. E. H. Burrage
Fatal Number. W. Shute
Fatal Past. Dora Russell
Fatal Picnic. Bernice Carey
Fatal Pit. J. W. Bobin
Fatal Pool. J. Rhode
Fatal Power. C. H. Bullivant
Fatal Prescription. N. Carter
Fatal Purchase. A. Rowe
Fatal Record. C. B. Booth
Fatal Relations. M. Erskine
Fatal Request. A. L. Harris
Fatal Resemblance. E. Ellerton
Fatal Resemblance. C. Faber
Fatal Revenge. Dennis J. Murphy
Fatal Ring. D. Donovan
Fatal Ruby. C. Garvice
Fatal Second. H. C. McNeile
Fatal Secret. Anonymous
Fatal Secret. E. Southworth
Fatal Shadows. D. C. Meade
Fatal Shadows. M. Peterson
Fatal Silence. F. Marryat
Fatal Song. F. Hume
Fatal Step. C. F. Cushman
Fatal Step. Wade Miller
Fatal Talisman. C. Brisbane
Fatal Thirteen. W. LeQueux
Fatal Three. M. E. Braddon
Fatal Undertaking. F. Kane
Fatal V Sign. M. Frazer
Fatal Venture. F. W. Crofts
Fatal Wager. A. Blair
Fatal Woman. D. Donovan
Fatal Woman. P. Quentin
Fatality in Fleet Street. C. S. Sprigg
Fate--and Drusilla. A. Askew
Fate and Fernand. P. Audemars
Fate and Four Sinners. H. L. Victor
Fate and the Man. T. W. Hanshew
Fate and the Watcher. M. Peterson
Fate at the Fair. M. Burton
Fate Laughs. H. Adams
Fate of Austin Craige. S. Campbell
Fate of Fay Delray. J. Wilstach
Fate of Felix. Mrs. C. Kernahan
Fate of Felix Brand. F. F. Kelly
Fate of Herbert Wayne. E. J. Goodman
Fate of Jane McKenzie. N. B. Mavity
Fate of Luke Ormerod. R. Dowling
Fate of Osmund Brett. H. G. Hutchinson
Fate of the Hara Diamond. T. W. Speight
Fate of the Immodest Blonde. P. Quentin
Fate of the Lying Jade. J. N. Chance
Fate of the Malous. G. Simenon
Fate Strikes Twice. C. Ashton
Fated Five. G. Biss
Fateful Abduction. M. A. Fleming
Fateful Departure. D. M. Disney
Fateful Hand. N. T. Oliver
Fateful Star Murder. H. Kerkow
Fate's Pendulum. G. Comley
Father Brown Omnibus. G. K. Chesterton
Father Hunt. R. Stout
"Father Pig." B. Hirschfeld
Father Pink. A. W. Barrett
Fatherless Fanny. T. P. Prest
Fathers and Daughters. S. Friedman
Fathers in Law. H. Cecil
Fauconberg. W. Magnay
Faulkner's Folly. C. Wells
Faust. G. W. M. Reynolds
Faust of the F.B.I. J. Mack
Fausta. P. J. Stead
Favourite Scratched. B. Hemyng
Faxon Secret. J. Ware
Fazackerley's Millions. F. Crisp
Fear! L. C. Douthwaite
Fear. T. Keneally
Fear. E. Nesbit
Fear. B. Sarto
Fear Among the Shadows. L. Hoffman
Fear and Miss Betony. D. Bowers

Fear and the Dead Man. L. Smith
Fear and the Guilt. W. Shaw
Fear and Trembling. B. Flynn
Fear Business. H. Hossent
Fear by Installments. Jonathan Burke
Fear by Night. P. Wentworth
Fear Came First. V. Kelsey
Fear Cay. K. Robeson
Fear Comes Calling. A. L. Martin
Fear Comes to Chalfont. F. W. Crofts
Fear Comes to Euston Road. R. Holmes
Fear Dealers. R. Cade
Fear Dealers. Jack Thomas
Fear Followed On. C. Kingston
Fear for Miss Betony. D. Bowers
Fear Fortune, Father. S. B. Hough
Fear Haunts the Fells. R. Goyne
Fear Haunts the Roses. C. Edwards
Fear Holds the Key. F. Duncan
Fear in a Desert Town. Roger Fuller
Fear in Borzano. W. Jay
Fear in the Forest. Reginald Campbell
Fear in the Wind. S. Jepson
Fear is a Weapon. F. Ford
Fear is My Shadow. Martin Thomas
Fear is the Key. Alistair MacLean
Fear is the Same. Carter Dickson
Fear Kissed My Lips. J. Ames
Fear Makers. D. L. Teilhet
Fear No Evil. L. Brackett
Fear No Evil. A. Brennan
Fear No More. L. Edgley
Fear of a Stranger. R. Foley
Fear of Death. C. Conte
Fear of Death. A. M. Wells
Fear of Fear. F. Ryerson
Fear of Felix Corder. J. Creasey
Fear of Heights. V. Coffman
Fear of Life. G. Maxwell
Fear of Mr. Taltry. E. G. Cousins
Fear of the Night. J. S. Fletcher
Fear Place. J. Ware
Fear Rides the Fog. E. C. Stone
Fear Round About. G. Bellairs
Fear Runs Softly. C. Franklin
Fear Shadowed. M. Peterson
Fear Sign. M. Allingham
Fear Stalks the City. N. MacKenzie
Fear Stalks the Footlights. Don Boyd
Fear Stalks the Village. Ethel L. White
Fear the Light. E. Ferrars
Fear to Tread. M. Gilbert
Fear Today--Gone Tomorrow. R. Bloch
Fear Treads Soft Shod. M. Clare
Fear Waits on Cypress Road. P. Wissmann
Fear Walked Behind. S. Horler
Fear Walks the Island. H. Desmond
Fear Without End. Noel Lee
Fearful Paradise. J. Ames
Fearful Passage. H. C. Branson
Fearful Thing. V. Gielgud
Fearful Way to Die. J. C. Nolan
Fearless Investigator. F. U. Eaton
Fearless Lovers. A. Applin
Fearsome Riddle. M. Ehrmann
Feast of Eggshells. F. Stevenson
Feast of Lanterns. M. Richmond
Feast of the Dead. G. M. Jay
Feast of the Scorpion. J. Pattinson
Feather Cloak Murders. D. L. Teilhet
Feather Your Nest. G. Greenaway
Feathered Octopus. K. Robeson
Feathered Serpent. E. Wallace
Feathers for the Toff. J. Creasey
Feathers in the Fire. C. Cookson
Feathers Left Around. C. Wells
Featherstone's Story. H. Wood
Featuring the Saint. L. Charteris
February Doll Murders. M. Avallone
February Plan. J. H. Roberts

Fed Up. G. A. Birmingham
Federal Agent. "G-Man"
Federal Agent. John Ross
Federal Bullets. G. F. Eliot
Fedora. A. Belot
Fedora of the Halls. A. Applin
Feedback. B. Copper
Feedback. H. Miller
Feeding the Wind. J. E. Gurdon
Feet of Death. B. Flynn
Feet of Death. M. Peterson
Feldisham Mystery. Gordon Holmes
Felicia. Mark Dane
Felix Boyd's Final Problems. S. Campbell
Felix Boyd's Revelations. S. Campbell
Felix Running. H. Ford
Felix Stone. A. Askew
Felix Walking. H. Ford
Fell Clutch. P. Motte
Fell Murder. E. C. R. Lorac
Fell of Dark. R. Hill
Fell of Dark. J. Judson
Fell Purpose. A. Derleth
Fellow of Trinity. A. St. Aubyn
Fellow Passenger. G. Household
Fellow Passengers. R. Pyke
Fellow-Traveler. D. Montross
Fellowship of Five. F. Johnston
Fellowship of the Feather. H. Pink
Fellowship of the Frog. E. Wallace
Fellowship of the Hand. E. D. Hoch
Felo De Se? R. A. Freeman
Felon Angel. C. Brown
Felon in Disguise. L. Southworth
Feloniously and Wilfully. Ernest Wood
Felonry of New South Wales. T. Walker
Felon's Daughter. J. Middlemass
Felony Squad. M. Avallone
Felony Tank. M. Braly
Female Bluebeard. E. Sue
Female Depravity. Anonymous
Female Depravity. O. Bradbury
Female Detective. A. Forrester
Female Detective. Old Sleuth
Female of the Species. H. C. McNeile
Female Spy. Emerson Bennett
Female Spy. Roland Daniel
Female Ventriloquist. Old Sleuth
Feminine for Spy. B. Sanders
Fen Tiger. C. Marchant
Fence. H. L. Nelson
Fence's Victim. D. Stuart
Fengriffin. D. Case
Fenland Mystery. C. A. Brandreth
Fennell's Tower. L. Tracy
Fenner. G. H. Coxe
Fennister Affair. J. Bell
Fenokee Project. R. Lewis
Fenton Affair. R. Quest
Fenton of the Foreign Office. M. Annesley
Fentons. R. Goyne
Fenton's Quest. M. E. Braddon
Fenwick Houses. C. A. Cookson
Fenwood Murders. G. E. Locke
Feo. M. Pemberton
Fer-de-Lance. R. Stout
Fer-de-Lance Contract. P. Atlee
Feral. B. Roueche
Feramontov. D. Cory
Ferguson. R. Kruger
Ferguson Affair. R. Macdonald
Fern Dead. R. H. R. Smithies
Fern Seed. H. M. Rideout
Fernande's Choice. F. Du Boisgobey
Fernwood. M. Thum
Ferret Detective. Anonymous
Ferrol Bond. J. Easton
Ferry Boat. F. Du Boisgobey
Ferrybridge Mystery. D. Vane
Ferryman, Take Him Across! V. Rath
Festival Death. R. Stephenson
Festival for Spies. David St. John

Title Index

Festival of Darkness. M. Garratt
Fetch. P. Everett
Fetch. J. Shearing
Fetch Me a Rope. R. Boyd
Fetish. K. Hewitt
Fetish Murders. A. Curry
Fettered. P. Trent
Fettered by Fate. G. W. Miller
Fettered by Fate. A. Wright
Fettered for Life. F. Barrett
Fettered Love. M. Richmond
Feud. "Capstan"
Feud. J. Templeton
Feud. D. Whitelaw
Feud of Fear. W. M. Graydon
Fever Grass. John Morris
Fever of Life. F. Hume
Feversham. Diane Davidson
Few Days in Endel. Diana Gordon
Few Days in Madrid. A. Roos
Few Die Well. S. Noel
Few Drops of Murder. I. Capeto
Few Fiends to Tea. V. Coffman
Few Small Bones. H. C. Rae
Fiasco in Fulham. J. Bell
Ficciones. J. L. Borges
Fickle Heart. F. Du Boisgobey
Fiddler's Place. R. Parker
Fiddlestrings. J. H. Vahey
Fiddling Cracksman. H. S. Keeler
Fidelio Score. G. Sinstadt
Fidgets. G. A. Birmingham
Field of Fire. P. Alding
Fiend. M. Millar
Fiend in Need. M. K. Ozaki
Fiend Incarnate. D. Malcolm
Fiends. P. Boileau
Fiends of the Family. P. Flower
Fiery Chariot. E. Everett-Green
Fiery Furnace. Lawrence Williams
Fiery Serpent. A. Mallory
Fiesta for Murder. P. O. McGuire
Fifteen Cells. Stuart Martin
Fifteen Keys. C. Dawe
Fifteen Streets. C. Cookson
Fifth Ace. D. Grant
Fifth Answer. M. Pereira
Fifth Caller. H. Nielsen
Fifth Cord. D. M. Devine
Fifth Dagger. D. Quick
Fifth Defector. P. Jones
Fifth Estate. Robin Moore
Fifth Finger. W. LeQueux
Fifth Form Detective. R. Walker
Fifth Freedom. A. O. Pollard
Fifth Grave. Jonathan Latimer
Fifth Horseman. N. M. Adams
Fifth House. J. Godey
Fifth Key. G. H. Coxe
Fifth Latchkey. N. S. Lincoln
Fifth Man. M. Coles
Fifth Must Die! R. Verron
5th of November. M. Franklin
Fifth Passenger. E. Young
Fifth Point of the Compass. M. Tripp
Fifth Seal. M. Aldanov
Fifth Tumbler. C. B. Clason
Fifth Victim. D. Collins
Fifth Woman. M. Fagyas
Fifty Candles. E. D. Biggers
Fifty-Five. G. Volk
55 Guineas Reward. F. C. Milford
₤50 Marriage Case. J. G. Brandon
Fifty Roads to Town. F. Nebel
Fifty Thousand Dollars Ransom. D. Malcolm
Fifty-Two Pickup. E. Leonard
Fight. V. Scannell
Fight for a Fortune. F. Du Boisgobey
Fight for a Soul. F. Warden
Fight for a Throne. N. Carter
Fight for Right. N. Carter
Fight for the Child. F. M. White
Fight for the Luck. J. Blyth
Fight to a Finish. W. G. Forbes
Fight to a Finish. G. Hackforth-Jones
Fight to a Finish. E. Phillpotts

Fight to a Finish. F. Warden
Fight with a Fiend. N. Carter
Fighter Pilot. R. Wilkes-Hunter
Fighting Against Millions. N. Carter
Fighting an Unknown Power. W. G. Forbes
Fighting Back. C. Alverson
Fighting Blood. J. Addiscombe
Fighting Byng. A. Stone
Fighting Cartoonist Detective. Hedley Trembath
Fighting Fool. G. Dilnot
Fighting Footballers. P. Gill
Fighting for a Fortune. Old Sleuth
Fighting Hearts. J. Dorrance
Fighting His Way. Old Sleuth
Fighting Lieutenant. J. G. Rowe
Fighting Snub Reilly. E. Wallace
Fighting the Red Shadow. Vigilant
Fighting Through. A. Abdullah
Fighting Tramp. P. Gill
Fighting Troubadour. A. C. Gunter
"Fightingcocks." W. P. Drury
Figure Away. P. A. Taylor
Figure Eight. S. Regester
Figure in the Corner and other stories. M. E. Braddon
Figure in the Dusk. J. Creasey
Figure in the Shadows. Dana Ross
Figure It Out for Yourself. J. H. Chase
Figure of Eight. C. Waye
Figure on the Terrace. A. R. Weekes
Figurehead. B. Knox
File for Death. J. Hart
File for Record. A. Tilton
File No. 115. H. Harper
File No. 114. E. A. Young
File No. 113. E. Garboriau
File of the Golden Goose. J. Watson
File on a Missing Redhead. L. Cameron
File on Bolitho Blane. D. Wheatley
File on Claudia Cragge. Q. Patrick
File on Death. K. Giles
File on Devlin. C. Gaskin
File on Fenton and Farr. Q. Patrick
File on Lester. A. Garve
File on Robert Prentice. D. Wheatley
File on Rufus Ray. H. Reilly
Filibusters. C. J. C. Hyne
Filibuster's Warning. G. Jerome
Filigree Ball. A. K. Green
Fillets on the Menu. J. Hague
Filly Wore Red. H. Janson
Film Mystery. A. B. Reeve
Film of Fear. A. Fredericks
Film Star Vanishes. D. Richmond
Film Studio Murder. C. Kenwood
Filthy Five. N. Carter
Final Agenda. E. Hyams
Final Appearance. J. C. Nolan
Final Approach. C. Hodder-Williams
Final Chance. P. Trent
Final Copy. J. Barbette
Final Count. H. C. McNeile
Final Crossroads. M. Parker
Final Curtain. W. H. L. Crauford
Final Curtain. F. Kane
Final Curtain. N. Marsh
Final Deduction. R. Stout
Final Ending of It. H. Wood
Final Exploits of Nick Carter. N. Carter
Final Exposure. P. H. Mansfield
Final Fear. L. M. Janifer
Final Judgement. P. Barrington
Final Night. R. Gaines
Final Notice. J. Gores
Final Payment. A. Applin
Final Payment. T. C. H. Jacobs
Final Portrait. V. Caspary
Final Proof. A. MacVicar
Final Proof. R. Ottolengui
Final Reckoning. L. Edgley
Final Run. D. Sanderson
Final Score. George Douglas

Final Score. G. Goodchild
Final Sentence. M. Maurice
Final Set. P. Harris
Final Steal. P. George
Final Triumph. Old Sleuth
Final War. L. Tracy
Final Witness. J. F. Straker
Finances of Sir John Kynnersley. A. C. Fox-Davies
Financier. J. B. Harris-Burland
Financier's Wife. F. Warden
Finch Takes to Crime. F. Lester
Find a Crooked Sixpence. E. Thompson
Find a Victim. J. R. Macdonald
Find Actor Hart. H. S. Keeler
Find Eileen Hardin--Alive! A. Frazer
Find Inspector West. J. Creasey
Find Me a Killer! Arthur MacLean
Find My Killer. M. W. Wellman
Find the Body. J. York
Find the Clock. H. S. Keeler
Find the Diamonds. J. Pattinson
Find the Don's Daughter. J. Jacks
Find the Innocent. Roy Vickers
Find the Lady. G. Barnett
Find the Lady. R. C. Finney
Find the Lady! G. Goodchild
Find the Lady! D. Walshe
Find the Motive. J. Woodford
Find the Professor. Mark Cross
Find the Woman. G. Burgess
Find the Woman. D. M. Disney
Find the Woman. J. S. Fletcher
Find the Woman. A. Hornblow
Find the Woman. H. J. Hultman
Find the Woman. A. S. Roche
Find This Woman. R. S. Prather
Find Tracy George. R. Owen
Findernes' Flowers. G. R. Preedy
Finders Keepers. G. Homes
Finders, Losers--. P. Muller
Finding Maubee. A. H. Z. Carr
Finding of the Gentian. A. W. Rollins
Findings is Keepings. J. B. Clarke
Fine and Private Place. M. Fitt
Fine and Private Place. E. Queen
Fine Day for Dying. J. T. MacCargo
Fine Day for Murder. J. Ingerson
Fine Feathers. W. LeQueux
Fine Night for Dying. M. Fallon
Fine Pair. C. Stratton
Finger. H. Kane
Finger. A. M. Stein
Finger! Finger! H. S. Keeler
Finger in the Sky Affair. P. Leslie
Finger Man and other stories. R. Chandler
Finger of Death. H. Connolly
Finger of Destiny and other stories. E. Snell
Finger of Fate. H. C. McNeile
Finger of Saturn. V. Canning
Finger of Smoke. R. M. Wells
Finger of Suspicion. N. Carter
Finger-Prints Never Lie! J. G. Brandon
Finger to Her Lips. E. Berckman
Fingered City. D. Hatch
Fingered Man. B. Fischer
Fingernail Beach. R. Butler
Fingerprint. Anthony Gilbert
Fingerprint. P. Wentworth
Fingerprints. H. Stinson
Fingerprints of Fate! L. H. Brooks
Fingers Before Forks. E. Woodward
Fingers for Ransom. N. Berrow
Fingers of Fate. L. G. Moberly
Fingers of Fear. P. MacDonald
Fingers of Fear. J. U. Nicolson
Finish Line. P. Kruger
Finish Me Off. H. Waugh
Finish of a Rascal. N. Carter

Finishing Stroke. E. Queen
Finishing Touch. A. Hocking
Finlay of the Sentinel. C. F. Gregg
Finnegan's Dilemma. C. Belmar
Finsbury Lot. G. Burnett
Finsbury Mob. E. Bruton
Fiona. C. Gaskin
Fire and the Clay. P. Audemars
Fire Ant. J. F. Drexler
Fire at Greycombe Farm. J. Rhode
Fire at Will. D. M. Disney
Fire Below. D. Yates
Fire Bomb. S. Jason
Fire-Bomb Jack. Old Sleuth
Fire Bug. E. Bruton
"Fire-Bug." R. St. Clair
Fire, Burn! J. D. Carr
Fire Circle. W. L. Marshall
Fire Engine That Disappeared. M. Sjowall
Fire Escape. T. S. Strachan
Fire Flingers. W. J. Neidig
Fire Goddess. S. Rohmer
Fire in Anger. A. Mars
Fire in His Hand. M. Grieg
Fire in the Flesh. D. Goodis
Fire in the Ice. A. D. Divine
Fire in the Snow. H. Innes
Fire in the Streets. J. Messmann
Fire in the Thatch. E. C. R. Lorac
Fire Island. G. M. Fenn
Fire Mountain. H. Hastings
Fire of Death. M. E. Cooke
Fire of the Witches. Lydia Belknap Long
Fire on Fear Street. S. Sterling
Fire on the Cliffs. C. Waynar
Fire on the Seven Peaks. R. Arnold
Fire on the Wind. D. Garth
Fire Opal. Robert Fraser
Fire Opal. P. Monnow
Fire over Baghdad. G. Griffith
Fire over India. W. H. Baker
Fire-Raiser. E. Trevor
Fire Rock. J. Wood
Fire-Tongue. S. Rohmer
Fire Trap. O. Cameron
Fire Trumpet. B. Mitford
Fire-Watcher's Night. H. Kaner
Fire Will Freeze. M. Millar
Fire Within. G. F. Gibbs
Fire Zone. J. Bogar
Fireball. H. Janson
Fireball Assignment. A. Sugar
Firebase. J. Crowther
Firebase Seattle. D. Pendleton
Firebrace and Father Kelly. Seafarer
Firebrand. S. R. Crockett
Firebug. R. Bloch
Firecrest. V. Canning
Firegold. J. R. Daniels
Firemen Hot. C. J. C. Hyne
Fires at Fairlawn. J. Bell
Fires at Fitch's Folly. K. Whipple
Fires of Ballymorris. V. Connolly
Fires of Brimstone. P. Gallagher
Fires of Fate. W. F. Fauley
Fires of Hate. R. Bridges
Fires of Kiwai. E. Lindall
Fires of Love. M. Leighton
Fires That Destroy. H. Whittington
Fireside Omnibus. Anonymous
Firework for Oliver. J. Sanders
Firm Hand. H. Bindloss
First a Murder. M. Halliday
First Blood. D. Morrell
First Body. L. Payne
First Born. R. M. Gilchrist
First-Born. G. Simenon
First-Born. P. Trent

First-Born Son. A. Murray
First Came a Murder. J. Creasey
First Case of Mr. Paul Savoy. J. Gregory
First Come, First Kill. F. Allan
First Come, First Kill. R. Lockridge
First Deadly Sin. L. Sanders
First Englishman. R. Thorndike
First False Step. T. P. Prest
First Flight. J. R. Daniels
First Immortals. E. L. Arch
First It Was Ordained. B. Thorne
First Law. G. Willets
First Man. A. Dick
First Mrs. Winston. R. Foley
First Night Murder. F. G. Parke
First of the English. A. C. Gunter
First Person Plural. R. Wiseman
First Person Singular. W. R. Benet
First Person Singular. D. C. Murray
First Round Murder. J. V. Turner
First Saint Omnibus. L. Charteris
First Steps Inside the Zoo. J. Lodwick
First Stone. M. S. Boyd
First Stone. M. Peterson
First Stop to Hell. M. Urquhart
First Team. J. Ball
First Television Murder. V. Gielgud
First Time He Died. Ethel L. White
First to Kill. F. Usher
First Train to Babylon. M. Ehrlich
First Waltz. J. L. Roberts
Fish and Company. R. Arnold
Fish and Kill. Macdonald Hastings
Fish Are So Trusting. N. Morland
Fish for Murder. Edward Lee
Fish Lane. L. Corkill
Fish on a Hook. P. MacTyre
Fish or Cut Bait. A. A. Fair
Fish Out of Water. G. Hackforth-Jones
Fisherman's End. K. D. Guinness
Fisherman's Gat. E. Noble
Fisherman's Luck. T. Pace
Fishers of Men. C. Dawe
Fishing is Dangerous. F. N. Millar
Fishport. G. Thorne
Fist in the Sky. M. Jopson
Fist of Fatima. H. Edwards
Fistful of Death. H. Kane
Fit as a Filly. Howard Mason
Fit to Kill. B. Halliday
Fit to Kill. M. Kane
Fit to Kill. L. Trimble
Fitch and His Fortunes. G. Dick
Five. T. Field
Five Aces. David Hume
Five Against the House. J. Finney
Five Alarm Funeral. S. Sterling
Five Arrows. Allan Chase
Five Assassins. O. F. Jerome
Five Brains. W. Sheridan
Five Bullets. L. Thayer
Five Came to Kill. R. Wilkes-Hunter
Five-Day Nightmare. F. Brown
Five Days. D. Raymond
Five Days Till Noon. Sheila Ross
Five Days to Kill. R. Wilkes-Hunter
Five Days to Oblivion. D. O. Woodbury
Five Dead Men. A. Skene
Five Deceivers. F. Armitage
Five Devils of Kilmainham. E. M. McCullough
Five Diamonds. W. M. Graydon
5.18 Mystery. J. J. Farjeon
Five Faces of Murder. J. Flynn
Five Fatal Days. J. Woodford
Five Fatal Letters. Dana Scott
Five Fatal Words. E. Balmer
Five Flamboys. F. Beeding
Five for Bridge. E. Ward
Five for One. L. Allan
5:45 to Suburbia. V. Packer
Five Fowlers. E. Morris
Five Fragments. G. Dyer
Five Frontiers. W. H. Murray
Five Gates to Armageddon. J. Christian

Five Hours From Isfahan. W. Copeland
520%. B. North
$500. H. Alger
Five Hundred Pounds Reward. Anonymous
Five Hundred Pounds Reward. A. O. Cooke
₺500 Reward. D. Vane
Five in Fear. G. H. Teed
Five Inns. R. Inchbald
Five Keys to Mystery. Donald Ross
Five Knots. F. M. White
Five-Leafed Clover. James Fraser
Five Little Pigs. A. Christie
Five Matchboxes. H. Blayn
Five Men Go to Prison. R. Straus
Five Million Francs. G. Schleifer
Five Million in Cash. O. B. King
Five Minutes, Sir Matthew. T. C. Worsley
Five Minutes with a Stranger. M. Tripp
Five Murderers. R. Chandler
Five Mutineers. J. Spenser
Five Nights in Singapore. M. Derby
Five of Hearts. V. Yorke
Five of My Best. M. G. Eberhart
Five of Spades. P. C. De Crespigny
Five Old Maids. G. Warden
Five Passengers from Lisbon. M. G. Eberhart
Five Pieces of Jade. J. Ball
Five Red Fingers. B. Flynn
Five Red Herrings. D. L. Sayers
Five Red Stars. B. Bolt
Five Roads Inn. R. Goyne
Five Roads to S'Agaro. K. G. Ballard
Five Roundabouts to Heaven. J. Bingham
Five Silver Buddhas. H. S. Keeler
Five Sinister Characters. R. Chandler
Five Star Fugitive. J. D. MacDonald
Five Survive. C. Graves
Five Suspects. R. A. J. Walling
Five Thousand a Year. H. Wood
$5000 Reward. G. Fleming
Five Thousand Dollars Reward. A. F. Pinkerton
5,000 Trojan Horses. L. T. White
Five Times Maigret. G. Simenon
Five to Five. D. E. Muir
Five to Kill. M. Halliday
Five Ways to Die. Richard Grant
Five Were Doomed. D. Dayle
Five Were Murdered! T. A. Plummer
Five Who Vanished. G. F. Worts
Five Years After. W. M. Graydon
Fives Wild. W. Winward
Fix. J. Gannold
Fix. J. Usher
Fix Like This. K. C. Constantine
Fixed Alibi. N. Carter
Fixer. M. B. Dix
Flag in the City. C. Landon
Flagdown. M. Muller
Flagellator. C. Brown
Flail and the Fish. F. Gerard
Flame. L. P. Greene
Flame. H. Zore
Flame and the Wind. J. Blackburn
Flame Breathers. K. Robeson
Flame Dancer. F. A. Mathews
Flame Eternal and the Maharajah's Son. W. E. Roys
Flame in the Air. A. Prior
Flame in the Heather. Agnes Russell
Flame in the Mist. P. Audemars
Flame Lily. C. K. MacKinnon
Flame of Evil. D. M. Disney
Flame of Folly. L. Noel
Flame of Murder. M. Neville
Flame of the Forest. A. Broome
Flame of the Forest. M. Peterson
Flame of the Khan. M. B. Dix
Flame Too Hot. K. Kramer
Flames Burn High. G. Usher

Flames of Velvet. M. Dekobra
Flames of Vengeance. M. S. Jones
Flames on the Bosphorus. L. Motta
Flaming Belt. H. H. C. Gibbons
Flaming Crescent. O. Binns
Flaming Falcons. K. Robeson
Flaming Jewel. R. W. Chambers
Flaming Man. M. E. Chaber
Flaming Wilderness. R. Cullum
Flaming Lake. J. D. White
Flamstock Mystery. J. S. Fletcher
Flanders Spy. A. O. Pollard
Flannelfoot, Phantom Crook. J. Henry
Flash. J. Ruegg
Flash Casey, Detective. G. H. Coxe
Flash D 13. V. K. Kaledin
Flash--Hold for Murder. P. Whelton
Flash of Green. J. D. MacDonald
Flash of Light. C. Frisbie
Flash of Lightning. J. Adye
Flash of Splendour. A. Stevenson
Flash Point. J. Bruce
Flash Point. M. Gilbert
Flashback. H. Carmichael
Flashback. R. Dooley
Flashpoint. H. Blayn
Flashpoint. H. Janson
Flashpoint. D. J. Marlowe
Flashpoint. A. A. Randall
Flashpoint for Treason. D. Reid
Flask for the Journey. F. L. Green
Flat Aback. E. L. Long
Flat Beneath. B. Delannoy
Flat No. 4. W. J. Bayfield
Flat 2. E. Wallace
Flat Tyre in Fulham. J. Bell
Flats Fixed--Among Other Things. D. Tracy
Flaw. J. Laflin
Flaw. A. Samarakis
Flaw in the Crystal. Godfrey Smith
Flaw in the Sapphire. C. M. Snyder
Flaxborough Crab. C. Watson
Fledgeling. D. Lee
Flee from Terror. Martin Brett
Flee from the Past. C. G. Hart
Flee the Night in Anger. D. Keller
Fleeced. Stuart Buchan
Fleet Hall Inheritance. R. Keverne
Fleeting Hour. Rona Randall
Fleetwood Mansions Mystery. M. B. Dix
Flemish Shop. G. Simenon
Flesh and Blood. J. Foss
Flesh and Blood. B. Palmer
Flesh and Fire. G. Arnaud
Flesh and Mr. Rawlie. Morton Cooper
Flesh and the Devil. E. Ford
Flesh Game. H. Spencer
Flesh is Strong. D. Doubtfire
Flesh of the Orchid. J. H. Chase
Flesh Peddlers. F. Boyd
Flesh Traders. Morton Cooper
Flesh was Cold. B. Fischer
Fletch. G. Mcdonald
Fleur de Lys. J. G. Sarasin
Fleur de Lys Affair. H. Ross
Fleur Macabre. I. S. Way
Flick of a Fin. G. Peters
Flickering Death. Robert MacLeod
Flier. M. Spillane
Flies in the Web. F. Hume
Flies on the Wall. Alex Hamilton
Flight by Night. D. Keene
Flight Errant. Laurence Kirk
Flight 409. S. Frazee
Flight from a Dark Equator. N. Lewis
Flight from a Firing Wall. B. Kendrick
Flight from a Throne. M. Richmond
Flight from Eden Key. Dorinne Moore
Flight from Fear. H. Janson
Flight from Fear. R. Owen
Flight from Montego Bay. A. Haig
Flight from Riversedge. M. K. Simmons
Flight from the Grave. R. J. Hogan
Flight in Darkness. S. Harvester
Flight into Danger. J. Castle
Flight into Danger. J. England
Flight into Darkness. P. Clark
Flight into Fear. J. Ames
Flight into Fear. F. Gerard
Flight into Fear. D. Kyle
Flight into Fear. P. Saxon
Flight into Love. J. Blackmore
Flight into Peril. D. Rutherford
Flight into Terror. L. White
Flight of a Fallen Angel. D. Winston
Flight of a Witch. Ellis Peters
Flight of an Angel. V. Chute
Flight of an Angel. J. F. W. Hannay
Flight of Chariots. J. Cleary
Flight of Dutchmen. N. Tranter
Flight of Faviel. R. E. Vernede
Flight of Hawks. M. Eden
Flight of the Bamboo Saucer. F. Gordon
Flight of the Bat. Donald Gordon
Flight of the Duchess, and other stories. B. Reynolds
Flight of the Falcon. D. Du Maurier
Flight of the Phoenix. E. Trevor
Flight of the Raven. R. Charles
Flight of the Stiff. Michael Brett
Flight One. C. Carpentier
Flight to a Finish. Valentine
Flight to Afar. W. L. Andersch
Flight to Darkness. G. Brewer
Flight to Takla-Ma. T. Thomey
Flight to the Villa Mistra. V. Maxwell
Flight Without Wings. M. Latham
Flighty Phyllis. R. A. Freeman
Flittermouse. J. G. Sarasin
Floater. B. Cassiday
Floating Cafe, and other stories. Margery Lawrence
Floating Dutchman. N. Bentley
Floating Game. J. Garforth
Floating Head. Old Sleuth
Floating Peril. E. P. Oppenheim
Floating Prison. G. Leroux
Flock of Ships. B. Callison
Flockmasters. N. Tranter
Flood. Lionel Black
Flood. J. Creasey
Flood Light. C. Massie
Flood of Fate. W. C. Tuttle
Flood's First Case. M. O'Driscoll
Floods of Fear. J. Hawkins
Floodwater. P. Meredith
Floozie Takes Lawman. B. Sarto
Floral Tribute. C. E. Vulliamy
Florence. E. A. Dupuy
Florentine Dagger. B. Hecht
Florentine Finish. C. Hirschberg
Florentine Ring. J. Stanley
Flotsam of the Line. O. Binns
Flow My Tears, the Policeman Said. P. K. Dick
Flower and Weed. M. E. Braddon
Flower-Bed Murder. C. P. Cleary
Flower-Covered Corpse. M. Avallone
Flower Forbidden. A. M. Williamson
Flower Gang. G. Radcliffe
Flower in the Desert. M. Richmond
Flower of Crime. A. Belot
Flower of Desire. H. Janson
Flower of Desire. A. Wood
Flower of Evil. D. Lyons
Flower of Fate. J. A. Dunn
Flower of the Forest. O. Bradbury
Flower of the Forest. C. Gibbon
Flower of the Gods. E. Phillpotts
Flower of the Gorse. L. Tracy
Flower o' the Orange, and other stories. A. Castle
Flower o' the Peach. W. A. MacKenzie
Flowering. A. S. Turnbull
Flowering Death. A. MacVicar
Flowering Shamrock. S. Pim
Flowers by Request. L. Holton
Flowers for a Dead Witch. M. Butterworth
Flowers for Teacher. Margaret Archer
Flowers for the Judge. M. Allingham
Flowers of Vengeance. M. A. Willis
Flush as May. P. M. Hubbard
Flutter in Kings. D. Whitelaw
Fluttered Dovecote. G. M. Fenn
Fly Away Death. P. Malloch
Fly by Night. M. Afford
Fly Country. Anthony Lang
Fly Girls. S. Friedman
Fly Me a Killer. F. Lester
Fly on the Wall. T. Hillerman
Flyaway Ned. Old Sleuth
Flyaway Peter. D. Rhodes
Flying Argosy. A. J. Rees
Flying Armada. D. T. Lindsay
Flying Arrow. M. Mizzen
Flying Beast. W. S. Masterman
Flying Beetle. G. E. Rochester
Flying Blind. A. Campbell
Flying Blood. T. Burtis
Flying Chinaman. H. H. Fein
Flying Clues. C. J. Dutton
Flying Cowboys. G. E. Rochester
Flying Crusader. D. T. Lindsay
Flying Dagger Murder. J. Cowdroy
Flying Death. S. H. Adams
Flying Death. E. Balmer
Flying Dutchman. M. Arlen
Flying Dutchman. W. C. Russell
Flying Eye. B. McKnight
Flying Fifty-Five. E. Wallace
Flying Finish. D. Francis
Flying Firs. A. M. Westwood
Flying Girl. R. Marsh
Flying Headhunter. T. Wallace
Flying Hooligans. Martin Kent
Flying Horse. S. Harvester
Flying Kidnappers. Martin Kent
Flying Palatine, and other stories. J. G. Sarasin
Flying Peter. P. Trent
Flying Red Horse. F. Crane
Flying Saucer Gambit. L. Maddock
Flying Squad. E. Wallace
"Flying Squad" Tragedy. W. J. Bayfield
Flying Visitor. A. Kennington
Flynn, A.B. E. L. Long
Flynn of the "Martagon." E. L. Long
Flynn's Sampler. E. L. Long
Flypaper War. R. Starnes
Foam on the River. Sheila Ross
Focus on Murder. Dale Clark
Focus on Murder. G. H. Coxe
Foe-Farrell. A. T. Quiller-Couch
Foe in the Shadow. C. E. Pearce
Foe of Barnabas Collins. Marilyn Ross
Foes of Justice. H. Hill
Fog. J. Remenham
Fog. V. Williams
Fog Comes. Mary Collins
Fog for a Killer. B. Graeme
Fog Hides the Fury. P. Minton
Fog Is a Shroud. M. Malmer
Fog Island. Marilyn Ross
Fog Island Secret. Marilyn Ross
Fog of Doubt. C. Brand
Fog Off Weymouth. H. Clandon
Fog on the Mountain. F. De Laguna
Fog Over Fundy. L. A. Cummingham
Fog Princes. F. Warden
Fogarty and Co. J. Flaherty
Fogbound. Clarissa Ross
Foggerty's Fairy and other tales. W. S. Gilbert
Foggy, Foggy Death. R. Lockridge

Foggy, Foggy Dew. C. Blackstock
Foggy Foggy Dew. A. Dean
Foggy Night at Offord. H. Wood
Foghorn. G. Atherton
Foiled. Anonymous
Foiled. T. W. Speight
Foiling a Counterfeiter. E. C. Derby
Folded Paper Mystery. H. Footner
Folio Forty-One. Michael Sinclair
Folio on Florence White. W. Oursler
Follow a Shadow. G. Greenaway
Follow a Shadow. J. Marshall
Follow a Shadow. W. Reyburn
Follow, as the Night. P. McGerr
Follow McLean. G. Goodchild
Follow Me. H. Reilly
Follow My Leader. G. Greenaway
Follow That Hearse! J. Gonzales
Follow the Blue Car. R. A. J. Walling
Follow the Lady. B. Gray
Follow the Little Pictures. Alan Graham
Follow the Saint. L. Charteris
Follow the Toff. J. Creasey
Follow This Fair Corpse. L. D. Smith
Follow Your Heart. A. Maybury
Follower. P. Quentin
Following a Chance Clew. N. Carter
Following Ann. K. R. G. Browne
Following Feet. E. C. Vivian
Following Footsteps. J. J. Farjeon
Folly Morrison. F. Barrett
Folly of Fear. K. C. Groom
Folly of the Wise. S. Paternoster
Folly's Gold. L. Scott
Fontego's Folly. A. Garve
Fontenay, the Swordsman: A Military Novel. F. Du Boisgobey
Foo Dog. T. Wells
Food for Felony. B. Cobb
Food for Fishes. R. Wills
Fool and His Money. E. Colles
Fool Beloved. J. Farnol
Fool Errant. P. Wentworth
Fool for a Client. R. Lewis
Fool From Down Under. R. Wilkes-Hunter
Fool Killer. H. Eustis
Fool of Nature. J. Hawthorne
Fool of the "Yard." T. A. Plummer
Fool the Toff. J. Creasey
Fool with Women. F. Whishaw
Foolish Cargo. N. Carta
Foolish Margaret. T. W. Speight
Foolish Virgin. N. Karta
Foolish Virgin Returns. N. Karta
Foolish Virgin Says No! N. Karta
Fool's Apple. S. Cardiff
Fool's Bet. M. K. Douglas
Fools Die on Friday. A. A. Fair
Fool's Fair. C. Campbell
Fools' Gold. D. Hitchens
Fool's Gold. S. H. Page
Fools in Town Are on Our Side. Ross Thomas
Fools' Parade. D. Grubb
Fool's Proof. A. S. Carter
Fools Walk In. B. Fischer
Foot in the Grave. E. Ferrars
Football Pool Murders. G. Verner
Football Pools Mystery. W. D. Maydwell
Football Racket. W. D. Maydwell
Football Racketeers. F. W. Gumley
Footbridge to Death. K. M. Knight
Footfall in the Mist. V. Black
Footfall of Fate. J. H. Riddell
Foothills of Fear. J. Creasey
Footlight Glare. A. Askew
Footlights. A. Applin
Footlights. M. McGrath

Footlight's Call. G. Goodchild
Footpath. L. Meynell
Footpath Murder. M. Bringle
Footprints. K. C. Strahan
Footprints in the Sand. W. J. Elliott
Footprints in the Sand. W. Richmond
Footprints in the Snow. Dora Russell
Footprints of Death. N. MacKenzie
Footprints of Satan. N. Berrow
Footprints on the Ceiling. C. Rawson
Footsteps. T. Du Bois
Footsteps at the Lock. R. A. Knox
Footsteps Behind Her. M. A. Wilson
Footsteps Behind Me. Anthony Gilbert
Footsteps Behind Them. S. Truss
Footsteps in the Air. S. Wells
Footsteps in the Dark. G. Heyer
Footsteps in the Dark. L. Mearson
Footsteps in the Night. C. Fraser-Simson
Footsteps in the Night. D. Hitchens
Footsteps of Death. V. Gunn
Footsteps of the Cat. L. A. Olmsted
Footsteps on the Stairs. L. Ford
Footsteps on the Stairs. J. Potts
Footsteps That Stopped. A. Fielding
For a Madman's Millions. N. Carter
For a Noble Cause. P. Boulle
For a Pawned Crown. N. Carter
For a Woman's Honour. Christopher Wilson
For a Young Queen's Bright Eyes. R. H. Savage
For Cash Only. J. Payn
For Conduct Unbefitting. D. Whitelaw
For Crying Out Shroud. O. Blakeston
For Dying You Always Have Time. S. M. Singer
For England. M. Gerard
For Ever Beloved. M. Richmond
For Ever You'll Be Mine. K. Lindsay
For Fear of Little Men. J. Blackburn
For France. M. Gerard
For Gain Not Glory. J. W. McGaw
For Godmother and Country. R. T. Larkin
For Goodness' Sake. C. Wells
For Her Dear Sake. M. C. Hay
For Her Life. R. H. Savage
For Her Sister's Sake. M. E. Cooke
For Her to See. J. Shearing
For Himself Alone. T. W. Speight
For His Brother's Crime. C. E. Blaney
For His Friend's Honor. S. Norris
For Honour and Life. W. Westall
For Honour or Death. D. Donovan
For Information Received. E. Wallace
For Jacques' Sake. J. Claretie
For Kicks. D. Francis
For Lack of Gold. C. Gibbon
For Liberty. H. Nisbet
For Life and After. G. R. Sims
For Life and Love. R. H. Savage
For Love and Honour. F. Barrett
For Love of a Bedouin Maid. Le Voleur
For Love of Her. G. Boothby
For Love of Imabelle. C. Himes
For Love or Crown. A. W. Marchmont
For Love or Money. M. Leighton
For Maimie's Sake. G. Allen
For Murder I Charge More. F. McAuliffe
For Murder Will Speak. J. J. Connington
For Old Crime's Sake. D. Ames
For One Season Only. R. Jocelyn
For Pete's Sake. B. Street
For Pete's Sake! G. Usher
For Reasons Unknown. G. Goodchild
For Richer, For Poorer, Til Death. P. McGerr
For Richer for Richer. D. Gray
For Sale--Murder. W. Levinrew
"For So Little": The Story of a Crime. Helen Davis
For the Asking. H. R. Daniels
For the Defence: Dr. Thorndyke. R. A. Freeman
For the Defense. B. L. Farjeon
For the Defense. F. Hume

For the Defense. J. Reach
For the Eyes of the President Only. P. Salinger
For the Hangman. J. S. Strange
For the Love of Murder. M. Scherf
For the President's Eyes Only. R. Sale
For the Queen. E. P. Oppenheim
For the Sake of Revenge. N. Carter
For Those in Peril. M. Richmond
For Us the Living. H. Chevalier
For Valour. F. R. Adams
For Value Received. T. Cobb
For Woman's Love. E. Southworth
For You, I Commit Murder. D. R. Sperduti
For Your Eyes Only. I. Fleming
Forbidden. A. Maybury
Forbidden Area. P. Frank
Forbidden by Law. A. Griffiths
Forbidden Cargo. S. Box
Forbidden Castle. W. E. D. Ross
Forbidden Cave. A. Furness
Forbidden Door. Herman Landon
Forbidden Door. E. C. Vivian
Forbidden Frontiers. L. Noel
Forbidden Frontiers. S. Maddock
Forbidden Garden. U. Curtiss
Forbidden Hour. M. Crossley
Forbidden Land. D. Cushman
Forbidden Road. V. Canning
Forbidden Road. G. Morton
Forbidden Room. Jaclen Steele
Forbidden Room. R. Thorndike
Forbidden Shrine. C. Dawe
Forbidden Territory. "Capstan"
Forbidden Territory. D. Wheatley
Forbidden Tower. E. Cook
Forbidden Valley. L. P. Greene
Forbidden Wine. F. A. Kummer
Forbidden Word. W. LeQueux
Forbidden Years. W. Camp
Force of Innocence. J. Weatherhead
Force 10 from Navarone. Alistair MacLean
Forced Apart. M. Redwing
Forced Landing. G. Goodchild
Fordham's Feud. B. Mitford
Ford's Folly, Ltd. A. Griffiths
Forecast--Murder. A. Tack
Foreign Bodies. R. Petrie
Foreign Bodies. S. Truss
Foreign Exchange. J. Sangster
Foreign Harry Complot. G. Hertz
Foreign Squad. G. Kent
Foreign Secretary Who Vanished. H. G. Hutchinson
Forest Affair. J. N. Chance
Forest and the Damned. R. Severn
Forest Exile. O. Binns
Forest Inn. H. L. V. Fletcher
Forest Mystery. N. Burnaby
Forest of Eyes. V. Canning
Forest of Fear. A. Rundle
Forest of Fortune. W. W. Sayer
Forest Officer. F. E. Penny
Forest Ranger. B. Bolt
Forests of the Night. Elliott Arnold
Forests of the Night. J. Cleary
Forests of the Night. I. R. G. Hart
Forever Glory. S. Fisher
Forever Is Today. Raymond Mason
Forever McLean. G. Goodchild
Forever Timeless. D. Rochester
Forfeit. R. Cullum
Forfeit. D. Francis
Forge and Furnace. F. Warden
Forged Evidence. A. O. Pollard
Forged Note. O. Micheaux
Forged in Strong Fires. J. Ironside
Forged Will. Emerson Bennett
Forged Note. H. M. Jones
Forger. E. Wallace
Forgers and Confidence Men. G. S. McWatters
Forget-Me-Not. J. Shearing

Title Index

Forget My Fate. R. S. Wallis
Forget What You Saw. J. Ashford
Forging the Blades. B. Mitford
Forging the Links. J. K. Stafford
Forgive Me, Lovely Lady. N. Easton
Forgotten Fleet Mystery. G. Coffin
Forgotten Honeymoon. D. Durham
Forgotten of Allah. G. Radcliffe
Forgotten Hills. M. L. Tyrrell
Forgotten Place. J. Fores
Forgotten Road. S. Harvester
Forgotten Story. Winston Graham
Forgotten Terror. Constance Rutherford
Foreign Affairs. H. Fleetwood
Foreign Body. Moira Field
Forked Lightning. M. Durham
Forked Tongue. R. L. De Havilland
Forlorn Hope. E. Yates
Form of Release. G. Petrie
Formula. S. Horler
Formula. G. Sager
Formula for Crime. Richard Grant
Formula for Murder. B. S. Ballinger
Formula for Murder. A. Reynolds
Forsaken. T. Kingsley-Smith
Forsaken Inn. A. K. Green
Forsythia Finds Murder. R. C. Payes
Port. J. Hale
Fort Minster, M.P. E. J. Reed
Fort Terror Murders. V. W. Mason
FORTEC Conspiracy. R. M. Garvin
Fortescue Candle. B. Flynn
Fortieth Victim. C. Franklin
Fortnight by the Sea. Emma Page
Fortnight of Fear. S. Drew
Fortnightly Club. H. G. Hutchinson
Fortress of Solitude. K. Robeson
Fortress of the Maquis. Stagg Green
Fortress of Yadasara. C. Lys
Fortunate Island. E. S. Russell
Fortunate Miss East. L. Meynell
Fortunate Prisoner. M. Pemberton
Fortunate Wayfarer. E. P. Oppenheim
Fortune A-Begging. T. Gallon
Fortune Cheats. N. Wray
Fortune Favors Fools. R. Arnold
Fortune for Four. D. H. Barber
Fortune for the Taking. C. Dixon
Fortune Hunters. Joan Aiken
Fortune Hunters and others. C. N. Williamson
Fortune in Death. L. St. Clair
Fortune in Peril. R. M. Wells
Fortune in the Sky. J. Pattinson
Fortune Is a Woman. Winston Graham
Fortune Must Follow. D. G. Waring
Fortune of Bridget Malone. M. B. Lowndes
Fortune Road. J. McCague
Fortune Seeker. E. Southworth
Fortune's Apprentice. L. Cargill
Fortune's Fool. J. Hawthorne
Fortune's Fool. F. E. Wynne
Fortunes of Conrad. S. Cobb
Fortunes of Flynn. E. L. Long
Fortunes of the Ashtons. G. W. M. Reynolds
Fortune's Sport. A. M. Williamson
Fortune's Wheel. M. Gerard
Fortune's Wheel. George Long
Forty Days. O. Wynd
48 Hours. H. Janson
Forty-Eight Short Stories. E. Wallace
Forty-First Passenger. K. Hopkins
Forty-First Thief. E. A. Pollitz
Forty-Nine Chances. J. Rhys-Williams
49 Days of Death. B. S. Ballinger
Forty Pieces of Alloy. P. Carlon
Forty Thieves. R. Wallace
Forty-Three Candles for Mr. Beamish. P. Barrington
42 Days for Murder. R. Torrey
Forty Whacks. G. Homes
Forty Years On. J. Owen
Forward from Youth. L. A. Pavey

Foss River Ranch. R. Cullum
Foul Deeds Will Arise. Mark Cross
Foul Deeds Will Rise. R. Harrison
Foul Hawsers. E. L. Long
Foul Play. J. Potter
Foul Play. C. Reade
Foul Play at Lentwood. H. Leyford
Foul Play Suspected. John Beynon
Foul Play Suspected. M. Halliday
Foul Weather. G. F. Gibbs
Found--Adventure. R. Hardinge
Found and Fettered: A Series of Thrilling Detective Stories. D. Donovan
Found Dead. C. Brooks
Found Dead. J. Payn
Found Dead. Hero Strong
Found Drowned. M. Burton
"Found Drowned." E. Phillpotts
Found Floating. F. W. Crofts
Found Guilty. F. Barrett
Found in Possession. P. Urquhart
Found in the Jungle. N. Carter
Found on the Beach. N. Carter
Found on the Road. Gret Lane
Found Out. H. B. Mathers
Found Shot. H. Willett
Founder Member. J. Gardner
Foundered Galleon. W. Chesney
Foundling. P. Trent
Fountain at Marlieux. C. Aveline
Fountain of Beauty. L. T. Meade
Fountain of Death. H. Nelson
Fountain of Green Fire. P. Brebner
Four-and-Twenty Blackbirds. H. V. O'Brien
Four and Twenty Virgins. J. McClure
Four Answers. J. Cobnor
Four Armourers. F. Beeding
Four at Bay. Mark Cross
Four Blind Mice. C. C. Lewis
Four Boys and a Gun. W. Wiener
Four Brains. W. J. Makin
Four Callers in Razor Street. S. Fowler
Four Came Back. M. Caidin
Four Chambered Villain. G. Madderom
Four Cornered Story. F. A. Chittenden
Four Corners. C. S. Raymond
Four Corners of the World. A. E. W. Mason
Four Corpses in a Million. J. Robb
Four Days. J. Buell
Four Days in a Lifetime. G. Simenon
Four Days to the Fireworks. P. Purser
Four Days' Wonder. A. A. Milne
Four Dead Men. S. Simpson
Four Dead Mice. T. B. Black
Four Defences. J. J. Connington
Four Doors to Death. J. Courage
Four Extra Daughters. J. Maconechy
Four Faces. W. LeQueux
Four Faces of Siva. R. J. Casey
Four False Weapons. J. D. Carr
Four Faultless Felons. G. K. Chesterton
Four Feet in the Grave. A. R. Long
4:50 from Paddington. A. Christie
Four Find Danger. M. Halliday
Four-Fingered Glove. N. Carter
Four Fingers. F. M. White
Four for the Money. D. J. Marlowe
Four Frightened Women. G. H. Coxe
Four Get Going. Mark Cross
Four Green Fish. E. Jepson
Four Guns to Carson City. Dan Morgan
Four Hoodoo Charms. N. Carter
Four Hours to Fear. F. Lockridge
Four in a Fairlead. E. L. Long
Four in Hand. J. Middlemass
Four Jealous Men. M. Frazer
Four Johns. E. Queen
Four Just Men. E. Wallace
Four Kings in the Street of Gold. F. H. Rose
Four Knocks on the Door. J. P. Seabrooke

Four Letter Crowd. P. Leslie
Four Liars. E. Murray
Four Lost Ladies. S. Palmer
Four Lost Ships. E. Spencer
Four Make Holiday. Mark Cross
Four Men and a Prayer. D. Garth
Four Men Called John. E. Queen
Four Million. O. Henry
Four Million a Year. C. Collins
Four Motives for Murder. B. Hope
Four of a Kind. Dan Morgan
Four of Hearts. E. Queen
4 P.M. Express. F. Hume
Four Past Four. Roy Vickers
Four Philanthropists. E. Jepson
Four Pitiful People. A. Wood
Four Plus One. J. H. Hurst
Four-Ply Yarn. M. Burton
Four Pools Mystery. Anonymous
Four-Pools Mystery. J. Webster
Four Red Nightcaps. W. Chesney
Four Roads to Death. B. Appel
Four Square Jane. E. Wallace
Four Stars for Danger. Jonathan Burke
Four Stragglers. F. Packard
Four Strange Women. E. R. Punshon
Four Strike Home. Mark Cross
Four-Time Loser. D. Lynch
Four Times a Widower. A. Bliss
Four Tragedies of Memworth. Ernest Hamilton
Four Trails. W. M. Graydon
Four Unfaithful Servants. G. Bellaire
Four Way Proof. R. A. Henriquez
Four Winds. H. Adams
Four Winds. S. Gluck
Four Winds. R. Pertwee
"Four Winds" Mystery. Norman Lee
Four Witnesses. M. Reisner
Four Women in the Case. Annie Thomas
Four Women Went. O. Cecil
Fourfingers. L. Brock
Fourflush Island. L. C. Douthwaite
Foursquare Murder. David Hume
Fourteen Points. A. B. Reeve
14 Seconds to Hell. N. Carter
Fourteen Years After! J. Hunter
14th Agent. D. C. Cooke
Fourteenth Key. C. Wells
Fourteenth Trump. J. Philips
Fourth Agency. J. Fredman
Fourth Bomb. J. Rhode
Fourth Challenge. R. H. Hutchinson
Fourth Chamber. G. R. Preedy
Fourth Dagger. L. Allan
Fourth Day of Fear. Berrie Davis
Fourth Degree. K. S. Daiger
Fourth Down to Death. B. Halliday
Fourth Finger. A. Wynne
Fourth Funeral. C. L. Leonard
Fourth Gambler. D. Castle
Fourth Grave. J. Boland
Fourth King. H. S. Keeler
Fourth Letter. F. Gruber
Fourth Man. W. McCarthy
Fourth Man. H. Mitchell
Fourth Man on the Rope. E. Berckman
Fourth Murder. D. M. Glew
Fourth of Forever. B. S. Ballinger
Fourth Plague. E. Wallace
Fourth Postman. C. Rice
Fourth Reich. M. Hale
Fourth Road. F. Hird
Fourth Seal. P. Groom
Fourth Shadow. R. Charles
Fourth Ship. E. C. Mayne
Fourth Side of the Triangle. E. Queen
Fourth Star. R. Burke

Fourth Theory. W. J. Bayfield
Fourth Victim. P. Barrington
Fourth Wall. A. A. Milne
Fowl Murder. R. H. Lindsay
Fowl Play. T. Du Bois
Fowler Formula. H. Dalmas
Fox from His Lair. E. Cadell
Fox in the Sea. R. Magowan
Fox-Magic Murders. R. Van Gulik
Fox of Maulen. H. H. Kirst
Fox Prowls. V. Williams
Fox Valley Murders. J. H. Vance
Foxfire Cove. K. Ostrander
Foxglove Manor. R. Buchanan
Foxhole. M. Urquhart
Fracas in the Foothills. Elliot Paul
Fractured Silence. F. Cowen
Fragment of Fear. J. Bingham
Fragment of Glass. F. L. Green
Frail Ghost. M. Maurice
Frail on North Circular. M. Urquhart
Frails Can Be So Tough. H. Janson
Frame for Murder. K. Mechem
Frame for Murder. R. Simons
Frame Is Beautiful. C. Brown
Frame the Baron. A. Morton
Frame-Up. J. G. Brandon
Frame-Up. C. Brooks
Frame-Up. A. Garve
Frame-Up. Neill Graham
Frame-Up. D. Whitelaw
Framed. E. Ellison
Framed. H. Janson
Framed Evidence. J. Cowdroy
Framed for Hanging. G. Cullingford
Framed in Blood. B. Halliday
Framed in Guilt. D. Keene
Framed in Guilt. J. Slate
Framework of Fate. N. Carter
Framing of Carol Woan. B. Cobb
Frampton--of "the Yard"! T. A. Plummer
Frampton Sees Red. T. A. Plummer
Frances. F. F. Kelly
Frances Hildyard. H. Wood
Francesca. S. Marlowe
Francesca. L. Snow
Franchise Affair. J. Tey
Francine. S. Shelley
Francis Quarles Investigates. J. Symons
Francois the Valet. G. W. Appleton
Frangipani. N. Easton
Frank James in St. Louis. W. B. Lawson
Frank Redland, Recruit. Mrs. C. Kernahan
Frank Sinclair's Wife, and other stories. J. H. Riddell
Frankenstein. M. W. Shelley
Frankenstein Factory. E. D. Hoch
Frankincense and Murder. B. Kendrick
Frantic. N. Calef
Frantic Boast. J. L. Rickard
Fraser Butts In. H. Clevely
Frass. J. Chancellor
Fratricides. M. Edelman
Fraud. Mrs. C. Kernahan
Frauds. M. Hastings
Fraulein. J. McGovern
Fraulein is Feline. C. Brown
Fraulein Spy. N. Carter
Fraser Acquittal. S. Ransome
Freak Island Murders. R. Verron
Freak Museum. R. R. Ryan
Freak of Fate. E. F. Spence
Freak of St. Freda's! G. E. Rochester
Freak-Out. M. Arrighi
Freak Racket. W. J. Elliott
Freaked Out Stranger. P. Morgan
Freckled Shark. K. Robeson
Fred Bennett, the Mormon Detective. F. E. Bennett
Fred Danford, the Skillful Detective. H. Rockwood
Fred in Situ. G. Hammond
Fred Travis, A. B. Taffrail
Frederick Lonton. D. W. Croft

Frederika and the Convict. L. M. Robertson
Free Agent. P. Murray
Free Are the Dead. S. Friedman
Free as Air. E. Kyle
Free Heart. E. C. Reed
Free-Lance Murder. V. Rodell
Free Lovers. R. W. Kauffman
Free Ride. J. M. Fox
Freebie and the Bean. Paul Ross
Freebody Heiress. E. Gordon
Freebooters. N. Tranter
Freedman. J. Pattinson
Freedom. A. Askew
Freedom for Two. J. Carr
Freedom from Fear. I. Perrot
Freedom Trap. D. Bagley
Freeloaders. E. Lacy
Freer's Cove. E. Gordon
Freeway to Murder. W. Sproule
Freeze Thy Blood Less Coldly. J. Wainwright
French Connection II. Robin Moore
French Doctor. L. Royer
French Doll. V. McConnor
French Farce. E. Greenwood
French for Murder. B. Mara
French for Trouble. L. T. Shortell
French Girl. A. Mills
French Hazard. W. Mills
French Inheritance. A. Stevenson
French Key. F. Gruber
French Killing. J. P. Cody
French Master. A. W. Barrett
French Powder Mystery. E. Queen
French Self-Instructor. G. W. M. Reynolds
French Strikes Oil. F. W. Crofts
Frenchman Must Die. K. Boyle
Frenzied Fiction. S. Leacock
Frenzy. J. O. Causey
Frenzy. A. La Bern
Frenzy in the Flesh. D. Reid
Frenzy of Evil. H. Kane
Frequent Hearses. E. Crispin
Fresh Waters and other stories. R. W. Child
Friarsmead. Laura Smith
Friday Before Bank Holiday. George Davis
Friday for Death. L. Lariar
Friday Market. C. Meadows
Friday Run. J. Wood
Friday the Rabbi Slept Late. H. Kemelman
Friday the 13th. J. J. Farjeon
Friday to Monday. W. Garrett
Friend of Mary Rose. E. Fenwick
Friendless Millionaire. H. L. Phillips
Friendly Fiends. P. Muller
Friendly Place to Die. M. P. Faur
Friends. H. Herlin
Friends. Godfrey Smith
Friends at Court. H. Cecil
Friends of Eddie Coyle. G. V. Higgins
Friend's Victim. A. Hurlba
Friendship of Veronica. T. Cobb
Firgate Captain. S. Styles
Fright. G. Hopley
Fright. J. Reach
Frightened Amazon. A. M. Stein
Frightened Bowerbird. F. Y. McIlugh
Frightened Brides. M. Cumberland
Frightened Chameleon. L. Gribble
Frightened Child. D. Lyon
Frightened Dove. P. Hardin
Frightened Eyes. Roland Daniel
Frightened Fiancee. G. H. Coxe
Frightened Fingers. S. Dean
Frightened Girl. M. Crombie

Frightened Heart. J. Ames
Frightened Ladies. B. Benson
Frightened Lady. W. H. Baker
Frightened Lady. E. Wallace
Frightened Man. D. Chambers
Frightened Man. L. Meynell
Frightened Man. G. Verner
Frightened Murderer. N. Rutledge
Frightened One. F. Gamble
Frightened Ones. M. Marlette
Frightened People. J. T. Story
Frightened Pigeon. R. Burke
Frightened Sailor. D. Sharp
Frightened Stiff. K. Roos
Frightened to Death. H. Gray
Frightened Village. N. Edwards
Frightened Widow. Bernice Carey
Frightened Widow. C. Robertson
Frightened Wife. M. R. Rinehart
Frighteners. R. Busby
Frighteners. P. Leslie
Frightening Talent. L. Golding
Frightful Sin of Cisco Newman. G. A. Ralston
Fringe of the Law. C. H. Bullivant
Frisco Detective. Anonymous
Frisco Hi-Jack. A. Capelli
'Frisco Rock. D. Spade
Fritz, the Bound Boy Detective. E. L. Wheeler
Fritz, the German Detective. T. Pastor
Fritz to the Front. E. L. Wheeler
Fritzi. A. Kennington
Frivolities. R. Marsh
Frog in the Moonflower. I. Drummond
Frog Murders. L. Serrester
Frog was Yellow. F. Vivian
Frogman Assassination. J. Seward
Froler Case. J. L. Jacolliot
From a Dark Place. L. Charbonneau
From a High Tower. T. Newman
From a Prison Cell. N. Carter
From a Surgeon's Diary. C. Ashdown
From A to Z. San Antonio
From All Blindness. H. Gibbs
From Behind the Arras. P. C. De Crespigny
From Blue to Capture. D. Donovan
From Clue to Climax. W. N. Harben
From Clue to Clue. N. Carter
From Dance Hall to Opium Den. Griff
From Death to Life. Old Sleuth
From Despair to Triumph. W. G. Forbes
From Doon with Death. R. Rendell
From Dusk Till Dawn. W. Garrett
From Exile. J. Payn
From Father to Son. P. Trent
From Information Received. D. Donovan
From Information Received. C. F. Gregg
From Information Received. E. Radford
From Lake to Wilderness. W. M. Graydon
From Laughter to Death. J. Sandys
From London Far. M. Innes
From Midnight to Morning. M. Leblanc
From Natural Causes. J. Bell
From 9 O'Clock to Jamaica Bay. D. Broun
From Nine to Nine. L. Perutz
From Now On. F. Packard
From Out the Vasty Deep. M. B. Lowndes
From Peril to Peril. N. Carter
From Post to Finish. H. Smart
From Russia, with Love. I. Fleming
From Satan, with Love. V. Coffman
From Scenes Like These. Gordon M. Williams
From Secret Places. M. Lynch
From Shadow to Light. G. Campbell
From Sing Sing to Liberty. H. C. Blaney
From Six to Six. W. B. Foster
From the Bosom of the Deep. J. E. Muddock

From the Cliffs of Croaghaun. R. Cromie
From the Hand of the Hunter. L. T. Meade
From the House of Bondage. R. Rodd
From the Scourge of the Tongue. B. Marchant
From the Valley of the Missing. Grace M. White
From the Vasty Deep. M. B. Lowndes
From Thief to Detective. F. Hume
From This Dark Stairway. M. G. Eberhart
From This Day Forth. Laura Smith
From This Death Forward. R. Bloomfield
Front Door Key. J. Brophy
Front for Murder. G. Emery
Front Man. F. Wallace
Front of Brass. F. M. White
Front Page Murder. J. Bentley
Front Page Murder. J. Powers
Front Page Murder. R. Trevor
Front Page Mystery. G. M. Dean
Front Page Woman. P. Saxon
Frontier. M. Leblanc
Frontier. P. Tabori
Frontier Detective. E. L. Wheeler
Frontier Incident. S. B. Hough
Frontier Mystery. B. Mitford
Frontier Mystery. J. Mowbray
Frontier of Fear. I. R. G. Hart
Frontiers of Death. J. Turner
Frontiers of Violence. C. Leader
Frontiersman. H. Bindloss
Frontiersmen. H. Bindloss
Frost. Andrew Hall
Frosted Death. K. Robeson
Frozen Death. Winifred Graham
Frozen Death. A. Weymouth
Frozen Deep. W. Collins
Frozen Fire. H. Hawton
Frozen Flame. M. E. Hanshew
Frozen Gold. A. J. Small
Frozen Ground. N. Hoult
Frozen Hearts. G. W. Appleton
Frozen Humor. R. P. Woodward
Frozen Inlet Post. J. B. Hendryx
Frozen Pirate. W. C. Russell
Frozen Slippers. A. M. Williamson
Frozen Stiff. R. Chapman
Fruit of Indiscretion. W. Magnay
Fruit of the Poppy. R. Wilder
Fu Manchu's Bride. S. Rohmer
Fuehrer Dies. H. Desmond
Fugitive. W. H. Baker
Fugitive. R. Bridges
Fugitive. R. L. Fish
Fugitive. G. Simenon
Fugitive Eye. C. Jay
Fugitive from Fear. T. E. Wilson
Fugitive from Murder. M. V. Heberden
Fugitive Men. R. Goyne
Fugitive Millionaire. A. Carlyle
Fugitive Pigeon. D. E. Westlake
Fugitive Sleuth. H. Footner
Fugitives. Morley Roberts
Fugitives. N. Sligh
Fugitives. Alan Thomas
Fugitives of Pearl Hill. E. A. Young
Fugitive's Road. A. MacVicar
Fugitive's Road. P. Malloch
Fulfilling of the Law. E. Gwynne
Fulfillment. Elsie Lee
Full Cargo. W. D. Steele
Full Circle. H. Cecil
Full Coverage. J. M. Ullman
Full Crash Dive. A. R. Bosworth
Full Fare for a Corpse. T. Davis
Full Fathom Five. H. S. Davies
Full Fathom Five. G. V. Galwey
Full Fury. R. Ormerod
Full Moon. T. Mundy
Full Moon. W. Spence
Full Moon for Murder. J. M. Spender
Full Stop. G. Mitcham
Full Term. P. Spencer

Full Treatment. R. S. Thorn
Fuller's Earth. C. Wells
Fullerton Case. R. Doubleday
Fully Dressed and in His Right Mind. M. Fessier
Fully Ripe. P. H. Irving
Fun and Deadly Games. D. Tracy
Fun City. H. Barron
Fun Fair. H. H. Lee
Fun House. P. Reid
Funeral for a Commissar. R. Magowan
Funeral for a Physicist. P. Bloxham
Funeral for Five. J. Stagge
Funeral in Berlin. L. Deighton
Funeral in Eden. P. McGuire
Funeral March of a Marionette. Winifred Duke
Funeral of Figaro. Ellis Peters
Funeral Rites. J. Hedges
Funeral was in Spain. E. McGirr
Funerals are Fatal. A. Christie
Funhouse. B. Appel
Funniest Killer in Town. Hampton Stone
Funny Bob. Old Sleuth
Funny Bone. J. MacLaren-Ross
Funny Money. R. Sapir
Fur Bringers. H. Footner
Fur Raiders. H. H. C. Gibbons
Furious Old Women. L. Bruce
Furnace for a Foe. C. Rushton
Furnished for Murder. E. Ferrars
Further Adventures of a Cowboy Detective. C. A. Sirengo
Further Adventures of Captain Kettle. C. J. C. Hyne
Further Adventures of Doctor Syn. R. Thorndike
Further Adventures of Jimmie Dale. F. Packard
Further Adventures of Quincy Adams Sawyer. C. F. Pidgin
Further Adventures of Romney Pringle. C. Ashdown
Further Adventures of the Black Pilgrim. G. Stanley
Further Evidence. A. Brock
Further Exploits of Nick Carter, Detective. N. Carter
Further Foolishness. S. Leacock
Further Outlook Unsettled. H. Clevely
Further Secrets of Potsdam. W. LeQueux
Further Side of Fear. H. McCloy
Furthest Fury. C. Wells
Furtive Flame. H. Janson
Furtive Men. L. Spencer
Fury on Sunday. R. Matheson
Fury with Legs. G. Lawrence
Fury Within. R. St. Clair
Futile Alibi. F. W. Crofts
Future Mrs. Dering. T. Cobb
Fuzz. E. McBain

G

"G.B." W. F. Morris
G is for Ghoul. M. Hervey
G Man. C. F. Coe
G Man at the Yard. P. Cheyney
G-Men on Murder Island. L. Jamieson
G-String Murders. G. R. Lee
Gabbart Destiny. E. L. Long
Gables Mystery. C. E. Perry
Gaboreau. P. Steward
Gaboreau the Terrible. P. Steward
Gabriel Comes to 24. R. Braddon
Gabriel Hounds. M. Stewart

Gabriel Praed's Castle. A. Jones
Gabriel Samara. E. P. Oppenheim
Gabriel Samara, Peacemaker. E. P. Oppenheim
Gabriel Sounds for Africa. C. Edwards
Gabrielle. J. Maass
Gabrielle. K. Norris
Gage. D. Chako
'Gainst Chink and Gunman. T. Lloyd
Galahad of the Air. T. Wallace
Galatea. J. M. Cain
Galaxy Lot. W. A. Ballinger
Gale Gallyon Takes a Hand. Spike Gordon
Gale of the World. Laurence Kirk
Gale Warning. H. Innes
Gale Warning. D. Yates
Gallant. C. Blackstone
Gallant Adventuress. Therese Benson
Gallant Affair. Hank Hobson
Gallant Tom. T. P. Prest
Galleon Gold. M. Drake
Galleon Rock. G. Volk
Galleon Treasure. A. B. Sherlock
Galleon's Gold. R. W. Sneddon
Galleys of St. John. E. L. Long
Galloping Dick. H. B. M. Watson
Galloping Gold. D. Learmonth
Galloping Gold. W. C. Tuttle
Galloway Case. A. Garve
Gallows Alley. A. Skene
Gallows Are High. H. Spencer
Gallows Are Waiting. J. York
Gallows Bait. S. Truss
Gallows-Bird. L. Storm
Gallows Child. P. G. Winslow
Gallows' Foot. V. Gielgud
Gallows for a Fool. C. Franklin
Gallows for the Groom. D. B. Olsen
Gallows' Fruit. H. Desmond
Gallows Garden. M. E. Chaber
Gallows Grange. H. Holt
Gallows in My Garden. R. Deming
Gallows in My Garden. J. Fleming
Gallows Inn. E. P. Thorne
Gallows March. G. Norham
Gallows of Chance. E. P. Oppenheim
Gallows Orchard. C. Spencer
Gallows Parade. F. Tyler
Gallows Seed. P. Troubetzkoy
Gallows Set. W. Rutherford
Gallows Wait. J. Corbett
Gallows Waits. J. Budd
Galmart Affair. S. Westall
Galton Case. R. Macdonald
Gambit. L. Kendall
Gambit. K. Lane
Gambit. R. Stout
Gambit for Mr. Groode. G. Griswold
Gamble My Last Game. R. W. Krepps
Gamble of Life. A. Applin
Gamble with Death. R. Simons
Gambler. C. Burdett
Gambler. O. Hogstrand
Gambler. W. Krasner
Gambler of the West. O. Harper
Gamblers. W. LeQueux
Gamblers. E. Woodward
Gambler's Choice. J. B. Hendryx
Gambler's Girl. J. Matcha
Gambler's Gold. A. Wright
Gambler's Last Throw. Anonymous
Gambler's Syndicate. N. Carter
Gambler's Throw. E. L. Adams
Gambler's Wax Finger and other startling detective experiences. G. S. McWatters
Gambling Man. C. Cookson
Gambling with Fire. D. Montrose
Game. M. Hastings
Game and the Candle. E. M. Ingram
Game and the Candle. K. Roche
Game Called Murder. J. Ingerson
Game for Eagles. O. M. Hall
Game for Hawks. R. Severn
Game for Heroes. J. Graham
Game for the Living. P. Highsmith

Game for Three Losers. E. Lustgarten
Game Keeper's Secret. W. M. Graydon
Game of Chance. A. Ferguson
Game of Craft. N. Carter
Game of Draw. D. Stewart
Game of Hazard. P. Allardyce
Game of Liberty. E. P. Oppenheim
Game of Life. Waters
Game of Life and Death. L. Colcord
Game of Love. G. Warden
Game of Murder. P. Barrington
Game of Murder. F. Durbridge
Game of Plots. N. Carter
Game of Shadows. M. Ruuth
Game of Statues. A. Stevenson
Game of the Golden Ball. Elizabeth Johnson
Game of Troy. J. M. White
Game of X. R. Sheckley
Game Show Girls. J. P. Radford
Game Well Played. N. Carter
Game Without Rules. M. Gilbert
Game Without Winners. D. Bennett
Gamecock Murders. F. Gruber
Games. H. Ellson
Game's Afoot. M. Hardwick
Games Murderers Play. C. Carpenter
Games of Chance. T. Hinde
Games of Chance with Strangers. M. Redfield
Gaming for Gold. A. Wright
Gamma Ray Murders. P. Yorke
Gammon and Espionage. N. Bentley
Gang. D. Whitelaw
Gang Buster. K. Roe
Gang Girl. Wenzell Brown
Gang Girls. C. Bingham
Gang Law. H. Clevely
Gang Rumble. E. Ronns
Gang Smasher. H. Clevely
Gang Smasher Again. H. Clevely
Gang that Couldn't Shoot Straight. J. Breslin
Gang War. J. G. Brandon
Gang War. G. H. Teed
Gangdom's Doom. M. Grant
Ganges Mud. E. P. Thorne
Gang's Deserter. C. Brisbane
Gang's Orders. M. Poole
Gang's Prisoners. L. Bidston
Gangster. Roland Daniel
Gangster and the Private Eye. Dale Clark
Gangster Girl. R. Campert
Gangster Girl. J. Lait
Gangster Lady. B. Sarto
Gangster War on Bar "G." G. C. Shedd
Gangsters. D. Chandler
Gangsters All. G. Stanley
Gangster's Daughter. Roland Daniel
Gangster's Deputy. S. Drew
Gangster's Girl. J. Hunter
Gangster's Girl. R. Starr
Gangsters' Glory. E. P. Oppenheim
Gangster's Isle. J. Brooke
Gangster's Last Shot. Roland Daniel
Gangsters of the Air. J. Noy
Gangsters Parade. G. Stanley
Gangster's Revenge. G. N. Philips
Gangway! D. E. Westlake
Gantry Episode. June Drummond
Gaol Breaker. E. Wallace
Gaol Gates Are Open. David Hume
Gaol in Conflict. James Preston
Gap in the Curtain. J. Buchan
Garden. A. Armstrong
Garden at No. 19. E. Jepson
Garden City Crime. D. Stuart
Garden Club Murders. D. Van Deusen
Garden Court Mystery. B. Delannoy
Garden Game. J. M. White
Garden in Asia. M. D. Post
Garden Murder Case. S. S. Van Dine
Garden o' Dreams. F. M. White

Garden of Evil. B. Stoker
Garden of Ghosts. Marilyn Ross
Garden of Grief. H. Arvonen
Garden of Memories. M. Richmond
Garden of Mystery. R. Marsh
Garden of Satan. C. Vincent
Garden of Shadows. V. Coffman
Garden of Silent Beasts. Gavin Holt
Garden of Swords. M. Pemberton
Garden of the Gods. E. M. Keate
Gardenias Bruise Easily. J. P. Carstairs
Gargantua Falls. P. Bair
Gargoni Girdle. N. Carter
Gargoyle Conspiracy. M. Albert
Gargoyle of Polgelly. R. Hardinge
Gargrave Mystery. H. C. Davidson
Garlands for Sylvia. Gavin Holt
Garment. C. Cookson
Garment of Immortality. A. Askew
Garments of Repentance. D. Whitelaw
Garmiscath. J. S. Clouston
Garnered. R. Marsh
Garnett Bell, Detective. C. H. Bullivant
Garrison Tales from Tonquin. James O'Neill
Garrity. Allan Nixon
Garston Murder Case. H. C. Bailey
Garstons. H. C. Bailey
Garth. J. Hawthorne
Garthoyle Gardens. E. Jepson
Garvock. C. Gibbon
Gas. B. Hirschfeld
Gas Light. P. Hamilton
Gas Mask Gang. H. Pink
Gas-Mask Murder. J. R. Warren
Gascoyne. S. Crawford
Gaslight. W. Drummond
Gaspar Trenchard. B. Hemyng
Gasparoni Detective. Aldine
Gastronomic Murder. A. Roudybush
Gat Heat. R. S. Prather
Gate Fever. J. B. O'Sullivan
Gate of Ivory, Gate of Horn. Philip Craig
Gate of Sinners. Mrs. C. Kernahan
Gate of Temptation. P. Brebner
Gates of Birth. R. Bridges
Gates of Brass. F. J. Kelly
Gates of Chance. V. Sutphen
Gates of Dawn. F. Hume
Gates of Flame. R. R. Hobbs
Gates of Montrain. W. D. Roberts
Gates of Sorrow. M. Leighton
Gates of Tien T'ze. L. H. Gordon
Gateway to Escape. N. Deane
Gateway to Hell. D. Wheatley
Gateway to the Grave. M. Lynch
Gathering of Eagles. E. Lindall
Gathering of Evil. Marilyn Ross
Gathering of Moondust. P. Morton
Gathering Storm. F. A. M. Webster
Gaudy Night. D. L. Sayers
Gaudy Shadows. J. Brunner
Gauge of Deception. K. G. Ballard
Gauges Steady. E. L. Long
Gaunt Stranger. E. Wallace
Gaunt Woman. J. Blackburn
Gauntlet of Alceste. H. Moorhouse
Gautran. B. L. Farjeon
Gay Adventure. A. Applin
Gay Captain. M. V. Victor
Gay-Cat. P. Casey
Gay Conspirators. P. Curtiss
Gay Deceiver. P. Leslie
Gay Deception. R. Harding
Gay Desperado. B. Gray
Gay Detective. V. Rand
Gay Gallant. L. Blake
Gay Ghastly Holiday. S. Blayne
Gay Head Conspiracy. C. Baker

Gay Lord Waring. H. Townley
Gay Mortician. M. M. Raison
Gay of Heart. A. Maybury
Gay Pilgrimage. B. Bolt
Gay Triangle. W. LeQueux
Gay World. J. Hatton
Gazebo. Alec Coppel
Gazebo. P. Wentworth
Gees' First Case. Jack Mann
Gelignite Gang. J. Creasey
Gem of a Murder. C. Keith
Gemini in Darkness. Clarissa Ross
Gemini Revenged. Charlotte Hunt
Gemini Smile, Gemini Kill. R. Lory
Gendarme's Report. G. Simenon
General Besserley's Puzzle Box. E. P. Oppenheim
General Besserley's Second Puzzle Box. E. P. Oppenheim
General Crack. G. R. Preedy
General Died at Dawn. C. G. Booth
General Goes too Far. L. Robinson
Generals. P. Wahloo
General's Will. G. Allen
Generous Heart. K. Fearing
Genesis 38. Brian Cooper
Genesta. A. Griffin
Geneva Mystery. F. Durbridge
Genghis Coppersmith. R. J. Griffin
Genial Stranger. D. MacKenzie
Genius in Murder. E. R. Punshon
Gentle Assassin. C. Richards
Gentle Binns. E. Jepson
Gentle Giant. A. Eichler
Gentle Grafter. O. Henry
Gentle Hangman. J. M. Fox
Gentle Highwayman. P. Allardyce
Gentle Killer. P. Barrington
Gentle Kiss of Murder. A. Barron
Gentle Murderer. D. S. Davis
Gentle Obsession. F. Cowen
Gentle Rain. Margaret Archer
Gentle Sex. Angus Hall
Gentle Thespians. R. M. Gilchrist
Gentleman Anonymous. M. B. Lowndes
Gentleman Called. D. S. Davis
Gentleman Crook. M. Crombie
Gentleman for the Gallows. S. Horler
Gentleman from Chicago. J. Cashman
Gentleman from Nowhere. G. Thorne
Gentleman from Portland. C. R. Gull
Gentleman from Texas. H. Balfour
Gentleman Garnet. H. B. Vogel
Gentleman George. J. G. Rowe
Gentleman Hangs. J. Dollond
Gentleman in Pajamas. C. N. Buck
Gentleman-in-Waiting. S. Horler
Gentleman Johnny. S. Styles
Gentleman Junkie and other stories of the Hung-Up Generation. H. Ellison
Gentleman Juror. C. L. Marsh
Gentleman of London. M. Gerard
Gentleman of Rio. A. Mills
Gentleman of the Road. H. Bleackley
Gentleman of Virginia. P. Brebner
Gentleman Pirate. Janette Radcliffe
Gentleman Thorne. Old Sleuth
Gentleman Traitor. Alan Williams
Gentleman Tramp. G. Wintle
Gentleman Who Vanished. F. Hume
Gentleman's Agreement. B. Von Hutten
Gentleman's Daughters. M. Masterman
Gentleman's Gentleman. M. Pemberton
Gentleman's Relish. H. Spencer
Gentlemen at Large. J. Boland
Gentlemen at Large. E. Woodward
Gentlemen Go By. L. Meynell
Gentlemen in Hades. F. A. Kummer
Gentlemen March. R. Pertwee
Gentlemen of Crime. A. Gask
Gentlemen of the Jury. H. Leyford

Title Index

Gentlemen of the Night. S. Maddock
Gentlemen of the Sea. P. Trent
Gentlemen Reform. J. Boland
Gently at a Gallop. A. Hunter
Gently by the Shore. A. Hunter
Gently Coloured. A. Hunter
Gently Continental. A. Hunter
Gently Does It. A. Hunter
Gently Down the Stream. A. Hunter
Gently Dust the Corpse. S. H. Courtier
Gently Floating. N. Berrow
Gently French. A. Hunter
Gently Go Man. A. Hunter
Gently in the Highlands. A. Hunter
Gently in the Sun. A. Hunter
Gently in Trees. A. Hunter
Gently North-West. A. Hunter
Gently Sahib. A. Hunter
Gently Through the Mill. A. Hunter
Gently Through the Woods. A. Hunter
Gently to the Summit. A. Hunter
Gently Where the Roads Go. A. Hunter
Gently with Love. A. Hunter
Gently with the Innocents. A. Hunter
Gently with the Ladies. A. Hunter
Gently with the Painters. A. Hunter
George and Georgina. E. Phillpotts
George Canterbury's Will. H. Wood
George Caulfield's Journey. M. E. Braddon
George Elvaston. Mrs. Lodge
Georgia Detective. Anonymous
Geraldine. T. P. Prest
Geraldine Walton--Woman! M. Leighton
Gerard. M. E. Braddon
German Helmet. P. McCutchan
German Spy. W. LeQueux
German Spy. B. Newman
German Spy System from Within. W. LeQueux
Gerrard Street Mystery and other weird tales. J. C. Dent
Gertrude Haddon. E. Southworth
Gertrude of the Rock. T. P. Prest
Gervase Castonel. H. Wood
Gestapo Dormouse. Frank King
Gestapo File. D. Cory
Gestapo Fugitive. A. O. Pollard
Gestapo Gauntlet. L. Cargill
Gustapo Trial. J. Petersen
Get a Load o' Dis. R. Drayton
Get Carter. T. Lewis
Get Clutha. H. Munro
Get Dumm! J. Brewer
Get Garrity. Allan Nixon
Get Me Headquarters. A. Capelli
Get Out and Stay Out. R. Angel
Get Out of Town. P. Connolly
Get Out of Town. H. V. Dixon
Get Out the Cuffs. David Hume
Get Ready to Die. B. Gray
Get-Rich-Quick Wallingford. G. R. Chester
Get Smart! W. Johnston
Get Smart Once Again! W. Johnston
Get That Man. R. Drayton
Get Wallace! A. Wilson
Get Your Man. E. Dorrance
Getaway. L. Charteris
Getaway. J. Harris
Getaway. J. Thompson
Getaway Gang. D. J. Gammon
Geth Straker. B. Mather
Getting Rid of Anne. T. Cobb
Getting the Boy. William Scott
Ghost. A. Bennett
Ghost and the Garnet. Marilyn Ross
Ghost at Ravenkill Manor. P. Warren
Ghost at Stagmere. A. Brennan
Ghost at the Wedding. Elna Stone
Ghost Blonde. M. Derby
Ghost Breaker. R. Goulart
Ghost Car. B. Knox
Ghost City. R. St. Clair
Ghost City Killings. W. Martyn

Ghost Comes Knocking. Marilyn Ross
Ghost Counts Ten. R. Trevor
Ghost Dancers. Angela Gray
Ghost Does a Richard III. R. B. Saxe
Ghost Fingers. C. Robertson
Ghost Flowers. M. Summerton
Ghost from the Past. Colin Hope
Ghost from the Past. A. M. Meadows
Ghost Girl. H. K. Webster
Ghost Guns. W. C. Tuttle
Ghost House. N. Berrow
Ghost House. F. Daingerfield
Ghost House. C. B. Pallen
Ghost House. R. St. Clair
Ghost House. G. Verner
Ghost-Hunter and His Family. O'Hara Family
Ghost Hunters. R. Aiken
Ghost Hunters. C. Brooks
Ghost Hunters. G. Meyrick
Ghost in the Belfry. P. Pray
"Ghost in the Glass." R. St. Clair
Ghost in the Making. N. Fitzgerald
Ghost in the Wall. R. St. Clair
Ghost It Was. R. Hull
Ghost Knows His Greengages. R. B. Saxe
Ghost Lane. E. P. Hoyt
Ghost Makers. M. Grant
Ghost Man. G. Verner
Ghost Murder. L. Allan
Ghost of a Cardinal. J. Maske
Ghost of a Chance. K. Roos
Ghost of a Chance. F. Usher
Ghost of a Clue. C. Barry
Ghost of a Clue. O. Mills
Ghost of Archie Gilroy. P. Allardyce
Ghost of Channing House. G. St. John
Ghost of Dark Harbor. C. Ross
Ghost of Downhill. E. Wallace
Ghost of Gaston Revere. M. Hansom
Ghost Mesa. T. Craig
Ghost of Glen George. Grace M. White
Ghost of Grand Canyon. R. H. Wilkinson
Ghost of Graveyard Hill. P. W. Fairman
Ghost of Greystone Grange. A. W. A'Beckett
Ghost of Lost Lover's Lake. J. A. Blackwood
Ghost of Megan. M. Lovell
Ghost of Oaklands. W. E. D. Ross
"Ghost of the Air." R. St. Clair
Ghost of the Dunsany. E. L. Long
Ghost of Truth. J. N. Chance
Ghost of Windy Hill. E. B. Cook
Ghost on the Balcony. D. Marfield
Ghost Party. H. Clandon
Ghost Plane. P. Conde
Ghost Plane. J. Corbett
Ghost Plane. A. Stringer
Ghost Pulls the Jackpot. R. B. Saxe
Ghost River. C. Hale
Ghost River Inn. C. Van Hazinga
Ghost Ship of Fog Island. Marilyn Ross
Ghost Song. D. Daniels
Ghost Squad. G. Verner
Ghost Stories and Mysteries. J. S. Le Fanu
Ghost Trail. L. C. Douthwaite
Ghost Trails. W. C. Tuttle
Ghost Train. Ruth Alexander
Ghost Train. A. Ridley
Ghost Voice. M. Hervey
Ghost Walks. C. Brogan
Ghost Walks. N. MacKenzie
Ghost Wanted. F. McDermid
Ghost Wore Black. F. Y. McHugh
Ghost Writer. D. Carter
"Ghostly Fingers." W. Spence
Ghostly Quarantine. R. St. Clair

Ghostly Strength. Winifred Graham
Ghosts. A. Crabb
Ghosts. K. Prichard
Ghosts Can't Kill. M. V. Heberden
Ghosts, Ghouls and Gallows. G. F. Marson
Ghosts' Gloom. I. G. Holmes
Ghosts' High Noon. J. D. Carr
Ghosts' High Noon. C. Wells
Ghosts I Have Met and Some Others. J. K. Bangs
Ghosts Never Die. R. Heed
Ghosts of Ballyduff. K. Ostrander
Ghosts of Grantmeer. Clarissa Ross
Ghosts of Harrel. W. D. Roberts
Ghosts of Kings. A. Pritchett
Ghosts of Perranprah. H. Lea
Ghosts of Slave Driver's Bend. H. H. Kroll
Ghosts of Society. A. Partridge
Ghost's Revenge, and other stories of modern Paris. R. H. Sherard
Ghost's Touch and other stories. W. Collins
Ghostwater. E. Phillpotts
Ghostwind. R. A. Payne
Ghoul. Frank King
Ghoul Goalie. F. W. Gumley
Ghouls in My Grave. J. Ray
Giant Athlete. Old Sleuth
Giant City Swindle. Anonymous
Giant City Swindle. G. N. Philips
Giant Detective. Anonymous
Giant Detective Among the Cowboys. Old Sleuth
Giant Detective Among the Italian Brigands. Old Sleuth
Giant Detective in France. Old Sleuth
Giant Detective in Ireland. Anonymous
Giant Hunchback. H. J. Wurr
Giant Kill. K. Platt
Giantkiller. C. Pincher
Giant's Chair. Winston Graham
Giant's Gate. M. Pemberton
Giants of Darkness. N. Thurley
Gibraltar Conspiracy. D. Betteridge
Gibralter Prisoner. B. Perowne
Gibralter Road. P. McCutchan
Gideon Drexel's Millions. N. Carter
Gideon Drexel's Millions and other stories. N. Carter
Gideon of Scotland Yard. J. J. Marric
Gideon's Art. J. J. Marric
Gideon's Badge. J. J. Marric
Gideon's Day. J. J. Marric
Gideon's Fear. J. J. Marric
Gideon's Fire. J. J. Marric
Gideon's Fog. J. J. Marric
Gideon's Lot. J. J. Marric
Gideon's March. J. J. Marric
Gideon's Men. J. J. Marric
Gideon's Month. J. J. Marric
Gideon's Night. J. J. Marric
Gideon's Power. J. J. Marric
Gideon's Press. J. J. Marric
Gideon's Ride. J. J. Marric
Gideon's Risk. J. J. Marric
Gideon's River. J. J. Marric
Gideon's Sport. J. J. Marric
Gideon's Staff. J. J. Marric
Gideon's Vote. J. J. Marric
Gideon's Week. J. J. Marric
Gideon's Wrath. J. J. Marric
Gift from Berlin. A. Barker
Gift Horse. M. R. Douglas
Gift Horse. F. Gruber
Gift in the Gauntlet. B. Reynolds

G

Gift of Death. E. Ronns
Gift of Hermes. C. W. Whitaker
Gift of the Desert. R. Parrish
Gift of the Gods. N. Carter
Gift of the Sea. R. M. Sears
Gift Shop. C. Armstrong
Gift Supreme. G. A. England
Gigantic Shadow. J. Symons
Giggling Ghosts. K. Robeson
Gigins Court. B. Graeme
Giglamps. Will Scott
Gilbert's Last Toothache. M. Scherf
Gilchrist Case. J. Barclay
Gilded Clique. E. Gaboriau
Gilded Fleece. N. Tranter
Gilded Fly. H. Payne
Gilded Jar. Margery Lawrence
Gilded Kiss. D. Enefer
Gilded Lady. W. M. Clemens
Gilded London. A. Aksew
Gilded Man. Carter Dickson
Gilded Nightmare. H. Pentecost
Gilded Sarcophagus. Charlotte Hunt
Gilded Serpent. D. Donovan
Gilded Snatch Caper. J. D. Lawrence
Gilded Witch. J. Webb
Gilead Balm, Knight Errant. B. Capes
Gillespie Suicide Mystery. L. Gribble
Gillingham Rubies. E. Jepson
Gilt Edge. K. A. Saddler
Gild-Edge Mystery. E. M. Channon
Gilt-Edge Tom, Conductor. E. L. Coolidge
Gilt-Edged Cockpit. D. Rutherford
Gilt-Edged Guilt. C. Wells
Gilt-Edged Traitor. M. Eden
Gilt Kid. J. Curtis
Gin and Ginger. J. F. W. Hannay
Gin and Murder. J. Pullein-Thompson
Ginger Cat. C. Reeve
Ginger Cat Mystery. R. Forsythe
Ginger Horse. J. F. Straker
Gingerbread House. M. Dobner
Gingerbread Man. R. Parker
Ginkgo Tree. C. Jarrett
Ginny. Morton Cooper
Ginzberg Circle. A. O'Neill
Gipsey Chief. H. M. Jones
Gipsey Chief. G. W. M. Reynolds
Gipsey Girl. H. M. Jones
Gipsey Mother. H. M. Jones
Gipsies Don't Have Them. G. M. Wilson
Gipsy Blair, the Western Detective. J. R. Taylor
Gipsy Boy. T. P. Prest
Gipsy in Evening Dress. W. J. Makin
Gipsy of the North. O. Binns
Gipsy or Gentleman? W. M. Graydon
Gipsy Reno, the Detective. Old Sleuth
Gipsy Rose, the Female Detective. Old Sleuth
Gipsy's Prophecy. E. Southworth
Gipsey's Warning. E. A. Dupuy
Girl Alone. J. Blackmore
Girl Alone. Howel Evans
Girl and the Bill. B. Merwin
Girl and the Detective. C. E. Blaney
Girl and the Miracle. R. Marsh
Cirl at Central. G. Bonner
Girl, a Man and a River. J. Hawkins
Girl at Pine Creek. G. Goodchild
Girl Behind the Keys. T. Gallon
Girl Between. B. Fischer
Girl by the Roadside. Roland Daniel
Girl by the Roadside. V. Vanardy
Girl Cage. J. Ehrlich
Girl Called Ann. Rona Randall
Girl Called Fathom. L. Forrester
Girl Champion. Old Sleuth
Girl Chase. D. Enefer
Girl Died Laughing. V. Paradise
Girl Died Singing. N. Morland
Girl for Danny. W. Ard
Girl Found Dead. M. Underwood

Girl Friday. D. Whitelaw
Girl from Alsace. B. E. Stevenson
Girl from Belfast. V. Bridges
Girl from Easy Street. R. Foster
Girl from H.A.R.D. J. Moffatt
Girl from Hateville. G. Brewer
Girl from Las Vegas. J. M. Flynn
Girl from Malta. F. Hume
Girl from Midnight. Wade Miller
Girl from Moscow. M. Corrigan
Girl from Nippon. C. Dawe
Girl from Nowhere. E. Bond
Girl from Nowhere. R. Foley
Girl from Nowhere. P. Minton
Girl from Outer Space. C. Brown
Girl from Peking. G. B. Mair
Girl from Scotland Yard. M. McGrath
Girl from Scotland Yard. E. Wallace
Girl from Taiping. H. C. James
Girl from Texas. C. E. Blaney
Girl from the East. D. Whitelaw
Girl from the Mimosa Club. L. Ford
Girl from the Sea. R. Abbey
Girl from Toronto. H. Clevely
Girl He Left Behind Him. H. F. Moulton
Girl Hunt. L. D. Smith
Girl Hunters. M. Spillane
Girl in a Big Brass Bed. P. Rabe
Girl in a Hurry. T. A. Plummer
Girl in a Mask. H. K. Maxwell
Girl in a Million. D. Enefer
Girl in a Net. John Marsh
Girl in a Shroud. C. Brown
Girl in a Thousand. J. Middlemass
Girl in Arms. D. Enefer
Girl in Asses' Milk. W. H. Baker
Girl in Black. V. Bridges
Girl in Black Velvet. L. De Jean
Girl in Blue Pants. R. Nettell
Girl in Cabin B54. L. Fletcher
Girl in Green. A. Carr
Girl in Hand. H. Janson
Girl in His House. H. McGrath
Girl in His Past. G. Simenon
Girl in Love. Rona Randall
Girl in 906. D. Hall
Girl in Ocean View. M. Symons
Girl in Shadow. C. Franklin
Girl in the Blue Dress. R. Marsh
Girl in the Cage. B. Benson
Girl in the Cage. C. Fitzsimmons
Girl in the Case. R. Barr
Girl in the Case. N. Carter
Girl in the Cellar. P. Wentworth
Girl in the Cockpit. M. Avallone
Girl in the Cop's Pocket. Robert Turner
Girl in the Crime Belt. J. N. Chance
Girl in the Crimson Cloak. R. Trevor
Girl in the Dark. Roland Daniel
Girl in the Dark. E. C. Vivian
Girl in the Death Seat. F. Nichols
Girl in the Fog. J. Gollomb
Girl in the Frame. W. Fuller
Girl in the Green Beret. N. Penley
Girl in the Killer's Bed. A. Curry
Girl in the News. Roy Vickers
Girl in the Other Seat. A. R. Weekes
Girl in the Plain Brown Wrapper. J. D. MacDonald
Girl in the Punchbowl. T. B. Dewey
Girl in the Rain. J. Reach
Girl in the Red Jaguar. J. Manor
Girl in the River. V. B. Miller
Girl in the Secret. A. M. Williamson
Girl in the Spy Racket. W. J. Blackledge
Girl in the Telltale Bikini. P. Morgan

Girl in the Tiffany Dress. M. Eyre
Girl in the Tower. J. Corby
Girl in the Train. B. Bolt
Girl in the Web. Mark Allerton
Girl in the Wet-Look Bikini. S. Mitchell
Girl in the White Mercedes. J. Usher
Girl in 304. H. R. Daniels
Girl in Waiting. A. Eyre
Girl in Waiting. G. Simenon
Girl Known as D 13. S. Kyle
Girl Meets Body. J. Iams
Girl Missing. E. Sherry
Girl Named Tamiko. R. Kirkbride
Girl Nobody Knows. M. McShane
Girl of Ghost Mountain. J. A. Dunn
Girl of Grit. A. Griffiths
Girl of Lost Island. W. H. Osborne
Girl of the Guard Line. C. C. Waddell
Girl of the Islands. J. M. Walsh
Girl of the Passion Play. A. M. Williamson
Girl of the Yellow Diamonds. M. Leighton
Girl of These Days. Roy Vickers
Girl on a High Wire. R. Foley
Girl on a Slay Ride. L. Trimble
Girl on Crown Street. D. Karp
Girl on the Beach. M. Cronin
Girl on the Beach. A. Holden
Girl on the Best Seller List. V. Packer
Girl on the Left Bank. Joan Shepherd
Girl on the Loose. G. G. Fickling
Girl on the M6. D. Enefer
Girl on the Prowl. G. G. Fickling
Girl on the Run. E. S. Aarons
Cirl on the Run. E. Hunt
Girl on the Run. J. Sibly
Girl on the Run. H. Waugh
Girl on the Waterfront. M. Urquhart
Girl on Zero. B. Perowne
Girl Out Back. C. Williams
Girl Out in Corsica. A. Philips
Girl Prisoner. N. Carter
Girl Raffles. C. E. Blaney
Girl Running. Adam Knight
Girl Stalker. Lawrence Trent
Girl, the City, and the Soldier. W. H. Baker
Girl, the Gold Watch & Everything. J. D. MacDonald
Girl Watcher's Funeral. H. Pentecost
Girl Who Cried Wolf. H. Waugh
Girl Who Dared. D. Durham
Girl Who Didn't Die. R. Jensen
Girl Who Died. K. Hopkins
Girl Who Failed Him. G. Goodchild
Girl Who Had Nothing. A. M. Williamson
Girl Who Had to Die. E. S. Holding
Girl Who Kept Knocking Them Dead. Hampton Stone
Girl Who Killed Things. T. Powell
Girl Who Knew Too Much. J. G. Brandon
Girl Who Never Was. Jan Alexander
Girl Who Never Was. T. B. Dewey
Girl Who Passed for Normal. H. Fleetwood
Girl Who Saw Too Much. D. Reid
Girl Who Wanted Experience. L. Shippey
Girl Who Was Possessed. C. Brown
Girl Who Wasn't There. T. B. Dewey
Girl Who Wasn't There. W. D. Roberts
Girl with a Golden Bar. B. Conrad
Girl with a Secret. C. Armstrong
Girl with Money. F. Warden
Girl with no Place to Hide. N. Quarry
Girl with Red Hair. Giles Gordon
Girl with Six Fingers. H. Pentecost
Girl with the Dynamite Bangs. L. Cameron
Girl with the Frightened Eyes. L. Lariar
Girl with the Green Eyes. M. Leblanc
Girl with the Haunting Eyes. F. Warden
Girl with the Hole in Her Head. Hampton Stone

Title Index

Girl with the Key. M. K. Simmons
Girl with the Leopard-Skin Bag. M. Halliday
Girl with the Long Green Heart. Lawrence Block
Girl with the Sweet Plump Knees. T. B. Dewey
Girl with the X-Ray Eyes. M. O'Nair
Girls at the Grange. F. Warden
Girl's Head. E. Jepson
Girls in White. Rona Randall
Girl's Number Doesn't Answer. T. Powell
Girl's Temptation. S. Warwick
Girls Who Came to Murder. K. Carr
Girls Will Be Girls. F. Warden
Giselle. Brian Cooper
Give a Corpse a Bad Name. E. Ferrars
Give a Man a Gun. J. Creasey
Give a Man Rope. Gavin Holt
Give Daddy the Knife, Darling. J. Lymington
Give Death a Name. Anthony Gilbert
Give 'em the Ax. A. A. Fair
Give It to Me Straight. S. Morelli
Give Me a Gun. R. Angel
Give Me a Little Something. W. L. Rohde
Give Me Back Myself. L. P. Davies
Give Me Death. I. B. Myers
Give Me Murder. G. Ashe
Give Me That Man. E. G. Cousins
Give Me the Knife. L. Meynell
Give Me the Lowdown. D. Linton
Give Me This Woman. W. Ard
Give Me Yesterday. G. Vaizey
Give Thanks to Death. H. Bailey
Give the Boys a Great Big Hand. E. McBain
Give the Devil His Due. P. Graaf
Give the Girl a Gun. R. Deming
Give the Little Corpse a Great Big Hand. G. Bagby
Give up the Body. L. Trimble
Give up the Ghost. M. Erskine
Give Us the World. F. L. Green
Giver in Secret. T. Cobb
Glad Eye. C. R. Gull
Glad Summer. J. Farnol
Glamour Girl. K. Lindsay
Glare. C. Dawe
Glass Alibi. L. Gribble
Glass Arrow. G. Verner
Glass Bottom Boat. B. Street
Glass Cage. E. Ronns
Glass Cage. G. Simenon
Glass Cage. Colin Wilson
Glass Cell. P. Highsmith
Glass Centipede. T. Painter
Glass Cipher. P. Winston
Glass Dagger. J. G. Brandon
Glass Dagger. C. J. C. Hyne
Glass Facade. J. B. Watney
Glass Fish. G. Stuart
Glass Heart. M. Holland
Glass House. Jan Alexander
Glass Houses. E. Thompson
Glass Interval. J. Turner
Glass Key. D. Hammett
Glass Knife. L. Thayer
Glass Ladder. P. W. Fairman
Glass Man. K. Robeson
Glass Mask. L. G. Offord
Glass Mountain. K. Robeson
Glass of Red Wine. M. Tripp
Glass on the Stairs. M. Scherf
Glass Painting. Jan Alexander
Glass Room. E. Rolfe
Glass-Sided Ants' Nest. P. Dickinson
Glass Slipper. M. G. Eberhart
Glass Spear. S. H. Courtier
Glass Too Many. Jack Mann
Glass Totem. D. Chandler
Glass Tower. D. Osborne

Glass Triangle. G. H. Coxe
Glass Village. E. Queen
Glass Virgin. C. Cookson
Gleam of Sapphire. D. Tower
Gleaming Rails. G. M. Dean
Gleave Mystery. L. Tracy
Glencairly Castle. H. G. Hutchinson
Glenlitten Murder. E. P. Oppenheim
Glenrannoch. Rona Randall
Glenvirgin's Ghost. Winifred Graham
Glimpse into Terror. Clarissa Ross
Glimpse of Evil. T. Irving-James
Glimpse of Paradise. John Marsh
Glint of Spears. A. Lejeune
Glitter-Gold Mountain. D. C. Steele
Glittering Desire. E. R. Punshon
Glittering Hour. A. Hodges
Glittering Isle. W. Collison
Glittering Prizes. B. Flynn
Glittering Road. W. A. MacKenzie
Global Globules Affair. S. Latter
Globe Hollow Mystery. H. Gartland
Gloria. E. Southworth
Gloriana. M. Sarsfield
Glorious Masquerade. K. Lindsay
Glory Box Mystery. G. W. Wicking
Glory Thrown In. Eric Lambert
Gloved Hand. L. Bryson
Gloved Hand. N. Carter
Gloved Hand. B. E. Stevenson
Gloved Saskia. W. C. MacDonald
Glover Undercover. G. Blumberg
Glow Job. H. Kane
Glow-Worm Tales. J. Payn
Glowering Gables. L. Churchill
Gloyne Murder. C. Clausen
Glut of Red Herrings. J. Bude
Glut of Virgins. B. Strutton
Glyphs of Gold. P. Edwards
Gnat. L. H. Brooks
Gnome Mine Mystery. P. De Mar
Go Ahead with Murder. M. Halliday
Go Away Death. J. Creasey
Go Away to Murder. J. Creasey
Go Back for Murder. A. Christie
Go-Between. Mrs. C. Kernahan
Go-Between. A. Maling
Go Down Dead. S. Stevens
Go Down, Death. S. B. Hays
Go Find a Shadow. K. Hewitt
Go for Broke. J. Welcome
Go for Garrity. Allan Nixon
Go for the Body. E. Lacy
Go Home, Stranger. C. Williams
Go, Honeylou. T. B. Dewey
Go, Lovely Rose. J. Potts
Go South, Go Crazy. K. Howard
Go to Sleep, Jeannie. T. B. Dewey
Go to Thy Death Bed. S. Forbes
Go with a Jerk. H. Janson
Goat. J. F. Straker
Goat Island. W. Fuller
Gobblecock Mystery. L. Austen-Leigh
Goblin Market. H. McCloy
God Bless America. S. Johnson
God for Tomorrow. M. Dibner
God Keepers. E. R. Johnson
God Machine. M. Caidin
God of the Labyrinth. Colin Wilson
God Save the Child. R. B. Parker
God Save the Mark. D. E. Westlake
God Save the Queen! A. Upward
God-Seeker. John Williams
God Speed the Night. D. S. Davis
God with Four Arms and other stories. H. T. W. Bousfield
Goddess. R. Marsh
Goddess Game. H. Barron
Goddess Gone Bad. C. Brown
Goddess of Terror. A. Gale

Goddesses Never Die. G. B. Mair
Godfather. M. Puzo
Godfather Killer. D. Brennan
Godfather Must Live. T. Halstead
Godkillers. T. Journet
Godmother. R. T. Larkin
Godmother Caper. J. D. Lawrence
Godolphin. E. Bulwer-Lytton
God's Back was Turned. H. Whittington
God's Clay. A. Askew
God's Gift to All Women. T. Rome
Gods in Green. W. D. Roberts
God's Winepress. A. Jenkinson
Godwulf Manuscript. R. B. Parker
Goggle-Box Affair. V. Gielgud
Going, Going, Gone. C. Hale
Going, Going, Gone. P. A. Taylor
Going Public. D. Westheimer
Going to St. Ives. Colver Harris
Going to the Bad. E. Yates
Going West. J. Potter
Golconda Necklace. H. St. J. Cooper
Gold. K. Perkins
Gold and Copper Delamonds. A. Autumn
Gold and Flesh. B. Appel
Gold and Gaiters. C. A. Alington
Gold and Glory. F. A. M. Webster
Gold and Guns on Halfaday Creek. J. B. Hendryx
Gold--and the Mounted. J. B. Hendryx
Gold and Thorns. M. Rittenberg
Gold and Wine. Roy Vickers
Gold at K-BAR-T. W. C. Tuttle
Gold Bag. C. Wells
Gold Bait. W. J. Sheldon
Gold Ballast. E. L. Long
Gold Bomb. K. Laumer
Gold Brick Island. J. J. Connington
Gold Bug. W. B. Hare
Gold Bullets. C. G. Booth
Gold Cat. A. Mills
Gold Coast Nocturne. H. Nielsen
Gold Comes in Bricks. A. A. Fair
Gold Comfit Box. V. Williams
Gold Cup Murder. F. Duke
Gold Digger, and fourteen other short stories. M. Hervey
Gold Door. Ardath Wise
Gold Drain. S. Johnson
Gold Dust Darrell. B. Brentford
Gold Express. J. Budd
Gold for My Girl. J. Blackmore
Gold for Prince Charlie. N. Tranter
Gold for the Bank of England. Ernest H. Robinson
Gold Game. Roy Vickers
Gold Gap. F. Gruber
Gold Girl. J. B. Hendryx
Gold, Gore and Gehenna. G. A. Birmingham
Gold Hijack. C. Eland
Gold-Hunters' Adventures. W. H. Thomes
Gold-Hunter's Adventures Between Melbourne and Ballarat. W. H. Thomes
Gold-Hunters in Europe. W. H. Thomes
Gold in Every Grave. H. L. Nelson
Gold Is King. O. Binns
Gold Is the Color of Blood. J. M. Patterson
Gold Is Where You Find It. J. B. Hendryx
Gold Is Where You Find It. H. C. James
Gold Island. N. West
Gold-Killer. J. Prosper
Gold Maker's Secret. E. C. Derby
Gold-Marked Charm. B. Marchant
Gold of Cathay. G. Wintle
Gold of Gabria. S. C. Mason

Gold of Lubra Rock. Michael Barrett
Gold of Malabar. B. Mather
Gold of Ophir. E. J. Lysaght
Gold of St. Matthew. D. Hart-Davis
Gold of the Gods. A. B. Reeve
Gold of the Sunset. F. Sleath
Gold of Vala. G. V. Morris
Gold Ogre. K. Robeson
Gold Out of China. G. Volk
Gold Pistol. J. Warren
Gold Plated Hearse. J. Hedges
Gold-Plated Sewer. O. Demaris
Gold Poison. P. Trent
Gold Run. D. Bickerton
Gold Skull Murders. F. Packard
Gold Slippers. F. P. Keyes
Gold-Spinner. D. Donovan
Gold Star Detective from Kentucky. Anonymous
Gold Star Line. L. T. Meade
Gold Trap. A. Applin
Gold-Trackers. D. Hart-Davis
Gold Treasure Mystery. J. Laurence
Gold Was Our Grave. Henry Wade
Gold Without Glitter. B. O'Keefe
Gold Worshippers. J. B. Harris-Burland
Golden Alaskan. J. Dorrance
Golden Angel. N. Brent
Golden Angel. M. Corrigan
Golden Ape. H. Adams
Golden Arrow. D. Clarke
Golden Arrow. C. Stoddard
Golden Ashes. F. W. Crofts
Golden Ball. L. Bennet-Thompson
Golden Ball and other stories. A. Christie
Golden Ballast. H. D. Stacpoole
Golden Barrier. A. M. Burrage
Golden Bat. F. M. White
Golden Beast. E. P. Oppenheim
Golden Belts. A. Murray
Golden Boats of Taradata Affair. S. Latter
Golden Bough. G. F. Gibbs
Golden Bowl. A. Joscelyn
Golden Box. F. Crane
Golden Bull. I. Brook
Golden Calf. M. E. Braddon
Golden Carpet. A. M. Williamson
Golden Casket. F. A. Symonds
Golden Cat. H. Long
Golden Cat. D. Newton
Golden Chalice. K. L. Meredith
Golden Clue. B. Wayde
Golden Cockatrice. G. Black
Golden Corn. C. Rodda
Golden Crystal. F. Hird
Golden Dagger. E. R. Punshon
Golden Dart. S. Jepson
Golden Dawns the Sun. E. Messenger
Golden Death. N. Deane
Golden Deed. A. Garve
Golden Door. B. Spicer
Golden Dress. I. Montgomery
Golden Drum. B. Freestone
Golden Dwarf. R. N. Silver
Golden Earnest. A. Bright
Golden Enchantress. M. Clare
Golden-Eyed Venus. M. Dekobra
Golden-Eyes. S. Jepson
Golden Face. W. LeQueux
Golden Face. B. Mitford
Golden Fear. S. Harvester
Golden Fleece. J. Boland
Golden Fleece. J. Hawthorne
Golden Fleece. N. Lofts
Golden Fleece. Ernest Paul
Golden Fluid. M. B. Dix
Golden Fool. D. Divine
Golden Foundling. S. Murray
Golden Frame. J. Chadwick
Golden Frame. M. Wolf
Golden Girl. A. Askew

Golden Girl and All. R. Dennis
Golden Gizmo. J. Thompson
Golden Glory. E. M. Channon
Golden Gloves. J. Ingersol
Golden Goddess. H. E. Hill
Golden Goddess Gambit. L. Maddock
Golden Goose. F. Mahannah
Golden Goose. E. Queen
Golden Goose Murders. A. McRoyd
Golden Guilt. F. Gerard
Golden Hades. E. Wallace
Golden Harvest. H. H. Hill
Golden Helmet. H. Bogue
Golden Hoard. E. Balmer
Golden Hole. J. Blyth
Golden Hooligan. T. B. Dewey
Golden Hooves. S. Grey
Golden Horn. B. Davidson
Golden Horse. A. Kennington
Golden Horseshoe. R. Aitken
Golden Imp. J. H. Chase
Golden Isle. H. H. Hill
Golden Keel. D. Bagley
Golden Key. W. O'Farrell
Golden Kill. M. Olden
Golden Knot. C. Gibbon
Golden Lady. B. Atkey
Golden Land. B. L. Farjeon
Golden Lantern. T. Warriner
Golden Legacy. Old Sleuth
Golden Lives. F. Wicks
Golden Lode. A. Davidson
Golden Lotus. A. W. Barrett
Golden Lotus. G. E. Locke
Golden Lure. C. Leader
Golden Man. F. Lockridge
Golden Milestone. Scott Graham
Golden Milestone. K. Hewitt
Golden Monkey. V. Gunn
Golden Murder. F. Lester
Golden Nightmare. W. Snow
Golden Oriole. P. Traill
Golden Oyster. Donald Gordon
Golden Packet. Angela Gray
Golden Panther. S. Gluck
Golden Pebble. M. Bennett
Golden Peril. K. Robeson
Golden Pheasant Mystery. M. Worth
Golden Pig. F. Du Boisgobey
Golden Plough. P. Merritt
Golden Precipice. H. B. M. Watson
Golden Quest. A. Askew
Golden Rapids of High Life. R. H. Savage
Golden Rat. P. Trent
Golden Reef. J. Pattinson
Golden Rendezvous. Alistair MacLean
Golden Rope. J. W. Brodie-Innes
Golden Rose. F. M. White
Golden Salamander. V. Canning
Golden Scarab. J. Adye
Golden Scarab. P. Goulden
Golden Scarab. B. Moorhouse
Golden Scorpion. S. Rohmer
Golden Sentinals. R. M. Sears
Golden Serpent. N. Carter
Golden Shadow. L. T. Meade
Golden Shroud. H. Arre
Golden Sickle. D. Grubb
Golden Slipper and Other Problems for Violet Strange. A. K. Green
Golden Soak. H. Innes
Golden Spaniard. D. Wheatley
Golden Spiders. R. Stout
Golden Spike. H. Ellson
Golden Spur. J. S. Fletcher
Golden Statuette. J. Pendower
Golden Stone. D. A. G. Pearson
Golden Stranger. Robin Temple
Golden Swan Murder. D. C. Disney
Golden Teddybear. John Marsh
Golden Temptress. H. Hill
Golden Thistle. J. L. Roberts
Golden Thread. T. Gallon

Golden Three. W. LeQueux
Golden Tooth. J. M. Cobban
Golden Torrent. Alan Graham
Golden Trap. H. Pentecost
Golden Tress. F. Du Boisgobey
Golden Triangle. M. Leblanc
Golden Triangle. C. Robertson
Golden Urge. R. Kyle
Golden Valley. D. Winston
Golden Venus Affair. A. MacVicar
Golden Violet. J. Shearing
Golden Virgin. A. Dipper
Golden Virgin. J. Rossiter
Golden Wang-Ho. F. Hume
Golden Web. E. P. Oppenheim
Golden Widow. F. Mahannah
Golden Witch. Gavin Holt
Golden Woman. R. Cullum
Golden Woman. E. Hatch
Golden Years Caper. R. Carson
Goldfinger. I. Fleming
Goldfish Have No Hiding Place. J. H. Chase
Goldfish Murders. W. Mitchell
Goldsmith's Row. Sheila Bishop
Golf Club Murder. O. F. Jerome
Golf-Course Murder. O. F. Jerome
Golf Course Mystery. C. K. Steele
Golf House Murder. H. Adams
Golf Links Mystery. P. Quiroule
Goliath Scheme. W. Arden
Gone to Ground. T. H. White
Gone Tomorrow. F. C. Davis
Good and Evil. W. Reyburn
Good and the Bad. J. Fleming
Good Books. R. Philmore
Good by Stealth. H. Clandon
Good-Bye and Amen. F. Clifford
Good-Bye to Life. David Hume
Good-Bye to Market. R. M. Gilchrist
Good-Bye Tomorrow. Griff
Good Children Don't Kill. L. Thomas
Good Citizens. J. Boland
Good Day to Die. T. Blackburn
Good Day to Die. J. Harrison
Good Day to Die. J. A. Hoffman
Good Evans! E. Wallace
Good Girls Don't Get Murdered. P. S. Parker
Good Knight, Sailor. T. C. H. Jacobs
Good Luck, Sucker. R. Telfair
Good Luck to the Corpse. M. Murray
Good Men and Bad. J. B. Hendryx
Good Men and True. S. Harvester
Good Men Do Nothing. J. Brunner
Good Morning, Mavis. C. Brown
Good-Natured Lady. J. E. Buckrose
Good Neighbor Murder. E. Pierson
Good Night, Irene. J. M. Ullman
Good Night, Ladies. V. Siller
Good Night, Sheriff. H. R. Steeves
Good Old Anna. M. B. Lowndes
Good Old Boys. W. L. Heath
Good Old Charlie. J. Bingham
Good Old Potts! C. N. Boyle
Good One. G. Tabori
Good Place for Murder. C. Mullen
Good Place to Die. B. Copper
Good Place to Die. R. Gaulden
Good Place to Work and Die. W. Van Atta
Good Recovery. A. Wright
Good Ship "Dove." F. Warden
Good Ship Rajah. E. L. Long
Good Thief. R. Rosenblum
Good-Time Girl. M. Richmond
Good Year for Dwarfs? C. Brown

Title Index

Goodbye, Aunt Charlotte! J. F. Straker
Goodbye, Aunt Elva. E. Fenwick
Goodbye, Dear Elizabeth. G. Hoster
Goodbye, Dr. Thorndyke. N. Donaldson
Goodbye, Friend. S. Japrisot
Goodbye Gemini. Jenni Hall
Goodbye, Gillian. Jonathan Burke
Goodbye Gorgeous. Keith Campbell
Goodbye Is Forever. M. Carroll
Goodbye Is Not Worthwhile. W. Mole
Goodbye Look. R. Macdonald
Goodbye, Miss Lizzie Borden. L. De La Torre
Goodbye, Mr. Shaft. E. Tidyman
Goodbye Piccadilly, Farewell Leicester Square. A. La Bern
Goodbye, Shirley. P. Muller
Goodbye, Stranger. D. Heyes
Goodbye, Sweet William. P. Flower
Goodbye to an Old Friend. B. Freemantle
Goodbye to Murder. D. Henderson
Goodey's Last Stand. C. Alverson
Goodnight, Garrity. Allan Nixon
Goose is Cooked. E. Hogarth
Gooseberry Fool. J. McClure
Gorgeous Ghoul. D. V. Babcock
Gorgeous Ghoul Murder Case. D. V. Babcock
Gorgon. J. L. Hamilton
Gorgon's Head. Ladbroke Black
Gorgon's Head. F. Hurd
Gorgonzola, Won't You Please Come Home? C. Ames
Gorilla. R. Spence
Gorilla Moll. B. Sarto
Goring's First Case. P. Kippax
Gory Details. D. Elias
Gory Dew. G. Mitchell
Gory Knight. M. R. Larminie
Gospel of Death. W. Harrington
Gospel of Death. M. Judd
Gossamer Thread. A. Lowing
Gossip to the Grave. Jonathan Burke
Gossip Truth. Jonathan Burke
Gouffe Case. J. Maass
Government Contract. B. Stanley
Government Official. J. H. Riddell
Government Special Detective. Anonymous
Government Spy. Lieut. Carlton
Government Trust. B. Wayde
Government's Man. E. C. Derby
Governor. Alan Thomas
Governor of Chi-Foo. E. Wallace
Governor of Kattowitz. G. Seton
Governors. E. P. Oppenheim
Gown and Shroud. K. Freeman
Gownsman's Gallows. K. Farrer
Grab. J. P. Heggy
Grab. P. Malloch
Grab. Zeno
Grab Operators. J. N. Chance
Grabbers. L. S. Taube
Grace Darling. G. W. M. Reynolds
Grace O'Malley, Princess and Pirate. R. Machray
Grace Walter. T. P. Prest
Gracie Allen Murder Case. S. S. Van Dine
Gracious Lily Affair. V. W. Mason
Graffiti Gambit. A. Wingard
Graft Town. Neill Graham
Grafter. J. Cassells
Grafters. N. Carter
Grafters. F. Lynde
Grammarian's Funeral. E. Acheson
Grand Babylon Hotel. A. Bennett
Grand Catch. G. Buhet
Grand Central Murder. P. MacTyre
Grand Central Murders. S. McGurk
Grand Duke. C. Dawe
Grand Duke's Finances. F. Heller
Grand Graft Hotel. B. Sarto
Grand Guignol. F. C. Witney
Grand Guignol Stories. M. Level

Grand Jury. E. Rose
Grand Man. C. Cookson
Grand Modena Murder. L. Gribble
Grand National Mystery, and other tales. T. S. Denham
Grand Ole Opry Murders. M. Kaye
Grand Prix Murders. D. Rutherford
Grand Street Collector. J. Arleo
Grandmother. M. Masterman
Grandmother Martin is Murdered. J. Courtney
Granduca. M. Brand
Grangerfjord Monks. R. M. Sears
Granite Folly. C. Farr
Granite Shadows. M. Warrick
Grant McKenzie. Old Sleuth
Grantham Mystery. M. Danvers
Grant's Overture. F. N. Millar
Granville Crypt Murders. Melville Burt
Grape From a Thorn. J. Payn
Grape Vine. H. Janson
Grapevine. Jonathan Starr
Graphics. H. M. Lyon
Grasp at Straws. J. Y. Dane
Grasp of the Sultan. Anonymous
Grass Spinster. C. C. Lewis
Grass-Widow's Tale. Ellis Peters
Grasshopper Summer. J. L. Cooper
Grassleyes Mystery. E. P. Oppenheim
Grave Affair. Shelley Smith
Grave Between Them. C. Boutelle
Grave can Wait. H. B. Kaye
Grave Case of Murder. R. Bax
Grave Consequences. M. Cumberland
Grave Danger. F. Kane
Grave Danger. K. Roos
Grave Descend. J. Lange
Grave-Digger of Monks Arden. A. Gask
Grave-Digger's Apprentice. V. M. Grayland
Grave Doubt. I. Baker
Grave for Coyotes. S. D. Frances
Grave for Madam. P. Cagney
Grave for Miss Carling. D. W. F. Hardie
Grave Gives Up. P. MacCormack
Grave Is Waiting. A. MacKenzie
Grave Journey. M. Hebden
Grave Lady Jane. F. Warden
Grave-Maker's House. R. Weber
Grave Matter. L. Vardre
Grave Matters. J. Rhode
Grave Matters. M. Yorke
Grave Must Be Deep. T. Roscoe
Grave of Green Water. J. Roffman
Grave of Heroes. J. Cross
Grave of Sand. D. Graham
Grave Undertaking. Lionel White
Grave Without Grass. D. C. Cameron
Gravedigger's Funeral. A. Arent
Gravel Patch. R. Goyne
Gravelhanger. V. Gielgud
Graven Image. J. D. Fitz
Graven Image. Mrs. C. Kernahan
Grave's Company. S. Nichols
Graves, I Dig! C. Brown
Grave's in the Meadow. M. L. Stokes
Graveswood. S. Lloyd
Graveyard. P. M. Hubbard
Graveyard Never Closes. F. C. Davis
Graveyard Plot. M. Erskine
Graveyard Rolls. M. Procter
Graveyard Shift. Harry Patterson
Graveyard to Let. Carter Dickson
Graveyard Watch. A. D. Divine

Graveyard Watch. J. Esteven
Gravy Train. W. Masterson
Gravy Train Hit. C. Stevens
Gray Amber. Basil Carey
Gray Canaan. D. Garth
Gray Charteris. Robert Simpson
Gray Creatures. Zorro
Gray Dusk. O. R. Cohen
Gray Eyes. S. Friedman
Gray Flannel Shroud. H. Slesar
Gray Gull. H. F. Granger
Gray Magic. Herman Landon
Gray Man Walks. H. Bellamann
Gray Mask. W. Camp
Gray Phantom. Herman Landon
Gray Phantom's Return. Herman Landon
Gray Sage. F. W. Hilton
Gray Stranger. F. Crane
Gray Terror. Herman Landon
Graymists. M. Lynch
Grayson Affair. S. Waldron
Great Abduction. A. S. Roche
Great Abduction Mystery. W. M. Graydon
Great Adams Express Robbery. A. F. Pinkerton
Great Adventure and Out of a Dark Sky. S. Horler
Great Aeroplane Mystery. J. Laurence
Great Affair. V. Canning
Great Air Swindle. J. Creasey
Great Airport Racket. J. Hunter
Great Airways Plot. J. Noy
Great Alone. G. Goodchild
Great Alternative. C. H. Bullivant
Great Amherst Mystery. W. Hubbell
Great Art-Gallery Crime. M. Osborne
Great Autumn Double. P. Trent
Great Awakening. E. P. Oppenheim
Great Bank Mystery. N. Ned
Great Bank Robbery. J. Hawthorne
Great Bank Robbery. Old Sleuth
Great Baruma Mystery. W. P. Brown
Great Bear. E. P. Oppenheim
Great Beckleswaithe Mystery. H. Herman
Great Berwyck Bank Burglary. J. G. Bethune
Great Betrayal. H. Wintle
Great Big Laughing Hannah. W. Rutherford
Great Billy. Old Sleuth
Great Black Kanba. Constance Little
Great Bluff. H. Hill
Great Boy. Old Sleuth
Great Brain Robbery. K. A. Saddler
Great Brighton Mystery. J. S. Fletcher
Great Buxton Mystery. Anonymous
Great Canal Plot. G. H. Teed
Great Capture. Old Sleuth
Great Circus Mystery. E. J. Murray
Great Circus Mystery. N. Ridley
Great Conspiracy. N. Carter
Great Conspiracy. A. Soutar
Great Court Scandal. W. LeQueux
Great Craneboro' Conspiracy. J. Oakley
Great Cronin Mystery. Anonymous
Great Currency Racket. G. Chester
Great Dandelion. J. L. Cooper
Great Day for Dying. J. Dillon
Great Debauch. Williams Forrest
Great Deception. M. K. Douglas
Great "Detectives." T. Mathieson
Great Diamond Bluff. J. W. Bobin
Great Diamond Robbery. S. O'Donnell
Great Diamond Syndicate. N. Carter
Great Dinosaur Robbery. D. Forrest
Great Dollar Fraud. A. Parsons
Great Dumping Mystery. W. Jardine
Great Dust. P. Traill
Great Elk. E. G. Cousins

Great Enigma. N. Carter
Great Explosion. A. Murray
Great Express Robbery. Grace M. White
Great Fear. R. Goyne
Great Feast. H. Wood
Great Flood. Louise Collis
Great Fog and other weird tales. H. F. Heard
Great Game. H. C. Bailey
Great Gay Road. T. Gallon
Great Gift. S. Paternoster
Great God Gold. W. LeQueux
Great Gorme. Colleen Cairus
Great Green Diamond. I. Stark
Great Green God. F. Whishaw
Great Hesper. F. Barrett
Great Hijack. A. Tack
Great Hold-Up Mystery. W. Usher
Great Hotel Murder. V. Starrett
Great House in the Park. A. Burr
Great Hush-Hush Mystery. M. B. Dix
Great Impersonation. E. P. Oppenheim
Great Indian Scout Detective. Old Sleuth
Great Insurance Murders. M. Propper
Great Ivory Swindle. G. H. Teed
Great Jekyll Diamond. J. L. Owen
Great Jewel Mystery. F. Du Boisgobey
Great Journey and other stories. M. E. Braddon
Great K & A Train Robbery. P. L. Ford
Great Ling Plot. W. Martyn
Great London Mystery. S. Gluck
Great London Mystery. C. Kingston
Great Magor Diamond, and the Creaking Door. H. C. McNeile
Great Mail Racket. G. Dilnot
Great Mail Robbery. C. B. Kelland
Great Marl-Pit. G. Ohnet
Great Mill Street Mystery. A. Sergeant
Great Mistake. M. R. Rinehart
Great Mogul. L. Tracy
Great Money Order Swindle. N. Carter
Great Museum Mystery. H. E. Hill
Great Mystery Solved. G. Vase
Great Newmarket Mystery. C. Rae-Brown
Great Opium Case. N. Carter
Great Orme Terror. G. Radcliffe
Great Pearl Secret. C. N. Williamson
Great Pimlico Mystery. K. Kingston
Great Pirate Syndicate. George Griffith
Great Plot. W. LeQueux
Great Porter Square. B. L. Farjeon
Great Portrait Mystery. R. A. Freeman
Great Pretender. J. Deane
Great Prince Shan. E. P. Oppenheim
Great "Push" Experiment. A. Pratt
Great Radio Mystery. C. K. Steele
Great Revenge. S. M. Sitwell
Great Revue Mystery. H. H. C. Gibbons
Great River Mystery. Old Sleuth
Great Ruby. T. W. Hanshew
Great Salvage Swindle. H. H. C. Gibbons
Great Secret. Roland Daniel
Great Secret. H. Nisbet
Great Secret. E. P. Oppenheim
Great Shakes. E. Moodie
Great Shipyard Mystery. J. Ascott
Great Skene Mystery. B. Capes
Great Snake Murder. L. D. Stranger
Great Southern Mystery. G. D. H. Cole
Great Spy Race. A. Diment
Great Stone Heart. M. Farnsworth
Great Stores Crime. W. Edwards
Great Stores Mystery. W. Edwards
Great Syndicate. George Griffith

Great Taxi-Cab Mystery. J. H. Collins
Great Taxi-Cab Ramp. J. G. Brandon
Great Temptation. R. Marsh
Great Temptation. S. Warwick
Great Tontine. H. Smart
Great "Tote" Fraud. J. W. Bobin
Great Train Hijack. W. Masterson
Great Train Robbery. M. Crichton
Great Travers Case. D. M. Merrick
Great Trunk Mystery. R. H. Poole
Great Trunk Tragedy. M. Redwing
Great Tunnel Mystery. A. Blair
Great Turf Fraud. D. J. Belgrave
Great Turf Fraud. A. Blair
Great Turf Fraud, and Other Notorious Crimes. D. Donovan
Great Turf Mystery. C. Frisbie
Great Van Suttart Mystery. G. A. Chamberlain
Great Wash. G. Kersh
Great Waxworks Crime. Gwyn Evans
Great Weather Syndicate. G. Griffith
Great White Army. M. Pemberton
Great Yant Mystery. A. B. Cunningham
Great Year for Dying. B. Copper
Greater Claim. A. Applin
Greater Crime. G. A. England
Greater Punishment. S. Chalmers
Greatest Fool. G. Hackforth-Jones
Greatest Game. C. L. Reid
Greatest Gift. A. W. Marchmont
Gredos Reckoning. C. Rougvie
Greed. M. Leighton
Greedy Fingers. T. Roan
Greedy Killers. E. Radford
Greedy Ones. V. Kelly
Greek Affair. F. Gruber
Greek Coffin Mystery. E. Queen
Greek Fire. Winston Graham
Greek God Affair. R. Deming
Greek Tragedy. G. D. H. Cole
Greek Virgin. J. Stark
Greek Wedding. J. A. Hodge
Green Ace. S. Palmer
Green Archer. Margery Lawrence
Green Archer. E. Wallace
Green Arrow. B. Bolt
Green Bag. A. Leaman
Green Bag. J. P. Seabrooke
Green Blot. S. Gluck
Green Bondage. F. Ogilvie
Green Bough. Margery Lawrence
Green Bracken. D. Lee
Green Bungalow. F. M. White
Green Cat. S. Guise
Green Circle. Mark Cross
Green Circle. C. Massie
Green Cloak. Y. Davis
Green Complex. H. MacGrath
Green Coral. H. D. Stacpoole
Green Cross. A. R. Weekes
Green Curtain. M. E. Braddon
Green Death. Elaine Hamilton
Green Death. K. Robeson
Green Death and other stories. B. Hutton
Green December Fills the Graveyard. M. Sarsfield
Green Diamond. Arthur Morrison
Green Diamond Mystery. F. Grierson
Green Diamonds. C. Robertson
Green Domino. K. Lindsay
Green Dragon. J. J. Farjeon
Green Eagle. K. Robeson
Green Eagle Score. R. Stark
Green Evil. F. Grierson
Green Eye of Death. J. Sandys
Green Eye of Goona. Arthur Morrison
Green-Eyed Monster. G. Bronson-Howard
Green-Eyed Monster. P. Quentin
Green Eyes. E. S. Brooks
Green Eyes Are Dangerous. E. L. MacKeag

Green Eyes of Bast. S. Rohmer
Green Fields of Eden. F. Clifford
Green Fire. A. Maybury
Green Flag and other stories of war and sport. A. C. Doyle
Green Flames of Aries. R. Lory
Green Flash and other tales of horror, suspense and fantasy. Joan Aiken
Green for a Grave. M. L. Stokes
Green for a Season. P. H. Irving
Green for Danger. C. Brand
Green for Danger. Gavin Holt
Green Gene. P. Kickinson
Green Ghost. Stuart Martin
Green Ghost. J. Reach
Green Ghost Murder. J. Ronald
Green Glare Murders. R. Wallace
Green Glove. J. L. Linklater
Green God. F. A. Kummer
Green Goddess. P. Edwards
Green Gold. Frank King
Green Goods Speculator. D. Stewart
Green Grass. M. Kenyon
Green Grassy Slopes. W. A. Ballinger
Green Grow the Graves. M. E. Chaber
Green Grow the Tresses-O. S. Hyland
Green Hazard. M. Coles
Green Hell Rampage. Dan Morgan
Green Hell Treasure. R. L. Fish
Green Ice. R. Whitfield
Green Ice Murders. R. Whitfield
Green Ink. J. S. Fletcher
Green Jacket. Jennette Lee
Green Jade Buddha. J. Gibbons
Green Jade God. Roland Daniel
Green Jade Hand. H. S. Keeler
Green Jade Necklace. J. H. Chase
Green Killer. C. Dawe
Green Killer. K. Robeson
Green Knife. A. Wynne
Green Knight. W. M. Duncan
Green Lane. Alec Brown
Green Lantern. B. Bolt
Green Lantern. Augustus Muir
Green Light. L. Landon
Green Light. R. St. Clair
Green Light for Death. F. Kane
Green Light, Red Catch. F. Ryck
Green Lipstick. G. C. Foster
Green Mandarin Mystery. G. Galcom
Green Mask. A. Skene
Green Mask. G. Verner
Green Mountain Murders. C. Culley
Green Mummy. F. Hume
Green Opal. H. C. James
Green Oranges. R. Masson
Green Orb. C. Massie
Green Orchard. A. Soutar
Green Overcoat. H. Belloc
Green Pack. Robert (G.) Curtis
Green Pack. E. Wallace
Green Parrot. B. Capes
Green Phantom. G. Meyrick
"Green Phantom." W. Spence
Green Plaid Pants. M. Scherf
Green Plush. J. E. Middleton
Green Ray. W. LeQueux
Green Ray. D. T. Lindsay
Green Ray. V. Thompson
Green Ribbon. E. Wallace
Green Room Crime. G. Chester
Green Rope. J. S. Fletcher
Green Rust. E. Wallace
Green Sandals. C. C. Lowis
Green Scarf. P. Fry
Green Scorpion. H. Hawton
Green Seal. C. E. Walk
Green Shade. H. Hill

Title Index

Green Shadow. J. E. Grant
Green Shadow. Herman Landon
Green Shadows. L. V. Stevens
Green Ship. G. Volk
Green Shiver. C. B. Clason
Green Silence. M. Hastings
Green Stone. S. Blanc
Green Stone. H. MacGrath
Green Stones of Evil. M. Peterson
Green Suns. Henry Ward
Green Swallows. F. Sleath
Green Tablets. B. Goldie
Green Tabloids. B. Goldie
Green Talons. Gavin Holt
Green Thermos. G. Simenon
Green to Pagan Street. J. T. Story
Green Toad. W. S. Masterman
Green Tree Mystery. R. Doubleday
Green Triangle. W. M. Duncan
Green Triangle Mystery. H. Pink
Green Tunnel. C. C. Lowis
Green Turban. W. M. Graydon
Green Turbans. J. M. Cobban
Green Windmill. I. Mercer
Green Wood. J. Phillips
Green Wood Burns Slow. M. Brice
Green Wound. P. Atlee
Green Wound Contract. P. Atlee
Green Wounds. P. P. Muir
Greene Murder Case. S. S. Van Dine
Greenface. Frank King
Greenfield Mystery. G. F. Worts
Greenhouse. A. Lamb
Greenmantle. J. Buchan
Greenmask. J. J. Farjeon
Greenmask. E. Linington
Greensea Island. V. Bridges
Greenstone Door. W. Satchell
Greenwell Mystery. E. C. R. Lorac
Greenwell's Glory Case. H. G. Hutchinson
Greenwood. F. Swann
Grell Mystery. F. Froest
Gremlin's Grampa. R. L. Pike
Grenfell Legacy. M. McEvoy
Grenson Murder Case. T. C. H. Jacobs
Gretna Green. H. M. Jones
Gretna Green. G. W. M. Reynolds
Grey Affair. J. Weeks
Grey Beast. J. Atholl
Grey Cat. J. B. Harris-Burland
Grey Doctor. F. Hume
Grey Domino. P. C. De Crespigny
Grey Face. J. Cassells
Grey Face. S. Rohmer
Grey Fair. M. Gerard
Grey Fish. W. V. Cook
Grey Gables. G. E. Locke
Grey Ghost. J. Cassells
Grey Man. M. Urquhart
Grey Mask. P. Wentworth
Grey Mask Gang. J. A. Jordan
Grey Mask Murders. Hugh C. McDonald
Grey Messengers. M. Storm
Grey Mist Murders. Constance Little
Grey Monk. T. W. Speight
Grey Moth. F. Warden
Grey Phantom's Triumph. Herman Landon
Grey Rat. O. Binns
Grey Room. E. Phillpotts
Grey Shadow. G. E. Rochester
Grey Shapes. Jack Mann
Grey Shepherds. A. MacVicar
Grey Sisters. M. D. Anderson
Grey Sombrero. P. Fry
Grey Studio. A. Scudder
Grey Timothy. E. Wallace
Grey Wolf's Daughter. G. Warden
Grey Woman. F. M. White
Greybreek. A. MacVicar

Greygallows. B. Michaels
Greyhound Murder Mystery. W. D. Maydwell
Greyhound Stadium Plot. E. T. Woodhall
Greymarsh. A. J. Rees
Greyslaer. Anonymous
Greystone Tavern. L. Bronte
Greystones. A. Lamb
Greystones. H. Leigh
Greyvale School Mystery. P. Manton
Grid Murder. E. Snell
Grierson Mystery. L. Osbourne
Grieve for the Past. S. Forbes
Grif. B. L. Farjeon
Griff. R. Weverka
Griffin Towers. J. Winslow
Griffith Case. J. Bentley
Grifters. J. Thompson
Grim Caretaker. E. Ascher
Grim Chancery. W. Mills
Grim Death. G. Verner
Grim Death and the Barrow Boys. J. Fleming
Grim Game. S. Horler
Grim Grow the Lilacs. M. Randolph
Grim Inheritance. H. Leyford
Grim Joker. G. Verner
Grim Justice. Rita
Grim Maiden. B. Flynn
Grim Rehearsal. R. Fenisong
Grim Smile of the Five Towns. A. Bennett
Grim Souvenir. J. Rowland
Grim Tales. E. Nesbit
Grim Tomorrow. M. Richmond
Grim Vengeance. J. J. Connington
Grimm Death. D. F. Brown
Grin and Dare It. R. Drayton
Grinder's Wheel. Morley Roberts
Grindle Nightmare. Q. Patrick
Grinning Avenger. E. Jepson
Grinning Ghoul. L. Churchill
Grinning Gismo. S. W. Taylor
Grinning Pig. N. Lombard
Grip Finds the Lady. J. Dory
Grip of Fear. S. H. Burchell
Grip of Fear. I. Lambot
Grip of Fear. M. Level
Grip of Sin. A. Askew
Grip of the Bookmaker. Percy White
Grip of the Four. Mark Cross
Grip of the Law. J. W. Bobin
Grip of the Strangler. J. C. Cooper
Grip of the Wolf. M. Gerard
Gripped by Drought. A. W. Upfield
Gristmill. G. S. Caldwell
Groaning Spinney. G. Mitchell
Groom Lay Dead. G. H. Coxe
Groote Park Murder. F. W. Crofts
Groovy Way to Die. R. Deming
Grossbeak Mansion. N. Buntline
Grosvenor Square Goodbye. F. Clifford
Grotto of Tiberius. F. E. Smith
Ground for Suspicion. M. Burton
Grounds for Indecency. M. H. Gropper
Grounds for Murder. J. Appleby
Grounds for Murder. T. D. Carroll
Grounds for Murder. V. Van Urk
Group Flashing Two. D. Howarth
Grouse Moor Murder. J. Ferguson
Grouse Moor Mystery. J. Ferguson
Grouser Investigates. E. S. Brooks
Grove of Doom. W. B. Gibson
Grow Cold Along with Me. M. Lynch
Grow Grey with Fear. N. Thurley
Grow Young and Die. W. O'Farrell
Growing Evil. E. Messenger
Grubstake Gold. J. B. Hendryx
Grudge. B. Hitchens
Grudge Mountain. A. P. Terhune
Grue of Ice. G. Jenkins
Guard the Girl. R. Cifford
Guarded Room. J. S. Fletcher
Guarded Soul. A. Dare

Guarded Woman. C. Cannell
Guardian. C. Dilke
Guardian. J. Hough
Guardian Angel in the Underworld. J. Wall
Guardian of the Cup. C. Cannell
Guardian of Willow House. D. Daniels
Guardians. W. H. Baker
Guardians. S. Brackeen
Guardians. R. Parkes
Guardian's Mystery. C. Faber
Guardians of the Treasure. H. C. McNeile
Guerrilla Girls. H. Whittington
Guess Who's Coming to Kill You? E. Queen
Guest in the House. P. MacDonald
Guest with the Scythe. Gret Lane
Guests of Chance. J. L. Rickard
Guile. H. Hill
Guile Wears a Coronet. G. Vaizey
Guilt. H. J. Forman
Guilt Edged. W. J. Burley
Guilt Edged. J. B. O'Sullivan
Guilt Edged. L. Thayer
Guilt-Edged Cage. C. Brown
Guilt-Edged Frame. F. Kane
Guilt-Edged Murder. L. Thayer
Guilt for Innocence. C. Franklin
Guilt Is Plain. D. Frome
Guilt Is Where You Find It. L. Thayer
Guilt Merchants. R. Harwood
Guilt of Innocence. M. Halliday
Guilt Without Proof. P. Alding
Guilty? J. W. Arctander
Guilty! L. Thayer
Guilty! D. Walshe
Guilty Accuser. A. Livingston
Guilty Are Afraid. J. H. Chase
Guilty as Hell. B. Halliday
Guilty Be Damned. G. J. Barrett
Guilty Bonds. W. LeQueux
Guilty, But--. S. Kyle
Guilty, But Insane. D. Stuart
Guilty But Not Insane. J. C. Lenehan
Guilty Bystander. Mike Brett
Guilty Bystander. Wade Miller
Guilty Gold. H. Hill
Guilty Governor. N. Carter
Guilty Hands. J. A. Jordan
Guilty House. F. Hume
Guilty House. C. Kingston
Guilty Man. F. Coppee
Guilty, My Lord. M. Peterson
Guilty, My Lord. I. Stefan
Guilty Ones. D. Telfer
Guilty or Innocent? M. Leighton
Guilty or Not Guilty? M. M. Bodkin
Guilty, or Not Guilty? W. G. Hamley
Guilty or Not Guilty? N. Ridley
Guilty or Not Guilty. G. Smythies
Guilty or Not Guilty. M. V. Victor
Guilty Party. John Burke
Guilty Party. R. Dolphin
Guilty Party. T. Herd
Guilty River. W. Collins
Guilty Silence. S. Warwick
Guilty Thing Surprised. R. Rendell
Guilty Witness. M. Hershman
Guilty You Must Be. C. Franklin
Guinea Pigs. L. Vaculik
Guinea Pig's Tail. F. Hope
Guinguette by the Seine. G. Simenon
Gulf Coast Girl. C. Williams
Gull Cove Murders. E. Colter
Gull Yard. Margaret Archer
Gulls Fly Low. V. Bridges

G

Gull's Kiss. P. Graaf
Gumshoe. N. Smith
Gun. M. T. Kaufman
Gun and Mr. Smith. J. Godey
Gun Before Butter. N. Freeling
Gun-Brand. J. B. Hendryx
Gun Business. G. Dickson
Gun Business. V. B. Miller
Gun Cotton. Rupert Grayson
Gun Cotton--Ace High. Rupert Grayson
Gun Cotton--Adventure Nine. Rupert Grayson
Gun Cotton--Adventurer. Rupert Grayson
Gun Cotton at Blind Man's Hood. Rupert Grayson
Gun Cotton Goes to Russia. Rupert Grayson
Gun Cotton in Hollywood. Rupert Grayson
Gun Cotton in Mexico. Rupert Grayson
Gun Cotton--Murder at the Bank. Rupert Grayson
Gun Cotton--Outside the Law. Rupert Grayson
Gun Cotton, Secret Agent. Rupert Grayson
Gun Cotton--Secret Airman. Rupert Grayson
Gun-Crasher. W. L. Rohde
Gun Feud. W. C. Tuttle
Gun Fever. E. Ellison
Gun for a God. N. Morland
Gun for Company. A. Bocca
Gun for Honey. G. G. Fickling
Gun for Inspector West. J. Creasey
Gun for Sale. G. Greene
Gun for Sale. D. Spade
Gun Fury. J. K. Baxter
Gun Garden. P. Stanton
Gun in Daniel Webster's Bust. M. Scherf
Gun in His Hand. V. Rosen
Gun in My Back. B. Edmunds
Gun Moll for Hire. H. Janson
Gun Rule. P. Urquhart
Gun-Runner. B. Mitford
Gunn-Runner. A. Stringer
Gun Runners. J. Crosbie
Gun to Play With. J. F. Straker
Gunboat Mystery. J. G. Brandon
Gunboat Mystery. J. A. Jordan
Gungu Sahib. T. Mundy
Gunman. C. F. Coe
Gunman at Large. George Douglas
Gunman of Gozo. H. C. Davis
Gunman's Bluff. E. Wallace
Gunman's Holiday. M. Knight
Gunmen, Gallants, and Ghosts. D. Wheatley
Gunner. E. Wallace
Gunners. G. H. Teed
Gunner's Island. A. Glanville
Gunning in England. W. J. Elliott
Gunpowder Alley. J. Rowland
Gunpowder Treason and Plot. Moira Field
Gunrunners. J. Murphy
Guns and Saddles. E. Ellison
Guns Covered with Flowers. S. Jackman
Guns for Achin. M. Leinster
Guns in the Desert. B. Netton
Guns of Calliope. N. W. Firth
Guns of Darkness. F. Clifford
Guns of Mazatlan. L. Parker
Guns of Navarone. Alistair MacLean
Guns of the Gods. T. Mundy
Guns over the Border. S. Brydon
Gunshot Grand Prix. D. Rutherford
Gunsmoke Haze. R. Wilkes-Hunter
Gunsmoke in Her Eyes. H. Janson
Gunston Cotton. Rupert Grayson
Gup Bahadur. T. Mundy
Gusher. J. Boland
Gutenberg Murders. G. Bristow
Gutter Gang. Jay De Bekker
Gutter Tragedies. S. Paternoster
Guttersnipe. G. Kersh
Guv'nor. E. Wallace
Guv'nor and other stories. E. Wallace

Guy Deverell. J. S. Le Fanu
Guy Fawkes Murder. E. C. Lester
Guy Garrick. A. B. Reeve
Guy Gets His. J. Cello
Guy Must Live. J. Dark
Gwendoline's Harvest. J. Payn
Gwenyth. R. Carol
Gwythyn Clay Mystery. M. Poole
Gyfford of Weare. J. Farnol
Gypsies and the Detectives. A. Pinkerton
Gypsum Flower. P. Bair
Gypsy Detective. Anonymous
Gypsy Detective. Old Sleuth
Gypsy, Go Home. W. O'Farrell
Gypsy Grove. M. K. Simmons
Gypsy in Amber. Martin Smith
Gypsy's Curse. R. Carol
Gypsy's Luck. J. Fairfax-Blakeborough
Gypsy's Warning. G. Kent
Gyrth Chalice Mystery. M. Allingham

H

H as in Hangman. L. Treat
H as in Hunted. L. Treat
H.M.S. Anonymous. Taffrail
Ha-Ha Case. J. J. Connington
Habeas Corpus and other stories. P. Green
Habits of Command. J. Rosner
Hacienda on the Hill. R. H. Savage
Hacienda Triste. F. Swann
Had. R. Gehman
Had I But Groaned. C. Brown
"Hades Belle." C. McManus
Hades Hello. W. Wright
Hadfield Mystery. M. E. Cooke
Haelstrom Manor. S. J. Treibich
Hagar. E. Southworth
Hagar, Called Hannah. A. Soutar
Hagar of the Pawn-Shop. F. Hume
Hagar's Castle. C. Matthews
Haggard's Cove. M. K. Simmons
Hag's Nook. J. D. Carr
Haight Is the Killer. J. K. Lucas
Hail, Hail, the Gang's All Here! E. McBain
Hail McLean! G. Goodchild
Hail to the Chief. E. McBain
Hail, Victor, Hail! Michael Kent
Hailey Street Murder. W. Jardine
Hair Divides. C. Houghton
Hair of the Dog. Jean Leslie
Hair of the Dog. D. Whitelaw
Hairpin Mystery. J. M. Walsh
Hair's Breadth. L. Thayer
Hairy Arm. E. Wallace
Haitian Legacy. S. Wagner
Haitian Vendetta. Don Smith
Haldane Station. F. E. Randall
Half a Bag of Stringer. P. McCutchan
Half a Chance. F. S. Isham
Half a Clew. R. H. Watkins
Half a Clue. J. R. Warren
Half a Corpse. R. Millar
Half a Million Insurance. H. W. Vrooman
Half Ace. J. M. Walsh
Half Angel. B. Jefferis
Half Brothers. E. P. Frankland
Half-Caste. A. Murray
Half Devil, Half Tiger. R. J. Fletcher
Half-Haunted Saloon. R. Shattuck
Half Hours of a Blind Man's Holiday. W. W. Fenn
Half Hunter. J. Sherwood
Half Interest in Murder. J. Creighton

Half Mast. P. Traill
Half-Mast for the Deemster. G. Bellairs
Half-Mast Murder. M. Kennedy
Half Moon Street. J. J. Lydecker
Half-Open Door. B. Gray
Half-Past Mortem. J. A. Saxon
Half-Sister's Secret. F. Du Boisgobey
Half-Smart Set. F. Warden
Half-Way to Murder. S. Troy
Halford's Adventure. H. Bindloss
Halfway House. E. Queen
Halfway to Hell. H. Whittington
Halfway to Horror. David Hume
Halfway to Paradise. Laurence Kirk
Hall of Death. N. Tyre
Hallam Moor Mystery. C. H. Barker
Hallelujah Corner. J. Harris
Hallowe'en Homicide. L. Thayer
Halloween Murder. D. M. Disney
Halloween Murders. J. N. Chance
Hallowe'en Party. A. Christie
Hallowmass Abbey. Winifred Graham
Halo for Nobody. H. Kane
Halo for Satan. John Evans
Halo in Blood. John Evans
Halo in Brass. John Evans
Halves, a Novel. J. Payn
Hamlet Problem. B. Jones
Hamlet, Revenge! M. Innes
Hammer in His Hand. W. Masterson
Hammer Island. S. Styles
Hammer Me Home. R. R. Werry
Hammer of Doom. F. Everton
Hammer of God. C. H. Bullivant
Hammer of God. N. De Mille
Hammer of Justice. S. Milne
Hammer of Thor. C. Brown
Hammer the Toff. J. Creasey
Hammerhead. D. Cory
Hammerhead. J. Mayo
Hammerhead Reef. K. Conway
Hammers of Fingal. A. MacVicar
Hammers of Hate. G. Thorne
Hammersmith Maggot. W. Mole
Hammersmith Murders. D. Frome
Hammett. J. Gores
Hammett Homicides. D. Hammett
Hampstead Mystery. F. Marryat
Hampstead Mystery. J. R. Watson
Hampton Mystery. Mrs. H. Lewis
Hamydal, the Vagabond Philosopher. M. Dekobra
Hand. J. Farrington
Hand. T. F. W. Hickey
Hand and Land. George Long
Hand and Ring. A. K. Green
Hand in Glove. M. G. Eberhart
Hand in Glove. N. Marsh
Hand in Murder. C. Dixon
Hand in Red. I. Stark
Hand in the Dark. A. J. Rees
Hand in the Game. G. Hunting
Hand in the Glove. R. Stout
Hand Me a Crime. C. M. Russell
Hand of a Killer. M. Seuffert
Hand of Allah. W. LeQueux
Hand of Doom. J. M. Walsh
Hand of Fear. G. Verner
Hand of Fu-Manchu. S. Rohmer
Hand of Horror. O. F. Jerome
Hand of Justice. F. Duncan
Hand of Mary Constable. P. Gallico
Hand of Peril. A. Stringer
Hand of Power. E. Wallace
Hand of Seeta. J. G. Brandon
Hand of Solange. M. Rippon
Hand of the Chimpanzee. R. Hare
Hand of the Four. Mark Cross
Hand of the Imposter. P. Minton

Title Index

Hand of the Mafia. J. Baynes
Hand of the Spoiler. S. Paternoster
Hand of the Unseen. M. Leighton
Hand of the Waverleys. B. Goldie
Hand of Vengeance. H. Desmond
Hand of Vengeance. G. H. Teed
Hand of Vengeance. G. F. Underhill
Hand on the Alibi. J. Bude
Hand on the Cobbler's Safe. S. Bailey
Hand on the Web. R. E. Salwey
Hand on the Window Sill. B. Wayde
Hand Out. J. Rathbone
Hand-Picked for Murder. Robert Martin
Hand-Picked to Die. R. Deming
Hand-Print Mystery. S. Fowler
Hand That Hid in Darkness. W. M. Graydon
Hand That Won. N. Carter
Hand to Hand. N. Carter
Hand Without Mercy. J. Sandys
Handcuff Wizard. N. Carter
Handful of Dominoes. J. L. Johnson
Handful of Murder. F. Findley
Handful of Silver. V. Canning
Handful of Silver. J. S. Strange
Handful of Sinners. C. Franklin
Handful of Stars. E. V. Zukas
Handkerchief Clue. H. Rockwood
Handle. R. Stark
Handle of Sin. E. Metcalfe
Handle with Care. H. Luger
Handle with Fear. T. B. Dewey
Hands in the Dark. M. Grant
Hands in the Darkness. A. Golsworthy
Hands of Cain. Martin Thomas
Hands of Clay. E. R. Beach
Hands of Death. A. Colin
Hands of Death. Eric Wood
Hands of Innocence. J. Ashford
Hands of Justice. B. Flynn
Hands of Justice. F. W. Robinson
Hands of Orlac. M. Renard
Hands of Terror. J. Crecy
Hands of the Shadow. S. Truss
Hands Off Bulldog Drummond. G. Fairlie
Hands Unseen. Herman Landon
Hands Up! J. G. Bethune
Hands Without Healing. P. Conway
Handsome, But Dead. A. H. Wahl
Handsome Phil, and other stories. J. H. Riddell
Handwriting on the Wall. D. Fox
Handwriting on the Wall. M. Propper
Handy Death. R. L. Fish
Hang by Your Neck. H. Kane
Hang Dead Hawaiian Style. P. Morgan
Hang the Hangman. M. L. Stokes
Hang the Little Man. J. Creasey
Hang the Man High. G. Household
Hang-Up. Sam Ross
Hang-Up Kid. C. Brown
Hanged by a Thread. D. Haddow
"Hanged by the Neck." F. G. Layton
Hanged for a Sheep. R. Gatenby
Hanged for a Sheep. F. Lockridge
Hanged I'll Be! R. Goyne
Hanged Man's House. E. Ferrars
Hanging. L. Halegua
Hanging Captain. Henry Wade
Hanging Heiress. R. Wormser
Hanging Judge. Gwyn Evans
Hanging Judge. B. Hamilton
Hanging Matter. M. H. Bradley
Hanging of Constance Hillier. S. Fowler
Hanging Rope. Martin Kent
Hanging Sword! A. Soutar

Hanging Waters. K. West
Hanging Woman. J. Rhode
Hanging Woman. J. Roffman
Hanging's Too Good. J. Ronald
Hanging's Too Good. L. Thayer
Hangman. G. Verner
Hangman Never Waits. M. Dekobra
Hangman Waits. Roland Daniel
Hangman Waits. H. Desmond
Hangman's Child. A. Wood
Hangman's Choice. C. Knight
Hangman's Curfew. G. Mitchell
Hangman's Daughter. W. Tyrer
Hangman's Dozen. David Alexander
Hangman's Guests. Stuart Martin
Hangman's Hands. C. Wogan
Hangman's Handyman. Hake Talbot
Hangman's Harvest. M. E. Chaber
Hangman's Hat. P. Ernst
Hangman's Hill. F. Pell
Hangman's Holiday. D. L. Sayers
Hangman's Honeymoon. C. H. Barker
Hangman's Knot. A. Gask
Hangman's Moon. L. Gribble
Hangman's Noose. G. Batson
Hangman's Noose. D. D. Green
Hangman's Tale. G. Griffith
Hangman's Tide. J. B. Hilton
Hangman's Tie. C. Hale
Hangman's Tree. D. C. Disney
Hangman's Whip. M. G. Eberhart
Hangover House. S. Rohmer
Hangover Murders. A. Hobhouse
Hangover Square. P. Hamilton
Hangsaman. S. Jackson
Hank of Hair. C. Jay
Hank Tries the Sidewalk. Griff
Hannah Massey. C. Cookson
Hannah Says Foul Play. D. V. Babcock
Hanno's Doll. E. Piper
Hanoi. N. Carter
Happening. E. Curry
Happy Alienist. W. Smith
Happy Anniversary, Harrison High. J. Farris
Happy Deathday. P. D. Westbrook
Happy Exile. F. M. White
Happy Harvest. J. Farnol
Happy Highwayman. L. Charteris
Happy Holiday! T. O'Finn
Happy Killers. K. Robeson
Happy Murderers. V. Bridges
Happy New Year, Herbie and other stories. E. Hunter
Happy Nightmare. P. Buranelli
Happy Now I Go. T. Charles
Happy Returns. F. Gaite
Happy Thieves. R. Condon
Harassed Hero. E. Dudley
Harbor of the Little Boats. W. E. Huntsberry
Harbour. P. MacDonald
Harbour of Refuge. F. M. White
Hard and Fast. U. S. Andersen
Hard Kill. L. Grex
Hard Knot. C. Gibbon
Hard Lines. H. Smart
Hard Liver. A. Weymouth
Hard Luck. A. W. A'Beckett
Hard Man. L. Katcher
Hard Man. W. J. White
Hard Man to Kill. Ritchie Perry
Hard Option. G. Moffat
Hard Pressed. F. M. White
Hard Rock Man. J. B. Hendryx
Hard Sell. W. Haggard
Hard to Get. A. S. Roche
Hard to Handle. J. Welcome
Hard to Kill. J. Marcott
Hard Trip. A. Dipper
Harden's Escape. H. Bindloss
Harder Than Steel. G. Thorne

Harder They Fall. A. Bocca
Hardican's Hollow. J. S. Fletcher
Hardiman's Landing. P. Malloch
Harding Mystery. A. J. Alderson
Harding Scandal. F. Barrett
Hardliners. W. Haggard
Hardly a Man is Now Alive. H. Brean
Hardly a Man is Now Alive. J. Ridgway
Hardman. D. Karp
Hardship Our Garment. L. Wood
Hardway Diamonds Mystery. M. Burton
Hare in March. V. Packer
Hare Sitting Up. M. Innes
Harem. L. Royer
Harem Mystery. A. Parsons
Hark, Hark, the Watchdogs Bark. T. Wells
Harlem Hit. R. Mallory
Harlem Is My Heaven. I. Gordon
Harlem Showdown. M. Barry
Harlem Underground. E. Lacy
Harlequin. M. L. West
Harlequin House. L. Hayes
Harlequin of Death. S. Horler
Harlequin of Doom. J. Sandys
Harlequin Opal. F. Hume
Harley Greenoak's Charge. B. Mitford
Harlingham Case. F. Warden
Harlot's Daughter. P. Hastings
Harlot's House. E. G. Cousins
Harm in Trying. M. Dedina
Harm Intended. R. Parker
Harmattan. T. Klop
Harmony in Autumn. K. Hewitt
Harne Grange Mystery. Colin Hope
Harness Bull. L. T. White
Harness of Death. W. S. Sykes
Harp of Life. F. H. Rose
Harper. Ross Macdonald
Harpinger's Hunch. H. Carstairs
Harpoon. F. Ponthier
Harpoon of Death. W. O'Farrell
Harriet. Elizabeth Jenkins
Harriet Farewell. M. Erskine
Harringay's Last Gamble. O. Williams
Harrington Street Mystery. W. P. Kelly
Harris in Wonderland. P. Reid
Harrison Keith and the Phantom Heiress. N. Carter
Harrison Keith at Bay. N. Carter
Harrison Keith, Magician. N. Carter
Harrison Keith, Sleuth. N. Carter
Harrison Keith--Star Reporter. N. Carter
Harrison Keith's Abduction Tangle. N. Carter
Harrison Keith's Battle of Nerve. N. Carter
Harrison Keith's Big Stakes. N. Carter
Harrison Keith's Cameo Case. N. Carter
Harrison Keith's Chance Clue. N. Carter
Harrison Keith's Chance Shot. N. Carter
Harrison Keith's Close Quarters. N. Carter
Harrison Keith's Crooked Trail. N. Carter
Harrison Keith's Cyclone Clue. N. Carter
Harrison Keith's Danger. N. Carter
Harrison Keith's Death Compact. N. Carter
Harrison Keith's Death Watch. N. Carter
Harrison Keith's Diamond Case. N. Carter
Harrison Keith's Dilemma. N. Carter
Harrison Keith's Double Cross. N. Carter
Harrison Keith's Double Mystery. N. Carter
Harrison Keith's Drag Net. N. Carter
Harrison Keith's Dual Role. N. Carter
Harrison Keith's Fight for Life. N. Carter
Harrison Keith's Greatest Task. N. Carter
Harrison Keith's Green Diamond. N. Carter

Harrison Keith's Haunted Client. N. Carter
Harrison Keith's Labyrinth. N. Carter
Harrison Keith's Lucky Strike. N. Carter
Harrison Keith's Mummy Mystery. N. Carter
Harrison Keith's Mystic Letter. N. Carter
Harrison Keith's Oath. N. Carter
Harrison Keith's Padlock Mystery. N. Carter
Harrison Keith's Perilous Contact. N. Carter
Harrison Keith's Poison Problem. N. Carter
Harrison Keith's Queer Clue. N. Carter
Harrison Keith's River Front Ruse. N. Carter
Harrison Keith's River Mystery. N. Carter
Harrison Keith's Sparkling Trail. N. Carter
Harrison Keith's Strange Summons. N. Carter
Harrison Keith's Struggle. N. Carter
Harrison Keith's Studio Crime. N. Carter
Harrison Keith's Tact. N. Carter
Harrison Keith's Time Lock Case. N. Carter
Harrison Keith's Triple Tragedy. N. Carter
Harrison Keith's Triumph. N. Carter
Harrison Keith's Wager. N. Carter
Harrison Keith's Warning. N. Carter
Harrison Keith's Weird Partner. N. Carter
Harrison Keith's Wireless Message. N. Carter
Harry Ambler. S. Marlow
Harry Ambler and How He Saved the Homestead. S. Marlow
Harry and the Bikini Bandits. B. Heatter
Harry Blount, the Detective. T. J. Flanagan
Harry Hogbin. D. W. MacArthur
Harry-O. L. Hays
Harry Pinkurten, the King of Detectives. H. Rockwood
Harry Sharpe, the New York Detective. H. Rockwood
Harry Williams, the New York Detective. F. L. Broughton
Harry's Game. G. Seymour
Harsh Evidence. R. Sheldon
Harsh Heritage. N. Tranter
Hart Hit. J. Wainwright
Hartinger's Mouse. P. McCutchan
Hartington's Luck. D. Walshe
Hartland Case. J. Bentley
Hartness Millions. G. Norsworth
Hartwell Case. R. L. Goldman
Harvest for Harpies. H. Luger
Harvard has a Homicide. T. Fuller
Harvest Home. T. P. Prest
Harvest Moon. J. S. Fletcher
Harvest Murder. J. Rhode
Harvest of Deceit. K. Lindsay
Harvest of Guilt. S. Warwick
Harvest of Hate. R. Goyne
Harvest of Hate. H. Leyford
Harvest of Javelins. B. Atkey
Harvest of Love. C. R. Gull
Harvest of Sin. M. Leighton
Harvest of Tares. M. Dalton
Harvest of Terror. A. Gale
Harvest of Violence. S. Brydon
Harvey Garrard's Crime. E. P. Oppenheim
Has Anyone Seen Jean? W. B. Hare
Hash. N. Fleming
Hashish. T. King
Hashknife of Stormy River. W. C. Tuttle
Hashknife of the Canyon Trail. W. C. Tuttle
Hashknife of the Double Bar 8. W. C. Tuttle
Hasty Heiress. P. Muller
Hasty Wedding. M. G. Eberhart
Hat of Authority. J. Sanders
Hat-Pin Murder. G. Dilnot
Hatchet Man. M. Arrighi
Hatchet Man. J. Cassells
Hatchet Man. San Antonio
Hatchet Man. W. Van Atta
Hatchet Murders. N. Morland
Hatchetman. D. Dodge
Hatchie, the Guardian Slave. W. J. Ashton
"Hate"! R. Gar
Hate. H. Janson
Hate Alley. M. L. Weiss
Hate Begins at Home. Joan Aiken
Hate Finds a Way. M. Cumberland
Hate for Sale. M. Cumberland
Hate Is for the Hunted. S. D. Frances
Hate Is My Livery. M. Durham
Hate Island. A. West
Hate Master. K. Robeson
Hate of Evil. K. Snowden
Hate of Man. H. Hill
Hate Ship. B. Graeme
Hate That Kills. N. Carter
Hate, the Destroyer. R. N. Silver
Hate Thy Neighbor. M. Lynch
Hate Thy Neighbor. John Marsh
Hate to Kill. M. Halliday
Hate Will Find a Way. M. Cumberland
Hated by All! J. Drummond
Hated Eight. P. Quiroule
Hated One. D. Tracy
Hated Therewith. D. G. Waring
Hateful Voyage. M. Neville
Hatfield-McCoy Feud. W. B. Lawson
Hatred's Web. P. Nottingham
Hats Off! A. H. Veysey
Hatter's Ghosts. G. Simenon
Hatter's Phantoms. G. Simenon
Hatton Garden Mystery. F. Marlowe
Haughton Diamond Robbery. Roland Daniel
Haunt of the "Queen" Makers. Lieut. Carlton
Haunted. Janice Bennett
Haunted. G. Warden
Haunted Abbey. H. Leyford
Haunted Bells. M. S. Buchanan
Haunted Bookshop. C. Morley
Haunted Castle. O. Bradbury
Haunted Chair. G. Leroux
Haunted Farm. L. Austen-Leigh
Haunted Garden. W. E. D. Ross
Haunted Hammock. E. Lockwood
Haunted Harbor. D. Douglas
Haunted Heart. T. Brun
Haunted Heart. Claudette Nicole
Haunted Hills. B. M. Bower
Haunted Hollow. B. Symons
Haunted Homestead. E. Southworth
Haunted Hotel. W. Collins
Haunted Hotel Mystery. A. Skene
Haunted House. H. Belloc
Haunted House. A. Bernede
Haunted House. Owen Davis
Haunted House at Kew. G. Warden
Haunted House of Marley. M. Somers
Haunted Ice Rink. E. R. Home-Gall
Haunted Island. H. Bourne
Haunted Lady. M. R. Rinehart
Haunted Light. E. Price
Haunted Lives. J. S. Le Fanu
Haunted Looking Glass. G. Darrell
Haunted Man. J. Gaunt
Haunted Monastery. R. Van Gulik
Haunted Ocean. K. Robeson
Haunted Pajamas. F. P. Elliott
Haunted Place. V. Coffman
Haunted Rectory. H. C. McNeile
Haunted Rock. R. C. Finney
Haunted Sea. J. Pattinson
Haunted Ship. Seafarer
Haunted Shore. M. Gerard
Haunted Station, and other stories. H. Nisbet
Haunted Strangler. J. C. Cooper
Haunted Suit. N. Mapple
Haunted Summer. Anne Edwards
Haunted Tower. H. Wood
Haunted Woman. Melissa Napier
Haunted Wood Hollow. V. Silliman
Haunting Cavalier. M. Thum
Haunting Fingers. Herman Landon
Haunting Hand. W. A. Roberts
Haunting Lights. T. A. Plummer
Haunting of Alan Mais. P. Saxon
Haunting of Cliffside. J. Letton
Haunting of Clifton Court. Dana Ross
Haunting of Drumroe. Claudette Nicole
Haunting of Fog Island. Marilyn Ross
Haunting of Helen Wren. Jan Alexander
Haunting of Hill House. S. Jackson
Haunting of Hill House. F. Andrew Leslie
Haunting of Kathleen Saunders. Reginald Campbell
Haunting of Low Fennel. S. Rohmer
Haunting of Toby Jugg. D. Wheatley
Haunting of Villa Gabriel. Clarissa Ross
Haunting Shadow. J. A. Jordan
Haunting Shadow. Old Sleuth
Hauser's Memory. C. Siodmak
Havana Hit. M. Barry
Havana Hotel Murders. F. Dudley
Havana Mystery. W. W. Sayer
Have a Change of Scene. J. H. Chase
Have a Lovely Funeral. A. T. Hopkins
Have Gat--Will Travel. R. S. Prather
Have His Carcase. D. L. Sayers
Have Mercy Upon Us. T. Wells
Have Nude, Will Travel. C. Allison
Have Patience, Delaney! B. Singer
Have This One on Me. J. H. Chase
Have You Seen This Man? G. Hurley
Haven for the Damned. S. Mitchell
Haven for the Damned. H. Whittington
Haven of St. Garth. E. L. Long
Haven of Unrest. G. Collins
Havenhurst. S. Wagner
Havenhurst Affair. A. O. Pollard
Havering Plot. R. Keverne
Haversham Legacy. D. Winston
Haviland's Chum. B. Mitford
Having No Hearts. G. Goodchild
Having Wonderful Crime. C. Rice
Havoc. E. P. Oppenheim
Havoc. F. F. Van De Water
Havoc by Accident. G. Simenon
Hawaii Five-O. M. Avallone
Hawaii for Danger. N. A. Hintze
Hawaiian Eye. F. Castle
Hawaiian Hellground. D. Pendleton
Hawk. R. Hardwick
Hawk. S. Kyle
Hawk of Rede. H. Harding
Hawk Watch. B. Bird
Hawkline Monster. R. Brautigan
Hawkmoor Mystery. W. H. L. Crauford
Hawks of Glenaerie. Ruth MacLeod
Hawksboll Manor. A. Grace
Hayes Hall Affair. W. Hunt
Hazard. G. A. Browne
Hazard. R. Chanslor
Hazard Chase. J. Potter
Hazard House. P. Warren
Hazard Island. P. Tabori

Hazard of the Snows. O. Binns
Hazardous Duty. David St. John
Hazardous Holiday. E. Nisot
Haze of Evil. K. Lowe
Hazel Verne. A. L. Halstead
Hazell and the Three Card Trick. P. B. Yuill
Hazell Plays Solomon. P. B. Yuill
He Arrived at Dusk. R. C. Ashby
He Came by Night. Anthony Gilbert
He Could Not Have Slipped. F. Beeding
He Could Stop the World. K. Robeson
He Dared Not Look Behind. Cledwyn Hughes
He Didn't Mind Danger. M. Gilbert
He Didn't Mind Hanging. N. B. Mavity
He Died Laughing. R. P. Connolly
He Died Laughing. L. Lariar
He Died of Murder! Shelley Smith
He Died Thrice. M. G. Hugi
He Died Twice. G. J. Barrett
He Died Twice. M. Hadley
He Dies and Makes No Sign. M. Thynne
He Fell Among Thieves. D. C. Murray
He Fell Down Dead. V. Perdue
He Found Himself Murdered. D. Ames
He Had It Coming to Him. F. Grierson
He Had to Die. A. Hocking
He Hanged His Mother on Monday. N. Morland
He Laughed at Murder. R. Keverne
He Liked Them Murderous. L. Dundas
He Loved Freedom. S. Fairway
He Never Came Back. H. McCloy
He Never Came Back. P. Tabori
He Ought to be Shot. J. Fleming
He Ran All the Way. Sam Ross
He Shot to Kill. P. Drax
He Should Have Been King. K. Lindsay
He Should Have Died Hereafter. C. Hare
He Travels Alone. P. Loring
He Walked in Her Sleep. P. Cheyney
He Walked in Her Sleep and other stories. P. Cheyney
He Walks by Night. F. Nichols
He Was Found in the Road. A. Armstrong
He Who Digs a Grave. D. Delman
"He Who Fights..." L. Gorell
He Who Hesitates. E. McBain
He Who Walked in Scarlet. N. Tom-Gallon
He Who Whispers. J. D. Carr
He Won't Need It Now. J. L. Docherty
He Would Provoke Death. C. G. Jarvis
He Wouldn't Kill Patience. Carter Dickson
He Wouldn't Stay Dead. F. C. Davis
Head. D. Cory
Head Crusher. B. Rossi
Head for Death. N. Longmate
Head Held High. C. B. Bass
Head Hunter. A. P. Morris
Head Hunter's Secret. A. Murray
Head of a Girl. E. O'Duffy
Head of a Traveler. N. Blake
Head of Medusa. A. Grace
Head of Pasht. W. B. Allen
Head of the Firm. J. H. Riddell
Head of the Household. T. Cobb
Head on the Sill. M. Neville
Head over Heels in Murder. I. S. Shriber
Headed for a Hearse. Jonathan Latimer
Headhunter. F. Scarpetta
Heading for a Wreath. David Hume
Headland House Affair. W. Martyn
Headless Beings. M. Malcolm
Headless Ghost. T. S. King

Headless Girl of the North River. Old Sleuth
Headless Hound, and other stories. R. H. Mottram
Headless Lady. C. Rawson
Headless Man. G. M. Wilson
Headless Mystery. Old Sleuth
Headline for Murder. E. Lanham
Headline--Murder! G. Rayne
Headlined for Murder. E. Lanham
Headlines Make Murder. O. Mills
Headlong for Murder. M. Mace
Headlong from Heaven. M. Valbeck
Headmaster. D. H. Landels
Headmaster's Secret. R. Hardinge
Headquarters Budapest. Robert Parker
Heads. E. Stewart
Heads for Death. L. Johnson
Heads I Win. Q. Downes
Heads Off at Midnight. F. Beeding
Heads or Tails. S. Jepson
Heads You Die. L. Gribble
Heads You Live. David Hume
Heads You Lose. C. Brand
Heads You Lose. L. Cargill
Heads You Lose. B. Halliday
Heads You Lose. B. Shannon
Heads You Lose. Jimmy Starr
Headsman. Austin Stone
Headsman's Holiday. D. Hawkins
Heap of Trouble. E. Messenger
Hear No Evil. N. Bowen
Hear No Evil. M. Carroll
Hear No Evil. S. Ransome
Hear Not My Steps. L. S. Thompson
Hear the Stripper Scream. P. Cagney
Heard in the Dark. N. Carter
Hearken to the Evidence. H. R. Wakefield
Hearse Class Male. F. Kane
Hearse for Cinderella. H. Howard
Hearse for McNally. G. J. Barrett
Hearse for the Boss. A. Eichler
Hearse Horse Snickered. C. Thomas
Hearse in May-Day. G. Mitchell
Hearse of a Different Color. M. Constiner
Hearse of Another Color. M. E. Chaber
Hearse of Dark Harbor. Clarissa Ross
Hearse Waiting. W. Wright
Hearse with Horses. E. McGirr
Hearsed in Death. M. Cumberland
Hearses Don't Hurry. S. Ransome
Heart and Science. W. Collins
Heart Cut Diamond. S. Horler
Heart in Exile. R. Garland
Heart in the Box. F. Grierson
Heart Merchants. L. Goldman
Heart of a Girl. F. Warden
Heart of a Hero. M. Gerard
Heart of a Man. G. Simenon
Heart of a Mystery. T. W. Speight
Heart of a Princess. W. LeQueux
Heart of Delilah. Christopher Wilson
Heart of Gold. R. H. Greenan
Heart of Ice. F. Hume
Heart of Noel. F. Whishaw
Heart of Oak Detective. E. S. Ellis
Heart of Oak Detective. E. L. Wheeler
Heart of Penelope. M. B. Lowndes
Heart of Stone. G. Warden
Heart of the Dancer. Percy White
Heart of the Dog. T. A. Roberts
Heart of the Matter. G. Greene
Heart of the Underworld. N. Carter
Heart of the West. O. Henry
Heart of Unaga. R. Cullum
Heart Specialist. P. Trent
Heart to Heart. P. Boileau
Heartache. H. Janson
Hearts. D. C. Murray
Hearts by the Tower. O. Sinclair
Heart's Delight. C. Gibbon

Heart's Delight. L. Tracy
Hearts in Turmoil. M. Richmond
Hearts of Gold and Hearts of Steel. H. Herman
Hearts or Diamonds. I. D. Hardy
Heart's Problem. C. Gibbon
Heat Lightning. W. Shaw
Heat Not a Furnace. H. Kemp
Heat of Night. H. Whittington
Heath Hover Mystery. B. Mitford
Heather. M. Dobner
Heather-Bells. R. Gover
Heather Mixture. M. Gerard
Heather Mystery. M. Gerard
Heat's On. R. Drayton
Heat's On. C. Himes
Heatwave. Ceasar Smith
Heaven-Kissed Hill. J. S. Fletcher
Heaven Ran Last. W. P. McGivern
Heaven-Sent Witness and other stories. J. S. Fletcher
Heaven Will Be Ours. K. Lindsay
Heavenly Bodies. T. Warriner
Heavenly Body. G. Morgan
Heaviest Pipe. A. M. Patterson
Heavy as Lead. M. Torrie
Heavy, Heavy Hangs. D. M. Disney
Heavy Stakes. M. K. Douglas
Hebrew Maiden. T. P. Prest
Hec Ramsey. D. Owen
Hecatomb. B. Palmer
Heckler. E. McBain
Hector Duval. H. Collinson
Hector Tumbler Investigates. S. Crabtree
He'd Rather Be Dead. G. Bellaire
Hedgerow. F. E. Randall
Hedri. H. B. Mathers
Heed the Thunder. J. Thompson
Heel. W. L. Rohde
Heel of Achilles. L. H. Fox
Heel of Achilles. E. Radford
Heel of Achilles. G. Verner
Height of Day. D. Cory
Heights of Zervos. C. Forbes
Heil Britannia. P. Long
Heil Harris! J. Garforth
Heil! Hollywood. Jack Preston
Heir Apparent. E. L. Withers
Heir Hunters. B. S. Ballinger
Heir of Ashly. H. Wood
Heir of Douglas. L. De La Torre
Heir of Grangerfjord Castle. R. M. Sears
Heir of Greymount. J. E. Cooke
Heir of Kings. Winifred Duke
Heir of Starvelings. E. Berckman
Heir of the Ages. J. Payn
Heir to Lucifer. M. Burton
Heir to Murder. M. Burton
Heir to Murder. M. Halliday
Heir to Polventon. Marjorie Watson
Heir to the Throne. A. W. Marchmont
Heiress Apparent. L. Conway
Heiress of Bayou Vache. Harriet Stone
Heiress of Bellefront. Emerson Bennett
Heiress of Densley Wold. F. Warden
Heiress of Frascati. J. Shearing
Heiress of Glen Gower. M. A. Fleming
Heiress of the Season. W. Magnay
Heiress to Evil. S. O'Brien
Heiress to Wolfskill. K. Kimbrough
Heirloom of Tragedy. E. Noone
Heirs of Cain. A. Rothberg
Heirs of Merlin. P. Atkey
Heirs to Kildrennan. A. Foxe
Heist Me Higher. B. S. Ballinger
Heisters. R. P. Jones
Held Apart. R. N. Silver

H

Held for Ransom. N. M. Murray
Held for Trial. N. Carter
Held in Suspense. N. Carter
Held in the Toils. J. K. Leys
Held in Thrall. B. Hemyng
Held in Trust! W. M. Graydon
Held Open for Death. E. Payne
Held to Ransom. R. Gover
Helen. E. V. Cunningham
Helen All Alone. W. Buchan
Helen Elwood, the Female Detective. B. and R.
Helen of All Time. W. Holt-White
Helen of London. J. Goodwin
Helen of the Moor. A. Askew
Helen Passes By. E. R. Punshon
Helen Vardon's Confession. R. A. Freeman
Helen Whitney's Edding, and other stories. H. Wood
Helena. H. S. Irwin
Helga's Web. J. Cleary
Helix File. W. D. Blankenship
Hell and High Water. R. Drayton
Hell and High Water. R. Garland
Hell-Bent for Danger. W. Grove
Hell-Black Night. S. Fisher
Hell-Bomb Floozies. Griff
Hell Can Wait. H. Whittington
Hell-Crazy Range. F. W. Hilton
Hell for Heather. P. Flower
Hell for Leather. A. Wood
Hell for Tomorrow. P. Leslie
Hell Gate. James Dawes
Hell-Gate Tides. L. Thayer
Hell Hath No Fury. L. Eby
Hell Hath No Fury. M. Richmond
Hell Hath No Fury. C. Williams
Hell House. R. Matheson
Hell in Harness. J. Auslander
Hell in the Afternoon. W. Sproule
Hell Is a City. W. Ard
Hell Is a City. M. Procter
Hell Is Always Today. Harry Patterson
Hell Is Empty. J. F. Straker
Hell Is My Destination. J. Conway
Hell Is Sold Out. M. Dekobra
Hell Is Too Crowded. Harry Patterson
Hell Is Where You Find It. J. Welcome
Hell Let Loose. F. Beeding
Hell of a Murder. W. Carrier
Hell of a Woman. J. Thompson
Hell on Friday. W. Bogart
Hell on the Way. J. M. Fox
Hell in Harness. J. Auslander
Hell! Said the Duchess. M. Arlen
Hell Ship to Kuma. C. Clements
Hell Street. M. Franklin
Hell to Pay! H. Clevely
Hell to Pay. W. R. Cox
Hell with Elaine. V. Siller
Hellbottom. E. Corder
Hellbound Flight. L. Derrick
Hellcat. C. Brown
Helldorado. H. Janson
Hellfire Conspiracy. Ralph Hayes
Hellgate Plantation. F. Swann
Hellions. R. T. Bickers
Hello Cruel World, Goodbye. J. Goodman
Hell's Above Us. Henry Ward
Hell's Acre. F. H. Rose
Hell's Angel. H. Janson
Hell's Belle. J. Fleming
Hell's Belles. R. Drayton
Hell's Belles. H. Janson
Bell's Brew. S. Horler
Hell's Harbour. H. P. Lee
Hell's Harvest. H. S. Banner
Hell's Harvest. Jos. N. Wilson
Hell's Kitchen. B. Appel

Hell's Loose. R. Pertwee
Hell's Our Destination. G. Brewer
Hell's Wenches. V. Norwood
Help from the Baron. A. Morton
Help I Am Being Held Prisoner. D. E. Westlake
Help, Please. E. Bahr
Help Wanted--for Murder. W. L. Rohde
Help Yourself to Happiness. F. R. Adams
Helping Hand. C. Dale
Helsinki Affair. M. Sariola
Hemlock Avenue Mystery. R. Doubleday
Hemlock Galore. A. Kennington
Hemlock Tree. E. Lottman
Henbane. C. Meadows
Hendon's First Case. J. Rhode
Hennessy. M. Franklin
Henrietta Who? C. Aird
Henry Broch, Old Sleuth's Assistant. Old Sleuth
Henry Cassland. H. Druce
Henry Dunbar. M. E. Braddon
Henry in a Silver Frame. J. Eastwood
Henry Massinger. R. Jocelyn
Henry Northcote. J. C. Snaith
Henry Prince in Action. C. F. Gregg
Henry the Sheriff. W. C. Tuttle
Hepsworth Millions. C. Lys
Her Assigned Husband. A. Pratt
Her Convict. M. E. Braddon
Her Convict Husband. Ladbroke Black
Her Convict Husband. M. Leighton
Her Crooked Lover. B. Delane
Her Demon Lover. L. Bronte
Her Empty Triumph. A. Askew
Her Fairy Prince. G. Warden
Her Faithful Knight. G. Warden
Her Fatal Sin. M. E. Holmes
Her Fate and His. M. Leighton
Her Father's Daughter. A. Askew
Her Foreign Conquest. R. H. Savage
Her Fugitive. C. Stanton
Her Garden of Eden. J. Chancellor
Her Grace at Bay. H. Hill
Her Great Moment. E. Balmer
Her Great Surprise. H. P. Halsey
Her Happy Face. L. T. Meade
Her Heart in Her Throat. Ethel L. White
Her Heart's Awakening. M. Leighton
Her Heart's Gift. O. Kent
Her Hidden Past. B. M. Clay
Her Highness. F. Whishaw
Her Highness's Secretary. C. Dawe
Her Honour. R. Machray
Her Ladyship. T. W. Speight
Her Ladyship's Jewels and What Became of Them. R. H. Gooch
Her Ladyship's Secret. W. Westall
Her Ladyship's Silence. M. Leighton
Her Lips Betrayed. D. Walshe
Her Lover's Peril. A. Eadie
Her Loving Slave. H. Nisbet
Her Majesty the Queen. J. E. Cooke
Her Majesty's Minister. W. LeQueux
Her Marriage Lines. M. Leighton
Her Month of Freedom. P. Trent
Her Mother's Child. A. Askew
Her Mother's Darling. J. H. Riddell
Her Own Affair. T. A. Plummer
Her Private Murder. J. Corbett
Her Private Passions. M. Holland
Her Reputation. T. Mundy
Her Right Divine. O. Kent
Her Royal Highness. W. LeQueux
Her Royal Highness's Love Affair. J. M. Cobban
Her Sacrifice. A. Applin
Her Second Murder. J. Corbett
Her Second Self. A. Wood
Her Secret Life. R. Machray
Her Senator. A. C. Gunter

Her Sentinel. A. W. Marchmont
Her Soul's Desire. A. M. Meadows
Her Splendid Sin. H. Hill
Her Stepfather's House. J. Wetherell
Her Two Millions. W. Westall
Her Ways Are Death. J. Mann
Her Weapon Is Passion. H. Janson
Her Wedding Night. M. Pemberton
Her Wild Oats. P. Trent
Herald of Death. M. Dalman
Herald of Doom. G. Ashe
Herald Personal and other stories. N. Carter
Herapath Property. J. S. Fletcher
Hercule and the Gods. P. Audemars
Hercule Poirot's Christmas. A. Christie
Hercule Poirot's Early Cases. A. Christie
Hercules and the Marionettes. R. M. Gilchrist
Hercules, Esq. Gwyn Evans
Hercules--Spotsman. B. Atkey
Here Come the Dead. R. P. Koehler
Here Comes a Candle. F. Brown
Here Comes a Candle. J. A. Hodge
Here Comes a Chopper. G. Mitchell
Here Comes a Hero. Lawrence Block
Here Comes the Copper. Henry Wade
Here Comes the Corpse. G. Bagby
Here Comes the Corpse. G. Brandon
Here Comes the Lady. M. P. Shiel
Here Comes the Toff. J. Creasey
Here in Eden. K. Lindsay
Here Is an S.O.S. S. Horler
Here Is Danger. G. Ashe
Here Is the Evidence. P. Vane
Here Lies. D. M. Disney
Here Lies Blood. M. M. Mannon
Here Lies Georgia Linz. P. Mason
Here Lies My Wife. E. McGirr
Here Lies Nancy Frail. Jonathan Ross
Here Lies the Body. R. Burke
Here Lies the Shadow. R. Foxall
Here There be Dragons. R. Bentley
Here to Die. M. Sadler
Here Today--Dead Tomorrow. J. W. Hornby
Here's a Villain! J. Mitchell
Here's Blood in Your Eye. Manning Long
Here's Murder Done. C. Ashton
Here's Why. F. Collins
Heresy. L. Snelling
Heretic. M. L. West
Herewith the Clues! D. Wheatley
Heritage in Trust. C. Davy
Heritage of Cain. I. Ostrander
Heritage of Danger. M. Lynch
Heritage of Fear. E. Bond
Heritage of Folly. C. Marchant
Heritage of Kid McCleod. H. Pink
Heritage of Mercy. P. Tabori
Heritage of Peril. A. W. Marchmont
Heritage of the Horned Steer. R. Wilkes-Hunter
Heritage of Trouble. N. Carter
Heritage Perilous. J. Farnol
Hermit Island. F. Swann
Hermit of Turkey Hollow. A. Train
Hermitage. M. K. Simmons
Hero. P. Haining
Hero by Proxy. H. Tolman
Hero for Leanda. A. Garve
Hero Game. W. H. Baker
Hero in the Tower. H. H. Kirst
Hero of a Summer's Day. J. Pudney
Hero of Romance. R. Marsh
Herod's Peal. R. Thorndike

Title Index

Heroes of Yuca. Michael Barrett
Heroin Triple Cross. J. Weisman
Heroine of the Desert. A. Eadie
Heron Tree. E. Kyle
Heronbrook. A. Rundle
Heronstroke Mystery. E. Everett-Green
Hero's Lust. K. Jaediker
Hers Is a Hearse. M. Brody
He's Late This Morning. C. Hale
Heseltine Mystery. H. E. Chapman
Hester and I. P. C. De Crespigny
Hester Strong's Life Work. E. Southworth
Hex. K. Robeson
Hex Marks the Spot. J. Dekker
Hex Murder. F. Hazard
Hi-Fi Fadeout. C. Brown
Hi-Jack for a Jill. C. Brown
Hi-Jack That Dame. Griff
Hi-Jacker's Lady. B. Sarto
Hi-Spy-Kick-the-Can. V. MacClure
Hibernation of Ginger Scrubb. A. Gardner
Hick Town Dame. F. Foden
Hickey and Boggs. P. Rock
Hickory Dickory Death. A. Christie
Hickory Dickory Dock. A. Christie
Hickory Hall. E. Southworth
Hidden and the Hunted. H. Swiggett
Hidden Answer. John Marsh
Hidden Blood. W. C. Tuttle
Hidden Chain. Dora Russell
Hidden Chapel. L. Ames
Hidden Cipher. A. O. Pollard
Hidden Clue. E. D. Pierson
Hidden Clues. D. Deane
Hidden Death. C. Goodall
Hidden Death. M. Grant
Hidden Death. E. W. Terris
Hidden Door. A. Gask
Hidden Door. F. Packard
Hidden Enemy. V. Lloyd
Hidden Eyes. E. Levison
Hidden Face. V. Canning
Hidden Fear. J. Blyth
Hidden Flame. R. Dowling
Hidden Foe. G. A. Henty
Hidden Foes. N. Carter
Hidden Gang. D. T. Hughes
Hidden Gold. W. Anthony
Hidden Gold. F. Barrett
Hidden Grave. P. Hardin
Hidden Hand. C. J. Daly
Hidden Hand. S. Horler
Hidden Hand. E. Phillpotts
Hidden Hand. E. Southworth
Hidden Hands. M. Leighton
Hidden Hands. W. LeQueux
Hidden Hoard. J. Creasey
Hidden Horror. M. Richmond
Hidden Hour. J. B. Harris-Burland
Hidden Hour. S. Ransome
Hidden House. J. C. Dane
Hidden Island. A. Rutherford
Hidden Key. G. H. Coxe
Hidden Kingdom. F. Beeding
Hidden Light. M. Dalman
Hidden Lives. C. H. Merritt
Hidden Lives. E. R. Punshon
Hidden Man. C. F. Pidgin
Hidden Mask. C. G. Mitford
Hidden Men. S. Truss
Hidden Menace! J. W. Bobin
Hidden Menace. D. Stuart
Hidden Message. A. Murray
Hidden Million. P. Merritt
Hidden, Not Lost. Anonymous
Hidden Out. H. Fielding
Hidden Paths. W. S. King
Hidden Perils. M. C. Hay
Hidden Portal. Garnett Weston
Hidden Record. E. W. Blaisdell

Hidden Sin. E. A. Dupuy
Hidden Submarine. C. Holland
Hidden Terror. Anonymous
Hidden Ways. F. F. Van De Water
Hidden Witness. H. C. McNeile
Hidden Woman. J. Hay
Hidden Wrath. S. Phillips
Hide and Go Seek. A. Garve
Hide and Go Seek. Colver Harris
Hide and Kill. J. York
Hide and Seek. W. Collins
Hide and Seek. Jacqueline Wilson
Hide Away. N. Bond
I'ide Her from Every Eye. H. Pentecost
Hide in the Dark. F. N. Hart
Hide My Body. F. Lester
Hide My Eyes. M. Allingham
Hide-Out. L. Holden
Hide the Baron. A. Morton
Hide the Body! M. Propper
Hide Those Diamonds! Roy Vickers
Hideaway. N. Content
Hideaway. J. Gardner
Hideaway. F. Nichols
Hideaway. M. Procter
Hiding Place. C. Keith
Hiding Place. C. Wilcox
High Adventure. J. Farnol
High Adventure. P. Groom
High Bid for Murder. A. O'Neill
High-Bouncing Lover. Angus Hall
High Bright Sun. I. S. Black
High Citadel. D. Bagley
High-Class Kill. J. Wainwright
High Class Swindler. Old Spicer
High Commissioner. J. Cleary
High Corniche. D. Dodge
High Cost of Murder. H. Barron
High Crystal. M. Caidin
High Dive. F. O'Rourke
High Doom. J. L. Morrissey
High Encounter. B. Wohl
High Explosive. N. Mapple
High Explosive. G. Phillips
High Fashion in Homicide. C. Brown
High Game. P. Geddes
High Game. S. Horler
High Hand. J. Futrelle
High Hazard. S. Horler
High Hazard. R. M. Stern
High Heel Homicide. F. C. Davis
High Heels and Homicide. D. Reid
High Jacker. H. E. O. Whitman
High Jump. V. Gielgud
High Kill. P. Ordway
High-Minded Murder. C. Sykes
High Noon to High Noon. E. L. Long
High on a Hill. F. Y. McHugh
High Pastures. H. L. V. Fletcher
High Pavement. E. Bonett
High Place. G. Household
High Red for Dead. W. L. Rohde
High Rendezvous. K. M. Knight
High Requiem. D. Cory
High Road to Hell. H. L. Gates
High Roller. F. Du Boisgobey
High School Confidential. Morton Cooper
High School Mystery. R. St. Clair
High Seas Murder. P. Drax
High Season. E. Kyle
High Sheriff. Henry Wade
High Sierra. W. R. Burnett
High Speed. C. H. Stagg
High Spirits. N. Tranter

High Spy. R. Trevor
High Stakes. L. Dent
High Stakes. D. Francis
High Stakes. S. Horler
High Stakes. L. L. Lynch
High Stakes. C. Riess
High Street. C. Edwards
High Summer Homicide. A. Kirby
High Tension. E. H. Clements
High Tension. T. Du Bois
High Tension. Alex Fraser
High Terrace. V. Coffman
High Tide. P. M. Hubbard
High Tide at Midnight. R. Cocking
High Tide for Hanging. G. Compton
High Tide Temptress. M. Brody
High Toby. H. B. M. Watson
High Treason. J. Bruce
High Treason. L. A. Knight
High Treason. A. Upward
High Valley. J. North
High Walk to Wandlemere. P. Sibley
High Wall. B. Copper
High Wall. S. Truss
High Water at Four. J. Tickell
High Water Mark. R. Dowling
High Water Mark. F. Hume
High Window. R. Chandler
High Wire. W. Haggard
High Wray. K. Hughes
Highbinders. O. Bleeck
Higher They Fly. C. Hodder-Williams
"Highest References." F. Warden
Highflight to Hell. C. H. Wallace
Highgate Mystery. C. Kingston
Highgrade Murder. C. H. Snow
Highland Fling. M. MacKintosh
Highland Gathering. J. Wood
Highland Homicide. J. Austwick
Highland Masquerade. M. Elgin
Highly Inflammable. M. Saltmarsh
Highly Unsafe. M. Saltmarsh
Highway of Fear. Donald Moore
Highway Robber's Derby. F. Johnston
Highway to Hell. D. Forde
Highway to Murder. H. Howard
Highwayman. G. Rawlence
Highways of Death. H. Desmond
Hijack. L. White
Hijacked. D. Harper
Hijacker's Morgue. L. Mantz
Hijacking Manhattan. L. Derrick
Hiker's Secret. W. Edwards
Hilary's Terms. H. Janson
Hilda, Take Heed. M. Halliday
Hilda Wade. G. Allen
Hildegarde Withers Makes the Scene. S. Palmer
Hill Fog. J. N. Chance
Hill Girl. C. Williams
Hill of Ashes. L. Ames
Hill of Riches. F. A. M. Webster
Hill of the Crows. F. Sleath
Hill of the Terrified Monk. G. Homes
Hill of the Wild Cat. Agnes Russell
Hillerway Letters. T. Cobb
Hilliare Henderson. N. Buntline
Hillman. E. P. Oppenheim
Hills of Fire. D. Daniels
Hills Were Higher Then. H. M. Kahler
Hilltop. J. Letton
Hilltop Murders. M. Baker
Hilma. W. T. Eldridge
Himalayan Assignment. V. W. Mason
Himself Again. R. E. Pickering
Hindoo Khan. M. J. Pemberton
Hinges of Hell. S. Sterling

Hint of Murder. N. Kent
Hippo's Coup. Sean Graham
Hippy Cult Murders. R. Stanley
Hire Me a Hearse. P. Marlowe
Hire Me a Rope. B. Sarto
Hire Purchase Crime. G. Chester
Hire-Purchase Fraud. W. Tyrer
Hired Girl. Mrs. C. Kernahan
Hired Girl's Millions. C. E. Blaney
Hired Target. W. Tucker
Hiroshima Reef. Eric Lambert
His Aunt Came Late. L. Meynell
His Beautiful Client. George Griffith
His Better Half. George Griffith
His Bones Are Coral. V. Canning
His Brother's Keeper. M. M. Bodkin
His Borther's Keeper. E. Phillpotts
His Burial Too. C. Aird
His Chinese Concubine. M. Dekobra
His Crooked Highness. K. Lindsay
His Cuban Sweetheart. R. H. Savage
His Dainty Whim. C. G. Mitford
His Darling Sin. M. E. Braddon
His Downward Path. Harry Mills
His Eminence, Death. Simon Quinn
His Evil Eye. H. I. Hancock
His Excellency, Governor Wallace. A. Wilson
His Excellency's Secret. A. Murray
His Fatal Success. M. Bell
His Father's Crime. W. M. Graydon
His Father's Crime. E. P. Oppenheim
His Father's Ghost. S. Davis
His Father's Honour. D. C. Murray
His Father's Son. B. Matthews
His Father's Wife. D. Keene
His Final Choice. A. Applin
His First Affair. D. Walshe
His First Offense. J. S. Clouston
His Fortunate Foe. A. S. Arnold
His Foster Sister. Albert Ross
His Friend the Enemy. W. W. Cook
His Great Revenge. F. Du Boisgobey
His Greatest "Shadow." Old Sleuth
His Hand Betrays. P. Conway
His Helpmate. F. Barrett
His Heritage. L. Gardiner
His Honor. C. E. Cleveland
His Kind of Woman. M. Morgan
His Last Bow. A. C. Doyle
His Lawful Wife. J. Middlemass
His Lordship the Crook. E. Louis
His Lordship the Judge. D. H. Landels
His Love or His Life. R. Marsh
"His Majesty." A. W. Marchmont
His Majesty--the Crook. Gwyn Evans
His Majesty's Peacock. W. A. MacKenzie
His Master's Voice. I. Litvinoff
His Mexican Wife. A. Applin
His Name Was Death. F. Brown
His Natural Life. M. Clarke
His Other Self. R. W. Cole
His Other Self. E. J. Goodman
His Other Wife. Roy Vickers
His Own Accuser. S. Hocking
His Own Accuser. H. Townley
His Own Appointed Day. D. M. Devine
His Own Funeral. G. J. Barrett
His Own Ghost. D. C. Murray
His Own Law. F. Barrett
His Patients Died. C. Lillingston
His Prey Was Man. A. Gask
His Reverence the Rogue. H. Desmond
His Robe of Honor. E. Dorrance
His Royal Highness. George Hastings
His Secret. M. E. Braddon
His Silence. I. D. Hardy
His Son's Honour. J. W. Bobin
His Terrible Secret. C. E. Blaney
His Unknown Wife. L. Tracy

His Weight in Gold. M. Procter
His Wife's Revenge. G. R. Sims
His Wife's Soul. J. F. Molloy
Histoire des Treize. H. D. Balzac
History of Edward Brown. E. C. Reed
Hit. R. Deming
Hit. B. Garfield
Hit and Run. J. Ashford
Hit and Run. J. Creasey
Hit and Run. R. Deming
Hit and Run. V. Kathrens
Hit and Run. R. Marshall
Hit and Run, Run, Run. A. Bodelsen
Hit It Rich. M. Bardsley
Hit Man. R. J. Flood
Hit Man. B. Rossi
Hit Me Hard. Neill Graham
Hit #29. Joey and Dave Fischer
Hit the Jackpot. R. Madison
Hit Woman. G. Blumberg
Hitchhike Killer. Paul Ross
Hitchhike to Hell. B. Grant
Hitchhiker. G. Simenon
Hitler Diamonds. D. Cory
Hitler Has Won. F. Mullally
Hitler Needs You. J. T. Story
Hive of Glass. E. Woodward
Hive of Glass. P. M. Hubbard
Hive of Suspects. S. Pim
Hobgoblin Murder. K. C. Strahan
Hochmann Miniatures. R. L. Fish
Hodak. T. Pendleton
Hoffman's Row. W. H. Carnahan
Hogdown Farm Mystery. M. Butcher
Hog's Back Mystery. F. W. Crofts
Holbein Mystery. A. Wynne
Hold Back the Night. D. Leslie
Hold Everything. D. Linton
Hold Out. E. Bruton
Hold That Tiger. D. Ambler
Hold-Up. W. F. Morris
Hole and Corner. P. Wentworth
Hole and Corner Marriage. F. Warden
Hole in the Ground. J. Bell
Hole in the Ground. A. Garve
Hole in the Mountain. "Capstan"
Hole in the Vault. N. Carter
Hole in the Wall. F. MacIsaac
Hole in the Wall. Arthur Morrison
Holes in the Wall. J. Bahr
Holiday Adventures of Mr. P. J. Davenant. F. S. Hamilton
Holiday at Half-Mast. J. J. Farjeon
Holiday Camp Murder. B. Francis
Holiday Camp Mystery. W. Tyrer
Holiday Express. J. J. Farjeon
Holiday for a Spy. B. Graeme
Holiday for Inspector West. J. Creasey
Holiday for Murder. A. Christie
Holiday Homicide. R. King
Holiday in a Manor House. E. Everett-Green
Holiday in Gaol. F. Martyn
Holiday of Fear. Gretchen Travis
Holiday with a Vengeance. Ritchie Perry
Holiday with Danger. E. Wilmot
Holiday with Murder. G. Carr
Holladay Case. B. E. Stevenson
Holland Suggestions. J. Dunning
Hollow. A. Christie
Hollow Ash Hall. M. Blount
Hollow Chest. A. Tilton
Hollow Crown Affair. D. McDaniel
Hollow House. U. Curtiss
Hollow Hub. K. West
Hollow Land. N. A. Temple-Ellis

Hollow Man. J. D. Carr
Hollow Man. J. Roeburt
Hollow Mountain. Alec Brown
Hollow Needle. G. H. Coxe
Hollow Needle. M. Leblanc
Hollow Sea. G. Jenkins
Hollow Shell. J. Farrimond
Hollow Skin. V. Swain
Hollow Stump Mystery. C. H. Snow
Hollow Sunday. R. Harling
Hollow Triumph. M. Forbes
Holly Ash. S. Youd
Hollywood and LeVine. A. Bergman
Hollywood Detective: Garrison. J. Rovin
Hollywood Detective: The Wolf. J. Rovin
Hollywood Hitman. V. Saxon
Hollywood Hoax. R. C. Frazer
Hollywood Love. A. M. Williamson
Hollywood Murder Mystery. H. Crooken
Hollywood Mystery. Anonymous
Hollywood Mystery! B. Hecht
Holm Oaks. P. M. Hubbard
Holocaust. A. McCall
Holocaust Auction. P. Edwards
Holy Disorders. E. Crispin
Holy Father's Navy. P. Purser
Holy Terror. L. Charteris
Holy Terror. R. Sapir
Hombre from Sonora. W. Charles
Home and Murder. A. M. Stein
Home at Seven. R. C. Sherriff
Home Guard Mystery. B. Cobb
Home Is the Hangman. R. Sale
Home Is the Heart. A. Meredith
Home Is the Prisoner. J. Potts
Home Is the Sailor. D. Keene
Home Is Where the Quick Is. William Johnston
Home of His Children. W. J. Bayfield
Home of Silence. L. T. Meade
Home Secretary Affair. C. Franklin
Home, Sweet Home. J. H. Riddell
Home Sweet Homicide. C. Rice
Home Sweet Homicide. J. T. Story
Home Through the Dark. Anthea Fraser
Home to Cypresswood. L. V. Stevens
Home to Our Valley. D. Lee
Home Town. G. Simenon
Homeward Tide. J. MacKenzie
Homeward Trail. G. Goodchild
Homicidal Colonel. R. Player
Homicidal Holiday. G. Brandon
Homicidal Lady. D. Keene
Homicidal Spy. A. O. Pollard
Homicidal Virgin. B. Halliday
Homicide. L. T. White
Homicide at Saxondale. E. Wilmot
Homicide at Yuletide. H. Kane
Homicide Blonde. M. Procter
Homicide Blues. D. Reid
Homicide Call. S. A. Krasney
Homicide Club. Gwyn Evans
Homicide Dragnet. R. Marlowe
Homicide for Hannah. D. V. Babcock
Homicide Handicap. B. McKnight
Homicide Harem and Felon Angel. C. Brown
Homicide Haven. J. V. Turner
Homicide Honeymoon. D. B. Hobart
Homicide Hotel. Joe Barry
Homicide House. D. Frome
Homicide Hoyden. C. Brown
Homicide Hussy. A. McGuire
Homicide Is My Game. S. Marlowe

Title Index

Homicide Johnny. S. Gould
Homicide Lost. W. Vance
Homicide Trinity. R. Stout
Homicide West. S. A. Krasney
Homicide with Charm. E. Ryley
Honduras Double Cross. K. Edgar
Honest Crook. A. S. Roche
Honest Davie. F. Barrett
Honest Dealer. F. Gruber
Honest Lawyer. G. V. McFadden
Honest Reliable Corpse. G. Bagby
Honest Rogue. M. Park
Honey Ain't So Sweet. M. Shane
Honey for Me. H. Janson
Honey for the Marshal. E. H. Clements
Honey, Here's Your Hearse! C. Brown
Honey, Hold That Scream. T. Angelo
Honey in the Flesh. G. G. Fickling
Honey on Her Tail. G. G. Fickling
Honey Siege. G. Buhet
Honey Take My Gun. H. Janson
Honeycombers. J. Laing
Honeyfall. W. Searle
Honeymoon Hate. A. M. Williamson
Honeymoon in Shanghai. M. Dekobra
Honeymoon Killers. P. Buck
Honeymoon Murder. R. C. Finney
Honeymoon Mystery. J. Laurence
Honeymoon with Death. H. Pentecost
Hong Kong Aftermath. Wenzell Brown
Hong Kong Airbase Murders. V. W. Mason
Hong Kong Caper. C. Brown
Hong Kong Incident. J. Dark
Hong Kong Kill. Bryan Peters
Hong Kong Nightstop. N. Shore
Honky in the Woodpile. J. Brunner
Honolulu Murder Story. L. Ford
Honolulu Murders. L. Ford
Honolulu Snatch. M. Corrigan
Honolulu Story. L. Ford
Honor of a Black Sheep. S. Campbell
Honor of the Name. E. Gaboriau
Honor Thy Godfather. T. P. Mulkeen
Honor Thy Godmother. R. T. Larkin
Honorable Gentleman and Others. A. Abdullah
Honorary Consul. G. Greene
Honour Among Thieves. H. C. Bailey
Honour Lost. E. V. De Fontmell
Honour of His House. F. M. White
Honeysuckle Rogue. R. M. Gilchrist
Honour of Thieves. C. J. C. Hyne
Honourable Algernon Knox, Detective. E. P. Oppenheim
Honourable Assassins. Geoffrey Davison
Honourable Mister Death and other stories. S. Gluck
Honour of the Family. P. Trent
Honourable Mr. Tawnish. J. Farnol
Honourable Pursuit. P. Wynnton
Honourable Roger. C. A. Brandreth
Hooch! C. F. Coe
Hood of Death. N. Carter
Hooded Asp. J. A. McManis
Hooded Man. W. M. Duncan
Hooded Monster. W. S. Masterman
Hooded Raider. D. Stuart
Hooded Riders. J. W. Bobin
Hooded Skull. P. Monnow
Hooded Snake. W. Phillips
Hooded Stranger. Harrington Strong
Hooded Vulture Murders. R. P. Koehler
Hoodlum. E. Lipsky
Hoodlum Was a Honey. C. Brown
Hoodlums. J. Eagle
Hoodmen's Bait. J. Bogar
Hoodoo Half-Back. F. W. Gumley
Hoods. H. Grey
Hoods Come Calling. N. Quarry
Hoods Incorporated. P. J. Andrews
Hoods Ride In. Wenzell Brown

Hoods Take Over. O. Demaris
Hoodwink. Robin Temple
Hook, Line and Sinker. K. Nicholson
Hooker-Smash Operation. J. Rosenberger
Hooky and the Crock of Gold. L. Meynell
Hooligan. D. Dodge
Hooligan Nights. C. Rook
Hop Thief. O. Blakeston
Hope Strange Mystery. E. Short
Hope to Die. H. Waugh
Hopeless Case. E. Fawcett
Hopjoy Was Here. C. Watson
Hopkinson and the Devil of Hate. P. McCutchan
Hopscotch. B. Garfield
Horace Steps Out. D. Whitelaw
Hordern Mystery. E. Finn
Hordes of the Red Butcher. G. Stockbridge
Horizon. H. MacInnes
Horizontal Man. H. Eustis
Horn. B. Flynn
Horn of Roland. Ellis Peters
Horned Cat. J. M. Cobban
Horned Owl. W. B. Cooke
Hornet's Nest. E. Bond
Hornet's Nest. B. Fischer
Hornet's Nest. J. R. Holden
Hornets' Nest. C. Landon
Hornets Nest. A. Soutar
Hornet's Nest. W. Woodrow
Horns of the Devil. L. Malley
Horns of Truth. T. B. Morris
Horrible Dummy and other stories. G. Kersh
Horrible Hat. R. Savage
Horrible Man. M. Avallone
Horrible Man in Heron's Wood. B. Cobb
Horrible Revenge. I. Crookenden
Horror at Gull House. P. Brisco
Horror at the Moated Mill. H. Desmond
Horror at Wardens Hall. C. Wogan
Horror Castle. R. Sharp
Horror Comes to Thripplands. G. Collins
Horror Hall. F. W. Irwin
Horror House. L. C. Douthwaite
Horror House. P. Warren
Horror House. C. Wells
Horror in the Dark. N. MacKenzie
Horror Medley. M. Hervey
Horror of the Juvenal Manse. K. Perkins
Horror on the Loch. D. Whitelaw
Horror on the Ruby X. F. Crane
Horror-7. R. Bloch
Horror's Head. S. Horler
Horrors of Smiling Manor. M. B. Gardner
Horse-Shoe Luck. W. C. Tuttle
Horse Under Water. L. Deighton
Horsehair Santa Claus and other stories. R. J. McLaughlin
Horseman of Death. A. Wynne
Horsemen of the Law. F. F. Van De Water
Horses. J. Helvick
Horse's Head. E. Hunter
Horses of Winter. A. A. T. Davies
Horstmann Inheritance. B. Healey
Hospital Homicides. E. S. De Puy
Hospital Murders. Means Davis
Hospital Thief. T. A. Plummer
Hospitality for Murder. Gerard Fisher
Hospitality of Miss Tolliver and other Stories. G. Kersh
Hospitality of the House. D. M. Disney
Host for Dying. P. Audemars
Host of Extras. J. Leasor
Hostage. E. Garth
Hostage. Charles Henry

Hostage. S. Horler
Hostage. Colin Mason
Hostage. R. Wilkes-Hunter
Hostage for a Hood. L. White
Hostage of Evil. W. Winthrop
Hostage to Death. H. Desmond
Hostages. S. Heym
Hostages. C. E. Israel
Hostages. C. Stratton
Hostages to Fortune. M. E. Braddon
Hostages to Fortune. P. Conway
Hostess to Death. H. R. Wakefield
Hostess to Murder. E. S. Holding
Hostile Valley. B. A. Williams
Hostile Witness. J. Roffey
Hosts of Midian. P. Capon
Hosts of the Flaming Death. C. Steele
Hot. F. Lorenz
"Hot Air" Clew. N. Carter
Hot and Cold. C. H. Ross
Hot as Fire, Cold as Ice. H. Whittington
Hot Blood--Cold Blood. J. W. Mason
Hot Body. M. Avallone
Hot Bullets for Love. G. Nyland
Hot Cargo. S. Coburn
Hot Cargo. G. H. Otis
Hot Chariot. J. M. Flynn
Hot Dam. N. MacNeil
Hot Dames--Cold Lead. C. Wheatley
Hot Dames Die Cold. B. Sarto
Hot Dames on Cold Slabs. M. Storm
Hot Day Hot Night. C. Himes
Hot Diary. H. J. Olmsted
Hot End of the Stick. A. Nuttall
Hot Fire. J. McKimmey
Hot-Foot. Bill Turner
Hot Freeze. Martin Brett
Hot Gold. F. MacIsaac
Hot Half-Million. R. Chapman
Hot House. H. Janson
Hot Ice. R. Angel
Hot Ice. R. J. Casey
Hot Ice. H. Seymour
Hot Ice. S. Waldron
Hot-Line. J. Bruce
Hot Line. H. Janson
Hot Line--Capricorn. D. E. Mandeville
Hot Line for a Honey. M. Brody
Hot Mods. Garrity
Hot Potato. R. Esser
Hot Prowl. H. D. Kastle
Hot Pursuit. L. Katcher
Hot Red Money. B. Kendrick
Hot Rock. D. E. Westlake
Hot Rod Gang Rumble. M. Dolinsky
Hot Season. G. Merrick
Hot Seat. W. E. Butterworth
Hot Seat. D. Weir
Hot Seat for a Honey. C. Brown
Hot-Shot Rita. Griff
Hot Spot. C. Williams
Hot Summer Killing. J. Philips
Hot Swag. H. Kaner
Hot Tip. J. Dolph
Hot Wind from Hell. H. McCutcheon
Hotel Cremona Mystery. Gret Lane
Hotel de Luxe. Rona Randall
Hotel for Scandal. R. Lacroix
Hotel Geneva. J. Notley
Hotel Homicide. A. Parsons
Hotel Murders. S. Sterling
Hotel Richelieu Murders. A. Blackmon
Hotel Sinister. D. Whitelaw

Hotel X. W. LeQueux
Hotels with Empty Rooms. H. Gilbert
Hotshot. F. Flora
Hotspur. M. T. Walworth
Hotsy, You'll be Chilled. H. Janson
Hound and the Fox and the Harper. S. Herron
Hound From the North. R. Cullum
Hound Island. M. Williams
Hound of Death. J. Corbett
Hound of Death and other stories. A. Christie
Hound of Heaven. J. D. White
Hound of the Baskervilles. A. C. Doyle
Hounded! M. Richmond
Hounded Down. D. Durham
Hounded Man. F. Carco
Hounded to Death. N. Carter
Hounds. V. Coffman
Hounds are Restless Tonight. L. T. Shortell
Hounds of Carvello. F. Cowen
Hounds of Justice. R. Forsythe
Hounds of Sparta. Barry Norman
Hounds of the Moon. E. O. Allen
Hounds of Vengeance. J. Creasey
Hound's Tooth. R. E. McDowell
Houndstooth. G. A. Ruse
Hour After Westerley. R. M. Coates
Hour Before Moonrise. N. Buckingham
Hour Before Zero. S. Harvester
Hour-Glass. Winifred Duke
Hour-Glass Mystery. H. Hill
Hour-Glass to Eternity. M. Hastings
Hour of Death. L. Morningstar
Hour of Destiny. M. Richmond
Hour of Evil. A. Grace
Hour of Maximum Danger. J. Barlow
Hour of Recognition. P. Quiroule
Hour of the Bishop. W. M. Duncan
Hour of the Harp. Lynna Cooper
Hour of the Wolf. N. Carter
Hour of the Wolf. R. Charles
Hour of Truth. D. Egerton
Hour Struck. D. E. L. Patch
Hours After Midnight. J. Hayes
Hours Before Dawn. C. Fremlin
Hours to Kill. U. Curtiss
House Above Hollywood. V. Johnston
House Above the River. J. Bell
House Across the River. M. Bonham
House Across the Street. N. Carter
House Across the Water. H. Bourne
House Across the Way. F. Daingerfield
House and the Tower. F. S. Smith
House at Ballyslane. C. E. R. Sinclair
House at Balnesmoor. H. C. Rae
House at Canterbury. F. Kent
House at Fern Canyon. W. D. Roberts
House at Hag's Curtain. P. Motte
House at Hawk's End. Claudette Nicole
House at Kilgallen. M. L. Roby
House at Norwood. W. P. Kelly
House at Pluck's Gutter. M. Coles
House at River's Bend. R. J. Jensen
House at Rose Point. Jan Alexander
House at Sandalwood. V. Coffman
House at Satan's Elbow. J. D. Carr
House at Serraville. R. Bagot
House at the Corner. A. M. Meadows
House at the Crossroads. N. Bell
House at the Estuary. A. MacKenzie
House Behind the Mint. L. Huffman

House Between the Trees. J. Russell Lane
House-Boat Mystery. J. K. Leys
House by Exmoor. C. Stafford
House by the Bay. J. Wetherell
House by the Bridge. M. G. Easton
House by the Bridge. Melissa Napier
House by the Canal. K. Hewitt
House by the Canal. G. Simenon
House by the Church-Yard. J. S. Le Fanu
House by the Common. T. Cobb
House by the Lake. Hugh Mills
House by the Lock. A. M. Williamson
House by the River. A. P. Herbert
House by the River. F. Warden
House by the Road. C. J. Dutton
House by the Sea. M. G. Eberhart
House by the Sea. M. B. Lowndes
House by the Tarn. R. Abbey
House Called Edenhythe. N. Buckingham
House Called Whispering Winds. M. M. Fletcher
House Cried Murder. F. Nash
House Dick. Gordon Davis
House for Sale. E. C. Vivian
House in Belmont Square. M. Erskine
House in Brook Street. R. Cocking
House in Cavendish Square. D. Whitelaw
House in Charlton Crescent. A. Haynes
House in Gowderdale. T. Lang
House in Greek Street. S. Horler
House in Harlem. M. S. Michel
House in Lordship Lane. A. E. W. Mason
House in Marsh Road. L. Meynell
House in Naples. P. Rabe
House in Paris. D. Ward
House in Queen Anne Square. W. D. Lyell
House in Ralston Place. A. B. Moody
House in Sinister Lane. T. A. Plummer
House in Spitalfields. G. Wolfenden
House in Spite Street. W. M. Duncan
House in Spring Gardens. A. Griffiths
House in the Country. D. M. Low
House in the Crescent. A. Sergeant
House in the Forest. M. Cumberland
House in the Hills. L. Meynell
House in the Hills. F. Warden
House in the Mist. A. K. Green
House in the Way. Colin Hope
House in the Wood. G. Chester
House in the Woods. J. Drummond
House in Tuesday Market. J. S. Fletcher
House in White Mist. Melissa Napier
House is Falling. N. Fitzgerald
House Malign. J. Wellsley
House Next Door. A. Askew
House Next Door. B. E. Stevenson
House Next Door. L. White
House of a Thousand Candles. M. Nicholson
House of a Thousand Lanterns. V. Holt
House of Anna. A. J. Evans
House of Athena. Janice Bennett
House of Black Magic. L. T. Meade
House of Blight. Mrs. C. Kernahan
House of Brass. E. Queen
House of Broken Dolls. D. Daniels
House of Cain. S. Roberts
House of Cain. A. W. Upfield
House of Candles. P. Brisco
House of Cards. S. Ellin
House of Cards. H. Gartland
House of Cards. J. M. Ullman
House of Carson. A. Mallory
House of Cellars. G. H. Teed
House of Certain Death. A. Cossery
House of Clouds. H. L. Poole
House of Clystevill. B. Atkey
House of Cobwebs. M. Reisner
House of Counted Hatreds. S. Jennifer
House of Creeping Horror. G. F. Worts
House of Crimson Shadows. H. D. Stacpoole

House of Curtains. G. H. Teed
House of Danger. G. Thorne
House of Dark Illusions. C. Farr
House of Dark Laughter. Melissa Napier
House of Dark Secrets. G. M. Allen
House of Dark Shadows. Marilyn Ross
House of Darkness. J. Hunter
House of Darkness. K. Laing
House of Darkness. A. MacKinnon
House of Deadly Calm. M. Farnsworth
House of Deadly Night. I. Barry
House of Dearth. V. MacClure
House of Death. C. Goodall
House of Death. L. Groc
House of Death. K. Robeson
House of Delusion. R. S. Holland
House of Destiny. C. Farr
House of Disappearance. J. J. Farjeon
House of Disappearances. C. K. Steele
House of Discord. M. E. Hanshew
House of Distant Voices. E. Bond
House of Dr. Edwardes. F. Beeding
House of Dogs. R. Elliott
House of Doom. N. Carter
House of Dread. R. Dorian
House of Echoes. John Marsh
House of En-Dor. A. Hocking
House of Evil. H. Clevely
House of Evil. W. LeQueux
House of Evil. C. Lipman
House of Evil. M. Lynch
House of Evil. J. Trinian
House of Faith. M. G. Kiddy
House of False Faces. D. Daniels
House of False Faces. H. G. Weston
House of Fand. A. Maybury
House of Fand. K. Troy
House of Fatal Mirrors. F. W. Gumley
House of Fear. W. Camp
House of Fear. M. Dalton
House of Fear. Jack Lewis
House of Fear. R. W. Service
"House of Fear." W. Spence
House of Fears. J. England
House of Fendon. R. Bridges
House of Flesh. B. Fischer
House of Fools. Jan Alexander
House of Fortune. M. Pemberton
House of Four Widows. D. Lyons
House of Fury. J. A. Creighton
House of Ghosts. L. H. Brooks
House of Ghosts. Marilyn Ross
House of Glass. G. Ferrand
House of Godwinsson. E. R. Punshon
"House of Greed." R. St. Clair
House of Green Turf. Ellis Peters
House of Haddon. L. Ames
House of Halliwell. H. Wood
House of Happy Mayhem. W. J. Sheldon
House of Hate. J. E. Ferris
House of Hate. Dorothy Fletcher
House of Hate. H. Mace
House of Horror. M. Crombie
House of Horror. R. Halifax
House of Horror. T. C. H. Jacobs
House of Horror. N. MacKenzie
House of Horror. Donald Ross
House of Horrors. J. Reach
House of Illusion. D. Quentin
House of Intrigue. L. Hoffman
House of Intrigue. C. Robertson
House of Intrigue. A. Stringer
House of Intrigue. Percy White
House of Iron Men. Jack Steele
House of Jackals. S. Horler
House of Jeffreys. R. Thorndike

Title Index

House of Lies. Austin Moore
House of Lies. S. Warwick
House of Living Death. T. Blore
House of Lyes. C. W. Whitaker
House of Malory. H. McElroy
House of Mammon. F. M. White
House of Many Doors. D. Daniels
House of Many Mirrors. V. Hunt
House of Many Shadows. B. Michaels
House of Many Voices. B. Capes
House of Marney. J. Goodwin
House of Masks. Barbara Cooper
House of Masques. F. Kent
House of Men. C. Marchant
House of Menace. A. Furness
House of Merrilees. A. Marshall
House of Mirror Images. D. Winston
House of Mist. M. L. Bolton
House of Moreys. P. Bentley
House of Murder. H. L. Gates
House of Murder. J. H. Wallis
House of Mystery. Will Irwin
House of Mystery. Hilary Lang
House of Mystery. R. Marsh
House of Mystery. W. J. Newton
House of Mystery. Grace M. White
House of Night. L. H. Gordon
House of Numbers. J. Finney
House of Ogilvie. Winifred Duke
House of Peril. M. B. Lowndes
House of Peril. L. Tracy
House of Rancour. S. Nichols
House of Ravensbourne. M. A. Gibbs
House of Retrogression. C. Patrick
House of Rhinestad. D. M. Parish
House of Rising Water. Melissa Napier
House of Rogues. C. B. Booth
House of Scorpio. P. Wallace
House of Seclusion. M. Harvey
House of Secrets. C. Farr
House of Secrets. S. Horler
House of Secrets. W. Martyn
House of Secrets. S. Noel
House of Secrets. H. L. Phillips
House of Shade. M. M. Kaye
House of Shadows. E. Bond
House of Shadows. J. J. Farjeon
House of Shadows. F. Hurd
House of Shadows. D. Martyn
House of Shayle. John Alexander
House of Silence. C. Collins
House of Silence. H. W. Jarvis
House of Silence. J. H. Robinson
House of Silence. G. H. Teed
House of Silence. L. Tracy
House of Silence. R. Trevor
House of Silence. C. N. Williamson
House of Sin. B. Sarto
House of Sin. A. Upward
House of Sleep. Michael Burt
House of Sleep. Frank King
House of Soldiers. A. Garve
House of Sorcery. C. Brown
House of Sorrows. F. M. White
House of Stolen Memories. D. Daniels
House of Storm. M. G. Eberhart
House of Storms. H. Bridges
House of Strange Guests. N. Brady
House of Strange Victims. B. Atkey
House of Strangers. M. Padget
House of Sudden Sleep. J. Hawk
House of Tears. E. Downey
House of Terror. E. Berckman

House of Terror. G. Biss
House of Terror. F. Swann
House of Terror. E. Woodward
House of the Apricots. H. Imber
House of the Arrow. A. E. W. Mason
House of the Bears. J. Creasey
House of the Black Ring. F. L. Pattee
House of the Cat. A. Roudybush
House of the Damned. A. M. Rud
House of the Dancing Dead. A. Vandergriff
House of the Enchantress. M. Erskine
House of the Fiery Cauldron. A. Brennan
House of the Four Winds. J. Buchan
House of the Fragrant Lotus. E. P. Thorne
House of the Hatchet and other tales of horror. R. Bloch
House of the Hawk. W. C. Tuttle
House of the Hunter. F. Taylor
House of the Lost. B. Gray
House of the Lost Court. M. D'Alpins
House of the Lost Court. D. T. De Savallo
House of the Lost Woman. Louise O'Flaherty
House of the Missing. S. Gluck
House of the Moving Room. J. J. Chichester
House of the Opal. J. Gregory
House of the Pines. J. Tempest
House of the Purple Stairs. J. Helm
House of the Secret. C. Farrere
House of the Seven Courts. D. Daniels
House of the Seven Flies. V. Canning
House of the Seven Keys. M. E. Hanshew
House of the Siren. J. Selborne
House of the Soul. J. B. Harris-Burland
House of the Spaniard. A. Behrend
House of the Sword. D. G. Browne
House of the Talisman. H. H. Ross
House of the Three Ganders. I. A. Bacheller
House of the Twelve Caesars. P. Hastings
House of the Uneasy Dead. S. Horler
House of the Vanishing Goblets. L. Edgley
House of the Weeping Women. C. Dawson
House of the Whispering Pines. A. K. Green
House of the Whispering Winds. E. McCrae
House of the White Shadows. B. L. Farjeon
House of the Wicked. W. LeQueux
House of the Winds. C. Hodge
House of the Winds. J. G. Sarasin
House of the Yellow Door. N. Carter
House of Tombs. C. Farr
House of Torment. C. R. Gull
House of Torture. L. C. Douthwaite
House of Tragedy. A. J. Fitzgerald
House of Treason. D. Allan
House of Two Green Eyes. S. Chalmers
House of Two Wives. D. Locke
House of Vengeance. R. St. Clair
House of Wailing Winds. W. M. Duncan
House of Whipplestaff. E. F. Boyd
House of Whispers. N. Carter
House of Whispers. W. A. Johnston
House of Whispers. W. LeQueux
House of Women. L. K. Scott
House of Wraith. E. J. Millward
House of Yesteryear. M. Lynch
House on Black Bayou. M. Sellers
House on Cabra. J. Wetherell
House on Charles Street. A. Burr
House on Cheyne Walk. P. Organ
House on Circus Hill. D. Daniels
House on Doubloon Inlet. J. A. Dunn
House on Gannet's Point. C. Van Hazinga
House on Greenapple Road. H. R. Daniels
House on K Street. L. White
House on Malador Street. P. Hastings
House on Mount Vernon Street. W. E. D. Ross

House on Q Street. R. Dietrich
House on Quai Notre Dame. G. Simenon
House on Rainbow Leap. R. M. Vale
House on Sixteenth Street. E. Thorne
House on Sky High Road. I. S. Way
House on Smith Square. A. Burr
House on Somber Lake. A. De Marquand
House on Telegraph Hill. D. Lyon
House on the Bay. Arthur MacLean
House on the Beach. E. E. Cameron
House on the Beach. E. L. Withers
House on the Black Moor. D. Polk
House on the Broads. Wilfrid Robertson
House on the Cliff. G. Batson
House on the Cliff. L. Meynell
House on the Cliffs. G. Chester
House on the Cliffs. C. Farr
House on the Downs. G. E. Locke
House on the Drive. B. Kingsley
House on the Fen. C. Rayner
House on the Fens. C. Cookson
House on the Fens. A. Gask
House on the Hard. A. Wynne
House on the Hill. J. Drummond
House on the Hudson. F. Powell
House on the Island. A. Gask
House on the Lake. J. Reach
House on the Left Bank. V. Johnston
House on the Mall. E. Jepson
House on the Marsh. J. J. Farjeon
House on the Marsh. H. R. Martin
House on the Marsh. F. Warden
House on the Moat. V. Coffman
House on the River. J. Drummond
House on the Rocks. T. Charles
House on the Roof. M. G. Eberhart
House on the Saltings. V. Bridges
House on the Strand. D. Du Maurier
House on the Thames. G. W. Appleton
House on Thunder Hill. S. Somers
House on Tollard Ridge. J. Rhode
House on Trevor Street. F. Hurd
House on Vickers' Island. J. St. Clair
House on Windswept Ridge. K. Kimbrough
House Opposite. J. J. Farjeon
House Opposite. E. Kent
House over the Tunnel. J. J. Farjeon
House over the Way. A. W. Barrett
House Party Murder. Colin Ward
House Party Murders. E. A. Poe
House-Party Mystery. G. Norsworthy
House Possessed. C. Blackstock
House Possessed. L. Paige
House 'Round the Corner. Gordon Holmes
House-Surgeon. I. Jefferies
House Surgeon at Luke's. Rona Randall
House Terrible. A. Towner
House that Berry Built. D. Yates
House that Chak Built. K. West
House that Died. H. Bordeaux
House that Died. Josephine Gill
House that Fear Built. C. Knye
House that Hate Built. S. E. Mason
House that Samael Built. R. Jensen
House that Stood Still. A. E. Van Vogt
House that Waited. C. Reeve
House that Whispered. S. Emery
House Upstairs. C. Rodda
House with a Bad Name. P. P. Sheehan
House with a History. F. Warden
House with a Past. J. Courage
House with Black Blinds. H. Bridges
House with Blind Eyes. H. Jobson
House with Crooked Walls. B. Graeme
House with Green Shutters. A. R. Long
House with No Address. E. M. Channon
House with No Address. E. Nesbit
House with Steel Shutters. A. Parsons
House with Strange Secrets. A. E. Bayly

House with the Blue Door. H. Footner
House with the Double Moat. E. S. Brooks
House with the Green Shutters. George Douglas
House with the High Wall. A. Gask
House with the Light. S. Horler
House with the Red Blinds. T. C. Wignall
House with the Stained Glass Windows. Winston Graham
House with the Watching Eyes. N. A. Hintze
House with Two Faces. Sheila Bishop
House Without a Door. T. Sterling
House Without a Key. E. D. Biggers
House Without the Door. E. Daly
House Without Windows. L. Constable
Houseboat Enigma. R. R. Hillman
Houseboat Killings. R. Simons
Houseboat Mystery. J. Edwards
Household of Hertz. W. J. Newton
Household Skeleton. G. L. Aiken
Household Traitors. J. Blackburn
Householders. Margaret Henry
Housekeeper's Secret. H. Fielding
Houseparty. K. P. Britton
Houses of Glass. W. Lloyd
Hovering Darkness. E. Berckman
How Awful About Allan. H. Farrell
How Bad Can They Be? N. Leslie
How Briggs Died. D. E. Harding
How Came He Dead? J. F. Molloy
How Can We Sing? A. Dick
How Could They? C. N. Boyle
How Dark Are the Dunes? C. Herbert
How Dead Can You Be? D. Linton
How Did Elmer Die? G. P. West
How Doth the Little Crocodile? P. Antony
How Goes the Murder? E. Queen
How Good a Detective Are You? A. Ripley
How Hard to Kill. T. B. Dewey
How He Did It. E. A. Dupuy
How He Won Her. E. Southworth
How He Won Her, and A False Friend. G. Fleming
How I Became Eminent. J. Middlemass
How I Made a Million Dollars. A. F. Taylor
How Like an Angel. M. Millar
How Many Cards? I. Ostrander
How Many Coupons for a Shroud? N. Morland
How Many to Kill? M. Halliday
How Murder Speaks. R. S. Holland
How Now, McLean? G. Goodchild
How Sleeps the Beast. D. Tracy
How Slow the Snooth. C. Herbert
How Still My Love. D. Siegel
How Strange a Thing. D. Bennett
How the Old Woman Got Home. M. P. Shiel
How to Kill a Man. T. Wells
How to Live Dangerously. J. Fleming
How to Murder Your Wife. Henry Williams
How to Steal a Million. Michael Sinclair
How to Succeed at Business Spying by Trying. S. Mead
How to Succeed at Murder Without Really Trying. D. Von Elsner
How Was It Done? Mark Cross
Howards of Saxondale. Rona Randall
Howling Dog. R. Drayton
Howling in the Woods. V. Johnson
Hoxton Mystery. T. W. Hanshew
Hoyland Intervenes. P. C. Williams
Hoyland Steps Out. P. C. Williams
Hubberthwaite Horror. J. Austwick
Hubschmann Effect. T. P. McMahon
Huddersfield Job. Angus Ross
Huddle. C. Wells
Hue and Cry. T. B. Dewey
Hue and Cry. B. Hamilton
Hue and Cry. J. B. O'Sullivan
Hue and Cry. P. Wentworth
Hugger-Mugger in the Louvre. Elliot Paul
Human Bacillus. R. Eustace
Human Bloodhound. E. S. Brooks
Human Cat. D. Stewart
Human Chase. E. P. Oppenheim
Human Element. J. Fores
Human Factor. Simon Quinn
Human Fiend. N. Carter
Human Mole. C. Collins
Human Nature. M. Leighton
Human Question Mark. D. Stewart
Human Time Bomb. N. Carter
Human Vampire. T. F. Elstow
Human Vultures. Roland Daniel
Humdrum House. M. Foster
Humming Box. H. Whittington
Humming Cliff. M. Tannock
Humming Top. D. Spicer
Hunch. R. Humphreys
Hunchback House. D. B. Hobart
Hunchback of Hatton Garden. G. Bowman
Hunchback of Hatton Garden! H. E. Hill
Hunchback of Soho. Roland Daniel
Hunchback of Westminster. W. LeQueux
Hundred Days. T. Mundy
Hundred-Dollar Girl. W. C. Gault
Hundred Per Cent. H. C. McNeile
Hundred Thousand Guineas. E. Jepson
Hundredth Acre. J. Campden
Hundredth Door. R. Foley
Hung by an Eyelash. L. Anson
Hung Until Dead. P. Johnson
Hungarian Game. Roy Hayes
Hunger and other stories. C. Beaumont
Hunger and the Hate. H. V. Dixon
Hungering Shame. R. V. Cassill
Hungry Dog. F. Gruber
Hungry Goblin. J. D. Carr
Hungry Heart. H. B. Kaye
Hungry House. L. Lauferty
Hungry Killer. M. O'Brine
Hungry Killer. E. Radford
Hungry One. G. Brewer
Hungry Sea. L. Ames
Hungry Spider. S. Jepson
Hunslett's Yard. E. L. Long
Hunt. W. Carrier
Hunt and Kill. R. T. Bickers
Hunt at Desolation. Michael Barrett
Hunt Ball Murder. F. W. Crofts
Hunt Ball Mystery. W. Magnay
Hunt Club. N. Daniels
Hunt for Danger. A. Curry
Hunt for Richard Thorpe. J. Tickell
Hunt in the Highlands. H. J. Wurr
Hunt Is Up. A. Hocking
Hunt the Body. P. Flower
Hunt the Evidence. R. Clifford
Hunt the Killer. D. Keene
Hunt the Lady! D. Reid
Hunt the Man. W. Pearson
Hunt the Man Down. W. Pearson
Hunt the Spy. M. McKenna
Hunt the Toff. J. Creasey
Hunt the Tortoise. E. Ferrars
Hunt to Kill. M. Russell
Hunt with the Hounds. M. G. Eberhart
Hunted. G. F. Gibbs
Hunted. J. Millard
Hunted! T. A. Plummer
Hunted. M. Reisner
Hunted and Haunted. I. Stark
Hunted Down. C. Dickens
Hunted Down. M. Hillary
Hunted Down. J. M'Govan
Hunted Down. R. H. Rohde
Hunted Down. R. A. Wainwright
Hunted Man. W. S. Masterman
Hunted to Death. W. S. Hayward
Hunted Woman. M. Albrand
Hunted Woman. J. Pendower
Hunter. R. Holland
Hunter. R. Stark
Hunter and the Trapped. J. Bell
Hunter at Large. T. B. Dewey
Hunter for Hire. W. Spann
Hunter Hunted. H. Treece
Hunter, Hunter, Get Your Gun. D. Macomber
Hunter in the Shadows. J. Melville
Hunter Is the Hunted. A. B. Cunningham
Hunter-Killer. G. Jenkins
Hunter of Men. N. Carter
Hunter of Men. C. H. Guenter
Hunters. J. Ambler
Hunter's Green. P. A. Whitney
Hunter's Mate. J. Blackmore
Hunter's Moon. N. Benchley
Hunters of Humans. V. M. Steele
Hunters Point. G. Sims
Hunter's Way. C. Reeve
Hunterstone Outrage. S. Truss
Hunting for Gold. H. Nisbet
Hunting-Ground. F. Clifford
Hunting Ground. M. Sutherland
Hunting of Hillary. E. Winch
Hunting Party. J. Millard
Huntingtower. J. Buchan
Huntress. H. Footner
Huntress. Williams Forrest
Huntress. C. C. Lowis
Huntress. M. A. Wilson
Huntress Is Dead. B. Benson
Huntress of Death. S. Horler
Huntsman. G. Verner
Hurricane. J. D. MacDonald
Hurricane Drift. J. N. Chance
Hurricane House. R. St. Clair
Hurricane Tex. G. Goodchild
Hurricane Warning! Richard Williams
Hurricane Williams' Vengeance. Gordon Young
Hurry the Darkness. M. Procter
Hurrying Feet. F. F. Van De Water
Hurt Me No More. I. Batista-Olivieri
Hurton Treasure Mystery. F. Hume
Husband. V. Caspary
Husband and Wife. M. Leighton
Husband of the Corpse. M. Judd
Husband's Secret. R. Dowling
Hush-a-Bye Murder. David Alexander
Hush, Gabriel! V. P. Johns
Hush Hush Johnson. N. Gates
Hush-Hush Murders. M. T. Yates
Hush, It's a Game. P. Carlon
Hush Money. P. Israel
Hush Money. J. Middlemass
Hushed Up! W. LeQueux
Hushed Up at German Headquarters. W. LeQueux
Husky Voice. Roland Daniel
Hustle. S. Shagan
Hustler Paul. J. Cleveland
Hustlers. Sam Ross
Hut. L. Meynell
Hyacinth Spell. F. Y. McHugh
Hyde Place. V. Coffman
Hydra-Head. S. Noel
Hydra with Six Heads. J. Bell

Title Index

Hymn Tune Mystery. G. A. Birmingham
Hypnotic Demon. M. E. Cooke
Hypnotist Detective. Anonymous
Hypnotized. M. Brandon
Hypocrite. C. R. Gull

I

I Accuse. C. Kingston
I Am a Smuggler. C. Evelyn
I Am Afraid. E. K. Lobaugh
I Am Being Poisoned. L. Phraile
I Am Death. R. Conner
I Am Death. G. Verner
I Am Gabriella! A. Maybury
I Am Jonathan Scrivener. C. Houghton
I Am Maud Latimer. J. Shard
I Am Saxon Ashe. S. Ashe
I Am the Captain. G. Hackforth-Jones
I Am the Cat. R. Kutak
I Am the Withered Man. N. Deane
"I, and I Alone." J. Weidman
I and My True Love. H. MacInnes
I Came to a Castle. V. Johnson
I Came to Kill. Gordon Davis
I Came to the Highlands. V. Johnston
I Can Cope. M. Cronin
"I Can't Die Here." J. C. Nolan
I Can't Stop Running. E. Ronns
I Charge You Both. A. M. Meadows
I Come to Kill You. B. Halliday
I Could a Tale Unfold. D. Whitelaw
I Could Murder Her. E. C. R. Lorac
I Crown Thee King. M. Pemberton
I Did It! Garret Smith
I Did Not Kill Osborne. V. Bridges
I Die Possessed. J. B. O'Sullivan
I Die Slowly. K. Millar
I Don't Die Easy. R. Drayton
I Don't Get It. Spike Gordon
I Don't Get It. Griff
I Don't Like Cats. L. Anson
I Don't Scare Easy. B. Dougall
I Escape. J. L. Hardy
I Fear the Greeks. A. M. Stein
I Fear You Not. B. Kerr
I Fell Among Thieves. B. Cobb
I for Intrigue. H. Janson
"I Forbid the Banns." F. Frankfort Moore
I Found Him Dead. G. Gallagher
I Gave at the Office. D. E. Westlake
I Get What I Want. Larry Heller
I Had to Kill Her. E. Connell
I Hate Actors! B. Hecht
I Hate Blondes. W. Kaufman
I Hate You to Death. K. Edgar
I Have Gloria Kirby. R. Himmel
I Have Killed a Man! C. F. Gregg
I Heard the Death Bell. C. M. Russell
I Hide, We Seek. R. M. Stern
I Keep My Word. J. M. Scott
I Kill 'Em Inch by Inch. B. Sarto
I Killed Stalin. S. Noel
I Killed the Count. Alec Coppel
I Knew MacBean. M. Erskine
I Knew Mrs. Lang. G. Barnett
I Know a Secret. P. Hambledon
I Know My Love. F. Nichols
I Know What You Did Last Summer. L. Duncan
"I.L.F." D. Dallas
I Let Him Go. J. Brophy
I Like a Good Murder. M. Magill
I Like Danger. M. Corrigan
I Like 'Em Tough. C. Cannon
I Like It Cool. Michael Lawrence
I Like It Tough. J. A. Howard

I Love, I Kill. J. Bingham
I Love You Again. O. R. Cohen
I, Lucifer. P. O'Donnell
I Married a Dead Man. W. Irish
I Married a Doctor. Rona Randall
I Married Mr. Richardson. J. Ames
I Met a Man. M. Blankfort
I Met Murder. S. Jepson
I Met Murder on the Way. M. Echard
I Never Killed. Max Gordon
I Never Miss Twice. B. Cobb
I.O.U. Murder. T. B. Dewey
I.O.U.--Murder. W. Francis
I Prefer Murder. B. Norton
"I!" Said the Demon. G. Baxt
I, Said the Fly. E. Ferrars
I, Savaran! D. Newton
I Saw Murder. G. Cobden
I Saw Three Ships, and other winter's tales. Q
I Say "No." W. Collins
I See Red. S. Noel
I See You. C. Armstrong
I Shall Avenge. J. Robb
I Should Have Stayed Home. H. McCoy
I Sit in Hanger Lane. J. T. Story
I Smell the Devil. C. Magoon
I Spit on Your Grave. Griff
I Spy. N. S. Lincoln
I, Spy. D. MacKenzie
I Spy. K. Medusa
I, Spy. S. Stone
I Spy. J. Tiger
I Start Counting. A. E. Lindop
I Stood in the Shadow of the Black Cap. J. Budd
I Take This Woman. G. Simenon
I Thank a Fool. A. E. Lindop
I, the Criminal. D. Sharp
I, the Executioner. S. Ransome
I, the Hangman. W. A. Ballinger
I, the Jury. M. Spillane
I Thought I'd Die. D. V. Reed
I, Victoria Strange. R. Willock
I Wake Screaming. B. Shannon
I Wake Up Screaming. S. Fisher
I Want a Policeman! R. King
I Want an Audience. John Gloag
I Want Out. T. Thomey
I Want to Be a Lady. M. Foster
I Want to go Home. R. Lockridge
I Want to Live! T. Rawson
I Wanted to Murder. C. F. Cushman
I Was a Spy in Britain. G. Usher
I Was Alone. K. David
I Was Following This Girl. D. Skirrow
I Was Going Anyway. R. Switzer
I Was Murdered. M. E. Longman
I Was Murdered. G. M. Wilson
I Was Walking Down Below. T. Gates
I Will Speak Daggers. M. Procter
I Wonder What Happened to Tom? B. Reade
I Would Rather Stay Poor. J. H. Chase
I Wouldn't Be in Your Shoes. W. Irish
Ibeza Syndicate. B. Reade
Ice-Axe Murders. G. Carr
Ice Before Killing. M. Strobel
Ice Bomb Zero. N. Carter
Ice-Cold in Alex. C. Landon
Ice Cold in Ermine. C. Brown
Ice-Cold Nude. C. Brown
Ice Forest. V. Coffman
Ice Goddess. P. Edwards
Ice Maiden. J. Vicary
Ice Maidens. J. N. Chance
Ice Pilot. H. Leverage

Ice Pond Mystery. J. Kipley
Ice Station Zebra. Alistair MacLean
Ice Trap Terror. N. Carter
Iceberg. C. Cussler
Iceman No. 7. J. Nazel
Icepick in Ollie Birk. E. Sudak
Icepick in the Spine. F. Scarpetta
I'd Crowns Resign. J. M. Cobban
Identical Strangers. V. Hawthorne
Identification Parade. P. N. Walker
Identity. Winifred Graham
Identity Crisis. L. Latham
Identity Unknown. T. C. H. Jacobs
Identity Unknown. R. Marlowe
Identity Unwanted. Jean Marsh
Ides of November. F. Stevenson
Idle Island. E. Hueston
Idle Tales. J. H. Riddell
Idol of Last Chance. Anonymous
Idol of the Blind. T. Gallon
Idol of the Town. W. LeQueux
Idol's Eye. H. E. Hill
If a Body. G. W. Yates
If a Body Kill a Body. P. Mortimer
If a Body Meet a Body. G. Malcolm-Smith
If Anything Happens to Hester. A. Morton
If Anything Should Happen. Kevin O'Hara
If Anything Should Happen to Me. A. Barker
If Death Ever Slept. R. Stout
If Dying Was All. R. Goulart
If Hate Could Kill. J. Bradley
If I Die Before I Wake. S. King
If I Die--It's Murder. M. Ervin
If I Kill Him. J. Hawkins
If I Knew What I Was Doing. Albert Ross
If I Live to Dine. H. Waugh
If I Should Die. P. Bannon
If I Should Die Before I Wake. W. Irish
If I Should Lose You. M. Richmond
If I Should Murder. P. Laing
If It Please You. Richard Marsh
If Laurel Shot Hardy the World Would End. S. Forbes
If Love Be Ours. K. Lindsay
If Murder Interferes with Business. A. Spiller
If She Should Die. M. L. Roby
If She Should Die. F. Rydell
If Sinners Entice Thee. W. LeQueux
If the Coffin Fits. D. Keene
If the Shoe Fits. Lee Roberts
If the Shroud Fits. P. Kruger
If the Shroud Fits. K. Roos
If They Fall--. V. MacClure
If This Be Murder. R. Darby
If This Be Treason. M. Echard
If Two of Them Are Dead. S. Forbes
If Two of Them Are Dead. M. Gregory
If Wishes Were Hearses. J. H. Bond
If Wishes Were Hearses. G. Cullingford
If You Can't Be Good. Ross Thomas
If You Have Tears. John Evans
If You Should Ever Need Me. B. Treynor
If You Want a Murder Well Done. M. Scherf
If You Want to See Your Wife Again. John Craig
If Your Cover Is Blown. J. Browning
Ilion Like a Mist. J. Mitchell
I'll Always Remember. M. Richmond
I'll Be Glad When You're Dead. D. Lyon
I'll Be Judge, I'll Be Jury. E. Hely
I'll Be Judge, I'll Be Jury. M. Kennedy

I'll Blackmail the World. A. Wood
I'll Bring Her Back. P. Cheyney
I'll Bury My Dead. J. H. Chase
I'll Come Quietly. T. McCoy
Ill Deeds Done. A. Hocking
I'll Die for You. S. Ransome
I'll Die Tonight. J. Laffin
I'll Do Anything. D. Bateson
I'll Eat You Last. H. C. Branson
I'll Find You. R. Himmel
I'll Fix Eye. H. Ellson
I'll Fry Yet. R. Angel
I'll Get By. B. Sarto
I'll Get Mine. Thurston Scott
I'll Get You for This. J. H. Chase
I'll Get You Yet. J. A. Howard
I'll Go Anywhere. D. Bateson
Ill Gotten Gains. A. Murray
I'll Grind Their Bones. T. Roscoe
I'll Hate Myself in the Morning, and Summer in December. Elliot Paul
I'll Kill You Last. H. C. Branson
I'll Kill You Next! Adam Knight
Ill Met by a Fish Shop on George Street. M. McShane
Ill Met by Moonlight. L. Ford
Ill Met in Mexico. C. M. Russell
I'll Never Leave You. E. Lustgarten
I'll Never Let You Go. F. Nichols
I'll Never Like Friday Again. S. Maddock
I'll Never Tell. Roy Vickers
I'll Say She Does! P. Cheyney
I'll See You in Hell. J. McPartland
I'll Sing at Your Funeral. H. Pentecost
I'll Sing You the Death of Bill Brown. B. Dexter
I'll Take What's Mine. N. Jones
I'll Tell You Everything. J. B. Priestley
Ill-Tempered Clavicord. S. J. Perelman
Ill Will. H. Brinton
Ill Wind. R. Fenisong
Ill Wind. M. Fitt
Ill Wind. W. L. Heath
Ill Wind Contract. P. Atlee
Illegal Entry. R. Bernard
Illegal Tender. D. M. Devine
Illegitimate Spy. R. Silverwood
Illicit Cargo. R. Lacroix
Illusion. F. Keinzley
Illusion at Haven's Edge. D. Daniels
Illusionist. S. D. Frances
Illustrious Corpse. T. Thayer
Illustrious Prince. E. P. Oppenheim
I'm Afraid I'll Live! K. S. Cole
I'm Cannon--for Hire. C. Cannon
I'm King of the Castle. Susan Hill
I'm No Hero. H. Howard
I'm No Murderer. B. Perowne
I'm Trying to Give It Up. D. Skirrow
I'm Waiting. S. Reese
Image in the Dust. Warwick Scott
Image in the Mirror. D. L. Sayers
Image Killer. W. Maner
Image Makers. B. V. Dryer
Image of a Ghost. D. Daniels
Image of a Murder. P. Capon
Image of Hell. S. Fisher
Image of Man. M. Tripp
Image of Stephanie. S. Sloan
Image Seller. K. Ostrander
Images of Han. J. M. Walsh
Images of Rose. Anna Gilbert
Imagine a Man. N. Fitzgerald
Imagine a Man in a Box. H. R. Wakefield
Imitation Thieves. M. Lovell
Immaterial Murder Case. J. Symons

Immediate Jewel. A. Applin
Immortal Dawn. R. Bridges
Immortal Error. E. Trevor
Immortals of the Mountain. C. V. Gheorghiu
Imogen Hartland. G. W. M. Reynolds
Impact. B. Copper
Impact. H. Olesker
Impact of Evidence. C. Carnac
Impact-20. W. F. Nolan
Impartial Eye. P. Boulle
Impeached! B. Graeme
Impeccable People. E. Fenwick
Impending Sword. H. A. Vachell
Impending Sword. E. Yates
"Impenetrable Mystery" of Zora Burns. Anonymous
Imperfect Alibi. M. Hervey
Imperfect Crime. B. Graeme
Imperfect Lover. R. Gore-Browne
Imperfect Lover. A. Soutar
Imperial Blue. E. Bond
Imperial Marriage. A. W. Marchmont
Imperial Treasure. V. Gielgud
Imperial Venus. A. Dick
Impersonators. E. S. Brooks
Impetuous Mistress. G. H. Coxe
Implacable Hunter. G. Kersh
Implied Immunity. D. F. Holmes
Implosion. J. Montgomerie
Import of Evil. J. N. Chance
Importance of Being Murdered. C. Wells
Impossible Apollo. T. Cobb
Impossible Crime. E. C. Vivian
Impossible Dream. L. Hoffman
Impossible Guest. J. J. Farjeon
Impossible Husband. F. Warden
Impossible Lover. B. Bolt
Impossible Virgin. P. O'Donnell
Impossibles. M. Phillips
Imposter. W. H. Baker
Imposter. M. Cumberland
Imposter. J. Jakes
Imposter. E. Keeley
Imposter. K. Steel
Imposter. D. Whitelaw
Impregnable City. M. Pemberton
Improbable Fiction. S. Woods
Impromptu Imposter. V. Vicas
Impulse. I. Ostrander
In a Bad Man's Grip. S. Warwick
In a Beautiful Pea-Green Boat. J. M. Scott
In a Deadly Vein. M. Culpan
In a Deadly Vein. B. Halliday
In a Fair Ground. L. G. Moberly
In a Glass Darkly. J. Caird
In a Glass Darkly. J. S. Le Fanu
In a House Unknown. D. Hitchens
In a Little House. T. Gallon
In a Lonely Place. D. B. Hughes
In a Silver Sea. B. L. Farjeon
In a Telephone Cabinet. G. D. H. Cole
In a Vain Shadow. R. Marshall
In a Vanishing Room. R. Colby
In Accordance with the Evidence. O. Onions
In After Years. J. K. Stafford
In All Shades. G. Allen
In All Simplicity. P. Capon
In an Alpine Valley. G. M. Fenn
In an Ancient Mirror. H. Flowerdew
In an Iron Grip. L. T. Meade
In and Out. Edgar Franklin
In Another Man's Shoes. M. L. Eades
In Any Case. R. G. Stern
In at the Death. F. Duncan
In at the Death. D. Frome

In at the Death. G. F. Underhill
In at the Kill. B. Knox
In at the Kill. E. McDowell
In Bad with Sinbad. A. Stringer
In Barracks and Wigwam. W. M. Graydon
In Black & Whitey. E. Lacy
In Brighton Waters. G. Volk
In Camera. John Gloag
In Camera. C. G. Mitford
In Case of Emergency. G. Simenon
In Chinatown. T. Burke
In Cold Blood. G. Bagby
In Cold Blood. T. Capote
In Cold Blood. A. Livingston
In Comes Death. P. Whelton
In Connection with Kilshaw. P. Driscoll
In Council Rooms Apart. John Craig
In Court. F. Andreas
In Crime's Disguise. F. C. Milford
In Cupid's Wars. C. Gibbon
In Dark Places. J. Russell
In Darkest Madras. H. E. Hill
In Deadly Peril. E. Gaboriau
In Deadly Peril. D. Lechmere
In Death's Grip. N. Carter
in Deep Abyss. G. Ohnet
In Deep Water. M. Richmond
In Defense of Mrs. Maxon. G. A. Chamberlain
In Direst Peril. D. C. Murray
In Double Disguise. W. M. Graydon
In Extremis. Mrs. Greenough
In Face of the Verdict. J. Rhode
In False Attire. G. Norway
In Fear of a Woman. Winifred Graham
In Fear of the Hangman. M. Richmond
In Fear of the Night. H. Desmond
In Fort and Prison. W. M. Graydon
In Friendship's Guise. W. M. Graydon
In Full Commission. E. L. Long
In Full Cry. J. Goodwin
In Full Cry. R. Marsh
In God's Good Time. M. Leighton
In Great Danger. N. MacKenzie
In Her Own Right. J. R. Scott
In High Places. M. E. Braddon
In His Blood. H. R. Daniels
In His Grip. D. C. Murray
In Honour Bound. C. Gibbon
In Hot Blood. M. B. Cook
In Jeopardy. V. Sutphen
In Jeopardy, and other stories of peril. G. M. Fenn
In Lands of Terror. D. Lenton
In League with Counterfeiters. E. C. Derby
In League with Satan. I. Stark
In Letters of Fire. N. Carter
In Like Flint. B. Street
In London's Heart. G. R. Sims
In Love and War. C. Gibbon
In Lovers' Lane. A. Askew
In Loving Memory. Emma Page
In Male Attire. J. Hutton
In Market Overt. J. Payn
In Memory of Murder. D. Hawkins
In Mid-Atlantic. B. Delannoy
In Minden Town. M. A. Curtois
In Muffled Night. D. E. Muir
In My Father's Den. M. Gee
In Pastures Green and other stories. C. Gibbon
In Peril of His Life. G. D. H. Cole
In Peril of His Life. E. Gaboriau
In Pursuit of a Million. F. Marlowe
In Pursuit of Evil. Hugh Mills
In Queer Quarters. N. Carter
In Queer Street. F. Hume
In re Sherlock Holmes. A. Derleth
In Record Time. N. Carter

In Satan's Bonds. C. E. Perry
In Savage Hayti. R. C. Armour
In Savage Surrender. W. Chambers
In Scarlet and Plain Clothes. T. M. Longstreth
In Search of a Villain. R. Gore-Browne
In Search of Emily Crew. A. Furness
In Search of Himself. N. Carter
In Search of Stephanie. K. Rhodes
In Secret. R. W. Chambers
In Secret. W. LeQueux
In Secret Places. S. Truss
In Secret Service. J. Rosmer
In Shadows of Desire. James Stevens
In Sheep's Clothing. H. Nisbet
In Sickness and in Health. R. Rendell
In Sin or Folly? A. Nestorien
In Spite of Thunder. J. D. Carr
In Spite of the Czar. G. Boothby
In Storm and Strife. J. Middlemass
In Strange Company. G. Boothby
In Strange Shoes. A. Askew
In Such a Night... V. Gielgud
In Suspicion's Shadow. N. Carter
In Terror's Grasp. Warren Miller
In the Absence of a Body. G. Bromley
In the Absence of Mrs. Petersen. N. Balchin
In the Balance. P. Wentworth
In the Best Families. R. Stout
In the Blood. L. Lamensdurf
In the Blood. A. Soutar
In the Bride's Mirror. M. Turnbull
In the Brooding Wild. R. Cullum
In the Cause of Freedom. A. W. Marchmont
In the Clutch of the Law. J. K. Stafford
In the Dark. S. Horler
In the Dark. D. Richberg
In the Dark Night. M. P. Hood
In the Days of Marlborough. George Long
In the Dead of Night. Mark Cross
In the Dead of Night. J. T. MacIntyre
In the Dead of Night. T. W. Speight
In the Dead of the Night. M. L. Roby
In the Death of a Man. L. Egan
In the Dentist's Chair. A. Armstrong
In the Depths of the First Degree. J. Doran
In the Emperor's Villa. R. H. Savage
In the Esbekieyeh Gardens, and other stories. R. H. Savage
In the Event of My Death. H. Bourne
In the Eye of the Law. W. D. Lyell
In the Face of Evidence. N. Carter
In the Face of Night. D. Donovan
In the Face of the Verdict. J. Rhode
In the First Degree. R. Scarlett
In the Flashlight. O. Binns
In the Fog. R. H. Davis
In the Force. Anonymous
In the Force. B. Hemyng
In the Gloom of Night. N. Carter
In the Grip of a Lie. M. Leighton
In the Grip of Destiny. C. E. Sterrey
In the Grip of Fate. N. Carter
In the Grip of the Brute. G. Radcliffe
In the Grip of the Dragon. M. Richmond
In the Grip of the Gestapo. S. Hope
In the Grip of the Kidnappers. N. Ridley
In the Grip of the Law. D. Donovan
In the Grip of the Tong. J. W. Bobin
In the Hag's Hands. C. C. Lowis
In the Halls of Evil. T. A. Waters
In the Hand of the Riffs. W. M. Graydon
In the Hands of Spies. J. G. Brandon
In the Hands of the Enemy. R. Sharp
In the Heat of the Night. J. Ball
In the Highest Tradition. E. F. Droge
In the Hour Before Midnight. J. Higgins
In the House of Another. B. Mantle

In the House of the Eye. W. A. MacKenzie
In the Key of Black. P. Broadley
"In the King's Name--!" H. D. Dearden
In the Labyrinth. A. Robbe-Grillet
In the Lamb White Days. F. H. Hall
In the Lap of Danger. N. Carter
In the Lap of Fortune. J. Hatton
In the Last Act. R. Goyne
In the Last Analysis. A. Cross
In the Lion's Den. J. Cotton
In the Mayor's Parlour. J. S. Fletcher
In the Meshes. F. Severne
In the Middle Watch. W. C. Russell
In the Midnight Express. A. Murray
In the Money. A. S. Roche
In the Name of a Woman. A. W. Marchmont
In the Name of Liberty. F. Marryat
In the Name of the Law. D. Stewart
In the Name of the People. A. W. Marchmont
In the Nick of Time. N. Carter
In the Nick of Time. N. Ridley
In the Night. L. Gorell
In the Night Watch. E. S. Brooks
In the Old Chateau. R. H. Savage
In the Onyx Lobby. C. Wells
In the Plotter's Web. M. Leighton
In the Potter's House. G. D. Eldridge
In the Queen's Service. D. Donovan
In the Red. J. Fleming
In the Russian Secret Service. Old Sleuth
In the Secret Vault. B. Wayde
In the Serpent's Coils. F. Du Boisgobey
In the Service of Love. R. Marsh
In the Shadow. Old Spicer
In the Shadow of Fear. N. Carter
In the Shadow of Guilt. M. Leighton
In the Shadow of Night. E. W. Alais
In the Shadow of the Cheka. J. D. Kennedy
In the Shadow of the Guillotine. J. W. Bobin
In the Shadow of the Hills. G. C. Shedd
In the Shadow of the Pyramids. R. H. Savage
In the Shadow of the Tower. R. M. Sears
In the Shadows. N. Harris
In the Still of the Night. H. Seymour
In the Street of the Angel. P. J. Stead
In the Swim. R. H. Savage
In the Teeth of the Evidence. D. L. Sayers
In the Tenth Moon. S. Williams
In the Thraldom of Fear. Maurice Scott
In the Tiger's Cage. C. Wells
In the Toils. J. T. MacIntyre
In the Toils. F. Trent
In the Toils of Fear. N. Carter
In the Tsar's Dominions. Le Voleur
In the Wake of a Stranger. I. S. Black
In the Whirl of the Rising. B. Mitford
In the Wrong Box. F. Russell
In Those Dark Woods. D. Ince
In Tight Places. A. Griffiths
In Time for Murder. R. A. J. Walling
In Triple Disguise. W. M. Graydon
In Two Latitudes. G. Simenon
In Walks Murder. C. Ryland
In White Raiment. W. LeQueux
In Whose Dim Shadow. J. J. Connington
Inca Death Squad. N. Carter
Ince Murder Case. E. J. Pond
Incendiary. W. A. Leahy

Incendiary Blonde. K. Edgar
Incense of Death. N. Deane
Inch of the C.I.D. J. Templeton
Inch of Time. James Norman
Incident. M. Avallone
Incident. A. Rives
Incident. E. Warman
Incident at a Corner. C. Armstrong
Incident at Hendon. J. Letton
Incident at La Junta. O. Lange
Incident at Naha. M. J. Bosse
Incident at 125th Street. J. E. Brown
Incident at the Merry Hippo. E. Huxley
Incident at Villa Rahmana. A. Eliot
Incident Closed. H. J. Dellar
Incident on a Summer's Day. D. Raymond
Incidental Bishop. G. Allen
Incidental Murder. J. Champion
Incitement to Murder. R. Amberley
Inclination to Murder. R. Ellerbeck
Inclination to Murder. H. Hunter
Inclining to Crime. A. Kent
Incognito. N. R. Nusbaum
Income Tax Conspiracy. A. Parsons
Incomparable Doll. K. Lindsay
Inconsistent Villains. N. A. Temple-Ellis
Inconvenient Bride. J. M. Fox
Inconvenient Corpse. E. P. Fenwick
Inconvenient Corpse. D. Sharp
Incredible Adventure. M. Richmond
Incredible Adventures of Rowland Hern. N. Olde
Incredible Crime. L. Austen-Leigh
Incredible Elopement of Lord Peter Wimsey. D. L. Sayers
Incredible Schlock Homes. R. L. Fish
Incredible Theft. A. Christie
Incredible Truth. C. Massie
Incredulity of Father Brown. G. K. Chesterton
Incubated Girl. F. T. Jane
Incumbent. P. Hill
Indecent Exposure. E. Berckman
"Independent." T. Newman
Independent Detective. Anonymous
Independent Means. F. Singleton
Independent Witness. H. Cecil
Index Finger. T. Abrojal
India. E. Southworth
India-Rubber Men. E. Wallace
Indian Bangle. F. Hume
Indian Drum. W. MacHarg
Indian Idol Mystery. H. J. Andrews
Indian Love Lyrics. M. Richmond
Indian Lullaby. M. Richmond
Indian Mystery. G. Allen
Indian Police. Richard Fisher
Indian Princess. A. M. Williamson
Indian Wizard. A. Lillie
Indigo Death. M. Saltmarsh
Indigo Necklace. F. Crane
Indigo Necklace Murders. F. Crane
Indiscretions of a Lady's Maid. W. LeQueux
Induna's Wife. B. Mitford
Inevitable Crime. H. Leyford
Inevitable Hour. M. Boggon
Inevitable Law. F. E. Penny
Inevitable Millionaires. E. P. Oppenheim
Inexpendable. W. H. Baker
Infallible System. C. Kingston
Infallible Witness. P. Luck
Infamous Conduct. H. A. Wrenn
Infamous Fame. E. C. Vivian
Infamous Gentleman. G. Goodchild
Infant. F. Wicks

Infatuation of Marcella. A. M. Meadows
Infernal Idol. H. Seymour
Infernal Light. E. Friend
Inferno. J. Creasey
Inferno. R. Dundee
Infidel. M. E. Braddon
Infiltrator. A. York
Infinite Morning. D. Newton
Infinity of Mirrors. R. Condon
Influenza Mystery. Sutherland Scott
Informant. The Gordons
Information Received. E. R. Punshon
Information Received and other stories. P. Cheyney
Informer. Ladbroke Black
Informer. Liam O'Flaherty
Informer. A. Takagi
Informer. F. Whishaw
Infra Blood. P. D. Westbrook
Ingenious Captain Cobbs. G. W. Appleton
Ingenious Mr. Stone. R. Player
Ingenious Strategem. N. Carter
Inherit the Darkness. W. D. Roberts
Inherit the Wind. G. Vaizey
Inheritance. Stuart Martin
Inheritance. D. Winston
Inheritors. J. Messmann
Initials Only. A. K. Green
Injured Lover. M. B. Lowndes
Ink Street Murder. F. Grierson
Inkosi-Carver Investigates. "Capstan"
Inland Passage. G. H. Coxe
Inn at the Red Oak. L. Griswold
Inn by the Shore. F. Warden
Inn Closes for Christmas. Cledwyn Hughes
Inn of Evil. J. A. Creighton
Inn of the Thirteen Swords. D. Graeme
Inn with the Wooden Door. N. MacSwan
Inner Circle. M. Harvey
Inner Circle. E. C. Mayne
Inner City Hoodlum. D. Goines
Inner Number. F. C. Williams
Inner Room. P. H. Irving
Inner Steps. S. Cardiff
Innocence. C. H. Bullivant
Innocence at Play. J. Middlemass
Innocence of Father Brown. G. K. Chesterton
Innocence of Rosamond Prior. A. Dick
Innocent. E. Piper
Innocent Accomplice. B. Reynolds
Innocent and Willing. Morton Cooper
Innocent Bottle. Anthony Gilbert
Innocent Bystander. B. Frost
Innocent Bystander. M. F. Page
Innocent Bystander. C. Rice
Innocent Bystanders. J. Munro
Innocent Criminal. J. D. Beresford
Innocent Flower. C. Armstrong
Innocent Guilt. E. C. Vivian
Innocent Gunman. J. P. Lacroix
Innocent House. F. Lockridge
Innocent Imposter and other stories. M. Grey
Innocent Mrs. Duff. E. S. Holding
Innocent Murder. L. D. Allen
Innocent Murderers. W. A. Johnston
Innocent One. J. Reach
Innocent Sinner. A. M. Meadows
Innocents. W. Archibald
Innocents. R. Savage
Innocents. G. Simenon
Innocents on Broadway. E. E. Saks

Inquest. H. Clandon
Inquest. R. Neumann
Inquest. M. K. Ozaki
Inquest. P. Wilde
Inquest Betraying. T. J. R. Sennocke
Inquest--Eleven Thirty. S. Darrell
Inquest on a Lady. T. J. R. Sennocke
Inquest on a Mistress. T. J. R. Sennocke
Inquest on Bouvet. G. Simenon
Inquest on Miriam. M. Dalton
Inquests by Jury. T. J. R. Sennocke
Inquests on the Deceased. T. J. R. Sennocke
Inquiries by the Yard. A. Brock
Inquisition. M. Olden
Inquisitory. R. Pinget
Inscrutable Miss Stone. A. Askew
Inside Information. N. Bentley
Inside Job. J. Boland
Inside Man. G. H. Coxe
Inside Man. E. R. Johnson
Inside Out. William Hughes
Inside Out. David Miles
Inside-Out Heist. T. B. Reagan
Inside Out Man. F. Cockain
Inside the Lines. E. D. Biggers
Inside Track. G. Dilnot
Insider. G. Joseph
Insiders. S. Morrow
Insiders. M. Pflaum
Insidious Dr. Fu-Manchu. S. Rohmer
Insoluble. F. Everton
Inspector Bedison and the Sunderland Case. T. Cobb
Inspector Bedison Risks It. T. Cobb
Inspector Burmann's Black-Out. B. Cobb
Inspector Burmann's Busiest Day. B. Cobb
Inspector Calls. J. B. Priestley
Inspector Cole. R. Batchelor
Inspector Dickins Retires. E. P. Oppenheim
Inspector Flagg and the Scarlet Skeleton. J. Cassells
Inspector French and the Cheyne Mystery. F. W. Crofts
Inspector French and the Starvel Tragedy. F. W. Crofts
Inspector French's Greatest Case. F. W. Crofts
Inspector Frost and Lady Brassingham. H. M. Smith
Inspector Frost and the Waverdale Fire. H. M. Smith
Inspector Frost and the Whitbourne Murder. H. M. Smith
Inspector Frost in Crevenna Cove. H. M. Smith
Inspector Frost in the Background. H. M. Smith
Inspector Frost in the City. H. M. Smith
Inspector Frost's Jigsaw. H. M. Smith
Inspector Ghote Breaks an Egg. H. R. F. Keating
Inspector Ghote Caught in Meshes. H. R. F. Keating
Inspector Ghote Goes by Train. H. R. F. Keating
Inspector Ghote Hunts the Peacock. H. R. F. Keating
Inspector Ghote Plays a Joker. H. R. F. Keating
Inspector Ghote Trusts the Heart. H. R. F. Keating
Inspector Ghote's Good Crusade. H. R. F. Keating
Inspector Henderson, the Central Office Detective. H. I. Hancock
Inspector Higgins Goes Fishing. C. F. Gregg
Inspector Higgins Hurries. C. F. Gregg

Inspector Higgins Sees It Through. C. F. Gregg
Inspector Hornleigh Investigates. H. W. Priwin
Inspector Jackson Goes North. D. T. Lindsay
Inspector Jackson Investigates. D. T. Lindsay
Inspector McLean's Casebook. G. Goodchild
Inspector McLean's Holiday. G. Goodchild
Inspector Maigret and the Burglar's Wife. G. Simenon
Inspector Maigret and the Dead Girl. G. Simenon
Inspector Maigret and the Killers. G. Simenon
Inspector Maigret and the Strangled Stripper. G. Simenon
Inspector Maigret in New York's Underworld. G. Simenon
Inspector Maigret Investigates. G. Simenon
Inspector Malone Sails In. David J. Murphy
Inspector Manson's Success. E. Radford
Inspector Morgan's Dilemma. J. Bingham
Inspector Queen's Own Case. E. Queen
Inspector Richardson C.I.D. B. Thomson
Inspector Rusby's Finale. V. Markham
Inspector Treadgold Investigates. A. Weymouth
Inspector West Alone. J. Creasey
Inspector West at Bay. J. Creasey
Insepctor West at Home. J. Creasey
Inspector West Cries Wolf. J. Creasey
Inspector West Kicks Off. J. Creasey
Inspector West Leaves Town. J. Creasey
Inspector West Makes Haste. J. Creasey
Inspector West Regrets. J. Creasey
Inspector West Takes Charge. J. Creasey
Inspector Wilkins Reads the Proofs. Murray Thomas
Inspector Wilkins Sees Red. Murray Thomas
Inspector's Holiday. R. Lockridge
Inspector's Opinion. M. Reybold
Inspector's Puzzle. C. Matthew
Instant Enemy. R. Macdonald
Instead of Murder. J. Goodman
Instigator. E. A. Treeton
Instinct at Fault. N. Carter
Instinctive Criminal. G. Coleridge
Instrument. P. Everett
Instrument of Destiny. J. D. Beresford
Instrument of Vengeance. H. McCutcheon
Instruments of Darkness. S. Horler
Insufficient Evidence. M. Hervey
Insulators. J. Creasey
Insurgent Love. M. Richmond
Insurrection! D. Brennan
Insurrection of Hippolytus Brandenberg. R. Friedman
"Intelligence" Game of Secret Service Cases and Problems. R. McKay
Intent to Kill. M. Bryan
Intent to Kill. H. Desmond
Intent to Murder. N. Deane
Intent to Murder. L. Sands
Intercept. K. Bernstein
Intercom Conspiracy. E. Ambler
Interface. J. Gores
Interference. R. Pertwee
Interloper. Gwendoline Butler
Interloper. E. P. Oppenheim
Interlopers. D. Hamilton

Interlude. S. P. B. Mais
Intermind. R. Luther
International Affair. B. Graeme
International Commando. J. Courage
International Crook League. N. Carter
International Spy. A. Upward
Interrogators. A. Prior
Interrupted Honeymoon. A. Swift
Interrupted Kiss. R. Marsh
Interrupted Wedding. M. Gerard
Interview. H. C. Rae
Interviewing's Killing. A. Tack
Intimate Journal of Warren Winslow. Jean Leslie
Intimate Relations. Fredrick Jackson
Intimate Stranger. E. Thomas
Intimate Victims. V. Packer
Intimidators. D. Hamilton
Into a Dark Mirror. K. Orvis
Into His Own Trap. J. K. Stafford
Into Nick Carter's Web. N. Carter
Into the Fog. Winston Graham
Into the Jaws of Death. W. G. Forbes
Into the Night. F. N. Greene
Into the Shade, and other stories. M. C. Hay
In the Shadow of the Bush. John Bell
Into Temptation. K. Lindsay
Into the Arena. E. Darby
Into the Void. F. Converse
Into Thin Air. H. Carmichael
Into Thin Air. J. Iams
Into Thin Air. G. Vaizey
Into Thin Air. H. Winslow
Into This Universe. Fredrick Jackson
Into Thy Hands. A. Applin
Intrigue. D. Cory
Intrigue. Clive Desmond
Intrigue. G. Usher
Intrigue and Matrimony. D. Vane
Intrigue for Empire. K. M. Knight
Intrigue in Paris. S. Noel
Intrigue in Tangier. H. Seymour
Intrigue Island. A. Mills
Intrigue on Halfaday Creek. J. B. Hendryx
Intrigue on the Upper Level. T. T. Hoyne
Intriguer. M. Parker
Intriguers. T. Cobb
Intriguers. D. Hamilton
Intriguers. W. LeQueux
Intrigues of a Prisoner. E. Gaboriau
Introducing Inspector Maigret. G. Simenon
Introducing Mr. Brandon. A. Morton
Introducing Mr. Robinson. Rupert Grayson
Introducing the Super. R. Goyne
Introducing the Toff. J. Creasey
Introducing William Allison. W. Hewlett
Intruder. O. R. Cohen
Intruder. M. Cronin
Intruder. C. Farr
Intruder. H. Horn
Intruder. S. Laforest
Intruder. Hadley Lawrence
Intruder. D. M. Low
Intruder. R. Maugham
Intruder. A. Myrer
Intruder at Maison Benedict. S. Richard
Intruder from the Sea. G. McDonell
Intruder in the Dark. G. Bellairs
Intruder in the Dust. W. Faulkner
Intruders. P. Montandon
Intrusion. E. McCrae
Intrusive Tourist. B. Reynolds
Invader. R. Wormser
Invaders. E. P. Frankland
Invaders. L. Tracy
Invaders from the Dark. G. La Spina
Invasion. H. Janson
Invasion. J. Wallace

Invasion Coast. J. G. Sarasin
Invasion of Privacy. H. Kurnitz
Invasion of the Yellow Warlords. C. Steele
Inverness Murder. C. A. Byers
Inverted Crime. L. Gribble
Investigation. S. Lem
Investigation. M. Urquhart
Investigation at Holman Square. N. M. Hopkins
Investigations are Proceeding. J. Ashford
Investigations of Colwin Grey. A. J. Rees
Investigations of John Pym. D. C. Murray
Investigators. J. S. Fletcher
Investment in Crime. J. C. Crowley
Invisibility Affair. Thomas Stratton
Invisible Border. Mildred Davis
Invisible Bridge. F. Allan
Invisible Companion and other stories. J. J. Farjeon
Invisible Cord. V. Castang
Invisible Cord. C. Cookson
Invisible Darkness. P. Paul
Invisible Death. B. Flynn
Invisible Empire. C. Steele
Invisible Enemy. G. C. Shedd
Invisible Evidence. P. Winn
Invisible Evil. R. Gaines
Invisible Eye. P. Tabori
Invisible Flamini. C. Brown
Invisible Foe. L. J. Miln
Invisible Hand. R. Dark
Invisible Host. G. Bristow
Invisible Image. F. Chabrey
Invisible Man Murders. R. Foster
Invisible Pickpocket. J. M'Govan
Invisible Red. M. Parker
Invisible Ships. Sea Lion
Invisible Verdict. R. Goyne
Invisible Weapons. J. Rhode
Invisible Worm. M. Millar
Invisibles. E. E. Christopher
Invisibles. J. Dark
Invitation. C. Cookson
Invitation to a Ball. P. Meredith
Invitation to a Dynamite Party. P. Lovesey
Invitation to a Funeral. T. Harknett
Invitation to a Murder. R. King
Invitation to a Murder. J. T. Story
Invitation to a Strangling. R. L. Brent
Invitation to Adventure. G. Ashe
Invitation to an Inquest. R. Hull
Invitation to Danger. F. Murray
Invitation to Death. A. R. Long
Invitation to Death. A. O. Pollard
Invitation to Die. F. French
Invitation to Evil. W. D. Roberts
Invitation to Kill. G. Low
Invitation to Kill. V. Warren
Invitation to Murder. Robert (G.) Curtis
Invitation to Murder. L. Ford
Invitation to Murder. Manning Long
Invitation to Murder. I. S. Shriber
Invitation to Murder. R. Stout
Invitation to Murder. R. Trevor
Invitation to Paradise. Lesley Howard
Invitation to Terror. P. Hambledon
Invitation to the Grave. David Hume
Invitation to Vengeance. K. M. Knight
Invitation to Violence. L. White
Invited. Z. Davis
Involved. Johnny Morgan

Involvement in Austria. J. N. Chance
Involvement of Arnold Wechsler. J. A. Graham
Inward Eye. P. Bacon
Inward Glance. L. Robinson
Ipcress File. L. Deighton
Ippletree Manor Mystery. D. W. Spurgeon
Irina. S. Friedman
Irina. Gavin Holt
Iris. T. Douglas
Iris the Avenger. F. Marryat
Irish Beauty Contract. P. Atlee
Irish Detective. Anonymous
Irish Detective. Old Sleuth
Irish Monte Cristo Abroad. A. Robertson
Irish Monte Cristo's Search. A. Robertson
Irish Monte Cristo's Trail. A. Robertson
Irish Police Officer. Robert Curtis
Irish Witch. D. Wheatley
Iron Apple. G. Bowman
Iron Box. C. R. Gull
Iron Burgess, the Government Detective. Anonymous
Iron Burgess, the Government Detective. Old Sleuth
Iron Chalice. O. R. Cohen
Iron Claw. F. A. Symonds
Iron Clew. A. Tilton
Iron Cobweb. U. Curtiss
Iron Cross. S. Cobb
Iron Cross. R. H. Sherard
Iron Curtain. A. O. Pollard
Iron Door. O. Martin
Iron Egg. D. W. F. Hardie
Iron Gates. M. Millar
Iron Grip. E. Wallace
Iron Hand. J. M. Cobban
Iron Hand. Howard Dean
Iron Hand. A. Tilton
Iron Hand. F. Warden
Iron Horse. R. M. Ballantyne
Iron Maiden. E. C. Brown
Iron Mask. F. Du Boisgobey
Iron Mask. Gwyn Evans
Iron Mask. J. G. Sarasin
Iron Orchid. J. Bentley
Iron Pirate. M. Pemberton
Iron Ring. H. S. Keeler
Iron Sanctuary. Robert MacLeod
Iron Skull. K. Robeson
Iron Spiders. B. Kendrick
Iron Spiders Murder. B. Kendrick
Iron Staircase. G. Simenon
Iron Tiger. Harry Patterson
Iron Tiger. M. L. Stokes
Iron Virgin. J. M. Fox
Iron Will. C. N. Buck
Ironmaster's Daughter. P. Trent
Ironmouth. C. Stanton
Ironside. J. Thompson
Ironsides Abroad. Anonymous
Ironsides' Lone Hand. V. Gunn
Ironsides of the Yard. V. Gunn
Ironsides on the Spot. V. Gunn
Ironsides Sees Red. V. Gunn
Ironsides Smashes Through. V. Gunn
Ironsides Smells Blood. V. Gunn
Ironwood. J. Melville
Irralie's Bushranger. E. W. Hornung
Irregular Marriage. S. Warwick
Irresistable Stranger. A. Applin
Irrespressible Peccadillo. F. Flora
Is and Was. W. Hewlett
Is He Dead, Miss Ffinch? J. N. Smith
Is He the Man? W. C. Russell
Is No One Innocent? M. H. Gropper

Is She Dead Too? Anthony Gilbert
Is Skin Deep, Is Fatal. H. R. F. Keating
Is There a Traitor in the House? P. McGerr
Is This Revenge? L. Gribble
Isa. A. W. Marchmont
Isabel Broderick--"Bubbles We Buy." A. Jones
Isabella Vincent. G. W. M. Reynolds
Ishmael. M. E. Braddon
Ishmael. E. Southworth
Ishmaelite. M. E. Braddon
Ishmael's Wife. Roy Vickers
Island. J. Matheson
Island. Mildred Nelson
Island Alert. J. M. Walsh
Island Doctor. Rona Randall
Island Feud. S. M. Parkman
Island Gold. V. Williams
Island Heirs. J. Judson
Island Murder. T. Stevenson
Island Murder. P. Trent
Island Mystery. G. A. Birmingham
Island Mystery. J. W. Bobin
Island Mystery. J. Bolton
Island of Atonement. H. Leyford
Island of Bitter Memories. D. Daniels
Island of Creeping Death. V. Norwood
Island of Dangerous Men. A. Drummond
Island of Death. A. Broome
Island of Death. D. Seaman
Island of Destiny. A. J. Rees
Island of Disaster. Michael Lewis
Island of Eden. B. Mitford
Island of Escape. H. L. Nelson
Island of Evil. D. Daniels
Island of Fear. J. D. Conway
Island of Fear. H. Footner
Island of Fog. M. Kingsbury
Island of Fu Manchu. S. Rohmer
Island of Galloping Gold. E. Wallace
Island of Ghosts. O. Sackville
Island of Intrigue. I. Ostrander
Island of Peril. J. Creasey
Island of Romance. D. Whitelaw
Island of Sheep. J. Buchan
Island of Spies. J. M. Walsh
Island of Surprises. W. B. M. Ferguson
Island of Terror. H. C. McNeile
Island of Test. A. Soutar
Island of the Accursed. W. Winthrop
Island of the Guilty. G. H. Teed
Island of the Pit. V. James
Island of the Seven Hills. Z. Cass
Island of Unrest. J. G. Sarasin
Island Princess. E. Southworth
Island Rescue. J. Tickell
Island Schooner. G. Volk
Island Secret. W. M. Graydon
Island Twilight. N. Tranter
Island Where Time Stands Still. D. Wheatley
Islands of the Condemned. F. A. M. Webster
Isle for a Stranger. D. W. Low
Isle of Confusion. D. Christie
Isle of Desire. Basil Carey
Isle of Desire. D. Christie
Isle of Dragons. Robert MacLeod
Isle of Enchantment. A. Wood
Isle of Hate. A. Dare
Isle of Horror. G. H. Teed
Isle of Innocence. L. Noel
Isle of Men. G. Volk
Isle of Peril. A. Wade
Isle of Strife. G. C. Shedd
Isle of Surrey. R. Dowling
Isle of the Dolphins. J. L. Roberts
Isle of the Drums. J. A. Dunn
Isle of the Seventh Sentry. F. Kent
Isle of the Snakes. R. L. Fish
Isle of the Undead. V. Coffman
Isoworg. H. Bentinck
Israel Rank. R. Horniman
Issue. E. Noble
Issue of the Bishop's Blood. T. P. McMahon
Istanbul. N. Carter
Istanbul Elopement. D. T. Hughes
It Adds Up to Trouble. A. Nuttall
It Ain't Hay. D. Dodge
It Always Happens. Robin Temple
It Always Rains on Sunday. A. La Bern
It Began in New York. M. Kennedy
It Began in Singapore. G. P. Willis
It Began in Vauxhall Gardens. K. Kellow
It Boils Down to Murder. P. D. Westbrook
It Came to Pass. S. Fairway
It Came to Pass. G. M. Fenn
It Can't Always be Caviar. J. M. Simmel
It Comes by Night. Clarissa Ross
It Could Happen to You. J. B. O'Sullivan
It Couldn't Be Caroline. D. Egerton
It Couldn't Be Murder. H. Austin
It Couldn't Be Murder. Mark Cross
It Couldn't Be Murder. R. B. Sinclair
It Couldn't Be Suicide. C. Francis
It Couldn't Happen to Me. J. Blackmore
It Couldn't Matter Less. P. Cheyney
It Doesn't Add Up. R. Drayton
It Had to Be You. V. Siller
It Happened at Midnight. J. Reach
It Happened at Night. Roland Daniel
It Happened at the Cape. K. Lindsay
It Happened at the Lake. J. T. Shaw
It Happened in Boston. R. H. Greenan
It Happened in Cairo. K. Rhodes
It Happened in Essex. V. Bridges
It Happened in Hamburg. W. H. Baker
It Happened in Melgrove Square. J. Hunter
It Happened in Vienna. T. B. Marle
It Happened in Wayland. F. Shroyer
It Happened on Halfaday Creek. J. B. Hendryx
It Happened to Susan. J. Blackmore
It Howls at Night. N. Berrow
"It Is Expedient..." K. Ingram
It Is No Wonder. J. F. Molloy
It Is Not Safe to Know. B. Reynolds
It Leaves Them Cold. Kevin O'Hara
It Makes a Nice Change. John Gloag
It Makes You Think. A. E. Jones
It Means Mischief. R. Pertwee
It Might Have Been. P. Trent
It Might Have Meant Murder. L. Cargill
It Might Lead Anywhere. E. R. Punshon
It Never Rains--. V. Bridges
It Never Rains in Los Angeles. C. Flowers
It Only Hurts a Minute. D. M. Mankiewicz
It Pays to Die. C. M. Wills
It Prowls at Dark. H. R. Taunton
It Rained that Friday. G. M. Wilson
It Shouldn't Happen to a Dog. E. Lanham
It Takes a Thief. D. Dillany
It Walks at Midnight. J. Reach
It Walks by Night. J. D. Carr
It Walks the Woods. Alan Grant
It Was Christmas Every Day. A. La Bern
It Was Locked. J. Hawk
It Was Murder, They Said. J. Bentley
It Wasn't a Nightmare. L. F. Hay
It Wasn't Me! I. Jefferies
"It Will Be All Right!" T. Gallon
It Will Be Warmer When It Snows. A. La Bern
It Won't Get You Anywhere. D. Skirrow
Italian. A. Radcliffe
Italian Bandit. Old Sleuth
Italian Called Mario. P. H. Irving
Italian Connection. Robin Moore
Italian Gadget. H. Calvin
Italian Job. T. K. Martin
Italian Maze. E. Lascelles
Item 7. Alan Nixon
It's a Battlefield. G. Greene
It's a Crime. R. Ellington
It's a Free Country. L. Brain
It's a Sin. H. Zore
It's a Sin to Kill. D. Keene
It's a Wise Child. T. Curley
It's About Crime. M. Kantor
It's All Yours. R. Angel
It's Always Eve That Weeps. H. Janson
It's Always too Late to Mend. P. V. Stern
It's an Ill Wind. D. Mayor
It's Bedtime, Baby! H. Janson
It's Cold Out There. M. Braly
It's Death, My Darling! A. R. Long
It's Different Abroad. H. Calvin
It's Different in July. K. Fitzgerald
It's Easier for Homicide. K. David
It's Easy to Kill. A. Wood
It's Her Own Funeral. C. Carnac
It's in the Bag. A. Spiller
It's Later Than You Think. M. M. Kaye
It's Loaded, Mr. Bauer. J. P. Marquand
It's Locked in with You. G. Mayo
It's Lonely on the Sidewalk. D. Bogard
It's Murder. R. Drayton
It's Murder! T. T. Flynn
It's Murder if You Say So! A. Aldous
It's Murder, McHugh. J. Flynn
It's Murder, Maguire. R. Himmel
It's Murder, Miss King. I. Waitt
It's Murder, Mr. Potter. R. Foley
It's Murder, Senorita. D. Bateson
It's Murder She Says. R. Angel
It's Murder to Live. E. Radford
It's Murder with Dover. J. Porter
It's My Funeral. P. Rabe
It's My Own Funeral. D. Lyon
It's Only Saps That Die. B. Toler
It's Quiet in the Country. H. Willett
It's Raining Violence. T. Du Bois
It's Safe in England. K. Fitzgerald
It's Your Funeral. A. Bocca
It's Your Funeral. Kevin O'Hara
It's Your Turn to Die. Gerard Fisher
Ivan Greet's Masterpiece. G. Allen
Ivan the Serf. S. Cobb
I've Found My Love. M. Richmond
Ivor's Chance. P. Trent
Ivory Ball. C. C. Hotchkiss
Ivory Dagger. P. Wentworth
Ivory Disc. P. Brebner
Ivory God. J. S. Fletcher
Ivory Goddess. W. H. L. Crauford
Ivory Grin. J. R. Macdonald
Ivory Ladies. Gavin Holt
Ivory Locket. M. Alan
Ivory Penguin. John Morgan
Ivory Queen. N. Hurst
Ivory Screen. G. H. Teed
Ivory Snuff Box. A. Fredericks
Ivory Talisman. F. A. M. Webster
Ivory Tower. M. Eatock
Ivory Trail. T. Mundy
Ivory Tusk. R. Hardinge
Ivory Valley. C. J. C. Hyne
Ivy Halls. B. H. Hyatt
Ivy Tree. M. Stewart
Izelle of the Dunes. C. G. Mitford

J

"J for Jennie" Murders. T. A. Plummer
J for Jupiter. T. Fuller
J. P. Dunbar: A Story of Wall Street. W. C. Hudson
Jacaranda Murders. H. Desmond
Jack Allyn's Friends. G. W. Appleton
Jack and Jill. Old Sleuth
Jack Breakaway. Old Sleuth
Jack Carter and the Law. T. Lewis
Jack Carter's Law. T. Lewis
Jack Chanty. H. Footner
Jack Curzon. A. C. Gunter
Jack Gordon, Night Errant, Gotham 1883. W. C. Hudson
Jack-in-the-Box. J. J. Connington
Jack Junk. T. P. Prest
Jack O'Judgment. E. Wallace
Jack O'Lantern. G. Goodchild
Jack o' the Cudgel. Anonymous
Jack of Clubs. J. Ironside
Jack of Hearts. D. Von Elsner
Jack on the Gallows Tree. L. Bruce
Jack Ranworth. J. Blyth
Jack Shepard, the Bandit King. Anonymous
Jack Sheppard. W. H. Ainsworth
Jack Sheppard, the Bandit King. O. Harper
Jack Spot. H. Janson
Jack the Juggler. Old Sleuth
Jack the Juggler's Ordeal. Old Sleuth
Jack the Juggler's Trial. Old Sleuth
Jack the Outlaw. K. Snowden
Jack the Rascal. G. M. Fenn
Jack the Ripper. S. James
Jack Vinton, the Boy Detective. Anonymous
Jack Warleigh. D. J. Belgrave
Jackal. D. Whitelaw
Jackals. C. Kernahan
Jackals and Others. F. E. Penny
Jackal's Head. B. Michaels
Jackal's Head. Elizabeth Peters
Jackals of the Secret Service. Operator 1384
Jackanapes Jacket. E. M. Keate
Jackdaw. C. Hill
Jackdaw Mystery. F. Grierson
Jack's Father, and other stories. W. E. Norris
Jack's Return Home. T. Lewis
Jacob Niemand. R. H. Sherard
Jacob Street Mystery. R. A. Freeman
Jacob's Ladder. E. P. Oppenheim
Jacob's Ladder, and other stories. W. B. Maxwell
Jacqueminot. K. Rich
Jade; and other stories. H. Wiley
Jade Cat. G. B. Mair
Jade Dragon. N. Buckingham
Jade Elephant. E. Fraser
Jade Elephants. T. Allen
Jade Eye. F. Hume
Jade Eye. J. Ingersol
Jade-Eyed Jinx. C. Brown
Jade-Eyed Jungle. C. Brown
Jade Figurine. L. Foxx
Jade Figurines. Jan Alexander
Jade for a Lady. M. E. Chaber
Jade God. A. Sullivan
Jade Green. D. Daniels
Jade Green Cats. E. Blake
Jade-Green Garter. D. Newton
Jade Green Judy. D. Enefer
Jade Hatpin. M. G. Kiddy
Jade in Aries. T. Coe

Jade Lizard. Taffrail
Jade of Death. R. Gar
Jade of Destiny. J. Farnol
Jade Rabbit. A. Blood
Jade Venus. G. H. Coxe
Jade Wind. J. Harris
Jade's Progress. J. S. Clouston
Jadoo. N. Newham-Davis
Jail and Farewell. M. Shane
Jail Bait! R. Angel
Jail Bait. S. Chayes
Jail Bait. J. W. Mason
Jail Break. D. Barton
Jail-Breakers. Roland Daniel
Jail-Breakers. B. Newman
Jail Gates Are Open. David Hume
Jailbait Jungle. Wenzell Brown
Jailbait Street. H. Ellson
Jailer, My Jailer. M. Gavin
Jailer's Pretty Wife. F. Du Boisgobey
Jake Canuke. J. Templeton
Jake of Diamonds. D. Von Elsner
Jamaica Inn. D. Du Maurier
James Ballingray, Murderer. J. Maconechy
James Cope. C. Barmby
James Joyce Murder. A. Cross
James Knowland: Deceased. H. Carmichael
James Tarrant, Adventurer. F. W. Crofts
James Whitaker's Dukedom. E. Jepson
Jamintha. Beatrice Parker
Jamo and the Bent Playboy. J. Vaughan
Jane Carberry and the Laughing Fountain. B. Symons
Jane Carberry: Detective. B. Symons
Jane Carberry Investigates. B. Symons
Jane Carberry's Week-End. B. Symons
Jane Shore. T. P. Prest
Jane the Ripper. W. Tyrer
Jane Ventures. P. Trent
Jane with Green Eyes. H. Janson
Janson, Go Home. H. Janson
Japanese Girl. Winston Graham
Japanese Jeopardy. P. Tabori
Japanese Mistress. R. Neely
Japanese Revenge. L. Tracy
Japanese Tales of Mystery and Imagination. E. Rampo
Japanese Umbrella and other stories. Francis King
Jarvis. R. W. Kauffman
Jarvis of Harvard. R. W. Kauffman
Jarwick the Prodigal. T. Gallon
Jasius Pursuit. D. Orgill
Jasmine Trail. H. J. Hagerty
Jason Affair. J. N. Chance
Jason and the Sleep Game. J. N. Chance
Jason Burr's First Case. D. Kent
Jason Goes West. J. N. Chance
Jason King. R. Miall
Jason Murders. J. N. Chance
Jasper Dane's Secret. M. E. Braddon
Java Jack. O. Binns
Javelin for Jonah. G. Mitchell
Jaws of Circumstance. C. Clausen
Jaws of Darkness. Mark Cross
Jaws of Death. G. Allen
Jaws of Death. L. Thayer
Jaws of the Watchdog. I. Drummond
Jazz Jungle. H. Janson
Jealous One. C. Fremlin
Jealous Woman. J. M. Cain
Jealousy. N. Karta
Jealousy. A. Robbe-Grillet
Jealousy Pulls the Trigger. M. E. Corne
Jean of the Lazy J Ranch. H. Pink
Jeanie with the Light Brown Corpse. J. Cello
Jeanne of the Marshes. E. P. Oppenheim
Jedcrow. Mark Elder
Jeff Clayton and the Outlaws. W. Ward

Jeff Clayton in the Heart of Trouble. W. Ward
Jeff Clayton's Blind Trail. W. Ward
Jeff Clayton's Brigand Foe. W. Ward
Jeff Clayton's Dancing Bubble. W. Ward
Jeff Clayton's Daring Leap. W. Ward
Jeff Clayton's Deal with Death. W. Ward
Jeff Clayton's Decoy. W. Ward
Jeff Clayton's Demon Pursuer. W. Ward
Jeff Clayton's Discovery. W. Ward
Jeff Clayton's Fatal Shot. W. Ward
Jeff Clayton's Golden Ladder. W. Ward
Jeff Clayton's Last Bullet. W. Ward
Jeff Clayton's Last Ship. W. Ward
Jeff Clayton's Long Chase. W. Ward
Jeff Clayton's Lost Clue. W. Ward
Jeff Clayton's Man-Trap. W. Ward
Jeff Clayton's Master Stroke. W. Ward
Jeff Clayton's Mexican Plot. W. Ward
Jeff Clayton's Pursuit. W. Ward
Jeff Clayton's Puzzle. W. Ward
Jeff Clayton's Red Mystery. W. Ward
Jeff Clayton's Riddle. W. Ward
Jeff Clayton's Strange Quest. W. Ward
Jeff Clayton's Surprise. W. Ward
Jeff Clayton's Thunder Bolt. W. Ward
Jeff Clayton's Triumph. W. Ward
Jeff Clayton's White Mission. W. Ward
Jeff Clayton's Winged Flight. W. Ward
Jefferson Boone, Handyman. J. Messmann
Jefferson Secret. R. Blaker
Jenkin's Green. R. Arnold
Jennerton & Co. E. P. Oppenheim
Jennie Barlowe, Adventuress. E. O'Donnell
Jennie Baxter, Journalist. R. Barr
Jennifer. J. Goodwin
Jennifer by Moonlight. Clarissa Ross
Jennifer Disappears. M. O'Nair
Jennifer Pontefracte. A. Askew
Jenny and I. J. Letton
Jenny Be Good. W. F. Fauley
Jenny Kissed Me. R. Fenisong
Jenny Newstead. M. B. Lowndes
Jenny Wren. R. Kirkbride
Jenny's Case. E. F. Pinsent
Jeopardy. M. Conte
Jeopardy Is My Job. S. Marlowe
Jeremiah and the Princess. E. P. Oppenheim
Jeremiah Painter. G. Wolk
Jeremy Takes a Hand. C. K. Rathbone
Jerry the Lag. P. Baron
Jersey Guns. D. Pendleton
Jersey Plunder. J. Chancellor
Jesmond Mystery. H. Hill
Jess. M. G. Lowe
Jessamy Court. A. Maybury
Jesse James, and His Band of Notorious Outlaws. W. Gordon
Jesse James at Coney Island. W. B. Lawson
Jesse James' Double. W. B. Lawson
Jesse James in New York. W. B. Lawson
Jesse James' Oath. W. B. Lawson
Jessica. A. Maybury
Jessie Trim. B. L. Farjeon
Jessie Vandeleur. E. C. Mayne
Jessop Bequest. A. Burr
Jest of Darkness. V. M. Grayland
Jesus Factor. E. Corley
Jesus II. F. Riley
Jet and Ivory. R. Thorndike
Jethro Hammer. M. Venning
Jetsam. V. Bridges
Jew Detective. Anonymous
Jew of Prague. A. W. Barrett
Jewel in the Crypt. O. Baster

Jewel Mysteries from a Dealer's Notebook. M. Pemberton
Jewel Mysteries I Have Known. M. Pemberton
Jewel of Death. E. Berckman
Jewel of Death. H. Mee
Jewel of Destiny. G. Davison
Jewel of Doom. N. Carter
Jewel of Seven Stars. B. Stoker
Jewel of the Java Sea. D. Cushman
Jewel Thief. A. Mills
Jeweled Cat. L. Rutland
Jeweled Dagger. J. Ellis
Jeweled Mummy. N. Carter
Jewels for a Shroud. W. De Steiguer
Jewels Go Back. E. C. Vivian
Jewels in Jeopardy. Ernest Paul
Jewels of Death. R. Halifax
Jewels of Death. M. Richmond
Jewels of Prince de Janville. Almhain
Jewels of Sin. B. Bolt
Jewels of Terror. J. L. Roberts
Jewels of Wu Ling. Jack Lewis
Jewels that Got Away. G. Madderom
Jew's House. F. Hume
"Jews" Pellegrini. B. Sarto
Jews Without Jehovah. G. Kersh
Jezebel's Daughter. W. Collins
Jig-Saw. E. Phillpotts
Jig-Saw Murder Case. R. Wallace
Jig-Saw Puzzle Murder. W. F. Eberhardt
Jig-Time Murders. C. G. Givens
Jigger Moran. J. Roeburt
Jigsaw. E. McBain
Jigsaw. Robin Sherman
Jigsaw. H. Waugh
Jill Fell Down. J. Tickell
Jilt. C. Reade
Jim. R. W. Kauffman
Jim Barnett Intervenes. M. Leblanc
Jim Brent. H. C. McNeile
Jim Crowshaw's Mary. F. M. White
Jim Cummings. F. Ferrars
Jim Cummings. A. F. Pinkerton
Jim Goes North. G. Goodchild
Jim Hanvey, Detective. O. R. Cohen
Jim Maitland. H. C. McNeile
Jim the Penman. C. H. Bullivant
Jim the Penman. D. Donovan
Jim the Penman. W. Gordon
Jim Trelawney. O. Binns
Jim Trent. R. W. Kauffman
Jimgrim. T. Mundy
Jimgrim and Allah's Peace. T. Mundy
Jimmie Dale and the Blue Envelope Murder. F. Packard
Jimmie Dale and the Missing Hour. F. Packard
Jimmie Dale and the Phantom Clue. F. Packard
Jimmie Rezaire. A. Armstrong
Jimmy Quixote. T. Gallon
Jimmy the Kid. D. E. Westlake
Jink. T. P. McMahon
Jinx Theatre Murder. Alexander Williams
Joan Mar, Detective. M. Leighton
Joan of the Hills. T. B. Clegg
Joan, the Curate. F. Warden
Joanna. J. Blackmore
Joanna Sets to Work. T. Cobb
Job Abroad. G. Bartram
Job Lot Sketches and Stories. J. P. Marsden
Job of Murder. F. Gruber
Jock MacKay, Crook. S. Grey
Jockey. G. Verner

Jockey Club Stories. F. Barrett
Jockey Died First. A. Mills
Jockey's Revenge. N. Gould
Joe Fuller, Detective. G. I. Colbron
Joe Jenkins' Case Book. P. Rosenhayn
Joe Jenkins: Detective. P. Rosenhayn
Joe Leslie's Wife. A. Robertson
Joe Phoenix, Private Detective. A. W. Aiken
Joe Phoenix Puzzled. Anonymous
Joe Phoenix, the Police Spy. A. W. Aiken
Joey Kills. Joey Fisher
John Allard. E. M. Ingram
John Ames, Native Commissioner. B. Mitford
John and Son. P. Trent
John Armiger's Revenge. P. H. Hunter
John Boddy. T. Thurston
John Brand, Fugitive. J. Creasey
John Brand's Will. H. Adams
John Brown & Larry Lohengrin. W. Westall
John Brown's Body. E. C. R. Lorac
John Carruthers: Indian Policeman. E. C. Cox
John Carstairs, Space Detective. F. B. Long
John Clutterbuck. J. Ruegg
John Dene of Toronto. H. Jenkins
John Dighton, Mystery Millionaire. M. Pemberton
John Doe--Murderer. W. Dale
John Fanning's Legacy. N. Royde-Smith
John Ford. F. Barrett
John Hazel's Vengeance. W. S. Hayward
John Heriot's Wife. A. Askew
John Horsleydown. T. L. Holt
John Jasper's Gatehouse. E. Harris
John Jenkin, Public Enemy. B. Graeme
John Jeremy--Cracksman. Jeffrey Montague
John Kyleing Died. E. Radford
John Lillibud. F. G. Hurrell
John Lisbon, Agent. J. Budd
John Macnab. J. Buchan
John Marchmont's Legacy. M. E. Braddon
John Montcalm. M. Gerard
John Needham's Double. J. Hatton
John o' the Green. J. Farnol
John Parmelee's Curse. J. Hawthorne
John Quinton's Secret. R. H. Poole
John Riddell Murder Case. J. Riddell
John Rutland's Romance. J. P. Bessell
John Silence. A. Blackwood
John Smith Hears Death Walking. W. Blassingame
John Solomon, Incognito. A. Hawkwood
John Thorndyke's Cases. R. A. Freeman
John Topp, Pirate. W. Chesney
John Traile: Smuggler. A. Salcroft
John Vale's Guardian. D. C. Murray
John Webb's End. F. Adams
Johnnie. D. B. Hughes
Johnnie Madison. J. Haslette
Johnny Blood. P. Malloch
Johnny Come Deadly. P. Race
Johnny Come Lately. F. Kane
Johnny Counterfeit. M. Y. Shapleigh
Johnny Danger. P. Allardyce
Johnny Death. W. Schnurr
Johnny Get Your Gun. J. Ball
Johnny Gets His! D. Ambler
Johnny Goes East. D. Cory
Johnny Goes North. D. Cory
Johnny Goes South. D. Cory
Johnny Goes West. D. Cory
Johnny Havoc. J. Jakes
Johnny Havoc and the Doll Who Had "It." J. Jakes
Johnny Havoc Meets Zelda. J. Jakes
Johnny Liddell's Morgue. F. Kane
Johnny Lost. P. Jones

Johnny Ludlow. H. Wood
Johnny Ludlow. Fifth Series. H. Wood
Johnny Ludlow. Fourth Series. H. Wood
Johnny Ludlow. Second Series. H. Wood
Johnny Ludlow. Sixth Series. H. Wood
Johnny Ludlow. Third Series. H. Wood
Johnny on the Spot. A. Dell
Johnny Staccato. F. Boyd
Johnny Under Ground. P. Moyes
Johnstown Stage, and other stories. R. H. Fletcher
Joker. E. Wallace
Joker Deals with Death. W. M. Duncan
Joker in the Deck. R. S. Prather
Joker in the Pack. J. H. Chase
Joker Takes Queen. B. Munslow
Jokers. M. Sands
Jolly Jess. Old Sleuth
Jolly Roger Mystery. P. Lancaster
Jonah Game. J. S. Abel
Jonah's Luck. F. Hume
Jonas Haggerley. J. J. Wray
Jonathan Bradford. T. P. Prest
Jonathan Guest. Margaret Archer
Jones, A., Finds the Body. H. McEvoy
Jones Men. V. E. Smith
Jones's Little Murders. E. Radford
Jordans Murder. S. Fowler
Joseph File. A. Harris
Joseph Prickett, the Scotland Yard Detective. I. Murray
Joseph Proctor's Money. W. H. L. Crauford
Joseph Stone. J. La Tourrette
Joseph Wilmot. G. W. M. Reynolds
Joseph's Coat. D. C. Murray
Joshua Haggard's Daughter. M. E. Braddon
Joshua Humble. E. R. Beach
Joss. R. Marsh
Josselin Takes a Hand. A. C. Brown
Journey Downstairs. R. Philmore
Journey from Baghdad. David Roberts
Journey in the Dark. J. Ames
Journey into Danger. J. M. Fox
Journey into Darkness. I. Mercer
Journey into Death. Jack Jones
Journey into Fear. E. Ambler
Journey into Stone. A. E. Lindop
Journey into Terror. D. Daniels
Journey into Terror. P. Rabe
Journey into Twilight. M. Lynch
Journey into Violence. D. Orgill
Journey into Violence. H. Whittington
Journey Past Repentance. G. Arnaud
Journey to Genoa. F. D. Fawcett
Journey to Happiness. M. Richmond
Journey to Love. Rona Randall
Journey to Nowhere. N. Tyre
Journey to Orassia. A. Caillou
Journey to Romance. L. Ames
Journey to the Hangman. A. W. Upfield
Journey with a Stranger. The Gordons
Journeying Boy. M. Innes
Journey's Eve. E. Cadell
Joy Boys. W. Grave
Joy House. D. Keene
Joy Ride. J. G. Brandon
Joy Ride. A. Prior
Joy Wheel. P. W. Fairman
Joyce Harrington's Trust. B. Marchant
Joyce Pleasantry and other stories. G. R. Sims
Joyful Jays. J. C. Lenehan

Title Index

Joyous Adventures of Aristide Pujol. W. J. Locke
Joyous Conspirator. G. F. Gibbs
Ju-Ju Man. A. Livingston
Juanita Carrington. R. Jocelyn
Judah Lion Contract. P. Atlee
Judas. E. R. Johnson
Judas! P. Van Greenway
Judas C.I.D. F. Grierson
Judas Cat. D. S. Davis
Judas Country. G. Lyall
Judas Cross. J. M. Wallmann
Judas Diary. W. H. Baker
Judas Freak. H. Pentecost
Judas Goat. B. Cleeve
Judas Goat. L. Edgley
Judas Gospel. P. Van Greenway
Judas Hour. Howard Hunt
Judas, Incorporated. K. Steel
Judas Journey. Lee Roberts
Judas Kiss. H. Adams
Judas Kiss. J. J. Dratler
Judas Mandate. C. Egleton
Judas Sheep. J. Roberts
Judas Spies. C. Robertson
Judas Spy. N. Carter
Judas Way. C. Whitton
Judas Window. Carter Dickson
Judd for the Defense. L. Goldman
Judge. E. W. Peattie
Judge. Alan Thomas
Judge and His Hangman. F. Duerrenmatt
Judge and the Hatter. G. Simenon
Judge Dee at Work. R. Van Gulik
Judge Is Reversed. F. Lockridge
Judge Me Not. J. D. MacDonald
Judge Not. C. H. Bullivant
Judge Priest Turns Detective. I. S. Cobb
Judge Robinson Murdered! R. L. Goldman
Judge Speaks. R. Monroe
Judge Sums Up. J. J. Farjeon
Judge Will Call It Murder. S. M. Lott
Judge's Chair. E. Phillpotts
Judge's Daughters. G. E. Mitton
Judge's Dilemma. S. Kyle
Judges of Hades, and other Simon Ark stories. E. D. Hoch
Judgment. T. Wicker
Judgment Castle. A. Wood
Judgment Day. R. Sapir
Judgment Deferred. G. Braddon
Judgment in Suspense. G. Bullett
Judgment Night. D. Honig
Judgment of Ann. P. Trent
Judgment of Death. A. Mills
Judgment of Death. M. Richmond
Judgement of Helen. T. Cobb
Judgment of Larose. A. Gask
Judgment on Deltchev. E. Ambler
Judgment Rock. L. A. Knight
Judicial Body. M. Scherf
Judith Lee. R. Marsh
Judson Murder Case. A. B. Leonard
Judy--and the Philosopher. T. Gallon
Judy Ashbane, Police Decoy. M. O'Nair
Judy of Bunter's Buildings. E. P. Oppenheim
Judy the Torch. A. P. Hankins
Jugger. R. Stark
Juggernaut. A. Campbell
Juggernaut. A. Hine
Juggler and the Soul. H. B. Mathers
Juggler of Nankin. S. Cobb
Juggling Fortune. T. W. Speight
Juice. S. Becker
Juke Box King. F. Kane
Julia. P. Straub
Julia Ballantyne. G. R. Preedy
Julia Bicknell. O. Bradbury
Julia Courtney. J. M. Cobban

Julie. A. L. Stone
Juliet Dies Twice. Lange Lewis
Juliet Room. G. Hall
Julius Caesar Murder Case. Wallace Irwin
Julius Vernon. P. L. MacDermott
July at Fritham. M. Home
July 14 Assassination. B. Abro
Jump Cut. R. R. Irvine
Jump for Glory. G. McDonell
Jump the Gun. M. Cronin
Jump the High Wall. C. Richardson
Jumping Jenny. A. Berkeley
June, Moon, and Murder. C. M. Russell
June 13. F. Vreeland
Jungle Crime. L. Allan
Jungle Goddess. O. Sackville
Jungle Heat. D. Wilmer
Jungle Hut. E. P. Thorne
Jungle Jest. T. Mundy
Jungle Kids. E. Hunter
Jungle Manhunt. J. Laffin
Jungle Murder. A. Amos
Jungle Night. Reginald Campbell
Jungle She. D. Cushman
Jungle Terror. H. Wickham
Junior League Murders. C. Canyon
Juniper Rock. P. Atkey
Junk Market. H. Janson
Jupiter Crisis. W. Harrington
Jupiter Missile Mystery. E. Beatty
Juror. M. Underwood
Juror in Waiting. H. Cecil
Juror No. 17. C. C. Waddell
Jurors. B. Siegal
Jury. G. Bullett
Jury. E. Phillpotts
Jury Disagree. G. Goodchild
Jury Is Out. D. W. Rimel
Jury of Angels. B. Strutton
Jury of Death. R. C. Washburn
Jury of Four. G. Vallings
Jury of Her Peers. S. Glaspell
Jury of His Peers. J. Pearl
Jury of One. M. G. Eberhart
Juryman. D. MacKenzie
Juryman. E. E. Sumner
Just a Corpse at Twilight. Robert Martin
Just a Matter of Time. J. H. Chase
Just a Song at Twilight. J. Lodwick
Just an Ordinary Case. B. Graeme
Just and the Unjust. N. Carter
Just and the Unjust. J. G. Cozzens
Just Another Murder. D. Furber
Just Another Sucker. J. H. Chase
Just Around the Coroner. S. Brock
Just as I Am. M. E. Braddon
Just Fate. G. Long
Just for the Bride. D. P. Clark
Just Killing Time. R. Ellington
Just Let Me Be. J. Cleary
Just Men of Cordova. E. Wallace
Just Murder, Darling. J. A. Brussel
Just Not Making Mayhem Like They Used To. D. Von Elsner
Just Off Bond Street. R. Quest
Just One Slip. N. Carter
Just Sheaffer, or Storms in the Troubled Heir. I. Mowatt
Just the Way It Is. R. Marshall
Just Vengeance. L. P. Greene
Just What the Doctor Ordered. C. Watson
Justice! C. F. Gregg
Justice! M. Leighton
Justice. G. Simenon
Justice Astray. S. Warwick
Justice Be Damned. A. Hilliard

Justice by Accident. V. Lester
Justice by Midnight. J. Farnol
Justice by Proxy. G. H. Davies
Justice-Clerk. W. D. Lyell
Justice Enough. H. Carmichael
Justice for a Dead Spy. J. Moffatt
Justice for Judas. I. Baker
Justice for Judy. C. E. Vulliamy
Justice for Julia. M. Richmond
Justice Has No Sword. M. Franklin
Justice in Jeopardy. C. M. Wills
Justice, Inc. K. Robeson
Justice Is Done. A. Soutar
Justice Is Minc. E. P. Thorne
Justice Limited. F. Duncan
Justice Never Sleeps. O. Williams
Justice of Revenge. George Griffith
Justice of Sanders. F. Gerard
Justice on Halfaday Creek. J. B. Hendryx
Justice on the Rocks. B. Knox
Justice Peeps over the Handkerchief. C. Herbert
Justice Returns. F. Duncan
Justice--Suspended. R. Marsh
Justification of Andrew Lebrun. F. Barrett
Justified Sinner. J. F. Molloy
Justin Bayard. J. Cleary
Justine. W. Calvert
Justus Wise. A. W. Barrett
Juve in the Dock. M. Allain
Juvenile Delinquent. R. Deming
Juvenile Hoods. J. Shallit
Juvenile Jungle. F. Counsel
Juvies. H. Ellison

K

"K." L. Waller
K Code Plan. G. Seton
KGB Frame. J. Rosenberger
KGB Is Here. C. Franklin
KKK. P. E. Walsh
K.O. for Keeps. R. Angel
K Section. T. Lilley
Ka of Gifford Hillary. D. Wheatley
Kabaka. C. Johnston
Kahuna Killer. J. Sheridan
Kaiser's Blonde Spy. G. Ladoux
Kak-Abdullah Conspiracy. M. Macao
Kalahari Kill. S. Dembo
Kalee's Shrine. G. Allen
Kaleidoscope. M. Avallone
Kamikaze Assignment. A. Sugar
Kanaga. K. R. Butler
Kane and Miss Able. Tod Conrad
Kanesbrake. J. Blair
Kang-He Vase. J. S. Fletcher
Kangaroo Shoots Man. A. Scobie
Kara. J. Ellis
Kara Yerta Tragedy. J. E. Harrison
Karadac, Count of Gerzy. K. Prichard
Karaman, the Bandit Chief. G. W. M. Reynolds
Karamanov Equations. M. Goldberg
Karamour. A. Pritchett
Karl Grier. L. Tracy
Karl, the Lion. S. Cobb
Kashmiri Love Song. M. Richmond
Kastle Krags. A. Martin
Kat and Copy-Cat. E. E. Steven
Kat Strikes. N. Spain

K

Katana. M. Olden
Kate Hannigan. C. Cookson
Kate Meredith, Financier. C. J. C. Hyne
Kate, Plus Ten. E. Wallace
Kate Scott, the Decoy Detective. Anonymous
Kath. K. Henshaw
Katherine and the Dark Angel. M. Reisner
Katharine Beresford. H. M. Jones
Kathleen. T. P. Prest
Katie Mulholland. C. Cookson
Katrina. R. Kirkbridge
Keane of Kalgoorlie. A. Wright
Kearny Died Twice. K. Howard
Keeban. E. Balmer
Keegan. B. Ball
Keep Away from Water! A. Campbell
Keep Back the Dark. A. McElfresh
Keep Cool, Mr. Jones. T. Fuller
Keep It a Secret. Philip Chambers
Keep It Crisp. S. J. Perelman
Keep It Quiet. R. Hull
Keep It Simple. L. Johnson
Keep Moving, Bud. D. Linton
Keep Murder Quiet. S. Jepson
Keep the Coffins Coming. J. Long
Keep This Door Shut. A. M. Williamson
Keep Your Fingers Crossed. S. Maddock
Keep Your Fingers Crossed. Kevin O'Hara
Keeper of Black Hounds. N. Carter
Keeper of Red Horse Pass. W. C. Tuttle
Keeper of the Keys. E. D. Biggers
Keeper of the Keys. F. W. Robinson
Keepers. Sam Ross
Keepers of Death. S. Jason
Keepers of the King's Peace. E. Wallace
Keepers of the People. E. Jepson
Keeps Death His Court. M. Durham
Keersboskloof. N. Giles
Kefton, the Detective. Old Sleuth
Kellogg Junction. B. Spicer
Kelly. Eric Lambert
Kemmler. Hawkshaw
Kennel Murder Case. S. S. Van Dine
Kennels Crime. M. Osborne
Kenneth. G. W. M. Reynolds
Kentucky Detective. Anonymous
Kentucky Moonshiner. I. Stark
Kenya Mystery. C. T. Stoneham
Kenya Tragedy. Roland Daniel
Kenyatta's Escape. A. C. Clark
Kenyatta's Last Hit. A. C. Clark
Kept Women Can't Quit. A. A. Fair
Kermanshah Transfer. E. Sigel
Kerrell. Taffrail
Kessler Legacy. R. M. Stern
Kestrel House Mystery. T. C. H. Jacobs
Kestrel Syndicate. Jack Lewis
Kestrel's Claw. Jack Lewis
Kestrel's Conspiracy. Jack Lewis
Kettel Mill Mystery. I. Oellrichs
Kettle of Fish. N. Tranter
Key. M. Aldanov
Key. B. Kevern
Key. M. B. Lowndes
Key. L. Thayer
Key. P. Wentworth
Key Diablo. D. Daniels
Key Major. T. S. Strachan
Key Man. C. B. Kelland
Key Man. V. Williams
Key Men. A. Feist
Key Ring Clew. N. Carter
Key to Death. F. Lockridge
Key to Hawthorn Heath. A. P. Huff
Key to Murder. L. Marshall
Key to Nicholas Street. S. Ellin
Key to the Case. K. Orbison
Key to the Morgue. H. Howard
Key to the Morgue. Robert Martin
Key to the Suite. J. D. MacDonald
Key Without a Lock. Jack Lloyd
Key Witness. F. Kane
Key Witness. W. D. Roberts
Keyhole Peeper. J. De Bekker
Keys for the Criminal. P. Hambledon
Keys from a Window. E. Berckman
Keys of Chance. Winston Graham
Keys of Hell. M. Fallon
Keys of My Prison. F. S. Wees
Keys of the Flat. E. C. Vivian
Keys to Crime. Richard Martin
Keys to the House. E. Marion
Khaki Mafia. Robin Moore
Kharduni. A. Soutar
Khufra Run. J. Graham
Kibbutz. Alan White
Kick a Tin Can. D. Doubtfire
Kick-In. W. Mack
Kick-In. D. Torbett
Kick Start. D. Rutherford
Kickback. P. Malloch
Kicked to Death by a Camel. C. J.-L. Jackson
Kid. P. McCutchan
Kid Was a Killer. C. Chessman
Kid Was Last Seen Hanging Ten. Hampton Stone
Kid Who Came Home with a Corpse. Hampton Stone
Kid with a Gun. R. Wilkes-Hunter
Kiddy. T. Gallon
Kidnap. J. Boland
Kidnap. I. Morris
Kidnap Castle. S. Styles
Kidnap Club. A. B. Reeve
Kidnap Island. Roy Vickers
Kidnap Kid. T. Kenrick
Kidnap Murder Case. S. S. Van Dine
Kidnap Murders. E. T. Woodhall
Kidnapped. A. S. Manly
Kidnapped Again. J. Crozier
Kidnapped Child. G. Ashe
Kidnapped Child. J. Creasey
Kidnapped for a Million. D. Dayle
Kidnapped for Revenge. C. E. Blaney
Kidnapped for Revenge. Grace M. White
Kidnapped Heiress. Old Sleuth
Kidnapped King. R. Arnold
Kidnapped Millionaire. R. A. Wainwright
Kidnapped Millionaires. F. U. Adams
Kidnapped President. G. Boothby
Kidnapped Prince. T. S. King
Kidnapped Scientist. M. B. Dix
Kidnapped Squatter and other Australian tales. Andrew Robertson
Kidnapped Wife. Roland Daniel
Kidnapped Witness. A. Blair
Kidnapper. C. Bishop
Kidnapper. R. Bloch
Kidnapper, and Railway Line Murder. W. G. Mack
Kidnapper of Women. M. J. Pemberton
Kidnappers. B. Thomson
Kidnappers. A. E. Ullman
Kidnapper's Victim. R. Goyne
Kidnapping of Lincoln and Other War Detective Stories. J. C. Harris
Kidnapping of Madame Storey. H. Footner
Kidnapping of the President. C. Templeton
Kidnapping Syndicate. C. B. Booth
Kidneyed Caper. Alan Chase
Kigi Sets a Trap. R. St. Clair
Kildallon Affair. D. Vallance
Kildhurm's Oak. J. Hawthorne
Kilgaren. I. Holland
Kill! F. Scarpetta
Kill a Wicked Man. K. Hunt
Kill All the Young Girls. B. Halliday
Kill and Be Damned. M. Carrel
Kill and Desire. D. Linton
Kill and Tell. H. Rigsby
Kill as Directed. E. Queen
Kill at Dusk. P. Ketchum
Kill-Box. M. Stark
Kill City. A. Sugar
Kill Cure. J. Rathbone
Kill Dog. J. George
Kill 'Em with Kindness. F. Dickenson
Kill for It. R. Hawkes
Kill for the Millions. H. Kane
Kill Gently, But Sure. S. Jason
Kill Her if You Can. H. Janson
Kill Her with Passion. H. Janson
Kill Her--You'll Like It! M. Avallone
Kill Him Gently, Nurse. K. Fitzgerald
Kill Him Quickly, It's Raining. Michael Brett
Kill Him Tonight. J. Lane
Kill Him Twice. R. S. Prather
Kill in the Ring. V. Loder
Kill Is a Four-Letter Word. A. M. Stein
Kill Jason King. R. Miall
Kill Joy. E. S. Holding
Kill Kissinger. G. De Villiers
Kill Me a Fortune. R. Colby
Kill Me a Priest. J. Farrimond
Kill Me Again. J. Bentley
Kill Me and Live. C. Franklin
Kill Me for Kicks. H. Janson
Kill Me in Atami. E. Norman
Kill Me In Shimbashi. E. Norman
Kill Me in Shinjuku. E. Norman
Kill Me in Tokyo. E. Norman
Kill Me in Yokohama. E. Norman
Kill Me in Yoshiwara. E. Norman
Kill Me on the Ginza. E. Norman
Kill Me, Sweet. J. Wilcox
Kill Me Tomorrow. R. S. Prather
Kill Me with Kindness. J. H. Bond
Kill My Love. K. Hunt
Kill Now--Pay Later. L. Grex
Kill Now, Pay Later. R. Kyle
Kill-Off. J. Thompson
Kill Once, Kill Twice. K. Hunt
Kill 1 Kill 2. W. W. Anderson
Kill One, Kill Two. R. Kelston
Kill or Be Killed. G. Ashe
Kill or Cure. E. Ferrars
Kill or Cure. J. Fleming
Kill or Cure. W. Francis
Kill or Cure. R. Sapir
Kill Petrosino! F. Nolan
Kill Quick or Die. S. Jason
Kill Squad. W. Bond
Kill, Sweet Charity, Kill. J. L. Potter
Kill the Boss Good-By. P. Rabe
Kill the Clown. R. S. Prather
Kill the Dragon. R. Hawkes
Kill the Girls and Make Them Cry. J. Wainwright
Kill the Hack! Michael Bradley
Kill the Toff. J. Creasey
Kill Them All. F. Scarpetta
Kill This Man. H. Janson
Kill 3. M. Shulman
Kill Time. S. Jason
Kill to Fit. B. Fischer
Kill Two Birds. P. Levene
Kill with Care. H. L. Nelson

Title Index

Kill with Kindness. R. Bloomfield
Kill with Kindness. D. Shannon
Kill with Style. H. Gulliver
Kill Your Own Snakes. A. Seifert
Killed by Scandal. S. Nash
Killer. Roland Daniel
Killer. L. C. Douthwaite
Killer. Wade Miller
Killer. R. Parker
Killer. C. Wells
Killer. Colin Wilson
Killer Aboard. G. H. Teed
Killer Among Us. Robert Martin
Killer Among Us. Ben Ames Williams
Killer and His Star. H. M. Stephenson
Killer and the Slain. H. Walpole
Killer at His Back. J. Godey
Killer at Large. D. Bannon
Killer at Large. Ladbroke Black
Killer at Large. N. MacKenzie
Killer at Large. M. Procter
Killer at Scotland Yard. G. Davison
Killer Bait. D. Linton
Killer Be Killed. K. Chase
Killer Boy Was Here. G. Bagby
Killer by Night. H. Keyworth
Killed by Proxy. S. Jepson
Killer Came Riding. James Preston
Killer Conference. J. Carrick
Killer Conquest. B. Gray
Killer Cop. F. Findley
Killer Corps. P. Leslie
Killer Dolphin. N. Marsh
Killer Elite. R. Rostand
Killer for a Song. J. Gardner
Killer for the Chairman. M. Hebden
Killer from the Grave. F. J. Lowe
Killer Grew Tired. George Davis
Killer in Canvas Jeans. M. McCracken
Killer in Dark Glasses. H. Treece
Killer in Love. B. Sarto
Killer in My Mind. G. Blumberg
Killer in Silk. H. V. Dixon
Killer in the House. B. Deal
Killer in the Kitchen. F. James
Killer in the Rain. R. Chandler
Killer in the Shade. P. Marlowe
Killer in the Straw. R. Lockridge
Killer in the Street. H. Nielsen
Killer in White. T. Thomey
Killer Inside Me. J. Thompson
Killer Is Kissable. C. Brown
Killer Is Loose. G. Brewer
Killer Is Loose. C. Nicolai
Killer Is Loose Among Us. R. Terrall
Killer Is Mine. T. Powell
Killer Kay. E. Wallace
Killer Keep. W. M. Duncan
Killer Loose! G. Holden
Killer Mine. H. Innes
Killer Mine. M. Spillane
Killer of Fort Norman. C. Stoddard
Killer of Sheep River. C. Stoddard
Killer on the Catwalk. J. Philips
Killer on the Keys. M. Avallone
Killer on the Line. A. Hyde
Killer on the Prowl. F. Scarpetta
Killer on the Run. B. Toler
Killer on the Track. D. Rutherford
Killer on the Turnpike. W. P. McGivern
Killer Pack. W. McNeilly
Killer Pine. L. Gutteridge
Killer Reaction. J. N. Chance

Killer Road. M. Hastings
Killer Squad. J. Creasey
Killer Take All. J. O. Causey
Killer Take All. M. Hampton
Killer Take All. P. Race
Killer to Come. Sam Merwin
Killer Touch. E. Queen
Killer Waiting. W. Sproule
Killer Warrior. M. Olden
Killer Watches the Manhunt. A. B. Cunningham
Killer Wind. R. Hiscock
Killer with a Badge. W. Masterson
Killer with a Golden Touch. A. Riefe
Killer with a Key. D. J. Marlowe
Killers. W. H. Fear
Killers Are My Meat. S. Marlowe
Killers Are on Velvet. Neill Graham
Killers at Sea. A. Joseph
Killers at Sea. J. Messmann
Killer's Bargain. D. Owen
Killer's Blade. P. Malloch
Killers Cannot Live. A. Kinlay
Killer's Cargo. S. Jason
Killer's Carnival. T. Field
Killer's Category. J. Armour
Killer's Choice. S. Brock
Killer's Choice. E. McBain
Killer's Choice. Wade Miller
Killers Come Cheap. E. I. English
Killer's Conscience. J. Ingersol
Killer's Contract. T. C. Bridges
Killers End. H. Luger
Killers from the Keys. B. Halliday
Killer's Game. E. Hudiburg
Killer's Highway. M. Avallone
Killers in the Sun. J. E. Dixon
Killer's Kiss. H. Ellson
Killer's Kiss. H. Kane
Killer's Laughter. I. Lambot
Killer's Manual. John Morgan
Killer's Mask. C. Robertson
Killer's Moon. H. McCutcheon
Killers Must Die. Roland Daniel
Killers Must Eat. M. O'Brine
Killers of Innocence. J. Creasey
Killers of Karawala. E. Lindall
Killer's Payoff. E. McBain
Killers Play Rough. A. Ring
Killer's Playground. E. Harrison
Killer's Progress. F. Griffin
Killer's Rope. J. Cassells
Killer's Wedge. E. McBain
Killigrew. A. Dare
Killing. L. White
Killing. David Wilson
Killing Affair. P. Baker
Killing at the Big Tree. D. McCarthy
Killing Bone. P. Saxon
Killing Bottle Murder. L. A. Fenn
Killing Business. A. Tack
Killing Chase. R. Simons
Killing Comes Easy. P. Chester
Killing Cousins. F. Flora
Killing Experiment. J. N. Chance
Killing for the Hawks. F. E. Smith
Killing Frost. M. Catto
Killing Frost. E. Burgess
Killing Game. P. Cheyney
Killing Game. B. Knox
Killing Game. L. Peters
Killing Gift. B. Wood
Killing Ground. S. Linakis
Killing in Black and White. M. Hastings
Killing in Hats. J. Davey
Killing in Malta. Robert MacLeod
Killing in the Market. N. Daniels
Killing in the Market. G. Goodman
Killing Is Easy. M. Cronin
Killing Jazz. C. B. Booth

Killing Kin. A. Hocking
Killing Machine. B. Rossi
Killing Match. R. Severn
Killing no Murder. Colin Howard
Killing no Murder. M. G. Kiddy
Killing no Murder. F. A. M. Webster
Killing of Alquin Judd. P. Monnow
Killing of Ezra Burgoyne. P. Luck
Killing of Francie Lake. J. Symons
Killing of Judge MacFarlane. M. Plum
Killing of Paris Norton. R. Garnett
Killing of R.F.K. D. Freed
Killing of the Golden Goose. R. J. Black
Killing of the King. D. R. Slavitt
Killing Run. M. Barry
Killing Season. J. Redgate
Killing Star. M. Avallone
Killing Strike. J. Creasey
Killing the Goose. F. Lockridge
Killing Time. T. Berger
Killing Time. D. E. Westlake
Killing Touch. W. Murray
Killing Wind. John Lee
Killing with Kindness. A. Morice
Killings. Clark Howard
Killings in Carter Cave. K. Whipple
Killing's No Murder. N. MacKenzie
Killings on Kersivay. A. MacVicar
Killraven. M. Bishop
Killtown. R. Stark
Killy. D. E. Westlake
Kilmeny in the Dark Wood. Florence Stevenson
Kilo Forty. M. Tripp
Kilroy Gambit. I. R. Blacker
Kim. R. Colby
Kim Ruff. R. Gover
Kind Lady. E. Chodorov
Kind Man. H. Nielsen
Kind of Anger. E. Ambler
Kind of Courage. J. Harris
Kind of Justice. R. Gaines
Kind of Justice. E. Lindall
Kind of Misfortune. R. Parker
Kind of Nightmare. E. Cannon
Kind of Prisoner. J. Creasey
Kind of Treason. R. S. Elegant
Kind Uncle Buckby. John Gloag
Kindest Use a Knife. L. Revell
Kindly Dig Your Grave, and other wicked stories. S. Ellin
Kinds of Love, Kinds of Death. T. Coe
King Against Anne Bickerton. S. Fowler
King Among Crooks. J. K. Stafford
King and the Corpse. H. Murray
King and Two Queens. M. MacKintosh
King Blood. J. Thompson
King by Night. E. Wallace
King Cobra. F. Dudley
King Cole. W. R. Burnett
King Comes Back. V. Bridges
King Coppersmith. R. J. Griffin
King Dan, the Factory Detective. G. W. Goode
King Diamond. E. Bruton
King Diamond. F. M. White
King Edward Intervenes. A. Kenealy
King Fritz's A.D.C. F. Hird
King in Babylon. B. E. Stevenson
King in Bohemia. H. Herman
King in Check. T. Mundy
King Is Dead. E. Queen
King Is Dead on Queen Street. F. Bonnamy
King Killers. T. B. Dewey
King Maker. K. Robeson
King Murder. C. R. Jones
King of Anarchists. B. Wayde

K

King of Bigamists. O. Harper
King of Crooks. W. H. Ainsworth
King of Crooks. C. H. Bullivant
King of Dancing Valley. W. C. Tuttle
King of Detectives. Anonymous
King of Diamonds. J. J. Chichester
King of Diamonds. L. Tracy
King of Fun. Old Sleuth
King of Gold. N. Ned
King--of Kearsarge. A. O. Friel
King of Scamps. D. Stewart
King of Spain's Daughter. E. Spencer
King of Terrors. J. D. Spooner
King of the Castle. G. M. Fenn
King of the Castle. V. Holt
King of the Detectives. Old Sleuth
King of the Khyber Rifles. T. Mundy
King of the Opium Ring. C. E. Blaney
King of the Opium Ring. Grace M. White
King of the Peak. S. Cranbrook
King of the Rainy Country. N. Freeling
King of the Rocks. A. Pratt
King of the Underworld. N. Carter
King of the Underworld. Gwyn Evans
King of the World. G. Morton
King of Tiger Bay. J. M. Walsh
King of White Lady. R. L. Hill
King Pin. H. Miller
King-Sized Murder. W. Herber
King Spiv. L. Grex
King Vagabond. A. Wood
King Versus Wargrave. J. S. Fletcher
King Waits. M. Gerard
King Who Preferred Moonlight. A. Weigall
Kingblood. S. Jason
Kingdom and the Wall, and other tales. B. Reynolds
Kingdom Lost. P. Wentworth
Kingdom of Death. M. Allingham
Kingdom of Death. H. Pentecost
Kingdom of Earth. A. Partridge
Kingdom of Hate. T. Gallon
Kingdom of Johnny Cool. J. McPartland
Kingdom of the Blind. E. P. Oppenheim
Kingdom's Castle. D. Winston
Kingdoms of the World. L. Osbourne
Kingmakers. B. E. Stevenson
King's Assegai. B. Mitford
King's Castle. L. Ames
King's Club Murder. I. Greig
King's Coil. C. B. Pallen
King's Crew. F. R. Adams
King's Detective. Old Sleuth
Kings Die Hard. C. G. Booth
King's Elm Mystery. J. Goodwin
King's Enemies. Reginald Campbell
King's Enemies. J. M. Walsh
King's Highway. H. B. M. Watson
Kings in Adversity. E. S. Van Zile
King's Incognito. W. LeQueux
King's Justice. L. Galletley
King's Messenger. J. M. Walsh
King's Pawn. W. D. Roberts
King's Prisoner. N. Carter
King's Ransom. E. McBain
King's Red-Haired Girl. S. Jepson
King's Secret. H. H. C. Gibbons
King's Secret. R. H. Poole
King's Secret. R. H. Savage
King's Signature. A. Askew
King's Signet. M. Gerard
King's Stockbroker. A. C. Gunter
King's Talisman. S. Cobb
Kingsclere Mystery. M. Dalton
Kingsford Mark. V. Canning
Kingsley the Detective. Old Sleuth
Kingston Black. R. East
Kink. L. Brock
Kinks. Anonymous
Kinsman. W. Haggard
Kiriov Tapes. O. Sela
Kirke Webbe, the Privateer Captain. Waters
Kirkland Revels. V. Holt
Kirsty Affair. D. Hall
Kiss a Day Keeps the Corpses Away. J. Yardley
Kiss and Kill. Joe Barry
Kiss and Kill. C. Brown
Kiss and Kill. R. Deming
Kiss and Kill. Adam Knight
Kiss and Kill. R. McCary
Kiss and Kill. M. Meyers
Kiss and Kill. E. Queen
Kiss and Kill. M. Strobel
Kiss Before Dying. I. Levin
Kiss for a Killer. G. G. Fickling
Kiss for a Killer. D. B. Hughes
Kiss for a Killer. B. Sanders
Kiss for a Killer. E. F. Stafford
Kiss Her Goodbye. Wade Miller
Kiss Kiss. R. Dahl
Kiss! Kiss! Kill! Kill! H. Kane
Kiss Me Again, Stranger. D. Du Maurier
Kiss Me as You Go. D. Spade
Kiss Me Deadly. C. Brown
Kiss Me, Deadly. M. Spillane
Kiss Me Hard. T. Brandt
Kiss Me, Kill Me. B. Sarto
Kiss Me Quick. K. Kramer
Kiss My Fist! J. H. Chase
Kiss of Death. L. P. Bachmann
Kiss of Death. C. Birkin
Kiss of Death. Malcom Knight
Kiss of Death. E. Lipsky
Kiss of the Enemy. H. Hill
Kiss-Off. D. Heyes
Kiss Off the Dead. Garrity
Kiss That Killed. G. Leroux
Kiss the Babe Goodbye. B. McKnight
Kiss the Blonde Goodbye. F. McDermid
Kiss the Blood Off My Hands. Gerald Butler
Kiss the Book. A. Spiller
Kiss the Boss Goodbye. R. Drawford
Kiss the Boys and Make Them Die. J. Yardley
Kiss the Corpse Goodbye. M. Storm
Kiss the Killer. J. Shallit
Kiss the Tiger. F. M. Davis
Kiss the Toff. J. Creasey
Kiss Tomorrow Goodbye. Griff
Kiss Tomorrow Goodbye. H. McCoy
Kiss Your Elbow. A. Handley
Kissed Corpse. A. Baker
Kissed Corpse. W. J. Elliott
Kisses Can Kill. Donnell Carey
Kisses from Satan. G. B. Mair
Kisses of Death. H. Kane
Kissing Covens. C. Watson
Kissing Gourami. K. Platt
Kissing the Rod. E. Yates
Kit. J. Payn
Kit Wyndham. F. Barrett
Kitchen Cake Murder. C. Bush
Kitten with a Whip. Wade Miller
Kitten with Blue Eyes. J. Godden
Kitty Atherton. M. Blount
Kitty Brown's Princess. E. Jepson
Kitty Shafton--Swindler. A. Askew
Kitty the Madcap. M. M. Bodkin
Kitty's Engagement. F. Warden
Kitty's Father. F. Barrett
Kiwi Club. N. Leslie
Kiwi Contract. P. Atlee
Kleinert Case. Jack Mann
Klondike Claim. N. Carter
Klondyke Kit's Revenge. G. Goodchild
Klondyker. B. Knox
Klute. W. Johnston
Knave of Diamonds. J. Karney
Knave of Diamonds. Percy Marks
Knave of Eagles. R. Wade
Knave of Hearts. D. Shannon
Knave Takes Queen. P. Cheyney
Knaves & Co. S. Horler
Knaves' Castle. C. Robertson
Knaves in High Places. N. Carter
Knaves of Diamonds. George Griffith
Knaves Rampant. W. Mills
Knavish Crows. S. Woods
Knee-Deep in Death. B. Fischer
Knife. H. Adams
Knife. H. Ellson
Knife at My Back. Adam Knight
Knife Behind the Curtain. V. Williams
Knife Behind You. J. Benet
Knife Edge. W. Ellis
Knife Edge. D. MacKenzie
Knife-Edged Thing. S. Mitchell
Knife for Celeste. E. Burgess
Knife for Harry Dodd. G. Bellairs
Knife for the Juggler. M. Coles
Knife for the Killer. N. Morland
Knife for the Toff. J. Creasey
Knife for Your Heart. P. Marlowe
Knife in My Back. Sam Merwin
Knife in the Dark. G. D. H. Cole
Knife in the Night. W. M. Duncan
Knife Is Feminine. C. Jay
Knife Is Silent. D. Kent
Knife Terror. A. West
Knife Will Fall. M. Cumberland
Knifeman. D. Craig
Knight and the Castle. J. N. Chance
Knight at Arms. S. Horler
Knight Errant. E. Jepson
Knight in Red Armor. D. Daniels
Knight Missing. S. Stone
Knight of Evil. D. Donovan
Knight of the Silver Star. C. Lys
Knight Reluctant. C. Headlam
Knight Sinister. S. Rattray
Knight Takes Queen. G. Goodchild
Knight Templar. L. Charteris
Knight's Gambit. G. Dickson
Knight's Gambit. W. Faulkner
Knight's Keep. Rona Randall
Knights of Arabia. San Antonio
Knightsbridge Affair. C. Dawe
Knives Have Edges. S. Woods
Knock and Come In. G. Goodchild
Knock and Wait a While. W. R. Weeks
Knock at Midnight. C. Blackstock
Knock Down. D. Francis
Knock 'Em Dead. J. Karney
Knock, Knock! Who's There? J. H. Chase
Knock, Knock, Who's There? Anthony Gilbert
Knock, Murderer, Knock! H. Rutland
Knock-Out. H. C. McNeile
Knock-Out Kavanagh. B. Stuart
Knock Softly on Death's Door. T. E. Wilson
Knock Three-One-Two. F. Brown
Knocked for a Loop. C. Rice
Knocker on Death's Door. Ellis Peters
Knockout. C. F. Coe
Knockover. N. Thornbug
Knots in the Noose. N. Carter
Knots Untied. G. S. McWatters
Knotted Silk. Monte Barrett

Know Then Thyself. H. Gibbs
Known as Z.1. G. Goodchild
Knuckles. C. B. Kelland
Knutsford Mystery. D. Donovan
Kocska Formula. F. Riley
Koheleth. L. A. Storrs
Kojak. Abby Mann
Kokoda Trail. R. Wilkes-Hunter
Kolchak's Gold. B. Garfield
Komani Mystery. V. Sampson
Komespi Affair. Ernest Paul
Konigsmark. P. Benoit
Kono Diamond. N. Daniels
Kontrol. E. Snell
Korean Tiger. N. Carter
Kosygin Is Coming. T. Ardies
Kowloon Contract. P. Atlee
Krakatao Cult. J. Prescot
Kregoff Necklace. N. Carter
Kremlin File. N. Carter
Kremlin Letter. N. Behn
Kreutzman Formula. V. Scott
Kriegspiel. F. H. Groome
Kristiana Killers. H. Burland
Kronstadt. M. Pemberton
Kruger's Wagon. F. H. Rose
Krush. H. Janson
Kubla Khan Caper. R. S. Prather
Kukri Killer. R. Gilmour
Kundu. M. L. West
Kung Fu Avengers. M. Minick
Kyle Contract. D. MacKenzie

L

L for Murder. M. Stand
"L" Mystery. D. Stewart
L.S.D. Dossier. Roger Harris
L.2002. E. Jepson
La Belle Laurine. B. Graeme
La Bora. P. Jones
La Casa Dorada. J. L. Roberts
La Masque. C. M. Carleton
Label It Murder. Neill Graham
Laboratory Murder and other stories. N. Morland
Labour of Hercules. M. B. Lowndes
Labours of Hercules. A. Christie
Labyrinth. R. M. Gilchrist
Labyrinth Makers. A. Price
Labyrinthine Ways. G. Greene
Labyrinths. J. L. Borges
Lace in the Mews. R. Glover
LaChance Mine Mystery. S. Carleton
Lackey and the Lady. T. Gallon
Lacquer Screen. R. Van Gulik
Lad of Mettle. N. Gould
Ladder of Cards. J. Chancellor
Ladder of Death. B. Flynn
Ladies Always Talk. S. Truss
Ladies' Bane. P. Wentworth
Ladies' Bar. W. Dinner
Ladies Can Be Dangerous. L. Marshall
Ladies in Boxes. G. Burgess
Ladies in Ermine. Gavin Holt
Ladies in Hades. F. A. Kummer
Ladies in Reitrement. E. Percy
Ladies in Retreat. B. Perowne
Ladies in the Case. E. C. Vivian
Ladies in the Dark. M. Neville
Ladies' Juggernaut. A. C. Gunter
Ladies Leave the Castle. A. Athen
Ladies' Man. Rupert Hughes
Ladies of Locksley. F. Vivian
Ladies Prefer Bruisers. A. Applin
Ladies Sleep Alone. L. Della
Ladies Won't Wait. P. Cheyney
Lady. C. Massie

Lady Adelaide's Oath. H. Wood
Lady Afraid. L. Dent
Lady All Alone. L. Noel
Lady and Her Doctor. E. Piper
Lady and Leader. J. G. Sarasin
Lady and the Arsenic. J. Shearing
Lady and the Burglar. E. Turner
Lady and the Cheetah. J. Flagg
Lady and the Giant. C. B. Kelland
Lady and the Pirate. P. Allardyce
Lady and the Prowler. J. Roeburt
Lady and the Snake. J. Farr
Lady and the Unicorn. P. H. Irving
Lady Anne's Trustee, and other stories. F. Warden
Lady at Bay. E. Maass
Lady at Lyon House. E. Marlow
Lady Audley's Secret. M. E. Braddon
Lady Bachelor. H. P. Halsey
Lady, Be Bad. B. Halliday
Lady, Be Careful. C. Reeve
Lady, Behave! P. Cheyney
Lady Beware. P. Cheyney
Lady Bites. B. Sarto
Lady Bites the Dust. M. Shane
Lady Borradale's Ordeal. A. Askew
Lady Called Nita. E. Wallace
Lady Came by Night. B. Halliday
Lady Came to Kill. M. E. Chaber
Lady Can Do. S. Merwin
Lady Clara. F. M. White
Lady Death. G. Braddon
Lady Detective. Anonymous
Lady Detective. Rebecca Marsh
Lady Detective. Old Sleuth
Lady Doctor--Woman Spy. B. Newman
Lady, Don't Die on My Doorstep. J. Shallit
Lady, Don't Shroud Me! M. Brody
Lady--Don't Turn Over. D. Glinto
Lady Dorothy's Indiscretion. A. Applin
Lady Doth Protest. B. Graeme
Lady, Drop Dead. L. Treat
Lady Eleanor, Lawbreaker. R. Barr
Lady Elverton's Emeralds. D. Conyers
Lady Evelyn. M. Pemberton
Lady Fell in Love. E. Woodward
Lady Finger. G. Malcolm-Smith
Lady for Botany Bay. K. Lindsay
Lady for Sale. N. Daniels
Lady Forgot. M. S. Marble
Lady from Hamburg. V. Hill
Lady from Lisbon. V. Blake
Lady from Long Acre. V. Bridges
Lady from Nowhere. F. Hume
Lady from Shanghai. S. King
Lady from the Air. C. N. Williamson
Lady from Tokyo. M. Corrigan
Lady, Get Your Gun. P. Ernst
Lady Gets Wise. R. Madison
Lady Gift. J. Crecy
Lady Gone Astray. K. Hewitt
Lady Grace and other stories. H. Wood
Lady Grace's Mistake. J. Gibbon
Lady Gwendoline. T. Cobb
Lady Had a Gun. N. Morland
Lady Had a Tiger. G. Brodie
Lady Has a Scar. H. Janson
Lady Has Claws. H. Desmond
Lady Has No Convictions. C. Brown
Lady Helena. G. Leroux
Lady, Here's Your Wreath. R. Marshall
Lady in a Cage. R. Durand
Lady in a Frame. J. N. Chance
Lady in a Million. S. Shane
Lady in a Veil. G. R. Preedy

Lady in a Wedding Dress. S. Shane
Lady in Armor. O. R. Cohen
Lady in Black. B. Graeme
Lady in Black. F. Warden
Lady in Blue. A. Groner
Lady in Blue. F. M. White
Lady in Cement. A. Rome
Lady in Danger. M. Afford
Lady in Danger. S. Shane
Lady in Darkness. E. Bond
Lady in Darkness. K. Booton
Lady in Distress. M. Richmond
Lady in Distress. Martin Thomas
Lady in Dread. R. Johnson
Lady in Furs. F. Warden
Lady in Green and other stories. P. Cheyney
Lady in Leicester Square. N. W. Firth
Lady in Lilac. S. Shane
Lady in Mink. V. Caspray
Lady in No. 4. R. Keverne
Lady in Peril. L. Dent
Lady in Peril. H. Desmond
Lady in Peril. B. A. Williams
Lady in Sables. G. W. Appleton
Lady in Scarlet. Roland Daniel
Lady in Shadows. A. Lamb
Lady in Tears and other stories. P. Cheyney
Lady in the Black Mask. T. Gallon
Lady in the Blue Veil. L. Clarke
Lady in the Car. W. LeQueux
Lady in the Car with Glasses and a Gun. S. Japrisot
Lady in the Case. J. Futrelle
Lady in the Lake. R. Chandler
Lady in the Lightning. K. Tobias
Lady in the Mist. T. Charles
Lady in the Morgue. Jonathan Latimer
Lady in the Veil. A. Abdullah
Lady in the Wood. J. Dellbridge
Lady-in-Waiting. W. LeQueux
Lady Incognito. J. M. Walsh
Lady Ingram's Retreat. J. Tattersall
Lady Ingram's Room. J. Tattersall
Lady Is a Spitfire. B. Carson
Lady Is a Spy. Lionel Black
Lady Is a Tramp. H. Zore
Lady Is a Vamp. M. Dekobra
Lady Is Afraid. G. H. Coxe
Lady Is Available. C. Brown
Lady Is Chased. C. Brown
Lady Is Dead. P. Laing
Lady Is in Danger. R. A. Eames
Lady Is Lethal. P. Muller
Lady Is Not Available. C. Brown
Lady Is Not Fooling. A. Redwood
Lady Is Poison. B. Gray
Lady Is Transparent. C. Brown
Lady Is Waiting. J. Mitchell
Lady Jezebel. F. Hume
Lady Jim of Curzon Street. F. Hume
Lady Joan's Companion. F. Warden
Lady Judas. F. Barrett
Lady Kate, the Dashing Female Detective. Anonymous
Lady Killer. G. H. Coxe
Lady Killer. Anthony Gilbert
Lady Killer. W. Hardy
Lady Killer. E. S. Holding
Lady Killer. E. McBain
Lady Killers. A. Riefe
Lady Kills. B. Fischer

Lady, Lady, I Did It!   E. McBain
Lady Lee.   F. Warden
Lady, Lie Low.   H. Janson
Lady Likes to Sin.   D. Spade
Lady Lisle.   M. E. Braddon
Lady Living Alone.   P. Curtis
Lady Lost.   D. Cory
Lady Lost Her Head.   M. L. Stokes
Lady Make-Believe.   K. Lindsay
Lady Makes News.   V. Kathrens
Lady Marked for Murder.   P. Bacon
Lady Mary of the Dark House.   A. M. Williamson
Lady Mary's Experiences.   R. Jocelyn
Lady Maude's Mania.   G. M. Fenn
Lady, Mind That Corpse.   H. Janson
Lady Mislaid.   C. Rayner
Lady Molly of Scotland Yard.   B. Orczy
Lady Muriel's Secret.   J. Middlemass
Lady Noggs, Peeress.   E. Jepson
Lady of Arlac.   S. Shulman
Lady of Ascot.   E. Wallace
Lady of Balmerino.   M. Leighton
Lady of Burlesque.   Gypsy Rose Lee
Lady of China Street.   M. Corrigan
Lady of Despair.   F. Grierson
Lady of Doom.   G. Verner
Lady of Little Hell.   E. Wallace
Lady of Longbourne.   P. Trent
Lady of Mallow.   D. Eden
Lady of Mystery House.   G. C. Shedd
Lady of Night.   Jerome Barry
Lady of No Compassion.   P. Malloch
Lady of Ravensedge.   Jack Lewis
Lady of Resource.   A. S. Roche
Lady of Shadows.   N. Carter
Lady of Storm House.   E. Bond
Lady of the Barge.   W. W. Jacobs
Lady of the Blue Motor.   S. Paternoster
Lady of the Cameo.   T. Gallon
Lady of the Guns.   Andrew Murray
Lady of the Ice.   J. De Mille
Lady of the Island.   G. Boothby
Lady of the Isle.   E. Southworth
Lady of the Hundred Dresses.   S. R. Crockett
Lady of the Lens.   F. C. Long
Lady of the Leopard.   C. L'Epine
Lady of the Lilacs.   E. D. Pierson
Lady of the Miniature.   O. Binns
Lady of the Night.   S. Horler
Lady of the Night.   B. Swift
Lady of the Night.   V. Vanardy
Lady of the North Star.   O. Binns
Lady of the Rifle.   F. E. Penny
Lady of the Shadows.   D. Daniels
Lady of the Shroud.   B. Stoker
Lady of the Swamp.   C. A. Brandreth
Lady of Wildersley.   J. Edgar
Lady on a Train.   L. Charteris
Lady on Fire.   J. M. Ullman
Lady on Loan.   E. Ellison
Lady on Platform One.   L. Meynell
Lady, or the Tiger, and other stories.   F. R. Stockton
Lady Ottoline.   Mrs. Lodge
Lady Pamela's Pearls.   J. Ironside
Lady Passenger.   A. W. Marchmont
Lady Pays.   S. Coburn
Lady Prefers Murder.   H. A. Wrenn
Lady Regrets.   J. M. Fox
Lady Richly Left.   M. B. Dix
Lady Rodway's Ordeal.   F. Warden
Lady Said No.   A. Allyson
Lady Sarah's Deed of Gift.   A. Griffin

Lady Saw Red.   A. R. Long
Lady Saxondale's Crimes.   G. W. M. Reynolds
Lady Says When.   D. Ambler
Lady Screams.   H. Kaner
Lady Shadower.   Old Sleuth
Lady Sharlow's Secret.   W. M. Graydon
Lady, Shed Your Head.   D. Foster
Lady So Innocent.   H. Adams
Lady So Silent.   L. Dent
Lady Sylvia's Imposter.   T. Cobb
Lady, Take Care.   C. Robertson
Lady Takes a Flyer.   E. Ronns
Lady Takes Care.   G. Goodchild
Lady, That's My Skull.   C. Shannon
Lady--This Is It!   H. Luger
Lady, This Is Murder.   Peter Chambers
"Lady, Throw Me a Curve."   G. Ross
Lady to Kill.   L. Dent
Lady, Toll the Bell.   H. Janson
Lady Turned Traitor.   Roland Daniel
Lady Turpin.   H. Herman
Lady Ursula's Husband.   F. Warden
Lady Vanishes.   Ethel L. White
Lady Varley.   D. Vane
Lady Velvet.   N. Carter
Lady Was a Spy.   Roland Daniel
Lady Was a Tramp.   H. Whittington
Lady Was Disturbed.   J. Warren
Lady Was Elusive.   L. Cargill
Lady Was Warned.   K. Rhodes
Lady Wept Alone.   C. B. Dawson
Lady, What's Your Game?   T. C. H. Jacobs
Lady, Where Are You?   H. Desmond
Lady with a Cool Eye.   G. Moffat
Lady with a Gun.   E. P. Thorne
Lady with a Rose.   F. Hay
Lady with the Dice.   J. T. Rogers
Lady with the Limp.   S. Horler
Lady Without Mercy.   R. McDougald
Lady Zia.   P. Wynnton
Ladybirds Are In.   H. Janson
Ladyfingers.   J. Gregory
Ladyfingers.   S. Rifkin
Lady's a Decoy.   K. T. McCall
Lady's Eyes Were Green.   A. Aldous
Lady's for Killing.   B. Shannon
Lady's in Danger.   N. Berrow
Lady's Mile.   M. E. Braddon
Lady's Not for Living.   D. St. Clair
Lagden's Luck.   T. Gallon
Laguna Contracts.   E. C. Allen
Laidlaw's Wife.   F. Warden
Lair of the Vampire.   G. E. Rochester
Lair of the White Worm.   B. Stoker
Laird.   Winifred Duke
Laird and the Lady.   J. Grant
Laird of Evil.   Martin Thomas
Lairds of Turriff Hall.   A. Jamison
Lairu Murders.   E. N. Mangat Rai
Lake District Murder.   J. Rhode
Lake Frome Monster.   A. W. Upfield
Lake House.   J. Rhode
Lake Loot.   H. Janson
Lake Lovers.   G. Wagner
Lake Mystery.   M. Dana
Lake of Darkness.   F. Cowen
Lake of Fire.   L. Houser
Lake of Fury.   Robert MacLeod
Lake of the Dead.   L. P. Greene
Lake of the Wind.   Lynn Williams
Lake of Wine.   B. Capes
Lakeland Tragedy.   J. Courage

Lakeside Murder.   C. H. Snow
Lakeside Zero.   D. Enefer
Lam to Slaughter.   D. Sanderson
Lam to the Slaughter.   A. A. Fair
Lama's Secret.   W. M. Graydon
Lamb to the Slaughter.   D. Eden
Lambert's Son.   A. Maling
Lambs of Fire.   P. Gascar
Lame Dog Murder.   M. Halliday
Lament for a Lonesome Corpse.   Ruth Reeves
Lament for a Lousy Lover.   C. Brown
Lament for a Lover.   P. Highsmith
Lament for a Maker.   M. Innes
Lament for a Virgin.   L. White
Lament for Four Brides.   E. Berckman
Lament for Julie.   R. Colby
Lament for Leto.   G. Mitchell
Lament for Lost Lovers.   Alanna Knight
Lament for the Bride.   H. Reilly
Lament for William.   C. M. Russell
Lammas Grove.   C. Dawe
Lamp Burns Blood.   Leslie Carroll
Lamp of God.   E. Queen
Lamp-Post 592.   S. Maddock
Lampton Dreamers.   L. P. Davies
Lanagan, Amateur Detective.   E. H. Hurlbut
Lancaster Triple Thousand.   W. B. Woods
Lancer Spy.   M. McKenna
Land at Last.   E. Yates
Land from the Sea.   S. Styles
Land God Gave to Cain.   H. Innes
Land o' the Leal.   H. B. Mathers
Land of Big Things.   L. H. Gordon
Land of Fear.   K. Robeson
Land of Hidden Death.   J. Atholl
Land of Long Juju.   K. Robeson
Land of Eldorado.   G. Goodchild
Land of No Escape.   G. Horne
Land of Promises.   S. P. Hyatt
Land of Seals.   J. M. Scott
Land of Terror.   K. Robeson
Land of the Free.   W. McNeilly
"Land of the Free."   W. Slater
Land Pirate.   J. Bogar
Landed at Last.   N. Gould
Landed Gently.   A. Hunter
Landfall.   D. W. MacArthur
Landfall Finesse.   D. Da Cruz
Landlady.   C. Rauch
Landor Case.   J. Bentley
Landru.   W. LeQueux
Landru.   R. Masson
Land's End, and other stories.   W. D. Steele
Landscape with Corpse.   D. Ames
Landscape with Corpses.   M. Barnes
Landscape with Dead Dons.   R. Robinson
Landscape with Violence.   J. Wainwright
Landslide.   D. Bagley
Lane of Darkness.   M. Clare
Langley Murder Case.   Roland Daniel
Lanier Riddle.   D. Daniels
Lansing Legacy.   A. Hyman
Lantern for Diogenes.   S. Harvester
Lantern Hill.   B. Worsley-Gough
Lantern House Affair.   Gret Lane
Lantern of Luck.   H. Douglas
Lapse of the Bishop.   G. Thorne
Larceny in Her Heart.   L. Grex
Large Type Killer.   Richard Williams
Larkspur Conspiracy.   J. Philips
Larrabee Heiress.   D. Daniels
Larry Lohengrin.   W. Westall
Las Vegas.   Arthur Moore
Las Vegas Strip.   M. Renek
Las Vegas Vengeance.   B. Rossi
Laser War.   J. Rosenberger
Lass That Loved a Soldier.   G. M. Fenn
Last Act in Bermuda.   D. Burnham

Title Index

Last Adventure. E. Wallace
Last Alive. J. M. Cobban
Last Appointment. H. Howard
Last Assignment. N. Fisher
Last Best Friend. G. Sims
Last Believers. D. Karp
Last Breath. H. Q. Masur
Last Bridge. B. Garfield
Last Bridge. D. Mariner
Last Buccaneer. J. Wainwright
Last Bus to Woodstock. C. Dexter
Last Cab on the Rank. H. Grisewood
Last Call. N. Carter
Last Call. R. Dowling
Last Call for Lissa. D. Mayor
Last Card. H. H. Kirst
Last Card. Mark Ross
Last Checkpoint. J. Quigley
Last Clear Chance. B. Wilkinson
Last Clue. W. J. Bayfield
Last Clue. Eugene Jones
Last Command. C. Houghton
Last Commandment. G. H. Coxe
Last Concubine. F. S. Wees
Last Contract. Clark Howard
Last Cop Out. M. Spillane
Last Coup. H. Smart
Last Cruise of the "Majestic." G. Goodchild
Last Day of Lincoln Charles. Gordon M. Williams
Last Days of Berlin. P. Saxon
Last Days of Louisiana Red. I. Reed
Last Days of Miss Jenkinson. N. Hoult
Last Deception. H. Howard
Last Deserter. J. Robb
Last Ditch. G. Goodchild
Last Ditch. V. Hunt
Last Ditch. M. McGrath
Last Door. O. Binns
Last Door. D. Enefer
Last Doorbell. J. Harrington
Last Doorbell. J. K. Vedder
Last Drop. B. Cobb
Last Enemy. Keith Ayling
Last Enemy. V. M. Methley
Last Enemy. B. Roueche
Last Escape. E. C. R. Lorac
Last Escape. M. Walker
Last Express. B. Kendrick
Last Fathom. M. Caidin
Last First. R. Hull
Last Flight. M. Land
Last Flowers. Michael Barrett
Last Frontier. Alistair MacLean
Last Galley. A. C. Doyle
Last Gamble. J. Fairfax-Blakeborough
Last Gamble. R. Foley
Last Gamble. H. Q. Masur
Last Hero. L. Charteris
Last Heroes. John Gill
Last Hope House. Wilma Forrest
Last House. G. Dessart
Last House. M. Maurice
Last Indictment. M. Cronin
Last Journey. Keith Campbell
Last Kill. Charlie Wells
Last King of Yewle. P. L. MacDermott
Last Known Address. J. Harrington
Last Lady. H. Janson
Last Lap. G. B. Savi
Last Laugh. C. Einstein
Last Laugh. Winifred Graham
Last Laugh and No Pictures for Cathy. P. Denver
Last Laugh for the Baron. A. Morton
Last Laugh, Mr. Moto. J. P. Marquand

Last Link. M. Gerard
Last Lord Avanley. G. Maxwell
Last Man at Arlington. J. Di Mona
Last Man Club. E. Queen
Last Man's Head. Jessica Anderson
Last Mayday. K. Wheeler
Last Meeting. B. Matthews
Last Miracle. M. P. Shiel
Last Move in the Game. N. Carter
Last Night. J. McPartland
Last Note for a Lovely. C. Brown
Last of Lysandra. E. Fenwick
Last of Mr. Moto. J. P. Marquand
Last of Mrs. Cheyney. D. G. Herriot
Last of Philip Banter. J. F. Bardin
Last of Sheila. Alexander Edwards
Last of the Country House Murders. E. Tennant
Last of the Crazy People. T. Findley
Last of the Darrells. C. E. Pearce
Last of the Grenvilles. B. Copplestone
Last of the Mansions. D. Daniels
Last of the Pleasure Gardens. Francis King
Last of the Van Slacks. E. S. Van Zile
Last One Kills. W. Masterson
Last Page. J. H. Chase
Last Parable. Alec Coppel
Last Place God Made. J. Higgins
Last Place Left. M. Pugh
Last Plane from Uli. C. Keary
Last Post for a Partisan. C. Egleton
Last Quarter Hour. J. Bruce
Last Redoubt. G. Goodchild
Last Refuge of a Scoundrel and other stories. W. Howard
Last Resort. V. Siller
Last Rites for the Vulture. Simon Quinn
Last Run South. R. Hiscock
Last Score. E. Queen
Last Scourge. W. Martyn
Last Secret. D. Chambers
Last Secret. G. Goodchild
Last Seen Alive. A. Mills
Last Seen Hitchhiking. B. Halliday
Last Seen in Samarra. J. G. Vermandel
Last Seen Wearing--. H. Waugh
Last Seven Hours. J. N. Chance
Last Shaft. E. Tidyman
Last Shot. L. Thayer
Last Shot and other stories. R. Goyne
Last Signal. Dora Russell
Last Spin and other stories. E. Hunter
Last Stop. W. Tucker
Last Stop Camp 7. H. H. Kirst
Last Straw. D. M. Disney
Last Straw. F. Hume
Last Straw. I. S. Shriber
Last Stroke. L. L. Lynch
Last Stronghold. J. Pattinson
Last Survivor. E. Dale
Last Suspect. J. Rhode
Last Tales. I. Dinesen
Last Tenant. B. L. Farjeon
Last Tiger. W. A. Ballinger
Last Time I Saw Hell. Simon Quinn
Last Train Out. E. P. Oppenheim
Last Train to Limbo. J. N. Chance
Last Train to Rock Ferry. D. Enefer
Last Traitor of Long Island. R. H. Savage
Last Trap. S. Gluck
Last Trump. L. Thayer
Last Trumpet. T. Downing

Last Twist of the Knife. M. Bonner
Last Vanity. H. Howard
Last War Dance. R. Sapir
Last Warning. W. Camp
Last Warning. T. Fallon
Last Warning. G. Verner
Last Will and Testament. G. D. H. Cole
Last Witness. W. Collison
Last Woman. R. Beeckman
Last Woman in His Life. E. Queen
Last Year at Marienbad. A. Robbe-Grillet
Last Year's Blood. H. C. Branson
Last Year's Snow. D. Tracy
Last Year's Wife. A. M. Williamson
Lastingham Murder. L. Tracy
Late and Cold. M. Torrie
Late Bill Smith. A. Garve
Late Boy Wonder. Angus Hall
Late Bride. T. Du Bois
Late Clara Beame. T. Caldwell
Late Demented. B. Carson
Late Edwina Black. W. Dinner
Late Final Blonde. M. Brody
Late for the Funeral. D. Stapleton
Late Harvest. K. Sunderland
Late into the Night. H. Bigden
Late Lamented. F. Brown
Late Lamented. A. A. Thomson
Late, Lamented Lady. M. Blizard
Late Last Night. J. Reach
Late Miss Trimming. C. Carnac
Late Mr. Beverly. T. Cobb
Late Mrs. D. H. Waugh
Late Mrs. Five. R. Wormser
Late Mrs. Fonsell. V. Johnston
Late Mrs. Lane. Rona Randall
Late Night Revel. H. Janson
"Late of London Wall..." Bruce Norman
Late Phoenix. C. Aird
Late Recovery. S. Fairway
Late Repentance. T. W. Speight
Late Tenant. Gordon Holmes
Late Uncle Max. M. Fitt
Late Unlamented. C. N. Boyle
Late Unlamented. H. Carmichael
Late Unlamented. D. L. Mathews
Late Unlamented. R. A. J. Walling
Lately Deceased. B. Picton
Later Than You Think. M. M. Kaye
Latigo. F. O'Rourke
Latter End. P. Wentworth
Lattimore Arch. Angela Gray
Laugh Was on Lazarus. J. Garforth
Laughing Bacchante. D. Yates
Laughing Buddha. C. Glick
Laughing Buddha. V. Starrett
Laughing Buddha Murders. R. Foster
Laughing Cat. S. Toye
Laughing Death. W. C. Brown
Laughing Death. P. Edwards
Laughing Dog. F. Vivian
Laughing Fish. L. Bell
Laughing Fish. S. Jepson
Laughing Fox. F. Gruber
Laughing Gangster. D. Newton
Laughing Ghost. D. Eden
Laughing Girl. R. W. Chambers
Laughing Girl. G. F. Worts
Laughing Grave. V. Gunn
Laughing Lightweight. P. Gill
Laughing Loon. J. E. Greene
Laughing Malefactor. C. West
Laughing Men. T. C. H. Jacobs
Laughing Mill and other stories. J. Hawthorne
Laughing Mountains. K. Lynn
Laughing Peril. H. L. Gates
Laughing Policeman. E. Bruton
Laughing Policeman. M. Sjowall
Laughing Rider. L. Y. Erskine

L

Laughing Whitefish. R. Traver
Laughing Widow. G. Warren
Laughter Came Screaming. H. Kane
Laughter in the Alehouse. H. Kane
Laughter in the Night. F. Ford
Laughter in the Ranks. M. Hervey
Laughter Trap. J. Philips
Launching of Roger Brook. D. Wheatley
Laura. V. Caspary
Laura Possessed. Anthea Fraser
Laura Sarelle. J. Shearing
Laurell'd Captains. G. R. Preedy
Laurels Are Poison. G. Mitchell
Laurels for McLean. G. Goodchild
Laurels for the Dreamer. W. M. Duncan
Laurine. B. Graeme
Lava Flow Murders. Max Long
Lavender Dagger. D. C. Calthrop
Lavender Gripsack. H. S. Keeler
Lavender's Inheritance. A. Askew
Lavenham Mystery. B. Bolt
Law. B. S. Ballinger
Law and Order. D. Uhnak
Law and Order on Halfaday Creek. J. B. Hendryx
Law and Order, Unlimited. W. C. MacDonald
Law and the Lady. W. Collins
Law Breakers. R. Cullum
Law-Breakers and other stories. Robert Grant
Law Courts Mystery. A. Blair
Law Not Justice. F. Warden
Law of Nemesis. A. Carlyle
Law of Probability. M. Sharman
Law of the Bolo. S. P. Hyatt
Law of the Four Just Men. E. Wallace
Law of the Gun. R. Cullum
Law of the Hills. O. Binns
Law of the Knife. C. Dawe
Law of the Land. F. M. White
Law of the River. F. Gerard
Law of the Streets. A. Le Breton
Law of the Talon. L. Tracy
Law of the Three Just Men. E. Wallace
Lawful Pursuit. M. Underwood
Lawless. C. Dawe
Lawless Hand. W. LeQueux
Lawless Justice. A. Edgar
Lawless Voyage. A. D. Divine
Lawrence Barclay File. B. Musto
Laws Be Their Enemy. F. E. Smith
Lawton Mystery. W. J. Burns
Lawyer and the Carpenter. E. Thompson
Lawyer Bell from Boston. R. L. Tyler
Lawyer-Detective. W. Warner
Lawyer Manton of Chicago. Le Jemlys
Lawyers Don't Hang. G. M. Barnes
Lawyer's Secret. M. E. Braddon
Lawyer's Secret. J. K. Leys
Lawyer's Secret. H. Lloyd
Lawyer's Story. J. A. Maitland
Lay Her Among the Lilies. J. H. Chase
Lay On, MacDuff! C. Armstrong
Lay-Over Town. D. Brennan
Lay That Pistol Down. R. Powell
Layers of Deceit. B. Jones
Laying on of Hands. A. Arent
Layoff. R. G. Dean
Layout for a Corpse. G. Goldsmith
Layout for Murder. J. Karney
Layton Court Mystery. A. Berkeley
Lazarus in London. F. W. Robinson
Lazarus Murder Seven. R. Sale
Lazarus #7. R. Sale
Lazy Detective. G. Dilnot
Lazy Lawrence Murders. T. Downing
Le Père Goriot. H. D. Balzac
Lead Astray. C. Brown
Lead Her Gently to the Grave. D. Bogard
Lead Him to Death. H. Windsor
Lead-Lined Coffin. E. McGirr
Lead Me into Temptation. F. Heller
Lead Me to the Gallows. F. Lester
Lead On, McLean! G. Goodchild
Lead with Your Left. E. Lacy
Leaden Bubble. H. C. Branson
Leading Lady. G. Bonner
Leading Lady. H. Herman
Leaf of a Lime Tree. P. Tabori
League of Counterfeiters. Old Sleuth
League of Crime. F. Balfour
League of Dark Men. J. Creasey
League of Discontent. F. Beeding
League of Five. D. Lenton
League of Frightened Men. R. Stout
League of Gentlemen. J. Boland
League of Guilt. I. Murray
League of Justice. F. Duncan
League of Life. M. Gerard
League of Light. J. Creasey
League of Matthias. B. Flynn
League of Missing Men. J. M. Walsh
League of Nameless Men. J. Cassells
League of St. Louis. D. Whitelaw
League of the Lotus. A. Eadie
League of the Ring and Torn Apart. M. O'Brien
League of the Triangle. L. Lurgan
League of the White Hand. O. Crawford
League of Three. Old Sleuth
League of Twelve. G. Boothby
League of Twelve. F. Stanley
Lean Years. H. Bindloss
Leaning Man. C. Bush
Leap Before You Look. S. Waldron
Leap in the Dark. Donald Gordon
Leap in the Dark. L. G. Moberly
Leap in the Dark. Rona Randall
Leap in the Dark. M. Richmond
Leap in the Dark. E. Southworth
Lease of Convict 308. E. W. Alais
Leases of Death. M. B. Gaunt
Least of All Evils. H. Arvonen
Leather Duke. F. Gruber
Leather Man. L. Treat
Leather Mask. A. Pratt
Leatherface. E. Dudley
Leatherface Lonergan Stakes a Claim. P. Renwick
Leatherjacket. Arthur Wise
Leathermouth. C. Dawe
Leathermouth's Luck. C. Dawe
Leave Her to Heaven. Ben Ames Williams
Leave Her to Hell! F. Flora
Leave It to Conquest. B. Gray
Leave It to Me. M. Cronin
Leave It to Me. G. Joseph
Leave It to Me. H. Luger
Leave It to the Hangman. B. Knox
Leave It to the Toff. J. Creasey
Leave Murder to Me. R. Powell
Leave of Absence. Eric Bailey
Leave the Dead Behind Us. P. McCutchan
Leavenworth Case. A. K. Green
Leavenworth Irregulars. W. D. Blankenship
Leaves from the Diary of a Law Clerk. Waters
Leaves from the Journal of a Custom-House Officer. Waters
Leaves from the Note Book of a Chief of Police. A. Hughes
Leaves from the Note-Book of a New York Detective. J. B. Williams
Leaves from the Notebook of a New York Detective. Anonymous
Leavetaking. G. Milner
Lebanon Paradise. E. Atiyah
Lecoq, the Detective's Daughter. W. Busnach
Led to the Light. M. A. Denison
Ledge. G. Schweitzer
Ledger. D. Uhnak
Ledger Is Kept. R. Postgate
Leech Club. G. W. Owen
Leeds Fiasco. Angus Ross
Leering House. B. Symons
Lees and Leaven. E. W. Townsend
Left for Dead. Basil Carey
Left Hand Left. M. Massey
Left Hand of God. J. Lane
Left-Handed Death. R. Hull
Left-Handed Murder. A. Carruthers
Left-Handed Passenger. F. Riesenberg
Left-Handed Sleeper. T. Willis
Left Leg. A. Tilton
Lefty Cuts Loose. B. Shannon
Lefty Hands It Out. B. Shannon
Lefty O'Connor Moves In. B. Shannon
Lefty Takes Over. B. Shannon
Legacy. A. Askew
Legacy in Blood. M. Allingham
Legacy in Green. D. Whitelaw
Legacy Lenders. H. Q. Masur
Legacy of a Spy. H. S. Maxfield
Legacy of Cain. W. Collins
Legacy of Danger. Richard Grant
Legacy of Danger. P. McGerr
Legacy of Death. M. Burton
Legacy of Death. R. A. J. Walling
Legacy of Doom. E. J. Murray
Legacy of Evil. Lydia Belknap Long
Legacy of Evil. A. Pritchett
Legacy of Fear. F. D. Hancock
Legacy of Fear. A. Skene
Legacy of Fear. Garnett Weston
Legacy of Hate. N. Carter
Legacy of Hate. T. Douglas
Legacy of Hate. R. Hardinge
Legacy of Loneliness. S. Wagner
Legacy of Mendoubia. J. Reddoch
Legacy of Redfern. J. Judson
Legacy of Shadows. R. Batchelor
Legacy of Shame. J. W. Bobin
Legacy of Terror. K. Cameron
Legacy of the Golden Key. W. H. Brown
Legacy of the Granite Hills. B. Mitford
Legacy of the Lost. J. Wetherell
Legacy of Vengeance. J. W. Bobin
Legacy of Vengeance. P. Trent
Legal Fiction. E. Ferrars
Legal Fire. O. Stanley
Legal Settlement. Harrington Strong
Legal Wreck. W. Gillette
Legend. Evelyn Anthony
Legend of Baverstock Manor. N. Buckingham
Legend of Crownpoint. M. Heath
Legend of Joseph Nokato. L. P. Bachmann
Legend of Monk's Court. Dorinne Moore
Legend of Piper's Hole. P. Farmer
Legend of the Grey Castle. R. Eldridge
Legend of the Loch. Alanna Knight
Legend of the Seventh Virgin. V. Holt
Legion. R. Bridges
Legion of the Lost. J. Creasey
Legionnaire Spy. W. B. Bannerman
Legions of the Death Master. C. Steele
Legislative Body. J. L. Hensley
Legs. W. Kennedy
Leighton Grange. M. E. Braddon

Title Index

Leila. G. W. M. Reynolds
Leila and Her Lover. M. Pemberton
Leipzig Affair. J. D. White
Leland Case. H. Somerville
Leland Legacy. D. Daniels
Lemmings. C. Blackstock
Lemon in the Basket. C. Armstrong
Lemons Never Lie. R. Stark
Lena Hates Men. M. Neville
Lend a Hand. J. S. Blazer
Lend a Hand to Murder. M. Halliday
Lend Me a Rod. D. Linton
Lenient Beast. F. Brown
Lenore. M. E. Edward
Leonard Harlowe. Waters
Leopard Cat's Cradle. Jerome Barry
Leopard Died Too. N. Brent
Leopard Man. R. C. Armour
Leopard-Paw Orchid. K. Allsop
Leopard Valley. C. K. MacKinnon
Leopard with a Thin Skin. J. B. Watney
Leopard's Spots. A. Soutar
Leopard's Spots. F. M. White
Leopold Contract. G. Wolk
Leper's Bell. M. Sparroy
Lepke. J. Pearl
Leprechaun Murders. A. Reynolds
Lerouge Case. E. Gaboriau
Less Black than We're Painted. J. Payn
Less Than the Dust. L. Crichton
Less Than the Dust. K. Lindsay
Lesser Antilles Case. R. King
Lesser Evil. R. Chambers
Lesser Evil. I. D. Hardy
Lessing Murder Case. S. Horler
Lessinger Comes Back. R. Essex
Lessinger Laughs Last. R. Essex
Lesson in Crime. G. D. H. Cole
Lesson in Crime and other stories. G. D. H. Cole
Lesson in Crime, and The Motive. G. D. H. Cole
Lesson in Murder. S. Claydon
Lester Affair. A. Garve
Lester Grayling, K.C. L. J. Lynwood
Lester's Secret. M. C. Hay
L'Estrange Case. J. Bentley
Let Dead Enough Alone. R. Lockridge
Let Him Die. E. H. Clements
Let Him Go Hang. B. Clifton
Let Him Go, Let Him Tarry. M. Penoyre
Let Him Have Judgment. B. Hamilton
Let Him Stay Dead. T. C. H. Jacobs
Let It Lie. J. Goodwin
Let Justice Be Done. Mark Allerton
Let Justice Be Done! M. Poole
Let Me Kill You, Sweetheart. K. Carr
Let Me Kill You, Sweetheart. F. Flora
Let My People Be. D. Reid
Let Not Thy Left Hand. L. Gorell
Let or Hindrance. E. H. Clements
Let or Hindrance. E. Lemarchand
Let Sleeping Girls Lie. J. Mayo
Let the Dead Past--. J. S. Strange
Let the Lady Die. B. Winter
Let the Man Die. S. H. Courtier
Let the Night Cry. Charlie Wells
Let the Skeletons Rattle. F. C. Davis
Let the Tiger Die. M. Coles
Let the Witness Die. I. Lambot
Let Them Eat Bullets. H. Schoenfeld
Let Them Pray. S. Harvester
Let Tomorrow Come. A. J. Barr
Let Well Alone. E. C. R. Lorac
Let X Be the Murderer. C. Witting
Let X Equal Murder. E. Healey
Lethal in Love. C. Brown
Lethal Lady. R. King
Lethal Playground. D. Franklin
Lethbridge of the Moor. M. Drake

Let's Ask Aunt. M. Godwyn
Let's Choose Executors. S. Woods
Let's Face It. A. Bocca
Let's Go Play at the Adams'. M. W. Johnson
Let's Hear It for the Deaf Man. E. McBain
Let's Kill George. L. Cores
Let's Kill Uncle. R. O'Grady
Let's Kill Uncle Lionel. J. York
Let's Not Get Smart. A. Bocca
Let's Shoot This Out. R. Angel
Let's Talk of Graves, of Worms, and Epitaphs. R. Player
Letter E. W. LeQueux
Letter for Obi. J. F. Straker
Letter from Spain. F. P. Keyes
Letter of Intent. U. Curtiss
Letter to a Dead Girl. S. Jepson
Letter to a Ghost. A. Furness
Letters for a Spy. A. C. Ley
Letters of Discredit. P. Harris
Letters of Marque. A. P. Terhune
Letty Lynton. M. B. Lowndes
Levanter. E. Ambler
Levity Hicks. T. Gallon
Levkas Man. H. Innes
Levy Caper. D. Shaw
Lewker in Norway. G. Carr
Lewker in Tyrol. G. Carr
Lexicon Murders. D. Whitelaw
Lezaire Mystery. A. Griffiths
Li Kwang's Dagger. F. Johnston
Li Ting of London and other stories. G. R. Sims
Liability Limited. J. A. Saxon
Liar Dice. J. S. Mosher
Libel. E. Wooll
Liberation. I. Ostrander
Liberators. J. Cleary
Liberators. J. Pattinson
Libertines. H. Clewes
Liberty Bar. G. Simenon
Library of Death. R. S. L. Harding
Library of Fiction. Anonymous
License to Kill. N. Daniels
Licensed for Murder. J. Rhode
Lid Off. John Aiken
Lidless Eye. P. Romsey
Lidy Takes Plenty. B. Sarto
Lie a Little, Die a Little. Michael Brett
Lie Down, I Want to Talk to You. W. P. McGivern
Lie Down in Darkness. H. R. Hays
Lie Down, Killer. R. S. Prather
Lie Fallow My Acre. G. Joseph
Lie Like a Lady. C. S. Cody
Lie Quiet in Your Grave. M. L. Roby
Lieutenant and Others. H. C. McNeile
Lieutenant Barnabas. P. Barrett
Lieutenant Bones. E. Wallace
Lieutenant Flynn, R.N. E. L. Long
Lieutenant Must Be Mad. H. H. Kirst
Lieutenant of the King. M. Gerard
Lt. Pascal's Tastes in Homicide. H. Pentecost
Lieutenant What's-His-Name. M. Futrelle
Life, Adventure and Opinions of a Liverpool Policeman and His Contemporaries. Anonymous
Life--and a Fortnight. M. Peterson
Life and Anecdotes of the Black Dwarf. Anonymous
Life and Death of a Tough Guy. B. Appel

Life and Death of Peter Wade. Lionel Black
Life and Mary Ann. C. Cookson
Life at Stake. P. Andreae
Life at Stake. I. Stark
Life Between. Roy Vickers
Life Experiences of a Detective. A. W. Scott
Life Fashionable. P. Traill
Life for a Death. G. Ashe
Life for a Life. A. Bloomfield
Life for a Life. H. Fanger
Life for a Life. M. M. Murray
Life for Ruth. W. Drummond
Life for Sale. S. Horler
Life Has No Price. D. O'Neill
Life He Stole. S. Kyle
Life in London. G. W. M. Reynolds
Life in New York. Old Sleuth
Life in Paris. G. W. M. Reynolds
Life in the Far West. C. H. Simpson
Life in the Mines. C. H. Simpson
Life Is No Bargain. P. Graham
Life Is Short. L. Della
Life Must Go On. M. Crombie
Life of a Nobody. Winifred Graham
Life of Anson Bunker, "The Bloody Hand." Anonymous
Life of Ease. P. De Polnay
Life of the Party. E. Jordan
Life on the Ocean Wave. G. Hackforth-Jones
Life Perilous. C. Dawe
Life Sentence. H. C. Bailey
Life Sentence. W. W. Burgess
Life Sentence. M. A. Hamilton
Life Sentence. O. Hesky
Life Sentence. A. Sergeant
Life Story of Madame Zelle, the World's Most Beautiful Spy. H. De Halsalle
Life That Kills. Grace M. White
Life to Lose. L. Hammond
Life We Live. G. R. Sims
Lifeline. P. Bottome
Lifer. J. Phelan
Life's Arrears. F. Warden
Life's Assize. J. H. Riddell
Life's Atonement. D. C. Murray
Life's Golden Web. J. B. Harris-Burland
Life's Secret. H. Wood
Lift and the Drop. G. V. Galwey
Lift Murder. R. Francis Foster
Lift Shaft Crime. W. Jardine
Lift up the Lid. Anthony Gilbert
Lifted Latch. T. Frank
Lifting of the Shadow. O. Binns
Lige Golden. W. W. Harvey
Light Above the Crossroads. J. L. Rickard
Light and a Dark Christmas. H. Wood
Light and the Shadows. R. W. Howe
Light Beyond. E. P. Oppenheim
Light Cavalry Action. J. Harris
Light Fingered Ladies. A. Livingston
Light from a Lantern. J. Stagge
Light in Dends Wood, and other stories. T. Dagless
Light in the Swamp. V. Johnston
Light in the Tower. M. Lynch
Light in the Tower. Marilyn Ross
Light in the Upper Storey. F. Warden
Light in the Window. M. Lynn
Light of Day. E. Ambler
Light on Murder. E. Messenger
Light Side of the Law. G. A. MacDonald
Light That Lies. J. L. Rickard
Light That Lures. P. Brebner

Lightbody on Liberty. N. Balchin
Lighted Way. E. P. Oppenheim
Lighter of Candles. O. Cecil
Lighthearted Quest. A. Bridge
Lighthouse Mystery. R. C. Armour
Lighthouse Mystery. G. Volk
Lightly Lost. H. Smart
Lightning Conductor Comes Back. A. M. Williamson
Lightning over Mayfair. J. Monmouth
Lightning Strikes Twice. J. Potts
Lightning Strikes Twice. L. Thayer
Lightning Tree. J. Crecy
Lightning's Eye. R. Savage
Lights, Camera, Murder. John Shepherd
Lights of Skaro. D. Dodge
Lights Out. J. Cello
Lights That Did Not Fail. M. Annesley
Lightship Murders. N. Wray
Ligny's Lake. S. H. Courtier
Like a Guilty Thing. B. Cobb
Like a Hole in the Head. J. H. Chase
Like a Man. J. Lane
Like a Rose. M. Peterson
Like an Evening Gone. J. Burrows
Like and Unlike. M. E. Braddon
Like Another Helen. G. Horton
Like Any Other Fugitive. J. Hayes
Like Crazy. H. Janson
Like Father, Like Son. J. Payn
Like Ice She Was. W. Ard
Like Lethal. H. Janson
Like Love. E. McBain
Like Poison. H. Janson
Like Shadows on the Wall. W. B. Maxwell
Like Water. I. R. G. Hart
Likely to Die. J. Roffman
Lil. J. Middlemass
Lil of the Slums. D. Donovan
Lila My Lovely. Dudley Dean
Lilac Bride Mystery. M. Crossley
Lilac Is for Sharing. J. Blackmore
Lilies for Madame. H. Austin
Lilies for My Lovely. H. Janson
Lilies in Her Garden Grew. F. C. Davis
Lilies That Fester. I. Wilson
Lilith. K. Kellow
Lilith. E. Southworth
Lilith. F. Warden
Lilli Marlene. K. Lindsay
Lillian's Vow. Mrs. E. B. Collins
Lily and the Devil. A. Askew
Lily Dale. P. Tabori
Lily Field. Constance Rutherford
Lily in Her Coffin. B. Benson
Lily Pond. D. Daniels
Lily-Pond Mystery. G. Davison
Limb of Satan. P. Souvestre
Limbo Affair. A. Firth
Limbo Line. V. Canning
Limbo Lover. H. Janson
Limbo Touch. J. Weeks
Limehouse Nights. T. Burke
Limey. J. Spenser
Limey Breaks In. J. Spenser
"Limited" Hold-Up. N. Carter
Limited Liability. H. H. C. Gibbons
Limmerston Hall. H. W. Chapman
Limner. P. D. Boles
Limping Death. A. Stapleton
Limping Goose. F. Gruber
Limping Man. M. Erskine
Limping Man. F. Grierson
Limping Sailor. J. Brooke
Limping Wolf. E. T. Portwine
Lincoln McKeever. E. Lipsky
Lincoln's Inn Tragedy. W. J. Bayfield
Lincoln's Inn Tragedy. A. Blair
Linda Walked Alone. J. MacKenzie
Linden Affair. M. Albrand

Linden Walk Tragedy. F. Daingerfield
Line Between. S. Toye
Line of Duty. E. Tidyman
Line of Fire. D. Hamilton
Line of Fire. R. Parkes
Line of Succession. B. Garfield
Line on Ginger. R. Maugham
Line-Up. F. Kane
Line Up. H. Luger
Line-Up. H. Reilly
Line-Up for Murder. F. C. Tickner
Lingala Code. W. Kiefer
Lingard. Colin Wilson
Lingo Dan. P. Pollard
Link. H. Carmichael
Link. P. MacDonald
Link. R. Maugham
Link by Link. J. W. Bobin
Link by Link. C. Courteney
Link by Link. D. Donovan
Link by Link. N. D. Urner
Linked by Peril. B. Bolt
Linked to Crime. B. North
Linked with Fate. J. L. Berry
Linkram Jewels. J. Laurence
Links in the Chain. S. Campbell
Links in the Chain. H. Hill
Links in the Chain. J. Rhode
Linnet. G. Allen
Linnet Estate. D. Polk
Linnet Singing. D. Eden
Linnet's Folly. J. Aeby
Lint House Mystery. N. Oakley
Linton Memorial. L. Lloyd
Lion and the Lamb. E. P. Oppenheim
Lion and the Mouse. A. Hornblow
Lion in the Cellar. P. Branch
Lion in Wait. D. Gardiner
Lion Men. J. Crosbie
Lion of Cooling Bay. P. Paul
Lion of Delos. A. Worboys
Lion of Petra. T. Mundy
Lion of the Law. S. Campbell
Lion? or Murder? D. Gardiner
Lion Trimphant. P. Carr
Lions at the Kill. S. Kent
Lion's Mouse. C. N. Williamson
Lion's Mouth. J. Corbett
Lion's Share. O. Thanet
Lip-Service. L. J. Vance
Lipstick Clue. R. Goyne
Lipstick Larceny. C. Brown
Liquid Death. Griff
Liquidated and The Seer. R. Lindau
Liquidator. R. L. Brent
Liquidator. N. Carter
Liquidator. J. Gardner
Liquor Is Quicker. H. Janson
Lisa Bastian. J. Wood
Lisping Man. F. Rawlings
List of Adrian Messenger. P. MacDonald
Listen for a Stranger. S. Devine
Listen for the Whisperer. P. A. Whitney
Listen, Lovely. Keith Campbell
Listen, Please Listen. N. A. Hintze
Listen to Danger. D. Eden
Listen to the Mocking Bird. S. H. Courtier
Listener. T. Du Bois
Listener. John Gill
Listening Boy. P. Hambledon
Listening Eye. P. Wentworth
Listening House. M. Seeley

Listening In. C. Moore
Listening Man. J. A. Moroso
Listening Silence. H. Lillie
Listening Walls. M. Millar
Listening Woman. M. Sparrow
Listerdale Mystery. A. Christie
Litany of Evil. A. Brennan
Litmore Snatch. Henry Wade
Little Anarchist. A. W. Marchmont
Little Blue Goddess. W. LeQueux
Little Boy Laughed. J. Dow
Little Brother Fate. M. C. Roberts
Little Brother of God. L. H. Gordon
Little Brothers. D. S. Davis
Little Caesar. W. R. Burnett
Little Caesars. E. De Roo
Little Captain. H. C. Bailey
Little Colonel. Old Sleuth
Little Comrade. B. E. Stevenson
Little Cowboy. Old Sleuth
Little Cowboy in New York. Old Sleuth
Little Crime. J. N. Chance
Little Dead-Sure. Old Sleuth
Little Dog Barked. A. Rowe
Little Dog's Day. J. T. Story
Little Doll. P. Garrod
Little Doves of Destruction. G. Wolfenden
Little Dragon from Peking. J. Eastwood
Little Drops of Blood. B. Knox
Little Ferret. R. Foxall
Little Fishes. Arthur Wise
Little Fortune. A. Fredericks
Little Game. F. Farrington
Little Gentleman from Okehampstead. E. P. Oppenheim
Little Giant. Old Sleuth
Little Girl Who Lives Down the Lane. L. Koenig
Little God Ben. J. J. Farjeon
Little Green Man. E. Wallace
Little Grey Man. W. Bouchier
Little Grey Mouse. F. Warden
Little Grey Shoe. P. Brebner
Little Hanging Men. P. Groom
Little Hangman. M. Elwin
Little Heiress. F. Cowen
Little Hercules. F. Gruber
Little Hercules. F. Wallace
Little Hour of Peter Wells. D. Whitelaw
Little Killer. G. Paul
Little Lady Linton. F. Barrett
Little Lady of Arrock. D. Whitelaw
Little Lady of Lagunitas. R. H. Savage
Little Lady of the Shot-Gun. L. H. Gordon
Little Less Than Kind. C. Armstrong
Little Lie. J. Potts
Little Lightning, the Shadow Detective. Police Captain James
Little Lost Lady. W. Morton
Little Man from Archangel. G. Simenon
Little Man Murders. V. Loder
Little Man Who Wasn't There. Mildred Gordon
Little Matter of Arson. L. Meynell
Little Men, Big World. W. R. Burnett
Little Miner. Old Sleuth
Little Miss Murder. M. Avallone
Little Miss Prim. F. Warden
Little Murder Music. D. Ramsay
Little Ned's Engagement. E. Southworth
Little Novels. W. Collins
Little Nugget. P. G. Wodehouse
Little Old Lady. Roland Daniel
Little Old Man of the Batignolles. E. Gaboriau
Little People. J. Christopher

Little Pig-Alee. Y. Audouard
Little Red Captain. C. J. C. Hyne
Little Red Monkey. E. Maschwitz
Little Rosebud's Lovers. L. J. Libbey
Little Saint. G. Simenon
Little Sin. W. Hardy
Little Sister. R. Chandler
Little Sister. Lee Roberts
Little Spot of Bother. M. Polland
Little Squaw Big Hurry. S. F. Griffin
Little Tales of Smethers, and other stories. Lord Dunsany
Little Terror. C. E. Blaney
Little Time to Stay. J. Garden
Little Tragedy at Tien-Tsin. F. A. Mathews
Little Tramp. G. Brewer
Little Treachery. P. Paul
Little Victims. T. P. McMahon
Little Victims Play. A. Hocking
Little Walls. Winston Graham
Little Wax Doll. P. Curtis
Little White God. E. Brock
Little White Hag. F. Beeding
Little White Hen. Robin Temple
Little White Nun. A. M. Williamson
Little Widow Murder. A. Wood
Little Woman in Black. M. E. Braddon
Littlejohn on Leave. G. Bellairs
Live Again, Love Again. D. Keene
Live and Let Die. I. Fleming
Live Bait. A. Mills
Live Bait. R. Wills
Live Bait for Murder. W. Herber
Live Cartridge. C. Dawe
Live Dangerously. A. Kielland
Live Gold. R. Sheckley
Live Like a Hero. Angus Hall
Live, Love, and Cry. G. B. Mair
Live Lumber. E. L. Long
Live Men's Shoes. R. Marsh
Live Now, Pay Later. J. T. Story
Live Till You Die. R. Angel
Live Wire. A. Allen
Live Wire. J. Bruce
Live Wire Clue. N. Carter
Lively Corpse. M. Millar
Lively Dead. P. Dickinson
Lively Form of Death. E. Lindall
Lively Game of Death. Marvin Kaye
Lively Luke. Old Sleuth
Lives and Times of Bernardo Brown. G. Household
Lives in a Box. Richard Grant
Lives to Give. S. De Gramont
Living Alibi. S. Truss
Living and the Dead. P. Boileau
Living Bomb. M. Avallone
Living Come First. J. Danvers
Living Dangerously. F. E. Penny
Living Dead Man. L. Scott
Living Death. N. Carter
Living Demons. R. Bloch
Living End. F. Kane
Living Fire Menace. K. Robeson
Living in Fear. A. Parsons
Living Link. J. De Mille
Living Mask. N. Carter
Living Mummy. A. Pratt
Living or Dead. H. Conway
Living Shadow. M. Grant
Living Shadow. W. W. Sayer
Living Skeleton. W. J. Fraser
Living Too Fast. W. T. Adams
Living's a Dying Game. R. Hamilton
Liz. F. Kane
Lizard in the Cup. P. Dickinson
Lizzie. S. Jackson
Lizzie and Caroline. Ruth Moore
Lizzie Borden. M. B. Lowndes

'Lo Sweeny Gang. Roland Daniel
Loaded Dice. E. H. Clark
Loaded Dice. M. Cumberland
Loaded Dice. E. Fawcett
Loaded Dice. P. Marlowe
Loaded Gun. F. Ryck
Loaded Orange. G. Jerome
Loadstone of Love. J. Middlemass
Loaves and Fishes. B. Capes
Lobelia Grove. A. Rolls
Lobster Guerrillas. W. Mole
Lobster Pick Murder. M. V. Heberden
Lobster Pot. G. Volk
Local Call. M. P. Berthold
Local Talent. W. Fuller
Local Talent. H. M. Kahler
Location Shots. J. F. Burke
Loch. J. Caird
Loch Sinister. Marilyn Ross
Loch Spy. D. Duff
Lock and Key. A. M. Stein
Lock and the Key. F. Gruber
Lock at Charenton. G. Simenon
Lock the Door, Mademoiselle. T. C. H. Jacobs
Locked Book. F. Packard
Locked Corridor. Marilyn Ross
Locked Door. J. Hawk
Locked Doors. M. R. Rinehart
Locked Room. Herbert Ashton, Jr.
Locked Room. M. Sjowall
Locked Tower. C. Carfax
Locked Up. A. Griffiths
Locust in the Wind. R. Collin
Lodestar. M. Pemberton
Lodestar. E. Wooll
Lodestar of Death. J. Sandys
Lodge Sinister. Dana Ross
Lodger. M. B. Lowndes
Lodger. G. Simenon
Lodging-House Mystery. R. Hardinge
Log Across the Road. Sheila Ross
Logan. A. Joseph
Lola Brought Her Wreath. H. Janson
Lola of the Isles. D. W. MacArthur
Lombard Street Mystery. A. Blair
Lombard Street Mystery. M. Robertson
Lona. John Evans
London Adventures of Mr. Collin. F. Heller
London After Midnight. M. Coolidge-Rask
London Assignment. Angus Ross
London, Bloody London. M. Avallone
London Bridge Mystery. J. Arnold
London by Night. Anonymous
London Calling. V. Gielgud
London Cobweb. P. Brebner
London Cobweb. C. Lys
London Detective's Thrilling Adventures. Anonymous
London Lamb. W. B. M. Ferguson
London Lights Were Shining. Robin Temple
London Nights of Belsize. V. Rendall
London, 1913. M. Stacpoole
London Particular. C. Brand
London Plot. C. Dawe
London Pride. M. E. Braddon
London Spy Murders. P. Cheyney
London Switch. Robin Moore
London's Heart. B. L. Farjeon
Lone Commando. J. Sandys
Lone Cottage. T. P. Prest
Lone Crook Murders. C. Ryland

"Lone Cross Manor" Mystery. M. Danvers
Lone Hand. H. Bindloss
Lone Hand. S. Warwick
Lone Hater. G. Thorne
Lone House by the Sea. Old Sleuth
Lone House Mystery. J. J. Farjeon
Lone House Mystery. E. Wallace
Lone Inn. F. Hume
Lone Isle. E. C. Vivian
Lone Kiwi. F. N. Millar
Lone Lodge Mystery. J. Hawk
Lone Vendetta. Jean Fraser
Lone Wolf. W. C. Tuttle
Lone Wolf. L. J. Vance
Lone Wolf Returns. L. J. Vance
Lone Wolf's Last Prowl. L. J. Vance
Lone Wolf's Son. L. J. Vance
Loneliest Girl in the World. K. Fearing
Lonely Beat. W. Keenan
Lonely Breeze. V. Siller
Lonely Bungalow. Taffrail
Lonely Cage. F. Usher
Lonely Church. F. Hume
Lonely God. C. Kernahan
Lonely Graves. C. Monig
Lonely Heritage. A. Furness
Lonely Hollow Mystery. T. A. Plummer
Lonely House. J. Blackmore
Lonely House. A. Gask
Lonely House. M. B. Lowndes
Lonely Hunter. C. Wilcox
Lonely Inn Mystery. L. Grex
Lonely Is the Grave. G. J. Barrett
Lonely Island. H. L. V. Fletcher
Lonely, Lovely Lady. J. Monmouth
Lonely Magdalen. Henry Wade
Lonely Man. G. Frankau
Lonely Man. J. T. Phillifent
Lonely Pathway. John Marsh
Lonely Place. R. M. Sears
Lonely Place to Die. C. Robertson
Lonely Road. J. Farnol
Lonely Shore. G. Volk
Lonely Shroud. S. Mitchell
Lonely Side of the River. D. MacKenzie
Lonely Skier. H. Innes
Lonely Steeple. Victor Wolfson
Lonely Stronghold. B. Reynolds
Lonely Subaltern. F. Hume
Lonely Target. H. Pentecost
Lonely Terror. S. Mayfield
Lonely Voyage. J. Harris
Lonely Walk. M. E. Chaber
Lonely Water. N. Thurley
Lonely Way to Die. H. Debrett
Lonely Years. Alan Thomas
Lonelyheart 4122. C. Watson
Loner. O. Friedrich
Loner. F. Nichols
Lonesome Badger. F. Gruber
Lonesome Road. P. Wentworth
Lonesome Town. E. Dorrance
Long and Living Shadow. D. Winston
Long Arm. H. Cecil
Long Arm. S. M. Gardenhire
Long Arm. E. P. Oppenheim
Long Arm of Fantomas. P. Souvestre
Long Arm of Mannister. E. P. Oppenheim
Long Arm of Murder. F. Gruber
Long Arm of the Mounted. J. Dorrance
Long Arm of the Mounted. W. B. Mowery
Long Arm of the Prince. E. Berckman
Long Baffled Capture. I. Stark
Long Body. H. McCloy
Long Branch Detective. Anonymous
Long Chance. D. Enefer

Long Chase. J. M. Eshleman
Long Coffin. N. Tranter
Long Cool Day in Hell. G. Kersh
Long Corridor. C. Cookson
Long Corridor. K. Royce
Long Dark Night. J. Hayes
Long Day's Dying. Alan White
Long Death. G. Dyer
Long Distance--Wrong Number. N. Gifford
Long Divorce. E. Crispin
Long Drop. Alan White
Long Echo. K. Hughes
Long Echo. D. Rutherford
Long Escape. D. Dodge
Long Farewell. M. Innes
Long Fast Ride. A. F. Libby
Long Fuse. Alan White
Long Goodbye. R. Chander
Long Goodnight. C. D. Burton
Long Green. B. Spicer
Long Green Gaze. V. Fuller
Long-Haired Bill. J. A. Dunn
Long Hand. W. Magnay
Long Hard Look. M. Gair
Long Hate. S. Forbes
Long Haul. M. Mills
Long Hot Night. D. Enefer
Long Island Murders. M. W. Glidden
Long Journey Home. M. F. Ford
Long Knife. E. S. De Puy
Long Lane. P. Trent
Long Lankin. J. Banville
Long Lavender Look. J. D. MacDonald
Long Leaf. R. Brock
Long Live the King. G. Boothby
Long Memory. H. Clewes
Long Memory. M. Cronin
Long Midnight. Alan White
Long Night. F. R. Adams
Long Night. O. Demaris
Long Night. B. Graeme
Long Night. H. Howard
Long Night. A. Lyttle
Long Night. S. Truss
Long Night of Fear. Marilyn Ross
Long Night Through. H. McCutcheon
Long Nightmare. J. Roeburt
Long Night's Journey. I. MacKersey
Long Night's Walk. Alan White
Long Odds. H. Smart
Long Overcoat. P. Fry
Long Patrol. H. A. Cody
Long Patrol. A. M. Treynor
Long Portage. H. Bindloss
Long Pursuit. J. Cleary
Long Reach. K. Hayles
Long Reconnaissance. J. Murphy
Long Revenge. J. Thomson
Long Ride. J. McKimmey
Long Ride Out. V. James
Long Road. A. Furness
Long Rope. F. W. Hilton
Long Run South. Alan Williams
Long Saturday Night. C. Williams
Long Search. G. Ashe
Long Shadow. F. Bryan
Long Shadow. J. Cleary
Long Shadow. C. Fremlin
Long Shadow. Anthony Gilbert
Long Shadow. J. Pendower
Long Shadow. H. W. Thomas
Long Shadows. J. Cannan
Long Shadows. C. Carnac
Long Shadows. Camilla Hope
Long Shadows. A. D. Sanderson
Long Short Cut. A. Garve
Long Shot. E. Hely
Long Silence. P. Costello
Long Silence. N. Freeling
Long Skeleton. F. Lockridge
Long Sleep. A. Bocca

Long Spoon. C. Bryce
Long Spoon. J. B. O'Sullivan
Long Straight Road. G. Horton
Long Summer. Alan White
Long Thrill. O. L. Rosmanith
Long Time No Leola. C. Brown
Long Time Sleeping. Michael Sinclair
Long Tunnel. S. Fairway
Long Vendetta. J. Gant
Long Wait. M. Spillane
Long Watch. Alan White
Long Way Down. E. Fenwick
Long Way Down. D. Hall
Long Way Down. C. Wilcox
Long Way from Shiloh. L. Davidson
Long Way Home. V. Norwood
Long Way Round. M. Maurice
Long Way to Fall. Angus Hall
Long Way to Pitt Street. D. Enefer
Long Week. P. Doncaster
Long White Night. Eric Lambert
Long Window. J. M. Eshleman
Longbow Murder. V. Luhrs
Longbridge Murders. M. Dalton
Longer Bodies. G. Mitchell
Longer the Thread. E. Lathen
Longest Second. B. S. Ballinger
Longstreet Legacy. D. Ashe
Loo Loo's Legacy. D. Dodge
Loo Sanction. Trevanian
Look Alive. M. Burton
Look at Murder. N. Deane
Look Back on Murder. D. M. Disney
Look Back to Love. V. Packer
Look Behind You. J. Barbette
Look Behind You, Lady. M. Erskine
Look Behind You, Lady. A. S. Fleischman
Look Down for Mercy. Max Gordon
Look Down on Her Dying. D. Tracy
Look for the Body. M. F. Christopher
Look in any Doorway. N. Morland
Look in at Murder. E. Radford
Look of Innocence. Anna Gilbert
Look Out Behind You. K. Lewis
Look Out for Lucifer! E. Dudley
Look Three Ways at Murder. J. Creasey
Look to the Dawn. M. Richmond
Look to the Lady. M. Allingham
Look to the Lady! J. L. Bonney
Look Upon the Prisoner. H. Desmond
Look Who's Talking. R. Adam
Look Your Last. J. S. Strange
Looker-On. W. LeQueux
Looking Glass Murder. Anthony Gilbert
Looking-Glass Murders. D. G. Browne
Looking Glass War. J. Le Carre
Looking Out for #1. M. Monsky
Lookout Cartridge. J. McElroy
Looks That Kill! W. B. Gibson
Loom. J. Remenham
Loom of Terror. P. Minton
Loom of the Law. Anonymous
Loophole. A. Maling
Loophole. R. Pollock
Loose End. M. Cronin
Loose Ends. P. Warner
Loose Lady Death. L. Marshall
Loose Rib. A. Allen
Loose Screw. G. Hammond
Loot! A. Murray
Loot. A. S. Roche
Loot! A. P. Terhune
Loot Curran, R. N. E. L. Long

Loot from the Temple of Fortune. H. A. Vachell
Loot of Cities. A. Bennett
Loot of France. A. Parsons
Loot of Nana Sahib. H. E. Hill
Loot of Pakistan. A. Parsons
Loot of the Lazy F. W. C. Tuttle
Looted Gold. G. E. C. Webster
Looters. J. Reese
Lopsided Man. B. S. Ballinger
Lord Alistair's Rebellion. A. Upward
Lord and Mary Ann. C. Cookson
Lord Arthur Savile's Crime, and other stories. O. Wilde
Lord Blackshirt. B. Graeme
Lord Cobleigh Disappears. J. C. Snaith
Lord Edgware Dies. A. Christie
Lord Have Mercy. Shelley Smith
Lord, I Was Afraid. N. Balchin
Lord John in New York. C. N. Williamson
Lord Lynmore's Life. I. Roy
Lord Mayor's Show Mystery. A. Blair
Lord Oakburn's Daughters. H. Wood
Lord of Irongray. J. B. Harris-Burland
Lord of Terror. M. Allain
Lord of Terror. S. Horler
Lord of the Dyke. W. Wood
Lord of the Far Island. V. Holt
Lord of the Gallows. J. Neil
Lord of the Manor. F. M. White
Lord of the Sorcerers. Carter Dickson
Lord Penworth's Daughter. F. Warden
Lord Peter. D. L. Sayers
Lord Peter Goes A-Wooing. J. Ronald
Lord Peter Views the Body. D. L. Sayers
Lord Quare's Visitor. F. Warden
Lord Satan. L. Bronte
Lord Saxondale. G. W. M. Reynolds
Lords and Ladies. R. M. Gilchrist
Lords of Human Kind. J. D. White
Lordship, the Passen, and We. F. T. Jane
Lorelei. L. P. Bachmann
Lorelei. D. Rico
Lorena Veiled. M. J. Ragosta
Lorie. Old Sleuth
Loring Affair. J. Sherry
Loring Mystery. J. Farnol
Lorry. P. Wahloo
Los Angeles Holocaust. M. Barry
Los Huecos Mystery. E. T. Sawyer
Lose This Gun. H. Janson
Loser Takes All. G. Greene
Loser Takes Nothing. M. Cronin
Losers. C. Irving
Losers, Weepers. E. Queen
Losers, Weepers. E. Silberstang
Losing Game. F. W. Crofts
Losing Game. H. Nisbet
Losing Game. W. Payne
Loss of a Head. J. Bude
Loss of the Jane Vosper. F. W. Crofts
Lost! A Day. F. C. Milford
Lost Ambassador. E. P. Oppenheim
Lost American. A. C. Gunter
Lost and Found Man. N. Guild
Lost and the Damned. W. Carrier
Lost Bank Note. H. Wood
Lost Bride. C. Augusta
Lost Bride. E. Southworth
Lost Caesar. R. Fenisong
Lost Casket. F. Du Boisgobey
Lost Cause. Winifred Duke
Lost Chittendens. N. Carter
Lost City of Light. F. A. M. Webster
Lost Countess Falka. R. H. Savage
Lost Despatch. N. S. Lincoln
Lost Diamond. D. G. Adee

Title Index

Lost Diamonds. F. Marryat
Lost Diary. H. Bleackley
Lost Discovery. B. Reynolds
Lost Duchess. J. G. Sarasin
Lost Eden. M. E. Braddon
Lost Emeralds of Zarinthia. H. Beauchamp
Lost Endeavor. G. Boothby
Lost Expedition. W. W. Sayer
Lost for Love. M. E. Braddon
Lost Fraulein. R. Meade
Lost Friday. E. J. Fredericks
Lost Gallows. J. D. Carr
Lost Garrison. J. Robb
Lost Generation. P. Trent
Lost Girl. J. Boswell
Lost Golfer. H. G. Hutchinson
Lost Hat. E. Percy
Lost Heir. S. Cobb
Lost Heir. G. A. Henty
Lost Heir of Linlithgow. E. Southworth
Lost Heiress. E. Southworth
Lost House Mystery. L. West
Lost Hyena. C. K. MacKinnon
Lost Identity. D. Hennessey
Lost Idol. A. Askew
Lost in Cambodia. W. M. Graydon
Lost in the Post, and other tales. H. Wood
Lost in the Slave Land. W. M. Graydon
Lost Inheritance. Scott Graham
Lost Island. P. A. Whitney
Lost Jewel. H. Spofford
Lost Judge. C. R. Gull
Lost Karim. E. Kyle
Lost Key. Forfex et Hesta
Lost Kingdom. J. G. Sarasin
Lost Lady. O. R. Cohen
Lost Lake. R. Kirk
Lost Lawyer. G. A. Birmingham
Lost Leader. E. P. Oppenheim
Lost Liner. R. Cromie
Lost Lotus. A. Rundle
Lost Man's Lane. A. K. Green
Lost Mark. P. Wynnton
Lost Million. W. Alden
Lost Million. W. LeQueux
Lost Mr. Linthwaite. J. S. Fletcher
Lost Moorings. G. Simenon
Lost Name. J. S. Le Fanu
Lost Naval Papers. B. Copplestone
Lost Oasis. K. Robeson
Lost Oasis. H. H. Ross
Lost One. A. Kennington
Lost One. D. Lyon
Lost Paradise. F. A. Kummer
Lost Parchment. F. Hume
Lost Pearl. F. Grierson
Lost Person. V. White
Lost Pibroch. N. Munro
Lost Provinces. L. Tracy
Lost Rapture. B. Poynter
Lost Sir Brian. F. Whishaw
Lost Sir Massingberd. J. Payn
Lost Souls in Bohemia. W. J. Elliott
Lost Square. L. T. Meade
Lost Stradivarius. J. M. Falkner
Lost Trooper. F. H. Dimmock
Lost Trooper. T. Mundy
Lost Vengeance. C. Portway
Lost Victim. T. A. Waters
Lost Viol. M. P. Shiel
Lost Will. H. Wood
Lost Without Trace. B. Cobb
Lost Witness. L. L. Lynch
Lost World. L. K. Vincent
Lot 41--Dead Auctioneer. M. Symons
Lottery. S. Jackson
Lottery Ticket. F. Du Boisgobey
Lottie, the Poor Saleslady. C. E. Blaney
Lotus Affair. T. Wells

Lotus for Miss Quon. J. H. Chase
Lotus Leaves and Larceny. Philip Chambers
Lotus Vellum. Charlotte Hunt
Loudwater Mystery. E. Jepson
Loudwater Tragedy. T. W. Speight
Louis Beretti. D. H. Clarke
Louisa Reignier. R. Watson
Louise. J. Dering
Louise Martin, the Village Maiden. O. Bradbury
Louse for the Hangman. L. Bruce
Lovable Man. David Fletcher
Love After Five. Raymond Mason
Love Against the World. W. S. Hayward
Love-All. J. Leasor
Love and a Title. H. Flowerdew
Love and Death in a Barn. Anonymous
Love and Dr. Maynard. Rona Randall
Love and Hatred. M. B. Lowndes
Love--and Helen. S. Jepson
Love and I. E. Aiken
Love and Lordship. F. Warden
Love and Mary Ann. C. Cookson
Love and the Law. H. Curties
Love and the Spy. C. N. Williamson
Love Bade Me Welcome. J. Lodwick
Love Besieged. C. E. Pearce
Love, Blood and Tears. N. Weaver
Love Calling. M. Dekobra
Love Camp. L. Royer
Love Can Be Dangerous. O. R. Cohen
Love Child. T. B. Clegg
Love Child. T. P. Prest
Love Clinic. M. Dekobra
Love Comes Lethal. L. Della
Love Cruisers. P. Trent
Love-Death Thing. T. B. Dewey
Love for Sale. M. Corrigan
Love Forbidden. J. Blackmore
Love from a Stranger. F. Vosper
Love from Elizabeth. M. Fitt
Love Has No Alibi. O. R. Cohen
Love-Hate Relationship. J. N. Chance
Love in a Mist. L. V. Stevens
Love in Amsterdam. N. Freeling
Love in Burma. R. Carr
Love in Danger. C. Talbot
Love in Fetters. R. Marsh
Love in Lilac-Land. C. G. Mitford
Love in Peril. S. Jepson
Love in Suburbia. J. Conway
Love in the Purple. M. Gerard
Love Insurance. E. D. Biggers
Love Is a Deadly Weapon. P. Quentin
Love Is a Fiend. E. Woodward
Love Is a Flame. M. B. Lowndes
Love Is a Spirit. J. Hawthorne
Love Is Enough. M. Peterson
Love Is for Hating. D. Telfer
Love Is for the Living. E. Kyle
Love Is Just a Word. J. M. Simmel
Love Is King. R. Sharp
Love Is the One with Wings. P. V. Stern
Love Letters. C. Massie
Love Lies Bleeding. E. Crispin
Love Like an Arrow. F. Y. McHugh
Love Like That. D. Garth
Love, Lust and Larceny. S. Evans
Love Makers. H. Janson
Love Me and Die. D. Keene
Love Me and Die. L. Trimble
Love Me, Hurt Me. N. Karta
Love Me in Death. D. B. Olsen
Love Me Now. J. McPartland
Love Me Now. F. Nichols
Love Me to Death. F. Diamond
Love Not Denied. K. Lindsay

Love of Lucifer. D. Winston
Love on the Set. A. Kennington
Love--or a Name. J. Hawthorne
Love Secretaries. H. Janson
Love Song. J. L. Roberts
Love Spell. Anonymous
Love Spy, Love. R. C. Kasper
Love Stone. A. Askew
Love Test. J. A. Jordan
Love That Believeth. O. Binns
Love That Kills. C. Stanton
Love That Lasts. F. Warden
Love That Spy. T. A. Waters
Love the Criminal. J. B. Harris-Burland
Love, the Foe. F. M. White
Love the Harvester. M. Pemberton
Love the Jester. A. Askew
Love, the Sportsman. S. Horler
Love, the Thief. H. B. Mathers
Love Thieves. P. Packer
Love Thing. H. Barron
Love to Cherish. Clarissa Ross
Love Trap. L. White
Love Under Smoke. T. Craig
Love Was Married. S. Kyle
Love with a Gun and other stories. P. Cheyney
Love Without Honour. M. Richmond
Loved and the Loving. N. Sligh
Loved Enemy. S. Coulter
Lovehead. Jackie Collins
Loveless Isle. N. Penley
Lovelies Are Never Lonely. M. Storm
Lovels of Arden. M. E. Braddon
Lovely and Lethal. F. Castle
Lovely and the Damned. O. Beeby
Lovely and the Damned. R. Collier
Lovely but Dangerous. Roland Daniel
Lovely--but Lethal! P. Saxon
Lovely but Lethal. D. Steel
Lovely Corpse. M. Cumberland
Lovely in Death. W. O'Farrell
Lovely Ladies. N. Freeling
Lovely Lady. M. Corrigan
Lovely Lady, Pity Me. R. Huggins
Lovely Mask for Murder. Gerry Travis
Lovely Mrs. Blake. R. Marsh
Lovely Mrs. Pemberton. F. Warden
Lover. C. Brown
Lover. H. Janson
Lover Come Home. D. Lee
Lover, Don't Come Back! C. Brown
Lover for Cindy. H. V. Dixon
Lover, Let Me Live. N. Daniels
Lover--Say It with Mink. Norma Lee
Lover Too Many. R. Lewis
Lover Who Lost Himself. D. Newton
Lovers Are Losers. Howard Hunt
Lovers at Fault. F. Whishaw
Lover's Feud. R. C. Finney
Lovers in the Dark. J. Ames
Lovers in Waiting. D. Whitelaw
Lovers of Astrea. J. G. Sarasin
Love's Atonement. K. Lindsay
Love's Burden. M. Peterson
Love's Challenge. J. Templeton
Love's Enemy. A. J. Small
Love's Great Surrender. C. H. Bullivant
Love's Harvest. B. L. Farjeon
Love's Labor Won. E. Southworth
Love's Legacy. R. Ashe King
Love's Lovely Counterfeit. J. M. Cain
Loves of the Harem. G. W. M. Reynolds

Loves Old and New. J. Middlemass
Love's Ordeal. D. Dayle
Love's Prisoner. R. C. Finney
Love's Revenge. M. B. Lowndes
Love's Sentinel. F. Warden
Love's Service. M. Peterson
Love's the Only Guide. M. Richmond
Love's Triumph. F. Du Boisgobey
Love's Victory. B. L. Farjeon
Loving a Dream, and One of His Inventions. C. Gibbon
Loving and the Dead. C. Brown
Loving Cup. A. Prior
Loving Cup. A. Wynne
Low Company. H. Atkinson
Low Road. H. Morrison
Lowdown. R. Chanslor
Lowdown. R. Jessup
Lowdown on G Men. K. Medusa
Lower Underworld. A. R. L. Gardner
Lowly Lover. F. Warden
Loxfinger. S. Weinstein
Loyal Lady. K. Lindsay
Loyalty of Peter Drayton, and Mrs. Peter Skeffington's Revenge. H. C. McNeile
Lucienne. M. Pemberton
Lucifer and Partner. J. Henry
Lucifer at Ponsfordville. J. Workman
Lucifer at Sunset. S. Harvester
Lucifer Cell. W. Fennerton
Lucifer Cult. L. Benedict
Lucifer Mask. K. Rich
Lucifer's Dream. J. L. Curtis
Lucile Clery. J. Shearing
Lucile Dare, Detective. M. Leighton
Lucinda. H. Rigsby
Lucius Davoreen. M. E. Braddon
Luck and a Lady. J. A. Dunn
Luck of Bella Barton. G. W. Appleton
Luck of Gerard Ridgeley. B. Mitford
Luck of Jocelyn Pinner, R.N. Bruce Norman
Luck of Luce. D. Deane
Luck of Norman Dale. B. Pain
Luck of St. Boniface. L. C. Douthwaite
Luck of the Darrells. A. Murray
Luck of the Darrells. J. Payn
Luck of the Golden Star. H. J. Andrews
Luck of the Irish. H. MacGrath
Luck of the Kid. R. Cullum
Luck of the Mounted. R. S. Kendall
Luck of the Secret Service. W. LeQueux
Luck of Udaipur. J. I. Emery
Luck Was No Lady. C. Brown
Lucky Jane. D. Ames
Lucky Mr. Loder. G. Thorne
Lucky Partners. W. C. Tuttle
Lucky Pierre. M. Endfield
Lucky Policeman. R. Penny
Lucky Shot. E. W. Elkington
Lucky Stiff. C. Rice
Lucretia. E. Bulwer-Lytton
Lucy and the Dark Gods. E. Jepson
Ludus Amoris. B. Swift
Luger Lullaby. R. Angel
Lugger Audace. E. L. Long
Lugs O'Leary. A. Kimmins
Luigi of Catanzaro. L. Golding
Luke Darby, the "World" Detective. E. A. Young
Luke Leighton, the Government Detective. H. Rockwood
Luke's Summer. D. Lee
Lukundoo, and other stories. Edward L. White
Lullaby with Lugers. J. Crockett
Lulu. M. T. Walworth
Lumber Ship. E. L. Long
Luminous Face. C. Wells
Lumley Wood Mystery. G. W. L. Banbury
Lunatic at Large. J. S. Clouston

Lunatic at Large Again. J. S. Clouston
Lunatic in Charge. J. S. Clouston
Lunatic in Love. J. S. Clouston
Lunatic Still at Large. J. S. Clouston
Lunatic, the Lover. B. Cobb
Lunatic Time. J. Roeburt
Lunatics at Large. J. Reach
Lunge Wire. J. B. O'Sullivan
Lure. C. Cavendish
Lure. G. Scarborough
Lure of Contraband. J. Wear-Gifford
Lure of Gold. N. Carter
Lure of Love. W. LeQueux
Lure of Mammon. D. Stewart
Lure of the Black Pool. Old Sleuth
Lure of the Bush. A. W. Upfield
Lured from Home. Grace M. White
Lures of Death. P. Whelton
Lurking Death. F. W. Gumley
Lurking Man. Gerald Butler
Lurking Policeman. G. Kent
Lurking Shadow. A. Askew
Lurking Shadow. J. Remenham
Lurking Terror. A. Peverett
Lurking Terror. E. Wilmot
Luscious Puritan. S. Friedman
Lust for Innocence. D. Doubtfire
Lust for Murder. H. Klinger
Lust for Vengeance. R. Bloomfield
Lust for Vengeance. H. Janson
Lust Is No Lady. M. Avallone
Lust of Hate. G. Boothby
Lust of Power. H. Kane
Lust of Treasure. H. C. Marksman
Lust to Kill. Edward Lee
Lustful Ape. R. Gray
Lustful Summer. R. V. Cassill
Lusting Drive. O. Demaris
Lustre Jug. F. Hird
Lusty Men. W. R. Cox
Lute and the Glove. K. W. Eyre
Luther Wing. M. Maurice
Luxury Tour. L. Handley
Lycanthia. F. Layland-Barratt
Lycanthrope, the Mystery of Sir William Wolf. E. Phillpotts
Lyddon House Mystery. G. Ellinger
Lydia. E. V. Cunningham
Lydia Trendennis. F. E. Smith
Lying at Death's Door. M. Cumberland
Lying Down Below. H. Carstairs
Lying Jade. L. Ford
Lying Ladies. R. Finnegan
Lying Lips. W. LeQueux
Lying Lips. T. A. Plummer
Lying Voices. E. Ferrars
Lynch Town. W. B. Murphy
Lynching of Orin Newfield. G. J. Goldberg
Lyndley Waters. G. R. Preedy
Lyndwood Affair. U. L. Silberrad
Lynmara Legacy. C. Gaskin
Lynne Court Spinney. J. S. Fletcher
Lynx, Counter Spy. Vigilant
Lynx, Spyflyer. Vigilant
Lynx, V.C. Vigilant
Lynx, V.C., Flies Again. Vigilant
Lyona Grimswood, Spinster. L. Higgin
Lyonesse Abbey. J. Tattersall
Lyonhurst. Rona Randall
Lyttleton Case. R. A. V. Morris

M

MacAlastair Looks On. A. Dick
Macall Gets Curious. G. Fairlie

McAllister and His Double. A. Train
McCabe. E. Naughton
McCabe and Mrs. Miller. E. Naughton
McCarthy, C.I.D. J. G. Brandon
McCarty, Incog. I. Ostrander
McCloud. C. Wilcox
McCreary Moves In. M. East
MacGilleroy's Millions. I. D. Hardy
McHugh. J. Flynn
McInnes of the N.I.D. Sea-Wrack
McKee of Centre Street. H. Reilly
Mackenzie Break. S. Shelley
Mackenzie's Glen. Janis Dawson
Mackintosh Man. D. Bagley
McLean at the Golden Owl. G. Goodchild
McLean Carries On. G. Goodchild
McLean Deduces. G. Goodchild
McLean Disposes. G. Goodchild
McLean Excels. G. Goodchild
McLean Finds a Way. G. Goodchild
McLean Incomparable. G. Goodchild
McLean Intervenes. G. Goodchild
McLean Investigates. G. Goodchild
McLean Invincible. G. Goodchild
McLean Keeps Going. G. Goodchild
McLean Knows Best. G. Goodchild
McLean Knows the Answers. G. Goodchild
McLean: Non-Stop. G. Goodchild
McLean of Scotland Yard. G. Goodchild
McLean Plays a Hand. G. Goodchild
McLean Predominant. G. Goodchild
McLean Prevails. G. Goodchild
McLean Remembers! G. Goodchild
McLean Scores Again. G. Goodchild
McLean Sees It Through. G. Goodchild
McLean Solves It. G. Goodchild
McLean Steps In. G. Goodchild
McLean Takes a Holiday. G. Goodchild
McLean Takes Charge. G. Goodchild
McLean Takes Over. G. Goodchild
McLean the Magnificent. G. Goodchild
McLean to the Dark Tower Came. G. Goodchild
McLoon of the South Seas. O. Sackville
Maclure Mystery. A. S. Swan
MacLurg Goes West. R. Petrie
McNeills Chase a Ghost. T. Du Bois
McQ. Alexander Edwards
McQuaid. S. Rifkin
MacStodger's Affinity. D. Whitelaw
MacTavish. P. Cheyney
McTodd. C. J. C. Hyne
M. L. Falkner
M.D.--Doctor of Murder. Donald Ross
M.F.H.'s Daughter. R. Jocelyn
M for Murder. J. G. Brandon
M.R.C.S. B. Delannoy
M.S. Bradford, Special. A. C. Gunter
M-Squad. D. Saunders
MW-XX.3. R. Pertwee
Mabel Seymour. C. Matthew
Macabre Manor. E. Grayson
Macabre Mansion. L. Churchill
Macao. N. Carter
Macedonian Mixup. J. Bentley
Machinations of Dr. Grue. H. M. Raleigh
Machinations of the Myo-ok. C. C. Lewis
Machine Gun McCann. O. Demaris
Machine Gun Murder. Jacques Thomas
Machine to Kill. G. Leroux
Macon Moore, the Southern Detective. J. R. Taylor
Macowen Murder. E. Y. Miller
Maculan's Daughter. S. Gainham

Title Index

Mad. G. M. Fenn
Mad Baxter. Wade Miller
Mad Doctor. F. J. Thwaites
Mad Doctor in Harley Street. F. J. Thwaites
Mad-Doctor Merciful. C. Brooks
"Mad Dog" Coll. S. Thurman
Mad Eyes. K. Robeson
Mad-Gun Mesa. F. W. Hilton
Mad Hatter Murder. F. Grierson
Mad Hatter Mystery. J. D. Carr
Mad Hatter's Holiday. P. Lovesey
Mad Hatter's Rock. V. Gunn
Mad Interlude. A. L. Martin
Mad Mesa. K. Robeson
Mad Mike. G. Goodchild
Mad Monk. R. T. M. Scott
Mad Murder. R. H. Wilkinson
Mad Scientist Affair. J. T. Phillifent
Mad Shepherdess. H. Brooke
Mad Sir Geoffrey. F. Warden
Mad with Much Heart. Gerald Butler
Madam Ambassador. N. Calmer
Madam and Eve. M. Corrigan
Madam Captain. E. L. Long
Madam Crowl's Ghost, and other tales of mystery. J. S. Le Fanu
Madam Is Dead. R. Terrall
Madam Julia's Tale and other queer stories. N. Royde-Smith
Madam Will Not Dine Tonight. H. Waugh
Madam, Will You Talk? M. Stewart
Madam You're Mayhem. C. Brown
Madame. E. P. Oppenheim
Madame and Her Twelve Virgins. E. P. Oppenheim
Madame Aubry and the Police. H. Travers
Madame Aubry Dines with Death. H. Travers
Madame Baltimore. H. Knowland
Madame Bluebeard. B. Sanders
Madame Flirt. C. E. Pearce
Madame Holle. Margery Lawrence
Madame Judas. M. Turnbull
Madame Knits. R. Rodd
Madame Lies Murdered. G. Wishart
Madame Lucien. A. Hodges
Madame Maigret's Friend. G. Simenon
Madame Maigret's Own Case. G. Simenon
Madame Midas. F. Hume
Madame "Q." N. Carter
Madame Shadow. F. Grierson
Madame Sly. M. Corrigan
Madame Spy. B. Graeme
Madame Storey. H. Footner
Madame X. M. Avallone
Madball. F. Brown
Madcap Betty. D. Whitelaw
Maddening Scar. D. R. Clinton
Maddon's Rock. H. Innes
Made for Murder. Elizabeth Anthony
Made for Murder. F. McGrew
Made to Murder. J. Courage
Made Up for Murder. K. Roos
Made Up to Kill. K. Roos
Madeleine Smith. Winifred Duke
Madeline Brown's Murderer. F. Adams
Madeline Payne, the Detective's Daughter. L. L. Lynch
Madeline Power. A. W. Marchmont
Mademoiselle B. M. Pons
Mademoiselle from Armentieres. J. Rhode
Mademoiselle of Monte Carlo. W. LeQueux
Madgwick Affair. D. Whitelaw
Madhouse. Angus Hall
Madhouse in Washington Square. David Alexander
Madigan. R. Dougherty
Madigan's Women. J. Conway
Madison Murder. L. Grex
Madman. M. Hansom

Madman of Bergerac. G. Simenon
Madman of the Marshes. W. Jardine
Madman on a Drum. N. R. De Mexico
Madman Theory. E. Queen
Madman's Bend. A. W. Upfield
Madman's Buff. K. Steel
Madman's Manor. F. Rushton
Madman's Whisper. Richard Grayson
Madmen Die Alone. J. E. Greene
Madness at the Castle. S. Claudia
Madness of Charlie Pierce. H. C. James
Madness of Gloria. F. Whishaw
Madness Opens the Door. C. F. Caunter
Madonna Creek Witch. J. La Tourrette
Madonna in Hollywood. M. Dekobra
Madonna of Hell. K. Lindsay
Madonna of the Music Halls. W. LeQueux
Madonna of the Seven Moons. Margery Lawrence
Madonna of the Sleeping Cars. M. Dekobra
Madrigal. J. Gardner
Madrone Tree. D. Duncan
Maelstrom. F. Froest
Maelstrom. Howard Hunt
Maelstrom. W. H. Murray
Maestro Murders. F. S. Wees
Mafalda. J. Goodwin
Mafia. N. Clad
Mafia Death Watch. B. Rossi
Mafia Fix. R. Sapir
Mafia Kiss. P. Loraine
Mafia Man. R. Posner
Mafia Massacre. F. Scarpetta
Mafia Vendetta. L. Sciascia
Mafia Wipe-Out. F. Scarpetta
Mafia Women. J. Cenni
Mafia's Victim. I. Stark
Mafioso. P. McCurtin
Maggie? F. Barrett
Maggie Rowan. C. Cookson
Magic Casket. R. A. Freeman
Magic Change Detective. Anonymous
Magic Dick, a Boy Detective. Old Sleuth
Magic Eardrums. H. S. Keeler
Magic for Murder. A. Livingston
Magic Grandfather. D. M. Disney
Magic in the Air. F. E. Penny
Magic Lantern Murders. Carter Dickson
Magic Makes Murder. H. R. Campbell
Magic Man. H. E. Rives
Magic Necklace. N. Carter
Magic Valley. W. E. D. Ross
Magic Year. J. Maass
Magician. F. L. Green
Magician. G. Simenon
Magician and the Widow. G. Simenon
Magician's Wife. J. M. Cain
Maginot Line Murder. B. Newman
Magistrate's Own Case. B. P. Rosenkrantz
Magnate Detective. Anonymous
Magnet. A. O. Crozier
Magnet for Danger. M. Richmond
Magnet for Murder. M. E. Corne
Magnet for Murder. B. Symons
Magnet of Doom. G. Simenon
Magnetic Girl. R. Marsh
Magnetic Man. N. Daniels
Magnetism of Sin. Aesculapius
Magnificent Hoax. E. P. Oppenheim
Magnificent Hobo. A. Wilson
Magnificent Moll. J. Gonzales
Magnolia Curse. L. Murfi
Magnolia Murder. W. Bell

Magnum for Schneider. J. Mitchell
Magnum Force. M. Valley
Magpie House. A. Soutar
Magpie Murder. G. Coverack
Magpie on the Gallows. J. G. Sarasin
Mahatma's Pupil. R. Marsh
Mahme Nousie. G. M. Fenn
Mahogany Murder. Lee Roberts
Mahoney Million. C. Townsend
Maid for Murder. C. Brown
Maid for Murder. C. Franklin
Maid for Murder. M. K. Ozaki
Maid in Paris. F. Kane
Maid Indomitable. L. T. Meade
Maid of Athens. M. Richmond
Maid of Honour. R. Aitken
Maid of Mansfield. P. Trent
Maid of Mystery. L. T. Meade
"Maid of Sussex." G. Volk
Maid to Murder. Roy Vickers
Maiden Armour. John Marsh
Maiden Fair and other stories. C. Gibbon
Maiden Possessed. J. N. Chance
Maiden Widow. E. Southworth
Maiden's Prayer. J. Fleming
Maigret Abroad. G. Simenon
Maigret Afraid. G. Simenon
Maigret and Monsieur Charles. G. Simenon
Maigret and Monsieur Labbe. G. Simenon
Maigret and the Bum. G. Simenon
Maigret and the Burglar's Wife. G. Simenon
Maigret and the Calame Report. G. Simenon
Maigret and the Dead Girl. G. Simenon
Maigret and the Dosser. G. Simenon
Maigret and the Enigmatic Lett. G. Simenon
Maigret and the Flea. G. Simenon
Maigret and the Gangsters. G. Simenon
Maigret and the Headless Corpse. G. Simenon
Maigret and the Hundred Gibbets. G. Simenon
Maigret and the Informer. G. Simenon
Maigret and the Killer. G. Simenon
Maigret and the Lazy Burglar. G. Simenon
Maigret and the Loner. G. Simenon
Maigret and the Madwoman. G. Simenon
Maigret and the Man on the Bench. G. Simenon
Maigret and the Man on the Boulevard. G. Simenon
Maigret and the Millionaires. G. Simenon
Maigret and the Minister. G. Simenon
Maigret and the Nahour Case. G. Simenon
Maigret and the Old Lady. G. Simenon
Maigret and the Reluctant Witnesses. G. Simenon
Maigret and the Saturday Caller. G. Simenon
Maigret and the Wine Merchant. G. Simenon
Maigret and the Young Girl. G. Simenon
Maigret at the Crossroads. G. Simenon
Maigret Cinq. G. Simenon
Maigret Goes Home. G. Simenon
Maigret Goes to School. G. Simenon
Maigret Has Doubts. G. Simenon
Maigret Has Scruples. G. Simenon
Maigret Hesitates. G. Simenon
Maigret in Court. G. Simenon
Maigret in Montmartre. G. Simenon
Maigret in New York's Underworld. G. Simenon
Maigret in Society. G. Simenon

Maigret in Vichy. G. Simenon
Maigret Keeps a Rendezvous. G. Simenon
Maigret Loses His Temper. G. Simenon
Maigret Meets a Milord. G. Simenon
Maigret Mystified. G. Simenon
Maigret Omnibus. G. Simenon
Maigret on Holiday. G. Simenon
Maigret on the Defensive. G. Simenon
Maigret Quartet. G. Simenon
Maigret Rents a Room. G. Simenon
Maigret Returns. G. Simenon
Maigret Right and Wrong. G. Simenon
Maigret Sets a Trap. G. Simenon
Maigret Sits It Out. G. Simenon
Maigret Stonewalled. G. Simenon
Maigret Takes a Room. G. Simenon
Maigret Takes the Waters. G. Simenon
Maigret to the Rescue. G. Simenon
Maigret Travels South. G. Simenon
Maigret Trio. G. Simenon
Maigret's Boyhood Friend. G. Simenon
Maigret's Dead Man. G. Simenon
Maigret's Failure. G. Simenon
Maigret's First Case. G. Simenon
Maigret's Little Joke. G. Simenon
Maigret's Memoirs. G. Simenon
Maigret's Mistake. G. Simenon
Maigret's Pickpocket. G. Simenon
Maigret's Revolver. G. Simenon
Maigret's Special Murder. G. Simenon
Mail for McNair. S. Lock
Mail Robber. J. E. Stewart
Mail Robbers' Syndicate. E. C. Derby
Mail Train. K. A. Dobson
Mail Van Mystery. J. G. Brandon
Main Attraction. S. Michaels
Main Experiment. C. Hodder-Williams
Main Line Kill. R. Busby
Main Street Morgue. Griff
Mainline Plot. J. Rosenberger
Maitland Inheritance. Laura Smith
Maitland Street Murder. Mark Allerton
Maitland's Master Mystery. M. Severy
"Majestic" Mystery. D. Mackail
Majesty of the Law. M. Danning
Majii. K. Robeson
Major. John Ross
Major. F. Warden
Major Adventures. L. P. Greene
Major Crime. O. Keystone
Major Developments. L. P. Greene
Major--Diamond Buyer. L. P. Greene
Major Exploits. L. P. Greene
Major Has Seven Guests. C. Wagner
Major Hazards. L. P. Greene
Major Incident. P. N. Walker
Major--Knight Errant. L. P. Greene
Major Occasions. L. P. Greene
Major Owen, and other tales. C. N. Johnston
Major Steps Out. John Ross
Major Washington. E. A. Shaffer
Major's Candlesticks. G. A. Birmingham
Make a Killing. H. Q. Masur
Make a Killing. B. Williams
Make-Believe Man. E. Fenwick
Make Do with Spring. E. Bonett
Make Every Kiss Count. Ronald Simpson
Make Fame a Monster. E. H. Clements
Make Haste to Live. The Gordons
Make It Lethal. R. Drayton
Make It Nylons. J. P. Heggy
Make Me a Murderer. Gwendoline Butler
Make Mine a Corpse. M. Storm
Make Mine a Harlot. M. Storm
Make Mine a Redhead. M. Storm

Make Mine a Virgin. M. Storm
Make Mine Beautiful. M. Storm
Make Mine Dangerous. M. Storm
Make Mine Maclain. B. Kendrick
Make Mine Mavis. W. Ard
Make Mine Mayhem. P. Muller
Make Mine Mink. H. Janson
Make Mine Murder. R. S. Bowen
Make Mine Murder. Neill Graham
Mike Mine Murder. M. Hervey
Make Mine Murder. B. Winter
Make Mine Vengeance. R. Colby
Make My Bed Soon. J. S. Strange
Make My Bed Soon. J. Webb
Make My Coffin Big. J. B. O'Sullivan
Make My Coffin Strong. W. R. Cox
Make Out with Murder. C. Harrison
Make Sure I'm Dead. D. Bogard
Make the Corpse Walk. R. Marshall
Make-Up for Murder. J. Wright
Make-Up for the Toff. J. Creasey
Make Way for a Sailor. Seafarer
Make Way for Murder. A. A. Marcus
Make Way for the Mourners. David Hume
Make with the Brains, Pierre. Dana Wilson
Maker of History. E. P. Oppenheim
Maker of Mischief. S. P. Hyatt
Maker of Nations. G. Boothby
Maker of Opportunities. G. F. Gibbs
Maker of Secrets. W. LeQueux
Maker of Shadows. Jack Mann
Maker of Ware. S. Edge
Making Crime Pay. P. Cheyney
Making Good Again. L. Davidson
Making Progress. A. Bailey
Makra Mystery. H. Campbell
Malabang Pearl. F. Archer
Malabar Magician. F. E. Penny
Malachi Breen Times Two. L. Pope
Malachite Jar. J. S. Fletcher
Malady in Madeira. A. Bridge
Malaret Mystery. O. Hartley
Malaspiga Exit. Evelyn Anthony
Malay Manhunt. A. S. Fleischman
Malay Woman. A. S. Fleischman
Malayan Rose. M. Derby
Malayan Story. G. Sheen
Malcolm Sage, Detective. H. Jenkins
Malcolm the Wonder. Old Sleuth
Malcontents. S. Franklin
Malefactor. E. P. Oppenheim
Malefactors. C. Blair
Malice Aforethought. F. Iles
Malice and the Maternal Instinct. M. Tripp
Malice Domestic. E. Cameron
Malice Domestic. P. Capon
Malice Domestic. R. Foley
Malice Domestic. S. Woods
Malice in Wonderland. N. Blake
Malice in Wonderland. R. King
Malice Matrimonial. J. Fleming
Malice of Monday. E. Burgess
Malice with Murder. N. Blake
Malicious Madonna. D. Romaine
Malicious Mischief. L. Egan
Maliday Mystery. A. Mills
Malignant Heart. C. Sibley
Malignant Snowman. K. Laing
Malignant Stars. Jerome Barry
Malinsay Massacre. D. Wheatley
Mallabec. D. Walker
Mallen Girl. C. Cookson
Mallen Litter. C. Cookson
Mallen Lot. C. Cookson
Mallen Streak. C. Cookson
Mallion's Pride. C. Salisbury
Mallison Mystery. T. W. Hanshew
Mallory. R. Marshall
Mallory Grange. C. Randell

Mallory of the Royal Mounted. C. Stoddard
Malloy's Tryst. P. C. De Crespigny
Mally Lee. E. Kyle
Malta Conspiracy. F. Mullally
Malta Mystery. S. G. Hedges
Maltese Cross. E. T. Sawyer
Maltese Falcon. D. Hammett
Maluti Murder. E. Haldane
Malverne Manor. H. York
Malvery Hold. J. S. Fletcher
Malvie Inheritance. P. Hill
Mama Doll. M. Woodhouse
Mambo to Murder. Dale Clark
Mamizelle Bon Voyage. G. Buhet
Mammon. P. C. Wren
Mammon of Righteousness. P. C. Wren
Mammon's Daughter. N. Tranter
Mammoth. S. P. Hyatt
Mammoth Mansions Mystery. H. Hill
Mamo Murders. J. Sheridan
M'amselle It's Murder. K. T. McCall
Man. M. Dinelli
Man. Will Scott
Man. B. Stoker
Man About a Dog. Alec Coppel
Man About Town. W. LeQueux
Man Above Suspicion. J. Mayo
Man Against Fear. M. Brewer
Man Against Man. N. Carter
Man Alive. M. Cronin
Man Alone. Shelley Smith
Man Alone. E. C. Vivian
Man and a Half. F. Gamble
Man and His Kingdom. E. P. Oppenheim
Man and His Money. F. S. Isham
Man and His Price. N. Carter
Man and Master. L. L. Lynch
Man and the Crime. H. Rockwood
Man and Two Gods. Jean Morris
Man and Wife. W. Collins
Man at Large. M. Cronin
Man at Six. L. De Leon
Man at the Carlton. E. Wallace
Man at the Manor. O. Sinclair
Man at the Window. N. Carter
Man at Willow Ranch. H. Bindloss
Man Beguiled. R. Rodd
Man Behind. A. Dax
Man Behind. J. Hunter
Man Behind Me. J. N. Chance
Man Behind the Chair. Winifred Graham
Man Behind the Curtain. A. Murray
Man Behind the Curtain. N. Tranter
Man Behind the Curtain. J. M. Walsh
Man Behind the Curtain. D. Walshe
Man Behind the Door. A. C. Gunter
Man Behind the Face. J. March
Man Behind the Mask. M. C. Cooke
Man Behind the Tinted Glasses. Diana Forbes
Man Between. W. A. Frost
Man Called Black. W. Manson
Man Called Eighty-Eighty. R. W. Hinds
Man Called Gillray. F. M. White
Man Called Harry Brent. F. Durbridge
Man Called Jones. J. Symons
Man Called Lenz. George Young
Man Called Spade. D. Hammett
Man Called Tempest. W. Shand
Man Could Get Killed That Way. Weldon Hill
Man Dead. S. Jepson
Man Died Here. G. Dessart
Man Died Talking. R. Garnett
Man Dormant. J. Lodwick
Man Drowning. H. Kuttner

Man Eater. H. M. Rideout
Man for Me. T. Charles
Man from Algiers. W. Jardine
Man from Arnheim. L. Jackson
Man from Atlantis. K. Robeson
Man from Australia. F. A. Symonds
Man from Australia. W. L. Whitehouse
Man from AVON. M. Avallone
Man from Bar Harbour. G. Mitcham
Man from Checkmate. W. R. Bennett
Man from Chicago. L. C. Douthwaite
Man from China. A. Parsons
Man from Chun King. R. Hardinge
Man from Dartmoor. Gwyn Evans
Man from Destiny. I. MacKintosh
Man from Dieppe. H. King
Man from Downing Street. W. LeQueux
Man from Dublin. A. Blair
Man from Egypt. H. Hill
Man from Everywhere. G. Simenon
Man from Fleet Street. J. Creasey
Man from Greek and Roman. J. Goldman
Man from Holland. R. Hardinge
Man from India. N. Carter
Man from Italy. J. G. Brandon
Man from Kabul. G. De Villiers
Man from Kenya. A. Parsons
Man from Kura-Kura. A. Murray
Man from Limbo. G. Endore
Man from London. N. Carter
Man from M.O.D. W. B. Day
Man from Madagascar. F. Grierson
Man from Madrid. P. Meriton
Man from Maloba. O. Binns
Man from Manchester. D. Donovan
Man from Manhattan. L. Grex
Man from Maybrick Road. A. Parsons
Man from Mexico City. D. Whitelaw
Man from Michigan. B. Graeme
Man from Mongolia. R. Hardinge
Man from Morocco. E. Wallace
Man from Moscow. G. Chester
Man from Moscow. P. McCutchan
Man from Moscow. F. Usher
Man from MOTHER. Harry Gregory
Man from Norway. G. Chester
Man from Nowhere. V. Bridges
Man from Nowhere. S. Ellin
Man from Nowhere. J. Fleming
Man from Nowhere. E. Huxley
Man from Occupied France. A. Parsons
Man from Pansy. D. Rico
Man from Paris. Roland Daniel
Man from Paris. L. Royer
Man from Pecos. D. Reid
Man from Persia. L. Jackson
Man from Prison. Roland Daniel
Man from Scapa Flow. Taffrail
Man from Scotland Yard. D. Frome
Man from Scotland Yard. S. Horler
Man from Sing Sing. E. P. Oppenheim
Man from Singapore. J. G. Brandon
Man from Space. R. Hardinge
Man from Texas. B. Wayde
Man from the Bomb. R. Chetwynd-Hayes
Man from the Chamber of Horrors. John Ross
Man from the Clouds. J. S. Clouston
Man from the Diner's Club. S. Barl
Man from the Far East. J. Hunter
Man from the Jungle. R. Hardinge
Man from the Lias River. R. Cullum
Man from the Mist. M. Elgin
Man from the Norlands. J. Buchan
Man from the Past. S. P. Hyatt
Man from the Past. A. MacKenzie
Man from the Rhine. L. Cargill
Man from the River. G. D. H. Cole
Man from the Rock. D. Bateson
Man from the Sea. M. Innes

Man from the South. J. R. Taylor
Man from the Turkish Slave. V. Canning
Man from the West. G. Goodchild
Man from the West, and other stories of Adventure. G. Goodchild
Man from Tibet. C. B. Clason
Man from Tokyo. W. Jardine
Man from Troy. J. G. Sarasin
Man from Whitehall. J. M. Walsh
Man from Yesterday. D. Daniels
Man Gets into His Tomb. L. Mercer
Man Himself. A. M. Williamson
Man; His Mark. W. C. Morrow
Man Hunt. G. Bettany
Man Hunt. O. Cameron
Man Hunt! L. Como
Man Hunt. T. Gallon
Man Hunt. G. Household
Man Hunt. L. A. Knight
Man-Hunter. D. Donovan
Man-Hunter. M. O. Rolfe
Man I Didn't Kill. N. Deane
Man I Killed. M. Halliday
Man in a Black Hat. T. Thurston
Man in a Mist. L. Lamb
Man in a Net. W. Butler
Man in a Net. P. Garrod
Man in Ambush. M. Procter
Man in Aspic. Andrew Hall
Man in Black. S. J. Weyman
Man in Blue. M. A. Denison
Man in Brown. W. Edwards
Man in Brown. M. Walsh
Man in Charge. R. Jessup
Man in Evening Clothes. J. R. Scott
Man in Gray. F. Crane
Man in Gray. B. Orczy
Man in Gray. E. C. Vivian
Man in Lower Ten. M. R. Rinehart
Man in Mail. Lieut. Carlton
Man in Motion. C. Williams
Man in Motley. T. Gallon
Man in My Chair. H. B. Kaye
Man in My Grave. W. Tucker
Man in My Shoes. J. N. Chance
Man in No. 3. J. S. Fletcher
Man in Question. J. Godey
Man in Ratcatcher, and other stories. H. C. McNeile
Man in Room 3. A. Carr
Man in Steel. J. S. Clouston
Man in Stripes. Lieut. Carlton
Man in the Auto. N. Carter
Man in the Basement. B. P. Rosenkrantz
Man in the Bird Cage. K. MacLean
Man in the Blue Mask. A. Morton
Man in the Bottle. B. Knox
Man in the Box. N. Worth
Man in the Brown Derby. W. S. Hastings
Man in the Brown Suit. A. Christie
Man in the Button Boots. Anthony Gilbert
Man in the Cage. J. H. Vance
Man in the Cape. H. C. Bailey
Man in the Car. A. Raleigh
Man in the Check Suit. T. W. H. Delf
Man in the Cloak. S. Horler
Man in the Corner. B. Orczy
Man in the Dark. W. Cook
Man in the Dark. J. Ferguson
Man in the Dark. D. Orgill
Man in the Dark. S. Scarlett
Man in the Dark. D. Stuart
Man in the Dark. A. P. Terhune

Man in the Driver's Seat. Ira Walker
Man in the Fog. H. Tighe
Man in the Fur Coat. J. S. Fletcher
Man in the Garden. P. Mason
Man in the Green Hat. M. Coles
Man in the Grey Cowl. A. Murray
Man in the Hood. S. Horler
Man in the Jury Box. R. O. Chipperfield
Man in the Lubianka. D. Vallance
Man in the Mews. J. Packer
Man in the Middle. H. Atkinson
Man in the Middle. M. E. Chaber
Man in the Middle. F. Findley
Man in the Middle. D. Wagoner
Man in the Mirror. F. Ayer
Man in the Mirror. H. Douglas
Man in the Mist. F. Bonnamy
Man in the Monkey Suit. A. Hathaway
Man in the Moonlight. R. S. Holland
Man in the Moonlight. H. McCloy
Man in the Net. P. Quentin
Man in the Night Mail Train. A. Philips
Man in the Pig Mask. C. T. Stoneham
Man in the Portrait. F. A. M. Webster
Man in the Purple Gown. C. Haddon
Man in the Queue. G. Daviot
Man in the Red Hat. R. Keverne
Man in the Red Mask. Roy Vickers
Man in the Rolls-Royce. Ilian Stuart
Man in the Sandhills. A. Marsden
Man in the Shadow. R. Foley
Man in the Shadow. S. Kyle
Man in the Shadow. H. Whittington
Man in the Shadows. C. Bidmead
Man in the Shadows. C. J. Daly
Man in the Shadows. S. Horler
Man in the Sopwith Camel. M. Butterworth
Man in the Spike. Michael Barrett
Man in the Tricorn Hat. D. Ames
Man in the Trilby Hat. R. Goyne
Man in the Turkish Bath. H. F. Moulton
Man in the Twilight. R. Cullum
Man in the Water. R. Sheckley
Man in the White Raincoat. R. Lebherz
Man in the White Slicker. L. H. Nason
Man in the Wood. M. S. Boyd
Man in White. S. Horler
Man in Yellow, and The Empty House. H. C. McNeile
Man Inside. M. E. Chaber
Man Inside. N. S. Lincoln
Man-Killer. T. Powell
Man Lay Dead. N. Marsh
Man, Let's Go On. P. McCutchan
Man Made Angry. H. Brooke
Man Made Law. C. Stanton
Man Made of Tin. Shane Martin
Man Missing. M. G. Eberhart
Man Must Live. H. Holland
Man Named Seraphin. R. Ray
Man Named Thin. D. Hammett
Man Next Door. M. G. Eberhart
Man No One Knew. L. Meynell
Man Nobody Knew. D. T. Lindsay
Man Nobody Saw. P. Cheyney
Man of a Hundred Faces. G. Leroux
Man of a Hundred Masks. G. Leroux
Man of Affairs. S. Horler
Man of Affairs. J. D. MacDonald
Man of Bronze. K. Robeson
Man of Character. D. H. Landels
Man of Cold Rages. Jordan Park
Man of Dangerous Secrets. M. March
Man of Dartmoor. O. Binns
Man of Death. A. Gask
Man of Evil. S. Horler
Man of Forty. G. Bullett

M

572/ Man of Iron   Bibliography of Crime Fiction

Man of Iron. N. Carter
Man of Last Resort. M. D. Post
Man of Little Evils. S. Dobyns
Man of Many Colours. D. Braza
Man of Many Faces. N. Carter
Man of Many Minds. E. E. Evans
Man of Miracles. M. Leblanc
Man of Mystery. N. Carter
Man of Mystery. Leon Lewis
Man of Mystery. J. Neil
Man of Mystery. Old Sleuth
Man of No Sorrows. C. Kernahan
Man of Power. J. Blackmore
Man of Riddles. N. Carter
Man of Sentiment. T. Cobb
Man of Silver Mount. M. Pemberton
Man of Substance. A. Hodges
Man of Talent. E. Kyle
Man of the Avenue. F. Dard
Man of the Crag. G. Boothby
Man of the Forty Faces. T. W. Hanshew
Man of the Hour. W. Magnay
Man of the Moment. M. Gerard
Man of the North. J. B. Hendryx
Man of the River. O. Sinclair
Man of Two Tribes. A. W. Upfield
Man of Wrath. P. Allardyce
Man on a Horse. H. Clewes
Man on a Leash. C. Williams
Man on a Nylon String. W. Masterson
Man on a Rope. G. H. Coxe
Man on a Short Leash. O. Jacks
Man on a String. M. Wolfe
Man on All Fours. A. Derleth
Man on His Shoulder. K. Methold
Man on Horseback. A. Abdullah
Man on the Balcony. M. Sjowall
Man on the Bench in the Barn. G. Simenon
Man on the Box. H. MacGrath
Man on the Bridge. I. S. Black
Man on the Couch. E. C. Derby
Man on the Crater's Edge. J. Gerson
Man on the Dole. P. Urquhart
Man on the Dover Road. D. Whitelaw
Man on the End of the Rope. Paul Townend
Man on the Marsh. D. Leach
Man on the Raffles Verandah. Lydia Kirk
Man on the Run. M. Halliday
Man on the Run! A. Kirby
Man on the Run. C. Williams
Man on the Spot. S. C. Mason
Man on the Stairs. Carnaby Brown
Man on the Tight Rope. N. Paterson
Man on the Twenty-Fourth Floor. L. Allan
Man on Watch. T. Filer
Man Out of Nowhere. L. P. Davies
Man Out of the Rain. P. MacDonald
Man Outside. S. Campbell
Man Outside. W. Martyn
Man Outside. D. Stuart
Man Overboard! F. W. Crofts
Man Overboard. A. MacKinnon
Man Pays. A. Applin
Man Peter. G. Goodchild
Man Pinches Bottom. J. T. Story
Man Running. S. Jepson
Man Running. E. West
Man That I Love. D. Egerton
Man the Devil Didn't Want. P. C. Wren
Man They Could Not Convict. R. Hardinge
Man They Could Not Kill. J. Corbett
Man They Couldn't Arrest. A. J. Small
Man They Couldn't Buy. Gilbert Chester
Man They Couldn't Escape. M. Fiaschetti
Man They Couldn't Hang. O. Martyn
Man They Couldn't Kill. R. L. Meyers
Man They Feared. T. A. Plummer
Man They Held Back. N. Carter
Man They Put Away. T. A. Plummer
Man to Be Feared. N. Carter

Man to Match the Hour. S. Truss
Man Trap. Anonymous
Man Trap. J. A. Dunn
Man-Trap. J. D. MacDonald
Man-Trap. W. Magnay
Man-Trapper. Old Sleuth
Man Under the Window. G. T. Ockley
Man Upstairs. P. Hamilton
Man Who Asked Why. Jessica Ryan
Man Who Awoke. M. I. Taylor
Man Who Backed Out! A. Parsons
Man Who Bailed Out. G. Chester
Man Who Bombed the World. J. Milton
Man Who Bought London. E. Wallace
Man Who Butted In. V. Bridges
Man Who Called Too Soon. A. M. Griffin
Man Who Came Back. J. Bryan
Man Who Came Back. W. M. Graydon
Man Who Came Back. M. Hastings
Man Who Came Back. E. Jepson
Man Who Came Back. H. W. Leggett
Man Who Came Back. A. Wood
Man Who Came Back from the Dead. G. Leroux
Man Who Cannot Kill. J. F. Straker
Man Who Caught the 4:15. A. Spiller
Man Who Changed Faces. N. Carter
Man Who Changed His Face. T. A. Plummer
Man Who Changed His Name. Robert (G.) Curtis
Man Who Changed His Name. E. Wallace
Man Who Changed His Plea. E. P. Oppenheim
Man Who Chose Death. E. Allen
Man Who Convicted Himself. D. Fox
Man Who Could Cheat Death. J. Sangster
Man Who Could Not Shudder. J. D. Carr
Man Who Could Still Laugh. C. Houghton
Man Who Could Stop War. W. Penmare
Man Who Couldn't Sleep. A. Stringer
Man Who Covered Mirrors. M. Cumberland
Man Who Crawled Away. L. Butler
Man Who Cried All the Way Home. D. Hitchens
Man Who Dealt in Blood. G. Wolk
Man Who Did Not Die. T. Harknett
Man Who Did Not Hang. S. Horler
Man Who Didn't Answer. I. Oellrichs
Man Who Didn't Count. G. M. Glaskin
Man Who Didn't Exist. G. Homes
Man Who Didn't Exist. A. West
Man Who Didn't Fly. M. Bennett
Man Who Didn't Mind Hanging. N. B. Mavity
Man Who Died on Friday. M. Underwood
Man Who Died Too Soon. G. H. Coxe
Man Who Died Twice. G. H. Coxe
Man Who Died Twice. Warren Dekobra
Man Who Died Twice. S. Horler
Man Who Died Twice. L. Paxton
Man Who Disappeared. E. Bohle
Man Who Disappeared. R. Pyke
Man Who Dreamed Right. W. Holt-White
Man Who Dressed to Kill. A. Spiller
Man Who Drove On. W. M. Graydon
Man Who Drove the Car. M. Pemberton
Man Who Escaped. S. Bedford
Man Who Fainted. N. Carter
Man Who Feared. P. Forsyth
Man Who Feared. W. F. Jenkins
Man Who Fell. M. Eden
Man Who Fell Through the Earth. C. Wells
Man Who Finally Died. John Burke
Man Who Followed Women. B. Hitchens
Man Who Forgot. R. C. Armour

Man Who Forgot. J. Hay
Man Who Forgot. H. Holt
Man Who Forgot. J. Mackie
Man Who Found Himself. M. Stacpoole
Man Who Found His Way. F. O'Rourke
Man Who Got Away. S. L. Elliott
Man Who Got Away with It. Bernice Carey
Man Who Grew Bulbs. J. M. Walsh
Man Who Grew Tomatoes. G. Mitchell
Man Who Guided Missiles. P. Denman
Man Who Had to Quit. A. Parsons
Man Who Had Too Much to Lose. Hampton Stone
Man Who Haunted Himself. Ralph Martin
Man Who Held Five Aces. Jean Leslie
Man Who Held the Queen to Ransom and Sent Parliament Packing. P. Van Greenway
Man Who Hid. D. Stewart
Man Who Killed. C. Farrere
Man Who Killed Fortescue. J. S. Strange
Man Who Killed Himself. J. Symons
Man Who Killed Me. Arthur MacLean
Man Who Killed the King. D. Wheatley
Man Who Killed Too Soon. M. Underwood
Man Who Knew. H. Leyford
Man Who Knew. M. O. Rolfe
Man Who Knew. E. Wallace
Man Who Knew. F. A. M. Webster
Man Who Knew All. M. Leighton
Man Who Knew the Date. S. Kerr
Man Who Knew Too Much. Ruth Alexander
Man Who Knew Too Much. W. H. Baker
Man Who Knew Too Much and other stories. G. K. Chesterton
Man Who Laughed. G. Fairlie
Man Who Laughed at Murder. G. Ashe
Man Who Left Home. L. Jackson
Man Who Left Well Enough. M. McShane
Man Who Liked to Look at Himself. K. C. Constantine
Man Who Limped. V. Bridges
Man Who Lived Twice. H. Shaw
Man Who Looked Back. J. Fleming
Man Who Looked Death in the Eye. Hampton Stone
Man Who Lost an Hour. F. Marlowe
Man Who Lost His Memory. A. Skene
Man Who Lost His Way. W. E. Johns
Man Who Lost His Wife. J. Symons
Man Who Loved Chocolates. D. Batchelor
Man Who Loved His Wife. V. Caspary
Man Who Loved Lions. Ethel L. White
Man Who Loved Spiders. S. Horler
Man Who Loved Zoos. M. J. Bosse
Man Who Made a King. R. Ladline
Man Who Made Diamonds. Warren Miller
Man Who Made Good. P. Trent
Man Who Made Money. B. Wayde
Man Who Made Monsters. J. Ronald
Man Who Made Roubles. J. Ingersol
Man Who Mislaid the War. S. Horler
Man Who Missed the War. D. Wheatley
Man Who Murdered Goliath. G. Homes
Man Who Murdered Himself. G. Homes
Man Who Never Blundered. G. Gluck
Man Who Never Laughed. A. Hare
Man Who Never Slept! Gwyn Evans
Man Who Never Was. S. Picard
Man Who Paid. N. Carter
Man Who Paid His Way. W. J. Sheldon
Man Who Played Patience. S. Truss
Man Who Played Thief. Don Smith
Man Who Plundered the City. S. Elvestad
Man Who Preferred Cocktails. S. Horler
Man Who Pulled the Strings. J. Haslette
Man Who Raised Hell. R. Sale

Title Index

Man Who Ran Away. D. B. Dodson
Man Who Rang the Bell. M. Kennedy
Man Who Said No. W. Grove
Man Who Saved London. J. K. Keith
Man Who Saw the Devil. J. Corbett
Man Who Saw Through Heaven. W. D. Steele
Man Who Shook the Earth. S. Horler
Man Who Shook the Earth. K. Robeson
Man Who Shook the World. J. Creasey
Man Who Shot Birds and other tales. M. Fitt
Man Who Slept All Day. M. Venning
Man Who Smiled No More. K. Robeson
Man Who Sold Death. N. Carter
Man Who Sold Death. J. Munro
Man Who Sold Secrets. Roland Daniel
Man Who Sought Trouble. Roland Daniel
Man Who Squealed. G. N. Philips
Man Who Stayed Alive. G. Ashe
Man Who Stayed at Home. B. Tinker
Man Who Stole Heaven. J. Ingersol
Man Who Stole Millions. N. Carter
Man Who Stole Millions and other stories. N. Carter
Man Who Stole the Crown Jewels. Augustus Muir
Man Who Stole the Earth. W. Holt-White
Man Who Stood Alone. P. Trent
Man Who Thought He Was a Pauper. E. P. Oppenheim
Man Who Tilted the Earth. J. Atholl
Man Who Turned King's Evidence. J. Hunter
Man Who Used Perfume. S. Horler
Man Who Vanished. V. Bridges
Man Who Vanished. N. Carter
Man Who Vanished. F. Hume
Man Who Vanished. Old Sleuth
Man Who Vanished. J. T. Smith
Man Who Walked Away. C. Jay
Man Who Walked Like a Dancer. R. Brennan
Man Who Walked on Diamonds. J. Quartermain
Man Who Walked with Death. S. Horler
Man Who Wanted to Die. A. MacKenzie
Man Who Wanted Tomorrow. B. Freemantle
Man Who Was Bormann. Derek Boyd
Man Who Was Chief. G. Horne
Man Who Was Cursed. N. Carter
Man Who Was Dead. A. W. Marchmont
Man Who Was Dead. W. S. Sykes
Man Who Was Guilty. F. H. Loughead
Man Who Was Murdered Twice. R. H. Leitfred
Man Who Was Nobody. E. Wallace
Man Who Was Not Himself. J. Graffy
Man Who Was Not There. Ethel L. White
Man Who Was Ten Years Late for Breakfast. C. Herbert
Man Who Was There. D. G. Barron
Man Who Was There. N. A. Temple-Ellis
Man Who Was Three Jumps Ahead. Hampton Stone
Man Who Was Thursday. G. K. Chesterton
Man Who Was Too Clever. Anthony Gilbert
Man Who Was Too Much. A. Gardner
Man Who Was Two. F. M. White
Man Who Wasn't. G. Goodchild
Man Who Wasn't Himself. L. Cargill
Man Who Wasn't Murdered. H. C. Davis
Man Who Wasn't There. Anthony Gilbert
Man Who Wasn't There. J. Sandys
Man Who Wasn't There. B. Whitaker
Man Who Watched the Trains Go By. G. Simenon
Man Who Went Away. K. David
Man Who Went Up in Smoke. M. Sjowall
Man Who Went Wrong. L. Jackson
Man Who Would Do Anything. I. T. Ross
Man Who Would Not Swim. B. E. Wallace
Man Who Wouldn't Quit. G. Chester
Man Who Wouldn't Talk. Q. Reynolds
Man Whose Dreams Came True. J. Symons
Man Will Be Kidnapped Tomorrow. J. Ashford
Man with a Background of Flames. R. Johns
Man with a Calico Face. Shelley Smith
Man with a Crutch. N. Carter
Man with a Double. N. Carter
Man with a Grievance. W. Jardine
Man with a Gun. Lieut. Carlton
Man with a Monocle. C. F. Gregg
Man with a Number. S. Blakesley
Man with a Paper Skull. D. Marfield
Man with a Past. J. M. Patterson
Man with a Scar. E. C. Vivian
Man with a Secret. F. Hume
Man with a Shadow. G. M. Fenn
Man with a Thumb. W. C. Hudson
Man with a Weak Heart. G. Gardiner
Man with Bated Breath. J. B. Carr
Man with Dry Hands. S. Horler
Man with Five Enemies. R. Hardinge
Man with Good Intentions. J. Barlow
Man with Half a Face. G. Davison
Man with His Back to the East. H. H. Ross
Man with Jitters. J. G. Brandon
Man with My Face. S. W. Taylor
Man with Nine Lives. J. Corbett
Man with Nine Lives. R. Marsh
Man with No Bones. P. Helm
Man with No Face. M. Armstrong
Man with No Face. J. N. Chance
Man with No Face. D. L. Sayers
Man with No Shadow. S. Marlowe
Man with Talent. G. Fairlie
Man with the Amber Eyes. E. Jepson
Man with the Amber Eyes. F. Warden
Man with the Big Head. M. Scrope
Man with the Black Cord. A. Groner
Man with the Black Feather. G. Leroux
Man with the Black Patch. F. E. Verney
Man with the Black Wallet. W. W. Sayer
Man with the Brooding Eyes. J. Goodwin
Man with the Brown Paper Face. I. Hamilton
Man with the Cane. J. Potts
Man with the Chocolate Egg. J. Noone
Man with the Clubfoot. D. Valentine
Man with the Crimson Box. H. S. Keeler
Man with the Crooked Arm. T. A. Plummer
Man with the Dark Beard. A. Haynes
Man with the Getaway Face. R. Stark
Man with the Glaring Eyes. A. Blair
Man with the Glass Eye. N. Leslie
Man with the Gloved Hand. J. McKimmey
Man with the Golden Gun. I. Fleming
Man with the Green Eyes. N. Goddard
Man with the Iron Chest. Richard Williams
Man with the Little Dog. G. Simenon
Man with the Lumpy Nose. L. Lariar
Man with the Magic Eardrums. H. S. Keeler
Man with the Magnetic Eyes. Roland Daniel
Man with the Million Pounds. R. M. Newman
Man with the Monocle. Garnett Weston
Man with the Opals. A. W. Barrett
Man with the Painted Head. H. Reilly
Man with the Parrots. A. E. Bayly
Man with the Rake. M. B. Lee
Man with the Red Beard. P. Cheyney
Man with the Red Beard. D. Whitelaw
Man with the Scar. J. Lomas
Man with the Scarlet Skull, and other tales. Gwyn Evans
Man with the Scarred Hand. H. K. Webster
Man with the Seared Hand. J. G. Rowe
Man with the Sixth Sense. L. Tracy
Man with the Squeaky Voice. R. A. J. Walling
Man with the Tattooed Face. M. Burton
Man with the Tiny Head. I. Drummond
Man with the Twisted Face. G. Davison
Man with the Vandyk Beard. F. M. White
Man with the Wax Face. R. Wormser
Man with the White Face. M. Gerard
Man with the Wooden Spectacles. H. S. Keeler
Man with the Yellow Eyes. A. S. Burrage
Man with Three Chins. D. Ames
Man with Three Jaguars. D. Ames
Man with Three Names. H. MacGrath
Man with Three Passports. D. Ames
Man with Three Witches. J. N. Chance
Man with Tin Trumpet. F. Mullally
Man with Two Clocks. W. Masterson
Man with Two Faces. S. Horler
Man with Two Heads. J. N. Chance
Man with Two Shadows. R. Maugham
Man with Two Souls. P. Quiroule
Man with Two Ties. H. Van Rensburg
Man with Two Wives. P. Quentin
Man with Two Wives and other stories. P. Cheyney
Man with Yellow Eyes. B. Atkey
Man with Yellow Shoes. A. Heckstall-Smith
Man. Within. G. Greene
Man Without a Conscience. N. Carter
Man Without a Face. A. Boissiere
Man Without a Face. J. E. Hasty
Man Without a Face. C. Robbins
Man Without a Head. J. Bowen
Man Without a Head. T. De Saix
Man Without a Head. W. S. Masterman
Man Without a Memory. A. W. Marchmont
Man Without a Mouth. J. Charles
Man Without a Name. S. Kyle
Man Without a Passport. A. Parsons
Man Without a Will. N. Carter
Man Without Friends. M. Echard
Man Without Friends. M. Tripp
Man Without Nerves. E. P. Oppenheim
Man Without Pity. S. Truss
Man, Woman and Sin. E. Jepson
Manacle and Bracelet. E. C. Strong
Manana Kid. F. W. Hilton
Manasco Road. V. Canning
Manchester Thing. Angus Ross
Manchu Blood. H. Wiley
Manchu Jade. S. Jepson
Manchurian Candidate. R. Condon
Mandarin Cypher. Adam Hall
Mandarin's Bride. M. Richmond
Mandarin's Dagger. L. Crichton
Mandarin's Fan. F. Hume
Mandarin's Pearl. Jeffrey Montague
Mandarin's Sapphire. D. Marfield
Mandarin's Seal. A. Murray
Manderley Mystery. B. Ketterer
Mandragora. J. Palmer
Mandrakes in the Cupboard. T. B. Morris
Mandura Mystery. I. Barry
Manfred the Magic Trick Detective. Anonymous
Mangrove Murder. Mary Scott
Manhandled. W. Chambers
Manhandled. A. Stringer
Manhattan Bombshell. N. W. Firth
Manhattan Cowboy. C. Brown

574/ Manhattan File

Manhattan File. I. K. Martin
Manhattan Masquerade. F. A. Kummer
Manhattan Massacre. P. McCurtin
Manhattan Murder. A. Train
Manhattan Night. W. A. Wolff
Manhattan North. M. Albrand
Manhattan Terrors. B. Sarto
Manhattan Wipeout. J. Rosenberger
Manhunt. D. MacKenzie
Manhunt. Mark Ross
Manhunt in Manhattan. J. Dekker
Manhunt in Murder. W. Martyn
Manhunt in Sicily. S. Brydon
Manhunt Is My Mission. S. Marlowe
Manhunting. D. Sliman
Mania for Blondes. S. A. Krasney
Maniac. A. MacVicar
Maniac Father. T. P. Prest
Maniac Rendezvous. M. Brandel
Maniac Responsible. R. Gover
Maniac's Dream. F. H. Rose
Manila Hemp. Elinor Chamberlain
Manila Masquerade. D. Garth
Manila Stranger. F. Crisp
Manipulators. W. Garner
Manipulators. J. Rossiter
Mannequin. V. Williams
Mannequin Doll. D. Glinto
Manning-Burke Murder. L. Tracy
Mannix. M. Avallone
Manoeuvres of Celeste. M. E. G.
Manor House Menace. J. Drummond
Manor House Mystery. J. S. Fletcher
Manor Inn. G. H. R. Dabbs
Manordale Mystery. Old Sleuth
Man's Blessing. L. Sciascia
Man's Enemies. L. Thayer
Man's Estate. J. Cleary
Man's Estate. N. Tranter
Man's Shadow. W. H. L. Crauford
Mansel Disappearance Mystery. G. Comley
Mansfield Mystery. J. C. Lenehan
Mansion House Mystery. S. Drew
Mansion of Deadly Dreams. G. Corren
Mansion of Evil. C. Farr
Mansion of Evil. J. Millard
Mansion of Lost Memories. D. Daniels
Mansion of Mystery. C. K. Steele
Mansion of Peril. C. Farr
Mansion of Shadows. E. J. Murray
Mansion of Smiling Masks. D. Winston
Mansion of the Golden Windows. Elsie Lee
Mansion on the Moor. J. Purley
Mansion on the Moors. W. E. D. Ross
Manslaughter. A. D. Miller
Mantis and the Moth. M. Weatherly
Mantle of Ishmael. J. S. Fletcher
Mantrackers. W. Mulvihill
Mantrap. J. N. Chance
Mantrap. A. Evans
Mantrap. D. Yarnell
Mantrapper. Anonymous
Manufacturer's Daughter. A. C. Gunter
Manuscript for Murder. R. M. Stern
Manuscript Murder. L. Robinson
Manuscripts from the Diary of a Physician. T. P. Prest
Manville Murders. C. Fitzsimmons
Manx Cat. F. Levon
Many a Flower. A. Dick
Many a Monster. R. Finnegan
Many a Murder. D. Van Deusen
Many a Slip. F. W. Crofts
Many a Slip. O. Mills
Many Brave Hearts. D. M. Douglass

Many-Coloured Thread. L. Allan
Many Deadly Returns. P. Moyes
Many Engagements. J. S. Fletcher
Many Happy Returns. Justin Scott
Many-Headed Monster. G. Lett
Many Murders. I. H. Irwin
Many Parts. John Marsh
Many Thanks, Ben Hassett. H. De Hamel
Many Ways of Death. F. Didelot
Many Worlds of Magnus Ridolph. J. Vance
Maori Murder Case. A. L. Albert
Map of Mistrust. A. MacKinnon
Maple Hall Mystery. E. Parmer
Maplethorpe Tangle. Elliot Bailey
Maracaibo Mission. V. W. Mason
Marakano Formula. J. Pattinson
Maras Affair. E. Reed
Maraskar Bound. R. T. Bickers
Marathon Man. W. Goldman
Marathon Mystery. B. E. Stevenson
Marauders by Night. A. Gask
Marbeau Cousins. Harry S. Edwards
Marble Angel. D. Daniels
Marble Arch Mystery. W. J. Bayfield
Marble Forest. T. Durrant
Marble Forest. E. K. Goldthwaite
Marble Heart. H. Luger
Marble Hills. D. Daniels
Marble Jungle. C. Richards
Marble Leaf. D. Daniels
Marble Orchard. B. Copper
Marble Tomb Mystery. C. Robertson
Marceau Case. H. S. Keeler
Marcel Levignet. E. Barron
March Hare Murders. E. Ferrars
March of Fate. B. L. Farjeon
March of the Flame Marauders. C. Steele
March of the Legion. J. Robb
March to the Gallows. M. Kelly
Marches of Honour. Ganpat
Marchester Royal. J. S. Fletcher
Marco. S. Cobb
Marcus Hay. S. P. Hyatt
Marcus Holbeach's Daughter. A. Jones
Mardi. K. Hewitt
Mardi Gras Massacre. L. Derrick
Mardi Gras Murders. G. Bristow
Mardi-Gras Mystery. H. Bedford-Jones
Mare's Nest. C. Coffin
Margaret. G. W. M. Reynolds
Margaret Benson's Vow. T. A. Plummer
Margaret Carmichael. C. Gibbon
Margaret Rutland. T. Cobb
Margaret the Peacemaker. W. Wood
Margate Murder Mystery. B. Delannoy
Margie. E. V. Cunningham
Margie and the Wolf Man. R. St. Clair
Margin for Doubt. M. Borgenicht
Margin for Error. Clare Booth
Margin for Terror. F. Kane
Margin of Terror. P. Capon
Margin of Terror. W. P. McGivern
Margot--and Her Judges. R. Marsh
Margot Leck. P. Piper
Margravine. J. Hiscott
Maria. Brian Cooper
Maria Marches On. J. Slate
Marianne. J. Dering
Marianne. F. Mullally
Marianne the Outcast. Anonymous
Marianne's Kingdom. P. J. Cooper
Maridu. S. Wagner
Marie Arnaud, Spy. F. Hope
Marie de Brinvilliers. E. Gaboriau
Marie Halkett. R. W. Chambers
Marie-Rose. F. Du Boisgobey
Marie, the Dancing Girl. Old Sleuth
Marie Vee. D. Newton
Mariella--Spy! C. Davy
Mariette. T. P. Prest

Marihuana. W. Irish
Marijuana Girl. N. R. De Mexico
Marijuana Mob. J. H. Chase
Marijuana Murder. M. Stimson
Marilyn K. L. White
Marine Residence, and other stories. J. Payn
Marinova of the Secret Service. R. Essex
Mario. J. Carrick
Marion. J. Bingham
Marjorie Daw and Other People. T. B. Aldrich
Marjorie Daw and other stories. T. B. Aldrich
Marjorie Daw and other tales. T. B. Aldrich
Mark. P. C. De Crespigny
Mark. C. E. Israel
Mark Castle--Cable Address: Roma. C. Marcus
Mark Danver's Sin, and The Madman of Coral Reef Lighthouse. H. C. McNeile
Mark Heffron. A. W. Bailey
Mark It for Murder. D. Sanderson
Mark Kilby and the Manhattan Murders. R. C. Frazer
Mark Kilby and the Miami Mob. R. C. Frazer
Mark Kilby and the Secret Syndicate. R. C. Frazer
Mark Kilby Solves a Murder. R. C. Frazer
Mark Kilby Stands Alone. R. C. Frazer
Mark Kilby Takes a Risk. R. C. Frazer
Mark Magic, the Detective. A. P. Morris
Mark of a Buoy. G. Peters
Mark of a Witch. H. Kemp
Mark of Cain. Andrew Lang
Mark of Cain. C. Wells
Mark of Cosa Nostra. N. Carter
Mark of Displeasure. E. Hely
Mark of Kane. C. Frankin
Mark of Murder. D. Shannon
Mark of Pak San Ri. W. Stroup
Mark of Satan. A. Loring
Mark of the Beast. R. W. Kauffman
Mark of the Broad Arrow. Maurice Scott
Mark of the Crescent. J. Creasey
Mark of the Dead. The Aresbys
Mark of the Dragon. M. Richmond
Mark of the Four. Mark Cross
Mark of the Hand. C. Armstrong
Mark of the Leech. J. Cassells
Mark of the Moccasin. K. Perkins
Mark of the Moon. F. Gerard
Mark of the Paw. Gavin Holt
Mark of the Rat. A. Fredericks
Mark of the Red Diamond. J. H. Chase
Mark of the Shadow. M. Grant
Mark of the Tong. J. G. Brandon
Mark of the Vulture. R. J. Hogan
Mark of Treachery. C. B. Kelland
Mark of Yekel. E. Y. Miller
Mark One: The Dummy. J. Ball
Mark Ryder's Vow. P. Trent
Mark Sutherland. E. Southworth
Mark the Sparrow. Clark Howard
Mark Three for Murder. R. P. Hansen
Mark Twain's A Double Barrelled Detective Story. R. St. Clair
Marked "Cancelled." N. S. Lincoln
Marked Cards. J. Addiscombe
Marked Dangerous. E. Y. Miller
Marked Down for Murder. S. Dean

Marked for a Victim. S. C. Cumberland
Marked for Death. N. Carter
Marked for Death. D. Plantz
Marked for Life. A. F. Pinkerton
Marked for Murder. Ronald Campbell
Marked for Murder. B. Halliday
Marked for Murder. J. R. Macdonald
Marked for Murder. V. B. Miller
Marked for Murder. W. Reed
Marked Hand. N. Carter
Marked Man. C. Barling
Marked Man. H. Carmichael
Marked Man. W. LeQueux
Marked Man. H. C. Wire
Marked Men. C. N. Buck
Marked "Personal." A. K. Green
Marked Pistol. J. C. Lenehan
Marked to Die. M. Cronin
Marked with a Cross. G. Monro
Marked Woman. M. Leighton
Marked Woman. D. Newton
Marked Woman. Grace M. White
Markenmore Mystery. J. S. Fletcher
Market for Murder. F. Gruber
Market for Murder. C. M. Russell
Market of Venus. M. Richmond
Markham Affair. S. P. Hyatt
Marksman. M. Cronin
Marksman. H. C. Rae
Marl-Pit Mystery. G. Ohnet
Marley's Empire. P. McCutchan
Marloe Mansions Murder. A. G. MacLeod
Marlowe. R. Chandler
Marnie. Winston Graham
Maroc 7. M. Sands
Marooned. M. Caidin
Marooned. M. Maurice
Marooned! A. Murray
Marooned with Murder. R. A. J. Walling
Marozia. A. G. Hales
Marquis. A. Soutar
Marquis of Loveland. C. N. Williamson
Marquis of Murray Hill. Baron
Marquis of Putney. R. Marsh
Marquise de Brinvilliers. E. Gaboriau
Marrendon Mystery, and other stories of crime and detection. J. S. Fletcher
Marriage and Mary Ann. C. Cookson
Marriage and Murder. D. Sharp
Marriage at a Venture. E. Gaboriau
Marriage Bed. H. V. Dixon
Marriage-Broker. M. B. Lowndes
Marriage Broker. F. Warden
Marriage by Capture. A. Stringer
Marriage by Mistake. W. Carter
Marriage Cage. W. Johnston
Marriage Chest. D. Eden
Marriage for the Defence. Roy Vickers
Marriage for Two. A. S. Roche
Marriage Has Been Arranged. P. Allardyce
Marriage Lines. J. S. Fletcher
Marriage Mystery. F. Hume
Marriage of Adventure. E. Gaboriau
Marriage of Captain Kettle. C. J. C. Hyne
Marriage of Esther. G. Boothby
Marriage of Inconvenience. T. Cobb
Marriage of Inconvenience. J. L. Roberts
Marriage of Kettle. C. J. C. Hyne
Marriage of Margot. A. Applin
Marriage of Meldrum Strange. T. Mundy
Marriage of Yussuf Khan. F. Heller
Marriage Pact. L. Cheatham
Married Beneath Him. J. Payn

Married by Stealth. F. Warden
Married for Love. F. Du Boisgobey
Married in Haste. M. E. Braddon
Married in Mask. M. T. Walworth
Married into Murder. Reginald Campbell
Married or Trapped. T. Walton
Married to a Spy. R. Starr
Married to Murder. E. Radford
Married to Murder. H. Whittington
Marriott Hall. D. Daniels
Marrowby Myth. W. Martyn
Marry in Haste. J. A. Hodge
Marry in May. M. Richmond
Marrying Beneath Your Station. H. Wood
Marseilles. A. Caillou
Marseilles Enforcer. Don Smith
Marsh. E. Raymond
Marsh Gang. H. N. Field
Marsh House. M. L. Roby
Marshmallow Pie. Graham Lord
Marshmead Murders. S. Taylor
Marston Murder Case. W. A. Stowell
Marta. Marilyn Ross
Martello Tower Mystery. G. H. Teed
Marten Mystery. J. Ironside
Martha Willis. T. P. Prest
Marthe and the Madman. J. De Bosschere
Martin Faber, The Story of a Criminal. W. G. Simms
Martin Hewitt, Investigator. Arthur Morrison
Martin Speed Versus "The Snatcher." M. G. Hugi
Martineau Murders. R. Hull
Martini Murders. Roger Fuller
Martinis and Murder. H. Kane
Martyn Ware's Temptation. H. Wood
Martyr or Criminal? I. L. Cassilis
Martyred Fool. D. C. Murray
Marune: Alastor 933. J. Vance
Marvellous Coincidence. K. Cornwallis
Marvelous Escape. Old Sleuth
Marvels and Mysteries. R. Marsh
Marworth Mystery. W. A. Frost
Mary. M. E. Braddon
Mary Ann and Bill. C. Cookson
Mary Ann's Angels. C. Cookson
Mary Clifford. T. P. Prest
Mary Deare. H. Innes
Mary Elizabeth--Adventuress. R. Starr
Mary Jane Married. George R. Sims
Mary Middleton. G. W. M. Reynolds
Mary Price. G. W. M. Reynolds
Mary Regan. L. Scott
Mary Roberts Rinehart's Crime Book. M. R. Rinehart
Mary Stuart, Queen of Scots. G. W. M. Reynolds
Maryjane Tonight at Angels Twelve. M. Caidin
Marylebone Miser. E. Phillpotts
Mascarada Pass. W. C. MacDonald
Masinglee Murders. M. B. Dix
Mask. J. Cowdroy
Mask. A. Hornblow
Mask. W. LeQueux
Mask. Will Scott
Mask and the Man. P. Andreae
Mask and the Man. Alan Thomas
Mask and the Moonflower. P. A. Whitney
Mask for Crime. Marion Roberts
Mask for Murder. M. Dalman
Mask for Murder. H. Kane
Mask for Murder. A. M. Stein
Mask for the Toff. J. Creasey
Mask of Alexander. M. Albrand
Mask of Danger. M. Clare
Mask of Dimitrios. E. Ambler
Mask of Evil. C. Armstrong
Mask of Evil. D. M. Disney

Mask of Fear. Ross Alexander
Mask of Fu Manchu. S. Rohmer
Mask of Fury. Arthur MacLean
Mask of Glass. H. Roth
Mask of Gold. A. S. Swan
Mask of Medusa. P. Minton
Mask of Memory. V. Canning
Mask of Mephisto. W. B. Gibson
Mask of Mephisto. M. Grant
Mask of Murder. E. Radford
Mask of Pursuit. J. N. Chance
Mask of Shadows. R. Owen
Mask of Terror. H. Desmond
Mask of the Andes. J. Cleary
Mask of Violence. M. Hebden
Mask of Words. J. Roffman
Masked Alibi. M. A. Clune
Masked Ball. A. Lowing
Masked Ball Murder. D. Fairfax
Masked Blackmailer. J. C. Lenehan
Masked Dancer. W. J. Bayfield
Masked Danger. B. Bolt
Masked Detective. Anonymous
Masked Detective. H. P. Halsey
Masked Dictator. W. M. Graydon
Masked Forgers. W. J. Bayfield
Masked Gunman. G. Ashe
Masked in Mystery. S. Rathbone
Masked Invasion. C. Steele
Masked Judgment. D. T. Lindsay
Masked Killer. G. H. Teed
Masked Lady. M. M. Murray
Masked Man. G. Leroux
Masked Man of the Desert. C. Brisbane
Masked Marauder. R. M. Graydon
Masked Motorist. Anonymous
Masked Murder. M. Alan
Masked Raiders. R. C. Armour
Masked Slayer. R. Hardinge
Masked Stranger. L. Allan
Masked Terror. H. Pink
Masked Terror. M. Richmond
Masked Venus. R. H. Savage
Masked Woman. J. McCulley
Masks. B. Fleming
Masks. A. Skene
Masks of Malevolence. L. Amino
Masks of Thespis. M. Richardson
Masks Off at Midnight. V. Williams
Masque by Gaslight. V. Coffman
Masque of a Savage Mandarin. P. Robinson
Masque of Mutiny. C. L. Reid
Masque of Satan. V. Coffman
Masque of the Red Death. Elsie Lee
Masquerade. W. Morton
Masquerade. M. Pereira
Masquerade at Monfalcone. Dorinne Moore
Masquerade in Blue. G. M. Barnes
Masquerade in Venice. V. Johnston
Masquerade into Madness. Samuel Merwin
Masquerade Mystery. F. Hume
Masquerade of Evil. E. Zumwalt
Masquerader. R. M. Graydon
Masquerader. K. C. Thurston
Mass for a Dead Witch. A. Grace
Mass of Death. J. Turner
Mass Radiography Murders. Sutherland Scott
Massacre in Milan. N. Carter
Massacre of Glencoe. G. W. M. Reynolds
Massingham Affair. E. Grierson
Massingham Butterfly. J. S. Fletcher
Master. M. Braly
Master. C. Brown
Master and Man. A. Askew
Master Criminal. N. Carter
Master Criminal. J. J. Farjeon

Master Criminal. S. Paternoster
Master Detective. P. Brebner
Master Hand. R. Dallas
Master Hand. J. Futrelle
Master Key. A. Soutar
Master-Key. F. Warden
Master Manhunters. J. Gollomb
Master Mind. M. Dana
Master-Mind. F. Hume
Master Mind. H. Janson
Master Mind. C. Moffett
Master Mummer. E. P. Oppenheim
Master Murderer. C. Wells
Master Mystery. A. B. Reeve
Master Mystery. Seamark
Master of Beechwood. A. Sergeant
Master of Blacktower. B. Michaels
Master of Blue Mire. V. Coffman
Master of Broken Men. C. Steele
Master of Charteris Towers. W. M. Graydon
Master of Crime. C. Williams
Master of Deception. R. Marsh
Master of Deviltry. N. Carter
Master of Evil. H. Long
Master of Evrington. V. Blake
Master of Fear. C. Rushton
Master of Fortune. C. J. C. Hyne
Master of Graylands. H. Wood
Master of High Beck. John Marsh
Master of His Fate. J. M. Cobban
Master of Malcarew. V. Black
Master of Men. E. P. Oppenheim
Master of Merlains. D. Whitelaw
Master of Merripit. E. Phillpotts
Master of Millions. G. C. Lorimer
Master of Money. F. Lady
Master of Montrolfe Hall. R. O'Grady
Master of Murder. T. Robbins
Master of Mysteries. G. Burgess
Master of Mysteries. L. T. Meade
Master of Penrose. J. A. Hodge
Master of Phoenix Hall. E. Marlow
Master of Rathkelly. H. Smart
Master of Revels. R. H. Watkins
Master of Shadows. Margery Lawrence
Master of Souls. M. Hansom
Master of the Ceremonies. G. M. Fenn
Master of the Dark. J. Cassells
Master of the Day of Judgment. L. Perutz
Master of the Macabre. R. Thorndike
Master of the Microbe. R. W. Service
Master of the Priory. A. Haynes
Master of the Skies. P. Trent
Master of Trenance. T. W. Speight
Master of Venom. S. Horler
Master Rogue. D. G. Phillips
Master Rogue. C. Somerville
Master Schemer. V. Campbell
Master Spirit. W. Magnay
Master Spy. R. J. Buckley
Master Spy. A. Gask
Master Spy. J. Pendower
Master Stroke. E. C. Derby
Master Timothy's Bookcase. G. W. M. Reynolds
Master Villain. N. Carter
Master Vorst. A. J. Small
Masterful Voice. H. Buchanan
Masterly Trick. N. Carter
Masterman's Mistake. T. Cobb
Masterpiece Affair. K. Royce
Masterpiece in Murder. R. Powell
Masterpiece of Crime. N. Carter
Masterpiece of Nice Mr. Breen. H. Hunvald
Masterpieces of Crime. A. D. Vandam
Masterpieces of Mystery. A. K. Green

Masters Affair. B. Hirschfeld
Masters of Kaolina. E. L. Long
Masters of the Parachute Mail. J. Carr
Masterstroke. J. Tiger
Matador Dies. J. Peyre
Matador's Fortune. J. W. Bobin
Matapan Affair. F. Du Boisgobey
Matapan Jewels. F. Du Boisgobey
Match for a Murderer. D. Halliday
Match Point for Murder. K. Platt
Matched with Mystery. J. A. Jordan
Matchless Detective. Anonymous
Material Witness. E. Messenger
Mathematician. W. Manson
Mathematics of Guilt. I. Ostrander
Mathematics of Murder. K. Bedford
Matheson Fever. J. Easton
Matheson Formula. J. S. Fletcher
Matheson Money. F. Warden
Matilda Hunter Murder. H. S. Keeler
Mating Call. W. Shaw
Mating Cry. A. E. Van Vogt
Mating in the Wilds. O. Binns
Mating of the Blades. A. Abdullah
Matlock Paper. R. Ludlum
Mato Grosso Horror. J. Rosenberger
Matorni's Vineyard. E. P. Oppenheim
Matrimonial Causes. Laurence Kirk
Matrimonial Mixture. C. J. C. Hyne
Matrimony Most Dangerous. L. Cargill
Matsu Dossier. W. Dainton
Matter of Accent. D. Keith
Matter of Blood. B. Whitaker
Matter of Business and other stories. J. Farnol
Matter of Confidence. B. Williams
Matter of Conscience. E. P. Hoyt
Matter of Conviction. E. Hunter
Matter of Diplomacy. W. Tute
Matter of Fact. H. Brean
Matter of Intelligence. G. Wittman
Matter of Iodine. D. Keith
Matter of Love and Death. T. Wells
Matter of Luck and other stories. P. Cheyney
Matter of Mandrake. Barry Norman
Matter of Millions. W. J. Bayfield
Matter of Millions. A. K. Green
Matter of Millions. F. M. White
Matter of Motive. G. Montrose
Matter of Murder. Neill Graham
Matter of Nerves. R. Hull
Matter of Opportunity. C. Arley
Matter of Paradise. B. Meggs
Matter of Policy. Sam Merwin
Matter of Scents. T. Fitzgerald
Matter of Sixpence. J. La Tourrette
Matter of Skill. N. Carter
Matter of Tar. H. C. McNeile
Matter of Taste. R. Lockridge
Matter of Thousands. Old Spicer
Matter of Witchcraft. A. Brennan
Matthew's Hand. C. Larson
Matty Doolin. C. Cookson
Matzohball. S. Weinstein
Maud Blackstone, the Millionaire's Daughter. R. R. Johnston
Maulever Hall. J. A. Hodge
Mauleverer Murders. A. C. Fox-Davies
Maumbury Rings. G. V. McFadden
Maundy. Julian Gloag
Maureen of the Island. Robin Temple
Maureen Versus Fate. R. Rodd
Maurice Mystery. J. E. Cooke
Maurizius Case. J. Wasserman
Mausoleum Key. N. Daniels
Mauve Front Door. L. Meynell
Mavde Baxter. C. C. Hotchkiss
Mawpeth Millions. W. Reynolds
Max. Mrs. G. Sheldon

Max Carrados. E. Bramah
Max Carrados Mysteries. E. Bramah
Max Fargus. O. Johnson
Max Logan. P. Trent
Max Smart and the Ghastly Ghost Affair. W. Johnston
Max Smart and the Perilous Pellets. W. Johnston
Max Smart Loses Control. W. Johnston
Max Smart--The Spy Who Went out to the Cold. W. Johnston
Maxims by a Man of the World. J. Payn
Maximum Game. E. Naughton
Maximus Zone. C. Keane
Maxine. P. Trent
Max's Marriage. E. Gaboriau
Maxwell Mystery. C. Wells
May Day Mystery. O. R. Cohen
May Grayson. T. P. Prest
May We Come Through? and other stories. R. Pertwee
May-Week Murders. D. G. Browne
May You Die in Ireland. M. Kenyon
Maya Temple. D. Daniels
Maybe a Trumpet. S. Harvester
Maybe He's Dead. S. Oakroyd
Maybe It's Murder. A. Barron
Mayday. T. P. McMahon
Mayfair Magician. G. Griffith
Mayfair Murder. H. Holt
Mayfair Mystery. L. Clarke
Mayfair Mystery. H. Holt
Mayfair Mystery. F. Richardson
Mayfair Nights. H. Duval
Mayfair Slayride. H. Janson
Mayhem in B-Flat. Elliot Paul
Mayhem in Greece. D. Wheatley
Maynard's Wives. H. Flowerdew
Mayor Harding of New York. S. Endicott
Mayor on Horseback. E. P. Oppenheim
Mayor's Wife. A. K. Green
Mazaroff Murder. J. S. Fletcher
Mazaroff Mystery. J. S. Fletcher
Maze. P. MacDonald
Maze. E. Orford
Maze of Crime. Anonymous
Maze of Death. P. K. Dick
Maze of Motives. N. Carter
Mazeppa. T. P. Prest
Mazeppa. F. Whishaw
Me and My Ghoul. M. Storm
Me and Rudolph. W. C. Tuttle
Me, Detective. L. T. White
Me--Gangster. C. F. Coe
Me, Hood! M. Spillane
Me Tanner, You Jane. Lawrence Block
Meadows of Tallon. E. Thompson
Mean Streets. T. B. Dewey
Meandering Corpse. R. S. Prather
Meanwhile Back at the Morgue. M. Avallone
Measure for Murder. C. Witting
Measured for Murder. Babs Lee
Meat for Murder. Lange Lewis
Mecca for Murder. S. Marlowe
Mechanic. L. J. Carlino
Mechanic's Son. Old Sleuth
Medal from Pamplona. C. Rougvie
Medallion. L. Johnson
Medallion. G. Sereny
Medbury Fort Murder. G. Limnelius
Meddle with the Mafia. Fiona Sinclair
Meddler and Her Murder. J. Porter

Title Index

Meddlers. C. Rayner
Medea Legend. E. York
Medical Examiner. W. H. A. Carr
Medical Witness. Richard Gordon
Medici Ring. N. St. John
Medicine Lady. L. T. Meade
Medicine Maker. W. C. Tuttle
Medicine-Man. W. C. Tuttle
Mediterranean Caper. G. Brewer
Mediterranean Caper. C. Cussler
Mediterranean Murder. A. Hocking
Mediterranean Murder. Rosa Lambert
Mediterranean Mystery. S. G. Hedges
Mediterranean Mystery. F. E. Wynne
Mediterranean Nights. D. Wheatley
Medium for Murder. G. Compton
Medusa. E. H. Visiak
Medusa Emerald. G. F. Gibbs
Medusa Kiss. M. Woodman
Medusa Touch. P. Van Greenway
Medusa's Head. J. D. Bacon
Meet a Body. J. Decrest
Meet a Body. D. Rutherford
Meet a Dark Stranger. L. Belvedere
Meet a Dark Stranger. T. E. Huff
Meet Desmond Drake. Sea Lion
Meet Doctor Death. R. Trevor
Meet Dr. Morelle. E. Dudley
Meet Dr. Morelle Again. E. Dudley
Meet in Darkness. S. Ransome
Meet Inspector Bourne. R. C. Finney
Meet Me at Philippi. C. Connell
Meet Me at the Morgue. J. R. Macdonald
Meet Me in Darkness. R. E. Banks
Meet Me in the Green Glen. R. P. Warren
Meet Me Tonight. M. Albrand
Meet Mike Desmond. J. V. Nolan
Meet Mr. Callaghan. G. Verner
Meet Mr. Fortune. H. C. Bailey
Meet Morocco Jones. J. Baynes
Meet Morocco Jones in the Case of the Syndicate Hoods. J. Baynes
Meet Murder, My Angel. C. Brown
Meet Nero Wolfe. R. Stout
Meet the Baron. A. Morton
Meet the Don. B. Gray
Meet the Dragon. David Hume
Meet the Dreamer. W. M. Duncan
Meet the Falcon. D. J. Gammon
Meet the Picaroon. J. Cassells
Meet the Rev. G. Pedrick
Meet the Tiger. L. Charteris
Meet You in Munich. R. Jansson
Meeting by Moonlight. R. Knotts
Meeting Her Fate. M. E. Braddon
Meeting in Casa. J. Kershaw
Meeting in Madrid. Dorothy Fletcher
Meeting Place and other stories. J. D. Beresford
Meeting with Murder. M. Lynch
Meg the Lady. T. Gallon
Megacull. D. Hart-Davis
Megan. M. K. Simmons
Megeve Mystery. J. Mowbray
Megstone Plot. A. Garve
Meirovity Plan. H. Arvay
Melamare Mystery. M. Leblanc
Melander's Millions. C. F. Gregg
Melbourne Mystery. J. G. Brandon
Melbourne Mystery. S. J. Stutley
Mellbridge Mystery. A. O. Cooke
Melmoth. C. R. Maturin
Melody Murders. R. Wallace
Melody of Death. T. A. Plummer
Melody of Death. E. Wallace
Melody of Terror. S. Forbes
Melon in the Cornfield. C. Blackstock
Melora. M. G. Eberhart
Melting Man. V. Canning
Melwood Mystery. J. Hay
Melyonen. A. Lowing
Member of Tattersall's. H. Smart
Member's Lobby. K. Thompson
Memo for Murder. D. Wilmer
Memo to a Firing Squad. F. H. Brennan
Memoirs of a Bow Street Runner. Henry Goddard
Memoirs of a Landlady. G. R. Sims
Memoirs of a Veteran Detective. M. Canler
Memoirs of an Aberdeen Detective. J. C. Philip
Memoirs of Arsene Lupin. M. Leblanc
Memoirs of Constantine Dix. B. Pain
Memoirs of J. (Paddy) MacDowell. M. J. Hobbs
Memoirs of Jane Cameron, Female Convict. F. W. Robinson
Memoirs of Monsieur Claude. M. Claude
Memoirs of Murder. R. C. Payes
Memoirs of Schlock Homes. R. L. Fish
Memoirs of Sherlock Holmes. A. C. Doyle
Memoirs of Solar Pons. A. Derleth
Memoirs of Vidocq. Vidocq
Memory Man. C. W. Sanders
Memory of a Scream. D. X. Manners
Memory of Darkness. M. Summerton
Memory of Evil. Marilyn Ross
Memory of Megan. M. Lovell
Memory of Murder. H. Pentecost
Memory of Passion. G. Brewer
Memory of Treason. H. Hossent
Memory of You. M. Richmond
Memos from Purgatory. H. Ellison
Men Are Strange Lovers. A. Rowe
Men Are What Women Make Them. A. Belot
Men Die at Cyprus Lodge. J. Rhode
Men for Counters. G. Fairlie
Men for Pieces. B. Flynn
Men from the Boys. E. Lacy
Men in Blue Glasses. S. P. B. Mais
Men in Her Death. M. Blizard
Men in Her Death. P. Marlowe
Men in Her Death. S. Ransome
Men in Knots. Richard Grant
Men, Maids and Murder. J. Creasey
Men of Affairs. R. Pertwee
Men of Career. J. Lorraine
Men of Mystery. W. Anthony
Men of Silence. J. Forgione
Men of the Bureau. E. Gaboriau
Men of the Mist. G. Stanley
Men on Foot. F. R. Adams
Men on the Dead Man's Chest. C. S. Raymond
Men Who Died Laughing. J. Creasey
Men Who Explained Miracles. J. D. Carr
Men Who Wrought. R. Cullum
Men with the Double Faces. V. Loder
Men with Three Eyes. L. Revell
Men Without Bones and other stories. G. Kersh
Men Without Faces. W. Martyn
Men, Women and Beasts. H. D. Stacpoole
Men, Women and Guns. H. C. McNeile
Menace. L. G. Blochman
Menace! J. Creasey
Menace. The Gordons
Menace. S. Horler
Menace. H. Janson
Menace. R. Keverne
Menace. P. MacDonald
Menace for Dr. Morelle. E. Dudley
Menace from the East. D. Holden
Menace in Siam. M. Corrigan
Menace of Death. E. Churchill
Menace of Li-Sin. N. Vane
Menace of Marble Hill. M. Farnsworth
Menace of the Silent Death. E. J. Murray
Menace of X. A. Kahn
Menace on the Downs. M. Burton
Menace to Mrs. Kershaw. A. Allen
Menacers. D. Hamilton
Menacing Darkness. S. Shulman
Menagerie. C. Cookson
Mendelov Conspiracy. M. Caidin
Mender of Images. N. Lorimer
Mendip Mystery. L. Brock
Mendon Mystery. J. Mary
Mendoza File. C. Matthews
Mene Tekel. A. Groner
Menfreya. V. Holt
Menfreya in the Morning. V. Holt
Menorah Men. L. Davidson
Mental Marvel. F. MacIsaac
Mental Wizard. K. Robeson
Mentons. C. F. R. Hayward
Mephisto Waltz. F. M. Stewart
Mercenaries. J. Harris
Mercenaries. D. E. Westlake
Mercenary. H. Barron
Mercenary. A. Marsden
Merchandise. R. Bridges
Merchandise Murders. A. Richards
Merchant of Menace. K. Bedford
Merchant of Murder. S. Dean
Merchants of Disaster. K. Robeson
Merchant's Secret. J. W. Bobin
Merciless Ladies. Winston Graham
Mercy Flight. A. MacVicar
Mercy of the Court. M. E. Porter
Mere Murder. C. M. Wills
Meredith Legacy. S. A. Salvato
Meredith Mystery. N. S. Lincoln
Merely Man. G. Warden
Merely Michael. M. Somers
Merely Murder. G. Heyer
Merely Players. J. F. Molloy
Merindol. F. Du Boisgobey
Merivale. J. Robertshaw
Meriweather Mystery. K. C. Strahan
Merlewood Mystery. Mrs. J. O. Arnold
Merlin's Forest. M. Wallenstein
Merlin's Furlong. G. Mitchell
Mermaid. O. Martin
Mermaid of Dark Mountain. Melissa Napier
Mermaid on the Rocks. B. Halliday
Merrily to the Grave. K. Sully
Merrivale Mystery. J. Corbett
Merriweather File. L. White
Merry Andrews. Rona Randall
Merry-Go-Round. J. Cowdroy
Merry Go Round. R. M. Stern
Merry-Go-Round of Murder. J. F. Dinneen
Merry Hippo. E. Huxley
Merry Men and other tales. R. L. Stevenson
Merry Mug. H. M. Raleigh
Merry Murder. S. Rubenstein
Merrylees Mystery. R. Goyne
Meryl. W. T. Eldridge
Mesalliance. W. F. Fauley
Mesh. J. Haslette
Meshes of Fear. H. Richards
Meshes of Mischance. G. Wintle
Mesmerists. B. L. Farjeon
Message. H. C. McNeile
Message. L. Tracy
Message Ends. D. Craig
Message from a Corpse. Sam Merwin
Message from a Ghost. Marilyn Ross

Message from a Spy. D. Helwig
Message from Absalom. A. A. Thompson
Message from Hong Kong. M. G. Eberhart
Message from Malaga. H. MacInnes
Message from Marise. P. Kruger
Message from Sirius. C. Jenkins
Message of the Mute Dog. C. M. Russell
Messenger. E. Robins
Messenger from Munich. N. Pierce
Messenger from the Unknown. J. Hawthorne
Messengers of Death. A. West
Messengers of Evil. P. Souvestre
Metal Box. T. Cobb
Metal Flask. B. Thomson
Metal Monster. K. Robeson
Metamorphosis. R. Marsh
Metcalfe Mystery. Elliot Bailey
Meteor Menace. K. Robeson
Methinks the Lady--. G. Endore
Method in His Murder. T. Warriner
Method in Madness. D. M. Disney
Methods of Dr. Scarlett. A. Laing
Methods of Maigret. G. Simenon
Methods of Mr. Ames. F. Carrel
Methods of Sergeant Cluff. G. North
Methods of Uncle Abner. M. D. Post
Methuselah Enzyme. F. M. Stewart
Methylated Murder. C. Robbins
Metropolitan Opera Murders. H. Traubel
Mexican Adventure. L. Oliver
Mexican Bill, the Cowboy Detective. N. Ned
Mexican Deadline. J. Grecco
Mexican Mourning. J. Hedges
Mexican Slayride. T. B. Dewey
Mexican Slay Ride. N. MacNeil
Mexican Slay Ride. S. Weintraub
Mexico Run. L. White
Mezzoni, the Brigand. M. M. Murray
Miami 59. D. Keene
Miami for Murder. B. Sarto
Miami Marauder. M. Barry
Miami Massacre. D. Pendleton
Miami Mayhem. A. Rome
Miami Mob and Mark Kilby Stands Alone. R. C. Frazer
Miami Murder-Go-Round. M. La France
Miami Undercover. E. L. Heyman
Miasma. E. S. Holding
Micah Faraday, Adventurer. L. T. Meade
Mice Are Not Amused. K. Hewitt
Michael and All Angels. N. Lofts
Michael Anonymous. J. M. Scott
Michael Bray. Taffrail
Michael Carmichael. M. Sandys
Michael Cassidy, Sergeant. H. C. McNeile
Michael Dred, Detective. M. Leighton
Michael Durrant. P. Trent
Michael Intervenes. G. Clifford
Michael Shayne Investigates. B. Halliday
Michael Shayne Takes a Hand. B. Halliday
Michael Shayne's 50th Case. B. Halliday
Michael Shayne's Long Chance. B. Halliday
Michael Shayne's Triple Mystery. B. Halliday
Michaelmas Girls. J. B. Barry
Michael's Crag. G. Allen
Michael's Evil Deeds. E. P. Oppenheim
Michael's Wife. M. Millhiser
Mick Cardby Works Overtime. David Hume
Micky's Hide. B. Sarto
Microbe Murders. F. G. Eberhard
Microbe of Crime. N. Carter
Microbe's Kiss. G. Braddon
Microbes of Power. A. Wilson
Mid-Atlantic. Taffrail
Mid-Ocean Tragedy. J. Hawk
Mid the Thick Arrows. M. Pemberton
Midas Coffin. Simon Quinn
Midas Man. K. Robeson
"Midas" Monkhouse, M.F.H. E. Woodward
Midas Touch. J. Boland
Midday Moon. D. Daniels
Middle Class Murder. B. Hamilton
Middle Distance. O. Martin
Middle Kingdom. W. L. Marshall
Middle Link. N. Carter
Middle of Midnight. W. G. Beymer
Middle of the Negro's Head. C. Brisbane
Middle of Things. J. S. Fletcher
Middle Temple Murder. J. S. Fletcher
Middle Wall. Edward Marshall
Middlefold Murders. E. Radford
Midge. P. MacTyre
Midget Marvel. P. Manton
Midnight. O. R. Cohen
Midnight. M. Strange
Midnight Adventure and other stories. J. J. Farjeon
Midnight Alibi. E. Ellison
Midnight and Percy Jones. V. Starrett
Midnight at Mallyncourt. T. E. Huff
Midnight at Mallyncourt. E. Marlow
Midnight at Mears House. H. J. Holt
Midnight Cavalier. R. Armstrong
Midnight Cry. J. M. Parker
Midnight Dancers. A. Maybury
Midnight Eye. M. Roscoe
Midnight Guest. F. M. White
Midnight Hag. J. Fleming
Midnight Hazard. B. Sanders
Midnight Hostess. Griff
Midnight House. Ethel L. White
Midnight House and other tales. W. F. Harvey
Midnight King. G. Delamare
Midnight Lace. W. Drummond
Midnight Lady. G. Leroux
Midnight Lady. H. Parker
Midnight Lady and the Mourning Man. D. Anthony
Midnight Lorry Crime. E. S. Brooks
Midnight Mail. H. Holt
Midnight Male. R. Drayton
Midnight Man. H. Kane
Midnight Men. N. Vane
Midnight Message. N. Carter
Midnight Minute. C. Herbert
Midnight Murder. P. Herring
Midnight Murder. John Morgan
Midnight Murder. K. Robeson
Midnight Murder. R. Rodd
Midnight Murder. D. Stuart
Midnight Mystery. Anonymous
Midnight Mystery. B. Atkey
Midnight Mystery. R. Hardinge
Midnight Mystery. F. Hume
Midnight Never Comes. M. Fallon
Midnight Oak. J. Tattersall
Midnight on the Place Pigalle. M. Dekobra
Midnight Passenger. R. H. Savage
Midnight Patient. E. Hostovsky
Midnight Plumber. M. Procter
Midnight Plus One. G. Lyall
Midnight Queen. Anonymous
Midnight Quest. Old Sleuth
Midnight Road. A. Wood
Midnight Sailing. L. G. Blochman
Midnight Sailing. S. Hufford
Midnight Sister. H. Luger
Midnight Sleep. Frank King
Midnight Special. B. Delannoy
Midnight Surrender. E. Nepean
Midnight Tales. W. F. Harvey
Midnight to High Noon. C. C. Waddell
Midnight Treasure. W. Rollins
Midnight Vigil. Warren Miller
Midnight Walker. Rona Randall
Midnight Walkers. K. Laing
Midnight Webs. G. M. Fenn
Midnight Wireless. C. A. Alington
Midst Balkan Perils. E. S. Brooks
Midsummer Lokki. E. Wuorio
Midsummer Madness. Langdon Dodge
Midsummer Madness. Morley Roberts
Midsummer Malice. N. Fitzgerald
Midsummer Masque. J. Tattersall
Midsummer Mischief. N. Mapple
Midsummer Murder. C. M. Wills
Midsummer Murder. C. Witting
Midsummer Mystery. G. H. Gerould
Midsummer Nightmare. C. Hale
Midsummer's Night Murder. L. Crosby
Midsummer's Nightmare. E. Shenkin
Midway to Murder. M. T. Yates
Miernik Dossier. C. McCarry
Might As Well Be Dead. R. Stout
Mighty Arm. C. Dawe
Mighty Blockhead. F. Gruber
Mignon. J. M. Cain
Mignonette. G. Norway
Mignonette. J. Shearing
Mignon's Peril. J. Middlemass
Mikado Jewel. F. Hume
Miklos Alexandrovitch Is Missing. Anne Edwards
Milady Charlotte. K. Kellow
Milady Took the Rap. H. Janson
Milan Grill Room. E. P. Oppenheim
Mild Case of Murder. G. Brandon
Mildred Arkell. H. Wood
Mildred Pierce. J. M. Cain
Mile-Away Murder. A. Armstrong
Mile Deep Grave. J. Hedges
Mile High. R. Condon
Mile High. H. C. Rowland
Milk Churn Murder. M. Burton
Milk of Human Kindness. E. Ferrars
Milkmaid's Millions. H. Austin
Mill. Mark Allerton
Mill House Murder. J. S. Fletcher
Mill House Mystery. F. Warden
Mill Mystery. A. K. Green
Mill of Fear. L. Bidston
Mill of Many Windows. J. S. Fletcher
Mill of Silence. B. Capes
Mill Pond Mystery. H. E. Hill
Mill Reef Hall. A. Pritchett
Mill Street Mystery. A. Sergeant
Millbank Case. G. D. Eldridge
Miller and His Men. T. P. Prest
Miller's Maid. T. P. Prest
Millie. E. V. Cunningham
Millie Lynn, Shop Investigator. C. H. Bullivant
Milliner's Hat Mystery. B. Thomson
Million a Minute. H. Douglas
Million Dollar Babe. C. Brown
Million Dollar Bloodhound. J. Millard
Million-Dollar Diamond. J. S. Fletcher
Million Dollar Gamble. F. Johnston
Million Dollar Mayhem. K. T. McCall
Million Dollar Murder. T. B. Black
Million Dollar Murder. E. Ronns
Million Dollar Murder. B. Sarto
Million Dollar Mystery. H. MacGrath
Million Dollar Snapshot. H. Howard
Million Dollar Snatch. J. Grecco

Million Dollar Story. E. Wallace
Million Dollar Suitcase. A. MacGowan
Million Dollar Tramp. W. C. Gault
Million Heiress. P. Trent
Million in Diamonds. N. Carter
Million in Diamonds. Old Sleuth
Million in Jewels. Old Sleuth
Million of Money. A. M. Meadows
Million Pound Cipher. R. Pertwee
Million Pound Deposit. E. P. Oppenheim
Million Pounds Reward. F. Lady
Million to Burn. M. S. Jones
Millionaire and the Lady. G. Warden
Millionaire and the Policeman's Wife. O. Harper
Millionaire Baby. A. K. Green
Millionaire Crook. Roland Daniel
Millionaire Detective. C. E. Blaney
Millionaire Gangster. J. Wallace
Millionaire Girl. A. W. Marchmont
Millionaire Mystery. F. Hume
Millionaire Mystery. A. W. Marchmont
Millionaire of Yesterday. E. P. Oppenheim
Millionaire Partner. N. Carter
Millionaire Tramp. S. C. Trebor
Millionaires. H. D. Kastle
Millionaire's Crime. J. K. Stafford
Millionaire's Fate. F. Du Boisgobey
Millionaire's Folly. J. Mooney
Millionaire's Folly. L. E. Smyles
Millionaire's Island. M. Pemberton
Millionaire's Love Story. G. Boothby
Millionaire's Mania. N. Carter
Millionaire's Nest Egg. A. Parsons
Millionaire's Revenge. O. Harper
Millionaire's Son. F. Warden
Millionairess. J. Ralph
Millions at Stake and other stories. N. Carter
Millions for Murder. F. MacIsaac
Millions of Mischief. H. Hill
Millions of Money. L. Clarke
Mills. M. O'Brine
Mills of the Law. N. Carter
Millstone Man. B. Healey
Milly Darrell and other tales. M. E. Braddon
Milly the Actress. A. Askew
Mimic a Murderer. S. H. Courtier
Mind Killers. N. Carter
Mind Killers. Martin Thomas
Mind-Masters. J. F. Rossmann
Mind of Dr. Morelle. E. Dudley
Mind of John Meredith. F. Gerard
Mind of Max Duvine. E. Trevor
Mind of Mr. J. G. Reeder. E. Wallace
Mind Over Murder. R. S. Hastings
Mind Poisoners. N. Carter
Mind Reader. M. Rittenberg
Mind Reader. W. A. Roberts
Mind Readers. M. Allingham
Mind to Murder. A. Clarke
Mind to Murder. P. D. James
Mind-Twisters Affair. Thomas Stratton
Mind Wreckers, Limited, and Other Adventures of Barrow--Ace Insurance Detective. F. J. Price
Mind Your Own Murder. Y. Foldes
Mindanao Pearl. A. Caillou
Mindbenders. J. Quinn
Mindy Lindy May Surprise. M. Erlanger
Mine. R. Jeffery
Mine Enemy My Friend. T. B. Morris
Mine in the Desert. D. Footman
Mine Is the Power. J. Lukens
Mine of Ill Omen. H. Lea
Mine Own Executioner. N. Balchin
Mine Sinister Host. W. W. Sayer
Mine to Avenge. T. Wills
Miner Detective. Anonymous

Minerva Stone. A. Maybury
Ming Vase Mystery. R. Dark
Ming Yellow. J. P. Marquand
Mini-Murders. C. Brown
Mini-Skirt Murders. Martin Thomas
Miniatures Frame. K. Royce
Minion of the Moon. T. W. Speight
Minister of Evil. W. LeQueux
Minister of Injustice. M. Culpan
Minister of Police. H. Mountjoy
Ministers of Vengeance. R. E. Conot
Ministers Too Are Mortal. F. Duncan
Ministry Murder. C. Dixon
Ministry of Fear. G. Greene
Mink and Murder. H. Holt
Mink-Lined Coffin. Jonathan Latimer
Mink Steel. M. Dedina
Minkie. L. Tracy
Minnesota Gothic. W. O'Meara
Minnie Santangelo's Mortal Sin. A. Mancini
Minor Operation. J. J. Connington
Minor Operation. Taffrail
Minority. F. T. Hill
Minos Magnificent. G. Seton
Minotaur Country. H. McCloy
Minotaur Garden. L. Hosegood
Minot's Folly. R. S. Holland
Mint Mystery. W. J. Bayfield
Minus a Shamus. Anthony Graham
Minus Man. R. Maxwell
Minus One Corpse. J. Cleveland
Minus X. S. Gluck
Minute for Murder. N. Blake
Minute Mysteries. A. Ripley
Minuteman Murder. J. Langton
Minutes of a Murder. M. Polland
Minutes to Impact. M. Gray
Minx Goes to the Front. C. N. Williamson
Minx Is Murder. C. Brown
Mirabilis Diamond. J. Odlum
Mirabil's Island. L. Tracy
Miracle Gold. R. Dowling
Miracle in the Drawing Room. E. Greenwood
Miracle Man. F. Packard
Mirador Collection. B. Flynn
Mirage. W. Ericson
Mirage. P. P. Muir
Miranda. J. Blackmore
Miranda. M. E. Braddon
Miranda. C. Larner
Miranda Clair. Phyllis Ross
Miranda Must Die. H. Calvin
Miranda Said Murder. M. Carroll
Miranda's Curse. Dorinne Moore
Miriam Lemaire, Money Lender. C. Stanton
Miriam Rozella. B. L. Farjeon
Mirk Abbey. J. Payn
Miro. S. Herron
Miro Papers. S. Herron
Mirror. E. C. Reed
Mirror and Knife. J. Rosenberg
Mirror Crack'd. A. Christie
Mirror Crack'd from Side to Side. A. Christie
Mirror Dance. E. Kyle
Mirror Image. M. Sadler
Mirror Lies. G. Vaizey
Mirror, Mirror on the Wall. S. Ellin
Mirror Murder. L. Z. Adams
Mirror of a Dead Lady. H. D. Irvine
Mirror of Delusion. M. Reisner
Mirror of Hell. L. Holton

Mirror of Silver. R. Bridges
Mirror Room. C. Landon
Mirror Train. J. N. Chance
Mirrored Murder. A. W. Eyles
Mis-Rule of Three. F. Warden
Misadventures of Athelstan Digby. W. F. Harvey
Misadventures of Mr. Larkin. D. Lynn
Miscarriage of Justice. N. Carter
Miscarriage of Justice. C. Kingston
Miscarriage of Murder. J. F. Straker
Miscast for Murder. R. Fenisong
Mischief. C. Armstrong
Mischief. B. A. Williams
Mischief in the Lane. A. Derleth
Mischief in the Offing. C. Witting
Mischief-Maker. E. P. Oppenheim
Mischief of a Glove. P. C. De Crespigny
Mischief Past. E. Thompson
Miser Farebrother. B. L. Farjeon
Miser Hoadley's Secret. A. W. Marchmont
Miser of Shoreditch. T. P. Prest
Miser's Money. E. Phillpotts
Miser's Will. F. Hume
Misfit. G. B. Savi
Misfits. G. F. Forrest
Misfortunes of Mr. Teal. L. Charteris
Misguided Angel. R. Angel
Misguided Missile. O. Mills
Misleading Lady. A. Wood
Misplaced Corpse. S. Rider
Misprision of Felony. Seaforth
Miss Agatha. H. L. V. Fletcher
Miss Agatha Doubles for Death. H. L. V. Fletcher
Miss Arnott's Marriage. R. Marsh
Miss Bantling Is Missing. J. W. Meagher
Miss Betty's Mistake. A. Sergeant
Miss Blake's Husband. E. Jordan
Miss Bones. J. Fleming
Miss Bracegirdle and others. S. Aumonier
Miss Brandt. Margery Lawrence
Miss Brown of X.Y.O. E. P. Oppenheim
Miss Cadogna. J. Hawthorne
Miss Callaghan Comes to Grief. J. H. Chase
Miss Called Murder. C. Brown
Miss Cayley's Adventures. G. Allen
Miss Devereux of the Mariquita. R. H. Savage
Miss Dividends. A. C. Gunter
Miss Doll, Go Home. D. Markson
Miss Dynamite. B. Gray
Miss Fenny. C. Blackstock
Miss Ferriby's Clients. F. Warden
Miss Frances Baird, Detective. R. W. Kauffman
Miss from S.I.S. R. Tralins
Miss Gascoigne. J. H. Riddell
Miss Gloria Gets Wise. E. Ellison
Miss Hamblett's Ghost. A. Brock
Miss Hogg and the Bronte Murders. A. Lee
Miss Hogg and the Covent Garden Murders. A. Lee
Miss Hogg and the Dead Dean. A. Lee
Miss Hogg and the Missing Sisters. A. Lee
Miss Hogg and the Squash Club Murder. A. Lee
Miss Hogg Flies High. A. Lee
Miss Hogg's Last Case. A. Lee
Miss Hurd. A. K. Green
Miss Ivory White. R. Haggard
Miss Madelyn Mack, Detective. H. C. Weir
Miss Maitland, Private Secretary. G. Bonner

M

Miss Maitland's Spy. G. A. Birmingham
Miss Malevolent. C. R. Gull
Miss Marple and the Thirteen Problems. A. Christie
Miss Martha Mary Crawford. C. Marchant
Miss Melbourn's Million. N. Penley
Miss Mephistopheles. F. Hume
Miss Merewether's Money. T. Cobb
Miss Milverton. A. Hocking
Miss Mitchell. H. Brooke
Miss Mystery. S. Horler
Miss Nobody of Nowhere. A. C. Gunter
Miss or Mrs? W. Collins
Miss Otis Blows Town. B. Sarto
Miss Otis Comes to Piccadilly. B. Sarto
Miss Otis Desires. B. Sarto
Miss Otis Gets Fresh. B. Sarto
Miss Otis Goes French. B. Sarto
Miss Otis Goes Up. B. Sarto
Miss Otis Has a Daughter. B. Sarto
Miss Otis Hits Back. B. Sarto
Miss Otis Makes a Date. B. Sarto
Miss Otis Makes Hay. B. Sarto
Miss Otis Moves In. B. Sarto
Miss Otis Plays Ball. B. Sarto
Miss Otis Plays Eve. B. Sarto
Miss Otis Relents. B. Sarto
Miss Otis Says Yes. B. Sarto
Miss Otis Takes the Rap. B. Sarto
Miss Otis Throws a Come-Back. B. Sarto
Miss Pauline of New York. St. George Rathborne
Miss Pegham. P. Conway
Miss Pill Is Missing. L. Gershe
Miss Pink at the Edge of the World. G. Moffat
Miss Pinkerton. M. R. Rinehart
Miss Pinnegar Disappears. Anthony Gilbert
Miss Private Eye. G. Batson
Miss Pym Disposes. J. Tey
Miss Rayburn's Diamonds. R. Jocelyn
Miss Rolling Stone. P. Loring
Miss Schuyler's Alias. G. Horton
Miss Seeton Bewitched. H. Carvic
Miss Seeton Draws the Line. H. Carvic
Miss Seeton Sings. H. Carvic
Miss Shumway Waves a Wand. J. H. Chase
Miss Silver Comes to Stay. P. Wentworth
Miss Silver Deals with Death. P. Wentworth
Miss Silver Intervenes. P. Wentworth
Miss Silver's Past. J. Skvorecky
Miss Turquoise. G. B. Mair
Miss White of Mayfair. G. W. Appleton
Miss Withers Regrets. S. Palmer
Miss X. S. Kyle
Missed It by That Much. W. Johnston
Missile. A. MacKenzie
Missile Mob. H. Janson
Missing! M. Avallone
Missing. M. Halliday
Missing. E. Hostovsky
Missing! S. Kyle
Missing! F. E. Penny
Missing--A Lady. N. MacKenzie
Missing--A Young Girl. F. Warden
Missing Ace. W. H. L. Crauford
Missing Agent. M. Annesley
Missing! and other tales. M. C. Hay
Missing Archduke. G. Leroux
Missing at Lloyds. G. H. Teed
Missing Aunt. G. D. H. Cole
Missing Background. L. Cargill
Missing Bank Manager. M. Poole
Missing Banker. C. Brandon
Missing Baronet. G. D. H. Cole
Missing, Believed Dead. N. MacKenzie
Missing Body. Roland Daniel
Missing Book-Keeper. C. Keith
Missing Bracelet. I. Stark
Missing Bride. E. Southworth
Missing Bridegroom. J. K. Leys
Missing Bullet. Warren Miller
Missing Cashier. E. D. Pierson
Missing Chancellor. J. S. Fletcher
Missing Chauffeur. H. C. McNeile
Missing Clue. C. Dawe
Missing Cotton King. N. Carter
Missing Cyclist and other stories. B. Delannoy
Missing Delora. E. P. Oppenheim
Missing Deputy Chief. N. Carter
Missing Doctor. R. J. Fletcher
Missing Elizabeth. A. Sergeant
Missing Finger. A. Boissiere
Missing Formula. J. Decrest
Missing from Her Home. Anthony Gilbert
Missing from His Home. Mark Cross
Missing from His Home. C. Hosken
Missing from His Home. J. R. Warren
Missing from Home. S. Green
Missing from Home. M. Halliday
Missing from Monte Carlo. B. Malim
Missing from the Shelf. M. Salkeld
Missing Gates. R. Francis Foster
Missing Grandfather. F. Y. McHugh
Missing Grave. M. Dalman
Missing Heiress. Bernice Carey
Missing Heiress. Roland Daniel
Missing Hoard. J. Creasey
Missing Hour. J. Blackmore
Missing Husband and other tales. G. R. Sims
Missing in Mexico. J. N. Pentelow
Missing Initial. N. S. Lincoln
Missing Lady. Roland Daniel
Missing Letter. H. Wood
Missing Link. K. Farrer
Missing Link. G. Varney
Missing Link. C. Wells
Missing Man. N. Carter
Missing Man. H. Sutherland Edwards
Missing Man. M. R. Hatch
Missing Man. H. Waugh
Missing Masterpiece. H. Belloc
Missing Matisse. B. Levy
Missing Mayor. T. S. King
Missing Men. G. Leroux
Missing Men. A. Skene
Missing Million. A. Askew
Missing Million. E. H. Burrage
Missing Million. G. Stanley
Missing Million. E. Wallace
Missing Millionaire. Christopher Wilson
Missing Miniature. E. Kastner
Missing Minx. R. Goyne
Missing Miss Randolph. M. Leighton
Missing Money-Lender. W. S. Sykes
Missing Note. Mrs. G. Corbett
Missing or Dead. G. Ashe
Missing or Murdered. R. Forsythe
Missing Partner. J. M. Cobban
Missing Partner. H. M. Stephenson
Missing Partners. Henry Wade
Missing Person. O. Millard
Missing Piece. P. C. De Crespigny
Missing, Presumed Dead. C. Keith
Missing Rajah. R. Gilmour
Missing Rope. C. Carnac
Missing Rubies. F. Du Boisgobey
Missing Scapegoat. B. Cobb
Missing Ships. A. Murray
Missing Spy. W. W. Sayer
Missing Treaty. C. Dawe
Missing Two. B. Reynolds
Missing Tycoon. H. B. Taylor
Missing Widow. Anthony Gilbert
Missing Witness. F. Barrett
Missing Witness. M. E. Braddon
Missing Witness. I. Cabot
Missing Witness. N. Daniels
Missing Witness. J. M. Hickman
Missing Witness. J. Reach
Missing Witness. D. W. Spurgeon
Mission Accomplished. J. Walker
Mission for Betty Smith. Brian Cooper
Mission for Vengeance. P. Rabe
Mission House Murder. Hank Hobson
Mission Impossible. J. Tiger
Mission in Black. G. Cotler
Mission in Guemo. S. B. Hough
Mission in Sparrow Brush Lane. A. Stanford
Mission in Tunis. J. Pendower
Mission into Auschwitz. K. Netzen
Mission of Death. M. T. Walworth
Mission of Doom. Gwyn Evans
Mission of Fear. G. H. Coxe
Mission of Menace. R. Hardinge
Mission of Mercy. J. Robb
Mission of Mercy. D. Torr
Mission of Murder. R. Charles
Mission of Vengeance. R. Hardinge
Mission: Police Action. M. Kurland
Mission River Justice. W. C. Tuttle
Mission: Tank War. M. Kurland
Mission: Third Force. M. Kurland
Mission to Beirut. E. Mannin
Mission to Majorca. I. Mercer
Mission to Malaspiga. Evelyn Anthony
Mission to Mexico. Arthur MacLean
Mission to Murder. R. Glendinning
Mission to Siena. R. Marshall
Mission to Vengeance. N. Carter
Mission to Venice. R. Marshall
Missioner. E. P. Oppenheim
Mississippi Outlaws and the Detectives. A. Pinkerton
Mist of Darkness. V. Coffman
Mist of Error. M. A. Dickens
Mist on the Saltings. Henry Wade
Mist on the Waters. F. L. Green
Mist over Talla. A. E. Lindop
Mistake Me Not. N. Easton
Mistakenly in Mallorca. R. Jeffries
Mr. Ace. H. Christy
Mr. Allen. H. A. Vachell
Mr. & Mrs. North. Owen Davis
Mr. & Mrs. North and the Poisoned Playboy. F. Lockridge
Mr. & Mrs. North Meet Murder. F. Lockridge
Mr. Angel Comes Aboard. C. G. Booth
Mr. Arkadin. O. Welles
Mr. Babbacombe Dies. M. Burton
Mr. Balkram's Band. Frank King
Mr. Ball of Fire. B. Gray
Mr. Barnes, American. A. C. Gunter
Mr. Barnes of New York. A. C. Gunter
Mr. Bazalgette's Agent. L. Merrick
Mr. Benson's Business. Elliot Bailey
Mr. Big. M. Kenyon
Mister Big. G. Verner
Mr. Billingham, the Marquis and Madelon. E. P. Oppenheim
Mr. Birdsall Breezes Through. W. H. Mack
Mr. Blessington's Imperialist Plot. J. Sherwood
Mr. Blessington's Plot. J. Sherwood
Mr. Bobadil. F. Beeding

Title Index

Mr. Bowling Buys a Newspaper. D. Henderson
Mr. Braddy's Safe and other humorous tales. R. Connell
Mister Brown's Bodies. J. Blackburn
Mr. Buckby Is Not at Home. John Gloag
Mr. Budd Again. G. Verner
Mr. Budd Investigates. G. Verner
Mr. Burnside's Responsibility. T. Cobb
Mr. Byculla. E. Linklater
Mr. Campion and Others. M. Allingham
Mr. Campion: Criminologist. M. Allingham
Mr. Campion's Falcon. Y. Carter
Mr. Campion's Farthing. Y. Carter
Mr. Campion's Quarry. Y. Carter
Mr. Capon. Jenni Hall
Mr. Caution--Mr. Callaghan. P. Cheyney
Mr. Chang of Scotland Yard. A. E. Apple
Mr. Chang's Crime Ray. A. E. Apple
Mr. Christopoulos. C. Blackstock
Mr. Clackworthy. C. B. Booth
Mr. Clackworthy, Con Man. C. B. Booth
Mr. Clerihew: Wine Merchant. W. Allen
Mr. Clunk's Text. H. C. Bailey
Mr. Collin Is Ruined. F. Heller
Mr. Commissioner Sanders. E. Wallace
Mr. Cooper's Frederika. L. M. Robertson
Mr. Coroner Presides. S. Truss
Mr. Cromwell Is Dead. L. Ford
Mr. Cronk's Cases. W. A. Darlington
Mr. Crook Lifts the Mask. Anthony Gilbert
Mr. Daddy-Detective. C. Brooks
Mr. Dass. B. Atkey
Mr. Death. C. Wallace
Mr. Death Walks Abroad. C. Wallace
Mr. Denning Drives North. Alec Coppel
Mr. Diabolo. A. Lejeune
Mr. Digweed & Mr. Lumb. E. Phillpotts
Mr. Dorillon. J. Middlemass
Mr. Dovecourt's Decoy. H. Tuite
Mr. Dunton's Invention, and other stories. J. Hawthorne
Mr. Essington in Love. J. S. Clouston
Mr. Evans. C. A. Alington
Mr. Fairlie's Final Journey. A. Derleth
Mr. Faraday's Formula. D. O. Woodbury
Mr. Fortescue. W. Westall
Mr. Fortune Explains. H. C. Bailey
Mr. Fortune Finds a Pig. H. C. Bailey
Mr. Fortune Here. H. C. Bailey
Mr. Fortune Objects. H. C. Bailey
Mr. Fortune, Please. H. C. Bailey
Mr. Fortune Speaking. H. C. Bailey
Mr. Fortune Wonders. H. C. Bailey
Mr. Fortune's Practice. H. C. Bailey
Mr. Fortune's Trials. H. C. Bailey
Mr. Forty-Five. R. Angel
Mr. Grantley's Idea. J. E. Cooke
Mr. Grex of Monte Carlo. E. P. Oppenheim
Mr. Guelpa. V. Thompson
Mr. Hedley's Private Hell. P. Barrington
Mr. Hercules. Gwyn Evans
Mr. Hire's Engagement. G. Simenon
Mr. Holmes and the Fair Armenian. C. V. Bark
Mr. Holmes and the Love Bank. C. V. Bark
Mr. Holmes at Sea. C. V. Bark
Mr. Holmes Goes to Ground. C. V. Bark
Mr. Holroyd Takes a Holiday. W. Stanley
Mr. Horrocks, Purser. C. J. C. Hyne
Mr. Hoyland Looks Round. P. C. Williams
Mr. J. G. Reeder Returns. E. Wallace
Mr. Jackson. H. Green
Mr. Jelly's Business. A. W. Upfield
Mr. Justice. A. Wilson
Mr. Justice Maxell. E. Wallace
Mr. Justice Philbank. P. Trent
Mr. Justice Raffles. E. W. Hornung
Mr. Kettle, Third Mate. C. J. C. Hyne
Mr. Kilmer Sees Red. P. Urquhart
Mr. Laxworthy's Adventures. E. P. Oppenheim
Mr. Lessingham Goes Home. E. P. Oppenheim
Mr. Lucky. Albert Conroy
Mr. Lyndon at Liberty. V. Bridges
Mr. Majestyk. E. Leonard
Mr. Malcolm Presents. G. Fairlie
Mr. Marlow Chooses Wine. J. Bentley
Mr. Marlow Stops for Brandy. J. Bentley
Mr. Marlow Takes to Rye. J. Bentley
Mr. Marx's Secret. E. P. Oppenheim
Mr. Meeson's Will. H. R. Haggard
Mr. Merston's Money. J. Welcome
Mr. Midnight. G. Verner
Mr. Mirakel. E. P. Oppenheim
Mr. Moon's Last Case. B. Patten
Mr. Mortimer Gets the Jitters. B. Gray
Mr. Moto Is So Sorry. J. P. Marquand
Mr. Moto Takes a Hand. J. P. Marquand
Mr. Munt Carries On. H. Clevely
Mr. Murray and the Boococks. W. F. Harvey
Mr. Nelson's Ladies. S. Styles
Mr. Nemesis. J. H. Vahey
Mr. Nobody of England. A. Soutar
Mr. Parker Pyne, Detective. A. Christie
Mr. Passingham. T. Cobb
Mr. Pendlebury and the Suicide Club. A. Webb
Mr. Pendlebury Makes a Catch. A. Webb
Mr. Pendlebury's Hat Trick. A. Webb
Mr. Pendlebury's Second Case. A. Webb
Mr. Pennington Barges In. J. G. Brandon
Mr. Pennington Comes Through. J. G. Brandon
Mr. Pennington Goes Nap. J. G. Brandon
Mr. Pennington Sees Red. J. G. Brandon
Mr. Penny. M. Moiseiwitsch
Mr. Penny at War. M. Moiseiwitsch
Mr. Penny Comes Down Heads. M. Moiseiwitsch
Mr. Pepper, Investigator. B. Thomson
Mr. Perkins of New Jersey. G. Parker
Mr. Peters. R. Stephens
Mr. Pidgeon's Island. A. Berkeley
Mr. Pinkerton and the Old Angel. D. Frome
Mr. Pinkerton at the Old Angel. D. Frome
Mr. Pinkerton Finds a Body. D. Frome
Mr. Pinkerton Goes to Scotland Yard. D. Frome
Mr. Pinkerton Grows a Beard. D. Frome
Mr. Pinkerton Has the Clue. D. Frome
Mr. Pinkerton: Passage for One. D. Frome
Mr. Polton Explains. R. A. Freeman
Mr. Potter of Texas. A. C. Gunter
Mr. Pottermack's Oversight. R. A. Freeman
Mr. Preed Investigates. Ladbroke Black
Mr. Preed's Gangster. Ladbroke Black
Mr. Preston's Daughter. T. Cobb
Mr. Priestley's Problem. A. B. Cox
Mr. Punt of Chelsea. H. G. Hutchinson
Mister Q33. G. Goodchild
Mr. Quentin Investigates. A. Morton
Mr. Quixley of the Gate House. P. Brebner
Mr. Ramosi. V. Williams
Mr. Reeder Returns. E. Wallace
Mr. Sandeman Loses His Life. E. P. Healey
Mister Scipio. T. Gates
Mr. Sefton, Murderer. F. W. Crofts
Mr. Simpson Finds a Body. D. Frome
Mr. Smith's Hat. H. Reilly
Mr. Snoop Is Murdered. J. Reach
Mr. South Burned His Mouth. G. Nyland
Mr. Spenyard's Two Experiments. T. W. Speight
Mr. Spirket Reforms. T. E. B. Clarke
Mr. Splitfoot. H. McCloy
Mr. Standfast. J. Buchan
Mr. Stimpson and Mr. Gorse. P. Hamilton
Mr. Strang. C. J. Daly
Mister Target. W. Harrington
Mr. Three. W. Butler
Mr. Tolefree's Reluctant Witnesses. R. A. J. Walling
Mr. Treadgold Cuts In. V. Williams
Mr. Trouble. W. Ard
Mr. Tutt Comes Home. A. Train
Mr. Tutt Finds a Way. A. Train
Mr. Tutt Takes the Stand. A. Train
Mr. Tutt's Case Book. A. Train
Mister Violence. V. Warren
Mr. Walker Wants to Know. E. Dudley
Mr. Watson Intervenes. D. Gardiner
Mr. Westerby Missing. M. Burton
Mr. Whimset Buys a Gun. B. Graeme
Mr. Whipple Explains. G. Verner
Mr. Wingrave, Millionaire. E. P. Oppenheim
Mr. Wray's Cash Box. W. Collins
Mr. Wu. L. J. Miln
Mr. X. C. Brooks
Mr. Zero. P. Wentworth
Mistigris. B. G. Quin
Mistress. C. Brown
Mrs. Balfame. G. Atherton
Mrs. Belfort's Strategem. T. Cobb
Mrs. Blarney from Ireland. C. E. Blaney
Mrs. Brown on the Tichborne Case. A. Sketchley
Mrs. Brown's Pearls. A. Crabb
Mistress Devon. V. Coffman
Mrs. Dimmock's Worries. B. L. Farjeon
Mrs. Donald Dyke, Detective. H. Rockwood
Mistress Dorothy Marvin. J. C. Snaith
Mrs. Druse's Case, and Maggie Houghtaling. Anonymous
Mrs. Dunbar's Secret. A. St. Aubyn
Mrs. Erricker's Reputation. T. Cobb
Mrs. Fitzherbert. G. W. M. Reynolds
Mrs. Fuller. Marguerite Bryant
Mrs. Gainsborough's Diamonds. J. Hawthorne
Mrs. Gray's Past. H. Flowerdew
Mrs. Greet's Story of the Golden Owl. Mrs. Greet
Mrs. Greystone--Murdered. Roland Daniel
Mrs. Grundy's Victim. G. Corbett
Mrs. Halliburton's Troubles. H. Wood
Mrs. Homicide. D. Keene
Mrs. Isaac. B. L. Farjeon
Mrs. John Foster. C. Granville
Mrs. Jonathan Abroad. George Hastings
Mrs. Knox's Profession. Jessica Mann
Mrs. Latham's Extravagance. T. Cobb
Mrs. Lygon's Husband. A. Sergeant
Mrs. McGinty's Dead. A. Christie
Mrs. Maitland's Affair. M. Lynn
Mrs. Marden's Ordeal. J. Hay
Mrs. Meeker's Money. D. M. Disney
Mrs. Munck. E. Leffland
Mistress Murder. P. Cheyney
Mistress Murder. B. Picton
Mrs. Murdock Takes a Case. G. H. Coxe
Mrs. Murphy's Underpants. F. Brown
Mrs. Musgrave--and Her Husband. R. Marsh
Mistress of Bonaventure. H. Bindloss
Mistress of Devil's Manor. F. Stevenson
Mistress of Falcon Hill. D. Daniels

Mistress of Farrondale. D. Nile
Mistress of Fear. H. Janson
Mistress of Ghosthaven. J. Bellamy
Mistress of Horror House. W. Woody
Mistress of Mellyn. V. Holt
Mistress of Moorwood Manor. Marilyn Ross
Mistress of Orion Hall. Claudette Nicole
Mistress of Ravenstone. M. Heath
Mistress of Ravenswood. Clarissa Ross
Mistress of Ravenswood. Marilyn Ross
Mistress of Tara. C. Laffeaty
Mistress of the Moor. A. Clements
Mrs. Pollifax, Spy. D. Gilman
Mrs. Pomeroy's Reputation. T. Cobb
Mrs. Pym of Scotland Yard. N. Morland
Mrs. Raffles. J. K. Bangs
Mrs. Sparks of Paris. A. C. Bond
Mrs. Starr Lives Alone. J. Godden
Mrs. Tenterden. Margerie Scott
Mistress to Murder. R. Dietrich
Mrs. Vanderstein's Jewels. C. Bryce
Mrs. Vannock. A. Griffin
Mrs. Waldegrave's Will and other tales. Inspector F
Mrs. Warrender's Profession. G. D. H. Cole
Mrs. Whiston's Party. T. Cobb
Mrs. Winterton's Rebellion. J. Dering
Mrs. W's Last Sandwich. E. Denby
Mrs. Wylde. L. Gardiner
Mists Came Down. E. Backhouse.
Mists of Dark Harbor. C. Ross
Mists of Fear. J. Creasey
Mists of Memory. C. Cookson
Mists of Mourning. S. Somers
Mists of Treason. J. N. Chance
Misty Curtain. L. Cores
Misty Pathway. H. Desmond
Mitcham Murder Mystery. G. H. Teed
Mitre Court. J. H. Riddell
Mix Me a Person. J. T. Story
Mix Yourself a Redhead. C. Williams
Mixed Bags. S. C. Westerham
Mixed-Up Mess. N. Carter
Mixer. E. Wallace
Mizmaze. M. Fitt
Moab Is My Washpot. E. G. Cousins
Moat Farm Mystery. M. E. Cooke
Moat House Mystery. B. M. Clay
Moat House Mystery. R. Francis Foster
Mob Says Murder. Albert Conroy
Mobile Library Murders. J. Austwick
Mobsmen on the Spot. M. Grant
Mobster. F. Arrigio
Mobster. J. Roeburt
Moccasin Men. John Ross
Moccasin Murders. K. Perkins
Mockery in Arms. J. Aldridge
Mocking Face of Murder. S. Horler
Moday Mystery. M. E. Hively
Model Corpse. M. B. Clark
Model Father. D. C. Murray
Model for Murder. P. Campion
Model for Murder. J. Fast
Model for Murder. R. Kyle
Model for Murder. S. Marlowe
Model for Murder. Jeanne Wilson
Model for the Toff. J. Creasey
Model in Mayhem. H. Janson
Model Is Murdered. Babs Lee
Model of No Virtue. C. Brown
Model Town and the Detectives. A. Pinkerton
Modeled in Murder. Manning Long
Moderate Murderer and The Honest Quack. G. K. Chesterton
Modern Cameos. A. Mills
Modern Circe. Maurice Scott
Modern Corsair. R. H. Savage
Modern Delilah. B. Bolt

Modern Dick Whittington. J. Payn
Modern Magician. J. F. Molloy
Modern Man-Hunt. P. H. Lockwood
Modern Mercenary. K. Prichard
Modern Portia. P. Trent
Modern Prometheus. E. P. Oppenheim
Modern Quixote. August Berkeley
Modern Robyn Hood. M. M. Bodkin
Modern Sorceress. I. Stark
Modern Ulysses. J. Hatton
Modern Wizard. R. Ottolengui
Modesty Blaise. P. O'Donnell
Mogul Men. P. Leslie
Mohawks. M. E. Braddon
Mohune's Nine Lives. P. Groom
Moina. L. L. Lynch
Moles of Death. J. Dellbridge
Mollie the Handful. F. Warden
Molls Mean Murder. Griff
Molly and the Confidence Man. S. Overholser
Molly Maguires. James O'Neill
Molly Maguires and the Detectives. A. Pinkerton
Molly on the Spot. Frank King
Molly's Aunt at Angmering. H. C. McNeile
Molly's Husband. R. Marsh
Molting Season. C. Ferguson
Moment. E. Davies
Moment After. R. Buchanan
Moment After. V. Tracy
Moment for Murder. A. Eichler
Moment for Murder. L. Marshall
Moment in Time. J. Wellard
Moment More. J. Laing
Moment of Danger. D. MacKenzie
Moment of Decision. S. B. Hough
Moment of Madness. C. J. Bellamy
Moment of Need. M. Coombs
Moment of Truth. W. M. Goeney
Moment of Truth. L. Snow
Moment of Untruth. E. Lacy
Moment of Violence. G. H. Coxe
Moment on Ice. N. Easton
Moment to Moment. Alec Coppel
Momentary Stoppage. A. F. Grey
Moment's Error. A. W. Marchmont
Mona. Lawrence Block
Monastery Mystery. G. Chester
Moncasket Mystery and How Tom Hardy Solved It. S. Marlow
Moncrieff. I. Holland
Monday Never Came. C. Ryland
Monday Night. K. Boyle
Monday Night Murder. R. Trevor
Monday the Rabbi Took Off. H. Kemelman
Mondo. A. De Stefano
Moneta Papers. J. Messmann
"Money." M. Leighton
Money Barons. J. H. Vahey
Money Buys Everything. Roy Vickers
Money by Menaces. S. Adams
Money for Murder. H. Carmichael
Money for Murder. Neill Graham
Money for the Taking. D. M. Disney
Money from Holme. M. Innes
Money from Rome. R. Holt
Money Goes Round and Round. J. T. Story
Money Harvest. Ross Thomas
Money Jugglers. B. Wayde
Money Lender. B. Delannoy
Money-Lender in Gloves. F. Blane
Money Means Murder. L. Marshall
Money Moon. J. Farnol
Money Movers. D. Minchin
Money Murder. J. Ingersol
Money, Murder and the McNeills. T. Du Bois

Money Murders. Eugene Franklin
Money Musk. C. Wells
Money Musk. B. A. Williams
Money on Murder. H. Gardiner
Money on the Black. A. MacKinnon
Money Order Murder. Stafford Edwards
Money People. L. Katcher
Money Sense. P. Trent
Money Spider. M. Leighton
Money-Spider. W. LeQueux
Money Spinners. S. Murray
Money Spinners and other stories. A. Soutar
Money That Money Can't Buy. J. Munro
Money to Burn. W. Douglas
Money to Burn. R. W. Kauffman
Money to Burn. H. Woodward
Money Trap. L. White
Money Walks. J. J. Farjeon
Money with Menaces and To the Public Danger. P. Hamilton
Money's Worth of Murder. C. Conrad
Mongol Mask. David St. John
Mongolian Interlude. L. Oliver
Mongolian Mystery. G. Collins
Mongo's Back in Town. E. R. Johnson
Monique. D. Blankfort
Monitor Affair. C. B. Kelland
Monk. M. G. Lewis
Monk of Cruta. E. P. Oppenheim
Monk of Hambleton. A. Livingston
Monkey and the Tiger. R. Van Gulik
Monkey Boat. N. Trott
Monkey Game. G. Kent
Monkey Murder, and other Hildegarde Withers stories. S. Palmer
Monkey on a Chain. C. Blackstock
Monkey on a Chain. E. J. Lanham
Monkey-Puzzle. B. Von Hutten
Monkey Trick. J. E. Gurdon
Monkey Wrench. J. Griffith
Monkey Wrench Gang. E. Abbey
Monkhurst Case. A. Stanley
Monkhurst Murder. F. Grierson
Monk's Bridge Mystery. W. G. Borth
Monk's Court. K. W. Eyre
Monk's Croft Mystery. T. S. King
Monk's Hollow. John Marsh
Monk's Hood Murders. L. Edgley
Monk's Retreat. Susannah Curtis
Monk's Treasure. G. Horton
Monksglade Mystery. H. Hill
Monkshood. E. Phillpotts
Monocled Man. J. Ronald
Monocled Monster. H. S. Keeler
Monomark Mystery. L. Carlton
Monopoly Menace. J. Hunter
Monopoly to Murder. R. Magowan
Monsieur Blackshirt. D. Graeme
Monsieur Brunner. D. A. Grant
Monsieur Faux-Pas. Rosa Lambert
Monsieur Jonquelle, Prefect of Police. M. D. Post
Monsieur Judas. F. Hume
Monsieur la Souris. G. Simenon
Monsieur Lecoq. E. Gaboriau
Monsieur Monde Vanishes. G. Simenon
Monsieur X. R. W. Sneddon
Monsieur Zenith. A. Skene
Monsieur Zero. N. Tom-Gallon
Monsoon Murder. Brian Cooper
Monster. H. Hext

Title Index

Monster. E. Saltus
Monster Club. R. Chetwynd-Hayes
Monster in the Pool. A. Livingston
Monster of Dagenham Hall. J. Corbett
Monster of Grammont. G. Goodchild
Monster of Lazy Hook. T. Lee
Monster of Mu. O. Rutter
Monster of Snowdon Hall. Grove Wilson
Monster of the Lagoon. G. F. Worts
Monster Wheel Affair. D. McDaniel
Monsters. K. Robeson
Monstrous Enemy. C. R. Gull
Monstrous Regiment. J. N. Chance
Montana Man. W. C. Tuttle
Monte Carlo Mission. V. Connell
Monte Carlo Stories. J. Barrett
Monte Cristo Cover-Up. J. M. Simmel
Monte Cristo in Khaki. R. H. Savage
Montenegrin Gold. B. Ball
Montezuma's Revenge. H. Harrison
Month of the Falling Leaves. B. Marshall
Month of the Pearl. P. Jones
Monument of Terror. V. Jones
Mood for Murder. F. Gruber
Mood for Murder. V. Siller
Moods and Tenses. W. F. Harvey
Moon Dance. E. P. Thorne
Moon Endureth. J. Buchan
Moon Express. N. Daniels
Moon Garden. Jan Alexander
Moon Gate. C. C. Estes
Moon in the Gutter. D. Goodis
Moon Is Red. S. Rohmer
Moon Killer. J. Corbett
Moon Killer. R. Verron
Moon Marriage. A. Rundle
Moon Murders. N. Morland
Moon of Darkness. M. Lynch
"Moon of Death!" R. Gar
Moon of Joy. Camilla Hope
Moon of Madness. S. Rohmer
Moon of the Wolf. L. H. Whitten
Moon of Valleys. D. Whitelaw
Moon of Violence. E. Douglas
Moon over Miami. J. Deane
Moon over the Danube. M. McEvoy
Moon over the Water. M. Greig
Moon over Willow Run. D. E. L. Patch
Moon Returns. Rona Randall
Moon Rock. A. J. Rees
Moon Saw Murder. G. Oliver
Moon-Spinners. M. Stewart
Moon Was Made for Murder. N. Morland
Moon Was Red. D. Sage
Moonbathers. R. Miles
Moonbeams. R. V. Beste
Moonblood. P. J. Cooper
Mooney Moves Around. K. O'Neil
Moonflower. B. Nichols
Moonflower. P. A. Whitney
Moonflower Murder. B. Nichols
Moonflowers. M. Peterson
Moonhill Mystery. W. Woodrow
Moonlake Manor. L. Churchill
Moonlight Flitting. M. Procter
Moonlight Gondola. Janette Radcliffe
Moonlight Madness. E. Nepean
Moonlight Path. K. Lindsay
Moonlight Red. D. Morel
Moonlighter. H. Kane
Moonlighters. S. Morrow
Moonlit Door. A. Maybury
Moonlit Trap. R. Willock
Moonlit Way. R. W. Chambers
Moonlit Way. A. Dwyer-Joyce
Moonmilk and Murder. A. M. Stein
Moonraker. I. Fleming

Moonrakers and Mischief. G. J. Feakes
Moonraker's Bride. M. Brent
Moonrise. T. Strauss
Moonrock. R. Weverka
Moons in Gold. C. S. Montanye
Moonshine. R. Carr
Moonshine Momma. C. Brown
Moonshine Mountain. C. Glore
Moonshine War. E. Leonard
Moonshiner's Dupe. Lieut. Carlton
Moonstone. W. Collins
Moonstone Jungle. S. Harvester
Moonstone Mystery. A. Marsden
Moonstone Spirit. J. Deweese
Moonwater. Claudia Nicole
Moonwind. S. Wagner
Moor. D. Whitelaw
Moor Barn Mystery. H. L. Phillips
Moor Fires Mystery. H. R. Campbell
Moor House Murders. G. Verner
Moorcroft Manor Mystery. R. Trevor
Moorhaven. D. Winston
Moorland Terror. H. Broadbridge
Moorlands Mystery. C. Jude
Moorsend Manor. F. Hurd
Moorwood Legacy. I. Foster
Morals and Millions. F. Warden
Morals and Mysteries. H. Aide
Morals Squad. S. A. Krasney
Moran Chambers Smiled. E. P. Oppenheim
Moran's Women. D. Keene
Mord Em'ly. W. P. Ridge
More About P.J., the Secret Service Boy. F. S. Hamilton
More Adventures of Ellery Queen. E. Queen
More Beautiful than Murder. O. R. Cohen
More Bitter than Death. K. Wilhelm
More Crook Stuff. R. Keverne
More Dangerous than the Moon. R. Butler
More Deadly than the Male. Ambrose Grant
More Deadly than the Male. L. Meynell
More Deaths for Sergeant Cluff. G. North
More Deaths than One. S. Engstrand
More Deaths than One. B. Fischer
More Deaths than One. R. Stout
More Educated Evans. E. Wallace
More Exploits of Sherlock Holmes. Adrian Conon Doyle
More Knaves than One. F. Packard
More Limehouse Nights. T. Burke
More Lives than One. C. Houghton
More Lives than One. C. Wells
More Murder in a Nunnery. E. Shepherd
More Mysteries of a Great City. W. LeQueux
More News from Middle East. Robert Mason
More Nightmares. R. Bloch
More Perfect Union. R. Stapp
More Secrets of Potsdam. W. LeQueux
More Stories from Thriller. T. Hart
More Tales of the Uneasy. V. Hunt
More Than All. M. Warby
More Than Flesh. L. A. Brennan
More Than Kisses, Baby. S. Morelli
More Than Once Upon a Time. G. Kersh
More Than One Serpent. R. A. J. Walling
More to Be Pitied Than Scorned. C. E. Blaney
More Trouble for Archer. H. Clevely
More Work for the Undertaker. M. Allingham
Moreton Mystery. E. Dejeans
Morgan of the Mounted. S. A. White

Morgan the Dauntless. J. K. Stafford
Morgan Trail. W. C. Tuttle
Morganatic Marriage. C. Dawe
Morganatic Marriage. M. Leighton
Morganatic Wife. L. Tracy
Morgan's Castle. J. Hilliard
Morgan's Horror. G. M. Fenn
Morgan's Mountain. A. Mayse
Morgan's Wife. V. James
Morgue Amour. C. Brown
Morgue for Venus. Jonathan Craig
Morgue Is Always Open. J. Odlum
Morgue the Merrier. J. Truesdell
Moriarty. J. Gardner
Morituri. W. J. Luddecke
Morlo. L. A. Knight
Morning After. J. B. Weiner
Morning After Death. N. Blake
Morning of the Tiger. D. J. Fretland
Moroccan. C. A. Haddad
Morocco Episode. W. P. Brothers
Morocco Jones and the Case of the Golden Angel. J. Baynes
Moron. M. Brandel
Morosco. R. Pertwee
Morris Hume, Detective. William Robertson
Mortal Coils. A. Huxley
Mortal Fire. H. Gibbs
Mortal Remains. M. Yorke
Mortal Stakes. R. B. Parker
Mortal Storm. P. Bottome
Mortgage for Murder. P. Costello
Mortgaged Lives. P. Trent
Mortimer Story. P. Barrington
Mortissimo. P. E. H. Durston
Mortlake. G. Taylor
Mortmain. H. C. Asterley
Mortmain. A. Train
Mortmorley's Estate. J. H. Riddell
Morton Mystery. E. D'Arcy
Mortover Grange Affair. J. S. Fletcher
Mortover Grange Mystery. J. S. Fletcher
Mosaic Earring. C. Boyer
Mosaic of Death. W. Keenan
Moscow. N. Carter
Moscow at Noon Is the Target. P. Richards
Moscow by Nightmare. J. L. Shub
Moscow Coach. P. McCutchan
Moscow File. E. P. Thorne
Moscow Intercept. H. Arvay
Moscow Interlude. C. W. Thayer
Moscow Manhunt. Philip Chambers
Moscow Murder. B. Newman
Moscow Mystery. I. Litvinoff
Moscow Road. S. Harvester
Mosque of the Mahdi. A. Murray
Mosquito Net. G. B. Savi
Mosquito Serenade. N. McGuire
Mosquitoes Don't Kill. R. Hamilton
Moss Mystery. C. Wells
Moss Rose. J. Shearing
Mossbank Murder. Harry Mills
Mosshaven. S. Hancock
Most Beautiful Lady. D. Brande
Most Contagious Game. C. Aird
Most Contagious Game. S. Grafton
Most Dangerous Game. G. Lyall
Most Deadly Game. E. Friend
Most Deadly Hate. H. Carmichael
Most Delicious Poison. C. Connell
Most Happy Con Man. J. P. Radford
Most Immoral Murder. H. Ashbrook
Most Likely to Love. F. Flora
Most Men Don't Kill. David Alexander
Most Private Intrigue. L. Rosten
Most Sacred of All. J. Farnol
Most Savage Animal. H. Atkinson
Most Secret. J. D. Carr
Most Secret...Most Immediate. H. Swiggett

Most Unnatural Murder. Fiona Sinclair
Mostly by Moonlight. D. Daniels
Mostly Murder. F. Brown
Mote House Mystery. H. A. Vachell
Moteley's Concession. C. N. Boyle
Moth. J. M. Cain
Moth and the Flame. A. M. Meadows
Moth and the Footlights. G. Warden
Moth in a Rag Shop. R. Chambers
"Moth" Murder. L. Blow
Moth-Watch Murder. M. Burton
Moth-Woman. F. Hume
Mother Finds a Body. G. R. Lee
Mother Hunt. R. Stout
Mother-in-Law. E. Southworth
Mother Mandarin. F. Hume
Mother Night. K. Vonnegut
Mother of the Year. B. B. Johnson
Mother's Day. J. M. Ryan
Mother's Sacrifice. C. Faber
Mother's Secret. E. Southworth
Motion Menace. K. Robeson
Motive. H. Carmichael
Motive. M. B. Lowndes
Motive. E. Piper
Motive for Murder. C. Barling
Motive for Murder. N. Brent
Motive for Murder. A. Griffin
Motive for Murder. E. T. Hamill
Motive for Murder. B. Manningham
Motive for Murder. W. Reed
Motive for Murder. D. W. Rimel
Motive for Revenge. P. Conway
Motive for the Crime. A. Soutar
Motive Not the Deed. A. Arden
Motives for Murder. G. Croudace
Motives of Nicholas Holtz. T. Painter
Motley and Murder. H. Holt
Motley Menace. L. Cargill
Motor Bus Murder. D. Stuart
Motor Coach Murder. L. Bidston
Motor Coach Mystery. A. Murray
Motor Coach Mystery. W. Tyrer
Motor Cracksman. Charles Carey
Motor-Gun. H. C. McNeile
Motor Horn Mystery. T. S. King
Motor Pirate. S. Paternoster
Motor Rally Mystery. J. Rhode
Motor Show Mystery. H. H. C. Gibbons
Motor Show Mystery. R. Hardinge
Motor Wizard's Mystery. B. L. Standish
Mottled Death. J. Creasey
Motto for Murder. M. Mace
Mouls House Mystery. C. Barry
Mound Hill Mystery. Max Burton
Mount Desolation. C. Dawe
Mount Despair, and other stories. D. C. Murray
Mount Royal. M. E. Braddon
Mountain Cabin Mystery. C. Bussell
Mountain Cat. R. Stout
Mountain Cat Murders. R. Stout
Mountain Fires. M. Sutherland
Mountain Gold. Basil Carey
Mountain Gold. G. Goodchild
Mountain House Mystery. R. St. Clair
Mountain Inn Mystery. N. Ridley
Mountain Justice. C. N. Buck
Mountain Limited. E. L. Coolidge
Mountain Madness. L. Ford
Mountain Man. H. C. Wire
Mountain Meadow. J. Buchan
Mountain Murder. J. T. Adams
Mountain Murder Case. C. H. Snow
Mountain Mystery. J. J. Farjeon
Mountain Mystery. L. L. Lynch
Mountain of Fear. Rona Randall
Mountain of Terror. H. S. Banner
Mountain of the Blind. J. Creasey
Mountain Terror. M. E. Cooke

Mountaineer Detective. Anonymous
Mountaineer Detective. C. W. Cobb
Mountaineers. H. Bindloss
Mountainhead. D. Cory
Mountains Have a Secret. A. W. Upfield
Mountains Have No Shadow. O. Cameron
Mountains of Fears. H. C. Rowland
Mountains West of Town. W. Downing
Mounted Justice. K. Mayo
Moura. V. Coffman
Mourn the Hangman. H. Whittington
Mourned on Sunday. H. Reilly
Mourner. R. Stark
Mourner's Voyage. Shane Martin
Mournful Demeanor of Lieutenant Boruvka. J. Skvorecky
Mourning After. T. B. Dewey
Mourning After. Z. Johnson
Mourning After. F. Kane
Mourning Raga. Ellis Peters
Mourning Trees. V. Johnston
Mouse in Eternity. N. Tyre
Mouse in the Mountain. N. Davis
Mouse Trap. M. Messer
Mouse Who Wouldn't Play Ball. Anthony Gilbert
Mouse with Red Eyes. E. Eastman
Mouseback. J. C. Woodiwiss
Mousetrap. A. Christie
Mouthpiece. Robert (G.) Curtis
Move. G. Simenon
Move Along. F. Castle
Move in the Dark. N. Carter
Move On, Miss Mayhem. M. Brody
Movement Toward Eden. Clark Howard
Movie Mystery. R. C. Armour
Moving Day. Charles Henry
Moving Eye. M. E. Cooke
Moving Finger. J. H. Barrington
Moving Finger. A. Christie
Moving Finger. C. Fitzsimmons
Moving Finger. N. S. Lincoln
Moving Finger. E. P. Oppenheim
Moving Graveyard. M. Avallone
Moving House of Foscaldo. C. Chadwick
Moving Picture Mystery. N. Carter
Moving Target. J. MacDonald
Moving Toyshop. E. Crispin
Mowbray Mystery. B. Holt
Mox. M. Grant
Mozart Fiddle. K. Bird
"Mozart" Leaves at Nine. H. Greene
M'Sango, the Witch Doctor. F. A. M. Webster
Much Ado About Murder. F. Levon
Much Ado About Something. B. Graeme
Much Darker Days. A. H. Longway
Much in Evidence. H. Cecil
Mud in His Eye. G. Hammond
Muddles of Solon Mudhen, the Blacksmith Detective. Anonymous
Muddy Leaf Mystery. T. B. Morris
Muertalma. M. Dey
Muffled Man. G. Ingram
Mufti. H. C. McNeile
Mugger. E. McBain
Mugs, Molls and Dr. Harvey. G. Malcolm-Smith
Mullenthorpe Thing. C. Hood
Mulligan's Pirates. D. Stanford
Mulligan's Seed. H. Burkholz
Multi-Million-Dollar Murders. V. W. Mason

Multi-Millionaire. A. Hodges
Multiple Murder. T. Macrae
Multitude of Shadows. A. Calin
Multitude of Sins. M. K. Wren
Mumbo Jumbo. I. Reed
Mummer Case Mystery. D. Morrah
Mummy. R. Stephens
Mummy Case. D. Morrah
Mummy Comes to Life. V. Van Der Elst
Mummy Moves. M. Gaunt
Mummy's Curse. T. S. King
Mummy's Hand. Mrs. C. Kernahan
Mum's the Word for Murder. A. Baker
Mumsy, Nanny, Sonny, and Girly. B. Comport
Mungo. G. Woden
Munich Involvement. F. Mullally
Munitions Master. K. Robeson
Mura, the Western Detective. Old Sleuth
Mura, the Western Lady Detective. Anonymous
Murder! John Arnold
Murder!! M. Crombie
Murder. H. Janson
Murder. Evelyn Johnson
Murder a Day! R. Avery
Murder a la Mode. P. Moyes
Murder a la Mode. E. K. Sellars
Murder a la Mozambique. A. Scobie
Murder a la Richelieu. A. Blackman
Murder a la Stroganoff. C. Brahms
Murder a Mile High. E. Dean
Murder, A Mystery, and A Marriage. M. Twain
Murder Abroad. W. C. Harvey
Murder Abroad. E. R. Punshon
Murder, Absolutely Murder. C. H. Cloutier
Murder Adrift. G. Bellairs
Murder After a Fashion. S. Dean
Murder After Christmas. R. Latimer
Murder After Dark. J. Gannett
Murder After Hours. A. Christie
Murder After the Blitz. P. Piper
Murder Against the Grain. E. Lathen
Murder Ahead. N. Deane
Murder al Fresco. Jennifer Jones
Murder All Over. C. F. Adams
Murder Amid Proofs. M. Bremner
Murder Among Children. T. Coe
Murder Among Friends. I. E. Cox
Murder Among Friends. E. Ferrars
Murder Among Friends. Lange Lewis
Murder Among Friends. Simon
Murder Among Members. C. Carnac
Murder Among the Angells. R. Scarlett
Murder Among the Nudists. P. Hunt
Murder Among Thieves. P. Alding
Murder Among Those Present. H. Mace
Murder--and Ariadne. I. Wray
Murder and Blueberry Pie. F. Lockridge
Murder & Co. B. Gray
Murder and Gardenias. M. Neville
Murder and Marigold. G. Brandon
Murder and Miss Ming. P. Hambledon
Murder and Music. G. Lee
Murder and Mystery. Evelyn Johnson
Murder and Poor Jenny. M. Neville
Murder and the Married Virgin. B. Halliday
Murder and the Red-Haired Girl. H. Balfour
Murder and the Secret Weapon. G. F. Worts
Murder and the Shocking Miss Williams. H. J. Kennedy
Murder and the Wanton Bride. B. Halliday

Murder Anonymous. Anthony Gilbert
Murder Arranged. B. Thomson
Murder as a Fine Art. F. Bonnamy
Murder as a Fine Art. C. Carnac
Murder as an Ornament. M. Boniface
Murder as Arranged. Mark Cross
Murder as Usual. O. F. Jerome
Murder Assured. M. Halliday
Murder at a Cottage. Roland Daniel
Murder at a Dog Show. D. F. Gardiner
Murder at a Police Station. A. Swift
Murder at Arondale Farm. J. Hawk
Murder at Arroways. H. Reilly
Murder at Auction. E. Beatty
Murder at Avalon Arms. O. F. Jerome
Murder at Bador. S. C. Mason
Murder at Barclay House. K. McKay
Murder at Bayside. R. Robins
Murder at Belle Butte. T. M. Longstreth
Murder at Belle Camille. Monte Barrett
Murder at Benfleet. G. Bettany
Murder at Brambles. G. Collins
Murder at Bratton Grange. J. Rhode
Murder at Bridge. Anne Austin
Murder at Brownhill. T. A. Plummer
Murder at Buzzards Bay. A. Abbot
Murder at Calamity House. A. Cardwell
Murder at Cambridge. Q. Patrick
Murder at Castle Deeping. W. E. Johns
Murder at Charters. J. Fethaland
Murder at Chartres Towers. M. Beard
Murder at City Hall. Dan Ross
Murder at Cloud Hospital. M. Stand
Murder at Coney Island. J. D. O'Hanlon
Murder at Constantia. C. M. Lindsay
Murder at Cost Price. L. H. Hart
Murder at Covent Garden. W. J. Makin
Murder at Crawford Notch. M. L. Burns
Murder at Crome House. G. D. H. Cole
Murder at Cypress Hall. O. Stacey
Murder at Daybreak. G. A. Mayhew
Murder at Deer Lick. A. B. Cunningham
Murder at Derivale. J. Rhode
Murder at Drake's Anchorage. E. L. Waddell
Murder at Eastover. A. Rutter
Murder at Eight Bells. E. L. McReay
Murder at Elstree. T. Burke
Murder at End House. M. Halliday
Murder at Endor. W. A. Wolff
Murder at Exbridge. V. L. Whitechurch
Murder at Fenwold. C. Bush
Murder at Fleet. E. B. Young
Murder at Four Dot Ranch. F. L. Gregory
Murder at Full Moon. W. J. Makin
Murder at Glen Athol. N. Lippincott
Murder at Government House. E. Huxley
Murder at Grand Bay. W. D. Roberts
Murder at Grassmere Abbey. M. B. Dix
Murder at H.Q. H. Hawton
Murder at Hazelmoor. A. Christie
Murder at Hermit's Cottage. R. Hardinge
Murder at Hide and Seek. E. O'Donnell
Murder at High Noon. P. McGuire
Murder at High Tide. C. G. Booth
Murder at Horsethief. J. D. O'Hanlon
Murder at King's Kitchen. M. Halliday
Murder at Le Touquet. R. Lacroix
Murder at Lancaster Gate. F. Grierson
Murder at Landred Hall. J. Turner
Murder at Lantern Corner. T. A. Plummer
Murder at Large. L. Frost
Murder at Leisure. J. G. Edwards
Murder at Leisure. H. Monteilhet
Murder at Liberty Hall. A. Clutton-Brock
Murder at Lilac Cottage. J. Rhode
Murder at Linpara. H. Horn
Murder at Lintercombe. I. Greig
Murder at Little Malling. Roland Daniel
Murder at Lover's Lake. M. Brucker
Murder at Maison Manche. H. Burleigh
Murder at Malibu. J. D. O'Hanlon
Murder at Maneuvers. R. Howes
Murder at Manor House. L. Gorell
Murder at Manson's. R. E. Young
Murder at Marble Arch. Gavin Holt
Murder at Markendon Court. H. H. Stanners
Murder at Marks Caris. M. Duncan
Murder at Marlington. T. A. Plummer
Murder at Marston Manor. R. Forsythe
Murder at Mavering. L. Gorell
Murder at Melton Peveril. C. Ashton
Murder at Mid-Day. A. Hocking
Murder at Midnight. L. Allan
Murder at Midnight. J. Blackburn
Murder at Midnight. M. Cumberland
Murder at Midnight. H. Desmond
Murder at Midnight. C. F. Gregg
Murder at Midnight. R. Sale
Murder at Midnight. R. A. J. Walling
Murder at Midyears. Marion Mainwaring
Murder at Mocking House. W. C. Brown
Murder at Monk's Barn. C. Waye
Murder at Montauk. D. Wheelock
Murder at Monte Carlo. E. P. Oppenheim
Murder at Moreby. A. Cartlidge
Murder at Morning Prayers. Hilary Landon
Murder at Mornington. C. Carnac
Murder at Mulberry Cottage. G. Norsworthy
Murder at Night. J. Corbett
Murder at Nightfall. E. Sherry
Murder at No. 3. L. G. Horsefield
Murder at Our House. C. J. Daly
Murder at Out-Patients. A. W. Eyles
Murder at Pirate's Head. I. Waitt
Murder at Plenders. F. Everton
Murder at Pringlehurst. J. Corbett
Murder at Puck's Cottage. M. Alan
Murder at Radio City. N. Morland
Murder at Red Grange. J. Corbett
Murder at Red Pass. The Aresbys
Murder at St. Dennis. M. A. Hubbard
Murder at School. G. Trevor
Murder at Scotland Yard. G. Dilnot
Murder at Sea. R. Connell
Murder at Shirttail Flats. K. Franklin
Murder at Stone House. E. Howie
Murder at Sundown. James Preston
Murder at Sunset Gables. D. Heffernan
Murder at Sunset Rock. D. P. Neeley
Murder at Tall Tip. E. G. Gless
Murder at 10,000 Feet. P. Conde
Murder at the Admiralty. Eric Bennett
Murder at the Angel. H. McCutcheon
Murder at the Arab Stud. S. Miles
Murder at the Bar. T. Stevenson
Murder at the Black Crook. C. H. Matschat
Murder at the "Black Swan." N. Walthew
Murder at the Blue Garter. C. Wheatley
Murder at the Boarding House. A. S. Bradshaw
Murder at the Bookstall. H. Holt
Murder at the Casino. C. Wells
Murder at the Class Reunion. C. Andrews
Murder at the Club. L. Allan
Murder at the Coffee Stall. B. Rogers
Murder at the College. V. L. Whitechurch
Murder at the Cookout. G. De Fraga
Murder at the DeSoto. J. Rand
Murder at the Dôme. G. Burgess
Murder at the Eclipse. John Alexander
Murder at the Eisteddfod. J. E. Williams
Murder at the Flea Club. M. Head
Murder at the Flood. M. E. Allan
Murder at the Flower Show. M. Beckett
Murder at the Gallop. A. Christie
Murder at the Hunting Club. M. Plum
Murder at the Inn. L. Brock
Murder at the Inn. R. Goyne
Murder at the Kentucky Derby. C. Parmer
Murder at the Keyhole. R. A. J. Walling
Murder at the Mardi Gras. E. M. Stone
Murder at the Met. F. G. Jarvis
Murder at the Microphone. D. Hogg
Murder at the Mike. C. Saxby
Murder at the Ministry. A. A. Thomson
Murder at the Miramar. E. Snell
Murder at the Moorings. M. Burton
Murder at the Motel. V. Gunn
Murder at the Motor Show. J. Rhode
Murder at the Movies. M. Hervey
Murder at the Munition Works. G. D. H. Cole
Murder at the New York World's Fair. Freeman Dana
Murder at the Nook. A. Fielding
Murder at the Old Stone House. C. M. Russell
Murder at the Open. A. MacVicar
Murder at the Pageant. V. L. Whitechurch
Murder at the Palace. J. Corbett
Murder at the Party. H. Willett
Murder at the Piano. G. Bagby
Murder at the Polls. M. Propper
Murder at the Red Cockatoo. A. Parsons
Murder at the Savoy. M. Sjowall
Murder at the Schoolhouse. A. B. Cunningham
Murder at the "Signal." M. Byrne
Murder at the Stadium. A. Parsons
Murder at the Varsity. F. L. Cary
Murder at the Varsity. Q. Patrick
Murder at the Vicarage. M. Charles
Murder at the Vicarage. A. Christie
Murder at the Wedding. F. Grierson
Murder at the White Tulip. D. Cole
Murder at the Wishing Well. A. Wood
Murder at the Women's City Club. Q. Patrick
Murder at the World's Fair. M. Plum
Murder at the Yard! J. G. Brandon
Murder at 300 to 1. J. D. O'Hanlon
Murder at 28:10. N. Gayle
Murder at Wrides Park. J. S. Fletcher
Murder Backstairs. Anne Austin
Murder Bait. D. Yarnell
Murder Beacon. L. P. Greene
Murder Beat. R. Drennen
Murder Beat. A. Lenton
Murder Before Breakfast. L. G. Offord
Murder Before Dinner. C. Franklin
Murder Before Marriage. M. Neville
Murder Before Midnight. A. B. Cunningham
Murder Before Tuesday. Elaine Hamilton
Murder Began Yesterday. L. Johnson
Murder Begets Murder. J. Corbett
Murder Begets Murder. M. G. Hugi
Murder Begins at Home. D. Ames
Murder Behind the Mike. R. L. Goldman
Murder Being Once Done. R. Rendell
Murder Belongs to Me! Roderic Wilkinson
Murder Below Wall Street. R. Delancey
Murder Besieged. D. Whitelaw
Murder Between Dark and Dark. Max Long
Murder Between Drinks. A. Gibbs
Murder Beyond the Pale. M. Neville
Murder Bicarb. D. Van Deusen
Murder, Bless It! N. Spain
Murder Blues. B. Edwards

Murder Bound. P. Anderson
Murder Breaks Trail. E. M. Boyd
Murder Breeds Murder. A. Willsdon
Murder Brewing. A. W. Eyles
Murder but Gently. F. Duncan
Murder--but Natch. M. Hagen
Murder Buttoned Up. P. A. Holmes
Murder by a Maniac. M. Richmond
Murder by Accident. L. Mason
Murder by Air. W. E. Johns
Murder by an Aristocrat. M. G. Eberhart
Murder--by an Idiot. T. A. Plummer
Murder by Appointment. E. Browne
Murder by Appointment. J. Paul
Murder by Arrangement. W. G. Beyer
Murder by Bamboo. D. Sabre
Murder by Bequest. R. Foley
Murder by Burial. S. Casson
Murder by Chance. P. Drax
Murder by Contract. Griff
Murder by Dart. B. Tempest
Murder by Degrees. J. B. Fearnley
Murder by Design. R. Simons
Murder by Experiment. L. A. Knight
Murder by Experts. Anthony Gilbert
Murder by Formula. J. H. Wallis
Murder by Gemini. R. Gallagher
Murder by Inches. S. Hopkins
Murder by Inspiration. E. H. Bierstadt
Murder by Installment. M. Hervey
Murder by Invitation. A. C. MacLean
Murder by Jury. R. B. Sanborn
Murder by Latitude. R. King
Murder by Legacy. W. A. Sweeney
Murder by Magic. J. Creasey
Murder by Magic. M. J. Freeman
Murder by Magic. W. B. Gibson
Murder by Magic. M. Grant
Murder by Magic. A. R. Long
Murder by Mail. F. McGrew
Murder by Marriage. R. G. Dean
Murder by Matchlight. E. C. R. Lorac
Murder by Mathematics. H. Hawton
Murder by Miss-Demeanour. C. Brown
Murder by Mistake. P. Urquhart
Murder by Moonlight. W. B. Gibson
Murder by Moonlight. D. Reid
Murder by Multiplication. M. Durham
Murder by Nail. J. Farnol
Murder by Neglect. Elizabeth Jenkins
Murder by Night. J. L. Rickard
Murder by Numbers. J. Phelan
Murder--by Persons Unknown. J. Rowland
Murder by Precedent. R. Petrie
Murder by Prescription. J. Stagge
Murder by Proxy. B. Boyer
Murder by Proxy. H. Carmichael
Murder by Proxy. P. Drax
Murder by Proxy. B. Halliday
Murder by Proxy. H. Nielsen
Murder by Proxy. Richard Williams
Murder by Reflection. H. F. Heard
Murder by Request. B. Nichols
Murder by Schedule. J. Hinckley
Murder by Scripture. A. R. Long
Murder by Stealth. J. W. Booth
Murder by Suggestion. E. Acheson
Murder by Telecopter. D. T. Hughes
Murder by Telephone. B. Herbert
Murder by the Arch. H. W. Higginson
Murder by the Book. H. Arre
Murder by the Book. F. Lockridge
Murder by the Book. R. Stout
Murder by the Clock. R. King

Murder by the Day. V. P. Johns
Murder by the Dozen. H. Wiley
Murder by the Lake. C. Coram
Murder by the Law. P. McGuire
Murder by the Mile. M. Russell
Murder by the Minute. A. Wood
Murder by the Pack. C. G. Hodges
Murder by the Way. M. Halliday
Murder by the Yard. M. T. Yates
Murder by Treason. A. R. Long
Murder by Twenty-Five. C. Robbins
Murder by Warrant. E. T. Collis
Murder by Wash of Light. G. De Fraga
Murder C.O.D. Donald Ross
Murder Calling. D. Whitelaw
Murder Calling "50." G. Bagby
Murder Calls Dr. Hailey. A. Wynne
Murder Calls the Tune. W. M. Duncan
Murder Calls the Tune. R. Verron
Murder Came Late. J. York
Murder Came Tumbling. Martin Brett
Murder Can Be Fun. F. Brown
Murder Can Be Such Fun! L. Beresford
Murder Cancels All Debts. M. V. Heberden
Murder Can't Stop. W. T. Ballard
Murder Can't Wait. R. Lockridge
Murder Can't Wait. M. L. Stokes
Murder Caravan. T. T. Flynn
Murder Case Number 33. L. Cornell
Murder Cave. H. Hawton
Murder Challenges Valcour. R. King
Murder Charge. Wade Miller
Murder Chase. E. Elton
Murder Cheats the Bride. Anthony Gilbert
Murder, Chop Chop. James Norman
Murder City. O. M. Hall
Murder City. A. Lenton
Murder Clear, Track Fast. J. Philips
Murder Club. Howel Evans
Murder Column. C. Franklin
Murder Come Home. M. Halliday
Murder Comes at Night. I. Oellrichs
Murder Comes Back. H. Ashbrook
Murder Comes Calling. M. Douglas
Murder Comes Calling! D. Reid
Murder Comes First. F. Lockridge
Murder Comes High. H. L. Nelson
Murder Comes Home. M. Chappell
Murder Comes Home. N. Child
Murder Comes Home. Anthony Gilbert
Murder Comes Smiling. G. Brandon
Murder Comes to Dinner. Robert Fleming
Murder Comes to Eden. L. Ford
Murder Comes to Rothesay. J. Cassells
Murder Could Not Kill. G. Baxter
Murder, Country Style. M. F. Ford
Murder Cries Out. A. Hocking
Murder Cruise. M. Keyes
Murder Cum Laude. J. Y. Dane
Murder Day by Day. I. S. Cobb
Murder Defies the Roman Emperor. C. E. Gray
Murder DeLuxe. R. King
Murder Disqualifies. Alan Graham
Murder Does Light Housekeeping. M. Bardon
Murder Doesn't Always Out. F. C. Davis
Murder Doll. M. K. Ozaki
Murder Doll. R. O. Saber
Murder, Double Murder. Neill Graham
Murder Down Below. J. Stagg
Murder Down South. L. Ford
Murder Down Under. A. W. Upfield
Murder Draws a Line. W. A. Barber
Murder Each Way. J. Brown
Murder En Route. B. Flynn
Murder Ends the Song. A. Meyers
Murder Enters the Picture. W. A. Barber
Murder Every Monday. P. Branch
Murder Expert. R. P. Koehler
Murder Fantastical. P. Moyes
Murder First Class. R. Simons

Murder--First Edition. T. Garrett
Murder Flies the Atlantic. S. H. Page
Murder Flight. K. Hemingway
Murder Follows Desmond Shannon. M. V. Heberden
Murder for a Hollow Shell. A. L. Albert
Murder for a Million. J. G. Brandon
Murder for a Million. C. B. Kelland
Murder for a Million. Roy Vickers
Murder for a Wanton. W. Chambers
Murder for Art's Sake. R. Lockridge
Murder for Breakfast. P. Hunt
Murder for Cash. J. Ronald
Murder for Charity. O. Dudley
Murder for Christmas. A. Christie
Murder for Christmas. F. Duncan
Murder for Christmas. E. Howie
Murder for Empire. K. M. Knight
Murder for Fun. R. Savage
Murder for Hannah. D. V. Babcock
Murder for Her Birthday. G. Cobden
Murder for His Money. G. Cobden
Murder for Love. D. E. Boocock
Murder for Love. S. Salt
Murder for Madame. Adam Knight
Murder for Millions. N. Rutledge
Murder for Missemily. J. F. Straker
Murder for Money. Jay Bennett
Murder for Money. H. Liggett
Murder for Real. M. Bardon
Murder for Sale. M. Bardsley
Murder for Sale. N. W. Firth
Murder for Sale. S. Horler
Murder for Tea. E. Howie
Murder for the Asking. G. H. Coxe
Murder for the Bride. J. D. MacDonald
Murder for the Holidays. H. Rigsby
Murder for the Million. R. Chapman
Murder for the Millions. H. Kane
Murder for Two. G. H. Coxe
Murder for Two. N. MacKenzie
Murder for Two Pins. R. Trevor
Murder for What? K. Steel
Murder Forestalled. P. Chester
Murder, Four Miles High. R. A. Braun
Murder from Beyond. R. Francis Foster
Murder from Heaven. P. Palmer
Murder from the East. C. J. Daly
Murder from the Grave. W. Levinrew
Murder from the Grave. Eric Wood
Murder from the Mind. P. Laing
Murder from Three Angles. V. Loder
Murder from Three Angles. J. R. Warren
Murder Game. R. Batchelor
Murder Game. J. S. Strange
Murder Gang. Roland Daniel
Murder Germ. A. O. Pollard
Murder Gets Around. R. S. Bowen
Murder Gives a Lovely Light. J. S. Strange
Murder-Go-Round. C. P. Donnel
Murder Goes Astray. M. V. Heberden
Murder Goes Fishing. T. Brace
Murder Goes Free. Roland Daniel
Murder Goes in a Trailer. T. Brace
Murder Goes Nap. R. Dolphin
Murder Goes Rolling Along. H. F. S. Moore
Murder Goes South. A. R. Long
Murder Goes to Bank Night. W. C. Clark
Murder Goes to College. K. Steel
Murder Goes to Press. Cicely Cairns
Murder Goes to Press. N. Loomis
Murder Goes to School. H. Farrar
Murder Goes to School. R. Savage
Murder Goes to Sea. A. R. Bosworth
Murder Goes to the Dogs. T. Brace

Title Index

Murder Goes to the World's Fair. T. Brace
Murder Goes West. L. C. Douthwaite
Murder Gone Mad. G. Bellairs
Murder Gone Mad. P. MacDonald
Murder Gone Mad. S. Stone
Murder Gone Minoan. C. B. Clason
Murder Gone to Earth. J. Stagge
Murder Greets Jean Holton. K. M. Knight
Murder Grows Roots. S. Taylor
Murder Half Baked. G. Bagby
Murder Happens. A. Ridley
Murder Has a Motive. F. Duncan
Murder Has an Echo. J. Notley
Murder Has Been Arranged. R. Trevor
Murder Has Been Arranged. Emlyn Williams
Murder Has Been Done. Neill Graham
Murder Has Its Points. F. Lockridge
Murder Has Many Faces. W. Grew
Murder Has No Friends. B. Jones
Murder Has No Tongue. Anthony Gilbert
Murder Has Three Dimensions. A. Spiller
Murder Hath Charms. M. Durham
Murder Helps. I. Oellrichs
Murder Hide-and-Seek. A. O. Pollard
Murder Hole Road. A. Douglas
Murder House. T. A. Plummer
Murder Humane. H. Kemp
Murder Hunt. P. Stadley
Murder in a Barge. P. Street
Murder in a Blue Moon. M. Neville
Murder in a Church. A. Wynne
Murder in a Dark Room. Neill Graham
Murder in a Haystack. D. Aldis
Murder in a Hurry. F. Lockridge
Murder in a Library. C. J. Dutton
Murder in a Lighter Vein. M. M. Raison
Murder in a Madhouse. C. B. Molyneaux
Murder in a Maze. M. Alan
Murder in a Muffler. G. Davison
Murder in a Nunnery. E. Lavery
Murder in a Nunnery. E. Shepherd
Murder in a Road Gang. M. Cresswell
Murder in a Shell. M. Beam
Murder in a Walled Town. K. Woods
Murder in Absence. M. Burton
Murder in Amber. Colver Harris
Murder in Angel Yard. F. Vivian
Murder in Any Degree. O. Johnson
Murder in Any Language. K. Roos
Murder in Baracoa. P. E. Walsh
Murder in Bavaria. C. Rushton
Murder in Beacon Street. W. Martyn
Murder in Berkeley Square. R. Dark
Murder in Berlin. Harold Trembath
Murder in Bermuda. W. Sharp
Murder in Bethnal Square. S. Fowler
Murder in Black. Mark Cross
Murder in Black. F. Grierson
Murder in Black and White. David Alexander
Murder in Black and White. E. Elder
Murder in Black Letter. P. Anderson
Murder in Blue. C. Witting
Murder in Blue Street. F. Crane
Murder in Bostall. P. McGuire
Murder in Brief. M. Trask
Murder in Bright Red. F. Crane
Murder in Broad Daylight. G. D. H. Cole
Murder in Camera. W. A. Ballinger
Murder in Canton. R. Van Gulik
Murder in Cardigan Square. N. MacKenzie
Murder in Chelsea. E. C. R. Lorac
Murder in Church. Babette Hughes
Murder in College. J. Y. Dane
Murder in Crown Passage. M. Burton
Murder in Dawson City. Roland Daniel
Murder in Devil's Hollow. L. N. Morgan
Murder in Disguise. C. Kingston
Murder in Duplicate. P. Conway
Murder in Duplicate. H. L. Victor
Murder in Earl's Court. N. Gordon
Murder in False Face. G. Childerness
Murder in False-Face. R. Lockridge
Murder in Fancy Dress. I. H. Irwin
Murder in Fiji. J. W. Vandercook
Murder in Five Columns. F. Diamond
Murder in Flat 14. A. G. E. Cromwell
Murder in Focus. D. Halliday
Murder in Four Degrees. J. S. Fletcher
Murder in Four Parts. G. D. H. Cole
Murder in Full Flight. M. Magill
Murder in Full View. J. D. Forbes
Murder in G-Sharp. K. Steel
Murder in Gay Ladies. J. Ronald
Murder in Haiti. J. W. Vandercook
Murder in Haste. E. P. Fenwick
Murder in Haste. H. Gardiner
Murder in Haste. B. Halliday
Murder in Haste. P. McGuire
Murder in Haste. Garnett Weston
Murder in Havana. G. H. Coxe
Murder in Hawthorn. J. Armour
Murder in Her Big Blue Eyes. J. Long
Murder in High Place. R. B. Dominic
Murder in Hollywood. C. Gibbons
Murder in Hospital. J. Bell
Murder in Hospital. A. W. Eyles
Murder in Jackson Hole. M. Parker
Murder in Las Vegas. J. Waer
Murder in Lima. R. A. Levey
Murder in Majorca. M. Bryan
Murder in Majorca. P. Tabori
Murder in Make-Up. C. Ashton
Murder in Makeup. Lorenz Heller
Murder in Man. F. Duncan
Murder in Manchuria. G. H. Teed
Murder in Manhattan. A. Procter
Murder in Manhattan. J. Roeburt
Murder in Manuscript. R. Strevens
Murder in Manuscript. G. Verner
Murder in Marble. J. Philips
Murder in Marrakech. C. Leader
Murder in Married Life. A. Morice
Murder in Marseilles. C. Lefevre
Murder in Maryland. L. Ford
Murder in Mayfair. J. G. Brandon
Murder in Mayfair. F. Goldsmith
Murder in Mayfair. R. J. Lawrence
Murder in Maytime. G. Brandon
Murder in Medora Mansions. J. S. Fletcher
Murder in Melancholy. W. Keenan
Murder in Melbourne. D. Gray
Murder in Mesopotamia. A. Christie
Murder in Mid-Air. D. Dayle
Murder in Mid-Atlantic. E. Antill
Murder in Midsummer. M. M. Atwater
Murder in Millenium VI. C. Gray
Murder in Mind. D. Gray
Murder in Mind. J. A. Howard
Murder in Miniature. E. Mack
Murder in Miniatures. S. Merwin Jr.
Murder in Mink. R. G. Dean
Murder in Mink. B. Iles
Murder in Mocking Valley. W. Crowell
Murder in Monaco. J. Flagg
Murder in Montana. Muriel Bradley
Murder in Montparnasse. J. Bude
Murder in Mortimer Square. F. Grierson
Murder in Moscow. A. Garve
Murder in Motley. D. Whitelaw
Murder in Mount Holly. P. Theroux
Murder in Mozambique. David Wilson
Murder in New Guinea. J. W. Vandercook
Murder in Newport. G. B. Lambert
Murder in November. M. Alan
Murder in Ocean Drive. Roland Daniel
Murder in Oil. J. Avrach
Murder in Oils. J. N. Chance
Murder in Okefenokee. C. H. Matschat
Murder in Paradise. R. Dana
Murder in Paradise. G. Joseph
Murder in Paradise. J. Laffin
Murder in Paradise. J. Shill
Murder in Paris. A. Campbell
Murder in Pastiche. Marion Mainwaring
Murder in Peking. V. Starrett
Murder in Piccadilly. Roland Daniel
Murder in Piccadilly. C. Kingston
Murder in Pimlico. J. G. Brandon
Murder in Plain Sight. G. Brown
Murder in Port Afrique. B. V. Dryer
Murder in Print. R. Sonin
Murder in Public. J. Crozier
Murder in Queer Street. C. Ryland
Murder in Red. F. Castle
Murder in Retrospect. A. Christie
Murder in Reverse. A. Webb
Murder in Rockwater. M. Neville
Murder in Romney Marsh. E. Jepson
Murder in Room 700. M. H. Bradley
Murder in Room 13. Albert Conroy
Murder in Rosemary Lane. H. M. Keynes
Murder in St. John's Wood. E. C. R. Lorac
Murder in Season. O. R. Cohen
Murder in Shinbone Alley. H. Reilly
Murder in Silence. G. Selmark
Murder in Silk. R. Trevor
Murder in Soho. J. G. Brandon
Murder in Space. D. V. Reed
Murder in Stained Glass. M. Armstrong
Murder in Strange Houses. R. Peckham
Murder in Style. E. L. Fetta
Murder in Style. R. Stout
Murder in Suffolk. A. Fielding
Murder in Sussex. G. Norsworthy
Murder in Switzerland. E. Snell
Murder in Sydney. L. Mann
Murder in Texas. A. E. Lingo
Murder in the Air. C. Brisbane
Murder in the Air. Mark Cross
Murder in the Air. J. Hunter
Murder in the Air. A. O. Pollard
Murder in the Air. D. L. Teilhet
Murder in the Atlantic. Carter Dickson
Murder in the Ballroom. K. Hewitt
Murder in the Bank. R. Essex
Murder in the Basement. A. Berkeley
Murder in the Bath. F. Didelot
Murder in the Bazaar. D. Lynn
Murder in the Bedroom. G. Leroux
Murder in the Blackout. J. R. Warren
Murder in the Bookshop. C. Wells
Murder in the Borough Library. J. Austwick
Murder in the Brownstone House. W. Collison
Murder in the Bud. P. Bottome
Murder in the Calais Coach. A. Christie
Murder in the Camp. M. Stand
Murder in the Cellar. L. Eppley
Murder in the Clinic. Edmond Hamilton
Murder in the Coalhole. M. Burton
Murder in the Cockpit. P. Conde
Murder in the Consulting Room. M. S. Michel
Murder in the Dark. C. J. Dutton
Murder in the Dentist Chair. M. Thynne
Murder in the Embassy. Diplomat
Murder in the Family. M. H. Bradley

Murder in the Family. D. Emerson
Murder in the Family. M. Leinster
Murder in the Family. J. Ronald
Murder in the Family. J. York
Murder in the Family Way. C. Brown
Murder in the Fifth Column. R. Trevor
Murder in the Fine Arts. C. Nicolai
Murder in the First Person. S. Adams
Murder in the Flagship. P. W. Taylor
Murder in the Fog. H. L. Gates
Murder in the Fog. Elaine Hamilton
Murder in the Fog. P. Thorne
Murder in the Fog. R. Worth
Murder in the French Room. H. J. Hultman
Murder in the Game Reserve. P. W. Taylor
Murder in the Garden. F. Grierson
Murder in the Gilded Cage. S. Spewack
Murder in the Green Sedan. R. P. Koehler
Murder in the Gunroom. H. B. Piper
Murder in the Harem Club. C. Brown
Murder in the Haunted Sentry-Box. N. Gayle
Murder in the Highlands. P. Manton
Murder in the Home Guard. R. Adam
Murder in the Hotel. H. P. Hanshew
Murder in the House of Commons. M. A. Hamilton
Murder in the House with the Blue Eyes. J. N. Darby
Murder in the Hurricane. E. L. Adams
Murder in the Key Club. C. Brown
Murder in the King's Road. J. Boyd
Murder in the Laboratory. T. L. Davidson
Murder in the Lady Chapel. S. Toye
Murder in the Madhouse. Jonathan Latimer
Murder in the Making. H. Petersen
Murder in the Maze. J. J. Connington
Murder in the Melody. N. Berrow
Murder in the Mews. A. Christie
Murder in the Mill. H. Reilly
Murder in the Mill-Race. E. C. R. Lorac
Murder in the Mills. H. S. Keeler
Murder in the Mind. K. T. Knoblock
Murder in the Mirror. W. W. Masters
Murder in the Mirror. L. Thayer
Murder in the Mist. W. Chambers
Murder in the Mist. H. L. Gates
Murder in the Mist. Z. Popkin
Murder in the Mobile Unit. Sutherland Scott
Murder in the Moonlight. F. Brown
Murder in the Moor. T. Kindon
Murder in the Morning. G. Pahlow
Murder in the Morning. C. Robertson
Murder in the Morning. A. Wynne
Murder in the Museum. F. W. Gumley
Murder in the Museum. E. Heath
Murder in the Museum. J. Rowland
Murder in the Navy. R. Marsten
Murder in the News Room. H. C. Beck
Murder in the Newspaper Guild. H. C. Beck
Murder in the Night. A. Gask
Murder in the North-West. C. W. Sanders
Murder in the O.P.M. L. Ford
Murder in the Old Jail. Michael Henry
Murder in the Opera House. Q. Mario
Murder in the Outlands. J. B. Hendryx
Murder in the Pallant. J. S. Fletcher
Murder in the Park. C. F. Gregg
Murder in the Pool. Mark Cross
Murder in the Procession. L. Cargill
Murder in the Radio Department. A. Eichler
Murder in the Rain. W. Collison
Murder in the Rain Forest. N. MacKenzie
Murder in the Raw. B. Fischer
Murder in the Raw. W. C. Gault
Murder in the Raw. B. Grant
Murder in the Rough. L. Allen
Murder in the Round. D. Halliday
Murder in the Rue Royale. M. Harrison
Murder in the Ruins. N. A. Temple-Ellis
Murder in the Sacristy. D. A. Lord
Murder in the Sanctuary. L. Grex
Murder in the Senate. G. Coffin
Murder in the Square. J. Smith
Murder in the Squire's Pew. J. S. Fletcher
Murder in the Stacks. M. Boyd
Murder in the Stars. M. Halliday
Murder in the Stars. J. Stagge
Murder in the State Department. Diplomat
Murder in the Stork Club. V. Caspary
Murder in the Stratosphere. G. Eldredge
Murder in the Stratosphere. J. Laurence
Murder in the Submarine Zone. Carter Dickson
Murder in the Suez Canal. P. W. Taylor
Murder in the Sun. H. Footner
Murder in the Sun. J. T. Story
Murder in the Surgery. J. G. Edwards
Murder in the Surgery. T. A. Plummer
Murder in the Taj Mahal. P. W. Taylor
Murder in the Telephone Exchange. J. Wright
Murder in the Temple. J. Brooke
Murder in the Theatre. E. M. McDuff
Murder in the Tomb. L. A. Osgood
Murder in the Top Drawer. E. G. Cousins
Murder in the Town. M. Richert
Murder in the Tropic Night. F. Arthur
Murder in the Vestry. M. Crossley
Murder in the Village. T. A. Plummer
Murder in the Village. J. Skinner
Murder in the WPA. Alexander Williams
Murder in the Walls. R. M. Stern
Murder in the Willett Family. R. King
Murder in the Wind. J. D. MacDonald
Murder in the Wind. V. Roser
Murder in the Zoo. E. Balneaves
Murder in the Zoo. Babette Hughes
Murder in Thin Air. A. Wynne
Murder in Three Acts. A. Christie
Murder in Three Moves. R. Watters
Murder in Time. L. Day
Murder in Time. E. Ferrars
Murder in Touraine. B. E. Wallace
Murder in Tow. C. Hale
Murder in Transit. W. R. Hutton
Murder in Trinidad. J. W. Vandercook
Murder in Triplicate. H. Austin
Murder in Triplicate. L. Marshall
Murder in Two Flats. Roy Vickers
Murder in Vegas. W. R. Cox
Murder in Venice. Anne-Mariel
Murder in Venice. T. Sterling
Murder in Vienna. E. C. R. Lorac
Murder in Vision. K. Bird
Murder in Waiting. M. G. Eberhart
Murder in Waiting. R. Murphy
Murder in Wardour Street. N. Morland
Murder in Wax. P. Baron
Murder in White Pit. J. H. Barrington
Murder in Whitehall. T. Hyde
Murder in Windy Coppice. T. A. Plummer
Murder in Wonderland. G. Bagby
Murder in Y Division. J. G. Brandon
Murder in Your Home. E. Cobb
Murder Incidental. M. Cronin
Murder Incidental. K. Trask
Murder Included. J. Cannan
Murder Incognito. M. Dare
Murder Inc. J. Eastwood
Murder Indicted. R. Verron
Murder Inherited. G. Cobden
Murder Insoluble. E. Wilmot
Murder Intended. F. Beeding
Murder Is a Best Seller. M. Judd
Murder Is a Collector's Item. E. Dean
Murder Is a Furtive Thing. R. Boyd
Murder Is a Gamble. G. M. Barnes
Murder Is a Gentle Kiss. A. Barron
Murder Is a Habit. B. Halliday
Murder Is a House Guest. I. Cabot
Murder Is a Kill-Joy. E. S. Holding
Murder Is a Maiden's Handicap. M. Brody
Murder Is a Package Deal. C. Brown
Murder Is a Serious Business. E. Dean
Murder Is a Shady Business. A. Spiller
Murder Is a Witch. J. Bingham
Murder Is Absurd. P. McGerr
Murder Is an Art. A. B. Correll
Murder Is an Art. M. Innes
Murder Is an Evil Business. M. Bramhall
Murder Is Announced. A. Christie
Murder Is Catching. M. Ainsworth
Murder Is Cheap. Anthony Gilbert
Murder Is Contagious. M. Bramhall
Murder Is Dangerous. S. Levinson
Murder Is Easy. A. Christie
Murder Is Easy! A. Livington
Murder Is for Keeps. Peter Chambers
Murder Is Forgetful. W. Bogart
Murder Is Grim. S. Rogers
Murder Is Incidental. D. Rutherford
Murder Is Infectuous. Sutherland Scott
Murder Is Insane. G. M. Barnes
Murder Is Justified. H. Desmond
Murder Is Lonely. U. Rothwell
Murder Is Mutuel. J. Dolph
Murder Is My Business. B. Halliday
Murder Is My Business. J. Reach
Murder Is My Business. V. Siller
Murder Is My Dish. S. Marlowe
Murder Is My Mistress. C. Brown
Murder Is My Mistress. H. Whittington
Murder Is My Racket. R. H. Leitfred
Murder Is My Shadow. C. Nash
Murder Is My Weakness. Neill Graham
Murder Is No Accident. Jerome Barry
Murder Is Not Enough. B. E. Wallace
Murder Is Not Enough. S. Wells
Murder Is Not Mute. A. Newell
Murder Is Out. L. Thayer
Murder Is Ruby Red. E. Radford
Murder Is Served. F. Lockridge
Murder Is So Easy. W. D. Roberts
Murder Is So Nostalgic! C. Brown
Murder Is So Simple. S. Horler
Murder Is Staged. A. Tack
Murder Is Suggested. F. Lockridge
Murder Is Swift. C. Fitzsimmons
Murder Is the Message. C. Brown
Murder Is the Pay-Off. L. Ford
Murder Is the Reason. L. Marshall
Murder Is Where You Find It. R. P. Hansen
Murder Is Where You Find It. A. Rutter
Murder Island. L. Jamieson
Murder Island. W. Martyn
Murder Isn't Cricket. E. Radford
Murder Isn't Easy. R. Hull
Murder Isn't Funny. J. H. Bond
Murder Isn't Private. J. Garden
Murder Jigsaw. E. Radford
Murder Joins the Chorus. R. Simons
Murder Kick. Wenzell Brown
Murder Knows No Master. S. Miles
Murder Lady. N. Chambers

Title Index

Murder Lands the Odds. R. Verron
Murder Las Vegas Style. W. T. Ballard
Murder Laughs Last. J. Ford
Murder Lays a Golden Egg. E. T. Hull
Murder Lays the Odds. J. Letherby
Murder League. R. L. Fish
Murder Leaves a Ring. F. G. Stanley
Murder Lies in Waiting. Neill Graham
Murder Lifts the Veil. R. Verron
Murder Limited. C. R. Gull
Murder Limps By. T. A. Plummer
Murder Line. P. Alding
Murder Link. H. T. Johnson
Murder Listens In. E. Daly
Murder, London-Australia. J. Creasey
Murder, London-Miami. J. Creasey
Murder, London-New York. J. Creasey
Murder, London-South Africa. J. Creasey
Murder Looks Back. M. Alan
Murder Loves Company. J. Mersereau
Murder, M.A. A. Kennington
Murder M.D. M. Burton
Murder Machine. F. Scarpetta
Murder Made Absolute. M. Underwood
Murder Made Easy. R. Goyne
Murder Made Easy. Neill Graham
Murder Made Easy. D. Reid
Murder Madness. M. Leinster
Murder, Maestro, Please. D. Ames
Murder, Maestro, Please. J. Sharkey
Murder Magnified. E. Radford
Murder Makers. J. Rossiter
Murder Makes a Call. F. C. Tickner
Murder Makes a Date. Neill Graham
Murder Makes a Deadline. S. Fuller
Murder Makes a Man. W. T. Walsh
Murder Makes a Marriage. S. Broocks
Murder Makes a Merry Widow. R. G. Dean
Murder Makes a Racket. M. V. Heberden
Murder Makes a Villain. Denis Scott
Murder Makes an Entrance. C. B. Kelland
Murder Makes By-Lines. K. Secrist
Murder Makes Haste. J. Creasey
Murder Makes It Certain. Neill Graham
Murder Makes Its Mark. M. Judd
Murder Makes Me Laugh. J. Jackson
Murder Makes Me Mad. F. Findley
Murder Makes Me Nervous. M. Scherf
Murder Makes Merry. F. W. Irwin
Murder Makes Mistakes. G. Bellairs
Murder Makes Murder. H. Ashbrook
Murder Makes Murder. M. Halliday
Murder Makes the Mare Go. J. Dolph
Murder Makes the News. Neill Graham
Murder Makes the Wheels Go Round. E. Lathen
Murder Makes Us Gay. I. Oellrichs
Murder Man. W. Bogart
Murder Man. W. M. Duncan
Murder Manana. S. Bandolier
Murder Maniac. R. S. L. Harding
Murder Manor. A. Eadie
Murder Manor. P. Manton
Murder Mansion. J. H. Barry
Murder Mansion. Herman Landon
Murder Mansion. J. H. Wallis
Murder Mansion. A. Wilson
Murder Maritime. C. Cranston
Murder Market. T. C. H. Jacobs
Murder Market. C. Rushton
Murder Mars the Tour. M. Fitt
Murder Mask. G. Begbie
Murder Mask. S. Horler
Murder Mask. J. A. Jordan
Murder Masks Miami. R. King
Murder Masquerade. G. Dilnot
Murder Masquerade. I. H. Irwin
Murder Matinee. B. Carson
Murder Matrix. E. J. Fredericks
Murder May Follow. S. Morrow

Murder May Pass Unpunished. F. Everton
Murder Maze. H. Liggett
Murder Me for Nickels. P. Rabe
Murder Me Never. C. Shannon
Murder Medley. M. Hervey
Murder Meets Mephisto. Q. Mario
Murder Melody. K. Robeson
Murder Melody. K. Secrist
Murder Memo to the Commissioner. W. Oursler
Murder: Men Only. B. Cobb
Murder Menagerie. J. Lane
Murder Minus Motive. J. Corbett
Murder Mirage. K. Robeson
Murder Mislaid. M. Cronin
Murder Mission! Al Conroy
Murder Mission. F. W. Irwin
Murder Mistaken. Janet Green
Murder Mistress. R. Colby
Murder Money. Jay Bennett
Murder Money. E. Ronns
Murder Money. R. Wallace
Murder Moon. P. H. Dobbins
Murder Moon. H. Leyford
Murder Most Artistic. W. Gore
Murder Most Black. R. Verron
Murder Most Fair. J. G. Vermandel
Murder Most Familiar. M. Bremner
Murder Most Foul. K. Ashe
Murder Most Foul. K. B. Coxe
Murder Most Foul. H. Hawton
Murder Most Fouled Up. T. Wells
Murder Most Ingenious. K. Chase
Murder Most Intimate. W. H. Baker
Murder Most Monstrous. R. Verron
Murder Most Opportune. R. G. Dean
Murder Moves In. E. Ferrars
Murder Moves On. J. Dall
Murder! Murder! J. Symons
Murder! Murder! L. Vail
Murder Muscles In. M. Franklin
Murder Must Advertise. D. L. Sayers
Murder Must Wait. J. Creasey
Murder Must Wait. A. W. Upfield
Murder Mutuel. B. McKnight
Murder, My Love. E. Atiyah
Murder, My Sweet. H. Holt
Murder Needs a Face. R. Fenisong
Murder Needs a Name. R. Fenisong
Murder Next Door. M. Alan
Murder Next Door. Jean Marsh
Murder Next Year. B. J. Farmer
Murder--Nine and Out. J. V. Turner
Murder '97. F. Gruber
Murder Noon and Night. K. Roos
Murder Now and Then. H. Brean
Murder Now, Pay Later. F. Bosworth
Murder of a Bad Man. H. Footner
Murder of a Banker. J. S. Fletcher
Murder of a Black Cat. Neill Graham
Murder of a Bookmaker. Roland Daniel
Murder of a Chemist. M. Burton
Murder of a Dead Man. W. H. L. Crauford
Murder of a Dead Man. K. Steel
Murder of a Diplomat. A. O. Pollard
Murder of a Film Star. H. Holt
Murder of a Headmistress. E. Pickering
Murder of a Lady. L. Marshall
Murder of a Lady. A. Wynne
Murder of a Magnate. M. Beckett
Murder of a Man Afraid of Women. A. Abbot
Murder of a Marriage. R. Armstrong
Murder of a Martinet. E. C. R. Lorac
Murder of a Matriarch. H. Austin
Murder of a Midget. M. J. Freeman
Murder of a Missing Man. A. M. Chase
Murder of a Mistress. H. Kuttner

Murder of a Mistress. J. Sherwood
Murder of a Mouse. M. Fitt
Murder of a Musician. "Capstan"
Murder of a Mystery Writer. J. Hawk
Murder of a Mystery Writer. E. Heath
Murder of a Novelist. S. Wood
Murder of a Nymph. M. Neville
Murder of a Painted Lady. Harold Ward
Murder of a Professor. J. Miller
Murder of a Quack. G. Bellairs
Murder of a Redhaired Man. M. Plum
Murder of a Snob. Roy Vickers
Murder of a Startled Lady. A. Abbot
Murder of a Student. P. Malloch
Murder of a Stuffed Shirt. M. V. Heberden
Murder of a Suicide. E. Ferrars
Murder of a Wife. H. Kuttner
Murder of Alonzo. P. Cheyney
Murder of an Initiate. M. Propper
Murder of an M.P. R. Gore-Browne
Murder of an M.P. B. H. Homersham
Murder of an Old Man. D. Frome
Murder of an Owl. G. Carr
Murder of an Unpopular Man. D. R. Forbes
Murder of Ann Avery. H. Kuttner
Murder of Augustin Dench. E. Jepson
Murder of Bishop Conrad. L. Hebach
Murder of Busy Lizzie. G. Mitchell
Murder of Caroline Bundy. A. Campbell
Murder of Cecily Thane. H. Ashbrook
Murder of Christine Wilmerding. W. Morton
Murder of Constable Cartwright. A. Blair
Murder of Convenience. R. G. Dean
Murder of Crows. P. Buchanan
Murder of Dave Brandon. T. Lund
Murder of Doctor Grey. T. A. Plummer
Murder of Edwin Drood. P. T. Carden
Murder of Eleanor Pope. H. Kuttner
Murder of Estelle Cantor. C. F. Gregg
Murder of Eve. M. Dalton
Murder of Geraldine Foster. A. Abbot
Murder of Guy Thorpe. Roland Daniel
Murder of Harvey Blake. R. L. Goldman
Murder of Jacob Canansey. P. Capon
Murder of Lalla Lee. H. Burnham
Murder of London Lew. H. S. Keeler
Murder of Love. D. Gray
Murder of Lydia. J. Cowdroy
Murder of Margaret. C. Ryland
Murder of Margot Midnight. P. Herring
Murder of Marion Mason. T. B. Dewey
Murder of Martin Fotherill. E. C. Lester
Murder of Mary Steers. Brian Cooper
Murder of Me. J. F. W. Hannay
Murder of Me. M. S. Michel
Murder of Me. F. A. Symonds
Murder of Miss Betty Sloan. S. Williams
Murder of Mr. Mallabee. Winifred Duke
Murder of Mrs. Davenport. Anthony Gilbert
Murder of Monsieur Fualdes. A. Praviel
Murder of My Aunt. R. Hull
Murder of My Patient. M. G. Eberhart
Murder of My Wife. Reginald Campbell
Murder of No Consequence. R. Verron
Murder of Olympia. M. Neville
Murder of Paul Rougier. V. Sampson
Murder of Quality. J. Le Carre
Murder of Roger Ackroyd. A. Christie
Murder of Sigurd Sharon. H. Ashbrook
Murder of Sir Edmund Godfrey. J. D. Carr
Murder of Some Importance. B. Graeme
Murder of Steven Kester. H. Ashbrook

Murder of Suzy Pommier. E. Bove
Murder of the Admiral. S. Gould
Murder of the Circus Queen. A. Abbot
Murder of the Clergyman's Mistress. A. Abbot
Murder of the Dainty-Footed Model. F. E. Hewens
Murder of the Fifth Columnist. L. Ford
Murder of the Honest Broker. W. Sharp
Murder of the Lawyer's Clerk. J. S. Fletcher
Murder of the Man Next Door. P. Malloch
Murder of the Missing Link. Vercors
Murder of the Night Club Lady. A. Abbot
Murder of the Ninth Baronet. J. S. Fletcher
Murder of the Only Witness. J. S. Fletcher
Murder of the Park Avenue Playgirl. H. Kane
Murder of the Pigboat Skipper. S. Fisher
Murder of the Prime Minister. L. Clark
Murder of the Secret Agent. J. S. Fletcher
Murder of the U.S.A. W. F. Jenkins
Murder of the Well-Beloved. M. Neville
Murder of Three Ghosts. E. Radford
Murder of Whistler's Brother. David Alexander
Murder Off Broadway. L. Falkner
Murder Off Broadway. H. Klinger
Murder Off Key. K. Sproul
Murder Off Miami. D. Wheatley
Murder Off Stage. Monte Barrett
Murder Off Stage. A. Eichler
Murder Off the Record. J. Bingham
Murder on a Bad Trip. June Drummond
Murder on a Monument. E. C. R. Lorac
Murder on a Saturday. D. Gray
Murder on a Shoestring. A. Spiller
Murder on a Tangent. D. M. Disney
Murder on Alternate Tuesdays. T. Davis
Murder on Angler's Island. H. Reilly
Murder on Arrival. G. Batson
Murder on "B" Deck. V. Starrett
Murder on Bag Hill. C. Ryland
Murder on Beacon Hill. G. Brown
Murder on Both Sides. A. Sideman
Murder on Broadway. H. Q. Masur
Murder on Cape Cod. F. Shay
Murder on Coney Island. Dan Morgan
Murder on Delivery. S. Dean
Murder on Demand. Neill Graham
Murder on Demand. R. Verron
Murder on Display. C. Hale
Murder on Duty. M. Burton
Murder on Every Floor. A. Demerest
Murder on Fifth Avenue. C. Cranston
Murder on Fire. M. Bardsley
Murder on Flight 354. John Laffin
Murder on 47th Street. B. Poynter
Murder on French Leave. A. Morice
Murder on Friday. H. Ashbrook
Murder on Ghost Tree Island. K. S. Daiger
Murder on Halfaday Creek. J. B. Hendryx
Murder on Her Mind. R. Dietrich
Murder on Her Mind. Vechel Howard
Murder on High. C. Brown
Murder on High Heels. R. Burke
Murder on His Mind. G. Goldsmith
Murder on Holiday. B. Malim
Murder on Honeymoon. D. Gray
Murder-on-Hudson. Jennifer Jones

Murder on Ice. M. Bardsley
Murder on Ice. V. Gunn
Murder on Largo Island. C. Hogarth
Murder on Leave. G. V. Galwey
Murder on Location. L. Thayer
Murder on Manoeuvres. S. C. Mason
Murder on Margin. R. G. Dean
Murder on Mitcham Common. R. Simmat
Murder on Monday. G. Barnett
Murder on Monday. C. Barry
Murder on Monday. C. Bush
Murder on Monday. R. P. Wilmot
Murder on Monday. G. M. Wilson
Murder on Monk's Wood. H. G. Hutchinson
Murder on Montmartre. N. Vexin
Murder on Mount Capita. L. W. Martin
Murder on My Conscience. E. Radford
Murder on My Hands. C. Franklin
Murder on My Hands. Neill Graham
Murder on My Street. E. Lanham
Murder on Parade. C. Wells
Murder on Paradise Island. R. Forsythe
Murder on Polopel. M. Wright
Murder on Queer Street. Gene Evans
Murder on Route 40. H. J. Hultman
Murder on Russian Hill. L. G. Offord
Murder on Safari. E. Huxley
Murder-on-Sea. R. Harrison
Murder on Shadow Island. Garnett Weston
Murder on Shark Island. J. De Witt
Murder on Show. M. Babson
Murder on Stage. Sutherland Scott
Murder on Stilts. G. Dean
Murder on Sundays. E. Gilzean
Murder-on-Thames. D. Fearon
Murder on the Aphrodite. R. B. Sanborn
Murder on the Beam. J. G. Brandon
Murder on the Blackboard. S. Palmer
Murder on the Bluff. E. Tyler
Murder on the Boat Express. R. Hardinge
Murder on the Brain. A. Heckstall-Smith
Murder on the Brain. E. M. Poate
Murder on the Bridge. L. Brock
Murder on the Broads. G. Chester
Murder on the Burrows. E. C. R. Lorac
Murder on the Bus. C. F. Gregg
Murder on the Camp. J. H. Waring
Murder on the Cattle Ranch. C. H. Snow
Murder on the Cliff. C. Ryland
Murder on the Common. C. Ryland
Murder on the Costa Brava. J. Bonett
Murder on the Day of Judgment. V. Rath
Murder on the Downbeat. R. Avery
Murder on the "Duchess." Neill Graham
Murder on the "Enriqueta." M. Thynne
Murder on the Face of It. E. L. Fetta
Murder on the Fell. H. D. Stacpoole
Murder on the Fourth Floor. J. G. Brandon
Murder on the Frontier. E. Haycox
Murder on the Glass Floor. V. B. Shore
Murder on the High Seas. J. G. Brandon
Murder on the High Seas. R. H. Wilkinson
Murder on the Ice Rink. J. G. Brandon
Murder on the Left Bank. Elliot Paul
Murder on the Line. J. Creasey
Murder on the Line. W. L. Rohde
Murder on the Links. A. Christie
Murder on the List. Neill Graham
Murder on the Loire. T. B. Morris
Murder on the Marsh. J. Ferguson
Murder on the Marshes. G. Chester
Murder on the Matterhorn. G. Carr
Murder on the Merry-Go-Round. J. Bell
Murder on the Mistral. V. G. Malo
Murder on the Monte. Ross Richards
Murder on the Moon. C. MacDaniel
Murder on the Moor. H. Desmond

Murder on the Moor. W. Edwards
Murder on the Moors. C. Campbell
Murder on the Mountain. C. N. Govan
Murder on the Mountain. A. H. Hill
Murder on the Mountain! F. W. Irwin
Murder on the Mountain. N. Rutledge
Murder on the Night Ferry. B. E. Wallace
Murder on the Nile. A. Christie
Murder on the Nose. G. Bagby
Murder on the Orient Express. A. Christie
Murder on the Pacific. D. K. Patton
Murder on the Pacific. L. Thayer
Murder on the Palisades. W. Levinrew
Murder on the Pier. G. Chester
Murder on the Pike. A. Nonweiler
Murder on the Program. M. M. Mannon
Murder on the Prowl. J. M. Spender
Murder on the Purple Water. F. Crane
Murder on the Ranch. F. C. Ryan
Murder on the River. R. Gar
Murder on the Rocks. R. Dietrich
Murder on the Roof. E. J. Doherty
Murder on the Salem Road. K. M. Roof
Murder on the Second Floor. C. Bishop
Murder on the Second Floor. F. Vosper
Murder on the Side. D. Keene
Murder on the Sixth Hole. D. Frome
Murder on the Square. D. Frome
Murder on the Stage. J. G. Brandon
Murder on the Stairs. D. Gray
Murder on the Ten-Yard Line. J. S. Strange
Murder on the Terrace. H. Waugh
Murder on the Thirty-First Floor. P. Wahloo
Murder on the Tropic. T. Downing
Murder on the Underground. W. Boggs
Murder on the Veld. R. Hardinge
Murder on the Way! T. Roscoe
Murder on the Wild Side. J. Jacks
Murder on the Wing. A. Eadie
Murder on the Yacht. R. King
Murder on Their Minds. G. H. Coxe
Murder on Tour. T. Downing
Murder on Trial. M. Underwood
Murder on Trust. C. Rushton
Murder on Tuesday. Mary Taylor
Murder on Vacation. Ruth MacLeod
Murder on Wall Street. J. B. Ethan
Murder on Wheels. S. Palmer
Murder on Wheels. K. Robeson
Murder on Wheels. L. Warden
Murder on Whispering Sands. V. Gunn
Murder One! M. E. Cohane
Murder One. F. Gruber
Murder One. H. Howard
Murder One. E. Lipsky
Murder: One, Two, Three. J. Creasey
Murder or Manslaughter. H. B. Mathers
Murder or Mercy. J. Stagge
Murder Out of Class. H. C. Davis
Murder Out of Court. J. Cowdroy
Murder Out of Court. R. B. Dominic
Murder Out of Mind. K. F. Crossen
Murder Out of School. M. Burton
Murder Out of School. I. T. Ross
Murder Out of Season. L. Gribble
Murder Out of the Past. J. Creasey
Murder Out of Tune. F. L. Cary
Murder Out of Tune. M. Magill
Murder Out of Tune. C. Rushton
Murder Out of Turn. F. Lockridge
Murder over Broadway. F. Malina
Murder over Dorval. D. Montrose
Murder over Karmak. N. MacKenzie
Murder--Paris Fashion. C. Brown
Murder Party. H. Bordeaux
Murder Party. F. L. Cary
Murder Paves the Way. S. Truss
Murder Pays a Call. B. Rogers

Title Index

Murder Pays No Dividends. C. Cookson
Murder Picks the Jury. Harrison Hunt
Murder, Plain and Fancy. Garland Lord
Murder Plan Six. J. Bingham
Murder Plays an Ugly Scene. L. A. G. Strong
Murder Pluperfect. K. Giles
Murder Plus. C. Wells
Murder Point. C. Dawson
Murder Points a Finger. David Alexander
Murder Points East. R. Verron
Murder Pool. E. Heath
Murder Premeditated. P. H. Powell
Murder Proof. J. B. O'Sullivan
Murder--Queen High. B. Wade
Murder R.F.D. H. Petersen
Murder Recalls Van Kill. S. Bayne
Murder Red-Handed. Richard Grayson
Murder Reflected. J. Caird
Murder Rehearsal. R. East
Murder Rehearsal. B. G. Quin
Murder Remote. J. Caird
Murder Rents a Room. S. E. Mason
Murder, Repeat Murder. A. MacKinnon
Murder Rides a Rocket. F. Diamond
Murder Rides the Campaign Train. The Gordons
Murder Rides the Express. H. Reilly
Murder Rings the Bell. Neill Graham
Murder Road. G. J. Barrett
Murder Room. P. E. Walsh
Murder Round the Corner. N. MacKenzie
Murder Roundabout. R. Lockridge
Murder Run Riot. J. Courage
Murder Run Wild. H. Desmond
Murder Runs a Fever. R. Fenisong
Murder Runs in the Family. H. Footner
Murder Runs Riot. S. Forbes
Murder Runs Wild. G. Morland
Murder Sails at Midnight. M. Babson
Murder Scholastic. J. Caird
Murder Secretary. W. G. Beyer
Murder Seeks an Agent. Wenzell Brown
Murder Set to Music. H. R. Campbell
Murder Sets the Pace. E. W. Freeman
Murder, She Said. A. Christie
Murder She Says! Reginald Campbell
Murder Ship. G. H. Teed
Murder Sits Pretty. C. Robertson
Murder!--So What? B. Shannon
Murder Solves a Problem. M. Bramhall
Murder, Somewhere in This City. M. Procter
Murder Speaks. E. Radford
Murder Special. F. MacIsaac
Murder Specialist. B. Clifton
Murder Spins the Wheel. B. Halliday
Murder Spoils Everything. J. Lane
Murder Stalks a Billion. R. Wallace
Murder Stalks the Bay. E. Messenger
Murder Stalks the Circle. L. Thayer
Murder Stalks the Mayor. R. T. M. Scott
Murder Stalks the Wakely Family. A. Derleth
Murder Starts from Fishguard. H. C. Davis
Murder Steals the Show. L. Hirsch
Murder Steps In. C. M. Russell
Murder Steps Out. C. Reeve
Murder Strikes an Atomic Unit. T. Du Bois
Murder Strikes at Dawn. H. Desmond
Murder Strikes North. N. Thurley
Murder Strikes Pink. J. Pullein-Thompson
Murder Strikes Three. D. MacDuff
Murder Strikes Thrice. C. G. Booth
Murder Strikes Twice. M. B. Dix
Murder Strikes Twice. J. V. Nolan
Murder, Sunny Side Up. R. B. Dominic
Murder Swings High. N. Brent
Murder Syndicate. J. Chancellor
Murder Takes a Honeymoon. E. Fleming
Murder Takes a Wife. J. A. Howard

Murder Takes No Holiday. B. Halliday
Murder Takes Over. A. Tack
Murder Takes the Baths. L. Priestley
Murder Takes the Stage. J. Reach
Murder Takes the Veil. M. A. Hubbard
Murder That Had Everything. H. Footner
Murder That Wouldn't Stay Solved. Hampton Stone
Murder Through Room 45. T. A. Plummer
Murder Through the Looking Glass. R. G. Dean
Murder Through the Looking Glass. A. Garve
Murder Through the Looking Glass. M. Venning
Murder Through the Window. F. Everton
Murder Thy Neighbor. M. Hervey
Murder Times Five. R. Colby
Murder Times 4. C. Nuetzel
Murder Times Three. A. R. Long
Murder Tips the Scales. J. Creasey
Murder to Follow. K. Field
Murder to Go. E. Lathen
Murder to Hounds. E. Acheson
Murder to Make You Grow Up Little Girl. L. Oriol
Murder to Measure. Robert Mason
Murder to Music. G. Burne
Murder to Music. G. Chester
Murder to Music. P. Colson
Murder to Music. W. H. L. Crauford
Murder to Music. L. Edgley
Murder to Music. J. Kilgore
Murder to Music. M. Newman
Murder to Order. L. Marshall
Murder to Type. A. R. Long
Murder to Welcome Her. M. Neville
Murder Today, Money Tomorrow. J. Messmann
Murder Too Late. G. Ashe
Murder Town. L. Marshall
Murder Trail. C. W. Sanders
Murder Trail. R. Wallace
Murder Train. Gavin Holt
Murder Trap. Howel Evans
Murder Trap. J. A. Jordan
Murder Trap. L. Livingston
Murder Trapp. Eugene Franklin
Murder Tree. L. McFarlane
Murder Trouble. L. Trimble
Murder Tunes In. C. Kingston
Murder Twice Removed. Muriel Bradley
Murder Twice Told. D. Hamilton
Murder Under Construction. P. MacTyre
Murder Under the Big Top. R. Wallace
Murder Under the Sun. L. O'Donnell
Murder Underground. W. Arden
Murder Underground. M. D. Hay
Murder Unleashed. D. Bennett
Murder Unlimited. N. Carter
Murder Unlimited. M. V. Heberden
Murder Unmourned. George Douglas
Murder Unplanned. E. A. St. Clair
Murder Unrecognized. M. Burton
Murder Unseen. J. York
Murder Unsolved. S. Adams
Murder Unsuspected. J. Cowdroy
Murder up My Sleeve. E. S. Gardner
Murder up the Glen. C. Campbell
Murder Upstairs. A. Bliss
Murder Very Dry! S. S. Baker
Murder Walks Alone. J. V. Nolan
Murder Walks Alone. C. Ripley
Murder Walks on Tiptoe. Neill Graham
Murder Walks the Corridors. J. D. Perry

Murder Walks the Deck. W. Martyn
Murder Walks the Stairs. G. M. Barnes
Murder Ward. R. Sapir
Murder Was My Neighbor. G. Cobden
Murder Was Never Bolder. L. G. Redmond-Howard
Murder Was Their Medicine. G. Cobden
Murder Wears a Mantilla. C. Brown
Murder Wears a Mummer's Mask. B. Halliday
Murder Wears Mukluks. E. M. Boyd
Murder Week-End. M. Halliday
Murder Well Begun. S. Adams
Murder Well Done. I. S. Shriber
Murder When Necessary. P. Levene
Murder While You Wait. J. Corbett
Murder While You Work. S. Scarlett
Murder Will. E. Wilmot
Murder Will Be Committed. G. Goodchild
Murder Will In. C. Wells
Murder Will Out. E. M. Bowen
Murder Will Out. M. Leinster
Murder Will Out. H. Leyford
Murder Will Out. G. E. Minot
Murder Will Out. Jeannette Covert Nolan
Murder Will Out. Roy Vickers
Murder Will Out. P. C. Williams
Murder Will Speak. G. Bellaire
Murder Will Speak. J. J. Connington
Murder Will Speak. Mark Cross
Murder with a Kiss. V. Gunn
Murder with a Past. E. Queen
Murder with a Theme Song. V. Rath
Murder with a Vengeance. R. Quest
Murder with Gloves. B. Huber
Murder with Impatience. R. Verron
Murder with Long Hair. H. D. Spatz
Murder with Love. Vechel Howard
Murder with Love. Garland Lord
Murder with Love. D. Shannon
Murder--with Love. J. T. Story
Murder with Magic. R. St. Clair
Murder with Minarets. C. Forsyte
Murder with Mirrors. A. Christie
Murder with Mushrooms. G. Ashe
Murder with Music. G. Riddell
Murder with Orange Blossoms. R. Darby
Murder with Pictures. G. H. Coxe
Murder with Relish. C. L. Taylor
Murder with Roses. A. McElfresh
Murder with Southern Hospitality. L. Ford
Murder with Variety. W. Arthur
Murder with Your Malted. Jerome Barry
Murder Within Murder. F. Lockridge
Murder Without Alibis. S. McPhellamy
Murder Without Clues. J. L. Bonney
Murder Without Crime. B. Healey
Murder Without Crime. J. Lee Thompson
Murder Without Icing. E. Lathen
Murder Without Makeup. E. Benjamin
Murder Without Malice. A. Spiller
Murder Without Men. T. B. Morris
Murder Without Morals. M. M. Marshall
Murder Without Motive. M. Carrel
Murder Without Motive. R. L. Goldman
Murder Without Mourners. Sutherland Scott
Murder Without Mystery. J. Playfair
Murder Without Regret. E. L. Cushing
Murder Without Regret. R. Trevor
Murder Without Risk. H. Adams
Murder Without Tears. L. Lupton
Murder Without Weapons. A. B. Cunningham
Murder Without Weapons. Means Davis
Murder Won't Out. P. Hobson
Murder Won't Wait. C. J. Daly
Murder Won't Wait. R. S. O'Connor

Murder Yet to Come. I. B. Myers
Murdered but Not Dead. Anne Austin
Murdered Cliche. J. Samuel
Murdered Man's Derby. E. A. St. Clair
Murdered Manservant. C. F. Gregg
Murdered Mathematician. H. S. Keeler
Murdered Millionaire. E. Queen
Murdered: One by One. F. Beeding
Murdered Sleep. G. Braddon
Murderer. W. Morton
Murderer. G. Simenon
Murderer Among Us. C. Brown
Murderer at Large. W. A. Ballinger
Murderer at Large. D. Henderson
Murderer at Large. S. Horler
Murderer in the House. K. Clugston
Murderer in This House. R. King
Murderer Invisible. P. Wylie
Murderer Is a Fox. E. Queen
Murderer of Sleep. M. Kennedy
Murderer Returns. E. D. Torgerson
Murderer Vine. S. Rifkin
Murderer Who Wanted More. B. Kendrick
Murderers. F. Brown
Murderers Are Silent. R. Clarke
Murderer's Bluff. F. Duncan
Murderer's Bride. H. Desmond
Murderer's Challenge. H. Footner
Murderer's Choice. A. M. Wells
Murderers Don't Smile. John Morgan
Murderer's Fen. A. Garve
Murderer's Holiday. D. H. Clarke
Murderers' Houses. J. Melville
Murderer's Island. Y. Tregarron
Murderer's Luck. H. Holt
Murderers Make Mistakes. F. W. Crofts
Murderer's Maze. R. Glover
Murderer's Maze. John Marsh
Murderers' Medicine. A. Train
Murderers Meet. Gwyn Evans
Murderer's Mistake. E. C. R. Lorac
Murderer's Moon. R. Dana
Murderer's Moon. R. Goyne
Murderer's Moon. G. Morgan
Murderers of Monty. R. Hull
Murderer's Row. R. Batchelor
Murderer's Row. D. Hamilton
Murderer's Stand-In. J. G. Brandon
Murderers Three. F. C. Tickner
Murderer's Trail. J. J. Farjeon
Murderer's Vanity. H. Footner
Murderer's Wench. P. Hoyt
Murdering Kind. Gwendoline Butler
Murdering Mr. Velfrage. Roy Vickers
Murderous Journey. E. McGirr
Murderous Suspense. G. M. Barnes
Murderous Welcome. J. Irwin
Murder's a Swine. N. Lombard
Murder's a Waiting Game. Anthony Gilbert
Murder's Always Final. Neill Graham
Murders at Crossby. E. P. Frankland
Murders at Hibiscus Key. V. Siller
Murders at Highbridge. R. Slingsby
Murders at Loon Lake. K. Whipple
Murders at Moon Dance. A. B. Guthrie
Murders at Scandal House. P. Hunt
Murders at the Crab Apple Cafe. G. Manners
Murders at the Lakes. G. L. Jennings
Murders at the Manor. C. Ryland
Murders at Turbot Towers. S. J. Peskett
Murder's Burning. S. H. Courtier
Murders by Moonlight. A. Hyde
Murder's Coming. D. C. Cameron
Murder's End. R. Kelston
Murders for Sale. A. Weston
Murders Form Fours. David Hume

Murders in Lovers' Lane. J. G. Dunton
Murders in Praed Street. J. Rhode
Murders in Sequence. M. Propper
Murders in Silk. M. Teagle
Murders in Surrey Wood. John Arnold
Murders in the Dispensary. J. Carr
Murders in the Mortuary. Austin Stone
Murders in Volume 2. E. Daly
Murders I've Seen. P. Mechem
Murder's Just for Cops. L. Marshall
Murder's Little Helper. G. Bagby
Murder's Little Helper. Garland Lord
Murder's Little Sister. F. Branch
Murder's Money. G. A. Ralston
Murders Near Mapleton. B. Flynn
Murder's No Accident. A. S. Fleischman
Murder's No Accident. F. Orpet
Murder's No Picnic. E. L. Cushing
Murder's No Picnic. P. Hambledon
Murder's No Picnic. P. Muat
Murder's Not an Odd Job. R. Dennis
Murders of Richard III. Elizabeth Peters
Murders on Fox Island. M. P. Hood
Murders on the Square. T. George
Murder's out of Season. L. Marshall
Murder's Rock. D. Reid
Murder's Shield. R. Sapir
Murder's So Permanent. E. Howie
Murder's Web. Dorothy Dunn
Murders While You Wait. C. Hunter
Murdoch Legacy. Irma Walker
Murdock's Acid Test. G. H. Coxe
Muriel Wins Through. G. Thorne
Murillo Mystery. A. Eadie
Murillo Mystery. B. Poynter
Murmansk Assignment. J. Pattinson
Murmur of Mutiny. M. Pugh
Murmuring Willow. Rona Randall
Murmurs in the Rue Morgue. M. Cumberland
Murphy Gang. Roland Daniel
Murphy's Game. M. Tarmey
Murphy's Master, and other stories. J. Payn
Murray Hill Mystery. N. Carter
Murray of the Scots Greys. L. Clarke
Murray, the Detective. Old Sleuth
Muscle Beach Party. Elsie Lee
Muscle Boy. B. Clifton
Muse Theatre Murder. T. A. Plummer
Museum Murder. J. T. MacIntyre
Museum Mystery. A. Soutar
Museum Piece No. 13. R. King
Mushalong. G. Goodchild
Mushroom Cave. R. Rosenblum
Mushrooms on Toast. Laurence Kirk
Music from the Past. K. Cameron
Music Gallery Murder. R. Francis Foster
Music Room. W. E. D. Ross
Music Tells All. E. R. Punshon
Musical Comedy Crime. Anthony Gilbert
Mussolini Murder Plot. B. Newman
Muster of the Vultures. G. Fairlie
Mustering of the Hawks. J. Harris
Mutable Many. R. Barr
Mutation Mink. P. Traill
Mute Witness. R. L. Pike
Muted Murder. S. Sinclair
Mutilators. B. Heatter
Mutiny. F. R. Bechdolt
Mutton Dressed as Lamb, and Live. J. M. Walsh
Muzzle Blast. B. Rossi
Muzzled Ox. C. Stanton
My Adventure in the Flying Scotsman. E. Phillpotts
My Bad Boy. M. Neville
My Body. R. Dietrich
My Bones Will Keep. G. Mitchell
My Bonny Lies Under the Sea. R. Alan
My Brother, Cain. V. Thiessen

My Brother Michael. M. Stewart
My Brother's Executioner. J. Laffin
My Brother's Killer. D. M. Devine
My Brother's Killer. J. Potts
My Brother's Killer. J. York
My Brother's Wife. Harry Davis
My Business Is Murder. H. Kane
My Child and I. F. Warden
My Coat Is Travel-Stained. F. Gamble
My Cousin Caroline's Wedding. H. Wood
My Cousin Cynthia, and others. P. C. De Crespigny
My Cousin Rachel. D. Du Maurier
My Darlin' Evangeline. H. Kane
My Darling Is Deadpan. C. Brown
My Darling's Ransom. R. Dowling
My Deadly Angel. J. Chelton
My Dear Heart. K. Lindsay
My Dear Miss Emma. P. Allardyce
My Dearest Elizabeth. A. Maybury
My Enemy--My Wife. A. Haden
My Enemy's Friend. H. Osborne
My Face Beneath the Stone. J. Crecy
My Fair Lady. Georgius
My Father Sleeps. G. Mitchell
My First Crime. G. Mace
My First Love. J. H. Riddell
My Flesh Is Sweet. D. Keene
My Foe Outstretch'd Beneath the Tree. V. C. Clinton-Baddeley
My Fourteen Cases. Anonymous
My Friend Charles. F. Durbridge
My Friend Judas. P. Barrington
My Friend Maigret. G. Simenon
My Friend Pasquale and other stories. J. S. Tait
My Friend the Murderer and other mysteries and adventures. A. C. Doyle
My Friend Tony. W. Johnston
My God How the Money Rolls In. J. Ripley
My Grave Is for the Living. S. Connor
My Guess Was Murder. G. Cobden
My Gun, Her Body. J. Bogar
My Gun Is Quick. M. Spillane
My Heart and Stephanie. R. W. Kauffman
My Heart Went Dead. A. McElfresh
My Husband's First Love. H. Wood
My Indian Queen. G. Boothby
My Japanese Prince. A. C. Gunter
My Killer Doesn't Understand Me. T. P. Mulkeen
My Kind of Game. A. Rome
My Kingdom for a Hearse. C. Rice
My Lady Bountiful. F. M. White
My Lady Caprice. J. Farnol
My Lady Cinderella. A. M. Williamson
My Lady Dangerous. S. Horler
My Lady Evil. P. J. Cooper
My Lady Mischief. J. L. Roberts
My Lady of the Yellow Domino. A. W. Marchmont
My Lady of Whims. F. Warden
My Lady Ruby and John Basileon, Chief of Police. G. F. Monkshood
My Lady Vamp. G. W. Gough
My Lady's Bath. C. N. Boyle
My Lady's Diamonds. A. Sergeant
My Lady's Garter. J. Futrelle
My Lady's Money. W. Collins
My Late Wives. Carter Dickson
My Lodger's Legacy. R. W. Hume
My Lord Duke. E. W. Hornung
M'Lord, I Am Not Guilty. F. S. Wees

My Lord the Felon. H. Hill
My Lost Self. A. W. Marchmont
My Love Has a Secret. A. Maybury
My Love Is Stone. C. Massie
My Love Is Violent. T. B. Dewey
My Love Noel. H. Nisbet
My Love Wears Black. O. R. Cohen
My Lovely Executioner. P. Rabe
My Mermaid Murmurs Murder. C. Brown
My Miscellanies. W. Collins
My Mother Was Hanged. E. S. Willards
My Mysterious Clients. H. Scribner
My Name Is Black! J. Nazel
My Name Is Celia. R. Kruger
My Name Is Death. C. Birkin
My Name Is Death. L. Egan
My Name Is Love. J. MacLaren-Ross
My Name Is Michael Sibley. J. Bingham
My Name Is Morgan. W. Woolfolk
My Neighbor's Wife. D. M. Disney
My Official Wife. R. H. Savage
My Old Man's Badge. F. Findley
My Own Murderer. R. Hull
My Pal, the Killer. C. Warwick
My Particular Murder. D. Sharp
My Path Belated. N. Ames
My Peril in a Pullman Car and other tales. A. Griffiths
My Poll and My Partner. T. P. Prest
My Private Hangman. N. Herries
My Rubies Are Blood Red. J. C. Crawley
My Search for Ruth. A. Clarke
My Shadow. P. Malloch
My Sister Erica. J. Blackmore
My Sister, Good Night. G. McDonell
My Sister, My Friend. K. Blake
My Sister Sophie. J. Edgar
My Sister's Confession and other stories. M. E. Braddon
My Son, the Murderer. P. Quentin
My Soul to Keep. E. Davis
My Strangest Case. G. Boothby
My Tattered Loving. G. R. Preedy
My Terrible Twin. F. Whishaw
My Tom-Boy Girl. C. E. Blaney
My True Love Lies. L. G. Offord
My Turn Next. Winston Graham
My Turn Now. Janet Green
My Turn to Die. K. Royce
My Two Wives and other stories. G. R. Sims
My Undiscovered Crimes. F. Wicks
My Wife Melissa. F. Durbridge
My Wife's Lover. J. Courage
My Word You Should Have Seen Us. J. Ripley
Mycroft Murder Case. A. Marsden
Myer for Hire. L. S. Taube
Mynns' Mystery. G. M. Fenn
Myopic Mermaid. C. Brown
Mysteries. W. LeQueux
Mysteries and Adventures. A. C. Doyle
Mysteries and Miseries of New Orleans. N. Buntline
Mysteries and Miseries of New York. N. Buntline
Mysteries of a Great City. W. LeQueux
Mysteries of Ann. Alice Brown
Mysteries of Black Valley. A. Mallory
Mysteries of Blair House. R. O. Eastman
Mysteries of Chicago. Anonymous
Mysteries of Crime, as Shown in Remarkable Capital Crimes. Anonymous
Mysteries of Heron Dyke. T. W. Speight
Mysteries of London. G. W. M. Reynolds
Mysteries of Modern London. G. R. Sims

Mysteries of Nashua. Anonymous
Mysteries of New Orleans. Anonymous
Mysteries of New York. Old Sleuth
Mysteries of Oakendale Abbey. Anonymous
Mysteries of Paris. E. Sue
Mysteries of Ryeburn Manor. J. Laurence
Mysteries of the City. J. M'Levy
Mysteries of the Court of France. G. W. M. Reynolds
Mysteries of the Court of London. G. W. M. Reynolds
Mysteries of the Court of Naples. G. W. M. Reynolds
Mysteries of the Marchmonts. G. W. M. Reynolds
Mysteries of the Riviera. E. P. Oppenheim
Mysteries of Udolpho. A. Radcliffe
Mysterious Abduction. G. S. Goodman
Mysterious Affair at Styles. A. Christie
Mysterious Aviator. N. Shute
Mysterious Beggar. A. A. Day
Mysterious Bohemian. A. M. Diehl
Mysterious Burglar. G. E. Walsh
Mysterious Cane of Dr. Chang. R. St. Clair
Mysterious Card. C. Moffett
Mysterious Case. K. F. Hill
Mysterious Castle. N. Carter
Mysterious Cavern. N. Carter
Mysterious Chinaman. J. S. Fletcher
Mysterious Chinese Mandrake, and other stories. I. D. Ekbergh
Mysterious Commission. M. Innes
Mysterious Crime at Burleigh Mansion. Anonymous
Mysterious Dagger. Anonymous
Mysterious Disappearance. L. Tracy
Mysterious Disappearance of a Bride. M. Danvers
Mysterious Disappearance of Helen St. Vincent. J. J. Flinn
Mysterious Disappearances. G. M. Winsor
Mysterious Dr. Oliver. J. B. Ellis
Mysterious Foe. N. Carter
Mysterious Game. N. Carter
Mysterious "Graft." N. Carter
Mysterious Inheritance. B. Marchant
Mysterious Journey. M. L. Tyrrell
Mysterious Juror. F. Du Boisgobey
Mysterious Madame S. S. D'Erigny
Mysterious Mademoiselle. F. Grierson
Mysterious Mail Robbery. N. Carter
Mysterious Marksman. Anonymous
Mysterious Marriage. E. Southworth
Mysterious Martin. T. Robbins
Mysterious Mickey Finn. Elliot Paul
Mysterious Millionaire. L. S. West
Mysterious Miss Cass. G. W. Appleton
Mysterious Miss Death. Gwyn Evans
Mysterious Miss Morrisot. V. Williams
Mysterious Missile. C. H. Snow
Mysterious Mr. Badman. W. F. Harvey
Mysterious Mr. Brent. G. Davison
Mysterious Mr. Frame. M. Merrick
Mysterious Mr. Garland. W. Martyn
Mysterious Mr. I. H. S. Keeler
Mysterious Mr. Jarvis. F. R. Giles
Mysterious Mr. Maynard. J. Hunter
Mysterious Mr. Miller. W. LeQueux
Mysterious Mr. Pickering. P. E. Curtiss
Mysterious Mr. Quin. A. Christie
Mysterious Mr. Reece. R. M. Graydon
Mysterious Mr. Rocco. J. Creasey
Mysterious Mr. Sabin. E. P. Oppenheim
Mysterious Mrs. Nutford. B. M. Clay
Mysterious Mrs. Nutford. J. Middlemass
Mysterious Mrs. Wilkinson and other stories. W. E. Norris
Mysterious Monsieur Moray. B. Stuart

Mysterious Murder of Pearl Bryan. Anonymous
Mysterious Office. Jennette Lee
Mysterious Partner. A. Fielding
Mysterious Stranger. C. H. Thorburn
Mysterious Suspect. J. Rhode
Mysterious Three. W. LeQueux
Mysterious Valley. G. W. Wicking
Mysterious Way. J. Boland
Mysterious Waye. P. C. Wren
Mysterious Wife. Grove Wilson
Mysterious Yankee. Old Sleuth
Mysteriouser and Mysteriouser. G. Bagby
Mystery. Anonymous
Mystery. G. S. Crosby
Mystery. M. Paris
Mystery. S. E. White
Mystery. H. Wood
Mystery and Minette. H. Adams
Mystery and other stories. Annie Thomas
Mystery at Angel's End. J. Chancellor
Mystery at Arden Court. E. C. Holt
Mystery at Butlin's. M. O'Nair
Mystery at Chillery. R. Francis Foster
Mystery at Collinwood. Marilyn Ross
Mystery at Crowstone. Colin Hope
Mystery at Folly Mill. J. Brooke
Mystery at Friar's Pardon. M. Porlock
Mystery at Furze Acres. D. Whitelaw
Mystery at Geneva. R. Macaulay
Mystery at Greenfingers. J. B. Priestley
Mystery at Greycombe Farm. J. Rhode
Mystery at Greystones. K. Lindsay
Mystery at Grimsdale. E. P. Frankland
Mystery at Hardacres. G. Morton
Mystery at Hermit's End. G. Morton
Mystery at Hidden Harbor. C. Fitzsimmons
Mystery at King's Grant. A. E. D.
Mystery at Lover's Cave. A. Berkeley
Mystery at Lynden Sands. J. J. Connington
Mystery at Manby House. J. Creasey
Mystery at Merrilees. M. Poole
Mystery at Moor Street. C. F. Gregg
Mystery at Olympia. J. Rhode
Mystery at Peak House. A. J. Rees
Mystery at Ramshackle House. H. Footner
Mystery at Spanish Hacienda. J. Gregory
Mystery at Stowe. V. Loder
Mystery at the Blue Villa. M. D. Post
Mystery at the Inn. J. H. Vahey
Mystery at the JHC Ranch. W. C. Tuttle
Mystery at the Rectory. A. Fielding
Mystery at Tudor Arches. L. Gribble
Mystery at Vellum. L. G. Horsefield
Mystery Blues and other stories. P. Cheyney
Mystery Box. W. W. Sayer
Mystery Car. M. Gerard
Mystery Castle. Elsie Lee
Mystery Chain. L. G. Moberly
Mystery Crime Cases. Anonymous
Mystery Crime Cases. N. W. Firth
Mystery Cruise. K. Langmaid
Mystery Cruise. Taffrail
Mystery DeLuxe. R. King
Mystery Evans. B. Baker
Mystery Flier. E. T. Woodhall
Mystery Flight. J. Davies
Mystery for Mary. V. Hanson
Mystery from the Air. J. Laurence
Mystery Gangster. G. Chester
Mystery Girl. C. Wells
Mystery Hand. B. Bolt

Mystery House. P. Hobson
Mystery House. K. Norris
Mystery House. J. M. Walsh
Mystery in Blue. G. E. Mallette
Mystery in Glass. E. Kilvington
Mystery in Green. A. Vinton
Mystery in Hawaii. R. St. Clair
Mystery in Kensington Gore. M. Porlock
Mystery in Minchin Mews. R. Gar
Mystery in Red. F. Grierson
Mystery in Red. S. Williams
Mystery in St. James Square. G. Collins
Mystery in the Channel. F. W. Crofts
Mystery in the Drood Family. M. Saunders
Mystery in the English Channel. F. W. Crofts
Mystery in the Mist. C. Kingston
Mystery in the Ritsmore. W. A. Johnston
Mystery in the Snow. G. Darwent
Mystery in the Woodshed. Anthony Gilbert
Mystery in White. J. J. Farjeon
Mystery Island. E. H. Hurst
Mystery Island. F. Whishaw
Mystery Island. Palmer White
Mystery Keepers. M. Fox
Mystery Killer. H. Desmond
Mystery Lady. R. W. Chambers
Mystery Lamp. M. R. Rinehart
Mystery Maker. Seamark
Mystery Man. S. Hocking
Mystery Man. J. M. Walsh
Mystery Man in the Tower. H. Chichester
Mystery Mandarin. J. W. Bobin
Mystery Manor. L. Gribble
Mystery Mansion. L. Archer
Mystery Mansion. Herman Landon
Mystery Message. T. C. Bridges
Mystery Mile. M. Allingham
Mystery Militiaman. Ladbroke Black
Mystery Mind. A. B. Reeve
Mystery Mission. S. Horler
Mystery Mission and other stories. S. Horler
Mystery Money. J. Laurence
Mystery Motive. M. Halliday
Mystery of a Bungalow. W. Chesney
Mystery of a Butcher's Shop. G. Mitchell
Mystery of a Hansom Cab. F. Hume
Mystery of a Madstone. Anonymous
Mystery of a Madstone. K. F. Hill
Mystery of a Millionaire. M. J. Pemberton
Mystery of a Millionaire's Grave. G. Stables
Mystery of a Moonlight Tryst. I. D. Hardy
Mystery of a Motor Cab. F. Hume
Mystery of a Motor-Car. W. LeQueux
Mystery of a Shipyard. R. H. Savage
Mystery of a Studio and other stories. R. H. Fletcher
Mystery of a Turkish Bath. Rita
Mystery of Airedale Hall. B. Bolt
Mystery of Alfred Doubt. W. Hay
Mystery of Allan Grale. I. F. Mayo
Mystery of Allanwold. E. Van Loon
Mystery of Alton Grange. E. Everett-Green
Mystery of an Omnibus. F. Du Boisgobey
Mystery of Angelina Frood. R. A. Freeman
Mystery of Arrowhead Hill. L. W. Douglas
Mystery of Ashton Hall. B. Nitsua
Mystery of Avenue Road. A. Parsons
Mystery of Bar Harbor. Alsop Leffingwell
Mystery of Barnard Hanson. U. L. Silberrad
Mystery of Beacon Hill. L. G. Redmond-Howard
Mystery of Beaton Craig. Mark Allerton
Mystery of Beckers' Brook. A. Blair
Mystery of Belgrave Square. Curtis Yorke
Mystery of Belvoir Mansions. B. Bolt
Mystery of Bent Cove. F. D. Holmgren
Mystery of Black Pit. Anonymous
Mystery of Blackmoor Prison. J. Creasey
Mystery of Blencarrow. M. Oliphant
Mystery of Bloomsbury Crescent. Mrs. Lodge
Mystery of Bullen Point. R. C. Armour
Mystery of Burnleigh Manor. W. Livingston
Mystery of Captain Burnaby. A. S. McNalty
Mystery of Cedar Valley. V. Henry
Mystery of Cell 13. G. H. Teed
Mystery of Central Park. N. Bly
Mystery of Choice. R. W. Chambers
Mystery of Clement Dunraven. J. Middlemass
Mystery of Cloomber. A. C. Doyle
Mystery of Clough Mills. Stuart Martin
Mystery of Colde Fell. C. M. Braeme
Mystery of "Crazy Canyon" Ranch. E. H. Ott
Mystery of Crooknose. L. W. Douglas
Mystery of DS 24. T. Wallace
Mystery of Dagget's Bank. N. Ned
Mystery of Daria Kane. M. V. Hunt
Mystery of Dark Hollow. E. Southworth
Mystery of Dead Man's Heath. J. J. Farjeon
Mystery of Devil's Canyon. C. H. Snow
Mystery of Dr. Fu-Manchu. S. Rohmer
Mystery of Dudley Horne. F. Warden
Mystery of Echo Caverns. R. C. Payes
Mystery of Edwin Drood. C. Dickens
Mystery of Enid Belairs. D. Whitelaw
Mystery of Evangeline Fairfax. E. Kunst
Mystery of Evelin Delorme. A. B. Paine
Mystery of Fell Castle. A. Gask
Mystery of Fernridge Manor. R. Bodwell
Mystery of Fifty-Two. W. S. Masterman
Mystery of Flat 60. A. J. Sarl
Mystery of Flying V Ranch. G. E. Rochester
Mystery of Fourways. F. Warden
Mystery of Frances Farrington. E. Banks
Mystery of Fury Castle. Dan Ross
Mystery of Fury Castle. Marilyn Ross
Mystery of Fyfe House. V. Nielsen
Mystery of Glyn Castle. L. H. Brooks
Mystery of "Golden Lotus." L. Gerard
Mystery of Gruden's Gap. Mark Cross
Mystery of Grudge Mountain. A. P. Terhune
Mystery of Hanging Sword Alley. W. J. Bayfield
Mystery of Hartley House. C. S. Raymond
Mystery of Helmsley Grange. A. Askew
Mystery of High Eldersham. M. Burton
Mystery of Holly Tavern. L. Collis
Mystery of Horseshoe Island. F. W. Gumley
Mystery of Hotel Brichet. E. Chavette
Mystery of Hunting's End. M. G. Eberhart
Mystery of Jamaica Terrace. D. Donovan
Mystery of Jessie Page, and other stories. H. Wood
Mystery of Joan Marryat. Mark Cross
Mystery of John Peppercorn. T. Gallon
Mystery of Judith. C. E. Pearce
Mystery of June 13. M. Severy
Mystery of Khufu's Tomb. T. Mundy
Mystery of Killard. R. Dowling
Mystery of King Cobra. D. Marfield
Mystery of King's Everard. C. Brandon
Mystery of Knickerbocker Towers. E. Thorne
Mystery of Kun-Ja-Muck Cave. G. F. Tibbitts
Mystery of Lady Chetwynd's Spectre. Anonymous
Mystery of Lady Chetwynd's Spectre. H. Lewis
Mystery of Lady Isobel. E. R. Punshon
Mystery of Ladyplace. P. Brebner
Mystery of Ladyplace. C. Lys
Mystery of Landy Court. F. Hume
Mystery of Leighton Grange. M. E. Braddon
Mystery of Lincoln's Inn. R. Machray
Mystery of Lostland Academy. A. M. Sholl
Mystery of Lucien Delorme. G. De Teramond
Mystery of Lynne Court. J. S. Fletcher
Mystery of Madeline Le Blanc. M. Ehrmann
Mystery of Mademoiselle. W. LeQueux
Mystery of Magdalen. Mrs. C. Kernahan
Mystery of Mandeville Square. G. Campbell
Mystery of Mar Saba. J. H. Hunter
Mystery of Margaret. O. Read
Mystery of Martha's Vineyard. G. Dyer
Mystery of Martin Guerre. J. G. Sarasin
Mystery of Mary Anne and other stories. G. R. Sims
Mystery of Mary Hamilton. Roland Daniel
Mystery of Maybury Manor. Eric Wood
Mystery of Mayfair. J. S. Winter
Mystery of Me...? W. J. Elliott
Mystery of Mere Hall. Mrs. C. Kernahan
Mystery of Merlyn Mansions. W. Shute
Mystery of Metropolisville. E. Eggleston
Mystery of Milford Haven. Taffrail
Mystery of Mirbridge. J. Payn
Mystery of Miriam. J. W. Johnston
Mystery of Miss Motte. C. A. Mason
Mystery of Mr. Bernard Brown. E. P. Oppenheim
Mystery of Mr. Cross. C. Robbins
Mystery of Mr. E. Drood. O. C. Kerr
Mystery of Mr. Jessop. E. R. Punshon
Mystery of Mr. Mock. R. A. J. Walling
Mystery of Mr. X. S. Horler
Mystery of Mr. X. M. Porlock
Mystery of Mrs. Blencarrow. M. Oliphant
Mystery of Mitcham Common. Gwyn Evans
Mystery of Moat Farm. J. Hunter
Mystery of Monkswood. Mrs. Lodge
Mystery of M. Felix. B. L. Farjeon
Mystery of Monte Carlo. W. M. Graydon
Mystery of Moor Manor. F. W. Irwin
Mystery of Mortimer Strange. A. W. Marchmont
Mystery of Mostyn Manor. A. W. A'Beckett
Mystery of Murray Davenport. R. N. Stephens
Mystery of Myrtle Cottage. O. Crawfurd
Mystery of Nelson's Coat. E. M. Keate
Mystery of New Orleans. W. M. H. Holcombe
Mystery of New York Bay. Old Sleuth
Mystery of Newton Ferry. L. Meynell
Mystery of Nine. W. LeQueux
Mystery of Norman's Court. J. Chancellor
Mystery of North Fortune. George Douglas
Mystery of Number Five. F. J. Whaley
Mystery of No. 47. J. S. Clouston
Mystery of No. 1. S. Horler
Mystery of No. 7 Bitton Court. P. Quiroule
Mystery of No. 13. H. B. Mathers
Mystery of No. 13 Cavendish Square. P. Quiroule
Mystery of Oldham. L. Bidston
Mystery of One Night. Old Sleuth
Mystery of Orchard House. J. Coggin

Mystery of Orcival. E. Gaboriau
Mystery of Orleton Manor. R. Jewell
Mystery of Paul Chadwick. J. W. Postgate
Mystery of Pauline's Lady. M. V. Woodgate
Mystery of Philip Bennion's Death. R. Marsh
Mystery of Pine Point. K. Norris
Mystery of Rapallo. Courtenay Pollock
Mystery of Redmarsh Farm. A. Marshall
Mystery of Roaring Meg. B. L. Farjeon
Mystery of Rodney's Cove. E. S. Brooks
Mystery of Roger Bullock. T. Gallon
Mystery of St. Dunstans. T. Wright
Mystery of St. James' Park. J. E. Bloundelle-Burton
Mystery of St. Martin's Copse. Beatrix Hughes
Mystery of St. Michael's. G. Thorne
Mystery of St. Rule's. E. F. Heddle
Mystery of Sett. J. Cowdroy
Mystery of Sherwood Towers. G. Verner
Mystery of Squadron X. W. Tyrer
Mystery of Stephen Claverton & Co. H. Knight
Mystery of Suicide Place. A. M. Miller
Mystery of Sun Dial Court. M. Wickes
Mystery of Swordfish Reef. A. W. Upfield
Mystery of Tara Heston. J. L. Rickard
Mystery of the Abandoned Cottage. W. M. Graydon
Mystery of the Abbe Montrose. S. Elvestad
Mystery of the African Expedition. R. Hardinge
Mystery of the African Farm. R. Hardinge
Mystery of the African Mine. R. Hardinge
Mystery of the "Agony." J. W. Bobin
Mystery of the Albanian Avenger. W. W. Sayer
Mystery of the American Envoy. J. Hunter
Mystery of the Amorous Music Master. G. Woden
Mystery of the Arab Agent. W. Jardine
Mystery of the Ashes. A. Wynne
Mystery of the Aztec Chain. John Norman
Mystery of the Baghdad Chest. A. Christie
Mystery of the Bankrupt Estate. A. Parsons
Mystery of the Barranca. H. Whitaker
Mystery of the Barren Lands. R. Cullum
Mystery of the Black Dagger. P. Elliott
Mystery of the Black Gate. B. G. Quin
Mystery of the Blackmailed Baronet. H. E. Hill
Mystery of the Blitzed Tower. A. Parsons
Mystery of the Blue Geranium, and Other Tuesday Club Murders. A. Christie
Mystery of the Blue Inns. E. Anstey
Mystery of the Blue Train. A. Christie
Mystery of the Body on the Cliff. R. Hardinge
Mystery of the Bombed Hotel. A. Skene
Mystery of the Bombed Monastery. A. Parsons
Mystery of the Bonanza Trail. F. J. Arkins
Mystery of the Boule Cabinet. B. E. Stevenson
Mystery of the Cairo Express. A. Parsons
Mystery of the Campagna, and A Shadow on a Wave. Von Degan
Mystery of the Cape Cod Players. P. A. Taylor
Mystery of the Cape Cod Tavern. P. A. Taylor
Mystery of the Cashiered Officer. G. H. Teed
Mystery of the Castle. M. S. Boyd
Mystery of the Centre-Forward. P. Gill
Mystery of the Championship Belt. A. Steffens Hardy
Mystery of the Clasped Hands. G. Boothby
Mystery of the Clock. A. Murray
Mystery of the Closed Car. K. Sproul
Mystery of the Common. J. Blyth
Mystery of the Condemned Cottage. G. Chester
Mystery of the Confiscated Ship. Gilbert Chester
Mystery of the Corbin Necklace. H. K. Webster
Mystery of the Corded Box. Mark Cross
Mystery of the Crashed Air Liner. G. Chester
Mystery of the Creek. J. J. Farjeon
Mystery of the Creeping Man. F. S. Wees
Mystery of the Crested Falcon. J. Noy
Mystery of the Crime in Cabin 66. A. Christie
Mystery of the Crimson Blind. F. M. White
Mystery of the Crooked Gift. A. Parsons
Mystery of the Crystal Skull. George M. White
Mystery of the "David M." D. W. MacArthur
Mystery of the Dead Man's Wallet. J. G. Brandon
Mystery of the Dead Police. M. Porlock
Mystery of the Demobilized Soldier. G. Chester
Mystery of the Derelict. J. G. Rowe
Mystery of the Deserted Camp. J. Drummond
Mystery of the Devil Mask. R. Hardinge
Mystery of the Docks. W. M. Graydon
Mystery of the Double Burglary. G. Chester
Mystery of the Dover Road. W. M. Graydon
Mystery of the Downs. J. R. Watson
Mystery of the East Wind. D. Marfield
Mystery of the Elms. S. W. Judge
Mystery of the Engraved Skull. S. Hope
Mystery of the Evil Eye. A. Wynne
Mystery of the Fast Mail. B. D. Adsit
Mystery of the Fiddling Cracksman. H. S. Keeler
Mystery of the Fifth Tulip. D. Deane
Mystery of the Film City. G. H. Teed
Mystery of the Five Guilty Men. J. Drummond
Mystery of the Flaming Hut. H. Best
Mystery of the Folded Paper. H. Footner
Mystery of the Forbidden Territory. R. Hardinge
Mystery of the Four Abreast. C. R. Cooper
Mystery of the Four Fingers. F. M. White
Mystery of the Four Rooms. H. H. C. Gibbons
Mystery of the Free Frenchmen. A. Parsons
Mystery of the French Milliner. B. Thomson
Mystery of the Frightened Lady. E. Wallace
Mystery of the Furlined Cloak. C. E. Pearce
Mystery of the German Prisoner. M. Frazer
Mystery of the Girl in Blue. F. Perry
Mystery of the Girl in Green. A. Parsons
Mystery of the Glass Bullet. B. Atkey
Mystery of the Golconda. W. N. Vaile
Mystery of the Gold Box. V. Williams
Mystery of the Golden Angel. F. Grierson
Mystery of the Golden Chalice. W. M. Graydon
Mystery of the Golden Wings. Rosa Lambert
Mystery of the Greek Exile. G. Chester
Mystery of the Green Bottle. J. G. Brandon
Mystery of the Green Car. A. Weissl
Mystery of the Green Caterpillars. J. M. Walsh
Mystery of the Green Garnet Murder. P. De Waal
Mystery of the Green Heart. M. Pemberton
Mystery of the Green Ray. W. LeQueux
Mystery of the Gregory Kotovsky. J. Pattinson
Mystery of the Grey Car. J. W. Bobin
Mystery of the Hasty Arrow. A. K. Green
Mystery of the Haunted Square. J. Drummond
Mystery of the Heart. O. Binns
Mystery of the Hidden Room. M. Harvey
Mystery of the Hope Diamond. H. L. Gates
Mystery of the Horse with the Wrong Harness. O. L. Miller
Mystery of the House of Commons. F. Hope
Mystery of the Human Bookcase. W. Morton
Mystery of the Hundred Chests. A. Murray
Mystery of the Hush-Hush Factory. G. Chester
Mystery of the Hushing Pool. J. S. Fletcher
Mystery of the Hypnotic Room. Simon
Mystery of the Indian Relic. A. Parsons
Mystery of the Inn by the Shore. F. Warden
Mystery of the Ironworks. D. Lenton
Mystery of the Isle of Fortune. R. C. Armour
Mystery of the Italian Ruins. D. Long
Mystery of the Kidnapped Munition Worker. G. Chester
Mystery of the Kneeling Woman. M. Dalton
Mystery of the Living Shadow. W. W. Sayer
Mystery of the Locked Door. E. Baird
Mystery of the Locks. E. W. Howe
Mystery of the Lodge. M. D. Chellis
Mystery of the London Banker. J. S. Fletcher
Mystery of the Lorry Driver. P. Urquhart
Mystery of the Lost Battle-Ship. W. W. Sayer
Mystery of the Lost Dauphin. E. P. Bazan
Mystery of the Lost Legionnaire. M. Osborne
Mystery of the Lost Loot. H. King
Mystery of the Lotus Queen. H. H. Ross
Mystery of the Louvre. A. Bernede
Mystery of the Luminous Ray. Arthur Russell
Mystery of the Lyons Mail. F. A. Edwards
Mystery of the Mad Millionaires. W. Tyrer
Mystery of the Man from Rio. G. H. Teed
Mystery of the Mandarin's Idol. R. M. Graydon
Mystery of the Mansion Fire. H. H. C. Gibbons
Mystery of the Marbletons. M. Mackin
Mystery of the Marchers. W. Edwards
Mystery of the Marshes. G. Prout
Mystery of the Mason's Arms. A. Parsons
Mystery of the Middle Temple. R. Machray
Mystery of the Miniature. R. K. Edwards
Mystery of the Missing Angler. W. Tyrer
Mystery of the Missing Aviator. W. W. Sayer
Mystery of the Missing Constable. A. Blair
Mystery of the Missing Corpses. G. Elliott

Mystery of the Missing Doctor. C. Brisbane
Mystery of the Missing Envoy. P. Quiroule
Mystery of the Missing Journalist. W. J. Bayfield
Mystery of the Missing Refugee. H. Scott
Mystery of the Moat. A. Sergeant
Mystery of the Moat House. D. Vane
Mystery of the Monkey-Gland Cocktail. R. East
Mystery of the Montauk Mills. E. L. Coolidge
Mystery of the Monument. A. Blair
Mystery of the Mud Flats. M. Drake
Mystery of the Murdered Blonde. J. G. Brandon
Mystery of the Murdered Chef. R. Hardinge
Mystery of the Murdered Ice Cream Man. J. G. Brandon
Mystery of the Murdered Sentry. J. G. Brandon
Mystery of the Myrtles. E. Jepson
Mystery of the New Tenant. J. Hunter
Mystery of the Old Age Pensioner. G. H. Teed
Mystery of the Old Curiosity Shop. G. Chester
Mystery of the One-Day Alibi. A. Parsons
Mystery of the "Opal." R. S. Holland
Mystery of the Open Window. Anthony Gilbert
Mystery of the Outlawed Black. R. Hardinge
Mystery of the Painted Nude. W. Gore
Mystery of the Papyrus. G. B. Vale
Mystery of the Patrician Club. A. D. Vandam
Mystery of the Peacock's Eye. B. Flynn
Mystery of the Phantom Billionaire. M. J. De Lauer
Mystery of the Phantom Blackmailer. G. Verner
Mystery of the Platinum Nugget! W. W. Sayer
Mystery of the "Polarlys." G. Simenon
Mystery of the Pot-Bank. W. J. Bayfield
Mystery of the Purple Cloak. E. W. Terris
Mystery of the Rabbit's Paw. S. Jepson
Mystery of the Rajah's Jewels. P. Urquhart
Mystery of the Rajah's Son. C. Brisbane
Mystery of the Ravenspurs. F. M. White
Mystery of the Red Chateau. J. Hunter
Mystery of the Red Cockatoo. A. Parsons
Mystery of the Red Flame. G. Barton
Mystery of the Red-Haired Valet. G. Davison
Mystery of the Red Suitcase. L. M. Day
Mystery of the Red Tower. C. Brisbane
Mystery of the Red Triangle. W. C. Tuttle
Mystery of the Reunion Dinner. R. Hardinge
Mystery of the Rio Star. W. Tyrer
Mystery of the Royal Mail. B. L. Farjeon
Mystery of the Rue de Babylone. J. N. Raphael
Mystery of the S. S. Timor. G. Grantham
Mystery of the Sabotaged Jet. J. Drummond
Mystery of the Sandal-Wood Box. M. C. Barnard
Mystery of the Scented Death. Roy Vickers
Mystery of the Sea. B. Stoker
Mystery of the Seaside Hotel. W. J. Bayfield
Mystery of the Second Shot. J. R. Gillies
Mystery of the Seine. G. H. Teed
Mystery of the Seven. W. Usher
Mystery of the 7 Bad Men. H. L. Gates
Mystery of the Seven Cafes. S. Horler
Mystery of the Shadow. F. Hume
Mystery of the Shadowed Footballer. M. Frazer
Mystery of the Shot P.C. G. N. Philips
Mystery of the Silver Dagger. R. Parrish
Mystery of the Silver Run. B. Marchant
Mystery of the Singing Walls. W. A. Stowell
Mystery of the Skating Rink. H. D. Dearden
Mystery of the Skeleton Key. B. Capes
Mystery of the Sleeping Car Express, and other stories. F. W. Crofts
Mystery of the Smiling Doll. H. Holt
Mystery of the Smoking Gun. C. J. Daly
Mystery of the Snow. K. Robeson
Mystery of the Stolen Despatches. A. Parsons
Mystery of the Stolen Hats. B. Graeme
Mystery of the Stolen Plans. M. Coles
Mystery of the Street Musician. J. G. Brandon
Mystery of the Suez Canal. C. H. Hillcoat
Mystery of the Summer-House. H. G. Hutchinson
Mystery of the Sunken Road. R. C. Armour
Mystery of the Swamp. W. M. Graydon
Mystery of the Swanley Viaduct. G. N. Philips
Mystery of the Swindler's Stooge. W. Tyrer
Mystery of the Sycamore. C. Wells
Mystery of the Tailor's Dummy. R. Sonin
Mystery of the Tarn. C. Wells
Mystery of the Thames. F. Warden
Mystery of the Third Parrot. M. Dana
Mystery of the Thirteenth Chest. P. Urquhart
Mystery of the 13th Floor. L. Thayer
Mystery of the Thousand Peaks. A. Murray
Mystery of the Three Acrobats. J. G. Brandon
Mystery of the Three B Syndicate. E. Begbie
Mystery of the Three City's. J. G. Brandon
Mystery of the Three Demobbed Men. W. Tyrer
Mystery of the Three Fingers. M. Leighton
Mystery of the Tower Room. L. Despard
Mystery of the Tramp Steamer. C. Brisbane
Mystery of the Tumbling V. D. T. Lindsay
Mystery of the Turkish Agreement. W. W. Sayer
Mystery of the Twin Rubies. A. Livingston
Mystery of the Two-Faced Man. F. Grierson
Mystery of the 250,000 Rupees. A. Parsons
Mystery of the Underground Factory. G. Chester
Mystery of the Unicorn. W. Magnay
Mystery of the Uninvited Guest. W. Shute
Mystery of the Unknown Victim. W. Jardine
Mystery of the Vanished Trainer. J. Hunter
Mystery of the Vanishing Aerodrome. P. Conde
Mystery of the Walled Garden. A. Salcroft
Mystery of the White Knight. C. MacLeod
Mystery of the Whitehall Bomb. A. Parsons
Mystery of the Woman in Red. Anthony Gilbert
Mystery of the Woman Overboard. W. Tyrer
Mystery of the Yellow Room. G. Leroux
Mystery of Theyne Manor. W. J. Passingham
Mystery of 31, New Inn. R. A. Freeman
Mystery of Tumbling Reef. B. Grimshaw
Mystery of Tumult Rock. C. P. Hauck
Mystery of Tunnel 51. A. Wilson
Mystery of Uncle Ballard. H. D. Stacpoole
Mystery of Vaucluse. J. H. Wallis
Mystery of Victor Grayson. R. Groves
Mystery of Villa Aurelia. B. E. Stevenson
Mystery of Villa Sineste. W. Livingston
Mystery of Vincent Dane. J. L. Rickard
Mystery of White Fell Gill. H. McKay
Mystery of Witch-Face Mountain. C. E. Craddock
Mystery of Wo-Sing. A. G. Hales
Mystery of Wolverston Grange. W. R. Sunman
Mystery of Woodcroft. Anonymous
Mystery of Woodleigh Grange. Anonymous
Mystery of X04. Jack Lewis
Mystery of X20. J. G. Brandon
Mystery on Southampton Water. F. W. Crofts
Mystery on the Broads. G. H. Teed
Mystery on the Centre Court. H. Willett
Mystery on the Clyde. W. M. Duncan
Mystery on the Moor. J. J. Farjeon
Mystery on the Moors. B. Michaels
Mystery on the Queen Mary. B. Graeme
Mystery on the River. B. O'Farrell
Mystery Plane. J. Bolton
Mystery Puzzle Book. L. Wren
Mystery Puzzles. A. Ripley
Mystery Queen. F. Hume
Mystery Reef. H. Bindloss
Mystery Road. E. P. Oppenheim
Mystery Still. F. Du Boisgobey
Mystery Stories. S. Ellin
Mystery Street. L. Noel
Mystery Tipster. F. Johnston
Mystery Tour. D. Rutherford
Mystery Under the Sea. K. Robeson
Mystery Underground. J. J. Farjeon
Mystery Villa. E. R. Punshon
Mystery Week-End. P. Wilde
Mystery Woman. A. MacGowan
Mystery Woman. C. Praed
Mystic Diagram. N. Carter
Mystic Manor. D. Daniels
Mystic Manor. H. G. Weston
Mystic Mullah. K. Robeson
Mystic Number Seven. Annabel Gray
Mystic Romances of the Blue and Grey. A. C. Branscomb
Myth Is Murder. Shane Martin
Mythmaker. S. Gainham

N

N or M? A. Christie
N3 Conspiracy. N. Carter
Nabob and Knave. N. Carter
Nabob's Jewel. C. A. Alington
Nadine. G. Bocca
Nail of Suspicion. F. Crisp
Nails. R. L. Hill
Nairobi Nightcap. D. Fearon
Naked and Alone. Michael Lawrence
Naked and the Innocent. W. Ard
Naked and the Lost. F. M. Davis
Naked Angel. J. Webb
Naked Blade. P. Saxon
Naked Canvas. Warwick Scott
Naked City. C. Einstein

Title Index — Nevada Alibi /597

Naked Country. M. East
Naked Crusader. F. Archer
Naked Ebony. D. Cushman
Naked Edge. M. Ehrlich
Naked Eye. H. Martin
Naked Face. S. Sheldon
Naked Fear. J. Farr
Naked Foot. H. Kaner
Naked from a Well. W. A. Ballinger
Naked Fury. D. Keene
Naked Hours. Wenzell Brown
Naked Hunter. W. Woolfolk
Naked in the Dark. G. Paul
Naked in the Night. J. Cleary
Naked Island. B. Heatter
Naked Jungle. H. Whittington
Naked Kiss. S. Fuller
Naked Lady. M. Corrigan
Naked Land. H. Innes
Naked Light. J. Moffatt
Naked Mistress. W. Deptula
Naked Morning. R. V. Cassill
Naked Murder. F. Erskine
Naked Murderer. E. Piper
Naked Nemesis. K. Conway
Naked Nuns. C. Watson
Naked Runner. F. Clifford
Naked She Died. D. Tracy
Naked Skier. C. Short
Naked Spur. A. Ullman
Naked Storm. S. Eisner
Naked Sun. I. Asimov
Naked Tide. Roderic Hastings
Naked to My Enemy. H. Jobson
Naked to My Pride. H. Rigsby
Naked to the Grave. H. Carmichael
Naked Villainy. C. G. Hodges
Naked Villany. J. Davey
Naked Year. P. Atlee
Nakia. L. Hays
Name for Evil. A. Lyttle
Name Is Archer. J. R. Macdonald
Name Is Chambers. H. Kane
Name Is Jordan. H. Q. Masur
Name Is Judas. R. Gaines
Name Is Malone. C. Rice
Name Is Smith. E. North
Name My Own. C. Holicker
Name of Action. G. Greene
Name of the Game. D. Cory
Name of the Game Is Death. D. J. Marlowe
Name of the Game Is Death. C. Richardson
Name of the Game Is Murder. E. Asinof
Name the Woman. A. M. Williamson
Name Your Poison. H. Reilly
Nameless Coffin. Gwendoline Butler
Nameless Crime. W. S. Masterman
Nameless Dread. J. K. Stafford
Nameless Five. A. Skene
Nameless Man. F. Du Boisgobey
Nameless Man. N. S. Lincoln
Nameless Ones. L. Egan
Nameless Ones. R. T. M. Scott
Nameless Ones. L. Vardre
Nameless Order. Dargon
Nameless Road. S. Harvester
Nameless Stranger and What Happened at Flaunce. B. Reynolds
Nameless Thing. M. D. Post
Name's Death, Remember Me? S. Forbes
Name's Maguire. R. Himmel
Nancy Lee, Mill Lass. H. E. Inman
Nancy Manoeuvres. C. Gleig
Nanny. E. Piper
Naomi, the Modern. C. H. Bullivant
Nap on Nighthawk. S. Horler
Napalm Bugle. E. Lacy
Naples, or Die! H. Chesham
Napoleon of the Press. M. Leighton
Napoleon Ring. A. Lowing

NARC. R. Hawkes
Narc. S. L. Stebel
Narcissus in the Way. G. V. McFadden
Narcissus Murders. XV8
Narracong Riddle. A. Derleth
Narrow Cell. Dale Clark
Narrow Escape. Annie Thomas
Narrow Exit. P. Henissart
Narrow Gauge to Murder. C. Thomas
Narrow House. H. Fernee
Narrow Search. A. Garve
Narrowing Circle. H. Hill
Narrowing Circle. J. Symons
Narrowing Lust. G. Baxter
Narrowing Lust. H. Kane
Nasty Cropper. G. F. Underhill
Nasty Name Murders. R. Howes
Nasty Piece of Work. R. Croft-Cooke
Nat Foster, the Boston Detective. H. Rockwood
Nat Wedgewood, Jockey. J. Fairfax-Blakeborough
Natalie Limited. P. Trent
Natasha. C. W. Thayer
Nation's Missing Guest. H. Footner
Nation's Peril. N. Carter
Native Superstition. H. C. McNeile
Natural Causes. H. Cecil
Nature of a Crime. J. Conrad
Naughty but Dead. G. G. Fickling
Naughty Girls. Arthur Wise
Naughty Maid of Mitcham. D. Donovan
Naval Adventuress. P. Trent
Naval Detective's Chase. Anonymous
Naval Detective's Chase. N. Buntline
Navy Colt. F. Gruber
Navy in Action. Taffrail
Navy Murders. W. Chambers
Navy Spy Murders. G. F. Eliot
Nazi Assassins. D. Cory
Nazi Hunter. B. Shaw
Nazi Overcoat. R. Lebherz
Nazi Shadows. E. L. Fleming
Nazi Speedway Plot. E. T. Woodhall
Nearest and Dearest. E. Southworth
Nearness of Evil. C. Mills
Neat Little Corpse. M. Murray
'Neath the Southern Cross. K. Lindsay
Nebuly Coat. J. M. Falkner
Necessary Action. P. Wahloo
Necessary Corpse. R. C. Woodthorpe
Necessary Doubt. Colin Wilson
Necessary End. V. Gielgud
Necessary End. S. Harper
Necessary Evil. K. Roos
Neck and Neck. L. Bruce
Neck in a Noose. E. Ferrars
Neck of Sinners. H. Spencer
Necklace and Calabash. R. Van Gulik
Necklace of Death. H. Holt
Necklace of Parmona. L. T. Meade
Necktie for Norman. J. L. Morrissey
Necromancer. G. W. M. Reynolds
Ned Bachman, the New Orleans Detective. A. Dale
Need a Body Tell? B. Cobb
Needful Journey. Winifred Duke
Needle. H. N. Field
Needle. Francis King
Needle in a Haystack. G. Joseph
Needle That Wouldn't Hold Still. Hampton Stone
Needle's Eye. Edward Lee
Needle's Kiss. Seamark
Needles of Death. P. Edwards
Needy Nine. N. Carter
Nefarious Quest. H. Janson

Negative in Blue. C. Brown
Negative Man. R. C. Galway
Negative of a Nude. C. E. Fritch
Negative Value. J. Boland
Negatives. P. Everett
Neglected Clue. I. Ostrander
Neglected Fire. H. Horn
Negotiator. C. Matthews
Negotiator. R. M. Rogers
Negro. G. Simenon
Negrohead. R. Bridges
Neighbors. M. Allwright
Neighbors. G. Simenon
Neil Nelson, the Veteran Detective. H. Rockwood
Neila Sen and My Casual Death. J. H. Connelly
Neither a Candle nor a Pitchfork. J. Porter
Neither do I Condemn Thee. A. Soutar
Neither Five nor Three. H. MacInnes
Neither Had I Rest. N. Cromarty
Neither Man nor Dog. G. Kersh
Neither the Sea nor the Sand. G. Honeycombe
Nell Alone. J. Melville
Nella Waits. M. Millhiser
Nelly Jocelyn, Widow. J. Middlemass
Nelson Lord--One of Our Agents. G. Windsor
Nelson's Blood. G. Kent
Nemesis. A. Christie
Nemesis. J. M. Cobban
Nemesis at Raynham Parva. J. J. Connington
Nemesis Club. W. W. Sayer
Nemesis Wife. C. L. Evans
Nemesis Wore Nylons. C. Brown
Nemo, the Shadow Detective. F. L. Broughton
Neon Haystack. J. M. Ullman
Neon Jungle. J. D. MacDonald
Neon Rainbow. C. Terrot
Neptune's Son. R. S. Holland
Nerve. D. Francis
Nerve Beat. J. B. O'Sullivan
Nerve Centre. H. Janson
Nerve of Foley, and other railroad stories. F. H. Spearman
Nervestorm. M. Sharland
Nesbit's Compact. P. Trent
Nest-Egg for the Baron. A. Morton
Nest of Fear. H. Ellson
Nest of Spies. Geoffrey Davison
Nest of Spies. P. Souvestre
Nest of Traitors. G. Ashe
Nest of Vipers. T. Claymore
Nest of Vipers. Wallace Crawford
Nest of Vultures. Robert MacLeod
Net. J. Pudney
Net. E. Ronns
Net Around Joan Ingilby. A. Fielding
Net of Cobwebs. E. S. Holding
Nether Millstone. F. M. White
Nets of Fate. O. Binns
Nets to Catch the Wind. D. Hitchens
Netta. F. M. White
Nettle. E. Wooll
Nettle Shade. J. Turner
Network. Godfrey Smith
Network. Roderic Wilkinson
Network of Crime. N. Carter
Network of Fear. A. Yudkoff
Neutron Beam Murder. T. J. King
Nevada Alibi. Dan Morgan

Nevada Detective. Anonymous
Nevada Gunslinger. V. Coffman
Never a Dull Moment. P. Cheyney
Never Again. Francis King
Never Ask a Policeman. D. J. Olivy
Never Be Caught. J. McKimmey
Never Bet Your Life. G. H. Coxe
Never by Chance. Sylvia Tate
Never Come Back. J. Mair
Never Contract. D. Gerrity
Never Die Alone. D. Goines
Never Die in Honolulu. I. Hamilton
Ne'er-Do-Well. D. Yates
Never-Fail Blake. A. Stringer
Never-Fail Detective. H. Holmes
Never Fight a Lady. S. Truss
Never Fire First. J. Dorrance
Never Forget, Never Forgive. C. Fox
Never Give a Millionaire an Even Break. H. Kane
Never Go Dark. E. Bonett
Never Had a Chance. R. Farran
Never Had a Spanner on Her. J. Leasor
Never in Vain. J. L. Hardy
Never Kill a Client. B. Halliday
Never Kill a Cop! M. Colton
Never Kill a Cop. L. Costigan
Never Kill a Cop. J. B. West
Never Leave My Bed. J. T. Rogers
Never Live Twice. D. J. Marlowe
Never Look Back. H. Carter
Never Look Back. M. G. Eberhart
Never Mind the Lady. D. Garth
Never Mix Business with Pleasure. B. Graeme
Never Need an Enemy. A. M. Stein
Never Put Off Till Tomorrow What You Can Kill Today. J. Godey
Never Say Dead. E. Kennedy
Never Say Die. M. Malmer
Never Say Die. M. K. Ozaki
Never Say Die. I. S. Shriber
Never Say Live! David Hume
Never Say No to a Killer. J. Gant
Never Shake a Skeleton. A. Flett
Never Shoot a Lady. E. Hale
Never Smile at Children. E. T. French
Never Step on a Rainbow. W. Wolfe
Never Summer Mystery. T. Perry
Never to Die. A. Brennan
Never to Me. A. Dick
Never Trust a Dame. C. Wheatley
Never Turn Your Back. A. Capelli
Never Turn Your Back. M. Scherf
Never Wake a Dead Man. B. Bird
Never Walk Alone. R. King
Never-Was Girl. C. Brown
Never Wed an Old Man. H. Caswell
Nevermore Affair. K. Wilhelm
Nevlo. K. Robeson
New Adventures of Ellery Queen. E. Queen
New Andromeda. C. Dawe
New Arabian Nights. R. L. Stevenson
New Bodies for Old. M. Renard
New Breed. L. Costigan
New Centurions. J. Wambaugh
New Chronicles of Don Q. K. Prichard
New Departure. K. Connor
New Detective Stories. G. Campbell
New England Gothic. A. J. Allen
New Exploits of Nick Carter. N. Carter
New Graves at Great Norne. Henry Wade
New Gun Runners. N. Gordon
New Idol. G. Leroux
New Jack Sheppard. E. A. Treeton
New Kind of Killer. J. Melville
New Kind of Killer, an Old Kind of Death. J. Melville
New Leaf, and other stories. J. Ritchie
New Lease of Death. R. Rendell
New Lease of Life. G. Simenon
New Lease on Life. G. Simenon
New Made Grave. H. Footner
New Magdalen. W. Collins
New Man in Lowuni. J. Fores
New Master. A. Golsworthy
New Mexico Connection. C. Wilcox
New Mistress. G. M. Fenn
New Moon. Taffrail
New Order. M. Gerard
New Orleans Holocaust. P. McCurtin
New Orleans Knockout. D. Pendleton
New Othello. I. D. Hardy
New People at the Hollies. J. Bell
New Race Diplomatist. J. B. Waterbury
New Rivers Calling. J. B. Hendryx
New Serpent in Eden. N. Carter
New Shining White Murder. D. Launay
New Shoe. A. W. Upfield
New Sonia Wayward. M. Innes
New Tenant. E. P. Oppenheim
New Terror. G. Leroux
New Vigilantes. J. D. Horan
New Year's Eve in Lan-Fang. R. Van Gulik
New York by Night. Grace M. White
New York Detective. Old Sleuth
Newgate. T. P. Prest
Newhaven-Dieppe. G. Simenon
News of Murder. A. Lejeune
News of Paul Temple. F. Durbridge
News Reel. R. J. Casey
News Reel Murder. P. Buranelli
News Travels by Night. B. Graeme
Newshound's Nemesis. R. Kirby
Newspaper Girl. A. M. Williamson
Newspaper Seller's Secret. W. Edwards
Next Door. F. Hume
Next Door to Danger. C. MacLeod
Next Door to Death. B. Cobb
Next Door to Murder. L. Cargill
Next O'Kin. W. M. Graydon
Next of Kin. G. Goodchild
Next One to Die. V. Gunn
Next, Please. J. M. Walsh
Next Saturday in Milan. W. Tute
Next Stop--the Morgue. B. Winter
Next Time I'll Pay My Own Fare. R. V. Beste
Next Time, You'll Wake up Dead. Philip Evans
Next to Die. J. Godey
Next to Die. G. Verner
Next-to-Last Train Ride. C. Dennis
Next Victim. D. Stuart
Nic Barker I.D.B. D. Brechin
Nic Revel. G. M. Fenn
Nice and Easy. David Miles
Nice Bloke. C. Cookson
Nice Class of People. A. La Bern
Nice Cup of Tea. Anthony Gilbert
Nice Day for a Funeral. H. Howard
Nice Day for a Murder. V. Gunn
Nice Day for Murder. F. Murray
Nice Derangement of Epitaphs. Ellis Peters
Nice Enough to Murder. E. S. Russell
Nice Fillies Finish Last. B. Halliday
Nice Friendly Town. H. Calvin
Nice Girl Like You. R. Wormser
Nice Girl's Story. Rosemary Harris
Nice Guys Don't Win. S. Mitchell
Nice Guys Finish Dead. Albert Conroy
Nice Guys Finish Last. R. Kyle
Nice Little Killing. Anthony Gilbert
Nice Neighborhood. E. Bahr
Nice People Don't Kill. F. W. Bronson
Nice People Murder. M. H. Bradley
Nice People Poison. M. H. Bradley
Nice Place to Die. M. Culpan
Nice Way to Die. H. Janson
Nice Young Man. W. L. Harter
Nicest Corpse. John Morgan
Nicholas Goade, Detective. E. P. Oppenheim
Nicholas Lattermole's Case. C. Barry
Nicholas Snatch. P. Malloch
Nick Carter and the Green Goods Men. N. Carter
Nick Carter and the Red Button. N. Carter
Nick Carter, Detective. N. Carter
Nick Carter Down East. N. Carter
Nick Carter's Auto Trail. N. Carter
Nick Carter's Chance Clue. N. Carter
Nick Carter's Chinese Puzzle. N. Carter
Nick Carter's Cipher. N. Carter
Nick Carter's Clever Protege. N. Carter
Nick Carter's Clever Ruse. N. Carter
Nick Carter's Close Call. N. Carter
Nick Carter's Close Finish. N. Carter
Nick Carter's Convict Client. N. Carter
Nick Carter's Counterplot. N. Carter
Nick Carter's Death Warrant. N. Carter
Nick Carter's Double Catch. N. Carter
Nick Carter's Egyptian Clew. N. Carter
Nick Carter's Fall. N. Carter
Nick Carter's Girl Detective. N. Carter
Nick Carter's Intuition. N. Carter
Nick Carter's Last Card. N. Carter
Nick Carter's Masterpiece. N. Carter
Nick Carter's Menace. N. Carter
Nick Carter's New Assistant. N. Carter
Nick Carter's Persistence. N. Carter
Nick Carter's Promise. N. Carter
Nick Carter's Retainer. N. Carter
Nick Carter's Roundup. N. Carter
Nick Carter's Star Pupils. N. Carter
Nick Carter's Subtle Foe. N. Carter
Nick Carter's Swim to Victory. N. Carter
Nick Carter's Treasure Chest Case. N. Carter
Nick Carter's Wildest Chase. N. Carter
Nick of Time. W. T. Hickman
Nick the Click. G. K. Wilkinson
Nickel Ride. M. T. Kaufman
Nicky Nimble. Anonymous
Nicola. A. E. Lindop
Nicolette of the Quarter. V. MacClure
Niece of Abraham Pein. J. H. Wallis
Nig-Nog. E. Wallace
Nigel Fortescue. W. Westall
Night-Action! S. M. Parkman
Night After Night. S. Thurman
Night Air Is Dangerous. Sutherland Scott
Night and Fog. A. Gask
Night and Fog. K. Netzen
Night & Green Ginger. D. Lockwood
Night and Morning. Old Sleuth
Night and No Moon. J. Odlum
Night and the City. G. Kersh
Night and the Judgement. L. Butler
Night Assassin. M. B. Dix
Night at Hogwallow. T. Strauss
Night at Krumlin Castle. Frank King
Night at Lost End. G. A. Chamberlain
Night at Sea Abbey. V. Coffman
Night at the Mocking Widow. Carter Dickson
Night at the Vulcan. N. Marsh
Night Attack. L. Crosby
Night Beat. Arthur MacLean
Night Before Murder. S. Fisher
Night Before the Wedding. The Gordons

Night Boat. T. Trent
Night Boat from Puerto Vedra. Donald MacKenzie
Night Boat to Paris. R. Jessup
Night Callers. F. Crisp
Night Child. C. De Blasis
Night Club. P. Cheyney
Night-Club Crime. A. Skene
Night Club Lady. A. Abbot
Night Club Murder. J. G. Brandon
Night Club Murder. Roland Daniel
Night Club Murder. J. A. Jordan
Night Club Mystery. E. Jordan
Night-Club Mystery. G. H. Teed
Night Coach. "Capstan"
Night Comer. Jack Wilson
Night-Comers. E. Ambler
Night Crossing. K. Kolb
Night Cry. W. L. Stuart
Night Darkens the Streets. A. La Bern
Night Drop. F. C. Davis
Night Drum. A. Abdullah
Night Encounter. Anthony Gilbert
Night Exercise. J. Rhode
Night Express Murder. L. A. Knight
Night Extra. W. P. McGivern
Night Falls at Bitterhill. P. Warren
Night Falls on the City. S. Gainham
Night Flight to Zurich. C. F. Gregg
Night Flower. W. C. Butler
Night for Evil. Jack Lewis
Night for Screaming. H. Whittington
Night for Treason. J. Jakes
Night Freight Murders. Robert Fleming
Night Frost. B. Copper
Night Ghouls. R. Chetwynd-Hayes
Night Has a Thousand Eyes. G. Hopley
Night Has Another Voice. G. Colizzi
Night Has Eyes. E. Backhouse
Night Has Eyes. A. Kennington
Night Has Red Eyes. J. Millson
Night Hawk. D. Cory
Night Hawk. J. R. Holden
Night Hawk. E. Jepson
Night Hawk. A. Stringer
Night Hunters. J. Crecy
Night Hunters. J. Miles
Night I Caught the Santa Fe Chief. E. Thorpe
Night I Died. W. Irish
Night in George Square. S. Fraser
Night in Glengyle. J. Ferguson
Night in Havana. R. Sylvester
Night Is a Child. R. Llewellyn
Night Is a Time for Listening. E. West
Night Is a Time to Die. J. Wainwright
Night Is for Screaming. Robert Turner
Night Is for Violence. D. Bateson
Night Journey. Winston Graham
Night Judgment at Sinos. J. Higgins
Night Jump--Cuba. P. Runyon
Night Lady. W. C. Gault
Night Lights. M. Pemberton
Night Mail. H. F. Wood
Night Man. A. Ullman
Night Moves. A. Sharp
Night Must Fall. W. Drummond
Night Must Fall. Emlyn Williams
Night My Enemy. A. Maybury
Night Never Ends. F. Lorenz
Night of Camp David. F. Knebel
Night of Clear Choice. D. M. Disney
Night of Crime. A. Livingston
Night of Dread. J. Creasey
Night of Errors. M. Innes
Night of Evil. G. St. John
Night of Fear. M. Dalton

Night of Fear. N. MacKenzie
Night of Four Hundred Rabbits. Elizabeth Peters
Night of Glass. P. Purser
Night of Horror. C. Buchanan
Night of Horror. A. Soutar
Night of Love. B. E. M. Ward
Night of May Third. A. M. Wells
Night of Murder. C. Rushton
Night of Mystery. J. C. Ellis
Night of Peril. H. Bleackley
Night of Reckoning. F. Barrett
Night of Reckoning. S. Horler
Night of Reckoning. P. Ordway
Night of Reckoning. J. S. Strange
Night of Secrets. S. Warwick
Night of Shadows. F. Lockridge
Night of Terror. Joy Brown
Night of Terror. H. Desmond
Night of Terror. R. H. Wilkinson
Night of the Assassin. Don Smith
Night of the Assassins. B. Rossi
Night of the Avenger. N. Carter
Night of the Black Horror. V. Norwood
Night of the Black Tower. Michael Sinclair
Night of the Bonfire. J. Blackmore
Night of the Bowstring. D. B. Olsen
Night of the Crime. H. Desmond
Night of the Crisis. J. Ingersol
Night of the Darkest Moon. J. Peart
Night of the Dead. Dana Ross
Night of the Eagles. R. Collin
Night of the Enchantress. K. Troy
Night of the Fog. Anthony Gilbert
Night of the Fox. J. Gannold
Night of the Full Moon. J. N. Chance
Night of the Funeral. H. C. Davis
Night of the Garter Murder. R. Howes
Night of the Generals. H. H. Kirst
Night of the Good Children. M. Carleton
Night of the Hawk. R. Raine
Night of the Hellebore. J. Reddoch
Night of the Horns. D. Sanderson
Night of the Hunter. D. Grubb
Night of the Jabberwock. F. Brown
Night of the Jackals. Ralph Hayes
Night of the Juggler. W. P. McGivern
Night of the Kill. Breni James
Night of the Letter. D. Eden
Night of the Living Dead. J. Russo
Night of the Long Shadows. H. St. Thomas
Night of the Moonrose. M. Lynch
Night of the Party. M. Cronin
Night of the Phantom. Marilyn Ross
Night of the Phoenix. N. De Mille
Night of the Picaroon. J. Cassells
Night of the Rape. L. White
Night of the Reaper. V. M. Grayland
Night of the Rose. H. Castillou
Night of the Ruby. L. Conway
Night of the Settlement. J. N. Chance
Night of the Shadow. M. Grant
Night of the Shooting Star. D. Vipond
Night of the Short Knives. B. Wilkinson
Night of the Storm. J. Dallas
Night of the Storm. A. Gask
Night of the Stranger. J. Blackmore
Night of the 3rd Ult. H. F. Wood
Night of the Thirteenth. S. Warwick
Night of the Tiger. D. C. Cooke
Night of the Tiger. M. Kistler
Night of the Toads. Michael Collins
Night of the Tribolites. P. Leslie
Night of the 12th-13th. A. Steeman
Night of the 23rd. L. Jackson
Night of the Visitor. R. Willock
Night of the Watchman. J. Creasey
Night of the Wedding. C. N. Williamson

Night of the Wolf. W. H. Baker
Night of the Wolf. J. Kersey
Night of the World. F. H. Rose
Night of Vengeance. A. W. Sherring
Night of Violence. P. Barrington
Night of Violence. L. Charbonneau
Night of Wenceslas. L. Davidson
Night of Wrath. Y. Smith
Night on Penwith. F. B. Clark
Night on the Bare Mountain. J. D. White
Night on the Devil's Pathway. C. M. Russell
Night on the Island. M. M. Kaye
Night on the Killer Reef. A. MacVicar
Night on the Pathway. C. M. Russell
Night Operator. F. Packard
Night over Fitch's Pond. C. Jarrett
Night over Mexico. T. Downing
Night over the Wood. H. Addis
Night Passage to Kano. M. K. Robertson
Night Patrol. Griff
Night Pieces. T. Burke
Night Pillow. H. C. Rae
Night Raider. M. Barry
Night Raiders. A. Skene
Night Ride. Mark Ross
Night Ride and Other Journeys. C. Beaumont
Night Riders. R. Cullum
Night Riders. N. Tranter
Night Run. E. Fenwick
Night Safe Mystery. L. Carlton
Night Scenes in New York. T. Pastor
Night Search. J. Mangione
Night Seekers. K. Royce
Night Shadows. C. Robertson
Night Shift. R. Blaker
Night Squad. D. Goodis
Night Stalker. J. Rice
Night Stands at the Door. K. Blake
Night Stop. E. Trevor
Night Strangler. J. Rice
Night Surprise. F. Warden
Night the Fog Came Down. J. Bude
Night, the Woman. S. Ransome
Night They Killed Joss Varran. G. Bellairs
Night Thorn. I. Gordon
Night Tide. G. Carpenter
Night Tide. J. R. Wilmot
Night Train. K. Millar
Night Train to Mombasa. J. Farrington
Night Train to Paris. M. Coles
Night Trap. C. Robertson
Night Visitor and other stories. A. Bennett
Night Walk. E. Daly
Night Walker. D. Hamilton
Night Walker. S. Stuart
Night Was Dark. J. Reach
Night Was Made for Murder. W. Cotton
Night Was Made for Murder. B. Winter
Night Watch. T. Walsh
Night-Watchman's Friend. M. Fitt
Night Wheeler. C. Brown
Night Winds. B. Cleeve
Night Wind's Promise. V. Vanardy
Night Wings. M. Gerard
Night Without Darkness. P. Audemars
Night Without Darkness. K. Orvis
Night Without End. F. Duncan
Night Without End. S. MacIvers
Night Without End. Alistair MacLean
Night Without Sleep. E. Moll
Night Without Stars. Winston Graham

Night-World. R. Bloch
Nightborn. L. Grex
Nightcap. M. Marcin
Nightcap and Plume. G. R. Preedy
Nightclimber. J. M. White
Nightclub Mystery. H. Clevely
Nightcomers. M. Hastings
Nightfall. D. Goodis
Nightfighter Spy. M. McKenna
Nighthawk. W. M. Duncan
Nighthawk Mops Up. S. Horler
Nighthawk of the Northwest. S. A. White
Nighthawk Strikes to Kill. S. Horler
Nighthawk Swears Vengeance. S. Horler
Nighthawk the Mountain Detective. Anonymous
Nighthawks! J. G. Brandon
Nightingale at Noon. M. Summerton
Nightingales Never Sing. J. Courage
Nightlight. M. Bardos
Nightlights. B. Goldie
Nightly Deadshade. John Aiken
Nightly She Sings. E. Olmstead
Nightmare. E. S. Aarons
Nightmare. A. Blaisdell
Nightmare. L. Brock
Nightmare. R. H. Greenan
Nightmare. W. Irish
Nightmare. A. La Bern
Nightmare. G. Mygatt
Nightmare. C. Woolrich
Nightmare Abbey. T. L. Peacock
Nightmare Abbey. W. E. D. Ross
Nightmare Alley. W. L. Gresham
Nightmare and Dawn. M. Aldanov
Nightmare at Dawn. J. Philips
Nightmare at Mountain Aerie. F. Hurd
Nightmare at Noon. S. Sterling
Nightmare at Riverview. Angela Gray
Nightmare Baby. L. Du Breuil
Nightmare Castle. W. Martyn
Nightmare Chase. E. Berckman
Nightmare Chessboard. T. B. Morris
Nightmare Conspiracy. Ralph Hayes
Nightmare Cottage. G. M. Wilson
Nightmare Cruise. Wade Miller
Nightmare Dance. M. Lynch
Nightmare Ends. F. Cowen
Nightmare Farm. Jack Mann
Nightmare Fiesta. D. Martyn
Nightmare for Dr. Morelle. E. Dudley
Nightmare Hall. A. L. McMurdie
Nightmare Honeymoon. R. Foley
Nightmare House. R. Foley
Nightmare House. B. Gray
Nightmare in Colour. R. H. Greenan
Nightmare in Copenhagen. M. Albrand
Nightmare in Dublin. P. Loraine
Nightmare in Eden. M. Asher
Nightmare in Manhattan. T. Walsh
Nightmare in Naples. J. Stagg
Nightmare in New York. D. Pendleton
Nightmare in Pink. J. D. MacDonald
Nightmare in Rust. P. Audemars
Nightmare Incident. S. Brydon
Nightmare Island. Ralph Hayes
Nightmare Kick. Jon Stevens
Nightmare of Eyes. D. Rico
Nightmare of Murder. Mildred Davis
Nightmare on the Nile. C. Leader
Nightmare Street. H. Ellson
Nightmare Town. D. Hammett
Nightmares. R. Bloch
Nightmares and Geezenstacks. F. Brown
Nightmare's Morning. M. Lynch

Night's Black Agent. J. Bingham
Night's Candles. A. Hocking
Night's Cloak. E. R. Punshon
Night's Dark Secret. J. Shearing
Night's Evil. M. McShane
Night's Moves. O. Blakeston
Nights of the Round Table. Margery Lawrence
Nights with an Old Lag. W. J. Wintle
Nightshade. G. M. Allen
Nightshade. I. Foster
Nightshade. H. Imbert-Terry
Nightshade. J. N. Makris
Nightshade. Derek Marlowe
Nightshade. J. H. Robinson
Nightshade & Damnations. G. Kersh
Nightshade Ring. L. Hardy
Nightspawn. J. Banville
Nightwalkers. B. Cross
Nightwalkers. James Norman
Nightwatchmen. B. Hannah
Nightwebs. C. Woolrich
Nightwind. S. Allis
Nightwitch Devil. K. Robeson
Nihilist's Vengeance. E. C. Derby
Nikki. S. Friedman
Nikki Revisited. S. Friedman
Nile Green. A. Hocking
Nile Green. D. Jordan
Nimble Dollar, with other stories. C. M. Thompson
Nimble Ike, the Detective. Old Sleuth
Nimble Ike, the Trick Ventriloquist. Old Sleuth
Nimble Ike's Mystery. Old Sleuth
Nimble Ike's Romance. Old Sleuth
Nina's Peril. A. M. Miller
Nine Against New York. Albert Leffingwell
Nine--and Death Makes Ten. Carter Dickson
Nine Bears. E. Wallace
Nine Bells. K. Davies
Nine Buck's Row. T. E. Huff
Nine Club. T. Clare
Nine Coaches Waiting. M. Stewart
Nine Commandments. J. Blackmore
Nine Cuts. B. Flynn
9 Dark Hours. L. G. Offord
Nine Days. E. C. Vivian
Nine Days' Murder. A. MacKinnon
Nine Days' Panic. R. Davis
Nine Doctors and a Madman. E. M. Curtiss
Nine Dragon Man. D. De Reszke
9:45. Owen Davis
Nine Green Bottles. J. Cowdroy
9 Had No Alibi. M. Silverman
Nine Holiday Adventures of Mr. P. J. Davenant in the Year 1915. F. S. Hamilton
Nine Horrors and a Dream. J. P. Brennan
Nine Lives Are Not Enough. J. Odlum
Nine Lives of Alphonse. J. L. Johnson
Nine Lives to Pompeii. W. Melton
Nine Men of Soho. J. MacLaren-Ross
Nine Men's Morrice. W. H. Pollock
Nine Mile Walk. H. Kemelman
Nine More Lives. M. Morgan
Nine Nicks. J. Farndale
Nine O'Clock Curtains. J. M. Hickman
Nine O'Clock Shadow. J. T. Story
Nine of Hearts. B. L. Farjeon
Nine of Hearts. E. C. Mayne
Nine Pine Street. J. Colton
Nine Pointed Star. C. W. Sykes
Nine Points of the Law. W. S. Jackson
Nine Seven Juliet. L. Lafore
Nine Singing Apes. H. Hawton
Nine-Spoked Wheel. J. R. L. Anderson

Nine Strings to Your Bow. M. Walsh
Nine Tailors. D. L. Sayers
9009. J. Hopper
Nine Times Nine. H. H. Holmes
Nine Unknown. T. Mundy
Nine Waxed Faces. F. Beeding
Nine Wrong Answers. J. D. Carr
19. Roger Hall
1946 MS. R. Maugham
Nineteen Impressions. J. D. Beresford
Nineteen Stories. G. Greene
Nineteen Thousand Pounds. B. Delannoy
Nineteenth Century Miracle. Z. Z.
Nineteenth Hole Mystery. H. Adams
98.4. C. Hodder-Williams
95 File. J. E. Martin
90 Gramercy Park. P. Dalton
Ninety in the Shade. A. R. Weekes
99 44/100% Dead. M. Franklin
99, Dark Street. F. W. Robinson
Ninety-Second Tiger. M. Gilbert
Ninon. M. Peterson
Ninth Candle. F. Ford
9th Directive. Adam Hall
Ninth Earl. J. Farnol
Ninth Earl of Whitby. N. Bell
Ninth Enemy. F. Vivian
Ninth Floor. K. O'Neil
Ninth Guest. G. Bristow
Ninth Guest. Owen Davis
Ninth Hour. B. Benson
Ninth Life. F. I. S. Eden
Ninth Life. E. Ferrars
Ninth Life. Jack Mann
Ninth Marquess. J. Cleary
Ninth Plague. D. T. Lindsay
Ninth Tentacle. M. Rippon
Ninth Week. Irene Alexander
Nipped in the Bud. S. Palmer
Nirvana Can Also Mean Death. H. Kane
Nita's Place. H. Whittington
Nitroglycerine League. I. Stark
Nixon Recession Caper. R. Maloney
No Alibi. B. Cobb
No Alibi. J. York
No Alibi for Murder. A. Parsons
No Angel. Morton Cooper
No Angels for Me. W. Ard
No Answer from a Corpse. R. Stahl
No Apparent Motive. E. C. Williams
No Bail for Dalton. M. Borgenicht
No Bail for the Judge. H. Cecil
No Beast so Fierce. E. Bunker
No Beast so Fierce. C. Rushton
No Better Fiend. E. McGirr
No Birds Sang. J. B. Hilton
No Blonde Is an Island. C. Brown
No Body She Knows. C. Brown
No Bones About It. J. Fleming
No Bones About It. R. S. Wallis
No Bouquets for Brandon. V. Warren
No Business for a Lady. J. L. Rubel
No Business of Mine. R. Marshall
No Case for the Crown. D. McLachlin
No Case for the Police. V. C. Clinton-Baddeley
No Castle of Dreams. M. McEvoy
No Cause for Dying. K. Evans
No Cause to Kill. D. Ramsay
No Chance in Hell. N. Quarry
No Charge for Framing. D. Sanderson
No Charge for the Poison. B. Cobb
No Choice for Sergeant Cluff. G. North
"No Clue!" J. Hay
No Clues. M. Leinster
No Clues for Dexter. B. Graeme
No Coffin for the Corpse. C. Rawson
No Coffins in China. C. Edwards
No Come-Back from Connie. D. Glinto
No Corpus Delecti. H. Bohnstedt

Title Index

No Coupons for a Shroud. N. Morland
No Crest for the Wicked. G. Morgan
No Crime for a Lady. Z. Popkin
No Crime Is Perfect. H. E. Wheeler
No Crime Like the Present. A. Gaines
No Crime Like the Present. M. Hervey
No Crime More Cruel. M. Halliday
No Crime So Great. Elliot Bailey
No Curtains for Cora. Gavin Holt
No Dame Wants to Die. M. Clinten
No Darker Crime. J. Creasey
No Diamonds for a Doll. P. Cagney
No Dice! A. Bocca
No Dignity in Death. R. Lockridge
No Doors, No Windows. H. Ellison
No Doubts After Friday. I. Waltmore
No Down Payment. J. McPartland
No Dust in the Attic. Anthony Gilbert
No Duty on a Corpse. M. Murray
No Earth for Foxes. M. O'Brine
No Easy Way Out. Robert Mason
No End of a Rogue. F. A. Clement
No End to Danger. M. Halliday
No End to Fear. H. Hossent
No Entry. M. Coles
No Epitaph for Mr. Zarke. C. I. D. Smith
No Escape. J. Bell
No Escape. E. Ellison
No Escape. C. B. Kelland
No Escape. M. Richmond
No Escape. R. R. Ryan
No Escape from Murder. N. MacKenzie
No Escape from Murder. P. Manton
No Evil Angel. E. Linington
No Excuse for Murder. M. Hervey
No Exit. G. Goodchild
No Exit. Winston Graham
No Exit. A. E. Redmond
No Face for a Killer. H. Spencer
No Face to Murder. E. Howie
No Fatherland. H. H. Kirst
No Fear or Favour. H. Cecil
No Flowers by Request. S. Palmer
No Flowers for the General. B. Copper
No Flowers in Brazlov. F. Usher
No Footprints in the Bush. A. W. Upfield
No Friendly Drop. Henry Wade
No Fury. F. Beeding
No Future Fair Lady. C. Brown
No Future for Luana. A. Derleth
No Gold When You Go. Peter Chambers
No Good from a Corpse. L. Brackett
No Grave for a Lady. J. Bonett
No Grave for March. M. E. Chaber
No Greater Love. W. LeQueux
No Guest at the Villa. D. Martyn
No Halo for Hedy. C. Brown
No Halo for Me. J. Manor
No Haloes for Hoods. Craig Cooper
No Haloes in Hell. W. Wright
No Hands on the Clock. G. Homes
No Harm Intended. E. S. Holding
No Harp for My Angel. C. Brown
No Head for Her Pillow. S. S. Taylor
No Hero. J. P. Marquand
No Hero. Desmond Martin
No Hiding Place. R. Foley
No Hiding Place. J. Lanham
No Higher Mountain. A. Armstrong
No Holiday for Crime. D. Shannon
No Holiday for Death. L. Thayer
"No Honour--." Colin Hope
No Honour Amongst Spies. H. T. Rothwell
No House Limit. S. Fisher
No Hurry to Kill. N. Deane
No Judges' Rules. D. MacDonald
No Kisses from the Kremlin. H. T. Rothwell
No Known Grave. E. Berckman
No Land Without Liberty. J. G. Sarasin

No Last Words. B. Cobb
No Law Against Angels. C. Brown
No Law in Illyria. T. S. Strachan
No Less Renowned. G. Hackforth-Jones
No Letters from the Grave. B. Copper
No Light Came On. A. Campbell
No Lilies. H. Holt
No Limit. A. Applin
No Little Enemy. O. W. Bayer
No Looking Back. G. Greenaway
No Love Lost. M. Allingham
No Love Lost. Robert Reeves
No Luck for a Lady. F. Mahannah
No Man Pursues. H. S. Davies
No Man's Hand. J. L. Bonney
No Man's Land. H. C. McNeile
No Man's Land. L. J. Vance
No Man's Laughter. K. Laing
No Man's Money. H. M. Rideout
No Man's Street. B. Nichols
No Man's Woman. A. Boyd
No Man's World. M. Caidin
No Mask for Murder. A. Garve
No Match for Murder. J. F. Webb
No Match for the Law. O. Mills
No Mean Tartar. L. F. Hay
No Medal if I Die. J. Ward
No Medals for Murder. H. Holt
No Medals for the Major. M. Yorke
No Medicine for Murder. Jeanne Wilson
No Mercy for Margaret. B. Cobb
No Mercy in the Sky. J. Fores
No Moon Tonight. J. Courage
No Moonlight. P. H. Powell
No More a Brother. T. Newman
No More a Corpse. L. Brent
No More A-Roving. S. Troy
No More Ancestors. L. Robinson
No More Dying Then. R. Rendell
No More Love. M. Hervey
No More Murders. M. Lang
No Mortgage on a Coffin. D. Glinto
No Motive for Murder. W. E. Johns
No Mourners Present. F. G. Presnell
No Mourning for the Matador. D. Ames
No Mourning in the Family. R. Philmore
No Murder. H. C. Bailey
No Murder of Mine. A. Campbell
No Name. W. Collins
No Need for Violence. J. Burrows
No Need to Die. G. Ashe
No News on Monday. R. Clapperton
No Next of Kin. D. M. Disney
No! No! the Woman! N. Klein
No Obelisk for Emily. S. H. Courtier
No One of That Name. W. Merrick
No One to Worry Us. T. S. Strachan
No Orchids for Miss Blandish. J. H. Chase
No Ordinary Cheyney. P. Cheyney
No Other Hunger. F. Mullally
No Other Killer. J. Corbett
No Other Tiger. A. E. W. Mason
No Other Victim. C. Franklin
No Other Way. L. Tracy
No Outlet. A. M. Chase
No Paradise. K. Royce
No Past Is Dead. J. J. Connington
No Peace for Archer. H. Clevely
No Peace for the Living. M. Hervey
No Peace for the Wicked. Peter Chambers
No Peace for the Wicked. E. Ferrars
No Percentage in Death. R. Angel
No Place for a Dame. M. Clinten
No Place for a Tickle. R. Cooper
No Place for Me. S. Morelli
No Place for Murder. G. H. Coxe
No Place for Strangers. W. H. Baker

No Place for the Young. E. Warman
No Place to Be a Cop. F. Nolan
No Place to Hide. E. Lindall
No Place to Hide. C. Runyon
No Place to Live. E. Ronns
No Pockets in a Shroud. H. McCoy
No Pockets in Shrouds. L. Revell
No Profit in Dying. O. Beeby
No Proof. L. L. Lynch
No Proud Chivalry. M. Procter
No Quarter for a Star. D. Gray
No Quarter Given. B. Rossi
No Question of Murder. P. Curtis
No Questions Asked. W. A. Frost
No Questions Asked. F. Rydell
No Questions Asked. E. Sherry
No Reason for Murder. E. Radford
No Red Herrings. Mary Scott
No Refuge. J. Boland
No Regrets for Clara. H. Janson
No Rehearsals for Murder. E. Ferrars
No Reprieve. H. Desmond
No Return Ticket. M. Russell
No Room at the Morgue. A. Bocca
No Ruined Castles. J. McGovern
No Safe Road. B. Munslow
No Sainted City. S. Bunce
No Sale. M. Cronin
No Sale for Haloes. Anthony Graham
No Scars to See. I. See
No Second Stroke. C. Rushton
No Sentiment. A. Dick
No Sentiment in Murder. M. Cumberland
No Shame for the Devil. B. Cobb
No Sign of Murder. W. Reed
No, Sir Jeremy. A. Weymouth
No Sky. N. Balchin
No Sleep at All. J. Warren
No Sleep for Elsa. T. C. H. Jacobs
No Sleep for Macall. G. Fairlie
No Slightest Whisper. D. Evans
No Smoke No Flame. Q. Downes
No Snow at Latching. M. Home
No Space for Murder. N. Brent
No Stockings. A. S. Roche
No Such Word. R. Pertwee
No Surrender. M. Albrand
No Sweet Aspersion. Y. Pickering
No Target for Bowman. H. Howard
No Tears Are Shed. S. Davis
No Tears at the Funeral. H. Arre
No Tears for Hilda. A. Garve
No Tears for Shirley Minton. K. Lowe
No Tears for Teddy. Surrey Smith
No Tears for the Dead. P. Audemars
No Tears for the Dead. S. Deane
No Tears for the Dead. R. Foley
No Tears from the Widow. C. Brown
No Tears Shed. A. B. Caldwell
No Thanks for the Shroud. J. P. Carstairs
No Thoroughfare. D. Egerton
No Through Road. B. Hector
No Through Road. M. Russell
No Time at All. C. Einstein
No Time for Corpses. R. Carni
No Time for Crime. C. M. Russell
No Time for Death. P. Capon
No Time for Terror. P. MacDonald
No Time to Die. R. Pape
No Time to Kill. J. Bonett
No Time to Kill. G. H. Coxe
No Time to Laugh. J. Norwood
No Time to Live. W. H. Baker
No Time to Play. K. Hewitt
No Traveller Returns. D. Ames

No Traveller Returns. A. Dean
No Trespassing. D. Tracy
No Trial--No Error. C. Robertson
No Turning Back. W. F. Morris
No Vacation for Maigret. G. Simenon
No Vacation from Murder. E. Lemarchand
No Vindication. Mrs. C. Kernahan
No Walls of Jasper. J. Cannan
No Way Back from Prague. P. Brent
No Way Home. G. R. Preedy
No Way Out. W. McNeilly
No Way Out. B. Musto
No Way Out. R. O. Saber
No Way to Treat a Lady. H. Longbaugh
No Weeds for the Widow. M. M. Raison
No Will to Die. W. Ellis
No Wind of Blame. G. Heyer
No Wings on a Cop. C. F. Adams
No Witness! C. Fitzsimmons
No Wooden Overcoat. J. P. Carstairs
No Wreath from Manuela. A. MacKinnon
No Wreaths for the Duchess. F. Grierson
Noah's Ark Murders. A. Douglas
Noble Blood. J. Hawthorne
Noble Error. M. L. Tyrrell
Noble Lord. E. Southworth
Noble Profession. P. Boulle
Nobleman's Wife. H. Wood
Nobody. L. J. Vance
Nobody Answered the Bell. R. Davies
Nobody Died for Honnie. D. Bogard
Nobody Heard the Shot. D. B. Chidsey
Nobody Is Safe. M. Cumberland
Nobody Knew They Were There. E. Hunter
Nobody Lives Forever. W. R. Burnett
Nobody Lives Forever. Peter Chambers
Nobody Loves a Dead Man. M. M. Raison
Nobody Loves a Loser. H. Kane
Nobody Needs a Corpse. M. Cronin
Nobody on the Road. G. Rose
Nobody Stops Me. E. North
Nobody Wore Black. D. Ames
Nobody's Daughter. C. Augusta
Nobody's Fortune. E. Yates
Nobody's Man. E. P. Oppenheim
Nobody's Perfect. Douglas Clark
Nobody's Vineyard. H. C. Bailey
Nobody's Widow. G. Warden
Nodding Canaries. G. Mitchell
Nodding Towers. Sam Hill
Noise in the Night. S. Jepson
Nomads of the Night. G. Leroux
Non-Murder. J. Ingersol
None But the Lethal Heart. C. Brown
None of Maigret's Business. G. Simenon
None of My Business. D. Sharp
None of Us Cared for Kate. J. Haythorne
None Shall Know. M. Albrand
None Shall Sleep Tonight. H. McCutcheon
None So Blind. M. A. Wilson
Nonsense Novels. S. Leacock
Noon Balloon to Rangoon. J. Haase
Noon Jury. Mark Ross
Noonday Devil. U. Curtiss
Noonday Devils. W. Martyn
Noose. P. MacDonald
Noose for a Lady. H. Carmichael
Noose for a Lady. G. Verner
Noose for Her. E. Crispin
Noose Is Drawn. W. A. Barber
Noose of Emeralds. B. Winter
Noose of Red Beads. T. J. King
Noose of Sin. F. Carco
Nor All Your Tears. L. Charbonneau
Nor Evil Dreams. Rosemary Harris
Nor Iron Bars. S. Dannett
Nor Spell nor Charm. Alicen White
Nora's Love Test. M. C. Hay

Norine's Revenge, and Sir Noel's Heir. M. A. Fleming
Norma Danton. Anonymous
Norroy, Diplomatic Agent. G. Bronson-Howard
Norslag. Michael Sinclair
North. J. B. Hendryx
North Beach Girl. J. Trinian
North Beat. J. Wood
North Cape. J. Poyer
North for Danger. C. Robertson
North from Rome. H. MacInnes
North from Singapore. D. Nabarro
North from Thursday. J. Cleary
North Kill. J. Wood
"North of 55°." A. Murray
North of the Law. S. A. White
North of the Stars. C. Stoddard
North of Welfare. W. Krasner
North Sea Mystery. H. Edmonds
North Sea Patrol. G. E. Rochester
North Star. H. Innes
North Walk Mystery. W. N. Harben
Northern Mission. J. Wood
Northing Tramp. E. Wallace
Norths Meet Murder. F. Lockridge
Northward the Coast. E. Lindall
Northwater. C. Crowe
Northwest! H. Bindloss
Northwest Contract. L. Derrick
Northwest Law. S. A. White
Northwest Patrol. S. A. White
Northwest Trouble. C. Stoddard
Norval, the Detective. Old Sleuth
Norwich Victims. F. Beeding
Norwood Mystery. J. K. Blades
Nose on My Face. L. Payne
Not a Bad Show. F. Beeding
Not a Clue. A. De Mirjian
Not a Dog's Chance. W. R. Hutton
Not a Leg to Stand On. M. Burton
Not a Nice Murder! E. Wilmot
Not After Midnight. D. Du Maurier
Not Comin' Home to You. P. Kavanagh
Not Dead Enough. Clay Henry
Not Dead Yet. D. Banko
Not Expected to Live. M. Cumberland
Not for a Curse. K. Kramer
Not for Export. M. Coles
Not Guilty. Anonymous
Not Guilty. W. E. Norris
Not Guilty. W. Phillips
Not Guilty, My Lord. H. Desmond
Not Herbert. H. I. Young
Not I, Said the Sparrow. R. Lockridge
Not I, Said the Vixen. B. S. Ballinger
Not in the Book. A. Watkyn
Not in the Newspapers. John Gloag
Not in the Script. J. Bonett
Not in Utter Nakedness. D. Ames
Not Killed, Just Dead. D. Ambler
Not Long to Live. Mark Cross
Not Me, Inspector. H. Reilly
"Not Mentioned..." A. Soutar
Not My Murder. John Marsh
Not Negotiable. M. Coles
Not Nice People. H. Clevely
Not on the Records. N. Carter
Not One of Us. J. Thomson
Not Proven. A. Askew
Not Proven. J. Dering
Not Proven. B. Graeme
Not Proven. P. Traill
Not Proven Castle. A. Wood
Not Quite Dead Enough. R. Stout
Not Quite So Black. D. G. Waring
Not Ready to Die. J. Monmouth
Not Safe to Be Free. J. H. Chase
Not Single Spies. D. Betteridge
Not So Evil as Eve. J. Creighton

Not So Quickly. K. Fitzgerald
Not Sufficient Evidence. J. L. Rickard
Not the Glory. P. Boulle
Not to Be Opened. L. Osbourne
Not to Be Taken. A. Berkeley
Not to the Swift. H. Gibbs
Not to the Swift. L. Harrison
Not Too Narrow--Not Too Deep. R. Sale
Not Wanted. F. Hume
Not Wanted on Voyage. N. Spain
Not with a Bang. C. Pincher
Not with My Neck. T. Van Dycke
Not Wooed, but Won. J. Payn
Notch on the Knife. W. Haggard
Notched Hairpin. H. F. Heard
Note of Enchantment. E. H. Clements
Notebooks. S. Picard
Notes of an Itinerant Policeman. J. Flynt
Nothing Barred. Johnny Morgan
Nothing but a Man. J. Thompson
Nothing but Blood. P. C. Smith
Nothing but the Night. J. Blackburn
Nothing but the Night. J. Yaffe
Nothing but the Truth. J. Rhode
Nothing Can Rescue Me. E. Daly
Nothing for Nothing. N. Easton
Nothing Happens to Children in Beverly Hills. Vi Wolfson
Nothing Hid. A. Marshall
Nothing in Her Way. C. Williams
Nothing Irredeemable. D. G. Waring
Nothing Is the Number When You Die. J. Fleming
Nothing Like Blood. L. Bruce
Nothing Man. J. Thompson
Nothing More Than Murder. J. Thompson
Nothing to Declare. M. Coles
Nothing to Declare. R. Mann
Nothing to Hide. M. Perelli
Nothing to Hide. D. Spade
Nothing to Lose. R. Charles
Nothing to Lose But My Life. L. Trimble
Nothing to Pretend. E. Thorne
Nothing to Report. R. McLaughlin
Nothing Venture. P. Wentworth
Notice to Quit. J. Quince
Notorious. D. Keene
Notorious Landlady. I. Shulman
Notorious Miss Lisle. B. Reynolds
Notorious Miss Walters. S. Kyle
Notorious Sophie Lang. F. I. Anderson
Notting Hill Murder. C. Ryland
Notting Hill Mystery. C. Felix
Noughts and Crosses. E. Woodward
November. G. Simenon
November Joe, the Detective of the Woods. H. Prichard
November 9th at Kersea. A. Swift
November Reef. R. Maugham
November Wind. P. Geddes
Now and for Never. H. A. Hoare
Now and on Earth. J. Thompson
Now, Gentlemen, Please. H. Fernee
Now I Lay Me Down to Die. E. Tebbetts-Taylor
Now Is the Time. L. Katcher
Now It's My Turn. M. E. Chaber
Now Like to Die. H. Brinton
Now Lying Dead. O. Norton
Now Lying Dead. P. H. Powell
Now or Never. M. Coles
Now Seek My Bones. S. H. Courtier
Now Try the Morgue. T. D. Smith
Now We Are Free. K. David
Now Will You Try for Murder? H. Olesker
Now You See It-Him-Them. G. DeWeese

Title Index

Nowhere Man. Ritchie Perry
Nowhere Place. J. Lymington
Nowhere to Go. D. MacKenzie
Nude in Mink. S. Rohmer
Nude in Nevada. T. B. Dewey
Nude on the Rocks. Clay Henry
Nude on Thin Ice. G. Brewer
Nude on Thin Ice. C. Williams
Nude Was Framed. R. Drayton
Nude--with a View. C. Brown
Nudist Murder. T. Stevenson
Number 18. C. M. Wills
Number 87. H. Hext
Number Fifteen. D. Whitelaw
No. 9 Belmont Square. M. Erskine
Number Nineteen. J. J. Farjeon
No. 19. E. Jepson
No. 19 State Street. D. G. Adee
No. 99. A. Griffiths
Number Nought. S. Truss
Number One. R. Masson
"No. 101." Wymond Carey
Number 1-2-3. F. Gerard
Number One with a Bullet. E. Jesmer
Number One's Last Crime. M. E. Cooke
Number Seven Queer Street. Margery Lawrence
No. 7, Saville Square. W. LeQueux
No. 17. J. J. Farjeon
Number Seventeen. L. Tracy
Number 70, Berlin. W. LeQueux
Number Seventy-Three. S. Kyle
Number Six. E. Wallace
Number 13. F. M. White
No. 13, Rue du Bon Diable. Arthur Sherburne Hardy
No. 13 Rue Marlot. R. De Pont-Jest
No. 13 Toroni. J. Regis
No. 13 Washington Square. L. Scott
"No. 3." L. K. Vincent
No. 3 the Square. F. Warden
Number Two, North Steps. J. Dering
Numbered Account. A. Bridge
Numbers for Lovers. A. J. Fitzgerald
Nun in the Closet. D. Gilman
Nun in the Cupboard. D. Gilman
Nun's Castle. J. Melville
Nun's Curse. J. H. Riddell
Nuplex Red. Simon Quinn
Nurse. A. Askew
Nurse Alice in Love. T. Charles
Nurse at Brooding Mansion. P. Warren
Nurse at Danger Mansion. D. Daniels
Nurse Elisia. G. M. Fenn
Nurse Lester's First Case. A. M. Griffin
Nurse Revel's Mistake. F. Warden
Nurse Stacey Comes Aboard. Rona Randall
Nurse to Dives. P. Trent
Nursemaid Who Disappeared. P. MacDonald
Nursery Rhyme Murders. G. Verner
Nursery Tea and Poison. A. Morice
Nursing Home. A. Applin
Nursing Home Crime. C. Brisbane
Nursing-Home Murder. N. Marsh
Nut-Browne Mayd. G. Warden
Nylon Nightmare. C. Matthews
Nylon Pirates. N. Monsarrat
Nymph at Bay. E. P. Frankland
Nymph in the Night. H. Janson
Nymph to the Slaughter. C. Brown
Nympho Named Silvia. H. Janson

O

O as in Omen. L. Treat
O Charitable Death. R. C. Payes
O Clouds Unfold. P. Capon

O.D. at Sweet Claude's. M. Gattzden
O Huge Angel. H. Baer
O Sweet McTavish. C. Brooks
Oak and Iron. J. B. Hendryx
Oakdale Affair. E. R. Burroughs
Oaks of Bashan. R. P. Pond
Oasis. J. Creasey
Oasis. P. Meredith
Oasis Nine. V. Canning
Oasis of Fear. K. Evans
Oasis of Sleep. J. Atholl
Oasis of Tears. M. Richmond
Oath of Fear. W. J. Bayfield
Oath of Vengeance. J. K. Stafford
Obeah Murders. H. Footner
Obelisk Conspiracy. G. Marton
Obelists at Sea. C. D. King
Obelists en Route. C. D. King
Obelists Fly High. C. D. King
Obi. Anonymous
Obit Deferred. L. Trimble
Obit Delayed. H. Nielsen
Obituary Club. H. Pentecost
Object of Jealousy. A. Rutledge
Obligations of Hercule. P. Audemars
Obliging Corpse. J. Courage
Obliging Husband. F. Barrett
Oblong Circle. H. P. Rednour
Obole of Paradise. A. Miller
Obols for Charon. S. Harvester
Obsequies at Oxford. E. Crispin
Observer Corps Mystery. R. Hardinge
Obsession. Alec Coppel
Obsession. M. Tripp
Obsession. L. White
Obsession for Two. J. Bentley
Obsession to Kill. M. Shane
Obsessions. T. Gurr
Obstinate Captain Samson. Gavin Douglas
Obstinate Girl. E. Jepson
Obstinate Murderer. E. S. Holding
Obstinate Virgin. S. Murray
Obvious Solution. C. F. Gregg
Occidental Sketches. B. C. Truman
Occupying Power. Evelyn Anthony
Ocean Knight. F. Du Boisgobey
Ocean Prize. J. Pattinson
Ocean Road. Jack Bennett
Ocean Secret. G. Boothby
Ocean Sleuth. M. Drake
Ocean Tragedy. W. C. Russell
Ocean's 11. G. C. Johnson
Octagon Crystal. P. Foley
Octagon House. G. Knevels
Octagon House. P. A. Taylor
Octangle. E. N. Sachs
October Circle. R. Littell
October Day. F. Griffin
October House. K. C. Strahan
October Men. John Mills
October Tea. A. Price
October Plot. C. Egleton
uctober Witch. Alanna Knight
Octopus of Crime. B. House
Octopus of Paris. G. Leroux
Octopus' Shadow. M. Carrel
Octopussy. I. Fleming
Octopussy and the Living Daylights. I. Fleming
Octoroon. M. E. Braddon
Odd--But Even So. P. C. Wren
Odd Flamingo. N. Bawden
Odd Issues. S. S. Sprigge
Odd Job. P. Flower
Odd Job No. 101, and other future crimes and intrigues. R. Goulart
Odd Man In. L. A. G. Strong
Odd Man Out. F. L. Green
Odd Man Pays. D. L. Teilhet
Odd One Out. L. D. Stranger
Odd Pairs. L. Housman

Odd Trick. A. M. Meadows
Odd Woman Out. George Douglas
Odd Woman Out. S. Fox
Odd Woman Out. J. L. Linklater
Oddest of Courtships. J. W. De Forrest
Odds Against. D. Francis
Odds Against Her. A. Wood
Odds Against Linda. S. Ward
Odds Against Tomorrow. W. P. McGivern
Odds On. J. Lange
Odds on Bluefeather. L. Meynell
Odds on Death. C. Drummond
Odds on Miss Seeton. H. Carvic
Odds-on-Murder. J. Dolph
Odds on Murder. M. Levien
Odds on the Hot Seat. J. Philips
Odds Run Out. H. Waugh
Oddways. H. Adams
Odean Theatre Mystery. D. Whitelaw
Odessa File. F. Forsyth
Odious Ones. J. Sohl
Odor of Bitter Almonds. J. G. Edwards
Odor of Violets. B. Kendrick
Odour of Decay. M. Jenson
Of All the Bloody Cheek. F. McAuliffe
Of Hidden Depths. A. Windsor-Richards
Of High Degree. C. Gibbon
Of High Descent. G. M. Fenn
Of Ladies Dead. A. Hasluck
Of Love and Hunger. J. MacLaren-Ross
Of Love and Intrigue. V. Coffman
Of Malicious Intent. L. Meynell
Of Masks and Minds. F. E. Smith
Of Mice and Murder. B. Whitaker
Of Midnight Honor. J. G. Vermandel
Of Missing Persons. D. Goodis
Of Royal Blood. W. LeQueux
Of Singular Purpose. R. Lewis
Of Six Suspects. D. Newton
Of Tender Sin. D. Goodis
Of the Deepest Dye. C. Larking
Of This Death. V. Campbell
Of Unsound Mind. H. Carmichael
Off-Islanders. N. Benchley
Off Lands End. W. Reid
Off Shore. Taffrail
Off the Beaten Track. F. St. Mars
Off the Track in London. G. R. Sims
Off to the Wilds. G. M. Fenn
Off with Her Head! G. D. H. Cole
Off with His Head. N. Marsh
Off with His Head. J. L. Morrissey
Offense Against the Persons. H. Gilbert
Office Scandal. F. A. Edwards
Office Secret. W. LeQueux
Officer! H. Footner
Officer and a Gentleman? and other stories. G. Thorne
Officer Factory. H. H. Kirst
Officer from Special Branch. T. Lilley
Officer 666. B. Currie
Officer, That's Your Man. P. G. Larbalestier
Official Chaperon. N. S. Lincoln
Official Secret. A. Duncan
Offshore! S. Coulter
"Oh, Joshua!" Taffrail
Oh, Murderer Mine. N. Davis
Oh, No, You Don't. H. Carstairs
Oh! Where Are Bloody Mary's Earrings? R. Player
Oh, Wicked Wanda. F. Mullally
Oil Bastards. P. McCutchan
Oil by Murder. J. Paul
Oil Slick. R. Sapir
Oil Under the Window. N. Berrow

Okewood of the Secret Service. D. Valentine
Oktoberfest. F. De Felitta
Old Admiral Death. R. Bridges
Old Age of Lecoq, the Detective. F. Du Boisgobey
Old Age of Monsieur Lecoq. F. Du Boisgobey
Old Anthony's Secret. W. J. Shaw
Old Bailey Mystery. A. Blair
Old Bank. W. Westall
Old Battle Ax. E. S. Holding
Old Blazer's Hero. D. C. Murray
Old Bones. H. Petersen
Old Corcoran's Money. R. Dowling
Old Dark House. J. B. Priestley
Old Detective's Pupil. Anonymous
Old Detective's Pupil. N. Carter
Old Ebbie. F. A. M. Webster
Old Ebbie Returns. F. A. M. Webster
Old Electricity, the Lightning Detective. Anonymous
Old Electricity, the Lighting Detective. Old Sleuth
Old English Baron. Clara Reeve
Old English Peep Show. P. Dickinson
Old Factory. W. Westall
Old-Fashioned Christmas. A. Dick
Old-Fashioned Murder. M. McIntire
Old Fires and Profitable Ghosts. A. T. Quiller-Couch
Old Fox. W. Fennerton
Old Friend. V. Siller
Old Goat. E. Greenwood
Old Granstock. J. Easton
Old Gumber's Mill. E. J. Kyle
Old Hall, New Hall. M. Innes
Old Harry Hawks. Anonymous
Old House at Sandwich. J. Hatton
Old House at the Corner. F. Warden
Old House by the Sea. S. E. Phipps
Old House of Fear. R. Kirk
Old House of West Street. T. P. Prest
Old Ironsides Among the Italian Brigands. Old Sleuth
Old Isaacs from the Bowery. C. E. Blaney
Old Jew Mystery. H. Adams
Old Judge Priest. I. S. Cobb
Old King Cole. S. P. B. Mais
Old King Cole. E. Shanks
Old Lady Dies. Anthony Gilbert
Old Lattimer's Legacy. J. S. Fletcher
Old Lover's Ghost. L. Ford
Old Madhouse. W. F. De Morgan
Old Maid's Vengeance. F. Powell
Old Man Dies. G. Simenon
Old Man in the Corner. B. Orczy
Old Man in the Corner Unravels the Mystery of the Fulton Gardens Mystery, and The Moorland Tragedy. B. Orczy
Old Man in the Corner Unravels the Mystery of the Pearl Necklace, and The Tragedy in Bishop's Road. B. Orczy
Old Man in the Corner Unravels the Mystery of the Russian Prince, and of Dog's Tooth Cliff. B. Orczy
Old Man in the Corner Unravels the Mystery of the White Carnation, and The Montmartre Hat. B. Orczy
Old Man Mystery. J. J. Farjeon
Old Man of the Moors. W. Jardine
Old Man Tutt. A. Train
Old Manor. C. F. Gregg
Old Manor Crime. W. Martyn
Old Manor House. Charlotte Smith
Old Man's Money. J. Reach
Old Masters. W. Haggard
Old Mill. P. W. Wilson
Old Mill Mystery. A. W. Marchmont
Old Miser's Mystery. Old Sleuth
Old Miser's Ward. Old Sleuth
Old Mr. Davenant's Money. F. Powell
Old Mrs. Camelot. E. Bonett
Old Mrs. Fitzgerald. A. Hocking
Old Mrs. Ommanney Is Dead. M. Erskine
Old Mrs. Warren. F. Wolseley
Old Murders Never Die. N. Carlson
Old Must Die. A. Gaines
Old Myddelton's Money. M. C. Hay
Old Offenders and a Few Old Scores. E. W. Hornung
Old Patch's Medley. M. Bowen
Old Puritan, the Old Time Detective. Anonymous
Old Quartz, the Nevada Detective. E. T. Sawyer
Old Reliable. P. G. Wodehouse
Old Rogue's Tragedy. Rita
Old Rowley. M. M. Bodkin
Old Sinners Never Die. D. S. Davis
Old Sins Have Long Shadows. J. L. Rickard
Old Sleuth, Detective. Anonymous
Old Sleuth, the Avenger. Old Sleuth
Old Sleuth, the Detective. Old Sleuth
Old Sleuth to the Rescue. Old Sleuth
Old Sleuth's Greatest Case. Old Sleuth
Old Sleuth's Triumph. Old Sleuth
Old Sleuth's Winning Hand. Old Sleuth
Old Sleuth's Wonderful Revelation. Old Sleuth
Old Specie, the Treasury Detective. M. Manly
Old Specie, the Treasury Detective. A. Robertson
Old Stone House and other stories. A. K. Green
Old Stonewall, the Colorado Detective. J. R. Taylor
Old Stonewall, the "Shadower." Anonymous
Old Students Never Die. I. T. Ross
Old Terrible. Old Sleuth
Old Terrible, the Iron Arm Detective. Anonymous
Old Tollgate Mystery. W. J. Bayfield
Old Trade of Killing. J. Harris
Old Transform, the Secret Special Detective. Anonymous
Old Ugly Face. T. Mundy
Oldest Confession. R. Condon
Oldest Profession. B. Sarto
Oldest Road. D. G. Waring
Olga Knaresbrook, Detective. H. Campbell
Olga's Crime. F. Barrett
Oliver Goldfinch. Emerson Bennett
Oliver Quendon's First Case. Cowdray Browne
Olivia. Gwendoline Butler
Olmec Head. D. Westheimer
Olura. G. Household
Om. T. Mundy
Omar Pasha. G. W. M. Reynolds
Omega-Minus. T. Allbeury
Omega Operation. N. Conway
Omega Terror. N. Carter
Omen. M. Eyre
Omerta. P. McCurtin
Ominous Star. R. Foley
Omit Flowers. S. Palmer
Omit Flowers, Please. A. Gaines
Omnibus Mystery. F. Du Boisgobey
Omnipotent Avenger. Old Sleuth
On a Blind Trail. J. K. Stafford
On a Crimson Trail. N. Carter
On a False Charge. S. W. Hopkins
On a Fated Night. D. Malm
On a Million-Dollar Trail. N. Carter
On a Still Night. C. D. Peel
On Appeal. P. Dewdney
On Circumstantial Evidence. F. Marryat
On Compassionate Leave. L. Jackson
On Dangerous Ground. E. S. Drewry
On Death's Trail. D. Stewart
On Desperate Seas. J. Pattinson
On Fortune's Wheel. R. M. Wells
On Government Service. F. A. M. Webster
On Hazardous Duty. David St. John
On Helle's Wave. H. Imber
On Her Majesty's Secret Service. Anonymous
On Her Majesty's Secret Service. I. Fleming
On Her Majesty's Service. A. Upward
On Ice. R. G. Dean
On Land and Sea. G. Simenon
On Schedule. E. L. Long
On Secret Service. R. Arnold
On Secret Service. J. Mowbray
On Secret Service. W. N. Taft
On Swan River. H. Footner
On the Bed of the Ocean. E. S. Brooks
On the Borderland. F. B. Austin
On the Brink. D. Batchelor
On the Brink. M. Endfield
On the Brink of a Chasm. L. T. Meade
On the Brink of Ruin. Old Spicer
On the Danger Line. G. Simenon
On the Danger List. M. Cumberland
On the Day of the Shooting. C. Franklin
On the Dead Run. W. B. Murphy
On the Double. Roger Fuller
On the Edge of the Sea. F. L. Green
On the 11:40 Down. H. King
On the Embankment. R. Dowling
On the Eve of Triumph. N. Carter
On the Fringe. T. W. Speight
On the Highest Hill. H. M. Stephenson
On the Hook. R. Powell
On the Inside. F. F. Kelly
On the Instructions of My Government. P. Salinger
On the Jury. R. Marsh
On the Jury. W. Phillips
On the Lightship. H. K. Viele
On the Line and Danger Signal. B. Hemyng
On the Make. J. D. MacDonald
On the Midnight Beat. J. G. Brandon
On the Night Express! H. H. C. Gibbons
On the Night Express. F. M. White
On the Night in Question. C. M. Wills
"On the Night of the 18th..." L. Meynell
On the Night of the Fire. F. L. Green
On the Night of the 14th. Mark Cross
On the Night of the Ninth. R. Trevor
On the Night of the Seventh Moon. V. Holt
On the Prime Minister's Account. O. Hogstrand
On the Rack. W. C. Hudson
On the Ragged Edge. N. Carter
On the Rank. B. Hemyng
On the Right Wrists. A. Livingston
On the Rim of the Arctic. J. B. Hendryx
On the Road. B. Hemyng
On the Run. E. M. Bowen
On the Run. Roland Daniel
On the Run. Angus Hall
On the Run. J. D. MacDonald
On the Scent. Anonymous
On the Secret Service of His Majesty, the Queen. S. Weinstein
On the Shady Side. F. Swinnerton
On the Shores of Night. A. Mans

On the Spot. E. Wallace
On the Stretch. J. Welcome
On the Stroke of Midnight. M. O. Rolfe
On the Stroke of Nine. A. Parsons
On the Track of Death. D. Rutherford
On the Trail of "Big Finger." S. Campbell
On the Way Out. John Williams
On the Wing. Old Sleuth
On the Wing of Occasions. J. C. Harris
On the Yard. M. Braly
On Their Track. Old Sleuth
On Ticket of Leave. S. Blake
On Ticket of Leave. J. G. Brandon
On Trial. E. L. Reizenstein
On Trial. D. Torbett
On Trial for His Life. Anonymous
On Trial for His Life. O. Harper
On Trust. T. Cobb
On Winding Waters. W. M. Graydon
Once a Copper. W. Terry
Once a Crook. E. Price
Once a Thief. Z. Marko
Once a Widow. Lee Roberts
Once Acquitted. A. R. Long
Once, and Then the Funeral. B. J. Farmer
Once Bit, Twice Hit. H. C. McNeile
Once Bitten, and What Ensued. G. M. Winsor
Once for All. M. Hillary
"Once I Was Blind." Andrew Stewart
Once in a Lifetime. J. Mayo
Once in a Red Moon. J. T. Rogers
Once in Tiger Bay. J. M. Walsh
Once More the Saint. L. Charteris
Once Off Guard. J. H. Wallis
Once over Deadly. F. Gruber
Once over Deadly. E. McNamara
Once too Often. W. Chambers
Once too Often. Mark Cross
Once too Often. F. Warden
Once upon a Christmas Time. G. R. Sims
Once upon a Crime. Mark Cross
Once upon a Crime. Michael Hall
Once upon a Crime. M. Kerrigan
Once upon a Crime. C. Monig
Once upon a Crime. R. Selman
Once upon a Friday. P. Moore
Once upon a Midnight. J. Reach
Once upon a Nightmare. Lynn Williams
Once upon a Private Eye. P. Quinn
Once upon a Time. E. Phillpotts
Once upon a Tombstone. E. Salter
Once You Stop, You're Dead. E. K. Goldthwaite
One. D. Karp
I-A Stranger. A. Guirdham
One Across, Two Down. R. Rendell
One Against the Earth. D. Mainwaring
One Against the Odds. N. Fagan
One Against Time. H. Janson
One Alone. V. Siller
One Among None. R. Stratton
One Angel Less. H. W. Roden
One Angry Man. N. Daniels
One-Armed Murder. R. Gallagher
One Away. A. Prior
One Between. F. Cowen
One Black Summer. B. Jefferis
One Blonde Died. L. Edgley
One Bright Day. E. S. Miller
One Bright Summer Morning. J. H. Chase
One by One. F. Nichols
One by One They Disappeared. M. Dalton
One Clear Call. F. N. Greene
One Corpse Missing. Z. H. Ross
One Cried Murder. S. H. Courtier
One Cried Murder. Jean Leslie
One Crime Too Many. J. Guil
One Dead Debutante. H. Gould
One Deadly Dawn. H. Whittington
One Down. A. Bodelsen
One Down and Two to Slay. H. Brinton
"One Dreadful Night." R. S. L. Harding
One Drop of Blood. Anne Austin
One Enchanted Evening. M. Richmond
One Endless Hour. D. J. Marlowe
One Evening I Shall Return. Anne-Mariel
One-Eyed King. E. Fadiman
One-Eyed Knave. Ganpat
One-Faced Girl. C. Armstrong
One Fair Enemy. C. Dawe
One False Move. R. Drayton
One False Move. K. Roos
One Fearful Yellow Eye. J. D. MacDonald
153 Oakland Street. D. Highland
One Fine Day. M. Richmond
One Foot in the Grave. M. Cumberland
One Foot in the Grave. D. Grubb
One for My Dame. J. Webb
One for My Money. E. Chaze
One for Sleep. F. Bonham
One for the Book. Neill Graham
One for the Death House. J. M. Flynn
One for the Devil. E. Leroux
One for the Road. F. Brown
One for the Road. R. Dietrich
One for the Road. B. Grant
One for the Road. W. J. White
144 Piccadilly. S. Fuller
One from Five. J. W. Lee
One Girl in a Million. L. Tracy
One Glorious Spring. M. Richmond
One Good Turn. N. Easton
One Got Away. H. Whittington
One Grave Too Many. R. Goulart
One Half of the World. J. Barlow
One Helluva Blow. G. Werner
One Horrible Night. E. Hayford
One Horse Race. T. H. Stone
One Hour to Kill. G. H. Coxe
100 Mysteries for Arm-Chair Detectives. J. C. Cannell
$106,000 Blood Money. D. Hammett
100 Kilo Club. S. Gandolfi
100 Megaton Kill. Ralph Hayes
$100,000 Kiss. N. Carter
£100,000 Insurance Swindle. W. W. Sayer
£100,000 versus Ghosts. R. Jocelyn
100,000 Welcomes. M. Kenyon
One Is a Lonely Number. B. Elliott
One Is One. A. Dick
One Is One. M. Tripp
One Jump Ahead. A. Armstrong
One Jump Ahead. R. Chapman
One Just Man. James Mills
One Kind and Another. B. Pain
One Last Chance. L. Noel
One Last Mad Embrace. J. T. Story
One Last Time. M. Carrel
One Life Between. A. M. Meadows
One Life, One Love. M. E. Braddon
One Lonely Night. M. Spillane
One Louisburg Square. W. E. D. Ross
One Mad Night. J. Reach
One Maid's Mischief. G. M. Fenn
One Man in His Time. H. Janson
One Man in the World. J. Barlow
One-Man Jury. S. Ransome
One Man Must Die. A. B. Cunningham
One Man Saw Them Die. A. Webb
One Man Show. M. Innes
One Man Too Many. V. Coffman
One Man's Awe. V. Carrington
One Man's Crime. L. W. Brent
One Man's Death. S. Truss
One Man's Enemies. S. Truss
One Man's Meat. W. H. L. Crauford
One Man's Muddle. E. B. Quinn
One Man's Murder. D. Delman
One Man's Poison. C. Fitzsimmons
One Man's Poison. S. Fox
One Man's Secret. S. Davis
One Man's Secret. A. Mills
One Man's War. B. Bavin
One Man's Wars. G. Hackforth-Jones
One Man's Woman. K. Hewitt
$1,000,000 in Corpses. E. Ronns
One Million Francs. A. Fredericks
£1,000,000 Film Murder. D. Stuart
£1,000,000 Plot. A. Skene
£1,000,000. W. J. Elliott
One Minus One. R. D. MacDougall
One-Minute Murder. J. G. Brandon
One Minute Past Eight. G. H. Coxe
One Minute to Eternity. R. Weverka
One Monday We Killed Them All. J. D. MacDonald
One More Bridge to Cross. A. Hale
One More Nice White Body. D. Glinto
One More River. Laurence Kirk
One More Time. M. Avallone
One More Time. Jay Bell
One More Unfortunate. E. Lustgarten
One Murder Too Many. G. H. Coxe
One Murder Too Many. F. C. Davis
One Murder Too Many. E. Lanham
One Murder Too Many. J. C. Lenehan
One Murdered, Two Dead. M. Propper
One Must Survive. R. Charles
One Night in Styria. D. Howarth
One Night Mystery. Old Sleuth
One Night of Fear. A. Crane
One Night of Murder. H. Boyd
One Night of Terror. M. Carleton
One Night Stand. W. B. Murphy
One Night to Kill. C. Franklin
One Night with Nora. B. Halliday
One Night's Mystery. M. A. Fleming
119 Great Porter Square. B. L. Farjeon
One Object in Life. N. Carter
One O'Clock at the Gotham. R. Foley
One of God's Dilemmas. A. Upward
One of Marlborough's Captains. M. Gerard
One of My Sons. A. K. Green
One of Our Agents Is Missing. David St. John
One of Our Dinosaurs Is Missing. D. Forrest
One of Our Grandmothers. E. C. Mayne
One of Our H-Bombs Is Missing. F. H. Brennan
One of Seven. R. Hardinge
One of the Bevans. R. Jocelyn
One of the Eleven. W. Tyrer
One of the Family. J. Payn
One of the Flying Squad. W. M. Graydon
One of the Guilty. W. L. George
One of the Ones. J. C. Snaith
One of These Seven. C. Logan
One of Those Things. P. Cheyney
One of Those Ways. M. B. Lowndes
One of Three. C. S. Raymond
One of Us Is a Murderer. A. Le May
One of Us Works for Them. J. D. Hunter
One-Off Job. A. Willsdon
One-One-One. G. Hackforth-Jones
One Page Missing. A. Soutar
One Remained Seated. J. Slate
One Rose Less. P. Flower
One Sane Man. F. Beeding
One Shall Be Taken. A. Hocking
One Shipwreck Too Many. N. Carter
One Shot for Sadie. M. Brody
One Step from Murder. L. Meynell
One Step Too Far. N. Carter

One Sunny Day. Joan Alexander
One Sword Less. C. D. Peel
One Tear for My Grave. M. Roscoe
One That Got Away. H. McCloy
One Thing Constant. V. B. Harris
One Thing Needful, and Cut by the County. M. E. Braddon
1001 Afternoons in New York. B. Hecht
One Thrilling Night. N. Berrow
One Thrilling Night. M. K. Douglas
One-Time Champ. Duff Johnson
One to Jump. George Douglas
One to Play. H. Adams
One Touch of Blood. S. S. Baker
One Touch of Murder. H. Fraser
One Traveller Returns. D. C. Murray
One Tropic Night. E. C. Vivian
One, Two, Buckle My Shoe. A. Christie
1-2-3 Murders. F. Gerard
One Way Only. L. A. Knight
One Way Out. G. H. Coxe
One Way Out. G. Simenon
One Way Street. P. H. Irving
One Way Street. D. Keller
One Way Street. N. Marino
One-Way Ticket. B. Hitchens
One-Way Ticket. H. Luger
One Way Ticket. A. Thackeray
One Way to Venice. J. A. Hodge
One-Way Trail. R. Cullum
One-Way Trip. R. Angel
One Who Kills. R. Cullum
One Who Passed By. T. Cobb
One Who Saw. H. Hill
One Wife's Ways. G. F. Fox
One Wonderful Night. L. Tracy
O'Neil McDarragh. Anonymous
O'Neil McDarragh, the Detective. T. Pastor
Onion Field. J. Wambaugh
Only a Bullet. J. K. Stafford
Only a Clod. M. E. Braddon
Only a Flirt. R. Jocelyn
Only a Girl's Heart. E. Southworth
Only a Headless Nail. D. Stewart
Only a Horse Dealer. R. Jocelyn
Only a Love Song. M. Richmond
Only a Love Story. R. Jocelyn
Only a Matter of Time. V. C. Clinton-Baddeley
Only a Photograph. Old Sleuth
Only a Shadow. D. C. Murray
Only a Woman. M. E. Braddon
Only at Sunset. D. Martyn
Only Couples Need Apply. D. M. Disney
Only Game in Town. C. Einstein
Only Gentlemen Can Play. H. McLeave
Only Girl in the Game. J. D. MacDonald
Only Good Body's a Dead One. T. Kenrick
Only Good Secretary. J. Potts
Only Half the Doctor Died. Frank King
Only Her Hairdresser Knew. C. Carpenter
Only in New England. T. Roscoe
Only Mugs Die Young. Griff
Only Mugs Work. W. Greenwood
Only on Tuesdays. T. B. Dewey
Only Security. Jessica Mann
Only Seven Were Hanged. Stuart Martin
Only Some Had Guns. R. Parker
Only Son. J. W. Bobin
Only the Good. Mary Collins
Only the Guilty. A. M. Stein
Only the Losers Win. G. M. Barnes
Only the Rich Die Young. H. Pentecost
Only the Ruthless Can Play. Jonathan Burke
Only the Unafraid. R. Kirkbridge
Only the Very Rich? C. Brown
Only Three Died. P. H. Powell
Only with a Bargepole. J. Porter
Only Witness. E. J. Goodman
Oonah. G. Payne
Opal Heart. M. Leighton
Opal Legacy. F. Kent
Opal Murder Case. B. Symons
Opal Pin. J. R. Gillies
Opal Serpent. F. Hume
Opal Street. J. Wetherell
Open City. H. Miller
Open Contract. F. Scarpetta
Open Door. E. A. Walcott
Open Door. F. M. White
Open Foe. A. Sergeant
Open House. M. Innes
Open Mouth. M. Urquhart
Open Prison. Lady A. Scott
Open Question. J. De Mille
Open Roadsteads. E. L. Long
Open Season. D. Osborn
Open Season. B. Thielen
Open Secret. T. Cobb
"Open, Sesame!" B. Reynolds
Open Verdict. M. E. Braddon
Open Verdict. F. L. Cary
Open Verdict. R. Keverne
Open Verdict. W. LeQueux
Open Verdict. J. Rhode
Open Your Hand and Close Your Eyes. P. Bair
Opener of the Way. R. Bloch
Opening Door. H. Reilly
Opening Night. N. Marsh
Opera House Murders. D. Billany
Opera Murders. K. Williams
Operation Alcestis. M. Rennert
Operation: Alpha Death. N. Conway
Operation Atlantis. M. G. Braun
Operation Ballerina. Selwyn
Operation Barbarossa. B. Newman
Operation Breakthrough. D. J. Marlowe
Operation Burning Candle. Blyden Jackson
Operation Carlo. J. Pendower
Operation Caroline. C. H. Gibbs-Smith
Operation Castanets. D. Martyn
Operation Che Guevara. N. Carter
Operation Checkmate. D. J. Marlowe
Operation Cicero. L. C. Moyzisch
Operation Cleansweep. D. Graham
Operation Cocaine. Don Romano
Operation Conquest. B. Gray
Operation Cuttlefish. D. R. Mounce
Operation Dancing Dog. J. M. Fox
Operation--Deadline. M. Dines
Operation Deathmaker. D. J. Marlowe
Operation Deep Sea. K. Stanton
Operation Delta. A. McCall
Operation Diamond. "Capstan"
Operation Doctors. H. Roth
Operation Dragnet. E. P. Thorne
Operation Drumfire. D. J. Marlowe
Operation Endless Hour. D. J. Marlowe
Operation Fireball. D. J. Marlowe
Operation Fireball. Sea Lion
Operation Flashpoint. D. J. Marlowe
Operation Godiva. L. Miller
Operation Goldkill. B. Cassiday
Operation Halter. Frank King
Operation Hammerlock. D. J. Marlowe
Operation Hijack. Don Romano
Operating Hit Man. Don Romano
Operation Homicide. E. Adams
Operation Honeymoon. Frank King
Operation Ice Cap. J. Dark
Operation Intrigue. W. Hermann
Operation Iscariot. B. Marshall
Operation Jealousy. M. G. Braun
Operation K. N. Daniels
Operation--Kill or Be Killed. M. Dines
Operation Kuwait. H. Arvay
Operation Loan Shark. Don Romano
Operation "M.O." Taffrail
Operation Malacca. J. Poyer
Operation Manhunt. M. Coles
Operation Megali. M. Dekobra
Operation Mermaid. K. Stanton
Operation Moon Rocket. N. Carter
Operation Mora. Christopher King
Operation--Murder. L. White
Operation N. N. Daniels
Operation New York. G. De Villiers
Operation Nightfall. J. Miles
Operation Nightmare. G. Fredrics
Operation Nuke. M. Caidin
Operation Octopus. J. Dark
Operation Overkill. D. J. Marlowe
Operation Overkill. J. Rosenberger
Operation Pax. M. Innes
Operation Piracy. P. Somers
Operation Porno. Don Romano
Operation Red Carpet. J. Boland
Operation Royal Family. G. Null
Operation S-L. N. Daniels
Operation Scorpio. D. Mariner
Operation Scuba. J. Dark
Operation Sea Monster. K. Stanton
Operation Sky Drop. D. Brennan
Operation Snake. N. Carter
Operation Snatch. John Marsh
Operation Starvation. N. Carter
Operation Steal. J. W. R. Morrison
Operation Steelfish. K. Stanton
Operation Stranglehold. D. J. Marlowe
Operation: Super Ms. A. Offutt
Operation Superman. H. Hawton
Operation T. N. Daniels
Operation Terror. The Gordons
Operation--To Kill a Man. M. Dines
Operation Tokyo. T. Middleton
Operation Urgent. Sutherland Scott
Operation VC. N. Daniels
Operation Vengeance. R. Crane
Operation Weatherkill. P. Edwards
Operation Whiplash. D. J. Marlowe
Operation: World War Three. J. Milton
Operator. D. Honig
Operator. D. E. Westlake
Operator. C. Williams
Operator from Chicago. Duff Johnson
Operator No. 19. G. Goodchild
Operator X. Mark Ross
Operators. A. Prior
Ophelia. F. Stevenson
Opium Clipper. E. L. Long
Opium Flower. D. Cushman
Opium Murders. P. Baron
Opium Smugglers of Frisco. O. Harper
Opperman Case. J. Bentley
Opportunist. S. Youd
Opportunity. A. Soutar
Opposite the Jail. M. A. Denison
Or Be He Dead. J. Byrom
...Or Be He Dead. H. Carmichael
Or By Default. G. Vaizey
Or Give Me Death! E. Spencer
--Or Murder for Free. J. L. Potter
Or Was He Pushed? R. Lockridge
Oracle of Maddox Street. L. T. Meade
Orange Axe. B. Flynn
Orange Blossoms. J. Shearing
Orange Divan. V. Williams
Orange Girl. B. Hemyng
Orange Necktie. P. Fry
Orange Ray. M. G. Kiddy

Title Index Outside the Law /607

Orange-Tree Mystery. J. Rowland
Orange Wednesday. Leslie Thomas
Orange-Yellow Diamond. J. S. Fletcher
Orator. E. Wallace
Orchard Close. A. Askew
Orchard of Tears. S. Rohmer
Orchids to Murder. H. Footner
Orchids with Murder. T. B. Morris
Ordeal. D. Collins
Ordeal. Roger Fuller
Ordeal by Fire. A. Upward
Ordeal by Innocence. A. Christie
Ordeal by Moonlight. H. Kaner
Ordeal of Alick Hillersdon. W. M. Graydon
Ordeal of Ann Curtis. A. Askew
Ordeal of Major Grigsby. J. Sherlock
Ordeal of Mark Bannister. H. Leyford
Ordeal of Mrs. Snow. P. Quentin
Order a Coffin. T. McCoy
Order of Battle. I. Melchoir
Order of the Octopus. S. Horler
Ordered South. A. M. Williamson
Orders to Kill. D. Downes
Ordinary Accident. R. Amberley
Ordinary Day. H. Brinton
Ordinary Lunacy. Jessica Anderson
Ordinary Man. M. Arrighi
Organ Speaks. E. C. R. Lorac
Organization. D. Anthony
Organization. O. Demaris
Organizer. D. MacDonald
Orient Express. G. Greene
Origin of Evil. E. Queen
Original Carcase. G. Bagby
Orion, the Gold Beater. S. Cobb
Orloff Diamond. G. H. Teed
Ormond. C. B. Brown
Orphan Ann. H. C. Bailey
Orphan-Monger. S. Paternoster
Orphan of the Shadows. P. Minton
Orphans of Brandenburg. H. Edmonds
'Orrible Murder. B. Trice
Orville College. H. Wood
Osage Bow. W. C. MacDonald
Oscar. Old Sleuth
Oscar Bertrand. M. E. Braddon
Oscar Montague--Paranoiac. G. L. Walton
Oscar Mooney's Head. W. E. Huntsberry
Oshawa Project. F. Nolan
Osiris Died in Autumn. L. Langley
Ossington Mystery. H. Richards
Ostenders. G. Simenon
Osterman Weekend. R. Ludlum
Ostrekoff Jewels. E. P. Oppenheim
Ostrich Man. A. Soutar
Oswald Gray. H. Wood
Otan Plot. B. Newman
Othello's Occupation. L. A. G. Strong
Other. T. Tryon
Other Body in Grant's Tomb. R. Starnes
Other Brown. A. Luehrmann
Other Bullet. N. B. Mavity
Other Cousin. D. Farrell
Other End. R. E. Roberts
Other Folks' Money. W. B. M. Ferguson
Other Gods. E. C. Vivian
Other Half. C. F. Coe
Other Half of the Orange. J. M. Scott
Other House. Henry James
Other House. C. Massie
Other Island. E. H. Clements
Other Juliet. A. Maybury
Other Man. F. Durbridge
Other Man. A. MacVicar
Other Man. E. Wallace
Other Man's Danger. M. March
Other Maritha. C. Leonard
Other Men's Shoes. A. Soutar
Other Miss Evans. E. Kyle
Other Mr. North. L. Beresford

Other One. C. Turney
Other Passenger. J. K. Cross
Other Paths to Glory. A. Price
Other People's Business. S. Pim
Other People's Money. E. Gaboriau
Other Person. F. Hume
Other Romilly. E. P. Oppenheim
Other Room. J. Blackmore
Other Side of Midnight. S. Sheldon
Other Side of the Door. L. Chamberlain
Other Side of the Door. H. Howard
Other Side of the Moon. J. M. Scott
Other Side of the Tunnel. C. Kendall
Other Side of the Wall. H. C. McNeile
Other Side of the Wall. S. Truss
Other Sins Only Speak. H. Kane
Other than Natural Causes. Mark Cross
Other Three. B. Bolt
Other Woman. O. R. Cohen
Other World. K. Robeson
Others. G. Simenon
Otley. M. Waddell
Otley Forever. M. Waddell
Otley Pursued. M. Waddell
Otley Victorious. M. Waddell
Ottawa Allegation. P. Geddes
Ould Flynn. E. L. Long
Our Admirable Betty. J. Farnol
Our Adversary. M. E. Braddon
Our Agent in Rome Is Missing. N. Carter
Our Doom Is Gone. R. Harrison
Our First Murder. T. Chanslor
Our Jubilee Is Death. L. Bruce
Our Lady of Darkness. B. Capes
Our Lady of Pain. J. Blackburn
Our Lady's Inn. J. S. Clouston
Our Man Flint. J. Pearl
Our Man in Camelot. A. Price
Our Man in Havana. G. Greene
Our Member Mr. Muttlebury. J. S. Clouston
Our Mother's House. Julian Gloag
Our Mysterious Passenger, and other
    stories. R. H. Savage
Our Second Murder. T. Chanslor
Our Share of Love. W. E. D. Ross
Our Spacecraft Is Missing! P. Richards
Our Very Best People. C. S. Raymond
Our Widow. F. Warden
Out Brief Candle. J. Rosenberg
Out, Brief Candle! L. Thayer
Out by the River. L. Peters
Out, Damned Tot! N. Spain
Out for a Killing. J. W. Vandercook
Out for Kicks. W. Shaw
Out for the Kill. Anthony Gilbert
Out for Vengeance. N. Carter
Out from Shanghai. S. M. Parkman
Out from the Night. A. M. Meadows
Out Goes She. R. Stout
Out Is Death. P. Rabe
Out of a Dark Sky. S. Horler
Out of Asia Alive. M. Derby
Out of Chaos. R. M. Wells
Out of Circulation. A. Bell
Out of Control. B. Kendrick
Out of Crime's Depths. N. Carter
Out of Death's Shadow. N. Carter
Out of Evil. Richard Fisher
Out of Evil. Ganpat
Out of Evil. D. G. Waring
Out of Focus. Peter Townend
Out of His Head. T. B. Aldrich
Out of It All. C. Saxby
Out of Order. P. A. Taylor
Out of Prison. M. A. Denison

Out of Reach of the Law. J. W. Bobin
Out of Satan's Grip. C. Frisbie
Out of Season. M. Kenyon
Out of Shape. L. Greenbaum
Out of the Ashes. F. Grierson
Out of the Ashes. E. W. Mumford
Out of the Blue. F. Archer
Out of the Blue. H. C. McNeile
Out of the Dark. U. Curtiss
Out of the Dark. G. F. Gibbs
Out of the Dark. G. Knevels
Out of the Dark. Seamark
Out of the Darkness. C. J. Dutton
Out of the Deep. H. Wood
Out of the Depths. L. Holton
Out of the Desert. A. Dare
Out of the Dog House. C. North
Out of the Dusk. B. Flynn
Out of the Fire. H. Howard
Out of the Foam. J. E. Cooke
Out of the Fog. J. C. Lincoln
Out of the Fog. Clarissa Ross
Out of the Fog. F. A. Symonds
Out of the Frying Pan. C. N. Boyle
Out of the Jaws of Death. F. Barrett
Out of the Labyrinth. L. L. Lynch
Out of the Night. B. Reynolds
Out of the Night. Dan Ross
Out of the Night. R. O. Saber
Out of the Night. M. White
Out of the Past. P. Wentworth
Out of the Running. A. Askew
Out of the Shadow. A. Glanville
Out of the Shadows. H. Curties
Out of the Shadows. M. Halliday
Out of the Storm. R. Braddon
Out of the Underworld. I. Stark
Out of the War? M. B. Lowndes
Out of the Whirlwind. W. T. Walsh
Out of This World. M. Cumberland
Out of This World. J. Pendower
Out of Time. C. Franklin
Out of Wild Hills. C. Campbell
Out on Bail. R. L. Goldman
Out There. D. Donovan
Out to Win. J. A. Jordan
Out Went the Taper. R. C. Ashby
Out with the Tide. N. Carter
Outbreak. Lionel Black
Outcast. M. E. Braddon
Outcast. H. Janson
Outcasts. A. Murray
Outcrop. Colin Cooper
Outer Gate. O. R. Cohen
Outer Ring. A. E. Lindop
Outfit. R. Stark
Outlaw. D. Hennessey
Outlaw and Lawmaker. C. Praed
Outlaw Empire. W. C. Tuttle
Outlaw Island. A. R. Hilliard
Outlaw Jess. A. Askew
Outlawed Guns. N. W. Firth
"Outlaws." Clarke Little
Outlaw's Bride. H. M. Jones
Outlaw's Oath. E. C. Derby
Outlaws of Halfaday Creek. J. B. Hendryx
Outlaws of the Blue. N. Carter
Outlaws of Yugo-Slavia. W. W. Sayer
Outpost of Eternity. H. Arvonen
Outrage. M. Tarmey
Outrage in Manchukuo. V. Gielgud
Outrage on Gallows Hill. G. Bellairs
Outrageous Fortune. P. Wentworth
Outrun the Constable. S. Jepson
Outside Job. A. Brede
Outside the Law. J. Barnes
Outside the Law. W. Dale
Outside the Law. H. Leyford

Outside the Law. P. Loraine
Outside the Law. M. McGrath
Outsider. L. Cameron
Outsider. I. Cleaton
Outsider. M. K. Douglas
Outsider. J. Letherby
Outsider. H. Smart
Outsider in Amsterdam. J. Van De Wetering
Outsiders. A. E. Martin
Outsider's Year. F. Warden
Outward Walls. John Burke
Outwitted. O. Bland
Outwitted. R. Marsh
Outwitted at Last. S. A. Gardner
Oval Table. J. J. Farjeon
Oven. G. Thorne
Over and Above. J. E. Gurdon
Over and Done With. E. H. Clements
Over Her Dear Body. R. S. Prather
Over My Dead Body. R. Angel
Over My Dead Body. F. Mayfair
Over My Dead Body. S. Mitchell
Over My Dead Body. M. Risco
Over My Dead Body. R. Stout
Over My Shoulder. Margery Lawrence
Over the Border. R. Barr
Over the Border. H. Whitaker
Over the Edge. David Miles
Over the Edge. L. Treat
Over the Edge. D. Westheimer
Over the Edge of the World. N. Carter
Over the Garden Wall. C. Carnac
Over the High Side. N. Freeling
Over the Hills. J. Farnol
Over the Hump. E. S. Gardner
Over the Line. Alec Coppel
Over the Top. D. Newton
Over the Tunnel. A. Rives
Over the Wall. T. D. Smith
Over Thin Ice. Mark Cross
Overboard. G. F. Worts
Overdose of Death. A. Christie
Overdrive. M. Gilbert
Overdue. F. Clifford
Overdue for Death. Z. H. Ross
Overkill. N. Daniels
Overkill. W. Garner
Overkill. J. Lange
Overload of Hope. J. Fores
Overlook House. W. Payne
Overlooked. B. Hawker
Overlord. O. Demaris
Overlords. N. Sligh
Overlords. W. Woolfolk
Overnight. R. Goyne
Overture to Death. H. Desmond
Overture to Death. N. Marsh
Overture to Trouble. S. Maddock
Owl. J. Gray
Owl. Frank King
Owl and the Pussycat. O. Cameron
Owl Flies Home. B. Rodney
Owl Hoots. B. Rodney
Owl in the Cellar. M. Scherf
Owl Is Abroad. R. Bridges
Owl Meets the Devil. B. Rodney
Owl of Darkness. M. Afford
Owl Sang Three Times. V. Kelsey
Owl Taxi. H. Footner
Owls Don't Blink. A. A. Fair
Owl's Warning. Herman Landon
Owner Lies Dead. T. Perry
Ownley Inn. J. C. Lincoln
Ox. J. Brothers
Oxford Murders. A. Broome
Oxford Mystery. G. D. H. Cole
Oxford Tragedy. J. C. Masterman
Oyster-Bed Mystery. A. Murray
Ozmar the Mystic. E. Hulme-Beaman

P

P.A. to Murder. A. Tack
P as in Police. L. Treat
P.C. Richardson's First Case. B. Thomson
P.J., the Secret Service Boy. F. S. Hamilton
P. Moran, Operative. P. Wilde
P.O. Detective. B. D. Adsit
P.P.C. N. S. Lincoln
P's Progress. F. O'Rourke
P.S. Your Cat Is Dead. J. Kirkwood
Pace Grows Hotter. B. Sarto
Pace That Kills. W. Fuller
Pace That Kills. Kevin O'Hara
Pace That Kills. E. Saltus
Pacific Blue. C. Dawe
Pacific North-West. D. Enefer
Pacific Pearl. M. Cronin
Pack of Cards. A. Dick
Pack of Lies. G. Ashe
Package Deal. E. Hely
Package Holiday Spy Case. D. Betteridge
Package Included Murder. J. Porter
Package to Spain. M. Polland
Packard Case. W. Merrick
Packed for Murder. J. Blackburn
Packet of Death. H. Metcalfe
Packet of Trouble. F. U. Ashford
Pact. J. A. Brown
Pact with Satan. L. Holton
Pact with the Devil. H. Desmond
Padded Cell. P. Conway
Padded Door. B. Flynn
Paddington Mystery. J. Rhode
Padgate Mystery. E. C. Reed
Padrone. Don Smith
Paduan Conspiracy. M. Walton
Pagan. W. F. Morris
Pagan Joe. T. A. Plummer
Pagan Madonna. H. MacGrath
Pagan Pagoda. M. Mundy
Pagans. A. Soutar
Pagan's Cup. F. Hume
Page Mr. Pomeroy. E. Jordan
Page Mr. Tutt. A. Train
Pageant, and other stories. E. H. W. Meyerstein
Pageant of Murder. G. Mitchell
Paging Blackshirt. R. Graeme
Pagoda. J. A. Phillips
Pagoda Mystery. M. Worth
Paid. M. Dana
Paid in Full. R. Bay
Paid in Full. M. Cronin
Paid in Full. E. Ellison
Paid in Full. J. Goodwin
Paid in Full. L. Meynell
Paid in His Own Coin. E. J. Goodman
Paid Out. J. P. Bessell
Paid with Death. N. Carter
Paignton Honour. A. Ashew
Painful Predicament of Sherlock Holmes. W. Gillette
Painswick Line. H. Cecil
Paint-Stained Flannels. P. Fry
Paint the Town Black. David Alexander
Painted Angel. G. R. Preedy
Painted Dagger. J. Drummond
Painted Death. D. Enefer
Painted Death. P. Quiroule
Painted Dog. V. Gunn
Painted Doll Affair. A. MacVicar
Painted Face. J. Stubbs
Painted Faces. C. Robertson
Painted for the Kill. L. Cores
Painted Honeymoon. S. H. Webb
Painted Lady. J. Boland
Painted Monster. A. Rowe
Painted on a Donkey Cart. J. Bogar
Painted Window. Lady A. Scott
Painted Woman. F. A. Kummer
Painter of Flowers. H. Fleetwood
Painter of Parma. S. Cobb
Pair of Knaves and A Few Trumps. M. D. Flattery
Pakistani Agent. P. Robinson
Palace. D. G. Compton
Palace and Prison. F. H. Rose
Palace of Chance. Old Spicer
Palace of Spies. H. Compton
Palace of Terror. E. J. Murray
Palais de Danse Tragedy. G. Chester
Pale Ape. M. P. Shiel
Pale Betrayer. D. S. Davis
Pale Blue Nightgown. L. Golding
Pale Door. Lee Roberts
Pale Gray for Guilt. J. D. MacDonald
Pale Hand of Danger. M. Lynch
Pale Horse. A. Christie
Pale Pink House. F. Y. McHugh
Palermo Affair. C. Forbes
Palermo Ambush. C. Forbes
Palgrave Mummy. F. M. Pettee
Palindrome. P. Conway
Paliser Case. E. Saltus
Pall for a Painter. E. C. R. Lorac
Pallard the Punter. E. Wallace
Palludia. A. Burr
Palm for Mrs. Pollifax. D. Gilman
Palomino Blonde. T. Allbeury
Palzer Experiment. A. Murray
Pamela and Her Lion Man. M. Peterson
Pamela's Honeymoon. R. Jocelyn
Pamela's Palace. A. J. Fitzgerald
Panama Plot. A. B. Reeve
Panama Portrait. S. Ellin
Panda One Investigates. P. N. Walker
Panda One on Duty. P. N. Walker
Pandemic. T. Ardies
Pandora. A. B. Reeve
Pandora Feature. I. Baker
Pandora's Box. T. Chastain
Pandora's Box. R. Dundee
Panelled Room. R. S. Holland
Panic! J. Creasey
Panic. H. McCloy
Panic! B. Pronzini
Panic in Box C. J. D. Carr
Panic in Needle Park. James Mills
Panic in Paradise. A. Amos
Panic in Philly. D. Pendleton
Panic in Pursuit. S. Dewes
Panic in the Night. J. Stagg
Panic in the Solomons. K. M. Stevens
Panic Party. A. Berkeley
Panic-Stricken. M. A. Wilson
Panther Face. E. Woodward
Panther Jones for President. S. Johnson
Panther's Moon. V. Canning
Pantomime Girl. A. Applin
Pantoufle. Fredrick Jackson
Papa. A. M. Williamson
Papa La-Bas. J. D. Carr
Papa Pontivy and the Maginot Murder. B. Newman
Paper Albatross. R. Croft-Cooke
Paper Bag. J. Rhode
Paper Bullet. O. Carney
Paper Chase. H. Balfour
Paper Chase. O. W. Bayer

Paper Chase. L. Egan
Paper Chase. R. Esser
Paper-Chase. A. Fielding
Paper Chase. J. Kennedy
Paper Chase. M. Saxton
Paper Chase. J. Symons
Paper Chase. R. Watkins
Paper-Chase Mystery. A. Fielding
Paper Circle. B. Fischer
Paper Coffin. L. Lamensdurf
Paper Doll. J. Lennox
Paper Dolls. L. P. Davies
Paper Ghost. E. Lindall
Paper Mistress. D. Malm
Paper Palace. R. Harling
Paper Pistol Contract. P. Atlee
Paper Prison. P. C. Wren
Paper Salvage Crime. G. Chester
Paper Thunderbolt. M. Innes
Paper Tomb. S. Donati
Paperback Thriller. L. Meyer
Paperchase Murder. H. Seymour
Papers Mean Peril. Noel Lee
Papers of Andrew Melmoth. H. S. Davies
Papyrus Murder. T. B. Morris
Parachute Murder. L. Mitchell
Parade of Cockeyed Creatures. G. Baxt
Parade of the Empty Boots. C. A. Seltzer
Paradigm Red. Harold King
Paradine Case. R. Hichens
"Paradise" Coal-Boat, and other tales. C. J. C. Hyne
Paradise Conspiracy. G. Tracey
Paradise Court. J. S. Fletcher
Paradise for Two. M. Richmond
Paradise Formula. A. Dipper
Paradise Garden. G. F. Gibbs
Paradise Gun. J. Flagg
Paradise Island. M. Caywood
Paradise Men. S. Harvester
Paradise Mystery. J. S. Fletcher
Paradise of Fools. D. Vane
Paradise Party. E. Hunter
Paradise Road. D. S. Milton
Paradise Smith. R. Johnston
Paradise Spells Danger. G. B. Mair
Paradise Trap. R. Crane
Paradiso. A. Prior
Paradoxes of Mr. Pond. G. K. Chesterton
Paragon. E. Trevor
Parajacker. J. A. Nelson
Parallax View. L. Singer
Parasite. O. Demaris
Parasites. T. E. Wilson
Parcel of Fortune. E. H. Clements
Parcel Post Murder. B. Herbert
Parcels for Inspector West. J. Creasey
Parchment Key. S. Hopkins
Pardon My Blood. P. Whelton
Pardon My Body. D. Bogard
Pardon My Gun. Keith Campbell
Pardon My Gun. J. P. Carstairs
Pardon My Return. D. Leslie
Paris Agent. A. Mills
Paris Bit. I. Marder
Paris in September. E. Randolph
Parisian Adventure. L. H. Brenning
Parisian Detective. F. Du Boisgobey
Parisian Love. L. H. Brenning
Parisian Nights. R. Goyne
Parisian Pigeon Drop. J. P. Radford
Park Avenue Executioner. David Wilson
Park Avenue Murder! N. Carter
Park Avenue Tramp. F. Flora
Park Lane Mystery. J. Hatton
Park Lane Mystery. L. Tracy
Park Mystery. H. L. Phillips
Parker Case. J. Courage
Parker Pyne Investigates. A. Christie
Parkwater. H. Wood
Parliament of Owls. P. Buchanan
Parole. J. Ehrlich
Parricide. G. W. M. Reynolds
Parrish for the Defense. H. Waugh
Parrot Faced Man. C. R. Gull
Parson o' Dumford. G. M. Fenn
Parson Thring's Secret. A. W. Marchmont
Part for a Poisoner. E. C. R. Lorac
Part for a Policeman. J. Creasey
Part of Virtue. R. Lewis
Part 35. J. N. Iannuzzi
Parted by Fate. L. J. Libbey
Partisan. M. Urquhart
Partisans Die Alone. R. Wilkes-Hunter
Partners in Crime. A. Christie
Partners in Crime. H. King
Partners in Peril. N. Carter
Partners of the Night. L. Scott
Party at No. 5. Shelley Smith
Party at the Penthouse. A. M. Chase
Party Every Night. F. Lorenz
Party for Lawty. M. Sarsfield
Party for the Shooting. L. Revell
Party Girl. M. Albert
Party in Dolly Creek. C. Blackstock
Party Man. C. B. Kelland
Party of Eight. L. Meynell
Party to Murder. R. Verron
Party to Murder. L. White
Party Was the Pay-Off. E. S. Holding
Pasang Run. E. Trevor
Pascal's Mill. B. A. Williams
Pasha's Web. H. Bradshaw
Pasquinado. J. S. Fletcher
Pass. R. G. Hubler
Pass Along, Madam! A. Webb
Pass Beyond Kashmir. B. Mather
Pass Key to Murder. B. Reed
Pass the Aspirin. C. L. Pancoast
Pass the Body. C. S. Sprigg
Pass the Gravy. A. A. Fair
Passage by Night. H. Marlowe
Passages from the Diary of a Late Physician. S. Warren
Passage in Park Lane. J. D. Rowley
Passage of Arms. E. Ambler
Passage Through Bohemia. F. Warden
Passage to Danger. E. Lanham
Passage to Samoa. D. Keene
Passage to Terror. E. Ronns
Passage to Violence. S. Kennedy
Passenger. E. Fenwick
Passenger from Calais. A. Griffiths
Passenger from Scotland Yard. H. F. Wood
Passenger List. O. L. Rosmanith
Passenger on the U. C. Aveline
Passenger to Folkestone. J. S. Fletcher
Passenger to Frankfurt. A. Christie
Passenger to Nowhere. Anthony Gilbert
Passengers for Painted Rock. W. C. Tuttle
Passerman's Hollow. Jane Stuart
Passers-By. A. Partridge
Passing of Charles Lanson. L. Tracy
Passing of Evil. M. McShane
Passing of Gloria Munday. J. Garforth
Passing of Mr. Quinn. G. R. McRae
Passing of Night. J. F. Bradley
Passing of Third Floor Back. C. Houghton
Passing of Tony Blount. S. M. Parkman
Passing Show. R. H. Savage
Passing Strange. R. Sale
Passing Stranger. L. Hoffman
Passion. R. Manvell
Passion and the Pity. E. Trevor
Passion Flower Puzzle. D. Rico
Passion Lighting the World. M. Dekobra
Passion Murders. D. Keene
Passion of Gabrielle. M. S. Boylan
Passion of the Beast. J. Lamarre
Passion of the President. J. Haslette
Passion Pact. H. Janson
Passion Pulls the Trigger. A. Wallace
Passion the Plaything. R. M. Gilchrist
Passionate. C. Brown
Passionate Adventure. F. Stayton
Passionate Atonement. M. Richmond
Passionate City. I. S. Black
Passionate City. J. L. Rickard
Passionate Invaders. J. Clare
Passionate Land. G. Wagner
Passionate Pagan. C. Brown
Passionate Particles. M. Peterson
Passionate Playmate. H. Janson
Passionate Quest. E. P. Oppenheim
Passionate Strangers. G. Wagner
Passionate Trail. A. Hillgarth
Passionate Victims. Lange Lewis
Passionate Waif. H. Janson
Passionate Youth. E. C. Reed
Passionless Quest. C. Cannell
Passions of Medora Graeme. Elsie Lee
Passion's Victim. H. Duval
Passive Crime, and other stories. The Duchess
Passport. R. Bagot
Passport. E. Voute
Passport for a Pilgrim. J. Leasor
Passport for a Renegade. K. Bennett
Passport in Suspense. J. Leasor
Passport into Fear. W. H. Baker
Passport Invisible. G. C. Shedd
Passport to Danger. J. Paull
Passport to Danger. M. Richmond
Passport to Danger. J. Stagg
Passport to Death. B. Home
Passport to Murder. E. Allen
Passport to Murder. Neill Graham
Passport to Oblivion. J. Leasor
Passport to Oblivion. Babs Lee
Passport to Panic. E. Reed
Passport to Paradise. C. Houghton
Passport to Peril. J. Leasor
Passport to Peril. S. Marlowe
Passport to Peril. Robert Parker
Passport to Terror. M. Daniels
Passport to Treason. M. O'Brine
Passports to Murder. P. Hambledon
Password. D. Kim
Past All Dishonor. J. M. Cain
Past Dies Hard. D. W. MacArthur
Past Finding Out. D. E. L. Patch
Past Master of Crime. D. J. MacKenzie
Past Praying For. S. Woods
Past Won't Die. M. Malmer
Pastime. A. Fowles
Pat. T. Cobb
Pat o' Nine Tales. M. M. Bodkin
Patched-Up Affair. F. Warden
Patchwork Man. D. Harper
Patchwork of Death. P. Nichols
Patchwork Palace. M. L. Tyrrell
Paternoster Ruby. C. E. Walk
Path of a Hundred Deaths. C. R. Gull
Path of a Star. A. Applin
Path of Fear. W. M. Graydon
Path of Ghosts. Robert MacLeod
Path of Ivory. W. R. Foran
Path of Lies. A. Askew
Path of the Spendthrift. N. Carter
Path of Virtue. G. Warden
Path to Glory. S. Styles
Path to the Bridge. Brian Cooper

Pathless Trail. A. O. Friel
Paths of the Dead. H. Nisbet
Pathway of Adventure. R. Tyrrell
Pathway to Fame. P. Trent
Patience of Maigret. G. Simenon
Patience Pettigrew's Perplexities. C. Augusta
Patient. A. Christie
Patient. G. Simenon
Patient in Room 18. M. G. Eberhart
Patient Is the Hunter. R. Wilkes-Hunter
Paton Street Case. J. Bingham
Patrick Butler for the Defense. J. D. Carr
Patriot. C. Durbin
Patriot. R. Seth
Patriot. A. E. Walter
Patriot Game. J. De St. Jorre
Patriotic Murders. A. Christie
Patriots. J. Barlow
Patriots. F. Whishaw
Patrol to Zaruse. J. Robb
Patron Saint and other stories. C. R. Gull
Pattern. M. G. Eberhart
Pattern for Destruction. P. W. Fairman
Pattern for Murder. D. Knight
Pattern for Murder. I. S. Shriber
Pattern for Murder. E. Warman
Pattern for Panic. R. S. Prather
Pattern for Perfidy. J. Bentley
Pattern in Beads. D. M. Bumpus
Pattern in Black and Red. F. Keene
Pattern in Poison-Ivy. G. Bowman
Pattern in Yellow. K. Hewitt
Pattern Is Murder. Jean Marsh
Pattern of Chalk. Dennis Miles
Pattern of Chance. G. Gardiner
Pattern of Conquest. K. Thompson
Pattern of Death. P. George
Pattern of Guilt. Gavin Holt
Pattern of Murder. M. G. Eberhart
Pattern of Murder. M. Symons
Pattern of Rape. H. Janson
Pattern of Violence. R. Busby
Patty's Partner. J. Middlemass
Paul Beck, Detective. M. M. Bodkin
Paul Beck, the Rule of Thumb Detective. M. M. Bodkin
Paul Burdon. W. Magnay
Paul Campenhaye, Specialist in Criminology. J. S. Fletcher
Paul Clifford. T. P. Prest
Paul Deverell. Anonymous
Paul Ferroll. Anonymous
Paul Jones's Alias. D. C. Murray
Paul Pry's Poison Pen. E. Baird
Paul Quentin. F. M. White
Paul Richards--Detective. D. Dallas
Paul Temple and the Front Page Men. F. Durbridge
Paul Temple and the Harkdale Robbery. F. Durbridge
Paul Temple and the Kelby Affair. F. Durbridge
Paul Temple Intervenes. F. Durbridge
Paul, the Sage. F. M. White
Paul Vargas, a Mystery, and other tales. F. J. Fargus
Paula. D. Kingery
Paulette. K. Lindsay
Pauline. J. Hawthorne
Pauline--A Mystery. N. Carter
Pauline's Lady. M. V. Woodgate
Paul's Apartment. V. Siller
Paulton Plot. H. Adams

Pauper of Park Lane. W. LeQueux
Pavement Artist Mystery. W. Jardine
Pavilion. Hilda Lawrence
Pavilion at Monkshood. A. Maybury
Pavilion by the Lake. A. J. Rees
Pavilion of Honour. G. R. Preedy
Pavilion on the Links. R. L. Stevenson
Paw in the Bottle. R. Marshall
Pawn. L. A. Knight
Pawn. F. Nichols
Pawn. N. P. Sutherland
Pawn in Jeopardy. S. Rattray
Pawn in the Game. J. L. Hardy
Pawn of Evil. A. Leech
Pawned. F. Packard
Pawnee Tom. Old Sleuth
Pawns and Kings. Seamark
Pawns Count. E. P. Oppenheim
Pawns of Fear. J. Manor
Pawns of Murder. W. Woodrow
Pawnshop Murder. J. G. Brandon
Paxton Plot. C. G. Mitford
Pay as You Die. R. Crawford
Pay-Day. H. Osborne
Pay-Grab Murders. P. Chester
Pay-Off. Joe Barry
Pay-Off. J. C. Barton
Pay Off. Neill Graham
Pay Off. K. Laing
Pay Off. A. W. Sherring
Pay-Off for a Dumb Dame. F. Duggan
Pay-Off in Blood. B. Halliday
Pay-Off in Calcutta. R. Collier
Pay on the Way Out. J. Murphy
Pay Out. P. Elliott
Pay the Devil. Harry Patterson
Pay to Bearer. M. S. Jones
Paydirt. L. Durie
Paying Guest. L. A. Knight
Paying the Price. N. Carter
Payment Deferred. C. S. Forester
Payment Down. J. H. Vahey
Payment for Silence. A. Rivers
Payment in Full. J. W. Bobin
Payment Suspended! J. W. Bobin
Payoff. N. Karta
Payoff. J. Mack
Payoff. Don Smith
Payoff for the Banker. F. Lockridge
Payoff in Black. W. G. Schofield
Payoff on Fever Street. J. Wolf
Payola. D. Keene
Payroll. D. Bickerton
Payroll of Fate. W. C. Tuttle
Pazenger Problem. J. Plain
Peace and Peter Lamont. N. Harman
Peace Bridge. W. A. Low
Peacemaker. J. Remenham
Peacemaker. P. Trent
Peacock Fan. H. S. Keeler
Peacock Feather Murders. Carter Dickson
Peacock House and other mysteries. E. Phillpotts
Peacock Is a Bird of Prey. R. Foley
Peacock of Jewels. F. Hume
Peacock's Feather. S. Esmond
Peak House. A. J. Rees
Peal of Ordnance. J. Lodwick
Peanut Butter & Jelly Is Not for Kids. B. Kelly
Pear-Tree. W. Hewlett
Pearl and Plain. A. Griffin
Pearl Choker. R. East
Pearl-Headed Pin. D. Durham
Pearl Island. H. C. Rowland
Pearl Necklace. A. Applin
Pearl of Blood. K. Netzen

Pearl of Great Price. A. Askew
Pearl Thief. B. Ruck
Pearls and Perjury. H. H. Lewis
Pearls Are a Nuisance. R. Chandler
Pearls Before Swine. M. Allingham
Pearls of Desire. A. J. Small
Pearls of Doom. G. H. Teed
Pearls of Pilolu. Alys Brown
Peccadilloes. F. Keene
Peccavi. E. W. Hornung
Peccavi. C. Massie
Peck of Salt. K. Royce
Peddler. D. Ring
Peddler. H. C. Rowland
Pedestal. G. Lanning
Pedigree. G. Simenon
Pedigree in Pawn. A. H. Veysey
Pedigreed Murder Case. J. S. Fletcher
Pedlar's Acre. T. P. Prest
Peel Rocke--Black Sheep. H. H. Ross
Peeping Tom Murders. J. Baynes
Peer and His Plunder. H. Hill
Peer and the Woman. E. P. Oppenheim
Peerage in Peril. R. E. Salwey
Peggy's Dilemma. T. Cobb
Peking Connection. Don Smith
Peking Dossier. N. Carter
Peking Incident. G. Atcheson
Peking Payoff. I. Stewart
Peking Plot. Ralph Hayes
Peking Switch. J. J. Marsh
Peking/The Tulip Affair. N. Carter
Pekoe Reef. F. Knight
Pelham. E. Bulwer-Lytton
Pelham Affair. L. Tracy
Pelham Murder Case. Monte Barrett
Pelican Island. A. D. Divine
Pelican Strikes Back. R. Arnold
Pelota Murder. J. Daymont
Peloton, Detective. H. A. Cartledge
Pembroke Mason Affair. G. Barton
Pen-Friend. A. Wykes
Penal Settlement. C. C. Lowis
Penalty Is Death! V. G. Kennedy
Penalty of Fate. M. E. Braddon
Penance of Brother Alaric. B. Graeme
Penance Was Death. L. B. McNamara
Pencil Points to Murder. W. A. Barber
Pendragon. M. Howe
Pendulum. J. Christopher
Penelope. E. V. Cunningham
Penelope of the Polyantha. E. Wallace
Penelope, the Damp Detective. W. C. Anderson
Penelope's Daughter. Dair Alexander
Penelve. R. H. Thomas
Pengard Awake. R. Straus
Penguin Island Murders. M. MacElwain
Penguin Pool Murder. S. Palmer
Penhallow. G. Heyer
Penknife in My Heart. N. Blake
Penman's Progress. S. Brydon
Penmarric. S. Howatch
Pennies for His Eyes. W. M. Duncan
Pennies from Hell. David Alexander
Pennies on Her Eyes. M. L. Roby
Penniless Millionaire. D. C. Murray
Pennington Case. R. H. Wilkinson
Penny for the Guy. J. Roffman
Penny to Spend. Edward Brown
Penny Whipp. C. Massie
Pennycross Murders. M. Procter
Pennygreen Street. A. La Bern
Pennyworth of Murder. G. Meyrick
Penrose Mystery. R. A. Freeman
Pentagon. H. Searls
Pentallion. V. Blake
Penthouse. A. S. Roche
Penthouse Conspirators. C. Pincher
Penthouse Killings. H. Brown

Penthouse Murders. R. P. Holden
Penthouse Mystery. E. Queen
Penthouse Passout. C. Brown
Penthouse Preview. M. Brody
People Against Nancy Preston. J. A. Moroso
People Against O'Hara. E. Lipsky
People Apart. L. T. Shortell
People Ask Death. G. Dyer
People in Cages. H. Ashton
People in Glass House. June Drummond
People in Glass House. J. Ridgway
People of the Night. V. Russell
People of the River. E. Wallace
People of the Twilight. H. Kaner
People on the Hill. V. Johnston
People vs. Withers and Malone. S. Palmer
People Will Talk. E. C. R. Lorac
People's Man. E. P. Oppenheim
Peplow's Paper-Chase. T. Gallon
Pepper-Pot Problem. O. Cecil
Perchance to Kill. C. Franklin
Perdida. F. W. Pangborn
Perdita's End. P. Tabori
Peregrination 22. P. Purser
Peregrine's Progress. J. Farnol
Perennial Boarder. P. A. Taylor
Perfect Alibi. J. Laurence
Perfect Alibi. A. A. Milne
Perfect Alibi. C. S. Sprigg
Perfect Assignment. J. Moffatt
Perfect Carrier. Sheila Ross
Perfect Crime. H. Kane
Perfect Crime. E. Queen
Perfect Crime, or Two. H. Monteilhet
Perfect Criminal. G. Furnivall
Perfect Fool. F. Warden
Perfect Frame. W. Ard
Perfect Frame. John Morgan
Perfect Murder. J. Atholl
Perfect Murder. H. R. F. Keating
Perfect Murder Case. C. Bush
Perfect Pigeon. R. Wormser
Perfect Plot. G. Canary
Perfect Round. H. Adams
Perfect Score. R. E. Cummins
Perfect Treasure. J. Payn
Perfect Victim. J. McKimmey
Perfect Wife. J. Pendower
Perfectionist. L. Kauffmann
Perfidious Lydia. F. Barrett
Perfume of the Lady in Black. G. Leroux
Perfumed Lure. M. St. Dennis
Perfumes of Arabia. E. Dewar
Perhaps a Little Danger. E. H. Clements
Perhaps I Look Simple. R. B. Amos
Perhaps the Prodigal. J. Courage
Perhaps to Kill. H. C. Davis
Peril. S. Horler
Peril. L. Osbourne
Peril Ahead. J. Creasey
Peril at Cranbury Hall. J. Rhode
Peril at Dune's Edge. D. Quick
Peril at End House. A. Christie
Peril at End House. A. Ridley
Peril at Journey's End. Norman Lee
Peril at Midnight. Elaine Hamilton
Peril at Polvellyn. M. McEvoy
Peril at Stone House. J. Corby
Peril at the Spy Nest. A. M. Chase
Peril in Darkness. H. Willett
Peril in Provence. R. Hugill
Peril in the Pyrenees. J. J. Farjeon
Peril Is My Pay. S. Marlowe
Peril Island. P. Brebner
Peril of Barnabas Collins. Marilyn Ross
Peril of Helen Marklove and other stories. W. LeQueux
Peril of Oliver Sargent. E. J. Bliss
Peril of Richard Pardon. B. L. Farjeon

Peril of the Course. M. K. Douglas
Peril of the Prince! E. S. Brooks
Peril of the Prince. H. Hill
Perilous Adventure. M. Richmond
Perilous Assignment. R. Marlowe
Perilous Country. J. Creasey
Perilous Crossways. J. S. Fletcher
Perilous Elopement. J. L. Rickard
Perilous Errand. M. Sutherland
Perilous Hazard. Mark Cross
Perilous Holiday. Don Smith
Perilous Parole. N. Carter
Perilous Passage. A. Mayse
Perilous Passport. E. Allen
Perilous Secret. D. Peacock
Perilous Sky. D. Rutherford
Perilous Transactions of Mr. Collin. F. Heller
Perilous Voyage. D. Quentin
Perilous Voyage. R. St. Clair
Perilous Waters. J. Blackmore
Perilous Waters. E. Nepean
Perilous Way. M. Cumberland
Perils in Persia. J. Bolton
Perils of Josephine. Ernest Hamilton
Perils of Pekin. W. M. Graydon
Perils of Petrograd. W. M. Graydon
Perils of the Red Box. H. Hill
Perimeter Fence. A. Crockett
Period of Evil. M. Halliday
Period Stuff. D. Yates
Perish by the Sword. P. Anderson
Perishable Goods. D. Yates
Perjured Alibi. W. S. Masterman
Permanent Eclipse. M. Maurice
Permanent Wave. V. Sullivan
Perrin Murder Case. G. Morton
Perris of the Cherry Trees. J. S. Fletcher
Persecuted. F. Whishaw
Persecutor. I. Hamilton
Persian Cat. J. Flagg
Persian Price. Evelyn Anthony
Persian Ransom. Evelyn Anthony
Persian Tassel. O. S. Cornelius
Person Called "Z." J. J. Farjeon
Person of Some Importance. L. Osbourne
Person Shouldn't Die Like That. A. D. Goldstein
Personal Adventures of a Detective. A. Carmichael
Personal Appearance of a Lioness. V. Tracy
Persons Unknown. P. MacDonald
Persons Unknown. H. Sutcliffe
Persons Unknown. L. Thayer
"Persons Unknown." V. Tracy
Persuaders #1. F. E. Smith
Persuaders #3. F. E. Smith
Persuaders #2. F. E. Smith
Perturbing Spirit. J. Caird
Peruvian Nightmare. M. Barry
Peruvian Printout. A. Haig
Perverted Village. A. Soutar
Pest. A. P. Terhune
Pester Finger. H. B. M. Watson
Peter Cornish's Revenge. H. C. McNeile
Peter Cotterell's Treasure. R. S. Holland
Peter Darington. Douglas V. Duff
Peter Grayleigh Flies High. C. Robertson
Peter Gunn. H. Kane
Peter Hyde, M.P. P. Trent
Peter in Peril. V. Bridges
Peter Intervenes. E. Jepson
Peter Krimsov. L. S. Taube
Peter Ruff. E. P. Oppenheim
Peter Ruff and the Double-Four. E. P. Oppenheim

Peter the Brazen. G. F. Worts
Peter's Pence. J. Cleary
Peter's Profession. C. L. Reid
Petersburg-Cannes Express. H. Koning
Petrodollar Takeover. P. Tanous
Petronov Plan. J. Pattinson
Petrovka 38. J. Semyonov
Petticoat Lane. G. Goodchild
Petticoat Lane Murders. V. Gunn
Phantasmagoria. Anonymous
Phantom. J. Sylvester
Phantom Airman. R. Walker
Phantom Alibi. H. Leverage
Phantom and Barnabas Collins. Marilyn Ross
Phantom Army. M. Pemberton
Phantom at Lost Lake. D. Lyons
Phantom Bat. R. C. Elliott
Phantom Bells. R. St. Clair
Phantom Bride. L. Ames
Phantom Bus. R. St. Clair
Phantom Canoe. W. B. Mowery
Phantom Car. F. M. White
Phantom Circus. A. Spiller
Phantom City. K. Robeson
Phantom Clue. G. Leroux
Phantom Cottage. V. Johnston
Phantom Death, and other stories. W. C. Russell
Phantom Detective Cases. N. W. Firth
"Phantom Dirigible." R. St. Clair
Phantom Empire. R. M. Sears
Phantom-Fighter. Seabury Quinn
Phantom Fingers. J. J. Farjeon
Phantom Fingers. L. Mearson
Phantom Flame of Wind House. K. Kimbrough
Phantom Fleet. Sea Lion
Phantom Footballer. F. W. Gumley
Phantom Fortune. M. E. Braddon
Phantom Fortune. K. C. Groom
Phantom Forward. S. Horler
Phantom Gondola. M. Dekobra
Phantom Greyhound. F. W. Gumley
Phantom Gunman. N. Morland
Phantom Holiday. M. Russell
Phantom Hollow. G. Verner
Phantom in the House. A. Soutar
Phantom in the Rainbow. S. La Master
Phantom in the Wings. Michael Elder
Phantom Island. R. Walker
Phantom Killer. Colin Hope
Phantom Killer. H. Taylor
Phantom Lady. W. Irish
Phantom Leg. F. Du Boisgobey
Phantom Light. E. Price
Phantom Lover. A. Eadie
Phantom Manor. Marilyn Ross
Phantom Millionaire. M. E. Longman
Phantom Miner. R. St. Clair
Phantom Murderer. B. G. Quin
Phantom Musketeer. C. Brandon
Phantom of Belle Acres. Marilyn Ross
Phantom of Dark Harbor. Clarissa Ross
Phantom of Fog Island. Marilyn Ross
Phantom of Forty-Second Street. M. M. Raison
Phantom of Glencourt. Clarissa Ross
Phantom of Meadow Creek. Old Sleuth
Phantom of the Creek. G. H. Teed
Phantom of the Films. A. Eadie
Phantom of the Mill. L. Bidston
Phantom of the Opera. G. Leroux
Phantom of the Pacific. W. W. Sayer
Phantom of the Swamp. Marilyn Ross
Phantom of the Temple. R. Van Gulik

Phantom of the Thirteenth Floor. Marilyn Ross
Phantom Passenger. Mansfield Scott
Phantom Pilot. P. Conde
Phantom 'Plane. A. O. Pollard
Phantom President. G. F. Worts
Phantom Raider. R. Trevor
Phantom Railway. A. Wood
Phantom Rustlers. F. W. Hilton
Phantom Scarlet. W. Mills
Phantom Slayer. D. Steele
Phantom Spy. M. Brand
Phantom Spy. F. Russell
Phantom Stockman. G. Boothby
"Phantom Tiger." R. St. Clair
Phantom Torpedo-Boats. A. Upward
Phantom Tourer. G. Collins
Phantom Train. D. Timins
Phantom Violin. J. Joseph-Renaud
Phantom Wedding. E. Southworth
Phantom Wife. M. V. Victor
Phantom Wires. A. Stringer
Phantom Wreck. Old Sleuth
Phantoms over Potsdam. R. Vacha
Pharoah with His Waggons and other stories. R. Croft-Cooke
Pharoah's Crown. F. H. Rose
Pharos, the Egyptian. G. Boothby
Phase of Darkness. Robin Moore
Phil and Me. M. Woodhouse
Phil Conway. A. C. Gunter
Phil Scott, the Indian Detective. J. R. Taylor
Philadelphia Blow-Up. M. Barry
Philadelphia Murder Story. L. Ford
Philanthropic Burglar. Rita
Phileas Fox, Attorney. A. T. Sadlier
Philip Bennion's Death. R. Marsh
Philip Derby, Reporter. W. J. Abbot
Philip Henson M.D. George Hastings
Philip, the Draftsman. F. X. J. Coleman
Philipp Steele of the Royal Northwest Mounted Police. J. O. Curwood
Phillida. T. Cobb
Phillip and the Flappers. D. Newton
Phillip in Particular. D. Newton
Philly. D. Greenburg
Philo Gubb, Correspondence School Detective. E. P. Butler
Philopena. H. K. Webster
Philosopher's Hemlock. M. Cranston
Philosopher's Murder Case. J. R. Crawford
Philosopher's Stone. Colin Wilson
Philosophy of the Marquise. M. B. Lowndes
Phoebe, the Miller's Daughter. T. P. Prest
Phoenix. L. P. Bachmann
Phoenix from the Ashes. H. Monteilhet
Phoenix from the Gutter. P. Motte
Phoenix in Castile. J. G. Sarasin
Phoenix in the Blood. Harry Patterson
Phoenix Inferno. M. Barry
Phoenix Sings. D. Cory
Phone Booth Mystery. J. Ironside
Phone Calls. L. O'Donnell
Phone for a Hearse. B. Carson
Phonies. W. B. M. Ferguson
Phonographic Mystery. L. Madreyhijo
Photo Finish. J. Bruce
Photo Finish. Howard Mason
Photo Game. Jack Lang
Photocrimes. M. Horton
Photogenic Soprano. D. Halliday
Photographer. P. Boulle
Photographer's Evidence. N. Carter
Photographs Have Been Sent to Your Wife. P. Loraine
Phreak-Out! C. Brown

Phryne. M. Dekobra
Phyllis. E. V. Cunningham
Physical Attraction. H. Janson
Physician, Heal Thyself. E. Phillpotts
Physician's Fare. C. G. Learoyd
Pianist Shoots First. G. Fairlie
Piano Box Mystery. N. Carter
Picaroon. E. Dudley
Picaroon Collects. J. Cassells
Picaroon Does Justice. Herman Landon
Picaroon Goes West. J. Cassells
Picaroon in Pursuit. Herman Landon
Picaroon: Knight Errant. Herman Landon
Picaroon Laughs Last. J. Cassells
Picaroon Resumes Practice. Herman Landon
Picaroons. G. Burgess
Piccadilly Ghost. E. Spencer
Piccadilly Murder. A. Berkeley
Piccadilly Puzzle. F. Hume
Pick and Run. J. Farrimond
Pick Up. J. B. O'Sullivan
Pick-Up on Noon Street. R. Chandler
Pick Up Sticks. E. Lathen
Pick Up the Pieces. J. F. Straker
Pick Your Victim. P. McGerr
Picked Up. A. Applin
Pickled Poodles. L. Harris
Pickup Alley. E. Ronns
Pickwick Abroad. G. W. M. Reynolds
Picture Frame. L. Lamb
Picture Her Missing. Lynn Williams
Picture Him Dead. F. A. Clement
Picture Miss Seeton. H. Carvic
Picture of Death. K. Giles
Picture of Death. E. C. R. Lorac
Picture of Death. R. Simons
Picture of Guilt. M. Innes
Picture of Innocence. H. Fleetwood
Picture of Millie. P. M. Hubbard
Picture of Murder. S. Curtis
Picture of the Victim. J. S. Strange
Picture on the Wall. J. Breckenridge Ellis
Pictures of Death. K. Robeson
Pidgin Island. H. MacGrath
Piece by Piece. J. K. Stafford
Piece of Action. E. Cannon
Piece of Resistance. C. Egleton
Piece of Something. Harry Reed
Piece of the Moon. Robert Lambert
Piece of the Moon Is Missing. J. L. Johnson
Pieces of Modesty. P. O'Donnell
Pieces of the Game. L. Gifford
Pied Piper of Helfenstein. E. V. McCarthy
Piedouche, a French Detective. F. Du Boisgobey
Pierce the Gloom. M. Clare
Pierce with a Pin. K. Hopkins
Pierced Ear Murders. T. A. Plummer
Pierhead 627. D. Enefer
Pig in a Poke. L. Thayer
Pig Is Fat. L. M. Maynard
Pig-Tail Murder. F. Durbridge
Pig That Got Up and Slowly Walked Away. J. Ripley
Pigeon Among the Cats. J. Bell
Pigeon Blood Rubies. M. M. Bodkin
Pigeon House. V. Williams
Pigeon Loft Crime. J. G. Brandon
Pigeon Parade. Maz
Pigeon Wins. E. Woodward
Pigeon's Blood. M. Pereira
Pigskin Bag. B. Fischer
Pilditch Puzzle. W. Morton

Pilebuck. J. Hawkins
Pilgrim at the Gate. D. Cory
Pilgrim Came Late. M. Purcell
Pilgrim Come Home. C. Rodda
Pilgrim on the Island. D. Cory
Pilgrim's End. L. B. McNamara
Pilgrims Meet Murder. Dexter Muir
Pilgrim's Rest. P. Wentworth
Pillar of Fire. M. Clare
Pillar of Light. L. Tracy
Pillars of Salt. A. Mills
Pillory. B. Fleming
Pilot's Graveyard. P. Conde
Pimp for the Dead. R. Dennis
Pimpernel 60. P. Kinsley
Pin Men. R. East
Pin to See the Peepshow. F. T. Jesse
Pinball Murders. T. B. Black
Pinch of Poison. F. Lockridge
Pinch of Snuff. M. Underwood
Pinchbeck Masterpiece. P. Cleife
Pincher Martin, O.D. Taffrail
Pinday and the "White Slaver." B. Sarto
Pinecastle. I. Manchester
Pinehurst. J. Rhode
Pink and the Brown. H. Atkinson
Pink Camellia. L. Bergstrom
Pink Carrara. Harris Evans
Pink Film. J. Bogar
Pink Panther. M. Albert
Pink Ribbon, as Told to the Police. O. Blakeston
Pink Shop. F. Hume
Pink Silk Alibi. D. Sanders
Pink Umbrella. F. Crane
Pink Umbrella Murder. F. Crane
Pinkerton Ferret. C. Morris
Pinned Man. G. Griswold
Pins and Needles. E. Greenwood
Pioneer. H. Bindloss
Pioneer Herd. F. W. Hilton
Pious Agent. J. Braine
Pipe Dream. P. Ferguson
Pipe Dream. J. Symons
Pipe Dream Finesse. D. Da Cruz
Pipeline to Death. A. Eichler
Piper of Arristoun. B. Goldie
Piper on the Mountain. Ellis Peters
Piperock Tales. W. C. Tuttle
Piping a Detective. Anonymous
"Piping Times." J. Farnol
Pippin's Journal. R. O'Grady
Piracies, Ltd. Bok
Piraeus Plot. H. Arvay
Pirate Airship. J. Noy
Pirate Love. M. Richmond
Pirate of Pittsburgh. H. E. O. Whitman
Pirate of the Pacific. K. Robeson
Pirates. Taffrail
Pirate's Ghost. K. Robeson
Pirate's Gold. D. Whitelaw
Pirates of the Air Way. R. C. Armour
Pirates of the Main. Stuart Martin
Pirate's Pack. J. G. Sarasin
Pirate's Purchase. B. A. Williams
Pirate's Retreat. Lieut. Carlton
Pirdale Island. A. O. Pollard
Pistol at My Head. A. Nuttall
Pistol for Miss Preedy. H. C. Davis
Pistols and Pedagogues. F. Evans
Pistols for Two. A. M. Stein
Pistols with Coffee. W. Du Bois
Pit. F. Merrilees
Pit and the Pundulum. L. Sheridan
Pit in the Garden. L. Meynell
Pit of Corruption. Winifred Graham
Pit of Death. Breton Lee
Pit-Prop Syndicate. F. W. Crofts

Title Index

Pit Town Coronet. C. J. Wills
Pitfall. J. J. Dratler
Pitfall. W. Magnay
Pitfall in August. H. Roman
Pitiful Rebellion. M. Peterson
Pitiless as Death. Anonymous
Pity for Pamela. M. Fitt
Pity Him Afterwards. D. E. Westlake
Pity My Love. D. Winston
Pity My Simplicity. C. Massie
Pity the Honest. E. Lacy
Pity Us All. J. Reese
Place at Whitten. T. Keneally
Place for a Poisoner. E. C. R. Lorac
Place for Murder. E. Lathen
Place for the Wicked. E. Trevor
Place in the Country. S. Gainham
Place of Execution. A. Curry
Place of Execution. M. Vinter
Place of Judgment. B. Levy
Place of Mists. Robert MacLeod
Place of Sapphires. F. E. Randall
Place of Shadows. K. Booton
Place of the Dragons. W. LeQueux
Place on Dark Island. G. Corren
Place to Hide. Clifford King
Place with Two Faces. Josephine Mann
Plague Court Murders. Carter Dickson
Plague Makers. J. Pattinson
Plague of Dragons. Michael Brett
Plague of Sailors. B. Callison
Plague of Silence. J. Creasey
Plague of Spies. M. Kurland
Plague of Violence. H. Pentecost
Plague on Both Your Causes. J. Brunner
Plague over London. T. Craig
Plague Panic. S. G. Hedges
Plague Spot. B. Tutton
Plaid Shroud. Marc Miller
Plain Case of Murder. L. Thayer
Plain Man. J. Symons
Plain Miss Cray. F. Warden
Plain Murder. C. S. Forester
Plain Unvarnished Murder. K. Klein
Plains of Silence. A. Askew
Plan for Escape. A. Bioy-Casares
Plan 79. C. F. Maxwell
Plan XVI. D. G. Browne
Planetoid 127 and The Sweizer Pump. E. Wallace
Planned Coincidence. B. Mortlock
Plant Me Now. M. Hagen
Plant Poppies on My Grave. A. Kent
Plantation Inn. P. Maxwell
Plantation Murder. C. N. Govan
Planter. H. Whitaker
Plaster Saints. F. A. Kummer
Plastic Kind of Death. T. D. Carroll
Plastic Magicians. P. Leslie
Plastic Nightmare. R. Neely
Plate of Red Herrings. R. Lockridge
Platinum Ass. A. Storey
Platinum Bullet. R. L. Graves
Platinum Cat. M. Burton
Platinum High School. I. Shulman
Platinum Jag. A. Storey
Platinum Smugglers. R. C. Armour
Play for Keeps. H. Whittington
Play for Millions. N. Carter
Play for Murder. N. Deane
Play It Casual. H. Janson
Play It Hard. G. Brewer
Play It Solo. Neill Graham
Play Like You're Dead. W. Masterson
Play Misty for Me. P. J. Gillette
Play Now--Kill Later! C. Brown
Play or Pay. H. Smart

Play the Roman Fool and Die. Richard Grayson
Play with Death. C. Franklin
Play with Fire. E. Percy
Play with Matches. F. Ford
Playback. R. Chandler
Playback. The Gordons
Playboy. P. W. Fairman
Played the Hard Way. Griff
Played to a Finish. N. Carter
Player. W. Downing
Player and the Guest. G. F. Newman
Player on the Other Side. E. Queen
Players. W. Magnay
Players and the Game. J. Symons
Players in a Dark Game. S. Coulter
Playgirl. H. Janson
Playgirl Wanted. Roy Vickers
Playing a Bold Game. N. Carter
Playing a Lone Hand. N. Carter
Playing for a Fortune. N. Carter
Playing for Time. R. Rand
Playing the Knave. F. Warden
Playing the Mischief. J. W. De Forrest
Playing with Fire. G. Sampson
Plaything of Fate. N. Carter
Plaza Mystery. M. Worth
Plea for Justice. N. Carter
Pleasant Dreams--Nightmares. R. Bloch
Pleasant Grove Murders. J. H. Vance
Pleasantries of Old Quong. T. Burke
Please Kill My Cousin. G. Fairlie
Please Omit Funeral. H. Dolson
Please Pass the Guilt. R. Stout
Pleasure Buyers. A. S. Roche
Pleasure Cruise Murder. W. Jardine
Pleasure Cruise Mystery. R. Forsythe
Pleasure Dome. E. Kyle
Pleasure Girl. B. Sarto
Pleasure House. P. Tabori
Pleasure Island. F. R. Adams
Pleasure of Your Death. M. Farhi
Pleasure Principle. P. McCurtin
Pleasant Rogue. L. Keith
Pleasure Seekers. H. V. Dixon
Pledge. F. Duerrenmatt
Pledged to the Dead. E. M. Poate
Plender. T. Lewis
Plenty Under the Counter. K. Hewitt
Plot. E. Hostovsky
Plot. E. Piper
Plot. Irving Wallace
Plot Against a Widow. R. C. Ashby
Plot Against Roger Rider. J. Symons
Plot and Counterplot. Anonymous
Plot and Counterplot. Old Sleuth
Plot Counter-Plot. A. Clarke
Plot for a Warship. N. Carter
Plot for an Empire. N. Carter
Plot for Millions'. S. Campbell
Plot for Murder. F. Brown
Plot in Private Life, and other tales. W. Collins
Plot It Yourself. R. Stout
Plot-Maker. W. Hewlett
Plot of the Yellow Emperor. A. Parsons
Plot That Failed. N. Carter
Plot to Kill the President. J. Pearl
Plot Uncovered. N. Carter
Plot Within a Plot. N. Carter
Plotters. A. Caillou
Plotters. R. Hardwick
Plotters. T. W. Speight
Plotters of Paris. E. Mitchell
Plucked. H. Smart

Plucky Bob. Old Sleuth
Plucky Girl. Old Sleuth
Plume of Smoke. E. Morris
Plumley Inheritance. C. Bush
Plunder. B. Appel
Plunder. P. Meriton
Plunder. A. S. Roche
Plunder. F. F. Van De Water
Plunder Bar. S. M. Parkman
Plunder for the Picaroon. J. Cassells
Plunder of the Sun. D. Dodge
Plunder Pit. K. Snowden
Plunder Ship. H. Hill
Plunder Squad. R. Stark
Plunderers. E. Lefevre
Plunderers. E. P. Oppenheim
Plunderers. Morley Roberts
Plunge. C. Brogan
Plunge into Crime. N. Carter
Plunge into Peril. W. Spann
"Plunger." H. Smart
Plush and Guilt. J. Foss
Plush-Lined Coffin. C. Brown
Plutonium Heist. W. M. Green
Poached Peerage. W. Magnay
Poacher. P. Baron
Pocket Full of Clues. J. R. Langham
Pocket Full of Rye. A. Christie
Pocket Hercules. E. Jepson
Pocketful of Clues. J. R. Langham
Pocock & Pitt. E. Baker
Pod, Bender & Co. G. A. England
Poellenberg Inheritance. Evelyn Anthony
Poet and the Lunatics. G. K. Chesterton
Poetic Justice. A. Cross
Poets and Murder. R. Van Gulik
Poet's Curse. M. Y. Halidom
Poindexter Crashes the Fifth Column. G. C. Foster
Point Blank. R. Stark
Point of a Gun. A. MacKenzie
Point of a Thousand Spears. L. P. Greene
Point of Death. N. Dun
Point of Death. I. Lambot
Point of Lost Souls. J. J. Toombs
Point of no Escape. M. Colton
Point of Peril. E. Ronns
Point of Violence. L. Duncan
Pointed Tower. V. Thompson
Pointer to a Crime. A. Fielding
Pointers to Crime. N. Carter
Pointing Finger. M. Richmond
Pointing Finger. Rita
Pointing Man. M. Douie
Points and Lines. S. Matsumoto
Poirot and the Regatta Mystery. A. Christie
Poirot Investigates. A. Christie
Poirot Knows the Murderer. A. Christie
Poirot Lends a Hand. A. Christie
Poirot Loses a Client. A. Christie
Poirot on Holiday. A. Christie
Poirot's Early Cases. A. Christie
Poison. A. Askew
Poison. L. Thayer
Poison and the Root. R. Savage
Poison at Plessis. M. Dekobra
Poison Case Number 10. L. Cornell
Poison Chasers. H. Calvin
Poison Cocktail Murders. C. B. Molyneaux
Poison Cross Mystery. I. H. Irwin
Poison Cupboard. John Burke
Poison Dealer. G. Ohnet
Poison Death. Glint Green
Poison Duel. P. Dingwall
Poison Eye. M. S. Buchanan
Poison Fly Murder. H. Rutland
Poison for One. J. Rhode
Poison for One. E. Wilmot
Poison for Teacher. N. Spain

Poison for the Toff. J. Creasey
Poison from a Wealthy Widow. P. Haggard
Poison Gang. D. Steele
Poison Gas Robberies. J. Creasey
Poison in a Garden Suburb. G. D. H. Cole
Poison in Jest. J. D. Carr
Poison in Kensington. C. Kingston
Poison in Paradise. A. Hocking
Poison in Pimlico. E. Ford
Poison in Play. N. Spain
Poison in Public. C. Barry
Poison in the Blood. P. Dolan
Poison in the Garden Suburb. G. D. H. Cole
Poison in the Parish. M. Kennedy
Poison in the Pen. P. Wentworth
Poison in the Shade. E. Benfield
Poison Is a Bitter Brew. A. Hocking
Poison Is Queen. J. L. Morrissey
Poison Island. A. T. Quiller-Couch
Poison Island. K. Robeson
Poison Ivy. C. Brown
Poison Ivy. P. Cheyney
Poison Ivy. J. P. Heggy
Poison Jasmine. C. B. Clason
Poison League. J. B. Harris-Burland
Poison Lockspur. C. W. Sanders
Poison of Asps. F. Marryat
Poison of Poppies. G. Brodie
Poison on the Menu. F. Ramsdale
Poison Oracle. P. Dickinson
Poison Party. M. Brucker
Poison Pen. H. Desmond
Poison-Pen at Pyford. D. Fisher
Poison Plague. W. Levinrew
Poison, Poker and Pistols. E. M. Stone
Poison Pool. G. Collins
Poison Ring. M. Y. Halidom
Poison Shadows. W. LeQueux
Poison Speaks Softly. D. P. Clark
Poison Summer. J. L. Hensley
Poison Trail. A. Armstrong
Poison Unknown. M. Dalman
Poison Unknown. C. J. Dutton
Poison War. Ladbroke Black
Poison Weed. M. Richmond
Poisoned Anemones. U. Sanford
Poisoned Arrow. Lieut. Carlton
Poisoned Arrows. J. Middlemass
Poisoned Chalice. A. Hocking
Poisoned Chocolates Case. A. Berkeley
Poisoned Fang. K. Bruce
Poisoned Glass. S. J. Stutley
Poisoned Goblet. A. Gask
Poisoned Letter. Anonymous
Poisoned Paradise. R. W. Service
Poisoned Pen. O. Binns
Poisoned Pen. A. B. Reeve
Poisoned Relations. G. Simenon
Poisoned Sleep. B. Graeme
Poisoned Stream. H. Habe
Poisoner. G. Verner
Poisoners. D. Hamilton
Poisoners. G. R. Preedy
Poisoner's Base. B. Cobb
Poisoner's Mistake. B. Cobb
Poisonous Angel. Griff
Poisonous Relations. J. Cannan
Poisons of Exili. N. Carter
Poisons Unknown. F. Kane
Poker Jim, Gentleman and other tales and sketches. G. F. Lydston
Poker King. M. Manly
Polar Treasure. K. Robeson
Poldrate Street. Garnett Weston
Pole of Inaccessibility. J. M. Scott
Pole Reaction. J. Bruce
Polferry Mystery. P. MacDonald
Polferry Riddle. P. MacDonald
Police at the Funeral. M. Allingham

Police Blotter. R. L. Pike
Police Detective Stories. L. Dexter
Police Murders. P. H. Powell
Police Sergeant C21. R. Barnett
Police Station Mystery. R. Hardinge
Police Your Planet. E. Van Lhin
Policeboat Mystery. A. Blair
Policeman at the Door. C. Carnac
Policeman Flynn. E. Flower
Policeman in Armour. R. Penny
Policeman's Dread. J. Creasey
Policeman's Evidence. R. Penny
Policeman's Holiday. R. Penny
Policeman's Lot. E. Linington
Policeman's Lot. Henry Wade
Policeman's Nightmare. M. Cumberland
Policeman's Progress. B. Picton
Policeman's Triumph. P. Manton
Policemen in the Precinct. E. C. R. Lorac
Polite Pirate. "Capstan"
Political Plotter. D. Stewart
Politics Is Murder. E. Lanham
Polkadot Murder. F. Crane
Polluted City. G. Thorne
Polly Put the Kettle On. J. Fleming
Polmarran Tower. C. Massey
Polo Ground Mystery. R. Forsythe
Pomeroy Abbey. H. Wood
Pomeroy, Deceased. G. Bellairs
Pomfret Mystery. A. D. Vinton
Pompeii Scroll. J. La Tourrette
Ponson Case. F. W. Crofts
Pontifex, Son & Thorndyke. R. A. Freeman
Pool. M. R. Rinehart
Pool of Death. K. Patrick
Pool of Flame. L. J. Vance
Poor Dear Esme. A. M. Burrage
Poor Devils. D. Ely
Poor Fellow! J. H. Riddell
Poor Harriet. E. Fenwick
Poor Man's Shilling. K. M. Knight
Poor Miss Finch. W. Collins
Poor, Poor Ophelia. C. Weston
Poor, Poor Yorick. F. C. Davis
Poor Prisoner's Defense. R. Sheldon
Poor Quail. D. Skirrow
Poor Roger Is Dead. M. Lynch
Pop Goes the Queen. B. Wade
Pope Joan. G. W. M. Reynolds
Poppies of Death. P. Edwards
Pop. 1280. J. Thompson
Porcelain Fish. H. R. Campbell
Porcelain Fish Mystery. H. R. Campbell
Porcelain Mask. J. J. Chichester
Porkchoppers. Ross Thomas
Pornbroker. C. Brown
Porro Palaver. A. Broome
Porson's Flying Service. G. E. Rochester
Port Afrique. B. V. Dryer
Port Allington Stories and others. R. E. Vernede
Port Angelique. R. Jessup
Port of Call. W. Reyburn
Port of Destination. E. L. Long
Port of Little Ships. A. Wood
Port of London Murders. J. Bell
Port of Lost Cargoes. M. Hastings
Port of Missing Men. M. Nicholson
Port of no Return. R. M. Sears
Port of Seven Strangers. K. M. Knight
Port Orient. D. Cushman
Portals. E. A. Mann
Portcullis Room. V. Williams
Portland Place Mystery. C. Kingston
Portland Place Mystery. E. D. Pierson
Portly Peregrine. P. Traill
Portrait in a Dusty Frame. M. Hebden

Portrait in Black. I. Goff
Portrait in Black. R. Vincent
Portrait in Smoke. B. S. Ballinger
Portrait Invisible. J. Gollomb
Portrait of a Beautiful Harlot. H. Howard
Portrait of a Beautiful Woman. C. Massie
Portrait of a Dead Heiress. T. B. Dewey
Portrait of a Judge and other stories. H. Cecil
Portrait of a Killer. C. D. E. Francis
Portrait of a Man with Red Hair. H. Walpole
Portrait of a Mobster. H. Grey
Portrait of a Murderer. A. Meredith
Portrait of a Scoundrel. E. Phillpotts
Portrait of a Spy. T. Thurston
Portrait of a Victim. R. E. McDowell
Portrait of Alison. F. Durbridge
Portrait of Death. W. Bannister
Portrait of Doubt. R. Abbey
Portrait of Emma. L. Cheatham
Portrait of Fear. M. Richardson
Portrait of Fear. F. Usher
Portrait of Jirjohn Cobb. H. S. Keeler
Portrait of Rene. Harry Davis
Portrait of Terror. P. Minton
Portrait of the Accused. F. A. Symonds
Portrait of the Artist as a Dead Man. F. Bonnamy
Portraits of the Past. K. Cameron
Portrush Mystery. G. L. Curry
Portuguese Diamonds. G. Horne
Portuguese Escape. A. Bridge
Portuguese Fragment. O. Sela
Portuguese Silver. C. N. Buck
Possess and Conquer. Wenzell Brown
Possess Me Not. F. Nichols
Possess the Land. Alan White
Possessed. D. Daniels
Possessed. C. Farr
Possessed. F. Hurd
Possessed. C. Moffett
Possessed. G. F. Scott
Possession. C. Fremlin
Possession of Elizabeth Calder. Melissa Napier
Possession of Joel Delaney. R. Stewart
Possession of Tracy Corbin. D. Daniels
Post After Post-Mortem. E. C. R. Lorac
Post-Mark Homicide. A. A. Marcus
Post Mortem. H. Carmichael
Post-Mortem. G. Collins
Post Mortem. G. Cullingford
Post-Mortem. M. Moiseiwitsch
Post-Mortem Evidence. S. Fowler
Post Office Burglars of the Shawangunk Mountains. L. A. Newcome
Post Office Case. D. M. Disney
Post Office Detective. Anonymous
Post-Office Detective. G. W. Goode
Post Road. W. D. Steele
Postage Stamp Murder. G. C. Bestor
Posted for Murder. V. Rath
Postern of Fate. A. Christie
Postman Always Rings Twice. J. M. Cain
Postman's Daughter, and other tales. H. Herman
Postman's Knock. J. F. Straker
Postmark Murder. M. G. Eberhart
Postmaster of Market Deignton. E. P. Oppenheim
Postmaster's Daughter. L. Tracy
Postscript for Malpas. P. Pearson
Postscript to a Dead Letter. D. MacKenzie
Postscript to a Death. M. Cumberland

Title Index

Postscript to Murder. P. Winn
Postscript to Nightmare. D. Hitchens
Postscript to Penelope. S. Gilruth
Postscript to Poison. D. Bowers
Pot of Trouble. D. Tracy
Pot Shot. L. Stallworth
Potentate. W. Fennerton
Potsdam Murder Plot. D. Betteridge
Potting Shed. G. Greene
Poulter's Passage. P. McCutchan
Pound of Flesh. B. Delannoy
Pour a Swindle Through a Loophole. D. Von Elsner
Powder Barrel. W. Haggard
Powder River. F. W. Hilton
Powder Train. W. Tute
Powdered Proof. M. S. Buchanan
Power. W. Harrington
Power. F. M. Robinson
Power. R. M. Stern
Power and the Glory. G. Greene
Power Bug. G. Osborne
Power Cube Affair. J. T. Phillifent
Power Failure. James Preston
Power Gods. B. Clifton
Power-House. B. Appel
Power-House. J. Buchan
Power House. W. Haggard
Power Kill. C. Runyon
Power Killers. J. Philips
Power of a Villain. Warren Miller
Power of Gold. C. Meyer
Power of the Borgias. W. LeQueux
Power of the Bug. I. Drummond
Power of the Unknown. A. Edgar
Power of Woman. A. C. Gunter
Power on the Scent. H. Clandon
Power Play. John Craig
Power Play. T. J. Culver
Power Play. The Gordons
Power Sellers. P. Hall
Power to Kill. R. Hichens
Powers and Maxine. C. N. Williamson
Powers of Darkness. D. Miall
Powers of Darkness. F. M. White
Powers of Mischief. W. Magnay
Powers That Prey. J. Flynt
Practice to Deceive. G. Bradshaw
Practice to Deceive. E. Linington
Practise to Deceive. R. Lockridge
Praed Street Dossier. A. Derleth
Praed Street Papers. A. Derleth
Prairie Detective. Anonymous
Prairie Detective. L. P. Richardson
Prairie Flowers. J. B. Hendryx
Prairie Gold. H. Bindloss
Prairie Patrol. H. Bindloss
Prairie Peril. C. Stoddard
Pray for a Brave Heart. H. MacInnes
Pray for a Miracle. A. Amos
Pray for the Dawn. E. Harding
Pray Silence. M. Coles
Prayer for the Dying. J. Higgins
Praying Mantis. Edgar Johnson
Praying Mantis. H. Monteilhet
Praying Mantises. H. Monteilhet
Praying Monkey. Gavin Holt
Preach No More. R. Lockridge
Preacher of the Lord. A. Askew
Preaching Jim. D. Donovan
Precious Company. J. Budd
Precious Porcelain. N. Bell
Precipice. F. Warden
Predator. A. York
Preface to a Killing. N. Ashe
Prelude for War. L. Charteris
Prelude to a Certain Midnight. G. Kersh
Prelude to a Killing. N. Ashe
Prelude to Blue Mountains. A. Hyder
Prelude to Crime. J. J. Farjeon

Prelude to Horror. W. B. M. Ferguson
Prelude to Murder. G. C. Bestor
Prelude to Murder. Anthony Gilbert
Prelude to Murder. N. Leslie
Prelude to Murder. S. Noel
Prelude to Passion. H. Luger
Prelude to Peril. J. Sohl
Prelude to Peril. S. Toye
Prelude to Trouble. J. Bentley
Premature Burial. M. H. Danne
Premedicated Murder. Douglas Clark
Premeditated Murder. P. Cheyney
Premier. G. Simenon
Premier's Daughter. A. Askew
Preparatory School Murder. R. Macnaughtan
Prepare for Action. J. Creasey
Prescription for Death. Desmond Martin
Prescription for Murder. H. Lees
Prescription for Murder. S. Miles
Prescription: Murder. D. M. Disney
Prescription: Murder. W. Link
Presence. M. Eyre
Presence in the House. M. Lovell
Presenting Inspector Flagg. J. Cassells
Presenting the Dreamer. W. M. Duncan
President Fu Manchu. S. Rohmer
President Has been Kidnapped! P. Richards
President Kettle. C. J. C. Hyde
President Plan. D. Meiring
President Vanishes. Anonymous
Presidential Plot. S. Johnson
President's Agent. J. Milton
President's Doctor. W. Woolfolk
President's Mystery Story. F. D. Roosevelt
President's Plane Is Missing. R. J. Serling
Press of Suspects. A. Garve
Pressing Peril. N. Carter
Pressure. C. F. Coe
Pressure-Gauge Murder. F. W. B. Von Linsingen
Pressure Man. Roderic Wilkinson
Pressure Point. L. Agniel
Preston Jayne. Old Sleuth
Presumed Dead. J. Larteguy
Presumed Dead. P. Urquhart
Presumed Dead. D. Whitelaw
Pretender. C. Hosken
Prettiest Girl I Ever Killed. C. Runyon
Pretty Boy. W. Cunningham
Pretty Fanny's Way. R. M. Gilchrist
Pretty Jailer. F. Du Boisgobey
Pretty Lady. M. Babson
Pretty Miss Murder. W. T. Ballard
Pretty Miss Smith. F. Warden
Pretty Ones. D. Eden
Pretty Pass. D. Footman
Pretty Poison. S. Geller
Pretty Sinister. F. Beeding
Pretty Stenographer Mystery. N. Carter
Prettybelle. Jean Arnold
Preventive Man. G. V. McFadden
Previous Lady. J. La Tourrette
Previously Reported Missing--Now? G. Chester
Prey by Dawn. H. Kane
Prey by Night. M. Douglas
Prey for a Newshawk. H. Janson
Prey for Me. T. B. Dewey
Prey for the Dreamer. W. M. Duncan
Prey for the Nightingale. H. McCutcheon
Prey for the Picaroon. J. Cassells
Prey of the Eagle. P. G. Leonard
Prey of the Strongest. Morley Roberts
Preying Mantis. N. Rutledge
Preying Streets. L. Baker
Price. D. Chacko

Price. A. Hornblow
Price. F. Lynde
Price. G. F. Newman
Price of a Secret. N. Carter
Price of a Secret. T. W. Speight
Price of a Soul. P. Trent
Price of Admiralty. M. B. Lowndes
Price of Admiralty. S. Stone
Price of an Impulse. J. P. Bessell
Price of an Orphan. P. Carlon
Price of Death. F. Usher
Price of Delusion. W. Magnay
Price of Exile. W. J. Makin
Price of Freedom. A. W. Marchmont
Price of Love. A. Applin
Price of Murder. J. D. MacDonald
Price of Pity. C. R. Gull
Price of Power. W. LeQueux
Price of Protection. Warren Miller
Price of Silence. M. Dalton
Price of Silence. S. Kyle
Price of Silence. F. Warden
Price of Silence. M. C. Weiner
Price of Treachery. N. Carter
Price Tag for Murder. S. Dean
Price Was High. G. Hackforth-Jones
Pricking Thumb. H. C. Branson
Pride of Dolphins. M. Hebden
Pride of Heroes. P. Dickinson
Pride of Life. W. Magnay
Pride of Overmoor. E. Woodward
Pride of Pigs. J. Wainwright
Pride of Place. W. P. McGivern
Pride of Race. B. L. Farjeon
Pride of the Paddock. H. Smart
Pride of the Ring. B. Bolt
Pride of the Stable. E. J. Murray
Pride of the Trevallions. C. Salisbury
Pride of Women. K. Platt
Prideful Woman. H. G. Hutchinson
Priest of Piccadilly. A. Applin
Priestess of the Damned. V. Coffman
Priests of the Abomination. I. Drummond
Priest's Secret. E. Finn
Priest's Secret. W. M. Graydon
Priest's Secret. A. Maxwell
Prillilgirl. C. Wells
Prim Windows. J. Chancellor
Prima Donna's Husband. F. Du Boisgobey
Prime Cut. M. Roote
Prime Minister and Mrs. Grantham. C. Dawe
Prime Minister Is Dead. H. Simpson
Prime Minister's Boat Is Missing. J. Dyson
Prime Minister's Pencil. C. Waye
Prime Minister's Pyjamas. F. Evelyn
Prime Minister's Secret. W. Holt-White
Prime Time Corpse. J. Babbin
Primrose Path. A. Mills
Primula. G. R. Preedy
Primus. B. Street
Prince and the Perjurer. A. Hillgarth
Prince and the Undertaker, and What They Undertook. R. Stephens
Prince Cinderella. G. Alexander
Prince for Inspector West. J. Creasey
Prince from Overseas. B. Thomson
Prince in Petrograd. E. Jepson
Prince in the Garret. A. C. Gunter
Prince Karl. M. Gerard
Prince Karl. A. C. Gunter
Prince of Balkistan. A. Upward
Prince of Blackmail. C. Bishop
Prince of Darkness. B. Michaels
Prince of Darkness. E. Southworth

Prince of Darkness. F. Warden
Prince of Fraud. E. T. Sawyer
Prince of Good Fellows. R. Barr
Prince of India. L. Clarke
Prince of Liars. N. Carter
Prince of Lovers. W. Magnay
Prince of Mischance. T. Gallon
Prince of Paradise. F. Gerard
Prince of Plunder. S. Horler
Prince of Poisoners. Ladbroke Black
Prince of Rogues. N. Carter
Prince of Romance. R. Pertwee
Prince of Sinners. E. P. Oppenheim
Prince of Spies. G. Davison
Prince of Swindlers. G. Boothby
Prince of the Blood. J. Payn
Prince of the Captivity. J. Buchan
Prince of the Palais Royal. M. Pemberton
Prince of Thieves. J. J. Lynx
Prince of Trouble. Colin Hope
Prince of Turf Crooks. F. Johnston
Prince of Ventriloquists. Old Sleuth
Prince of Wales's Garden-Party, and other stories. J. H. Riddell
Prince or Clown. M. Dekobra
Prince Punnie. A. W. Marchmont
Prince Saroni's Wife. J. Hawthorne
Prince Schamyl's Wooing. R. H. Savage
Prince Zaleski. M. P. Shiel
Princely Detective. Anonymous
Princely Quartet. J. Budd
Prince's Darling. G. R. Preedy
Prince's Diamond. E. Hulme-Beaman
Princes of Peele. W. Westall
Princess After Dark. S. Horler
Princess Brinda. M. Dekobra
Princess Galva. D. Whitelaw
Princess in Mufti. H. T. Johnson
Princess Kate. L. Tracy
Princess Maritza. P. Brebner
Princess Mary's Locked Book. A. M. Williamson
Princess Mazaroff. J. Hatton
Princess of Alaska. R. H. Savage
Princess of Copper. A. C. Gunter
Princess of Crime. N. Carter
Princess of Happy Chance. T. Gallon
Princess of Jutedom. C. Gibbon
Princess of Paradise. Stuart Martin
Princess of Paris. A. C. Gunter
Princess of Persia. J. D. White
Princess of the Purple Palace. W. M. Graydon
Princess' Own. Roland Daniel
"Princess Proxy." J. R. Warren
Princess Stakes Murder. K. Platt
Princess Sunshine, and other stories. J. H. Riddell
Princess Zara. R. Beeckman
Printer's Devil. B. Barclay
Printer's Devil. C. Dane
Printer's Error. G. Mitchell
Prinvest-London. V. Gielgud
Prior Betrothal. Elsie Lee
Priority for Death. P. Vane
Priority Murder. L. Ford
Priscilla Darling. Maz
Priscilla to the Rescue. T. Cobb
Prison. G. Simenon
Prison Breakers. R. H. Poole
Prison Breakers. E. Wallace
Prison Feud. James Preston
Prison Girl. Wenzell Brown
Prison House. D. F. Gardiner
Prison Murder. R. Dark
Prison Princess. A. Griffiths
Prisoner. P. Bouileau
Prisoner. Roland Daniel

Prisoner. T. M. Disch
Prisoner. M. Gerard
Prisoner. D. McDaniel
Prisoner. D. St. Michaels
Prisoner at the Bar. J. Ashford
Prisoner Born. C. Aveline
Prisoner Go Free. D. Lee
Prisoner in the Hold. A. Parsons
Prisoner in the Mask. D. Wheatley
Prisoner in the Opal. A. E. W. Mason
Prisoner in the Skull. C. Dye
Prisoner in the Square. D. Quentin
Prisoner #3. H. Stine
Prisoner #2. D. McDaniel
Prisoner of Ellis Island. W. M. Graydon
Prisoner of Garve. S. Shulman
Prisoner of Ingecliff. J. Bellamy
Prisoner of Lost Island. J. Hunter
Prisoner of Love. H. Monteilhet
Prisoner of Love. M. Richmond
Prisoner of Malville Hall. D. Daniels
Prisoner of Ornith Farm. F. Powell
Prisoner of the Buddha. R. C. Armour
Prisoner of the Chateau. G. H. Teed
Prisoner of the Garret. B. Reynolds
Prisoner of the Kremlin. A. Murray
Prisoner of the Manor. R. Abbey
Prisoner of the Manor. R. Hardinge
Prisoner of the Mountains. W. M. Graydon
Prisoner of the Priory. C. Goodall
Prisoner of the Pyramid. F. Gerard
Prisoner of War. Grace M. White
Prisoner Pleads "Not Guilty." L. Thayer
Prisoners. M. Cholmondeley
Prisoner's Base. C. Fremlin
Prisoner's Base. R. Stout
Prisoner's Friend. A. Garve
Prisoner's Friend. G. Goodchild
Prisoners in the Wall. G. Radcliffe
Prisoners of Devil's Claw. E. H. Hawkins
Prisoners of Fear. M. Broughton
Prisoners of Peru. Gwyn Evans
Prisoners of the Desert. S. Blake
Prisoner's Plea. H. Waugh
Prisoner's Secret. J. K. Leys
Private and Confidential. P. Trent
Private Anger, and Flight and Pursuit. F. O'Rourke
Private Carter's Crime. J. Creasey
Private Death. M. Urquhart
Private Detective. A. Forrester
Private Detective. R. Machray
Private Detective. J. D. Shea
Private Detective No. 39. J. W. Postgate
Private Enquiry. C. H. Ross
Private Enterprise, and other stories. R. Standish
Private Eye. C. F. Adams
Private Eye. E. Dudley
Private Eyeful. H. Kane
Private Face of Murder. J. Bonett
Private I. J. Sangster
Private Inquiries. Dorothy Johnson
Private Killing. J. Benet
Private Life. P. Selver
Private Life of Sherlock Holmes. M. Hardwick
Private Line. S. Maddock
Private Party. W. Ard
Private Pavilion. J. G. Edwards
Private Practice of Michael Shayne. B. Halliday
Private Report. K. Roberts
Private Sector. J. Hone
Private Undertaking. H. T. Teilhet

Private Vendetta. B. Jones
Private View. M. Innes
Private Wire to Washington. H. MacGrath
Private Worlds. S. Gainham
Private Wound. N. Blake
Privateer Captain. Waters
Privateers. H. B. M. Watson
Privateer's Defiance. B. Wayde
Privateersman's Legacy. F. Du Boisgobey
Privilege. John Burke
Privileged Character. J. Laborde
Prize of Gold. M. Catto
Prize of Traitors. D. Vallance
Prizewinner. F. Mullally
Pro. B. Hamilton
Pro Patria. M. Pemberton
Probability Factor. W. Kempley
Probation. M. L. Storer
Probationer! E. Price
Problem at Pollensa Bay and Christmas Adventure. A. Christie
Problem by Rail. E. C. Vivian
Problem Club. B. Pain
Problem for Superintendent Flagg. J. Cassells
Problem for the Dreamer. W. M. Duncan
Problem in Angels. L. Holton
Problem in Ciphers. "Capstan"
Problem in Ciphers. R. Hardinge
Problem Island. C. E. R. Sinclair
Problem of Cell 13. J. Futrelle
Problem of the Derby Favorite. J. W. Bobin
Problem of the Green Capsule. J. D. Carr
Problem of the Purple Maculas. J. C. Iraldi
Problem of the Wire Cage. J. D. Carr
Procane Chronicle. O. Bleeck
Proceed at Will. B. Wilkinson
Proceed with Caution. J. Rhode
Procession of the Damned. W. Tucker
Procession of Two. R. Philmore
Procession--to Prison. D. Henderson
Procrastination of Sergeant Cluff. G. North
Prodigal, and other stories. A. Soutar
Prodigal Soldier. F. H. Rose
Prodigals of Monte Carlo. E. P. Oppenheim
Prodigal's Portion. C. C. Lewis
Prodigal's Progress. F. Barrett
Produce the Body. R. Goyne
Professional. J. D. Buchanan
Professional Guest. W. Garrett
Professional Jealousy. C. F. Gregg
Professional Prince. E. Jepson
Professional Thieves and the Detective. A. Pinkerton
Professionals. J. Harris
Professor. Roland Daniel
Professor. J. Lynn
Professor. Alan Thomas
Professor Dies. J. Rowland
Professor Knits a Shroud. W. Van Arsdale
Professor on the Case. J. Futrelle
Prof. Slagg of London. D. E. Marvin
Professor's Christmas Party, and A Student of the Obvious. H. C. McNeile
Professor's Last Experiment. H. Edmonds
Professor's Mystery. W. S. Hastings
Professor's Poison. N. Gordon
Professor's Sister. J. Hawthorne
Profile in Gilt. J. C. Nolan
Profile of a Murder. R. King
Profit for the Picaroon. J. Cassells
Profiteers. E. P. Oppenheim
Profligate. A. Hornblow
Progeny of the Adder. L. H. Whitten
Programmed for Death. L. Gribble
Programmed Man. W. D. Blankenship
Progress of a Crime. J. Symons

Title Index

Progress of Rachel. A. Sergeant
Project X. C. Robertson
Projects Section. T. Lilley
Prologue to Murder. M. B. Dix
Prologue to the Gallows. P. McGuire
Prom Concert Murders. A. Wood
Prominent Among the Mourners. C. Thomas
Promise. J. B. Hendryx
Promise for Death. J. Messmann
Promise for Tomorrow. E. Woodward
Promise of Diamonds. G. Ashe
Promise of Murder. M. G. Eberhart
Promise of the Phoenix. F. Gerard
Promise to Kill. P. Marlowe
Promise(s) of Marriage. E. Gaboriau
Promotion Tour. T. Harknett
Proof, Counter Proof. E. R. Punshon
Proof of the Poison. A. A. Thomson
Proof of the Pudding. P. A. Taylor
Proof Positive. John Drummond
Proper Carve-Up. M. Cronin
Property in Cyprus. Robert MacLeod
Property of a Gentleman. C. Gaskin
Prophet of Fire. J. Creasey
Prophet's Mantle. F. Bland
Prose Romances of Edgar A. Poe. E. A. Poe
Prosecutor. B. Botein
Prosecutor. James Mills
Prosecutor. P. R. Van Zyl
Prospect's Dead. A. Tack
Protagonists. J. Barlow
Protection for a Lady. M. Delaney
Protection for a Lady. J. T. Story
Protector. L. Harris
Protectors. W. Haggard
Protectors. R. Miall
Protectors. W. Pine
Protege. C. Armstrong
Proteus Pact. G. St. George
Protocol for a Kidnapping. O. Bleeck
Proud Adversary. Howard Mason
Proud Citadel. T. Charles
Prove It, Mr. Tolefree. R. A. J. Walling
Provenance of Death. K. Giles
Proverbial Murder Case. W. Sutherland
Providence Hall. C. Rodda
Province of Darkness. P. Morton
Provincial Crime. Lionel Black
Provincial Papers. J. Hatton
Proving Flight. D. Beaty
Prowl Cop. G. Jones
Prowl No More, Lady. J. Warren
Prowler. F. Rickett
Prowler in the Night. J. Matcha
Prowling Terror. C. T. Stoneham
Pruneface. C. Gould
Prussian Blue. A. Hocking
Prynter's Devil. J. Wainwright
Psalm Stone. F. M. White
Psychedelic Spy. T. A. Waters
Psychiatric Murders. M. S. Michel
Psychiatrist Says Murder. L. Freeman
Psycho. R. Bloch
Psycho. P. Moore
Psycho in Focus. L. Smith
Psychotron Plot. J. Rosenberger
Pub Crawler. M. Procter
Pub on the Pool. A. D. Divine
Public Defender. G. Goodchild
Public Enemies. A. Bracey
Public Enemy. H. Clevely
Public Enemy. K. Glasmon
Public Enemy--No. 1. B. Graeme
Public Ghost Number One. A. Soutar
Public Mischief. S. Maddock
Public School Murder. R. C. Woodthorpe

Publicity for Anne. A. M. Williamson
Publicity for Murder. E. Messenger
Publish and Perish. F. M. Nevins
Puck of Crooks' Hill. San Antonio
Pulitzer Prize Murders. D. Heyward
Pull the House Down. M. L. Tyrrell
Pulled Down. P. Paul
Pulling the Strings. F. E. Penny
Pulpit in the Grill Room. E. P. Oppenheim
Pulse of Danger. J. Cleary
Punch and Judy Murders. Carter Dickson
Punch with Care. P. A. Taylor
Punctual Rape. C. Black
Punitive Action. J. Robb
Punt Murder. A. Griffin
Puppet-Masters. W. Garner
Puppet on a Chain. Alistair MacLean
Puppets of Chance. R. P. Koehler
Puppets of Fate. S. Jepson
Puppets of Father Bouvard. W. M. Duncan
Puppets Part. D. Carew
Purchase Price. R. Cullum
Pure as the Lily. C. Cookson
Pure Poison. H. Waugh
Pure Sweet Hell. M. Douglas
Purgatory Street. R. McDougald
Puritan. C. Watson
Puritan's Wife. M. Pemberton
Purity League. Alan Williams
Purloined Prince. E. Turner
Purloined Prince. Ian Wallace
Purple Aces. R. J. Hogan
Purple Ball. F. Packard
Purple Claw. H. Horn
Purple Dressing Gown. P. Fry
Purple Fern. H. Hume
Purple Jacaranda. Nancy Graham
Purple Legion. G. F. Eliot
Purple Limited. H. Leverage
Purple Love. M. Gerard
Purple Mask. L. J. Miln
Purple Mist. G. E. Locke
Purple Onion Mystery. H. Ashbrook
Purple Parrot. C. B. Clason
Purple Pearl. A. Pryde
Purple Place for Dying. J. D. MacDonald
Purple Plague. D. Steele
Purple Pony Murders. S. E. Porcelain
Purple Rock. A. MacVicar
Purple Shadow. E. Snell
Purple Shadows. A. V. Bartram
Purple Sheba. K. Hayles
Purple Shells. R. L. Goldman
Purple Sickle Murders. F. W. Crofts
Purple-6. H. Brinton
Purple Spot. N. Carter
Purple Stain. J. M. Walsh
Purple Threat. D. Dayle
Purple Trident. C. Whitton
Purple Zombie. K. Robeson
Purse Which Was Found and other stories. R. Marsh
Purser's Mate. E. L. Long
Pursue the Wind. L. Richards
Pursued. A. Mills
Pursued by the Law. J. M. Cobban
Pursuer. L. Golding
Pursuing Shadow. J. Laurence
Pursuit. L. G. Blochman
Pursuit. M. McLaren
Pursuit. R. Pertwee
Pursuit. F. Saville
Pursuit. A. Soutar
Pursuit. R. Unekis
Pursuit in Peru. C. L. Leonard
Pursuit of a Parcel. P. Wentworth
Pursuit of Agent M. D. Copp
Pursuit of Mr. Faviel. R. E. Vernede
Pursuit of the House Boat. J. K. Bangs

Pursuit Till Morning. A. Wykes
Pursuit to Algeria. Arthur MacLean
Push-Button Spy. L. James
Pushbutton Butterfly. K. Platt
Pusher. E. McBain
Put Back the Clock. M. Richmond
Put on the Spot. J. Lait
Put Out That Star. H. Carmichael
Put Out the Light. H. Desmond
Put Out the Light. S. Truss
Put Out the Light. Ethel L. White
Put Yourself in Her Place. M. Leighton
Puzzle. L. Thayer
Puzzle for Fiends. P. Quentin
Puzzle for Fools. P. Quentin
Puzzle for Inspector West. J. Creasey
Puzzle for Pilgrims. P. Quentin
Puzzle for Players. P. Quentin
Puzzle for Puppets. P. Quentin
Puzzle for Wantons. P. Quentin
Puzzle in Paint. Kootz
Puzzle in Paisley. E. Gresham
Puzzle in Parchment. E. Gresham
Puzzle in Parquet. E. Gresham
Puzzle in Patchwork. E. Gresham
Puzzle in Pearls. G. Ashe
Puzzle in Petticoats. Kootz
Puzzle in Pewter. R. Grey
Puzzle in Poison. A. Berkeley
Puzzle in Porcelain. R. Grey
Puzzle in Pyrotechnics. J. Rowland
Puzzle Lock. R. A. Freeman
Puzzle of the Blue Banderilla. S. Palmer
Puzzle of the Briar Pipe. S. Palmer
Puzzle of the Five Pistols and other stories. N. Carter
Puzzle of the Happy Hooligan. S. Palmer
Puzzle of the Pepper Tree. S. Palmer
Puzzle of the Red Stallion. S. Palmer
Puzzle of the Silver Persian. S. Palmer
Puzzled Policeman. G. Woden
Puzzling Shadow. Old Sleuth
Pyramid of Death. N. MacKenzie
Pyramid of Lead. Atkey
Pyramids of Snow. E. Metcalfe
Pyrrha. P. Grayson
Python Project. V. Canning
Pyx. J. Buell

Q

Q as in Quicksand. L. Treat
QBI: Queen's Bureau of Investigation. E. Queen
Q Document. J. H. Roberts
Q.E.D. L. Brock
Q.E.D. L. Thayer
QED: Queen's Experiments in Detection. E. Queen
"Q" Squad. G. Verner
Q's Mystery Stories. A. T. Quiller-Couch
Q33. G. Goodchild
Q33--Spy Catcher. G. Goodchild
Quadraphone Homicide. J. Weisman
Quaking Widow. R. Colby
Qualified Adventurer. S. Jepson
Quality Bill's Girl. C. W. Tyler
Quality of Mercy. R. Carson
Qualtrough. Angus Hall
Quarrel. C. Houghton
Quarrel with Murder. M. Halliday
Quarrelling Room. J. B. Watney
Quarry. F. Duerrenmatt
Quarry. J. A. Moroso
Quarry. R. L. Pike

Quarry House. J. Ware
Quarter to Four. W. W. Cook
Quartet. E. Phillpotts
Quartet of Three. M. Tripp
Quartz Eye. H. K. Webster
Quayle of the Yard. P. Trent
Quayle's First Case. P. Trent
Que Viva Guevera. G. De Villiers
Queen Against Owen. A. Upward
Queen and the Corpse. M. Murray
Queen Anne's Gate Mystery. R. Arkwright
Queen City Murder Case. W. Bogart
Queen Dies First. I. Lambot
Queen from Mars. R. St. Clair
Queen in Danger. S. Rattray
Queen of a Day. J. S. Fletcher
Queen of America. R. H. Greenan
Queen of Blackmailers. M. O. Rolfe
Queen of Bohemia. J. Hatton
Queen of Chance. D. Stewart
Queen of Clubs. H. Footner
Queen of Crookdom. M. Welford
Queen of Crooks. Detective Dunn
Queen of Crook's Harem. B. Sarto
Queen of Diamonds. N. Carter
Queen of Hearts. W. Collins
Queen of Hearts. L. Paige
Queen of Knaves and other stories. N. Carter
Queen of My Heart. M. Richmond
Queen of Night. H. Hill
Queen of Spades. H. C. Bailey
Queen of Spades. M. McEvoy
Queen of Spies. T. Coulson
Queen of the Black Hand. H. C. Davidson
Queen of the Gangsters. J. Fairfax-Blakeborough
Queen of the Highway. Old Sleuth
Queen of the Jesters. M. Pemberton
Queen of the Meadow. C. Gibbon
Queen of the Mirage. K. Lindsay
Queen of the Night. K. Perkins
Queen of the Outlaw's Camp. Anonymous
Queen of the Riffs. Operator 1384
Queen of the Secret Seven. Anonymous
Queen of the Secret Seven. O. Harper
Queen of the Stage. F. M. White
Queen of the Underworld. J. W. Booth
Queen of the White Slaves. Grace M. White
Queen of the World. George Weston
Queen Street. M. Gant
Queen Sweetheart. A. M. Williamson
Queen Victoria's Revenge. H. Harrison
Queen Wasp. J. Middlemass
Queenie. W. F. Fauley
Queenie's Terrible Secret. A. M. Miller
Queen's Advocate. A. W. Marchmont
Queen's Desire. H. Nisbet
Queen's Error. H. Curties
Queen's Evidence. E. Kyle
Queen's Falcon. E. E. Blau
Queens Full. E. Queen
Queen's Gate Mystery. H. Adams
Queen's Gate Mystery. H. Curties
Queen's Grace. N. Tranter
Queen's Hall Murder. A. Broome
Queen's Hand. B. Reynolds
Queen's Justice. Edwin Arnold
Queen's Mate. H. Adams
Queen's Mate. M. Gerard
Queen's Pawn. V. Canning
Queen's Revenge. S. Cobb
Queen's Scarf. D. C. Murray
Queen's Scarlet. G. M. Fenn
Queen's Treasure. C. Ashdown

Queer Affair. G. Boothby
Queer Bag of Bodies. A. Webb
Queer Face. G. Verner
Queer Fish. J. Boland
Queer Folk Next Door. G. Woden
Queer Kind of Death. G. Baxt
Queer Looking Box, and other stories. M. Hervey
Queer Mr. Quell. W. J. Makin
Queer Partners. S. Murray
Queer Race. W. Westall
Queer Things at Queechy. P. Gurney
Queerest Man Alive, and other stories. G. H. Hepworth
Quella. G. N. Farmer
Quest. N. De Mille
Quest. N. A. Temple-Ellis
Quest for Alexis. N. Buckingham
Quest for Gold. G. Horne
Quest for Superintendent Flagg. J. Cassells
Quest for the Bogeyman. F. Lockridge
Quest for the Picaroon. J. Cassells
Quest of Douglas Holmes. H. E. Inman
Quest of El Dorado. A. Askew
Quest of Geoffrey Darrell. A. Sergeant
Quest of John Clare. Sea Lion
Quest of Julian Day. D. Wheatley
Quest of Juror 19. David Davidson
Quest of Krang. C. Van Horn
Quest of Mr. Sandyman. Neill Graham
Quest of Nigel Rex. G. Goodchild
Quest of Qui. K. Robeson
Quest of the Crooked. H. Maxwell
Quest of the Emerald. M. Seville
Quest of "The Lost Hope." N. Carter
Quest of the Sacred Slipper. S. Rohmer
Quest of the Seeker. J. T. Elton
Quest of the Spider. K. Robeson
Quest of the "Stormalong." D. W. MacArthur
Quest of the Vanishing Star. R. Ladline
Quest of the Yellow Pearl. P. C. MacFarlane
Quest of Youth. J. Farnol
Quest of Youth. J. G. Sarasin
Quest Sinister. S. P. B. Mais
Quest to Kill. R. Severn
Questing Hound. G. Hackforth-Jones
Questing Man. M. Home
Question. M. Peterson
Question of Character. J. Hougron
Question of Coercion. G. Norham
Question of Degree. R. Lewis
Question of Evidence. Old Spicer
Question of Identity. H. C. McNeile
Question of Judgment. P. B. Young
Question of Loyalty. N. Freeling
Question of Mud. H. C. McNeile
Question of Murder. Anthony Gilbert
Question of Negligence. H. McLeave
Question of Policy. M. Wayde
Question of Proof. N. Blake
Question of Queens. M. Innes
Question of Taste. F. Bamford
Question of Time. H. Carmichael
Question of Time. N. Carter
Question of Time. F. Duncan
Question of Time. H. McCloy
Questionable Shape. M. Cumberland
Questor Tapes. D. C. Fontana
Quests of Paul Beck. M. M. Bodkin
Queue Here for Murder. N. MacKenzie
Queue Up to Listen. A. Spiller
Quick and the Dead. Griff
Quick and the Dead. E. Queen
Quick and the Dead. V. Starrett

Quick and the Wed. G. Bowman
Quick Brown Fox. W. R. Burnett
Quick Curtain. A. Melville
Quick Red Fox. J. D. MacDonald
Quick Tempo. N. Easton
Quickie Mysteries. A. Badger
Quickly Dead. B. Cobb
Quickness of the Hand. J. Mayo
Quicksand. M. Land
Quicksands of London. C. H. Bullivant
Quicksilver. Roland Daniel
Quicksilver Pool. P. A. Whitney
Quickthorn. Lanora Miller
Quid Est. E. Mariner-Scarritt
Quidnunc County. R. M. Stern
Quiet American. G. Greene
Quiet City. Mark Ross
Quiet Fear. M. Halliday
Quiet Game of Bambu. R. Gouze
Quiet Horror. S. Ellin
Quiet Killer. D. MacKenzie
Quiet Mrs. Fleming. R. Pryce
Quiet Murder. V. R. Muzzey
Quiet Ones. B. Graeme
Quiet Passion. L. Hoffman
Quiet Place in the Country. H. Clement
Quiet River. J. D. White
Quiet Sound of Fear. L. Paxton
Quiet Under the Sun. K. Fitzgerald
Quiet Violence. D. M. Disney
Quiet Waits the Grave. H. Janson
Quiet War. J. Browning
Quiet Woman. H. Carmichael
Quietly She Lies. E. M. D. Hawthorn
Quiller Memorandum. Adam Hall
Quincunx Case. W. D. Pitman
Quinn. N. Scanlon
Quinn and the Desert Oil. N. Scanlon
Quinn of the "Fury." S. Styles
Quinneys'. H. A. Vachell
Quinney's Adventures. H. A. Vachell
Quin's Hide. M. Summerton
Quinta Affair. N. Grey
Quinton Clyde, Private Investigator. T. McCoy
Quintus Oakes. C. R. Jackson
Quirindi. K. R. Butler
Quislings over Paris. M. Cumberland
Quite by Accident. K. Booton
Quite Like Old Days. V. Bridges
Quittance in Full. T. W. Speight
Quixote of Magdalen. Mrs. C. Kernahan
Quoth the Raven. B. Fischer

R

R. Holmes & Co. J. K. Bangs
R.I.P. P. MacDonald
R.I.S.C. R. C. Frazer
R in the Month. N. Spain
R.O.F. Murders. H. Varley
R.S.V.P. Murder. M. G. Eberhart
Ra-Ta-Plan--! D. Ogburn
Rabbitfoot. A. W. Grahame
Rabbit's Paw. S. Jepson
Rabble of Rebels. G. Ashe
Race Against the Sun. D. Rutherford
Race for a Fortune. R. S. Holland
Race for a Wife. H. Smart
Race for Life. A. F. Pinkerton
Race for Life. J. Remy
Race for Life. F. Whishaw
Race for Life and other tales. Anonymous
Race for Millions. D. C. Murray
Race for Ten Thousand. N. Carter
Race for Wealth. J. H. Riddell
Race Gang. E. Woodward
Race of Life. G. Boothby

Title Index

Race Toward Death. N. MacKenzie
Race Track Crooks. N. Ridley
Race Track Gamble. N. Carter
Race with Death. D. Stewart
Race with Ruin. H. Hill
Race with the Sun. G. Church
Race with the Sun. L. T. Meade
Racecourse Tragedy. N. Gould
Rachel Weeping. Shelley Smith
Racing Axes. James Preston
Racing Crazy. Duff Johnson
Racing Ramp. A. J. Sarl
Racing Rubber. H. Smart
Racing Yacht Mystery. B. Graeme
Racket Busters, Incorporated. H. H. Lee
Racketeers. R. Sharp
Racketeers of the Turf. Carlton Ross
Racketeer's Will. W. P. Vickery
Rackets Incorporated. Griff
Racoon Lake Mystery. N. M. Hopkins
Radcliffe Case. J. Bentley
Radford Shone. H. Hill
Radingham Mystery. Roy Vickers
Radio Blackmail. L. G. Redmond-Howard
Radio Crook. R. Hardinge
Radio Detective. A. B. Reeve
Radio Mystery. J. Mowbray
Radio Studio Murder. C. Wells
Radioactive Camel Affair. P. Leslie
Radium Profiteer. G. N. Philips
Radium Terrors. A. Dorrington
Rafferty. B. S. Ballinger
Rafferty. L. White
Rafferty and the Gold Dust Twins. Lillian Roberts
Raffles. E. W. Hornung
Raffles After Dark. B. Perowne
Raffles and the Key Man. B. Perowne
Raffles' Crime in Gibralter. B. Perowne
Raffles in Pursuit. B. Perowne
Raffles Revisited. B. Perowne
Raffles, the Amateur Cracksman. E. W. Hornung
Raffles Under Sentence. B. Perowne
Raffles vs. Sexton Blake. B. Perowne
Raft of Swords. D. Kyle
Rag and a Bone. H. Waugh
Rag Pickers. H. V. Dixon
Rage. P. Friedman
Rage. L. V. Roper
Rage at Sea. F. Lorenz
Rage in Babylon. S. Mitchell
Rage in Harlem. C. Himes
Rage to Die. R. Jessup
Rage to Kill. B. E. Lovell
Ragged Edge. J. Karney
Ragged Edge. J. T. MacIntyre
Ragged Robin Murders. G. Morton
Raging Waters. D. Daniels
Ragland. J. Van Orsdell
Rags. A. Applin
Raid. W. E. Johns
Raid. J. B. O'Sullivan
Raid on the Mint. F. Putnam
Raid on the Villa Joyosa. R. Hopkins
Raid over England. N. Leslie
Raiders of the Southern Seas. T. Wallace
Raiders Passed! J. Hunter
Rail-Road Forger and the Detectives. A. Pinkerton
Railroad Murder Case. R. M. Laurenson
Railway Detective. Anonymous
Railway Detective. H. Rockwood
Railway Hotel Murder. A. Compton-Rickett
Railway Tragedy. F. Du Boisgobey
Rain Before Seven. J. August
Rain Before Seven. M. Brandel
Rain Before Seven. C. Buckley
Rain Islands. J. Wood
Rain of Death. J. D. Kennedy
Rain of Terror. M. Douglas
Rain on the Roof. G. Goodchild
Rain on the Roof. K. Lipky
Rain with Violence. D. Shannon
Rainbird Pattern. V. Canning
Rainbow Affair. D. McDaniel
Rainbow Coloured Hearse. K. Bird
Rainbow Coloured Shroud. J. Hedges
Rainbow Conspiracy. D. Lee
Rainbow Feather. F. Hume
Rainbow Glass. A. Dwyer-Joyce
Rainbow Gold. D. C. Murray
Rainbow Island. L. Tracy
Rainbow Mystery. W. LeQueux
Rainbow Nights, and other stories. A. Soutar
Rainbow Puzzle. E. C. Vivian
Rainbow/Seagreen Case. P. K. Palmer
Rainbow's End. J. M. Cain
Rainbrother. C. Edwards
Rajah of Dah. G. M. Fenn
Rajah of Ghanapore. H. E. Hill
Rajah's Casket. D. Christie
Rajah's Fortress. W. M. Graydon
Rajah's Revenge. A. Murray
Rajah's Ruby. N. Carter
Rajah's Sapphire. M. P. Shiel
Rajah's Second Wife. H. Hill
Rakehell. A. Rundle
Raking for the Moon. M. G. Lowe
Rally to Kill. B. Knox
Rally to the Death. D. Rutherford
Ralph Norbreck's Trust. W. Westall
Ralph Ryder of Brent. F. Warden
Ralph the Bailiff and other tales. M. E. Braddon
Ralph Wildhawk. Anonymous
Ram Dass. C. Felix
Ramona. M. Risco
Ramsden. T. Mundy
Ramsden Case. D. Chandler
Ramsey, the Detective. Old Sleuth
Ramshackle House. H. Footner
Ramshackle Inn. G. Batson
Randolph Mason, Corrector of Destinies. M. D. Post
Randolph Mason: The Clients. M. D. Post
Randolph Mason: The Strange Schemes. M. D. Post
Random Army. M. Polland
Randy Inheritance. J. N. Chance
Range Justice. R. Wilkes-Hunter
Ranger of the Susquehannock. R. W. Kauffman
Ranger of the Tomb. Wilhelmina Johnson
Ranger of the Tomb. T. P. Prest
Rank Outsider. J. Fairfax-Blakeborough
Ransom. J. Cleary
Ransom. C. F. Coe
Ransom. C. Hume
Ransom! J. Messmann
Ransom! A. S. Roche
Ransom. R. K. Smith
Ransom. P. Wheeler
Ransome Castle. M. Farnsworth
Ransom for a Nude. Lionel Black
Ransom for London. J. S. Fletcher
Ransom of the Angel. D. Dodge
Ransom Racket. L. Thayer
Ransomed Madonna. L. White
Rape. L. Trevor
Rape of a Quiet Town. D. Lee
Rape of a Town. N. Daniels
Rape of Berlin. W. H. Baker
Rape of Europa. G. Sager
Rape of Sun Lee Fong. M. Macao
Rape of Venice. D. Wheatley
Raper. J. McCready
Raphael, M.D. Augustus Muir
Raphael "Resurrection." T. Newman
Rapid Fire. J. Butler
Rapidan. J. Gregory
Rapist. S. A. Krasney
Rapist. D. Logan
Rapt in Glory. E. Silberstang
Rapture Beyond. K. N. Burt
Rare Adventure. B. Fergusson
Rare Coin Score. R. Stark
Rascal of Quality. N. Carter
Rascals and Co. N. Carter
Rascal's Nerve. M. O. Rolfe
Rash Conclusions. G. W. Appleton
Rasp. P. MacDonald
Raspberry Jam. C. Wells
Rasprava. E. J. Harrison
Rasputin the Rascal Monk. W. LeQueux
Rasputinism in London. W. LeQueux
Rat. P. Bottome
Rat Alley. H. Robison
Rat Began to Gnaw the Rope. C. W. Grafton
Rat in a Trap. M. Vinter
Rat Pack. S. Stevens
Rat Race. D. Francis
Rat Trap. W. LeQueux
Rather a Common Sort of Crime. J. Porter
Rather a Vicious Gentleman. F. McAuliffe
Rather Cool for Mayhem. L. G. Blochman
Rather Like. J. Castier
Ratman's Notebooks. S. Gilbert
Rats. A. Christie
Rats' Castle. R. Bridges
Rattle His Bones. J. Shore
Rattler. J. Cassells
Rattlesnake. H. Pink
Rattlesnake. K. Tynan
Ravaged. S. Friedman
Ravagers. D. Hamilton
Rave for a Roughneck. H. Janson
Raven. M. E. Cooke
Raven. B. Goldie
Raven. E. Sudak
Raven Is a Blood Red Bird. D. J. Marlowe
Raven Never More. G. Marton
Ravencroft Mystery. W. H. L. Crauford
Ravenelle Riddle. E. B. Black
Ravenhurst. Marilyn Ross
Ravenkill. P. Warren
Raven's Causeway. C. Hodge
Raven's Eye. E. Bond
Raven's Feathers. D. Carey
Raven's Forge. J. Melville
Ravenscroft. D. Eden
Ravenscroft Affair. C. R. Gull
Ravenscroft Horror. C. R. Gull
Ravensdale Mystery. G. E. Locke
Ravensdene Court. J. S. Fletcher
Ravensgill. W. Mayne
Ravenshaw of Rietholine. B. Mitford
Ravensmount. M. McEvoy
Ravenswood. E. W. Gilliam
Ravenswood. J. L. Roberts
Ravenswood Hall. Angela Gray
Ravenswood Mystery. J. S. Fletcher
Raventree. S. Sloan
Ravine. K. Young
Ravishing Idiot. C. Exbrayat
Ravishing of Lady Mary Ware. D. Wheatley
Raw Deal for Dames. M. Hampton
Raw Edge. B. Appel
Raw Gold. J. B. Hendryx
Raw Material. G. B. Savi
Raw Summer. J. Blackmore

Rawdon Murder Case. J. H. Acott
Rawhide Vixen. Tod Conrad
Rawson of the Mounted. E. Dorrance
Raxl, Voodoo Princess. D. Daniels
Ray of Doom. W. S. Sykes
Rayner Case. R. Wray
Rayner-Slade Amalgamation. J. S. Fletcher
Ray's Adventure. Old Sleuth
Rays of Darkness. L. Bamburg
Re-Enter Arnholt. G. Latta
Re-Enter Dr. Fu Manchu. S. Rohmer
Re-Enter Fu Manchu. S. Rohmer
Re-Enter Sir John. C. Dane
Reach for the Shadows. A. Dwyer-Joyce
Reach of Fear. D. L. Mathews
Reaching Hand. A. MacKenzie
Reader Is Warned. Carter Dickson
Ready for Death. H. J. Hultman
Ready for the Tiger. Sam Ross
Ready or Not. I. S. Shriber
Ready Revenge. C. Arley
Ready to Burn. C. J. Daly
Ready to Die. J. Frederics
Real Cool Killers. C. Himes
Real Detective. G. Dilnot
Real Estate Skeleton Caper. W. J. Jones
Real Gold. G. M. Fenn
Real Gone Goose. G. Bagby
Real Gone Guy. F. Kane
Real Life. A. R. Weekes
Real Mrs. Daybrook. F. Warden
Real Serendipitous Kill. Hampton Stone
Real Thing. A. Philips
Realist. H. Flowerdew
Realization of Justus Moran. F. Carrel
Reap the Whirlwind. M. L. Roby
Reaper. G. Fairlie
Reaping the Whirlwind. Anonymous
Reaping the Whirlwind. N. Carter
Reardon. R. L. Pike
Reason for Loving. A. Furness
Reason for Madness. T. S. Drachman
Reason for Murder. A. Hocking
Reason for Murder. J. Usher
Reason for Violence. D. Doubtfire
Reason Why. M. B. Lowndes
Reasonable Doubt. Edgar Smith
Reasonable Doubt. J. S. Strange
Reasonable Man. R. Busby
Rebecca. D. Du Maurier
Rebecca of the Snatch Racket. B. Sarto
Rebecca's Pride. D. N. Douglass
Rebel Chief. H. Nisbet
Rebel Heart. A. Maybury
Rebel Lady. K. Lindsay
Rebel Wife. Rona Randall
Rebel Woman. H. Whittington
Rebellion. W. A. Ballinger
Rebellion. N. Harman
Rebellion. S. P. B. Mais
Rebels' Triumph. J. F. W. Hannay
Rebound. J. Mayo
Recalled by the Double-Four. E. P. Oppenheim
Recalled to Life. G. Allen
Receipt for Murder. Gwendoline Butler
Recess. H. Grisewood
Recipe for Diamonds. C. J. C. Hyne
Recipe for Homicide. L. G. Blochman
Recipe for Murder. A. Ridley
Reckless. R. Angel
Reckless Angel. M. B. Lowndes
Reckless Coulson. Jack Mann
Reckless Lady. R. Foley
Reckoning. H. Atkinson
Reckoning in Ice. J. R. L. Anderson
Reclining Figure. H. Kurnitz
Reclining Figure. M. Page
Reclining Nude. Maurice Watson
Recluse of Fifth Avenue. W. Martyn
Recoil. K. C. Groom
Recoil. J. L. Hardy
Recoil. B. How
Recoil. J. Thompson
Recoiling Vengeance. F. Barrett
Recollections of a Detective. Waters
Recollections of a Detective Police-Officer. Waters
Recollections of a Glasgow Detective Officer. T. P. MacNaught
Recollections of a Physician. W. H. Hillyard
Recollections of a Policeman. Waters
Recollections of a Relieving Officer. E. P. Rowsell
Recollections of a Sheriff's Officer. Waters
Recollections of an Irish Police Magistrate and Other Reminiscences of the South of Ireland. H. R. Addison
Reconnaissance. G. Gardiner
Reconnoitre Krellig. J. J. Deegan
Record No. 33. I. C. Clarke
Record of Jeffrye Cranfield. G. C. Keech
Record of the Case. W. M. Graydon
Records of Vincent Trill of the Detective Service. D. Donovan
Recover or Kill. L. Butler
Rectory Governess. F. Hume
Recurrent Melody. R. Pinget
Red Account. V. Gielgud
Red Aces. E. Wallace
Red Alert. P. Bryant
Red Altars. J. G. Brandon
Red Anger. G. Household
Red Bamboo. E. P. Thorne
Red Band. F. Du Boisgobey
Red Beard. P. Costello
Red Bicycle. F. Hume
Red Bishop. Howard Mason
Red Boomerang. J. G. Brandon
Red Boulders Mystery. P. Sebastian
Red Box. R. Stout
Red Box Clue. J. B. Ellis
Red Bridal. W. Westall
Red Bull. R. Stout
Red Button. Will Irwin
Red Camarilla. E. J. Harrison
Red Camelia. F. Du Boisgobey
Red Canyon Mystery. W. B. Lawson
Red Carnation. Augustus Muir
Red Carnation. B. E. Stevenson
Red Carnelian. A. Whitney
Red Carpet for the Shah. P. Ritner
Red Castle. H. C. Bailey
Red Castle Mystery. H. C. Bailey
Red Castle Women. M. Widdemer
Red Cavalier. G. E. Locke
Red Cecil, the Detective. Old Sleuth
Red Chancellor. W. Magnay
Red Chindvit Conspiracy. H. W. Holzer
Red Christmas. P. Ruell
Red Claws. M. Richmond
Red Club. H. R. Taunton
Red Coats Galloping. J. Welcome
Red Cobra. H. S. Banner
Red Cobra. F. Grierson
Red Colonel. G. Edgar
Red Colonel. G. Seton
Red Court Farm. H. Wood
Red Crescent. A. Murray
Red Cripple. C. Bradley
Red Dagger. J. Corbett
Red Dancer of Moscow. H. L. Gates
Red Danger. P. Wentworth
Red Darkness. A. B. Sherlock
Red Darkness. G. F. Worts
Red Dawning. M. Richmond
Red Death. G. Collins
Red Derelict. B. Mitford
Red Desert. H. Edmonds
Red Devil of the Air Police. J. Noy
Red Diamonds. J. H. McCarthy
Red Dice. Norman Lucas
Red Domino. W. W. Sayer
Red Dragon. W. Curtis
Red Dwarf. F. A. Symonds
Red Dwarf. M. Thynne
Red Eagle. Gavin Holt
Red Emerald. J. R. Scott
Red Emeralds. S. Gluck
Red Ending. H. Hervey
Red Escapade. R. Bax
Red Eye for the Baron. A. Morton
Red Eyes of Kali. T. C. H. Jacobs
Red Farm Mystery. J. Corbett
Red Fate. E. Forbes
Red Fathom. R. E. Alter
Red File for Callan. J. Mitchell
Red Flame of Erinpura. T. Mundy
Red Flower Kill. W. J. Sheldon
Red Flowers of Death. C. Rudd
Red Flows the Barada. D. Weir
Red for Danger! E. Price
Red for Murder. H. Kemp
Red Gardenias. Jonathan Latimer
Red Gate. R. Burke
Red Geranium. V. Siller
Red Glen. C. Campbell
Red Glove. D. Grant
Red God of Tragedy. N. Carter
Red Gold. M. Leighton
Red Greed. Marion Roberts
Red, Green and Amber. P. Traill
Red Guard. N. Carter
Red Hair. S. Kyle
Red-Haired Alibi. W. Collison
Red-Haired Death. S. Horler
Red-Haired Girl. C. Wells
Red Hand. S. Cobb
Red-Handed. L. Thayer
Red-Handed They Came. A. Wood
Red Harvest. D. Hammett
Red Hat. W. LeQueux
Red Hazard. A. O. Pollard
Red Head Herring. B. Healey
Red Head of the Red Sea. W. J. Makin
Red-Headed Dames and Murder. Roland Daniel
Red-Headed Man. F. Hume
Red Heart of the Incas. Jack Lewis
Red Heroin. W. Curtis
Red Herring. E. Acheson
Red Herring. W. Tucker
Red Herring Murder. P. D. Westbrook
Red Herrings. C. J. C. Hyne
Red Herrings Ltd. Laurence Kirk
Red Hill Tragedy. E. Southworth
Red Horsemen. K. Laing
Red, Hot and Deadly. M. Clinten
Red Hot and Morgue Bound. M. Brody
Red Hot Dollar and other stories from The Black Cat. H. D. Umbstaetter
Red Hot Ice. F. Kane
Red-Hot Murder. S. Levinson
Red Hotel. H. Hervey
Red House. G. A. Chamberlain
Red House. Mrs. Hungerford
Red House. Derek Lambert
Red House. E. Nesbit
Red House Mystery. Mrs. Hungerford
Red House Mystery. A. A. Milne

Red House on Rowan Street. R. Doubleday
Red Ice. J. Dallas
Red Idol. L. P. Greene
Red in the Morning. D. Yates
Red Invader. H. Edmonds
Red Is for Killing. G. Bagby
Red Is for Murder. P. A. Whitney
Red Jaguar. N. McFather
Red Jaguar. J. Manor
Red January. W. Chamberlain
Red Judas. D. Newton
Red Kite Clue. O. F. Jerome
Red Knight. J. N. Chance
Red Lacquer Case. H. R. Jorgensen
Red Lacquer Case. P. Wentworth
Red Lady. K. N. Burt
Red Lady. A. Wynne
Red Lamp. M. R. Rinehart
Red League. N. Carter
Red Ledger. F. Packard
Red Light. N. MacKenzie
Red-Light Will, the River Detective. Anonymous
Red Lights. G. Simenon
Red Lilac. L. Gorell
Red Lion. D. Tower
Red Lodge. V. Bridges
Red Lottery Ticket. F. Du Boisgobey
Red Mammon. D. Learmonth
Red Mark, and other stories. J. Russell
Red Mask. W. J. Makin
Red Masquerade. L. J. Vance
Red Mass. V. Williams
Red Menace. M. Grant
Red Mill Mystery. Detective Dunn
Red Mirage. P. Trent
Red Mirror Mystery. Gret Lane
Red Mist. J. Borgen
Red Money. F. Hume
Red Moon. J. B. Harris-Burland
Red Moon. K. Robeson
Red Morn. M. Pemberton
Red Mountain. W. W. Sayer
Red Mountain, Limited. E. A. Clancy
Red Mouse. W. H. Osborne
Red Murchison. Roland Daniel
Red Murder File. C. Dixon
Red Net. T. C. H. Jacobs
Red Nights of Paris. M. F. Goron
Red on Wight. D. Winsor
Red Owl. W. Gillette
Red Painted Box. M. Leighton
Red Paper. C. C. Hotchkiss
Red Paste Murders. A. Gask
Red Pavilion. M. Summerton
Red Pavilion. R. Van Gulik
Red Pawns. G. Griswold
Red Peril. C. Kernahan
Red Plague. N. Carter
Red Plague in Bolivia. M. Macao
Red Queen Club. A. Broome
Red Rafferty. H. B. Kaye
Red Rain Mystery. H. Hill
Red Raincoat. H. Bourne
Red Rajah. F. Whittaker
Red Rat's Daughter. G. Boothby
Red Rays. N. Carter
Red Rebellion. N. Carter
Red--Red--Red. A. Kent
Red, Red Rose. M. McEvoy
Red Redmaynes. E. Phillpotts
Red Revenge. C. E. Pearce
Red Revenge. G. A. Ralston
Red Rhapsody. C. Fitzsimmons
Red Riding Hood. E. Jordan
Red Right Hand. J. T. Rogers
Red Rivington. W. Westall
Red Road. S. Harvester

Red Rods. Dale Clark
Red Room. W. LeQueux
Red Rope. F. Gerard
Red Rose for Annabel. Agnes Russell
Red Rose for Maria. D. Downes
Red Sap. J. Easton
Red Saunders Bites the Dust. P. Renwick
Red Scar. A. Wynne
Red Scarf. G. Brewer
Red Scorpion. C. Buchanan
Red Sea Spy. W. J. Makin
Red Seal. M. Gerard
Red Seal. N. S. Lincoln
Red Shadow. P. Wentworth
Red Signal. N. Carter
Red Skull. F. Hume
Red Skull. K. Robeson
Red Sky. V. James
Red Sky at Night. H. McCutcheon
Red Sky in the Morning. R. Johnston
Red Slayer. E. Leslie
Red Snow at Darjeeling. L. G. Blochman
Red Spider. E. S. Brooks
Red Spider Web. B. Newman
Red Spinner. E. Snell
Red Square. A. Wood
Red Stain. A. Abdullah
Red Stain. S. Campbell
Red Stain. V. Loder
Red Stain. W. Magnay
Red Stands for Danger. R. Trevor
Red Star Mystery. C. Barry
Red Star of Night. W. A. MacKenzie
Red Stefan. P. Wentworth
Red Stilleto. A. Skene
Red Stockings. P. Fry
Red Stranger. Netley Lucas
Red Streak. P. Trent
Red Sun of Nippon. H. O. Yardley
Red Symbol. J. Ironside
Red Tape Murders. G. Verner
Red Tassel. D. Dodge
Red Threads. R. Stout
Red Thumb Mark. R. A. Freeman
Red Tiger. R. Carr
Red Token. O. Binns
Red Tower. L. V. Stevens
Red Triangle. N. Carter
Red Triangle. Arthur Morrison
Red Van. A. St. Aubyn
Red Van Mystery. G. Chester
Red Vulture. F. Sleath
Red War. J. Philips
Red Warning. V. Markham
Red Widow. W. LeQueux
Red Widow Murders. Carter Dickson
Red Wind. R. Chandler
Red Window. F. Hume
Red-Winged Angel. A. MacKinnon
Redbeard. L. A. Knight
Redbird Affair. L. V. Stevens
Redcap. P. McCutchan
Redding Straik. R. Aitken
Reddy Brant, His Adventures. W. C. Tuttle
Redeemed. C. R. B.
Redemption of Grace Milroy. C. Dawe
Redemption of Richard. Marguerite Bryant
Redemption Range. Gavin Holt
Redfern's Miracle. E. Trevor
Redfingers. W. M. Duncan
Redhead. W. L. Andersch
Redhead. J. Creasey
Redhead for Danger. Arthur MacLean
Redhead for Free. K. T. McCall
Redhead for Mike Shayne. B. Halliday

Redhead from Chicago. L. Royer
Redhead from Sun Dog. W. C. Tuttle
Redheads Are Poison. B. Winter
Redheads Cool Fast. B. Winter
Redheads Die Young. B. Diamond
Redman Cave Murder. E. Barker
Redmaynes. G. E. Locke
Redoubtable Dexter. G. Hackforth-Jones
Reduction of Staff. F. J. Whaley
Reeds in the Wind. C. Gleig
Reef of Gold. M. H. Hervey
Reef Pearlers. S. M. Parkman
Reefer Boy. H. Ellson
Reel of Death. R. Simons
Reference to Death. L. R. Davis
Reflection of Evil. J. Roffman
Reformation of Royce Remington. W. M. Graydon
Reformatory Girls. N. Tyre
Reformed Highwayman. G. W. M. Reynolds
Regan. I. K. Martin
Regan and the Manhattan File. I. K. Martin
Regarding Sherlock Holmes. A. Derleth
Regatta Mystery. A. Christie
Regent Street Raid. J. G. Brandon
Regent's Candlesticks. E. Kyle
Reginald Vernon. W. H. Hillyard
Regular Fraud. R. Jocelyn
Rehabilitated Man. Eric Lambert
Rehearsal for Death. G. Batson
Rehearsal for Death. Theodora Benson
Rehearsal for Murder. F. Bunce
Rehearsal for the Funeral. E. Colter
Reign of Terror. H. Desmond
Reimann Curse. J. Deweese
Reincarnation of Peter Proud. M. Ehrlich
Reins of Chance. C. R. Gull
Reivaulx Abbey. N. Davison
Rejected Bride. E. Southworth
Rejuvenation of Mrs. Semaphore. H. Godfrey
Relative Murder. A. Hocking
Relative Stranger. A. Stevenson
Relative to Death. S. Forbes
Relative to Murder. E. Warman
Relative to Poison. E. C. R. Lorac
Relative Values. H. C. McNeile
Release the Prisoner. A. Wood
Released for Death. Henry Wade
Relentless. B. Garfield
Relentless Current. M. E. Charlesworth
Relentless Storm. C. Lorrimer
Religious Body. C. Aird
Reluctant Assassin. J. Godey
Reluctant Assassin. A. Reynaud-Fourton
Reluctant Bride. C. Laffeaty
Reluctant Cloak and Dagger Man. Ernest Paul
Reluctant Duchess. M. Richmond
Reluctant Executioner. John Marsh
Reluctant Gunman. W. H. Baker
Reluctant Hangman and other stories of crime. G. Allen
Reluctant Heiress. G. H. Coxe
Reluctant Hostess. H. Janson
Reluctant Hussy. R. Burke
Reluctant Medium. L. Vardre
Reluctant Murderer. Bernice Carey
Reluctant Prodigal. H. L. V. Fletcher
Reluctant Rebel. M. Richmond
Reluctant Sleuth. F. Crane

Reluctant Spy. J. Blackburn
Reluctant Spy. T. D. Calnan
Reluctant Spy. J. Laflin
Reluctant Spy. H. Wood-Hill
Reluctant Transgressor. M. Kane
Remains to Be Seen. M. Cumberland
Remarkable Adventures of Christopher Poe. R. C. Brown
Remarkable Case of Burglary. H. R. F. Keating
Remarkable Feat. Old Sleuth
Remarkable "Shadow." Old Sleuth
Rembrandt Murder. H. J. Forman
Remember! J. G. Sarasin
Remember That Face. F. Findley
Remember the Summer We Lived at the Pad. A. Lamb
Remember with Tears. H. Arvonen
Remembered Anger. M. Albrand
Remembered Death. A. Christie
Remind Me to Forget. C. B. Dawson
Reminiscences of a Great French Detective. Anonymous
Reminiscences of a Rogue. F. Martyn
Reminiscences of Chief-Inspector Littlechild. J. G. Littlechild
Reminiscences of Solar Pons. A. Derleth
Remittance-Woman. A. Abdullah
Remote Control. H. Carmichael
Remote Journey. L. Handley
Remove the Bodies. E. Ferrars
Remover. Roland Daniel
Remover Returns. Roland Daniel
Removers. D. Hamilton
Render unto Caesar. K. Lindsay
Rendezvous. Evelyn Anthony
Rendezvous in Amsterdam. E. Randolph
Rendezvous in Australia. W. E. D. Ross
Rendezvous in Black. C. Woolrich
Rendezvous in Peking. Anne-Mariel
Rendezvous in Rio. G. Fallon
Rendezvous in Rio. Vince Howard
Rendezvous of Mysteries. K. S. Nakagawa
Rendezvous Off Newport. H. R. Simpson
Rendezvous on an Island. T. Claymore
Rendezvous with a Dead Man. N. Carter
Rendezvous with Danger. J. Corbett
Rendezvous with Danger. M. Pemberton
Rendezvous with Danger. Lynn Williams
Rendezvous with Death. J. Bentley
Rendezvous with Death. J. Corbett
Rendezvous with Death. J. Paull
Rendezvous with Fear. N. Davis
Rendezvous with the Past. K. M. Knight
Renegade Cop. Jonathan Craig
Renegade from Russia. H. C. Davis
Renegade Sheriff. W. C. Tuttle
Reno Rendezvous. L. Ford
Renshaw Fanning's Quest. B. Mitford
Repaid in Like Coin. N. Carter
Reparation. O. Williams
Repeat Performance. W. O'Farrell
Repeat the Instructions. R. V. Beste
Repent at Leisure. R. Foley
Reply Paid. H. F. Heard
Report for a Corpse. H. Kane
Report from Argyll. A. MacKinnon
Report from Group 17. R. C. O'Brien
Report to the Commissioner. James Mills
Reporter. J. Stearn
Reporter. E. Wallace
Reporter Detective. D. J. MacKenzie
Reporter's Triumph. S. Campbell
Reporting Murder. D. Maggs
Reprieve of Roger Maine. G. McDonell
Reprisal. Arthur Gordon
Reprisal. W. P. McGivern
Reprisal. E. Vance

Reputation for a Song. E. Grierson
Requiem for a Blonde. K. Roos
Requiem for a Chaser. J. Conway
Requiem for a Cop. V. B. Miller
Requiem for a Loser. J. Wainwright
Requiem for a Rat. J. Godwin
Requiem for a Redhead. A. Bocca
Requiem for a Redhead. L. Hardy
Requiem for a Schoolgirl. I. T. Ross
Requiem for Charles. H. Carmichael
Requiem for Redheads. W. H. Baker
Requiem for Robert. M. Fitt
Requiem for Rogues. David Hume
Requiem for Two Sisters. J. Turner
Requiem in Utopia. R. Starnes
Requiem of Sharks. P. Buchanan
Rescuing Rupert. G. Thorne
Reservation for Murder. J. Wright
Reservations for Death. B. Kendrick
Resident. W. Tute
Resident Magistrate. B. Marnan
Resolute Jack. Old Sleuth
Resolved to be Rich. E. H. Cooper
Resort to War. G. Revelli
Resources of Mycroft Holmes. C. Andrews
Respectable Miss Parkington-Smith. P. Allardyce
Respectable Woman. David Fletcher
Rest Hollow Mystery. R. N. Porter
Rest in Agony. I. Jorgenson
Rest Is Silence. P. Barrington
Rest Is Silence. V. Coffman
Rest Must Die. R. Foster
Restless Corpse. A. Pruitt
Restless Hands. B. Fischer
Restless Quiet. D. O'Connor
Results of a Duel. F. Du Boisgobey
Results of an Accident. T. C. H. Jacobs
Resurrection Day. K. Robeson
Resurrection Man. T. Walsh
Resurrection Murder Case. S. H. Page
Resurrection of His Grace. C. Rae-Brown
Resurrection Rock. E. Balmer
Retake. R. Hubbard
Retaliation. H. Flowerdew
Retired from the Yard. A. Parsons
Retreat from Oblivion. D. Goodis
Retreat into Night. R. Glendinning
Retribution. D. Essex
Retribution. C. R. Gull
Retribution. T. P. Prest
Retribution. E. Southworth
Return. D. Winston
Return a Gain for Murder. R. Verron
Return from the Ashes. H. Monteilhet
Return from the Dead. M. Burton
Return from Vorkuta. David St. John
Return of A. J. Raffles. G. Greene
Return of Anthony Trent. W. Martyn
Return of Arsene Lupin. M. Leblanc
Return of Blackshirt. B. Graeme
Return of Blue Mask. A. Morton
Return of Bulldog Drummond. H. C. McNeile
Return of Cardannesley. G. Ellinger
Return of Clubfoot. V. Williams
Return of Colonel Pho. Ronald Simpson
Return of Dick Barton. Anonymous
Return of Dr. Fu-Manchu. S. Rohmer
Return of Frank Clamart. H. C. Rowland
Return of Frass. J. Chancellor
Return of George Washington. L. Brent
Return of Grey Shadow. G. E. Rochester
Return of Henry Prince. C. F. Gregg
Return of Hercules, Esq. Gwyn Evans
Return of Jennifer. H. Upshaw
Return of Jenny Weaver. M. Turnbull
Return of Mick Cardby. David Hume
Return of Mr. Budd. G. Verner
Return of Moriarty. J. Gardner

Return of Nighthawk. S. Horler
Return of Raffles. B. Perowne
Return of Sanders of the River. F. Gerard
Return of Sherlock Holmes. A. C. Doyle
Return of Solar Pons. A. Derleth
Return of Sumuru. S. Rohmer
Return of the Assassin. A. Tack
Return of the Black Gang. G. Fairlie
Return of the Ceteosaurus, and other tales. G. Radcliffe
Return of the Continental Op. D. Hammett
Return of the Cornish Soldier. Michael Barrett
Return of the Hood. M. Spillane
Return of the Night Wind. V. Vanardy
Return of the Opium Wars. M. Macao
Return of the Shadow. W. B. Gibson
Return of the Shadow. M. Grant
Return of the Vagabond. G. M. Cohan
Return of Van Weik. C. Evelyn
Return of Wu Fang. Roland Daniel
Return of Yesterday. K. Ingram
Return They Must. John Marsh
Return to a Traitor. T. B. Morris
Return to Adventure. N. Deane
Return to Aylforth. A. Eliot
Return to Ballyrock. A. Furness
Return to Clerycastle. M. Heath
Return to Cottington. F. Bamford
Return to Darkness. W. D. Roberts
Return to Glenshael. M. Elgin
Return to Gravesend. M. Eyre
Return to Hawkeston Hall. L. Whitaker
Return to Love. J. Blackmore
Return to Octavia. D. Macomber
Return to Terror. M. Albrand
Return to Terror. T. Charles
Return to Terror. F. Hurt
Return to the Alcazar. E. Kyle
Return to the River. K. Hewitt
Return to the Scene. Q. Patrick
Return to Tiger Bay. J. M. Walsh
Return to Vienna. N. Buckingham
Return to Vikki. J. Tomerlin
Return to Violence. W. Spann
Reuben Foreman, the Village Blacksmith. D. Dale
Reunion. W. Kuhns
Reunion in Florida. T. Claymore
Reunion in Renfrew. W. E. D. Ross
Reunion with Murder. T. Fuller
Revealed by Lightning. I. Stark
Revelations of a Detective. A. Forrester
Revelations of a Lady Detective. Anonymous
Revelations of a Police Court Interpreter. J. Jacobsen
Revelations of a Private Detective. A. Forrester
Revelations of Inspector Morgan. O. Crawford
Revelations of the Secret Service. W. LeQueux
Revellers. L. Tracy
Revenge! R. Barr
Revenge. J. Ehrlich
Revenge at Indy. L. Kenyon
Revenge at Nightfall. Elliot Bailey
Revenge Can Wait. Irene Alexander
Revenge in a Convent. C. B. Boyd
Revenge Incorporated. Dennis Phillips
Revenge of Annie Charlie. A. Fry
Revenge of Fantomas. M. Allain
Revenge of Gilbert Strange. W. Wood

Title Index

Revenge of Moriarty. J. Gardner
Revenge of Taurus. R. Lory
Revenge of Valerie. H. Nisbet
Revenge with a Vengeance. C. L. Reid
Revenger. J. Messmann
Revenue Detective. Anonymous
Revenue Detective. Police Captain James
Rev. Captain Kettle. C. J. C. Hyne
Reverend Gentleman. J. M. Cobban
Rev. Miles Latimer. L. Gardiner
Reverend Randolph and the Wages of Sin. C. M. Smith
Reverse the Charges. B. Flynn
Revised Proof. P. Conway
Revolt from Bondage. H. D. Dearden
Revolt in the Desert. J. Robb
Revolt of Beatrix. F. Whishaw
Revolt of Jill Braddock. S. Friedman
Revolution Script. B. Moore
Revolutionist. E. Garth
Revue Girl. A. Applin
Reward. Michael Barrett
Reward for a Defector. M. Underwood
Reward for the Baron. A. Morton
Reward for Treason. T. C. H. Jacobs
Rexworth Mystery. S. Cummings
Rhapsody in Fear. J. N. Chance
Rhea. R. De Pont-Jest
Rhine Replica. M. Albrand
Rhinemann Exchange. R. Ludlum
Rhino for Rosamund. D. Fearon
Rhino in the Kitchen. D. W. MacArthur
Rhodesia. N. Carter
Rhododendron Man. J. A. Tyson
Ribs of Death. Joan Aiken
Rich and Dangerous Game. L. White
Rich and the Damned. R. Himmel
Rich Die Hard. B. Nichols
Rich Get It All. F. Huston
Rich, Hip and Deadly. H. Paul
Rich Husband. J. H. Riddell
Rich Is the Treasure. M. Procter
Rich Man. G. Simenon
Rich Man, Dead Man. H. Waugh
Rich Man, Murder. H. Waugh
Rich Man, Poor Man. M. Foster
Rich Man's Daughter. J. H. Riddell
Rich Man's Wife. D. Donovan
Rich to Die. B. Tutton
Rich Uncle. C. Keith
Rich Way to Die. K. Evans
Richard. Marguerite Bryant
Richard Arbour. J. Payn
Richard Parker. T. P. Prest
Richardson Goes Abroad. B. Thomson
Richardson Scores Again. B. Thomson
Richardson Solves a Dartmoor Mystery. B. Thomson
Richardson's Second Case. B. Thomson
Richest Corpse in Show Business. Dan Morgan
Richest Girl in the World. V. Coffman
Richest Man. E. Shanks
Richlands. A. S. Turnbull
Richmond. Anonymous
Rick. D. G. Falk
Rickerby's Folly. T. Gallon
Ricksha Clue. G. Ellinger
Rickshaw Bend. H. Arvonen
Ricochet. B. Copper
Ricochet. J. F. Straker
Riddle, and other stories. W. De La Mare
Riddle Me This. M. Roscoe
Riddle of a Lady. Anthony Gilbert
Riddle of Big Ben. A. Parsons
Riddle of Crocodile Creek. W. M. Graydon
Riddle of Crooked Creek. J. W. Booth
Riddle of Cubicle 7. A. Parsons
Riddle of Dead Man's Mine. M. Frazer
Riddle of Dead Man's Pit. R. C. Armour
Riddle of Double Island. M. Corrigan
Riddle of Five Needle Creek. A. Blair
Riddle of Garth. Augustus Muir
Riddle of Helena. C. Houghton
Riddle of Identities. N. Carter
Riddle of John Rowe. Winston Graham
Riddle of Loch Lemman. A. O. Pollard
Riddle of Nap's Hollow. L. A. Knight
Riddle of Rainbow Mountain. J. A. Rennie
Riddle of Riverdale. J. W. Bobin
Riddle of Samson. A. Garve
Riddle of the Amber Room. H. E. Hill
Riddle of the Amber Ship. M. E. Hanshew
Riddle of the Black Racketeers. J. Hunter
Riddle of the Blazing Bungalow. S. Blakesley
Riddle of the Body on the Road. E. S. Brooks
Riddle of the Book-Mark. W. J. Lomax
Riddle of the Burmese Curse. A. Parsons
Riddle of the Cambrian Venus. D. W. F. Hardie
Riddle of the Captured Quisling. A. Parsons
Riddle of the Cloisters. E. Burton
Riddle of the Crooked Gambler. R. Hardinge
Riddle of the Dead. L. Bamburg
Riddle of the Dead Cats. A. Blackmon
Riddle of the Dead Man's Bay. J. G. Brandon
Riddle of the Disguised Greek. A. Parsons
Riddle of the Eighth Guest. B. Wheeler
Riddle of the Emeralds. P. C. De Crespigny
Riddle of the Escaped P.O.W. A. Parsons
Riddle of the Evil Eye. P. Quiroule
Riddle of the Film Star's Jewels. L. Jackson
Riddle of the Florentine Folio. E. S. Liddon
Riddle of the Forest. B. Tozer
Riddle of the French Alibi. W. Tyrer
Riddle of the Frozen Flame. M. E. Hanshew
Riddle of the Gambling Den. A. Parsons
Riddle of the Garage. H. H. C. Gibbons
Riddle of the Gas Meter. G. Chester
Riddle of the Golden Fingers. E. J. Murray
Riddle of the Great Art Exhibition. R. C. Armour
Riddle of the Greek Financier. J. G. Brandon
Riddle of the Green Cylinder. W. Jardine
Riddle of the Highwayman's Stone. R. Hardinge
Riddle of the Indian Alibi. A. Parsons
Riddle of the Invisible Menace. R. Hardinge
Riddle of the Italian Prisoner. J. Hunter
Riddle of the Keys. J. A. Kolbe
Riddle of the Kidnapped Pensioner. G. Chester
Riddle of the Lascar's Head. L. H. Brooks
Riddle of the Leather Bottle. J. Drummond
Riddle of the Lost Emigrant. R. C. Armour
Riddle of the Lost Ship. J. Hunter
Riddle of the Marsh. J. Blyth
Riddle of the Million Pound Bet. W. J. Bayfield
Riddle of the Missing Fire Watcher. G. Chester
Riddle of the Mummy Case. J. Drummond
Riddle of the Murdered Fisherman. G. Chester
Riddle of the Mysterious Light. M. E. Hanshew
Riddle of the Night. T. W. Hanshew
Riddle of the Night Garage. G. Chester
Riddle of the Phantom Plague. G. Verner
Riddle of the Prince's Stooge. A. Parsons
Riddle of the Purple Emperor. T. W. Hanshew
Riddle of the Rail. F. M. White
Riddle of the Rajah's Curios. A. Parsons
Riddle of the Ranch. W. Jardine
Riddle of the Ravens. L. Gribble
Riddle of the Receiver's Hoard. J. Drummond
Riddle of the Red Dragon. Gwyn Evans
Riddle of the Registry Office. H. H. C. Gibbons
Riddle of the Ring. W. LeQueux
Riddle of the River. J. Wear-Gifford
Riddle of the Roost. L. Brock
Riddle of the Rose. W. B. M. Ferguson
Riddle of the Rovers. A. B. Maurice
Riddle of the Ruins. L. Jackson
Riddle of the Runaway Cat. H. H. C. Gibbons
Riddle of the Russian Bride. A. Parsons
Riddle of the Russian Gold. G. H. Teed
Riddle of the Russian Princess. E. S. Liddon
Riddle of the Sands. E. Childers
Riddle of the Sealed Room. R. Hardinge
Riddle of the Smiling Man. J. Hunter
Riddle of the Spanish Circus. M. Corrigan
Riddle of the Spinning Wheel. M. E. Hanshew
Riddle of the Straits. H. Edmonds
Riddle of the Sunken Garden. D. Stuart
Riddle of the Three Marked Men. G. N. Philips
Riddle of the Traveling Skull. H. S. Keeler
Riddle of the Turkish Baths. Gwyn Evans
Riddle of the Ugly Face. P. Quiroule
Riddle of the Uncensored Letter. J. Hunter
Riddle of the West End Hairdresser. H. H. C. Gibbons
Riddle of the Winged Death. H. P. Hanshew
Riddle of the Workman Squire. L. Jackson
Riddle of the Yellow Zuri. H. S. Keeler
Riddle of the Yukon. L. C. Douthwaite
Riddle of Three-Way Creek. R. Cullum
Riddle of Wraye. J. Laurence
Riddles of Hildegarde Withers. S. Palmer
Riddles Read. D. Donovan
Ride a Dead Horse. B. Edmunds
Ride a High Horse. R. S. Prather
Ride a Paper Tiger. W. Ash
Ride a Tiger. D. Orgill
Ride a Tiger. A. A. Randall
Ride a White Dolphin. A. Maybury
Ride for a Fall. V. Gielgud
Ride on a Tiger. D. Gray
Ride out the Storm. John Harris
Ride the Dark Storm. N. Jones
Ride the Gold Mare. O. Demaris
Ride the Man Down. R. Dolphin
Ride the Nightmare. F. Dudley
Ride the Nightmare. R. Matheson
Ride the Pink Horse. D. B. Hughes
Ride the Roller Coaster. C. Brown

R

Ride West of the Law. R. Wilkes-Hunter
Ride with Terror. Charles Henry
Rider in the Sky. L. A. Knight
Rider of Waroona. G. Firth Scott
Riders of the Sands. W. W. Sayer
Ridgway Woman. R. Neely
Rififi in New York. A. Le Breton
Rifled Gold. W. C. Tuttle
Rigdale Puzzle. C. Kingston
Rigging the Evidence. C. Carnac
Right and Wrong. B. Z. Spencer
Right for Murder. L. White
Right for Trouble. N. Easton
Right Hand Opposite. R. M. Stern
Right Honourable Corpse. M. Murray
Right Murder. C. Rice
Right of Reply. J. Harris
Right to Die. R. Stout
Right to Kill. R. R. Ryan
Right Turn for Murder. R. Verron
Right You Are, Mr. Moto. J. P. Marquand
Righted Wrong. E. Yates
Righteous Abel. J. Remenham
Rights of Mallaroche. C. N. Boyle
Rigoville Match. D. Walker
Riley of the Special Branch. L. Gribble
Rim-Fire, Detective. C. Ballew
Rim of Terror. H. T. Teilhet
Rim of the Pit. Hake Talbot
Rim Rider. W. C. Tuttle
Rim-World Legacy. F. A. Javor
Rimfire Murders. Frank O'Brian
Rinaldi Rinaldini, Captain of Banditti. C. A. Vulpius
Ring-a-Ding-Ding. F. Kane
Ring-a-Ding Girl. D. Rico
Ring-a-Ding UFO's. R. Tralins
Ring and the Lamp. W. Rollins
Ring and Walk In. M. Borgenicht
Ring Around a Rogue. J. M. Flynn
Ring Around a Murder. G. Bagby
Ring Around Rosa. W. C. Gault
Ring Around Rosy. Gordon Davis
Ring for a Noose. Anthony Gilbert
Ring for Luck. J. Pudney
Ring in Meiji. W. Butler
Ring o' Bells. G. R. Sims
Ring of Darkness. K. Ostrander
Ring of Dust. N. Carter
Ring of Eyes. H. Footner
Ring of Innocent. B. Flynn
Ring of Iron. I. Stark
Ring of Liars. J. N. Chance
Ring of Mischief. M. Summerton
Ring of Rascals. N. Carter
Ring of Roses. J. Blackburn
Ring of Truth. G. H. Coxe
Ring the Bell at Zero. H. L. Nelson
Ring the Bell, Sister! L. Bell
Ring Twice for Murder. A. Spiller
Ring Up Nighthawk. S. Horler
Ringed with Fire. A. Campbell
Ringer. D. Shannon
Ringer. E. Wallace
Ringer Returns. E. Wallace
Ringing Sands. O. Binns
Ringnecker. S. H. Courtier
Rings on Her Finger. Laurence Kirk
Rio Casino Intrigue. V. W. Mason
Rio d'Oro. N. Tranter
Rio Rustlers. J. Dorrance
Riot Act. R. Philmore
Riot '71. L. Peters
Rip-Off! B. J. Hurwood
Rip-Off. W. C. Ulsh
Ripe for Development. John Gloag
Ripe for Rapture. H. Janson
Ripe Fruit. J. McPartland
Ripley Under Ground. P. Highsmith
Ripley's Game. P. Highsmith

Ripper. M. Procter
Ripper File. Elwyn Jones
Ripper Murders. M. Procter
Ripper Returns. A. Skene
Ripple on the Water. D. M. Low
Rippling Ruby. J. S. Fletcher
Rise and Fall of Legs Diamond. O. H. Gaylord
Rise at Dawn. N. Fisher
Rise of Ruderick Clowd. J. Flynt
Rise with the Wind. A. C. Marin
Risifi's Daughter. A. K. Green
Rising of the Lark. S. Styles
Rising of the Moon. G. Mitchell
Rising Sea. M. Hastings
Rising Star. D. C. Murray
Rising Storm. D. Wheatley
Rising Sun. H. L. V. Fletcher
Rising Suns. John Gloag
Risk. L. Earl
Risk All for Love. M. Richmond
Risky! L. Della
Risky Game. H. Bindloss
Risky Way to Kill. R. Lockridge
Rissole Mystery. S. Fowler
Rita Makes a Killing. E. Ellison
Rita Takes a Ride. N. Perrelli
Rites for a Killer. J. M. Fox
Ritter Double-Cross. F. Nolan
Ritual in the Dark. Colin Wilson
Rival Claimants. E. P. Palmer
Rival Detectives. L. L. Lynch
Rival Detectives. H. Rockwood
Rival Lovers. Anonymous
Rival Lovers. O. Bradbury
Rival Millionaires. L. Fitzhamon
Rival Stables. M. K. Douglas
Rivals. T. P. Prest
River and the Rose. S. Abbott
River Detective and the Wharf Rat's Game. Old Sleuth
River Gang. Roland Daniel
River Gets Wider. R. L. Gordon
River Girl. C. Williams
River Grown Deep. M. Pereira
River House. Mrs. Mary Armat
River House Mystery. G. Verner
River House Mystery. S. Warwick
River in the Dark. M. Latham
River Men. G. Verner
River Mystery. A. J. Rees
River of Diamonds. T. Craig
River of Diamonds. G. Jenkins
River of Fear. Leslie T. White
River of Ice. K. Robeson
River of Marriage. A. Furness
River of No Return. L. T. White
River of Pearls. R. De Pont-Jest
River of Stars. E. Wallace
River of Unrest. B. Mitford
River Passage. E. L. Long
River Pirate. C. F. Coe
River Rising. J. North
River Secrets. B. Hemyng
River Syndicate. C. E. Carryl
River Tragedy. Old Sleuth
River Will Hide Me. A. Wood
Riverport Mail. O. Wright
Rivers to Cross. G. Goodchild
Rivers to Cross. R. Pertwee
Riverside Club Murder. A. Skene
Riverside Mystery. J. G. Brandon
Riverside 90. D. Enefer
Riverside Villas Murder. K. Amis
Riverslea. G. Norway
Riverton Wagers. H. Collinson Owen
Rivertown. J. L. Roberts
Riverwood. J. Corby

Riverwood. M. Lynch
Riviera Love Story. S. Jepson
Riviera Nights. B. Sarto
Riviera Showdown. H. Janson
Roach & Co., Pirates, and other stories. H. Fuller
Road. V. Siller
Road and the Star. B. Mather
Road Back. B. M. Scott
Road Back. S. Warwick
Road Block. H. Waugh
Road End. W. Morrison
Road Floozie. D. Glinto
Road from Chilanga. D. W. MacArthur
Road Home. G. Vaizey
Road House Murder. A. Skene
Road House Murders. R. P. Koehler
Road Through the Wall. S. Jackson
Road to Bagdad. G. F. Gibbs
Road to Ballarat. K. Lindsay
Road to Canossa. J. Wood
Road to Desperation. M. H. Bradley
Road to El Saida. Paul Townend
Road to Folly. L. Ford
Road to Fortune. F. A. Kummer
Road to Gandolfo. M. Shepherd
Road to Glenfairlie. D. Garth
Road to Hell. E. Jackson
Road to Hell. H. Monteilhet
Road to London. D. S. Foster
Road to Marrakesh. G. Goodchild
Road to Midnight. M. Lynch
Road to Murder. V. Gunn
Road to Rhuine. S. Troy
Road to Romance. A. Soutar
Road to Ruin. Anonymous
Road to the Coast. J. Harris
Road to the Moon. W. C. Tuttle
Road to the Snail. W. P. McGivern
Road Winds Back. P. Conway
Roadblock. M. Borgenicht
Roadhouse Girl. D. Reid
Roadhouse Mystery. J. G. Brandon
Roadknight. R. M. Gilchrist
Road's End. Albert Conroy
Roads of Destiny. O. Henry
Roadside Night. E. N. Nistler
Roag's Syndicate. George Davis
Roanleigh. G. Mockler
Rob the Lady. Jonathan Burke
Robber Countess. S. Cobb
Robber King. P. Tyrell
Robberies Co., Ltd. N. Lloyd
Robbery at Portage Bend. T. Lund
Robbery at Rudwick House. V. L. Whitechurch
Robbery Blue. R. Busby
Robbery of the Orphans. F. Du Boisgobey
Robbery Under Arms. R. Boldrewood
Robbery with Violence. J. Rhode
Robe of Lucifer. F. M. White
Robert Ainsleigh. M. E. Braddon
Robert Ashton's Wedding Day, and other stories. H. Wood
Robert Bruce, the Hero King of Scotland. G. W. M. Reynolds
Robert Macaire. Anonymous
Robert Macaire in England. G. W. M. Reynolds
Robert the Devil. G. Warden
Roberta Died. G. M. Wilson
Robespierre Serial. N. Luard
Robin and the 7 Hoods. J. Pearl
Robin Grey. C. Gibbon
Robin Hoodwinker, V.C. G. Davison

Robin Redbreast in a Cage. Myrtle
    Johnston
Robineau Look. K. M. Knight
Robineau Murders. K. M. Knight
Robinson. M. Spark
Robot Detective. M. Billett
Robthorne Mystery. J. Rhode
Rochemer Hag. L. W. King
Rock. H. Ellson
Rock! C. Stratton
Rock Ahead. E. Yates
Rock Baby. M. Woodhouse
Rock Harvest. H. C. Rae
Rock in the Baltic. R. Barr
Rock of Ages. F. H. Rose
Rock of Diamond. J. Quartermain
Rock of Justice. H. M. Richardson
Rock Rude. E. Stewart
Rockabilly. H. Ellison
Rockabye Contract. P. Atlee
Rocket for the Toff. J. Creasey
Rocket to the Morgue. H. H. Holmes
Rockets--Operation Manhattan. H.
    Edmonds
Rocking Chair. F. Y. McHugh
Rockingham Diamond. H. Collinson Owen
Rocklitz. G. R. Preedy
Rocks and Ruin. H. J. Calin
Rocksburg Railroad Murders. K. C.
    Constantine
Rocky Libido in San Francisco. L. Folder
Rocky Mountain. Duff Johnson
Rocky Rhodes. W. C. Tuttle
Rococo Coffin. Richard Brown
Rod of Anger. D. Nabarro
Rod of Justice. A. Askew
Rod of the Snake. V. Shortt
Rodeo Murder Mystery. H. Pink
Roderick of Kildare. S. Cobb
Rodriguez Affair. J. Pattinson
Roger Bennion's Double. H. Adams
Roger Quinney. P. H. Irving
Roger Sheringham and the Vane Mystery.
    A. Berkeley
Roger Sinclair's Treasure. N. Worth
Rogue. T. W. H. Crosland
Rogue. W. E. Norris
Rogue Aunt. J. N. Chance
Rogue by Compulsion. V. Bridges
Rogue Cop. W. P. McGivern
Rogue Haven. B. Home
Rogue in Ambush. H. Hill
Rogue in Love. T. Gallon
Rogue Male. G. Household
Rogue of Afganistan. W. M. Graydon
Rogue of Quality. N. Carter
Rogue of Rye. W. W. Dixon
Rogue Ransome--Manhunter. Dan Morgan
Rogue Ransome--Racket Buster. Dan Morgan
Rogue Ransome--Triggerman. Dan Morgan
Rogue Royal. Gwyn Evans
Rogue Running. M. Procter
Rogue with a Past. R. Wesley
Rogue Worth Trapping. N. Carter
Rogues. R. H. Sherard
Rogues and Company. I. A. R. Wylie
Rogues and Diamonds. S. Jepson
Rogues and Vagabonds. G. R. Sims
Rogue's Badge. C. N. Buck
Rogue's Castle. S. Stanley
Rogue's Coat. T. Du Bois
Rogue's Conscience. D. C. Murray
Rogues Fall Out. H. Adams
Rogues Fall Out. F. Warden
Rogue's Gambit. A. Caillou
Rogue's Harbour. J. T. Story

Rogue's Harvest. N. Cromarty
Rogues' Haven. R. Bridges
Rogue's Heiress. T. Gallon
Rogue's Holiday. M. March
Rogues in Arcady. W. Magnay
Rogues in Clover. P. Wilde
Rogues in the Forest. C. T. Stoneham
Rogues' Island. B. Perowne
Rogue's Life. W. Collins
Rogues Ltd. C. R. Gull
Rogue's Luck. A. Wright
Rogues' March. G. Dilnot
Rogue's March. E. W. Hornung
Rogues' March. M. Turnbull
Rogue's Murder. W. Ard
Rogues of Fortune. J. J. Chichester
Rogues of Ransom. G. H. Teed
Rogues of Society, and The Doctor of
    Duddlestone. G. F. Underhill
Rogues of the Desert. W. M. Graydon
Rogues of the North. A. M. Treynor
Rogues' Paradise. E. Pugh
Rogue's Progress. E. Oliver
Rogues Rampant. G. Ashe
Rogue's Ransom. G. Ashe
Rogue's Reach. N. Carter
Rogues' Republic. G. H. Teed
Rogues' Syndicate. F. Froest
Rogue's Tragedy. B. Capes
Rokewood Tragedy. M. Pinkerton
Roland Yorke. H. Wood
Roles and Relations. D. Sarmiento
Roll Film Mystery. M. Poole
Roll, Jordan, Roll. D. P. Clark
Roll-Top Desk Mystery. C. Wells
Rollicking Rogue. J. McCulley
Rolling Stone. P. Wentworth
Rolling Stones. O. Henry
Rollo of Normandy. S. Cobb
Roman Collar Detective. G. Johnson
Roman Gold. Michael Lewis
Roman Hat Mystery. E. Queen
Roman Mystery. R. Bagot
Roman Ring. C. P. Bracken
Roman Way. G. V. McFadden
Romance at Hillyard House. K. Norris
Romance at Random. H. B. M. Watson
Romance Comes to Scotland Yard. H. Black
Romance in Crimson. O. R. Cohen
Romance in the First Degree. O. R. Cohen
Romance of a Common Life. Waters
Romance of a Coward. M. Dekobra
Romance of a Madhouse. A. M. Meadows
Romance of a Maid of Honour. R. Marsh
Romance of a Million Dollars. E. Dejeans
Romance of a Pretty Girl. R. De Pont-
    Jest
Romance of a Queen. W. Chesney
Romance of a Salvation Army Girl. Old
    Sleuth
Romance of a Spy. E.7.
Romance of an Alter Ego. L. Bryce
Romance of Elaine. A. B. Reeve
Romance of Hellerism. A. S. Gifford
Romance of Lilies. C. H. Montague
Romance of Nikko Cheyne. R. Pertwee
Romance of Poisons. R. Cromie
Romance of Politics. A. Upward
Romance of the Forest. A. Radcliffe
Romance of the Ruby. G. Campbell
Romance of the Woods. F. Whishaw
Romance on the Rhine. Elsie Lee
Romances of Crime. J. M'Levy
Romances of Mayfair. Anonymous
Romances of the Law. R. E. Francillon
Romances of the Road. Thormanby
Romanoff Jewels. M. Grant
Romanov Succession. B. Garfield

Romantic Assignment. Elsie Lee
Romantic Road. G. Rawlence
Romantic Stories of the Legal Profession.
    R. E. Francillon
Romany Curse. S. Somers
Rome Express. Ruth Alexander
Rome Express. A. Griffiths
Romelle. W. R. Burnett
Ronald o' the Moors. G. E. Locke
Ronald Standish. H. C. McNeile
Roof. D. Whitelaw
Rook Takes Knight. S. Palmer
Rookery. H. C. Rae
Rookery Detective. Anonymous
Rookies. C. Parker
Rook's Gambit. S. Rattray
Rook's Nest. G. W. Appleton
Rooksmiths. S. Truss
Room at the Bottom. J. L. Potter
Room at the Hotel Ambre. A. Armstrong
Room Beneath the Stairs. K. St. Clair
Room Five. H. Drummond
Room for a Body. J. Bell
Room for a Ghost. Winifred Duke
Room for Murder. T. B. Dewey
Room for Murder. D. M. Disney
Room 14. M. Annesley
Room in Quiver Court. J. Cassells
Room in the Tower. J. Blackmore
Room in the Tower and other stories.
    E. F. Benson
Room Nineteen. F. Warden
Room Number 6. J. J. Farjeon
Room Number 3 and other stories. A. K.
    Green
Room of Mirrors. N. Carter
Room of Mirrors. H. Flowerdew
Room of Secrets. W. LeQueux
Room Opposite, and other tales of
    mystery and imagination. F. M. Mayor
Room Service. Alan Williams
Room 13. E. Wallace
Room 37. H. Howard
Room to Die In. E. Queen
Room to Swing. E. Lacy
Room 12a. A. Marsh
Room Under the Stairs. Herman Landon
Room Upstairs. Mildred Davis
Room Upstairs. M. Dickens
Room with Dark Mirrors. V. Johnston
Room with No Escape. A. Barber
Room with the Iron Shutters. A. Wynne
Room with the Tassels. C. Wells
Room Without a Key. W. E. D. Ross
Rooming House. B. Roueche
Rooms at Mrs. Oliver's. K. Kellow
Rooney. C. Cookson
Root and Branch. N. Tranter
Root of All Evil. J. S. Fletcher
Root of All Evil. F. Marryat
Root of All Evil. D. Shannon
Root of All Evil. I. Stark
Root of Evil. J. Cross
Root of Evil. E. K. Goldthwaite
Root of His Evil. W. Ard
Root of His Evil. J. M. Cain
Rooted Sorrow. P. M. Hubbard
Roots of Fury. I. Shulman
Rope. P. Hamilton
Rope. A. Hitchcock
Rope Began to Hang the Butcher. C. W.
    Grafton
Rope Broke. D. Barr
Rope by Arrangement. H. Clandon
Rope-Dancer. V. Marchetti
Rope Enough. J. S. Strange
Rope Fodder. O. Thomas
Rope for a Convict. R. C. Woodthorpe
Rope for a Lady. B. Sarto
Rope for an Ape. D. Chambers

Rope for Breakfast. A. Spiller
Rope for Christmas. F. Griffin
Rope for General Dietz. J. Rossiter
Rope for the Baron. A. Morton
Rope for the Hanging. N. Morland
Rope for the Judge. H. Hawton
Rope of Sand. F. Bonnamy
Rope of Sand. C. Franklin
Rope of Sand. P. Traill
Rope of Slender Threads. N. Carter
Rope over Jezebel. R. Harrison
Rope to Spare. P. MacDonald
Rope Waits. L. Dean
Rope Which Hangs. G. Fairlie
Rope's End. P. Hamilton
Rope's End--Rogue's End. E. C. R. Lorac
Rosa at Ten O'Clock. M. Denevi
Rose and the Key. J. S. Le Fanu
Rosa Lambert. G. W. M. Reynolds
Rosalie. T. P. Prest
Rosalie Du Pont. Emerson Bennett
Rosaline Woodbridge. H. M. Jones
Rosamunda. Marjory Hall
Rosaria. M. K. Robertson
Rosario Murder Case. Roland Daniel
Rosario, the Female Monk. M. G. Lewis
Rose Bath Riddle. A. M. Rud
Rose Brocade. P. C. De Crespigny
Rose Can Kill. J. Ingersol
Rose Foster. G. W. M. Reynolds
Rose from the Dead. P. Ernst
Rose in the Dark. Roy Vickers
Rose Lodge. H. Wood
Rose of Algiers. C. H. Bullivant
Rose of Allandale. G. Stables
Rose of Blenheim. M. Gerard
Rose of Death. W. S. Masterman
Rose of Kantara. A. Richardson
Rose of Life. M. E. Braddon
Rose of Tibet. L. Davidson
Rose Petal Murders. C. G. Givens
Rose Seymour. N. Buntline
Rose Window. S. Blanc
Roseanna. M. Sjowall
Rosebud. J. Hemingway
Rosecrest Cell. V. Caspray
Roseheath. K. Troy
Rosemary for Death. Dexter Muir
Rosemary's Baby. I. Levine
Rosery Folk. G. M. Fenn
Roses from a Haunted Garden. J. F. Webb
Rose's Last Summer. M. Millar
Rosevean. I. Bromige
Rosewell Heritage. M. F. Ford
Ross Forgery. W. H. Hallahan
Rossano. G. Lett
Rostron Outfit. Dan Morgan
Rostron Outfit in Chicago. Dan Morgan
Rostron Outfit in Mexico. Dan Morgan
Rostron Outfit in Rio. Dan Morgan
Rostron Outfit to Texas. Dan Morgan
Rostron Outfit--Undercover Agents. Dan Morgan
Rosy Pastor. N. Fitzgerald
Rothhaven. W. E. D. Ross
Rotten with Honour. Derek Robinson
Rotterdam Delivery. E. A. O'Neill
Rouge. H. McFall
Rough Company. D. Hamilton
Rough Going. G. Goodchild
Rough Justice. M. E. Braddon
Rough on Rats. W. Francis
Rough Passage. Gavin Douglas
Rough Passage. G. Hackforth-Jones
Rough Passage. A. Wright
Rough Seas to Sunrise. J. Ames
Rough Shoot. G. Household
Rough Trade. L. Rand
Roughneck. J. Thompson
Roumanian Envoy. G. N. Philips
Round Robin. G. W. Bain
Round Table Murders. P. Baron
Round Table Murders. A. Reynolds
Round the Block. Anonymous
Round the Clock at Volari's. W. R. Burnett
Round the Fire Stories. A. C. Doyle
Round the Red Lamp. A. C. Doyle
Round the World for a Quarter. N. Carter
Round Tower. C. Cookson
Round Trip. D. Tracy
Round Trip in the Year 2000. W. W. Cook
Round Trip to Nowhere. J. T. MacCargo
Roundabout. M. Allwright
Rout of the Oliver Samuelsons. H. C. McNeile
Route of the Red Gold. D. J. Marlowe
Routine Investigation. H. Howard
Roving Hearts. K. Prichard
Rox Hall Illuminated. P. Paul
Roxy by Proxy. H. Janson
Roy of Roy's Court. W. Westall
Royal Abduction. A. W. Upfield
Royal Affair and other stories. G. Boothby
Royal Alliance. C. Dawe
Royal Bed for a Corpse. M. Murray
Royal Bluejacket. F. T. Jane
Royal Box. F. P. Keyes
Royal Chase. C. Buckley
Royal Exchange. J. M. Cobban
Royal Exchange. H. M. Raleigh
Royal Flush Murders. G. Verner
Royal Heritage. R. Pertwee
Royal Hoax. F. Whishaw
Royal Indiscretion. R. Marsh
Royal Ishmael. Winifred Duke
Royal Outlaw. S. Cobb
Royal Prisoner. P. Souvestre
Royal Rascal. A. Griffiths
Royal Special, and other stories. E. Burton
Royal Street. F. Swann
Royal Thief. N. Carter
Royal Twins. T. P. Prest
Royal Wrong. F. M. White
Royston Affair. D. M. Devine
Rub-a-Dub-Dub. R. L. Fish
Rub-Out Specialty. Griff
Rubbed Out. R. Barnett
Rubber Band. R. Stout
Rubber Mask. F. L. Stickney
Rubber Smugglers. G. H. Teed
Rubber Stamp, and A Matter of Voice. H. C. McNeile
Rubberface. G. Stanley
Rubberneck. B. Shannon
Rubbish. S. Barrett
Rube Burrows League. M. Manly
Rubies, Emeralds and Diamonds. B. Chetwynd
Rubies of Rajmar. E. Eastwick
Ruby. F. Lorenz
Ruby. J. Siegal
Ruby Beyond Price. G. Campbell
Ruby Cup. L. K. Vincent
Ruby Heart of Kishgar. A. W. Marchmont
Ruby Maclaine. J. Roeburt
Ruby of a Thousand Dreams. Roland Daniel
Ruby Pin. N. Carter
Ruby Sword. B. Mitford
Rude Awakening. H. Brinton
Rude Justice. L. Austen-Leigh
Rue Bargain. R. M. Gilchrist
Rue the Day. M. Alan
Rue the Reservoir. Annabelle Melville
Rugged Way. E. W. Elkington
Ruin. E. S. West
Ruined Map. K. Abe
Ruled off the Turf. Grace M. White
Rules Don't Apply. R. Hamilton
Rules of the Game. S. Morrow
Ruling Passion. R. Hill
Ruling the Planets. M. E. Burton
Ruling Vice. P. Trent
Rum Alley. A. O. Pollard
Rum and Coca-Cola Murders. Wenzell Brown
Rum Row Murders. C. R. Jones
Rum Week. N. Tranter
Rumble. H. Ellison
Rumble Murders. M. Deal
Rumble on the Docks. F. Paley
Rumor Hath It. C. Hale
Rumour at Nightfall. G. Greene
Run. M. Shedd
Run! P. Wentworth
Run Away to Murder. J. York
Run, Brother, Run! T. Brandt
Run by Night. H. Innes
Run, Chico, Run. Wenzell Brown
Run Corpse, Run. G. Pember-Hiller
Run Down. Robert Garrett
Run Far, Run Fast. L. A. Goldstone
Run, Fool, Run. F. Gruber
Run for Cover. J. Welcome
Run for Doom. H. Kane
Run for Lover. H. Janson
Run for the Money. Dale Clark
Run for the Money. R. Colby
Run for Your Death. H. Hossent
Run for Your Life. B. Fischer
Run for Your Life. R. Foley
Run for Your Life! S. Noel
Run for Your Life! M. Stark
Run for Your Money. G. Nyland
Run for Your Money. H. Seymour
Run from Death. J. P. Duff
Run from the Hunter. K. Grantland
Run from the River. L. Barth
Run from the Sheep. E. Capit
Run if You Can. O. Dudley
Run if You're Guilty. J. McKimmey
Run in Diamonds. A. Saxon
Run, Killer, Run. N. Deemster
Run, Killer, Run. W. C. Gault
Run, Killer, Run. L. White
Run Lethal. R. Stark
Run Like a Thief. M. Niall
Run Man Run. C. Himes
Run, Mann, Run! J. Keenan
Run, Mongoose. B. Wilkinson
Run...Run...Run. F. Taubes
Run Scared. M. G. Eberhart
Run, Shadow, Run. H. B. Cave
Run, Spy, Run. N. Carter
Run, Thief, Run. F. Gruber
Run to Death. P. Quentin
Run to Earth. M. E. Braddon
Run to Earth. N. Carter
Run to Earth. P. Grayson
Run to Evil. L. Egan
Run to Ground. R. Jocelyn
Run to Morning. J. Graham
Run, Traitor, Run. R. Pierce
Run When I Say Go. H. Waugh
Run While You Can. W. Woolfolk
Run with the Fox. Craig Cooper
Run with the Hare. K. Abbey
Run with the Killer. J. Armour
Run with the Weasel. R. Wilkes-Hunter
Runagate. C. C. Lowis
Runagates Club. J. Buchan
Runaround. V. Warren
Runaway. M. Halliday

Title Index

Runaway. Old Sleuth
Runaway. J. Peter
Runaway. C. Stratton
Runaway Bag. A. P. Terhune
Runaway Black. R. Marsten
Runaway Corpse. J. Warren
Runaway from Love. Rona Randall
Runaway Home! K. Booton
Runaway Match. H. Wood
Runaway Pigeon. L. Edgley
Runaway Wife. S. O'Donnell
Rung In. A. Wright
Runner Is Red. J. B. Kovalsky
Running. R. Shaw
Running Amok. G. M. Fenn
Running Blind. D. Bagley
Running Deep. R. Petrie
Running Down a Double. Anonymous
Running Fight. E. P. Oppenheim
Running Killer. W. J. Elliott
Running Lions. J. D. White
Running Man. B. Benson
Running Man. L. Dietz
Running Man. A. Ferguson
Running Nun. B. Flynn
Running Sand. J. Wade
Running Scared. J. Burmeister
Running Scared. Craig Cooper
Running Scared. Gregory McDonald
Running Scared. B. McKnight
Running Special. F. Packard
Running Spy. J. Milton
Running Target. S. Frazee
Running the Blockade. W. H. Thomes
Running the Gauntlet. E. Yates
Running Water. A. E. W. Mason
Running Woman. P. Carlon
Runway Zero-Eight. J. Castle
Rupert Godwin. M. E. Braddon
Rupert Hall. H. Wood
Ruse of the Vanished Women. V. Gielgud
Rush Hour Crime. A. Skene
Rush on the Ultimate. H. R. F. Keating
Russian Coward. F. Whishaw
Russian Interpreter. M. Frayn
Russian Judas. F. Whishaw
Russian Roulette. T. Ardies
Russian Roulette. A. Bloomfield
Russian Roulette. J. Mitchell
Russian Roulette. B. Picton
Rust of Murder. J. March
Rustle of Spring. K. Lindsay
Rustlers' Roost. W. C. Tuttle
Rustling End. D. G. Browne
Rusty Sword. J. H. Riddell
Ruth. V. Caspary
Ruth Anstey. J. Middlemass
Ruth of the U.S.A. E. Balmer
Rutherford. E. Fawcett
Rutland Mystery. C. F. Gregg
Rx for Murder. J. Layhew
Ryan Affair. D. MacDonald
Rye House Plot. G. W. M. Reynolds
Rynox. P. MacDonald
Rynox Murder Mystery. P. MacDonald
Rynox Mystery. P. MacDonald

S

S.O.S. S. Horler
S.P.Q.R. P. H. Bonner
S.P.Y.S. T. R. Joyce
S.S. Murder. Q. Patrick
S.S. Mystery. L. A. Knight
"S-S-S-Sh!" K. Carmel
Saba's Treasure. D. M. Douglass
Sabath Quest. I. Foster
Sabbath Slayer. B. Heygate

Saberlegs. E. Pace
Sable in the Rain. W. E. D. Ross
Sable Lorcha. H. Hazeltine
Sable Messenger. F. Vivian
Sable Night. A. Roy
Sables Spell Trouble. S. Mitchell
Sabotage. C. F. Adams
Sabotage. J. Creasey
Sabotage. R. C. Elliott
Sabotage. O. John
Sabotage at Sea. J. Davies
Sabotage Broadcast. H. Innes
Sabotage Murder Mystery. M. Allingham
Sabotage Unlimited. P. Groom
Saboteurs. June Drummond
Saboteurs. J. W. Mason
Sabre Squadron. S. Raven
Sabre-Tooth. P. O'Donnell
Sabres on the Sand. G. Household
Sack of Monte Carlo. W. Frith
Sackcloth and Broadcloth. J. Middlemass
Sacked City. G. R. Preedy
Sacrament of Death. S. Esmond
Sacred City. W. W. Sayer
Sacred Crescents. W. Westall
Sacred Edifice. John Gloag
Sacred Eye. J. Creasey
Sacred Herb. F. Hume
Sacred Shaft. J. Weatherhead
Sacred Skull. George Griffith
Sacrifice. C. H. Merrett
Sacrifice. G. Simenon
Sacrifice. P. Trent
Sacrifice & Co. Winifred Graham
Sacrificial Pawn. F. Ryck
Sad Adventurers. M. Rutledge
Sad and Tender Flesh. S. D. Frances
Sad Cypress. A. Christie
Sad-Eyed Seductress. C. Brown
Sad Road to the Sea. G. Kersh
Sad Song Singing. T. B. Dewey
Sad Sontag Plays His Hunch. W. C. Tuttle
Sad, Sudden Death of My Fair Lady. S. Forbes
Sad Variety. N. Blake
Sad Wind from the Sea. Harry Patterson
Saddle a Killer. N. Wylie
Saddle and Sabre. H. Smart
Saddle the Storm. H. Whittington
Saddled with Murder. S. Miles
Saddleroom Murder. N. K. McKechnie
Sadie, Don't Cry Now. H. Janson
Sadie Swings the Blues. B. Shannon
Sadie When She Died. E. McBain
Safari for Spies. N. Carter
Safari with Fear! R. Hardinge
Safari with Fear. J. York
Safe Behind Bars. Andrew Hall
Safe Conduct. J. England
Safe Custody. D. Yates
Safe House. J. Cleary
Safe Job. D. Vallance
Safe Number Sixty-Nine. J. S. Fletcher
Safe Place. A. Rider
Safe Road. K. N. Burt
Safe Secret. H. Carmichael
Safer Dead. J. H. Chase
Safety First Murders. E. Radford
Safety Last. G. Goodchild
Safety Last. J. Gray
Safety Pin. J. S. Fletcher
Saffron Robe. J. Browning
Saffron Summer. M. Summerton
Saffron's War. F. E. Smith

Saga of a Scoundrel. P. Barrington
Saga of Halfaday Creek. J. B. Hendryx
Saga of the Cliffs. E. L. Long
Sagas of the Mounted Police. W. B. Mowery
Sahara Road. S. Harvester
Sahara Survival. Burt Cole
Said Dr. Spendlove. Hilda Lewis
Said the Spider to the Fly. R. Shattuck
Said with Flowers. A. Nash
Saigon. N. Carter
Saigon Singer. V. W. Mason
Sail a Crooked Ship. N. Benchley
Sail into Silence. D. Marble
Sailcloth Shroud. C. Williams
Sailor and the Widow. E. L. Long
Sailor and the Widow. Seafarer
Sailor, Take Warning. K. Roos
Sailor, Take Warning. R. Sale
Sailor's Bride. G. Boothby
Sailor's Luck. B. Heatter
Sailor's Rendezvous. G. Simenon
Saint Abroad. L. Charteris
Saint: Ace of Knaves. L. Charteris
Saint and Mr. Teal. L. Charteris
Saint and the Fiction Makers. L. Charteris
Saint and the Last Hero. L. Charteris
Saint and the People Importers. L. Charteris
Saint and the Sizzling Saboteur. L. Charteris
Saint Around the World. L. Charteris
Saint at a Thieves' Picnic. L. Charteris
Saint at Large. L. Charteris
Saint Bids Diamonds. L. Charteris
Saint Cleans Up. L. Charteris
Saint Closes the Case. L. Charteris
St. Cloud Affair. B. Baskerville
St. Cuthbert's Tower. F. Warden
Saint Errant. L. Charteris
Saint-Fiacre Affair. G. Simenon
St. George Manor. R. M. Sears
Saint Goes On. L. Charteris
Saint Goes West. L. Charteris
Saint in Action. L. Charteris
Saint in England. L. Charteris
Saint in Europe. L. Charteris
Saint in Miami. L. Charteris
Saint in Mufti. C. Dawe
Saint in New York. L. Charteris
Saint in Pursuit. L. Charteris
Saint in the Sun. L. Charteris
Saint Intervenes. L. Charteris
St. Ives. O. Bleeck
St. Ives Murders. R. Wincor
St. Louis Showdown. D. Pendleton
Saint Maker. L. Holton
Saint-Malo Mystery. J. Maske
St. Martin's Eve. H. Wood
Saint Meets His Match. L. Charteris
Saint Meets the Tiger. L. Charteris
Saint of the Speedway. R. Cullum
Saint on Guard. L. Charteris
Saint on TV. L. Charteris
Saint on the Spanish Main. L. Charteris
Saint Overboard. L. Charteris
St. Peter's Finger. G. Mitchell
Saint Plays with Fire. L. Charteris
Saint Returns. L. Charteris
Saint Sees It Through. L. Charteris
Saint Steps In. L. Charteris
Saint--The Brighter Buccaneer. L. Charteris
Saint--The Happy Highwayman. L. Charteris
Saint to the Rescue. L. Charteris
Saint: Two in One. L. Charteris

St. Valentine's Day Massacre. B. O'Hara
Saint vs. Scotland Yard. L. Charteris
Saint--Wanted for Murder. L. Charteris
Saints Are Sinister. B. Flynn
Saint's Getaway. L. Charteris
Saintsbury Affair. R. Doubleday
Saladin! A. Osmond
Salamander. M. L. West
Salazar Grant. E. L. Withers
Salesman of Death. C. Leader
Salisbury Manuscript. W. M. Green
Sally. E. V. Cunningham
Sally. W. B. M. Ferguson
Sally of Scotland Yard. L. Gribble
Sally of the Underworld. Roland Daniel
Sally's in the Alley. N. Davis
Salt and Pepper. Alex Austin
Salt for the Tiger. W. C. Tuttle
Salt Is Leaving. J. B. Priestley
Salt of the Earth. F. M. White
Salter's Folly. A. Marsden
Saltmarsh Murders. G. Mitchell
Salute Blue Mask. A. Morton
Salute for the Baron. A. Morton
Salute from a Dead Man. Donald MacKenzie
Salute Inspector Flagg. J. Cassells
Salute Mr. Sandyman. Neill Graham
Salute the Dreamer. W. M. Duncan
Salute the Picaroon. J. Cassells
Salute the Toff. J. Creasey
Salute to Bazarada and other stories. S. Rohmer
Salute to Blackshirt. R. Graeme
Salute to Murder. Neill Graham
Salute to Murder. R. P. Koehler
Salute to the Gods. Malcolm Campbell
Salute to Tomorrow. J. Nicholas
Salvage. H. Smart
Salvage of the Sea. W. M. Graydon
Salvage Pirates. G. Chester
Salvation. A. Askew
Salvation of Pisco Gabar and other stories. G. Household
Salvator. P. Gibbon
Salvatore. P. Tabori
Salving of a Derelict. M. Drake
Salzburg Connection. H. MacInnes
Sam Benedict: Cast the First Stone. Elsie Lee
Sam Casanova. M. Catto
Samantha. J. Carew
Samantha. E. V. Cunningham
Samantha. D. Eden
Samara. N. Lewis
Samarai Affair. A. Behrend
Same Difference. H. Janson
Same Lie Twice. R. Goulart
Sammy. D. Enefer
Samson. E. C. Vivian
Samson's Surrender. T. Lloyd
Samuel Boyd of Catchpole Square. B. L. Farjeon
Samuel Lyle, Criminologist. A. Crabb
Samurai. G. MacBeth
San Diego Siege. D. Pendleton
San Francisco Vendetta. R. Mallory
Sanctuary. W. Faulkner
Sanctuary Club. L. T. Meade
Sanctuary Island. Robert (G.) Curtis
Sanctuary Isle. B. Knox
Sand and Satin. S. Rohmer
Sand Dollar. G. Sims
Sand Pit. H. Jobson
Sand Rose. M. Summerton
Sandal Wood Slipper. N. Carter
Sandalwood Fan. K. W. Eyre
Sandalwood Fan. T. McMorrow
Sandbar Sinister. P. A. Taylor

Sandcliff Mystery. Scott Graham
Sanders. E. Wallace
Sanders of the River. E. Wallace
Sanderson: Master Rogue. J. J. Chichester
Sanderson's Diamond Loot. J. J. Chichester
Sandi, the King Maker. E. Wallace
Sandlappers. A. Rutherford
Sandling Case. L. Tracy
Sandover Goes Gay. D. Lee
Sandra Rifkin's Jewels. R. Doliner
Sands of Fear. Augustus Muir
Sands of Khali. M. Hastings
Sands of Lilliput. S. Dembo
Sands of Oro. B. Grimshaw
Sands of the Desert. P. Meredith
Sands of Windee. A. W. Upfield
Sands Street. W. Bogart
Sandwiches Are Not My Business. B. Kelly
Sandycroft Mystery. T. W. Speight
Sanfield Scandal. R. Keverne
Sant of the Secret Service. W. LeQueux
Santa Ana Wind. S. Ashton
Santa Claus Bank Robbery. A. C. Greene
Santa Dolores Stage. W. C. Tuttle
Santa Klaus Murder. M. D. Hay
Santa Maria. Seafarer
Santos, Border Detective. W. B. Bannerman
Sappers and Miners. G. M. Fenn
Sapphire. E. G. Cousins
Sapphire. A. E. W. Mason
Sapphire Conference. P. Graaf
Sapphire Cross. G. M. Fenn
Sapphire King, and other stories. R. Dowling
Sapphire Ring. C. Granville
Sapphires on Wednesday. M. Gair
Saraband for a Smuggler. S. Brydon
Saracen Gardens. M. K. Simmons
Saracen Shadow. Shane Martin
Sarah Brown, Detective. Anonymous
Sarah Brown, Detective. K. F. Hill
Sarah Mandrake. M. Wadelton
Saranoff Murder. M. L. Luther
Saratoga Lady. F. Y. McHugh
Saratoga Mantrap. D. St. Clare
Sardia. C. L. Daniels
Sargasso Ogre. K. Robeson
Sargasso People. Wade Miller
Sargasso Secret. K. Stanton
Sarita, the Carlist. A. W. Marchmont
Sark Street Chapel Murder. T. Cobb
Sarnia. H. Ford
Sarsen Place. Gwendoline Butler
Sartoroe. J. A. Maitland
Satan Bug. I. Stuart
Satan Buys a Wreath. M. Storm
Satan Comes Across. B. Barlay
Satan Has Six Fingers. V. Kelsey
Satan in High Heels. N. Chandler
Satan Is a Woman. G. Brewer
Satan Is Blonde. B. Sarto
Satan Ltd. Gwyn Evans
Satan Strike. J. Rosenberger
Satan Takes the Helm. B. Clements
Satan Was a Man. E. H. Bierstadt
Satanic Power. V. Van Der Elst
Satanic Sex. A. J. Fitzgerald
Satanist. D. Wheatley
Satan's Acres. S. Wagner
Satan's Angel. S. Fisher
Satan's Apt Pupil. N. Carter
Satan's Child. P. Saxon
Satan's Children. G. Simenon
Satan's Coach. F. Du Boisgobey
Satan's Coast. Elsie Lee
Satan's Island. Marilyn Ross
Satan's Mistress. B. Graeme

Satan's Rock. Marilyn Ross
Satan's Satellite. G. Davison
Satan's Secret. B. Stacey
Satan's Sister. T. Angelo
Satan's Spring. S. Nichols
Satan's Widow. H. Whittington
Saturday Epic. H. C. Rae
Saturday Games. B. Meggs
Saturday Night Town. H. Whittington
Saturday Out. L. Meynell
Saturday the Rabbi Went Hungry. H. Kemelman
Saturn over the Water. J. B. Priestley
Satyr. J. McKimmey
Satyr Mask. Augustus Muir.
Savage. N. Clad
Savage Affair. V. Scott
Savage Breast. Manning Long
Savage Breast. J. Trinian
Savage Bride. C. Woolrich
Savage Chase. F. Lorenz
Savage Day. J. Higgins
Savage Encounter. G. Goodchild
Savage Game. J. Trevor
Savage Gentleman. P. Wylie
Savage Height. J. Trevor
Savage Interlude. D. Cushman
Savage Night. J. Thompson
Savage Salome. C. Brown
Savage Sequel. H. Janson
Savage Siren. H. Zore
Savage Slaughter. B. Rossi
Savage Squeeze. Arthur MacLean
Savage Streets. W. P. McGivern
Savage Streets. F. C. Miller
Savage Triangle. L. Royer
Savage Venture. W. A. Ballinger
Savannah Purchase. J. A. Hodge
Savant's Vendetta. R. A. Freeman
Savaran and the Great Sand. D. Newton
Savarin's Shadow. R. Goyne
Save a Lady. W. Collison
Save a Rope. H. C. Bailey
Save Me from My Friends. E. F. Knight
Save the Witness. P. McGerr
Save Them for Violence. J. M. Fox
Save Your Pity. M. Hervey
Save Your Tears. R. Madison
Saved at the Scaffold. A. F. Pinkerton
Saved by a Ruse. N. Carter
Saved from the Harem. F. Du Boisgobey
Saverstall. J. Vicary
Saving a Rope. H. C. Bailey
Saving Clause. H. C. McNeile
Saving Face. P. Boulle
Saving of Christian Sergison. E. A. Treeton
Sawdust Angel. G. Bowman
Sawn Off. G. M. Fenn
Sawney Bean, the Man Eater of Midlothian. T. P. Prest
Saxon Ashe...Secret Agent. S. Ashe
Saxon's Ghost. S. Fisher
Say It with Bullets. R. Powell
Say It with Candy. H. Janson
Say It with Flowers. G. C. Foster
Say It with Flowers. G. Mitchell
Say It with Homicide. B. Diamond
Say It with Murder. Neill Graham
Say It with Murder. E. Ronns
Say It with Violence. D. Eames
Say No to Death. D. Cusack
Say Yes to Murder. W. T. Ballard
Sayle Case. T. Freeman-Hilton
Scales of Chance. H. Curties

Scales of Justice. B. Delannoy
Scales of Justice. G. L. Knapp
Scales of Justice. N. Marsh
Scales of Justice. F. M. White
Scallywag. G. Allen
Scalpel. H. McCoy
Scalps. M. Leinster
Scamp Hunter. D. Stewart
Scamp's Law. P. A. Foxall
Scandal. F. Nichols
Scandal at High Chimneys. J. D. Carr
Scandal at School. G. D. H. Cole
Scandal at Scotland Yard. B. Cobb
Scandal at the Home Office. F. A. Clement
Scandal Has Two Faces. M. E. Campbell
Scandal in Eden. G. Rogers
Scandal in the Chancery. Diplomat
Scandal-Monger. W. LeQueux
Scandal of Father Brown. G. K. Chesterton
Scandal Street. W. H. Baker
Scandalize My Name. Fiona Sinclair
Scapegoat. D. Du Maurier
Scapegoat. P. Orum
Scapegoat Dances. M. Benney
Scapegoats for Murder. A. Wilson
Scar. D. Vane
Scar of Crime. J. Corey
Scar on a Corpse. L. Paradise
Scar 77. G. Seton
Scarab Clue. H. H. Ross
Scarab Murder Case. S. S. Van Dine
Scarabaeus. C. Lanza
Scarborough House. S. A. Salvato
Scarborough Romance. F. Warden
Scarbrow. G. Bettany
Scare the Gentle Citizen. I Crawford
Scarecrow. A. Fielding
Scarecrow. E. K. Goldthwaite
Scarecrow Murders. F. A. Kummer
Scarecrow Rides. R. Thorndike
Scared Nymph. A. Applin
Scared Stiff. P. J. Rainier
Scared to Death. G. Bagby
Scared to Death. R. Foley
Scarf. R. Bloch
Scarf. F. Durbridge
Scarf of Passion. R. Bloch
Scarf on the Scarecrow. M. J. Freeman
Scarface. A. Trail
Scarfaced Killer. B. Rossi
Scarhaven Keep. J. S. Fletcher
Scarlatti Inheritance. R. Ludlum
Scarlet Bat. F. Hume
Scarlet Bee. Tanjong
Scarlet Bikini. G. Croudace
Scarlet Blossoms. M. Peterson
Scarlet Button. Anthony Gilbert
Scarlet Car. R. H. Davis
Scarlet Circle. J. Stagge
Scarlet Cloak. P. Fry
Scarlet Clue. S. Hocking
Scarlet Death. Roger Randall
Scarlet Fan. H. L. Gates
Scarlet Feather. H. Adams
Scarlet Feather. F. Gruber
Scarlet Feather. H. Townley
Scarlet Flower. T. Rourke
Scarlet Flush. C. Brown
Scarlet Fortune. H. Herman
Scarlet Fountains. G. Milner
Scarlet Fox. E. H. Ball
Scarlet Gargoyle. T. F. Elstow
Scarlet Handkerchief. Le Jemlys
Scarlet Imperial. D. B. Hughes
Scarlet Impostor. D. Wheatley
Scarlet Iris. V. Thompson
Scarlet Lady. A. St. Aubyn
Scarlet Letters. E. Queen
Scarlet Lily. N. Brent
Scarlet Livery. Rupert Grayson
Scarlet Macaw. G. E. Locke
Scarlet Mask. W. E. Groves
Scarlet Mask. C. Rodda
Scarlet Messenger. H. Holt
Scarlet Runner. C. N. Williamson
Scarlet Ruse. J. D. MacDonald
Scarlet Saint. M. Sarne
Scarlet Scarab. L. C. Douthwaite
Scarlet Scissors. B. Fischer
Scarlet Scourge. J. McCulley
Scarlet Scourge. Harrington Strong
Scarlet Seal. D. Donovan
"Scarlet Ship." R. C. Finney
Scarlet Sign. W. LeQueux
Scarlet Sin. A. Askew
Scarlet Sin. F. Marryat
Scarlet Sinners. D. Donovan
Scarlet Slippers. J. M. Fox
Scarlet Spade. E. K. Goldthwaite
Scarlet Spot. D. Stewart
Scarlet Squadron. G. E. Rochester
Scarlet Starlet. D. Warren
Scarlet Surf at Makaha. P. Morgan
Scarlet Tanager. J. A. Tyson
Scarlet Thread. D. Downes
Scarlet Thread. M. P. Hood
Scarlet Thumb. J. March
Scarlet Thumb Print. G. Morton
Scarlet Town. A. Askew
Scarlet Venus. C. Green
Scarlet Widow. R. Rioti
Scarlet Widow. B. Sanders
Scarlet X. H. Wickham
Scarlett Gets the Kidnapper. S. Horler
Scarlett Murder. W. Martyn
Scarlett--Special Branch. S. Horler
Scarred Chin. W. Payne
Scarred Hand. E. H. Robinson
Scarred Jungle. H. Footner
Scarred Man. B. Heatter
Scarred Wrists. V. M. Steele
Scars of Dracula. Angus Hall
Scarthroat. Roland Daniel
Scarweather. A. Rolls
Scattered Death. I. Somerville
Scattergood Baines. C. B. Kelland
Scattergood Pulls the Strings. C. B. Kelland
Scattergood Returns. C. B. Kelland
Scavenger Kill. Ralph Hayes
Scavengers. B. Knox
Scavengers. Allan Nixon
Scavengers. D. O'Callaghan
Scavengers at War. C. Leader
Scenario for Murder. Dana Wilson
Scend of the Sea. G. Jenkins
Scene for Death. N. Hoult
Scene in the Ice-Blue Eyes. P. Winner
Scene of the Crime. J. Creasey
Scenes from the Show. G. R. Sims
Scent from Heaven. H. Janson
Scent of Danger. E. Kyle
Scent of Danger. D. MacKenzie
Scent of Death. Morley Roberts
Scent of Fear. S. Dean
Scent of Lilacs. Carolyn Wilson
Scent of Mayhem. R. T. Bickers
Scent of Mystery. K. Roos
Scent of New-Mown Hay. J. Blackburn
Scent of Roses. H. Bourne
Scent of Sandalwood. C. Coleman
Scent of the Rose. M. Peterson
Scent of White Poppies. J. Christopher
Scented Danger. F. Cowen
Scented Death. A. Drummond
Scented Flesh. R. O. Saber
Schack Job. H. Kane
Schamyl, the Sultan, Warrior and Prophet of the Caucasus. T. P. Prest
Scheherazade. F. Warden
Scheme for One. A. Roberts
Schemer. W. E. Groves
Schemers. R. Fenisong
Schirmer Inheritance. E. Ambler
School for Liars. O. Norton
School for Murder. H. Carmichael
School for Murder. D. Scanlon
School for Scoundrels. A. Bracey
School on Lone Island. B. E. M. Ward
Schoolboys Three. W. P. Kelly
Schooled to Kill. D. Shannon
Schoolgirl Murder Case. Colin Wilson
Schoolmaster's Daughters. D. Eden
Schooner "Sybil." E. L. Long
Schulsinger Affair. R. Temple
Schultz Money. M. Gair
Schwartz. D. C. Murray
Science Traps the Criminal. J. W. Booth
Scientific Forger. N. Carter
Scientific Sprague. F. Lynde
Scientists. E. Lipsky
Scipio. T. Gates
Scissors Cut Paper. G. Fairlie
Scobie in September. B. Craig
Scoop. L. Meynell
Scorch. N. Williams
Score. R. Stark
Score for Superintendent Flagg. J. Cassells
Score for the Toff. J. Creasey
Score of Arms. R. Meade
Scornful Corpse. M. Kennedy
Scornful Man. Muriel Harris
Scorpio. M. Roote
Scorpio 5. W. Harrington
Scorpio Letters. V. Canning
Scorpion. D. Carey
Scorpion. C. Hill
Scorpion. W. Penmare
Scorpion of Chateau Laverria. M. M. Fletcher
Scorpion Reef. C. Williams
Scorpion's Nest. J. Angus
Scorpion's Nest. H. McCutcheon
Scorpion's Suicide. F. Dale
Scorpion's Tale. W. Haggard
Scorpion's Trail. T. C. H. Jacobs
Scotch on the Rocks. D. Hurd
Scotland Expects. J. S. Clouston
Scotland Yard Alibi. D. Betteridge
Scotland Yard Can Wait! D. Frome
Scotland Yard: Department of Queer Complaints. Carter Dickson
Scotland Yard Experiences. G. H. Greenham
Scotland Yard Takes a Holiday. L. Allan
Scots Wha Ha'e. J. S. Clouston
Scottish Chieftains. H. M. Jones
Scoundrel. M. Aldanov
Scoundrel Mark. F. Dilnot
Scoundrel or Saint? G. Warden
Scoundrels & Co. C. Kernahan
Scoundrels Rampant. N. Carter
Scourge of Damascus. S. Cobb
Scourge of the Desert. Operator 1384
Scourge of the Wizard. N. Carter
Scourged by Fear. N. Carter
Scout Grey--Detective. R. L. Bellamy
Scrambled Yeggs. O. R. Cohen
Scrambled Yeggs. D. Knight
Scrap-Metal Mystery. W. Tyrer
Scrap of Black Lace. N. Carter

Scrap of Paper. H. C. McNeile
Scratch a Lover. J. G. Vermandel
Scratch a Thief. Z. Marko
Scratch a Thief. J. Trinian
Scratch on the Dark. B. Copper
Scratch on the Surface. T. Harknett
Scratch One. J. Lange
Scream. D. Launay
Scream at Midnight. J. P. Brennan
Scream at Midnight. T. A. Plummer
Scream Bloody Murder. R. Telfair
Scream for Sarah. V. Heley
Scream in Soho. J. G. Brandon
Scream in the Dark. N. Ridley
Scream in the Night. H. Desmond
Scream in the Sky. N. McCallum
Scream in the Storm. C. Farr
Scream of Murder. G. Ashe
Scream of the Doll. S. K. Wilson
Scream of the Dove. R. Charles
Scream Street. Mike Brett
Screaming Bride. H. T. Teilhet
Screaming Cargo. J. M. Flynn
Screaming Dead Balloons. P. McCutchan
Screaming Fog. J. N. Chance
Screaming Gull. A. MacVicar
Screaming Mimi. F. Brown
Screaming Orchid. D. Enefer
Screaming Portrait. F. L. Fraser
Screaming Rabbit. H. Carmichael
Screaming Skull and other stories. S. Horler
Screams from a Penny Dreadful. J. Fleming
Screen for Murder. A. Jeffers
Screen for Murder. E. C. R. Lorac
Screened. F. Wolseley
Scrimshaw Millions. L. Thayer
Scrope. F. B. Perkins
Scruples. T. Cobb
Sculptor's Daughter. F. Du Boisgobey
Scum in the Pot. W. A. Miller
Scutari. M. Zarubica
Scylla. Malden Grange Bishop
Sea Angel. K. Robeson
Sea Case. G. Volk
Sea Change. E. H. Clements
Sea Could Tell. A. M. Williamson
Sea Dust. E. L. Long
Sea Fog. J. S. Fletcher
Sea Fox. N. Carter
Sea Fury. J. Pattinson
Sea Gold. J. Remenham
Sea House. M. Summerton
Sea Jade. P. A. Whitney
Sea King's Daughter. B. Michaels
Sea Lavender. R. Gover
Sea Loot. A. D. Divine
Sea Magician. K. Robeson
Sea Monks. A. Garve
Sea Mystery. F. W. Crofts
Sea of Death. H. H. Ross
Sea of Fortune. R. Jocelyn
Sea of Troubles. Sea Lion
Sea Officer. S. Styles
Sea Raiders. A. B. Sherlock
Sea Range. E. L. Long
Sea Scamps. H. C. Rowland
Sea Scrape. J. Dark
Sea Shall Not Have Them. J. Harris
Sea Shroud. S. Gluck
Sea, Spray and Spindrift. Taffrail
Sea Spy. E. K. Chatterton
Sea Tigers. P. Saxon
Sea Tower. K. Ostrander
Sea Trap. N. Carter
Sea Troll. S. Blanc
Sea Urchin. A. Q. Roby

Sea Vengeance. R. Charles
Sea Vermin. K. Henshaw
Sea Whispers. W. W. Jacobs
Sea Wolves. M. Pemberton
Sea-Wyf. J. M. Scott
Sea-Wyf and Biscuit. J. M. Scott
Seacliffe. J. W. De Forrest
Seacliffe. E. Noone
Seafire. B. Knox
Seaford's Snake. B. Mitford
Seagull Said Murder. M. Neville
Seajet Spies. N. Rich
Seal of Confession. H. A. Bulley
Seal of Death. N. Carter
Seal of Silence. N. Carter
Sealed Book. A. Livingstone
Sealed by a Kiss. J. Middlemass
Sealed Door. N. Carter
Sealed Envelope. B. Bolt
Sealed Envelope. Lady A. Scott
Sealed Lips. S. Campbell
Sealed Lips. F. Du Boisgobey
Sealed Lips. M. Leighton
Sealed Lips. V. Yorke
Sealed Message. F. Hume
Sealed Orders. A. E. Carey
Sealed Orders. N. Carter
Sealed Orders. R. Gover
Sealed Orders. E. J. Lysaght
Sealed Room Murder. M. Crombie
Sealed-Room Murder. R. Penny
Sealed Trunk. H. K. Webster
Sealed Valley. H. Footner
Sealed Verdict. L. L. Lynch
Sealed Verdict. L. Shapiro
Sealed with Blood. S. Jason
Sealer. J. Wood
Seals. P. Dickinson
Seamew Abbey. F. Warden
Seamstress. G. W. M. Reynolds
Seance. M. McShane
Seance for the Dead. F. Hurd
Seance for Two. M. McShane
Seance on a Wet Afternoon. M. McShane
Search. R. Weverka
Search and Destroy. I. R. Blacker
Search and Destroy. J. P. Cody
Search for a Dead Nympho. P. W. Fairman
Search for a Motive. D. Stewart
Search for a Scientist. C. L. Leonard
Search for a Secret. G. A. Henty
Search for a Sultan. M. Coles
Search for Basil Lyndhurst. R. N. Carey
Search for Bruno Heidler. S. Marlowe
Search for Elizabeth Brandt. W. Harrington
Search for Geoffrey Goring. David Wilson
Search for Joseph Tully. W. H. Hallahan
Search for Miss Sylvester. W. V. Cook
Search for My Great-Uncle's Head. P. Coffin
Search for Rita. Barry Cole
Search for Sergeant Baxter. B. Cobb
Search for Tabitha Garr. R. M. Stern
Search for the Blue Sedan. Gavin Douglas
Search for Tomorrow. E. Lindall
Search for X-Y-Z. H. S. Keeler
Search in the Dark. A. MacKenzie
Search Party. G. A. Birmingham
Search the Dark Woods. M. Land
Search the Lady. H. Duval
Search Through the Mist. L. V. Stevens
Search Warrant. J. Pattinson
Search Will Find It Out. B. Harraden

Searchers. John Foster
Searching Spectre. S. Claudia
Searchlight on Hambledon. J. Dellbridge
Seared Hand. J. G. Rowe
Sea's Fool. F. Knight
Seaside Cafe Crime. W. Jardine
Seaside Comedy. I. Jerrold
Seaside Crime. W. Jardine
Seaside Mystery. C. B. Booth
Season for Death. A. Roudybush
Season for Love. W. Chambers
Season for Murder. H. L. Nelson
Season for Violence. T. B. Dewey
Season of Assassins. G. Wagner
Season of Danger. R. Gatenby
Season of Desire. A. W. Lyons
Season of Doubt. J. Cleary
Season of Evil. Elsie Lee
Season of Evil. S. Morrow
Season of Nerves. J. Mayo
Season of Snows and Sins. P. Moyes
Season of the Skylark. J. T. Story
Season of the Stranger. S. Becker
Season to Be Deadly. R. Hardwick
Seasons of God. Edythe Latham
Seat of the Scornful. J. D. Carr
Seaward for the Foe. H. Hill
Seaway Tombstone. K. Klein
Seawife. J. M. Scott
Sebastian Strome. J. Hawthorne
Second Baffle Book. L. Wren
Second Baronet. L. Tracy
Second Best. C. Stanton
Second Bounce. M. Cronin
Second Bout with the Mildew Gang. S. Fowler
Second Bullet. R. O. Chipperfield
Second Bullet. C. J. Dutton
Second Bullet. L. Thayer
Second Bureau. C. R. Dumas
Second Burial. A. M. Stein
Second Case of Mr. Paul Savoy. J. Gregory
Second Chance. P. Trent
Second Chance. E. Trevor
Second Chance. W. Woodrow
Second Class Passenger and other stories. P. Gibbon
Second Confession. R. Stout
Second Count. S. Pearson
Second Cousin Removed. S. Troy
Second Cousin Twice Removed. M. Pereira
Second Curtain. Roy Fuller
Second Dandy Chater. T. Gallon
Second Death of Ramon Mercader. J. Semprun
Second Elopement. H. Flowerdew
Second Floor Mystery. E. D. Biggers
Second Front--First Spy. B. Newman
Second Guess. W. C. Brown
Second-Hand Death. E. E. Sumner
Second-Hand Nude. B. Fischer
Second-Hand Tomb. R. J. White
Second House. Jan Alexander
Second-in-Command. G. Hackforth-Jones
Second in the Field. T. Cobb
Second Key. M. B. Lowndes
Second Knife. H. J. Gill
Second Latchkey. C. N. Williamson
Second Longest Night. S. Marlowe
Second Love. T. W. Speight
Second Maigret Omnibus. G. Simenon
Second Man. E. Grierson
Second Mr. Carstairs. N. Carter
Second Mrs. Locke. J. Cassells
Second Mrs. Lynton. W. Collison
Second Mrs. Savenage. H. W. Leggett
Second Officer. Taffrail
Second Opinion. R. S. Thorn
Second Plan. C. G. Hope
Second Red Dragon. C. V. Bark

Second Romance. Elsie Lee
Second Saint Omnibus. L. Charteris
Second Seal. D. Wheatley
Second Season. Elsie Lee
Second Secret. E. Noone
Second Shot. A. Berkeley
Second Shot. L. Thayer
Second Sickle. U. Curtiss
Second Storey Sinner. M. Brody
Second Storm. M. Sutherland
Second String. H. Janson
Second Stroke. F. Leslie
Second Tablet. C. E. Simon
Second Thoughts. M. Le Bas
Second Thursday. Elspeth Taylor
Second Tigress. Ganpat
Second Victory. M. L. West
Second Wager. H. R. Taunton
Seconds. D. Ely
Seconds and Thirds. E. L. Long
Secrecy at Sandhurst. C. Barry
Secrecy Essential. V. Bridges
Secrecy Street. M. Crossley
Secret. L. De Breuil
Secret. E. P. Oppenheim
Secret Adventure. O. Binns
Secret Adversary. A. Christie
Secret Agent. J. Conrad
Secret Agent. S. Horler
Secret Agent: Ashton-Kirk. J. T. MacIntyre
Secret Agent in Africa. Rupert Grayson
Secret Agent in Port Arthur. W. O. Greener
Secret Agent Number One. F. Frost
Secret Agents of Brazil. N. Carter
Secret Arena. E. Trevor
Secret at Sixty-Six Fathoms. S. Hope
Secret Attic. F. R. Adams
Secret Barrier. C. Kingston
Secret Betrothal. D. Essex
Secret Beyond the Door. R. King
Secret Brotherhood. J. G. Brandon
Secret Brotherhood. H. Campbell
Secret Cargo. S. Esmond
Secret Cargo. J. S. Fletcher
Secret Ceremony. W. Hughes
Secret Chamber at Chad. E. Everett-Green
Secret Citadel. M. Heath
Secret Command. J. Hawkins
Secret Compact. J. B. Williams
Secret Corridors. H. Pentecost
Secret Dancer. N. Berrow
Secret Door. R. St. Clair
Secret Door. D. Vane
Secret Dragnet. B. Sanders
Secret Emerald Mines. G. H. Teed
Secret Enemy. E. O'Duffy
Secret Enemy. M. K. Robertson
Secret Enterprise. Basil Carey
Secret Errand. N. Deane
Secret Establishment. R. Quest
Secret Fear. A. E. W. Mason
Secret Fear. W. O'Farrell
Secret Fear. R. Underwood
Secret Foe. G. Warden
Secret Formula. W. LeQueux
Secret Formula. A. Peters
Secret Formula. A. O. Pollard
Secret Fortune. M. E. Cooke
Secret Front. P. Gallico
Secret Gold. A. M. Williamson
Secret Guest Mystery. M. Welford
Secret Hand. Roland Daniel

Secret Hand. C. G. L. Du Cann
Secret Hand. S. Horler
Secret Hand. D. Valentine
Secret Harbour. S. A. White
Secret History of Today. A. Upward
Secret: Hong Kong. F. M. Davis
Secret Hour. M. Richmond
Secret House. E. Wallace
Secret House of Death. R. Rendell
Secret in Seven Fathoms. M. Frazer
Secret in the Hill. B. Capes
Secret Information. R. Hichens
Secret Inheritance. B. L. Farjeon
Secret Inquest. A. Blair
Secret Inquiry. B. Cobb
Secret Island. J. Fores
Secret Journal of Charles Dunbar. J. Maconechy
Secret Journey. R. Kirkbridge
Secret Judges. F. Grierson
Secret Kingdom. F. Richardson
Secret Life of Algernon Pendleton. R. H. Greenan
Secret Life of the Ex-Tsaritza. W. LeQueux
Secret Listeners. L. Goldman
Secret Listeners of the East. D. G. Mukerji
Secret Lover. E. Nepean
Secret Loving Shadows. M. E. Atkins
Secret Marriage. A. W. Barrett
Secret Masters. G. Kersh
Secret Meeting. J. Rhode
Secret Melody. P. Minton
Secret Menace. Wilfred Barclay
Secret Millionaire. H. H. C. Gibbons
Secret Ministry. D. Cory
Secret Mission: Angola. Don Smith
Secret Mission: Athens. Don Smith
Secret Mission: Cairo. Don Smith
Secret Mission: Corsica. Don Smith
Secret Mission: Istanbul. Don Smith
Secret Mission: Morocco. Don Smith
Secret Mission: Munich. Don Smith
Secret Mission: North Korea. Don Smith
Secret Mission of Colonel Death. J. Rapier
Secret Mission: Peking. Don Smith
Secret Mission: Prague. Don Smith
Secret Mission: The Kremlin Plot. Don Smith
Secret Mission: Tibet. Don Smith
Secret Mission to Bangkok. V. W. Mason
Secret Monitor. G. Thorne
Secret Mountains. J. Appleby
Secret Murder. G. Ashe
Secret of a Letter. G. Warden
Secret of Awen Castle. F. Hurd
Secret of Ayanora. Basil Carey
Secret of Barnabas Collins. Marilyn Ross
Secret of Baron's Folly. H. M. Webster
Secret of Benjamin Square. J. Plum
Secret of Berry Pomeroy. F. Whishaw
Secret of Bogey House. H. Adams
Secret of Canfield House. F. Hurd
Secret of Capri. W. Jardine
Secret of Castle Ferrara. G. Farr
Secret of Castle Voxzel. A. O. Pollard
Secret of Chateau Kendall. S. Richard
Secret of Chauville. D. Whitelaw
Secret of Chimneys. A. Christie
Secret of Devil's Cave. Jennifer Hale
Secret of Draker's Folly. A. Murray
Secret of Dresden Farm. G. St. John
Secret of Enoch Seal. J. B. Harris-Burland
Secret of Father Brown. G. K. Chesterton
Secret of Ferrars. R. Mattheson
Secret of Frontellac. F. K. Scribner
Secret of Gaunt House. F. H. Dimmock

Secret of Gnome Head. B. Strong
Secret of Graytowers. E. Randolph
Secret of Greylands. A. Haynes
Secret of Harbor House. Claudette Nicole
Secret of Haverly House. C. Bauman
Secret of Hayworth Hall. F. Hurd
Secret of Hedges Hall. Lynn Williams
Secret of High Eldersham. M. Burton
Secret of Holm Peel and other strange stories. S. Rohmer
Secret of Kensington Manor. G. St. John
Secret of Kyriels. E. Nesbit
Secret of Lonesome Cove. S. H. Adams
Secret of Lucifer's Island. M. Lynch
Secret of Lynndale. F. Warden
Secret of MI6. L. Smith
Secret of Mallet Castle. Clarissa Ross
Secret of Matchams. N. Burnaby
Secret of Maxshelling. E. Everett-Green
Secret of Mirror House. P. Maxwell
Secret of Mohawk Pond. N. S. Lincoln
Secret of Moor House. D. Stuart
Secret of Musterton House. G. Granby
Secret of Oil Creek. A. Parsons
Secret of Providence Lodge. R. E. Salwey
Secret of Room No. 13. C. E. Pearce
Secret of Saraband. M. Floyd
Secret of Sarek. M. Leblanc
Secret of Scotland Yard. A. E. Bayly
Secret of Sea-Dream House. A. P. Terhune
Secret of Secrets. J. S. Fletcher
Secret of Seven. D. Stuart
Secret of Seven Oaks. J. Coulson
Secret of Sheen. J. Laurence
Secret of Shower Tree. V. Coffman
Secret of Simon Cornell. H. Howard
Secret of Sir George Hartley. A. M. Diehl
Secret of Skye. A. S. Swan
Secret of Stark Island. Colin Desmond
Secret of Stillwater Mere. G. Chester
Secret of Superintendent Manning. B. Cobb
Secret of Sylvia. Lee Borden
Secret of Tangles. L. Gribble
Secret of Tarn-End House. C. Randell
Secret of the African Settler. R. Hardinge
Secret of the African Trader. R. Hardinge
Secret of the Armaments King. P. Quiroule
Secret of the Ashes. A. Ornstien
Secret of the Balkan Heiress. C. Brisbane
Secret of the Baltic. T. C. Bridges
Secret of the Barbican. J. S. Fletcher
Secret of the Bayou. F. Davenport
Secret of the Black Mere. Anonymous
Secret of the Black Wallet. W. W. Sayer
Secret of the Blue Macaw. I. L. Forrester
Secret of the Blue Vase. H. Tuite
Secret of the Bucket Shop. J. G. Jones
Secret of the Bungalow. R. J. Casey
Secret of the Burma Road. A. Parsons
Secret of the Carpathians. H. H. C. Gibbons
Secret of the Cask. R. C. Armour
Secret of the Castle Ruins. A. Parsons
Secret of the Cellar. W. Edwards
Secret of the Chateau. C. Farr
Secret of the Chinese Jar. F. Hume
Secret of the Circle. P. Quiroule
Secret of the Coconut Groves. G. H. Teed
Secret of the Cove. H. L. Deakin
Secret of the Crater. H. H. Hill
Secret of the Creek. V. Bridges
Secret of the Dark Room. R. J. Casey
Secret of the Dead. L. T. Meade
Secret of the Dead. I. Stark
Secret of the Dead Convict. M. B. Dix

Secret of the Dead Man. P. Urquhart
Secret of the Demolition Worker. J. Hunter
Secret of the Dental Surgeon. R. Hardinge
Secret of the Desert. R. Hardinge
Secret of the Diamond. E. D. Pierson
Secret of the Diamonds. C. W. Greatorex
Secret of the Doubting Saint. L. Holton
Secret of the Downs. W. S. Masterman
Secret of the Evacuee. P. Urquhart
Secret of the Everglades. B. Marchant
Secret of the Farm. G. Chester
Secret of the Fated Family. R. Hardinge
Secret of the Flames. W. M. Graydon
Secret of the Flames. R. Rodd
Secret of the Frozen North. W. W. Sayer
Secret of the Garden. A. Gask
Secret of the Ghostly Shroud. N. Buckingham
Secret of the Glacier. W. Jardine
Secret of the Glacier. A. Murray
Secret of the Glen. C. Brisbane
Secret of the Gold Locket. R. C. Armour
Secret of the Golden Horse. A. Parsons
Secret of the Grange. Mark Cross
Secret of the Grave. J. Hunter
Secret of the Graveyard. J. Addiscombe
Secret of the Green Lagoon. A. Murray
Secret of the Hills. W. Garrett
Secret of the Hold. J. Hunter
Secret of the Hulk. A. Murray
Secret of the Hulk. D. Stuart
Secret of the Hunger Desert. A. Murray
Secret of the Identification Parade. W. Edwards
Secret of the Indian Lawyer. A. Parsons
Secret of the Jungle. R. Hardinge
Secret of the Jungle. G. Rees
Secret of the Lagoon. R. C. Armour
Secret of the Lake House. J. Rhode
Secret of the Lebombo. B. Mitford
Secret of the Little Flea. B. Munslow
Secret of the Little Gods. K. H. Taylor
Secret of the Living Skeleton. J. Drummond
Secret of the Loch. C. Brisbane
Secret of the Locket. E. St. Clair
Secret of the Man Who Died. R. Hardinge
Secret of the Mansions. W. J. Bayfield
Secret of the Marble Mantle. N. Carter
Secret of the Marionettes. E. D. Pierson
Secret of the Marsh. O. Warner
Secret of the Marshbanks. K. Norris
Secret of the Marshes. M. Richmond
Secret of the Mere. D. Peacock
Secret of the Mere. J. J. Wray
Secret of the Midway Plaza. A. E. Dramond
Secret of the Mine. A. Steffens Hardy
Secret of the Missing Checks. H. Rockwood
Secret of the Moat. H. Desmond
Secret of the Monastery. S. G. Shaw
Secret of the Moor. M. Gerard
Secret of the Moor Cottage. H. R. Cromarsh
Secret of the Morgue. F. G. Eberhard
Secret of the Moroccan Bazaar. A. Parsons
Secret of the Night. G. Leroux
Secret of the Oblong Chest. W. W. Sayer
Secret of the Old Lighthouse. J. G. Rowe
Secret of the Pale Lover. Clarissa Ross
Secret of the Past. W. M. Graydon
Secret of the President's Daughter. G. H. Teed
Secret of the Priory. S. O. Bryan
Secret of the Priory. M. Richmond
Secret of the Raft. H. Townley
Secret of the Red Mountain. W. W. Sayer
Secret of the River. Dora Russell
Secret of the Roman Temple. A. Parsons
Secret of the Russian Refugees. W. M. Graydon
Secret of the Safe. A. Edgar
Secret of the Sale Room. R. Hardinge
Secret of the Saltings. V. Bridges
Secret of the Sanatorium. C. Brisbane
Secret of the Sandbanks. J. Plain
Secret of the Sandhills. A. Gask
Secret of the Sandhills. F. Marlowe
Secret of the Sands. W. Tyrer
Secret of the Sands. F. M. White
Secret of the Sapphire Ring. M. V. Woodgate
Secret of the Scarlet Bomber. P. Conde
Secret of the Screen. S. Fowler
Secret of the Sea. W. Allison
Secret of the Sea. C. M. Parsons
Secret of the Sea. T. W. Speight
Secret of the Sealed Room. D. Stuart
Secret of the Second Door. R. Colby
Secret of the Seven Sisters. John Marsh
Secret of the Seven Spiders. G. Stanley
Secret of the Sheba. R. Hardinge
Secret of the Siding. J. Brooke
Secret of the Siegfried Line. M. B. Dix
Secret of the Silver Car. W. Martyn
Secret of the Six Black Dots. W. W. Sayer
Secret of the Sixty Steps. J. Drummond
Secret of the Sky. K. Robeson
Secret of the Smuggler's Cove. R. Hardinge
Secret of the Snows. G. Chester
Secret of the Snows. H. H. C. Gibbons
Secret of the Snows. J. Plain
Secret of the Snows. W. Tyrer
Secret of the Spa. C. L. Leonard
Secret of the Spectre's Nest. W. E. Groves
Secret of the Sphinx. H. Carew
Secret of the Square. W. LeQueux
Secret of the Stage. N. Ridley
Secret of the Stargazer's Club. Jack Carew
Secret of the Steps. G. Chester
Secret of the Storm County. Grace M. White
Secret of the Strong Room. G. H. Teed
Secret of the Sudan. W. Jardine
Secret of the Suez Canal. G. Rees
Secret of the Sunken Ships. G. Chester
Secret of the Surgery. J. W. Bobin
Secret of the Surgery. W. Jardine
Secret of the Swamp. G. Bettany
Secret of the Swinging Boom. E. M. Robinson
Secret of the Ten Bales. A. Parsons
Secret of the Thieves' Kitchen. G. H. Teed
Secret of the Tomb. W. J. Bayfield
Secret of the Tong. A. Edgar
Secret of the Tower. Anthony Hope
Secret of the Two Blackmailed Men. W. M. Graydon
Secret of the Vampire Actress. W. M. Graydon
Secret of the Vault. G. Verner
Secret of the Veld. R. Hardinge
Secret of the Villa Como. S. Marvin
Secret of the Vineyard. M. Heath
Secret of the Weeping Monk. B. McMikle
Secret of the White Thug. R. Francis Foster
Secret of the Willows. Elna Stone
Secret of the Woods. P. Quiroule
Secret of the Zodiac. J. Sterne
Secret of Thirty-Seven Hardy Street. R. J. Casey
Secret of Thirty Years! W. W. Sayer
Secret of Thurlston Towers. L. H. Brooks
Secret of Torre Island. R. C. Armour
Secret of Trescobell. J. Hocking
Secret of Tso Feng. L. C. Douthwaite
Secret of Villa Vanesta. E. Glen
Secret of Wardale Court and other stories. Andree Hope
Secret of Weir House. F. Cowen
Secret of Wold Hall. E. Everett-Green
Secret of Wyvern Towers. T. W. Speight
Secret Orchards. Michael Burt
Secret Pact. A. O. Pollard
Secret Panel. N. Carter
Secret Panel. A. S. Swan
Secret Paper. W. Wood
Secret Passage. F. Hume
Secret Pathway. A. Askew
Secret Pearls. O. Binns
Secret People. H. H. C. Gibbons
Secret Pilot. G. E. Rochester
Secret Police. John Lang
Secret Power. T. C. H. Jacobs
Secret Power. V. Van Der Elst
Secret Quest. G. M. Fenn
Secret Road. J. Ferguson
Secret Sceptre. F. Gerard
Secret Sea-Plane. G. Thorne
Secret Search. E. R. Punshon
Secret Servant. B. Newman
Secret Service. C. T. Brady
Secret Service. A. Forrester
Secret Service. W. Gillette
Secret Service. W. LeQueux
Secret Service. P. Sebastian
Secret Service Girl. Roland Daniel
Secret Service Girl. J. M. Walsh
Secret Service Man. G. Dilnot
Secret Service Man. S. Horler
Secret Service Mystery. H. Pink
Secret Service Operator 13. R. W. Chambers
Secret Service Ship. C. E. Averill
Secret Service Smith. R. T. M. Scott
Secret Service Submarine. G. Thorne
Secret Service Woman. H. De Halsalle
Secret Services. G. Frankau
Secret Session. H. Janson
Secret Shame of the Kaiser. W. LeQueux
Secret Ship. E. K. Chatterton
Secret Sin. W. LeQueux
Secret Singing. R. Lewis
Secret Sister. A. Applin
Secret Six. F. Marion
Secret Soldier. J. Quigley
Secret Spring. P. Benoit
Secret Squadron in Germany. G. E. Rochester
Secret Square. E. Jepson
Secret Super-Charger. P. Gill
Secret Suspicion. M. O. Rolfe
Secret Syndicate. R. C. Frazer
Secret Syndicate. F. Whishaw
Secret Telephone. W. LeQueux
Secret Temple. C. Brisbane
Secret Terror. F. Hird
Secret That Was Kept. E. Robins
Secret Thread. E. Vance
Secret Toll. P. Thorne
Secret Tomb. M. Leblanc
Secret Tontine. R. M. Gilchrist
Secret Traffic. B. Tozer
Secret Trail. A. Armstrong
Secret Tunnel. R. C. Finney
Secret Understanding. Merle Miller

Title Index — Servant of Satan /633

Secret Valley. Elliot Bailey
Secret Vanguard. M. Innes
Secret Vendetta. A. O. Pollard
Secret Voice. H. Desmond
Secret Voyage. Basil Carey
Secret Voyage. H. Edmonds
Secret War. N. Daniels
Secret War. D. Wheatley
Secret Way. J. S. Fletcher
Secret Ways. Alistair MacLean
Secret Ways. A. Soutar
Secret Weapon. F. Beeding
Secret Weapon. B. Newman
Secret Weapon. A. O. Pollard
Secret Weapons. J. M. Walsh
Secret Witness. G. F. Gibbs
Secret Woman. V. Holt
Secretary. Anonymous
Secretary of Frivolous Affairs. M. Futrelle
Secretary of State for Death. H. Carstairs
Secrets. B. Hirschfeld
Secrets Can Be Fatal. M. Heath
Secrets Can't Be Kept. E. R. Punshon
Secrets for Sale. C. L. Leonard
Secrets for Sale. J. H. Vahey
Secrets of a Dark Plot in New York Society. A. S. Manly
Secrets of a Private Enquiry Office. Mrs. G. Corbett
Secrets of a Private Enquiry Office. J. Peddie
Secrets of Cromwell Crossing. D. Winston
Secrets of Dr. Taverner. D. Fortune
Secrets of Hillyard House. K. Norris
Secrets of Monte Carlo. W. LeQueux
Secrets of Potsdam. W. LeQueux
Secrets of Sedbury Manor. Marilyn Ross
Secrets of the Coast. S. Cobb
Secrets of the Courts of Europe. A. Upward
Secrets of the Dead-Letter Office. B. Hemyng
Secrets of the Foreign Office. W. LeQueux
Secrets of the Police. Grace M. White
Secrets of the River. B. Hemyng
Secrets of the Turf. B. Hemyng
Secrets of the White Tsar. W. LeQueux
Section 558. J. Hawthorne
Security Risk. G. Hackforth-Jones
Security Risk. T. C. H. Jacobs
Security Secrets Sold Here. B. Cobb
Sedan Murder Mystery. J. Wallace
Seduce and Destroy. J. Eastwood
Seducer. F. Flora
Seduction of a Tall Man. R. Gadney
Seductress. C. Brown
Sedulous Ape. D. Batchelor
See How They Run. A. Kennington
See How They Run. D. M. Mankiewicz
See How They Run. W. Shaw
See Naples and Die. J. Davies
See No Evil. W. Hughes
See No Evil. F. McDermid
See Nothing--Say Nothing. P. Carlon
See Rome and Die. L. Revell
See the Living Crocodiles. C. V. Bark
See the Red Blood Run. N. N. Peebles
"See the Woman." D. Barnes
See Them Die. E. McBain
See Who's Dying. S. H. Courtier
See You at the Morgue. L. G. Blochman
Seed of Doubt. D. Keene
Seed of Empire. F. M. White
Seed of Envy. J. Remenham
Seed of Evil. P. Crawford
Seed of Violence. Williams Forrest
Seed Was Kind. D. Macardle

Seeds of Corruption. J. Knowler
Seeds of Destruction. R. V. Beste
Seeds of Destruction. D. Nabarro
Seeds of Hate. H. Carmichael
Seeds of Murder. V. W. Mason
Seeds of Murder. J. York
Seeds of Suspicion. J. Roffman
Seeds of Violence. M. Sharman
Seeing Double. E. Ferrars
Seeing Eye. J. Bell
Seeing Is Believing. Carter Dickson
Seeing Life. E. P. Oppenheim
Seeing Red. T. Du Bois
Seek and Destroy. R. Owen
Seek and Destroy. M. K. Robertson
Seek, Strike and Destroy. K. Stanton
Seeker to the Dead. A. M. Burrage
Seen and the Unseen. R. Marsh
Seen Dimly Before Dawn. N. Balchin
Seen in the Shadow. F. Hume
Seersucker Whipsaw. Ross Thomas
Seidlitz and the Super-Spy. C. Brown
Seine Fishers. J. Wood
Seine Mystery. C. Moffett
Self-Appointed Saint. A. E. Lindop
Self-Convicted. H. Wood
Self-Doomed. B. L. Farjeon
Self-Made. E. Southworth
Self-Made Thief. H. Footner
Self-Made Widow. P. Race
Self-Portrait of Murder. F. Bonnamy
Self-Raised. E. Southworth
Selicombe Murder. N. Islay
Sellers of Death. W. W. Sayer
Selling's Murder! A. Tack
Sellout. D. Jewell
Selmin of Selmingfold. B. Mitford
Selminster Murders. C. Ryland
Seminar in Evil. D. Winston
Semonov Impulse. J. Meldrum
Semper Inheritance. C. Carfax
Sempinski Affair. W. S. Kuniczak
Senator's Nude. B. Goode
Senator's Plot. N. Carter
Senator's Ransom. K. Bernstein
Send Another Coffin. J. Grecco
Send Another Coffin. F. G. Presnell
Send Another Hearse. H. Q. Masur
Send Danger. M. Sutherland
Send for Angel. G. Montrose
Send for Paul Temple. F. Durbridge
Send for Paul Temple Again! F. Durbridge
Send Him Victorious. D. Hurd
Send Inspector West. J. Creasey
Send No Flowers. Gavin Holt
Send-Off. R. Hiscock
Send-Off. C. Leach
Send Superintendent West. J. Creasey
Seneca, U.S.A. J. Roeburt
Senior Partner. J. H. Riddell
Senor Saint. L. Charteris
Sensation at Blue Harbour. J. L. Rickard
Sensational Case. F. Warden
Sensational Trance. F. Dawson
Sense of Danger. E. Cannon
Sense of Guilt. G. Simenon
Sense of Reality. G. Greene
Sense of Survival. K. Casey
Sensualists. B. Hecht
Sent to His Account. E. Dillon
Sentence Deferred. A. Derleth
Sentence for Sin. H. Janson
Sentence of Death. J. York
Sentence of Life. Julian Gloag
Sentence of the Court. H. Hill
Sentence of the Court. F. M. White
Sentence of the Six-Gun. A. M. Rud
Sentenced! S. Gibney

Sentenced to Death. R. Machray
Sentenced to Life. M. A. Hamilton
Sentiment, and other stories. V. O'Sullivan
Sentimental Crook. A. Wilson
Sentimental Season. T. Cobb
Sentimental Sex. G. Warden
Sentimental Warrior. E. Jepson
Sentinel. J. Konvitz
Sentries. E. McBain
Sentry-Box Murder. N. Gayle
September Can Be Dangerous in Edinburgh. B. Craig
September Comes In. F. M. McGuire
September Story. R. Inchbald
Septimus and the Danedyke Mystery. Stephen Chance
Septimus and the Minister Ghost. Stephen Chance
Sequel to Don Juan. G. W. M. Reynolds
Sequel to Opposite the Jail. M. A. Denison
Sequin Syndicate. O. Hesky
Sequins Lost Their Lustre. S. Harvester
Serbian Assignment. Andrew Moore
Serenade. J. M. Cain
Serenade for Murder. A. Wood
Serenade to the Hangman. M. Dekobra
Sergeant and the Queen. R. Crane
Sergeant Cluff and the Day of Reckoning. G. North
Sergeant Cluff and the Madmen. G. North
Sergeant Cluff and the Price of Pity. G. North
Sergeant Cluff Goes Fishing. G. North
Sergeant Cluff Rings True. G. North
Sergeant Cluff Stands Firm. G. North
Sgt. Corbin's War. R. Crane
Sergeant Cork's Casebook. A. Swinson
Sergeant Cork's Second Casebook. A. Swinson
Sergeant Death. D. G. Browne
Sergeant Death. F. P. Grady
Sergeant Death. J. Mayo
Sergeant Gray's Crime. J. Hunter
Sergeant Lancey Carries On. L. P. Greene
Sergeant Lancey Reports. L. P. Greene
Sergeant Lancey Tells the Tale. L. P. Greene
Sergeant Michael Cassidy, R.E. H. C. McNeile
Sergeant Ross in Disguise. B. Cobb
Sergeant Sir Peter. E. Wallace
Sergeant Verity and the Cracksman. F. Selwyn
Sergeant Verity and the Imperial Diamond. F. Selwyn
Sergeant Von. Anonymous
Sergeant Whatisname. L. P. Greene
Serious Investigation. L. Egan
Serle's Secret. F. Warden
Sern Charter. F. Ryck
Serpent-Headed Stick. J. Hawk
Serpent Heart. M. A. Taylor
Serpent in the Shadows. A. Barron
Serpent Sleeping. E. Weismuller
Serpent Stirs. Richard Grant
Serpent Under It. E. Taylor
Serpentine Murder. L. Gribble
Serpent's Egg. D. Duncan
Serpent's Fang. B. Stuart
Serpent's Smile. O. Hesky
Serpent's Tooth. S. Woods
Servant of Death. J. H. Wallis
Servant of Satan. L. Berard

Servant of the King. A. Griffin
Servants of the Goddess. H. Campbell
Servants of the Skull. B. House
Servant's Problem. V. P. Johns
Set a Spy. M. McKenna
Set a Thief. L. Thayer
Set of Flats. A. Griffiths
Set of Rogues. F. Barrett
Set of Six. J. Conrad
Set to Partners. G. Warden
Set-Up. J. K. Baxter
Set-Up. R. Carni
Set-Up. B. E. Miller
Set-Up. Robin Moore
Set Up for Danger. R. Madison
Set-Up for Murder. P. Cheyney
Seth Bond. Old Sleuth
Settled Out of Court. H. Cecil
Settled Out of Court. R. A. Knox
Settler or Slaver. A. Murray
Setup for Murder. L. A. Olmsted
Seven Against Greece. N. Carter
Seven Agate Devils. K. Robeson
Seven Black Chessmen. J. Huntingdon
Seven Bloodhounds. M. Richmond
Seven Blue Diamonds. C. B. Stilson
Seven Chose Murder. Roy Vickers
Seven Clues. G. Verner
Seven Clues in Search of a Crime. B. Graeme
Seven Conundrums. E. P. Oppenheim
Seven Dawns to Death. B. Gray
Seven Days Before Dying. H. Nielsen
Seven Days for Hanging. J. M. Spender
Seven Days from Midnight. Rona Randall
Seven Days' Hard. S. M. Parkman
Seven Days in a Pullman Car. A. Towner
Seven Days in May. F. Knebel
Seven Day's Mystery. F. R. Burton
Seven Days' Secret. J. S. Fletcher
Seven Days to a Killing. C. Egleton
Seven Days to Death. N. MacKenzie
Seven Days to Death. J. J. Marric
Seven Days to Never. P. Frank
Seven Dead. J. J. Farjeon
Seven Deadly Sisters. P. McGerr
Seven Dials Mystery. A. Christie
Seven Died. G. Homes
711--Officer Needs Help. W. Masterson
Seven Elms Mystery. H. B. Harris
Seven File. W. P. McGivern
Seven Footprints to Satan. A. Merritt
Seven Gothic Tales. I. Dinesen
Seven Green Stones. P. Wentworth
Seven Guests of Fear. I. Barry
Seven Hells. C. Brooks
Seven Keys to Baldpate. E. D. Biggers
Seven Keys to Baldpate. G. M. Cohan
Seven Lamps. G. Verner
Seven Lean Years. C. Fremlin
Seven Lies South. W. P. McGivern
Seven Looked On. B. Malim
Seven Men. T. Roscoe
Seven Men Are Murdered. R. Wallace
7 Murders. R. H. May
7 Must Die. J. W. Bellah
Seven of Hearts. M. Leblanc
Seven-Per-Cent Solution. N. Meyer
Seven Pillars to Hell. H. Marlowe
Seven Red-Headed Men. F. Marlowe
Seven Red Herrings. E. P. Thorne
Seven Saints. G. Stanley
Seven Schemers. N. Carter
Seven Screens. G. Dickson
Seven Seas Murders. V. W. Mason
Seven Seats to the Moon. C. Armstrong
Seven Secrets. W. LeQueux
Seven Shadows. G. Stanley

Seven Sins. S. Rohmer
Seven Sirens. C. Brown
Seven Sisters. W. T. Ballard
Seven Sisters. R. Chapman
Seven Sisters. J. Lilly
Seven Slayers. P. Cain
Seven Sleepers. F. Beeding
Seven Sleepers. E. Ferrars
Seven Stabs. J. Cameron
Seven Stars. V. Bridges
Seven Steps East. B. Benson
Seven Suspects. M. Innes
Seven Suspects. F. Ryerson
Seven Tears for Apollo. P. A. Whitney
7.30 Victoria. P. McGuire
Seven Thunders. R. Croft-Cooke
Seven Thunders. M. M. Lawrence
Seven Tickets to Singapore. Ared White
Seven Times Seven. J. Creasey
Seven to Die. H. Long
7 to 12. A. K. Green
Seven-Ups. R. Posner
Seven Votes for Death. P. Bannister
Seven Were Suspect. R. Goyne
Seven Were Suspect. K. M. Knight
Seven Were Veiled. K. M. Knight
Seven Who Waited. A. Derleth
Seven Women. Winifred Duke
Seven Year Secret. F. Hurt
Seven Years Dead. S. Truss
17 and Black. J. Waer
Seventeen Cards. F. C. Vivian
Seventeen Thieves of El-Kabil. T. Mundy
Seventeen Widows of Sans Souci. C. Armstrong
17th Letter. D. C. Disney
Seventeenth Stair. B. Paul
Seventh. R. Stark
Seventh All Hallow's Eve. R. Jensen
Seventh Chasm. O. Gard
Seventh Entanglement. E. Leslie
Seventh Fury. J. Castle
Seventh Juror. F. Didelot
Seventh Man. Wilson Barclay
Seventh Man. J. Scotland
Seventh Mask. H. Slesar
Seventh Mourner. D. Gardiner
Seventh Passenger. P. Capon
Seventh Passenger. A. MacGowan
Seventh Postcard. H. Flowerdew
Seventh Shot. H. Coverdale
Seventh Sign. B. Flynn
Seventh Sinner. Elizabeth Peters
Seventh Vial. F. Sleath
Seventh Wife of Prince Hasson. M. Dekobra
Seventy Fathom Treasure. A. D. Divine
Seventy North--70°N. Taffrail
71 Hours. M. Mason
77 Rue Paradis. G. Brewer
77 Sunset Strip. R. Huggins
77 Willow Road. H. D. Irvine
77th Day. H. Possendorf
70 Sutton Place. J. Di Mona
70,000 Witnesses. C. Fitzsimmons
Severed Hand. F. Du Boisgobey
Severed Hand. E. Lecale
Severed Key. H. Nielsen
Severence. T. Cobb
Severing Line. S. Cardiff
Severith Style. D. Honig
Severn Affair. G. Warden
Sevier Secrets. D. Daniels
Sex Angle. H. Janson
Sex Castle. E. Lacy
Sex Clinic. C. Brown

Sex Marks the Spot. S. Browning
Sex Trap. C. Brown
Sex Trap. Bill Turner
Sexton Blake in Silesia. W. M. Graydon
Sexton Blake--Special Constable. J. W. Bobin
Sexton Blake's Vow. A. Steffens Hardy
Sexton Woman. R. Neely
Sexy Vixen. H. Janson
Shabby Eagles. B. Gaston
Shack-Up. A. Curry
Shackled. M. Crossley
Shackleton Called Sheila. D. Mariner
Shade of Darkness. M. Torrie
Shade of Time. D. Duncan
Shades and Shadows. L. Churchill
Shades of Evil. S. Wagner
Shadow. H. Bedford-Jones
Shadow. W. B. Gibson
Shadow. V. Kelly
Shadow. M. Level
Shadow. P. Mason
Shadow. A. Stringer
Shadow. D. Stuart
Shadow. P. Urquhart
Shadow Acres. F. Y. McHugh
Shadow Agent. W. Martyn
Shadow, and other stories. J. Farnol
Shadow and the Blot. N. D. Lobell
Shadow and the Fear. J. Corby
Shadow and the Stone. L. Meynell
Shadow and the Web. Mary Allerton
Shadow Before. L. P. Davies
Shadow Before. W. Rollins
Shadow Behind. F. Warwick
Shadow Behind the Throne. O. Harper
Shadow Between. R. Pattison
Shadow Beware. M. Grant
Shadow Box. V. Coffman
Shadow Buttress. S. Styles
Shadow Called Janet. J. N. Chance
Shadow Crook. A. De Brune
Shadow Crook. G. H. Teed
Shadow Crusade. W. Mills
Shadow--Destination Moon. M. Grant
Shadow Detective. Old Sleuth
Shadow 81. L. Nahum
Shadow Falls. C. Lorrimer
Shadow Falls. G. Simenon
Shadow for a Lady. J. L. Linklater
Shadow from the Bogue. C. Wood
Shadow Game. M. Underwood
Shadow Glen. D. Daniels
Shadow--Go Mad! M. Grant
Shadow Guest. H. Waugh
Shadow Hall. J. P. Seabrooke
Shadow in the Corner. M. E. Braddon
Shadow in the Courtyard. G. Simenon
Shadow in the House. S. Gluck
Shadow in the House. M. March
Shadow in the Sea. O. John
Shadow in the Sun. L. Meynell
Shadow in the Wild. W. Masterson
Shadow Knows. Diane Johnson
Shadow Laughs! M. Grant
Shadow Man. J. Goodwin
Shadow Mansion. Wilma Forrest
Shadow Men. D. Richberg
Shadow Men. G. Verner
Shadow of a Cat. P. Nottingham
Shadow of a Crime. H. Caine
Shadow of a Crime. J. Rhode
Shadow of a Crime. Mrs. C. Sheldon
Shadow of a Dead Man. T. W. Hanshew
Shadow of a Doubt. H. Judd
Shadow of a Gun. Martin Thomas
Shadow of a Hair. D. C. Meade
Shadow of a Hawk. M. Carrel
Shadow of a Hero. Allan Chase
Shadow of a Killer. W. Mole

Shadow of a Lady. H. Roth
Shadow of a Man. D. Daniels
Shadow of a Man. D. M. Disney
Shadow of a Man. E. W. Hornung
Shadow of a Past Love. W. D. Roberts
Shadow of a Rope. E. W. Hornung
Shadow of a Sin. H. Zore
Shadow of a Spy. A. MacKenzie
Shadow of a Stranger. A. Maybury
Shadow of a Tiger. Michael Collins
Shadow of a Vendetta. A. C. Gunter
Shadow of a Witch. P. Minton
Shadow of a Witch. M. Paradise
Shadow of an Alibi. J. Rhode
Shadow of an Assassin. I. Stark
Shadow of an Unknown Woman. D. Winston
Shadow of Ashlydyat. H. Wood
Shadow of Chu-Sheng. E. Thomas
Shadow of Death. G. Ashe
Shadow of Dr. Ferrari. E. P. Thorne
Shadow of Doctor Syn. R. Thorndike
Shadow of Doom. J. Creasey
Shadow of Doubt. A. S. Roche
Shadow of Egypt. H. H. Ross
Shadow of Evil. M. Black
Shadow of Evil. C. Dawe
Shadow of Evil. D. Donovan
Shadow of Evil. C. J. Dutton
Shadow of Fear. R. C. Payes
Shadow of Fear. B. Spicer
Shadow of Fear. N. Toye
Shadow of Fu Manchu. S. Rohmer
Shadow of Gilsland. M. Gerard
Shadow of Guilt. R. Bloomfield
Shadow of Guilt. Old Spicer
Shadow of Guilt. P. Quentin
Shadow of Hampton Mead. E. Van Loon
Shadow of Himself. M. Delving
Shadow of His Crime. J. W. Bobin
Shadow of John Wallace. L. Clarkson
Shadow of Larose. A. Gask
Shadow of Li Tong Su. C. Bishop
Shadow of Madness. H. Pentecost
Shadow of Malreward. J. B. Harris-Burland
Shadow of Monte Carlo and other stories. C. Kingston
Shadow of Murder. C. Blackstock
Shadow of Murder. M. F. Ford
Shadow of Murder. P. Laing
Shadow of My Brother. D. Grubb
Shadow of Peril. A. I. Zhdanov
Shadow of Polperro. F. Cowen
Shadow of Quong Lung. C. W. Doyle
Shadow of Ravenscliffe. J. S. Fletcher
Shadow of Salvador. J. Haslette
Shadow of Shame. Austyn Granville
Shadow of Sheila Ann. P. Wissmann
Shadow of Tarleton Manor. B. M. Clay
Shadow of the Bars. E. D. Pierson
Shadow of the Bear. H. Hill
Shadow of the Caravan. S. O'Brien
Shadow of the Cobra. D. Dalheath
Shadow of the Condor. J. Grady
Shadow of the Czar. J. R. Carling
Shadow of the Four. Mark Cross
Shadow of the Gallows. M. Richmond
Shadow of the Guillotine. G. E. Rochester
Shadow of the Hunter. C. Kerr
Shadow of the Killer. J. N. Chance
Shadow of the Lynx. V. Holt
Shadow of the Mafia. L. Malley
Shadow of the Monsoon. W. Manchester
Shadow of the Past. M. Richmond
Shadow of the Rock. G. Hackforth-Jones
Shadow of the Rope. I. Stark
Shadow of the Sun. S. Wagner
Shadow of the Truth. H. Arvonen
Shadow of the Unseen. B. Pain
Shadow of the Volcano. D. Rowan
Shadow of the Wolf. R. A. Freeman
Shadow of the Yemen. B. Bolt
Shadow of Theale. F. Cowen
Shadow of Thirteen. J. J. Farjeon
Shadow of Time. C. Landon
Shadow of Tyburn Tree. D. Wheatley
Shadow of Wrong. C. Gibbon
Shadow on Capricorn. Clarissa Ross
Shadow on Mercer Mountain. D. Winston
Shadow on Mockways. M. Bowen
Shadow on Spanish Swamp. G. St. John
Shadow on the Cliff. M. Burton
Shadow on the Course. B. Strong
Shadow on the Downs. R. C. Woodthorpe
Shadow on the Glass. C. J. Dutton
Shadow on the Hearth. F. Halsey
Shadow on the House. A. W. Barrett
Shadow on the House. F. Ford
Shadow on the House. M. Hansom
Shadow on the House. F. Stevenson
Shadow on the House. E. C. Vivian
Shadow on the Left. Augustus Muir
Shadow on the Moon. L. Churchill
Shadow on the Purple. Anonymous
Shadow on the Sea. M. Pemberton
Shadow on the Steppe. M. Billett
Shadow on the Threshold. M. C. Hay
Shadow on the Wall. H. C. Bailey
Shadow on the Wall. M. E. Coleridge
Shadow on the Wall. M. Dalton
Shadow on the Water. H. Ainsworth
Shadow on the Wind. A. Lowing
Shadow on the Window. G. Bagby
Shadow over Elveron. M. J. Kingsley
Shadow over Emerald Castle. Marilyn Ross
Shadow over Europe. N. Leslie
Shadow over Fairholme. S. Kyle
Shadow over Grove House. M. L. Roby
Shadow over Mount Sharon. F. Y. McHugh
Shadow over Pleasant Heath. K. Kimbrough
Shadow over the Garden. C. Ross
Shadow Passes. E. Phillpotts
Shadow Passes. Y. Pickering
Shadow People. K. Laing
Shadow Play. C. Phillips
Shadow Play. L. Powell
Shadow Shooter. W. C. Tuttle
Shadow Strikes. M. Grant
Shadow Syndicate. C. Hosken
Shadow That Caught Fire. H. Jobson
Shadow the Baron. A. Morton
Shadow Wife. D. Eden
Shadow Witness. A. A. Thomson
Shadowbox. S. Noyes
Shadowboxer. N. Behl
Shadowed! H. Belloc
Shadowed. M. Cumberland
Shadowed by a Detective. V. Champlin
Shadowed by the C.I.D. T. A. Plummer
Shadowed by Three. L. L. Lynch
Shadowed by 2. Old Sleuth
Shadowed from Europe. Hawkshaw
Shadowed Lives. A. Applin
Shadowed Lives. W. M. Graydon
Shadowed Love. F. M. White
Shadowed Place. V. Scannell
Shadowed Porch. E. Moor
Shadowed Round the World. J. K. Stafford
Shadowed to Europe. Le Jemlys
Shadowed to His Doom. Old Sleuth
Shadowed Victory. A. Stringer
Shadowers. D. Hamilton
Shadowland. Elaine Evans
Shadowless Men. B. Jones
Shadows. Jan Alexander
Shadows. Winifred Duke
Shadows. F. Ryerson
Shadows. Will Scott
Shadows at Noon. M. M. Goldsmith
Shadows Before. D. Bowers
Shadows by the Sea. J. J. Farjeon
Shadows Don't Bleed. W. Wright
Shadows from the Past. D. Daniels
Shadows from the Thames. E. Noble
Shadows in a Hidden Land. S. Harvester
Shadows in Succession. E. K. Lobaugh
Shadows in the Fire. Eva Dane
Shadows in the Moonlight. Elizabeth Peters
Shadows in the Night. J. Reach
Shadows in the Sun. J. Edgar
Shadows of Evil. G. La Spina
Shadows of Life. C. Meyer
Shadows of One Another. T. R. Cox
Shadows of the House. M. E. Atkins
Shadows of the Past. M. Craig
Shadows of Tomorrow. D. Daniels
Shadows of Violence. K. Evans
Shadows on a Wall. C. E. Israel
Shadows on Abu Simbel. T. B. Morris
Shadows on the Hill. M. Carleton
Shadows on the Landing. G. M. Wilson
Shadows on the River. A. MacKenzie
Shadows on the Sand. G. Greenaway
Shadows on the Sand. Rona Randall
Shadows on the Wall. M. Reisner
Shadows on the Water. Dorothy Fletcher
Shadows over Seascape. Lynn Williams
Shadow's Revenge. M. Grant
Shadow's Shadow. L. Ragsdale
Shadows Sometimes Scream. L. Della
Shadows Tonight. A. Seifert
Shadows Waiting. A. Eliot
Shadowy Thing. H. B. Drake
Shadowy Third. M. Page
Shady Doings. V. P. Johns
Shady Lady. C. F. Adams
Shady Lady. C. Brown
Shady Place to Die. J. Savage
Shaft. E. Tidyman
Shaft Among the Jews. E. Tidyman
Shaft Has a Ball. E. Tidyman
Shaft's Big Score. E. Tidyman
Shaft's Carnival of Killers. E. Tidyman
Shaggy Dog and other murders. F. Brown
Shaggy Dog and other stories. F. Brown
Shake a Crooked Town. D. J. Marlowe
Shake Hands for Ever. R. Rendell
Shake Hands for Ever. E. Woodward
Shake Him Till He Rattles. M. Brady
Shake-Up. H. Edmiston
Shake-Up. Breni James
Shakedown. R. Ellington
Shakedown. B. Kerr
Shakedown. J. Mack
Shakedown. R. Scott
Shakedown for Murder. E. Lacy
Shakedown Hotel. E. J. Fredericks
Shakedown Kid. N. Singer
Shaken Down. A. MacGowan
Shaken Leaf. D. Cory
Shakeout. K. Follett
Shakespeare Curse. J. Boland
Shakespeare Murders. N. Gordon
Shakespeare Murders. A. R. Long
Shaking Shadow. Elizabeth Stuart
Shaking Spear. B. Flynn
Shall Do No Murder. H. Alexander
Shallow Grave. J. Quinn
Shallow Runs the River. E. Moore
Sham Detective. Anonymous
Shamballah. J. F. Rossmann
Shame. R. Himmel

Shame Dance, and other stories. W. D. Steele
Shame of Arizona. W. C. Tuttle
Shame of Silence. M. Leighton
Shamelady. J. Mayo
Shameless. J. M. Cain
Shamus. R. Giles
Shamus. J. Mack
Shamus, Your Slip Is Showing. C. Brown
Shandon Hall. J. L. Rickard
Shanghai Bund Murders. V. W. Mason
Shanghai Flame. A. S. Fleischman
Shanghai Honeymoon. M. Dekobra
Shanghai Incident. S. Dodge
Shanghai Jezebel. M. Corrigan
Shanghai Jim. F. Packard
Shanghai Lily. M. S. Jones
Shankill Road Contract. P. Atlee
Shannon. P. Gallagher
Shannon Terror. T. Du Bois
Shannondale. E. Southworth
Shanty Sled. H. Footner
Shape of a Stain. E. Ferrars
Shape of Danger. A. Kielland
Shape of Fear. L. B. Long
Shape of Fear. H. Pentecost
Shape of Illusion. W. E. Barrett
Shape of Murder. J. F. Straker
Shapes in the Fire. M. P. Shiel
Shapes of Sleep. J. B. Priestley
Shapes That Creep. M. Bonner
Shard's Rock. D. Justin
Share and Share Alike. R. W. Kauffman
Shares in Murder. J. L. Waten
Sharing Her Crime. M. A. Fleming
Shark Among Herrings. G. Milner
Shark Hunters. W. A. Ballinger
Shark River. R. Powell
Sharkbait. R. Butler
Sharks of Society. B. Hemyng
Sharkskin Book. H. S. Keeler
Sharp Edge. R. Himmel
Sharp Edge. W. Wright
Sharp Night's Work. J. F. Fitts
Sharp Practice. J. Farris
Sharp Quillet. B. Flynn
Sharper's Downfall. N. Carter
Shattered. K. R. Dwyer
Shattered. P. Trent
Shattered Affair. B. Palmer
Shattered Halo. A. McElfresh
Shattered Hopes. Roland Daniel
Shattered Raven. E. D. Hoch
Shattered Steel. James Preston
Shayne Case. W. B. M. Ferguson
She Ain't Got No Body. J. T. Story
She Asked for Adventure. A. Applin
She Asked for It. E. Berckman
She Asked for Murder. E. Sherry
She Ate Her Cake. B. Treynor
She Came Back. P. Wentworth
She Came by Night. J. Pendower
She Could Take Care. S. Truss
She Deserved to Die. F. Griffin
She Didn't Like Dying. N. Morland
She Died a Lady. Carter Dickson
She Died Because... K. Hopkins
She Died Dancing. K. Roos
She Died Downtown. B. Carson
She Died Laughing. L. Gribble
She Died, of Course. T. Warriner
She Died on the Stairway. K. Rhoades
She Died Without Lights. N. Mathews
She Died Young. A. Kennington
She Drew the Bolt. E. Elton
She Faded into Air. Ethel L. White
She Fell Among Actors. J. Warren
She Fell Among Thieves. Gretchen Travis
She Fell Among Thieves. D. Yates
She Gave Me Hell and... D. Glinto
She Got What She Asked For. J. Ronald
She Had a Little Knife. J. L. Linklater
She Had It Coming--. Griff
She Had My Number. M. Delaney
She Had to Have Gas. R. Penny
She Kept on Dying. G. M. Wilson
She Left a Silver Slipper. F. Stevens
She Let Him Continue. S. Geller
She Married Raffles. B. Perowne
She, Me, and Murder. Robert Martin
She Means Trouble. Spike Gordon
She Met Murder. H. Desmond
She Modelled Her Coffin. D. Launay
She Never Grew Old. Garland Lord
She Never Reached the Top. E. K. Lobaugh
She Paid 'Em Off. Griff
She Painted Her Face. D. Yates
She Posed for Death. Russell Gordon
She Ruled with a Rod. B. Sarto
She Saw the Murderer. E. M. Crawford
She Screamed Blue Murder. K. Secrist
She Sees Things. G. M. Wilson
She Sent Her Mother to the Scaffold. W. Tyrer
She Shall Die. Anthony Gilbert
She Shall Have Murder. D. Ames
She Shark. J. Farr
She Should Have Cried on Monday. E. S. Russell
She Sleeps to Conquer. H. Janson
She Sure Slipped. M. Perelli
She, the Accused. M. Moiseiwitsch
She Vamped a Strangler. H. Duval
She Vanished in the Dawn. Anthony Gilbert
She Walked in Fear. Roy Vickers
She Walks Alone. H. McCloy
She Walks in Shadow. L. Paige
She Wanted a Guy. R. Rand
She Was a Lady. L. Charteris
She Was His Secretary. A. Demerest
She Was My Beloved. K. Lindsay
She Was No Angel. B. E. M. Ward
She Was No Lady. A. Bocca
She Was Only the Sheriff's Daughter. S. Forbes
She Who Sleeps. S. Rohmer
She Who Was Helena Cass. L. Rising
She Who Will Not--. E. C. Vivian
She Woke to Darkness. B. Halliday
She Wore Pink Gloves. M. Dekobra
She Wouldn't Say Who. D. Ames
Shear the Black Sheep. D. Dodge
Shears of Destiny. Winifred Duke
Shears of Destiny. L. Scott
Shed a Bitter Tear. H. F. S. Moore
"Shed No Tears." Don Martin
Sheep and the Wolves. G. Burnett
Sheep in Wolf's Clothing. W. M. Graydon
Sheep May Safely Graze. S. Harvester
Sheep's Clothing. A. Lee
Sheep's Clothing. L. J. Vance
Sheer Bluff. John Collins
Sheer Silk. W. J. Elliott
Sheets in the Wind. R. Cullum
Sheikh Bill. A. M. Williamson
Sheikh Stuff. H. M. Raleigh
Sheikh Touch, and other stories. B. Reynolds
Sheikh's Son. A. Murray
Sheik's Capture. Old Sleuth
Sheilah McLeod. G. Boothby
She'll Be Dead by Morning. D. Chambers
Shell Game. R. Powell
She'll Hate Me Tomorrow. R. Deming
She'll Love You Dead. C. Franklin
Shell of Death. N. Blake
Shell Scott Sampler. R. S. Prather
Shell Scott's Seven Slaughters. R. S. Prather
Shelter. L. Meynell
Sheltered Garden. S. Pim
Sheltering Night. S. Fisher
Shelton Conspiracy. R. Foley
Shem's Demise. M. Underwood
Shen's Pigtail, and Other Cues of Anglo-China Life. Mr. M--
Shepherd File. C. V. Bark
Shepherd's Crook. E. C. R. Lorac
Sheridan Road Mystery. P. Thorne
Sheriff of Angel Gulch. C. E. Blaney
Sheriff of Dyke Hole. R. Cullum
Sheriff of Wasco. C. R. Jackson
Sheriff Olson. M. G. Chute
Sheriff's Deputy. G. V. McFadden
Sherlock Holmes. W. Gillette
Sherlock Holmes in Tibet. R. Wincor
Sherlock Holmes versus Arsene Lupin. M. Leblanc
Sherlock Holmes vs. Jack the Ripper. E. Queen
Sherlock Holmes's War of the Worlds. M. W. Wellman
She's a Cop, Ain't She? I. King
She's Fooling Thee! J. Middlemass
She's No Lady. J. Grecco
Shetland Plan. Taffrail
Shield and Sword. V. Kozhevnikov
Shield for Murder. W. P. McGivern
Shield of His Honor. R. H. Savage
Shield of Love. B. L. Farjeon
Shield of Silence. E. Balmer
Shield of the Law. W. M. Graydon
Shield Project. D. R. Mounce
Shift of Guilt. J. Bude
Shilling for Candles. J. Tey
Shills Can't Cash Chips. A. A. Fair
Shining Head. J. Madeley
Shining Mischief. B. Levy
Shining Trail. O. Binns
Shining Trap. D. Enefer
Ship Ashore. S. M. Parkman
Ship of Death. J. Creasey
Ship of Secrets. V. Loder
Ship of Spies. G. Sinstadt
Ship of the Damned. J. Hilton
Ship That Died of Shame, and other stories. N. Monsarrat
Ships Aflame! J. Toussaint-Samat
Shipwrecked. G. Greene
Shipwrecked Detective. W. M. Graydon
Shipwrecked Schoolship. John Marsh
Shipyard Menace. J. Stamper
Shirley. E. V. Cunningham
Shivering Bough. N. Burke
Shivering Mountain. P. Somers
Shivering Sands. V. Holt
Shoal Water. D. Yates
Shock! V. Markham
Shock Corridor. M. Avallone
Shock Tactics. J. Bruce
Shock to Society. F. Warden
Shock Treatment. J. H. Chase
Shock Treatment. W. Van Atta
Shock-Wave. B. Copper
Shock Wave. D. S. Davis
Shocking Pink Hat. F. Crane
Shocking Secret. H. Roth
Shockwave. D. Cory
Shoe Fits. R. Ladline
Shoes for My Love. Jean Leslie
Shoes That Had Walked Twice. J. Toussaint-Samat
Sholto Budd. M. Cobb

Title Index

Shoot. D. Fairbairn
Shoot! B. Newman
Shoot. E. Trevor
Shoot a Sitting Duck. David Alexander
Shoot at the Moon. W. F. Temple
Shoot If You Must. R. Powell
Shoot It. P. Tyner
Shoot It Again. E. Lacy
Shoot It Again, Sam. M. Avallone
Shoot Me Dacent. A. M. Stein
Shoot the Piano Player. D. Goodis
Shoot the Scene. E. Queen
Shoot the Works. R. Ellington
Shoot the Works. B. Halliday
Shoot to Kill. J. Dekker
Shoot to Kill. B. Halliday
Shoot to Kill. Wade Miller
Shoot to Live. Griff
Shoot When Ready. W. H. Baker
Shoot Your Enemies. Richard Grant
Shooter Man. T. Barling
Shooting Gallery. H. C. Rae
Shooting Made Easy. K. Howard
Shooting of Dan McGrew. M. Kenyon
Shooting of Sergius Leroy. Roland Daniel
Shooting of the Green. J. Poyer
Shooting Script. G. Lyall
Shooting Star. R. Bloch
Shop at Sly Corner. E. Percy
Shop-Girl. C. N. Williamson
Shop in Loch Street. J. Wood
Shop Window Murders. V. Loder
Shoplifter. R. H. R. Smithies
Shore House Mystery. Jean Marsh
Shorecliff. Marilyn Ross
Short Bier. F. Kane
Short Cases of Inspector Maigret. G. Simenon
Short Circuit. H. Miller
Short Circuit. L. Oriol
Short Cut. D. Blunt
Short End of the Stick, and other stories. I. Shulman
Short List. R. Philmore
Short Madness. A. Manning
Short Night. R. Kirkbridge
Short Night. Russell Turner
Short of Murder. P. Ernst
Short of Murder. T. T. Ness
Short Reaction. J. Gale
Short Shrift. Manning Long
Short-Term Wife. H. Janson
Short Walk to the Stars. Eric Lambert
Short Wave. J. Bruce
Short Weekend. T. S. Strachan
Shortest Night. G. B. Stern
Shortly Before Midnight. E. Nisot
Shorty Bill. H. C. McNeile
Shot. S. Creed
Shot at Dawn. J. Rhode
Shot at Dawn. G. M. Wilson
Shot at Night. T. A. Plummer
Shot from Above. J. K. Stafford
Shot from the Dark. Philip Chambers
Shot from the Door. C. Barry
Shot in Question. M. Gilbert
Shot in the Dark. G. Fairlie
Shot in the Dark. L. Ford
Shot in the Dark. H. Kurnitz
Shot in the Dark. R. Powell
Shot in the Dark. F. Usher
Shot in the Night. B. Bolt
Shot in the Pulpit. S. M. Woodward
Shot in the Woods. O. Binns
Shot of Murder. J. Iams
Shot on Location. H. Nielsen
Shot on the Downs. V. L. Whitechurch

Shot-Silk. W. J. Elliott
Shot Silk. M. Maguire
Shot That Killed Graeme Andrews. H. L. Deakin
Shotgun. E. McBain
Shotgun Gold. W. C. Tuttle
Should a Corpse Tell? G. Dugdale
Should Auld Acquaintance. D. M. Disney
Should She Have Left Him? W. C. Hudson
Should She Have Spoken? A. Forbes
Show Business. B. Ford
Show Girl. M. Pemberton
Show House--Sold. R. Thorndike
Show Must Go On. G. Verner
Show No Mercy. L. Hardy
Show of Violence. S. Woods
Show Red for Danger. R. Lockridge
Showdown. R. Carni
Showdown in Sydney. D. Reid
Showman's Daughter. Scott Graham
Shown on the Screen. N. Carter
Shred of Evidence. R. C. Sherriff
Shrew Is Dead. Shelley Smith
Shrewsdale Exit. J. Buell
Shriek in the Midnight Tower. K. Kimbrough
Shriek of Tyres. D. Rutherford
Shrieking Pit. A. J. Rees
Shrine of Kali. H. E. Hill
Shriveling Murders. Zorro
Shroud for a Lady. E. Daly
Shroud for a Nightingale. P. D. James
Shroud for Grandmama. D. Ashe
Shroud for Jesso. P. Rabe
Shroud for Mr. Bundy. J. M. Fox
Shroud for My Sugar. C. Brown
Shroud for Rowena. V. Rath
Shroud for Shylock. S. Ransome
Shroud for Unlac. S. H. Courtier
Shroud 9. Robert Turner
Shroud of Canvas. I. Lambot
Shroud of Darkness. E. C. R. Lorac
Shroud of Fog. W. D. Roberts
Shroud of Silence. N. Buckingham
Shroud of Snow. A. Mills
Shroud off Her Back. S. Ransome
Shroud Society. R. Crawford
Shrouded Death. H. C. Bailey
Shrouded Room. T. Charles
Shrouded Walls. S. Howatch
Shrouded Way. J. Caird
Shrouded Woman. M. L. Bolton
Shrunken Head. R. L. Fish
Shuddering Castle. W. F. Fauley
Shuddering Fair One. P. J. Cooper
Shudders. A. Abbot
Shudders. L. E. Austin
Shulamite. A. Askew
Shut out the Sun. L. Alroy
Shuttered House. K. Roche
Shuttered Room. C. A. Sherman
Shuttered Room. J. Withers
Shuttle of Hate. R. Harrison
Shy Plutocrat. E. P. Oppenheim
Shylock Holmes: His Posthumous Memoirs. J. K. Bangs
Shylock of the River. F. Hume
Shyster Lawyer. L. F. Schmitt
Si-Fan Mysteries. S. Rohmer
Siamese Cat. J. Dekker
Siamese Coup Affair. S. Weintraub
Siamese Twin Mystery. E. Queen
Sibylla. J. H. Robinson
Sic Transit Gloria. M. Kennedy
Sicilian Affair. M. MacKintosh

Sicilian Defense. J. N. Iannuzzi
Sicilian Heritage. J. Higgins
Sicilian Romance. A. Radcliffe
Sicilian Slaughter. Jim Peterson
Sicilian Specialist. N. Lewis
Sicily Street. R. Masson
Sick Fox. P. Brodeur
Sick Heart River. J. Buchan
Sick to Death. Douglas Clark
Sickness of the Soul. H. E. Fuller
Sidewalk Caesar. D. Honig
Sidewalk Floozie. B. Sarto
Siege. V. B. Miller
Siege of Scotland Yard. L. G. Redmond-Howard
Siege of the Seven Suitors. M. Nicholson
Siege of Trencher's Farm. Gordon M. Williams
Siegfried Spy. B. Newman
Sigh for a Drum-Beat. P. Doncaster
Sight of Death. J. York
Sight Unseen. A. E. Lindop
Sight Unseen, and The Confession. M. R. Rinehart
Sign at Six. S. E. White
Sign in the Sky. A. Edgar
Sign of Arnim. G. Seton
Sign of Blood. P. Street
Sign of Evil. A. Wynne
Sign of Fear. A. Derleth
Sign of Seven. G. Stanley
Sign of Silence. W. LeQueux
Sign of the Black Feather. H. E. Hill
Sign of the Blue Triangle. S. Hope
Sign of the Burning Ship. L. A. Cunningham
Sign of the Cobra. N. Carter
Sign of the Coin. N. Carter
Sign of the Crescent. D. Stewart
Sign of the Crossed Knives. N. Carter
Sign of the Dagger. N. Carter
Sign of the Dagger. H. O. Cooke
Sign of the Dagger. J. L. Jacolliot
Sign of the Death Circle. C. H. Snow
Sign of the Four. A. C. Doyle
Sign of the Four. W. Spence
Sign of the Glove. C. Dawe
Sign of the Golden Goose. R. Danton
Sign of the Grinning Dragon. M. Grimshaw
Sign of the Knotted String. H. Harper
Sign of the Nine. F. Grierson
Sign of the Ram. M. Ferguson
Sign of the Saracen. Gwyn Evans
Sign of the Scorpion. E. Snell
Sign of the Serpent. J. Goodwin
Sign of the Serpent. W. M. Graydon
Sign of the Seven Sins. W. LeQueux
Sign of the Skull. J. A. Dunn
Sign of the Snake. D. Vane
Sign of the Spider. E. L. MacKeag
Sign of the Spider. B. Mitford
Sign of the Stranger. W. LeQueux
Sign of the Swan. M. Baillie-Saunders
Sign of the Tiger. O. Williams
Sign of the Triangle. J. Hocking
Sign on for Tokyo. A. Haig
Signal. Roland Daniel
Signal for Danger. T. Harnan
Signal for Death. J. Rhode
Signal for Invasion. H. Adams
Signal Thirty-Two. M. Kantor
Signature. B. Goldie
Signature to a Crime. O. L. Rosmanith
Signed in Yellow. E. H. Loban
Signet of Death. L. Grey
Signing Off. J. T. MacIntyre
Signora. P. Andreae
Signpost to Fear. M. Drin
Signpost to Murder. M. Doyle
Signpost to Murder. D. Folliott

Silas Sharp, the Silent Detective. Anonymous
Silecroft Case. J. C. Lenehan
Silence. S. Kyle
Silence! A. Soutar
Silence After Dinner. C. Witting
Silence for the Murderer. F. W. Crofts
Silence in Court. P. Wentworth
Silence in Crete. E. Ayrton
Silence Is Golden. Elsie Lee
Silence Observed. M. Innes
Silence of a Purple Shirt. R. C. Woodthorpe
Silence of Dr. Duveen. M. Leighton
Silence of Herondale. Joan Aiken
Silence of Jeremy Langton. H. H. Ross
Silence of Mrs. Harrold. S. M. Gardenhire
Silence of the Night. R. Ormerod
Silence So Deadly. C. Dekker
Silence Under Threat. B. Cobb
Silence with Voices. C. Carfax
Silenced. L. T. Meade
Silenced Witnesses. N. C. Rosenthal
Silencers. D. Hamilton
Silent Accuser. A. Soutar
Silent Are the Dead. G. H. Coxe
Silent Barrier. L. Tracy
Silent Battle. G. F. Gibbs
Silent Battle. A. M. Williamson
Silent Bell. Elaine Hamilton
Silent Bullet. P. Elliott
Silent Bullet. A. B. Reeve
Silent Clue. M. Leighton
Silent Conquest. M. Gerard
Silent Cousin. E. Fenwick
Silent Cracksman. J. J. Chichester
Silent Cry. H. Jobson
Silent Dead. A. Gask
Silent Death. H. Leyford
Silent Dust. B. Fischer
Silent Five. T. M. Longstreth
Silent Force. Harry Goddard
Silent Four. T. A. Plummer
Silent Guardian. N. Carter
Silent Guests. A. E. Forrest
Silent Halls of Ashenden. D. Daniels
Silent Hostage. S. Gainham
Silent House. J. G. Brandon
Silent House. N. Deane
Silent House. F. Hume
Silent House. L. Tracy
Silent House in Pimlico. F. Hume
Silent Jury. Gwyn Evans
Silent Kind of War. J. Laflin
Silent Liars. M. Underwood
Silent Loom. P. Inman
Silent Man. J. M. Walsh
Silent Men. C. Bidmead
Silent Menace. A. Skene
Silent Mountain. G. Bettany
Silent Murders. N. Gordon
Silent Murders. Ernest Paul
Silent One. O. Cameron
Silent Partner. L. Brackett
Silent Partner. N. Carter
Silent Partner. K. M. Knight
Silent Partner. Augustus Muir
Silent Passenger. G. W. Appleton
Silent Passenger. N. Carter
Silent Place. R. C. Payes
Silent Pool. P. Wentworth
Silent Scream. Michael Collins
Silent Seven. M. Grant
Silent Shore. J. E. Bloundelle-Burton
Silent Shot. C. H. Snow
Silent Signal. F. Hume
Silent, Silken Shadows. P. Dalton
Silent Siren. T. Sterling
Silent Sisters. Margaret Archer
Silent Six. Seamark
Silent Slain. C. Pilgrim
Silent Slayer. G. Verner
Silent Speaker. R. Stout
Silent Stranger. H. G. Harper
Silent Street. G. Barnett
Silent Syndicate. L. Bidston
Silent Terror. L. C. Douthwaite
Silent Terror. T. C. H. Jacobs
Silent Thunder. Rona Randall
Silent Tragedy. J. H. Riddell
Silent Voice. S. Claudia
Silent Voyage. J. Pattinson
Silent Walls. M. L. Roby
Silent Watcher. F. Stevenson
Silent Watchers. I. D. Hardy
Silent Watchers. Dora Russell
Silent Witness. G. H. Coxe
Silent Witness. J. Dering
Silent Witness. H. Desmond
Silent Witness. M. F. Ford
Silent Witness. R. A. Freeman
Silent Witness. J. Hunter
Silent Witness. M. D. Post
Silent Witness. J. Walworth
Silent Witness. A. Yates
Silent Witness. M. Yorke
Silent Witnesses. J. S. Strange
Silent Women. M. P. Hood
Silhouette. E. Trevor
Silhouette Symbol. P. Quiroule
Silinski, Master Criminal. E. Wallace
"Silk!" W. J. Elliott
Silk and Cordite. D. Spade
Silk Purse. J. Tickell
Silk Road. S. Harvester
Silk Rope. G. Mountford
Silk Scarf Murders. J. Addiscombe
Silk Stocking Murders. A. Berkeley
Silk Stocking Murders. G. Chester
Silken Baroness. P. Atlee
Silken Baroness Contract. P. Atlee
Silken Nightmare. C. Brown
Silken Shroud. J. Sandys
Silken Snare. H. Janson
Silken Threads. G. Afterem
Silken Web. M. Lynch
Silky Ones Sting. Richard Grant
Silver and Death. R. Simons
Silver Arrow. A. Wynne
Silver Arrow Murder. T. Stevenson
Silver Bag. T. Cobb
Silver Bar Mystery. W. C. Tuttle
Silver Basilisk. S. Warwick
Silver Bears. P. E. Erdman
Silver Blade. C. E. Walk
Silver Buckshot. W. C. Tuttle
Silver Bugle. G. McDonell
Silver Bullet. F. Hume
Silver Bullet. P. H. Hunter
Silver Bullet Gang. J. Miles
Silver Butterfly. W. Woodrow
Silver Canyon. G. M. Fenn
Silver Chest. Herman Landon
Silver Circle. A. Skene
Silver Cobweb. B. Benson
Silver Cord. G. A. Chamberlain
Silver Cord. Rona Randall
Silver Death. G. F. Gibbs
Silver Death. M. Hervey
Silver Doll. B. Treynor
Silver Eagle. W. R. Burnett
Silver Fang. G. F. Worts
Silver Forest. B. A. Williams
Silver Fox. R. Hansard
Silver Goblet. R. Foxall
Silver Grass. G. Croudace
Silver Greyhound. B. Newman
Silver Greyhound. J. M. Walsh
Silver Hair Clue. N. Carter
Silver Horseshoe. G. Verner
Silver Jackass. C. K. Boston
Silver Key. Griff
Silver Key. E. Wallace
Silver King. A. W. Barrett
Silver King Mystery. I. Greig
Silver King's Vengeance, and other stories. H. Herman
Silver Ladies. M. Erskine
Silver Lady. J. Facos
Silver Land. J. M. Scott
Silver Leopard. W. S. Masterman
Silver Leopard. H. Reilly
Silver Medallion. P. Brebner
Silver Mirror. M. V. Woodgate
Silver Mistress. P. O'Donnell
Silver Panther. W. J. Elliott
Silver Peril. M. Rutledge
Silver Phantom Murder. B. Stuart
Silver Pin. A. W. Barrett
Silver Pineapple. E. Kyle
Silver Poppy. A. Stringer
Silver Puma. A. Riefe
Silver Sandals. C. H. Stagg
Silver Scale Mystery. A. Wynne
Silver Shadow. L. Noel
Silver Shamrock. H. Curties
Silver Sickle Case. L. Brock
Silver Slave. G. Stanley
Silver Spade. L. Revell
Silver Spoon. A. Griffiths
Silver Stair. M. Leighton
Silver Street. E. R. Johnson
Silver Street Killer. E. R. Johnson
Silver Tom, the Detective. Anonymous
Silver Tombstone. F. Gruber
Silver Tombstone Mystery. F. Gruber
Silver Urn. F. Daingerfield
Silver Venus. H. McElroy
Silver-Voiced Murder. G. Morton
Silver Wood. D. Rowan
Silvered Cage. H. Blayn
Silverface. H. Long
Silverface Surrenders. H. Long
Silverhill. P. A. Whitney
Silvermead. J. Middlemass
Silverskull. P. Edwards
Simba Bwana. D. W. MacArthur
Simon. J. S. Clouston
Simon Lash, Detective. F. Gruber
Simon Lash, Private Detective. F. Gruber
Simon of Hangletree. A. J. Rees
Simon Takes "the Rap." T. A. Plummer
Simon Wheeler, Detective. M. Twain
Simple Art of Murder. R. Chandler
Simple Case of Ill-Will. E. Berckman
Simple Case of Susan. J. Futrelle
Simple Justice. T. B. Morris
Simple Life. N. Balchin
Simple Peter Cradd. E. P. Oppenheim
Simple Way of Poison. L. Ford
Simple Way of Poison. A. Hocking
Simpson of Snells. W. Hewlett
Simultaneous Equations. L. Halley
Simultaneous Man. Ralph Blum
Sin. A. Applin
Sin and Johnny Inch. J. F. Straker
Sin and Sand. H. H. Ross
Sin and the Sinners. F. E. Smith
Sin and the Woman. D. Vane
Sin File. S. Ransome
Sin for Me. G. Brewer
Sin Has No Future. J. Cello
Sin in Their Blood. E. Lacy

Sin in Time. J. Conway
Sin Is Her Mantle. J. Cello
Sin Mark. M. P. Hood
Sin of Angels. A. M. Wells
Sin of David. M. Cumberland
Sin of Hong Kong. M. Corrigan
Sin of Joost Avelingh. M. Maartens
Sin of Laban Routh. A. Sergeant
Sin of Olga Zassoulich. F. Barrett
Sin of Preaching Jim. D. Donovan
Sin of Silence. O. Binns
Sin of the Duchess. H. Townley
Sin That Was His. F. Packard
Since There's No Help. A. Kennington
Sinews of War. E. Phillpotts
Sinful Stones. P. Dickinson
Sinful Woman. J. M. Cain
Sinfully Rich. H. Footner
Sinfully Yours. C. Brown
Sing a Dark Song. W. D. Roberts
Sing a Song of Cyanide. N. Morland
Sing a Song of Homicide. J. R. Langham
Sing a Song of Murder. P. Drax
Sing a Song of Murder. R. P. Koehler
Sing a Song of Murder. J. R. Langham
Sing a Song of Murder. A. Spiller
Sing, Clubman, Sing! Kevin O'Hara
Sing Me a Murder. H. Nielsen
Sing Out, Sweet Homicide. J. Roeburt
Sing Sing Nights. H. S. Keeler
Sing Softly, Stranger. G. Greenaway
Sing Witch, Sing Death. R. Gellis
Singapore. W. Bogart
Singapore Downbeat. M. Corrigan
Singapore Exile Murders. V. W. Mason
Singapore Kate. Roland Daniel
Singapore Set-Up. J. Dekker
Singapore Wink. Ross Thomas
Singing Bone. R. A. Freeman
Singing Cave. J. Appleby
Singing Clock. V. Perdue
Singing Corpse. B. Dougall
Singing Diamonds. H. McCloy
Singing Ghost. R. St. Clair
Singing Head. F. Hume
Singing in the Shrouds. N. Marsh
Singing Kid. W. C. Tuttle
Singing Lizard. J. Knowler
Singing Masons. F. Vivian
Singing Millionaire. M. Pereira
Singing River. W. C. Tuttle
Singing Room. N. Berrow
Singing Sands. J. Tey
Singing Soul. A. J. Foxall
Singing Spider. A. MacVicar
Singing Swans. A. Manners
Singing Sword. P. G. Larbalester
Singing Widow. V. P. Johns
Single Clue. Old Sleuth
Single File. N. Fruchter
Single Hair. H. Adams
Single Pilgrim. N. Lewis
Single Ticket to Death. G. Bellairs
Single to Hong Kong. K. Royce
Single Track. D. Grant
Singleton's Mill. Sinclair Buchan
Singular Case of the Multiple Dead. M. McShane
Singular Conspiracy. B. Perowne
Singular Crime. H. Nisbet
Singular Fury. H. L. Oleck
Singular Sinner. C. R. Harker
Sinister Abbey. Elsie Lee
Sinister Alibi. C. Wallace
Sinister Assignment. R. Fenisong
Sinister Cargo. M. Black
Sinister Cargo. S. H. Page
Sinister Castle. Gwyn Evans
Sinister Civility. W. Croyland
Sinister Craft. R. Ladline

Sinister Crag. N. Gayle
Sinister Creek. J. Rowland
Sinister Eden. B. Cotterell
Sinister Encounter. J. Brooke
Sinister Errand. P. Cheyney
Sinister Garden. Marilyn Ross
Sinister Gardens. W. D. Roberts
Sinister House. C. G. Booth
Sinister House. L. C. Douthwaite
Sinister House. L. Hall
Sinister House. G. Verner
Sinister Inn. J. J. Farjeon
Sinister Island. W. Camp
Sinister Island. A. Wood
Sinister Lady. D. M. Disney
Sinister Legacy. D. Martyn
Sinister Light. Frank King
Sinister Light. Ethel L. White
Sinister Love. L. Ames
Sinister Lovely. N. Karta
Sinister Madonna. W. Jackson
Sinister Madonna. S. Rohmer
Sinister Man. E. Wallace
Sinister Mark. L. Thayer
Sinister Moonlight. C. Robertson
Sinister Murders. P. Cheyney
Sinister Playhouse. R. Armstrong
Sinister Quest. T. C. H. Jacobs
Sinister River. A. Soutar
Sinister Sanctuary. E. P. Thorne
Sinister Scourge. B. House
Sinister Secret. F. Gerard
Sinister Secret. A. Nettleton
Sinister Secret. A. O. Pollard
Sinister Service. W. E. Johns
Sinister Shadow. S. Hocking
Sinister Shadow. H. Holt
Sinister Shelter. C. L. Leonard
Sinister Sister. M. Brody
Sinister Smith. H. Atkins
Sinister Stars. J. Pattinson
Sinister Station. R. St. Clair
Sinister Stone. D. Winston
Sinister Stones. A. W. Upfield
Sinister Strangers. C. B. Kelland
Sinister Street. R. Burke
Sinister Street. S. Horler
Sinister Talent. J. Pendower
Sinister Valley. G. Stanley
Sinister Voice. G. St. John
Sinister Warning. M. S. Michel
Sinister Widow. R. Armstrong
Sinister Widow Again. R. Armstrong
Sinister Widow at Sea. R. Armstrong
Sinister Widow Comes Back. R. Armstrong
Sinister Widow Down Under. R. Armstrong
Sinister Widow Returns. R. Armstrong
Sinister Wooing. B. Sarto
Sink Me the Ship. Sea Lion
Sinless Crime. G. Fleming
Sinner. D. Linton
Sinner Take All. Wade Miller
Sinner Takes All. A. Bocca
Sinner Takes All. M. Corrigan
Sinner Takes All. D. Holt
Sinner, You Slay Me! C. Brown
Sinners. E. S. Aarons
Sinners. C. Brown
Sinners. D. Torbett
Sinners and Shrouds. Jonathan Latimer
Sinners Beware. E. P. Oppenheim
Sinners' Castle. A. Wood
Sinners Go Secretly. A. Wynne
Sinners in Clover. S. Toye
Sinners Never Die. A. E. Martin
Sinner's Shroud. T. Angelo
Sinners' Syndicate. C. Stanton
Sinnings of Seraphine. Mrs. C. Kernahan
Sino-Variant. A. Ind
Sin's Half Mile. D. Linton
Sins of Billy Serene. W. Ard
Sins of Severac Bablon. S. Rohmer
Sins of Society. C. Raleigh
Sins of Sumuru. S. Rohmer
Sins of the City. W. LeQueux

Sins of the Fathers. A. Applin
Sins of the Fathers. C. Houghton
Sins of the Fathers. R. Rendell
Sins of the Fathers. T. Walton
Sir Adam Disappeared. E. P. Oppenheim
Sir Anthony. A. Sergeant
Sir Anthony's Secret. A. Sergeant
Sir Christopher Leighton. M. L. Storer
Sir Devil. S. Styles
Sir Gregory's Silence. A. W. Marchmont
Sir Hector. R. Machray
Sir Hector's Watch. C. Granville
Sir Hilton's Sin. G. M. Fenn
Sir Jaffray's Wife. A. W. Marchmont
Sir Jasper's Tenant. M. E. Braddon
Sir John Dering. J. Farnol
Sir John Magill's Last Journey. F. W. Crofts
Sir Julian's Crime. F. Warden
Sir Morecambe's Marriage. F. Warden
Sir Penywern's Wife. F. Warden
Sir Peter's Arm. M. Cobb
Sir Ralph's Secret. J. M. Cobban
Sir Richard Penniless. C. Edwards
Sir Theodore's Guest and other stories. G. Allen
Sir Vincent's Patient. H. Hill
Sir, You Bastard. G. F. Newman
Sirdar's Oath. B. Mitford
Siren. T. A. Trollope
Siren in Satin. D. Walshe
Siren in the Night. L. Ford
Siren on the Skids. M. Brody
Siren Signs Off. C. Brown
Siren Song. D. Beaty
Sirocco. A. Betteridge
Sister at Sea. Rona Randall
Sister Disciple. W. LeQueux
Sister, Don't Hate Me. H. Janson
Sister of Cain. Mary Collins
Sister Satan. G. Dilnot
Sister Simon's Murder Case. M. A. Hubbard
Sister Sinister. B. Diamond
Sister Susie--Spinster. A. Applin
Sister Theatre. G. Vaizey
Sisters of Sorrow. A. Vandergriff
Sister's Sacrifice. G. Fleming
Sit-In. G. Anderson
Sittaford Mystery. A. Christie
Sitting Duck. M. Carr
Sitting Emperor. E. N. Willett
Sitting Target. L. Henderson
Sitting Up Dead. A. M. Stein
Situation, Grave! H. Janson
Situation Vacant. M. Burton
Situations Vacant. Norman Lucas
Six Bars at Seven. Mollie Kaye
Six Black Camels. E. Lanham
Six Came to Dinner. Roy Vickers
Six Cent Sam's. J. Hawthorne
Six Curtains for Stroganova. C. Brahms
Six-Day Loving. W. A. Ballinger
Six-Day Week. A. Gardner
Six Days' Grace. W. R. Burnett
Six Days of the Condor. J. Grady
Six Days to Death. P. Alding
Six Dead Men. A. Steeman
Six Deadly Dames. F. Nebel
Six Feet of Dynamite. B. Gray
Six Foot Deep. H. Luger
Six Foot of Rope. H. R. Taunton
Six for the Toff. J. Creasey
Six Golden Angels. M. Brand
Six Graves to Munich. M. Cleri
Six Green Bottles. A. Hocking
Six Gun Empire. R. Wilkes-Hunter
Six-Gun Judgment. E. Z. Frank
Six-Hour Mystery. A. Marsden
Six Iron Spiders. P. A. Taylor
Six-Letter Word for Death. T. R. Frierson
Six Lines. N. A. Temple-Ellis
Six Lives and a Book. C. Houghton
Six Men. E. Radford

Six Men Died. G. Verner
Six-Mile Face. H. Gibbs
Six Minutes Past Twelve. Gavin Holt
Six Murders in the Suburbs. Roy Vickers
Six Nights of Mystery. W. Irish
Six Nuns and a Shotgun. C. Watson
Six of One. P. Traill
Six Other Days. A. Meisels
Six Proud Walkers. F. Beeding
Six Queer Things. C. S. Sprigg
Six Ropes for Glory. J. G. Sarasin
Six Rubies. J. M. Forman
Six Seconds of Darkness. O. R. Cohen
Six Seconds to Kill. B. Halliday
Six Sign-Post Murder. C. Robbins
Six Silver Handles. G. Homes
633 Squadron. F. E. Smith
633 Squadron, Operation Rhine Maiden. F. E. Smith
Six Times Death. W. Irish
Six to Kill. B. Gray
6 to 10. J. Garden
Six Under Suspicion. C. Kingston
Six Weeks. L. Saunders
Six Weeks South of Texas. L. T. White
Six Were Present. E. R. Punshon
Six Were to Die. J. Ronald
Six Who Ran. M. E. Chaber
Sixes and Sevens. O. Henry
Sixpenny Dame. E. K. Goldthwaite
16 Beans. H. S. Keeler
Sixteen Bells. G. Hackforth-Jones
Sixteenth Stair. E. C. R. Lorac
Sixth Column. P. Fleming
Sixth Commandment. Howel Evans
Sixth Commandment. C. Wells
Sixth Director. D. Newton
Sixth Directorate. J. Hone
"Sixth Key." R. St. Clair
Sixth Seal. M. Wesley
Sixth Sense Is Death. J. Garforth
Sixth Victim. W. M. Graydon
Sixty Days to Live. D. Wheatley
Sixty-First Second. O. Johnson
64 Thousand Murder. V. Gunn
60 Hours of Darkness. A. Sederberg
69 Babylon Park. H. Whittington
Sixty-Nine Diamonds. J. Lord
Skater's Waltz. E. Kyle
Skein Well Tangled. J. K. Stafford
Skeleton at the Feast. C. Wells
Skeleton at the Villa Wolkonsky. C. Pincher
Skeleton Clew. D. Stewart
Skeleton Coast Contract. P. Atlee
Skeleton Finger. H. Hill
Skeleton in Concrete. J. E. Barry
Skeleton in Every House. Waters
Skeleton in the Clock. Carter Dickson
Skeleton in the Closet. A. B. Cunningham
Skeleton in the Closet. E. Southworth
Skeleton in the Cupboard. H. Hawton
Skeleton Island. G. Mitchell
Skeleton Key. B. Capes
Skeleton Key. R. Dowling
Skeleton Key. L. G. Offord
Skeleton out of the Cupboard. V. Williams
Skeleton Staff. E. Ferrars
Skeleton Talks. F. G. Eberhard
Skeletons and Cupboards. R. Arnold
Skeleton's Clutch. T. P. Prest
Skeleton's Holiday. L. Ashley
Sketches of Gotham. I. Swift
Skin and Bone. E. Greenwood
Skin Dealer. M. Tripp
Skin Deep. P. Dickinson
Skin Deep. J. Gautier
Skin for Skin. Winifred Duke
Skin for Skin. D. Rutherford
Skin Game. F. Bonham

Skin o' My Tooth. B. Orczy
Skin Trap. W. Mole
Skinman. M. Tarmey
Skinner. H. C. Rae
Skirmish. C. Egleton
Skirts Bring Me Sorrow. H. Janson
Skirts of the Dead Night. W. W. Seward
Skuldoggery. F. Flora
Skull. J. Buffer
Skull Beneath the Eaves. H. Best
Skull Mountain. D. Hawkins
Skull of Kanaima. V. Norwood
Skull of the Marquis de Sade and other stories. R. Bloch
Skull of the Waltzing Clown. H. S. Keeler
Skull Still Bone. J. Wyllie
Skullduggery on Halfaday Creek. J. B. Hendryx
Sky Bandits. G. E. Rochester
Sky Block. S. Frazee
Sky-Blue Life. M. Moiseiwitsch
Sky Divers. L. Cameron
Sky Fever, and other stories. W. E. Johns
Sky High. M. Gilbert
Sky High. W. E. Johns
Sky-High Terror. J. Trevor
Sky Kill. D. Da Cruz
Sky-Rocket. M. Fitt
Sky Steward. K. Attiwill
Sky Walker. K. Robeson
Sky Wolves. G. Radcliffe
Skyborne Sapper. H. Chesham
Skye Cameron. P. A. Whitney
Skye Manor. J. Blair
Skyjacked. D. Harper
Skylark Mission. I. MacAlister
Skyline Message. N. Carter
Skyline Riders. F. W. Hilton
Skyprobe. P. McCutchan
Skyriders. T. Wallace
Sky's the Limit. R. Ladline
Sky's the Limit. E. Woodward
Skyscraper Murder. S. Spewack
Skytip. E. Reed
Skyway Vampire. P. Conde
Slab Happy. R. S. Prather
Slack Tide. G. H. Coxe
Slack Water. A. D. Divine
Sladd's Evil. P. McCutchan
Slade of the Yard. R. Essex
Slade, Range Detective. G. Tuttle
Slade Scores Again. R. Essex
Slag. D. McGibeny
"Slag." J. T. MacIntyre
Slam the Big Door. J. D. MacDonald
Slander. A. S. Roche
Slander of Witches. R. Gehman
Slander Villa. C. Kingston
Slane's Long Shots. E. P. Oppenheim
Slant Eye. Roland Daniel
Slashed Portrait. J. Hines
Slasher. O. Demaris
Slasher. H. Desmond
Slate Landscape. J. Turner
Slaughter. H. Clement
Slaughter Horse. M. Maguire
Slaughter in Satin. A. Bocca
Slaughter in Satin. C. Brown
Slaughter in the Sun. S. Christie
Slaughter Street. L. Falstein
Slaughtered Lovelies. D. Stanford
Slaughterhouse. F. Scarpetta
Slaughter's Big Rip-Off. A. Kane
Slave Bangle. G. Leroux
Slave Brain. D. Reid
Slave Junk. F. Packard
Slave of Circumstances. E. D. Pierson

Slave of Crime. N. Carter
Slave of Silence. F. M. White
Slave of the Mill. O. Harper
Slave Safari. R. Sapir
Slave Women of England. G. W. M. Reynolds
Slavemaster. N. Carter
Slaver. D. Reid
Slavers. R. Telfair
Slaver's Secret. P. Quiroule
Slaves of Ishtar. Richard Grant
Slaves of Paris. E. Gaboriau
Slaves of Sumuru. S. Rohmer
Slaves of the Lamp. G. Bronson-Howard
Slay Me Suddenly. Antony Brown
Slay-Ride. D. Francis
Slay Ride. F. Kane
Slay Ride for a Lady. H. Whittington
Slay-Ride for Cutie. H. Janson
Slay the Loose Ladies. P. Quentin
Slay the Murderer. H. Holman
Slay Time. P. Muller
Slayer. Roland Daniel
Slayer and the Slain. H. McCloy
Slayer of Souls. T. S. King
Slayground. R. Stark
Slaying in September. I. MacKintosh
Slaying of Julian Summers. Richard Williams
Slaying on the 16th Floor. Arthur MacLean
Slaying Squad. Robert Mason
Sledgehammer. W. Wager
Sleep. J. Creasey
Sleep and His Brother. P. Dickinson
Sleep, and the City Trembles. J. Garforth
Sleep for the Wicked. H. Howard
Sleep If You Dare. G. Usher
Sleep in the Woods. D. Eden
Sleep Is Deep. H. L. Nelson
Sleep Is for the Rich. D. MacKenzie
Sleep Long, My Love. H. Waugh
Sleep Long, My Lovely. B. Winter
Sleep, My Love. Robert Martin
Sleep, My Pretty One. H. Howard
Sleep No More. M. Erskine
Sleep No More. F. Ryerson
Sleep No More. G. Sims
Sleep No More. S. S. Taylor
Sleep of Reason. C. P. Snow
Sleep of the Unjust. L. Meynell
Sleep Well, Christine. A. Brennan
Sleep with Nightmares. D. C. Cooke
Sleep with Slander. D. Hitchens
Sleep with Strangers. D. Hitchens
Sleep with the Devil. D. Keene
Sleep Without Dreams. H. Kane
Sleep Without Morning. R. Foley
Sleeper. J. Browning
Sleeper. H. Roth
Sleeper Agent. I. Melchior
Sleeper Wakes. G. F. Gibbs
Sleepers Can Kill. S. Jay
Sleepers East. F. Nebel
Sleeping Bacchus. H. S. Saunders
Sleeping Beauty. P. Boileau
Sleeping Beauty. R. Macdonald
Sleeping Beauty Murders. L. O'Donnell
Sleeping Beauty's Daughter. A. Dick
Sleeping Bomb. J. Moffatt
Sleeping Bride. D. Eden
Sleeping Car Murders. S. Japrisot
Sleeping Cat. I. Ostrander
Sleeping Cop. I. Ostrander
Sleeping Cupid. E. G. Whitney
Sleeping Death. G. D. H. Cole
Sleeping Dogs. E. Ferrars

Title Index

Sleeping Dogs. C. Wells
Sleeping Dogs Laugh. H. C. Danby
Sleeping Dogs Lying. Kenneth O'Hara
Sleeping Draught. H. Adams
Sleeping Draught. C. E. Simon
Sleeping House Party. Elisabeth Lambert
Sleeping Island. F. Vivian
Sleeping Memory. E. P. Oppenheim
Sleeping Mountain. J. Harris
Sleeping Partner. Winston Graham
Sleeping Salamander. C. Carfax
Sleeping Sphinx. J. D. Carr
Sleeping Tiger. D. M. Devine
Sleeping Tiger. M. Moiseiwitsch
Sleeping Witness. M. V. Heberden
Sleepless Eye. Warren Miller
Sleepless Man. Gwyn Evans
Sleepless Men. E. Nisot
Sleepwalker. H. McCloy
Sleepy Death. G. Ashe
Sleepy-Eyed Blonde. J. Monmouth
Sleeve of Night. P. Traill
Sleight of Hand. C. Carpenter
Slender Chance. D. O'Connor
Slender Clue. L. L. Lynch
Slender Margin. B. Francis
Slender Thread. P. J. Merrill
Slender Thread. S. Silliphant
Sleuth. A. Shaffer
Sleuth and the Liar. J. Sherwood
Sleuth Hound. G. Leroux
Sleuth o' the World. R. Rodd
Sleuth of St. James's Square. M. D. Post
Slice of Death. B. McKnight
Slice of Hell. M. Roscoe
Slick and the Dead. A. Bocca
Slick and the Dead. P. Cleife
Slick Detective Yarns. Anonymous
Slick-Fingered Kate. Roland Daniel
Slick Revenge. J. Nazel
Sliding Death. K. Bruce
Sliding Scale of Life. J. M'Levy
Slight Case of Murder. H. Desmond
Slight Case of Murder. D. Runyon
Slight Mourning. C. Aird
Slightly Bitter Taste. H. Carmichael
Slightly Disjointed Affair. I. L. Dunn
Slightly Imperfect. Ann
Slime Beast. G. N. Smith
Sling and the Arrow. S. Engstrand
Slings and Arrows. C. Dawe
Slings and Arrows and other tales. F. J. Fargus
Slingshot. S. Jackman
Slinky Jane. C. Cookson
Slip-Carriage Mystery. L. Brock
Slip Coach. C. Baines
Slip of a Girl. S. Warwick
Slippery Ann. H. C. Bailey
Slippery as Sin. P. Souvestre
Slippery Dick. H. Adams
Slippery Hitch. Gerald Butler
Slippery Staircase. E. C. R. Lorac
Slips Sees Red. P. Boyd
Slit My Throat, Gently. Michael Brett
Sloan Square Mystery. H. Adams
Sloan Square Scandal and other stories. Annie Thomas
Slocombe Dies. L. A. G. Strong
Sloth and Heathen Folly. E. L. Robinson
Slow. John Gloag
Slow Burn. J. Ehrlich
Slow Burner. W. Haggard
Slow Death at Geneva. Diplomat
Slow Poison. P. Barrington
Slow Poison. J. Rowland

Slow Vengeance. J. Bude
Slowly the Poison. June Drummond
Slug It Slay. E. Lanham
Slugger. P. Malloch
Sly as a Serpent. M. Halliday
Slyboots. P. Flower
Slype. R. Thorndike
Smack Man. N. De Mille
Small and Deadly. John Marsh
Small Back Room. N. Balchin
Small Change. Carnaby Brown
Small Hotel. Edward Morris
Small Hours of the Morning. M. Yorke
Small-Part Lady, and other stories. G. R. Sims
Small Tawny Cat. V. Coffman
Small Time Crooks. K. Howard
Small Town Corpse. Clarence Hunt
Small-Town D.A. R. Traver
Small Town in Germany. J. Le Carre
Small Town Murder. B. W. Jefferson
Small Venom. W. Mole
Small War Made to Order. N. Lewis
Small Wilderness. M. Summerton
Small World of Murder. E. Ferrars
Smallbone Deceased. M. Gilbert
Smaller Penny. C. Barry
Smart-Aleck Kill. R. Chandler
Smart Girls Don't Talk. H. Janson
Smartest Grave. R. J. White
Smash a Glass Image. K. Bird
Smash and Grab. V. McCall
Smash and Grab. C. Robbins
Smasher. T. Powell
Smashers. H. Paul
Smashers. D. E. Westlake
Smear Job. J. Mitchell
Smell of Evil. C. Birkin
Smell of Fear. R. Chandler
Smell of Fear. S. Dean
Smell of Garbage. V. Castang
Smell of Money. M. Head
Smell of Murder. S. S. Van Dine
Smell of Peardrops. J. P. Carstairs
Smell of Smoke. M. Burton
Smell of Trouble. L. Trimble
Smile and Be a Villain. H. Jobson
Smile and Murder. F. A. Symonds
Smile of Cheng Su. E. P. Thorne
Smile on the Face of the Tiger. D. Hurd
Smiler Bunn Brigade. B. Atkey
Smiler Bunn, Byewayman. B. Atkey
Smiler Bunn, Gentleman-Adventurer. B. Atkey
Smiler Bunn, Gentleman-Crook. B. Atkey
Smiler Bunn, Manhunter. B. Atkey
Smiler with the Knife. N. Blake
Smiling Corpse. Anonymous
Smiling Corpse. H. C. Bailey
Smiling Death. F. Grierson
Smiling Dogs. K. Robeson
Smiling Mask. Frank King
Smiling Medusa. Jean Muir
Smiling Spider. L. Halliday
Smiling the Boy Fell Dead. M. Delving
Smiling Tiger. L. G. Offord
Smiling Willie and the Tiger. J. Harris
Smith & Jones. N. Monsarrat
Smith Conspiracy. R. Neely
Smith of the Secret Service. R. T. M. Scott
Smith Slayer. "Burmar"
Smithfield Slayer. E. Bruton
Smith's Dream. C. K. Stead
Smith's Odyssey. G. D. Hooker
Smog. J. Creasey
Smoke-Filled Boudoir. Lawrence Williams
Smoke Screen. C. Hale

Smoke Screen. L. Saunders
Smoke-Screen. D. Walshe
Smokers of Hashish. N. Berrow
Smokes of Spring. A. M. Burrage
Smokescreen. D. Francis
Smoking Leg and other stories. J. Metcalfe
Smoky Cell. Robert (G.) Curtis
Smoldering Sea. U. S. Andersen
Smooth Killing. W. H. L. Crauford
Smooth Runs the Water. M. Hill
Smooth Silence. M. Billett
Smouldering Fire. M. Clare
Smouldering Fire. G. Franklin
Smouldering Fuse. F. French
Smuggled Atom Bomb. P. Wylie
Smuggled Masterpiece. E. Jepson
Smuggler of King's Cove. S. Cobb
Smugglers. F. Goldsmith
Smuggler's Ally. B. Wayde
Smugglers at Odds. J. K. Stafford
Smuggler's Bride. R. Laker
Smuggler's Buoy. A. O. Pollard
Smuggler's Fate. E. C. Derby
Smuggler's Ghost. H. Wood
Smugglers' Moon. C. Robertson
Smugglers' Moon. C. Springer
Smuggler's Pay for Firebrace. Seafarer
Smuggler's Secret. F. Barrett
Snaggletooth. S. Jepson
Snags and Shallows. C. C. Lewis
Snail-Watcher and other stories. P. Highsmith
Snake. J. McClure
Snake. M. Spillane
Snake and the Arrow. M. Hastings
Snake Doctor and other stories. I. S. Cobb
Snake Face. Roland Daniel
Snake Hips. B. Sarto
Snake in the Grass. Anthony Gilbert
Snake in the Grass. J. Wellard
Snake Is Living Yet. S. Gilruth
Snake of Luvercy. M. Renard
Snake on 99. S. Farrar
Snake on the Grave. G. Beare
Snake Walk. Johnny Dark
Snake Water. Alan Williams
Snakes and Ladders. A. Broome
Snakes Have Fangs. D. Lee
Snakes of St. Cyr. W. O'Farrell
Snake's Pass. B. Stoker
Snake's Picnic. T. Herd
Snap. Jacqueline Wilson
Snap and Jenny. Old Sleuth
Snapdragon. Margery Lawrence
Snappy Vendetta. H. H. Lee
Snapshot Chap. B. Lebhar
Snapshot Mystery. B. Bolt
Snare. J. A. Brown
Snare. N. Calef
Snare and the Game. N. Carter
Snare Andalucian. A. M. Stein
Snare for Sinners. R. Fenisong
Snare for Witches. Elinor Chamberlain
Snare of Circumstance. E. E. Buckley
Snare of the Fowler. C. R. Gull
Snare of the Hunter. H. MacInnes
Snark Was a Boojum. R. Shattuck
Snarl of the Beast. C. J. Daly
Snarled Identities. N. Carter
Snatch. R. Airth
Snatch. G. Ashe
Snatch. H. R. Daniels
Snatch. R. L. Goldman
Snatch. L. Mantz
Snatch. V. Markham
Snatch. B. Pronzini
Snatch. D. Scanlon
Snatch an Eye. H. Kane

Snatch Game. J. G. Brandon
Snatch of Music. L. Peters
Snatch the Lady. Craig Cooper
Snatched Dame. W. J. Elliott
Snatchers. L. White
Sneaky People. T. Berger
Sneeze on a Monday. P. Tabori
Sneeze on Monday. S. Carver
Snide Man. Roland Daniel
Snipe Hunt. A. Dean
Sniper. N. De Mille
Sniper. P. Malloch
Sniper. H. Pentecost
Sniper. M. Stratford
Sniper. Richard Williams
Sniper. B. Wynne
Sniper Jackson. F. Sleath
Sniper Murders. Richard Grant
Snipe's Spinster. J. Nuttall
Snow Along the Border. R. H. Sawkins
Snow Among the Stars. A. K. George
Snow Blind. A. M. Treynor
Snow Falcon. Ganpat
Snow Heroine. M. Gerard
Snow in Essex. J. Clappen
Snow in June. J. Blackmore
Snow in Paradise. R. H. Sawkins
Snow in the Desert. A. Soutar
Snow Job. M. Gair
Snow Leopard. S. Miller
Snow on High Ground. R. H. Sawkins
Snow on the Ben. I. Stuart
Snow Tiger. D. Bagley
Snow Upon the Desert. J. R. Warren
"Snow" Vogue. D. Glinto
Snow Was Black. G. Simenon
Snow-White Murder. L. Ford
Snowball. T. Allbeury
Snowbird. O. Binns
Snowbound. B. Pronzini
Snowboys. F. Webb
Snowdrift. J. B. Hendryx
Snowfall and Other Chilling Events. E. Walter
Snowfire. P. A. Whitney
Snowflake and Shaky. C. Gould
Snowline. B. Mather
Snowman. A. Maling
Snowman Cometh. D. Reid
Snowstone. J. M. Scott
So Bad a Death. J. Wright
So Blue Marble. D. B. Hughes
So Cold, My Bed. S. S. Taylor
So Cold the Night. R. L. Yorck
So Dark a Shadow. F. Hurt
So Dark the Mirror. J. Blackmore
So Dead My Love! H. Whittington
So Dead My Lovely. D. Keene
So Dead, So Sweet. D. Linton
So Dead the Rose. M. E. Chaber
So Deadly a Web. R. Owen
So Deadly Fair. Gertrude Walker
So Deadly My Love. S. Ransome
So Deadly, Sinner! C. Brown
So Death Came. C. Ryland
So Dies the Dreamer. U. Curtiss
So Difficult to Die. J. Matheson
So Disdained. N. Shute
So Evil My Love. J. Shearing
So Fair, So Evil. P. Connolly
So Help Me God. Felix Jackson
So Hurt and Humiliated and other stories. Francis King
So I Killed Her. L. O. Mosley
So I'm a Heel. M. Heller
So It Goes On. H. Willett
So Late, Monsieur Calone. A. Page
So Like a Woman. G. M. Fenn

So Long at the Fair. A. Thorne
So Long at the Fair. J. G. Vermandel
So Long, Sucker. M. Clinten
So Lovely She Lies. C. Brown
So Lovely to Kill. Harrison Wade
So Lush, So Deadly. B. Halliday
So Many Dangers. T. B. Morris
So Many Doors. O. M. Hall
So Many Doors. A. Hocking
So Many Doors. L. Meynell
So Many Doors. E. R. Punshon
So Many Steps to Death. A. Christie
So Move the Body. C. Brown
So Much Blood. B. Fischer
So Much Blood. Z. Popkin
So Much for Gennaro. J. Palmer
So Much in the Dark. J. Bude
So Near and Yet. C. Farr
So Near to Love. K. Lindsay
So Nude, So Dead. E. Hunter
So Pale, So Cold, So Fair. C. Birkin
So Pretty a Problem. F. Duncan
So Quiet a Death. N. Morland
So Rich, So Dead. G. Brewer
So Rich, So Lovely, and So Dead. H. Q. Masur
So Sad, So Fresh. B. Hamilton
So Sharp the Razor. B. Graeme
So Sits the Turtle. P. Traill
So Slender a Thread. C. Dixon
So Soon to Die. J. York
So Speed We. G. V. McFadden
So Sweet, So Deadly. D. Rico
So the Lady Died. E. Hale
So Thin Is the Veil. D. E. Bordeaux
So This Is Love! E. Woodward
So What Happens to Me? J. H. Chase
So What Killed the Vampire? C. Brown
So Wicked My Love. B. Fischer
So Young a Body. F. Bunce
So Young, So Cold, So Fair. J. Creasey
So Young, So Wicked. Jonathan Craig
So Young to Burn. J. Creasey
So Young to Die. G. Tree
Sob-Sister Cries Murder. C. Brown
Sober as a Judge. H. Cecil
Soccer League Scandal. W. D. Maydwell
Social Buccaneer. F. S. Isham
Social Evil. P. Grayson
Social Gangster. A. B. Reeve
Social Kaleidoscope. G. R. Sims
Social Sinner. R. Bacon
Social Sinners. H. Smart
Social Storming. W. Martyn
Socialism of Lady Jim. F. Warden
Society Detective. Anonymous
Society Detective. O. Maitland
Society Editor. H. C. Beck
Society Intrigues I Have Known. W. LeQueux
Society Jezebel. F. M. White
Society Marriage. A. Askew
Society of Nobles. I. Tattersall
Society of the Spiders. Roland Daniel
Society Scare. F. Warden
Society's Prodigal. P. Crowe
Sock-It-to-Em Murders. R. Deming
Soeur Angele and the Bell Ringer's Niece. H. Catalan
Soeur Angele and the Embarrassed Ladies. H. Catalan
Soeur Angele and the Ghosts of Chambord. H. Catalan
Soft Arms of Death. R. Hayward
Soft as Silk. M. C. McDougall
Soft at the Centre. E. Warman
Soft Cargo. H. Janson
Soft Centre. J. H. Chase
Soft-Footed Moor. K. Royce
Soft Guy. V. Hill

Soft in the Middle. M. Storey
Soft Sell. J. Bruce
Soft Talkers. M. Millar
Soft Touch. J. D. MacDonald
Softcover Kill. T. Harknett
Softly as I Kill You. C. Nuetzel
Softly Dust the Corpse. S. H. Courtier
Softly in the Night. M. E. Chaber
Softly, Softly Casebook. A. Yarrow
Softly Treads Danger. M. McEvoy
Soho Cafe Crime. W. W. Sayer
Soho Jungle. D. Bateson
Soho Racket. G. Dickson
Soho Spiv. B. Sarto
Soho Spy. C. Robertson
Solander Box Mystery. L. A. Knight
Solange Stories. F. T. Jesse
Soldato! Al Conroy
Solden's Women. Bill Turner
Soldier and a Gentleman. J. M. Cobban
Soldier from the Wars Returning. J. Tickell
Soldier of the Legion. O. Binns
Soldier of the Legion. C. N. Williamson
Soldier Who Came Back. G. Chester
Soldier's Love. A. W. Barrett
Soldiers' Revolt. H. H. Kirst
Soldier's Wife. G. W. M. Reynolds
Sole Agent. K. Benton
Sole Survivor. L. Falstein
Sole Survivor. G. Hackforth-Jones
Sole Survivor. Gavin Holt
Sole Survivor and The Kynsard Affair. Roy Vickers
Solemn High Murder. B. N. Byfield
Solent Intrigue. M. Easton
Solitary Child. N. Bawden
Solitary Farm. F. Hume
Solitary House. E. R. Punshon
Solitary Witness. R. Collier
Solitude Island. J. Brophy
Solitude Limited. J. H. Vahey
Solo for No Voices. W. Paddon
Solo for Several Players. B. Jefferis
Solomon Isaacs. B. L. Farjeon
Solomon's Story. W. J. Shaw
Solomon's Vineyard. Jonathan Latimer
Solution of a Mystery. J. S. Fletcher
Solved in Thirty-Six Hours! H. H. C. Gibbons
Solved Mysteries. J. M'Govan
Solver of Mysteries and other stories. R. H. Todd
Solving a Mystery. D. Miall
Somber Memory. V. Siller
Some Avenger, Rise! L. Egan
Some Beasts No More. K. Giles
Some Beckoning Wraith. P. Warren
Some Buried Caesar. R. Stout
Some Cases of Sherwood Lang, Detective. C. D. Warren
Some Crime Stories. C. Windust
Some Dame. N. Karta
Some Dames Are Deadly. Jonathan Latimer
Some Dames Die Young. D. Foster
Some Dames Don't. P. Muller
Some Dames Don't. M. Perelli
Some Dames Play Rough. S. Mitchell
Some Day I'll Kill You. D. Chambers
Some Die Hard. N. Quarry
Some Die in Their Beds. M. L. Roby
Some Die Running. N. Daniels
Some Die Slow. W. Herber
Some Die Young. J. P. Duff
Some Die Young. J. Kilgore
Some Died Laughing! R. Dolphin

Some Further Adventures of Mr. P. J. Davenant. F. S. Hamilton
Some Geese Lay Golden Eggs. B. Graeme
Some Get It. B. Shannon
Some Kind of Grace. R. Jenkins
Some Kind of Hero. J. Kirkwood
Some Lie and Some Die. R. Rendell
Some Like 'Em Shot. F. Malina
Some Like It Cool. R. Kyle
Some Like It Hot. S. Marshall
Some Like It Tough. J. Karney
Some Look Better Dead. H. Janson
Some Men and Women. M. B. Lowndes
Some Mischief Still. J. E. Hasty
Some Must Die. G. Brewer
Some Must Die. L. Moody
Some Must Watch. B. Cobb
Some Must Watch. S. Ransome
Some Must Watch. Ethel L. White
Some Names Are Dangerous. M. Latham
Some of Your Blood. T. Sturgeon
Some Other Place, the Right Place. D. Harington
Some Persons Unknown. E. W. Hornung
Some Persons Unknown. R. Trevor
Some Poisoned by Their Wives. S. Forbes
Some Put Their Trust in Chariots. A. Grey
Some Queer Stories. Anonymous
Some Rats Have Two Legs. Griff
Some Rise by Sin. C. Houghton
Some Rogues and Daphne. R. Tremayne
Some Slips Don't Show. A. A. Fair
Some Take a Lover. P. Traill
Some Tommies. M. Dekobra
Some Try Murder. R. P. Koehler
Some Unknown Hand. Elaine Hamilton
Some Village Borgia. S. H. Courtier
Some Women Won't Wait. A. A. Fair
Somebody at the Door. R. Postgate
Somebody Has to Lose. Peter Chambers
Somebody Just Grabbed Annie. C. Dennis
Somebody Killed Kelvin. H. Clevely
Somebody Killed Milner. G. P. Willis
Somebody Knew. M. Montgomery
Somebody on the Phone. W. Irish
Somebody Owes Me Money. D. E. Westlake
Somebody Shot the Captain. G. Pahlow
Somebody Wants Me Dead. Richard Williams
Somebody's Done For. D. Goodis
Somebody's Sister. D. Marlowe
Somebody's Story. H. Conway
Somebody's Walking Over My Grave. R. Arthur
Someday I'll Kill You. H. Desmond
Someone and Felicia Warwick. Raymond Mason
Someone Else's War. J. Burmeister
Someone Falling. D. Ambler
Someone from the Past. M. Bennett
Someone Is Bleeding. R. Matheson
Someone Like You. P. Dahl
Someone Lying, Someone Dying. Jonathan Burke
Someone Must Die. M. Cumberland
Someone Waiting. A. Maybury
Someone Waiting. K. Troy
Someone Walked over My Grave. J. B. O'Sullivan
Someone Will Die Tonight in the Caribbean. R. Puissesseau
Someone's Death. C. Larson
Someone's Sleeping in My Bed. J. Gonzales
Someone's Stolen Nellie Grey. Ira Walker
Somerset Murder Case. B. Flynn
Somerville Case. J. Corbett
Something About Midnight. D. B. Olsen

Something Between. M. Cockrell
Something Blue. C. Armstrong
Something Burning. N. Daniels
Something Doing. V. Vanardy
Something Evil. D. Quick
Something for Nothing. H. V. Dixon
Something for Nothing. J. T. Story
Something for the Birds. A. Dean
Something for the Birds. T. S. Drachman
Something in the Air. J. A. Graham
Something in the City. F. Warden
Something in the Heart. J. Lodwick
Something in the Shadows. V. Packer
Something Nasty in the Woodshed. Anthony Gilbert
Something Occurred. B. L. Farjeon
Something on the Stairs. S. Maddock
Something or Nothing. J. W. Conway
Something Rich. J. Butler
Something to Hide. M. Burton
Something to Hide. P. MacDonald
Something to Hide. N. Monsarrat
Something to Hide. L. Sands
Something to His Advantage. W. F. Morris
Something to Kill About. D. Reid
Something Up a Sleeve. R. Lockridge
Something Wicked. H. McCutcheon
Something Wicked. C. Runyon
Something Worth Fighting For. R. Gadney
Something Wrong. E. Linington
Something Wrong. E. Nesbit
Something Wrong at Chillery. R. Francis Foster
Something's Happened to Kate. G. Holden
Sometime Wife. C. Brown
Sometimes Life's Funny. J. J. Farjeon
Somewhere a Voice Is Calling. J. Lodwick
Somewhere in England. R. Gadney
Somewhere in Sark. A. Philips
Somewhere in the House. E. Daly
Somewhere in the Night. B. Barclay
Somewhere in This City. M. Procter
Somewhere in This House. R. King
Somewhere off Borneo. W. B. M. Ferguson
Somewhere Within This House. J. F. Webb
Somnambulist and the Detective. A. Pinkerton
Son. G. Simenon
Son-in-Law Syndicate. F. Marlowe
Son of Blackshirt. B. Graeme
Son of Desolation. M. Y. Halidom
Son of Flynn. E. L. Long
Son of His Father. R. Cullum
Son of Ishmael. L. T. Meade
Son of Mars. A. Griffiths
Son of the Flying Tiger. M. Macao
Son of the Gods. Mrs. Lodge
Son of the Immortals. L. Tracy
Son of Three Fathers. G. Leroux
Son of Wallingford. G. R. Chester
Son of Wu Fang. Roland Daniel
Song for a Prince. R. Foxall
Song for a Siren. V. B. Harris
Song for the Angels. F. L. Green
Song of Corpus Juris. J. L. Hensley
Song of Doom. V. Markham
Song of India. M. Richardson
Song of Sixpence. F. A. Kummer
Song of the Dawn. K. Lindsay
Song of the Flea. G. Kersh
Song of the Scorpions. P. Tabori
Song of the Undersea. R. Kirkbridge
Sonntag. Michael Sinclair
Sons and the Daughters. P. Gallagher
Sons of Belial. W. Westall
Sons of Fire. M. E. Braddon
Sons of Nippon. Bryan Peters
Sons of Satan. J. Creasey
Sons of Satan. W. LeQueux
Sons of Seven. C. B. Dignan

Sons of the Legion. G. E. Rochester
Sons of the Morning. J. Cassells
Sons of the Mounted Police. T. M. Longstreth
Sons of the Wolf. B. Michaels
Sontag of Sundown. W. C. Tuttle
Sookey. D. Newton
Sooper's Cases. N. Morland
Sophisticates. G. Atherton
Sophy Bunce. T. Cobb
Sorcerer of the Castle. F. Stevenson
Sorcerers. David St. John
Sorcerer's Broth. R. Garland
Sorcerer's Chessman. M. Hansom
Sorcerer's House. G. Verner
Sorcerers of Set. Martin Thomas
Sorcerer's Shaft. F. Gerard
Sorceress of the Strand. L. T. Meade
Sore Temptation. J. K. Leys
Sorrow for Angels. H. Arvonen
Sorrow of a Secret. M. C. Hay
Sorry, Chief. W. Johnston
Sorry State. M. Kenyon
Sorry Wrong Number. M. Simpson
Sorry, Wrong Number. A. Ullman
Sorry Wrong Number, and The Hitchhiker. L. Fletcher
Sorry You've Been Shot. A. Bocca
Sorry You've Been Troubled. P. Cheyney
Sort of Madness. E. B. Ronald
Sort of Traitors. N. Balchin
Sorting Van Murder. Mander Ross
Soul Destroyers. N. Carter
Soul Laid Bare. J. K. Egerton
Soul of a Man. D. Vane
Soul of a Shop Girl. C. E. Pearce
Soul of Phyllis Fabian. Mrs. C. Kernahan
Soul of the Sword. R. Bridges
Soul Scar. A. B. Reeve
Soul Stealer. C. R. Gull
Souls Adrift. A. Askew
Souls in Bondage. P. Gibbon
Souls in Hell. John O'Neill
Souls on Fire. L. Tracy
Sound Alibi. M. Edwin
Sound an Alarm. G. Holden
Sound Machine. E. Snell
Sound of a Voice. L. Gardiner
Sound of Dying Roses. J. De Pre
Sound of Footsteps. L. Ford
Sound of Hasty Footsteps. B. La Force
Sound of Insects. Mildred Davis
Sound of Murder. J. Bonett
Sound of Murder. W. Fairchild
Sound of Murder. K. Fearing
Sound of Murder. R. Stout
Sound of Murder. Martin Thomas
Sound of Revelry. O. R. Cohen
Sound of Rowlocks. W. D. Steele
Sound of the Weir. M. Ingate
Sound of Water. M. S. Gerry
Sound of Winter. F. L. Green
Sounder of Swine. P. Buchanan
Soundless Scream. M. Butterworth
Soundless Years. M. Home
Sour Apple Tree. J. Blackburn
Sour Cream with Everything. J. Porter
Sour Grapes. H. Bindloss
Sour Lemon Score. R. Stark
Source of Death. H. Windsor
Source of Fear. B. S. Ballinger
Sourdough Gold. J. B. Hendryx
South by Java Head. Alistair MacLean
South Coast Mystery. J. Drummond
South Coast Mystery. H. H. C. Gibbons
South Coast of Danger. V. Connolly
South Foreland Murder. J. S. Fletcher
South of Heaven. J. Thompson

South of Hell's Gates. R. Butler
South of the Line. G. Volk
South of the Sun. Wade Miller
South Pacific Affair. E. Lacy
South Pole Terror. K. Robeson
South Sea Bubble. R. Pertwee
South Sea Gold. C. Rodda
South Sea Sarah, and Murder in Paradise. B. Grimshaw
Southarn Folly. P. Allardyce
Southern Daughter. D. Keene
Southern Fires. J. G. Sarasin
Southern Electric Murder. F. J. Whaley
Souvenir. P. Carlon
Souvenir from Qam. M. Connelly
Souvenir of Monique. M. Z. Bradley
Soviet Marriage. P. Trent
Sow the Wind. D. M. Disney
Space Beam. J. Robb
Space for Hire. W. F. Nolan
Space Raiders. B. Beverley
Spades at Midnight. S. Maddock
Spahis. M. McCracken
Spandau Quid. O. Fleming
Spandau Warrant. A. Morgan
Spaniard. P. Pettit
Spaniard's House. Robin Temple
Spaniard's Thumb. N. Berrow
Spanish Blood. R. Chandler
Spanish Cape Mystery. E. Queen
Spanish Chapel. D. Daniels
Spanish Connection. N. Carter
Spanish Cove. L. A. Knight
Spanish Crown Affair. C. Conte
Spanish Death. E. R. G. R. Evans
Spanish Duet. F. Clifford
Spanish Galleon. N. Tranter
Spanish Heels. D. Whitelaw
Spanish House. H. Bourne
Spanish Interlude. Margery Lawrence
Spanish Lady. M. Cronin
Spanish Lady. A. Fredericks
Spanish Prisoner. P. C. De Crespigny
Spanish Prisoner. F. Gruber
Spanish Prisoner. F. Tilden
Spanish Season. B. Oldsey
Spanish Steps. G. Goodchild
Spanish Steps. P. McGuire
Spare the Vanquished. M. F. Page
Spare Time for Murder. J. Gale
Spargo. J. D. Scott
Sparkling Cyanide. A. Christie
Sparrows of Paris. M. Pei
Sparta Medallion. H. L. Lawrence
Spawn of Satan. C. Birkin
Spawn of the Desert. W. C. Tuttle
Spawn of the Hawk. P. Conde
Spawn of the Vampire. N. W. Firth
Speak Ill of the Dead. Peter Chambers
Speak Ill of the Dead. Richard Williams
Speak Justly of the Dead. E. C. R. Lorac
Speak no Evil. M. G. Eberhart
Speak no Evil of the Dead. M. L. Roby
Speak of the Devil. E. S. Holding
Speak Softly to the Dead. D. Bogard
Speaker. G. Ashe
Speaking Eye. Clark Smith
Speaking of Murder. A. Roos
Speaking of Murder. V. Van Urk
Spear Gun Murders. B. Kendrick
Spearhead. F. M. Davis
Spearhead Death. M. Procter
Special Agent. Roland Daniel
Special Agent. J. R. McCarthy
Special Collection. T. Allbeury
Special Delivery. V. Gielgud
Special Detective: Ashton-Kirk. J. T. MacIntyre
Special Duty. P. N. Walker
Special Edition--Murder. A. Kent
Special Murders. A. Douglas
Special Orders for Commander Leigh. R. H. Savage
Special Providence. M. A. Hamilton
Special Relationship. W. Clark
Specialist in Crime. G. G. Bolton
Specialists. Lawrence Block
Specimen Case. E. Bramah
Speck of the Motley. F. Hume
Speckled Swan. Dexter Muir
Spectacle. R. Kruger
Spectacles of Mr. Cagliostro. H. S. Keeler
Specter of the Dunes. K. Ostrander
Spectral Bride. W. Shearing
Spectral Evidence. R. Hare
Spectral Mist. C. Ross
Spectre Bullet. T. Mack
Spectre Gold. H. Hill
Spectre in Brown. H. Adams
Spectre Lover. E. Southworth
Spectre of Dolphin Cove. K. Kimbrough
Spectre of the Camera. J. Hawthorne
Spectre's Secret. S. Cobb
Sped Arrow. V. Watkinson
Speed King. J. Addiscombe
Speed Queens. J. Bogar
Speedo! M. Urquhart
Speedwell. T. Claymore
Speedy Death. G. Mitchell
Speight Street Angle. O. Norton
Spell of Sarnia. B. Reynolds
Spell of the Devil. F. E. Penny
Spell of the Snow. C. G. Mitford
Spellbound. F. Beeding
Spellbound. C. Vincent
Spells of Evil. P. Boileau
Spencer Blair, G-Man. Roland Daniel
Spencer's Bag. W. M. Green
Spend the Night. Grant Lane
Sphinx. F. Converse
Sphinx's Lawyer. F. Danby
Spice Route Contract. P. Atlee
Spicy Lady. J. A. Daley
Spider. Elliot Bailey
Spider. F. Hume
Spider. F. Oursler
Spider. G. Oursler
Spider and the Fly. Graham Lord
Spider and the Fly. R. A. J. Walling
Spider at the Elvira. L. Dundas
Spider Ballet. A. G. Wilson
Spider Flies Again. J. R. Holden
Spider Girls. D. Walshe
Spider House. V. W. Mason
Spider in the Cup. J. Shearing
Spider in the Morning. D. Hart-Davis
Spider in the Web. N. Brent
Spider Joe. F. Johnston
Spider Lily. B. Fischer
Spider Man. T. A. Plummer
Spider Never Falls. Winifred Graham
Spider of Soho. S. Cranbrook
Spider of Truxillo. R. H. Savage
Spider on the Belly. W. Rabon
Spider Run Alive. B. Munslow
Spider Spinning. P. Troubetzkoy
Spider Stone. E. E. Cameron
Spider Strikes. M. Innes
Spider Strikes! R. T. M. Scott
Spider Underground. K. Royce
Spider Woman. J. Goodwin
Spider's Debt. J. McCulley
Spider's Den. J. McCulley
Spider's Den. Harrington Strong
Spider's Eye. W. LeQueux
Spider's Fury. J. McCulley
Spiders in the Night. B. Edmunds
Spider's Parlor. N. Carter
Spider's Parlour. P. Wynnton
Spider's Touch. V. Williams
Spider's Web. A. Christie
Spider's Web. Roland Daniel
Spider's Web. Winifred Duke
Spiders' Web. S. Harvester
Spider's Web. R. W. Kauffman
Spider's Web. S. Rathbone
Spider's Web. Mansfield Scott
Spiderweb. R. Bloch
Spiderweb. A. Campbell
Spiderweb Clues. P. Thorne
Spies. T. Von Harbou
Spies Abounding. M. Annesley
Spies Abroad. Anonymous
Spies Against Them. C. R. Dumas
Spies Along the Severn. S. Maddock
Spies and Rebels. Operator 1384
Spies Are Abroad. J. M. Walsh
Spies Die at Dawn. H. Hossent
Spies from the Skies. J. M. Walsh
Spies Go Running. O. Quinn
Spies Have No Friends. H. Hossent
Spies in Action. M. Annesley
Spies in Amber. A. Armstrong
Spies in Ambush. J. H. Vahey
Spies in Concert. R. Stephenson
Spies in Pursuit. J. M. Walsh
Spies in Spain. J. M. Walsh
Spies in the Web. M. Annesley
Spies, Inc. J. D. Hunter
Spies Left! D. Betteridge
Spies Ltd. G. H. Teed
Spies Never Return. J. M. Walsh
Spies of Good Intent. G. Veraldi
Spies of Peace. W. Martyn
Spies of Peenemunde. D. Betteridge
Spies of the Kaiser. W. LeQueux
Spies of the Secret Police. J. G. Rowe
Spies on the Wight. H. Hill
Spies on the Roof. O. Quinn
Spies over France. James Stewart
Spies' Vendetta. J. M. Walsh
Spies Within. B. Wynne
Spiked Heel. R. Marsten
Spiked Lion. B. Flynn
Spill the Jackpot! A. A. Fair
Spin a Coin for Murder. V. B. Hoyt
Spin a Dark Web. A. Barron
Spin a Dark Web. M. Clare
Spin of the Coin. E. R. Punshon
Spin the Glass Web. M. Ehrlich
Spin the Web Tight. D. Lyon
Spin Your Crime. J. Carol
Spin Your Web, Lady! R. Lockridge
Spinach Jade. James Bennett
Spindrift. P. A. Whitney
Spine. H. Imber
Spinner of Death. N. Carter
Spinners of Life. V. Thompson
Spinning Target. J. Nazel
Spinsters. John Williams
Spinsters in Jeopardy. N. Marsh
Spinster's Secret. Anthony Gilbert
Spiral. Robert Garrett
Spiral Path. Richard Grayson
Spiral Staircase. Ethel L. White
Spiral Web. J. M. Wallmann
Spirit Murder Mystery. R. Forsythe
Spirit of Cove Island. R. M. Sears
Spirit Smugglers. G. H. Teed
Spiritualists and the Detectives. A. Pinkerton
Spitting Image. M. Avallone

Title Index

Spiv's Mistake. J. Hunter
Splash of Red. A. MacKenzie
Splendid Adventure of Hannibal Tod. E. Jepson
Splendid Blackguard. R. Pocock
Splendid Coward. H. Townley
Splendid Crime. G. Goodchild
Splendid Exile. L. P. Greene
Splendid Imposter. F. Whishaw
Splendid Love. H. S. Cooper
Splendid Outcast. G. F. Gibbs
Splendid Sin. G. Allen
Splendor and the Dust. H. Gibbs
Splendour Falls. K. Lindsay
Splinter of Glass. J. Creasey
Splinter of Ice. B. Marriner
Splintered Man. M. E. Chaber
Splintered Sunglasses Affair. P. Leslie
Splinters of Fear. N. W. Erickson
Split. G. F. Newman
Split. R. Stark
Split Bamboo. L. Phillips
Split down the Middle. David Miles
Split Peas. H. Hill
Split Scene. F. Mullally
Spoil! E. G. Perrault
Spoil of the Desert. H. H. Hill
Spoiler of Men. R. Marsh
Spoilers. D. Bagley
Spoilers and the Spoils. N. Carter
Spoils of Chance. N. Carter
Spoilt Girl. F. Warden
Spoilt Kill. M. Kelly
Spoletta Story. J. D. White
Spoofs. R. B. Glaenzer
Spook Hole. K. Robeson
Spook Legion. K. Robeson
Spook Who Sat by the Door. S. Greenlee
Spooks Sometimes Sing. J. Courage
Spooky Hollow. C. Wells
Spooky Riders. W. C. Tuttle
Spoonful of Luger. R. Ormerod
Sport for Inspector West. J. Creasey
Sport for the Baron. A. Morton
Sport of Chance. T. W. Speight
Sport of Fate. L. Clarke
Sport of Fate. R. Dowling
Sport of Fate. Old Spicer
Sport of Kings. A. S. Roche
Sport of the Gods. Grove Wilson
Sporting Chance. A. Askew
Sporting Deacon. C. E. Blaney
Sporting Offer. F. Warden
Sporting Proposition. J. Aldridge
Sportsman-Detective. Mansfield Scott
Spot Marked X. B. Gray
Spot of Murder and other stories. P. Cheyney
Spot the Lady. L. Powell
Spotlight. J. Korotkin
Spotlight. P. Wentworth
Spotlight on Murder. F. A. Symonds
Spotlight on Murder. Martin Thomas
Spotlight on Murder. J. Wellard
Spotted Hemlock. G. Mitchell
Spread of Sail. J. D. White
Spreewald Collection. D. MacKenzie
Spriggs the Cracksman. H. Hill
Spring Came Late. G. Greenaway
Spring Cruise. L. A. Knight
Spring Darkness. J. Metcalfe
Spring Fire. V. Packer
Spring Harrowing. P. A. Taylor
Spring of Malice. J. Harris
Spring of Violence. D. Shannon
Spring Term. B. Hamilton
Springboard. J. Fores
Springers. B. Mather
Springs of Violence. E. Lindall
Spun Silk. W. J. Elliott

Spur of Danger. C. C. Hotchkiss
Spurious Note Maker. J. K. Stafford
Spurs of Troodos. W. H. Murray
Spy. J. F. Cooper
Spy. S. Horler
Spy. P. Thomas
Spy. T. Von Harbou
Spy Against the Reich. M. Annesley
Spy and the Thief. E. D. Hoch
Spy at Angkor Wat. B. S. Ballinger
Spy at No. 10. B. Newman
Spy at the Villa Miranda. Elsie Lee
Spy Business. J. Pendower
Spy Castle. N. Carter
Spy Catchers. N. MacNeil
Spy Catchers. B. Newman
Spy Company. A. C. Gunter
Spy Converted. P. Boulle
Spy Corner. M. Annesley
Spy-Counter Spy. M. Annesley
Spy-Counter Spy. D. Betteridge
Spy Flyers. W. E. Johns
Spy for a Spy. B. Mather
Spy for Churchill. R. Vacha
Spy for England. Martin Kent
Spy for Germany. E. Gimpel
Spy for Mr. Crook. Anthony Gilbert
Spy for Sale. L. Payne
Spy from Spain. J. G. Brandon
Spy from the Grave. J. Dark
Spy Gang. P. Sebastian
Spy Ghost. N. Daniels
Spy Hunt. N. Daniels
Spy Hunter. W. LeQueux
Spy Hunters. J. Bolton
Spy-In. R. Deming
Spy in Bangkok. B. S. Ballinger
Spy in Black. J. S. Clouston
Spy in Black. C. Weston
Spy in Camera. Richard Grayson
Spy in Chancery. K. Benton
Spy in Damascus. N. Vange
Spy in Khaki. M. McKenna
Spy in the Brown Derby. B. Newman
Spy in the Hand. Henry Talbot
Spy in the Java Sea. B. S. Ballinger
Spy in the Jungle. B. S. Ballinger
Spy in the Navy. D. Lenton
Spy in the Nude. R. Seth
Spy in the Ointment. D. E. Westlake
Spy in the Room. D. Clift
Spy in the Tunnel. John Morgan
Spy in the Vodka. Ross Thomas
Spy in White Gloves. J. Laflin
Spy Is a Dirty Word. R. Temple
Spy Is Forever. R. P. French
Spy Island. M. Annesley
Spy Kill. L. W. Blanco
Spy Meets Spy. C. V. Frost
Spy Net. Ared White
Spy Now, Pay Later. N. Rich
Spy No. 13. R. W. Chambers
Spy of Osawatomie. M. E. Jackson
Spy on Approval. R. Child
Spy or Die. B. Graham
Spy Paramount. E. P. Oppenheim
Spy Puppets. Geoffrey Davison
Spy Story. L. Deighton
Spy Trap. B. Graham
Spy 222. R. Dark
Spy Was Born. M. McKenna
Spy Who Came Home to Die. J. Weil
Spy Who Came in from the Cold. J. Le Carré
Spy Who Didn't. J. Laflin

Spy Who Died in Bed. G. Wolfenden
Spy Who Died of Boredom. G. Mikes
Spy Who Died Twice. M. Bar-Zohar
Spy Who Got Off at Las Vegas. D. Savage
Spy Who Hated Licorice. R. L. Hershatter
Spy Who Liked Fudge. R. L. Hershatter
Spy Who Loved America. J. Laflin
Spy Who Loved Me. I. Fleming
Spy Who Sat and Waited. R. W. Campbell
Spy Who Spoke Porpoise. P. Wylie
Spy Who Swopped Shoes. Geoffrey Davison
Spy Who Was Three Feet Tall. P. Rabe
Spy Who Wasn't Exchanged. A. Tack
Spy with a Cold Nose. R. Galton
Spy with the Scar. J. Rowland
Spying at the Fountain of Youth. W. Butler
Spying Blind. J. Dark
Spying Blind. M. McKenna
Spylight. J. Leasor
Spylight. W. Taylor
Spymaster. P. Freund
Spymaster. E. P. Oppenheim
Spyrocket. W. Taylor
Squaberry Canyon. A. Rutherford
Squadron Without a Number. G. E. Rochester
Square Dance. J. Wainwright
Square Deal. G. Goodchild
Square Emerald. F. Johns
Square Emerald. E. Wallace
Square in the Middle. W. C. Gault
Square Mark. Grace M. White
Square of Many Colours. J. Blackmore
Square One. H. Janson
Square Peg. G. Malcolm-Smith
Squaring the Triangle, and other stories. H. Kaner
Squaw Point. R. H. Shimer
Squeaker. E. Wallace
Squeaking Goblin. K. Robeson
Squealer. J. Dark
Squealer. G. Verner
Squealer. E. Wallace
Squealer's Secret. D. Stuart
Squeeze. G. Brewer
Squeeze. D. Craig
Squeeze Play. J. McKimmey
Squeeze Play. T. H. Stone
Squire Errant. R. Foxall
Squire of Death. R. Lockridge
Squire of Kilderman. F. Burdon
Squire of Landrewn. G. V. Vosper
Squire Trevlyn's Heir. H. Wood
Squire's Fatal Will. M. Danvers
Squire's Heir. E. Everett-Green
Squire's Legacy. M. C. Hay
Stab in the Back. H. Adams
Stab in the Back. C. Drummond
Stab in the Dark. J. Rayter
Stab in the Dark. L. Trimble
Stable Mystery, and other stories. N. Gould
Stables Crime. M. Osborne
Stables to £1,000,000. Gordon Holt
Stacked Deck. F. Kane
Staffordshire Assassins. C. Stokes
Staffordshire Knot. J. Ruegg
Stag Party. W. Krasner
Stage Door. A. Applin
Stage Door Crime. G. Chester
Stage-Struck. A. Applin
Stages of Terror. B. Kingsley
Stain. F. Halsey
Stain of Suspicion. C. Williams
Stain on the Snow. G. Simenon
Stainless Steel Rat. H. Harrison

Stainless Steel Rat Saves the World. H. Harrison
Stainless Steel Rat's Revenge. H. Harrison
Stainless Steel Wreath. J. Hedges
Staircase 4. H. Reilly
Staircase of Surprise. F. A. Mathews
Staircase to the Sea. J. Turner
Stairs Lead Nowhere. H. Swiggett
Stairs of Sand. E. D. Pierson
Stairway. U. Curtiss
Stairway to an Empty Room. D. Hitchens
Stairway to Death. B. Fischer
Stairway to Murder. A. Kent
Stairway to Murder. O. Mills
Stairway to Murder. F. Usher
Stairway to Nowhere. H. Ellson
Stake in the Game. E. Berckman
Stalag Mites. L. Grex
Stalemate. E. Berckman
Stalk a Long Shadow. R. Severn
Stalk the Hunter. M. A. Wilson
Stalk to Kill. R. Adam
Stalker. B. Pronzini
Stalkers. P. Ketchum
Stalkers of the Sea. K. Stanton
Stalking Horse. V. Gielgud
Stalking Horse. A. Rothberg
Stalking Lamb. M. Babson
Stalking Man. W. Tucker
Stalking of Adrian Lawford. Roderick Grant
Stalking Stranger. C. Robertson
Stalking Terror. V. Coffman
Stamboul Intrigue. R. Charles
Stamboul Train. G. Greene
Stamp Me Mortal. J. Lodwick
Stamped for Death. E. McDowell
Stamped for Murder. B. Benson
Stampede. L. Sieveking
Stampeders. J. B. Hendryx
Stand and Deliver. G. Warden
Stand By! Taffrail
Stand By for Danger. P. Manton
Stand By--London Calling. H. S. Keeler
Stand By to Shoot. E. Cannon
Stand In. B. Kingsley
Stand-In. E. Piper
Stand-In for Danger. K. Hewitt
Stand-In for Danger. R. Rayner
Stand-In for Death. M. Echard
Stand-In for Murder. L. Gribble
Stand-In for Murder. A. C. MacLean
Stand-In for Murder. D. Reid
Stand Up and Die. R. Lockridge
Stand Up and Fight. David Hume
Standard-Bearers. K. Mayo
Standish Gaunt Case. I. Patterson
Standish Place. I. Holland
Stanhope Gate Mystery. R. Machray
Stanhope of Chester. P. Andreae
Stanton Wins. E. M. Ingram
Star Above Paris. J. G. Sarasin
Star Crossed. M. Mead
Star-Crossed Love. Elsie Lee
Star-Crossed Lover. C. Brown
Star Detective. D. Essex
Star Dust. J. Ronald
Star-Gazers. G. M. Fenn
Star in a Mist. A. Stringer
Star in the Forest. M. Frazer
Star Is Falling. M. Richmond
Star of Danger. Elsie Lee
Star of Death. M. Gillen
Star of Earth. O. R. Cohen
Star of Evil. L. Noel
Star of Hollywood. E. Stilgebauer
Star of Ill-Omen. D. Wheatley
Star of Midnight. A. S. Roche
Star of Persia. R. Adams
Star of the East. C. E. Pearce
Star of the Goddess. M. Clare
Star Ruby Contract. P. Atlee
Star Stalker. R. Bloch
Star Trap. R. Colby
Star Witness. R. Madison
Starbuck. Bryan Peters
Starcrossed Road. M. Farnsworth
Starfish Affair. J. N. Chance
Staring Eyes! T. A. Plummer
Stark Murder. L. Thayer
Stark Naked. L. R. Bourne
Starlet for a Penny. W. A. Ballinger
Starlight Motel Incident. J. Weisman
Starling Street. D. Palmtag
Starr Bedford Dies. R. Garnett
Starrbelow. C. Thompson
Starry-Eyed Chipmonk. S. M. Schley
Starry Eyed Murder. T. A. Plummer
Stars and Stripes. M. Dekobra
Stars Are Dark. P. Cheyney
Stars Cannot Tell. A. Maybury
Stars for the Toff. J. Creasey
Stars Give Warning. B. Conrad
"Stars I'd Give--." A. Soutar
Stars in the Heather. O. Wynd
Stars in the Water. J. Appleby
Stars of Evil. D. E. Stitt
Stars Scream Murder. A. B. Reeve
Stars Spell Death. J. Stagge
Starstruck. E. Tidyman
Start Screaming Murder. T. Powell
Starting Gun. G. Bagby
Startling and Thrilling Narrative of the Dark and Terrible Deeds of Henry Medison, and His Associate and Accomplice, Miss Ella Stevens, Who Was Executed by the Vigilance Committee of San Francisco, on the 20th September Last. S. Drury
Startling Crimes and Notorious Criminals. D. Donovan
Startling Discovery. Old Sleuth
Starved. A. Thompson
Starvel Hollow Tragedy. F. W. Crofts
Stash Spots a Murder. R. Peters
State Department Cat. M. Plum
State Department Murders. E. Ronns
State of Emergency. J. Robb
State of Emergency. Sheila Ross
State of Fear. D. Reid
State of Siege. E. Ambler
State Puppet. D. Bennett
State Secrets. W. B. Home-Gall
State Torch. J. G. Sarasin
State Trooper. N. B. Gerson
State vs. Elinor Norton. M. R. Rinehart
State vs. Elna Jepson. N. B. Mavity
Stately Homicide. G. Milner
Stateroom Opposite. A. H. Veysey
Statesman's Game. J. Aldridge
Station Master's Secret. A. Murray
Station Wagon in Spain. F. P. Keyes
Station Wagon Murder. M. Propper
Station X. G. M. Winsor
Statue. E. Phillpotts
Statue and the Lady. S. M. Wick
Stay Dead, Sweetheart. R. Drayton
Stay of Execution. H. Desmond
Stay of Execution. M. Gilbert
Stay of Execution. L. Halliday
Stay of Execution. E. C. Williams
Stay Out of Menchis. B. Sarto
Stay Until Tomorrow. A. Maybury
Steadfast Heart. M. Richmond
Steady, Boys, Steady. J. Mitchell
Steal Big. L. White
Stealing Lillian. T. Kenrick
Stealthy Death. M. Richmond
Stealthy Steve, the Six-Eyed Sleuth. N. Newkirk
Stealthy Terror. J. Ferguson
Steam Packet. G. W. M. Reynolds
Steam Pig. J. McClure
Steamboatmen. C. J. C. Hyne
Stedman Gang. Roland Daniel
Steel and Jade. A. Abdullah
Steel Balloon. H. McLeave
"Steel" Callaghan. M. Chesney
Steel Casket and other stories. N. Carter
Steel Crown. F. Hume
Steel Face. Gwyn Evans
Steel Garrotte. J. Ingersol
Steel Hit. R. Stark
Steel Mask. M. Carrel
Steel Mirror. D. Hamilton
Steel Necklace. F. Du Boisgobey
Steel Noose. A. Drake
Steel Shutters. Gavin Holt
Steel Spring. P. Wahloo
Steele Bey's Revenge. T. Lund
Steeley Flies Again. W. E. Johns
Steeltown Strangler. H. S. Keeler
Steelyard Blues. Timothy Harris
Steep Steps. K. Ingram
Stella Buys a Shroud. M. Storm
Stella Nash. Ganpat
Stella Shall Die. H. Desmond
Step Aside to Death. S. Maddock
Step by Step. C. Collins
Step in the Dark. F. Cowen
Step in the Dark. K. Eyre
Step in the Dark. Ethel L. White
Step in the House. R. Ramsay
Step into Murder. S. Curtis
Step into Quicksand. L. Treat
Step into Terror. Marilyn Ross
Step Light, Lady. Margery Lawrence
Step on the Stair. A. K. Green
Step Softly on My Grave. M. A. Hubbard
Step Up, Sucker. G. Ross
Stepfather. C. Jay
Stepford Wives. I. Levin
Stephen Vale. P. Trent
Stepmother's House. C. Bramwell
Stepping Blindfold. T. W. Speight
Steps Going Down. J. T. MacIntyre
Steps in Mystery. T. R. Morden
Steps in the Dark. M. Black
Steps in the Dark. M. Cumberland
Steps to Murder. R. King
Steps to Murder. R. P. Koehler
Steps to Nowhere. C. Leonard
Stern Chase. G. Hackforth-Jones
Sterne of the Secret Service. J. A. Jordan
Steve. G. Goodchild
Steve Bentley's Calypso Caper. R. Dietrich
Stevedore Mystery. B. North
Steward. E. Wallace
Stewardess Strangler. R. Gallagher
Stick at Nothing. A. Wood
Stick 'Em Up! F. Ryerson
Stick or Bust. R. Drayton
Sticking Place. Jessica Mann
Sticking Point. K. Jackson
Stiff as a Broad. G. G. Fickling
Stiff Silk. S. Milne
Stiffs Can't Squeal. Griff
Stiffs Don't Vote. G. Homes
Stiffsons, and other stories. H. Jenkins
Stigma for Valor. Williams Forrest
Stiletto. B. Rossi

Title Index

Stiletto Signature. J. Messmann
Still as the Grave. M. L. Roby
Still Dead. R. A. Knox
Still No Answer. L. Thayer
Still of Night. L. Powell
Still the World Is Young. K. Hewitt
Still They Smile. P. Conway
Still Water. K. N. Burt
Still Waters. Dorothy Fletcher
Still Waters. E. C. R. Lorac
Still Waters. F. F. Van De Water
Stillwater Tragedy. T. B. Aldrich
Stillwell Murder. M. T. Dawson
Sting. W. LeQueux
Sting. R. Weverka
Sting of Death. P. D. Westbrook
Sting of the Adder. N. Carter
Stingaree. E. W. Hornung
Stingaree Murders. W. S. Pleasants
Stink of Murder. W. Spann
Stinson's Reef. C. J. C. Hyne
"Stir." G. Ingram
"Stir" Crazy. B. Shannon
Stir of Echoes. R. Matheson
"Stir" Train. G. Ingram
Stirring Adventures. F. A. M. Webster
Stirrup Cup. J. A. Tyson
Stitch in Time. E. Lathen
Stoat. L. Brock
Stockade. W. C. Tuttle
Stockbroker's Wife, and other sensational tales. B. Hemyng
Stockholders in Death. K. Robeson
Stoenberg Affair. R. A. Goodwin
Stoke Silver Case. L. Brock
Stolen Bacillus, and other incidents. H. G. Wells
Stolen Boat-Train. D. G. Browne
Stolen Brain. N. Carter
Stolen Bride. E. Klein
Stolen Budget. J. S. Fletcher
Stolen Cellini. Alan Thomas
Stolen Cipher. Sea Lion
Stolen Crown. J. W. Bobin
Stolen Death. L. Grex
Stolen Fiddle. W. H. Mayson
Stolen Formula Mystery. M. E. Cooke
Stolen Gold. J. Chancellor
Stolen Goods. C. B. Kelland
Stolen Heiress. C. Merrick
Stolen Home Secretary. L. Gribble
Stolen Honeymoon. M. Leighton
Stolen Horse Race. N. Carter
Stolen Husband. R. D. Andrews
Stolen Identity. N. Carter
Stolen Idols. E. P. Oppenheim
Stolen Jewels. Old Spicer
Stolen Laces. J. W. Postgate
Stolen Laces. D. Simmons
Stolen Lady. A. Askew
Stolen Letter. C. Morris
Stolen Liberty Bonds. N. Ridley
Stolen Life. M. M. Bodkin
Stolen Like Magic Away. P. Audemars
Stolen Man. Mrs. C. Kernahan
Stolen Mask. W. Collins
Stolen Millionaire. S. Truss
Stolen Name. N. Carter
Stolen Necklace. Roland Daniel
Stolen Nugget of Gold. N. Ridley
Stolen or Strayed. D. Collins
Stolen Partnership Papers. J. W. Bobin
Stolen Pay Train. N. Carter
Stolen Pay Train and other stories. N. Carter
Stolen Pearl. G. Warden
Stolen Peer. G. Boothby
Stolen Plans. R. Gar
Stolen Race. N. Gould
Stolen Race Horse. N. Carter

Stolen Scar. Gret Lane
Stolen Signet. F. M. Smith
Stolen Singer. M. Bellinger
Stolen Souls. W. LeQueux
Stolen Squadron. C. L. Leonard
Stolen Statesman. L. Gribble
Stolen Statesman. W. LeQueux
Stolen Strychnine. B. Cobb
Stolen Submarine. R. Bacon
Stolen Submarine. S. Hope
Stolen Sweets. W. LeQueux
Stolen Test-Tube. W. Jardine
Stolen Virtue. C. Kingston
Stolen White Elephant. M. Twain
Stolen Will. W. S. Hayward
Stolen Will. M. Pinkerton
Stolen Woman. Wade Miller
Stone. N. Tranter
Stone Around Her Neck. B. McKnight
Stone Baby. B. Healey
Stone Blunts Scissors. G. Fairlie
Stone Carnation. N. A. Hintze
Stone Cold Blonde. Adam Knight
Stone Cold Dead. R. Ellington
Stone Cold Dead in the Market. C. Landon
Stone-Cold-Dead in the Market Affair. P. Leslie
Stone-Cold Dead in the Market Affair. J. Oram
Stone Dead. C. Ashton
Stone Dead. P. Laing
Stone Dead. San Antonio
Stone Dead. F. A. Symonds
Stone Dormitory. J. Turner
Stone Dragon and Other Tragic Romances. R. M. Gilchrist
Stone for His Head. B. Cobb
Stone House. D. Daniels
Stone Killer. J. Gardner
Stone Killer. F. Scarpetta
Stone Leopard. C. Forbes
Stone Maiden. A. Manners
Stone of Blood. J. Coulson
Stone Roses. S. Gainham
Stone Walls. C. Heath
Stoned Cold Soldier. C. Dennis
Stones of Enchantment. W. Martyn
Stones of Khor. D. Whitelaw
Stones of Satan. R. Wallace
Stonewall Steevens Investigates. M. G. Kiddy
Stoneware Monkey. R. A. Freeman
Stool Pigeon. Roland Daniel
Stool Pigeon. L. Malley
Stop at Nothing. J. Welcome
Stop-at-Nothing Man. Roland Daniel
Stop at the Red Light. A. A. Fair
Stop on the Green Light! M. Barrington
Stop-Over Danger. V. Warren
Stop Press. M. Innes
Stop, Press! E. Spencer
Stop Press--Homicide! R. Dolphin
Stop Press in Scarlet. M. Brody
Stop Press Murder. G. Ramsey
Stop Press--Murder! P. Stirling
Stop That Man. C. Franklin
Stop That Man! R. Ladline
Stop Thief! G. C. Jenks
Stop Thief! C. Moore
Stop This Man! P. Rabe
Stopover for Murder. M. Mahannah
Stopover for Murder. T. H. Stone
Stopover: Tokyo. J. P. Marquand
Stopped Clock. J. T. Rogers
Store of Wrath. S. Truss
Storefront Lawyers. A. L. Conroy
Stories and Interludes. B. Pain
Stories and Sketches. J. Payn

Stories Cops Only Tell Each Other. G. Radano
Stories from Scotland Yard. M. Moser
Stories from the Diary of a Doctor. L. T. Meade
Stories from the Note-Book of a Detective. D. Donovan
Stories in Black and White. G. R. Sims
Stories in Grey. B. Pain
Stories in the Dark. B. Pain
Stories of a World Renown Detective. Anonymous
Stories of Darkness and Dread. J. P. Brennan
Stories of Donald Shoubridge. D. Shoubridge
Stories of East and West. H. D. Stacpoole
Stories of Fear. J. McLaren
Stories of the Broadmoor Patient, and the Poor Clerk. F. Wicks
Stories of the Railroad. J. A. Hill
Stories of the Railway. V. L. Whitechurch
Stories of the Seen and the Unseen. M. Oliphant
Stories of Three Burglars. F. R. Stockton
Stories of Today and Yesterday. P. C. De Crespigny
Stories Weird and Wonderful. H. Nisbet
Storm. H. L. V. Fletcher
Storm. Gavin Holt
Storm Against the Wall. L. Meynell
Storm and the Silence. D. Walker
Storm-Bound. J. G. Sarasin
Storm Breaks. A. Gask
Storm Canvas. E. L. Long
Storm Center. B. E. Stevenson
Storm Centre. B. Musto
Storm Cloud over Vienna. O. L. Rosmanith
Storm Driven. A. Applin
Storm Evil. J. Robb
Storm Fear. C. Seeley
Storm Gang. Richard Grant
Storm Girl. J. C. Lincoln
Storm House. F. Hurd
Storm in a Sanctuary. K. Ingram
Storm in an Inkpot. C. Franklin
Storm in Harbour. G. Hackforth-Jones
Storm in the Family. J. Blackmore
Storm in the Mountains. N. Buckingham
Storm in the Sand. T. B. Morris
Storm Is Rising. G. Dyer
Storm Knight. F. E. Smith
Storm Lady. J. H. Vahey
Storm Maiden. K. Lindsay
Storm Music. D. Yates
Storm of Spears. A. C. Marin
Storm over Bitterhill. P. Warren
Storm over Fox Hill. G. Addison
Storm over Hollywood. J. Reach
Storm over Paris. S. Noel
Storm over Rockall. W. H. Baker
Storm over Roseheath. K. Troy
Storm Signals. R. H. Savage
Storm South. P. McCutchan
Storm Squad. P. Leslie
Storm Tarn. P. Troubetzkoy
Storm Tide. A. MacVicar
Storm Tossed. M. S. Jones
Storm Wind Rising. J. Rouverol
Storm-Wrack. H. Hill
Stormberg Jewel Case. K. M. Sheahan
Stormcliff. M. T. Walworth
Stormhaven. Jennifer Hale
Stormlight. J. N. Chance
Storm's End. Rebecca James
Stormtide. B. Knox

Stormy Night. C. Hale
Stormy Paradise. K. Lindsay
Story Behind the Verdict. F. Danby
Story of a Dark Crime. Hawkshaw
Story of a Great Sin. M. Leighton
Story of a Killer. D. Spade
Story of a Sin. H. B. Mathers
Story of Antony Grace. G. M. Fenn
Story of Barbara. M. E. Braddon
Story of Charles Strange. H. Wood
Story of Clovelly's Wife. W. J. Newton
Story of Dorothy Grape, and other tales. H. Wood
Story of Dorothy Stanfield. O. Micheaux
Story of Ivy. M. B. Lowndes
Story of Joan Courage. R. Rodd
Story of Leland Gay. A. R. Weekes
Story of Professor X. J. Budd
Story of Rachel. R. Abbey
Story of the Fast Mail. C. Thornton
Story of the Foss River Ranch. R. Cullum
Story of the Stage. C. R. Gull
Story on Crime. J. T. Story
Story Teller. G. Buhet
Story-Teller. P. Highsmith
Story That Could Not Be Told. M. Albrand
Story to Tell. P. Fleming
Story Without a Name. A. Stringer
Stout Cortez. G. Goodchild
Stowaway. R. Johnston
Stowaway. A. Mills
Stowaway. G. Simenon
Stowaway. L. Tracy
Stowaway Girl. L. Tracy
Stowaway of the S. S. Wanderer. A. Parsons
Stowmarket Mystery. L. Tracy
Straight Ahead for Danger. W. M. Duncan
Straight and Crooked. M. McShane
Straight Clue. Old Sleuth
Straight Crooks. H. Fielding
Straight Furrow. Constance Rutherford
Straight-Out Detective. Old Sleuth
Straight Road. G. Radcliffe
Straight Shooting. W. C. Tuttle
Straight Time. E. Bunker
"Straight to the Mark." Old Sleuth
Straight-Up Girl. D. Glinto
Stranded. E. R. Beach
Stranded in Arcady. F. Lynde
Strands of Red...Hair! Glint Green
Strange Adventure of Roger Wilkins and other stories. R. Andom
Strange Adventures of a Magistrate. T. R. Threlfall
Strange Adventures of Bromley Barnes. G. Barton
Strange Adventures of Handel Archimedes. C. W. Sykes
Strange Adventures of Miss Brown. R. Buchanan
Strange Adventures of Mr. Collin. F. Heller
Strange Adventures of Mr. Middleton. W. A. Curtis
Strange Adventures of Richard Conway Bowen. C. R. Benstead
Strange Affair. B. Toms
Strange Affair at Greylands. Mark Cross
Strange Affair of the Shot Gun Sniper. W. Tyrer
Strange Affair of the Widow's Diamonds. H. Clevely
Strange Affection. G. Des Cars
Strange Bargain. H. Whittington
Strange Bedfellow. E. Berckman
Strange Blue Yawl. L. Fletcher
Strange Boarders of Palace Crescent. E. P. Oppenheim
Strange Capers. A. Meeker
Strange Caravan. Margery Lawrence
Strange Career of Bishop Sterling. S. Endicott
Strange Cargo. M. Richmond
Strange Case. Anonymous
Strange Case of Cavendish. R. Parrish
Strange Case of Deacon Brodie. F. Bramble
Strange Case of Dr. Bruno. F. E. Daniel
Strange Case of Dr. Earle. F. W. Crofts
Strange Case of Dr. Jekyll and Mr. Hyde. R. L. Stevenson
Strange Case of Edgar Heriot. F. Grierson
Strange Case of Eleanor Cuyler. K. Crosby
Strange Case of Habberton's Mile. W. J. Bayfield
Strange Case of Harriet Hall. M. Dalton
Strange Case of Henry Toplass and Capt. Shiers. J. W. Postgate
Strange Case of John R. Graham. V. Kutchin
Strange Case of Lucile Clery. J. Shearing
Strange Case of Mary Page. F. Lewis
Strange Case of Mr. Henry Marchmont. J. S. Fletcher
Strange Case of Mr. Jocelyn Thew. E. P. Oppenheim
Strange Case of Mr. Pelham. A. Armstrong
Strange Case of Mortimer Fenley. L. Tracy
Strange Case of Pamela Wilson. Mark Cross
Strange Case of Peter the Lett. G. Simenon
Strange Case of Sir Merton Quest. A. Soutar
Strange Case of the Antlered Man. E. S. Brooks
Strange Case of the Footman's Crime. G. Chester
Strange Case of Vincent Hume. D. Miall
Strange Case of Vintrix Polbarton. I. Marshall
Strange Case of William Cook. R. Keverne
Strange Cases of Dr. Stanchon. J. D. Bacon
Strange Cases of Magistrate Pao. L. Comber
Strange Cases of Mason Brant. N. M. Hopkins
Strange Citadel. R. Spain
Strange Clues. J. M'Govan
Strange Code of Justice. R. K. Isely
Strange Conflict. D. Wheatley
Strange Corner. Mildred Davis
Strange Corpse on Murder Mile. D. Boyle
Strange Countess. E. Wallace
Strange Crime in Bermuda. E. S. Holding
Strange Crimes. W. Westall
Strange Death of a Doctor. L. Landon
Strange Death of Manny Square. A. B. Cunningham
Strange Death of Martin Green. D. Frome
Strange Destiny. C. Dawe
Strange Disappearance. A. K. Green
Strange Disappearance of Eugene Comstocks. M. R. Hatch
Strange Disappearance of John Haversham. I. D. Hardy
Strange Disappearance of Lady Delia. L. Tracy
Strange Disappearance of Mary Young. M. Propper
Strange Doctor and other mystic stories. V. Van Der Elst
Strange Doings on Halfaday Creek. J. B. Hendryx
Strange Enchantment. B. L. Farjeon
Strange Enchantment. P. Webling
Strange Ending. E. R. Punshon
Strange Experiences of Mr. Verschoyle. T. W. Speight
Strange Experiment. Valentine
Strange Face of Murder. W. A. Ballinger
Strange Fate. R. S. L. Harding
Strange Fellowship of Maxwell Gale. W. Bouchier
Strange Flaw. H. S. Wilcox
Strange Fugitive. M. Callaghan
Strange Happening. N. MacKenzie
Strange Harmony. A. Carr
Strange Heritage. M. A. Clune
Strange Heritage. T. Uphill
Strange History of Ambrose Hinkle. T. McMorrow
Strange Holiday. E. Gill
Strange Houses. C. Jarrett
Strange Hunger. M. Hervey
Strange Infatuation. L. Harrison
Strange Inheritance. G. Simenon
Strange Inheritance. P. Trent
Strange Instrument. N. Rennie
Strange Journeys. B. Hemyng
Strange Land. H. Innes
Strange Landing. L. Meynell
Strange Legacy. A. Barron
Strange Legacy. L. Bergstrom
Strange Legacy. E. M. Williams
Strange Little Snakes. J. Turner
Strange Lovers. J. Trinian
Strange Mansion. T. Rook
Strange Manuscript Found in a Copper Cylinder. J. De Mille
Strange Message. Dora Russell
Strange Money. Mark Ross
Strange Motives. R. Goyne
Strange Murder of Hatton, K.C. H. Adams
Strange Murders at Greystones. E. N. Wright
Strange Occupation. J. A. Park
Strange Occurrences. L. Davis
Strange Paradise. D. Daniels
Strange Partner. D. Lee
Strange Partners. G. Wintle
Strange Prisoner. M. Home
Strange Pursuit. N. R. De Mexico
Strange Pursuit. P. Wynnton
Strange Quartet. K. Rhodes
Strange Relations. Jerome Barry
Strange Rendezvous. H. D. Dearden
Strange Report. John Burke
Strange Return. A. B. Cunningham
Strange Ritual. H. Janson
Strange Romance. B. Herbert
Strange Salvation. K. Hewitt
Strange Sanctuary. E. Butler
Strange Schemes of Randolph Mason. M. D. Post
Strange Sin. C. Kernahan
Strange Sisters. F. Flora
Strange Smell of Murder. L. Dundas
Strange Stories. G. Allen
Strange Stories from a Chinese Studio. H. A. Giles
Strange Stories of a Detective. Anonymous
Strange Stories of a Detective. Waters
Strange Stories of Strange People. O. Dale
Strange Story. E. Bulwer-Lytton
Strange Story. Hilda Lewis
Strange Story in The Falconer Papers. U. L. Silberrad
Strange Story of Linda Lee. D. Wheatley

Title Index

Strange Sylvester Affair. L. Thayer
Strange Tales of a Nihilist. W. LeQueux
Strange Tangle. A. King
Strange Visitor. H. Elsna
Strange Welcome. F. A. Chittenden
Strange Will. H. S. Keeler
Strange Witness. D. Keene
Strange Witness. B. Symons
Strange Wooing. C. Gibbon
Strange Wooing. R. Marsh
Strange Wooing of Mary Bowler. R. Marsh
Strange World. M. E. Braddon
Strange Young Man. L. Gerard
Strangely She Died. N. Morland
Stranger Among Friends. E. Lindall
Stranger and Afraid. E. Ferrars
Stranger and Afraid. M. Hardt
Stranger at Christmas. A. MacVicar
Stranger at Home. G. Sanders
Stranger at Pembroke. A. Eliot
Stranger at Plantation Inn. P. Maxwell
Stranger at the Gate. J. Edgar
Stranger at the Gates. Evelyn Anthony
Stranger Beware. R. Madison
Stranger by Night. M. Lynn
Stranger by the Lake. Beatrice Parker
Stranger Called the Blues. S. Coulter
Stranger Came Back. C. Franklin
Stranger Came to Dinner. A. Soutar
Stranger in a Dark Land. J. Wellsley
Stranger in Galah. Michael Barrett
Stranger in Her House. H. Arvonen
Stranger in His Grave. D. Bennett
Stranger in My Grave. M. Millar
Stranger in the Dark. H. Nielsen
Stranger in the House. A. Caballero
Stranger in the House. S. Mayfield
Stranger in the Land. M. Pereira
Stranger in These Parts. E. F. Boyd
Stranger in Town. R. Bloomfield
Stranger in Town. B. Halliday
Stranger in Town. J. D. White
Stranger of the Glen. H. M. Jones
Stranger on the Cliff. J. Bell
Stranger on the Highway. H. R. Hays
Stranger Than Fiction. C. Dawe
Stranger Than Fiction. H. Desmond
Stranger Than Truth. V. Caspary
Stranger to Herself. B. Williams
Stranger to Myself. S. Shubin
Stranger to Town. L. P. Davies
Stranger, Tread Light. Jean Muir
Stranger with My Face. P. McGerr
Stranger Within the Gates. C. N. Boyle
Strangers Among the Dead. G. Bellairs
Strangers and Afraid. T. Sterling
Strangers and Pilgrims. M. E. Braddon
Strangers at Collins House. Marilyn Ross
Strangers from the Sea. A. MacVicar
Stranger's Gate. E. P. Oppenheim
Strangers in Company. J. A. Hodge
Strangers in Flight. M. G. Eberhart
Strangers in 7-A. F. Farrington
Strangers in the House. G. Simenon
Strangers in the Night. G. St. John
Strangers Meeting. Winston Graham
Stranger's Meeting. R. Savage
Strangers on a Train. P. Highsmith
Strangers on Friday. H. Whittington
Strangest Grand National. F. Johnston
Strangle Hold! Al Conroy
Strangle Hold. M. McMullen
Strangled Witness. L. Ford
Stranglehold. H. Carmichael
Stranglehold. D. Cory
Stranglehold. J. Creighton
Stranglehold. A. Hocking
Stranglehold. G. C. Knapp

Stranglehold. D. T. Lindsay
Stranglehold. B. Reynolds
Strangler. D. Black
Strangler. H. Desmond
Strangler. L. Marshall
Strangler. T. A. Plummer
Strangler. E. C. Reed
Strangler. San Antonio
Strangler. Hampton Stone
Strangler. M. Thynne
Strangler Fig. J. S. Strange
Strangler Who Couldn't Let Go. Hampton Stone
Strangler's Holiday. K. Steel
Strangler's Moon. C. Leader
Stranglers of Bombay. S. James
Strangler's Serenade. W. Irish
Strasbourg Legacy. W. Craig
Strasburg Collection. E. L. McGinnis
Straus. A. Bodelsen
Straw Donkey Case. A. S. Fleischman
Straw Man. D. M. Disney
Straw Virgin. A. Barker
Strawberry Marten. P. G. Winslow
Straws in the Wind. D. Dawe
Straws in the Wind. P. C. De Crespigny
Straws in the Wind. W. C. Tuttle
Strawstack. D. C. Disney
Strawstack Murders. D. C. Disney
Stray Bullet. D. Franklin
Streaked-Blond Slave. C. Brown
Streaked Peril. N. Carter
Streaked with Crimson. C. J. Dutton
Stream Sinister. K. M. Knight
Streamlined Dragon. L. C. Goldsmith
Streamlined Murder. P. MacTyre
Street of Fear. J. Fast
Street of Fortune. M. L. Tyrrell
Street of Grass. P. Audemars
Street of No Return. D. Goodis
Street of Painted Lips. M. Dekobra
Street of Strange Faces. L. J. Vance
Street of the Crying Woman. G. Homes
Street of the Leopard. N. Morland
Street of the Lost. D. Goodis
Street of the Serpent. F. Beeding
Street of the Singing Fountain. Rona Randall
Street of the Small Steps. R. Willock
Street Paved with Water. Robin Temple
Street Players. D. Goines
Street Singer. J. T. MacIntyre
Street That Died. W. Reyburn
Streetcar to Hell. J. Dekker
Streets of Shadow. L. McFarlane
Strelsen Castle Mystery. H. Pink
Strength of the Weak. D. Stewart
Stretelli Case and other mystery stories. E. Wallace
Strethcairn. C. A. Collins
Stretton Case. H. Howard
Stretton Darknesse Mystery. M. Dalton
Stretton Street Affair. W. LeQueux
Strictly a Loser. E. Sherry
Strictly Business. O. Henry
Strictly for Cash. J. H. Chase
Strictly for Felony. C. Brown
Strictly Illegal. M. Clinten
Strictly Legitimate. M. Cronin
Strictly Private. Therese Benson
Strictly Private Business. M. Cronin
Striding Folly. D. L. Sayers
Strike Deep. A. North
Strike for a Kingdom. M. Gallie
Strike for Death. J. Creasey
Strike for Freedom. N. Carter
Strike Force 7. I. MacAlister
Strike Force Terror. N. Carter
Strike North. W. H. Baker
Strike of Millions. E. T. Sawyer

Strike Out Where Not Applicable. N. Freeling
Strike Terror. H. Steirman
Strike Zone. Richard Curtis
Strikeback! R. Crane
Strikefast. R. Charles
Striker Portfolio. Adam Hall
Strikers, Communists, Tramps and Detectives. A. Pinkerton
Striking Force. D. Christie
String Glove Mystery. H. R. Campbell
String of Pearls. T. P. Prest
Strip Death Naked. N. Longmate
Strip for Murder. R. S. Prather
Strip for Violence. E. Lacy
Strip Jack Naked. W. Garner
Strip Tease. J. Bruce
Strip Tease Angel. D. Linton
Strip-Tease Macabre. L. Gribble
Strip-Tease Murders. G. R. Lee
Strip Without Tease. C. Brown
Stripe for a Stripe. J. Sandys
Striped Majesty. Reginald Campbell
Striped Suitcase. C. Carnac
Stripped for Murder. R. Blake
Stripped for Murder. B. Fischer
Stripped to Kill. R. Drayton
Stripper. C. Brown
Stripper, You've Sinned. C. Brown
Striptease. G. Simenon
Striptease for Murder. P. Denver
Strode Venturer. H. Innes
Stroke of a Knife. Burnham F. Mason
Stroke of Eight. J. L. Hardy
Stroke of One. R. A. J. Walling
Stroke of Policy. N. Carter
Stroke of Seven. R. Wade
Stroke Sinister and other stories. S. Horler
Strolling Players. A. Dwyer-Joyce
Strong Arm. R. Barr
Strong-Arm. B. Copper
Strong as Death. F. Adams
Strong Dose of Poison. H. Desmond
Strong Man. H. R. F. Keating
Strong Man's Way. C. H. Bullivant
Strong Poison. D. L. Sayers
Strong Right Arm. P. Trent
Strong Room. R. A. J. Walling
Strong Room of the Sutro. E. L. Long
Strongarm. D. J. Marlowe
Strongbox. H. Swiggett
Stronger Hand. J. Goodwin
Stronghold. S. Ellin
Stroud Case. E. C. Williams
Struck Dead. Anonymous
Struck Down. J. G. Rowe
Struck Down. H. Smart
Struggle. Gavin Douglas
Struggle for Fame. J. H. Riddell
Struggle to Win. Old Sleuth
Struggle with Destiny. N. Carter
Strumpet's Fool. F. Griffin
Strychnine for One. T. A. Plummer
Strychnine Tonic, and A Dose of Cyanide. G. D. H. Cole
Stryker. William Crawford
Stuart Legacy. R. Kerr
Stubble. Winifred Duke
Studd. A. Cullen
Studdingly Stables Mystery. B. Strong
Student Body. N. Fitzgerald
Student Body. M. R. Hodgkin
Student Fraternity Murder. M. Propper
Studies in Black and Red. J. Forster

Studio Crime. G. Chester
Studio Crime. I. Jerrold
Studio Model. B. Delannoy
Studio Murder Mystery. L. Edgley
Studio Mystery. R. C. Armour
Studio Mystery. F. Aubrey
Studio One Murder. W. A. Ballinger
Study in Scarlet. A. C. Doyle
Study in Suspense. A. Soutar
Study in Terror. E. Queen
Study of Death. F. Leslie
Stuff to Give the Troops. J. MacLaren-Ross
Stuffed Man. J. B. O'Sullivan
Stuffed Men. A. M. Rud
Stuffed Swan. J. Appleby
Stumble on the Threshold. J. Payn
Stumbling. D. E. Smalley
Stunt Man. P. Brodeur
Sturgeon's West. T. Sturgeon
Sturgis Wager. E. Morette
Sturmer. I. F. Romer
Stuttering Death. L. Como
Stylist. G. Cullingford
Sub. Taffrail
Sub Killers. San Antonio
Sub Rosa. C. T. Murray
Subaltern, the Policeman, and the Little Girl. B. Fforde
Subject--Murder. C. Witting
Subject of Harry Egypt. D. Broun
Subjugated Beast. R. R. Ryan
Submarine at Bay. A. Mars
Submarine Flotilla. G. Hackforth-Jones
Submarine Girl. E. Turner
Submarine Mystery. K. Robeson
Submarine Signalled...Murder! A. R. Bosworth
Submarine Trail. N. Carter
Submariner. E. Stephens
Subscription to Murder. M. V. Heberden
Substitute Millionaire. H. Footner
Substitute Prisoner. M. Marcin
Subterranean Brotherhood. J. Hawthorne
Subterranean Club. L. Geoghegan
Subtle Adversary. C. Scofield
Subtle Minotaur. A. Alderson
Subtle Trail. J. Gollomb
Suburban Saraband. R. Harrison
Suburban Vendetta. J. K. Leys
Subway in the Sky. B. Birch
Subway Murder. M. S. Buchanan
Subway Mystery. B. Bolt
Subways Are for Killing. W. B. Murphy
Successful Alibi. M. E. Cooke
Successful "Shadow." Old Sleuth
Such a Gorgeous Kid Like Me. H. Farrell
Such an Enmity. R. Pertwee
Such Bitter Business. E. Ford
Such Bright Disguises. B. Flynn
Such Friends Are Dangerous. W. Tyrer
Such Is Death. L. Bruce
Such Men Are Dangerous. B. Diamond
Such Men Are Dangerous. P. Kavanagh
Such Men Are Dangerous. Martin Thomas
Such Natural Deaths. L. Anson
Such Nice People. Mary Scott
Such Power Is Dangerous. D. Wheatley
Such Women Are Dangerous. J. Webb
Sucker Bait. R. O. Saber
"Sucker for a Red-Head." M. Storm
Sucker Money. R. H. Rohde
Sucker Punch. Duff Johnson
Sucker Punch. R. Marshall
Sucker Trap. M. Kane
Sucking Pit. G. N. Smith
Sudden Darkness. E. McCrae
Sudden Death! A. Bocca
Sudden Death. F. W. Crofts
Sudden Death. D. Delman
Sudden Death. B. C. Skottowe
Sudden Death. L. Thayer
Sudden Death at Scotland Yard. G. Begbie
Sudden Death of the M.F.H. E. Welden
Sudden Fear. E. Sherry
Sudden Lady. M. G. Lowe
Sudden Silence. C. Fitzsimmons
Sudden Squall. J. C. Nolan
Sudden Storm. V. Siller
Sudden Vengeance. E. Crispin
Suddenly a Corpse. H. Q. Masur
Suddenly a Shroud. M. Kerrigan
Suddenly a Widow. G. H. Coxe
Suddenly at His Residence. C. Brand
Suddenly, at Singapore... G. Black
Suddenly by Shotgun. N. Daniels
Suddenly by Violence. C. Brown
Suddenly He Knew. W. Vinn
Suddenly in Paris. A. Roudybush
Suddenly, in the Air. Karen Campbell
Suddenly, in Vienna. H. McCutcheon
Suddenly It's Murder. J. T. Story
Suddenly It's Sin. H. Janson
Suddenly One Night. K. Roos
Suddenly You're Dead. W. Wright
Sue for Mercy. V. Heley
Suez Patrol. J. R. Holden
Suez Side Ace. J. R. Holden
Suffer a Witch. N. Fitzgerald
Suffer a Witch. R. Foley
Suffer a Witch to Die. E. Davis
Sufficient Rope. C. F. Gregg
Sugar. G. Brewer
Sugar and Vice. H. Janson
Sugar Cuts the Corners. L. Marshall
Sugar for the Lady. L. Marshall
Sugar Man's Dead. J. Franklin
Sugar on the Carpet. L. Marshall
Sugar on the Cuff. L. Marshall
Sugar on the Kill. L. Marshall
Sugar on the Loose. L. Marshall
Sugar on the Prowl. L. Marshall
Sugar on the Target. L. Marshall
Sugar Shannon. Adam Knight
Sugar, You're a Scoop! M. Brody
Sugarplum Staircase. R. English
Suicide Academy. Daniel Stern
Suicide Alibi. J. Rowland
Suicide Can Be Murder. Roland Daniel
Suicide Circle. W. J. Elliott
Suicide Clause. H. Carmichael
Suicide Club. R. L. Stevenson
Suicide Excepted. C. Hare
Suicide Fleet. H. Desmond
Suicide House. E. Snell
Suicide in San Juan. S. Jason
Suicide Passage. A. A. Randall
Suicide Spies. M. Annesley
Suicide Squad. Richard Curtis
Suicide Squad. R. Goyne
Suitable for Framing. M. Holbrook
Suitable for Framing. J. A. Phillips
Suitcase Full of Money. W. C. Thompson
Sullen Sky Mystery. H. C. Bailey
Sultana. H. C. Rowland
Sultan's Daughter. D. Wheatley
Sultan's Pearls. N. Carter
Sultan's Skull. W. K. Smith
Sultry Avenger. H. Janson
Sulu Sea Murders. V. W. Mason
Sumatra Seven Zero. O. Wynd
Summer Adventure. Alan Thomas
Summer Assassin. J. Melville
Summer Book. M. Pemberton
Summer Camp Mystery. N. Blake
Summer for Witches. M. Lynch
Summer Holiday. G. Simenon
Summer Lightning. G. F. Hummel
Summer Moon. G. Goodchild
Summer of Evil. H. Arvonen
Summer of Sighs. P. Gallagher
Summer of the Red Wolf. M. L. West
Summer School Mystery. J. Bell
Summer Shock. T. Lee
Summer Showers. H. Arthur
Summer Stranger. G. Wagner
Summer Street. H. Ellson
Summer Sunday. D. Eden
Summer Velvet. F. Y. McHugh
Summerhouse. P. Wentworth
Summer's Cloud. J. Tattersall
Summer's Day. I. Jerrold
Summer's Lease. C. Larner
Summit. S. Marlowe
Summit Chase. R. Sapir
Summit House Mystery. L. Dougall
Summit Kill. Clark Howard
Summons. A. E. W. Mason
Summons from Baghdad. A. MacKinnon
Sumuru. S. Rohmer
Sun Dance Murders. P. McCurtin
Sun Dog Loot. W. C. Tuttle
Sun God. R. C. Armour
Sun in the Hunter's Eyes. M. Derby
Sun Is a Witness. A. M. Stein
Sun Queen. H. Kaner
Sun Virgin. R. Charles
Sunburned Corpse. Adam Knight
Sunburst. D. Cory
Sunday. G. Simenon
Sunday Evening. M. Lynn
Sunday Fix. J. Nazel
Sunday Pigeon Murders. C. Rice
Sunday the Rabbi Stayed Home. H. Kemelman
Sunday Woman. C. Fruttero
Sundial. S. Jackson
Sundial. F. M. White
Sundial Clue. B. Bolt
Sundial Drug Mystery. J. Ronald
Sundown Gun. D. Owen
Sundry Fell Designs. O. Mills
Sunk Island. J. B. Harris-Burland
Sunk Without Trace. S. M. Parkman
Sunken Sailor. P. Moyes
Sunlight and Gloom. G. Fleming
Sunlit Ambush. M. Derby
Sunningdale Mystery. A. Christie
Sunny Draper. C. Phillips
Sunny Stories, and some shady ones. J. Payn
Sunset at Sheba. J. Harris
Sunset Express. F. Marlowe
Sunset Hour. M. Summerton
Sunset over Soho. G. Mitchell
Sunset Strip. J. Reach
Sunshine and Snow. H. Smart
Sunshine Corpse. M. Murray
Sup with the Devil. S. Troy
Super-Barbarians. C. Dawe
Super-Cinema Murder. L. A. Knight
Super Fly. P. Fenty
Super-Gangster. F. G. Eberhard
Super Man Chu. S. M. Sullivan
Super Spy. C. Brown
Super Spy. W. Holt-White
Superdoll. L. August
Superdude. John Craig
Superintendent Slade Investigates. L. Gribble
Superintendent Wakley's Mistake. G. D. H. Cole
Superintendent Wilson's Holiday. G. D. H. Cole
Superintendent's Room. J. Ashford

Title Index

Superkill. J. Tiger
Supermind. M. Phillips
Supernatural Clue. S. Campbell
Supersonic. Basil Jackson
Supplanter. P. Trent
Suppressed Evidence. V. Yorke
Suppressed Sensations. Anonymous
Suppression. W. Hallatt
Surakarta. W. MacHarg
Sure Thing. R. S. Prather
Surf Queen. Stuart Martin
Surfeit of Lampreys. N. Marsh
Surfeit of Sun. Sean Graham
Surfeit of Suspects. G. Bellairs
Surfside Caper. L. Trimble
Surfside 6. J. M. Flynn
Surgeon. Alan Thomas
Surgeon of Gaster Fell. A. C. Doyle
Surgeons. S. Friedman
Surgeons Adrift. E. L. Long
Surly Sullen Bell. R. Kirk
Surprise for the Four. Mark Cross
Surprise of His Life. Old Sleuth
Surprise! Surprise! A. Christie
Surprise, Surprise. H. McCloy
Surprises of an Empty Hotel. A. C. Gunter
Surprising Experiences of Mr. Shuttlebury Cobb. R. A. Freeman
Surprising Husband. R. Marsh
Surprising Sanctuary. L. Cargill
Surregar's Raft. P. Kenley
Surrendered. R. Rand
Surrey Wood Mystery. J. Arnold
Surrounded. B. Coffey
Survival of the Fittest. E. Sherry
Survival Zero. M. Spillane
Survivor. T. Keneally
Survivor. E. P. Oppenheim
Survivor. J. Q.
Survivor of Darkness. V. Coffman
Survivor of Darkness. D. Daniels
Survivors. Anne Edwards
Survivors. H. Innes
Survivors. G. Simenon
Survivor's Secret. J. G. Brandon
Susan Drummond. J. H. Riddell
Susan Turnbull. A. C. Gunter
Susanna, Don't You Cry! M. Plum
Susannah Screaming. C. Weston
Susie Comes to Soho. B. Sarto
Suspect. G. Fairlie
Suspect. M. Ilacruz
Suspect. H. L. Nelson
Suspect. E. Percy
Suspect Scientist. L. Meynell
Suspected. G. Dilnot
Suspected. F. P. Rathbun
Suspected. L. Stratenus
Suspected Four. W. D. Roberts
Suspected Governess. Anonymous
Suspected Six. H. Scott
Suspects All. M. Page
Suspects--Nine. E. R. Punshon
Suspense. B. Graeme
Suspense. K. Lindsay
Suspense. I. Ostrander
Suspense. R. M. Stern
Suspension of Mercy. P. Highsmith
Suspicion. P. Brebner
Suspicion. M. Hervey
Suspicion. E. J. Landon
Suspicion. V. Loder
Suspicion. C. Lys
Suspicion. F. Riddell
Suspicion. Lee Roberts
Suspicion Aroused. D. Donovan
Suspicion in Triplicate. B. Cobb
Suspicion Was Aroused. A. Brock
Suspicious Characters. D. L. Sayers
Suspicious Circumstances. P. Quentin

Suspicious Company. M. Richmond
Sussex Cuckoo. B. Flynn
Sussex Downs Murder. J. Bude
Sutter House. E. Orford
Sutter's Sands. M. C. Donahue
Sutton Papers. S. Jepson
Sutton Place Murders. R. G. Dean
Suva Harbour Mystery. F. Arthur
Suvarov Adventure. D. Kyle
Swag. C. F. Coe
Swallowed Up. W. Woodrow
Swami's Curse. F. E. Penny
Swamp Fever. B. Sarto
Swamp Fire. D. Kingery
Swamp Kill. W. Harrison
Swamp Man. D. Goines
Swamp of Cardelli. T. Craig
Swamp Sanctuary. B. McKnight
Swamp Sister. R. E. Alter
Swampers. H. Nisbet
Swamps of Death. Hawkshaw
Swan Island Murders. V. Lincoln
Swan River Story. P. Hastings
Swan Sang Once. M. Carleton
Swan Song. E. Crispin
Swan Song. H. Robertson
Swan Song for a Siren. C. Brown
Swan Song for a Thrush. G. Joseph
Swansong for a Rare Bird. A. Draper
Swap. W. Wager
Swarthmoor Tragedy. E. P. Frankland
Swashbuckler, and other tales. B. Reynolds
Swastika Hunt. D. Cory
Swastika Rises. C. Short
Sway of Sin. N. Carter
Swaying Corpse. R. Platt
Swaying Pillars. E. Ferrars
Swaying Rock. A. J. Rees
Sweat of Fear. R. C. Dennis
Sweeney. I. K. Martin
Sweepstake Murders. J. J. Connington
Sweepstake Winner. E. Jepson
Sweet and Deadly. V. Chute
Sweet and Deadly. M. Corrigan
Sweet and Deadly. D. Duncan
Sweet and Deadly. P. MacDonald
Sweet and Low. E. Lathen
Sweet and Low. N. Perrelli
Sweet and Low-Down. J. Waer
Sweet Blond Trap. W. C. Gault
Sweet Charlie. H. Kane
Sweet Cheat. H. Crooker
Sweet Danger. M. Allingham
Sweet Death. F. Hurt
Sweet Enemy. Robin Temple
Sweet Epitaph. M. Lynn
Sweet Evil. J. D. White
Sweet Hostage. N. Benchley
Sweet Inisfail. R. Dowling
Sweet Is Revenge. J. F. Molloy
Sweet Is the Rose. H. D. Irvine
Sweet Justice. C. Robertson
Sweet Lady Death. P. Malloch
Sweet Mace. G. M. Fenn
Sweet Money Girl. B. Appel
Sweet Murder. M. S. Michel
Sweet Night for Murder. M. Neville
Sweet Poison. Douglas Clark
Sweet Poison. M. Fitt
Sweet Poison. T. C. H. Jacobs
Sweet Poison. R. Penny
Sweet Racket. John Gloag
Sweet Reason. R. Littell
Sweet Revenge. S. Gilruth
Sweet Revenge. J. C. Shaffer

Sweet Ride. R. S. Prather
Sweet Shame of Fury. S. D. Frances
Sweet Sinner. H. Nisbet
Sweet Sister Seduced. S. B. Hough
Sweet Smelling Death. V. Gunn
Sweet, Sweet Summer. J. Gaskill
Sweet Talk. H. Janson
Sweet Water. M. Cronin
Sweet Wild Wench. W. C. Gault
Sweet William Is Dead. L. O'Brien
Sweetbriar in Town, and other tales. D. C. Murray
Sweetcrab. M. Summerton
Sweeter for His Going. S. Truss
Sweeter Than Honey. A. Applin
Sweetheart and Wife. Anonymous
Sweetheart, Here's Your Grave! H. Janson
Sweetheart of the Razors. P. Cheyney
Sweetheart Submarine. G. Thorne
Sweetheart, This Is Homicide. C. Brown
Sweetheart with a Wreath. M. Storm
Sweethearts and Wives. G. Hackforth-Jones
Sweetie, Hold Me Tight. H. Janson
Sweets and Sinners. A. Griffin
Swell Garrick. J. Spencer
Swell-Looking Babe. J. Thompson
Swell Night for Murder! G. Brandon
Swift Hand of Vengeance. Clifton Yorke
Swift Solution. F. J. Whaley
Swift Summer. John Burke
Swift to Its Close. S. Troy
Swifter Than a Weaver's Shuttle. J. W. Gambier
Swiftly to Evil. B. Arthur
Swimming Frog. C. Brooks
Swimming Pool. M. R. Rinehart
Swimming Pool Murder. J. Bolton
Swing Away, Climber. G. Carr
Swing, Brother, Swing. N. Marsh
Swing High, Sweet Murder. S. H. Courtier
Swing It, Death. Gavin Holt
Swing Low, Sweet Death. R. T. Campbell
Swing Low, Sweet Harriet. G. Baxt
Swing Low, Swing Dead. F. Gruber
Swing Music Murder. Harlan Reed
Swinger Who Swung by the Neck. Hampton Stone
Swinging Corpse. D. Linton
Swinging Death. B. Flynn
Swinging Murder. Lionel Black
Swinging Shutter. C. Fraser-Simson
Swinging Virgin. D. Rico
Swirling Waters. M. Rittenberg
Swiss Arrangement. W. Fairchild
Swiss Legacy. A. A. Thompson
Swiss Secret. J. Messmann
Swiss Shot. Michael Bradley
Switch. P. Ridgeway
Switched Out. R. Lait
Switcheroo. E. McDowell
Swooning Venus. A. Marsden
Sword and Dragon. R. Pocock
Sword and the Scales. H. McLeave
Sword for Mr. Fitton. S. Styles
Sword for the Baron. A. Morton
Sword in the Air. A. C. Gunter
Sword in the Pool. D. Marfield
Sword of Allah. C. L. Clifford
Sword of Allah. M. Olden
Sword of Damocles. A. K. Green
Sword of Fate. H. Herman
Sword of Fate. D. Wheatley
Sword of Fortune. B. Bolt
Sword of Ganelon. R. Parker
Sword of Genghis Khan. J. Dark
Sword of Harlequin. J. K. Keith
Sword of Honour. D. Beaty

Sword of Justice. F. Duncan
Sword of Monsieur Blackshirt. D. Graeme
Sword of Peace. A. Askew
Sword of Silk. M. Carrel
Sword of Vengeance. G. Chester
Sword-Points of Love. M. Peterson
Sword Swallower. R. Goulart
Swordlight. A. Rundle
Swords Reluctant. M. Pemberton
Swordsman of Fortune. L. P. Greene
Swordsman of Warsaw. T. Pastor
Sworn to Silence. A. M. Miller
Sybaritic Death. A. Roudybush
Sybil Brotherton. E. Southworth
Sybil, Trapper of Men. M. Barbour
Sydney for Sin. M. Corrigan
Sylvanian Adventure. F. Wheeler
Sylvia. E. V. Cunningham
Sylvia Arden. O. Crawfurd
Sylvia in Flowerland. L. Gardiner
Sylvia's Chauffeur. L. Tracy
Symbol of the Cat. Neill Graham
Symbol of Vengeance. D. Mariner
Symphony in Murder. A. R. Long
Symphony in Two Time. A. Irving
Syncopated Love. W. J. Makin
Syndic. C. M. Kornbluth
Syndicate. P. McCurtin
Syndicate. A. Masters
Syndicate Girl. F. Kane
Syndicate Murders. W. R. Randall
Syndicate of Death. F. Foden
Syndicate of Death. H. E. Wheeler
Syndicate of Evil. W. R. D. McLaughlin
Syndicate of Rascals. N. Carter
Syndicate of Sinners. G. Warden
Synonym for Murder. R. Clarke
Synthetic Gentleman. Channing Pollock
Synthetic Philanthropist. J. H. Wallis
System. H. Calvin
System's Hand. M. T. Jones

T as in Trapped. L. Treat
T. Racksole and Daughter. A. Bennett
TNT for Two. J. Byron
Table. Robert (G.) Curtis
Table Near the Band, and other stories. A. A. Milne
Tabloid Murders. C. Wood
Tachi Tree. L. O'Donnell
Tag Murders. C. J. Daly
Tail Job. H. Kane
Tail of Gold. D. Hennessey
Tail of the "Dozing Cat." E. Messenger
Tail Spin Morgan. T. Wallace
Tail Sting. H. Janson
Tailwind to Danger. C. H. Wallace
Taint of Innocence. M. Childs
Taint of Plague. B. Jones
Tainted Gold. P. Trent
Tainted Gold. H. N. Williams
Tainted Money. A. Manning
Tainted Power. C. J. Daly
Tainted Token. K. M. Knight
Tainted Turf. D. Learmonth
Take a Body. M. Halliday
Take a Dark Journey. M. Erskine
Take a Murder, Darling. R. S. Prather
Take a Pair of Private Eyes. J. T. McIntosh
Take a Step to Murder. D. Keene
Take All You Can Get. S. Fisher
Take Any City. G. Joseph
Take-Away Girl. G. Tracey
Take Away the Lady. Gavin Holt
Take Care. N. Bond
Take Death for a Lover. W. H. Baker
Take Death for a Lover. A. Berry

Take It and Like It. S. Morelli
Take It Crooked. F. Beeding
Take It Easy. M. Perelli
Take It on the Lam. R. Drayton
Take Me Alive. B. Tutton
Take Me Home. F. Flora
Take My Drum to England. D. Cory
Take My Face. P. Held
Take My Life. Winston Graham
Take-Off. W. Ash
Take One Ambassador. A. Broinowski
Take One for Murder. M. E. Chaber
Take Only as Directed. J. Byrom
Take-Over. V. B. Miller
Take Over, Angel. B. Sarto
Take-Over Man. J. Wainwright
Take the War to Washington. P. Van Greenway
Take Thee a Sharp Knife. R. T. Campbell
Take This Gun. R. Wilkes-Hunter
Take This Life. S. Bunce
Take This My Heart. K. Lindsay
Take This--Sweetie. H. Janson
Take Two at Bedtime. M. Allingham
Take Two Popes. H. Calvin
Take Up the Bodies. K. T. Knoblock
Take What's Coming. B. Sarto
Take Your Last Look. M. Brady
Taken at the Flood. G. Bonner
Taken at the Flood. M. E. Braddon
Taken at the Flood. A. Christie
Taken at the Flood. B. Newman
Taken by Assault. Morley Roberts
Taken by Force. K. Stellier
Taken for Dollars. Spike Gordon
Takeoff. C. M. Kornbluth
Takeover. R. Wormser
Takeover Bid. S. Gainham
Takers. M. Ehrlich
Takers. H. J. Taub
Taking Gary Feldman. S. Cohen
Taking Life Easy. Kevin O'Hara
Taking of Pelham One Two Three. J. Godey
Talatala. G. Simenon
Talbott Agreement. R. M. Garvin
Tale for Midnight. F. Prokosch
Tale of a Physician. A. J. Davis
Tale of Fleur. E. C. Vivian
Tale of Pimlico. Gavin Douglas
Tale of Sin, and other tales. H. Wood
Tale of the Lazy Dog. Alan Williams
Tale of the Town. George Hastings
Tale of Twenty-Five Hours. B. Matthews
Tale of Two Murders. H. C. Asterley
Tale of Two Murders. E. Ferrars
Tale of Two Thieves. G. Beardmore
Tale Untold. E. Morrison
Talent for Murder. J. L. Benton
Talent for Murder. J. Wainwright
Talent for Murder. A. M. Wells
Talent for Violence. W. Manson
Talented Mr. Ripley. P. Highsmith
Tales. E. A. Poe
Tales by a Female Detective. A. Forrester
Tales for the Marines. R. Blatchford
Tales from a Rolltop Desk. C. Morley
Tales from Two Pockets. K. Capek
Tales in a Jugular Vein. R. Bloch
Tales in Eccentric Life. W. A. Hammond
Tales in Prose and Verse. T. E. Heath
Tales in Prose and Verse. D. C. Murray
Tales of a Cruel Country. G. Cumberland
Tales of a Government Official. A. Griffiths
Tales of Adventure. R. H. Savage
Tales of Adventurers. G. Household
Tales of Chinatown. S. Rohmer
Tales of East and West. S. Rohmer

Tales of Fantasy and Fact. B. Matthews
Tales of Heroism and Records of Strange and Wonderful Adventures. Anonymous
Tales of Intrigue and Revenge. S. McKenna
Tales of Mynheer Amayat. H. D. Stacpoole
Tales of Mystery and Crime. W. Wallace
Tales of Mystery and Horror. M. Level
Tales of Mystery and Horror. C. D. Pamely
Tales of Mystery and Revenge. N. Langley
Tales of Romance and Mystery. H. Rockwood
Tales of Secret Egypt. S. Rohmer
Tales of Suspense. W. Collins
Tales of Terror. D. Donovan
Tales of Terror. E. Sudak
Tales of Terror and Mystery. A. C. Doyle
Tales of Terror and the Supernatural. W. Collins
Tales of the Black Widowers. I. Asimov
Tales of the Coast Guard. L. Warneford
Tales of the Coastguard and other stories. Anonymous
Tales of the Mounted Police. W. B. Mowery
Tales of the R.I.C. Anonymous
Tales of the Rock. M. Anderson
Tales of the Strong Room. F. Denison
Tales of the Uneasy. V. Hunt
Tales of Today. G. R. Sims
Tales of Two Continents. R. Barr
Tales Out of Court. F. T. Hill
Tales Told to the Magistrate. R. E. Corder
Talika, the Geisha Girl. N. Carter
Talk of the Town. J. Payn
Talk of the Town. C. Williams
Talkative Policeman. R. Penny
"Talkie" Murder Mystery. W. Shute
Talking Clock. F. Gruber
Talking Clues. R. C. Finney
Talking of Murder. L. N. Morgan
Talking Skull and other selected short stories grave and gay. G. H. R. Young
Talking Sparrow Murders. D. L. Teilhet
Talking Turkey. K. A. Saddler
Tall, Balding, Thirty-Five. A. Firth
Tall, Dark and Dead. K. Jaediker
Tall, Dark, and Deadly. H. Q. Masur
Tall Dark Man. A. Chamberlain
Tall Dolores. M. Avallone
Tall Headlines. A. E. Lindop
Tall House Mystery. A. Fielding
Tall Man. Gavin Douglas
Tall Man. John Ross
Tall Man Walking. K. Wolffe
Tall Pines in Paddington. C. Edwards
Tall Timber. G. Goodchild
Tallants of Barton. J. Hatton
Talleyrand Maxim. J. S. Fletcher
Tallyman. B. Knox
Tallyman's Fate. L. Jackson
Talons of the Hawk. J. Hines
Tamara. M. L. Dodge
Tamarind. F. Hurd
Tamarind Seed. Evelyn Anthony
Tamer of Men. O. Binns
Tamiko. R. Kirkbridge
Taming of Carney Wilde. B. Spicer
Taming of Nancy. G. Goodchild
Taming of Neville Ibbetson. W. M. Graydon
Taming of Sydney Marsham. H. C. McNeile
Tan and Sandy Silence. J. D. MacDonald
Tanagra Affair. P. Kenny
Tancredi. L. Cameron
Tandra. Robert Mason
Tangier Assignment. C. Rougvie
Tangle. W. S. Masterman

Title Index

Tangle. H. L. Phillips
Tangle. H. A. Wrenn
Tangle of Terror. E. J. Murray
Tangled Case. N. Carter
Tangled Cord. F. Lockridge
Tangled Destinies. D. Donovan
Tangled Evidence. P. C. De Crespigny
Tangled Flags. A. C. Gunter
Tangled in Crime. N. Carter
Tangled Lives. T. W. Speight
Tangled Marriage. C. Dawe
Tangled Miracle. H. Herne
Tangled Skein. N. Carter
Tangled Threads. N. Carter
Tangled Trails. W. M. Raine
Tangled Web. N. Blake
Tangled Web. J. D. Levick
Tangled Web. L. G. Moberly
Tangled Web. G. Vaizey
Tangles Unravelled. E. K. Johnson
Tanglewood Mystery. C. E. Pearce
Tango. C. Rodda
Tango Briefing. Adam Hall
Tanker. R. Kruger
Tannahill Tangle. C. Wells
Tanner's Tiger. Lawrence Block
Tanner's Twelve Swingers. Lawrence Block
Tap on the Shoulder. M. Dupree
Tapestry Odyssey. N. Conway
Tapestry of Death. D. M. Bowick
Tapestry of Terror. M. Ruuth
Tapestry Room Murder. C. Wells
Tapping on the Wall. H. Hull
Taps, Colonel Roberts. H. Gibbs
Tarakian. L. Peters
Target. W. W. Haines
Target Doomsday Island. N. Carter
Target Five. C. Forbes
Target for Conquest. B. Gray
Target for Malice. Barbara Cooper
Target for Murder. G. E. Giles
Target for Terror. M. Hershman
Target for Terror. T. C. H. Jacobs
Target for Their Dark Desire. C. Brown
Target for Tonight. R. Telfair
Target in Taffeta. B. Benson
Target Is H. L. Derrick
Target Manhattan. D. Mallory
Target Manhattan. D. Pitts
Target: Mike Shayne. B. Halliday
Target Practice. N. Meyer
Tarn House. R. Brock
Tarnham Connection. W. Tute
Tarnished Angel. H. Pentecost
Tarnished Gold. W. Mills
Tarnished Love. Gerry Travis
Tarnished Woman. H. Thompson
Tarot Spell. W. D. Roberts
Tarry and Be Hanged. S. Woods
Tashkent Crisis. W. Craig
Task Demolition. R. Wilkes-Hunter
Task of Destruction. Michael Barrett
Taste for Blood. J. B. West
Taste for Brilliants. N. Clad
Taste for Cognac. B. Halliday
Taste for Death. P. O'Donnell
Taste for Honey. H. F. Heard
Taste for Murder. H. F. Heard
Taste for Violence. B. Halliday
Taste of Ashes. H. Browne
Taste of Blood. D. Batchelor
Taste of Blood. Ralph Hayes
Taste of Brass. R. D. Locke
Taste of Death. Richard Grayson
Taste of Death. F. McGrew
Taste of Fears. M. Millar
Taste of Fears. S. Woods
Taste of Murder. J. Cannan
Taste of Murder. I. Lambot
Taste of Poison. R. Ullmann
Taste of Power. W. J. Burley
Taste of Proof. B. Knox
Taste of Sangria. C. Keith
Taste of Sin. G. Brewer
Taste of Sin. R. V. Cassill
Taste of Treasure. H. Ashe
Taste of Vengeance. L. R. Davis
Tatterley. T. Gallon
Tattershall Castle. B. Gilbert
Tattoo Mystery. W. LeQueux
Tattooed Arm. I. Ostrander
Tattooed Man. T. C. H. Jacobs
Tattooed Triangle. J. G. Brandon
Tattooed Wrist. Old Spicer
Tau Cross Mystery. J. J. Connington
Taurus Trip. T. B. Dewey
Tavern. G. M. Cohan
Tavern and the Arrows. A. Carlyle
Taverns in Terrazzo. M. J. Ragosta
Tavistocks. A. Griffin
Tawny Menace. B. Sanders
Taxed to Death. R. Simons
Taxi-Cab Murder. J. G. Brandon
Taxi Man's Quest. G. Chester
Taxicab Riddle. N. Carter
Tea at Four. R. H. Wilkinson
Tea at the Abbey. C. E. Vulliamy
Tea on Sunday. Lettice Cooper
Tea-Shop in Limehouse. T. Burke
Tea Time Tragedy. M. Beckett
Tea Tray Murders. C. Bush
Teach You a Lesson. J. Hollis
Teach Yourself Treachery. Jonathan Burke
Teacher Goes Abroad. E. Randolph
Teacher's Blood. I. T. Ross
Teak Forest. P. Ordway
Team of Crooks. A. Steffens Hardy
Tears Are for Angels. P. Connolly
Tears for Jessie Hewitt. E. Sherry
Tears for the Bride. Robert Martin
Tears in Paradise. J. Blackmore
Tears of Angels. H. Curties
Tears of Autumn. C. McCarry
Tears of Blood. M. Carrel
Tears of Hate. G. Thorne
Tease. G. Brewer
Tease. R. H. R. Smithies
Teaser Set to Kill. M. Brody
Technique for Treachery. S. Truss
Teddington Tragedy. D. H. Landels
Teddy Bear. G. Simenon
Teddy-Boy Mystery. J. Drummond
Teen-Age Jungle. H. Whittington
Teen-Age Mafia. Wenzell Brown
Teen-Age Mobster. B. Appel
Teen-Age Terror. Wenzell Brown
Teeth of the Dragon. M. Grant
Teeth of the Tiger. M. Leblanc
Tejera Secrets. M. Orr
Telefair. C. Rice
Telefon. W. Wager
Telegram from Le Touquet. J. Bude
Telegraph Clue. I. Stark
Telegraph Secrets. B. Hemyng
Telemann Touch. W. Haggard
Telephone Call. J. Rhode
Telephone Girl. A. Askew
Television Murders. W. A. Ballinger
Television Mystery. R. St. Clair
Tell Death to Wait. A. Boutell
Tell Her It's Murder. H. Reilly
Tell It to the Birds. J. H. Chase
Tell It to the Dead. L. Vardre
Tell No Tales. G. Day
Tell No Tales. G. Limnelius
Tell-Tale Clock Mystery. J. Carmack
Tell-Tale Photographs. N. Carter
Tell-Tale Tart. P. Duncan
Tell-Tale Watch. G. Hocker
Tell Them Nothing. H. Ellson
Tell Them What's-Her-Name Called. Mildred Davis
Tell You What I'll Do. H. Cecil
Telling of Murder. D. Rutherford
Telling the Truth. W. Hewlett
Telltale Print. C. B. Booth
Telltale Tattoo. J. Sharp
Telltale Telegram. H. Burnham
Tempania Mystery. J. M. Walsh
Temperamental Journey. P. Groom
Tempering Steel. S. Jepson
Tempest. R. V. Cassill
Tempest at Dawn. M. Richmond
Tempest Driven. R. Dowling
Tempest in a Tea-Cup. W. Shand
Tempest Weaves a Shroud. W. Shand
Tempestuous Wooer. G. T. Ockley
Temple at Ilumquh. J. Laflin
Temple Dogs Guard My Fate. D. Sinclair
Temple Falls. A. MacVicar
Temple Murder. H. M. Richardson
Temple of Dawn. C. Robertson
Temple of Death. F. Du Boisgobey
Temple of Death. E. Mitchell
Temple of Fear. N. Carter
Temple of Slumber. Neill Graham
Temple of the Dead. V. Norwood
Temple of the Flaming God. D. T. Lindsay
Temple of Vice. N. Carter
Temple Tower. H. C. McNeile
Temple Tree. D. Beaty
Temple's Trial. E. Everett-Green
Templeton Case. V. L. Whitechurch
Templeton Memoirs. D. Daniels
Tempt a Tigress. C. Brown
Tempt Me Not. A. Weymouth
Temptation in a Private Zoo. A. Dekker
Temptation of Father Anthony. G. Horton
Temptation of Gideon Holt. Mrs. C. Kernahan
Temptation of Mary Gordon. S. Horler
Temptation of Selma. C. Dawe
Temptation of Tavernake. E. P. Oppenheim
Temptation to Steal. N. B. Gerson
Temptations of Hercule. P. Audemars
Temptations of Valerie. H. Whittington
Tempter. A. Bloomfield
Tempting Anne Brayton. A. Applin
Tempting of Paul Chester. A. Askew
Tempting of Tavernake. E. P. Oppenheim
Temptress. C. Brown
Temptress. W. LeQueux
Temptress. S. Shulman
Temptress on Trial. J. Laffin
Ten Against Nura. Michael Barrett
Ten Black Pearls. C. F. Gregg
Ten Commandments. G. R. Sims
Ten Crowded Hours. C. A. Alington
Ten Dangerous Hours. G. B. Jenkins
Ten Day Mystery. Old Sleuth
Ten Day's Leave. W. M. Graydon
Ten Days to Oblivion. M. Cooney

Ten Days Wonder. E. Queen
Ten Faces of Cornell Woolrich. C. Woolrich
Ten Fathoms Deep. J. Templeton
Ten Grand Story. B. Carson
Ten Grand Tallulah and Temptation. C. Brown
Ten Green Brothers. A. MacVicar
Ten Holy Horrors. F. Beeding
Ten Hours. H. S. Keeler
Ten Jewels. P. Wynnton
Ten Little Indians. A. Christie
Ten Little Niggers. A. Christie
Ten Million. M. Hellinger
Ten Minute Alibi. A. Armstrong
Ten Peacocks. A. Wood
Ten Per Cent of Your Life. S. Winchester
Ten Plus One. E. McBain
Ten Seconds to Hell. L. P. Bachmann
Ten Seconds to Zero. K. Stanton
Ten Star Clues. E. R. Punshon
Ten Steps to the Gallows. J. Wainwright
Ten Teacups. Carter Dickson
Ten Thirteen. C. Edwards
10:30 from Marseilles. S. Japrisot
Ten-Thirty Sharp. H. Gibbs
$10,000 Reward. C. B. Booth
Ten Thousand Passports to Hell. H. P. Lees
£10,000 Trophy Race. P. Gill
Ten Thousand Several Doors. M. Craig
Ten-Tola Bars. B. Wohl
Ten Trails to Tyburn. B. Graeme
Ten True Secret Service Stories. D. B. Shaw
Ten Were Missing. M. Allingham
Ten Words of Poison. B. Perowne
Ten Years After. J. W. Bobin
Ten Years Among the Mail Bags. J. Holbrook
Tenacity. G. Cottar
Tenant. John Gill
Tenant. R. Topor
Tenant for Death. C. Hare
Tenant for the Tomb. Anthony Gilbert
Tenant of No. 13. L. Jackson
Tenant of the Grange. M. Gerard
Tenants of Malory. J. S. Le Fanu
Tendency to Corrupt. R. Barker
Tender Conspiracy. Eric Lambert
Tender Is the Knife. Joan Shepherd
Tender Killer. S. B. Hough
Tender Leaves. Robert Mason
Tender Poisoner. J. Bingham
Tender to Danger. E. Reed
Tender to Moonlight. E. Reed
Tennessee Tess. C. E. Blaney
Tennis Club Mystery. J. Reach
Tension. H. Janson
Tentacles. D. Lyon
Tenth Commandment. V. Bridges
Tenth Leper. F. Didelot
Tenth Point. T. Walsh
Tenth Session. R. Quilty
Tenth Victim. R. Sheckley
Tenth Year of the Ship. N. Lewis
Tents of Shame. E. C. Reed
Tents of Shem. G. Allen
Terence O'Rourke, Gentleman Adventurer. L. J. Vance
Term of Silence. F. Halsey
Term of Terror. P. Flower
Term of Trial. J. Barlow
Terminators. D. Hamilton
Terminators. B. Mather
Terms of Surrender. L. Tracy
Terrace Suicide Mystery. L. Gribble
Terracotta Palace. A. Maybury

Terrible Baron, and other stories. B. Reynolds
Terrible Crime. E. G. Jones
Terrible Door. G. Sims
Terrible Family. F. Warden
Terrible Hand. L. F. Hay
Terrible Hobby of Sir Joseph Londe, Bt. E. P. Oppenheim
Terrible Inheritance. G. Allen
Terrible Island. B. Grimshaw
Terrible Legacy. G. W. Appleton
Terrible Night. P. Cheyney
Terrible Ones. N. Carter
Terrible People. E. Wallace
Terrible Performance. J. Bergner
Terrible Pictures. B. Healey
Terrible Secret. G. Fleming
Terrible Secret. M. A. Fleming
Terrible Thing Has Happened to Miss Dupont. P. Hobson
Terrible Thirteen. N. Carter
Terrible Threat. N. Carter
Terrible Youth. Old Sleuth
Terribly Wild Flowers. G. Kersh
Terrified Heart. A. Grace
Terrified Society. H. T. Teilhet
Terrified Target. A. Grace
Terriford Mystery. M. B. Lowndes
Terror. R. Bloch
Terror. J. Creasey
Terror. E. Wallace
Terror at Dark Harbor. Clarissa Ross
Terror at Deepcliff. D. Nile
Terror at Nelson Woods. S. Richard
Terror at Staups House. Frank King
Terror at Tansey Hill. S. Roberts
Terror at Tree Tops. A. Parsons
Terror by Day. G. Ashe
Terror by Night. R. D. Bunnell
Terror by Night. R. Chetwynd-Hayes
Terror by Night. J. M. Cobban
Terror by Night. L. Crosby
Terror by Night. P. W. Fairman
Terror by Night. G. W. Gough
Terror by Night. C. R. Gull
Terror by Night. N. Klein
Terror by Night. P. Luck
Terror by Night. M. Richmond
Terror by Twilight. K. M. Knight
Terror Catches Up. H. Kaner
Terror Comes Creeping. C. Brown
Terror Comes to London. C. Bishop
Terror Comes to Twelvetrees. S. Horler
Terror Factor. E. Wuorio
Terror for the Toff. J. Creasey
Terror-Go-Round. J. Moffatt
Terror in Exton. Molly Nelson
Terror in Taos. L. Derrick
Terror in the Fog. N. Berrow
Terror in the Navy. K. Robeson
Terror in the Night. S. Blayne
Terror in the Night. Old Sleuth
Terror in the Night and other stories. R. Bloch
Terror in the Sun. M. Avallone
Terror in the Sun. R. Glendinning
Terror in the Thames. A. D. Divine
Terror in the Town. E. Ronns
Terror in Times Square. A. Handley
Terror in Tokyo. N. Perrelli
Terror Is My Trade. S. Marlowe
Terror Island. R. C. Armour
Terror Island. M. E. Longman
Terror Keep. E. Wallace
Terror Loch. W. McNeilly
Terror Lurks in Darkness. D. Hitchens

Terror Manor. M. E. Edward
Terror of Gold-Digger Creek. G. H. Teed
Terror of Lonely Tor. D. Stuart
Terror of Stormcastle. A. Leech
Terror of Tangier. G. H. Teed
Terror of the Air. W. LeQueux
Terror of the Handless Corpse. W. Dale
Terror of the Moat House. L. C. Douthwaite
Terror of the Pacific. J. G. Brandon
Terror of the Shape. C. Jude
Terror of the Tenements. A. Skene
Terror of the Tongs. J. Sangster
Terror of Thunder Creek. S. Hope
Terror of Tongues. Roy Vickers
Terror of Torlands. T. C. H. Jacobs
Terror of Toynham Hall. H. K. McDonnell
Terror of Tregarwith. J. Sylvester
Terror on Broadway. David Alexander
Terror on Compass Lake. T. Davis
Terror on Duncan Island. C. Farr
Terror on Halfaday Creek. J. B. Hendryx
Terror on the Island. J. Ferguson
Terror on Tip-Toe. S. Horler
Terror over London. G. F. Fox
Terror Package. R. Chavis
Terror Rides the West Wind. R. Madison
Terror Ship. C. Edwards
Terror Squad. R. Sapir
Terror Stalks Abroad. M. Richmond
Terror Stalks by Night. N. W. Firth
Terror Touches Me. S. Forbes
Terror Tournament. J. M. Flynn
Terror Tower. F. W. Irwin
Terror Tower. C. Rushton
Terror Tower. G. Verner
Terror Trap. J. Creasey
Terror Trap. W. D. Roberts
Terror Walks by Night. H. Desmond
Terror Wave. H. S. Banner
Terror Wears a Smile. L. Grex
Terrorists. N. De Mille
Terrors and other stories. A. Marshall
Terror's Cradle. D. Kyle
Terrors of the Earth. S. Forbes
Terry of Tangistan. D. Christie
Test. M. M. Bodkin
Test Case. B. D. Ashe
Test Match Murder. D. Batchelor
Test Match Murder. A. Tack
Test Match Mystery. H. Pink
Test of Anarchy. E. C. Derby
Test of Courage. N. Carter
Test of Love. E. Southworth
Testament. D. Moreell
Testament of Cairo, 1898. R. Maugham
Testament of Caspar Schultz. M. Fallon
Testament of Death. Norman Lucas
Testament of Evil. B. Jones
Testament of John Hastings. A. C. Fox-Davies
Testimony by Silence. D. M. Disney
Testing of Olive Vaughn. P. Brebner
Testing of Tony. M. Cumberland
Tether's End. M. Allingham
Texan. J. B. Hendryx
Texas Bank Murders. Christopher Culley
Texas by the Tail. J. Thompson
Texas Storm. D. Pendleton
Text for Murder. P. Fielding
Thameside Gold. M. Welford
Thanesworth House. K. Kimbrough
Thank You, Mr. Conquest. B. Gray
Thank You, Mr. Moto. J. P. Marquand
Thank You, Mr. Pendlebury. A. Webb
Thanks for the Apple. K. Hewitt
Thanks for the Felony. L. Grex
Thanks to Dr. Molly. S. Fairway
Thanks to Murder. J. Krumgold
Thanks to the Saint. L. Charteris

Title Index

That Affair at Elizabeth. B. E. Stevenson
That Affair at Portstead Manor. G. E. Locke
That Affair at St. Peter's. E. A. Brown
That Affair at the Cedars. L. Thayer
That Affair Next Door. A. K. Green
That American Girl. S. Warwick
That Awful Mess on Via Merulana. C. E. Gadda
That Brain Again. H. Janson
That Bullet Hole Has a History! H. C. McNeile
That Charming Crook. Frank King
That Cold Day in the Park. R. Miles
That Dame Sal. D. Linton
That Dark Inn. S. Nichols
That Darn Cat. The Gordons
That Dinner at Bardolph's. R. A. J. Walling
That Evening in Shanghai. P. Thorne
That Fatal Feeling. E. Kennedy
That Fatal Night. M. Richmond
That Fatal Touch. M. L. Roby
That Fatal Tree. V. Day
That Feeds on Men. I. Wilson
That Fellow MacArthur. S. Jepson
That Fiddler Fellow. H. G. Hutchinson
That Followed After. J. G. Lockhart
That French Girl. J. Hilton
That Frenchman. A. C. Gunter
That Gay Nineties Murder. F. Daingerfield
That Girl from Istanbul. M. G. Braun
That Girl in the Alley. M. Kelly
That Glover Woman. H. Ellson
That He May Die. G. Braddon
That Mainwaring Affair. A. M. Barbour
That Man Bolt. P. Crowcraft
That Man Returns. G. Fairlie
That Nairobi Affair. B. Leslie-Melville
That Night. J. Blackmore
That Night at Nine. D. R. Sperduti
That Night It Rained. H. Waugh
That Room in Camden Town. Griff
That Royle Girl. E. Balmer
That Strange Sylvester Affair. L. Thayer
That Summer's Earthquake. M. Bennett
That Villain, Romeo! J. F. Molloy
That Was No Lady. Keith Campbell
That Was Yesterday. M. Home
That Washington Affair. J. Hay
That We Might Live. Alan Thomas
That Which Is Crooked. D. M. Disney
That Which Is Crooked. Warren Hill
That Which Is Hidden. R. Hichens
That Wilmslow Girl! J. Oakley
That Yew Tree's Shade. C. Hare
That's All I Need. D. Spade
That's Her Problem. M. Hampton
That's Mark Avery. M. L. Tyrrell
That's No Way to Die. L. Kelley
That's Piracy, My Pet. C. Brown
That's the House, There. L. Singer
That's the Spirit. M. V. Heberden
That's the Way the Money Goes. S. Miller
That's Where the Cat's At, Baby. B. B. Johnson
That's Your Man, Inspector! D. Frome
Theatre Crime. F. Andreas
Theatre of Life. G. R. Sims
Theban Mysteries. A. Cross
Theft in Kind. M. Summerton
Theft of Magna Carta. J. Creasey
Theft of the Crown Jewels. E. Jepson
Theft of the Iron Dogs. E. C. R. Lorac
Their Flowers Were Always Black. P. Hastings
Their Great Adventure. W. M. Graydon
Their Man in the White House. T. Ardies
Their Nearest and Dearest. Bernice Carey
Their Rainbow Had Black Edges. Gerald Butler
Their Wife. D. Walshe
Thelma. V. Caspary
Theme Is Murder. M. A. De Ford
Theme Is Murder. Gavin Holt
Then Came Bronson. W. Johnston
Then Came the Police. C. M. Wills
Then Came Two Women. C. Armstrong
Then There Were Three. G. Homes
Theodora. K. Lindsay
Therapy In Dynamite. V. B. Miller
There Ain't No Justice. J. Curtis
There Are Dead Men in Manhattan. J. Roeburt
There Are Giants. E. Woodward
There Are More Ways of Killing... M. Fitt
There Are Thirteen. F. Beeding
There Are Worse Jungles. N. Tranter
There Came Both Mist and Snow. M. Innes
There Could Be Trouble. B. Carson
There Goes Davey Cohen. W. Owen
There Goes Death. G. Ashe
There Goes His Ghost. J. Atholl
There Goes Shorty Higgins. J. Karney
There Goes the Bride. W. Maner
There Has Been a Murder. H. Holt
There Is a Death, Elizabeth. Gerald Butler
There Is a Green Hill. Robert Mason
There Is a Tide... A. Christie
There Is a Tide--. E. Wooll
There Is No Justice. R. B. Dominic
There Is No Ogpu. A. Wood
There Is No Return. A. Blackmon
There Is No Silence. M. Dolinsky
There Is No Yesterday. K. Lindsay
There Is One S.O.S. J. B. O'Sullivan
There Is Something About a Dame. M. Avallone
There Lies Your Love. J. Melville
There Must Be Some Mistake. M. Babson
There Must Be Victims. M. Cumberland
There None Embrace. F. Shroyer
There Sits Death. P. McGuire
There Was a Crooked Man. D. Keene
There Was a Crooked Man. K. Roos
There Was a Crooked Man. C. Witting
There Was a Crooked Man. G. W. Yates
There Was a Door. T. Mundy
There Was a Little Man. C. Conrad
There Was a Witness. E. Salter
There Was an Old Man. E. Phillpotts
There Was an Old Woman. E. Davis
There Was an Old Woman. E. Phillpotts
There Was an Old Woman. E. Queen
There Was No Island. L. Handley
There Was No Moon. F. Hay
There Were No Asper Ladies. E. Ascher
There Were No Windows. N. Hoult
Thereby Hangs a Corpse. C. Mullen
Thereby Hangs a Tale. G. M. Fenn
Therefore I Killed Him. H. Jobson
There's a Hippie on the Highway. J. H. Chase
There's a Reason for Everything. E. R. Punshon
There's Always a Dame. B. Sarto
There's Always a Murder. K. Parker
There's Always a Payoff. R. P. Hansen
There's Always a Price Tag. J. H. Chase
There's Always Time to Die. O. R. Cohen
There's Always Tomorrow. A. Meredith
There's Been Murder Done. K. T. Knoblock
There's Danger, Miss Minden! A. Jackson
There's Death in the Churchyard. W. Gore
There's Death in the Cup. A. Hocking
There's Money in Murder. G. Barnett
There's No One in the Village. O. Rees
There's Trouble Brewing. N. Blake
Theresa. T. P. Prest
These Arrows Point to Death. W. O'Farrell
These Cliffs Are Dangerous. L. March
These Haunted Streets. John Burke
These Lonely, These Dead. R. Colby
These Lonely Victories. E. West
These Names Make Clues. E. C. R. Lorac
These Men and Women. S. Horler
These Small Glories. J. Cleary
These Unlucky Deeds. R. M. Stern
These Within. L. K. Vincent
Thespian Detective and other theatrical stories. B. Delannoy
They All Bleed Red. R. Sted
They All Came Back. J. Courage
They All Ran Away. E. Ronns
They Being Dead Yet Speak. C. Massie
They Blocked the Suez Canal. A. D. Divine
They Buried a Man. Mildred Davis
They Burn for Me. B. Sarto
They Call It Murder. Peter Chambers
They Called Him Death. David Hume
They Called Him Nighthawk. S. Horler
They Came by Night. S. Truss
They Came to Baghdad. A. Christie
They Came to Kill. M. Scherf
They Came to London. P. Tabori
They Can Only Hang You Once. D. Hammett
They Can't All Be Guilty. M. V. Heberden
They Can't Hang Me! J. Mallett
They Can't Hang Me! J. Ronald
They Can't Hang Caroline. Roy Vickers
They Carry a Torch. J. Blackmore
They Couldn't Go Wrong. R. Armstrong
They Cracked Her Glass Slipper. Gerald Butler
They Died in Death. R. Terrall
They Died in the Spring. J. Pullein-Thompson
They Died Laughing. A. Green
They Do It with Mirrors. A. Christie
They Don't Always Hang Murderers. B. Herbert
They Don't Dance Much. James Ross
They Don't Live Long. J. Cello
They Don't Make Them Like That Any More. J. Leasor
They Drive by Night. J. Curtis
They Found Atlantis. D. Wheatley
They Found Each Other. G. Fairlie
They Found Him Dead. G. Heyer
They Hadn't a Clue. Q. Downes
They Hang Them in Gibraltar. B. Perowne
They Hunted a Fox. A. Campbell
They Journey by Night. D. Ames
They Kidnapped Stanley Matthews. L. Gribble
They Kill by Night. K. Medusa
They Killed a Spy. M. Hastings
They Liked Entwhistle. R. A. J. Walling
They Lived with Death. H. Desmond
They Love Not Poison. S. Woods
They Met at Mrs. Bloxom's. H. Norwood
They Never Came Back. B. Flynn
They Never Came Back. David Hume
They Never Come Back. E. P. Thorne
They Never Looked Inside. M. Gilbert
They Never Say When. P. Cheyney
They Rang Up the Police. J. Cannan
They Rubbed Him Out. J. L. Cora
They Sailed on a Friday. T. C. Paynter
They Say I'm Bad. B. Shannon
They See in Darkness. Ethel L. White

They Shoot Horses, Don't They? H. McCoy
They Stand Accused. G. Braddon
They Stole a Ship. C. H. Barker
They Stuck at Nothing. R. Ladline
They Talked of Poison. M. Evermay
They Tell No Tales. M. Coles
They Tell No Tales. A. Spiller
They Tell No Tales. L. Thayer
They Thought He Was Dead. S. Horler
They Used Dark Forces. D. Wheatley
They Used to Play on Grass. Gordon M. Williams
They Vanish at Night. Frank King
They Voted Me to Die. J. Laffin
They Waited for the Night. V. Dale
They Walk in Darkness. G. Verner
They Want Me Dead. P. Bannon
They Wanted Him Dead! L. Eyles
They Watched by Night. J. Rhode
They Went Thataway. D. A. Brown
They Were Seven. E. Phillpotts
They Wetted His Head. H. Fernee
They Who Sin. J. Roeburt
They Won't Believe Me. G. McDonell
They Won't Lie Down. M. Annesley
They Wouldn't Be Chessmen. A. E. W. Mason
They'll Never Find Out. F. Duncan
They're Coming to Kill You, Jane. K. Carr
They're Going to Kill Me. K. M. Knight
They're Not Home Yet. F. Rydell
They've Got Me Again. D. Linton
They've Shot the President's Daughter. E. Stewart
Thick Blue Sweater. P. Fry
Thickening Light. G. Ferrand
Thicker Than Water. M. Halliday
Thicker Than Water. J. Payn
Thicker Than Water. M. Polland
Thicker Than Water. J. Sandys
Thicker Than Water. W. C. Tuttle
Thicket. P. Gallagher
Thief. R. Croft-Cooke
Thief. M. L. Tyrrell
Thief by Night. D. Peacock
Thief in the Night. N. Carter
Thief in the Night. E. W. Hornung
Thief in the Night. P. Manton
Thief in the Night. E. Wallace
Thief in the Night. T. Walsh
Thief Is an Ugly Word. P. Gallico
Thief of Clubs. G. Johns
Thief Taker. J. Sturrock
Thief Who Came to Dinner. T. L. Smith
Thief Who Couldn't Sleep. Lawrence Block
Thief Who Painted Sunlight. O. Bleeck
Thief Who Was Robbed. N. Carter
Thieves. Aix
Thieves Fall Out. C. Kay
Thieves' Highway. Ruth Grayson
Thieves' Hole. D. Howarth
Thieves' Honour. S. Gluck
Thieves' Justice. A. Marsden
Thieves Like Us. R. E. Alter
Thieves Like Us. E. Anderson
Thieves' Nights. H. S. Keeler
Thieves of Alexandria. J. Hunter
Thieves of Enchantment. P. Audemars
Thieves' Picnic. L. Charteris
Thieves' Wit. H. Footner
Thieving Fingers. F. Du Boisgobey
Thin Air. H. Browne
Thin Air. J. Pudney
Thin Edge of Mania. M. Macklin
Thin Edge of Violence. W. O'Farrell
Thin Ice. M. Richmond
Thin Line. E. Atiyah
Thin Man. D. Hammett
Thin Red Line. A. Griffiths

Thin-Spun Thread. A. Hocking
Thing at the Door. H. Slesar
Thing at Their Heels. H. Hext
Thing from the Lake. E. M. Ingram
Thing in the Brook. P. Storme
Thing in the Night. K. Virden
Thing in the Road. T. M. White
Thing in the Woods. Harper Williams
Thing That Happens to You. E. Berckman
Thing to Love. G. Household
Things as They Are. W. Godwin
Things Happen. R. Glover
Things Men Do. R. Marshall
Things That Are Caesar's. R. W. Kauffman
Things That No One Tells. E. C. Mayne
Things That Women Do. F. Warden
Think Fast, Mr. Moto. J. P. Marquand
Think Inc. A. Diment
Think of a Number. A. Bodelsen
Think of Death. R. Lockridge
Thinking Machine. J. Futrelle
Thinking Machine Affair. Joel Bernard
Thinking Machine on the Case. J. Futrelle
Third Alibi. M. Dalman
Third Assassin. H. C. Davis
Third Attempt. H. E. Wheeler
Third Baffle Book. L. Wren
Third Bullet. Carter Dickson
Third Bullet and other stories. J. D. Carr
Third Case for Mr. Paul Savoy. J. Gregory
Third Child. A. Nichols
Third Crime Lucky. Anthony Gilbert
Third Day. J. Hayes
Third Degree. Joe Barry
Third Degree. M. B. Dix
Third Degree. C. Franklin
Third Degree. A. Hornblow
Third Degree. C. R. Jackson
Third Diamond. J. B. Ellis
Third Ear. C. Siodmak
Third Encounter. S. Woods
Third Eye. E. Leroux
Third Eye. Ethel L. White
Third Figure. C. Wilcox
Third Force. H. Matheson
Third Girl. A. Christie
Third Half. Mildred Davis
Third Horseman. J. B. O'Sullivan
Third Hour. G. Household
Third Key. H. H. C. Gibbons
Third Key. G. Verner
Third Kiss. H. Flowerdew
Third Man. J. G. Bethune
Third Man and The Fallen Idol. G. Greene
Third Messenger. P. Wynnton
Third Miracle. L. Tracy
Third Mistake. A. W. Barrett
Third Murderer. C. J. Daly
Third on a Seesaw. N. MacNeil
Third Owl. R. J. Casey
Third Party Risk. N. Bentley
Third Party Risk. G. Cullingford
Third Policeman. Flann O'Brien
Third Possibility. S. Jepson
Third Robin Featherstone. L. C. Douthwaite
Third Round. H. C. McNeile
Third Shadow. D. Nile
Third Shot. F. W. Irwin
Third Side of the Coin. F. Clifford
Third Skin. J. Bingham
Third Spectre. W. E. D. Ross
Third Statue. Shane Martin
Third Time Unlucky. Mark Cross

Third Time Unlucky! L. Meynell
Third Time Unlucky. T. B. Morris
Third Truth. M. Bar-Zohar
Third Twin. Clay Henry
Third Victim. J. J. Farjeon
Third Victim. D. Stuart
Third Volume. F. Hume
Third Warning. Augustus Muir
Third Woman. J. De Pre
Thirsty Evil. P. M. Hubbard
Thirsty Evil. G. Verner
Thirteen. F. B. Austin
13. P. Loraine
Thirteen at Dinner. A. Christie
13 Clues for Miss Marple. A. Christie
Thirteen Days. I. Jefferies
13 for Luck! A. Christie
13 French Street. G. Brewer
Thirteen Guests. J. J. Farjeon
Thirteen in a Fog. B. Graeme
Thirteen Men. T. Thayer
Thirteen Moons. M. L. Tyrrell
Thirteen O'Clock. E. Bond
Thirteen Problems. A. Christie
Thirteen Stannergate. G. M. Wilson
Thirteen Steps. W. Chambers
13 Steps to Lime Street. D. Enefer
13 Thirteenth Street. N. S. Lincoln
Thirteen Toy Pistols. E. E. Halleran
Thirteen Trumpeters. L. Meynell
13 West Street. L. Brackett
13 White Tulips. F. Crane
Thirteen Winston Street. J. Wetherell
Thirteenth Bed in the Ballroom. E. H. Fonseca
Thirteenth Chair. B. Veiller
13th Chime. T. C. H. Jacobs
13th Code. W. Jardine
13th Doll. A. Loring
Thirteenth Floor. J. F. W. Hannay
Thirteenth Guest. F. Hume
Thirteenth Guest. A. Trail
13th Hour. S. Horler
Thirteenth House. C. Barry
Thirteenth Juror. F. T. Hill
Thirteenth Letter. N. S. Lincoln
Thirteenth Lover. R. Clarke
13th Lover. M. Dekobra
Thirteenth Man. Mrs. C. Kernahan
13th Mummy. G. Radcliffe
13th Murder. F. G. Eberhard
13th Spy. N. Carter
Thirteenth Treasure. Charlotte Hunt
Thirteenth Trick. R. Braddon
Thirty Days. H. Wales
Thirty Days Hath July. A. Brennan
Thirty Days Hath September. P. Capon
30 Days Hath September. D. C. Disney
Thirty Days Hath September. O. John
Thirty Days to Live. Anthony Gilbert
.38. W. Ard
.38 Automatic. E. C. Vivian
Thirty-Eighth Floor. C. Irving
Thirty Famous Chinese Stories. W. I-Ting
Thirty-First Bullfinch. H. Reilly
Thirty-First Floor. P. Wahloo
Thirty-First of February. J. Symons
Thirty-Four East. Alfred Coppel
"30" Manhattan East. H. Waugh
Thirty-Nine Steps. J. Buchan
Thirty Pieces of Silver. A. Soutar
Thirty Seconds over New York. R. Buchard
36 Hours. C. K. Hittleman
.32 Caliber. D. McGibeny
Thirty Years After. W. M. Graydon
This Ancient Evil. D. Daniels
This Animal Is Dangerous. Reginald Campbell

Title Index

This Animal Must Die. F. Scarpetta
This Body of Death. A. Sergeant
This Business of Bomfog. M. Donne
This Chequered Floor. F. Bamford
This City Is Ours. D. Pitts
This Creeping Evil. Sea Lion
This Crowded Earth & Ladies' Day. R. Bloch
This Dame Dies Soon. H. Janson
This Dame Spells Death. C. Wheatley
This Dark Desire. J. Conway
This Dark Monarchy. F. Leary
This Day's Madness. D. G. Waring
This Deadly Dark. L. Wilson
This Deadly Grief. P. Power
This Death Was Murder. M. Evermay
This Delicate Murder. H. Clandon
This Doll Is Dangerous. Frank King
This Drakotny--. P. McCutchan
This Fearful Paradise. J. Ames
This Fell Sergeant. D. Garner
This Fortress. M. Coles
This Game of Murder. R. Deming
This Girl for Hire. G. G. Fickling
This Gun for Gloria. B. Mara
This Gun for Hire. G. Greene
This Hood for Hire. H. Janson
This House Is Haunted. R. Bridges
This House to Let. W. LeQueux
This Inward Horror. J. R. Warren
This Is Death Calling. J. Sandys
This Is Dynamite. Richard Grant
This Is for Keeps. G. Joseph
This Is for Real. J. H. Chase
This Is Harry Flynn. J. Jost
This Is It. H. Ellson
This Is It, Michael Shayne. B. Halliday
This Is Jezebel. D. Cory
This Is Mr. Fortune. H. C. Bailey
This Is Murder. W. Ard
This--Is Murder! C. Fitzsimmons
This Is Murder. C. J. Kenny
This Is Murder. P. Muller
This Is Murder, Lady! N. W. Firth
This Is Murder, Mr. Herbert and other stories. D. Keene
This Is Murder, Mr. Jones. T. Fuller
This Is My Murder. M. B. Dix
This Is My Night. R. Deming
This Is the Castle. N. Freeling
This Is the House. Shelley Smith
This Is What Happened. T. Claymore
This Is Your Life. B. Newman
This Kill Is Mine. D. Evans
This Land Turns Evil Slowly. M. L. Roby
This Little Measure. S. Woods
This Little World. D. C. Murray
This Man Belongs to Me. M. Richmond
This Man Dawson. H. E. Helseth
This Man Did I Kill? M. Halliday
This Man I Love. W. E. D. Ross
This Man Is a Spy. D. L. David
This Man Is a Stranger. H. B. Kaye
This Man Is Dangerous. P. Cheyney
This Man Is Death. A. Capelli
This Man Is Mine. K. Lindsay
This Man Must Die! W. A. Ballinger
This Man's Doom. L. Thayer
This Man's Wife. G. M. Fenn
This Mortal Coil. G. Allen
This Mortal Coil. J. R. Warren
This Murderous Shaft. H. J. Hultman
This New Corn. D. G. Waring

This Path Is Dangerous. F. J. Whaley
"This Road Is Dangerous!" H. D. Dearden
This Road Is Dangerous. M. Richmond
This Rough Magic. M. Stewart
This Shrouded Night. Dana Ross
This Side Murder. J. Bonett
This Side of Hell. R. Charles
This Side of Terror. D. Bateson
This Side of the Sky. J. Barlow
This Side Up. H. Luger
This Spy Must Die. P. Saxon
This Suitcase Is Going to Explode. T. Ardies
This Sweet Sickness. P. Highsmith
This Tangled Web. E. O. Allen
This Traitor, Death. D. Cory
This Troublesome World. L. T. Meade
This Undesirable Residence. M. Burton
This Unnecessary Murder. F. S. Wees
This Was a Woman. H. Zore
This Was Ivor Trent. C. Houghton
This Was No Accident. J. A. Saxon
This Way for a Shroud. J. H. Chase
This Way for Hell. S. Morelli
This Way for Hell. G. Ross
This Way Out. J. Ronald
This Way Out. A. M. Sholl
This Way to Evil. H. P. Lees
This Witch. W. Tucker
This Woman Is Dangerous. Mark Ross
This Woman Is Death. S. D. Frances
This Woman Is Death. H. Janson
This Woman Is Wanted. Roland Daniel
This Woman Is Wanted. G. Goodchild
This Woman to This Man. C. N. Williamson
This Woman Wanted. R. Foley
This Won't Hurt You. N. Fitzgerald
This World Is Wide Enough. G. Greenfield
This Year's Death. J. Godey
This Yellow Slave. L. Durie
This'll Kill You. Peter Chambers
This'll Kill You. M. Randolph
This'll Slay You. A. Payne
Thistle Sifters. C. R. Burke
Thomas Crown Affair. E. L. Heyman
Thompson the Detective. J. L. Hempstead
Thompson's Progress. C. J. C. Hyne
Thorn in the Dust. P. Audemars
Thorne House. J. Ware
Thorne in the Flesh. R. Petrie
Thorne Theatre Mystery. Joshua Willard
Thornley Colton, Blind Detective. C. H. Stagg
Thornley Colton, Blind Reader of Hearts. C. H. Stagg
Those on the List. A. Parsons
Those Other Days. E. P. Oppenheim
Those Seven Alibis. C. G. Booth
Those That Have Eyes. P. Conway
Those Westerton Girls. F. Warden
Those Who Have Come Back. P. C. MacFarlane
Those Who Prey Together Slay Together. D. Von Elsner
Those Who Return. M. Level
Those Who Smiled, and other stories. P. Gibbon
Those Who Walk Away. P. Highsmith
Those Who Walk in Darkness. G. C. Shedd
Thou Art the Man. M. E. Braddon
Thou Shalt Not Kill. B. Heygate
"Thou Shalt Not Kill." M. B. Lowndes
Thou Shell of Death. N. Blake
Though I Know She Lies. S. Woods
Thoughtless Yes. H. H. Gardener
Thousand and One Afternoons in Chicago. B. Hecht
Thousand and Second Night. F. Heller
Thousand Coffins Affair. M. Avallone
Thousand Doors. A. Rothberg
Thousand Faces of Night. Harry Patterson

Thousand Francs Reward. E. Gaboriau
Thousand Hands. Bruce Norman
Thousand-Headed Man. K. Robeson
Thousand Secrets. J. Selborne
Thousand Witnesses. G. Beardmore
Thousandth Case. G. Dilnot
Thousandth Woman. E. W. Hornung
Thread of Evidence. B. Picton
Thread of Proof. H. Hill
Threads of Gold. L. V. Stevens
Threads of Intrigue. Lynn Williams
Threads of Love. E. Randolph
Threat of Dragons. L. R. Davis
Threat of the Cloven Hand. Richard Grant
Threatening Eye. E. F. Knight
Threatening Shadows. C. Robertson
Three. F. Hume
Three Act Tragedy. A. Christie
Three Against Fate. M. A. Hamilton
Three Alibis. J. F. W. Hannay
Three Amateurs. Michael Lewis
Three Among Mountains. H. Slater
Three at the Angel. M. Procter
Three at Wolfe's Door. R. Stout
Three Bad Nights. B. Buckingham
Three Beans. M. Coles
Three Beds in Manhattan. G. Simenon
Three Black Bags. M. P. Angellotti
Three Black Dots. O. Binns
Three Blind Mice. V. Bridges
Three Blind Mice. A. Christie
3 Blind Mice. A. Seifert
Three Blind Mice. J. Wood
Three Blue Anchors. O. Binns
Three Boy Detectives. Old Sleuth
Three Brass Balls. G. R. Sims
Three Brass Elephants. Herman Landon
Three Bright Pebbles. L. Ford
Three Cheers for Treason! Robert Mason
Three Coffins. J. D. Carr
Three-Coloured Pencil. S. P. B. Mais
Three-Cornered Cover. G. Marton
Three-Cornered Murder. Jean Leslie
Three-Cornered Wound. G. Dyer
Three Corners to Nowhere. M. Caidin
Three Corpse Trick. M. Burton
Three Couriers. C. MacKenzie
Three Cousins Die. J. Rhode
Three Crimes. M. Burton
Three Crows. J. Hunter
Three Daggers. C. F. Gregg
Three Dates with Death. V. Gunn
Three Daughters of Night. D. Vane
Three Day Alliance. H. R. Simpson
Three Day Pass--to Kill. J. W. Burke
3-Day Terror. V. Packer
Three Days in Hong Kong. F. Crane
Three Days of the Condor. J. Grady
Three Days' Terror. J. S. Fletcher
Three Days Terror. P. Manton
Three Days to Catastrophe. Douglas Clark
Three Days to Live. R. Charles
Three Dead. D. Magarshack
Three Dead Men. P. McGuire
Three Dead, One Hurt. S. Mackenzie
Three Die at Midnight. J. Hunter
Three Die at Midnight. P. Meriton
Three Died Beside the Marble Pool. C. M. Chapin
Three Died for Morson. C. Ryland
Three Died That Night. Gret Lane
3 Died Variously. G. E. Giles
Three Doors to Death. R. Stout
Three Down Vulnerable. Z. H. Ross
Three Envelopes. H. Drummond

Three Exploits of M. Parent. J. Lermina
Three Faces of Death. J. Weisman
Three Fair Philanthropists. A. M. Muzzy
Three Fantastic Tales. C. Houghton
Three Fears. J. Stagge
Three Finger Marks. Old Spicer
Three Fingered Death. G. M. Wilson
Three Fishers. F. Beeding
Three for a Killing. D. Leach
Three for Adventure. M. Halliday
Three for the Chair. R. Stout
Three for the Gallows. E. McDowell
Three for the Money. W. T. Ballard
Three for the Money. Joe Barry
Three for the Money. J. McConnaughey
Three Freaks. T. Robbins
Three Frightened Men. B. Gray
Three Gentlemen from New Caledonia. R. D. Hemingway
3 Girls and a Killer. H. D. Spatz
Three Glass Eyes. W. LeQueux
Three Gnomes. G. Verner
Three Gold Coins. K. Robeson
Three Graces. P. Hobson
Three Green Bottles. D. Devine
Three Ha-Pence to the Angel. Charles Harris
Three Hostages. J. Buchan
Three Hours to Hang. A. MacKenzie
Three Hundred Grand. J. Pattinson
361. D. E. Westlake
Three Hunting Horns. M. Fitt
Three Impostors. A. Machen
Three in a Cell. R. Croft-Cooke
Three Inquisitive People. D. Wheatley
Three Jolly Vagabonds. J. Budd
Three Judges. H. Maxwell
Three Just Men. E. Wallace
Three Keys. F. Ormond
Three Keys to Murder. M. Holloway
Three Knaves. S. L. Greenleaf
Three Knaves. E. Phillpotts
Three Knots. W. LeQueux
Three Knots. R. Parker
Three Layers of Guilt. J. Ashford
Three Lepers' Heads. P. Quiroule
Three Letters to Pan. J. Blackmore
Three Lights Went Out. R. G. Dean
Three Little Tramps. Old Sleuth
Three Lost Ladies. H. R. Campbell
Three Lovers and One Lass. A. M. Meadows
Three Masked Men. J. N. Pentelow
Three Masks of Death. J. N. Chance
Three Men and a God, and other stories. N. Newham-Davis
Three Men and a Maid. Robert Fraser
Three Men Die. S. G. Millin
Three Men for the Job. D. Ambler
Three Men in a Plane. C. Winchester
Three Men Murdered. A. A. Archer
Three Men Out. R. Stout
$3 Million Turn-Over. Richard Curtis
Three Millions! W. T. Adams
Three Minus Two. D. MacKenzie
Three Minutes to Midnight. Mildred Davis
Three Must Die! D. Gregory
Three Mysteries. T. Douglas
Three Names for Murder. H. R. Campbell
Three Nights. E. Hostovsky
Three Oak Mystery. E. Wallace
Three of a Kind. J. M. Cain
Three of a Kind, and The Haunting of Jack Burnham. H. C. McNeile
Three of Clubs. V. Williams
Three of Diamonds. K. M. Knight
Three of Hearts. J. M. Cain
Three on the Road. S. Ryder
Three People's Secret. G. M. Fenn
Three-Pipe Problem. J. Symons
Three Plots for Asey Mayo. P. A. Taylor
Three Point Murder. R. C. Finney
Three Problems for Solar Pons. A. Derleth
3 Professional Ladies. G. F. Newman
Three Quick and Five Dead. G. Mitchell
Three R's. Ganpat
Three Rainbows. K. Hewitt
Three Recruits, and the Girls They Left Behind Them. J. Hatton
Three Roads. K. Millar
Three Roads to a Star. D. Garth
"Three Rounds Rapid--." R. Hardinge
Three Saw the Murder. H. L. Blair
Three Sentinels. G. Household
3-7-9 Murder. G. Morton
Three Sevens. P. P. Sheehan
Three Short Biers. J. Starr
Three Short Men. F. Vivian
Three Shots. O. Gray
Three Silent Men. E. P. Thorne
Three Silver Birches. R. M. Sears
Three Sisters Flew Home. M. Fitt
Three Sisters of Briarwick. K. Kimbrough
Three Sisters of No End House. M. Farnsworth
Three Slips to a Noose. Fiona Sinclair
Three Spies for Glory. M. McKenna
Three Steps to Hell. V. Warren
Three Steps to Murder. N. MacKenzie
Three Strangers. M. Dalman
Three Strangers. G. Joseph
Three Straw Men. A. Derleth
Three Strings. N. S. Lincoln
Three Sundays to Live. Roland Daniel
Three Taps. R. A. Knox
Three Taps at Twelve. A. Saunders
Three Thirds of a Ghost. T. Fuller
3-13 Murders. T. B. Black
Three Thousand Dollars. A. K. Green
Three Tiers of Fantasy. N. Berrow
Three-Time Losers. G. Bagby
Three Times a Victim. F. L. Wallace
Three Times Dead. M. E. Braddon
Three to Be Read. P. Wylie
Three to Make Murder. V. Patrick
Three-Toed Pussy. W. J. Burley
Three Trails. W. M. Graydon
Three Trials of Manirema. J. J. Veiga
Three Verdicts. F. I. Katzenberger
Three-Way Split. G. Brewer
Three Wayward Girls. F. Warden
Three Went In. N. A. Temple-Ellis
Three Were to Die. F. C. Tickner
Three Who Died. A. Derleth
Three Who Paid. D. Stuart
Three Widows. Bernice Carey
Three--with Blood. A. M. Stein
Three Witnesses. S. Fowler
Three Witnesses. R. Stout
Three Wives. Alex Fraser
Three Women. W. Reyburn
Three Women in Black. H. Reilly
Three Women in the House. E. Thompson
Three Wooden Overcoats. H. Clevely
Three Worlds of Johnny Handsome. J. Godey
Three Yards of Cord. C. Brooks
Three Years After. N. Buntline
Threefold Cord. F. Vivian
Threefold Disappearance. N. Carter
Threefold Threat. D. Miall
Threepence to Marble Arch. P. McGuire
Threepersons Hunt. B. Garfield
Three's a Crowd. D. M. Disney
Three's a Shroud. R. S. Prather
Threescore Years. P. Capon
Threshing Floor. J. S. Fletcher
Threshold. S. Coulter
Threshold of Fear. A. J. Rees
Thrice Captive. A. Griffiths
Thrice Judas. F. Grierson
Thrice Past the Post. H. Smart
Thrice Upon a Killing Spree. P. Quinn
Thrifty Abe. Old Sleuth
Thrill a Minute with Jack Albany. J. Godey
Thrill Kids. V. Packer
Thrill Killers. R. Novak
Thrill Machine. I. Hamilton
Thriller. T. Hart
Thrilling Adventures of a New York Detective. Anonymous
Thrilling Detective Stories. T. P. MacNaught
Thrilling Mystery. Old Sleuth
Thrilling Stories. Anonymous
Thrilling Stories of the Railway. V. L. Whitechurch
Throbbing Dark. F. Arthur
Throne of Bayonets. K. Fitzgerald
Throne of Peril. C. M. Hincks
Throne of Satan. J. Dark
Through a Glass Darkly. Anonymous
Through a Glass Darkly. T. Blakemore
Through a Glass Darkly. V. Gielgud
Through a Glass, Darkly. H. McCloy
Through a Glass Darkly. E. Phillpotts
Through a Glass Darkly. B. Symons
Through Another Gate. R. Bridges
Through Another Gate. G. Vaizey
Through Devil's Gate. D. P. Neeley
Through Fire and Water. R. C. Armour
Through Folly's Mill. A. Askew
Through the Bamboo Curtain. M. Urquhart
Through the Cellar Wall. N. Carter
Through the Dark and Hairy Wood. S. Herron
Through the Dark Curtain. P. Saxon
Through the Eyes of the Judge. B. Graeme
Through the Lens. M. Massey
Through the Night. F. Ryerson
Through the Wall. C. Moffett
Through the Wall. K. Sully
Through the Wall. P. Wentworth
Through War to Peace. Benjamin F. Mason
Throw. A. Bloomfield
Throw Back the Little Ones. P. Colombo
Thug Executive. J. N. Chance
Thugs and Bottles. San Antonio
Thumb-Mark. Warren Hill
Thumb Stroke. F. Du Boisgobey
Thunder Above. A. J. Wallis
Thunder Ahead. Malcolm Campbell
Thunder at Dawn. H. Gibbs
Thunder at Noon. Harry Patterson
Thunder Dragon Gate. T. Mundy
Thunder Heights. P. A. Whitney
Thunder in Europe. J. Creasey
Thunder Island. J. Hunter
Thunder Island. G. Volk
Thunder of the Roses. M. Peyrou
Thunder on Sunday. Karen Campbell
Thunder on the Right. M. Stewart
Thunder over South Parish. A. J. Allen
Thunder over the Reefs. P. Minton
Thunderball. I. Fleming
Thunderbird. D. Garth
Thunderbird Range. W. C. Tuttle
Thunderbolt. J. G. Sarasin
Thunderbolt and Lightfoot. J. Millard
Thunderbolt Collects. J. McCulley
Thunderbolt's Jest. J. McCulley

Thursday at Dawn. W. J. Luddecke
Thursday Island. M. Keck
Thursday Turkey Murders. C. Rice
Thursday's Blade. F. C. Davis
Thursday's Folly. J. Philips
Thurtell's Crime: The Story of a Strange Tragedy. D. Donovan
Thus Far. J. C. Snaith
Thy Arm Alone. J. Slate
Thy First Begotten. N. Bell
Thy Guilt Is Great. C. I. D. Smith
Tiara. Anthony Mann
Tic-Tac. D. Learmonth
Tick of Death. P. Lovesey
Tick of the Clock. H. Asbury
Tick...Tick...Tick. P. Rock
Tickencote Treasure. W. LeQueux
Ticker-Tape Murder. M. Propper
Ticket. C. Stratton
Ticket for Death. E. M. Bowen
Ticket of Leave. G. Simenon
Ticket-of-Leave Girl. A. M. Meadows
Ticket-of-Leave Man. C. H. Bullivant
Ticket-of-Leave Man. Tom Taylor
Ticket-of-Leave Man. H. C. Williams
Ticket San Diego. A. Bocca
Ticket to Buffalo. A. Dean
Ticket to Eternity. G. Shayne
Ticket to Hell. H. Whittington
Ticket to Oblivion. Robert Parker
Ticket to Ride. Ritchie Perry
Tickets for Death. B. Halliday
Ticking Clock. F. Lockridge
Ticking Heart. D. B. Olsen
Ticking Terror Murders. D. L. Teilhet
Tickletoby. H. Wayne
Tidal Wave. G. Simenon
Tide Can't Wait. L. Trimble
Tide of Death. J. M. Hickman
Tide of Fortune. M. Gerard
Tide Rip. Robin Temple
Tide Waits for No Man. H. La Garde
Tide Watchers. S. M. Parkman
Tideless Sea. G. Volk
Tidemill. D. Daniels
Tidewrack. N. Tranter
Tidings of Joy. G. Goodchild
Tidy Death. N. Lombard
Tie and Trick. H. Smart
Tied for Murder. C. Fitzsimmons
Tied up in Tinsel. N. Marsh
Tiffany Caper. J. Purtell
Tiger Among Us. L. Brackett
Tiger at Bay. B. Picton
Tiger by the Tail. J. H. Chase
Tiger by the Tail. L. Goldman
Tiger Claws. F. Packard
Tiger Dawn. S. Jepson
Tiger from the Shadows. B. Jones
Tiger-Heart. J. G. Sarasin
Tiger Hill. Ardath Wise
Tiger House. R. St. Clair
Tiger in the Bed. M. Catto
Tiger in the Night. R. Kyle
Tiger in the Night. J. M. Walsh
Tiger in the North. J. Harvester
Tiger in the Smoke. M. Allingham
Tiger in the Streets. L. Malley
Tiger Kittens. A. Zuckerman
Tiger Lily. G. Dilnot
Tiger Lily. G. M. Fenn
Tiger Lily. C. N. Williamson
Tiger Mark. P. Graham
Tiger Milk. D. Garth

Tiger of Baragunga. J. I. Emery
Tiger of Canton. G. H. Teed
Tiger of Cloud River. R. Cullum
Tiger of Karan. D. Lenton
Tiger of Mayfair. H. Holt
Tiger Reef. M. Hastings
Tiger River. A. O. Friel
Tiger Snake. H. S. Keeler
Tiger Sniffs the Rose. H. G. Carlisle
Tiger Standish. S. Horler
Tiger Standish Comes Back. S. Horler
Tiger Standish Does His Stuff. S. Horler
Tiger Standish Has a Party. S. Horler
Tiger Standish Steps on It. S. Horler
Tiger Standish Takes the Field. S. Horler
Tiger Street. E. Trevor
Tiger Strikes Again. C. M. Wills
Tiger, Tiger. G. Goodchild
Tiger Tooth. E. Woodward
Tigerman of Terrahpur. E. Lecale
Tigers Are Hungry. C. Early
Tiger's Back. J. W. Mason
Tiger's Claw. A. P. Terhune
Tiger's Claws. C. Robertson
Tiger's Coat. E. Dejeans
Tiger's Cub. E. Phillpotts
Tiger's Cub. G. Seton
Tigers Fight Alone. F. Duncan
Tigers Have Claws. B. Graeme
Tiger's Head Mystery. E. T. Sawyer
Tiger's Necklace. R. St. Clair
Tiger's Wife. Wade Miller
Tight Circle. J. F. Straker
Tight Corner. A. W. Marchmont
Tight Corner. Sam Ross
Tight Rope. A. L. Burks
Tight Squeeze. W. Fuller
Tightening of the Coils. Old Spicer
Tightening String. A. Bridge
Tightrope. J. Legaret
Tightrope Men. D. Bagley
Tightrope Minor. T. Topor
Tigress. J. Bogar
Tigress. C. Brown
Tigress. M. Derby
Tigress. H. Janson
Tigress of Brazil. B. Sarto
'Til Death. E. McBain
'Til Death Do Us Part. A. Hynd
Tiled House Mystery. W. M. Duncan
Till Death Do Us Part. J. D. Carr
Till Death Do Us Part. L. Trimble
Till Doomsday. Robin Temple
Till It Hurts. N. Quarry
Till Murder Do Us Part. W. H. L. Crauford
Till the Clock Stops. J. J. Bell
Till the Dying Day. A. Watkins
Tilsit Inheritance. C. Gaskin
Tilted Moon. B. Perowne
Tim Frazer Again. F. Durbridge
Timber Beasts. C. Stoddard
Timber Wolf. J. Templeton
Timberjack. D. Cushman
Time and the Torture. N. Sligh
Time at Tarragon. J. Tattersall
Time Bargains. T. W. Speight
Time Before This. N. Monsarrat
Time Bomb. H. Howard
Time Bomb. W. Tucker
Time Clock of Death. N. Carter
Time Enough to Die. P. Rabe
Time for a Murder. G. Coverack
Time for Caution. P. Cheyney
Time for Crime. P. C. Williams
Time for Killing. J. Rowland
Time for Murder. P. O. McGuire
Time for Murder. H. P. Martin
Time for Murder. R. O. Saber
Time for Murder. J. Stagg
Time for Passion. H. Rigsby

Time for Pirates. G. Black
Time for Scandal. H. H. Kirst
Time for Sleeping. J. Moffatt
Time for Survival. P. McCutchan
Time for Tea. J. Coates
Time for Treason. P. Deane
Time for Treason. O. Hesky
Time for Truth. H. H. Kirst
Time for Vengeance. G. Osborne
Time in the End. F. M. McGuire
Time Is an Ambush. F. Cifford
Time Is an Enemy. S. J. Baker
Time Limit. R. Sheckley
Time Lock. C. E. Walk
Time, Murderer, Please. C. Dyer
Time of Assassins. R. Batchelor
Time of Day. F. Durbridge
Time of Dreaming. J. Edgar
Time of Killing. W. Hardy
Time of Predators. J. Gores
Time of Temptation. P. Audemars
Time of Terror. H. Pentecost
Time of Terror. L. White
Time of the Crime. D. Stuart
Time of the Fire. M. Brandel
Time Off for Death. G. Braddon
Time Off for Murder. Z. Popkin
Time Out. D. Ely
Time Remembered, Time Lost. Rona Randall
Time Right Deadly. S. Gainham
Time Running Out. K. Booton
Time Running Out. R. Crane
Time to Change Hats. M. Bennett
Time to Die. George Douglas
Time to Die. Hilda Lawrence
Time to Hate. S. Truss
Time to Kill. C. Barling
Time to Kill. Alec Brown
Time to Kill. G. Household
Time to Kill. R. Ormerod
Time to Kill. W. Reed
Time to Kill. C. Robertson
Time to Kill. T. Spain
Time to Kill. J. M. Walsh
Time to Kill. G. Ward
Time to Kill. J. Weeks
Time to Kill...A Time to Die. J. Pearl
Time to Prey. F. Kane
Time to Prey. F. Keinzley
Time to Retreat. Brian Cooper
Time to Run. S. Waldron
Time Too Soon. E. Lindall
Time-Worn Town. J. S. Fletcher
Timeless Serpent. Roger Fuller
Timeless Sleep. R. C. Galway
Timelock. D. Cory
Time's Hour Glass. A. E. Carey
Time's Revenges. D. C. Murray
Timetable for the General. B. Frizell
Timetable Murder. R. Denbie
Timid Tycoon. R. C. Frazer
Timothy Twill's Secret. F. J. Proctor
Tin Bath Murder. M. G. Hugi
Tin Cowrie Dass. H. M. Rideout
Tin God of Twisted River. W. C. Tuttle
Tin Hats. F. MacIsaac
Tin Tree. J. Quince
Tin Trumpets at Dawn. J. Appleby
Tincture of Murder. Sutherland Scott
Tinker, Tailor, Soldier, Spy... J. Le Carré
Tinker's Kitchen. A. R. L. Gardner
Tinker's Lone Hand. A. Murray
Tinker's Pride. N. Tranter
Tinkletop's Crime and other tales. G. R. Sims

Tinkling Symbol. P. A. Taylor
Tinman. T. Gallon
Tinsley's Bones. P. Wilde
Tinted Vapours. J. M. Cobban
Tiny Carteret. H. C. McNeile
Tiny Diamond. C. M. Russell
Tiny Luttrell. E. W. Hornung
Tip and Run. W. Tait
Tip Off. A. W. Sherring
"Tipster." Roland Daniel
Tipster. G. Verner
Tiptoe thro' a Graveyard. M. Storm
Tirana Assignment. C. Portway
Tired Spy. D. Stone
Tisket, a Casket. J. L. Linklater
Titanic Hotel Mystery. J. Hawk
Tithe War Mystery. G. Chester
Title Is Murder. H. L. Nelson
Titled Counterfeiter. N. Carter
Titty's Dead. P. Hobson
To a Blindfold Lady. J. Purtell
To Any Lengths. G. Simenon
To Be a Hero. J. McCague
To Be Hanged. B. Hamilton
To Bed at Noon. V. Gielgud
To Bed at Noon. J. Shearing
To Borrow Trouble. M. Borgenicht
To Burgundy and Back. D. M. Low
To Cache a Millionaire. M. Scherf
To Catch a Crooked Girl. P. W. Fairman
To Catch a Shadow. B. Jones
To Catch a Spy. A. A. Randall
To Catch a Spy. B. Sanders
To Catch a Thief. M. Burton
To Catch a Thief. D. Dodge
To Catch a Thief. D. Sanders
To Catch a Thief. L. Thayer
To Cease Upon the Midnight. A. Hocking
To Comfort the Signora. E. G. Cousins
To Defeat the Ends of Justice. H. Compton
To Die a Little. C. Carfax
To Die in California. N. Thornbug
To Die or Not to Die. H. Kane
To Dream of Evil. L. Hoffman
To Dusty Death. H. McCutcheon
To Fear a Painted Devil. R. Rendell
To Find a Killer. L. White
To Hang a Witch. P. Wissmann
To Have and to Hold. M. Richmond
To Have and to Kill. Robert Martin
To Hell for Half-a-Crown. J. Cross
To Hell in a Basket. I. R. Blacker
To Hell Together. H. V. Dixon
To Hell with the Law. E. Martin
To Hide a Rogue. T. Walsh
To Keep or Kill. W. Tucker
To Kill a Cat. W. J. Burley
To Kill a Cat. R. Pertwee
To Kill a Corpse. E. Ascher
To Kill a Hero. John Morgan
To Kill a House. S. Roberts
To Kill a Killer. K. Hunt
To Kill a Witch. A. Brennan
To Kill a Witch. B. Knox
To Kill Again. R. Stout
To Kill or Die. J. York
To Kill or to Die. J. York
To Kill the Pope. K. Wlaschin
To Kiss, or Kill. D. Keene
To Let, Furnished. J. Bell
To Live and Die in Dixie. T. Roscoe
To Live in Danger. B. Magee
To Love a Dark Stranger. V. Coffman
To Love a Stranger. L. A. Olmsted
To Love Again. A. Furness
To Love and Be Wise. J. Tey
To Love and to Perish. E. Dudley
To Love and Yet to Die. S. D. Frances
To Make You Mine. M. Richmond
To Market, to Market. A. Richards
To Meet Mr. Stanley. Dorothy Johnson
To Meet the Law. F. A. M. Webster
To Play the Devil. Angus Hall
To Protect the Guilty. J. Ashford
To Reach a Dream. N. C. Heard
To Save His Life. K. Roos
To See a Stranger. M. Lynn
To See Ourselves. G. C. Pollock
To Shadow Our Love. L. Ames
To Sleep No More. R. Angel
To Spite Her Face. H. Dolson
To Study a Long Silence. V. C. Clinton-Baddeley
To the Adventurous. E. Nesbit
To the Bitter End. M. E. Braddon
To the Bitter End. J. M. Simmel
To the Castle. D. Malm
To the Dark Tower. M. S. Cross
To the Dark Tower. Francis King
To the Dark Tower. L. B. Long
To the Devil--a Daughter. D. Wheatley
To the Ends of the Earth. N. Carter
To the Gallows I Must Go. T. S. Matthews
To the Minute and Scarlet and Black. A. K. Green
To the Tombaugh Station. W. Tucker
To the Tune of Murder. H. M. Ballard
"To This End." B. Malim
To This Favour. S. Gilruth
To Venus in Five Seconds. F. T. Jane
To Wake the Dead. J. D. Carr
To Walk the Night. J. Mangione
To Walk the Night. W. Sloan
To What Dread End. M. V. Heberden
To Win and to Lose. K. Netzen
To Win the Love He Sought. E. P. Oppenheim
To Windward. H. C. Rowland
Toast Is Death! F. W. Gumley
Toast to a Corpse. David Hume
Toast to Tomorrow. M. Coles
Toasted Blonde. C. Reeve
Tobacco Auction Murders. Robert Turner
Tobey's First Case. C. L. Burnham
Toby Jug Murders. H. A. Wrenn
Toby Scuffell. P. Capon
Toby Shad. Taffrail
Tocsin. A. Askew
Todd Dossier. C. Young
Todmanhawe Grange. J. S. Fletcher
Toff. J. Creasey
Toff Among the Millions. J. Creasey
Toff and Old Harry. J. Creasey
Toff and the Curate. J. Creasey
Toff and the Deadly Parson. J. Creasey
Toff and the Deep Blue Sea. J. Creasey
Toff and the Fallen Angels. J. Creasey
Toff and the Golden Boy. J. Creasey
Toff and the Great Illusion. J. Creasey
Toff and the Kidnapped Child. J. Creasey
Toff and the Lady. J. Creasey
Toff and the Runaway Bride. J. Creasey
Toff and the Sleepy Cowboy. J. Creasey
Toff and the Spider. J. Creasey
Toff and the Stolen Tresses. J. Creasey
Toff and the Teds. J. Creasey
Toff and the Terrified Tax Man. J. Creasey
Toff and the Trip-Trip-Triplets. J. Creasey
Toff at Butlin's. J. Creasey
Toff at the Fair. J. Creasey
Toff Breaks In. J. Creasey
Toff Down Under. J. Creasey
Toff Goes Gay. J. Creasey
Toff Goes On. J. Creasey
Toff Goes to Market. J. Creasey
Toff in New York. J. Creasey
Toff in Town. J. Creasey
Toff in Wax. J. Creasey
Toff Is Back. J. Creasey
Toff on Board. J. Creasey
Toff on Fire. J. Creasey
Toff on Ice. J. Creasey
Toff on the Farm. J. Creasey
Toff on the Trail. J. Creasey
Toff Proceeds. J. Creasey
Toff Steps Out. J. Creasey
Toff Takes Shares. J. Creasey
Together Brothers. J. Robinson
Toilers of Babylon. B. L. Farjeon
Toilers of the Thames. B. Hemyng
Token. L. Tracy
Token. G. Verner
Token of Evil. E. Grayson
Tokyo Doll. J. McPartland
Tokyo Intrigue. W. Bender
Tokyo Purple. L. Derrick
Told at Monte Carlo. A. M. Williamson
Told in the East. T. Mundy
Told in the Marketplace. F. B. Austin
Told in the Rockies. A. M. Barbour
Told in the Twilight. H. Wood
Toledano. George Davis
Toledo Dagger. R. Brennan
Toledo Sword. M. L. Tyrrell
Toll. M. L. Fowler
Toll for the Brave. Harry Patterson
Toll-House Murder. A. Wynne
Toll the Bell for Murder. G. Bellairs
Tolliver Case. R. A. J. Walling
Toltec Cup. Anonymous
Tom and Jerry. Anonymous
Tom and Jerry. T. Pastor
Tom Brown's Body. G. Mitchell
Tom Chester's Sweetheart. J. Hatton
Tom Dawson. F. Warden
Tom Fox. Anonymous
Tom Gerrard. L. Becke
Tom Harris. S. Themerson
Tom Ossington's Ghost. R. Marsh
Tom Rocket. A. Fonblanque
Tom Sawyer, Detective, and other stories. M. Twain
Tom, the Young Explorer. Old Sleuth
Tom Tiddler's Island. J. J. Connington
Tomb for Mr. Lee. R. Wilkes-Hunter
Tomb of T'sin. E. Wallace
Tomb with a View. L. Sieveking
Tomboy. H. Ellson
Tombs of Blue Ice. R. Faust
Tombstone for a Troubleshooter. W. C. MacDonald
Tombstone Treasure. F. Hume
Tombstones Are Free to Quitters. B. Sarto
Tommy Weston, Adventuress. W. Sheridan
Tomorrow a Stranger. E. M. Williams
Tomorrow and a Day. H. Janson
Tomorrow and Yesterday. N. Sligh
Tomorrow Country. Jack Wilson
Tomorrow Is Murder. C. Brown
Tomorrow Plus X. W. Tucker
Tomorrow--the Chair. R. Angel
Tomorrow Trap. M. Borgenicht
Tomorrow We Die. K. Lindsay
Tomorrow We'll Be Sober. M. Cranston
Tomorrow Will Be Monday. M. Marlette
Tomorrow's Another Day. W. R. Burnett

Title Index

Tomorrow's Harvest. M. Richmond
Tomorrow's Horizon. G. E. Meagher
Tomorrow's Yesterday. B. Graeme
Tong. Bok
Tong Men and a Million. A. P. Hankins
Tongking! D. Cushman
Tongue of Treason. R. Crane
Tongue-Tied Canary. N. Bentley
Toni Diamonds. G. Latta
Tonight and Tomorrow. S. Troy
Tonight in Sacarra. Michael Barrett
Tonight Is for Death. Gavin Holt
Tonight They Die to Mendelssohn. F. Gordon
"Tontine Bell." E. Kyle
Tontine Treasure. H. M. Webster
Tony Rome. A. Rome
Too Beautiful to Die. M. Carroll
Too Black for Heaven. D. Keene
Too Busy to Die. H. W. Roden
Too Clever by Half. L. Meynell
Too Close for Comfort. M. Carr
Too Curious. E. J. Goodman
Too Dangerous to Be Free. J. H. Chase
Too Dangerous to Live. David Hume
Too Dead to Run. J. Manor
Too Dead to Talk. A. E. Jones
Too Fast We Live. R. Glendinning
Too French and Too Deadly. H. Kane
Too Friendly, Too Dead. B. Halliday
Too Good to Be True. M. Halliday
Too Good to Be True. J. F. Hutton
Too Hot for Hawaii. T. B. Dewey
Too Hot for Hell. K. Vining
Too Hot to Handle. I. Fleming
Too Hot to Handle. F. G. Presnell
Too Hot to Handle. S. Sterling
Too Hot to Hold. D. Keene
Too Hot to Kill. S. Sterling
Too Innocent to Kill. D. M. Disney
Too Late for Death. D. Linton
Too Late for Mourning. R. Foster
Too Late for Tears. H. Carmichael
Too Late for Tears. P. Henneker
Too Late for Tears. R. Huggins
Too Late to Mend. T. Rainham
Too Late to Shout. R. Drayton
Too Late to Talk. N. Carter
Too Late! Too Late! The Maiden Cried. J. Fleming
Too Like the Dead. D. Chambers
Too Like the Lightning. D. Chambers
Too Lively to Live. A. Damer
Too Lively to Live. R. Fenisong
Too Long Endured. L. Thayer
Too Many Boats. C. L. Clifford
Too Many Bones. R. S. Wallis
Too Many Bottles. E. S. Holding
Too Many Chiefs. S. Marlowe
Too Many Clients. R. Stout
Too Many Clues. C. Henderson
Too Many Cooks. R. Stout
Too Many Cousins. D. G. Browne
Too Many Crooks. R. S. Prather
Too Many Crooks. E. J. Rath
Too Many Crooks. I. Trent
Too Many Doctors. H. Roth
Too Many Doors. L. Crosby
Too Many Enemies. W. Haggard
Too Many Ghosts. P. Gallico
Too Many Innocents. O. Beeby
Too Many Magicians. Randall Garrett
Too Many Murderers. G. Childerness
Too Many Murderers. G. Compton

Too Many Murderers. M. L. Stokes
Too Many Sinners. S. Stark
Too Many Suspects. J. Rhode
Too Many Women. M. K. Ozaki
Too Many Women. R. Stout
Too Many Yesterdays. D. Linton
Too Many Yesterdays. K. Rogers
Too Married. A. Applin
Too Mini Murders. P. Morgan
Too Much Ambition. E. Ellison
Too Much for Mr. Jellipot. S. Fowler
Too Much of Water. B. Hamilton
Too Much Poison. A. Rowe
Too Old to Die. Gretchen Travis
Too Rich to Die. H. V. Dixon
Too Sharp by Half. B. Hemyng
Too Small for His Shoes. L. Payne
Too Smart to Live. E. Ellison
Too Soon for Daisies. W. Dinner
Too Soon to Die. H. Janson
Too Soon to Die. Henry Wade
Too Strange a Hand. D. Quick
Too Sweet to Die. R. Goulart
Too Tough for Death. D. Steel
Too Tough to Die. G. Bruce
Too Tough to Die. R. Gadhart
Too Tough to Die. F. Gruber
Too Tough to Live. Griff
Too Young to Die. R. O. Saber
Too Young to Die. L. White
Tooth and Nail. N. Carter
Tooth and the Nail. B. S. Ballinger
Tooth Merchant. C. L. Sulzberger
Top Assignment. G. H. Coxe
Top Bloody Secret. S. Hyland
Top Boot. M. Kennedy
Top Dog. F. Hume
Top Floor Back. G. Radcliffe
Top-Floor Killer. W. A. Roberts
Top Landing. P. Brebner
Top of the Heap. A. A. Fair
Top Secret. J. Bruce
Top Secret. L. Halliday
Top Secret Kill. J. P. Cody
Top Secret No. 1. W. Jardine
Top Steal. A. Tack
Top Storey Murder. A. Berkeley
Top Ten. H. Janson
Topaz. L. Uris
Topaz for My Lady Fair. J. J. Toombs
Toper's End. G. D. H. Cole
Topkapi. E. Ambler
Topless Dancer Hangup. P. Morgan
Topless Tulip Caper. C. Harrison
Topsy and Evil. G. Baxt
Torch Bearers. B. V. Dryer
Torch for a Dark Journey. L. Shapiro
Torch Murder. C. R. Jones
Torhaven Mystery. J. B. Harris-Burland
Torment for Trixy. H. Janson
Torment Was a Redhead. Richard Williams
Torment Was a Woman. B. Carson
Tormented. D. Daniels
Tormented. F. E. Smith
Tormented. C. Weston
Tormenter. B. Swift
Tormentors. G. Bellairs
Torn Curtain. R. Wormser
Torn Letter. E. Balmer
Torn-Out Page. Dora Russell
Torrid Temptress. H. Janson
Torrington Square Mystery. M. L. Eades
Tortoiseshell Cat. N. Royde-Smith
Tortuous Trails. H. Footner
Torture Chamber and other stories. V. Van Der Elst

Torture Contract. F. Scarpetta
Torture Island. I. R. G. Hart
Torture Machine. D. Dayle
Torture Machine. P. Tabori
Torture Trust. B. House
Tortured Angel. D. Garth
Tortured Boy. H. C. Davis
Tortured Heart. E. Southworth
Tortured Love. H. Duval
Tortured Path. K. F. Crossen
Torturer. P. Saxon
Torturer's Horse. R. Inman
Torvick Affair. M. Sariola
Toss of a Coin. N. Carter
Toss of a Penny. N. Carter
Touch a French Pom-Pom. J. P. Carstairs
Touch and Go. L. Della
Touch and Go. J. Middlemass
Touch and Go. E. C. Vivian
Touch and Go. P. Wentworth
Touch of Danger. James Jones
Touch of Darkness. J. Crowe
Touch of Death. J. Creasey
Touch of Death. C. Williams
Touch of Drama. G. Cullingford
Touch of Evil. Arthur MacLean
Touch of Evil. W. Masterson
Touch of Fear. J. Ware
Touch of Jonah. L. Holton
Touch of Malice. J. Wainwright
Touch of Murder. J. B. Cearley
Touch of Myrrh. Charlotte Hunt
Touch of Purple. E. Trevor
Touch of Red. W. Fennerton
Touch of Stagefright. J. Davey
Touch of the Child, and other stories. T. Gallon
Touch of the Nettle. J. M. Scott
Touch of the Sun. H. B. Kaye
Touch of the Witch. J. Wetherell
Touch of Thunder. Brian Cooper
Touch Pitch. L. Peck
Touch the Lion's Paw. Derek Lambert
Touchfeather. J. Sangster
Touchfeather, Too. J. Sangster
Touching Evil. N. S. Rosen
Touchstone. E. Bradford
Tough and the Tender. A. MacLeod
Tough and the Toughs. J. Creasey
Tough Company. C. Dawe
Tough Cop. J. Roeburt
Tough Die Hard. Robert Martin
Tough for You, Hazel. D. Foster
Tough Ghosts. W. J. Elliott
Tough Guys. M. Spillane
Tough Justice. San Antonio
Tough on the Wops. B. Toler
Tough One to Lose. T. Kenrick
Tough Spot for Cupid and other stories. P. Cheyney
Tough Town. J. Karney
Toughs Afloat. M. Hervey
Toughs Ashore. M. Hervey
Tour. D. Ely
Tour de Force. C. Brand
Tour de Force. P. Cleife
Tour of Terror. J. W. Bobin
Touring Company Crime. A. Steffens Hardy
Tourist Trap. Ted Stratton
Tournament. J. Q.
Tournelles Plot. H. Drummond
Towards Tomorrow. J. Blackmore
Towards Zero. A. Christie
Towards Zero. G. Verner
Tower. P. M. Hubbard
Tower. R. M. Stern
Tower Hill Mystery. A. W. Barrett
Tower Mystery. P. McGuire
Tower of Babel. M. L. West
Tower of Darkness. H. Hawton
Tower of Evil. J. Rhode

Tower of Hate. F. Shroyer
Tower of Kilraven. C. Crowe
Tower of Monte Rado. Sheila Ross
Tower of Strength. N. Carter
Tower of Terror. J. I. Lawrence
Tower of the Crow. D. Polk
Tower Room. D. Daniels
Tower Room. M. L. Roby
Tower Room. D. Spicer
Tower Room Mystery. R. St. Clair
Towers of Fear. C. Farr
Towers of Love. S. Birmingham
Towers of Silence. David St. John
Towers of Terror. D. Dayle
Town Cried Murder. L. Ford
Town Hall Crime. A. Blair
Town Is Full of Rumors. R. Wilson
Town Lady and Country Lass. F. Warden
Town of Masks. D. S. Davis
Town of Shadows. J. Drummond
Town Parole. Alex Hamilton
Town That Went Sick. S. Truss
Townsend Murder Mystery. O. R. Cohen
Toy. K. Booton
Toy Lamb. B. Flynn
Toying with Fate. N. Carter
Toyland. Mark Smith
Toys of Death. G. D. H. Cole
Toys of Desperation. A. Crockett
Traced and Tracked. J. M'Govan
Traced Through a Dream. C. Courteney
Tracer of Lost Persons. R. W. Chambers
Traces of Brillhart. H. Brean
Traces of Merrilee. H. Brean
Track of Midnight. G. F. Scott
Track of the Beast. Ralph Hayes
Track of the Slayer. B. Strong
Tracked Across the Atlantic. N. Carter
Tracked Across the Seas. Wilfred Barclay
Tracked and Taken. D. Donovan
Tracked by a Female Detective. Old Sleuth
Tracked by a Pin. R. Hackstaff
Tracked by a Tattoo. F. Hume
Tracked by a Woman. "Goldey"
Tracked by a Woman. Old Sleuth
Tracked by Fate. F. Hume
Tracked by the Ogpu. E. Jepson
Tracked by Wireless. W. LeQueux
Tracked Down. L. Edgley
Tracked Down. H. Hill
Tracked on a Wheel. Old Sleuth
Tracked Out. A. W. A'Beckett
Tracked to Death. M. Redwing
Tracked to Doom. D. Donovan
Tracked to His Doom. J. K. Stafford
Tracked to the West. N. Ridley
Tracker Tracked. G. Furnivall
Tracker Tracked. B. Wayde
Tracking of K.K. D. Grey
Trackless Death. A. Livingston
Trackless Thing. J. Atholl
Tracks in the Snow. G. R. Benson
Trade-Off. V. B. Miller
Trade Wind. M. M. Kaye
Trademark of a Traitor. K. M. Knight
Trader Brook. K. Hayles
Trader Random. O. Binns
Trader's Daughter. W. M. Graydon
Trader's Licence. J. England
Trading with Bodies. Griff

Trafalgar Square. Gavin Holt
Trafalgar Square Mystery. C. Brisbane
Traffic in Souls. E. H. Ball
Traffic with Evil. A. Johns
Tragedies of Oak Hurst. B. Marean
Tragedy After Tea. C. Ashton
Tragedy and Strategy. Old Sleuth
Tragedy at Beechcroft. A. Fielding
Tragedy at Blue Aloes. M. Richmond
Tragedy at Cumberland Park. Arthur Russell
Tragedy at Draythorpe. L. Grex
Tragedy at Freyne. Anthony Gilbert
Tragedy at Law. C. Hare
Tragedy at Ravensthorpe. J. J. Connington
Tragedy at the Beach Club. W. A. Johnston
Tragedy at the Thirteenth Hole. M. Burton
Tragedy at the Unicorn. J. Rhode
Tragedy at Twelvetrees. A. J. Rees
Tragedy at Wembley. C. F. Gregg
Tragedy in a Brick Box. J. Budd
Tragedy in Blue. M. Bramhall
Tragedy in E Flat. L. Gribble
Tragedy in Pewsey Chart. H. Willett
Tragedy in the Dark. Elaine Hamilton
Tragedy in the Hollow. F. W. Crofts
Tragedy in the Rue de la Paix. A. Belot
Tragedy in Turquoise. L. Trimble
Tragedy Indeed. A. Belot
Tragedy Near Tring. J. K. Ryland
Tragedy of a Flirtation. H. B. Vogel
Tragedy of an Indiscretion. J. W. Brodie-Innes
Tragedy of Andrea. E. P. Oppenheim
Tragedy of Ascot Mills. S. Campbell
Tragedy of Brinkwater. M. L. Moodey
Tragedy of Captain Harrison. R. C. J.
Tragedy of Featherstone. B. L. Farjeon
Tragedy of Ida Noble. W. C. Russell
Tragedy of Redmount. M. E. Holmes
Tragedy of the Bromleigh's. R. Hardinge
Tragedy of the Chinese Mine. I. Greig
Tragedy of the Great Emerald. W. Chesney
Tragedy of the Silver Moon. A. Gask
Tragedy of the West End Actress. J. G. Brandon
Tragedy of Windyridge. R. Hardinge
Tragedy of X. B. Ross
Tragedy of Y. B. Ross
Tragedy of Z. B. Ross
Tragedy on the Line. J. Rhode
Tragic Case of John Renold. H. Allan
Tragic Case of the Station Master's Legacy. J. Drummond
Tragic Curtain. S. H. Page
Tragic Lesson. J. H. Vahey
Tragic Mystery. J. Hawthorne
Tragic Mystery. Old Sleuth
Tragic Quest. F. W. Irwin
Tragic Quest. Old Sleuth
Tragic Target. M. V. Heberden
Trail from Devil's Country. A. M. Treynor
Trail of a Human Tiger. N. Carter
Trail of a Tramp. N. Quarry
Trail of Adventure. O. Binns
Trail of Blood. J. Potter
Trail of Blood. C. Rushton
Trail of Death. W. M. Graydon
Trail of Deceit. W. C. Tuttle
Trail of Doom. R. C. Armour
Trail of Fear. A. Armstrong
Trail of Fu Manchu. S. Rohmer
Trail of Raider No. 1. S. Blakesley
Trail of the Axe. R. Cullum
Trail of the Barrow. Anonymous
Trail of the Barrow. J. Mooney
Trail of the Beast. A. Abdullah
Trail of the Black King. A. Armstrong
Trail of the Catspaw. N. Carter
Trail of the Cloven Hoof. A. Eadie
Trail of the Dead. B. F. Robinson

Trail of the Dope Chief. J. Hunter
Trail of the Fingerprints. N. Carter
Trail of the Ghosts. N. Thurley
Trail of the Hunted. R. Wilkes-Hunter
Trail of the Lonely River. H. Edmonds
Trail of the Lotto. A. Armstrong
Trail of the Missing Scientist. A. Parsons
Trail of the Old Lag. W. J. Bayfield
Trail of the Ruby. W. Proudfoot
Trail of the Serpent. M. E. Braddon
Trail of the Serpent. T. E. B. Clarke
Trail of the Serpent. E. Southworth
Trail of the Serpent. C. Worth
Trail of the Shadow. H. Bedford-Jones
Trail of the Shadow. S. M. Parkman
Trail of the Skull. Gavin Holt
Trail of the Squid. H. Wickham
Trail of the Tiger. R. C. Armour
Trail of the White Knight. B. Graeme
Trail of the White Turban. C. Brisbane
Trail of the Yoshiga. N. Carter
Trail to Death. R. Wallace
Trail to Kingdom Come. W. C. Tuttle
Trail to the End. J. K. Stafford
Trail to Treason. C. Dixon
Trail Under the Sea. R. H. Poole
Trailer Mystery. R. St. Clair
Trailer Park. J. Vaughn
Trailing Death. G. Begbie
Trailing of the Picaroon. Herman Landon
Train. G. Simenon
Train a Fast Gun. R. Wilkes-Hunter
Train from Katanga. Wilbur Smith
Trainer's Secret. A. Steffens Hardy
Trains That Met in the Blizzard. R. P. Woodward
Traitor. L. Allan
Traitor! W. H. Baker
Traitor. S. Horler
Traitor. G. Sheen
Traitor. H. Wouk
Traitor and Loyalist. A. R. Weekes
Traitor and Spy. A. Steffens Hardy
Traitor Betrayed. O. Mills
Traitor Dragoon. W. M. Graydon
Traitor Game. D. McLeish
Traitor in London. F. Hume
Traitor in the Fleet. E. L. MacKeag
Traitor Mask. F. A. Smith
Traitor Spy. T. C. H. Jacobs
Traitor Unmasked. G. Davison
Traitors. P. Chester
Traitors. E. P. Oppenheim
Traitor's Bridge. N. Sligh
Traitor's Crime. R. Jeffries
Traitor's Cross. F. Grierson
Traitor's Doom. J. Creasey
Traitor's Exit. J. Gardner
Traitors' Gate. S. Harvester
Traitor's Gate. G. Osborne
Traitor's Gate. E. Wallace
Traitor's Gate. D. Wheatley
Traitor's Gate and other stories. G. M. Fenn
Traitor's Harvest. M. Richmond
Traitor's Island. F. Hay
Traitor's Island. J. Pendower
Traitor's Market. G. Dickson
Traitor's Mountain. S. Styles
Traitor's Pass. D. Duff
Traitor's Purse. M. Allingham
Traitor's Road. D. Daniels
Traitor's Rock. G. E. Rochester
Traitor's Tide. R. Goyne
Traitor's Way. B. Hamilton

Traitor's Wife. D. Montross
Traitor's Wooing. H. Hill
Tramp. E. Wallace
Trample an Empire. W. Mole
Tramplers. J. Manor
Tramp's Evidence. E. C. Vivian
Transactions of Lord Louis Lewis. R. Pertwee
Transactions of Oliver Prince. R. E. Forbes
Transatlantic Ghost. D. Gardiner
Transatlantic Puzzle. M. O. Rolfe
Transatlantic Trouble. L. Grex
Transcendental Murder. J. Langton
Transformation of Timothy. T. Cobb
Transformation Scene. C. Houghton
Transgressing the Law. F. Whittaker
Transgressor. F. Thompson
Transgressors. J. Thompson
Transient Guest, and Other Episodes. E. Saltus
Transit of the Red Dragon, and other tales. E. Phillpotts
Transome Murder Mystery. P. Luck
Transparent Traitor. F. Gerard
Transplant. J. Weatherhead
Transport Murders. J. G. Brandon
Transvection Machine. E. D. Hoch
Trap. J. Beckett
Trap. D. Billany
Trap. John Burke
Trap. J. L. Cotte
Trap. D. Donovan
Trap. M. Foster
Trap. George E. Jones
Trap. E. Jordan
Trap. N. Karta
Trap. Mrs. C. Kernahan
Trap. J. Knowler
Trap. D. Winston
Trap for a Redhead. S. Palmer
Trap for Bellamy. P. Cheyney
Trap for Cinderella. S. Japrisot
Trap for Fools. J. Pendower
Trap for Lovers. J. Blackmore
Trap in the Tunnel. G. Ellinger
Trap #6. S. Ransome
Trap of Fate. I. D. Hardy
Trap of Tangled Wire. N. Carter
Trap Spider. K. Royce
Trap the Baron. A. Morton
Trapeze. M. Catto
Trapped. R. Hayward
Trapped. J. Hougron
Trapped. H. Innes
Trapped. L. Mantz
Trapped by a Female Detective. Old Sleuth
Trapped by a Woman. N. Carter
Trapped in His Own Net. N. Carter
Trapped Ones. L. Charbonneau
Trapper of Rat River. C. Stoddard
Trapper's Victim. C. Brisbane
Trapping the Moonshiners. Old Sleuth
Trappings Are Gorgeous. H. D. Dearden
Traps. F. Duerrenmatt
Traps Need Fresh Bait. A. A. Fair
Trash Stealer. J. Potts
Travel the Hard Way. M. Hervey
Traveling Butcher. P. Campbell
Traveling Corpse. K. Steel
Traveling Horseman. N. Luard
Traveling Skull. H. S. Keeler
Traveller Returns. P. Wentworth
Travelling Deadman. J. Varnam
Travelling Executioners. B. Newman
Travels with a Duchess. M. Gallie
Travels with My Aunt. G. Greene
Travers, a Mystery Story. R. B. Siddall
Trawl Adrift. E. L. Long
Treacherous Border. N. Thurley

Treacherous Road. S. Harvester
Treachery. K. Lindsay
Treachery at Guadamonte. D. Martyn
Treachery in Trieste. C. L. Leonard
Tread Gently, Death. R. P. Koehler
Tread Lightly, Angel. F. C. Davis
Tread Softly. B. Flynn
Tread Softly. P. Malloch
Tread Softly. F. Rickett
Tread Softly in This Place. B. Cleeve
Tread Softly, Nurse Scott. Marilyn Ross
Tread Warily. Hilary Mason
Tread Warily at Midnight. M. Carr
Treason at Home. Mrs. Greenough
Treason by Truth. W. H. Baker
Treason-Felony. J. Hill
Treason in My Breast. Anthony Gilbert
Treason in the Egg. L. A. G. Strong
Treason Line. D. Torr
Treason Remembered. W. H. Baker
Treason Under Seal. W. V. Cook
Treasure. A. E. Hotchner
Treasure at Greyladies. H. Leyford
Treasure for Treasure. Justin Scott
Treasure House of Martin Hews. E. P. Oppenheim
Treasure Hunt. T. Pace
Treasure Hunters. W. H. Baker
Treasure Nets. G. Fairlie
Treasure of Big Waters. R. Cullum
Treasure of Captain Scarlett. A. Sergeant
Treasure of Caricar. R. W. Hinds
Treasure of Christophe. O. Binns
Treasure of Scarland. M. B. Dix
Treasure of the Cosa Nostra. J. Ridgway
Treasure of the Manchus. R. C. Armour
Treasure of the Sun. H. McCutcheon
Treasure of Wycliffe House. J. Judson
Treasure on Camise. Alan Graham
Treasure on Earth. Laurence Kirk
Treasure on the Broads. W. G. Elliott
Treasure Royal. W. Garrett
Treasure Trail. R. Pertwee
Treasure Train. A. B. Reeve
Treasury-Officer's Wooing. C. C. Lewis
Treasury's Millions. B. Wayde
Treble Chance Murder. V. Gunn
Treble Cross. H. Howard
Tree Frog. M. Woodhouse
Tree of Evil. R. Morrison
Tree of Heaven. E. Raymond
Treen and Wild Horses. P. F. Gaye
Tregaron's Daughter. M. Brent
Tregarthen. G. Norway
Tregarthen's Wife. F. M. White
Tregear's Treasure. J. Remenham
Trelawny. I. Holland
Trelawny's Fell. I. Holland
Tremayne Case. Alan Thomas
Tremayne's Wife. Charlotte Hunt
Trembling Earth. F. Clifford
Trembling Earth Contract. P. Atlee
Trembling Flame. L. J. Vance
Trembling Hills. P. A. Whitney
Trembling Thread. C. Franklin
Tremendous Event. M. Leblanc
Tremlett Diamonds. A. St. Aubyn
Tremlow Murder Case. R. Dark
Tremolo. E. Borneman
Tremor of Forgery. P. Highsmith
Tremor of Intent. A. Burgess
Trench's Wives. Anonymous
Trent Fights Again. W. Martyn
Trent Intervenes. E. C. Bentley
Trent of the Lone Hand. W. Martyn
Trent Trail. W. Martyn

Trent's Last Case. E. C. Bentley
Trent's Own Case. E. C. Bentley
Trespass. A. Askew
Trespass. F. Knebel
Trespass. N. Tranter
Trespass in the Sun. J. Pudney
Trespassers. A. Coburn
Trespassers Will Die. M. Seuffert
Trevayne. J. Ryder
Treveryan. A. Du Maurier
Trevlyn Hold. H. Wood
Trevor Case. N. S. Lincoln
Trewinnot of Guy's. Mrs. C. Kernahan
Triad. M. Leader
Trial. W. Harrington
Trial. D. M. Mankiewicz
Trial and Error. A. Berkeley
Trial and Terror. L. Treat
Trial and Triumph. Anonymous
Trial at Bannock. J. Bier
Trial by Ambush. L. Ford
Trial by Desire. K. G. Ballard
Trial by Fury. C. Rice
Trial by Murder. E. S. Holding
Trial by Murder. G. Hoster
Trial by Ordeal. O. Mills
Trial by Perjury. J. Creighton
Trial by Slander. T. Macrae
Trial by Terror. P. Gallico
Trial by Terror. R. Lockridge
Trial by Water. H. Footner
Trial by Wilderness. T. M. Longstreth
Trial from Ambush. L. Ford
Trial of Alvin Boaker. J. Reywall
Trial of Bebe Donge. G. Simenon
Trial of Billy Jack. H. Liebling
Trial of Callista Blake. E. Pangborn
Trial of Gideon, and Countess Almara's Murder. J. Hawthorne
Trial of Gregor Kaska. F. Andreas
Trial of John and Henry Norton. R. Puccetti
Trial of Lizzie Borden and other radio plays. D. Henderson
Trial of Lobo Icheka. D. Creed
Trial of Mary Dugan. B. Veiller
Trial of Mary Dugan. W. A. Wolff
Trial of Parson Finch. S. Gibney
Trial of Scotland Yard. Stuart Martin
Trial of Soren Qvist. Janet Lewis
Trial of the Golden Girl. R. Dolphin
Trial of Vincent Doon. W. Oursler
Trial of Vivienne Ware. K. M. Ellis
Triall Case. L. Durie
Trials and Tribulations of Aaron Amsted. K. A. Lapatine
Trials of a City Detective. Anonymous
Trials of Commander McTurk. C. J. C. Hyne
Trials of Love. H. M. Jones
Trials of O'Brien. R. L. Fish
Trials of the Phideas. E. L. Long
Triangle. M. Leighton
Triangle Has Four Sides. P. Barrington
Triangle Man. G. F. Gibbs
Triangle Murder. R. Batchelor
Triangle of Fear. J. N. Chance
Triangle of Terror. Gwyn Evans
Triangle of the Grey Wolf. J. Addiscombe
Tribal Town. H. Munro
Tribunal. P. Bair
Trick of Time. F. Hume
Trick or Treat. D. M. Disney
Trick, Trial and Triumph. A. Cheviot
Tricked and Trapped. I. Stark
Tricks and Triumphs. Old Sleuth
Tricks of the Trade. R. L. Fish
Tried for Her Life. E. Southworth
Tried for His Life. Anonymous

Tried for His Life. B. Hemyng
Trieste. D. Cory
Trificante Treasure. D. Winston
Trigger Finger. C. R. Cooper
Trigger Man. R. Posner
Trigger Mortis. F. Kane
Trigger of Conscience. R. O. Chipperfield
Triggerman. B. Rossi
Triggerman! G. Usher
Triggers Are Trumps. W. J. Elliott
Trilogy in Jeopardy. H. Kane
Trimmed Lamp. O. Henry
Trinity. R. Bridges
Trinity in Violence. H. Kane
Trio for Blunt Instruments. R. Stout
Trip to Eternity. G. Monro
Trip Trap. J. Rathbone
Triple Bite. B. Flynn
Triple Crime. N. Carter
Triple Cross. Joe Barry
Triple Cross. J. Roeburt
Triple Cross. J. K. Stafford
Triple Cross Murders. A. R. Long
Triple Death. C. Carnac
Triple Identity. N. Carter
Triple Jeopardy. R. Stout
Triple Knavery. N. Carter
Triple Knock. N. Carter
Triple Mirror. J. D. Gautier
Triple Mirror. L. James
Triple Murder. Colin Hughes
Triple Murder. C. Wells
Triple Mystery. A. Luehrmann
Triple Quest. E. R. Punshon
Triple Slay. Adam Knight
Triple Terror. H. Kane
Triple Threat. K. Roos
Triple Zero. A. Whitney
Tripwire. B. Garfield
Triumph. C. F. Coe
Triumph for Inspector West. J. Creasey
Triumph of Elaine. A. B. Reeve
Triumph of Evil. P. Kavanagh
Triumph of Hilary Blackland. B. Mitford
Triumph of Inspector Maigret. G. Simenon
Triumph of John Kars. R. Cullum
Triumph of McLean. G. Goodchild
Triumph of Manhood. M. Leighton
Triumphal Chariot. P. H. Irving
Triumphant Defeat. B. Christianson
Triumphant Prodigal. W. Martyn
Triumphs of Eugene Valmont. R. Barr
Triumphs of Fabian Field: Criminologist. D. Donovan
Triumvirate. H. Baldwin Taylor
Trixy. Mrs. G. Sheldon
Trodmore Turf Mystery. F. Johnston
Troika. S. Harvester
Troika. D. Montross
Trojan Cow. G. Tippette
Trojan Hearse. R. S. Prather
Trojan Horse. H. Innes
Trooper MacLean. C. Stoddard
Trooper O'Neill. G. Goodchild
Tropic Moon. G. Simenon
Trot. D. Ely
Trotter. B. Fforde
Trouble! B. Graeme
Trouble A-Brewing. J. Bude
Trouble Aboard. T. Muir
Trouble Ahead. E. Gunton
Trouble at Glaye. B. Reynolds
Trouble at Hanard. V. Beynon-Harris

Trouble at Harrison High. J. Farris
Trouble at Moon Dance. A. B. Guthrie
Trouble at Number Seven. G. Bullett
Trouble at Pinelands. E. M. Poate
Trouble at Saxby's. J. Creasey
Trouble at the Inn. Roland Daniel
Trouble at the JHC. W. C. Tuttle
Trouble at the Top. C. B. Flood
Trouble at Turkey Hill. K. M. Knight
Trouble at Wrekin Farm. J. Bell
Trouble Buster. N. W. Firth
Trouble Calling. A. Bocca
Trouble Comes Double. R. P. Hansen
Trouble Follows Me. K. Millar
Trouble in Burma. V. W. Mason
Trouble in College. F. J. Whaley
Trouble in Paradise. R. L. Fish
Trouble in the Air. K. Kay
Trouble in the Bank. H. C. Davis
Trouble in Thor. J. Valentine
Trouble in Tokyo. J. Bruce
Trouble in Triplicate. R. Stout
Trouble in West Two. K. Fitzgerald
Trouble Is a Dame. C. Brown
Trouble Is My Business. R. Chandler
Trouble Is My Name. R. Dolphin
Trouble Is My Name. S. Marlowe
Trouble Makers. C. Fremlin
Trouble Man. J. D. Black
Trouble on the Frontier. D. Christie
Trouble on the Thames. V. Bridges
Trouble on Tuesday. S. Carver
Trouble Rides Tall. H. Whittington
Trouble Trailer. W. C. Tuttle
Trouble with Ava. S. Friedman
Trouble with Fidelity. G. Malcolm-Smith
Trouble with Harry. J. T. Story
Trouble with Love. B. Heatter
Trouble with Murder. R. Bax
Trouble with Penelope. B. Healey
Trouble with Product X. Joan Aiken
Trouble with Ruth. R. Rayner
Trouble with Series Three. M. Kenyon
Trouble with Tycoons. H. B. Taylor
Trouble with Women. J. P. Heggy
Troublecross. Jessica Mann
Troubled Harvest. E. Woodward
Troubled Heritage. M. Richmond
Troubled House. K. Booton
Troubled Journey. R. Lockridge
Troubled Midnight. R. Garland
Troubled Mind. S. Davis
Troubled Night. R. Drayton
Troubled Star. J. August
Troubled Tranton. W. E. Norris
Troubled Waters. H. Hill
Troublemaker. J. Hansen
Troublemaker. J. Potts
Troubles of Colonel Marwood. A. C. Fox-Davies
Troubles of Doctor Cortland. S. Friedman
Troubleshooter. D. Dodge
Troupe of Star-Crossed Killers. T. Journet
Trout in the Milk. H. Holman
Trout in the Milk. M. Underwood
Trout Inn Mystery. W. Greenleaves
Trout Inn Tragedy. W. Greenleaves
Truce of the Bear. H. C. McNeile
True Adventures of the Secret Service. C. E. Russell
True Blue, the Detective. Old Sleuth
True Detective Stories. A. L. Drummond
True Detective Stories. M. Moser
True Detective Stories from the Archives of the Pinkertons. C. Moffett
True Son of the Beast! C. Brown
True Stories of Celebrated Crimes. G. Barton
True Tales of the D.C.I. K. Detzer

Truly Remarkable Life of the Beautiful Helen Jewett. Anonymous
Trump Card. D. Vane
Trumpets of November. W. S. Thurston
Trunk Call. J. J. Farjeon
Trunk Call Mystery. J. J. Farjeon
Trunk Call to Murder. E. Radford
Trunk Crime. E. Percy
Trunk Crime Number Three. W. Tyrer
Trust a Woman? R. Foley
Trust McLean. G. Goodchild
Trust-Money. W. Westall
Trust the Police. P. Elliott
Trust the Saint. L. Charteris
Trust Them and Die. Jeffry Scott
Trusted Like the Fox. R. Marshall
Trusted Like the Fox. S. Woods
Trusted Rogue. N. Carter
Trusting Victim. D. Lyon
Trusty Servant. G. V. McFadden
Truth About Belle Gunness. L. De La Torre
Truth About Claire Veryan. S. Truss
Truth About Lord Tench. D. Stuart
Truth About My Father. P. Martens
Truth About the Case. M. F. Goron
Truth About Unicorns. B. J. Reynolds
Truth Came Out. E. R. Punshon
Truth Comes Limping. J. J. Connington
Truth Game. D. Hurd
Truth of the Matter. J. Lutz
Truth or Dare. Jacqueline Wilson
Truth with Her Boots On. H. Cecil
Truxton Cipher. H. Gruppe
Try Anything Once. A. A. Fair
Try Anything Once. J. Pendower
Try Anything Twice. P. Cheyney
Trying Patient. J. Payn
Tryst for a Tragedy. E. C. R. Lorac
Tryst with Terror. W. Winthrop
Tsing-Boum. N. Freeling
Tube. P. Boileau
Tudor Garden Mystery. G. Verner
Tuesday Club Murders. A. Christie
Tuesday the Rabbi Saw Red. H. Kemelman
Tule Marsh Murder. N. B. Mavity
Tulip Tree. H. Rigsby
Tumbled House. Winston Graham
Tumbling River Range. W. C. Tuttle
Tumult and the Shouting. H. Gibbs
Tumult in San Benito. John Arnold
Tumult in the North. G. R. Preedy
Tumulto. B. Williams
Tuna Is Not for Eating. B. Kelly
Tundra Trail. C. Stoddard
Tune to a Corpse. P. Drax
Tuned for Murder. K. Robeson
Tunnel. A. Bristowe
Tunnel. B. Kendrick
Tunnel from Calais. A. D. Divine
Tunnel Mystery. J. C. Lenehan
Tunnel Mystery and Its Solution. A. W. A'Beckett
Tunnel 13. M. M. Raison
Tunnel to Doom. R. W. Hinds
Turbulence. C. Hodder-Williams
Turbulent Duchess. P. Brebner
Turbulent Tales. R. Sabatini
Turf and Veldt. D. J. Belgrave
Turf Bandits. E. Woodward
Turf Conspiracy. N. Gould
Turf Crook. F. Johnston
Turf Mystery. J. Fairfax-Blakeborough
Turf Racketeers. F. Johnston
Turkish Mafia Conspiracy. Ralph Hayes
Turkish Spy. Charles Cooper

Title Index

Turmoil at Brede. S. Truss
Turmoil in Zion. G. Bellairs
Turn Back from Death. H. Desmond
Turn Blue, You Murderers. Michael Brett
Turn Killer. B. Lecomber
Turn Left for Danger. B. Gray
Turn Left for Murder. S. Marlowe
Turn Left or Be Killed. N. Ashbaugh
Turn of a Card. N. Carter
Turn of a Wheel. A. Rowe
Turn of the Screw. Henry James
Turn of the Table. J. Stagge
Turn of the Tide. F. M. White
Turn on the Heat. A. A. Fair
Turn up a Stone. A. Cade
Turncoat. H. G. Evart
Turncoat. G. Langelaan
Turning Point. H. Clevely
Turning Point. L. Tracy
Turning Sword. S. Bayne
Turning Sword. G. V. McFadden
Turning Wheel. D. Donovan
Turnpike House. F. Hume
Turns of Time. P. Audemars
Turnstile of Night. W. Allison
Turnstile of Night. A. M. Williamson
Turquoise Clues. A. Cecil
Turquoise Hazard. A. B. Caldwell
Turquoise Lament. J. D. MacDonald
Turquoise Mask. P. A. Whitney
Turquoise Shop. F. Crane
Turquoise Spike. F. Archer
Turquoise Talisman. S. Wagner
Turquoise Trail. W. C. Tuttle
Turquoise/Yellow Case. P. K. Palmer
Turret Room. C. Armstrong
Tuscany Madonna. M. Canfield
Tut, Tut! Mr. Tutt. A. Train
Tutt and Mr. Tutt. A. Train
Tutt for Tutt. A. Train
Twana. A. Du Camp
Tweak the Devil's Nose. R. Deming
Tweedledum and Tweedledee. Alec Coppel
Tween Snow and Fire. B. Mitford
Twelfth Crime. S. Cross
Twelfth Mile. E. G. Perrault
Twelfth Night Murders. C. Ryland
12th of Never. D. Heyes
Twelve Apostles. G. Verner
Twelve Chinamen and a Woman. J. H. Chase
Twelve Chinks and a Woman. J. H. Chase
Twelve Disguises. F. Beeding
Twelve Girls in the Garden. Shane Martin
Twelve Horses and the Hangman's Noose. G. Mitchell
Twelve in a Grave. N. Carter
Twelve Maidens. S. Farrar
Twelve Midnight Street. R. Davis
12 Must Die. Zorro
Twelve on Endurance. Michael Hastings
Twelve Steps at Miramar. M. Reisner
Twelve Tales. G. Allen
Twelve Tales of Suspense and the Supernatural. D. Grubb
12:30 from Croydon. F. W. Crofts
Twelve Tin Boxes. N. Carter
Twelve to Dine. E. Nisot
Twelve Trains to Babylon. A. Connable
Twelve Wise Men. N. Carter
20th of July. H. H. Kirst
Twenty East of Greenwich. J. Lodwick
2835 Mayfair. F. Richardson
Twenty-Fifth Hour. C. V. Gheorghiu
Twenty-Fifth Hour. M. Kelly
Twenty-First Burr. V. Lauriston
Twenty-Five Sanitary Inspectors. R. East
Twenty-Four Hours. L. T. Meade
24 Hours to Kill. J. McKimmey
24th Horse. H. Pentecost
24th Level. K. Benton
Twenty Minutes to Kill. A. M. Chase

Twenty-One Clues. J. J. Connington
Twenty-One Stories. G. Greene
Twenty Per Cent. T. Macrae
Twenty Plus Two. F. Gruber
27th Ride. A. D. Welton
Twenty-Six Clues. I. Ostrander
26 Three-Minute Thrillers. N. Morland
Twenty-Third Man. G. Mitchell
Twenty-Thousand Thieves. Eric Lambert
22 Brothers. D. Sage
Twenty-Two Windows. Roland Daniel
Twenty Years of Hate. D. Stuart
Twentymen. P. Purser
Twice American. E. M. Ingram
Twice as Dead. D. Spade
Twice Broken. M. Peterson
Twice Checked. Graham Hastings
Twice Dead. J. Bude
Twice Dead. E. M. Channon
Twice Dead. J. Rhode
Twice Dead. C. Robertson
Twice Lost. P. Paul
Twice Murdered. C. H. Snow
Twice Murdered Man. N. Toye
Twice Retired. R. Lockridge
Twice Round the Clock. B. Houston
Twice So Fair. N. Tyre
Twice Ten Thousand Miles. F. Lynch
Twice Times Murder. M. Peterson
Twice-Told Tales. N. Hawthorne
Twice Tried. W. LeQueux
Twice Upon a Crime. P. Quinn
Twice Wronged! J. W. Bobin
Twickenham Peerage. R. Marsh
Twig Is Bent. E. Thompson
Twilight at Dawn. M. Murray
Twilight Man. F. Gruber
Twilight of Death. L. Langley
Twilight People. R. Batchelor
Twilight Web. W. E. D. Ross
'Twill Soon Be Dark. Ethel L. White
Twillford Mystery. G. F. Scott
Twin Athletes. Old Sleuth
Twin Detectives. Anonymous
Twin Detectives. K. F. Hill
Twin Killing. G. Bagby
Twin Mystery. N. Carter
Twin Serpents. R. S. Thorn
Twin Sisters. R. Marsh
Twin Tales. A. Stringer
Twin Ventriloquists. Old Sleuth
Twinkleface, the Merry Elf. M. Peterson
Twins Murder Case. H. G. Hutchinson
Twins of Suffering Creek. R. Cullum
Twist and other stories. J. J. Farjeon
Twist for Two. H. Janson
Twist in the Trail. W. J. Bayfield
Twist of a Stick. G. Peters
Twist of Sand. G. Jenkins
Twist of the Knife. V. Canning
Twist of the Rope. J. Bude
Twist of Yarn. E. Lookabee
Twist the Knife Slowly. K. Clugston
Twisted Cameo. K. Kimbrough
Twisted Cross. A. Pinchot
Twisted Evidence. M. B. Dix
Twisted Face. F. A. Kummer
Twisted Face Defends His Title. G. Davison
Twisted Face Strikes Again. G. Davison
Twisted Face, The Avenger. G. Davison
Twisted Foot. H. M. Rideout
Twisted Grin. A. Salcroft

Twisted Mirror. L. Lee
Twisted Nerve. Peter Evans
Twisted Ones. V. Packer
Twisted People. J. Philips
Twisted Tales. L. H. Fox
Twisted Tales. Christopher Ward
Twisted Thing. M. Spillane
Twisted Thread. J. Moffatt
Twisted Tongues. Jonathan Burke
Twisted Trails. W. C. Tuttle
Twisted Wire. R. Falkirk
Twister. E. Wallace
Twister's Double. C. Davy
Twittering Bird Mystery. H. C. Bailey
'Twixt Devil and Deep Sea. A. M. Williamson
Twixt Sword and Glove. A. C. Gunter
Two. C. Trieschman
Two After Malic. L. Peters
Two Against Scotland Yard. D. Frome
Two and Two Make Five. T. E. B. Clarke
Two and Two Make Five. B. Graeme
Two and Two Make Twenty-Two. G. Bristow
Two Apaches of Paris. A. Askew
Two Aunts and a Grandmother. T. B. Morris
Two Black Pearls. M. Leighton
Two Bullets for Briggs. D. MacDonald
Two by Day and One by Night. V. Bell
Two by Tricks. E. Yates
Two Clues. E. S. Gardner
Two Conspirators. Old Sleuth
Two Conspirators. M. O. Rolfe
Two Crosses. W. J. Newton
Two Dames Too Many. M. Perelli
Two Days, Two Nights. P. O. Sundman
Two Dead. V. Loder
Two Dead Charwomen. N. Morland
Two Dead Men. J. Anker
Two Deaths for a Penny. N. Burnaby
Two Deaths Must Die. R. Himmel
Two Destinies. W. Collins
Two Died at Three. C. F. Gregg
Two Died in Singapore. J. Sherwood
Two Ends to the Town. J. Bude
Two-Face. E. Dudley
Two-Faced Man. V. Vanardy
Two Faced Murder. Jean Leslie
Two Faces of Death. W. Wright
Two Faces of Fear. J. Wellsley
Two Faces of January. P. Highsmith
Two False Moves. J. Middlemass
Two Feet from Heaven. P. C. Wren
Two-Five to Mardon. B. Field
Two Flights Up. M. R. Rinehart
Two-Fold Inheritance. G. Boothby
Two for a Pair. D. Walshe
Two for Inspector West. J. Creasey
Two for Tanner. Lawrence Block
Two for the Grave. R. B. Houston
Two for the Money. M. Halliday
Two for the Price of One. T. Kenrick
Two Forces. E. W. Elkington
Two Gay Sleuths. H. R. Kaye
Two Girls and a Saint. G. Warden
Two Goodwins. R. M. Gilchrist
Two Graphs. J. Rhode
Two Gun Hedgehopper. T. Wallace
Two-Gun Sue. D. Grant
Two Guns for Hire. N. MacNeil
Two Hot to Handle. E. Lacy
Two Hours to Doom. P. Bryant
Two Houses on the Cliff. M. V. Woodgate
£250 Marriage Case. J. G. Brandon
Two Hundred Ghost. H. Hamilton
200% Rule. E. A. Pollitz
Two Hundred Pounds Reward, and other tales. J. Payn

Two If by Sea. R. Bax
Two Imposters. P. Audemars
Two in a Tangle. W. LeQueux
Two in Shadow. J. Blackmore
Two in the Bush. G. Blumberg
Two in the Dark. G. G. Magnus
Two Kinds of Murder. D. MacDonald
Two Kisses. H. Smart
Two Knaves and a Queen. F. Barrett
Two Knocks for Death. W. Jackson
2 L.O. W. S. Masterman
Two Ladies in Verona. Lionel Black
Two Lads and a Lass, and other stories. F. Warden
Two Legacies. Mrs. C. Kernahan
Two Little Children and How They Grew. D. M. Disney
Two Little Rich Girls. M. G. Eberhart
Two Little Ships. E. L. Long
Two Lives in Parenthesis. George Long
Two Living and One Dead. S. Christiansen
Two London Fairies. G. R. Sims
Two Lovers Too Many. J. Fleming
Two Magics. Henry James
Two Meet Trouble. M. Halliday
Two Men from the East. T. A. Plummer
Two Men in Twenty. M. Procter
Two Men Missing. G. Ashe
Two Million. H. B. Vogel
Two Minute Warning. G. La Fountaine
Two Mrs. Carrolls. H. Arvonen
Two Mrs. Farrells. John Marsh
Two Moods of a Man. H. G. Hutchinson
Two Much! D. E. Westlake
Two Must Die. H. Kane
Two Must Die. C. Robertson
Two Mysteries. G. H. Teed
Two Names for Death. E. P. Fenwick
Two O'Clock Courage. G. Burgess
Two of Diamonds. L. Brock
Two on the Trail. H. Footner
Two Pardons. H. S. Vince
Two Pinches of Snuff. W. Westall
Two Plus Two. N. Carter
Two Plus Two Equals Minus Seven. J. F. Adams
Two Red Capsules. D. T. Lindsay
Two Sets to Murder. L. Peters
Two Shadows for Death. J. Wolf
Two Shadows Pass. Clifford King
Two Shots. P. Luck
Two Sisters. E. Southworth
Two Smart Dames. G. Ross
2 Spruce Lane. Gretchen Travis
Two-Star Pigeon. M. Wolfe
Two Stolen Idols. F. Packard
Two Strange Adventures. K. Cornwallis
Two Strange Ladies. H. S. Keeler
Two Strange Men. J. S. Clouston
Two Strokes of the Bell. C. H. Montague
Two Tales of the Occult. M. Eliade
Two-Thirds of a Ghost. H. McCloy
Two Thousand Maniacs! H. G. Lewis
Two Tickets Puzzle. J. J. Connington
Two Tickets to Destruction. G. S. Foster
Two Tickets to Tangier. V. W. Mason
Two-Timing Blonde. C. Brown
Two to Slay. H. Brinton
Two to Tangle. F. Kane
Two Undertakers. F. Beeding
Two Villains in One. N. Carter
Two-Way Frame. T. Harknett
Two-Way Mirror. D. Launay
Two-Way Witness. D. Franklin

Two Ways to Die. L. Thayer
Two Ways to Murder. E. Radford
Two Weeks Before Murder. W. Metcalfe
Two Weeks to Find a Killer. C. Davis
Two White Elephants. A. H. Veysey
Two Who Talked. Frank King
Two with a Gun. P. Malloch
Two Women. M. Pemberton
Two Women in Black. J. W. Postgate
Two Wonderful Detectives. Old Sleuth
Two Worlds of Peggy Scott. D. Daniels
Twopence for a Rat's Tail. S. M. Lott
Twopenny Box. J. N. Chance
Two's Company. M. Kennedy
Two's Two. J. S. Clouston
Tycoon and the Tigress. W. R. Cox
Tycoon of Crime. R. Wallace
Tycoon's Death-Bed. G. Bellairs
Tyger! Tyger! R. C. K. Ginn
Tyler Mystery. P. Temple
Typed for a Corpse. A. Pruitt
Typewritten Letter. R. H. Sherard
Typhoon. J. W. McConaughy
Typhoon Shipments. K. Klose
Typhoon's Secret. S. N. Sheridan
Tyson Murder Case. T. J. O'Connell

U

U-Boat in the Hebrides. A. D. Divine
Ubiquitous Yank. Old Sleuth
Ugly Customer. C. F. Gregg
Ugly Face of Love and other stories. G. Kersh
Ugly Woman. M. Cameron
Ugly Woman. W. O'Farrell
Uist Project. J. Wood
Ukridge. P. G. Wodehouse
Ullman Code. R. Bernhard
Ultimate Act. L. P. Bachmann
Ultimate Client. M. Avallone
Ultimate Conclusion. A. C. Fox-Davies
Ultimate Island. L. Sieveking
Ultimate Solution. E. Norden
Ultimatum. B. Meyer
Ultimatum. R. Rohmer
Ultraviolet Widow. F. Crane
Ultus, the Man from the Dead. R. Hodder
Umbrella Murder. C. Wells
Umgasi Diamonds. E. De Caire
Un Mystere (A Mystery). H. Greville
Unaccepted Death. H. Gilson
Unaccountable Crook. N. Carter
Unafraid. Gerald Butler
Unafraid. E. M. Ingram
Unaltered Cat. A. Lewin
Unappointed Rounds. D. M. Disney
Unbaited Trap. C. Cookson
Unbarred Door. C. H. Bullivant
Unbecoming Habits. T. Heald
Unbegotten. J. Creasey
Unbidden. R. Chetwynd-Hayes
Unbidden Guests. D. Stewart
Unbriefed Mission. L. Bridgemont
Unbroken Barriers. K. Lindsay
Uncanny Adventures. E. Ascher
Uncanny Stories. May Sinclair
Uncas Island Murders. F. W. Bronson
Uncertain Agent. S. Donald
Uncertain Death. Anthony Gilbert
Uncertain Glory. H. Meadow
Uncertain Judgement. G. Mitcham
Uncertain Quest. E. Messenger
Uncertain Treasure. D. Lee
Uncertain Voyage. D. Gilman
Uncharted. S. M. Parkman
Uncharted Island. S. M. Parkman
Uncharted Seas. D. Wheatley
Unclaimed Daughter. Anonymous

Unclaimed Letter. A. M. Sholl
Unclaimed Million. H. Maxwell
Uncle Abner, Master of Mysteries. M. D. Post
Uncle from India. E. D. Pierson
Uncle James's Golf Match. H. C. McNeile
Uncle Joe's Legacy and other stories. G. Boothby
Uncle Oscar's Niece. G. Goodchild
Uncle Paul. C. Fremlin
Uncle Sagamore and His Girls. C. Williams
Uncle Sam, Detective. W. A. Dupuy
Uncle Sam's Bad Boys. B. D. Adsit
Uncle Silas. J. S. Le Fanu
Uncle Simon. M. Stacpoole
Uncle William and other stories. D. G. Browne
Uncle Xavier. D. H. Landels
Unclean. G. Des Cars
Uncle's Advice. W. Hewlett
Uncle's Crime. J. H. Robinson
Uncommitted Man. R. E. Pickering
Uncommon Cold. E. H. Clements
Uncommon Danger. E. Ambler
Uncommon Market. H. Janson
Uncomplaining Corpses. B. Halliday
Unconfessed. M. H. Bradley
Unconquerable. H. MacInnes
Unconscious Crime. N. T. Oliver
Unconscious Witness. R. A. Freeman
Uncounted Hour. W. Allen
Uncover Agent. H. Janson
Uncrowned Prince. J. J. Farrington
Uncut Diamonds. D. Brechin
Undaunted. J. Harris
Undefeated. J. Thompson
Under a Ban. Mrs. Lodge
Under a Black Veil. N. Carter
Under a Cloud. J. K. Ludlum
Under a Cloud. V. Siller
Under a Cloud. T. W. Speight
Under a Mask. J. K. Leys
Under a Mask. J. B. Williams
Under a Strange Mask. F. Barrett
Under a Veil. Old Sleuth
Under Cover. W. Martyn
Under Cover. R. C. Megrue
Under Cover Man. J. Wilstach
Under Cover of Night. R. M. Gilchrist
Under Cover of Night. M. L. Stokes
Under Dog and other stories. A. Christie
Under Dogs. H. Footner
Under Egyptian Skies. S. Rathbone
Under False Colors. N. Carter
Under False Pretenses. A. Sergeant
Under Fate's Wheel. L. L. Lynch
Under Fire. R. Parker
Under Groove. A. Stringer
Under His Thumb. Anonymous
Under His Thumb. D. J. MacKenzie
Under Lock and Key. T. W. Speight
Under London. V. Gielgud
Under Love's Rule. M. E. Braddon
Under Masks. H. F. Wood
Under Observation. D. Christie
Under One Roof. J. Payn
Under Police Observation. G. Chester
Under Police Protection. J. G. Brandon
Under St. Paul's. R. Dowling
Under Seal of the Confessional. Mrs. C. Kernahan
Under Sealed Orders. G. Allen
Under Secret Orders. J. G. Brandon
Under-Secretary. W. LeQueux
Under Sentence. Mary Cross
Under Sentence of Death. Old Sleuth
Under Suspicion. H. W. Leggett

Title Index

Under Suspicion. A. MacVicar
Under Suspicion. A. Sergeant
Under Suspicion. R. Trevor
Under the Black Eagle. A. W. Marchmont
Under the Broad Arrow. M. Leighton
Under the Cherry Tree. P. Traill
Under the Dragon Throne. L. T. Meade
Under the Eagle's Wing. G. H. Teed
Under the Fourth--? P. Luck
Under the Goad. C. A. Brandreth
Under the Golden Bough. G. F. Gibbs
Under the Great Seal. J. Hatton
Under the Influence. G. Kerr
Under the Lens. F. B. Austin
Under the Long Barrow. C. Haddon
Under the Quiet Water. F. S. Wees
Under the Red Flag. M. E. Braddon
Under the Red Flag. M. J. Pemberton
Under the Red Star. M. Gerard
Under the Rose. H. Wood
Under the Shadow. H. L. Jones
Under the Skin. Dorothea Bennett
Under the Sunset. B. Stoker
Under the Surface. J. K. Stafford
Under the Tiger's Claws. N. Carter
Under the Will, and other tales. M. C. Hay
Under the Willows. E. Van Loon
Under Three Flags. B. L. Taylor
Under Twelve Stars. H. S. Keeler
Under Two Skies. E. W. Hornung
Under Western Eyes. J. Conrad
Under-World. L. Osbourne
Undercover Agent. E. Ellison
Undercover Cat. The Gordons
Undercover Cat Prowls Again. The Gordons
Undercover Cutie. M. Brody
Undercover Girl. Roland Daniel
Undercover Man. H. H. Kirst
Undercover Woman. D. Herzog
Undercurrent. J. Bogar
Undercurrent. M. Boggon
Undercurrent. B. Jefferis
Undercurrent. B. Pronzini
Underdog. W. R. Burnett
Underground. J. J. Farjeon
Underground. J. K. Leys
Underground. C. Stratton
Underground Cities Contract. P. Atlee
Underground Man. R. Macdonald
Underground Men. M. Carrel
Underground Mystery. R. H. Sherard
Underground Syndicate. A. M. Williamson
Underhandover. Kenneth O'Hara
Understrike. J. Gardner
Understudy. D. H. Landels
Understudy to Murder. D. Gray
Undertaker Dies. Garnett Weston
Undertaker Wind. W. Masterson
Undertaker's Field. H. Compton
Undertow. D. Cory
Underwood Mystery. C. J. Dutton
Underworld of Zello. J. J. Deegan
Undesirable Company. F. Ryck
Undetective. B. Graeme
Undine. P. B. Young
Undiplomatic Exit. J. Sherwood
Undisclosed Client. E. Wallace
Undiscovered Crimes. Waters
Undivided Light. C. Massie
Undoing of Mrs. Cransby. H. C. McNeile
Undoubted Deed. J. Davey
Undressed to Kill. P. Cheyney
Undying Serpent. T. B. Morris
Une Ténébreuse Affaire. H. D. Balzac
Unearthly. D. Daniels
Uneasily to Bed. D. Ames
Uneasy Alibi. N. Karta
Uneasy Freehold. D. Macardle
Uneasy Is the Grave. J. S. Strange
Uneasy Lies the Dead. M. E. Chaber

Uneasy Lies the Head. W. L. Rohde
Uneasy Money. M. Tannock
Uneasy Street. B. Chetwynd
Uneasy Street. S. Coburn
Uneasy Street. Wade Miller
Uneasy Street. A. S. Roche
Uneasy Sun. M. Butterworth
Uneasy Terms. P. Cheyney
Uneasy Virtue. Reginald Campbell
Uneasy Virtue. Dana Wilson
Uneasy Years. L. Noel
Unending Track. J. Farrimond
Unexpected. F. Hume
Unexpected Adventure. T. F. W. Hickey
Unexpected Angel. J. B. Watney
Unexpected Corpse. E. L. Cushing
Unexpected Daughter. P. Trent
Unexpected Death. D. Shannon
Unexpected Guest. A. Christie
Unexpected Legacy. E. R. Punshon
Unexpected Mrs. Pollifax. D. Gilman
Unexpected Move. S. Campbell
Unexpected Night. E. Daly
Unfair Exchange. M. Babson
Unfair Fare Affair. P. Leslie
Unfair Lady. G. Fairlie
Unfeeling Sky. P. Saxon
Unfinished Business. C. Lucas
Unfinished Clue. G. Heyer
Unfinished Crime. E. S. Holding
Unfinished Crime. H. McCloy
Unfinished Letter. N. Carter
Unfinished Murder. E. W. Lyon
Unfit to Plead. J. Dellbridge
Unfolding Years. A. Gask
Unforbidden Sin. Roy Vickers
Unforeseen. D. Macardle
Unforeseen. J. C. Snaith
Unforgetting Heart. Margery Lawrence
Unforgivable Sin. A. Applin
Unforgiving Moment. F. Cowen
Unforgiving Wind. J. Harris
Unforgotten. L. Conway
Unforgotten. D. Winston
Unfortunate Murderer. R. Hull
Unfortunate Replacement. M. Jahn
Unfortunate Rogue. Warren Miller
Unfriendly Persuasion. W. A. Ballinger
Ungilded Lily. Morton Cooper
Unguarded. D. Daniels
Unguarded Hour. A. W. Marchmont
Unguarded Hour. D. Vane
Unguarded Moment. H. A. Wrenn
Unhallowed Murder. S. Nash
Unhandsome Corpse. S. Campion
Unhappy Hooligan. S. Palmer
Unhappy Hophead. Spike Gordon
Unhappy Lady and other stories. P. Cheyney
Unhappy New Year. C. C. Estes
Unhappy Parting. Elsie Lee
Unhappy Rendezvous. A. Nash
Unhappy Ship. E. L. Long
Unheeded Warning. D. Stewart
Unholy Crusade. D. Wheatley
Unholy Dying. R. T. Campbell
Unholy Flame. O. L. Rosmanith
Unholy Matrimony. Winifred Graham
Unholy Sanctuary. M. Higgins
Unholy Spell. C. Vincent
Unholy Three. T. Robbins
Unholy Trio. H. Kane
Unholy Trio. J. Ronald
Unholy Wife. J. Roeburt

Unholy Wish, and other stories. H. Wood
Unicorn. C. Goodall
Unicorn Murders. Carter Dickson
Unidentified Woman. M. G. Eberhart
Uniformed Killers. R. Wallace
Uninhabited House. J. H. Riddell
Uninvited. F. A. Chittenden
Uninvited. D. Macardle
Uninvited Corpse. P. Whelton
Uninvited Guest. G. H. Coxe
Uninvited Guests. J. J. Farjeon
Union Bust. R. Sapir
Union Down. S. Campbell
Unique Hamlet. V. Starrett
Unjust Jury. Winifred Duke
Unjustly Branded. R. H. Poole
Unkindly Cup. H. McElroy
Unkindness of Ravens. T. B. Reagan
Unknown. J. Barclay
Unknown. E. Southworth
Unknown Agent. M. Annesley
Unknown Assailant. P. Hamilton
Unknown Countess. Emerson Bennett
Unknown Enemy. Gret Lane
Unknown Foe. J. K. Stafford
Unknown Goddess. A. Philips
Unknown Hand. M. Peterson
Unknown Man, Seen in Profile. Kenneth O'Hara
Unknown Menace. D. Stuart
Unknown Mission. N. Deane
Unknown Murderer. H. Liggett
Unknown Path. Lady A. Scott
Unknown Quantity. M. G. Eberhart
Unknown Quantity. W. E. Johns
Unknown River. J. M. Scott
Unknown Seven. H. Coverdale
Unknown Terror. H. Holt
Unknown Tomorrow. W. LeQueux
Unknown Woman. L. Hoffman
Unlamented. D. Daniels
Unlatched Door. L. Thayer
Unlawful. C. Turner
Unlawful Justice. John Gloag
Unlawful Occasions. H. Cecil
Unlawful Occasions. P. Wentworth
Unleashed Will. C. Clark
"Unless a Child Is Born--." B. Heygate
Unlighted House. J. Hay
Unloved. D. Birkley
Unloved Wife. E. Southworth
Unlucky Break. O. Mills
Unlucky Dip. Margaret Henry
Unlucky for Some. A. Behrend
Unlucky Number. E. Phillpotts
Unmasked at Last. H. Hill
Unnamed. W. LeQueux
Unnatural Break. T. Girtin
Unnatural Causes. H. Hawton
Unnatural Causes. P. D. James
Unnatural Death. M. Richmond
Unnatural Death. D. L. Sayers
Unnatural Deeds. E. Nisot
Unneutral Murder. H. Footner
Unofficial Executor. H. F. Moulton
Unofficial Spy. A. O. Pollard
Unorthodox Corpse. C. Brown
Unpardonable Crime. D. B. Miller
Unpardonable Sin. A. D. Vinton
Unpleasantness at the Bellona Club. D. L. Sayers
Unprofessional Spy. M. Underwood
Unprotected. I. Barry
Unpublishable Memoirs. A. S. W. Rosenbach
Unquenchable Flame. A. J. Rees
Unquiet Corpse. W. Sloan
Unquiet Grave. J. S. Strange

U

Unquiet Night. P. Carlon
Unquiet Night. M. Cronin
Unquiet Sleep. W. Haggard
Unraveled Knots. B. Orczy
Unreasonable Doubt. E. Ferrars
Unrelenting. C. W. Dodge
Unrepentant. C. Phillips
Unrepentant Sinners. L. Royer
Unscrupulous Mr. Callaghan. P. Cheyney
Unseen! A. P. Terhune
Unseen. Ethel L. White
Unseen Assassin. H. Janson
Unseen Barrier. M. Gerard
Unseen Ear. N. S. Lincoln
Unseen Enemy. C. Landon
Unseen Foes. N. Carter
Unseen Hand. L. L. Lynch
Unseen Hand. C. H. New
Unseen Hand. I. Stark
Unseen Hand. Valentine
Unseen Hands. R. O. Chipperfield
Unseen Torment. K. Kimbrough
Unseen Witness. B. Bolt
Unsheltered. D. Ward
Unsolved. B. Graeme
Unsolved Mysteries. V. Tweedale
Unsought Adventure. H. A. Kennedy
Unspeakable. S. Ransome
Unspeakable Turk. G. Horton
Unspoken Word. M. Gerard
Unsuitable Job for a Woman. P. D. James
Unsung Road. S. Harvester
Unsuspected. C. Armstrong
Unsuspected Chasm. M. Innes
Unsuspected Evil. D. M. Disney
Untamed. V. Norwood
Untaxed Whiskey. B. Wayde
Untidy Murder. F. Lockridge
Until Death. S. Somers
Until She Dies. W. Wright
Until She Was Dead. R. Hull
Until Temptation Do Us Part. C. Brown
Until the Day She Dies. J. MacLaren-Ross
Until They Are Dead. John Lloyd
Until You Are Dead. H. Kane
Untimely Death. C. Hare
Untimely Frost. E. G. Cousins
Untimely Ripped. M. McShane
Untimely Slain. J. Gray
Unto Death Utterly. M. Cumberland
Unto the Third Generation. M. P. Shiel
Untold Tale. L. K. Vincent
Untouchable Juli. J. Aldridge
Unwanted Child. P. Conway
Unwanted Corpse. M. Burton
Unwanted Witness. George Douglas
Unwashed Gods. E. C. Vivian
Unwelcome Corpse. B. Frost
Unwelcome Rapture. M. Richmond
Unwelcome Visitor. A. Corliss
Unwilling Adventurer. John Gloag
Unwilling Angel. A. Stuart
Unwilling Bride. F. Hume
Unwilling Guest. E. Ellison
Unwilling Rebel. M. Lynch
Unwilling to Wed. M. Richmond
Unwise Virgin. Mrs. C. Kernahan
Up a Winding Stair. H. V. Dixon
Up Against It. V. Vanardy
Up for Grabs. A. A. Fair
Up from the Grave. D. Craig
Up Jumped the Devil. C. F. Adams
Up, McLean! G. Goodchild
Up North. T. Lund
Up North. J. H. Vahey
Up the Garden Path. M. Burton
Up the Garden Path. J. Rhode
Up the Ladder of Gold. E. P. Oppenheim
Up This Crooked Way. H. Holman
Up-Tight Blonde. C. Brown
Up to Her Neck. J. N. Chance
Up to No Good. A. M. Stein
Up to the Hilt. A. Rowe
Upfold Farm Mystery. A. Fielding
Upfold Witch. J. Bell
Upland Mystery. M. R. Hatch
Upmarket Affair. T. Harknett
Upper Case. M. Merrick
Upside Down Murders. H. Austin
Upstairs. J. L. Rickard
Upstairs and Downstairs. C. Carnac
Upstairs and Downstairs. R. S. Thorn
Upstairs, Downstairs. C. Carnac
Upstart. P. P. Read
Uranian Jewel Case. R. Dark
Uranium Murders. J. E. Barry
Urban District Lover. J. T. Story
Urbane Guerilla. S. Johnson
Urgent Action. N. Forde
Urgent Delivery. N. Forde
Urgent Enquiry. N. Forde
Urgent Hangman. P. Cheyney
Urgent Private Affairs. H. F. Moulton
Urn Burial. P. Ruell
Ursula Lenorme. T. W. Speight
Ursula Vanet. A. Mills
Us or Them War. W. Garner
Used in Evidence. P. Froud
Utmost Ebb. R. Harrison
Utopia Affair. D. McDaniel
Utter Death. J. Hymers
Uttermost Farthing. R. A. Freeman
Uttermost Farthing. M. B. Lowndes

V

V as in Victim. L. Treat
V.C. D. C. Murray
"V" for Vengeance. D. Wheatley
V for Vitality. H. Janson
V.I.P. W. L. Rohde
V.I.P. E. Trevor
V Plan. G. Seton
V2 Expert. A. J. Evans
Vacancy. P. Mann
Vacancy with Corpse. M. Burton
Vacant Possession. M. Butcher
Vacation with Fear. J. T. Story
Vagabond Nights. H. S. Keeler
Vagabond Sonata. L. Geoghegan
Vagabond Vamp. H. Janson
Vagabond's Honor. E. D. Pierson
Vagrant Bride. Mrs. C. Kernahan
Vagrant Duke. G. F. Gibbs
Vagrant Wife. F. Warden
Vaia's Lord. J. Middlemass
Vail's Gate. J. Cabot
Vain Ambitions. R. Gaines
Vain Escape. E. C. Vivian
Vain Pride. C. Kingston
Vain Sacrifice. N. Carter
Vaivaisukko's Brude. D. Scott-Moncrieff
Val Strange. D. C. Murray
Valazy Family and other narratives. Waters
Valcour Meets Murder. R. King
Valdez Is Coming. E. Leonard
Valentine Estate. S. Ellin
Valentine Victim. D. McLeish
Valhalla. George Long
Valiant Jester. M. Edwin
Valiant View. T. Mundy
Valkyrie Mandate. R. Vaughan
Vallency Tradition. G. Merrick
Valley. C. Irving
Valley and the Shadow. W. H. Boore
Valley of Achor. P. C. De Crespigny
Valley of Bells. D. Whitelaw
Valley of Creeping Men. R. Crawley
Valley of Death. W. R. Hutton
Valley of Death. S. Jason
Valley of Death. Paul Ross
Valley of Doom. M. Richmond
Valley of Fear. J. Creasey
Valley of Fear. A. C. Doyle
Valley of Fear. R. Gar
Valley of Fear. F. A. Symonds
Valley of Ghosts. E. Wallace
Valley of Green Shadows. L. A. Knight
Valley of Hanoi. I. R. Blacker
Valley of Headstrong Men. J. S. Fletcher
Valley of Lies. G. Goodchild
Valley of Lost Gold. G. Bettany
Valley of Night. J. Farnol
Valley of No Escape. James Preston
Valley of Poppies. J. Hatton
Valley of Shadows. D. Lyons
Valley of Skulls. O. Sackville
Valley of Smugglers. A. W. Upfield
Valley of Suspicion. F. Riddell
Valley of Suspicion. W. C. Tuttle
Valley of Terror. D. Stuart
Valley of the Assassins. I. MacAlister
Valley of the Damned. V. Norwood
Valley of the Ravens. N. Buckingham
Valley of the Shadow. W. LeQueux
Valley of the Shadow. H. C. McNeile
Valley of the Shadow. M. Richmond
Valley of Twisted Trails. W. C. Tuttle
Valley of Vanishing Herds. W. C. Tuttle
Valley of Vultures. P. Edwards
Valparaiso. F. R. E. Nicolas
Valrose Mystery. W. LeQueux
Valse Caprice. Gavin Holt
Valse Macabre. K. M. Knight
Value for Murder. Craig Cooper
Vamp Till Ready. T. Rieman
Vampire. R. Hodder
Vampire. S. Horler
Vampire Abroad. M. Dalman
Vampire Affair. D. McDaniel
Vampire, and sixteen other stories. L. H. Fox
Vampire Bat. R. St. Clair
Vampire Cameo. D. Nile
Vampire City. T. S. King
Vampire Contessa. Marilyn Ross
Vampire Curse. D. Winston
Vampire in the Shadows. M. Lovell
Vampire Man. G. Verner
Vampire Murders. R. Wallace
Vampire of N'Gobi. R. Cullum
Vampire of the Andes. H. Carew
Vampire of the Skies. J. Corbett
Vampires of Finistere. P. Saxon
Vampires of the China Coast. Bok
Vampires of Vengeance. J. A. Kolbe
Vampires Overhead. A. Hyder
Vampire's Trail. N. Carter
Vampyre of Moura. V. Coffman
Van Alstine Case. N. Carter
Van Beck Will. H. W. Jessup
Van Dreisen Affair. H. Roth
Van Dylk Diamonds. A. Applin
Van Langeren Girl. Brian Cooper
Van Norton Murders. C. R. Jones

Title Index

Van Peltz Diamonds. Anonymous
Van Roon. J. C. Snaith
Van Suyden Sapphires. Charles Carey
Van, the Government Detective. H. P. Halsey
Vandekkers. R. Thorndike
Vanderlyn's Adventure. M. B. Lowndes
Vandersley. Edward Brown
Vandor Mystery. C. F. Gregg
Vanessa. K. Martin
Vanish in an Instant. M. Millar
Vanished. M. Carleton
Vanished. F. Knebel
Vanished. B. Pronzini
Vanished Emperor. P. Andreae
Vanished Guest. O. Binns
Vanished Messenger. E. P. Oppenheim
Vanished Million. W. W. Sayer
Vanished Prospector. T. Lund
Vanished Squadron. J. R. Holden
Vanished Stamps Mystery. M. Poole
Vanished Vice-Counsel. M. Annesley
Vanished Yacht. E. H. Burrage
Vanisher. K. Robeson
Vanishing Act. M. Butterworth
Vanishing Celebrities. A. Alington
Vanishing Cheques. B. Capes
Vanishing Clue. H. K. McDonnell
Vanishing Corpse. Anthony Gilbert
Vanishing Corpse. E. Queen
Vanishing Death. W. M. Graydon
Vanishing Death. N. Vane
Vanishing Diamond. G. Campbell
Vanishing Diary. J. Rhode
Vanishing Emerald. N. Carter
Vanishing Gold Truck. H. S. Keeler
Vanishing Hand. E. L. Wilson
Vanishing Heiress. N. Carter
Vanishing Idol. G. F. Gibbs
Vanishing Ladies. R. Marsten
Vanishing Man. R. A. Freeman
Vanishing Men. R. W. Child
Vanishing Men. W. B. M. Ferguson
Vanishing Men. G. M. Winsor
Vanishing Murderer. C. J. Dutton
Vanishing of Betty Varian. C. Wells
Vanishing of Ira Bouck. J. St. David
Vanishing of Tera. F. Hume
Vanishing Point. C. Dawson
Vanishing Point. P. Flower
Vanishing Point. P. Wentworth
Vanishing Professor. F. MacIsaac
Vanishing Senator. J. Philips
Vanishing Shadows. J. Maconechy
Vanishing Smuggler. S. Chalmers
Vanishing Trick. H. Carmichael
Vanishing Vixen. R. B. Sparkia
Vanishing Yacht. E. Anstey
Vanity Box. A. M. Williamson
Vanity Case. C. Wells
Vanity Dies Hard. R. Rendell
Vanity Row. W. R. Burnett
Vanity's Daughter. H. Smart
Vantage Hall. C. Gluyas
Vantage Point. K. Rogers
Vantage Striker. H. Simpson
Vantine Diamonds. Seamark
Varanoff Tradition. O. Panbourne
Vardy. J. Harris
Variation on a Theme of Murder. C. G. Jarvie
Variety. R. Connell
Variety Jack. Old Sleuth
Variety of Weapons. R. King
Varney the Vampire. T. P. Prest

Vase Mystery. V. Loder
Vasiliko Affair. M. Culpan
Vasty Deep. S. C. Cumberland
Vatican Vendetta. N. Carter
Vats of Tyre. R. Bridges
Vault of Doom. A. Skene
Vaults of Blackarden Castle. A. Gask
Vavel, the Wonderful Treasure Seeker. Old Sleuth
Veetols. Anthony Graham
Vegas Trap. H. Kantor
Vegas Vendetta. D. Pendleton
Vegetable Duck. J. Rhode
Veil of Death. B. Simons
Veil of Islam. L. Noel
Veil of Silence. A. Seilaz
Veil Withdrawn. B. J. Maddux
"Veiled Beauty." Old Sleuth
Veiled Hand. F. Wicks
Veiled Lady. H. Sealis
Veiled Lady. F. Warden
Veiled Lady and The Mystery of the Baghdad Chest. A. Christie
Veiled Man. W. LeQueux
Veiled Murder. A. Campbell
Veiled Picture. E. J. Lysaght
Veiled Prisoner. G. Leroux
Veiled Vampire. A. Eadie
Veiled Woman. A. Abdullah
Veils of Death. N. Vane
Veils of Fear. G. Mark
Veils of Fear. V. Meik
Vein of Violence. W. C. Gault
Veins of Compassion. P. Audemars
Veldt Official. B. Mitford
Veldt Vendetta. B. Mitford
Vellum. B. Goldie
Velvet Ape. D. C. Holmes
Velvet Black. R. W. Child
Velvet Claw. A. Dorrington
Velvet Fleece. L. Eby
Velvet Hammer. D. Franklin
Velvet Hand. H. Footner
Velvet Hand. H. Reilly
Velvet Johnnie and other stories. P. Cheyney
Velvet Lawn. C. Felix
Velvet Mask and other stories. L. Gribble
Velvet Target. G. Holden
Velvet Trap. J. Blackmore
Velvet Vixen. C. Brown
Velvet Well. J. Gearon
Venables. G. Wagner
Vendetta. J. Boland
Vendetta. H. Carmichael
Vendetta. C. Durbin
Vendetta. J. Gilmore
Vendetta. J. L. Haas
Vendetta. P. McCurtin
Vendetta. N. Quarry
Vendetta! Richard Williams
Vendetta Con Brio. B. De Bilio
Vendetta Contract. J. Messmann
Vendetta for the Saint. L. Charteris
Vendetta in Spain. D. Wheatley
Veneered Scamp. J. Middlemass
Venetian Affair. H. MacInnes
Venetian Bird. V. Canning
Venetian Blind. W. Haggard
Venetian Blonde. A. S. Fleischman
Venetian Key. A. Upward
Venetian Mask. C. Robertson
Venetian Secret. E. Bond
Venetian Swimmer Mystery. S. G. Hedges
Venetian Trelawney. G. W. M. Reynolds
Venetians. M. E. Braddon
Vengeance. A. Murray
Vengeance. B. Tozer
Vengeance Business. Jim Ryan
Vengeance Due. J. Sandys

Vengeance in the Air. Colin Hope
Vengeance Is Mine. D. Dane
Vengeance Is Mine. M. Leighton
Vengeance Is Mine. R. Marlowe
Vengeance Is Mine. J. Middlemass
Vengeance Is Mine. Mark Richards
Vengeance Is Mine! M. Spillane
Vengeance Is Ours! P. Saxon
Vengeance Is the Spur. H. Whittington
Vengeance Man. M. Coles
Vengeance Man. D. J. Marlowe
Vengeance of ? J. Wallace
Vengeance of Blue Pete. L. Allan
Vengeance of Five. H. K. McDonnell
Vengeance of Flynn. E. L. Long
Vengeance of Henry Jarroman. Roy Vickers
Vengeance of Hurricane Williams. Gordon Young
Vengeance of Kali. I. Marshall
Vengeance of Larose. A. Gask
Vengeance of Li-Sin. N. Vane
Vengeance of Mrs. Danvers. S. Kyle
Vengeance of Monsieur Blackshirt. D. Graeme
Vengeance of Mortimer Daly. M. Locke
Vengeance of Mynheer Van Lok and other stories. H. D. Stacpoole
Vengeance of Science. J. Dalmaine
Vengeance of Sheevra. O. Williams
Vengeance of the Ivory Skull. M. Harvey
Vengeance of the Tong. B. Rogers
Vengeance of Three. W. M. Graydon
Vengeance of Valdone. B. Ferm
Vengeance Pulls the Trigger. S. M. Schley
Vengeance Run. R. Rostand
Vengeance Street. R. Bloomfield
Vengeance Under Law. F. Castle
Vengeance with a Twist and other stories. P. Cheyney
Vengeful Sinner. H. Whittington
Vengeful Virgin. G. Brewer
Venice of the Black Sea. H. Robertson
Venice Preserve Me. J. Appleby
Venice Train. G. Simenon
Venner Crime. J. Rhode
Venom Business. J. Lange
Venom House. A. W. Upfield
Venom in Eden. M. Boniface
Venom in the Cup. G. Joseph
Ventilated Head. A. Nuttall
Ventriloquist. E. Belasyse
Ventriloquist Detective. Old Sleuth
Venture. R. N. Grisewood
Venturers All. L. Gorell
Venturous Lady. G. H. Coxe
Venus Afflicted. F. Mullally
Venus Besieged. E. C. Reed
Venus Death. B. Benson
Venus Died at Dawn. L. H. Hart
Venus Disarmed. J. Dole
Venus in Plastic. J. Mitchell
Venus Makes Three. H. Janson
Venus of Samos. R. Quest
Venus on Wheels. M. Dekobra
Venus Probe. David St. John
Venus Trap. J. M. Ullman
Venus Unarmed. C. Brown
Venus Unarmed. L. Treat
Venus with Pistol. G. Lyall
Vera Gerard Case. J. C. Cooke
Vera the Medium. R. H. Davis
Verboten. S. Esmond
Verdict. A. Christie
Verdict. L. Martin
Verdict Afterwards. D. Ensor
Verdict in Question. S. Jepson
Verdict of Twelve. R. Postgate

Verdict of You All. Henry Wade
Verdict Suspended. H. Nielsen
Verdict Without Jury. A. Webb
Verner's Pride. H. Wood
Veron Mystery. H. C. Bailey
Verona's Father. D. C. Murray
Veronica Died Monday. G. Trotta
Veronica's Room. I. Levin
Veronique. V. Coffman
Verrall Street Affair. M. E. Cooke
Versus Inspector Maigret. G. Simenon
Versus the Baron. A. Morton
Versus the C.I.A. G. De Villiers
Vertigo. P. Boileau
Very Big Bang. P. McCutchan
Very Black Deed. W. Manson
Very Breath of Hell. G. Beare
Very Cold for May. W. P. McGivern
Very Dead of Winter. S. Nichols
Very Deadly Game. V. B. Miller
Very Dry with a Twist. D. Banko
Very Good Hater. R. Hill
Very Long Odds and A Strange Finish. C. Rae-Brown
Very Private Island. Z. Z. Smith
Very Private Secretary. B. Reynolds
Very Queer Business, and other stories. W. Westall
Very Quiet Murder. F. Crane
Very Quiet Place. A. Garve
Very Rough Diamond. F. Warden
Very Special Agent. G. Napier
Very Thin Line. M. Borgenicht
Very Welcome Death. D. L. Mathews
Very Wicked. Clifton Adams
Very Young Couple. B. L. Farjeon
Vesey Inheritance. Gwendoline Butler
Vesper Bells. B. H. Hyatt
Vesper Service Murders. V. W. Mason
Vespucci Papers. B. Healey
Vessel May Carry Explosives. S. Harvester
Vestibule Limited Mystery. M. Manly
Vestibule Limited Mystery. A. Robertson
Vestry Murder. T. A. Plummer
Vet It Was That Died. M. Silverman
Veterans. Eric Lambert
Via Berlin. C. Marriott
Viaduct Murder. R. A. Knox
Vial of Death. N. Carter
Vial with the White Powder. J. B. Williams
Vibart Affair. G. M. Fenn
Vicar. J. Hatton
Vicar in Hell. A. Melville
Vicar of Moura. V. Coffman
Vicar's Experiments. A. Rolls
Vicar's People. G. M. Fenn
Vicar's Secret. C. E. Jeffery
Vice and Its Victim. T. P. Prest
Vice City. B. Sarto
Vice Cop. R. Deming
Vice Czar Murders. F. Charles
Vice Isn't Private. B. Cleeve
Vice Net. M. Carey
Vice Queens on Broadway. Griff
Vice Squad. H. Spencer
Vice Squad. J. Van Raalte
Vice Squad. L. T. White
Vice Squad Cop. M. Carey
Vice Trap. E. Gilbert
Vice Volcano. B. Sarto

Viceroy's Protege. G. Boothby
Vicious Breed. B. Sarto
Vicious Circle. A. Evans
Vicious Circle. Manning Long
Vicious Circuit. C. G. Jarvie
Vicious Circuit. J. Langdon
Vicious Pattern. M. V. Heberden
Vicious Virtuoso. L. Lombard
Vicky Van. C. Wells
Victim. J. Bell
Victim! C. Brown
Victim. W. Drummond
Victim. T. Journet
Victim. D. Winston
Victim Died Twice. H. Liggett
Victim Must Be Found. A. Hocking
Victim Needs a Nurse. J. Redfern
Victim of Black Magic. G. H. Teed
Victim of Circumstances. N. Carter
Victim of Deceit. N. Carter
Victim of Fashion. H. M. Jones
Victim of His Clothes. H. Fielding
Victim of the Combine. G. Chester
Victim of the Crooked Hypnotist. J. Hunter
Victim of the Cult. W. Jardine
Victim of the Devil's Bowl. R. Hardinge
Victim of the Gang. G. H. Teed
Victim of the Girl Spy. M. B. Dix
Victim of the Occult. I. Stark
Victim of the Red Mask. S. Hope
Victim of the Secret Service. J. G. Brandon
Victim of the Thieves' Den. J. G. Brandon
Victim of the Waterway. G. N. Philips
Victim of Villainy. F. L. Broughton
Victim Unknown. D. Reid
Victim Was Important. J. Rayter
Victims. P. Boileau
Victims. T. Gift
Victims. J. Pearl
Victims. J. Rossiter
Victim's Niece. B. Hector
Victims of Devil's Alley. P. Urquhart
Victims of Villainy. Andrew Murray
Victims Unknown. R. Clapperton
Victor. D. Kirby
Victor and Vanquished. M. C. Hay
Victor Maury, the French Detective. G. Reynolds
Victor Versus Verhasst. D. Kirby
Victoria Pruitt Comes to Town. R. G. Cochran
Victoria Winters. Marilyn Ross
Victorian Album. E. Berckman
Victorian Crown. E. Noone
Victorine. F. P. Keyes
Victors. J. Harris
Victor's Spoils. I. Stark
Victory Murders. F. Johns
Victory Song. H. Adams
Vidocq of New York. C. Fulton
Vidocq, the Police Spy. Vidocq
Vienna Pursuit. A. Goddard
View from Daniel Pike. B. Knox
View from the Terrace. L. Meynell
View of the Mountain. G. Greenaway
View to a Death. Kenneth O'Hara
Viewless Winds. M. C. Morgan
Vigorous Daunt, Billionaire. A. Pratt
Viking Feast Mystery. L. A. Knight
Viking's Skull. J. R. Carling
Villa Aurelia. B. E. Stevenson
Villa Caprice. Irene Alexander
Villa Fountains. V. Coffman
Villa Jane. J. Laing
Villa Mimosa. J. Tickell
Villa Mystery. H. Flowerdew
Villa Nova. C. Selden
Villa of Shadows. C. Farr
Villa on the Shore. M. Butterworth

Villa Petroff. D. Whitelaw
Villa Rossignol. M. L. Storer
Village Affairs. R. Armfelt
Village Afraid. M. Burton
Village Blacksmith. D. Dale
Village Called Death. P. Motte
Village East. R. Chambers
Village Gentleman, and The Attorney at Law. A. Duncombe
Village Mystery. Mrs. C. Kernahan
Village Mystery. Benjamin F. Mason
Village Never Knew. B. Goldie
Village of Fear. F. Cowen
Village of Fear. M. Jenson
Village of Fear. D. Stuart
Village of Rogues. J. Sturrock
Village of Stars. P. Stanton
Village Pub Murders. F. Krull
Village Scandal. H. M. Jones
Village Temptress. F. Whishaw
Villain and the Virgin. J. H. Chase
Villainous Company. R. Fenisong
Villainous Saltpetre. C. Witting
Villainous Scheme. N. Carter
Villains. J. Rossiter
Villains Galore. G. Bell
Villain's Work. D. Stewart
Villainy. G. Bettany
Villainy at Vespers. J. Cockin
Villiers Touch. B. Garfield
Vindicator. E. P. Oppenheim
Vinegar--and Cream. H. T. W. Bousfield
Vines of Yarrabee. D. Eden
Vintage Murder. N. Marsh
Vintage So Evil. M. Vinter
Vintage Stuff. A. Brede
Violante. G. R. Preedy
Viola's Dilemma. T. S. King
Violator. H. Kane
Violence. C. Woolrich
Violence in Paradise. D. Buttenshaw
Violence in Quiet Places. J. T. Story
Violence in Velvet. M. Avallone
Violence Is Golden. B. Halliday
Violence Is Golden. C. H. Thames
Violence Is My Business. S. Marlowe
Violence of Hate. H. P. Lees
Violent Brink. A. Beever
Violent Brothers. E. Bruton
Violent City. J. Hawkins
Violent Dark. L. Gribble
Violent Dawn. C. Rudd
Violent Death. W. Sproule
Violent Death of a Bitter Englishman. B. Cleeve
Violent End. V. Kathrens
Violent Ends. G. Simenon
Violent Enemy. H. Marlowe
Violent Holiday. R. Wilkes-Hunter
Violent Hours. F. Castle
Violent Hours. P. Saxon
Violent Hours. R. Walsh
Violent Keepsake. L. Grex
Violent Night. W. Harrison
Violent Night. R. Jackson
Violent Ones. Howard Hunt
Violent Ones. P. Saxon
Violent Saturday. W. L. Heath
Violent Security. G. Burnett
Violent World of Hugh Greene. Colin Wilson
Violent World of Michael Shayne. B. Halliday
Violet Forster's Lover. R. Marsh
Viper. H. Footner

Title Index

Viper in Her Bosom. P. Muller
Viper of Luxor. G. Seton
Viper Three. W. Wager
Viper's Bite. J. D. Fitz
Viper's Brood. B. Sarto
Viper's Game. R. Rostand
Viper's Sting. H. Desmond
Viper's Vengeance. R. Trevor
Viper's Vengeance. B. E. M. Ward
Virgin Cay. B. Heatter
Virgin Collector. D. Ambler
Virgin Fortress. M. Pemberton
Virgin Heiresses. E. Queen
Virgin Huntress. E. S. Holding
Virgin in Flames. S. Rohmer
Virgin Kills. R. Whitfield
Virgin Luck. L. Meynell
Virginia. C. Dawe
Virginia. K. Lindsay
Virginia and Magdalene. E. Southworth
Virginia Box and the "Unsatisfied." J. Moffatt
Virginia's Quest. M. Caywood
Virginia's Quest. J. Templeton
Virginia's Thing. H. Woodfin
Virgins Die Lonely. N. Perrelli
Virgin's Vendetta. N. Perrelli
Virility Factor. H. Kane
Virtues of Hell. P. Boulle
Virtuous Vamp. J. S. Clouston
Virus X. S. Horler
Visa for Violence. M. Risco
Visa to Death. E. Lacy
Viscount Lacklands. A. Griffiths
Visibility Nil. P. Conde
Visibility Nil. M. Elgin
Visible and Invisible. E. F. Benson
Vision of Beauty. J. Hatton
Vision of Murder. J. M. Brillant
Vision of the Foam. J. McEnery
Visit. J. Matheson
Visit from a Broad. H. Janson
Visiting Villain. C. Wells
Visitor. Anthony Gilbert
Visitor. C. Randau
Visitor. K. White
Visitors for Venning. C. Ryland
Vitriol Thrower. F. Du Boisgobey
Viva McHugh. J. Flynn
Vivanti. S. Horler
Vivanti Returns. S. Horler
Vivero Letter. D. Bagley
Vivia. E. Southworth
Vivian Bertram. G. W. M. Reynolds
Vivian Morgan's First Case. F. Curtis
Vivienne--Gently Where She Lay. A. Hunter
Vivier of Vivier, Longman & Company, Bankers. W. C. Hudson
Vixen. M. E. Braddon
Vixen. C. Brown
Vixen. L. Fitzhamon
Vodka on Ice. H. McLeave
Voice. Anthony Gilbert
Voice at Johnnywater. B. M. Bower
Voice from the Cell. A. MacKenzie
Voice from the Dark. E. Phillpotts
Voice from the Dead. B. Copper
Voice from the Grave. D. M. Disney
Voice from the Grave. Clarissa Ross
Voice from the Grave. Clifton Yorke
Voice from the Night. C. E. Sterrey
Voice from the Past. N. Carter

Voice from the Void. W. LeQueux
Voice from Yesterday. F. Crisp
Voice in the Closet. Herman Landon
Voice in the Dark. C. Lorrimer
Voice in the Fog. H. MacGrath
Voice Like Velvet. D. H. Landels
Voice of Air. E. Berckman
Voice of Armageddon. D. Lippincott
Voice of Bethia. T. Cobb
Voice of Murder. M. Erskine
Voice of the Charmer. L. T. Meade
Voice of the City. O. Henry
Voice of the Corpse. M. Murray
Voice of the Crab. G. Halls
Voice of the Dolls. D. Eden
Voice of the House. M. Erskine
Voice of the Lobster. R. J. Casey
Voice of the Murderer. G. Walsh
Voice of the Peacock. E. Salter
Voice of the Seven Sparrows. H. S. Keeler
Voice of Vice. R. Angel
Voice on the Telephone. Mildred Davis
Voice on the Wind. D. Daniels
Voice on the Wire. E. H. Ball
Voice out of Darkness. U. Curtiss
Voiceless Ones. J. Creasey
Voiceless Victims. G. Thorne
Voices. G. J. Brenn
Voices from the Bottom of the World. T. M. Walker
Voices in an Empty Room. P. Loraine
Voices in the Fog. K. Cameron
Voices in the Wind. E. V. Allen
Voices of the Storm. J. Sandys
Volcano. K. Hayles
Volcano Island. A. Wood
Volcanoes Above Us. N. Lewis
Volcanoes of San Domingo. Adam Hall
Voodoo. J. Esteven
Voodoo Death. W. B. Gibson
Voodoo Drum. P. Saxon
Voodoo Drums. E. Wilmot
Voodoo Goat. A. Gaines
Voodoo Island. G. H. Teed
Voodoo Murders. M. Avallone
Voodoo Violence. H. Janson
Voodoo'd. K. Perkins
Vorovich Affair. S. L. Stebel
Vortex. F. Whishaw
Vote Against Poison. J. Sherwood
Vote for Death. N. Longmate
Vote for Murder. Richard Martin
Vote for the Toff. J. Creasey
Vote for Violence. G. Johns
Vote to Kill. D. Hurd
Vote X for Treason. B. Cleeve
Vow. P. Trent
Vow of Love. F. Y. McHugh
Vow of Vengeance. A. Carlyle
Voyage Home. Alan Graham
Voyage into Nowhere. J. Wood
Voyage into Peril. Seafarer
Voyage into Violence. F. Lockridge
Voyage of Fear. R. Hardinge
Voyage of the "San Marcos." M. Hastings
Voyage of the Secret Duchess. F. Hurd
Voyage with Murder. J. York
Voyeur. A. Robbe-Grillet
Vrouw Grobelaar and Her Leading Cases. P. Gibbon
Vrouw Grobelaar's Leading Cases. P. Gibbon
Vulcan Bulletins. S. Gulliver
Vulcan's Hammer. D. Da Cruz
Vulnerable. D. Collins

Vulture. J. Carrick
Vulture. C. Heath
Vulture. G. Scott-Heron
Vulture. Harold Ward
Vulture in the Sun. J. Bingham
Vulture Is a Patient Bird. J. H. Chase
"Vulture" Strikes. Harold Ward
Vultures Gather. A. Hocking
Vultures in the Sky. T. Downing
Vultures in the Smoke. P. A. Foxall
Vultures, Ltd. B. Gray
Vultures of Desolate Island. G. E. Rochester
Vultures of Erin. N. J. Dunn
Vultures of the Dark. R. E. Enright
Vultures of the Sky. P. Conde
Vultures of the White Death. R. J. Hogan
Vulture's Prey. T. De Saix
Vye Murder. I. Wray
Vyvyans. Andree Hope

W

W.H.O.R.E. C. Brown
W.I.L. One to Curtis. P. Loraine
WO$_2$. M. Drake
W.1. P. McGuire
W Plan. G. Seton
Waddington Cipher. W. A. Johnston
Wade House. F. Hurd
Wager. R. L. Fish
Wager, and The House at Fernwood. F. Oursler
Wages of Fear. G. Arnaud
Wages of Peril. J. Bechdolt
Wages of Rascality. N. Carter
Wages of Sin. M. E. Braddon
Wages of Sin. E. Yates
Wagoner's Halt Mystery. M. Poole
Waif of the River. J. Farnol
Waifs and Strays. O. Henry
Waifs of Circumstance. L. Tracy
Waikiki Widow. J. Sheridan
Wail for the Corpses. L. Treat
Wailing Frail. R. S. Prather
Wailing Rock Murders. C. Orr
Wailing Woman. D. Shattuck
Wait. E. Berckman
Wait for Death. G. Ashe
Wait for Death. J. Veitch
Wait for It, Pal. A. Bocca
Wait for Me, Wendy. J. Marie
Wait for the Corpse. M. Murray
Wait for the Dawn. M. Albrand
Wait for the Wake. M. Carr
Wait for the Wedding. C. Fremlin
Wait, Just You Wait. E. Berckman
Wait Long, Wait Still. M. M. Thomas
Wait Until Dark. F. Knott
Wait Until the Evening. H. Bennett
Waiting Darkness. W. D. Roberts
Waiting for a Tiger. B. Healey
Waiting for Oliver. S. Troy
Waiting for the News. L. Litwak
Waiting for the Police and other stories. J. J. Farjeon
Waiting for Willa. D. Eden
Waiting Game. M. Powell
Waiting Game. P. Wayland
Waiting Race. E. Yates
Waiting Room Mystery. A. Blair
Waiting Sands. S. Howatch
Waiting to Hear from William. B. H. Deal
Wake All the Dead. S. Kilpatrick
Wake for a Lady. H. W. Roden
Wake for Mourning. Shane Martin
Wake in Fright. K. Cook
Wake of the Icarus. N. Benchley
Wake of the Setting Sun. W. A. Stowell

Wake the Sleeping Wolf. R. Foley
Wake the Sleeping Wolf. T. McCoy
Wake Up and Scream. M. K. Ozaki
Wake Up Dead. W. Wall
Wake Up Screaming! A. Kent
Wake Up to Murder. D. Keene
Wake Up with a Stranger. F. Flora
Wakefield Witches. D. Winston
Walbury Case. A. Hilliers
Walde-Warren; a Tale of Circumstantial Evidence. Emerson Bennett
Waldo. L. Kauffmann
Walk a Black Wind. Michael Collins
Walk a Crooked Mile. R. Deming
Walk a Crooked Mile. R. P. Hansen
Walk a Crooked Mile. J. Philips
Walk a Crooked Mile. S. Truss
Walk a Tightrope. J. Ellis
Walk Around the Square. D. Winston
Walk at a Steady Pace. N. Fisher
Walk at Night. D. Craig
Walk in, Death. P. Malloch
Walk in Fear. W. H. Baker
Walk in Fear. W. T. Ballard
Walk in Shadow. J. Fast
Walk in the Dark. C. Phillips
Walk in the Dark. J. Roffman
Walk in the Jungle. G. Canary
Walk in the Paradise Garden. A. Maybury
Walk in the Shadows. R. Dolphin
Walk into Murder. P. Helm
Walk into My Parlour. D. Eden
Walk into My Parlour. A. Hocking
Walk into My Parlour. Rona Randall
Walk into Yesterday. Mildred Davis
Walk of the Devil. M. Kane
Walk on the Blind Side. J. T. MacCargo
Walk out on Death. C. Armstrong
Walk Softly. W. Sproule
Walk Softly in Fear. M. Butterworth
Walk Softly, Men Praying. O. Wynd
Walk Softly, Walk Deadly. L. Bergman
Walk Softly Witch! C. Brown
Walk Softly, Witch. C. Brown
Walk the Bloody Boulevard. A. A. Marcus
Walk the Dark Bridge. W. O'Farrell
Walk the Dark Streets. W. Krasner
Walk to the River. W. Hoffman
Walk to Your Grave. N. M. Newland
Walk with Care. P. Wentworth
Walk with Evil. R. Wilder
Walker of the Secret Service. M. D. Post
Walking Corpse. G. D. H. Cole
Walking Dead. M. Hervey
Walking Dead Man. H. Pentecost
Walking Shadow. L. G. Offord
Walking Shadow. J. M. Walsh
Walking Stick. Winston Graham
Walking Tall. D. Warren
Walking Tall: Part 2. Webster Carey
Walking the Dusk. L. J. Webb
Walking Trip. H. Buckmaster
Walking Wounded. J. Laffin
Wall. M. R. Rinehart
Wall in the Long Dark Night. O. Wynd
Wall of Eyes. M. Millar
Wall of Jeopardy. W. Spann
Wall of Masks. B. Coffey
Wall of Men. W. Rollins
Wall Street and the Woods. W. J. Flagg
Wall Street Haul. Anonymous
Wall Street Haul. N. Carter
Wall Street Murders. D. M. Hoffecker
Wall Street Swindlers. J. Sharp
Wall Street Wonder. D. J. MacKenzie
Wallace at Bay. A. Wilson
Wallace Intervenes. A. Wilson
Wallace of the Secret Service. A. Wilson
Wallace, the Hero of Scotland. G. W. M. Reynolds
Walled Parrot. J. Weston
Wallingford and Blackie Daw. G. R. Chester
Wallingford in His Prime. G. R. Chester
Walls Are High. J. Van Raalte
Walls Came Tumbling Down. B. H. Deal
Walls Came Tumbling Down. J. Eisinger
Walls of Silence. D. Hawkins
Walt Wheeler, the Scout Detective. H. Rockwood
Walter Syndrome. R. Neely
Walter's Word. J. Payn
Walton Mystery. L. Reynolds
Waltz Across Texas. M. Crawford
Waltz in Scarlet. Muriel Bradley
Waltz into Darkness. W. Irish
Waltz of Death. P. B. Maxon
Waltz of My Heart. M. Richmond
Wandering Dogies. W. C. Tuttle
Wandering Knife. M. R. Rinehart
Wandering Romanoff. B. Kennedy
Wandering Widows. E. Ferrars
Wanderings of Asaf. Afghan
Want to Stay Alive? J. H. Chase
Wanted! C. Dawe
Wanted! D. Donovan
Wanted. W. M. Graydon
Wanted: A Clew. N. Carter
Wanted: A Fool. P. E. Curtiss
Wanted: A Murderess. M. Holbrook
Wanted at His Office. Leonard Cooper
Wanted by the Gestapo. A. O. Pollard
Wanted by the Police. O. Harper
Wanted by Two Clients. N. Carter
Wanted: Danny Fontaine. W. Ard
Wanted: Dead Men. M. E. Chaber
Wanted: Dead or Alive. M. Hervey
Wanted Dead or Alive! M. Leinster
Wanted for Killing. J. Welcome
Wanted for Murder. L. Charteris
Wanted for Murder. R. Gilmour
Wanted for Murder. H. Holt
Wanted for Murder. N. Rutledge
Wanted for Questioning. Mark Cross
Wanted for Questioning. W. McNeilly
Wanted Man. H. Cecil
Wanted--One Body! C. Dyer
Wanted: Someone Innocent. M. Allingham
Wanton. C. Brown
Wanton for Murder. H. Klinger
Wanton Princess. D. Wheatley
Wanton Venus. M. Leblanc
Wantons Die Hard. L. Gribble
Wapping Butt. L. Blake
War Against the Mafia. D. Pendleton
War and the Woman. M. Pemberton
War Bride. Roy Vickers
War Dog Stirs. H. Hastings
War in the Gates. L. A. B. Cooke
War Maker. A. Hillgarth
War of Brains. N. Carter
War of Nerves. P. Brickhill
War of the Dons. P. Rabe
War Runners. W. McNeilly
War Terror. A. B. Reeve
Ward of Navarre. M. Gerard
Warden of the North. L. C. Douthwaite
Wardour Street Mystery. R. Dark
Ware Case. G. Pleydell
'Ware Danger. G. Ashe
Warehouse Murder. Davies
Warlock. M. Olden
Warlock. W. Tucker
Warlock's Daughter. Angela Gray
Warlock's Woman. J. De Pre
Warm and Golden War. N. Luard
Warmaster. P. McCutchan
Warn the Baron. A. Morton
Warned Off. J. Fairfax-Blakeborough
Warned Off. N. Gould
Warned Off! J. Hunter
Warning Bell. S. Ransome
Warning Bell. Grace M. White
Warning Shot. W. Masterson
Warning to Critics. A. Melville
Warrant for a Wanton. M. Gillian
Warrant for Arrest. F. Didelot
Warrant for X. P. MacDonald
Warrant No. 113. E. Gaboriau
Warrielaw Jewel. W. Peck
Warring Sky. P. Saxon
Warrior's Playtime. G. Hackforth-Jones
Wars Within Wars. Sheila Ross
Warsaw Document. Adam Hall
Warwick. M. T. Walworth
Wary Transgressor. R. Marshall
Was Ever Woman in This Humor Wooed? C. Gibbon
Was He Guilty? E. A. Dupuy
Was He Severe? H. Wood
Was It a Ghost? Anonymous
Was It Montelli? L. Cargill
Was It Murder? F. Du Boisgobey
Was It Murder? G. Trevor
Was It Murder? J. H. Waring
Was Murder Done? S. Fowler
Was She Justified? F. Barrett
Was She Poison? D. Linton
Was She Worth It? M. Leighton
Was the Mayor Murdered? T. A. Plummer
Washington IOU. D. Pendleton
Washington Legation Murders. V. W. Mason
Washington Payoff. Gordon Davis
Washington Square Enigma. H. S. Keeler
Washington Whispers Murder. L. Ford
Washington Woman. D. Varnado
Wasp. J. Cleft-Addams
Wasp. U. Curtiss
Wasp in the Web. R. B. Amos
Waste Lands. C. Dawe
Wasted Crime. D. C. Murray
Wasted Fires. H. Nisbet
Wastrel Goes West. J. Street
Watch Across the Channel. M. McKenna
Watch Below. Taffrail
Watch Dog. A. Hornblow
Watch McLean. G. Goodchild
Watch Mr. Moh. J. Cowdroy
Watch of Evil. P. Le Bailly
Watch on the Bridge. D. Garth
Watch on the Wall. H. Burnett
Watch Sinister. M. Blizard
Watch the Wall. L. Meynell
Watch the Wall, My Darling. J. A. Hodge
Watched Out. E. A. Clancy
Watcher. D. Hitchens
Watcher. G. Verner
Watcher and other weird stories. J. S. Le Fanu
Watcher at the Door. G. H. Hall
Watcher by the Threshold. J. Buchan
Watcher in the Dark. D. Daniels
Watcher in the Shadows. G. Household
Watcher in the Wood. M. G. Kiddy
Watcher on the Shore. I. Lambot
Watchers. A. E. W. Mason
Watchers. W. D. Roberts
Watchers. V. Siller

Watchers in the Hills. W. R. Foran
Watchers of the Plains. R. Cullum
Watches of the Night. G. R. Sims
Watchful at Night. J. Fast
Watching Brief. J. Pattinson
Watchmaker. G. Simenon
Watchmaker of Everton. G. Simenon
Watchman. D. Grubb
Watchman's Stone. Rona Randall
Water for the Fire. J. Fores
Water Horse. G. Scott
Water on the Brain. C. MacKenzie
Water Trail. I. Stark
Water Weed. A. Campbell
Water Witch. R. Thorndike
Waterfront. F. Findley
Waterfront Cop. W. P. McGivern
Watering Place of Good Peace. G. Jenkins
Waterloo. F. E. Smith
Waterman. Eric Lambert
Watermead Affair. R. Barr
Waters of Madness. W. A. Ballinger
Waters of Sadness. J. Cassells
Waters of the North. L. C. Douthwaite
Watershed. N. Tranter
Watersplash. P. Wentworth
Watertown Mystery. H. Rockwood
Watson's Choice. G. Mitchell
Watson's Revenge. R. Mallett
Wave Hangs Dark. A. Dipper
Wave of Fatalities. M. Delving
Waves Behind the Boat. Francis King
Wax. Ethel L. White
Wax Apple. T. Coe
Wax Flowers for Gloria. P. Flower
Waxworks Murder. J. D. Carr
Waxworks Spies. H. C. Davis
'Way Aloft. E. L. Long
Way Back. J. Mitchell
Way Beyond. J. Farnol
Way of a Maid. C. Dawe
Way of a Wanton. R. S. Prather
Way of an Eagle. D. Potter
Way of Deception. L. Beresford
Way of Escape. C. Stanton
Way of Sinners. M. Leighton
Way of the Cardines. S. P. Hyatt
Way of the Four. Mark Cross
Way of the North. J. B. Hendryx
Way of the Strong. R. Cullum
Way of the Tamarisk. V. Maxwell
Way of the Weasel. J. Mowbray
Way of the Wicked. N. Carter
Way of the Wicked. W. Woolfolk
Way of the World. W. T. Adams
Way of the World. D. C. Murray
Way of These Women. E. P. Oppenheim
Way Out. B. Graeme
Way Out Wanton. H. Janson
Way Some People Die. J. R. Macdonald
Way the Cookie Crumbles. J. H. Chase
Way to Adventure, and two other stories. J. G. Dunbar
Way to Dusty Death. Alistair MacLean
Way to Go, Doll Baby! W. R. Cox
Way to Gold. W. D. Steele
Way to Nowhere. M. McShane
Way to Win. W. LeQueux
Way We Die Now. M. Z. Lewin
Way We Love. S. Friedman
Waylaid by Wireless. E. Balmer
Waylaid in Boston. Elliot Paul
Wayland of the Guides. B. Bolt
Wayland 13. F. Shroyer
Ways and Means. H. Cecil
Ways of Death. Hans C. Owen
Ways of Men. H. Flowerdew
Ways of the Millionaire. O. Crawfurd
Ways That Are Wary. L. De Bra
Wayward. C. Brown

Wayward Angel. V. Chute
Wayward Blonde. M. Corrigan
Wayward Blonde. J. Creighton
Wayward Girl. B. Reynolds
Wayward Girl's Fate. Hawkshaw
Wayward Heart. J. MacKenzie
Wayward Nymph. C. H. Barker
Wayward Wahine. C. Brown
Wayward Widow. W. C. Gault
Wayward Woman. A. Griffiths
We All Killed Grandma. F. Brown
We Are for the Dark. D. Eden
We Died in Bond Street. J. Ward
We Don't Want to Lose You. V. Bridges
We Have Always Lived in the Castle. S. Jackson
We Haven't Seen Her Lately. E. Ferrars
We Never Die in the Winter. A. Manning
We Saw Him Die. A. M. Stein
We Shall See. E. Wallace
We Shot an Arrow. G. Goodchild
We, the Accused. E. Raymond
We the Condemned. N. Karta
We, the Condemned. J. Robb
We, the Killers. Michael Brett
We the Unworthy. J. Courage
We Walk with Death. H. Desmond
We Who Survived. S. Noel
We Will Meet Again. J. Hawkins
Weak and the Strong. A. Kent
Weak-Eyed Bat. M. Millar
Weak-Kneed Rogue. N. Carter
Weaker Vessel. D. C. Murray
Weapon Heavy. J. Reese
Weapon of Night. N. Carter
Weapons of Mystery. J. Hocking
Wear the Butcher's Medal. J. Brunner
Weather of My Fate. P. Conway
Weathercock. E. H. Clements
Weatherel Affair. J. W. De Forrest
Weatherman Guy. J. Burmeister
Weave a Rope of Sand. E. Trevor
Weave a Wicked Web. P. Kruger
Weaver Webb. Old Sleuth
Weavers. A. Askew
Weavers and Weft, and other tales. M. E. Braddon
Weaving the Web. N. Carter
Weaving the Web. H. Mee
Web. Rolf Bennett
Web. H. Brooke
Web. F. T. Hill
Web. S. Horler
Web. F. A. Kummer
Web. F. Urquhart
Web in Childhood. Winifred Duke
Web of Deceit. C. A. Smith
Web of Destiny. Seamark
Web of Enchantment. M. Richmond
Web of Evil. L. Emerick
Web of Fate. T. W. Speight
Web of Fear. M. Reisner
Web of Hate. L. Thayer
Web of Horror. C. Farr
Web of Love. W. E. D. Ross
Web of Murder. Seamark
Web of Murder. H. Whittington
Web of Peril. D. Daniels
Web of Salvage. B. Callison
Web of Shadows. E. Backhouse
Web of Silence. J. Wainwright
Web of Spies. N. Carter

Web of the Golden Spider. F. O. Bartlett
Web of the Spider. H. B. M. Watson
Web of Wan Li. L. Beresford
Web to Catch a Spider. C. Joyce
Webs in the Way. G. M. Fenn
Wed for Wealth. A. Wood
Wedded but Not a Wife. F. Warden
Wedderburn's Will. T. Cobb
Wedding Bargain. A. S. Turnbull
Wedding-Chest Mystery. A. Fielding
Wedding Day. C. N. Williamson
Wedding Eve Murder. B. M. Dix
Wedding Guest Sat on a Stone. R. Shattuck
Wedding March Murder. Monte Barrett
Wedding Night Murder. C. Bush
Wedding Ring. H. M. Jones
Wednesday at Noon. J. Corbett
Wednesday the Tenth. G. Allen
Weed. C. L. Cooper
Weed. J. Pattinson
Weeds. H. Imbert-Terry
Weeds of Hate. O. Binns
Weed-End at Green Trees. M. Meynell
Weed-End at Thrackley. A. Melville
Week-End Crime Book. J. M. Walsh
Week-End Murder. N. Brady
Week-End Murders. A. A. Archer
Week-End with Death. H. Gray
Week-Ends for Harry. H. Holland
Week of Love. J. Leasor
Week of Passion. Edward Jenkins
Week of Suspense. G. Greenaway
Week of Suspense. A. MacKenzie
Week to Kill. D. Delman
Weekend at the Villa. D. G. Quintano
Weekend Girls. Jonathan Burke
Weekend in Baghdad. R. Wadham
Weekend Mystery. R. A. Simon
Weekend with Death. P. Wentworth
Weekend with Maxwell. E. G. Cousins
Weep for a Blonde. B. Halliday
Weep for a Wanton. L. Treat
Weep for Me. J. D. MacDonald
Weep for Willow Green. P. Kruger
Weep No More, Lady. R. Cocking
Weeping and the Laughter. V. Caspary
Weeping Lady. J. L. Roberts
Weeping Tower. C. Randell
Weeping Willow Murders. C. Koonce
Weighed in the Balance. N. Carter
Weight of the Cross. F. M. White
Weight of the Evidence. M. Innes
Weighted Scales. B. Musto
Weir Boyd Mystery. S. G. Hedges
Weird Adventures of the Shadow. M. Grant
Weird Courtship. Old Sleuth
Weird Gift. G. Ohnet
Weird Legacy. F. Johnston
Weird of Deadly Hollow. B. Mitford
Weird o' It. M. P. Shiel
Weird Picture. J. R. Carling
Weird Sea Mystery. Old Sleuth
Weird Sisters. J. Blyth
Weird Sisters. R. Dowling
Weird Stories. J. H. Riddell
Weird Treasure. N. Carter
Weird Wedlock. R. M. Gilchrist
Weird World of Wes Beattie. J. N. Harris
Welcome Back to Wayland. F. Shroyer
Welcome, Danger! J. Reach
Welcome Danger. Robert Simpson
Welcome Death. G. Daniel
Welcome for a Hero. Robin Perry
Welcome Home! H. Adams
Welcome Home, Lily Glow. Clay Henry

Welcome, My Dear, to Belfry House. S. Forbes
Welcome, Proud Lady. June Drummond
Welcome to Xanadu. N. Benchley
Welded Lives. G. Ingram
Welding the Chain. D. Stewart
Welfleet Mystery. Mrs. G. Sheldon
Well-Born Corpse. E. Benjamin
Well Caught. A. Armstrong
Well Caught, McLean! G. Goodchild
Well-Dressed for Murder. Laverne Rice
Well-Dressed Skeleton. B. Williams
Well-Furnished Life. E. McCrae
Well, I'll Be Hanged! Kevin O'Hara
Well-Known Face. J. Bell
Well Now, My Pretty--. J. H. Chase
Well-Told Lie. C. Hobhouse
Wellspring. E. H. Hawkins
Wench Is Dead. F. Brown
Wench Is Dead. R. Fenisong
Wench Is Wicked. C. Brown
Wentworth Hall. A. O'Neill-Barna
Wentworth Mystery. W. Phillips
We're All Guilty. J. Reach
Were Death Denied. D. Yates
Were They Justified? A. Philips
Werewolf. C. L. Swem
Werewolf Among Us. D. Koontz
Werewolf by Moonlight. G. N. Smith
Werewolf of Elphinstone. R. C. Armour
Werewolf of Paris. G. Endore
Werewolf Walks Tonight. M. Avallone
West End. J. G. Brandon
West Highland Spirits. C. J. C. Hyne
West of Aztec Pass. W. C. Tuttle
West of Jerusalem. G. De Villiers
West of Rio Grande. T. Craig
West of the Moon. A. Burr
West Pier. P. Hamilton
West Point Lieutenant. Old Sleuth
West Shore Mystery. Old Sleuth
West Side Jungle. J. Ridgway
Westbound Murder. C. S. Wallace
Western Express Robbery. N. Ridley
Western Ferret. I. Stark
Westgate Mystery. Darby St. John
Westhorpe Mystery. I. D. Hardy
Westlade Murders. T. A. Plummer
Westlakes. T. Cobb
Westminster Mystery. Elaine Hamilton
Westminster One. T. Willis
Weston of the North-West Mounted Police. T. Lund
Weston of the Royal North-West Mounted Police. T. Lund
Westwood Mystery. C. J. Dutton
Westwood Mystery. A. Fielding
Wetback. W. O'Farrell
Wettermark. E. Chaze
We've Been Waiting for You. E. Thornbury
Wharf Sinister. A. Grace
What a Body! A. Green
What a Tangled Web. A. Hocking
What Are the Bugles Blowing For? N. Freeling
What Are Your Angels Now? P. Groom
What Became of Alex Bretherton? P. Harris
What Became of Eugene Ridgewood? P. James
What Became of Mr. Desmond. C. N. Boyle
What Beckoning Ghost. D. G. Browne
What Befell a Bristol Trader. J. Johnson
What Can You Lose? R. B. Saxe

What Changed Charley Farthing. M. Hebden
What Crime Is It? D. Gardiner
What Dark Secret. D. Dudley
What Did Hattie See? K. Roos
What Did I Do Tomorrow? L. P. Davies
What Do I Care? D. Linton
What Dread Hand. C. Brand
What Dread Hand? E. Gill
What Else Could I Do? T. Claymore
What Ever Happened to Baby Jane? H. Farrell
What Fools Men Are! S. Murray
What Fools Women Are! D. Vane
What Gentleman Strangles a Lady? R. G. Dean
What Happened at Andals? John Arnold
What Happened at Hazelwood. M. Innes
What Happened Is This. B. Von Hutten
What Happened to Forester. E. P. Oppenheim
What Happened to Hammond? H. Blayn
What Happened to Mary? R. C. Brown
What Hast Thou Done? J. F. Molloy
What Have They Done to You, Ben? B. Reade
What He Cost Her. J. Payn
What He Least Expected. Holworthy Hall
What Immortal Hand. J. Curtis
What Is This Mystery? M. E. Braddon
What Is Your Verdict? T. J. R. Sennocke
What Lies Beneath. B. Swift
What Mrs. McGillicuddy Saw! A. Christie
What News of Kitty? D. Quentin
What Next? Winifred Graham
What Next? J. T. Patterson
What Night Will Bring. H. Bailey
What--No Body? Mary Archer
What--No Witnesses? Mary Archer
What Now My Love. F. Salas
What of Terry Conniston? B. Garfield
What Old Father Thames Said. C. Nelson
What Price Doubloons? Frank King
What Price Murder. C. F. Adams
What Price Paradise? A. Hillgarth
What Really Happened. B. Halliday
What Really Happened. M. B. Lowndes
What Rhymes with Murder? J. Iams
What Rough Beast. J. Trench
What Say the Jury? C. M. Wills
What Shall I Cry. A. Binkley
What Shall It Profit? H. E. Inman
What She Ought to Be. F. Warden
What Should a Man Do? H. G. Hutchinson
What Should You Know of Dying. T. Wells
What Stranger Cause? F. Bamford
What the Doctor Ordered. V. Bridges
What the Peeper Saw. J. Gratus
What Thinkest Thou, Simon? Winifred Graham
What Timmy Did. M. B. Lowndes
What to Do Until the Undertaker Comes. T. Wells
What Was It? and other stories. Fitz-James O'Brien
What Will the World Say? C. Gibbon
What Would You Have Done? L. Tracy
Whatever Dies. P. Woodruff
Whatever Goes Up. B. Millhauser
Whatever Happened to Aunt Alice? U. Curtiss
Whatever Happened to Ruby? W. Owen
What's at the End? L. Beresford
What's Become of Screwloose? and other stories. R. Goulart
What's Better than Money? J. H. Chase
What's Bred in the Bone. G. Allen
What's Funny About Murder. Craig Cooper
What's in a Name? A. Spiller
What's in the Dark? E. Queen
What's Past Is Prologue. M. McKenna

What's the Matter with Helen? R. Deming
What's with You? D. Ambler
What's Wrong at Pyford? D. Fisher
What's Ya Problem? H. Zore
Whatsoever a Man Soweth. W. LeQueux
Whatsoever Things Are True. S. Harvester
Wheat and Tares. P. Trent
Wheatstack. J. S. Fletcher
Wheel. Alan White
Wheel Fortune. Karen Campbell
Wheel Is Fixed. J. M. Fox
Wheel o'Fortune. L. Tracy
Wheel of Circumstance. D. W. Spurgeon
Wheel of Death. R. T. M. Scott
Wheel of Fire. K. M. Middlemass
Wheel of Fortune. Karen Campbell
Wheel Spins. Ethel L. White
Wheel That Turned. K. M. Knight
Wheelchair Corpse. W. Levinrew
Wheeler, Dealer! C. Brown
Wheeler Fortune. C. Brown
Wheeling Light. F. Hume
Wheels. J. Spenser
Wheels Beneath. G. Kelton
Wheels in the Forest. J. N. Chance
Wheels of Anarchy. M. Pemberton
Wheels Within Wheels. H. Mee
Wheels Within Wheels. C. Wells
When a Man Yields. N. Carter
When a Rogue's in Power. N. Carter
When All Is Staked. N. Carter
When Ape Is King. O. Wynd
When Beggars Choose. K. N. Burt
When Brave Men Tremble. N. Carter
When Carruthers Laughed. H. C. McNeile
When Clews Are Hidden. N. Carter
When Cold Steel Clashed. C. Frisbie
When Conscience Sleeps. W. J. Bayfield
When Crook Meets Crook. A. Spiller
When Dames Get Tough. H. Janson
When Danger Threatens. Mark Cross
When Danger Threatens. Sea Lion
When Dead Men Tell Tales. J. Goodwin
When Death Walks. J. Corbett
When Destruction Threatens. N. Carter
When Dorinda Dances. B. Halliday
When Duty Calls. M. I. Burke
When Eight Bells Toll. Alistair MacLean
When Emmalyn Remembers. E. Marlow
When England Slept. H. Curties
When Fell the Night. E. Queen
"When First We Practise." W. Cheame
When Fools Endanger Us. R. Ladline
When Footsteps Echo. B. Copper
When Greek Meets Greek. J. Hatton
When Greek Meets Greek. P. Trent
When Honors Fall. N. Carter
When I Grow Rich. J. Fleming
When I Was Czar. A. W. Marchmont
When in Greece. E. Lathen
When in Rome. N. Marsh
When It Was Dark. G. Thorne
When Jealousy Spurs. N. Carter
When Johnny Died. C. Rougvie
When Last I Died. G. Mitchell
When London Sleeps. H. T. Johnson
When Love Called. A. W. Marchmont
When Michael Calls. J. Farris
When My Ship Comes Home. C. Massie
When Necessity Drives. N. Carter
When No Man Pursueth. M. B. Lowndes
When No Man Pursueth. D. Sharp
When One Door Shuts. M. Pereira
When Rogues Conspire. N. Carter
When Rogues Fall Out. R. A. Freeman

Title Index

When Rogues Fall Out. J. Hatton
When Satan Ruled. C. R. Gull
When Scholars Fall. T. Robinson
When Shall I Sleep Again? N. W. Firth
When She Was Bad. W. Ard
When Spy Meets Spy. R. Walker
When Strangers Meet. R. Bloomfield
When the Bells Rang. A. Armstrong
When the Case Was Opened. J. Bude
When the Cat's Away. G. Bullett
When the Clews Point Wrong. D. Stewart
When the Devil Drives. F. Warden
When the Devil Was Sick. C. Carnac
When the Empire Crashed. A. W. Marchmont
When the Gallows Is High. P. Hastings
When the Gangs Came to London. E. Wallace
When the Gods Laughed. P. Audemars
When the Gunmen Came. J. Hunter
When the Heart Is Young. A. M. Meadows
When the Jury Disagreed! J. Hunter
When the Moon Died. R. Savage
When the Police Failed. R. Ladline
When the Quarry Turns. I. Stark
When the Rainbow Is Pale. G. Joseph
When the Sea Gives Up Its Dead. Mrs. G. Corbett
When the Sun Goes Down. C. Blackstock
When the Trap Was Sprung. N. Carter
When the Wicked Man... J. F. W. Hannay
When the Wicked Man. G. Thorne
When the Wicked Prosper. N. Carter
When the Wind Blows. C. Hare
When the Witch Is Dead. M. L. Roby
When the World Reeled. G. Thorne
When the World Was Younger. M. E. Braddon
When Thief Meets Thief. H. S. Keeler
When Thieves Fall Out. Mark Cross
When Thieves Fall Out. J. K. Stafford
When Thieves Fall Out. B. Thomson
When Threads Get Tangled. J. K. Stafford
When Three Makes Two. H. Carstairs
When Tragedy Grins. Grace M. White
When Trails Cross. J. K. Stafford
When Trails Were New. T. Mundy
When Tutt Meets Tutt. A. Train
Where All the Girls Are Sweeter. R. Butler
Where Angel Treads. G. Montrose
Where Angels Fear... B. Heming
Where Are the Children? M. H. Clark
Where Are You Going? A. Applin
Where Dead Men Walk. H. Leverage
Where Did Charity Go? C. Brown
Where Did the Girls Go? M. Cousin
Where Eagles Dare. Alistair MacLean
Where Every Prospect Pleases. R. Halket
Where Evil Waits. M. Lynch
Where Ignorance Is Bliss. R. Greene
Where Is Barbara Prentice? M. Burton
Where Is Bianca. E. Queen
Where Is Evie Alton? H. Bourne
Where Is Jane? Lynn Williams
Where Is Janice Gantry? J. D. MacDonald
Where Is Jenny Now? F. S. Wees
Where Is Jenny Willet? W. H. L. Crauford
Where Is Nancy Bostwick? R. Foley
Where Is She Now? L. Meynell
Where Is the Withered Man? N. Deane
Where Murder Waits. Gordon Davis
Where No Fire Burns. M. Garratt
Where No Flags Fly. F. Ayer, Jr.
Where Nothing Ever Happens. L. Shippey
Where Peril Beckons. N. Carter
Where Satan Dwells. F. Stevenson
Where Secrecy Begins. J. C. Nolan
Where Shadows Lie. M. Lynch
Where Some Men Are Men. G. F. Worts
Where Terror Stalked. C. Birkin
Where the Clue Leads. I. Stark
Where the Dark Streets Go. D. S. Davis

Where the Desert Ends. W. LeQueux
Where the East Wind Blows. A. Mair
Where the Fresh Grass Grows. Brian Cooper
Where the Heart Is. A. Hale
Where the Pavement Ends. J. Russell
Where the River Bends. J. M. Scott
Where the Shoe Pinches. L. T. Meade
Where the Snow Was Red. H. Pentecost
Where the Spies Are. J. Leasor
Where the Trail Ended. W. M. Graydon
Where There Are Vultures. A. Heckstall-Smith
"Where There Is a Will..." A. Griffin
Where There Was Smoke. B. Flynn
Where There's a Head. L. Gorell
Where There's a Will. K. Chase
Where There's a Will. R. S. Hastings
Where There's a Will. Ellis Peters
Where There's a Will. M. R. Rinehart
Where There's a Will. R. Stout
Where There's Smoke. C. B. Kelland
Where There's Smoke. E. McBain
Where There's Smoke. S. Sterling
Where Was Trail Murdered? T. A. Plummer
Where You Throw Blood. B. Sarto
Whereabouts Unknown. B. Reynolds
Where's Emily. C. Wells
Where's Mr. Chumley? S. Truss
Where's Zenobia? F. Du Boisgobey
Wherever Lynn Goes. Beatrice Parker
Which Doctor? E. Candy
Which I Never. L. A. G. Strong
Which--Innocent or Guilty? E. S. Clem
Which Mrs. Bennett? A. Littlefield
Which Mrs. Torr? M. Parker
Which of Them? P. Black
Which of Us Is Safe? M. Cumberland
Which One? R. A. Bennet
Which the Justice, Which the Thief. W. Harrington
Which Way Came Death? F. Wolseley
Which Way to Die? E. Queen
Whiff of Death. I. Asimov
Whiff of Money. J. H. Chase
While Guy Was in France. T. Cobb
While London Sleeps. R. Dowling
While Love Lay Sleeping. R. Neely
While Murder Waits. B. Cassiday
While Murder Waits. J. Esteven
While of Sound Mind. S. McKenna
While She Sleeps. Ethel L. White
While Still We Live. H. MacInnes
While the Bells Rang. C. L. Clifford
While the City Sleeps. C. Einstein
While the Coffin Waited. J. Sheridan
While the Fetters Were Forged. N. Carter
While the Patient Slept. M. G. Eberhart
While the Wind Howled. A. Gaines
Whilst the Crowd Roared. S. Horler
Whim to Kill. D. Shannon
Whip. S. E. Mason
Whip. R. Parker
Whip and the Tongue. H. L. V. Fletcher
Whip Hand. V. Canning
Whip Hand. R. Crawford
Whip Hand. I. Gordon
Whip Hand. W. F. Sanders
Whip of the Will. Mrs. C. Kernahan
Whip-Poor-Will Mystery. H. Footner
Whiplash. H. Janson

Whiplash. R. W. Taylor
Whipping Boy. P. Orum
Whipping Boys. G. Cullingford
Whipping Girl. R. Rodd
Whips of Time. N. Giles
Whirl of a Bird. G. Peters
Whirligig. R. L. Fish
Whirligig of Time. D. De Jong
Whirligigs. O. Henry
Whirling Death. N. Carter
Whirlpool. J. L. Henderson
Whirlpool. D. Lamson
Whirlpool. V. Morton
Whirlwind Beneath the Sea. K. Stanton
Whiskered Footman. E. Jepson
Whiskey Drips. J. J. Brooks
Whisky Johnny. C. McManus
Whisper Her Name. Howard Hunt
Whisper His Sin. V. Packer
Whisper If You Dare! A. MacKenzie
Whisper in a Lonely Place. G. Sinstadt
Whisper in the Dark. A. Maybury
Whisper in the Dark. K. Troy
Whisper in the Darkness. T. E. Huff
Whisper in the Forest. N. Ames
Whisper in the Glen. P. M. Hubbard
Whisper in the Gloom. N. Blake
Whisper Murder! V. Kelsey
Whisper Murder Softly. P. Bannon
Whisper of Danger. Clarissa Ross
Whisper of Darkness. M. Lynn
Whisper of Death. V. Siller
Whisper of Fear. C. Randell
Whisper of Fear. Elna Stone
Whisper of Heather. L. Benedict
Whisper of Love. F. Flora
Whisper of Shadows. J. L. H. Whitney
Whisper on the Stair. L. Mearson
Whisper Town. J. Philips
Whisperer. W. M. Duncan
Whisperer. Mrs. C. Kernahan
Whisperer. J. M. Walsh
Whispering Buddha. J. C. Cowles
Whispering Caverns. A. Winter
Whispering Chorus. P. P. Sheehan
Whispering Corpse. W. P. McGivern
Whispering Cracksman. B. Perowne
Whispering Cup. M. Seeley
Whispering Dead. A. Ganachilly
Whispering Death. D. Carnay
Whispering Death. J. Pattinson
Whispering Death. J. Spencer
Whispering Ear. C. B. Clason
Whispering Gables. S. Abbott
Whispering Galleries. B. Goldie
Whispering Gallery. W. E. D. Ross
Whispering Ghost. S. Chalmers
Whispering Hill. M. Albrand
Whispering House. M. Erskine
Whispering Island. N. McFather
Whispering Lane. F. Hume
Whispering Lodge. S. Murray
Whispering Man. W. M. Duncan
Whispering Man. H. Holt
Whispering Man. H. K. Webster
Whispering Master. F. Gruber
Whispering Money. Richard Bennett
Whispering Riders. W. B. Bannerman
Whispering Shadows. Herman Landon
Whispering Steel. J. Nicholas
Whispering Tongues. Laurence Kirk
Whispering Wall. P. Carlon
Whispering Walls. W. Spence
Whispering Window. C. Fitzsimmons
Whispering Windows. T. Burke
Whispering Wires. H. Leverage

Whispering Woman. G. Verner
Whispers. Louis Dodge
Whispers in the Dark. J. M. Walsh
Whispers in the Night. Clarissa Ross
Whispers in the Night. W. E. D. Ross
Whispers in the Sun. M. Greig
Whispers of the Flesh. F. Flora
Whistle and I'll Come. P. McCutchan
Whistle at My Window. H. Arvonen
Whistle Me over the Water. W. Leighton
Whistle of Fate. R. Marsh
Whistle Past the Graveyard. R. Deming
Whistle Up the Devil. Derek Smith
Whistler's Lane. Anthea Fraser
Whistling Hangman. B. Kendrick
Whistling in the Dark. H. K. Carpenter
Whistling in the Dark. L. Gross
Whistling Key. V. Gunn
Whistling Legs. R. McDougald
Whistling Man. M. Foster
Whistling Sands. E. Dudley
Whistling Shadow. M. Seeley
Whistling Wires. P. Groom
White Alley. C. Wells
White Angel. J. Corbett
White Arab. E. P. Thorne
White Arrow. A. Wynne
White August. J. Boland
White Badger. C. Talbot
White Bikini. C. Brown
White Bird, and other stories. W. J. Newton
White Blackbird. H. Douglas
White Bride. F. M. White
White Cad Cross-Up. W. F. Nolan
White Camellia. F. Grierson
White Castello. M. McEvoy
White Cat. G. Burgess
White Chalet. L. Cross
White Cipher. H. Leverage
White Circle. C. J. Daly
White Cockatoo. M. G. Eberhart
White Cottage Mystery. M. Allingham
White Countess. F. Warden
White Cowl. F. H. Harrison
White Crash Helmet. P. Fry
White Crow. P. MacDonald
White Crown and other stories. H. D. Ward
White Cruiser. N. Buntline
White Crusaders. A. W. Halse
White Death. W. M. Graydon
White Death. R. Sheckley
White Desert. C. R. Cooper
White Dominoes. F. M. Pettee
White Dress. M. G. Eberhart
White Eagle. Roland Daniel
White Face. E. Wallace
White-Faced Man. Gavin Holt
White Feather Mystery. M. Williamson
White Feathers. G. I. Cervus
White for a Shroud. D. C. Cameron
White Friar. D. Stuart
White Gas. R. Keverne
White Gauntlet. P. Brebner
White Ghost of Fenwick Hall. A. Wharton
White Girls Eastward. T. Craig
White Glove. W. LeQueux
White Glove. F. M. White
White Gold. O. Binns
White Gold. M. D. Orr
White Hand and the Black. B. Mitford
White Hand Mystery. M. E. Campbell
White Hand of Athene. J. Thorne
White Hands of Justice. O. Binns
White Hen. P. Traill
White Horse to Banbury Cross. R. Llewellyn
White Horseman. C. Stanton
White House. M. E. Braddon
White Island. N. Lansdale
White Jade. Jan Alexander
White Jade. W. D. Roberts
White Jade Fox. A. Norton
White King of Africa. W. M. Graydon
White Lady. E. Kyle
White Lady. G. W. M. Reynolds
White Lady of Khaminavatka. R. H. Savage
White Leaves of Death. P. Audemars
White Lie. W. LeQueux
White Lie and No Glory. D. Mariner
White Lie Assignment. P. Driscoll
White Lie Company, and The Woman with the Green Eyes. A. Soutar
White Lie the Dead. P. Loraine
White Line Fever. J. Kaplan
White Magic. M. M. Bodkin
White Man's Chance. J. McCulley
White Man's Justice: Black Man's Grief. D. Goines
White Man's Prestige. E. Leslie
White Man's Stride. L. P. Greene
White Mask. J. M. Walsh
White Mazurka. B. Boyer
White Menace. J. Rhode
White Menace. C. Robertson
White Mercenary. P. Saxon
White Mice. R. H. Davis
White Moll. F. Packard
White Motley. M. Pemberton
White Negro. A. Mills
White Nigger. F. A. M. Webster
White Night. F. Rosaire
White Owl. E. Snell
White Panthers. D. Vane
White Pavilion. V. Johnston
White Peacock. M. L. Roby
White Phantom. M. E. Braddon
White Phantom. J. Hunter
White Pierrot. P. Barrington
White Prior. F. Hume
White Priory Murders. Carter Dickson
White Raiment. C. H. Bullivant
White Raven. Roy Vickers
White Refugees. R. C. Armour
White Rider. L. Charteris
White Rook. J. B. Harris-Burland
White Rook. H. M. Kahler
White Room. P. Davies
White Rose. Alanna Knight
White Rose Mystery. G. Biss
White Sapphire. L. F. Hartman
White Satin. J. L. Rickard
White Savage. A. W. Upfield
White Shield. B. Mitford
White Shroud. R. Nicholas
White Sin. A. Wood
White Siren. S. Maddock
White Snake. A. Mills
White South. H. Innes
White Stacks. W. Hewlett
White Streak. S. Gluck
White Trails over London. R. Wilkes-Hunter
White Tuareg. Operator 1384
White Velvet. S. Rohmer
White Violets. E. Crandall
White Virgin. G. M. Fenn
White Walls. M. Pemberton
White Wig. G. Verner
White Witch. T. Douglas
White Witch. F. Warden
White Witch of Mayfair. George Griffith
White Witch of the Matabele. F. Whishaw
White Witch of the South Seas. D. Wheatley
White Witch's Warning. Anonymous
White Wizard. N. Buntline
White Wolverine Contract. P. Atlee
Whitebird Murders. T. B. Black
Whitechapel Murder. F. Allen
Whitechapel Murders. A. F. Pinkerton
Whitechapel Mystery. N. T. Oliver
Whiteoakes Murder. J. Laurence
Whitewater. B. Knox
Whither Do You Wander? J. Tickell
Whither Thou Goest. W. LeQueux
Whitney Case. J. Bentley
Whitton's Folly. P. Hill
Who? P. Baron
Who? A. Budrys
Who? E. Kent
Who? A. W. Marchmont
Who? A. J. Palermo
Who Are You, Linda Condrick? P. Carlon
Who Benefits? L. Thayer
Who Called Diamonds? G. Brodie
Who Calls the Tune. N. Bawden
Who Closed the Casement? T. Cobb
Who Cries for a Loser? R. Owen
Who Cut the Colonel's Throat? W. L. Hay
Who Dialled 999? C. F. Gregg
Who Did It. Anonymous
Who Did It? N. Gould
Who Died at the Grange? M. Halliday
Who Dies? S. P. B. Mais
Who Dies for Me? S. H. Courtier
Who Dies Next? H. J. Wurr
Who Dies There? J. P. Duff
Who Dies There? H. Kane
Who Do Women?... M. Corrigan
Who Else but She? S. Fowler
Who Evil Thinks. R. Glendinning
Who Fired the Factory? T. A. Plummer
Who Giveth This Woman? W. LeQueux
Who Goes Hang? S. Hyland
Who Goes Home? R. Curle
Who Goes There? B. K. Benson
Who Goes There? L. Paxton
Who Goes There? D. Vane
Who Has Wilma Lathrop? D. Keene
Who Is Elissa Sheldon? D. Montross
Who Is Guilty? P. Woolf
Who Is John Noman? C. H. Beckett
Who Is Lewis Pinder? L. P. Davies
Who Is Mary Stark? L. Kropp
Who Is My Enemy? Barbara Cooper
Who Is My Neighbor? N. Balchin
Who Is Nemo? R. Douglas
Who Is the Ace? N. Anthony
Who Is the Heir? M. Collins
Who Is the Man? J. S. Tait
Who Is the Next? H. K. Webster
Who Is This Girl? H. T. Miller
Who Is This Man? A. MacGowan
Who Keeps the Keys? F. Leslie
Who Kill to Live. H. Harris
Who Killed Alfred Snowe? J. S. Fletcher
Who Killed Amanda? G. Monro
Who Killed Ann Gage? R. St. Clair
Who Killed Aunt Maggie? Medora Field
Who Killed Beau Sparrow? Roger Fuller
Who Killed Brother Treasurer? C. M. Wills
Who Killed Caldwell? C. Wells
Who Killed Carson? H. H. C. Gibbons
Who Killed Cavelotti? A. Newell
Who Killed Charmian Karslake? A. Haynes
Who Killed Chloe? M. Allingham

Title Index

Who Killed Cock Robin? H. Hext
Who Killed Coralie? The Aresbys
Who Killed Diana? H. Hext
Who Killed Dick Whittington? E. Radford
Who Killed Dr. Sex? C. Brown
Who Killed Enoch Powell? Arthur Wise
Who Killed Frankie Leash? M. Echard
Who Killed Gatton? E. C. Vivian
Who Killed Gerald Cruden? Alan Graham
Who Killed Gregory? Eugene Jones
Who Killed Henry Wickenstrom. Mark Cross
Who Killed Honeybee? Craig Cooper
Who Killed Jefferson Broome? H. M. Keynes
Who Killed Lady Poynder? R. Marsh
Who Killed Lord Brixham? G. De Jeans
Who Killed Lord Henry Rollestone? J. Daye
Who Killed Lord Luxmore? M. Leighton
Who Killed Madcap Millicent? Roger Fuller
Who Killed Mr. Fisk? J. Brooke
Who Killed Mr. Garland's Mistress? R. Forrest
Who Killed My Wife? R. Goyne
Who Killed Netta Maul? F. Arthur
Who Killed Oliver Cromwell? L. Gribble
Who Killed Peter Trueman? Anonymous
Who Killed Pretty Becky Low? A. B. Cunningham
Who Killed Rebecca? M. Halliday
Who Killed Robert Prentice? D. Wheatley
Who Killed Robin Cockland? P. Luck
Who Killed Roger Whitely? B. Allerton
Who Killed Rosa Gray? F. Usher
Who Killed Stella Pomeroy? B. Thomson
Who Killed Stephen Tennant? T. S. King
Who Killed Sweet Sue? H. Kane
Who Killed the Chauffeur? G. V. Vosper
Who Killed the Count? B. Delane
Who Killed the Crooner? R. Trevor
Who Killed the Curate? J. Coggin
Who Killed the Doctor? M. Burton
Who Killed the Doctors? A. Peters
Who Killed the Husband? H. Footner
Who Killed the Pie Man? P. Lore
Who Killed Trainer Lincoln? A. Steffens Hardy
Who Killed William Drew? Harrington Strong
Who Killed You, Cindy Castle? K. Carr
Who Lies Bleeding? H. Carstairs
Who Lies Here? Ellis Peters
Who Maimed Spurto? J. Fairfax-Blakeborough
Who Murdered Reynard? S. Fowler
Who Murdered Westaway? G. Comley
Who Needs Enemies? G. Kent
Who Needs Forever? E. I. English
Who Opened the Door? T. Cobb
Who Owned the Jewels? M. V. Victor
Who Pays the Piper? P. Wentworth
Who Plays with Sin. A. Spiller
Who Poisoned Hetty Duncan? and other detective stories. D. Donovan
Who Put It There? Mary Scott
Who Rides a Tiger. D. M. Disney
Who Rides a Tiger? C. Robertson
Who Rides on a Tiger. M. B. Lowndes
Who Said Murder? M. Halliday
Who Saw Her Die? P. Moyes
Who Saw Him Die? M. Halliday
Who Saw Maggie Brown? K. Roos
Who Says a Corpse Has to Be Dull. D. Von Elsner
Who Screamed? J. Courage
Who Shall Be Victor? E. A. Dupuy
Who Shall Condemn? J. C. Shannon
Who Shall Hang? M. Magill
Who Shot the Bull? B. Knox
Who Shot the Spy? Anonymous
Who Should Have Died? M. Silverman

Who Spies, Who Kills? E. Queen
Who Spoke Last? J. V. Turner
Who Steals My Name. C. Richards
Who Stole Sassi Manoon? D. E. Westlake
Who Strikes by Night. Richard Grant
Who Sups with the Devil? P. McCartney
Who Told Clutha. H. Munro
Who Walk in Fear. N. Bell
Who Walks by Moonlight? M. McEvoy
Who Was Claire Jallu? P. Boileau
Who Was Ellen Smith? K. Ayling
Who Was He? P. Little
Who Was He? M. V. Victor
Who Was Lady Thurne? F. Warden
Who Was the Jester? G. Ashe
Who Was the Killer? J. Corbett
Who Was the Killer? N. Wray
Who Was This Woman? Two Photographs, and The King of Hearts. H. C. McNeile
Who Were You with Last Night? F. Raphael
Who Will Watch the Watchers. E. Fadiman
Who Wins? M. A. Fleming
Who'd Shoot a Genius? S. M. Schley
Whole Hog. M. Kenyon
Who'll Buy My Evil? A. Caillou
Whom God Hath Joined. F. Hume
Whom Gods Destroy. Clifton Adams
Whom Nobody Owns. A. Spiller
Whom the Gods Would Destroy. N. Carter
Whore-Mother. S. Herron
Whoreson. D. Goines
Who's Afraid? E. S. Holding
Who's Been Sitting in My Chair? C. Armstrong
Who's Been Sleeping in My Grave? J. Hart
Who's Calling? H. McCloy
Who's for Dying. M. MacQuade
Who's in Charge Here? H. H. Kirst
Who's Sorry Now? D. Linton
Who's the Guy? A. J. Evans
Who's the Target? M. Carr
Whose Body? D. L. Sayers
Whose Corpse? S. Ransome
Whose Hand? V. Loder
Whose Hand? W. G. Willis
Whose Head? W. E. Huntsberry
Whose Little Girl Are You? D. Craig
Whose Millions? Joseph Montague
Whose the Hand? Diana Forbes
Whose Was the Crime? G. Warden
Whose Was the Hand? W. J. Bayfield
Whose Was the Hand? M. E. Braddon
Whose Was the Hand? J. E. Muddock
Whose Wife? C. H. Bullivant
Whoso Findeth a Wife. W. LeQueux
Whosoever Loveth. W. LeQueux
Why? E. D. Bartlett
Why Be Lonely? M. B. Lowndes
Why Call It Homicide? R. Kirby
Why Did He Do It? B. Capes
Why Did She Die? J. Coggin
Why Did Trethewy Die? R. A. J. Walling
Why Didn't They Ask Evans? A. Christie
Why It Happened. M. B. Lowndes
Why Jane Matcham Disappeared. M. Carane
Why Kill a Butler? P. H. Powell
Why Kill Johnny? H. Carmichael
Why Murder? N. Deane
Why Murder Mrs. Hope? J. Courage
Why Murder the Judge? C. S. Hammock

Why Not? George Scott
Why Pick on Me? R. Marshall
Why Pick on Me? P. Muller
Why Pick on Pickles? M. Durham
Why She Cries, I Do Not Know. W. Masterson
Why She Left Him. F. Warden
Why Shoot a Butler? G. Heyer
Why Should Sylvia? H. Janson
Why Slug a Postman? S. Truss
Why So Dead? E. Queen
Why Squeal on Me? Max Gordon
Why They Married. M. B. Lowndes
Wicked. A. Applin
Wicked Angel. T. Caldwell
Wicked as the Devil. M. Halliday
Wicked Flee. A. Hocking
Wicked Girl. M. C. Hay
Wicked Guardian. Elsie Lee
Wicked Lord. R. Foxall
Wicked Marquis. E. P. Oppenheim
Wicked Pack of Cards. Rosemary Harris
Wicked Pack of Cards. H. R. Williamson
Wicked Saint. E. Bruton
Wicked Shall Flourish. H. Desmond
Wicked Streets. Wenzell Brown
Wicked Uncle. P. Wentworth
Wicked Way to Die. J. Sturrock
Wicked Woman. Anne Austin
Wicked World. A. M. Meadows
Wickedest Man. J. Millard
Wide Arch. D. Stivens
Wide Boy! M. Hervey
Wide Girl. M. Hervey
Wide Open Door. T. E. B. Clarke
Widening Stain. W. B. Johnson
Wider Sea of Love. F. E. Smith
Widow. C. Blackstock
Widow. Francis King
Widow. G. Simenon
Widow and the Cavalier. R. Armstrong
Widow and the Web. Robert Martin
Widow Barony. W. R. Burnett
Widow Bewitched. C. Brown
Widow Cherry. B. L. Farjeon
Widow from Spain. J. Pendower
Widow Gay. A. A. Marcus
Widow Had a Gun. G. H. Coxe
Widow in White. E. Bond
Widow in White. F. A. Chittenden
Widow Lerouge. E. Gaboriau
Widow Maker. F. Diamond
Widow-Makers. M. Blankfort
Widow Mortimer. T. P. Prest
Widow of Bath. M. Bennett
Widow Watchers. F. Archer
Widow with the Pink Gloves. M. Dekobra
Widow Wondered Why. W. J. Coughlin
Widow Wore Red. R. Wormser
Widow Wore White. C. P. Cleary
Widower. V. Siller
Widower. G. Simenon
Widower's Wife. T. Charles
Widowmaker. M. Fagyas
Widowmaster. L. Bergson
Widows' Blackmail. R. Fenisong
Widows Can Be Dangerous. N. Leslie
Widow's Cruise. N. Blake
Widow's Might. M. Dekobra
Widow's Mite. E. S. Holding
Widow's Necklace. E. Davies
Widows of Broome. A. W. Upfield
Widows of the Magistrate. K. West
Widows Ought to Weep. D. B. Olsen
Widow's Peak. J. Nicholas

Widow's Pique. B. Treynor
Widow's Plight. R. Fenisong
Widow's Son. E. Southworth
Widow's Walk. Anonymous
Widow's Walk. M. Bishop
Widow's Walk. S. Nichols
Widow's Walk. C. Rabou
Widow's Walk. M. Yates
Widows Wear Weeds. A. A. Fair
Widow's Web. U. Curtiss
Widows Won't Wait. D. Hitchens
Wieland. C. B. Brown
Wife at Sea. G. Simenon
Wife by Purchase. P. Trent
Wife He Never Saw. M. Marcin
Wife in the Dark. H. Desmond
Wife in Toledo. J. Budd
Wife Next Door. R. V. Cassill
Wife of Baal. M. Dalton
Wife of Elias. E. Phillpotts
Wife of Ronald Sheldon. P. Quentin
Wife of the Red-Haired Man. B. S. Ballinger
Wife or Death. E. Queen
Wife or No Wife? and A Close Shave. T. W. Speight
Wife Who Died Twice. E. Bohle
Wife Who Disappeared. B. Flynn
Wife Who Ran Away. T. Mascott
Wife Whom God Forgot. C. H. Bullivant
Wife's Dream. T. P. Prest
Wife's Honor. E. A. Young
Wife's Victory. E. Southworth
Wilberforce Legacy. J. Bell
Wilby Conspiracy. P. Driscoll
Wild. G. Brewer
Wild Abyss. John Gunn
Wild and Weird. G. Campbell
Wild Apple Orchard. D. Lee
Wild Beauty. D. Donovan
Wild Bird. H. Footner
Wild Card. R. Hawkey
Wild-Cat Scheme. E. M. Keate
Wild-Catters. C. J. C. Hyne
Wild Darrie. D. C. Murray
Wild Dreams. Michael Sinclair
Wild Duck Murders. T. Du Bois
Wild Flame. Winifred Duke
Wild Georgie. J. Middlemass
Wild Girl. H. Janson
Wild Girl. D. Keene
Wild Grapes. B. Jefferis
Wild Horse Valley. W. C. Tuttle
Wild Hunt. J. Tattersall
Wild Is My Heart. T. Thomas
Wild Justice. G. A. Birmingham
Wild Justice. F. Clifford
Wild Justice. T. B. Morris
Wild Justice. J. Pattinson
Wild Man of Cape Cod. F. MacIsaac
Wild Midnight Falls. M. E. Chaber
Wild Night. R. Foley
Wild Onion. Loren Carroll
Wild Party. J. McPartland
Wild Pitch. A. B. Guthrie
Wild Reckoning. M. Richmond
Wild Secret. M. Clare
Wild Sheba. A. Askew
Wild Summer. Jack Wilson
Wild to Possess. G. Brewer
Wild Town. J. Thompson
Wild Track. Alex Hamilton
Wild Trip. M. Arrighi
Wild Turkey. R. L. Simon

Wild Week-End. T. C. H. Jacobs
Wild Wooing. F. Warden
Wildcat. D. Ambler
Wildcat. C. Brown
Wildcat. S. Gluck
Wilder Curse. K. Robeson
Wilderness. T. B. Clegg
Wilderness. R. Donaldson
Wilderness Patrol. H. Bindloss
Wilderness Patrol. C. Stoddard
Wilderness Road. A. Davidson
Wilders Walk Away. H. Brean
Wildfire. N. Carter
Wildfire at Midnight. M. Stewart
Wildwater Terrace. R. E. Salwey
Wiles of the Wicked. W. LeQueux
Wiles of Wilhelmina. F. Warden
Wilful and Premeditated. F. W. Crofts
Wilful Lady. J. Sturrock
Wilful-Missing. D. G. Waring
Wilful Murder. J. York
Wilful Susie. A. Applin
Wilful Ward. F. Warden
Wilful Way. H. Compton
Will and the Deed. D. Ogburn
Will and the Deed. Ellis Peters
Will and the Way. B. Capes
Will and the Way. J. M. Scott
Will and the Willful. M. Webb
Will Anyone Who Saw the Accident... J. Ashford
Will He Betray Her? H. Wood
Will in the Way. M. Burton
Will-o'-the-Wisp. P. Wentworth
Will of the Tribe. A. W. Upfield
Will on the Watch. Ernest H. Robinson
Will-Power. H. Janson
Will to Kill. R. Bloch
Will to Kill. G. Brodie
Will to Survive. E. Salter
Will You Walk a Little Faster. R. Braddon
Willard and His Bowling Trophies. R. Brautigan
William Allair. H. Wood
William Conrad. P. Boulle
William Cook--Antique Dealer. R. Keverne
William Jordan Junior. J. C. Snaith
Willing to Die. J. S. Le Fanu
Willing Transgressor, and other stories. A. G. Plympton
Willing Witness. B. Cobb
Willoughby Affair. G. W. Appleton
Willoughby Manor. J. Wetherell
Willow Herb. Rona Randall
Willow Pattern. R. Van Gulik
Willow Pond. M. K. Simmons
Willow Weep. D. Daniels
Willowbrake. R. M. Gilchrist
Willowford Woods. R. M. Gilchrist
Wills of Jane Kanwhistle. S. Fowler
Wilson and Some Others. G. D. H. Cole
Wilson Calling. G. D. H. Cole
Wilt Thou Have This Woman? J. M. Cobban
Wilton's Silence. P. Trent
Wily Widow. A. Bouvier
Wimbledon Common Trap. J. Hunter
Win, Place and Die! L. Lariar
Wind Blows Death. C. Hare
Wind Chill Factor. T. Gifford
Wind from Nowhere. O. Micheaux
Wind in His Fists. K. Murphy
Wind in Our Hands. M. Duston
Wind in the Cypress. R. M. Sears
Wind in the East. A. Burr
Wind in the East. H. Edmonds
Wind in the Snottygobble Tree. J. T. Story
Wind of Death. G. Black
Wind of Desire. K. Lindsay
Wind Off the Sea. D. Beaty

Wind Over the Citadel. L. Ames
Wind Over the Citadel. W. E. D. Ross
Wind Tunnel. D. Buckingham
Wind-Up Doll. C. Brown
Wind Was Cold. H. Clevely
Wind Without Rain. G. McDonell
Windblow Mystery. E. Gellibrand
Windfall. A. Leslie
Windfall. M. Pflaum
Windfall Harvest. M. Edwin
Windfellow. C. Edwards
Winding Road. C. Dawe
Winding Stair. J. A. Hodge
Winding Stair. A. E. W. Mason
Winding Way. J. S. Fletcher
Windmill Mystery. J. J. Farjeon
Window. K. Ingram
Window. J. Reach
Window at the White Cat. M. R. Rinehart
Window Episode. E. Geller
Window Hack. R. Standish
Window in Chungking. S. H. Courtier
Window in the Dark. E. Kilvington
Window in the Dark. F. O'Rourke
Window on the Seine. F. Y. McHugh
Window on the Square. P. A. Whitney
Window Over the Way. G. Simenon
Window with the Sleeping Nude. R. L. Bellem
Windows Facing West. V. MacFadyen
Wind's End. H. Asquith
Winds of April. I. D. Baharav
Winds of Evil. A. W. Upfield
Winds of Fear. J. Ames
Winds of Fortune. J. Farnol
Winds of Midnight. J. Blackburn
Winds of Night. A. Maybury
Winds of Terror. P. H. Howell
Winds of the World. T. Mundy
Winds of Time. H. Gibbs
Windscreen Weepers and other stories of horror and suspense. Joan Aiken
Windswept Farm. W. Hewlett
Windy Side of the Law. S. Woods
Wine of Vengeance. J. Wellsley
Wine of Violence. N. S. Boardman
Wine of Violence. L. Egan
Wine of War. E. G. Cousins
Wine Room Murder. S. Vestal
Wine, Women, and Death. W. Deptula
Wine, Women, and Murder. Desmond Martin
Wine, Women and Murder. J. Roeburt
Winegarden. Elsie Lee
Winged Danger. A. Foxe
Winged Death. J. R. Holden
Winged Murderer. F. MacIsaac
Winged Mystery. A. W. Upfield
Winged Victory. N. Leslie
Winged Witnesses. H. Robertson
Wingrave Case. P. Luck
Wings. A. Abdullah
Wings Above the Claypan. A. W. Upfield
Wings Above the Diamantina. A. W. Upfield
Wings Behind Bars. P. Trent
Wings of Adventure. A. Whitehouse
Wings of Chance. M. Leinster
Wings of Darkness. P. Audemars
Wings of Death. M. Boniface
Wings of Desire. M. Dekobra
Wings of Destiny. W. F. Moore

Title Index

Wings of Destiny. George Weston
Wings of Destiny. Christopher Wilson
Wings of Doom. G. E. Rochester
Wings of Fear. M. G. Eberhart
Wings of Love. C. R. Gull
Wings of Love. P. Trent
Wings of Madness. J. Philips
Wings of Mystery. W. Gavine
Wings of Peace. J. Creasey
Wings of Revolution. J. R. Holden
Wings of Romance. W. E. Johns
Wings of the Black Death. G. Stockbridge
Wings of the Morning. L. Tracy
Wings of Tomorrow. P. Traill
Wings of Victory. F. M. White
Wings Over Africa. D. T. Lindsay
Wings Over Panama. G. Church
Wings Over the Amazon. D. T. Lindsay
Wings Over the Atlantic. A. D. Divine
Wings Without Freedom. J. G. Sarasin
Wink. K. Bennett
Winking at the Brim. G. Mitchell
Winner Take All. G. Fairlie
Winner Take All. J. McKimmey
Winner Takes All. R. Douglas
Winners. J. Mitchell
Winnifred's Way. A. Griffiths
Winning a Princess. Old Sleuth
Winning Clue. J. Hay
Winning of Winifred. L. Tracy
Winning Through. A. Applin
Winning Through. J. Templeton
Winning Trick. N. Brand
Winny Darling. E. Southworth
Winsome Lass. K. Lindsay
Winston Affair. H. Fast
Winston Churchill Murder. K. Netzen
Winston of the Prairie. H. Bindloss
Winter. G. Horne
Winter After This Summer. S. Ellin
Winter Keeper. J. Crecy
Winter Kill. S. Fisher
Winter Kills. R. Condon
Winter Landscape. N. Brand
Winter Murder Case. S. S. Van Dine
Winter of Discontent. G. Frankau
Winter of Fear. S. Tempest
Winter of Madness. D. Walker
Winter of the Fox. J. Roffman
Winter People. P. A. Whitney
Winter Pride. Winifred Duke
Winter Wears a Shroud. R. Chapman
Winter Wheat. E. Woodward
Winter's Tale. Robert Hardy
Winter's Tales. I. Dinesen
Wintershade. E. Evans
Winterton Hotel Mystery. J. Corbett
Winterwood. D. Eden
Winton Street Mystery. H. Carstairs
Wipeout. J. Tiger
Wire Devils. F. Packard
Wire Tappers. A. Stringer
Wired for Scandal. F. L. Wallace
Wireless Call. Mrs. C. Kernahan
Wiretap! C. Einstein
Wisdom of Father Brown. G. K. Chesterton
Wise and Foolish Virgin. G. Warden
Wise Fool. S. Jepson
Wise Fool. E. C. Reed
Wise Man of Welby. N. Worth
Wise Virgin. G. Goodchild
Wise Virgin. M. McGrath
Wish-Bone. Ethel L. White
Wish Me Dead. D. West
Wish You Were Dead. R. Chapman
Wish You Were Dead. H. McCloy
Wishful Think. B. Newman
Wishing Smith. C. J. C. Hyne
Wisteria Cottage. R. M. Coates
Wistful Wanton. P. Muller
Witch. B. Michaels
Witch Alone. M. Higgins
Witch at the Funeral. F. Hurt
Witch Door. E. Ogilvie
Witch from the Sea. P. Carr
Witch Haven. L. Churchill
Witch Hunt. S. Harvester
Witch-Hunt! D. Reid
Witch Man. M. B. Houston
Witch Miss Seeton. H. Carvic
Witch of Bralhaven. Marilyn Ross
Witch of Chelsea. O. Hartley
Witch of Goblin's Acres. W. E. D. Ross
Witch of Manhattan. Old Sleuth
Witch of Nun. D. Newton
Witch of the Hills. F. Warden
Witch of the Low-Tide. J. D. Carr
Witch or Wife. S. Rathbone
Witch Temple. Alan Graham
Witch Tree. L. B. Long
Witch Wood. C. Hale
Witchcraft Murder. J. Ingersol
Witchdance in Bavaria. Robert MacLeod
Witches. C. Brown
Witches. P. Curtis
Witches' Cove. Marilyn Ross
Witches' Holiday. M. Lynch
Witches' Moon. G. Verner
Witches of All Saints. J. Tattersall
Witches of Brimstone Hill. H. Arvonen
Witches of Notting Hill. W. A. Ballinger
Witches of Omen. A. Leech
Witches of Windlake. M. Lynch
Witches' Pond. F. Hurd
Witches' Pond. S. Wells
Witches' Sabbath. P. Allardyce
Witchfinder. M. Hilliard
Witching Hill. E. W. Hornung
Witching Hour. Rona Randall
Witching Hour. F. Stevenson
Witching Night. C. S. Cody
Witch's Castle. D. Daniels
Witch's Cauldron. E. Phillpotts
Witch's Crossing. F. Stevenson
Witch's Doing. A. Dick
Witch's Hammer. C. Farr
Witch's House. C. Armstrong
Witch's Island. D. Daniels
Witch's Mark. June R. Lewis
Witch's Moon. G. Jackson
Witch's Song. M. Lynch
Witch's Suckling. G. Hall
Witch's Web. D. Spicer
Witchstone. V. Graham
Witchwater. G. M. Wilson
With a Bare Bodkin. C. Hare
With a Madman Behind Me. T. Powell
With a Vengeance. D. Shannon
With a View to Matrimony, and other stories. J. Blyth
With All John's Love. M. B. Lowndes
With Bated Breath. A. Campbell
With Blood and Kisses. R. Shattuck
With Bullet and Steel. J. K. Stafford
With Cause Enough? S. Fowler
With Chains of Brass. I. Stark
With Clipped Wings. M. S. Boyd
With Cossack and Convict. W. M. Graydon
With Criminal Instinct. R. Hardinge
With Dead Bodies. J. Cadman
With Extreme Prejudice. B. Mather
With Gauge and Swallow, Attorneys. A. Tourgee
With Hoops of Steel. F. F. Kelly
With Intent. L. Henderson
With Intent to Deceive. M. Coles
With Intent to Destroy. K. Rogers
With Intent to Kill. B. Cobb
With Intent to Kill. G. H. Coxe
With Intent to Kill. D. Shannon
With Intent to Kill. E. C. Vivian
With Links of Steel. N. Carter
With Love from Rachel. S. Murray
With Murder for Some. H. C. Huston
With Murder in Mind. E. Ferrars
With Murder in Mind. J. Roffman
With Murder in Mind. J. Rothman
With My Friends. B. Matthews
With My Knives I Know I'm Good. J. Rathbone
With My Little Eye. D. Durrant
With My Little Eye. Roy Fuller
With One Stone. R. Lockridge
With Option to Die. R. Lockridge
With Shackles of Fire. N. Carter
With Sirens Screaming. Ernest Booth
With Soul So Dead. G. Mason
With the Unhanged. R. Dowling
With This Ring. M. G. Eberhart
With What Motive? T. C. H. Jacobs
Withdraw Thy Foot. C. R. Sumner
Withered Garland. H. Gibbs
Withered Man. N. Deane
Withered Murder. A. Shaffer
Withering Fires. M. Bowen
Within an Inch of His Life. E. Garboriau
Within Four Walls. E. Baulsir
Within Fourteen Days. W. M. Graydon
Within Sound of the Weir. T. S. Hake
Within the Bubble. J. Shearing
Within the Labyrinth. N. Lewis
Within the Law. M. Dana
Within the Law. B. Veiller
Within the Maze. H. Wood
Within the Vault. L. Thayer
Within This Circle. G. Beaumont
Within This House. F. Crisp
Within Twenty-Four Hours. H. Leyford
Without a Clue. N. Carter
Without a Grave. P. Nottingham
Without a Name. D. Stewart
Without a Trace. S. Ransome
Without a Warrant. H. Brooks
Without Clues. J. Helm
Without Gloves. J. B. Hendryx
Without Issue. H. Cresswell
Without Judge or Jury. R. Rodd
Without Justification. J. L. Rickard
Without Lawful Authority. M. Coles
Without Love or Licence. H. Smart
Without Malice. B. Graeme
Without Mercy. J. J. Dratler
Without Mercy. J. Goodwin
Without Motive. Winston Graham
Without Motive. C. Robertson
Without Music. G. Fox
Without Orders. M. Albrand
Without the Law. H. F. Moulton
Without the Option. A. Hocking
Without Trace. C. Goodall
Without Trace. W. LeQueux
Without Trumpet or Drum. J. Sanders
Without Warning. W. H. Baker
Without Witness. A. Armstrong
Witness. R. G. Toepfer
Witness. D. Uhnak

Witness at Large. M. G. Eberhart
Witness at the Window. C. Barry
Witness Box. V. Karsland
Witness for the Crown. Richard Gordon
Witness for the Defence. A. E. W. Mason
Witness for the Prosecution. A. Christie
Witness in Peril. M. Marlette
Witness in Support. J. H. Vahey
Witness of the Sun. H. S. Williams
Witness on the Roof. A. Haynes
Witness This Woman. G. F. Fox
Witness to Murder. E. Harrison
Witness to the Crime. J. Hunter
Witness to the Deed. G. M. Fenn
Witness Tree. H. C. Wire
Witnesses. A. Holden
Witnesses. G. Simenon
Witnesses and the Watchmaker. G. Simenon
Wits' End. W. Spence
Wives to Burn. L. G. Blochman
Wizard Detective. Old Sleuth
Wizard of Berner's Abbey. M. Hansom
Wizard of the Cue. N. Carter
Wizard Tramp. Old Sleuth
Wizard's Aunt. J. Laing
Wizard's Spyglass. E. Kinsburn
Wobble to Death. P. Lovesey
Wolf. H. Holt
Wolf at the Door. F. Warden
Wolf by the Ears. R. Lewis
Wolf Cop. R. Jessup
Wolf Creek Valley. W. C. Tuttle
Wolf Hollow Bubbles. D. H. Keller
Wolf Howls Murder. M. L. Stokes
Wolf in Man's Clothing. M. G. Eberhart
Wolf in Sheep's Clothing. J. K. Leys
Wolf in the Fold. V. Loder
Wolf Man. A. Machard
Wolf Mountain. P. L. Sandberg
Wolf-Net. Winifred Graham
Wolf of Corsica. W. J. Elliott
Wolf of the Evenings. Winifred Graham
Wolf Pack. R. Cullum
Wolf Pack of Lobo Butte. W. C. Tuttle
Wolf Shows His Teeth. B. Sarto
Wolf Swept Down. R. Ladline
Wolf That Follows. H. Clevely
Wolf to the Slaughter. R. Rendell
Wolf Tone. L. Goldman
Wolf Troubleth Not. B. M. Scott
Wolf Within. N. Carter
Wolf Woman. A. Stringer
Wolfe's Cloister. B. Plagemann
Wolf's Claw. H. Holt
Wolf's Crag. D. Whitelaw
Wolves and the Lamb. J. S. Fletcher
Wolves and the Lamb. A. Soutar
Wolves of Chaos. H. MacGrath
Wolves of Craywood. Jan Alexander
Wolves of New York. A. W. Aiken
Wolves of the Night. S. Horler
Wolves of the Sea. G. Leroux
Wolves of Washington. Anonymous
Woman Accused. D. Durham
Woman Accused. J. Templeton
Woman Against the World. George Griffith
Woman Against Woman. M. A. Holmes
Woman Always Knows. J. Cleft-Addams
Woman Always Wins. C. H. Bullivant
Woman and Her Master. J. F. Smith
Woman and the Prowler. S. Friedman
Woman and the Wheel. T. B. Morris
Woman Aroused. E. Lacy
Woman at Bay. N. Carter
Woman at Bay. G. H. Coxe
Woman at Kensington. W. LeQueux
Woman at Risk. M. Tripp
Woman Bars the Way. M. Leighton
Woman Cain. M. Richmond
Woman Delia. P. Piper

Woman Dominant. E. C. Vivian
Woman from A.U.N.T. B. Negulesco
Woman Ayisha. T. Mundy
Woman from Outside. H. Footner
Woman from the East. E. Wallace
Woman He Chose. J. H. Wallis
Woman Hunt. F. Ryck
Woman in Armour. D. C. Murray
Woman in Black. H. Adams
Woman in Black. E. C. Bentley
Woman in Black. N. Carter
Woman in Black. L. Ford
Woman in Black. M. Y. Halidom
Woman in Black. M. Heath
Woman in Black. W. Spence
Woman in Grey. A. M. Williamson
Woman in Marble. C. Dekker
Woman in Mauve. G. MacMillan
Woman in 919. J. P. Seabrooke
Woman in Number Five. L. Meynell
Woman in Purple Pajamas. W. Kent
Woman in Question. J. R. Scott
Woman in Red. S. Campbell
Woman in Red. Anthony Gilbert
Woman in Red. R. St. Clair
Woman in the Alcove. A. K. Green
Woman in the Car. R. Marsh
Woman in the Case. Mark Allerton
Woman in the Case. C. R. Gull
Woman in the Case. H. Malot
Woman in the Case. F. P. Rathburne
Woman in the Case. N. Thurley
Woman in the Case. L. Tracy
Woman in the Case. Bessie Turner
Woman in the Dark. D. Hammett
Woman in the Dark. F. W. Robinson
Woman in the Maze. M. Dobner
Woman in the Mirror. Winston Graham
Woman in the Picture. J. August
Woman in the Sea. Shelley Smith
Woman in the Shadow. L. J. Vance
Woman in the Wardrobe. P. Antony
Woman in the Way. W. LeQueux
Woman in the Window. J. H. Wallis
Woman in the Woods. C. Blackstock
Woman in White. W. Collins
Woman in Whitehall. R. Walker
Woman Intervenes. R. Barr
Woman Is Dead. R. King
Woman Missing and other stories. H. Nielsen
Woman Named Anne. H. Cecil
Woman Named Smith. M. C. Oemler
Woman of Action. P. Trent
Woman of Business. A. Griffiths
Woman of Cairo. J. Flagg
Woman of Character. Julian Gloag
Woman of Danger. N. W. Firth
Woman of Death. G. Boothby
Woman of Death. Old Sleuth
Woman of Destiny. S. Maddock
Woman of Evil. N. Carter
Woman of Kronstadt. M. Pemberton
Woman of Mystery. N. Carter
Woman of Mystery. A. K. Green
Woman of Mystery. M. Leblanc
Woman of Mystery. G. Ohnet
Woman of Nerve. N. T. Oliver
Woman of Nerve. R. M. Wells
Woman of Paris. G. Des Cars
Woman of Saigon. P. Saxon
Woman of Shanghai. M. L. Berges

Woman of Sorek. A. Gould
Woman of Steel. N. Carter
Woman of Straw. C. Arley
Woman of the Grey House. G. Simenon
Woman of the Iron Bracelets. F. Barrett
Woman on Her Own. J. Blackmore
Woman on the Place. H. Whittington
Woman on the Roof. M. G. Eberhart
Woman on the Roof. H. Nielsen
Woman on the Spot. J. Hunter
Woman Out of Nowhere. L. Hoffman
Woman Pays. S. Warwick
Woman Possessed. C. Randell
Woman Question. D. Malm
Woman Racket. G. Lawrence
Woman Spy. H. De Halsalle
Woman Stealer. Harry Mills
Woman Tempted Him. W. Westall
Woman, the Man, and the Monster. C. Dawe
Woman, the Mystery. H. Herman
Woman: The Sphinx. F. Hume
Woman Under the Mountain. R. McDougald
Woman Who Dared. L. L. Lynch
Woman Who Dared. A. M. Williamson
Woman Who Held On. F. Hume
Woman Who Knew. M. Pemberton
Woman Who Saved the World. W. Holt-White
Woman Who Stole Everything and other stories. A. Bennett
Woman Who Tempted. G. Warden
Woman Who Understood. Mrs. C. Kernahan
Woman Who Waited. T. C. H. Jacobs
Woman Who Was. P. Boileau
Woman Who Was No More. P. Boileau
Woman Who Was Not. A. Applin
Woman Wins. R. Barr
Woman Wins. C. H. Bullivant
Woman Wins. R. Machray
Woman with a Gun. G. H. Coxe
Woman with a "Record." L. Jackson
Woman with a Secret. R. Ferguson
Woman with Claws. Williams Forrest
Woman with One Hand, and Mr. Ely's Engagement. R. Marsh
Woman with the Diamonds. F. Warden
Woman with the Portuguese Basket. E. Wuorio
Woman with the Yellow Hair and Other Modern Mysteries. Anonymous
Woman with Two Smiles. M. Leblanc
Woman Without a Name. L. M. Janifer
Woman Without a Name. G. Lenotre
Woman Worth Winning. G. M. Fenn
Womanhunt. M. Derby
Woman's Burden. F. Hume
Woman's Calvary. J. Middlemass
Woman's Courage. F. Wicks
Woman's Debt. W. LeQueux
Woman's Devotion. J. W. Postgate
Woman's Eyes. G. Weill
Woman's Face. F. Warden
Woman's Fate. E. Southworth
Woman's Footprint. E. R. Punshon
Woman's Friend. M. Storm
Woman's Hand. N. Carter
Woman's Hand. J. R. Coryell
Woman's Honor. E. A. Young
Woman's House. H. L. V. Fletcher
Woman's Ransom. F. W. Robinson
Woman's Revenge. M. Pinkerton
Woman's Story. F. Warden
Woman's Tragedy. L. L. Lynch
Woman's Vengeance. M. A. Holmes
Woman's Vengeance. J. Payn
Woman's View. H. Flowerdew
Woman's World. A. Askew

Title Index

Women Are Like That. T. C. H. Jacobs
Women Are Like That. E. Woodward
Women Are Skin Deep. P. Whelton
Women at Belguardo. M. Erskine
Women--Dope--and Murder. Roland Daniel
Women Hate Till Death. H. Janson
Women in White. J. Reach
Women Like to Know. Kevin O'Hara
Women of London. B. Hemyng
Women of Paris. B. Hemyng
Women of Peasenhall. R. J. White
Women Swore Revenge. I. H. Irwin
Women to Love. S. Drago
Women's Battalion. W. A. Ballinger
Won by Magic. N. Carter
Wonder Jack. Old Sleuth
Wonderful Career of Ebenezer Lobb. A. Upward
Wonderful Detective. Old Sleuth
Wonderful Scheme. H. S. Keeler
Wonderful Scheme of Mr. Christopher Thorne. H. S. Keeler
Wondering Moon. George Weston
Wood and the Trees. M. Elgin
Woodchuck Jerry. Old Sleuth
Woodchuck Jerry, the Country Detective. Old Sleuth
Woodcutter Operation. K. Royce
Wooden Hand. F. Hume
Wooden Indian. C. Wells
Wooden Overcoat. P. Branch
Wooden Spectacles. H. S. Keeler
Woodley Lane Ghost and other stories. M. V. Dahlgren
Wooing of a Fairy. G. Warden
Wooing of Esther Gray. L. Tracy
Wooing of Grey Eyes, and other stories. R. Stephens
Wooing of Martha. C. G. Mitford
Woolf Sarason, Special Agent. M. Moiseiwitsch
Woollen Monkey. G. Goodchild
Word and the Will. J. Payn
Word for Word and Letter for Letter. A. J. D. Biddle
Word of Honour. H. C. McNeile
Word of Six Letters. H. Adams
Word of the Sorceress. B. Mitford
Words for Murder Perhaps. E. Candy
Words Have Wings. N. Berrow
Work for the Hangman. B. Graeme
Work of Darkness. J. Karney
Work of Her Hands. A. Askew
Workers All. P. Trent
Workers in Darkness. J. B. Harris-Burland
Working for the Man. R. Dennis
Working Man Detective. D. J. MacKenzie
Works of the Late Edgar Allan Poe. E. A. Poe
World Championship Mystery. W. J. Passingham
World Grabbers. P. W. Fairman
World in My Pocket. J. H. Chase
World Masters. George Griffith
World of Crime. M. F. Goron
World of Sin. H. T. Johnson
World of Tim Frazer. F. Durbridge
World of Violence. Colin Wilson
World Outside. H. MacGrath
World Rapers. B. Von Block
World-Shakers. D. Reid

World Stood Still. W. Holt-White
World, the Flesh, and the Devil. M. E. Braddon
World Under Snow. D. K. Broster
World Without Dreams. R. Garland
Worldbreaker. J. Milton
Worldly Goods. A. Soutar
World's a Stage. K. Kellow
World's Blackmail. L. Cleeve
World's Fair Goblin. K. Robeson
World's Fair Murders. J. Ashenhurst
World's Finger. T. W. Hanshew
World's Great Snare. E. P. Oppenheim
Worm of Death. N. Blake
Worms Must Wait. J. Wainwright
Worse and More of It. N. E. Henshaw
Worse Than a Crime. F. Crane
Worse Than Death. L. Lamb
Worse Than Murder. E. Berckman
Worse Than Murder. D. Duncan
Worst Case on Record. N. Carter
Worst Enemy. G. Hackforth-Jones
Worst Man in the World. S. Horler
Worst Squadron in France. G. E. Rochester
Worst Way to Die. B. Rossi
Worsted Viper. G. Mitchell
Wotan's Wedge. F. Gerard
Would You Kill Him? G. P. Latham
Wound and the Scar. V. Scannell
Wound of Love. R. V. Cassill
Wounded and the Slain. D. Goodis
Wounds of Treason. M. Vinter
Woven Web. P. Audemars
Wrack. M. Drake
Wraith. P. MacDonald
Wraith of Olverstone. F. Warden
Wraithwood. L. Churchill
Wrap It Up. A. Dean
Wrath of Fu Manchu and other stories. S. Rohmer
Wrath of God. J. Graham
Wrath of the Lion. Harry Patterson
Wrath to Come. E. P. Oppenheim
Wraxton Marne. R. Ray
Wreath for a Dead Angel. H. Kimberley
Wreath for a Lady. M. Baroni
Wreath for a Redhead. C. Brown
Wreath for a Redhead. Peter Chambers
Wreath for a Spy. R. Tashkent
Wreath for America. R. Raine
Wreath for Jenny's Grave. Charlotte Hunt
Wreath for Rebecca. C. Brown
Wreath for Rivera. J. Marsh
Wreath for the Bride. M. Lang
Wreath for the Lady. H. Holt
Wreath from Bangkok. C. Leader
Wreath of Bones. J. N. Chance
Wreath of Camellias. G. B. Mair
Wreath of Lords and Ladies. James Fraser
Wreath of Poppies. C. Leader
Wreath of Roses. J. Blackburn
Wreath of Water-Lilies. P. Flower
Wreck of the Chinook. L. Tracy
Wreck of the Grey Cat. Winston Graham
Wreck of the Mary Deare. H. Innes
Wreck of the Redwing. B. Grimshaw
Wrecked in Port. E. Yates
Wrecker. Ruth Alexander
Wrecker. A. Ridley
Wrecker. R. L. Stevenson
Wreckers. F. Lynde
Wreckers Must Breathe. H. Innes
Wrecking Crew. D. Hamilton
Wrecking of Offshore Five. R. Johnston
Wrecking Ray. G. E. C. Webster
Wrenfield Mystery. G. Woden
Wrist Mark. J. S. Fletcher
Write It Murder. H. Arre
Write Me a Murder. F. Knott
Write Murder Down. R. Lockridge
Write-Off. P. Malloch

Write Off the Redhead. M. Brody
Write on Both Sides of the Paper. M. Kelly
Writing on the Wall. H. Adams
Written in Blood. N. Carter
Written in Dust. M. Burton
Written in Red. C. H. Montague
Wrong Body. Anthony Gilbert
Wrong Body. V. A. Van Sickle
Wrong Box. G. Napier
Wrong Box. R. L. Stevenson
Wrong Case. J. Crumley
Wrong House. C. F. Gregg
Wrong Letter. W. S. Masterman
Wrong Man. H. C. Bailey
Wrong Man in the Mirror. P. Loraine
Wrong Mr. Chamberlain and other stories. P. Herring
Wrong Move. A. Burr
Wrong Road. A. Griffiths
Wrong Murder. C. Rice
Wrong Murder Mystery. C. Barry
Wrong Murderer. H. Clevely
Wrong Number. P. Luck
Wrong Ones. J. McKimmey
Wrong Road by Hook or Crook. A. Griffiths
Wrong Saturday. E. Thompson
Wrong Side of the Sky. G. Lyall
Wrong Slant of Red. H. L. Skalland
Wrong That Was Done. John Marsh
Wrong That Was Done. F. W. Robinson
Wrong Turning. T. E. B. Clarke
Wrong Venus. C. Williams
Wrong Verdict. W. S. Masterman
Wrong Verdict. A. O. Pollard
Wrong Way Down. E. Daly
Wrong Way to Die. E. Messenger
Wrong Wife. A. S. Roche
Wrongdoer. A. Upward
Wrychester Paradise. J. S. Fletcher
Wu Fang. Roland Daniel
Wu Fang's Revenge. Roland Daniel
Wulfheim. M. Furey
Wyatt's Hurricane. D. Bagley
Wych Stone. M. McEvoy
Wycherly Woman. R. Macdonald
Wychford Poisoning Case. A. Berkeley
Wycliffe and the Pea-Green Boat. W. J. Burley
Wycliffe-Pepin Case. A. Fane
Wye Valley Mystery. Essex Smith
Wylder's Hand. J. S. Le Fanu
Wyllard's Weird. M. E. Braddon
Wyndham's Pal. H. Bindloss
Wyndham's Partner. H. Bindloss
Wyndspelle. A. Vandergriff
Wynnum. D. Hennessey
Wyoming Tragedy. W. B. M. Ferguson
Wyss Pursuit. Adam Hamilton
Wyvern Mystery. J. S. Le Fanu

X. E. Sudak
X Esquire. L. Charteris
X14. G. Lennox
X. Jones. H. S. Keeler
X. Jones of Scotland Yard. H. S. Keeler
X Marks the Dot. Muriel Stafford
X Marks the Spot. L. Thayer
X-Rated Corpse. M. Avallone
X-Ray Murders. M. S. Michel
X v. Rex. M. Porlock
XX--A Fatal Clue. Anonymous

XYY Man. K. Royce
XYZ. A. K. Green
Xander Pursuit. Adam Hamilton
Xavier Affair. R. L. Fish
Xelucha and Others. M. P. Shiel
X's Page. N. Miller

Y

Y. Cheung, Business Detective. H. S. Keeler
Yacht of Mystery. W. M. Graydon
Yakuza. L. Schrader
Yang Meridian. J. Leasor
Yank. A. Sugar
Yank in Fleet Street. R. McLoughlin
Yankee Lawyer--Autobiography of Ephraim Tutt. A. Train
Yankee Napoleon. J. F. Macpherson
Yankee Poodle. C. H. Gibbs-Smith
Yankey Rue, the Ex-Pugilist Detective. Old Sleuth
Yaroslav Incident. D. Mariner
Yard Lengths. D. Shoubridge
Yashar Pursuit. Adam Hamilton
Yasmin. A. Lowing
Yatton Murders. L. Galletley
Yawning Lion. M. Warrick
Yazoo Mystery. I. Craddock
Year and a Day. G. Thorne
Year of August. M. Saxton
Year of Miracle. F. Hume
Year of the Golden Ape. C. Forbes
Year of the Rat. M. Zarubica
Year of the Rooster. M. K. Simmons
Year of the Tiger. M. Fallon
Years Between. P. Trent
Years of the Hungry Tiger. J. G. Davis
Yell Bloody Murder. J. Shallit
Yell Ruddy Murder. J. Shallit
Yellerlegs. L. C. Douthwaite
Yellow Angels. H. E. Helseth
Yellow Arrow Murders. V. W. Mason
Yellow Badge. J. Middlemass
Yellow Beetle. A. B. Sherlock
Yellow Brand. N. Carter
Yellow Brick Road. E. Cadell
Yellow Bungalow Mystery. L. Gribble
Yellow Card Mystery. P. G. Larbalestier
Yellow Cat. H. H. C. Gibbons
Yellow Cat. C. Knight
Yellow Circle. P. Foley
Yellow Circle. C. E. Walk
Yellow Claw. S. Rohmer
Yellow Claws of Wong. E. H. Robinson
Yellow Cloud. K. Robeson
Yellow Corsair. James Bennett
Yellow Crayon. E. P. Oppenheim
Yellow Crystal. A. Wynne
Yellow Danger. M. P. Shiel
Yellow Death. U. Key
Yellow Devil. Roland Daniel
Yellow Devil. J. J. Farjeon
Yellow Diamond. G. F. Gibbs
Yellow Diamond. A. Sergeant
Yellow Disc Murder. N. Carter
Yellow Disc Murders. T. A. Plummer
Yellow Document. M. Allain
Yellow Door. D. Whitelaw
Yellow Dove. G. F. Gibbs
Yellow Dragon. A. Mills
Yellow Dusk. B. Bedwell
Yellow Face. W. M. Graydon
Yellow Face. F. M. White
Yellow Fangs. T. F. Elstow
Yellow Fiend. Mrs. Alexander
Yellow Fiend. W. J. Elliott
Yellow Flag. I. S. Black
Yellow Flag. E. Yates

Yellow Gods. J. G. Brandon
Yellow Gold of Tiryns. H. Osborne
Yellow Hand. A. Upward
Yellow Hearse. F. Mahannah
Yellow Hibiscus. J. Templeton
Yellow Hoard. K. Robeson
Yellow Holly. F. Hume
Yellow House. E. P. Oppenheim
Yellow Hunchback. F. Hume
Yellow Is for Fear and other stories. D. Eden
Yellow Jacket. E. Snell
Yellow Journalist. M. Michelson
Yellow Label. N. Carter
Yellow Letter. W. A. Johnston
"Yellow--Like Gold!" D. Christie
Yellow Magic. E. Thomas
Yellow Man. C. Dawe
Yellow Mask. J. G. Brandon
Yellow Mask. W. Collins
Yellow Mistletoe. W. S. Masterman
Yellow Munro. G. Fairlie
Yellow Music Kill. W. J. Sheldon
Yellow Overcoat. S. Acre
Yellow Peril. G. Hackforth-Jones
Yellow Peril. M. P. Shiel
Yellow Phantom. L. Cargill
Yellow Rat. F. Grierson
Yellow Ribbon. W. LeQueux
Yellow Robe Murders. Melville Burt
Yellow Robed Wago. Marion Roberts
Yellow Rock. D. Footman
Yellow Room. M. R. Rinehart
Yellow Room. G. Shipway
Yellow Satchel. F. Whishaw
Yellow Scourge. C. Steele
Yellow Seven. E. Snell
Yellow Shadows. S. Rohmer
Yellow Shadows of Death. R. Wallace
Yellow Shop. F. MacIsaac
Yellow Skull. G. H. Teed
Yellow Snake. E. Wallace
Yellow Spider. J. C. Beecham
Yellow Stockings. D. W. MacArthur
Yellow Strangler. C. Robertson
Yellow Streak. V. Williams
Yellow Stub. E. Lynn
Yellow Taxi. J. Stagge
Yellow Terror. R. Hardinge
Yellow Ticket. V. Morton
Yellow Tiger! G. H. Teed
Yellow Triangle. Margery Lawrence
Yellow Trousers. P. Fry
Yellow Turban. C. Jay
Yellow Typhoon. H. MacGrath
Yellow Vengeance. P. Urquhart
Yellow Villa. S. Blanc
Yellow Violet. F. Crane
Yellow Viper. S. Fairway
Yellow Wagon. C. Edwards
Yellow Will Out! Warren Hill
Yellow Wolf. T. S. King
Yellow Yoke. A. Askew
Yellowing Hay. A. Dick
Yellowleaf. S. Gregory
Yellowstones. G. Goodchild
Yellowthread Street. W. L. Marshall
Yermakov Transfer. Derek Lambert
Yes, Inspector McLean. G. Goodchild
Yesterday Walkers. S. Harvester
Yesterday's Bones. S. Tower

Yesterday's Enemy. M. Moiseiwitsch
Yesterday's Love. J. L. Rickard
Yesterday's Murder. C. Rice
Yesterday's Murder. J. York
Yesterday's Poison. Ruth Grayson
Yesterday's Spy. L. Deighton
Yesteryear Phantom. W. E. D. Ross
Yet She Must Die. H. McCutcheon
Yet She Must Die. S. Phillips
Yet She Must Die. S. Woods
Yetta the Magnificent. J. F. Macpherson
Yield to the Night. J. Karney
Yo-Ho, and a Bottle of Rum! H. M. Stephenson
Yoga Mist. E. P. Thorne
Yogi Shrouds Yolanda and Poison Ivy. C. Brown
Yokohama Hood. J. R. Fernandes
Yolan. J. Tickell
Yolan of the Plains. J. Tickell
Yonder. M. B. Houston
Yonder Grow the Daisies. W. Lipman
Yoris. R. Ingham
Yorkshire Moorland Murder. J. S. Fletcher
Yoshar the Soldier. W. Harrington
You Asked For It. I. Fleming
You Belong to Me. Sam Ross
You Can Always Duck. P. Cheyney
You Can Call It a Day. P. Cheyney
You Can Help Me. M. Birmingham
You Can Keep the Corpse. C. Robertson
You Can Run So Far. M. Barnes
You Can't Believe Your Eyes. J. Fleming
You Can't Call It Murder. Neill Graham
You Can't Catch Me. L. Lariar
You Can't Die Here. S. Coburn
You Can't Die Laughing. A. A. Fair
You Can't Die Tomorrow. L. Gribble
You Can't Do Business with Murder. D. Von Elsner
You Can't Escape. L. M. Janifer
You Can't Gag the Dead. M. Propper
You Can't Get Away by Running. W. Chambers
You Can't Get Away with Murder! A. Spiller
You Can't Hang the Dead. Leslie Carroll
You Can't Hit a Woman and other stories. P. Cheyney
You Can't Ignore Murder. R. Teague
You Can't Keep the Change. P. Cheyney
You Can't Kill a Corpse. L. Trimble
You Can't Kill Shadows. R. Goyne
You Can't Kill the Dead. E. Bowen-Rowlands
You Can't Live Forever. H. Q. Masur
You Can't See Around Corners. J. Cleary
You Can't Stop Me. W. Ard
You Can't Trust Duchesses and other stories. P. Cheyney
You Could Die Laughing, and The Swingers. J. Adams
You Did It. E. K. Goldthwaite
You Die in Valpaso. B. Sarto
You Die Next, Jill Baby! K. Carr
You Die Today. B. Kendrick
You Don't Die Twice. R. Angel
You Don't Need an Enemy. R. M. Stern
You Don't Say! H. Luger
You Find Him--I'll Fix Him. R. Marshall
You Gotta Be Rough. M. Fiaschetti
You Have Yourself a Deal. J. H. Chase
You Kill Me. J. D. MacDonald
You Kill Me! P. Muller
You Know the Way It Is. A. E. Jones
You Leave Me Cold! S. Rogers
You Live Once. J. D. MacDonald

Title Index

You Murdered Me. R. Tarne
You Must Never Go Back. B. Cleeve
You Never Know with Women. J. H. Chase
You Never Learn. M. Cronin
You Nice Bastard. G. F. Newman
You Only Die Once. H. B. Kaye
You Only Hang Once. H. W. Roden
You Only Live Twice. I. Fleming
You Only Live Until You Die. S. Weinstein
You Pay for Pity. W. Mole
You Pay the Price. Griff
You Pay Your Money. M. Cronin
You Play the Black and the Red Comes Up. R. Hallas
You Remember the Case. T. Claymore
You Shall Know Them. Vercors
You Slay Me. D. Spade
You Stand Accused. D. Hughston
You Take the Rap. Spike Gordon
You Talk Too Much. B. Shannon
You, the Jury. J. M. Liebeler
You, the Jury. J. Reach
"You Took Me...Keep Me." D. Glinto
You Want to Die, Johnny? G. Black
You Will Die Today! R. I. Wakefield
You Won't Let Me Finish. J. Fleming
You Won't Need a Coat. E. Messenger
You'd Be Surprised. P. Cheyney
You'll Be Better Off Dead. M. Storm
You'll Be Sorry! S. Rogers
You'll Catch Your Death. David Hume
You'll Die Laughing. Craig Cooper
You'll Die Laughing. B. Elliott
You'll Die Next! H. Whittington
You'll End Up Dead. L. H. Hart
You'll Fry Tomorrow. M. V. Heberden
You'll Get Yours. T. Wills
You'll Hang, My Love. F. Swann
You'll Have to Talk. D. Steel
You'll Like My Mother. N. A. Hintze
You'll Never Get Me. S. Morelli
You'll Never Get to Heaven. S. Mitchell
You'll Never See Me Again. W. Irish
You'll Play This My Way. D. Spade
Young Accused. A. Furness
Young Alladin. Old Sleuth
Young and Deadly. J. Carrick
Young and Violent. V. Packer
Young and Wild. Morton Cooper
Young Archduchess. W. LeQueux
Young Beck. M. M. Bodkin
Young Blood. E. W. Hornung
Young Blood. F. Lynde
Young Buffalo. C. E. Blaney
Young Buffalo in New York. C. E. Blaney
Young Can Die Protesting. T. Wells
Young Cardinaud. G. Simenon
Young Chauncey. Old Sleuth
Young Chevalier. D. W. MacArthur
Young Dash. Old Sleuth
Young Detective. R. Abbott
Young Dillinger. S. Stuart
Young Don't Cry. R. Jessup
Young Duchess. G. W. M. Reynolds
Young Engineer. Old Sleuth
Young Eve and Old Adam. T. Gallon
Young Flynn. E. L. Long
Young Gingers. Old Sleuth
Young Girl's Bondage. J. R. Wilmot
Young Girl's Life. B. L. Farjeon
Young Harold. Old Sleuth
Young Lord Folliot. N. H. Romanes
Young Love. J. G. Brandon
Young Lucifer. C. Blackstock
Young Magician. Old Sleuth

Young Man from Lima. J. Blackburn
Young Man, I Think You're Dying. J. Fleming
Young Man in Question. J. L. Rickard
Young Man on a Bicycle. V. Canning
Young Man with a Scythe. A. Kennington
Young Men May Die. D. Craig
Young Mr. Gibbs. J. L. Rickard
Young Mrs. Barter's Repentence. D. C. Murray
Young Mrs. Caudle. G. R. Sims
Young Mrs. Henniker. J. L. Rickard
Young Prey. H. Waugh
Young Savages. E. Hunter
Young Sleuth's Victory. A. Kutch
Young Vanish. F. Everton
Young Vigilance. Old Sleuth
Young Villain with Wings. R. Kruger
Young Wallingford. G. R. Chester
Young Widow. E. E. Cameron
Young Wife's Trial. F. Warden
Young Wolves. H. Janson
Younger Venus. N. Royde-Smith
Youngest Miss Brown. F. Warden
Youngest Soldier of the Grand Armee. F. Du Boisgobey
Your Casket Awaits, Madame. M. Lynch
Your Daughter Will Die! J. P. Cody
Your Deal, My Lovely. P. Cheyney
Your Friendly Neighborhood Death Pedlar. J. Sangster
Your Golden Jugular. W. Squerent
Your Loving Victim. P. McGerr
Your Money and Your Life. G. Milner
Your Money and Your Wife. Ritchie Perry
Your Move, Delaney! B. Singer
Your Neck in a Noose. E. Ferrars
Your Number Is Up. A. Mills
Your Red Wagon. E. Anderson
Your Secret Friend. M. Torrie
Your Shot, Darling! L. Bergquist
Your Turn, Mr. Moto. J. P. Marquand
You're a Long Time Dead. R. Clapperton
You're Better Off Dead. Peter Chambers
You're Dead, My Lovely. G. Ross
You're Dead Without Money. J. H. Chase
You're Fairly Welcome. J. Ditton
You're Hired: You're Dead. K. Carr
You're in the Racket, Too. J. Curtis
You're Lonely When You're Dead. J. H. Chase
You're My Man! C. C. Waddell
You're Never Too Old to Die. A. D. Goldstein
You're No Lady. Spike Gordon
You're Welcome to Ulster! M. Gallie
You're Wrong, Delaney. B. Singer
Yours Truly, Angus MacIvor. N. Harman
Yours Truly, Jack the Ripper. R. Bloch
Youth at Bay. L. Vincent
Youth Hostel Murders. G. Carr
Youth Without Glory. B. Von Hutten
Youthful Imposter. G. W. M. Reynolds
You've Bet Your Life. G. Ashe
You've Got Him Cold. T. B. Dewey
You've Got It Coming. J. H. Chase
You've Had Your Chance. J. Cairo
Yu-Chi Stone. E. Snell
Yu-Malu, the Dragon Princess. T. Leslie
Yu'an Hee See Laughs. S. Rohmer
Yuki. R. Kirkbridge
Yukon Kid. J. B. Hendryx

Z

Z Cars Again. A. Prior
"Z" Case. Roland Daniel
Z Effect. M. Laurens
Z for Zaborra. E. Wuorio
"Z" Murders. J. J. Farjeon
"Z" Ray. E. Snell
Zadda Street Affair. W. Jackson
Zadig. Voltaire
Zahara. M. T. Walworth
Zaharan Pursuit. Adam Hamilton
Zakari's Skull. Michael Barrett
Zakhov Mission. A. Gulyashki
Zalea. R. C. Garland
Zaleski's Percentage. D. MacKenzie
Zambra the Detective. H. Hill
Zantelli. Old Sleuth
Zanzibar Intrigue. V. W. Mason
Zebra-Striped Hearse. R. Macdonald
Zelda. C. Brown
Zen There Was Murder. H. R. F. Keating
Zenobie Capitaine. F. Du Boisgobey
Zeph and other stories. G. R. Sims
Zeppelin Destroyer. W. LeQueux
Zeppelin's Passenger. E. P. Oppenheim
Zero Always Wins. P. Gascoigne
Zero at the Bone. E. Ferrars
Zero Cool. J. Lange
Zero Hour. L. C. Douthwaite
Zero Hour. C. Robertson
Zero in the Gate. S. Farrar
Zero Minus Nine. E. P. Thorne
Zero 08.00. B. Gaston
Zero Ray Terrors. E. T. Portwine
Zero Take All. H. Janson
Zero the 14th. H. Clevely
Zhukov Briefing. A. Trew
Zia. P. Wynnton
Zig-Zag Man. J. C. Goodwin
Zig-Zag the Clown. F. Du Boisgobey
Zilov Bombs. D. G. Barron
Zinzin Road. F. Knebel
Zion Road. S. Harvester
Zodiac. D. Lees
Zoe's Revenge. M. Y. Halidom
Zola's Thirteen. G. Morton
Zolotov Affair. R. H. Rimmer
Zombie. E. Lecale
Zombie. D. Lynn
Zombie. R. St. Clair
Zone of Fire. H. Hill
Zone Zero. J. Robb
Zoo Gang. P. Gallico
Zoo Murder. F. Grierson
Zoo Murders. J. Farr
Zoo Ship. S. Volk
Zoom! Peter Townend
Zoraida. W. LeQueux
Zurich/AZ 900. M. Albrand

Series Index

This index lists alphabetically all series and series characters that are identified in the Author Index. Following each series (character) name is the byline under which books about that series are cited in the Author Index. The bylines are given in abbreviated form—initials and last name only—except when that would lead to ambiguity. In addition, although some series (characters) were created by two authors in collaboration under a joint byline, only the first author is given here, since that is how it will be found in the Author Index.

Series Index

A

Abbot, John; B. Whitaker
Abbott, Pat and Jean; F. Crane
Abbott, Samuel G.; J. R. Langham
Abner, Uncle; M. D. Post
"Ace," The; S. Horler
Acton, Kit (Marsden); M. Bramhall
Adam 12; M. Stratford, C. Stratton
Adams, Insp.; L. Hollingsworth
Adams, Adelaide; A. Blackmon
Adams, Anthony; T. Brace
Adams, Bradley; M. Dekobra
Adams, Hilda; M. R. Rinehart
Adjusters, The; P. Winston
Adkins, Harry; R. Foxall
Adrano, Johnny; Michael Bradley
Adrian, Christopher; M. R. Silverman
Albany, Jack; J. Godey
Allain, Insp.; B. Graeme
Allan, Rocky; V. Rath
Allen, Peter; L. Anson
Alleyn, Roderick; N. Marsh
Allison, John; R. Meade
Allport, Det.-Insp.; F. Everton
Ames, Martin; A. Eichler
Ames, Sid; H. W. Roden
Ames, William; L. Freeman
Amsterdam, Johnny; Michael Lawrence
Anders, Inspector; H. Jobson
Anderson, Ben; G. Compton
Anderson, Everett; K. S. Daiger
Angele, Soeur; H. Catalan
Annesley, George; F. Everton
Annie, Polack; J. Lait
Anstruther, Colin; J. Plain
Anthony, Wade; Eric Heath
Antonio, San; San Antonio
Antony, Mark; C. Curzon
Appleby, John; M. Innes
Appleby, Pecos; R. P. Koehler
April, Johnny; M. Roscoe
Arbuthnot, Montrose; N. A. Temple-Ellis
Archer, Lew; John Macdonald
      John Ross Macdonald
      Ross Macdonald
Archer, Matt; Clay Henry
Archer, Maxwell; H. Clevely
Archer, Oceola; Joseph Baker Carr
Aristo Autos; J. Leasor
Ark, Simon; E. D. Hoch
Armitage, Bryan; B. Cobb
Armstrong, Inspector; A. White
Arnholt; G. Latta
Arnold, Inspector; Miles Burton
Arrest and Trial; N. Daniels
Arrow, Frank; W. Deptula
Artifex, Simon; R. Keverne
Asch, Jacob; Arthur Lyons
Ash, Andrew; F. Grierson
Ashe, Saxon; Saxon Ashe
Ashe, Steve; J. A. Howard
Ashley, Robert Lee; Chester K. Steele
Ashton, Simon; E. Antill
Assassin, The; P. McCurtin
Aubry, Madame; H. Travers
Audley, David; A. Price
Austen, William; A. Hocking
Austin, Steve; M. Caiden
Autos, Aristo; J. Leasor
Avenger, The; K. Robeson
Avengers, The; N. Daniels
      J. Garforth
      K. Laumer
      P. MacNee
Aveyard, William; James Fraser
Aylwin, Jerome; A. Curry

B

Bailey, Hilary Dunsany III; H. Bailey
Bailey, Hilea; H. Bailey
Bailey, Stuart; R. Huggins
Bain, Joe; J. H. Vance
Baines, Scattergood; C. B. Kelland
Baird, Frances; R. W. Kauffman
Baker, Inspector; O. Mills
Baker, Charles A.; H. C. Huston
Baker, Larry; Carter Brown
Baker, Paul; B. Norman
Baley, Elijah; I. Asimov
Balzic, Mario; K. C. Constantine
Banacek; D. Romano
Banion, Dan; R. Finnegan
Banner, Rex; Robert Chapman
Banning, Bill; N. Easton
Bannion, Burns; E. Norman
Bannister, Guy; M. Crossley
Barcello, Lee; S. Ransome
Barclay, George; Ernest Paul
Barlach, Hans; F. Duerrenmatt
Barlow, Supt.; Elwyn Jones
Barlowe, Inspector; C. I. D. Smith
Barnard, Inspector; T. C. H. Jacobs
Barne, Richard; E. G. Cousins
Barnes, Berkeley; Eugene Franklin
Barnes, Bromley; G. Barton
Barnes, John; R. Ottolengui
Barney, Al; J. H. Chase
Baron, The; A. Morton
Baron, Bruce; N. Daniels
Baron, Hugo; Michael Brett
Barrie, Dennis; A. Reynolds
Barrin, John; Gret Lane
Barron, Peter and Janet; R. Darby
Barrow, Jake; N. Quarry
Barrows, Winston; M. L. Eades
Barry, Inspector; A. Rowe
Barry, Alun; Kenneth O'Hara
Bartlett, Nell; D. Elias
Bartley, John; C. J. Dutton
Basil, Inspector; P. Hobson
Bass, Inspector; S. Truss
Bassett, Inspector; C. Ryland
Bassett, Justin; R. Stratton
Bastion, Professor; Gavin Holt
Bastion, William; R. Harrison
Bathurst, Anthony; B. Flynn
Batman; W. Lyon
Batts, Singer; T. B. Dewey
Bawtry, Sam; D. Enefer
Baynes, Dr.; V. Bell
Beagle, Lutie and Amanda; T. Chanslor
Beagle, Otis; C. K. Boston, F. Gruber
Beale, Edward; F. R. Penny
Beck, Martin; M. Sjowall
Beck, Paul; M. M. Bodkin
Beckett, Lee; J. Crowe
Beef, Sergeant; L. Bruce
Beeke, William; E. S. Brooks
Belcourt, Robert; N. Rougvie
Beldrum, Archibald; L. F. Hay
Bell; E. R. Punshon
Bell, Garnett; C. H. Bullivant
Bellamy, Harker; S. Horler
Bellamy, John; T. C. H. Jacobs
Bellecroix, Stephen; D. Craig
Belot, Frederic; C. Aveline
Ben the Tramp; J. J. Farjeon
Benasque, Mike; A. Caillou
Bencolin, Henri; J. D. Carr
Bendilow, Edmund; Carlton Wallace
Benedict, Sam; H. L. Oleck
      Brad Williams
Benjamin, Paul; B. Garfield
Bennett, Jim; Robert Martin
Bennion, Roger; H. Adams
Bent, John; H. C. Branson
Bentiron, Dr.; E. M. Poate
Bentley, Steve; R. Dietrich
Beresford, Tommy & Tuppence; A. Christie
Berkley, George Stanhope; L. Meynell
Bernard, Paul; S. Gluck
Best, Petunia; B. Chetwynd
Beverley, Jim; A. Marsden
Bey, Nur; J. Rathbone
Bignon, Orestes; F. Didelot
Birdseye, Miriam; N. Spain
Birge, Sam; W. Krasner
Birkett, Sam; L. Payne
Birtley, Mr.; C. A. Alington
Bishop, Hugo; S. Rattray
Bishop, Robin; G. Homes
Black, Supt.; J. N. Chance
Black; W. Manson
Black; J. Nazel
Black, Capt.; M. Pemberton
Black, Jonathan; R. Garnett
Blackburn; Jeffery; M. Afford
Blackwood, Riley; V. Starrett
Blackshirt; B. Graeme, R. Graeme
Blackshirt, Lord; B. Graeme
Blackshirt, Monsieur; D. Graeme
Blackstone; R. Falkirk
Blade, Jud; K. Jackson
Blair, Margot; K. M. Knight
Blair, Nigel; L. F. Hay
Blair, Major Peter; J. R. L. Anderson
Blaise, Modesty; P. O'Donnell
Blake, Arab & Andy; Richard Powell
Blake, Jonathan; J. N. Chance
Blake, Red; Edward Lee
Blake, Sexton; D. Ames
      R. C. Armour
      W. Arthur
      J. Ascott
      W. H. Baker
      W. A. Ballinger
      W. J. Bayer
      L. Bidston
      Ladbroke Black
      A. Blair
      S. Blake
      S. Blakesley
      J. W. Bobin
      G. Bowman
      J. G. Brandon
      T. C. Bridges
      C. Brisbane
      E. S. Brooks
      L. H. Brooks
      Jonathan Burke
      Lewis Carlton
      Philip Chambers
      Gilbert Chester
      S. Christie
      H. Clevely
      J. Creasey
      G. Dilnot
      M. B. Dix
      Rex Dolphin
      L. C. Douthwaite
      S. Drew
      J. Drummond
      A. Edgar
      W. Edwards
      R. C. Elliott
      L. Essex
      Gwyn Evans
      F. D. Fawcett
      R. Francis Foster
      M. Frazer
      C. Vernon Frost
      C. Gates
      H. C. Gibbons
      N. Goddard
      R. Goyne
      B. Gray
      R. M. Graydon
      W. M. Graydon
      V. J. Hanson
      R. Hardinge
      A. S. Hardy
      Edwin Harrison
      Harry Egbert Hill
      C. M. Hincks
      W. B. Home-Gall
      S. Hood
      S. Hope
      D. H. Hyde
      L. Jackson

Blake, Sexton; W. Jardine
    G. Johns
    J. G. Jones
    A. Kent
    Hilary King
    A. Kirby
    Jack Lewis
    D. Long
    Arthur MacLean
    W. McNeilly
    A. Maxwell
    M. Mead
    P. Meriton
    O. Merland
    H. C. Miln
    Andrew Murray
    Edgar Joyce Murray
    M. Osborne
    A. Parsons
    W. J. Passingham
    J. N. Pentelow
    G. N. Philips
    M. Poole
    R. H. Poole
    J. Purley
    P. Quiroule
    G. Rees
    Desmond Reid
    W. Reynolds
    Ross Richards
    P. Saxon
    W. W. Sayer
    H. Scott
    Stanley Gordon Shaw
    W. Shute
    A. Skene
    J. Stagg
    J. Stamper
    W. E. Stanton-Hope
    J. T. Story
    D. Stuart
    G. Sydney
    J. Sylvester
    F. A. Symonds
    G. H. Teed
    Martin Thomas
    H. Townley
    W. Tyrer
    P. Urquhart
    G. Verner
    W. P. Vickery
    T. C. Wignall
    Richard Williams
Bland, Inspector; J. Symons
Blatchington, Everard; G. D. H. Cole
Blaze, Joe; R. Novak
Blessington, Charles; J. Sherwood
Blinkwell, Prof.; S. Fowler
Bliss, Inspector; J. Remenham
Blixen, Nils-Frederik; C. Larson
Blood; A. Morgan
Bloom, John Isidore; E. Warman
Blow, Dr.; K. Hopkins
Blunt, Mortimer; M. Cranston
Bognor, Simon; T. Heald
Bolan, Mack; D. Pendleton
    Jim Peterson
Bolt, Dave; Richard Curtis
Bolt, John; R. Hawkes
Bonaparte, Napoleon; A. W. Upfield
Bond, Christoper; W. Martyn
Bond, James; Ian Fleming
    R. Markham
Bondurant, Victor; J. G. Edwards
Bonner, Dol; R. Stout
Boone, Jefferson; J. Messmann
Booth, Silas; J. L. Linklater
Borden, Steve; B. Dougall
Borges, Inspector; J. & E. Bonett
Bounty, Peter; T. Downing
Bourne, Inspector; R. C. Finney

Bourne, "Daddy"; G. V. Galwey
Bowman, Glenn; Hartley Howard
Boyd, Danny; Carter Brown
Boyd, Felix; S. Campbell
Boyne, Jerry; A. MacGowan
Bracken, Donald; J. S. Blazer
Bradbury, Insp.; N. Longmate
Brade, Simon; H. R. Campbell
Bradford, Peter; C. Witting
Bradley, Supt.; Colin Robertson
Bradley, Adela Beatrice Lestrange;
    G. Mitchell
Bradley, Ben; W. G. Forbes
Bradley, Bill; G. Tree
Bradley, Luke; H. Pentecost
Bradley, Rupert "Brad"; E. B. Ronald
Bradshaw, Noah; Madeleine Johnston
Brady, Franklin; A. McRoyd
Bragg, John; Henry Wade
Brain, Big; G. Brandner
Brand, Jake; R. L. Brent
Brand, Mark; J. J. Connington
Brandon, Anthony; Bryan Peters
Brandon, Mark; V. Warren
Brandstetter, Dave; J. Hansen
Brannigan, Supt.; Andrew MacKenzie
Branson, Al; R. P. Koehler
Brant, Mason; N. M. Hopkins
Breck, Adam; K. Orvis
Bredder, Joseph; L. Holton
Bredon, Miles; R. A. Knox
Breed, Barr; B. S. Ballinger
Breen, Jim; J. Karney
Breeze, Benedict; I. Bayne
Brendel, Ernest; J. C. Masterman
Brent, Carey; M. W. Glidden
Brent, Dudley; D. Marfield
Brent, Jimmy; H. Kemp
Brett, Alan; Robert Garrett
Brett, Brian; C. Monig
Brett, Chester; Gwyn Evans
Brett, Chico; Kevin O'Hara
Brett, Dixon; T. Stanleyan King
Brett, Mike; Keith Campbell
Brett, Reginald; L. Tracy
Brewer, William; H. McElroy
Brews, Inspector; V. Loder
Brewster, Amy; S. Merwin, Jr.
Brierly, Herman; W. Levinrew
Briggs; R. L. Fish
Briggs; D. MacDonald
Bright, Rosie; Judge Ruegg
Brindle, Max; A. S. Fleischman
Britain, William; J. Courage
Brock, John; D. Skirrow
Brook, Roger; D. Wheatley
Brooke, Clay; H. Crooker
Brooks, Mike; H. T. Rothwell
Broom, Herbert; F. Hurt
Brown, Father; G. K. Chesterton
Brown, Angel; G. Montrose
Brown, Benvenuto; E. Gill
Brown, Jane and Dagobert; D. Ames
Brown, Vee; C. J. Daly
Browne, Freddie; M. Poole
Bryant, John; Richard Grayson
Bryce, Emily & Henry; M. Scherf
Bryden, Avis; E. Phillpotts
Buck, Inspector; A. Marsden
Buckby, Lionel; John Gloag
Buckle, Ebenezer; N. Brady
Budd, Robert; G. Verner
Buell, Martin; M. Scherf
Bull, George; M. Kennedy
Bull, Homer; L. Lariar
Bullion, Simon; M. B. Dix
Bunce, Dr.; E. M. Curtiss
Bunker, Terry; Paul Ross
Bunn, Smiler; B. Atkey
Burford, Archie; V. MacClure
Burgess, Inspector; C. Franklin
Burke, Eleanora; V. Perdue
Burke, Jerry; Asa Baker
Burke's Law; R. Fuller
Burmann, Cheviot; B. Cobb
Burnell, John; F. Vivian
Burr, Jason; D. Kent
Burrell, Jacob; G. Boothby

Burrill, William; Adam Gordon MacLeod
Burton, Inspector; G. E. Locke
Burton, Major; M. Beckett
Butcher, The; S. Jason
Butler, Patrick; J. D. Carr
Byrnes, Inspector; J. Hawthorne

C

Cabot, Philip; R. McDougald
Cadee, Don; S. Dean
Cadman, Inspector; C. Rushton
Cage, Huntington; A. Riefe
Cain, Cabot; A. Caillou
Cainsforth, Duncan; J. Maske
Cairn, Donald; V. Loder
Caldwell, Prof.; M. K. Ozaki
Cale, Martyn; P. Long
Callaghan, Slim; P. Cheyney
Callaghan, "Steel"; M. Chesney
Callahan, Brock; W. C. Gault
Callan, David; J. Mitchell
Cam, Inspector; J. Cockin
Camberwell, Ronald; J. S. Fletcher
Cameron, Janice; J. Sheridan
Campbell, Humphrey; G. Homes
Campbell, Pat; E. Colter
Campion, Albert; Margery Allingham
    Youngman Carter
Cane, David; J. Courage
Cannon; R. Gallagher
Cannon, Curt; Curt Cannon
Cannon, Dave; M. Delving
Canuck, Johnny; J. Moffatt
Carberry, Jane; B. Symons
Carbo; J. Quartermain
Cardby, Mick; David Hume
Cardiff, Insp.; D. Gray
Cardigan, Burgess (Buzz); D. Rico
Cardigan, Peter; Monte Barrett
Carding, Hugh; G. Collins
Carlisle, Kenneth; Carolyn Wells
Carmichael, Justine; K. Chase
Carnaby; P. N. Walker
Carnellion, Richard; J. Rosenberger
Carner, Mary; Z. Popkin
Carolus, Lucian; E. Ascher
Carpenter, Chips; G. Eldredge
Carr, Dan; Willard K. Smith
Carradine, Steve; M. K. Robertson
Carrados, Max; E. Bramah
Carrick, Webb; B. Knox
Carrington, Derek; B. Netton
Carrington, F. T.; J. S. Clouston
Carroll, David; O. R. Cohen
Carroll, Jimmy; H. McCutcheon
Carruthers; R. L. Fish
Carruthers, John; E. C. Cox
Carson, Arthur; B. Jones
Carson, Don; A. Pruitt
Carstairs; N. Davis
Carstairs, "Apples"; S. Myles
Carter; E. R. Punshon
Carter, Jack; T. Lewis
Carter, Nick; Nicholas Carter
    Nick Carter
Carter, Ralph; T. Lilley
Carter, Steve; A. R. Long
Carter, Tony; David Hume
Cartwright, Bill; P. Morgan
Carvel, Kelly; N. Daniels
Carver, Rex; V. Canning
Caryll, Victor; G. Fairlie
Casey, Flash; P. Ayres
    G. H. Coxe
Castang, Henri; N. Freeling
Castle, Peter; G. Davison
Castleman, Marc; R. Kutak
Castleton, James; C. A. Alington
Cauldron, Insp.; S. Fowler
Caution, Lemmy; P. Cheyney
Cellini, Dr. Emmanuel; M. Halliday
Chace, Inspector; V. Loder

Chadwick, John; G. Cobden
Chalice, Harry; Donald MacKenzie
Challis, Professor; Shane Martin
Challis, Bart; W. F. Nolan
Chambers, Peter; H. Kane
Chambrun, Pierre; H. Pentecost
Champnell, Augustus; Richard Marsh
Chan, Charlie; E. D. Biggers
    D. Lynds
Chance, John Newton; J. N. Chance
Chandos; D. Yates
Chang, Mr.; A. E. Apple
Chantecoq; A. Bernede
Chaos, Jacob; Shelley Smith
Chard, Peter; G. Verner
Chard, Simon; B. Malim
Charlesworth, Inspector; C. Brand
Charlton, Inspector; C. Witting
Chase; N. Daniels
Chavasse, Paul; M. Fallon
Cheri-Bibi; G. Leroux
Cherington, Richard; G. Daniel
    D. Rees
Chipstead, "Bunny"; S. Horler
Chisholm, Paul; A. W. Eyles
Chopper Cop; Paul Ross
Christie, Bob; James Preston
Christopher, James; Curtis Steele
Circle, Secret; G. Null
Cirret, Antoine; E. Hely
Clackworthy, Amos; Christopher B. Booth
Clancy, Lt.; R. L. Pike
Clancy, Peter; L. Thayer
Clane, Terry; E. S. Gardner
Claremont, Clarice; C. Cranston
Clark, Clark Clark; S. S. Baker
Clarkson-Parry; B. G. Quin
Clay, Lucien; R. Gore-Browne
Clay, Stephen; S. E. Porcelain
Claymore, Tod; T. Claymore
Clayton; S. Gluck
Clayton, Jeff; W. Ward
Cleek, Hamilton; H. P. Hanshew
    M. E. Hanshew
    T. W. Hanshew
Cleveland, Insp.; S. Fowler
Clifford, Bob; Leroy Scott
Clinton, Hortense; M. Hagen
Clown, Crimson; J. McCulley
Club, Catalyst; G. Dyer
Clubfoot; D. Valentine
    V. Williams
Cluff, Sgt.; G. North
Clune, Asaph; R. L. Goldman
Clunk, Joshua; H. C. Bailey
Cluthra; H. Munro
Clymping, Viscount; V. Gielgud
Cockrill, Inspector; C. Brand
Coffee, Dr.; L. G. Blochman
Coffin, John; Gwendoline Butler
Colby, Al; D. Dodge
Cole, Schyler; Frederick C. Davis
Collier, Hugh; M. Dalton
Collin, Mr.; F. Heller
Collins; B. Hitchens
Collins, Barnabas; Marilyn Ross
Colt, Thatcher; A. Abbot
Colton, Thornley; C. H. Stagg
Columbo; H. Clement
    A. Lawrence
Cominsec, Agent of; Ralph Hayes
Commandos, Israeli; A. Sugar
Conacher, Steve; Adam Knight
Condon; D. Jordan
Condor, The; J. Grady
Connell, Jim; J. Foxx
Connor, Doc; J. Dolph
Conquest, Norman; B. Gray
Considine, Steve; R. P. Wilmot
Constantine, Dr.; M. Thynne
Conway, Brian Dinsmore; Simon Stone
Cool, Bertha; A. A. Fair
Cop, Chopper; Paul Ross
Coppersmith; R. J. Griffin
Corbin, Ben; R. Crane
Cord, Talos; Robert MacLeod
Cordry, Jason; J. D. O'Hanlon
Cork, Sgt.; A. Swinson

Cork, Montague; MacDonald Hastings
Cornelius, Jerry; M. Moorcock
Cornford, Inspector; M. Kennedy
Cornish, Katherine (Kay); Virginia Hanson
Corridon, "Brick Top"; R. Marshall
Corrigan, "Biff"; W. Morton
Corrigan, Mark; M. Corrigan
Corrigan, Tim; E. Queen
Costaine, Tony; N. MacNeil
Cotten, Neal; Sam S. Taylor
Cotterell, Martin; J. Trench
Cotton, Gunston; Rupert Grayson
Coulson, Rex; J. Mann
Courtenay, Det.-Insp.; N. Berrow
Coyle; J. Philips
Crader, Carl; E. D. Hoch
Craft, Sebald; I. Patterson
Crag, Osborne; S. Elvestad
Cragg, Sam; F. Gruber
Craggs, John; C. A. Alington
Craig, Professor; Babette Hughes
Craig, John; J. Munro
Craig, Peter; K. Benton
Craig, Steve; B. Winter
Craig, Tom; V. Van Urk
Craine, Paul; E. P. Healy
Cramer, Inspector; R. Stout
Crammond, Roger; T. Muir
Crane, Bill; Jonathan Latimer
Crane, Lionel; D. Stuart
Crane, Paul; Wade Curtis
Cranfurd, Liane; R. S. Gilruth
Cranston, Lamont; W. B. Gibson
    M. Grant
Crawford; D. Cushman
Creevy, Winston; J. Lord
Creighton, Peter; A. Livingston
Crewe; John R. Watson
Crewe; V. Vanardy
Cribb, Sgt.; P. Lovesey
Crichton, Tessa; A. Morice
Criddle, Adrian; B. Strong
Crole, Simon; R. H. Leitfred
Crombie, Sam; G. H. Coxe
Cromwell, Bill "Ironsides"; V. Gunn
Crook, Arthur; Anthony Gilbert
Crosley, Lee; R. Tralins
Crow, Inspector; R. Lewis
Crow, Anderson; G. B. McCutcheon
Crowder, George; H. Pentecost
Crown, John; T. Harknett
Cullinan, Timothy; O. Martin
Cummings, Inspector; Paul McGuire
Cunningham, "Brains"; E. P. Thorne
Curfew, Max; J. Brunner
Curtis, Hugh; P. Somers
Curtis, Lyle; E. L. Fetta
Cutting, Samuel; P. D. Westbrook

D

Dain, Stephen; R. Sheckley
Dakkers, Sam; Mike Brett
Dakota; G. A. Ralston
Dale, Jimmie; F. Packard
Dalgliesh, Adam; P. D. James
Dalton Boys, The; W. B. Lawson
Dalziel, Andrew; Reginald Hill
Dancer, April; M. Avallone
    S. Latter
    P. Leslie
Dane, Bartholomew; Rex Dark
Dane, Timothy; W. Ard
Dangerfield, Maxine; C. Franklin
Daniels, Superintendent; G. Baxter
Daniels, Charmian; J. Melville
Daniels, Webster; Terrence Lore Smith
Danning, David; D. Von Elsner
Darby, Parrish; The Aresby's

Dark Shadows; Marilyn Ross
Darling, Kiss; J. Yardley
Darroch, Mike; A. MacKinnon
Davenant, P. J.; F. S. Hamilton
Davie, Dr.; V. C. Clinton-Baddeley
Davies, Bill; Sara Elizabeth Mason
Davis, John George; J. Ripley
Davison, Gilbert; R. J. Fletcher
Davvie, Anne Davenport McLean; Margaret Tayler Yates
Dawlish, Patrick; G. Ashe
Dawson, Chief Inspector; B. Copplestone
Dax, Saturnin; M. Cumberland
Day, Julian; D. Wheatley
de la Bath, Hubert Bonisseur; J. Bruce
de Lancey, Marka; B. Frost
De Prundis; R. L. Graves
de Richleau, Duke; D. Wheatley
de Silva, Jose; R. L. Fish
Dean, Garry; P. Whelton
Dean, Paul; B. Francis
Deane, Robert; J. W. Vandercook
Death, Dr.; Zorro
Death Merchant, The; J. Rosenberger
Decker, Bill; L. Treat
Decker, Paul; A. I. Albert
Decker, Paul; G. Hackforth-Jones
Dee, Judge; R. Van Gulik
Deene, Carolus; L. Bruce
Defenders, The; R. Fuller
DeHavilland, Mr.; J. N. Chance
Delaney; B. Singer
Delaney, Al; T. B. Black
Delaney, Joe; F. Archer
Dene, Dorcas; George R. Sims
Dene, Michael; G. Verner
Dene, Trevor; V. Williams
Department of Dead Ends; R. Vickers
d'Espinal, Harcourt; B. Healey
Destroyer, The; R. Sapir
Devereaux, Johnny; J. Roeburt
Deville, Rufus; J. Noy
Devlin, Brock; Scott Mitchell
DeWitt, Manny; P. Rabe
Dexter, Charles; J. Fredman
di Ganzarello, Alessandro; I. Drummond
Di Gris, Jim; H. Harrison
Diavolo, Don; S. Towne
Dickerson, Joseph; E. K. Goldthwaite
Digburn, Howard; B. Sanders
DiMarco, Jeff; D. M. Disney
Dingle, James; G. Osborne
Disher; Will Scott
Dixon, George; T. Willis
Doan; N. Davis
Dobbs, John; R. B. Saxe
Dodds, Septimus; Sutherland Scott
Docker, Inspector; H. Pink
Doight, Henry; B. Symons
Dolan, Brad; W. Fuller
Donahue, Lorna; Katharine Hill
Donavan, Paul; Carter Brown
Doner, Dan (DeeDee); F. Shay
Donovan; L. Parker
Donovan; J. Philips
Donovan, Dick; Dick Donovan
Dormouse, The; The Frank King
Dortmunder; D. E. Westlake
Douglas, Brian; John Lee
Downey, Corporal; J. B. Hendryx
Downs, Inspector; V. Sampson
Draco, Pete; Richard Foster
Dragnet; R. Deming
    D. Knight
    R. Tralins
    D. Vowell
Dragoon, Ransome; F. Diamond
Drake, Desmond; Sea-Lion
Drake, Dexter; E. Barker
Drake, Earl; Dan J. Marlowe
Drake, Simon; M. Maguire
Drake, Stephen; C. Wilcox
Drake, Steve; R. Ellington
Dreamer, The; W. M. Duncan

Drew, Adam; Virginia Hanson
Drewer, Timothy; Hilary Landon
Drewry, Chief Inspector; N. Burnaby
Drex, Quentin; Gwyn Evans
Drexel, Michael; G. Usher
Driffield, Sir Clinton; J. J. Connington
Drum, Chester; S. Marlowe
Drummond, Bulldog; G. Fairlie, H. C. McNeile, H. Reymond
Drury, Inspector; W. S. Sykes
Drury, Dynamite; L. P. Greene
Drury, Frank; P. Marlowe
Du Cas, Inspector; H. Imbert-Terry
Duane, Stephen; J. L. Benton
Duff, MacDougal; C. Armstrong
Duffy, Insp./Supt.; N. Fitzgerald
Duker, Casson; W. Mole
Duluth, Peter; P. Quentin
Dundas, Michael; V. Rath
Dundee, James F. "Bonnie"; Anne Austin
Dunn, Jim; H. L. Nelson
Dupin, C. Auguste; M. Harrison, E. A. Poe
Dupuy, M.; Anthony Gilbert
Durell, Sam; E. S. Aarons
Dust, Joe; P. Graaf
DuVivien, Johnny; N. Spain
Dyke, Toby; E. (X.) Ferrars
Dynes, Lathom; H. Robertson

E

Eady, Quentin; E. P. Thorne
Eagle, John; P. Edwards
East, Floyd; C. Rushton
East, Mark; Hilda Lawrence
Easy, John; R. Goulart
Eddie, Crying; Donald MacKenzie
Eddison, Bob; M. Delving
Edwards, Jane Amanda; Charlotte Murray Russell
Egerton, Scott; Anthony Gilbert
Egg, Montague; D. L. Sayers
Egypt, Harry; D. Broun
87th Precinct; E. McBain
Eldon, Bill; E. S. Gardner
Elk, Inspector; E. Wallace
Ellis, Tony; R. P. Koehler
Elton, Fox; Ared White
Elver, Horace Augustus; G. Dilnot
Emery, Val; G. Dilnot
Emory, Jason; Kootz
Emp, H.; S. Horler
Enforcer, The; A. Sugar
Entwhistle, Ebbie; F. A. M. Webster
Erridge, Matt; A. M. Stein
Evans, Inspector; W. J. Makin
Evans, Educated; E. Wallace
Evans, Homer; Elliot Paul
Everhard; P. Steward
Ewart, Edgar; A. E. Walter
Executioner, The; D. Pendleton
    Jim Peterson
Expediter, The; P. Edwards

F

Face, Twisted; G. Davidson
Fair, Prosper; B. Atkey
Fairbanks, Hank; E. Dean
Fairfield, Peggy; E. S. Liddon
Fairr, Melville; M. Venning
Falcon; J. Crozier
Falcon, Supt.; D. Yates
Falcon, The; D. Drake
Falkenstein, Jesse; L. Egan
Fane, Martin & Richard; M. Halliday
Fang, Wu; Roland Daniel
Fanks, Octavius; F. Hume
Fannin, Harry; D. Markson
Fanshaw, Jim; M. Poole
Fansler, Kate; A. Cross
Fantomas; M. Allain
    P. Souvestre
Faraday, Mike; B. Copper

Farrant, Michael; P. G. Larbalestier
Farrel, John; B. Hitchens
Farrell, Mike; Carter Brown
Farrow, Marcus Aurelius; Angus Ross
Faulkner, Reggie; E. Snell
Fedora, Johnny; D. Cory
Fell, Gideon; J. D. Carr
Fellows, Fred; H. Waugh
Felse Family; E. Pargeter
    Ellis Peters
Feltham, Peter; B. Mather
Felton, Ray; John Marsh
Fen, Gervase; E. Crispin
Fenn, Christopher; M. L. Stokes
Fennell, Geoff; E. P. Thorne
Fenner, Dave; J. H. Chase
Fenner, Jack; G. H. Coxe
Fenner, Maxwell; L. F. Booth
Fenton, Lawrie; M. Annesley
Ferenc, Dr.; Richard Savage
Ferrars, Francis; L. L. Lynch
Fielding, Henry Arthur; D. Sharp
Fillinger, Inspector; Paul McGuire
Finch, Inspector; J. Thomson
Finch, Martyn; P. Cleife
Finch, Septimus; M. Erskine
Finnegan, John; N. Forrest
Finney, Mary; M. Head
Firebrace, Captain; Seafarer
Firth, Ian; Ludovic Peters
Fitzgerald, Homer; Charlotte Murray Russell
Flack, Jeremy; J. Maske
Flagg, Inspector; J. Cassells
Flagg, Conan; M. K. Wren
Flagg, Webster; V. P. Johns
Flamm, Greg; I. Wilson
Flecker, James; Josephine Pullein-Thompson
Fleming, Inspector; J. Cameron
Fletcher, Johnny; F. Gruber
Flick, Robert; J. Ehrlich
Flicker, Gil; E. J. Millward
Flower, Insp.; Moira Field
Flute, Adam; D. Launay
Flynn, Captain; E. L. Long
Folly, Supt.; J. York
Fontaine, Danny; W. Ard
Force, Check; Ralph Hayes
Ford, Alan; Carolyn Wells
Ford, Brad; Hank Hobson
Fordinghame, Brian; S. Horler
Forge, Barney; R. Starnes
Fortescue, John; C. Brandon
Fortune, Dan; Michael Collins
Fortune, Hannibal; L. Maddock
Fortune, Reggie; H. C. Bailey
Fortune, Temple; T. C. H. Jacobs
Four Just Men; E. Wallace
Fowler, Dan; G. F. Eliot
Fowler, Timothy; C. Harris
Fox, Tecumseh; R. Stout
Frame, Reynold; H. Brean
Frampton, Andrew; T. A. Plummer
Frant, Arabella; D. Fearon
Fraser, Alan; H. Desmond
Fraser, Geoffrey; Elliot Bailey
Frass; J. Chancellor
Frayne, Ambrose and Dominique;
    J. T. McIntosh
Frazer, Tim; F. Durbridge
Freeman, John; J. Ironside
Freeman, Jub; L. Treat
French, Bill; C. Hale
French, Joseph; F. W. Crofts
Frend, Max; B. Chetwynd
Frere, Royston; W. J. Elliott
Frost, Inspector; H. Maynard Smith
Frost, Gerald; S. Horler
Frost, Henry; Josephine Bell
Fry, Pete; Pete Fry
Fu Manchu; S. Rohmer
Furling, Richard; F. Grierson

Furneaux, Inspector; G. Holmes
    L. Tracy
Furnival, Inspector; A. Haynes
Furnival, Matthew; S. Phillips
Fusil, Inspector; P. Alding

G

G-8; R. J. Hogan
Gaden, Supt.; P. H. Powell
Gail, John; S. D. Frances
Gaines, Vicky; F. Diamond
Galbreath, District Attorney; W. McCully
Gale, Simon; G. Verner
Gall, Joe; P. Atlee
Gallagher, Gale; Gale Gallagher
Galt; J. Gollomb
Gamadge, Henry; E. Daly
Gannon, Mike; D. Ballenger
Gantian, Colonel; C. Dawe
Gantt, Barney; J. S. Strange
Garden, Ben; T. Pace
Garfield, Grant; C. Franklin
Garfin, Mike; Martin Brett
Garnett, Inspector; R. Philmore
Garnett, David; C. Egleton
Garrison, Roger; J. Rovin
Garrison, Victor; D. Kirby
Garrity; Allan Nixon
Garstang; R. A. J. Walling
Garth, Inspector; H. Blayn
Gates, Ben; R. Kyle
Gaunt, Jonathan; Robert MacLeod
Gaunt, Michael; G. Braddon
Gaylord, Supt.; W. M. Duncan
Gently, Insp./Supt.; A. Hunter
Gethryn, Anthony; P. MacDonald
Ghost, The; R. B. Saxe
Ghote, Ganesh; H. R. F. Keating
Gibson; Hampton Stone
Gibson, Christopher; I. Montgomery
Gibson, Glen; J. Bentley
Gideon, George; J. J. Marric
Gidleigh, Inspector; S. Truss
Gifford, Adam; A. Lejeune
Gilette, Jenny; E. Gresham
    R. Grey
Gill, Eve; S. Jepson
Gilles, M.; J. Decrest
Gilliant, Supt.; J. Wainwright
Gilly, Mr.; W. M. Duncan
Gilmartin, Lawrence; C. Barry
Girl from H.A.R.D.; J. Moffatt
Girl from U.N.C.L.E.; M. Avallone
    S. Latter
    P. Leslie
Girland, Mark; J. H. Chase
Glenne, Al; M. G. Braun
Gloom, Insp.; Frank King
Glover, Inspector; M. Evermay
Glover, Insp.; L. Lamb
Glover, Derek; S. C. Mason
Goddin, Haggai; O. John
Godfrey, Jim; B. E. Stevenson
Godwin, Cynthia; G. Beare
Golden, Sammy; Jack Webb
Good, Carl; R. O. Saber
Good, Simon; George Davis
Goodwin, Archie; R. Stout
Gordon, Ben; I. T. Ross
Gordon, Chet; K. Millar
Gore, Colonel; L. Brock
Gorham, Inspector; J. Cowdroy
Gorse, Mr.; P. Hamilton
Goss, Nathaniel; C. Willock
Gould, Bart; J. Milton
Grady, Bill; I. S. Shriber
Graham, Richard; J. Welcome
Grainger, Paul; F. Sinclair
Gramport, Inspector; G. Barnett
Granby, Colonel; F. Beeding
Grant, Alan; G. Daviot
    J. Tey
Grant, Casey; D. Rico

Grant, David; G. B. Mair
Grant, Douglas, F. N. Millar
Grant, Duncan; G. Seton
Grant, Laurie; M. MacKintosh
Grant, Michael; Roland Daniel
Grant, Patrick; M. Yorke
Grant, Victor; J. B. Ethan
Granville, Clive; M. McKenna
Graves, Inspector; W. J. Makin
Gray, Inspector; P. Piper
Gray, Lt.; E. Lanham
Gray, Michael; H. Kuttner
Graydon, Kendal; H. E. Wheeler
Grayleigh, Peter; Colin Robertson
Great Merlini, The; C. Rawson
Greaves, Emma; Lionel Black
Green, Gregory George Gordon; J. Mann
Green, Horatio; B. Nichols
Green, Jeff; C. Keith
Greene, "Tubby"; R. Goyne
Greer, James; N. Gayle
Gregg, Avery; R. P. Koehler
Gregory, Scott; R. Stratton
Grey, Colwin; A. J. Rees
Grey, Roman; Martin Smith
Grey, Scout; R. L. Bellamy
Griddle, L. F. "Scoop"; T. Polsky
Grigson, Denzil; A. Broome
Grofield, Alan; R. Stark
Grogan, Inspector; M. Neville
Groode, Mr.; G. Griswold
Grundt, Adolph; D. Valentine
        V. Williams
Gryce, Ebenezer; A. K. Green
Guelpa, Mr.; V. Thompson
Gunning, Ed; W. J. Elliott
Guttman, Max; A. D. Goldstein
Guy, Brian; J. Ridgway

H

Haig, Alec; Alec Haig
Haig, "Digger"; S. H. Courtier
Haig, Leo; C. Harrison
Hailey, Eustace; A. Wynne
Hale, Max; G. H. Coxe
Hale, Max; K. Sandford
Hall, Satan; C. J. Daly
Hall, "Tubby"; P. Hambledon
Hallan, Insp.; George Douglas
Halliday, David; H. Baldwin Taylor
Halstead, Arthur; W. E. Hayes
Hambledon, Rupert; J. Dellbridge
Hambledon, Tommy; M. Coles
Hamilton, Anthony; J. Frost
Hammer, Mike; M. Spillane
Hanaud, Inspector; A. E. W. Mason
Hand, Christopher; S. H. Page
Handyman, The; J. Messmann
Hanlon, Red; Mollie Merrick
Hannasyde, Supt.; G. Heyer
Hannay, Richard; J. Buchan
Hanvey, Jim; O. R. Cohen
Hardin, Bart; David Alexander
Hardin, Mark; L. Derrick
Harding, Professor; H. H. Stanners
Hardman, Jim; Ralph Dennis
Hardy, Bren; W. J. Elliott
Harland, John; R. Foley
Harley, John; A. Tack
Harley, Paul; S. Rohmer
Harman, Mike; J. M. Walsh
Harmas, Steve; J. H. Chase
Harpe, Angela; James D. Lawrence
Harper, Bill; P. Ernst
Harper, Stephen; Walter C. Brown
Harrigan; P. O'Malley
Harrington Convent; E. Shepherd
Harris, Albie; A. Dean
Harris, Jim and Kate; T. MacRae
Harris, Paul; G. Black
Harrison, Clay; Clifton Robbins
Harrow, Inspector; Shipley Adams
Harry-O; L. Hays
Hartley, Hashknife; W. C. Tuttle
Hartley, Roger; G. Ellinger

Harty, Cass; J. Y. Dane
Harvard, Bingham; V. Vanardy
Hastings, Bill and Coco; L. G. Offord
Hastings, Frank; C. Wilcox
Hastings, Jefferson; J. Hay
Hastings, Jimmy; C. G. Givens
Haswell, Jimmie; H. Adams
Hatch, Cyrus; Frederick C. Davis
Hatfield, Professor; S. Rogers
Havilland, Antony; V. Gielgud
Havoc, Johnny; J. Jakes
Hawaii Five-O; M. Avallone
Hawkehurst, Valentine; M. E. Braddon
Hawkes, A. B. C.; Ephesian
Hawkins, Tony; H. Harrison
Hawks, Joaquin; B. S. Ballinger
Hayes, Lee; E. Lacy
Hazard, Bill; P. Marlowe
Hazard, Eric; L. Crosby
Hazell, James; P. B. Yuill
Hazelrigg, Insp.; M. Gilbert
Head, Inspector; E. C. Vivian
Headcorn, Inspector; A. Campbell
Headhunters, The; J. Weisman
Headley, Inspector; T. B. Morris
Heald, Max; H. Hossent
Hearne, Bunjy; T. Craig
Hedley, Paul; B. Healey
Heffernan (or Hefferman), Hooky;
 L. Meynell
Heimrich, Merton; F. & R. Lockridge
        R. Lockridge
        R. & F. Lockridge
Heldar, Sally and Johnny; H. Hamilton
Helm, Ben; B. Fischer
Helm, Matt; D. Hamilton
Hemingway, Clarence E.; J. Maske
Hemlock, Jonathan; Trevanian
Hemyock, Maurice; D. G. Browne
Hemmingway, Inspector; G. Heyer
Henry, George Herbert; J. Sharkey
Henry, Gil; C. W. Grafton
Henry, Rush; Joe Barry
Hepburn, Maurice; Lord Gorell
Hero, Pepperoni; B. Kelly
Heron, Felix; G. Verner
Heron, Patrick; C. Brogan
Herring, Timothy; M. Torrie
Herrivell, Richard; J. Bentley
Hewes-Bradford, Barrington; A. Hamilton
Hewitt, Martin; Arthur Morrison
Heysen, Pete; I. Hamilton
Higgins, Cuthbert; C. F. Gregg
Higgins, Matthew; Means Davis
Highway; Garnett Weston
Hillary, Charles; F. McGrew
Hiller, Gregory; Jack Laflin
Hiscock, Inspector; Jeremy Potter
Hite, Quinny; R. Burke
Hodson, Mr.; Margaret Bidwell
Hoeffler; P. O'Malley
Hogg, Miss; A. Lee
Holliday, Felix; Arthur E. Jones
Holliday, Hiram; P. Gallico
Holman, Rick; Carter Brown
Holmes, Sherlock; Adrian Conan Doyle
        Arthur Conan Doyle
Holmes, William; C. V. Bark
Holton, Paul; Charlotte Hunt
Homes, Schlock; R. L. Fish
Honegger, George; J. S. Strange
Hood, Charles; W. Tucker
Hood, Mark; James Dark
Hook, Inspector; Gret Lane
Hook, Sam; H. T. Teilhet
Hopkins, Sgt.; V. Sampson
Hopkins, John; Roland Daniel
Hopton, Inspector; J. C. Woodiwiss
Horne, Charles; W. Tucker
Horne, Harry; J. Gonzales
Hornsley, Michael; E. Salter

Horowitz, Jacob & Helen; D. Delman
Houghton, Bill; M. Culpan
Houston, Sam; E. S. De Puy
Howard, Anthony; H. McCutcheon
Howe, Larry; Eugene Franklin
Hoyland, Mr.; P. C. Williams
Hubbard, Mike; M. Seuffert
Huff, Percy Aloysius; C. Edwards
Hughes, Elwyn; D. W. F. Hardie
Hughes, Matt; Aylwin Lee Martin
Huish, Martin; S. Horler
Hume, Laurie; W. M. Duncan
Hunt, Elsie Mae; A. M. Stein
Hunt, Frederick; Lillian Day
Hunter, The; Ralph Hayes
Hunter, Adam; N. Conway
Hunter, Ed and Am; F. Brown
Hunter, Max; W. T. Ballard
Hunter, Pete; A. A. Marcus
Hunter, Philip; M. Procter
Hunter, Tony; R. G. Dean
Hunters, The; P. Tabori
Huuygens, Kek; R. L. Fish
Hyde, Barney; N. Brent
Hyer, Hank; K. Steel

I

I Spy; J. Tiger
Iceman; J. Nazel
Ike, Nimble; Old Sleuth
Inch, Johnny; J. F. Straker
Inquisitor, The; Simon Quinn
Invaders, The; P. Leslie
Irish, Jeremiah; N. Child
Ironside; J. Thompson
Irving, Paul; L. Grex
Irving, Rip; O. Mills
Iskirlak, Nuri; Joan Fleming
Israeli Commandos; A. Sugar
It Takes a Thief; G. Brewer

J

Jack the Juggler; Old Sleuth
Jacks, Wilton; J. H. Wallis
Jackson, Inspector; D. T. Lindsay
Jackson, Juliet; M. Turnbull
Jackson, Kane; W. Arden
Jackson, William; W. B. Murphy
Jagger, Mick; W. Garner
James, Harry; K. Giles
James, Jesse; W. B. Lawson
James, Mike; Denis Scott
Jason; J. N. Chance
Jason, Alex; A. Sugar
Jaxon, Wood; M. S. Michel
Jazine, Earl; E. D. Hoch
Jellipot, Mr.; S. Fowler
Jenkins, Joe; P. Rosenhayn
Jensen, Peter; P. Wahloo
Jeremy, John; Jeffrey Montague
Jericho, John; H. Pentecost
Jerningham, Peter; I. B. Myers
Johnson, Coffin Ed; C. Himes
Johnson, Johnson; D. Halliday
Johnson, Dr. Sam; L. de la Torre
Johnson, Steve; H. L. Nelson
Jones, Barnaby; M. L. Stokes
Jones, Cleopatra; R. Goulart
Jones, Glyn; G. Osborne
Jones, Grave Digger; C. Himes
Jones, Jupiter; T. Fuller
Jones, Morocco; J. Baynes
Jones, Russell; M. Mundy
Jordan, Dan; Harlan Reed
Jordan, Jack; William Du Bois
Jordan, Marc; R. M. Laurenson
Jordan, Scott; H. Q. Masur
Joyce, Michael; L. Cornell
Judd for the Defense; L. Goldman

Judd, George; E. Bruton
Justice, Peter; F. Duncan
Justus, Jake and Helene; C. Rice

K

Kane, Andy; Carter Brown
Kane; D. Jordan
Kane, Inspector; R. Scarlett
Kane, Sugar; L. Marshall
Kavanagh, Knock-Out; B. Stuart
Kay, Bromley; J. M. Walsh
Kearney, Daniel, Associates; J. Gores
Keate, Sarah; M. G. Eberhart
Keats, Colin; V. B. Shore
Keeble, Magnus; A. Wood
Keefe, Michael; Michael Wolfe
Keen, Franklyn; H. Long
Keen, James; B. Jones
Keene, Arnold; Eric Wood
Keene, Gregory; L. Hardy
Keene, Max; R. O. Saber
Keene, Oliver; J. M. Walsh
Keith, Harrison; Nicholas Carter
Keith, John; N. Daniels
Kellaway, Bill; Gwyn Evans
Keller; N. De Mille
Keller, Konstantin; H. H. Kirst
Kellogg, Casey; C. Weston
Kells, Michael; P. Cheyney
Kelly, Homer; J. Langton
Kelly, Joe; R. Avery
Kelly, Joseph; L. Ford
Kelly, Samuel Moses; J. F. Burke
Kendrick, Don; A. MacKinnon
Kennedy, Craig; A. B. Reeve
Kenny, Mike; E. Dillon
Kent, Addison; H. Moorhouse
Kent, Brice; G. E. Giles
Kent, Christopher; J. Boswell
Kenton, Malcolm; S. Harvester
Kenworthy, Supt.; John Buxton Hilton
Kenyatta; Al C. Clark
Kerr, Constable; P. Alding
Kerrigan, Lt.; J. Harrington
Kerrigan, Peter; N. Gordon
Kerry, Daniel "Red"; S. Rohmer
Kerry, Don; J. Ashford
Ker(r)wood, Charles Douglas; Allan Duncan
Kettle, Owen; C. J. C. Hyne
Keyne, Skelton; C. Wood
Kham, Chin Kwang; Richard Foster
Khan, Asaf; Afghan
Kharduni; A. Soutar
Kidnadze, Gyp; K. Vincent
Kilby, Inspector; J. C. Lenehan
Kilby, Mark; R. C. Frazer
Kilgerrin, Paul; Charles L. Leonard
Killain, Johnny; Dan J. Marlowe
Killers, The; K. Netzen
Killinger, Jedediah, III; P. K. Palmer
Kilpi, Osmo; M. Sariola
Kincaid, Rogan; H. Talbot
King, Frank; Frank King
King, Jason; R. Miall
King, Reefe; A. Barker
King, Sam; R. E. Banks
King, Wylie; L. Saunders
Kirby, Grant; C. Richards
Kirby, Jacqueline; Elizabeth Peters
Kirby, William; S. Horler
Kirk, Ashton; J. T. MacIntyre
Knickman, Inspector; A. Eichler
Knight, Clarence; Frank King
Knollis, Gordon; F. Vivian
Knowles, Colin; R. East
Knox, Jonathan; R. E. McDowell
Koa, Komako; Max Long
Kojak; Abby Mann
 V. B. Miller
Kolchak, Carl; J. Rice
Kollin, Lars; O. Hogstrand
Koregorvsky; A. Wood
Koval, Stash; R. Peters
Kozminski, Abraham; Q. Downes
Krag, Asbjorn; S. Elvestad
Kramer, Lt.; J. McClure
Kramer, Phil; P. Kruger
Kreutzemark, Professor; F. Beeding
Krim, Major; D. Marfield
Krim, Harvey; E. V. Cunningham
Krug, Al; C. Weston
Kusak, Handsome; C. Rice

L

Lacaita, Nigel; W. A. MacKenzie
Lacy, A. Lincoln; M. Strobel
Laing, Patrick; P. Laing
Lam, Donald; A. A. Fair
Lamb, Johnny; J. Donavan
Lancey, Sgt.; L. P. Greene
Land, Marty; David Alexander
Landon, Geoffrey; G. Sinstadt
Landon, Harvey; J. Pattinson
Lane, Drury; B. Ross
Lane, Jimmy; F. Ryerson
Lane, Lorimer; Carolyn Wells
Lane, Paul; F. & R. Lockridge
Langley, Bill; P. Meriton
Langley, Tom; J. Monmouth
Langry, Jimmy; Francis Leslie
Lanson, Mike; J. H. Bond
Lantz, Tony; C. Mullen
Lanyard, Michael; L. J. Vance
Largo, Lou; W. Ard
Larkin, Jim; M. Russell
Larose, Gilbert; A. Gask
Larren, Simon; R. Charles
Larrimore, Tracy; J. Paull
Larson, Abe; S. A. Krasney
Lash, Simon; F. Gruber
Latham, Grace; L. Ford
Latimer, Charles; E. Ambler
Latimer, Charles and James; F. Gaite
Lavender, Jimmie; V. Starrett
Layton, Anne and David; Marion Roberts
Le Breton, Miles; J. Esteven
Leaphorn, Joe; T. Hillerman
Leather, Danny; D. Lawrence
Leathermouth; C. Dawe
Lecain, Inspector; F. Didelot
Lecoq, Monsieur; E. Gaboriau
Lee, Gerry; K. Hopkins
Lee, Gypsy Rose; Gypsy Rose Lee
Lee, Judith; Richard Marsh
Lee, Norma "Nicky"; Norma Lee
Left, Richard; C. Forsyte
Leighton, Shirley; P. Ernst
Leith, Gwynn; V. B. Shore
Leithen, Edward; J. Buchan
Leland, Quinn; Franklin M. Davis
Lennox, Inspector; J. Wainwright
Lennox, Bill; W. T. Ballard
Lennox, Bill; John Shepherd
Leric, Detective-Inspector; R. Busby
Lessinger; R. Essex
Lester, Edward; E. Levison
LeVine, Jack; A. Bergman
Lewis, Gregory; D. Frome
Lewis, Jenny and Hunter; E. Gresham
 R. Grey
Lewker, Abercrombie; G. Carr
 S. Styles
Li-Sin; N. Vane
Liberator, The; N. Deane
Lincoln, John Abraham; D. Dodge
Lincoln, Matt; E. Garth
Lindsay, Ralph; Ben Benson
Linge, Malko; G. De Villiers
Link, Barry; Vigilant
Lintott, Inspector; J. Stubbs
Lissendale, Gerald; S. Horler
Little, Jim; Maude Parker
Littlejohn, Thomas; G. Bellairs

Llorca, Juan; D. Ames
Lloyd, Bill; W. Reed
Locke, Kim; K. F. Crossen
 C. Richards
Locken, Mike; R. Rostand
Logan; A. Joseph
Logan, Mike; Henry Holt
Logan, Richard; H. McCutcheon
Lone Wolf, The; M. Barry
Lone Wolf, The; L. J. Vance
Long, Chester; C. Carpenter
Long, Lydford; H. Carstairs
Lord, Michael; C. Daly King
Louis, Ben; E. S. Russell
Love, Jason; J. Leasor
Love, Pharoah; G. Baxt
Lovick, Inspector; G. M. Wilson
Lowe, Trevor; G. Verner
Luccan, Rory; N. Morland
Lucias, Ben; R. Howes
Luckraft, Inspector; A. J. Rees
Ludlow, Adam; S. Nash
Lund, Eric; R. S. Wallis
Lundberg, Nels; L. Saunders
Lupin, Arsene; M. Leblanc
Lydney, George; S. Fox
Lyle, Samuel; A. Crabb
Lynch, Bertram; J. W. Vandercook
Lynx; Vigilant
Lyon, Inspector; P. Winn

M

McAlpin, Inspector; R. H. R. Smithies
McAlpine, Philip; A. Diment
MacArthur, Ian; S. Jepson
McArthur, Kendall "Dizzy"; Mansfield Scott
McBain, Vicky; Colin Robertson
McBride, Rex; C. F. Adams
McCale, Duke; Gerald Brown
McCall, Andrew; M. Carrel
McCall, Bert; N. MacNeil
McCall, Mike; E. Queen
MacCallum, Duncan; A. MacKinnon
McCarthy, Patrick Aloysius; G. Brandon
 J. G. Brandon
McCarty, Timothy; I. Ostrander
McCloud; C. Wilcox
 David Wilson
McClue, Ferris; H. Wickham
McCorkle; Ross Thomas
McCoy, Ross; S. Gluck
MacCray, Philip; O. F. Jerome
McCunn, Duncan; J. Buchan
MacDonald, Inspector; E. C. R. Lorac
MacDonald, Lynn; K. C. Strahan
McGee, Travis; John D. MacDonald
McGinty, Slade; J. Pendower
McGrath, Peter; Michael Brett
McGregory; H. Kane
M'Guire, Inspector; G. Coverack
 J. Russell Warren
McGurk, Gail; D. Marfield
McHugh; Jay Flynn
McIntyre, Mac; M. E. Corne
MacKay, Inspector; E. L. Cushing
McKay, Ellis; L. A. G. Strong
McKay, Robin; John Morris
McKechnie; B. Hitchens
McKee, Inspector; H. Reilly
McKeene, Deville; R. Walker
McKellar, Ross; N. N. Peebles
McKelvie, Graydon; M. Harvey
McKinnon, Todd; L. G. Offord
Maclain, Duncan; B. Kendrick
McLean, Inspector; G. Goodchild
McLean, Anne Davenport; Margaret
 Tayler Yates
MacLean, Roy; B. Gaston
MacLeod, Neil; Allan Campbell McLean
MacLurg, Marcus; R. Petrie
McMurdo, Andy; N. Morland

MacNab, Francis; J. Ferguson
MacNeill, Supt.; W. M. Duncan
McNeill, Anne & Jeffrey; T. Du Bois
Macomber, Elisha; K. M. Knight
Macrae, Hawk; A. Barker
Macready, Sheriff; H. Holman
Macsporran, Inspector; L. Hill
MacTavish, Alonzo; P. Cheyney
McTavish, O. Swete; C. Brooks
MacVeigh, Andy and Sue; S. MacVeigh
MacWhorter, Angus; H. S. Keeler
MacWilliams, Eve; M. Blizard
M-Squad; D. Saunders
Maasten, Nicholas; O. Sela
Mac; Hampton Stone
Macall, Johnny G. Fairlie
Macauley, Mike; N. Marino
Mace, Inspector; R. Keverne
Madden, David; D. M. Disney
Madden, Joseph; V. J. Santiago
Maddox, Ivor; E. Linington
Madigan, Lt.; E. Lanham
Magellan, Philip; F. Scarpetta
Magic, Mark; Anthony P. Morris
Magill, Moss; Dorothy Gardiner
Maguire, Joe; J. P. Radford
Maguire, Johnny; R. Himmel
Mahon, Ambrose; S. H. Courtier
Mahoun, Nicky; Clark Smith
Maidment, Richard; M. Cronin
Maitland, Antony; S. Woods
Maitland, George; M. Severy
Major, The; John Ross
Major, Aubrey St. John; L. P. Greene
Malcolm, Mr.; G. Fairlie
Malcolm, James "Solo"; N. Graham
Malcolm, Richard; J. Grady
Malins, Tommy; M. B. Dix
Mallaby, James; Bruce Norman
Mallard, "Duck"; A. Spiller
Mallett, Inspector; M. Fitt
Mallett, Inspector; C. Hare
Mallett, William; D. Orgill
Mallory; C. Stoddard
Mallory, Sgt.; T. J. R. Sennocke
Mallory, Vic; J. H. Chase
Malloy, Chance; L. Dent
Malone, Jim; T. C. H. Jacobs
Malone, John J.; L. M. Harris
    C. Rice
Malone, Kenneth; M. Phillips
Malone, Scobie; J. Cleary
Malone, Steven; N. Morland
Man from U.N.C.L.E.; M. Avallone
    Joel Bernard
    J. Hunter Holly
    P. Leslie
    D. McDaniel
    J. Oram
    J. T. Phillifent
    Thomas Stratton
    H. Whittington
Manchenil, Bolivar; D. M. Douglass
Mandell-Essington, Francis; J. S. Clouston
Mandrake, Professor; J. & E. Bonett
Mandrell, Augustus; F. McAuliffe
Manfred, Judge; A. R. Hilliard
Mann, Tiger; M. Spillane
Mannering, John; A. Morton
Manners, Harley; C. J. Dutton
Manners, Silas; J. Moffatt
Manning, Supt.; B. Cobb
Mannix; M. Avallone
    J. T. MacCargo
Mansel, Jonah; D. Yates
Manson, Doctor; E. Radford
Manton, Simon; M. Underwood
Mappin, Amos Lee; H. Footner
March, Colonel; J. D. Carr
March, Erik; G. G. Fickling
March, Milo; M. E. Chaber
March, Septimus; L. Bamburg

Maria, Black; J. Slate
Markham; Lawrence Block
Marks, Jonathan; G. M. Barns
Marksman, The; P. McCurtin
    F. Scarpetta
Marley, Lawrence; J. Walker
Marlow, "Cissie"; G. Dickson
Marlow, Dick; J. Bentley
Marlow, Peter; J. Hone
Marlowe, Greg; Greg Marlowe
Marlowe, Philip; R. Chandler
Marne, John; W. Keenan
Marple, Jane; A. Christie
Marquis, Sir Henry; M. D. Post
Marrell, Peter; Stanley Hopkins, Jr.
Marsden, Eric; Anthony Graham
Marsh, Emma; E. Dean
Marsh, Kate; Gret Lane
Marshall, George; C. Barling
    P. Barrington
Marshall, John and Suzy; J. M. Fox
Marshall, Nick; G. Mitcham
Martin, Inspector; R. Amberley
Martin, Anthony; W. Francis
Martin, Ben; J. Messmann
Martin, Clancy; Wallace Jackson
Martin, George; F. Beeding
Martin, John; Colin Robertson
Martin, Tavy; D. Winsor
Martin, William; K. Stanton
Martineau, Inspector; M. Procter
Martini, David; R. Raine
Martinson, Arthur; C. Fitzsimmons
Martinson, John; H. Clevely
Martiny, Paul; W. Haggard
Mason, Perry; E. S. Gardner
Mason, Randolph; M. D. Post
Massey, Richard; V. Siller
Master, Murder; J. Rosenberger
Masters, George; Douglas Clark
Masters, J. C. K. "Jiggers"; A. Rud
Mata, Hoani; V. M. Grayland
Mather, Robert; B. Graeme
Matson, Gunnar; Breni James
Matthews, James; W. Oursler
Max, Gaston; S. Rohmer
Mayberry, Noel; G. Tree
Mayhew, Stephen; D. B. Olsen
Mayo, Asey; Phoebe Atwood Taylor
Mead, Selena; P. McGerr
Meatyard, Chief Constable; S. Horler
Medford, Inspector; H. Roth
Medford, Joe; J. Starr
Meldrum, "Tiny"; A. Glanville
Melrose, John; W. Mills
Mendoza, Julian; J. Ronald
Mendoza, Luis; D. Shannon
Menendez, Inspector; S. Blanc
Mercer, Penny & Vincent; H. Clandon
Meredith, Inspector; J. Bude
Meredith, Lt.; D. Ramsay
Meredith, John; F. Gerard
Merlini, Great; C. Rawson
Merlotti, Nick; J. Deane
Merrion, Desmond; Miles Burton
Merrivale, Henry; J. D. Carr
    C. Dickson
Mersey, Supt.; F. A. Clement
Micklem, Don; R. Marshall
Mildmay, Geoffrey; B. Wilkinson
Miles, Don; L. Kenyon
Miller, Alan; P. Hunt
Miller, Doc; H. Petersen
Miller, James; M. B. Dix
Miller, Nick; Harry Patterson
Milton, Arthur; L. Henderson
Mind-Masters; J. F. Rossmann
Minter, Supt.; E. Wallace
Miro; S. Herron
Mission Impossible; J. Tiger
    M. Walker
Mitchell, Inspector; N. S. Lincoln
Mitchell, Lt.; W. A. Wolff
Mitchell, Robert Leroy; R. Ottolengui
Mitchell, Steven; Josephine Bell
Mitchell, William; H. A. Wrenn
Mod Squad; R. Deming
    William Johnston

Moh, Li; J. Cowdroy
Mohune, Peter; P. Groom
Montero, Inspector; S. Nash
Montgomery, Kirke; A. Mallory
Montigny, Pierre; E. D. Torgerson
Moody, Nathaniel; E. C. Lester
Moon, Manville; R. Deming
Mooney, Supt.; D. Magarshack
Mooney, Jerry; K. O'Neil
Moore, Toussaint M.; E. Lacy
Moran, Jigger; J. Roeburt
Moreau, Birge; V. Vanardy
Morelle, Dr.; E. Dudley
Morgan, Connie; J. B. Hendryx
Morgan, Elwyn; S. Farrar
Morgan, Glyn; Rosa Lambert
Morganthau, Molly; G. Bonner
Moriarty, Prof.; J. Gardner
Morini, Johnny; Al Conroy
Mornington, Anthony; M. B. Dix
Morrison, Dan; J. Shallit
Morrison, Nigel; N. Fisher
Morthoe, Julian; P. M. Wilson
Moss, Phil; B. Knox
Mosson, Major; L. Cargill
Most Deadly Game, The; R. Gallagher
Mostyn, Colonel; M. Hebden
Moto, Mr.; J. P. Marquand
Mott, Daisy Jane; Jennifer Jones
Muir, George; F. Grierson
Mulcahaney, Norah; L. O'Donnell
Muldoon, Hart; J. Flagg
Muldrew, Gordon; L. Allan
Muller, "Dusty"; A. Glanville
Muller, Joe; G. I. Colbron
    A. Groner
Muller, Paul; Paul Muller
Mulligan, Tim; A. M. Stein
Mundy, Al; G. Brewer
Murder Master; J. Rosenberger
Murdoch, Bruce; N. Deane
Murdock, Kent; G. H. Coxe
Murdock, Rachel and Jennifer; D. B. Olsen
Murgatroyd, William; W. H. Osborne
Murmur, Heron; S. Harvester
Murphy, Captain; G. Bristow
Murray, Bill; A. Colin
Mustard, Buddy; Roland Daniel
Mycroft, Mr.; H. F. Heard

Nash, Aubrey; T. Davis
Nash, Monty; R. Telfair
Nelson, Gridley; R. Fenisong
Newberry, Millicent; Jennette Lee
Nicholson; M. Kelly
Nicolson, Lloyd; P. Wayland
Nighthawk; S. Horler
Nightingale, Inspector; M. Kelly
Nightingale, Amanda; G. Revelli
Nikola, Dr.; G. Boothby
Noble, Branders; A. Richard Martin
Noble, Stewart; M. MacKintosh
Nolan, Frank; Max Collins
Nolan, John; C. Nicolai
Noon, Ed; M. Avallone
Norrington, Jennifer; I. Drummond
Norris, Mrs.; D. S. Davis
Norroy, Yorke; G. Bronson-Howard
Norse, Rae; J. Esteven
North, Mr. & Mrs.; F. & R. Lockridge
North, Edward; Colin Robertson
North, Hugh; Van Wyck Mason
North, Pam and Jerry; F. & R. Lockridge

O

Oakes, Boysie; J. Gardner
O'Breen, Fergus; A. Boucher

O'Brien, Patrick; I. H. Irwin
O'Brien, Sarah; M. Marlett
O'Connor, Lefty; B. Shannon
O'Day, Chauncey; A. Gaines
O'Day, Double; Gwyn Evans
O'Dell, Barry; R. O. Chipperfield
Odell, Philip; L. Powell
Odom, Hiram; M. Boniface
O'Hannay, James; C. Rushton
O'Hara, Terence; P. Costello
O'Kelly, Michael the; M. O'Brine
Old Man in the Corner; B. Orczy
Old Sleuth; Anonymous, Old Sleuth
O'Leary, Lance; M. G. Eberhart
O'Malley, Supt.; M. Kenyon
O'Malley, Brian; Roland Daniel
O'Mara, Shaun; P. Cheyney
O'Neill, Jim; D. M. Disney
Op, Continental; D. Hammett
Opara, Christie; D. Uhnak
Operator 5; Curtis Steele
Ord, Inspector; Austen Allen
Ormiston, Colonel; J. M. Walsh
Ormsberry, Van Dusen; J. S. Strange
Ortiz, Johnny; R. M. Stern
O'Shaunnessey; Jessica Ryan
Otis, Miss; B. Sarto
Otley; M. Waddell
Owen, Bobby; E. R. Punshon
Oy-Oy-7; S. Weinstein
Ozmar; E. Hulme-Beaman

P

Pace, Quentin; R. Denbie
Padillo; Ross Thomas
Padre, The; R. Goyne
Palfrey, Dr.; J. Creasey
Palmer, Harry; L. Deighton
Pancho, Don; B. Buckingham
Pardoe, Chief Inspector; D. Bowers
Parew, Thibault; G. Eldredge
Paris, Wade; Ben Benson
Parker, Inspector; J. Austwick
Parker; R. Stark
Parnell, Tim; Don Smith
Parr, Deputy; F. I. Anderson
Parrott, Liz; Manning Long
Parry, Lane; M. Sarsfield
Pascal, Lt.; H. Pentecost
Paternoster, Colonel; R. Inchbald
Paterson, Ross; K. Field
Patras, Commissaire; F. Grierson
Patten, Roger; A. A. Randall
Pavlov, Gregory (Grischa); Jessica Ryan
Payne, Detective; Old Sleuth
Payne, Sham; K. Secrist
Peacemaker, The; A. Hamilton
Peachy, St. George; R. Starnes
Pearson, Jack; Roland Daniel
Peck, Judge; A. Derleth
Pedley, Ben; S. Sterling
Pellew, Gregory; V. Gielgud
Pemberty, Dick; P. Conde
Pendlebury, Mr.; A. Webb
Penetrator, The; L. Derrick
Penk, Inspector; W. Gore
Pennington, Arthur Stukeley; G. Brandon
    J.G. Brandon
Pennington, Peter; E. Snell
Penny, Mrs.; A. Bliss
Penny, Archibald; Wallace Jackson
Pennyfeather, A.; D. B. Olsen
Pepper, Supt.; Frank A. Smith
Perkins, Bruce; J. Lilly
Perkins, Douglas; M. Babson
Perkins, R. I.; R. Garnett
Perks, Matilda; R. C. Woodthorpe
Perrin, Christopher; C. Waye
Pete, Blue; L. Allan
Petersen, Brian; J. P. Cody

Petrella, Patrick; M. Gilbert
Petrie, Amos; J. V. Turner
Pettengill, Inspector; A. Rowe
Pettigrew, Francis; C. Hare
Phantom Detective, The; Robert Wallace
Phantom, Gray; Herman Landon
Phelan, Lt.; M. K. Ozaki
Phelan, Sam; T. Kyd
Phelps, Chet; G. Childerness
Phibes, Dr.; W. Goldstein
Philis; Ritchie Perry
Philpotts, Freddy; A. B. Caldwell
Phoenix, Joe; A. W. Aiken
    Anonymous
Pibble, James; P. Dickinson
Picaroon, The; J. Cassells
Picaroon, The; Herman Landon
Pilgrim, Mr.; D. Cory
Pilgrim, Black; G. Stanley
Pinaud, Monsieur; P. Audemars
Pine, Paul; H. Browne
    J. Evans
Pink, Norman; M. McShane
Pinkerton, Evan; D. Frome
Piper, John; H. Carmichael
Piper, "Peter"; A. R. Long
Piper, Peter; N. B. Mavity
Piron; E. McGirr
Pitt, Inspector; J. F. Straker
Place, Thackeray; K. Williams
Pleydell, Bertram; D. Yates
Plotkin, Sylvia; G. Baxt
Plummer, Jeff; D. Lees
Plush, Paul; O. Keystone
Poggioli, Henry; T. S. Stribling
Pointer, Inspector; A. Fielding
Poirot, Hercule; A. Christie
Policewoman; L. Trevor
Pollard, Insp.; E. Lemarchand
Pollifax, Mrs.; E. Gilman
Pons, Solar; A. Derleth
Ponsonby, Peter; Jean Leslie
Pontivy, Papa; B. Newman
Poole, Inspector; Henry Wade
Port, Daniel; P. Rabe
Potter, Hiram; R. Foley
Power, William; H. Clandon
Powers, Johnny; J. Rayter
Powledge, Lt.; M. P. Rea
Poynings, Roger; Michael Burt
Precinct, 87th; E. McBain
Preed, Mr.; Ladbroke Black
Prentiss, Agatha Welch; V. P. Johns
Prescot, Julian; Julian Prescot
Preston, Johnny; P. Chester
Preston, Mark; Peter Chambers
Price, Jimmy "Wiggly"; J. J. Chichester
Price, Ronald; J. Cannan
Pride, Duncan; A. Frazer
Pride, Jeff; A. O'Neill
Priest, Judge; I. S. Cobb
Priestley, Dr.; J. Rhode
Prike, Leonidas; L. G. Blochman
Primrose, John; L. Ford
Prince, Henry; C. F. Gregg
Pringle, Romney; C. Ashdown
Prisoner, The; T. M. Disch
    H. Stine
Private Eye; B. Pronzini
Probyn, Julia; A. Bridge
Prye, Paul; M. Millar
Puma, Joe; W. C. Gault
Purbright, Inspector; C. Watson
Pym, Henry; W. J. Burley
Pym, Nicholas; J. Sanders
Pym, Mrs. Palmyra; N. Morland
Pyne, Parker; A. Christie

Q

Q, Don; K. Prichard
Q33; G. Goodchild
Quade, Oliver; F. Gruber
Quaile, Inspector; J. M. Walsh
Quan, Samuel; G. Begbie
Quane, Crispin; E. Kilvington
Quarles, Christopher; P. Brebner

Quarles, Francis; J. Symons
Quarshie, Dr.; J. Wyllie
Quayle, Hilary; M. Kaye
Quayle, Kit; J. Aldridge
Quayle, Peter; P. Trent
Quayne, Maxwell; F. A. Symonds
Queen, Ellery; E. Queen
Queen, Richard; E. Queen
Quentin, Peter; R. Quest
Quest, Philip; Peter Townend
Quest, Philip; N. Vane
Quill, Inspector; C. Brahms
Quill, Supt.; L. Lamb
Quiller; Adam Hall
Quin, Harley; A. Christie
Quin, Sebastian; S. Horler
Quinn; H. Carmichael
Quinn; N. Scanlon
Quint, Peter; H. Austin
Quintain, Richard; W. H. Baker
    W. A. Balinger
Quinto, Gimiendo Hernandez; James Norman
Quist, Gregory; W. C. MacDonald
Quist, Julian; H. Pentecost
Qwilleran, Jim; L. J. Braun

R

Radcliff; R. Mallory
Radnitz, Herman; J. H. Chase
Raeburn, Mark; M. Gair
Raffles; E. W. Hornung
    B. Perowne
Ramsay, Andrea Reid; C. H. Matschat
Ramsay, David; C. H. Matschat
Ramsay, Steve; C. H. Wallace
Ramsdale, Lucy; H. Dolson
Ramsey, Hec; D. Owen
Randall, D. C.; The Gordons
Raneleigh, Arthur; M. L. Luther
Rankin, Tommy; M. Propper
Ransome, Rogue; Dean Morgan
Ransome, Steve; S. Ransome
Rant, Stephen; H. E. Wheeler
Rason, Det. Insp.; D. Durham
    S. Kyle
    R. Vickers
Ravel, Claude; B. Jones
Ravenhill, Anthony; R. Francis Foster
Raymond, Sgt.; N. Longmate
Razoni, Ed; W. B. Murphy
Read, Anthony; S. Toye
Reamer, Donald; W. M. Duncan
Reardon, Lt. Jim; R. L. Pike
Reed, Sgt.; C. Drummond
Reed, Lal; C. Wood
Reeder, J. G.; E. Wallace
Reeder, Paul; Robert C. Dennis
Regan, Jack; I. K. Martin
Regan, Michael; E. Hale
Register, Mark; Arthur Douglas
Rehm, Jimmy; W. Herber
Reid, Andrea; C. H. Matschat
Remington, J. A.; R. Ladline
Remover, The; Roland Daniel
Remsen; D. Montross
Renard, Hercule; P. Audemars
Rennert, Hugh; T. Downing
Revel, Michael; N. Berrow
Revenger, The; J. Messmann
Rex, Nigel; G. Goodchild
Reynolds, Insp.; Elaine Hamilton
Rezaire, Jimmie; A. Armstrong
Rhoden, Steve; I. Walker
Rhymer, Arnold; U. Key
Riam, George; D. O. Woodbury
Rice, Bill; M. Stand
Rice, Stan; B. Kendrick
Richardson, P. C.; B. Thomson
Richmond, Frank; Anthony Graham
Rickman, Roy; D. Craig
Ridgway, Martin; P. Helm
Ridley, Nat; N. Ridley, Jr.
Riggs, Bingo; C. Rice

Rillington, Anthony; N. Orde-Powlett
Rim-Fire; C. Ballew
Ringer, The; E. Wallace
Ringway, Stephen; S. M. Lott
Ringwood, Richard; K. Farrer
Ripley, Charles; J. Wainwright
Ripley, John; The Gordons
Ripley, Tom; P. Highsmith
Rivers, Ed; T. Powell
Rivers, Julian; C. Carnac
Roath, Sheila; D. Craig
Robak, Donald; J. L. Hensley
Roberts, George; M. Symons
Roberts, Randy; Carter Brown
Robins, Constable; M. Stand
Rock, Johnny; B. Rossi
Rockwell, Rocky; J. Iams
Roden, Jess; A. B. Cunningham
Rodway, Inspector; J. K. Ryland
Rogers, Bull; A. Brede
Rogers, Huntoon; C. Knight
Rogers, John; Jonathan Ross
Rogers, Pogy; Z. H. Ross
Roharik, Larry; J. M. Eshleman
Rolfe, Helga; J. H. Chase
Rolfe, Simon; J. L. Bonney
Rollison, Richard; J. Creasey
Rome, Tony; A. Rome
Rook, Howie; S. Palmer
Roper, Max; K. Platt
Roque, Konrad; G. Morton
Ross, Supt.; J. J. Connington
Ross, Mike; K. Carr
Rostetter, Tommy; A. Campbell
Roston Outfit; Dean Morgan
Rouletabille, Joseph; G. Leroux
Rourke, Timothy; J. Wolf
Rowlands, Bill; Norman Lucas
Royce, Rupert; J. Aldridge
Rudd, Inspector; J. Thomson
Rudd, Hugh; H. C. Davis
Ruff, Peter; E. P. Oppenheim
Russell, Alan; N. Fitzgerald
Russell, Charles; W. Haggard
Russell, Franklin; R. M. Baker
Ryan, Charlie; J. C. Lenehan
Ryan, Jim; P. Ernst
Ryan, Sean; B. Cleeve
Ryder, Dick; H. B. M. Watson
Rye, Bill; J. Spain
Ryker; N. De Mille
    E. T. Hamill
Ryvet, Inspector; C. Carnac

S

Saber, Joel; Gavin Holt
Sader, Jim; D. Hitchens
Safford, Ben; R. B. Dominic
Sage, Malcolm; H. Jenkins
Saint, The; L. Charteris
St. Amand, Jean Henri; D. L. Teilhet
St. Cyr, Claudine; Ian Wallace
St. Ives, Philip; O. Bleeck
St. Vincent, Britt; J. F. Rossmann
Sallust, Gregory; D. Wheatley
Salmond, Andrew; L. Dundas
Samson, Captain; Gavin Douglas
Samson, Albert; Michael Z. Lewin
San Antonio; San Antonio
Sand, Robert; M. Olden
Sanders, Commissioner; F. Gerard
    E. Wallace
Sanderson, Insp.; David Hume
Sanderson, Maxwell; J. J. Chichester
Sanderson, Phil; L. Grex
Sands, Inspector; M. Millar
Sands, Jim; R. J. Casey
Sandyman, Mr.; N. Graham

Santos; W. B. Bannerman
Sarel, Richard; J. Bryan
Sargeant, Peter; E. Box
Sargent, Jock; D. Da Cruz
Sark, Mortimer; J. Hawk
Sasha; A. Wood
Saumarez, John; C. Dane
Saunders, Inspector; V. M. Steele
Savage, Doc; K. Robeson
Savage, John; J. Trevor
Savage, Mark; M. Eden
Savage, Matt; Craig Cooper
Savage, Myra; M. McShane
Savage, Rampion; James Turner
Saville, Bill; Roland Daniel
Savoy, Paul; J. Gregory
Sawyer, Quincy Adams; C. F. Pidgin
Saxe, Christopher; S. Shane
Saxon, Ludovic; J. Cassells
Scant, Jerry; L. A. Knight
Scarf, Paul; Raymond Boyd
Scarfe, Det.-Sgt.; J. Goodwin
Scarlett, Doctor; A. Laing
Scarlett, Peter; S. Horler
Schmidt, Inspector; G. Bagby
Schofield, Pete; T. B. Dewey
Scipio, Danny; T. Gates
Scott, John; S. Picard
Scott, Philip; Hartley Howard
Scott, Shell; D. Knight
    R. S. Prather
Scott, Spider; K. Royce
Scotter, Mr.; T. Warriner
Scudamore, Laura; R. Armstrong
Search; R. Weverka
Seary, Major; John Ross
Sebastian; J. L. Johnson
Secret Agent; W. H. Baker
    W. A. Ballinger
    P. Leslie
    W. McNeilly
Secret Circle; G. Null
Seeton, Miss; N. Carvic
Seidlitz, Mavis; Carter Brown
Selby, Doug; E. S. Gardner
Selby, Pete; Jonathan Craig
Seldon, Dick; W. S. Masterman
Sessions, Frank; H. Waugh
Seton, Mike; T. C. H. Jacobs
Severance, Grace; M. Scherf
Severn, Inspector; G. Bromley
Severson, Knute; T. Wells
Sevrel, Inspector; C. Worth
Shadow, The; W. B. Gibson
    M. Grant
Shadowers, The; D. Fox
Shadows, Dark; Marilyn Ross
Shaft, John; E. Tidyman
Shand, Dale; D. Enefer
Shane, Inspector; S. Truss
Shane, Peter; F. Bonnamy
Shanley, Joseph; Jack Webb
Shannon, Supt.; C. Ryland
Shannon, Clinton; Lee Roberts
Shannon, Desmond; I. M. V. Heberden
Shannon, John J.; C. F. Adams
Shannon, Michael; G. Bowman
Shannon, Patrick; J. Quinn
Shapiro, Nathan; F. & R. Lockridge
    R. Lockridge
Shard, Simon; P. McCutchan
Shark, Tiger; K. Stanton
Sharpe, Morrison; L. Cargill
Sharpshooter, The; B. Rossi
Shaw, Esmonde; P. McCutchan
Shaw, Paul; M. Sadler
Shayne, Michael; B. Halliday
Shelley, Inspector; John Rowland
Sheringham, Roger; Anthony Berkeley
Sherman, Phil; Don Smith
Shimoni, Tami; O. Hesky
Shirley, Patrick C.; O. Mills
Shock, Ben; P. Buchanan
Shomar, Shomri; H. Klinger
Shrig, Jasper; J. Farnol
Silence, John; A. Blackwood
Silk, Dorian; S. Harvester
Silk, Lou; J. H. Chase

Silk, Steve; J. B. O'Sullivan
Silver, Inspector; Henry Holt
Silver Maud; P. Wentworth
Silvestri, Guy; M. Rennert
Simmons, Bernard; F. & R. Lockridge
    R. Lockridge
Simon, Benjamin; G. Dean
Simon, Grant; H. Pentecost
Simpson; R. L. Fish
Simpson, Arthur Abdel; E. Ambler
Sims, Det. Insp.; F. Grierson
Sinclair, Arthur; W. S. Masterman
Skane, Inspector; D. Marfield
Slade, Anthony; L. Gribble
Slade, Geoffrey; F. Lester
Slade, John; R. Essex
Slade, Nicholas; R. C. Woodthorpe
Slane, Inspector; S. Maddock
Sleuth, Satan; M. Avallone
Sloan, Inspector; C. Aird
Slone, Maggie; Elizabet M. Stone
Small, David; H. Kemelman
Smarles, Inspector; M. Urquhart
Smart, Maxwell; William Johnston
Smiley, George; J. Le Carre
Smith, Detective; The Edingtons
Smith, Inspector; S. Troy
Smith, Aurelius; R. T. M. Scott
Smith, Beau; Z. H. Ross
Smith, Cellini; Robert Reeves
Smith, Daye; F. Usher
Smith, John; H. Pentecost
Smith, John; M. Plum
Smith, John; J. Sangster
Smith, Kim; J. Boland
Smith, Lancelot Carolus; N. Berrow
Smith, Nayland; S. Rohmer
Smith, T. B.; E. Wallace
Smyth, Millard; E. M. Boyd
Sneed, Terry; G. F. Newman
Snow, John; R. H. Sawkins
Solo, Napoleon; M. Avallone
    Joel Bernard
    J. Hunter Holly
    P. Leslie
    D. McDaniel
    J. Oram
    J. T. Phillifent
    Thomas Stratton
    H. Whittington
Spade, Danny; D. Ambler
Spade, Richard; B. B. Johnson
Spade, Sam; D. Hammett
Speare, Luke; Frederick C. Davis
Spearpoint, Inspector; F. Arthur
Spears, Simon; V. Gielgud
Speed, Martin; M. G. Hugi
Speer, Giff; D. Tracy
Spenser; Robert B. Parker
Spicer, Robert; M. Danvers
Spider, The; J. McCulley
Spider, The; R. T. M. Scott
    G. Stockbridge
Spinnet, Phineas; A. Soutar
Spratt, Sgt.; George Douglas
Springfield, Mr.; J. Sandys
Squad, Ms.; M. Endfield
Stallard, Vincent; G. Beare
Standish, Ronald; H. C. McNeile
Standish, Tiger; S. Horler
Stannard, Rand; R. L. Hershatter
Stanton, Hugh; R. Vickers
Star, Black; J. McCulley
Stark, John; T. Harknett
Starte, Roger and Kate; Eric Williams
Stash; R. Peters
Staveley; Clifton Robbins
Steel, Alan; Colin Robertson
Steel, Raeburn; C. Brooks
Steele, Argus; Babs Lee
Steele, Jim; D. Chambers
Steele, Malcome; Mansfield Scott
Steele, Rocky; John B. West
Steevens, Stonewall; M. G. Kiddy
Stevens, Insp.; B. Graeme

Stevens, Dave; K. A. Saddler
Stevens, Gavin; W. Faulkner
Stewart, Allan; V. Siller
Steytler, Det. Sgt.; S. Milne
Stoddart, Inspector; A. Haynes
Stone, Curt; J. Seward
Stone, Fleming; Carolyn Wells
Stone, J. Rockingham; R. Armstrong
Stone, "Rolling"; K. Laing
Stone, Shep; J. Jacks
Storey, Rosika; H. Footner
Storm, Inspector; J. M. Walsh
Storm, Christopher; W. A. Barber
Straight, Ricky; G. Morgan
Strang, Jim; G. Dilnot
Strang, John and Sally; H. Brinton
Strange, James; E. B. Quinn
Strange Report; John Burke
Strange, Violet; A. K. Green
Strangely, Peter; E. B. Black
Strangeways, Nigel; N. Blake
Stratton, Mark; R. T. Bickers
Straussman; G. Davison
Stricken; M. J. Bosse
Strickland, Insp.; G. Dilnot
Strickland, Jack; H. Balfour
Strong, Philip; W. Oursler
Strong, Robert; Colin Robertson
Stryker, Colin; William Crawford
Stryker, John; Q. Barnes
Stuart, Scott; G. Coffin
Stubbs, John; R. T. Campbell
Sturrock, Jeremy; Jeremy Sturrock
Styles, Peter; J. Philips
Sullivan, Bob; F. Mullally
Sultan, Wm. (Sultan's Harem); H. Austin
Summers, "Doc"; F. Marlowe
Summers, Steve; J. Manor
Sumuru; S. Rohmer
Sutherland, Chief of Police; F. Eberhard
Swain, Ape; D. Da Cruz
Swan; R. Philmore
Swift, Leighton; C. R. Jones
Swinton, Inspector; I. Greig
Syn, Dr.; R. Thorndyke

T

Talbot, Clem; T. P. Mulkeen
Tallis, Roger; J. Rossiter
Tancred, Dr.; G. D. H. Cole
Tandy, Michael "Napper"; N. Shepherd
Tanner, Evan; Lawrence Block
Tarleton, John; F. F. Van de Water
Taylor, Pete; R. D. Abrahams
Teed, Russell; D. Montrose
Telefair, Kitty; F. Stevenson
Tempest, Bill; W. Shand
Templar, Simon; L. Charteris
Temple, Paul; F. Durbridge
 Paul Temple
Templeton, Paul; R. Goyne
Terhune, Theodore I.; B. Graeme
Tern, Bill; B. E. Wallace
Terrel, Timothy; S. Maddock
Terrell, Frank; J. H. Chase
Terrence, Michael and "Terry"; G. Brandon
Thackeray, Constable; P. Lovesey
Thane, Colin; B. Knox
Thatcher family; P. Yates
Thatcher, John Putnam; E. Lathen
Then Came Bronson; William Johnston
 C. Stratton
Thew, Inspector; D. G. Browne
Thomas, Ethel; C. Fitzsimmons
Thompson, Chief Insp.; Peter Drax
Thompson, Jake; Evelyn Cameron
Thompson, Mike; J. Paull
Thorndyke, John; J. H. Dirckx
 N. Donaldson
 R. A. Freeman
Thorne, Tommy; Charles H. Snow
Thunderbolt, The; J. McCulley
Thursby, Roger; H. Cecil
Thursday, Max; Wade Miller
Tibbett, Henry and Emmy; P. Moyes

Tibbs, Virgil; J. Ball
Tiger Shark; K. Stanton
Tintagel, Lord and Lady; F. Draco
Titterton, Adrian; Edward Brown
Tobin, Inspector; Dorothy B. Hughes
Tobin, Mitchell; T. Coe
Toby, Quentin; S. M. Schley
Todd, Inspector; J. Halstead
Todd, Fraser; H. L. Jones
Todd, Irving; P. Conde
Todd, Jerry; M. J. Freeman
Toff, The; J. Creasey
Tolefree, Philip; R. A. J. Walling
Tonelli, Pietro; Alexander Williams
Tong, Harry; E. Burgess
Tope, Inspector; Ben Ames Williams
Tope, Edward; H. C. Davis
Toplitt, Kingsley; G. Stockwell
Torrent, Andrew; L. Cores
Torreyton, Dick; E. F. Charles
Torry, Derek; J. Gardner
Touchfeather, Katy; J. Sangster
Townsend, Schuyler; F. Gordon
Townshend, Mr.; J. M. Cobban
Tracy, Dick; C. Gould
 William Johnston
Tracy, Noel; Alex Fraser
Tracy, Philip "Spike"; H. Ashbrook
Train, Rick; B. Fischer
Trant, Timothy; Q. Patrick
Travers, Ludovic; C. Bush
Treadgold, Inspector; A. Weymouth
Treadgold, Mr.; V. Williams
Tredennick, Angeline; R. B. Sanborn
Trees, Peter; John Q.
Trelawny, Edward; A. R. Long
Treloar, Septimus; Stephen Chance
Tremayne, Charles; N. MacKenzie
Trent, Anthony; W. Martyn
Trent, Gregory; A. Seifert
Trent, Marla; H. Kane
Trent, Philip; E. C. Bentley
Trenton, Garaway; J. P. Carstairs
Trenton, Hilda; D. Lyon
Trevor, Carole; J. Philips
Treynor, Jimmy; A. Livingston
Trothe, Edmund; R. Llewellyn
Trotter, Tuddleton; H. S. Keeler
Troy, David; Alan Gardner
Troy, Jeff and Haila; K. Roos
Tuck, Richard; Lange Lewis
Tucker, Charity; P. Buchanan
Tucker, Coleridge, III; I. Drummond
Tucker, Mike; B. Coffey
Tudor, Mark; A. Nash
Tuke, Harvey; D. G. Browne
Tully, Jasper; D. S. Davis
Tumbler, Hector; S. Crabtree
Turnbull, Roger; J. Tyndall
Tutt, Mr.; A. Train
Twins, Avenging; J. McCulley
Twombley, Jabez; Sidney Williams
Twotoes, Tommy; David Alexander
Tyler, Dennis; Diplomat
Tyler, Jeff; J. L. Potter
Tyler, Julia; L. Revell
Tyson, Henry; F. A. Kummer

U

U.N.C.L.E., Girl from; M. Avallone
 S. Latter
 P. Leslie
U.N.C.L.E., Man from; M. Avallone
 Joel Bernard
 J. Hunter Holly
 P. Leslie
 D. McDaniel
 J. Oram
 J. T. Phillifent
 Thomas Stratton
 H. Whittington
Urizar, Miguel; H. McCloy

Ursula, Sister; H. H. Holmes
Usher, Ambrose; J. Davey

V

Vachell, Supt.; E. Huxley
Valcour, Lt.; Rufus King
Vallance, Bill; W. Proudfoot
Vallon, Johnny; P. Cheyney
Van der Valk, Inspector; N. Freeling
Van Dusen, S. F. X.; J. Futrelle
Van Kill, Hendrik; S. Bayne
Van Larsen, Max; G. Baxt
Van Loan, Richard Curtis; Robert Wallace
Vance, Philo; J. Riddell
 S. S. Van Dine
Vaness, Richard; M. Black
Vanessa, Sarah; J. Storm
Vanner, Rick; M. V. Heberden
Varallo, Vic; L. Egan
Varney, Chick; Jerome Barry
Venable, Tessie; H. Holley
Venables, Charles; C. St. John Sprigg
Vereker, Anthony; R. Forsythe
Verity, Sgt.; F. Selwyn
Vernon, Larry; D. Bateson
Veseloffsky, Baron; S. Horler
Vickary, Grant; R. Hobart
Vigilante, The; V. J. Santiago
Villiers, Francis; B. Rodney
Vine, Gil; S. Sterling
Vivanti, Paul; S. Horler
von Kaz, Baron; D. L. Teilhet
von Kopf, Olga; H. De Halsalle
Vorobeitchik, Wenceslas; A. Steeman
Voss, Abelard; D. C. Cameron
Vulture, The; Harold Ward

W

Wace, Fadiman; Roger Simons
Wake, Inspector; C. Kingston
Wallace, Leonard; Alexander Wilson
Wallace, Michael; Roland Daniel
Wallingford, James Rufus; George Randolph Chester
Wallion, Maurice; J. Regis
Ward, Peter; David St. John
Ware, Anthony; S. Wells
Ware, Drexel; C. Andrews
Waring, Scarsdale; T. Stanleyan King
Warlock, Mike; P. Haggard
Warren, James; James Warren
Warrender, Mrs.; G. D. H. Cole
Warrington-Reeve, Claude; Josephine Bell
Warwick, John; J. McCulley
Watchman, Sam; B. Garfield
Waterlow, Roger; C. MacKenzie
Watson, Mr.; Dorothy Gardiner
Wayne, Morgan; M. Blood
Wayne, Rodney; A. G. E. Cromwell
Wayne, Steve; T. Harknett
Wayward, Carl; L. Treat
Weaver, T. S.; D. Keith
Webb, John and Anne; F. G. Presnell
Webley; L. Maddock
Webster, Dallas; D. Stanford
Weigand, Bill; F. & R. Lockridge
Welch, Agatha; V. P. Johns
Wells, Professor; F. Grierson
Wells, Clifford; N. S. Bortner
Welpton, Sam; J. A. Saxon
Wentworth, Richard; R. T. M. Scott
 G. Stockbridge
Wesley, Sheridan; H. Waugh
West, Ambrose; P. Levene
West, Henry Highland; J. Nazel

West, Honey; G. G. Fickling
West, Roger; J. Creasey
Westborough, Theocritus Lucius;
  C. B. Clason
Westlake, Hugh; J. Stagge
Weston, Mrs. Caywood; E. Thomas
Weston, Dick; T. Lund
Weston, James; James Warren
Wexford, Inspector; R. Rendell
Wharton, Sam; D. Buckingham
Wheat, Whitney; J. Lane
Wheeler, Al; Carter Brown
Whelan, Dick; Laurence Dwight Smith
White, Al; G. Holden
White, George; M. M. Mannon
White, Lace; Jeannette Covert Nolan
Whitney, Whit; D. Dodge
Wick, Christer; Maria Lang
Widgeon, Inspector; Alan Thomas
Wield, Inspector; Glint Green
Wigan, James; B. J. Farmer
Wiggin, Gramps; E. S. Gardner
Wilde, Carney; B. Spicer
Wilde, Jonas; A. York
Wilkins, Inspector; Murray Thomas
Williams, Chief Inspector; H. Clevely
Williams, Race; C. J. Daly
Williams, Remo; R. Sapir
Willing, Basil; H. McCloy
Wilson, Supt.; G. D. H. Cole
Wilson, Dick; K. Sproul
Wimble, "One Week"; H. Burnham
Wimsey, Lord Peter; D. L. Sayers
Wine, Moses; Roger L. Simon
Winkley, Mr.; H. Rutland
Winkman, Jake; D. Von Elsner
Winters, Matt; I. Oellrichs
Wintino, Dave; E. Lacy
Wintringham, David; Josephine Bell
Wise, Pennington; Carolyn Wells
Witherall, Leonidas; A. Tilton
Withers, Hildegarde; S. Palmer
Woar, Hazlitt; G. W. Yates
Wolfe, Nero; R. Stout
Woodhead, Alister; E. H. Clements
Woodward, James Rowland, VII; J. S. Blazer
Woolfe, Miss; Winifred Graham
Woolrich, Tony; M. M. Raison
Wraithlea, Commander; P. Walker Taylor
Wrayne, Daphne; Mark Cross
Wright, Eddie; C. Mullen
Wu, Lily; J. Sheridan
Wulff, Burt; M. Barry
Wycliffe, Charles; W. J. Burley
Wynnton, Robert; S. Horler

X

X, Secret Agent; B. House

Y

Yamamura, Trygve; P. Anderson
Yard, John; Ralph Hayes
Yates, Susan; E. L. Fetta
Yeoman, Giles; M. Woodhouse
York, Inspector; M. Durham
York, Sherrett; Gavin Holt
Young, Bernard; Eric Wood

Z

Z, Department; J. Creasey
Zambra, Sebastian; Headon Hill
Zane, Thornton; M. Massey
Zimmerman, Arnold; T. George
Zondi, Sgt.; J. McClure
Zordan, Anna; J. Eastwood

Ref
Z
2014
F4
H82

JAN 10 1980

RAYMOND H. FOGLER LIBRARY
DATE DUE

BOOKS ARE SUBJECT TO
AFTER TWO WEEKS